HALLIWELL'S

The Movies That Matter

FROM BOGART TO BOND AND ALL
THE LATEST FILM RELEASES

DAVID GRITTEN

HarperCollins*Publishers*

David Gritten writes about and reviews films for the *Daily Telegraph,* and for *Saga* magazine. He was a London-based film correspondent for the *Los Angeles Times* for fifteen years. He is the author of a 2002 book about celebrity culture, *Fame: Stripping Celebrity Bare* and has just completed a two-year term as chairman of the London Film Critics' Circle.

HarperCollins*Publishers*
77–85 Fulham Palace Road
Hammersmith
London W6 8JB

Previous editions in 1977, 1979, 1981, 1983, 1985, 1987, 1989, 1991, 1992, 1993, 1994, 1995, 1996, 1997, 1998, 1999, 2000, 2001, 2002, 2003, 2004, 2005, 2006, 2007

This edition published in 2008

Copyright © HarperCollins*Publishers* 1977, 1979, 1981, 1983, 1985, 1987, 1989, 2008

1 3 5 7 9 8 6 4 2

A CIP catalogue record for this book is available from the British Library

ISBN-13 978–0–00–727106–1
ISBN-10 0–00–727106–9

Typeset by RefineCatch Limited, Bungay, Suffolk
Printed and bound in China by Leo Paper Products Ltd

The HarperCollins website address is www.harpercollins.co.uk

Photographs courtesy of Getty Images (page 30), PA Photos (page 522) and the MovieStore Collection Ltd (pages 80, 140, 200, 292, 370, 450, 638)

Contents

Introduction

Welcome to the 2009 edition of *Halliwell's*, which represents a significant change of emphasis from previous guides in this series. This is a smaller-format volume, containing some 2,800 carefully selected films; as such, it is a response not only to feedback from readers but also to the future of film-guide publishing in the early 21st century.

The accumulation of new film entries over the years has led to *Halliwell's* guides becoming bulky; last year's edition, containing more than 24,000 entries, ran to almost 1,400 pages and weighed around 5 lb. Many regular buyers have voiced concerns about handling such a heavy, large volume and accommodating it on their bookshelves; ironically, many readers have also warned us that the print in these guides was as small as they could tolerate. Clearly, these two problems were irreconcilable in the existing format.

Then there's the question of how people now access information about films. It's largely a generational issue; most of those who came of age before the internet arrived still find automatic comfort in the printed page, while for lots of younger readers it is easier simply to click on a screen than to wade through the pages of a dense, formidable-looking tome. *Halliwell's* needs a future involving both the printed word and the digital world; we are currently discussing this topic with some urgency.

We believe this edition represents a way of sustaining *Halliwell's* through a transition period; a volume that is more accessible and reader-friendly for first-time buyers but an invaluable companion work to those who peruse the guide each year.

The edition lists all films in alphabetical order, but consists of three elements. Firstly, it includes new UK releases, some 350 for the year ending June 2008. These exclude only Bollywood movies, re-releases of classics and a handful of films that received a tiny release (sometimes on one screen), were barely seen in cinemas and are primarily intended for the DVD market. But all this past year's major titles are in the 350.

Secondly, the bulk of this volume comprises 2,000 titles from the past 20 years, each one with a brand new review; for good or bad, most films seen today, whether on television, or bought or rented on DVD, come from this period.

We believe almost all the significant films of these last two decades are here. Many others are underrated or simply neglected. Inclusion in the 2,000 does not necessarily imply a hearty endorsement: titles such as *Showgirls* and *Striptease* confirm as much. Some films make the list only because they were a talking point at the time, even if it involved hand-wringing at the state of the film business.

Box-office success does not confer automatic selection: you will look in vain here for the two most recent *Star Wars* films, and for a few *Harry Potters*. We also judge each film on individual merit, rather than as part of a series: clearly, *Lord of the Rings* enthusiasts will have seen the entire trilogy, but we feel if you're neutral about the first, you could skip the second and head straight for the last one.

The third and final category is a group of 500 earlier films selected by myself. They range from early silents to the latter part of the 1980s; from *Intolerance* to *Blue Velvet*, if you will. It's a purely subjective list, and anyone can argue the merit or otherwise of any entry; but it's safe to say that acquainting yourself with all, or even most of them, would give you a solid grounding in film history.

Leslie Halliwell, the founder of these guides, wrote the original reviews for these 500 films. Some of his pithy assessments, especially for the older entries, are virtually unimprovable and appear here in their original form or close to it. But tastes change, reputations of films rise and fall, and many of these older entries, especially those from the 70s and 80s, have been given new reviews.

Speaking of Halliwell, he is the subject of one of 10 features sprinkled throughout this volume, most of them about people or subjects that were topical this last year. We hope you enjoy the innovative elements in this new edition.

My grateful thanks go to Belinda Budge and Tom Whiting at HarperCollins; my agent Rosemary Sandberg; my stalwart contributors Tim Robey, Mike McCahill, Neil Smith, Stafford Hildred, Alan Jones and Richard Mowe; Gary Holmes and David Balls at RefineCatch for the long hours; and to Rose Harrow and Daniel Gritten for their diligent, invaluable research.

David Gritten
July 2008

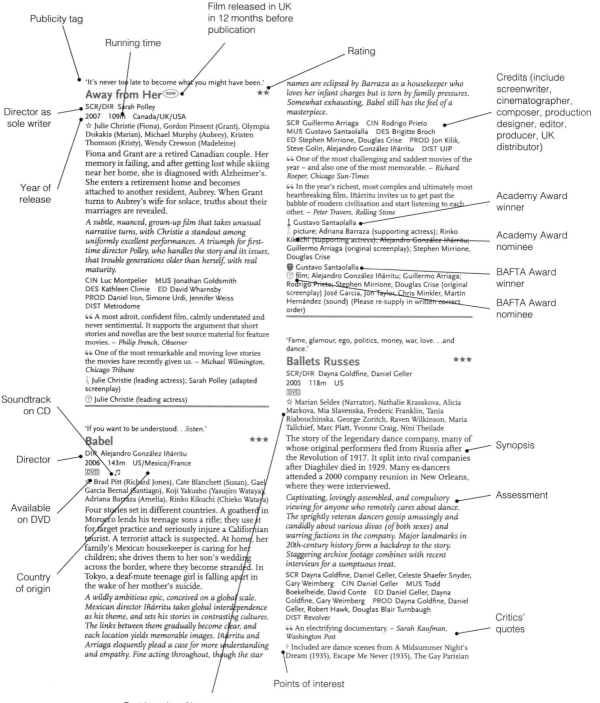

Publicity tag

Running time

Film released in UK in 12 months before publication

Rating

Credits (include screenwriter, cinematographer, composer, production designer, editor, producer, UK distributor)

Director as sole writer

Year of release

Soundtrack on CD

Director

Available on DVD

Country of origin

Academy Award winner

Academy Award nominee

BAFTA Award winner

BAFTA Award nominee

Synopsis

Assessment

Critics' quotes

Points of interest

Cast in order of importance (*italics* for standout performance)

'It's never too late to become what you might have been.' ★★

Away from Her (new)

SCR/DIR Sarah Polley
2007   109m   Canada/UK/USA
☆ Julie Christie (Fiona), Gordon Pinsent (Grant), Olympia Dukakis (Marian), Michael Murphy (Aubrey), Kristen Thomson (Kristy), Wendy Crewson (Madeleine)

Fiona and Grant are a retired Canadian couple. Her memory is failing, and after getting lost while skiing near her home, she is diagnosed with Alzheimer's. She enters a retirement home and becomes attached to another resident, Aubrey. When Grant turns to Aubrey's wife for solace, truths about their marriages are revealed.

A subtle, nuanced, grown-up film that takes unusual narrative turns, with Christie a standout among uniformly excellent performances. A triumph for first-time director Polley, who handles the story and its issues, that trouble generations older than herself, with real maturity.

CIN Luc Montpelier   MUS Jonathan Goldsmith
DES Kathleen Climie   ED David Wharnsby
PROD Daniel Iron, Simone Urdi, Jennifer Weiss
DIST Metrodome

66 A most adroit, confident film, calmly understated and never sentimental. It supports the argument that short stories and novellas are the best source material for feature movies. – *Philip French, Observer*

66 One of the most remarkable and moving love stories the movies have recently given us. – *Michael Wilmington, Chicago Tribune*

Julie Christie (leading actress); Sarah Polley (adapted screenplay)

Julie Christie (leading actress)

'If you want to be understood. . .listen.'

Babel ★★★

DIR Alejandro González Iñárritu
2006   143m   US/Mexico/France
♫
Brad Pitt (Richard Jones), Cate Blanchett (Susan), Gael Garcia Bernal (Santiago), Koji Yakusho (Yasujiro Wataya), Adriana Barraza (Amelia), Rinko Kikuchi (Chieko Wataya)

Four stories set in different countries. A goatherd in Morocco lends his teenage sons a rifle; they use it for target practice and seriously injure a Californian tourist. A terrorist attack is suspected. At home, her family's Mexican housekeeper is caring for her children; she drives them to her son's wedding across the border, where they become stranded. In Tokyo, a deaf-mute teenage girl is falling apart in the wake of her mother's suicide.

A wildly ambitious epic, conceived on a global scale. Mexican director Iñárritu takes global interdependence as his theme, and sets his stories in contrasting cultures. The links between them gradually become clear, and each location yields memorable images. Iñárritu and Arriaga eloquently plead a case for more understanding and empathy. Fine acting throughout, though the star

names are eclipsed by Barraza as a housekeeper who loves her infant charges but is torn by family pressures. Somewhat exhausting, Babel still has the feel of a masterpiece.

SCR Guillermo Arriaga   CIN Rodrigo Prieto
MUS Gustavo Santaolalla   DES Brigitte Broch
ED Stephen Mirrione, Douglas Crise   PROD Jon Kilik, Steve Golin, Alejandro González Iñárritu   DIST UIP

66 One of the most challenging and saddest movies of the year – and also one of the most memorable. – *Richard Roeper, Chicago Sun-Times*

66 In the year's richest, most complex and ultimately most heartbreaking film, Iñárritu invites us to get past the babble of modern civilisation and start listening to each other. – *Peter Travers, Rolling Stone*

Gustavo Santaolalla
picture; Adriana Barraza (supporting actress); Rinko Kikuchi (supporting actress); Alejandro González Iñárritu; Guillermo Arriaga (original screenplay); Stephen Mirrione, Douglas Crise

Gustavo Santaolalla
film; Alejandro González Iñárritu; Guillermo Arriaga; Rodrigo Prieto; Stephen Mirrione, Douglas Crise (original screenplay) José Garcia, Jon Taylor, Chris Minkler, Martín Hernández (sound) (Please re-supply in written correct order)

'Fame, glamour, ego, politics, money, war, love. . .and dance.'

Ballets Russes ★★★

SCR/DIR Dayna Goldfine, Daniel Geller
2005   118m   US
DVD
☆ Marian Seldes (Narrator), Nathalie Krasskova, Alicia Markova, Mia Slavenska, Frederic Franklin, Tania Riabouchinska, George Zoritch, Raven Wilkinson, Maria Tallchief, Marc Platt, Yvonne Craig, Nini Theilade

The story of the legendary dance company, many of whose original performers fled from Russia after the Revolution of 1917. It split into rival companies after Diaghilev died in 1929. Many ex-dancers attended a 2000 company reunion in New Orleans, where they were interviewed.

Captivating, lovingly assembled, and compulsory viewing for anyone who remotely cares about dance. The sprightly veteran dancers gossip amusingly and candidly about various divas (of both sexes) and warring factions in the company. Major landmarks in 20th-century history form a backdrop to the story. Staggering archive footage combines with recent interviews for a sumptuous treat.

SCR Dayna Goldfine, Daniel Geller, Celeste Shaefer Snyder, Gary Weimberg   CIN Daniel Geller   MUS Todd Boekelheide, David Conte   ED Daniel Geller, Dayna Goldfine, Gary Weimberg   PROD Dayna Goldfine, Daniel Geller, Robert Hawk, Douglas Blair Turnbaugh
DIST Revolver

66 An electrifying documentary. – *Sarah Kaufman, Washington Post*

† Included are dance scenes from A Midsummer Night's Dream (1935), Escape Me Never (1935), The Gay Parisian

Explanatory Notes

Alphabetical order   This guide lists entries on a one-word-at-a-time basis. Thus for instance all titles starting with the word 'On' are listed together; *On the Waterfront* goes before *Once Upon A Time in America*. Definite and indefinite articles are not counted as part of the title.

Individual entries   All entries follow the order below.

Publicity taglines   The phrase or phrases used by distributors to promote the film at the time of release. They appear above the title.

Title   This is given in full, even though the film may be known by an abbreviated title. See *Dr Strangelove*. There is one departure from the custom of recent editions, which we hope will simplify matters for readers: if a foreign-language film was released in the UK under the English translation of its original title, that English title is listed here. So look under *All About My Mother*, not *Todo Sobre Mi Madre*.

New   This refers to films that had a UK release within 12 months of publication of this current edition.

Ratings   These range from zero to four stars. Many of this past year's films rate zero; this does not make them automatically unwatchable but indicates there is nothing of excellence to distinguish them. *Halliwell's* traditionally prides itself on the stinginess of the stars it awards, and this edition is no exception – even though this last year also provided a relatively high number of four-star titles. The rating bestowed represents a consensus between the editor and his contributors.

Writer credit (SCR)   This means the author of the screenplay. If the script is adapted from a different source (for instance, a book, short story, magazine article, or play) this is mentioned separately.

Director credit (DIR)   If the director also wrote the screenplay, the joint credit will appear (SCR/DIR).

Year of release   Determining this has been an imprecise science up to now. 'Year of release' can mean many things, including the year that shooting of a film was completed, the year it was first seen at a festival, or its first commercial release. For older films, this might mean any of those things, but for films of the last two or three years, we have generally pinpointed the year they were first seen by paying customers anywhere in the world, not including festivals or film markets.

Running time   This is given in minutes. It generally refers to the length of the film when first released, rather than 'director's cut' versions. Bear in mind that the length includes the end titles, which have become longer in recent years.

Country of origin   Singular or plural.

Colour   Assume a film is in colour, unless it has a 'bw' notation, indicating black-and-white.

DVD DVD   This indicates that a film is available on DVD, though it does not differentiate between Region 1 and Region 2. The availability of a recent film on DVD may well have changed since the time of writing; suffice it to say that the vast majority of recent films are available on DVD six months after their theatrical release, and frequently sooner.

Soundtrack ♫   This indicates that the soundtrack is available in a recorded format, usually CDs for more recent films.

Cast ☆   A list of the leading actors is given, usually five or six of them and more or less according to the prominence of the role. Names in *italics* indicate a contribution of a notably high standard.

Synopsis   A brief description of a film's plot or theme.

Assessment   A review of the film's qualities, usually concise but often slightly longer in the case of significant films. Individual assessments are anonymous, but represent a *Halliwell's* consensus between the editor and contributors.

Photography credit (CIN)   This means the cinematographer or lighting cameraman, known in the business as the DP, rather than the camera operator(s).

Music credit (MUS)   The composer of the score. If songs of note are performed in a film, or have been specially composed for it, they appear under † .

Production credit (PROD and DIST)   The production company or companies involved are listed, along with the British distributor and the name(s) of the producer(s). Only people with an unadorned 'producer' credit are named: executive producers, associate producers and co-producers are not.

Other credits   These include screenwriter (**SCR**), production designer (**DES**), editor (**ED**).

Critical comments 66   Quotes from other British and/or American critics, where added, may indicate a range of opinion about a film, or in some cases confirm a near-unanimous consensus about its qualities or lack of them.

Annotations †   These are points of interest about the film, not covered in the above categories.

Awards   Oscar awards ♟ and nominations ♙ in leading categories are listed. Major BAFTA awards ⬭ and nominations Ⓣ also appear.

A Bout de Souffle ★★★★

DIR *Jean-Luc Godard*
1960 90m France
DVD ♫

☆ *Jean-Paul Belmondo* (Michel Poiccard/Laszlo Kovacs), *Jean Seberg* (Patricia Franchini), Daniel Boulanger (Police Inspector), Jean-Pierre Melville (Parvulesco), Jean-Luc Godard (Informer), Liliane Robin (Minouche)

In Paris, a young petty crook kills a policeman and goes on the run with his American girlfriend, a newspaper vendor.

A film that literally changed the way the world viewed cinema. The debutant Godard's use of location shooting, jump-cuts, hand-held camera work and sly homages to other directors seem familiar today; at the time they were revolutionary. As for his stars, Belmondo and Seberg both seem cool, chic and modern nearly half a century later. This was arguably the most influential film of the French New Wave.

SCR Jean-Luc Godard   CIN *Raoul Coutard*   MUS Martial Solal   ED Cécile Decugis   PROD Georges de Beauregard

66 A film all dressed up for rebellion but with no real tangible territory on which to stand and fight. – *Peter John Dyer*

† An American re-make, Breathless, was released in 1983.
† Godard dedicated the film to the Hollywood studio company Monogram, which specialised in Westerns and, significantly, crime melodramas.
† The film was partly inspired by Gun Crazy (1949).

A Comedy of Power (new) ★

DIR Claude Chabrol
2006 110m France/Germany

☆ Isabelle Huppert (Jeanne Charmant-Killman), François Berléand (Michel Humeau), Patrick Bruel (Jacques Sibaud), Robin Renucci (Philippe Charmant-Killman), Maryline Canto (Erika), Thomas Chabrol (Felix), Jean-François Balmer (Boldi)

A female magistrate investigates a businessman accused of misusing company funds.

Talky character study, inspired by a notorious French case; those unable to make that connection, however, will be left scratching their heads.

SCR Odile Barski, Claude Chabrol   CIN Eduardo Serra
MUS Matthieu Chabrol   DES Françoise Benoit-Fresco
ED Monique Fardoulis   PROD Patrick Godeau
DIST ICA

66 As always, helmer Chabrol delights in the permutations of human stupidity. – *Lisa Nesselson, Variety*

66 After a strong start, this movie progressively loses focus and dramatic point. – *Peter Bradshaw, Guardian*

'Journey To A World Where Robots Dream And Desire.'

A.I. Artificial Intelligence ★★

SCR/DIR *Steven Spielberg*
2001 146m US
DVD ♫

☆ *Haley Joel Osment* (David), Jude Law (Gigolo Joe), Frances O'Connor (Monica Swinton), Brendan Gleeson (Lord Johnson-Johnson), Sam Robards (Henry Swinton), William Hurt (Professor Hobby), Jake Thomas (Martin Swinton), Ken Leung (Syatyoo-Sama), Michael Mantell (Dr Frazier), Michael Berresse (Stage Manager), Kathryn Morris (Teenage Honey), Adrian Grenier (Teen in Van)

A robot boy programmed to have feelings is abandoned by his flesh-and-blood mother and tries to find her.

Ambitious, overblown, hugely interesting futuristic fable, a technically dazzling riff on Pinocchio with debts to Kubrick. Whole sections misfire, but the overall thrust is a darkly imaginative quest into the subconscious, and the twists of the fairytale narrative are less consoling than they initially appear.

CIN *Janusz Kaminski*   MUS *John Williams*   DES Rick Carter   ED *Michael Kahn*   PROD Kathleen Kennedy, Steven Spielberg, Bonnie Curtis   DIST Warner

66 Spielberg exercises his usual skills – a no-nonsense pace, huge bursts of sound and action, eye-popping special effects – with a nod to Kubrick-style images. – *Philip Strick, Sight & Sound*

66 Those gagging on the glut of cinematic junk food should welcome this brilliantly made visionary work that's bursting with provocative ideas. – *Todd McCarthy, Variety*

† Stanley Kubrick had planned to make this from Brian Aldiss's script, but decided that special effects technology wasn't adequate at the time.

⚲ John Williams; visual effects (Dennis Muren, Scott Farrar, Michael Lantieri)

Ⓣ special visual effects (Dennis Muren, Scott Farrar, Stan Winston, Michael Lantieri)

A la Place du Coeur ★

DIR Robert Guédiguian
1998 113m France

☆ Ariane Ascaride (Marianne Patché), Christine Brücher (Francine Lopez), Jean-Pierre Darroussin (Joel Patché), Gérard Meylan (Franck Lopez), Alexandre Ogou (François Lopez), Laure Raoust (Clémentine Patché), Véronique Balme (Sophie Patché), Pierre Banderet (Mr d'Assas)

DVD Available on DVD   ☆ Cast in order of importance   66 Critics' Quotes   ⚲ Academy Award / Academy Award nomination   Ⓑ BAFTA / Ⓣ BAFTA nomination
♫ Soundtrack on CD   † Points of interest

A pregnant white teenage girl in Marseille embarks on an affair with the young black father of her child, who is jailed on a rape charge.

Downbeat slice-of-life story transposed from the Harlem of Baldwin's righteously indignant novel to the director's home town, where the story's racial tensions remain intact but some indefinable magic gets lost.

SCR Jean-Louis Milesi, Robert Guédiguian **CIN** Bernard Cavalié **MUS** Jacques Menichetti **DES** Michel Vandestien **ED** Bernard Sasia **PROD** Gilles Sandoz, Michel Saint-Jean, Robert Guédiguian **DIST** Artificial Eye

66 Crucially, the film maker treats his characters with genuine compassion, and handles the various issues – racism, mixed-race relationships, alcoholism, unemployment – with a refreshing lightness of touch. – *Tom Dawson, BBC*

A Secret (new) ★★

SCR/DIR Claude Miller
2008   105m   France
DVD   ♫

☆ *Mathieu Amalric* (François Grimbert), Valentin Vigourt (Young François), *Cécile de France* (Tania), *Patrick Bruel* (Maxime Grimbert), Julie Depardieu (Louise), Ludivine Sagnier (Anna)

In 1955 François, a lonely Jewish boy, invents a brother and re-imagines his parents' past in World War II. But he later discovers a secret, tying his family's past to the Holocaust, that finally helps him develop a sense of self.

Based on a fact-inspired novel, Miller's finely-wrought drama deals with simple people caught up in forces beyond their control. Amalric offers a well-judged performance as the troubled adult François, with de France and Bruel as parents with a knack for survival.

CIN Gérard de Battusta **MUS** Zbigniew Preisner **DES** Jean-Pierre Kohut-Svelko **ED** Veronica Lange **PROD** Yves Marmion **DIST** Arrow

66 It's a gripping story, extremely well acted, far superior to Truffaut's bogus The Last Metro, but not quite in the same class as Malle's Au Revoir les Enfants and Lacombe Lucien. – *Philip French, Observer*

66 A blue-chip cast and handsome stagings do little to prevent this French movie being a muddled, pretentious wash-out. – *Peter Bradshaw, Guardian*

† "I was born in 1942. There weren't many survivors in my family: most of my uncles, aunts and grandparents didn't come back from the concentration camps. As a boy, then a teenager, I was haunted by this traumatising, stressful story." – Claude Miller

Abouna ★★★

SCR/DIR *Mahamat-Saleh Haroun*
2002   84m   Chad/France/Netherlands
DVD

☆ *Ahidjo Mahamat Moussa* (Tahir), Hamza Moctar Aguid (Amine), Zara Haroun (Achta), Mounira Khalil (Mute Girl), Koulsy Lamko (Father), Garba Issa (Headmaster)

Two young boys in Chad are abandoned by their father and set about trying to find him.

Tender comedy of inter-generational strife, almost perfectly directed and played, and with many magical touches; the wonderful music is performed by Ali Farka Touré.

CIN Abraham Haile Biru **MUS** *Diego Moustapha Ngarade* **DES** Laurent Cavero **ED** Sarah Taouss Matton **PROD** Guillaume De Seille

66 It's hard to imagine that any European film-maker would have the audacity to end on such a note of unforced, minor-key optimism. – *Philip Kemp, Sight & Sound*

'Growing up has nothing to do with age.'

About a Boy ★

DIR Paul and Chris Weitz
2002   101m   GB/US/Germany/France
DVD   ♫

☆ Hugh Grant (Will), Toni Collette (Fiona), Rachel Weisz (Rachel), Nicholas Hoult (Marcus), Isabel Brook (Angie), Sharon Small (Christine), Victoria Smurfit (Suzie), Augustus Prew (Ali)

A womanising trustafarian learns to become responsible when forced to look after a forlorn 12 year-old schoolboy.

A pleasant idea and breezy production which somehow comes out smug and forced, perhaps because its leading man is better feigning sincerity than convincing us of it.

SCR Peter Hedges, Chris Weitz, Paul Weitz **CIN** Remi Adefarasin **MUS** *Badly Drawn Boy* **DES** Jim Clay **ED** Nick Moore **PROD** Jane Rosenthal, Robert De Niro, Brad Epstein, Tim Bevan, Eric Fellner **DIST** UIP

66 This is a serious, intelligent and committed performance from Grant, however without some of the champagne-fizz of his comic stuff with Richard Curtis: and you can be mature without jettisoning the gags.' I – *Peter Bradshaw, Guardian*

⚲ Peter Hedges, Chris Weitz, Paul Weitz (adapted screenplay)

Ⓣ Toni Colette (supporting actress); Peter Hedges, Chris Weitz, Paul Weitz (adapted screenplay)

'Schmidt Happens.'

About Schmidt ★★

DIR Alexander Payne
2002   125m   US
DVD   ♫

☆ *Jack Nicholson* (Warren Schmidt), Hope Davis (Jeannie), Dermot Mulroney (Randall Hertzel), *Kathy Bates* (Roberta Hertzel), Len Cariou (Ray), Howard Hesseman (Larry), June Squibb (Helen Schmidt)

An ageing actuary retires, is suddenly widowed and interferes in his daughter's wedding plans.

Nicholson scores in a scalding and often hilarious portrait of end-of-life crisis; but the film has a somewhat condescending way with its lesser characters, and the cruel satire and sentimentality are uneasy bedfellows.

SCR Alexander Payne, Jim Taylor **CIN** James Glennon **MUS** Rolfe Kent **DES** Jane Ann Stewart **ED** Kevin Tent **PROD** Michael Gittes, Harry Besman **DIST** Entertainment

66 The bleakness and poignancy are inescapable in About

DVD Available on DVD   ☆ Cast in order   66 Critics' Quotes   ⚲ Academy Award   Ⓣ BAFTA
♫ Soundtrack on CD   of importance   † Points of interest   ⚲ Academy Award nomination   Ⓣ BAFTA nomination

Schmidt, a character study that has the emotional richness of the great Italian and Eastern European films of the 1960s, in which humour and pathos rode up and down on the seesaw together. – *John Powers, L.A. Weekly*

66 Sublimely funny and exquisitely sad, this might just turn out to be an American classic. – *Peter Bradshaw, Guardian*

⚐ Jack Nicholson (leading actor); Kathy Bates (supporting actress)

Ⓣ Jack Nicholson (leading actor)

'Sometimes you can't wake from a nightmare, even if you do. . .'

Abre Los Ojos ★★★

DIR *Alejandro Amenábar*
1997   117m   Spain/France/Italy
DVD   ♫

☆ Eduardo Noriega (Cesar), Penelope Cruz (Sofia), Chete Lera (Antonio), Fele Martinez (Pelayo), Najwa Nimri (Nuria), Gérard Barray (Duvernois), Jorge de Juan (Department head)

A handsome playboy has his face disfigured in a car crash; surgeons rebuild it, but he is traumatised by apparitions of an alternative self.

Sophisticated and disturbing thriller about different planes of reality, skilfully realised and often jolting when it pulls away the façade.

SCR Alejandro Amenábar, Matteo Gil   CIN Hans Burmann   MUS Alejandro Amenábar, Mariano Marin   ED Maria Elena Sainz de Rojas   PROD José Luis Cuerda, Fernando Bovaira   DIST Redbus

66 The most successful moments are not those which cite Hitchcock but those that reveal Amenábar's distinctively chilly style. – *Paul Julian Smith, Sight & Sound*

† Remade in the US as Vanilla Sky.

'Corrupts Absolutely.'

Absolute Power ★

DIR Clint Eastwood
1997   121m   US
DVD   ♫

☆ Clint Eastwood (Luther Whitney), Gene Hackman (President Richmond), Ed Harris (Seth Frank), Laura Linney (Kate Whitney), *Judy Davis* (Gloria Russell), Scott Glenn (Bill Burton), Dennis Haysbert (Tim Collin), E.G. Marshall (Walter Sullivan), Melora Hardin (Christy Sullivan)

A career thief witnesses a murder in which the US President is complicit.

Ludicrous guff which manages to get even sillier as it goes along; but there's some fun to be had in the performances.

SCR William Goldman   CIN Jack N. Green   MUS Lennie Niehaus   DES Henry Bumstead   ED Joel Cox   PROD Clint Eastwood, Karen Spiegel   DIST Columbia/Castle Rock/Malpaso

66 A first-rate thriller about arrogance at the top, a showdown between two kinds of Americans: the evil, omnipotent bureaucrat and the enterprising, mind-his-own-business loner. – *Mick LaSalle, San Francisco Chronicle*

'A place on earth more awesome than anywhere in space.'

The Abyss ★★

SCR/DIR *James Cameron*
1989   138m   US
DVD   ♫

☆ *Ed Harris* (Virgil 'Bud' Brigman), *Mary Elizabeth Mastrantonio* (Lindsey Brigman), Michael Biehn (Lt. Hiram Coffey), Leo Burmester (Catfish De Vries), Todd Graff (Alan 'Hippy' Carnes), John Bedford Lloyd (Jammer Willis), J. C. Quinn (Arliss 'Sonny' Dawson), Kimberly Scott (Lisa 'One Night' Standing)

A crew of oil rig divers experience disaster while attempting the emergency recovery of a nuclear submarine, and find that they may not be alone in the ocean.

A tense and immersive underwater epic, with human interest in the embattled relationship between a couple on the verge of divorce: it is almost terrific, but badly damaged by a gormless and overblown finale.

CIN Mikael Salomon   MUS Alan Silvestri   DES Leslie Dilley   ED Joel Goodman, Conrad Buff, Howard Smith   PROD Gale Anne Hurd   DIST Fox

66 Stupendously exciting and emotionally engulfing. – *Peter Travers, Rolling Stone*

66 Ends with a whimper. But it starts out with a bang. – *Entertainment Weekly*

⚐ visual effects
⚐ Mikael Salomon (cinematography); Leslie Dilley, Anne Kuljian (art direction); sound

'Falling in love. . .even the expert is confused.'

The Accidental Husband (new)

DIR Griffin Dunne
2008   90m   US
DVD

☆ Uma Thurman (Dr. Emma Lloyd), Colin Firth (Richard Bratton), Jeffrey Dean Morgan (Patrick Sullivan), Sam Shepard (Wilder), Isabella Rossellini (Mrs. Bollenbecker), Lindsay Sloane (Marcy)

A radio agony aunt finds herself married to a New York fireman, much to the chagrin of her stuffy fiancé.

Feeble romantic comedy with a preposterous premise and a script that gives its stars nothing to work with.

SCR Mimi Hare, Clare Naylor, Bonnie Sikowitz   CIN William Rexer II   MUS Andrea Guerra   DES Mark Ricker   ED Suzy Elmiger   PROD Jennifer Todd, Suzanne Todd, Jason Blum, Uma Thurman, Bob Yari   DIST Momentum

66 A plot of insufferable silliness contrives to keep the lovers on tenterhooks and the audience in a permanent cringe. – *Anthony Quinn, Independent*

66 Uma Thurman grins, mugs and capers like a whippet on crack. – *Peter Bradshaw, Guardian*

DVD Available on DVD   ☆ Cast in order of importance   66 Critics' Quotes   ⚐ Academy Award   Ⓑ BAFTA
♫ Soundtrack on CD   † Points of interest   ⚐ Academy Award nomination   Ⓣ BAFTA nomination

3

The Accidental Tourist ★★

DIR Lawrence Kasdan
1988 121m US
DVD ♫

☆ William Hurt (Macon Leary), Kathleen Turner (Sarah Leary), Geena Davis (Muriel Pritchett), Amy Wright (Rose Leary), Bill Pullman (Julian), Robert Gorman (Alexander Pritchett), David Ogden Stiers (Porter Leary), Ed Begley Jnr (Charles Leary)

A repressed travel writer is abandoned by his wife and falls in love with a quirky dog trainer.

A rather glum romantic comedy, well-enough acted, and finding room for plenty of quietly observational scenes, though the lead character is arguably too morose.

SCR Frank Galati, Lawrence Kasdan CIN John Bailey
MUS John Williams DES Bo Welch ED Carol Littleton
PROD Lawrence Kasdan, Charles Okun, Michael Grillo
DIST Warner

66 I've never seen a movie so sad in which there was so much genuine laughter. – *Roger Ebert, Chicago Sun-Times*

66 Hell to sit through. – *Pauline Kael, New Yorker*

⚊ Geena Davis (supporting actress)
⚊ picture; Frank Galati, Lawrence Kasdan (adapted screenplay); John Williams (music)
ⓣ Frank Galati, Lawrence Kasdan (adapted screenplay)

The Accompanist ★

DIR Claude Miller
1992 111m France
♫

☆ *Richard Bohringer* (Charles Brice), *Elena Safonova* (Irene Brice), Romane Bohringer (Sophie Vasseur), Bernard Verley (Jacques Ceniat), Samuel Labarthe (Jacques Fabert), Nelly Borgeaud (Madame Vasseur), Julien Rassam (Benoit Weizman), Jean-Pierre Kohut Svelko (General Heller)

In 1942, in occupied Paris, a young woman is hired as an accompanist to a singer whose husband is a collaborator with the Nazis.

Complex, thoughtful performances lift this otherwise ordinary wartime story.

SCR Claude Miller, Luc Béraud, Claude Rich CIN Yves Angelo MUS Alain Jomy DES Jean-Pierre Kohut Svelko
ED Albert Jurgenson PROD Jean-Louis Livi
DIST Gala/Film Par Film/De la Boissière Orly/Sedif France/3 Cinema

66 Even the archive wartime footage, which Miller has added to give an air of moral seriousness to the film, serves to reinforce the feeling you've seen it all before. – *Martin Bright, Sight and Sound*

The Accused ★★

DIR Jonathan Kaplan
1988 111m US
DVD

☆ Kelly McGillis (Kathryn Murphy), *Jodie Foster* (Sarah Tobias), Bernie Coulson (Ken Joyce), Ann Hearn (Sally Fraser), Steve Antin (Bob Joiner), Tom O'Brien (Larry)

A rape victim, whose attackers received light sentencing because of her provocative dance in a sleazy bar, persuades her female attorney to prosecute the bystanders who cheered them on.

A crude, issue-led drama on an important subject, but one elevated above mediocrity by the fire and conviction of Foster's performance.

SCR Tom Topor CIN Ralf Bode MUS Brad Fiedel
DES Richard Kent Wilcox ED Jerry Greenberg, O. Nicholas Brown PROD Stanley R. Jaffe, Sherry Lansing
DIST UIP/Paramount

66 Not a brilliant film, but an intelligent and thoughtful one. – *Jonathan Rosenbaum, Chicago Reader*

† The film is based on an incident that occurred at a bar in New Bedford, Massachusetts in 1983.

⚊ Jodie Foster (leading actress)
ⓣ Jodie Foster (leading actress)

Ace in the Hole ★★★

DIR *Billy Wilder*
1951 111m US

☆ *Kirk Douglas* (Chuck Tatum), Jan Sterling (Lorraine), *Porter Hall* (Boot), Bob Arthur (Herbie), Richard Benedict (Leo), Ray Teal (Sheriff), Frank Cady (Federber)

A cynical journalist delays the rescue of a man trapped in a cave, in order to prolong the story, boost his newspaper's sales and advance his career.

An incisive, compelling melodrama taking a sour look at the American scene; one of its director's masterworks. This was Wilder at his most disenchanted; it surveys the dark, unattractive underbelly of post-war American affluence and optimism, and remains a ferocious attack on human avarice, and on tabloid news values.

SCR *Billy Wilder, Lesser Samuels, Walter Newman*
CIN Charles B. Lang Jnr. MUS Hugo Friedhofer
PROD Billy Wilder DIST Paramount

LORRAINE TO TATUM: I've met some hard-boiled eggs, but you – you're twenty minutes!

LORRAINE: I don't go to church. Kneeling bags my nylons.

TATUM TO EDITOR: I've done a lot of lying in my time. I've lied to men who wear belts. I've lied to men who wear suspenders. But I'd never be so stupid as to lie to a man who wears both belt and suspenders.

TATUM, DYING, TO EDITOR: How'd you like to make a thousand dollars a day, Mr Boot? I'm a thousand-dollar-a-day newspaperman. You can have me for nothing.

66 Few of the opportunities for irony, cruelty and horror are missed. – *Gavin Lambert*

66 Style and purpose achieve for the most part a fusion even more remarkable than in Sunset Boulevard. – *Penelope Houston*

† Locations were at Gallup, New Mexico.

⚊ script

'All you need is love.'

Across the Universe (new)

DIR Julie Taymor
2007 133m US
♫

☆ Evan Rachel Wood (Lucy), Jim Sturgess (Jude), Joe Anderson (Max), Dana Fuchs (Sadie), Martin Luther McCoy (Jo-Jo), Eddie Izzard (Mr. Kite), Bono (Dr. Robert)

DVD Available on DVD ☆ Cast in order of importance 66 Critics' Quotes † Points of interest ⚊ Academy Award ⚊ Academy Award nomination ⓦ BAFTA ⓣ BAFTA nomination
♫ Soundtrack on CD

A Liverpudlian dock worker falls in love with a young radical in 1960s America.

Florid, ambitious attempt to string 30-odd Beatles numbers into a coherent narrative. Individual sequences dazzle; as a whole, though, the film is uneven, kitsch and risibly over-literal.

SCR Dick Clement, Ian La Frenais   CIN Bruno Delbonnel   MUS Elliot Goldenthal   DES Mark Friedberg   ED Françoise Bonnot   PROD Suzanne Todd, Jennifer Todd, Matthew Gross   DIST Sony Pictures

66 Hard to dislike but hard to take seriously. – *Justin Chang, Variety*

66 Taymor has mistaken a clichéd view of the late '60s for a radical slice of the zeitgeist. – *Dave Calhoun, Time Out*

Adam's Rib ★★

DIR George Cukor
1949   101m   US
DVD

☆ *Spencer Tracy, Katharine Hepburn, David Wayne, Tom Ewell, Judy Holliday, Jean Hagen*, Hope Emerson, Clarence Kolb

Husband and wife lawyers find themselves on opposing sides in a trial for attempted murder.

A sophisticated, blue-chip 'battle of the sexes' comedy, with razor-sharp dialogue from Gordon and Kanin and real sexual chemistry between Tracy and Hepburn. Yet they are all equalled by Holliday, in her film debut, as the ditzy defendant. A complete delight.

SCR *Ruth Gordon, Garson Kanin*   CIN George J. Folsey   MUS Miklos Rozsa   PROD Lawrence Weingarten   DIST MGM

66 Hepburn and Tracy are again presented as the ideal US Mr and Mrs of upper-middle income. This time, as well as being wittily urbane, both are lawyers. – *Time*

66 It isn't solid food but it certainly is meaty and juicy and comically nourishing. – *Bosley Crowther*

† A 1972 TV series of the same title provided a boring imitation, with Ken Howard and Blythe Danner.

⚖ Ruth Gordon and Garson Kanin

'Charlie Kaufman writes the way he lives. . .With Great Difficulty. His Twin Brother Donald Lives the way he writes. . .with foolish abandon. Susan writes about life. . .But can't live it. John's life is a book. . .Waiting to be adapted. One story. . .Four Lives. . .A million ways it can end.'

Adaptation ★★★

DIR *Spike Jonze*
2002   114m   US
DVD   ♫

☆ *Nicolas Cage* (Charlie Kaufman/Donald Kaufman), *Meryl Streep* (Susan Orlean), *Chris Cooper* (John Laroche), *Tilda Swinton* (Valerie), Cara Seymour (Amelia), Brian Cox (Robert McKee), Judy Greer (Alice the Waitress), Maggie Gyllenhaal (Caroline)

A depressive screenwriter has difficulty adapting a non-fiction book about orchids, while his dunce of a brother works on a gimmicky serial-killer movie.

Impressively deft comedy about writer's block, hardly an inherently cinematic subject; the obsessive self-referentiality is rewarding and revealing, and the performances wonderful, though the deliberately clunky final act will strike some as a clever conceit too far.

SCR *Charlie Kaufman, Donald Kaufman*   CIN *Lance Acord*   MUS *Carter Burwell*   DES KK Barrett   ED Eric Zumbrunnen   PROD Edward Saxon, Vincent Landay, Jonathan Demme   DIST Columbia

66 Like no movie before it, Adaptation risks everything – its cool, its credibility, its very soul – to expose the horror of making art for the business of entertainment. – *Wesley Morris, Boston Globe*

66 Spellbindingly original – like the wild orchid, Adaptation is a marvel of adaptation, entwined with its hothouse environment and yet stunningly unique. – *Peter Rainer, New York Magazine*

† Both Charlie Kaufman and 'Donald Kaufman', his fictional brother in the film, were nominated for the Best Adapted Screenplay Oscar.

⚖ Chris Cooper (supporting actor)
⚖ Nicolas Cage (leading actor); Meryl Streep (supporting actress); Charlie Kaufman, Donald Kaufman (adapted screenplay)
Ⓑ adapted screenplay
Ⓣ Chris Cooper (supporting actor); Meryl Streep (supporting actress)

'Creepy. Kooky. Spooky. Ooky.'

The Addams Family ★

DIR Barry Sonnenfeld
1991   99m   US
DVD   ♫

☆ Anjelica Huston (Morticia Addams), Raul Julia (Gomez Addams), Christopher Lloyd (Uncle Fester / Gordon Craven), Dan Hedaya (Tully Alford, Addams' Attorney), Elizabeth Wilson (Abigail Craven / Dr. Greta Pinder-Schloss), Judith Malina (Grandma), Carel Struycken (Lurch), Dana Ivey (Margaret Alford / Margaret Addams), Christina Ricci (Wednesday Addams), Paul Benedict (Judge Womack), Christopher Hart (whose hand appears as The Thing)

Con artists try to fleece the Addams family, using an impostor who claims to be their long-lost Uncle Fester.

With the barest slip of a plot, it relies too much on interchangeable one-liners for laughs.

SCR Caroline Thompson, Larry Wilson   CIN Owen Roizman   MUS Marc Shaiman   DES *Richard MacDonald*   ED Dede Allen, Jim Miller   PROD Scott Rudin   DIST Columbia TriStar/Paramount/Orion

66 There are a lot of little smiles, and many chuckles and grins, but they don't add up to much. – *Roger Ebert, Chicago Sun-Times*

† A sequel, Addams Family Values, was released in 1993.

⚖ Ruth Myers (costume design)
Ⓣ Richard MacDonald (production design); makeup

DVD Available on DVD   ☆ Cast in order of importance   66 Critics' Quotes   † Points of interest   ⚖ Academy Award   ⚖ Academy Award nomination   Ⓑ BAFTA   Ⓣ BAFTA nomination   ♫ Soundtrack on CD

5

'The dark is their sunlight. What makes them different is what keeps them alive.'

The Addiction ★★

DIR *Abel Ferrara*

1995   82m   US

DVD

☆ Lili Taylor (Kathleen Conklin), Christoper Walken (Peina), Annabella Sciorra (Casanova), Edie Falco (Jean), Paul Calderon (Professor), Fredro Star (Black), Kathryn Erbe (Anthropology Student), Michael Imperioli (Missionary)

A New York philosophy student is bitten by a vampire, and discovers a new perspective on human evil.

A serious attempt to explore the metaphorical implications of bloodlust, invoking parallels to mass murder and the Holocaust; it risks crashing pretension in scene after scene, but the unnerving black-and-white imagery gives it a freaky charge.

SCR Nicholas St John   CIN Ken Kelsch   MUS Joe Delia   DES Charlie Lagola   ED Mayin Lo   PROD Denis Hann, Fernando Sulichin   DIST Guild/Fast Films

66 Macabre and provocative. – *Desson Howe, Washington Post*

66 It's mesmerising to watch Ferrara go for broke. – *Rolling Stone*

'Sex . . . Power . . . Obsession.'

The Adjuster ★★

SCR/DIR *Atom Egoyan*

1991   102m   Canada

DVD

☆ Elias Koteas (Noah Render), Arsinée Khanjian (Hera), Maury Chaykin (Bubba), Gabrielle Rose (Mimi), Jennifer Dale (Arianne), David Hemblen (Bert, the Head Censor), Rose Sarkisyan (Seta, Hera's Sister), Armen Kokorian (Simon, Hera's Child)

An insurance loss adjuster and his wife, a censor of pornographic videos, become involved with a couple who want to make a film in their house.

Intriguingly perverse art-house drama about characters who take a creepy interest in the lives of others.

CIN *Paul Sarossy*   MUS *Mychael Danna*   DES Linda Del Rosario, Richard Paris   ED Susan Shipton   PROD Atom Egoyan   DIST Metro/Ego Film Arts/Téléfilm Canada/Ontario Film Development Corp.

66 Finds strange comedy in familiar things. – *Roger Ebert, Chicago Sun-Times*

'After Kidulthood comes. . .'

Adulthood (new)

DIR Brian Tufano   SCR/DIR Noel Clarke

2008   99m   UK

☆ Noel Clarke (Sam Peel), Scarlett Alice Johnson (Lexi), Jacob Anderson (Omen), Ben 'Plan B" Drew (Dabs), Don Klass (Blammy), Adam Deacon (Jay), Danny Dyer (Hayden)

Six years on from the events of Kidulthood, a young killer leaves jail to find his old life returning to haunt him.

Earnest follow-up to a cult success that lacks the humour and vivacity of its predecessor.

MUS Chad Hobson   DES Murray McKeown   ED Tom Hemmings   PROD Damian Jones, George Isaac   DIST Pathe

66 Tense, tough, troubling. – *Simon Crook, Empire*

66 A vivid sequel-snapshot of yoof-life on the mean streets of West London. – *Jonathan Crocker, Total Film*

'Remarkable. Unbelievable. Impossible. And true.'

Adventures of Baron Munchausen ★

DIR Terry Gilliam

1988   126m   GB/West Germany

DVD   ♫

☆ John Neville (Hieronymus Karl Frederick Baron von Munchausen), Eric Idle (Desmond/ Berthold), Sarah Polley (Sally Salt), Oliver Reed (Vulcan), Charles McKeown (Rupert/Adolphus), Winston Dennis (Bill/ Albrecht), Jack Purvis (Jeremy/ Gustavus), Valentina Cortese (Queen Ariadne/ Violet), Jonathan Pryce (The Right Ordinary Horatio Jackson), Bill Paterson (Henry Salt), Peter Jeffrey (Sultan), Uma Thurman (Venus/Rose)

A 17th-century German aristocrat recounts his fantastical exploits.

A notorious flop in its day, this is one of those fitfully entertaining follies which seem dwarfed by its own spectacular production values.

SCR Charles McKeown, Terry Gilliam   CIN Giuseppe Rotunno   MUS Michael Kamen, Eric Idle   DES *Dante Ferretti*   ED Peter Hollywood   PROD Thomas Schühly   DIST Prominent Features/Laura Film/Columbia-Tri Star

66 A wondrous feat of imagination. In terms of sheer inventiveness, it makes the other movies around these days look paltry and underfed. The worlds Gilliam has created here are like the ones he created in his animations for Monty Python – they have a majestic peculiarity. And you're constantly amazed by the freshness and eccentricity of what is pushed in front of your eyes. – *Hal Hinson, Washington Post*

† The film went wildly over budget, and cost an estimated $46m. It grossed just $8m in the US.

⚖ Dante Ferretti; Gabriella Pescucci (costume design); Ricahrd Conway, Kent Houston (visual effects); Maggie Weston, Fabrizio Sforza (makeup)

🎭 Dante Ferretti; Gabriella Pescucci (costume design); Ricahrd Conway, Kent Houston (special visual effects); Maggie Weston, Fabrizio Sforza (makeup)

'Finally, a comedy that will change the way you think, the way you feel and, most importantly, the way you dress.'

The Adventures of Priscilla Queen of the Desert ★★

SCR/DIR *Stephan Elliott*

1994   104m   Australia

DVD   ♫

☆ *Terence Stamp* (Ralph / Bernadette Bassenger), Hugo Weaving (Anthony 'Tick' Belrose / Mitzi Del Bra), Guy

Pearce (Adam Whitely / Felicia Jollygoodfellow), Bill Hunter (Bob), Sarah Chadwick (Marion), Mark Holmes (Benji), Julia Cortez (Cynthia)

Two drag queens and a transsexual travel from Sydney to Alice Springs by bus for a cabaret gig.

An enjoyably bitchy road movie with vivid performances and a warmly inclusive spirit beneath all the squabbling.

CIN Brian J. Breheny   MUS Guy Gross   DES Owen Paterson   ED Sue Blainey   PROD Al Clark, Michael Hamlyn   DIST Rank/Polygram/AFFC/Latent Image/Specific Films

66 Presents a defiant culture clash in generous, warmly entertaining ways. – *Janet Maslin, New York Times*

66 A one-note pleasure. – *Desson Howe, Washington Post*

⚊ Lizzy Gardiner, Tim Chappell (costume design)

⬟ Stephan Elliot (original screenplay); Terence Stamp (leading actor); Brian J. Breheny (cinematography); make up/hair; Lizzy Gardiner, Tim Chappell (costume design); Guy Gross; production design

---

'Only the rainbow can duplicate its brilliance!'

The Adventures of Robin Hood ★★★★

DIR *William Keighley, Michael Curtiz*

1938   102m   US

DVD ♫

☆ *Errol Flynn* (Sir Robin of Locksley), *Basil Rathbone* (Sir Guy of Gisbourne), *Claude Rains* (Prince John), Olivia de Havilland (Maid Marian), *Alan Hale* (Little John), Patric Knowles (Will Scarlet), *Eugene Pallette* (Friar Tuck), *Ian Hunter* (King Richard), Melville Cooper (Sheriff of Nottingham), Una O'Connor (Bess), Herbert Mundin (Much the Miller's Son), Montagu Love (Bishop of Black Canons), Howard Hill (Captain of Archers)

Rebel outlaw Robin Hood outwits Guy of Gisborne and the Sheriff of Nottingham, and saves the throne for the absent King Richard.

A splendid adventure story, rousingly operatic in treatment, with dashing action highlights, fine comedy balance, and incisive acting all round. Historically notable for its use of early three-colour Technicolor; also for convincingly re-creating Britain in California.

SCR *Seton I. Miller, Norman Reilly Raine*   CIN *Tony Gaudio, Sol Polito, W. Howard Greene*   MUS *Erich Wolfgang Korngold*   ED *Ralph Dawson*   PROD *Hal B. Wallis*   DIST Warner

PRINCE JOHN: Any objections to the new tax, from our Saxon friends?

ROBIN TO GISBOURNE DURING DUEL: Did I upset your plans?

GISBOURNE: You've come to Nottingham once too often!

ROBIN: When this is over, my friend, there'll be no need for me to come again!

PRINCE JOHN: Ho, varlets, bring Sir Robin food! Such insolence must support a healthy appetite!

ROBIN: It's injustice I hate, not the Normans!

66 Magnificent, unsurpassable. . .the film is lavish, brilliantly photographed, and has a great Korngold score. – *NFT, 1974*

66 Mostly the picture is full of movement, some of it

---

dashing in fine romantic costume style, some of it just sprightly. The excitement comes from fast action – galloping steeds, men swinging Tarzan-like from the trees, hurling tables and chairs, rapid running swordplay, the sudden whiz of Robin's arrows coming from nowhere to startle his enemies – more than from any fear that Robin might be worsted. Somehow the whole thing has the air of being a costume party, a jolly and rather athletic one, with a lot of well-bred Englishmen playing at being in the greenwood. – *James Shelley Hamilton, National Board of Review*

† At the time of its release this was Warner's most expensive film, costing more than $2m. Chico, California, stood in for Sherwood Forest; the archery contest was shot at Busch Gardens, Pasadena. Curtiz took over direction when it was felt that the action lacked impact.

⚊ Erich Wolfgang Korngold; Carl Jules Weyl; Ralph Dawson
⚊ picture

Ae Fond Kiss ★★

DIR Ken Loach

2004   104m   GB/Italy/Germany/Spain/Belgium

☆ *Atta Yaqub* (Casim Khan), *Eva Birthistle* (Roisin Hanlon), *Ahmad Riaz* (Tariq Khan), Shabana Bakhsh (Tahara Khan), Shamshad Akhtar (Sadia Khan), Ghizala Avan (Rukhsana Khan), Pasha Bocarie (Amar), Gerard Kelly (Parish Priest)

A Pakistani DJ in Glasgow starts seeing an Irish Catholic music teacher.

A passionate and charmingly acted romance across divides of racism and misunderstanding; its social significance gets a little exhausting.

SCR Paul Laverty   CIN Barry Ackroyd   MUS George Fenton   DES Martin Johnson   ED Jonathan Morris   PROD Rebecca O'Brien

66 English-language East–West domestic dramas usually tip the scales in favor of modernity. . .But Ae Fond Kiss is equally sympathetic to each side. – *Stephen Holden, New York Times*

† The film's title is a phrase from a poem by Robert Burns.

'Wade Whitehouse is frightened to death of following in his father's footsteps.'

Affliction ★★

SCR/DIR Paul Schrader

1997   114m   US

DVD ♫

☆ *Nick Nolte* (Wade Whitehouse), Sissy Spacek (Margie Fogg), *James Coburn* (Glen Whitehouse), Willem Dafoe (Rolfe Whitehouse), Mary Beth Hurt (Lillian Whitehouse Horner), Jim True (Jack Hewitt), Marian Seldes (Alma Pittman), Holmes Osborne (Gordon LaRiviere), Brigid Tierney (Jill Whitehouse), Sean McCann (Evan Twombley), Wayne Robson (Nick Wickham)

A small-town sheriff in wintry New Hampshire finds himself inexorably following in the footsteps of his vicious, alcoholic father.

A potentially depressing tract about the sins of the father, elevated to searing drama by an outstanding lead performance; Schrader's direction can be a little on the remote side, but the bleak psychology is socked home.

CIN *Paul Sarossy*   MUS Michael Brook   DES Anne

DVD Available on DVD   ☆ Cast in order of importance   66 Critics' Quotes   ⚊ Academy Award   ⬟ BAFTA
♫ Soundtrack on CD   † Points of interest   ⚊ Academy Award nomination   ⬟ BAFTA nomination

7

Pritchard   ED Jay Rabinowitz   PROD Linda Reisman
DIST Largo

66 Affliction is a harsh experience, but the harshness isn't a matter of punishing the audience or of the director, Schrader, showing off his toughness: That unvarnished harshness is the very essence of the material. – *Charles Taylor, Salon.com*

⚱ James Coburn (supporting actor)
⚱ Nick Nolte (leading actor)

'You can't escape what you can't see.'

Afraid of the Dark ★

SCR/DIR Mark Peploe
1991   91m   GB/France
DVD

☆ James Fox (Frank), Fanny Ardant (Miriam), Paul McGann (Tony Dalton), Clare Holman (Rose), Ben Keyworth (Lucas)

A policeman attempts to protect his small son and his blind wife from a psychotic criminal who attacks women.

This psychological thriller has a twist of sorts, though it trades in an eerie, uneasy atmosphere rather than specific shocks. Still, a stylish, intelligent exercise.

SCR Frederick Seidel   CIN Bruno de Keyzer
MUS Richard Hartley   DES Caroline Ames   ED Scott Thomas   PROD Simon Bosanquet
DIST Rank/Sovereign/Telescope/Les Films Ariane/Cine Cinq

66 There's a faint academicism at work which militates against real suspense. – *Geoff Andrew, Time Out*

'They never dreamed of being in each other's arms, yet the mystic spell of the jungle swept them to primitive, hungry embrace! The greatest adventure a man ever had. . .with a woman!'

The African Queen ★★★

DIR *John Huston*
1951   103m   GB
DVD

☆ *Humphrey Bogart* (Charlie Allnutt), *Katharine Hepburn* (Rose Sayer), Robert Morley (The Rev. Samuel Sayer), Peter Bull (Captain), Theodore Bikel (2nd Officer)

In 1915, a gin-drinking river trader and a prim missionary make odd companions for a boat trip down a dangerous river, culminating in an attack on a German gunboat.

Despite some unfortunate studio sets mixed in with real African footage, achieved through great hardship by all concerned, this is one of those surprising films that really work: a splendidly successful mixture of comedy, character and adventure.

SCR *James Agee*   CIN *Jack Cardiff*   MUS Allan Gray
ED Ralph Kemplen   PROD Sam Spiegel
DIST IFD/Romulus-Horizon

ROSE: I never dreamed that any experience could be so stimulating!

66 Entertaining but not entirely plausible or original. – *Robert Hatch*

66 The movie is not great art but it is great fun, essentially one long, exciting, old-fashioned movie chase. – *Time*

† Peter Viertel's book, White Hunter Black Heart, filmed by Clint Eastwood, is basically about Huston during the making of this film.

⚱ Humphrey Bogart (leading actor)
⚱ Katharine Hepburn (leading actress); John Huston (direction); James Agee (screenplay)

'Seduced Beyond The Limits Of Deception. Betrayed Beyond The Limits Of Desire.'

After Dark, My Sweet ★

DIR James Foley
1990   114m   US
DVD   ♫

☆ Jason Patric (Kevin 'Kid' Collins), Rachel Ward (Fay Anderson), Bruce Dern (Garrett 'Uncle Bud' Stoker), George Dickerson (Doc Goldman), James Cotton (Charlie)

An ex-boxer with mental problems falls in with a widow and an ex-cop, and they plan the kidnapping of a rich youngster.

Not the most successful Jim Thompson adaptation, uninvitingly cast and baggily plotted; but the noir atmospherics are some consolation.

SCR Bob Redlin   CIN Mark Plummer   MUS Maurice Jarre   DES David Brisbin   ED Howard Smith
PROD Ric Kidney, Bob Redlin   DIST Virgin/Avenue

† Other films from Thompson's novels include both versions of The Getaway, The Grifters and Coup de torchon.

'What Is The One Memory You Would Take With You?'

After Life ★★★

SCR/DIR *Hirokazu Kore-Eda*
1998   118m   Japan
DVD

☆ Arata (Takashi Mochizuki), Erika Oda (Shiori Satonaka), Susumu Terajima (Satoru Kawashima), Taketoshi Naito (Ichiro Watanabe), Kyoko Kagawa (Kyoko Watanabe), Kei Tani (Ken-nosuke Nakamura), Takashi Naito (Takuro Sugie), Sadao Abe (Ichiro Watanabe, as student)

The recently dead are allowed to take one memory into eternity, which is re-created for them on film at a special counselling facility.

Elegant premise, elegantly handled, with traces of the Albert Brooks comedy Defending Your Life. The film is full of poignant melancholy and unexpected humour.

CIN Yutaka Yamazaki, Masayoshi Sukita   MUS Yasuhiro Kasamatsu   DES Hideo Gunji, Toshihiro Isomi
ED Hirokazu Kore-Eda   PROD Shiho Sato, Masayuki Akieda   DIST ICA

66 Slyly humorous, utterly original and generous-hearted. – *Derek Elley, Variety*

'Champagne is poured. . .secrets are spilled.'

After the Wedding ★★

DIR Susanne Bier
2006   120m   Denmark/UK/Sweden
DVD   ♫

☆ Mads Mikkelsen (Jacob), Rolf Lassgård (Jorgen), Sidse Babett Knudsen (Hélène)

DVD Available on DVD   ☆ Cast in order of importance   66 Critics' Quotes   ⚱ Academy Award   BAFTA
♫ Soundtrack on CD   † Points of interest   ⚱ Academy Award nomination   BAFTA nomination

A Danish aid worker in India is invited to Copenhagen by a tycoon, who promises him a fortune for his cash-strapped orphanage. Invited to the tycoon's daughter's wedding, he realises that her mother is his ex-lover.

Intriguing film that unfolds faster than it should – too many life-changing incidents occur over the space of a weekend. This brings it awfully close to soap opera, but the quality of the acting and the story's themes redeem it.

SCR Susanne Bier, Anders Thomas Jensen   CIN Morten Søborg   MUS Johan Soderqvist   DES Søren Skjær   ED Pernille Bech Christensen, Morten Hølbjerg   PROD Sisse Graum Jørgensen   DIST Soda

66 A thrilling – and harrowing, and beautiful – celebration of the unpredictability of life. – *Joe Morgenstern, Wall Street Journal*

⚱ Foreign language film

Afterglow ★

SCR/DIR Alan Rudolph
1997   119m   US
DVD   ♫

☆ *Julie Christie* (Phyllis Mann), Nick Nolte (Lucky Mann), Lara Flynn Boyle (Marianne Byron), Jonny Lee Miller (Jeffrey Byron)

Two dissatisfied couples in Montreal seek solace in infidelity with each other.

Odd, elusive and frustrating study of floundering relationships and lost love, in which only Christie truly rises above the wispy material.

CIN Toyomichi Kurita   MUS Mark Isham   DES François Séguin   ED Suzy Elmiger   PROD Robert Altman   DIST Entertainment/Moonstone/Sandcastle 5/Elysian Dreams

66 Christie radiates a mature sexuality that's a rare treat. – *Walter Addiego, San Francisco Examiner*

⚱ Julie Christie (leading actress)

'In a world of tradition. In an age of innocence. They dared to break the rules.'

The Age of Innocence ★★

DIR Martin Scorsese
1993   139m   US
DVD   ♫

☆ Daniel Day-Lewis (Newland Archer), *Michelle Pfeiffer* (Ellen Olenska), Winona Ryder (May Welland), Richard E. Grant (Larry Lefferts), Alec McCowen (Sillerton Jackson), Geraldine Chaplin (Mrs. Welland), Mary Beth Hurt (Regina Beaufort), Stuart Wilson (Julius Beaufort), Miriam Margolyes (Mrs. Mingott), Sian Phillips (Mrs. Archer), Michael Gough (Henry van der Luyden), Alexis Smith (Louisa van der Luyden), Jonathan Pryce (Rivière), Robert Sean Leonard (Ted Archer)

A wealthy lawyer in 1870s New York falls scandalously in love with his wife's cousin, the disreputable wife of a Polish count.

Handsome but oddly muted, the film succeeds as a gorgeously costumed recreation of its era, but fails on the level of adaptation: it feels corseted by its own design, and the emotional agony of the story doesn't fully come through, even in the performances.

SCR Jay Cocks, Martin Scorsese   CIN *Michael Ballhaus*   MUS *Elmer Bernstein*   DES *Dante Ferretti*   ED *Thelma Schoonmaker*   PROD Barbara de Fina   DIST Columbia

66 A gravely beautiful fairy tale of longing and loss. – *Richard Corliss, Time*

66 As beautifully mounted as this production is, Scorsese has a habit of letting the decor take over, so that Wharton's tale of societal constraints comes over only in fits and starts. But it's a noble failure. – *Jonathan Rosenbaum, Chicago Reader*

† Its release was delayed for almost 12 months to allow Scorsese and his editor Thelma Schoonmaker to complete the film as they desired.

⚱ Winona Ryder (supporting actress); Jay Cocks, Martin Scorsese (adapted screenplay); Elmer Bernstein (music); Dante Ferretti (art direction); Gabriella Pescucci (costume design)

Ⓑ Miriam Margolyes (supporting actress)
Ⓣ Winona Ryder (supporting actress); Dante Ferretti; Michael Ballhaus

Aguirre, Wrath of God ★★★★

SCR/DIR *Werner Herzog*
1972   95m   West Germany
DVD   ♫

☆ *Klaus Kinski* (Don Lope de Aguirre), Ruy Guerra (Don Pedro de Ursua), Helena Rojo (Inez), Cecilia Rivera (Flores), Del Negro (Brother Gaspar de Carvajal), Peter Berling (Don Fernando de Guzman), Alejandro Repulles (Gonzalez Pizarro)

In 1560 in the Andes, the lieutenant of a Spanish conquistador, searching for the lost city of El Dorado, takes a 40-strong party down river by raft, and in a fever, suffers delusions of grandeur.

Absorbing melodrama, vividly assembled and impossible to forget.

CIN Thomas Mauch   MUS Popol Vuh   ED Beate Mainka-Jellinghaus   DIST Hessicher Rundfunk/Werner Herzog

66 It ingeniously combines Herzog's gift for deep irony, his strong social awareness, and his worthy ambition to fashion a whole new visual perspective on the world around us via mystical, evocative, yet oddly direct imagery. It is a brilliant cinematic achievement. – *David Sterritt, Christian Science Monitor*

† Director Herzog's relationship with his leading man declined to the extent of threatening to shoot Kinski if he quit the unfinished film.

Aileen: Life and Death of a Serial Killer ★★★

DIR *Nick Broomfield, Joan Churchill*
2003   89m   GB/US
DVD

The final days of Aileen Wuornos, America's most notorious female serial killer, as she sabotages her own appeal on the eve of execution.

DVD Available on DVD	☆ Cast in order of importance	66 Critics' Quotes	⚱ Academy Award
♫ Soundtrack on CD		† Points of interest	⚱ Academy Award nomination

Ⓑ BAFTA
Ⓣ BAFTA nomination

9

The second of Broomfield's documentaries about Wuornos, and one of the strongest pieces of work in his long career; a stark and upsetting close-up portrait which raises serious doubts about the quality of psychiatric assessment for those on Death Row.

CIN Joan Churchill   **MUS** Rob Lane   **ED** Claire Ferguson
PROD Jo Human

66 Immensely moving. – *Manohla Dargis, New York Times*

† Charlize Theron won an Oscar for playing Wuornos in the biopic Monster (2004).

Un Air de Famille ★

DIR Cédric Klapisch
1996   110m   France
[DVD]   ♫

☆ Jean-Pierre Bacri (Henri), Jean-Pierre Darroussin (Denis), Catherine Frot (Yolande), Agnès Jaoui (Betty), Claire Maurier (the Mother), Wladimir Yordanoff (Philippe)

A fractured French family get together for a reunion in a Paris café to bury several hatchets, but three siblings refuse to shoulder the blame for their own failings.

Witty family drama with delightful dialogue – an early example of the Jaoui-Bacri writing team's way with words – and generally superior acting.

SCR Agnès Jaoui, Jean-Pierre Bacri, Cédric Klapisch
CIN Benoît Delhomme   **MUS** Philippe Eidel
DES François Emmanuelli   **ED** Francine Sandberg
PROD Charles Gassot
DIST Metro/Tartan/Téléma/Canal/France2

66 The film was shot on the dark side, and viewers may find themselves squinting, but every character lights up the screen in funny ways making Un Air de Famille an affectionate glimpse at humankind. – *Peter Stack, San Francisco Chronicle*

'To err is human. To air guitar, divine.'

Air Guitar Nation (new) ★

DIR Alexandra Lipsitz
2007   81m   US
[DVD]

☆ David 'C-Diddy' Jung (Himself), Dan 'Björn Türoque' Crane (Himself), Gordon 'Krye Tuff' Hintz (Himself)

Two rock fans compete to represent America at the World Air Guitar Championships in Finland.

Agreeably daft documentary that's in on its own joke; even at this slender length, though, it starts to wear thin.

CIN Anthony Sacco   **MUS** Dan Crane   **ED** Conor O'Neill, Clark Vogeler   **PROD** Dan Cutforth, Jane Lipsitz, Anna Barber   **DIST** Contender

DAVID 'C-DIDDY' JUNG: 'I never fear the audience. . .I fear for the audience.'

66 The wild performances and droll humour are tough to resist. – *Matt Zoller Seitz, New York Times*

66 Despite the film's admirable brevity it's still hard to maintain a wry ironic grin for a full 81 minutes. – *Kevin Maher, The Times*

'Sometimes the things we can't change end up changing us.'

The Air I Breathe (new)

DIR Jieho Lee
2007   95m   Mexico/US

☆ Kevin Bacon (Love), Julie Delpy (Gina), Brendan Fraser (Pleasure), Andy Garcia (Fingers), Sarah Michelle Gellar (Sorrow), Emile Hirsch (Tony), Forest Whitaker (Happiness)

Four strangers – a gambling businessman, a psychic hit-man, a singer and a doctor – find their lives intersecting.

Pretentious crime drama, divided into four sections and governed by preposterous contrivance.

SCR Jieho Lee, Bob DeRosa   **CIN** Walt Lloyd
MUS Marcello Zarvos   **DES** Bernardo Trujillo
ED Robert Hoffman   **PROD** Emilio Diez Barroso, Darlene Caamano Loquet, Paul Schiff   **DIST** Pathe

HAPPINESS: 'When a butterfly leaves the safety of its cocoon, does it realise how beautiful it has become? Or does it still just see itself as a caterpillar?'

66 A flashy example of the everything-is-connected mode of filmmaking embodied by movies like Short Cuts, Crash and Babel. – *Stephen Holden, New York Times*

66 A stew of cheap irony, ponderous but meaningless allegory, violence and pretension. – *Carina Chocano, Los Angeles Times*

† The film is based on a Chinese proverb that says happiness, pleasure, sorrow and love are the four cornerstones of life.

† Entirely shot in Mexico City.

The Air Up There ★

DIR Paul M. Glaser
1994   107m   US
[DVD]   ♫

☆ Kevin Bacon (Jimmy Dolan), Charles Gitonga Maina (Saleh), Yolanda Vasquez (Sister Susan), Winston Ntshona (Urudu), Mabutho 'Kid' Sithole (Nyaga), Sean McCann (Ray Fox), Dennis Patrick (Father O'Hara), Nigel Miguel (Halawi), Ilo Mitumbo (Mifundo)

In Africa, a US basketball coach wants to sign up a new star, and must train a local team to win a game as part of the deal.

Underrated, sweet-natured sports comedy, with a different slant and an agreeable message about values and perspective.

SCR Max Apple   **CIN** Dick Pope   **MUS** David Newman
DES Roger Hall, Brent Thomas   **ED** Michael E. Polakow, Tom McMurtry   **PROD** Ted Field, Rosalie Swedlin, Robert W. Cort   **DIST** Buena Vista/Hollywood/Interscope/Polygram

'Neo-Tokyo is about to E.X.P.L.O.D.E.'

Akira ★★★

DIR Katsuhiro Otomo
1988   124m   Japan
[DVD]   ♫

☆ Mitsuo Iwata (Shôtarô Kaneda (voice)), Nozomu Sasaki (Tetsuo Shima (voice)), Mami Koyama (Kei (voice)),

[DVD] Available on DVD   ☆ Cast in order   66 Critics' Quotes   ↓ Academy Award   🇺 BAFTA
♫ Soundtrack on CD   of importance   † Points of interest   ↓ Academy Award nomination   🇺 BAFTA nomination

Tetsusho Genda (Ryûsaku (voice)), Hiroshi Ôtake (Nezu (voice))

A gang of slum kids in post-apocalyptic Tokyo band together to counter the scheming of a friend turned bad.

Stunningly executed animated film, adapted from a comic-strip, that generates so much audience adrenalin that the uneven narrative is easy to overlook.

SCR Katsuhiro Otomo, Izo Hashimoto   CIN Katsuji Misawa   MUS Shoji Yamashiro   DES Koji Ohno, Yuji Ikehata, Kazuo Ebisawa   ED Takeshi Seyama   PROD Ryohei Suzuki, Shunzo Kato, Haruyo Kanesaku, Hiroe Tsukamoto   DIST ICA/Akira Committee

66 Simply put, no Akira, no Matrix. It's that important. – *Kim Newman, Empire*

66 A phenomenal work of animation with all the hallmarks of an instant cult classic. – *Janet Maslin, New York Times*

'The past, present, and future. The thoughts and images of one man. . .for all men. One man's dreams. . .for every dreamer.'

Akira Kurosawa's Dreams   ★

SCR/DIR Akira Kurosawa
1990   119m   US/Japan
[DVD]

☆ Mitsuko Baisho (Mother of 'I'), Toshihiko Nakano ('I' as a young child), Mitsunori Isaki ('I' as a boy), Mie Suzuki ('I''s sister), Akira Terao (I), Mieko Harada (The Snow Fairy), Yoshitaka Zushi (Pvt. Noguchi), Martin Scorsese (Vincent Van Gogh), Chosuke Ikariya (The crying demon), Chishu Ryu (Old Man)

Eight short sequences based on actual dreams of the master director. They're linked by a concern for the environment, though the standout is the dream about the paintings of Vincent Van Gogh.

Kurosawa was 80 years old when he directed this minor offering, which has delightful moments – and in the case of the Van Gogh film, a startlingly vivid colour palette.

CIN Takao Saito, Masaharu Ueda   MUS Shinichiro Ikebe   DES Akira Sakuragi, Yoshirô Muraki   ED Tome Minami   PROD Hisao Kurosawa, Mike Y. Inoue   DIST Warner/Akira Kurosawa USA

66 Dreams will knock your eyes out without ignoring the mind and heart. – *Peter Travers, Rolling Stone*

'Imagine if you had three wishes, three hopes, three dreams and they all could come true.'

Aladdin   ★★★

DIR John Musker, Ron Clements
1992   90m   US
[DVD]   ♫

☆ Voices of: Scott Weinger (Aladdin), Brad Kane (Aladdin's singing), Robin Williams (Genie), Linda Larkin (Jasmine), Lea Salonga (Jasmine's singing), Jonathan Freeman (Jafar), Frank Welker (Abu/Narrator), Gilbert Gottfried (Iago), Douglas Seale (Sultan)

A street urchin discovers a magic lamp which allows him the win the favour of a princess.

Splendidly spry and enjoyable romp, a return to near-peak form for Disney which lets loose Robin Williams's improvisatory flair in the role of the Genie, while showing off some great animation. But it's a shame about the songs.

SCR John Musker, Ron Clements, Ted Elliott, Terry Rossio   MUS Alan Menken   DES R.S. Vander Wende   ED H. Lee Peterson, Mark A. Hester   PROD John Musker, Ron Clements   DIST Buena Vista/Walt Disney

66 Floridly beautiful, shamelessly derivative and infused with an irreverent, sophisticated comic flair. – *Variety*

66 A rollicking, bodaciously choreographed fantasy right out of Busby Berkeley. – *Rita Kempley, Washington Po*

† It was followed by two sequels released direct to video: Return of Jafar, edited from an animated TV series, and Aladdin and the King of Thieves.

⚊ Alan Menken (music, original score); Alan Menken (m), Tim Rice (ly) (music, original song – Whole New World)

⚊ Alan Menken (m), Howard Ashman (ly) (music original song – Friends like Me); Terry Porter, Mel Metcalfe, David J. Hudson, Doc Kane (sound); Mark A. Mangini (sound effects editing)

Ⓣ Alan Menken; Don Paul, Steve Goldberg (special effects)

'Deliberate sacrifice for deliberate gain.'

Albino Alligator   ★

DIR Kevin Spacey
1996   97m   US/France
[DVD]

☆ Matt Dillon (Dova), Faye Dunaway (Janet), Gary Sinise (Milo), William Fichtner (Law), Viggo Mortensen (Guy), John Spencer (Jack), Skeet Ulrich (Danny), M. Emmet Walsh (Dino), Joe Mantegna (G.D. Browning)

In this hostage thriller, three members of an amateurish gang hole themselves up in an all-night bar while armed police outside wait for them to surrender.

It feels more like a play than a film, with a single main location, overwrought dialogue and theatrical flourishes. But it's enjoyable watching the ensemble cast strut their stuff.

SCR Christian Forte   CIN Mark Plummer   MUS Michael Brook   DES Nelson Coates   ED Jay Cassidy   PROD Brad Krevoy, Steve Stabler, Brad Jenkel   DIST Miramax/UGC DA/Motion Picture Corp

66 The tension revs along nicely and – if you're not heisted out already – there's some suspense to be had. – *Kim Newman, Empire*

'Fortune favors the bold.'

Alexander

DIR Oliver Stone
2004   175m   France/GB/Netherlands/Germany/Italy
[DVD]   ♫

☆ Colin Farrell (Alexander), Angelina Jolie (Olympias), Val Kilmer (Philip), Christopher Plummer (Aristotle), Jared Leto (Hephaistion), Rosario Dawson (Roxane), Anthony Hopkins (Old Ptolemy), Jonathan Rhys Meyers (Cassander), Brian Blessed (Wrestling trainer), Tim Pigott-Smith (Omen Reader)

The life, loves and campaigns of Alexander the Great, as recounted by the elder Ptolemy.

[DVD] Available on DVD   ☆ Cast in order of importance   66 Critics' Quotes   ⚊ Academy Award   Ⓣ BAFTA
♫ Soundtrack on CD   † Points of interest   ⚊ Academy Award nomination   Ⓣ BAFTA nomination

11

Bloated, sometimes spectacular, but chronically embarrassing cod-epic, portraying its hero as a neurotic driven by his demons – but driven more often to tantrums and camp histrionics than feats of conquest. The soporific narration and near-universal miscasting don't help.

SCR Oliver Stone, Christopher Kyle, Laeta Kalogridis. CIN *Rodrigo Prieto* MUS Vangelis DES Jan Roelfs ED Tom Nordberg, Yann Herve, Alex Marquez, Gladys Joujou PROD Thomas Schuhly, Jon Kilik, Iain Smith, Moritz Borman DIST Warner

66 There's something overbearing, almost bullying, about this abbreviated tour through a decade-long campaign, pinpointing loud, emotional moments rather than dramatically satisfying ones. – *Ian Nathan, Empire*

66 A monument to egomania – and I don't mean Alexander's. – *Michael Sragow, Baltimore Sun*

† The film cost an estimated $155m and took $34m at the US box office.

† A director's cut was released on DVD, trimming eight minutes from the running time and removing some of the overt hints of homosexuality.

† Though Jolie is cast as Farrell's mother, the two actors were born less than a year apart.

Alexander Nevsky ★★★★

DIR *Sergei Eisenstein*
1938 112m USSR
DVD ♫

☆ *Nikolai Cherkassov* (Prince Alexander Yaroslavich Nevsky), Nikolai Okhlopkov (Vassily Buslai), Andrei Abrikosov (Gavrilo Olexich), Dmitri Orlov (Ignat, Master Armourer), Vasili Novikov (Pavsha, Governor of Pskov)

In 1242, Prince Alexander Nevsky defeats the invading Teutonic Knights in a battle on the ice of Lake Peipus.

A splendid historical pageant which shows the director at his most inventively pictorial, and climaxes in a superb battle sequence using music instead of natural sound.

SCR Pyotr Pavlenko, Sergei Eisenstein CIN *Edouard Tissé* MUS *Sergei Prokofiev* DIST Mosfilm

66 The picture will meet with good results wherever its political sentiments find established adherents. Otherwise it's almost nil for general appeal. – *Variety*

66 Superb sequences of cinematic opera that pass from pastoral to lamentation and end in a triumphal cantata. – *Georges Sadoul*

'What's it all about?'

Alfie ★★

DIR Charles Shyer
2004 103m US/GB
DVD ♫

☆ Jude Law (Alfie), Marisa Tomei (Julie), Omar Epps (Marlon), Nia Long (Lonette), Jane Krakowski (Dorie), Sienna Miller (Nikki), Susan Sarandon (Liz)

A laddish Cockney limo driver in Manhattan learns the down-side of his lothario ways.

Far from the disaster many expected – though the attempt to update 1960s sexual politics is decidedly superficial, it's engaging and even touching on its own terms.

SCR Elaine Pope, Charles Shyer CIN *Ashley Rowe* MUS Mick Jagger, David A. Stewart, John Powell DES Sophie Becher ED Padraic Mckinley PROD Elaine Pope, Charles Shyer DIST Paramount

66 Breezy, sexy romp with a conscience that reflects in obvious but interesting ways on societal changes over the intervening 38 years. – *Todd McCarthy, Variety*

66 Doesn't chase social significance, it just wants us to have a good time. – *Manohla Dargis, New York Times*

Alfie ★★

DIR Lewis Gilbert
1966 114m GB
DVD ♫

☆ *Michael Caine*, Vivien Merchant, Shirley Anne Field, Millicent Martin, Jane Asher, Julia Foster, *Shelley Winters*, Eleanor Bron, Denholm Elliott

A Cockney Lothario is proud of his amorous conquests, but near-tragedy finally makes him more mature.

Garish sex comedy, an immense box-office success because of its frankness and an immaculate performance from its star.

SCR *Bill Naughton* CIN Otto Heller MUS Sonny Rollins PROD Lewis Gilbert DIST Paramount

66 Paramount thought it was a good bet because it was going to be made for $500,000, normally the sort of money spent on executives' cigar bills. – *Lewis Gilbert*

† The film was re-made in 2004, set in New York and starring Jude Law as a cockney chauffeur.

♪ picture; Bill Naughton; Michael Caine (leading actor); Vivien Merchant (supporting actress); Burt Bacharach (m), Hal David (ly) (music, original song – Alfie)

♣ Vivien Merchant (leading actress)

'He Shook Up The World.'

Ali ★★

DIR Michael Mann
2001 157m US
DVD ♫

☆ *Will Smith* (Cassius Clay/Muhammad Ali), Jamie Foxx (Drew 'Bundini' Brown), Jon Voight (Howard Cosell), Mario Van Peebles (Malcolm X), Ron Silver (Angelo Dundee), Jeffrey Wright (Howard Bingham), Mykelti Williamson (Don King), Jada Pinkett Smith (Sonji), Nona Gaye (Belinda), Michael Michele (Veronica), Joe Morton (Chauncy Eskridge), Giancarlo Esposito (Cassius Clay Sr), LeVar Burton (Martin Luther King Jr), Albert Hall (Elijah Muhammad)

Biopic spanning the ten years during which Muhammad Ali became world heavyweight boxing champion, lost the title for draft evasion, and then regained it in the 'Rumble in the Jungle' against George Foreman.

Respectable and engrossing, but never wholly enlightening biopic, buoyed up by Smith's charisma and Mann's sequence-to-sequence technique; but given

DVD Available on DVD ☆ Cast in order 66 Critics' Quotes ♪ Academy Award ♣ BAFTA
♫ Soundtrack on CD of importance † Points of interest ♪ Academy Award nomination ♥ BAFTA nomination

its considerable length the movie feels oddly sketchy and incomplete.

SCR Stephen J. Rivele, Christopher Wilkinson, Eric Roth, Michael Mann CIN *Emmanuel Lubezki* MUS *Lisa Gerrard, Pieter Bourke* DES John Myhre ED *William Goldenberg, Stephen Rivkin, Lynzee Klingman, Stuart Waks* PROD Jon Peters, James Lassiter, Paul Ardaji, Michael Mann, A. Kitman Ho DIST Columbia

66 Quite accomplished but finally distant. – *Kenneth Turan, Los Angeles Times*

66 To show Ali being scared is a blasphemy quite alien to this handsomely mounted hagiography. – *Peter Bradshaw, Guardian*

Will Smith (leading actor); Jon Voight (supporting actor)

Alice ★

SCR/DIR Woody Allen
1990 102m US
DVD

☆ Mia Farrow (Alice Tate), Joe Mantegna (Joe), Alec Baldwin (Ed), Blythe Danner (Dorothy), Judy Davis (Vicki), William Hurt (Doug Tate), Keye Luke (Dr Yang), Bernadette Peters (Muse), Cybill Shepherd (Nancy Brill), Gwen Verdon (Alice's mother)

A frustrated, underachieving housewife contemplates an affair and lets her fantasies wander.

Chamber piece with Farrow centre stage as a rich man's wife longing to find herself. Unhappily, the performances around her are all more compelling than her own. Great things were still automatically expected of Allen back then, so this was counted a disappointment. Yet in retrospect it has its amusing moments.

CIN Carlo di Palma DES Santo Loquasto ED Susan E. Morse PROD Robert Greenhut DIST Orion/Jack Rollins, Charles H. Joffe

66 It is hilarious and romantic, serious and exuberantly satiric. – *Vincent Canby, New York Times*

original screenplay

Alice ★★

SCR/DIR *Jan Svankmajer*
1988 86m GB/Switzerland/West Germany
DVD

☆ Kristyna Kohoutova (Alice)

An animated version of Lewis Carroll's story that takes Alice into Wonderland.

Modern-day version that blends live action with animation, introducing dark and occasionally erotic elements into the story. Ironically, all this brings it close in spirit to Carroll's original work.

CIN Svatoluk Maly DES Jan Svankmajer ED Marie Drvotova PROD Peter-Christian Fueter DIST Condor-Hessisches/SRG/Film Four

66 Though [Jan Svankmajer] strips away all sweetness and light, he does not violate Lewis Carroll's story. – *Caryn James, New York Times*

'In space, no one can hear you scream!'

Alien ★★★★

DIR *Ridley Scott*
1979 117m GB
DVD ♫

☆ Tom Skerritt (Dallas), *Sigourney Weaver (Ripley), John Hurt (Kane)*, Veronica Cartwright (Lambert), Harry Dean Stanton (Brett), Ian Holm (Ash), Yaphet Kotto (Parker)

Astronauts returning to Earth visit an apparently dead planet and are infected by a violent being with unpredictable behaviour patterns, which starts to eliminate them one by one.

One of director Scott's career highlights: a terrific-looking, genuinely scary story in a claustrophobic space. It's both a horror flick and a sci-fi B-movie, set in space. The moment when the legendary H.R. Giger's creature first makes its appearance is a classic movie moment.

SCR Dan O'Bannon CIN *Derek Vanlint* MUS Jerry Goldsmith DES *Michael Seymour* ED Terry Rawlings, Peter Weatherley PROD Walter Hill, Gordon Carroll, David Giler DIST TCF

66 A sort of inverse relationship to The Thing invites unfavourable comparisons. – *Sight & Sound*

66 Empty bag of tricks whose production values and expensive trickery cannot disguise imaginative poverty. – *Time Out*

† This was the first of four related films, all featuring Sigourney Weaver: Aliens, Alien3 and Alien Resurrection.

H. R. Giger, Carlo Rambaldi and others (visual effects)
art direction

Michael Seymour (production design)

'It's been more than 200 years. . .The beginning has just started.'

Alien Resurrection ★★

DIR Jean-Pierre Jeunet
1997 109m US
DVD ♫

☆ *Sigourney Weaver (Ellen Ripley)*, Winona Ryder (Annalee Call), Ron Perlman (Johner), Dominique Pinon (Vriess), Michael Wincott (Frank Elgyn), Dan Hedaya (Gen. Martin Perez), Gary Dourdan (Christie), Kim Flowers (Sabra Hillard), J.E. Freeman (Dr. Mason Wren), Brad Dourif (Dr. Jonathan Gediman)

A clone of Ellen Ripley tries to prevent the alien species reaching Earth, despite having hybrid DNA that makes her part-monster.

Nice try at reviving the franchise, with some nifty conceits, stylish sequences and a star having the time of her life; but it becomes disappointingly generic in the second half.

SCR Joss Whedon CIN *Darius Khondji* MUS John Frizzell DES *Nigel Phelps* ED Herve Schneid PROD Bill Badalato, Gordon Carroll, David Giler, Walter Hill DIST TCF/Brandywine

66 Weaver battles slimy monsters with a command only enhanced by middle age. – *Lisa Schwarzbaum, Entertainment Weekly*

66 The filmmaker's ghoulishly fecund imagination makes this tale so murky that even the screen's toughest woman

DVD Available on DVD   ☆ Cast in order   66 Critics' Quotes   Academy Award   BAFTA
♫ Soundtrack on CD   of importance   † Points of interest   Academy Award nomination   BAFTA nomination

13

warrior remains largely stuck in the mud. – *Janet Maslin, New York Times*

Aliens ★★

DIR James Cameron
1986 137m US
DVD ♫

☆ Sigourney Weaver, Carrie Henn, Michael Biehn, Paul Reiser

The sole survivor of the space team in Alien goes back with a Marine squadron to the mystery planet, and finds more monsters.

James Cameron took over the directing reins from Ridley Scott for this second film, and Sigourney Weaver established herself as the series star. This was a vastly different, and more expensive film than its predecessor: with its dialogue-heavy first half setting up the relentless action of the remainder – a fight to the death between the aliens and their human adversaries. Well-executed and technically brilliant, if not as memorable as Scott's effort.

SCR James Cameron, Walter Hill, David Giler CIN Adrian Biddle MUS James Horner DES Peter Lamont ED Ray Lovejoy PROD Gale Anne Hurd DIST TCF/Brandywine

66 Audiences will be riveted to their seats with drooling dread in anticipation of the next horrifying attack. – *Variety*

66 I'm giving the movie a high rating for its skill and professionalism, and because it does the job it says it will do. I am also advising you not to eat before you see it. – *Roger Ebert*

† A 'director's cut' version of the film runs an extra 17 minutes.

⚐ Robert Skotak, Stan Winston, John Richardson, Suzanne Benson (special visual effects)

⚐ Sigourney Weaver (leading actress); music; production design; Ray Lovejoy

'This Christmas there will be no peace on Earth.'

Aliens vs. Predator - Requiem (new) ★

DIR Colin Strause, Greg Strause
2007 86m US
♫

☆ Steven Pasquale (Dallas), Reiko Aylesworth (Kelly), John Ortiz (Morales), Johnny Lewis (Ricky), Ariel Gade (Molly)

A warrior Predator speeds to Earth to clean up the bloody havoc caused when a spaceship crashes near a small Colorado town with the hybrid PredAlien aboard.

A tension-free, repetitive melange of familiar shock tactics drawn from the far better previous entries in both space monster franchise series. A tiresome trudge through rigid mutant Martian mayhem conventions.

SCR Shane Salerno CIN Daniel C. Pearl MUS Brian Tyler DES Andrew Neskoromny ED Dan Zimmerman PROD John Davis, David Giler, Walter Hill DIST Twentieth Century Fox

66 Provides enough cheap thrills and modest suspense. – *Joe Leydon, Variety*

66 The world's most illogical and boring horror grudge-

match between two dull trademarked franchise monsters is back on. – *Peter Bradshaw, Guardian*

'The most provocative picture of the year!'

All About Eve ★★★★

SCR/DIR *Joseph L. Mankiewicz*
1950 138m US
DVD

☆ *Bette Davis* (Margo Channing), *George Sanders* (Addison de Witt), Anne Baxter (Eve), Celeste Holm (Karen Richards), Thelma Ritter (Birdie), Gary Merrill (Bill Sampson), Hugh Marlowe (Lloyd Richards), Gregory Ratoff (Max Fabian), Marilyn Monroe (Miss Caswell), Barbara Bates (Phoebe), Walter Hampden (Speaker at dinner)

An ageing Broadway star's status is undermined by a self-effacing but secretly ruthless and ambitious young actress.

A basically unconvincing story with thin characters is transformed by a screenplay scintillating with savage wit and a couple of waspish performances into a movie experience to treasure.

CIN *Milton Krasner* MUS Alfred Newman ED Barbara McLean PROD Darryl F. Zanuck DIST TCF

MARGO: Fasten your seat belts, it's going to be a bumpy night!
ADDISON: That I should want you at all suddenly strikes me as the height of improbability. . .you're an improbable person, Eve, but so am I. We have that in common. Also a contempt for humanity, an inability to love or be loved, insatiable ambition – and talent. We deserve each other.
BIRDIE: The bed looks like a dead animal act.
ADDISON: That's all television is, dear – just auditions.
BIRDIE: What a story! Everything but the bloodhounds snappin' at her rear end!
ADDISON: I have lived in the theatre as a Trappist monk lives in his faith. In it I toil not, neither do I spin. I am a critic and a commentator. I am essential to the theatre – as ants to a picnic, as the boll weevil to a cotton field.

66 The wittiest, the most devastating, the most adult and literate motion picture ever made that had anything to do with the New York stage. – *Leo Mishkin*

66 The dialogue and atmosphere are so peculiarly remote from life that they have sometimes been mistaken for art. – *Pauline Kael, 1968*

† The idea for the film came from a short story, 'The Wisdom of Eve', by Mary Orr.

⚐ picture; George Sanders (supporting actor); Joseph L. Mankiewicz (screenplay); Joseph L. Mankiewicz (direction)

⚐ Bette Davis (leading actress); Anne Baxter (leading actress); Celeste Holm (supporting actress); Thelma Ritter (supporting actress); Milton Krasner; Alfred Newman; art direction; editing

🎭 picture

'Part of every woman is a mother/actress/saint/sinner. And part of every man is a woman.'

All About My Mother ★★★★

SCR/DIR *Pedro Almodóvar*
1999 101m Spain/France
DVD ♫

☆ *Cecilia Roth* (Manuela), Eloy Azorin (Esteban), *Marisa*

DVD Available on DVD ☆ Cast in order of importance 66 Critics' Quotes ⚐ Academy Award 🎭 BAFTA
♫ Soundtrack on CD † Points of interest ⚐ Academy Award nomination 🎭 BAFTA nomination

Paredes (Huma Rojo), Penelope Cruz (Sister Rosa), Candela Pena (Nina), *Antonia San Juan* (La Agrado), Rosa Maria Sarda (Rosa's Mother), Toni Canto (Lola)

A mother sees her son killed in a car accident and heads for Barcelona to break the news to the boy's father, a transsexual prostitute.

Emotional Spanish drama that includes a re-working of the Bette Davis classic All About Eve, and refers constantly to Hollywood's 'women's movies' of the 1940s and 50s so beloved of this director. A melodrama, certainly, but utterly true to itself and its cast of extravagant characters. The final confirmation that Almodóvar had matured into a world-class director with a humane, mature world view – and a sense of his own place on film history, both as a disciple and as a new master.

CIN Affonso Beato   MUS Alberto Iglesias   ED Jose Salcedo   PROD Agustin Almodóvar   DIST Pathé

66 The last masterpiece of the century. – *Philip French, Observer*

66 I can't say it made me cry even though it is drenched with death and mourning what might have been. I simply couldn't avoid the feeling that I was witnessing and old story retold from a universe parallel to my own with an intervening layer of high camp. – *Andrew Sarris, New York Observer*

⚱ foreign language film

Ⓣ Pedro Almodóvar (director); film not in the English language

Ⓣ Pedro Almodóvar (original screenplay)

All or Nothing   ★★

SCR/DIR Mike Leigh
2002   128m   GB/France
[DVD]

☆ Timothy Spall (Phil Bassett), *Lesley Manville* (Penny Bassett), Alison Garland (Rachel Bassett), James Corden (Rory Bassett), Ruth Sheen (Maureen), Marion Bailey (Carol), Paul Jesson (Ron), Sally Hawkins (Samantha)

A couple on a working-class housing estate struggle to rekindle their love for each other and their children.

Leigh at his bleakest, with rare moments of hope and forgiveness shining through the general gloom. It's tough going, but the acting makes it worthwhile.

CIN Dick Pope   MUS Andrew Dickson   DES Eve Stewart
ED Lesley Walker   PROD Simon Channing Williams
DIST UGC

66 Leigh succeeds in delivering a dramatic slap in the face that's simultaneously painful and refreshing. – *Jamie Russell, BBC*

66 An exhilarating movie about sadness and renewal. – *Michael Sragow, Baltimore Sun*

All Quiet on the Western Front

★★★★

DIR *Lewis Milestone*
1930   130m   US
[DVD]

☆ Lew Ayres (Paul Baumer), Louis Wolheim (Katczinsky),

Slim Summerville (Tjaden), John Wray (Himmelstoss), Raymond Griffith (Gerard Duval), Russell Gleason (Muller), Ben Alexander (Kemmerick), Beryl Mercer (Mrs. Baumer)

In 1914, a group of German teenagers volunteer for action on the Western Front, but they become disillusioned, and none of them survives.

A landmark of American cinema and Universal's biggest and most serious undertaking until the 1960s, this highly emotive war film, with its occasional outbursts of bravura direction, fixed in millions of minds the popular image of what it was like in the trenches, even more so than Journey's End which had shown the Allied viewpoint. Despite dated moments, it retains its overall power and remains a great pacifist work.

SCR Lewis Milestone, Maxwell Anderson, Del Andrews, George Abbott   CIN *Arthur Edeson*   MUS David Broekman   ED Milton Carruth, Edgar Adams
PROD Carl Laemmle Jnr.   DIST Universal

TJADEN: Me and the Kaiser, we are both fighting. The only difference is, the Kaiser isn't here.
KATCZINSKY: At the next war let all the Kaisers, Presidents and Generals and diplomats go into a big field and fight it out first among themselves. That will satisfy us and keep us at home.
PAUL: We live in the trenches out there. We fight. We try not to be killed, but sometimes we are. That's all.

66 A magnificent cinematic equivalent of the book. . .to Mr Milestone goes the credit of effecting the similitude in united and dynamic picture terms. The sound and image mediums blend as one, as a form of artistic expression that only the motion screen can give. – *National Board of Review*

66 Nothing passed up for the niceties; nothing glossed over for the women. Here exhibited is war as it is, butchery. The League of Nations could make no better investment than to buy up the master-print, reproduce it in every language to be shown to every nation every year until the word war is taken out of the dictionaries. – *Variety*

⚱ picture; Lewis Milestone (direction)
⚱ Lewis Milestone, Maxwell Anderson, Del Andrews, George Abbott; Arthur Edeson

'Together again. . .surpassing their performances in "Magnificent Obsession"

All that Heaven Allows   ★★★

DIR *Douglas Sirk*
1955   89m   US

☆ *Jane Wyman*, Rock Hudson, Agnes Moorehead, Conrad Nagel, Virginia Grey, Charles Drake

A sad widow falls in love with the gardener at her winter home, and marries him despite local prejudice when she returns home.

Standard tearjerker in the tradition of Magnificent Obsession, reuniting the same stars, producer and director. At the time, critics failed to grasp the suggested gay subtext in the story, and dismissed it as a routine soap. But modern audiences get the point, through its atmosphere of barely suppressed hysteria and the framing of Wyman as a prisoner in her own home.

SCR Peg Fenwick   CIN Russell Metty   MUS Frank Skinner   PROD Ross Hunter   DIST U-I

---

† The story was re-worked in 1974 in Fassbinder's *Fear Eats the Soul*. In 2002, Todd Haynes used the narrative device of an affluent woman falling for her gardener in *Far From Heaven*.

All that Money Can Buy ★★★★

DIR *William Dieterle*
1941   106m   US
DVD

☆ *Walter Huston* (Mr. Scratch), James Craig (Jabez Stone), Anne Shirley (Mary Stone), Simone Simon (Belle), *Edward Arnold* (Daniel Webster), Jane Darwell (Ma Stone), Gene Lockhart (Squire Slossum), John Qualen (Miser Stevens), H.B. Warner (Justice Hawthorne)

A hard-pressed farmer gives in to the Devil's tempting, but is saved from the pit by a famous lawyer's pleading at his 'trial'.

A brilliant Germanic Faust set in 19th-century New Hampshire and using historical figures, alienation effects, comedy asides and the whole cinematic box of tricks which Hollywood had just learned again through Citizen Kane. *A magic act in more ways than one.*

SCR *Dan Totheroh*   CIN *Joseph August*   MUS *Bernard Herrmann*   ED Robert Wise   PROD Charles L. Glett   DIST RKO

MR SCRATCH: A soul. A soul is nothing. Can you see it, smell it, touch it? No. Think of it – this soul – your soul – a nothing, against seven whole years of good luck! You will have money and all that money can buy.

❝ Some of those in the movie industry who saw it restively called it a dog; but some of them cried it was another catapult hurling the cinema up to its glorious destiny. – *Cecilia Ager*

⚱ Bernard Herrmann (music)
⚱ Walter Huston (leading actor)

'Everyone is dying to be with her.'

All The Boys Love Mandy Lane (new) ★★

DIR Jonathan Levine
2008   88m   US

☆ Amber Heard (Mandy Lane), Anson Mount (Garth), Whitney Able (Chloe), Michael Welch (Emmet), Aaron Himmelstein (Red)

Guests at a weekend ranch party start turning up dead, slaughtered by a mysterious stalker ensuring no one will ever get close to popular cheerleader Mandy Lane.

A skilful recreation of exploitation aesthetics, this is a tightly wound, twisty and gory shocker.

SCR Jacob Forman   CIN Darren Genet   MUS Mark Schulz   DES Thomas S. Hammock   ED Josh Noves   PROD Joe Neurauter, Felipe Marino, Chad Feehan   DIST Optimum

❝ Smart in how it neatly catches the petty, hurtful, sexy and druggy aspects of high school life, dumb in how it makes absolutely no sense once its resolution is known. – *Todd McCarthy, Variety*

❝ It's the inspired finale that makes it stand out from the slasher pack. – *Andrew Williams, Metro*

'The most devastating detective story of the century!'

All the President's Men ★★★★

DIR Alan J. Pakula
1976   138m   US
DVD

☆ *Robert Redford* (Bob Woodward), *Dustin Hoffman* (Carl Bernstein), Jason Robards Jnr. (Ben Bradlee), Martin Balsam (Howard Simons), Hal Holbrook (Deep Throat), Jack Warden (Harry Rosenfeld), Jane Alexander (Bookkeeper), Meredith Baxter (Debbie Sloan)

A reconstruction of the discovery of the White House link with the Watergate affair by two young reporters from the Washington Post, whose dogged investigations hastened the resignation of President Nixon.

An absorbing drama, which despite its many excellences would have been better with a more audible dialogue track, less murky photography and a clearer introduction of the characters concerned. The acting, however, is a treat.

SCR William Goldman   CIN Gordon Willis   MUS David Shire   DES George Jenkins   ED Robert L. Wolfe   PROD Robert Redford, Walter Coblenz   DIST Warner

❝ It works as a detective thriller (even though everyone knows the ending), as a credible (if occasionally romanticized) primer on the prosaic fundamentals of big league investigative journalism, and best of all, as a chilling tone poem that conveys the texture of the terror in our nation's capital during that long night when an aspiring fascist regime held our democracy under siege. – *Frank Rich, New York Post*

⚱ William Goldman; Jason Robards Jnr.; art direction; Arthur Piantadosi, Les Fresholtz, Dick Alexander, Jim Webb (sound)
⚱ picture; Jane Alexander (supporting actress); Alan J. Pakula; Robert L. Wolfe

---

'Some passions can never be tamed.'

All the Pretty Horses ★

DIR Billy Bob Thornton
2000   116m   US
DVD   ♫

☆ Matt Damon (John Grady Cole), Henry Thomas (Lacey Rawlins), *Lucas Black* (Jimmy Blevins), Penélope Cruz (Alejandra), Ruben Blades (Rocha), Robert Patrick (Cole), Julio Oscar Mechoso (Captain), Miriam Colon (Alfonsa), Bruce Dern (Judge), Sam Shepard (J.C. Franklin)

Two Texan cowboys ride into Mexico in 1949, but their search for adventure brings them up against heartbreak and imprisonment.

Somehow both slavish and rushed as the rendering of a beautifully episodic novel; only one performance really comes alive, and there's a sense of missing fire throughout the whole photogenic business.

SCR Ted Tally   CIN Barry Markowitz   MUS Marty Stuart, Larry Paxton and Kristin Wilkinson   DES Clark Hunter   ED Sally Menke   PROD Robert Salerno, Billy Bob Thornton   DIST Columbia

❝ A boy's adventure story that has mistaken itself for an epic, and rattles around in its own ambitions like a child's head in a 10-gallon hat. – *A.O. Scott, New York Times*

| DVD | Available on DVD | ☆ | Cast in order of importance | ❝ | Critics' Quotes | ⚱ | Academy Award | 🏆 | BAFTA |
| ♫ | Soundtrack on CD | | | † | Points of interest | ⚱ | Academy Award nomination | 🏆 | BAFTA nomination |

† Miramax, who handled the film's US distribution, forced Thornton to halve the length of his original four-hour cut.

'Love is a puzzle. These are the pieces.'

All the Real Girls ★★
SCR/DIR David Gordon Green
2003 108m US
DVD ♫

☆ Paul Schneider (Paul), *Zooey Deschanel* (Noel), Patricia Clarkson (Elvira Fine), Maurice Compte (Bo), Danny McBride (Bust-Ass), Benjamin Mouton (Leland), Shea Whigham (Tip)

A notorious cad in small-town North Carolina starts seeing the teenage sister of his best friend, to the latter's dismay.

Lovely, sensitive and astute little picture about the awkwardness of genuinely romantic entanglement between young people; the director's fondness for magic-hour reverie does occasionally get the better of him.

CIN *Tim Orr* MUS David Wingo, Michael Linnen DES Richard Wright ED Zene Baker, Steven Gonzales PROD Jean Doumanian, Lisa Muskat DIST Columbia Tristar

66 A deeply accomplished and intelligent film about the fragility and perishability of love. – *Peter Bradshaw, Guardian*

'Experience it. Enjoy it. Just don't fall for it.'

Almost Famous ★★
SCR/DIR Cameron Crowe
2000 122m US
DVD ♫

☆ Billy Crudup (Russell Hammond), *Frances McDormand* (Elaine Miller), Kate Hudson (Penny Lane), Jason Lee (Jeff Bebe), Patrick Fugit (William Miller), Anna Paquin (Polexia Aphrodisia), Fairuza Balk (Sapphire), Noah Taylor (Dick Roswell), Zooey Deschanel (Anita Miller), John Fedevich (Ed Vallencourt), Bijou Phillips (Estrella Starr), *Philip Seymour Hoffman* (Lester Bangs), Eion Bailey (Jann Wenner), Terry Chen (Ben Fong-Torres)

A teenager obsessed with rock music is given the chance to follow an up-and-coming band on tour for Rolling Stone.

Sparky, amusing, but naggingly synthetic re-creation of the post-hippie era, based on Crowe's own break as a music journalist. He portrays his younger self in an idealised light. Rarely less than entertaining, it all comes across as rather cute and sanitised.

CIN John Toll MUS Nancy Wilson ED Joe Hutshing, Saar Klein PROD Cameron Crowe, Ian Bryce DIST DreamWorks

66 A sweet-minded, picaresque story, woolly with some of its dramatic details, but stacked with attractions. – *Geoff Andrew, Time Out*

♟ Cameron Crowe (original screenplay)
♟ Kate Hudson (supporting actress); Frances McDormand (supporting actress); Joe Hutshing, Saar Klein
♟ Cameron Crowe (original screenplay); Jeff Wexler, D.M. Hemphill, Rick Kline, Paul Massey, Mike Wilhoit (sound)
♟ film; Kate Hudson (supporting actress); Frances McDormand (supporting actress); Nancy Wilson

Almost Peaceful ★★
SCR/DIR Michel Deville
2002 94m France
DVD

☆ Simon Abkarian (Albert), Zabou Breitman (Lea), Denis Podalydes (Charles), Vincent Elbaz (Leon), Lubna Azabal (Jacqueline), Stanislas Merhar (Maurice), Clotilde Courau (Simone), Julie Gaynet (Mme Andree)

In post-war Paris, a group of Jewish tailors establish a workshop and try to build up their business once more.

A discreet, low-key essay about survival and a quest for happiness, tinged with feelings of grief and guilt for friends and family who perished. Touching and telling.

SCR Rosalinde Deville CIN Andre Diot MUS Giovanni Bottesini DES Arnaud de Moleron ED Andrea Sedlackova, Judith Rivière Kawa PROD Rosalinde Deville

66 You become aware of how few movies about survivors of the Holocaust show them going about their lives, as opposed to acting out someone's idea of a Holocaust Survivor. – *Ella Taylor, L.A. Weekly*

66 This is a film of half-notes and nuances, and as a chronicle of emotional survival it is infinitely inspiring. – *Andrew Sarris, New York Observer*

Alphaville ★★
SCR/DIR Jean-Luc Godard
1965 98m France/Italy
DVD ♫

☆ Eddie Constantine, Anna Karina, Akim Tamiroff, Howard Vernon, Laszlo Szabo

A trench-coated private eye travels across space to find out what happened to his predecessor, and finds himself in a loveless, robotic society.

A rather chill futuristic fantasy on the lines of 1984 but with an outer space background. It's a peculiar hybrid of film noir and science-fiction that does not always work; yet it's agreeable enough, and accessible by Godard's standards.

CIN Raoul Coutard MUS Paul Misraki PROD André Michelin DIST Chaumiane/Filmstudio
† Godard wanted to title the film Tarzan v IBM.

'Things are going to get messy.'

Alvin and the Chipmunks (new)
DIR Tim Hill
2007 91m US
♫

☆ Jason Lee (Dave Seville), David Gross (Ian Hawk), Cameron Richardson (Claire), Justin Long (Voice of Alvin), Matthew Gray Gubler (Voice of Simon), Jesse McCartney (Voice of Theodore), Jane Lynch (Gail)

A luckless songwriter is inspired by a trio of singing chipmunks who become unlikely overnight pop sensations.

Aggravating comedy in the Garfield mould, built around three computer-generated rodents; there is no sign of whatever charm the original cartoon series

possessed, though generous fans may appreciate the satirical updates.

SCR Jon Vitti, Will McRobb, Chris Viscardi   CIN Peter Lyons Collister   MUS Christopher Lennertz   DES Richard Holland   ED Peter Berger   PROD Janice Karman, Ross Bagdasarian Jr., Steve Waterman   DIST TCF

66 This partially animated, charm-free atrocity is awful enough to instantly cure any remaining nostalgia for the rodent trio. – *Lou Lumenick, New York Post*

66 More than hyperactive enough to engage small fry with microscopic attention spans. – *Joe Leydon, Variety*

'They couldn't hear him. They couldn't see him. But he was there when they needed him. . .Even after he was gone'

Always   ★

DIR Steven Spielberg
1989   122m   US
DVD   ♪

☆ Richard Dreyfuss (Pete Sandich), Holly Hunter (Dorinda Durston), Brad Johnson (Ted Baker), John Goodman (Al Yackey), Audrey Hepburn (Hap), Roberts Blossom (Dave), Keith David (Powerhouse), Ed Van Nuys (Nails)

A firefighter pilot returns from the dead to facilitate a budding romance between his girlfriend and a flying colleague.

Minor-league Spielberg film, though it was in part a response to criticism that the director was uncomfortable making films for grown-ups, seeking instead to locate the 'inner child' in his audiences. This straight remake of the Spencer Tracy film A Guy Named Joe from 1943 might have been judged delightful from other directors not carrying such a weight of expectation.

SCR Jerry Belson   CIN Mikael Salomon   MUS John Williams   DES James Bissell   ED Michael Kahn   PROD Steven Spielberg, Frank Marshall, Kathleen Kennedy   DIST UIP/Amblin/Steven Spielberg, Frank Marshall, Kathleen Kennedy

66 Spielberg's confident direction is particularly effective in the aerial sequences, but he gets carried away in an overblown conclusion. – *Geoff Andrew, Time Out*

† This was the final screen role for Audrey Hepburn, playing an angel guide.

'The Man. . .The Music. . .The Madness. . .The Murder. . .The Motion Picture. . .Everything you've heard is true.'

Amadeus   ★★★

DIR *Milos Forman*
1984   160m   US
DVD   ♪

☆ *F. Murray Abraham* (Antonio Salieri), *Tom Hulce* (Wolfgang Amadeus Mozart), Elizabeth Berridge (Constanze Mozart), Simon Callow (Emanuel Schikaneder), Roy Dotrice (Leopold Mozart), Christine Ebersole (Katerina Cavalieri)

Dying in 1823, the jealous composer Salieri claims to have murdered Mozart.

A musical legend performed with success and economy on stage now becomes an exciting baroque film, like an

opera in high-pitched dialogue. The brilliance of its conceit is that the story is more about Salieri's mediocrity and failure in the shadow of Mozart's genius. It is lavish, spectacular, and great to look at; Hulce and Abraham never again played roles of this stature.*

SCR *Peter Shaffer*   CIN *Miroslav Ondricek*   DES *Patrizia Van Brandenstein*   ED Nena Danevic, Michael Chandler   DIST Saul Zaentz

† It was shot in Prague, standing in for Vienna; director Forman thus returned to his native land after 16 years in exile in the West.

⚊ picture; F. Murray Abraham (leading actor); Milos Forman (direction); Peter Shaffer (adapted screenplay); Paul LeBlanc, Dick Smith (make up)

⚊ Tom Hulce (leading actor); photography; editing; art direction

Ⓣ Miroslav Ondricek

'Romance... In a most unlikely place.'

Les Amants du Pont-Neuf   ★

SCR/DIR Leos Carax
1991   125m   France
DVD

☆ Juliette Binoche (Michèle Stalens), Denis Lavant (Alex), Klaus-Michael Gruber (Hans)

A curious romance on the oldest bridge in Paris, the Pont-Neuf, between a female artist threatened with blindness and an injured fire-eater who sleeps rough.

An expensive and hugely controversial film in France that exemplified the cinema du look, an extravagant pop-video-inspired style favouring visual impact over textual substance. The film is a paradox: it aims to be hard-hitting about deprivation in France at the bicentennial of the Revolution, but its soaring, glorious set-pieces rather undermine its aims.

CIN Jean-Yves Escoffier   DES Michael Vandestien   ED Nelly Quettier   PROD Christian Fechner   DIST Artificial Eye/Christian Fechner

66 Ultimately, the problem with Carax's film is one of mismatch between exciting and innovative aesthetics and conservative politics. – *Ginette Vincendeau, Sight & Sound*

Ⓣ film not in the English language

Amarcord   ★★★

DIR *Federico Fellini*
1973   123m   Italy/France
DVD   ♪

☆ Pupella Maggio (Miranda Biondi, Titta's Mother), Magali Noel (Gradisca), Armando Brancia (Aurelio Biondi, Titta's Father), Ciccio Ingrassia (Uncle Teo)

A recollection of childhood in an Italian seaside town during the Fascist era, with colourful characters congregating to swap anecdotes and mock Mussolini.

A bizarre, intriguing mixture of fact, fantasy and obscurity, pleasing to watch.

SCR Federico Fellini, Tonino Guerra   CIN Giuseppe Rotunno   MUS *Nino Rota*   ED Ruggero Mastroianni

DVD Available on DVD   ☆ Cast in order of importance   66 Critics' Quotes   † Points of interest   ⚊ Academy Award   ⚊ Academy Award nomination   Ⓣ BAFTA   Ⓣ BAFTA nomination
♪ Soundtrack on CD

PROD Franco Cristaldi   DIST FC Produzione/PECF

66 A rich surface texture and a sense of exuberant melancholia. – *Michael Billington, Illustrated London News*

66 Peaks of invention separated by raucous valleys of low comedy. – *Sight & Sound*

† The title means 'I remember'.

⚊ foreign film

⚊ script; direction

'Accountancy, Murder, Amnesia, Torture, Ecstasy, Understanding, Redemption.'

Amateur   ★★

SCR/DIR Hal Hartley

1994   105m   US/France/GB

DVD   ♫

☆ *Isabelle Huppert* (Isabelle), *Martin Donovan* (Thomas Ludens), Elina Lowensohn (Sofia Ludens), Damian Young (Edward), Pamela Stewart (Officer Patsy Melville), David Simonds (Kurt), Chuck Montgomery (Jan)

An ex-nun who has turned to writing pornographic novels helps an amnesiac criminal reconstruct his identity.

Deadpan stab at a wry, cerebral thriller, in which smart performances provide most of the fun. The writer-director's skewed vision remains an acquired taste.

CIN Michael Spiller   MUS Ned Rifle, Jeffrey Taylor   DES Steve Rosenzweig   ED Steven Hamilton   PROD Ted Hope, Hal Hartley   DIST UGC/Zenith/True Fiction

66 A sharp-witted thriller that takes off into dark and uncharted territory. – *Peter Travers, Rolling Stone*

'Behind the song you love is a story you will never forget.'

Amazing Grace   ★

DIR Michael Apted

2007   118m   UK/US

DVD   ♫

☆ Ioan Gruffudd (William Wilberforce), Romola Garai (Barbara Spooner), Benedict Cumberbatch (William Pitt), Albert Finney (John Newton), Michael Gambon (Lord Charles Fox), Youssou N'Dour (Olaudah Equiano), Rufus Sewell (Thomas Clarkson)

In 18th-century England, campaigner William Wilberforce battles to push anti-slavery legislation through Parliament.

Sturdy, well-made biopic compromised by the worthiness of its protagonist and absence of actual slaves; the director is to be commended, though, for making a fusty historical subject dramatic.

SCR Steven Knight   CIN Remi Adefarasin   MUS David Arnold   DES Charles Wood   ED Rick Shaine   PROD Edward Pressman, Terrence Malick, Patricia Heaton, David Hunt, Ken Wales   DIST Momentum

66 A detailed, affecting biography of one of the great souls who moved humanity forward. – *Mick LaSalle, San Francisco Chronicle*

66 Marinaded in good intentions and served up with a garnish of complacency and condescension. – *Peter Bradshaw, Guardian*

---

† Not to be confused with The Amazing Grace, a 2007 DVD title starring Nick Moran that concentrated on the early life of John Newton, Albert Finney's character.

'She'll change your life.'

Amélie   ★★★

DIR *Jean-Pierre Jeunet*

2001   122m   France/Germany

DVD   ♫

☆ *Audrey Tautou* (Amélie), Mathieu Kassovitz (Nino Quincampoix), Rufus (Raphael Poulain), Yolande Moreau (Madeleine Wallace), Artus Penguern (Hipolito), Urbain Cancellier (Collignon), Dominique Pinon (Joseph), Maurice Benichou (Bretodeau), Andre Dussollier (Narrator)

A lonely young Parisian woman decides to improve the lives of those around her, eventually coming to find true love.

Its arc is that of one gigantic swoon, and more cynical viewers may well resist; those with the appropriate sweet tooth will surely fall head over heels with its compendium of small pleasures, tourist-board evocation of Montmartre and wide-eyed heroine, as large audiences did.

SCR Guillaume Laurant, Jean-Pierre Jeunet   CIN Bruno Delbonnel   MUS Yann Tiersen   DES Aline Bonetto   ED Herve Schneid   PROD Claudie Ossard, Jean-Marc Deschamps   DIST Momentum

66 You see it, and later when you think about it, you smile. – *Roger Ebert, Chicago Sun-Times*

66 The very dictionary definition of 'feel-good' – its irresistible charms will dispel the heaviest clouds hanging over the head of the gloomiest misanthrope. – *Alan Morrison, Empire*

† The lead role was originally offered to Emily Watson, who declined it because she did not speak French and had already committed to Gosford Park.

† It became the top-grossing French-language film in history. In its first month of release in France, it sold an unprecedented 4.2 million tickets.

⚊ foreign language film; Guillaume Laurant, Jean-Pierre Jeunet (original screenplay); Bruno Delbonnel; Aline Bonetto; Vincent Arnardi, Guillaume Leriche, Jean Umansky (sound)

Ⓣ Guillaume Laurant, Jean-Pierre Jeunet (original screenplay); Aline Bonetto

Ⓣ film; film not in the English language; Audrey Tatou (leading actress); Jean-Pierre Jeunet; Bruno Delbonnel; Herve Schneid; Yann Tiersen

---

Amen   ★★

DIR Costa-Gavras

2002   132m   France/Germany

DVD

☆ *Ulrich Tukur* (Kurt Gerstein), Mathieu Kassovitz (Riccardo Fontana), *Ulrich Mühe* (The Doctor), Michel Duchaussoy (The Cardinal), Ion Caramitru (Count Fontana), Marcel Iures (The Pope), Friedrich von Thun (Gerstein's Father), Antje Schmidt (Mrs Gerstein)

DVD Available on DVD   ☆ Cast in order of importance   66 Critics' Quotes   † Points of interest   ⚊ Academy Award   ⚊ Academy Award nomination   Ⓣ BAFTA   Ⓣ BAFTA nomination

♫ Soundtrack on CD

19

A Jesuit priest and an SS officer try to convince the Pope about the extermination of Jews during WWII.

Often cumbersome thriller, in which the fictional character of the priest weakens the other fact-based material; but it's forceful all the same, exposing a chilling bureaucracy of evil without a single shot inside the gas chambers.

SCR Costa-Gavras, Jean-Claude Grumberg **CIN** Patrick Blossier **MUS** Armand Amar **DES** Ari Hantke **ED** Yannick Kergoat **PROD** Andrei Boncea, Michèle Ray-Gavras **DIST** Pathé

&& Powerful, awkward, dramatically uneven. – *Patrick Z. McGavin, Chicago Tribune*

† Kurt Gerstein was arrested by the Allies and died, either by his own hand or at the hands of others, while in custody. His name was cleared in 1965, when it was acknowledged that he had done much to document Nazi atrocities and to try to prevent them.

'. . .look closer.'

American Beauty ★★★

DIR *Sam Mendes*
1999 122m US
DVD ♫

☆ *Kevin Spacey* (Lester Burnham), *Annette Bening* (Carolyn Burnham), Thora Birch (Jane Burnham), Wes Bentley (Ricky Fitts), Mena Suvari (Angela Hayes), Peter Gallagher (Buddy Kane), Allison Janney (Barbara Fitts), Scott Bakula (Jim Olmeyer), Sam Robards (Jim Berkley), Chris Cooper (Colonel Fitts)

A depressed suburban father recalls the events leading up to his own murder.

Rampantly skewering the hypocrisies of bourgeois American life, the movie was hailed, somewhat paradoxically, as an instant modern classic for its painterly veneer and mordant acting. It's immensely well crafted, but a lurking archness infects the tone on repeat viewings.

SCR *Alan Ball* **CIN** *Conrad L. Hall* **MUS** Thomas Newman **DES** Naomi Shohan **ED** Tariq Anwar, Christopher Greenbury **PROD** Bruce Cohen, Dan Jinks **DIST** DreamWorks

&& A film of incredible flair and formal, compositional brilliance. – *Peter Bradshaw, Guardian*

&& Hilarious, painful and brutally frank. – *Desson Thomson, Washington Post*

⌁ picture; Kevin Spacey (leading actor); Sam Mendes; Alan Ball (original screenplay); Conrad L. Hall

⌁ Annette Bening (leading actress); Thomas Newman; Tariq Anwar, Christopher Greenbury

⬯ film; Kevin Spacey (leading actor); Annette Bening (leading actress); Conrad L. Hall; Tariq Anwar, Christopher Greenbury; Thomas Newman

⬯ Sam Mendes; Alan Ball (original screenplay); Wes Bentley (supporting actor); Thora Birch (supporting actress); Mena Suvari (supporting actress); Naomi Shohan (production design); Scott Martin Gershin, Scott Milan, Bob Beemer, Richard Van Dyke (sound); Tania McComas, Carol A. O'Connell (make up/hair)

'They had a plan. It wasn't worth a nickel.'

American Buffalo ★★

DIR Michael Corrente
1996 88m US, GB
DVD ♫

☆ *Dustin Hoffman* (Walt 'Teach' Teacher), *Dennis Franz* (Don 'Donny' Dubrow), Sean Nelson (Bob 'Bobby')

A petty thief decides to muscle in on the plans of a junkshop owner to burgle the home of a coin collector.

It never quite leaves its stage origins behind, and Mamet's distinctive dialogue is purely theatrical, but the interplay between the actors is riveting.

SCR David Mamet **CIN** Richard Crudo **MUS** Thomas Newman **DES** Daniel Talpers **ED** Kate Sanford **PROD** Gregory Mosher **DIST** Film Four/Capitol/Samuel Goldwyn/Channel 4/Punch

'Education in love.'

American Friends ★

DIR Tristram Powell
1991 95m GB

☆ Michael Palin (Reverend Francis Ashby), Trini Alvarado (Miss Elinor Hartley), *Connie Booth* (Miss Caroline Hartley), Bryan Pringle (Haskell), Fred Pearson (Hapgood), Alfred Molina (Oliver Syme), Susan Denaker (Mrs. Cantrell), Robert Eddison (Rushden – The President)

In 1866, a shy Oxford academic bachelor confronts a work/life dilemma when he falls in love with an American woman.

This personal project of Palin's has sweetness and charm to burn, without ever becoming a film of any great distinction.

SCR Michael Palin, Tristram Powell **CIN** Philip Bonham-Carter **MUS** Georges Delerue **DES** Andrew McAlpine **ED** George Akers **PROD** Patrick Cassavetti **DIST** Virgin/British Screen/Millennium/Mayday/Prominent Features

† Palin has claimed the character he plays is based on his great-grandfather.

'There are two sides to the American dream.'

American Gangster (new) ★★

DIR Ridley Scott
2007 156m US
DVD ♫

☆ Denzel Washington (Frank Lucas), Russell Crowe (Richie Roberts), Chiwetel Ejiofor (Huey Lucas), Cuba Gooding Jr. (Nicky Barnes), Josh Brolin (Detective Trupo), Ruby Dee (Mama Lucas), Ted Levine (Lou Toback), Armand Assante (Dominic Cattano)

In 1970s Harlem, drug baron Frank Lucas makes a killing by shipping pure heroin from Thailand. He is stalked by Richie Roberts, a principled New Jersey narcotics cop who finally causes Lucas's downfall.

Sleek film with epic ambitions, fluently directed and brisk-moving despite its long running time. But Washington is uncomfortably cast as a brutal crime

DVD Available on DVD ♫ Soundtrack on CD ☆ Cast in order of importance && Critics' Quotes † Points of interest ⌁ Academy Award ⌁ Academy Award nomination ⬯ BAFTA ⬯ BAFTA nomination

boss, while Crowe's Roberts comes across as dull and self-righteous. Finally, one wonders if these two real-life characters were worth all the huge effort and time expended to depict them.

SCR Steven Zaillian   CIN Harris Savides   MUS Marc Streitenfeld   DES Arthur Max   ED Pietro Scalia   PROD Brian Grazer, Ridley Scott   DIST Universal

66 We see (Lucas) go from humble chauffeur to very rich businessman, and he does it by hard work, taking risks and selling a superior product (good heroin) at half the price charged by the competition (the mafia). The film gives us only a cursory look at the consequences – dead black people. – *Cosmo Landesman, Sunday Times*

66 The movie isn't quite enthralling; it's more like the ghost version of a '70s classic. – *Owen Gleiberman, Entertainment Weekly*

🎞 Ruby Dee (supporting actress); Arthur Max

Ⓣ Film; Steven Zaillian (original screenplay); Harris Savides; Pietro Scalia; Marc Streitenfeld

---

'Where were you in '62?'

American Graffiti ★★★

SCR/DIR George Lucas
1973   110m   US
DVD   🎵

☆ *Richard Dreyfuss* (Curt), Ronny Howard (Steve), Paul le Mat (John), Charlie Martin Smith (Terry), Cindy Williams (Laurie), *Candy Clark* (Debbie), Mackenzie Phillips (Carol)

In 1962 California, four young men about to leave for college gather for a night's girl-chasing and police-baiting.

Nostalgic comedy recalling many sights and sounds of the previous generation and carefully crystallizing a particular time and place. Hugely successful itself, it led to many imitations.

CIN Ron Eveslage, Jan D'Alquen   MUS popular songs   ED Verna Fields, Marcia Lucas   PROD Francis Ford Coppola, Gary Kurtz   DIST Universal/Lucasfilm/Coppola Company

66 A very good movie, funny, tough, unsentimental... full of marvellous performances. – *Roger Greenspun, New York Times*

† The film cost $750,000, and grossed $55 million.
† Harrison Ford had a small role in the film.

🎞 picture; George Lucas (screenplay); George Lucas (direction); Candy Clark

---

'His father taught him to hate. His friends taught him rage. His enemies gave him hope.'

American History X ★★

DIR Tony Kaye
1998   119m   US
DVD   🎵

☆ *Edward Norton* (Derek Vinyard), Edward Furlong (Danny Vinyard), Fairuza Balk (Stacey), Stacy Keach (Cameron Alexander), Elliott Gould (Murray), Avery Brooks (Dr Bob Sweeney), *Beverly D'Angelo* (Doris Vinyard), Paul Le Mat (McMahon)

A neo-Nazi skinhead sees the error of his ways in prison, and tries to prevent his brother following in his footsteps.

Jolting melodrama about an intelligent racist, which engineers his redemption too cheaply and gets suckered by its own lyric power. The movie often seems at war with itself, but that's precisely the quality that makes Norton's performance so riveting.

SCR David McKenna   CIN Tony Kaye   MUS Anne Dudley   DES Jon Gary Steele   ED Jerry Greenberg, Alan Heim   PROD John Morrissey   DIST Entertainment/New Line

66 An inflated yet gut-slugging film. – *Janet Maslin, New York Times*

† Tony Kaye disowned the released version, and claimed that Edward Norton had altered and edited the film to give his role more prominence.

🎞 Edward Norton (leading actor)

An American in Paris ★★★★

DIR Vincente Minnelli
1951   113m   US
DVD   🎵

☆ *Gene Kelly* (Jerry Mulligan), *Oscar Levant* (Adam Cook), *Nina Foch* (Milo Roberts), *Leslie Caron* (Lise Bouvier), *Georges Guetary* (Henri Baurel)

A struggling young artist scorns a rich woman's patronage and wins the love of an innocent young French girl.

Altogether delightful musical holiday, one of the high spots of the Hollywood genre, with infectious enthusiasm and an unexpected sense of the Paris that was. The climactic ballet is breath-taking in its virtuosity and artistic ambition.

SCR Alan Jay Lerner   CIN Al Gilks, John Alton   MUS ED Adrienne Fazan   PROD Arthur Freed   DIST MGM

66 Too fancy and overblown, but the principal performers are in fine form and the Gershwin music keeps everything good-spirited. – *New Yorker, 1977*

† Chevalier was originally paged for the Georges Guetary role, but turned it down because he lost the girl. The production cost $2,723,903, of which $542,000 went on the final ballet
† 'I Got Rhythm'; 'Embraceable You'; 'By Strauss'; 'Swonderful'; 'Tra La La'; 'Our Love Is Here to Stay'; 'Stairway to Paradise'; 'Concerto in F' (instrumental); 'An American in Paris' (ballet)

🎞 picture; Alan Jay Lerner (screenplay); Al Gilks, John Alton; Saul Chaplin, Johnny Green (musical arrangement); art direction; Walter Plunkett, Irene Sharaff (costume design)
🎞 Vincente Minnelli; Adrienne Fazan

'Why can't the most powerful man in the world have the one thing he wants most?'

The American President ★★

DIR Rob Reiner
1995   114m   US
DVD

☆ Michael Douglas (President Andrew Shepherd), Annette Bening (Sydney Ellen Wade), Martin Sheen (A.J. MacInerney), Michael J. Fox (Lewis Rothschild), David Paymer (Leon Kodak), Samantha Mathis (Janie Basdin), Richard Dreyfuss (Senator Bob Rumson)

A widowed US president begins dating an environmental lobbyist, which gives the press and his rivals a field day.

Tartly scripted confection, not set in any world we truly recognise, but thoroughly engaging as a romantic fantasy, and offering passing comment of an impeccably liberal variety on a few hot-button issues.

SCR *Aaron Sorkin* CIN John Seale MUS *Marc Shaiman* DES Lilly Kilvert ED Robert Leighton PROD Rob Reiner DIST Columbia/Castle Rock/Wildwood

66 As bustling and impassioned as the best Sturges and Capra movies. – *Richard Schickel, Time*

66 A rather wonderful crock. – *Desson Howe, Washington Post*

† The film was a precursor to the successful, long-running TV series The West Wing, also created by Aaron Sorkin. Martin Sheen, the chief of staff in this film, was 'promoted' to playing the President in the series.

⚮ Marc Shaiman (music)

'Killer looks.'

American Psycho ★★

DIR *Mary Harron*
2000   101m   US/Canada
DVD   ♫

☆ *Christian Bale* (Patrick Bateman), Willem Dafoe (Donald Kimball), Jared Leto (Paul Allen), Reese Witherspoon (Evelyn Williams), Samantha Mathis (Courtney Rawlinson), Chloe Sevigny (Jean), Justin Theroux (Timothy Bryce), Josh Lucas (Craig McDermott), Guinevere Turner (Elizabeth), Matt Ross (Luis Carruthers), Bill Sage (David Van Patten), Cara Seymour (Christie)

A Wall Street investment banker struggles to hide his homicidal tendencies from colleagues.

Grisly satire which literalises cut-throat capitalism with a smirk: impeccably mounted, oddly refined, and not on any account to be taken too seriously.

SCR Mary Harron, Guinevere Turner CIN *Andrzej Sekula* MUS *John Cale* DES *Gideon Ponte* ED Andrew Marcus PROD Edward R. Pressman, Chris Hanley, Christian Halsey Solomon DIST Entertainment

66 The carnage, like the sex scenes, is shot so pristinely that it becomes a nouvelle-cuisine feast; this is a splatter film Martha Stewart could love. – *Richard Corliss, Time*

'At last, a comic book hero that we can all relate to. . .'

American Splendor ★★

SCR/DIR Shari Springer Berman, Robert Pulcini
2003   101m   US
DVD   ♫

☆ *Paul Giamatti* (Harvey Pekar), Harvey Pekar (Real Harvey), Shari Springer Berman (Interviewer), Earl Billings (Mr Boats), James Urbaniak (Robert Crumb), *Judah Friedlander* (Toby Radloff), Toby Radloff (Real Toby), *Hope Davis* (Joyce Brabner), Joyce Brabner (Real Joyce)

A filing clerk in Cleveland finds success with his underground comic books.

Self-reflexive look at the humdrum being turned into art, in which the acted sections are wittily commented on by the real-life figures depicted. It's droll and often novel, but there's a faint lack of overall point.

CIN Terry Stacey MUS Mark Suozzo DES Therese DePrez ED Robert Pulcini PROD Ted Hope DIST Optimum

66 Hilarious, moody and cantankerous. – *A.O. Scott, New York Times*

66 Sad, tender, wise and beautiful film. . .It's a profound tribute to lives lived on the fringes of society – to the introspective loners who are the most observant chroniclers of our times. – *Scott Foundas, Variety*

⚮ Shari Springer Berman, Robert Pulcini (adapted screenplay)

'A comedy about celebrity, family and other forms of insanity.'

America's Sweethearts

DIR Joe Roth
2001   102m   US
DVD   ♫

☆ Julia Roberts (Kiki Harrison), Billy Crystal (Lee Phillips), Catherine Zeta-Jones (Gwen Harrison), John Cusack (Eddie Thomas), Hank Azaria (Hector), Stanley Tucci (Dave Kingman), Christopher Walken (Hal Weidmann), Alan Arkin (Wellness Guide), Seth Green (Danny Wax), Scot Zeller (Davis)

A studio publicist embarks on damage limitation when the two stars of an upcoming movie split up.

Grating insider farce, satirising celebrity obsession and the media circus with a smug and heavy hand, and giving its all-star cast little to do but look pleased with themselves.

SCR Billy Crystal, Peter Tolan CIN Phedon Papamichael MUS James Newton Howard DES Garreth Stover ED Stephen A. Rotter PROD Billy Crystal, Susan Arnold, Donna Arkoff Roth DIST Columbia

66 Turns the kleig lights around to produce a wry and dead-on commentary on the film industry and the journalists who cover it. – *Michael Sragow, Baltimore Sun*

† Released the month after 9/11, and a box-office flop; the world was decidedly not in the mood for bitchy humour about grasping celebrities.

'Freedom is not given. It is our right at birth. But there are some moments when it must be taken.'

Amistad ★

DIR Steven Spielberg
1997   152m   US
DVD   ♫

☆ Matthew McConaughey (Baldwin), Anthony Hopkins (John Quincy Adams), Morgan Freeman (Theodore Joadson), Nigel Hawthorne (Martin Van Buren), *Djimon Hounsou* (Cinque), David Paymer (Secretary of State John Forsyth), Pete Postlethwaite (Holabird), Stellan Skarsgård (Tappan), Anna Paquin (Queen Isabella II), Tomas Milian (Calderon), Austin Pendleton (Prof. Gibbs)

A slave-ship uprising in 1839 becomes a cause célèbre when an American abolitionist lawyer takes up the Africans' case.

Forceful only in its flashbacks to the mutiny, this mostly hidebound courtroom drama overflows with 'importance' and noble rhetoric, but adopts a thoroughly white perspective on black suffering; there's one majestic performance.

SCR David Franzoni CIN Janusz Kaminski MUS John Williams DES Rick Carter ED Michael Kahn

---

DVD Available on DVD   ☆ Cast in order   66 Critics' Quotes   ⚮ Academy Award   🅣 BAFTA
♫ Soundtrack on CD   of importance   † Points of interest   ⚮ Academy Award nomination   🅥 BAFTA nomination

PROD Steven Spielberg, Debbie Allen, Colin Wilson
DIST DreamWorks/HBO

66 Prestige filmmaking bereft of inspiration. – *Charles Taylor, Salon.com*

⚱ Anthony Hopkins (supporting actor); Janusz Kaminski; John Williams; Ruth E. Carter (costume design)

'Some heights can only be reached by the heart.'

Among Giants   ★

DIR Sam Miller
1998 93m GB

☆ Pete Postlethwaite (Raymond), Rachel Griffiths (Gerry), James Thornton (Steven), Rob Jarvis (Weasel), Andy Serkis (Bob), Lennie James (Shovel), Alan Williams (Frank), Emma Cunniffe (Barmaid)

In the north of England, an Australian backpacker becomes the only woman in a group of electricity pylon painters, and her arrival causes romantic complications.

This was screenwriter Simon Beaufoy's first script after his astonishing success with The Full Monty. That film's warmth and camaraderie are present, but there is little at stake otherwise.

SCR Simon Beaufoy CIN Witold Stok MUS Tim Atack DES Luana Hanson ED Paul Green, Elen Pierce Lewis PROD Stephen Garrett DIST Kudos/British Screen/Capitol/Arts Council/YMPA/BBC

66 The picture's most impressive assets are the electrical towers that dominate the landscape, turning an inherently small picture into towering entertainment, at least where the scenery is concerned. – *David Sterritt, Christian Science Monitor*

'Love. Betrayal. Death.'

Amores Perros   ★★★★

DIR *Alejandro Gonzalez Inarritu*
2000 154m Mexico
[DVD] ♫

☆ *Emilio Echevarria* (El Chivo), *Gael Garcia Bernal* (Octavio), Goya Toledo (Valeria), Alvaro Guerrero (Daniel), Vanessa Bauche (Susana), Jorge Salinas (Luis), Marco Pérez (Ramiro)

A car crash in Mexico city changes the lives of a young adulterer, a model who loses her leg and an ageing contract killer.

Startlingly successful debut from a director and screenwriter whose colliding storylines have since become shop-worn; here they came blazing off the screen in sensationally well achieved, operatic style.

SCR *Guillermo Arriaga* CIN *Rodrigo Prieto* MUS *Gustavo Santaolalla* DES *Brigitte Broch* ED *Alejandro Gonzalez Inarritu, Luis Carballar, Fernando Perez Unda* PROD Alejandro Gonzalez Inarritu DIST Optimum

66 A truly prodigious piece of work, resembling a career summation far more than a maiden voyage. – *Peter Rainer, New York Magazine*

66 One of the great films of our time, or any other. – *Joe Morgenstern, Wall Street Journal*

⚱ foreign language film

🇹 film not in the English language

'Be glad you're afraid. It means you're still alive.'

Amsterdamned   ★

SCR/DIR Dick Maas
1988 105m Netherlands

☆ Huub Stapel (Eric Visser), Monique Van de Ven (Laura), Serge-Henri Valcke (Vermeer), Tanneke Hartsuiker (Potter), Wim Zomer (John), Hidde Maas (Ruysdael)

A determined killer is wreaking havoc in the area round Amsterdam's canals.

Outstanding mainly for its inspired use of locations. It makes one wonder why Amsterdam's canals, portrayed here as both sinister and picturesque, are not used more often on film.

CIN Marc Felperlaan MUS Dick Maas DES Dick Schillemans ED Hans Van Dongen PROD Laurens Geels, Dick Maas DIST Vestron/First Floor Features

'You try telling him his 50 minutes are up.'

Analyze This   ★★

SCR/DIR Harold Ramis
1999 103m US/Australia
[DVD] ♫

☆ Robert De Niro (Paul Vitti), Billy Crystal (Dr. Ben Sobel), Lisa Kudrow (Laura MacNamara Sobel), Joe Viterelli (Jelly), Chazz Palminteri (Primo Sidone), Bill Macy (Isaac Sobel), Leo Rossi (Carlo Mangano), Kyle Sabihy (Michael Sobel), Rebecca Schull (Dorothy Sobel), Molly Shannon (Caroline), Max Casella (Nicky Shivers), Pat Cooper (Salvatore Masiello)

A psychiatrist helps a top mafioso deal with his anxiety attacks.

Patchy farce, giving De Niro a nice opportunity to send up his Godfather persona, but also letting him mug his way through fits of blubbing. Crystal milks the shrink's wholly understandable anxiety for all it's worth. The plot is an afterthought.

SCR Peter Tolan, Kenneth Lonergan CIN Stuart Dryburgh MUS Howard Shore DES Wynn Thomas ED Christopher Tellefsen, Craig P. Herring PROD Paula Weinstein, Jane Rosenthal DIST Warner/Village Roadshow/NPV/Baltimore/Spring Creek/Face/Tribeca

66 An intermittently funny, one-joke vaudeville. – *J. Hoberman, Village Voice*

66 Think of it as an offer you can't refuse – *Janet Maslin, New York Times*

† It was followed by a sequel, Analyze That.

'Last year's number one best seller. This year's (we hope) number one motion picture!'

Anatomy of a Murder   ★★★

DIR Otto Preminger
1959 161m US
[DVD] ♫

☆ James Stewart (Paul Biegler), Ben Gazzara (Lt. Frederick Manion), Lee Remick (Laura Manion), Eve Arden (Maida), Arthur O'Connell (Parnell McCarthy), George C. Scott (Claude Dancer), Kathryn Grant (Mary Pilant), Orson Bean (Dr. Smith), Murray Hamilton (Alphonse Paquette)

A small-town lawyer successfully defends an army officer accused of murdering a bartender who had assaulted his wife.

Overlong and over-faithful version of a highly detailed courtroom bestseller. The plot is necessarily equivocal, the characterizations overblown, but the trial commands some interest. It was Scott's first notable role, as the prosecutor, and his scenes with Stewart, a totally different kind of actor, are hugely compelling.

SCR Wendell Mayes   CIN Sam Leavitt   MUS Duke Ellington   DES Boris Leven   ED Louis R. Loeffler   DIST Columbia/Carlyle/Otto Preminger

† The trial judge was played by Joseph N. Welch, a real-life judge who had gained fame in 1954 by representing the army against Senator McCarthy.

⚐ picture; James Stewart (leading actor); Arthur O'Connell (supporting actor); George C. Scott (supporting actor); Wendell Mayes (adapted screenplay; Sam Leavitt; editing

And Life Goes On. . .   ★★★
SCR/DIR Abbas Kiarostami
1992   108m   Iran
☆ Ferhed Kherdamend (Film director), Buba Bayour (Puya)

A film director (an actor playing Kiarostami) and his son visit a region of Iran hit by an earthquake to see whether the cast of his recent film survived the disaster.

Deeply affecting road movie that fulfils one of Kiarostami's ongoing preoccupations: establishing a,bridge between cinema and real life. It switches seamlessly from drama and documentary and leaves an indelible impression.

CIN Homayun Payvar, Changiz Sayad   MUS Vivaldi   ED Abbas Kiarostami   PROD Ali Reza Zarrin   DIST ICA/I.I.D.C.Y.A.

66 It's still one of the very best Iranian features I've seen. – *Jonathan Rosenbaum, Chicago Reader*

† Non-professional actors were used to re-stage real events.

'A threat no one dared face. A word no one wanted to speak. A fight for many, fought by few.'

And the Band Played On   ★
DIR Roger Spottiswoode
1993   141m   US
DVD   ♫
☆ Matthew Modine (Dr. Don Francis), Alan Alda (Dr. Robert Gallo), Richard Gere (The Choreographer), Patrick Bauchau (Dr. Luc Montagnier), Nathalie Baye (Dr. Françoise Barre), Christian Clemenson (Dr. Dale Lawrence), Phil Collins (Eddie Papasano), Bud Cort (Antique shop owner), Alex Courtney (Dr. Mika Popovic), David Dukes (Dr. Mervyn Silverman), David Clennon (Mr. Johnstone), Anjelica Huston (Dr. Betsy Reisz), Steve Martin (The Brother), Ian McKellen (Bill Kraus), Lily Tomlin (Dr. Selma Dritz)

In the 1980s, American doctors investigate a disease affecting gay men. Theirs are the first researches into Aids.

A sprawling and unfocused adaptation of Randy Shilts's book. It's overstuffed with distracting stars and its narrative veers all over the place. But at least it plainly demonstrates the US government's denials and inactivity when confronted with the scale of the disease.

SCR Arnold Schulman   CIN Paul Elliott   MUS Carter Burwell   DES Victoria Paul   ED Lois Freeman-Fox   PROD Midge Sanford, Sarah Pillsbury .   DIST ITC/Odyssey/HBO

† The film was made for the US cable network HBO, but opened in cinemas in Britain.

† Shilts voiced criticisms of the film shortly before he died in 1994.

'A parent and a child. The past and the present. Memories and secrets. Can you know someone for a lifetime.... and not know them at all? The life of a father. Through the journey of a son.'

And When Did You Last See Your Father? (new)   ★
DIR Anand Tucker
2007   92m   UK/Ireland
DVD   ♫
☆ *Jim Broadbent* (Arthur Morrison), Colin Firth (Blake Morrison), Juliet Stevenson (Kim), Gina McKee (Kathy), Sarah Lancashire (Beaty), Elaine Cassidy (Sandra), Claire Skinner (Gillian), *Matthew Beard* (Blake as teenager)

An adult author tries to achieve an uneasy reconciliation with his overbearing, emotionally withholding father, who has enraged him since his childhood.

A handsome, well-acted piece, with Broadbent in splendid form as the bluff, bullying patriarch; but it winds its way towards a last act of closure with not a single unpredictable moment.

SCR David Nicholls   CIN Howard Atherton   MUS Barrington Pheloung   DES Alice Norrington   ED Trevor Waite   PROD Elizabeth Karlsen, Stephen Woolley   DIST Buena Vista

66 It's a great song of innocence and embarrassment, with a lively, gregarious performance at its centre by Jim Broadbent as Arthur and a quieter but no less effective one by debutant Beard. – *Anthony Quinn, Independent*

66 This deeply felt film by Anand Tucker deserves to be seen. – *Peter Bradshaw, Guardian*

Andrei Rublev   ★★★★
DIR *Andrei Tarkovsky*
1966   181m   USSR
DVD   ♫
☆ *Anatoly Solonitsin* (Andrei Rublev), *Ivan Lapikov* (Kirill), Nikolai Grinko (Daniel Chorny), Nikolai Sergeyev (Theophanes the Greek)

Imaginary episodes from the life of a 15th-century icon painter.

A superb recreation of mediaeval life dramatizes the eternal problem of the artist: whether to take part in the life around him or merely comment on it. This showed a brisk Tarkovsky, lighter on his feet than when directing his later, more stately films.

DVD Available on DVD	☆ Cast in order of importance
♫ Soundtrack on CD	† Points of interest
66 Critics' Quotes	⚐ Academy Award / Academy Award nomination
⚐ BAFTA / BAFTA nomination	

SCR Andrei Mikhalkov-Konchalovsky, Andrei Tarkovsky
CIN *Vadim Yusov*   MUS *Vyacheslav Tcherniaiev*
ED Ludmila Feyganova   DIST Mosfilm

66 The one indisputable Russian masterpiece of the last decade. – *Nigel Andrews, Monthly Film Bulletin, 1973*

66 With the exception of the great Eisenstein, I can't think of any film which has conveyed a feeling of the remote past with such utter conviction. . .a durable and unmistakable masterpiece. – *Michael Billington, Illustrated London News*

An Angel at My Table ★★
DIR Jane Campion
1990   158m   New Zealand/Australia
DVD ♫

☆ *Kerry Fox* (Janet Frame), Alexia Keogh (Janet Frame as adolescent), *Karen Fergusson* (Janet Frame as a child), Iris Churn (Mother), K.J. Wilson (Father), Melina Bernecker (Myrtle), Glynis Angell (Isabel), Sarah Smuts-Kennedy (June), Colin McColl (John Forrest)

A reclusive poet is misdiagnosed as mentally ill and institutionalised.

Impressionistic biopic of the New Zealand writer Janet Frame's troubled life, depicted acutely and without sentimentality. Its cinematic scale successfully disguises its TV origins.

SCR Laura Jones   CIN *Stuart Dryburgh*   MUS Don McGlashan   DES Grant Major   ED Veronica Haussler
PROD Bridget Ikin, Grant Major   DIST Hibiscus Films/N.Z. Film Commission/TV New Zealand/ABC

66 Strangely engrossing from beginning to end. – *Roger Ebert, Chicago Sun-Times*

† The film was originally made as a three-part TV miniseries.

Angel-A ★★
SCR/DIR Luc Besson
2005   91m   France
DVD ♫

☆ Jamel Debbouze (Andre), Rie Rasmussen (Angel-A), Gilbert Melki (Franck), Serge Riaboukine (Pedro), Akim Chir (Chief Malfrat)

A would-be suicide is taught life lessons by his guardian angel.

Overly repetitive and rather obvious, but the bittersweet charms of the 'light fantastic' conceit build towards a touching and delightful poignancy.

CIN Thierry Arbogast   MUS Anja Garbarek   DES Jaques Bufnoir   ED Christine Lucas Navarro, Frederic Thoraval
PROD Luc Besson   DIST Optimum

66 An achingly sincere but protracted effort. – *Lisa Nesselson, Variety*

'The Hopes of a Mother. The Dreams of a Father. The Fate of a Child.'
Angela's Ashes ★
DIR Alan Parker
1999   145m   US/GB/Ireland
DVD ♫

☆ Emily Watson (Angela), Robert Carlyle (Dad), Joe Breen (Young Frank), Ciaran Owens (Middle Frank), Michael Legge (Older Frank), Ronnie Masterson (Grandma Sheehan), Pauline McLynn (Aunt Aggie), Liam Carney (Uncle Pa Keating), Eanna Macliam (Uncle Pat), Andrew Bennett (Narrator)

An Irish Catholic lad grows up amid unspeakable hardship in pre-war Limerick.

An acclaimed misery memoir gets almost operatically grim screen treatment. As drama it's both soggy and hectoring – you feel beaten into submission.

SCR Laura Jones, Alan Parker   CIN Michael Seresin, Chris Connier   MUS John Williams   DES *Geoffrey Kirkland*
ED Gerry Hambling   PROD Scott Rudin/David Brown/Alan Parker   DIST Universal/Paramount

66 This is the kind of film about hardship in which nobody has indoor plumbing, but everyone has clean hair. – *Janet Maslin, New York Times*

♪ John Williams

Ⓣ Emily Watson (leading actress); Michael Seresin, Chris Connier, Geoffrey Kirkland

'An elegant seduction. An erotic deception. A stunning revelation.'
Angels & Insects ★★
DIR *Philip Haas*
1995   116m   GB/US
DVD ♫

☆ Mark Rylance (William Adamson), *Kristin Scott-Thomas* (Matty Crompton), Patsy Kensit (Eugenia Alabaster Adamson), Jeremy Kemp (Sir Harald Alabaster), *Douglas Henshall* (Edgar Alabaster), Annette Badland (Lady Alabaster), Chris Larkin (Robin), Anna Massey (Miss Mead), Saskia Wickham (Rowena Alabaster)

A working-class entomologist marries his rich patron's daughter, and unearths some alarming family secrets.

Verbose, somewhat unwelcoming, but peculiarly fascinating period drama, told with a scientific detachment comparable to that of its hero, and dissecting witty parallels between insect and human societies.

SCR *Belinda Haas, Philip Haas*   CIN Bernard Zitzermann
MUS Alexander Balanescu   DES Jennifer Kernke
ED Belinda Haas   PROD Joyce Herlihy, Belinda Haas,
DIST Film Four/Samuel Goldwyn/Playhouse

66 A work of clarity, ambition and intelligence. – *Geoff Andrew, Time Out*

♪ Paul Brown (costume design)

Angels with Dirty Faces ★★★
DIR *Michael Curtiz*
1938   97m   US
DVD

☆ *James Cagney* (Rocky Sullivan), *Pat O'Brien* (Jerry Connelly), *Humphrey Bogart* (James Frazier), *The Dead End Kids* (as themselves), *Ann Sheridan* (Laury Ferguson), George Bancroft (Mac Keefer), Edward Pawley (Guard Edwards)

A Brooklyn gangster is admired by slum boys, but for their sake pretends to be a coward when he goes to the electric chair.

DVD Available on DVD   ☆ Cast in order of importance   66 Critics' Quotes   † Points of interest   ♪ Academy Award   Academy Award nomination   Ⓑ BAFTA   Ⓣ BAFTA nomination

25

A shrewd, slick entertainment package and a seminal movie for all kinds of reasons. It combined gangster action with fashionable social conscience; it confirmed the Dead End Kids as stars; it provided archetypal roles for its three leading players and catapulted the female lead into stardom. It also showed the Warner style of film-making, all cheap sets and shadows, at its most effective.

SCR John Wexley, Warren Duff CIN Sol Polito MUS Max Steiner ED Owen Marks PROD Sam Bischoff DIST Warner

66 Should do fair business, but the picture itself is no bonfire. – *Variety*

66 A rousing, bloody, brutal melodrama. – *New York Mirror*

⚍ James Cagney (leading actor); Rowland Brown (original screenplay); Michael Curtiz (direction)

'On the Inside the Rules Are Brutal And the Stakes Are High.'

Animal Factory ★★

DIR Steve Buscemi
2000 94m US
DVD

☆ *Willem Dafoe* (Earl Copen), *Edward Furlong* (Ron Decker), Seymour Cassel (Lt Seeman), Mickey Rourke (Jan the Actress), Steve Buscemi (A.R. Hosspack), Tom Arnold (Buck Rowan), John Heard (James Decker), Danny Trejo (Vito), Edward Bunker (Buzzard)

A privileged young man is sent to jail for marijuana possession and taken under the wing of a dangerous skinhead.

Terse and rewarding prison drama, never sensationalising the brutalities of inmate life. Though less hard-hitting than it might have been, it works very well as an actors' piece.

SCR Edward Bunker, John Steppling CIN Phil Parmet MUS John Lurie DES Steve Rosenzweig ED Kate Williams PROD Julie Yorn, Elie Samaha, Steve Buscemi, Andrew Stevens DIST Optimum

66 Unsettlingly plausible. – *Gene Seymour, Los Angeles Times*

Anita and Me ★

DIR Metin Huseyin
2002 92m GB
DVD ♫

☆ Chandeep Uppal (Meena Kumar), Anna Brewster (Anita Rutter), Sanjeev Bhaskar (Meena's father), Ayesha Dharker (Meena's mother), Kathy Burke (Anita's mother), Lynn Redgrave (Shopkeeper), Max Beesley (Rocker), Meera Syal (Meena's aunt)

A Punjabi teenager growing up in an East Midlands village in 1972 befriends a local gang leader.

Well-meaning Anglo-Indian nostalgia piece that's unfortunately over-familiar, though not without charm.

SCR Meera Syal CIN Cinders Forshaw MUS Nitin Sawhney, Barry Blue and Lynsey De Paul DES Caroline Hanania ED Annie Kocur PROD Paul Raphael DIST Icon

66 Stutters through what are now screen clichés. – *Demetrios Matheou, Independent on Sunday*

Annie Hall ★★★★

DIR Woody Allen
1977 93m US
DVD

☆ *Woody Allen* (Alvy Singer), Diane Keaton (Annie Hall), Tony Roberts (Rob), Carol Kane (Allison), Paul Simon (Tony Lacey), Shelley Duvall (Pam), Colleen Dewhurst (Mom Hall), Christopher Walken (Duane Hall)

Against the neuroses of New York and Los Angeles, a Jewish comedian has an affair with a mid-western girl.

Semi-serious collage of jokes and bits of technique, some of the former very funny and some of the latter very successful. A hugely appealing film, it was a box-office smash, and turned its creator, of whom it is very typical, from a cult performer to a superstar.

SCR Woody Allen, Marshall Brickman CIN Gordon Willis MUS various ED Wendy Greene Bricmont, Ralph Rosenblum PROD Fred T. Gallo DIST UA

ALVY: Hey, don't knock masturbation. It's sex with someone I love.

ALVY: (AFTER ANNIE PARKS THE CAR): Don't worry. We can walk to the kerb from here.

66 The film's priceless vignettes about the difficulties in chitchatting with strangers, the awkward moments in family visits, and the frequent breakdowns in communication and failures in intimacy, its reminiscences about the palpable horrors of growing up in Brooklyn, and its comic encounters with lobsters in the kitchen or spiders in the bathroom, all seem like snapshots from Allen and Keaton's own romance. – *Les Keyser, Hollywood in the Seventies*

† The narrative supposedly mirrors the real-life affair of the stars, who separated before the film came out. (Diane Keaton's family name is Hall.)

⚍ picture; Diane Keaton (leading actress); Woody Allen, Marshall Brickman (original screenplay); Woody Allen (direction)

⚍ Woody Allen (leading actor)

Ⓣ picture; Diane Keaton (leading actress); Woody Allen, Marshall Brickman (original screenplay); Woody Allen (direction)

'We live at the abyss.'

Another Day in Paradise ★★

DIR Larry Clark
1997 100m US
DVD ♫

☆ *James Woods* (Mel), *Melanie Griffith* (Sid), Vincent Kartheiser (Bobbie), Natasha Gregson Wagner (Rosie), James Otis (Reverend), Peter Sarsgaard (Ty), Paul Hipp (Richard Johnson), Brent Briscoe (Clem), Branden Williams (Danny), Kim Flowers (Bonnie Johnson)

A drug dealer and his girlfriend team up with a young junkie couple and hit the road in 1970s Oklahoma.

Shaggy-dog crime saga with a genial slacker vibe, despite the explicit violence and drug-taking. As the heads of this makeshift family, Woods and Griffith are on vital form.

DVD Available on DVD ♫ Soundtrack on CD ☆ Cast in order of importance 66 Critics' Quotes † Points of interest ⚍ Academy Award ⚍ Academy Award nomination Ⓣ BAFTA Ⓣ BAFTA nomination

SCR Christopher Landon, Stephen Chin CIN Eric Edwards DES Aaron Osborne ED Luis Colina PROD Stephen Chin, Larry Clark, James Woods DIST Metrodome

66 Scrambles squalor, comedy, mayhem and pathos. – *Owen Gleiberman, Entertainment Weekly*

† Lou Diamond Phillips appears uncredited as Jewels.

Another Woman ★★

SCR/DIR *Woody Allen*
1988 81m US
DVD

☆ *Gena Rowlands* (Marion Post), Mia Farrow (Hope), Ian Holm (Ken), Blythe Danner (Lydia), Gene Hackman (Larry Lewis), Betty Buckley (Kathy), Martha Plimpton (Laura), John Houseman (Marion's Father), *Sandy Dennis* (Claire)

A philosophy professor rents an apartment next to a psychiatrist's office, and becomes absorbed in the problems of a patient.

Both minor and minor-key Allen, in serious Bergmanesque mode. The literary style can be mannered, but there are haunting insights about regret and disappointment.

CIN *Sven Nykvist* DES Santo Loquasto ED Susan E. Morse PROD Robert Greenhut DIST Rank/Orion/Jack Rollins, Charles H. Joffe

66 Takes the breath away, both for the intensity of its grand aspirations and for the thoroughness of its windy failure. – *Vincent Canby, New York Times*

'The Good is the Evil in it.'

Antibodies ★★

SCR/DIR Christian Alvart
2005 127m Germany
DVD

☆ Wotan Wilke Mohring (Michael Martens), Andre Hennicke (Gabriel Engel), Norman Reedus (Schmitz), Christian von Aster (Wagner), Hauke Diekamp (Christian Martens)

A country cop is drawn into the sick world of an imprisoned serial killer as he investigates the murder of a local girl.

A gripping, stylish study in evil using faith and moral dilemmas as provocative, compelling plot motors.

CIN Hagen Bogdanski MUS Michl Britsch DES Christian Goldbeck ED Philipp Stahl PROD Theo Baltz, Boris Schonfelder DIST Tartan

66 Fairly riveting, thanks to Alvart's command of craft and tone. – *Chuck Wilson, LA Weekly*

'A motion picture that celebrates everything you love about life.'

Antonia's Line ★★★

SCR/DIR *Marleen Gorris*
1995 102m Netherlands/Belgium/GB
DVD ♫

☆ Willeke van Ammelrooy (Antonia), Els Dottemans (Danielle), Jan Decleir (Bas), Mil Seghers (Crooked Finger), Marina de Graaf (DeeDee), Jan Steen (Loony

Lips), Veerle van Overloop (Therese), Dora van der Groen (Allegonde)

After World War II, a vibrant woman returns to her Dutch village and gives shelter to what becomes her extended family over four decades.

A life-affirming of community values, feminism and determination in the face of hardships. An immensely popular film that deservedly won the foreign language Oscar.

CIN Willy Stassen MUS Ilona Sekacz ED Michiel Reichwein, Wim Louwrier PROD Hans de Weers, Hans de Wolf and Gerard Cornelisse DIST Guild/Antonia's Line/Bergen/Prime Time/Bard/NPS

66 Written and directed with quirky charm by Marleen Gorris. – *Janet Maslin, New York Times*

⚱ foreign language film

Ⓣ film not in the English language

'Fight fear. Face truth. Embrace life.'

Antwone Fisher ★

DIR Denzel Washington
2002 120m US
DVD ♫

☆ Derek Luke (Antwone Fisher), Joy Bryant (Cheryl Smolley), Denzel Washington (Jerome Davenport), Salli Richardson (Berta), Earl Billings (James), Kevin Connolly (Slim), *Viola Davis* (Eva)

A volatile US Navy recruit submits to mandatory sessions with a counsellor, who becomes a surrogate father.

An autobiographical saga of child abuse, behavioural problems and inspirational recovery, directed as a blandly heartwarming exercise in therapy and closure.

SCR Antwone Fisher CIN Philippe Rousselot MUS Mychael Danna DES Nelson Coates ED Conrad Buff PROD Todd Black, Randa Haines, Denzel Washington DIST TFC

66 Glib and as slow-moving as bank holiday traffic. – *Philip French, Observer*

66 A successful if modest debut film. – *Kirk Honeycutt, Hollywood Reporter*

'See the world from a whole new perspective.'

Antz ★★

DIR Eric Darnell, Tim Johnson
1998 83m US
DVD ♫

☆ the voices of: Woody Allen, Dan Aykroyd, Anne Bancroft, Jane Curtin, Danny Glover, Gene Hackman, Jennifer Lopez, John Mahoney, Paul Mazursky, Sylvester Stallone, Sharon Stone, Christopher Walken

A neurotic worker ant struggles to escape the oppressive yoke of his society, and to woo an ant princess.

Whizzy computer animation and a witty, sarcastic script, well-delivered, enliven what is otherwise a standard fable about individuality versus tyranny. It's enjoyable, but just a tiny bit pleased with itself.

SCR Todd Alcott, Chris Weitz, Paul Weitz MUS Harry

Gregson-Williams, John Powell **DES** John Bell **ED** Stan Webb **PROD** Brad Lewis, Aron Warner, Patty Wooton **DIST** DreamWorks/PDI

66 It halfway works, but there is no magic in the air. – *Kenneth Turan, Los Angeles Times*

66 The trip to Insectopia sticks in the mind as the one sequence that matches Toy Story's inspiration and existential wit. – *Tom Charity, Time Out*

Ⓣ Ken Bielenberg, Philippe Gluckman, John Bell, Kendal Crankhite (special visual effects)

'Life Is A Contact Sport. Play. Or Be Played.'

Any Given Sunday ★★

DIR Oliver Stone
1999 150m US
[DVD] ♫

☆ Al Pacino (Tony D'Amato), Cameron Diaz (Christina Pagniacci), Dennis Quaid (Jack 'Cap' Rooney), James Woods (Dr Harvey Mandrake), Jamie Foxx (Willie Beamen), LL Cool J (Julian Washington), Dr Ollie Powers (Matthew Modine), Jim Brown (Montezuma Monroe), Charlton Heston (AFFA Commissioner), Ann-Margret (Margaret Pagniacci), Aaron Eckhart (Nick Crozier), John C. McGinley (Jack Rose), Lauren Holly (Cindy Rooney)

When a star quarterback is knocked out of his American football team, the ageing coach and female co-owner clash with different strategies for getting back to the top.

Cranked up to within an inch of its life with hyperbolic editing and sound, Stone's attempt to take on the rabid commercialism of US sports constantly seems to be shouting its head off, but some occasional insights are scored.

SCR John Logan, Oliver Stone, Daniel Pyne **CIN** Salvatore Totino **MUS** Robbie Robertson, Paul Kelly, Richard Horowitz **DES** Victor Kempster **ED** Tom Nordberg, Keith Salmon, Stuart Waks, Stuart Levy **PROD** Lauren Shuler Donner, Clayton Townsend, Dan Halsted **DIST** Warner

TONY D'AMATO: I don't know what to say, really. Three minutes to the biggest battle of our professional lives all comes down to today. Either we heal as a team or we are going to crumble. Inch by inch play by play till we're finished. We are in hell right now, gentlemen, believe me and we can stay here and get the shit kicked out of us or we can fight our way back into the light. We can climb out of hell. One inch, at a time.

66 A rambunctious, hyperkinetic, testosterone-and-adrenaline-drenched look at that American obsession known as professional football. – *Todd Mccarthy, Variety*

66 The film's cumulative effect is as exhausting as it is exciting. – *Owen Gleiberman, Entertainment Weekly*

† Pacino's rabble-rousing speech to his failing team has been used as a motivational tool by several sports coaches.

'In any relationship, one person always does the heavy lifting.'

Anything Else

SCR/DIR Woody Allen
2003 108m US
[DVD]

☆ Woody Allen (David Dobel), Jason Biggs (Jerry Falk),

Christina Ricci (Amanda), Danny DeVito (Harvey), Stockard Channing (Paula), KaDee Strickland (Brooke)

A budding comedy writer seeks advice from his elderly teacher about an impossible relationship with an actress who's cheating on him.

Sour and superficial contemporary romantic comedy, not Allen's worst from this period, but betraying a suspicious view of women that borders on paranoid.

CIN Darius Khondji **DES** Santo Loquasto **ED** Alisa Lepselter **PROD** Letty Aronson **DIST** DreamWorks

66 The film isn't really a romantic comedy, more a stand-up tragedy with jokes thrown in for pacing. – *Wendy Ide, The Times*

66 Everything looks dated, adrift and obsolete. – *Peter Bradshaw, Guardian*

'Movie-wise, there has never been anything like it – laugh-wise, love-wise, or otherwise-wise!'

The Apartment ★★★★

DIR *Billy Wilder*
1960 125m US
[DVD]

☆ *Jack Lemmon* (C. C. Baxter), *Shirley MacLaine* (Miss Kubelik), *Fred MacMurray* (Jeff D. Sheldrake), Ray Walston (Joe Dobisch), Jack Kruschen (Dr Dreyfuss), Joan Shawlee (Sylvia), Edie Adams (Miss Olsen), David Lewis (Al Kirkeby)

A lonely, ambitious clerk rents out his apartment to philandering executives and finds that one of them is after his own girl.

Agreeably mordant and cynical comedy with a sour view of city office life and some deftly handled individual sequences. Intriguing because of the timing of its release: Wilder delivered this slap at America's corporate ethos at a time when the country and its businesses were at a peak of self-confidence. In retrospect, he got it right.

SCR *Billy Wilder, I. A. L. Diamond* **CIN** Joseph LaShelle **MUS** Adolph Deutsch **ED** Daniel Mandell **PROD** Billy Wilder **DIST** UA/Mirisch

BAXTER'S OPENING NARRATION: On November 1st, 1959, the population of New York City was 8,042,753. If you laid all these people end to end, figuring an average height of five feet six and a half inches, they would reach from Times Square to the outskirts of Karachi, Pakistan. I know facts like this because I work for an insurance company – Consolidated Life of New York. We are one of the top five companies in the country. Last year we wrote nine point three billion dollars worth of policies. Our home office has 31,259 employees, which is more than the entire population of Natchez, Mississippi, or Gallup, New Mexico. I work on the 19th floor – Ordinary Policy department – Premium Accounting division – Section W – desk number 861.

BAXTER: Miss Kubelik, one doesn't get to be a second administrative assistant around here unless he's a pretty good judge of character, and as far as I'm concerned you're tops. I mean, decency-wise and otherwise-wise.

BAXTER: You know, I used to live like Robinson Crusoe – shipwrecked among eight million people. Then one day I saw a footprint in the sand and there you were. It's a wonderful thing, dinner for two.

MISS KUBELIK (LAST LINE OF FILM): Shut up and deal.

66 Without either style or taste, shifting gears between

[DVD] Available on DVD   ☆ Cast in order of importance   66 Critics' Quotes   ▮ Academy Award   Ⓑ BAFTA
♫ Soundtrack on CD   † Points of interest   ▯ Academy Award nomination   Ⓣ BAFTA nomination

pathos and slapstick without any transition. – *Dwight MacDonald*

66 Billy Wilder directed this acrid story as if it were a comedy, which is a cheat, considering that it involves pimping and a suicide attempt and many shades of craven ethics. – *New Yorker, 1980*

↟ picture; Billy Wilder (direction); Billy Wilder, I. A. L. Diamond (original screenplay)
↟ Jack Lemmon (leading actor); Shirley MacLaine (leading actress); Jack Kruschen (supporting actor); Joseph LaShelle; art direction; editing
Ⓣ picture; Jack Lemmon (leading actor); Shirley MacLaine (leading actress)

Apocalypse Now ★★★★

DIR *Francis Ford Coppola*
1979   153m   US
DVD   ♫

☆ *Martin Sheen* (Capt. Willard), *Robert Duvall* (Lt. Col. Kilgore), *Frederic Forrest* (Chef), Marlon Brando (Col. Kurtz), Sam Bottoms (Lance), Dennis Hopper (Photojournalist)

During the Vietnam War, a US captain is sent up the Mekong river with a small crew to terminate 'with extreme prejudice' the command of a colonel who, suffering delusions of grandeur, is ruling his own 'kingdom' in the jungle.

A fever dream of a war movie, a hallucinogenic experience that aims to replicate the dislocation and hellishness of the Vietnam conflict. It's easily disparaged as an expensive folly that got out of control, both in the logistical and budgetary sense. But it remains a series of dazzling, sometimes macabre set-pieces, held together by a river journey into the unknown. Based loosely on Joseph Conrad's novel Heart of Darkness, it shares that book's sense of horror and insanity. Even the film's harshest critics would concede that it is unforgettable.

SCR John Milius, Francis Ford Coppola   **CIN** *Vittorio Storaro*   **MUS** Carmine Coppola, Francis Ford Coppola   **DES** *Dean Tavoularis*   **ED** Richard Marks, Walter Murch, Gerald B. Greenberg, Lisa Fruchtman   **PROD** Francis Ford Coppola   **DIST** Omni Zoetrope

LT-COL KILGORE (ROBERT DUVALL): I love the smell of napalm in the morning. It smells like. . .victory!

66 The characters are living through Vietnam as pulp adventure fantasy, as movie, as stoned humour. – *New Yorker*

† Coppola's wife Eleanor published a book about the filming experience, titled Notes on the Making Of Apocalypse Now. She also shot behind-the-scenes footage during shooting, which ended up in the documentary Hearts of Darkness: A Film-Maker's Apocalypse, (1991), for which she won an Emmy award.
† Coppola offered the role of Willard to Al Pacino, James Caan and Jack Nicholson, and the role of Kurtz to Steve McQueen, Robert Redford and Nicholson. Brando finally agreed to play Kurtz. Harvey Keitel was hired as Willard before being replaced by Sheen.
† Apocalypse Now Redux, a version that added an extra 50 minutes of footage, was released in 2001.

↟ Vittorio Storaro; Walter Murch, Mark Berger, Richard Beggs, Nat Boxer (sound)

↟ picture; Robert Duvall (supporting actor); John Milius, Francis Ford Coppola (adapted screenplay); Francis Ford Coppola (direction); art direction; editing
Ⓣ Francis Ford Coppola (direction); Robert Duvall (supporting actor)

'No one can outrun their destiny.'

Apocalypto ★

DIR Mel Gibson
2006   138m   US
DVD   ♫

☆ Rudy Youngblood (Jaguar Paw), Dalia Hernandez (Seven), Jonathan Brewer (Blunted), Raoul Trujillo (Zero Wolf), Rodolfo Palacios (Snake Ink), Morris Birdyellowhead (Flint Sky)

In the last days of the ancient Mayan civilisation, a young warrior is earmarked for human sacrifice.

Audacious historical epic told entirely in subtitled Yucatec and as brutally violent as we have come to expect from Gibson; for all its exotic trappings and gruesome detail, it finally becomes a simple, if well-directed, chase movie.

SCR Mel Gibson, Farhad Safinia   **CIN** Dean Semler   **MUS** James Horner   **DES** Tom Sanders   **ED** John Wright   **PROD** Mel Gibson, Bruce Davey   **DIST** Icon

66 A trip to a place one's never been before, offering hitherto unseen sights of exceptional vividness and power. – *Todd McCarthy, Variety*

66 It is, above all, a muscular and kinetic action movie, a drama of rescue and revenge. – *A.O. Scott, New York Times*

† The film's release was overshadowed by Gibson's anti-Semitic outburst during a drink-driving arrest in California in July 2006.
† The film was accused by some indigenous groups of misrepresenting Mayan culture.

↟ Aldo Signoretti, Vittorio Sodano (makeup); Sean McCormack, Kami Asgar (sound editing); Kevin O'Connell, Greg P. Russell, Fernando Cámara (sound mixing)
Ⓣ film not in the English language

'Houston, we have a problem.'

Apollo 13 ★★

DIR Ron Howard
1995   140m   US
DVD   ♫

☆ Tom Hanks (Jim Lovell), Bill Paxton (Fred Haise), Kevin Bacon (Jack Swigert), Ed Harris (Gene Kranz), Gary Sinise (Ken Mattingly), Kathleen Quinlan (Marilyn Lovell), Mary Kate Schellhardt (Barbara Lovell), Emily Ann Lloyd (Susan Lovell)

The Apollo space launch to the moon in 1970 is crippled by an explosion, and Mission Control communicates in a frenzy with the astronauts to bring them back safely.

Utterly straight re-creation of a narrowly averted catastrophe, but one which achieves genuine suspense in its focus on the nuts and bolts. A shame that there's not much room for characters or context.

DVD Available on DVD   ☆ Cast in order   66 Critics' Quotes   ↟ Academy Award   Ⓣ BAFTA
♫ Soundtrack on CD   of importance   † Points of interest   ↟ Academy Award nomination   Ⓣ BAFTA nomination

29

In the same way we connect the name Wisden with the cricketers' almanac, Pevsner with architectural guides and Jane with fighting ships, so Halliwell automatically brings to mind film encyclopaedias. Named after their chroniclers, these are the pre-eminent works of reference in their particular field; *Halliwell's* reflects this indisputable fact with the phrase 'the only film guide that matters'.

This seems an appropriate time to look back on the life of Leslie Halliwell, who started this series of guides in 1965, with the publication of the first *Filmgoer's Companion*. To call Halliwell a film buff would be something of an understatement. That first volume grew out of a casual conversation at a cocktail party, when Halliwell suggested to a publisher the need for such a general film encyclopaedia. He was given the go-ahead to compile the book, the presumption being that he would surround himself with a large team of contributors, experts and assistants. To the surprise of his publishers, Halliwell wrote every word of the volume himself.

Astonishingly, he managed to maintain the *Filmgoer's Companion*, along with an ever-growing range of complementary reference books – *Halliwell's Film Guide* (from 1977), *The Filmgoer's Book of Quotes*, *Halliwell's Movie Quiz*, and others – for the next 23 years, until his death. He was sole author of all these titles.

As a body of first-person scholarship, it is a remarkable body of work. What makes it almost uncanny is that it represented just one of two outstanding parallel careers. His other life, inevitably, also had to do with movies: from 1968 to 1987, he was the programme buyer of films and TV series for ITV.

This second role made him a hugely important and influential figure; back then, ITV was part of an unchallenged duopoly with the BBC, and commanded an enormous share of Britain's TV audience. Twice a year, Halliwell would visit Los Angeles to inspect the new wares of the US television networks, and negotiate broadcast deals for films from Hollywood studios. He happened upon this job at a fortunate time, when the studios were just starting to open up their archives for television rights.

Yet while his ITV duties made him a formidable figure in the TV industry, he found it increasingly difficult to find and buy films suitable for consumption by family audiences seated around the television. He came to feel that films of the 1970s and 1980s were too dependent on violence, coarse language and sexuality for effect.

His real love was the cinema of the Golden Age – films from the 1930s and 1940s, up to the mid-1950s – about which he was deeply knowledgeable. This expertise proved invaluable when he programmed seasons of classic and forgotten films for the then relatively new Channel 4. This worked extremely well for both sides. Channel 4, with its limited budgets, could not afford to enter into bidding wars for blockbuster films with ITV and the BBC, and were happy to settle for more specialised titles, which were far cheaper. For his part, Halliwell justifiably regarded these seasons of older gems as a National Film Theatre for people's homes, via the medium of TV.

He was born in Bolton in 1929, and first attended a cinema, to keep his mother company, when he was four years old. He was allowed to go to the pictures on his own when he was nine. As he recalled in his autobiography, *Seats in All Parts*, there were no less than 47 cinemas to choose from in the Bolton area of his childhood, some of them beautiful, extravagant buildings in the midst of a somewhat grim industrial setting. His extreme devotion to movies first manifested itself when he was 11, and he began maintaining a critical diary of each film he saw.

He ran the film society at his local grammar school, again at Cambridge, and in the Army during his National Service. The screenwriter and playwright Frederic Raphael, a near-contemporary of his at Cambridge, recalls that Halliwell was not one of the fashionable set; socially he was rather reserved. But fellow students admired his encyclopaedic knowledge of film, and were truly impressed when he returned to Cambridge as manager and booker of the Rex Cinema, where he showed foreign language films, 'golden oldies' (*The Philadelphia Story*, one of his all-time favourites, was regularly screened) and comedies from the Marx Brothers and Laurel and Hardy. Under Halliwell, the Rex occasionally pulled off a coup: it was the first British cinema to exhibit *The Wild One*, starring Marlon Brando, which was still banned at the time.

In 1959 he joined Granada as a film researcher. There, his prodigious knowledge of film helped him rise swiftly through the ranks; within nine years he was programme buyer for the whole ITV network. He also put his stamp on Granada's film output; the long-running series *Cinema* was his idea, as was a companion series for children, *Clapperboard*. He sometimes appeared on this latter show, explaining in simple terms to a young audience how films were made.

> ' His extreme devotion to movies first manifested itself when he was 11, and he began maintaining a critical diary of each film he saw. '

As ITV's film buyer he made a real mark. He was shrewd enough to buy up rights for half a dozen James Bond films relatively early on, calculating correctly that they would work ideally for TV audiences, especially families.

He brought this same confidence to creating his film guides and encyclopaedias; there were, of course, no precedents for this work, and he could shape them precisely as he wished.

One quality he brought to these volumes, especially the *Film Guide*, was critical rigour. He decided that all films could be assessed within a tough star system ranging from zero to four stars, with most films being consigned to the lower end of that scale. (Compare the plethora of gushing five-star reviews in many other guides, magazines and newspapers today.)

Halliwell also liked conciseness in reviews; it became his trademark

Whatever one's feelings about the films he reviewed, it had to be admitted that he told the truth as he saw it, plainly and simply. Halliwell was no academic film historian; he was interested in communicating his passion about films and his opinion of them to a broad audience. These populist tendencies extended to the films he bought for ITV and the successful guides he authored.

Those less enamoured of his approach to film criticism found all this rather curmudgeonly. He was certainly hard on films dating from the last 20 years of his life, much preferring titles from 1935 to 1955. A friend and film critic, the late Tom Hutchinson, remarked affectionately of Halliwell on his death in 1989: 'I don't think he liked any film after *Gone With The Wind*.'

That's an exaggeration, yet it's true that you could search long and hard for films after the late 1960s which he awarded the maximum four stars. (His successor John Walker undertook revisions of his reviews, especially those of films released in the 1970s and 1980s.)

Halliwell admitted this prejudice himself. He was no fan of sex and brutality in movies, and in the 1980s described modern films as 'crude, violent, pretentious'. It is probably as well he did not live to see the advent of the recent, unlovely 'torture porn' movement, or even the broad comedies (such as *Knocked Up*) that spring from Judd Apatow's comedy factory.

Still, any critic is entitled to prejudices and preferences; they are what make us individuals. Happily, Halliwell was also a great fan of films from before World War II that sadly are all but lost to us today. They are almost never seen on television; they may very occasionally be part of a season or retrospective at the BFI Southbank; but mostly they stay lodged in the British Film Institute's archives. He insisted, correctly, that they had intrinsic worth; as a result, this is the only leading film guide that features so many titles from that far-off era.

What Leslie Halliwell bequeathed in these volumes (which continue today, revised, updated but still recognisable) was a labour of love – an attempt to list and codify a history of films released in this country, for the benefit of succeeding generations. His works will long remain a starting point for academic researchers delving into cinema's past – and a trustworthy guide for all film lovers.

SCR William Broyles Jnr, Al Reinert   CIN Dean Cundey
MUS James Horner   DES Michael Corenblith   ED Mike
Hill, Dan Hanley   PROD Brian Grazer   DIST Imagine

66 A nail-biter and knuckle-whitener of the first rank. –
Michael Wilmington, Chicago Tribune

66 Plays boringly safe. . .The drama proceeds in a narrow
line that leaves no room for poetry, surprise or true
excitement. – *Geoff Brown, The Times*

Mike Hill, Dan Hanley; Rick Dior, Steve Pederson, Scott
Millan, David MacMillan (sound)

picture; Ed Harris (supporting actor); Kathleen Quinlan
(supporting actress); Michael Corenblith; William Broyles
Jnr, Al Reinert (original screenplay); Robert Legato, Michael
Kanfer, Leslie Ekker, Matt Sweeney (visual effects)

Robert Legato, Michael Kanfer, Leslie Ekker, Matt
Sweeney (special visual effects)

Dean Cundey; Mike Hill, Dan Hanley; Rick Dior, Steve
Pederson, Scott Millan, David MacMillan (sound)

'Lust, Obsession, Revenge... Redemption'

The Apostle ★★

SCR/DIR Robert Duvall
1997   134m   US
DVD   ♫

☆ *Robert Duvall* (Euliss Dewey), Farrah Fawcett (Jessie
Dewey), Todd Allen (Horace), John Beasley (Brother
Blackwell), June Carter Cash (Mrs Dewey), Walton
Goggins (Sam), Billy Joe Shaver (Joe), Billy Bob Thornton
(Troublemaker), Miranda Richardson (Toosie)

A Southern evangelical preacher assaults his wife's
love with a baseball bat, changes his name, and goes
on the run, establishing a new church in rural
Louisiana.

*Absorbing drama about a complicated man driven by
his faith; it becomes a somewhat shameless excuse for
Duvall to strut his stuff in this plum role, but strut it he
does.*

CIN Barry Markowitz   MUS David Mansfield   DES Linda
Burton   ED Stephen Mack   PROD Rob Carliner
DIST Universal/October/Butchers Run

66 Avoiding the clichés and condescension that
characterize many films on religious figures, the movie is
at once a compelling drama and a thoughtful look at faith-
related issues on personal, social, and cultural levels. –
David Sterritt, Christian Science Monitor

66 Duvall's performance is so passionate, so energized,
that it's almost eerie: is Sonny acting him or is he acting
Sonny? – *Daphne Merkin, New Yorker*

† Duvall wrote the script in the 1980s, but after being
turned down by several studios, bankrolled the film
himself to the tune of $4 million. Its success (it grossed
$20 million in the US alone) allowed him to get his money
back from distributors.

Robert Duvall (leading actor)

The Apple ★★★

DIR *Samirah Makhmalbaf*
1997   86m   Iran/France
DVD

☆ Massoumeh Naderi (Massoumeh), Za Naderi (Zahra),
Ghorban Ali-Naderi (Father), Azizeh Mohamadi (Azizeh)

After being imprisoned all their lives by their
elderly, conservative father and blind mother, 12-
year-old twin sisters in Tehran are released into the
outside world by social workers.

*One of the first vital Iranian pictures, based on real
events with the cast playing themselves: it collapses the
boundaries between documentary and drama, and has
a clear-eyed candour that's wonderfully fresh.*

SCR *Mohsen Makhmalbaf, Samirah Makhmalbaf*
CIN Ebrahim Ghafouri, Mohamad Ahmadi   ED Mohsen
Makhmalbaf   DIST Artificial Eye/MK2

66 You rarely come across a film this inquisitive about the
world, and about film. – *Jonathan Romney, Guardian*

† Samirah Makhmalbaf was just 17 when she directed
this, her first feature film.

Après l'Amour ★

DIR Diane Kurys
1992   104m   France
DVD

☆ Isabelle Huppert (Lola), Bernard Giraudeau (David),
Hippolyte Girardot (Tom), Lio (Marianne), Yvan Attal
(Romain), Judith Reval (Rachel), Ingrid Held (Anne),
Laure Killing (Elisabeth), Mehdi Ioossen (Simon), Florian
Billon (Olivier)

A year in the sexual lives of sophisticated
Parisians.

*A novelist, an architect and a pop star couple and
uncouple over a 12-month period. There's an
appealingly wry, knowing air about it all, even if no
profound insights are offered up.*

SCR Diane Kurys, Antoine Lacomblez   CIN Fabio
Conversi   MUS Yves Simon   DES Tony Egry   ED Hervé
Schneid   PROD Jean-Bernard Fetoux
DIST Mayfair/Alexandre/TF1/Prodeve

66 Après l'amour seems. . .at ease with itself. It copes
with agony, bluster, lies and voyeurism in a cynically
relaxed spirit that places it firmly in the French
'relationship movie' genre. – *Amanda Lipman, Sight
and Sound*

Aprile ★

SCR/DIR Nanni Moretti
1998   78m   Italy/France
DVD

☆ Nanni Moretti, Silvio Orlando, Silvia Nono, Pietro
Moretti, Agata Apicella Moretti, Nuria Schoenberg, Angelo
Barbagallo, Silvia Bonucci, Quentin de Fouchecour,
Renato De Maria, Daniele Luchetti, Andrea Molaioli,
Nicola Piepoli, Corrado Stajano

An Italian film director works on a musical
and considers shooting a documentary about
his country's politics, all the while musing
on fatherhood, nationality and his own
mortality.

*It's no wonder that Nanni Moretti was once tagged the
Italian Woody Allen. Few film-makers have inserted
their lives into their films to quite such an extent. This
blend of fact and fiction even surpasses the introspection
of Dear Diary. But it's entertaining enough, especially*

for those who care about Italy's politics and the workings of its film industry.

CIN Giuseppe Lanci **MUS** Ludovico Einaudi **DES** Marta Maffucci **ED** Angelo Nicolini, Daniele Sordoni **PROD** Angelo Barbagallo, Nanni Moretti, Jean Labadie **DIST** Metro Tartan

Apt Pupil ★★

DIR Bryan Singer
1997 111m US/France
DVD ♫

☆ *Ian McKellen* (Kurt Dussander), *Brad Renfro* (Todd Bowden), Bruce Davison (Richard Bowden), Elias Koteas (Archie), Joe Morton (Dan Richler), Jan Triska (Isaac Weiskopf), Michael Byrne (Ben Kramer), Heather McComb (Becky Trask), David Schwimmer (Edward French)

A precocious high-school boy obsessed with the Holocaust blackmails an ageing Nazi into sharing his experiences.

Audacious and undeniably creepy drama about evil begetting evil; the pas de deux is well written and played, but the plot frays badly towards the end.

SCR Brandon Boyce **CIN** *Newton Thomas Sigel* **MUS** *John Ottman* **DES** Richard Hoover **ED** *John Ottman* **PROD** Jane Hamsher, Don Murphy, Bryan Singer **DIST** Columbia TriStar/Phoenix/Bad Hat Harry/Canal+

❝ Brought off with such skill and commitment that there isn't any time to snicker at its obviousness. – *Mick LaSalle, San Francisco Chronicle*

❝ I didn't like my character. He didn't seem very deep. He just seemed a representative of evil. – *Ian McKellen*

† An earlier version of Stephen King's story was shot in 1987, starring Rick Schroder and Nicol Williamson, but ran over budget and was never finished. When King heard Bryan Singer wanted to re-film it, he sold the rights for $1.

† Brad Renfro died in January 2008, due to an accidental drugs overdose. He was 25.

'Eight legs. Two fangs. And an attitude.'

Arachnophobia ★★

DIR Frank Marshall
1990 103m US
DVD ♫

☆ Jeff Daniels (Dr. Ross Jennings), Harley Jane Kozak (Molly Jennings), John Goodman (Delbert McClintock), Julian Sands (Doctor James Atherton), Stuart Pankin (Sheriff Lloyd Parsons), Brian McNamara (Chris Collins), Mark L. Taylor (Jerry Manley), Henry Jones (Doctor Sam Metcalf)

A deadly South American spider stows away in a crate to rural California, breeds in the house of a newly arrived doctor, and thousands of its offspring overrun the town.

Rather expert horror comedy, best enjoyed by spider-phobes through slitted fingers.

SCR Don Jacoby, Wesley Strick **CIN** Mikael Salomon **MUS** Trevor Jones **DES** James Bissell **ED** Michael Kahn **PROD** Kathleen Kennedy, Richard Vane **DIST** Hollywood Pictures/Amblin/Tangled Web

❝ Designed to reduce the audience to a squirming mass. – *Colette Maude, Time Out*

† Steven Spielberg was executive producer on the film.

'A real adventure in the coolest place on earth.'

Arctic Tale (new)

DIR Adam Ravetch, Sarah Robertson
2007 86m US
♫

☆ Queen Latifah (Storyteller)

A polar bear cub and a walrus calf face similar hardships as they attempt to survive in the inhospitable North Pole.

Family-friendly documentary with impressive wildlife footage, an informal narrator and a rather heavy-handed environmental message.

SCR Linda Woolverton, Mose Richards, Kristin Gore **CIN** Adam Ravetch **MUS** Joby Talbot **ED** Beth Spiegel **PROD** Adam Leipzig, Keenan Smart **DIST** Paramount

❝ An expertly assembled docu with an underlying message about multiple species threatened by man's pigheaded behaviour. – *Ken Eisner, Variety*

❝ Queen Latifah's gooey narration, coupled with the preachy and insincere message about global warming, made me want to head out to the ice floes with my trusty culling club. – *Peter Bradshaw, Guardian*

Ariel ★★

SCR/DIR *Aki Kaurismäki*
1988 73m Finland

☆ Turo Pajala (Taisto Olavi Kasurinen), Susanna Haavisto (Irmeli Katariina Pihlaja), Matti Pellonpää (Mikkonen), Eetu Hilkamo (Riku), Erkki Pajala (Miner), Matti Jaaranen (Assaulter), Hannu Viholainen (Henchman)

A miner in Lapland loses his job and sets off in his Cadillac in search of adventure. He hooks up with a female traffic warden and considers the notion of getting rich through crime.

For those who appreciate this director's bone-dry humour and his meditations on Americanisation and existential angst, this is a real treat. Kaurismaki has a great gift for droll juxtaposition: on this occasion the downbeat ending is accompanied by the strains of Somewhere Over the Rainbow – sung in Finnish.

CIN *Timo Salminen* **DES** Risto Karhula **ED** Raija Talvio **PROD** Aki Kaurismäki **DIST** Electric/Villealfa

'A rebellious young man. With his own vision of the future. And his own fantasy of love.'

Arizona Dream ★

DIR Emir Kusturica
1991 142m US/France
DVD ♫

☆ Johnny Depp (Axel Blackmar), Faye Dunaway (Elaine Stalker), *Jerry Lewis* (Leo Sweetie), Lili Taylor (Grace Stalker), Paulina Porizkova (Millie), Vincent Gallo (Paul Leger), Candyce Mason (Blanche)

A young drifter in New York takes a trip to Arizona where his favourite uncle urges him to settle down.

DVD Available on DVD ☆ Cast in order of importance ❝ Critics' Quotes † Points of interest ⚐ Academy Award ⚐ Academy Award nomination ⚐ BAFTA ⚐ BAFTA nomination
♫ Soundtrack on CD

33

Instead he falls in love with an older, child-like woman.

A curious, skewed view of America by this talented, tempestuous Bosnian director. The thought occurs more than once during this overlong trek that he misses the point of the whole country. The film's calculated quirkiness overwhelms its few good moments, though Jerry Lewis and Faye Dunaway turn out to be surprising, inspired casting. Another example of Depp taking the art-house route by portraying an impenetrable oddball.

SCR David Atkins   CIN Vilko Filac   MUS Goran Bregovic   DES Miljen Kljakovic   ED Andrija Zafranovic   PROD Claudie Ossard, Yves Marmion   DIST Electric/Constellation/UGC/Hachette

66 There is so much to like in Arizona Dream that you can't help wondering why you don't like it better. Director Emir Kusturica. . .behaves as if he has a patent on whimsy. – *Barbara Shulgasser, San Francisco Examiner*

† The film opened in mainland Europe with a 142-minute running time, but was cut by more than 20 minutes for US and UK release.

'How Well Do You Know Your Neighbour?'

Arlington Road ★★

DIR Mark Pellington
1998   117m   US/GB
DVD   ♫

☆ Jeff Bridges (Michael Faraday), Tim Robbins (Oliver Lang), Joan Cusack (Cheryl Lang), Hope Davis (Brooke Woolfe), Robert Gossett (Whit Carver), Mason Gamble (Brady Lang), Spencer Treat Clark (Grant Faraday), Stanley Anderson (Dr. Archer Scobee)

A college history professor begins to suspect that his neighbour is a terrorist.

A contrived but ingenious paranoid thriller, often stretching credulity but ultimately justifying its hysterics.

SCR Ehren Kruger   CIN Bobby Bukowski   MUS *Angelo Badalamenti*   DES Therese Deprez   ED Conrad Buff   PROD Peter Samuelson, Tom Gorai, Marc Samuelson   DIST Sony/Screen Gems/Lakeshore Entertainment

66 Deceptively keen as both a paranoid political thriller and a caveat against the trustworthiness of your friends and neighbours. – *Wesley Morris, Boston Globe*

The Army in the Shadows ★★★★

SCR/DIR *Jean-Pierre Melville*
1969   143m   France/Italy

☆ *Lino Ventura* (Philippe Gerbier), *Simone Signoret* (Mathilde), *Jean-Pierre Cassel* (Jean Francois), Paul Meurisse (Luc Jardie), Claude Mann (Le Masque), Paul Crauchet (Felix), Christian Barbier (Le Bison)

In 1942, a French resistance leader in Lyon is determined to discover who betrayed him to the Nazis.

Utterly riveting thriller fuelled by one man's vengeance. Brilliantly filmed, appropriately long on shadows, with a moody, unbearably tense atmosphere. No film is more

calculated to leave audiences with sweaty palms – and that is a warm recommendation.

CIN *Pierre L'homme*   MUS Eric de Marsan   ED Françoise Bonnot   PROD Jacques Dorfman   DIST Films Corona/Fono Roma

66 Gerbier flees his captors along empty night-time streets, slows to a walk, and slips into the only shop where the lights still burn. It happens to be a barber's, so he sits and has a shave, still panting from his exertions, and not knowing whether the man with the razor will help him out or slit his throat. There is no backchat, no music: nothing but the scraping of the blade. For the first, and maybe the only, time this year, you are in the hands of a master, and you follow every cut. – *Anthony Lane, New Yorker*

'It's a wonderful world, if you'll only take the time to go around it!'

Around the World in Eighty Days ★★★

DIR Michael Anderson, Kevin McClory
1956   178m   US
DVD   ♫

☆ *David Niven* (Phileas Fogg), *Cantinflas* (Passepartout), *Robert Newton* (Inspector Fix), Shirley MacLaine (Princess Aouda), Charles Boyer (Monsieur Casse), Joe E. Brown (Station Master), Martine Carol (Tourist), John Carradine (Col. Proctor Stamp), Charles Coburn (Clerk), *Ronald Colman* (Railway Official), Melville Cooper (Steward), *Noël Coward* (Hesketh-Baggott), Finlay Currie (Whist Partner), Reginald Denny (Police Chief), Andy Devine (First Mate), Marlene Dietrich, Luis Dominguin, Fernandel, John Gielgud, Hermione Gingold, Jose Greco, Cedric Hardwicke, Trevor Howard, Glynis Johns, Buster Keaton, Evelyn Keyes, Beatrice Lillie, Peter Lorre, Edmund Lowe, A. E. Matthews, Mike Mazurki, Tim McCoy, Victor McLaglen, John Mills, Alan Mowbray, Robert Morley, Jack Oakie, George Raft, Gilbert Roland, Cesar Romero, Frank Sinatra, Red Skelton, Ronald Squire, Basil Sidney, Harcourt Williams, Ed Murrow

A Victorian gentleman and his valet win a bet that they can go round the world in eighty days.

Amiable large-scale pageant resolving itself into a number of sketches, which could have been much sharper, separated by wide-screen spectacle. What was breath-taking at the time seems generally slow and blunted in retrospect, but the fascination of recognizing 44 cameo stars remains. The film is less an exercise in traditional skills than a tribute to producer Mike Todd's energy.

SCR James Poe, John Farrow, S. J. Perelman   CIN *Lionel Lindon*   MUS *Victor Young*   ED Gene Ruggiero, Paul Weatherwax   PROD *Michael Todd*   DIST UA

66 Michael Todd's 'show', shorn of the ballyhoo and to critics not mollified by parties and sweetmeats, is a film like any other, only twice as long as most. . .the shots of trains and boats seem endless. – *David Robinson*

⚱ picture; James Poe, John Farrow, S. J. Perelman; Lionel Lindon; Victor Young
⚱ Michael Anderson; art direction; editing

DVD Available on DVD   ☆ Cast in order of importance   66 Critics' Quotes   ⚱ Academy Award   🅑 BAFTA
♫ Soundtrack on CD   † Points of interest   ⚱ Academy Award nomination   🅣 BAFTA nomination

'A comedy from the heart that goes for the throat.'

As Good as It Gets ★★

DIR James L. Brooks
1997 139m US
DVD ♫

☆ Jack Nicholson (Melvin Udall), *Helen Hunt* (Carol Connelly), *Greg Kinnear* (Simon Bishop), Cuba Gooding Jnr (Frank Sachs), Skeet Ulrich (Vincent), Shirley Knight (Beverly), Yeardley Smith (Jackie), Lupe Ontiveros (Nora)

A bigoted, obsessive-compulsive writer tries to redeem himself by helping a struggling waitress and his vulnerable gay neighbour.

Cracklingly nasty one-liners from an implausible main character can't quite sustain this whole film, and it comes dangerously close to collapsing into its own gooey centre; somehow it doesn't. File under trite but effective.

SCR Mark Andrus, James L. Brooks   CIN John Bailey
MUS Hans Zimmer   DES Bill Brzeski   ED Richard Marks   PROD James L. Brooks, Bridget Johnson, Kristi Zea   DIST Columbia TriStar/Gracie

66 Wicked, but it works. – *Janet Maslin, New York Times*

Ⅰ Jack Nicholson (leading actor); Helen Hunt (leading actress)

Ⅰ picture; Greg Kinnear (supporting actor); Mark Andrus, James L. Brooks (original screenplay); Richard Marks; Hans Zimmer

'Romance. . .or something like it.'

As You Like It (new) ★

SCR/DIR Kenneth Branagh
2006 127m USA/UK
DVD ♫

☆ Brian Blessed (Duke Senior, Duke Frederick), Bryce Dallas Howard (Rosalind), Romola Garai (Celia), Adrian Lester (Oliver de Boys), Alfred Molina (Touchstone), Kevin Kline (Jaques), David Oyelowo (Orlando de Boys), Richard Briers (Adam), Janet McTeer (Audrey)

Shakespeare's leading characters are banished from the court in a Japanese treaty port in the 1880s, into a forest exile.

The decorative Japanese touches soon fall away for a relatively straightforward version of the play. The humour depends too heavily on pratfalls, but the overall atmosphere is agreeably playful. Well-spoken throughout.

CIN Roger Lancer   MUS Patrick Doyle   DES Tim Harvey
ED Neil Farrell   PROD Kenneth Branagh, Judy Hofflund, Simon Moseley   DIST Lionsgate UK

66 The setting doesn't help the production. There are major longueurs. Little of the comedy comes off. – *Philip French, Observer*

66 Rather stodgy version of the Bard's wise comedy. . .It's rather a long haul. – *Trevor Johnston, Time Out*

† The Forest of Arden scenes were shot at Wakehurst Place, West Sussex.

Ashes and Diamonds ★★★★

SCR/DIR *Andrzej Wajda*
1958 104m Poland
DVD

☆ *Zbigniew Cybulski* (Maciek), Ewa Krzyzanowska

(Krystyna), Adam Pawlikowski (Andrzej), Waclaw Zastrzezynski (Szczuka), Bogumil Kobiela (Drewnowski)

At the close of World War II, a Polish partisan who fought in the Resistance feels ambivalent about a new assignment: to assassinate a Communist Party boss considered too sympathetic to the Soviet Union.

A dazzling performance by the charismatic Cybulski, who was briefly hailed as Europe's new James Dean, in a work that blends noir elements with the texture of a war film. Haunting, moving, and suffused with the fatigue felt by a man who suffered through a long, gruelling conflict.

CIN Jerzy Wojcik   MUS Aroclaw Radio Quintet
ED Halina Nawrocka   DIST Film Polski

† This was the final part of an acclaimed trilogy of war films by Wajda, who himself fought in the Polish Resistance: A Generation and Kanal were its predecessors.

Ask the Dust ★

SCR/DIR Robert Towne
2005 117m Germany/US/South Africa

☆ Colin Farrell (Arturo Bandini), Salma Hayek (Camilla Lopez), Donald Sutherland (Hellfrick), Eileen Atkins (Mrs. Hargraves), Idina Menzel (Vera Rivkin)

In Depression-era 1930s Los Angeles, an impoverished writer, holed up in a shabby boarding-house, dreams of greatness. He embarks on a stormy affair with an upwardly mobile Mexican waitress.

Brave stab at adapting a legendary novel, but John Fante's haunting prose and narrative subtlety lose their power when adapted for the screen. Undercurrents of hostility between Anglos and Hispanics in LA are well observed, and period details, including the city's orange sunsets, are captured perfectly. An interesting failure which confirms Towne's talent is for screenwriting rather than directing.

CIN Caleb Deschanel   MUS Ramin Djawadi, Heitor Pereira   DES Dennis Gassner   ED Robert K. Lambert
PROD Don Granger, Jonas McCord, Tom Cruise, Paula Wagner   DIST Pathé

66 Ask the Dust requires an audience with a special love for film noir, with a feeling for the loneliness and misery of the writer. – *Roger Ebert, Chicago Sun-Times*

† The look and atmosphere of 1930s Los Angeles was captured entirely on South African sets.

The Asphalt Jungle ★★★

DIR *John Huston*
1950 112m US

☆ *Sterling Hayden* (Dix Handley), Louis Calhern (Alonzo D Emmerich), *Sam Jaffe* (Doc Erwin Riedenschneider), Jean Hagen (Doll Conovan), James Whitmore (Gus Minissi), John McIntire (Police Commissioner Hardy), Marc Lawrence (Cobby), Marilyn Monroe (Angela Phinlay), Barry Kelley (Lt. Ditrich)

An elderly crook comes out of prison and assembles a gang for one last robbery.

Probably the very first film to show a 'caper' from the

DVD Available on DVD   ☆ Cast in order   66 Critics' Quotes   Ⅰ Academy Award   Ⓑ BAFTA
♫ Soundtrack on CD   of importance   † Points of interest   Ⅰ Academy Award nomination   Ⓑ BAFTA nomination

35

criminals' viewpoint (a genre which has since been done to death several times over), this is a clever character study rather than a thriller, extremely well executed and indeed generally irreproachable, yet somehow not a film likely to appear on many top ten lists; perhaps writer-director Huston stands too far back from everybody, or perhaps he just needed Humphrey Bogart.

SCR Ben Maddow, John Huston   CIN Harold Rosson   MUS Miklos Rozsa   ED George Boemler   PROD Arthur Hornblow Jnr   DIST MGM

RIEDENSCHNEIDER: Crime is a left-handed form of human endeavour.

66 Where this film excels is in the fluency of its narration, the sharpness of its observation of character and the excitement of its human groupings. – *Dilys Powell*

66 That Asphalt Pavement thing is full of nasty, ugly people doing nasty things. I wouldn't walk across the room to see a thing like that. – *Louis B. Mayer (who was head of the studio which made it)*

† Apart from imitations, the film has been directly remade as The Badlanders, Cairo and A Cool Breeze.

⚖ Sam Jaffe (supporting actor); John Huston (direction); Ben Maddow, John Huston (screenplay); Harold Rosson

The Assassination of Jesse James by the Coward Robert Ford (new) ★★★★

SCR/DIR *Andrew Dominik*
2007   160m   US/Canada
DVD   ♫

☆ *Brad Pitt* (Jesse James), *Casey Affleck* (Robert Ford), Sam Shepard (Frank James), Mary-Louise Parker ('Zee' James), *Paul Schneider* (Dick Liddil), *Sam Rockwell* (Charley Ford), Jeremy Renner (Wood Hite), Zooey Deschanel (Dorothy Evans)

An account of the final years of the outlaw Jesse James, how he came to be slain by a member of his own gang, and the curious aftermath of his death.

Ravishing looking, in muted tones that recall sepia-tinted photos, the story has a modern resonance: Affleck's grinning, sycophantic Ford is like a celebrity stalker-fan who goes to extremes. Pitt's Jesse verges on psychosis, switching from charm to cold fury in an instant. This slow moving film, all snowy vistas, fields of waving corn and fast-moving clouds, aims for epic grandeur. But Dominik also stages a night-time train robbery thrillingly. An elegy for the Old West, it is touched with brilliance throughout.

CIN *Roger Deakins*   MUS Nick Cave, Warren Ellis   ED Dylan Tichenor, Curtiss Clayon   PROD Brad Pitt, Dede Gardner, Ridley Scott, Jules Daly, David Valdes   DIST Warners

66 The nervy style of this newfangled Western, with its eerie, insinuating score by Nick Cave and Warren Ellis, is so effective that long after Pitt and Affleck have left the screen, emotional disturbance lingers like gun smoke. – *Lisa Schwarzbaum, Entertainment Weekly*

66 Andrew Dominik's sensational film debags a cherished idol. Tyrone Power, Robert Wagner and Roy Rogers famously played Jesse James like Robin Hood. Brad Pitt plays him like a poisonous Mr Hyde. – *James Christopher, The Times*

⚖ Casey Affleck supporting actor (supporting actor); Roger Deakins

'The mad story of a true man.'

The Assassination of Richard Nixon ★

DIR Niels Mueller
2004   95m   US
DVD

☆ *Sean Penn* (Samuel Bicke), Don Cheadle (Bonny Simmons), Jack Thompson (Jack Jones), *Michael Wincott* (Julius Bicke), *Mykelti Williamson* (Harold Mann), Naomi Watts (Marie Bicke), Nick Searcy (Tom Ford)

A depressed salesman plots to hijack a plane in 1974 and crash it into the White House.

Curious true-life case history of a disturbed individual driven to desperate measures by his failed relationships and the pressure to meet quotas at work: it is a rather self-conscious throwback to American films of the era such as Taxi Driver.

SCR Niels Mueller, Kevin Kennedy   CIN Emmanuel Lubezki   MUS Steven Stern   DES Lester Cohen   ED Jay Cassidy   PROD Alfonso Cuaron, Jorge Vergara   DIST Metrodome

66 Has a creepy, meticulous exactitude. – *Owen Gleiberman, Entertainment Weekly*

66 Overheated and overacted, but very watchable for all that. – *Aaron Hillis, Premiere*

'A White Hot Night of Hate!'

Assault on Precinct 13 ★★★

SCR/DIR *John Carpenter*
1976   91m   US
DVD   ♫

☆ *Austin Stoker* (Bishop), Darwin Joston (Wilson), Laurie Zimmer (Leigh), Martin West (Lawson), Tony Burton (Wells), Nancy Loomis (Julie)

Gang members with a grudge attack a police station in Los Angeles.

Violent, basically efficient and old-fashioned programmer, which shows that not all the expertise of the 40s in this then-familiar field has been lost. Director Carpenter has spoken of his original ambitions to make Westerns, and how he ended up making 'hidden Westerns.' This is one of them.

CIN Douglas Knapp   MUS John Carpenter   ED John T. Chance (John Carpenter)   PROD Joseph Kaufman   DIST CKK

66 One of the most effective exploitation movies of the last ten years. . .Carpenter scrupulously avoids any overt socio-political pretensions, playing instead for laughs and suspense in perfectly balanced proportions. – *Time Out*

'Every sacrifice deserves to be immortalized.'

Assembly (new) ★

DIR Feng Xiaogang
2007   123m   China/Hong Kong
DVD

☆ Zhang Hanyu (Capt. Gu Zidi), Yuan Wenkang (Wang

DVD Available on DVD   ☆ Cast in order of importance   66 Critics' Quotes   ⚖ Academy Award   🏆 BAFTA
♫ Soundtrack on CD   † Points of interest   ⚖ Academy Award nomination   🏆 BAFTA nomination

Jincun), Hu Jun (Liu Zeshui), Deng Chao (Er Dou), Tang Yan (Sun Guiqin)

The sole survivor of a Chinese Civil War battle fights to have his comrades' sacrifice recognised.

Compelling if overlong melodrama whose visceral combat sequences raise expectations not satisfied by a meandering second half.

SCR Liu Heng   CIN Lu Yue   MUS Wang Liguang   ED Liu Miaomiao   PROD Wang Zhongjun, Ren Zhonglun, John Chong, Wang Tongyuan   DIST Metrodome

66 A potent anti-war epic in the guise of a patriotic, and presumably state-sanctioned, salute to the Chinese military. – *Xan Brooks, Guardian*

Asterix at the Olympic Games (new)

DIR Frédéric Forestier, Thomas Langmann
2008   116m   France/Germany/Spain/Italy/Belgium
♫

☆ Gérard Depardieu (Obelix), Clovis Cornillac (Asterix), Benoît Poelvoorde (Brutus), Alain Delon (Caesar), Stéphane Rousseau (Alafolix), Vanessa Hessler (Princess Irina), Jamel Debbouze (Numérobis), Zinedine Zidane (Numérodix), Amélie Mauresmo (Amélix), Michael Schumacher (Schumix)

Astérix and Obélix accompany a love-struck Gaul to Greece so he can compete at the Olympics against the Romans and win the hand of a princess.

Aggravating live-action caper that attempts to replace the sublime wit of the original comic books with extravagant sets and baffling cameos from international sports stars.

SCR Alexandre Charlot, Franck Magnier, Olivier Dazat, Thomas Langmann   CIN Thierry Arbogast
MUS Frédéric Talgorn   DES Aline Bonetto   ED Yannick Kergoat   PROD Jérôme Seydoux, Thomas Langmann
DIST Pathé

66 Every cent is visible onscreen. Shame more coin wasn't spent on the scrappy script. – *Leslie Felperin, Variety*

66 The thin plot and cartoonish Looney Tunes aesthetic seem little more than an excuse to put famous figures in sandals and tunics. – *Wendy Ide, The Times*

† With a budget of 78m euros ($123m), the film was reported to be the most expensive ever produced in France.

'Passion knows no boundaries.'

Asylum ★

DIR David Mackenzie
2005   99m   US/Ireland
DVD

☆ *Natasha Richardson* (Stella Raphael), Ian McKellen (Dr Peter Cleave), Marton Csokas (Edgar Stark), Hugh Bonneville (Max Raphael), Judy Parfitt (Brenda Raphael), Sean Harris (Nick), Gus Lewis (Charlie), Joss Ackland (Dr Jack Straffen)

The wife of an asylum doctor in the 1950s falls in love with one of his patients, who murdered and mutilated his ex-wife.

Unfortunate adaptation of a much better novel, which

fails to translate the clever narration into successful screen drama, despite one good performance.

SCR Patrick Marber, Chrys Balis   CIN Giles Nuttgens
MUS Mark Mancina   DES Laurence Dorman   ED Colin Monie, Steven Weisberg   PROD Laurence Borg, David E. Allen, Mace Neufeld   DIST Momentum

66 Irredeemable tosh of the ripest sort. – *Martin Hoyle, Financial Times*

66 Mackenzie and his screenwriter, Patrick Marber, have captured the essence of McGrath's novel and skilfully rethought it in cinematic terms. – *Philip Kemp, Sight & Sound*

† The film had a chequered journey to the screen. Liam Neeson was originally due to play Dr Cleave, with a script first written by Stephen King.

At the Height of Summer ★

SCR/DIR Tran Anh Hung
2000   112m   France/Germany/Vietnam
DVD

☆ Tran Nu Yen Khe (Lien), Nguyen Nhu Quynh (Suong), Le Khanh (Khanh), Ngo Quang Hai (Hai), Chu Hung (Quoc), Tran Manh Cuong (Kien), Le Tuan Anh (Tuan), Le Ngoc Dung (Huong)

Three sisters in Vietnam, devastated by the death of their mother, share dark secrets with their brother.

Gorgeous-looking family drama, psychologically fascinating, dream-like and complex, but finally too convinced of its own importance.

CIN Mark Lee   MUS Ton That Tiet   DES Benoit Barouh
ED Mario Battistel   PROD Christophe Rossignon
DIST Artificial Eye

66 A delicious, dreamy excursion into an erotic state. – *Peter Bradshaw, The Guardian*

Atanarjuat the Fast Runner ★★★★

DIR Zacharias Kunuk
2000   168m   Canada
DVD

☆ Natar Ungalaaq (Atanarjuat), Sylvia Ivalu (Atuat), Peter Henry Arnatsiaq (Oki), Lucy Tulugarjuk (Puja), Pakkak Innushuk (Amaqjuaq), Madeline Ivalu (Panikpak), Paul Qulitalik (Qulitalik)

An Inuit tribesman gets caught up in internecine struggles for power, possession of women and revenge.

Spectacular and strange folkloric epic, driven by basic human impulses that make it remarkably gripping, even over a running time of almost three hours. Utterly distinctive and original.

SCR Paul Apak Angilirq   CIN *Norman Cohn*   MUS Chris Crilly   DES James Ungalaaq   ED Zacharias Kunuk, Norman Cohn, Marie-Christine Sarda   PROD Paul Apak Angilirq, Norman Cohn, Zacharias Kunuk   DIST ICA

66 Captures an amazingly eerie sense of place and light. – *Anthony Quinn, Independent*

66 Spellbinding as storytelling, it also prompts admiration for the Inuit people's patience, resilience and their overriding concern for harmony with the world around them. – *Trevor Johnston, Time Out*

| DVD Available on DVD | ☆ Cast in order of importance | 66 Critics' Quotes | Academy Award / Academy Award nomination | BAFTA / BAFTA nomination |
| ♫ Soundtrack on CD | | † Points of interest | | |

37

Atlantic City ★★★

DIR *Louis Malle*

1981   105m   Canada/France

[DVD] ♫

☆ *Burt Lancaster* (Lou), *Susan Sarandon* (Sally), Kate Reid (Grace), Michel Piccoli (Joseph), Hollis McLaren (Chrissie)

An elderly small-time hoodlum, trading on anecdotes about his past glories, tries to run a gambling racket in a faded seaside casino resort, and romances a local woman in vain.

A delicate, melancholy work, much of it a two-hander between Lancaster and Sarandon, with a background of a town being energised, and spoiled by new money. Understated but devastatingly effective.

SCR John Guare   CIN Richard Ciupka   MUS Michel Legrand   DES Anne Pritchard   ED Suzanne Baron   PROD Denis Heroux   DIST Cine-Neighbour/Selta Films

⚲ picture; John Guare (original screenplay); Burt Lancaster (leading actor); Susan Sarandon (leading actress); Louis Malle (direction)

Ⓣ Louis Malle (direction); Burt Lancaster (leading actor)

'You can only imagine the truth.'

Atonement (new) ★★★★

DIR *Joe Wright*

2007   130m   UK/US/France

[DVD] ♫

☆ *James McAvoy* (Robbie Turner), Keira Knightley (Cecilia Tallis), Romola Garai (Bryony, aged 18), *Saoirse Ronan* (Bryony, aged 13), Vanessa Redgrave (Bryony, older), Brenda Blethyn (Grace Turner), Peter Wight (Police inspector), Harriet Walter (Emily Tallis), Gina McKee (Sister Drummond)

On a hot summer's day in the 1930s in the grounds of an English manor house, Briony Tallis (Ronan), a budding author aged 13, tells a damaging lie about Robbie (McAvoy), the lover of her older sister Cecilia (Knightley). The lie changes all their lives, with consequences that extend beyond World War II.

This remarkably lavish, visually ravishing film does full justice to Ian McEwan's brilliant, detailed source novel. Director Wright skilfully evokes the atmosphere of languid lust in the first act, and surpasses himself with a nightmarish evocation of the chaos and misery on the beach at Dunkirk, brought to life in a single five-minute tracking shot. A short triumphant coda with Redgrave as an older, successful Bryony, voicing her regrets, confirms Atonement as a rarity: a sumptuous spectacle with vast reserves of intelligence. Dario Marianelli's lush, romantic score includes a theme featuring the tapping of typewriter keys, a reminder that this is a story about storytelling.

SCR Christopher Hampton   CIN *Seamus McGarvey*   MUS *Dario Marianelli*   DES Sarah Greenwood   ED Paul Tothill   PROD Tim Bevan, Eric Fellner, Paul Webster   DIST Universal

❝ Hampton and director Joe Wright are really thinking big, in every sense, and the result is exhilarating. – *Peter Bradshaw, Guardian*

❝ It is ambitious, terrifically acted, moving and for the most part transcends its status as a historical drama. – *Sukhdev Sandhu, Daily Telegraph*

'People always called Nancy the little woman. . .They'll never do that again.'

Attack of the 50 Ft. Woman ★

DIR Christopher Guest

1993   90m   US

[DVD]

☆ Daryl Hannah (Nancy Archer), Daniel Baldwin (Harry Archer), William Windom (Hamilton Cobb), Frances Fisher (Dr. Theodora Cushing), Paul Benedict (Dr. Victor Loeb), O'Neal Compton (Sheriff Denby), Cristi Conaway (Louise 'Honey' Parker)

An abused, unhappy wife grows to an enormous size after being zapped by a UFO ray – and avenges herself on her cheating husband and bossy father.

Some critics griped that this was a pallid remake of the 1958 original – as if that film boasted anything beyond a terrific poster. This time around, everyone concerned knows it's a cheesy enterprise, which is all to the good.

SCR Joseph Dougherty   CIN Russell Carpenter   MUS Nicholas Pike, Christopher Guest, Michael McKean   DES Joseph T. Garrity   ED Harry Keramidas   PROD Debra Hill   DIST Entertainment/HBO/Bartleby

---

Au Coeur du Mensonge ★

DIR Claude Chabrol

1998   113m   France

☆ Sandrine Bonnaire (Vivianne Sterne), Jacques Gamblin (Rene Sterne), Valeria Bruni-Tedeschi (Frederique Lesage), Antoine de Caunes (Germain-Roland Desmot), Bernard Verley (Detective Loudun), Bulle Ogier (Evelyne Bordier), Pierre Martot (Regis Marchal), Noel Simsolo (M Bordier), Adrienne Pauly (Anna)

A ten-year-old girl is found raped and murdered in Brittany, and her art teacher is pegged as the prime suspect.

Moderate Chabrol murder mystery, predictably elegant and witty, but not up to his best work.

SCR Odile Barski, Claude Chabrol   CIN Eduardo Serra   MUS Matthieu Chabrol   DES Françoise Benoît-Fresco   ED Monique Fardoulis   PROD Marin Karmitz   DIST Cinéfrance

❝ This movie's chill has not been satisfactorily refrigerated. – *Peter Bradshaw, Guardian*

Au Revoir Les Enfants ★★★★

SCR/DIR *Louis Malle*

1987   104m   France/ Germany/ Italy

[DVD]

☆ Gaspard Manesse (Julien Quentin), Raphaël Fejtö (Jean Bonnet), Francine Racette (Mme Quentin), Stanlislas Carre de Malberg (François Quentin), Philippe Morier-Genoud (Father Jean), François Berleand (Father Michel), François Negret (Joseph)

A Catholic boy in occupied France betrays his friend's Jewish identity by mistake.

Carefully controlled and intensely moving semi-autobiographical drama, a late masterpiece from a

[DVD] Available on DVD   ☆ Cast in order of importance   ❝ Critics' Quotes   ⚲ Academy Award   Ⓑ BAFTA
♫ Soundtrack on CD   † Points of interest   ⚲ Academy Award nomination   Ⓣ BAFTA nomination

remarkable director. It achieves an amazing particularity in its portrait of childhood, yet the themes of loyalty, friendship and belonging are universal.

CIN Renato Berta **DES** Willy Holt **ED** Emmanuelle Castro **PROD** Louis Malle **DIST** Nouvelles éditions de Films/MK2/Stella Films

66 Sombre, lovingly detailed. . .its emotional power remains undeniable. – *Geoff Andrew, Time Out*

⌁ foreign film; Louis Malle (original screenplay)

� Louis Malle (direction)

Ⓣ film not in the English language; Louis Malle (original screenplay)

'She always gets a part.'

Audition ★

DIR Takashi Miike
1999 115m Japan/Korea
DVD

☆ Ryo Ishibashi (Shigeharu Aoyama), Eihi Shiina (Asami Yamasaki), Jun Kunimura (Yoshikawa), Miyuki Matsuda (Ryoko Aoyama), Ren Osugi (Shimada), Tetsu Sawaki (Shigehiko Aoyama), Renji Ishibashi (Old Man)

Seven years after losing his wife to cancer, a TV producer finds a potential dream bride when he holds auditions for a non-existent movie, and lives to regret it.

Harrowing horror drama that begins like an affecting romantic comedy, and ends up suspiciously close to torture porn. Only for those with the strongest of stomachs, particularly during its eye-popping finale.

SCR Daisuke Tengan **CIN** Hideo Yamamoto **MUS** Koji Endo **DES** Tatsuo Ozeki **ED** Yasushi Shimamura **PROD** Akemi Suyama, Satoshi Hukushima **DIST** Metro Tartan

66 It turns into a hallucinatory nightmare of female revenge that will pin back the audience's eyelids. – *Bob Graham, San Francisco Chronicle*

66 It has a climax that leaves many males crawling to the exits. – *Time Out*

'You can live a whole lifetime in a single weekend. . .'

August ★

DIR Anthony Hopkins
1996 94m GB/ US/Japan
DVD ♫

☆ Anthony Hopkins (Ieuan Davies), Leslie Phillips (Professor Alexander Blathwaite), Kate Burton (Helen Blathwaite), Gawn Grainger (Dr Michael Lloyd), Hugh Lloyd (Thomas Prosser), Rhoda Lewis (Mair Davies), Menna Trussler (Gwen), Rhian Morgan (Sian Blathwaite)

Chekhov's Uncle Vanya is transposed to 1890s Wales, where a boozy, discontented estate manager's emotions are thrown into disarray by the arrival of his brother-in-law's younger wife.

A decent version of Chekhov, and a highly personal project for Welshman Hopkins, making his directorial debut. Its stage origins are evident, with more care expended on the clarity of dialogue than the fluidity of on-screen action.

SCR Julian Mitchell **CIN** Robin Vidgeon **MUS** Anthony

Hopkins **DES** Eileen Diss **ED** Edward Mansell **PROD** June Wyndham Davies, Pippa Cross **DIST** Film Four/Majestic/Newcomm/Granada

† Screenwriter Julian Mitchell had already written a version of August for the stage before this film's release.

'An incredible journey moving at the speed of sound.'

August Rush ⁽ⁿᵉʷ⁾

DIR Kirsten Sheridan
2007 113m US/Korea
DVD ♫

☆ Freddie Highmore (Evan Novacek, 'August Rush'), Keri Russell (Lyla Novacek), Jonathan Rhys Meyers (Louis Connelly), Terrence Howard (Richard Jeffries), Robin Williams ('Wizard' Wallace), William Sadler (Thomas Novacek), Marian Seldes (The Dean), Mykelti Williamson (Reverend James)

A troubled boy with an uncanny gift for music escapes from a boys' home and sets off for New York to find his lost parents.

Whimsical, treacly film that falls flat on every front it encounters: as a cloying romance between the young hero's musician parents; a sentimental orphan tale that grates unbearably; and an inspirational fable, triggered by the presence of Robin Williams as a Fagin-style leader of musical youths.

SCR Nick Castle, James V. Hart **CIN** John Mathieson **MUS** Mark Mancina, Hans Zimmer **DES** Michael Shaw **ED** William Steinkamp **PROD** Richard Barton Lewis **DIST** Entertainment

66 Feeble-headed tribute to the power of love and music. – *Peter Whittle, Sunday Times*

66 The plot is preposterous. Particularly the part about a kid who has never before played an instrument, but can pick up a guitar and play like Eric Clapton and belly up to a church organ and perform like Mozart. – *Carrie Rickey, Philadelphia Inquirer*

'"Shall we shag now, or shall we shag later?" – Austin Powers'

Austin Powers: International Man of Mystery ★★

DIR Jay Roach
1997 94m US
DVD ♫

☆ *Mike Myers* (Austin Powers/Dr Evil), Elizabeth Hurley (Vanessa Kensington), Michael York (Basil Exposition), Mimi Rogers (Mrs Kensington), Robert Wagner (Number Two), Seth Green (Scott Evil), Fabiana Udenio (Alotta Fagina), Charles Napier (Commander Gilmour)

A 1960s hipster spy is brought out of cryofreeze to stop his old nemesis taking over the world.

Spoofing what's already half a spoof – the James Bond movies – sounds like a terrible idea, but it works, largely thanks to Myers's irresistibly cheesy personae.

SCR Mike Myers **CIN** Peter Deming **MUS** George S. Clinton **DES** Cynthia Charette **ED** Debra Neil-Fisher **PROD** Suzanne Todd, Demi Moore, Jennifer Todd, Mike

DVD Available on DVD ☆ Cast in order of importance 66 Critics' Quotes ⌁ Academy Award Ⓦ BAFTA ⌁ Academy Award nomination Ⓣ BAFTA nomination

♫ Soundtrack on CD

39

Myers   DIST Guild/New Line/Capella/KC Medien/Eric's Boy

66 Silly but spirited comedy. – *Jonathan Rosenbaum, Chicago Reader*

66 Definitely lives up to its promise of being smashing, groovy, baby. – *Leonard Klady, Variety*

'A day without sex is a day wasted.'

Auto Focus ★★

DIR Paul Schrader
2002   105m   US
[DVD]   ♫

☆ *Greg Kinnear* (Bob Crane), *Willem Dafoe* (John Carpenter), Rita Wilson (Anne Crane), Maria Bello (Patricia Crane), Ron Leibman (Lenny), Kurt Fuller (Werner Klemperer/Klink), Ed Begley Jnr (Mel Rosen)

A TV sitcom star is lured into amateur pornography and sex addiction by his video technician friend.

A bizarre real-life case history of sex and death is treated in Schrader's unduly clinical style; but the performances are excellent, and the director's usual theme of male narcissism gets some purchase here.

SCR Michael Gerbosi   CIN Fred Murphy, Jeffrey Greeley   MUS Angelo Badalamenti   DES James Chinlund   ED Kristina Boden   PROD Scott Alexander, Larry Karaszewski, Todd Rosken, Pat Dollard, Alicia Allain, Brian Oliver   DIST Columbia TriStar

66 A cautionary tale about socially induced satyriasis. – *Philip French, Observer*

66 Schrader's objectification of sad and stupid material is neither tragic nor transgressive. It is just undramatic and uninvolving. – *Richard Corliss, Time*

† Bob Crane played the lead role in Hogan's Heroes, a TV sitcom set in a German POW camp. It ran for six seasons.

Autobus ★★★

SCR/DIR *Eric Rochant*
1991   95m   France
♫

☆ *Yvan Attal* (Bruno Fournier), Kristin Scott-Thomas (L'Institutrice), Marc Berman (Le Chauffeur), Charlotte Gainsbourg (Juliette Mangin), Renan Mazeas (Sam)

An emotionally unstable man hijacks a school bus as a means of impressing his girlfriend.

It starts out as a potentially routine hostage thriller, then becomes something quite different as Attal's naive Bruno gets acquainted with his captives. Writer-director Rochant handles the shift of gears expertly.

CIN Pierre Novion   MUS Gérard Torikian   ED Catherine Quesemand   PROD Alain Rocca   DIST Artificial Eye/Les Productions Lazennec/FR3/SGGC/La Générale d'Images/Canal

Autumn Moon ★★

DIR *Clara Law*
1992   108m   Hong Kong/Japan
[DVD]

☆ Masatoshi Nagase (Tokio), Li Pui Wai (Li Pui Wai), Maki Kiuchi (Miki), Choi Siu Wan (Granny), Suen Ching Hung (Wai's boyfriend), Sung Lap Yeung (Wai's father)

A teenage Hong Kong girl, about to emigrate and leave her ailing grandmother, becomes involved with a serious Japanese boy.

A light handling of serious themes, including social mobility, new ways of life replacing the old, and contrasts in attitudes between Asian nations. Delightfully executed.

SCR *Eddie Ling Ching Fong*   CIN Tony Leung Siu Hung   MUS Lau Lee Tat   ED Eddie Ling Ching Fong   PROD Clara Law/Eddie Ling Ching Fong   DIST ICA/Trix

66 Lately the word 'fading' keeps coming back to me. – *Clara Law (director's statement)*

66 Shot in a water-pale light, Autumn Moon is most obviously an elaboration on that waning process. – *Lizzie Francke, Sight & Sound*

'Three generations of family. They shared a dream called America in a place called Avalon.'

Avalon ★

SCR/DIR Barry Levinson
1990   128m   US
[DVD]   ♫

☆ Armin Mueller-Stahl (Sam Krichinsky), Elizabeth Perkins (Ann Kaye), Joan Plowright (Eva Krichinsky), Kevin Pollak (Izzy Kirk), Aidan Quinn (Jules Kaye), Leo Fuchs (Hymie Krichinsky), Eve Gordon (Dottie Kirk), Lou Jacobi (Gabriel Krichinsky)

Half a century in the lives of a Polish-Jewish family in Baltimore.

Appealing but undistinguished immigrant saga which bathes the past in a golden glow.

CIN Allen Daviau   MUS Randy Newman   DES *Norman Reynolds*   ED Stu Linder   PROD Mark Johnson, Barry Levinson   DIST Columbia TriStar/Baltimore Pictures

66 A shamelessly sentimental interpretation of history. – *Colette Maude, Time Out*

66 This movie is an elegy to a mythical past. That's probably why people emerge from the theatre sniffling. – *Pauline Kael, New Yorker*

⚖ Barry Levinson (original screenplay); Allen Daviau; Randy Newman (music); Gloria Gresham (costume design)

'Some men dream the future. He built it.'

The Aviator ★★★

DIR *Martin Scorsese*
2004   170m   US
[DVD]   ♫

☆ *Leonardo DiCaprio* (Howard Hughes), *Cate Blanchett* (Katharine Hepburn), Kate Beckinsale (Ava Gardner), John C. Reilly (Noah Dietrich), Alec Baldwin (Juan Trippe), *Alan Alda* (Sen Ralph Owen Brewster), Ian Holm (Professor Fitz), Danny Huston (Jack Frye), Gwen Stefani (Jean Harlow), Jude Law (Errol Flynn), Kelli Garner (Faith Domergue), Stanley DeSantis (Louis B. Mayer), Edward Herrmann (Joseph Breen), Willem Dafoe (Roland Sweet)

Howard Hughes becomes a Hollywood

[DVD] Available on DVD   ♫ Soundtrack on CD   ☆ Cast in order of importance   66 Critics' Quotes   † Points of interest   ⚖ Academy Award   ⚖ Academy Award nomination   Ⓑ BAFTA   Ⓑ BAFTA nomination

entrepreneur, then an aviation pioneer, and is crippled by private compulsions and phobias.

Smashing and inspiring take on Hughes's early years, often glossed-over in the focus on his notorious dotage as a paranoid recluse, as in Melvin and Howard: Scorsese's film explores these problems in embryo, but fashions Hughes's achievements and contradictions into a surprisingly spirited, big-hearted entertainment.

SCR *John Logan* CIN *Robert Richardson* MUS Howard Shore DES *Dante Ferretti* ED *Thelma Schoonmaker* PROD Sandy Climan, Charles Evans Jr., Michael Mann

66 When it flies, it soars. – *Peter Travers, Rolling Stone*

66 An occasionally brilliant but eccentrically structured and finally unsatisfying demi-epic, which, at almost three hours, fails to give us a complete biopic of Hughes, and fails to convince that his early life works as a self-contained story. – *Peter Bradshaw, Guardian*

⚲ Cate Blanchett (supporting actress); Dante Ferretti (art direction); Thelma Schoonmaker (editing)

⚲ film; Martin Scorsese; John Logan (original screenplay); Leonardo DiCaprio (leading actor); Alan Alda (supporting actor); Robert Richardson (cinematography); Sandy Powell (costume design); Tom Fleischman, Petur Hliddal (sound mixing)

Ⓣ film; Cate Blanchett (supporting actress); make up; Dante Ferretti;

Ⓣ Howard Shore; visual effects; Robert Richardson; Sandy Powell; Thelma Schoonmaker; Alan Alda; Leonardo DiCaprio; John Logan; sound; Martin Scorsese (direction)

'Every year, one in 700 people wake up during surgery. When they planned her husband's murder, they never thought he'd be the one.'

Awake (new)

SCR/DIR Joby Harold
2007 84m US
DVD

☆ Hayden Christensen (Clayton Beresford Jr.), Jessica Alba (Samantha Lockwood), Lena Olin (Lilith Beresford), Arliss Howard (Dr. Jonathan Neyer), Terrence Howard (Dr. Jack Harper), Christopher McDonald (Dr. Larry Lupin), Fisher Stevens (Dr. Puttnam)

A wealthy scion undergoing a heart transplant wakes up on the operating table to find his surgeon is plotting to murder him.

Preposterous, unpleasantly graphic thriller with a gormless lead who deserves everything he gets.

CIN Russell Carpenter MUS Samuel Sim DES Dina Goldman ED Craig McKay PROD Joana Vicente, Jason Kilot, John Penotti, Fisher Stevens DIST Icon

DR. JONATHAN NEYER: 'My hands have been inside Presidents!'

66 If you are one of those who viewed Hayden Christensen's portrayal of Anakin Skywalker as the ne plus ultra of lifelessness, prepare to be proven wrong. – *Jeannette Catsoulis, New York Times*

66 In the end it all becomes quite hilarious, despite the overload of squishy organs. – *Christopher Tookey, Daily Mail*

'There is no such thing as a simple miracle.'

Awakenings ★

DIR Penny Marshall
1990 121m US
DVD ♫

☆ Robert De Niro (Leonard Lowe), Robin Williams (Dr. Malcolm Sayer), Julie Kavner (Eleanor Costello), Ruth Nelson (Mrs Lowe), John Heard (Dr. Kaufman), Penelope Ann Miller (Paula), Alice Drummond (Lucy), Judith Malina (Rose), Barton Heyman (Bert), Max von Sydow (Dr. Peter Ingham)

A shy neurologist treats the catatonic victims of encephalitis in the hope of reviving them.

Offers terribly lachrymose, heart-tugging drama where there was room for something more thoughtful.

SCR Steven Zaillian CIN Miroslav Ondricek MUS Randy Newman DES Anton Furst ED Jerry Greenberg, Battle Davis PROD Walter F. Parkes, Lawrence Lasker DIST Columbia TriStar

66 We are deep in Rain Man territory, a terrain notable for its squashiness. – *Brian Case, Time Out*

⚲ picture; Robert De Niro (leading actor); Steven Zaillian (adapted screenplay)

'It's never too late to become what you might have been.'

Away from Her ★★

SCR/DIR Sarah Polley
2007 109m Canada/UK/USA

☆ Julie Christie (Fiona), Gordon Pinsent (Grant), Olympia Dukakis (Marian), Michael Murphy (Aubrey), Kristen Thomson (Kristy), Wendy Crewson (Madeleine)

Fiona and Grant are a retired Canadian couple. Her memory is failing, and after getting lost while skiing near her home, she is diagnosed with Alzheimer's. She enters a retirement home and becomes attached to another resident, Aubrey. When Grant turns to Aubrey's wife for solace, truths about their marriages are revealed.

A subtle, nuanced, grown-up film that takes unusual narrative turns, with Christie a standout among uniformly excellent performances. A triumph for first-time director Polley, who handles the story and its issues, that trouble generations older than herself, with real maturity.

CIN Luc Montpelier MUS Jonathan Goldsmith DES Kathleen Climie ED David Wharnsby PROD Daniel Iron, Simone Urdi, Jennifer Weiss DIST Metrodome

66 A most adroit, confident film, calmly understated and never sentimental. It supports the argument that short stories and novellas are the best source material for feature movies. – *Philip French, Observer*

66 One of the most remarkable and moving love stories the movies have recently given us. – *Michael Wilmington, Chicago Tribune*

⚲ Julie Christie (leading actress); Sarah Polley (adapted screenplay)

Ⓣ Julie Christie (leading actress)

DVD Available on DVD ☆ Cast in order 66 Critics' Quotes ⚲ Academy Award Ⓑ BAFTA
♫ Soundtrack on CD of importance † Points of interest ⚲ Academy Award nomination Ⓣ BAFTA nomination

41

'In A World Of Make Believe Stella Is About To Discover The Difference Between True Love. . .And Real Life.'

An Awfully Big Adventure ★

DIR Mike Newell

1994   112m   GB/ Ireland/ France/US

DVD   ♫

☆ Georgina Cates (Stella), Hugh Grant (Meredith Potter), Alan Rickman (P.L. O'Hara), *Peter Firth* (Bunny), Alun Armstrong (Uncle Vernon), Prunella Scales (Rose), Rita Tushingham (Aunt Lily), Edward Petherbridge (St Ives), Nicola Pagett (Dotty Blundell), Alan Cox (Geoffrey), Carol Drinkwater (Dawn Allenby), Clive Merrison (Desmond Fairchild), Gerard McSorley (George)

Romantic entanglements between the members of a British repertory company rehearsing Peter Pan in the late 1940s centre around a naive teenage girl, an egocentric director and an ageing matinee idol.

Workmanlike adaptation of Beryl Bainbridge's novel, with sharply observed behaviour of theatre types. But the malice and back-biting is laid on a little thick. This was Grant's first film to be released after Four Weddings and a Funeral and some fans of his from that film were disappointed by the dark tone of this one. For all that, it's highly entertaining.

SCR Charles Wood   **CIN** Dick Pope   **MUS** Richard Hartley   **DES** Mark Geraghty   **ED** Jon Gregory
PROD Hilary Heath, Philip Hinchcliffe
DIST TCF/Portman/British Screen/BBC/Wolfhound

66 With its flawed characters and disturbingly dark centre, this fragile gem of a movie sparkles with intelligence and glows with feeling. – *Nigel Floyd, Time Out*

Azur & Asmar: The Princes' Quest (new) ★★

SCR/DIR Michel Ocelot

2006   95m   France/Belgium/Spain/Italy

DVD   ♫

☆ Azur (Steven Kyman), Asmar (Nigel Pikington), Jeanne (Suzanna Nour), Crapoux (Nigel Lambert), Princess Chamsous Sabah (Imogen Bailey), The Djinn Fairy (Emma Tate), The Elf Fairy (Suzanne David), Wise Man Yadoa (Sean Barrett), The Father (Keith Wickham)

Two boys growing up in the same household hear the story of a fairy waiting to be rescued. As adults, both set out to find her. Set in a colourful Arabian world of princesses, scarlet lions, thieves and bandits, wise men and fairies, animator Ocelot embarks on a journey of discovery against a backdrop of exotic lands and mystical tales.

A charming fable with each frame like a work of art. Ocelot delves behind the story of the boyhood pals becoming arch-rivals, to field serious points about racism and xenophobia. Such concerns do not go unmissed amid the ravishing visuals.

MUS Gabriel Yared   **PROD** Christophe Rossignon
DIST Soda Pictures

66 It's an enchanting piece in the graphic manner of early 20th-century children's books of Oriental yarns. – *Philip French, Observer*

† Shown in the UK in an English dubbed version. The original was in French and Arabic.

'A father. A son. A revolution.'

Baadasssss! ★★

DIR Mario Van Peebles
2003   109m   US
DVD   ♫

☆ Mario Van Peebles (Melvin Van Peebles), Joy Bryant (Priscilla), Terry Crews (Big T), Ossie Davis (Grandad), David Alan Grier (Clyde Houston), Nia Long (Sandra)

An account of an Afro-American writer-director's problems in making and getting distribution for a 1970s film about a radical street hustler.

Impressive recounting of the genesis of Melvin Van Peebles' ground-breaking Sweet Sweetback's Baadasssss Song, with his son Mario playing him respectfully but without sentiment. Hugely appealing, and an intriguing insight into how blaxploitation movies came to be regarded as commercially viable.

SCR Mario Van Peebles, Dennis Haggerty   CIN Robert Primes   MUS Tyler Bates   DES Alan E. Muraoka   ED Anthony Miller, Nneka Goforth   PROD Mario Van Peebles   DIST BFI

66 Mario Van Peebles creates what can only be called a lucid fantasia; the movie quickly reaches a pitch of manic activity and stays there. It's an exhausting, and exhaustingly pleasurable, entertainment. – *David Denby, New Yorker*

'In the heart of the city, a pig with heart.'

Babe: Pig in the City ★

DIR George Miller
1998   97m   Australia
DVD   ♫

☆ Magda Szubanski (Mrs. Esme Cordelia Hoggett), James Cromwell (Farmer Arthur Hoggett), Mary Stein (The Landlady), Mickey Rooney (Fugly Floom, the Speechless Man in Hotel), Julie Godfrey (Suspicious Neighbour), the voices of: E.G. Daily, Danny Mann, Glenne Headly, Steven Wright, James Cosmo, Roscoe Lee Browne

Following his victory in the sheep-herding trials, Babe goes to New York to rescue the impounded animals from the cash-strapped Hoggett farm.

Not as fine as the exquisite original, but an intriguingly dark tone prevails, exemplified by the sinister urban sets. Babe is a less dominant character, but there are compensations, notably a surreal moment when a trio of mice sing 'Je ne regrette rien'.

SCR George Miller, Judy Morris, Mark Lamprell   CIN Andrew Lesnie   MUS Nigel Westlake   DES Roger Ford   ED Jay Friedkin, Margaret Sixel   PROD George Miller, Doug Mitchell, Bill Miller   DIST Universal

66 There is plenty of fun in this cinematic menagerie, consummate screen magic and a series of well-intentioned messages that sidestep the cloying and saccharine. – *Leonard Klady, Variety*

† The film's surreal tone, less child-friendly than Babe, panicked studio executives into cancelling preview screenings. On its release, it was an expensive box-office failure.

♪ Randy Newman (music, original song – That'll Do)

Ⓣ Bill Westenhofer, Neal Scanlan, Chris Godfrey, Grahame Andrew (special visual effects)

'A Little Pig Goes a Long Way.'

Babe ★★★★

DIR *Chris Noonan*
1995   89m   Australia/US
DVD   ♫

☆ *James Cromwell* (Arthur Hoggett), Magda Szubanski (Esme Hoggett), Roscoe Lee Browne (Narrator), the voices of Christine Cavanaugh, Miriam Margolyes, Danny Mann, Hugo Weaving

A pig raised by sheepdogs learns to herd their flock, with a little help from the farmer.

Magical children's film which could hardly be bettered, achieving the double feat of making animals look like they're talking and giving them entirely apt things to say. It must be one of the most straightforwardly charming pictures of its kind ever made.

SCR George Miller, Chris Noonan   CIN *Andrew Lesnie*   MUS Nigel Westlake   DES Roger Ford   ED Marcus D'Arcy, Jay Friedkin   PROD George Miller, Doug Mitchell, Bill Miller   DIST Universal/Kennedy Miller

66 A captivating comic allegory. – *Rita Kempley, Washington Post*

66 I've seen nothing like it for sustained invention. – *Alexander Walker, Evening Standard*

† Followed by a sequel, Babe: Pig in the City

♪ Scott E. Anderson, Charles Gibson, Neal Scanlan, John Cox (visual effects)

♪ picture; James Cromwell (supporting actor); Chris Noonan; George Miller, Chris Noonan (adapted screenplay); Marcus D'Arcy, Jay Friedkin; Roger Ford

Ⓣ film; special visual effects; adapted screenplay; editing; art direction

'If you want to be understood. . .listen.'

Babel ★★★

DIR Alejandro González Iñárritu
2006   143m   US/Mexico/France
DVD   ♫

☆ Brad Pitt (Richard Jones), Cate Blanchett (Susan),

DVD Available on DVD   ☆ Cast in order of importance   66 Critics' Quotes   † Points of interest   ♪ Academy Award   ♪ Academy Award nomination   Ⓣ BAFTA   Ⓣ BAFTA nomination

♫ Soundtrack on CD

43

Gael Garcia Bernal (Santiago), Koji Yakusho (Yasujiro Wataya), Adriana Barraza (Amelia), Rinko Kikuchi (Chieko Wataya)

Four stories set in different countries. A goatherd in Morocco lends his teenage sons a rifle; they use it for target practice and seriously injure a Californian tourist. A terrorist attack is suspected. At home, her family's Mexican housekeeper is caring for her children; she drives them to her son's wedding across the border, where they become stranded. In Tokyo, a deaf-mute teenage girl is falling apart in the wake of her mother's suicide.

A wildly ambitious epic, conceived on a global scale. Mexican director Iñárritu takes global interdependence as his theme, and sets his stories in contrasting cultures. The links between them gradually become clear, and each location yields memorable images. Iñárritu and Arriaga eloquently plead a case for more understanding and empathy. Fine acting throughout, though the star names are eclipsed by Barraza as a housekeeper who loves her infant charges but is torn by family pressures. Somewhat exhausting, Babel still has the feel of a masterpiece.

SCR Guillermo Arriaga CIN Rodrigo Prieto
MUS Gustavo Santaolalla DES Brigitte Broch
ED Stephen Mirrione, Douglas Crise PROD Jon Kilik, Steve Golin, Alejandro González Iñárritu DIST UIP

66 One of the most challenging and saddest movies of the year – and also one of the most memorable. – *Richard Roeper, Chicago Sun-Times*

66 In the year's richest, most complex and ultimately most heartbreaking film, Iñárritu invites us to get past the babble of modern civilisation and start listening to each other. – *Peter Travers, Rolling Stone*

⚊ Gustavo Santaolalla

⚊ picture; Adriana Barraza (supporting actress); Rinko Kikuchi (supporting actress); Alejandro González Iñárritu; Guillermo Arriaga (original screenplay); Stephen Mirrione, Douglas Crise

Ⓣ Gustavo Santaolalla
Ⓣ film; Alejandro González Iñárritu; Guillermo Arriaga (original screenplay); Rodrigo Prieto; Stephen Mirrione, Douglas Crise, José Garcia, Jon Taylor, Chris Minkler, Martín Hernández (sound)

Babette's Feast ★★

SCR/DIR *Gabriel Axel*
1987 103m Denmark
DVD ♫

☆ *Stéphane Audran* (Babette Harsant), Jean-Philippe Lafont (Achille Papin), Jarl Kulle (Old Lorens Lowenhielm), Bibi Andersson (Swedish Court Lady-in-waiting), Bodil Kjer (Old Philippa), Birgitte Federspiel (Old Martina)

In 1870s Denmark, a French housekeeper in a pious household exerts a life-affirming influence on an austere community, and finally prepares a magnificent celebratory banquet.

Delicate, subtly amusing fable of liberation that reaches a joyous climax of release from self-denial with the arrival of the extraordinary food.

CIN Henning Kristiansen MUS Per Norgard DES Jan Peterson, Sven Wichmann ED Finn Henriksen
PROD Just Betzer, Bo Christensen
DIST Panorama/Nordisk/Danish Film Institute

66 Still the gold standard of food movies. – *Jeffrey M. Anderson, San Francisco Examiner*

⚊ foreign film

Ⓣ film in a foreign language
Ⓣ film; Stéphane Audran (leading actress); Gabriel Axel (direction); Gabriel Axel (adapted screenplay)

'J.C. Wiatt, corporate powerhouse, just received an inheritance. And it sucks.'

Baby Boom ★

DIR Charles Shyer
1987 110m US
DVD

☆ *Diane Keaton* (J.C. Wiatt), Harold Ramis (Steven Bochner), Sam Wanamaker (Fritz Curtis), Sam Shepard (Dr. Jeff Cooper), James Spader (Ken Arrenberg), Pat Hingle (Hughes Larabee), Britt Leach (Verne Boone)

A high-flying Manhattan executive is forced to alter her entire life when she becomes foster-mother to a relative's orphaned baby.

Amusing comedy, generally well executed, and very much of its time: it lands a few satirical jabs at 80s yuppie myths about having it all. Keaton, who later became unbearable playing affluent characters with a Big Dilemma, is charming and funny here.

SCR Nancy Meyers, Charles Shyer CIN William A. Fraker
MUS Bill Conti DES Jeffrey Howard ED Lynzee Klingman PROD Bruce A. Block, Nancy Meyers
DIST UIP/MGM

66 Like a Frank Capra film, Baby Boom shows us a little of the darkness and a lot of the dawn. – *Roger Ebert, Chicago Sun-Times*

† The film was later adapted for a short-lived TV series.

The Baby of Macon

SCR/DIR Peter Greenaway
1993 122m GB/Netherlands/France/Germany
♫

☆ Julia Ormond (The Daughter), Ralph Fiennes (The Bishop's Son), Philip Stone (The Bishop), Jonathan Lacey (Cosimo Medici), Don Henderson (The Father Confessor), Celia Gregory (Mother Superior), Jeff Nuttall (The Majordomo), Kathryn Hunter (The Second Midwife), Gabrielle Reidy (The Third Midwife), Jessica Stevenson (The First Midwife), Frank Egerton (The Prompter)

In a 17th-century theatre, a play is performed in which an elderly woman gives birth to a 'miracle baby', but one of her daughters claims the child as her own. At this point, the play and reality merge, and the performance becomes an actual religious ritual.

Director Greenaway certainly knows how to polarise audiences: this is a confusing, maddening piece, remarkable to look at, but cold, alienating and repetitive. It feels as if it were made for an audience of one – the director himself.

DVD Available on DVD ☆ Cast in order of importance 66 Critics' Quotes ⚊ Academy Award Ⓣ BAFTA
♫ Soundtrack on CD † Points of interest ⚊ Academy Award nomination Ⓣ BAFTA nomination

CIN Sacha Vierny   MUS Henry Purcell, Matthew Locke and others   DES Jan Roelfs, Ben van Os   ED Chris Wyatt PROD Kees Kasander   DIST Allarts/UGC/La Sept/Cine Electra II/Channel 4/Filmstiftung/Canal

66 As close to a formulaic picture as Greenaway could come to making. – *Geoffrey Macnab, Sight and Sound*

Back to the Future   ★★★★

DIR *Robert Zemeckis*
1985   116m   US
DVD   ♫

☆ *Michael J. Fox* (Marty McFly), *Christopher Lloyd* (Dr. Emmett Brown), Crispin Glover (George McFly), Lea Thompson (Lorraine Baines), Claudia Wells (Jennifer Parker), Thomas F. Wilson (Biff Tannen)

In the 1980s, a teenager travels 30 years back in time to act as a matchmaker for his future parents, using a gull-winged DeLorean car as a time machine.

One of the founding films in the special-effects action blockbuster genre, though few of its successors have half its wit, charm or grace. There are some truly good jokes at the expense of both the 1950s and the 1980s, and a lovely plot, which actually holds together logically about changing the present via tweaking the past. The eager, likable Fox proved to be a perfect Marty; Lloyd, as the irascible, sardonic Dr. Brown, offered sterling support.

SCR *Robert Zemeckis, Bob Gale*   CIN Dean Cundey MUS Alan Silvestri   DES Lawrence G. Paull   ED Arthur Schmidt, Harry Keramidas   PROD Bob Gale, Neil Canton DIST Universal/Steven Spielberg

66 Accelerates with wit, ideas, and infectious, wide-eyed wonder. – *Variety*

† Two sequels followed in 1989 and 1990.

⅄ Robert Zemeckis (original screenplay); Chris Hayes, Johnny Colla (m), Huey Lewis (ly) (music, original song – The Power of Love); sound

'Getting back was only the beginning.'
Back to the Future II

DIR Robert Zemeckis
1989   108m   US
DVD   ♫

☆ Michael J. Fox (Marty McFly/Marty McFly, Jr./Marlene McFly), Christopher Lloyd (Dr. Emmett Brown), Lea Thompson (Lorraine), Thomas F. Wilson (Biff Tannen/Griff), Harry Waters Jnr. (Marvin Berry), Charles Fleischer (Terry), Joe Flaherty (Western Union Man)

The eccentric Dr. Brown and Marty McFly get back from their time-travelling in their De Lorean to discover that the present is now in urgent need of attention.

The weak link in this generally splendid trilogy. It's overstuffed with ideas, some of which misfire. Still, the special effects are outstanding. The climax functions blatantly as a cliff-hanger for the final film in the series.

SCR Bob Gale   CIN Dean Cundey   MUS Alan Silvestri DES Rick Carter   ED Arthur Schimdt, Harry Keramidas PROD Bob Gale, Neil Canton   DIST UIP/Amblin Entertainment

⅄ Ken Ralston, Michael Lantieri, John Bell, Steve Gawley (visual effects)

'They've saved the best trip to the last. But this time they may have gone too far.'

Back to the Future III   ★★

DIR *Robert Zemeckis*
1990   118m   US
DVD   ♫

☆ Michael J. Fox (Marty McFly/Seamus McFly), Christopher Lloyd (Dr. Emmett Brown), Mary Steenburgen (Clara Clayton), Thomas F. Wilson (Buford 'Mad Dog' Tannen/Biff Tannen), Lea Thompson (Maggie McFly/Lorraine McFly), Elisabeth Shue (Jennifer), Matt Clark (Bartender), Richard Dysart (Barbed Wire Salesman), James Tolkan (Marshal Strickland)

Marty McFly travels back to the Wild West of 1885, where Dr. Emmett Brown's life is in danger. They must then work out how to power up the De Lorean to return to the present for the last time.

A delightful climax to this franchise that works on several fronts: as an affectionate spoof of Western movies, as an ingenious time-travel story – and even as a romance, when Dr. Brown finds himself falling for an attractive Wild West schoolmarm.

SCR Bob Gale   CIN Dean Cundey   MUS Alan Silvestri DES Rick Carter   ED Arthur Schmidt, Harry Keramidas PROD Bob Gale, Neil Canton   DIST UIP/Amblin

66 There's real movie magic at work here. – *Leonard Maltin*

'He Had To Choose Between His Best Friend. . .The Woman He Loved. . .And The Greatest Rock 'n' Roll Band In the World.'

Backbeat   ★

DIR Iain Softley
1994   100m   GB/Germany
DVD   ♫

☆ Sheryl Lee (Astrid Kirchherr), Stephen Dorff (Stuart Sutcliffe), Ian Hart (John Lennon), Gary Bakewell (Paul McCartney), Chris O'Neill (George Harrison), Scot Williams (Pete Best), Kai Wiesinger (Klaus Voormann), Jennifer Ehle (Cynthia Powell)

Stuart Sutcliffe, a friend of John Lennon, joins the Beatles and performs with them in Hamburg. But when he falls in love with a beautiful bohemian German photographer, he chooses a career as a painter over music.

Softley's film captures the heady excitement of Hamburg's music and arts scenes in the early 60s, though tellingly Hart's performance as Lennon overshadows the two lead roles.

SCR Iain Softley, Michael Thomas, Stephen Ward CIN Ian Wilson   MUS Don Was   DES Joseph Bennett ED Martin Walsh   PROD Finola Dwyer, Stephen Woolley DIST Rank/Polygram/Scala/Channel 4 Films/Royal

66 Does not encourage the viewer to sympathise with the Hamburg sophisticates –probably because it is most at ease as a restive pop romp. – *Robert Yates, Sight & Sound*

† Sutcliffe died of a cerebral haemorrhage, aged 21.
† American actress Sheryl Lee, who played Astrid Kirchherr, was herself born in Germany.

🅣 Don Was
🅣 British film; Glenn Freemantle, Chris Munro, Robin O'Donoghue (sound)

'One breath of oxygen and it explodes in a deadly rage.'

Backdraft ★

DIR Ron Howard
1991 132m US
[DVD] ♫

☆ Kurt Russell (Stephen 'Bull' McCaffrey/Dennis McCaffrey), William Baldwin (Brian McCaffrey), Robert De Niro (Donald 'Shadow' Rimgale), Donald Sutherland (Ronald Bartel), Jennifer Jason Leigh (Jennifer Vaitkus), Scott Glenn (John 'Axe' Adcox), Rebecca DeMornay (Helen McCaffrey), Jason Gedrick (Tim Krizminski), J.T. Walsh (Alderman Marty Swayzak)

Two warring brothers, whose fire-fighter father died at work, cope with a series of fires set by an arsonist.

Overwrought, masculine, full of gritted-teeth conviction, but undermined by a routine plot. Notable only for its astonishing special fire effects; these constitute a pyromaniac's dream.

SCR Gregory Widen **CIN** Mikael Salomon **MUS** Hans Zimmer **DES** Albert Brenner **ED** Daniel Hanley, Michael Hill **PROD** Richard B. Lewis, Pen Densham, John Watson **DIST** UIP/Trilogy/Imagine

66 What I regret is that all of the expertise lavished on this movie couldn't have been put at the service of a more intelligent story about real firemen, real working conditions, real heroism, and the real craft and art of fire-fighting. – *Roger Ebert, Chicago Sun-Times*

Mikael Salomon, Allen Hall, Clay Pinney, Scott Farrar (visual effects); Gary Summers, Randy Thorn, Gary Rydstrom, Glenn Williams (sound); Gary Rydstrom, Richard Hymns (sound effects)
🅣 Mikael Salomon, Allen Hall, Clay Pinney, Scott Farrar (special visual effects)

'The Mother, The Planner And The Gobshite.'

Bad Behaviour ★

DIR Les Blair
1993 104m GB
[DVD]

☆ Stephen Rea (Gerry McAllister), Sinead Cusack (Ellie McAllister), Philip Jackson (Howard Spink), Clare Higgins (Jessica Kennedy), Phil Daniels (The Nunn Brothers), Saira Todd (Sophie Bevan), Mary Jo Randle (Winifred Turner)

Complacent Irish couple in north London find their relationship undermined by external factors, not least the invasion of their home by builders renovating their bathroom.

Improvised comedy in the Mike Leigh fashion that presents wry little domestic dilemmas. Hardly world-shattering but Rea and Cusack both exhibit a low-key, shambling charm; they're all the better for seeming faintly ill-suited as actors.

CIN Witold Stok **MUS** John Altman **DES** Jim Grant **ED** Martin Walsh **PROD** Sarah Curtis **DIST** First Independent/Channel 4/British Screen/Parallax

66 Brilliantly credible screen partnership between Rea and Cusack, their relaxed intimacy and bantering humour suggesting a relationship as familiar as a favourite pair of socks. – *Claire Monk, Sight & Sound*

'All he needs is love.'

Bad Boy Bubby ★★

SCR/DIR *Rolf de Heer*
1993 114m Australia/Italy
[DVD]

☆ *Nicholas Hope* (Bubby), Claire Benito (Mam), Ralph Cotterill (Pop), Sid Brisbane (Yobbo), Norman Kaye (The Scientist), Carmel Johnson (Angel), Bridget Walters (Angel's mother)

An abused, child-like man of 35, who has been imprisoned in his home and never allowed to meet anyone outside his family, finally cuts loose in a shocking manner.

Jolting black comedy of an unfortunate man's squalid life. Understandable, it polarised opinions sharply; its best sequences are riveting, though director De Heer sometimes revels in his capacity to shock.

CIN Ian Jones **MUS** Graham Tardiff **DES** Mark Abbott **ED** Suresh Ayyar **PROD** Domenico Procacci, Giorgio Draskovic, Rolf de Heer
DIST Entertainment/Fandango/Bubby

66 Technically the film is as fascinating as in its theme and lack of inhibition. . .admittedly unforgettable. – *David Robinson, Sight & Sound*

† 31 cameramen were separately employed on the film to reflect Bubby's ever-changing vision.

'Watcha Gonna Do?'

Bad Boys ★

DIR Michael Bay
1995 118m US
[DVD] ♫

☆ Martin Lawrence (Det. Marcus Burnett), Will Smith (Det. Mike Lowrey), Téa Leoni (Julie Mott), Tcheky Karyo (Fouchet), Theresa Randle (Theresa Burnett), Marg Helgenberger (Capt. Alison Sinclair), Joe Pantoliano (Captain C. Howard)

Two Miami cops with contrasting lifestyles hunt down an audacious gang of heroin robbers.

Noisy, frantic buddy movie that announced debut director Michael Bay's distinctive approach to film-making. Smith and Lawrence make a plausible team, though the wholesale mayhem and destruction on display overshadows their sometimes witty repartee.

SCR Michael Barrie, Jim Mulholland, Doug Richardson **CIN** Howard Atherton **MUS** Mark Mancina **DES** John Vallone **ED** Christian Wagner **PROD** Don Simpson, Jerry Bruckheimer **DIST** Columbia

66 The bad boys achieve something a budget can't buy: an easy, natural rapport that makes you root for them. For comedy and thrills, Lawrence and Smith are a dream team. – *Peter Travers, Rolling Stone*

[DVD] Available on DVD ☆ Cast in order of importance 66 Critics' Quotes † Points of interest Academy Award Academy Award nomination 🅣 BAFTA 🅣 BAFTA nomination
♫ Soundtrack on CD

† Producer Don Simpson was reportedly struggling to make the film economically viable, so replaced his original white leads with two black actors, whose fees were lower. Ironically, Bad Boys opened doors for other black actors to be leads in action movies.

Bad Day at Black Rock ★★★★

DIR *John Sturges*
1955 81m US
DVD

☆ *Spencer Tracy* (John J. MacReedy), *Robert Ryan* (Reno Smith), Dean Jagger (Tim Horn), Walter Brennan (Doc Velie), Ernest Borgnine (Coley Trimble), Lee Marvin (Hector David), Anne Francis (Liz Wirth), John Ericson (Pete Wirth), Russell Collins (Mr. Hastings)

A one-armed stranger gets off the train at a sleepy desert hamlet and is greeted with hostility by the townsfolk, who have something to hide.

Seminal suspense thriller – the 'guilty town' motif became a cliché – with a terse script and professional presentation. The moments of violence, long awaited, are electrifying.

SCR *Millard Kaufman* CIN *William C. Mellor*
MUS André Previn ED Newell P. Kimlin PROD Dore Schary DIST MGM

66 A very superior example of motion picture craftsmanship. – *Pauline Kael*

66 The movie takes place within 24 hours. It has a dramatic unity, an economy of word and action, that is admirable in an age of flabby Hollywood epics that maunder on forever. – *William K. Zinsser, New York Herald Tribune*

Ⅰ Spencer Tracy (leading actor); Millard Kaufman (screenplay); John Sturges (direction)

Bad Education ★★

SCR/DIR Pedro Almodóvar
2004 106m Spain
DVD

☆ Fele Martinez (Enrique Goded), *Gael Garcia Bernal* (School Friend/Zahara), Daniel Gimenez Cacho (Father Manolo), Lluis Homar (Sr Berenguer), Javier Camara (Paca), Petra Martinez (Mother), Raul Garcia Forneiro (Young Enrique)

A struggling actor pitches an idea for a film to a well-known director, claiming they were lovers when at school together. The director makes the film – about a schoolboy being abused by a priest.

Almodóvar tips his hat to Hollywood melodramas in this hugely complex story that incorporates sexual abuse, blackmail and cross-dressing. It's finally a little too clever for its own good. Bernal is wildly convincing as a transvestite.

CIN José Luis Alcaine MUS Alberto Iglesias ED José Salcedo PROD Agustin Almodóvar, Pedro Almodóvar DIST Pathé

66 Almodóvar is famous for his great women's roles. But here, for the first time, there are no significant women's parts – though there's Bernal in drag, which is almost as good. – *David Ansen, Newsweek*

Ⓣ film not in the English language

'Gambler. Thief. Junkie. Killer. Cop.'

Bad Lieutenant ★★

DIR Abel Ferrara
1992 96m US
DVD

☆ *Harvey Keitel* (The Lieutenant), Frankie Thorn (The Nun), Zoe Lund (Zoe), Anthony Ruggiero (Lite), Eddie Daniels (Jersey Girl (driver)), Bianca Bakija (Jersey Girl (passenger))

A corrupt cop, who is also a lapsed Catholic and addicted to drugs and gambling, has a chance to redeem himself when he investigates the rape of a nun who refuses to press charges.

An extraordinary essay about self-loathing and Catholic guilt, with Keitel superb as one of the most flawed individuals ever to appear on a film screen. Ferrara does not shirk from lurid exploitation and deliberate shock tactics. But it's memorable, if gruelling viewing.

SCR Zoe Lund, Abel Ferrara, Paul Calderon, Victor Argo CIN Ken Kelsch MUS Joe Delia DES Charles Lagola ED Anthony Redman PROD Edward R. Pressman, Mary Kane DIST Guild/Pressman

66 When Abel Ferrara calls something bad, better believe it: he means business. – *Janet Maslin, New York Times*

'One thing the aliens hadn't counted on was Derek, and Dereks don't run!'

Bad Taste

DIR Peter Jackson
1987 91m New Zealand
DVD ♫

☆ Terry Potter (Ozzy), Pete O'Herne (Barry), Craig Smith (Giles), Mike Minett (Frank), Peter Jackson (Derek/Robert), Doug Wren (Lord Crumb)

Invading alien fast-food entrepreneurs stalk humans as potential menu choices.

The title could hardly be clearer: it's a gross-out comedy in which blood and guts quite literally dominate. It happily and deliberately sets out to disgust. Still, it's intriguing as the debut film of Peter Jackson, director of the Lord of the Rings trilogy, and a revered mainstream film-maker.

SCR Peter Jackson, Tony Hiles, Ken Hammon CIN Peter Jackson MUS Michelle Scullion ED Peter Jackson, Jamie Selkirk PROD Peter Jackson DIST Blue Dolphin/Wing Nut Films/Peter Jackson

66 A climatic rebirth-by-chainsaw scene almost makes it all worthwhile. – *Mark Kermode, Time Out*

'In 1959 a lot of people were killing time. Kit and Holly were killing people.'

Badlands ★★★★

SCR/DIR *Terrence Malick*
1973 94m US
DVD

☆ *Martin Sheen* (Kit), *Sissy Spacek* (Holly), *Warren Oates* (Father), Ramon Bieri (Cato), Alan Vint (Deputy), Gary Littlejohn (Sheriff)

| DVD Available on DVD | ☆ Cast in order | 66 Critics' Quotes | Ⅰ Academy Award | Ⓑ BAFTA |
| ♫ Soundtrack on CD | of importance | † Points of interest | Ⅰ Academy Award nomination | Ⓑ BAFTA nomination |

47

A teenage girl and a young garbage collector take to the road, and wander across several states of America on a vengeful murder spree.

If a film can be defined by its influence, the status of Badlands as a cult classic is deserved. The template of two kids on the run has served any number of subsequent film-makers, who have gazed enviously on its elusive power. Its story is filtered through the feelings of Spacek's Holly, who views Kit's actions as hopelessly romantic; she is blinded by her adolescent crush on him, and the dislocation between her dreamy acquiescence and the horror of the couple's actions lends the film a unique tone, fluctuating between lyricism and jolting reality.

CIN *Brian Probyn, Tak Fujimoto, Stevan Larner*
MUS George Tipton, James Taylor   ED Robert Estrin
PROD Terrence Malick
DIST Warner/Pressman/Williams/Badlands

66 One of the finest literate examples of narrated cinema since the early days of Welles and Polonsky. – *Jonathan Rosenbaum*

66 Kit is played by Martin Sheen, in one of the great modern film performances. – *Roger Ebert, Chicago Sun-Times*

'Stuck between a rock and a hot plate.'
Bagdad Café   ★★
DIR *Percy Adlon*
1987   91m   West Germany
DVD   ♫

☆ *Marianne Sägebrecht* (Jasmin Munchgstettner), Jack Palance (Rudi Cox), C.C.H. Pounder (Brenda), Christine Kaufmann (Debby), Monica Calhoun (Phyllis), Darron Flagg (Sal Junior)

A frumpy German woman tourist is stranded in the California desert, and makes friends at a roadside diner.

Low-key, almost plot-free story that has great charm, and makes a few telling points about racism and America's cultural melting pot.

SCR Percy and Eleonore Adlon, Christopher Doherty
CIN Bernd Heinl   MUS Bob Telson   ED Norbert Herzner   PROD Percy and Eleonore Adlon
DIST Mainline/Pelemele/Pro-Ject

66 Its charm is that every character and every moment is unanticipated, obscurely motivated, of uncertain meaning and vibrating with life. – *Roger Ebert, Chicago Sun-Times*

† Whoopi Goldberg starred in a TV series based on the film.

♪ Bob Telson (music, original song – Calling You)

'One girl, one gun, one hitman. . . A killer comedy.'
The Baker (new)
SCR/DIR Gareth Lewis
2008   86m   UK
DVD

☆ Damian Lewis (Milo), Kate Ashfield (Rhiannon), Michael Gambon (Leo), Nikolaj Coster-Waldau (Bjorn), Annette Badland (Martha), Anthony O'Donnell (Rhys)

A professional killer goes undercover as a baker in a small Welsh village, only to find its residents clamouring for his services.

Bland black comedy peopled by caricatures; one of several films released at the time (see also In Bruges and You Kill Me) that invited audiences to warm to troubled assassins.

CIN Sean Bobbitt   MUS Alex Wurman   DES Jennifer Kernke   ED Alan Strachan   PROD Damian Lewis, Daniel Shepherd, Adrian Sturges, Justin Williams   DIST Verve Pictures

66 A slow, dim affair. . . it lacks dramatic yeast. – *Philip French, Observer*

66 The jokes are flat, a chaotic sex scene is anything but sexy, and the infuriating Latin-lite soundtrack would be better suited to an advert for carpet shampoo. – *Wendy Ide, The Times*

† Gareth and Damian Lewis are brothers.

The Ballad of Jack and Rose   ★
SCR/DIR Rebecca Miller
2004   112m   US
DVD

☆ Daniel Day-Lewis (Jack Slavin), Camilla Belle (Rose Slavin), Catherine Keener (Kathleen), Paul Dano (Thaddius), Ryan McDonald (Rodney), Jena Malone (Red Berry), Jason Lee (Gray), Beau Bridges (Marty Rance)

A dying eco-warrior, still living on the island site of a commune with his teenage daughter, receives a surprise visit from his old flame with teenage children of her own.

No film featuring Day-Lewis will be without merit, but this fuzzy, unfocused drama starts down too many narrative paths, changes its mind and re-starts. Well-acted across the board, it's too sombre and earnest by half, and never leaves a shred of doubt that it will end badly.

CIN Ellen Kuras   MUS Michael Rohatyn   DES Mark Ricker   ED Sabine Hoffman   PROD Lemore Syvan
DIST Entertainment

66 Has density enough for several films. What's missing is spontaneity, and variety. And, throughout most of the narrative, velocity. – *Joe Morgenstern, Wall Street Journal*

'In 1866, A Woman Had Two Choices . . . She Could Be A Wife Or She Could Be A Whore. Josephine Monaghan Made The Boldest Choice Of All. She Chose To Be A Man.'
The Ballad of Little Jo   ★
SCR/DIR Maggie Greenwald
1993   121m   US
DVD   ♫

☆ Suzy Amis (Josephine 'Jo' Monaghan), Bo Hopkins (Frank Badger), Ian McKellen (Percy Corcoran), David Chung (Tinman Wong), Carrie Snodgress (Ruth Badger), Rene Auberjonois (Streight Hollander), Heather Graham (Mary Addie), Sam Robards (Jasper Hill), Tom Bower (Lyle Hogg)

A New York socialite, driven out of town by a scandal, poses as a man and becomes a rancher in a frontier town.

Based on a true story, this film was heralded as a woman's Western, but falls short of the definition. It's not as if Jo the heroine is born to the frontier; instead, the story concentrates on misogyny and racism in the Wild West, and the impossibility of women being regarded as equals in such an environment.

CIN Declan Quinn   MUS David Mansfield   DES Mark Friedberg   ED Keith Reamer   PROD Fred Berner, Brenda Goodman   DIST Rank/Fine Line/Polygram/Joco

66 The Ballad of Little Jo may not quite be a Western, but moments of astuteness compensate for plenty. – *Claire Monk, Sight & Sound*

† The real Jo Monaghan lived undetected as a man until her death.

'Fame, glamour, ego, politics, money, war, love. . .and dance.'

Ballets Russes   ★★★

SCR/DIR Dayna Goldfine, Daniel Geller

2005   118m   US

[DVD]

☆ Marian Seldes (Narrator), Nathalie Krasskova, Alicia Markova, Mia Slavenska, Frederic Franklin, Tania Riabouchinska, George Zoritch, Raven Wilkinson, Maria Tallchief, Marc Platt, Yvonne Craig, Nini Theilade

The story of the legendary dance company, many of whose original performers fled from Russia after the Revolution of 1917. It split into rival companies after Diaghilev died in 1929. Many ex-dancers attended a 2000 company reunion in New Orleans, where they were interviewed.

Captivating, lovingly assembled, and compulsory viewing for anyone who remotely cares about dance. The sprightly veteran dancers gossip amusingly and candidly about various divas (of both sexes) and warring factions in the company. Major landmarks in 20th-century history form a backdrop to the story. Staggering archive footage combines with recent interviews for a sumptuous treat.

SCR Dayna Goldfine, Daniel Geller, Celeste Shaefer Snyder, Gary Weimberg   CIN Daniel Geller   MUS Todd Boekelheide, David Conte   ED Daniel Geller, Dayna Goldfine, Gary Weimberg   PROD Dayna Goldfine, Daniel Geller, Robert Hawk, Douglas Blair Turnbaugh   DIST Revolver

66 An electrifying documentary. – *Sarah Kaufman, Washington Post*

† Included are dance scenes from A Midsummer Night's Dream (1935), Escape Me Never (1935), The Gay Parisian (1941), Spanish Fiesta (1942) and Tonight and Every Night (1945).

'A huge comedy with tiny balls.'

Balls of Fury (new)

DIR Robert Ben Garant

2007   90m   US

[DVD] ♫

☆ Dan Fogler (Randy Daytona), Christopher Walken (Feng), George Lopez (Agent Rodriguez), Maggie Q

(Maggie), James Hong (Master Wong), Terry Crews (Freddy), Robert Patrick (Sgt. Pete Daytona)

A former Olympic ping-pong player is recruited by the CIA to enter a table tennis tournament run by Chinese gangsters.

Oafish parody of Enter the Dragon and The Karate Kid, fitfully energised by a scene-stealing Christopher Walken.

SCR Robert Ben Garant, Thomas Lennon   CIN Thomas Ackerman   MUS Randy Edelman   DES Jeff Knipp   ED John Refoua   PROD Roger Birnbaum, Gary Barber, Jonathan Glickman, Thomas Lennon   DIST Universal

66 Fairly tame and not all that funny. – *Walter Addiego, San Francisco Chronicle*

66 A crude, almost painfully unfunny comedy. – *Philip French, Observer*

Balzac and the Little Chinese Seamstress   ★★

DIR Dai Sijie

2002   110m   France/China

[DVD]

☆ Ziiou Xun (Little Chinese Seamstress), Chen Kun (Luo), Liu Ye (Ma), Wang Shuangbao (Village Head), Cong Zhijun (Old Tailor), Wang Hongwei (Four Eyes)

In the period of China's Cultural Revolution, two educated city dwellers are exiled to a rural community as part of a re-education scheme, and read western literature to the peasants.

Writer-director Dai Sijie based this film on his own largely autobiographical novel, and asserts the subtly liberating power of literature in an oppressive regime. Gentle and lyrical in tone, it has passages of striking beauty.

SCR Dai Sijie, Nadine Perront   CIN Jean Marie Drejou   MUS Wang Pujian   DES Cao Juiping   ED Julia Gregory, Luc Barnier   PROD Lise Fayolle   DIST Soda

66 In the end, it's a lovely little movie about very big things, and the smallness both illuminates it and keeps it from greatness. – *Ty Burr, Boston Globe*

Bamako   ★★

SCR/DIR Abderrahmane Sissako

2006   117m   France/Mali/US

[DVD] ♫

☆ Aïssa Maïga (Melé), Tiécoura Traoré (Chaka), Hélène Diarra (Saramba), Habib Dembele (Falai)

A young couple, Melé and Chaka, are breaking up, while in their home backyard in Bamako, Mali, a courtroom is established to hold a trial against such institutions as the International Monetary Fund and World Bank.

Warm, vibrant, entertaining essay about global politics and economics woven into a personal story of a young couple. Maïga and Traoré give excellent accounts of their characters; Mauritanian director Sissako never preaches, and lightens the story with humour and wry observation.

CIN Jacques Besse   DES Mahamadou Kouyaté
ED Nadia Ben Rachid   PROD Denis Freyd/Abderrahmane
Sissako   DIST Artificial Eye

† A spoof Western battle features 'cowboys' Danny Glover, an executive producer and Palestinian director Elia Suleiman.

Bambi ★★★★

DIR David D. Hand
1942   72m   US
DVD   ♫

☆ voices of: Bobby Stewart (Bambi), Peter Behn (Thumper), Paula Winslowe (Bambi's Mother), Stan Alexander (Flower), Cammie King (Faline)

The story of a forest deer, from the book by Felix Salten.

Anthropomorphic cartoon feature, one of Disney's most memorable and brilliant achievements, with a great comic character in Thumper the rabbit and a climactic forest fire sequence which is genuinely thrilling. The off-screen death of Bambi's mother is extraordinarily moving. A triumph of the animator's art.

SCR Larry Morey, Perce Pearce   MUS Frank Churchill, Edward Plumb   DIST Walt Disney

⚱ Frank Churchill, Edward Plumb; Frank Churchill (m), Larry Morey (ly) (music, original song – Love Is a Song); Sam Slyfield (sound recording)

'Starring the great negroe actors.'

Bamboozled ★

SCR/DIR Spike Lee
2000   135m   US
DVD   ♫

☆ Damon Wayans (Pierre Delacroix), Savion Glover (Manray/Mantan), Jada Pinkett-Smith (Sloan Hopkins), Tommy Davidson (Womack/Sleep 'N Eat), Michael Rapaport (Thomas Dunwitty), Thomas Jefferson Byrd (Honeycutt), Paul Mooney (Junebug), Sarah Jones (Dot), Gillian Iliana Waters (Verna), Susan Batson (Orchid Dothan), Mos Def (Big Black)

The only black executive at a network TV station tries to get himself fired by creating a politically correct minstrel show, portraying blacks as half-witted. But his plan misfires.

Not an entirely successful essay on racist attitudes in the media, but Lee is as provocative as ever and there are savagely amusing moments.

CIN Ellen Kuras   MUS Terence Blanchard   DES Victor Kempster   ED Sam Pollard   PROD John Kilik, Spike Lee
DIST Entertainment

❝ Starts out hilarious and then turns very, very grim. – *Michael Wilmington, Chicago Tribune*

❝ What the movie lacks in clarity, it makes up for in honesty, toughness, relentlessness and passion. – *Stephen Hunter, Washington Post*

The Band Wagon ★★★★

DIR Vincente Minnelli
1953   112m   US
DVD   ♫

☆ *Fred Astaire* (Tony Hunter), *Jack Buchanan* (Jeffrey Cordova), *Oscar Levant* (Lester Marton), Cyd Charisse (Gaby Gerard), Nanette Fabray (Lily Marton)

A has-been Hollywood dancer joins forces with a temperamental stage producer to put on a Broadway musical.

Simple but sophisticated musical with the bare minimum of plot, told mostly in jokes, and the maximum of music and song, including a spoof Mickey Spillane ballet finale. The level of technical accomplishment is very high.

SCR *Adolph Green, Betty Comden*   CIN Harry Jackson
MUS Adolph Deutsch   ED Albert Akst   PROD Arthur Freed   DIST MGM

❝ The best musical of the month, the year, the decade, or for all I know of all time. – *Archer Winsten*

† The Jack Buchanan character, Jeffrey Cordova, was first offered to Clifton Webb. It was loosely based on José Ferrer, who in the early fifties produced four Broadway shows all running at the same time, and acted in a fifth

† 'A Shine on Your Shoes', 'By Myself', 'That's Entertainment', 'Dancing in the Dark', 'Triplets', 'New Sun in the Sky', 'I Guess I'll Have to Change My Plan', 'Louisiana Hayride', 'I Love Louisa', 'Girl Hunt' ballet.

⚱ Adolph Green, Betty Comden (screenplay); Adolph Deutsch; Mary Ann Nyberg (costume design)

Bandit Queen ★

DIR Shekhar Kapur
1994   119m   GB/India
DVD   ♫

☆ Seema Biswas (Phoolan Devi), Nirmal Pandey (Vikram Mallah), Manoj Bajpai (Man Singh), Rajesh Vivek (Mustaquim), Raghuvir Yadav (Madho), Saurabh Shukla (Kailash), Govind Namdeo (SriRam)

When an Indian woman, Phoolan Devi, is gang-raped by bandits, she forms a band of outlaws and embarks on a mission of revenge before turning herself in.

Judged purely as a film, it's a mess, and there's always the sense Kapur has one eye on the global market. Yet as a polemical piece, it's a damning condemnation of the place of women in Indian society and a caste system that effectively imprisons everyone.

SCR Mala Sen, Ranjit Kapoor   CIN Ashok Mehta
MUS Nusrat Fateh Ali Khan, Roger White   DES Eve Mavrakis   ED Renu Saluja   PROD Sundeep Singh Bedi
DIST Mainline/Kaleidoscope/Channel 4

❝ An astonishing, overpowering piece of rabble-rousing, consciousness-raising, epic-scale filmmaking. – *Kevin Thomas, Los Angeles Times*

❝ An exciting movie that brings Devi's story to life with passion but without passing judgment. – *Richard Corliss, Time*

† This remarkably controversial film's Indian release was held up after widespread protests – and a lawsuit from Pholan Devi, who claimed her privacy had been invaded and her trial for murder prejudiced. She later entered politics, but was assassinated in 2001.

DVD Available on DVD   ☆ Cast in order of importance   ❝ Critics' Quotes   ⚱ Academy Award   ⊕ BAFTA
♫ Soundtrack on CD   † Points of interest   Academy Award nomination   BAFTA nomination

'Two's Company, Three's A Crime.'

Bandits ★

DIR Barry Levinson
2001   123m   US
[DVD] ♫

☆ Bruce Willis (Joe Blake), Billy Bob Thornton (Terry Collins), Cate Blanchett (Kate Wheeler), Troy Garity (Harvey Pollard), Brian F. O'Byrne (Darill Miller), Stacey Travis (Cloe Miller), Bobby Slayton (Darren Head), January Jones (Claire), William Converse-Roberts (Charles Wheeler)

A pair of bank robbers break out of jail, then fall for a bored housewife who they have kidnapped.

Shambling, jokey thriller with a fair share of laughs and some enjoyable interplay between the three leads.

SCR Harley Peyton   CIN Dante Spinotti
MUS Christopher Young   DES Victor Kempster   ED Stu Linder   PROD Michael Birnbaum, Michele Berk, Barry Levinson, Paula Weinstein, Ashok Amritraj, David Hoberman, Arnold Rifkin   DIST TCF

66 Levinson's quirky caper is rich with laughs. – *Michael Sragow, Baltimore Sun*

66 An amusing tale of larceny triumphant, Bandits is an entertainment with a rogue's imagination. – *Kenneth Turan, Los Angeles Times*

'Once, not long ago, a small Egyptian police band arrived in Israel. Not many remember this. It wasn't that important.'

The Band's Visit (new) ★★

SCR/DIR Eran Kolirin
2007   87m   Israel/US/France
☆ Sasson Gabai (Tawfiq), Ronit Elkabetz (Dina), Saleh Bakri (Haled), Khalifa Natour (Simon)

An Egyptian ceremonial police band arrives in Israel to perform at an Arab cultural centre, but find themselves stranded in a remote town.

Good-hearted, amiable parable about overcoming differences between mutually hostile communities. Modest but charming and eager to please.

CIN Shai Goldman   MUS Habib Shehadah Hanna
DES Eitan Levi   ED Arik Leibovitz   PROD Ehud Bleiberg, Eilon Ratzkovsky, Yossi Uzrad, Koby Gal-Raday, Guy Jacoel   DIST Sony

66 A beautifully controlled piece, it marks the impressive debut of director and screenwriter Eran Kolirin, who handles the delicate shades of politics with subtle tones. – *Jason Solomons, Observer*

† The US Academy ruled the film ineligible for the foreign language Oscars because a proportion of its screenplay is in English.

The Bank Dick ★★★

DIR Edward F. Cline
1940   73m   US
[DVD]

☆ W. C. Fields (Egbert Sousè), Franklin Pangborn (J. Pinkerton Snoopington), Una Merkel (Myrtle Souse), Shemp Howard (Joe Guelpe), Jack Norton (A. Pismo Clam), Grady Sutton (Og Oggilby), Cora Witherspoon (Agatha Souse)

In Lompoc, California, a ne'er-do-well accidentally stops a hold-up, is made a bank detective, acquires deeds to a worthless mine and interferes in the production of a film.

Imperfect, but probably the best W.C. Fields vehicle there is: the jokes sometimes end in mid-air, but there are delicious moments and very little padding. The character names are sometimes funnier than the script: they include Egbert Sousè, J. Pinkerton Snoopington, Ogg Oggilby and Filthy McNasty.

SCR Mahatma Kane Jeeves (W. C. Fields)   CIN Milton Krasner   ED Arthur Hilton   DIST Universal

66 One of the great classics of American comedy. – *Robert Lewis Taylor*

66 When the man is funny he is terrific . . . but the story is makeshift, the other characters are stock types, the only pace discernible is the distance between drinks or the rhythm of the fleeting seconds it takes Fields to size up trouble coming and duck the hell out. – *Otis Ferguson*

† Fields's writing nom-de-plume was allegedly borrowed from noble characters in old English plays he squirmed through as a youth. They kept saying: 'M'hat, m'cane, Jeeves.'

'The true story of a heist gone wrong. . .in all the right ways.'

The Bank Job (new)

DIR Roger Donaldson
2008   111m   UK
[DVD]

☆ Jason Statham (Terry Leather), Saffron Burrows (Martine), Stephen Campbell Moore (Kevin), Daniel Mays (Dave), James Faulkner (Guy Singer), David Suchet (Lew Vogel), Peter Bowles (Miles Urquhart), Keeley Hawes (Wendy Leather)

In 1971 London, criminals are hired to break into a bank vault and retrieve photographs of a misbehaving royal.

Breezy crime caper, supposedly based on truth, with a retro feel that seems forced and bouts of violence that feel out of place.

SCR Dick Clement, Ian LaFrenais   CIN Michael Coulter
MUS J. Peter Robinson   DES Gavin Bocquet   ED John Gilbert   PROD Steven Chasman, Charles Roven
DIST Lionsgate

66 A lumbering thriller that feels like it belongs on the telly. – *Chris Hewitt, Empire*

66 A back-to-basics Brit flick that tells a good story with a minimum of pretension. – *David Edwards, Mirror*

'A provocative new comedy about sex, friendship, and all other things that invade our lives.'

The Barbarian Invasions ★

SCR/DIR Denys Arcand
2003   99m   Canada/France
[DVD]

☆ Remy Girard (Remy), Stephane Rousseau (Sebastien), Marie-Josée Croze (Nathalie), Marina Hands (Gaelle), Dorothee Berryman (Louise), Johanne Marie Tremblay (Sister Constance), Dominique Michel (Dominique), Louise Portal (Diane)

[DVD] Available on DVD   ☆ Cast in order   66 Critics' Quotes   🏆 Academy Award   🎭 BAFTA
♫ Soundtrack on CD   of importance   † Points of interest   Academy Award nomination   BAFTA nomination

51

A dying leftist academic in Montreal is reconciled with his son, a rich city type.

Despite its class and pedigree, this is an exasperatingly self-satisfied account of deathbed rapprochements; the literary banter is pompous, the attitude to America horribly snobbish. It hides a blatant sentimentality, too, behind its veil of brittle wit.

CIN Guy Dufaux   MUS Pierre Aviat   DES Francois Seguin   ED Isabelle Dedieu   PROD Denise Robert, Daniel Louis   DIST UIP

66 A pungently funny and heartfelt piece of wish fulfilment. – *David Edelstein, Slate*

66 A total, suppurating pain... Arcand has the same respect for plausibility that Jack the Ripper had for chivalry. – *Nigel Andrews, Financial Times*

† Many of the characters also feature in Arcand's 1986 film The Decline of the American Empire.
† Marie-Josée Croze won the best actress award, and Denys Arcand was named best screenwriter at the 2003 Cannes Film Festival.

⚭ foreign language film
⚭ Denys Arcand (original screenplay)

Ⓣ Denys Arcand (original screenplay); film not in the English language

---

'Some people never go crazy. What truly horrible lives they must lead.'

Barfly ★

DIR Barbet Schroeder
1987   97m   US
[DVD]

☆ Mickey Rourke (Henry Chinaski), Faye Dunaway (Wanda Wilcox), Alice Krige (Tully Sorenson), Jack Nance (Detective)

Writer Charles Bukowski's reminiscences of 'heroic' drinking bouts in murky LA bars.

Not much fun, and more 'drunk' acting than one might ever wish to see again. Yet it captures Bukowski's milieu accurately.

SCR Charles Bukowski   CIN Robby Muller   MUS Jack Baran   DES Bob Ziembicki   ED Eva Gardos   PROD Tom Luddy, Fred Roos, Barbet Schroeder   DIST Cannon/Barbet Schroeder, Fred Roos, Tom Luddy

---

Barry Lyndon ★★

SCR/DIR Stanley Kubrick
1975   187m   GB
[DVD]   ♫

☆ Ryan O'Neal, Marisa Berenson, Patrick Magee, Hardy Kruger, Steven Berkoff, Gay Hamilton, Marie Kean, Murray Melvin, André Morell, Leonard Rossiter, Philip Stone, Michael Hordern

Adventures of an 18th-century Irish gentleman of fortune.

A curiously cold-hearted enterprise, like an art gallery in which the backgrounds are sketched in loving detail and the human figures totally neglected; there is much to enjoy, but script and acting are variable, to say the least, and the point of it all is obscure, as it certainly does not tell a rattling good story. O'Neal is frankly miscast. It is,

however, one of the most ravishingly beautiful films in cinema history.

CIN John Alcott   DES Ken Adam   PROD Stanley Kubrick   DIST Warner

66 The motion picture equivalent of one of these very large, very expensive, very elegant and very dull books that exist solely to be seen on coffee tables. – *Charles Champlin, Los Angeles Times*

66 Watching the movie is like looking at illustrations for a work that has not been supplied. – *John Simon*

⚭ John Alcott; Leonard Rosenman; Ken Adam; Britt Soderlund, Milena Canonero (costume design)
⚭ picture; Stanley Kubrick (adapted screenplay); Stanley Kubrick (direction)

Ⓣ Stanley Kubrick (direction); John Alcott

'There's Only One Thing Stranger Than What's Going On Inside His Head. What's Going On Outside.'

Barton Fink ★★★

DIR Joel Coen
1991   116m   US
[DVD]   ♫

☆ *John Turturro* (Barton Fink), *John Goodman* (Charlie Meadows), Judy Davis (Audrey Taylor), *Michael Lerner* (Jack Lipnick), John Mahoney (W.P. Mayhew), Tony Shalhoub (Ben Geisler), Jon Polito (Lou Breeze), Steve Buscemi (Chet)

In the 1940s, a serious-minded radical playwright ends up in Hollywood. Beset by writer's block, he is ordered to script a vapid wrestling picture.

A delicious satire on Hollywood excess and insensitivity, and a sharp jab at worthy social realist writers such as Clifford Odets. But the film really takes off with the arrival of Goodman as Fink's murderous neighbour, and starts on a pleasing crescendo into delirium.

SCR Ethan and Joel Coen   CIN Roger Deakins   MUS Carter Burwell   DES Dennis Gassner   ED Roderick Jaynes   PROD Ethan Coen   DIST Rank/Circle

CHARLIE: 'Look upon me! I'll show you the life of the mind!'

66 Stimulating entertainment, as rigorously challenging and painfully funny as anything the Coens have done. But it's necessary to meet the Coens halfway. If you don't, Barton Fink is an empty exercise that will bore you breathless. If you do, it's a comic nightmare that will stir your imagination like no film in years. – *Peter Travers, Rolling Stone*

66 Creepily beautiful, acted with relish, Barton Fink is a savagely original work. It lodges in your head like a hatchet. – *David Ansen, Newsweek*

⚭ Michael Lerner (supporting actor); Dennis Gassner

'Flesh seduces. Passion kills.'

Basic Instinct ★

DIR *Paul Verhoeven*
1992   128m   US/ France
[DVD]   ♫

☆ Michael Douglas (Det. Nick Curran), *Sharon Stone* (Catherine Tramell), George Dzundza (Gus Moran), Jeanne Tripplehorn (Dr. Beth Garner), Denis Arndt (Lt. Philip Walker), Leilani Sarelle (Roxy), Dorothy Malone (Hazel Dobkins)

A bisexual woman novelist is a suspect in a murder case, but the investigating detective becomes sexually infatuated with her.

Erotic thriller unburdened by notions of taste and restraint, but directed with brio. A guilty pleasure that finally made Stone a star; quite a sensation in its time.

SCR Joe Eszterhas   CIN Jan de Bont   MUS Jerry Goldsmith   DES Terence Marsh   ED Frank J. Urioste   PROD Alan Marshall   DIST Guild/Carolco/Canal

66 Beneath its heavy-breathing fripperies, though, Basic Instinct is mechanical and routine, a muddle of Hitchcockian red herrings and standard cop-thriller ballistics. – *Owen Gleiberman, Entertainment Weekly*

Jerry Goldsmith; Frank J. Urioste

'The true story of the death of innocence and the birth of an artist. . .'

The Basketball Diaries   *

DIR Scott Kalvert
1995   102m   US
DVD   ♫

☆ Leonardo DiCaprio (Jim Carroll), Bruno Kirby (Swifty), Lorraine Bracco (Jim's Mother), Ernie Hudson (Reggie), Patrick McGaw (Neutron), James Madio (Pedro), Mark Wahlberg (Mickey), Michael Rapaport (Bald Punk)

A teen rebel at a Catholic school takes to the streets and becomes addicted to heroin.

Thin gruel, rarely convincing in its details, and glossing over much of the headier material in Jim Carroll's cult memoir.

SCR Brian Goluboff   CIN David Phillips   MUS Graeme Revell   DES Christopher Nowak   ED Dana Congdon   PROD Liz Heller, John Bard Manulis   DIST New Line/Island

66 Too lame and too tame. – *Jay Carr, Boston Globe*

66 It's an energetic, watchable mess. – *Owen Gleiberman, Entertainment Weekly*

'In 1981, A Nineteen-Year-Old Unknown Graffiti Writer Took The New York Art World By Storm. The Rest Is Art History.'

Basquiat   *

SCR/DIR Julian Schnabel
1996   108m   US
DVD   ♫

☆ Jeffrey Wright (Jean Michel Basquiat), David Bowie (Andy Warhol), Dennis Hopper (Bruno Bischofberger), Gary Oldman (Albert Milo), Claire Forlani (Gina Cardinale), Michael Wincott (Rene Ricard), Parker Posey (Mary Boone), Elina Löwensohn (Annina Nosei), Tatum O'Neal (Cynthia Kruger), Benicio Del Toro (Benny Dalmau), Christopher Walken (The Interviewer), Courtney Love (Big Pink), Paul Bartel (Henry Geldzahler), Willem Dafoe (The Electrician)

New York graffiti artist Jean-Michel Basquiat becomes a key member of Andy Warhol's coterie and achieves recognition but overdoses on heroin.

A tragic story of a talented artist who died at age 27. It's not made clear why Basquiat should be remembered two decades after his death; the best sequences portray

denizens of the Manhattan art scene embracing a hot new talent who despised everything they stood for.

CIN Ron Fortunato   MUS John Cale, Julian Schnabel   DES Dan Leigh   ED Michael Berenbaum   PROD Jon Kilik, Randy Ostrow, Sigurjon Sighvatsson   DIST Guild/Eleventh Street/Miramax

66 It's smart and good-hearted and boasts an amazingly good score, but the film is limited by the very private nature of the man it portrays. – *Edward Guthmann, San Francisco Chronicle*

† Director Schnabel was a friend and contemporary of Basquiat.

'Trapped behind enemy lines. A whole army after him. . .And only one man can save him.'

Bat 21   ★★

DIR Peter Markle
1988   105m   US
DVD   ♫

☆ Gene Hackman (Lt. Col. Iceal Hambleton), Danny Glover (Capt. Bartholomew Clark), Jerry Reed (Col. George Walker), David Marshall Grant (Ross Carver), Clayton Rohner (Sgt. Harley Rumbaugh), Erich Anderson (Maj. Jake Scott), Joe Dorsey (Col. Douglass)

In Vietnam an American intelligence expert crashes behind enemy lines, and a helicopter pilot tries to track him down.

Two good lead performances lift this fact-based drama.

SCR William C. Anderson, George Gordon   CIN Mark Irwin   MUS Christopher Young   DES Vincent Cresciman   ED Stephen E. Rivkin   PROD David Fisher, Gary A. Neill, Michael Balson   DIST Tri-Star/Vision/Eagle

---

Batman   ★★

DIR Tim Burton
1989   126m   US
DVD   ♫

☆ Michael Keaton (Batman/Bruce Wayne), *Jack Nicholson* (The Joker), Kim Basinger (Vicki Vale), Robert Wuhl (Alexander Knox), Pat Hingle (Commissioner James Gordon), Billy Dee Williams (Harvey Dent), Michael Gough (Alfred Pennyworth), Jack Palance (Carl Grissom), Jerry Hall (Alicia Grissom)

Batman, traumatised since seeing his parents murdered, grows up to don a mask and combat the criminal antics of the equally disturbed Joker.

Tim Burton jettisoned the flippant comic-strip approach of the TV series and catapults us into a dark, troubled world. The episodic narrative would work better if Nicholson's Joker did not upstage Keaton's Batman at every turn. Still, Anton Furst's Metropolis sets look terrific.

SCR Sam Hamm, Warren Skaaren   CIN Roger Pratt   MUS *Danny Elfman*   DES *Anton Furst*   ED Ray Lovejoy   PROD Jon Peters, Peter Guber   DIST Warner

66 It has so many unpredictable spins that what's missing doesn't seem to matter much. The images sing. – *Pauline Kael, New Yorker*

† Prince contributed six songs to the soundtrack.

Anton Furst

DVD Available on DVD   ☆ Cast in order of importance   66 Critics' Quotes   Academy Award   Academy Award nomination   BAFTA   BAFTA nomination

† Points of interest   ♫ Soundtrack on CD

53

Jack Nicholson (supporting actor); Anton Furst; Derek Meddings, John Evans (special effects); Don Sharpe, Tony Dawe, Bill Rowe (sound); Bob Ringwood (costume design); Paul Engelen, Nick Dudman (make up)

'It's not who he is underneath but what he does that defines him.'

Batman Begins ★★★

DIR *Christopher Nolan*
2005   140m   US
DVD   ♫

☆ *Christian Bale* (Bruce Wayne/Batman), Michael Caine (Alfred), Liam Neeson (Ducard), Katie Holmes (Rachel Dawes), Gary Oldman (Jim Gordon), Cillian Murphy (Dr. Jonathan Crane), Tom Wilkinson (Carmine Falcone), Rutger Hauer (Thomas Wayne), Morgan Freeman (Lucius Fox), Gus Lewis (Bruce Wayne, age 8)

As a child, Bruce Wayne sees his parents killed by a criminal, and grows up uneasily to assume the mantle of crime fighter.

Easily the best Batman picture in 20 years, with director Nolan and leading man Bale doing sterling work. Nolan has taken the franchise back to its basics, clinically tracing Batman's personal history and psyche. Shot on an epic scale, it's both thoughtful and exciting, though perhaps too intense and complex for kids.

SCR Christopher Nolan, David S. Goyer   **CIN** *Wally Pfister*
MUS Hans Zimmer, James Newton Howard
DES *Nathan Crowley*   **ED** Lee Smith   **PROD** Charles Roven, Emma Thomas, Larry Franco   **DIST** Warner

66 A carefully thought out and consummately well-made piece of work, a serious comic-book adaptation that is driven by story, psychology and reality, not special effects. – *Kenneth Turan, Los Angeles Times*

66 In a year when the franchise watchword is 'dark', this delivers the full noir with a side order of dementia. – *Kim Newman, Empire*

Wally Pfister

Nathan Crowley; Janek Sirrs, Dan Glass, Chris Corbould, Paul J. Franklin (special visual effects); David Evans, Stefan Henrix, Peter Lindsay (sound)

'The Bat, the Cat, the Penguin.'

Batman Returns ★

DIR Tim Burton
1992   126m   US
DVD

☆ Michael Keaton (Batman/Bruce Wayne), Danny DeVito (Penguin/Cobblepot), Michelle Pfeiffer (Catwoman/Selina Kyle), Christopher Walken (Max Shreck), Michael Gough (Alfred Pennyworth), Michael Murphy (The Mayor), Cristi Conaway (Ice Princess), Pat Hingle (Commissioner James Gordon)

Batman finds new criminal enemies: Penguin and Catwoman.

Burton's second stab at Batman repeats the virtues and vices of the first: it's great to look at and imaginatively realised, but if anything its script is even more incoherent. Pfeiffer's cat-suit is pretty distracting, though.

SCR Daniel Waters   **CIN** Stefan Czapsky   **MUS** Danny Elfman   **DES** *Bo Welch*   **ED** Chris Lebenzon, Bob Badami
PROD Denise Di Novi, Tim Burton   **DIST** Warner

66 More of the same, but nowhere near as good (funny, disturbing, obsessive) as the uneven original, revealing arrested development on every level. – *Jonathan Rosenbaum, Chicago Reader*

† Two other Batman films were released by Warners in the 1990s as part of this franchise: Batman Forever (1995) and Batman and Robin (1997). Neither one is recommended viewing.

Michael L. Fink, Craig Barron, John Bruno, Dennis Skotak (visual effects); Ve Neill, Ronnie Spector, Stan Winston (make up)

Michael L. Fink, Craig Barron, John Bruno, Dennis Skotak (special visual effects); Ve Neill, Ronnie Spector, Stan Winston (make up)

'There are many ways to see the same story.'

Battle for Haditha (new) ★

DIR Nick Broomfield
2007   96m   UK
DVD

☆ Elliot Ruiz (Cpl. Ramirez), Falah Flayeh (Ahmad), Yasmine Hanani (Hiba), Andrew McClaren (Capt. Sampson), Eric Mehalacopoulos (Sgt. Ross), Duraid A. Ghaieb (Rashied), Matthew Knoll (Cpl. Matthews)

When their convoy is attacked by a roadside bomb, US marines take revenge by slaughtering Iraqi civilians.

Powerful dramatisation of a contested outrage from a British filmmaker better known for his documentaries; though the result feels overly emotive and polemical, it is certainly to be commended for striving to show both sides of a sorry story.

SCR Nick Broomfield, Marc Hoeferlin, Anna Telford
CIN Mark Wolf   **MUS** Nick Laird-Clowes   **DES** David Bryan   **ED** Ash Jenkins, Stuart Gazzard   **PROD** Nick Broomfield   **DIST** Contender

66 A brutally effective docudrama. – *Michael Rechtshaffen, Hollywood Reporter*

66 A moving, even-handed and often revelatory account of a military campaign that deforms soldiers and civilians alike. – *Sukhdev Sandhu, Daily Telegraph*

'The Revolt That Stirred The World!'

The Battle of Algiers ★★★★

DIR *Gillo Pontecorvo*
1965   135m   Algeria/Italy
DVD

☆ Brahim Haggiag (Ali La Pointe), Jean Martin (Colonel), Yacef Saadi (Kader), Tommaso Neri (Captain), Samia Kerbash (One of the Girls), Ugo Paletti (Captain)

In 1954 Algiers, an ex-convict joins the terrorists in rebellion against the French government.

Politically-oriented reconstruction of a bitter period of French colonial history, astonishingly angry, tense and powerful, and made more convincing by its wealth of effective detail.

SCR Franco Solinas   **CIN** *Marcello Gatti*   **MUS** Ennio Morricone, Gillo Pontecorvo   **DES** Sergio Canevari

DVD Available on DVD	☆ Cast in order	66 Critics' Quotes	Academy Award	BAFTA
♫ Soundtrack on CD	of importance	† Points of interest	Academy Award nomination	BAFTA nomination

ED Mario Morra, Mario Serandrei **PROD** Antonio Musi, Yacef Saadi **DIST** Casbah/Igor

66 It's one of the best movies about revolutionary and anti-colonial activism ever made, convincing, balanced, passionate, and compulsively watchable as storytelling. – *Jonathan Rosenbaum, Chicago Reader*

66 Has any movie ever made a more concise and reasonable argument for the "low-intensity," low-resource warfare referred to by powerful nations as terrorism? – *Michael Atkinson, Village Voice*

foreign film; Gillo Pontecorvo (direction); Franco Solinas (original screenplay)

'The Kids Definitely Aren't Alright!'

Battle Royale ★★

DIR Kinji Fukasaku
2000 114m Japan
DVD ♫

☆ Tatsuya Fujiwara (Shuya), Aki Maeda (Noriko), Taro Yamamoto (Kawada), Masanobu Ando (Kiriyama), Kou Shibasaki (Mitsuko), Chiaki Kuriyama (Chigusa), Beat Takeshi (Kitano)

In this futuristic story, a class of unruly schoolchildren are taken to a remote island, armed with weapons and given three days in which to eliminate one another until the sole survivor is allowed to rejoin society.

Terrific, cruel and compelling premise, along the lines of William Golding's Lord of the Flies, that pre-dates the conventions of reality TV. It's quite a thrill ride, and in its own way savagely funny.

SCR Kenta Fukasaku **CIN** Katsumi Yanagijima **MUS** Masamichi Amano **DES** Kyoko Heya **ED** Hirohide Abe **PROD** Masao Sato, Masumi Okada, Teruo Kamaya, Tetsu Kayama **DIST** Metro Tartan

66 Some will be uncomfortable or appalled, and the mix of humour and horror is uneasy, but this isn't a film you'll forget easily. – *Kim Newman, Empire*

The Battleship Potemkin ★★★★

SCR/DIR *Sergei Eisenstein*
1925 75m USSR
DVD

☆ A. Antonov (Vakulinchuk), Grigori Alexandrov (Senior Officer Gilyarovsky), Vladimir Barsky (Commander Golikov), Aleksandr Levshin (Petty Officer), Ivan Bobrov (Humiliated Soldier), Mikhail Gomorov (Sailor Matyushenko)

A partly fictitious account of the mutiny at Odessa, an episode in the 1905 revolution. (The film was made as part of the 20th anniversary celebrations.)

A textbook cinema classic, and masterpiece of creative editing, especially in the famous Odessa Steps sequence in which innocent civilians are mown down in the bloodshed; the happenings of a minute are drawn into five by frenzied cross-cutting. The film contains 1,300 separate shots, and in 1948 and 1958 was judged the best film ever made by a panel of international judges.

CIN *Edouard Tissé, V. Popov* **ED** *Sergei Eisenstein* **DIST** Goskino

---

'You name it, we shoot it.'

Be Kind Rewind (new)

SCR/DIR Michel Gondry
2008 100m US/France/UK
DVD ♫

☆ Jack Black (Jerry), Mos Def (Mike), Danny Glover (Mr. Fletcher), Mia Farrow (Miss Falewicz), Melonie Diaz (Alma)

At a struggling video rental store in a small New Jersey town, all the tapes get erased in a freak accident. In the absence of the owner, two store clerks shoot their own low-tech versions of films like Ghostbusters and Rush Hour 2 to satisfy customer demand.

A delightful little idea that amounts to a sketch; extended to feature length it feels like a massive overdose of whimsy. Black, one of nature's sidekicks, is especially irritating in the lead role, mugging frantically for no good reason.

CIN Ellen Kuras **MUS** Jean-Michel Bernard **DES** Dan Leigh **ED** Jeff Buchanan **PROD** Georges Bermann **DIST** Pathé

66 Be kind. Erase. – *Anthony Lane, New Yorker*

66 A sentimental, whimsical embarrassment. – *Philip French, Observer*

'Somewhere on this planet it must exist.'

The Beach ★★

DIR Danny Boyle
2000 119m US/GB/Thailand
DVD ♫

☆ Leonardo DiCaprio (Richard), Tilda Swinton (Sal), Virginie Ledoyen (Francoise), Guillaume Canet (Etienne), Paterson Joseph (Keaty), Robert Carlyle (Daffy), Peter Youngblood Hills (Zeph), Jerry Swindall (Sammy), Lars Arentz Hansen (Bugs)

An American backpacker in Thailand is told about the existence of a perfect beach on a secret island that has been colonised by radical travellers.

An initially seductive tale of paradise and danger, gripping for an hour before losing its way; DiCaprio is naggingly miscast, and the dynamics of the community are increasingly hard to believe.

SCR John Hodge **CIN** *Darius Khondji* **MUS** Angelo Badalamenti **DES** Andrew McAlpine **ED** Masahiro Hirakubo **PROD** Andrew Macdonald **DIST** TCF

66 An edgy, hypnotic entertainment that's like a Club Med production of Lord of the Flies. – *Wesley Morris, Boston Globe*

66 Relentlessly beautiful and wholly annoying. – *Stephen Hunter, Washington Post*

† On the set in Thailand, environmental protesters picketed the film because crew members had moved shrubbery and plants from their natural location.
† Ewan McGregor was originally set to play the lead role of Richard, thus reuniting with director Boyle, producer Macdonald and writer John Hodge, his colleagues from Shallow Grave and Trainspotting. But Fox insisted on a bigger star, and DiCaprio replaced McGregor, who has not worked with his former colleagues since.

DVD Available on DVD   ☆ Cast in order   66 Critics' Quotes   Academy Award   BAFTA
♫ Soundtrack on CD   of importance   † Points of interest   Academy Award nomination   BAFTA nomination

55

B

'The Friendship You'll Always Remember. . .In The Film You'll Never Forget'

Beaches ★

DIR Garry Marshall

1988 123m US

DVD

☆ Bette Midler (Cecilia 'CC' Carol Bloom), Barbara Hershey (Hillary Whitney Essex), John Heard (John Pierce), Spalding Gray (Dr. Richard Milstein), Lainie Kazan (Leona Bloom), James Read (Michael Essex), Grace Johnston (Victoria Cecilia Essex), Mayim Bialik (Cecilia 'CC' Carol Bloom (age 11)), Marcie Leeds (Hillary Whitney Essex (age 11))

A forthright, egocentric singing star visits her friend from childhood, who is dying, and they revisit the ups and downs of their relationship.

Melodramatic and sentimental 'women's picture' carried off with a certain grace and belief. As always, Midler's larger-than-life personality tends to dominate everyone else on screen, and she sings impressively.

SCR Mary Agnes Donoghue   CIN Dante Spinotti   MUS Georges Delerue   DES Albert Brenner   ED Richard Halsey   PROD Bonnie Bruckheimer-Martell, Bette Midler, Margaret Jennings South   DIST Warner/Touchstone/An All Girl Production

66 Pure soap from beginning to end. – *Janet Maslin, New York Times*

⚬ art direction

'The Ultimate Disaster Movie.'

Bean

DIR Mel Smith

1997 90m GB

DVD

☆ Rowan Atkinson (Mr Bean), Peter MacNicol (David Langley), Pamela Reed (Alison Langley), Harris Yulin (George Grierson), Burt Reynolds (General Newton), John Mills (Chairman), Richard Gant (Lt Brutus), Tricia Vessey (Jennifer Langley), Andrew Lawrence (Kevin Langley), Peter Egan (Lord Walton), Peter Capaldi (Gareth)

The bumbling Bean, a clumsy attendant at the National Gallery, travels to Los Angeles to see the unveiling of the newly acquired Whistler's Mother.

Notable mainly because it was such a huge global hit. Atkinson's millions of fans love it: the rest of us find it shoddily constructed, with a less than likeable central character.

SCR Richard Curtis, Robin Driscoll, Rowan Atkinson   CIN Francis Kenny   MUS Howard Goodall   DES Peter Larkin   ED Chris Blunden   PROD Tim Bevan, Eric Fellner, Peter Bennett-Jones   DIST Polygram/Working Title/Tiger Aspect

† The film grossed over $200 million worldwide, half of which was recouped even before it opened in the US.

The Bear ★★

DIR Jean-Jacques Annaud

1988 98m France

DVD ♫

☆ Bart, Youk, Jack Wallace, Tcheky Karyo, André Lacombe

A newly orphaned bear cub teams up with an adult male to avoid human hunters in the wild.

Engaging minimalist adventure with next to no human participation in front of the camera, and a slightly idealised, National Geographic flavour.

SCR Gérard Brach   CIN Philippe Rousselot   MUS Philippe Sarde   DES Toni Ludi   ED Noelle Boisson   PROD Claude Berri   DIST Tri-Star/Renn/Price Entertainment

66 Simply a ripping yarn. – *Geoff Andrew, Time Out*

⚬ Noelle Boisson (editing)

Ⓣ Philippe Rousselot

The Beat That My Heart Skipped ★★★

DIR *Jacques Audiard*

2005 107m France

DVD ♫

☆ *Romain Duris* (Thomas), Niels Arestrup (Robert), Linh-Dan Pham (Miao-Lin), Aure Atika (Aline), Emmanuelle Devos (Chris), Jonathan Zaccai (Fabrice)

A scummy real-estate developer in Paris, in danger of turning into his father, nurses an urge to become a concert pianist, like his mother.

Jittery and compelling drama of redemption and artistic ambition, based on James Toback's 1978 Fingers, and making an Oedipal neurosis its central point of characterisation. There's technique in spades, and Duris is hard to take your eyes off.

SCR Jacques Audiard, Tonino Benacquista   CIN Stéphane Fontaine   MUS *Alexandre Desplat*   DES François Emmanuelli   ED *Juliette Welfling*   PROD Pascal Caucheteux

66 Audiard's film is a rigorous study in counterpoint, evoking two parallel worlds that play off each other, then finally come together with an elliptical flash-forward ending. – *Lanie Goodman, Guardian*

66 Fevered, immediate, and hopeful – a story of a man recovering his soul. – *David Edelstein, Slate*

Ⓣ foreign film

Beau Travail ★

DIR Claire Denis

1999 93m France

DVD

☆ Denis Lavant (Galoup), Michel Subor (Commandant Bruno Forestier), Grégoire Colin (Sentain), Richard Courcet (Legionnaire)

A French Foreign Legion sergeant in a remote unit forms a hatred for a new recruit.

Herman Melville's Billy Budd is transplanted to the North African desert. Handsome to look at, it's shot in a studied manner that emphasises the story's homoerotic elements.

SCR Jean-Pol Fargeau, Claire Denis   CIN *Agnes Godard*   MUS *Eran Tzur, Charles Henri de Pierrefeu*   DES Arnaud de Moleron   ED Nelly Quettier   PROD Jerome Minet, Patrick Grandperret   DIST Artificial Eye

| DVD Available on DVD | ☆ Cast in order of importance | 66 Critics' Quotes | ⚬ Academy Award | Ⓣ BAFTA |
| ♫ Soundtrack on CD | | † Points of interest | ⚬ Academy Award nomination | Ⓣ BAFTA nomination |

66 Claire Denis is good with bodies, and in this most spectacularly somnambulant of narratives they do a lot of work. – *Charlotte O'Sullivan, Sight & Sound*

Beaufort (new)   ★★

DIR Joseph Cedar
2008   125m   Israel
DVD

☆ Oshri Cohen (Liraz Liberti), Itay Tiran (Koris), Eli Eltonyo (Oshri), Ohad Knoller (Ziv), Itay Turgeman (Zitlawy), Arthur Faradjev (Shpitzer)

A personal diary of a unit commander chronicles the daily routine of a group of Israeli soldiers based at Beaufort Castle (a fortress built during the Crusades) just before the end of the South Lebanon conflict.

With Hezbollah and the Lebanon kept firmly in the background, director Cedar concentrates powerfully on the inner turmoil and conflicts of the soldiers as the Israeli forces prepare to take their leave from the "invisible enemy." Stands comparison with such striking war movies as Das Boot and Paths of Glory.

SCR Joseph Cedar, Ron Leshem   **CIN** Ofer Inov
MUS Ishai Adar   **DES** Miguel Merkin   **ED** Zohar M Sela
PROD David Silber, David Mandil   **DIST** Trinity Filmed Entertainment

66 Even if it does not entirely rise above cliché, Beaufort has an earnest, sober intelligence that makes it hard to shake. It suggests that, for those who fight, the futility of war is inseparable from its nobility. – *A. O. Scott, The New York Times*

† Winner of the Silver Bear for best director at the 2007 Berlin Film Festival

⌂ foreign language film

'Good times never seemed so good.'

Beautiful Girls   ★

DIR Ted Demme
1996   112m   US
DVD

☆ Matt Dillon (Tommy 'Birdman' Rowland), Noah Emmerich (Michael 'Mo' Morris), Tim Hutton (Willie Conway), *Natalie Portman* (Marty), Annabeth Gish (Tracy Stover), Lauren Holly (Darian Smalls), Rosie O'Donnell (Gina Barrisano), Max Perlich (Kev), Mira Sorvino (Sharon Cassidy), Uma Thurman (Andera), Martha Plimpton (Jan)

A New York-based pianist, on the verge of getting married, returns to his small working-class home town, and finds his married friends stuck in routine, mundane lives.

Acutely observed story with a hard-working cast, from which Portman stands out as a precocious, worldly wise teenager. Minor, but appealing.

SCR Scott Rosenberg   **CIN** Adam Kimmel   **MUS** David A. Stewart   **DES** Dan Davis   **ED** Jeffrey Wolf
PROD Cary Woods   **DIST** Buena Vista/Miramax

66 The sensibility's very Diner, and rather smart-alecky, but this is a picture worth listening to. You don't have to check your brain at the box-office, just your PC sensibilities. – *Tom Charity, Time Out*

'He Saw The World In A Way No One Could Have Imagined.'

A Beautiful Mind   ★

DIR Ron Howard
2001   135m   US
DVD   ♫

☆ Russell Crowe (John Nash), Ed Harris (William Parcher), Jennifer Connelly (Alicia Larde Nash), Paul Bettany (Charles Herman), Adam Goldberg (Sol), Judd Hirsch (Helinger), Josh Lucas (Hansen), Anthony Rapp (Bender), Christopher Plummer (Dr Rosen), Austin Pendleton (Thomas King)

Hollywood biopic of maths genius John Forbes Nash, whose brilliant career was blighted by schizophrenia and paranoid delusions.

Ascribes a great deal less intelligence to its audience than it does to its subject, approaching his life through a prism of dubious narrative gimmickry and with much overrated acting. A feeling of Oscar-grab mendacity is hard to shake off.

SCR Akiva Goldsman   **CIN** *Roger Deakins*   **MUS** James Horner   **DES** Wynn Thomas   **ED** Mike Hill, Dan Hanley   **PROD** Brian Grazer, Ron Howard   **DIST** Universal

66 Consistently engrossing as an unusual character study and as a trip to the mysterious border-crossing between rarified brilliance and madness. – *Todd McCarthy, Variety*

66 The governing dynamic of A Beautiful Mind is sentimentality of a familiar and not altogether unwelcome kind. The movie can – indeed, should – be intellectually rejected, but you can't quite banish it from your mind. – *A.O. Scott, New York Times*

⌂ picture; Jennifer Connelly (supporting actress); Ron Howard; Akiva Goldsman (adapted screenplay)
⌂ Russell Crowe (leading actor); Mike Hill, Dan Hanley; James Horner (editing); Greg Cannom, Colleen Callaghan (makeup)
Ⓣ Russell Crowe (leading actor); Jennifer Connelly (supporting actress)
Ⓣ film; Akiva Goldsman (adapted screenplay)

'A comic collision of chaos and coincidence.'

Beautiful People   ★★

SCR/DIR *Jasmin Dizdar*
1999   107m   GB
DVD   ♫

☆ Charlotte Coleman (Portia Thornton), Charles Kay (George Thornton), Rosalind Ayres (Nora Thornton), Roger Sloman (Roger Midge), Heather Tobias (Felicity Midge), Danny Nussbaum (Griffin Midge), Siobhan Redmond (Kate Higgins), Gilbert Martin (Jerry Higgins), Steve Sweeney (Jim), Linda Bassett (Sister), Nicholas Farrell (Dr Mouldy), Edin Dzandzanovic (Pero Guzina)

Intertwining stories in 1990s London that illustrate the city's complicated cultural cross-currents. Serbs and Croats from Bosnia are among those trying to carve out new lives.

An impressive debut from a director who sadly failed to follow up on this small triumph. Dizdar has an eye (and an ear) for the teeming, confusing cultural landscape of modern London – and while some of his stories work better than others, there's intelligent observation here.

CIN Barry Ackroyd MUS Garry Bell DES Jon Henson
ED Justin Krish PROD Ben Woolford DIST Warner

66 For Dizdar, it's political and cultural conflict, rather than narcissism, that shapes the human comedy. – *Amy Taubin, Village Voice*

'An urban fairytale.'

Beautiful Thing ★

DIR Hettie Macdonald
1996 90m GB
DVD ♫

☆ Linda Henry (Sandra Gangel), Glen Berry (Jamie Gangel), Scott Neal (Ste Pearce), Ben Daniels (Tony), Tameka Empson (Leah Russell)

Two teenage neighbours on a London housing estate realise they are gay.

Low-key romance, often amusing and all the more charming for being contrasted with a harsh environment. The sunny, optimistic music of the Mama Cass Elliot nails the tone.

SCR Jonathan Harvey CIN Chris Seager MUS John Altman DES Mark Stevenson ED Don Fairservice
PROD Tony Garnett, Bill Shapter DIST Film Four/World

66 The movie takes the rosiest possible view of a ticklish situation. – *Stephen Holden, New York Times*

'The most beautiful love story ever told.'

Beauty and the Beast ★★★

DIR Gary Trousdale, Kirk Wise
1991 84m US
DVD ♫

☆ The voices of Paige O'Hara, Robby Benson, Jerry Orbach, Angela Lansbury, Richard White, David Ogden Stiers, Jesse Corti, Rex Everhart, Bradley Michael Pierce, Jo Anne Worley, Kimmy Robertson

Inspired by the fairy tale, a story about a prince, turned into a beast, who keeps a beautiful girl prisoner in his castle.

A turning point in the history of Disney animation, it is conceived along the lines of a Broadway musical. Excellent, rousing score and a thoughtful, satisfying script contribute to its triumph.

SCR *Linda Woolverton* ED John Carnochan PROD Don Hahn DIST Buena Vista/Walt Disney/Silver Screen Partners IV

66 There's enough wit and ingenuity in Roger Allers's story and Howard Ashman and Alan Menken's songs to give the CGI whizzkids a run for their money. – *Peter Bradshaw, Guardian*

† It was the first feature-length animated film to be nominated for the best picture Oscar.
† It spawned a Broadway musical, a US TV series and two straight-to-video sequels.

⫚ Alan Menken (music, original score); Alan Menken (m), Howard Ashman (ly) (music, original song – Beauty and the Beast)
⫚ picture; Alan Menken (m), Howard Ashman (ly) (music, original song – Belle); Alan Menken (m), Howard Ashman (ly) (music, original song – Be Our Guest); Terry Porter, Mel Metcalfe, David J. Hudson, Doc Kane (sound)

Ⓣ Alan Menken (music, original score); Randy Fullmer (special effects)

Beavis and Butthead Do America ★

DIR Mike Judge
1996 81m US
DVD ♫

☆ The voices of: Mike Judge, Cloris Leachman, Robert Stack, David Spade, Eric Bogosian, Richard Linklater, Bruce Willis (uncredited), Demi Moore (uncredited)

Two dim-witted teenagers travel from Las Vegas to Washington DC, unaware they are carrying a lethal weapon.

Adapted from the sniggering pair's series on MTV, this is gross, lowbrow, crude – and occasionally, it must be said, drop-dead funny.

SCR Mike Judge, Joe Stillman CIN David J. Miller
MUS John Frizzell ED Terry Kelley, Gunter Glinka, Neil Lawrence PROD Abby Terkuhle
DIST Paramount/Geffen/MTV

66 Their monumentally stupid and childish observations burst like water balloons over the heads of everyone they encounter; the movie plays like a dumbed-down "Animal House," and its idiocy is irresistible. – *Bruce Diones, New Yorker*

'Becoming a woman. Becoming a legend.'

Becoming Jane ★★

DIR Julian Jarrold
2007 120m UK/Ireland/US
DVD ♫

☆ Anne Hathaway (Jane Austen), James McAvoy (James Lefroy), Julie Walters (Mrs. Austen), James Cromwell (Rev. Austin), Maggie Smith (Lady Gresham), Ian Richardson (Judge Langlois), Helen McCrory (Mrs. Radcliffe)

The young Jane Austen harbours ambitions to be a novelist. Defying her parents' wishes to wed a 'suitable' husband, she falls for a poor but handsome lawyer.

An ingenious way to present another Jane Austen story for the screen, this literate script tracks her path to becoming a writer, suggesting sources in Austen's life that inspired Pride and Prejudice. It looks ravishing; American Hathaway acquits herself well, buttressed by a strong supporting cast of British veterans. A low-key delight.

SCR Sarah Williams, Kevin Hood CIN Eigil Bryld
MUS Adrian Johnston DES Eve Stewart ED Emma E. Hickox PROD Graham Broadbent, Robert Bernstein, Douglas Rae DIST Buena Vista

MRS. AUSTEN: 'Affection is desirable. Money is absolutely indispensable!'

66 Austen's fans will recognise something of the author's playful wit in the film, and forgive the dramatic liberties. – *Wendy Ide, The Times*

† Though the action takes place in England, all exterior scenes were shot in Ireland.

DVD Available on DVD ☆ Cast in order 66 Critics' Quotes ⫚ Academy Award Ⓑ BAFTA
♫ Soundtrack on CD of importance † Points of interest ⫚ Academy Award nomination Ⓣ BAFTA nomination

'Born to bee wild.'

Bee Movie (new) ★

DIR Simon J. Smith, Steve Hickner
2007 91m US
DVD ♪

☆ Jerry Seinfeld (Barry B. Benson), Renee Zellweger (Vanessa Bloome), Matthew Broderick (Adam Flayman), John Goodman (Layton T. Montgomery), Patrick Warburton (Ken), Chris Rock (Mooseblood)

Barry, an individualistic bee, shuns joining the workforce at the honey plant and devotes himself to suing the human race for stealing honey.

Amiable but minor, with a smattering of jokes from Seinfeld, in decidedly less acid mood than on his TV series. But the film is neither memorable nor especially child-friendly.

SCR Jerry Seinfeld, Spike Ferestein, Barry Marder, Andy Robin MUS Rupert Gregson-Williams DES Alex McDowell ED Nick Fletcher PROD Jerry Seinfeld, Christina Steinberg DIST Paramount

NARRATOR: 'According to all known laws of aviation, there is no way a bee should be able to fly. Bees, of course, fly anyway, because bees don't care what humans think is impossible.'

66 'There's no real jeopardy. The stakes are low. It's a bee movie about nothing. – *Carina Chocano, Los Angeles Times*

66 The best we can award is bee minus. – *Nigel Andrews, Financial Times*

'Say it once. . .Say it twice. . .But we dare you to say it THREE TIMES.'

Beetlejuice ★

DIR Tim Burton
1988 92m US
DVD ♪

☆ Alec Baldwin (Adam), Geena Davis (Barbara), Michael Keaton (Beetlejuice), Catherine O'Hara (Delia), Glenn Shadix (Otho)

A freelance exorcist is called in to help frighten off unlikable new buyers from a dead couple's home.

Over-frenetic and resolutely zany horror-comedy with exhausting special effects. Yet it helped cement director Burton's reputation.

SCR Michael McDowell, Warren Skaaren CIN Thomas Ackerman MUS Danny Elfman DES Bo Welch ED Jane Kurson PROD Michael Bender, Richard Hashimoto, Larry Wilson DIST Warner Bros/Geffen

66 Gets off to a start that's so charming it never lives it down. The movie is all anti-climax once we realize it's going to be about gimmicks, not characters. – *Roger Ebert, Chicago Sun-Times*

Ⅰ Ve Neill, Steve LaPorte, Robert Short (makeup)

Ⓣ Peter Kuran, Alan Munro, Robert Shore, Ted Rae (special effects); Ve Neill, Steve LaPorte, Robert Short (makeup)

Before Night Falls ★★

DIR Julian Schnabel
2000 133m US
DVD ♪

☆ Javier Bardem (Reinaldo Arenas), Olivier Martinez (Lazaro Gomez Carilles), Andrea Di Stefano (Pepe Malas), Johnny Depp (Bon Bon/Lieutenant Victor), Sean Penn (Cuco Sanchez), Michael Wincott (Herberto Zorilla Ochoa), Najwa Nimri (Fina Ochoa), Hector Babenco (Virgilio Pinera), Olatz Lopez Garmendia (Reinaldo's mother), Vito Maria Schnabel (Teenage Reinaldo), Jerzy Skolimowski (Professor)

Account of the life of poet Reinaldo Arenas, a marked man in Castro's Cuba because of his homosexuality, who finally succumbed to Aids in New York.

As with this director's Basquiat, also about a tormented artist, this is a fragmented, episodic and overlong account of a life. Yet Bardem's carefully studied performance, at times electrifying, partially redeems the structural faults.

SCR Cunningham O'Keefe, Lazaro Gomez Carilles, Julian Schnabel CIN Xavier Perez Grobet, Guillermo Rosas MUS Carter Burwell, Lou Reed, Laurie Anderson DES Salvador Parra ED Michael Berenbaum PROD Jon Kilik DIST TCF

66 Emotionally, it's all over the place, and so, deliberately, is the movie. – *Peter Rainer, New York magazine*

Ⅰ Javier Bardem (leading actor)

'When love can come as a complete surprise.'

Before Sunrise ★★

DIR Richard Linklater
1995 105m US/Austria
DVD ♪

☆ Ethan Hawke (Jesse), Julie Delpy (Celine)

An American slacker meets a French student on a train bound for Vienna, and they spend one eventful night together – mostly talking.

An ambitious two-hander that stand or falls on the strength of its talky script. It's charming and smart enough, yet more is needed at feature length. Still, a decent stab at reinventing the romance.

SCR Richard Linklater, Kim Krizan CIN Lee Daniel MUS Fred Frith DES Florian Reichmann ED Sandra Adair, Sheri Galloway PROD Anne Walker-McBay DIST Rank/Castle Rock/Detour/Filmhaus

66 An intoxicatingly romantic idea. – *Janet Maslin, New York Times*

66 Funny, poignant and perceptive, this is a brilliant gem. – *Geoff Andrew, Time Out*

'What if you had a second chance with the one that got away?'

Before Sunset ★

DIR Richard Linklater
2004 77m US
DVD ♪

☆ Ethan Hawke (Jesse), Julie Delpy (Celine), Vernon Dobtcheff (Book Store Manager), Louise Lemoine Torres (Journalist #1), Rodolphe Pauly (Journalist #2), Marianne Plasteig (Waitress), Diabolo (Philippe)

Nine years after they met fleetingly en route to Vienna, an American author and a French woman reunite by accident in Paris.

DVD Available on DVD   ☆ Cast in order of importance   66 Critics' Quotes   Ⅰ Academy Award   Ⓑ BAFTA
♪ Soundtrack on CD   † Points of interest   Ⅰ Academy Award nomination   Ⓣ BAFTA nomination

59

Charming sequel to *Before Sunrise* with identical virtues and vices, and an extra ruefulness about possibly missed opportunities. The lengthy conversation between the couple is played out in real time.

SCR Richard Linklater, Julie Delpy, Ethan Hawke   **CIN** Lee Daniel   **DES** Baptiste Glaymann   **ED** Sandra Adair   **PROD** Anne Walker-McBay, Richard Linklater

66 Although there isn't a single kiss in this love story, it's intensely erotic – and more to the point, it's not afraid of eroticism's juicier and more forthright twin, carnality. – *Stephanie Zacharek, Salon.com*

⚱ original screenplay

'No-one was supposed to get hurt.'

Before The Devil Knows You're Dead (new)   ★★★★

DIR *Sidney Lumet*
2007   117m   UK/US
[DVD]

☆ *Philip Seymour Hoffman* (Andy Hanson), *Ethan Hawke* (Hank Hanson), Marisa Tomei (Gina Hanson), Albert Finney (Charles Hanson), Michael Shannon (Dex), Amy Ryan (Martha), Brian O'Byrne (Bobby), Rosemary Harris (Nanette Hanson)

Two siblings, both in financial difficulties, decide to rob their parents' jewellery store in what they hope will be a victimless crime.

An astonishingly assured film that in any other year would have been garlanded with major awards. It creates an extraordinary degree of tension, even though we know its two unsavoury anti-heroes – Hoffman in his usual imperious form, and Hawke, who has never been better – will screw up their master plan. A jewel of a script from debutant Masterson, and a terrific achievement for Lumet; one needs to go back to Dog Day Afternoon *to find a film by this veteran that felt so accomplished.*

SCR *Kelly Masterson*   **CIN** Ron Fortunato   **MUS** Carter Burwell   **DES** Christopher Nowak   **ED** Tom Swartwout   **PROD** Michael Cerenzie, Brian Linse, Paul Parmar, William S. Gilmore   **DIST** Entertainment

66 The performances are big and entertaining, and Sidney Lumet, now in his eighties, directs with youthful force. – *Edward Porter, Sunday Times*

66 Superb heist thriller. . .after this film was over, I needed to relax my tensed-up muscles. – *Peter Bradshaw, Guardian*

'Once You Know The Faces You Will Begin To Understand The Story.'

Before the Rain   ★★★

SCR/DIR Milcho Manchevski
1994   113m   GB/France/Macedonia
♫

☆ *Katrin Cartlidge* (Anne), Rade Serbedzija (Aleksandar), Gregoire Colin (Kiril), Labina Mitevska (Zamira), Jay Villiers (Nick), Silvija Stojanovska (Hana), Phyllida Law (Anne's Mother)

Three separate but linked stories, concerning the newly independent republic of Macedonia.

This drama only yields its connections and its majestic structure in its final moments. But even before then, it's a chilling statement about poverty and poisonous ethnic rivalries.

CIN Manuel Teran   **MUS** Goran Trajkoski, Zoran Spasovski, Zlatko Origjanski   **DES** Sharon Lamofsky, David Munns   **ED** Nicolas Gaster   **PROD** Judy Counihan, Cedomir Kolar, Sam Taylor, Cat Villiers   **DIST** Electric/Aim/Noe/Vardar

66 This is one of the year's best films, a brilliant directorial debut. – *Roger |Ebert, Chicago Sun-Times*

⚱ foreign film

Behind the Sun   ★★

DIR *Walter Salles*
2001   105m   Brazil/France/Switzerland
[DVD]   ♫

☆ José Dumont (Father), Rodrigo Santoro (Tonho), Rita Assemany (Mother), Luiz Carlos Vasconcelos (Salustiano), Ravi Ramos Lacerda (Pacu), Flavia Marco Antonio (Clara), Othon Bastos (Mr Lourenco)

Rival families in the hinterlands of Brazil engage in a 'blood feud' over long-held grudges..

In the wake of Central Station *director Salles takes to Brazil's remotest regions again. This gorgeously composed film sets its frustrating, futile pattern of killings in a golden-hued landscape that curiously evokes misty-eyed nostalgia. There's a hint of magical realism about the proceedings, which raises some narrative uncertainties. But its exquisite look trumps its weaknesses.*

SCR Walter Salles, Sergio Machado, Karim Ainouz   **CIN** *Walter Carvalho*   **MUS** Antonio Pinto, Ed Cortes, Beto Villares   **DES** Cassio Amarante   **ED** Isabelle Rathery   **PROD** Arthur Cohn   **DIST** Buena Vista

66 Carvalho's superb cinematography, Antonio Pinto's score and a dedicated cast and crew admirably sustain this poetic and uncompromising film. – *Kevin Thomas, Los Angeles Times*

Ⓣ film not in the English language

'Ever wanted to be someone else? Now you can.'

Being John Malkovich   ★★★

DIR *Spike Jonze*
1999   112m   US
[DVD]

☆ *John Cusack* (Craig Schwartz), Cameron Diaz (Lotte Schwartz), Catherine Keener (Maxine), Orson Bean (Dr. Lester), Mary Kay Place (Floris), Charlie Sheen (Charlie), John Malkovich (John Horatio Malkovich)

A struggling puppeteer finds work in an office where a door hidden behind a filing cabinet leads to a tunnel, and a portal into the head of film actor John Malkovich. He and a colleague start charging people big money for the chance to be Malkovich for a few minutes at a time.

A dazzling, surreal comedy from screenwriter Kaufman, whose Kafkaesque plot twists make this a cerebral thrill-ride. No-one else writes screenplays quite like him, and in director Jonze he finds a sympathetic accomplice. Cusack brings exactly the right tone as a

---

[DVD] Available on DVD   ☆ Cast in order of importance   66 Critics' Quotes   † Points of interest   ⚱ Academy Award   ⚱ Academy Award nomination   Ⓑ BAFTA   Ⓣ BAFTA nomination
♫ Soundtrack on CD

doleful man, incredulous at his discovery, but with a quick glint in his eye. It falls short of perfection only in its inability to sustain its wonderful conceit to the end.

SCR *Charlie Kaufman*   CIN Lance Acord   MUS Carter Burwell   DES *K.K. Barrett*   ED Eric Zumbrunnen   PROD Michael Stipe, Sandy Stern, Steve Golin, Vincent Landay   DIST UIP

CRAIG: Nobody's looking for a puppeteer in today's wintry economic climate.

CRAIG: There's a tiny door in my office, Maxine. It's a portal and it takes you inside John Malkovich. You see the world through John Malkovich's eyes. . .and then after about 15 minutes, you're spit out. . .into a ditch on the side of the New Jersey Turnpike.

66 Either Being John Malkovich gets nominated for best picture, or the members of the Academy need portals into their brains. – *Roger Ebert, Chicago Sun-Times*

66 I don't know how a movie this original got made today, but thank God for wonderful aberrations. – *David Ansen, Newsweek*

⚮ Catherine Keener (supporting actress), Spike Jonze (direction); Charlie Kaufman (original screenplay)

Ⓣ Charlie Kaufman (original screenplay)

Ⓣ Cameron Diaz (supporting actress); Eric Zumbrunnen

'Passion. Obsession. Revenge. Prepare for the performance of a lifetime.'

Being Julia ★

DIR Istvan Szabo
2004   104m   Canada/GB/Hungary/US
DVD   🎵

☆ *Annette Bening* (Julia Lambert), Jeremy Irons (Michael Gosselyn), Bruce Greenwood (Lord Charles), Miriam Margolyes (Dolly de Vries), Juliet Stevenson (Evie), Michael Gambon (Jimmie Langton), Shaun Evans (Tom Fennel), Leigh Lawson (Archie Dexter), Rosemary Harris (Mrs Lambert), Rita Tushingham (Aunt Carrie)

In the 1930s, a star actress in her 40s embarks on a turbulent affair with a young American who is clearly after her money.

Acidly amusing script enhances a solid, professionally crafted film. Bening's actressy histrionics are perfectly pitched.

SCR *Ronald Harwood*   CIN Lajos Koltai   MUS Mychael Danna   DES Luciana Arrighi   ED Susan Shipton   PROD Robert Lantos

66 Annette Bening may not be the obvious choice to play an ageing British stage actress in the 1930s, but she does a good job of holding this slightly rambling comedy-drama together. – *Anna Smith, Empire*

⚮ Annette Bening (leading actress)

The Believer ★★

SCR/DIR Henry Bean
2001   102m   US
DVD   🎵

☆ *Ryan Gosling* (Danny Balint), Summer Phoenix (Carla Moebius), Glenn Fitzgerald (Drake), Theresa Russell (Lina Moebius), Billy Zane (Curtis Zampf), Garret Dillahunt (Billings), Kris Eivers (Carleton), Joel Garland (O. L.)

A young Jewish student becomes a neo-Nazi skinhead.

Skilful, unsettling account of an extreme identity crisis, ratcheted up by a blazingly persuasive performance from Gosling.

CIN Jim Denault   MUS Joel Diamond   DES Susan Block   ED Mayin Lo, Lee Percy   PROD Christopher Roberts, Susan Hoffman   DIST Pathé

66 One of the year's most thought-provoking, hard-hitting films, gutsily opening up a subject rarely done with this kind of all-out chutzpah. – *Michael Wilmington, Chicago Tribune*

66 A dynamite performance in a unique, and uniquely troubling, role. – *Todd McCarthy, Variety*

† Winner of the grand jury prize at Sundance in 2001.

'They exist. Fear them.'

The Believers ★

DIR John Schlesinger
1987   114m   US
DVD

☆ Martin Sheen (Cal Jamison), Helen Shaver (Jessica Halliday), Harley Cross (Chris Jamison), Robert Loggia (Lieutenant Sean McTaggert), Elizabeth Wilson (Kate Maslow), Harris Yulin (Robert Calder)

When a voodoo cult holds New York in a grip of terror, a psychiatrist tries to save his son from satanic rituals.

MA thriller that is genuinely frightening, but melodramatic to the point of hysteria. You have to love a film with a first scene that shows the mother of a young son electrocuted by her own coffee machine.

SCR Mark Frost   CIN Robby Müller   MUS J. Peter Robinson   DES Simon Holland   ED Peter Honess   PROD John Schlesinger, Michael Childers, Beverly J. Camhe   DIST Orion/John Schlesinger, Michael Childers, Beverly J. Camhe

Belle de Jour ★★★

DIR *Luis Buñuel*
1967   100m   France/Italy
DVD

☆ *Catherine Deneuve* (Severine Serizy), Jean Sorel (Pierre Serizy), Michel Piccoli (Henri Husson), Genevieve Page (Madame Anais), Pierre Clémenti (Marcel)

A virginal, newly-married surgeon's wife has sado-masochistic fantasies, and finds herself drawn to afternoon work in a Paris brothel.

Fascinating Buñuel mixture of reality and dream, impeccably woven into a rich fabric.

SCR *Luis Buñuel, Jean-Claude Carrière*   CIN *Sacha Vierny*   MUS none   ED Louisette Hautecoeur, Walter Spohr   PROD Robert and Raymond Hakim   DIST Paris Film/Five Film

† In 1967, it won the Golden Lion for best film at the Venice Film Festival.

Belle Epoque ★

DIR Fernando Trueba
1992   109m   Spain
DVD   🎵

☆ Fernando Fernán Gómez (Manolo), Jorge Sanz

DVD Available on DVD   ☆ Cast in order   66 Critics' Quotes   ⚮ Academy Award   Ⓑ BAFTA
🎵 Soundtrack on CD   of importance   † Points of interest   ⚮ Academy Award nomination   Ⓣ BAFTA nomination

61

(Fernando), Maribel Verdú (Rocio), Ariadna Gil (Violeta), Miriam Diaz-Aroca (Clara), Penélope Cruz (Luz), Gabino Diego (Juanito), Michel Galabru (Danglard)

In 1931, during Spain's pre-Franco era, an army deserter is sheltered by an anarchist artist with four winsome daughters.

A warm, nostalgic view of an optimistic time in Spanish history, with a story that affirms life's varied pleasures, notably food and sex.

SCR Rafael Azcona   CIN *José Luis Alcaine*   MUS Antoine Duhamel   ED Carmen Frias   PROD Fernando Trueba   DIST Mayfair/Lola/Animatografo/French Production/Fernando Trueba

66 A recipe for sensual self-expression. – *Rita Kempley, Washington Post*

† The film was also garlanded with several awards in Spain.

⚱ foreign film

🅣 film not in the English Language

La Belle Noiseuse ★★★

DIR *Jacques Rivette*
1991   236m   France
DVD

☆ Michel Piccoli (Edouard Frenhofer), Jane Birkin (Liz), *Emmanuelle Béart* (Marianne), Marianne Denicourt (Julienne), David Bursztein (Nicolas), Gilles Arbona (Porbus)

A young man volunteers his girlfriend to pose for a world-famous artist while he completes a painting of his wife he had abandoned many years before.

A painstakingly detailed study in the politics of painting and the creation of a masterpiece: less a story about real people than an extended discourse on the history and philosophy of art, with a pair of thoroughly committed performers – filmmaker-substitute Piccoli and a mostly naked Béart – assuming the archetypal roles of 'artist' and 'model'.

SCR *Pascal Bonitzer, Christine Laurent, Jacques Rivette*   CIN *William Lubtchansky*   DES Emmanuel de Chauvigny   ED Nicole Lubtchansky   PROD Martine Marignac   DIST Artificial Eye/Pierre Grise

66 The camera regards the artist's hand for minutes at a time, which may sound boring, but when the process of art and the process of life come into such fascinating conflict, it is more thrilling than a car chase. – *Roger Ebert, Chicago Sun-Times*

66 Rarely have 240 minutes been better spent than in the company of this magisterial study of the agonising process of creation. – *David Parkinson, Empire*

† Frenhofer's paintings were created for the film by the artist Bernard Dufour.

Belleville Rendez-vous ★★

SCR/DIR *Sylvain Chomet*
2002   80m   France/Canada/Belgium/GB
DVD ♫

☆ Voices of: Jean-Claude Donda, Michel Robin, Monica Viegas

After a cyclist is kidnapped by the Mafia during the Tour de France, the search-and-rescue mission is led by the cyclist's grandma, faithful dog and an ageing song-and-dance trio.

One-of-a-kind animation, of the sort one might stumble across on TV in the middle of the night and wonder what on earth was going on. Chomet has an extraordinary facility for original characterisations; his numerous subtle flourishes of the pen flash by too quickly in a film of perpetual motion, and may only truly be appreciated on DVD.

MUS Benôit Charest   ED Dominique Brune, Chantal Colibert Brunner, Dominique Lefever   PROD Didier Brunner, Viviane Vanfleteren   DIST Metro Tartan

66 To call it weird would be a cowardly evasion. It is creepy, eccentric, eerie, flaky, freaky, funky, grotesque, inscrutable, kinky, kooky, magical, oddball, spooky, uncanny, uncouth and unearthly. Especially uncouth. – *Roger Ebert, Chicago Sun-Times*

66 A pure, streamlined delight, the advent of a talent with no exact equal in modern film. – *Shawn Levy, Portland Oregonian*

⚱ animated film; song 'The Triplets of Belleville' (m/l Benôit Charest, Sylvain Chomet)

🅣 film not in the English language

'The past has a life of its own.'

Beloved ★

DIR Jonathan Demme
1998   172m   US
♫

☆ *Oprah Winfrey* (Sethe), Danny Glover (Paul D. Garner), Thandie Newton (Beloved), Kimberly Elise (Denver), Beah Richards (Baby Suggs), Lisa Gay Hamilton (Younger Sethe), Albert Hall (Stamp Paid), Irma P. Hall (Ella), Carol Jean Lewis (Janey Wagon), Kessia Kordelle (Amy Denver), Jason Robards (Mr Bodwin)

A former slave in 1870s America kills her daughter to prevent her being sold into slavery. But years later a young woman arrives at her door who seems to share many of her daughter's characteristics.

Respectful adaptation of a great novel, but one that cannot escape the charge of being too worthy and fatally overlong. Winfrey acquits herself well in the difficult lead role.

SCR Akosua Busia, Richard LaGravenese, Adam Brooks   CIN Tak Fujimoto   MUS Rachel Portman   DES Kristi Zea   ED Carol Littleton, Andy Keir   PROD Edward Saxon, Jonathan Demme, Gary Goetzman, Oprah Winfrey, Kate Forte   DIST Buena Vista/Touchstone/Harpo/Clinica Estetico

66 They should have called it Belaboured. – *Tom Shone, Sunday Times*

66 Something rare: a brave film about the emotional toll of slavery, the anguish of memory and the cruel divisions that still sear African American lives. – *Edward Guthmann, San Francisco Chronicle*

⚱ Colleen Atwood (costume design)

DVD Available on DVD   ☆ Cast in order of importance   66 Critics' Quotes   ⚱ Academy Award   🅑 BAFTA
♫ Soundtrack on CD   † Points of interest   ⚱ Academy Award nomination   🅣 BAFTA nomination

'Who wants to cook Aloo Gobi when you can bend a ball like Beckham?'

Bend It Like Beckham ★★

DIR Gurinder Chadha
2002   112m   US/GB/Germany
[DVD]   ♫

☆ Parminder Nagra (Jess Bhamra), Keira Knightley (Jules Paxton), Jonathan Rhys Meyers (Joe), Anupam Kher (Mr Bhamra), Archie Panjabi (Pinky Bhamra), Shaznay Lewis (Mel), Frank Harper (Alan Paxton), Juliet Stevenson (Paula Paxton)

An 18-year-old London girl, in thrall to England's football captain David Beckham, wants to take up the game professionally, to the horror of her Punjabi Sikh parents.

Amiable, feelgood comedy with a light touch that dwells, not too long, on difficult cultural differences, and settles for a conciliatory ending.

SCR *Gurinder Chadha, Guljit Bindra, Paul Mayeda Berges*
CIN Jong Lin   **MUS** Craig Pruess   **DES** Nick Ellis
ED Justin Krish   **PROD** Deepak Nayar, Gurinder Chadha
DIST Helkon SK

◖◗ I'm still smiling as I recall Jess, the soccer star-to-be, standing behind her straitlaced mother in the kitchen and casually bouncing a head of lettuce on her knee. – *Joe Morgenstern, Wall Street Journal*

◖◗ Delightfully upbeat, it will send you back out onto the street grinning from ear to ear. – *Alan Morrison, Empire*

† This was the breakthrough film for Keira Knightley, who was just 16 when the film was shot.

Ⓣ British film

Ben-Hur ★★

DIR *William Wyler, Andrew Marton*
1959   217m   US
[DVD]   ♫

☆ Charlton Heston (Judah Ben Hur), Haya Harareet (Esther), Jack Hawkins (Quintus Arrius), Stephen Boyd (Messala), Hugh Griffith (Sheik Ilderim), Martha Scott (Miriam), Sam Jaffe (Simonides), Cathy O'Donnell (Tirzah), Finlay Currie (Balthasar), Frank Thring (Pontius Pilate), Terence Longdon (Drusus), André Morell (Sextus), George Relph (Tiberius)

At the time of Christ, a Palestinian Jewish prince battles against the might of the Roman Empire.

Not as exciting or as rousing as one might wish, and its excessive running time makes for a number of longueurs, but this was the state-of-the art epic of the 1950s, and it's pleasingly apparent where the vast budget went. It's a spectacle rather than an actor's film; the action sequences are the whole point, and the 20-minute chariot race that vindicates Ben-Hur is rightly regarded as a classic.

SCR Karl Tunberg   **CIN** Robert L. Surtees   **MUS** Miklos Rozsa   **ED** Ralph E. Winters, John D. Dunning
PROD Sam Zimbalist   **DIST** MGM

◖◗ Watching it is like waiting at a railroad crossing while an interminable freight train lumbers by, sometimes stopping altogether. – *Dwight MacDonald*

◖◗ A Griffith can make a hundred into a crowd while a Wyler can reduce a thousand to a confused cocktail party. – *Ibid.*

† The production cost $4 million, twice the maximum at the time. Rock Hudson, Marlon Brando and Burt Lancaster were all sought in vain for the lead before Heston was selected.

† This version was subtitled 'A Tale of the Christ'.

⬦ picture; Charlton Heston (leading actor); Hugh Griffith (supporting actor); William Wyler (direction); Robert L. Surtees; Miklos Rozsa; art direction; Elizabeth Haffenden (costume design); editing; Arnold Gillespie, Robert MacDonald, Milo Lory (special effects); Franklin Milton (sound)

⬦ Karl Tunberg (adapted screenplay)

Ⓣ film

'Benny's breaking up his sister Joon's romance. Isn't that what big brothers are for?'

Benny and Joon

DIR Jeremiah Chechik
1993   98m   US
[DVD]   ♫

☆ Johnny Depp (Sam), Mary Stuart Masterson (Joon), Aidan Quinn (Benny), Julianne Moore (Ruthie), Oliver Platt (Eric), C.C. H. Pounder (Dr Garvey), Dan Hedaya (Thomas), Joe Grifasi (Mike)

A silent man-child woos a mentally unstable artist, despite her strait-laced brother's wishes.

Whimsical, fey and exasperating romance, notable only for an eccentric turn by Depp that encouraged him to proceed in resolutely offbeat roles.

SCR Barry Berman, Leslie McNeil   **CIN** John Schwartzman   **MUS** Rachel Portman   **DES** Neil Spisak
ED Carol Littleton   **PROD** Susan Arnold, Donna Roth
DIST MGM

◖◗ If you can accept it on its fable-like terms, the wishfully rosy resolution will seem heavenly; more sceptical viewers may have an allergic reaction to the whole concept. Your call. – *David Ansen, Newsweek*

Bent

DIR Sean Mathias
1996   105m   GB/US/Japan
[DVD]

☆ Lothaire Bluteau (Horst), Clive Owen (Max), Brian Webber (Rudy), Ian McKellen (Uncle Freddie), Mick Jagger (Greta/George), Nikolaj Waldau (Wolf), Jude Law (Stormtrooper), Suzanne Bertish (Half woman, half man)

In a Nazi concentration camp, two prisoners embark on a gay relationship.

A perfect example of a play that seemed electrifying on stage losing all its impact en route to the big screen. Be warned: it's a disappointment.

SCR Martin Sherman   **CIN** Giorgos Arvanitis
MUS Philip Glass   **DES** Stephen Brimson Lewis
ED Isabelle Lorente   **PROD** Michael Solinger, Dixie Linder
DIST Film Four/NDF/Ask Kodansha/Channel 4/Nippon

◖◗ The sad fact of the film is that its semi-realistic elaboration of a drama that was staged as sparsely as a

[DVD] Available on DVD   ☆ Cast in order of importance   ◖◗ Critics' Quotes   ⬦ Academy Award   Ⓣ BAFTA
♫ Soundtrack on CD   † Points of interest   ⬦ Academy Award nomination   Ⓣ BAFTA nomination

63

Samuel Beckett play has reduced it from an anguished historical meditation into mawkish, overwrought kitsch with a pornographic gloss. – *Stephen Holden, New York Times*

† Rainer Werner Fassbinder was at one point scheduled to film the 1979 play with Richard Gere in the lead. Costa-Gavras was also briefly attached to the project.

'Pride is the Curse'

Beowulf (new) ★★★

DIR *Robert Zemeckis*

2007   114m   US

♫

☆ Ray Winstone (Beowulf), Anthony Hopkins (Hrothgar), John Malkovich (Unferth), Robin Wright Penn (Wealthow), Brendan Gleeson (Wiglaf), Crispin Hellion Glover (Grendel), Angelina Jolie (Grendel's Mother)

After destroying the demon Grendel, a Viking warrior incurs the undying wrath of the creature's ruthlessly seductive mother who uses all means to ensure revenge.

Using performance-capture animation, the epic Old English poem is smartly and literately transformed into a thrilling fantasy adventure, with visual pizzazz and breathtaking action.

SCR *Neil Gaiman, Roger Avary*   CIN Robert Presley   MUS Alan Silvestri   DES Doug Chiang   ED Jeremiah O'Driscoll   PROD Robert Zemeckis, Steve Starkey, Jack Rapke   DIST Warner Bros

❝ A muscular, sometimes stirring but ultimately soulless reinterpretation. – *Justin Chang, Variety*

❝ Once you have acclimatised yourself to the animation style, it tells a cracking good story, and the screenplay by Neil Gaiman and Roger Avary conjures a secret history of vulnerability and human weakness behind the legend. – *Peter Bradshaw, Guardian*

Besieged ★★

DIR Bernardo Bertolucci

1998   93m   Italy/GB

DVD

☆ Thandie Newton (Shandurai), David Thewlis (Jason Kinsky), Claudio Santamaria (Agostino)

In Rome, a reticent British pianist falls in love with his African maid and agrees to help her husband, who is being held as a political prisoner by an oppressive regime.

Uunderrated minor work by Bertolucci, and intriguingly a chamber piece: a deliberate step back from his expansive epics such as The Last Emperor and The Sheltering Sky. Much of it takes place in the confines of an apartment. Still, it is seamlessly constructed and boasts engrossing dramatic sequences.

SCR Clare Peploe, Bernardo Bertolucci   CIN Fabio Cianchetti   MUS Alessio Vlad   DES Gianni Silvestri   ED Jacopo Quadri   PROD Massimo Cortesi   DIST Fiction/Navert/Mediaset

❝ This is cinema with music's fluid purity of form – indeed, it runs for 15 minutes before Bertolucci has

recourse to anything so base as the spoken word. – *Tom Charity, Time Out*

'Some pets deserve a little more respect than others.'

Best in Show ★★

DIR Christopher Guest

2000   90m   US

DVD ♫

☆ Bob Balaban (Dr. Theodore W. Millbank III), Jennifer Coolidge (Sherri Ann Ward Cabot), Christopher Guest (Harlan Pepper), John Michael Higgins (Scott Donlan), Michael Hitchcock (Hamilton Swan), Eugene Levy (Gerry Fleck), Jane Lynch (Christy Cummings), Michael McKean (Stefan Vanderhoof), Catherine O'Hara (Cookie Fleck), Parker Posey (Meg Swan), Fred Willard (Buck Laughlin), Patrick Cranshaw (Leslie Cabot), Don Lake (Graham Chissolm), Jim Piddock (Trevor Beckwith), Ed Begley Jnr (Hotel Manager)

Dog-lovers from across America bring their pets to Philadelphia for the Mayflower Kennel Club's annual competition.

Dry, sporadically hilarious mock-documentary distinguished by an excellent comic ensemble, though Guest's subjects remain broad targets for satire.

SCR Christopher Guest, Eugene Levy   CIN Roberto Schaefer   MUS Jeffery C.J. Vanston   DES Joseph T. Garrity   ED Robert Leighton   PROD Karen Murphy   DIST Warner

❝ Has both bark and bite. – *Kenneth Turan, L.A. Times*

❝ You giggle every so often, but you never give yourself over to the characters. – *Owen Gleiberman, Entertainment Weekly*

The Best Intentions ★★★

DIR *Bille August*

1992   181m   Sweden/ Germany/Italy/GB/France

☆ Samuel Fröler (Henrik Bergman), *Pernilla August* (Anna Akerblom-Bergman), Max von Sydow (Johan Akerblom, Anna's Father), Ghita Norby (Karin Akerblom, Anna's Mother), Lennart Hjulström (Nordenson, Landowner and Owner of the Works), Mona Malm (Alma Bergman, Henrik's Mother), Lena Endre (Frida Strandberg, Henrik's First Fiancee), Keve Hjelm (Fredrik Bergman, Henrik's Paternal Grandfather)

In Sweden in the early 1900s, a poor theology student marries a young woman from a more prosperous family, against her strict father's wishes.

A beautifully made, partly biographical account by Ingmar Bergman of his parents' courtship and marriage. Their relationship is tempestuous; emotional intensity and angst are the prevailing moods in this magisterial film.

SCR *Ingmar Bergman*   CIN Jörgen Persson   MUS Stefan Nilsson, Björn Linnman   DES Anna Asp   ED Janus Billeskov Jansen   PROD Ingrid Dahlberg   DIST Artificial Eye/STV1/ZDF/Channel 4/RAIDU/La Sept/DR/YLE 2/NRK/RUV

† At the Cannes Film Festival in 1992, the film won the Palme D'Or for best film. Pernilla August was named best actress.

† A six-hour version was shown on Swedish television.

The Best of Youth ★★

DIR Marco Tullio Giordana
2003 383 (2 parts)m Italy
DVD

☆ Luigi Lo Cascio (Nicola Carati), Alessio Boni (Matteo Carati), Adriana Asti (Adriana Carati), Sonia Bergamasco (Giulia Monfalco), Fabrizio Gifuni (Carlo Tommasi), Maya Sansa (Mirella Utano), Jasmine Trinca (Giorgia), Andrea Tidona (Angelo Carati)

Two Italian brothers of opposing political temperament thrash out their differences over the decades.

Mammoth Italian soap, originally a TV mini-series, which offers a thoroughly absorbing account of Italy's changing social landscape in the last decades of the 20th century, even if there are credibility problems along the way, and especially near its end.

SCR Sandro Petraglia, Stefano Rulli CIN Roberto Forza
DES Franco Ceraolo ED Roberto Missiroli
PROD Angelo Barbagallo, Donatella Botti

66 A satisfying and (very) generously proportioned piece of work. – *Peter Bradshaw, Guardian*

'Three wonderful loves in the best picture of the year!'

The Best Years of Our Lives ★★★★

DIR *William Wyler*
1946 182m US
DVD ♫

☆ Fredric March (Al Stephenson), Myrna Loy (Milly Stephenson), Teresa Wright (Peggy Stephenson), Dana Andrews (Fred Derry), Virginia Mayo (Marie Derry), Cathy O'Donnell (Wilma Cameron), *Hoagy Carmichael* (Butch Engle), *Harold Russell* (Homer Parrish), Gladys George (Hortense Derry), Roman Bohnen (Pat Derry), Ray Collins (Mr. Milton)

Three men come home from war to a small middle-American community, and find it variously difficult to start up where they left off.

The situations and even some of the characters now seem a little obvious, but this was a superb example of high-quality film-making in the 1940s, with smiles and tears cunningly spaced, and a film which said what was needed on a vital subject. The three leads all stand out, but honours go to Harold Russell, a non-professional actor but a real wartime amputee who lost both hands in World War II. He won two Oscars – one for acting and one for the inspirational hope he gave to others in a similar plight.

SCR *Robert Sherwood* CIN *Gregg Toland* MUS Hugo Friedhofer ED Daniel Mandell DIST Samuel Goldwyn

66 One of the best pictures of our lives! – *Variety*
66 The result is a work of provocative and moving insistence and beauty. – *Howard Barnes*

⌁ picture; Fredric March (leading actor); Harold Russell (supporting actor); William Wyler (direction); Robert Sherwood (screenplay); Hugo Friedhofer; Daniel Mandell

⊕ picture

'The wedding picture doesn't always tell the whole story.'

Betsy's Wedding ★

SCR/DIR *Alan Alda*
1990 94m US

☆ *Alan Alda* (Eddie Hopper), Joey Bishop (Eddie's father), *Madeline Kahn* (Lola Hopper), Anthony LaPaglia (Stevie Dee), Catherine O'Hara (Gloria Henner), Joe Pesci (Oscar Henner), *Molly Ringwald* (Betsy Hopper), Ally Sheedy (Connie Hopper), Burt Young (Georgie)

An Italian-American father, sniping at his Jewish wife, is determined to give his daughter a lavish wedding.

Good-hearted domestic comedy trading on ethnic stereotypes. Alda, Kahn and Ringwald are pitch-perfect in this sentimental outreach to mature audiences.

CIN Kelvin Pike MUS Bruce Broughton DES John Jay Moore ED Michael Polakow PROD Martin Bregman, Louis A. Stroller DIST Warner/Touchstone/Silver Screen Partners IV

66 A warm, wordy, middle-brow crowd-pleaser. – *Wally Hammond, Time Out*

'Crimes of passion are not always between lovers.'

Betty Fisher et Autres Histoires ★

SCR/DIR Claude Miller
2001 103m France/Canada
DVD

☆ Sandrine Kiberlain (Betty Fisher), Nicole Garcia (Margot Fisher), Mathilde Seigner (Carole Novacki), Luck Mervil (François Diembele), Edouard Baer (Alex Basato), Stephane Freiss (Edouard)

A young writer grieving the death of her son becomes ensnared in her mother's plans to kidnap another child.

Watchable French adaptation of a Ruth Rendell novel, marshalled with Hitchcockian efficiency and a touch of Clouzot-like cruelty. Miller draws intriguing parallels between his female characters; the acute social observation narrowly trumps the plot holes.

CIN Christophe Pollock MUS Francois Dompierre, Thom Yorke DES Jean-Pierre Kohut-Svelko ED Veronique Lange PROD Annie Miller, Yves Marmion
DIST Optimum

66 Endows Rendell's novel with the fascination of an exotic, spiky, poisonous flower. – *Peter Bradshaw, Guardian*
66 A deftly wrought suspense yarn whose richer shadings work as colouring rather than substance. – *Stephen Holden, New York Times*

'Truth has a witness. . .'

Beyond Rangoon ★★

DIR John Boorman
1995 100m US
DVD ♫

☆ Patricia Arquette (Laura Bowman), Frances McDormand (Andy Bowman), Spalding Gray (Jeremy Watt), U Aung Ko (U Aung Ko), Victor Slezak (Mr. Scott), Adelle Lutz (Aung San Suu Kyi)

An American doctor in Burma is thrown into the

DVD Available on DVD ☆ Cast in order of importance 66 Critics' Quotes ⌁ Academy Award / Academy Award nomination ⊕ BAFTA / BAFTA nomination ♫ Soundtrack on CD † Points of interest

65

conflict between the oppressive regime and dissident pro-democracy protesters.

Boorman's films remain intriguing even when he over-reaches, and here is a case in point: an awkward blend of suspense thriller and political tract that is utterly watchable.

SCR Alex Lasker, Bill Rubenstein CIN John Seale
MUS Hans Zimmer DES Anthony Pratt ED Ron Davis
PROD Barry Spikings, Eric Pleskow, John Boorman, Sean Ryerson DIST Columbia/Castle Rock

66 It's as if a civil war had been concocted just to take Laura [Patricia Arquette] outside of her not-unjustified misery. – *Barbara Shulgasser, San Francisco Examiner*

Beyond the Clouds ★

DIR Michelangelo Antonioni, Wim Wenders
1995 112m France/Italy/Germany
DVD

☆ Sophie Marceau (The Girl), Vincent Perez (Niccolo), Irène Jacob (The Girl), Marcello Mastroianni (The Man of All Vices), Fanny Ardant (Patricia), John Malkovich (The Director), Kim Rossi Stuart (Silvano), Chiara Caselli (Mistress), Jean Reno (Carlo), Peter Weller (Husband), Jeanne Moreau (Friend), Ines Sastre (Carmen)

Between films, an internationally renowned director mulls over past love affairs.

Good-looking, starry, but fundamentally listless romantic meandering; evidence of a sad decline in this once-great filmmaker's powers. Antonioni completists will be intrigued.

SCR Wim Wenders, Michelangelo Antonioni, Tonino Guerra CIN Alfio Contini, Robby Müller MUS Laurent Petitgang, Van Morrison, U2 DES Thierry Flamand
ED Claudio di Mauro, Michelangelo Antonioni, Peter Przygodda, Luciano Segura PROD Stéphane Tchal Gadjieff, Philippe Carcassonne, Arlette Danys
DIST Artificial Eye/Sunshine/Cine B/France 3/Cecchi Gori/Road Movies

66 Antonioni's dreamy, pretentious fickle-finger-of-fate mini-tales struggle to wrestle with love and desire, but truck in adolescent ideas and delight in nothing so much as undressing their many young actresses. – *Michael Atkinson, Village Voice*

66 Two parts meaningful, three parts sublime, and five parts a load of old cobblers. I enjoyed it enormously. – *Anne Billson, Sunday Telegraph*

'In the era of cool, he was the soundtrack.'

Beyond the Sea ★

DIR Kevin Spacey
2004 118m US/GB/Germany
DVD ♫

☆ Kevin Spacey (Bobby Darin), Kate Bosworth (Sandra Dee), John Goodman (Steve Blauner), Bob Hoskins (Charlie Maffia), Brenda Blethyn (Polly), Greta Scacchi (Mary), Caroline Aaron (Nina Cassotto Maffia)

An account of the life of rock 'n' roller Bobby Darin, who became a successful Sinatra-style crooner and joined Hollywood's A-list by marrying teen star Sandra Dee before succumbing to rheumatic fever in his 30s.

A labour of love for Spacey, who wrote, co-produced and impersonated Darin's voice effectively. Yet the structure of the script is over-complicated, and Spacey's efforts amount to little more than a valiant stab at portraying an elusive personality.

SCR Kevin Spacey, Lewis Colick CIN Eduardo Serra
DES Andrew Laws ED Trevor Waite PROD Andy Paterson, Kevin Spacey, Jan Fantl, Arthur E. Friedman
DIST Entertainment

66 Ambitious and unexpected, with stylish musical numbers and a sympathetic performance from Spacey. – *Angie Errigo, Empire*

'A Day To Set Yourself Free!'

Bhaji on the Beach ★

DIR Gurinder Chadha
1993 101m GB
DVD ♫

☆ Kim Vithana (Ginder), Jimmi Harkishin (Ranjit), Sarita Khajuria (Hashida), Mo Sesay (Oliver), Lalita Ahmed (Asha), Shaheen Khan (Simi), Zohra Sehgal (Pushpa), Amer Chadha-Patel (Amrik), Nisha Nayar (Ladhu)

Asian women from Birmingham, young and old, face up to their problems during a day trip to Blackpool.

Rough and ready at times, this cheerfully enthusiastic escapade was the first success for a generous-spirited British director.

SCR Meera Syal CIN John Kenway MUS Craig Pruess, John Altman, Kuljit Bhamra DES Derek Brown ED Oral Norrie Otley PROD Nadine Marsh-Edwards DIST First Independent/Umbi/Channel 4

66 The kind of made-for-TV film in which characters are forever lecturing each other or telling us what they feel. It makes Neighbours look subtle. – *Christopher Tookey, Daily Mail*

66 A good-hearted double whammy, a bull's-eye for anti-racism and feminism. – *George Perry, Sunday Times*
Ⓣ British film

Bicycle Thieves ★★★★

DIR *Vittorio de Sica*
1948 90m Italy
DVD

☆ *Lamberto Maggiorani* (Antonio Ricci), *Enzo Staiola* (Bruno Ricci)

An Italian workman, long unemployed, is robbed of the bicycle he needs for his new job, and he and his small son search Rome for it.

To the rest of the world, this beloved film became the jewel in the crown of the post-war Italian neo-realist movement: a film shot with urgency and immediacy that did not shirk harsh economic realities, yet also emphasised the touching relationship between father and son, and the shame and guilt that easily creep into desperate lives. That the two lead actors were non-professionals only makes the film seem more believable and authentic. Unquestionably a masterpiece.

SCR *Cesare Zavattini*   CIN Carlo Montuori
MUS Alessandro Cicognini   ED Eraldo Da Roma
PROD Umberto Scarparelli   DIST PDS-ENIC

66 A film of rare humanity and sensibility. – *Gavin Lambert*

66 A memorable work of art with the true flavour of reality. To see it is an experience worth having. – *Richard Mallett, Punch*

⚲ foreign film
⚲ Cesare Zavattini
Ⓣ picture

'Have you ever had a really big secret?'

Big ★★

DIR *Penny Marshall*
1988   104m   US
[DVD]   ♫

☆ *Tom Hanks* (Josh), Elizabeth Perkins (Susan), John Heard (Paul), Jared Rushton (Billy), Robert Loggia (MacMillan), David Moscow (Young Josh)

A teenager comes of age overnight after an encounter with a fairground wish-granting machine.

Enjoyable fantasy, infinitely preferable to the knock-offs it spawned; its charm resides in the performances, the zest of Marshall's direction, and a script displaying insight into what it means to be a kid in a grown-up world, and what we leave behind as adults.

SCR *Gary Ross, Anne Spielberg*   CIN Barry Sonnenfeld
MUS Howard Shore   DES Santo Loquasto   ED Barry Malkin   PROD James L. Brooks, Robert Greenhut
DIST TCF

66 Big features believable young teenage mannerisms from the two real boys in its cast, and this only makes Mr. Hanks's funny, flawless impression that much more adorable. This really is the performance to beat. – *Janet Maslin, The New York Times*

⚲ Tom Hanks (leading actor); Gary Ross, Anne Spielberg (original screenplay)

The Big Blue

DIR Luc Besson
1988   119m   France
[DVD]   ♫

☆ Rosanna Arquette (Johana Baker), Jean-Marc Barr (Jacques Mayol), Jean Reno (Enzo Molinari)

Two rival deep-sea divers team up to rescue a dolphin.

Vapid, new-agey aquatic fantasy without much to recommend it.

SCR Luc Besson, Robert Garland, Marilyn Goldin, Jacques Mayol, Marc Perrier   CIN Carlo Varini   MUS Eric Serra, Bill Conti   DES Dan Weil   ED Olivier Mauffroy
PROD Patrice Ledoux   DIST TCF

66 Predictably lachrymose. – *Mark Holcomb, Village Voice*

Big Business ★★★★

DIR James W. Horne
1929   20m   US
[DVD]

☆ *Stan Laurel, Oliver Hardy, James Finlayson*

A Laurel and Hardy short, in which Stan and Ollie fail to sell a Christmas tree to a belligerent householder.

Classic silent comedy consisting largely of a brilliant tit-for-tat routine of reciprocal destruction, to which scripting, acting and editing equally combine.

SCR Leo McCarey, H. M. Walker   ED Richard Currier
DIST Hal Roach

The Big Combo ★★★

DIR *Joseph H. Lewis*
1955   80m   US

☆ *Cornel Wilde, Richard Conte, Jean Wallace*, Brian Donlevy, Robert Middleton, Lee Van Cleef, Ted de Corsia, Helen Walker, John Hoyt

A tough police detective maintains a vengeful obsession with a mobster running a crime syndicate.

A top-notch example of violent, hard-boiled film noir from director Lewis, one of the genre's most eminent exponents. Shot moodily and atmospherically, it wears its artfulness modestly.

SCR Philip Yordan   CIN *John Alton*   MUS David Raksin
PROD Sidney Harmon   DIST Allied Artists/Security-Theodora

'Her Life Was In Their Hands. Now Her Toe Is In The Mail.'

The Big Lebowski ★★★★

DIR *Joel Coen*
1998   117m   US/GB
[DVD]   ♫

☆ *Jeff Bridges* (Jeffrey Lebowski - The Dude), *John Goodman* (Walter Sobchak), *Julianne Moore* (Maude Lebowski), Steve Buscemi (Theodore Donald 'Donny' Kerabatsos), Peter Stormare (Nihilist #1, Uli Kunkel / 'Karl Hungus'), *David Huddleston* (Jeffrey Lebowski - The Big Lebowski), Sam Elliott (The Stranger), *John Turturro* (Jesus Quintana), David Thewlis (Knox Harrington), *Ben Gazzara* (Jackie Treehorn), *Philip Seymour Hoffman* (Brandt), Jimmie Dale Gilmore (Smokey)

A slobbish resident of Los Angeles is mistaken for his namesake, a disabled millionaire whose bimbo wife has been kidnapped, and seeks restitution for his ruined rug with the help of his bowling buddies.

A wide-eyed, one-of-a-kind comedy of genius, with the structure of a shaggy-dog Raymond Chandler pastiche. No surprise that it has ripened over the years and become a beloved cult favourite: it is the Coen Brothers' most exuberantly wacky and inventive film, but also their most affectionate, and the performances are a joy.

SCR *Joel and Ethan Coen*   CIN *Roger Deakins*
MUS *Carter Burwell*   DES Rick Heinrichs   ED Roderick Jaynes, Tricia Cooke   PROD Ethan Coen
DIST Polygram/Working Title

MAUDE LEBOWSKI: What do you do for recreation?
THE DUDE: Oh, the usual. I bowl. Drive around. The occasional acid flashback.

66 The Coens have defined and mastered their own bizarre subgenre. – *Desson Thomson, Washington Post*

66 Feels almost completely haphazard, thrown together

[DVD] Available on DVD   ☆ Cast in order   66 Critics' Quotes   ⚲ Academy Award   Ⓣ BAFTA
♫ Soundtrack on CD   of importance   † Points of interest   ⚲ Academy Award nomination   Ⓣ BAFTA nomination

without much concern for organising intelligence. – *Alexander Walker, London Evening Standard*

† So persuasive is the cult that gradually grew up around this film that 'Big Lebowski conventions' are regularly held in the US and Britain, typically in bowling alleys, where attendees dress up as characters in the film.

'Nothing hits as hard as the things that are really worth fighting for...'

The Big Man ★★

DIR David Leland
1990 116m GB
DVD

☆ Liam Neeson (Danny Scoular), Joanne Whalley-Kilmer (Beth Scoular), Billy Connolly (Frankie), Ian Bannen (Matt Mason), Maurice Roeves (Cam Colvin), Kenny Ireland (Tony), John Beattie (Beth's Father), Amanda Walker (Beth's Mother)

An unemployed Scottish miner becomes a bare-knuckle fighter, in the employ of a gang boss.

Neeson's first starring role, in an underrated film with genuinely interesting themes and textures, far beyond those of the average sports drama.

SCR Don MacPherson CIN Ian Wilson MUS Ennio Morricone DES Carol Amies ED George Akers
PROD Stephen Woolley
DIST Palace/Miramax/BSB/British STV Film Enterprises

❝ One of Britain's finest existential thrillers for ages. – *Geoff Andrew, Time Out*

'Comedy with Taste.'

Big Night ★★★

DIR Stanley Tucci, Campbell Scott
1996 107m US
DVD ♫

☆ Minnie Driver (Phyllis), Ian Holm (Pascal), Isabella Rossellini (Gabriella), *Tony Shalhoub* (Primo), *Stanley Tucci* (Secondo), Caroline Aaron (Woman in restaurant), Marc Anthony (Cristiano), Allison Janney (Ann)

New Jersey, the late 1950s: two temperamental brothers attempt to save their struggling Italian restaurant by preparing a feast for visiting bandleader Louis Prima.

A cordon bleu entry in the foodie subgenre, with Tucci and Shalhoub acting their aprons off at the head of a fine ensemble cast. For best enjoyment, keep sustenance of your own close at hand throughout, and await for the masterly, wordless extended final scene.

SCR Stanley Tucci, Joseph Tropiano CIN Ken Kelsch
MUS Gary DeMichele DES Andrew Jackness ED Suzy Elmiger PROD Jonathan Filley DIST Rysher/Timpano

❝ One of the great food movies, and yet it is so much more. It is about food not as a subject but as a language – the language by which one can speak to gods, can create, can seduce, can aspire to perfection. There is a moment in the movie when an Italian casserole is sliced open and the audience sighs with simple delight. – *Roger Ebert, Chicago Sun-Times*

❝ A movie that is both as real as food on the table and as hauntingly evanescent as its taste on one's tongue. – *Richard Schickel, Time*

The Big Parade ★

DIR Chen Kaige
1986 103m China

☆ Wang Xueqi (Li Weicheng), Sun Chun (Sun Fang), Lu Lei (Jiang Junbiao), Wu Ruofu (Lu Chun), Guan Qiang (Liu Guoqiang), Kang Hua (Hao Xiaoyuan)

In China, 400 volunteers from the People's Liberation Army volunteer for eight-months' training to participate in the National Day Parade in Tiananmen Square.

An intriguing glimpse, cunningly filmed as if genuinely behind real scenes, of the gruelling training and dedication involved.

SCR Gao Lili CIN Zhang Yimou MUS Qu Xiasong, Zhao Jiping DES He Qun ED Zhou Xinxia
PROD Chen Liguo DIST ICA/Guangxi Film Studio

† The People's Army ordered the director to edit the training scenes, so they focused on the unit as a whole rather than individuals, and also insisted on a more triumphalist ending.

'The epic of the American doughboy!'

The Big Parade ★★★

DIR *King Vidor*
1925 115m US

☆ John Gilbert (James Apperson), Renee Adoree (Melisande), Hobart Bosworth (Mr. Apperson), Karl Dane (Slim), George K. Arthur

A young American enlists in 1917, learns the realities of war, is wounded but survives.

Enormously successful commercially, this 'anti-war' film survives best as a thrilling spectacle and a well-considered piece of film-making.

SCR Laurence Stallings, Harry Behn CIN *John Arnold*
MUS William Axt, David Mendoza ED Hugh Wynn
DIST MGM

❝ The human comedy emerges from a terrifying tragedy. – *King Vidor*

❝ A cinegraphically visualized result of a cinegraphically imagined thing. . .something conceived in terms of a medium and expressed by that medium as only that medium could properly express it. – *National Board of Review*

† The biggest grossing silent film of all.

The Big Picture ★★

DIR *Christopher Guest*
1988 100m US
DVD

☆ *Kevin Bacon* (Nick Chapman), Emily Longstreth (Susan Rawlings), J. T. Walsh (Allen Habel), Jennifer Jason Leigh (Lydia Johnson), Martin Short (Neil Sussman, Nick's Agent), Michael McKean (Emmet Sumner), Kim Miyori (Jenny Sumner), Teri Hatcher (Gretchen)

A student film school graduate goes to Hollywood, and soon makes compromises in order to get his first picture made.

No-one would mistake this Hollywood satire for Robert Altman's cool, polished The Player, yet Christopher Guest's debut feature has some smart things to say

about the film biz, and it's full of insider jokes and hard-learned wisdom. Bacon, as usual, is splendid as the kid ready to sell out his integrity to nearest bidder.

SCR *Michael Varhol, Christopher Guest, Michael McKean* **CIN** Jeff Jur **MUS** David Nichtern **DES** Joseph T. Garrity **ED** Martin Nicholson **PROD** Michael Varhol **DIST** Hobo/Columbia

The Big Red One ★★★

SCR/DIR *Samuel Fuller*

1980 111m US

[DVD]

☆ Lee Marvin (Sergeant), Mark Hamill (Griff), Robert Carradine (Zab), Bobby DiCicco (Vinci), Kelly Ward (Johnson), Stéphane Audran (Walloon), Serge Marquand (Ransonnet)

Five foot-soldiers survive action in several theatres of war between 1940 and 1945.

Outstanding war drama, all the more effective for being as understated about heroism as the soldiers themselves..

CIN *Adam Greenberg* **MUS** Dana Kaproff **ED** David Bretherton, Morton Tubor **PROD** Gene Corman **DIST** UA/Lorimar

66 A picture of palpable raw power which manages both intense intimacy and great scope at the same time. – *Variety*

66 Like all Fuller movies, about an inch from cliché all the way. – *Guardian*

† Director Fuller died in 1997, but his posthumous reputation grew to the extent that the film was reconstructed with a 162-minute running time. Though somewhat overlooked at the time of its original release, it is now regarded as a classic war movie.

† Fuller himself served in The Big Red One, an infantry division in World War II, and the film is partly autobiographical.

The Big Sleep ★★★

DIR *Howard Hawks*

1946 114m US

[DVD]

☆ *Humphrey Bogart* (Philip Marlowe), *Lauren Bacall* (Vivian Sternwood Rutledge), John Ridgely (Eddie Mars), Martha Vickers (Carmen Sternwood), Dorothy Malone (Proprietress), Regis Toomey (Bernie Ohls), Charles Waldron (General Sternwood), Charles D. Brown (Norris), Elisha Cook Jnr (Harry Jones), Louis Jean Heydt (Joe Brody), Bob Steele (Canino), Peggy Knudsen (Mona Mars), Sonia Darrin (Agnes)

Private eye Philip Marlowe is hired to protect General Sternwood's wild young daughter from her own indiscretions, and finds several murders later that he has fallen in love with her elder sister.

Inextricably complicated, moody thriller from a novel whose author claimed that even he did not know 'who done it'. The film is nevertheless vastly enjoyable along the way for its slangy script, outbursts of violence, suspense, sheer fun, and star performances; it was clearly tweaked to accommodate Bogart and Bacall's chemistry on and off screen.

SCR *William Faulkner, Leigh Brackett, Jules Furthman* **CIN** Sid Hickox **MUS** *Max Steiner* **ED** Christian Nyby **PROD** Howard Hawks **DIST** Warner

MARLOWE: My, my, my. Such a lot of guns around town and so few brains.

GENERAL: You may smoke, too. I can still enjoy the smell of it. Nice thing when a man has to indulge his vices by proxy.

VIVIAN: So you're a private detective. I didn't know they existed, except in books – or else they were greasy little men snooping around hotel corridors. My, you're a mess, aren't you?

MARLOWE: I don't mind if you don't like my manners. I don't like 'em myself. They're pretty bad. I grieve over 'em on long winter evenings.

GENERAL: If I seem a bit sinister as a parent, Mr Marlowe, it's because my hold on life is too slight to include any Victorian hypocrisy. I need hardly add that any man who has lived as I have and indulges for the first time in parenthood at the age of 55 deserves all he gets.

MARLOWE: Speaking of horses . . . you've got a touch of class, but I don't know how far you can go.

VIVIAN: A lot depends on who's in the saddle. Go ahead Marlowe. I like the way you work. In case you don't know it, you're doing all right.

66 A sullen atmosphere of sex saturates the film, which is so fast and complicated you can hardly catch it. – *Richard Winnington*

66 A violent, smoky cocktail shaken together from most of the printable misdemeanours and some that aren't. – *James Agee*

Biggie and Tupac ★★

SCR/DIR Nick Broomfield

2001 107m GB

[DVD]

☆ Tupac Shakur (Himself (archive footage)), The Notorious B.I.G (Himself (archive footage))

Investigation of the murders of rappers Biggie Smalls and Tupac Shakur, tracing links between leading American record-industry figures and Los Angeles Police Department officers.

One of Broomfield's most rigorous films, building a compelling case against suspects in the murders, while unpeeling layers of gangster posturing to make a distinction between the rappers' stage personae and their (tragically curtailed) real lives. The pay-off is a memorably tense prison-yard interview with incarcerated Death Row Records boss Suge Knight.

CIN Joan Churchill **MUS** Christian Henson **ED** Mark Atkins, Jaime Estrada Torres **PROD** Michele D'Acosta, Nick Broomfield **DIST** Film4

66 At best, a half-finished puzzle, but Broomfield leaves you with questions that few investigators have even dared to ask. – *Owen Gleiberman, Entertainment Weekly*

66 It plays like a suspense thriller because that's exactly what it is. – *Manohla Dargis, Los Angeles Times*

'Once. . .they made history. Now. . .they are history.'

Bill & Ted's Bogus Journey ★

DIR Peter Hewitt

1991 93m US

[DVD] ♫

| [DVD] Available on DVD | ☆ Cast in order | 66 Critics' Quotes | ⌁ Academy Award | ⬤ BAFTA |
| ♫ Soundtrack on CD | of importance | † Points of interest | ⌁ Academy Award nomination | ⬤ BAFTA nomination |

69

☆ Alex Winter (Bill S. Preston, Esq./Granny Preston/Evil Robot Bill), Keanu Reeves (Ted Logan/Evil Ted), Jeff Miller (Stunt double for Alex Winter), David Carrera (Stunt double for Keanu Reeves), George Carlin (Rufus), Joss Ackland (Chuck De Nomolos), William Sadler (Grim Reaper/English Family Member)

Killed by evil robot replicas of themselves, our two teenage heroes find themselves stuck in their own personal hells before a Battle of the Bands competition.

More innocent fun, hard to dislike; fondly remembered in certain circles for its homage to The Seventh Seal, in which the Grim Reaper is challenged to games of Twister and Battleships.

SCR Ed Solomon, Chris Matheson   CIN Oliver Wood   MUS David Newman   DES David L. Snyder   ED David Finfer   PROD Scott Kroopf   DIST Columbia TriStar/Orion/Nelson Entertainment

66 A riot of visual invention and weird humour that works on its chosen sub-moronic level, and on several others as well, including some fairly sophisticated ones. – *Roger Ebert, Chicago Sun-Times*

66 One more sequel and they'll qualify as the Hope and Crosby of the 90s. – *Leonard Maltin*

† 'God Gave Rock And Roll To You II.'

'History is about to be rewritten by two guys who can't spell.'

Bill and Ted's Excellent Adventure ★

DIR Stephen Herek
1988   90m   US
DVD   ♫

☆ Keanu Reeves (Ted Logan), Alex Winter (Bill S Presley Esq.), Robert V. Barron (Abraham Lincoln), Terry Camilleri (Napoleon), Clifford David (Beethoven), Al Leong (Genghis Khan), Rod Loomis (Dr. Sigmund Freud), Dan Shor (Billy the Kid), Tony Steedman (Socrates), Jane Wiedlin (Joan of Arc)

Two dimwitted high-school students employ a time-travelling phone box to help them with their history projects.

Cult teen movie that scores big laughs from its affectionate interactions between latter-day Californian airheads and figures from the past.

SCR Chris Matheson, Ed Solomon   CIN Timothy Suhrstedt   MUS David Newman   DES Roy Forge Smith, Lynda Paradise   ED Larry Bock, Patrick Rand   PROD Scott Kroopf, Michael S. Murphey, Joel Soisson   DIST Castle Premier/Interscope Communications/Soisson-Murphey Productions/De Laurentiis Film Partners

66 Meant to be funny, but it only swells the sinus passages. – *Vincent Canby, The New York Times*

'Surfing doesn't get any bigger than this!'

Billabong Odyssey ★

DIR Philip Boston
2003   88m   US
DVD

☆ Shawn 'Barney' Barron (Himself), Fred Basse (Himself), Layne Beachley (Herself)

An account of surfers who go globe-hopping in search of the ultimate wave.

Competent surfer documentary, with some terrific footage. But nothing tops the film's very first minute, in which a lone surfer straddles and stays abreast of a frighteningly huge wave.

CIN Mike Prickett   MUS Dorian Cheah   ED Todd Busch, Andrew Marcus, Lars Woodruff   PROD Vincent Leone

'A seductive look at a notorious gangster's dazzling and decadent empire about to crumble.'

Billy Bathgate ★

DIR Robert Benton
1991   106m   US
DVD   ♫

☆ Dustin Hoffman (Dutch Schultz), Nicole Kidman (Drew Preston), Loren Dean (Billy Bathgate), Bruce Willis (Bo Weinberg), Steven Hill (Otto Berman), Steve Buscemi (Irving), Billy Jaye (Mickey)

In the 1930s, a teenage boy becomes involved with Dutch Schultz, a gangster whose power and influence are on the wane.

Stylish attempt by Benton and Stoppard to do something different with the gangster genre. It's handsome and graceful, but oddly lacking any excitement.

SCR Tom Stoppard   CIN Nestor Almendros   MUS Mark Isham   DES Patrizia von Brandenstein   ED Alan Heim, Robert Reitano, David Ray   PROD Arlene Donovan, Robert F. Colesberry   DIST Warner/Touchstone

66 It has a grace and gravity rare just now in American films. – *Richard Corliss, Time*

66 Too often Billy Bathgate looks like a new Disney attraction – Gangsterland. – *Henry Sheehan, Sight and Sound*

'Inside every one of us is a special talent waiting to come out. The trick is finding it.'

Billy Elliot ★★★

DIR *Stephen Daldry*
2000   110m   GB
DVD   ♫

☆ *Julie Walters* (Mrs Wilkinson), *Gary Lewis* (Dad), *Jamie Bell* (Billy), Jamie Draven (Tony), Jean Heywood (Grandmother), Stuart Wells (Michael), Nicola Blackwell (Debbie)

County Durham, 1984: a young boy in a community of striking miners defies gender expectations by taking up ballet.

Crowd-pleasing drama rushes through its plot points (and pirouettes over the miners' strike) in order to better deliver an upbeat experience; still, the direction is sharp, the choices of music striking and the lead performances engaging enough that most viewers won't mind.

SCR Lee Hall   CIN Brian Tufano   MUS Stephen Warbeck   DES Maria Djurkovic   ED John Wilson   PROD Greg Brenman, Jon Finn   DIST UIP

DVD Available on DVD   ☆ Cast in order of importance   66 Critics' Quotes   † Points of interest   ♪ Soundtrack on CD   ⚊ Academy Award   ⚊ Academy Award nomination   BAFTA   BAFTA nomination

66 An exquisite, ecstatic film, crude in its characterisations and plotting, yes, but extraordinary in its capacity for elation and its hard-earned sentimentality. – *Shawn Levy, Portland Oregonian*

66 In its determination to overdo surefire material, Billy Elliot becomes as impossible to wholeheartedly embrace as it is to completely reject. – *Kenneth Turan, Los Angeles Times*

† The film was adapted as a West End musical in 2005, with melodies by Elton John.

♟ Julie Walters (supporting actress); Stephen Daldry; Lee Hall (original screenplay)

🛡 British film; Jamie Bell (leading actor); Julie Walters (supporting actress)

🇹 film; Gary Lewis (supporting actor); Stephen Daldry; Lee Hall (original screenplay); Brian Tufano; John Wilson; Stephen Warbeck; Mark Holding, Mike Prestwood Smith, Zane Haywood (sound)

'The Army made Eugene a man. But Daisy gave him basic training!'

Biloxi Blues ★

DIR Mike Nichols
1988 106m US
DVD

☆ Matthew Broderick (Eugene Morris Jerome), Christopher Walken (Sgt. Toomey), Matt Mulhern (Joseph Wykowski), Corey Parker (Arnold B. Epstein)

Second film, after Brighton Beach Memoirs, about playwright Simon's alter ego Eugene Jerome, called into active service just as World War Two was winding down.

Amusing, touching rites-of-passage story, enlivened by Simon's reliably punchy dialogue and a sweet central performance.

SCR Neil Simon CIN Bill Butler MUS Georges Delerue DES Paul Sylbert ED Sam O'Steen PROD Ray Stark DIST Universal/Rastar

66 A very classy movie, directed and toned up by Mike Nichols so there's not an ounce of fat in it. – *Vincent Canby, New York Times*

'"There are no second acts in American lives." - F. Scott Fitzgerald.'

Bird ★

DIR Clint Eastwood
1988 161m US
DVD ♫

☆ Forest Whitaker (Charlie Parker), Diane Venora (Chan Parker), Michael Zelniker (Red Rodney)

Biopic of Charlie Parker, jazz saxophonist.

Ambitious free-form portrait of a virtuoso performer and a troubled man that – despite its director's usual technical polish – will be hard work for all but the most committed jazz buffs.

SCR Joel Oliansky CIN Jack N. Green MUS Lennie Niehaus DES Edward C. Carfagno ED Joel Cox PROD Clint Eastwood DIST Warner/Malpaso

66 The most serious, conscientious, and accomplished jazz biopic ever made, and almost certainly Eastwood's best picture as well. – *Jonathan Rosenbaum, Chicago Reader*

---

66 A rat's nest of a movie – all flashbacks and rain. – *Pauline Kael, New Yorker*

♟ Les Fresholtz, Rick Alexander, Vern Poore, Willie D. Burton (sound)

🇹 Lennie Niehaus; Alan Robert Murray, Robert G. Henderson, Willie D. Burton, Les Fresholtz (sound)

'What could possibly come between a match made in heaven? The parents. Dinner. And a nightclub called...'

The Birdcage ★

DIR Mike Nichols
1996 117m US
DVD ♫

☆ Robin Williams (Armand Goldman), Nathan Lane (Albert Goldman), Gene Hackman (Sen. Kevin Keeley), Dianne Wiest (Louise Keeley), Christine Baranski (Katherine Archer), Hank Azaria (Agador), Dan Futterman (Val Goldman), Calista Flockhart (Barbara Keeley)

A gay club-owner's son, who wants to get married, persuades his father to put up a heterosexual front for his straitlaced future in-laws at dinner.

Broad American remake of the French farce La Cage aux Folles, with a lively spirit and fun moments; but it also seems to be clapping itself on the back for smashing taboos, and all the giggly camp becomes rather relentless.

SCR Elaine May CIN Emmanuel Lubezki MUS Jonathan Tunick, Steven Goldstein DES Bo Welch ED Arthur Schmidt PROD Mike Nichols DIST United Artists

66 One of the loopiest, most hysterical family-values comedies ever made. – *Hal Hinson, Washington Post*

66 If it weren't so darned "sincere" this would be an unmitigated bird-brained delight, but it undoubtedly remains a genial crowd-pleaser. – *Angie Errigo, Empire*

♟ Bo Welch (art direction)

'Suspense and shock beyond anything you have ever seen or imagined!'

The Birds ★★★

DIR Alfred Hitchcock
1963 119m US
DVD

☆ Rod Taylor (Mitch Brenner), Tippi Hedren (Melanie Daniels), Jessica Tandy (Lydia Brenner), Suzanne Pleshette (Annie Hayworth), Ethel Griffies (Mrs Bundy), Charles McGraw (Sebastian Sholes), Ruth McDevitt (Mrs MacGruder), Doodles Weaver (Fisherman)

In a Californian coastal area, flocks of birds unaccountably make deadly attacks on human beings.

A curiously absorbing work which begins as light comedy and ends as apocalyptic allegory, this piece of Hitchcockery has no visible point except to tease the audience and provide plenty of opportunity for shock, offbeat humour and special effects (which are not quite as good as might be expected). The actors are pawns in the master's hand.

| DVD Available on DVD | ☆ Cast in order | 66 Critics' Quotes | ♟ Academy Award | 🛡 BAFTA | 71 |
| ♫ Soundtrack on CD | of importance | † Points of interest | ♟ Academy Award nomination | 🇹 BAFTA nomination | |

SCR Evan Hunter CIN *Robert Burks* MUS Bernard Herrmann DES Robert Boyle ED George Tomasini DIST Universal/Alfred Hitchcock

66 Enough to make you kick the next pigeon you come across. – *Judith Crist*

66 The dialogue is stupid, the characters insufficiently developed to rank as clichés, the story incohesive. – *Stanley Kauffmann*

'Careful What You Wish For. . .'

Birth ★★

DIR Jonathan Glazer
2004 100m US
DVD ♫

☆ Nicole Kidman (Anna), Cameron Bright (Sean), Danny Huston (Joseph), Lauren Bacall (Eleanor), Alison Elliot (Laura), Arliss Howard (Bob), Anne Heche (Clara), Peter Stormare (Clifford)

A jogger dies in New York's Central Park. A decade later his widow is approached by a 10-year-old boy who insists he is her dead husband.

Strong, stylish film that demands a leap of imagination from audiences, without which some narrative elements may seem merely preposterous.

SCR Jean-Claude Carrière, Milo Addica, Jonathan Glazer. CIN Harris Savides MUS Alexandre Desplat DES Kevin Thompson ED Sam Sneade, Claus Wehlisch PROD Jean-Louis Piel, Nick Morris, Lizie Gower DIST Entertainment

66 Glazer's lowering drama demonstrates his firm grasp of psychological disorientation. – *Graham Fuller, Sight & Sound*

† Birth sharply polarised opinion at its premiere at the 2004 Venice Film Festival. Some in the audience booed, while its supporters tried to hush the hecklers.

'The dawn of a new art!'

The Birth of a Nation ★★★★

DIR *D. W. Griffith*
1915 185m US
DVD ♫

☆ Henry B. Walthall (Col. Ben Cameron), Mae Marsh (Flora Cameron), Miriam Cooper (Margaret Cameron), Lillian Gish (Elsie), Robert Harron (Tod), Wallace Reid (Jeff), Donald Crisp (Gen U.S. Grant), Joseph Henabery (Abraham Lincoln), Raoul Walsh (John Wilkes Booth), Eugene Pallette (Union Soldier), Walter Long (Gus)

Northern and Southern families are caught up in the Civil War.

The cinema's first and still most famous epic, many sequences of which retain their mastery, despite Afro-American villains, Ku Klux Klan heroes, and white actors in blackface. Originally shown as The Clansman; a shorter version with orchestral track was released in 1931. A brilliant piece of film-making, though its political attitudes understandably cast long shadows over its reputation.

SCR D. W. Griffith, Frank E. Woods CIN G. W. Bitzer PROD D. W. Griffith, Harry E. Aitken DIST Epoch

66 A film version of some of the melodramatic and inflammatory material contained in The Clansman . . . a great deal might be said concerning the sorry service rendered by its plucking at old wounds. But of the film as a film, it may be reported simply that it is an impressive new illustration of the scope of the motion picture camera. – *New York Times*

'Some lovers never know when to stop. . .'

Bitter Moon ★

DIR Roman Polanski
1992 140m GB/France
DVD ♫

☆ Peter Coyote (Oscar), Emmanuelle Seigner (Mimi), Hugh Grant (Nigel), Kristin Scott-Thomas (Fiona), Victor Banerjee (Mr Singh), Sophie Patel (Amrita Singh), Stockard Channing (Beverly)

A paralysed writer and his wife draw an innocent English couple into their sexual fantasies on an ocean voyage.

Lurid drama with sketchy psychological overtones, played with deadly seriousness when dark comedy might have been more appropriate; an intriguing glimpse into this director's world view.

SCR Roman Polanski, Gérard Brach, John Brownjohn CIN Tonino Delli Colli MUS Vangelis DES Willy Holt, Gérard Viard ED Hervé de Luze PROD Roman Polanski DIST Columbia Tristar/Les Films Alain Sarde/Canal/R.P. Productions/Timothy Burrill Productions

66 The cool, poised Ms. Scott-Thomas has the film's hardest job, that of maintaining a calm veneer while everyone else goes off the deep end. – *Janet Maslin, New York Times*

'When doing right goes very, very wrong.'

A Bittersweet Life ★

SCR/DIR Kim Jee-woon
2005 120m Korea
DVD

☆ Byung-Hun Lee (Sun Woo), Yeong-cheol Kim (Boss Kang), Shin Min-ah (Heui-su), Hwang Jeong-min (Boss Baek), Roe-ha Kim (Mun-suk), Mun Chong-hyuk (Tae-gu), Gi-yeong Lee (Mu-sung), Ku Jin (Min-gi)

A hitman gets caught in the clash between two rival gangs.

Strikingly stylish mob thriller from Korea, grippingly plotted in a conventional sort of way, but weakened by odd traces of sentimentality and a gratuitous bloodbath at the end.

CIN *Kim Ji-yong* MUS Dalpalan, Jang Yeong-gyu DES Ryu Seong-heui ED Choi Jae-geun PROD Oh Jeong-wan, Yo-jin Lee DIST Tartan

66 Tour de force of noirish style and Korean ultra-violence that will have genre fans nailed to their seats. – *Derek Elley, Variety*

'One man's conviction divided a nation.'

Black and White ★

DIR Craig Lahiff
2002 99m Australia/GB
DVD

☆ Robert Carlyle (David O'Sullivan), Charles Dance

B

(Roderic Chamberlain), Kerry Fox (Helen Devaney), Colin Friels (Father Tom Dixon), Ben Mendelsohn (Rupert Murdoch), David Ngoombujarra (Max Stuart), Roy Billing (Det. Sgt. Paul Turner), John Gregg (Rohan Rivett), Chris Haywood (Det. Sgt. Karskens)

In late 50s Adelaide, a defence lawyer is assigned to the case of an Aborigine unjustly accused of raping and murdering a young white girl.

By-the-numbers courtroom drama which seems constructed scene-for-scene from others of its type; Dance's nefarious-prosecutor turn and Mendelsohn as the young Rupert Murdoch briefly raise a flicker of interest.

SCR Louis Nowra **CIN** Geoffrey Simpson **MUS** Cezary Skubiszewski **DES** Murray Picknett **ED** Lee Smith **PROD** Helen Leake, Nik Powell **DIST** Tartan

66 Watchable, in a television-drama sort of way. . .however, there isn't much to think about on the way home. – *Edward Porter, Sunday Times*

Black and White ★

SCR/DIR James Toback
1999   99m   US
DVD   ♫

☆ Scott Caan (Scotty), Robert Downey Jnr (Terry), Stacy Edwards (Sheila King), Allan Houston (Dean), Gaby Hoffman (Raven), Kidada Jones (Jesse), Jared Leto (Casey), Marla Maples (Muffy), Joe Pantoliano (Bill King), Bijou Phillips (Charlie), Power (Rich Bower), Raekwon (Cigar), Claudia Schiffer (Greta), Brooke Shields (Sam), William Lee Scott (Will King), Ben Stiller, Mike Tyson

Rich white teens hook up with a would-be rap artist with a criminal past.

Irreverent and provocative look at racial politics from either side of the divide.

CIN David Ferrara **MUS** American Cream Team **DES** Anne Ross **ED** Myron Kerstein **PROD** Michael Mailer, Daniel Bigel, Ron Rotholz **DIST** Columbia TriStar

Black Beauty ★

SCR/DIR Caroline Thompson
1994   88m   GB/US
DVD   ♫

☆ Alan Cumming (voice), Sean Bean (Farmer Grey), David Thewlis (Jerry Barker), Jim Carter (John Manly), Peter Davison (Squire Gordon), Eleanor Bron (Lady Wexmire), Alun Armstrong (Reuben Smith), John McEnery (Mr York), Peter Cook (Lord Wexmire)

An old horse relates the ups and downs of his life in flashback.

The best screen version of this classic children's tale, solid, English and somewhat conservative, save for the horse's appealing narration voiced by Cumming.

CIN Alex Thomson **MUS** Danny Elfman **DES** John Box **ED** Claire Simpson **PROD** Robert Shapiro, Peter MacGregor-Scott **DIST** Warner

66 It plays like a cross between New Age mysticism and anthropomorphism run amok. – *Roger Ebert, Chicago Sun-Times*

Black Book ★★

DIR Paul Verhoeven
2006   145m   Netherlands/Germany/UK/Belgium
DVD

☆ Carice van Houten (Rachel Steinn/Ellis de Vries), Sebastian Koch (Ludwig Muntze), Thom Hoffman (Hans Akkermans), Halina Reijn (Ronnie), Waldemar Kobus (Gunther Franken), Derek de Lint (Gerben Kuipers), Christian Berkel (General Kautner)

Dutch-Jewish cabaret singer Rachel Steinn aims to survive World War II by joining the Resistance and fraternising with Nazi officers to gain information. When her plans misfire, she becomes persona non grata to both sides.

Paul Verhoeven's first film in his native Holland after a 20-year exile in Hollywood questions legends about Dutch resistance heroism and denials about collaboration. No-one emerges from the story wholly clean, not even its resourceful heroine. For her, moral ambiguity is a vital tool to survive so many narrow escapes. Verhoeven is as hard on the Dutch resistance as on the Nazis. The fast-paced, powerful story is directed with real flair and even a welcome dash of vulgarity. Rachel would be a demanding role for any actress; van Houten is equal to the challenge.

SCR Gerard Soeterman, Paul Verhoeven **CIN** Karl Walter Lindenlaub **MUS** Anne Dudley **DES** Wilbert van Dorp **ED** Job ter Burg, James Herbert **PROD** San Fu Maltha, Jens Meurer, Teun Hilte, Jos van den Linden, Frans von Gestel, Jeroen Beker **DIST** Tartan

66 As subversive as it is traditional, both enamoured of conventional notions of heroism and frankly contemptuous of them. – *Kenneth Turan, Los Angeles Times*

66 A strange mix indeed: Verhoeven's exaggerations as applied to the Nazi occupations of the Netherlands. It's implausible and outrageously comic, but equally memorable and passionate. Worth seeing. – *Ian Nathan, Empire*

† Verhoeven claims he and co-screenwriter Gerard Soeterman spent 20 years working on the script. They insist the film's heroine Rachel is a composite of several real people.
† The Black Book of the title was a collection of names, compiled by corrupt Resistance figures, of wealthy Dutch Jews whose possessions the Nazis might wish to plunder.

Ⓣ film not in the English language

Black Cat, White Cat ★

DIR Emir Kusturica
1998   127m   France/Germany/Yugoslavia
DVD

☆ Bajram Severdzan (Matko Destanov), Florijan Ajdini (Zare Destanov), Salija Ibraimova (Afrodita), Branka Katic (Ida), Srdan Todorovic (Dadan Karambolo), Zabit Memedov (Zarije Destanov), Sabri Sulejman (Grga Pitic), Jasar Destani (Grga Veliki), Ljubica Adzovic (Sujka)

Personal and professional squabbles amongst Yugoslavian criminals result in an unlikely marriage of convenience.

Kusturica's everything-goes aesthetic is an acquired taste, and this typically raucous comedy is no exception:

DVD Available on DVD   ☆ Cast in order   66 Critics' Quotes   🏆 Academy Award   Ⓑ BAFTA
♫ Soundtrack on CD   of importance   † Points of interest   Academy Award nomination   Ⓑ BAFTA nomination

73

the kind of movie where the camera will pan to show a pig eating a rusted car, as if it were the most normal thing in the world. 'This is chaos!,' one character remarks. He's not far wrong.

SCR Gordan Mihic, Emir Kusturica   CIN Thierry Arbogast, Michel Amathieu   MUS D. Nele Karajilic, Vajislav Aralica, Dejo Sparavalo   DES Milenko Jeremic   ED Svetolik Mika Zajc   PROD Karl Baumgartner   DIST October/Ciby 2000/Pandora/Komuna

66 The perfect film for anyone who finds the Keystone Cops a little too understated, and I mean that as a compliment. – *Chris Kaltenbach, Baltimore Sun*

66 Kusturica so overcrowds his film – is there a single shot of this movie that doesn't contain a flock of geese? – that you end up desperate to clear your head of its clutter. – *Tom Shone, Sunday Times*

'Inspired by the most notorious unsolved murder in California history.'

The Black Dahlia ★★

DIR Brian de Palma
2006   120m   US/Germany
DVD

☆ Josh Hartnett (Dwight ('Bucky') Bleichert), Aaron Eckhart (Lee Blanchard), Scarlett Johansson (Kay Lake), Hilary Swank (Madeleine Linscott), Mia Kershner (Elizabeth Short), Fiona Shaw (Ramona Linscott)

In the 1940s, two LA cops who are boxing rivals set out to find a murderer when a young woman's mutilated corpse is discovered.

Sepia-tinted attempt to re-create the classic period of film noir, with varied results. Director de Palma stages terrific set-pieces and, as usual with James Ellroy's stories, the dialogue is fast, slangy and obscure. Johansson and the two male leads constitute a scrappy, photogenic love triangle, though overall the acting is decidedly mixed. Finally, the film falls short of its ambitions.

SCR Josh Friedman   CIN Vilmos Zsigmond   MUS Mark Isham   DES Dante Ferretti   ED Bill Pankow   PROD Art Linson, Avi Lerner, Moshe Diamant, Rudy Cohen   DIST Entertainment

66 The second half feels heavy and unfulfilled, potential greatness reduced to a good movie plagued with problems. – *Kirk Honeycutt, Hollywood Reporter*

† k.d. lang appears uncredited, singing Love for Sale in a night club.
† Los Angeles in the 1940s was re-created entirely on sets in Bulgaria.
♪ Vilmos Zsigmond

'Your coffee will never taste the same again.'

Black Gold ★★

DIR Marc Francis
2006   78m   UK
☆ Tadesse Meskela (Himself)

This exploration of the inequities of the coffee trade travels to Ethiopia, the original birthplace of coffee, where farmers earn a pittance, while western middlemen get rich and consumers gladly pay high prices for their latte.

A heartfelt examination of an unfair trade. Ethiopian farmers earn just 2p from a cappuccino that costs £3 in Britain. Troubling scenes show them huddled together deciding if they can afford to build a community school, while coffee traders make fortunes off their labour. Imperfect research leaves several unanswered questions, but this powerful, angry work makes the case for fair trade indisputable. Its unquestioned star is the tenacious Ethiopian activist Tadesse Meskela, who travels the world trying to secure his farmers a fair price for their coffee.

SCR Lisa Ko, Eric Martin, Charlie Pearson, Lois Vossen   CIN Nick Francis, Ben Cole   MUS Andreas Kapsalis   ED Hugh Williams   PROD Marc Francis, Nick Francis   DIST Dogwoof

66 Adds a welcome shot of conscience to your daily cup of Java. – *Trevor Johnston, Time Out*

66 Full of stark statistics and painful juxtapositions between the back-breaking labour of Ethiopian coffee producers and comfy Western consumers. . .it would work well as a teaching aid. – *Sukhdev Sandhu, Daily Telegraph*

† After the film's warmly received world premiere at the 2006 Sundance Festival, a member of the audience wrote a cheque for $10,000 on the spot, so the Ethiopian farmers in the film could build their community school.

'Leave No Man Behind.'

Black Hawk Down ★

DIR Ridley Scott
2001   144m   US
DVD   ♪

☆ Josh Hartnett (Ranger Staff Sgt. Matt Eversmann), Ewan McGregor (Ranger Spec Grimes), Tom Sizemore (Ranger Lt. Col. Danny McKnight), Eric Bana (Delta Sgt. First Class 'Hoot' Gibson), William Fichtner (Delta Sgt. First Class Jeff Sanderson), Ewen Bremner (Specs Sgt. Shawn Nelson), Sam Shepard (Maj. Gen. William F. Garrison), Gabriel Casseus (Ranger Spec Mike Kurth), Ron Eldard (Chief Warrant Officer Mike Durant), Ioan Gruffudd (Ranger Beales), Jeremy Piven (Chief Warrant Officer Cliff Wolcott), Kim Coates (Delta Master Sgt. Chris Wexler), Hugh Dancy (Ranger Sgt. First Class Kurt Schmid)

American troops dropped into Mogadishu in 1993 to capture a warlord find themselves surrounded and under heavy fire.

A true-life account displaying its director's usual meticulous attention to technical and logistical detail, to the detriment of much human interest: the soldiers are merely interchangeable pawns whose extremities are blown off at regular intervals; more regrettably, the Somali casualties are reduced to a footnote after all the flag-waving is over.

SCR Ken Nolan   CIN Slawomir Idziak   MUS Hans Zimmer   DES Arthur Max   ED Pietro Scalia   PROD Jerry Bruckheimer, Ridley Scott   DIST Columbia

66 A triumph of pure filmmaking, a pitiless, unrelenting, no-excuses war movie so thoroughly convincing it's frequently difficult to believe it is a staged recreation. – *Kenneth Turan, Los Angeles Times*

66 It's a Jerry Bruckheimer art film, perhaps the most extravagantly aestheticised combat movie ever made. – *J. Hoberman, Village Voice*

DVD Available on DVD   ☆ Cast in order   66 Critics' Quotes   ♪ Academy Award   BAFTA
♪ Soundtrack on CD   of importance   † Points of interest   ♪ Academy Award nomination   BAFTA nomination

🏆 Pietro Scalia; Mike Minkler, Myron Nettinga, Chris Munro (sound)

👤 Ridley Scott; Slawomir Idziak

Ⓣ Slawomir Idziak; Pietro Scalia; Mike Minkler, Myron Nettinga, Chris Munro (sound)

Black Narcissus ★★★

SCR/DIR *Michael Powell, Emeric Pressburger*
1947   100m   GB
DVD

☆ Deborah Kerr (Sister Clodagh), David Farrar (Mr. Dean), Sabu (Young General), Jean Simmons (Kanchi), Kathleen Byron (Sister Ruth), Flora Robson (Sister Philippa), Esmond Knight (Old General), Jenny Laird (Sister Honey), May Hallatt (Angu Ayah), Judith Furse (Sister Briony), Nancy Roberts (Mother Dorothea), Eddie Whaley Jnr. (Joseph Anthony), Shaun Noble (Con)

Passions start to run unpredictably high when an order of British nuns stationed in Calcutta travel to a remote Himalayan village and open a school and hospital in an old palace that was once a bordello, with examples of erotic art still on the walls.

A film of unusual beauty and an unlikely theme – that of barely suppressed desire, the treatment of which itself needed to be downplayed. Best known for its extraordinary visual power, its exotic Himalayan look was created entirely on sets at Pinewood Studios.

CIN *Jack Cardiff*   MUS Brian Easdale   DES *Alfred Junge*
ED Reginald Mills   PROD Michael Powell, Emeric Pressburger   DIST GFD/The Archers

🏆 Jack Cardiff

'An American Cop in Japan. Their country. Their laws. Their game. His rules.'

Black Rain ★

DIR Ridley Scott
1989   125m   US
DVD ♫

☆ Michael Douglas (Nick), Andy Garcia (Charlie), Ken Takakura (Masahiro), Kate Capshaw (Joyce), Yusaku Matsuda (Sato), Shigeru Koyama (Ohashi), John Spencer (Oliver)

A disgraced New York city cop and his laid-back partner escort a yakuza gangster to Japan, but he escapes en route.

Conventional, but decent thriller, though as always with this director, every shot is glossy and perfectly composed, while every small dramatic moment is milked mercilessly. Osaka is made to look like a suburb of Scott's Blade Runner city set.

SCR Craig Bolotin, Warren Lewis   CIN Jan de Bont
MUS Hans Zimmer   DES Norris Spencer   ED Tom Rolf
PROD Stanley R. Jaffe, Sherry Lansing
DIST UIP/Paramount/Stanley R. Jaffe, Sherry Lansing

66 Black Rain may be dumb but it's pretty. – *Vincent Canby, New York Times*

🏆 Donald O. Mitchell, Kevin O'Connell, Greg P. Russell, Keith A. Wester (sound); Milton C. Burrow, William L. Manger (sound effects)

Black Robe ★★

DIR *Bruce Beresford*
1991   101m   Canada/Australia
DVD ♫

☆ *Lothaire Bluteau* (Father Laforgue), Aden Young (Daniel), Sandrine Holt (Annuka), August Schellenberg (Chomina), Tantoo Cardinal (Chomina's Wife), Frank Wilson (Father Jerome)

In the forests of Quebec in the 1600s, a Jesuit priest attempts to convert the native Indians.

Intense, brooding, thoughtfully directed piece, epic in theme if not in budget, with a clash of two deeply ingrained cultures leading inexorably to tragedy. Bluteau's priest is a standout.

SCR *Brian Moore*   CIN Peter James   MUS Georges Delerue   DES Herbert Pinter   ED Tim Wellburn
PROD Robert Lantos, Stephane Reichel, Sue Milliken
DIST Samuel Goldwyn/Alliance/Samson/Telefilm Canada

66 A fiercely realistic drama of frontier Quebec, "Black Robe" mucks about where the new age western "Dances With Wolves" dared not put its pretty paw. – *Rita Kempley, Washington Post*

'Get Ready For The Violence Of The Lambs'

Black Sheep (new) ★★

SCR/DIR Jonathan King
2007   87 minsm   New Zealand/Korea
DVD

☆ Nathan Meister (Henry Oldfield), Peter Feeney (Angus Oldfield), Danielle Mason (Experience), Tammy Davis (Tucker), Glenis Levestam (Mrs Mac)

A genetically mutated toxic lamb foetus infects a New Zealand farm, turning the flock into rampaging bloodthirsty monsters, their bite turning humans into were-sheep.

Deliriously silly and hilariously gory, its refusal to take itself seriously gives this low-budget madcap shocker an engaging anything-goes atmosphere.

CIN Richard Bluck   MUS Victoria Kelly   DES Kim Sinclair   ED Chris Plummer   PROD Philippa Campbell
DIST Icon Film Distribution

66 Exhilarating and self-deprecating, knowledgeable without being fannish, clever but not too clever. – *Sam Adams – Los Angeles Times*

'What would you do?'

Black Water (new) ★

SCR/DIR Andrew Traucki, David Nerlich
2008   90m   Australia/UK
DVD

☆ Diana Glenn (Grace), Maeve Dermody (Lee), Andy Rodorenda (Adam), Ben Oxenbould (Ben)

An Australian couple in their 20s and a younger sister are left up a crocodile-infested creek, then a tree, without a paddle.

The two directors calibrate the tension skilfully in this efficient thriller.

DVD Available on DVD	☆ Cast in order of importance	66 Critics' Quotes	🏆 Academy Award	Ⓑ BAFTA
♫ Soundtrack on CD		† Points of interest	Academy Award nomination	Ⓣ BAFTA nomination

CIN John Biggins   MUS Rafael May   DES Aaron Crothers   ED Rodrigo Balart   PROD Michael Robertson, Andrew Traucki, David Nerlich   DIST The Works

66 Unspectacular but entertaining creature feature. – *Edward Porter, Sunday Times*

'I'm a teacher. My pupils are the kind you don't turn your back on, even in class!'

The Blackboard Jungle ★★

SCR/DIR Richard Brooks
1955   101m   US

☆ Glenn Ford, Anne Francis, Louis Calhern, Margaret Hayes, John Hoyt, Richard Kiley, Emile Meyer, Warner Anderson, Basil Ruysdael, *Sidney Poitier, Vic Morrow*, Rafael Campos

In a slum school in the mid-1950s, a teacher finally gains the respect of his class of young hooligans.

Seminal 1950s melodrama notable for its introduction of 'Rock Around the Clock' behind the credits and its embrace of rock 'n'roll rebel culture. It doesn't truly stand the test of time, but every high-school drama since owes it a debt.

CIN Russell Harlan   MUS *Bill Haley and the Comets*   ED Ferris Webster   PROD Pandro S. Berman   DIST MGM

66 It could just as well have been the first good film of this kind. Actually, it will be remembered chiefly for its timely production and release. – *G. N. Fenin, Film Culture*

⚲ Richard Brooks (screenplay); Russell Harlan; art direction; editing

Blackboards ★

DIR Samirah Makhmalbaf
2000   84m   Iran/Italy/Japan
DVD

☆ Bahman Ghobadi (Reeboir), Said Mohamadi (Said), Behnaz Jafari (Halaleh)

Two teachers, carrying blackboards on their backs, scour the harsh countryside of Kurdistan in search of employment.

Elusive, ambiguous portrayal of life during wartime, weighing education through repetition of facts against education through lived experience.

SCR Mohsen Makhmalbaf, Samirah Makhmalbaf   CIN Ebrahim Ghafori   MUS Monamed Reza Darvishi   ED Mohsen Makhmalbaf   PROD Mohsen Makmalbaf, Marco Muller   DIST Artificial Eye

66 Like so much Iranian cinema, Blackboards is a work of lyrical propaganda. But its metaphors are opaque enough to avoid didacticism, and the film succeeds as an emotionally accessible, almost mystical work. – *Wesley Morris, Boston Globe*

'Sex+Drugs+Alcohol+'

The Blackout

DIR Abel Ferrara
1997   98m   US/France
DVD

☆ Matthew Modine (Matty), Claudia Schiffer (Susan), Dennis Hopper (Mickey Wayne), Béatrice Dalle (Annie 1), Sarah Lassez (Annie 2)

A hedonistic Hollywood celebrity refuses to rein in his wild lifestyle, despite suffering blackouts – periods when he cannot recall his deeds.

No-one's finest hour, this, but Ferrara completists (and they do exist) will warm to this lesser-seen example of the director's self-indulgent whims.

SCR Marla Hanson, Chris Zois, Abel Ferrara   CIN Ken Kelsch   MUS Joe Delia   DES Richard Hoover   ED Anthony Redman   PROD Edward R. Pressman, Clayton Townsend   DIST Feature/Films Number One/CIPA/MDP

'One Man Still Has The Edge.'

Blade II

DIR Guillermo del Toro
2002   117m   US/Germany
DVD ♫

☆ Wesley Snipes (Blade), Kris Kristofferson (Whistler), Ron Perlman (Reinhardt), Leonor Varela (Nyssa), Norman Reedus (Scud), Thomas Kretschmann (Damaskinos), Luke Goss (Nomak), Donnie Yen (Snowman)

Vampire-slayer Blade has to deal with a virus sweeping through Prague's undead community.

Flimsy sequel with a narrative that falls away into senseless betrayals and double-crosses. Del Toro's bold visual sense offers a modicum of pleasure, but once you've seen one vampire explode in a hail of sparks against yet another grimy post-industrial backdrop, you really have seen them all.

SCR David S. Goyer   CIN Gabriel Beristain   MUS Marco Beltrami, Danny Saber   DES Carol Spier   ED Peter Amundson   PROD Peter Frankfurt, Wesley Snipes, Patrick Palmer   DIST Entertainment

66 Even del Toro can't wake the conceptually dead. – *Manohla Dargis, LA Weekly*

† Director del Toro inherited this second feature in the franchise from Stephen Norrington, who made the first Blade film in 1998.

'A chilling, bold, mesmerizing, futuristic detective thriller.'

Blade Runner ★★★

DIR *Ridley Scott*
1982   117m   US
DVD ♫

☆ *Harrison Ford* (Rick Deckard), *Rutger Hauer* (Roy Batty), Sean Young (Rachael), Edward James Olmos (Gaff), M. Emmet Walsh (Bryant), Daryl Hannah (Pris)

In a futuristic Chinatown district of Los Angeles, an ex-cop with carte blanche to kill is charged with tracking down and eliminating a group of androids, who escaped from a remote colony, hijacked a space shuttle and made their way to Earth.

A film with a cult following that has gradually grown since it opened to distinctly mixed reviews and moderate box-office success. A huge influence on subsequent attempts to re-create science-fiction on film; its production design, all urban grunge and slick, acid-rainy streets, was widely copied, not least by Scott himself. Its story is just the right combination of

DVD Available on DVD   ☆ Cast in order of importance   66 Critics' Quotes   † Points of interest   ⚲ Academy Award   ⚲ Academy Award nomination   BAFTA   BAFTA nomination
♫ Soundtrack on CD

coherent but elusive to inspire multiple readings; the film's appeal to successive generations seems limitless.

SCR Hampton Fancher, David Peoples **CIN** Jordan Cronenweth **MUS** Vangelis **DES** *Lawrence G. Paull* **ED** Terry Rawlings **PROD** Michael Deeley, Ridley Scott **DIST** Warner/Ladd/Blade Runner Partnership

66 Glitteringly and atmospherically designed; but ultimately mechanics win out over philosophizing. – *Sight & Sound*

66 A richly detailed and visually overwhelming trip to 2019 which sticks with you like a recurrent nightmare. – *Sunday Times*

† A supposedly definitive version, Blade Runner: The Final Cut was released in 2007. A 'director's cut' received a theatrical release in 1992. Scott's major change was to lose Ford's voice-over narration.

⚱ art direction; Douglas Trumbull, Richard Yuricich, David Dryer (visual effects)

🏆 Jordan Cronenweth; Lawrence G. Paull

'Kick some ice.'

Blades of Glory ★★

DIR Will Speck, Josh Gordon
2007   93m   US
DVD ♫

☆ Will Ferrell (Chazz Michael Michaels), Jon Heder (Jimmy MacElroy), Will Arnett (Stranz Van Waldenberg), Amy Poehler (Fairchild Van Waldenberg), William Fichtner (Darren MacElroy), Jenna Fischer (Katie), Craig T. Nelson (Coach)

Two male ice-skaters, banned after brawling at a championship, team up as a duo.

A goofy premise, which this odd couple (Ferrell a strutting tattooed sex addict, Heder a fey, squeaky-clean orphan) exploit to the full. The film shows its affection for ice-skating, while stressing its absurdities. Laughs, some of them surprisingly dark, arrive regularly. The leads are almost upstaged by Arnett and Poehler as a creepy pair of skating siblings with appallingly tasteless routines – one involving JFK, Marilyn Monroe and sleeping pills. Overall the casual air masks real comic expertise.

SCR Jeff Cox, Craig Cox, John Altschuler, Dave Krinsky **CIN** Stefan Czapsky **MUS** Theodore Shapiro **DES** Stepohen Lineweaver **ED** Richard Pearson **PROD** Ben Stiller, Stuart Cornfeld, John Jacobs **DIST** Paramount

JIMMY: 'Spandex, glitter and egos. . .it's the only place that life makes sense.'

66 I can't remember a time when I have laughed so long and hard at a decapitation gag. – *Wendy Ide, The Times*

'In October of 1994 three student filmmakers disappeared in the woods near Burkittsville, Maryland, while shooting a documentary...A year later their footage was found.'

The Blair Witch Project ★★★

SCR/DIR Daniel Myrick, Eduardo Sanchez
1999   86m   US
DVD

☆ Heather Donahue (herself), Michael Williams (himself), Joshua Leonard (himself), Bob Griffith (Short Fisherman), Jim King (Interviewee), Sandra Sanchez (Waitress (as Sandra Sanchez)), Ed Swanson (Fisherman With Glasses), Patricia Decou (Mary Brown)

Three film students head out into a Maryland forest to shoot a documentary about the local legend of a witch; they disappear, and their footage is found a year later.

Startlingly effective horror on a shoestring, which took the world by storm, convincing many audiences they were actually watching a documentary; it achieves some truly frightening effects on the bare minimum of resources.

CIN Neal Fredericks **ED** Daniel Myrick, Eduardo Sanchez **PROD** Gregg Hale, Robin Cowie **DIST** Pathé

66 Stunningly effective and brilliant in its sheer macabre clarity and simplicity. – *Peter Bradshaw, Guardian*

66 Forgoes a literal bogeyman in favour of the unseen, which in this case is as scarily bone-chilling as anything they could show you. – *Wesley Morris, San Francisco Examiner*

† A sequel, Book of Shadows: Blair Witch 2, was released in 2000.

Blame It On Fidel (new) ★★

SCR/DIR Julie Gavras
2006   98m   France/Italy
DVD

☆ Nina Kervel (Anna), Julie Depardieu (Marie), Stefano Accorsi (Fernando), Benjamin Feuillet (François), Martine Chevaillier (Granny), Olivier Perrier (Grandad)

In the early 1970s, a nine year old Parisian girl's life is thrown into disarray when her affluent bourgeois parents suddenly become radicals.

Charming and often amusing story of a young girl's bewilderment when her parents swap her comfortable house for a flat, where crowds of socialist radicals congregate. Deftly directed by Gavras, who teases a complex, delightful performance from her young lead.

CIN Nathalie Durand **MUS** Armand Amar **DES** Laurent Deroo **ED** Pauline Dairou **PROD** Sylvie Pialat **DIST** ICA

66 A deft, original, entertaining and thoughtful look at that moment when we realise the world's just that bit more complicated than we thought. – *Trevor Johnston, Time Out*

66 Gavras is an experienced maker of documentaries, but this assured, intelligent film marks an auspicious beginning to her career in fictional features. – *Karl French, Financial Times*

† Writer-director Julie Gavras is the daughter of the distinguished director Constantin Costa-Gavras.

'She was a woman of the world. He had never been around the block.'

Blast from the Past ★★

DIR Hugh Wilson
1999   112m   US
DVD ♫

☆ *Brendan Fraser* (Adam Webber), *Alicia Silverstone* (Eve Rustikoff), *Christopher Walken* (Calvin Webber), *Sissy Spacek* (Helen Thomas Webber), Dave Foley (Troy), Joey

DVD Available on DVD   ☆ Cast in order   66 Critics' Quotes   ⚱ Academy Award   🏆 BAFTA
♫ Soundtrack on CD   of importance   † Points of interest   Academy Award nomination   BAFTA nomination

77

Slotnick (Soda Jerk/Archbishop Melker), Dale Raoul (Mom)

A young boy shut in a nuclear shelter at the time of the Cuban Missile Crisis emerges as an innocent 35-year-old in contemporary LA, sweeping a cynical city girl off her feet.

Delightful comedy, consistently clever in the manner in which it develops its higher-than-high-concept premise while remaining true to some old-fashioned virtues: wit, charm and romance. Fraser's light comic gifts have never been more evident, but the performances are excellent all round.

SCR *Bill Kelly, Hugh Wilson* CIN Jose Luis Alcaine MUS Steve Dorff DES Robert Ziembicki ED Don Brochu PROD Renny Harlin, Hugh Wilson DIST New Line/Midnight Sun

66 You can see how the treatment might have been darker – how Adam could have been much more a lamb to the Lala-land slaughter. But playing it fresh and sweet is possibly tougher to pull off, and Wilson manages it beautifully. – *Jonathan Romney, Guardian*

Blaze ★
DIR Ron Shelton
1989 117m US

☆ Paul Newman (Gov. Earl K. Long), Lolita Davidovich (Blaze Starr), Jerry Hardin (Thibodeaux), Gailard Sartain (LaGrange), Jeffrey DeMunn (Eldon Tuck), Garland Bunting (Doc Ferriday)

In the 1950s, Louisiana governor Earl Long embarks on a scandalous affair with a New Orleanian stripper.

Lightweight fun, enlivened by Shelton's facility with ornate speech and the relish with which Newman approaches his role as a shameless good ol' boy.

SCR *Ron Shelton* CIN Haskell Wexler MUS Bennie Wallace DES Armin Ganz ED Robert Leighton, Adam Weiss PROD Gil Friesen, Dale Pollock DIST Warner/Touchstone/Silver Screen Partners IV/A&M

66 Shelton still shows some flair for dialogue, and the material–mostly drawn from Starr's as-told-to autobiography–is certainly ripe and colourful. – *Jonathan Rosenbaum, Chicago Reader*

† Earl Long was the brother of the infamous Huey Long, the subject of All the King's Men
† The real Blaze Starr has a cameo role – as a stripper.
⚱ Haskell Wexler

Bleeder ★
SCR/DIR Nicolas Winding Refn
1999 98m Denmark
DVD

☆ Kim Bodnia (Leo), Mads Mikkelsen (Lenny), Rikke Louise Andersson (Louise), Liv Corfixen (Lea), Levino Jensen (Louis), Zlatko Buric (Kitjo), Claus Flygare (Joe), Ole Abildgaard (Video shop customer)

A Copenhagen video store worker's disdainful treatment of his pregnant girlfriend has violent consequences.

Tough, uncompromising drama that reveals a genuine morality beneath its murky surface.

CIN Morten Soborg MUS Peter Peter DES Peter De Neergaard ED Anne Osterud PROD Henrik Danstrup, Thomas Falck, Nicolas Winding Refn DIST Metrodome

66 Further underscores that Refn is shaping up into an intriguing director. – *Chris Darke, Sight and Sound*

Blind Flight ★
DIR John Furse
2003 97m GB
DVD

☆ Ian Hart (Brian Keenan), Linus Roache (John McCarthy), Bassem Breish (Joker), Ziad Lahoud (Said)

A dramatised account of teacher Brian Keenan and journalist John McCarthy's four-year spell as hostages in Beirut.

Two contrasting actors near the top of their game power this carefully composed chamber piece.

SCR John Furse, Brian Keenan CIN Ian Wilson MUS Stephen McKeon DES Andrew Sanders ED Kristina Hetherington PROD Sally Hibbin DIST Optimum

66 A suitably spartan testament to an unimaginably grim ordeal, and finally moving in the extreme. – *Tim Robey, Daily Telegraph*

'There is no honor amongst thieves.'
Blood & Wine ★
DIR Bob Rafelson
1996 98m US/ GB
DVD ♫

☆ Jack Nicholson (Alex Gates), Michael Caine (Victor 'Vic' Spansky), Stephen Dorff (Jason), Jennifer Lopez (Gabby), *Judy Davis* (Suzanne), Harold Perrineau Jnr (Henry)

A wine merchant's best laid plans for a jewellery heist are scuppered by his estranged wife and stepson.

Watchable – if somewhat insincere – attempt at hard-boiled modern noir that turns into soft-centred Freudian melodrama halfway through: the fiercely compelling Davis is the only one who seems to be taking it seriously.

SCR Nick Villiers, Alison Cross CIN Newton Thomas Sigel MUS Michel Lorenc DES Richard Sylbert ED Steven Cohen PROD Jeremy Thomas DIST TCF/Blood & Wine/Marmont/Recorded Picture/Majestic

66 Rafelson's most assured genre exercise: the plot twists like an eel, but action stems directly from character, with results that are both unforeseen and inevitable. . .A supple, atmospheric entertainment which doesn't pull its punches. – *Tom Charity, Time Out*

66 Too crude and plot-driven to be a character study, and too downbeat to pack a thriller's punch. – *Anthony Quinn, Mail on Sunday*

'Two Cats. . . One Car. . . And A World Of Hurt.'
Blood Guts Bullets & Octane ★
SCR/DIR Joe Carnahan
1997 87m US
DVD

☆ Joe Carnahan (Sid French), Dan Leis (Bob Melba), Ken

Rudulph (FBI Agent Jared), Dan Harlan (Danny Woo), Hugh McChord (Mr Reich), Kurt Johnson (Hillbilly Sniper), Mark S. Allen (FBI Agent Franks), Kellee Benedic (FBI Agent Littel)

Two car dealers, given money to look after a Pontiac Le Mans, decide to steal the car instead, not knowing that the FBI believe it contains drugs and was used by a serial killer.

Sprightly low-budget directorial debut, hardly original, but executed with all the spirit and verve the title suggests.

CIN John Alexander Jimenez   MUS Mark Priolo, Martin Birke   ED Joe Carnahan   PROD Dan Leis, Leon Corcos, Patrick Lynn, Arye Flex II, Joe Carnahan   DIST Downtown

66 Carnahan has a splendid ear for dialogue and a broad and outrageous sense of humour. – *Kevin Thomas, Los Angeles Times*

'An epic story of three brothers. Bound by blood. Divided by fate. Driven by destiny.'

Blood In, Blood Out   ★★

DIR Taylor Hackford
1992   180m   US
DVD   ♫

☆ Jesse Borrego (Cruz), Benjamin Bratt (Paco), Enrique Castillo (Montana), Damian Chapa (Miklo), Delroy Lindo (Bonafide), Teddy Wilson (Wallace), Karmin Murcelo (Dolores), Ving Rhames (Ivan), Jenny Gago (Lupe)

Three young Mexican-American men get involved with street life in gang-dominated East Los Angeles, then end up in San Quentin prison.

A gruelling journey as described by someone who actually lived it: the flipside of the Californian dream, depicting impoverished lives in which brutality and violence inevitably intrude. Long and occasionally preachy, but with individual storylines that command attention.

SCR *Jimmy Santiago Baca, Jeremy Iacone, Floyd Mutrux*
CIN Gabriel Beristain   MUS Bill Conti   DES Bruno Rubeo   ED Fredric Steinkamp, Karl F. Steinkamp   PROD Taylor Hackford, Jerry Gershwin   DIST Buena Vista/Hollywood Pictures/Touchstone Pacific Partners I

66 Though it's not the epic it means to be, it is not a failure. – *Vincent Canby, New York Times*

Blood Simple   ★★★

DIR *Joel Coen*
1983   99m   US
DVD   ♫

☆ John Getz, *Frances McDormand, Dan Hedaya*, M. Emmet Walsh

A saloon owner hires a sleazy hit man to kill his unfaithful wife and her lover, but the plot rebounds on him.

A debut that announces itself with great style: the Coen brothers' sense of playfulness is in evidence, what with their flamboyant tracking shots and inspired use of light and sound. The final shot, cutting away abruptly to the Four Tops' hit It's The Same Old Song over the end titles, authoritatively confirmed that two prodigious

talents had arrived. *Combining elements of classic noir with the look of a cheap horror movie, it's not as relaxed as their later work, and far less fun: this is a genuinely grim story.*

SCR *Joel and Ethan Coen*   CIN Barry Sonnenfeld
MUS Carter Burwell   DES Jane Musky   ED Roderick Jaynes, Don Wiegmann, Peggy Connolly   PROD Ethan Coen   DIST Palace/River Road

† Coens' regular Frances McDormand, who is married to Joel Coen, made her film debut here.

Bloody Angels   ★

DIR Karin Julsrud
1998   100m   Norway/GB

☆ Reidar Sørensen (Nicholas Ramm), Gaute Skjegstad (Niklas Hartmann), Trond Høvik (Holger), Laila Goody (Victoria), Stig Henrik Hoff (Dwayne Karlson), Simon Norrthon (Cato)

Townsfolk impede the investigation into the rape and murder of a girl with Down's syndrome.

Norwegian crime drama set in a morally bleak universe. Minor, but full of grim conviction.

SCR Kjetil Indegaard, Finn Gjerdum   CIN Philip Ogaard
MUS Kjetil Bjerkestrand, Magne Furuholmen   DES Billy Johansson   ED Sophie Hesselberg   PROD Tom Remlov, Finn Gjerdum   DIST United Media

66 Crisply made crime thriller that makes excellent use of wintry locations in rural Norway. . .filled with sardonic humor and sharp observation. – *David Stratton, Variety*

Bloody Sunday   ★★★

SCR/DIR *Paul Greengrass*
2002   110m   GB/Ireland
DVD

☆ *James Nesbitt* (Ivan Cooper), Tim Pigott-Smith (Major General Ford), Nicholas Farrell (Brigadier Maclellan), Gerard McSorley (Chief Supt Lagan), Kathy Kiera Clarke (Frances), Allan Gildea (Kevin McCorry), Gerard Crossan (Eamonn McCann), Mary Moulds (Bernadette Devlin), Carmel McCallion (Bridget Bond), Declan Duddy (Gerry Donaghy)

Reconstruction of the events of January 30, 1972, when British paratroopers opened fire on a civil rights march through the streets of Derry.

An early indicator of this director's formidable talents: a passionately political docudrama more interested in human lives than dogmatic debate, and a searing depiction of a community unravelled by the strangers in their midst.

CIN Ivan Strasburg   MUS Dominic Muldowney
DES John Paul Kelly   ED Clare Douglas   PROD Mark Redhead

66 Surges forward with barely a respite. It's like watching a propane factory burn, waiting for the tanks inside to explode, and when they do, we're right in the middle of it. – *Jack Mathews, New York Daily News*

66 Most of what you see has a brutal, you-are-there immediacy. You're not merely watching history, you're engulfed by it. – *Wesley Morris, Boston Globe*

† The film was first seen on British television before it opened in cinemas.

DVD Available on DVD   ☆ Cast in order of importance   66 Critics' Quotes   † Points of interest   🎓 Academy Award   🎓 Academy Award nomination   🏆 BAFTA   🏆 BAFTA nomination

79

Daniel Day-Lewis, in a scene from *There Will be Blood*, as Daniel Plainview, a man who becomes a vastly wealthy oil tycoon but loses his humanity in the process. The film's dark tone typifies this year's leading awards contenders.

If you had to use a single word to characterise the films of the past year, that word would be 'dark'. It's true that we are living in difficult times, what with terrorist attacks, conflicts in Iraq and Afghanistan, a tsunami, floods, earthquakes, famine, global warming and widespread human rights abuses. But it's hard to recall another year in which films reflected this gloom and misery quite so wholeheartedly.

For proof, one need look no further than this year's leading Academy Award nominees. *No Country For Old Men*, the year's overall Oscar winner, is a merciless film that relentlessly reflects a blood-drenched world of mindless, nihilistic violence and greed. *Michael Clayton* is about a flawed, struggling law-firm fixer, battered and wearied by the corruption he sees around him. The much-admired *There Will Be Blood* is about a man who becomes rich beyond his dreams, but loses any vestiges of humanity he may once have possessed.

Other movies admired by the Academy this year included *Sweeney Todd*, a stylised Victorian blood-bath; *Away From Her* and *The Savages*, both of which tackled the distressing issue of Alzheimer's; and *The Diving Bell and the Butterfly*, which at least attempts to bring optimism to a terrible story, about a stroke victim reduced to communicating in code by blinking one eye.

And this is before we survey the rash of movies directly or indirectly about the war on terror, or US military adventures in the Middle East: *Lions for Lambs*, *Rendition*, *Redacted*, *In the Valley of Elah*, *Stop Loss*, *The Kingdom* and *Battle for Haditha*. You may notice one thing these films have in common; none was a box-office hit. *The Kingdom* did moderate business in the United States, while all the others did virtually no business at all.

Indeed, in the case of *In the Valley of Elah* (an excellent film in which Tommy Lee Jones gives a superlative performance as the father of a young ex-soldier who dies shortly after arriving home from Iraq) the film was unceremoniously dumped by its studio, Warner Bros., after early indications that the public could not be cajoled into seeing such a downbeat story.

Even more astonishing, on the face of it, was *Lions for Lambs*. Certainly, it was a preachy, somewhat tiresome airing of arguments for and against the US military presence in Afghanistan. But one might have thought the star wattage of its cast – Tom Cruise, Meryl Streep, Robert Redford – might have attracted sizeable audiences.

As for Brian de Palma's renegade account of a military unit in Iraq who resort to violence and rape, it received wildly mixed reviews, but was barely released in the US or Britain. Clearly, it was too jolting for most people's tastes.

But then, so were other serious-minded films that had nothing to do with war. One of the year's very best, *The Assassination of Jesse James by the Coward Robert Ford*, was also effectively dumped by Warner Bros. when it failed to attract sizeable audiences shortly after its US release. Forget that this was a startlingly beautiful movie that boasted Brad Pitt in the lead role as the famous outlaw; none of that could overcome its long running time, Jesse James's psychopathic mood swings, and the script's grim, brooding perspective on fame, betrayal and life outside the law.

And remember that even the big serious-minded Oscar-winning films could not convert all those accolades, and the free publicity that accompanies them, into box-office success. *No Country For Old Men* was only the 36th most watched film seen in the US in 2007. *Michael Clayton* came in at number 55, while *There Will Be Blood* struggled at number 66.

All this is regrettable. People have stayed away from films that, taken together, stand as the best crop in any single year since the 1970s. Something certainly kept audiences away from the sober realities they portrayed, but it wasn't the quality of the films themselves.

> '**People have stayed away from films that, taken together, stand as the best crop in any single year since the 1970s.**'

Surprisingly, in the US, it may have been the quality of television. Since the success of *The Sopranos*, American TV cable channels, immune from network restrictions on bad language and depictions of sexuality and violence, have commissioned several series of a serious, dark nature that have captured the imaginations of those very people who might reasonably have been expected to see comparable material in cinemas. Shows such as *The Wire*, *Mad Men*, *Dexter* and *The Shield* have all met with critical acclaim and explore the darker side of human nature. So, it must be said, do two of the most enduring network TV series, *Law and Order* and the *CSI* franchise.

This was a real turnaround. For years, intelligent, provocative films have functioned as a refuge for audiences tired of the predictable rhythm ploys and premises of television schedules. It's an irony that once American TV finally raised its game by gambling on series aimed at sophisticated grown-ups, it caused problems for the very films those series were designed to complement, rather than supplant. Quality television may not have been the only reason for the failure of those films, but people certainly stayed away from them.

What are we to make of all this? It's often mentioned on these occasions that while the Iraq war is unpopular, so was Vietnam — yet audiences flocked to see *Apocalypse Now*, *The Deer Hunter* and *Platoon*. But that's hardly a valid parallel. Those Vietnam-themed films opened well after the war was over, and the public had processed it into recent history. (In Britain, of course, we were not directly involved in Vietnam.) The Iraq conflict grinds on, and the overall feeling about it, from both supporters and opponents of the war, has diminished from, respectively, enthusiasm and anger, into a kind of helplessness. That's not a sentiment you want to embrace more tightly by a visit to the cinema.

It's no surprise, then, that the most successful films have been those that steered away from seriousness: action-adventure flicks like *Indiana Jones and the Crystal Skull*, those aimed at younger audiences, such as *Iron Man*, *Chronicles of Narnia: Prince Caspian* and *Kung Fu Panda*; and light-hearted family fare including *Ratatouille* and *Enchanted*.

The only mystery is that films that promise a taste of gloom, misery and angst are promoted as such by distributors. *Iron Man*, we were told, was 'darker' than most comic book adventure adaptations. All you need to know about the new Batman film, *The Dark Knight* is right there in its title. Darkness, it seems, stands for a certain virtue and integrity, though clearly it doesn't make films one bit more appealing to the general public.

> '**Even the big serious-minded Oscar-winning films could not convert all those accolades, and the free publicity that accompanies them, into box-office success.**'

This is why this past year of 'dark' films will surely come to be seen as some kind of aberration – a blip that reflected the desire of dedicated film-makers to tell stories that reflected the difficult times we live in.

The problem with that kind of idealism, of course, is that someone has to foot the bill for such films to be made. One would not bet that the Hollywood studios will be going out of their way to encourage new scripts about Iraq, or indeed any ideas for films that peddle too gloomy a view of life.

Blue   ★

SCR/DIR Derek Jarman
1993   76m   GB
[DVD]

☆ The voices of John Quentin, Derek Jarman, Nigel Terry, Tilda Swinton

Over a still blue image, a number of disembodied voices – including that of a dying filmmaker – consider life, death, AIDS, sight and sightlessness.

A highly personal account of its director's physical deterioration, perhaps best engaged with as radio; visually, a little Yves Klein goes a very long way.

MUS Simon Fisher Turner   PROD James Mackay, Takashi Asai   DIST Basilisk/Uplink

66 A minimalist experiment, carried out with the nerveless daring of someone who has nothing to lose. You don't exactly watch Blue – you expose yourself to it and wait for the results. – *Stuart Klawans, New Republic*

66 Has moments of power, but its many digressions prompt the mind to wander, giving one the chance to think about anything – Jarman's other films, how other artists have reacted to their own AIDS, what's playing down the street. – *Variety*

† Before opening in cinemas, Blue was first broadcast simultaneously on television and stereo radio in Britain.

The Blue Angel   ★★★★

DIR Josef von Sternberg
1930   98m   Germany
[DVD]

☆ *Emil Jannings* (Prof. Immanuel Rath), *Marlene Dietrich* (Lola Frohlich), Kurt Gerron (Kiepert), Hans Albers (Mazeppa), Rosa Valetti (Guste)

A fuddy-duddy professor is infatuated with a tawdry night-club singer. She marries him, but is soon bored and contemptuous; humiliated, he leaves her and dies in his old classroom.

A masterwork of late 1920s German grotesquerie, and after a slowish beginning an emotional powerhouse, set in a dark nightmare world which could be created only in a studio. Shot also in English, it was highly popular and influential in Britain and America. It instantly catapulted Dietrich to international stardom.

SCR Robert Liebmann, Carl Zuckmayer, Karl Vollmoeller   CIN Günther Rittau, Hans Schneeberger   MUS Frederick Hollander (inc 'Falling in Love Again', 'They Call Me Wicked Lola')   ED S.K. Winston   PROD Erich Pommer   DIST UFA

66 It will undoubtedly do splendidly in the whole of Europe and should also appeal strongly in the States. . .only fault is a certain ponderousness of tempo which tends to tire. – *Variety*

66 At the time I thought the film was awful and vulgar and I was shocked by the whole thing. Remember, I was a well brought-up German girl. – *Marlene Dietrich*

'Tamed by a brunette – framed by a blonde – blamed by the cops!'

The Blue Dahlia   ★★

DIR George Marshall
1946   99m   US
☆ Alan Ladd, Veronica Lake, William Bendix, Howard da

Silva, Doris Dowling, Tom Powers, Hugh Beaumont, Howard Freeman, Will Wright

A returning war veteran finds his faithless wife has been murdered and he becomes the chief suspect.

Hailed on its first release as sharper than average, this suspense thriller is now only moderately compelling despite Chandler's screenplay credit; the direction and editing lack urgency and the acting lacks bounce.

SCR Raymond Chandler   CIN Lionel Lindon   MUS Victor Young   PROD John Houseman   DIST Paramount

66 It threatens to turn into something, but it never does. – *New Yorker, 1978*

66 The picture is as neatly stylized and synchronized, and as uninterested in moral excitement, as a good ballet; it knows its own weight and size perfectly and carries them gracefully and without self-importance; it is, barring occasional victories and noble accidents, about as good a movie as can be expected from the big factories. – *James Agee*

⚱ Raymond Chandler (original screenplay)

'Just Over The Bridge, Around The Corner From Reality Is A Place That's Out Of This World. Welcome To Planet Brooklyn.'

Blue in the Face   ★

SCR/DIR Wayne Wang, Paul Auster
1995   89m   US
[DVD] ♫

☆ Harvey Keitel (Auggie Wren), Lou Reed (Man with Strange Glasses), Roseanne (Dot), Michael J. Fox (Pete Maloney), Jim Jarmusch (Bob), Lily Tomlin (Waffle Eater), Mel Gorham (Violet), Jared Harris (Jimmy Rose), Giancarlo Esposito (Tommy Finelli), Victor Argo (Vinnie), Madonna (Singing Telegram), Keith David (Jackie Robinson), Mira Sorvino (Young Lady)

The manager of a Brooklyn cigar shop tries to secure his establishment's future while dealing with a variety of interruptions.

A joshing, amiable companion piece to Smoke finds a starry line-up of new players improvising with many of the first film's characters. Several funny moments, notably Jarmusch's diatribe against the wastefulness of movie cops.

CIN Adam Holender   MUS John Lurie   DES Kalina Ivanov   ED Christopher Tellefsen   PROD Greg Johnson, Peter Newman, Diana Phillips   DIST Miramax

66 Of the film's ninety minutes, a total of about twenty succeeds. – *Stanley Kauffmann, New Republic*

66 Good-humored, try-anything fun. – *Elvis Mitchell, New York Times*

The Blue Kite   ★★★

DIR Tian Zhuangzhuang
1993   138m   China
[DVD] ♫

☆ Zhang Wenyao (Tietou, as a child), Chen Xiaoman (Tietou, as a teenager), Lu Liping (Mum (Chen Shujuan)), Pu Quanxin (Dad (Lin Shaolong)), Li Xuejian (Uncle Li (Li Guodong)), Guo Baochang (Stepfather (Lao Wu)), Zhong Ping (Chen Shusheng), Chu Qhuangzhong (Chen Shuyan), Song Xiaoying (Sis), Zhang Hong (Zhu Ying)

[DVD] Available on DVD	☆ Cast in order	66 Critics' Quotes	⚱ Academy Award	🎭 BAFTA
♫ Soundtrack on CD	of importance	† Points of interest	⚱ Academy Award nomination	🎭 BAFTA nomination

In a story based on the director's own memories, a young boy recounts his family history over two decades, his mother's multiple marriages and the political turmoil of those times.

Banned by the authorities in China, the story traces the devastating effects Mao's era, particularly the Cultural Revolution, had on ordinary Chinese lives. It combines a sharp sense of anger at the seemingly arbitrary political upheavals, and sorrowful sympathy for lives that are wasted or ruined.

SCR Xiao Mao   CIN Hou Yong   MUS Yoshihide Otomo
DES Liansheng Wang   ED Qian Lengleng
DIST Longwick/Beijing Film Studio

66 Tian combines lucidity of vision with a novelistic richness and complexity of narrative. – *Philip Kemp, Sight & Sound*

'For a rookie cop, there's one thing more dangerous than uncovering a killer's fantasy. Becoming it.'

Blue Steel ★

DIR Kathryn Bigelow
1990 102m US
[DVD]

☆ Jamie Lee Curtis (Megan Turner), Ron Silver (Eugene Hunt), Clancy Brown (Nick Mann), Elizabeth Pena (Tracy Perez), Louise Fletcher (Shirley Turner), Philip Bosco (Frank Turner)

A rookie female cop is compromised when her weapon falls into the hands of a serial killer.

Typically savvy genre piece from a much underrated director, slow in places, but edged along by two committed lead performances.

SCR Kathryn Bigelow, Eric Red   CIN Amir Mokri
MUS Brad Fiedel   DES Tony Corbett   ED Lee Percy
PROD Edward R. Pressman, Oliver Stone
DIST Vestron/Lightning Pictures/Precision Films/Mack-Taylor Productions

66 What I like most about Blue Steel. . .is that the heroine is strengthened and ennobled by her ordeal, and her soul is never sacrificed to the spectacle. Kathryn Bigelow and Jamie Lee Curtis have thus imaginatively collaborated on a work of art of both style and substance. – *Andrew Sarris, New York Observer*

Blue Velvet ★★★★

SCR/DIR *David Lynch*
1986 120m US
[DVD] ♫

☆ Kyle MacLachlan (Jeffrey Beaumont), *Isabella Rossellini* (Dorothy Vallens), *Dennis Hopper* (Frank Booth), Laura Dern (Sandy Williams), Hope Lange (Mrs. Williams), Dean Stockwell (Ben)

A young man in a small town finds a severed ear and, in trying to track its owner, finds himself entangled in murder, perversion and ways of life he never imagined.

The opening scene is a classic: white picket fences, smiling small-town firemen waving from their truck, a man tending his garden. But then he suffers a stroke, the camera dips below ground, and we see teeming insect life under the lawn. It's a perfect metaphor for what is to come: a young man playing amateur sleuth and ending up on the dark side of town. Hopper is superb as the local criminal mastermind (complete with inhaler) while Rossellini suffers for her art as his bruised chanteuse girlfriend. A shocking, confident, stylish piece of work, and for aspiring screenwriters, maybe the seminal film of the 1980s: certainly Lynch's notion of weirdness and malice lurking behind the cheery face of small towns has since been thoroughly explored.

CIN Frederick Elmes   MUS Angelo Badalamenti
DES Patricia Norris   ED Duwayne Dunham
PROD Richard Roth   DIST De Laurentiis

66 Horrifying in ways that genre horror movies never are. . .Lynch's nightmare has a sort of irregular, homemade quality, as if it had been cooked up with familiar but not entirely wholesome ingredients – a fresh apple pie with a couple of worms poking through the crust. – *Terrence Rafferty, Nation*

† Lynch has claimed that Bobby Vinton, who sang the innocent pop song that gave the film its title, asked to audition for the role of Frank Booth.

⚐ David Lynch

Bob Le Flambeur ★★★

DIR Jean-Pierre Melville
1956 95m France
[DVD]

☆ Roger Duchesne (Bob), Isabelle Corey (Anne), Daniel Cauchy (Paolo), Howard Vernon (McKimmie), Guy Decomble (Inspector Ledru), Claude Cerval (Jean)

A weary French gambler and ex-gangster, past his peak, plans one last heist against apparently insuperable odds: to rob the casino at Deauville with a group of henchmen.

The curiously honourable, principled Bob is an ambivalent anti-hero; amoral, certainly, but capable of kindness and honour. This downbeat thriller has a loose, jazzy feel, while Bob relates directly to American post-war noir heroes – men who had seen human behaviour at its worst, and internalised it. A film whose reputation has steadily grown.

SCR Auguste Le Breton, Jean-Pierre Melville   CIN Henri Decaë   MUS Eddie Barclay, Jean Boyer   ED Monique Bonnot

66 Its dark-toned cinematography by Henri Decaë still packs a wallop, and the screenplay has a refreshing sense of humour, reflecting Melville's concept of the picture as less a straightforward cops-and-robbers story than a scruffy comedy of manners. – *David Sterritt, Christian Science Monitor*

66 A sort of lyrical documentary thriller. – *David Thomson*

† It was remade by Neil Jordan in 2002 as The Good Thief.

'More amazing than Watergate.'

Bob Roberts ★★

SCR/DIR *Tim Robbins*
1992 102m US
[DVD]

☆ Tim Robbins (Bob Roberts), Giancarlo Esposito (Bugs Raplin), Alan Rickman (Lukas Hart III), Ray Wise (Chet

[DVD] Available on DVD   ☆ Cast in order   66 Critics' Quotes   ⚐ Academy Award   ⚐ BAFTA
♫ Soundtrack on CD   of importance   † Points of interest   ⚐ Academy Award nomination   ⚐ BAFTA nomination

83

MacGregor), Brian Murray (Terry Manchester), Gore Vidal (Senator Brickley Paiste), Rebecca Jenkins (Delores Perrigrew), Harry J. Lennix (Franklin Dockett), Susan Sarandon (Tawna Titan), John Cusack (Cutting Edge Host), Bob Balaban (Michael Janes)

Mock-documentary portrait of an ultra-conservative folk singer as he moves from show business to campaigning for a seat in the US Senate.

Primary Colors meets Don't Look Back: a smart American satire, authentic in both form and content, that finds room for numerous familiar faces and several spot-on pop pastiches along its way to a chilling punchline.

CIN Jean Lépine   MUS David Robbins   DES Richard Hoover   ED Lisa Churgin   PROD Forrest Murray
DIST Rank/Polygram/Working Title/Live Entertainment

66 A wry exploration of the relationship between political reality and manufactured image, showing how far contemporary politics has been reduced to the media to the level of easy-to-handle entertainment. It does have flaws, but its confidence and courage in going against the grain of an increasingly conservative America is impressive. – *Geoff Andrew, Time Out*

'He saw wrong and tried to right it. He saw suffering and tried to heal it. He saw war and tried to stop it.'

Bobby ★

SCR/DIR Emilio Estevez
2006   116m   US
DVD   ♫

☆ Harry Belafonte (Nelson), Emilio Estevez (Tim), Laurence Fishburne (Edward Robinson), Heather Graham (Angela), Anthony Hopkins (John Casey), Helen Hunt (Samantha), Ashton Kutcher (Fisher), Lindsay Lohan (Diane), William H. Macy (Paul Ebbers), Demi Moore (Virginia Fallon), Martin Sheen (Jack), Christian Slater (Daryl Timmons), Sharon Stone (Miriam Ebbers), Elijah Wood (William), Shia La Beouf (Cooper)

Intertwining stories about fictional characters in the Ambassador Hotel in Los Angeles on the day of Senator Robert Kennedy's assassination in 1968.

High-minded but flawed cross between Grand Hotel and Nashville. All the stories strive to suggest RFK's almost saintly influence at a tumultuous time in American history. Predictably, some stories work better than others. The strongest part is the depiction of Kennedy's death, which at least confirms that few politicians in 40 subsequent years could inspire such a tribute.

CIN Michael Barrett   MUS Mark Isham   DES Patti Podesta   ED Richard Chew   PROD Michael Litvak, Edward Bass, Holly Wiersma   DIST Momentum

66 Few of the characterisations could fill the back of a matchbook, and in refusing to see RFK as anything but a liberal messiah, the film meanders through its political context with a white stick and a dopey smile. – *Tim Robey, Daily Telegraph*

66 So keenly felt and deeply imagined, I couldn't help but be moved, even grateful, for its bleeding-heart nostalgia. – *Jonathan Rosenbaum, Chicago Reader*

Body and Soul ★★★

DIR *Robert Rossen*
1947   104m   US

☆ *John Garfield*, Lilli Palmer, Hazel Brooks, Anne Revere, William Conrad, Joseph Pevney, Canada Lee

A hugely ambitious young boxer from a poor Brooklyn neighbourhood stops at nothing to become champ, but finds he has sold his soul.

Garfield's intensity as a man determined to escape poverty is something to see, and director Rossen makes the most of limited resources, aided by superb photography and razor-sharp editing. It's a melodrama, but one that delivers.

SCR *Abraham Polonsky*   CIN *James Wong Howe*
MUS Hugo Friedhofer   ED *Francis Lyon, Robert Parrish*
PROD Bob Roberts   DIST Enterprise

66 Here are the gin and tinsel, squalor and sables of the depression era, less daring than when first revealed in Dead End or Golden Boy but more valid and mature because shown without sentiment or blur. – *National Board of Review*

⚐ Francis Lyon, Robert Parrish
⚐ John Garfield (leading actor); Abraham Polonsky (original screenplay)

'Never let her out of your sight. Never let your guard down. Never fall in love.'

The Bodyguard

DIR Mick Jackson
1992   130m   US
DVD   ♫

☆ Kevin Costner (Frank Farmer), Whitney Houston (Rachel 'Rach' Marron), Gary Kemp (Sy Spector), Bill Cobbs (Bill Devaney), Ralph Waite (Herb Farmer), Tomas Arana (Greg Portman), Michele Lamar Richards (Nicki Marron), Mike Starr (Tony Scipelli)

A former Secret Service agent is hired as a bodyguard by a singer who has received death threats from a stalker.

Straightforward star pairing, a commercial success despite its total shortage of originality or verve.

SCR Lawrence Kasdan   CIN Andrew Dunn   MUS Alan Silvestri, Allan Dennis Rich   DES Jeffrey Beecroft
ED Richard A. Harris, Donn Cambern   PROD Lawrence Kasdan, Jim Wilson, Kevin Costner
DIST Warner/Tig/Kasdan Pictures

66 A multimedia circus of music videos, entertainment journalism, action thriller and '60s movie melodrama carried by the dream couple of the '90s. – *Rita Kempley, Washington Post*

† Dolly Parton's song 'I Will Always Love You,' sung by Whitney Houston in the film, became a huge hit. Parton, then a struggling young unknown, had written it in the 1970s. Elvis Presley wanted to record it, but Parton refused because Presley's manager Col. Tom Parker insisted on taking half the publishing rights. In the wake of the film's release, it became the best-selling song of the 1990s, and within a year Parton was $6 million richer.

⚐ Jud Friedmann (m), Allan Rich (ly) (music, original songs – I Have Nothing, Run to You)

DVD Available on DVD   ☆ Cast in order of importance   66 Critics' Quotes   ⚐ Academy Award   🏆 BAFTA
♫ Soundtrack on CD   † Points of interest   ⚐ Academy Award nomination   🏆 BAFTA nomination

'Welcome to the New American Dream.'

Boiler Room ★

SCR/DIR Ben Younger

2000   118m   US

[DVD]   ♫

☆ Giovanni Ribisi (Seth), Vin Diesel (Chris), Nia Long (Abby), Nicky Katt (Greg), Scott Caan (Richie), Ron Rifkin (Seth's Father), Jamie Kennedy (Adam), Taylor Nichols (Harry Reynard), Tom Everett Scott (Michael), Ben Affleck (Jim Young)

A young recruit at a high-profile brokerage firm is encouraged to sell his clients failing shares.

Shouty study in brokering ethics, updating Glengarry Glen Ross for an age of hothouse corporate capitalism; the urge this time round is to sell short.

CIN Enrique Chediak   MUS The Angel   DES Anne Stuhler   ED Chris Peppe   PROD Suzanne Todd, Jennifer Todd   DIST Entertainment

66 A classic Sundance resume movie – texturally interesting, bubbling with ideas, and as structurally predictable as a cardboard box. – *Michael Atkinson, Mr. Showbiz*

Bombón El Perro ★★

DIR Carlos Sorin

2004   97m   Argentina/Spain

[DVD]

☆ Juan Villegas (Juan), Walter Donado (Walter), Rosa Valsecchi (Susana), Gregorio (Bombon (the dog))

The life of an unemployed Argentinian mechanic is subtly transformed when he is given a large, appealing dog.

Amateur actors and documentary-style shooting give this gently enjoyable, understated shaggy dog story a feeling of reassuring realism.

SCR Santiago Calori, Salvador Roselli, Carlos Sorin   CIN Hugo Colace   MUS Nicolas Sorin   DES Margarita Jusid   ED Mohamed Rajid   PROD Oscar Kramer, José María Morales   DIST TCF

66 Though this slim but likeable tale is light on surprises, there's a terrific one in store when Bombon finally comes of age. – *Matthew Leyland, BBC*

Bon Voyage

DIR Jean-Paul Rappeneau

2003   114m   France

[DVD]

☆ Isabelle Adjani (Viviane), Gerard Depardieu (Beaufort), Virginie Ledoyen (Camille), Yvan Attal (Raoul), Gregori Derangere (Frederic Roger), Peter Coyote (Winckler), Jean-Marc Stehle (Kopolski), Nicolas Pignon (Andre Arpel)

1940: with the German army approaching Paris, a convoy of unlikely travelling companions sets out for the relative calm of Bordeaux.

Glossily frenetic period piece that never seems to get anywhere; its star wattage is impressive, but it basically amounts to a series of light comic fist-fights and hissy-fits, with no real sense of the invading army's threat.

SCR Jean-Paul Rappeneau, Patrick Modiano, Jerome Tonnerre, Gilles Marchand, Julien Rappeneau

CIN Thierry Arbogast   MUS Gabriel Yared   DES Jacques Rouxel   ED Maryline Monthieux   PROD Michele Petin, Laurent Petin

66 Arrives like one of those old soldiers who stumbles from his hiding place unaware that the war is over and the world has changed – and, with it, French cinema. – *Lisa Schwarzbaum, Entertainment Weekly*

66 It's just plain exhausting to watch the admirably game cast members running around like headless chickens in chic period clothes, surrendering their dignity to the task of navigating the plot's frenetic contrivances. – *Maitland McDonagh, TV Guide*

'Take one Wall Street tycoon, his Fifth Avenue mistress, a reporter hungry for fame, and make the wrong turn in The Bronx . . . then sit back and watch the sparks fly'

The Bonfire of the Vanities

DIR Brian de Palma

1990   125m   US

[DVD]   ♫

☆ Tom Hanks (Sherman McCoy), Bruce Willis (Peter Fallow), Melanie Griffith (Maria Ruskin), Kim Cattrall (Judy McCoy), Saul Rubinek (Jed Kramer), Morgan Freeman (Judge Leonard White), F. Murray Abraham (D.A. Abe Weiss), John Hancock (Reverend Bacon), Kevin Dunn (Tom Killian), Clifton James (Albert Fox)

A Wall Street trader and his mistress take a wrong turn in the Bronx one night, igniting a media frenzy when he is arrested for a hit-and-run accident.

Notoriously misjudged, horribly miscast adaptation of a fine, much-read novel, pushing the satire into realms of contempt and condescension that are hard to bear.

SCR Michael Cristofer   CIN Vilmos Zsigmond   MUS Dave Grusin   DES Richard Sylbert   ED David Ray, Bill Pankow, Beth Jochem Besterveld   PROD Brian de Palma   DIST Warner

66 Totally misguided. – *Jeffrey M. Anderson, San Francisco Examiner*

66 The beauty of the Wolfe book was the way it saw through its time and place, dissecting motives and reading minds. The movie sees much, but it doesn't see through. – *Roger Ebert, Chicago Sun-Times*

† Wall Street Journal reporter Julie Salamon wrote a best-selling account of this troubled production, The Devil's Candy: The Bonfire of the Vanities Goes to Hollywood .
† The film's budget was an extravagant $47 million. It grossed only $15 million in the US.

'They're young. . .they're in love. . .and they kill people!'

Bonnie and Clyde ★★★★

DIR Arthur Penn

1967   111m   US

[DVD]

☆ *Warren Beatty* (Clyde Barrow), *Faye Dunaway* (Bonnie Parker), Gene Hackman (Buck Barrow), Estelle Parsons (Blanche), *Michael J. Pollard* (C.W. Moss), Dub Taylor (Ivan Moss), Denver Pyle (Frank Hamer), Gene Wilder (Eugene Grizzard)

In the early 1930s, a car thief and the daughter of his intended victim team up to become America's most feared and ruthless bank robbers.

[DVD] Available on DVD   ☆ Cast in order of importance   66 Critics' Quotes   † Points of interest   Academy Award   Academy Award nomination   BAFTA   BAFTA nomination

85

Technically brilliant evocation of sleepy mid-America at the time of the 'Public Enemies,' using every kind of cinematic trick including fake snapshots, farcical interludes, dreamy soft-focus and a jazzy score. It failed to draw sizeable audiences or overwhelmingly positive reviews on its immediate release, and the studio effectively dumped it. But among it champions, it became a huge talking point: no-one had seen such glamorisation of criminals in a mainstream studio film, nor the abrupt switches of mood between comic moments and murderous brutality. Penn drew on the French New Wave auteurs for his visual style, and to earlier American B-movies (notably Gun Crazy) that had in turn inspired them. Bonnie and Clyde looked chic, cool and ground-breaking, and eventually audiences – and awards – came its way. It remains a landmark American film.

SCR *David Newman, Robert Benton* CIN *Burnett Guffey* MUS *Charles Strouse, using 'Foggy Mountain Breakdown' by Flatt and Scruggs* ED Dede Allen PROD *Warren Beatty* DIST Warner/Seven Arts/Tatira/Hiller

66 It is a long time since we have seen an American film so perfectly judged. – *Monthly Film Bulletin*

66 It works as comedy, as tragedy, as entertainment, as a meditation on the place of guns and violence in American society. – *Roger Ebert*

† Before Beatty committed to playing Clyde, Penn reputedly wanted Bob Dylan to take the role.
† Both Jean-Luc Godard and François Truffaut were offered a chance to write the script.

⚊ Estelle Parsons (supporting actress); Burnett Guffey
⚊ picture; Warren Beatty (leading actor); Faye Dunaway (leading actress); Gene Hackman (supporting actor); Michael J. Pollard (supporting actor); Arthur Penn (direction); David Newman, Robert Benton (original screenplay); Theodora Van Runkle (costume design)

Ⓣ Faye Dunaway; Michael J. Pollard

'The life of a dreamer, the days of a business and the nights in between.'

Boogie Nights ★★★

SCR/DIR *Paul Thomas Anderson*
1997 156m US
DVD ♫

☆ *Mark Wahlberg* (Eddie Adams – 'Dirk Diggler'), *Burt Reynolds* (Jack Horner), *Julianne Moore* (Amber Waves-Maggie), John C. Reilly (Reed Rothchild), Don Cheadle (Buck Swope), Heather Graham (Brandy 'Rollergirl'), Luis Guzman (Maurice T.T. Rodriguez), *Philip Seymour Hoffman* (Scotty J), *William H. Macy* (Little Bill), Alfred Molina (Rahad Jackson)

A boyish young waiter makes it big as a performer in the adult film industry of the 1970s, only to succumb to excess a decade later.

Anderson announced himself in sensational style with a sub-cultural epic that (un)covers both porn's heyday and its demise into videotaped product throughout the 1980s. With half-a-dozen or so performances that might have won Oscars were the clips not so R-rated, it's surprisingly sweet in its portrayal of an extended family

of porno-folk, while never far from harsh truths about human desires.

CIN *Robert Elswit* MUS *Michael Penn* DES Bob Ziembicki ED *Dylan Tichenor* PROD Lloyd Levin, Paul Thomas Anderson, John Lyons, Joanne Sellar DIST Entertainment/New Line/Ghoulardi/Lawrence Gordon

66 Has the quality of many great films, in that it always seems alive. – *Roger Ebert, Chicago Sun-Times*

66 Turns retro-chic into a highly evocative, superbly designed, amusing and affectionate chronicle of one of the last great [sex] parties of the century. – *Wally Hammond, Time Out*

† Porn actor John Holmes was the inspiration for the film's Dirk Diggler character.

⚊ Burt Reynolds (supporting actor); Julianne Moore (supporting actress); Paul Thomas Anderson (original screenplay)

Ⓣ Burt Reynolds (supporting actor); Paul Thomas Anderson (original screenplay)

'Imagine having all the power, passion and pleasure money can buy. Now imagine losing them.'

The Boost ★

DIR Harold Becker
1988 95m US
DVD

☆ James Woods (Lenny Brown), Sean Young (Linda Brown), John Kapelos (Joel Miller), Steven Hill (Max Sherman), Kelle Kerr (Rochelle), John Rothman (Ned), Amanda Blake (Barbara), Grace Zabriskie (Sheryl)

A hot-shot salesman and his wife become addicted to cocaine, and their lives and marriage are ruined.

Underrated account of a chilling descent, propagandist in tone but played with real conviction.

SCR Darryl Ponicsan CIN Howard Atherton MUS Stanley Myers DES Waldemar Kalinowski ED Maury Winetrobe PROD Daniel H. Blatt DIST Hemdale/Becker-Blatt-Ponicsan

---

Das Boot ★★★

SCR/DIR *Wolfgang Petersen*
1981 149m West Germany
DVD ♫

☆ *Jürgen Prochnow*, Herbert Grönemeyer, Klaus Wennemann, Hubertus Bengsch, Martin Semmelrogge

Adventures of a German U-boat during World War II.

Arguably the best submarine movie of all, conveying brilliantly the claustrophobic atmosphere on board, and genuinely tense when it comes to stand-offs below the waves.

CIN *Jost Vacano* MUS Klaus Doldinger DES Rolf Zehetbauer PROD Gunter Röhrbach DIST Columbia/Bavaria Atelier/Radiant Film

⚊ Wolfgang Petersen (direction); Wolfgang Petersen (adapted screenplay); cinematography; editing; sound; sound editing

---

DVD Available on DVD ☆ Cast in order of importance 66 Critics' Quotes † Points of interest ⚊ Academy Award ⚊ Academy Award nomination Ⓣ BAFTA Ⓣ BAFTA nomination

'High five!'

Borat: Cultural Learnings of America for Make Benefit Glorious Nation of Kazakhstan ★

DIR Larry Charles
2006 84m US/UK
[DVD] ♫
☆ Sacha Baron Cohen (Borat), Ken Davitian (Azamat), Luenell (Luenell)

In this spoof, Borat, a Kazakh TV presenter, is ordered by his government to travel to the US and report on its way of life. He interviews Americans about feminism, sex, etiquette, humour, politics and religion. He also falls for Baywatch star Pamela Anderson, who he tries to kidnap.

A clever premise, with a straight-faced, apparently naïve foreigner coaxing outrageous, embarrassing comments from innocent, well-meaning Americans not in on the gag. Yet the film trades on gross-out humour, and picks on easy targets: evangelical Christians, rodeo rednecks, unsmiling feminists. Essentially, this is Candid Camera – with the unwelcome addition of anti-Semitic jokes. One wonders at Baron Cohen's motives: Is this a smug in-joke, a tilt at political correctness, or a cynical attempt to shock? Exasperatingly, it's a little bit of all three.

SCR Sacha Baron Cohen, Peter Baynham, Anthony Hines, Dan Mazer **CIN** Anthony Hardwick, Luke Geissbuhler **MUS** Erran Baron Cohen **ED** Peter Teschner, James Thomas **PROD** Sacha Baron Cohen, Jay Roach **DIST** TCF

BORAT: 'Jak sie masz? (How are you?) My name-a Borat. I like you. I like sex. Is nice!'

BORAT: [about women seated beside him at dinner] 'In my country, they would go crazy for these two.' [indicates minister's wife] 'This one. . .not so much. . .'

66 The brilliance of Borat is that its comedy is as pitiless as its social satire, and as brainy. – *Manohla Dargis, New York Times*

† Pamela Anderson appears uncredited as herself.
† The film was criticised by the Kazakhstan government, Jewish and gypsy groups.

⚱ Sacha Baron Cohen, Peter Baynham, Anthony Hines, Dan Mazer, Todd Phillips (adapted screenplay)

Born and Bred (new) ★★

DIR Pablo Trapero
2006 100m Argentina/Italy/UK
☆ Guillermo Pfening (Santiago), Federico Esquerro (Robert), Martina Gusman (Milli), Tomás Lipán (Cacique)

When a fashionable Buenos Aires interior designer is involved in a horrific car crash, he heads for a bleak, remote region of Patagonia and hunts animals for their skins.

Understated but unsettling account of a comfortable, affluent existence ripped apart by tragedy and guilt.

SCR Pablo Trapero, Mario Rulloni **CIN** Guillermo Nieto **MUS** Palo Pandolfo, Luis Chomicz, Las Voces Blancas

ED Ezequiel Borovinsky, Pablo Trapero **PROD** Pablo Trapero, Douglas Cummins **DIST** Axiom

66 The theme of bourgeois life being turned on its head....speaks particularly to the social and economic upheavals that Argentine has gone through in recent years. – *Sukhdev Sandhu, Daily Telegraph*

66 Trapero creates a cinematic eco-system that moment, scene by subtle scene, completely unfolds you. – *Peter Bradshaw, Guardian*

Born into Brothels ★★

SCR/DIR Zana Briski, Ross Kaufmann
2004 85m US/Canada
☆ Shanti Das, Avijit, Suchitra, Manik, Gour, Puja Merkerjee, Tapasi, Mamuni, Kochi

A documentary chronicle of photographer Zana Briski's project to put cameras (and career options) in the hands of those children living in Calcutta's red-light areas.

Somewhat unfocused where the contextualising information needs to be, but otherwise an uplifting account of social work which has had a significant effect on its young subjects' lives.

CIN Zana Briski, Ross Kaufmann **MUS** John McDowell **ED** Nancy Baker, Ross Kaufmann **PROD** Zana Briski, Ross Kaufmann **DIST** ICA

66 Designed to be "inspirational," yet it shortchanges the complex reality of the lives it makes such a show of saving. – *Owen Gleiberman, Entertainment Weekly*

⚱ documentary

'A true story of innocence lost and courage found.'

Born on the Fourth of July ★★★

DIR Oliver Stone
1989 145m US
[DVD] ♫
☆ *Tom Cruise* (Ron Kovic), Bryan Larkin (Young Ron), Raymond J. Barry (Mr. Kovic), Caroline Kava (Mrs. Kovic), Josh Evans (Tommy Kovic), Seth Allan (Young Tommy), Jamie Talisman (Jimmy Kovic), Sean Stone (Young Jimmy), Anne Bobby (Susanne Kovic), Jenna von Oy (Young Susanne)

Biopic of Ron Kovic, an all-American boy who returned from Vietnam in a wheelchair and became a pivotal figure in the anti-war movement.

Not for the first time, Stone risks alienating audiences with his methodology, although here his faith in his own wilder instincts looks more like bold, gutsy filmmaking. He draws a commanding central performance from his young lead, who stretches himself as far as Kovic's plight will allow.

SCR Oliver Stone, Ron Kovic **CIN** Robert Richardson **MUS** John Williams **DES** Bruno Rubeo **ED** David Brenner, Joe Hutshing **PROD** A Kitman Ho, Oliver Stone **DIST** UIP/Ixtlan

66 Kovic's book is simple and explicit; he states his case in plain, angry words. Stone's movie yells at you for two hours and twenty-five minutes. – *Pauline Kael, New Yorker*

66 Few recent movies have covered so much ground with such aplomb, fewer still have packed such a punch to the heart. – *Barry McIlheney, Empire*

[DVD] Available on DVD ♫ Soundtrack on CD ☆ Cast in order of importance 66 Critics' Quotes † Points of interest ⚱ Academy Award Academy Award nomination Ⓑ BAFTA Ⓣ BAFTA nomination

87

⚲ Oliver Stone; David Brenner, Joe Hutshing

⚲ picture; Tom Cruise (leading actor); John Williams; Oliver Stone, Ron Kovic (adapted screenplay); Robert Richardson

Ⓣ Tom Cruise (leading actor); Oliver Stone, Ron Kovic (adapted screenplay)

'Small Is Awesome.'

The Borrowers ★★

DIR Peter Hewitt

1997 89m GB

[DVD] ♬

☆ John Goodman (Ocious P. Potter), Jim Broadbent (Pod Clock), Mark Williams (Exterminator Jeff), Hugh Laurie (Police Officer Steady), Bradley Pierce (Pete 'Petey' Lender), Flora Newbigin (Arrietty 'Ett' Clock), Tom Felton (Peagreen Clock), Raymond Pickard (Spud Spiller), Celia Imrie (Homily Clock)

A shady lawyer intends to demolish a house where a family of tiny people live under the floorboards.

Delightful family film, with a crowd of British comic talent in its cast, and wizard special effects.

SCR Gavin Scott, John Camps **CIN** John Fenner, Trevor Brooker **MUS** Harry Gregson-Williams **DES** Gemma Jackson **ED** David Freeman **PROD** Tim Bevan, Eric Fellner, Rachel Talalay **DIST** Polygram/Working Title

66 Exemplary entertainment. – *Trevor Johnston, Time Out*

Ⓣ British film; Peter Chiang (special effects)

The Boss of It All (new) ★

SCR/DIR Lars von Trier

2006 99m Denmark/Sweden/France/Italy

[DVD]

☆ Jens Albinus (Kristoffer), Peter Gantzler (Ravn), Fridrik Thór Fridriksson (Finnur), Iben Hjejle (Lise), Sofie Grabol (Kisser), Jean-Marc Barr (Spencer), Casper Christensen (Gorm), Louise Mieritz (Mette)

An actor is hired to impersonate the non-existent head of an IT firm in order that it can be sold off to a rival.

Playful satire from a director more usually associated with grimmer fare; the result, though undeniably slight, is witty enough to make the self-referential humour forgivable.

CIN 'Automavision' **ED** Molly Marlene Stensgaard **PROD** Meta Louise Foldager, Vibeke Windelov, Signe Jensen **DIST** Diffusion Pictures

66 Pic is helmer's least pretentious and most sheerly enjoyable for years. – *Leslie Felperin, Variety*

66 A very conventional comedy of office life. – *Peter Bradshaw, Guardian*

† The cinematography was entrusted to Automavision, a computer program designed to tilt, pan and make other adjustments at random. According to von Trier, the system was designed to 'limit human influence by inviting chance in from the cold.'

Le Bossu ★

DIR Philippe de Broca

1997 128m France/Italy/Germany

[DVD]

☆ Daniel Auteuil (Lagardère/Le bossu), Fabrice Luchini (Gonzague), Vincent Perez (Duc de Nevers), Marie Gillain (Aurore), Yann Collette (Peyrolles), Jean-François Stevenin (Cocardasse), Didier Pain (Passepoil), Philippe Noiret (Philippe d'Orléans)

A swordsman poses as a hunchback in the court of a dastardly Count in order to avenge his master's death.

Old-fashioned, amusing swashbuckler in which floppy-haired knights rescue fair maidens from irredeemable schemers; mostly enjoyable, though the final duel is somewhat underwhelming.

SCR Jean Cosmos, Jerome Tonnerre, Philippe de Broca **CIN** Jean-François Robin **MUS** Philippe Sarde **DES** Bernard Vezat **ED** Henri Lanoë **PROD** Patrick Godeau **DIST** Aliceleo/TFI/CGG Tiger/Gemini

66 Consistently enjoyable, if rarely exceptional, mass entertainment. – *Variety*

Ⓣ film not in the English language

'A heist needs skill, planning and a little bit of luck. Theirs just ran out.'

Botched (new)

DIR Kit Ryan

2008 94m UK/US/Germany/Ireland

[DVD]

☆ Stephen Dorff (Ritchie Donovan), Jaime Murray (Anna), Jamie Foreman (Peter), Sean Pertwee (Mr. Groznyi), Hugh O'Conor (Dmitry), Bronagh Gallagher (Sonya), Geoff Bell (Boris)

An American thief on a job in Moscow finds himself at the mercy of a psychopathic killer.

Inane horror comedy done on a visibly low budget; laughs and scares are in short supply, though the players are game enough.

SCR Derek Boyle, Eamon Friel, Raymond Friel **CIN** Bryan Loftus **MUS** Tom Green **DES** Jon Bunker **ED** Jeremy Gibbs **PROD** Terence Ryan, Ken Tuohy, Leonid Minkovski, Serge Konoy, Alan Balladur, Thomas Fischer, Steve Richards **DIST** Optimum Releasing

66 Director Kit Ryan's attempts to walk a tonal tightrope fail dismally. – *Nigel Floyd, Time Out*

66 Unfunny and badly acted. – *Philip French, Observer*

Le Boucher ★★★★

SCR/DIR *Claude Chabrol*

1969 94m France/Italy

[DVD]

☆ *Stéphane Audran* (Helene), *Jean Yanne* (Popaul), Antonio Passalia (Angelo), Mario Beccaria (Leon Hamel)

Murders in a small French town are traced to an inoffensive-seeming young butcher who is courting the local schoolmistress.

Curious, mainly charming film which can't make up its mind whether to be an eccentric character study or a Hitchcock thriller, but works on both levels. Chabrol again does what he likes best: peering behind the bland, polite surface of the French bourgeoisie and finding ugliness and twisted desires.

CIN *Jean Rabier* **MUS** Pierre Jansen **ED** Jacques Gaillard **PROD** André Génoves **DIST** La Boétie/Euro International

[DVD] Available on DVD ♬ Soundtrack on CD ☆ Cast in order of importance 66 Critics' Quotes † Points of interest ⚲ Academy Award ⚲ Academy Award nomination Ⓑ BAFTA Ⓑ BAFTA nomination

66 A thriller, but a superlative example of the genre. – *The Times*

'A Trust So Deep It Cuts Both Ways.'

Bound ★★

SCR/DIR *Andy Wachowski, Larry Wachowski*
1996 108m US
DVD 🎵

☆ Jennifer Tilly (Violet), Gina Gershon (Corky), Joe Pantoliano (Caesar), John P. Ryan (Micky Malnato), Christopher Meloni (Johnnie Marzzone), Richard C. Sarafian (Gino Marzzone), Barry Kivel (Shelly)

A handywoman and the moll next door team up to relieve a mobster of his blood money.

Stylish latter-day noir, updated with explicit (Sapphic) sex and bloody violence: plotting is taut, camerawork fluid, the casting more or less perfect.

CIN Bill Pope   MUS Don Davis   DES Eve Cauley
ED Zach Staenberg   PROD Andrew Lazar, Stuart Boros
DIST Guild/Dino de Laurentiis/Summit/Newmarket

66 It's pure cinema, spread over several genres. It's a caper movie, a gangster movie, a sex movie and a slapstick comedy. – *Roger Ebert, Chicago Sun-Times*

66 Lovingly designed in black and white, and played with a nice sense of irony, this offers the not unappealing spectacle of gorgeous, funny, clever women making fools of hard-boiled Mafia guys. – *Kim Newman, Empire*

'He was the perfect weapon until he became the target.'

The Bourne Identity ★★

DIR Doug Liman
2002 119m US
DVD 🎵

☆ Matt Damon (Jason Bourne), Franka Potente (Marie Kreutz), Chris Cooper (Ted Conklin), Clive Owen (The Professor), Brian Cox (Ward Abbott), Adewale Akinnuoye-Agbaje (Nykwana Wombosi), Gabriel Mann (Zorn), Julia Stiles (Nicolette)

Left for dead, an American intelligence agent wakes with no memory, and attempts to piece together who he really is.

Solid, proficient action-thriller that rarely seems to strain for effect: the second hour – which has the hero chasing a paper trail across Europe, while the CIA tries to tie up its loose ends – isn't nearly as much fun as the first, but there's an unexpectedly classy cast for this kind of thing.

SCR Tony Gilroy, William Blake Herron   CIN Oliver Wood
MUS John Powell   DES Dan Weil   ED Saar Klein
PROD Doug Liman, Patrick Crowley, Richard N. Gladstein
DIST Universal

66 The movie is a generic paranoid espionage fantasy, but its proportions are refreshingly correct. It moves quickly, adroitly, and without fuss. – *David Edelstein, Slate*

'They should have left him alone.'

The Bourne Supremacy ★★★

DIR *Paul Greengrass*
2004 108m US/Germany
DVD 🎵

☆ Matt Damon (Jason Bourne), Franka Potente (Marie),

Brian Cox (Ward Abbott), Julia Stiles (Nicky), Karl Urban (Kirill), Gabriel Mann (Danny Zorn), Joan Allen (Pamela Landy)

A former CIA hitman fights to prove his innocence after being framed for the murder of two informants.

The spy franchise propelled itself into the 21st century with this second instalment, which – despite Damon's necessarily blank performance – benefits from the immediacy of Greengrass's camera, several truly exhilarating set-pieces and the continued employment of blue-chip acting talent.

SCR Tony Gilroy   CIN Oliver Wood   MUS John Powell
DES Dominic Watkins   ED Christopher Rouse, Richard Pearson   PROD Frank Marshall, Patrick Crowley, Paul L. Sandberg   DIST Universal

66 A conventionally heightened series of escapes and clashes and hide-and-seek gambits, yet the way the film has been made, nothing that happens seems inevitable - which is to say, anything seems possible. There's a word for that sensation. It's called excitement. – *Owen Gleiberman, Entertainment Weekly*

66 Rarely does pop come with such sizzle. – *Manohla Dargis, Los Angeles Times*

'Remember everything. Forgive nothing.'

The Bourne Ultimatum (new) ★★★

DIR *Paul Greengrass*
2007 115m US/Germany
DVD

☆ Matt Damon (Jason Bourne), Julia Stiles (Nicky Parsons), David Strathairn (Noah Vosen), Scott Glenn (Ezra Kramer), Paddy Considine (Simon Ross), Albert Finney (Dr. Albert Hirsch), Joan Allen (Pam Landy)

Jason Bourne, still suffering from memory loss, is determined to uncover his past and discover how he became an assassin, while a US agent tries to track him down.

The best of the Bourne trilogy, with a logical, grounded narrative and a relentless pace enhanced by quick cutting and razor-sharp editing. Two sequences, one at London's Waterloo station, the other a chase over rooftops in Tangier, represent visceral film-making at its most accomplished.

SCR Tony Gilroy, Scott Z. Burns, George Nolfi   CIN Oliver Wood   MUS John Powell   DES Peter Wenham
ED Christopher Rouse   PROD Frank Marshall, Patrick Crowley, Paul. L. Sandberg   DIST Universal

66 The only action-thriller franchise of the past decade that actually thrills. – *Sukhdev Sandhu, Daily Telegraph*

⌁ Christopher Rouse; Scott Millan, David Parker, Kirk Francis, (sound); Karen M. Baker, Per Hallberg (sound editing)

🅣 Editing; sound
🅣 British film; Paul Greengrass; Oliver Wood; visual effects

'They're going to lie, cheat and steal – but in a nice way.'

Bowfinger ★

DIR Frank Oz
1999 97m US
DVD 🎵

☆ Steve Martin (Bobby Bowfinger), Eddie Murphy (Kit

DVD Available on DVD   ☆ Cast in order   66 Critics' Quotes   ⌁ Academy Award   🅣 BAFTA
🎵 Soundtrack on CD   of importance   † Points of interest   ⌁ Academy Award nomination   🅣 BAFTA nomination

89

Ramsey/Jiff Ramsey), Heather Graham (Daisy), Christine Baranski (Carol), Jamie Kennedy (Dave), Adam Alexi-Malle (Afrim), Kohl Sudduth (Slater), Barry Newman (Kit's Agent), Robert Downey Jnr (Jerry Renfro), Terence Stamp (Terry Stricter)

A Z-grade producer covertly films an A-list star, hoping to incorporate the footage into his latest production.

Easy-going Hollywood satire, a last hurrah for its stars before their subsequent descent into family-orientated schlock.

SCR Steve Martin   CIN Ueli Steiger   MUS David Newman   DES Jackson DeGovia   ED Richard Pearson   PROD Brian Grazer   DIST Universal

66 One of those comedies where everything works. – *Roger Ebert, Chicago Sun-Times*

'Are we a nation of gun nuts or are we just nuts?'

Bowling for Columbine ★★★

SCR/DIR *Michael Moore*
2002   120m   Canada/Germany/US
DVD

Documentary response to the shootings at Columbine High School, exploring America's enduring fascination with guns.

Moore elects for a typically contentious, scattershot editorial approach, but his joined-up thinking impresses, and whole segments represent wildly funny, passionate and compassionate filmmaking. A final, botched confrontation with National Rifle Association chairman Charlton Heston aside, the director's targets are the right ones.

CIN Brian Danitz, Michael McDonough   MUS Jeff Gibbs   ED Kurt Engfehr   PROD Charles Bishop, Michael Donovan, Kathleen Glynn, Jim Czarnecki, Michael Moore   DIST Momentum

66 A brave and important piece of filmmaking that dares to ask questions that many people would prefer remain unsaid. This isn't just about guns: it's about the psychology of a nation whose every move has global implications. – *Alan Morrison, Empire*

66 Impressively reframes the gun-control debate in terms that advocates of both sides might find fruitful, but Moore doesn't do anything to shed his reputation as a snot. – *Shawn Levy, Portland Oregonian*

documentary

'Some people have a hard time unwinding.'

Box of Moonlight ★

SCR/DIR Tom DiCillo
1996   112m   US
DVD

☆ *John Turturro* (Al Fountain), Sam Rockwell (Kid), Catherine Keener (Floatie Dupre), Lisa Blount (Purlene Dupre), Annie Corley (Deb Fountain), Rica Martens (Doris), Ray Aranha (Soapy), Alexander Goodwin (Bobby Fountain), Dermot Mulroney (Wick)

A stressed construction engineer takes off for the countryside and learns how to unwind from a boyish forest-dweller.

Gentle, uplifting tale of self-fulfilment from a director clearly relishing the opportunity to get out in the fresh air.

CIN Paul Ryan   MUS Jim Farmer   DES Thérèse DePrez   ED Camilla Toniolo   PROD Marcus Viscidi, Thomas A. Bliss   DIST First Independent/Lakeshore/Largo/JVC/Lemon Sky

66 One of the best independent films of the year. . . Turturro has never been better. – *Derek Malcolm, Guardian*

'Love is always worth fighting for.'

The Boxer ★

DIR Jim Sheridan
1997   113m   GB/Ireland/US
DVD   ♫

☆ *Daniel Day-Lewis* (Danny Flynn), *Emily Watson* (Maggie), Brian Cox (Joe Hamill), Ken Stott (Ike Weir), Gerard McSorley (Harry), Eleanor Methven (Patsy), Ciaran Fitzgerald (Liam), Kenneth Cranham (Matt MaGuire)

Upon his release from prison, an ex-IRA man opens a gym for young people, and attempts to rekindle an old romance.

Redemption drama of a kind often seen in American pictures; its grasp of the Troubles is less convincing than the two lead performances.

SCR Jim Sheridan, Terry George   CIN Chris Menges   MUS Gavin Friday, Maurice Seezer   DES Brian Morris   ED Gerry Hambling, Clive Barrett   PROD Jim Sheridan, Arthur Lappin   DIST Universal/Hell's Kitchen

66 The movie's acts of violence and betrayal may be familiar, but the filmmakers' obvious contempt for people given over to fanaticism is enormously welcome – a call for the most elementary kind of sanity. – *David Denby, New York Magazine*

66 A well-meaning, competent effort that will look good on television. On the big screen, it's let down by worthiness and a tendency to preach. – *Christpher Tookey, Daily Mail*

† Day-Lewis trained for his role with the Irish former boxing champion Barry McGuigan, and became hugely proficient in the ring.

'A True Story About Finding The Courage To Be Yourself.'

Boys Don't Cry ★★★

DIR Kimberly Peirce
1999   118m   US
DVD   ♫

☆ *Hilary Swank* (Brandon Teena), *Chloe Sevigny* (Lana), Peter Sarsgaard (John), Brendan Sexton III (Tom), Alison Folland (Kate), Alicia Goranson (Candace), Matt McGrath (Lonny), Rob Campbell (Brian), Jeannetta Arnette (Lana's Mom)

Nebraska, the early 1990s: young Teena Brandon chooses, with tragic consequences, to pass herself off as a boy in order to pick up other girls in bars.

One of the most singular debut films of recent years: a heartrending, harrowing work that plays like a true-life Jerry Springer story without any of the attendant sensationalism or sleaze. Instead, Pierce covers Teena's final fling with intelligence, great heart and vivid performances from her up-and-coming cast.

DVD Available on DVD   ☆ Cast in order of importance   66 Critics' Quotes   † Points of interest   Academy Award   Academy Award nomination   ♫ Soundtrack on CD   BAFTA   BAFTA nomination

SCR Kimberly Peirce, Andy Bienen   CIN Jim Denault
MUS Nathan Larson   DES Michael Shaw   ED Lee Percy,
Tracy Granger   PROD Jeffrey Sharp, John Hart, Eva
Kolodner, Christine Vachon   DIST TCF

66 An amazing work, a film that seems to gurgle up from
the American heartland, resonant and fully formed, ripe
with possibilities. – *Marjorie Baumgarten, Austin Chronicle*

66 The longest, hardest sit of the season – you are stuck
there, a single tube of puckered muscle, waiting for the
extremely ugly violence to occur – but it is driven by
performances of such luminous humanity that they break
your heart. – *Stephen Hunter, Washington Post*

Ⓘ Hilary Swank (leading actress)
Ⓘ Chloe Sevigny (supporting actress)
Ⓣ Hilary Swank (leading actress)

'Increase The Peace.'

Boyz N the Hood   ★★★

SCR/DIR *John Singleton*
1991   112m   US
DVD   ♫

☆ Ice Cube (Darin 'Doughboy' Baker), *Cuba Gooding Jnr*
(Tre Styles), Morris Chestnut (Ricky Baker), *Larry
Fishburne* (Jason 'Furious' Styles), Nia Long (Brandi), Tyra
Ferrell (Brenda Baker)

Several boyhood friends come of age against the
backdrop of South Central Los Angeles.

*Powerhouse social drama, the most impressive of the
films emanating from the New Black Cinema of the
early 90s: Singleton's scenes of street life are dotted with
moments of humour and poignancy, before tragedy
sweeps in with full emotional force.*

CIN Charles Mills   MUS Stanley Clarke, Roger Troutman
ED Bruce Cannon   PROD Steve Nicolaides
DIST Columbia TriStar

66 There are no cheap shots, nothing is thrown in for
effect, realism is placed ahead of easy dramatic payoffs,
and the audience grows deeply involved. – *Roger Ebert,
Chicago Sun-Times*

† Singleton was just 22 at the time of the film's
production.

Ⓘ John Singleton (as director); John Singleton (screenplay)

'A romantic comedy about a boy, a girl and their power
tools.'

Braindead   ★

DIR Peter Jackson
1992   104m   New Zealand
DVD   ♫

☆ Timothy Balme (Lionel Cosgrove), Diana Penalver
(Paquita Maria Sanchez), Elizabeth Moody (Mum), Ian
Watkin (Uncle Les), Brenda Kendal (Nurse McTavish),
Stuart Devenie (Father McGruder), Jed Brophy (Void)

A 25-year-old virgin's attempts at finding true love
are hampered by his overbearing mother and a
cellar full of zombies.

*Gory comedy of manners that often feels like Abigail's
Party as directed by a George A. Romero wannabe; a
few engaging cultural observations can be made out
beneath its orgiastic splatter.*

SCR Stephen Sinclair, Frances Walsh, Peter Jackson
CIN Murray Milne   MUS Peter Dasent   DES Kenneth
Leonard-Jones   ED Jamie Selkirk   PROD Jim Booth
DIST Polygram/Wingnut Films

LIONEL: That's my mother you're pissing on!

66 A gonzo splatterfest from New Zealand that manages to
stay breezy and good-natured even as you're watching
heads get snapped off of spurting torsos. – *Owen
Gleiberman, Entertainment Weekly*

66 It's a good job the director grew out of making this
stuff. – *Christopher Tookey, Daily Mail*

'Love Never Dies.'

Bram Stoker's Dracula

DIR Francis Ford Coppola
1992   128m   US
DVD   ♫

☆ Gary Oldman (Count Dracula), Winona Ryder (Mina
Murray), Anthony Hopkins (Van Helsing), Keanu Reeves
(Jonathan Harker)

15th-century Romanian king Vlad the Impaler
denounces God and turns to evil; as the immortal
Count Dracula, he chances across the image of his
lost love in Victorian London.

*Sexed-up, wildly overblown updating of Stoker's novel –
some nice touches in the production design, but the cast
sink collectively under the weight of their director's most
pretentious flourishes.*

SCR James V. Hart   CIN Michael Ballhaus
MUS Wojciech Kilar   DES Thomas Sanders
ED Nicholas C. Smith, Glen Scantlebury, Anne Goursaud
PROD Francis Ford Coppola, Fred Fuchs, Charles Mulvehill
DIST Columbia TriStar/American Zoetrope/Osiris

66 A lovingly made, gorgeously realised, meticulously
crafted failure. It has big names, a big budget, big sets, a
big, thundering score and even big hair. But it doesn't do
it. It doesn't excite or fascinate but just lies there on the
screen. – *Mick LaSalle, San Francisco Chronicle*

66 The eye and the ear are dazzled, but the nose must be
held. – *John Simon, National Review*

Ⓘ Tom C. McCarthy, David E. Stone (sound effects editing);
Greg Cannon, Michele Burke, Matthew W. Mungle
(makeup); Eiko Ishioka (costume design)
Ⓘ Thomas Sanders

Ⓣ Thomas Saunders; Roman Coppola, Gary Gutierrez,
Michael Lantien, Gene Warren Jr. (special effects); Eiko
Ishioka (costume); Greg Cannon, Michele Burke, Matthew
W. Mungle (makeup)

'Fed up with the system. Ticked off at the establishment.
And mad about. . .each other.'

Brassed Off   ★★★

SCR/DIR *Mark Herman*
1996   107m   GB
DVD   ♫

☆ *Pete Postlethwaite* (Danny), Tara Fitzgerald (Gloria),
Ewan McGregor (Andy), Jim Carter (Harry), *Stephen
Tompkinson* (Phil), Ken Colley (Greasely), Stephen Moore
(Mackenzie), Peter Gunn (Simmo), Mary Healey (Ida),
Melanie Hill (Sandra), Philip Jackson (Jim), Sue Johnston
(Vera)

DVD Available on DVD   ☆ Cast in order   66 Critics' Quotes   Ⓘ Academy Award   Ⓑ BAFTA
♫ Soundtrack on CD   of importance   † Points of interest   Ⓘ Academy Award nomination   Ⓣ BAFTA nomination

91

A brass band from a struggling mining community attempt to win a national competition.

An entertaining and skilfully played ensemble piece, not so far removed from minor-key Ken Loach: like the music the band play, it has grit and humour, melancholy and heart.

CIN Andy Collins **MUS** Trevor Jones **DES** Don Taylor
ED Michael Ellis **PROD** Steve Abbott **DIST** Film Four/Miramax/Prominent Features

66 Trimmed to an hour, and tucked between a documentary on snails and an episode of Coronation Street, writer-director Mark Herman's Brassed Off could prove lively watching indeed. As it is, however, his pedestrian if sweetly well-meaning inspirational. . .is too long, too laborious and 15 years too late. – *Manohla Dargis, LA Weekly*

66 Comes close to turning into a rant, not so much Brassed Off as Sounding Off. But it survives through its never-failing sense of humour. . .It is a triumph of ensemble acting, of authentic grit and wit. – *Quentin Curtis, Daily Telegraph*

ⓣ British film; Mark Herman (original screenplay); Trevor Jones

---

'Get ready. Get glam. Get real.'

Bratz (new)

DIR Sean McNamara
2007   101m   US
DVD   ♫

☆ Nathalia Ramos (Yasmin), Janel Parrish (Jade), Logan Browning (Sasha), Skyler Shaye (Cloe), Chelsea Staub (Meredith), Jon Voight (Principal Dimly), Lainie Kazan (Bubbie)

Four girlfriends drift apart in a high school whose students are segregated into mutually exclusive cliques.

Abrasive, obnoxious teen fare inspired by a range of dolls; one wonders whether the originals might have given more authentic performances.

SCR Susan Estelle Jansen **CIN** Christian Sebaldt
MUS John Coda **DES** Rusty Smith **ED** Jeff W. Canavan
PROD Avi Arad, Steven Paul, Isaac Larian
DIST Momentum

66 A high school story that feels hastily composed from fragments of much better movies. – *Jeannette Catsoulis, New York Times*

66 Excruciatingly inane. – *Lou Lumenick, New York Post*

† Paula Abdul was originally hired as a choreographer and designer, only to be sacked during production.

'How many wrongs to make it right?'

The Brave One (new)

DIR Neil Jordan
2007   122m   US
DVD   ♫

☆ Jodie Foster (Erica Bain), Terrence Howard (Det. Sean Mercer), Naveen Andrews (David Kirmani), Nicky Katt (Det. Vitale), Mary Steenburgen (Carol), Carmen Ejogo (Jackie)

A New York radio host takes revenge against the gang that killed her fiancé, and anyone else who gets in her way.

Glum, ponderous stab at a vigilante thriller from a director and star from which one expects more. The plot holes outnumber the bullet holes by a considerable margin.

SCR Roderick Taylor, Bruce A. Taylor, Cynthia Mort
CIN Philippe Rousselot **MUS** Dario Marianelli
DES Kristi Zea **ED** Tony Lawson **PROD** Joel Silver, Susan Downey **DIST** Warner Bros

66 Trapped in a no man's land between seriousness and pulp trash, it plays like a combination of Death Wish and The Hours. – *Kenneth Turan, Los Angeles Times*

66 A pro-lynching movie that even liberals can love. – *A.O. Scott, New York Times*

'His passion captivated a woman. His courage inspired a country. His heart defied a king.'

Braveheart   ★★

DIR *Mel Gibson*
1995   177m   US
DVD   ♫

☆ Mel Gibson (William Wallace), Sophie Marceau (Princess Isabelle), Patrick McGoohan (Longshanks, King Edward I), Catherine McCormack (Murron), Brendan Gleeson (Hamish), James Cosmo (Campbell), Alun Armstrong (Mornay), Angus Macfadyen (Robert the Bruce), Ian Bannen (The Leper)

Scottish rebel William Wallace rallies an army of various clans against English king Edward I.

A historically questionable account of Wallace's life and death with a hackneyed script. But it undoubtedly makes for stirring widescreen cinema, heading off Hollywood glamour with a mixture of mud, blood and guts.

SCR Randall Wallace **CIN** *John Toll* **MUS** James Horner **DES** Tom Sanders **ED** Steven Rosenblum
PROD Mel Gibson, Alan Ladd Jnr, Bruce Davey
DIST TCF/Icon/Ladd

66 Doesn't have enough on its mind to sustain our full attention over that span. Freedom, Wallace keeps telling everyone, is a good thing, worth dying for. Tyranny, on the other hand, is a bad thing. It leads to rape and pillage, and besides, its soldiers always march in straight lines, which is stupid. – *Richard Schickel, Time*

66 At its best, it's an exhilaratingly grandiose Highland fling. – *Michael Wilmington, Chicago Tribune*

⚎ picture; Mel Gibson; John Toll; Lon Bender, Per Hallberg (sound effects editing); Peter Frampton, Paul Pattison, Lois Burwell (makeup)
⚎ Randall Wallace (original screenplay); James Horner; Steven Rosenblum; Andy Nelson, Scott Millan, Anna Behlmer, Brian Simmons (sound); Charles Knode (costume design)

ⓑ John Toll; Per Hallberg, Lon Bender, Brian Simmons, Andy Nelson, Scott Millan, Anna Behlmer (sound); Charles Knode (costume design)
ⓣ Mel Gibson; James Horner; Thomas E. Sanders; Peter Frampton, Paul Pattison, Lois Burwell (make up/hair)

DVD Available on DVD   ☆ Cast in order   66 Critics' Quotes   ⚎ Academy Award   ⓑ BAFTA
♫ Soundtrack on CD   of importance   † Points of interest   ⚎ Academy Award nomination   ⓣ BAFTA nomination

Brazil ★★★★

DIR *Terry Gilliam*
1985   142m   GB
DVD   ♫

☆ *Jonathan Pryce*, Robert De Niro, Michael Palin, Kim Greist, Katherine Helmond, Ian Holm, Ian Richardson, Peter Vaughan, Bob Hoskins

A dutiful clerk in a bureaucratic, futuristic police state stays out of trouble – until he gets a glimpse of his dream girl and springs into action.

A brilliantly inventive science-fiction fantasia, with a striking 'retro-futuristic' production design, a garbled plot and a strange amalgam of black comedy, violence and arresting visual images. It may have been too rich by half for studio suits, but it's one of this erratic director's finest moments.

SCR *Terry Gilliam, Tom Stoppard, Charles McKeown* CIN *Roger Pratt* MUS Michael Kamen DES Norman Garwood ED *Julian Doyle* PROD Arnon Milchan DIST Embassy

66 It will not be everybody's cup of poisoned tea. – *Variety*

66 Exuberantly violent, cruelly funny and sometimes sickeningly scatological. . .the whole is wrapped up in a melancholy wistfulness. – *Sight & Sound*

† Gilliam fell out badly with senior Universal executive Sid Sheinberg over Brazil: Sheinberg wanted to cut it, while Gilliam insisted it remain unedited. The director took out ads in the trade press, protesting against Sheinberg's inflexibility. He held a series of secret screenings around Hollywood, and finally showed it to members of the Los Angeles Critics' Association, who promptly named it the year's best film, and also gave it awards for best director and screenplay, even though it had not been released. Universal gave in, and gave it a modest release – uncut.

⚲ original screenplay; art direction

🛡 production design

Breach (new) ★★

DIR *Billy Ray*
2007   110m   US
DVD   ♫

☆ *Chris Cooper* (Robert Hanssen), Ryan Philippe (Eric O'Neill), Laura Linney (Kate Burroughs), Dennis Haybert (Dean Plesac), Gary Cole (Rich Garces)

A young FBI agent spies on a veteran colleague accused of selling secrets to the Soviets.

Based on a true story, this cerebral battle of wits is arguably too understated for its own good. It's nevertheless intriguing and intelligent.

SCR Adam Mazer, William Rotko, Billy Ray   CIN Tak Fujimoto   MUS Mychael Danna   DES Wynn Thomas ED Jeffrey Ford   PROD Bobby Newmyer, Scott Strauss, Scott Kroopf   DIST TCF

66 Tense, fascinating, worthwhile. – *Trevor Johnston, Time Out*

66 Breach resembles Hitchcock's supreme masterpiece Notorious, a thriller devoid of violence but packed with suspense. – *Philip French, Observer*

† In 2001, FBI agent Robert Hanssen was arrested for passing US government secrets to the Soviets. His treachery, now regarded as the worst security leak in FBI history, had remained undetected for two decades.

'The Balance Of Power Is About To Change.'

Bread and Roses ★★

DIR Ken Loach
2000   110m   GB/Germany/Spain/Italy/France
DVD

☆ Pilar Padilla (Maya), Adrien Brody (Sam), Elpidia Carrillo (Rosa), Jack McGee (Bert), George Lopez (Perez), Alonso Chavez (Ruben), Monica Rivas (Simona), Frank Davila (Luis)

Office cleaners in Los Angeles band together to join a union and protest against their low pay and poor working conditions.

For years Ken Loach resisted the temptation to make a film in America, and when he did typically gravitated towards a very different side of Los Angeles from those usually portrayed by Hollywood. This is a heart-on-sleeve account of underpaid workers, almost invisible to their affluent bosses, struggling to be heard and represented. Brody has good moments as an impassioned union worker, but it's Loach's shrewd deployment of a mostly non-professional cast that makes the film distinctive.

SCR Paul Laverty   CIN Barry Ackroyd, Haskell Wexler MUS George Fenton   DES Martin Johnson ED Jonathan Morris   PROD Rebecca O'Brien

66 The keen sense of moral responsibility informing the production makes most current cinema look fatuously self-absorbed by comparison. – *Peter Matthews, Sight & Sound*

'Imagine your life. Now go live it.'

Bread and Tulips ★★

DIR Silvio Soldini
2000   114m   Italy/Switzerland
DVD

☆ *Licia Maglietta* (Rosalba), Bruno Ganz (Fernando), Giuseppe Battiston (Costantino), Marina Massironi (Grazia), Antonio Catania (Mimmo)

Inadvertently abandoned by her insensitive family on a cheap-rate coach tour, a middle-aged Italian housewife makes her way to Venice and starts a new life there, finding romance and a very different set of friends.

Unapologetically aimed at older audiences, this slight but appealing comedy has distinct charm, and Maglietta inhabits her character with graceful authority.

SCR Doriana Leondeff, Silvio Soldini   CIN Luca Bigazzi MUS Giovanni Venosta   DES Paola Bizzarri   ED Carlotta Cristiani   PROD Daniele Maggioni

66 Actresses such as Maglietta are why movies were invented: You never get tired of her mercurial personality or of her infinitely compelling face. – *Carrie Rickey, Philadelphia Inquirer*

66 With its dream sequences, eccentric supporting characters and bitter-sweet sensibilities, it follows its own singular path, whilst mostly retaining a fairy-tale charm. – *Tom Dawson, BBC*

DVD Available on DVD   ☆ Cast in order   66 Critics' Quotes   ⚲ Academy Award   🛡 BAFTA
♫ Soundtrack on CD   of importance   † Points of interest   ⚲ Academy Award nomination   🛡 BAFTA nomination

'A cross-country trip. An unexpected breakdown. The trap has been set.'

Breakdown ★★

DIR *Jonathan Mostow*

1997 95m US

DVD

☆ *Kurt Russell* (Jeff), *J.T. Walsh* (Red), Kathleen Quinlan (Amy Taylor), M.C. Gainey (Earl), Jack Noseworthy (Billy), Rex Linn (Sheriff Boyd), Ritch Brinkley (Al), Moira Harris (Arleen Barr)

After their car breaks down in the middle of nowhere, a man finds that his wife has disappeared.

An expert suspense thriller, carried manfully by its star.

SCR Jonathan Mostow, Sam Montgomery **CIN** Doug Milsome **MUS** Basil Poledouris **DES** Victoria Paul **ED** Derek Brechin, Kevin Stitt **PROD** Martha De Laurentiis, Dino De Laurentiis **DIST** TCF/Dino de Laurentiis/Spelling

66 Feels at first so casual, so comfortable with its own small expectations (a good but unglamorous cast, a sturdy but unspectacular plot), that the authentic feelings of suspense are a surprise. – *Lisa Schwartzbaum, Entertainment Weekly*

66 A tough, vigorous exercise in pure action, shot with throwback expertise and, most refreshingly, without special effects. – *Elvis Mitchell, New York Times*

'When they speak of heroes – of villains – of men who look for action, who choose between honour and revenge – they tell the story of "Breaker" Morant.'

'Breaker' Morant ★★★

DIR Bruce Beresford

1980 107m Australia

DVD

☆ *Edward Woodward* (Lt. Harry Morant), *Jack Thompson* (Maj. J.F. Thomas), *Bryan Brown* (Lt. Peter Handcock), Charles Tingwell (Lt. Col. Denny), Terence Donovan (Capt. Simon Hunt), Vincent Ball (Lt. Ian (Johnny) Hamilton), John Waters (Capt. Alfred Taylor)

During the Boer War, three Australian officers are court-martialled for murdering prisoners.

Careful, moving, well-acted military drama which gives a more sympathetic view of the facts than history suggests. This was a commercial success in many territories, thus reinforcing the boom in Australia's film industry at the time.

SCR Jonathan Hardy, Bruce Beresford, David Stevens **CIN** Donald McAlpine **ED** William Anderson **PROD** Matthew Carroll **DIST** South Australian Film Corporation

66 It is impossible to suppress a feeling that the spirit of Stanley Kramer is abroad on the veldt. – *Tim Pulleine, Monthly Film Bulletin*

⚲ screenplay

Breakfast at Tiffany's ★

DIR Blake Edwards

1961 115m US

DVD ♫

☆ Audrey Hepburn (Holly Golightly), George Peppard

(Paul Varjak), Patricia Neal (2-E), Buddy Ebsen (Doc Golightly), Martin Balsam (O.J. Berman), *John McGiver* (Tiffany salesman), Mickey Rooney (Mr. Yunioshi)

A young New York writer has as a neighbour the volatile Holly Golightly, an unstable but extrovert call-girl with an exotic social and emotional life.

Director Edwards skilfully re-creates the milieu of an amusing New York social scene in which the young and glamorous look better off than they really are. The adaptation of Truman Capote's novel has been cleansed of any tough-mindedness and insalubrious elements, to the extent it's unclear what Holly actually does. The film's lasting legacy is the image of Hepburn, in a long black dress and with a cigarette holder, looking fabulous.

SCR *George Axelrod* **CIN** Franz Planer **MUS** Henry Mancini **ED** Howard Smith **PROD** Martin Jurow, Richard Shepherd **DIST** Paramount

⚲ Henry Mancini; Henry Mancini (m), Johnny Mercer (ly) (music, original song – Moon River)

⚲ Audrey Hepburn (leading actress); George Axelrod (adapted screenplay); art direction

---

'Love is no ordinary crime.'

Breaking and Entering ★

SCR/DIR Anthony Minghella

2006 118m UK/US

DVD ♫

☆ Jude Law (Will Francis), Juliette Binoche (Amira), Robin Wright Penn (Liv), Marti Freeman (Sandy Hoffman), Ray Winstone (Bruno Fella), Vera Farmiga (Oana), Rafi Gavron (Miro), Poppy Rogers (Bea)

An affluent London landscape architect's brush with a young burglar leads him into an affair with the boy's mother, a Bosnian refugee.

This state-of-the-nation story delivers less than it promises. It tackles big themes: immigration, class, parenthood, infidelity and the cost of urban renewal. But Minghella, striving for parallels, over-reaches himself: Will and Liv's marriage, foundering on benign mutual neglect, is made to mirror Britain's indifference to its refugees. The script buckles under this weight, and many characters are just embodiments of an idea. Yet the film perfectly captures the gleam of London's Kings Cross, once a slum but now ordered and aesthetically pleasing.

CIN Benoit Delhomme **MUS** Gabriel Yared, Underworld **DES** Alex McDowell **ED** Lisa Gunning **PROD** Sydney Pollack, Anthony Minghella, Timothy Bricknell **DIST** Buena Vista

AMIRA: 'You steal someone's heart, that's a crime.'

AMIRA: 'No story from Sarajevo is simple.'

WILL: 'When did we stop looking at each other?'

66 Flawed but complex and ambitious, a watchable, good-looking film. – *Peter Bradshaw, Guardian*

† This was the final feature film written and directed by Minghella, who died in March 2008. But his TV film The No. 1 Ladies' Detective Agency was broadcast by the BBC only days after his death.

Breaking Away ★

DIR *Peter Yates*

1979   101m   US

☆ *Dennis Christopher*, Dennis Quaid, Daniel Stern, Jackie Earle Haley, *Barbara Barrie*, Paul Dooley

A teenager from America's mid-west has trouble settling on his life's ambition, but is meanwhile besotted by cycling and the Italians who are legends at the sport.

Charming comedy about Middle American values and a boy's instinct to look for something beyond small-town life. The parents' bemusement when Christopher starts affecting an Italian accent is joyous to behold.

SCR *Steve Tesich*   CIN *Matthew F. Leonetti*   MUS Patrick Williams   PROD Peter Yates   DIST TCF

66 Affection for the middle classes, the landscapes of Indiana, and bicycle racing. – *New Yorker*

66 Here's a sunny, goofy, intelligent little film about coming of age in Bloomington, Indiana. – *Roger Ebert*

⚖ Steve Tesich (original screenplay)

⚖ picture; Barbara Barrie (supporting actress); Peter Yates (direction); Patrick Williams

Ⓣ Dennis Christopher (leading actor)

'An amateur thief and a professional robber team up for an outrageous comic heist.'

Breaking In ★

DIR Bill Forsyth

1989   94m   US

DVD

☆ Burt Reynolds (Ernie Mullins), Casey Siemaszko (Mike Lafeve), Sheila Kelley (Carrie aka Fonatine), Lorraine Toussaint (Delphine the Hooker), Albert Salmi (Johnny Scot), Harry Carey (Shoes), Maury Chaykin (Vincent Tucci)

An ageing burglar teaches his tricks to a younger man.

Hardly a career highlight for its director or writer, both hugely gifted; but an agreeably warm comedy.

SCR John Sayles   CIN Michael Coulter   MUS Michael Gibbs   DES Adrienne Atkinson, John Willett   ED Michael Ellis   PROD Harry Gittes   DIST Castle Premier/Breaking In Productions/Sam Goldwyn Company

66 Forsyth doesn't so much resolve his story as suspend it; it just hangs there. It's just possible that he's a master. But something in you pulls back from the highest praise. – *Hal Hinson, Washington Post*

'Love is a mighty power.'

Breaking the Waves ★★

DIR *Lars von Trier*

1996   159m   Denmark/Sweden/France/Netherlands

DVD   ♫

☆ *Emily Watson* (Bess), Stellan Skarsgård (Jan), Katrin Cartlidge (Dodo), Jean-Marc Barr (Terry), Udo Kier (Man on the Trawler), Adrian Rawlins (Dr. Richardson), Jonathan Hackett (The Minister), Sandra Voe (Bess' Mother)

A young Scotswoman who claims to converse with God is invited by her injured oil-rigger husband to take new lovers for herself.

A working definition of love-it-or-loathe-it cinema: a latter-day religious parable shot on the nascent digital video format, with its lead actress enduring a fair amount of sex and suffering. Everyone involved is at least taking risks, and even if you have cause to doubt von Trier's sincerity, there is cause for wonder in the natural imagery his camera seeks out.

SCR *Lars von Trier, Peter Asmussen*   CIN *Robby Müller*   MUS Joachim Holbek   DES Karl Júlíusson   ED Anders Refn   PROD Vibeke Windelöv, Peter Aalbaek Jensen   DIST Guild/Zentropa/Trust/Liberator/Argus/Northern Lights

66 True art is a journey to somewhere you've never been, and there has never been a movie quite like Breaking the Waves. – *Owen Gleiberman, Entertainment Weekly*

66 A narrative path leading from the sincere to the ludicrous. . .culminating in a final image of flabbergasting transcendance. – *Elvis Mitchell, New York Times*

† The film won the Grand Jury Prize at the Cannes Film Festival in 1996.

⚖ Emily Watson (leading actress)

Ⓣ Emily Watson (leading actress)

'A detective story.'

Brick ★

SCR/DIR *Rian Johnson*

2005   117m   US

DVD   ♫

☆ Joseph Gordon-Levitt (Brendan Frye), Nora Zehetner (Laura), Lukas Haas (The Pin), Noah Fleiss (Tugger), Matt O'Leary (The Brain), Noah Segan (Dode)

A loner high-school student rubs up against a local kingpin and a femme fatale while investigating the death of his ex-girlfriend.

Shot-on-a-shoestring Sundance festival fave transposes noir conventions onto the teen movie; ultimately, it knows more about other films than it does about real life, but Johnson brings a fresh eye to his LA locations, and there's a cherishably eccentric soundtrack.

CIN Steve Yedlin   MUS *Nathan Johnson*   DES Jodie Tillen   PROD Ram Bergman, Mark G. Mathis   DIST Optimum

66 A smart, original neo-noir that works as an ingenious mindgame as well as a slick Hollywood calling card. – *Damon Wise, Empire*

66 All in all, this twerpy little movie is one of the most entertaining pictures to be released so far this year. – *David Denby, The New Yorker*

'Love is a mighty power.'

Brick Lane (new) ★

DIR *Sarah Gavron*

2007   101m   UK

DVD   ♫

☆ Tannishtha Chatterjee (Nazneen), *Satish Kaushik* (Chanu), Christopher Simpson (Karim), Naeema Begum (Shahana), Lana Rahman (Bibi)

A young Bangladeshi woman leaves behind her beloved sister to live in London's East End with her demanding, under-achieving husband, with who she has two children. Disillusioned with her life,

---

she takes on work as a seamstress and starts a tryst with her young boss.

A decent, thoughtfully shot account of the external incidents from Monica Ali's novel, but the film denies Chatterjee's Nazneen an inner voice; as a result it lacks the emotional punch it should rightfully pack.

SCR Abi Morgan, Laura Jones   **CIN** *Robbie Ryan*
MUS Jocelyn Pook   **DES** Simon Elliott   **ED** Melanie Oliver   **PROD** Alison Owen, Christopher Collins
DIST Optimum

66 A lovely movie. If only it were a little more exciting. – *David Denby, New Yorker*

66 The romance at the heart of Brick Lane never comes alive. Chatterjee is doleful and weepy, Simpson enervated. – *Sukhdev Sandhu, Daily Telegraph*

🏆 Sarah Gavron (Most promising newcomer)

'Bollywood meets Hollywood. . .And it's a perfect match.'
Bride and Prejudice ★★
DIR Gurinder Chadha
2004   110m   GB
DVD   🎵

☆ Aishwarya Rai (Lalita Bakshi), Martin Henderson (Will Darcy), Anupam Kher (Mr Bakshi), Nadira Babbar (Mrs Bakshi), Naveen Andrews (Raj), Namrata Shirodkar (Jaya Bakshi), Daniel Gillies (Johnny Wickham)

An Indian wife is desperate to find suitable spouses for all her four eligible daughters.

Director Chadha has transposed Jane Austen's story to a dull Indian town, but turns it into a multi-coloured Bollywood extravaganza. It's a delightful conceit, though there's zero chemistry between her stiff leads: Rai as the Elizabeth Bennet equivalent Lalita, and Henderson as Darcy.

SCR Paul Mayeda Berges, Gurinder Chadha   **CIN** Santosh Sivan   **MUS** Craig Pruess   **DES** Nick Ellis   **ED** Justin Krish   **PROD** Deepak Nayar, Gurinder Chadha
DIST Pathé

66 Gurinder Chadha's film has all the feminist clout of a giant blancmange. – *James Christopher, The Times*

'The monster demands a mate!'
The Bride of Frankenstein ★★★★
DIR *James Whale*
1935   90m   US
DVD   🎵

☆ *Boris Karloff* (The Monster), Colin Clive (Henry Frankenstein), *Ernest Thesiger* (Dr Septimus Praetorius), Valerie Hobson (Elizabeth Frankenstein), *E. E. Clive* (Burgomaster), Dwight Frye, O. P. Heggie (Hermit), Una O'Connor (Minnie), *Elsa Lanchester* (Mary Shelley and the monster's mate), Gavin Gordon (Byron), Douglas Walton

Baron Frankenstein is blackmailed by Dr Praetorius into reviving his monster and building a mate for it.

Frankenstein was startlingly good in a primitive way; this sequel is the screen's sophisticated masterpiece of black comedy, with all the talents working deftly to one end. Every scene has its own delights, and they are woven together into a superb if wilful cinematic narrative which, of its gentle mocking kind, has never been surpassed.

SCR *John L. Balderston, William Hurlbut*   **CIN** *John Mescall*
MUS *Franz Waxman*   **ED** Ted Kent   **PROD** Carl Laemmle Jnr   **DIST** Universal

FRANKENSTEIN: I've been cursed for delving into the mysteries of life!

66 It is perhaps because Whale was by now master of the horror film that this production is the best of them all. – *John Baxter, 1968*

66 An extraordinary film, with sharp humour, macabre extravagance, and a narrative that proceeds at a fast, efficient pace. – *Gavin Lambert, 1948*

† The regular release version runs 75m, having dropped part of the Mary Shelley prologue and a sequence in which the monster becomes unsympathetic by murdering the burgomaster

† The title was originally to have been The Return of Frankenstein.

🎬 Gilbert Kurland (sound recording)

The Bridesmaid ★
DIR Claude Chabrol
2004   111m   France/Germany/Italy
DVD

☆ Benoît Magimel (Philippe Tardieu), Laura Smet (Stéphanie 'Senta' Bellange), Aurore Clément (Christine), Bernard Le Coq (Gérard Courtois), Solène Bouton (Sophie Tardieu), Anna Mihalcea (Patricia Tardieu)

A mother-fixated young man has a deadly liaison with a bridesmaid at his sister's wedding.

Silly thriller, less than psychologically convincing, in which the femme fatale is so obviously deranged from the word go that the male lead comes over as dumb even by the standards of the noir hero. Best for Chabrol completists.

SCR Pierre Leccia, Claude Chabrol   **CIN** Eduardo Serra
MUS Matthieu Chabrol   **DES** Françoise Benoît-Fresco
ED Monique Fardoulis   **PROD** Patrick Godeau
DIST Cinéfrance

66 Middling Chabrol, not as tight and suspenseful as his best work. – *Marjorie Baumgarten, Austin Chronicle*

† The film is Chabrol's second pass at the works of Ruth Rendell, after 1998's La Ceremonie.

'It spans a whole new world of entertainment!'
The Bridge on the River Kwai ★★★
DIR *David Lean*
1957   161m   GB
DVD   🎵

☆ *Alec Guinness* (Colonel Nicholson), William Holden (Shears), Jack Hawkins (Major Warden), Sessue Hayakawa (Colonel Saito), James Donald (Major Clipton), Geoffrey Horne (Lieut. Joyce), Andre Morell (Col. Green), Percy Herbert (Grogan)

British POWs in Burma are employed by the Japanese to build a bridge; meanwhile British agents seek to destroy it.

Ironic adventure epic with many fine moments but too many centres of interest and an unforgivably confusing climax. It is distinguished by Guinness's portrait of the

DVD Available on DVD   ☆ Cast in order of importance   66 Critics' Quotes   † Points of interest   🏆 Academy Award   🏆 Academy Award nomination   🎬 BAFTA   🎬 BAFTA nomination
🎵 Soundtrack on CD

English CO who is heroic in his initial stand against the enemy but finally cannot bear to see his bridge blown up: and the physical detail of the production is beyond criticism.

SCR Carl Foreman, Michael Wilson   CIN Jack Hildyard
MUS Malcolm Arnold   ED Peter Taylor
DIST Columbia/Sam Spiegel

66 It may rank as the most rousing adventure film inspired by the last World War. – *Alton Cook, New York World Telegram*

† Cary Grant was originally sought for the William Holden role

† Michael Wilson should also have been credited for the script, but he was blacklisted at the time.

⚊ picture; adaptation (now credited to Carl Foreman, Michael Wilson and Pierre Boulle); David Lean; Jack Hildyard; Malcolm Arnold; Alec Guinness; editing
⚊ Sessue Hayakawa
Ⓣ film; British film; Alec Guinness; Pierre Boulle

The Bridges of Madison County ★★

DIR Clint Eastwood
1995   135m   US
DVD ♫

☆ Clint Eastwood (Robert Kincaid), Meryl Streep (Francesca Johnson), Annie Corley (Carolyn Johnson), Victor Slezak (Michael Johnson), Jim Haynie (Richard Johnson)

While her husband is away, a bored housewife in rural Iowa enjoys an affair with a passing photojournalist.

Faithful, adaptation of a best-selling tear-jerker, superior to its source and staged with a burnished handsomeness; it is admirable in its focus on older protagonists seeking one more shot at happiness, but too often the performers are let down by solemn, cornball, unintentionally humorous dialogue.

SCR Richard LaGravenese   CIN Jack N. Green
MUS Lennie Niehaus   DES Jeannine Oppewall   ED Joel Cox   PROD Clint Eastwood, Kathleen Kennedy
DIST Warner/Amblin/Malpaso

66 Given the intelligent restraint of the treatment, this is about as fine an adaptation of this material as one could hope for, although there is still something of a gap between the impressive skill of the filmmaking and the ultimately irredeemable aspects of the source. – *Todd McCarthy, Variety*

66 Brief Encounter with pick-up trucks. . .immaculately photographed, tastefully directed, memorably acted, and it far outclasses the novel with several moments of searing honesty and emotional power. – *Christpher Tookey, Daily Mail*

⚊ Meryl Streep (leading actress)

'For anyone who's ever been set up, stood up or felt up.'

Bridget Jones's Diary ★

DIR Sharon Maguire
2001   97m   US/France/GB
DVD ♫

☆ Renée Zellweger (Bridget Jones), Colin Firth (Mark Darcy), Hugh Grant (Daniel Cleaver), Gemma Jones (Bridget's Mum), Jim Broadbent (Bridget's Dad), Embeth

Davidtz (Natasha), Shirley Henderson (Jude), Sally Phillips (Shazza), James Callis (Tom)

A thirtysomething singleton finds her affections torn between a safe but dull barrister and an altogether more roguish suitor.

Something of a mess – big on silly sight gags, pratfalls, 'songs inspired by the film' and dubious celebrity cameos – though its protagonist's plight clearly struck chords with many viewers.

SCR Helen Fielding, Andrew Davies, Richard Curtis
CIN Stuart Dryburgh   MUS Patrick Doyle   DES Gemma Jackson   ED Martin Walsh   PROD Tim Bevan, Eric Fellner, Jonathan Cavendish   DIST Universal

66 Really rather good – funny, engaging and winning in its self-deprecating modesty, albeit in a big-budget sort of way. – *Leslie Felperin, Sight & Sound*

66 An idiot's guide to Helen Fielding's depressing bestseller. But it's more unoriginal, unfunny and insultingly trite than anyone had a right to expect. – *Jack Seale, The Horse*

⚊ Renée Zellweger (leading actress)
Ⓣ British film; Renée Zellweger (leading actress); Colin Firth (supporting actor); Helen Fielding, Andrew Davies, Richard Curtis (adapted screenplay)

Brief Encounter ★★★★

DIR *David Lean*
1945   86m   GB
DVD

☆ *Celia Johnson* (Laura Jesson), *Trevor Howard* (Alec Harvey), Stanley Holloway (Albert Godby), Joyce Carey (Myrtle Bagot), Cyril Raymond (Fred Jesson)

A suburban housewife meets a local doctor at a railway station, and they embark on a subdued love affair.

A lovely, affecting film beloved in Britain, because it asserts values on which the British middle classes like to pride themselves – dignity, restraint and not a hint of improper conduct. Its craftsmanship is sublime, and its sense of place inspired: Carnforth railway station has become an unlikely Mecca for the film's fans.

SCR *Noël Coward, David Lean, Ronald Neame, Anthony Havelock-Allan*   CIN *Robert Krasker*   MUS Rachmaninov
ED Jack Harris   PROD Anthony Havelock-Allan, Ronald Neame   DIST Eagle-Lion/Cineguild

66 Both a pleasure to watch as a well-controlled piece of work, and deeply touching. – *James Agee*

66 Polished as is this film, its strength does not lie in movie technique, of which there is plenty, so much as in the tight realism of its detail. – *Richard Winnington*

⚊ Celia Johnson (leading actress); Anthony Havelock-Allan, Ronald Neame, David Lean (screenplay); David Lean (direction)

'Where did the universe come from? Will time ever come to an end? Which came first, the chicken or the egg?'

A Brief History of Time ★★

SCR/DIR Errol Morris
1992   80m   GB/US
DVD

☆ Isobel Hawking (Herself-–Stephen's mother), Stephen

DVD Available on DVD   ☆ Cast in order   66 Critics' Quotes   ⚊ Academy Award   Ⓣ BAFTA
♫ Soundtrack on CD   of importance   † Points of interest   ⚊ Academy Award nomination   Ⓣ BAFTA nomination

97

Hawking (Himself), Janet Humphrey (Herself—Stephen's aunt), Mary Hawking (Herself–Stephen's sister)

Documentary on British cosmologist Stephen Hawking, who attempts to explain the origins and nature of the universe in layman's terms.

A brave attempt to clarify theoretical concepts. Hawking suffers from amyotrophic lateral sclerosis, is almost totally paralysed and speaks through a voice synthesiser. He sits inert in his wheelchair, while blue-screen projections of the cosmos whizz around him. It's easier going than his bestselling book, which defeated many readers.

CIN John Bailey, Stefan Czapsky   MUS Philip Glass   DES Ted Bafaloukos   ED Brad Fuller   PROD David Hickman

66 A kind of adventure that seldom reaches the screen, and it's a tonic. – *Vincent Canby, New York Times*

Bright Lights, Big City

DIR James Bridges
1988   107m   US
[DVD] ♫

☆ Michael J. Fox (Jamie Conway), Kiefer Sutherland (Tad Allagash), Phoebe Cates (Amanda), Frances Sternhagen (Clara), Dianne Wiest (Mother), Swoosie Kurtz (Megan), John Houseman (Mr Vogel), Jason Robards (Rich Vanier), Tracy Pollan (Vicky)

A would-be novelist, temporarily working as a researcher on a Manhattan magazine, goes through a drug-induced life crisis.

It looks like a museum piece now, but this was the prototype 1980s New York movie: sleek clothes, jaded demeanours, minimalist decor – and of course, loads of money and cocaine. Fox, a decent light comic actor, is miscast.

SCR Jay McInerney   CIN Gordon Willis   MUS Donald Fagen   DES Santo Loquasto   ED John Bloom, George Berndt   PROD Mark Rosenberg, Sydney Pollack, Jack LArson   DIST UIP/United Artists

66 Unfortunately, the point seems to be that shoving half of Colombia's main export up your nose is not a good idea when all is said and done. – *Channel 4*

A Brighter Summer Day   ★★★

DIR *Edward Yang*
1991   237m   Taiwan

☆ Lisa Yang (Ming), Zhang Zhen (Xiao Si'r), Zhang Guozhu (Father), Elaine Jin (Mother), Wang Juan (Older Sister), Chang Han (Older Brother)

A Taiwanese teenager in the 1960s encounters gang rivalries, violence and first love.

A remarkable story, loosely based on fact, set in a nation still trying to find its way in the shadow of Communist China. As always with this director, the wealth of accumulated detail contributes to the emotionally satisfaction of the story.

SCR Edward Yang, Alex Yang, Hung Hung, Lai Mingtang   CIN Longyu Zhang, Huigong Li   DES Yu Weiyan Yang   ED Chen Bowen   PROD Yu Weiyan   DIST ICA/Yang and His Gang

66 On a deeper level, it's about a society in transition and in search of an identity, forever aware of its isolation from mainland China, and increasingly prey to Americanisation. – *Geoff Andrew, Time Out*

† In some territories, the film was released in a 185-mnute version, though Edward Yang prefers the original 235-minute cut.

† The film's original title translates as Juvenile Murder on Kuling Street.

Brighton Rock   ★★★★

DIR *John Boulting*
1947   92m   GB
[DVD]

☆ *Richard Attenborough* (Pinkie Brown), Hermione Baddeley (Ida Arnold), *Harcourt Williams* (Prewitt), William Hartnell (Dallow), Alan Wheatley (Fred Hale), Carol Marsh (Rose Brown), Nigel Stock (Cubitt)

The vicious teenage leader of a Brighton racetrack gang uses a waitress as alibi to cover a murder, and marries her. He later decides to be rid of her, but fate takes a hand in his murder plot.

A properly 'seedy' version of Graham Greene's 'entertainment', very flashily done for the most part, and with a stellar turn by Attenborough as the baby-faced psychopath. It is one of the most enduring films Britain has produced, and features an inspired, chilling ending, different from Greene's.

SCR Graham Greene, Terence Rattigan   CIN *Harry Waxman*   MUS Hans May   ED Peter Scott   PROD Roy Boulting   DIST Associated British/Charter Films

66 The film is slower, much less compelling, and, if you get me, less cinematic than the book, as a child's guide to which I hereby offer it. – *Richard Winnington*

66 It proceeds with the efficiency, the precision and the anxiety to please of a circular saw. – *Dilys Powell*

Bringing Out the Dead   ★★★

DIR *Martin Scorsese*
1999   121m   US
[DVD] ♫

☆ *Nicolas Cage* (Frank Pierce), Patricia Arquette (Mary Burke), John Goodman (Larry), Ving Rhames (Marcus), Tom Sizemore (Tom Wolls), Marc Anthony (Noel), Mary Beth Hurt (Nurse Constance), Cliff Curtis (Cy Coates), Nestor Serrano (Dr. Hazmat), Aida Turturro (Nurse Crupp)

A burned-out New York paramedic approaches breaking point over a series of night shifts.

Rich, darkly comic vision of a city in an almost irreparable state of disrepair; there's at least as much angst in this reuniting of director Scorsese and writer Schrader as there was in their previous Taxi Driver, but more laughs, too.

SCR *Paul Schrader*   CIN *Robert Richardson*   MUS Elmer Bernstein   DES *Dante Ferretti*   ED *Thelma Schoonmaker*   PROD Scott Rudin, Barbara De Fina   DIST Buena Vista/Paramount

66 Blazes up constantly with a stunning, off-kilter brilliance, an incandescent force that sometimes explodes

the space between us and the screen. – *Michael Wilmington, Chicago Tribune*

Bringing Up Baby ★★★

DIR *Howard Hawks*

1938   102m   US

DVD

☆ *Katharine Hepburn* (Susan Vance), *Cary Grant* (David Huxley), *May Robson* (Aunt Elizabeth), *Charles Ruggles* (Maj. Horace Applegate), *Walter Catlett* (Constable Slocum), *Fritz Feld* (Dr. Fritz Lehman), Jonathan Hale, Barry Fitzgerald (Mr. Gogarty)

A madcap young woman causes a palaeontologist to lose a dinosaur bone and a pet leopard in the same evening.

Outstanding, relentless screwball comedy which barely pauses for romance, and ends up with the whole splendid cast in jail.

SCR *Dudley Nichols, Hagar Wilde*   CIN *Russell Metty*   MUS Roy Webb   ED George Hively   PROD Howard Hawks   DIST RKO

66 It may be the American movies' closest equivalent to Restoration comedy. – *Pauline Kael*

66 I am happy to report that it is funny from the word go, that it has no other meaning to recommend it. . .and that I wouldn't swap it for practically any three things of the current season. – *Otis Ferguson*

† The dog George was played by Asta from The Thin Man movies.

† The 'Baby' of the title is the leopard.

'It's the story of their lives.'

Broadcast News ★★

SCR/DIR *James L. Brooks*

1987   133m   US

DVD

☆ William Hurt (Tom Grunick), Albert Brooks (Aaron Altman), *Holly Hunter* (Jane Craig), Robert Prosky (Ernie Merriman), Lois Chiles (Jennifer Mack), Joan Cusack (Blair Litton), Jack Nicholson (uncredited cameo) (Bill Rorich)

A TV news producer is torn, personally and professionally, between two very different reporters.

One of the ten best screenplays of the 1980s offers a rare, entirely unpredictable love triangle, eyefuls of the behind-the-scenes wrangling that goes into live news and dialogue that deserves to be quoted more than it is. All this, plus a genuine distaste for the way news is being turned into an entertainment, results in a truly sophisticated entertainment.

CIN Michael Ballhaus   MUS Bill Conti   DES Charles Rosen   ED Richard Marks   PROD James L. Brooks   DIST UKFD/Fox/Gracie Films

66 As knowledgeable about the TV news-gathering process as any movie ever made, but it also has insights into the more personal matter of how people use high-pressure jobs as a way of avoiding time alone with themselves. The movie was described as being about a romantic triangle, but that's only partly true. It is about three people who toy with the idea of love, but are obsessed

by the idea of making television. – *Roger Ebert, Chicago Sun-Times*

⚲ picture; William Hurt (leading actor); Holly Hunter (leading actress); Albert Brooks (supporting actor); James L. Brooks (original screenplay); Michael Ballhaus; Richard Marks

Broadway Bound ★

DIR Paul Bogart

1991   89m   US

☆ Anne Bancroft (Kate Jerome), Hume Cronyn (Ben), Corey Parker (Eugene Morris Jerome), Jonathan Silverman (Stanley Jerome), Jerry Orbach (Jack Jerome), Michele Lee (Blanche)

Two brothers aiming to become script-writers, devise a version of their quarrelsome family for a radio script, then leave home to hit the big time.

Based on events in the life of dramatist Neil Simon, and his brother Danny, this is gently humorous, though not this writer's best work.

SCR Neil Simon   CIN Isidore Mankofsky   MUS David Shire   DES Ben Edwards   ED Andy Zall   PROD Terry Nelson   DIST Blue Dolphin/ABC Productions

66 An enjoyable enough rehash of familiar themes. – *Geoffrey Macnab, Sight & Sound*

† The last segment of Simon's autobiographical trilogy that also includes Brighton Beach Memoirs and Biloxi Blues.

† The film was originally made for American television, and ran 120 minutes with commercials.

Broadway Danny Rose ★★★

SCR/DIR *Woody Allen*

1984   84m   US

♫

☆ *Woody Allen*, Mia Farrow, Nick Apollo Forte, Craig Vandenburgh, Herb Reynolds

An artists' agent and former comic falls foul of the Mafia while promoting a client.

A delight from its opening scene, featuring old comedians sitting in a New York deli, cracking wise, and relating the story of the legendary but hapless Danny Rose. Allen's affection for this under-exposed, slightly seedy side of showbiz is palpable, and if the film's gags are corny, they're at least true to the milieu in which they're told.

CIN Gordon Willis   DES Mel Bourne   ED Susan E. Morse   PROD Robert Greenhut   DIST Orion

⚲ Direction; original screenplay

Ⓣ original screenplay

'Love Is A Force Of Nature.'

Brokeback Mountain ★★★★

DIR *Ang Lee*

2005   134m   US/Canada

DVD   ♫

☆ *Heath Ledger* (Ennis Del Mar), *Jake Gyllenhaal* (Jack Twist), Linda Cardellini (Cassie), Anna Faris (Lashawn Malone), Anne Hathaway (Lureen Newsome), *Michelle*

DVD Available on DVD   ☆ Cast in order of importance   66 Critics' Quotes   ⚲ Academy Award   Ⓑ BAFTA
♫ Soundtrack on CD   † Points of interest   ⚲ Academy Award nomination   Ⓣ BAFTA nomination

99

Williams (Alma), Randy Quaid (Joe Aguirre), Graham Beckel (L.B. Newsome)

Wyoming, 1963: two young male ranchhands enter into a relationship while tending sheep on a mountain, and find it hard to adjust to married reality once they come down off the hillside.

A major achievement, but a supremely delicate piece of filmmaking, sensitive to a particular moment, place, set of attitudes, even to those viewers who might be left queasy by the thought of two cowboys sharing more than just a tent. Lee gets performances of staggering maturity from his young cast, and the prevailing mood is exceptionally vivid: time passes by under vast blue skies, sweeping the characters further and further away from a brief instant of happiness.

SCR *Larry McMurtry, Diana Ossana*   **CIN** *Rodrigo Prieto*   **MUS** *Gustavo Santaolalla*   **DES** Judy Becker   **ED** Geraldine Peroni, Dylan Tichenor   **PROD** Diana Ossana, James Schamus   **DIST** Entertainment

66 Brokeback Mountain is that rare thing, a big Hollywood weeper with a beautiful ache at its centre. It's a modern-day Western that turns into a quietly revolutionary love story. – *Owen Gleiberman, Entertainment Weekly*

66 The whole movie is a rich, spacious, passionate way of showing, not telling, feelings that dare not speak their name – and doing so with superb intelligence and magnificent candour. – *Peter Bradshaw, Guardian*

⚱ Ang Lee; Larry McMurtry, Diana Ossana; Gustavo Santaolalla

⚱ picture; Heath Ledger (leading actor); Jake Gyllenhaal (leading actor); Michelle Williams (supporting actress); Rodrigo Prieto

film; Jake Gyllenhaal (leading actor); Ang Lee; Larry McMurtry, Diana Ossana

Heath Ledger (leading actor); Michelle Williams (supporting actress); Rodrigo Prieto; Geraldine Peroni, Dylan Tichenor; Gustavo Santaolalla

---

'Prepare To Go Ballistic!'

Broken Arrow

DIR John Woo

1996   108m   US

DVD ♫

☆ John Travolta (Maj. Vic 'Deak' Deakins), Christian Slater (Capt. Riley Hale), Samantha Mathis (Terry Carmichael), Delroy Lindo (Colonel Max Wilkins), Bob Gunton (Pritchett), Frank Whaley (Giles Prentice), Howie Long (Kelly), Vondie Curtis-Hall (Chief Sam Rhodes), Jack Thompson (Chairman, Joint Chief of Staff)

A stealth bomber pilot pursues a colleague who's absconded with nuclear weapons.

Preposterous action-thriller, not helped by Travolta's OTT performance: the script consists of lines written specifically with the trailer in mind, and plot logic is non-existent.

SCR Graham Yost   **CIN** Peter Levy   **MUS** Hans Zimmer   **DES** Holger Gross   **ED** John Wright, Steve Mirkovich, Joe Hutshing   **PROD** Mark Gordon, Bill Badalato, Terence Chang   **DIST** TCF/WCG

66 About as abysmal as abysmal gets. – *Desson Howe, Washington Post*

'The language of love, honour and betrayal.'

Broken English   ★★

DIR Gregor Nicholas

1996   92m   New Zealand

☆ Rade Serbedzija (Ivan), Aleksandra Vujcic (Nina), Julian Arahanga (Eddie), Marton Csokas (Darko), Madeline McNamara (Mira), Zhoa Jing (Clara), Yang Li (Wu), Temuera Morrison (Manu)

A Romeo and Juliet-derived story set in New Zealand, where a young Maori falls for a colleague in the restaurant where he works: a Croatian woman with a violent father.

Ethnic drama with a real kick, though director Nicholas lingers too long in making every scene look good, sometimes at the expense of his material's gritty realism.

SCR Gregor Nicholas, Johanna Pigott, Jim Salter   **CIN** John Toon   **MUS** Murray Grindlay, Murray McNabb   **DES** Michael Kane   **ED** David Coulson   **PROD** Robin Scholes   **DIST** First Independent/Communicado/Village Roadshow

66 The film gets by on its energy and self-belief. – *Wally Hammond, Time Out*

'One Man Lives In The Neighborhood. Another Man Owns It.'

A Bronx Tale   ★★

DIR Robert De Niro

1993   121m   US

DVD

☆ Robert De Niro (Lorenzo Anello), Chazz Palminteri (Sonny LeSpeccio), Lillo Brancato (Calogero 'C' Anello (age 17)), Francis Capra (Calogero 'C' Anello (age 9)), Taral Hicks (Jane Williams), Katherine Narducci (Rosina Anello), Clem Caserta (Jimmy Whispers), Joe Pesci (Bobby Bars), Alfred Sauchelli Jnr

In New York's Little Italy in the 60s, the impressionable young son of a decent, law-abiding bus driver becomes attracted to the life and style of a fast-talking, sharp-suited gangster.

A thoughtful portrait of a specific place and time with a story that dares to question the fascination that mobsters exert.

SCR Chazz Palminteri   **CIN** Reynaldo Villalobos   **MUS** Butch Barbella   **DES** Wynn Thomas   **ED** David Ray, R.Q. Lovett   **PROD** Jane Rosenthal, Jon Kilik, Robert De Niro   **DIST** Rank/Price/Tribeca

66 A wonderfully vivid snapshot of a colorful place and time, as well as a very satisfactory directorial debut. – *Variety*

† Chazz Palminteri's screenplay, and the play from which it evolved, are both strongly autobiographical.

Brotherhood of the Wolf   ★

DIR Christophe Gans

2001   142m   France

DVD ♫

☆ Samuel Le Bihan (Grégoire de Fronsac), Mark Dacascos (Mani), Émilie Dequenne (Marianne de Morangias), Vincent Cassel (Jean-François de Morangias), Monica Bellucci (Sylvia), Jérémie Rénier (Thomas d'Apcher), Jean

Yanne (Le Comte de Morangias), Jean-François Stévenin (Henri Sardis)

In 18th century France, King Louis XIV sends a naturalist to a rural area to catch a savage, wolf-like beast that has been killing women and children.

An extravagant, superficial fantasy that does not take itself too seriously. A knowing mish-mash of styles, it incorporates martial arts, comic book imagery, and sequences that would not look misplaced in classic horror films. Still, it's fun on its own limited terms.

SCR Christophe Gans, Stéphane Cabel **CIN** Dan Laustsen **MUS** Joseph LoDuca **DES** Guy Claude François **ED** David Wu, Sébastien Prangère, Xavier Loutreuil **PROD** Richard Grandpierre, Samuel Hadida **DIST** Pathé

66 Brotherhood has its goofy side – it's a sleek, creepily atmospheric popcorn entertainment. – *Ella Taylor, L.A. Weekly*

66 The perfect film for anyone who likes their head-butting and kickboxing dressed up in gold brocade, frilly collars, and tri-cornered caps. And isn't that all of us?. – *Steven Rea, Philadelphia Inquirer*

Brothers ★

DIR Susanne Bier

2004 117m Denmark/GB/Sweden/Norway
[DVD]

☆ Connie Nielsen (Sarah), *Ulrich Thomsen* (Michael), Nikolaj Lie Kaas (Jannik), Bent Mejding (Henning), Solbjorg Hojfeldt (Else)

A woman learns her soldier husband has gone AWOL in Afghanistan; she takes consolation from his younger brother, only for her spouse to return home a changed man.

Sudsy modern-day melodrama lent credibility by the fine work of its cast.

SCR Anders Thomas Jensen, Susanne Bier **CIN** Morten Soborg **MUS** Johan Soderqvist **DES** Viggo Bentzon **ED** Pernille Bech Christensen, Adam Nielsen **PROD** Sisse Graum Jorgensen, Peter Aalbaek Jensen **DIST** Soda

66 It's all a little contrived, but Bier shows a refreshing interest in giving audiences the longed-for pleasure of an engrossing story. – *Peter Bradshaw, Guardian*

66 Arty close-ups of blinking eyes and ponderous cross-cutting make the drama seem creakier and more cliched than it actually is. – *Tim Robey, Daily Telegraph*

'Eliminating Evil Since 1812.'

The Brothers Grimm ★

DIR Terry Gilliam

2005 118m USA/Czech republic
[DVD] ♫

☆ Matt Damon (Wilhelm Grimm), Heath Ledger (Jacob Grimm), Peter Stormare (Cavaldi), Lena Headey (Angelika), Jonathan Pryce (Delatombe), Monica Bellucci (Mirror Queen)

In 19th-century Germany, two fraternal con men are rounded up by the authorities and asked to investigate the disappearance of local children in an enchanted forest.

Broken-backed fantasy piece, whose production troubles were well documented at the time: the idea – to return the Grimms' tales to their Mitteleuropean roots – is an intriguing one, and Gilliam throws himself into doodling around it; the finished result has brilliant images and moments, but lacks any real coherence. A fondness for Python might help.

SCR Ehren Kruger **CIN** Newton Thomas Sigel **MUS** Dario Marianelli **DES** Guy Hendrix Dyas **ED** Leslie Walker **PROD** Charles Roven, Daniel Bobker **DIST** MGM

66 A bit of a mess: sometimes delightful, sometimes tedious, always creative. – *Jami Bernard, New York Daily News*

66 A work of limitless invention, but it is invention without pattern, chasing itself around the screen without finding a plot. – *Roger Ebert, Chicago Sun-Times*

† Gilliam clashed with his producers over Damon's make-up, and wanted Samantha Morton to play the Headey role.

'A story of survival and belonging.'

Brothers in Trouble ★

DIR Udayan Prasad

1996 102m GB

☆ Om Puri (Hussein Shah), Pavan Malhotra (Amir), Angeline Ball (Mary), Ahsen Bhatti (Irshad), Bhasker Patel (Gholam), Pravesh Kumar (Sakib), Badi Uzzaman (Old Ram)

An account of immigrants from Pakistan, living in London in overcrowded conditions, and taking low-paid jobs while sending money home to their families.

A brave stab at conveying a specific experience of life in Britain for new arrivals, especially the appalling conditions of multi-occupation, with 18 illegal immigrants in a single house. But this keen observation finally gives way to melodrama.

SCR Robert Buckler **CIN** Alan Almond **MUS** Stephen Warbeck **DES** Chris Townsend **ED** Barrie Vince **PROD** Robert Buckler **DIST** BFI/BBC/Renegade/Kinowelt/Mikado

66 Explores little-charted territory with admirable compassion. – *Channel 4*

'Jack is Trying to Save His Marriage. Patrick is in a Hopeless Relationship. But Their Biggest Problem is Barry's Brotherly Advice.'

The Brothers McMullen ★★

SCR/DIR *Edward Burns*

1995 98m US
[DVD] ♫

☆ Jack Mulcahy (Jack McMullen), Mike McGlone (Patrick McMullen), Edward Burns (Barry / Finbar McMullen), Connie Britton (Molly McMullen), Maxine Bahns (Audrey), Elizabeth P. McKay (Ann), Shari Albert (Susan), Jennifer Jostyn (Leslie)

Three Irish-American brothers on Long Island wrestle with the various dilemmas their love lives present them with.

[DVD] Available on DVD   ☆ Cast in order of importance   66 Critics' Quotes   ▯ Academy Award   ▯ BAFTA
♫ Soundtrack on CD   † Points of interest   ▯ Academy Award nomination   ▯ BAFTA nomination

A likable, laid-back romantic comedy, insightfully written and engagingly played by its cast of unknowns.

CIN Dick Fisher **MUS** Seamus Egan **ED** Dick Fisher **PROD** Edward Burns, Dick Fisher **DIST** TCF/Marlboro Road Gang/Videography/Good Machine

66 Good old-fashioned virtues of three-dimensional characters, fine dialogue, recognisable life situations and meat-and-potatoes content. – *Todd McCarthy, Variety*

'They want to put a baby in you.'

The Brothers Solomon (new)

DIR Bob Odenkirk

2007 92m US

♫

☆ Will Arnett (John Solomon), Will Forte (Dean Solomon), Chi McBride (James), Kristen Wiig (Janine), Malin Akerman (Tara), Lee Majors (Ed Solomon), Jenna Fischer (Michelle)

Two gormless brothers with no social skills try to father a child in order to wake their own father from a coma.

Asinine, ill-conceived farce from the Dumb and Dumber school, built around a couple of grinning comedians who are more creepy than funny.

SCR Will Forte **CIN** Tim Suhrstedt **MUS** John Swihart **DES** John Paino **ED** Tracey Wadmore-Smith **PROD** Tom Werner, Matt Berenson **DIST** Sony Pictures

JOHN SOLOMON: 'Our plan is to blanket your ovarian walls with our sperm!'

66 Faux Farrelly brothers that should have gone straight to video. – *Lou Lumenick, New York Post*

66 The kind of thing you watch with disbelief, mounting horror and some degree of actual physical pain. – *Wendy Ide, The Times*

'The greatest lessons in life are the ones learned by the heart.'

The Browning Version ★

DIR Mike Figgis

1994 97m GB

DVD ♫

☆ Albert Finney (Andrew Crocker-Harris), Greta Scacchi (Laura Crocker-Harris), Matthew Modine (Frank Hunter), Julian Sands (Tom Gilbert), Michael Gambon (Dr. Frobisher), Ben Silverstone (Taplow), James Sturgess (Bryant), Joe Beattie (Wilson), Mark Bolton (Grantham), Heathcote Williams (Dr. Lake)

An emotionally closed, unpopular classics teacher faces enforced retirement, and, with rumours rife of his wife having a fling with a colleague, comes to ponder the value of his life.

A handsome, even lavish updating of the 1951 film, but despite the efforts of screenwriter Harwood to make this anti-Goodbye Mr. Chips story more modern, it still feels like an old-fashioned period piece with little to say to contemporary audiences. It's an average weepie, no more.

SCR Ronald Harwood **CIN** Jean-François Robin **MUS** Mark Isham **DES** John Beard **ED** Hervé Schneid **PROD** Ridley Scott, Mimi Polk Gitlin **DIST** UPI/Percy Main

66 Finney makes a doleful, sonorous classics teacher, but, for all the pathos he squeezes out of the part, he is too sturdy and monolithic a figure to seem especially tortured by his plight. – *Geoffrey Macnab, Sight & Sound*

Ⓣ Ronald Harwood (adapted screenplay)

'The King of Rock vs The King of the Dead.'

Bubba Ho-tep ★★

SCR/DIR Don Coscarelli

2002 92m US

DVD ♫

☆ *Bruce Campbell* (Elvis), Ossie Davis (Jack), Ella Joyce (The Nurse), Heidi Marnhout (Callie), Bob Ivy (Bubba-Ho-tep)

In a nursing home, the aged Elvis Presley and a black co-resident claiming to be JFK battle against a soul-sucking mummy.

A one-of-a-kind movie premise, put across with schlocky glee and an unexpectedly affecting sincerity with regard to matters of old age: wherever The King is watching from these days, you suspect he'd probably love it.

CIN Adam Janeiro **MUS** Brian Tyler **DES** Daniel Vecchione **ED** Donald Milne, Scott J. Gill **PROD** Don Coscarelli, Jason R. Savage **DIST** Anchor Bay

66 Authentically wacky and poignantly funny. – *Peter Bradshaw, Guardian*

'When he closed his eyes, his heart was opened.'

The Bucket List (new)

DIR Rob Reiner

2007 96m US

DVD ♫

☆ Jack Nicholson (Edward Cole), Morgan Freeman (Carter Chambers), Sean Hayes (Thomas), Rob Morrow (Dr. Hollins), Beverly Todd (Virginia Chambers), Alfonso Freeman (Roger Chambers), Rowena King (Angelica)

Two terminally ill cancer patients spend their last months achieving unrealised ambitions.

Mawkish vehicle for two aging stars clearly delighted to be in each other's company; the feeling, alas, is not mutual.

SCR Justin Zackham **CIN** John Schwartzman **MUS** Marc Shaiman **DES** Bill Brzeski **ED** Robert Leighton **PROD** Craig Zadan, Neil Meron, Alan Greisman, Rob Reiner **DIST** Warner Bros

EDWARD COLE: 'Never pass up a bathroom, never waste a hard-on, and never trust a fart.'

66 A feel-good film about death, a sitcom about mortality, Ikiru for meatheads. – *Todd McCarthy, Variety*

66 A hot contender for most vomit-inducing picture of the year. – *Christopher Tookey, Daily Mail*

† Morgan Freeman's son Alfonso plays his character's son in the film.

'In Havana, music isn't a pastime. . .it's a way of life.'

Buena Vista Social Club ★★

DIR Wim Wenders

1999 105m Germany

DVD ♫

☆ Ry Cooder, Compay Segundo, Ruben Gonzalez,

Ibrahim Ferrer, Eliades Ochoa, Omara Portuondo, Manuel 'Guajiro' Mirabal, Orlando 'Cachaito' Lopez, Barbarito Torres, Manuel 'Puntillita' Licea, Raul Planes, Felix Valoy, Maceo Rodriguez, Richard Eques, Joaquim Cooder

Documentary portrait of a generation of ageing Cuban musicians reunited by guitarist Ry Cooder to collaborate on new projects.

Absorbing record of a major musical rediscovery, which gave its subjects – individuals who have lived full, often extraordinary lives – a second spell in the spotlight.

CIN Jorg Widmer, Robby Muller, Lisa Rinzler   ED Brian Johnson   PROD Ulrich Felsberg, Deepak Nayar   DIST Film Four

66 Comes closer to pure happiness than anything else in the theatres at the moment. – *David Denby, New Yorker*

66 The players and their stories are as wonderful as the music, and the filmmaking is uncommonly sensitive and alert. – *Jonathan Rosenbaum, Chicago Reader*

🎞 documentary

Ⓣ film not in the English language; Ry Cooder, Nick Gold (music); Martin Müller, Jerry Boys (sound)

'Billy Brown just got out of jail. Now he's going to serve some real time. He's going home.'

Buffalo '66   ★

DIR Vincent Gallo
1998   110m   US
DVD   🎵

☆ Vincent Gallo (Billy Brown), Christina Ricci (Layla), Anjelica Huston (Jan Brown), Ben Gazzara (Jimmy Brown), Kevin Corrigan (Rocky the Goon), Mickey Rourke (The Bookie), Rosanna Arquette (Wendy Balsam), Jan-Michael Vincent (Sonny)

A passive-aggressive ex-con pressgangs a young girl into posing as his girlfriend during a visit to his parents.

A noodly, meandering directorial debut and more conventional in its comedy of dysfunctional families than it would like to appear; viewers will also need a high level of tolerance for its editor-writer-composer-director-star.

SCR Vincent Gallo, Alison Bagnall   CIN Lance Acord   MUS Vincent Gallo   DES Gideon Ponte   ED Curtiss Clayton   PROD Chris Hanley   DIST Lions Gate/Cinepix/Muse

66 Alive to cinematic ideas, generous to its actors and peppered with unexpected humour. – *Todd McCarthy, Variety*

66 Every scene sours over with scuzzy resentment, none of the other characters seems to get a word in edgeways, and the treatment of Ricci – tarted up throughout as a post-pubescent sex doll – is simply an insult. – *Tom Shone, Sunday Times*

'Steal all that you can steal. A story so outrageous you couldn't make it up.'

Buffalo Soldiers   ★

DIR Gregor Jordan
2001   98m   GB/Germany
DVD

☆ Joaquin Phoenix (Ray Elwood), *Ed Harris* (Col. Wallace

Berman), *Scott Glenn* (Sgt. Robert Lee), Anna Paquin (Robyn Lee), Gabriel Mann (Knoll), Leon Robinson (Stoney), Dean Stockwell (Gen. Lancaster), *Elizabeth McGovern* (Mrs Berman)

A fixer at a US Army base in Germany attempts to keep a black-marketeering operation from his superiors.

Essentially several episodes' worth of M*A*S*H or Bilko; in this case, the anti-authoritarian satire counts as no more than friendly fire, but there is fun to be had from the performances.

SCR Gregor Jordan, Eric Alex Weiss, Nora MacCoby   CIN Oliver Stapleton   MUS David Holmes   DES Steve Jones-Evans   ED Lee Smith   PROD Rainer, Grupe, Ariane Moody   DIST Pathé

66 A pleasingly disreputable trifle. – *Stephanie Zacharek, Salon*

† The film was first shown at the Toronto Film Festival in September 2001, but was not released for another two years because it was felt to be 'unpatriotic'.

'Sometimes it takes more than just good looks to kill.'

Buffy the Vampire Slayer

DIR Fran Rubel Kuzui
1992   86m   US
DVD   🎵

☆ Kristy Swanson (Buffy Summers), Donald Sutherland (Merrick Jamison-Smythe), Paul Reubens (Amilyn), Rutger Hauer (Lothos), Luke Perry (Oliver Pike), Michele Abrams (Jennifer Walkens), Hilary Swank (Kimberly Hannah), Paris Vaughan (Nicole Bobittson), David Arquette (Benny Jacks)

A dim Los Angeles teenage girl discovers to her surprise that she alone can save the city from marauding vampires.

Fitfully amusing, but interesting only as the predecessor to a remarkably successful TV series which made its debut five years after its release, and became a cult hit.

SCR Joss Whedon   CIN James Hayman   MUS Carter Burwell   DES Lawrence Miller   ED Camilla Toniolo, Jill Savitt, Richard Candib   PROD Kaz Kazui, Howard Rosenman   DIST TCF/Sandollar/Kuzui

66 Buffy isn't heinous, just disposable. As a friend tells Buffy while she eyes a fashion purchase, "It's so five minutes ago." – *Peter Travers, Rolling Stone*

66 Actress Kristy Swanson provides the ideal combination of energy and comic disdain that characterize a most unlikely saviour. While it would be a mistake to oversell Buffy the Vampire Slayer, the sad and/or happy truth is that you could do worse on a warm summer night. A lot worse. – *Kenneth Turan, Los Angeles Times*

† The TV series, also created by Whedon, starred Sarah Michelle Gellar as Buffy.

'First they send in their drone. Then they find their queen.'

Bug (new)   ★★

DIR William Friedkin
2007   101m   US/Germany
DVD

☆ Ashley Judd (Agnes White), Michael Shannon (Peter Evans), Lynn Collins (R.C.), Brian F. O'Byrne (Dr. Sweet), Harry Connick Jr. (Jerry Goss)

DVD Available on DVD   ☆ Cast in order of importance   66 Critics' Quotes   † Points of interest   🏅 Academy Award   Academy Award nomination   Ⓑ BAFTA   Ⓣ BAFTA nomination

🎵 Soundtrack on CD

103

A lonely bar waitress woman meets a drifter and takes him back to her motel room. Convinced he has been bitten by a bug, he strips the bed then deliriously explains the army carried out mysterious experiments on him. His paranoia about bugs in his blood escalates to a nightmarish climax.

A story that starts on a note of suppressed hysteria and graduates to intense, yelling hysteria. Its stage roots are apparent, but its lack of inhibitions and eventual utter madness are hugely enjoyable.

SCR Tracy Letts CIN Michael Grady MUS Brian Tyler DES Franco Carbone ED Darrin Navarro PROD Kimberley C. Anderson, Michael Burns, Gary Huckabay, Malcolm Petal, Andreas Schart, Holly Wiersma DIST Lionsgate UK

66 Has the feverish compression of live theatre and the moody expansiveness of film. The mix is insanely powerful. – *David Edelstein, New York Magazine*

66 It starts off like a horror film, or like a modern-day Tennessee Williams piece and then transmutes into. . .something very different indeed. – *Peter Bradshaw, Guardian*

A Bug's Life ★★

DIR John Lasseter
1998 96m US
DVD ♫

☆ The voices of: Dave Foley, Kevin Spacey, Julia Louis-Dreyfus, Hayden Panettiere, Phyllis Diller, Richard Kind, David Hyde Pierce, Joe Ranft, Denis Leary, Jonathan Harris, Madeline Kahn, Bonnie Hunt, Michael McShane, John Ratzenberger, Roddy McDowall

A misfit ant recruits a ragtag group of insects to try and save his colony from marauding grasshoppers.

Borrowing its plot from Seven Samurai, this early Pixar feature doesn't have the wit or sophistication of their best work, but children are unlikely to mind. The animation is top-notch.

SCR Andrew Stanton, Donald McEnery, Bob Shaw, John Lasseter, Joe Ranft CIN Sharon Calahan MUS Randy Newman DES William Cone ED Lee Unkrich PROD Darla K. Anderson, Kevin Reher DIST Buena Vista/Walt Disney/Pixar

66 Makes jaunty, imaginative use of both extraordinary technology and bold storytelling possibilities within the insect world. – *Janet Maslin, New York Times*

66 A pale imitation of Disney's best. – *Derek Malcolm, Guardian*

† Antz, also released in 1998, is another computer-animated film on a similar theme.

⚖ Randy Newman

Ⓣ Bill Reeves, Eben Ostby, Rick Sayre, Sharon Calahan (special visual effects)

'Glamour was the Disguise.'

Bugsy ★★

DIR Barry Levinson
1991 134m US
DVD ♫

☆ *Warren Beatty* (Ben 'Bugsy' Siegel), Annette Bening (Virginia Hill), Harvey Keitel (Mickey Cohen), Ben

Kingsley (Meyer Lansky), Elliott Gould (Harry Greenberg), Joe Mantegna (George Raft), Bebe Neuwirth (Countess di Frasso), Wendy Phillips (Esta Siegel), Richard Sarafian (Jack Dragna), Bill Graham (Charlie Luciano)

A mobster moves from Los Angeles to Vegas with the dream of building a casino in the desert.

Ravishing-looking if sanitised account of a psychopathic mob boss who could turn on both charm and rage at will. Not as good as its collection of awards might suggest, but it's executed with class and style, with a big screen always in mind. Beatty stretches himself beyond his usual 'handsome leading man' territory.

SCR James Toback CIN *Allen Daviau* MUS Ennio Morricone DES *Dennis Gassner* ED Stu Linder PROD Mark Johnson, Barry Levinson, Warren Beatty DIST Columbia TriStar/Mulholland/Baltimore

66 Warren Beatty, who is one of the film's co-producers, has found the role of his career in this sly, evasive schemer with the manipulative instincts of a born ladies' man. – *Janet Maslin, New York Times*

† Beatty and Bening, who later married, began their relationship on the set of the film.

⚖ Dennis Gassner; Albert Wolsky (costume design)
⚖ film; Warren Beatty (leading actor); Harvey Keitel (supporting actor); Ben Kingsley (supporting actor); Barry Levinson; James Toback (original screenplay); Allen Daviau; Ennio Morricone

'A Major League Love Story in a Minor League Town.'

Bull Durham ★★

SCR/DIR *Ron Shelton*
1988 108m US
DVD ♫

☆ *Kevin Costner* (Crash Davis), *Susan Sarandon* (Annie Savoy), *Tim Robbins* (Ebby Calvin 'Nuke' LaLoosh), Trey Wilson (Joe Riggins), Robert Wuhl (Larry Hockett), William O'Leary (Jimmy), David Neidorf (Bobby), Danny Gans (Deke)

Two players on the same struggling baseball team vie for the affections of the team's most ardent supporter, and English teacher.

Salty, grown-up sports romance, its bases – head, heart, body and soul – nimbly negotiated by the excellent central trio.

CIN Bobby Byrne MUS Michael Convertino DES Armin Ganz ED Robert Leighton, Adam Weiss PROD Thom Mount, Mark Burg DIST Rank/Orion/Mount Company

66 Shelton has written the wittiest, busiest screenplay since Moonstruck, and his three stars do their very best work. – *Richard Corliss, Time*

66 It eases up on you, lazy as a cloud, and carries you off in a mood of exquisite delight. – *Hal Hinson, Washington Post*

⚖ Ron Shelton (original screenplay)

'You only get one shot at life.'

Bullet Boy ★

DIR Saul Dibb
2004 89m GB
DVD

☆ *Ashley Waters* (Ricky), *Luke Fraser* (Curtis), Claire Perkins (Beverly), Leon Black (Wisdom)

DVD Available on DVD   ☆ Cast in order   66 Critics' Quotes   ⚖ Academy Award   Ⓑ BAFTA
♫ Soundtrack on CD   of importance   † Points of interest   ⚖ Academy Award nomination   Ⓣ BAFTA nomination

Upon his release from prison, a young man is drawn back into criminal activity, dragging his 12-year-old brother with him.

Commendable British attempt to do the same kind of urban morality play America staged fifteen years earlier with Boyz N the Hood; fine location work contrasts the wide-open spaces of Hackney Downs with cramped throughfares and tower blocks offering no easy way out.

SCR Saul Dibb, Catherine R. Johnson   **CIN** Marcel Zyskind   **MUS** Neil Davidge, Robert Del Naja, Massive Attack   **DES** Melanie Allen   **ED** Masahiro Hirakubo, John Mister   **PROD** Ruth Caleb, Marc Boothe   **DIST** Verve

66 Canny enough to know that preaching won't work, but responsible enough to put the hazards of gun ownership up on screen for all to see. . .in the quietly magnetic Walters, it finds a star presence well worth nurturing. – *Tim Robey, Daily Telegraph*

'A killer comedy!'

Bullets over Broadway ★★

DIR *Woody Allen*
1994   98m   US
DVD   ♫

☆ John Cusack (David Shayne), Jack Warden (Julian Marx), *Chazz Palminteri* (Cheech), Joe Viterelli (Nick Valenti), Jennifer Tilly (Olive Neal), Rob Reiner (Sheldon Flender), Mary-Louise Parker (Ellen), *Dianne Wiest* (Helen Sinclair), Harvey Fierstein (Sid Loomis), Jim Broadbent (Warner Purcell), Tracey Ullman (Eden Brent)

New York, the 1920s: a struggling playwright's latest opus is financed by a Mob boss, with one caveat – that his moll be cast as one of the leading ladies.

An undoubted highpoint of Allen's 1990s output, juggling inspired characterisation, witty dialogue and unexpected plot twists with a renewed film-making flair.

SCR *Woody Allen, Douglas McGrath*   **CIN** Carlo Di Palma   **DES** Santo Loquasto   **ED** Susan E. Morse   **PROD** Robert Greenhut   **DIST** Buena Vista/Magnolia/Sweetland

66 Teems with vividly beautiful period atmosphere, sparkling vignettes, wicked dialogue and detail, making this a charming, clever addition to [Allen's] already considerable canon. – *Angie Errigo, Empire*

66 Just when you wonder how much life is left in these stereotypes, Allen pulls off a doozy of a dramatic switch which takes the farce to unexpected, dizzy heights. – *Tom Charity, Time Out*

⚲ Dianne Wiest (supporting actress)
⚲ Chazz Palminteri (supporting actor); Jennifer Tilly (supporting actress); Woody Allen (direction); Woody Allen, Douglas McGrath (original screenplay); Santo Loquasto; Jeffrey Kurland (costume design)
Ⓣ Woody Allen, Douglas McGrath (original screenplay)

Bullitt ★★★

DIR *Peter Yates*
1968   113m   US
DVD   ♫

☆ *Steve McQueen* (Bullitt), Jacqueline Bisset (Cathy), Robert Vaughn (Chalmers), Don Gordon (Delgetti), Robert Duvall (Weissberg), Simon Oakland (Capt. Bennett)

A San Francisco police detective conceals the death

of a Mob witness in his charge, and goes after the killers himself.

Cop thriller with undoubted charisma, distinguished by what is arguably the greatest car chase in the movies, with Bullitt's Ford Mustang tearing up and down the vertiginous hills of San Francisco for nine minutes. Otherwise, it's brisk and efficient, with McQueen commanding as usual in the title role.

SCR Harry Kleiner, Alan R. Trustman   **CIN** *William A. Fraker*   **MUS** Lalo Schifrin   **ED** Frank P. Keller   **PROD** Philip D'Antoni   **DIST** Warner/Solar

66 It has energy, drive, impact, and above all, style. – *Hollis Alpert*
⚲ Frank P. Keller

'It's 4 a.m. . .do you know where your kids are?'

Bully ★

DIR Larry Clark
2001   113m   US/France
DVD   ♫

☆ Brad Renfro (Marty Puccio), Rachel Miner (Lisa Connelly), Nick Stahl (Bobby Kent), Bijou Phillips (Ali Willis), Michael Pitt (Donny Semenec), Kelli Garner (Heather Swaller), Daniel Franzese (Derek Dzvirko), Leo Fitzpatrick (Hitman)

Sexed-up teenagers murder one of their own in the Florida swamps.

Jolting account of a true-life event, made more unsettling by the dead-eyed gaze of its director: it often seems less interested in the state of America's youth than in the lead actresses' crotches.

SCR Zachary Long, Roger Pullis   **CIN** Steve Gainer   **DES** Linda Burton   **ED** Andrew Hafitz   **PROD** Chris Hanley, Don Murphy, Fernando Sulichin   **DIST** Film4

66 If you stick with Bully through its seemingly endless repetition of themes and its hurl-inducing hand-held camerawork, it does build a crude, indefinable power. – *Andrew O'Hehir, Salon*

66 A riot of sleazy camera moves, bad acting, and maladroit profane dialogue. – *David Edelstein, Slate*

'Brace yourself. This politician is about to tell the truth!'

Bulworth ★★★

DIR *Warren Beatty*
1998   108m   US
DVD

☆ Warren Beatty (Sen. Jay Billington Bulworth), Halle Berry (Nina), Don Cheadle (L.D.), Oliver Platt (Dennis Murphy), Paul Sorvino (Graham Crockett), Jack Warden (Eddie Davers), Isaiah Washington (Darnell), Joshua Malina (Bill Feldman), Christine Baranski (Constance Bulworth), Richard Sarafian (Vinnie), Amiri Baraka (Rastaman), Sean Astin (Gary)

A troubled Democrat senator arranges for his own assassination, and thus frees himself to speak the awful political truth.

More complex in its thinking than either Primary Colors or Wag the Dog, this tough, tricky satire seems to be an expression of a profound political disillusionment on Beatty's part; for the most part, it is brutally, often

DVD Available on DVD   ♫ Soundtrack on CD   ☆ Cast in order of importance   66 Critics' Quotes   † Points of interest   ⚲ Academy Award   ⚳ Academy Award nomination   Ⓑ BAFTA   Ⓣ BAFTA nomination

105

hilariously honest about the role money and public image have to play in modern politics.

SCR *Warren Beatty, Jeremy Pikser* CIN Vittorio Storaro MUS Ennio Morricone DES Dean Tavoularis ED Robert C. Jones, Billy Weber PROD Warren Beatty, Pieter Jan Brugge DIST TCF

66 This is a great liberal movie, which is to say, it will be loved most passionately by great liberals, and despised by the conservatives it contemptuously fails to notice. – *Stephen Hunter, Washington Post*

66 An experience akin to watching an attempt at romantic comedy co-written by Tony Benn, Tariq Ali and Diane Abbott. I don't mean that to be a totally pejorative statement. It's interesting and unusual, but more than slightly embarrassing. – *Chris Tookey, Daily Mail*

⌇ Warren Beatty, Jeremy Pikser (original screenplay)

'A comedy about one nice guy who gets pushed too far.'

The 'burbs ★★

DIR *Joe Dante*
1988 101m US
DVD

☆ Tom Hanks (Ray Peterson), Bruce Dern (Mark Rumsfield), Carrie Fisher (Carol Peterson), Rick Ducommun (Art Weingartner), Corey Feldman (Ricky Butler), Wendy Schaal (Bonnie Rumsfield), Henry Gibson (Dr. Werner Klopek), Brother Theodore (Uncle Reuben Klopek), Courtney Gains (Hans Klopek), Gale Gordon (Walter Seznick)

On one American street, a group of neighbours club together to investigate strange goings-on at the new family's house across the way.

Savvy black comedy that mines regular chuckles from the idea all is not what it seems behind white picket fences.

SCR Dana Olsen CIN Robert Stevens MUS Jerry Goldsmith DES James Spencer ED Marshall Harvey PROD Michael Finnell, Larry Brezner DIST UIP/Imagine

66 Not just an interesting attempt at subverting the normality-centred likes of Parenthood or Look Who's Talking, but a wickedly inventive comedy, crammed full of sly gags and bizarre characterisations. – *Kim Newman, Empire*

'For those who were burnt by the sun of the revolution.'

Burnt by the Sun ★★

DIR Nikita Mikhalkov
1994 135m Russia/France
DVD ♫

☆ Nikita Mikhalkov (Serguei Petrovitch Kotov), Oleg Menchikov (Dimitri (Mitia)), Ingeborga Dapkunaité (Maroussia), Nadya Mikhalkov (Nadia), Viacheslav Tikhonov (Vsevolod Konstantinovich), Svetlana Kriuchkova (Mokhova), Vladimir Ilyin (Kirik)

During an idyllic summer in mid-1930s Russia, a flamboyant colonel's household is thrown into turmoil by the arrival of a figure from the past.

The ugly betrayals of the Stalin era are documented in as pretty and lulling as any picture to have emerged from Russia in recent times; an advanced degree of

historical and political scholarship may be required to grasp all the film's resonances.

SCR Nikita Mikhalkov, Rustam Ibragimbekov CIN *Vilen Kalyuta* MUS Eduard Artemiev DES Vladimir Aronin, Aleksandr Samulekin ED Enzo Meniconi, Joëlle Hache PROD Nikita Mikhalkov, Michel Seydoux DIST Studio Trite/Camera One

66 That rarity: a film that feels as if the people who made it lived through the period it describes. – *Alexander Walker, Evening Standard*

⌇ foreign film

ⓣ film not in the English language

Bus 174 ★★

SCR/DIR Jose Padilha
2002 150m Brazil
DVD

☆ Yvonne Bezerra de Mello (Herself), Sandro do Nascimento (Himself), Rodrigo Pimentel (Himself)

Documentary centring on the hijacking of a bus by Sandro do Nascimento, a Rio street kid, and the five-hour stand-off that resulted.

A stark illustration of the gulf between rich and poor in a country where social mobility only comes when the dispossessed take violent action against those better off than them. With great compassion, Padilha pulls back from the electrifying live-TV coverage of the hijack to set the material in context; in so doing, he lends credibility to one interviewee's assertion that 'nothing in Brazil works right'.

CIN Cesar Moraes, Marcelo 'Guru' Duarte MUS Joao Nabuco, Sasha Ambak ED Felipe Lacerda PROD Marcos Prado, Jose Padilha

66 Tense, engrossing and superbly structured, Bus 174 is not just unforgettable drama but a skilfully developed argument. – *J. Hoberman, Village Voice*

The Business of Strangers ★

SCR/DIR Patrick Stettner
2001 84m US
DVD

☆ *Stockard Channing* (Julie Styron), Julia Stiles (Paula Murphy), Frederick Weller (Nick Harris)

When a confident, assertive career woman, on an overnight stay in an airport hotel, meets a young corporate assistant who claims she has been raped, the two women join forces to plot revenge.

Chilly, well-observed, but finally melodramatic piece that touches on the difficulties women face in adjusting to the heartless rhythms of male-dominated American business life.

CIN Teodoro Maniaci MUS Alexander Lasarenko DES Dina Goldman ED Keiko Deguchi PROD Susan A. Stover, Robert H. Nathan DIST Momentum

66 Looking back at the film, I don't buy all this, but no matter; Channing is so stormy, so keen to unleash her resentments, that for an hour or so you do believe in Julie. – *Anthony Lane, New Yorker*

66 Mr. Stettner has a serious subject here – how the hurts that women suffer at the hands of men can be internalized

---

more deeply than the victims know – and his film is graced with a stunning performance by Ms. Channing. – *Joe Morgenstern, Wall Street Journal*

'Not that it matters, but most of it is true!'

Butch Cassidy and the Sundance Kid ★★★★

DIR *George Roy Hill*

1969 110m US

DVD ♫

☆ *Paul Newman* (Butch Cassidy), *Robert Redford* (The Sundance Kid), Katharine Ross (Etta Place), Strother Martin (Paercy Garris), Henry Jones (Bike Salesman), Jeff Corey (Sheriff Bledsoe), Cloris Leachman (Agnes), Ted Cassidy (Harvey Logan), Kenneth Mars (Marshal)

A hundred years ago, two Western train robbers keep one step ahead of the law until finally tracked down to Bolivia.

Humorous, cheerful, poetic, cinematic account of two semi-legendary outlaws, winningly acted and directed. Newman and Redford made a superb, handsome, dry-humoured double act, and every Hollywood studio wanted to reunite them after this outing. (It finally happened in 1973 in The Sting.) One of the decade's great commercial successes, not least because of the song 'Raindrops Keep Fallin' on My Head'.

SCR *William Goldman* CIN *Conrad Hall* MUS *Burt Bacharach* ED John C. Howard PROD John Foreman DIST TCF/Campanile

66 The film does wonderful things with mood and atmosphere. The touches are fleeting, but they are there. – *Hollis Alpert, Saturday Review*

⚊ William Goldman (screenplay); Conrad Hall; Burt Bacharach; Burt Bacharach (m), Hal David (ly) (music, original song – Raindrops Keep Fallin' on My Head)
⚊ picture; George Roy Hill (direction); William Edmondson, David Dockendorf (sound)

🇹 picture; Robert Redford (leading actor); Katharine Ross (supporting actress); George Roy Hill (direction); Conrad Hall; Burt Bacharach; William Goldman (screenplay); sound track

Butcher Boy ★★

DIR Neil Jordan

1997 109m Ireland/US

DVD ♫

☆ Stephen Rea (Benny Brady, 'Da'), Fiona Shaw (Mrs Nugent), *Eamonn Owens* (Francie Brady), Alan Boyle (Joe Purcell), Brendan Gleeson (Father Bubbles), Milo O'Shea (Father Sullivan), Ian Hart (Uncle Alo), Sinead O'Connor (Our Lady/Colleen), Patrick McCabe (Jimmy-the-Skite)

Ireland, the 1960s: a teenager runs amok through his hometown, eventually turning to murder.

Shifts between the darkly comic and the outright disturbing in ways that don't make for smooth viewing, though the young lead gives a masterclass in insouciant superiority.

SCR Neil Jordan, Patrick McCabe CIN Adrian Biddle

MUS Elliot Goldenthal DES Anthony Pratt ED Tony Lawson PROD Redmond Morris, Stephen Woolley DIST Warner/Geffen

66 A film that makes you crack up with laughter in the shadows of the gallows. – *Alexander Walker, Evening Standard*

66 Caustic, compelling and really quite different. – *Geoff Andrew, Time Out*

'A story of love and redemption.'

Butterfly Kiss ★

DIR Michael Winterbottom

1995 88m GB

DVD

☆ Amanda Plummer (Eunice), Saskia Reeves (Miriam), Kathy Jamieson (Wendy), Des McAleer (Eric McDermott), Freda Dowie (Elsie), Lisa Jane Riley (Danielle), Ricky Tomlinson (Robert)

A lesbian serial killer and a dim service-station assistant join forces and go on a killing spree.

A less than likable British road movie without much joy or redemption, which did at least announce its fledgling director as a talent worth watching.

SCR Frank Cottrell Boyce CIN Seamus McGarvey MUS John Harle DES Rupert Miles ED Trevor Waite PROD Julie Baines, Sarah Daniel DIST Electric/Dan/British Screen

66 Ms. Plummer's brave, blazing performance (executed with a perfect Lancashire accent) is the heart of a disturbing road movie that suggests a twisted British answer to Thelma and Louise spiced with dashes of Heavenly Creatures and Natural Born Killers. – *Stephen Holden, New York Times*

66 A film unlikely to do much for either the serial killer genre or motorway services tourist trade. – *Clark Collis, Empire*

'A magical tale about growing up in country growing apart.'

Butterfly's Tongue ★

DIR José Luis Cuerda

1998 96m Spain

☆ Fernando Fernan Gomez (Don Gregorio), Manuel Lozano (Moncho), Uxía Blanco (Rosa), Gonzalo Uriarte (Ramon), Alexis de los Santos (Andres), Jesus Castejon (Don Avelino), Guillermo Toledo (O'lis), Elena Fernandez (Carmina), Tamar Novas (Roque), Tatan (Roque Padre), Roberto Vidal (Boal)

In pre-Civil War Spain, a young boy becomes aware of the political tensions gathering force around him.

Beautifully photographed and charmingly innocent account of a fraught historical era, seen from an innocent's viewpoint.

SCR Rafael Azcona, José Luis Cuerda, Manuel Rivas CIN *Javier G. Salmones* MUS Alejandro Amenábar DES Josep Rosell ED Ignacio Cayetano Rodriguez, Nacho Ruiz Capillas PROD Mónica Martínez, Myriam Mateos DIST Metrodome

DVD Available on DVD ☆ Cast in order 66 Critics' Quotes ⚊ Academy Award 🇹 BAFTA
♫ Soundtrack on CD   of importance † Points of interest ⚊ Academy Award nomination 🇹 BAFTA nomination

107

'A divinely decadent experience!'

Cabaret ★★★★

DIR *Bob Fosse*
1972 123m US
[DVD] ♫

☆ *Liza Minnelli* (Sally Bowles), *Joel Grey* (Master of Ceremonies), *Michael York* (Brian Roberts), Helmut Griem (Maximilian von Heune), Fritz Wepper (Fritz Wendel), Marisa Berenson (Natalia Landauer), Elisabeth Neumann-Viertel

In the early 1930s, Berlin is a hot-bed of vice and anti-Semitism. In the Kit Kat Klub, singer Sally Bowles shares her English lover with a homosexual German baron, and her Jewish friend Natalia has troubles of her own.

This version of Isherwood's Berlin stories regrettably follows the plot line of the play I Am a Camera rather than the Broadway musical on which it is allegedly based, and it lacks the incisive remarks of the MC, but the very smart direction creates a near-masterpiece of its own, and most of the terrific songs are intact. Minnelli's subsequent career is inseparable from her portrayal of Sally, which made her famous for life.

SCR Jay Presson Allen CIN *Geoffrey Unsworth* DES *Rolf Zehetbauer* ED David Bretherton PROD Cy Feuer
DIST ABC Pictures/Allied Artists

66 A stylish, sophisticated entertainment for grown-up people. – *John Russell Taylor*

66 Film journals will feast for years on shots from this picture; as it rolled along, I saw page after illustrated page from a not-too-distant book called The Cinema of Bob Fosse. – *Stanley Kauffmann*

⚊ Liza Minnelli (leading actress); Joel Grey (supporting actor); Bob Fosse (direction); Geoffrey Unsworth; Ralph Burns

⚊ picture; Jay Presson Allen

Ⓣ film; Liza Minnelli (leading actress); Joel Grey (supporting actor); Bob Fosse (direction); Rolf Zehetbauer; Geoffrey Unsworth

---

'See the sleepwalker, floating down the street, ripped from some nightmare! A street of misshapen houses with brooding windows, streaked by dagger strokes of light and darkened by blots of shadow! You will immediately feel the terror in the movements of that floating grotesque!'

The Cabinet of Dr Caligari ★★★

DIR *Robert Wiene*
1919 90m Germany
[DVD]

☆ *Werner Krauss, Conrad Veidt*, Lil Dagover, Friedrich Feher, Hans von Twardowski

A fairground showman uses a sleep-walker for the purpose of murder.

Faded now, but a silent classic, a film of immense influence on the dramatic art of cinema, with its odd angles, stylized sets and exaggerated acting, not to mention the sting in the tail of its story, added by the producer.

SCR *Carl Mayer, Hans Janowitz* CIN *Willy Hameister*
PROD Erich Pommer DIST Decla-Bioscop

66 The first hundred shocks are the hardest. – *New York Evening Post, 1924*

† The film cost $18,000 to make.

Café Lumière

DIR Hou Hsiao-Hsien
2004 103m Japan/Taiwan
[DVD]

☆ Yo Hitoto (Yoko), Tadanobu Asano (Hajime), Masato Hagiwara (Seiji), Kimiko Yo (Yoko No Kieba), Nenji Kobayashi (Yoko No Otosan)

A young female student returns to her hometown to research a project about a deceased Taiwanese composer.

Static drama, conceived as an homage to Yasujiro Ozu; stubbornly opposed to the frantic pace of modern life, its inertia nevertheless proves more trying than stirring.

SCR Hou Hsiao-Hsien, Chu T'ien-Wen CIN Lee Pin-Bing
DES Tashiharu Aida ED Liao Ching-song
PROD Hideshi Miyajima, Liao Ching-song, Ichiro Yamamoto, Fumiko Osaka DIST ICA

66 A great deal goes on beneath the film's placid, uneventful surface. . .Beyond the sociological observation, beyond the psychological insights, beyond the patterns of repetition and variation, there's a sense that Hou is reaching for some Platonic essence of cinema itself. – *Tony Rayns, Sight and Sound*

66 With its exasperatingly aimless scenes and deeply unrewarding dullness, it's more like a homage to Hou Hsiao-hsien, bordering on malign parody. – *Peter Bradshaw, Guardian*

Calamity Jane ★★★

DIR David Butler
1953 101m US
[DVD] ♫

☆ *Doris Day, Howard Keel*, Allyn McLerie, Phil Carey, Dick Wesson, Paul Harvey

Calamity helps a saloon owner friend find a star attraction, and wins the heart of Wild Bill Hickok.

Agreeable, cleaned-up, studio-set Western musical, a riposte to Annie Get Your Gun (which also starred Keel), but a much friendlier film, helped by an excellent score. Yet it's Doris Day's movie, from the moment she is first seen on the Deadwood stage, right up to her moving performance of the great Secret Love.

SCR James O'Hanlon   CIN Wilfrid Cline   PROD William Jacobs   DIST Warner

♪ Sammy Fain (m), Paul Francis Webster (ly) (music, original song – Secret Love)
♪ Ray Heindorf

Calendar ★

SCR/DIR Atom Egoyan
1993   75m   Canada/Germany/Armenia

☆ Arsinée Khanjian (Translator), Ashot Adamian (Driver), Atom Egoyan (Photographer)

A photographer and his translator girlfriend travel through Armenia to take photos of churches for a calendar.

Director Egoyan, himself Canadian-Armenian, ponders the dilemma of being part of two divergent cultures, and uses both video footage and striking colour film to illustrate aspects of his past life. A fascinating essay about (among other things) the pros and cons of various media to convey personal stories.

CIN Norayr Kasper   ED Atom Egoyan   PROD Atom Egoyan   DIST ZDF/Ego Film Arts

66 Calendar is still more a thesis than a true journey into the soul of an image-maker. – *Rita Kempley, Washington Post*

'They dropped everything for a good cause.'

Calendar Girls ★

DIR Nigel Cole
2003   108m   GB/US
DVD   ♪

☆ *Helen Mirren* (Chris Harper), *Julie Walters* (Annie Clark), John Alderton (John Clark), Linda Bassett (Cora), Annette Crosbie (Jessie), Philip Glenister (Lawrence), Ciaran Hinds (Rod), Celia Imrie (Celia), Geraldine James (Marie), Penelope Wilton (Ruth)

Members of a Women's Institute group in Yorkshire decide to pose naked for a charity calendar, becoming celebrities in the process.

Lively, well-played true-life tale adheres to the established Brit-script template of enthusiastic amateurs finding strength through mild comic nudity; as Disney-sponsored gerontophilia goes, it's absolutely fine, though the story dissipates when the WI heroines hit Hollywood.

SCR Juliette Towhidi, Tim Firth   CIN Ashley Rowe
MUS Patrick Doyle   DES Martin Childs   ED Michael Parker   PROD Nick Barton, Suzanne Mackie
DIST Buena Vista

66 Amongst the most heartwarming movies of many years, because it tackles issues such as middle age, bereavement and female friendship with a humour and depth that are not so much rare in modern cinema, as non-existent. – *Chris Tookey, Daily Mail*

66 An overly long, overly cute film that is far too tickled with its own naughtiness. – *Shawn Levy, Portland Oregonian*

California Dreamin' (Endless) (new) ★★

DIR Cristian Nemescu
2007   155m   Romania
DVD

☆ Armand Assante (Captain Jones), Marco Assante (American soldier), Sabina Branduse (Despina), Maria Dinulescu (Monica), Alexandru Dragoi (Rodriguez), Jamie Elman (David McLaren), Radu Gabriel (Stelica), Razvan Vasilescu (Doiaru)

In 1999, during the Kosovo war, in a small Romanian village, the chief of the railway station chief, who is also the local gangster, stops a NATO train transporting military equipment, supervised by American soldiers but without official documents.

The only movie by the late Romanian director Nemescu emerges as a poignant tale of the long-awaited arrival of the Americans. With a free-wheeling camera style, he stages the culture clash between Romanians and Americans as brash, broad comedy: one side is gung-ho and arrogant, the other ravaged by years of deprivation, corruption and bureaucratic dysfunction.

SCR Tudor Voican, Cristian Nemescu   CIN Liviu Marghidan   ED Catalin Cristutiu   PROD Andrei Boncea

66 This isn't just an excellent satire about crossed cultural wires but a parable, at length, about America's blundering exit strategy. – *Tim Robey, Daily Telegraph*

† Director Cristian Nemescu was killed in a car accident along with his sound editor, Andrei Toncu, on August 24, 2006. He was 27 and this first feature was not yet completed; it was awarded the Un Certain Regard prize at the Cannes Film Festival in 2007.
† The Romanian title Nesfasit means not only 'endless,' but 'unfinished,' a reference to the state in which Nemescu left the film at the time of his death.

'You who are so young – where can you have learned all you know about women like me?'

Camille ★★

DIR George Cukor
1937   108m   US
DVD

☆ *Greta Garbo*, Robert Taylor, Lionel Barrymore, *Henry Daniell*, Elizabeth Allan, Lenore Ulric, Laura Hope Crews, Rex O'Malley, Jessie Ralph, E. E. Clive

A dying courtesan, torn between two lovers, falls for an innocent young man and dies in his arms.

This old warhorse is an unsuitable vehicle for Garbo but magically she carries it off, and the production is elegant and pleasing. In its day, the quintessential tear-jerker.

SCR Frances Marion, James Hilton, Zoe Akins
CIN William Daniels   MUS Herbert Stothart
PROD Irving Thalberg, Bernard Hyman   DIST MGM

66 Pretty close to the top mark in showmanship, direction, photography and box office names. – *Variety*

DVD Available on DVD   ☆ Cast in order   66 Critics' Quotes   ♪ Academy Award   🏆 BAFTA
♪ Soundtrack on CD   of importance   † Points of interest   ♪ Academy Award nomination   🏆 BAFTA nomination

The slow, solemn production is luxuriant in its vulgarity: it achieves that glamour which MGM traditionally mistook for style. – *Pauline Kael, 1968*

† A 1927 silent version starred Norma Talmadge with Gilbert Roland.

⚲ Greta Garbo (leading actress)

Canadian Bacon

SCR/DIR Michael Moore
1995 91m US
[DVD]

☆ Alan Alda (U.S. President), John Candy (Sheriff Bud Boomer), Rhea Perlman (Deputy Pearlman), Kevin Pollak (Stuart Smiley), Rip Torn (General Dick Panzer), Bill Nunn (Kabral Jabar), Kevin J. O'Connor (Roy Boy), G.D. Spradlin (R.J Hacker), Carlton Watson (Clarence Thomason), James Belushi (Charles Jackal), Dan Aykroyd (OPP Officer)

A US President declares war on Canada in order to boost his poll ratings.

Director Moore is certainly a master at documentaries, but the film's sole point of interest here is to see what a leaden hand he brings to an indifferent comedy script.

CIN Haskell Wexler MUS Elmer Bernstein, Peter Bernstein DES Carol Spier ED Wendy Stanzler, Michael Berenbaum PROD Michael Moore, David Brown, Ron Rotholz DIST Polygram/Propaganda/Maverick

There are some interesting ideas in Canadian Bacon, but most of them fall flat because of Moore's screenwriting and lazy direction. – *Kevin Laforest, Montreal Film Journal*

'We Dare You To Say His Name Five Times!'

Candyman ★

SCR/DIR *Bernard Rose*
1992 99m US
[DVD]

☆ Virginia Madsen (Helen Lyle), Tony Todd (The Candyman), Xander Berkeley (Trevor Lyle), Kasi Lemmons (Bernie), Vanessa Williams (Anne-Marie McCoy), DeJuan Guy (Jake), Michael Culkin (Professor Phillip Purcell), Stanley DeSantis (Dr Burke), Gilbert Lewis (Detective Frank Valento)

An anthropology student writing a thesis on urban myths investigates the legend of a hook-handed serial killer.

Skilful modern horror that uses its inner-city location as a crucible for atmosphere and resonant themes, and a backdrop for some gory, suspenseful sequences.

CIN Anthony B. Richmond MUS *Philip Glass* DES *Jane Ann Stewart* ED Dan Rae PROD Steve Golin, Sigurjon Sighvatsson, Alan Poul DIST Columbia TriStar/Polygram/Propaganda

Cuts with a bloody hook through the superficiality of most recent horror movies, and demonstrates that you don't have to be stupid to be scary. – *Kim Newman, Empire*

'There is nothing in the dark that isn't there in the light. Except fear.'

Cape Fear ★★

DIR *Martin Scorsese*
1991 128m US
[DVD] ♫

☆ *Robert De Niro* (Max Cady), Nick Nolte (Sam Bowden), Jessica Lange (Leigh Bowden), Juliette Lewis (Danielle Bowden), Joe Don Baker (Claude Kersek), Robert Mitchum (Lieutenant Elgart), Gregory Peck (Lee Heller), Martin Balsam (Judge), Illeana Douglas (Lori Davis)

A lawyer and his family are menaced by a psychopathic ex-convict.

Technically superior entertainment, directed and played at full strength, though the appearance of Mitchum, Peck and Balsam in cameo roles only serve to remind the viewer of the altogether more contained and composed original.

SCR Wesley Strick CIN Freddie Francis DES Henry Bumstead ED Thelma Schoonmaker PROD Barbara de Fina DIST Universal/Amblin/Cappa/Tribeca

A spectacularly bad film for Scorsese to have made. . .a piece of hack work. – *Pauline Kael, New Yorker*

Everyone concerned with this repellent attempt to make a great deal of money out of a clumsy plunge into sexual pathology should be thoroughly ashamed of himself. – *J. Hoberman, Sight & Sound*

⚲ Robert De Niro (leading actor); Juliette Lewis (supporting actress)

Capote ★★★★

DIR *Bennett Miller*
2005 114m US/Canada
[DVD] ♫

☆ *Philip Seymour Hoffman* (Truman Capote), *Catherine Keener* (Nelle Harper Lee), Clifton Collins Jnr (Perry Smith), Chris Cooper (Alvin Dewey), Bruce Greenwood (Jack Dunphy), Bob Balaban (William Shawn), Amy Ryan (Mary Dewey), Mark Pellegrino (Dick Hickock)

The writer Truman Capote investigates the Kansas murders that would come to form the basis of In Cold Blood.

A rare biopic that seeks not to sanctify its protagonist, or excuse his many failings, instead turning close attention to the collateral damage that can flow from the creative process; powered by Hoffman's exceptional performance, it has much the same cold, hard crunch of verisimilitude as would have struck readers of Capote's book upon first publication.

SCR Dan Futterman CIN *Adam Kimmel* MUS Mychael Danna DES Jess Gonchor ED Christopher Tellefsen PROD Caroline Baron, William Vince, Michael Ohoven DIST Columbia TriStar

Honors its subject by doing just what Truman Capote did. It teases, fascinates, and haunts. – *Owen Gleiberman, Entertainment Weekly*

How often does one see a masterpiece about a masterpiece? – *Robert Wilonsky, Dallas Observer*

⚲ Philip Seymour Hoffman (leading actor)
⚲ picture; Catherine Keener (supporting actress); Bennett Miller; Dan Futterman

⚑ Philip Seymour Hoffman (leading actor)
⚑ film; Catherine Keener (supporting actress); Bennett Miller; Don Futterman (adapted screenplay)

[DVD] Available on DVD ☆ Cast in order 66 Critics' Quotes ⚲ Academy Award ⚑ BAFTA
♫ Soundtrack on CD of importance † Points of interest ⚲ Academy Award nomination ⚑ BAFTA nomination

Caramel (new)   ★★

DIR *Nadine Labaki*

2007   95m   France/Lebanon

DVD ♫

☆ Nadine Labaki (Layale), Yasmine Al Masri (Nisrine), Joanna Moukarzel (Rima), Gisele Aouad (Jamale), Adel Karam (Youssef), Sihame Haddad (Rose), Aziza Semaan (Lili)

The staff and clients of a Beirut beauty salon grapple with life, love and growing old.

Charming tale of romance and friendship that offers some revealing insights into a Lebanese woman's lot.

SCR Nadine Labaki, Jihad Hojeily, Rodney Al Haddad CIN Yves Sehnaoui   MUS Khaled Mouzanar DES Cynthia Zahar   ED Laurie Gardette   PROD Anne-Dominique Toussaint   DIST Momentum

66 Not especially original but always diverting. – *Jay Weissberg, Variety*

66 Sentimental, warm-hearted and occasionally irreverent. – *Wendy Ide, The Times*

Carandiru   ★★

DIR *Hector Babenco*

2003   145m   Brazil/US

DVD

☆ Luiz Carlos Vasconcelos (Doctor), Milhem Cortaz (Dagge), Milton Goncalves (Chico), Ivan de Almeida (Ebony), Ailton Graca (Highness), Aida Lerner (Rosirene), Rodrigo Santoro (Lady Di)

A doctor hears the stories of inmates in Brazil's most notorious prison, where overcrowding is rife and the tensions are mounting.

An Arabian Nights-like structure allows Babenco to tell a variety of tough, funny, absorbing, unpredictable tales of life on both sides of the prison walls until a bravura final half-hour in which all hell breaks loose.

SCR *Victor Nava, Hector Babenco, Fernando Bonassi* CIN Walter Carvalho   MUS Andre Abujarrura DES Clovis Bueno   ED Mauro Alice   PROD Hector Babenco, Oscar Kramer   DIST ColumbiaTriStar

66 For a film that is so full of death, Carandiru feels extraordinarily alive: its squalor is mixed with an irrepressible sense of carnival. – *Jenny McCartney, Sunday Telegraph*

† The film is based on an account of a real-life prison riot which left 111 prisoners dead.

'All Hannah wanted was a roommate. . .instead she got a best friend.'

Career Girls   ★

SCR/DIR *Mike Leigh*

1997   87m   GB

DVD

☆ Katrin Cartlidge (Hannah Mills), Lynda Steadman (Annie), Kate Byers (Claire), Mark Benton (Ricky Burton), Andy Serkis (Mr Evans), Joe Tucker (Adrian Spinks), Margo Stanley (Mrs Burton), Michael Healy (Lecturer)

After six years apart, two former college friends meet up for a day in London to reminisce about old times.

It's far from pretty – a film full of tics and scars, with flashbacks that all appear to have been shot at five in the morning – but the director's eye for social interactions remains reasonably sharp. Minor Leigh.

CIN Dick Pope   MUS Marianne Jean-Baptiste, Tony Remy DES Eve Stewart   ED Robin Sales   PROD Simon Channing-Williams   DIST Film Four/Thin Man/Matrix

66 The coincidental encounters with former friends in the film's last third do seem rather stagey, but given its unflattering wit and humanity, you'd forgive Career Girls an awful lot more. – *Anthony Quinn, Mail on Sunday*

66 Improvised study of endlessly whining women with annoying voices. . .the dialogue – apart from an occasional smart one-liner – is dysfunctional ranting. – *Anne Billson, Sunday Telegraph*

'A dream called freedom. A nightmare called Nicaragua.'

Carla's Song   ★★

DIR Ken Loach

1996   127m   GB/Germany/Spain

DVD

☆ Robert Carlyle (George Lennox), Oyanka Cabezas (Carla), Scott Glenn (Bradley), Salvador Espinoza (Rafael), Louise Goodall (Maureen), Richard Loza (Antonio), Gary Lewis (Sammy)

Glasgow, 1987: a bus driver falls for a Nicaraguan refugee, and accompanies her back to her war-torn homeland.

The first of several collaborations between director Loach and screenwriter Laverty displays the pair's ability to combine affecting personal drama with a commitment to harsh political realities.

SCR Paul Laverty   CIN Barry Ackroyd   MUS George Fenton   DES Martin Johnson   ED Jonathan Morris PROD Sally Hibbin   DIST Polygram/Channel 4/GFF/Parallax/Road Movies/Tornasol

66 Combines some of the most truthful, touching work that Ken Loach has done. – *Ryan Gilbey, Independent*

ⓣ British film; Ken Loach

Carlito's Way   ★★

DIR *Brian de Palma*

1993   145m   US

DVD ♫

☆ *Al Pacino* (Carlito 'Charlie' Brigante), *Sean Penn* (David Kleinfeld), Penelope Ann Miller (Gail), *John Leguizamo* (Benny Blanco), Ingrid Rogers (Steffie), Luis Guzman (Pachanga), James Rebhorn (District Attorney Norwalk), Viggo Mortensen (Lalin)

Released from jail, a reformed drug dealer struggles to escape the reach of those hoods who came through in his wake.

Supercharged rejig of gangster-movie motifs, rather overdone in its romantic subplot, but put over with all this director's usual flair and several colourful performances.

SCR David Koepp   CIN Stephen H. Burum   MUS Patrick Doyle   DES Richard Sylbert   ED Bill Pankow, Kristina Boden   PROD Martin Bregman, Willi Baer, Michael A. Bregman   DIST Universal

---

66 Inflated as the first two hours feel, the movie's final thirty minutes are an expert spiral of doom. – *J. Hoberman, Village Voice*

66 Too long and ultimately no more than a showpiece, but Pacino looks every inch a movie star. – *Tom Charity, Time Out*

'More than your eyes have ever seen!'

Carousel ★★

DIR Henry King
1956   128m   US
DVD   ♫

☆ *Gordon MacRae, Shirley Jones*, Cameron Mitchell, Gene Lockhart, Barbara Ruick, Robert Rounseville

A reprobate dies while committing a holdup. Fifteen years later he returns from heaven to earth to set his family's affairs in order and ensure his daughter is on the right path.

This super-wide-screen version of an effective stage musical does not make much of a film; the direction is creaky and lacking in verve. Worth seeing, though, for MacRae's and Jones's fine interpretation of the songs, some of the finest Rodgers and Hammerstein ever composed.

SCR *Phoebe and Henry Ephron, from the musical based on Ferenc Molnar's play Liliom*   CIN Charles G. Clarke   PROD Henry Ephron   DIST TCF

Carrie ★★

DIR *Brian de Palma*
1976   98m   US
DVD   ♫

☆ *Sissy Spacek, Piper Laurie*, Amy Irving, William Katt, John Travolta, Betty Buckley, Nancy Allen, P. J. Soles

A neurotic teenage girl with telekinetic powers avenges herself on classmates who taunt and persecute her, turning her school prom into a slaughter.

A horror film with a reputation that holds up well, in part because director de Palma takes time building sympathy for his unhappy young heroine, which makes the climactic bloodbath more dramatically satisfying.

SCR Lawrence D. Cohen   CIN Mario Tosi   MUS Pino Donaggio   ED Paul Hirsch   PROD Paul Monash   DIST UA/Red Bank

66 Combining Gothic horror, offhand misogyny and an air of studied triviality, Carrie is de Palma's most enjoyable movie in a long while, and also his silliest. – *Janet Maslin, Newsweek*

66 The horror is effective only once, and the attempts at humour are never very successful and come almost when one is inclined to be moved by somebody's plight, so that the non-jokes yield authentic bad taste. – *John Simon, New York*

⚖ Sissy Spacek (leading actress); Piper Laurie (supporting actress)

'A Love Story So Unusual It Has To Be True.'

Carrington ★

SCR/DIR Christopher Hampton
1995   121m   GB/France
DVD   ♫

☆ Emma Thompson (Carrington), *Jonathan Pryce* (Lytton Strachey), Steven Waddington (Ralph Partridge), Samuel West (Gerald Brenan), Rufus Sewell (Mark Gertler), Penelope Wilton (Lady Ottoline Morrell), Janet McTeer (Vanessa Bell), Peter Blythe (Philip Morrell)

An androgynous woman artist and a gay writer, both part of the Bloomsbury group, embark on an unlikely chaste affair.

Solidly directed in the 'heritage movie' tradition, but its conservative style is at odds with the tumultuous subject matter; considering the sexual shenanigans portrayed here, the tone remains resolutely staid. The main dramatic mis-step is centring events around the title character; the effete but charismatic Strachey (splendidly played by Pryce) is the story's heartbeat. Still, an absorbing account of an intriguing literary set.

CIN Denis Lenoir   MUS Michael Nyman   DES Caroline Amies   ED George Akers   PROD Ronald Shedlo, John McGrath   DIST Polygram/Freeway/Shedlo/Dora

STRACHEY: 'I must say I find those new young people wonderfully refreshing. They have no morals and they never speak. It's an enchanting combination.'

66 Thanks to the character's nonstop bons mots and an expertly clever, wonderfully sympathetic performance by Jonathan Pryce, Carrington is Strachey's film. – *Janet Maslin, New York Times*

† The film won the Special Jury Prize and Jonathan Pryce the Best Actor award at the 1995 Cannes Film Festival. It was originally to have been directed by Herbert Ross, and then by Mike Newell. Hampton wrote his original script in the mid-70s.

Ⓣ British film; Jonathan Pryce (leading actor);

'Ahhh. . .it's got that new movie smell.'

Cars ★★

DIR John Lasseter
2006   121m   US
DVD   ♫

☆ Owen Wilson (Lightning McQueen), Paul Newman (Doc Hudson), Bonnie Hunt (Sally Carrera), Larry the Cable Guy (Mater), Tony Shalhoub (Luigi), Cheech Marin (Ramone)

In a fantasy world, every character is a motor vehicle. Lightning McQueen, an arrogant stock car, cares only about himself and winning. En route to a big race, he gets trapped in a small, sleepy town, and re-thinks his life.

A story about common decency trumping naked ambition, and a winner-takes-all philosophy being put firmly in its place. A rare animation film that adults and children can enjoy, if for different reasons: kids will be amused by the characters and jokes, while grown-ups may reflect on its nostalgia for the values of a bygone age. Includes typically Pixar visual touches: cloud formations resembling car parts; a pile of tyres on the

---

DVD Available on DVD   ☆ Cast in order   66 Critics' Quotes   ⚖ Academy Award   Ⓑ BAFTA
♫ Soundtrack on CD   of importance   † Points of interest   ⚖ Academy Award nomination   Ⓣ BAFTA nomination

forecourt of a garage 'owned' by an Italian car, stacked like the Leaning Tower of Pisa.

SCR Dan Fogelman, John Lasseter, Joe Ranft, Kiel Murray, Phil Lorin, Jorgen Klubien CIN Jermey Lasky, Jean-Claude Kalache MUS Randy Newman DES William Cone, Bob Pauley ED Ken Schretzmann PROD Darla K. Anderson DIST Buena Vista International

66 If Cars is something of a letdown, that is not because of the moral messages that it delivers, but because of the heavy hand with which it cranks them out. – *Anthony Lane, New Yorker*

† The voice of the Ferrari in the film was dubbed by Formula 1 ace Michael Schumacher.

⚱ animated feature film; Randy Newman (music, original song – Our Town)

Ⓣ animated feature film

'As big and timely a picture as ever you've seen! You can tell by the cast it's important! gripping! big!'

Casablanca ★★★★

DIR *Michael Curtiz*
1942 102m US
DVD ♫

☆ *Humphrey Bogart* (Rick Blaine), *Ingrid Bergman* (Ilse Lund), Paul Henreid (Victor Laszlo), *Claude Rains* (Captain Louis Renault), Sydney Greenstreet (Ferrari), Peter Lorre (Ugarte), S.Z. Sakall (Carl), *Conrad Veidt* (Major Strasser), *Dooley Wilson* (Sam), *Marcel Dalio* (Croupier), Joy Page, John Qualen, Ludwig Stossel, Leonid Kinskey, Helmut Dantine, Ilka Gruning

Rick's Café in Casablanca is a centre for war refugees awaiting visas for America. Rick abandons his cynicism to help an old flame escape the Nazis with her husband, a heroic Resistance leader.

Cinema par excellence: a studio-bound Hollywood melodrama which after various chances just fell together impeccably into one of the outstanding entertainment experiences of cinema history, with romance, intrigue, excitement, suspense and humour cunningly deployed by master technicians and a perfect cast.

SCR *Julius J. Epstein, Philip G. Epstein, Howard Koch* CIN *Arthur Edeson* MUS *Max Steiner* ED *Owen Marks* PROD *Hal B. Wallis* DIST *Warner*

RICK: I stick out my neck for nobody. I'm the only cause I'm interested in.
LOUIS: How extravagant you are, throwing away women like that. Someday they may be scarce.
RICK: Ilse, I'm no good at being noble, but it doesn't take much to see that the problems of three little people don't amount to a hill of beans in this crazy world. Someday you'll understand that. Not now. Here's looking at you, kid.
RICK: I came to Casablanca for the waters.
LOUIS: What waters? We're in the desert.
RICK: I was misinformed.
RICK: Louis, I think this is the beginning of a beautiful friendship.
LOUIS: Major Strasser has been shot. Round up the usual suspects.

66 A picture which makes the spine tingle and the heart take a leap. . .they have so combined sentiment, humour

and pathos with taut melodrama and bristling intrigue that the result is a highly entertaining and even inspiring film. – *New York Times*

66 Its humour is what really saves it, being a mixture of Central European irony of attack and racy Broadway-Hollywood Boulevard cynicism. – *Herman G. Weinberg*

† Originally named for the leads were Ronald Reagan, Ann Sheridan and Dennis Morgan

† 'As Time Goes By', 'Knock on Wood'

⚱ picture; Julius J. and Philip G. Epstein, Howard Koch (screenplay); Michael Curtiz (direction)

⚱ Humphrey Bogart (leading actor); Claude Rains (supporting actor); Arthur Edeson; Max Steiner; Owen Marks

---

'Sometimes love is hiding between the seconds of your life.'

Cashback ⓝⓔⓦ

SCR/DIR Sean Ellis
2007 102m UK
DVD

☆ Sean Biggerstaff (Ben Willis), Emilia Fox (Sharon Pintley), Shaun Evans (Sean Higgins), Michelle Ryan (Suzy)

An arts school student, dumped by his girl-friend works the graveyard shift at a supermarket, where he daydreams about love, women and having the ability to freeze time.

Slight, superficial, resolutely unfunny British comedy, extended from a short to a grotesquely long running time for no apparent reason.

CIN Angus Hudson MUS Guy Farley DES Morgan Kennedy ED Scott Thomas, Carlos Domeque PROD Sean Ellis, Lene Bausager DIST The Works

66 For all its slickness, it's an unforgivably shallow film. – *Cath Clarke, Guardian*

† Writer-director Ellis made an 18-minute short version of Cashback, which was Oscar-nominated in 2004.

'You don't stay at the top forever.'

Casino ★★★

DIR *Martin Scorsese*
1995 178m US/France
DVD ♫

☆ *Robert De Niro* (Sam 'Ace' Rothstein), *Sharon Stone* (Ginger McKenna), Joe Pesci (Nicky Santoro), James Woods (Lester Diamond), Don Rickles (Billy Sherbert), Alan King (Andy Stone), Kevin Pollak (Phillip Green), L.Q. Jones (Pat Webb), Dick Smothers (Senator)

A gambler assumes managership of a Mob-run Vegas casino, only for dealings with his former call-girl wife and a petulant bodyguard to expose him to his enemies.

A film of excess in both content and form, bloated at almost three hours. One could argue that voiceover and soundtrack to bridge the gaps between set-pieces, but those set-pieces are masterful. Pesci's performance – a hyperactive retread of his Goodfellas schtick – is a weak spot, but De Niro and Stone (the real revelation here) are very good indeed. Arguably Scorsese's most underrated movie.

DVD Available on DVD   ☆ Cast in order   66 Critics' Quotes   ⚱ Academy Award   Ⓑ BAFTA
♫ Soundtrack on CD   of importance   † Points of interest   ⚱ Academy Award nomination   Ⓣ BAFTA nomination

113

SCR Nicholas Pileggi, Martin Scorsese CIN Robert Richardson DES Dante Ferretti ED Thelma Schoonmaker PROD Barbara de Fina
DIST Universal/Syalis/Legende/De Fina/Cappa

66 Possesses a stylistic boldness and verisimilitude that is virtually matchless. – *Variety*

66 It constantly dazzles with visual, auditory and thematic stimuli. – *Jonathan Romney, Sight & Sound*

♫ Sharon Stone (leading actress)

Casino Royale ★★

DIR Martin Campbell
2006   144m   UK/US/Czech Republic/Germany
DVD
☆ Daniel Craig (James Bond), Eva Green (Vesper Lynd), Mads Mikkelsen (Le Chiffre), Giancarlo Giannini (Mathis), Jeffrey Wright (Felix Leiter), Judi Dench (M)

MI6 despatches James Bond to track down and destroy Le Chiffre, a villainous banker to terrorist organisations. The chase continues over three continents.

The best Bond film since Sean Connery quit the role, with Craig a saviour of a tired franchise that creatively had long overstayed its welcome. It jettisons the infantilism and flippancy that dogged Bond movies for years, and restores a welcome touch of cruelty and toughness. A ruthless, stripped-down, modern Bond, Craig rises above the role's stereotypical traps. The script is coherent while finding room for splendid stunt-driven set-pieces, notably a chase on a construction site. The opening scene, a bloody murder in a public lavatory, sets the mood; a grim torture scene confirms this is neither for kids nor for the squeamish. Here's a Bond film that Ian Fleming might have enjoyed.

SCR Neal Purvis, Robert Wade, Paul Haggis CIN Phil Meheux MUS David Arnold DES Peter Lamont ED Stuart Baird PROD Michael G. Wilson, Barbara Broccoli DIST Sony

BOND: 'Vodka Martini.'
WAITER: 'Shaken or stirred?'
BOND: 'Do I look like I give a damn?'

66 Contrary to pre-release nay-sayers, Daniel Craig has done more with James Bond in one film than some previous stars have done in multiple reprises. This is terrific stuff, again positioning 007 as the action franchise to beat. – *Kim Newman, Empire*

66 There's clearly life in the old dog yet. – *Tom Charity, CNN.com*

† The last remaining Bond novel by Fleming to be filmed by Eon Productions. Casino Royale was previously made in 1967, in a poorly received version starring David Niven and Deborah Kerr.

Ⓣ Ian Munro, Eddy Joseph, Mike Prestwood Smith, Martin Cantwell, Mark Taylor (sound)

Ⓣ British film; Daniel Craig (leading actor); Neal Purvis, Robert Wade, Paul Haggis; Peter Lamont, Phil Meheux, Stuart Baird; David Arnold; Steve Begg, Chris Corbould, John Paul Docherty, Ditch Doy (special visual effects)

'How far will you go to make your dreams come true?'

Cassandra's Dream (new)

SCR/DIR Woody Allen
2007   108m   UK/France
DVD   ♫
☆ Colin Farrell (Terry Blaine), Ewan McGregor (Ian Blaine), Tom Wikinson (Uncle Howard), Hayley Atwell (Angela Stark), Sally Hawkins (Kate), John Benfield (Mr. Blaine), Phil Davis (Martin Burns)

Two London brothers, both seriously short of money, are tempted when their shady uncle offers to pay them to murder a man.

The London portrayed here feels so wrong, so unrecognisable, the film might as well have been shot in Latvia. Nor do the two leads convince as brothers; after three films set in Britain, Allen is no nearer to understanding the structures and nuances of British society. His insistence on making a film every year is leading him to cut corners in his scripts; he needs to concentrate harder.

CIN Vilmos Zsigmond MUS Philip Glass DES Maria Djurkovic ED Alisa Lepselter PROD Letty Aronson, Stephen Tenenbaum, Gareth Wiley DIST Optimum

66 Allen, who stays behind the camera, brings too little wit and too much contrivance to material that quickly dissolves into warmed-over Dostoevsky. – *Peter Travers, Rolling Stone*

66 This is (Allen's) third mediocre London movie in a row – a run that would have destroyed lesser reputations, and should probably be deleted from the records. – *Steve Rose, Guardian*

'At the edge of the world, his journey begins.'

Cast Away ★

DIR Robert Zemeckis
2000   143m   US
DVD   ♫
☆ *Tom Hanks* (Chuck Noland), Helen Hunt (Kelly Frears), Nick Searcy (Stan), Lari White (Bettina Peterson), Michael Forest (Pilot Jack), Viveka Davis (Pilot Gwen)

A clockwatching FedEx executive is forced to reassess his priorities in life after being marooned on a tropical island.

Has the feel of a Hollywood exercise or conceit – just how long will audiences watch nothing but Tom Hanks? – yet Zemeckis and his leading man get surprisingly close to a real and affecting sense of disconnection and isolation.

SCR William Broyles Jnr CIN Don Burgess MUS Alan Silvestri DES Rick Carter ED Arthur Schmidt PROD Steve Starkey, Tom Hanks, Robert Zemeckis, Jack Rapke DIST TCF/Dreamworks

66 Here is a strong and simple story surrounded by needless complications, and flawed by a last act that first disappoints us and then ends on a note of forced whimsy. – *Roger Ebert, Chicago Sun-Times*

66 It's mournful and troubling in a way that goes beyond ordinary movie manipulation. – *Stephanie Zacharek, Salon*

⚖ Tom Hanks (leading actor); Randy Thom, Tom Johnson, Dennis Sands, William B. Kaplan (sound)

Ⓣ Tom Hanks (leading actor)

'Ordinary Family. Extraordinary Story.'

The Castle ★★

DIR Rob Sitch
1997   82m   Australia
[DVD]

☆ *Michael Caton* (Darryl Kerrigan), Anne Tenney (Sal Kerrigan), Sophie Lee (Tracy Kerrigan), Anthony Simcoe (Steve Kerrigan), Stephen Curry (Dale Kerrigan), Wayne Hope (Wayne Kerrigan), Eric Bana (Con Petropoulous), Tiriel Mora (Dennis Denuto), Charles (Bud) Tingwell (Lawrence Hammill), Robyn Nevin (Federal Court Judge), Costas Kilias (Farouk)

A family of eccentrics attempt to save their home from being bought up by developers looking to expand a nearby airport.

Bright, good-spirited comedy pitting David against Goliath, and dressing the former in gaudy sportswear for much of its duration; the whole is cheap, cheerful and quite irresistible.

SCR Rob Sitch, Santo Cilauro, Tom Gleisner, Jane Kennedy   CIN Miriana Marusic   MUS Craig Harnath   DES Carrie Kennedy   ED Wayne Hyett   PROD Debra Choate   DIST UIP/Village Roadshow/Working Dog/Frontline TV

❝ It pisses on The Piano. – *Phillip Adams, The Australian*

'Even in war. . .murder is murder.'

Casualties of War ★★★

DIR Brian de Palma
1989   113m   US
[DVD] ♫

☆ Michael J. Fox (PFC Eriksson), Sean Penn (Sgt. Tony Meserve), Don Harvey (Cpl. Thomas E. Clark), John C. Reilly (PFC. Herbert Hatcher), John Leguizamo (PFC. Antonio Diaz), Thuy Thu Le (Tran Thi Oanh/Girl on Train), Erik King (Cpl. Brown), Jack Gwaltney (PFC. Rowan)

A young Vietnamese woman is kidnapped and raped by four American soldiers. Another GI observes the incident, does nothing to stop it, but tells his superiors what happened.

Based on real events, this provocative story dwells on how soldiers are brutalised to prepare them for battle. The clash of wills between the decent soldier (Fox) and the chief culprit (Penn) is simplistic, but de Palma shoots with conviction and blistering energy.

SCR David Rabe   CIN Stephen H. Burum   MUS Ennio Morricone   DES Wolf Kroeger   ED Bill Pankow   PROD Art Linson   DIST Columbia TriStar

❝ This new film is the kind that makes you feel protective. When you leave the theatre, you'll probably find that you're not ready to talk about it. You may also find it hard to talk lightly about anything. – *Pauline Kael*

❝ Casualties of War moves toward its climax so inevitably and surely that the courts-martial, which are the film's penultimate sequence, are no less riveting for the theatrical way in which they have been compressed. – *Vincent Canby, New York Times*

† Screenwriter David Rabe distanced himself from the film, complaining that director de Palma had not been faithful to his script.
† Brian de Palma used an almost identical story for Redacted, his 2007 film that was set in the Iraq conflict.

'In the heat of passion lies the coldest desire.'

Cat Chaser ★

DIR Abel Ferrara
1988   98m   US

☆ Peter Weller (George Moran), Kelly McGillis (Mary DeBora), Charles Durning (Jiggs Scully), Frederic Forrest (Nolen Tyner), Tomas Milian (Andre DeBoya), Juan Fernandez (Rafi), Phil Leeds (Jerry Shea), Kelly Jo Minter (Loret), Tony Bolano (Corky)

A motel owner with a military past reunites with an old flame, now the wife of a sadistic Dominican ex-police chief with a stash of hidden cash.

Though Elmore Leonard co-scripted this adaptation of his novel, the results are patchy. The first-rate cast deliver uniformly sound performances, but somewhere in the mix, Leonard's artful blend of passion, wit and sardonic resignation gets lost. An interesting failure.

SCR James Borelli, Elmore Leonard   CIN Anthony B. Richmond   MUS Chick Corea   DES Dan Leigh   ED Anthony Redman   PROD Peter A. Davis, William Panzer   DIST Whiskers Productions

❝ There's more than enough going on to warrant an hour and a half of your time. – *Channel 4*

† This was a troubled production, with several re-writes of the script, and re-cutting ordered by the studio.

'The true story of a real fake.'

Catch Me If You Can ★

DIR *Steven Spielberg*
2002   141m   US
[DVD] ♫

☆ *Leonardo DiCaprio* (Frank Abagnale Jnr), *Tom Hanks* (Carl Hanratty), *Christopher Walken* (Frank Abagnale), Martin Sheen (Roger Strong), Nathalie Baye (Paula Abagnale), Amy Adams (Brenda Strong), James Brolin (Jack Barnes)

The true story of Frank Abagnale Jr, a young con artist in the 1960s who – on the run from a broken home – posed as a pilot, a doctor and a lawyer, all the while pursued by the FBI.

Zesty caper movie that suggests it's possible to get away with anything in America if you put a pretty face in the right suit. Spielberg shies away from his hero's philandering, but delivers a light, crowdpleasing work, rich in period detail.

SCR Jeff Nathanson   CIN Janusz Kaminski   MUS *John Williams*   DES Jeannine Oppewall   ED Michael Kahn   PROD Steven Spielberg, Walter F. Parkes   DIST DreamWorks

❝ Spielberg must have felt that he owed us some fun, and the movie has a sleek and carefree look – the lightness of a sixties comedy, made with the extraordinary speed and panache of our most fluent director. – *David Denby, New Yorker*

| [DVD] Available on DVD | ☆ Cast in order | ❝ Critics' Quotes | ⚖ Academy Award | Ⓑ BAFTA |
| ♫ Soundtrack on CD | of importance | † Points of interest | ⚖ Academy Award nomination | Ⓣ BAFTA nomination |

66 Isn't a Spielberg masterpiece, but it cheers you up twice over: by being downright entertaining, and by reassuring us that its director has lost neither the ability nor the inclination to make this kind of movie. – *Edward Porter, Sunday Times*

👤 Christopher Walken (supporting actor); John Williams

🎭 Christopher Walken (supporting actor)

Ⓓ Jeff Nathanson (adapted screenplay); John Williams; Mary Zophres (costume design)

'When murder is your business, you'd better not fall in love with your work.'

Catchfire ★

DIR Alan Smithee
1989 98m US
[DVD]

☆ Dennis Hopper (Milo), Jodie Foster (Anne Benton), Dean Stockwell (John Luponi), Vincent Price (Mr Avoca), John Turturro (Pinella), Joe Pesci (Leo Carelli), Fred Ward (Pauling), Julie Adams (Martha), G. Anthony Sirico (Greek)

A Mob hitman is ordered to kill a woman who witnessed a gangland murder, but instead they fall for each other.

Given the problems this film endured during and after production, it's no surprise that it's chaotic and uneven. The surprise is that's also curiously compelling.

SCR Rachel Kronstadt Mann, Ann Louise Bardach
CIN Ed Lachman   MUS Curt Sobel, Michel Colombier
DES Ron Foreman   ED David Rawlins   PROD Dick Clark, Dan Paulson   DIST Vestron/Precision Films/Mack-Taylor Productions

† Director Dennis Hopper disowned the final cut, and insisted on the 'Alan Smithee' credit for his work. The director's cut is titled Backtrack.
† Bob Dylan has an uncredited walk-on role.

'The Whisper Told Most Often. . .'

The Cat's Meow ★

DIR Peter Bogdanovich
2001 114m Germany/GB/USA
[DVD]   ♪

☆ Kirsten Dunst (Marion Davies), Cary Elwes (Thomas Ince), Edward Herrmann (William Randolph Hearst), Eddie Izzard (Charlie Chaplin), Joanna Lumley (Elinor Glyn), Victor Slezak (George Thomas), Jennifer Tilly (Louella Parsons), James Laurenson (Dr. Goodman)

A voyage on board a yacht owned by media magnate William Randolph Hearst ends in the murder of one of the guests.

Adapted from a stage play drawing on old Hollywood gossip, this is essentially a decent episode of Poirot, as suspects with familiar faces shout 'Charleston!' whenever events threaten to get too talky; the material elicits diverting impersonations of real people, and is at its strongest in the run-up to the crime itself, where the literary allusions – to Othello and The Rime of the Ancient Mariner – can finally drop into place.

SCR Steven Peros   CIN Bruno Delbonnel   DES Jean-

Vincent Puzos   ED Edward Norris   PROD Kim Bieber, Carol Lewis, Dieter Meyer, Julie Baines   DIST Lions Gate

66 Good gossip, entertainingly delivered, yet with a distinctly musty odour, its expiry date long gone. – *Rick Groen, Toronto Globe and Mail*

66 A diverting and mordant picture of muddled, well-meaning souls and cynical hedonists adrift on a sea of danger and spite. – *Peter Bradshaw, Guardian*

† Though the action is set in California, the film was shot entirely in Berlin.

Cave of the Yellow Dog ★★

SCR/DIR Byambasuren Davaa
2005 93m Mongolia/Germany
☆ Urjindorj Batchuluun (Father), Buyandulam Batchuluun (Mother), Nansaal Batchuluun (Nansal), Nansalla Batchhuluun (Nansalmaa)

The young daughter of a nomadic family of Mongolian sheepherders brings home a stray dog. But her father worries it may have been running with wolves who kill the family's sheep.

Besides the adorable children at its heart, this subtle story is of a harsh culture threatened by progress on Mongolia's remote steppes. A scene of the family dismantling their yurt and moving on is masterfully realised.

CIN Daniel Schonauer   MUS Ganpurev Dagvan
ED Sarah Clara Weber   PROD Stephan Schesch
DIST Tartan

66 More successful as a documentary than as a drama, this offers a gently absorbing glimpse into nomadic Mongolian life. – *Anna Smith, Empire*

'A rap-to-riches comedy.'

CB4

DIR Tamra Davis
1993 89m US
[DVD]   ♪

☆ Chris Rock (Albert/MC Gusto), Allen Payne (Euripides/Dead Mike), Deezer D (Otis/Stab Master Arson), Phil Hartman (Virgil Robinson), Arthur Evans (Albert Snr.), Theresa Randle (Eve), Willard E. Pugh (Trustus), Richard Gant (Baa Baa Ack), Charlie Murphy (Gusto), Chris Elliott (A. White)

Respectable young African-Americans reinvent a past for themselves as tough street kids, and form a rap group CB4, short for Cell Block 4.

One of Hollywood's first attempts to find a way to exploit rap music for mainstream consumption. An amusing parody of the posturing and fake machismo in hip-hop culture, it's like a rap version of This Is Spinal Tap.

SCR Chris Rock, Nelson George, Robert LoCash   CIN Karl Walter Lindenlaub   MUS John Barnes   DES Nelson Coates   ED Earl Watson   PROD Nelson George
DIST Universal

66 Sending up the macho, misogynistic postures of rap isn't easy, because so much of the real thing already borders on knowing self-parody. – *David Ansen, Newsweek*

'Long Live Guerilla Film Making!'

Cecil B. Demented ★

SCR/DIR John Waters
2000   88m   US/ France
[DVD] ♫

☆ *Melanie Griffith* (Honey Whitlock), Stephen Dorff (Cecil B. Demented), Alicia Witt (Cherish), Larry Giliard Jnr (Lewis), Maggie Gyllenhaal (Raven), Eric M. Barry (Fidget), Zenzele Uzoma (Chardonnay), Erika Lynn Rupli (Pam), Harriet Dodge (Dinah), Adrian Grenier (Lyle), Jack Noseworthy (Rodney), Mink Stole (Mrs Mallory), Ricki Lake (Libby), Patricia Hearst (Fidget's Mom), Eric Roberts (Honey's Ex-husband)

An underground director and his guerrilla film crew kidnap a Hollywood actress to star in their latest work of propaganda.

A trashy delight, rough around the edges, but with smart, funny things to say about the inanity of bad studio movies: whether bullying those execs responsible for greenlighting films based on video games, or slaughtering the audience of Patch Adams: The Director's Cut, Waters remains on the side of all that is right and good in cinema.

CIN Robert Stevens   **MUS** Basil Poledouris, Zoe Poledouris   **DES** Vincent Peranio   **ED** Jeffrey Wolf   **PROD** John Fielder, Joe Caracciolo Jr, Mark Tarlov

66 Waters at his most cheerful and thematically focused. – *Wesley Morris, San Francisco Examiner*

66 Appears to have been written and directed by a grade-school dropout snorting aeroplane glue. – *Michael Atkinson, Mr. Showbiz*

'A new comedy about people who will do anything to get famous. . .or stay famous.'

Celebrity

SCR/DIR Woody Allen
1998   113m   US
[DVD] ♫

☆ Hank Azaria (David), Kenneth Branagh (Lee Simon), Judy Davis (Robin Simon), Leonardo DiCaprio (Brandon Darrow), Melanie Griffith (Nicole Oliver), Famke Janssen (Bonnie), Michael Lerner (Dr Lupus), Joe Mantegna (Tony Gardella), Bebe Neuwirth (Nina), Winona Ryder (Nola), Charlize Theron (Supermodel)

A showbiz journalist attempts to get through an acrimonious divorce by pursuing the rich and famous.

Bitter, mean-spirited satire, full of oft-heard aphorisms about the pressures of celebrity and media intrusion; there are flashes of the old Woody wit, but too many scenes end with resistible characters screaming blue blazes at one another. Unhappily, Branagh chooses – or is perhaps encouraged – to impersonate Allen's delivery.

CIN Sven Nykvist   **DES** Santo Loquasto   **ED** Susan E. Morse   **PROD** Jean Doumanian   **DIST** Buena Vista/Sweetland

66 The story feels febrile and unhappy, and Allen seems to take his dissatisfaction out on his helpless characters – especially the women. – *Anthony Lane, The New Yorker*

66 Cheap, muddled and thoroughly devoid of insight. – *David Edelstein, Slate*

'The eerie, chilling tale of one child's terror.'

Celia ★

SCR/DIR Ann Turner
1988   103m   Australia

☆ Rebecca Smart (Celia Carmichael), Nicholas Eadie (Ray Carmichael), Victoria Longley (Alice Tanner), Mary-Anne Fahey (Pat Carmichael)

Rites-of-passage drama, set in 1950s Melbourne, in which a grief-stricken nine-year-old girl retreats into a fantasy world.

Low-key but effective story about a child learning to distinguish fact from imagination, with a surprising sub-text about anti-Communist attitudes in Australia at the time.

CIN Geoffrey Simpson   **MUS** Chris Neal   **DES** Peta Lawson   **ED** Ken Sallows   **PROD** Timothy White, Gordon Glenn   **DIST** BCB/Seon

The Celluloid Closet ★★

DIR *Rob Epstein, Jeffrey Friedman*
1995   102m   US/GB/Germany
[DVD]

☆ Tony Curtis (Himself), Armistead Maupin (Himself), Susie Bright (Herself), Whoopi Goldberg (Herself), Quentin Crisp (Himself), Harvey Fierstein (Himself), Arthur Laurents (Himself), Gore Vidal (Himself), Farley Granger (Himself), Paul Rudnick (Himself), Shirley MacLaine (Herself), Tom Hanks (Himself), John Schlesinger (Himself), Lily Tomlin (narrator)

Documentary examining the representation of gay and lesbian characters in the American cinema.

An enlightening film, lovingly curated with clips from classics such as Ben-Hur and cult items like Cruising, and boasting informed commentary from scholars and thespians alike; its aim is to identify both the homophobia and the gay subtexts in hitherto straight-acting productions.

SCR *Rob Epstein, Jeffrey Friedman, Sharon Wood, Armistead Maupin*   **CIN** Nancy Schreiber   **MUS** *Carter Burwell*   **DES** Scott Chambliss   **ED** Jeffrey Friedman, Arnold Glassman   **PROD** Rob Epstein, Jeffrey Friedman   **DIST** Electric/Reflective/Telling Pictures/HBO/Channel 4/ZD

66 It's interesting to see how gay and lesbian themes began to be treated openly in films, but it's fascinating to see how – earlier – those themes were used subtextually in films that make no overt reference to the real subject. – *Stanley Kauffmann, New Republic*

'He was looking for the father he never knew. She was looking for a second chance.'

Central Station ★★★★

DIR *Walter Salles*
1998   110m   Brazil/France
[DVD] ♫

☆ *Fernanda Montenegro* (Dora), Marilia Pera (Irene), Vinicius de Oliveira (Josue), Soia Lira (Ana), Othon Bastos (Bastos), Otavio Augusto (Pedrao), Stela Freitas (Yolanda), Matheus Nachtergaele (Isaias), Caio Junqueria (Moises)

In Rio, a cynical retired teacher, who writes letters for illiterate peasants separated from their families,

[DVD] Available on DVD   ☆ Cast in order   66 Critics' Quotes   🏆 Academy Award   🏆 BAFTA
♫ Soundtrack on CD   of importance   † Points of interest   🏆 Academy Award nomination   🏆 BAFTA nomination

117

accompanies a young boy into remote regions of Brazil in a search for his absent father.

A conventional but heart-warming, tale of bonding between an old grump and a young cherub is lifted by the director's remarkable eye for the imagery of his homeland – and his concern for the beleaguered state of its distant outposts.

SCR João Emanuel Carneiro, Marcos Bernstein **CIN** Walter Carvalho **MUS** Antonio Pinto, Jaques Morelenbaum **DES** Cassio Amarante, Carla Caffe **ED** Isabelle Rathery, Felipe Lacerda **PROD** Arthur Cohn, Martine de Clermont-Tonnerre **DIST** MACT/Videofilms/Riofilme/Canal+

66 Normally, the sound in movie theatres is of popcorn crunching. But the sound at theatres where Central Station is showing is of hearts breaking. – *Jami Bernard, New York Daily News*

66 A richly tender and moving experience. – *Owen Gleiberman, Entertainment Weekly*

† A Region 1 DVD has commentary by Walter Salles, Fernanda Montenegro, and Arthur Cohn.

⚱ foreign language film; Fernanda Montenegro (leading actress)

🎭 film not in the English language

Century ★

SCR/DIR Stephen Poliakoff
1993   112m   GB
♫

☆ Charles Dance (Professor Mandry), Clive Owen (Paul Reisner), Miranda Richardson (Clara), Robert Stephens (Mr Reisner), Joan Hickson (Mrs Whitweather), Lena Headey (Miriam), Neil Stuke (Felix), Liza Walker (Katie)

The roots of eugenics and female emancipation are explored at the dawn of the 20th century.

Stuffed with genuinely interesting ideas, but as so often with this writer-director, ideas can prove hard to translate successfully to screen.

CIN Witold Stok **MUS** Michael Gibbs **DES** Michael Pickwoad **ED** Michael Parkinson **PROD** Therese Pickard **DIST** Electric/BBC/Beambright

66 A big theme that got away. – *Brian Case, Time Out*

La Cérémonie ★★

DIR Claude Chabrol
1995   112m   France/Germany
DVD

☆ Sandrine Bonnaire (Sophie), Isabelle Huppert (Jeanne), Jean-Pierre Cassel (Georges Lelievre), Jacqueline Bisset (Catherine Lelievre), Virginie Ledoyen (Melinda), Jean-François Perrier (Priest)

Two women, a small-town postmistress and a housekeeper newly arrived in a middle-class family, to find they have dark secrets in their past, and form a conspiratorial friendship that ends tragically.

Director Chabrol likes nothing better than to undermine the prejudices and condescension of the bourgeoisie, and he's at it again here with Bonnaire and Huppert making mincemeat of a family's weakness and

snobbery. *A finely-wrought thriller that encourages sympathy with the two put-upon underlings.*

SCR Claude Chabrol, Caroline Eliacheff **CIN** Bernard Zitzermann **MUS** Matthieu Chabrol **DES** Daniel Mercier **ED** Monique Fardoulis **PROD** Marin Karmitz **DIST** Gala/MK2/France3/Prokino/Olga/ZDF

66 Fits nicely with a recent spate of films about transgressive female outsiders, particularly those dealing with class. – *Lizzie Francke, Sight & Sound*

C'est la Vie ★

DIR Diane Kurys
1990   96m   France

☆ Nathalie Baye (Lena), Richard Berry (Michel), Zabou (Bella), Jean-Pierre Bacri (Leon), Vincent Lindon (Jean-Claude), Valéria Bruni-Tedeschi (Odette), Didier Benureau (Ruffier), Julie Bataille (Frederique), Candice Lefranc (Sophie)

A bitter-sweet reminiscence of a summer holiday, when two young sisters gradually realise that their parents' marriage is crumbling.

Delightful small-scale autobiographical story, laced with humour and sadness. The child actors are particularly well directed.

SCR Diane Kurys, Alain Le Henry **CIN** Giuseppe Lanci, Fabio Conversi **MUS** Philippe Sarde **DES** Tony Egry **ED** Raymonde Guyot **PROD** Alexandre Arcady, Diane Kurys **DIST** Electric/Contemporary/Alexandre/SGGC/A2/CNC

'One Wrong Turn Deserves Another.'

Changing Lanes ★★

DIR *Roger Michell*
2002   99m   US
DVD   ♫

☆ *Ben Affleck* (Gavin Banek), *Samuel L. Jackson* (Doyle Gipson), Toni Collette (Michelle), Sydney Pollack (Delano), William Hurt (Sponsor), *Amanda Peet* (Cynthia Banek), Richard Jenkins (Walter Arnell), Kim Staunton (Valerie Gipson), John Benjamin Hickey (Carlyle), Jennifer Dundas Lowe (Mina Dunne), Dylan Baker (Finch), Matt Malloy (Ron Cabot)

After a minor road accident, a hotshot lawyer and a struggling single father are driven to commit increasingly vindictive acts against each other.

Striking modern morality play on the theme of personal responsibility versus our prevailing blame culture: Michell adopts a cool, intelligent, understated approach to the material, while shaking his two lead actors out of several years of professional complacency.

SCR *Chap Taylor, Michael Tolkin* **CIN** Salvatore Totino **MUS** David Arnold **DES** Kristi Zea **ED** Christopher Tellefsen **PROD** Scott Rudin **DIST** Paramount

66 Glossy, big-budget thriller that qualifies as the season's biggest and most rewarding surprise. – *Lou Lumenick, New York Post*

66 A thoughtful film that by its very existence shames studio movies that have been dumbed down into cat-and-mouse cartoons. . .It lays these guys out and X-rays them, and by the end of the day, each man's own anger scares him more than the other guy's. This is one of the best movies of the year. – *Roger Ebert, Chicago Sun-Times*

Les chansons d'amour (new) ★

SCR/DIR Christophe Honoré
2007 100m France
[DVD] ♫

☆ Louis Garrel (Ismaël), Ludivine Sagnier (Julie), Chiara Mastroianni (Jeanne), Clotilde Hesme (Alice), Grégoire Leprince-Ringuet (Erwann), Brigitte Roüan (The mother)

A journalist gets involved in a ménage-à-trois with his girl-friend and another woman. Confusingly, his emotions are then also stirred by a smitten young man. These characters, increasingly unable to project their feelings toward one another, resort to songs as emotional outlets.

French cinema has an honourable musical tradition, of which Honoré clearly sees himself as a part; his characters meet, part and fall in love again, while making nostalgic nods towards the New Wave. This flawed work at least does not lack sincerity or ambition.

CIN Rémy Chevrin DES Samuel Deshors ED Chantal Hymans PROD Paulo Branco DIST Artificial Eye

66 The songs are poor, the faddishness (folk parading books passim, à la Godard) and Garrel's performance are irritating, and only Chiara Mastroianni as a grieving sister brings any real sense of conviction to her role. – *Geoff Andrew, Time Out*

† Honoré has known composer Beaupain since they were students and have enjoyed parallel artistic careers. Both are fans of musicals, and after the release of Honoré's Inside Paris, they agreed to collaborate on a modern film musical.

'When the system breaks down. . .someone is about to get rich.'

Chaos

SCR/DIR Tony Giglio
2007 98m Canada/GB/US
[DVD]

☆ Jason Statham (Quentin Conners), Ryan Phillippe (Shane Dekker), Wesley Snipes (E. Lorenz), Henry Czerny (Capt. Jenkins), Justine Waddell ('Teddy' Galloway), Nicholas Lea (Vincent)

A mismatched detective partnership – gnarled veteran and eager-beaver newcomer – team up to probe a bank heist that has ended in a stand-off with hostages.

Mostly unpretentious, slightly predictable thriller that is actually harmed by its supposedly unique selling point: a young detective's familiarity with chaos theory, which leads him to make unlikely connections in crime-solving.

CIN Richard Greatrex MUS Trevor Jones DES Chris August ED Sean Barton PROD Huw Penalt Jones, Gavin Wilding, Michael Derbas, Mark Williams

---

'He made the whole world laugh and cry. He will again.'

Chaplin ★★

DIR Richard Attenborough
1992 143m GB/US/France/Italy
[DVD] ♫

☆ *Robert Downey Jnr* (Charles Spencer Chaplin), Dan Aykroyd (Mack Sennett), Geraldine Chaplin (Hannah Chaplin), Kevin Dunn (J. Edgar Hoover), Anthony Hopkins (George Hayden), Milla Jovovich (Mildred Harris), Kevin Kline (Douglas Fairbanks), Diane Lane (Paulette Goddard), Penelope Ann Miller (Edna Purviance), Paul Rhys (Sydney Chaplin), John Thaw (Fred Kamo), Marisa Tomei (Mabel Normand), Nancy Travis (Joan Barry), James Woods (Joseph Scott)

Charlie Chaplin recounts his life story, from childhood poverty in London to dazzling success in Hollywood – to an attentive biographer.

A labour of love for director Attenborough, who is hampered by an over-comprehensive script. Not even lives as intriguing as Chaplin's have natural dramatic arcs, and the cutting back and forth between the chronological events and the interview with biographer becomes tedious. Yet Downey has just the right spring-heeled verve to play Chaplin, and its attention to detail (it was shot in California and London) is laudable. It may have worked better as a multi-part TV series.

SCR William Boyd, Bryan Forbes, William Goldman CIN Sven Nykvist MUS John Barry, Jose Padilla DES *Stuart Craig* ED Anne V. Coates PROD Richard Attenborough, Mario Kassar DIST Guild/Lambeth/Carolco/Studio Canal

66 With this reverential biopic, director Richard Attenborough has cranked out a many-reel, talky talkie. – *Duane Byrge, Hollywood Reporter*

66 For all the love and money that went into Chaplin, one cannot fail to note that the big laughs and choicest bits come with the excerpts of the real Chaplin at his best in The Kid, City Lights, Modern Times and others, inescapably suggesting that the only thing one really needs to know about him is his inimitable work. – *Angie Errigo, Empire*

Ⓐ Robert Downey Jnr (leading actor); John Barry; Stuart Craig

Ⓑ Robert Downey Jnr (leading actor)

Ⓣ Stuart Craig; John Mollo, Ellen Mirojnick (costume design); Wally Schneiderman, Jill Rockow, John Caglione Jr (make up)

Character ★

DIR Mike van Diem
1997 122m Netherlands
[DVD]

☆ Jan Decleir (Dreverhaven), Fedja van Huêt (Katadreuffe), Betty Schuurman (Joba), Tamar van den Dop (Lorna Te George), Victor Löw (De Gankelaar), Hans Kesting (Jan Maan)

Arrested for the murder of a bailiff, a young lawyer recounts the story of how he came to commit the crime.

Reasonably absorbing period drama, literary in tone, with a few neat twists towards the end.

SCR Mike van Diem, Laurens Geels, Ruud van Megen CIN Rogier Stoffers MUS Paleis van Boem DES Jelier & Schaaf ED Jessica de Koning PROD Laurens Geels DIST Gala/Almerica/NPS Made

66 Dark, demanding and very Dutch. – *David Parkinson, Empire*

Ⓐ foreign language film

[DVD] Available on DVD ☆ Cast in order 66 Critics' Quotes Ⓐ Academy Award Ⓑ BAFTA
♫ Soundtrack on CD   of importance † Points of interest Academy Award nomination Ⓣ BAFTA nomination

119

The Charge of the Light Brigade ★★

DIR Tony Richardson
1968 141m GB
DVD

☆ *Trevor Howard, John Gielgud*, David Hemmings, Vanessa Redgrave, Jill Bennett, Harry Andrews, Peter Bowles, Mark Burns

An historical fantasia with comic, sociological and cartoon embellishments.

This version of history for the Swinging Sixties has a few splendid moments but it is desperately uneven, and polarised audiences and critics alike. On the plus side, it finds new directions for historical narrative aside from run-of-the-mill costume dramas. And while Richardson locates the futility and failure of this historical incident accurately enough, the attempts at innovation for its own sake seem strained.

SCR Charles Wood   CIN David Watkin, Peter Suschitzky
MUS John Addison   PROD Neil Hartley
DIST UA/Woodfall

66 Considering the lucid book on which it is largely based, it is almost as inexcusably muddled as the British commanders at Balaclava. – *John Simon*

66 The point of the film is to recreate mid-Victorian England in spirit and detail. – *Stanley Kauffmann*

'Two men chasing dreams of glory!'

Chariots of Fire ★★★

DIR *Hugh Hudson*
1981 121m GB
DVD ♫

☆ *Ben Cross* (Harold Abrahams), *Ian Charleson* (Eric Liddell), Nigel Havers (Lord Andrew Lindsay), Nicholas Farrell (Aubrey Montague), Daniel Gerroll (Henry Stallard), Cheryl Campbell (Jennie Liddell), Alice Krige (Sybil Gordon), John Gielgud (Master of Trinity), Lindsay Anderson (Master of Caius), Nigel Davenport (Lord Birkenhead), *Ian Holm* (Sam Mussabini), Patrick Magee (Lord Cadogan)

In the 1924 Paris Olympics, angst-ridden, Jewish Harold Abrahams and devout Scot Eric Liddell compete for Britain.

A film of subtle qualities, rather like those of a BBC classic serial. In Welland's thoughtful script, both men encounter and overcome prejudice and adversity, and find their own kinds of victories. A surprise Oscar winner, but in fairness, all the elements are in place: some classic scenes (including the slo-mo dawn training session on the beach) – and Vangelis's throbbing electronic score, which surprisingly suits the material to perfection.

SCR *Colin Welland*   CIN *David Watkin*   MUS Vangelis
ED Terry Rawlings   PROD David Puttnam
DIST TCF/Allied Stars/Enigma

66 The whole contradictory bundle is unexpectedly watchable. – *Jo Imeson, MFB*

66 A piece of technological lyricism held together by the glue of simple-minded heroic sentiment. – *Pauline Kael*

⌁ picture; Colin Welland (original screenplay); Vangelis; Milena Canonero (costume design)

⌁ Ian Holm (supporting actor); Hugh Hudson (direction); Terry Rawlings;

Ⓣ picture; Ian Holm (supporting actor); Milena Canonero (costume design)

'Willy Wonka is semi-sweet and nuts.'

Charlie and the Chocolate Factory ★★

DIR *Tim Burton*
2005 115m GB/US/Australia
DVD ♫

☆ Johnny Depp (Willy Wonka), Freddie Highmore (Charlie Bucket), David Kelly (Grandpa Joe), Helena Bonham Carter (Mrs Bucket), Noah Taylor (Mr Bucket), Missi Pyle (Mrs Beauregarde), James Fox (Mr Salt), Christopher Lee (Dr Wonka), Deep Roy (Oompa-Loompa)

A young boy from an impoverished household is one of several children to win a tour of a chocolate factory, guided by the factory's reclusive owner.

Dahl purists may be alarmed by the Americanisation of the author's tale – 'chocolate bar' becomes 'candy bar' in places – and a script that imposes cod-psychology on events, but the basic story makes a good match for Burton's left-of-centre sensibilities, and there's plenty of weird, surreal, eye-popping spectacle.

SCR John August   CIN *Philippe Rousselot*   MUS *Danny Elfman*   DES *Alex McDowell*   ED Chris Lebenzon
PROD Richard D. Zanuck, Brad Grey   DIST Warner

66 Burton's finest movie since Ed Wood: a madhouse kiddie musical with a sweet-and-sour heart. – *Owen Gleiberman, Entertainment Weekly*

66 A white chocolate space egg of a picture that has a giddy hallucinatory quality in some places and an overcalculated glossiness in others. . .For better or worse, it's fascinating. – *Stephanie Zacharek, Salon*

† A previous version of this Dahl story, Willy Wonka and the Chocolate Factory, is widely judged inferior to Burton's film.

⌁ Gabriella Pescucci (costume design)

Ⓣ Alex McDowell; Nick Davis, Jon Thum, Chas Jarrett, Joss Williams (special visual effects); Gabriella Pescucci (costume design); Peter Owen, Ivana Primorac (make up/hair)

'People like you are the reason people like me need medication.'

Charlie Bartlett ⓝⓔⓦ

DIR Jon Poll
2008 96m US
DVD ♫

☆ Anton Yelchin (Charlie Bartlett), Hope Davis (Marilyn Bartlett), Kat Dennings (Susan Gardner), Robert Downey Jnr (Principal Gardner), Tyler Hilton (Murphey Bivens), Mark Rendall (Kip Crombwell), Dylan Taylor (Len Arbuckle)

A high school misfit finds a niche handing out advice, and prescription medication, to his fellow students.

Arch comedy reminiscent of Rushmore; riddled with inconsistencies, it suffers from a less than endearing

hero and a romantic subplot that even John Hughes would find uninspired.

SCR Gustin Nash   **CIN** Paul Sarossy   **MUS** Christophe Beckl   **DES** Tamera Deverell   **ED** Alan Baumgarten   **PROD** David Permut, Barron Kidd, Jay Roach, Sidney Kimmel   **DIST** Verve Pictures

66 Such a smart, likeable teen comedy that you wish it had the courage of its convictions to break free from convention. – *Henry Fitzherbert, Express*

66 A cross between Pump Up the Volume, Thumbsucker and Ferris Bueller's Day Off, it's not a patch on any of the above. – *David Edwards, Mirror*

'Based on a true story. You think we could make all this up?'

Charlie Wilson's War (new)   ★

DIR Mike Nichols
2007   101m   US
DVD   ♫

☆ Tom Hanks (Charlie Wilson), Julia Roberts (Joanne Herring), *Philip Seymour Hoffman* (Gust Avrakotos), Amy Adams (Bonnie Bach), Ned Beatty (Doc Long), Om Puri (President Zia of Pakistan), Emily Blunt (Jane Liddle), Ken Stott (Zvi Rafiah)

In the 1980s, a raffish U.S. congressman engineers support for Afghan partisans resisting the Soviet Union.

Hanks is in breezy, hail-fellow-well-met form as roguish, politically incorrect Wilson, first glimpsed sharing a hot tub with three deeply available looking women. If only the film had the same air of insouciance; but apart from Hoffman's turn as a cynical CIA agent, it tries to be perceived as patriotic too. Sorkin's trademark staccato dialogue serves its purpose, but the story is no more plausible than one of Wilson's tall tales. And there's an oddly unspoken subtext: Wilson's Afghan pals later mutated into the Taliban and other anti-western groups, leaving the world worse off than it was when these events occurred.

SCR Aaron Sorkin   **CIN** Stephen Goldblatt   **MUS** James Newton Howard   **DES** Victor Kempster   **ED** John Bloom, Antonia Van Drimmelen   **PROD** Tom Hanks, Gary Goetzman   **DIST** Universal

66 Extremely enjoyable. Although it's a little tonally unsure, whenever Hanks and Hoffman are on screen, any misgivings are forgiven. – *Chris Hewitt, Empire*

66 It's nice to watch a political movie that, for a change, isn't trying to save our souls. It's possible to have a good time with this movie while, at the same time, regretting all that it isn't. – *Peter Rainer, Christian Science Monitor*

⚱ Philip Seymour Hoffman (supporting actor)
Ⓣ Philip Seymour Hoffman (supporting actor)

'Sex Is Easy. Love Is Hard.'

Chasing Amy   ★

SCR/DIR Kevin Smith
1997   113m   US
DVD

☆ Ben Affleck (Holden McNeil), Joey Lauren Adams (Alyssa Jones), Jason Lee (Banky Edwards), Dwight Ewell (Hooper X), Jason Mewes (Jay), Kevin Smith (Silent Bob)

A male comic-book artist falls for a female friend, who is gay.

Overlong and finally inconclusive romantic roundelay, though all Smith's usual virtues – frank, witty dialogue, cherishable pop-cultural asides, credible interpersonal relationships – are present, and there are even signs of a new-found directorial maturity.

CIN David Klein   **MUS** David Pirner   **DES** Robert 'Ratface' Holtzman   **ED** Kevin Smith, Scott Mosier   **PROD** Scott Mosier   **DIST** Metrodome/Miramax/View Askew

66 A true movie rarity: a brutally honest romance. If you loved Sleepless in Seattle, you'll just hate it. – *Richard Schickel, Time*

'In three days, his resurrection will be complete. . .'

Chemical Wedding (new)

DIR Julian Doyle
2008   106m   UK
DVD   ♫

☆ Simon Callow (Haddo), Kal Weber (Mathers), John Shrapnel (Aleister Crowley), Lucy Cudden (Lia), Paul McDowell (Symons), Jud Charlton (Victor)

Futuristic technology is used to reincarnate the occultist Aleister Crowley in the body of a Cambridge academic.

Camp horror built on a ludicrous premise; a thoroughly unholy union between its anarchic subject and co-writer Bruce Dickinson, of rock band Iron Maiden fame.

SCR Bruce Dickinson, Julian Doyle   **CIN** Brian Herlihy   **MUS** Andre Jacquemin   **DES** Mark Tanner   **ED** Bill Jones   **PROD** Malcolm Kohll, Justin Peyton, Ben Timlett   **DIST** Warner Music Entertainment

66 The picture is an absolute shambles but nevertheless achieves a kind of greatness. – *Henry Fitzherbert, Express*

66 An anomaly most notable for Callow's off-the-rails performance. – *Derek Adams, Time Out*

† Bruce Dickinson personally flew a plane of friends, backers and journalists from London to Cannes for the film's 2008 festival screening.

'If you can't be famous. . .be infamous.'

Chicago   ★

DIR Rob Marshall
2002   113m   US/Germany
DVD   ♫

☆ Catherine Zeta-Jones (Velma Kelly), Renée Zellweger (Roxie Hart), Richard Gere (Billy Flynn), Queen Latifah (Matron 'Mama' Morton), John C. Reilly (Amos Hart), Christine Baranski (Mary Sunshine), Lucy Liu (Kitty), Taye Diggs (Bandleader), Colm Feore (Martin Harrison), Dominic West (Fred Casely)

Chicago, the 1920s: a chorine shoots her lover and finds herself in the middle of a media storm.

A fitful filming of the Kander and Ebb musical in which, as the libretto tells us, old-school razzle-dazzle can help us to overlook creative faults. Casting in the central roles is timid and commercially minded, and there's a lack of modulation: starting with a

---

DVD Available on DVD   ☆ Cast in order of importance   66 Critics' Quotes   ⚱ Academy Award   ⚱ Academy Award nomination   Ⓣ BAFTA   Ⓣ BAFTA nomination
♫ Soundtrack on CD   † Points of interest

C

121

showstopper like *All That Jazz* barely leaves the filmmakers with anywhere to go.

SCR Bill Condon   **CIN** Dion Beebe   **MUS** Danny Elfman **DES** John Myhre   **ED** Martin Walsh   **PROD** Martin Richards   **DIST** Buena Vista

66 Isn't just the most explosively entertaining movie musical in a couple of decades. It's going to be the most influential: the one that inspires the rebirth of the Hollywood musical. – *David Edelstein, Slate*

66 Sophisticated, brash, sardonic, completely joyful in its execution. It gives anyone who ever loved movie musicals, and lamented their demise, something to live for. – *Stephanie Zacharek, Salon*

† Maurine Watkins' play was first filmed in 1927 with Phyllis Haver, and again in 1942 as *Roxie Hart*, starring Ginger Rogers.

† 'And All That Jazz'; 'When You're Good to Mama'; 'Cell Block Tango'; 'Roxie'; 'Me and My Baby'; 'Razzle Dazzle'; 'Funny Honey'; 'All I Care About Is Love'; 'We Both Reached For the Gun'; 'I Can't Do It Alone'; 'Mr Cellophane'; 'Nowadays'; 'I Move On'.

⚍ picture; Catherine Zeta-Jones (supporting actress); Martin Walsh; John Myhre (with Gordon Sim); Colleen Atwood (costume design); Michael Minkler, Dominic Tavella, David Lee (sound)

⚍ Renée Zellweger (leading actress); John C. Reilly (supporting actor); Queen Latifah (supporting actress); Rob Marshall; Bill Condon; Dion Beebe; John Kander (m), Fred Ebb (ly) (music, original song I Move On)

⚍ Catherine Zeta-Jones (supporting actress); (Michael Minkler, Dominic Tavella, David Lee, Maurice Schell (sound)

⚍ film; Renée Zellweger (leading actress); Queen Latifah (supporting actress); Dion Beebe; Martin Walsh; Danny Elfman, John Kander, Fred Ebb (music, original score); Colleen Atwood (costume design); John Myhre; Jordan Samuel, Judi Cooper-Sealy (hair and make up); Martin Richards

---

'This Ain't No Chick Flick.'

Chicken Run ★★

DIR Peter Lord, Nick Park
2000   84m   US/GB
DVD   ♫

☆ Voices of: Mel Gibson (Rocky), Julia Sawalha (Ginger), Miranda Richardson (Mrs Tweedy), Jane Horrocks (Babs), Lynn Ferguson (Mac), Imelda Staunton (Bunty), Benjamin Whitrow (Fowler), Tony Haygarth (Mr Tweedy), Timothy Spall (Nick), Phil Daniels (Fetcher)

On a British farm, a cocky American rooster urges a coop of chickens to evade their intended fate as filling for pies.

A poultry version of The Great Escape finds the animators at Aardman attempting the transition from short to long-form storytelling: the results are largely enjoyable, though the central relationship proves less engaging than the clucking support cast, and the best jokes are all in the trailer.

SCR Karey Kirkpatrick   **CIN** Tristan Oliver, Frank Passingham   **MUS** John Powell, Harry Gregson-Williams **DES** Phil Lewis   **ED** Mark Solomon, Tamsin Parry, Robert Francis   **PROD** Peter Lord, David Sproxton, Nick Park **DIST** Pathé

66 Never loses its priceless stamp of individuality. Reduced to its essence, this is a joke told by a person, not a corporation – and that makes all the difference. – *Kenneth Turan, Los Angeles Times*

66 It is not only an amazing technical accomplishment, it's also the wittiest and best-voiced animated movie to come along in years. – *Jonathan Foreman, New York Post*

⚍ British film; Paddy Eason, Mark Nelmes, Dave Alex Riddett (special effects)

The Child ★★★

SCR/DIR Jean-Pierre Dardenne, Luc Dardenne
2005   100m   France/Belgium
DVD

☆ Jeremie Renier (Bruno), Deborah Francois (Sonia), Jeremie Segard (Steve), Fabrizio Rongione (Young Thug), Olivier Gourmet (Plainclothes Officer)

In a small Belgian industrial town, a young petty criminal leaves behind his new-born baby as collateral during a business deal, then makes attempts to retrieve the child.

A powerful, gripping study of a world where everything is a transaction, shot in its directors' usual ultra-observant fashion; it is ultimately less about the immature lead character doing the wrong thing than his coming to do the right thing – trying to get his son back, a long shot at redemption – and features one car-versus-motorcycle chase that, in its pace and tension, a Hollywood action movie would kill for.

CIN Alain Marcoen   **ED** Marie-Helene Dozo
PROD Jean-Pierre Dardenne, Luc Dardenne, Denis Freyd **DIST** Artificial Eye

66 One of the greatest films of recent years. – *Andrew O'Hehir, Salon*

66 Astonishingly vivid. . .the screen becomes a perfectly transparent window on lives hanging in the balance. – *Joe Morgenstern, Wall Street Journal*

† The film won the Palme D'Or for best film at the Cannes festival in 2005.

'A nation rose. Then all was quiet.'

Children of Glory (new) ★

DIR Krisztina Goda
2006   120m   Hungary

☆ Kata Dobo (Viki Falk), Ivan Fenyo (Karcsi Szabo), Sandor Csanyi (Tibi Vamos), Zsolt Huszar (Jancsi Gal), Viktoria Szavai (Eszter Hanak), Tamas Jordan (Karcsi's Grandfather), Peter Haumann ('Uncle Feri')

Following the Hungarian revolution of 1956, the country's water polo team faces off against their Soviet counterparts at the Melbourne Olympics.

Glossy blend of soap opera and history lesson, released in Hungary to mark the 50th anniversary of the country's abortive uprising.

SCR Joe Eszterhas, Eva Gardos, Geza Beremenyi, Reka Divinyi   **CIN** Buda Gulyas, Janos Vecsernyes   **MUS** Nick Glennie-Smith   **DES** Janos Szabolcs   **ED** Eva Gardos, Annamaria Komlossy   **PROD** Andrew G. Vajna **DIST** Lionsgate

66 Joe Eszterhas brings his sledgehammer touch to this

DVD Available on DVD   ☆ Cast in order of importance   66 Critics' Quotes   † Points of interest   ⚍ Academy Award   ⚍ Academy Award nomination   ⚍ BAFTA   ⚍ BAFTA nomination
♫ Soundtrack on CD

heartfelt movie about Hungary. – *Peter Bradshaw, Guardian*

66 Doctor Zhivago with water sports. – *Sam Wigley, Total Film*

† Both Andrew G. Vajna and Joe Eszterhas were born in Hungary.

'No children. No future. No hope.'

Children of Men ★★★

DIR Alfonso Cuaron

2006   109m   UK/US/Japan

DVD ♫

☆ Clive Owen (Theo), Julianne Moore (Julian), Michael Caine (Jasper), Chiwetel Ejiofor (Luke), Danny Huston (Nigel), Claire-Hope Asitey (Kee), Peter Mullan (Syd), Pam Ferris (Miriam)

In 2027, humanity is infertile, and doomed to extinction. In Britain, immigrants are imprisoned in cages, bombings are commonplace and lawless gangs run free. Theo, an ex-activist and bureaucrat, is kidnapped by a resistance group and told to secure exit papers for a girl who turns out to be pregnant.

Electrifying, brilliantly shot film with a downbeat story that oddly contains a final glimpse of hope. It portrays a future London that is recognisable, if seedier and gloomier. Cuaron stages outstanding set-pieces: a gang attacking a car containing the principal characters, an action sequence in a refugee detention camp. Extraordinary film-making.

SCR Alfonso Cuaron, Timothy J. Sexton, David Arata, Mark Fergus, Hawk Ostby   CIN Emmanuel Lubezki   MUS John Tavener   DES Jim Clay, Geoffrey Kirkland   ED Alex Rodriguez, Alfonso Cuaron   PROD Hilary Shor, Marc Abraham, Tony Smith, Eric Newman, Iain Smith   DIST UIP

66 Made with palpable energy, intensity and excitement, it compellingly creates a world gone mad that is uncomfortable close to the one we live in. It is a Blade Runner for the 21st century, a worthy successor to that epic of dystopian decay. – *Kenneth Turan, Los Angeles Times*

⚱ Emmanuel Lubezki, Alfonso Cuaron, Timothy J. Sexton, David Arata, Mark Fergus, Hawk Ostby (adapted screenplay); Alex Rodriguez, Alfonso Cuaron

---

Chinatown ★★★★

DIR Roman Polanski

1974   131m   US

DVD ♫

☆ *Jack Nicholson* (J.J. Gittes), Faye Dunaway (Evelyn Mulwray), John Huston (Noah Cross), Perry Lopez (Escobar), John Hillerman (Yelburton), Roman Polanski (Man with Knife), Darrell Zwerling (Hollis Mulwray), Diane Ladd (Ida Sessions)

In 1937 Los Angeles, a grasping tycoon takes control of the city's water supply and causes a drought, while a private eye takes on a case involving the tycoon's daughter, which entangles him in a major scandal.

A brilliant mystery, written with an astute sense of narrative architecture and played to the hilt by a terrific cast, including Nicholson, who has never done better

work than his portrayal of the insouciant Gittes. It's a rare thriller, one that addresses itself to serious moral and public policy issues while remaining gripping, exciting and finally heartbreaking.

SCR Robert Towne   CIN John A. Alonso   MUS Jerry Goldsmith   DES Richard Sylbert   ED Sam O'Steen   PROD Robert Evans   DIST Paramount/Long Road

66 Polanski is everywhere in the film, greedy for detail. – *David Thomson*

⚱ Robert Towne (original Screenplay)

⚱ picture; Jack Nicholson (leading actor); Faye Dunaway (leading actress); Roman Polanski (direction); John A. Alonso; Jerry Goldsmith

🏆 Jack Nicholson (leading actor); Roman Polanski (direction); Robert Towne (original screenplay)

Chop Suey ★

SCR/DIR Bruce Weber

2001   98m   US

☆ Peter Johnson, Frances Faye, Rickson Gracie, Robert Mitchum, Jan Michael Vincent, Diana Vreeland, Sir Wilfred Thesiger

Photographer Bruce Weber films his social circle and sheds light on his obsessions.

An undisciplined mess and entirely a vanity project – which doesn't mean it's not watchable. Weber's friends and acquaintances included Robert Mitchum and Diana Vreeland, though he lavishes most of the film's running time on a young hunk named Peter Johnson, a wrestler Weber resolved to turn into a male model. Eerily fascinating glimpse of a self-regarding world.

CIN Lance Acord, Douglas Cooper, Jim Fealy   MUS John Leftwich   ED Angelo Corrao

66 It is the most personal and accomplished of the several documentaries Weber has made over the years, and, like the dish for which it is named, it contains many ingredients. – *Kevin Thomas, Los Angeles Times*

'The Truth, The Half Truth And Nothing Like The Truth.'

Chopper ★

SCR/DIR Andrew Dominik

2000   94m   Australia

DVD

☆ Eric Bana (Mark 'Chopper' Read), Vince Colosimo (Neville Bartos), Simon Lyndon (Jimmy Loughnan), Kate Beahan (Tanya), David Field (Keithy George), Dan Wyllie (Bluey), Bill Young (Detective Downey), Kenny Graham (Keith Read), Gary Waddell (Kevin Darcy), Fred Barker (Governor Beasley)

The true(ish) stories of 'Chopper' Read, noted Australian criminal, killer and best-selling author.

'This is not a biography', states the opening title card of this uncomfortable, grisly, knife-edge picture, though there remains some question as to whether the subsequent film panders to, or debunks, Read's cheerily psychotic self-image; there's no denying Bana's skill in the title role, however.

CIN Geoffrey Hall, Kevin Hayward   MUS Mick Harvey

DES Paddy Reardon   ED Ken Sallows   PROD Michele Bennett   DIST Metrodome

66 You'll laugh, you'll gag, you'll leave the cinema mentally calculating the distance between your place and Chopper's Tasmanian home. – *Margaret Ambrose, The Lounge*

The Chorus ★

DIR Christophe Barratier
2004   96m   France/Switzerland/Germany
DVD   ♫

☆ Gerard Jugnot (Clement Mathieu), François Berleand (Rachin), Kad Merad (Chabert), Jacques Perrin (Pierre Morhange as adult), *Jean-Baptiste Maunier* (Pierre Morhange as child), Marie Bunel (Violette Morhange), Jean-Paul Bonnaire (Maxence), Philippe Du Janerand (Langlois)

A conductor recalls his days at boarding school, when he and his fellow troublemakers were taken under the wing of a kindly new choirmaster.

A hymn to the abiding power of music and the selflessness of those who teach it, proving creaky in its construction and sentimentality; still, if it's singing an old familiar song, at least it sings its heart out.

SCR Christophe Barratier, Philippe Lopes-Curval, CIN Carlo Varini, Dominique Gentil, Jean-Jacques Bouhon   MUS *Bruno Coulais*   DES François Chauvaud   ED Yves Deschamps   PROD Jacques Perrin, Arthur Cohn, Nicolas Mauvernay   DIST Pathé

66 A movie you've seen many times before, but the setting is different, its characters are well drawn, and it delivers its uplifting message with succinctness, sincerity and skill. – *William Arnold, Seattle Post-Intelligencer*

66 Does it by the numbers, so efficiently this feels more like a Hollywood wannabe than a French film. Where's the quirkiness, the nuance, the deeper levels? – *Roger Ebert, Chicago Sun-Times*

⚱ foreign language film; Bruno Coulais (m), Christophe Barratier (ly) (music – original song Look to your path/Vois sur ton chemin)

Ⓣ film not in the English language; Christophe Barratier, Philippe Lopes-Curval (adapted screenplay); Bruno Coulais

A Chorus of Disapproval ★

DIR Michael Winner
1989   99m   GB
DVD

☆ *Anthony Hopkins* (Dafydd Ap Llewellyn), Jeremy Irons (Guy Jones), Richard Briers (Ted Washbrook), Gareth Hunt (Ian Hubbard), Patsy Kensit (Linda Washbrook), Alexandra Pigg (Bridget Baines), *Prunella Scales* (Hannah Ap Llewellyn), Jenny Seagrove (Fay Hubbard), Peter Lee-Wilson (Crispin Usher), Barbara Ferris (Enid Washbrook), Lionel Jeffries (Jarvis Huntley-Pike), Sylvia Syms (Rebecca Huntley-Pike), David King (Mr Ames)

A shy widower moves to a seaside town, joins an amateur theatrical group, and inadvertently becomes an object of desire.

Amusing adaptation of a wittily observed play, generally well performed, but sunk by clumsy directing.

SCR Michael Winner, Alan Ayckbourn   CIN Alan Jones   MUS John Du Prez   ED Arnold Crust, Chris Barnes   PROD Michael Winner, Elliott Kastner   DIST Hobo/Curzon/Palisades Entertainment

'For Every Credit There Must Be A Debit'

Christie Malry's Own Double-Entry ★★

DIR Paul Tickell
2000   94m   GB/Netherlands/Luxembourg
DVD

☆ Nick Moran (Christie Malry), Neil Stuke (Headlam), Kate Ashfield (Carol), Mattia Sbragia (Leonardo), Marcello Mazzarella (Pacioli), Salvatore Lazzaro (Giacomo), Sergio Albelli (Duke Ludovico), Francesco Giuffrida (Salai), Shirley Anne Field (Mary)

A humble book-keeper with a twisted view of humanity devises his own unique accounting system, committing deadly crimes to balance out perceived slights against him.

Pitch-black comedy, adapted from an experimental novel long presumed unfilmable. But it's strikingly inventive and original.

SCR Simon Bent   CIN Reinier van Brummelen   MUS Luke Haines   DES Wilbert Van Dorp   ED Chris Wyatt   PROD Kees Kasander   DIST Ian Rattray

66 Engagingly truculent black comedy, as original as anything that's come out of British cinema this year. – *Philip Kemp, Sight & Sound*

† The film's opening was delayed for two years because of the lack of a willing distributor. It then received a minimal release.

Ⓣ Simon Bent (Most Promising Newcomer)

Chromophobia (new) ★

SCR/DIR Martha Fiennes
2006   136m   UK/France
DVD

☆ Ben Chaplin (Trent Masters), Penelope Cruz (Gloria), Ralph Fiennes (Stephen Tulloch), Ian Holm (Edward Aylesbury), Rhys Ifans (Colin), Damian Lewis (Marcus Aylesbury), Kristin Scott Thomas (Iona Aylesbury), Harriet Walter (Penelope Aylesbury)

Every family has secrets to hide. Marcus Aylesbury has them by the bucket load. His wife Iona and his son Orlando both have psychological problems. Meanwhile the boy's gay godfather lies half beaten to death in hospital. Marcus's stepmother finds her dogs better company than his father and a journalist friend decides to sell out to success and celebrity.

Director Fiennes has assembled an ambitious, starry ensemble drama which aims to reveal the shallow concerns of her bored protagonists via a litany of psychoanalysis, cosmetic surgery, retail therapy, yoga and adultery. Set in London, it has a New York sensibility. She founders with too many plot lines and totally unsympathetic characters.

CIN George Tiffin   MUS Magnus Fiennes   DES Tony Burrough   ED Tracy Granger   PROD Tarak Ben Ammar, Ron Rotholz   DIST Momentum Pictures

DVD Available on DVD   ☆ Cast in order of importance   66 Critics' Quotes   ⚱ Academy Award   † Points of interest   ♫ Soundtrack on CD   Academy Award nomination   Ⓑ BAFTA   Ⓣ BAFTA nomination

66 A fine cast scuttles around, to rapidly diminishing returns, in...an over-long ensembler set among a bunch of self-absorbed neurotics that starts as a wannabe comedy and later expects audiences to sympathise with its characters' plight. – *Derek Elley, Variety*

† Actress Kristin Scott Thomas was angry that a film she made in 2004 and premiered at the Cannes Film Festival the following year, was only released in the UK in 2007. She said: 'It was a great role for me – a lunatic mother, completely self-obsessed. I gave a lot of time for a cut-rate fee.'

'A new adventure begins'

The Chronicles of Narnia: Prince Caspian (new)

DIR Andrew Adamson
2008   143m   UK/US
♫

☆ Georgie Henley (Lucy Pevensie), Skandar Keynes (Edmund Pevensie), William Moseley (Peter Pevensie), Anna Popplewell (Susan Pevensie), Ben Barnes (Prince Caspian), Sergio Castellito (King Miraz), Peter Dinklage (Trumpkin), Warwick Davis (Nikabrik), Liam Neeson (Voice of Aslan), Eddie Izzard (Voice of Reepicheep), Tilda Swinton (White Witch)

The Pevensie children are summoned back to the magical realm of Narnia to help a young prince claim his rightful throne.

Epic follow-up to The Lion, the Witch and the Wardrobe based on familiar precepts of good and evil; all very wholesome but strangely unnecessary, with significantly less of the first film's religious symbolism.

SCR Andrew Adamson, Christopher Markus, Stephen McFeely   CIN Karl Walter Lindenlaub   MUS Harry Gregson-Williams   DES Roger Ford   ED Sim Evan Jones   PROD Mark Johnson, Andrew Adamson, Philip Steuer   DIST Walt Disney

66 A worthy if less wondrous successor, several shades darker than the previous edition. – *Michael Rechtshaffen, Hollywood Reporter*

66 You leave feeling covered in a blanket of bland. – *Peter Travers, Rolling Stone*

'Evil Has Reigned For 100 Years. . .'

The Chronicles of Narnia: The Lion, the Witch and the Wardrobe ★

DIR Andrew Adamson
2005   143m   US
DVD ♫

☆ *Tilda Swinton* (White Witch), *Georgie Henley* (Lucy Pevensie), Skandar Keynes (Edmund Pevensie), William Moseley (Peter Pevensie), Anna Popplewell (Susan Pevensie), James McAvoy (Mr Tumnus), Jim Broadbent (Professor Kirke), James Cosmo (Father Christmas), voices of: Liam Neeson (Aslan), Ray Winstone (Mr Beaver), Dawn French (Mrs Beaver), Rupert Everett (Mr Fox)

Four siblings evacuated from the London Blitz take refuge in an old country house, where one of the wardrobes opens onto a magical kingdom.

A classic of children's literature is efficiently but rather joylessly converted into a shiny, glossy, effects-ridden cash machine: a couple of the human performers lend interest, but the voice you hear coming through loudest is that of the producers, not the director or the original author.

SCR Ann Peacock, Andrew Adamson, Christopher Markus, Stephen McFeely   CIN Donald M. McAlpine   MUS Harry Gregson-Williams   DES Roger Ford   ED Sim Evan-Jones, Jim May   PROD Mark Johnson, Philip Steuer   DIST Buena Vista

66 Well told, handsome, stirring and loads of fun. – *Stephen Hunter, Washington Post*

66 More prosaic than inspiring. – *Todd McCarthy, Variety*

⚱ Howard Berger, Tami Lane (makeup)
⚱ Terry Porter, Dean Zupancic, Tony Johnson (sound); Dean Wright, Bill Westenhofer, Jim Berney, Scott Farrar (visual effects)

Ⓣ Howard Berger, Gregory Nicotero, Nikki Gooley (make up/hair)
Ⓣ Dean Wright, Bill Westenhofer, Jim Berney, Scott Farrar (special visual effects); Isis Mussenden (costume design)

'When Does A Close Friend Become Too Close?'

Chuck & Buck ★

DIR Miguel Arteta
2000   96m   US
DVD

☆ Mike White (Buck), Chris Weitz (Chuck), Lupe Ontiveros (Beverly), Beth Colt (Carlyn), Paul Weitz (Sam), Maya Rudolph (Jamilla), Mary Wigmore (Diane), Paul Sand (Barry), Gino Buccola (Tommy)

After the death of his mother, a 27-year-old oddball heads to LA and stalks a record executive who was once his childhood friend.

Weirdo black comedy that takes in child abuse, sexual perversity and deep-rooted self-loathing; viewers will have to weigh up whether it's worth negotiating the queasier stretches to get to a handful of somewhat discomforting laughs.

SCR Mike White   CIN Chuy Chavez   MUS Joey Waronker, Tony Maxwell, Smokey Hormel   DES Renee Davenport   ED Jeff Betancourt   PROD Matthew Greenfield   DIST Metrodome

66 The Citizen Kane of twisted-geek movies. – *Stephen Hunter, Washington Post*

66 A true original. . .Won't make for the most relaxed evening's entertainment, but it is funny and daring, and well worth the occasional shudder. – *Colin Kennedy, Empire*

† Both leads subsequently became better known for their work off-camera: White as the writer of School of Rock, Weitz as the director of The Golden Compass.

'If my memory of her has an expiration date, let it be 10,000 years. . .'

Chungking Express ★★★

SCR/DIR *Wong Kar-Wai*
1994   102m   Hong Kong
DVD

☆ Brigitte Lin (Woman in Blonde Wig), Takeshi Kaneshiro (He Zhiwu, Cop 223), Tony Leung Chiu Wai (Cop 663), Faye Wong (Faye), Valerie Chow (Air Hostess)

DVD Available on DVD   ☆ Cast in order   66 Critics' Quotes   ⚱ Academy Award   Ⓣ BAFTA
♫ Soundtrack on CD   of importance   † Points of interest   ⚱ Academy Award nomination   Ⓣ BAFTA nomination

125

A lovelorn cop unknowingly enters into a relationship with a heroin smuggler; meanwhile, another officer attempts to get over his failed liaison with an air stewardess.

Consider it Love in the Time of Convenience Food: a swoony, neon-lit, ultra-modern fable of young romantic obsessives taking what they can get from life and pining when it falls short of expectations. There's perhaps less to it than ravishes the eye, but it's mostly irresistible, the film equivalent of a perfect bubblegum pop record.

CIN *Christopher Doyle, Lau Wai-Keung* **MUS** Frankie Chan, Roel A. Garcia, Michael Galasso **DES** William Chang **ED** William Chang, Hai Kit-Wai, Kwong Chi-Leung **PROD** Chan Yi-Kan **DIST** ICA/Jet Tone

66 You enjoy it because of what you know about film, not because of what it knows about life. – *Roger Ebert, Chicago Sun-Times*

66 This is what Godard movies were once like: fast, hand-held and very, very catchy. – *Tony Rayns, Time Out*

† The film was the first title acquired for release by Quentin Tarantino's Rolling Thunder video label.

'A story about how far we must travel to find the place where we belong.'

The Cider House Rules ★

DIR Lasse Hallström
1999   126m   US
DVD   ♫

☆ *Tobey Maguire* (Homer Wells), Charlize Theron (Candy Kendall), Delroy Lindo (Mr Rose), Paul Rudd (Wally Worthington), *Michael Caine* (Dr. Wilbur Larch), Jane Alexander (Nurse Edna), Kathy Baker (Nurse Angela), Erykah Badu (Rose Rose), Kieran Culkin (Buster), Kate Nelligan (Olive Worthington)

An orphaned young man is taken in by a kindly doctor who runs an abortion clinic in the heart of New England.

Tasteful, chocolate-box Americana with a couple of decent performances at its heart, though after ninety minutes of patting the viewer on the head, its last-reel lurch into melodrama comes to feel like a clip around the ear.

SCR John Irving **CIN** *Oliver Stapleton* **MUS** Rachel Portman **DES** David Gropman **ED** Lisa Zeno Churgin **PROD** Richard N. Gladstein

66 A deliberately old-fashioned picture that succeeds in nearly everything it tries to do. – *Michael Wilmington, Chicago Tribune*

66 Impeccably crafted and utterly impersonal. – *Dave Kehr, Chicago Reader*

⚊ Michael Caine (supporting actor); John Irving (adapted screenplay)

⚊ picture; Lasse Hallström; Lisa Zeno Churgin; Rachel Portman; David Gropman

Ⓣ Michael Caine (supporting actor)

Cinderella ★★

DIR Wilfred Jackson, Hamilton Luske, Clyde Geronimi
1950   75m   US
♫

☆ the voices of Ilene Woods, William Phipps, Eleanor

Audley, Rhoda Williams, Lucille Bliss, Verna Felton

When Cinderella's stepmother prevents her from attending the royal ball, her fairy godmother and two friendly mice come to her help.

A feature cartoon rather short on inspiration, though with all Disney's solid virtues. The mice are lively and the villainous cat the best character.

MUS Oliver Wallace, Paul J. Smith **DIST** Walt Disney

⚊ Oliver Wallace, Paul J. Smith; Mack David, Al Hoffman, Jerry Livingston (m), (ly) (music, original song – Bibbidy Bobbidy Boo)

'One man's extraordinary fight to save the family he loved.'

Cinderella Man ★

DIR Ron Howard
2005   144m   US
DVD   ♫

☆ *Russell Crowe* (Jim Braddock), Renée Zellweger (Mae Braddock), *Paul Giamatti* (Joe Gould), Craig Bierko (Max Baer), Paddy Considine (Mike Wilson), Bruce McGill (Jimmy Johnston)

In the late 1920s, up-and-coming boxer James J. Braddock is laid low by the Depression, only to stage a remarkable professional fightback.

A handsome, serviceable biopic of a popular hero who, despite his successes, never lost touch with his roots. Howard's film is strong on historical context – the emasculation of America during the Depression years – but more effective at ringside than when taking sappy snapshots of life within the Braddock family home.

SCR Cliff Hollingsworth, Akiva Goldsman **CIN** *Salvatore Totino* **MUS** Thomas Newman **DES** *Wynn Thomas* **ED** Mike Hill, Dan Hanley **PROD** Brian Grazer, Ron Howard, Penny Marshall **DIST** Buena Vista

66 It's a crowd-pleasing, artful and convincing movie that just misses being great but nevertheless gratifies. – *Shawn Levy, Portland Oregonian*

⚊ Paul Giamatti (supporting actor); Mike Hill, Dan Hanley; David LeRoy Anderson, Lance Anderson (make up)

Ⓣ Cliff Hollingsworth, Akiva Goldsman

Cinema Paradiso ★★★★

SCR/DIR *Giuseppe Tornatore*
1989   122m   Italy/France
DVD   ♫

☆ Antonelli Attli (Young Maria), Enzo Cannavale (Spaccafico), Isa Danieli (Anna), Leo Gullotta (Bill Sticker), Marco Leonardi (Toto as a Teenager), Pupella Maggio (Older Maria), Agnese Nano (Elena), Leopoldo Trieste (Fr. Adelfio), Salvatore Cascio (Toto as a Child), Jacques Perrin (Toto as an Adult), *Philippe Noiret* (Alfredo)

A famous film director returns to his Sicilian village for the funeral of its cinema projectionist, and recalls their friendship that gave him a love for movies.

An affectionate, nostalgic film that trades on its love for cinema, and particularly for cinema-going in a bygone era. It's effective as a rites-of-passage piece, as an affable study of village characters, and later, in a melancholy aside, as a reminder that fame and success can make

one's emotional life more complicated than movies often suggest.

CIN Blasco Giurato MUS Ennio Morricone, Andrea Morricone DES Andrea Crisanti ED Mario Morra DIST Palace/Films Ariana/RAI TRE/Forum/Franco Cristaldi

† A four-disc DVD box-set, featuring the 172-minute director's cut, was released in 2007.

⚊ foreign film

⚏ foreign film; Philippe Noiret (leading actor); Salvatore Cascio (supporting actor); Giuseppe Tornatore (original screenplay); Ennio and Andrea Morricone

Citizen Kane ★★★★

DIR *Orson Welles*
1941 119m US
`DVD` ♫

☆ *Orson Welles* (Kane), *Joseph Cotten* (Jedediah Leland), *Dorothy Comingore* (Susan Alexander), *Everett Sloane* (Bernstein), *Ray Collins* (Boss Jim Geddes), *Paul Stewart* (Raymond), *Ruth Warrick* (Emily Norton), *Erskine Sanford* (Herbert Carter), *Agnes Moorehead* (Kane's mother), *Harry Shannon* (Kane's father), *George Coulouris* (Walter Parks Thatcher), *William Alland* (Thompson), *Fortunio Bonanova* (music teacher)

A newspaper tycoon dies, and a magazine reporter interviews his friends in an effort to discover the meaning of his last word: 'Rosebud.'

A brilliant piece of Hollywood cinema, using all the resources of the studio; despite lapses of characterization and gaps in the narrative, almost every shot and every line is utterly absorbing both as entertainment and as craft.

SCR *Herman J. Mankiewicz, Orson Welles* CIN *Gregg Toland* MUS *Bernard Herrmann* ED *Robert Wise* PROD *Orson Welles* DIST RKO

SONG: What is his name? It's Charlie Kane! I'll bet you five you're not alive if you don't know his name!
NEWSREEL: Then, last week, as it must to all men, death came to Charles Foster Kane.
BERNSTEIN: Old age. . .it's the only disease you don't look forward to being cured of.
THOMPSON: Mr Kane was a man who got everything he wanted, and then lost it. Maybe Rosebud was something he couldn't get, or something he lost. Anyway, I don't think it would have explained everything. I don't think any word can explain a man's life. No, I guess Rosebud is just a piece in a jigsaw puzzle. . .a missing piece.
SUSAN: Forty-nine acres of nothing but scenery and statues. I'm lonesome.
KANE: You're right, Mr Thatcher, I did lose a million dollars last year. I expect to lose a million dollars this year. I expect to lose a million dollars next year. You know, Mr Thatcher, at the rate of a million dollars a year, I'll have to close this place – in sixty years.
KANE: I run a couple of newspapers. What do you do?
BERNSTEIN: One day back in 1896 I was crossing over to Jersey on the ferry, and as we pulled out, there was another ferry pulling in, and on it there was a girl waiting to get off. A white dress she had on. She was carrying a white parasol. I only saw her for one second. She didn't see me at all, but I'll bet a month hasn't gone by since that I haven't thought of that girl.

❝ On seeing it for the first time, one got a conviction that if the cinema could do that, it could do anything. – *Penelope Houston*

❝ What may distinguish Citizen Kane most of all is its extracting the mythic from under the humdrum surface of the American experience. – *John Simon, 1968*

† Raising Kane by Pauline Kael, adapted from her 1971 New Yorker essay about the film, is recommended reading.

⚊ Herman J. Mankiewicz, Orson Welles (original screenplay)
⚍ picture; Orson Welles (leading actor); Orson Welles (directoin); Gregg Toland; Bernard Herrmann; art direction; Robert Wise

---

'It Started With A Shootout On A Rainswept Street And Ended In A Scandal That Shattered New York.'

City Hall ★

DIR Harold Becker
1996 111m US
`DVD` ♫

☆ Al Pacino (Mayor John Pappas), John Cusack (Deputy Mayor Kevin Calhoun), Bridget Fonda (Marybeth Cogan), Danny Aiello (Frank Anselmo), Martin Landau (Judge Walter Stern), David Paymer (Abe Goodman), Tony Franciosa (Paul Zapatti), Lindsay Duncan (Sydney Pappas)

After a shootout involving an off-duty cop on the streets of Brooklyn results in the death of a child, the deputy mayor of New York uncovers a web of corruption.

Classy but flawed attempt to ride the insider line of East Coast politics; Pacino's shouty, overbearing performance and too many sore-thumb scenes stuck in for commercial reasons comprise the flaws, but at least one of the writers was attempting to define unusually complex power structures.

SCR Ken Lipper, Paul Schrader, Nicholas Pileggi, Bo Goldman CIN Michael Seresin, John Corso MUS Jerry Goldsmith DES Jane Musky ED Robert C. Jones, David Bretherton PROD Edward R. Pressman, Ken Lipper, Charles Mulvehill, Harold Becker DIST Rank/Castle Rock

MAYOR JOHN PAPPAS: 'There was a palace that was a city. It was a PALACE! It was a PALACE and it CAN BE A PALACE AGAIN! A PALACE, in which there is no king or queen, or dukes or earls or princes, but subjects all: subjects beholden to each other, to make a better place to live. Is that too much to ask?'

❝ Moderately absorbing, and somehow, somewhere, the movie does care; it's just that the notion of corruption being endemic in the US system ain't hot news. – *Trevor Johnston, Time Out*

City Lights ★★★

SCR/DIR *Charles Chaplin*
1931 87m US
`DVD` ♫

☆ Charles Chaplin (A Tramp), Virginia Cherrill (A Blind Girl), Florence Lee (Her Grandmother), Harry Myers (An Eccentric Millionaire)

A tramp befriends a millionaire and falls in love with a blind girl.

Sentimental comedy with several delightful sequences in Chaplin's best manner. A masterpiece that effectively proved a fitting climax to cinema's silent era.

`DVD` Available on DVD   ☆ Cast in order   ❝ Critics' Quotes   ⚊ Academy Award   ⚏ BAFTA
♫ Soundtrack on CD   of importance   † Points of interest   ⚍ Academy Award nomination   ⚎ BAFTA nomination

CIN Rollie Totheroh   **MUS** Charles Chaplin
DIST UA/Charles Chaplin

66 Chaplin has another good picture, but it gives indications of being short-winded, and may tire fast after a bombastic initial seven days. . .he has sacrificed speed to pathos, and plenty of it. – *Variety*

66 Even while laughing, one is aware of a faint and uneasy feeling that Chaplin has been pondering with more than a bit of solemnity on conventional story values, and it has led him further than ever into the realms of what is often called pathetic. – *National Board of Review*

'She Didn't Believe In Angels Until She Fell In Love With One.'

City of Angels ★

DIR Brad Silberling
1998   114m   US/Germany
DVD   ♫

☆ Nicolas Cage (Seth), Meg Ryan (Dr. Maggie Rice), Andre Braugher (Cassiel), Dennis Franz (Nathaniel Messinger), Colm Feore (Jordan Ferris), Robin Bartlett (Anne), Joanna Merlin (Teresa Messinger), Sarah Dampf (Susan)

An angel circling Los Angeles considers becoming mortal after falling for a heart surgeon.

Better than expected remake of Wings of Desire transforms the original into no more than a glossy star vehicle with philosophical pretensions, but it's earnestly performed and beautifully shot.

SCR Dana Stevens   **CIN** *John Seale*   **MUS** Gabriel Yared
DES Lilly Kilvert   **ED** Lynzee Klingman   **PROD** Charles Roven, Dawn Steel   **DIST** Warner/Regency/Atlas

66 A fascinating hybrid. A Hollywood fantasy at its most fantastic, the film is equal parts true innocence and shameless calculation. Deciding whether the glass is half-empty or half-full depends on which part you are willing to embrace. – *Kenneth Turan, Los Angeles Times*

66 [There are] so many sweeping aerial shots that you start wishing the helicopter carrying the camera would crash, preferably on the two leading characters. – *Anne Billson, Sunday Telegraph*

'Fight and you'll never survive. . .Run and you'll never escape.'

City of God ★★★

DIR Fernando Meirelles, Katia Lund
2002   130m   Brazil/Germany/France
DVD   ♫

☆ Matheus Nachtergaele (Sandro Cenoura), Seu Jorge (Mane Galinha), Alexandre Rodrigues (Buscape), Leandro Firmino da Hora (Ze Pequeno), Phellipe Haagensen (Bene), Jonathan Haagensen (Cabeleira), Douglas Silva (Dadinho), Roberta Rodrigues (Berenice)

A promising young photographer attempts to stay out of a gang war unfolding between his contemporaries in the slums of Rio de Janeiro.

A little too in thrall to certain American crime epics, particularly in its occasionally jokey approach to violence, but possessed of such raw, vital energy that these and other faults are liable to pass most viewers by.

The result is a breakneck tour of one of the world's most forbidding neighbourhoods.

SCR Braulio Mantovani   **CIN** Cesar Charlone
MUS Antonio Pinto, Ed Cortes   **DES** Tule Peak
ED *Daniel Rezende*   **PROD** Andrea Barata Ribeiro, Mauricio Andrade Ramos   **DIST** Buena Vista

66 Contains enough indelible characters and unforgettable stories to fill several good films. – *Colin Kennedy, Empire*

66 Seductive, disturbing, enthralling - a trip to hell that gives the passengers a great ride. – *Richard Corliss, Time*

⚖ Fernando Meirelles; Braulio Mantovani; Cesar Charlone; Daniel Rezende

🛡 Daniel Rezende
Ⓣ film not in the English Language

City of Hope ★★★★

SCR/DIR *John Sayles*
1991   129m   US

☆ Vincent Spano (Nick Rinaldi), Joe Morton (Wynn), Tony Lo Bianco (Joe Rinaldi), Barbara Williams (Angela), Stephen Mendillo (Yoyo), Chris Cooper (Riggs), Charlie Yanko (Stavros), Jace Alexander (Bobby), Todd Graff (Zip), Scott Tiler (Vinnie), John Sayles (Carl), Frankie Faison (Levonne), Gloria Foster (Jeanette), Tom Wright (Malik)

Building contractors, politicians, crime bosses and racist cops all contribute to this kaleidoscopic analysis of a New Jersey city riddled with corruption.

Masterly deconstruction of the power plays, vested interests and spheres of influence that run, and often ruin American cities. Unrivalled in its sheer scope and ambition until the TV series The Wire, which it almost certainly influenced. Sayles's most satisfactory film.

CIN Robert Richardson   **MUS** Mason Daring   **DES** Dan Bishop, Dianna Freas   **ED** John Sayles   **PROD** Sarah Green, Maggie Renzi   **DIST** Mainline/Esperanza

66 Sayles brings something rare to American movies: a keen sense of purpose. The result is gutsy, knockdown entertainment. – *Peter Travers, Rolling Stone*

66 Epic, masterly, urgent, adult and unforgettable. Put simply – which is grossly unfair to its complexity – it is Bonfire of the Vanities without the vanities. – *Alexander Walker, Evening Standard*

City of Lost Children ★★

DIR Jean-Pierre Jeunet, Marc Caro
1995   112m   France/Spain/Germany
DVD   ♫

☆ Ron Perlman (One), Daniel Emilfork (Krank), Judith Vittet (Miette), Dominique Pinon (le scaphandrier /les clones), Jean-Claude Dreyfus (Marcello), Genevieve Brunet (La Pieuvre), Odile Mallet (La Pieuvre), Ticky Holgado (Ex-acrobat), Jean-Louis Trintignant (Uncle Irvin (voice))

A circus strongman strives to rescue his brother from a mad inventor who lives on an oil rig and steals children's dreams.

This one-of-a-kind industrial fairy tale is most likely too dark for real-world children, and favours visual invention over narrative coherence: it absolutely creates

its own world, though, and makes a bold attempt to immerse the viewer.

SCR Gilles Adrien, Jean-Pierre Jeunet, Marc Caro
CIN *Darius Khondji*　MUS Angelo Badalamenti
ED Hervé Schneid　PROD Claudie Ossard
DIST Entertainment/Lumiere/Canal Plus/France 3

66 A hugely inventive blend of dream, fairy-tale and myth. – *Geoff Andrew, Time Out*

66 Its creators have a prodigious eye for memorable grotesques but a lousy facility for making them drive the story, which leaves the characters with nothing much to do except gurn at the camera. – *Tom Shone, Sunday Times*

A City of Sadness ★★

DIR Hou Hsiao-Hsien
1989　157m　Taiwan

☆ Ikuyo Nakamura (Shisuko), Jack Kao (Wen Leung), Wou Yifang (Hinioei)

Life in Taiwan between the Japanese withdrawal in 1945 and the Chinese nationalist takeover of the mainland four years later.

Set in a single household undergoing turbulent changes that mirror those in the outside world, it's a meticulous study of a specific period in Taiwanese history.

SCR Wu Nianjen, Chu Tianwen　CIN Chen Huai'en
PROD Chiu Fusheng　DIST Artificial Eye/3-H/Era International

† The film won the Golden Lion at the Venice Film Festival in 1989.

'Three urban hombres heading west, seeking adventure, craving excitement. . .and longing for room service.'

City Slickers ★★

DIR Ron Underwood
1991　112m　US
DVD ♫

☆ Billy Crystal (Mitch Robbins), Daniel Stern (Phil Berquist), Bruno Kirby (Ed Furillo), Patricia Wettig (Barbara Robbins), Helen Slater (Bonnie Rayburn), *Jack Palance* (Curly), Josh Mostel (Barry Shalowitz), David Paymer (Ira Shalowitz), Noble Willingham (Clay Stone)

Three male friends on the brink of turning 40 face up to their issues while on a cattle drive.

Nicely played ensemble piece has fun with Western conventions, though its success inadvertently spawned a tiresome mini-genre: the New Age male midlife crisis movie.

SCR *Lowell Ganz, Babaloo Mandel*　CIN Dean Semler
MUS Marc Shaiman, Thomas Richard Sharp
DES Lawrence G. Paull　ED O. Nicholas Brown
PROD Irby Smith　DIST First Independent/Castle Rock/Nelson/Face

MITCH ROBBINS: 'Value this time in your life kids, because this is the time in your life when you still have your choices, and it goes by so quickly. When you're a teenager you think you can do anything, and you do. Your twenties are a blur. Your thirties, you raise your family, you make a little money and you think to yourself, "What happened to my twenties?" Your forties, you grow a little pot belly you

grow another chin. The music starts to get too loud and one of your old girlfriends from high school becomes a grandmother. Your fifties you have a minor surgery. You'll call it a procedure, but it's a surgery. Your sixties you have a major surgery, the music is still loud but it doesn't matter because you can't hear it anyway. Seventies, you and the wife retire to Fort Lauderdale, you start eating dinner at two, lunch around ten, breakfast the night before. And you spend most of your time wandering around malls looking for the ultimate in soft yogurt and muttering "how come the kids don't call?" By your eighties, you've had a major stroke, and you end up babbling to some Jamaican nurse who your wife can't stand but who you call mama. Any questions?'

66 Could reasonably be accused of being "mechanical", but only in the way that a Rolls Royce is mechanical: it's elegantly designed and immaculately crafted. – *Christopher Tookey, Daily Mail*

⚱ Jack Palance (supporting actor)

'Justice has its price.'

A Civil Action ★★

SCR/DIR Steven Zaillian
1998　115m　US
DVD ♫

☆ *John Travolta* (Jan Schlichtmann), Robert Duvall (Jerome Facher), Tony Shalhoub (Kevin Conway), William H. Macy (James Gordon), Zeljko Ivanek (Bill Crowley), *James Gandolfini* (Al Love), John Lithgow (Judge Walter J. Skinner), Kathleen Quinlan (Anne Anderson), Stephen Fry (Pinder), Sydney Pollack (Al Eustis)

A hot-shot litigator sues two corporations for deaths caused by dumping toxic waste, but the case proves so expensive and difficult it threatens to bankrupt his firm.

Unusually sober legal drama, based on the terrific non-fiction bestseller, which contemplates the prospect of failure in a class-action suit: a tad hammily acted, but well crafted as far as it goes.

CIN *Conrad L. Hall*　MUS Danny Elfman　DES David Gropman　ED Wayne Wahrman　PROD Scott Rudin, Robert Redford, Rachel Pfeffer　DIST Buena Vista/Paramount/Touchstone

66 A solid and intelligent legal thriller that may be too complex in its issues, and too low-key and unexciting in its style, for today's market demands. – *Emanuel Levy, Variety*

⚱ Robert Duvall (supporting actor); Conrad L. Hall

'Everything has a price.'

The Claim ★★

DIR *Michael Winterbottom*
2000　120m　GB/Canada/France
DVD ♫

☆ *Peter Mullan* (Dillon), Wes Bentley (Dalglish), Milla Jovovich (Lucia), Nastassja Kinski (Elena), *Sarah Polley* (Hope), Julian Richings (Bellinger), Sean McGinley (Sweetley)

The sheriff of a Sierra Nevada mining town is undone when his estranged wife and daughter show up unexpectedly.

It isn't just the snowy locations that make this rethink of

DVD Available on DVD　☆ Cast in order of importance　66 Critics' Quotes　⚱ Academy Award　Ⓦ BAFTA
♫ Soundtrack on CD　† Points of interest　Academy Award nomination　Ⓣ BAFTA nomination

129

The Mayor of Casterbridge a somewhat chilly proposition, but the unavoidable tragedy of Hardy's text is granted a rare and remarkable scale here, and Winterbottom elicits surprisingly assured performances from a diverse cast.

SCR *Frank Cottrell Boyce* **CIN** *Alwin Kuchler* **MUS** Michael Nyman **DES** *Mark Tildesley, Ken Rempel* **ED** Trevor Waite **PROD** Andrew Eaton

66 One of those rare literary adaptations that finds its fidelity in freedom, that stands as both a fitting version of its source material and as its own creation. – *Charles Taylor, Salon*

66 Stark, haunting, epic and mournful. . .a mountain of a film. – *Jay Carr, Boston Globe*

Claire Dolan ★

SCR/DIR Lodge Kerrigan
1998　95m　France/US
DVD

☆ *Katrin Cartlidge* (Claire Dolan), Vincent D'Onofrio (Elton Garrett), Colm Meaney (Roland Cain), John Doman (Cain's friend), Maryanne Plunkett (Mary Egan), Miranda Stuart-Rhyne (Angela), Kate Skinner (Madeline Garrett), David Little (Man in Chicago Cafe), Lola Pashalinski (Salon Client), Jim Frangione (Man in Bar), Ed Hodson (Driver)

In New York, a repressed prostitute attempts to begin a new chapter in her life, away from her brutal pimp.

Writer-director Kerrigan signalled his interest in people operating on society's margins in this debut feature. Its style is as closed as its struggling heroine, but it repays the effort, and Cartlidge delivers an exceptional honest, raw performance.

CIN Teodoro Maniaci **MUS** Ahrin Mishan, Simon Fisher Turner **DES** Sharon Lomofsky **ED** Kristina Boden **PROD** Ann Ruark **DIST** ICA

66 If a movie like this had a neat ending, the ending would be a lie. We do not want answers, but questions and observations. – *Roger Ebert, Chicago Sun-Times*

66 Cartlidge's beautifully still performance, mournful one moment, defiant the next, lets you see into Claire's soul without editorializing or begging for our empathy. – *Stephen Holden, New York Times*

'Nothing Personal. It's Just Father vs Daughter in The Fight Of Their Lives.'

Class Action ★

DIR Michael Apted
1990　110m　US
DVD　♫

☆ Gene Hackman (Jedediah Tucker Ward), Mary Elizabeth Mastrantonio (Maggie Ward), Colin Friels (Michael Grazier), Joanna Merlin (Estelle Ward), Larry Fishburne (Nick Holbrook), Donald Moffat (Fred Quinn), Jan Rubes (Alexander Pavel), Matt Clark (Judge R. Symes)

A liberal father and his conservative, ambitious daughter do battle in court.

Far better than its predictable sounding premise suggests. Well acted and thoughtfully directed, it insults no-one's intelligence.

SCR Carolyn Shelby, Christopher Ames, Samantha Shad **CIN** Conrad L. Hall **MUS** James Horner **DES** Todd Hallowell **ED** Ian Crafford **PROD** Ted Field, Scott Kroopf, Robert W. Cort **DIST** TCF/Interscope

66 Hackman is the one thing that keeps you watching. His performance, playing a man of dignity and honour with a veneer of vanity, is the only evidence of class on show here. – *Channel 4*

Class Trip ★

DIR Claude Miller
1998　96m　France
DVD

☆ Clement Van Den Bergh (Nicolas), Lokman Nalcakan (Hodkann), François Roy (The Father), Yves Verhoeven (Patrick), Emmanuelle Bercot (Mlle Grimm), Tina Sportolaro (The Mother), Chantal Banlier (Marie Ange), Benoit Herlin (Ribotton), Julien Le Mouel (Lucas)

An anxious boy on holiday at a school ski camp suffers crippling fears of death.

Thriller with an acute psychological edge, made creepier by its picturesque snowy backdrop. It finally doesn't amount to much, though Miller sustains an atmosphere of undefined dread to good effect.

SCR Emmanuel Carrere, Claude Miller **CIN** Guillaume Schiffman **MUS** Henri Texier **DES** Jean-Pierre Kohut-Svelko **ED** Anne Lafarge **PROD** Annie Miller **DIST** Warner

66 Few actors have conveyed the clamped-down angst that Van der Bergh does as Nicolas, whose dark home life propels him into a fantasy world. – *Kirven Blount, Entertainment Weekly*

Clean, Shaven ★★

SCR/DIR *Lodge Kerrigan*
1993　79m　US
DVD

☆ *Peter Greene* (Peter Winter), Robert Albert (Jack McNally), Megan Owen (Mrs Winter), Molly Castelloe (Melinda Frayne), Jennifer MacDonald (Nicole Winter), Alice Levitt (Girl with ball)

A schizophrenic sets out to reclaim his adopted daughter while a detective closes in on him, certain his quarry has killed another child.

A raw, compelling experience charting one man's mental disintegration through fractured images and a heightened soundtrack of white noise and half-heard conversations; it's by no means an easy film, but it is a brave and compassionate one, attempting to portray schizophrenia from the inside out.

CIN Teodoro Maniaci **MUS** Hahn Rowe **DES** Tania Ferrier **ED** Jay Rabinowitz **PROD** Lodge Kerrigan **DIST** ICA/DSM III

66 Few movie portraits of the paranoid experience have

been so detailed or, for that matter, so harrowing. – *Geoff Andrew, Time Out*

'Thirty remarkable days in the life of an ordinary man.'

Clean and Sober ★★

DIR Glenn Gordon Caron
1988   124m   US
DVD

☆ *Michael Keaton* (Daryl Poynter), Kathy Baker (Charlie Standers), Morgan Freeman (Craig), Tate Donovan (Donald Towle), Henry Judd Baker (Xavier), Claudia Christian (Iris), M. Emmet Walsh (Richard Dirks), Luca Bercovici (Lenny)

An estate agent facing embezzlement charges decides to lay low in a rehab clinic rather than face the music. He remains in denial about his alcoholism and drug dependency.

Keaton's first major big-screen detour into serious drama proves surprisingly effective. This full-blooded drama is more clear-eyed and level-headed about addiction than most.

SCR Tod Carroll   CIN Jan Kiesser   MUS Gabriel Yared
DES Joel Schiller   ED Richard Chew   PROD Tony Ganz, Deborah Blum   DIST Warner/Imagine Entertainment

66 I only wish there were some honest way of describing this movie that would make everyone go and see it. – *Philip French, Observer*

'Truth needs a soldier.'

Clear and Present Danger ★

DIR Phillip Noyce
1994   141m   US
DVD   ♫

☆ Harrison Ford (Jack Ryan), Willem Dafoe (John Clark), Anne Archer (Cathy Muller Ryan), Henry Czerny (Robert Ritter), Joaquim de Almeida (Col. Felix Cortez), Harris Yulin (James Cutter), Donald Moffat (President Bennett), Miguel Sandoval (Ernesto Escobedo), James Earl Jones (Adm. James Greer)

CIA agent Jack Ryan investigates the death of an associate of the President, uncovering links to Colombian drug cartels.

Over-plotted and over-populated action thriller, unsure whether it wants to be a techno-babble-filled spy picture or something more active; the leading man alternates between suit and tracksuit accordingly. Still, it's effective if undemanding entertainment

SCR Donald Stewart, Steven Zaillian, John Milius
CIN Donald McAlpine   MUS James Horner
DES Terence Marsh   ED Neil Travis   PROD Mace Neufeld, Robert Rehme   DIST Paramount

66 Enjoyable, but it's a shallow enjoyment. – *James Berardinelli, ReelViews*

66 Takes a slow route between short bursts of excitement. – *Lisa Schwarzbaum, Entertainment Weekly*

⚲ Donald O. Mitchell, Michael Herbick, Frank A. Montaño,

Art Rochester (sound); Bruce Stambler, John Leveque (sound effects editing)

'What if you had a universal remote. . .that controlled your universe?'

Click ★★

DIR Frank Coraci
2006   107m   US
DVD

☆ *Adam Sandler* (Michael Newman), *Kate Beckinsale* (Donna Newman), *Christopher Walken* (Morty), *David Hasselhoff* (Ammer), *Henry Winkler* (Ted), Julie Kavner (Trudy), Sean Astin (Bill)

A workaholic architect is given a magic universal remote allowing him to freeze time, mute noise and fast-forward through his schedule. Problems occur when the gizmo operates on its own, skipping key moments of his life.

Sandler's goofy charm saves a crudely sentimental fable in the It's A Wonderful Life vein – full of cheap gags, heartfelt emotion and terrific futuristic design.

SCR Steve Koren, Mark O'Keefe   CIN Dean Semler
MUS Rupert Gregson-Williams   DES Perry Andelin Blake   ED Jeff Gourson   PROD Adam Sandler, Jack Giarraputo, Neal H. Moritz, Steve Koren, Mark O'Keefe
DIST Sony

66 Once we get the idea, there are no more surprises, only variations on the first one. – *Roger Ebert, Chicago Sun-Times*

⚲ Bill Corso, Kazuhiro Tsuji (makeup)

'A district attorney out for a conviction. A new lawyer out of her league. A young boy who knew too much.'

The Client ★

DIR Joel Schumacher
1994   119m   US
DVD   ♫

☆ *Susan Sarandon* (Regina 'Reggie' Love), Tommy Lee Jones ('Reverend' Roy Foltrigg), Mary-Louise Parker (Dianne Sway), Anthony LaPaglia (Barry 'The Blade' Muldano), J. T. Walsh (Jason McThune), Anthony Edwards (Clint Von Hooser), Brad Renfro (Mark Sway), Will Patton (Sergeant Hardy), Ossie Davis (Judge Harry Roosevelt)

A female lawyer takes the case of a young boy, a witness to a Mob-related death. He is then hounded by a Mafia hitman, while she incurs the wrath of an federal attorney.

A decent adaptation of an efficient Grisham story, all lawyers, bluff and double bluffs, and fast-paced action. Sarandon elevates it above the merely average in her portrayal of a tender, caring relationship with her young charge.

SCR Akiva Goldsman, Robert Getchell   CIN Tony Pierce-Roberts   MUS Howard Shore   DES Bruno Rubeo
ED Robert Brown   PROD Arnon Milchan, Steven Reuther
DIST Warner/Regency/Alcor

⚲ Susan Sarandon (leading actress)

Ⓣ Susan Sarandon (leading actress)

DVD Available on DVD   ☆ Cast in order   66 Critics' Quotes   ⚲ Academy Award   Ⓣ BAFTA
♫ Soundtrack on CD   of importance   † Points of interest   ⚲ Academy Award nomination   Ⓣ BAFTA nomination

131

'Hang on.'
Cliffhanger ★
DIR Renny Harlin
1993 112m US
DVD ♫

☆ Sylvester Stallone (Gabe Walker), John Lithgow (Eric Qualen), Michael Rooker (Hal Tucker), Janine Turner (Jessie Deighan), Rex Linn (Richard Travers, Treasury Agent), Caroline Goodall (Kristel, Jetstar Pilot), Leon (Kynette), Craig Fairbrass (Delmar), Gregory Scott Cummins (Ryan), Paul Winfield (Walter Wright, Treasury Agent), Ralph Waite (Frank)

A tormented rescue expert leads a team in pursuit of a gang of bank robbers whose escape vehicle crashed in the Rocky Mountains.

Near-perfect post-pub entertainment, displaying a commendable faith in its own ludicrousness. The lead would appear to have been carved out of the scenery.

SCR Michael France, Sylvester Stallone **CIN** Alex Thomson **MUS** Trevor Jones **DES** John Vallone **ED** Frank J. Urioste **PROD** Alan Marshall, Renny Harlin **DIST** Carolco/Canal/Pioneer/RCS Video

66 Lithgow alone, gleefully sadistic, seems to grasp the fundamental silliness of a film where Sly repeatedly outwits everyone and recovers amazingly quickly from brutal beatings without so much as a scar. – *Geoff Andrew, Time Out*

⚲ Neil Krepela, John Richardson, John Bruno, Pamela Easley (visual effects); Michael Minkler, Bob Beemer, Tim Cooney (sound); Wylie Stateman, Gregg Baxter (sound effects editing)

Climates ★★★
SCR/DIR Nuri Bilge Ceylan
2006 102m Turkey/France/Netherlands
DVD

☆ Ebru Ceylan (Bahar), Nuri Bilge Ceylan (Isa), Nazan Kirilmis (Serap), Mehmet Eryilmaz (Mehmet)

Over three seasons in Turkey, a couple's relationship gradually disintegrates. He is a stolid, middle-aged professor and photographer, while she is an impulsive, fiery young woman who works in TV.

Ceylan astutely portrays two not particularly likable people with evident faults, yet manages to sustain sympathy for them both. A conventional Western film would raise hopes for the couple's reunion; here, we hope they will part, and wish them well separately. Ceylan's sense of composition is flawless, and he tells his story gradually, with relatively little dialogue. Emotionally subtle and shot through with helpless melancholy.

CIN Gokhan Tiryaki **ED** Ayhan Ergursel, Nuri Bilge Ceylan **PROD** Zeynep Ozbatur **DIST** Artificial Eye

66 Finds magnificence in the everyday and doesn't allow one single word or action to stray from a complete vision of what it means to be living and loving in [director] Ceylan's home city of Istanbul. – *Dave Calhoun, Time Out*

66 A surprisingly fond and tender portrait of the breakdown of a relationship and the ensuing sense of desolation. – *Ryan Gilbey, Sight & Sound*

† Director/actor Nuri Bilge Ceylan and lead actress Ebru Ceylan are man and wife.

'When there's murder on the streets, everyone is a suspect.'
Clockers ★★
DIR Spike Lee
1995 128m US
DVD ♫

☆ Harvey Keitel (Det. Rocco Klein), John Turturro (Det. Larry Mazilli), Delroy Lindo (Rodney Little), *Mekhi Phifer* (Ronald 'Strike' Dunham), Isaiah Washington (Victor Dunham), Keith David (André the Giant), Pee Wee Love (Tyrone 'Shorty' Jeeter), Regina Taylor (Iris Jeeter), Sticky Fingaz (Scientific)

A New York detective investigating the murder of a pusher comes to believe that a man who confesses to the crime is shielding his younger brother – a clocker, a low-level drug dealer working the streets.

Spike Lee makes clear his hostility to the gun culture of inner cities, which causes so many needless African-American deaths. He strikes a melancholy mood, shooting Brooklyn in shadows and muted light, sometimes using hand-held cinema verité techniques to enhance the immediacy of dramatic scenes. First-rate acting enhances a mature, contemplative work.

SCR Richard Price, Spike Lee **CIN** Malik Hassan Sayeed **MUS** Terence Blanchard **DES** Andrew McAlpine **ED** Sam Pollard **PROD** Martin Scorsese, Spike Lee, Jon Kilik **DIST** UIP/Universal/40 Acres and a Mule

66 A kaleidoscopic vision of a community mired in betrayal, psychosis, and murder. The images are like something out of a nightmare newsreel, raw and grainy and pulsatingly alive. – *Owen Gleiberman, Entertainment Weekly*

66 Confirms Lee's position as the cinema's great surgeon-general, alternately taking the pulse of America and probing its open wounds. But it is still, in many ways, a bad film – so full of holes you can see right through it. – *Tom Shone, Sunday Times*

† Originally, the film was to have been directed by Martin Scorsese. But he decided to make Casino instead, and Lee took over as director, rewriting the script to change its emphasis: in Price's novel, the protagonist is the Brooklyn detective played by Harvey Keitel.

'Being the adventures of a young man whose principal interests are rape, ultra-violence, and Beethoven!'
A Clockwork Orange ★★★
SCR/DIR Stanley Kubrick
1971 136m GB
DVD ♫

☆ *Malcolm McDowell* (Alex), Michael Bates (Chief Guard), Adrienne Corri (Mrs. Alexander), Patrick Magee (Mr. Alexander), Warren Clarke (Dim)

In a future Britain of desolation and violence, a young gangster guilty of rape and murder obtains a release from prison after being experimentally brainwashed: he finds society more violent than it was in his time.

DVD Available on DVD ☆ Cast in order of importance 66 Critics' Quotes † Points of interest ⚲ Academy Award ⚲ Academy Award nomination Ⓑ BAFTA Ⓑ BAFTA nomination
♫ Soundtrack on CD

A film that has been overshadowed by its reputation. As a portrayal of amorality, it was always likely to be shocking, though the scenes of rape (to Singin' in the Rain) and 'ultra-violence' by Alex and his 'droogs' in the first half seem excessive. Yet time has proved Kubrick right, and the world depicted in the film bears a startling resemblance to parts of Britain's inner cities. It remains a brilliant series of set-pieces, strung together by arguments about free will that now seem slightly dull.

CIN John Alcott MUS Walter Carlos DES John Barry ED Bill Butler PROD Bernard Williams DIST Warner

66 Very early there are hints of triteness and insecurity, and before half an hour is over it begins to slip into tedium. . .Inexplicably the script leaves out Burgess' reference to the title. – *Stanley Kauffmann*

66 The first punk tragicomedy, a chain-whipped cartoon meditation on Good, Evil, and Free Will that is as seductive as it is tasteless. That Kubrick misjudged the distance between comedy and cruelty seems to be unarguable. – *Michael Atkinson, Village Voice*

† Concerned that the film's subject matter was influencing the spread of violent incidents involving young people in Britain, Kubrick had the film withdrawn from distribution in the UK in 1973. It was re-released in 1999, the year of his death.

⚲ picture; Stanley Kubrick (direction); Stanley Kubrick (adapted screenplay)

Close My Eyes

SCR/DIR Stephen Poliakoff
1991 108m GB
DVD

☆ Alan Rickman (Sinclair), Saskia Reeves (Natalie), Clive Owen (Richard), Karl Johnson (Colin), Lesley Sharp (Jessica), Kate Gartside (Paula), Karen Knight (Philippa), Niall Buggy (Geof)

A brother and sister, estranged for years, reunite as adults and start an incestuous affair one hot summer in London.

Oddly overwrought, with a weak, implausible narrative that must bear the weight of pondering on universal truths as well a state-of-the-nation address about the 1980s – a decade of excess. Poliakoff has gone on to become one of Britain's most respected TV dramatists, but not a word of this feels true or real.

CIN Witold Stok MUS Michael Gibbs DES Luciana Arrighi ED Michael Parkinson PROD Thérèse Pickard DIST Artificial Eye/Beambright/Film Four

66 Should have a solid career ahead of it and is a major plus for all concerned. – *Variety*

66 Drags itself across the screen. After much huffing and puffing, the script refuses to become the sum of its many, many scholarly observations about life, love, the universe. The lack of feeling is fatal. – *John Lyttle, Independent*

Close to Eden ★

DIR Sidney Lumet
1992 110m US
☆ Melanie Griffith (Emily Eden), Eric Thal (Ariel), John

Pankow (Levine), Tracy Pollan (Mara), Lee Richardson (Rebbe), Mia Sara (Leah), Jamey Sheridan (Nick), Jake Weber (Yaakov Klausman)

In an attempt to hunt down a killer, a female New York cop goes undercover in a Hasidic Jewish community.

Flawed but potentially fascinating material about a rarely observed community. Director Lumet works the thriller aspects with practised ease, though the casting is disastrous: the notion of Griffith infiltrating Hasids is literally laughable.

SCR Robert J. Avrech CIN Andrzej Bartkowiak MUS Jerry Bock DES Philip Rosenberg ED Andrew Mondshein PROD Steve Golin, Sigurjon Sighvatsson, Howard Rosenman DIST Rank/Propaganda/Sandollar/Isis

66 With its Fiddler on the Roof score and some sneakily hypocritical espousing of deeply conservative religious values, this is little more than a 111-minute love letter to Sidney Lumet's rabbi. – *Kim Newman, Empire*

Closely Observed Trains ★★★

SCR/DIR Jiri Menzel
1966 92m Czechoslovakia
DVD

☆ Vaclav Neckar (Trainee Milos Hrma), Jitka Bendova (Conductor Masa), Vladimir Valenta (Stationmaster Max), Josef Somr (Train Dispatcher Hubicka)

During World War II in German-occupied Czechoslovakia, a dim-witted young railway guard at a country station tries to lose his virginity, and becomes a partisan saboteur.

Droll, affectionate comedy with a hearty, raucous attitude to sexuality and a serious ending.

CIN Jaromir Sofr MUS Jiri Pavlik ED Jirina Lukesova PROD Zdenek Oves DIST Ceskoslovensky Film

66 Like (Milos) Forman, Menzel seems incapable of being unkind to anybody. – *Tom Milne*

⚲ foreign film

'If you believe in love at first sight, you never stop looking.'

Closer ★

DIR Mike Nichols
2004 104m US
DVD

☆ Julia Roberts (Anna), Jude Law (Dan), Natalie Portman (Alice), *Clive Owen (Larry)*

A London journalist engineers a meeting between the woman who rebuffed him and a sexually rapacious dermatologist, with tragic consequences.

An altogether chilly experience, falling down not specifically because its characters are so dislikable (though they are), but because nobody appears to learn anything from tryst to trust and scene to scene. Casting Owen against the weak-willed Law creates a handful of dramatic sparks, but the women receive considerably shorter, borderline-misogynist shrift.

DVD Available on DVD ☆ Cast in order of importance 66 Critics' Quotes ⚲ Academy Award ♫ Soundtrack on CD † Points of interest Academy Award nomination 🅑 BAFTA 🅣 BAFTA nomination

133

A film that genuinely polarises audiences; some find it starkly real, others dismiss it as chic nonsense.

SCR Patrick Marber CIN Stephen Goldblatt DES Tim Hatley ED John Bloom, Antonia Van Drimmelen PROD Mike Nichols, John Calley, Cary Brokaw DIST Columbia

66 If you're the sort of person who laughs at funerals, train wrecks, earnest political documentaries and stories about the rape of nature, you'll love Closer. – *Stephen Hunter, Washington Post*

66 The film of the year. – *David Thomson, Independent on Sunday*

Clive Owen (supporting actor); Natalie Portman (supporting actress)

Clive Owen (supporting actor)

Natalie Portman (supporting actress); Patrick Marber

The Closet ★

SCR/DIR Francis Veber
2001 84m France
DVD

☆ Daniel Auteuil (Francois Pignon), Gerard Depardieu (Felix Santini), Thierry Lhermitte (Guillaume), Michele Laroque (Miss Bertrand), Michel Aumont (Belone), Jean Rochefort (Kopel), Alexandra Vandernoot (Christine)

On the verge of being fired, a company man pretends to be gay and seeks refuge under anti-discrimination law.

The stars do what they can, but the farce is slackened by too many supporting parts, and a feeling the set-up isn't all that funny to begin with.

CIN Luciano Tovoli MUS Vladimir Cosma DES Hugues Tissandier ED Georges Klotz PROD Patrice Ledoux DIST Optimum

66 By the end, we are left with a mildly amusing comedy, and the lingering memory of a sterling cast that deserved better material. – *John Petrakis, Chicago Tribune*

Close-Up ★

SCR/DIR Abbas Kiarostami
1989 90m Iran
DVD

☆ Hossain Sabzian (Himself/Makhmalbaf), Mohsen Makhmalbaf (Himself), Abolfazi Ahankhah (Himself), Mehrdad Ahankhah (Himself), Manoochehr Ahankhah (Himself), Hossein Farazmand (Reporter), Abbas Kiarostami (Himself (voice))

A young Iranian who posed as the director Mohsen Makhmalbaf to elicit money from a Tehran family recounts his story during his trial.

Intercutting documentary footage of the trial with interviews and reconstructions of true-life events – using the actual participants – this is a doodle that takes on more significance the longer one thinks about it: a self-reflexive exercise in which the illusory nature of cinema itself is put on trial.

CIN Ali Reza Zarrin-Dast ED Abbas Kiarostami DIST BFI/IIDCYA

66 Takes questions about movies and makes them feel like

questions of life, death and meaning. – *Michael Atkinson, Village Voice*

66 A masterpiece. . .absolutely wonderful. – *Geoff Andrew, Time Out*

'Discover the love of a lifetime.'

Closing the Ring (new) ★

DIR Richard Attenborough
2007 117m UK/Canada

☆ Shirley Maclaine (Ethel Ann Roberts), *Christopher Plummer* (Jack Etty), Mischa Barton (Young Ethel Ann), Stephen Amell (Teddy Gordon), Neve Campbell (Marie), Pete Postlethwaite (Michael Quinlan), Brenda Fricker (Granny), Gregory Smith (Young Jack), Martin McCann (Jimmy Reilly)

In World War II, a young US airman secretly marries his home-town sweetheart, but then dies when his plane crashes near Belfast. Fifty years later, an Irish boy finds the airman's ring and traces his widow.

Tremendously sincere and well-intentioned, this complex, time-hopping story is not for those who recoil from weepies.

SCR Peter Woodward CIN Roger Pratt MUS Jeff Danna DES Tom McCullagh ED Lesley Walker PROD Richard Attenborough, Jo Gilbert DIST The Works

66 Even once you accept the soppiness as part and parcel of the genre, there is no way anything here can be taken seriously. – *Edward Porter, Sunday Times*

'Some Thing Has Found Us.'

Cloverfield (new) ★

DIR Matt Reeves
2008 84m US
DVD

☆ Lizzy Caplan (Marlena Diamond), Jessica Lucas (Lily Ford), T.J. Miller (Hudson 'Hud' Platt), Michael Stahl-David (Rob Hawkins), Mike Vogel (Jason Hawkins), Odette Yustman (Beth McIntyre)

A giant lizard's attack on Manhattan is filmed on video by a group of friends trying to find a way out of the city.

Godzilla retooled for the YouTube generation, effectively launched under a veil of secrecy on an expectant audience seduced by its drip-feed marketing. The shaky camerawork is likely to induce nausea while the characterisation is non-existent; those seeking vicarious thrills, though, will not be disappointed.

SCR Drew Goddard CIN Michael Bonvillain DES Martin Whist ED Kevin Stitt PROD J.J. Abrams, Bryan Burk DIST Paramount

66 An old-fashioned monster movie dressed up in trendy new threads. – *Todd McCarthy, Variety*

66 Cinematic pleasure at its purest. – *Olly Richards, Empire*

† The film's first trailer did not reveal its title, only its release date.

† The film has no score besides an end credits theme composed by Michael Giacchino.

DVD Available on DVD ☆ Cast in order of importance 66 Critics' Quotes Academy Award BAFTA
♫ Soundtrack on CD † Points of interest Academy Award nomination BAFTA nomination

'The only remedy for love is to love more.'

Clubland (new) ★

DIR Cherie Nowlan
2007 105m Australia
♫

☆ *Brenda Blethyn* (Jean Dwight), Khan Chittenden (Tim), Emma Booth (Jill), Richard Wilson (Mark), Frankie J. Holden (John), Rebecca Gidney (Lana), Philip Quast (Ronnie)

An egocentric cockney comedienne on the Sydney club circuit interferes with the lives of her teenage sons.

In a role written specifically for her, Blethyn excels as the narcissistic, needy Jean, who sacrificed her career to raise her sons. It's an intermittently affecting drama about family tensions, though it isn't clear if Jean was ever talented at raunchy comedy. The plot meanders somewhat before focusing on this unsympathetic matriarch.

SCR Keith Thompson   CIN Mark Wareham
MUS Martin Armiger   DES Nell Hanson   ED Scott Gray
PROD Rosemary Blight   DIST Warners

66 Amiable, if directionless little Australian picture which is part coming-of-age comedy and part mid-life crisis. . .Blethyn always commands attention. – *Peter Bradshaw, Guardian.*

'Sex. Clothes. Popularity. Is there a problem here?'

Clueless ★★

SCR/DIR *Amy Heckerling*
1995 97m US
DVD ♫

☆ *Alicia Silverstone* (Cher Horowitz), Stacey Dash (Dionne), Brittany Murphy (Tai), Paul Rudd (Josh), Dan Hedaya (Mel Horowitz), Donald Faison (Murray), Elisa Donovan (Amber), Wallace Shawn (Mr. Wendell Hall)

A Beverly Hills teenager, adept at shopping and makeovers, proves helpless when it comes to settling on Mr. Right.

Peppy comedy, loosely based on Jane Austen's Emma, that gets in a few satirical shots at Californian mores in the space between pop songs and changing-room montages; it briefly made a star of its bright, funny young lead.

CIN Bill Pope   MUS David Kitay   DES Steve Jordan
ED Debra Chiate   PROD Robert Lawrence, Scott Rudin
DIST Paramount

66 Turns out to have more to it than anyone could anticipate. – *Kenneth Turan, Los Angeles Times*

66 A fresh, disarmingly bright and at times explosively funny comedy well worth a trip to the mall, even if it eventually runs out of gas. – *Brian Lowry, Variety*

'It begins on the street. It ends here.'

Coach Carter ★

DIR Thomas Carter
2004 136m US/Germany
DVD ♫

☆ Samuel L. Jackson (Coach Ken Carter), Robert Ri'chard

(Damien Carter), Rob Brown (Kenyon Stone), Ashanti (Kyra), Debbi Morgan (Tonya), Rick Gonzalez (Timo Cruz), Antwon Tanner (Worm), Nana Gbewonyo (Junior Battle)

An unconventional basketball coach in a high school courts unpopularity by throwing players off the team if they ignore their academic responsibilities.

An unusual sports-team movie that asserts there is more to life than sport, and especially winning. Adapted from a true story, and enlivened by an energetic, shouty performance from Jackson.

SCR Mark Schwahn, John Gatins   CIN Sharone Meir
MUS Trevor Rabin   DES Carlos Barbosa   ED Peter
Berger   PROD Brian Robbins, Mike Tollin, David Gale
DIST Paramount

66 A smart entertainment that trades on Mr. Jackson's forceful presence, a cast of extremely likable young actors and lots of basketball action. – *Joe Morgenstern, Wall Street Journal*

'Everyone hated this baseball legend. And he loved it.'

Cobb ★

SCR/DIR Ron Shelton
1994 128m US
DVD

☆ *Tommy Lee Jones* (Ty Cobb), Robert Wuhl (Al Stump), Lolita Davidovich (Ramona), Stephen Mendillo (Mickey Cochrane), Lou Myers (Willie), J. Kenneth Campbell (William Herschel Cobb), William Utay (Jameson), Rhoda Griffis (Amanda Chitwood Cobb)

A sportswriter accompanies baseball legend Ty Cobb to a Hall of Fame induction ceremony, and witnesses at first hand the icon's less heroic side.

Warts-and-all biopic that never backs away from its subject's abusive misanthropy; like Jones's central performance, it has an admirably abrasive quality, but becomes very hard to sit with after a while.

CIN Russell Boyd   MUS Elliot Goldenthal   DES Armin
Ganz, Scott Ritenour   ED Paul Seydor, Kimberly Ray
PROD David V. Lester   DIST Warner/Regency/Alcor

66 Like an exploding cigar: an in-your-face experience. – *Alexander Walker, Evening Standard*

66 A movie to see, if nothing else for Jones's screen-bulging performance: the film never sentimentalises the old swine as it explores the nature of his genius. Terrific ballplayer, miserable human being. Unworthy subject, great movie. – *Kim Newman, Empire*

'Because everyone loves an accurate period piece.'

A Cock and Bull Story ★★

DIR Michael Winterbottom
2005 94m GB
DVD

☆ Steve Coogan (Tristram Shandy, Walter Shandy, 'Steve Coogan'), Rob Brydon (Toby Shandy, 'Rob Brydon'), Keeley Hawes (Elizabeth Shandy, 'Keeley Hawes'), Shirley Henderson (Susannah, 'Shirley Henderson'), Dylan Moran (Dr Slop, 'Dylan Moran'), David Walliams (Parson), Jeremy Northam (Mark)

An attempt to film Laurence Sterne's Tristram

DVD Available on DVD   ☆ Cast in order   66 Critics' Quotes   Ⓘ Academy Award   Ⓑ BAFTA
♫ Soundtrack on CD   of importance   † Points of interest   Ⓐ Academy Award nomination   Ⓣ BAFTA nomination

135

Shandy is beset by clashes of egos and general confusion.

Witty, Altmanesque bit of cinematic horseplay, offering a postmodern style of 'adaptation' in which the impossibility of doing justice to the book is the whole point. The joke does wear a little thin at times.

SCR Martin Hardy CIN Marcel Zyskind MUS Edward Nogria DES John Paul Kelly ED Peter Christelis PROD Andrew Eaton DIST Redbus

66 This is not just a movie-within-a-movie, but a movie-within-a-movie-within-a-movie, something that sounds unbearably arch but that is swift, funny and surprisingly unpretentious. – *A.O. Scott, New York Times*

† The screenwriter's credit 'Martin Hardy' is a pseudonym. The script was written largely by Frank Cottrell Boyce, who asked for his name to be removed.

Ⓣ British film

'How do you solve a crime when the last thing you want to know is the truth?'

Code 46 ★

DIR Michael Winterbottom
2003 92m GB
DVD ♫

☆ Tim Robbins (William Geld), Samantha Morton (Maria), Jeanne Balibar (Sylvie Geld), Om Puri (Bahkland), Essie Davis (Doctor), Shelley King (William's boss)

The near-future: a married American security agent is sent to Shanghai to investigate a set of forged identity papers, only to fall for the accused.

One of its director's sporadic misfires: a thin sliver of sub-Gattaca coffee-table sci-fi, with a glossily seductive look and atmosphere. The little-and-large leads lack chemistry and flail badly.

SCR Frank Cottrell Boyce CIN Alwin Kuchler, Marcel Zyskind MUS Steve Hilton, David Holmes DES *Mark Tildesley* ED Peter Christelis PROD Andrew Eaton

66 Commits a Code 1 violation: it's boring. – *Stephen Hunter, Washington Post*

66 Code 46 has a noirish fatalism that renders it a close cousin to 'Blade Runner,' but Winterbottom's film, shot mostly in the light, uses the theme of memory erasure to peer into the eternal sunshine of tragically altered minds. – *Owen Gleiberman, Entertainment Weekly*

'In a dirty world, he's our only hope.'

Code Name: The Cleaner (new)

DIR Les Mayfield
2007 91m US
DVD ♫

☆ Cedric the Entertainer (Jake Rodgers), Lucy Liu (Gina), Nicollette Sheridan (Diane), Will Patton (Riley)

A janitor awakes in a hotel room beside a suitcase full of money and a dead FBI agent. He is suffering from memory loss, and does not know his name.

Dim plot laced with hopelessly lame gags.

SCR Robert Adetuyi, George Gallo CIN David Franco MUS George S. Clinton DES Douglas Higgins ED Michael Matzdorff PROD Jay Stewrn, Eric C. Rhone, Brett Ratner, Cedric the Entertainer DIST Verve

---

Code Unknown ★★★

SCR/DIR Michael Haneke
2000 117m France/Germany/Romania
DVD

☆ Juliette Binoche (Anne), Thierry Neuvic (Georges), Luminita Gheorghiu (Maria), Ona Lu Yenke (Amadou), Helene Diarra (Aminate), Sepp Bierbichler (Farmer), Alexandre Hamidi (Jean)

Scenes from the modern world, including the stories of street people in Paris, families in Kosovo and the children at an inner-city school for the deaf.

Mosaic drama in the Crash or Short Cuts mode, although considerably more austere and clinical in its study of contemporary dislocation. Like most Haneke films, it's a bumpy ride that doesn't let the viewer off easily – accusing the West of moral blindness when confronted with the problems of others – but superbly staged; you might not like having the argument, but at least there's one to be had here.

CIN Jurgen Jurges MUS Giba Gonçalves DES Emmanuel de Chauvigny ED Andreas Prochaska, Karin Hartusch, Nadine Muse PROD Marin Karmitz, Alain Sarde DIST Artificial Eye

66 The kind of art film that's rarely seen any more – the kind that trusts the audience to be as intelligent as the director. – *Ella Taylor, L.A. Weekly*

66 Haneke's most expansive and, oddly, hopeful work – not a gaze into the void, but a fierce attempt to scramble out of it. – *Jessica Winter, Village Voice*

Un Coeur en Hiver ★

DIR Claude Sautet
1992 105m France
DVD ♫

☆ Daniel Auteuil (Stéphane), Emmanuelle Béart (Camille), André Dussollier (Maxime), Elisabeth Bourgine (Hélène), Brigitte Catillon (Régine), Maurice Garrel (Lachaume)

A beautiful young violinist is just about to move in with her violin maker when she falls passionately in love with his friend and partner.

An unusual love triangle, with Emmanuelle Béart outstanding as a woman caught between two men. Paradoxically, the film feels highly intimate, yet there's a distance about all these characters, which makes them even more enigmatic. Sautet seems to be exploring the unknowable quality of human passions; if so, he succeeds.

SCR Claude Sautet, Jacques Fieschi, Jérôme Tonnerre CIN Yves Angelo MUS Philippe Sarde DES Christian Marti ED Jacqueline Thiedot PROD Jean-Louis Livi, Philippe Carcassonne DIST Artificial Eye/Film Par Film/Cinea/Orly/Sedif/Paravision/DA Films/FR 3

66 It has the intensity and delicacy of a great short story. It reveals how superficial most movie romances are— because they make love too simple and too easy a solution. – *Roger Ebert, Chicago Sun-Times*

Ⓣ film not in the English language

DVD Available on DVD ☆ Cast in order of importance 66 Critics' Quotes † Points of interest ⚊ Academy Award ⚊ Academy Award nomination Ⓑ BAFTA Ⓑ BAFTA nomination
♫ Soundtrack on CD

'Find Your Way Home.'

Cold Mountain ★

SCR/DIR Anthony Minghella
2003   154m   US
[DVD] ♫

☆ Jude Law (Inman), Nicole Kidman (Ada Monroe), Renée Zellweger (Ruby Thewes), Donald Sutherland (Reverend Monroe), Ray Winstone (Teague), Brendan Gleeson (Stobrod), Philip Seymour Hoffman (Veasey), Natalie Portman (Sara), Kathy Baker (Sally Swanger), Giovanni Ribisi (Junior), Eileen Atkins (Maddy), Charlie Hunnam (Bosie)

In 1864, a Confederate soldier leaves the Civil War behind him to make the long journey home to his beloved.

A mountain made of molehills, cutting tiresomely between one star taking an extended stroll and another doing her best Vivien Leigh impersonation while tilling a cabbage patch. Odd celebrity cameos occupy some of the extenuated running time, and it is handsomely shot. But the whole is severely lacking in unifying passion – and the less said about Zellweger's cartoon yokel, the better.

CIN *John Seale*   **MUS** Gabriel Yared   **DES** Dante Ferretti   **ED** Walter Murch   **PROD** Ron Yerxa, Sydney Pollack, William Horberg, Albert Berger   **DIST** Buena Vista

66 A grand and poignant movie epic about what is lost in war and what's worth saving in life. It is also a rare blend of purity and maturity – the year's most rapturous love story. – *Richard Corliss, Time*

66 There are not one, but two wars waging inside this adaptation: one between the North and the South, and another, more calamitous war between art and middlebrow entertainment. – *Manohla Dargis, Los Angeles Times*

⚱ Renée Zellweger (supporting actress)
⚱ Jude Law (leading actor); John Seale; Walter Murch; Gabriel Yared (music, original score); Sting (music, original song – You Will Be My Ain True Love); T-Bone Burnett, Elvis Costello (music, original song – Scarlet Tide)

Ⓣ Renée Zellweger (supporting actress); Gabriel Yared, T-Bone Burnett (music)
Ⓣ British film; Jude Law (leading actor); Anthony Minghella (direction); Anthony Minghella (screenplay); John Seale; Walter Murch; Dante Ferretti; Eddy Joseph, Ivan Sharrock, Walter Murch, Mike Prestwood Smith, Matthew Gough (sound); Ann Roth, Carlo Poggioli (costume design); Paul Engelen, Ivana Primorac (make up/hair)

'It started like any other night.'

Collateral ★★★

DIR *Michael Mann*
2004   120m   US
[DVD] ♫

☆ *Tom Cruise* (Vincent), *Jamie Foxx* (Max), Jada Pinkett Smith (Annie), Mark Ruffalo (Fanning), Peter Berg (Richard Weidner), Bruce McGill (Pedrosa), Irma P. Hall (Ida), Barry Shabaka Henley (Daniel), Javier Bardem (Felix)

A Los Angeles cabbie is forced to play chauffeur for a hitman, in town for a night on murderous business.

The Hollywood action-comedy at its most experimental, shot on a high-definition digital video that blurs and plays strange tricks with LA's light and space. For all its conceptual play, the basic set-up is terrifically entertaining and (until the final 20 minutes) surprisingly gripping, with both leading men on revelatory form. Los Angeles by night has never been captured on film more perfectly.

SCR Stuart Beattie   **CIN** *Dion Beebe, Paul Cameron*   **MUS** James Newton Howard   **DES** David Wasco   **ED** Jim Miller, Paul Rubell   **PROD** Michael Mann, Julie Richardson   **DIST** Paramount

66 In the homestretch, the thrills get too generic and far-fetched for their own good. But the first two thirds are a knockout. – *David Ansen, Newsweek*

66 Straight-up entertainment, not something to see and then talk about a month later, but definitely something to enjoy. – *Mick LaSalle, San Francisco Chronicle*

⚱ Jamie Foxx (leading actor); Jim Miller, Paul Rubell
Ⓣ Dion Beebe, Paul Cameron
Ⓣ Jamie Foxx (leading actor); Stuart Beattie; Jim Miller, Paul Rubell; Elliott Koretz, Lee Orloff, Michael Minkler, Myron Nettinga (sound)

'70,000 gang members. One million guns. Two cops.'

Colors ★

DIR Dennis Hopper
1988   120m   US
[DVD] ♫

☆ *Sean Penn* (Officer Danny McGavin), *Robert Duvall* (Officer Bob Hodges), Maria Conchita Alonso (Louisa Gomez), Randy Brooks (Ron Delaney), Grand Bush (Larry Sylvester), Don Cheadle (Rocket), Damon Wayans (T-Bone)

A veteran LA beat cop provides his young partner with a first-hand lesson in the city's gang culture.

Tough-cookie drama benefits from a keen observational eye behind the camera and the contrast between its respectively impulsive and sagacious stars; once you work out where it's heading, though, interest does tail off.

SCR Michael Schiffer   **CIN** Haskell Wexler   **MUS** Herbie Hancock   **DES** Ron Foreman   **ED** Robert Estrin   **PROD** Robert H. Solo   **DIST** Rank/Orion

66 A special movie – not just a police thriller, but a movie that has researched gangs and given some thought to what it wants to say about them. – *Roger Ebert, Chicago Sun-Times*

Come and See ★★★★

DIR *Elem Klimov*
1985   142m   USSR
[DVD]

☆ Aleksei Kravchenko (Florya Gaishun), Olga Mironova (Glasha), Lyubomiras Lautsiavitchus (Kosach), Vladas Bagdonas, Victor Lorentz

In Belarus during World War II, a teenage partisan witnesses the cruel destruction of several villages by the Nazis, and joins the resistance movement before going off optimistically to fight as a soldier.

[DVD] Available on DVD   ☆ Cast in order of importance   66 Critics' Quotes   ⚱ Academy Award   Ⓣ BAFTA
♫ Soundtrack on CD   † Points of interest   Academy Award nomination   BAFTA nomination

A film with a largely word-of-mouth reputation that has grown steadily since its release. It follows a shocking narrative trajectory, starting with a young, naive boy happy to be defending his country, but becoming a man hollowed and traumatised by war. Serious-minded and carrying great moral authority, it ranks as one of the best films about war ever made.

SCR Elem Klimov, Ales Adamovich   CIN Alexi Rodionov
MUS Oleg Yanchenko   ED Valeriya Belova

66 It's apocalypse caught in the act, a spellbinding, dangerous excursion to hell. – *Philip Horne, Daily Telegraph*

'In 1942, over 100,000 Americans were interned in prison camps. . .In America.'

Come See the Paradise ★

SCR/DIR Alan Parker
1990   133m   US
DVD   ♫

☆ Dennis Quaid (Jack McGurn), Tamlyn Tomita (Lily Yuriko Kawamura/McGann), Sab Shimono (Hiroshi Kawamura), Shizuko Hoshi (Mrs. Kawamura), Stan Egi (Charlie Kawamura), Ronald Yamamoto (Harry Kawamura), Akemi Nishino (Dulcie Kawamura), Naomi Nakano (Joyce Kawamura), Brady Tsurutani (Frankie Kawamura), Elizabeth Gilliam (Younger Mini McGann)

Like thousands of other Japanese-Americans, a woman married to a drafted US soldier is interned with her family in the wake of Pearl Harbor.

A single family story is made to carry the weight of a huge, complex issue, and proves insufficient for the task.

CIN Michael Seresin   MUS Randy Edelman
DES Geoffrey Kirkland   ED Gerry Hambling
PROD Robert F. Colesberry   DIST Fox

The Comfort of Strangers ★

DIR Paul Schrader
1990   107m   Italy/GB
DVD   ♫

☆ Christopher Walken (Robert), Rupert Everett (Colin), Natasha Richardson (Mary), Helen Mirren (Caroline), Manfredi Aliquo (Concierge)

An English couple holidaying in Venice to work out their problems are befriended by a curious local pair.

As befits a work by three very different authors – a Pinter adaptation of a McEwan novel, directed by Schrader – a film of often uncertain tone, though it can just about be enjoyed as a bizarre black comedy, blending elegance and eccentricity.

SCR Harold Pinter   CIN *Dante Spinotti*   MUS *Angelo Badalamenti*   DES Gianni Quaranta   ED Bill Pankow
PROD Angelo Rizzoli
DIST Rank/Erre/Sovereign/Reteitalia

66 The Rocky Horror Show, minus the laughs. – *Christopher Tookey, Daily Mail*

66 Moves with the speed of a gondola through sludge. – *Simon Rose, Essential Film Guide*

'They Had Absolutely Nothing. But They Were Willing To Risk It All.'

The Commitments ★★★

DIR Alan Parker
1991   118m   US/GB
DVD   ♫

☆ Robert Arkins (Jimmy Rabbitte), Michael Aherne (Steven Clifford, Piano), Angeline Ball (Imelda Quirke, Backup Singer), Maria Doyle (Natalie Murphy, Backup Singer), Dave Finnegan (Mickah Wallace, Drums), Bronagh Gallagher (Bernie McGloughlin, Backup Singer), Félim Gormley (Dean Fay, Sax), Glen Hansard (Outspan Foster, Guitar), Dick Massey (Billy Mooney, Drums), Johnny Murphy (Joey 'The Lips' Fagan, Trumpet), Kenneth McCluskey (Derek Scully, Bass), Andrew Strong (Deco Cuffe)

In Dublin, an unemployed young man attempts to assemble a soul group.

A couple of slow numbers threaten the pace; otherwise, this latter-day musical, a substantial box-office hit, keeps hitting rousing high notes all the way through to a bittersweet finale.

SCR *Dick Clement, Ian La Frenais, Roddy Doyle*   CIN Gale Tattersall   MUS *Wilson Pickett*   DES Brian Morris
ED *Gerry Hambling*   PROD Roger Randall-Cutler, Lynda Myles   DIST TCF/Beacon/First Film/Dirty Hands

66 A gritty, naturalistic comedy blessed with a wry, affectionate eye for the absurdities of the band's various rivalries and ambitions; and the songs are matchless. – *Geoff Andrew, Time Out*

66 A pop musical in the way Cliff's films or Elvis's 50s vehicles were, this is one liable to sneak by even the most committed Parker-phobe. Highly recommended. – *Jack Yeovil, Empire*

🏆 Gerry Hambling

🎬 film; Alan Parker; Dick Clement, Ian La Frenais, Roddy Doyle (adapted screenplay); Gerry Hambling
🎬 Andrew Strong (supporting actor); Clive Winter, Eddy Joseph, Andy Nelson, Tom Perry, Steve Pederson (sound)

The Company ★

DIR Robert Altman
2003   112m   US/Germany
DVD

☆ Neve Campbell (Ry), *Malcolm McDowell* (Alberto Antonelli), James Franco (Josh), Barbara Robertson (Harriet), William Dick (Edouard), Susie Cusack (Susie), Marilyn Dodds Frank (Ry's Mother), John Lordan (Ry's Father)

An up-and-coming ballerina gets her big break during one season in the life of Chicago's Joffrey Ballet company.

By its director's standards, a restrained affair, not especially revealing, satirical or funny; ballet fans will no doubt be delighted to have their rarefied scene addressed this comprehensively, but the result is so close to being a documentary as for any fictional pliés to be almost negligible.

SCR Barbara Turner   CIN Andrew Dunn   MUS Van Dyke Parks   DES Gary Baugh   ED Geraldine Peroni

---

DVD Available on DVD   ☆ Cast in order   66 Critics' Quotes   🏆 Academy Award   🎬 BAFTA
♫ Soundtrack on CD   of importance   † Points of interest   Academy Award nomination   BAFTA nomination

PROD David Levy, Joshua Astrachan, Neve Campbell, Robert Altman, Christine Vachon, Pamela Koffler, David Ley

66 Enjoyably lithe and droll. – *Elvis Mitchell, New York Times*

66 Essentially a doodle interrupted by nouveau ballet performances, the entire contraption assembled to please the ego of Neve Campbell. – *Michael Atkinson, Village Voice*

A Complete History of My Sexual Failures (new)

DIR Chris Waitt

2008 93m UK

A film-maker interviews his ex-partners to learn why his relationships never worked out.

Is it really a documentary, or a cunning comedy masquerading as one? It's certainly an exercise in self-exposure. It's sporadically funny, though as the Waitt on screen is mopey and irritating, it ceases to matter whether he's the real thing.

CIN Steven Mochrie ED Chris Dickens, Mark Atkins PROD Mary Burke, Henry Trotter, Robin Gutch, Mark Herbert DIST Optimum

66 In Waitt, the Me Generation has found its own Michael Moore. – *Cosmo Landesman, Sunday Times*

'Buckle up. . .and hang on.'

Con Air ★★

DIR Simon West

1997 115m US

DVD ♫

☆ Nicolas Cage (Cameron Poe), John Cusack (Vince Larkin), John Malkovich (Cyrus Grissom), Steve Buscemi (Garland Greene), Ving Rhames (Diamond Dog), Colm Meaney (Duncan Malloy), Mykelti Williamson (Baby-O), Rachel Ticotin (Sally Bishop), Monica Potter (Tricia Poe), Dave Chappelle (Pinball), M.C. Gainey (Swamp Thing)

A parolee returning home to his family is forced to take action when his flight is hijacked by a criminal mastermind.

The ne plus ultra of a particular school of high-octane filmmaking, gamely blowing up as much of America as the budget will allow while keeping its tongue very firmly in cheek, with witty exchanges.

SCR *Scott Rosenberg* CIN David Tattersall MUS Mark Mancina, Trevor Rabin ED Chris Lebenzon, Steve Mirkovich, Glen Scantlebury PROD Jerry Bruckheimer DIST Buena Vista/Touchstone

66 Ugly, vacuous and vicious. A high-concept massacre for the moron market. – *Alexander Walker, Evening Standard*

66 Starts out as a no-brainer and goes downhill. – *Anne Billson, Sunday Telegraph*

♫ Dianne Warren (music, original song – How Do I Live); Kevin O'Connell, Greg P. Russell, Art Rochester (sound)

Le Confessional ★★

SCR/DIR Robert Lepage

1995 100m Canada/GB/France

☆ Lothaire Bluteau (Pierre Lamontagne), Patrick Goyette (Marc Lamontagne), Kristin Scott-Thomas (Assistant to Hitchcock), Jean-Louis Millette (Raymond Massicotte), Richard Fréchette (André Lamontagne), François Papineau (Paul-Émile Lamontagne), Marie Gignac (Françoise Lamontagne), Ron Burrage (Alfred Hitchcock)

An exiled artist returns to Quebec for his father's funeral, and artist helps his adopted brother search for his real father, whose identity was once revealed by his unmarried teenage mother under the protection of the confessional.

Intriguingly structured thriller that trades in themes of faith and identity. It moves between 1952, when Alfred Hitchcock, in Quebec to shoot I Confess, is angry that the Catholic Church has made cuts in his film, and 1989, when the brothers bury their father. Lepage, a strikingly individual stage director, does full justice to these inter-linked stories, displaying a mastery of cinematic style and a feeling for film's history and traditions.

CIN Alain Dostie MUS Sacha Puttnam DES François Laplante ED Emmanuelle Castro PROD Denise Robert, David Puttnam, Philippe Carcassonne DIST Artificial Eye/Téléfilm Canada/Cinémaginaire/Enigma/Cinéa

'Some things are better left top secret.'

Confessions of a Dangerous Mind ★★

DIR George Clooney

2002 113m US/Germany/GB

DVD ♫

☆ *Sam Rockwell* (Chuck Barris), Drew Barrymore (Penny), George Clooney (Jim Byrd), Julia Roberts (Patricia), Rutger Hauer (Keeler), Maggie Gyllenhaal (Debbie), Kristen Wilson (Loretta), Jennifer Hall (Georgia)

The true story of Chuck Barris, creator of TV's The Gong Show, who claimed implausibly to have been a CIA hitman.

Told in the trademark offbeat style of its screenwriter, this starts with a barely believable premise and builds an almost-credible tissue of corroborating evidence to support it; with clever plot points and an eclectic ensemble cast, it marked a promising debut for its actor-turned-director.

SCR *Charlie Kaufman* CIN Newton Thomas Sigel MUS Alex Wurman DES James D. Bissell ED Stephen Mirrione PROD Andrew Lazar DIST Buena Vista

66 A picture that is surely one of the oddest ever made. – *Stephen Hunter, Washington Post*
66 An attractive, charming film that has fun with its period settings, its goofy plot and its off-kilter performances. – *Shawn Levy, Portland Oregonian*

The Conformist ★★★★

SCR/DIR Bernardo Bertolucci

1969 108m Italy/France/West Germany

♫

☆ *Jean-Louis Trintignant* (Marcello Clerici), *Stefania Sandrelli* (Giulia), Gastone Moschin (Manganiello), Enzo Taroscio (Professor Quadri), *Dominique Sanda* (Anna Quadri), Pierre Clementi (Lino Semirama, the Chauffeur)

| DVD | Available on DVD | ☆ | Cast in order | 66 | Critics' Quotes | ⚱ | Academy Award | Ⓑ | BAFTA |
| ♫ | Soundtrack on CD | | of importance | † | Points of interest | ⚱ | Academy Award nomination | Ⓣ | BAFTA nomination |

139

If ever the organisers of the Academy Awards and the BAFTAs changed the way they did things, and decided to reward actors for the totality, breadth and versatility of their work in a year rather than for just a single performance, there's no doubt that Cate Blanchett would have been the big winner in this past year's awards season.

It's hard to recall an actor of either gender being nominated by these august bodies in one year for two such striking and diverse performances. In the past 12 months, Blanchett reprised her role as Queen Elizabeth I in *Elizabeth: The Golden Age* and portrayed Bob Dylan in *I'm Not There*, director Todd Haynes's wildly ambitious, impressionistic filmed essay about the legendary singer.

At both the Oscars and the BAFTA ceremonies, the Australian Blanchett had to be content with nominations rather than awards. Yet in their different ways, these were both remarkable performances.

In *Elizabeth: The Golden Age,* she faced an intriguing challenge: revisiting a character she had played almost a decade previously. In *Elizabeth* (1998), she played the legendary British monarch as a spirited, relatively carefree young woman who finally enters adulthood and accepts the sobering responsibility of ruling a great nation. When director Shekhar Kapur enticed her to return for the sequel, Blanchett was required to execute a feat of subtle virtuosity: playing that same woman in later life, now an imperious, formidable monarch, but a woman still capable of flirtatiousness and sexual jealousy when confronted by the charms of Clive Owen's Sir Walter Raleigh. She even conveyed a sense of fleeting regret for a romantic life she had forsaken in assuming a title of such overwhelming political significance.

It says much for Blanchett's skill that she managed all this within the context of *Elizabeth: The Golden Age* proving such a disappointing film, especially when compared to its predecessor. Some of the first film's virtues remained intact: its production design and costumes were impeccably vivid, and the overall standard of the acting remained high. Yet *The Golden Age* felt faintly strained; one had the sense that apart from returning to the well to explore the new film's commercial potential, there was no urgent reason for it to be made.

Certainly audiences and critics thought so. *Elizabeth: The Golden Age* grossed an indifferent $16 million in the US, about half the takings of the first film. Even in Britain, the most obvious box-office territory for a film about an English queen, it made its opening weekend debut at a disappointing number four in the box-office charts, never rose higher, and finally took only £5 million over the next 16 weeks. Critical reaction can be gauged by the fact the leading reviewers on the Metacritic website gave it a consensus rating of 45 out of 100 – compared with the previous film's 75.

Yet even from this gloomy perspective, Blanchett's portrayal of the Virgin Queen shone brightly. It is only unfortunate that more people did not see the film on the big screen, where her giant performance truly belonged.

No-one would have expected Haynes's *I'm Not There* to attract mass audiences. It is an art-house film, and one squarely aimed at Bob Dylan's devotees. Furthermore, it is structured in a manner likely to alienate mass audiences: six actors play versions of Dylan in various personae at different stages of his life and career. Five of them, as one might expect, are men. And then there's Blanchett.

She takes on the role for the best-known and most mythologised era of Dylan's career – the period in the mid-1960s, when he shocked his folk music fans by switching to electric music. Blanchett eerily evokes the Dylan of this time, impenetrable behind dark glasses, with his unkempt, corkscrew-curly hair, his jittery, amphetamine-fuelled body language, his slurred speech and defiant attitude. Her five male counterparts merely portrayed the different Dylans; Blanchett seemed to be channelling him.

It is a jaw-dropping, audacious performance, and no-one sums up its virtues better than Haynes, who said at the time of the film's release: 'Obviously, Cate's a woman playing Dylan. It's the elephant in the room, and no-one in those scenes mentions it. But a great performer can make the most obvious thing immediately disappear. And that's what Cate does.'

As if to underline her versatility and unpredictability, she turned up yet again this past year in (of all films) *Indiana Jones and the Crystal Skull*, playing an icy Russian baddie named Colonel Dr Irina Spalko. Blanchett portrays her like an old-style villainess from a James Bond movie, with a pitch-perfect Russian accent, and a brunette Louise Brooks-style bob. The film could have used more of her; it's a very funny performance, though of course Blanchett knew enough to play it with a perfectly straight face.

For a trio of widely diverse roles, this could hardly be matched. Yet Blanchett has done this before. A couple of years back, she proved herself capable of almost anything a challenging script might throw at her, in three films that opened within a couple of months of each other.

In Alejandro Gonzáles Iñárritu's *Babel*, she was an American tourist in an unhappy marriage, shot and seriously injured while in the hinterlands of Morocco. In Steven Soderbergh's World War II story *The Good German*, she played a Berlin woman, the old flame of an American journalist, now turned to prostitution and desperate to get out of town. And in Richard Eyre's *Notes on a Scandal* she was completely believable as a flighty, attractive but thoughtless school teacher in north London, who triggers a catastrophic series of events when she unwisely embarks on an affair with one of her teenage boy students.

> '*All this would add up to an impressive lifetime's work for almost any other actress: for Blanchett, it only includes films in which she has worked in the past four years.*'

All this would add up to an impressive lifetime's work for almost any other actress: for Blanchett, it only includes films in which she has worked in the past four years. It's odd to reflect that her first full-length feature film, *Paradise Road*, was released as recently as 1997; since then, she has won an Oscar (for her portrayal of Katharine Hepburn in *The Aviator*) and two BAFTAs (for *The Aviator* and *Elizabeth*), with both awards bodies nominating her a further three times. She is as feted by the film industry now as Meryl Streep was in the 1980s and 1990s. And Blanchett is still under 40.

It sometimes seems that her stellar career has crept upon the world by stealth. If so, this has much to do with her personal preferences about privacy and dignity. In an age of celebrity overload, when many actors seem to want to exist largely to be photographed, Blanchett remains resolutely private; she will not attend a function because her presence might provide her with a publicity opportunity.

Such a choice gives her an air of mystery; she is in no danger of becoming over-familiar on screen through constant appearances in gossip magazines. Indeed, Blanchett is something of a chameleon; she is one of those actresses who could walk down a crowded city street without passers-by being sure they have recognised her. This ability makes it easier for her to lose herself inside roles; if audiences did not know her name, could they be sure that the middle-aged Queen Elizabeth is played by the same actress as Irina Spalko or the electric-era Bob Dylan? They could not.

Instead of subordinating her private life to the demands of the media and public, Blanchett prioritises it and works her career around it. She has dropped out of at least two films, *The Merchant of Venice* and *Closer* (both 2004), because she was pregnant. She and her husband, playwright and screenwriter Andrew Upton, now have three children and they put family first; if Blanchett's films seem to come in clusters with gaps in between, it is to accommodate her role as a mother.

It's a laudable, uncompromising way to live a private life and a career, and it has not hurt her one bit; she is surely the pre-eminent film actress of our times, and because she makes a virtue of being unpredictable, one constantly waits to see what roles she chooses to embark on next. There will be many more years for her like this last one.

In 1938 a repressed young man tries to conform to the prevailing mood of Fascism, but gets out of his depth when he turns informer.

Psychologically astute and brilliantly realized re-creation of an age; it's no accident that the Fascist-era architecture looks so imposing and tempting. An exquisitely photographed and conceived film that recounts the moral cowardice of its central character unflinchingly.

CIN *Vittorio Storaro* MUS *Georges Delerue* ED Franco Arcalli PROD Giovanni Bertolucci DIST Mars/Marianne/Maran

66 It's a triumph of feeling and of style – lyrical, flowing, velvety style, so operatic that you come away with sequences in your head like arias. – *New Yorker*

66 Last Tango In Paris won Bertolucci the headlines, and The Last Emperor won him the Oscars, but it is this 1970 movie that deserves to be called his masterpiece. . .a beautifully imagined portrait of moral and political cowardice. – *Anthony Quinn, The Independent*

Bernardo Bertolucci (adapted screenplay)

Conquest of the South Pole ★

DIR Gillies Mackinnon
1989 92m GB

☆ Stefan Rimkus (Sloopianek), Ewen Bremner (Penguin), Leonard O'Malley (Butcher), Alastair Galbraith (Frankieboy)

A group of out-of-work Scottish youths attempt to re-create Amundsen's expedition to Antarctica in an attempt to forget the misery of their lives.

An adaptation of a play that premiered in Edinburgh, this was shot in and around the tenement blocks and dockside area of nearby Leith. A strong sense of place enhances the drama in this striking low-budget feature by a debutant director.

CIN Sean Van Hales MUS Guy Woolfenden DES Andy Harris ED Stephen Singleton PROD Gareth Wardell DIST Jam Jar Films/Channel 4

The Consequences of Love ★★

SCR/DIR *Paolo Sorrentino*
2004 100m Italy
DVD ♫

☆ Toni Servillo (Titta Di Girolamo), Olivia Magnani (Sofia), Adriano Giannini (Valerio), Angela Goodwin (Isabella), Raffaele Pisu (Carlo)

A nondescript middle-aged man is tempted out of seclusion in a Swiss hotel by the attentions of his favourite waitress.

Simultaneously a striking puzzle piece and a study of an individual who, for reasons only gradually revealed, has no discernible life: the result is directed with notable precision, but also, like its lead character, somewhat remote.

CIN Luca Bigazzi MUS *Pasquale Catalano* DES Lino Fiorito ED Giogio Franchini PROD Domenico Procacci, Nicola Giuliano, Francesca Cima, Angelo Curti DIST Artificial Eye

66 Contrives to blend comedy, suspense and understated sentiment to intriguing and witty effect. – *Geoff Andrew, Time Out*

66 Just as an exercise in style, Consequences would be exceptional, but in its second half, as events gather momentum, it creates a compelling sense of existential vertigo. – *Philip Kemp, Sight and Sound*

'Love. At Any Cost.'

The Constant Gardener ★★★

DIR *Fernando Meirelles*
2005 129m US/GB/Canada/Germany
DVD ♫

☆ *Ralph Fiennes* (Justin Quayle), *Rachel Weisz* (Tessa Quayle), Danny Huston (Sandy Woodrow), Bill Nighy (Sir Bernard Pellegrin), Pete Postlethwaite (Lorbeer), Hubert Koundé (Dr Arnold Bluhm), Gerard McSorley (Sir Kenneth Curtiss)

A British diplomat investigates the circumstances of his wife's death in Kenya.

Intelligent adaptation of rock-solid source material lent an immediacy by vivid camerawork, although it sometimes seems more interested in an idea of Englishness than the exploitation of sick Africans by trans-national corporations; in the end, it's really only as much about the chain the West has around Africa's neck as it is about getting Ralph Fiennes to loosen his collar.

SCR Jeffrey Caine CIN *César Charlone* MUS Alberto Iglesias DES Mark Tildesley ED Claire Simpson PROD *Simon Channing Williams* DIST UIP

66 The movie is smart, serious, and adult about something that matters, but not at the expense of a kind of awful, sensual revelry as le Carre's capacious plot hurtles to its big finish. – *Lisa Schwarzbaum, Entertainment Weekly*

66 A supremely well-executed piece of popular entertainment that is likely to linger in your mind and may even trouble your conscience. – *Dana Stevens, New York Times*

Rachel Weisz (supporting actress)
Jeffrey Caine; Claire Simpson; Alberto Iglesias

Claire Simpson
film; British film; Ralph Fiennes (leading actor); Rachel Weisz (supporting actress); Fernando Meirelles; Jeffrey Caine (adapted screenplay); César Charlone; Alberto Iglesias; Joakim Sundström, Stuart Wilson, Mike Prestwood Smith, Sven Taits (sound)

'A message from deep space. Who will be the first to go? A journey to the heart of the universe.'

Contact

DIR Robert Zemeckis
1997 153m US
DVD ♫

☆ Jodie Foster (Ellie Arroway), Matthew McConaughey (Palmer Joss), James Woods (Michael Kitz), John Hurt (S.R. Hadden), Tom Skerritt (David Drumlin), Angela Bassett (Rachel Constantine)

An astronomer picks up signs of extraterrestrial life

and seeks to convince the sceptical authorities as to her findings.

It had its adherents, some of them fervent, but what starts as becalmed and thoughtful science fiction, playing off the vastness of the universe against more immediate, earthly concerns, soon tails off into ultra-longwinded Californian clap-trap.

SCR James V. Hart, Michael Goldenberg   CIN Don Burgess   MUS Alan Silvestri   DES Ed Verreaux   ED Arthur Schmidt   PROD Robert Zemeckis, Steve Starkey   DIST Warner/South Side Amusement

66 Proceeds very slowly through many banal deliberations about cosmic enigmas to a comfortably reassuring conclusion in which scientific humanism and vaguely uplifting religiosity are squishly reconciled. – *Richard Schickel, Time*

66 You realise that it's not aliens with whom Zemeckis has yet to make contact; it's humans. – *Tom Shone, Sunday Times*

Randy Thom, Tom Johnson, Dennis S. Sands, William B. Kaplan (sound)

Conte D'Automne   ★

SCR/DIR Eric Rohmer
1998   112m   France
DVD

☆ Marie Riviere (Isabelle), Béatrice Romand (Magali), Alain Libolt (Gérald), Didier Sandre (Etienne), Alexia Portal (Rosine), Stéphane Darmon (Léo), Aurélia Alcais (Emilia), Matthieu Davette (Grégoire), Yves Alcais (Jean-Jacques)

A married woman attempts to find a suitable match for her single best friend.

The final entry in Rohmer's Four Seasons series is a gentle exploration of well-cultivated individuals finding love at a mature age, nicely played against attractive Rhone Valley backdrops.

CIN Diane Baratier   MUS Claude Marti, Gérard Pansanel, Pierre Peyras, Antonello Salis   ED Mary Stephen   PROD Françoise Etchegaray   DIST Artificial Eye

66 A beautiful, witty and serene film. – *Ginette Vincendeau, Sight and Sound*

Conte de Printemps   ★★

SCR/DIR Eric Rohmer
1990   108m   France

☆ Anne Teyssedre (Jeanne), Hugues Quester (Igor), Florence Darel (Natacha), Eloise Bennett (Eve), Sophie Robin (Gaelle)

A teenage girl from a broken home goes to stay with her father and falls out with his new girlfriend.

The first of a quartet of filmed stories based on seasons; Rohmer establishes a tone here of talky, witty worldliness.

CIN Luc Pages   MUS Beethoven, Schumann   ED Maria Luisa Garcia   PROD Margaret Ménégoz   DIST Roissy Films/Films du Losange

Conte d'hiver   ★

SCR/DIR Eric Rohmer
1992   114m   France

☆ Charlotte Very (Felicie), Frederic Van Den Driessche (Charles), Michel Voletti (Maxence), Hervé Furic (Loic), Ava Loraschi (Elise), Christiane Desbois (Mother), Rosette (Sister), Jean-Luc Revol (Brother-in-Law)

A Parisian hairdresser is torn between three men, including the memory of her holiday romance, who fathered her daughter before disappearing.

Rohmer is here admirably honest about, and compassionate towards, a single mother who is characterised chiefly by an intellectual insecurity; the film around her goes big on the static talkiness you either love or hate in this director's work, but much of it does ring true.

CIN Luc Pages   MUS Sebastian Erms   DES Pierre-Jean Larroque   ED Mary Stephen   PROD Margaret Ménégoz   DIST Artificial Eye/Films du Losange

66 It's a small work, but nearly perfect. – *Hal Hinson, Washington Post*

Control (new)   ★★★

DIR *Anton Corbijn*
2007   122m   UK/Japan/Australia
DVD ♫

☆ *Sam Riley* (Ian Curtis), Samantha Morton (Deborah Curtis), Alexandra Maria Lara (Annik), Joe Anderson (Hooky), Toby Kebbell (Rob Gretton), Craig Parkinson (Tony Wilson)

An account of the doomed life of Ian Curtis, lead singer of the British cult band Joy Division.

An exemplary biopic that does not whitewash Curtis's life or his weaknesses. Starkly shot in black-and-white, it frames the band as outsiders and northern underdogs taking on the music establishment. Lead actor Riley uncannily captures the spirit and body language of Curtis in performance.

SCR Matt Greenhalgh   CIN Martin Ruhe   MUS New Order   DES Chris Roope   ED Andrew Hulme   PROD Orian Williams, Anton Corbijn, Todd Eckert   DIST Momentum

ANNIK: 'Tell me about Macclesfield.'

66 The film has an unerring eye for kitchen-sink mundanity. – *Jonathan Romney, Sight & Sound*

66 Everybody should see Control. – *Sukhdev Sandhu, Daily Telegraph*

Ⓣ British film; Samantha Morton (supporting actress)

The Conversation   ★★★

SCR/DIR *Francis Ford Coppola*
1974   113m   US
DVD

☆ *Gene Hackman* (Harry Caul), John Cazale (Stan), Allen Garfield (Bernie Moran), Frederic Forrest (Mark), Cindy Williams (Ann)

A surveillance expert, who uses bugging devices,

DVD Available on DVD   ☆ Cast in order   66 Critics' Quotes   ▯ Academy Award   Ⓣ BAFTA
♫ Soundtrack on CD   of importance   † Points of interest   ▯ Academy Award nomination   Ⓣ BAFTA nomination

143

lives only for his work but finally develops a conscience.

Absorbing but challenging to follow, this personal, timely (in view of Watergate), Kafkaesque suspense story depends almost entirely on its director and leading actor, both of whom have a field day.

CIN Bill Butler   MUS David Shire   DES Dean Tavoularis   ED *Walter Murch, Richard Chew*   DIST Paramount/Francis Ford Coppola

66 A private, hallucinatory study in technical expertise and lonely guilt. – *Sight & Sound*

66 A terrifying depiction of a ransacked spirit. – *New Yorker, 1977*

🏆 picture; Francis Ford Coppola (original screenplay)

'Where there's a will, there's a way.'

Cookie's Fortune ★★

DIR Robert Altman
1999   118m   US
DVD   ♫

☆ Glenn Close (Camille Orcutt), Julianne Moore (Cora Duvall), Liv Tyler (Emma Duvall), Chris O'Donnell (Jason Brown), *Charles S. Dutton* (Willis Richland), Patricia Neal (Jewel Mae 'Cookie' Orcutt), Ned Beatty (Lester Boyle), Courtney B. Vance (Otis Tucker), Donald Moffat (Jack Palmer), Lyle Lovett (Manny Hood), Danny Darst (Billy Cox), Ruby Wilson (Josie Martin)

Two sisters in a gossipy Southern town keep secret the suicide of an elderly aunt, while feverishly trying to get their hands on her inheritance.

Not vintage Altman, but not a disaster either, as Close and Moore offer fruity, over-the-top performances in a shambling, agreeably dark comedy.

SCR Anne Rapp   CIN Toyomichi Kurita   MUS David A. Stewart   DES Stephen Altman   ED Abraham Lim   PROD Robert Altman, Etchie Stroh   DIST Alliance/October

66 May or not be Robert Altman's best film in years, but it is certainly his most pleasurable. – *Todd McCarthy, Variety*

'What we've got here is a failure to communicate.'

Cool Hand Luke ★★

DIR *Stuart Rosenberg*
1967   126m   US
DVD   ♫

☆ Paul Newman, George Kennedy, Jo Van Fleet, J.D. Cannon, Lou Antonio, Robert Drivas, Strother Martin, Clifton James

Sentenced to two years' hard labour with the chain gang, a cocky rebel becomes a legend of invulnerability.

A not so radical updating of chain-gang genre movies, this labours slightly from Luke being portrayed as a Christ-like figure. But Newman seizes the role with relish, arguably making more of it than it deserves. A scene involving an egg-eating contest is firmly ensconced in film lore.

SCR Donn Pearce, Frank R. Pierson   CIN *Conrad Hall*

MUS Lalo Schifrin   PROD Gordon Carroll   DIST Warner/Jalem

66 May be the best American film of 1967. – *John Simon*

🏆 George Kennedy (supporting actor)

🏆 Paul Newman (leading actor); Donn Pearce, Frank R. Pierson (adapted screenplay); Lalo Schifrin

---

'Love. . .you have to play to win.'

The Cooler ★

DIR Wayne Kramer
2002   101m   US
DVD   ♫

☆ *William H. Macy* (Bernie Lootz), *Alec Baldwin* (Shelly Kaplow), *Maria Bello* (Natalie Belisario), Shawn Hatosy (Mikey), Ron Livingston (Larry Sokolov), Paul Sorvino (Buddy Stafford), Estella Warren (Charlene)

One of life's perpetual losers, employed by a bullying Vegas casino boss to cast bad luck upon nearby gamblers, enjoys a change of fortune when a waitress falls for him.

Quirky indie piece, better written and performed than directed, that sprawls like a Nevada desert town; ultimately shying away from the plotting's philosophical dimensions, it provides a platform for some fun, fleshy character studies and audition pieces.

SCR Frank Hannah, Wayne Kramer   CIN James Whitaker   MUS *Mark Isham*   DES Toby Corbett   ED Arthur Coburn   PROD Michael Pierce, Sean Furst

66 Look for realism, and you'll find The Cooler disappointing. Look for a far-fetched yarn that's as unpredictable as a throw of the dice, though, and you'll find it engaging fun. – *David Sterritt, Christian Science Monitor*

66 A good, simple idea, well executed. And you even get an acting masterclass from the three leads thrown in. – *Kim Newman, Empire*

🏆 Alec Baldwin (supporting actor)

'When a cop cares too much, how far is too far.'

Cop ★

SCR/DIR James B. Harris
1988   110m   US
DVD

☆ *James Woods* (Lloyd Hopkins), Lesley Ann Warren (Kathleen McCarthy), Charles Durning (Dutch Peltz), Charles Haid (Delbert 'Whitey' Haines), Raymond J. Barry (Captain Fred Gaffney), Randi Brooks (Joanie Pratt), Steven Lambert (Bobby Franco), Christopher Wynne (Jack Gibbs), Jan McGill (Jen Hopkins)

An obsessive policeman, who cares only about his work, hunts down a serial killer.

It wouldn't be much without Woods, but if malevolent intensity is called for, Woods is your go-to guy. He single-handedly lifts this routine thriller into something more memorable.

CIN Steve Dubin   MUS Michel Colombier   DES Gene Rudolf   ED Anthony Spano   PROD James B. Harris, James Woods   DIST Entertainment/Atlantic

'No One Is Above The Law.'

Cop Land ★★

SCR/DIR *James Mangold*
1997 104m US
[DVD] ♫

☆ *Sylvester Stallone* (Freddy Heflin), Harvey Keitel (Ray Donlan), Ray Liotta (Gary Figgis), Robert De Niro (Moe Tilden), Peter Berg (Joey Randone), Janeane Garofalo (Deputy Cindy Betts), Robert Patrick (Jack Rucker), Michael Rapaport (Murray Babitch), Annabella Sciorra (Liz Randone), Noah Emmerich (Deputy Bill Geisler), Cathy Moriarty (Rose Donlan)

A sheriff in a small New Jersey town is caught between an Internal Affairs investigator and the off-duty activities of the Manhattan cops who reside under his jurisdiction.

It doesn't always come together in the manner one might like, but Mangold provides his heavyweight cast with meaty dramatic material to be going on with. Stallone makes a surprisingly deft contribution as the vulnerable lawman.

CIN Eric Edwards MUS Howard Shore DES Lester Cohen ED Craig McKay PROD Cary Woods, Cathy Konrad, Ezra Swerdlow DIST Buena Vista/Woods Entertainment

66 Dense, meandering, ambitious yet jarringly pulpy, this tale of big-city corruption in small-town America has competence without mood or power – a design but not a vision. – *Owen Gleiberman, Entertainment Weekly*

66 Everywhere the camera turns in this tense and volatile drama, it finds enough interest for a truckload of conventional Hollywood fare. Whatever its limitations, Cop Land has talent to burn. – *Elvis Mitchell, New York Times*

'The passion behind the genius.'

Copying Beethoven (new)

DIR *Agnieszka Holland*
2006 104m UK/Germany/Hungary
[DVD] ♫

☆ Ed Harris (Ludwig van Beethoven), Diane Kruger (Anna Holtz), Matthew Goode (Martin Bauer), Ralph Riach (Schlemmer), Phyllida Law (Mother Canisius)

A fictional account of the great composer's last year of life, when a young female music student arrives to transcribe parts for his new Ninth Symphony as his music copyist.

A harmless fantasia marred by a flimsy script and over-ripe acting. But director Holland at least conveys how shocking and ground-breaking the Ninth must have seemed in 1824.

SCR Stephen J. Rivele, Christopher Wilkinson CIN Ashley Rowe MUS Antoni Lazarkiewicz DES Caroline Amies ED Alex Mackie PROD Sidney Kimmel, Michael Taylor, Stephen J. Rivele, Christopher Wilkinson DIST Verve

66 If the composer's shade could hear the words this script has put in his mouth it really would be a case of 'roll over, Beethoven', right there in his grave. – *Anthony Quinn, Independent*

66 A great example of that time-honoured genre, the biopic so silly it plays like a spoof.' – *Tim Robey, Daily Telegraph*

The Cottage (new) ★★

SCR/DIR *Paul Andrew Williams*
2008 92m UK

☆ Reece Shearsmith (Peter), Andy Serkis (David), Jennifer Ellison (Tracey), Dave Legeno (The Farmer)

Inept kidnappers hide out in a farm owned by a deformed cannibal psycho.

A good example of how to cross genres sneakily to provide a consistently entertaining laughter-and-slaughter ride through familiar Friday the 13th terrain.

CIN Christopher Ross MUS Laura Rossi ED Tom Hemmings PROD Ken Marshall DIST Pathe

66 An anarchic, gory horror-comedy. – *Peter Bradshaw, The Guardian*

† This was writer-director Williams's follow-up to the highly acclaimed, very different London To Brighton

'It takes a clever man to make money. It takes a genius to stay alive.'

The Counterfeiters (new) ★★★

SCR/DIR *Stefan Ruzowitzky*
2007 98m Austria/Germany/France
[DVD] ♫

☆ *Karl Markovics* (Salomon Sorowitsch), August Diehl (Adolf Burger), Devid Striesow (Sturmbannführer Herzog), Martin Brambach (Hauptscharführer Holst)

A group of Jewish forgers in a Nazi concentration camp are forced to create fake currency for the Third Reich.

Intriguing story that hints at moral ambivalence, self-loathing and survival guilt. Outstanding performance by Karl Markovics as Salomon, the playboy and master counterfeiter.

CIN Benedict Neuenfels MUS Marius Ruhland DES Isidor Wimmer ED Britta Nahler PROD Josef Aicholzer, Nina Bohlmann, Babette Schröder DIST Metrodome

66 A very thoughtful and imaginative effort. – *Tim Robey, Daily Telegraph*

66 Manages to be both gripping and to pose moral questions as relevant to our own times as then. – *Cosmo Landesman, Sunday Times*

⚱ foreign language film

Country Life ★

SCR/DIR *Michael Blakemore*
1994 114m Australia
[DVD]

☆ Greta Scacchi (Deborah Voysey), Sam Neill (Dr. Max Askey), John Hargreaves (Jack Dickens), Kerry Fox (Sally Voysey), Michael Blakemore (Alexander Voysey), Googie Withers (Hannah), Patricia Kennedy (Maud Dickens), Ron Blanchard (Wally Wells), Maurie Fields (Fred Livingstone)

[DVD] Available on DVD   ☆ Cast in order of importance   66 Critics' Quotes   † Points of interest   ⚱ Academy Award   ⚱ Academy Award nomination   🎭 BAFTA   🎭 BAFTA nomination

145

In Australia in 1919, a failed writer returns to his brother-in-law's sheep farm with his new wife, who becomes an object of desire with unhappy sequences.

A decent adaptation of Chekhov, imaginatively transplanted and generally well played.

CIN Stephen F. Windon **MUS** Peter Best **DES** Laurence Eastwood **ED** Nicholas Beauman **PROD** Robin Dalton **DIST** Metro Tartan/AFFC/Robin Dalton

66 A very funny film with a rippling undercurrent of imminent melancholy. It does more than entertain, with an observant view of humanity's pardonable frailties. – *Alexander Walker, Evening Standard*

'A movie for everyone who's ever struggled to love a brother. . .Or strangle one.'

Coupe de Ville ★★

DIR *Joe Roth*
1990 99m US
♫

☆ *Patrick Dempsey* (Robert 'Bobby' Libner), *Arye Gross* (Buddy Libner), *Daniel Stern* (Marvin Libner), Annabeth Gish (Tammy), Rita Taggart (Betty Libner), Joseph Bologna (Uncle Phil), *Alan Arkin* (Fred Libner)

In the early 1960s, three squabbling brothers are entrusted by their father to deliver a Cadillac Coupe de Ville car to their mother's birthday celebrations in Florida.

Well-crafted ensemble piece puts a sharply observed script in the hands of some fine, underrated actors; the result – playing out to frequent bursts of The Kingsmen's divine Louie Louie – is something of a small gem.

SCR *Mike Binder* **CIN** Reynaldo Villalobos **MUS** James Newton Howard **DES** Angelo Graham **ED** Paul Hirsch **PROD** Larry Brezner, Paul Schiff **DIST** Warner/Morgan Creek

66 Spotlights perfect performances from a trio of young actors who have individually paid their dues in enough bad movies to fill the world's biggest video store, but here are given material they can soar with. – *Kim Newman, Empire*

Courage Under Fire ★

DIR Edward Zwick
1996 117m US
DVD ♫

☆ Denzel Washington (Lt. Colonel Nathaniel Serling), Meg Ryan (Captain Karen Emma Walden), Lou Diamond Phillips (Staff Sergeant John Monfriez), Michael Moriarty (Brigadier General Hershberg), Matt Damon (Specialist Ilario), Bronson Pinchot (Bruno), Scott Glenn (Tony Gartner, Washington Post), Sean Astin (Patella)

A guilt-ridden colonel investigates the events that led to the death of a female helicopter pilot during the Gulf War.

Hollywood's first take on this conflict, and the first film to address the role of women in the military with any degree of seriousness. It ultimately raises more interesting ideas than it knows what to do with; there also seems little point in doubting the conduct of an officer played by Meg Ryan.

SCR Patrick Sheane Duncan **CIN** Roger Deakins **MUS** James Horner **DES** John Graysmark **ED** Steven Rosenblum **PROD** Joseph M. Singer, David T. Friendly, John Davis **DIST** TCF/Fox 2000/Davis Entertainment

66 It would like to be a thoughtful meditation on bravery, honour, truth – the big topics. But it's really just a crudely manipulated mystery story, building suspense by arbitrarily withholding pertinent information. It's hard to take its thoughts on integrity seriously when it exhibits so little of that quality in its own storytelling. – *Richard Schickel, Time*

Couscous ⓝⓔⓦ ★★

SCR/DIR Abdellatif Kechiche
2008 151m France
DVD ♫

☆ Habib Boufares (Slimane), Hafsia Herzi (Rym), Faridah Benkhetache (Karima), Abdelhamid Aktouche (Hamid), Bouraouia Marzouk (Souad), Alice Houri (Julia), Leila D'Issernio (Lila), Abelkader Djeloulli (Kader)

Ensemble comedy-drama set in the Mediterranean fishing port of Sète, and centred on the North African dockside community. An elderly shipyard worker, demoralised after being laid off, decides to pursue his long-cherished dream of opening a fish-and-couscous restaurant .

Tunis-born French director Kechiche takes a leisurely exploration of an immigrant family struggling to make ends meet. Overlong and rambling, but it does provide intriguing insights into old and new cultures.

SCR Abdellatif Kechiche, Ghalia Lacroix **CIN** Lubomir Bakchev **DES** Benoît Barouh **ED** Ghalia Lacroix **PROD** Nathalie Rheims / Pierre Grunstein / Claude Berri **DIST** Artificial Eye

66 Kechiche tells his tale with admirable detail, like a chef adding ingredient after ingredient until the mix is just right. – *Jason Solomons, Observer*

† The film was the undisputed winner at the 2008 Césars, winning four awards: best film, best director, best young actress [Hafsia Herzi] and best original screenplay.

'Who Knew Deception, Treachery And Revenge Could Be This Much Fun. . .'

Cousin Bette ★

DIR Des McAnuff
1998 108m US
DVD ♫

☆ Jessica Lange (Cousin Bette), Elisabeth Shue (Jenny Cadine), Bob Hoskins (Cesar Crevel), Hugh Laurie (Baron Hector Hulot), Kelly Macdonald (Hortense Hulot), Aden Young (Count Wenceslas Steinbach), Geraldine Chaplin (Adeline Hulot), Toby Stephens (Victorin Hulot), John Sessions (Musical Director)

A penniless seamstress takes revenge against her well-to-do cousins.

Balzac rejigged as pantomime, essentially, but it's a fun pantomime, with all the characters huffing and puffing to get into or out of their corsetry. A few footnotes

on the importance of age and beauty to both men and women remain, and it never takes itself remotely seriously.

SCR Lynn Siefert, Susan Tarr   **CIN** Andrzej Sekula
MUS Simon Boswell   **DES** Hugo Luczyc-Wyhowksi
ED Tariq Anwar, Barry Alexander Brown   **PROD** Sarah Radclyffe   **DIST** Fox Searchlight

66 Moves along at a cracking pace, packing a host of horrendous characters into a sumptuous dish of exquisite malice. – *Giala Murray, Empire*

66 The movie is not respectful like a literary adaptation, but wicked with gossip and social satire. – *Roger Ebert, Chicago Sun-Times*

'They already have a lot in common. Her husband is sleeping with his wife.'

Cousins ★

DIR Joel Schumacher
1989   109m   US
[DVD] ♫

☆ Ted Danson (Larry Kozinski), Isabella Rossellini (Maria Hardy), Sean Young (Tish Kozinski), William Petersen (Tom Hardy), Lloyd Bridges (Vincent Kozinski), Norma Aleandro (Edie Hardy Kozinski), Keith Coogan (Mitch Kozinski), Gina DeAngelis (Aunt Sofia), George Coe (Phil Kozinski)

Two couples meet at a wedding of distant relatives and change partners.

An example of that universally despised species the Hollywood remake of a French film. Admittedly, this isn't in the same league as Cousin, Cousine, yet it isn't without charm. Danson plays a dance instructor with easy grace, while Young is perfectly cast as a flirtatious schemer.

SCR Stephen Metcalfe   **CIN** Ralf Bode   **MUS** Angelo Badalamenti   **DES** Mark S. Freeborn   **ED** Robert Brown
PROD William Allyn   **DIST** UIP/Paramount

66 Combines satire, near-farce, and incipient fantasy with great dexterity. – *Tim Pulleine, MFB*

'Art is never dangerous – unless it tells the truth.'

Cradle Will Rock ★★

SCR/DIR *Tim Robbins*
1999   132m   US
[DVD] ♫

☆ Hank Azaria (Marc Blitzstein), Ruben Blades (Diego Rivera), Joan Cusack (Hazel Huffman), John Cusack (Nelson Rockefeller), Cary Elwes (John Houseman), Philip Baker Hall (Gray Mathers), Cherry Jones (Hallie Flanagan), Angus Macfadyen (Orson Welles), Bill Murray (Tommy Crickshaw), Vanessa Redgrave (Comtesse LaGrange), Susan Sarandon (Margherita Sarfatti), Jamey Sheridan (John Adair), John Turturro (Aldo Silvano), Emily Watson (Olive Stanton), Bob Balaban (Harry Hopkins), Barnard Hughes, Barbara Sukowa, John Carpenter, Gretchen Mol, Harris Yulin

New York, 1936: under the aegis of the socialist Federal Theatre Project, director Orson Welles, producer John Houseman and playwright Marc Blitzstein make efforts to stage a performance of the latter's The Cradle Will Rock.

Occasionally lumpy but illuminating drama which gives very specific historical subject matter – the rise and fall of leftwing theatre groups – a contemporary resonance by employing a cast of familiar faces and a multi-stranded structure familiar from Short Cuts, Go and Magnolia. It accomplishes Blitzstein's mandate to educate and entertain, conveying a rich sense of the era's artistic and political concerns.

CIN Jean Yves Escoffier   **MUS** David Robbins
DES Richard Hoover   **ED** Geraldine Peroni   **PROD** Jon Kilik, Lydia Dean Pilcher, Tim Robbins   **DIST** Buena Vista

66 Succeeds far more often than not in delivering a credible, kaleidoscopic portrait of creative, and often famous, individuals. – *Todd McCarthy, Variety*

'Poison in his veins. Vengeance in his heart.'

Crank ★★

SCR/DIR Mark Neveldine, Brian Taylor
2006   83m   US
[DVD] ♫

☆ *Jason Statham* (Chev Chelios), Amy Smart (Eve), Jose Pablo Cantillo (Verona), *Efren Ramirez* (Kaylo), *Dwight Yoakam* (Doc Miles)

A hit man is injected with a lethal drug that will shut down his system in one hour. Pumping himself full of stimulants, he tracks down the crime syndicate responsible for his attempted murder.

Outrageous nonsense, but this gore-drenched, high-octane action kitsch is a thrill-a-minute adrenalin rush, graced with a deliciously deadpan Jason Statham performance.

CIN Adam Biddle   **MUS** Paul Haslinger   **DES** Jerry Fleming   **ED** Brian Berdan   **PROD** Michael Davis, Gary Lucchesi, Tom Rosenberg, Skip Williamson, Richard Wright
DIST UIP

66 The film is so jubilantly over the top and aware of its own failings, it's hard not to laugh. – *Anna Smith, Time Out*

'The most controversial film you will ever see.'

Crash ★★

SCR/DIR *David Cronenberg*
1996   100m   Canada
[DVD] ♫

☆ James Spader (James Ballard), Holly Hunter (Helen Remington), Elias Koteas (Vaughan), Deborah Unger (Catherine Ballard), Rosanna Arquette (Gabrielle), Peter MacNeill (Colin Seagrave)

In the wake of a car crash, a photographer and a doctor fall in with a group who find sexual excitement in road traffic accidents.

An icily fascinating study of unfathomable desires, in which a series of beautifully shot yet largely detached sex scenes take the place of conventional narrative development. Crack the surface, and you'll find grim, pessimistic (but always moral) messages about the direction human sexuality is heading in; like it or loathe it, as many have, it is absolutely and uncompromisingly its own film.

CIN *Peter Suschitzky* MUS *Howard Shore* DES *Carol Spier* ED Ronald Sanders PROD David Cronenberg DIST Columbia TriStar/Alliance

66 Promulgates a twisted morality of its own: namely that life is about the pursuit of sexual gratification, whatever the consequences. It is the morality of the satyr, the nymphomaniac, the rapist, the paedophile, the danger to society. – *Christopher Tookey, Daily Mail*

66 A film that is immoral by any standard, unsafe at any speed. – *Alexander Walker, Evening Standard*

† Despite a great deal of controversy and media opposition, the film was released in Britain without cuts.

'You think you know who you are. You have no idea.'

Crash ★

DIR Paul Haggis
2004 112m US/ Germany / Australia
DVD ♫

☆ *Sandra Bullock* (Jean), *Don Cheadle* (Graham), Matt Dillon (Officer Ryan), Jennifer Esposito (Ria), Brendan Fraser (Rick), Terrence Howard (Cameron), Chris Bridges (Anthony), Thandie Newton (Christine), *Michael Pena* (Daniel)

In post-9/11, pre-Christmas Los Angeles, the lives of various, racially diverse Californians intersect around one road traffic accident.

Not a remake of the Cronenberg film of the same title, although its underlying concern – our increasingly desperate need to make contact with others – isn't all that dissimilar. Haggis compiles memorable performances, scenes and lines, but the whole tends towards the simplistic, wondering at some length why we all can't just get along.

SCR Paul Haggis, Bobby Moresco CIN *J. Michael Muro* MUS *Mark Isham* DES Laurence Bennett ED Hughes Winborne PROD Cathy Schulman, Don Cheadle, Paul Haggis, Mark Harris, Bobby Moresco, Bob Yari DIST Pathé

66 Crash succeeds in spite of itself. Its colour war starts to feel obvious and schematic. Its coincidences and clichés become like a pile-up on the 405 freeway, but there it is – you find yourself rubbernecking and can't manage to look away. – *Joanne Kaufmann, Wall Street Journal*

⚊ movie; Paul Haggis, Bobby Moresco (original screenplay); Hughes Winborne

⚊ Matt Dillon (supporting actor); Paul Haggis; Kathleen York (m/ly), Michael Becker (m) (music, original song – In the Deep)

⬤ Thandie Newton (supporting actress); Paul Haggis, Bobby Moresco (original screenplay)

⬤ film; J. Michael Muro; Hughes Winborne; Don Cheadle (supporting actor); Matt Dillon (supporting actor); Richard Van Dyke, Sandy Gendler, Adam Jenkins, Marc Fishman (sound); Paul Haggis

---

Creature Comforts ★★★

DIR *Nick Park*
1989 5m GB
DVD

Animated animals give 'candid' interviews about their living conditions in a zoo.

The Aardman animation house has made bigger, longer and more expensive films (notably those starring Wallace and Gromit) but has never surpassed this tiny masterpiece, with dialogue drawn from vox-pop interviews, then rendered in stop-go animation. It's a delight, ranging from roaringly funny to melancholy; and its influence on British animation is incalculable.

ED William Ennals PROD Sara Mullock DIST Aardman Animations/Channel 4

⚊ animated short
⬤ animated film

Cries and Whispers ★★★★

SCR/DIR *Ingmar Bergman*
1972 91m Sweden
DVD

☆ *Harriet Andersson* (Agnes), *Kari Sylwan* (Anna), *Ingrid Thulin* (Karin), *Liv Ullmann* (Maria/Her Mother)

A young woman dying of cancer in her family home is tended by her two sisters.

Quiet, chilling, classical chapter of doom which variously reminds one of Chekhov, Tolstoy and Dostoevsky but is also essential Bergman. Tough but important viewing, it lingers afterwards in the mind like a picture vividly painted in shades of red.

CIN *Sven Nykvist* MUS Chopin, Bach ED Siv Lundgren PROD Ingmar Bergman DIST Cinematograph

66 Harrowing, spare and perceptive, but lacking the humour that helps to put life and death into perspective. – *Michael Billington, Illustrated London News*

⚊ Sven Nykvist (cinematography)
⚊ picture; Ingmar Bergman (original screenplay); Ingmar Bergman (director)

'Some kids have lots of time to kill.'

Crime + Punishment in Suburbia ★

DIR Rob Schmidt
2000 100m US
DVD

☆ Monica Keena (Roseanne Skolnik), Vincent Kartheiser (Vincent), Ellen Barkin (Maggie Skolnik), Jeffrey Wright (Chris), James DeBello (Jimmy), Michael Ironside (Fred Skolnik), Christian Payne (Dean), Conchata Ferrell (Bella), Marshall Teague (Coach), Nicki Aycox (Cecil), Brad Greenquist (Calvin Berry), Lucinda Jenney (Vincent's Mom)

A popular high-school student recruits her boyfriend to murder her abusive stepfather, only for her mother to be charged with the crime.

Unusual entry in the teenpics-based-on-classics cycle, fashioning a dark, brooding, not always successful but certainly ambitious film out of Dostoyevsky's novel.

SCR *Larry Gross* CIN Bobby Bukowski MUS Michael Brook DES Ruth Ammon ED Gabriel Wrye PROD Pamela Koffler, Larry Gross, Christine Vachon DIST United Artists

66 A cut above the usual teenage-wasteland movie. – *John Patterson, L.A. Weekly*

'Lead us not into temptation. . .'

The Crime of Father Amaro ★

DIR Carlos Carrera

2002　118m　Mexico/Spain/Argentina/France

DVD

☆ Gael Garcia Bernal (Father Amaro), Sancho Gracia (Father Benito), Ana Claudia Talancon (Amelia), Damian Alcazar (Father Natalio), Angelica Aragon (Sanjuanera), Luisa Huertas (Dionisia), Ernesto Gomez Cruz (Obispo/Bishop), Gaston Melo (Martin)

In a rural parish, a handsome young new Mexican priest succumbs to sexual temptation and fights corruption.

This straight-faced drama, with its by-the-numbers script, nevertheless reinforced the global star appeal of Bernal in the wake of Amores Perros and Y Tu Mama Tambien.

SCR Vicente Lenero　**CIN** Guillermo Granillo **MUS** Rosino Serrano　**DES** Carmen Gimenez Cacho **ED** Oscar Figueroa　**PROD** Alfredo Ripstein, Daniel Birman Ripstein　**DIST** Columbia TriStar

66 Fantastic cinematic storytelling. – *Glenn Kenny, Premiere*

⚖ foreign film

Crimes and Misdemeanors ★★★

SCR/DIR *Woody Allen*

1989　104m　US

DVD

☆ Caroline Aaron (Barbara), Alan Alda (Lester), Woody Allen (Cliff Stern), Claire Bloom (Miriam Rosenthal), Mia Farrow (Halley Reed), Joanna Gleason (Wendy Stern), Anjelica Huston (Dolores Paley), *Martin Landau* (Judah Rosenthal), Jenny Nichols (Jenny), Jerry Orbach (Jack Rosenthal)

In latter-day New York, an opthalmologist hires a hitman to dispose of his mistress, while a documentary maker worries over the direction of his latest project.

More of an intellectual exercise – illustrating comedy and tragedy as flipsides of the same coin – than a wholly cinematic achievement, it nonetheless works through its premise with wit and rigour up to an inconclusive finale.

DES Santo Loquasto　**ED** Susan E. Morse　**PROD** Robert Greenhut　**DIST** Rank/Orion

66 Sometimes the joins in the movie's carpentry are awkward, sometimes its mood swings are jarring. But they also stir us from our comfortable stupor and vivify a true, moral, always acute and often hilarious meditation on the psychological economy of the Reagan years. – *Richard Schickel, Time*

66 Dramatically, the film seldom fulfils its promise, and its pessimistic 'moral' – that good and evil do not always meet with their just deserts – looks contrived and hollow. – *Geoff Andrew, Time Out*

⚖ Martin Landau (supporting actor); Woody Allen (direction); Woody Allen (original screenplay)

Ⓣ film; Alan Alda (supporting actor); Angelica Huston (supporting actress); Woody Allen (original screenplay); Susan E. Morse

'Danger runs deep.'

Crimson Tide ★★

DIR *Tony Scott*

1995　116m　US

DVD ♫

☆ *Denzel Washington* (Lt. Commander Ron Hunter), *Gene Hackman* (Capt. Frank Ramsey), George Dzundza (Chief of the Boat), Viggo Mortensen (Lt. Peter 'WEAPS' Ince), James Gandolfini (Lt. Bobby Dougherty), Matt Craven (Lt. Roy Zimmer, USS Alabama Communications Officer), Rick Schroder (Lt. Paul Hellerman), Jason Robards (uncredited) (Rear Admiral Anderson)

The captain of a US submarine and his executive officer disagree over orders after a Russian dictator seizes control of several missile bases.

A taut, gripping, forcefully acted post-Cold War thriller in which the real conflict is played out between two men who are ostensibly on the same side.

SCR Michael Schiffer　**CIN** *Dariusz Wolsky*　**MUS** Hans Zimmer　**DES** Michael White　**ED** *Chris Lebenzon* **PROD** Don Simpson, Jerry Bruckheimer　**DIST** Buena Vista/Hollywood

66 Has everything you could want from an action thriller and a few other things you usually can't hope to expect: an excellent script, first-rate performances, and a story that has more to do with individuals than explosions. – *Mick LaSalle, San Francisco Chronicle*

† A curious sequence involving an argument about the merits of the comic book hero The Silver Surfer was written by an uncredited Quentin Tarantino. A minor character, Petty Officer Vossler, gets his surname from a former colleague of Tarantino's in a video store.

⚖ Chris Lebenzon; Kevin O'Connell, Rick Kline, Gregory H. Watkins, William B. Kaplan (sound); George WaltersII (sound effects editing)

Criss Cross ★★★

DIR *Robert Siodmak*

1948　87m　US

☆ Burt Lancaster, *Yvonne de Carlo*, Dan Duryea, Stephen McNally, Richard Long, Tom Pedi, Alan Napier

A law-abiding armoured car guard starts courting his treacherous ex-wife, who is involved with a wealthy mobster – and both of them get drawn into plans for a dangerous heist.

Classic film noir with all the trimmings: foreboding music, flashback, a gritty urban setting and dark, shadowy atmospheres – not to mention a first-rate femme fatale. An outstanding example of the genre.

SCR Daniel Fuchs　**CIN** *Franz Planer*　**MUS** *Miklos Rozsa* **ED** Ted J. Kent　**PROD** Michel Kraike　**DIST** U-I

66 Siodmak's talent for brooding violence and the sombre urban setting gives the film a relentlessly mounting tension. – *Peter John Dyer*

† This marked Tony Curtis's debut in film.

† Steven Soderbergh remade the story in 1995, with the title Underneath.

DVD Available on DVD　☆ Cast in order of importance　66 Critics' Quotes　† Points of interest　⚖ Academy Award / Academy Award nomination　Ⓑ BAFTA　Ⓣ BAFTA nomination

149

Cronos ★★

SCR/DIR *Guillermo del Toro*
1992 94m Mexico
[DVD]

☆ Federico Luppi (Jesus Gris), Ron Perlman (Angel de la Guardia), Claudio Brook (De la Guardia), Margarita Isabel (Mercedes), Tamara Shanath (Aurora)

An elderly antiques dealer discovers a clockwork device that grants the bearer eternal life – but requires human blood to fully function.

Del Toro's breakthrough film: a clever, stylish updating of vampire legend that gave fresh life to certain long-dead genre cliches, while creating its own rich new universe.

CIN *Guillermo Navarro*   MUS Javier Álvarez   DES Tolita Figueroa   ED Raul Davalos   PROD Arthur H. Gorson, Bertha Navarro   DIST October Films/Iguana/Ventana

66 An enormously enjoyable gothic yarn from Mexico [that] transfuses the genre with wry grotesquerie, but retains respect for the old, classic films. – *Desson Thomson, Washington Post*

66 This film's reflective, even stately style elevates it from the ranks of ordinary stake-through-the-heart vampire dramaturgy, turning it into something much more exotic. – *Janet Maslin, New York Times*

'A sweet concoction of 70's soul and fun, fun, fun!'

Crooklyn ★

DIR Spike Lee
1994 115m US
[DVD] ♫

☆ Alfre Woodard (Carolyn Carmichael), Delroy Lindo (Woody Carmichael), Spike Lee (Snuffy), Zelda Harris (Troy), Carlton Williams (Clinton), Sharif Rashed (Wendell)

In 1970s Harlem, a 10-year-old African-American girl, one of five children, witnesses the tensions in her family.

Spike Lee wrote the script with two siblings, and the result is a subjective attempt to chart the problems of black inner-city life in the wake of a turbulent decade in American history. It is a minor entry on Lee's CV, though it has compensations: graceful performances from Woodard and Lindo, and a splendid, soul-drenched soundtrack.

SCR Joie Susannah Lee, Cinqué Lee, Spike Lee
CIN Arthur Jafa   MUS Terence Blanchard   DES Wynn Thomas   ED Barry Alexander Brown   PROD Spike Lee
DIST Electric Triangle/40 Acres and a Mule/Child Hoods

66 The juke-box principle of film-making was never applied so enthusiastically, with practically every scene anchored by a song. But it's all too tempting to shut your eyes and pretend you're listening to The Best Soul Album Ever, since the film's dramatic content is so confused. – *Jonathan Romney, Guardian*

'Sensational? No, it's dynamite!'

Crossfire ★★★

DIR *Edward Dmytryk*
1947 86m US

☆ *Robert Young* (Finlay), Robert Mitchum (Keeley), *Robert Ryan* (Montgomery), Gloria Grahame (Ginny), *Paul Kelly* (The Man), Sam Levene (Joseph Samuels), Jacqueline White (Mary Mitchell), Steve Brodie (Floyd)

When a Jewish man is found murdered in a Washington hotel, a group of ex-soldiers come under suspicion.

A ground-breaking noir thriller that was the first Hollywood film to make a stand against anti-Semitism. It audaciously bucked the spirit of the times by portraying post-war America, still basking in the glory of victory, as a place where sinister attitudes held sway. It looked the part, too, with dark, shadowy lighting complementing the mood. A hard-hitting, brilliant, uncomfortable film.

SCR John Paxton   CIN J. Roy Hunt   MUS Roy Webb
ED Harry Gerstad   PROD Adrian Scott   DIST RKO

66 Another murder story that holds its own with any on the basis of suspense and speed. – *Richard Winnington*

† After the film was nominated for five Oscars, producer Scott and director Dmytryk were summoned by the House Un-American Activities Committee, but refused to name names of suspected communists. They became members of the 'Hollywood Ten.' Scott never produced another film. Dmytryk spent a year in jail, then had a spell in exile in Britain before returning to the US, testifying and resuming work as a director.

⚱ picture; Robert Ryan (supporting actor); Gloria Grahame (supporting actress); Edward Dmytryk (direction); John Paxton (screenplay)

'A funny movie about getting serious.'

Crossing Delancey ★

DIR Joan Micklin Silver
1988 97m US
[DVD] ♫

☆ Amy Irving (Isabelle Grossman), Peter Riegert (Sam Posner), Reizl Bozyk (Bubbie Kantor), Jeroen Krabbe (Anton Maes), Sylvia Miles (Hannah Mandelbaum), George Martin (Lionel), John Bedford Lloyd (Nick)

In New York City, a pickle maker woos a sophisticated Jewish bookstore manager who in her turn has eyes for an egocentric novelist.

A sweet-natured comedy that harks back to days when matchmakers still held some sway in courtship matters. It is shrewd and funny, while retaining a certain innocence.

SCR Susan Sandler   CIN Theo Van de Sande   MUS Paul Chihara   DES Dan Leigh   ED Rick Shaine
PROD Michael Nozik   DIST Warner

The Crossing Guard ★★

SCR/DIR Sean Penn
1995 111m US
[DVD]

☆ *Jack Nicholson* (Freddy Gale), David Morse (John Booth), Anjelica Huston (Mary), Robin Wright (Jojo), Piper Laurie (Helen Booth), Richard Bradford (Stuart Booth), Robbie Robertson (Roger), John Savage (Bobby)

A grief-stricken man has waited six years to wreak revenge on a prisoner, about to be released, who was responsible for his daughter's death in a drink-drive accident.

A truly sorrowful film, with Nicholson's Freddy waiting for the act of vengeance that only he believes will soothe his raging, desperate feelings. Penn exploits this sorrow in intimate detail, and Nicholson is the perfect collaborator in making it seem real. A raw, deeply emotional piece.

CIN Vilmos Zsigmond   MUS Jack Nitzsche   DES Michael Haller   ED Jay Cassidy   PROD Sean Penn, David S. Hamburger   DIST Buena Vista/Miramax

66 The current of bereavement never flags even when the dramatic flood becomes stagnant. In every scene, Penn seems to know precisely where the nugget of feeling is hidden, and he doesn't let up until it's uncovered. – *Hal Hinson, Washington Post*

Crossing the Bridge: The Sound of Istanbul ★

SCR/DIR Fatih Akin
2005   90m   Germany
DVD   ♫

☆ Alexander Hacke, Baba Zula, Orient Expressions, Duman, Replikas, Erkin Koray, Istanbul Style Breakers, Orhan Gencebay

Alexander Hacke, bassist for industrial rock band Einsturzende Neubaten, visits Turkey to investigate Istanbul's music scene.

It might have been better served up as a soundtrack sampler, or an extra on the DVD of its director's Head-On, but Hacke proves a surprisingly genial tour guide, and what we hear and see lends credence to the thesis that Istanbul, city of bridges, serves as a musical bridge between Europe and the East.

CIN Herve Dieu   ED Andrew Bird   PROD Fatih Akin, Klaus Maeck, Andreas Thiel, Sandra Harzer-Kux, Christian Kux   DIST Soda

66 Does more than offer a wide variety of entertaining and intoxicating Turkish music. It also uses music to paint a portrait of a vibrant, cosmopolitan city and provide a window into a rich and varied national culture. – *Kenneth Turan, L.A. Times*

Crouching Tiger, Hidden Dragon ★★

DIR *Ang Lee*
2000   120m   Hong Kong/Taiwan/US
DVD   ♫

☆ Chow Yun-fat (Li Mu Bai), *Michelle Yeoh* (Yu Shu Lien), *Zhang Ziyi* (Jen), Chang Chen (Lo), Lung Sihung (Sir Te), Cheng Pei-pei (Jade Fox), Li Fazeng (Governor Yu), Gao Xian (Bo), Hai Yan (Madam Yu), Wang Deming (Tsai), Li Li (May)

Two warriors with a tangled romantic history investigate the disappearance of a fabled sword, tracking it down to a feisty governor's daughter and an old witch.

Lee juggles romantic melodrama with often staggering martial-arts work that did as much to revivify its genre

as Fred Astaire or Gene Kelly did with the musical a half-century before: these characters are fighters and lovers, and the director makes exhilarating play of the connection between the wires that permit such counter-gravitational movement and the emotional ties binding the characters.

SCR James Schamus, Wang Hui Ling, Tsai Kuo Jung   CIN *Peter Pau*   MUS *Tan Dun*   DES *Tim Yip*   ED *Tim Squyres*   PROD Bill Kong, Hsu Li Kong, Ang Lee   DIST Columbia TriStar

66 High art meets high spirits in a rapturously romantic epic that really kicks butt. – *Richard Corliss, Time*

66 Sexy and sublime, a feast for the senses and 100 per cent sheer cinema. – *Tom Charity, Time Out*

† In 2001, this became the highest-grossing foreign-language film to date in the United States.

⚱ foreign language film; Peter Pau; Tan Dun; Tim Yip

⚱ picture; Ang Lee; Wang Hui Ling, James Schamus, Tsai Kuo Jung (adapted screenplay); Tim Squyres; Jorge Calandrelli (m), Tan Dun (m), James Schamus (ly) (music – original song A Love Before Time); Tim Yip (costume design)

🏆 film not in the English language; Ang Lee; Tan Dun; Tim Yip (costume design)

🏆 film; Michelle Yeoh (leading actress); Ziyi Zhang (supporting actress); Hui-Ling Wang, Kuo Jung Tsai (adapted screenplay); Peter Pau; Tim Squyres; Tim Yip; Rob Hodgson, Leo Lo, Jonathan P. Styrlund, Bessie Cheuk Travis Baumann (special visual effects); Drew Kunin, Reilly Steele, Eugene Grearty, Robert Fernandez (sound); make up/hair

'He hates cheats.'

Croupier ★★

DIR Mike Hodges
1997   94m   GB/Ireland/France/Germany
DVD

☆ *Clive Owen* (Jack Manfred), *Kate Hardie* (Bella), *Alex Kingston* (Jani de Villiers), *Gina McKee* (Marion Neil), Nicholas Ball (Jack Manfred Snr), Nick Reding (Giles Cremorne), Alexander Morton (David Reynolds)

A struggling writer seeks inspiration by taking a job in a casino, and is seduced by a South African gambler.

A cool, cerebral thriller that follows the flow of its writer-hero's imagination into pulpy territory, complete with artificial-sounding dialogue; the women are interesting, though, and Owen and his hand double are mesmerising.

SCR Paul Mayersberg   CIN Michael Garfath   MUS Simon Fisher Turner   DES Jon Bunker   ED Les Healey   PROD Jonathan Cavendish   DIST BFI

66 Has style and atmosphere, but I longed for a leaner, tighter script. – *Peter Bradshaw, Guardian*

66 Superbly played – Owen has never been better – and directed with a mature, imperturbable calm, this is cinema well worth seeking out. – *Tom Charity, Time Out*

† After a limited release and poor box-office in Britain, the film received high praise on the US art-house circuit and was re-released in Britain two years later.

DVD Available on DVD   ☆ Cast in order of importance   66 Critics' Quotes   ⚱ Academy Award   🏆 BAFTA
♫ Soundtrack on CD   † Points of interest   ⚱ Academy Award nomination   🏆 BAFTA nomination

151

'Believe In Angels.'

The Crow ★

DIR Alex Proyas
1994   102m   US
DVD   ♫

☆ Brandon Lee (Eric Draven), Ernie Hudson (Sergeant Albrecht), Michael Wincott (Top Dollar), Angel David (Skank), David Patrick Kelly (T-Bird), Rochelle Davis (Sarah), Laurence Mason (Tin Tin), Bai Ling (Myca), Tony Todd (Grange), Jon Polito (Gideon, Pawn Shop Owner)

A murdered rock star returns to Earth to reap his revenge upon those responsible for his death.

Comic-book adaptation that looks as though directed by a 14-year-old Goth, taking in Halloween, violent death, heavy metal, heavier rain, love beyond the grave, scores of moshing extras and a colour palette which ranges from the darkest grey to jet black. Morbid entertainment, to say the least.

SCR David J. Schow, John Shirley   CIN Dariusz Wolski
MUS Graeme Revell, Trent Reznor   DES Alex McDowell
ED Dov Hoenig, Scott Smith   PROD Edward R. Pressman, Jeff Most   DIST Entertainment/Jeff Most/Edward R. Pressman

66 We've been through this smoky urban wasteland one too many times. – *Owen Gleiberman, Entertainment Weekly*

† Brandon Lee died during filming after a shooting accident. His scenes were completed using the actor's on-set stand-in and digital techniques in post-production.
† The film spawned one theatrically released sequel, The Crow: City of Angels, in 1996, and two further straight-to-video releases.

The Crowd ★★★

DIR *King Vidor*
1928   98m   US
☆ *James Murray* (John), Eleanor Boardman (Mary), Bert Roach (Bert), Estelle Clark (Jane)

Episodes in the life of a city clerk.

A deliberately humdrum silent story, chosen to show that drama can exist in the lowliest surroundings. It retains much of its original power, though some of the director's innovations have become clichés.

SCR King Vidor, John V. A. Weaver, Harry Behn
CIN Henry Sharp   ED Hugh Wynn   PROD King Vidor
DIST MGM

66 No picture is perfect, but this comes as near to reproducing reality as anything you have ever witnessed. – *Photoplay*

⚖ King Vidor (direction); Unique and Artistic Picture

'What Some Hearts Desire They Must Possess.'

The Crucible ★★

DIR *Nicholas Hytner*
1996   124m   US
DVD   ♫

☆ *Daniel Day-Lewis* (John Proctor), Winona Ryder (Abigail Williams), *Paul Scofield* (Judge Thomas Danforth), *Joan Allen* (Elizabeth Proctor), Bruce Davison (Reverend Parris), Rob Campbell (Reverend Hale), Jeffrey Jones (Thomas Putnam), Peter Vaughan (Giles Corey), Karron

Graves (Mary Warren), Charlayne Woodard (Tituba), George Gaynes (Judge Samuel Sewall)

Salem, Massachusettes, the 1690s: a community is torn apart by allegations of witchcraft.

A forceful filming of a landmark play that permits persuasive performances, though by the mid-90s, its immediate relevance had somewhat dissipated.

SCR *Arthur Miller*   CIN Andrew Dunn   MUS George Fenton   DES Lilly Kilvert   ED Tariq Anwar
PROD Robert A. Miller, David V. Picker   DIST TCF

66 Audiences can attend this movie and enjoy the rare sensation of being treated with respect by the people who made it. – *Ralph Novak, People Weekly*

66 Offers solid workmanship and familiar epiphanies. – *Richard Corliss, Time*

⚖ Joan Allen (supporting actress); Arthur Miller (adapted screenplay)

🏆 Paul Scofield (supporting actor)
🏆 Arthur Miller (adapted screenplay)

A Crude Awakening (new) ★

SCR/DIR Basil Gelpke, Ray McCormack
2007   85m   Switzerland

A documentary in 10 chapters about the planet's depleting oil reserves.

Intriguing, sobering account of an urgent problem by two investigative journalists.

CIN Frank Messmer   MUS Philip Glass   ED Georgia Wyss   PROD Basil Gelpke, Ray McCormack
DIST Dogwoof

66 An informative and unashamedly apocalyptic documentary about the world's obsession with oil that makes An Inconvenient Truth look positively chipper. – *Kevin Maher, The Times*

'What You Can't Have, You Can't Resist.'

Cruel Intentions ★

SCR/DIR Roger Kumble
1999   97m   US
DVD   ♫

☆ Sarah Michelle Gellar (Kathryn Merteuil), Ryan Phillippe (Sebastian Valmont), Reese Witherspoon (Annette Hargrove), Selma Blair (Cecile Caldwell), Louise Fletcher (Helen Rosemond), Joshua Jackson (Blaine Tuttle), Eric Mabius (Greg McConnell), Sean Patrick Thomas (Ronald Clifford), Swoosie Kurtz (Dr. Greenbaum), Christine Baranski (Bunny Caldwell)

A Manhattan rich girl offers herself to her stepbrother, on the grounds that he seduces a committed virgin.

Slick, sheeny teen version of Dangerous Liaisons, in which the emotional betrayals are all played out in parentless, seemingly rentless apartment blocks on the Upper East Side; easy to watch, though nothing cuts too deep.

CIN Theo Van de Sande   MUS Edward Shearmur
DES Jon Gary Steele   ED Jeff Freeman   PROD Neal H. Moritz   DIST Columbia

66 A witty, raunchy comedy, which proves that a well-written piece of business – oozing with sex, wit and nasty

intrigue – works for any generation. – *Desson Thomson, Washington Post*

66 Never shocks or even offends by ascribing fully adult cruelties and erotic activities to obnoxious kids; such harshness wouldn't flatter a cast this moussed and magazine-layout-ready. – *Lisa Schwarzbaum, Entertainment Weekly*

The Cruel Sea ★★
DIR *Charles Frend*
1953   126m   GB
DVD

☆ *Jack Hawkins* (Capt. Ericson), Donald Sinden (Lt Lockhart), Stanley Baker (Bennett), John Stratton (Ferraby), Denholm Elliott (Sub-Lt Morell), John Warner (Baker), Bruce Seton (Bob Tallow), Virginia McKenna (Julie Hallam), Moira Lister (Elaine Morell), June Thorburn (Doris Ferraby), Alec McCowen (Tonbridge), Glyn Houston (Phillips)

Life and death on a British warship in the Atlantic during World War II.

Competent transcription of a bestselling book, cleanly produced and acted; a huge box-office success, perhaps because it portrayed Britons of all ranks pulling together in adverse conditions. A superior British war film.

SCR Eric Ambler   CIN Gordon Dines   MUS Alan Rawsthorne   ED Peter Tanner   PROD Leslie Norman   DIST Ealing

66 This is a story of the battle of the Atlantic, a story of an ocean, two ships and a handful of men. The men are the heroes. The heroines are the ships. The only villain is the sea – the cruel sea – that man has made even more cruel. – *opening narration*

66 One is grateful nowadays for a film which does not depict war as anything but a tragic and bloody experience, and it is this quality which gives the production its final power to move. – *John Gillett*

⚲ Eric Ambler (screenplay)

'Weird sex. Obsession. Comic books.'

Crumb ★★
DIR *Terry Zwigoff*
1994   120m   US
DVD ♫

☆ Robert Crumb (Himself), Charles Crumb (Himself, Robert's Older Brother), Maxon Crumb (Himself, Robert's Younger Brother), Aline Kominsky (Herself, Robert's Wife), Dana Crumb (Herself, Robert's First Wife), Beatrice Crumb (Herself, Robert's Mother)

A profile of counter-cultural cartoonist Robert Crumb, featuring interviews with his friends, family, admirers and the man himself as he prepares to leave America to live with his wife and daughter in France.

Zwigoff achieves remarkable levels of intimacy with his subject in a compellingly messy documentary that's part hagiography, part reality television and so much tabloid tittle-tattle. It's been made by a fan: the film is finally evasive on some of the more troubling elements of Crumb's work, and you may come away thinking of the

cartoonist as a pervert who got lucky with good draughtsmanship skills.

CIN Maryse Alberti   ED Victor Livingston   PROD Lynn O'Donnell, Terry Zwigoff, David Lynch   DIST Artificial Eye/Superior

66 Zwigoff not only presents a complex human being and the range of his art, but also guides us through a profound and unsettling consideration of what it means to be an American artist. Essential viewing. – *Jonathan Rosenbaum, Chicago Reader*

66 An acute but creepy bit of American gothic. – *Alexander Walker, Evening Standard*

Crush ★
DIR Alison Maclean
1992   97m   New Zealand
DVD

☆ Marcia Gay Harden (Lane), William Zappa (Colin Iseman), Donogh Rees (Christina), Caitlin Bossley (Angela Iseman), Pete Smith (Horse), Jon Brazier (Arthur)

A young American woman usurps her best friend, a journalist, in the affections of a famous writer.

Revenge is on the menu in this three-way relationship; it starts out as a taut thriller but spills over into melodrama. Still, a decent debut feature from director Maclean.

SCR Alison Maclean, Anne Kennedy   CIN Dion Beebe   MUS Antony Partos   DES Meryl Cronin   ED John Gilbert   PROD Bridget Ikin   DIST Metro/Hibiscus/NZFC/NFU/NZ On Air/Movie Partners

66 Often as murky as the bubbling New Zealand mud springs Maclean cuts to in order to underscore the otherworldly ambience. – *Empire*

'A family torn apart. A public filled with outrage. A woman accused of murder.'

A Cry in the Dark ★★
DIR Fred Schepisi
1988   121m   Australia/GB
DVD   ♫

☆ *Meryl Streep* (Lindy Chamberlain), Sam Neill (Michael Chamberlain), Dale Reeves (Aiden, 6 years), David Hoflin (Aiden, 8 years), Jason Reason (Aiden, 11 years), Michael Wetter (Reagan, 4 years), Kane Barton (Reagan, 6 years), Trent Roberts (Reagan, 9 years), Brian James (Cliff Murchison), Dorothy Alison (Avis Murchison)

The baby daughter of a Seventh Day Adventist couple is snatched in the outback, and the mother, who claims a dingo carried off the child, is tried for murder.

Probing reconstruction of a real-life cause célèbre, in which Meryl Streep's daringly unsympathetic performance provides one reason for the media turning against her character; the couple's religious convictions are another.

SCR Robert Caswell, Fred Schepisi   CIN Ian Baker   MUS Bruce Smeaton   DES Wendy Dickson, George Liddle   ED Jill Bilcock   PROD Verity Lambert   DIST Pathé/Evil Angels/Cannon International

DVD Available on DVD   ☆ Cast in order   66 Critics' Quotes   ⚲ Academy Award   Ⓑ BAFTA
♫ Soundtrack on CD   of importance   † Points of interest   ⚲ Academy Award nomination   Ⓣ BAFTA nomination

153

66 May be the most quietly uncondescending film ever made about religious fundamentalists. – *Peter Rainer, Los Angeles Herald Examiner*

Meryl Streep (leading actress)

C

'Too young to be square. . .Too tough to be shocked. . .Too late to be saved'

Cry-Baby ★

SCR/DIR John Waters

1990 85m US

DVD ♫

☆ Johnny Depp (Wade 'Cry-Baby' Walker), Amy Locane (Allison Vernon-Williams), Susan Tyrrell (Ramona Rickettes), Polly Bergen (Mrs. Vernon-Williams), Iggy Pop (Uncle Belvedere Rickettes), Ricki Lake (Pepper Walker), Traci Lords (Wanda Woodward), Kim McGuire (Hatchet-Face), Darren E. Burrows (Milton Hackett)

A rock 'n' roll rebel seduces an all-American good girl.

Waters' second display of early pop nostalgia after the superior Hairspray; his affection for the period sometimes tips over into kitsch and/or grotesquerie, but there's a typically idiosyncratic cast to marvel at.

CIN David Insley MUS Patrick Williams DES Vincent Peranio ED Janice Hampton PROD Rachel Talalay DIST UIP/Imagine Entertainment

66 Entertaining as a rude joyride through another era, full of great clothes and hairdos. – *Variety*

66 Still Waters runs shallow. – *Christopher Tookey, Daily Mail*

'Desire Is A Danger Zone.'

The Crying Game ★

SCR/DIR Neil Jordan

1992 112m GB/Japan

DVD ♫

☆ Stephen Rea (Fergus), Miranda Richardson (Jude), Forest Whitaker (Jody), Jim Broadbent (Col), Ralph Brown (Dave), Adrian Dunbar (Maguire), Jaye Davidson (Dil), Tony Slattery (Deveroux)

An IRA man assigned to murder a British soldier becomes involved with the woman his target was obsessed by.

Bafflingly overrated melodrama that labours from one hokey scenario to the next, the serious intent of its revelations continually undermined by problems of tone, heavy-handed symbolism, and Forest Whitaker's accent.

CIN Ian Wilson MUS Anne Dudley DES Jim Clay ED Kant Pan PROD Stephen Woolley DIST Palace/Channel 4/Eurotrustees/NDF/British Screen

66 By the time The Crying Game is over, you'll never look at beauty in quite the same way. – *Owen Gleiberman, Entertainment Weekly*

66 Enthralls and amazes us. It deserves to be called great. – *Hal Hinson, Washington Post*

† Harvey Weinstein, whose Miramax company distributed the film in the US, urged critics not to give away the crucial plot twist in the film.

† It was released first in Britain, and fared badly at the box-office, but after opening successfully in the US and benefiting from a splashy, aggressive awards season campaign by Miramax, it was re-released in Britain and attracted larger audiences.

Neil Jordan (original screenplay)

picture; Neil Jordan (direction); Stephen Rea (leading actor); Jaye Davidson (supporting actor); Kant Pan

film; British film; Stephen Rea (leading actor); Jaye Davidson (supporting actor); Miranda Richardson (supporting actress); Neil Jordan (direction); Neil Jordan (original screenplay)

'Buddhism is their philosophy. Soccer is their religion.'

The Cup ★★

SCR/DIR Khyentse Norbu

1999 93m Australia

☆ Jamyang Lodro (Orgyen), Orgyen Tobgyal (Geko), Neten Chokling (Lodo), Lama Chonjor (Abbot), Lama Godhi (Old lama)

Two young Tibetan Buddhist monks are such fervent football fans that they petition their abbot to let them start a fund-raising drive so they can buy satellite equipment and watch their hero Ronaldo in the World Cup final.

Delightfully amusing story about an apparent culture clash, which slyly emphasises that football is a universal force for unity in ways that religion strives to be. The film is so infectiously cheerful, it functions like an anti-depressant.

CIN Paul Warren MUS Douglas Mills DES Raymond Steiner ED John Scott PROD Malcolm Watson, Raymond Steiner DIST Alliance

66 A delightful demonstration of how spirituality can coexist quite happily with an intense desire for France to defeat Brazil. – *Roger Ebert, Chicago Sun-Times*

† The film uses a non-professional cast of real Buddhist monks. It is directed by a Tibetan lama.

† This was Bhutan's first feature film, though the kingdom has been used as a location by foreign productions.

Cyclo ★★

DIR *Tran Anh Hung*

1995 123m France/Vietnam

DVD ♫

☆ Le Van Loc (Cyclo), Tony Leung (Poet), Tran Nu Yen Khe (Sister), Nguyen Nhu Quynh (Madam), Nguyen Hoang Phuc (Tooth), Ngo Vu Quang Hal (Knife)

In Ho Chi Minh City, the driver of a pedicab falls in with a gang of toughs after his vehicle is stolen.

Vivid and atmospheric translation of Bicycle Thieves to the streets of Vietnam, in which all the characters are hurting in some way; perhaps a little overlong, it has enough weird plot tropes and arresting images to keep one watching.

SCR Nguyen Trung Binh, Tran Anh Hung CIN *Benoit Delhomme, Laurence Trémolet* MUS Ton That Tiet DES Benoît Barouh ED Nicole Dedieu, Claude Ronzeau PROD Christophe Rossignon DIST Entertainment/Lazannec/Lumière/La Sept/La SFP

66 With its dazzling camerawork, feverish energy and dark, visceral power, this admirably unsentimental film paints a compelling portrait of moral derailment and

salvation in a city in social and spiritual turmoil. . .It'll have you reeling. – *Geoff Andrew, Time Out*

† Director Anh Hung Tran's previous film was the Oscar-nominated Scent of Green Papaya. This title was voted best film at the 1995 Venice Film Festival.

Cyrano de Bergerac ★★★

DIR *Jean-Paul Rappeneau*
1990 137m France
DVD ♪

☆ *Gérard Depardieu* (Cyrano de Bergerac), Anne Brochet (Roxane), Vincent Perez (Christian de Neuvillette), Jacques Weber (Count DeGuiche), Roland Bertin (Ragueneau), Philippe Morier-Genoud (Le Bret), Philippe Volter (Viscount of Valvert), Pierre Maguelon (Carbon de Castel-Jaloux)

A soldier and poet, cursed by his abnormally long nose, employs a handsome friend to woo the woman he loves.

Tremendously spirited and perfectly cast adaptation of Rostand's novel that sweeps viewers off their feet with a combination of wit, charm, beauty and eloquence.

SCR Jean-Paul Rappeneau, Jean-Claude Carrière
CIN *Pierre Lhomme* **MUS** Jean-Claude Petit **DES** Ezio Frigerio **ED** Noëlle Boisson **PROD** Rene Cleitman, Michael Seydoux **DIST** Hachette Première/Camera One/Films A2/D.D. Productions/UGC

66 Other actors have given more flamboyant interpretations of the role, but Depardieu is the definitive romantic Cyrano. . .It's a towering performance, magnificent and moving, that does just what any honest telling of the Cyrano legend should strive to do: set us all dreaming. – *Peter Travers, Rolling Stone*

66 Truly the Greatest Love Story Ever Told. – *Phillipa Bloom, Empire*

† The English subtitles were written by Anthony Burgess.

⚱ Franca Squarciapino (costume design)
⚱ foreign film; Gérard Depardieu (leading actor); Ezio Frigerio; Michèle Burke, Jean-Pierre Eychenne (make up)

Pierre Lhomme; Jean-Claude Petit; Franca Squarciapino (costume design); Michèle Burke, Jean-Pierre Eychenne (make up)

film not in the English language; Gérard Depardieu (leading actor); Jean-Paul Rappeneau, Jean-Claude Carrière (adapted screenplay); Ezio Frigerio

Czech Dream

SCR/DIR Vít Klusák, Filip Remunda
2004 90m Czech Republic/GB
DVD

☆ Varhan Orchestrovich Bauer (Himself), Jaromír Kalina (Himself), Vít Klusák (Himself), Martin Prikryl (Himself), Filip Remunda (Himself), Eva Williams (Herself)

Two Czech film students receive a state grant to advertise the opening of a fictitious supermarket. Citizens flock to it.

Cruel hoax that toys with the aspirations of a nation still struggling to emerge from the yoke of Communism. Yet the hoax has a legitimate satirical point.

CIN Vít Klusák, Filip Remunda **MUS** Varhan Orchestrovic Bauer **ED** Zdenek Marek **PROD** Vít Klusák, Filip Remunda **DIST** Soda

DVD Available on DVD   ☆ Cast in order   66 Critics' Quotes   ⚱ Academy Award   BAFTA
♪ Soundtrack on CD   of importance   † Points of interest   ⚱ Academy Award nomination   BAFTA nomination

155

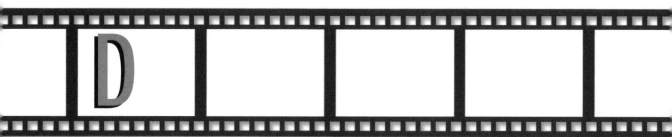

'Someone poisoned Dexter Cornell. He's got to find out who. He's got to find out why. He's got to find out now. In 24 hours, he'll be Dead On Arrival.'

D.O.A. ☆

DIR Rocky Morton, Annabel Jankel

1988   96m   US

DVD   ♫

☆ Dennis Quaid (Dexter Cornell), Meg Ryan (Sydney Fuller), Charlotte Rampling (Mrs. Fitzwaring), Daniel Stern (Hal Petersham), Jane Kaczmarek (Gail Cornell), Christopher Neame (Bernard), Robin Johnson (Cookie Fitzwaring), Rob Knepper (Nicholas Lang), Jay Patterson (Graham Corey)

A man learns that he has been poisoned, and finds himself in a race against the clock to solve his own murder.

Enjoyable remake of a noir classic, with Quaid a credible leading man. The colour drains out of the film as his health worsens; it's an appealing, if gimmicky touch.

SCR Charles Edward Pogue   **CIN** Yuri Neyman
MUS Chaz Jankel   **DES** Richard Amend   **ED** Michael R. Miller, Raja Gosnell   **PROD** Ian Sander, Laura Ziskin
DIST Warner/Touchstone/Silver Screen Partners III

Da ☆

DIR Matt Clark

1988   102m   US

DVD

☆ *Barnard Hughes* (Da), Martin Sheen (Charlie), William Hickey (Drumm), Doreen Hepburn (Mother), Karl Hayden (Young Charlie), Hugh O'Conor (Boy Charlie), Ingrid Craigie (Polly), Joan O'Hara (Mrs Prynne), Jill Doyle (Mary 'The Yellow Peril')

A successful Irish-American playwright returns from New York to the old country to bury his father, and recalls him in a series of flashbacks..

It never quite shakes off its stage origins, but its virtues run deep: it's an emotionally honest, deeply felt work.

SCR Hugh Leonard   **CIN** Alar Kivilo   **MUS** Elmer Bernstein   **DES** Frank Conway   **ED** Nancy Nuttal Beyda
PROD Julie Corman   **DIST** Premier/Film Dallas/A. J. Corman-Sheen/Greenblatt/Auerbach

'Seek the Truth.'

The Da Vinci Code

DIR Ron Howard

2006   149m   US

DVD   ♫

☆ Tom Hanks (Robert Langdon), Audrey Tautou (Sophie Neveu), Ian McKellen (Sir Leigh Teabing), Jean Reno (Captain Bezu Fache), Paul Bettany (Silas), Alfred Molina (Bishop Aringarosa), Jurgen Prochnow (Vernet), Jean-Yves Berteloot (Remy Jean)

An American cryptologist in Paris, framed for murder, goes on the run with a female detective and uncovers a conspiracy pertaining to the Catholic Church.

Very dull, occasionally silly, and – above all else – very long adaptation of a massive bestseller, with a plot that piles bunkum (high-flown conspiracy) on top of something only marginally less contentious (organised religion) and thus requires everyone involved to sit down at five-minute intervals to explain what's going on. It's hard to know what's worse: Hanks's haircut? Tautou's mangled English? Or Brown's invocation of maths, science and art history, all of which struggle to meet even GCSE levels?

SCR Akiva Goldsman   **CIN** Salvatore Totino   **MUS** Hans Zimmer   **DES** Allan Cameron   **ED** Dan Hanley, Mike Hill
PROD Brian Grazer, John Calley, Ron Howard
DIST Columbia TriStar

❝ An acceptable but uninspired simulacrum: an overly faithful multiplex translation of a very, very popular airport novel. – *Ty Burr, Boston Globe*

❝ The most controversial thriller of the year turns out to be about as exciting as watching your parents play Sudoku. – *Ann Hornaday, Washington Post*

† The film's distributors were widely criticised for arranging for this critically panned film to receive its world premiere at the 2006 Cannes Film Festival.

'The summer is going to be in tents.'

Daddy Day Camp (new)

DIR Fred Savage

2007   89m   US

DVD

☆ Cuba Gooding Jr. (Charlie Hinton), Lochlyn Munro (Lance), Richard Gant (Buck Hinton), Brian Doyle-Murray (Uncle Morty)

A children's day care centre owner accompanies his son to day camp.

Dismally unfunny, unless one finds breaking wind and bed-wetting intrinsically amusing.

SCR Geoff Rodkey, J. David Stern, David N. Weiss
CIN Geno Salvatori   **MUS** Jim Dooley   **DES** Eric Weller
ED Michael Aller   **PROD** William Sherak, Jason Shuman
DIST Sony

❝ Parents! Hire a bouncy castle. Put on clown paint and make balloon animals. You need not see this. – *Tim Robey, Daily Telegraph*

DVD Available on DVD   ☆ Cast in order   ❝ Critics' Quotes   ♫ Academy Award   ♥ BAFTA
♫ Soundtrack on CD   of importance   † Points of interest   ♀ Academy Award nomination   ♥ BAFTA nomination

66 Never work with children or animals. Unless you're a child or an animal, in which case, never work with Cuba Gooding Jnr. – *Jamie Russell, BBC*

† Director Fred Savage, now 32, is best known as the adolescent lead character in the TV series The Wonder Years.

† The film is a sequel to Daddy Day Care (2003), starring Eddie Murphy.

Daddy Nostalgie ★★

DIR Bertrand Tavernier
1990   105m   France
♫
☆ *Dirk Bogarde* (Daddy), Jane Birkin (Caroline), Emmanuelle Bataille (Juliette), Charlotte Kady (Barbara), Michele Minns (Caroline, as a child)

A screenwriter returns home to be close to her invalid father.

Gently understated domestic drama.

SCR Colo Tavernier O'Hagan   **CIN** Denis Lenoir
MUS Antoine Duhamel   **DES** Jean-Louis Poveda
ED Ariane Boeglin   **PROD** Adolphe Viezzi
DIST Clea/Little Bear/Solyfic Eurisma

66 A miniature jewel of a film . . . acted and directed with great subtlety. – *Variety*

The Dam Busters ★★★

DIR Michael Anderson
1954   125m   GB
DVD
☆ *Michael Redgrave* (Dr B. N. Wallis), Richard Todd (Wing Commander Guy Gibson), Basil Sydney (Air Chief Marshal Sir Arthur Harris), Derek Farr (Group Capt J. N. H. Whitworth), Patrick Barr (Capt. Joseph Summers), Ernest Clark (Air Vice-Marshal the Hon Ralph Cochrane), Raymond Huntley (Official), Ursula Jeans (Mrs Wallis), Brewster Mason (Flight Lt R. D. Trevor-Roper), Anthony Doonan (Flight Lt R. E. G. Hutchison), Nigel Stock (Flying Officer F. M. Spafford), Brian Nissen (Flight Lt A. T. Taerum), Robert Shaw (Flight Sgt J. Pulford), Peter Assinder (Flying Officer G. A. Deering)

In 1943 the Ruhr dams in Germany are destroyed by Dr Barnes Wallis's bouncing bombs.

Calculatedly understated British war epic with additional scientific interest and good acting and model work. It still commands enormous affection in Britain, where the bouncing bomb scenes have become part of a national folklore.

SCR R. C. Sherriff   **CIN** Erwin Hillier   **MUS** *Leighton Lucas, Eric Coates*   **ED** Richard Best   **PROD** Robert Clark
DIST ABPC

'Desire. Deceit.'

Damage ★

DIR Louis Malle
1992   111m   GB/France
DVD   ♫
☆ Jeremy Irons (Dr. Stephen Fleming), Juliette Binoche (Anna Barton), *Miranda Richardson* (Ingrid Fleming), Rupert Graves (Martyn Fleming), Leslie Caron (Elizabeth Prideaux), Ian Bannen (Edward Lloyd), Gemma Clarke

(Sally Fleming), Julian Fellowes (Donald Lyndsay), Tony Doyle (Prime Minister), Benjamin Whitrow (Civil Servant)

A Tory politician's life falls apart when he becomes besotted by his son's girlfriend.

Handsome film that looks and sounds better than its essentially lurid subject matter. Richardson is a knockout as the spurned wife.

SCR David Hare   **CIN** Peter Biziou   **MUS** Zbigniew Preisner   **DES** Brian Morris   **ED** John Bloom
PROD Louis Malle
DIST Entertainment/Skreba/NEF/Canal

66 A cold, brittle film about raging, traumatic emotions. – *Variety*

66 A carefully controlled picture about uncontrollable passion, in which precise camera movements and unobtrusive editing subtly complement the immaculate acting. – *Philip French, Observer*

⚲ Miranda Richardson (supporting actress)

Ⓣ Miranda Richardson (supporting actress)

'Something's happening to Dan. It's confusing. It's awkward. It's family.'

Dan in Real Life (new) ★★

DIR Peter Hedges
2007   98m   US
DVD   ♫
☆ Steve Carell (Dan Burns), Juliette Binoche (Marie), Dane Cook (Mitch Burns), Dianne Wiest (Nana Burns), John Mahoney (Poppy Burns), Emily Blunt (Ruthie Draper)

A widowed father falls in love with his brother's girlfriend during his annual weekend away with his extended family.

Winning, humane comedy that wrings a surprising amount of observant humour from its somewhat familiar conceit.

SCR Pierce Gardner, Peter Hedges   **CIN** Lawrence Sher   **MUS** Sondre Lerche   **DES** Sarah Knowles   **ED** Sarah Flack   **PROD** John Shestack, Brad Epstein   **DIST** Icon

66 Blissfully funny and touching. – *Peter Travers, Rolling Stone*

66 What Hedges does here so brilliantly is allow us to see two people fall madly in love in a situation where no one else can be aware of their passion. – *Kirk Honeycutt, Hollywood Reporter*

'You don't need eyes to see.'

Dancer in the Dark ★

SCR/DIR Lars Von Trier
2000   140m   Denmark/Sweden/France/Italy/Germany
DVD   ♫
☆ *Björk* (Selma), Catherine Deneuve (Kathy), David Morse (Bill), Peter Stormare (Jeff), Joel Grey (Oldrich Novy), Vincent Paterson (Samuel), Cara Seymour (Linda), Jean-Marc Barr (Norman), Vladica Kostic (Gene), Udo Kier (Doctor), Zeljko Ivanek (D.A.)

A Czech factory worker in small-town America is threatened with blindness and is trying to raise money for an operation to save her son from the same fate. But she also faces losing her job and home, and standing trial for killing a man who robbed her.

DVD Available on DVD   ☆ Cast in order   66 Critics' Quotes   ⚲ Academy Award   Ⓣ BAFTA
♫ Soundtrack on CD   of importance   † Points of interest   ⚱ Academy Award nomination   Ⓣ BAFTA nomination

Few films in recent years have polarised audiences like this one. Von Trier has called it an attempt to subvert the American musical, but he shows little understanding of the elusive crafts that make the best musicals magical. Its bold but grossly sentimental misery-memoir story, melodramatic in the extreme, features a lead actress who often looks out of her depth, while the camera work – relentlessly hand-held and shaky for no discernible reason – literally induces nausea and dizziness among some viewers. Beneath its angst-ridden veneer, it's a mess.

CIN Robby Muller DES Karl Juliusson ED Molly Malene Stensgaard, Francois Gediger PROD Vibeke Windelov DIST Film4

66 Occasionally riveting folly. – Adam Mars-Jones, The Times

66 I was simultaneously struck by the film's preposterousness and astounded by its intensity and audacity. – Edward Porter, Sunday Times

♪ Björk (m), Lars von Trier, Sjon Sigurdsson (ly), (music, original song – I've Seen It All)

'An honest man caught in a world of intrigue, power and passion.'

The Dancer Upstairs ★★

DIR John Malkovich
2001 132m US/Spain
DVD ♫

☆ Javier Bardem (Rejas), Juan Diego Botto (Sucre), Laura Morante (Yolanda), Elvira Minguez (Llosa), Alexandra Lencastre (Sylvina), Oliver Cotton (General Merino), Abel Folk (Ezequiel Duran), Marie-Anne Verganza (Laura)

In an unnamed Latin American country plagued by terrorist activity, a married cop investigating the activities of a guerrilla leader falls for his daughter's dance teacher.

Survive a shaky opening twenty minutes – which confront the audience with a set of non-English leads speaking in English, and a questionably absurd sense of humour – and Malkovich's directorial debut reveals itself as a carefully paced, skilfully acted thriller about personal and political corruption.

SCR Nicholas Shakespeare CIN Jose Luis Alcaine MUS Alberto Iglesias DES Pierre-François Limbosh ED Mario Battistel PROD Andres Vicente Gomez, John Malkovich DIST TCF

66 A haunting and often beautiful work. – Andrew O'Hehir, Salon

66 Far from perfect but completely unique, the film could best be described as a paranoid South American metaphysical political thriller – you heard me – and whatever its failures, they're not ones of nerve or imagination. – Ty Burr, Boston Globe

'Inside everyone is a frontier waiting to be discovered.'

Dances with Wolves ★★

DIR Kevin Costner
1990 180m US
DVD ♫

☆ Kevin Costner (Lt. John J. Dunbar), Mary McDonnell (Stands With A Fist), Graham Greene (Kicking Bird), Rodney A. Grant (Wind In His Hair), Floyd Red Crow Westerman (Ten Bears), Tantoo Cardinal (Black Shawl), Robert Pastorelli (Timmons), Charles Rocket (Lieutenant Elgin), Maury Chaykin (Major Fambrough), Jimmy Herman (Stone Calf), Nathan Lee Chasing His Horse (Smiles A Lot)

A disenchanted US cavalry officer and Civil War hero finds fulfilment living with Sioux Indians.

An epic award-winning western with a sentimental script and a tendency to labour obvious points. Still, it remains a powerful labour of love (on Costner's part), a passionate story of the oppression of native American decency. Serious-minded acting and stunning cinematography cannot disguise its excessive length.

SCR Michael Blake CIN Dean Semler MUS John Barry DES Jeffrey Beecroft ED Neil Travis, Stephen Potter, Chip Masamitsu, William Hoy PROD Kevin Costner, Jim Wilson DIST Guild/Tig Productions/Jim Wilson, Kevin Costner

66 Sincere, capable, at times moving, but overextended, this picture is seriously hampered by its tendency to linger over everything – especially landscapes with silhouetted figures and not excluding its own good intentions. – Jonathan Rosenbaum, Chicago Reader

66 In his directorial debut, Kevin Costner brings a rare degree of grace and feeling to this elegiac tale of a hero's adventure of discovery. – Amy Dawes, Variety

† .

♦ picture; Kevin Costner; Michael Blake (adapted screenplay); Dean Semler; Neil Travis; John Barry; Russell Williams II, Jeffrey Perkins, Bill W. Benton, Gregory H. Watkins (sound)

♦ Kevin Costner (leading actor); Graham Greene (supporting actor); Mary McDonnell (supporting actress); Jeffrey Beecroft; Elsa Zamparelli (costume design)

♦ film; Kevin Costner (leading actor); Kevin Costner (director); Michael Blake (adapted screenplay); Dean Semler; Neil Travis; John Barry; Russell Williams II, Jeffrey Perkins, Bill W. Benton, Gregory H. Watkins (sound); Francisco X. Pérez (make up)

'Five sisters embrace the spirit of a people.'

Dancing at Lughnasa

DIR Pat O'Connor
1998 92m Ireland/GB/US
DVD ♫

☆ Meryl Streep (Kit), Michael Gambon (Father Jack Mundy), Catherine McCormack (Chrissy), Kathy Burke (Maggie), Sophie Thompson (Rosie), Brid Brennan (Aggie), Rhys Ifans (Gerry Evans), Darrell Johnston (Mike), Lorcan Cranitch (Danny Bradley), Peter Gowen (Austin Morgan)

A missionary returns home to rural Ireland from Africa, and disturbs the lives of his five unmarried sisters.

Even with its stellar cast, the moody magic of Brian Friel's award-winning play fails to survive the switch to the screen. O'Connor opens up the play to include some pleasant scenery, but its magic just dissipates.

SCR Frank McGuinness CIN Kenneth MacMillan MUS Bill Whelan DES Mark Geraghty ED Humphrey Dixon PROD Noel Pearson DIST Ferndale/Capitol/Sony/Channel 4 Films

66 Pat O'Connor's film is a failure. It fails because it is pallid and emotionless. It never comes close to generating real feeling, to harnessing the forces that worked on stage. – *Gerry McCarthy, Sunday Times*

66 The movie is no more than a delicate whisper as each sister reveals her grieving heart, but it's no less extraordinary for that. – *Peter Travers, Rolling Stone*

'Lust. Seduction. Revenge. The Game As You've Never Seen It Played Before.'

Dangerous Liaisons ★★★

DIR Stephen Frears
1988   120m   US
DVD ♫

☆ *Glenn Close* (Marquise de Merteuil), John Malkovich (Vicomte de Valmont), *Michelle Pfeiffer* (Madame de Tourvel), Swoosie Kurtz (Madame de Volanges), Keanu Reeves (Chevalier Danceny), Mildred Natwick (Madame de Rosemonde), Uma Thurman (Cecile de Volanges)

Amorous aristocrats orchestrate historical hanky-panky.

A fine adaptation of 18th-century sexual power games in a corrupt French high society. The tone is one of jaded cynicism, and Frears adroitly moves his cameras right into the middle of exchanges, showing us the palpable lies that facilitate seduction. It leaves you breathless and feeling somewhat chilly.

SCR Christopher Hampton   **CIN** Philippe Rousselot   **MUS** George Fenton   **DES** Stuart Craig   **ED** Mick Audsley   **PROD** Norma Heyman, Hank Moonjean   **DIST** Warner/Lorimar/NFH

66 This incisive study of sex as an arena for manipulative power games takes too long to catch fire. – *Variety staff*

⚲ Christopher Hampton (adapted screenplay); Stuart Craig; James Acheson (costume design)

⚲ picture; Glenn Close (leading actress); Michelle Pfeiffer (supporting actress); George Fenton

Ⓣ Michelle Pfeiffer (supporting actress); Christopher Hampton (adapted screenplay)

Ⓣ Glenn Close (leading actress); Stephen Frears; Philippe Rousselot; Mick Audsley; George Fenton; Stuart Craig; James Acheson (costume design); Jean-Luc Russier (make up)

'She Broke The Rules. . .And Changed Their Lives.'

Dangerous Minds ★

DIR John N. Smith
1995   99m   US
DVD ♫

☆ Michelle Pfeiffer (Louanne Johnson), George Dzundza (Hal), Courtney B. Vance (George Grandey), Robin Bartlett (Carla), Bruklin Harris (Callie), Renoly Santiago (Raul), John Neville (Waiter)

An ex-marine turned teacher Johnson gets tough with her difficult, disruptive students and wins them over with determination, charisma and poetry.

A great-looking blonde teacher turns around the lives of deprived inner-city kids with the poems of Dylan Thomas? The original story may be rooted in fact, but it feels like a Hollywood liberal wet dream, and Pfeiffer

does not readily spring to mind as an actor to portray a Marine veteran. Yet it's executed skilfully, and it's not the fault of this film that its success spawned any number of inferior variations.

SCR Ronald Bass   **CIN** Pierre Letarte   **MUS** Wendy & Lisa   **DES** Donald Graham Burt   **ED** Tom Rolf   **PROD** Don Simpson, Jerry Bruckheimer   **DIST** Buena Vista/Hollywood

66 A respectable piece of work with an impressive tough-love performance by Michelle Pfeiffer. – *John N. Smith, Time Out*

66 Dangerous Minds doesn't drop the sentimental aspects of the good-teacher Hollywood drama but reconstitutes them with strong performances, sensitive direction and a firm conviction that teachers can make a difference in a person's life. – *Edward Guthman, San Francisco Chronicle*

'The truth hurts. But a lie can kill.'

A Dangerous Woman ★

DIR Stephen Gyllenhaal
1993   102m   US

☆ *Debra Winger* (Martha Horgan), Barbara Hershey (Anita Bell), Gabriel Byrne (Mackey), David Strathairn (Getso), John Terry (Steve Bell), Chloe Webb (Birdie), *Laurie Metcalf* (Anita)

A frumpy, emotionally disturbed woman finds it impossible to lie – a trait that places her in jeopardy with the law.

Winger is outstanding in a challenging role that almost defies audiences to sympathise with her. An intriguing drama that fails to press all the intended buttons, but highlights genuine moral predicaments.

SCR Naomi Foner   **CIN** Robert Elswit   **MUS** Carter Burwell   **DES** David Brisbin   **ED** Harvey Rosenstock, Angelo Carrao   **PROD** Naomi Foner   **DIST** First Independent/Amblin/Island World/Gramercy/Rollercoaster

66 The film tilts towards an uneasy and disruptive conclusion, its own power being in its oddness, its refusal to be categorised. – *Lizzie Francke, Sight & Sound*

Danny the Champion of the World ★

DIR Gavin Millar
1989   99m   GB
DVD

☆ Jeremy Irons (William Smith), Robbie Coltrane (Victor Hazell), Samuel Irons (Danny), Cyril Cusack (Doc Spencer), Michael Hordern (Lord Claybury), Lionel Jeffries (Mr Snoddy), Ronald Pickup (Captain Lancaster), Jean Marsh (Miss Hunter), Jimmy Nail (Rabbetts), William Armstrong (Springer), John Woodvine (Tallon)

In the 1950s, a resourceful young boy cleverly outwits a grasping local landowner.

A pleasant, straightforward story for family audiences, well acted, with an effortless blend of drama and light comedy.

SCR John Goldsmith   **CIN** Oliver Stapleton   **MUS** Stanley Myers   **DES** Don Homfray   **ED** Peter

DVD Available on DVD   ☆ Cast in order   66 Critics' Quotes   ⚲ Academy Award   Ⓣ BAFTA
♫ Soundtrack on CD   of importance   † Points of interest   ⚲ Academy Award nomination   Ⓣ BAFTA nomination

159

Tanner, Angus Newton **PROD** Eric Abraham **DIST** Portobello Productions

66 Colourful comedy-drama. – *Hal Erickson, New York Times*

† Roald Dahl frequently insisted this was his favourite film adaptation of his children's books.

† Jeremy and Samuel Irons, who play father and son in the film, are father and son in real life.

Daratt (new) ★★

SCR/DIR Mahamat Saleh Haroun
2006 96m Chad/France/Belgium/UK/Austria
DVD

☆ Ali Bacha Barkai (Atim), Youssouf Djaoro (Nassara), Aziza Hisseine (Aicha), Khayar Oumar Défallah (Grandfather)

In Chad in 2006, a teenager boy from a remote village is sent by his grandfather to the city to avenge his father's death.

A quietly telling drama about civil war at domestic and national level, and cycles of violence that can only be ended by forgiveness and reconciliation. Profound and modest in equal measures.

CIN Abraham Haile Biru **MUS** Wasis Diop **ED** Marie-Hélène Dozo **PROD** Abderrahmane Sissako, Mahamat-Saleh Haroun **DIST** Soda

66 Daratt is shot in a carefully composed style and communicates through small gestures and physical interactions rather than striking visual effects. – *Roy Armes, Sight & Sound*

66 A subtly enthralling drama, styled as a sophisticated take on a Western revenge thriller. – *Sukhdev Sandhu, Daily Telegraph*

† The title, Daratt, means 'dry season.'

The Darjeeling Limited (new) ★★

DIR Wes Anderson
2007 91m UK/USA
DVD ♫

☆ Owen Wilson (Francis), Adrien Brody (Peter), Jason Schwartzman (Jack), Anjelica Huston (Sister Patricia), Irrfan Khan (The father), Bill Murray (The businessman)

Three affluent brothers, estranged since their father's death a year earlier, take a train journey through India to re-discover their relationship. They encounter tragedy on the way.

Quirky, sweet-natured and finally touching story about three wounded souls. Yet the suspicion lingers that Anderson is repeating himself, using a canvas of family dysfunction. This eccentric work smacks of an extended in-joke.

SCR Wes Anderson, Jason Schwartzman, Roman Coppola **CIN** Robert Yeoman **DES** Mark Friedberg **ED** Andrew Weisblum **PROD** Wes Anderson, Scott Rudin, Roman Copola, Lydia Dean Pilcher **DIST** TCF

66 Spiritual journeys, even if they're comedies, don't really lend themselves to the extreme, anal-retentive formalism found in every frame. – *Michael Phillips, Chicago Tribune*

66 For all Anderson's pleasing, refreshing auteur tendencies, the overwhelming feeling delivered is of

frustration, déjà vu and little progression. – *Dave Calhoun, Time Out*

† In cinemas, the film was preceded by Hotel Chevalier, a 13-minute short directed by Anderson, and featuring Schwarzman (as Jack) and Natalie Portman. It was billed as 'Part 1 of The Darjeeling Limited'.

'Sworn to protect/Sworn to serve/Sworn to secrecy.'

Dark Blue ★

DIR Ron Shelton
2003 118m US/GB/Germany
DVD ♫

☆ *Kurt Russell* (Eldon Perry), Brendan Gleeson (Jack Van Meter), Scott Speedman (Bobby Keough), Michael Michele (Beth Williamson), Lolita Davidovich (Sally Perry), Ving Rhames (Arthur Holland), Dash Mihok (Gary Sidwell)

Unscrupulous LA cop gives rookie partner a lesson in the grim reality of fighting crime as riots loom.

Kurt Russell shines as an old-school law enforcer, and the pace rarely falters, but the attempts to merge fact and fiction are not always successful.

SCR David Ayer **CIN** Barry Peterson **MUS** Terence Blanchard **DES** J. Dennis Washington **ED** Paul Seydor, Patrick Flannery **PROD** Caldecot Chubb, David Blocker, James Jacks, Sean Daniel **DIST** Momentum

66 If Dark Blue lived up to its star Kurt Russell's turn it would be superb. As it is it's an engaging, tough movie that's far from uniform but only a must-watch for genre aficionados. – *Nev Pierce, BBC*

66 So many things go wrong – stunningly, breathtakingly wrong – throughout so much of Dark Blue that the movie is, somewhat like a spectacular auto wreck, perversely fascinating. – *Joe Leydon, San Francisco Examiner*

† The DVD release includes an audio commentary by Ron Shelton.

Dark Blue World

DIR Jan Sverak
2001 112m Czech Republic/GB
DVD ♫

☆ Ondrej Vetchy (Lt. Frantisek Slama), Krystof Hadek (Karel Vojtisek), Oldrich Kaiser (Machaty), Tara Fitzgerald (Susan Whitmore), Hans- Jorg Assmann (Doctor), Charles Dance (Wing Commander Bentley), Anna Massey (English teacher)

Two Czech pilots join the RAF in World War Two and fall in love with the same English woman.

Watchable if old-fashioned wartime romance, helped off the ground by a well-crafted script and a disturbing finale.

SCR Zdenek Sverak **CIN** Vladimir Smutny **MUS** Ondrej Soukup **DES** Jan Vlasak **ED** Alois Fisarek **PROD** Eric Abraham, Jan Sverak **DIST** Columbia TriStar

66 Dark Blue World has a real emotional pulse. . .it is a fitting requiem for heroes forgotten. – *Michael Wilmington, Chicago Tribune*

† Footage of aerial combat from The Battle of Britain has been used in the film.

DVD Available on DVD	☆ Cast in order of importance	66 Critics' Quotes	⚊ Academy Award	ⓑ BAFTA
♫ Soundtrack on CD		† Points of interest	Academy Award nomination	BAFTA nomination

Dark Days ★★

DIR Marc Singer
2000 94m US
DVD

☆ Marc Singer (Himself)

Documentary exploring the lives of social casualties, driven to exist in an underground community in the railroad tunnels below New York City.

A jolting film that reveals astonishing humour and self-help among the tunnel dwellers as well as human tragedies.

CIN Marc Singer MUS DJ Shadow ED Melissa Neidich PROD Marc Singer, David Wike DIST Optimum

66 It's a near-great film, reminiscent of the early Frederick Wiseman movies like Welfare and Hospital, that left you both aghast and exhilarated at what human beings are capable of. – *Peter Rainer, New York Magazine*

'Even the smallest of light...shines in the darkness.'

The Dark Is Rising (new)

DIR David L. Cunningham
2007 99m US
DVD

☆ Alexander Ludwig (Will Stanton), Christopher Eccleston (The Rider), Ian McShane (Merriman Lyon), Frances Conroy (Miss Greythorne), James Cosmo (Dawson)

A boy is told he is a fabled Signseeker and must collect six signs scattered throughout time and space to stop darkness winning the age-old battle over light.

A confusing, dull, mediocre Harry Potter knock-off with a sketchy plot and fragmented action.

SCR John Hodge CIN Joel Ransom MUS Christophe Beck DES David Lee ED Geoffrey Rowland, Eric Sears PROD Marc Platt DIST Fox

66 "A colourful, juvenile adventure whose clichés and silliness will be acceptable to younger viewers". – *Dennis Harvey, Variety*

66 Occult horror for kids, Dennis Wheatley for the wee ones and fun for the 10-12s. – *Philip French, Observer*

'From The Creators of Japan's Acclaimed RINGU, Inspiration for the hit phenomenon THE RING.'

Dark Water ★

DIR Hideo Nakata
2002 101m Japan
DVD

☆ Hitomi Kuroki (Yoshimi Matsubara), Rio Kanno (Ikuko), Mirei Oguchi (Mitsuko Kawai), Asami Mizukawa (Ikuko, age 16)

Young Japanese mother moves into a new apartment with her daughter to put her traumatic past behind her. But water, spookily dripping from the ceiling, heralds new terrors.

This ponderous horror film takes time to enthral its audience, but it's worth the wait: the climax delivers spine-chilling shocks.

SCR Yoshihiro Nakamura, Ken'ichi Suzuki CIN Junichiro Hayashi MUS Kenji Kawai, Shikao Suga DES Katsumi Nakazawa ED Nobuyuki Takahashi PROD Taka Ichise DIST Metro Tartan

66 The most disturbing spell in the cinema I've had in a very long time. – *Peter Bradshaw, Guardian*

'This Season, The Mystery Of The Darkness Will Consume Your Life.'

Dark Water

DIR Walter Salles
2005 105m US/Japan
DVD ♫

☆ Jennifer Connelly (Dahlia Williams), Dougray Scott (Kyle Williams), Tim Roth (Jeff Platzer), Pete Postlethwaite (Veeck), Ariel Gade (Cici Williams)

When a hard-up young mother is forced to move into rundown New York apartment with her young daughter after a bitter divorce, her troubles really start.

Horror movie without the shocks. Quality cast cannot overcome a disappointing drama.

SCR Rafael Yglesias CIN Affonso Beato MUS Angelo Badalamenti DES Thérèse DePrez ED Daniel Rezende PROD Doug Davison, Roy Lee, Bill Mechanic DIST Buena Vista

66 This re-make of the Japanese original is a solid piece of entertainment that is very watchable, but it is about as frightening as an episode of Little House on the Prairie. – *David Edwards, Daily Mirror*

Dark Wind

DIR Errol Morris
1991 111m US
DVD

☆ Lou Diamond Phillips (Jim Chee), Gary Farmer (Albert Dashee), Fred Ward (Joe Leaphorn), Guy Boyd (Agent Johnson), John Karlen (Jake West), Jane Loranger (Gail Pauling), Gary Basaraba (Larry), Blake Clark (Ben Gaines)

A Navajo cop investigates drugs-related murders which cause angry confrontation with another tribe.

Thriller with an unusual hero, but largely excitement-free. Lou Diamond Phillips seems strangely subdued in the leading role.

SCR Neal Jimenez, Eric Bergren CIN Stefan Czapsky MUS Michel Colombier DES Ted Bafaloukos ED Susan Crutcher, Freeman Davies PROD Patrick Markey DIST Guild/Carolco/North Face Motion Picture Company

66 Dark Wind lacks the suspense necessary to fuel the whodunnit plot and offers disappointingly little insight into the native American lifestyle. – *Channel 4*

The Darkest Light ★★

DIR *Bille Eltringham, Simon Beaufoy*
1999 92m GB/France
DVD

☆ Stephen Dillane (Tom), Kerry Fox (Sue), Keri Arnold (Catherine), Kavita Sungha (Uma), Jason Walton (Matthew), Nisha K. Nayar (Nisha), Nicholas Hope (Father Mark)

While playing on the Yorkshire Dales, two young schoolgirl friends experience a blinding white light, filling one with hope and the other with despair.

A sombre, ambitious film about faith, far removed from the lightweight concerns of most recent British cinema, and rooted in its landscape; perhaps too foreboding for most, it is intriguing, affecting, and, best of all, different.

D

SCR *Simon Beaufoy*   CIN *Mary Farbrother*   MUS *Adrian Johnston*   DES *Chris Townsend*   ED *Ewa J. Lind*   PROD *Mark Blaney*   DIST *Pathé*

66 Impressively thoughtful, thoroughly humane, robust in its drama, alert to its times; one means nothing but praise in asserting it's as valuable as a vintage BBC Play for Today. – *Richard Kelly, Sight and Sound*

66 Everyone who saw The Darkest Light found the film very moving, but hardly anyone did see it. It was only in cinemas for two weeks and that was it: three years of work just gone. I won't keep doing that. It's a waste of time and creativity. I'd rather go off and be a potter instead. – *Simon Beaufoy*

'They destroyed everything he had, everything he was. Now, crime has a new enemy, and justice has a new face.'

Darkman ★

DIR *Sam Raimi*

1990   96m   US

DVD   ♫

☆ Liam Neeson (Peyton Westlake/Darkman), Frances McDormand (Julie Hastings), Colin Friels (Louis Strack Jr.), Larry Drake (Robert G. Durant), Nelson Mashita (Yakitito), Jesse Lawrence Ferguson (Eddie Black), Rafael H. Robledo (Rudy Guzman)

Scientist disfigured by sadistic attackers recovers, using his synthetic skin invention to impersonate and destroy his enemies.

Would-be horror movie that makes up in energy and imagination what it lacks in credibility. Frequently hilarious.

SCR *Chuck Pfarrer, Sam Raimi, Ivan Raimi, Daniel Goldin, Joshua Goldin*   CIN *Bill Pope*   MUS *Danny Elfman*   DES *Randy Ser*   ED *David Stiven, Bud S. Smith*   PROD *Robert Tapert*   DIST *UIP/Universal*

66 Darkman is a frenetic funhouse ride that has you laughing and screaming at the same time. – *Joe Brown, Washington Post*

† The film spawned two sequels.

Darkness in Tallinn ★★

DIR *Ilkka Järvilaturi*

1993   99m   Finland/USA/Sweden/Estonia

☆ Ivo Uukkivi (Toivo), Milena Gulbe (Maria), Enn Klooren (Mikhail), Jüri Järvet (Anton), Väino Laes (Andres), Peeter Dja (Dimitri), Monika Mäger (Terje)

Russian gangsters plot to steal a billion dollars worth of gold in Estonia by persuading a local electrician to cut off the city's electricity. But during the blackout his wife goes into labour and he must restore the power to save the premature baby.

Hugely entertaining bungled-heist movie, laced with dark humour and dynamic camera work.

SCR *Paul Kolsby*   CIN *Rein Kotov*   MUS *Mader*   ED *Christopher Tellefsen*   PROD *Lasse Saarinen*   DIST *Metro/FilmZolfo/Upstream/FilmLance/Teknik/EXITfilm*

66 A gritty and often hilarious crime film. – *Mark Savlov, Austin Chronicle*

66 A funny, suspenseful movie with a properly sharp moral/political edge. – *Time Out*

'When she was good she was very very good. When she was bad, she was. . .'

Darling ★★★

DIR *John Schlesinger*

1965   127m   GB

DVD

☆ *Julie Christie* (Diana Scott), Dirk Bogarde (Robert Gold), Laurence Harvey (Miles Brand), Roland Curram (Malcolm), Alex Scott (Sean Martin), Basil Henson (Alec Prosser-Jones), Pauline Yates (Estelle Gold)

An ambitious young woman deserts her journalist mentor for a company director, an effeminate photographer and an Italian prince.

Fashionable mid-1960s concoction of smart people and their amoral doings. An influential film, presented with high style: many critics of the time made the mistake of assuming it was vacuous because its characters were vacuous. Yet Schlesinger and screenwriter Raphael were clearly critiquing the unconsidered lives of those who inhabited the fashionable circles of Swinging London. The clothes may have dated, but Darling has real resonance in today's celebrity-obsessed era. Christie is splendid as the superficial model who bed-hops her way to the top.

SCR *Frederic Raphael*   CIN *Ken Higgins*   MUS *John Dankworth*   DES *Ray Simm*   ED *James B. Clark*   PROD *Joseph Janni, Victor Lyndon*   DIST *Anglo-Amalgamated/Vic/Appia*

BOGARDE TO CHRISTIE: Your idea of being fulfilled is having more than one man in bed at the same time.

66 As empty of meaning and mind as the empty life it's exposing. – *Pauline Kael*

⚊ Julie Christie (leading actress); Frederic Raphael (original screenplay)

⚊ picture; John Schlesinger (direction)

⚊ Dirk Bogarde (leading actor); Julie Christie (leading actress); Frederic Raphael (original screenplay); Ray Simm

---

Daughters of the Dust ★

SCR/DIR *Julie Dash*

1991   112m   US

DVD

☆ Adisa Anderson (Eli Peazant), Barbara-O (Yellow Mary), Cheryl Lynn Bruce (Viola Peazant), Cora Lee Day (Nana Peazant), Geraldine Dunston (Viola's Mother), Vertamae Grosvenor (Hair Braider), Trula Hoosier (Trula), Kaycee Moore (Haagar Peazant), Alva Rodgers (Eula Peazant), Bahni Turpin (Iona Peazant)

An African-American family prepare to make a journey in 1902 from their simple but idyllic home in the South Carolina Sea Islands to a new life in the industrialised north of the US.

DVD Available on DVD   ☆ Cast in order of importance   66 Critics' Quotes   † Points of interest   ⚊ Academy Award   ⚊ Academy Award nomination   ⚊ BAFTA   ⚊ BAFTA nomination

Eloquent, impressionistic picture of the descendants of slaves struggling to come to terms with a changing world. At times difficult to follow, but always worth the effort.

CIN Arthur Jafa   MUS John Barnes   DES Kerry Marshall   ED Amy Carey, Joseph Burton   PROD Julie Dash, Arthur Jafa, Steven Jones   DIST BFI/American Playhouse/WMG/Geechee Girls

66 This is an astonishing, vivid portrait not only of a time and place, but of an era's spirit. – *Rita Kempley, Washington Post*

'In a country where anybody can become President, anybody just did.'

Dave ★★

DIR Ivan Reitman
1993   110m   US
DVD   ♫

☆ Kevin Kline (Dave Kovic), Sigourney Weaver (Ellen Mitchell), Frank Langella (Bob Alexander), Kevin Dunn (Alan Reed), Ben Kingsley (VP Nance), Charles Grodin (Murray Blum), Ving Rhames (Dueane Stevenson), Faith Prince (Alice), Laura Linney (Randi)

When a US President has a stroke while in bed with one of his aides, an Everyman lookalike is recruited by scheming deputies to impersonate him.

Kevin Kline revels in the role of presidential stand-in, adding gentle humour to a deft, charming script.

SCR *Gary Ross*   CIN Adam Greenberg   MUS James Newton Howard   DES J. Michael Riva   ED Sheldon Kahn   PROD Lauren Schuler-Donner, Ivan Reitman   DIST Warner

66 While this is a light movie it pulls off the impressive feat of blending old-fashioned romance with gentle comedy and a sprinkling of modern satire. – *Almar Haflidason, BBC*

66 Writer Gary Ross clearly knows how to capture the public fancy without dumbing down his work. – *Denver Post*

⚱ Gary Ross

'When there's no more room in hell, the dead will walk the earth.'

Dawn of the Dead ★★

DIR Zack Snyder
2004   101m   US
DVD

☆ Sarah Polley (Ana), Ving Rhames (Kenneth), Jake Weber (Michael), Mekhi Phifer (Andre), Ty Burrell (Steve), Michael Kelly (C J), Kevin Zegers (Terry)

When an apocalyptic plague grips the world, the dead arise from their graves to attack the living.

Higher-budget remake of Romero's 1978 zombie horror classic sees survivors gathering in a shopping mall, and surprisingly generates more wit, emotional depth and scary moments than the original.

SCR James Gunn   CIN Matthew F. Leonetti   MUS Tyler Bates   DES Andrew Neskoromny   ED Niven Howie

PROD Eric Newman, Richard P Rubinstein, Marc Abraham   DIST Universal

66 A terrifying, perfectly executed piece of grade-A horror that transcends its genre roots even as it resolutely nourishes them. – *Brent Simon, Entertainment Today*

'His war will never end. Her love will never die.'

The Dawning ★

DIR Robert Knights
1988   97m   GB
DVD

☆ Trevor Howard (Grandfather), Hugh Grant (Harry), Anthony Hopkins (Cassius aka Angus Barrie), Rebecca Pidgeon (Nancy Gulliver), Jean Simmons (Aunt Mary), Adrian Dunbar (Capt. Rankin), Tara MacGowran (Maeve)

In pre-Partition Ireland a teenage girl, who feels her life is stifling, encounters a persuasive older man who tries to recruit her to the Irish Republican cause.

A tidy little rites-of-passage story, set at a stage of a young woman's life where experience suddenly banishes innocence.

SCR Moira Williams   CIN Adrian Biddle   MUS Simon May   DES Mike Porter   ED Max Lemon   PROD Sarah Lawson   DIST Enterprise/TVS

† This was Trevor Howard's final film appearance.

'Whoever said "Tomorrow is another day". . .didn't check the weather.'

The Day After Tomorrow ★★

DIR *Roland Emmerich*
2004   124m   US
DVD   ♫

☆ Dennis Quaid (Jack Hall), Jake Gyllenhaal (Sam Hall), Ian Holm (Terry Rapson), Emmy Rossum (Laura Chapman), Sela Ward (Dr. Lucy Hall), Dash Mihok (Jason Evans), Kenneth Welsh (Vice President Becker)

A small band of survivors huddle together after the Earth is struck by a second Ice Age.

The first Hollywood blockbuster ever to feature the phrase 'critical desalination point' (and the first to be backed by Al Gore), care of a narrative that cleverly preys on growing concerns about real-world climate change; among the large-scale carnage common to the disaster movie, there's some unusually credible and informed discussion of the most viable response to the mounting crisis, and odd scenes, moments and images that really do send a shiver down the spine.

SCR *Roland Emmerich, Jeffrey Nachimanoff*   CIN Ueli Steiger   MUS Harald Kloser   DES Barry Chusid   ED David Brenner   PROD Roland Emmerich, Mark Gordon   DIST TCF

66 The spectacle, which is colossal and at times staggering to behold, begins within two minutes of the fade-in and keeps coming until the finish. I thought I'd seen it all. I hadn't. – *Mick LaSalle, San Francisco Chronicle*

66 A fast-moving pageant of end-of-the-world eye candy. – *Megan Lehmann, New York Post*

DVD Available on DVD   ☆ Cast in order of importance   66 Critics' Quotes   † Points of interest   ⚱ Academy Award   ⚱ Academy Award nomination   Ⓑ BAFTA   Ⓑ BAFTA nomination

163

Ⓣ Karen E. Goulekas, Neil Corbould, Greg Strause, Remo Balcells (special visual effects)

'Positively The Most Hilarious Picture You've Ever Seen!!!'

A Day at the Races ★★★★

DIR *Sam Wood*
1937   109m   US
DVD

☆ *Groucho Marx* (Dr. Hugo Z. Hackenbush), *Chico Marx* (Tony), *Harpo Marx* (Stuffy), *Margaret Dumont* (Mrs. Upjohn), Maureen O'Sullivan (Judy), Allan Jones (Gil), *Douglass Dumbrille* (Morgan), *Esther Muir* ('Flo'), *Sig Rumann* (Dr. Steinberg)

The Marx Brothers help a girl who owns a sanatorium and a racehorse.

Fashions in Marxism change, but this top quality production, though lacking their zaniest inspirations, does contain several of their funniest routines and a spectacularly well integrated racecourse climax. The musical and romantic asides are a matter of taste but delightfully typical of their time.

SCR *Robert Pirosh, George Seaton, George Oppenheimer* **CIN** *Joseph Ruttenberg* **MUS** Franz Waxman **ED** Frank E. Hull **PROD** Lawrence Weingarten **DIST** MGM

❝ The money is fairly splashed about; the capitalists have recognized the Marx Brothers; ballet sequences, sentimental songs, amber fountains, young lovers. Easily the best film to be seen in London, but all the same I feel a nostalgia for the old cheap rickety sets. – *Graham Greene*

† 'All God's Chillun Got Rhythm'; 'On Blue-Venetian Waters'; 'A Message From the Man in the Moon', 'Tomorrow Is Another Day'

🏆 Dave Gould

The Day I Became A Woman ★★

DIR Marziyeh Meshkini
2000   78m   Iran
DVD

☆ Fatemeh Cherag Akhar (Hava), Shabnam Toloui (Ahoo), Azizeh Sedighi (Hoora)

Three stories, set on an Iranian island, all highlight society's restrictions on women of all ages: a girl who turns nine and can thus no longer play with boys; a woman cyclist being strongly persuaded not to compete in a race; and an old woman compensating for a life of drudgery by buying all the household appliances she has been denied.

This thoughtful trio of mini-movies offers insight into everyday life in Iran, and discreetly celebrates female resilience and good humour under pressure.

SCR Mohsen Makhmalbaf, Marziyeh Meshkini **CIN** Ebrahim Ghafori, Mohammad Ahmadi **MUS** Mohammad Reza Darvishi **ED** Maysam Makhmalbaf, Shahrzad Poya **PROD** Mohsen Makhmalbaf **DIST** Artificial Eye

❝ Eloquent and deeply uplifting, this is foreign film-making at its most accessible and transcendingly joyous. – *Empire*

'From out of space – a warning and an ultimatum!'

The Day the Earth Stood Still ★★

DIR *Robert Wise*
1951   92m   US
♫

☆ *Michael Rennie*, Patricia Neal, Hugh Marlowe, Sam Jaffe, Billy Gray

A flying saucer arrives in Washington and its alien occupant, aided by a robot, demonstrates his intellectual and physical power, warns the world what will happen if wars continue.

Cold-war wish-fulfilment fantasy, impressive rather than exciting but very capably presented with the minimum of trickery and the maximum of sober conviction.

SCR Edmund H. North **CIN** *Leo Tover* **MUS** *Bernard Herrmann* **PROD** Julian Blaustein **DIST** TCF

❝ Quite wry and alarmingly smooth. – *New Yorker, 1977*

Days of Being Wild ★★

SCR/DIR *Kar Wai Wong*
1991   94m   Hong Kong
DVD

☆ Leslie Cheung (Yuddy), Maggie Cheung (Su Lizhen), Andy Lau (Tide), Carina Lau (Leung Fung-Ling), Jacky Cheung (Zeb), Rebecca Pan (Rebecca), Tony Leung (Mo-Wan Chan)

An appealing matinee-idol romance develops into a grimmer story of painful suffering as a womanising playboy creates emotional havoc from Hong Kong to the Phillippines in 1960.

Haunting, brilliantly constructed movie which uses scenes of extreme sensuality and alarming violence to follow the passionate and rootless lives of beautiful people.

CIN Christopher Doyle **DES** William Chang **ED** Kit-Wai Kai, Patrick Tam **PROD** Rover Tang **DIST** Made in Hong Kong/In-Gear

❝ A masterpiece. – *Ty Burr, Boston Globe*

❝ It may have been released in the olden days of 1991 but Kar Wai Wong's Days of Being Wild remains pulsatingly contemporary. . .it's a fascinating ride. – *Desson Thomson, Washington Post*

'The true story of World War II's forgotten heroes.'

Days of Glory ★★★

DIR Rachid Bouchareb
2006   123m   France/Belgium/Morocco/Algeria
DVD

☆ Jamel Debbouze (Saïd), Samy Naceri (Yassir), Roschdy Zem (Messaoud), Sami Bouajila (Abdelkader)

In 1943, four North African men enlist to join the French army and fight in World War II. But in the military, they encounter racial discrimination.

This would be a superior war movie, even without the intriguing subtext that its conscript heroes are marginalised within the ranks. A scene with the quartet

DVD Available on DVD   ☆ Cast in order of importance   ❝ Critics' Quotes   † Points of interest   🏆 Academy Award   🏆 Academy Award nomination   Ⓣ BAFTA   Ⓣ BAFTA nomination
♫ Soundtrack on CD

entering a deserted French village to ward off a German assault is brilliantly executed. More memorable still is the interplay between the four men, with their prickly camaraderie. The irony of their loyalty to a country that despised them is a constant, niggling undercurrent in this outstanding drama.

SCR Olivier Lorelle, Rachid Bouchareb   **CIN** Patrick Blossier   **MUS** Armand Amar, Khaled   **DES** Dominique Douret   **ED** Yannick Kergoat   **PROD** Jean Bréhat   **DIST** Metrodome

66 A passionate, historically important film. – *Jonathan Romney, Sight & Sound*

66 A movingly acted, terrifically old-fashioned World War II picture, re-thought as a post-colonial rebuke. – *Wesley Morris, Boston Globe*

† At the 2006 Cannes Film Festival, the ensemble cast jointly received the Best Actor award.
† After the film's release in France, legislation was passed to allow full pensions to surviving colonial war veterans.

⚱ Foreign language film

'Your eyes – your ears – your senses will be overwhelmed!'

Days of Heaven ★★★

SCR/DIR *Terrence Malick*
1978   95m   US
DVD

☆ Richard Gere (Bill), Brooke Adams (Abby), Sam Shepard (The Farmer), Linda Manz (Linda), Robert Wilke (Farm Foreman), Jackie Shultis (Linda's Friend), Stuart Margolin (Mill Foreman)

In the early 20th century, three young people – two lovers and the man's younger sister – work in the wheat fields of a terminally ill farmer, whose money they aim to take on his death.

Visually a superb slice of period life that turns into a complicated, tragic love triangle. But Malick seems uninterested in the plot; the look's the thing. Unfortunately, it's not quite enough, no matter how gorgeous the images concocted by cinematographer Almendros. In narrative terms, the film finally leaves viewers high and dry.

CIN *Nestor Almendros*   **MUS** Ennio Morricone   **ED** Billy Weber   **PROD** Bert and Harold Schneider   **DIST** Paramount/OP

66 It's serious, yes, very solemn, but not depressing. – *Roger Ebert*

⚱ Nestor Almendros
⚱ Ennio Morricone
Ⓣ Ennio Morricone

'What a day. What a trip.'

The Daytrippers ★★

SCR/DIR *Greg Mottola*
1996   87m   US
DVD

☆ *Hope Davis* (Eliza Malone D'Amico), Pat McNamara (Jim Malone), Anne Meara (Rita Malone), Parker Posey (Jo Malone), Liev Schreiber (Carl Petrovic), Stanley Tucci (Louis D'Amico), Campbell Scott (Eddie Masler), Marcia Gay Harden (Libby), Andy Brown (Ronnie)

A Long Island housewife discovers a love letter apparently addressed to her husband, and sets off with her family to confront him at his workplace in Manhattan.

Spirited ensemble comedy, with a fine cast striking sparks off one another within the confines of a small car.

CIN John Inwood   **MUS** Richard Martinez   **DES** Bonnie J. Brinkley   **ED** Anne McCabe   **PROD** Nancy Tenenbaum, Steven Soderbergh   **DIST** Metrodome/Fiasco/Trick Films

66 Indie cinema and Neil Simon intersect on the corner of pathos and farce. – *Tom Charity, Time Out*

66 Low-budget perfection, a comedy without a false note and without a flat joke. – *Mick LaSalle, San Francisco Chronicle*

'It was the last day of school in 1976, a time they'd never forget. . .if only they could remember.'

Dazed and Confused ★★

SCR/DIR *Richard Linklater*
1993   103m   US
DVD   ♫

☆ Jason London (Randall 'Pink' Floyd), Wiley Wiggins (Mitch Kramer), Milla Jovovich (Michelle Burroughs), Rory Cochrane (Ron Slater), Shawn Andrews (Kevin Pickford), Adam Goldberg (Mike Newhouse), Anthony Rapp (Tony Olsen), Sasha Jenson (Don Dawson), Matthew McConaughey (David Wooderson), Ben Affleck (Fred O'Bannion)

A group of 1976 high-school leavers mark their exit by tormenting and bullying luckless younger kids.

Hip teenage movie which perceptively highlights the humour of adolescents determined to avoid growing up at all costs.

CIN Lee Daniel   **DES** John Frick   **ED** Sandra Adair   **PROD** James Jacks, Sean Daniel, Richard Linklater   **DIST** Feature/Universal/Gramercy/Alphaville

66 Seriously funny and shorn of any hint of nostalgia or wish fulfilment, this is pretty much where it's at. – *Time Out*

† The film takes its title from a track on Led Zeppelin's 1969 debut album, written by Jake Holmes.
† Though it now enjoys cult status, Dazed and Confused grossed less than $10 million in the US on its release.

The Dead ★★★

DIR *John Huston*
1987   83m   GB
♫

☆ Anjelica Huston (Gretta Conroy), Donal McCann (Gabriel Conroy), Rachel Dowling (Lily), Cathleen Delany (Aunt Julia Morkan), Dan O'Herlihy (Mr. Browne), Helena Carroll (Aunt Kate Morkan), Donal Donnelly (Freddy Malins)

Two Irish spinster sisters throw a winter dinner for their relatives and friends.

Director Huston's last film, a moving swan song to a remarkable career, is a warm and somehow invigorating reminiscence of things past.

SCR Tony Huston CIN Fred Murphy MUS Alex North
DES Stephen Grimes, Dennis Washington ED Roberto
Silvi PROD Wieland Schulz-Keil, Chris Sievernich
DIST Vestron/Zenith/Liffey Films

66 A delicate coda in a minor key to an illustrious 46-year
career. – *Daily Variety*

66 A small masterpiece, perfectly achieved. – *Time
Out*

⚱ Tony Huston (adapted screenplay); Dorothy Jeakins
(costume design)

'A Voyage Into Fear.'

Dead Calm ★

DIR Phillip Noyce
1988 96m Australia
DVD

☆ Nicole Kidman (Rae Ingram), Sam Neill (John Ingram),
Billy Zane (Hughie Warriner), Rod Mulliner (Russell
Bellows), Joshua Tilden (Danny), George Shevtsov
(Doctor), Michael Long (Doctor)

A married couple go sailing to try to get over the
death of their son, but their lives are threatened by a
sinister stranger.

*Chilling but uneven thriller that just managed to stay
afloat despite some improbable action and helped
launch Nicole Kidman's career.*

SCR Terry Hayes CIN Dean Semler MUS Graeme
Revell, Tim O'Connor, SPK, The Tokens DES Graham
'Grace' Walker ED Richard Francis-Bruce PROD Terry
Hayes, Doug Mitchell, George Miller
DIST Warner/Kennedy Miller Productions

66 Dead Calm generates genuine tension because the
story is so simple and the performances are so
straightforward. – *Roger Ebert, Chicago Sun-Times*

'No One Can Survive Becoming A Legend.'

Dead Man ★

SCR/DIR Jim Jarmusch
1995 121m US/Germany
DVD ♫

☆ Johnny Depp (William Blake), Gary Farmer (Nobody),
Lance Henriksen (Cole Wilson), Robert Mitchum (John
Dickinson), Crispin Glover (Train Fireman), Gabriel Byrne
(Charlie Dickinson), John Hurt (John Schofield), Alfred
Molina (Trading Post Missionary), Michael Wincott
(Conway Twill), Mili Avital (Thel Russell), Iggy Pop
(Salvatore 'Sally' Jenko), Jared Harris (Benmont Trench),
Billy Bob Thornton (Big George Drakoulious)

An accident-prone accountant goes into the Wild
West of the late 19th century where he is wrongly
accused of murder. A noble Indian comes to the
rescue.

*Watchable Western with a thoughtful, inventive script
and a memorable central performance by Depp. High
on originality, low on pace.*

CIN Robby Müller MUS Neil Young DES Robert
Ziembicki ED Jay Rabinowitz PROD Demetra J.
MacBride DIST Electric/12-Gauge/Pandora

66 Jim Jarmusch movies are so laconic, slow-moving and
cold that if they were human you'd wonder if they weren't
victims of extremely low blood pressure. Even with the

wonderful Johnny Depp starring Dead Man suffers the
usual circulatory problems. – *Barbara Shulgasser, San
Francisco Examiner*

Dead Man Walking ★★★

SCR/DIR *Tim Robbins*
1995 122m US/GB
DVD ♫

☆ *Susan Sarandon* (Sister Helen Prejean), *Sean Penn*
(Matthew Poncelet), Robert Prosky (Hilton Barber),
Raymond J. Barry (Earl Delacroix), R. Lee Ermey
(Clyde Percy), Celia Weston (Mary Beth Percy), Lois
Smith (Helen's mother), Scott Wilson (Chaplain
Farley)

A Catholic nun reaches out to a savage double
murderer on Death Row and inspires
repentance.

*A thoughtful, well-crafted confrontation between good
and evil with two outstanding central performances. In
the wrong hands, this material could have made for a
dreadful, cloying movie; instead it is richly rewarding,
though never easy viewing.*

CIN *Roger A. Deakins* MUS David Robbins
DES Richard Hoover ED Lisa Zeno Churgin, Ray Hubley
PROD John Kilik, Tim Robbins, Rudd Simmons
DIST Polygram/Working Title/Havoc

66 An intelligent, balanced, devastating movie. – *Hal
Hinson, Washington Post*

66 Absorbing, surprising, technically superb and worth
talking about for a long time afterward. – *Roger Ebert,
Chicago Sun-Times*

⚱ Susan Sarandon (leading actress)
⚱ Sean Penn (leading actor); Tim Robbins; Bruce
Springsteen (music, original song 'Dead Man
Walking')

'He's in all of us.'

Dead Man's Shoes ★★

DIR Shane Meadows
2004 90m GB
DVD ♫

☆ Paddy Considine (Richard), Gary Stretch (Sonny), Toby
Kebbell (Anthony), Stuart Wolfenden (Horbie), Neil Bell
(Soz), Paul Sadot (Tuff), Jo Hartley (Marie), Seamus
O'Neill (Big Al)

A bitter ex-soldier returns to his dismal English
home town to take a cruel yet deserved revenge
on the local thugs who tortured his retarded
brother.

*There's a grim fascination about the central character's
determination to mete out his brand of rough justice in
this brutally realistic film.*

SCR Paddy Considine, Shane Meadows, Paul Fraser
CIN Daniel Cohen MUS Aphex Twin ED Chris Wyatt,
Lucas Roche, Celia Haining PROD Mark Herbert
DIST Optimum

66 Death Wish comes to the streets of Derbyshire. – *Jamie
Russell, BBC*

66 There's a hint of Shakespeare's goriest tragedies here,
sucked dry of any attendant heart or compelling human
interest. – *Jessica Reaves, Los Angeles Times*

DVD Available on DVD ☆ Cast in order 66 Critics' Quotes ⚱ Academy Award Ⓑ BAFTA
♫ Soundtrack on CD of importance † Points of interest ⚱ Academy Award nomination Ⓑ BAFTA nomination

'He was their inspiration. He made their lives extraordinary.'

Dead Poets Society ★★

DIR Peter Weir

1989 128m US

DVD ♫

☆ Robin Williams (John Keating), Robert Sean Leonard (Neil Perry), Ethan Hawke (Todd Anderson), Josh Charles (Knox Overstreet), Gale Hansen (Charlie Dalton), Dylan Kussman (Richard Cameron), Allelon Ruggiero (Steven Meeks), James Waterston (Gerard Pitts), Norman Lloyd (Mr. Nolan)

A free-thinking new English teacher encourages pupils at his New England school to ignore tradition and express themselves.

Powerful Robin Williams performance dominates, but a decent supporting cast and shrewd script contribute to the whole. A succession of lesser films of this ilk make it seem more hackneyed now than on its release.

SCR Tom Schulman CIN John Seale MUS Maurice Jarre DES Wendy Stites ED William Anderson PROD Steven Haft, Paul Junger Witt, Tony Thomas DIST Warner/Touchstone/Silver Screen Partners IV/Witt-Thomas Productions

❝ Solid, smart entertainment. – *Desson Howe, Washington Post*

❝ Sings whenever Williams is on screen. – *Variety.*

🗲 Tom Schulman (original screenplay)

🗲 picture; Robin Williams (leading actor); Peter Weir

🛡 film; Maurice Jarre

Ⓣ Robin Williams (leading actor); Peter Weir; Tom Schulman (original screenplay); William Anderson

---

'Dirty Harry Just Learned A New Game'

The Dead Pool ★

DIR Buddy Van Horn

1988 91m US

DVD

☆ Clint Eastwood (Insp. 'Dirty' Harry Callahan), Patricia Clarkson (Samantha Walker), Liam Neeson (Peter Swan), Evan C. Kim (Insp. Al Quan), David Hunt (Harlan Rook / Ed Butler), Michael Currie (Capt. Donnelly), Michael Goodwin (Lt. Ackerman), Darwin Gillett (Patrick Snow), Anthony Charnota (Lou Janero)

'Dirty' Harry Callahan investigates a demented film fan who appears to be killing off minor celebrities to win the 'Dead Pool' game, in which people bet on which star will die next.

The fifth outing for Dirty Harry, and it's by no means a classic; yet Eastwood, as always, has his moments, Neeson has an amusing turn as a British director of horror movies – and the Dead Pool game sounds like genuine, if tasteless fun.

SCR Steve Sharon CIN Jack N. Green MUS Lalo Schifrin DES Edward C. Carfagno ED Ron Spang PROD David Valdes DIST Warner/Malpaso

---

'In this daring heist, the only colour that counts is green.'

Dead Presidents ★★

DIR Allen Hughes, Albert Hughes

1995 119m US

DVD ♫

☆ Larenz Tate (Anthony Curtis), Keith David (Kirby), Chris Tucker (Skip), Freddy Rodriguez (Jose), Rose Jackson (Juanita Benson), N'Bushe Wright (Delilah Benson), Bokeem Woodbine (Cleon), Martin Sheen (uncredited) (The Judge)

An Afro-American Vietnam vet returns to the US to find a pimp controlling his girlfriend and child, and turns to crime.

Gritty, pessimistic thriller packed with violence and unpleasant characters. Yet it has the tang of realism. Impeccably chosen soundtrack of period r&b tracks.

SCR Michael Henry Brown CIN Lisa Rinzler MUS Danny Elfman DES David Brisbin ED Dan Lebental PROD Allen Hughes, Albert Hughes DIST Buena Vista/Hollywood/Caravan/Underworld

❝ A grim, extremely violent and uneven story. – *Peter Stack, San Francisco Chronicle*

'Two bodies. Two minds. One soul. Separation can be a terrifying thing.'

Dead Ringers ★★

DIR David Cronenberg

1988 115m Canada

DVD

☆ *Jeremy Irons* (Beverly Mantle/Elliot Mantle), Geneviève Bujold (Claire Niveau), Heidi von Palleske (Cary), Barbara Gordon (Danuta), Shirley Douglas (Laura), Stephen Lack (Anders Wolleck), Nick Nicholas (Leo), Lynne Cormack (Arlene)

Identical twin gynaecologists happily share everything, until a beautiful woman comes between them.

Resolutely weird and disturbing psychological chiller which requires effort to sustain suspension of disbelief, though it's based on a true story. Irons' virtuoso double act is what lingers in the memory.

SCR David Cronenberg, Norman Snider CIN Peter Suschitzky MUS Howard Shore DES Carol Spier ED Ronald Sanders PROD David Cronenberg, Marc Boyman DIST Rank/The Mantle Clinic II/Morgan Creek Productions

❝ An astonishing tour de force, especially for Irons, whose sense of nuance is so refined that one can tell in a matter of seconds which twin he is playing. – *Jonathan Rosenbaum, Chicago Reader*

'You scream. You die.'

Dead Silence (new)

DIR James Wan

2007 90m US

DVD ♫

☆ Ryan Kwanten (Jamie Ashen), Amber Valletta (Ella Ashen), Donnie Wahlberg (Det. Jim Lipton), Bob Gunton (Edward Ashen), Laura Regan (Lisa Ashen), Judith Roberts (Mary Shaw)

A young man comes to suspect a possessed ventriloquist's dummy of murdering his wife.

DVD Available on DVD   ☆ Cast in order   ❝ Critics' Quotes   🗲 Academy Award   🛡 BAFTA
♫ Soundtrack on CD   of importance   ✝ Points of interest   🗲 Academy Award nomination   Ⓣ BAFTA nomination

An old-fashioned throwback in the vein of Magic and the Michael Redgrave section of Dead of Night; the result is bizarre without being remotely scary.

SCR Leigh Whannell **CIN** John R. Leonetti **MUS** Charlie Clouser **DES** Julie Berghoff **ED** Michael N. Knue **PROD** Gregg Hoffman, Oren Koules, Mark Burg **DIST** Universal

66 You'd need an extravagant love of hokum not to feel mildly bored. – *Anthony Quinn, Independent*

66 To say the dummy has more personality than the live cast would be an overstatement. – *John Anderson, Variety*

† At one point the Jigsaw doll from the director's earlier film Saw can briefly be seen sitting on the floor.

Dear Diary ★★

SCR/DIR *Nanni Moretti*
1994   100m   Italy/France
♫

☆ Nanni Moretti (Himself), Jennifer Beals (Herself), Alexandre Rockwell (Himself), Renato Carpentieri (Gerardo), Antonio Neiwiller (Mayor of Stromboli)

A highly personal filmed essay which moves from a trip around Rome on a Vespa and a meeting with actress Jennifer Beals, to a voyage around the Aeolian Isles with a TV-obsessed friend, to a disturbing experience of cancer treatment in the Italian health service.

Three-part autobiographical movie in which Moretti reveals with charm, humour and perception a great deal about Italy and even more about himself. He's strongest on the subject of personal morality, though at times his self-regard is exhausting.

CIN Giuseppe Lanci **MUS** Nicola Piovani **DES** Marta Maffucci **ED** Mirco Garrone **PROD** Angelo Barbagallo, Nanni Moretti, Nella Banfi **DIST** Artificial Eye/Sacher/Banfilm/La Sept/Canal

66 As Moretti travels around, investigating and commenting, he manages to provoke not only laughter, but the sense that we are seeing Italy anew. – *Time Out*

66 Dear Diary makes it clear why Nanni Moretti is often called the Woody Allen of Italy. – *Marjorie Baumgarten*

'Tonight, mercy will be buried with the past.'

Death and the Maiden ★★

DIR *Roman Polanski*
1994   103m   GB/US/France
DVD   ♫

☆ *Sigourney Weaver* (Paulina Escobar), Ben Kingsley (Dr. Roberto Miranda), Stuart Wilson (Gerardo Escobar), Krystia Mova (Dr. Miranda's Wife)

In an unnamed South American country a woman captures the man she believes raped and tortured her in the days of a previous, oppressive regime. She puts him on trial at gunpoint.

Tense psychological thriller, expertly written, acted and directed at close quarters.

SCR *Rafael Yglesias, Ariel Dorfman* **CIN** Tonino delli Colli **MUS** Wojciech Kilar **DES** Pierre Guffroy **ED** Herve de Luze **PROD** Thom Mount, Josh Kramer **DIST** Electric/Capitol/Channel 4/Flach/Canal

66 Director Roman Polanski restores the play to the pulse-pounding political thriller it is. His electrifying film nearly jumps off the screen. – *Peter Travers, Rolling Stone*

'Last rites. . .and wrongs.'

Death at a Funeral (new)

DIR Frank Oz
2007   90m   US/UK/Germany
DVD

☆ Matthew Macfadyen (Daniel), Rupert Graves (Robert), Peter Dinklage (Peter), Jane Asher (Sandra), Keeley Hawes (Jane), Daisy Donovan (Martha), Kris Marshall (Troy), Alan Tudyk (Simon), Peter Vaughan (Uncle Alfie), Ewen Bremner (Justin)

Attempts to bury the head of an extended English family are confounded by his male ex-lover, a relative on drugs and an incontinent geriatric.

Strained black comedy with a large cast; some amusing moments but largely irritating.

SCR Dean Craig **CIN** Oliver Curtis **MUS** Murray Gold **DES** Michael Howells **ED** Beverley Mills **PROD** Sidney Kimmel, Share Stallings, Laurence Malkin, Diana Phillips **DIST** Verve Pictures

SANDRA: 'Tea can do many things, Jane, but it can't bring back the dead.'

66 Complications, confusion, desperation and embarrassment, all spiked with a twist of blackmail. – *Jonathan Crocker, Time Out*

66 A fine British cast is wasted on feeble material. – *Philip French, Observer*

'Your basic black comedy.'

Death Becomes Her ★

DIR Robert Zemeckis
1992   104m   US
DVD   ♫

☆ Meryl Streep (Madeline Ashton), Goldie Hawn (Helen Sharp), Bruce Willis (Dr Ernest Menville), Isabella Rossellini (Lisle von Rhoman), Ian Ogilvy (Chagall), Adam Storke (Dakota), Nancy Fish (Rose), Alaina Reed Hall (Psychologist), Michelle Johnson (Anna), Mary Ellen Trainor (Vivian Adams)

Two women, friends from childhood, become bitter rivals as they compete for the same man and the mysterious elixir of eternal life.

Fast-moving, amusing, and often barbed comedy that relies a little too heavily on eye-popping special effects.

SCR Martin Donovan, David Koepp **CIN** Dean Cundey **MUS** Alan Silvestri **DES** Rick Carter **ED** Arthur Schmidt **PROD** Robert Zemeckis, Steve Starkey **DIST** UIP/Universal

66 A clumsy but nonetheless amusing satire on the desperation of the beauty obsessed movie industry. – *Matt Ford, BBC*

⚬ Ken Ralston, Doug Chiang, Douglas Smythe, Tom Woodruff Jr. (visual effects)

Ⓣ Michael Lantien, Ken Ralston, Alec Gillis, Tom Woodruff Jr., Doug Chiang, Douglas Smythe (special effects)

DVD Available on DVD   ☆ Cast in order of importance   66 Critics' Quotes   ⚬ Academy Award   Ⓣ BAFTA
♫ Soundtrack on CD   † Points of interest   Academy Award nomination   BAFTA nomination

'The human whose name is written in this note shall die.'

Death Note (new)   ★★

DIR Shusuke Kaneko

2008   126m   Japan

DVD

☆ Tatsuya Fujiwara (Light Yagami), Ken'ichi Matsuyama (L), Asaka Seto (Naomi Misora), Shigeki Hosokawa (FBI Agent Ray)

A law student finds a notebook that kills the person whose name is written on its pages. Using this supernatural gift, he starts killing all unpunished criminals and becomes a national hero.

Low-key horror and constantly twisting action, with the accent on psychological and philosophical chills rather than easy scares.

SCR Tetsyua Oishi   CIN Hiroshi Takase   MUS Kenji Kawai   DES Hajime Oikawa   ED Yosuke Yafune   PROD Toyoharu Fukuda, Takahiro Kobashi, Takahiro Sato   DIST Blue Dolphin

66 "A little overlong, but clever and gripping". – *Philip French, Observer*

The Death of Mr. Lazarescu   ★★

DIR Cristi Puiu

2005   154m   Romania

DVD

☆ Ioan Fiscuteanu (Dante Lazarescu), Luminita Gheorghiu (Mioara), Doru Ana (Sandu Sterian)

An old man calls the ambulance service to complain about a headache. He is shuttled between hospitals, and his condition gradually deteriorates.

An appalling, though darkly funny story about the hellishness of health service bureaucracies and the indifference of staff contrasted with the life-or-death condition of one patient. Engaging and eloquent.

SCR Cristi Puiu, Razvan Radulescu   CIN Oleg Mutu   ED Dana Bunescu   PROD Bobby Paunescu, Anca Puiu   DIST Tartan

66 For all its terrible matter-of-factness, [it] produces tumultuous feelings of amazement and revolt. – *David Denby, New Yorker*

66 I suspect medical professionals would see much they recognise in this movie. – *Roger Ebert, Chicago Sun-Times*

'These 8 women are about to meet 1 diabolical man!'

Death Proof   ★

SCR/DIR Quentin Tarantino

2007   111m   US

☆ Kurt Russell (Stuntman Mike), Rosario Dawson (Abernathy), Zoe Bell (Herself), Tracie Thoms (Kim), Rose McGowan (Pam), Sydney Tamila Poitier (DJ Jungle Julia), Jordan Ladd (Shanna), Vanessa Ferlito (Arlene), Mary Elizabeth Winstead (Lee), Omar Doom (Nate), Eli Roth (Dov), Quentin Tarantino (Chili Parlour proprietor), Michael Parks (Texas Ranger Earl McGraw)

In Texas, three women go out on the town, unaware they are being stalked by Mike, a scarred stuntman who uses his car as a murderous weapon. Months later in Tennessee, Mike tries his lethal game on four other women, two of them in the stunt game. They decide to get their revenge.

There are watchable elements here: stuntwoman Zoe Bell straddling her car's bonnet in a thrilling high-speed chase, and decent work by Russell as the homicidal Mike. Yet Tarantino has lost the edge and verve that made him so cool and compelling. Here he salutes cheap, trashy 1970s exploitation films that never outstayed their welcome, yet he pads out his film with dreary, rambling speeches; this from a man whose snappy, smart dialogue was once a trademark. Equally tedious is the way he imposes his taste on audiences with gratuitous name-checks for records or films: a control freakery that allows no dissenting opinion.

CIN Quentin Tarantino   DES Steve Joyner, Caylah Eddlebute   ED Sally Menke   PROD Quentin Tarantino, Erica Steinberg, Elizabeth Avellan, Robert Rodriguez   DIST Momentum

66 The movie won't do much for anyone who doesn't have an academic or fanboy absorption in junk. – *David Denby, New Yorker*

66 Long-winded and juvenile. – *Mick LaSalle, San Francisco Chronicle*

† In the US, Death Proof was part of Grindhouse, a two-in-one homage to 1970s exploitation movies, along with Robert Rodriguez's Planet Terror. The two films were separated by trailers for spoof movies. In the UK, the two films were released separately; Tarantino added to the length of Death Proof for its individual release.

Death Sentence (new)

DIR James Wan

2007   105m   US

DVD

☆ Kevin Bacon (Nick Hume), Garrett Hedlund (Billy Darley), Kelly Preston (Helen Hume), John Goodman (Bones Darley)

When an insurance executive sees his son murdered in a gas-station hold-up, he vows revenge on the guilty gang.

An unholy mess, with Bacon as a mild-mannered family man becoming a cut-price Robocop, shaving his head, brandishing huge weapons and outrunning gang members half his age before gunning them down.

SCR Ian Mackenzie Jeffers   CIN John R. Leonetti   MUS Charlie Clouser   DES Julie Berghoff   ED Michael N.Knue   PROD Ashok Amritraj, Howard Baldwin, Karen Baldwin   DIST Entertainment

66 The movie has nothing to offer except titillation. – *Michael Sragow, Baltimore Sun*

'Some debts can never be paid.'

The Debt Collector

SCR/DIR Anthony Neilson

1999   109m   GB

DVD

☆ Billy Connolly (Dryden), Ken Stott (Keltie), Francesca Annis (Val), Iain Robertson (Flipper), Annette Crosbie (Lana), Alastair Galbraith (Colouhdun)

DVD Available on DVD   ☆ Cast in order   66 Critics' Quotes   Academy Award   BAFTA
♫ Soundtrack on CD   of importance   † Points of interest   Academy Award nomination   BAFTA nomination

169

In Glasgow, a reformed gangster's best-selling crime books attract the attentions of both a grudge-bearing detective and an aspirant young hoodlum.

Violent melodrama with semi-interesting ideas about class resentment, though these are quickly drowned out by histrionic acting and a wildly overwrought score.

CIN Dick Pope   MUS Adrian Johnston   DES Mark Geraghty   ED John Wilson   PROD Graham Broadbent, Damian Jones

66 A creditable addition to the long line of hard, mean, atmospheric British thrillers. – *Angie Errigo, Empire*

66 Relentlessly grim rather than inevitably tragic and none too enlightening. To be brutally candid, it made me sick. – *Alexander Walker, Evening Standard*

'After that summer nothing would ever be the same again.'

December Boys (new)

DIR Rod Hardy
2007   105m   Australia/US

☆ Daniel Radcliffe (Maps), Lee Cormie (Misty), Christian Byers (Spark), James Fraser (Spit), Jack Thompson (Bandy McAnsh), Teresa Palmer (Lucy), Sullivan Stapleton (Fearless), Victoria Hill (Teresa)

Four Australian teens in an orphanage, sent to the seaside for the summer, compete to be adopted by a likable couple.

Well-intentioned but teeth-grindingly earnest story, with a voice-over that seems to consist entirely of clichés. Daniel Radcliffe, in his first departure role since his debut as Harry Potter, looks understandably ill-at-ease throughout.

SCR Marc Rosenberg   CIN David Connell   MUS Carlo Giacco   DES Leslie Binns   ED Dany Cooper   PROD Richard Becker   DIST Warners

66 Quite the most pretentious piffle I've seen all year. – *Anthony Quinn, Independent*

66 A little more bit would have done December Boys a power of good. – *Derek Malcolm, Evening Standard*

Deception (new)

DIR Marcel Langenegger
2008   107m   US

☆ *Hugh Jackman* (Wyatt Bose), *Ewan McGregor* (Jonathan McQuarry), Michelle Williams (S), Lisa Gay Hamilton (Detective Russo), Maggie Q (Tina)

Meek accountant is lured by a sinister playboy into a twilight world of lurid sex clubs, fraud and murder.

Overwrought, contrived suspense-and-suspenders thriller.

SCR Mark Bomback   CIN Dante Spinotti   MUS Ramin Djawadi   DES Patrizia von Brandenstein   ED Douglas Crise, Christian Wagner   PROD Robbie Brenner, Hugh Jackman, David L. Bushell, Christopher Eberts, John Palermo, Arnold Rifkin, Marjorie Skik
DIST Entertainment

66 "Mildly titillating but not very good". – *Kim Newman, Empire*

66 Everything is wrong pretty much from the start of this misbegotten adventure in Adrian Lyne territory, including but not limited to the strained mind games that drive the plot, and the tentative New York accents on the actors from Australia and Scotland. – *Lisa Schwarzbaum, Entertainment Weekly*

'Harry Block Wrote A Bestseller About His Friends. Now, His Best Friends Are About To Become His Worst Enemies.'

Deconstructing Harry ★★

SCR/DIR Woody Allen
1997   96m   US
DVD

☆ Woody Allen (Harry Block), Caroline Aaron (Doris), Kirstie Alley (Joan), Bob Balaban (Richard), Richard Benjamin (Hen/Harry's character), Eric Bogosian (Burt), Billy Crystal (Larry/The Devil (Harry's Character)), Judy Davis (Lucy), Hazelle Goodman (Cookie), Mariel Hemingway (Beth Kramer), Amy Irving (Jane), Julie Kavner (Grace/Harry's character), Julia Louis-Dreyfus (Leslie/Harry's character), Tobey Maguire (Harvey Stern/Harry's character), Demi Moore (Helen/Harry's character), Elisabeth Shue, Stanley Tucci, Robin Williams

A sexually prolific writer upsets his friends and family by persistently using their private lives as material for his novels.

Sour, witty, sometimes self-indulgent comedy, crafted from a writer's chaotic life. It rattles along fast enough that if a joke falls flat, there's another one along any second.

CIN Carlo Di Palma   DES Santo Loquasto   ED Susan E. Morse   PROD Jean Doumanian   DIST Fine Line

66 A scathing look at one man's disastrous experiences with marriage, adultery and the literary life. – *Kenneth Turan, Los Angeles Times*

⚱ Woody Allen (original screenplay)

'Until Now We've Only Touched The Surface.'

Deep Blue ★★

DIR Alastair Fothergill, Andy Byatt
2003   83m   GB/Germany
DVD

☆ Michael Gambon (Narrator)

Documentary look at life under water which uses visuals shot for the BBC wildlife television series Blue Planet.

From savage killer whales in the Arctic's freezing depths to jellyfish lazily sunning themselves on a coral reef, all undersea life seems to be here. Fascinating for nautical nature lovers.

SCR Alastair Fothergill, Andy Byatt, Tim Ecott
CIN Michael deGruy, Rick Rosenthal   MUS George Fenton   ED Martin Elsbury   PROD Alix Tidmarsh, Sophokles Tasioulis

66 The big screen adds extra impact to inspiring images which capture all the brutality, camaraderie and absurdity of the ocean. – *Empire*

'He'd be the perfect criminal if he wasn't the perfect cop.'

Deep Cover ★★

DIR *Bill Duke*
1992   107m   US
DVD   ♫

☆ *Larry Fishburne* (Russell Stevens, Jr./John Hull/Narrator), *Jeff Goldblum* (David Jason), Victoria

---

Dillard (Betty McCutcheon), Charles Martin Smith (DEA Agent Gerald Carver), Gregory Sierra (Felix Barbosa), Clarence Williams III (Taft), Sydney Lassick (Gopher)

Gnarled mid-West undercover cop struggles to infiltrate a Californian drugs ring with powerful connections.

Suspenseful but faintly shambling thriller that constantly surprises with its energy and originality.

SCR Michael Tolkin, Henry Bean   CIN Bojan Bazelli   MUS Michel Colombier   DES Pam Warner   ED John Carter   PROD Pierre David, Henry Bean   DIST First Independent/Image Organisation

66 What emerges is a powerhouse thriller full of surprises, original touches, and rare political lucidity, including an impressive performance by Jeff Goldblum. – *Jonathan Rosenbaum, Chicago Reader*

66 A convoluted and mostly unconvincing portrait of the drug underworld, Deep Cover still carries some resonance due to its vivid picture of societal decay and a heavyweight performance by Larry Fishburne. – *Variety*

The Deep End ★

SCR/DIR Scott McGehee, David Siegel
2001   101m   US
[DVD]   ♫

☆ Tilda Swinton (Margaret Hall), Goran Visnjic (Alek Spera), Jonathan Tucker (Beau Hal), Raymond Barry (Carlie Nagle), Josh Lucas (Darby Reese), Peter Donat (Jack Hall), Tamara Hope (Paige Hall), Jordan Dorrance (Dylan Hall)

A loving mother covers up a death caused by her gay son, only for a blackmailer to show up on the family's doorstep.

Clever-clever thriller, strong on watery symbolism, but rather implausible when it gets round to wheeling on that rarest of cinematic beasts: the extortionist with a heart of gold.

CIN *Giles Nuttgens*   MUS Peter Nashel   DES Kelly McGehee, Christopher Tandon   ED Lauren Zuckerman   PROD Scott McGehee, David Siegel   DIST TCF

66 Displays a promise it doesn't, in the end, live up to. – *Owen Gleiberman, Entertainment Weekly*

† The source novel had been filmed once before, as the Max Ophuls picture The Reckless Moment (1949).

'The search for her son was over. The search for her family was just beginning.'

The Deep End of the Ocean ★★

DIR Ulu Grosbard
1999   106m   US
[DVD]   ♫

☆ *Michelle Pfeiffer* (Beth Cappadora), *Treat Williams* (Pat Cappadora), Whoopi Goldberg (Candy Bliss), Jonathan Jackson (Vincent Cappadora), Ryan Merriman (Sam), John Kapelos (George Karras), Michael McElroy (Ben Cappadora), Cory Buck (Vincent Cappadora, aged 7), Alexa Vega (Kerry Cappadora), Michael McGrady (Jimmy Daugherty), Brenda Strong (Ellen), Rose Gregorio (Rosie)

Nine years after their toddler is kidnapped, a family suspects that a 12 year old boy come to mow their lawn is their missing son.

The sort of domestic drama premise that is churned out weekly in TV movies, but the fine acting here and the emotional complexities depicted, lift it into a higher category altogether. Pfeiffer conveys a mother's grief and guilt with great skill.

SCR Stephen Schiff   CIN Stephen Goldblatt   MUS Elmer Bernstein   DES Dan Davis   ED John Bloom   PROD Kate Guinzberg, Steve Nicolaides   DIST Columbia/Mandalay/Via Rosa

66 So finely crafted, so alive with wonderful acting and an extraordinary commitment to realism that most audiences will be happy to surrender themselves to its improbable ride. – *Andrew O'Hehir, Salon.com*

'Oceans Rise. Cities Fall. Hope Survives.'

Deep Impact ★

DIR Mimi Leder
1998   120m   US
[DVD]   ♫

☆ Robert Duvall (Capt. Spurgeon 'Fish' Tanner), Téa Leoni (Jenny Lerner), Elijah Wood (Leo Beiderman), Vanessa Redgrave (Robin Lerner), Maximilian Schell (Jason Lerner), Morgan Freeman (President Tom Beck), James Cromwell (Alan Rittenhouse), Ron Eldard (Dr. Oren Monash), Jon Favreau (Dr. Gus Partenza)

Earth is threatened by a huge meteor and astronauts are despatched to destroy it while politicians plot self-preservation strategies.

Spectacular scenes of the planet facing destruction from a gigantic asteroid tend to overwhelm the mundane human dramas being played out in its path.

SCR Bruce Joel Rubin, Michael Tolkin   CIN Dietrich Lohmann   MUS James Horner   DES Leslie Dilley   ED David Rosenbloom, Paul Cichocki   PROD Richard D. Zanuck, David Brown   DIST Paramount/DreamWorks

66 Despite flaws, Deep Impact is worth seeing as a decent first step on the road to a more mature crop of high style action movies. – *Margaret A. McGurk, Cincinnati Enquirer*

The Deer Hunter ★★★

DIR *Michael Cimino*
1978   182m   US
[DVD]   ♫

☆ *Robert De Niro*, John Cazale, John Savage, *Christopher Walken*, *Meryl Streep*

Three friends from a small Pennsylvania town go to fight in Vietnam.

The three-hour running time is taken up with cross-cutting of a wedding, a deer hunt and, in Vietnam, an enforced game of Russian roulette. The film has a lurid, manipulative side, but that does not make it inauthentic or insincere. On the contrary, its simple, unadorned truths would be the sort appreciated by the very young men it sets out to commemorate. A moving, hugely ambitious epic.

SCR Deric Washburn   CIN *Vilmos Zsigmond*   MUS Stanley Myers   ED Peter Zinner   PROD Barry Spikings, Michael Deeley, Michael Cimino, John Peverall   DIST Universal/EMI

66 A hollow spectacle, less about war than its effect on a community, full of specious analogies, incoherent sentimentality and belief in its own self-importance. – *Time Out*

66 A big, awkward, crazily ambitious, sometimes breathtaking motion picture that comes as close to being a popular epic as any movie about this country since "The Godfather." – *Vincent Canby, New York Times*

⊥ picture; Christopher Walken (supporting actor); Michael Cimino (direction); Peter Zinner; Richard Portman, William L. McCaughey, Aaron Rochin, C. Darin Knight (sound)

⅄ Robert De Niro (leading actor); Meryl Streep (supporting actress); Deric Washburn; Vilmos Zsigmond

Ⓣ Vilmos Zsigmond

'The First True Story Of What Happens After You Die.'

Defending Your Life ★

SCR/DIR Albert Brooks

1991 112m US

DVD ♫

☆ Albert Brooks (Daniel Miller), Meryl Streep (Julia), Rip Torn (Bob Diamond), Lee Grant (Lena Foster), Buck Henry (Dick Stanley), Michael Durrell (Agency Head), James Eckhouse (Jeep owner), Gary Beach (Car salesman), Julie Cobb (Tram guide)

An advertising man is killed in a car crash and finds himself on trial in Judgement City where he must defend his lifelong lack of assertiveness.

Pleasantly undemanding fantasy comedy with a few thoughtful messages about modern priorities. Unhappily, it's not the ideal vehicle for Brooks's customary deadpan humour.

CIN Allen Daviau **MUS** Michael Gore **DES** Ida Random
ED David Finfer **PROD** Michael Grillo
DIST Warner/Geffen

66 The movie is lavishly designed and assembled. However, the sometimes muddled, sometimes boring, and definitely overlong screenplay, lacking subtlety and definition, disappoints the expectations of enjoyment that are set up in the first 15 minutes. – *Robyn Karney, Empire*

'Three relationships. Three disasters. One last chance.'

Definitely, Maybe (new)

SCR/DIR Adam Brooks

2008 111m UK/US/France

DVD ♫

☆ Ryan Reynolds (Will Hayes), Isla Fisher (April Hoffman), Derek Luke (Russell McCormack), Abigail Breslin (Maya Hayes), Elizabeth Banks (Emily), Rachel Weisz (Summer Hartley), Kevin Kline (Hampton Roth)

A soon-to-be-divorced father tells his daughter about the three loves of his life, challenging her to guess which one became her mother.

Overlong romantic comedy steeped in melancholy; though the film is not short on charm, it has a conspicuous paucity of amusing situations.

CIN Florian Ballhaus **MUS** Clint Mansell
DES Stephanie Carroll **ED** Peter Teschner **PROD** Tim Bevan, Eric Fellner **DIST** Universal

66 Everything a good rom-com should be. – *Sam Toy, Empire*

---

66 It is, I suppose, a premise of sorts, but not a particularly romantic or comedic one. – *Richard Schickel, Time*

'A futuristic comic feast.'

Delicatessen ★★★

SCR/DIR Jean-Pierre Jeunet, Marc Caro

1990 99m France

DVD

☆ Dominique Pinon (Louison), Marie-Laure Dougnac (Julie Clapet), Jean-Claude Dreyfus (Clapet), Karin Viard (Miss Plusse), Ticky Holgado (Mr. Tapioca), Anne-Marie Pisani (Mrs. Tapioca), Jacques Mathou (Roger Kube)

In a bizarre city of the future, vegetarian freedom fighters declare war on a malevolent butcher who kills his workers and sells their flesh.

Brash, brutal and often brilliant, this vibrant movie might not be for the squeamish, but its giddy cartoonish exuberance announces the arrival of two gifted film-makers.

SCR Gilles Adrien **CIN** Darius Khondji **MUS** Carlos D'Alessio **DES** Marc Caro **ED** Hervé Schneid
PROD Claudie Ossard
DIST Electric/Constellation/UGC/Hachette Première

66 A fair bet for cultdom, a lot more likeable than its subject matter suggests, and simply essential viewing for vegetarians. – *Jack Yeovil, Empire*

66 A hugely enjoyable film, Delicatessen welds comedy and magic into a bizarre, grotesque fantasy of an oddball dystopian future. – *Matt Ford, BBC*

Ⓣ film not in the English language

'What did happen on the Cahulawassee River?'

Deliverance ★★★

DIR *John Boorman*

1972 109m US

DVD ♫

☆ Burt Reynolds (Lewis), Jon Voight (Ed), Ned Beatty (Bobby), Ronny Cox (Drew), James Dickey (Sheriff Bullard), Billy McKinney (Mountain Man)

Four businessmen spend a holiday weekend canoeing down a dangerous river, but find that the real danger to their lives comes from themselves and other humans.

A nerve-shredding, almost apocalyptic vision of man's inhumanity, disguised as a thrilling adult adventure. This remarkably well-made, intelligent work caused controversy, which might have been foreseen, because of a jaw-droppingly violent rape scene. Unhappily it also inspired several low-budget horror movies about city types tramping through the backwoods and being accosted by voracious mountain men.

SCR *James Dickey* **CIN** Vilmos Zsigmond **MUS** Eric Weissberg **ED** Tom Priestley **PROD** John Boorman
DIST Warner/Elmer Enterprises

66 There is fundamentally no view of the material, just a lot of painful grasping and groping. – *Stanley Kauffmann*

⅄ picture; John Boorman (direction)

DVD Available on DVD	☆ Cast in order	66 Critics' Quotes	⊥ Academy Award	Ⓣ BAFTA
♫ Soundtrack on CD	of importance	† Points of interest	⅄ Academy Award nomination	Ⓣ BAFTA nomination

'The future isn't big enough for the both of them.'

Demolition Man ★

DIR *Marco Brambilla*

1993   115m   US

`DVD`   ♫

☆ Sylvester Stallone (John Spartan), Wesley Snipes (Simon Phoenix), Sandra Bullock (Lt. Lenina Huxley), Nigel Hawthorne (Dr. Raymond Cocteau), Benjamin Bratt (Alfredo Garcia), Bob Gunton (Chief George Earle), Denis Leary (Edgar Friendly)

In a peaceful, politically correct future society, a devious violent psychopath escapes from his frozen incarceration, and a flawed cop is thawed out to help catch him.

A decent thriller with a self-consciously absurd premise that also satirises the pieties of a po-faced society. Undeniably good fun.

SCR Daniel Waters, Robert Reneau, Peter M. Lenkov   CIN Alex Thomson   MUS Elliot Goldenthal   DES David L. Snyder   ED Stuart Baird   PROD Joel Silver, Michael Levy, Howard Kazanjian   DIST Warner/Silver Pictures

66 The script is fuelled by genuine wit, everyone turns in fine performances and, beginning to end, the film actually shows some thought, if little originality. – *Louis Black, Austin Chronicle*

'Lies. Betrayal. Sacrifice. How far will you take it?'

The Departed ★★★

DIR Martin Scorsese

2006   151m   US/Hong Kong

`DVD`   ♫

☆ Leonardo di Caprio (William 'Billy' Costigan Jr.), Matt Damon (Colin Sullivan), Jack Nicholson (Frank Costello), Mark Wahlberg (Staff Sergeant Dignam), Martin Sheen (Captain Queenan), Ray Winstone (Mr. French), Vera Farmiga (Madolyn), Alec Baldwin (Ellerby)

A young criminal is ordered by a Boston mobster to operate undercover within the State police, while a young cop infiltrates the mobster's gang.

Scorsese has made half a dozen better films, but finally he has his Oscar and Academy voters have spared their own blushes. Yet this is worth the plaudits: a great crime thriller with a deft, relentless plot that grips throughout. It vastly improves the 2003 Hong Kong thriller Infernal Affairs, clarifying a complex story and adding subtlety to characters. Scorsese coaxes superlative work from his actors: di Caprio and Damon are at their peak, Wahlberg is a real surprise in a relatively minor role, and Nicholson's profanely funny mobster Frank Costello marks his best work in years. Superbly staged set-pieces add to the film's visceral appeal; it's both a hoot and kick in the guts.

SCR William Monahan   CIN Michael Ballhaus   MUS Howard Shore   DES Kristi Zea   ED Thelma Schoonmaker   PROD Graham King, Brad Pitt, Brad Grey   DIST Entertainment

66 Scorsese's most purely enjoyable movie in years. But it's not for the faint of heart. It's rude, bleak, violent and defiantly un-PC. – *David Ansen, Newsweek*

66 A picture of grand gestures and subtle intricacies, a movie that, even at more than two hours long, feels miraculously lean. It's a smart shot of lucid storytelling. – *Stephanie Zacharek, salon.com*

⚖ picture; Martin Scorsese; William Monahan (adapted screenplay); Thelma Schoonmaker

⚖ Mark Wahlberg (supporting actor)

Ⓣ picture; Leonardo di Caprio (leading actor); Jack Nicholson (supporting actor); William Monahan (adapted screenplay); Thelma Schoonmaker

'Scream your last breath.'

The Descent ★★

SCR/DIR *Neil Marshall*

2005   99m   GB

`DVD`   ♫

☆ Shauna Macdonald (Sarah), Natalie Jackson Mendoza (Juno), Alex Reid (Beth), Saskia Mulder (Rebecca), MyAnna Buring (Sam), Nora-Jane Noone (Holly)

A group of young women run into physical, psychological and supernatural trouble during a potholing expedition.

Well-sustained exercise in subterranean suspense, distinguished from its genre peers by superb production design and a lively female ensemble.

CIN *Sam McCurdy*   MUS *David Julyan*   DES *Simon Bowles*   ED Jon Harris   PROD Christian Colson   DIST Pathé

66 A sensationally entertaining escalation of frights, the kind that make you wiggle and squirm as you alternately laugh at your own gullibility and marvel at the filmmaker's cunning and craft. – *Manohla Dargis, New York Times*

'He came back to settle the score with someone. Anyone. Everyone.'

Desperado

SCR/DIR Robert Rodriguez

1995   106m   US

`DVD`   ♫

☆ Antonio Banderas (El Mariachi), Salma Hayek (Carolina), Joaquin de Almeida (Bucho), Cheech Marin (Short Bartender), Steve Buscemi (Buscemi), Carlos Gomez (Right Hand), Quentin Tarantino (Pick-Up Guy), Tito Larriva (Tavo), Carlos Gallardo (Campa)

Armed with a guitar case full of weapons a man walks into a small Mexican town determined to avenge his girlfriend's death.

This remake of Rodriguez's low-budget tour de force El Mariachi is little more than one long carefully choreographed gunfight with occasional shafts of humour. Still, the action is passable throughout.

CIN Guillermo Navarro   MUS Los Lobos   DES Cecilia Montiel   ED Robert Rodriguez   PROD Bill Borden, Robert Rodriguez   DIST Columbia/Los Hooligans

66 Mr. Rodriguez may be good enough to make a film about anything, but Desperado would collapse if its characters had to do anything but play with guns. – *Janet Maslin, New York Times*

66 It's big, it's daft, but Desperado is confident and hugely entertaining film-making. – *Bob McCabe, Empire*

† El Mariachi is included in the film's DVD release.

`DVD` Available on DVD   ☆ Cast in order of importance   66 Critics' Quotes   † Points of interest   ⚖ Academy Award   ⚖ Academy Award nomination   Ⓣ BAFTA   Ⓣ BAFTA nomination   ♫ Soundtrack on CD

'They make the fighting sinful west blaze into action before your eyes!'

Destry Rides Again ★★★★

DIR *George Marshall*

1939   94m   US

DVD

☆ *James Stewart* (Tom Destry), *Marlene Dietrich* (Frenchy), *Brian Donlevy* (Kent), *Charles Winninger* ('Wash' Dimsdale), *Samuel S. Hinds* (Judge Slade), *Mischa Auer* (Boris Callahan), Irene Hervey (Janice Tyndall), Jack Carson (Jack Tyndall), *Una Merkel* (Lily Belle Callahan), Allen Jenkins (Bugs Watson), Warren Hymer (Gyp Watson), *Billy Gilbert* (Loupqerou)

A mild-mannered sheriff finally gets mad at local corruption and straps on his guns.

Classic Western which manages to encompass suspense, comedy, romance, tenderness, vivid characterization, horseplay, songs and standard Western excitements, without moving for more than a moment from a studio main street set. It starts with a sign reading 'Welcome to Bottleneck' and an outburst of gunfire; it ends with tragedy followed by a running joke. Hollywood expertise at its very best.

SCR Felix Jackson, Gertrude Purcell, Henry Myers   CIN *Hal Mohr*   MUS Frank Skinner   ED Milton Carruth   PROD Joe Pasternak   DIST Universal

66 Makes the b.o. grade in a big way. . .just plain, good entertainment. – *Variety*

66 I think it was Lord Beaverbrook who said that Marlene Dietrich standing on a bar in black net stockings, belting out See What the Boys in the Back Room Will Have, was a greater work of art than the Venus de Milo. – *Richard Roud*

† An early sound version in 1932 starred Tom Mix; Frenchie (1950) was a slight variation. See also Destry.

'Suspense As Startling As A Strangled Scream!'

Detour ★★★

DIR *Edgar G. Ulmer*

1945   68m   US

DVD

☆ Tom Neal, Ann Savage, Claudia Drake, Edmund MacDonald, Tim Ryan

On his way to Hollywood to meet a girlfriend, a night-club pianist accidentally causes a man's death, and gets involved with a blackmailing woman.

Now regarded as a bona fide noir classic, this hard-bitten B-movie has pace, style and energy to burn. A bleak, sour little story with spare dialogue and a lot of night scenes; in retrospect, it chimed perfectly with its time, for people who lived through it in desperation.

SCR Martin Goldsmith   CIN Benjamin H. Kline   MUS Leo Erdody   PROD Leon Fromkess   DIST PRC

† Ulmer shot the film in just six days.

'Private detective Easy Rawlins has been caught on the wrong side of the most dangerous secret in town.'

Devil in a Blue Dress ★★

SCR/DIR *Carl Franklin*

1995   102m   US

DVD ♫

☆ *Denzel Washington* (Ezekiel 'Easy' Rawlins), Tom Sizemore (DeWitt Albright), Jennifer Beals (Daphne Monet), Don Cheadle (Mouse Alexander), Maury Chaykin (Matthew Terell), Terry Kinney (Todd Carter), Mel Winkler (Joppy), Albert Hall (Degan Odell)

A black private eye disturbs white society in Los Angeles in the late 40s as he hunts for the mayor's missing mistress.

Complex, rewarding Chandleresque thriller that relies on characterisation instead of car chases and subtly alludes to pressing social concerns. Washington makes it look all look appropriately easy. A class act.

CIN Tak Fujimoto   MUS Elmer Bernstein   DES Gary Frutkoff   ED Carole Kravetz   PROD Jesse Beaton, Gary Goetzman   DIST TriStar/Clinica Estetico/Mundy Lane

66 Writer-director Carl Franklin's cool, expert adaptation of Walter Mosley's novel Devil in a Blue Dress evokes the spirit of '40s film noir more effectively than any movie since Chinatown. – *Richard Schickel, Time*

'Hell on heels.'

The Devil Wears Prada ★★

DIR David Frankel

2006   109m   US

DVD ♫

☆ Meryl Streep (Miranda Priestly), Anne Hathaway (Andy Sachs), Emily Blunt (Emily), Stanley Tucci (Nigel), Simon Baker (Christian Thompson)

A dowdy, brainy young woman gets a job in a cut-throat world as assistant to a New York fashion magazine's tyrannical editor.

Streep utterly dominates as the imperious Miranda. The plot is cursory: can Hathaway's fish-out-of-water Andrea survive in a viper's nest where assistants typically quit in tears? But the fun lies with Streep, pale, silver-haired, uttering crushing one-liners in a whispered, fatigued voice. Not exactly profound, certainly no more so than the fashion industry itself, but shrewd, witty entertainment.

SCR Aline Brosh McKenna   CIN Florian Ballhaus   MUS Theodore Shapiro   DES Jess Gonchor   ED Mark Livolsi   PROD Wendy Fineman   DIST TCF

MIRANDA: 'By all means move at a glacial pace. You know how that thrills me.'

66 It wants to hitch a free ride on all the high-speed excitement of the wicked fashion biz - before finally growing up and deciding it's way too superficial. – *Peter Bradshaw, Guardian*

⌕ Meryl Streep (leading actress); Patricia Field (costume design)

⌕ Maryl Streep (leading actress); Emily Blunt (supporting actress); Aline Brosh McKenna (adapted screenplay); Patricia Field (costume design); Nicki Ledermann, April de Angelis (make up and hair)

'Evil Has Its Winning Ways.'

Devil's Advocate ★

DIR Taylor Hackford
1997 144m US
DVD 🎵

☆ Keanu Reeves (Kevin Lomax), Al Pacino (John Milton), Charlize Theron (Mary Ann Lomax), Jeffrey Jones (Eddie Barzoon), Judith Ivey (Edith Lomax), Connie Neilsen (Christabella Andreoli), Craig T. Nelson (Alexander Cullen), Delroy Lindo (uncredited) (Phillipe Moyez)

A hotshot young Florida defence lawyer with integrity is lured away to join a big New York firm run by the Devil.

Fast-paced, imaginative thriller that often crosses the line into hilarity. Pacino dominates in playfully bombastic mode. Enjoyable, but not to be taken remotely seriously.

SCR Jonathan Lemkin, Tony Gilroy   CIN Andrzej Bartkowiak   MUS James Newton Howard   DES Bruno Rubeo   ED Mark Warner   PROD Arnon Milchan, Arnold Kopelson, Anne Kopelson   DIST Warner

66 The Devil's Advocate is a sharp, suspenseful and completely satisfying movie. – *Mick LaSalle, San Francisco Chronicle*

Devil's Island ★★

DIR Fridrik Thor Fridriksson
1996 99m Iceland/Norway/Germany/Denmark
☆ Baltasar Kormakur (Baddi), Sveinn Geirsson (Danni), Gisli Halldorsson (Thomas), Sigurveig Jonsdottir (Karolina), Halldora Geirhardsdottir (Dolly)

Slum dwellers of Reykjavik move into abandoned US army barracks and struggle to deal with the disruptive return of an affluent relative from America.

A curious, caustic but appealing tragicomedy set among the Icelandic underclass.

SCR Einar Kárason   CIN Ari Kristinsson   MUS Hilmar örn Hilmarsson, Björgvin Helgi Halldórsson   DES Arni Páll Jóhanson   ED Steingrimur Karlsson, Skule Eriksen   PROD Fridrik Thor Fridricksson, Egil ödergaard, Peter Rommel, Peter Aalbæk Jensen   DIST Theatrical Experience/IFC/Zentropa

66 Off-kilter and conflicted tale about family and change. . .directed by Fridrik Thor Fridriksson with the same eye for stark landscapes and human quirks he brought to his road movie Cold Fever. – *Gary Dauphin, Village Voice*

Les Diaboliques ★★★

DIR Henri-Georges Clouzot
1954 114m France
DVD

☆ Simone Signoret (Nicole Horner), Vera Clouzot (Christina Delasalle), Charles Vanel (Inspector Fichet), Paul Meurisse (Michel Delasalle)

A sadistic headmaster's wife and mistress conspire to murder him; but his body disappears and evidence of his presence haunts them.

Highly influential, suspenseful and scary thriller with a much-copied twist typical of its authors. Slow to start and shabby-looking as befits its grubby school setting, it gathers momentum with the murder and turns the screw with fine professionalism.

SCR Henri-Georges Clouzot, G. Geronimi   CIN Armand Thirard   MUS Georges Van Parys   ED Madeleine Gug   PROD Henri-Georges Clouzot   DIST Filmsonor

66 Scary, but so calculatedly sensational that it's rather revolting. – *New Yorker, 1978*

66 It depends very much on the intimate details of the seedy fourth-rate school, with its inadequate education and uneatable food, its general smell of unwashed children, hatred and petty perversions. – *Basil Wright, 1972*

† It received an unsuccessful American re-make in 1996 as Diabolique, with Sharon Stone and Isabelle Adjani in the lead roles.

'If a woman answers. . .hang on for dear life!'

Dial M For Murder ★★

DIR *Alfred Hitchcock*
1954 105m US
🎵

☆ *Ray Milland* (Tony Wendice), *John Williams* (Chief Inspector Hubbard), Grace Kelly (Margot Wendice), Robert Cummings (Mark Halliday), Anthony Dawson (Capt. Swan Lesgate), Patrick Allen (Pearson), George Leigh (Williams), Leo Britt (narrator)

An ageing tennis champion tries to arrange the death of his wife so that he will inherit, but his complex plan goes wrong.

Hitchcock did not try very hard to adapt this highly commercial play for the cinema, nor did he exploit the possibilities of 3-D. But for a one-room film with a not very exciting cast the film holds its grip pretty well.

SCR *Frederick Knott*   CIN Robert Burks   MUS Dimitri Tiomkin   ED Rudi Fehr   PROD Alfred Hitchcock   DIST Warner

66 All this is related with Hitchcock's ghoulish chic but everyone in it seems to be walking around with tired blood. – *Pauline Kael, 1968*

† Although shot in 3-D, it was never released in that form.

The Diary of a Country Priest ★★★

SCR/DIR *Robert Bresson*
1950 120m France
DVD

☆ *Claude Laydu* (Priest of Ambricourt), Jean Riveyre (Count), Armand Guibert (Priest of Torcy), Nicole Ladmiral (Chantal)

A lonely young priest fails to make much impression in his first parish; and, falling ill, he dies alone.

Striking, bleak, slow and austere, with little dialogue but considerable visual beauty; a very typical work of its director.

CIN L. Burel   MUS Jean-Jacques Grunenwald   ED Paulette Robert   PROD Léon Carré   DIST Union Générale Cinématographique

---

DVD Available on DVD	☆ Cast in order of importance	66 Critics' Quotes	Academy Award	🏆 BAFTA
🎵 Soundtrack on CD		† Points of interest	Academy Award nomination	BAFTA nomination

'Shoot the dead.'

Diary of the Dead (new)

SCR/DIR George A. Romero
2008   94m   US
DVD

☆ Michelle Morgan (Debra), Josh Close (Jason), Shawn Roberts (Tony), Amy Lalonde (Tracy), Joe Dinicol (Eliot), Scott Wentworth (Andrew), Philip Riccio (Ridley), Chris Violette (Gordo), Tatiana Maslany (Mary)

Film students shooting a low-budget horror are on hand to record the beginning of a zombie apocalypse.

More allegorical horror from a self-styled maestro content to parody his earlier cult successes.

CIN Adam Swica   MUS Norman Orenstein   DES Rupert Lazarus   ED Michael Doherty   PROD Peter Grunwald, Art Spigel, Sam Englebardt, Ara Katz   DIST Optimum

66 Romero has his finger squarely on the pulse of the younger generation's facile relationship with media and technology. – *Eddie Cockrell, Variety*

† Follows Night of the Living Dead, Dawn of the Dead, Day of the Dead and Land of the Dead.

'I'm on my way.'

Dick Tracy ★

DIR Warren Beatty
1990   103m   US
DVD   ♫

☆ Warren Beatty (Dick Tracy), Charlie Korsmo (Kid), Glenne Headly (Tess Trueheart), Madonna (Breathless Mahoney), Al Pacino (Big Boy Caprice), Dustin Hoffman (Mumbles), William Forsythe (Flattop), Charles Durning (Chief Brandon), Mandy Patinkin (88 Keys), Paul Sorvino (Lips Manlis), R.G. Armstrong (Pruneface), Dick Van Dyke (D.A. Fletcher)

Old-fashioned good-versus-evil adventure as ace detective Dick Tracy tangles with a master criminal.

Brilliantly realised re-creation of comic-strip cartoon and stellar cast help to compensate for predictable storylines. Not much of a coherent movie, but definitely a cinematic event.

SCR Jim Cash, Jack Epps Jnr   CIN Vittorio Storaro   MUS Danny Elfman   DES *Richard Sylbert*   ED Richard Marks   PROD Warren Beatty   DIST Touchstone/Silver Screen Partners IV

66 A spectacular movie whose technical achievements – notably the sharp editing – will surely provide a gauge by which subsequent comic strip films are judged. – *Time Out*

66 Summer hasn't officially arrived yet, but it's unlikely to offer a big budget commercial movie as thoroughly entertaining as this stylish real-life cartoon. – *Vincent Canby, New York Times*

⚖ Richard Sylbert; Stephen Sondheim (music, original song Sooner or Later); John Caglione Jr. Doug Drexler (makeup)
⚖ Al Pacino (supporting actor); Thomas Causey, Chris Jenkins, David E. Campbell, Doug Hemphill (sound); Vittorio Storaro, Milena Canonero (costume design)
🏆 Richard Sylbert; John Caglione Jr., Doug Drexler (make up)
🏆 Al Pacino (supporting actor); costume; Richard Marks;

special visual effects; Thomas Causey, Chris Jenkins, David E. Campbell, Doug Hemphill (sound); Milena Canonero (costume design)

'40 Stories Of Sheer Adventure!'

Die Hard ★★

DIR John McTiernan
1988   131m   US
DVD

☆ Bruce Willis (Officer John McClane), Bonnie Bedelia (Holly Gennaro McClane), Reginald VelJohnson (Sgt. Al Powell), Paul Gleason (Deputy Police Chief Dwayne T. Robinson), De'Voreaux White (Argyle), William Atherton (Richard Thornburg), Hart Bochner (Harry Ellis), James Shigeta (Joseph Yoshinobu Takagi), Alan Rickman (Hans Gruber), Alexander Godunov (Karl)

A New York cop battles with terrorists who have dared to derail his planned reconciliation with his wife by occupying a skyscraper and taking hostages.

First-rate special effects, sharp one-liners and enthralling action make this a memorable if overlong movie. At the time, it was a state-of-the-art action thriller. But subtle it is not.

SCR Jeb Stuart, Steven E. de Souza   CIN Jan de Bont   MUS Michael Kamen   DES Jackson DeGovia   ED Frank J. Urioste, John F. Link   PROD Lawrence Gordon, Joel Silver   DIST Fox/Gordon Company/Silver Pictures

66 Great pace, great gun battles, great fun. – *Channel 4*

† The film spawned three sequels, all starring Willis, in the two decades after its release

⚖ Frank J. Urioste, John F. Link; Richard Edlund, Al Di Sarro, Brent Boates, Thaine Morris (visual effects); Stephen Hunter Flick, Richard Shorr (sound effects); John J. Bassman, Kevin F. Cleary, Richard Overton, Al Overton Jr. (sound)

'He's not half the man she used to be.'

Different for Girls ★

DIR Richard Spence
1996   97m   GB
DVD   ♫

☆ Rupert Graves (Paul Prentice), Steven MacKintosh (Karl/Kim Foyle), Saskia Reeves (Jean), Neil Dudgeon (Neil Payne), Charlotte Coleman (Alison), Miriam Margolyes (Pamela), Ian Dury (Recovery Agent)

London motorcycle courier falls in love with the gentle schoolboy friend he used to protect from bullies, who has changed sex.

An ambitious, sensitive attempt to portray transsexual romance. Partly successful, but hampered by a meandering, implausible plot.

SCR Tony Marchant   CIN Sean Van Hales   MUS Stephen Warbeck   DES Grenville Horner   ED David Gamble   PROD John Chapman   DIST NTFC/X Pictures/BBC

66 This irrepressible and sensitive romance brings new flavour to the term odd couple. – *Rita Kempley, Washington Post*

66 The subtlety with which Steven Mackintosh conveys a complicated mixture of vulnerability, defensiveness and pride makes Karl/Kim one of the most fully realised

characters to be portrayed on screen in a long time. –
Stephen Holden, New York Times

'What they wanted most wasn't on the menu'

Diner ★★★

SCR/DIR *Barry Levinson*
1982 110m US
[DVD] ♫

☆ Steve Guttenberg (Edward 'Eddie' Simmons), Daniel
Stern (Laurence 'Shrevie' Schreiber), *Mickey Rourke*
(Robert 'Boogie' Sheftell), *Kevin Bacon* (Timothy Fenwick,
Jr.), Timothy Daly (William 'Billy' Howard), *Ellen Barkin*
(Beth), Paul Reiser (Modell), Kathryn Dowling (Barbara),
Michael Tucker (Bagel), Jessica James (Mrs. Simmons)

In 1959 Baltimore, college students congregate at
their old meeting place and find themselves more
occupied by adult problems than they used to be.

*Generally amusing group character study, with some
tender, wholehearted performances and a knowing,
funny, rueful script, full of well-observed detail. This
hugely enjoyable movie kick-started the careers of several
young actors, notably Bacon, Rourke and Barkin.*

CIN Peter Sova **MUS** Bruce Brody, Ivan Kral **DES** Leon
Harris **ED** Stu Linder **PROD** Jerry Weintraub
DIST MGM/SLM

🏆 Barry Levinson (original screenplay)

Le Diner de Cons ★★

SCR/DIR *Francis Veber*
1998 80m France
[DVD] ♫

☆ *Jacques Villeret* (François Pignon), *Thierry Lhermitte*
(Pierre Brochant), Francis Huster (Leblanc), Alexandra
Vandernoot (Christine), Daniel Prévost (Cheval),
Catherine Frot (Marlène), Edgar Givry (Cordier), Christian
Pereira (Sorbier)

A book publisher invites a slow fellow over to
dinner as part of an 'idiots' game' played by him and
his snobbish society pals, only to have his guest turn
the tables.

*A French farce in the best tradition, and with a
pleasingly moral sting; it is meticulously constructed
and beautifully played.*

CIN Luciano Tovoli **MUS** Vladimir Cosma **DES** Hugues
Tissandier **ED** Georges Klotz **PROD** Alain Poiré
DIST Pathé

66 No one would claim that the film is a distinguished
contribution to cinema, but it would be churlish to resist
its geniality and speed. – *Anthony Lane, The New Yorker*

66 A little classic. – *Peter Bradshaw, Guardian*

'Revenge is a dish best served cold.'

Dinner Rush ★★

DIR *Bob Giraldi*
2000 99m US
[DVD]

☆ Danny Aiello (Louis Cropa), Edoardo Ballerini (Udo),
Vivian Wu (Nicole), Mike McGlone (Carmen), Kirk
Acevedo (Duncan), Sandra Bernhard (Jennifer Freely),
John Corbett (Ken), Jamie Harris (Sean), Summer Phoenix

(Marti), Polly Draper (Natalie), Mark Margolis (Fitzgerald)

On a nightmare evening for the manager of a hip
Tribeca restaurant, an eminent food critic arrives,
gangsters invade and the chef rebels.

*The food looks good but the expertly orchestrated, multi-
strand drama is equally appetising. Modestly enjoyable.*

SCR Brian Kalata, Rick Shaughnessy **CIN** *Tim Ives*
MUS Alexander Lasarenko **DES** *Andrew Bernard*
ED Allyson C. Johnson **PROD** Lou DiGiaimo, Patti
Greaney **DIST** Pathé

66 There's a sorrowful undertow to this film's frenzied
multiple story lines. – *David Jays, Sight & Sound*

'You don't assign him to murder cases – you just turn him
loose!'

Dirty Harry ★★

DIR *Don Siegel*
1971 103m US
[DVD] ♫

☆ *Clint Eastwood* (Harry Callahan), Harry Guardino (Lt.
Bressler), Reni Santoni (Chico), John Vernon (The Mayor),
Andy Robinson (Killer), John Larch (Chief), John
Mitchum (De Georgio), Mae Mercer (Mrs. Russell)

A violently inclined San Francisco police inspector
is the only cop who can bring to book a mad sniper.
When the man is released through lack of evidence,
he takes private revenge.

*The inspiration for a spate of 'dirty cop' movies, widely
criticised at its time for its reactionary attitudes. But
while Eastwood's Harry has little patience for civil rights
for criminals, the film itself passes no judgement either
way. Yet it does offer audiences a guilty thrill of pleasure
to see bad guys banged up without formality,
impartiality or courtesy.*

SCR Harry Julian Fink, Rita M. Fink, Dean Riesner
CIN Bruce Surtees **MUS** Lalo Schifrin **ED** Carl
Pingitore **PROD** Don Siegel **DIST** Warner/Malpaso

HARRY CALLAHAN (CLINT EASTWOOD): I know what you're
thinking, punk. You're thinking, "Did he fire six shots or
only five?" Now, to tell you the truth I've forgotten myself
in all this excitement. But being this being a .44 Magnum,
the most powerful handgun in the world, and will blow
your head clean off, you've gotta ask yourself a question,
"Do I feel lucky?" Well, do ya, punk?

† It spawned four sequels, Magnum Force, The Enforcer,
Sudden Impact and The Dead Pool.

'Some things are too dangerous to keep secret.'

Dirty Pretty Things ★★

DIR *Stephen Frears*
2002 97m GB
[DVD] ♫

☆ Chiwetel Ejiofor (Okwe), Audrey Tautou (Senay), Sergi
Lopez (Sneaky), Sophie Okonedo (Juliette), Benedict Wong
(Guo Yi), Sotigui Kouyate (Shinti), Abi Gouhad (Shinti's
son), Jean-Philippe Ecoffey (Jean Luc)

Two illegal immigrants, a Nigerian taxi driver who
moonlights as a hotel night porter, and a Turkish
asylum seeker, struggle to carve out a decent life in
an unforgiving criminal London underworld.

D

Brilliantly observed slice of life all too rarely seen in British films: a shady world inhabited by hard-working immigrants in service industries, virtually invisible to mainstream society. The thriller element of the story feels needlessly tacked on, but for the most part this is trenchant, urgent drama.

SCR *Steven Knight* **CIN** *Chris Menges* **MUS** Nathan Larson **DES** Hugo Luczyc-Wyhowski **ED** Mick Audsley **PROD** Tracey Seaward, Robert Jones **DIST** Buena Vista

❝ Director Stephen Frears strikes a perfect balance between social commentary and melodrama while nudging his actors to turn potentially stereotypical figures into three-dimensional people. – *Philip French, Observer*

❝ A film with marvellous delicacy, humanity and charm. – *Peter Bradshaw, Guardian*

⚊ Steven Knight (original screenplay)

Ⓣ British film; Steven Knight (original screenplay)

'Sex is power.'

Disclosure ★

DIR Barry Levinson
1994 128m US
DVD ♫

☆ Michael Douglas (Tom Sanders), Demi Moore (Meredith Johnson), Donald Sutherland (Bob Garvin), Caroline Goodall (Susan Hendler), Dylan Baker (Phillip Blackburn), Roma Maffia (Catherine Alvarez), Dennis Miller (Mark Lewyn), Allan Rich (Ben Heller)

A married executive is sued for sexual harassment by his ex-lover and colleague after he rejects her advances.

This glossily crafted film plays cleverly on switched sexual stereotypes and races along like a thriller. Absolutely preposterous, but a first-rate guilty pleasure.

SCR Paul Attanasio **CIN** Tony Pierce-Roberts **MUS** Ennio Morricone **DES** Neil Spisak **ED** Stu Linder **PROD** Barry Levinson, Michael Crichton **DIST** Warner/Baltimore/Constant c

❝ The overheated sexual atmosphere of the modern workplace is used as the backdrop for a whooping satire on cutthroat corporate ambition. . .juicy, smashingly entertaining. – *Hal Hinson, Washington Post*

❝ Genuinely gripping. Demi Moore makes an awesome femme fatale. – *Ian Nathan, Empire*

The Discreet Charm of the Bourgeoisie ★★★★

DIR *Luis Buñuel*
1972 105m France/Spain/Italy
DVD

☆ *Fernando Rey* (Don Raphael, Ambassador of Miranda), *Delphine Seyrig* (Simone Thevenot), *Stéphane Audran* (Alice Senechal), Bulle Ogier (Florence), Jean-Pierre Cassel (Henri Senechal), Paul Frankeur (Francois Thevenot), Julien Bertheau (Bishop Dufour)

The efforts of a group of friends to dine together are continually frustrated.

A frequently hilarious, sometimes savage surrealist fable which makes all its points beautifully and then goes on twenty minutes too long. The performances are a joy.

SCR *Luis Buñuel, Jean-Claude Carrière* **CIN** Edmond Richard **ED** Hélène Plemiannikov **PROD** Serge Silberman **DIST** Greenwich

❝ A perfect synthesis of surreal wit and blistering social assault. – *Jan Dawson, Monthly Film Bulletin*

❝ Extraordinarily funny and brilliantly acted. – *Vincent Canby, New York Times*

⚊ foreign film

⚊ Luis Buñuel, Jean-Claude Carrière (screenplay)

Ⓣ Stéphane Audran (leading actress); screenplay

'As Neil Armstrong set foot on the moon, our only link was a satellite dish in rural Australia with a few bugs. (And a few hundred sheep.)'

The Dish ★★

DIR *Rob Sitch*
2000 101m Australia
DVD ♫

☆ *Sam Neill* (Cliff Buxton), Kevin Harrington (Ross 'Mitch' Mitchell), Tom Long (Glenn Latham), Patrick Warburton (Al Burnett), Genevieve Mooy (May McIntyre), Tayler Kane (Rudi Kellerman), Bille Brown (Prime Minister), Roy Billing (Mayor Bob McIntyre)

Engineers at a relay station in the Australian outback have to overcome major electrical failures to bounce pictures of the Apollo II moon landing to homes around the world.

Nostalgic comedy, set to a soundtrack of superior period hits, which marvels at the astronauts' out-of-this-world endeavours, but prefers the genial company of those back on the ground: a down-to-earth approach that proves thoroughly winning.

SCR Santo Cilauro, Tom Gleisner, Jane Kennedy, Rob Sitch **CIN** Graeme Wood **MUS** Edmund Choi **DES** Carrie Kennedy **ED** Jill Bilcock **PROD** Santo Cilauro, Tom Gleisner, Jane Kennedy, Rob Sitch, Michael Hirsh **DIST** Icon

❝ A comedy with a human face, warmth and spirit. – *Michael Wilmington, Chicago Tribune*

❝ Larkish, good-humoured and impossible to dislike, this is the kind of movie where you should treat with suspicion anyone who leaves the theatre unmoved. – *Colin Kennedy, Empire*

Distant Voices, Still Lives ★★★

SCR/DIR *Terence Davies*
1988 85m GB
DVD

☆ Freda Dowie (Mother), *Pete Postlethwaite* (Father), Angela Walsh (Eileen)

Moving and disturbing memories of working-class family life in post-war Liverpool.

Postlethwaite's jolting portrayal of a violent father sears itself on the memory, but this impoverished family's history is recounted painstakingly, in a visually poetic and unexpectedly warm manner, by one of Britain's most gifted, distinctive film-makers.

CIN William Diver, Patrick Duval **DES** Miki van Zwanenberg, Jocelyn James **ED** William Diver **PROD** Colin MacCabe **DIST** BFI/Film Four International

66 Few British film-makers have dared to attempt such a thoroughly poetic treatment of their native land and Terence Davies is the only one to have succeeded so spectacularly. . .this film is a masterpiece. – *Andrew Pulver, Guardian*

66 If there is such a thing as anthropological poetry, this is it. – *Ian Johns, The Times*

'Welcome to District 13. Welcome to the future.'

District 13 ★

DIR Pierre Morel
2004 84m France
DVD ♫

☆ Cyril Raffaelli (Damien), David Belle (Leito), Larbi Naceri (Taha), Dany Verissimo (Lola), Francois Chattot (Kruger)

In a lawless, politically restless Paris ghetto, a young ex-gang member teams up with a police officer to destroy the neutron bomb that threatens the neighbourhood.

A naïve, preposterous plot, but that misses the point. The highlights here are the two phenomenally athletic heroes in stunning free-running sequences – off balconies, along rooftops and between dizzyingly high buildings. The exhilaration trumps a lack of logic. For action fans rather than connoisseurs of political drama, it's a guilty pleasure.

SCR Luc Besson, Bibi Naceri CIN Manuel Teran
MUS Da Octopuss DES Hugues Tissandier
ED Frederic Thoraval DIST Momentum

'Every killer lives next door to someone.'

Disturbia (new) ★

DIR D.J. Caruso
2007 105m US
DVD

☆ Shia LaBeouf (Kale Brecht), David Morse (Robert Turner), Sarah Roemer (Ashley), Viola Davis (Detective Parker), Carrie-Ann Moss (Julie Brecht)

Teenager Kale (LaBeouf), sentenced to house arrest with an electronic tag for hitting a teacher, snoops from his bedroom window on the activities of a neighbour and starts to suspect him of murder.

Loose remake of Hitchcock's Rear Window for a younger, less demanding audience. Yet while it panders to teens, Kale's growing unease is skilfully charted, and the 100-foot boundary that he dare not cross (for fear of being sent to jail) is deftly exploited for dramatic purposes. The reliable LaBeouf gives the clueless Kale some charm, and David Morse is credibly sinister as his neighbour.

SCR Christopher Landon, Carl Ellsworth CIN Rogier Stoffers MUS Geoff Zanelli DES Tom Southwell
ED Jim Page PROD Joe Medjuck, E. Bennett Walsh, Jackie Marcus DIST Paramount

66 Despite the interesting set-up, the action degenerates into obvious implausibility and silliness – fatal for a suspense thriller – and boredom sets in. – *Peter Bradshaw, Guardian*

Divine Intervention ★★★

SCR/DIR *Elia Suleiman*
2002 92m France/Morocco/Germany
DVD

☆ Elia Suleiman (ES), Manal Khader (The woman), Nayef Fahoum Daher (Father), George Ibrahim (Santa Claus), Georges Khleifi (Collaborator), Avi Kleinberger (Officer)

A checkpoint manned by Israeli soldiers divides Palestinian lovers, and helps convey the dispiriting aspects of life in the occupied territories.

Black humour is the dominant mode here, but it masks a great deal of anguish and distress. The film's pessimism is also leavened by touches of quirky wit and an unforgettable image: a red balloon floating over Jerusalem, bearing the face of Yasser Arafat.

CIN Marc-Andre Batigne DES Miguel Markin, Denis Renault, ED Veronique Lange PROD Humbert Balsan
DIST Artificial Eye

66 Palestinian writer-director Elia Suleiman places a dainty flower in the gun barrel of Israeli occupation: a flower with dangerous spores. This is a deadpan comedy of sorts, almost silent, with touches of Tati and Keaton – and certainly quite unlike anything you'll see on the news. But it has a steely and very un-comic retributive message. – *Peter Bradshaw*

† The film was disbarred from Oscar consideration, because Palestine was not a nation recognised by the American Academy.
† Its bears the sub-title A Chronicle of Love and Pain.

'Let your imagination set you free.'

The Diving Bell and the Butterfly (new) ★★★

DIR *Julian Schnabel*
2007 111m France/US
DVD

☆ *Mathieu Amalric* (Jean-Dominique Bauby), Emmanuelle Seigner (Céline Desmoulin), Marie-Josée Croze (Henriette Roi), Anne Consigny (Claude), Patrick Chesnais (Doctor Lepage)

A French magazine editor suffers a serious stroke, and is left paralysed – except for his left eye, which he uses to communicate by blinking. Through a laborious process of using his blinks as code for letters of the alphabet, he dictates his autobiography.

An original, experimental film that comes close to capturing the imprisonment of a man barely able to interact with others, but who retained his memory, humour and imagination. Harwood's script initially means the audience sees only what Bauby sees – a radical device. Amalric performs nobly as the stricken author, and Schnabel finds a way of representing his plight in visual, poetic terms. But there's a faint air of self-importance here, and it's hard not to conclude that it's the book, not the film that merits the real applause.

SCR *Ronald Harwood* CIN *Janusz Kaminski* MUS Paul Centalon DES Michel Eric, Laurent Ott ED Juliette Welfing PROD Kathleen Kennedy, Jon Kilik DIST Pathé

DVD Available on DVD   ☆ Cast in order   66 Critics' Quotes   Ⓘ Academy Award   Ⓑ BAFTA
♫ Soundtrack on CD   of importance   † Points of interest   Ⓘ Academy Award nomination   Ⓑ BAFTA nomination

179

66 The movie has done what those who've cherished the book might have thought impossible – intensified its singular beauty by roving as free and fearlessly as Bauby's mind did. – *Joe Morgenstern, Wall Street Journal*

66 A tender and sensuously sad film, at once empathic and expressionist in its immersion in Bauby's bathysphere. – *Dave Calhoun, Time Out*

⚟ Julian Schnabel; Ronald Harwood; Janusz Kaminski; Juliette Welfing

Ⓣ Ronald Harwood (adapted screenplay)

Ⓣ foreign film

Divorcing Jack ★★

DIR David Caffrey

1998 120m GB/France

DVD

☆ David Thewlis (Dan Starkey), Rachel Griffiths (Lee Cooper), Robert Lindsay (Michael Brinn), Jason Isaacs (Cow Pat Keegan), Laura Fraser (Margaret), Richard Gant (Charles Parker), Bronagh Gallagher (Taxi Driver)

An outspoken Northern Ireland journalist is forced to go on the run after being accused of murder.

Madcap comedy-thriller, following the plight of a boozy columnist who finds biting sarcasm none too effective a weapon against pursuing gunmen.

SCR Colin Bateman CIN James Welland MUS Adrian Johnston DES Claire Kenny ED Nick Moore
PROD Robert Cooper DIST BBC/Winchester/Scala

66 The Brit gangster thing has been done to death, but here at least it has some wit and originality, thanks largely to its source material. – *Channel 4*

'It's the hottest day of the summer. You can do nothing, you can do something, or you can. . .'

Do the Right Thing ★★★★

SCR/DIR *Spike Lee*

1989 120m US

DVD ♫

☆ Danny Aiello (Sal), Ossie Davis (Da Mayor), Ruby Dee (Mother Sister), Richard Edson (Vito), Giancarlo Esposito (Buggin Out), Spike Lee (Mookie), Bill Nunn (Radio Raheem), John Turturro (Pino), John Savage (Clifton), Rosie Perez (Tina)

A mouthy Italian-American pizza parlour owner sparks a riot in a black neighbourhood of Brooklyn.

The sweltering heat on the streets explodes into rage and anger in this vibrant, dynamic film about the complexities of racism. Beautifully shot, intricately written and boasting a killer soundtrack.

CIN *Ernest Dickerson* MUS Bill Lee DES Wynn Thomas
ED Barry Alexander Brown PROD Spike Lee
DIST UIP/Forty Acres And A Mule Filmworks/Spike Lee

66 A pulsating homage to life on New York's streets, achieved thanks to Spike Lee's sleepless eye, but a passionate-yet-dignified study of racism, too. – *Lloyd Bradley, Empire*

⚟ Spike Lee (original screenplay); Danny Aiello (leading actor)

'He's a big city plastic surgeon. . .in a small town that doesn't take plastic.'

Doc Hollywood ★

DIR Michael Caton-Jones

1991 104m US

DVD ♫

☆ Michael J. Fox (Dr. Benjamin Stone), Julie Warner (Vialula/'Lou'), Barnard Hughes (Dr. Aurelius Hogue), Woody Harrelson (Hank Gordon), George Hamilton (Doctor Halberstrom), Bridget Fonda (Nancy Lee Nicholson)

A highly paid plastic surgeon, on his way to a new job in Los Angeles, crashes his car in rural South Carolina and is sentenced to work at the local hospital.

A charming, folksy, Capraesque hymn to small-town values, with Fox more than adequate as a young hotshot medic. But a limp, predictable script hampers the whole project.

SCR Jeffrey Price, Peter S. Seaman, Daniel Pyne
CIN Michael Chapman MUS Carter Burwell
DES Lawrence Miller ED Priscilla Nedd-Friendly
PROD Susan Solt, Deborah D. Johnson

66 A pleasurably low-key comedy that pits small-town values against big-city excess. – *Peter Travers, Rolling Stone*

† The animated film Cars used an almost identical narrative premise.

Doctor Mabuse the Gambler ★★★

DIR *Fritz Lang*

1922 270m Germany

DVD

☆ Rudolf Klein-Rogge (Dr. Mabuse), Alfred Abel (Graf Told), Gertrude Welcker (Graefin Told), Lil Dagover, Paul Richter (Edgar Hull)

A criminal mastermind uses hypnotism and blackmail in his efforts to obtain world domination, but when finally cornered is discovered to be maniacal.

A real wallow in German post-war depression and melodrama, in the form of a detective thriller. Fascinating scene by scene, but its extreme length makes it hard to endure with enthusiasm.

SCR Thea von Harbou, Fritz Lang CIN Carl Hoffman
PROD Erich Pommer DIST UFA

Dr. No ★★★

DIR Terence Young

1962 111m GB

DVD ♫

☆ *Sean Connery* (James Bond), *Ursula Andress* (Honey), Jack Lord (Felix Leiter), Joseph Wiseman (Dr. No), John Kitzmiller (Quarrel), Bernard Lee ('M'), Lois Maxwell (Miss Moneypenny), Zena Marshall (Miss Taro), Eunice Gayson (Sylvia), Anthony Dawson (Prof. Dent)

A British secret service agent foils a master criminal operating in the West Indies.

First of the phenomenally successful James Bond

DVD Available on DVD ☆ Cast in order of importance 66 Critics' Quotes † Points of interest ⚟ Academy Award Academy Award nomination Ⓣ BAFTA Ⓣ BAFTA nomination

♫ Soundtrack on CD

movies, mixing sex, violence and campy humour against expensive sets and exotic locales. Toned down from the original novels, they initially expressed a number of 1960s attitudes, and have proved unstoppable box-office attractions for almost half a century. This first one was representative of the series, and felt new and fresh at the time. It's mainly recalled now for the alluring scene of a bikini-clad Andress emerging from the sea. But there's more to it than that, notably Connery's confident, roguish debut as a character with real menace beneath the wisecracks.

SCR *Richard Maibaum, Johanna Harwood, Berkely Mather* CIN Ted Moore   MUS *Monty Norman*   ED Peter Hunt PROD Harry Saltzman, Albert R. Broccoli   DIST UA/Eon

---

'One elephant. One world. One story.'

Dr. Seuss' Horton Hears a Who! (new)

DIR Jimmy Hayward, Steve Martino
2008   86m   US
[DVD] ♫

☆ (voices), Jim Carrey (Horton), Steve Carell (Mayor of Whoville), Will Arnett (Mr. Vladikov), Seth Rogen (Morton)

An elephant fights to protect a community of microscopic creatures from his neighbours, who do not believe it exists.

Workmanlike, amusing adaptation; certainly better then previous attempts to convey the spirit of the delectable Seuss on film.

SCR Cinco Paul   MUS John Powell   ED Tim Nordquist PROD Bob Gordon, Bruce Anderson   DIST Fox

66 Fox Animation Studios favour a blandly cutesy visual style that isn't wildly appealing, but that's my only caveat about this clever and winning holiday entertainment. – *Tim Robey, Daily Telegraph*

66 An author's vision is seldom captured as delightfully on film as by this CGI escapade. – *Saadeya Shamsuddin, Sunday Times*

'The hot line suspense comedy!'

Dr Strangelove; or, How I Learned to Stop Worrying and Love the Bomb ★★★★

DIR Stanley Kubrick
1963   93m   GB
[DVD]

☆ *Peter Sellers* (Lionel Mandrake/Merkin Muffley/Dr. Strangelove), *George C. Scott* (Gen. 'Buck' Turgidson), Peter Bull (Ambassador de Sadesky), Sterling Hayden (Gen. Jack D. Ripper), Keenan Wynn (Col. 'Bat' Guano), Slim Pickens (Maj. T.J. 'King' Kong), James Earl Jones (Lt. Lothar Zogg), Tracy Reed (Miss Scott)

A mad US air force general launches a nuclear attack on Russia, and when recall attempts fail, and retaliation is inevitable, all concerned sit back to await the destruction of the world.

Black comedy resolving itself into a series of sketches, with the versatile Sellers playing three parts: the US president, an RAF captain, and a demented German-

American scientist. Historically important in its timing, its nightmares being those of the early 60s, it once more has genuine and chilling resonance in the early 21st century.

SCR Stanley Kubrick, Terry Southern, Peter George CIN Gilbert Taylor   MUS Laurie Johnson   ED Anthony Harvey   PROD Victor Lyndon   DIST Columbia

GENERAL (GEORGE C. SCOTT): I don't say we wouldn't get our hair mussed, but I do say no more than ten to twenty million people killed.

RIPPER (STERLING HAYDEN): War is too important to be left to politicians. They have neither the time, the training or the inclination for strategic thought. I can no longer sit back and allow Communist infiltration, Communist subversion and the international Communist conspiracy to sap and impurify all of our precious bodily fluids.

66 Scarcely a picture of relentless originality; seldom have we seen so much made over so little. – *Joan Didion*

† Fail Safe, which took the same theme more seriously, was released almost simultaneously.

⅃ picture; adapted screenplay; Stanley Kubrick (as director); Peter Sellers (leading actor)

Ⓣ picture; British film; Ken Adam (art direction)

'Grab life by the ball.'

Dodgeball: A True Underdog Story ★★

SCR/DIR Rawson Marshall Thurber
2004   92m   US/Germany
[DVD]

☆ Vince Vaughn (Peter La Fleur), Christine Taylor (Kate Veatch), Ben Stiller (White Goodman), Rip Torn (Patches O'Houlihan), Justin Long (Justin), Stephen Root (Gordon), Joel David Moore (Owen), Missi Pyle (Fran), Lance Armstrong (Himself), Chuck Norris (Himself), William Shatner (Dodgeball Chancellor), David Hasselhoff (German Coach)

The owner of a ramshackle gym assembles a team of no-hopers to take on the swaggering boss of his rival in a dodgeball competition.

Unpretentious comedy that pokes fun at the straight-faced pieties of sports movies, while also delivering belly laughs with laudable efficiency.

CIN Jerzy Zielinksi   MUS Theodore Shapiro   DES Maher Ahmad   ED Alan Baumgarten, Peter Teschner PROD Ben Stiller, Stuart Cornfield   DIST TCF

66 Crude, daft and hilarious, Dodgeball is the best mainstream American comedy for years. – *Nev Pierce, BBC*

66 Strangely exhilarating. – *Stephanie Zacharek, Salon.com*

Dog Day Afternoon ★★★

DIR Sidney Lumet
1975   130m   US
[DVD]

☆ *Al Pacino* (Sonny Wortzik), John Cazale (Sal), *Charles Durning* (Det. Sgt. Moretti), Sully Boyar (Mulvaney), James Broderick (Sheldon), *Chris Sarandon* (Leon)

Two robbers are besieged in a New York bank after their heist, the takings of which were to pay for a sex-change operation, goes badly wrong.

[DVD] Available on DVD   ☆ Cast in order of importance   66 Critics' Quotes   ⅃ Academy Award   ⅃ Academy Award nomination   Ⓣ BAFTA   Ⓣ BAFTA nomination
♫ Soundtrack on CD   † Points of interest

181

Recreation of a tragi-comic episode from the newspaper headlines; a largely fascinating and acutely observed film, with Pacino in peak form.

SCR Frank Pierson   CIN Victor J. Kemper   MUS none
ED Dede Allen   PROD Martin Bregman, Martin Elfand
DIST Warner/AEC

66 There is plenty of Lumet's vital best here in a film that at least glancingly captures the increasingly garish pathology of our urban life. – Jack Kroll

66 Scattered moments of wry humour, sudden pathos and correct observation. – John Simon

⚊ Frank Pierson (original screenplay)
⚊ picture; Sidney Lumet; Al Pacino (leading actor); Chris Sarandon (supporting actor)
Ⓣ Al Pacino (leading actor)

Dog Days   ★★

DIR Ulrich Seidl
2001   121m   Austria/Germany
DVD

☆ Maria Hofstatter (Hitchhiker), Christine Jirku (Teacher), Viktor Hennemann (Teacher), Georg Friedrich (The Lover's friend), Alfred Mrva (Security Guard), Erich Finsches (Old Man), Gerti Lehner (Housekeeper), Franziska Weiss (Young Girl)

Affluent Austrians leading dreary and increasingly cruel lives are revealed in this strange, observational movie.

Everyday happenings in suburban Vienna are recorded with documentary-style concentration. Sexual antics, physical abuse and perversions leave audiences feeling like voyeurs.

SCR Ulrich Seidl, Veronika Franz   CIN Wolfgang Thaler
DES Andreas Donhauser, Renate Martin   ED Andrea Wagner, Christof Schertenlieb   PROD Helmut Grasser, Philippe Bober   DIST Metro Tartan

66 The darkly comic Dog Days uncovers the seedy underside of suburban life in Vienna – and plays like arthouse Big Brother. – Richard Falcon, Sight and Sound

'Get "touched" by an angel.'

Dogma   ★

SCR/DIR Kevin Smith
1999   130m   US
DVD   ♫

☆ Ben Affleck (Bartleby), Matt Damon (Loki), Linda Fiorentino (Bethany), Salma Hayek (Serendipity), Jason Lee (Azrael), Jason Mewes (Jay), Alan Rickman (Metatron), Chris Rock (Rufus), George Carlin (Cardinal Glick), Bud Cort (John Doe Jersey), Alanis Morissette (God), Kevin Smith (Silent Bob), Janeane Garofalo (Liz)

Two unlikely fallen angels plan to trick their way back to heaven via a theological technicality. But if their plan succeeds it will mean the end of the world.

An ambitious yet sadly confused comedy that attempts to get laughs out of the dumbing down of religious faith as well as ridiculing institutional hypocrisy. Not entirely successful, but gleefully outrageous.

CIN Robert Yeoman   MUS Howard Shore   DES Robert 'Ratface' Holtzman   ED Kevin Smith, Scott Mosier
PROD Scott Mosier   DIST Miramax

66 Too talky, too fond of in-jokes, too caught up (especially during the dismally weak climax) in its crass comic-strip ethos, and not, finally, as funny, subversive or thought-provoking as it would like to be. – Geoff Andrew, Time Out

† Catholic groups in America voiced angry protests about the film on its release.

'A Film About The Birth Of The Now.'

Dogtown and Z-Boys   ★

DIR Stacy Peralta
2001   91m   US
DVD   ♫

☆ Sean Penn (Narrator)

Documentary on the golden age of US skateboarding, the 1970s.

Terrific archive footage is spliced with soft interviews with the legendary Z-Boys, Jay Adams, Tony Alva and director Stacy Peralta, all now chubbier and balder but still full of enthusiasm and self-regard.

SCR Stacy Peralta, Craig Stecyk   CIN Peter Pilafian, Sebastian Jungwirth   DES C. R. Stecyk   ED Paul Crowder
PROD Agi Orsi   DIST Columbia Tri-Star

66 Although devoid of objectivity and full of nostalgic comments from the now middle aged participants, Dogtown and Z-Boys has a compelling story to tell. – Laura Bushell, BBC

† Peralta wrote the screenplay for Lords of Dogtown, a 2005 feature film that covers the same ground. subject.

'A quiet little town not far from here.'

Dogville   ★★

DIR   SCR/DIR Lars von Trier
2003   178m
Denmark/Sweden/France/GB/Germany/Finland/Italy/Netherlands
DVD

☆ Nicole Kidman (Grace), Harriet Anderson (Gloria), Lauren Bacall (Ma Ginger), Jean-Marc Barr (The Man With the Big Hat), Paul Bettany (Tom Edison), Blair Brown (Mrs Henson), James Caan (The Big Man), Patricia Clarkson (Vera), Jeremy Davies (Bill Henson), Ben Gazzara (Jack McKay), Philip Baker Hall (Tom Edison Snr), Udo Kier (The Man in the Coat), Chloe Sevigny (Liz Henson), Stellan Skarsgard (Chuck), John Hurt (Narrator)

Back in the 1930s a fugitive from gangsters is first sheltered by the inhabitants of a remote small town in the American Rockies, but then they turn against her.

A piece of experimental minimalist filmed theatre, provocative and at least partly successful thanks to Nicole Kidman's commanding performance as a woman on the run who becomes enslaved. It takes place on a soundstage, with buildings and streets delineated by lines on the floor.

CIN Anthony Dod Mantle   DES Peter Grant   ED Molly Marlene Stensgard   PROD Vibeke Windeløv   DIST Icon

66 Ambitious, intriguing but fatally self-important

account of how an archetypal small town in the Rockies turns against a woman apparently on the run from a gangster. – *Time Out*

66 As movies go, Dogville's no dog. But it's no thoroughbred either. – *Peter Bradshaw, Guardian*

† The first of a projected trilogy by von Trier of films about America. Manderlay was released in 2005, and Wasington (sic) is expected to open in 2009.

La Dolce Vita ★★★★

DIR *Federico Fellini*
1960   173m   Italy/France
DVD ♫

☆ *Marcello Mastroianni*, *Anita Ekberg*, Anouk Aimée, Alain Cuny, Yvonne Furneaux, Magali Noel, Nadia Gray, Lex Barker

A journalist mixes in Rome's high society in 1960, and is alternately bewitched and sickened by the excess he sees.

Episodic satirical melodrama that was a ground-breaking film for Italian cinema, a critical favourite roundly condemned by the Vatican. It depicted a country arising from post-war humiliations, Fascism, and poverty – and embracing new, materialistic, hedonistic values that flew counter to the church's teachings. It has some astonishing set-pieces, most notably Ekberg splashing alluringly in the Trevi fountain. Most significantly, it hints at a template for celebrity worship that holds good half a century later; this, remember, was the film that coined the word 'paparazzi.' It is simply essential viewing for students of film.

SCR *Federico Fellini, Tullio Pinelli, Ennio Flaiano, Brunello Rondi* CIN *Otello Martelli* MUS Nino Rota ED Leo Catozzo PROD Giuseppe Amato DIST Riama/Pathé Consortium

66 Its personification of various familiar symbols – love, death, purity, sin, reason and so on – never succeeds in reflecting human values or creating intellectual excitement. . .Its actual significance rests in the way its (albeit specious) social attack has stirred the imagination of other Italian film-makers, as well as public interest in their work. – *Robert Vas, Monthly Film Bulletin*

66 It remains a work of moral force and a visual delight. – *Philip French, Observer*

⚱ Federico Fellini (direction); Federico Fellini, Tullio Pinelli, Ennio Flaiano, Brunello Rondi (original screenplay)

Dolls ★★

SCR/DIR Takeshi Kitano
2002   114m   Japan
DVD

☆ Miho Kanno (Sawako), Hidetoshi Nishijima (Matsumoto), Tatsuya Mihashi (Hiro), Chieko Matsubara (Woman in the park), Kyoko Fukada (Haruna), Tsutomu Takeshige (Nukui)

Preceded by a puppet show, a trio of tales from Japan opens with a young couple walking tied together by a red cord. Next an old man returns to the park where he used to meet his girlfriend only to

find she continues their ritual; finally a disfigured pop star meets her number one fan.

The stories are exquisitely filmed and crammed with riddles, irony and intricate symbolism. Slow-paced but intriguing.

CIN Katsumi Yanagishima MUS Joe Hisaishi DES Norihiro Isoda ED Takeshi Kitano PROD Masayuki Mori, Takio Yoshida DIST Artificial Eye

66 The stories themselves are loosely linked and feel slightly incomplete; however the film itself is beautiful. – *David Parkinson, Empire*

'They Were Separated By A Death. . .And Reunited By A Murder.'

Dolores Claiborne ★★

DIR Taylor Hackford
1995   132m   US
DVD ♫

☆ *Kathy Bates* (Dolores Claiborne), Jennifer Jason Leigh (Selena St. George), Judy Parfitt (Vera Donovan), *Christopher Plummer* (Det. John Mackey), David Strathairn (Joe St. George), Eric Bogosian (Peter), John C. Reilly (Frank Stamshaw), Bob Gunton (Mr. Pease)

A housekeeper is charged with murder when her elderly employer is found dead. The retired cop who previously tried to convict her of killing the dead woman's husband is convinced that this time he's got his woman.

Kathy Bates, sour possessed, and with all the best lines, effortlessly steals the show as the murder suspect in this entertaining, cleverly constructed thriller.

SCR Tony Gilroy CIN Gabriel Beristain MUS Danny Elfman DES Bruno Rubeo ED Mark Warner PROD Taylor Hackford, Charles Mulvehill DIST Rank/Castle Rock

DOLORES CLAIBORNE: 'Sometimes being a bitch is the only thing a woman has to hang on to.'

66 All the performances are good, the script is subtle and waste-free and Danny Elfman's score is evocative and appropriate, but Taylor Hackford's direction is what gives the movie its sweep. – *Barbara Shulgasser, San Francisco Examiner*

'The story of a man who thought he was the greatest lover in the world. . .and the people who tried to cure him of it!'

Don Juan de Marco ★

SCR/DIR Jeremy Leven
1995   97m   US
DVD

☆ Marlon Brando (Dr. Jack Mickler), *Johnny Depp* (Don Juan), Faye Dunaway (Marilyn Mickler), Geraldine Pailhas (Doña Ana), Bob Dishy (Dr. Paul Showalter), Rachel Ticotin (Doña Inez), Talisa Soto (Doña Julia), Richard Sarafian (Detective Sy Tobias)

A handsome young man, complete with mask and cape, claims to be the legendary lover Don Juan, and finds himself examined by a psychiatrist.

Curious, lyrical fantasy that dwells, but not for too long,

DVD Available on DVD   ☆ Cast in order   66 Critics' Quotes   ⚱ Academy Award   🏆 BAFTA
♫ Soundtrack on CD   of importance   † Points of interest   Academy Award nomination   🏆 BAFTA nomination

183

on the nature of love. Astutely written, it's delivered with panache by two great silver-screen seducers in the lead roles.

CIN Ralf Bode   MUS Michael Kamen, Robert John Lange   DES Sharon Seymour   ED Tony Gibbs   PROD Francis Ford Coppola, Fred Fuchs, Patrick Palmer   DIST Entertainment/New Line/American Zoetrope

66 What jump-starts the film is the casting of Johnny Depp as Don Juan and Marlon Brando as his shrink. They bring a playfully romantic touch to a drama that could have been dead weight in clumsier hands. – *Peter Travers, Rolling Stone*

♪ Michael Kamen, Bryan Adams, Robert John Lange (music, original song – Have You Ever Really Loved A Woman)

'1978. The US Government Waged A War Against Organised Crime. One Man Was Left Behind The Lines.'

Donnie Brasco   ★★★

DIR *Mike Newell*
1997   127m   US
DVD   ♪

☆ *Al Pacino* (Lefty Ruggiero), *Johnny Depp* (Donnie Brasco/Joe Pistone), Michael Madsen (Sonny Black), Bruno Kirby (Nicky), James Russo (Paulie), Anne Heche (Maggie Pistone), Zeljko Ivanek (Tim Curley), Gerry Becker (Dean Blandford), Zach Grenier (Dr. Berger)

A young FBI undercover agent successfully infiltrates the Mob, then finds his loyalties torn between his employers and the gangster who has taken him under his wing.

This tense thriller is based on a true story, and Donnie's gradual seduction by the brutal criminal he is meant to be investigating comes to feel totally convincing. With its terrific evocation of the styles and textures of the 1970s, this is director Newell's most satisfying film.

SCR *Paul Attanasio*   CIN Peter Sova   MUS Patrick Doyle   DES *Donald Graham Burt*   ED Jon Gregory   PROD Mark Johnson, Barry Levinson, Louis DiGiaimo, Gail Mutrux   DIST Entertainment/Mandalay/Baltimore

66 Pacino's outstanding work elevates this to the crime movie pantheon. – *Kim Newman, Empire*

⚖ Paul Attanasio (adapted screenplay)

'Dark, Darkest, Darko'

Donnie Darko   ★★★

SCR/DIR *Richard Kelly*
2001   113m   US
DVD   ♪

☆ *Jake Gyllenhaal* (Donnie Darko), Jena Malone (Gretchen Ross), Drew Barrymore (Karen Pomeroy), James Duval (Frank), Maggie Gyllenhaal (Elizabeth Darko), Mary McDonnell (Rose Darko), Holmes Osborne (Eddie Darko), Katharine Ross (Dr Lillian Thurman), Patrick Swayze (Jim Cunningham), Noah Wyle (Dr Monnitoff)

In the late 1980s, a disturbed, introverted teenager is visited by a giant rabbit who convinces him the world is about to end and commands him to destroy property while sleepwalking.

Dark, provocative and often muddled comedy, constantly brightened by sudden shafts of originality and humour. The film became a word-of-mouth cult hit and made Gyllenhaal a star, while writer-director Kelly also became a hot name for a while.

CIN Steven Poster   MUS Michael Andrews   DES Alexander Hammond   ED Sam Bauer, Eric Strand   PROD Sean McKittrick, Nancy Juvonen, Adam Fields   DIST Metrodome

66 Donnie Darko has plenty of problems. But most stem from a young film-maker over-swinging on his first time up to the plate and hitting a deep fly out rather than a home run. – *Todd McCarthy, Variety*

† When Kelly was allowed to release a director's cut, in 2004, containing 20 extra minutes of material, fans and critics of the film were divided in their opinions, and lively on-line exchanges of opinion ensued. For some, the new cut made clear some ambiguities in the original film, while others resented having the meaning spelled out.

† Kelly's long-awaited follow-up film Southland Tales was so badly received at the Cannes Film Festival that he was forced to make extensive cuts. It finally surfaced in 2007, when it failed dismally at the box-office.

† Mad World, an obscure-20-year-old Tears for Fears song from the film's soundtrack, became a number one hit in Britain for Michael Andrews and Gary Jules in the wake of the film's DVD release.

Don't Look Back   ★★★★

DIR *D.A. Pennebaker*
1967   95m   US
DVD

A documentary account of Bob Dylan's ground-breaking tour of Britain in 1965.

A seminal film about popular music, shot at a time when Dylan, then just 23, was starting to cast off his mantle as a folk troubadour whose songs could put the world to rights. Pennebaker's camera got up close and personal, even into a private conversation in which Dylan is behaving petulantly to his lover Joan Baez. He was the subject of intense media scrutiny, and he dealt with the press either brusquely or entertainingly, by coining vague, amusing aphorisms to keep them at bay. It's a remarkable portrait of a charismatic artist as a young man, and watching it now, it's hard to know which is more wondrous: that Dylan would be at yet another of his creative peaks more than 40 years on, or that he is still alive at all; he had the look of a doomed genius written all over him.

ED D.A. Pennebaker   PROD John Court, Albert Grossman
DYLAN: Keep a clear head and carry a light bulb.

66 Certain moments impart the flavour of freewheeling friendship more precisely than anything else I know of in an English-language movie. Pennebaker seems to have the born film-maker's quality of attentiveness. – *Penelope Gilliatt, New Yorker*

† The film was a major source of inspiration for Cate Blanchett's portrayal of the young Dylan in I'm Not There (2007)

Don't Look Now

★★★★

DIR *Nicolas Roeg*
1973   110m   GB
DVD   ♫

☆ *Donald Sutherland* (John Baxter), *Julie Christie* (Laura Baxter), Hilary Mason (Heather), Clelia Matania (Wendy), Massimo Serrato (Bishop)

After the death of their small daughter, a church restorer and his wife travel to Venice and meet two old sisters who claim a connection with the girl. The husband scorns the idea, but repeatedly sees a little red-coated figure in shadowy passages by the canals and decides to track it down.

A macabre short story that in Roeg's hands became a brilliant exploration of loss, grief, betrayal and eroticism. The celebrated sex scene between Sutherland and Christie sets the tone for a mystery of strange supernatural connections and unknowable truths, while Venice looks like a place with brooding, shadowy secrets and dark, nightmarish alleys. A masterpiece of suggestion and terror.

SCR Allan Scott, Chris Bryant   CIN *Anthony Richmond*
MUS Pino Donaggio   ED Graeme Clifford   PROD Peter Katz   DIST BL/Casey/Eldorado

❝ The fanciest, most carefully assembled enigma yet seen on the screen. – *New Yorker*

❝ A powerful and dazzling visual texture. – *Penelope Houston*

🎭 Anthony Richmond (cinematography)

Don't Touch the Axe (new)

★★★

DIR Jacques Rivette
2007   137m   France/Italy
DVD

☆ Jeanne Balibar (Antoinette de Langeais), Guillaume Depardieu (Armand de Montriveau), Michel Piccoli (Vidame de Parniers), BulleOgier (Princesse de Blamont-Chauvry), Barbet Schroeder (Le duc de Grandlieu), Anne Cantineau (Clara de Sérizy)

New Wave veteran Rivette adapts a Balzac novel about a society dominated by hypocrisy and the importance of appearances and money. Set in the aristocratic salons of 1820s Paris, it tells of emotional shenanigans between general Armand de Montriveau and socialite Antoinette de Langeais. It is framed in flashback: she has fled to a convent in Majorca and her general comes to seek her out.

Rivette delivers a hypnotic treatise on love and chance, sumptuously set and costumed. Stand-out performances from Balibar and Depardieu, who create verbal and physical fireworks. Veterans Michel Piccoli and Bulle Ogier flesh out their slight roles to perfection.

SCR Pascal Bonitzer, Christine Laurent, Jacques Rivette
CIN William Lubtchansky   MUS Pierre Allio
DES Emmanuel de Chauvigny   ED Nicole Lubtchansky
PROD Roberto Cicutto, Ermanno Olmi   DIST Artificial Eye

❝ It's slow but not intolerably so, subtle and beautifully mounted. – *Philip French, Observer*

'Survive this.'

Doomsday (new)

SCR/DIR Neil Marshall
2008   108m   UK/US/South Africa
♫

☆ Rhona Mitra (Eden Sinclair), Bob Hoskins (Bill Nelson), Adrian Lester (Norton), David O'Hara (Michael Canaris), Malcolm McDowell (Kane), Alexander Siddig (John Hatcher), Sean Pertwee (Talbot)

A female commando ventures into Scotland 30 years after a deadly plague outbreak and finds herself caught between two warring tribes.

Deliberately derivative throwback to such post-apocalyptic action thrillers as Mad Max 2 and Escape from New York; the irony of spending millions to ape films made for peanuts appears to be lost on its British writer-director.

CIN Sam McCurdy   MUS Tyler Bates   DES Simon Bowles   ED Andrew MacRitchie   PROD Steven Paul, Benedict Carver   DIST Universal

❝ Neil Marshall's flair for visceral action more than compensates for his script's lack of conceptual novelty. – *Dennis Harvey, Variety*

❝ Homage without innovation isn't homage, it's karaoke. – *Matt Zoller Seitz, New York Times*

'The most dangerous secrets are the ones we're afraid to tell ourselves.'

The Door in the Floor

★

SCR/DIR Tod Williams
2004   111m   US
DVD   ♫

☆ Jeff Bridges (Ted Cole), Kim Basinger (Marion Cole), Jon Foster (Eddie O'Hare), Mimi Rogers (Evelyn Vaughn), Elle Fanning (Ruth Cole), Bijou Philips (Alice)

While on work experience at the home of an arrogant children's writer, a teenager begins an affair with his host's wife, who's mourning the loss of her sons in a road accident.

Callow adaptation of a John Irving novel, often risible in its attempts to disguise a prosaic ordinariness with the most florid of orchestral scores. Performances are solid, and in most cases better than the film deserves.

CIN Terry Stacey   MUS Marcelo Zarvos   DES Therese DePrez   ED Affonso Goncalves   PROD Ted Hope, Anne Carey, Michael Corrente

❝ By turns absorbing, unsettling and, for lack of a better word, icky. – *Karen Karbo, Portland Oregonian*

❝ For all its handsomeness and its occasional moments of piercing intelligence, it's a fundamentally depressing piece of work - not because it deals with tragic events and memories, but because the characters seem hapless and even stupid, and the writer-director can't, or won't, take control. – *David Denby, New Yorker*

The Doors ★

DIR Oliver Stone
1991 140m US
DVD ♫

☆ Val Kilmer (Jim Morrison), Frank Whaley (Robby Krieger), Kevin Dillon (John Densmore), Meg Ryan (Pamela Courson), Kyle MacLachlan (Ray Manzarek), Billy Idol (Cat), Dennis Burkley (Dog), Josh Evans (Bill Siddons), Michael Madsen (Tom Baker), Michael Wincott (Paul Rothchild), Kathleen Quinlan (Patricia Kennealy)

The young Jim Morrison quits film school, fronts a band and becomes a famous rock star.

Given that the film is based on the autobiography of Doors drummer John Densmore, it seems effrontery on Oliver Stone's part to focus so closely on the group's admittedly charismatic singer. It doesn't work, though; Kilmer does a great impersonation of Morrison, but there's no sense he managed to capture his personality. The result is an overlong, disappointing biopic that sheds little light on the familiar arc of fame, celebrity and expensive bad habits.

SCR J. Randal Johnson, Oliver Stone **CIN** Robert Richardson **MUS** The Doors **DES** Barbara Ling **ED** David Brenner, Joe Hutshing **PROD** Bill Graham, Sasha Harari, A. Kitman Ho **DIST** Guild/Carolco/Imagine

'You can't kiss away a murder!'

Double Indemnity ★★★★

DIR *Billy Wilder*
1944 107m US
DVD

☆ *Fred MacMurray* (Walter Neff), *Barbara Stanwyck* (Phyllis Dietrichson), *Edward G. Robinson* (Barton Keyes), Tom Powers (Mr. Dietrichson), Porter Hall (Mr. Jackson), Jean Heather (Lola Dietrichson), Byron Barr (Nino Zachette), Richard Gaines (Mr. Norton)

An insurance agent connives with the glamorous wife of a client to kill her husband and collect the money.

Archetypal film noir of the forties, brilliantly filmed and incisively written, perfectly capturing the decayed Los Angeles atmosphere of a Chandler novel but using a simpler story and more substantial characters. At the time, the hero/villain was almost a new concept.

SCR *Billy Wilder, Raymond Chandler* **CIN** *John Seitz* **MUS** *Miklos Rozsa* **ED** Doane Harrison **PROD** Joseph Sistrom **DIST** Paramount

66 The sort of film which revives a critic from the depressive effects of bright epics about the big soul of America or the suffering soul of Europe and gives him a new lease of faith. – *Richard Winnington*

66 The most pared-down and purposeful film ever made by Billy Wilder. – *John Coleman, 1966*

⚲ picture; script, direction; Barbara Stanwyck (leading actress); John Seitz (cinematography); Miklos Rozsa (music); Loren L. Ryder (sound recording)

'Each of us is matched somewhere in the world, by our exact double – someone who shares our thoughts and dreams.'

The Double Life of Véronique ★★

DIR Krzysztof Kieślowski
1991 98m France/Poland
DVD ♫

☆ Irène Jacob (Weronika/Véronique), Halina Gryglaszewska (La Tante), Kalina Jedrusik (La femme barjolée), Aleksander Bardini (Conductor), Wladyslaw Kowalski (Weronika's father), Jerzy Gudejko (Antek)

A young woman in Krakow, seeking a sign she is not alone in this world, discovers she has a doppelganger in France.

Kieślowski's crossover film found the director leaving behind Poland to seek his destiny in the West, in collaboration with increasingly photogenic actresses; cast in the same divine light used in the artworld to signify religious ecstasy, the result is an intriguing, quasi-philosophical puzzle piece, albeit with an alarming tendency to treat its heroine as the most exquisite of inanimate objects, evidence of a double life but no inner life.

SCR Krzysztof Kieślowski, Krzysztof Piesiewicz **CIN** Slawomir Idziak **MUS** Zbigniew Preisner **DES** Patrice Mercier **ED** Jacques Witta **PROD** Leonardo de la Fuente **DIST** Gala/Sidéral/Canal Plus/TOR/Norsk Film

66 Kieślowski may not proffer the lucid moral insights of his earlier Dekalog series, but it's hard to imagine anyone else making a more mesmerising study of spiritual disquiet. – *Geoff Andrew, Time Out*

66 Could it be that our two, mirrored heroines were the product of a divided continent, and that, with the melting of borders, only one of them was now required? – *Anthony Lane, New Yorker*

Down from the Mountain ★★

DIR Nick Doob, Chris Hegedus, D.A. Pennebaker
2000 98m US
DVD

☆ John Hartford, *Dr. Ralph Stanley*, Fairfield Four, Emmylou Harris, The Cox Family, Chris Thomas King, Alison Kraus and Union Station, Colin Linden, The Nashville Bluegrass Band, The Peasall Sisters, Gillian Welch, Ethan Coen, Joel Coen, T-Bone Burnett, Tim Blake Nelson

Concert documentary featuring the vintage American music from the Coen brothers' film O Brother, Where Art Thou?

Watchable document (by the legendary D.A. Pennebaker) of the country and bluegrass musicians whose soundtrack album became an enormous hit worldwide. Highlights include the venerable veteran Ralph Stanley, and one of the last recorded performances by singer-songwriter and fiddle-player John Hartford, who died soon afterwards.

CIN Joan Churchill, Jim Desmond, Doob, Chris Hegedus, Bob Neuwirth, Jehane Noujaim, D.A. Pennebaker, John Paul Pennebaker **ED** Nick Doob, D.A. Pennebaker

PROD Bob Neuwirth, Frazer Pennebaker
DIST Momentum

66 The country melodies and lyrics of love, death and hard-earned wisdom, not to mention ace banjo and guitar work, connect back to roots from which blues and soul also sprang. – *Time Out*

'Sometimes it's hard to find your way. . .'

Down in the Valley ★

SCR/DIR David Jacobson
2005   114m   US
DVD ♫

☆ Edward Norton (Harlan), Evan Rachel Wood (Tobe), David Morse (Wade), Rory Culkin (Lonnie), John Diehl (Steve), Bruce Dern (Charlie), Geoffrey Lewis (Sheridan)

A San Fernando Valley sheriff is alarmed when his feisty 18-year-old stepdaughter falls for a smooth-talking would-be cowboy.

Norton's adolescent rebel from the wrong side of the tracks, with a head full of ideals about the Wild West, may look attractive to a headstrong girl. But he represents a series of unpleasant accidents waiting to happen. Values of past and present collide with a thud in a story that starts amusingly, but gradually turns a darker hue.

CIN Enrique Chediak   MUS Peter Salett   DES Franco-Giacomo Carbone   ED Lynzee Klingman, David Jacobson, Edward Harrison   PROD Holly Wiersma, Adam Rosenfelt, Edward Norton, Stavros Merjos   DIST Icon
66 The traffic-clogged landscape of the Sam Fernando Valley is overlaid with the values of the Old West in this lyrical, offbeat, indie movie, and the effect is distinctive and intriguing. – *Steve Rose, Guardian*

'The ultimate catch has met his match.'

Down with Love ★

DIR Peyton Reed
2003   101m   US
DVD ♫

☆ Renée Zellweger (Barbara Novak), Ewan McGregor (Catcher Block), Sarah Paulson (Vicki Hiller), David Hyde Pierce (Peter McMannus), Rachel Dratch (Gladys), Jack Plotnick (Maurice), Tony Randall (Theodore Banner)

Back in the early 60s, a sex-obsessed journalist wagers he can bed the outspoken author of the bestselling book about the arrival of a new kind of independent woman.

McGregor and Zellweger do their best with this misguided reinvention of Rock Hudson/Doris Day screen romances. Director Reed gets the clothes, the decor, the Technicolor palette and the social conventions right, but there's a faintly suggestive, knowing smirk to the script that undermines the project.

SCR Eve Ahlert, Dennis Drake   CIN Jeff Cronenweth
MUS Marc Shaiman   DES Andrew Laws   ED Larry Bock
PROD Bruce Cohen, Dan Jinks   DIST TCF
66 This gave me a migraine so bad I virtually had to be hospitalised. – *Peter Bradshaw, Guardian*

'April 1945, a nation awaits its. . .'

Downfall ★★★★

DIR Oliver Hirschbiegel
2004   156m   Germany/Austria/Italy
DVD ♫

☆ *Bruno Ganz* (Adolf Hitler), Alexandra Maria Lara (Traudl Junge), *Corinna Harfouch* (Magda Goebbels), *Ulrich Matthes* (Joseph Goebbels), Juliane Koehler (Eva Braun), Heino Ferch (Albert Speer), Christian Berkel (Dr Schenck), Matthias Habich (Werner Haase), Thomas Kretschmann (Hermann Fegelein)

After World War II, Hitler's vivacious secretary Traudl Junge recalls the last grim days in the Berlin bunker before the leader of the Third Reich killed himself, as Russian troops advanced on the city.

A fascinating film, featuring arguably the best portrayal on film of Adolf Hitler, by Bruno Ganz. It charts the delusional hysteria in the bunker with clinical clarity, yet the film has the same vulgar, voyeuristic appeal as the best reality TV: Eva Braun and her friends are literally seen dancing on table-tops and swigging champagne, trying to blot out the prospect of utter defeat and certain death. In contrast, a scene showing Magda Goebbels efficiently poisoning her young children is memorably chilling. Altogether a superb re-creation of events.

SCR *Bernd Eichinger*   CIN Rainer Klausmann
MUS Stephan Zacharias   DES Bernd Lepel   ED Hans Funck   PROD Bernd Eichinger   DIST Momentum
66 Watching the movie is like experiencing three hours in a madhouse – and it's a pleasure to escape at the end. – *Time Out*
66 Claustrophobic, tense and often riveting. . .Oliver Hirschbiegel's meticulous film is no sensational shockfest, but a living, breathing historical re-creation of Hitler's downfall. – *Jamie Russell, BBC*
† The film created controversy in Germany for its calm, neutral, non-judgemental portrayal of the Third Reich's leading players.
♟ foreign film

'Next Time Take The Stairs.'

Downtime ★

DIR Bharat Nalluri
1997   90m   GB/France
DVD ♫

☆ Paul McGann (Rob), Susan Lynch (Chrissy), Tom Georgeson (Jimmy), David Roper (Mike), Denise Bryson (Jan), Adam Johnston (Jake), David Horsefield (Kevin), Stephen Graham (Jacko), Birdy Sweeney (Pat)

A psychologist finds himself trapped in the derelict lift of a high-rise tower block on a crime-raddled Newcastle sink estate. With him are a suicidal woman, who he loves, her son and an older epileptic man.

Modest, claustrophobic thriller, all the better for its lack of pretension.

SCR Caspar Berry   CIN Tony Imi   MUS Simon Boswell
DES Chris Townsend   ED Les Healey   PROD Richard

DVD Available on DVD   ☆ Cast in order   66 Critics' Quotes   ♟ Academy Award   🅑 BAFTA
♫ Soundtrack on CD   of importance   † Points of interest   ♟ Academy Award nomination   🅑 BAFTA nomination

187

Johns **DIST** Film Four/Scala/Channel 4/Arts Council/Moving Image/Pandora

66 Tense, gritty and enthralling. – *Liverpool Echo*

The Draughtsman's Contract ★★★

SCR/DIR *Peter Greenaway*
1982 108m GB
[DVD] ♫

☆ Anthony Higgins, *Janet Suzman*, Anne Louise Lambert, Neil Cunningham, Hugh Fraser, Dave Hill

In 1694 a young draughtsman receives a curious commission from a country gentlewoman, his rewards to include sex. But when he agrees, it appears a murder mystery may be involved.

Pleasantly unusual, stylized, visually dazzling puzzle film which involves both sex and murder while maintaining a detached attitude to both. The period costumes help to give it a distancing air of fantasy.

CIN Curtis Clark **MUS** *Michael Nyman* **ED** John Wilson **PROD** David Payne **DIST** BFI/Channel 4

66 Mannered and idiosyncratic, the speeches are so arch and twitty that they seem to be pitched higher than a dog whistle. – *Pauline Kael, New Yorker*

66 Perhaps the four-hour version which may one day become available is clearer if not more concise. – *Guardian*

'This morning they were playing ping-pong in the hospital rec room. Now they're lost in New York and framed for murder. This was never covered in group therapy.'

The Dream Team ★

DIR Howard Zieff
1989 113m US
[DVD]

☆ Michael Keaton (Billy Caufield), Christopher Lloyd (Henry Sikorsky), Peter Boyle (Jack McDermott), Stephen Furst (Albert Ianuzzi), Dennis Boutsikaris (Dr. Weitzman), Lorraine Bracco (Riley), Milo O'Shea (Dr. Newald), Philip Bosco (O'Malley), James Remar (Gianelli)

On a day trip to Yankee Stadium, four inmates of a psychiatric hospital are separated from the doctor who is guarding them, witness a crime and set about bringing the perpetrators to justice.

Imagine a comedy version of One Flew Over the Cuckoo's Nest, and you're not far off. Yet the film is better than it may sound: Keaton plays a persuasive fast-talker to perfection, and Lloyd has fun portraying a patient convinced he is a doctor. It flirts with outright bad taste, while never truly embracing it, and is often amusing.

SCR Jon Connolly, David Loucka **CIN** Adam Holender **MUS** David McHugh **DES** Todd Hallowell **ED** C. Timothy O'Meara **PROD** Christopher W. Knight **DIST** UIP/Imagine Entertainment

The Dreamers ★★

DIR Bernardo Bertolucci
2003 115m France/Italy/GB
[DVD] ♫

☆ Michael Pitt (Matthew), Eva Green (Isabelle), Louis Garrel (Theo), Robin Renucci (Father), Anna Chancellor (Mother), Florian Cadiou (Patrick)

Paris, 1968: a young American exchange student falls into a relationship with quasi-incestuous French siblings.

Superficially seductive drama that crucially retreats from the evenements taking place on the streets outside to focus on a steamy love triangle with occasional film-buff references.

SCR Gilbert Adair **CIN** Fabio Cianchetti **DES** Jean Rabasse **ED** Jacopo Quadri **PROD** Jeremy Thomas **DIST** TCF

66 Ablaze with poetry and danger, and suffused with an odd kind of intellectual kitsch. – *Michael Wilmington, Chicago Tribune*

66 Fans of film and gorgeous naked people of either sex will find much here to interest them. But it also has moments that make you want to throw stones. – *Kim Newman, Empire*

† The film opened in the US with an NC-17 certificate for its scenes of sexual explicitness, under strong protests from its producer Thomas.

'Fame comes and goes, stars rise and fall, but dreams live forever.'

Dreamgirls ★

SCR/DIR Bill Condon
2006 130m US
[DVD] ♫

☆ Jamie Foxx (Curtis Taylor, Jr.), Beyonce Knowles (Deena Jones), Eddie Murphy (James 'Thunder' Early), Danny Glover (Marty Madison), Jennifer Hudson (Effie White), Anika Noni Rose (Lorrell Robinson), Hinton Battle (Wayne)

In the early 1960s, a female soul trio negotiate the pitfalls of fame, going mainstream and internal squabbling.

Its first half-hour is a fine, exciting, zestful evocation of rough-and ready soul revues, the breeding ground for groups like the fictional Dreams. But then the story, effectively a rehash of the Supremes being moulded for crossover superstardom by their Svengaliesque manager Berry Gordy, sags alarmingly. The songs simply do not pass muster and would never have survived Gordy's rigorous quality control at Motown. The story cries out for Deena, its Diana Ross surrogate, to become a shrewish diva, but Beyonce Knowles lacks the requisite acting range. Jamie Foxx, as the Dreams' manipulative manager, is a one-note baddie – a disservice to Gordy's genius.

CIN Tobias Schliessler **MUS** Henry Krieger **DES** John Myhre **ED** Virginia Katz **PROD** Laurence Mark **DIST** TCF

66 A glossy, gleaming Cadillac of a film, with a vintage rhythm-and-blues engine tuned to perfection. The cast is dressed to kill. – *James Christopher, The Times*

66 The problem with Dreamgirls – and it is not a small one – lies in those songs, which are not just lyrically and musically pedestrian, but historically and idiomatically disastrous. – *A.O. Scott, New York Times*

⚊ Jennifer Hudson (supporting actress); Michael Minkler, Bob Beemer, Willie D. Burton (sound mixing)

[DVD] Available on DVD   ☆ Cast in order of importance   66 Critics' Quotes   ⚊ Academy Award   🅱 BAFTA
♫ Soundtrack on CD   † Points of interest   ⚊ Academy Award nomination   🅱 BAFTA nomination

Eddie Murphy (supporting actor); John Myhre; Sharen Davis (costume design); Henry Krieger (m), Anne Preven (ly) (music, original song – Listen); Henry Krieger (m), Siedah Garrett (ly) (music, original song – Love You I Do); Henry Krieger (m), Willie Reafe (ly) (music, original song – Patience)

Jennifer Hudson (supporting actress)

Henry Krieger (music)

The Dreamlife of Angels ★★

DIR *Erick Zonca*
1998   113m   France
DVD ♫

☆ *Elodie Bouchez* (Isa), *Natacha Regnier* (Marie), Gregoire Colin (Chriss), Jo Prestia (Fredo), Patrick Mercado (Charly)

A young woman arriving in Lille strikes up a friendship, and comes to share a flat, with a more fragile contemporary.

Clear-eyed study of a couple of everyday lives going nowhere, and the limited choices two women can be presented with; though desperately sad, bleak even, it is impeccably performed by its lead actresses.

SCR Erick Zonca, Roger Bohbot   CIN Agnes Godard, Dominique Le Rigoleur   MUS Yann Thiersen
DES Jimmy Vansteenkiste   ED Yannick Kergoat
PROD François Marquis
DIST Bagheera/Diaphana/France3

66 A beautifully insightful movie which views its characters (the type of 'marginal' folk rarely shown in the cinema) sympathetically but unsentimentally, and after the scene setting of the first half-hour, it grips like a vice as it proceeds to a shocking and profoundly moving conclusion. – *Geoff Andrew, Time Out*

66 A wonderful example of humanist cinema, and a guaranteed future classic. – *Richard Williams, Guardian*

† Elodie Bouchez and Natacha Regnier shared the best actress award at the 1998 Cannes Film Festival.

The Dressmaker ★

DIR Jim O'Brien
1988   92m   GB
☆ *Joan Plowright* (Nellie), *Billie Whitelaw* (Margo), Jane Horrocks (Rita), Tim Ransom (Wesley), Peter Postlethwaite (Jack), Pippa Hinchley (Val), Rosemary Martin (Mrs. Manders), Tony Haygarth (Mr. Manders)

In Liverpool in 1944, the arrival of amorous American soldiers rocks the foundations of a family presided over by a genteel, respectable dressmaker.

A meticulous period drama with touches of wry humour about social pretensions. Plowright and Whitelaw are both excellent as sisters who could scarcely be more different.

SCR John McGrath   CIN Michael Coulter   MUS George Fenton   DES Caroline Amies   ED William Diver
PROD Ronald Shedlo   DIST Rank/Film Four International/British Screen

Judy Moorcroft (costume design)

Drifting Clouds ★★

SCR/DIR Aki Kaurismäki
1996   96m   Finland
DVD

☆ Kati Outinen (Ilona), Kari Väänänen (Lauri), Elina Salo (Mrs. Sjöholm), Sakari Kuosmanen (Melartin), Matti Onnismaa (Forsström), Markku Peltola (Lajunen)

A hard-up Helsinki couple are both thrown out of work, and decide to open a restaurant. But troubles are on the menu.

Dark, deadpan humour, the trademark of this wonderfully off-centre director, sets the tone here; but there is also warmth and affection for these characters, acute observation of character and a surprisingly optimistic ending.

CIN Timo Salminen   MUS Shelley Fisher   DES Jukka Salmi, Markku Pätilä   ED Aki Kaurismäki   PROD Aki Kaurismäki   DIST Metro/Tartan/Sputnik Oy/YLE TV-1/Pandora/Pyramide

66 In addition to achieving a paradoxical balance of mirth and melancholy, Drifting Clouds is a dark, mostly interior movie with a colour scheme as big as all outdoors. – *Mark Jenkins, Washington Post*

'You get what you pay for'

Drillbit Taylor (new)

DIR Steven Brill
2008   102m   US
☆ Owen Wilson (Drillbit Taylor), Nate Hartley (Wade), Troy Gentile (Ryan), Ian Roberts (Jim), Leslie Mann (Lisa)

A homeless army deserter is hired by three high school kids for playground protection.

A threadbare private-joke comedy geared around another tiresomely flaky Owen Wilson performance.

SCR Kristofor Brown, Seth Rogan   CIN Fred Murphy
MUS Christophe Beck   DES Jackson De Govia
ED Brady Heck, Thomas J. Nordberg   PROD Judd Apatow, Susan Arnold, Donna Roth   DIST Paramount Pictures

66 As clunky and humourless as its title. – *Claudia Puig, USA Today*

'All Ben wanted was a job. All Evie wanted was a friend.'

Driving Lessons ★

SCR/DIR Jeremy Brock
2005   98m   UK/USA
DVD

☆ Julie Walters (Evie), Rupert Grint (Ben), Laura Linney (Laura), Nicholas Farrell (Robert)

A teenage boy becomes assistant to an elderly eccentric actress.

Rites-of-passage story set in north London suburbia, with Walters as a foul-mouthed, boozy stage diva. On a road trip, she offers life lessons to the deadpan Grint, making a promising departure from the Harry Potter series. Linney has a nice turn as his overbearing mother. Amiable and surprisingly moving.

CIN David Katznelson   MUS John Renbourn, Clive Carroll   DES Amanda McArthur   ED Trevor Waite   PROD Julia Chasman   DIST Tartan

---

DVD Available on DVD   ☆ Cast in order   66 Critics' Quotes   Academy Award   BAFTA
♫ Soundtrack on CD   of importance   † Points of interest   Academy Award nomination   BAFTA nomination

66 A great turn from Julie Walters, and a likable film. – *Peter Bradshaw, Guardian*

'The comedy that won a Pulitzer Prize.'

Driving Miss Daisy ★

DIR Bruce Beresford
1989 99m US
DVD ♫

☆ Morgan Freeman (Hoke Colburn), Jessica Tandy (Daisy Werthan), Dan Aykroyd (Boolie Werthan), Patti LuPone (Florine Werthan)

Events draw an affluent, spirited Jewish matron into a dependent relationship with her black chauffeur, as the civil rights movement puts America through profound changes.

Gentle, old-fashioned comedy that veers towards schmaltz, but benefits from fine acting by its leads. Not everyone has found themselves enthralled by the balance of power in this inter-racial relationship, but it feels well intentioned.

SCR Alfred Uhry **CIN** Peter James **MUS** Hans Zimmer **DES** Bruno Rubeo **ED** Mark Warner **PROD** Lili Fini Zanuck, Richard D. Zanuck **DIST** Warner/Zanuck Company/Richard Zanuck, Lili Fini Zanuck

66 It gets to its hugely emotional destination without ever having to put the foot down; a poignant and provocative road movie. – *Philip Thomas, Empire*

⚊ picture; Jessica Tandy (leading actress); Alfred Uhry (adapted screenplay); Manlio Rocchetti, Lynn Barber, Kevin Haney (make up)
⚊ Morgan Freeman (leading actor); Dan Aykroyd (supporting actor); Mark Warner; Bruno Rubeo, Elizabeth McBride (costume design)
Ⓣ Jessica Tandy (leading actress)
Ⓣ film; Bruce Beresford; Alfred Uhry (adapted screenplay)

'If Looks Could Kill. . .'

Drop Dead Gorgeous ★

DIR Michael Patrick Jann
1999 97m US/Germany
DVD ♫

☆ Kirsten Dunst (Amber Atkins), Ellen Barkin (Annette Atkins), Allison Janney (Loretta), Denise Richards (Becky Leeman), Kirstie Alley (Gladys Leeman), Sam McMurray (Lester Leeman), Amy Adams (Leslie Miller), Tara Redepenning (Molly Howard), Shannon Nelson (Tess Weinhaus), Sarah Stewart (Jenelle Betz), Michael McShane (Harold Vilmes)

A team of documentary film-makers cover a beauty contest and discover a bitter world behind the smiles.

Patchy comedy about big ambitions in small-town life, with wickedly funny moments framed by long dull sequences. Barkin and Alley take the plaudits as two of the contestants' bitchy, wildly competitive mothers.

SCR Lona Williams **CIN** Michael Spiller **MUS** Mark Mothersbaugh **DES** Ruth Ammon **ED** David Codron, Janice Hampton **PROD** Gavin Pallone, Judy Hofflund **DIST** New Line

66 Occasionally heavy-handed and overdone – and scarcely free from a self-congratulatory tone – this latest beauty contest spoof is nonetheless lots of fun, clever and fearless, and loaded with wicked lines and touches. – *Kevin Thomas, Los Angeles Times*

'The great death game.'

Drowning by Numbers ★★

SCR/DIR Peter Greenaway
1988 119m GB
♫

☆ Bernard Hill (Madgett), Joan Plowright (Cissie Colpitts 1), Juliet Stevenson (Cissie Colpitts 2), Joely Richardson (Cissie Colpitts 3), Jason Edwards (Smut)

Three generations of women, all called Cissie Colpitts, drown their husbands and conspire with the local coroner to escape justice.

Sardonic, pitch-black, multi-layered comedy, with a gorgeous score and full of idiosyncratic allusions to numbers, word games and lists. It still manages to be moving, funny and largely comprehensible.

CIN Sacha Vierny **MUS** *Michael Nyman* **DES** Ben Van Os, Jan Roelfs **ED** John Wilson **PROD** Denis Wigman, Kees Kasander **DIST** Film Four International/Elsevier Vendex

66 Elegantly scored and luminously shot, it's a modernist black comedy filled with arcane, archaic and apocryphal lore, and hugely enjoyable. – *Time Out*

Drugstore Cowboy ★★

DIR *Gus Van Sant*
1989 102m US
DVD ♫

☆ Matt Dillon (Bob), Kelly Lynch (Dianne), James Remar (Gentry), James Le Gros (Rick), Heather Graham (Nadine)

Four junkies, who survive by holding up pharmacies in Oregon, hit trouble with the local law and head across America.

Low-budget, low-key look at lowlife at least attempts to explain addiction as well as condemn it. Director Van Sant contributes a gritty visual style, interspersed with drifting clouds of fantasy.

SCR Gus Van Sant, Daniel Yost **CIN** Robert Yeoman **MUS** Elliot Goldenthal **DES** David Brisbin **ED** Curtiss Clayton, Mary Bauer **PROD** Nick Wechsler, Karen Murphy **DIST** Avenue Pictures

66 For once a movie, even one that lurches and stumbles, sees the war on drugs honestly by recognising the enemy's power and allure. – *Peter Travers, Rolling Stone*

† William S. Burroughs, author of the drug-themed classic The Naked Lunch, has a cameo role as a junkie ex-priest.

A Dry White Season

DIR Euzhan Palcy
1989 107m US
DVD

☆ Donald Sutherland (Ben du Toit), Janet Suzman (Susan du Toit), Zakes Mokae (Stanley Makhaya), Jurgen Prochnow (Captain Stolz), Susan Sarandon (Melanie Bruwer), *Marlon Brando* (Ian McKenzie), Winston Ntshona (Gordon Ngubene), Thoko Ntshinga (Emily Ngubene), Leonard Maguire (Bruwer)

A white teacher in South Africa is newly politicised when the police brutally beat the son of his black gardener.

Stiff tract about racism and apathy under apartheid. The importance of the drama is stifled by TV-movie visuals, and the black characters are pushed to the margins. Brando, playing a barrister, seems more engaged than in most of his later films.

SCR Colin Welland, Euzhan Palcy   **CIN** Kelvin Pike, Pierre William Glenn   **MUS** Dave Grusin   **DES** John Fenner   **ED** Sam O'Steen, Glenn Cunningham   **PROD** Paula Weinstein   **DIST** UIP/MGM/Star Partners II

⚲ Marlon Brando (supporting actor)

Ⓣ Marlon Brando (supporting actor)

Duck Soup ★★★★

DIR *Leo McCarey*

1933   68m   US

DVD

☆ *Groucho Marx* (Rufus T. Firefly), *Chico Marx* (Chicolini), *Harpo Marx* (Pinky), *Zeppo Marx* (Bob Roland), *Margaret Dumont* (Mrs Teasdale), Louis Calhern (Ambassador Trentino), Edgar Kennedy (Lemonade man), Raquel Torres (Vera Marcal)

An incompetent becomes President of Freedonia and wages war on its scheming neighbour, having paid a month's advance rent on the battlefield.

The satirical aspects of this film are fascinating but appear to have been unintentional. Never mind, it's also the most satisfying and undiluted Marx Brothers romp, although the one without instrumental interludes. It includes the lemonade stall scene, the astonishing mirror sequence and an endless array of one-liners and comedy choruses.

SCR *Bert Kalmar, Harry Ruby, Arthur Sheekman, Nat Perrin*   **CIN** Henry Sharp   **ED** LeRoy Stone   **DIST** Paramount

❝ Practically everybody wants a good laugh right now, and this should make practically everybody laugh. – *Variety*

❝ So much preliminary dialogue is necessary that it seems years before Groucho comes on at all; and waiting for Groucho is agony. – *E. V. Lucas, Punch*

† Hail. Hail Freedonia; His Excellency is Due; Just Wait 'til I Get Through With It; Freedonia's Going to War.

Duel in the Sun ★★

DIR *King Vidor (and others)*

1946   138m   US

DVD

☆ Jennifer Jones, Joseph Cotten, Gregory Peck, Lionel Barrymore, Lillian Gish, Walter Huston, Herbert Marshall, Charles Bickford, Tilly Losch, Joan Tetzel, Harry Carey, Otto Kruger, Sidney Blackmer

A young mixed-race woman causes trouble between two brothers of contrasting character.

Massive Western with a lurid storyline, dominated and fragmented by producer Selznick, who saw it as a chance to emulate his astonishing success with Gone With the Wind. He bought the best talent and proceeded to interfere with it, so that while individual scenes are

marvellous, the narrative has little flow. The final gory shoot-up between two lovers was much discussed at the time, and the sexuality portrayed did not escape the attention of censors or religious groups. It's a spectacle, no question, and something of a guilty pleasure, but an unhappy occasion for its actors, especially Peck, miscast as a primal brute.*

SCR David O. Selznick, Oliver H. P. Garrett   **CIN** Lee Garmes, Harold Rosson, Ray Rennahan   **MUS** Dimitri Tiomkin   **DES** J. McMillan Johnson   **DIST** David O. Selznick

❝ A knowing blend of oats and aphrodisiac. – *Time*

❝ Cornographic is a word that might have been coined for it. – *Daily Mail*

† The uncredited directors included Josef von Sternberg, William Dieterle, B. Reeves Eason, and Selznick himself.

† The film was widely known by the nickname 'Lust in the Dust.'

⚲ Jennifer Jones (leading actress); Lillian Gish (supporting actress)

'Some friendships are wilder than others.'

Duma ★

DIR Carroll Ballard

2005   100m   US

DVD   ♫

☆ Alexander Michaletos (Xan), Eamonn Walker (Ripkuna), Campbell Scott (Peter), Hope Davis (Kristin)

A young white farmer's boy in South Africa adopts an abandoned cheetah cub. But a crisis looms when his family move to the city.

Heart-warming but unsentimental family drama that relies more on fine photography than originality.

SCR Karen Janszen, Mark St. Germain, Carol Flint   **CIN** Werner Maritz   **MUS** John Debney   **DES** Johnny Breedt   **ED** T.M. Christopher   **PROD** John Wells, Hunt Lowry, Stacey Cohen, E.K. Gaylord II, Kristin Harms   **DIST** Warner

❝ Too suspenseful for the youngest children but for anyone older than eight or nine it evokes nothing less than awe at the harsh beauty of the natural world. – *Ty Burr, Boston Globe*

Dumbo ★★★

DIR Ben Sharpsteen

1941   64m   US

DVD   ♫

☆ the voices of Sterling Holloway, Edward Brophy, Verna Felton, Herman Bing, Cliff Edwards

A baby circus elephant, mocked for his big ears, finds they have a use after all.

Delightful and touching cartoon feature, notable for set-pieces such as the crows' song, and the drunken nightmare, with the extraordinary pink elephants on parade. Walt Disney is said to have personally supervised every scene, and the quality control is apparent.

SCR Joe Grant, Dick Huemer   **MUS** Frank Churchill, Oliver Wallace   **DIST** Walt Disney

---

DVD Available on DVD   ☆ Cast in order of importance   ❝ Critics' Quotes   † Points of interest   ⚲ Academy Award   ⚲ Academy Award nomination   Ⓑ BAFTA   Ⓣ BAFTA nomination

♫ Soundtrack on CD

♪ Frank Churchill, Oliver Wallace (music)
♫ Frank Churchill (m), Ned Washington (ly) (music, original song – Baby Mine)

'He's not a serial killer. He's much worse.'

Dust Devil: The Final Cut ★

SCR/DIR Richard Stanley
1992   103m   GB/US
DVD

☆ Robert Burke (Dust Devil), Chelsea Field (Wendy Robinson), Zakes Mokae (Ben Mukurob), John Matshikiza (Joe Niemand), Marianne Sagebrecht (Dr. Leidzinger), William Hootkins (Capt. Beyman), Rufus Swart (Mark Robinson)

A battered wife driving away from her husband on an African desert road stops to pick up a hitch-hiker who is hiding a terrible secret.

Powerful sci-fi thriller that mixes masterful visual moments with leaden dialogue and a demanding, atmospheric script, but still commands the attention.

CIN Steven Chivers   **MUS** Simon Boswell   **DES** Joseph Bennett   **ED** Derek Trigg, Paul Carlin; Jamie Macdermott   **PROD** JoAnne Sellar   **DIST** Polygram/Palace/Film Four/Richard Stanley

❝ The non-linear storyline relies more on atmosphere than forward momentum and the tone veers wildly between dream-like mysteriousness and indulgent incomprehensibility. – *Time Out*

❝ The edges might be ragged and the story may not entirely convince, but there is still much to recommend Dust Devil. – *Richard Luck, Channel 4*

† Director Stanley financed the 'final cut' version of the film himself.

† The film's striking vistas were shot in Namibia.

Dust ★

SCR/DIR Milcho Manchevski
2001   127m   GB/Germany/Italy/Macedonia
DVD

☆ Joseph Fiennes (Elijah), David Wenham (Luke), Adrian Lester (Edge), Anne Brochet (Lilith), Nikolina Kujaca (Neda), Rosemary Murphy (Angela)

An elderly woman holds a would-be burglar at gunpoint in her New York apartment and narrates her agonising and complex family history – which opens with her father and his brother leaving America to fight in Macedonia.

An over-ambitious, wayward, confusing revenge saga that ranges over time and place so wildly it becomes bewildering. Yet its manic energy and self-belief are curiously compelling.

CIN Barry Ackroyd   **MUS** Kiril Dzajkovski   **DES** David Munns   **ED** Nicolas Gaster   **PROD** Chris Auty, Vesna Jovanoska, Domenico Procacci   **DIST** Pathé

❝ The bloodthirsty Dust lurches so wildly and meaninglessly between genres and time frames that all it creates is motion sickness. – *Megan Lehmann, New York Post*

E.T. The Extra-Terrestrial ★★★★

DIR *Steven Spielberg*
1982 115m US
DVD ♫

☆ Dee Wallace (Mary), Henry Thomas (Elliott), Peter Coyote (Keys), Robert MacNaughton (Michael), Drew Barrymore (Gertie), K. C. Martel (Greg), Sean Frye (Steve), Tom Howell (Tyler)

When an alien spacecraft is disturbed in a Los Angeles suburb, one of its crew members is left behind and befriended by a small boy.

Stupefyingly successful box-office fairy tale by Spielberg, many of whose family films work so brilliantly because he taps into the child-like sense of wonder that lies at the heart of everyone's earliest movie-going experiences. This one could hardly be simpler, but it is literally unimprovable, and works at all levels for all audiences.

SCR Melissa Mathison CIN Allen Daviau MUS *John Williams* DES James D. Bissell ED Carol Littleton
PROD Steven Spielberg, Kathleen Kennedy
DIST Universal

⚲ John Williams; Carlo Rambaldi, Dennis Murren, Kenneth F. Smith (visual effects); Buzz Knudson, Robert Glass, Don Digirolamo, Gene Cantamessa (sound); Charles L. Campbell, Ben Burtt (sound effects editing)

⚲ picture; Steven Spielberg; Melissa Matheson (original screenplay); Allen Daviau (cinematography); Carol Littleton (film editing)

Ⓣ John Williams

'Love is blind. . .luckily.'

Eagle Vs Shark (new)

SCR/DIR *Taika Waititi*
2007 88m New Zealand
DVD

☆ Loren Horsley (Lily), Jemaine Clement (Jarrod), Joel Tobeck (Damien), Brian Sergent (Jonah), Craig Hall (Doug), Rachel House (Nancy)

A socially inept waitress falls for a self-absorbed gaming enthusiast who scarcely acknowledges her presence.

Offbeat comedy laced with deadpan humour but short on actual laughs. Its deluded protagonists clearly deserve each other; whether we deserve them is another matter entirely.

CIN Adam Clark MUS Phoenix Foundation DES Joe Bleakley ED Jonathan Woodford-Robinson
PROD Ainsley Gardiner, Cliff Curtis DIST Optimum Releasing

---

66 A kind of cinematic coconut shy, piled high with trashy decor, uglied-up actors and broad comic stereotypes. – *Xan Brooks, Guardian*

66 A small, intermittently charming, sometimes tiresome celebration of quirkiness. – *A.O. Scott, New York Times*

† The title refers to the costumes the lead characters wear to a fancy dress party.

Earth ★★★

SCR/DIR *Alexander Dovzhenko*
1930 63m USSR
DVD

☆ Semyon Svashenko (Basil), Stephan Shkurat (Opanas), Mikola Nademsky (Grandfather Simon), Yelena Maximova (Basil's Fiancee)

Trouble results in a Ukrainian village when a landowner refuses to hand over his land for a collective farm.

The melodramatic plot takes second place to lyrical, radiant sequences of rustic beauty, illustrating life, love and death in the countryside, of a quality that at the time had never before been seen on film.

CIN Danylo Demutsky ED Alexander Dovzhenko
DIST VUFKU

66 Stories in themselves do not interest me. I choose them in order to get the greatest expression of essential social forms. – *Dovzhenko*

66 A picture for filmgoers who are prepared to take their cinema as seriously as Tolstoy took the novel. – *James Agate*

Earth (new) ★

SCR/DIR *Alastair Fothergill, Mark Linfield*
2007 99m UK/Germany
DVD ♫

☆ Patrick Stewart (Narrator)

Natural history documentary showing the effects of seasons and climate on various species worldwide.

Epic work that deserves a big-screen release. But the subject was explored more fully and satisfyingly on the BBC's Planet Earth series.

SCR Leslie Megahey, Alastair Fothergill, Mark Linfield
CIN 30 various MUS George Fenton ED Martin Elsbury PROD Alix Tidmarsh, Sophokles Tasoulis
DIST Lionsgate

---

66 Earth isn't especially subtle in the way it rings out its environmental message. – *Jane Lamacraft, Sight & Sound*

Easter Parade ★★★

DIR Charles Walters
1948   109m   US
[DVD]   ♫

☆ *Fred Astaire, Judy Garland*, Ann Miller, Peter Lawford, Clinton Sundberg, Jules Munshin

A song and dance man quarrels with his female partner, and trains a new young protegée in order to spite her.

A musical without much of a story; essentially it exists as a vehicle for Irving Berlin's songs. Happily, most of them are sublime.

SCR Sidney Sheldon, Frances Goodrich, Albert Hackett **CIN** Harry Stradling   **PROD** Arthur Freed   **DIST** MGM

66 The important thing is that Fred Astaire is back, with Irving Berlin calling the tunes. – *Newsweek*

† Fred Astaire was actually second choice, replacing Gene Kelly who damaged an ankle.

† 'Happy Easter'; 'Drum Crazy'; 'It Only Happens When I Dance With You'; 'A Fella with an Umbrella'; 'I Love a Piano'; 'When the Midnight Choo-Choo Leaves for Alabama'; 'Steppin' Out With My Baby'; 'A Couple of Swells'; 'Easter Parade'

⚖ Roger Edens, Johnny Green (music)

'Every sin leaves a mark.'

Eastern Promises (new) ★★

DIR David Cronenberg
2007   100m   UK/Canada/US
[DVD]   ♫

☆ *Viggo Mortensen* (Nikolai Luzhin), Naomi Watts (Anna), Vincent Cassel (Kirill), Armin Mueller-Stahl (Semyon), Sinéad Cusack (Helen), Donald Sumpter (Yuri)

A London midwife cares for a pregnant 14-year-old Russian prostitute who dies in childbirth. Her diary implicates a Russian gang boss in her death, and the midwife confronts him.

Brutal and blood-spattered from the first scene, but a gripping story that delves into a mysterious underworld. Mortensen is excellent as the Russian gang's enigmatic enforcer; less familiar views of London are shot in a sombre light.

SCR Steve Knight   **CIN** Peter Suchitzky   **MUS** Howard Shore   **DES** Carol Spier   **ED** Ronald Sanders **PROD** Paul Webster, Robert Lantos   **DIST** Pathé

66 An exciting story about hypocrisy, decency and different kinds of honour, and about the dark side of globalisation and multi-culturalism. – *Philip French, Observer*

66 Promises more than it delivers. – *Sukhdev Sandhu, Daily Telegraph*

† Screenwriter Steve Knight also explored a little-known area of London life in Dirty Pretty Things.

⚖ Viggo Mortensen (leading actor)

Ⓣ British film; Viggo Mortensen (leading actor)

'A man went looking for America and couldn't find it anywhere!'

Easy Rider ★★★★

DIR Dennis Hopper
1969   94m   US
[DVD]   ♫

☆ Peter Fonda (Captain America/Wyatt), Dennis Hopper (Billy), *Jack Nicholson* (George Hanson), Antonio Mendoza (Jesus), Phil Spector (Connection), Robert Walker (Jack)

Two hippie drop-outs ride from California to New Orleans, looking for the soul of America and hoping to conclude a drug deal.

A film that sent shock waves through Hollywood, opening up possibilities for a new, young, dissident generation of film-makers, actors and film audiences. Essentially, it's a great soundtrack held together by attractive landscape imagery, some rambling conversational set-pieces and a wildly melodramatic ending, but it chimed with the spirit of its turbulent times to a remarkable extent. Fonda and Hopper don't have to say or do much, so it's left to Nicholson, as a drink-sodden attorney, to voice the sour dissatisfaction with America that lies at the story's heart. It would be his major breakthrough movie.

SCR Peter Fonda, Dennis Hopper, Terry Southern **CIN** Laszlo Kovacs   **MUS** various recordings   **ED** Donn Cambern   **PROD** Peter Fonda **DIST** Columbia/Pando/Raybert

66 Cinéma-vérité in allegory terms. – *Peter Fonda*

66 Ninety-four minutes of what it is like to swing, to watch, to be fond, to hold opinions and to get killed in America at this moment. – *Penelope Gilliatt*

⚖ screenplay; Jack Nicholson (supporting actor)

Easy Street ★★★★

SCR/DIR *Charles Chaplin*
1917   22m   US
[DVD]

☆ *Charles Chaplin*, Edna Purviance, Albert Austin, Eric Campbell

In a slum street, a tramp is reformed by a dewy-eyed missionary, becomes a policeman, and tames the local bully.

Quintessential Chaplin short film, combining sentimentality and social comment with hilarious slapstick.

CIN William C. Foster, Rollie Totheroh **DIST** Mutual/Charles Chaplin

'They were fighting over a woman until the plane went down. Now, their only chance for survival is each other.'

The Edge ★

DIR Lee Tamahori
1997   117m   US
[DVD]   ♫

☆ Anthony Hopkins (Charles Morse), Alec Baldwin (Robert Green), Elle Macpherson (Mickey Morse), Harold Perrineau (Stephen), L.Q. Jones (Styles), Kathleen Wilhoite (Ginny)

After a plane crash, a millionaire and the photographer he suspects of having an affair with his model wife are stranded in a forest and forced to work together to evade a hungry bear.

The (somewhat self-serious) psychological duel of the first half gives way to conventional action-adventure business; Hopkins appears energised by all the fresh air, but it's Bart the bear who walks off with a good-looking, solidly entertaining picture.

SCR David Mamet   **CIN** *Donald M. McAlpine*   **MUS** *Jerry Goldsmith*   **DES** Wolf Kroeger   **ED** Neil Travis   **PROD** Art Linson   **DIST** TCF

66 An action movie with that little bit extra to sink your teeth into. – *Tom Charity, Time Out*

66 Merits a modest cheer as an action film that celebrates not brute force but survival of the smartest. – *Richard Corliss, Time*

The Edge of Heaven (new)   ★★

SCR/DIR Fatih Akin
2007   120m   Germany/Turkey
DVD   ♫

☆ Baki Davrak (Nejat Aksu), Nursel Köse (Yeter Öztürk), Hanna Schygulla (Susanne Staub), Tunzel Kurtiz (Ali Aksu), Nurgül Yesilcay (Ayten Öztürk), Patrycia Ziolkowska (Lotte Staub)

Three families are linked by the death of a prostitute in Bremen and a student's murder in Istanbul.

Intricate, touching fable with a humanist message from a Turkish-German filmmaker keen to explore the differences and similarities between his two host cultures.

CIN Rainer Klausmann   **MUS** Shantel   **DES** Tamo Kunz, Sirma Bradley   **ED** Andrew Bird   **PROD** Andreas Thiel, Klaus Maek, Fatih Akin

66 An utterly assured, profoundly moving [and] superbly cast drama. – *Derek Elley, Variety*

66 A passionate, ambitious and charismatically performed work that tackles issues as diverse as the psychology of diaspora, cross-generational kinship and Turkey's entry into the EU. – *Sukhdev Sandhu, Telegraph*

† This and Head-On form the first two parts of the writer-director's loosely connected 'Love, Death and the Devil' trilogy.

'Wife. Husband. Friend. Lover.'

The Edge of Love (new)   ★★

DIR John Maybury
2008   110m   UK
♫

☆ Keira Knightley (Vera Phillips), *Sienna Miller* (Caitlin Thomas), Cillian Muphy (Capt. William Killick), *Matthew Rhys* (Dylan Thomas)

In London during the Blitz, Welsh poet Dylan Thomas reunites with his teenage sweetheart Vera Lewis, now a nightclub singer. She and his spirited wife Caitlin start a friendship before Vera is courted by Killick, an intense young soldier, who goes off to fight. The other three move to rural Wales, and on Killick's return he suspects betrayal.

This speculative account of an interesting story remains unfocused and lacks dramatic thrust. It veers between routine melodrama and an over-glamorised account of good times during the Blitz – director Maybury zeroes in frequently on Vera's bright red lips at a microphone as she sings. Still, the cast acquit themselves well, especially Miller as the life-force Caitlin, and Rhys as her boozy, petulant poet husband.

SCR Sharman Macdonald   **CIN** Jonathan Freeman   **MUS** Angelo Badalamenti   **DES** Alan MacDonald   **ED** Emma E. Hickox   **PROD** Sarah Radclyffe, Rebekah Gilbertson   **DIST** Lionsgate

66 While the period drama has several redeeming features, tonally it's all over the map, veering between artsy stylization and hum-drum, sometimes almost twee melodrama. – *Leslie Felperin, Variety*

66 Doesn't quite know what it's trying to do or say, but is darkly seductive and entertaining none the less. – *Sukhdev Sandhu, Daily Telegraph*

† Producer Rebekah Gilbertson is the grand-daughter of William Killick and Vera Phillips.

'The Story Of A Nobody Everybody Is Watching!'

EdTV   ★

DIR Ron Howard
1999   122m   US
DVD   ♫

☆ Matthew McConaughey (Ed Pekurny), Jenna Elfman (Shari), Woody Harrelson (Ray Pekurny), Ellen DeGeneres (Cynthia Topping), Sally Kirkland (Al), Martin Landau (Jeanette), Rob Reiner (Mr Whitaker), Dennis Hopper (Henry Pekurny), Elizabeth Hurley (Jill), Clint Howard (Ken)

A shop worker's life is turned upside down after he agrees to be filmed round the clock by a cable TV channel.

Thoughtful but light-hearted movie reflecting perceptively on the hidden perils and massive complications of life in the public eye. Not as profound as The Truman Show but far funnier – and a story that foreshadows the upsurge of reality TV.

SCR Lowell Ganz, Babaloo Mandel   **CIN** John Schwartzman   **MUS** Randy Edelman   **DES** Michael Corenblith   **ED** Mike Hill, Dan Hanley   **PROD** Brian Grazer, Ron Howard, Jeffrey T. Barabe   **DIST** Universal/Imagine

66 Despite the film's superficial similarity to The Truman Show, it is a much different animal. Where Truman was cerebral and foreboding, EdTV is boisterous and irreverent. Truman was the kind of the movie that could make you shed a tear, EdTV is the kind of movie that could make you squirt milk out of your nose. – *Margaret A. McGurk, Cincinnati Enquirer*

The Edukators   ★★

DIR Hans Weingartner
2004   127m   Germany/Austria
DVD   ♫

☆ Daniel Bruhl (Jan), Julia Jentsch (Jule), Stipe Erceg (Peter), Burghart Klaussner (Hardenberg)

A trio of young political activists, who break into the homes of the wealthy in order to rearrange their

DVD Available on DVD   ☆ Cast in order of importance   66 Critics' Quotes   † Points of interest   Academy Award   Academy Award nomination   BAFTA   BAFTA nomination
♫ Soundtrack on CD

furniture, are forced to kidnap an industrialist when one of their stunts goes awry.

Appealing romantic drama, contrasting the ideals of past and present; rather than batter an audience over the head with its heroes' anti-capitalist rhetoric, it permits both kidnappers and kidnapped time to air their views, and advocates simply hanging out, the procrastination that comes with listening and which allows for learning, as a viable political position.

SCR *Katharina Held, Hans Weingartner* **CIN** Matthias Schellenberg, Daniela Knapp **MUS** Andreas Wodraschke **DES** Christian M. Goldbeck **ED** Dirk Oetelshoven, Andreas Wodraschke **PROD** Hans Weingartner, Antonin Svoboda **DIST** UGC

66 An engaging entertainment that packages its thought-provoking ideas in a combination of political thriller, comic adventure and romantic triangle. – *Andrew O'Hehir, Salon*

66 If you can look beyond the simple-minded Socratic discourse, The Edukators reveals itself as warm, humane and sad, a movie that genuinely wants you to think about how idealism eventually collides with human frailty, and about what upstarts and sell-outs might teach one another. – *M.E. Russell, Portland Oregonian*

'A Classic Tale of Sex, Revenge, and Love.'

Edward II ★★

DIR *Derek Jarman*
1991 90m GB
DVD ♫

☆ Steven Waddington (Edward II), Kevin Collins (Lightborn), Andrew Tiernan (Piers Gaveston), John Lynch (Spencer), Dudley Sutton (Bishop of Winchester), Tilda Swinton (Isabella), Jerome Flynn (Kent), Jody Graber (Prince Edward), Nigel Terry (Mortimer), Annie Lennox (singer)

Edward II's overwhelming passion for commoner Piers Gaveston causes chaos at court and leads to his downfall.

Director Jarman concentrates on the gay aspects of Marlowe's play in this powerful modern-dress re-working, which in his hands doubles as a rant against homophobia.

SCR Derek Jarman, Stephen McBride, Ken Butler **CIN** Ian Wilson **MUS** Simon Fisher Turner **DES** Christopher Hobbs **ED** George Akers **PROD** Steve Clark-Hall, Antony Root **DIST** Palace/Edward II/Working Title/British Screen/BBC

66 This modern dress adaptation of Marlowe's play excites through its sheer guts and combativeness. – *Time Out*

'His scars run deep.'

Edward Scissorhands ★

DIR Tim Burton
1990 105m US
DVD ♫

☆ Johnny Depp (Edward), Winona Ryder (Kim), Dianne Wiest (Peg), Anthony Michael Hall (Jim), Alan Arkin (Bill), Kathy Baker (Joyce), Robert Oliveri (Kevin), Conchata Ferrell (Helen), Vincent Price (The Inventor)

A mad scientist dies, leaving a boy with shears instead of hands and a struggle to find acceptance in suburbia.

Moving modern fairy-tale, with nods to Beauty and the Beast; its highlights include an imaginative script and a surreal view of America's suburbs.

SCR Caroline Thompson **CIN** Stefan Czapsky **MUS** Danny Elfman **DES** *Bo Welch* **ED** Richard Halsey, Colleen Halsey **PROD** Denise de Novi, Tim Burton **DIST** Fox

66 Enchantment on the cutting edge, a dark, yet heartfelt portrait of the artist as a young mannequin. – *Rita Kempley, Washington Post*

⬩ Ve Neill, Stan Winston (make up)

⬩ Bo Welch

⬩ Stan Winston (special visual effects); Colleen Atwood (costume); Ve Neill, Stan Winston (make up)

The Eel ★★

DIR Shohei Imamura
1996 117m Japan
DVD

☆ Koji Yakusho (Takuro Yamashita), Misa Shimizu (Keiko Hattori), Fujio Tsuneta (Jiro Nakajima), Mitsuko Baisho (Misako Nakajima), Makoto Sato (Jukichi Takada), Akira Emoto (Tamotsu Takasaki), Sho Aihara (Yuji Nozawa), Ken Kobayashi (Masaki Saito), Sabu Kawahara (Seitaro Misato), Etsuko Ichihara (Fumie Hattori)

After a man serves a prison sentence for murdering his adulterous wife, he opens a barber's shop, tries to re-integrate into society, and hires a suicidal young woman to help him.

Unusual, intriguing, at times almost upbeat account of a taciturn, closed-off man coming to terms with a new phase of his life, and reaching out to engage with others, maybe even more unfortunate than him. The progression from its bloody opening to its end is marked by cautious optimism.

SCR Motofumi Tomikawa, Daisuke Tengan, Shohei Imamura **CIN** Shigeru Komatsubara **MUS** Shinichiro Ikebe **DES** Hisao Inagaki **ED** Hajime Okayasu **PROD** Hisa Iino **DIST** Artificial Eye/KSS/Eisei Gekijo/Groove/Shochiku

66 It's a film with all the rough edges that Hollywood routinely smoothes away. – *Tony Rayns, Sight & Sound*

† The film won the Palme d'Or at the 1997 Cannes Film Festival.

8 and a Half ★★★

DIR *Federico Fellini*
1963 138m Italy
DVD

☆ *Marcello Mastroianni* (Guido Anselmi), Claudia Cardinale (Claudia), Anouk Aimée (Luisa Anselmi), Sandra Milo (Carla), Rossella Falk (Rossella), Barbara Steele (Gloria Morin), Madeleine Lebeau (French Actress)

A successful film director, on the verge of a nervous breakdown and in crisis over his career, has conflicting fantasies about his life.

A Fellini self-portrait: a coruscating, melancholy, self-reflecting spectacle of a man close to his wits' end, and

wondering how to sustain his creativity and reputation – whether to repeat the style of his successes or strive for new areas of endeavour. Necessarily self-indulgent, but heartfelt and true to itself, none the less.

SCR Federico Fellini, Ennio Flaiano, Tullio Pinelli, Brunello Rondi   CIN Gianni di Venanzo   MUS Nino Rota   ED Leo Catozzo   PROD Angelo Rizzoli   DIST Cineriz

66 The whole may add up to a magnificent folly, but it is too singular, too candid, too vividly and insistently alive to be judged as being in any way diminishing. – Peter John Dyer, Monthly Film Bulletin

66 Fellini's intellectualizing is not even like dogs dancing; it is not done well, nor does it surprise us that it is done at all. It merely palls on us, and finally appals us. – John Simon

⫶ foreign film; Piero Gherardi (costume design)
⫶ Federico Fellini (as director); original screenplay; Piero Gherardi (art direction)

'When sexual desire becomes an obsession, it's every man for himself.'

Eight and a Half Women   ★

SCR/DIR Peter Greenaway
1999   118m   Netherlands/GB/Luxembourg/Germany
DVD

☆ John Standing (Philip Emmenthal), Matthew Delamerie (Storey Emmenthal), Vivian Wu (Kito), Shizuka Inoh (Simato), Barbara Sarafian (Clothilde), Kirina Mano (Mio), Toni Collette (Griselda/Sister Concordia), Amanda Plummer (Beryl), Natacha Amal (Giaconda the Baby Factory), Manna Fujiwara (Giulietta/Half Woman), Polly Walker (Palmira)

A wealthy English businessman and his playboy son are inspired to create their own private brothel on their Swiss estate.

Interesting mainly because of Greenaway's insistence that this was a tribute to Fellini. Some tribute. It certainly has style to burn, but its lip-smacking male fantasies leave a bad taste, even when they are finally thwarted.

CIN Sacha Vierny, Reinier Van Brummelen   DES Wilbert Van Dorp, Emi Wada   ED Elmer Leupen   PROD Kees Kasander   DIST Pathé

66 Peter Greenaway's latest foray into highbrow elitism will test the endurance of even his most fervent admirers. – Jeremiah Kipp, Filmcritic.com

---

'The Scandal That Rocked A Nation.'

Eight Men Out   ★★★

DIR John Sayles
1988   119m   US
DVD

☆ John Cusack (Buck Weaver), Clifton James (Charles Comiskey), Michael Lerner (Arnold Rothstein), Christopher Lloyd (Bill Burns), John Mahoney (Kid Gleason), Charlie Sheen (Hap Felsch), David Strathairn (Eddie Cicotte), D.B. Sweeney ('Shoeless' Joe Jackson)

Baseball's darkest moment, when eight members of the 1919 Chicago White Sox took bribes to lose the World Series, is brought back to life.

This drama about corruption in sport makes enthralling viewing, even for non-baseball fans. As one would expect from this director, the social temperature of the time and its economic pressures are thoroughly explored.

SCR John Sayles   CIN Robert Richardson   MUS Mason Daring   DES Nora Chavooshian   ED John Tintori   PROD Sarah Pillsbury, Midge Sandford   DIST Rank/Orion

BOY WHITE SOX FAN (TO 'SHOELESS' JOE JACKSON: 'Say it ain't so, Joe.'

66 Perhaps the saddest chapter in the annals of professional American sport is recounted in absorbing fashion. – Variety

---

'Every moment is another chance.'

8 Mile   ★★

DIR Curtis Hanson
2002   110m   US/Germany
DVD   ♫

☆ Eminem (Jimmy Smith Jnr), Kim Basinger (Stephanie), Brittany Murphy (Alex), Mekhi Phifer (Future), Evan Jones (Cheddar Bob), Omar Benson Miller (Sol George)

A trailer-trash white boy comes good by winning a rap contest.

The hip-hop Rocky formula works well in the electrifying duels on stage, less so when off it. Even with his persona tamped down, Eminem's a hypnotic presence, and working-class Detroit is unforgettably captured by crew and director.

SCR Scott Silver   CIN Rodrigo Prieto   MUS Proof   DES Philip Messina   ED Jay Rabinowitz, Craig Kitson   PROD Brian Grazer, Curtis Hanson, Jimmy Iovine   DIST Universal

66 The rough power, as well as the humor and sensitivity, of pop phenom Eminem is delivered intact. – Todd McCarthy, Variety

66 Because it rejects easy victories, this may be one of the few inspirational movies that could actually inspire someone, somewhere, sometime. – Richard Shickel, Time

⫶ Eminem, Jeff Bass (m), Luis Resto (ly) (music, original song – Lose Yourself) Eminem

---

'Living in a house full of women can be murder'

8 Women   ★

DIR François Ozon
2001   111m   France/ Italy
DVD   ♫

☆ Catherine Deneuve (Gaby), Isabelle Huppert (Augustine), Emmanuelle Béart (Louise), Fanny Ardant (Pierrette), Virginie Ledoyen (Suzon), Danielle Darrieux (Mamy), Ludivine Sagnier (Catherine), Firmine Richard (Mme Chanel)

A man is murdered in a snowed-in country mansion, and his family try to nail the culprit.

Deliberately flimsy pastiche of an old-school whodunit, with three generations of French actresses vamping it up – some better than others – and often breaking out in song. The studied artificiality is an acquired taste.

DVD Available on DVD   ☆ Cast in order of importance   66 Critics' Quotes   ⫶ Academy Award   🎭 BAFTA
♫ Soundtrack on CD   † Points of interest   ⫶ Academy Award nomination   🎭 BAFTA nomination

SCR François Ozon, Marina de Van   CIN Jeanne Lapoirie
MUS Krishna Levy   DES Arnaud de Moleron
ED Laurence Bawedin   PROD Olivier Delbosc, Marc
Missonnier   DIST UGC

66 Indefensible, cynical, even grotesque; it is also pure –
that is to say innocent and uncorrupted – fun. – *A.O. Scott,
New York Times*

The Eighth Day ★

SCR/DIR Jaco Van Dormael
1996   118m   France/Belguim/GB
DVD   ♫

☆ *Daniel Auteuil* (Harry), *Pascal Duquenne* (Georges),
Miou-Miou (Julie), Isabelle Sadoyan (Georges' Mother),
Henri Garcin (Bank Director), Michele Maes (Nathalie)

A stressed executive is befriended by a young man
with Down's syndrome.

*An affecting, nicely performed study of the relationship
between two men out on their own in the world,
compromised by irritating fantasy sequences and an
absolute howler of an ending.*

CIN Walther Van den Ende   MUS Pierre Van Dormael
DES Hubert Pouille   ED Susana Rossberg
PROD Philippe Godeau   DIST Polygram/Pan-
Europééne/Home Made/TF1/RTL/TVI/Working
Title/DA

66 May need a certain willingness to swallow its cartoon-
like sweetness, but it errs on the right side of innocence
and remains a heartening experience. – *Alexander Walker,
Evening Standard*

66 Simultaneously sentimental and – ultimately –
unnecessarily negative in its attitude towards Down's
syndrome. – *Anne Billson, Sunday Telegraph*

† The two leads shared the prize for best actor at the 1996
Cannes Film Festival.

'Reading. Writing. Revenge.'

Election ★★★

DIR *Alexander Payne*
1999   103m   US
DVD   ♫

☆ *Matthew Broderick* (Jim McAllister), *Reese Witherspoon*
(Tracy Flick), Chris Klein (Paul Metzler), Jessica Campbell
(Tammy Metzler), Mark Harelik (Dave Novotny), Phil
Reeves (Walt Hendricks), Molly Hagan (Diane McAllister),
Delaney Driscoll (Linda Novotny), Colleen Camp (Judith
R. Flick)

A bitter teacher sets out to derail the plans of an
obsessively ambitious teenage girl, an academic star
who wants to be student president at a Midwest
high school.

*Brilliant comedic fun, underscored by obvious parallels
with electioneering in national politics. Witherspoon
plays her young over-achiever to a T, but Broderick,
playing somewhat against type, matches her as a
diligent teacher trying to rein her in. There's not a dull
moment.*

SCR *Alexander Payne, Jim Taylor*   CIN James Glennon
MUS Rolfe Kent   DES Jane Ann Stewart   ED Kevin Tent
PROD Albert Berger, Ron Yerxa, David Gale, Keith Samples
DIST Paramount

66 This remarkable film may be set in high school, but
its satiric take on moral corruption, political chicanery,
adultery and seduction is anything but juvenile. – *Time
Out*

66 Irresistibly sarcastic. – *Jeff Millar, Houston Chronicle*
⚱ Alexander Payne, Jim Taylor (adapted screenplay)

'An ordinary high school day. Except that it's not.'

Elephant ★★

SCR/DIR Gus Van Sant
2003   81m   US
DVD

☆ *Alex Frost* (Alex), Eric Deulen (Eric), John Robinson
(John McFarland), Elias McConnell (Elias), Jordan Taylor
(Jordan), Carrie Finklea (Carrie), Nicole George (Nicole),
Brittany Mountain (Brittany)

Two disaffected high school students massacre
fellow pupils and teachers in a school in Portland,
Oregon

*This slow, inexorable depiction of a shocking incident
was based on the Columbine high-school killings.
Director Van Sant chooses to portray the intense
boredom of a huge, impersonal high school, where
slights and taunts between pupils can have tragic
consequences. It's alienating and riveting at the same
time.*

CIN Harris Savides   ED Gus Van Sant   PROD Dany Wolf
DIST Optimum

66 Elephant is pseudo-important posturing without either
original thought or the excitement of an unashamed
exploitation movie. – *Nev Pierce, BBC*

66 Gripping and superbly made. – *Peter Bradshaw,
Guardian*

† In 2003, Elephant won the Palme D'Or at the Cannes
Film Festival. Van Sant was named best director.

'11 directors, 11 stories, 1 film.'

11' 09" 01 September 11 ★★

2002   134m   France/Iran/Egypt/Bosnia-Herzegovina/
Burkina Faso/GB/Mexico/Israel/India/US/Japan
DVD

11 directors from around the world respond to
the 9/11 attacks, in films that are each 9 minutes,
11 seconds and one frame long.

*As with most portmanteau films, this is a hugely
mixed proposition, its segments ranging in tone from
the stark and polemical (Ken Loach recalling 9/11/73,
when the US government backed the coup in Chile) to
the careful and pensive (Samira Makhmalbaf) to the
nakedly arty (Alejandro González Iñárritu). In the
worst ones, Sean Penn throws in gooey magic realism,
and Claude Lelouch ash-covered romantic sentiment.
It's provoking in ways both good and bad.*

DIST Artificial Eye

66 A bold attempt to define the terrorist attack as a
global event, and a global tragedy. – *Peter Bradshaw,
Guardian*

'Turn mankind's darkest hour into its finest.'

The 11th Hour (new)

DIR Leila Conners Petersen, Nadia Conners
2007 92m US
`DVD` ♫

☆ Leonardo DiCaprio (Narrator), Stephen Hawking (Himself), Mikhail Gorbachev (Himself), Andy Revkin (Himself), Lester Brown (Himself), Tim Carmichael (Himself), Wes Jackson (Himself)

How climate change and unsustainable living is destroying the planet, and what can be done to save it.

Eco-conscious documentary that bombards the viewer with so many dire predictions it makes An Inconvenient Truth look like a comedy. Its message is a sound one, even if it is being preached to the choir.

SCR Leonardo DiCaprio, Leila Conners Peterson, Nadia Conners **CIN** Peter Youngblood Hills, Andrew Rowland, Brian Knappenberger **MUS** Jean Pascal Beintus, Eric Avery **DES** Nadia Conners **ED** Pietro Scalia, Luis Alvarez y Alvarez **PROD** Leonardo DiCaprio, Leila Conners Petersen, Chuck Castleberry, Brian Gerber **DIST** Warner Brothers

66 An unnerving, surprisingly affecting documentary about our environmental calamity. . .essential viewing. – *Manohla Dargis, New York Times*

66 There's something a little off about an actor who reportedly earns some $20 million for one film fronting a movie that blames rapacious consumerism for the parlous state of our planet's ecosystems. – *Wendy Ide, The Times*

Elisa ★

DIR Jean Becker
1995 114m France
`DVD`

☆ *Vanessa Paradis* (Marie Desmoulin), Gérard Depardieu (Jacques 'Lébovitch' Desmoulin), Clothilde Courau (Solange), Sekkou Sall (Ahmed), Florence Thomassin (Elisa Desmoulin)

A cunning femme fatale blames her absent father for the tragic death of her mother and plots revenge.

Vanessa Paradis looks determined to prove she can act as well as sing, and narrowly convinces in this competently related account of a family vendetta.

SCR Jean Becker, Fabrice Carazo **CIN** Etienne Becker **MUS** Zbigniew Preisner, Michel Colombier **DES** Thérèse Ripaud **ED** Jacques Witta **PROD** Henri Brichetti, Christian Fechner **DIST** Gala/Christian Fechner/Solo/TF1

'Woman. Warrior. Queen.'

Elizabeth: The Golden Age (new) ★★

DIR Shekhar Kapur
2007 114m UK/US/Germany/France
`DVD` ♫

☆ *Cate Blanchett* (Queen Elizabeth), Geoffrey Rush (Sir Francis Walsingham), Clive Owen (Sir Walter Raleigh), Rhys Ifans (Robert Reston), Jordi Mollá (King Philip of Spain), Abbie Cornish (Bess Throckmorton)

In the middle years of her rein, Queen Elizabeth I continues to ward off plots against her. The Spanish monarch Philip II launches a naval attack against England. She begins a flirtation with the adventurer Walter Raleigh, but he begins an affair with her lady-in-waiting.

Disappointing sequel to the first Elizabeth film from this creative team. It looks equally sumptuous, and Blanchett plays the middle-aged monarch with imperious skill. But Elizabeth's romance with Raleigh feels implausible, and too many liberties are taken with historical fact.

SCR William Nicholson, Michael Hirst **CIN** Remi Adefarasin **MUS** Craig Armstrong, A.R. Rahman **DES** Guy Hendrix Dyas **ED** Jill Bilcock **PROD** Tim Bevan, Eric Fellner, Jonathan Cavendish **DIST** Universal

66 Making soap of statecraft, the film has plenty of juicy moments, but offers an inconsistent rather than complex view of Elizabeth. – *Ben Walters, Time Out*

66 Despite Blanchett's continuing excellence, The Golden Age only fitfully gleams. – *Geoffrey Macnab, Sight & Sound*

⚊ Alexandra Byrne (costume design)
⚊ Cate Blanchett (leading actress)

Ⓣ Cate Blanchett (leading actress); Guy Hendrix Dyas; Alexandra Byrne (costume design); Jenny Shircore (make up and hair)

'Declared Illegitimate Aged 3. Tried For Treason Aged 21. Crowned Queen Aged 25.'

Elizabeth ★★★

DIR Shekhar Kapur
1998 124m GB
`DVD` ♫

☆ *Cate Blanchett* (Elizabeth I), *Geoffrey Rush* (Sir Francis Walsingham), Christopher Eccleston (Duke of Norfolk), Joseph Fiennes (Robert Dudley, Earl of Leicester), Richard Attenborough (Sir William Cecil), Fanny Ardant (Mary of Guise), Kathy Burke (Queen Mary Tudor), Eric Cantona (Monsieur de Foix), James Frain (Alvaro de la Quadra), Vincent Cassel (Duc d'Anjou), Daniel Craig (John Ballard), John Gielgud (The Pope), Angus Deayton (Waad, Chancellor of the Exchequer), Edward Hardwicke (Earl of Arundel), Terence Rigby (Bishop Gardiner)

Historical drama following the life of Queen Elizabeth from innocent young woman to England's legendary Virgin Queen.

Bold attempt to re-create the massive political turmoil in 16th-century Britain while focussing on Elizabeth's astonishing personal growth from shy, withdrawn girl to motivated and powerful queen. Blanchett shows remarkable authority in her regal role, while the occasional rewriting of history seems acceptable and scarcely spoils the spectacle.

SCR Michael Hirst **CIN** Remi Adefarasin **MUS** David Hirschfelder **DES** John Myhre **ED** Jill Bilcock **PROD** Alison Owen, Eric Fellner, Tim Bevan **DIST** Polygram/Channel 4/Working Title

66 Director Kapur can't decide if he's making an art movie or a melodrama, an opera or a soap opera. – *David Denby, New Yorker*

E

At the climax of the 2008 awards season, the Oscar winners for acting, (left to right) Daniel Day-Lewis, Tilda Swinton, Marion Cotillard and Javier Bardem, compare the size of their statuettes.

A strange thing happened on 14 January 2008. Life went on as normal. The clocks did not stop. People went about their normal business. Somehow the world kept turning – despite the fact that the glitzy televised Golden Globes awards ceremony, scheduled for the previous night, had to be cancelled because of the Hollywood writers' strike.

Yes, humankind pulled through, hard though that may be to believe. Or at least it might be hard to believe if you toil in one of a wide variety of jobs supporting the bloated charade that is now the film industry's awards season. But it was true: the actors, glamorous or otherwise, who are the centrepiece of such events, declared their solidarity with the striking screenwriters, and boycotted the ceremony. And so those TV viewers who cared enough to know the names of the Golden Globes winners were treated (if that's the word) to a notably dull press conference to announce them.

Stripped of the presence of celebrities, one saw this event for what it is: no different from the annual gathering of trade associations that pack ballrooms in big London hotels like the Dorchester and the Grosvenor House on most nights of the year. Getting an award from the Hollywood Foreign Press Association, the startlingly small body of obscure journalists that doles out the Golden Globes, is equivalent to being named Innovator of the Year by the National Widget Manufacturers Association. Except, of course, you wear a designer tuxedo for the occasion.

The cancellation of the Globes did not result in riots in the streets. But then, why would it? The televised film awards ceremony is one of the dreariest forms of 'entertainment' yet devised. The parade of frocks, the tearful speeches of thanks, the grinning celebrities moving at a funereal pace along the red carpet to accommodate photographers and give banal interviews about their prospects: the smug insincerity of the whole business is all too apparent. No wonder TV audiences for such events are lower than ever.

It was all too good to be true, and though the next month's Academy Awards ceremonies seemed likely to be threatened by the lengthy writers' strike, few were surprised that a settlement was reached in time for the event to proceed in its customary format. Too much was at stake on both sides: writers, along with actors, directors and behind-the-camera craftspeople, know their fees will increase substantially if they are awarded an Oscar. The studios, meanwhile, regard the Oscar telecast as an invaluable marketing tool for the entire industry's output.

This last point is hard to over-emphasise. When you watch the Oscars on television, you are watching three hours (only three, if you're lucky) of thinly-veiled advertising for Hollywood. It is, if you will, the annual high point of the studio system's global media blitz. Since its foundation in 1922 the Motion Picture Association of America (the studios, basically) has co-operated closely with the US State Department in facilitating the distribution and exhibition of Hollywood films in far-flung corners of the globe. The deal was simple: the studios would make more money from selling its films in as many foreign territories as possible, while the State Department reaped a cultural benefit: people everywhere saw Hollywood movies and as a result they liked America a little bit more.

Broadly, this has worked – which is why for many years the American Academy boasted that the Oscar telecast was seen by a billion people all over the world. When a couple of years ago enough media commentators started sniping that this claim was clearly preposterous, the Academy changed its tune, claiming merely that 'several hundred million' TV viewers caught the Oscars. Even this is an exaggeration – but the fact that the Academy and the studios feel the need to make such claims has more to do with a desire for increased revenues than a love of verifiable fact.

> ' The cancellation of the Globes did not result in riots in the streets. But then, why would it? The televised film awards ceremony is one of the dreariest forms of "entertainment" yet devised. '

Still, the settlement failed to lift the gloom many of us feel about film awards ceremonies. To digress for a moment, is there any industry that arranges its annual output in such a bizarre manner as the film business? It has two peak periods: summer, when it releases the kid-friendly blockbusters that account for the bulk of studios' profits; and awards season, when all the grown-up, serious dramas and 'worthy' films see the light of day.

In both these periods, similar types of films compete in an overcrowded marketplace for a decent share of the audience. But that audience is finite, and this high-risk strategy ensures there will be big losers. Not much can be done about the warring blockbusters: summer is the season of long vacations, when school-age kids flock to cinemas. For those films even remotely likely to pick up awards, it's a different matter.

The veteran *Los Angeles Times* columnist Patrick Goldstein has written of 'the Oscar Follies, offering a legitimate batch of award contenders surrounded by a scrum of hapless pretenders being released at year's end only because of studio delusions, blind adherence to conventional wisdom and arm-twisting by narcissistic stars and filmmakers'. It's hard to improve on that assessment.

This past year has seen a welcome abundance of substantial films, all of which should have found appreciative adult audiences. But several of them were hurt by being released at a time that announced them as awards contenders, and were edged out of a crowded marketplace in which only so many films can prosper.

Victims of this overcrowding included Ang Lee's provocative but exquisite *Lust, Caution* – which was already an outside bet for awards recognition because it is a foreign-language film, and contains explicit sexual content. Another was *Before The Devil Knows You're Dead*, a brilliant, tense crime thriller, and veteran director Sidney Lumet's best work in years. Competing with higher-profile Oscar-chasing films, it failed to win a single major award; it didn't help that it was also a box-office flop, grossing less than $10 million in the US.

The same applied to *In the Valley of Elah*, except that Tommy Lee Jones got an Oscar nomination for his great lead performance. The film failed to find an audience, was unfortunately lumped in with a bunch of other serious movies about the conflicts in Iraq and the Middle East, and was effectively dumped by its studio.

All these films would have fared better had they been released at a time that removed them from awards consideration. Still, one can't single out the studios for blame. Everyone concerned with a film – producers, actors, directors and yes, writers – likes to see their work acknowledged, if only by the recognition that they're likely contenders for statuettes.

And so it goes on – the endless 'For Your Consideration' ads that studios and distributors place in the trade press to tout for awards, sometimes for the most implausible films and performances, primarily to massage the egos of everyone concerned. The six months of white noise that issues from the blogosphere about who's hot and who's not in the horse races for various awards categories. And the faux suspense about which actress will be wearing which designer's frock – and afterwards, did she look frumpish, or what?

It's harmless entertainment, of course, however irritating it gets. But when it gets in the way of decent films being seen as widely as they deserve, is awards-season hysteria really worth it?

66 It's a mark of how thoroughly Blanchett makes the role her own that we're reminded more of Diana and Thatcher than Glenda Jackson or Bette Davis. – *Tom Charity, Time Out*

⚲ Jenny Shircore (make up)

⚲ picture; Cate Blanchett (leading actress); Remi Adefarasin; David Hirschfelder; John Myhre; Alexandre Byrne (costume design)

🆃 British film; Cate Blanchett (leading actress); Geoffrey Rush (supporting actor); Remi Adefarasin; David Hirschfelder; Jenny Shircore (make up)

🆃 film; Shekhar Kapur; Michael Hirst (original screenplay); Jill Bilcock; John Myhre; Alexandre Byrne (costume design)

'They're packed and ready for the greatest adventure of their lives. All they have to do is get out of the house.'

Elling ★★

DIR Petter Naess
2001 89m Norway
DVD

☆ Per Christian Ellefsen (Elling), Sven Nordin (Kjell Bjarne), Per Christensen (Alfons Jorgensen), Jorgen Langhelle (Frank Asli), Marit Pia Jacobsen (Reidun Nordsletten)

Two men with mental-health problems leave hospital and move into a flat together in an attempt to deal with the outside world.

Mummy's boy meets slob, in a surprisingly affecting odd-couple comedy that rarely slips into sentimentality.

SCR Axel Hellstenius CIN Svein Krovel MUS Lars Lillo Stenberg DES Jan Sundberg ED Inge-Lise Langfeldt PROD Dag Alveberg DIST UIP

66 A witty and sophisticated sensibility brings individuality to the classic odd-couple comedy. – *Kevin Thomas, Los Angeles Times*

† A stage adaptation of the film opened in London's West End in 2007.

⚲ foreign language film

Éloge De L'Amour ★★

SCR/DIR Jean-Luc Godard
2001 97m France/Switzerland
DVD

☆ Bruno Putzulu (Edgar), Cecile Camp (Elle), Jean Davy (Grandfather), Françoise Verney (Grandmother), Audrey Klebaner (Eglantine), Jeremie Lippmann (Perceval), Claude Baigneres (Mr Rosenthal)

A writer and film-maker conceives a work about the love lives of three couples of different ages. But after his leading actress dies he realises he met her before in discussions about a Hollywood movie.

Godard returns to his earlier styles in this surreal, challenging film about love, history, memory and the effects of Hollywood on world culture. It's a bracing experience.

CIN Christophe Pollock, Julien Hirsch ED Raphaele Urtin PROD Ruth Waldburger, Alain Sarde DIST Optimum

66 It's the intellectual ride of your life, as far as movie-going goes. – *Desson Thomson, Washington Post*

'A new comedy from Jane Austen's timeless classic.'

Emma ★

SCR/DIR Douglas McGrath
1996 121m GB/US
DVD ♫

☆ *Gwyneth Paltrow* (Emma Woodhouse), Toni Collette (Harriet Smith), Jeremy Northam (Mr Knightly), Alan Cumming (Mr Elton), Ewan McGregor (Frank Churchill), Greta Scacchi (Mrs Weston), Juliet Stevenson (Mrs Elton), Polly Walker (Jane Fairfax), Sophie Thompson (Miss Bates), Phyllida Law (Mrs Bates)

In this latest Jane Austen adaptation, Emma's meddling matchmaking creates mayhem, but events turn out happily for her – almost against the odds.

Workmanlike and well-organised adaptation with perhaps slightly too much of an eye on the American market. Yet Paltrow throws herself gleefully into the role, capturing her heroine's perverse nature and nailing an English accent perfectly.

CIN Ian Wilson MUS Rachel Portman DES Michael Howells ED Lesley Walker PROD Patrick Cassavetti, Steven Haft DIST Buena Vista/Matchmaker/Miramax/Haft

66 Gwyneth Paltrow makes a resplendent Emma, gliding through the film with an elegance and patrician wit that bring the young Katharine Hepburn to mind – *Janet Maslin, New York Times*

⚲ Rachel Portman
⚲ Ruth Myers (costume design)

'To survive in a world at war, he must find a strength greater than all the events that surround him.'

Empire of the Sun ★★★

DIR *Steven Spielberg*
1987 154m US
DVD ♫

☆ *Christian Bale* (Jim Graham), John Malkovich (Basie), Miranda Richardson (Mrs. Victor), Nigel Havers (Dr. Rawlins), Joe Pantoliano (Frank Demarest)

Autobiographical story of an 11-year-old English boy stranded in a Japanese internment camp in China at the outbreak of World War II.

Enthralling movie that looks at the horrors of war through a child's eyes. Bale's remarkable portrayal of the boy was a memorable start to a considerable film career, but this well-judged film is the result of first-rate collaboration in all departments.

SCR *Tom Stoppard* CIN *Allen Daviau* MUS John Williams DES Norman Reynolds ED Michael Kahn PROD Steven Spielberg, Kathleen Kennedy, Frank Marshall DIST Robert Shapiro/Amblin

66 With an edgy, intelligent script by playwright Tom Stoppard, Mr Spielberg has made an extraordinary film out of Mr Ballard's extraordinary war experience. – *Julie Salamon, Wall Street Journal*

⚲ Allen Daviau; Michael Kahn; John Williams; Norman Reynolds; Bob Ringwood (costume design); Robert Knudson, Don Digirolamo, John Boyd, Tony Dawe (sound)

🆃 Allen Daviau; John Williams; Robert Knudson, Don Digirolamo, John Boyd, Tony Dawe (sound)

DVD Available on DVD	☆ Cast in order	66 Critics' Quotes	⚲ Academy Award	🆃 BAFTA
♫ Soundtrack on CD	of importance	† Points of interest	⚲ Academy Award nomination	🆃 BAFTA nomination

(T) Tom Stoppard (adapted screenplay); Norman Reynolds; Bob Ringwood (costume design)

'The real world and the animated world collide.'

Enchanted (new)   ★★★

DIR Kevin Lima

2007   107m   US

DVD   ♫

☆ *Amy Adams* (Giselle), Patrick Dempsey (Robert Philip), James Marsden (Prince Edward), Timothy Spall (Nathaniel), Idina Menzel (Nancy)

An animated fairy-tale princess in a magic kingdom is pushed down a well by an evil hag, and re-emerges as a live-action human being in modern-day New York City. There she becomes involved with a divorced lawyer who is a single father.

Delightful self-mocking spoof of traditional Disney movies that turns into an engaging, first-class romantic musical. Amy Adams plays the princess just knowingly enough.

SCR *Bill Kelly*   CIN Don Burgess   MUS Alan Menken DES Stuart Wurtzel   PROD Barry Josephson, Barry Sonnenfeld   DIST Buena Vista Intl.

ROBERT: 'I don't know if you're kidding or being ironic. It's like you escaped from a Hallmark card, or something.' GISELLE: 'Is that a bad thing?'

66 It may sound like faint praise to say that Enchanted is the movie of the year for smart and spirited 11-year-old girls. But a movie that genuinely respects that audience is not to be belittled. – *Peter Rainer, Christian Science Monitor*

66 Enchanting, fantastic fun for all the family. – *Christopher Tookey, Daily Mail*

† Jodi Benson, Paige O'Hara and Judy Kuhn, three actresses who have voiced princesses in earlier Disney animated films, have small parts in the live-action part of Enchanted.

♪ Alan Menken (m), Stephen Schwartz (ly), (music, – original songs Happy Working Song, So Close and That's How You Know)

'Escaping From Winter In London, They Planned A Holiday In Paradise. . .Everything Was Going Perfectly, Until The Men Arrived.'

Enchanted April   ★

DIR Mike Newell

1992   95m   GB

DVD

☆ Miranda Richardson (Rose Arbuthnot), Josie Lawrence (Lottie Wilkins), Polly Walker (Caroline Dester), Joan Plowright (Mrs. Fisher), Alfred Molina (Mellersh Wilkins), Michael Kitchen (George Briggs), Jim Broadbent (Frederick Arbuthnot)

Four bored, upper-crust Englishwomen take a break in an Italian castle in 1922.

A subtle, genteel drama with performances of practised professionalism.

SCR Peter Barnes   CIN Rex Maidment   MUS Richard Rodney Bennett   DES Malcolm Thornton   ED Dick Allen PROD Ann Scott   DIST Curzon/Miramax/BBC/Greenpoint

66 It's a jewel of a movie that brims with the pleasures of the unexpected. – *Peter Travers, Rolling Stone*

66 Period is tastefully evoked and loving care has gone into the visuals; but crucially a weak script lets down any spirit of adventure. – *Time Out*

† After performing moderately at the box-office in Britain, it opened in the US to critical acclaim and a better showing commercially.

♪ Joan Plowright (supporting actress); Peter Barnes (adapted screenplay); Sheena Napier (costume design)

'The end was just the beginning.'

The End of the Affair   ★★

SCR/DIR *Neil Jordan*

1999   102m   United Germany/ USA

DVD   ♫

☆ Ralph Fiennes (Maurice Bendrix), *Julianne Moore* (Sarah Miles), *Stephen Rea* (Henry Miles), Ian Hart (Mr Parkis), Samuel Bould (Lance Parkis), Jason Isaacs (Father Smythe), James Bolam (Mr Savage), Deborah Findlay (Miss Smythe)

A writer reflects on how he came to woo a married woman away from her civil-servant husband, and wonders why the affair came to naught.

Handsome, passionately performed period drama replaces the novel's ideas about religious faith with a more contemporary and affecting belief in love as the greatest miracle of all.

CIN *Roger Pratt*   MUS *Michael Nyman*   DES Anthony Pratt   ED Tony Lawson   PROD Stephen Woolley, Neil Jordan   DIST Columbia

66 Handsomely mounted, literate, emotionally sophisticated, The End of the Affair has everything a period romance should have. – *Kenneth Turan, Los Angeles Times*

66 The best and most graceful Greene adaptation since The Third Man. – *Janet Maslin, New York Times*

♪ Julianne Moore (leading actress); Roger Pratt

(T) Neil Jordan (adapted screenplay)

(T) film; Ralph Fiennes (leading actor); Julianne Moore (leading actress); Neil Jordan (direction); Roger Pratt; Michael Nyman; Anthony Pratt; Sandy Powell (costume design); Christine Beveridge (make up)

'Nothing Lasts Forever.'

The End of Violence   ★

DIR Wim Wenders

1997   122m   US/Germany/France

DVD   ♫

☆ Bill Pullman (Mike Max), Andie MacDowell (Page), Gabriel Byrne (Ray Bering), Loren Dean ('Doc' Dean Brock), Traci Lind (Cat), Daniel Benzali (Brice Phelps), K. Todd Freeman (Six O One), Pruitt Taylor Vince (Frank Cray), Peter Horton (Brian), Udo Kier (Zoltan Kovacs), Samuel Fuller (Louis Bering)

The lives of a big-shot Hollywood producer and a reclusive surveillance expert intersect after the former is almost killed during an attempted kidnapping.

A pondering on issues of movie and real-world violence, surveillance culture, and the spaciousness of Los

---

DVD Available on DVD   ☆ Cast in order   66 Critics' Quotes   ♪ Academy Award   (T) BAFTA
♫ Soundtrack on CD   of importance   † Points of interest   ♪ Academy Award nomination   (T) BAFTA nomination

Angeles; its atmosphere of dread is persuasive, but several characters get lost, and the narrative goes nowhere in particular.

SCR Nicholas Klein   CIN Pascal Rabaud   MUS Ry Cooder, DJ Shadow   DES Patricia Norris   ED Peter Przygodda   PROD Deepak Nayar, Wim Wenders, Nicholas Klein   DIST Artificial Eye/CiBy 2000/Road Movies/Kintop

66 The themes are certainly worth exploring, but you expect something more provocative from Wenders than contrasting violent images on Big Brother surveillance monitors with those on cinema/TV screens. – *David Parkinson, Empire*

66 The entire cast walk around with a slightly dazed expression as if they have just been hit over the head with a very large concept. The concept is violence. – *Tom Shone, Sunday Times*

'An extraordinary event brought them together. A deadly obsession will tear them apart.'

Enduring Love ★★

DIR Roger Michell
2004   100m   GB/US
[DVD]   ♫

☆ Daniel Craig (Joe Rose), Rhys Ifans (Jed), Samantha Morton (Claire), Bill Nighy (Robin), Susan Lynch (Rachel), Helen McCrory (Mrs Logan), Andrew Lincoln (TV Producer), Corin Redgrave (Professor)

A university lecturer is about to propose marriage to his sculptor girlfriend in a country field, when trouble floats into their lives from an out-of-control hot air balloon.

An unusual love triangle takes shape, as a disturbed stalker disrupts the smug lives of a seemingly perfect couple. An acid little story, as unsentimental about love as it could possibly be. First-class performances throughout the cast, and the jolting first scene is directed with consummate skill.

SCR Joe Penhall   CIN Haris Zambarloukos
MUS Jeremy Sams   DES John-Paul Kelly   ED Nicolas Gaster   PROD Kevin Loader   DIST Pathé

66 An intelligent and gripping thriller, Enduring Love is a real rarity: a film better than the book it is adapted from. – *Nev Pierce, BBC*

Enemies, a Love Story ★

DIR Paul Mazursky
1989   119m   US
[DVD]   ♫

☆ Anjelica Huston (Tamara Broder), Ron Silver (Herman Broder), *Lena Olin* (Masha), Margaret Sophie Stein (Yadwiga), Judith Malina (Masha's Mother), Alan King (Rabbi Lembeck), Rita Karin (Mrs. Schreier), Phil Leeds (Pesheles)

In New York, a Polish Holocaust survivor becomes passionately involved with three different women.

An affecting story of a bizarre emotional juggling act, told with warmth and empathy. Director Mazursky marshals his ensemble cast with flair.

SCR Roger L. Simon, Paul Mazursky   CIN Fred Murphy
MUS Maurice Jarre   DES Pato Guzman   ED Stuart H

Pappe   PROD Paul Mazursky   DIST Fox/Morgan Creek Productions

66 An intriguing film. . .about the tumult of the heart. – *Roger Ebert, Chicago Sun-Times*

⚱ Anjelica Huston (supporting actress), Lena Olin (supporting actress); Roger L. Simon, Paul Mazursky (adapted screenplay)

An Enemy of the People ★

SCR/DIR Satyajit Ray
1989   99m   India

☆ Soumitra Chatterjee (Dr Ashok Gupta), Dhritiman Chatterjee (Nishrith Gupta), Ruma Guhathakurta (Maya Gupta), Mamata Shankar (Indrani Gupta), Dipankar Dey (Haridas Bagghi), Subhendu Chatterjee (Biresh)

An Indian doctor tries to close down a temple when he discovers its water supply has been contaminated.

Ibsen's play is transposed to contemporary India for no compelling reason. A curio.

CIN Barun Raha   MUS Satyajit Ray   DES Ashoke Bose
ED Dulal Dutta   DIST Contemporary/Electric/National Film Development Corp of India

† Director Satyajit Ray was returning to work after a heart attack and was advised by doctors not to work on location. Thus the film was shot within a studio.

'It's not paranoia if they're really after you.'

Enemy of the State ★

DIR Tony Scott
1998   132m   US
[DVD]   ♫

☆ Will Smith (Robert Clayton Dean), Gene Hackman (Brill), Jon Voight (Reynolds), Lisa Bonet (Rachel Banks), Regina King (Carla Dean), Stuart Wilson (Congressman Albert), Tom Sizemore (Boss Paulie Pintero), Loren Dean (Hicks), Barry Pepper (Pratt), Ian Hart (Bingham), Jake Busey (Krug), Scott Caan (Jones), Jason Lee (Zavitz), Gabriel Byrne (Brill), James Le Gros (Jerry Miller)

A successful lawyer receives evidence of a politically motivated murder and finds himself targeted by ruthless Government agents.

Hi-tech thriller that leans heavily on advanced surveillance techniques to ramp up the frenetic speed of the action. A classy turn from Hackman adds humanity and humour to a thought-provoking premise.

SCR David Marconi   CIN Dan Mindel   MUS Trevor Rabin, Harry Gregson-Williams   DES Benjamin Fernandez   ED Chris Lebenzon   PROD Jerry Bruckheimer   DIST Buena Vista/Touchstone/Scott Free

66 It has a hurtling pace, non-stop intensity and a stylish, appealing performance by Will Smith in his first starring role. – *Elvis Mitchell, New York Times*

Les Enfants du Paradis ★★★★

DIR *Marcel Carné*
1945   195m   France
[DVD]

☆ *Arletty, Jean-Louis Barrault, Pierre Brasseur, Marcel Herrand, Maria Casarès, Louis Salou, Pierre Renoir, Gaston Modot, Jane Marken*

In the 'theatre street' of Paris in the 1840s, a mime falls in love with the legendary but elusive actress Garance, but her problems with other men keep them apart.

A magnificent evocation of a place and a period, this thoroughly enjoyable epic melodrama is flawed only by its lack of human warmth and of a real theme. It remains nevertheless one of the cinema's most memorable films.

SCR *Jacques Prévert* CIN *Roger Hubert* MUS Maurice Thiriet, Joseph Kosma, G. Mouque ED Henri Rust, Madeleine Bonin PROD Fred Orain, Raymond Borderic DIST Pathé

66 A magnificent scenario. . .Prévert is as adept with wit as with poignancy. . .I don't believe a finer group of actors was ever assembled on film – *John Simon*

⚲ Jacques Prévert (original screenplay)

'In memory, love lies forever.'

The English Patient ★★★

SCR/DIR *Anthony Minghella*
1996 162m US
DVD ♫

☆ *Ralph Fiennes* (Count Laszlo de Almásy), *Juliette Binoche* (Hana), Willem Dafoe (David Caravaggio), *Kristin Scott-Thomas* (Katharine Clifton), Naveen Andrews (Kip), Colin Firth (Geoffrey Clifton), Julian Wadham (Madox), Jürgen Prochnow (Major Muller)

In the aftermath of the Second World War, a dying Hungarian count recalls the affair he had with a married British woman while stationed in the Sahara some years before.

In equal parts, a glorious epic and a guilty pleasure, vacillating over the course of its two-and-a-half-hour plus running time between the romantic, the sombre and the camp. Minghella's direction successfully encompasses broad-canvas set-pieces and affecting human drama, though the film's David Lean-isms and its characters' stiff upper lips – the routine stuff of 1950s pictures, but an anachronism by the late twentieth century – may prove a matter for individual taste.

CIN *John Seale* MUS *Gabriel Yared* DES Stuart Craig ED *Walter Murch* PROD Saul Zaentz DIST Buena Vista/Tiger Moth/Miramax

66 All year we've seen mirages of good films. Here is the real thing. To transport picturegoers to a unique place in the glare of the earth, in the darkness of the heart – this, you realise with a gasp of joy, is what movies can do. – *Richard Corliss, Time*

66 Awfully close to a masterpiece. – *Anthony Lane, New Yorker*

† Juliette Binoche won the best actress award at the Berlin Film Festival in 1997.

⚲ picture; Juliette Binoche (supporting actress); Anthony Minghella (direction); John Seale; Walter Murch; Gabriel Yared; Stuart Craig; Walter Murch, Mark Berger, David Parker, Christopher Newman (sound); Ann Roth (costumes design)

⚲ Kristin Scott-Thomas (leading actress); Ralph Fiennes (leading actor); Anthony Minghella (adaptor screenplay)

🎭 film; Juliette Binoche (supporting actress); Anthony Minghella (adapted screenplay); John Seale; Walter Murch; Gabriel Yared

🎭 Ralph Fiennes (leading actor); Kristin Scott-Thomas (leading actress); Anthony Minghella (direction); Stuart Craig; Mark Berger, Pat Jackson, Walter Murch, Christopher Newman, David Parker, Ivan Sharrock (sound); Ann Roth (costume design); Fabrizio Sforza, Nigel Booth (make up/hair)

'Crack the Code.'

Enigma ★

DIR Michael Apted
2001 119m GB/US/Netherlands/Germany
DVD ♫

☆ Dougray Scott (Tom Jericho), Kate Winslet (Hester Wallace), Saffron Burrows (Claire Romilly), Jeremy Northam (Wigram), Nikolaj Coster Waldau (Puck), Tom Hollander (Logie), Corin Redgrave (Admiral Trowbridge), Matthew MacFadyen (Cave), Robert Pugh (Skynner)

A wartime maths genius at the headquarters of British intelligence in 1943 struggles to crack a new German code while distracted by two love affairs.

Exciting yet old-fashioned movie that uses historic deciphering success as the backdrop for an engaging thriller. The combination of breaking codes and breaking codes is not always completely convincing.

SCR Tom Stoppard CIN Seamus McGarvey MUS John Barry DES John Beard ED Rick Shaine PROD Lorne Michaels, Mick Jagger DIST Buena Vista

66 Enigma is not for everyone, but the thoughtful (and the historically minded) will find it an absorbing and extremely well-textured experience. – *Richard Schickel, Time*

66 Preposterous Boy's Own stuff. – *Peter Bradshaw, Guardian*

'Everyone Has A Dark Side. Henry's About To Meet His.'

Equinox ★

SCR/DIR Alan Rudolph
1992 110m US
♫

☆ *Matthew Modine* (Henry Petosa/Freddy Ace), Lara Flynn Boyle (Beverly Franks), Marisa Tomei (Rosie Rivers), Fred Ward (Mr. Paris), Tyra Ferrell (Sonya Kirk), Kevin J. O'Connor (Russell Franks), Tate Donovan (Richie Nunn), Lori Singer (Sharon Ace), M. Emmet Walsh (Pete Petosa), Gailard Sartain (Dandridge)

Twins separated at birth grow up very differently. One is a shy garage mechanic, hopeless with women, while the other is a brutal gangster. They join forces to make a claim for a $4 million legacy.

Matthew Modine is a stand-out as the chalk-and-cheese twins, yet this is more than the high-concept premise it sounds: Rudolph has assembled a classy ensemble cast, and he concentrates as much on character studies as on plot. It's a stylish piece from a distinctive film-maker who also writes elegant dialogue.

CIN Elliot Davis DES Steven Legler ED Michael Ruscio PROD David Blocker DIST Metro Tartan/SC Entertainment

---

DVD Available on DVD ☆ Cast in order 66 Critics' Quotes ⚲ Academy Award 🎭 BAFTA
♫ Soundtrack on CD   of importance † Points of interest ⚲ Academy Award nomination 🎭 BAFTA nomination

205

66 Equinox gives you the sensation of free-falling in a dream that's impossible to shake. It's an exhilarating workout. – *Peter Travers, Rolling Stone*

'She brought a small town to its feet and a huge corporation to its knees.'

Erin Brockovich ★★★

DIR *Steven Soderbergh*
2000 131m US
[DVD] ♫

☆ *Julia Roberts* (Erin Brockovich), Albert Finney (Ed Masry), Aaron Eckhart (George), Marg Helgenberger (Donna Jensen), Cherry Jones (Pamela Duncan), Veanne Cox (Theresa Dallavale), Conchata Ferrell (Brenda), Tracey Walter (Charles Embry), Peter Coyote (Kurt Potter), Scotty Leavenworth (Matthew), Gemmenne De la Pena (Katie), Jamie Harrold (Scott)

A spirited single mother lands a menial job in a small law firm, then confronts and defeats a giant public utility company responsible for contaminating the water supply in a small community.

A true story is given a inspirational Hollywood airing as one courageous woman flatly refuses to swallow poisoned water or corporate lies. Julia Roberts, playing Brockovich as brassy, outspoken and sexually candid, extends her range notably in triumphant style.

SCR *Susannah Grant* **CIN** Ed Lachman **MUS** Thomas Newman **DES** Phil Messina **ED** Anne V. Coates **PROD** Danny DeVito, Michael Shamberg, Stacey Sher **DIST** Columbia TriStar

66 If Julia Roberts' delightful performance, shaded with a depth and complexity unprecedented in her career, is the centrepiece of Erin Brokovich, considerable praise is also due to Steven Soderbergh's restrained, respectful direction. – *Andrew O'Hehir, Sight and Sound*

66 As the brisk, concise storytelling excises the fat, so Erin cuts through the crap. – *Time Out*

† Erin Brockovich herself appears briefly as a waitress in a coffee shop.

† Roberts was reportedly paid $20 million for playing Brockovich, the highest fee at the time ever paid to an actress.

⚊ Julia Roberts (leading actress)
⚊ picture; Albert Finney (supporting actor); Steven Soderbergh; Susannah Grant (original screenplay)

🅣 Julia Roberts (leading actress)
🅣 film; Albert Finney (supporting actor); Steven Soderbergh; Susannah Grant (original screenplay); Anne V. Coates

Ermo ★★

DIR Zhou Xiaowen
1994 98m China/Hong Kong

☆ Ai Liya (Ermo), Liu Peiqi (Xiazi, Blindman), Ge Zhijun (Village Chief, Ermo's Husband), Zhang Haiyan (Xiazi's Wife), Yan Zhenguo (Huzi, Ermo's Son)

A bored Chinese housewife goes to extraordinary lengths to buy a big-screen TV set to impress her neighbours.

A delightful satire that contrasts urban life with the poverty of a rural peasant existence. Unusually for Chinese films, it openly poses questions about life's meaning as well as the relentless march of materialism.

SCR Lang Yun **CIN** Lu Gengxin **MUS** Zhoi Xiaowen, Yi Hang **DES** Zhang Daqian **ED** Zhong Furong **PROD** Jimmy Tan, Chen Kunming **DIST** ICA/Ocean/Shanghai Studio

66 A marvellously astute morality tale that uses humour and warmth to make its comment on society. – *Channel 4*

The Escapist (new)

DIR Rupert Wyatt
2008 102m UK/Ireland

☆ Brian Cox (Frank Perry), Joseph Fiennes (Lenny Drake), Liam Cunningham (Brodie), Seu Jorge (Viv Baptista), Dominic Cooper (James Lacey), Steven Mackintosh (Tony), Damian Lewis (Rizza)

A lifer plots an elaborate escape with the help of a motley crew of associates.

Gritty prison break caper with a clear eye for jail's seamier side and a fractured structure that is more confusing than it needs to be.

SCR Rupert Wyatt, Daniel Hardy **CIN** Philipp Blaubach **MUS** Benjamin Wallfisch **DES** Jim Furlong **ED** Joe Walker **PROD** Adrian Sturges, Alan Moloney **DIST** Vertigo Films

66 What appears to be a straightforward gruff and grimy clinker about a prison break turns out to have more in common with Memento than The Shawshank Redemption, with an arresting expressionistic sound design, a jack-knifed plot and an existential twist. – *Siobhan Synnot, Scotland on Sunday*

† Partly filmed at Kilmainham Jail in Ireland.

'They can erase someone from your mind. Getting them out of your heart is another story.'

Eternal Sunshine of the Spotless Mind ★★

DIR Michel Gondry
2004 108m US
[DVD] ♫

☆ Jim Carrey (Joel Barish), Kate Winslet (Clementine Kruczynski), Kirsten Dunst (Mary), Mark Ruffalo (Stan), Elijah Wood (Patrick), Tom Wilkinson (Dr. Howard Mierzwiak), Jane Adams (Carrie), David Cross (Rob)

A man attempts to have all memories of his former lover erased from his mind, but the past is not as easy to jettison as he expected.

A surreal take on emotional overload that explores the bewildering horror of being trapped inside a deluded mind. Voluntarily erasing portions of one's memory is an intriguing notion, but the apparently random chronology of Kaufman's script makes the story more complex than necessary.

SCR Charlie Kaufman **CIN** Ellen Kuras **MUS** Jon Brion **DES** Dan Leigh **ED** Valdis Oskarsdottir **PROD** Steve Golin, Anthony Bregman **DIST** Momentum

66 It is not as fiendishly cunning as Being John Malkovich or as savage as Adaptation but the surreal romantic twists are pure Kaufman at his neurotic worst. – *James Christopher, The Times*

66 A sort of existential love story in reverse. . .a white-hot starburst of extravagant emotionalism. – *Brent Simon, Entertainment Today*

‡ Charlie Kaufman (original screenplay)
Ⅱ Kate Winslet (leading actress)
Ⓣ Charlie Kaufman (original screenplay); Valdis Oskarsdottir
Ⓣ film; Jim Carrey (leading actor); Kate Winslet (leading actress); Michel Gondry

Eternity and a Day ★★★

DIR Theo Angelopoulos
1998 132m Greece/France/Italy/Germany
DVD ♫

☆ Bruno Ganz (Alexandre), Isabelle Renauld (Anna), Achileas Skevis (The Child), Despina Bebedeli (Alexandre's Mother), Iris Chatziantoniou (Alexandre's Daughter), Helene Gerasimidiou (Urania), Fabrizio Bentivoglio (The Poet), Vassilis Siemenis (Son-in-Law)

A celebrated Greek author recalls his earlier egocentric days, and faces up to his terminal illness by helping a young Albanian refugee return home.

A slow and melancholy meditation on the meaning of life, with an epic sweep. Beautifully shot in lengthy, fluid takes, it has a personal intimacy that sometimes eludes this film-maker's work.

SCR Theo Angelopoulos, Tonino Guerra, Petros Markaris
CIN Giorgos Arvanitis, Andreas Sinanos MUS Eleni Karaindrou ED Yannis Tsitsopoulos PROD Theo Angelopoulos, Eric Heumann, Giorgio Silvagni, Amedeo Pagani DIST Theo Angelopoulos/Greek Film Centre/ERT/Paradis/La Sept/Intermedias

66 A gorgeous elegy of a film. – *Edward Guthmann, San Francisco Chronicle*

† In 1998, it won the Palme d'Or for best film in competition at the Cannes Film Festival.

Être et Avoir ★★★★

DIR *Nicolas Philibert*
2002 104m France
DVD

☆ Georges Lopez (teacher), Alize (student), Axel (student), Guillaume (student)

A documentary that traces a year in the life and career of 55-year-old Georges Lopez, a traditionally minded teacher, and his mixed-age class of 13 pupils in rural France.

Assiduous, patient documentary that assembles the life of a small school over a year in its charming detail. Director Philibert obtains relaxed, candid footage from its charming children; in Lopez he has unearthed a gem of a subject.

CIN Nicolas Philibert, Katell Djian, Laurent Didier, Hugues Gemignani MUS Philippe Hersant ED Nicolas Philibert PROD Gilles Sandoz DIST Metro Tartan

66 In its humanity and its quietly passionate idealism, this film is a tonic. – *Peter Bradshaw, Guardian*

66 To Be and To Have is a movie every teacher should

see, and every parent, too. – *Stephen Rea, Philadelphia Inquirer*

Ⓣ film not in the English language

Europa ★★

DIR Lars von Trier
1991 112m Denmark/France/Germany/Sweden
DVD

☆ Jean-Marc Barr (Leopold Kessler), Barbara Sukowa (Katharina Hartmann), Udo Kier (Lawrence Hartmann), Ernst-Hugo Järegàrd (Uncle Kessler), Erik Mørk (Pater), Jørgen Reenberg (Max Hartmann), Henning Jensen (Siggy), Eddie Constantine (Colonel Harris), Max von Sydow (Narrator)

An idealistic young American, determined to play a part in rebuilding Germany in 1945, falls for a wealthy woman who turns out to be a Nazi sympathizer.

It's a dark joke, even by the standards of provocateur von Trier: a Nazi partisan seducing an innocent American on a train that once shipped Jews to death camps. We get the point: European sophistication trumps American naivety. But beyond that shocking scenario, the script runs out of steam.

SCR Lars von Trier, Niels Vîrsel CIN Henning Bendtsen, Jean-Paul Meurisse, Edward Klosinsky MUS Joachim Holbek DES Henning Bahs ED Herve Schneid PROD Peter Aalbaek Jensen, Bo Christensen DIST Electric/Nordisk/Eurimages

66 A strange, haunting, labrynthine film about a naïve American in Germany just after the end of World War II. – *Roger Ebert, Chicago Sun-Times*

Europa Europa ★★

SCR/DIR Agnieszka Holland
1990 110m France/Germany
DVD

☆ Marco Hofschneider (Salomon 'Solly' 'Salek' Perel/Josef 'Jupp' Peters), Julie Delpy (Leni), André Wilms (Soldier Robert Kellerman), Aschley Wanninger (Gerd), Hanns Zischler (Captain von Lerenau), Klaus Kowatsch (Schulz)

As World War Two approaches, a teenage Jewish boy flees to Soviet-occupied Poland pretends to be a loyal Nazi in order to stay alive, and becomes a hero in the Hitler Youth movement

This story, all the more remarkable for being true, is recounted sensitively, and zeroes in on the young man's dilemma: how young Salomon became Josef before finding himself lost between two identities.

CIN Jacek Petrycki MUS Zbigniew Priesner DES Allan Starski ED Ewa Smal PROD Margaret Menegoz, Artur Brauner DIST Les Films du Losange/CCC Filmkunst/Perspektywa

66 There are a great many movies about the tragic experience of the Jews during the Second World War, but only a handful as passionate, as subtly intelligent, as universal as this one. – *Hal Hinson, Washington Post*

Ⅱ Agnieszka Holland (adapted screenplay)
Ⓣ film not in the English language

E

| DVD Available on DVD | ☆ Cast in order of importance | 66 Critics' Quotes | ‡ Academy Award | Ⓣ BAFTA |
| ♫ Soundtrack on CD | | † Points of interest | Ⅱ Academy Award nomination | Ⓣ BAFTA nomination |

207

'A Comedy of Biblical Proportions.'

Evan Almighty (new)

DIR Tom Shadyac
2007   96m   US
DVD   ♫

☆ Steve Carell (Evan Baxter), Morgan Freeman (God), Lauren Graham (Joan Baxter), John Goodman (Congressman Long), John Michael Higgins (Marty Stringer), Jimmy Bennett (Ryan Baxter), Wanda Sykes (Rita Daniels)

God orders a newly elected congressman to build an ark to protect his suburb from an impending flood.

A sequel to Bruce Almighty with the spotlight moved on to an aggravating subordinate character; what little divine inspiration the original possessed left with Jim Carrey.

SCR Steve Oedekerk   **CIN** Ian Baker   **MUS** John Debney   **DES** Linda DeScenna   **ED** Scott Hill   **PROD** Tom Shadyac, Gary Barber, Roger Birnbaum, Neal H. Moritz, Michael Bostick   **DIST** Universal

❛❛ The most expensive Hollywood comedy ever made. Problem? It's not that funny. – *Peter Travers, Rolling Stone*

❛❛ A comedic disaster of biblical proportions. – *Christopher Tookey, Daily Mail*

† The film narrowly recouped its reported $175m budget only at the end of its run in international territories.

'Her greatest secret was her greatest gift.'

Evening (new)   ★

DIR Lajos Koltai
2007   117m   US/Germany
DVD   ♫

☆ Vanessa Redgrave (Ann Lord), Claire Danes (Ann (younger)), Toni Collette (Nina), Patrick Wilson (Harris Arden), Natasha Richardson (Constance), Mamie Gummer (Lila (younger)), Eileen Atkins (The Night Nurse), Meryl Streep (Lila), Glenn Close (Mrs. Wittenborn), Hugh Dancy (Buddy)

A New England matriarch on her deathbed recalls a thwarted love affair from 50 years previously.

Resolutely unfashionable; nothing here would be out of place in a film from the 1950s, when it would have been called 'a women's picture'. A stellar cast of actresses act out a story that is often moving; but the exquisite camera work disguises its triviality, excessive length and lack of humour.

SCR Susan Minot, Michael Cunningham   **CIN** *Gyula Pados*   **MUS** Jan A.P. Kaczmarek   **DES** Caroline Hanania   **ED** Allyson C. Johnson   **PROD** Jeffrey Sharp   **DIST** Icon

❛❛ There are few things more depressing than a weeper that doesn't make you weep. Evening creeps through its dolorous paces as prudently as an undertaker. – *Roger Ebert, Chicago Sun-Times*

† Two sets of real-life mothers and daughters appear in Evening: Vanessa Redgrave with Natasha Richardson, and Meryl Streep with Mamie Gummer.

Everyone Says I Love You   ★★

SCR/DIR Woody Allen
1996   101m   US
DVD   ♫

☆ Woody Allen (Joe Berlin), Alan Alda (Bob Dandridge), Drew Barrymore (Skylar Dandridge), Goldie Hawn (Steffi Dandridge), Julia Roberts (Von Sidell), Tim Roth (Charles Ferry), Lukas Haas (Scott Dandridge), Gaby Hoffman (Lane Dandridge), Edward Norton (Holden Spence), Natalie Portman (Laura Dandridge), David Ogden Stiers (Arnold Spence), Natasha Lyonne (Djuna 'D.J.' Berlin)

Over the space of a year, a teenage girl observes the complex love affairs of her mother, father and brothers and sisters.

An old-fashioned musical with a modern twist: it features rather too many stars (notably Norton) understandably not known for their singing voices. There are some good jokes and plenty of nostalgic appeal, but it still looks curiously like a work in progress. For all that, it's endearing.

CIN Carlo Di Palma   **MUS** Dick Hyman   **DES** Santo Loquasto   **ED** Susan E. Morse   **PROD** Robert Greenhut

❛❛ No one seeing Everyone Says I Love You, Woody Allen's latest film, will wonder what's in it for him. What's in it for audiences is more problematical. – *Kenneth Turan, Los Angeles Times*

❛❛ This sweet conceit ought to glue a grin on your face until its crucial next-to-last scene hits a clunker note. – *Mike Clark, USA Today*

'Leave Normal Behind.'

Everything is Illuminated   ★★

SCR/DIR Liev Schreiber
2005   106m   US
DVD   ♫

☆ Elijah Wood (Jonathan Safran Foer), *Eugene Hutz* (Alex), Boris Leskin (Grandfather), Laryssa Lauret (Lista)

A geeky young Jewish New Yorker travels to the Ukraine to discover the truth about his family's past on a chaotic road trip.

Whimsical version of a wild and wonderful novel that often misses its elusive humour and mangled language, and settles for a grossly sentimental ending. But Eugene Hutz, as a Ukrainian tour guide obsessed with all things American, is perfectly cast.

CIN Matthew Libatique   **MUS** Paul Cantelon   **DES** Mark Geraghty   **ED** Craig McKay, Andrew Marcus   **PROD** Marc Turtletaub, Peter Saraf   **DIST** Warner

❛❛ Funky black comedy is set aside in favour of a sentimental resolution that does not quite do justice to the subject's cultural and historical mass. – *Peter Bradshaw, Guardian*

Everything Put Together   ★

DIR Marc Forster
2000   87m   US
DVD

☆ Radha Mitchell (Angie), Megan Mullally (Barbie), Justin Louis (Russ), Catherine Lloyd Burns (Judith), Alan Ruck (Kessel), Michele Hicks (April), Matt Malloy (Dr Reiner)

A distraught young wife tries to come to terms with the sudden death of her newborn baby and the collapse of her marriage.

Low-budget, high-intensity tearjerker makes uncomfortable viewing, but succeeds largely thanks to Radha Mitchell's convincing portrayal of the bereaved mother's grief.

SCR Adam Forgash, Catherine Lloyd Burns, Marc Forster CIN Roberto Schaefer MUS Thomas Koppel DES Paul Luther Jackson ED Matt Chessé PROD Sean Furst DIST ICA

'The secrets that hold us together can also tear us apart.'

Eve's Bayou ★★

SCR/DIR Kasi Lemmons
1997 109m US
DVD ♫

☆ Jurnee Smollett (Eve Batiste), Meagan Good (Cisely Batiste), Samuel L. Jackson (Louis Batiste), Lynn Whitfield (Roz Batiste), Debbi Morgan (Mozelle Batiste Delacroix), Jake Smollett (Poe Batiste), Diahann Carroll (Elzora), Ethel Ayler (Gran Mere), Vondie Curtis Hall (Julian Grayraven)

A 10-year-old girl in 1960s Louisiana decides to kill her womanising father.

There are riveting sequences in this good-looking, emotional family saga, during which new shades of truth come to the surface. Jackson, the biggest star on view, is marginalised, and rightly: this is a story about women, and a promising debut from writer-director Lemmons.

CIN *Amy Vincent* MUS Terence Blanchard DES Jeff Howard ED Terilyn A. Shropshire PROD Caldecot Chubb, Samuel L. Jackson DIST Alliance/Trimark

❝ A swamp of a picture, hardly worth slogging through. – *Mick LaSalle, San Francisco Chronicle*

Evita ★

DIR Alan Parker
1996 134m US
DVD ♫

☆ *Madonna* (Eva Peron), Antonio Banderas (Ché), Jonathan Pryce (Juan Perón), Jimmy Nail (Agustín Magaldi), Victoria Sus (Doña Juana), Julian Littman (Brother Juan), Olga Merediz

The rise of Eva Duarte from poverty to fame, fortune and power as a model, film actress and wife of the president of Argentina.

To call this Madonna's best film is to damn it with faint praise, though she sings well enough. Yet the problem with this musical is that no more than a handful of its songs are memorable. Parker directs ably, and many scenes are lavish and impressive. But his decision to dispense with dialogue and make it a sung-through piece makes it feel relentless.

SCR Alan Parker, Oliver Stone CIN *Darius Khondji* DES Brian Morris ED *Gerry Hambling* PROD Alan Parker, Andrew G. Vajna, Robert Stigwood DIST Entertainment/Cinergi/Robert Stigwood/Dirty Hands

❝ It is long, it is loud, it has enough extras to fit a small country, and it has more costumes than a New Orleans Mardi Gras, For 130 minutes it bludgeons you into submission; when it's over you are numb. – *Megan Rosenfeld, Washington Post*

† Many exterior scenes depicting Buenos Aires were shot in Budapest.

♪ Andrew Lloyd-Webber (m), Tim Rice (ly) (music, original song – You Must Love Me)

♪ Darius Khondji; Gerry Hambling; Brian Morris; Andy Nelson, Anna Behlmer, Ken Weston (sound)

Ⓣ Alan Parker, Oliver Stone (adapted screenplay); Darius Khondji; Gerry Hambling; Andrew Lloyd-Webber, Tim Rice (music); Brian Morris; Penny Rose (costume design); Sarah Monzani, Martin Samuel (make up/hair); Andy Nelson, Anna Behlmer, Ken Weston (sound)

Exiles ★

SCR/DIR Tony Gatlif
2004 104m France/Japan
DVD

☆ Romain Duris (Zano), *Lubna Azabal* (Naima), Leila Makhlouf (Leila), Habib Cheik (Habib)

A French couple in Paris decide to travel to Algeria, from where their parents hailed. On their arrival, they discover that not all the locals are friendly.

Road movie without much of a plot, but an enjoyable enough ride that sheds light on the immigrant experience in reverse. It's accompanied by striking world music on the soundtrack.

CIN Celine Bozon MUS Tony Gatlif, Delphine Mantoulet DES Brigitte Brassart ED Monique Dartonne PROD Tony Gatlif DIST Swipe

❝ Writer-director-composer Gatlif embroiders the travellers' sensory journey with rich aural textures. – *Rise Keller, Movie Habit*

'Play It. Live It. Kill For It.'

eXistenZ ★

SCR/DIR David Cronenberg
1999 97m US
DVD ♫

☆ Jennifer Jason Leigh (Allegra Geller), Jude Law (Ted Pikul), Willem Dafoe (Gas), Ian Holm (Kiri Vinokur), Don McKellar (Yevgeny Nourish), Callum Keith Rennie (Hugo Carlaw), Sarah Polley (Merle), Christopher Eccleston (Seminar Leader)

A video-game designer is threatened with genuine violence while demonstrating artificial mayhem on her latest creation.

Bizarre thriller involving cutting-edge video-game carnage techniques, contrasting them with the real thing. Most of the effects are special enough, but the multi-layered drama approaches the ludicrous and goes beyond. It has its moments, but no-one would mistake it for this gifted director's best work.

CIN Peter Suschitzky MUS Howard Shore DES Carol Spier ED Ronald Sanders PROD Robert Lantos, Andras Hamori, David Cronenberg DIST Miramax/Alliance Atlantis/Serendipity Point/Natural Nylon

❝ Like the virtual game he plays on us, the film is weird, it's addictive, Lord, it's alive! – *Richard Corliss, Time*

DVD Available on DVD   ☆ Cast in order of importance   ❝ Critics' Quotes   † Points of interest   ♪ Academy Award   ♪ Academy Award nomination   Ⓑ BAFTA   Ⓣ BAFTA nomination

209

The Exorcist ★

DIR William Friedkin
1973 122m US
DVD ♫

☆ Ellen Burstyn, Max von Sydow, Jason Miller, Linda Blair, Lee J. Cobb, Kitty Winn, Jack MacGowran

Two Catholic priests are called in to help a young girl, unaccountably possessed by the Devil and turned into a repellent monster who causes several violent deaths.

Great claims are made for this macabre horror story, with its gruesome special effects. Certainly it's influential, judging by the number of films directly inspired by it, but despite director Friedkin's careful stress on its alleged religious allegories, it can still be viewed as little more than a cynical exercise in exploitation.

SCR William Peter Blatty **CIN** Owen Roizman **MUS** Jack Nitzsche **DES** Bill Malley **ED** Jordan Leandopoulos, Evan Lottman, Norman Gay, Bud Smith **PROD** William Peter Blatty **DIST** Warner

66 No more nor less than a blood and thunder horror movie, foundering heavily on the rocks of pretension. – *Tom Milne*

66 The Exorcist makes no sense, [but] if you want to be shaken, it will scare the hell out of you. – *Stanley Kauffmann*

† Published 1974: The Story Behind the Exorcist by Peter Travers and Stephanie Reiff.
† The film was re-issued in 2000, with an extra 11 minutes of footage added.

⌶ William Peter Blatty (screenplay); Robert Knudson, Chris Newman (sound)
⌶ picture; Ellen Burstyn (leading actress); Jason Miller (supporting actor); Linda Blair (supporting actress); William Friedkin (direction); Owen Roizman; Bill Malley; editing

---

'In a world of temptation, obsession is the deadliest desire.'

Exotica ★★

SCR/DIR Atom Egoyan
1994 103m Canada
DVD ♫

☆ Bruce Greenwood (Francis Brown), *Elias Koteas* (Eric), Don McKellar (Thomas Pinto), Mia Kirshner (Christina), Arsinée Khanjian (Zoe), Sarah Polley (Tracey Brown)

For various reasons that become apparent, five people are brought together in the establishment of the title, a strip club.

Gradually unfolding drama, where the links between characters are explained and intertwined plots are slowly revealed. As always with Egoyan, there's a cerebral, distanced feel to the story, but it's worth persevering.

CIN Paul Sarossy **MUS** Mychael Danna **DES** Linda del Rosario, Richard Paris **ED** Susan Shipton **PROD** Atom Egoyan, Camelia Frieberg, Robert Lantos **DIST** Artificial Eye/Alliance/Ego

66 In the form of a taut psychological thriller, director Egoyan plumbs the violence of the mind in ways that are unique and unnerving. – *Peter Travers, Rolling Stone*

'They never imagined it would go this far.'

Das Experiment ★

DIR Oliver Hirschbiegel
2000 119m Germany
DVD

☆ Moritz Bleibtreu (Tarek Fahd, No 77), Maren Eggert (Dora), Christian Berkel (Robert Steinhoff, No 38), Justus von Dohnanyi (Berus), Oliver Stokowski (Günther Schütte, No 82), Andrea Sawatzki (Dr Jutta Grimm), Edgar Selge (Professor Dr Klaus Thon), Timo Dierkes (Eckert)

Volunteers take part in a controlled experiment into human behaviour in a mock prison. A 'prisoner' with a secret motive helps to arouse sadism in the 'guards'.

Inspired by the Stanford University Prison Experiment of 1971, which revealed how quickly power corrupts, this German film makes for enthralling, if uncomfortable viewing. A brutal rape scene is enough to test the strongest stomach.

SCR Mario Giordano, Christoph Darnstaedt, Don Bohlinger **CIN** Rainer Klausmann **MUS** Alexander Bubenheim **DES** Andrea Kessler **ED** Hans Funck **PROD** Norbert Preuss, Marc Conrad, Friedrich Wildfeuer **DIST** Metrodome

66 A sustained symphony of psychological and physical horrors, this isn't comforting but it is gripping, with the most exciting last act you'll see in a long time. – *Kim Newman, Empire*

The Exterminating Angel ★★★★

SCR/DIR *Luis Buñuel (story assistance from Luis Alcoriza)*
1962 95m Mexico

☆ Silvia Pinal (Letitia–"The Valkyrie"), Enrique Rambal (Esmundo Nobile), Jacqueline Andere (Senora Alicia Roc), Jose Baviera (Leandro)

High society dinner guests find themselves unable to leave the room, stay there for days, and lapse into neurosis before the strange spell is broken; when they go to church to give thanks, they find themselves unable to leave.

Fascinating surrealist fantasia on themes elaborated with even more panache in The Discreet Charm of the Bourgeoisie. Nevertheless, one of its director's key films.

CIN Gabriel Figueroa **ED** Carlos Savage Jr. **PROD** Gustavo Alatriste **DIST** Uninci Films 59

66 An unsound and unsightly mixture of spurious allegory and genuine craziness. – *John Simon*

'You won't believe her eyes.'

The Eye (new)

DIR David Moreau, Xavier Palud
2008 96m US
DVD

☆ Jessica Alba (Sydney Wells), Alessandro Nivola (Dr. Paul Faulkner), Parker Posey (Helen Wells), Rade Serbedzija (Simon McCullough), Fernanda Romero (Ana Christina Martinez), Rachel Ticotin (Rosa Martinez), Obba Babatundé (Dr. Haskins)

A blind violinist regains her sight after a cornea transplant, only to find she can now see ghosts.

DVD Available on DVD ☆ Cast in order of importance 66 Critics' Quotes ⌶ Academy Award ⌶ Academy Award nomination ♫ Soundtrack on CD † Points of interest 🎭 BAFTA 🎭 BAFTA nomination

Overblown reprise of the Hong Kong original that lacks its predecessor's unsettling mystery.

SCR Sebastian Gutierrez CIN Jeffrey Jur MUS Marco Beltrami DES James H. Spencer ED Patrick Lussier PROD Paula Wagner, Don Granger, Michelle Manning DIST Lionsgate

66 Once more a perfectly good foreign horror is remade into something that falls well short of the mark. – *David Edwards, Mirror*

66 Reasonably entertaining. – *Peter Bradshaw, Guardian*

Eyes Wide Shut ★

DIR Stanley Kubrick
1999 159m US/GB
DVD ♫

☆ Tom Cruise (Dr. William Harford), Nicole Kidman (Alice Harford), Sydney Pollack (Victor Ziegler), Marie Richardson (Marion), Rade Sherbedgia (Milich), Todd Field (Nick Nightingale), Vinessa Shaw (Domino), Alan Cumming (Desk Clerk), Sky Dumont (Sandor Szavost), Fay Masterson (Sally), Leelee Sobieski (Milich's Daughter), Thomas Gibson (Carl), Madison Eginton (Helena Harford)

A New York doctor becomes obsessed with having new sexual experiences after his wife confesses to fantasies about a man she briefly encountered.

One of Kubrick's least convincing films, with the buttoned-down Cruise miscast as the doctor who seeks wild sexual adventures as revenge for his wife's lurid fantasies. It has a curiously dated feel, especially its orgy scenes, which look very much like an old man's fond notions of what uninhibited sex looks like.

SCR Stanley Kubrick, Frederic Raphael CIN Larry Smith MUS Jocelyn Pook DES Les Tomkins, Roy Walker ED Nigel Galt PROD Stanley Kubrick DIST Warner

66 A riveting, thematically probing, richly atmospheric and just occasionally troublesome work, deeply inquisitive consideration of the extent of trust and mutual knowledge between a man and a woman. – *Todd McCarthy, Variety*

66 Kubrick left one more brilliantly provocative tour de force as his epitaph. – *Elvis Mitchell, New York Times*

† This was Kubrick's final film. He died in 1999, four months before its world premiere.

DVD Available on DVD   ☆ Cast in order   66 Critics' Quotes   Academy Award   BAFTA
♫ Soundtrack on CD   of importance   † Points of interest   Academy Award nomination   BAFTA nomination

211

'For 31 years it's been just the Fabulous Baker Boys. . .but times change.'

The Fabulous Baker Boys ★★★

SCR/DIR *Steve Kloves*
1989 114m US
DVD ♫

☆ *Jeff Bridges* (Jack Baker), *Michelle Pfeiffer* (Susie Diamond), *Beau Bridges* (Frank Baker), Ellie Raab (Nina), Jennifer Tilly (Blanche 'Monica' Moran)

Two piano-playing brothers recruit a escort-turned-chanteuse to pep up their failing act.

Mesmerising character study plays a long, slow, cool game, allowing everyone involved to make the most of one of the few recent American screenplays to carry the authentic whiff of cigarette smoke and cheap perfume about it.

CIN Michael Ballhaus **MUS** *Dave Grusin* **DES** Jeffrey Townsend **ED** William Steinkamp **PROD** Paula Weinstein, Sydney Pollack, Mark Rosenberg **DIST** Rank/Gladden

❝ Doesn't do anything very original, but what it does, it does wonderfully well. – *Roger Ebert, Chicago Sun-Times*

❝ With more than enough witty, well-observed details, it's a little charmer. – *Geoff Andrew, Time Out*

⚖ Michelle Pfeiffer (leading actress); Michael Ballhaus; Dave Grusin; William Steinkamp

🏆 J. Paul Huntsman, Stephan von Hase, Chris Jenkins, Gary Alexander, Doug Hemphill (sound)
🏆 Michelle Pfeiffer (leading actress); Dave Grusin

'The blag to kill for. Only one of them meant it for real.'

Face ★

DIR Antonia Bird
1997 105m GB
DVD

☆ Robert Carlyle (Ray), Ray Winstone (Dave), Steven Waddington (Stevie), Philip Davis (Julian), Damon Albarn (Jason), Lena Headey (Connie), Peter Vaughan (Sonny), Sue Johnston (Alice), Gerry Conlon (Vince)

A gang of villains turn angrily on each other after their haul from a violent raid goes mysteriously missing.

Pacy British gangster movie with snarling streetwise dialogue, credible action and enough nervous energy to revive the National Grid.

SCR Ronan Bennett **CIN** Fred Tamms **MUS** Adrian Corker, Andy Roberts, Paul Conboy **DES** Chris Townsend **ED** St John O'Rorke **PROD** David M. Thompson, Elinor Day **DIST** UIP

❝ It's muscular, raw and aggressive. – *Time Out*

A Face in the Crowd ★★★

DIR *Elia Kazan*
1957 126m US

☆ *Andy Griffith* (Lonesome Rhodes), *Lee Remick* (Betty Lou Fleckum), *Walter Matthau* (Mel Miller), *Patricia Neal* (Marcia Jeffries), Anthony Franciosa (Joey Kiely), Percy Waram (Colonel Hollister), Marshall Neilan (Sen. Fuller)

A small-town hick becomes a megalomaniac when TV turns him into a famous homespun philosopher.

Brilliantly cinematic melodrama of its time which only flags in the last lap. It now looks prescient in its portrayal of fame and celebrity as corrupting influences in a media-obsessed, inner-directed society.

SCR Budd Schulberg **CIN** *Harry Stradling, Gayne Rescher* **MUS** Tom Glazer **PROD** (Warner) Newton (Elia Kazan)

❝ Savagery, bitterness, cutting humour. – *Penelope Houston*

❝ If Kazan and Schulberg had been content to make their case by implication, it might have been a completely sophisticated piece of movie-making. Instead, everything is elaborately spelled out, and the film degenerates into preposterous liberal propaganda. – *Andrew Sarris*

'In order to catch him, he must become him.'

Face/Off ★★

DIR John Woo
1997 138m US
DVD ♫

☆ John Travolta (Sean Archer/Castor Troy), Nicolas Cage (Castor Troy/Sean Archer), Joan Allen (Dr. Eve Archer), Alessandro Nivola (Pollux Troy), Gina Gershon (Sasha Hassler), Dominique Swain (Jamie Archer), Nick Cassavetes (Dietrich Hassler), Harve Presnell (Victor Lazarro), Colm Feore (Dr. Malcolm Walsh)

A dedicated FBI man has his face replaced by a terrorist's in a desperate bid to find a deadly bomb ticking away somewhere in Los Angeles.

John Travolta and Nicolas Cage play ruthless rivals and then each other as this ambitious thriller goes for broke. It just about comes off amid some spectacular Woo-trademark violence, though it can also be viewed as ludicrously, riotously funny.

SCR Mike Werb, Michael Colleary **CIN** Oliver Wood **MUS** John Powell **DES** Neil Spisak **ED** Christian Wagner, Steven Kemper **PROD** David Permut, Barrie M. Osborne, Terence Chang, Christopher Godsick **DIST** Buena Vista/Douglas/Reuther/WCG

DVD Available on DVD ☆ Cast in order ❝ Critics' Quotes ⚖ Academy Award 🏆 BAFTA
♫ Soundtrack on CD of importance † Points of interest ⚖ Academy Award nomination 🏆 BAFTA nomination

66 Style overwhelms any hope of discerning story or acting through the haze of burning, crashing, bleeding and exploding. – *Barbara Shulgasser, San Francisco Examiner*

66 It's a fascinating film in so many ways. – *Martyn Glanville, BBC*

⌕ Mark P. Stoekinger, Per Hallberg (sound effects editing)

'What matters most is how you well you walk through the fire.'

Factotum ★

DIR Bent Hamer
2005   94m   Norway/US/Germany/Italy/France
DVD ♫

☆ Matt Dillon (Henry Chinaski), Lili Taylor (Jan), Marisa Tomei (Laura), Fisher Stevens (Manny), Didier Flammand (Pierre), Adrienne Shelly (Jerry)

A writer tries to drink his way through life as he drifts aimlessly from one dead-end job to another and his rejection slips pile up.

Matt Dillon is excellent in this meandering, undemanding movie, loosely based on the boozy life of celebrated literary wild man Charles Bukowski. But bottle fatigue wins in the end.

SCR Bent Hamer, Jim Stark   CIN John Christian Rosenlund   MUS Kristin Asbjornsen   DES Eve Cauley Turner   ED Pal Gengenbach   PROD Jim Stark, Bent Hamer   DIST Icon

66 What starts as a bittersweet tale of a man railing against the tyranny of small-minded managers swiftly descends into a desultory, rambling, go-nowhere biopic. – *David Edwards, Daily Mirror*

† Barfly is another film about Bukowski's life.

'Six students are about to find out their teachers really are from another planet.'

The Faculty ★

DIR Robert Rodriguez
1998   104m   US
DVD ♫

☆ Jordana Brewster (Delilah Profitt), Clea DuVall (Stokely 'Stokes' Mitchell), Laura Harris (Marybeth Louise Hutchinson), Josh Harnett (Zeke Tyler), Shawn Hatosy (Stan Rosado), Salma Hayek (Nurse Rosa Harper), Famke Janssen (Miss Elizabeth Burke), Piper Laurie (Mrs. Karen Olson), Chris McDonald (Mr. Frank Connor), Bebe Neuwirth (Principal Valerie Drake), Robert Patrick (Coach Joe Willis), Usher Raymond (Gabe Santora), Jon Stewart (Prof. Edward Furlong), Daniel von Bargen (Mr. John Tate), Elijah Wood (Casey Connor)

High-school students become aware of an alien presence in their midst.

Knowing teeny-bop reworking of the old Body Snatchers legend, with a bright cast and the odd moment of suspense.

SCR Kevin Williamson   CIN Enrique Chediak   MUS Marco Beltrami   DES Cary White   ED Robert Rodriguez   PROD Elizabeth Avellan   DIST Dimension/Los Hooligans

66 Results may not be Nobel Prize material, but they're zesty and cogent. – *Dennis Harvey, Variety*

66 Exactly the kind of sporadically clever, button-pushing fright-fest that keeps genre fans hanging on until something more fulfilling comes along. – *Maitland McDonagh, TV Guide*

'Italy 1948. Orson Welles is making a new film. . .Sex, corruption, murder. . .Get the picture?'

Fade to Black (new)

SCR/DIR Oliver Parker
2007   104m   UK

☆ Danny Huston (Orson Welles), Diego Luna (Tommaso), Paz Vega (Lea), Christopher Walken (Brewster), Anna Galiena (Aida), Nathaniel Parker (Viola), Kwame Kwei-Armah (Joe Black)

Orson Welles investigates a murder while making a film in post-war Italy.

Elaborate cinema in-joke with a labyrinthine plot; unlikely to appeal to anyone besides Welles aficionados, if them.

CIN John de Borman   MUS Charlie Mole   DES Luciana Arrighi   ED Guy Bensley   PROD Barnaby Thompson, Jonathan Olsberg, Massimo Pacilio   DIST Lionsgate

66 This shaggy dog outing is all fur and no tale. – *Xan Brooks, Guardian*

† John Sayles made a contribution to the screenplay.

'The temperature where freedom burns!'

Fahrenheit 9/11 ★★★

SCR/DIR Michael Moore
2004   122m   US
DVD ♫

Documentary investigating the legitimacy of George W. Bush's presidency, his links to the Bin Laden family and his decision to invade Iraq after pursuing the Taliban in Afghanistan in the wake of 9/11.

Angry, bitter but often amusing polemic that scorns notions of fairness and balance to pile up accusations on the Bush administration that director Moore clearly despises. Even if some of his facts are insufficiently researched (a perennial failing of Moore's) it makes riveting viewing.

CIN Mike Desjarlais   MUS Jeff Gibbs   ED Kurt Engfehr, Christopher Seward, T. Woody Richman   PROD Jim Czarnecki, Kathleen Glynn, Michael Moore   DIST Lions Gate

66 Strident, passionate, sometimes outrageously manipulative and often bafflingly selective. – *Peter Bradshaw, Guardian*

† In 2004, the film won the Palme D'Or at the Cannes Film Festival.

'It will have you sitting on the brink of eternity!'

Fail-Safe ★★★

DIR *Sidney Lumet*
1964   111m   US
DVD

☆ *Henry Fonda* (The President), Walter Matthau (Groeteschele), Dan O'Herlihy (Gen. Black), Frank Overton (Gen. Bogan), Fritz Weaver (Col. Cascio), Edward

Binns (Col. Grady), Larry Hagman (Buck), Russell Collins (Knapp)

Owing to a blunder at the Pentagon, an American plane with an atomic bomb on board is dispatched to destroy Moscow, and the US President must offer to destroy New York to atone for the deed.

A film that is the flip-side of the contemporaneous Dr Strangelove which treated the same theme, Cold War brinkmanship, as black comedy. The details in this deadly earnest melodrama are both terrifying and convincing.

SCR Walter Bernstein   CIN Gerald Hirschfeld
MUS none   ED Ralph Rosenblum   DIST Columbia/Max E. Youngstein/Sidney Lumet

† Fail-Safe was remade for US network TV in 2000, starring George Clooney and Richard Dreyfuss. Directed by Stephen Frears, it was broadcast live, in one take, and in black-and-white.

Faithless ★★

DIR Liv Ullmann
2000   154m   Sweden/Norway/Finland/Italy/Germany
DVD

☆ Lena Endre (Marianne Vogler), Erland Josephson (Bergman), Krister Henriksson (David), Thomas Hanzon (Markus), Michelle Gylemo (Isabelle), Juni Dahr (Margareta), Philip Zanden (Martin Goldman), Therese Brunnander (Petra Holst), Marie Richardson (Anna Berg)

Alone in a coastal cottage, an elderly film-maker tries to write a script about infidelity and finds himself confronting his conscience over a past affair.

Strong autobiographical echoes resonate from writer Ingmar Bergman throughout this relentlessly intense drama of marital crisis and revenge. Quietly absorbing.

SCR Ingmar Bergman   CIN Jorgen Persson   ED Sylvia Ingemarsson   PROD Kaj Larsen, Johan Mardell
DIST Metro Tartan

❝ A probing look at love, marriage, fidelity, rivalry, and other deep-rooted emotional issues. – *David Sterritt, Christian Science Monitor*

Fallen Angels ★★

SCR/DIR Wong Kar-Wai
1995   96m   Hong Kong
DVD   ♫

☆ Leon Lai (Wong Chi-Ming/Killer), Michele Reis (The Killer's Agent), Takeshi Kaneshiro (He Zhiwu), Charlie Young (Charlie/Cherry), Karen Mong (Punkie/Blondie/Baby)

A disillusioned hitman and a former convict look for love amidst the frenetic street life of Hong Kong.

Speedy, adrenalin-filled journey through neon-drenched Hong Kong, and encounters with its beautiful people. The film's style trumps its story and, fittingly, first impressions count for everything.

CIN Christopher Doyle   MUS Frankie Chan, Roel A. Garcia   DES William Chang   ED William Chan, Wong Ming-Lam   PROD Jeffrey Lau   DIST Electric/Jet Tone

❝ An exhilarating rush of a movie, with all manner of go-for-broke visual bravura that expresses the free spirits of bold young people. – *Kevin Thomas, Los Angeles Times*

The Fallen Idol ★★★

DIR Carol Reed
1948   94m   GB

☆ *Ralph Richardson* (Baines), Michèle Morgan (Julie), *Bobby Henrey* (Felipe), Sonia Dresdel (Mrs. Baines), Jack Hawkins (Detective Ames)

An ambassador's small son nearly incriminates his friend the butler in the accidental death of his shrewish wife.

A near-perfect piece of small-scale cinema, built up from clever nuances of acting and cinematic technique.

SCR Graham Greene   CIN Georges Périnal
MUS William Alwyn   ED Oswald Haffenrichter
PROD Carol Reed   DIST British Lion/London Films

❝ A short story has become a film which is compact without loss of variety in pace and shape. – *Dilys Powell*
❝ It's too deliberate and hushed to be much fun. . .you wait an extra beat between the low-key lines of dialogue. – *Pauline Kael, 70s*

♟ Carol Reed (direction); Graham Greene (screenplay)
Ⓣ British film

'The adventures of an ordinary man at war with the everyday world.'

Falling Down ★★

DIR *Joel Schumacher*
1993   113m   US
DVD

☆ Michael Douglas (William 'D-Fens' Foster), *Robert Duvall* (Detective Martin Prendergast), Barbara Hershey (Elizabeth 'Beth' Travino), Rachel Ticotin (Detective Sandra Torres), Tuesday Weld (Amanda Prendergast), Frederic Forrest (Nick, The Nazi Surplus Store Owner), Lois Smith (Mrs. Foster/William's Mother)

A sacked defence worker suddenly flips over the problems of urban life, turns into a one-man terrorist force and strikes out at rude car drivers, violent gangs, snooty golfers and, unwisely, against a homophobic neo-Nazi.

A flawed yet fascinating look at the results of personal overload triggering disproportionate reactions from an ordinary guy pushed too far. Michael Douglas makes a brave stab at unfamiliar acting territory, though the whiff of racism in his character cannot be dismissed easily.

SCR *Ebbe Roe Smith*   CIN Andrzej Bartkowiak
MUS James Newton Howard   DES Barbara Ling
ED Paul Hirsch   PROD Arnold Kopelson, Herschel Weingrod, Timothy Harris   DIST Warner

❝ Sometimes funny, sometimes touching, and certainly unnerving. – *Time Out*
❝ There is no denying the power of the tale or Douglas's riveting performance—-his best and riskiest since Wall Street. – *Peter Travers, Rolling Stone*

Fanny and Alexander ★★★★

SCR/DIR *Ingmar Bergman*
1982   188m   Sweden/France/West Germany
`DVD`

☆ Gunn Walgren (Helena Ekdahl), Ewa Fröling (Emilie Ekdahl), Jarl Kulle (Gustav-Adolph Ekdahl), Erland Josephson (Isak Jacobi), Allan Edwall (Oscar Ekdahl), Börje Ahlstedt (Prof. Carl Ekdahl), Mona Malm (Alma Ekdahl), Gunnar Björnstrand (Filip Landahl), Jan Malmsjö (Bishop Edvard Vergerus)

Two years in the life of an affluent Swedish family around 1910, from the viewpoint of a small boy.

By some distance Bergman's most accessible film, it manages to be simultaneously epic and intimate: it marks the transition of a faintly bohemian family, with a theatre director and his actress wife at its head, to a different setting and mood, in which the deceased patriarch is replaced by a devout pastor. Affecting and enthralling, and largely based on the lives of the director and his own parents.

CIN *Sven Nykvist*   MUS Daniel Bell   DES *Anna Asp*
ED Sylvia Ingemarsson   PROD *Jörn Donner*   DIST AB Cinematograph/Swedish Film Institute/Swedish TV One/Gaumont/Persona Film/Tobis

66 It's as if Bergman's neuroses had been tormenting him for so long that he cut them off and went sprinting back to Victorian health and domesticity. – *New Yorker*

⚚ foreign language film; Sven Nykvist (cinematography); Anna Asp, Susanne Lingheim (art direction); Marik Vos-Lundh (costume design)

⚚ Ingmarr Bergman (original screenplay, director)

🅱 Sven Nykvist (cinematography)

Fantasia ★★★

1940   135m   US
`DVD` 🎵

☆ Leopold Stokowski, the Philadelphia Orchestra, Deems Taylor

A concert of classical music is given cartoon interpretations.

An eccentric dialogue-free extravaganza, brilliantly inventive for the most part, the cartoons having become classics in themselves: the Sorcerer's Apprentice sequence, starring Mickey Mouse, is a rightly acknowledged masterpiece, and the dancing hippos are almost in the same league.

DIST Walt Disney

66 Dull as it is towards the end, ridiculous as it is in the bend of the knee before Art, it is one of the strange and beautiful things that have happened in the world. – *Otis Ferguson*

66 It is ambitious, and finely so, and one feels that its vulgarities are at least unintentional. – *James Agate*

† Multiplane cameras, showing degrees of depth in animation, were used for the first time.

⚚ Special Award to Walt Disney, Leopold Stokowski

'What imprisons desires of the heart?'

Far from Heaven ★★★★

SCR/DIR *Todd Haynes*
2002   107m   US/France
`DVD` 🎵

☆ *Julianne Moore* (Cathy Whitaker), Dennis Quaid (Frank Whitaker), *Dennis Haysbert* (Raymond Deagan), Patricia Clarkson (Eleonor Fine), Viola Davis (Sybil), James Rebhorn (Dr Bowman), Celia Weston (Mona Lauder)

A wife in a wealthy Connecticut suburb in 1957 discovers her husband is homosexual. Secretly, she embarks on a relationship with her black gardener.

A devastatingly clever device: director Haynes has shot the story in the lush colours and style of a melodramatic Douglas Sirk 'women's picture'. But all the grace notes in such films are ushered centre stage, and it becomes an acutely observed study of racial and sexual bigotry in 1950s America. A beautifully made, brilliantly thought through and genuinely moving piece of work.

CIN Edward Lachman   MUS Elmer Bernstein
DES Mark Friedberg   ED James Lyons   PROD Christine Vachon, Jody Patton   DIST Entertainment

66 Exultant in both its artifice and its cruel honesty. . .it's quite brilliant. – *Geoff Andrew, Time Out*

66 Heart-breaking and uncannily accurate. – *Phillip French, Observer*

⚚ Julianne Moore (leading actress); Todd Haynes (original screenplay); Edward Lachman; Elmer Bernstein

---

'A far off land, a far off journey, a far off adventure.'

A Far Off Place ★

DIR Mikael Salomon
1993   100m   US
`DVD` 🎵

☆ Reese Witherspoon (Nonnie Parker), Ethan Randall (Harry Winslow), Jack Thompson (John Ricketts), Sarel Bok (Xhabbo), Robert Burke (Paul Parker), Patricia Kalember (Elizabeth Parker), Maximilian Schell (Col. Mopani Theron)

A Kalahari bush guide leads two teenagers across the African desert, safe from the grasp of a malevolent ivory hunter.

Good looking children's film (director Salomon is primarily a cinematographer), though the source books' plot is softened somewhat. Notable as Witherspoon's first lead role.

SCR Robert Caswell, Jonathan Hensleigh, Sally Robinson
CIN *Juan Ruiz-Anchia*   MUS James Horner
DES Gemma Jackson   ED Ray Lovejoy   PROD Eva Monely, Elaine Sperber   DIST Buena Vista/Walt Disney/Amblin

66 There is just enough white-man's intrigue to make the trip engrossing, and just enough wildlife to make it diverting. – *Desson Howe, Washington Post*

† Though van der Post's original books were specifically set in Botswana, the film was shot in neighbouring Namibia.

Faraway, So Close ★

DIR Wim Wenders
1993 144m Germany
[DVD] ♫

☆ Otto Sander (Cassiel), Peter Falk (Himself), Bruno Ganz (Damiel), Horst Buchholz (Tony Baker), Nastassja Kinski (Raphaela), Heinz Rühmann (Chauffeur Konrad), Solveig Dommartin (Marion), Rudiger Vogler (Phillip Winter), Lou Reed (Himself), Willem Dafoe (Emit Flesti), Henri Alekan (Captain), Mikhail Gorbachev (Himself)

An angel who is tired of watching over Berlin wants to come down to earth and be human.

This sad, redundant sequel to Wings of Desire disappoints from the start. It's corny, sentimental – and hopelessly confused by the time Mikhail Gorbachev arrives, playing himself none too convincingly.

SCR Wim Wenders, Ulrich Zieger, Richard Reitinger **CIN** Jürgen Jürges **MUS** Laurent Petitgand, Graeme Revell, David Darling **DES** Albrecht Konrad **ED** Peter Pryzgodda **PROD** Wim Wenders, Ulrich Felsberg **DIST** Columbia TriStar/Road Movies/Tobis

66 Faraway. . .is vaguely deflating, a film that doesn't build to a powerful climax so much as gradually run out of air. – *Desson Thomson, Washington Post*

Farewell My Concubine ★★★

DIR *Chen Kaige*
1993 171m Hong Kong/China
[DVD] ♫

☆ *Leslie Cheung* (Cheng Dieyi), *Zhang Fengyi* (Duan Xiaolou), Gong Li (Juxian), Lu Qi (Guan Jifa), Ying Da (Manager), Ge You (Master Yuan), Li Chun (Xiao Si (teenager)), Lei Han (Xiao Si (adult)), Tong Di (Zhang the Eunuch)

Two young orphaned boys join the Peking Opera and form a lifelong relationship. But love drives them apart in a bitter split and they are forced into denouncing each other.

An engaging epic that traces the extraordinary changes in 50 years of Chinese history in comprehensive and fascinating detail.

SCR Lilian Lee, Lu Wei, Bik-Wa Lei **CIN** *Gu Changwei* **MUS** Zhao Jiping **ED** Pei Xiaonan **PROD** Hsu Feng **DIST** Artificial Eye/Thomson/China Film/Beijing Film

66 Farewell My Concubine is a demonstration of how a great epic can function. – *Roger Ebert, Chicago Sun-Times*

66 Intelligent, enthralling, rhapsodic. – *Time Out*

† In 1993, the film jointly won the Palme d'Or at the Cannes Film Festival, with Jane Campion's The Piano. It was the first Chinese film to do so.
† The film was initially banned in China, but the ban was lifted when it attracted international acclaim.

⚖ foreign language film; Gu Changwei

Ⓣ film not in the English language

'Small Town. . .Big Crime. . .Dead Cold.'

Fargo ★★★★

DIR *Joel Coen*
1996 98m US
[DVD] ♫

☆ *Frances McDormand* (Marge Gunderson), *William H.*

Macy (Jerry Lundegaard), Steve Buscemi (Carl Showalter), *Peter Stormare* (Gaear Grimsrud), Harve Presnell (Wade Gustafson), Kristin Rudrüd (Jean Lundegaard), Tony Denman (Scotty Lundegaard)

A cash-strapped Minnesota car salesman pays two bungling crooks to kidnap his wife in order to demand a ransom from his wealthy father-in-law. But his scheme goes disastrously wrong.

Off-centre masterpiece with Frances McDormand in luminous form as a decent, heavily pregnant police chief whose slow, discursive style of speech disguises the sharpness of her brain. This may be the Coens' most satisfying film: a mixture of droll humour, gory murder, quick wit and bumbling stupidity. The snowy wastes make a striking visual counterpoint for the madcap action and jolting violence.

SCR *Joel and Ethan Coen* **CIN** *Roger Deakins* **MUS** Carter Burwell **DES** Rick Heinrichs **ED** *Roderick Jaynes* **PROD** Ethan Coen **DIST** Polygram/Working Title

66 The beauty of the film is in the subtle detail of the dialogue and performances which continue to enchant on repeat viewings. – *George Perry, BBC*

66 Fargo is a strikingly mature, unique entertainment that plays on many levels. . .all satisfying. – *Leonard Klady, Variety*

† The Oscar-nominated Roderick Jaynes, supposedly an elderly Englishman living in Haywards Heath, is a pseudonym for the Coen Brothers.

⚖ Frances McDormand (leading actress); Ethan and Joel Coen (original screenplay)
⚖ picture; William H. Macy (supporting actor); Joel Coen; Roger Deakins; Roderick Jaynes

Ⓣ Joel Coen
Ⓣ film; Frances McDormand (leading actress); Ethan and Joel Coen (screenplay); Roderick Jaynes; Roger Deakins

Farinelli Il Castrato ★

DIR Gérard Corbiau
1994 111m Italy/Belgium/France/Germany
[DVD] ♫

☆ Stéfano Dionisi (Carlo Broschi (Farinelli)), Enrico Lo Verso (Riccardo Broschi), Elsa Zylberstein (Alexandra), Caroline Cellier (Margareth Hunter), Marianne Basler (Countess Mauer), Jeroen Krabbé (George Frideric Handel), Graham Valentine (Prince of Wales), Omero Antonutti (Nicola Porpora)

The most celebrated singer in Europe, a castrato whose high voice makes him a heart-throb to women, embarks on feuds with his less famous (but more manly) brother and the composer Handel.

Camp, colourful biopic on the extraordinary life of 18th-century singing sensation Carlo Broschi. Stunning soundtrack and vibrant visuals. An agreeable oddity.

SCR André Corbiau, Gérard Corbiau, Marcel Beaulieu **CIN** Walther van den Ende **DES** Gianni Quaranta **ED** Joelle Hache **PROD** Vera Belmont **DIST** Guild/Stephan/Alinea/Canal/France 2/Images/K2/RTL/TV1

66 Farinelli is in the grand European tradition of the sweeping, epic, historical romance, heady and histrionic,

F

replete with sumptuous costumes and décor. – *Kevin Thomas, Los Angeles Times*

⚮ foreign language film

'On the other side of drinks, dinner and a one night stand, lies a terrifying love story.'

Fatal Attraction ★★

DIR *Adrian Lyne*
1987   119m   US
DVD   ♫

☆ *Michael Douglas* (Dan Gallagher), *Glenn Close* (Alex Forrest), Anne Archer (Beth Gallagher), Fred Gwynne (Arthur)

A married man enjoys a one night stand, but his lover refuses to be cast aside and wreaks havoc in his life.

Stylish treatment of an extramarital fling that turns into a nightmare. It truly caught the mood of the moment, thanks to fine, full-on performances all round, with Close a stand-out as the avenging mistress from hell.

SCR James Dearden   CIN Howard Atherton
MUS Maurice Jarre   DES Mel Bourne   ED Michael Kahn
PROD Stanley Jaffe, Sherry Lansing
DIST Paramount/Jaffe-Lansing

66 Director Adrian Lyne takes a brilliantly manipulative approach to what might have been a humdrum subject and shapes a soap opera of exceptional power. – *Janet Maslin, New York Times*

66 One of the most effective thrillers in years, Attraction did an excellent job of mixing its suspense with trendy issues of sexual paranoia and monogamy. – *Edward Guthmann, San Francisco Chronicle*

† The film bequeathed a colourful phrase to the language: 'bunny-boiler' is now widely understood to mean a spurned, vengeful woman.

⚮ picture; Glenn Close (leading actress); Anne Archer (supporting actress); Adrian Lyne; James Dearden (original screenplay); Michael Kahn

Ⓑ Michael Kahn
Ⓣ Michael Douglas (leading actor); Anne Archer (supporting actress)

'You can close your eyes. You can turn away. But you will never forget.'

Fateless ★★★

DIR *Lajos Koltai*
2005   140m   Hungary/Germany/GB
DVD   ♫

☆ *Marcell Nagy* (György Köves), Aron Dimeny (Bandi Citrom), Andras M. Kecskes (Finn), Jozsef Gyabronka (Unlucky man), Endre Harkanyi (Old Kollmann), Daniel Craig (American Soldier)

A young Jewish Hungarian boy survives the Nazi death camps of World War II, then struggles to re-build his life.

An intensely powerful film, based on the auto-biographical novel of a Nobel Prize winner. It suggests hauntingly that the torment of war continues after fighting has finished, especially for a boy who only

partially understands the full horror of what he witnessed.

SCR *Imre Kertesz*   CIN *Gyula Pados*   MUS Ennio Morricone   DES Tibor Lazar   ED Hajnal Sello
PROD Andras Hamori, Peter Barbalics, Ildiko Kemeny, Jonathan Olsberg   DIST Dogwood

66 Fateless looks man's inhumanity to man square in the eye and pronounces it standard operating procedure, and that may be the greater horror. – *Ty Burr, Boston Globe*

66 It's a work that sears the heart and conscience. The events are annihilating, the way they're told, both beautiful and terrifying. – *Michael Wilmington, Chicago Tribune*

'The bride gets the thrills! Father gets the bills!'

Father of the Bride ★★★

DIR Vincente Minnelli
1950   93m   US

☆ *Spencer Tracy*, Joan Bennett, Elizabeth Taylor, Don Taylor, Billie Burke, Moroni Olsen, Leo G. Carroll, Taylor Holmes, Melville Cooper

A dismayed but happy father surveys the cost and chaos of his daughter's marriage.

Minor Minnelli in terms of film artistry, but a massive popular hit, this fragmentary but delightful lightweight comedy benefits from a strong, affecting performance by Tracy as a father with torn emotions.

SCR *Frances Goodrich, Albert Hackett*   CIN John Alton
MUS Adolph Deutsch   PROD Pandro S. Berman
DIST MGM

66 The idealization of a safe sheltered existence, the good life according to MGM: 24 carat complacency. – *New Yorker, 1980*

† Jack Benny badly wanted the Tracy role but was thought unsuitable.

† A vastly inferior re-make starring Steve Martin was released in 1991, with a sequel appearing in 1995.

⚮ picture; Frances Goodrich, Albert Hackett (original screenplay); Spencer Tracy (leading actor)

'Buy the ticket, take the ride.'

Fear and Loathing in Las Vegas ★

DIR Terry Gilliam
1998   118m   US
DVD   ♫

☆ Johnny Depp (Raoul Duke), Benicio Del Toro (Dr. Gonzo/Oscar Z. Acosta), Craig Bierko, Ellen Barkin (Waitress at North Star Cafe), Gary Busey (Highway Patrolman), Cameron Diaz (Blonde TV Reporter), Flea (Musician), Mark Harmon (Magazine Reporter at Mint 400), Katherine Helmond (Desk Clerk at Mint Hotel), Michael Jeter (L. Ron Bumquist), Penn Jillette (Carnie Talker), Lyle Lovett (Road Person), Tobey Maguire (Hitchhiker), Christina Ricci (Lucy), Harry Dean Stanton (Judge), Tim Thomerson

In 1971, a journalist and his eccentric lawyer make a road trip to Las Vegas for a spectacular drugs orgy.

Director Gilliam tries to capture Hunter S. Thompson's adrenalin-rush prose in this film, which fairly whizzes by. But as an epitaph for a heroically stoned generation, it fails to come alive, despite much wild raving, bizarre

DVD Available on DVD	☆ Cast in order of importance	66 Critics' Quotes	† Points of interest	⚮ Academy Award / Academy Award nomination	Ⓑ BAFTA / Ⓣ BAFTA nomination

217

behaviour and Depp's studious impersonation of Thompson.

SCR Terry Gilliam, Tony Grisoni, Tod Davies, Alex Cox **CIN** Nicola Pecorini **MUS** Ray Cooper **DES** Alex McDowell **ED** Lesley Walker **PROD** Laila Nabulsi, Patrick Cassavetti, Stephen Nemeth **DIST** Universal/Rhino

66 Gilliam's film is a spectacular wipeout, a visionary mess that is so unrelentingly dissolute that it may prove to be impenetrable viewing for most tastes. – *David Kronke, Los Angeles Times*

† Alex Cox was replaced as director by Gilliam before shooting began.

Fear and Trembling ★

SCR/DIR Alain Corneau
2003   107m   France
DVD

☆ Sylvie Testud (Amélie), Kaori Tsuji (Fubuki Mori), Taro Suwa (Mr Saito), Bison Katayama (Mr Omochi), Yasunari Kondo (Mr Tenshi)

Amelie, a Belgian translator, lands a job in the head office of a Tokyo firm and suffers at the hands of her rigid bosses and the subtle hierarchies within Japanese office politics.

Neat, observational comedy of culture clashes which is based on a true story and laudably takes a neutral view of racial differences.

CIN Yves Angelo **DES** Philippe Taillefer, Valerie Leblanc **ED** Thierry Derocles **PROD** Alain Sarde

66 Fear and Trembling offers a mostly fascinating look at Japanese culture as seen through narrowly focused Western eyes. – *Robert Denerstein, Denver Rocky Mountain News*

Fear Eats the Soul ★★★

SCR/DIR Rainer Werner Fassbinder
1974   92m   West Germany

☆ Brigitte Mira, El Hedi Ben Salem, Barbara Valentin, Irm Hermann, Rainer Werner Fassbinder

A 60-year-old German widow who works as a cleaner marries a younger Moroccan immigrant in Munich, and the couple encounter prejudice, mainly from her racist family.

An unusual, well-told moral fable, which Fassbinder deploys to emphasise the degree of prejudices existing in Germany at the time.

CIN Jürgen Jürges **ED** Thea Eymèsz **PROD** Christian Hohoff **DIST** Tango Film

'Some people are afraid of nothing.'

Fearless ★★★

DIR Peter Weir
1993   122m   US
DVD ♫

☆ *Jeff Bridges* (Max Klein), Isabella Rossellini (Laura Klein), Rosie Perez (Carla Rodrigo), Tom Hulce (Brillstein), John Turturro (Dr. Bill Perlman), Deirdre O'Connell (Nan Gordon), Benicio del Toro (Manny Rodrigo)

A man survives a near-death experience in a plane crash, and loses all sense of fear.

Difficult subject matter handled with great delicacy by Weir, who directs the terrifying opening scenes with aplomb. The real theme here is post-traumatic stress, which distances Bridges from his family also spurs his affinity with a fellow survivor. Intriguing, almost arcane material that might have been disastrous in lesser hands. Bridges does some of the best work of a distinguished career.

SCR Rafael Yglesias **CIN** Allen Daviau **MUS** Maurice Jarre **DES** John Stoddart **ED** William Anderson, Lee Smith, Armen Minasian **PROD** Paula Weinstein, Mark Rosenberg **DIST** Warner/Spring Creek

66 Fearless is like a short story that shines a bright light, briefly, into a corner where you usually do not look. – *Roger Ebert, Chicago Sun-Times*

⚲ Rosie Perez (supporting actress)

'A story for anyone with an appetite for love.'

Feast of Love (new)

DIR Robert Benton
2007   102m   US
♫

☆ Morgan Freeman (Professor Harry Stevenson), Greg Kinnear (Bradley), Radha Mitchell (Diana), Billy Burke (David Watson), Selma Blair (Kathryn), Alexa Davalos (Chloe), Toby Hemingway (Oscar), Jane Alexander (Esther Stevenson), Fred Ward (Bat)

A coffee-shop owner's romantic misfortunes fascinate an ageing university professor, though his intervention is not enough to stop another love affair ending tragically.

Sentimental, plodding drama, based on a novel; if there is a point it appears to have been mislaid, for all the explicatory narration.

SCR Allison Burnett **CIN** Kramer Morgenthau **MUS** Stephen Trask **DES** Missy Stewart **ED** Andrew Mondshein **PROD** Tom Rosenberg, Gary Lucchesi, Richard S. Wright **DIST** Entertainment

66 Benton juggles the multiple narratives with considerable grace and succeeds in creating a warm (if somewhat improbable) sense of community among the principal characters. – *Justin Chang, Variety*

66 Syrupy, drivelly, snively nonsense. – *Peter Bradshaw, Guardian*

Felicia's Journey ★★

SCR/DIR *Atom Egoyan*
1999   116m   GB/Canada
DVD ♫

☆ *Bob Hoskins* (Hilditch), Elaine Cassidy (Felicia), Arsinee Khanjian (Gala), Peter McDonald (Johnny), Gerard McSorley (Felicia's Father), Brid Brennan (Mrs Lysaght), Danny Turner (Young Hilditch), Claire Benedict (Miss Calligary)

An innocent young Irish girl arrives in England looking for the father of her unborn baby. She is taken in by a lonely, middle-aged catering manager with questionable motives.

William Trevor's novel is expertly adapted by Egoyan into an uncomfortable drama, with Hoskins a compelling but sinister Samaritan.

CIN Paul Sarossy MUS Mychael Danna DES Jim Clay
ED Susan Shipton PROD Bruce Davey DIST Icon

66 So elegantly layered and emotionally restrained, it makes the horror at its centre all the more disturbing. – *Desson Thomson, Washington Post*

Fellow Traveller ★★

DIR Philip Saville
1989 97m GB/US

☆ Ron Silver (Asa Kaufman), Imogen Stubbs (Sarah Atchison), Hart Bochner (Clifford Byrne), Daniel J. Travanti (Jerry Leavy), Katherine Borowitz (Joan Kaufman), Julian Fellowes (D'Arcy), Richard Wilson (Sir Hugo Armstrong), Doreen Mantle (Landlady), David O'Hara (Ronnie Wilson)

In London in 1954, an American scriptwriter who fled from the McCarthyite witch-hunts is shattered by the news of the suicide of a friend in Hollywood.

Tense, complex thriller which shrewdly employs the making of the then new Robin Hood TV series in Britain as a backdrop to contemporary political upheavals in America. A fresh, oblique take on an historical theme that had seemed well-aired.

SCR *Michael Eaton* CIN John Kenway MUS Colin Towns DES Gavin Davies, John Kenway ED Greg Miller PROD Michael Wearing DIST BFI/BBC Films/HBO

66 The clever script touches on politics, paranoia and betrayal, and director Saville clearly understands more than the surface complexities of this dark period. – *Channel 4*

66 A moody, gripping, suspense drama, reminiscent of classic film noir. – *Time Out*

† The film was originally made for the US cable channel HBO, but received a release in British cinemas.

'D-Day depends on them.'

Female Agents (new) ★

DIR Jean-Paul Salomé
2008 116m France

☆ Sophie Marceau (Louise Desfontaine), Julie Depardieu (Jeanne Faussier), Marie Gillain (Suze Desprez), Deborah Francois (Gaelle Lemenech), Maya Sansa (Maria Luzzato), Moritz Bleibtreu (Colonel Heindrich), Julien Boisselier (Pierre Desfontaine)

A member of the French Resistance is recruited by British intelligence to lead an all-female mission to assassinate a Nazi colonel in Paris.

Old-fashioned espionage yarn with some well-staged set-pieces, a strong cast and a surfeit of WWII clichés.

SCR Jean-Paul Salomé, Laurent Vachaud CIN Pascal Ridao MUS Bruno Coulais DES Francoise Dupertuis PROD Eric Névé DIST Revolver Entertainment

66 A period adventure that radiates star wattage but doesn't exactly shine in the script department. – *Jay Weissberg, Variety*

66 An old-fashioned action flick with a feminist slant. – *Bernard Besserglik, Hollywood Reporter*

La Femme Infidèle ★★★

SCR/DIR *Claude Chabrol*
1968 98m France/Italy
DVD

☆ *Stéphane Audran* (Helene Desvallees), *Michel Bouquet* (Charles Desvallees), Maurice Ronet (Victor Pegala)

A middle-aged insurance broker, set in his ways, murders his wife's lover; when she suspects the truth, they are drawn closer together.

Almost a Buñuel-like black comedy, spare and quiet, with immaculate performances – especially from Audran, Chabrol's leading muse. The director's debt to Hitchcock is fully in evidence in this claustrophobic story.

CIN Jean Rabier MUS Pierre Jansen ED Jacques Gaillard PROD André Génovès DIST La Boëtie/Cinegay

66 On any level, this bizarre murder framed by whiskies emerges as Chabrol's most flawless work to date. – *Jan Dawson, Monthly Film Bulletin*

The Fencing Master ★★★

DIR *Pedro Olea*
1992 88m Spain

☆ *Omero Antonutti* (Don Jaime Astarloa), *Assumpta Serna* (Adela de Otero), Joaquim de Almeida (Luis de Ayala), José Luis Lopez Vázquez (Jenaro Campillo), Alberto Closas (Álvaro Salanova), Miguel Rellán (Agapito Cárceles)

In Madrid in 1868, a fencing master is asked to teach his skills to a beautiful woman, and reluctantly agrees. Their agreement lands him in political intrigue, including murder.

A stylish costume drama that starts at a steady pace, but accelerates into melodrama territory. It's sustained by the considerable screen presence of its two leads.

SCR Antonio Larreta, Francisco Prada, Pedro Olea CIN Alfredo Mayo MUS José Nieto DES Luis Valles ED José Salcedo PROD Antonio Cardenal, Pedro Olea DIST Mayfair/Majestic/Origen/Altube Filmeak/ICAA

66 The film's chief fault is that it's a little too neat and thought-out. – *Philip Kemp, Sight & Sound*

'Every family has a secret.'

Festen ★★★

DIR Thomas Vinterberg
1998 105m Denmark
DVD

☆ Ulrich Thomsen (Christian), Henning Moritzen (Helge), Thomas Bo Larsen (Michael), Paprika Steen (Helene), Birthe Neumann (Mother), Trine Dyrholm (Pia), Helle Dolleris (Mette), Therese Glahn (Michelle), Klaus Bondam (Master of Ceremonies), Bjarne Henriksen (Cook), Gbatokai Dakinah (Gbatokai)

A family dinner to mark a Danish father's 60th birthday descends into chaos when his son accuses him of sexual abuse and blames him for the suicide of his twin sister.

A jolting experience, made more so by the in-your-face quality of hand-held video shooting. It's tremendously compelling material, yet it might feel like superior

DVD Available on DVD ☆ Cast in order 66 Critics' Quotes 🏆 Academy Award 🎭 BAFTA
🎵 Soundtrack on CD   of importance † Points of interest 🏆 Academy Award nomination 🎭 BAFTA nomination

219

melodrama if its stylistic trappings were stripped away.

SCR Thomas Vinterberg, Mogens Rukov   CIN Anthony Dod Mantle   ED Valdis Oskarsdottir   PROD Brigitte Hald   DIST October/Nimbus/DR TV/SVT Drama

66 The Celebration may be a conventional blend of melodrama and black comedy, but it is presented with the thrilling force of a fresh discovery. – *Liam Lacey, Globe and Mail, Canada*

† This was the first film was made under the 'vow of chastity' agreed upon by the signatories to the Dogme 95 school of film-making.

ⓣ film not in the English language

Festival ★

SCR/DIR Annie Griffin
2005   107m   GB
DVD

☆ Kevin Masson (The P), Lyndsey Marshal (Faith Myers), Paddy Bonner (Man on Street), Selina Cadell (Estate Agent), Daniela Nardini (Joan Gerard)

Artistic egos clash at the Edinburgh Fringe as street performers, comedians and actors compete to grab their moment of fame.

Chaotic observational comedy set behind the scenes of the famous festival. The script has a ring of truth but also an unfortunate surfeit of in-jokes. One joltingly explicit sex scene sits uneasily with the light-hearted tone.

CIN Daniel Cohen   MUS Jim Sutherland   DES Tom Sayer   ED William Webb   PROD Christopher Young   DIST Pathé

66 While it fails to tug your heartstrings, Festival will surely tickle your funny bone. – *Stella Papamichael, BBC*

† Writer-director Griffin made her name on TV, with the Scottish-based Channel 4 series The Book Group.

ⓣ British film; Annie Griffin (writer/director, promising newcomer)

'Life Gets Complicated When You Love One Woman and Worship Eleven Men.'

Fever Pitch ★

DIR David Evans
1996   102m   GB
DVD   ♫

☆ Colin Firth (Paul Ashworth), Ruth Gemmell (Sarah Hughes), Neil Pearson (Paul's dad), Lorraine Ashbourne (Paul's mum), Mark Strong (Steve), Holly Aird (Jo), Ken Stott (Ted), Stephen Rea (Ray)

Football fanatic teacher tries to interest his girlfriend in the real love of his life, Arsenal.

Weak attempt to turn Nick Hornby's brilliant, witty take on soccer obsession into a romantic comedy. Despite Firth's best efforts, it's about as much fun as a 0–0 draw in the driving rain.

SCR Nick Hornby   CIN Chris Seager   MUS Boo Hewerdine, Neil MacColl   DES Michael Carlin   ED Scott Thomas   PROD Amanda Posey   DIST Film Four/Wildgaze

66 Just because a first person analysis of a socio-cultural phenomenon is fascinating in print, it should not necessarily be turned into a movie. – *Anita Gates, New York Times*

† Many scenes were shot outside Highbury, Arsenal's former stadium. Hornby was an extra in crowd scenes.

A Few Days in September (new)

SCR/DIR Santiago Amigoréna
2006   110m   France/Italy

☆ Juliette Binoche (Irène), Nick Nolte (Elliot), John Turturro (William Pound), Sara Forestier (Orlando), Tom Riley (David)

In the first week of September 2001, a French secret service agent (Binoche) arranges a reunion between a shadowy ex-colleague (Nolte) and his estranged children. He has apparent foreknowledge of a major disaster.

Misjudged spy thriller with a gimmicky premise that relegates the appalling events of 9/11 to a lurid plot twist. The three stars are all miscast, especially John Turturro as a poetry-quoting assassin who calls his analyst whenever he kills someone.

CIN Christophe Beaucarne   MUS Laurent Martin   DES Emmanuelle Duplay   ED Sarah Turoche   PROD Paulo Branco   DIST Transmedia

66 The bemused viewer is likely to wonder how such starry actors could have ended up in such a godawful pickle. – *Kieron Corless, Sight & Sound*

66 Savvy thriller for conspiracy buffs with star performances by Binoche and Turturro. – *Ray Bennett, Hollywood Reporter*

'In the heart of the nation's capital, in a courthouse of the U.S. government, one man will stop at nothing to keep his honor, and one will stop at nothing to find the truth.'

A Few Good Men ★★

DIR Rob Reiner
1992   138m   US
DVD   ♫

☆ Tom Cruise (Lt. Daniel Kaffee), *Jack Nicholson* (Col. Nathan R. Jessep), Demi Moore (Lt. Cdr. JoAnne Galloway), *Kevin Bacon* (Capt. Jack Ross), Kiefer Sutherland (Lt. Jonathan Kendrick), Kevin Pollak (Lt. Sam Weinberg), James Marshall (Pfc. Louden Downey), J.T. Walsh (Lt. Col. Matthew Andrew Markinson), Christopher Guest (Dr. Stone), J.A. Preston (Judge Julius Alexander Randolph)

A cocky lawyer and his team defend two US Marines charged with the first-degree murder of a comrade, and come up against the might of the military machine.

Glossy all-star package, entertainingly absurd in the best Hollywood manner. The characters are all glib stereotypes with snappy lines, but it charges along unstoppably, and the cast are clearly having a ball.

SCR *Aaron Sorkin*   CIN Robert Richardson   MUS Marc Shaiman   DES J. Michael Riva   ED Robert Leighton, Steve Nevius   PROD David Brown, Rob Reiner, Andrew Scheinman   DIST Columbia TriStar/Castle Rock

66 A big-time, mainstream Hollywood movie par excellence. – *Variety*

DVD Available on DVD   ☆ Cast in order   66 Critics' Quotes   ⚊ Academy Award   ⓑ BAFTA
♫ Soundtrack on CD   of importance   † Points of interest   ⚊ Academy Award nomination   ⓣ BAFTA nomination

66 A slick, entertaining, flashily-acted courtroom drama replete with all the standard ingredients. – *Philip French, Observer*

⚱ Best picture; Jack Nicholson; Robert Leighton

'An unforgettable story of power and passion from the producer and director of My Left Foot.'

The Field ★

SCR/DIR Jim Sheridan
1990   107m   GB
DVD

☆ Richard Harris ('Bull' McCabe), John Hurt (Bird' O'Donnell), Tom Berenger (The American), Sean Bean (Tadgh McCabe), Frances Tomelty (Widow), Brenda Fricker (Maggie McCabe)

An Irish tenant farmer will stop at nothing to hang on to the patch of land that generations of his family have worked.

There's more than a touch of King Lear in this drama, which constantly asserts the importance of land, and its importance in maintaining a man's identity. In establishing a specific sense of time, place and tradition, the film assumes real power, though Harris's acting is somewhat overheated, compared with its overall tone.

CIN Jack Conroy   MUS Elmer Bernstein   DES Frank Conway   ED J. Patrick Duffner   PROD Noel Pearson
DIST Granada

66 Most of the burden of developing a tragic character is down to Harris, and he layers it richly. – *Brian Case, Time Out*

⚱ Richard Harris (leading actor)
Ⓣ John Hurt (supporting actor)

'All his life, Ray Kinsella was searching for his dreams. Then one day, his dreams came looking for him.'

Field of Dreams ★★

SCR/DIR Phil Alden Robinson
1989   107m   US
DVD ♫

☆ Kevin Costner (Ray Kinsella), Amy Madigan (Annie Kinsella), James Earl Jones (Terence Mann), Timothy Busfield (Mark), Ray Liotta (Shoeless Joe Jackson), Burt Lancaster (Dr. 'Moonlight' Graham), Gaby Hoffman (Karin Kinsella), Frank Whaley (Archie Graham), Dwier Brown (John Kinsella)

An Iowa farmer heeds voices telling him to build a baseball pitch to summon the ghosts of past players, including his late father.

Charming, sentimental fantasy with a universal appeal, even those who don't know a home run from a home help.

CIN John Lindley   MUS James Horner   DES Dennis Gassner   ED Ian Crafford   PROD Lawrence Gordon, Charles Gordon   DIST Guild/Universal/Carolco

THE VOICE: 'If you build it, he will come.'

66 No other film better captures the true spirit of baseball as does Field of Dreams, a true tear-jerking spectacle. – *Phil Villareal, Arizona Daily Star*

⚱ picture; Phil Alden Robinson (adapted screenplay); James Horner

'250 years in the future, all will be lost unless the fifth element is found.'

The Fifth Element

DIR Luc Besson
1997   126m   France
DVD ♫

☆ Bruce Willis (Korben Dallas), Gary Oldman (Zorg), Ian Holm (Cornelius), Milla Jovovich (Leeloo), Chris Tucker (Ruby Rhod), Luke Perry (Billy), Brion James (General Munro)

In the middle of an intergalactic war, a supreme being drops into the back of a weary driver's cab.

Tiresome fantasia in which the performances are almost as loud as some of the colouring; a prime example of a type of cinema that values spectacle at the expense of everything else.

SCR Luc Besson, Robert Mark Kamen   CIN Thierry Arbogast   MUS Eric Serra   DES Dan Weil   ED Sylvie Landra   PROD Patrice Ledoux
DIST Columbia/Gaumont

66 Too long by half, burdened with shabby effects and offering up some seriously weird performances, this pricey foray into science fiction is a muddle of miscues and narrative bloat – along with a lot of frivolous fun. – *Manohla Dargis, L.A. Weekly*

66 May or may not be the worst movie ever made, but it is one of the most unhinged. – *David Edelstein, Slate*

† The film began life as a script Besson wrote when he was just 16.

⚱ Mark A. Mangini (sound effects editing)
Ⓣ Mark Stetson, Karen E. Goulekas, Nick Allder, Neil Corbould, Nick Dudman (special effects)

'Mischief. Mayhem. Soap.'

Fight Club ★★★

DIR David Fincher
1999   139m   US
DVD ♫

☆ Brad Pitt (Tyler Durden), Edward Norton (Narrator), Helena Bonham Carter (Marla Singer), Meat Loaf (Robert Paulsen), Jared Leto (Angel Face)

A jaded businessman sets up secret fighting clubs where men can forget the rules of polite society and beat the living daylights out of each other.

The political incorrectness arrives like a well-judged upper-cut, but this harsh, often violent movie packs all sorts of surprising punches – including a late revelation about its two lead characters. It polarises opinion but remains bold, exciting and unmissable.

SCR Jim Uhls   CIN Jeff Cronenweth   MUS Dust Brothers
DES Alex McDowell   ED James Haygood   PROD Art Linson, Cean Chaffin, Ross Grayson Bell   DIST TCF

66 The film does everything short of rattling your seat to get a reaction. You can call that irresponsible. Or you can call that the only essential Hollywood film of 1999. – *Time Out*

66 The movie is not only anti-capitalism but anti-society, and, indeed, anti-God. – *Alexander Walker, This is London*

⚱ Ren Klyce, Richard Hymns (sound effects editing)

F

'A Sex Pistols film – uncut, unseen, unbelievable.'

The Filth and the Fury ★

DIR Julien Temple

2000 108m GB/US

DVD ♫

☆ Paul Cook (himself), Steve Jones (himself), Glen Matlock (himself), Johnny Rotten (himself), Sid Vicious (himself)

Documentary account of the rise and fall of punk group the Sex Pistols, in the band's own words.

A messy, scrapbook approach yields the occasional insight into the group's influences, but Temple buys into Pistols legend too easily: Sid Vicious's penchant for swastika T-shirts goes unexplored, and shooting the band's surviving members with their faces blacked out, as though wanted criminals, comes across as a sop (and a stylistic tic) too far. A useful corrective to the Temple-directed but Malcolm McLaren-controlled The Great Rock 'n' Roll Swindle, nonetheless.

ED Niven Howie   PROD Anita Camarata, Amanda Temple   DIST FilmFour

66 A clumsy bid for atonement. . .panders to all the participating survivors as they retrospectively recast their stories. This time round our blithely revisionist director makes sure he's 'in' with the 'lads'. – *Mark Sinker, Sight & Sound*

66 Funny and at times moving – despite all the ugliness and stupidity it depicts. – *Jonathan Foreman, New York Post*

'Fish are just like people, only flakier.'

Finding Nemo ★★★

DIR Andrew Stanton

2003 100m US

DVD ♫

☆ Voices of: Albert Brooks (Marlin), Ellen DeGeneres (Dory), Alexander Gould (Nemo), Willem Dafoe (Gill), Brad Garrett (Bloat), Allison Janney (Peach), Austin Pendleton (Gurgle), Geoffrey Rush (Nigel), Barry Humphries (Bruce), Eric Bana (Anchor), Bruce Spence (Chum), Bill Hunter (Dentist)

When Nemo the clown fish is captured and imprisoned in a Sydney aquarium, his worried father sets off to rescue him.

Astonishing animation, with underwater life stunningly captured by computer-generated means. There's a mythic quality to the story, which remains the focus of attention, rather than the usual tiresome, distracting pop-culture gags that scar too many animated films.

SCR Andrew Stanton, Bob Peterson, David Reynolds
CIN Sharon Calahan, Jeremy Lasky   DES Ralph Eggleston
ED David Ian Salter   PROD Graham Walters
DIST Buena Vista

66 A visual marvel, every frame packed to the gills with clever details. – *David Ansen, Newsweek*

66 Quality family entertaining is what this outstanding animation delivers. – *Peter Bradshaw, Guardian*

⚡ animated feature

⚡ Andrew Stanton, Bob Peterson, David Reynolds (original screenplay); Thomas Newman; Gary Rydstrom, Michael Silvers (sound editing)

Ⓣ Andrew Stanton, Bob Peterson, David Reynolds (original screenplay)

'Unlock your imagination.'

Finding Neverland ★★★

DIR *Marc Forster*

2004 106m US

DVD ♫

☆ *Johnny Depp* (Sir James Matthew Barrie), Kate Winslet (Sylvia Llewelyn Davies), Julie Christie (Mrs Emma du Maurier), Radha Mitchell (Mary Ansell Barrie), Dustin Hoffman (Charles Frohman), Kelly Macdonald (Peter Pan), Ian Hart (Sir Arthur Conan Doyle), Freddie Highmore (Peter Llewelyn Davies)

A lonely playwright finds inspiration in a widow and her four young sons he meets at play in London's Kensington Gardens and writes Peter Pan, the story about a boy who will not grow up.

Gentle, touching drama about the birth of a classic children's favourite, highlighted by a thoughtful script and an amusing, imaginative portrayal of J.M. Barrie by the chameleon-like Depp.

SCR David Magee   CIN Roberto Schaefer   MUS *Jan A.P. Kaczmarek*   DES Gemma Jackson   ED Matt Chesse
PROD Richard N. Gladstein, Nellie Bellflower
DIST Buena Vista

66 A rewarding piece of film-making that has all the makings of a classic weepie. – *Ray Bennett, Hollywood Reporter*

66 Finding Neverland does its job: it makes you cry. – *Tim Robey, Daily Telegraph*

⚡ Jan A.P. Kaczmarek

⚡ picture; Johnny Depp (leading actor); David Magee (original screenplay); Matt Chesse; Gemma Jackson; Alexandra Byrne (costume design)

Ⓣ Jan A.P. Kaczmarek

Ⓣ film; Johnny Depp (leading actor); Kate Winslet (leading actress); Julie Christie (supporting actress); David Magee (original screenplay); Roberto Schaefer; Gemma Jackson; Alexandra Byrne (costume design); Christine Blundell (make up/hair)

Fiorile ★

DIR Paolo and Vittorio Taviani

1993 122m Italy/France/Germany

DVD ♫

☆ Claudio Bigagli (Corrado/Alessandro), Galatea Ranzi (Elisabette/Elisa), Michael Vartan (Jean/Massimo), Renato Carpentieri (Massimo as an old Man), Lino Capolicchio (Luigi), Costanze Engelbrecht (Juliette), Chiara Caselli (Chiara), Athina Cenci (Gina)

Three stories that help explain a devastating 200-year-old curse on an Italian family are recounted to children on a long road trip.

Complex historical drama that resorts to frequent flashbacks to reveal its story. Still, it's told with the skill and elegance one expects from these fraternal film-makers.

SCR Sandro Petraglia, Paolo and Vittorio Taviani
CIN Giuseppe Lanci   MUS Nicola Piovani   DES Gianni Sbarra   ED Roberto Perpignani   PROD Grazia Volpi
DIST Arrow/Filmtre-Gierre/Pemnta/Flordia/La Sept/Canal/Roxy/KS

66 This is a film about passion, but it is curiously lacking. . .more a history lesson than a thrilling tale. – *Roger Ebert, Chicago Sun-Times*

'Beneath the surface lies a burning secret.'

Fire ★

SCR/DIR Deepa Mehta
1996   104m   India
[DVD]

☆ Shabana Azmi (Radha), Nandita Das (Sita), Kulbushan Kharbanda (Ashok), Jaaved Jaaferi (Jatin), Ranjit Chowdhry (Mundu), Kushal Rekhi (Biji), Alice Poon (Julie), Ram Gopal Bajaj (Swamiji)

Indian sisters-in-law, frustrated by the lack of love and affection from their husbands, begin a sexual relationship together.

Taboo-shattering movie with its treatment of adultery, masturbation and lesbianism. But from a western viewpoint, it's a competently assembled story of powerful romantic passions.

CIN Giles Nuttgens   MUS A.R. Rahman, Merlyn D'Souza
DES Aradhana Seth   ED Barry Farrell   PROD Bobby Bedi, Deepa Mehta

66 Audacious, yet sensitive, Fire may shock traditionalists but might well win Indian cinema a whole new audience. – *David Parkinson, Empire*

† The film was banned in India.
† It was conceived as the first of a trilogy named after elements: Earth and Water also dealt with facets of Indian life and culture.

'Hollywood's Coolest Dog Just Got Hotter.'

Firehouse Dog (new)

DIR Todd Holland
2007   111m   US
[DVD] ♫

☆ Josh Hutcherson (Shane Fahey), Bruce Greenwood (Captain Connor Fahey), Dash Mihok (Trey Falcon), Steven Culp (Zachary Hayden), Bill Nunn (Joe Musto), Bree Turner (Liz Knowles)

A movie star mutt saves a dilapidated fire station from closure.

Four-legged frolics with a sprinkling of Tinseltown satire and fireman heroics; entertaining enough for children but far too long.

SCR Claire-Dee Lim, Mike Werb, Michael Colleary
CIN Victor Hammer   MUS Jeff Cardoni   DES Tamara Deverell   ED Scott James Wallace   PROD Michael Colleary, Mike Werb   DIST TCF

66 A mixed breed of obvious humour, gently moving father-son drama and sub-Backdraft trial by fire. – *Justin Chang, Variety*

66 The sentimentality is ghastly. – *James Christopher, The Times*

The Firemen's Ball ★★★

DIR *Milos Forman*
1967   73m   Czechoslovakia/Italy
☆ Jan Vostrcil, Josef Kolb, Josef Svet, Frantisek Debelka
In a small provincial town, arrangements for the firemen's annual ball get bogged down in procedural problems and accidents.

Amusing comedy with a point to make: its bumbling committee members are stand-ins for the officials in the then communist government in Czechoslovakia. It was banned there, while enjoying international success.

SCR *Milos Forman, Ivan Passer, Jaroslav Papousek*
CIN *Miroslav Ondricek*   MUS *Karel Mares*
DIST Barrandov/Carlo Ponti

66 A compendium of superb items. – *Philip Strick*
⚲ foreign film

'Power can be murder to resist.'

The Firm ★

DIR Sydney Pollack
1993   154m   US
[DVD] ♫

☆ Tom Cruise (Mitch McDeere), Jeanne Tripplehorn (Abby McDeere), Gene Hackman (Avery Tolar), Hal Holbrook (Oliver Lambert), Terry Kinney (Lamar Quinn), Wilford Brimley (William Devasher), Ed Harris (Wayne Tarrance), Holly Hunter (Tammy Hemphill), David Strathairn (Ray McDeere), Gary Busey (Eddie Lomax), Steven Hill (F. Denton Voyles), Tobin Bell (The Nordic Man)

An ambitious young lawyer gets a plum job with a prestigious law firm, only to find strings attached: it offers other unspecified services for the Mob. He then finds himself caught between organised crime heavies and suspicious federal agents.

A decently scripted adaptation of Grisham's best-seller, even if it evades a couple of dark subplots. It bowls along efficiently if conventionally, but its real glory is its supporting cast, a long list of truly talented names doing seriously good work. They're enough to see the film past the finishing line.

SCR David Rabe, Robert Towne, David Rayfiel   CIN John Seale   MUS David Grusin   DES Richard Macdonald
ED William Steinkamp, Frederic Steinkamp
PROD Sydney Pollack, Scott Rudin, John Davis
DIST Paramount

66 No one is going to confuse The Firm with art, but its high-cholesterol virtues – a story that keeps you guessing, a dozen meaty character turns – are enough to send you home sated. – *Owen Gleiberman, Entertainment Weekly*

66 An average movie improved by Cruise's star appeal and accomplished supporting cast. – *Matt Mueller, Empire*

⚲ Holly Hunter (supporting actress); Dave Grusin
Ⓣ Holly Hunter (supporting actress)

'Keep the Faith. Steal the Rest.'

First Sunday (new)

SCR/DIR David E. Talbert
2008   98m   USA
☆ Ice Cube (Durell Washington), Katt Williams (Rickey), Loretta Devine (Sister Doris McPherson), Regina Hall (Omunique)

Two petty crooks go to church to rob the donations box and end up in a hostage situation.

[DVD] Available on DVD   ☆ Cast in order   66 Critics' Quotes   ⚲ Academy Award   Ⓑ BAFTA
♫ Soundtrack on CD   of importance   † Points of interest   ⚲ Academy Award nomination   Ⓣ BAFTA nomination

223

Embarrassing racial and religious stereotypes populate a hackneyed and overly sentimental heist romp.

CIN Alan Caso   **MUS** Stanley Clarke   **DES** Dina Lipton   **ED** Jeffrey Wolf   **PROD** David E. Talbert, Ice Cube, Matt Alvarez, David McIlvain, Julie Yom   **DIST** Sony Pictures

66 It plods along at a sluggard's pace through a weak premise with crude execution. – *Kirk Honeycutt, The Hollywood Reporter*

'Don't get mad. Get Everything.'

The First Wives Club ★

DIR Hugh Wilson
1996   103m   US
[DVD]   ♫

☆ Goldie Hawn (Elise Elliot), Bette Midler (Brenda Cushman), Diane Keaton (Annie Paradis), Maggie Smith (Gunilla Garson Goldberg), Dan Hedaya (Morton Cushman), Victor Garber (Bill Atchison), Bronson Pinchot (Duarto Feliz), Marcia Gay Harden (Dr. Leslie Rosen), Eileen Heckart (Catherine MacDuggan), Philip Bosco (Uncle Carmine Morelli), Elizabeth Berkley (Phoebe LaVelle)

Three women, estranged since college days, reunite at a friend's funeral, share tales of marital woe about their husbands chasing younger women, and decide to take revenge.

A women's movie without question – and specifically a movie for women who have suffered insensitivity or worse from men. It's slightly less shrewish than it sounds, and the three leads get to deliver some one-liners that have snap and wit. But it fails to maintain its pace, and gets soggier as it progresses. Adapted for the screen by Robert Harling, author of another work mostly featuring women, Steel Magnolias: that's a tip-off, right there.

SCR Robert Harling   **CIN** Donald Thorin   **MUS** Marc Shaiman   **DES** Peter Larkin   **ED** John Bloom   **PROD** Scott Rudin   **DIST** UIP/Paramount

66 We're here for catty one-liners, movie-star camaraderie and fur-flying vengeance, and, in spite of a regrettable wimpiness that creeps in toward the end, that's what we get. – *David Ansen, Newsweek*

66 What starts out so promisingly with some witty one-liners loses itself in the middle and finally descends into a slapstick routine that cries out for a touch of sophistication. – *Deborah Brown, Empire*

⚬ Marc Shaiman (music)

A Fish Called Wanda ★★★

DIR *Charles Crichton*
1988   108m   US
[DVD]   ♫

☆ *John Cleese* (Archie Leach), Jamie Lee Curtis (Wanda), Kevin Kline (Otto), Michael Palin (Ken Pile), Maria Aitken (Wendy)

Diamond-heist comedy depending on Anglo-American rivalries for its laughs.

Skilful, relentless comedy, with Cleese in top form as a stuffy barrister, smitten by Curtis's wily American crook and exasperated by her moronic boyfriend (Kline).

Ingeniously pitched somewhere between an Ealing comedy and an extended Monty Python sketch, it easily stands the test of time.

SCR *John Cleese, Charles Crichton*   **CIN** Alan Hume   **MUS** John Du Prez   **DES** Roger Murray-Leach   **PROD** Michael Shamberg   **DIST** MGM

† Crichton directed the film and received his Oscar nomination at age 78.
† Archie Leach, Cleese's character, is the real name of Cary Grant.

⚬ Kevin Kline (supporting actor)
⚬ Charles Crichton; (original screenplay)
Ⓣ John Cleese (leading actor); Michael Palin (supporting actor)

'A Modern Day Tale About The Search For Love, Sanity, Ethel Merman And The Holy Grail.'

The Fisher King ★★

DIR *Terry Gilliam*
1991   137m   US
[DVD]   ♫

☆ Robin Williams (Parry), *Jeff Bridges* (Jack Lucas), *Amanda Plummer* (Lydia Sinclair), *Mercedes Ruehl* (Anne Napolitano), Michael Jeter (Homeless cabaret singer)

A depressed New York radio DJ is saved from suicide by a tramp, who is a former professor of mediaeval history. Together the two men go in search of a mythical Holy Grail.

When one considers how awful this story might have been in the wrong hands, it's clear Gilliam wrought miracles, injecting the story with pace, humour, romance and, when called for, a decidedly spooky quality. He even manages to rein in Williams, whose holy-fool hobo could have been unbearable. As it is, this folk tale in modern dress is furnished handsomely by the director's ever-fertile visual imagination.

SCR Richard LaGravenese   **CIN** Roger Pratt   **MUS** George Fenton   **DES** *Mel Bourne*   **ED** Lesley Walker   **PROD** Debra Hill, Linda Obst   **DIST** Columbia TriStar

66 A modern epic that fuses myth with hard-edged reality, it's a one-of-a-kind, thoroughly engaging experience. – *Desson Thomson, Washington Post*

66 If you treasure Gilliam at his best and take his ideas seriously, you'll probably be infuriated as well as delighted. – *Jonathan Rosenbaum, Chicago Reader*

⚬ Mercedes Ruehl (supporting actress)
⚬ Robin Williams (leading actor); Richard LaGravenese (original screenplay); George Fenton (music); Mel Bourne
Ⓣ Amanda Plummer (supporting actress); screenplay

A Fistful of Dollars ★★★

DIR *Sergio Leone*
1964   100m   Italy/Germany/Spain
[DVD]   ♫

☆ *Clint Eastwood* (The Man with No Name), Gian Maria Volonte (Ramon Rojo), Marianne Koch (Marisol), Wolfgang Lukschy (John Baxter)

A vengeful mercenary, hired to bring order to a border town, pits rival families against each other and watches them destroy themselves.

This film was the first 'spaghetti Western', a European variation on a quintessentially American genre. Director Leone, plucking his star from a US TV series, devised a scenario of dramatic close-ups, sparse dialogue (especially from Eastwood) and explicit violence, all to Ennio Morricone's exquisite music. It became a pan-European hit, turned Eastwood into a global star – and despite snobbish criticism at the time about its lurid, melodramatic tone and Eastwood's TV origins, it reinvigorated the Western and launched a sub-genre whose influence is still being felt. Leone would go on to do more sophisticated work within this format – but this was a decent start.

SCR Sergio Leone, Duccio Tessari CIN Massimo Dallamano MUS *Ennio Morricone* ED Roberto Cinquini
PROD Arrigo Colombo, Georgio Papi
DIST UA/Jolly/Constantin/Ocean
† The film's plot was lifted directly from Akira Kurosawa's Yojimbo.

'The greatest Western ever made. . .in Somerset.'

A Fistful of Fingers ★

SCR/DIR Edgar Wright
1995 78m GB

☆ Graham Low ('No-Name'), Martin Curtis (Running Sore), Oliver Evans (The Squint), Quentin Green (Jimmy James), William Cornes (Sheriff Marshall), Jeremy Beadle (Himself)

The Man With No Name pursues an outlaw named Squint across the Mendips.

An ultra-low-budget Western spoof of spaghetti westerns; the horses are of the pantomime variety and the jokes are inspired by Airplane! As the debut effort of Edgar Wright, who later directed Shaun of the Dead and Hot Fuzz, it has rarity value.

CIN Alvin Leong MUS François Evans DES Simon Bowles ED Giles Harding PROD Daniel Figuero
DIST Blue Dolphin/Wrightstuff

❝ Its strong sense of fun is something that's rare in the modern commercial cinema. – *Tom Tunney, Sight & Sound*
† Wright, who was just 20 when he directed the film, shot it in Wells, Somerset for under £10,000.

Fitzcarraldo ★★★★

SCR/DIR *Werner Herzog*
1982 158m West Germany
DVD

☆ *Klaus Kinski* (Brian Sweeney Fitzgerald/Fitzcarraldo), Claudia Cardinale (Molly), José Lewgoy (Don Aquilino), Paul Hittscher (Capt. Orinoco Paul), Miguel Angel Fuentes (Cholo the Mechanic), Huerequeque Enrique Bohorquez (Cook)

In Peru in the early 20th century, an eccentric Irishman, who is a fervent Caruso fan, resolves to accomplish an extraordinary feat against all odds: establishing an opera house in the jungle.

A strange, brilliant, unforgettable film centring on the hero's successful attempt to drag his massive boat from one river to another; clearly in Herzog's mind, a

Herculean task comparable to getting a film made that reflects a director's artistic vision.

CIN *Thomas Mauch* MUS *Popol Vuh* ED Beata Mainka-Jellinghaus PROD Werner Herzog, Lucki Stipetic
DIST Werner Herzog/ProjectFilmproduktion/Zweite Deutsches Fernsehen/Wildlife Films, Peru

❝ A fine, quirky, fascinating movie. It's a stunning spectacle, an adventure-comedy not quite like any other, and the most benign movie ever made about nineteenth century capitalism running amok. – *Vincent Canby, New York Times*
† 'Fitzcarraldo' is the nearest the Peruvians can get to 'Fitzgerald'.
† An excellent feature-length documentary by Les Blank, Burden of Dreams (1982), captured the chaotic circumstances in which Fitzcarraldo was shot.

Five Corners ★

DIR Tony Bill
1988 90m US
DVD

☆ Jodie Foster (Linda), Tim Robbins (Harry), Todd Graff (Jamie), John Turturro (Heinz), Elizabeth Berridge (Melanie), Rose Gregorio (Mrs. Sabantino), Gregory Rozakis (Mazola), John Seitz (Sullivan)

When a convicted rapist is released from prison, he reunites with old friends from his neighbourhood.

Set in the Bronx in 1964, it begins well as a sprightly rites-of-passage tale before losing its way dramatically. The best reason to see it is the young cast with bright futures: Foster, Robbins and Turturro all went on to better things.

SCR John Patrick Shanley CIN Fred Murphy
MUS James Newton Howard DES Adrianne Lobel
ED Andy Blumenthal PROD Tony Bill, Forest Murray
DIST Handmade Films

❝ An odd mixture of the conventional and the unexpected, this is an unusual but enjoyable ensemble piece that contains elements of comedy, action and period drama. – *Channel 4*

Five Easy Pieces ★★★

DIR *Bob Rafelson*
1970 98m US
DVD

☆ *Jack Nicholson*, Karen Black, Susan Anspach, Lois Smith, Billy 'Green' Bush, Fannie Flagg

A middle-class drifter jilts his pregnant mistress for his brother's fiancée, but finally leaves both and hitches a ride to nowhere in particular.

Echoes of Easy Rider and The Graduate abound in this compelling drama about a dissatisfied young rebel straddling two worlds: his cerebral family home, where he learned to be a talented classical musician, and the rough, tough, blue-collar world of oil rigs. Nicholson is forcefully believable as yet another late 60s American screen character who does not want what his country has to offer.

SCR *Adrien Joyce* CIN *Laszlo Kovacs* MUS various
PROD Bob Rafelson, Richard Wechsler
DIST Columbia/Bert Schneider

DVD Available on DVD   ☆ Cast in order   ❝ Critics' Quotes   ⚱ Academy Award   🇧 BAFTA
♫ Soundtrack on CD   of importance   † Points of interest   ⚱ Academy Award nomination   🇧 BAFTA nomination

225

picture; Adrien Joyce (screenplay); Jack Nicholson (leading actor); Karen Black (supporting actress)

5 x 2 ★★

DIR François Ozon
2004 90m France
`DVD` ♫

☆ *Valeria Bruni-Tedeschi* (Marion), Stéphane Freiss (Gilles), Géraldine Pailhas (Valérie), Françoise Fabian (Monique), Michael Lonsdale (Bernard), Antoine Chappey (Christophe), Marc Ruchmann (Mathieu)

A marriage told in reverse, starting with the couple's divorce and backtracking in stages to their first meeting.

An ambitious and skilfully told relationship drama with problems of balance. It's thrown off from the start with an ill-advised rape scene, and the standout star performance continues to claim the lion's share of our sympathies.

SCR François Ozon, Emmanuèle Bernheim **CIN** Yorick Le Saux **MUS** Philippe Rombi **DES** Katia Wyszkop **ED** Monica Coleman **PROD** Olivier Delbosc, Marc Missonier

66 Shrewd, compassionate and quite brilliant essay in the secret theatre of relationships. – *Peter Bradshaw, Guardian*

Flags of Our Fathers ★★

DIR Clint Eastwood
2006 131m US
`DVD` ♫

☆ Ryan Philippe (John 'Doc' Bradley), Jesse Bradford (Rene Gagnon), Adam Beach (Ira Hayes), Barry Pepper (Mike Strank), Jamie Bell (Iggy), Paul Walker (Hank Hansen), Robert Patrick (Colonel Johnson), Tom McCarthy (James Bradley)

The stories of the six men who raised the Stars and Stripes on the Japanese island of Iwo Jima. An iconic photo of the event becomes a sensation in America, and three surviving soldiers return home for a huge publicity tour to sell war bonds and restore public faith in the war effort.

It seemed surprising that the conservative Eastwood would approach this story in anything but patriotic terms. Instead, the second half focuses on the cynical exercise with three Iwo Jima veterans being exploited to whip up support for the war. Yet Eastwood has already made his patriotic case: detailed, gory scenes depicting the taking of Iwo Jima show exactly what heroism entails. They also explain the three men's reluctance to embrace the fame being thrust upon them, or to act as cheerful heroes to a public unaware of the trauma they suffered. A thoughtful, moving film that pays tribute to the fraternal impulses of fighting men.

SCR William Broyles Jr., Paul Haggis **CIN** Tom Stern **MUS** Clint Eastwood **DES** Henry Bumstead **ED** Joel Cox **PROD** Clint Eastwood, Steven Spielberg **DIST** Warner Bros.

JAMES BRADLEY: 'Heroes are something we create, something we need. It's a way for us to understand what is almost incomprehensible, how people could sacrifice so much for us.'

66 Here, the feelings run very deep and as dark as dried blood, with Clint aware that some things don't need to be said and others shouldn't be shown. – *Geoff Andrew, Time Out*

66 Flags of our Fathers is touched by greatness. It argues that soldiers may go into battle for country and glory, but they always end up fighting for the survival of themselves and their comrades. – *Peter Bradshaw, Guardian*

† The Japanese government refused permission for combat scenes to be shot on Iwo Jima itself, so they were filmed in an area of Iceland that also has beaches of black sand, owing to volcanic activity. Eastwood shot his companion film Letters from Iwo Jima back-to-back with Flags of Our Fathers.

Alan Robert Murray, Bub Asman (sound editing); John Reitz, Dave Campbell, Gregg Rudloff, Walt Martin (sound mixing)

Flanders new ★★

SCR/DIR Bruno Dumont
2006 91m France
`DVD`

☆ Adélaïde Leroux (Barbe), Samuel Boidin (Demester), Henri Crétel (Blondel), Jean-Marie Bruveart (Briche), David Poulain (Leclercq), Patrice Venant (Mordac), David Legay (Lieutenant)

A farmer goes to fight in an unspecified conflict where he witnesses various atrocities. Back home, his girlfriend has an abortion before being committed to a psychiatric hospital.

Bleak, nearly wordless drama with a non-professional cast; austerity prevails, though some powerful moments emerge.

CIN Yves Cape **ED** Guy Lecorne **PROD** Jean Bréhat, Rachid Bouchareb **DIST** Soda Pictures

66 A sombre, beautifully acted reflection on the barbarity of war and the bestiality of man. – *Deborah Young, Variety*

66 An extraordinary and raw piece of work. – *James Christopher, The Times*

† Winner of the Grand Jury Prize at the 2006 Cannes Film Festival.

Flashbacks of a Fool new

SCR/DIR Baillie Walsh
2008 103m
`DVD` ♫

☆ Daniel Craig (Joe Scot), Harry Eden (Young Joe), *Olivia Williams* (Grace Scot), Jodhi May (Evelyn Adams), Helen McCrory (Peggy Tickell), Miriam Karlin (Mrs. Rogers), Felicity Jones (Young Ruth), Claire Forlani (Adult Ruth), Max Deacon (Boots)

When a washed-up, lonely, debauched British film star in Hollywood hears of the death of a childhood friend, he returns home to find direction in his life.

An uneven story, veering between Hollywood glamour and cosy 1970s British insularity. The uncertainty of tone complements a self-indulgent hero who never develops into anyone more interesting.

`DVD` Available on DVD	☆ Cast in order of importance	66 Critics' Quotes
♫ Soundtrack on CD		† Points of interest

Academy Award	BAFTA
Academy Award nomination	BAFTA nomination

CIN John Mathieson   MUS Liz Gallacher   DES Laurence Dorman   ED Struan Clay   PROD Lene Bausager, Damon Bryant, Genevieve Hofmeyr, Calus Clausen   DIST Disney

66 An ambitious but disappointing, regret-filled psychodrama. – *Wally Hammond, Time Out*

66 Walsh's tracing of Joe's rites of passage has moments of tenderness and warmth, but the film has a problem linking the past to the present. – *Anthony Quinn, Independent*

† The film's British coastal scenes were filmed on beaches in South Africa.

'They couldn't like each other less, or need each other more.'

Flawless   ★

SCR/DIR Joel Schumacher
1999   112m   US
DVD   ♫

☆ Robert De Niro (Walt Koontz), Philip Seymour Hoffman (Rusty), Barry Miller (Leonard Wilcox), Chris Bauer (Jacko), Skipp Sudduth (Tommy), Wilson Jermaine Heredia (Cha-Cha), Nashom Benjamin (Amazing Grace), Scott Allen Cooper (Ivana), Rory Cochrane (Pogo), Daphne Rubin-Vega (Tia), Wanda De Jesus (Karen)

When a macho security guard suffers a stroke and needs to improve his speech, he takes singing lessons from his drag artiste neighbour who needs money for a sex-change operation.

Good-natured, connect-the-dots comedy about opposites coming to understand and even respect each other. A long shadow of wishful thinking hangs heavy over the script, though De Niro and Hoffman give it their considerable all.

CIN Declan Quinn   MUS Bruce Roberts   DES Jan Roelfs   ED Mark Stevens   PROD Joel Schumacher, Jane Rosenthal   DIST MGM

66 A lively entertainment that manages some deft consciousness-raising. – *Kevin Thomas, Los Angeles Times*

'Evil is patient.'

Flesh and Bone   ★

SCR/DIR *Steve Kloves*
1993   126m   US
DVD   ♫

☆ Dennis Quaid (Arlis Sweeney), Meg Ryan (Kay Davies), James Caan (Roy Sweeney), Gwyneth Paltrow (Ginnie), Scott Wilson (Elliot), Christopher Rydell (Reese Davies)

A boy witnesses his psychotic father murdering a family when a robbery goes wrong. Some 25 years later he falls in love with a girl who was the sole survivor of the massacre.

Moody, noirish thriller, underrated and little seen at the time of release, but boasting excellent performances from Quaid and Ryan.

CIN Philippe Rousselot   MUS Thomas Newman   DES Jon Hutman   ED Mia Goldman   PROD Mark Rosenberg, Paula Weinstein   DIST Paramount/Mirage/Spring Creek

66 Director Kloves sometimes lets the film bog down in the Freudian muck. But stick with the seductively twisted Flesh and Bone. It slaps you like a raw wind. – *Peter Travers, Rolling Stone*

† Quaid and Ryan were husband and wife at the time the film was shot.

Flight of the Red Balloon (new)   ★

DIR Hou Hsiao Hsien
2008   115m   France/Taiwan

☆ Juliette Binoche (Suzanne), Simon Iteanu (Simon), Hippolyte Girardot (Marc), Fang Song (Song), Louise Margolin (Louise)

A single mother hires a Taiwanese film student to care for her young son while she works on a puppet show.

Elegant if somewhat directionless look at urban ennui and dislocation that re-creates imagery from famous short The Red Balloon.

SCR Hou Hsiao Hsien, Francois Margolin   CIN Mark Lee Ping Bing   MUS Camille, Constance Lee   DES Paul Fayard, Hwarng Wern Ying   ED Jean-Christophe Hym, Liao Ching Sung   PROD Francois Margolin, Kristina Larsen   DIST Park Circus

66 While nothing really happens in the leisurely French debut of lauded filmmaker Hou Hsiao-Hsien, it doesn't happen in the most beguiling of ways. – *Sam Wigley, Total Film*

66 Filmed with the Taiwanese director's characteristic sensitivity, this eloquent study of loneliness and postmodern drift will be received with more admiration than rapture. – *Justin Chang, Variety*

† Commissioned by the Musée d'Orsay in Paris.

'Yabba Dabba Do!'

The Flintstones

DIR Brian Levant
1994   91m   US
DVD   ♫

☆ John Goodman (Fred Flintstone), Elizabeth Perkins (Wilma Flintstone), Rick Moranis (Barney Rubble), Rosie O'Donnell (Betty Rubble), Elizabeth Taylor (Pearl Slaghoople), Kyle MacLachlan (Cliff Vandercave), Halle Berry (Rosetta Stone), Jonathan Winters (Grizzled Man), Sam Raimi (Cliff Look-A-Like)

In the Stone Age town of Bedrock, quarry worker Fred Flintstone is promoted to vice-president so that he can be the fall guy for his boss's crooked schemes.

This was a disastrous idea: a live-action version of Hanna-Barbera's old TV sitcom about a Stone Age family. Certainly the sets look just cartoonish enough, but the script is appalling. Famously, no less than 32 writers were hired to work on it at some point. Clearly not one of them got close to getting it right; the dialogue is utterly witless and dumb. The interest in seeing it now is how profligate Hollywood studios can be, even in the absence of a coherent script, without which no film can succeed.

SCR Tom S. Parker, Jim Jennewein, Steven E. de Souza   CIN Dean Cundey   MUS David Newman   DES *William*

Sandell **ED** Kent Beyda **PROD** Bruce Cohen
DIST Universal/Amblin/Hanna-Barbera

66 Yabba Dabba Doo-doo. – *Philadelphia Inquirer*

66 Yabba Dabba Don't. – *USA Today*

'Here's to risks.'

Flirting ★

SCR/DIR *John Duigan*
1990   99m   Australia
DVD

☆ *Noah Taylor* (Danny Embling), Thandie Newton
(Thandiwe Adjewa), Nicole Kidman (Nicola),
Bartholomew Rose ('Gilby' Fryer), Felix Nobis (Jock Blair),
Josh Picker ('Backa' Bourke), Kiri Paramore ('Slag' Green)

An Australian boarding school boy falls for
sophisticated Anglo-African girl at a neighbouring
college; the couple defy school rules to be
together.

*Above average teen drama, genuinely touching and
with occasional flashes of welcome humour. It marked
the first substantial film roles for both Nicole Kidman
and Thandie Newton.*

CIN Geoff Burton   **DES** Roger Ford   **ED** Robert Gibson
PROD George Miller, Doug Mitchell, Terry Hayes
DIST Warner/Kennedy Miller

66 One of the funniest, affecting institutional-life stories
to bolt out of the gates for a long time. – *Desson Thomson,
Washington Post*

† This was a sequel to Duigan's The Year My Voice Broke,
which also starred Noah Taylor.

'Have you flirted yet?'

Flirting with Disaster ★

SCR/DIR David O. Russell
1996   92m   US
DVD   ♫

☆ Ben Stiller (Mel Coplin), Patricia Arquette (Nancy
Coplin), Téa Leoni (Tina Kalb), Mary Tyler Moore
(Pearl Coplin), George Segal (Ed Coplin), Alan Alda
(Richard Schlichting), Lily Tomlin (Mary Schlichting),
Richard Jenkins (Paul Harmon), Josh Brolin (Tony
Kent)

A neurotic orphan who grows up and becomes a
father insists he cannot name his child until he
finds his biological parents who gave him up for
adoption.

*A deeply dysfunctional family is gradually
discovered – and partly re-assembled – in the course
of a chaotic, sometimes riotously funny road movie.
This confirmed director Russell as an original, if
wayward talent.*

CIN Eric Edwards   **MUS** Stephen Endelman   **DES** Kevin
Thompson   **ED** Christopher Tellefsen   **PROD** Dean
Silvers   **DIST** Buena Vista/Miramax

66 Flirting With Disaster is positively wacky, as a
crisscross-country reunion between parent and child turns
into something akin to a French bedroom farce, social
satire and The Three Stooges, all rolled into one. – *Steve
Davis, Austin Chronicle*

The Flower of Evil ★★

DIR *Claude Chabrol*
2003   104m   France
DVD

☆ *Nathalie Baye* (Anne), Benoit Magimel (François),
Suzanne Flon (Aunt Line), Bernard Le Coq (Gerard),
Mélanie Doutey (Michele), Thomas Chabrol
(Matthieu)

In Bordeaux, a woman from an affluent family runs
for election as mayor, and several skeletons come
tumbling out of the closet.

*Chabrol likes nothing better than tweaking the noses
of the French bourgeoisie, and he's at it again here –
though the story goes up several notches when the
family scandals come to incorporate collaboration with
the Nazis. Still, it's mischievously entertaining.*

SCR Caroline Eliacheff, Louise L. Lambrichs, Claude
Chabrol   **CIN** Eduardo Serra   **MUS** Matthieu Chabrol
DES Françoise Benoit-Fresco   **ED** Monique Fardoulis
PROD Marin Karmitz

66 Stealing the show is Suzanne Flon's immaculate
display as the matriarch whose good-natured
indulgence of her ghastly relations belies a guilty
secret. Mercilessly acute and quietly devastating. –
Patrick Peters, Empire

66 I feel such an affection for Chabrol and his work that
I probably can't see The Flower of Evil as it would be
experienced by a first-time viewer. Would that newcomer
note the elegance, the confidence, the sheer joy in
the way he treasures the banalities of bourgeois life
on his way to the bloodshed? – *Roger Ebert, Chicago
Sun-Times*

The Flower of My Secret ★★

SCR/DIR Pedro Almodóvar
1995   103m   Spain/France
DVD   ♫

☆ *Marisa Paredes* (Leo Macías), Juan Echanove (Ángel),
Imanol Arias (Paco), Carmen Elias (Betty), Rossy de Palma
(Rosa), Chus Lampreave (Madre de Leo), Joaquin Cortes
(Antonio)

A middle-aged writer, beset by problems personal
and professional, takes to drink, drugs and ever
more erratic behaviour.

*Minor-key Almodóvar that creates a credible
character trying to locate renewed interest in her
own life, but lacks the spark of the director's previous
comedies.*

CIN Affonso Beato   **MUS** Alberto Iglesias   **DES** Esther
García   **ED** José Salcedo   **PROD** Esther Garcia
DIST Electric/CiBy 2000/El Deseo

66 Propelled by stellar performances and a script that
resonates with intelligence, subtlety and surprises, this is
by far Almodóvar's best film in years. – *David Rooney,
Variety*

66 Almodóvar lets rip with a story of great emotional
intensity, while retaining his signature stunning visual
style and a central performance quite unlike anything
previously seen in his work. A potent and strikingly
well-delivered combination. – *Emma Cochrane,
Empire*

DVD Available on DVD   ☆ Cast in order   66 Critics' Quotes   ♙ Academy Award   Ⓑ BAFTA
♫ Soundtrack on CD   of importance   † Points of interest   ♙ Academy Award nomination   Ⓣ BAFTA nomination

'A family of orphaned geese who lost their way. A 14 year old kid who will lead them home. To achieve the incredible, you have to attempt the impossible.'

Fly Away Home ★

DIR *Carroll Ballard*

1996   107m   US

[DVD] ♫

☆ Jeff Daniels (Thomas 'Tom' Alden), Anna Paquin (Amy Alden), Dana Delany (Susan Barnes), Terry Kinney (David Alden), Holter Graham (Barry Stickland), Jeremy Ratchford (DNR Officer)

A young girl goes to live with her eccentric estranged father in Canada after her mother dies. Her grief is alleviated when she adopts a family of motherless goslings.

The charming story of a child dealing with bereavement is strictly routine; as ever with Ballard and Deschanel, the film's trump card is their skill at photographing the natural world.

SCR Robert Rodat, Vince McKewin   CIN *Caleb Deschanel*   MUS Mark Isham   DES Seamus Flannery   ED Nicholas C. Smith   PROD John Veitch, Carol Baum   DIST Columbia/Sandollar

66 Although the film seems a little long and tests credibility from time to time, Fly Away Home is a lovely adventure – and, not least, a visually captivating study of flight. – *Peter Stack, San Francisco Chronicle*

⏐ Caleb Deschanel

'Hope made him a dreamer. Heart made him a hero.'

The Flying Scotsman ★★

DIR Douglas Mackinnon

2006   102m   UK/Germany

☆ Jonny Lee Miller (Graeme Obree), Laura Fraser (Anne Obree), Billy Boyd (Marky McGovern), Brian Cox (Douglas Baxter), Steven Berkoff (Ernst Hagermann)

The true story of cyclist Graeme Obree, who designed and built his own bike from scrap metal, and became a world champion before succumbing to depression.

A remarkable story, and a rare sports film that asserts life is about more than winning and glory. Obree's psychological battles offer the most interest, though the cycling scenes are expertly shot. Miller acquits himself well as Obree: square-jawed, utterly determined and largely unknowable.

SCR John Brown, Simon Rose, Declan Hughes   CIN Gavin Finney   MUS Martin Phipps   DES Mike Gunn   ED Neil Comin   PROD Sara Giles, Peter Gallagher, Peter Broughan   DIST Verve

66 It's an underdog story with teeth. – *Kyle Smith, New York Post*

'This February true love takes a dive.'

Fool's Gold (new)

DIR Andy Tennant

2008   112m   US

[DVD]

☆ Matthew McConaughey (Ben 'Finn' Finnegan), Kate Hudson (Tess Finnegan), Donald Sutherland (Nigel Honeycutt), Ewen Bremner (Alfonz), Alexis Dziena

(Gemma Honeycutt), Kevin Hart (Bigg Bunny), Ray Winstone (Moe Fitch)

A fortune hunter joins forces with his estranged wife and a billionaire to locate a buried treasure.

Tedious caper that quickly wears out its welcome, thanks in part to a hand-me-down plot that is almost as skimpy as its stars' beach outfits.

SCR Andy Tennant, John Claflin, Daniel Zelman   CIN Don Burgess   MUS George Fenton   DES Charles Wood   ED Troy Takaki, Tracey Wadmore-Smith   PROD Donald DeLine, Bernie Goldmann, Jon Klane   DIST Warner Brothers

66 If only this hodgepodge offered more fun and less of the kind of frantic creative desperation that tries to pass itself off as giddy comic exuberance. – *A.O. Scott, New York Times*

66 The film is completely dead behind the eyes. – *James Christopher, The Times*

† McConaughey and Hudson previously co-starred in How to Lose a Guy in 10 Days.

For Your Consideration ★

DIR Christopher Guest

2006   86m   US

[DVD]

☆ Bob Balaban (Philip Koontz), Jennifer Coolidge (Whitney Taylor Brown), Christopher Guest (Jay Berman), John Michael Higgins (Corey Taft), Eugene Levy (Morley Orfkin), Jane Lynch (Cindy), Michael McKean (Lane Iverson), Catherine O'Hara (Marilyn Hack), Parker Posey (Callie Webb), Harry Shearer (Victor Allan Miller), Fred Willard (Chuck)

The cast of a creaky low-budget film become excited when they hear it is being tipped as an Oscar contender.

Disappointing by the remarkably high standards Guest's gifted comedy troupe set themselves. Hollywood vanity is more familiar territory than their previous excursions – into folk music (A Mighty Wind) or pedigree dog shows (Best in Show). As a result, the material feels faintly stale. Some scenes from the hapless movie-within-a-movie, Home for Purim, are priceless, notably the Jewish family dinner. Yet no-one would ever deem Home for Purim award-worthy, a fact that weakens the satire.

SCR Christopher Guest, Eugene Levy   CIN Roberto Schaefer   MUS C.J. Vanston   DES Joseph T. Garrity   ED Robert Leighton   PROD Karen Murphy   DIST Warner Bros.

COREY TAFT: 'In every actor there lives a tiger, a pig, an ass and a nightingale.'

MARILYN HACK (IN HOME FOR PURIM): 'Is that my sweet Rachel's voice I heard, or am I just going meshuga?'

66 The best jokes are the true jokes, and truth has not been best served here. – *Anthony Quinn, Independent*

Force of Evil ★★★

DIR *Abraham Polonsky*

1948   80m   US

[DVD]

☆ *John Garfield* (Joe Morse), *Thomas Gomez* (Leo Morse),

[DVD] Available on DVD   ☆ Cast in order   66 Critics' Quotes   ⏐ Academy Award   🅑 BAFTA
♫ Soundtrack on CD   of importance   † Points of interest   ⏐ Academy Award nomination   🅣 BAFTA nomination

229

Beatrice Pearson (Doris Lowry), Roy Roberts (Ben Tucker), Marie Windsor (Edna Tucker), Howland Chamberlain (Freddy Bauer), Barry Kelley (Egan), Paul Fix (Bill Ficco)

Two brothers, one a lawyer, fall foul of mobsters who are trying to gain control of a city's numbers racket.

A great example of film noir, about two brothers operating outside the law and the tension between them when mobsters threaten. A bleak condemnation of capitalism and greed, its visual compositions are wonderful, with a look reportedly influenced by Edward Hopper's paintings, while some of the dialogue verges on the poetic and Garfield is at his hyper-intense best.

SCR Abraham Polonsky, Ira Wolfert   CIN *George Barnes*
MUS *David Raksin*   ED Art Seid   PROD Bob Roberts
DIST MGM/Enterprise

66 It credits an audience with intelligence in its ears as well as its eyes. – *Dilys Powell*

† This was Polonsky's debut film as a director, but after being black-listed at the McCarthyite hearings, he did not direct again until 1969.

'A Comedy About Love. . .After Marriage.'

Forget Paris ★

DIR Billy Crystal
1995   101m   US
DVD   ♫

☆ Billy Crystal (Mickey Gordon), Debra Winger (Ellen Andrews Gordon), Joe Mantegna (Andy), Julie Kavner (Lucy), Richard Masur (Craig), Cathy Moriarty (Lois), William Hickey (Arthur), Cynthia Stevenson (Liz)

An American basketball referee goes to Paris to bury his father and falls for a sympathetic airline employee. But they encounter difficulties after moving in together.

Quirky, uneven romantic comedy with its share of decent one-liners dotted throughout a script that loses its way. The chemistry between Crystal and Winger seems forced; comedy is not the forte of this substantial actress.

SCR Billy Crystal, Lowell Ganz, Babaloo Mandel   CIN Don Burgess   MUS Marc Shaiman   DES Terence Marsh
ED Kent Beyda   PROD Billy Crystal   DIST Rank/Castle Rock/Face

66 This is a wonderful movie, filled with romantic moments that ring true, and great big laughs. – *Roger Ebert, Chicago Sun-Times*

'The ultimate romantic disaster movie.'

Forgetting Sarah Marshall (new)

DIR Nicholas Stoller
2008   111m   US
☆ Jason Segel (Peter Bretter), Kristen Bell (Sarah Marshall), Mila Kunis (Rachel Jansen), Russell Brand (Aldous Snow)

A homely slacker who composes music for a TV series dates the show's star, and is devastated when she dumps him. Then he finds himself at the same Hawaiian resort where she is staying with her new beau, a British rock star.

A typical template from the Judd Apatow comedy factory: nerdy man romances a fetching career woman. But all the characters here are unengaging and less than likable; the products from the factory's assembly line needs stricter quality control.

SCR Jason Segel   CIN Russ T. Alsobrook   MUS Lyle Workman   DES Jackson de Govia   ED William Kerr
PROD Judd Apatow, Shauna Robertson   DIST Universal

66 There are some laughs, but not that many, and a weird, nagging undertow of self-pity and resentment of beautiful women making honest guys' lives a misery. – *Peter Bradshaw, Guardian*

'The world will never be the same once you've seen it through the eyes of Forrest Gump.'

Forrest Gump ★

DIR *Robert Zemeckis*
1994   142m   US
DVD   ♫

☆ Tom Hanks (Forrest Gump), Robin Wright (Jenny Curran), Gary Sinise (Lt. Dan Taylor), Sally Field (Mrs. Gump), Mykelti Williamson (Pvt. Benjamin Buford 'Bubba' Blue), Michael Conner Humphreys (Young Forrest Gump), Hanna R. Hall (Young Jenny Curran)

Slow-witted boy grows up to become a sporting star, a Vietnam hero and a shrimp tycoon, while his one true love is not nearly so fortunate.

Ignorance really is bliss for simpleton Forrest, played with conviction by Hanks. But behind the story of a dimwit becoming an accidental success, a few pointed questions are posed about the American dream. The special effects that place Gump next to great historical figures are clever enough, yet the suspicion lingers that this is an inferior take on Woody Allen's Zelig – one that lacks its acerbic take on fame and success. Time has not been kind to this film, which now looks overrated and over-garlanded with awards.

SCR Eric Roth   CIN Don Burgess   MUS Alan Silvestri
DES Rick Carter   ED Arthur Schmidt   PROD Wendy Finerman, Steve Starkey, Steve Tisch

MRS. GUMP: 'Life is like a box of chocolates. You never know what you're gonna get.'

66 Manages the difficult feat of being an intimate, even delicate tale played with an appealingly light touch against an epic backdrop. – *Todd McCarthy, Variety*

66 It's a long drink of water at the fountain of pop-social memory. – *Richard Corliss, Time*

⌁ picture; Robert Zemeckis; Tom Hanks (leading actor); Eric Roth (adapted screenplay); Arthur Schmidt; Ken Ralston, George Murphy, Stephen Rosenblum, Allen Hall (visual effects)

⌁ Gary Sinise (supporting actor); Alan Silvestri; Rick Carter; Don Burgess; Randy Thorn, Tom Johnson, Dennis S. Sands, William B. Kaplan (sound); Gloria S. Borders, Randy Thorn (sound effects editing) Daniel C. Striepeke, Hallie D'Amore, Judith A. Cory (make up)

⬛ Ken Ralston, George Murphy, Stephen Rosenbaum, Doug Chiang, Allen Hall (special effects)

⬜ film; Tom Hanks (leading actor); Sally Field (supporting actress); Robert Zemeckis; Eric Roth (adapted screenplay); Don Burgess; Arthur Schmidt

DVD Available on DVD   ☆ Cast in order of importance   66 Critics' Quotes   † Points of interest   ⌁ Academy Award   ⌁ Academy Award nomination   ⬛ BAFTA   ⬜ BAFTA nomination
♫ Soundtrack on CD

Forty Shades of Blue ★★★

DIR Ira Sachs

2005   109m   US

[DVD]   ♫

☆ Rip Torn (Alan James), Dina Korzun (Laura), Darren Burrows (Michael James)

A glamorous but unhappy Russian wife of a wealthy, boorish Memphis music producer looks for warmth and understanding from her stepson.

Exquisitely subtle, moody character study; a seemingly blank Russian trophy wife emerges as a heartbreaking character. The hierarchies of the Memphis soul music scene are acutely observed. This sophisticated portrait of a crumbling relationship gradually gets under the skin. An astonishing performance by Korzun, who hints at her character's isolation and loneliness with great poise.

SCR Michael Rohatyn, Ira Sachs   CIN Julian Whatley   DES Teresa Mastropierro   ED Alfonso Goncalves   PROD Mary Bing, Jawal Nga, Donald Rosenfeld, Margot Bridger, Ira Sachs   DIST Artificial Eye

❝ Sachs has pulled off a film of inferences and intimations, thanks largely to the casting of accomplished actors. – *Kevin Thomas, Los Angeles Times*

† The film won the top prize at the Sundance Film Festival in 2005.

'Mightier than Broadway ever beheld.'

42nd Street ★★★

DIR *Lloyd Bacon*

1933   89m   US

[DVD]

☆ *Warner Baxter* (Julian Marsh), *Ruby Keeler* (Peggy Sawyer), *Bebe Daniels* (Dorothy Brock), George Brent (Pat Denning), Una Merkel (Lorraine Fleming), Guy Kibbee (Abner Dillon), Dick Powell (Billy Lawler), *Ginger Rogers* (Anytime Annie), *Ned Sparks* (Thomas Barry), George E. Stone (Andy Lee), Allen Jenkins (Mac Elory)

A Broadway musical producer has troubles during rehearsal but reaches a successful opening night.

Archetypal Hollywood putting-on-a-show musical in which the leading lady is indisposed and a chorus girl is told to get out there and come back a star. The clichés are written and performed with great zest, the atmosphere is convincing, and the numbers, when they come, are dazzlers.

SCR *James Seymour, Rian James*   CIN *Sol Polito*   ED Thomas Pratt   PROD Hal B. Wallis   DIST Warner

(WARNER BAXTER): Sawyer, you listen to me, and you listen hard. Two hundred people, two hundred jobs, two hundred thousand dollars, five weeks of grind and blood and sweat depend upon you. It's the lives of all these people who've worked with you. You've got to go on, and you've got to give and give and give. They've got to like you. Got to. Do you understand? You can't fall down. You can't because your future's in it, my future and everything all of us have is staked on you. All right, now I'm through, but you keep your feet on the ground and your head on those shoulders of yours and go out, and Sawyer, you're going out a youngster but you've got to come back a star!

❝ The story has been copied a hundred times since, but never has the backstage atmosphere been so honestly and felicitously caught. – *John Huntley, 1966*

❝ It gave new life to the clichés that have kept parodists happy. – *New Yorker, 1977*

† 'Forty-Second Street'; 'It Must Be June'; 'Shuffle Off to Buffalo'; 'Young and Healthy'; 'You're Getting to Be a Habit with Me'

⚱ picture

The Four Hundred Blows ★★★★

SCR/DIR *François Truffaut*

1959   94m   France

[DVD]

☆ *Jean-Pierre Léaud*, Claire Maurier, Albert Rémy

A 13-year-old boy, unhappy at home, finds himself in a detention centre but finally escapes and keeps running.

Little more in plot terms than a piece of character observation, this engaging film, Truffaut's partly autobiographical debut, is so controlled and lyrical as to be totally refreshing, and it offers a vivid picture of the Paris streets. The final freeze-frame is one of cinema's most eloquent moments.

CIN *Henri Decaë*   MUS Jean Constantin   ED Marie-Josèph Yoyotte   PROD Georges Charlot   DIST Films du Carrosse/SEDIF

❝ The narrative is boldly fluent. Sympathetic, amused, reminded, occasionally puzzled, you are carried along with it. I don't think you will get away before the end. – *Dilys Powell*

⚱ François Truffaut, Marcel Moussy (original screenplay)

Four Minutes (new) ★★

SCR/DIR Chris Kraus

2007   112m   Germany

[DVD]   ♫

☆ Monica Bleibtreu (Traude Krüger), Hannah Herzsprung (Jenny von Loeben), Sven Pippig (Mütze), Richy Müller (Kowalski), Jasmin Tabatabai (Ayse)

An elderly piano teacher has long taught music at a women's prison. But she is challenged by a talented new inmate, given to outbursts of violence, but a contender to win a prestigious piano contest.

Shunning any tendency to melodrama, writer-director Kraus deftly marshals his tale of redemption in the face of overwhelming odds. The film's success rests mainly on the shoulders of its lead actresses Bleibtreu and Herzsprung.

CIN Judith Kaufmann   MUS Annette Focks   DES Silke Buhr   ED Uta Schmidt   PROD Meike Kordes, Alexandra Kordes   DIST Peccadillo Pictures

❝ It's a marvellous piece of cinema that hides its secrets like a Russian doll. – *James Christopher, The Times*

† Four Minutes has won 32 international awards and drawn more than 500,000 moviegoers in Germany alone. It received its most significant honours at the German Film Awards in May 2007, winning the Golden Lola for Best Picture, while Monica Bleibtreu took the award for Best Lead Performance.

[DVD] Available on DVD	☆ Cast in order	❝ Critics' Quotes	⚱ Academy Award	Ⓦ BAFTA
♫ Soundtrack on CD	of importance	† Points of interest	⚱ Academy Award nomination	Ⓣ BAFTA nomination

4 Months, 3 Weeks and 2 Days (new) ★★★

SCR/DIR *Cristian Mungiu*

2007 113m Romania/Matherlands/France/Germany

DVD

☆ *Anamaria Marinca* (Otilia), Laura Vasiliu (Gabita), *Vlad Ivanov* (Bebe), Luminita Gheoghiu (Mrs. Radu), Alexandru Potocean (Adi Radu)

In Ceaucescu-era Romania in 1987, a young female student helps a friend to procure an illegal abortion.

A shattering experience: a story set in a bleak society, deprived of hope, in which a deed of self-sacrifice, however awful the circumstances in which it occurs, finally comes to be seen as a small reason for optimism. It is gruelling to watch, but eminently worth the discomfort.

CIN Oleg Mutu DES Mihaela Poenaru ED Dana Bunescu PROD Oleg Mutu, Cristian Mungiu DIST Artificial Eye

66 This brutal masterwork. – *Peter Bradshaw, Guardian*

66 An extraordinarily realised drama. – *Sukhdev Sandhu, Daily Telegraph*

† It won the Palme d'Or at the 2007 Cannes Film Festival.

† Its failure to be nominated for best foreign film at the Oscars led to controversy within the Academy, with strong calls for the reform of nomination criteria.

'Twelve outrageous guests. Four scandalous requests. And one lone bellhop, in his first day on the job, who's in for the wildest New Year's Eve of his life.'

Four Rooms

SCR/DIR Allison Anders, Alexandre Rockwell, Robert Rodriguez, Quentin Tarantino

1995 98m US

DVD ♫

☆ Tim Roth (Ted the Bellhop), Jennifer Beals (Angela), David Proval (Sigfried), Antonio Banderas (Man), Kathy Griffin (Betty), Marc Lawrence (Sam the Bellhop), Marisa Tomei (Margaret), Sammi Davis (Jezebel), Amanda de Cadenet (Diana), Valeria Golino (Athena), Madonna (Elspeth), Quentin Tarantino (Chester Rush), Lawrence Bender (Long Hair Yuppy Scum)

On New Year's Eve in a New York hotel, an overworked bell hop has to take care of a coven of witches, an angry husband with a gun, two misbehaving kids and some Hollywood executives involved in a drunken bet.

Four preposterous ideas come together in one disastrous, ill-conceived movie. Limp, ludicrous and not remotely funny – though Tarantino completists will find it indispensable.

CIN Andrzej Sekula, Phil Parmet, Guillermo Navarro, Rodrigo García MUS Combustible Edison DES Gary Frutkoff ED Margaret Godspeed, Sally Menke, Robert Rodriguez, Elena Maganini PROD Lawrence Bender DIST Buena Vista/Miramax

66 Anthology films never work; Tarantino is not infallible; casting Madonna as a lesbian witch and Bruce Willis in a silly party hat doesn't necessarily make for great entertainment. – *Mark Salisbury, Empire Magazine*

'Five Good Reasons To Stay Single.'

Four Weddings and a Funeral ★★★

DIR *Mike Newell*

1994 117m GB

DVD ♫

☆ *Hugh Grant* (Charles), Andie MacDowell (Carrie), *Kristin Scott Thomas* (Fiona), Simon Callow (Gareth), James Fleet (Tom), David Bower (David), Charlotte Coleman (Scarlett), John Hannah (Matthew), Anna Chancellor (Henrietta), Robert Lang (Lord Hibbott), Jeremy Kemp (Sir John Delaney), Rosalie Crutchley (Mrs. Beaumont), Rowan Atkinson (Father Gerald)

A hapless would-be bridegroom chases the woman he wants to marry from one ceremony to another.

Amusing, deftly written episodic British comedy which got away with shamelessly recycling old jokes and familiar situations thanks to ruthlessly paced direction and fine comic acting. It has an indefinable quality that guarantees audiences' affections, while the perfection of Grant's casting as the dithering Charles almost defies belief.

SCR *Richard Curtis* CIN Michael Coulter MUS Richard Rodney Bennett DES Maggie Gray ED Jon Gregory PROD Duncan Kenworthy DIST Rank/Polygram/Channel 4/Working Title

66 A British comedy that's classy and commercial and, most important, very funny. – *Geoff Andrew, Time Out*

66 Courting stardom, Hugh Grant delivers an engaging performance in Mike Newell's romantic comedy about the horrors of flying solo in a married world. – *Thomas Delapa, Boulder Weekly*

† It was released in the United States, where it briefly topped the box-office charts and grossed a reasonable $50 million, before opening in Britain, where it was marketed as a US hit.

† The film's extraordinary popularity even caused a brief resurgence of interest in poet W.H. Auden, whose Funeral Blues ('Stop all the clocks. . .') is recited by John Hannah. It was included in a volume of love poems by Auden, re-published hurriedly.

† The lead female role was due to be played by Jeanne Tripplehorn, who had to withdraw two weeks before shooting began, due to the death of her mother.

picture; Richard Curtis (original screenplay)

film; Hugh Grant (leading actor); Kristin Scott Thomas (supporting actress); Mike Newell

Simon Callow (supporting actor); John Hannah (supporting actor); Charlotte Coleman (supporting actress); Richard Curtis (original screenplay); Jon Gregory; Richard Rodney Bennett; Lindy Hemming (costume design)

'The Dolphin Hotel invites you to stay in any of its stunning rooms. Except one.'

1408 (new) ★★

DIR Mikael Hafström

2007 104m US

DVD ♫

☆ *John Cusack* (Mike Enslin), Samuel L. Jackson (Gerald Olin), Mary McCormack (Lily), Tony Shalhoub (Sam Farrell), Len Cariou (Father)

A sceptical writer, who debunks myths about

haunted houses and rooms, resolves to spend a night in a hotel suite where many people have met grisly ends.

Cusack, who is in almost every scene, makes this run-of-the-mill film, with its efficiently established premise, seem better than it is. His sardonic persona disintegrates gradually as the room plays its malevolent tricks on him.

SCR Matt Greenberg, Scott Alexander, Larry Karaszewski CIN Benoit Delhomme MUS Gabriel Yared DES Andrew Laws ED Peter Boyle PROD Lorenzo di Bonaventura DIST Paramount

66 Sharp little psychological thriller. – *Kyle Smith, New York Post*

66 Cusack's edgy, likeable performance carries this paranormal chiller. – *Anthony Quinn, Independent*

'Centuries Before The Exploration Of Space, There Was Another Voyage Into The Unknown.'

1492: Conquest of Paradise ★

DIR Ridley Scott

1992 154m UK/US/France/Spain

DVD ♫

☆ Gérard Depardieu (Christopher Columbus), Armand Assante (Sanchez), Sigourney Weaver (Queen Isabella I), Loren Dean (Older Fernado Columbus), Angela Molina (Beatrix Enriquez), Fernando Rey (Antonio de Marchena), Michael Wincott (Adrian de Moxica), Tcheky Karyo (Martin Alonso Pinzón), Kevin Dunn (Captain Mendez), Frank Langella (Luis de Santángel)

With the backing of the Spanish court, Christopher Columbus sails west and discovers the Americas, only to find peaceful co-existence with the natives impossible.

Ravishing but empty, Scott's film taxes the patience with its insistence on Columbus's idealism, the running time is murder and a miscast Depardieu, labouring in English, doesn't help. A box-office fiasco, and not without reason.

SCR Roselyne Bosch CIN *Adrian Biddle* MUS Vangelis DES Norris Spencer ED William Anderson, Françoise Bonnot PROD Ridley Scott, Alain Goldman DIST Guild/Touchstone

† It was released, like the same year's Christopher Columbus: The Discovery, to coincide with the 500th anniversary of America's colonisation.

'To have seen it is to wear a badge of courage!'

Frankenstein ★★★★

DIR *James Whale*

1931 71m US

DVD

☆ *Boris Karloff* (The Monster), *Colin Clive* (Henry Frankenstein), *Mae Clarke* (Elizabeth), John Boles (Victor Moritz), *Edward Van Sloan* (Dr. Waldman), *Frederick Kerr* (Baron Frankenstein), *Dwight Frye* (Fritz, the Dwarf)

A research scientist creates a living monster from corpses, but it runs amok.

Whole books have been written about this film and its sequels. Apart from being a fascinating if primitive cinematic work in its own right, it set its director and star on interesting paths and established a Hollywood attitude towards horror (mostly borrowed from German silents such as The Golem). A seminal film indeed, which at each repeated viewing belies its age.

SCR *Garrett Fort, Francis Edwards Faragoh, John L. Balderston* CIN *Arthur Edeson* MUS David Broekman ED *Clarence Kolster, Maurice Pivar* PROD Carl Laemmle Jnr. DIST Universal

66 Still the most famous of all horror films, and deservedly so. – *John Baxter, 1968*

66 The horror is cold, chilling the marrow but never arousing malaise. – *Carlos Clarens*

† Direct sequels by the same studio include The Bride of Frankenstein, Son of Frankenstein, Ghost of Frankenstein, Frankenstein Meets the Wolf Man, House of Frankenstein, House of Dracula, Abbott and Costello Meet Frankenstein. The later Hammer series, which told the story all over again in gorier vein, includes The Curse of Frankenstein, The Revenge of Frankenstein, The Evil of Frankenstein, Frankenstein Created Woman, Frankenstein Must be Destroyed, Horror of Frankenstein, Frankenstein and the Monster from Hell.

Frankenstein Unbound ★

DIR Roger Corman

1990 82m US

DVD

☆ John Hurt (Dr. Joe Buchanan/Narrator), Raul Julia (Dr. Victor Frankenstein), Bridget Fonda (Mary Wollstonecraft Godwin), Nick Brimble (The Monster), Catherine Rabett (Elizabeth Levenza, Victor's Fiancee), Jason Patric (Lord George Gordon Byron), Michael Hutchence (Percy Bysshe Shelley)

A scientist designing modern super-weapons is sent back in time to Switzerland in 1817 when an experiment goes wrong, and he meets Dr Frankenstein and his monster.

This ambitious cocktail of sci-fi, horror and humour is hard to swallow wholesale, but it has a sense of its own silliness and includes some entertaining passages.

SCR Roger Corman, F.X. Feeney CIN Armando Nannuzzi, Michael Scott MUS Carl Davis DES Enrico Tovaglieri ED Jay Cassidy, Mary Bauer PROD Roger Corman, Thom Mount, Kabi Jaeger DIST Fox/Mount Company

66 This metaphysical reflection on technology with science fiction and monster movie trimmings is packed with wit, originality and eccentricity. – *Jonathan Rosenbaum, Chicago Reader*

† This film marked Corman's return to directing after 19 years.

'He's no knight in shining armor. She's no princess. But who says life is a fairytale anyway?'

Frankie and Johnny ★

DIR Garry Marshall

1991 118m US

DVD ♫

☆ Al Pacino (Johnny), Michelle Pfeiffer (Frankie), Hector Elizondo (Nick), Nathan Lane (Tim), Jane Morris

DVD Available on DVD ☆ Cast in order of importance 66 Critics' Quotes † Points of interest 🏆 Academy Award 🏆 Academy Award nomination 🏆 BAFTA 🏆 BAFTA nomination

233

(Nedda), Greg Lewis (Tino), Al Fann (Luther), Glenn Plummer (Peter), Sean O'Bryan (Bobby), Kate Nelligan (Cora)

An ex-prisoner, working as a short-order cook in a restaurant, aggressively courts a shy waitress.

Sharply scripted romance with Pacino and Pfeiffer both justifying their star status by making the most of their roles.

SCR Terrence McNally   CIN Dante Spinotti
MUS Marvin Hamlisch   DES Albert Brenner   ED Battle Davis, Jacqueline Cambas   PROD Garry Marshall
DIST UIP/Paramount

66 In its celebration of cautious optimism, Frankie and Johnny becomes the perfect love story for these troubled times. – *Peter Travers, Rolling Stone*

66 Frankie and Johnny is a lot of fun when it aims to charm; when it asks to be taken seriously as a realistic look at urban romance, it seems as evanescent as television airwaves. – *David Ansen, Newsweek*

Ⓣ Kate Nelligan (supporting actress)

'They've taken his wife. Now he's taking action.'

Frantic ★

DIR *Roman Polanski*
1988   115m   US
DVD   ♫

☆ Harrison Ford (Dr. Richard Walker), Betty Buckley (Sondra Walker), Emmanuelle Seigner (Michelle), John Mahoney (US Embassy Official), Jimmy Ray Weeks (Shaap), Yorgo Voyagis (Kidnapper), David Huddleston (Peter)

An American heart surgeon, whose wife suddenly goes missing in Paris, becomes involved with terrorists.

Above-average thriller, with Ford gamely playing a worried man out of his depth, and director Polanski nodding in Hitchcock's direction as he carefully builds tension.

SCR Roman Polanski, Gérard Brach   CIN Witold Sobocinski   MUS Ennio Morricone   DES Pierre Guffroy   ED Sam O'Steen   PROD Thom Mount, Tim Hampton
DIST Warner/Mount

66 A tense, paranoid thriller as only Polanski can make them. – *Jeffrey M. Anderson, San Francisco Examiner*

'Every teenager's nightmare. . .turning into her mother.'

Freaky Friday ★

DIR Mark Waters
2003   97m   US
DVD   ♫

☆ *Jamie Lee Curtis* (Tess Coleman), Lindsay Lohan (Anna Coleman), Mark Harmon (Ryan), Harold Gould (Grandpa), Chad Michael Murray (Jake), Stephen Tobolowsky (Mr. Bates), Christina Vidal (Maddie)

A fortune cookie spell causes a bickering mother and daughter to inhabit each other's bodies.

An amiable re-make, far superior to the 1976 body-swap original. Its success hinges on Curtis playing a teenage girl with such gusto.

SCR Heather Hach, Leslie Dixon   CIN Oliver Wood
MUS Rolfe Kent   DES Cary White   ED Bruce Green
PROD Andrew Gunn   DIST Buena Vista

66 Cute and innocently funny, with engaging turns from a beautifully silly Jamie Lee Curtis and Lindsay Lohan as a 21st century high school heroine. – *Angie Errigo, Empire Magazine*

'Santa's brother is coming to town.'

Fred Claus (new)

DIR David Dobkin
2007   115m   US
♫

☆ Vince Vaughn (Fred Claus), Paul Giamatti (Nick 'Santa' Claus), Miranda Richardson (Annette Claus), John Michael Higgins (Willie), Elizabeth Banks (Charlene), Rachel Weisz (Wanda), Kathy Bates (Mother Claus), Kevin Spacey (Clyde Northcut)

Santa's deadbeat older brother comes to the North Pole, causing havoc on the run-up to Christmas.

Obnoxious, mean-spirited attempt to broaden its leading man's appeal; the result is all the more disappointing for the calibre of actors involved.

SCR Dan Fogelman   CIN Remi Adefarasin
MUS Christophe Beck   DES Allan Cameron   ED Mark Livolsi   PROD Joel Silver, David Dobkin, Jessie Nelson
DIST Warner Bros

66 A complete bust: derivative and uninspired, boring and dull, not funny, not moving and about a half hour too long. – *Mick LaSalle, San Francisco Chronicle*

66 With Santa Claus movies like Fred Claus, who needs Ebenezer Scrooge? – *Kirk Honeycutt, Hollywood Reporter*

† At one point Kevin Spacey – Lex Luthor in Superman Returns – dons a Superman cape.

'A 12 Year Old Street Kid. A 3 Ton Killer Whale. A Friendship You Could Never Imagine. An Adventure You'll Never Forget.'

Free Willy ★

DIR Simon Wincer
1993   112m   US
DVD   ♫

☆ Jason James Richter (Jesse), Lori Petty (Rae), Jayne Atkinson (Annie), August Schellenberg (Randolph), Michael Madsen (Glen), Michael Ironside (Dial), Keiko (Willy)

An abandoned young boy develops a bond with a killer whale facing a death sentence.

Tear-jerker with a portrayal of friendship that adroitly ticks all the boxes for pre-teens.

SCR Keith A. Walker, Corey Blechman   CIN Robbie Greenberg   MUS Basil Poledouris   DES Charles Rosen
ED O. Nicholas Brown   PROD Jennie Lew Tugend, Lauren Shuler-Donner   DIST Warner/Canal/Regency/Alcor

66 Free Willy has all the ingredients of a good family drama and will especially win the hearts of animal lovers. – *Almar Haflidason, BBC*

66 The kids' movie of the season. – *Hal Hinson, Washington Post*

† Two Free Willy sequels followed, in 1995 and 1997.

'Doyle is bad news . . . but a good cop!'

The French Connection ★★★

DIR *William Friedkin*
1971   104m   US
DVD

☆ *Gene Hackman* (Jimmy 'Popeye' Doyle), Roy Scheider (Buddy Russo), *Fernando Rey* (Alain Charnier), Tony Lo Bianco (Sal Boca), Marcel Bozzufi (Pierre Nicoli)

New York police track down a consignment of drugs entering the country in a car.

Lively police thriller based on the true exploits of a tough cop named Eddie Egan who liked to break a few rules. Most memorable for a car chase scene involving an elevated railway, for showing the seamy side of New York more or less as it is.

SCR Ernest Tidyman   CIN Owen Roizman   MUS Don Ellis   ED Jerry Greenberg   DIST TCF/Philip D'Antoni

66 There is only one problem with the excitement generated by this film. After it is over, you will walk out of the theatre and, as I did, curse the tedium of your own life. I kept looking for someone who I could throw up against a wall. – *Gene Siskel, Chicago Tribune*

⚊ picture; Ernest Tidyman (adapted screenplay); William Friedkin; Gene Hackman (leading actor)

⚊ Owen Roizman; Roy Scheider (supporting actor)

Ⓣ Gene Hackman

'A scorned wife. An outrageous affair. The perfect marriage.'

French Twist ★★

SCR/DIR *Josiane Balasko*
1995   104m   France
DVD

☆ *Victoria Abril* (Loli), *Josiane Balasko* (Marijo), Alain Chabat (Laurent Lafaye), Ticky Holgado (Antoine), Miguel Bosé (Diego), Catherine Hiegel (Dany), Catherine Samie (Sopha)

The married life of a young couple from Avignon is disrupted by the chance arrival of a passing lesbian musician.

A frank, funny French comedy, a huge hit in its native country, with a cheating husband as the butt of most of the humour.

SCR Patrick Aubrée   CIN Gérard de Battista   MUS Manuel Malou   DES Carlos Conti   ED Claudine Merlin   PROD Pierre Grunstein   DIST Guild/Renn/TF1/Les Films Flam

66 This is French farce, with a familiar emphasis on sexual appetites and domestic abuses, all played as broad comedy. – *Cindy Fuchs, Philadelphia City Paper*

'An innocent kid. An experienced mobster. This could be the start of a beautiful friendship.'

The Freshman ★★

SCR/DIR *Andrew Bergman*
1990   102m   US
DVD

☆ Marlon Brando (Carmine Sabatini, aka Jimmy The Toucan), Matthew Broderick (Clark Kellogg / Narrator), Bruno Kirby (Victor Ray, Carmine's Nephew), Penelope Ann Miller (Tina Sabatini), Frank Whaley (Steve Bushak, Clark's Roommate), Jon Polito (Agent Chuck Greenwald, Dept. of Justice Fish & Game Division), Paul Benedict (Arthur Fleeber, NYU Professor / Clark's Faculty Advisor), Richard Gant (Agent Lloyd Simpson, Dept. of Justice Fish & Game Division), Kenneth Welsh (Dwight Armstrong, Clark's Step-father), Pamela Payton-Wright (Liz Armstrong)

A film student with a taste for gangster movies takes a job as a delivery boy for a small-time mobster who resembles Don Corleone from The Godfather.

It's quite a self-referential joke, having Marlon Brando play the man who looks like Brando. But nothing is to be taken that seriously in this amiable send-up of gangster films and those who love them. Writer-director Bergman shoots off some snappy gags about film-school pretensions, Broderick looks suitably keen and confused, and it's all good, lightweight fun.

CIN William A. Fraker   MUS David Newman   DES Ken Adam   ED Barry Malkin   PROD Mike Lobell   DIST Tri-Star/Mike Lobell, Andrew Bergman

'Prepare to be seduced.'

Frida ★★

DIR Julie Taymor
2002   123m   US
DVD   ♫

☆ *Salma Hayek* (Frida Kahlo), Alfred Molina (Diego Rivera), Geoffrey Rush (Leon Trotsky), Ashley Judd (Tina Modotti), Antonio Banderas (David Alfaro Siqueiros), Edward Norton (Nelson Rockefeller), Valeria Golino (Lupe Marin), Mia Maestro (Cristina Kahlo), Roger Rees (Guillermo Kahlo)

Account of the tempestuous life of Mexican artist Frida Kahlo and her stormy relationships with fellow artist Diego Rivera (who she married twice) and Leon Trotsky, among others.

A labour of love for Hayek, who spent years shepherding this film to the screen. She works extraordinarily hard to portray Kahlo from her teen years to her death. Pleasingly, the vivid primary colours that dominated her work form the basis of its colour palette. But it has the fault of so many biopics, attempting to cram in every possible detail of a pained, passionate life, and any sense of a dramatic arc gets buried.

SCR Clancy Sigel, Diane Lake, Gregory Nava, Anna Thomas   CIN *Rodrigo Prieto*   MUS Elliot Goldenthal   DES *Felipe Fernández del Paso*   ED Francoise Bonnot   PROD Sarah Green, Salma Hayek, Jay Polstein, Lizz Speed, Nancy Hardin, Roberto Sneider, Lindsay Flickinger   DIST Buena Vista

66 There's something remote and stagy about Frida; though it was shot in Mexico, you feel as if the cast is just down there on a visit. – *David Ansen, Newsweek*

66 While Frida is no masterpiece, it's nevertheless worth the price of admission to see Hayek master her craft. – *Stella Papamichael, BBC*

† Before Hayek was confirmed in the role, actresses Madonna, Jennifer Lopez and Laura San Giacomo of declared their interest in playing Frida Kahlo.

† The film hit trouble in pre-production, with Miramax

DVD Available on DVD   ♫ Soundtrack on CD   ☆ Cast in order of importance   66 Critics' Quotes   † Points of interest   ⚊ Academy Award   ⚊ Academy Award nomination   Ⓣ BAFTA   Ⓣ BAFTA nomination

235

F

boss Harvey Weinstein demanding a 10-minute cut from director Taymor, who initially refused.

Elliot Goldenthal; John E. Jackson, Beatrice De Alba (make up)

Salma Hayek (leading actress); Julie Weiss (costume design); Elliot Goldenthal (m), Julie Taymor (ly) (music, original song – Burn It Blue) (with Hannia Robledo)

Judy Chin, Beatrice De Alba, John E. Jackson, Regina Reyes (make up/hair)

Alfred Molina (supporting actor); Salma Hayek (leading actress); Julie Weiss (costume design)

'Hope comes alive on Friday nights.'

Friday Night Lights ★★

DIR Peter Berg, Josh Pate

2004   118m   Germany/US

DVD   ♫

☆ Billy Bob Thornton (Coach Gary Gaines), Derek Luke (Boobie Miles), Jay Hernandez (Brian Chavez), Lucas Black (Mike Winchell), Garrett Hedlund (Don Billingsley), Tim McGraw (Charles Billingsley), Lee Thompson Young (Chris Comer)

In 1988, the depressed Texas town of Odessa is heartened by the unlikely success of the local high-school football team.

That rarity, a truly enthralling American sports film, based on a best-selling book. It focuses closely on the small town's young sportsmen and their charismatic coach, all briefly experiencing glory days.

SCR David Aaron Cohen, Peter Berg   CIN Tobias Schliessler   MUS Explosions in the Sky, David Torn, Brian Reitzell   DES Sharon Seymour   ED David Rosenbloom, Colby Parker Jnr   PROD Brian Grazer   DIST Universal

66 Its script is pure corn, drenched in syrupy sentiment and topped with prize ham in the shape of Billy Bob Thornton's tub-thumping coach. – *Neil Smith, BBC*

† The film was adapted for a network TV series in the US.

'The secret of life? The secret's in the sauce.'

Fried Green Tomatoes at the Whistle Stop Café ★

DIR Jon Avnet

1991   130m   US

DVD   ♫

☆ *Kathy Bates* (Evelyn Couch), Jessica Tandy (Ninny Threadgoode), Mary-Louise Parker (Ruth Jamison), Mary Stuart Masterson (Idgie Threadgoode), Cicely Tyson (Sipsey), Gailard Sartain (Ed Couch), Stan Shaw (Big George)

Two women form a friendship that unlocks a dark yet heart-warming story of life in Georgia in the 1930s.

Agreeable comedy-drama, pitched squarely at older audiences, and trading on nostalgia for simpler times, even when they involved bigotry. Bates handles her character's shift from shyness to self-assertiveness with enjoyable relish.

SCR Fannie Flagg, Carol Sobieski   CIN Geoffrey Simpson   MUS Thomas Newman   DES Barbara Ling   ED Debra

Neil   PROD Jordan Kerner, Jon Avnet   DIST Rank/Act III/Electric Shadow

66 Fried Green Tomatoes is fairly predictable, and the flashback structure is a distraction, but the strength of the performances overcomes the problems. – *Roger Ebert, Chicago Sun-Times*

Jessica Tandy (supporting actress); Fannie Flagg, Carol Sobieski (original screenplay)

Kathy Bates (leading actress); Jessica Tandy (supporting actress)

Friends with Money ★★

SCR/DIR Nicole Holofcener

2006   88m   US

DVD   ♫

☆ Jennifer Aniston (Olivia), Joan Cusack (Franny), Catherine Keener (Christine), Frances McDormand (Jane), Jason Isaacs (David), Scott Caan (Mike)

Four female friends in Los Angeles, three of them comfortably wealthy, one forced to work as a house cleaner, examine their relationships.

A telling script with believably discontented characters that tackles a theme rarely found in American movies – the lack of money in a circle of richer friends. It offers the unlikely spectacle of Jennifer Aniston on her hands and knees with a scrubbing brush. But despite its witty dialogue, delivered with killer timing by an excellent cast, it never finds a satisfactory resolution to the questions it poses, and settles for an easy, unearned ending.

CIN Terry Stacey   MUS Craig Richey   DES Amy Ancona   ED Robert Frazen   PROD Anthony Bregman   DIST Columbia TriStar

66 It could well be the best relationships drama of the year. It's that good. – *David Edwards, Daily Mirror*

† It was the opening film at the 2006 Sundance Festival.

'No Rest for the Wicked.'

The Frighteners ★★

DIR *Peter Jackson*

1996   110m   New Zealand/US

DVD   ♫

☆ Michael J. Fox (Frank Bannister), Trini Alvarado (Dr. Lucy Lynskey), Peter Dobson (Ray Lynskey), John Astin (The Judge), Jeffrey Combs (Milton Dammers), Dee Wallace Stone (Patricia Ann Bradley)

A phony psychic, who investigates supernatural occurrences with the aid of three friendly ghosts, is pitted against a malevolent spirit spooking a small town to death.

Very enjoyable effects comedy that retains its own oddball personality amid computerised phantasmagoria.

SCR Fran Walsh, Peter Jackson   CIN Alun Bollinger, John Blick   MUS Danny Elfman   DES *Grant Major*   ED Jamie Selkirk   PROD Jamie Selkirk, Peter Jackson   DIST UIP/Universal/Wingnut

66 A deeply sick, weird and enjoyable romp. – *Adam Smith, Empire*

'A terrifying evil has been unleashed. And five strangers are our only hope to stop it.'

From Dusk till Dawn ★

DIR Robert Rodriguez
1995 108m US
DVD ♫

☆ Harvey Keitel (Jacob Fuller), George Clooney (Seth Gecko), Quentin Tarantino (Richard Gecko), Juliette Lewis (Kate Fuller), Salma Hayek (Santanico Pandemonium), Brenda Hillhouse (Hostage Gloria Hill), Marc Lawrence (Old Timer Motel Owner), Cheech Marin (Border Guard/Chet Pussy/Carlos), Michael Parks (Texas Ranger Earl McGraw), Kelly Preston (Newscaster Kelly Houge), Fred Williamson (Frost), John Saxon (FBI Agent Stanley Chase), Tom Savini (Sex Machine), Ernest Liu (Scott Fuller)

Two malevolent brothers kidnap a preacher and his children and head for Mexico, where they wander into a nest of vampires.

A very odd movie indeed, starting out as a tense, pumped-up, then making an abrupt left turn to become a gory vampire flick. It's so colourfully choreographed that it has a certain grim fascination, but quite what Rodriguez and Tarantino were thinking is anyone's guess.

SCR Quentin Tarantino CIN Guillermo Navarro
MUS Graeme Revell DES Cecilia Montiel ED Robert Rodriguez PROD Gianni Nunnari, Meir Teper
DIST Dimension/Los Hooligans/A Band Apart

66 The sickest, most perverted movie within memory. Guiltily, I liked it. But what the hell is it? – *Joe Baltake, Sacramento Bee*

† Two sequels followed, in 1999 and 2000.

'You Think You Know Terror But You Don't Know Jack.'

From Hell ★

DIR Allen Hughes, Albert Hughes
2001 122m US
DVD ♫

☆ Johnny Depp (Insp. Fred Abberline), Heather Graham (Mary Kelly), Ian Holm (Sir William Gull), Robbie Coltrane (Sgt Peter Godley), Ian Richardson (Sir Charles Warren), Jason Flemyng (Netley), Katrin Cartlidge ('Dark Annie' Chapman), Terence Harvey (Ben Kidney), Susan Lynch (Liz Stride), Lesley Sharp (Kate Eddowes), Annabelle Apsion (Polly)

Detective film set in Victorian London following an unstable police inspector who learns that the serial killer Jack the Ripper has royal connections.

Foggy, sinister 1880s London is re-imagined (in Prague) with some success, though its leading characters are not so convincing. Depp seems literally clueless as the dope-fiend cop. Lurid and overwrought, but not easy to dismiss totally.

SCR Terry Hayes, Rafael Yglesias CIN Peter Deming
MUS Trevor Jones DES Martin Childs ED Dan Lebental, George Bowers PROD Don Murphy, Jane Hamsher DIST TCF

66 Many of the ideas that were sophisticated in the original graphic novel by Alan Moore and Eddie Campbell look shop-worn on screen. – *Peter Bradshaw, Guardian*

'The Boldest Book Of Our Time . . . Honestly, Fearlessly On The Screen!'

From Here to Eternity ★★★

DIR *Fred Zinnemann*
1953 118m US
DVD

☆ Burt Lancaster (Sgt. Milton Warden), *Deborah Kerr* (Karen Holmes), *Frank Sinatra* (Angelo Maggio), Donna Reed (Alma Lorene), Ernest Borgnine (Sgt. 'Fatso' Judson), *Montgomery Clift* (Robert E. Lee Prewitt), Philip Ober (Capt. Dana Holmes), Mickey Shaughnessy (Sgt. Leva)

Life in a Honolulu barracks in the days before the Japanese attack on Pearl Harbor, including the dilemma of a young pacifist in uniform and a clandestine affair between an officer's wife and a sergeant.

Cleaned up and streamlined version of a bestseller, turned into a star-heavy melodrama that proved a popular hit. Sinatra and Kerr did arguably their best screen work on this picture, though the same cannot be said for anyone else. In the end, it's a decent film with an eye on the box-office – though the scene with Kerr and Lancaster, making love as eaves crash around them, is regarded as a classic portrayal of sex, mainstream Hollywood style.

SCR Daniel Taradash CIN Burnett Guffey MUS George Duning ED William Lyon PROD Buddy Adler
DIST Columbia

66 This is not a theme which one would expect Zinnemann to approach in the hopeful, sympathetic mood of his earlier films; but neither could one expect the negative shrug of indifference with which he seems to have surrendered to its hysteria. – *Karel Reisz, Sight & Sound*

† The story was remade for TV in 1979 as a six-hour mini-series.
† Frank Sinatra got his key role after Eli Wallach dropped out.

♫ best picture; Daniel Taradash; Fred Zinnemann; Burnett Guffey (cinematography); Frank Sinatra (supporting actor); Donna Reed (supporting actress); William Lyon (film editing)
♫ Burt Lancaster (leading actor); Deborah Kerr (leading actress); Montgomery Clift (leading actor); George Duning (music)

From Russia with Love ★★

DIR Terence Young
1963 118m GB
DVD ♫

☆ *Sean Connery* (James Bond), *Robert Shaw* (Red Grant), *Pedro Armendariz* (Kerim Bey), Daniela Bianchi (Tatiana Romanova), *Lotte Lenya* (Rosa Klebb), Bernard Lee ('M'), Eunice Gayson (Sylvia), Lois Maxwell (Miss Moneypenny)

A Russian spy joins an international crime organization and develops a plan to kill James Bond and steal a coding machine.

The second Bond adventure, more spectacular than Dr. No, with Istanbul and Venice for backdrops, and climaxes involving a speeding train and a helicopter.

DVD Available on DVD   ☆ Cast in order   66 Critics' Quotes   ♫ Academy Award   ♥ BAFTA
♫ Soundtrack on CD   of importance   † Points of interest   ♫ Academy Award nomination   ♥ BAFTA nomination

237

Agreeable nonsense with tongue in cheek, on a big budget.

SCR *Richard Maibaum, Johanna Harwood*   **CIN** *Ted Moore*   **MUS** John Barry   **ED** Peter Hunt   **PROD** Harry Saltzman, Albert Broccoli   **DIST** UA/Eon

🏆 Ted Moore (cinematography)

Frontier(s) (new)   ★

SCR/DIR Xavier Gens

2008   108m   France/Switzerland

☆ Karina Testa (Yasmine), Simon Le Bihan (Goetz), Estelle Lefebure (Gilberte), Aurelien Wilk (Alex), David Saracino (Tom)

Young Paris thieves hide in a border guest house run by degenerate neo-Nazi cannibals, looking to breed a new master race.

Texas Chainsaw Massacre French-style. It ticks all the boxes for extreme splatter and blatant offensiveness, but despite piling on the disgust and spectacular gore, it makes little sense and becomes cartoon carnage.

CIN Laurent Bares   **MUS** Jean-Pierre Taieb   **DES** Jeremie Streliski   **ED** Carlo Rizzo   **PROD** Laurent Tolleron   **DIST** Optimum Films

66 Can a movie be an adrenalin-fueled, blood-gushing thrill ride and still be as boring as dirt? Apparently. – *John Anderson, Variety*

66 It is the hatred of humanity in movies displayed such as this that takes your breath away. – *Peter Whittle, Sunday Times*

'A murdered wife. A one-armed man. An obsessed detective. The chase begins.'

The Fugitive   ★★★

DIR *Andrew Davis*

1993   130m   US

DVD   ♫

☆ Harrison Ford (Dr. Richard Kimble), *Tommy Lee Jones* (Deputy US Marshal Samuel Gerard), Sela Ward (Helen Kimble), Joe Pantoliano (Cosmo Renfro), Jeroen Krabbé (Dr. Charles Nichols), Andreas Katsulas (Sykes, 'The One-Armed Man'), Julianne Moore (Dr. Ann Eastman)

Accused of his wife's murder, a doctor goes on the run, hunting down the real killer while a cop pursues him in turn.

The 1960s television series is updated into an expansive action-adventure movie, powered – even through its less coherent stretches – by lead performances of an old-school solidity and rigour.

SCR Jeb Stuart, David Twohy   **CIN** Michael Chapman   **MUS** James Newton Howard   **DES** Dennis Washington   **ED** Dennis Virkler, David Finfer, Dean Goodhill, Don Brochu, Richard Nord, Dov Hoenig   **PROD** Arnold Kopelson   **DIST** Warner

66 Turns out to be a smashing success, a juggernaut of an action-adventure saga that owes nothing to the past. – *Elvis Mitchell, The New York Times*

66 Pure energy, a perfect orchestration of heroism, villainy, suspense and comic relief. – *Desson Thomson, Washington Post*

---

† The original TV series, starring David Janssen, ran from 1963 to 1967.

⚱ Tommy Lee Jones (supporting actor)

⚱ picture; Michael Chapman (cinematography); James Newton Howard (music); editing; sound; sound effects editing

🏆 sound

🅣 Tommy Lee Jones (supporting actor); editing; special effects

---

'Everybody Needs A Release.'

Full Frontal

DIR Steven Soderbergh

2002   101m   US

DVD

☆ David Duchovny (Bill/Gus), Nicky Katt (Hitler), Catherine Keener (Lee), Mary McCormack (Linda), David Hyde Pierce (Carl), Julia Roberts (Francesca/Catherine), Blair Underwood (Calvin/Nicholas)

Twenty-four hours in Hollywood as the lives of assorted workers in the entertainment industry criss-cross.

A failed experiment, of interest solely to Soderbergh's many admirers. Shot on digital video and looking deliberately cheap, it's his answer to the dictates of Denmark's Dogme 95 movement. Yet he undermines those austere principles by casting a major star, Julia Roberts, as if to hedge his bets. Distressingly self-indulgent.

SCR Coleman Hough   **CIN** Peter Andrews   **MUS** Jacques Davidovici   **ED** Sarah Flack   **PROD** Scott Kramer, Gregory Jacobs   **DIST** Miramax

66 A boring, amateurish, incomprehensible and stupefyingly pretentious pile of swill. – *Rex Reed, New York Observer*

'The year's most revealing comedy.'

The Full Monty   ★★★

DIR *Peter Cattaneo*

1997   91m   GB

DVD   ♫

☆ Robert Carlyle (Gaz), Tom Wilkinson (Gerald), Mark Addy (Dave), Lesley Sharp (Jean), Emily Woof (Mandy), Steve Huison (Lomper), Paul Barber (Horse), Hugo Speer (Guy), Deirdre Costello (Linda)

Six unemployed Sheffield steelworkers turn to striptease as a way of making some money.

A thoroughly entertaining, often hilarious, and touchingly played comedy that also digs towards deeper truths about masculinity in a modern, specific world, while retaining enough universality to go over big with audiences everywhere.

SCR *Simon Beaufoy*   **CIN** John de Borman   **MUS** *Anne Dudley*   **DES** Max Gottlieb   **ED** David Freeman, Nick More   **PROD** Uberto Pasolini   **DIST** TCF

66 So seamlessly buoyant and enjoyable that it's easy to miss how carefully and sensitively it's made. – *Laura Miller, Salon*

66 Yet another solid entry in the much appreciated wave of no-fuss, low-budget British films designed to genuinely entertain. – *Deborah Brown, Empire*

† The story was turned into a Broadway musical in 2000, with the action relocated to Buffalo, N.Y.

♪ Anne Dudley (music)

picture; Peter Cattaneo; Simon Beaufoy (original screenplay)

film; Robert Carlyle (leading actor); Tom Wilkinson (supporting actor)

British film; Peter Cattaneo; Mark Addy (supporting actor); Lesley Sharp (supporting actress); Anne Dudley; Nick Moore, David Freeman (editing); Simon Beaufoy (original screenplay); sound

---

'One family, one murder, too many lies.'

The Funeral ★

DIR Abel Ferrara
1996   99m   US
DVD ♪

☆ Christopher Walken (Ray Tempio), Chris Penn (Chez Tempio), Annabella Sciorra (Jean), Isabella Rossellini (Clara Tempio), Vincent Gallo (Johnny), Benicio del Toro (Gaspare)

In 1930s New York, two gangster brothers seek revenge for a third brother's murder.

Brooding, full-strength Mob drama, agonising over its themes of faith and loyalty; undeniably well-acted, and brimming over with big ideas, it lacks only one thing: any semblance of a heart.

SCR Nicholas St John   **CIN** Ken Kelsch   **MUS** Joe Delia
DES Charles M. Lagola   **ED** Mayin Lo, Bill Pankow
PROD Mary Kane   **DIST** Guild/October/MDP/C&P

66 A brilliant, very visceral piece of filmmaking with an infectious strain of morbid humour. – *Geoffrey Macnab, Time Out*

'Beware. Comic geniuses at work.'

Funny Bones ★

DIR Peter Chelsom
1995   128m   US/GB
DVD ♪

☆ Oliver Platt (Tommy Fawkes), Lee Evans (Jack Parker), Richard Griffiths (Jim Minty), Oliver Reed (Dolly Hopkins), George Carl (Thomas Parker), Leslie Caron (Katie Parker), Jerry Lewis (George Fawkes)

When a struggling stand-up comic flops in Vegas, he heads back to his childhood home of Blackpool to rediscover his roots and rescue his act.

A bold, original story with a strong sense of place, this provides a bright, unusual film debut for the talented Evans, but it's too discursive to make a real impact. And given the subject matter, it might have been funnier.

SCR Peter Chelsom, Peter Flannery   **CIN** Eduardo Serra
MUS John Altman   **DES** Caroline Hanania   **ED** Martin Walsh   **PROD** Simon Fields, Peter Chelsom   **DIST** Buena Vista/Hollywood Pictures

66 Writer/director Peter Chelsom's follow-up to Hear My Song throws plenty of comic ideas around, but only one or two stick. – *Time Out*

66 Provocative entertainment that blends mirth and malice with startling results. – *Peter Travers, Rolling Stone*

Funny Face ★★★

DIR Stanley Donen
1956   103m   US
DVD

☆ *Fred Astaire, Audrey Hepburn, Kay Thompson*, Michel Auclair, Robert Flemyng

A fashion editor and photographer choose a shy bookstore attendant as their 'quality woman'.

Stylish, wistful musical, elegantly designed and beautifully photographed in Technicolor, with an amusing script that pokes fun at the fashion business and its fixation with Parisian chic. Hepburn's is the face in question, discovered in (of all places) a Greenwich Village book store. Thompson set the benchmark for all future portrayals of dictatorial fashion magazine editors.

SCR Leonard Gershe   **CIN** Ray June   **PROD** Roger Edens
DIST Paramount

Leonard Gershe (original screenplay); Ray June (cinematography); art direction

---

Funny Games ★

SCR/DIR Michael Haneke
1997   108m   Austria
DVD

☆ Susanne Lothar (Anna Schober), Ulrich Mühe (Georg Schober), Frank Giering (Peter), Arno Frisch (Paul), Stefan Clapczynski (Georgie Schober)

An Austrian family on holiday in their home in the country is targeted by two terrifying psychopaths.

This well-acted but queasy drama claims to strike a blow against the use of gratuitous movie violence by making the audience complicit, and then showing the pain involved. The legitimacy of the argument fails to dampen the suspicion that it's merely an ingenious justification for exploitation.

CIN Jurgen Jurges   **DES** Christoph Kanter   **ED** Andreas Prochaska   **PROD** Veit Heiduschka   **DIST** Metro Tartan/Wega

66 The basic puzzle is why this sophisticated director chose this tired formula. – *Stanley Kauffman, New Republic*

† An English-language version was released in 2008.

'You must admit, you brought this on yourself.'

Funny Games (new)

SCR/DIR Michael Haneke
2008   111m   US/UK/France/Germany/Italy

☆ Naomi Watts (Ann), Tim Roth (George), Michael Pitt (Paul), Brady Corbet (Peter), Devon Gearhart (Georgie)

A family's lakeside home is invaded by two clean-cut young strangers who bet them they will all be dead by the morning.

A shot-for-shot, English-language remake of the director's 1997 thriller, presumably made for audiences resistant to subtitles. The experience is no less unpleasant; this time, though, the casting feels less effective.

DVD Available on DVD   ☆ Cast in order   66 Critics' Quotes   Academy Award   BAFTA
♪ Soundtrack on CD   of importance   † Points of interest   Academy Award nomination   BAFTA nomination

239

F

CIN Darius Khondji   DES Kevin Thompson   ED Monika Willi   PROD Chris Coen, Hamish McAlpine

66 As shocking and deliberately manipulative as the original movie and – some may reckon – even more pointless. – *Derek Elley, Variety*

66 Ugly in any language. – *David Ansen, Newsweek*

Funny Girl ★★

DIR William Wyler
1968   169m   US
DVD   ♫

☆ *Barbra Streisand*, Omar Sharif, Walter Pidgeon, Kay Medford, Anne Francis, Lee Allen, Gerald Mohr, Frank Faylen

Fanny Brice, a vaudeville performer, becomes a big Broadway star, but her marriage falls apart in the process.

A meandering musical drama that needed trimming for screen purposes. Yet it is handsomely produced, and has some excellent songs. Above all it has Streisand, who became an overnight movie star as a result. If she has a fault here, it's that her presence is so potent that no other actor even competes.

SCR Isobel Lennart   CIN Harry Stradling   DES *Gene Callahan*   PROD Ray Stark   DIST Columbia/Rastar

🏆 Barbra Streisand (leading actress)
🏅 picture; Kay Medford (supporting actress); Harry Stradling (cinematography); Walter Scharf (music, score); Jule Styne (m), Bob Merrill (ly) (music, original song – Funny Girl)

Funny Ha Ha ★★

SCR/DIR Andrew Bujalski
2005   90m   US
DVD

☆ Kate Dollenmayer (Marnie), Christian Rudder (Alex), Myles Paige (Dave), Andrew Bujalski (Mitchell)

In Boston, a young female graduate spends the summer drifting between dead-end jobs to pay the rent, trying out ill-judged relationships and writing lists of ideas to improve her life.

A throwback to how American indie films used to be in the 1990s, before they all started resembling calling cards for studio employment. Yet its primary influence, John Cassavetes, goes back 40 years or more. Director Bujalski, using an amateur cast and crew, shoots on 16mm, with a script that feels partly improvised. His young, anxious, commitment-phobic characters are tentative, inarticulate and frequently exasperating. Yet the film feels fresh and amusing. Bujalski may never become a mainstream name, but could well acquire a cult reputation via DVD.

CIN Matthias Grunsky   ED Andrew Bujalski   PROD Ethan Vogt   DIST Diffusion/Miracle

66 An ebullient sliver of a movie. – *Owen Gleiberman, Entertainment Weekly*

66 Refreshingly unpolished, the film uses pained silences like punctuation. – *Wendy Ide, The Times*

† The film has had a long, chequered career. It was completed in 2002, was shown at various US festivals, and received a limited US release in 2005 before opening in the UK in 2007.

'The Show Was Cancelled. . .But The Adventure Has Only Begun.'

Galaxy Quest ☆

DIR Dean Parisot
1999 104m US
DVD

☆ Tim Allen (Jason Nesmith), Sigourney Weaver (Gwen DeMarco), Alan Rickman (Alexander Dane), Tony Shalhoub (Fred Kwan), Sam Rockwell (Guy Fleegman), Daryl Mitchell (Tommy Webber), Enrico Colantoni (Mathesar), Robin Sachs (Sarris), Patrick Breen (Quellek), Missi Pyle (Laliari)

Actors from a long-cancelled cult TV sci-fi series are asked by alien fans to help them combat an interstellar enemy.

Space dramas such as Star Trek are gently satirised in this charming comedy, clearly aimed at obsessive, convention-haunting fans.

SCR David Howard, Robert Gordon   CIN Jerzy Zielinski
MUS David Newman   DES Linda DeScenna   ED Don Zimmerman   PROD Mark Johnson, Charles Newirth
DIST DreamWorks

66 A sparkling blend of sci-fi and comedy that affectionately spoofs every Star Trek cliché known to man, Romulan or Klingon. – *Neil Smith, BBC*

'Are You Ready To Play?'

The Game ★★★

DIR *David Fincher*
1997 128m US
DVD ♫

☆ *Michael Douglas* (Nicholas Van Orton), Sean Penn (Conrad), Deborah Kara Unger (Christine), James Rebhorn (Jim Feingold), Peter Donat (Samuel Sutherland), Carroll Baker (Ilsa), Anna Katarina (Elizabeth), Armin Mueller-Stahl (Anson Baer)

A rich control freak receives an unusual birthday present from his brother: entry into a live-action game which unfolds in the course of the player's everyday existence.

Darkly comic thriller that toys skilfully with different levels of reality, asking us – like the film's hero – to question what we're seeing at every stage; the ending allows disappointingly little room for doubt, but Douglas unravels in such tremendous fashion en route that we get right behind an initially unsympathetic character. The direction is impeccable.

SCR John Brancato, Michael Ferris   CIN Harris Savides

MUS Howard Shore   DES Jeffrey Beecroft   ED James Haygood   PROD Steve Golin, Cean Chaffin
DIST Polygram/Propaganda

66 An intensely exciting puzzle-gimmick thriller, the kind of movie that lets you know from the start that it's slyly aware of its own absurdity. – *Owen Gleiberman, Entertainment Weekly*

66 It's formulaic, yet edgy. It's predictable, yet full of surprises. How far you get through this tall tale of a thriller before you give up and howl is a matter of personal taste. – *Desson Thomson, Washington Post*

'Joe Kingman had the perfect game plan to win the championship. . .but first, he has to tackle one little problem.'

The Game Plan (new)

DIR Andy Fickman
2007 110m US
DVD

☆ Dwayne 'The Rock' Johnson (Joe Kingman), Kyra Sedgwick (Stella Peck), Morris Chestnut (Travis Sanders), Roselyn Sanchez (Monique Vasquez), Madison Pettis (Peyton Kelly), Hayes Macarthur (Kyle Cooper), Brian White (Jamal Webber), Jamal Duff (Clarence Monroe)

An arrogant American Football player is forced to care for the eight-year-old daughter he never knew he had.

Sucrose comedy whose attempts to humanise its wrestler-cum-action star lead are as laboured as they are cynical.

SCR Nichole Millard, Kathryn Price   CIN Greg Gardiner
MUS Nathan Wang   DES David J. Bomba   ED Michael Jablow   PROD Gordon Gray, Mark Ciardi   DIST Buena Vista

66 An unfunny comedy, as embarrassing as it's overlong. . . Three Men and a Little Lady on the gridiron. – *Philip French, Observer*

66 Ruthlessly inoffensive family entertainment. – *Kevin Maher, The Times*

'His goal was freedom . . . his strategy was peace . . . his weapon was his humanity!'

Gandhi ★★★

DIR *Richard Attenborough*
1982 188m GB
DVD

☆ *Ben Kingsley* (Mahatma Gandhi), Candice Bergen (Margaret Bourke-White), Edward Fox (Gen. Dyer), John Mills (The Viceroy), John Gielgud (Lord Irwin), Trevor Howard (Judge Broomfield), Martin Sheen (Walker), Ian

DVD Available on DVD	☆ Cast in order	66 Critics' Quotes	🏆 Academy Award	🏆 BAFTA
♫ Soundtrack on CD	of importance	† Points of interest	🏆 Academy Award nomination	🏆 BAFTA nomination

Charleson (Charlie Andrews), Athol Fugard (Gen. Smuts), Saeed Jaffrey (Sardar Patel)

The life of the young Indian advocate who became a revolutionary, a saint and a martyr.

A straightforward treatment with the odd twists and turns expected of this director; but the remarkable things about the film are first, that it was made at all in an age which regarded inspirational epics as outdated; and secondly, that it brought into life so splendid a leading performance. Beside these factors the sluggish pace and the air of schoolbook history seem comparatively unimportant.

SCR John Briley CIN Billy Williams, Ronnie Taylor MUS George Fenton DES Stuart Craig ED John Bloom PROD *Richard Attenborough* DIST Columbia/Goldcrest/Indo-British/International Film Investors/National Film Development Corporation of India

66 It reminds us that we are, after all, human, and thus capable of the most extraordinary and wonderful achievements, simply through the use of our imagination, our will, and our sense of right. – *Roger Ebert*

† Opening dedication: 'No man's life can be encompassed in one telling . . . what can be done is to be faithful in spirit to the record and try to find one's way to the heart of the man.'

⚖ picture; Ben Kingsley (leading actor); Richard Attenborough (as director); John Briley (original screenplay); Billy Williams, Ronnie Taylor (cinematography); John Mollo, Bhanu Athalya (costume design); Stuart Craig, Bob Laing (art direction); John Bloom (editing)

⚖ Ravi Shanker, George Fenton (music)

🎭 film; direction; Ben Kingsley (leadiing actor); Rohini Hattangady (supporting actress); Ben Kingsley (outstanding newcomer)

'America Was Born In The Streets.'

Gangs of New York ★★★

DIR Martin Scorsese

2002 167m US

DVD ♫

☆ Leonardo DiCaprio (Amsterdam Vallon), *Daniel Day-Lewis* (William 'Bill the Butcher' Cutting), Cameron Diaz (Jenny Everdeane), Liam Neeson (Priest Vallon), Jim Broadbent (William 'Boss' Tweed), John C. Reilly (Happy Jack), Henry Thomas (Johnny Sirocco), Brendan Gleeson (Walter 'Monk' McGinn), Gary Lewis (McGloin), Stephen Graham (Shang), Alec McCowe (Reverend Raleigh)

In mid-19th-century New York, a young boy battles to avenge the death of his father, while native New Yorkers and Irish indulge in brutal gang warfare.

Huge, stirring epic thriller that writes a history of Manhattan's criminal underclass. Day-Lewis delivers a masterful performance as the terrifying 'Bill the Butcher', and Scorsese gives the film a grandiose, breathtaking sweep, neutralising a faint suspicion that the script could be more orderly and simple.

SCR Jay Cocks, Steven Zaillian, Kenneth Lonergan CIN *Michael Ballhaus* MUS Howard Shore DES *Dante Ferretti* ED Thelma Schoonmaker PROD Harvey Weinstein, Alberto Grimaldi DIST Entertainment

66 Wonderful spectacle, terrific acting and toweringly great film-making. – *Peter Bradshaw, Guardian*

66 A triumph of pure craft and passionate heart. – *Peter Travers, Rolling Stone*

⚖ picture; Daniel Day-Lewis (leading actor); Martin Scorsese; Jay Cocks, Steven Zaillian, Kenneth Lonergan (original screenplay); Michael Ballhaus; Thelma Schoonmaker; Sandy Powell (costume design); Bono, The Edge, Adam Clayton, Larry Mullen Jnr (music, original song – The Hands that Built America); Dante Ferretti (with Francesca LoSchiavo); Tom Fleischman, Eugene Gearty, Ivan Sharrock (sound)

🎭 Daniel Day-Lewis (leading actor)

🎭 film; Martin Scorsese; Jay Cocks, Steven Zaillian, Kenneth Lonergan (original screenplay); Michael Ballhaus; Thelma Schoonmaker; Howard Shore; Dante Ferretti (with Francesca LoSchiavo); R. Bruce Steinheimer, Michael Owens, Edward Hirsh, Joe Alexander (special visual effects); Tom Fleischman, Eugene Gearty, Ivan Sharrock (sound); Sandy Powell (costume design); Manlio Rocchetti, Aldo Signoretti (make up/hair)

'It's Not Who You Know, It's Who You Kill.'

Gangster No. 1 ★

DIR Paul McGuigan

2000 103m GB/Germany/Ireland

DVD

☆ Malcolm McDowell (Gangster 55), David Thewlis (Freddie Mays), Paul Bettany (Young Gangster), Saffron Burrows (Karen), Kenneth Cranham (Tommy), Jamie Foreman (Lennie Taylor), Razaaq Adoti (Roland), Doug Allen (Mad John), Eddie Marsan (Eddie Miller), David Kennedy (Fat Charlie), Andrew Lincoln (Maxie King), Cavan Clerkin (Billy), Johnny Harris (Derek), Anton Valensi (Trevor)

A treacherous act of betrayal in the distant past comes back to haunt a ruthless London gangster.

An uncomfortably violent thriller, but far superior to most British gangland movies at the turn of the century. It efficiently captures the scary glamour of London's violent underworld and boasts several creditable portrayals of tough guy; but McDowell's is the most compelling.

SCR Johnny Ferguson CIN Peter Sova MUS John Dankworth DES Richard Bridgland ED Andrew Hulme PROD Norma Heyman, Jonathan Cavendish DIST FilmFour

66 It's a handsomely ugly affair, well dressed enough to make a few friends, but tough enough to make just as many enemies. – *Mark Kermode, Sight and Sound*

66 Stylish and moody and exceptionally well acted. – *Shawn Levy, Oregonian*

Garage (new) ★

DIR Lenny Abrahamson

2007 84m Ireland

DVD

☆ Pat Shortt (Josie), Anne-Marie Duff (Carmel), Conor J. Ryan (David), Tommy Fitzgerald (Declan), Don Wycherley (Breffni), George Costigan (Dan)

DVD Available on DVD ☆ Cast in order of importance 66 Critics' Quotes † Points of interest ⚖ Academy Award ⚖ Academy Award nomination 🎭 BAFTA 🎭 BAFTA nomination ♫ Soundtrack on CD

The carefree life of a village simpleton in rural Ireland is upset when he is assigned a teenage apprentice to work alongside him at a rundown petrol station.

Quiet, affecting character study with a tragic undertow; the result is as unassuming as its unlikely hero.

SCR Mark O'Halloran CIN Peter Robertson MUS Stephen Rennicks DES Padraig O'Neill ED Isobel Stephenson PROD Ed Guiney DIST Soda Pictures

BREFFNI: 'A rising tide lifts all boats, isn't that right? Except for Josie's.'

66 Films like Garage come along all too rarely. – *Sukhdev Sandhu, Daily Telegraph*

66 A gentle and elegiac lament for lives wasted and lives on the brink of waste. – *Peter Bradshaw, Guardian*

The Garden ★★

SCR/DIR Derek Jarman
1990 92m GB/Germany/Japan
DVD ♫

☆ Kevin Collins (Lover), Roger Cook (Christ), Jody Graber (Young Boy), Pete Lee-Wilson (Devil), Philip Macdonald (Joseph), Johnny Mills (Lover), Tilda Swinton (Madonna)

Director Derek Jarman uses the garden of his home at Dungeness, on the Kent coast, as a starting point for images relating to other gardens – Gethsemane and Eden included – and stories that arose from them.

This film feels like a check-list of Jarman's main preoccupations: gay rights, the threat of Aids, the persecution of gay priests. It's completely fascinating; never has Jarman's uniqueness been more apparent on film.

CIN Christopher Hughes MUS Simon Fisher Turner DES Derek Brown ED Peter Cartwright PROD James McKay DIST Artificial Eye/Basilisk/Channel 4/British Screen/ZDF/Uplink

Garden State ★

SCR/DIR Zach Braff
2003 102m US
DVD ♫

☆ Zach Braff (Andrew Largeman), Ian Holm (Gideon Largeman), Ron Leibman (Dr Cohen), Method Man (Diego), Natalie Portman (Samantha), Ann Dowd (Olivia), Denis O'Hare (Albert), Peter Sarsgaard (Mark)

A miserable, struggling Hollywood actor returns home to New Jersey for his mother's funeral and falls in love.

Patchy comic drama, with a moping, ultra-sensitive twentysomething hero, and stacked with clichés about conformist suburbia. Predictably he finds the one girl in town who feels his pain. The very prototype of a Sundance movie, this is presumably aimed at younger audiences who may not have seen all this a dozen times before.

CIN Lawrence Sher MUS Chad Fisher DES Judy Becker ED Myron Kerstein PROD Pamela Abdy, Richard Klubeck, Gary Gilbert, Dan Halsted DIST Beuna Vista

'It was a dangerous time to be young. An impossible time to be a hero.'

Gardens of Stone ★

DIR Francis Coppola
1987 111m US
DVD

☆ James Caan (Sgt. Clell Hazard), Anjelica Huston (Samantha Davis), James Earl Jones (Sgt. Maj.'Goody' Nelson), D.B. Sweeney (Jackie Willow), Dean Stockwell (Capt. Homer Thomas), Mary Stewart Masterson (Rachel Feld), Dick Anthony Williams (Slasher Williams)

An army veteran trains young soldiers to prepare them for combat in the Vietnam War despite his overwhelming doubts about it.

A far more low-key Vietnam film from Coppola than Apocalypse Now. It's a thoughtful drama that airs the rights and wrongs of US involvement, and still has a resonance in the light of more recent military operations.

SCR Ronald Bass CIN Jordan Cronenweth MUS Carmine Coppola DES Dean Tavoularis ED Barry Malkin PROD Michael I. Levy, Francis Coppola DIST Tri-Star/ML Delphi

66 A quiet, respectful film filled with emotional power, exceptional acting and technical virtuosity. – *TV Guide's Movie Guide*

'When Shade's good, she's very good. But when Trudi's bad, she's better.'

Gas Food Lodging ★★

SCR/DIR Allison Anders
1991 101m US
DVD ♫

☆ Brooke Adams (Nora), Ione Skye (Trudi), Fairuza Balk (Shade), James Brolin (John Evans), Robert Knepper (Dank), David Lansbury (Hamlet Humphrey), Jacob Vargas (Javier), Donovan Leitch (Darius), Chris Mulkey (Raymond)

A single mother struggles to raise two unhappy daughters in a trailer park while holding down a job at a diner.

Claustrophobic yet absorbing domestic drama, shot by writer-director Anders on a low budget, but well observed both socially and psychologically.

CIN Dean Lent MUS J. Mascis DES Jane Ann Stewart ED Tracy S. Granger PROD Daniel Hassid, Seth M. Willenson, William Ewart DIST Mainline/Cineville Partners

66 The movie is about survivors, not about heroines. It's a great movie about making do. – *Hal Hinson, Washington Post*

'There Is No Gene For The Human Spirit.'

Gattaca

SCR/DIR Andrew Niccol
1997 106m US
DVD ♫

☆ Ethan Hawke (Vincent), Uma Thurman (Irene), Alan Arkin (Detective Hugo), Jude Law (Jerome/Eugene), Loren Dean (Anton), Gore Vidal (Director Josef), Ernest

DVD Available on DVD ☆ Cast in order of importance 66 Critics' Quotes † Points of interest 🏆 Academy Award 🏆 Academy Award nomination 🎭 BAFTA 🎭 BAFTA nomination

Borgnine (Caesar), Blair Underwood (Geneticist), Xander Berkeley (Lamar), Tony Shalhoub (German)

In a future time, when biologically created superior beings are in charge of the world, a humble janitor decides to do some sneaky genetic engineering of his own.

Engaging futuristic drama, visually arresting, with a generous airing for arguments about the moral issues surrounding scientific research.

CIN Slawomir Idziak   MUS Michael Nyman   DES *Jan Roelfs*   ED Lisa Zeno Churgin   PROD Danny DeVito, Michael Shamberg, Stacey Sher   DIST Columbia TriStar/Jersey

66 This is a thought-provoking film, an effective wake-up call to those who glorify science. – *Kevin N. Laforest, Montreal Film Journal*

⚱ Jan Roelfs

'The gayest of mad musicals!'

The Gay Divorcee   ★★★

DIR *Mark Sandrich*
1934   107m   US

☆ *Fred Astaire* (Guy Holden), *Ginger Rogers* (Mimi Glossop), *Edward Everett Horton* (Egbert Fitzgerald), *Alice Brady* (Hortense Ditherwell), *Erik Rhodes* (Rodolfo Tonetti), *Eric Blore* (Waiter), Lillian Miles (Hotel Guest), Betty Grable (Hotel Guest)

A would-be divorcee in an English seaside hotel mistakes a dancer who loves her for a professional co-respondent.

Wildly and hilariously dated comedy musical with splendidly archaic comedy routines supporting Hollywood's great new dance team in their first big success. Not much dancing, but 'The Continental' is a show-stopper.

SCR George Marion Jnr, Dorothy Yost, Edward Kaufman   CIN David Abel   ED William Hamilton   PROD Pandro S. Berman   DIST RKO

66 Cinch box office anywhere and certain of big foreign grosses. – *Variety*

66 The plot is trivial French farce, but the dances are among the wittiest and most lyrical expressions of American romanticism on the screen. – *New Yorker, 1977*

⚱ Con Conrad (m), Herb Magidson (ly) (music, original song – The Continental)

⚱ picture; Ken Webb, Samuel Hoffenstein (score); art direction

The General   ★★

SCR/DIR *John Boorman*
1998   124m   Ireland/GB
DVD

☆ *Brendan Gleeson* (Martin Cahill), Adrian Dunbar (Noel Curley), Sean McGinley (Gary), Maria Doyle Kennedy (Frances), Angeline Ball (Tina), *Jon Voight* (Inspector Ned Kenny)

A biopic of Martin Cahill, the Dublin gangster and popular hero who in the early 1990s pulled off a number of daring robberies, continually evading the police, until his death at the hands of an IRA gunman.

Shot in a monochrome that recalls the Warner Bros. crime pictures of the 1930s and 40s, an episodic, often witty account of its subject's life, alert to Cahill's vulnerability and hubris, his fierce loyalty as well as his fearsome brutality.

CIN *Seamus Deasy*   MUS Richie Buckley   DES Derek Wallace   ED Ron Davis   PROD John Boorman   DIST Warner/Merlin Films/J&M

66 A fulsome, fascinating piece of 20th century Irish folklore. – *Ian Nathan, Empire*

66 Notable for its deft characterisations and authenticity: while Cahill's sentiments and actions are appreciated as the exploits of a canny born rebel, we're never allowed to forget that he's also volatile, violent and, whatever his feelings for his family, ultimately self-obsessed. – *Geoff Andrew, Time Out*

† Boorman won the prize for best director at the Cannes Film Festival in 1998.

'Everybody laughs but Buster!'

The General   ★★★★

DIR *Buster Keaton, Clyde Bruckman*
1926   80m   US
DVD

☆ *Buster Keaton* (Johnnie Gray), Marion Mack (Annabelle Lee), Glen Cavander (Captain Anderson)

A Confederate train driver gets his train and his girl back when they are stolen by Union soldiers.

Slow-starting, then hilarious action comedy, often voted one of the best ever made. Its sequence of sight gags, each topping the one before, is an incredible joy to behold.

SCR Al Boasberg, Charles Smith   CIN J. Devereux Jennings, Bert Haines   ED Harry Barnes, J. Sherman Kell   PROD Joseph M. Schenck   DIST UA/Buster Keaton

66 It has all the sweet earnestness in the world. It is about trains, frontier America, flower-faced girls. – *New Yorker, 1977*

66 The production itself is singularly well mounted, but the fun is not exactly plentiful . . . here he is more the acrobat than the clown, and his vehicle might be described as a mixture of cast iron and jelly. – *Mordaunt Hall, New York Times*

† The story is based on an actual incident of the Civil War, treated more seriously in The Great Locomotive Chase.
† The screenplay with 1,400 freeze frames was issued in 1976 in the Film Classics Library (editor, Richard Anobile).

Genevieve   ★★★

DIR *Henry Cornelius*
1953   86m   GB
DVD

☆ *Dinah Sheridan* (Wendy McKim), *John Gregson* (Alan McKim), *Kay Kendall* (Rosalind Peters), *Kenneth More* (Ambrose Claverhouse), *Geoffrey Keen* (1st Speed Cop), *Joyce Grenfell* (Hotel Proprietress), *Reginald Beckwith* (J.C. Callahan), *Arthur Wontner* (Elderly Gentleman)

Two friendly rivals engage in a race on the way back from the Brighton veteran car rally.

One of those happy films in which a number of modest elements merge smoothly to create an aura of high style and memorable moments. A charmingly witty script, carefully pointed direction, attractive actors and locations, an atmosphere of light-hearted British sex and a lively harmonica theme turned it, after a slowish start, into one of Britain's biggest commercial hits and most fondly remembered comedies.

SCR *William Rose* **CIN** Christopher Challis **MUS** *Larry Adler (who also played it)* **ED** Clive Donner **PROD** Henry Cornelius **DIST** GFD/Sirius

66 One of the best things to have happened to British films over the last five years. – *Gavin Lambert*

♟ William Rose (original screenplay); Larry Adler (music)

T British film

'Now! It comes to the screen with nothing left unsaid and no emotion unstressed!'

Gentleman's Agreement ★★

DIR Elia Kazan

1947   118m   US

☆ *Gregory Peck*, Dorothy McGuire, *John Garfield*, Celeste Holm, *Anne Revere*, June Havoc, Albert Dekker, Jane Wyatt, Dean Stockwell

A magazine journalist passes himself off as Jewish in order to write about anti-Semitic prejudice in American high society.

A laudable but not exactly hard-hitting attempt to tackle a genuine social issue. Peck is outstanding in the lead role, but compared with the lower-budget Crossfire, released just a few weeks previously, which also addressed anti-Jewish prejudice, this worthy mainstream film pulls its punches. Still, it was praised widely on its release; its heart is in the right place.

SCR Moss Hart **CIN** Arthur Miller **MUS** Alfred Newman **ED** Harmon Jones **PROD** Darryl F. Zanuck **DIST** TCF

♔ picture; Elia Kazan; Celeste Holm (supporting actress)
♘ Moss Hart (original screenplay); Gregory Peck (leading actor); Dorothy McGuire (leading actress); Anne Revere (supporting actress); Harmon Jones (editing)

'Watch out!'

George of the Jungle ★

DIR Sam Weisman

1997   92m   US

[DVD]   ♫

☆ Brendan Fraser (George of the Jungle), Leslie Mann (Ursula Stanhope), Thomas Haden Church (Lyle van der Groot), Richard Roundtree (Kwame), Greg Cruttwell (Max), John Cleese (voice of 'Ape')

An appealing ape-man, raised by gorillas, meets humans for the first time, falls for a woman, and travels with her to America.

Amiable parody of the old Tarzan movies, with Fraser's talent for deadpan humour skilfully deployed. But much of the humour is pure slapstick; perfectly suitable for family viewing.

SCR Dana Olsen, Audrey Wells **CIN** Thomas Ackerman **MUS** Marc Shaiman **DES** Stephen Marsh **ED** Stuart Pappé, Roger Bondelli, Kent Beyda **PROD** David Hoberman, Jordan Kerner, Jon Avnet **DIST** Buena Vista/Walt Disney/Mandeville

---

66 Surprisingly, much of George of the Jungle is entertaining. It is lowbrow humour to be sure, but quality lowbrow humour. – *Louis B Parks, Houston Chronicle*

† A 2003 sequel went straight to video; Fraser absented himself.

'Down this twisted road, please watch over my soul and lift me up so gently so as not to touch the ground.'

George Washington ★

SCR/DIR David Gordon Green

2000   90m   US

[DVD]   ♫

☆ Candace Evanofski (Nasia), Donald Holden (George), Curtis Cotton III (Buddy), Eddie Rouse (Damascus), Paul Schneider (Rico), Damian Jewan Lee (Vernon), Rachel Handy (Sonya), Jonathan Davidson (Euless), Janet Taylor (Aunt Ruth)

A group of black kids in a poor North Carolina town try to hide the accidental death of a young boy.

Slow, almost wistful, drama about troubled teenagers, young love and growing up. As it progresses gently, it fails to live up to its early promise. But it has a lyrical charm.

CIN Tim Orr **MUS** Michael Linnen, David Wingo **DES** Richard Wright **ED** Steven Gonzales, Zene Baker **PROD** David Gordon Green, Sacha Mueller, Lisa Muskat **DIST** BFI

66 Amid languorous style the story gets lost, which is a pity because it could have been a nice, quirky one. – *Jason Solomons, Observer*

Germinal ★★★

DIR *Claude Berri*

1993   160m   France/Italy/Belgium

☆ *Gérard Depardieu* (Maheu), *Miou-Miou* (Maheude), Renaud (Etienne Lantier), Jean Carmet (Bonnemort), Judith Henry (Catherine Maheu), Jean-Roger Milo (Chaval), Laurent Terzieff (Souvarine)

French miners in the 1870s organise themselves into a union and strike in protest against their horrific working conditions. But the military is called in, and the strike is brutally put down.

This excellent, epic portrayal of Zola's hugely influential novel is highlighted by stirring acting performances and impressive reconstructions of the dreaded mines.

SCR Claude Berri, Arlette Langmann **CIN** *Yves Angelo* **MUS** Jean-Louis Roques **DES** *Thanh At Hoang, Christian Marti* **ED** Hervé de Luze **PROD** Claude Berri **DIST** AMLF/Renn/France 2/DD/Alternative Films/Nuova Artisti

66 This adaptation of Zola's novel looks superb, as befits the most expensive French film to date. – *Time Out*

'A Warrior. A Leader. A Legend.'

Geronimo: An American Legend ★

DIR Walter Hill

1994   115m   US

[DVD]   ♫

☆ Wes Studi (Geronimo), Gene Hackman (Brig. Gen. George Crook), Jason Patric (1st Lt. Charles B. Gatewood),

---

[DVD] Available on DVD   ☆ Cast in order   66 Critics' Quotes   ♔ Academy Award   T BAFTA
♫ Soundtrack on CD   of importance   † Points of interest   ♘ Academy Award nomination   T BAFTA nomination

245

Robert Duvall (Chief of Scouts Al Sieber), Matt Damon (2nd Lt. Britton Davis), Rodney A. Grant (Mangas), Kevin Tighe (Brig. Gen. Nelson Miles), Steve Reevis (Chato)

The US cavalry relentlessly hunt down the last great Apache leader.

Action-packed but thoughtful treatment of this story of the Indian hero. It is told with surprising frankness, including both the racism of the white men and the ferocity of the Indians.

SCR John Milius, Larry Gross CIN Lloyd Ahern MUS Ry Cooder DES Joe Alves ED Freeman Davies, Carmel Davies, Donn Aron PROD Walter Hill, Neil Canton DIST Columbia

66 A film of great beauty and considerable intelligence. – *Roger Ebert, Chicago Sun-Times*

⚱ Chris Carpenter, Doug Hemphill, Bill W. Benton, Lee Orloff (sound)

Gerry

DIR Gus Van Sant
2001 103m US
DVD

☆ Casey Affleck (Gerry), Matt Damon (Gerry)

Two guys called Gerry get lost in the desert.

The scenery in this movie, shot in Argentina, Death Valley and Utah's Great Salt Lake is captivating. Unfortunately two guys called Gerry keep getting in front of it. Totally bewildering. For extreme Van Sant fans only.

SCR Casey Affleck, Matt Damon, Gus Van Sant CIN Harris Savides MUS Arvo Part ED Casey Affleck, Matt Damon, Gus Van Sant PROD Dany Wolf DIST Pathé

66 Mind-numbing. – *Philip French, Observer*

Get Back

DIR Richard Lester
1991 89m GB
DVD

☆ Paul McCartney, Linda McCartney

Documentary of ex-Beatle Paul McCartney's 1989–90 world tour.

Richard Lester came out of retirement to create this respectful tale of the tour. It's a long way from his jaunty Beatles collaborations A Hard Day's Night and Help! For McCartney fans only, though there are plenty of them.

CIN Jordan Cronenweth, Robert Paynter ED John Victor Smith PROD Henry Thomas, Philip Knatchbull DIST Entertainment/Allied Filmmakers/Front Page/MPL

66 Nostalgia rules and there were some magical moments. – *Time Out*

Get Carter ★★★

SCR/DIR Mike Hodges
1971 112m GB
DVD ♫

☆ Michael Caine (Jack Carter), John Osborne (Cyril Kinnear), Ian Hendry (Eric Paice), Britt Ekland (Anna Fletcher)

A London racketeer goes to Newcastle to avenge his brother's death at the hands of gangsters.

Another film with a reputation that has grown with time. It boasts a taut script, a laconic, menacing performance by Caine, some fine work from supporting actors and a grimly accurate sense of place. Much of its dialogue, all brisk dry wit, is eminently quotable.

CIN Wolfgang Suschitzky MUS Roy Budd ED John Trumper DIST MGM

CARTER: You're a big man, but you're in bad shape. With me it's a full time job. Now behave yourself.

66 TV on the big screen – more sex, more violence, but no more attention to motivation or plot logic. – *Arthur Knight*

66 So calculatedly cool and soulless and nastily erotic that it seems to belong to a new era of virtuoso viciousness. – *Pauline Kael*

'On October 16, 1996, the one year anniversary of the Million Man March, Spike Lee invites you to lift your head, raise your voice, and. . .get on the bus.'

Get On the Bus ★★

DIR Spike Lee
1996 120m US
DVD ♫

☆ Richard Belzer (Rick), DeAundre Bonds (Junior aka 'Smooth'), Andre Braugher (Flip), Thomas Jefferson Byrd (Evan Thomas Snr.), Gabriel Casseus (Jamal), Albert Hall (Craig), Ossie Davis (Jeremiah), Charles S. Dutton (George)

A bus load of Afro-American men journey across America from Los Angeles to Washington for the Million Man March, called by the Black Muslim leader Louis Farrakhan, in October 1995.

Director Spike Lee has a wide range of attitudes on board his bus and he does well to provide some documentary-style balance to this controversial rolling talk-show that proves surprisingly entertaining.

SCR Reggie Rock Blythewood CIN Elliot Davis MUS Terence Blanchard DES Ina Mayhew ED Leander T. Sales PROD Reuben Cannon, Bill Borden, Barry Rosenbush DIST Columbia/40 Acres & A Mule

66 This is a film with a full message for heart and mind. – *Roger Ebert, Chicago Sun-Times*

'Get Dumped. Get Pumped. Get Even!'

Get Over It ★★

DIR Tommy O'Haver
2001 87m US
DVD ♫

☆ Kirsten Dunst (Kelly), Ben Foster (Berke Landers), Melissa Sagemiller (Allison McAllister), Sisqo (Dennis), Shane West (Bentley), Colin Hanks (Felix), Swoosie Kurtz (Beverly Landers), Ed Begley Jnr (Frank Landers), *Martin Short* (Dr Oates), Carmen Electra (Mistress Moira)

A teenage boy is traumatised after being dumped by his girlfriend. He tries to win her back by landing the key role in a rock version of Shakespeare's A Midsummer Night's Dream.

A sadly underrated teen comedy that demonstrates real wit and bounce from its zany opening scene – Foster

walking down his street singing the Captain and Tennille's Love Will Keep Us Together, with neighbours and passers-by falling in behind him and joining in. An agreeable treat, stuffed with funny one-liners, mostly from Short as a camp drama teacher.

SCR R. Lee Fleming Jnr   CIN Maryse Alberti   MUS Steve Bartek   DES Robin Standefer   ED Jeff Betancourt   PROD Michael Burns, Marc Butan, Paul Feldsher   DIST Miramax

66 It's the sort of show Judy Garland and Mickey Rooney would have bounced through 60 years ago. The nice thing is that it still comes up fresh. – *Peter Preston, Observer*

'What if you can't avoid sexuality virginity bigotry stupidity insecurity hormones heavies prats liars rumours confusion and big big trouble? Don't get angry. . .'

Get Real ★

DIR Simon Shore
1998   108m   GB/South Africa
DVD   ♫

☆ Ben Silverstone (Steven Carter), Brad Gorton (John Dixon), Charlotte Brittain (Linda)

A gay sixth-former in Basingstoke tentatively starts a secret fling with the school's head boy.

Small-scale but well-executed drama. Not exactly earth-shattering, but earnest, decent and occasionally funny. Silverstone is a winning presence.

SCR Patrick Wilde   CIN Alan Almond   MUS John Lunn   DES Bernd Lepel   ED Barrie Vince   PROD Stephen Taylor   DIST Paramount

66 Its knowing humour served it well. I laughed like a drain. – *Trevor Johnston, Time Out*

'Attitude Plays a Part.'

Get Shorty ★★★

DIR Barry Sonnenfeld
1995   105m   US
DVD   ♫

☆ John Travolta (Chili Palmer), Gene Hackman (Harry Zimm), René Russo (Karen Flores), Danny DeVito (Martin Weir), Dennis Farina (Ray 'Bones' Barboni), Delroy Lindo (Bo Catlett), James Gandolfini (Bear), Jon Gries (Ronnie Wingate), David Paymer (Leo Devoe)

A Miami loan shark goes to Hollywood to collect on a bad debt from a producer of trashy movies, and finds his devious talents qualify him as a film producer.

It comes as close to any other film adaptation of Elmore Leonard's work in capturing the novelist's elusive blend of malevolence, fast-paced action and insouciant wit. Travolta does his best work since Pulp Fiction, locating Chili Palmer's charm and brutality almost in the same breath. An entertaining, amusing story that suggests Leonard's long struggles with Hollywood have left him deeply cynical about the sort of people who produce and green-light films.

SCR Scott Frank   CIN Don Peterman   MUS John Lurie   DES Peter Larkin   ED Jim Miller   PROD Danny DeVito, Stacey Sher, Michael Shamberg   DIST MGM/Jersey

66 Hollywood has been in love with mobsters since the

beginning of movies. But the other side of the equation has seldom been considered. That is, until now. – *David Ansen, Newsweek*

'Witness History.'

Gettysburg ★★

SCR/DIR Ronald F. Maxwell
1993   259m   US
DVD   ♫

☆ Tom Berenger (Lt. Gen. James Longstreet), Martin Sheen (Gen. Robert E. Lee), Stephen Lang (Maj. Gen. George E. Pickett), Richard Jordan (Brig. Gen. Lewis A. Armistead), Jeff Daniels (Col. Joshua Lawrence Chamberlain), Sam Elliott (Brig. Gen. John Buford), C. Thomas Howell (Lt. Thomas D. Chamberlain), Kevin Conway (Sgt. 'Buster' Kilrain), Andrew Prine (Brig. Gen. Richard B. Garnett), Maxwell Caulfield (Col. Strong Vincent), James Lancaster (Lt. Col. Arthur Fremantle), Royce Applegate (Brig. Gen. James L. Kemper), Brian Mallon (Maj. Gen. Winfield Scott Hancock), Buck Taylor (Col. William Gamble), James Patrick Stuart (Col. E. Porter Alexander)

A detailed account of the American Civil War's pivotal battle in July 1863, in which three days of fierce fighting left thousands of soldiers dead but finally secured victory for the Union.

A comprehensive reconstruction of the battle which outlines military strategies and shows the fighting and slaughter in disturbing detail. Laudably, it takes the time to air opposing viewpoints, but there are long stretches that will appeal only to Civil War buffs.

CIN Kees van Oostum   MUS Randy Edelman   DES Cary White   ED Corky Ehlers   PROD Robert Katz, Moctesuma Esparza   DIST Mayfair/Turner

66 Gettysburg manages to make us reflect on concepts like duty, honour, loyalty and friendship – even God – almost lost to memory in our cynical age. – *Ken Ringle, Washington Post*

† Media mogul Ted Turner, whose company produced the film, has a cameo role as a Confederate colonel.
† Extras included 13,000 volunteer Civil War re-enactors, who paid their own way to the set to take part in the film.

'A love that will last forever.'

Ghost ★

DIR Jerry Zucker
1990   128m   US
DVD   ♫

☆ Patrick Swayze (Sam Wheat), Demi Moore (Molly Jensen), Tony Goldwyn (Carl Bruner), Whoopi Goldberg (Oda Mae Brown), Stanley Lawrence (Elevator man), Christopher J. Keene (Elevator man), Susan Breslau (Susan), Martina Degnan (Rose)

A murdered banker comes back as a ghost to get revenge on his killers and save his widow from becoming their next victim.

A shrewd blend of romance and the supernatural, wrapped up in a revenge motif. But Swayze and Moore are awfully wooden, and Ghost seems desperately eager to please everyone, even tossing in broad humour from Goldberg as a psychic. It's hard to believe this maudlin effort was a huge global hit. The similarly themed

---

DVD Available on DVD   ☆ Cast in order of importance   66 Critics' Quotes   † Points of interest   ⚊ Academy Award   ⚊ Academy Award nomination   🅑 BAFTA   Ⓣ BAFTA nomination

British film *Truly, Madly, Deeply*, also from 1990, is far superior.

SCR Bruce Joel Rubin   CIN Adam Greenberg
MUS Maurice Jarre   DES Jane Musky   ED Walter Murch
PROD Lisa Weinstein   DIST UIP/Paramount/Howard W. Koch

66 Ghost succeeds only at being insubstantial. – *Peter Travers, Rolling Stone*

66 Demi Moore, as the grieving girlfriend, displays the animation of a dishcloth. – *Time Out*

⚲ Whoopi Goldberg (supporting actress); Bruce Joel Rubin (original screenplay)

⚱ picture; Maurice Jarre; Walter Murch

♆ Whoopi Goldberg (supporting actress)

Ⓣ Bruce Joel Rubin (original screenplay); special visual effects; Ben Nye Jr (make up)

'All assassins live beyond the law. Only one follows the code.'

Ghost Dog: The Way of the Samurai ★★

SCR/DIR Jim Jarmusch
1999   116m   US/Japan/France/Germany
DVD   ♫

☆ Forest Whitaker (Ghost Dog), John Tormey (Louie), Cliff Gorman (Sonny Valerio), Henry Silva (Vargo), Isaach de Bankolé (Raymond), Tricia Vessey (Louise Vargo), Victor Argo (Vinny), Gene Ruffini (Old Consigliere), Richard Portnow (Handsome Frank), Camille Winbush (Pearline)

A lonely assassin for the Mob lives his life by a Samurai code of honour in his rooftop shack where he keeps pigeons. But after a difficult job goes wrong, he becomes the target for a hit.

This quirky Mob thriller turns on the differences between two rigidly traditional codes of behaviour in a ruthless, cruel world. While played straight-faced, there is humour in the story, thought it remains deeply buried. Jarmusch fans will embrace his oblique approach to the narrative, while neutrals are likely to be left cold.

CIN Robby Muller   MUS RZA   DES Ted Berner   ED Jay Rabinowitz   PROD Richard Guay, Jim Jarmusch
DIST Film4

66 This is a picture by turns amusing and melancholic, sweet-centred and dark-edged. – *Xan Brooks, Sight and Sound*

'It found a voice. . .now it needs a body.'

Ghost in the Shell ★

DIR Mamoru Oshii
1995   82m   Japan/GB
DVD   ♫

☆ Voices of: Richard George, Mimi Woods, William Frederick, Abe Lasser, Christopher Joyce, Mike Sorich, Ben Isaacson

Opposing anti-terrorist police forces clash in 21st-century Japan, while the Puppet Master, a strange formless self-generated secret agent, proves himself able to take over people's identities.

Explosive animation, replete with car chases, shoot-outs, a sex scene or two and even philosophical musings. All this in a grim setting that recalls Blade Runner. Best enjoyed as a visceral experience than as a coherent narrative.

SCR Kazunori Ito   CIN Hisao Shirai   MUS Kenji Kawai
DES Takashi Watabe   ED Shuichi Kakesu
PROD Shigeru Watanabe, Yoshimasa Mizuo, Ken Matsumoto, Ken Iyadomi, Mitsuhisa Ishikawa

66 If you try focusing on the plot particulars, Ghost in the Shell is frustrating and, despite the gunfire, not entirely dramatic. But as a piece of dark art, it's substantial and successful. This Shell isn't hollow. – *Barry Walters, San Francisco Examiner*

† A sequel, Ghost in the Shell 2: Innocence, followed in 2004.

'Accentuate the negative.'

Ghost World ★★

DIR Terry Zwigoff
2001   111m   US/GB/Germany
DVD   ♫

☆ Thora Birch (Enid), Scarlett Johansson (Rebecca), *Steve Buscemi (Seymour), Brad Renfro (Josh), Illeana Douglas (Roberta), Bob Balaban (Dad), Teri Garr (Maxine)*

Two best friend teenage girls leave their suburban American high school and struggle to make their mark in the adult world.

This deadpan comedy delves beneath the angst of adolescent misfits, and becomes a critique of an increasingly bland, uniform adult world where other eccentrics still exist and even flourish. Buscemi excels as a maladjusted, obsessive collector of vintage vinyl records.

SCR Daniel Clowes, Terry Zwigoff   CIN Affonso Beato
MUS David Kitay   DES Edward T. McAvoy   ED Carole Kravetz, Michael R. Miller   PROD Lianne Halfon, John Malkovich, Russel Smith

66 A true original, with sharp humour, subtle detail and painfully realistic characters. – *Angie Errigo, Empire*

66 For all its weirdness and weightless suburban ennui, this is actually a very plausible, understated account of late adolescent pain. – *Peter Bradshaw, Guardian*

⚲ Daniel Clowes, Terry Zwigoff (adapted screenplay)

Ghosts ★★★

DIR Nick Broomfield
2007   99m   UK
DVD

☆ Ai Qin Lin (Ai Qin), Zhan Yu (Mr Lin), Zhe Wei (Xiao Li), Man Qin Wei (Chio)

In rural China, a young mother leaves her small son with her mother and pays $25,000 to be smuggled to Britain to make money. After a gruelling six-month journey she finds work cockle-picking at Morecambe Bay, where disaster strikes her and her co-workers.

Documentarian Broomfield changes tack, using non-professional actors, staying off screen and offering a sober story – based on facts, but technically fictional.

This moving, appalling narrative of exploitation, told with sincerity and muted rage, haunts the memory.

SCR Nick Broomfield, Jez Lewis CIN Mark Wolf
MUS Molly Nyman, Harry Escott ED Peter Christelis
PROD Nick Broomfield, Jez Lewis DIST Tartan

66 Broomfield has made a film surprising in its intensity and compassion. – *Anthony Quinn, Independent*

Ghosts of Cité Soleil (new) ★★★

SCR/DIR Asger Leth
2007 88m US/Denmark
DVD ♫

☆ Winson '2Pac' Jean (Himself), James 'Bily' Petit Frère (Himself), Éleonore Senlis (Herself), Wyclef Jean (Himself)

The reality of poverty, despair and violence in Haiti is seen through the eyes of brothers 2Pac and Bily, gang leaders who strive to make better choices for their beleaguered families.

Danish director Leth's arresting documentary is set against the 2004 Haitian coup d'état that toppled the government of President Aristide. It shows a society in violent chaos, blending cinema vérité and newsreel footage to capture a modern, all set to a thumping rap soundtrack.

MUS Wyclef Jean, Jerry "Wonda" Duplessis ED Adam Nielsen PROD Mikael Chr. Rieks, Tomas Radoor, Seth Kanegis DIST Revolver

66 A raw, painful Danish documentary about gangsters in a Port-au-Prince slum in 2004. – *Philip French, Observer*

'The Only Witness To The Crime Was Not Even There.'

The Gift

DIR Sam Raimi
2000 112m US
DVD ♫

☆ Cate Blanchett (Annie Wilson), Giovanni Ribisi (Buddy Cole), Keanu Reeves (Donnie Barksdale), Katie Holmes (Jessica King), Greg Kinnear (Wayne Collins), Hilary Swank (Valerie Barksdale), Michael Jeter (Gerald Weems), Kim Dickens (Linda), Gary Cole (David Duncan), Rosemary Harris (Annie's Granny), J. K. Simmons (Sheriff Pearl Johnson), Chelchie Ross (Kenneth King), John Beasley (Albert Hawkins)

A single mother working as a psychic in a Deep South backwater is called in to help when the young wife of the local schoolmaster goes missing.

Individual scenes and performances in this Gothic stew are striking, but there's no magic in the mix, only creaking plot twists that are some way past their sell-by date.

SCR Billy Bob Thornton, Tom Epperson CIN Jamie Anderson MUS Christopher Young DES Neil Spisak
ED Arthur Coburn, Bob Murawski PROD Tom Rosenberg, Gary Lucchesi, James Jacks DIST Redbus

66 Too much hokum and too little suspense. – *David Sterritt, Christian Science Monitor*

66 Blanchett gives it all she's got, but there's a fundamental flaw here: if your beleaguered heroine has second sight, how come everybody in the entire audience is streets ahead of her? – *Tom Charity, Time Out*

Gigi ★★★

DIR Vincente Minnelli
1958 119m US
DVD ♫

☆ Leslie Caron (Gigi), Louis Jourdan (Gaston Lachaille), Maurice Chevalier (Honore Lachaille), Hermione Gingold (Mme Alvarez), Isabel Jeans (Aunt Alicia), Jacques Bergerac (Sandomir), Eva Gabor (Liane D'Exelmans), John Abbott (Manuel)

In 1890s Paris, a young girl is trained by her aunt to be a courtesan.

A gorgeous, opulent musical, with some splendid songs, costumes and sets. It reins in its cynical subject matter, and manages to be sophisticated and joyous all at once; a neat trick. Chevalier, winking and twinkling, does what Chevalier does, while the film further reinforced Caron's gamine appeal, seven whole years after An American in Paris. A feast for the ears, but even more so for the eyes.

SCR Alan Jay Lerner CIN Joseph Ruttenberg
ED Adrienne Fazan PROD Arthur Freed DIST MGM

66 It has the sureness expected when a group of the most sophisticated talents are able to work together on material entirely suited to them. – *Penelope Houston*

† 'Thank Heaven for Little Girls'; 'It's a Bore'; 'The Parisians'; 'Gossip'; 'She is Not Thinking of Me'; 'The Night They Invented Champagne'; 'I Remember It Well'; 'Gigi'; 'I'm Glad I'm Not Young Anymore'; 'Say a Prayer for Me Tonight'

⚊ picture; Alan Jay Lerner (adapted screenplay); Vincente Minnelli; Joseph Ruttenberg; André Previn (music); Cecil Beaton (costume design); Adrienne Fazan (editing); Preston Ames, William A. Horning (art direction); Frederick Loewe (m), Alan Jay Lerner (ly) (song – Gigi); Maurice Chevalier (special award)

'There never was a woman like Gilda!'

Gilda ★★★

DIR Charles Vidor
1946 110m US
DVD ♫

☆ Rita Hayworth (Gilda), Glenn Ford (Johnny Farrell), George Macready (Ballin Mundson), Steve Geray (Uncle Pio), Joseph Calleia (Obregon), Joe Sawyer (Casey), Gerald Mohr (Capt. Delgado), Ludwig Donath (German)

A gambler in a South American city resumes a love-hate relationship with an old flame . . . but she is now married to his dangerous new boss.

Archetypal Hollywood film noir, wholly studio-bound and the better for it, with dialogue that would seem risible if it did not happen to be dealt with in this style and with these actors, who keep the mood balanced between suspense and absurdity. Superb, sexually alive performance by Hayworth, whose star status it sealed. For years after, she was known as the 'Love Goddess.'

SCR Marion Parsonnet CIN Rudolph Maté MUS Hugo Friedhofer ED Charles Nelson PROD Virginia Van Upp
DIST Columbia

66 From a quietly promising opening the film settles into an intractable obscurity of narrative through which as in a

DVD Available on DVD ☆ Cast in order 66 Critics' Quotes ⚊ Academy Award 🅑 BAFTA
♫ Soundtrack on CD of importance † Points of interest ⚊ Academy Award nomination 🅑 BAFTA nomination

249

fog three characters bite off at each other words of hate. – *Richard Winnington*

The Gingerbread Man

DIR Robert Altman
1997   114m   US
DVD

☆ Kenneth Branagh (Rick Magruder), Embeth Davidtz (Mallory Doss), Robert Downey Jnr (Clyde Pell), Daryl Hannah (Lois Harlan), Robert Duvall (Dixon Doss), Tom Berenger (Pete Randle), Famke Janssen (Leeanne Magruder), Clyde Hayes (Carl Alden), Mae Whitman (Libby Magruder)

A lawyer picks up a poor waitress, only to fall foul of her eccentric cult leader father.

Altman attempts to bend the rules of the courtroom thriller, to no avail: his fondness for incidental details and characters comes over as so much pointless noodling in this instance, while his utter disregard for Grisham's plot conventions manifests itself in long stretches of tedium, if not incomprehensibility.

SCR Al Hayes   CIN Changwei Gu   MUS Mark Isham
DES Stephen Altman   ED Geraldine Peroni
PROD Jeremy Tannenbaum
DIST Polygram/Island/Enchanter

66 The lesson of this barely stylish crime thriller is that a dull story is not improved by withholding information about characters' motives from the audience as long as possible. – *Lisa Alspector, Chicago Tribune*

66 Built on one of those particularly ludicrous plots in which, just before the end, we are meant to believe that a long succession of coincidences was really a diabolical scheme. – *Stanley Kauffman, The New Republic*

'Six Is For Sex. . .'

Girl 6   ★

DIR Spike Lee
1996   108m   US
DVD   ♫

☆ *Theresa Randle* (Judy, aka Girl 6), Isaiah Washington (Shoplifter), Spike Lee (Jimmy), Jenifer Lewis (Lil), Debi Mazar (Girl #39), Peter Berg (Bob), Michael Imperioli (Scary caller), Naomi Campbell (Girl #75), Quentin Tarantino (QT), Madonna (Boss #3), John Turturro (Murray), Ron Silver (Director 2, LA)

An unemployed women finds a job at a phone sex agency, and proves accomplished at talking dirty. But her life is endangered when she unwisely agrees to meet an unbalanced client.

Spike Lee has yet to make a dull film, though his judgement sometimes teeters. Here he narrowly triumphs with a story that could be sunk by its political incorrectness. Randle is bracingly funny, and helped by a script that elicits guilty laughter over society's double-edged views about sexuality.

SCR Suzan-Lori Parks   CIN Malik Hassan Sayeed, John Corso   DES Ina Mayhew   ED Sam Pollard   PROD Spike Lee   DIST TCF/Fox Searchlight/40 Acres and a Mule

66 Girl 6 is glossy, technically proficient and a glib waste of time. – *Edward Guthmann, San Francisco Chronicle*

The Girl from Paris   ★

DIR Christian Carion
2001   103m   France/Belgium
DVD

☆ Michel Serrault (Adrien Rochas), Mathilde Seigner (Sandrine Dumez), Jean-Paul Roussillon (Jean Farjon), Frederic Pierrot (Gérard Chauvin), Marc Berman (Stéphane), Françoise Bette (Sandrine's mother)

A Parisian woman leaves her IT job and sets out to become a mountain farmer in the south. There she befriends an old farmer and buys his property.

This rural idyll was a huge hit in France, confirming the strong lure of all things pastoral in that country. Not much else apart from the luscious scenery can account for the film's success, because precious little happens, though Seigner and the grouchy Serrault make a charming odd couple.

SCR Christian Carion, Eric Assous   CIN Antoine Heberle
MUS Philippe Rombi   DES Jean-Michel Simonet
ED Andrea Sedlackova   PROD Christophe Rossignon
DIST Artificial Eye

'Sometimes the only way to stay sane is to go a little crazy.'

Girl, Interrupted   ★

DIR James Mangold
1999   127m   US/Germany
DVD   ♫

☆ Winona Ryder (Susanna), Angelina Jolie (Lisa), Clea Duvall (Georgina), Brittany Murphy (Daisy), Elisabeth Moss (Polly), Jared Leto (Tobias Jacobs), Jeffrey Tambor (Dr Potts), Vanessa Redgrave (Dr Wick), Whoopi Goldberg (Valerie), Mary Kay Place (Mrs Gilcrest)

A teenage girl is sent to a mental hospital in 1960s New England after a suicide attempt. There she meets new friends who are even more disturbed.

This commendable portrait of a traditional, impersonal mental institution will not erase One Flew Over The Cuckoo's Nest, from audiences' memories, but it has its moments. Director Mangold conveys Ryder's brittle state of mind effectively, and Jolie gets to chew the scenery as a subversive young patient.

SCR James Mangold, Lisa Loomer, Anna Hamilton Phelan
CIN Jack Green   MUS Mychael Danna   DES Richard Hoover   ED Kevin Tent   PROD Douglas Wick, Cathy Konrad   DIST Columbia/Red Wagon

66 Perhaps the problem with director James Mangold's movie is not that it fails to press the right buttons, it's just they've been worn out with overuse. – *Liese Spencer, Sight and Sound*

⌕ Angelina Jolie (supporting actress)

The Girl on the Bridge   ★

DIR Patrice Leconte
1998   90m   France
DVD

☆ Daniel Auteuil (Gabor), Vanessa Paradis (Adele), Demetre Georgalas (Takis), Isabelle Petit-Jacques (The Bride), Frederic Pfluger (The Contortionist)

A circus knife-thrower rescues a suicidal young woman from a bridge and recruits her as an assistant for his stage act.

A thin slip of a romance, but one that more often than not dazzles with its light comic touch and luminous photography.

SCR Serge Frydman   CIN *Jean-Marie Dreujou*   DES Ivan Maussion   ED Joelle Hache   PROD Christian Fechner   DIST Pathé

66 Gorgeously silly. – *David Edelstein, Slate*

66 A tangy frappe of a movie - preposterously comic, deliriously romantic, outrageously stylish. – *Richard Schickel, Time*

'Beauty inspires obsession.'

Girl with a Pearl Earring ★

DIR Peter Webber
2003   100m   GB/Luxembourg/US
DVD   ♫

☆ Colin Firth (Vermeer), Scarlett Johansson (Griet), Tom Wilkinson (Van Ruijven), Judy Parfitt (Maria Thins), Cillian Murphy (Pieter), Essie Davis (Catharina), Joanna Scanlan (Tanneke), Alakina Mann (Cornelia)

In 17th-century Holland, the artist Vermeer is struggling until he becomes inspired by the arrival of a pretty young maid in the household.

Vermeer is a daunting role model, and Webber's film is appropriately ravishing to gaze upon. Yet otherwise, it's something of a still life: the dialogue is stilted and the action slowed down, as if to give it more significance. Tracy Chevalier's novel spoke more directly to audiences' imaginations.

SCR Olivia Hetreed   CIN *Eduardo Serra*   MUS Alexandre Desplat   DES *Ben van Os*   ED Kate Evans   PROD Andy Paterson, Anand Tucker   DIST Pathé

66 This film doesn't just appeal to budding Vermeers but to anyone who likes serious intelligent drama and gentle erotic tension. – *Susan Hodgetts, BBC*

⌁ Eduardo Serra; Ben van Os, Cecile Heideman (art direction); Dien van Straalen (costume design)

ⓣ film; Scarlett Johansson (leading actress); Judy Parfitt (supporting actress); Peter Webber; Olivia Hetreed (adapted screenplay); Eduardo Serra; Alexandre Desplat; Ben van Os; Dien van Straalen (costume design); Jenny Shircore (make up/hair)

'Prove Them Wrong.'

Girlfight ★★

SCR/DIR *Karyn Kusama*
2000   110m   US
DVD   ♫

☆ *Michelle Rodriguez* (Diana), Jaime Tirelli (Hector), Paul Calderon (Sandro), Santiago Douglas (Adrian), Ray Santiago (Tiny), Elisa Bocanegra (Marisol), Shannon Walker Williams (Veronica), Iris Little-Thomas (Ms Martinez), John Sayles (Science Teacher)

A tough, lonely inner-city high school girl finds a outlet for her violent aggression by taking up boxing.

No punches pulled, but what lifts this gender twist on a

Rocky-style template is a knockout performance from Michelle Rodriguez.

CIN Patrick Cady   MUS Theodore Shapiro, Gene McDaniels   DES Stephen Beatrice   ED Plummy Tucker   PROD Sarah Green, Martha Griffin, Maggie Renzi   DIST Columbia TriStar

66 A powerful and empathic melodrama with feminist underpinnings. – *Kenneth Turan, Los Angeles Times*

'What We Do In Life Echoes In Eternity.'

Gladiator ★★★

DIR *Ridley Scott*
2000   155m   US
DVD   ♫

☆ *Russell Crowe* (Maximus), Joaquin Phoenix (Commodus), Connie Nielsen (Lucilla), *Oliver Reed* (Proximo), Derek Jacobi (Gracchus), Djimon Hounsou (Juba), Richard Harris (Marcus Aurelius), David Schofield (Falco), John Shrapnel (Gaius), Tomas Arana (Quintus), Ralf Moeller (Hagen), Spencer Treat Clark (Lucius), David Hemmings (Cassius)

A second-century Roman general is condemned to death by the Emperor but escapes to become a slave and a gladiator before wreaking a spectacular revenge and restoring the moral compass of the Roman Empire.

Expensive, elaborate, action movie that became the first bona fide sword-and-sandals epic in four decades. The pace never falters thanks to Scott's attentive direction, buttressed by an astronomical budget. Crowe, alternating between hand-to-hand combat and grave contemplation, is hugely credible in the title role. A massive hit for wholly understandable reasons.

SCR David Franzoni, John Logan, William Nicholson   CIN *John Mathieson*   MUS Hans Zimmer, Lisa Gerrard   DES *Arthur Max*   ED Pietro Scalia   PROD Douglas Wick, David Franzoni, Branko Lustig   DIST Universal/DreamWorks

66 Meaty and satisfying. – *Daniel Etherington, Channel 4*

66 Director Ridley Scott's sword and sandal spectacular is a bloody good yarn, packed with epic pomp and pageantry, dastardly plots, massed action and forthright, fundamental emotions. – *Geoff Andrew, Time Out*

⌁ picture; Russell Crowe (leading actor); Scott Millan, Bob Beemer, Ken Weston (sound); Janty Yates (costume design); John Nelson, Neil Corbould, Tim Burke, Rob Harvey (visual effects)

⌁ Joaquin Phoenix (supporting actor); Ridley Scott; David Franzoni, John Logan, William Nicholson (original screenplay); John Mathieson; Pietro Scalia; Hans Zimmer; Arthur Max, Crispian Sallis

ⓣ film; John Mathieson; Pietro Scalia; Arthur Max
ⓣ Russsell Crowe (leading actor); Joaquin Phoenix (supporting actor); Oliver Reed (supporting actor); Ridley Scott; David Franzoni, John Logan, William Nicholson (original screenplay); John Nelson, Neil Corbould, Tim Burke, Rob Harvey (speical visual effects); Scott Millan, Bob Beemer, Ken Weston (sound); Janty Yates (costume design); Paul Engelen, Graham Johnston (make up/hair)

G

DVD Available on DVD   ☆ Cast in order of importance   66 Critics' Quotes   ⌁ Academy Award   ⓑ BAFTA
♫ Soundtrack on CD   † Points of interest   ⌁ Academy Award nomination   ⓣ BAFTA nomination

251

The Glass Menagerie ★

DIR Paul Newman
1987 134m US

☆ *Joanne Woodward* (Amanda Wingfield), John Malkovich (Tom Wingfield), *Karen Allen* (Laura Wingfield), James Naughton (Jim O'Connor (the gentleman caller))

In Depression-era St. Louis, a family comprising a mother, her son and daughter are depressed and discontented with their lot in life, and fret about their prospects.

Newman's treatment of the stage play is respectful, with Woodward remarkably powerful as the manipulative mother. Yet it's Karen Allen who is the revelation here, as her crippled daughter, dutifully polishing her collection of glass animals and awaiting the day a 'gentleman caller' arrives to free her.

SCR Tennessee Williams **CIN** Michael Ballhaus
MUS Henry Mancini, Paul Bowles **DES** Tony Walton
ED David Ray **PROD** Burtt Harris **DIST** Cineplex

'A Story For Everyone Who Works For A Living.'

Glengarry Glen Ross ★★★

DIR James Foley
1992 100m US
DVD ♫

☆ *Al Pacino* (Ricky Roma), *Jack Lemmon* (Shelley Levene), Alec Baldwin (Blake), Ed Harris (Dave Moss), Alan Arkin (George Aaronow), Kevin Spacey (John Williamson), Jonathan Pryce (James Lingk)

Four pressurised real-estate salesmen in Chicago compete ruthlessly to clinch enough deals to save their jobs.

Superb acting from all concerned, especially Lemmon and Pacino, facilitates a riveting stage-to-screen transfer. Mamet's idiosyncratic language, used here within the context of a specific profession, has never seemed more appropriate. A sobering account of desperation overwhelming decency.

SCR *David Mamet* **CIN** Juan Ruiz Anchia **MUS** James Newton Howard **DES** Jane Musky **ED** Howard Smith
PROD Jerry Tokofsky, Stanley R. Zupnik
DIST Rank/Zupnik Enterprises

66 The pleasure of this unique film comes in watching superb actors dine on Mamet's pungent language like the feast it is. – *Peter Travers, Rolling Stone*

66 Glengarry Glen Ross is a hard sell, a wrenchingly claustrophobic tale about screwing up and getting screwed. – *Rita Kempley, Washington Post*

⚍ Al Pacino (supporting actor)

La Gloire de Mon Père ★

DIR Yves Robert
1990 105m France
DVD ♫

☆ Philippe Caubère (Joseph Pagnol), Nathalie Roussel (Augustine), Didier Pain (Uncle Jules), Thérèse Liotard (Aunt Rose), Julien Ciamaca (Marcel (11 years old)), Victorien Delamare (Paul), Joris Molinas (Lili des Bellons), Paul Crauchet (Mond des Parpaillouns), Jean-Pierre Darras (narrator)

When an 11 year old boy takes a family holiday in Provence, he becomes enthralled by its people and natural beauty.

Gorgeous landscapes dominate this self-consciously charming story, based in part on the memoirs of film-maker Marcel Pagnol. It's too sugary and nostalgic for large doses of reality to intrude, but it coasts by on its charm.

SCR Jérôme Tonnerre, Louis Nucera, Yves Robert
CIN Robert Alazraki, Paco Wiser, Eric Vallée, Guillaume Schiffman, Christophe Beaucarne, **MUS** Vladimir Cosma
DES Jacques Dugied **ED** Pierre Gillette **PROD** Alain Poiré **DIST** Palace/Gaumont International/La Guéville/TF1

'Their innocence. Their heritage. Their lives. Nothing would be spared in the fight for their freedom.'

Glory ★★

DIR Edward Zwick
1989 122m US
DVD ♫

☆ Matthew Broderick (Col. Robert Gould Shaw), *Denzel Washington* (Pvt. Trip), Cary Elwes (Maj. Cabot Forbes), Morgan Freeman (Sgt. Maj. John Rawlins), Jihmi Kennedy (Pvt. Jupiter Sharts), Andre Braugher (Cpl. Thomas Searles), John Finn (Sgt. Maj. Mulcahy), Donovan Leitch (Capt. Charles Fessenden Morse), John David Cullum (Henry Sturgis Russell)

During the American Civil War, a young white officer finds himself in charge of the first black regiment to fight in combat.

Intriguing tribute to heroes unsung for too long. Broderick does most of the heavy lifting as a well-meaning young man (from an anti-slavery family) who is resented by his troops and left to rot by his superiors. But Washington, as an escaped slave with a bad attitude, steals all his scenes. Veteran cinematographer Francis invests proceedings with a shimmering beauty.

SCR Kevin Jarre **CIN** *Freddie Francis* **MUS** James Horner **DES** Norman Garwood **ED** Steven Rosenblum
PROD Freddie Fields **DIST** Columbia TriStar

66 Richly plotted, alternately inspiring and horrifying, Glory is an enlightening and entertaining tribute to heroes too long forgotten. – *TV Guide*

⚍ Denzel Washington (leading actor); Freddie Francis; Donald O. Mitchell, Gregg Rudloff, Elliot Tyson, Russell Williams II (sound)
⚍ Steven Rosenblum; Norman Garwood
Ⓣ Freddie Francis

'A weekend wasted is never a wasted weekend.'

Go ★★

DIR Doug Liman
1999 103m US
DVD ♫

☆ Desmond Askew (Simon Baines), Taye Diggs (Marcus), William Fichtner (Burke), J.E. Freeman (Victor Sr), Katie Holmes (Claire Montgomery), Breckin Meyer (Tiny), Jay Mohr (Zack), Timothy Olyphant (Todd Gaines), *Sarah Polley* (Ronna Martin), Scott Wolf (Adam)

The lives of four sets of strangers intersect for bizarre reasons on a wild weekend in Las Vegas and LA.

Intricate, amusingly implausible script is kept afloat by intense directorial energy, the wide-eyed appeal of the youthful cast, and welcome occasional flashes of real humour. Its madcap quality and razor-sharp timing approaches the quality of farce. A chic, eclectic soundtrack, ranging from Massive Attack to Dean Martin, enhances the sense that Liman knows just what he's about.

SCR John August CIN Doug Liman MUS BT, Moby DES Thomas Wilkins ED Stephen Mirrione PROD Paul Rosenberg, Mickey Liddell, Matt Freeman DIST Columbia

66 Here is a picture that has wit, a hairpin-turn narrative, high pizzazz and ensemble star quality. Ready, set, Go. – *Richard Corliss, Time*

'The girl is out there.'

Go Fish ★

DIR Rose Troche
1994 83m US
DVD

☆ V.S. Brodie (Ely), Guinevere Turner (Camille 'Max' Turner), T. Wendy McMillan (Kia), Migdalia Melendez (Evy), Anastasia Sharp (Daria)

Five lesbians look for love and happiness as they interact at university.

Low-budget, almost documentary-style film about a community of gay women who spend much of their time talking about sex, but amusingly and engagingly.

SCR Guinevere Turner, Rose Troche CIN Ann T. Rossetti, Arthur C. Stone MUS Brendan Dolan, Jennifer Sharpe, Scott Aldrich ED Rose Troche PROD Rose Troche, Guinevere Turner DIST Mainline/Islet/Can I Watch Pictures/KVPI

66 A lively romantic set in Chicago, which blows fresh air on the fusty conventions applied to the representation of lesbian and gay lives. – *Time Out*

66 The film is honest, forthright and affectionate and it portrays the everyday worlds of these ordinary gay women with what I sense is accuracy. – *Roger Ebert, Chicago Sun-Times*

The Go-Between ★★★

DIR Joseph Losey
1970 116m GB

☆ Alan Bates (Ted Burgess), Julie Christie (Marian Maudsley), Michael Redgrave (The Older Leo), Dominic Guard (Leo Colston), Michael Gough (Mr. Maudsley), Margaret Leighton (Mrs. Maudsley), Edward Fox (Hugh Trimingham)

Staying at a stately home around the turn of the last century, a 12-year-old boy carries love letters from a farmer to his friend's sister.

A secret affair at the story's heart provides the opportunity to explore class prejudice in Britain, wrapped up in what is otherwise a workmanlike, handsomely photographed period drama.

SCR Harold Pinter CIN Geoffrey Fisher MUS Michel

Legrand ED Reginald Beck PROD John Heyman, Norman Priggen DIST EMI/World Film Services

66 It's an almost palpable recreation of a past environment, and that environment is the film's real achievement, not the drama enacted within it. – *Stanley Kauffmann*

† In 1971, the film won the Palme D'Or at the Cannes Film Festival.

⌕ Margaret Leighton (supporting actress)

⊕ Harold Pinter (screenplay); Edward Fox (supporting actor); Margaret Leighton (supporting actress); Dominic Guard

The Godfather ★★★★

DIR *Francis Ford Coppola*
1972 175m US
DVD ♫

☆ *Marlon Brando* (Don Vito Corleone), *Al Pacino* (Michael Corleone), *Robert Duvall* (Tom Hagen), James Caan (Sonny Corleone), Richard Castellano (Clemenza), *Diane Keaton* (Kay Adams), Talia Shire (Connie Rizzi), Richard Conte (Barzini), John Marley (Jack Woltz)

When, after ruling for two generations, the Mafia's New York Don dies, his youngest son takes over reluctantly, but later learns the ruthlessness and brutality required to maintain his position.

A brilliantly-made film with all the fascination of a snake pit: a warm-hearted family saga except that the members are thieves and murderers. Its position as one of the great films of the last century is secure, in part because it works on so many levels: as a father-and-son story, as an epic account of the Mob's overt power and clandestine business empires in America; and as an apparently authentic glimpse into a closed world, with its own distinct and deadly codes of behaviour.

SCR Francis Ford Coppola, Mario Puzo CIN *Gordon Willis* MUS *Nino Rota* DES *Dean Tavoularis* ED Paul Zinner, Marc Laub, William Reynolds, Murray Solomon PROD Albert S. Ruddy DIST Paramount

DON CORELEONE: I'm going to make him an offer he can't refuse.

66 One of the most brutal and moving chronicles of American life ever designed within the limits of popular entertainment. – *Vincent Canby, New York Times*

66 A handbook on cinematic lucidity. All events are described clearly. Motives of all the characters are set right there on the table next to the pasta for our consideration. – *Barbara Shulgasser, San Francisco Examiner*

⌕ picture; Francis Ford Coppola, Mario Puzo (adapted screenplay); Marlon Brando (leading actor)

⌕ Francis Ford Coppola (director); Al Pacino (supporting actor); Robert Duvall (supporting actor); James Caan (supporting actor); Anna Hill Johnstone (costume design); Charles Grenzbach, Richard Portman, Christopher Newman (sound)

⊕ Nino Rota

The Godfather Part II ★★★★

DIR *Francis Ford Coppola*
1974 200m US
DVD ♫

☆ *Al Pacino* (Michael Corleone), *Robert DeNiro* (Vito

DVD Available on DVD ☆ Cast in order of importance 66 Critics' Quotes † Points of interest ⌕ Academy Award ⌕ Academy Award nomination ⊕ BAFTA ⊕ BAFTA nomination

253

Corleone), *Diane Keaton* (Kay Adams), *Robert Duvall* (Tom Hagen), *John Cazale* (Fredo), *Lee Strasberg* (Hyman Roth), Michael V. Gazzo (Frank Pentangeli), Talia Shire (Connie Rizzi), Troy Donahue (Merle Johnson)

In 1958, Michael Corleone reflects on the problems of being a Mafia don, and those of his father before him.

One of those rare sequels that genuinely eclipses the original film – quite an achievement, in this instance. But Part II fleshes out the history of the Corleone clan, showing the rise of young Don Vito and reflecting on the increasingly icy demeanour of his son Michael as he accommodates himself to becoming a ruthless don. The scenes in Sicily, beautifully shot, have a lyrical, almost Edenic quality, tinged with foreboding: we all know this idyll cannot last. De Niro is spellbinding as young Vito, while Pacino almost visibly transforms himself into the man Michael Corleone is becoming. An astonishing popular masterpiece.

SCR Francis Ford Coppola, Mario Puzo   CIN *Gordon Willis*
MUS *Nino Rota, Carmine Coppola*   DES *Dean Tavoularis*
ED Peter Zinner, Richard Marks, Barry Malkin
PROD Francis Ford Coppola   DIST Paramount/the Coppola Company

66 The daring of Part II is that it enlarges the scope and deepens the meaning of the first film . . . It's an epic vision of the corruption of America. – *Pauline Kael, New Yorker*

66 I think Godfather II is simply one of the great American movies. – *Pauline Kael*

† The two films were eventually combined and extended for television into a ten-hour serial, The Godfather Saga.
† It was the first sequel ever to win a best picture Oscar.

⚏ picture; Francis Ford Coppola, Mario Puzo (adapted screenplay); Francis Ford Coppola (director); Nino Rota, Carmine Coppola (music); Robert DeNiro (supporting actor); art direction

⚏ Al Pacino; Lee Strasberg; Michael V. Gazzo; Talia Shire; Theodara Van Runkle

🎭 Al Pacino

'Real Power Can't Be Given. It Must Be Taken.'

The Godfather Part III   ★

DIR Francis Ford Coppola
1990   162m   US
DVD   🎵

☆ Al Pacino (Michael Corleone), Diane Keaton (Kay Adams), Talia Shire (Connie Rizzi), Andy Garcia (Vincent Mancini), Eli Wallach (Don Altobello), Joe Mantegna (Joey Zasa), George Hamilton (B.J. Harrison), Bridget Fonda (Grace Hamilton), Sofia Coppola (Mary Corleone), Raf Vallone (Cardinal Lamberto), Franc D'Ambrosio (Tony Corleone), Donal Donnelly (Archbishop Gilday), Richard Bright (Al Neri), Helmut Berger (Frederick Keinszig), Don Novello (Dominic Abbandando)

While attempting to conclude a real-estate deal with the Vatican that might confer legitimacy on his business affairs, Michael Corleone is distracted by the behaviour of his violent and ambitious nephew.

The greatest anti-climax in American cinema: a plodding third instalment that makes mistakes and poor choices from the word go, compounded by Coppola's

sudden lack of confidence around set-pieces and actors. Some small pleasure can be taken from seeing the loose ends tied up, but if this was a Corleone brother, it'd be the sickly Fredo, the one you want to see put out of his misery as soon as possible.*

SCR Mario Puzo, Francis Ford Coppola   CIN Gordon Willis   MUS Carmine Coppola   DES Dean Tavoularis
ED Barry Malkin, Lisa Fruchtman, Walter Murch
PROD Francis Ford Coppola   DIST Paramount/Zoetrope

MICHAEL CORLEONE: Just when I thought I was out... they pull me back in.

66 In this brilliantly sustained climax, Coppola unveils a vision of corruption that embraces the entire world, but he's also revelling in sheer theatrical magic in a way that only a master can. – *Owen Gleiberman, Entertainment Weekly*

66 It's the most thoughtful of the three films, and its climax brings the entire series into sharper focus. – *Mick LaSalle, San Francisco Chronicle*

⚏ picture; Francis Ford Coppola; Andy Garcia (supporting actor); Carmine Coppola (m), John Bettis (ly) (music, original song – Promise Me You'll Remember); art direction; cinematography, film editing

---

'The nation's heart was touched by. . .'

Gods and Generals

SCR/DIR Ronald F. Maxwell
2003   231m   US
DVD   🎵

☆ Jeff Daniels (Lt. Col. Joshua Lawrence Chamberlain), Stephen Lang (Gen. Stonewall Jackson), Robert Duvall (Gen. Robert E. Lee), Mira Sorvino (Fanny Chamberlain), Kevin Conway (Sgt. Buster Kilrain), C. Thomas Howell (Sgt. Thomas Chamberlain), Frankie Faison (Jim Lewis), William Sanderson (Maj. Gen. A.P. Hill)

The three main early battles of the American Civil War are recreated in enormous detail.

Another Civil War epic from media mogul Ted Turner but, unlike Gettysburg, there's little here for those not obsessed by the fortunes of Yankees and Confederates.

CIN Kees Van Oostrum   MUS John Frizzell, Randy Edelman   DES Michael Z. Hanan   ED Corky Ehlers
PROD Ronald F. Maxwell   DIST Warner

66 This incredibly boring and badly acted film about the American Civil War is almost four hours long and feels like four days. – *Peter Bradshaw, Guardian*

66 Swapping politics for crass platitudes, Gods and Generals is a monumental folly. – *Jamie Russell, BBC*

'Sometimes It's Hard To Tell Them Apart.'

Gods and Monsters   ★★

SCR/DIR Bill Condon
1998   105m   US/ GB
DVD

☆ *Ian McKellen* (James Whale), Brendan Fraser (Clayton Boone), Lynn Redgrave (Hanna), Lolita Davidovich (Betty), Kevin J. O'Connor (Harry), David Dukes (David Lewis), Brandon Kleyla (Young Whale), Jack Plotnick (Edmund Kay)

The celebrated Frankenstein film director James Whale looks back on his life and career in his twilight years, while trying to bed his handsome heterosexual young gardener.

A melancholy account of the decline of a director hounded out of Hollywood for being openly homosexual and a box-office liability. It is considerably enhanced by McKellen's flamboyant acting, yet Fraser, in a quieter role, is a match for him.

CIN Stephen M. Katz   MUS Carter Burwell   DES Richard Sherman   ED Virginia Katz   PROD Paul Colichman, Gregg Fienberg, Mark Harris   DIST Regent

66 Some of McKellen's bitchy line readings are worth their weight in gold. – *Jeff Millar, Houston Chronicle*

66 McKellen. . .reaches a remarkable new plateau here. – *Kenneth Turan, Los Angeles Times*

⚐ Bill Condon (adapted screenplay)

⚐ Ian McKellen (leading actor); Lynn Redgrave (supporting actress)

Ⓣ Lynn Redgrave (supporting actress)

'In love and life there's only one way to go.'

Going All the Way   ★

DIR Mark Pellington
1997   103m   US
DVD   ♫

☆ Jeremy Davies (Williard 'Sonny' Burns), Ben Affleck (Tom 'Gunner' Casselman), Amy Locane (Buddy Porter), Rose McGowan (Gale Ann Thayer), Rachel Weisz (Marty Pilcher), John Lordan (Elwood Burns), Bob Swan (Luke), Jill Clayburgh (Alma Burns), Lesley Ann Warren (Nina Casselman)

Two young post-Korea GIs struggle to come to terms with life as civilians.

Indianapolis in the 1950s is the unusual setting for this patchy rites-of-passage drama with two heroes, one introverted, the other full of sexual swagger. It has a pleasant nostalgic air.

SCR Dan Wakefield   CIN Bobby Bukowski
MUS Tomandandy   DES Thérèse DuPrez   ED Leo Trombetta   PROD Tom Gorai, Sigurjon Sighvatsson
DIST Polygram

66 If there were a juvenile detention hall for self-indulgent movie directors, you'd want to put Mark Pellington in it. – *Jeff Millar, Houston Chronicle*

Gold Diggers of 1935   ★★

DIR Busby Berkeley
1934   95m   US

☆ Dick Powell, Adolphe Menjou, Gloria Stuart, Alice Brady, Hugh Herbert, Glenda Farrell, Frank McHugh, Grant Mitchell, Wini Shaw

A socialite puts on a Broadway show at her country home, and is taken in by a swindler.

Heavy-handed but laugh-provoking comedy with familiar faces of the day, climaxed by big numbers including 'Lullaby of Broadway'. Easily the best in Berkeley's Gold Diggers series.

SCR Manuel Seff, Peter Milne, Robert Lord   CIN *George Barnes*   PROD Robert Lord   DIST Warner

66 Busby Berkeley, the master of scenic prestidigitation,

continues to dazzle the eye and stun the imagination. – *André Sennwald, New York Times*

66 A decidedly heady mixture. – *Pare Lorentz*

⚐ Harry Warren (m), Al Dubin (ly) (music, original song – Lullaby of Broadway)

⚐ Busby Berkeley (choreography)

The Gold Rush   ★★★

SCR/DIR *Charles Chaplin*
1925   72m   US
DVD

☆ *Charles Chaplin* (The Lone Prospector), Georgia Hale (Georgia), Mack Swain (Big Jim), Tom Murray (Black Larson)

A lone prospector in the Yukon becomes rich after various adventures.

Essentially a succession of slowly but carefully built visual gags, this is Chaplin's finest example of comedy drawn from utter privation; as such it appealed vastly to the poor of the world. As a clown, Chaplin himself is near his best, though as usual there is rather too much straining for pathos.

CIN Rollie Totheroh   MUS Charles Chaplin   ED Harold McGhean (1942 version)

⚐ Max Terr (music)

Golden Balls   ★

DIR Bigas Luna
1993   95m   Spain/France/Italy
DVD

☆ Javier Bardem (Benito González), Maria de Medeiros (Marta), Maribel Verdú (Claudia), Elisa Touati (Rita), Raquel Bianca (Ana), Maria Martin (The producer's wife), Francisco Casares (The producer)

A sex-obsessed Spanish businessman wants to build the biggest skyscraper in Benidorm to honour his alleged virility. But his over-complicated sex life proves a letdown.

No-one could accuse this comedy about male appetites of over-subtlety, but its satirical thrusts are well judged and entertaining.

SCR Cuca Canals, Bigas Luna   CIN José Luis Alcaine
MUS Nicola Piovani   DES Irene Montcada   ED Carmen Frias
DIST UIP/Lolafilms/Ovideo/Filmauro/Hugo/Lumiere

66 The film's heavy-handed symbolism and melodramatic plot just come across as forced. – *Erin Richter, Entertainment Weekly*

'It is the Alethiometer. It tells the truth. As for how to read it, you'll have to learn by yourself.'

The Golden Compass (new)   ★

SCR/DIR Chris Weitz
2007   113m   UK/US
DVD   ♫

☆ Nicole Kidman (Mrs. Coulter), Daniel Craig (Lord Asriel), Dakota Blue Richards (Lyra Belacqua), Sam Elliott (Lee Scoresby), Eva Green (Serafina Pekkala), Tom Courtenay (Farder Coram), Derek Jacobi (Magisterial Emissary)

G

DVD Available on DVD   ☆ Cast in order   66 Critics' Quotes   ⚐ Academy Award   Ⓑ BAFTA
♫ Soundtrack on CD   of importance   † Points of interest   ⚐ Academy Award nomination   Ⓣ BAFTA nomination

255

In a parallel reality, Lyra, a headstrong 12-year-old girl grows up in the confines of an Oxford college. Her uncle goes on a voyage to the North Pole to find other parallel worlds, and Lyra escapes the clutches of her conservative guardian to follow him, and investigate the location of kidnapped children. She is assisted in her quest by an armoured polar bear.

Almost certainly the year's best-looking film – a sumptuous CGI re-creation of Pullman's parallel universe, with its cunning blend of ancient and modern. Yet the intellectual thrust of Pullman's compelling story-telling gets lost in all the special effects, specifically the sceptical attitude towards organised religion and its potential to close minds. Re-invented as a linear action-adventure story without the cerebral underpinning, it feels as if less is at stake. On the plus side, the re-imagining of the daemons, the alter egos of each character, is a tour de force, and the armoured polar bears are genuine show-stoppers.

CIN *Henry Braham* **MUS** Alexandre Desplat **DES** *Dennis Gassner* **ED** *Peter Honess, Anne V. Coates, Kevin Tent* **PROD** Deborah A. Forte, Bill Carraro **DIST** Entertainment

66 Lavish and somewhat loony adaptation of the first book in Philip Pullman's acclaimed fantasy sequence....in truth, The Golden Compass, however sophisticated in design and breathless in plotting, is not a very exciting film. This fairy tale has a super-abundance of good guys. – *Anthony Quinn, Independent*

66 If Darth Vader wore a blond wig, a slinky dress and a dab of Chanel behind each ear, he could hardly be as evil as Nicole Kidman, playing the gorgeous villainess Mrs. Coulter. – *Peter Bradshaw, Guardian*

† Originally planned as the first of three films, each corresponding to a book in Pullman's His Dark Materials trilogy. The Golden Compass cost a reported $180 million, and grossed $70 million in the US, and some $300 million in other territories – a disappointing return for such a huge outlay. Early in 2008, its producing studio New Line was folded into its parent company Warner Bros., and at the time of writing no sequels have been green-lighted.
† Before the film's release, some Catholic groups in the US objected to the story's rejection of organised religion, a strong theme in Pullman's book. 'He wants to sell atheism to kids,' said Bill Donohue, Catholic League president.

⸸ Michael L. Fink, Bill Westenhofer, Ben Morris, Trevor Wood (visual effects)

⸸ Dennis Gassner; Anna Pinnock

Ⓣ Michael L. Fink, Bill Westenhofer, Ben Morris, Trevor Wood (visual effects)

The Golden Door (new) ★★

SCR/DIR *Emanuele Crialese*
2006   118m   Italy/France/Germany
DVD

☆ Charlotte Gainsbourg (Lucy), *Vincenzo Amato* (Salvatore Mancuso), Aurora Quattrocchi (Donna Fortunata), Francesco Casisa (Angelo), Filippo Pucillo (Pietro)

In the early 20th century, a poor Sicilian widower sells all his family's possessions to emigrate to America, a land of plenty. On the voyage they encounter bad weather and terrible living conditions. On arriving in America they are quizzed about their mental and medical suitability to enter the US.

Visually arresting, with a story of mythical, even Biblical dimensions. It is in three acts: the 'sign from God' that the family should emigrate, their troubled sea journey, and the humiliation they undergo to set foot in the New World. The ending manages to be charming, guardedly optimistic and faintly surreal. The presence of Lucy, a genteel young Englishwoman in steerage among desperate peasants, strikes the only false note. Otherwise, another triumph for this talented director.

CIN *Agnès Godard* **MUS** Antonio Castrignano **ED** Maryliune Monthieux **PROD** Alexandre Mallet-Guy, Fabrizio Mosca, Emanuele Crialese **DIST** Optimum

66 The film is touching, imaginative and makes the best of its cash through a minimalist skill that shows Crialese to be a genuinely original director. – *Derek Malcolm, Evening Standard*

66 A timely reminder that economic migrants have long been the backbone of Western civilisation. – *Mark Kermode, Observer*

'No limits. No fears. No substitutes.'

GoldenEye ★★

DIR Martin Campbell
1995   130m   US/ GB
DVD   ♫

☆ Pierce Brosnan (James Bond), Sean Bean (Alec Trevelyan/Janus), Izabella Scorupco (Natalya Fyodorovna Simonova), Famke Janssen (Xenia Zirgavna Onatopp), Joe Don Baker (Jack Wade), Judi Dench (M), Robbie Coltrane (Valentin Dmitrovich Zukovsky), Tcheky Karyo (Defense Minister Dmitri Mishkin), Gottfried John (General Arkady Grigorovich Ourumov), Alan Cumming (Boris Grishenko), Desmond Llewelyn (Q), Samantha Bond (Miss Moneypenny), Michael Kitchen (Bill Tanner)

James Bond goes to Russia to defeat a sinister villain with an awesome space weapon capable of global destruction.

The audience-tested assembly-line formula (stunts, girls, chases, action, knowing quips) remains unchanged. Brosnan makes a competent debut as Bond – suave, if vaguely stiff. Judi Dench's appearance as the first female M is little more than a distraction. But there's nothing here to disturb the equilibrium of this interminable money-machine franchise.

SCR Jeffrey Caine, Bruce Feirstein **CIN** Phil Meheux **MUS** Eric Serra **DES** Peter Lamont **ED** Terry Rawlings **PROD** Michael G. Wilson, Barbara Broccoli **DIST** UIP/United Artists/Danjaq/Eon

66 It isn't a great movie, but it's great, preposterous fun. – *Hal Hinson, Washington Post*

66 Most crucially, Brosnan makes the grade as 007. He handles the action capably and gets the standard quips out in a commendably straightforward way that's wry but not dismissive. – *Todd McCarthy, Variety*

Ⓣ Chris Corbould, Derek Meddings, Brian Smithies (special effects); Jim Shields, David John, Graham V. Hartstone, John Hayward, Michael A. Carter (sound)

'James Bond 007 Back In Action!'

Goldfinger ★★★

DIR *Guy Hamilton*

1964   112m   GB

DVD ♫

☆ *Sean Connery* (James Bond), *Honor Blackman* (Pussy Galore), Gert Frobe (Goldfinger), Harold Sakata (Oddjob), Shirley Eaton (Jill Masterson), Bernard Lee ('M'), Lois Maxwell (Moneypenny), Desmond Llewelyn ('Q')

James Bond prevents an international gold smuggler from robbing Fort Knox.

Lively, amusing, extravagantly budgeted Bond spy caper, with a more coherent plot than usual between action sequences.

SCR *Richard Maibaum, Paul Dehn*   CIN *Ted Moore*
MUS *John Barry*   DES *Ken Adam*   ED *Peter Hunt*
PROD *Harry Saltzman, Albert R. Broccoli*   DIST UA/Eon

66 A dazzling object lesson in the principle that nothing succeeds like excess. – *Penelope Gilliatt*

66 A diverting comic strip for grown-ups. – *Judith Crist*

'Everyone wants the truth. Until they find it.'

Gone Baby Gone (new) ★★★

DIR *Ben Affleck*

2007   113m   US

DVD

☆ *Casey Affleck* (Patrick Kenzie), Michelle Monaghan (Angie Gennaro), *Amy Ryan* (Helene McCready), Ed Harris (Remy Bressant), Morgan Freeman (Captain Jack Doyle), John Ashton (Nick Poole), Amy Madigan (Bea McCready), *Titus Welliver* (Lionel McCready)

When a young girl, the daughter of a dissolute single mother, goes missing from a working-class Boston suburb, her family, distrustful of the police's efforts, hire two private investigators to trace her.

Moody, taut crime thriller, and a promising directing debut by Ben Affleck, who keeps his splendid cast on a tight rein and skilfully conveys a strong sense of place and milieu. The going's great until the melodramatic last act, which is burdened by complex moral dilemmas.

SCR Ben Affleck, Aaron Stockard   CIN *John Toll*
MUS Harry Gregson-Williams   DES Sharon Seymour
ED William Goldenberg   PROD Alan Ladd Jr., Dan Rissner, Sean Bailey   DIST Buena Vista Intl.

66 An atmospheric and richly textured procedural. – *Sukhdev Sandhu, Daily Telegraph*

66 In some way superior to Scorsese's not dissimilar The Departed, Gone Baby Gone is a compelling film, the dynamic action sequences alternating with contemplative moments. – *Philip French, Observer*

† The film's UK release was postponed for six months because of its story's superficial resemblance to a hugely publicised real-life story: the kidnap of a four year old British girl, Madeline McCann, while she was holidaying with her parents in May 2007.

† Novelist Lehane also wrote Mystic River, another story set in working-class Boston that was adapted for film.

⌐ Amy Ryan (supporting actress)

'The most magnificent picture ever!'

Gone with the Wind ★★★★

DIR *Victor Fleming (and George Cukor, Sam Wood)*

1939   220m   US

DVD

☆ *Clark Gable* (Rhett Butler), *Vivien Leigh* (Scarlet O'Hara), Olivia de Havilland (Melanie Hamilton), Leslie Howard (Ashley Wilkes), Thomas Mitchell (Gerald O'Hara), Barbara O'Neil (Ellen O'Hara), *Hattie McDaniel* (Mammy), *Butterfly McQueen*, Victor Jory, Evelyn Keyes, Ann Rutherford, Laura Hope Crews, Harry Davenport, Jane Darwell, Ona Munson, Ward Bond

An egotistic Southern girl survives the Civil War but finally loses the only man she cares for.

The only film in history which could be profitably revived for half a century. Whole books have been written about it; in essence, its appeal is that of a romantic story with strong characters and an impeccable production.

SCR *Sidney Howard (and others)*   CIN *Ernest Haller, Ray Rennahan*   MUS *Max Steiner*   DES *William Cameron Menzies*   ED Hal C. Kern, James E. Newcom
PROD *David O. Selznick*   DIST MGM/Selznick International

66 A major event in the history of the industry but only a minor event in motion picture art. There are moments when the two categories meet on good terms, but the long stretches between are filled with mere spectacular efficiency. – *Franz Hoellering, The Nation*

66 Forget it, Louis, no Civil War picture ever made a nickel. – *Irving Thalberg to Louis B. Mayer, 1936*

† The best account of the film's making is in Gavin Lambert's 1975 book, GWTW

† In the early 1970s a stage musical version toured the world, with music by Harold Rome.

⌐ picture; Vivien Leigh (leading actress); Hattie McDaniel (supporting actress); Victor Fleming; Sidney Howard (original screenplay); Ernest Haller, Ray Rennahan (cinematography); Lyle Wheeler (art direction); Hal C. Kern, James E. Newcom (film editing); William Cameron Menzies (special award)

⌐ Clark Gable (leading actor); Olivia de Havilland (supporting actress); Max Steiner (music); special effects

---

The Good, the Bad and the Ugly ★★★

DIR *Sergio Leone*

1966   180m   Italy

DVD ♫

☆ Clint Eastwood (Joe), Eli Wallach (Tuco), Lee Van Cleef (Setenza), Luigi Pistilli (Father Pablo Ramirez), Rada Rassimov (Maria), Antonio Casas (Stevens)

During the American Civil War, three men seek hidden loot.

The last and most assured of Leone's 'spaghetti Western' trilogy starring Eastwood, this introduces a routine plot – mercenaries hunting money – and sets it against the murderous slaughter of the Civil War. Leone had been ratcheting up the emotional impact of his narratives as his trilogy progressed, and this one concludes with a sensational, widely admired three-way shoot-out in a cemetery.

SCR Age Scarpelli, Luciano Vincenzoni, Sergio Leone
CIN Tonino delli Colli   **MUS** *Ennio Morricone*
ED Eugenio Alabiso, Nino Baragli   **PROD** Alberto Grimaldi   **DIST** PEA

66 The most expensive, pious and repellent movie in the history of its peculiar genre. – *Renata Adler, New York Times*

66 A curious amalgam of the visually striking, the dramatically feeble and the offensively sadistic. – *Variety*

'The German Democratic Republic lives on – in 79 square meters!'

Good Bye, Lenin!   ★★

DIR Wolfgang Becker

2003   121m   Germany

DVD   ♫

☆ *Daniel Bruehl* (Alex), Katrin Sass (Christiane Kerner), Maria Simon (Ariane), Chulpan Khamatova (Lara), Florian Lukas (Denis), Alexander Beyer (Rainer), Burghard Klaussner (Robert Kerner), Michael Gwisdek (Principal Dr Klapprath)

A young Berliner, whose mother has just awakened from a coma in 1989, pretends that that her beloved East Germany still exists to protect her from the shock.

An appealingly bittersweet satire about the German inclination towards 'Ostalgie' – a kind of sentimental longing for its communist past. The re-creations of décor and even fake news broadcasts, all to conserve a mother's delicate health, raise a lot of smiles.

SCR Bernd Lichtenberg, Wolfgang Becker   **CIN** Martin Kukula   **MUS** *Yann Tiersen*   **DES** Lothar Holler
ED Peter R. Adam   **PROD** Stefan Arndt, Katja De Bock, Andreas Schreitmüller   **DIST** UGC

66 Funny but not a comedy, serious but never overbearing. – *Kenneth Turan, Los Angeles Times*

66 A remarkable film that makes you laugh and leaves you thinking. – *Philip French, Observer*

ⓣ film not in the English Language

'If war is hell, then what comes after?'

The Good German   ★

DIR Steven Soderbergh

2006   107m   US

DVD   ♫

☆ George Clooney (Jake Geismer), Cate Blanchett (Lena Brandt), Tobey Maguire (Tully), Beau Bridges (Colonel Muller), Tony Curran (Danny), Jack Thompson (Congressman Breimer)

A US war correspondent arrives in Berlin in 1945 to cover the Potsdam Conference, and reunites with a woman who was his pre-war lover.

Soderbergh conceived this as a tribute to 1940s classics like Casablanca and The Maltese Falcon, using back projections, boom mikes and vintage lenses on a single camera, thus re-creating shooting conditions of the period. It's an impressive exercise in style, but Attanasio's script fails to measure up. Each of the story's

three acts is introduced by a different character (morally confused Jake, innocent-looking but vicious Tully, femme fatale Lena) and its emotional centre is hard to locate. It looks gorgeous: all dark, expressionistic shadows in Berlin's post-war rubble; but the actors look lost, and it's hard to care about or engage with any of them.

SCR Paul Attanasio   **CIN** Peter Andrews   **MUS** Thomas Newman   **DES** Philip Messina   **ED** Mary Ann Bernard
PROD Ben Cosgrove, Gregory Jacobs   **DIST** Warner Bros.

66 A prime example of a movie made by highly skilled and intelligent film-makers that nevertheless seems misguided from the get-go. – *Peter Rainer, Christian Science Monitor*

66 Soderbergh has tried to resurrect the magic of classical Hollywood, principally by sucking all the air, energy and pleasure from his own film-making. – *Manohla Dargis, New York Times*

† Steven Soderbergh edited and photographed the film, using two pseudonyms.

♪ Thomas Newman (music, original score)

'True love is a blessing and a curse. She's the blessing. He's cursed.'

Good Luck Chuck ⓝⓔⓦ

DIR Mark Helfrich

2007   99m   US/Canada

DVD   ♫

☆ Dane Cook (Charlie), Jessica Alba (Cam Wexler), Dan Fogler (Stu), Ellia English (Reba), Lonny Ross (Joe), Chelan Simmons (Carol), Jodie Stewart (Eleanor Skipple)

A bachelor whose one-night stands all find true love with their next partner faces a quandary when he falls in love himself with an accident-prone penguin keeper.

A sex comedy that manages to be crass, coarse, misogynist and puerile, even when it is trying to be charming.

SCR Josh Stolberg   **CIN** Anthony B. Richmond
MUS Aaron Zigman   **DES** Mark Freeborn   **ED** Julia Wong   **PROD** Mike Karz, Barry Katz, Brian Volk-Weiss
DIST Lionsgate

66 The dirty movie of the year, slimy and scummy. – *Roger Ebert, Chicago Sun-Times*

66 Cross the street to avoid this one. Cross a dual carriageway. Cross the Limpopo. – *Peter Bradshaw, Guardian*

Good Morning, Night   ★★

SCR/DIR Marco Bellocchio

2003   106m   Italy

DVD

☆ Maya Sansa (Chiara), Luigi Lo Cascio (Mariano), Roberto Herlitzka (Aldo Moro), Paolo Briguglia (Enzo), Pier Giorgio Bellocchio (Ernesto), Giovanni Calcagno (Primo)

A female member of an Italian communist group guards the leading politician they have kidnapped.

Sober, unsensationalistic account of Aldo Moro's abduction in 1978, which grapples thoughtfully with the tragic flaws in revolutionary ideology.

CIN Pasquale Mari   MUS Riccardo Giagni   DES Marco Dentici   ED Francesca Calvelli   PROD Marco Bellocchio, Sergio Pelone

66 A curious mixture of obliqueness and intensity. – *Dana Stevens, New York Times*

'Time to rock it from the Delta to the DMZ!'

Good Morning, Vietnam ★

DIR Barry Levinson
1987   121m   US
DVD ♫

☆ Robin Williams (Adrian Cronauer), Forest Whitaker (Edward Garlick), Tung Thanh Tran (Tuan), Chintara Sukapatana (Trinh), Bruno Kirby (Lt. Steven Hauk)

A loose-cannon DJ shakes things up when he's given an slot on US Armed Forces Radio in Saigon.

Entertaining if glib vehicle for Williams's frenzied improvisations; his character's disillusionment with the American war effort is less convincing.

SCR Mitch Markowitz   CIN Peter Sova   MUS Alex North   DES Roy Walker   PROD Mark Johnson, Larry Brezner   DIST Touchstone

66 Williams' potshots rattle off faster than an M-16. – *Duane Byrne, Hollywood Reporter*

⚱ Robin Williams (leading actor)

Ⓣ Robin Williams (leading actor); Bill Phillips, Clive Winter, Terry Porter (sound)

'Dreaming is believing.'

The Good Night (new)

SCR/DIR Jake Paltrow
2007   93m   US/UK/Germany
♫

☆ Penelope Cruz (Anna/Melodia), Martin Freeman (Gary), Gwyneth Paltrow (Dora), Simon Pegg (Paul), Danny DeVito (Mel), Michael Gambon (Alan Weigert)

An unhappily married musician falls in love with an exotic beauty he can only see in his dreams.

Downbeat, metaphysical comedy in the Charlie Kaufman vein; all concerned seem oddly subdued.

CIN Giles Nuttgens   MUS Alec Puro   DES Eve Stewart   ED Rick Lawley   PROD Donna Gigliotti, Bill Johnson   DIST Momentum

66 Derivative, tonally uncertain and often misjudged. – *Peter Bradshaw, Guardian*

66 As becalmed and refreshing as a good night's sleep. – *Justin Chang, Variety*

† The director is Gwyneth Paltrow's younger brother.

'We will not walk in fear of one another.'

Good Night, and Good Luck ★★

DIR George Clooney
2005   93m   US/France/GB
DVD ♫

☆ *David Strathairn* (Edward R. Murrow), Patricia Clarkson (Shirley Wershba), George Clooney (Fred Friendly), Jeff Daniels (Sig Mickelson), Robert Downey Jnr (Joe Wershba), *Frank Langella* (William Paley), *Ray Wise* (Don Hollenbeck), Dianne Reeves (Jazz Singer)

In 1954, CBS news journalist Edward R. Murrow and his team take on the right-wing scare-mongering of Senator Joseph McCarthy.

Finely-made and acted encomium to a more principled age of journalism, intoning dire warnings about the trivialisation of our mass media. Its liberal credentials are impeccable, and its hero worthy of tribute; but there's a sense that Clooney and company are clapping themselves on the back, too.

SCR George Clooney, Grant Heslov   CIN Robert Elswit   DES James Bissell   ED Stephen Mirrione   PROD Grant Heslov   DIST Redbus

66 Passionate, serious, impeccably crafted movie tackling a subject Clooney cares about deeply: the duty of journalism to speak truth to power. – *David Ansen, Newsweek*

66 It all has a slightly inert, docudrama quality. – *Peter Bradshaw, Guardian*

⚱ picture; David Strathairn (leading actor); George Clooney; George Clooney, Grant Heslov (original screenplay); Robert Elswit; James Bissell

Ⓣ film; David Strathairn (leading actor); George Clooney (supporting actor); George Clooney; George Clooney, Grant Heslov (original screenplay); Stephen Mirrione

---

'Edward Wilson loved America, and he would sacrifice everything he loved to protect it.'

The Good Shepherd ★★★

DIR Robert De Niro
2006   166m   US
DVD ♫

☆ Matt Damon (Edward Wilson), Angelina Jolie (Margaret 'Clover' Russell), Alec Baldwin (Sam Murach), Billy Crudup (Arch Cummings), Robert De Niro (General Bill Sullivan), Michael Gambon (Dr. Fredericks), William Hurt (Philip Allen), Timothy Hutton (Thomas Wilson), Joe Pesci (Joseph Palmi)

Edward Wilson, a Yale graduate, enters the intelligence business during World War II and stays with the CIA through the early days of the Cold War right up to the Bay of Pigs incident, aimed at toppling Fidel Castro.

An assiduous, detailed film with a director who can hold his nerve: De Niro makes no concessions to making any characters likable. Indeed, its 'hero' Wilson is closed-off, unemotional and unknowable: the perfect CIA operative. Damon plays him with almost heroic restraint. Much of the film deals with the dull, unglamorous side of espionage: men sitting at desks, trying to break codes or analyse intelligence. That this is realistic does not make the film more enjoyable. But it's a riveting insight into a world that civilians might prefer to know little about.

SCR Eric Roth   CIN Robert Richardson   MUS Marcelo Zarvos, Bruce Fowler   DES Jeannine Oppenwall   ED Tariq Anwar   PROD James G. Robinson, Jane Rosenthal, Robert De Niro   DIST Universal

CLOVER (TO EDWARD): 'You don't say very much, do you?'

66 Not a film everyone will like. But those who do will appreciate De Niro's insistence on accurate detail. – *Derek Malcolm, Evening Standard*

DVD Available on DVD   ☆ Cast in order of importance   66 Critics' Quotes   † Points of interest   ⚱ Academy Award   ⚱ Academy Award nomination   Ⓣ BAFTA   Ⓣ BAFTA nomination

G

259

66 It's a film for fans of John le Carré rather than Ian Fleming. – *Nicholas Barber, Independent on Sunday*

⚱ Jeannine Oppenwall, Gretchen Rau, Leslie E. Rollins (art direction)

'He doesn't want money. He wants what money can't buy.'

The Good Thief ★★

SCR/DIR Neil Jordan

2002 108m GB/France/Ireland

DVD ♫

☆ *Nick Nolte* (Bob), Tcheky Karyo (Roger), Said Taghmaoui (Paulo), Gerard Darmon (Raoul), Emir Kusturica (Vladimir), Marc Lavoine (Remi), Ouassini Embarek (Said)

In Nice, an American thief, gambler and drug addict signs up to take part in a casino heist, and rescues a teenage girl from prostitution before going cold turkey to concentrate on the robbery.

Jordan came in for a lot of snobbish sniping merely for attempting a re-make of Jean-Pierre Melville's Bob Le Flambeur, but in truth it's pretty good – largely because Nolte is quite wonderful in the title role, as a man who has been around the block enough times to know the value, and beauty of incidental kindnesses. It may not be as good as the original, but it isn't negligible, either.

CIN Chris Menges MUS Elliot Goldenthal
DES Anthony Pratt ED Tony Lawson PROD Stephen Woolley, John Wells, Seaton McLean DIST Momentum

66 Nolte's gambler-bandit Bob Montagnet is a triumph of imagination, touched with electric existential poetry. – *Michael Sragow, Baltimore Sun*

66 Bob is a marvellous creation–a faker who is also the genuine article. He's the perfect hero for a movie about the world as one big scam. – *Peter Rainer, New York Magazine*

'Some people can never believe in themselves, until someone believes in them.'

Good Will Hunting ★★

DIR Gus Van Sant

1997 126m US

DVD ♫

☆ Matt Damon (Will Hunting), Robin Williams (Sean Maguire), Ben Affleck (Chuckie Sullivan), Minnie Driver (Skylar), Stellan Skarsgard (Prof. Gerald Lambeau), Casey Affleck (Morgan O'Mally), Cole Hauser (Billy McBride)

A troubled maths genius working as a janitor tries to turn his life around with the help of a kindly psychologist.

A cannily packaged self-help story, written by two young stars desperate to get a leg up, and handled smoothly by a director with his own sights on the mainstream. It's commercial schmaltz in indie clothing, but it wears it well.

SCR Matt Damon, Ben Affleck CIN Jean Yves Escoffier
MUS Danny Elfman DES Melissa Stewart ED Pietro Scalia PROD Lawrence Bender DIST Miramax

66 Stuffed – indeed, overstuffed – with heart, soul, audacity and blarney. – *Owen Gleiberman, Entertainment Weekly*

66 Schematic, predictable and somewhat tedious. – *Alexander Walker, Evening Standard*

† William Goldman was widely rumoured to have rewritten the script extensively, but denied this in his memoir Which Lie Did I Tell?

⚱ Robin Williams (supporting actor); Matt Damon, Ben Affleck (original screenplay)

⚱ picture; Matt Damon (leading actor); Minnie Driver (supporting actress); Gus Van Sant; Pietro Scalia; Danny Elfman (music, original score); Elliott Smith (music, original song – Miss Misery)

Goodbye Charlie Bright ★

DIR Nick Love

2001 87m GB

DVD ♫

☆ Paul Nicholls (Charlie), Roland Manookian (Justin), Phil Daniels (Eddie), Jamie Foreman (Tony Immaculate), Danny Dyer (Francis), Dani Behr (Blondie), Richard Driscoll (Hector), David Thewlis (Charlie's dad), Alexis Rodney (Damien), Sid Mitchell (Tommy), Frank Harper (Tommy's dad)

Two delinquent pals on a South London housing estate find their paths diverging one hot summer.

Small but sparky debut owing a debt to Mean Streets, and providing a good sense of the boredom underlying random acts of hooliganism.

SCR Nick Love, Dominic Eames CIN Tony Imi
MUS Ivor Guest DES Eve Stewart ED Patrick Moore
PROD Charles Steel, Lisa Bryer DIST Metrodome

66 An excellent cast, fluid direction and perceptive writing make it rattle persuasively. – *Alexander Walker, Evening Standard*

Goodbye Mr Chips ★★★

DIR Sam Wood

1939 114m GB

DVD

☆ *Robert Donat* (Charles Chipping), *Greer Garson* (Katherine Ellis), *Paul Henreid* (Max Staefel), Lyn Harding (Dr. Wetherby), Austin Trevor (Ralston), Terry Kilburn (John/Peter Colley), John Mills (Peter Colley as a young man), Milton Rosmer (Charteris), Judith Furse (Flora)

The life of a shy, beloved schoolmaster, from his first job to his death.

Sentimental romance in MGM's best style, a long-standing favourite for its performances and humour. It now feels very dated, though it is always welcome to hear of teaching praised as vocational. Donat does a tricky job splendidly, ageing 60 years from callow youth to wrinkly veteran.

SCR R. C. Sherriff, Claudine West, Eric Maschwitz
CIN Frederick A. Young MUS Richard Addinsell
ED Charles Frend PROD Victor Saville DIST MGM

66 Charming, quaintly sophisticated . . . more for the big situations than the smaller towns. – *Variety*

66 The whole picture has an assurance, bears a glow of popularity like the face of a successful candidate on election day. And it is wrong to despise popularity in the cinema. – *Graham Greene*

⚱ Robert Donat (leading actor)

---

picture; Greer Garson (leading actress); Sam Wood; Eric Maschwitz, R. C. Sherriff, Claudine West (original screenplay); Charles Frend (editing)

'Three Decades of Life in the Mafia.'

Goodfellas ★★★★

DIR *Martin Scorsese*
1990 146m US
[DVD] ♫

☆ Robert De Niro (James Conway), *Ray Liotta* (Henry Hill), *Joe Pesci* (Tommy DeVito), Lorraine Bracco (Karen Hill), Paul Sorvino (Paul Cicero), Frank Sivero (Frankie Carbone), Tony Darrow (Sonny Bunz), Mike Starr (Frenchy), Frank Vincent (Billy Batts), Chuck Low (Morris Kessler)

A Brooklyn boy works his way up the mafia hierarchy, until everything goes sour.

A scorching saga of criminality run amok, dictating every handshake and tainting every relationship. Cinematically it is lethal and seductive, drawing us into the evilly glamorous embrace of the mob lifestyle – but, like, Faust, these characters have hell to pay.

SCR Martin Scorsese, Nicholas Pileggi **CIN** *Michael Ballhaus* **DES** Kristi Zea **ED** *Thelma Schoonmaker, James Kwei* **PROD** Irwin Winkler **DIST** Warner

66 An incredible, relentless experience about the single-minded pursuit of crime. – *Desson Thomson, Washington Post*

66 Is it a great movie? I don't think so. But it's a triumphant piece of filmmaking – journalism presented with the brio of drama. – *Pauline Kael, New Yorker*

† More than a decade later, no less than 22 members of the cast would be featured in the acclaimed Mob-themed TV series The Sopranos.

⚲ Joe Pesci (supporting actor)
⚲ picture; Lorraine Bracco (supporting actress); Martin Scorsese; Martin Scorsese, Nicholas Pileggi (adapted screenplay); Thelma Schoonmaker
🛡 film; Martin Scorsese; Martin Scorsese, Nicholas Pileggi (adapted screenplay); Thelma Schoonmaker; Robert Bruno (costume design)
Ⓣ Robert De Niro (leading actor); Michael Ballhaus

'In a land of beauty, wonder and danger, she would follow a dream, fall in love and risk her life to save the mountain gorillas from extinction.'

Gorillas in the Mist ★

DIR Michael Apted
1988 129m US
[DVD] ♫

☆ *Sigourney Weaver* (Dian Fossey), Bryan Brown (Bob Campbell), Julie Harris (Roz Carr), John Omirah Miluwi (Sembagare), Iain Cuthbertson (Dr. Louis Leakey), Constantin Alexandrov (Van Veeten), Waigwa Wachira (Mukara), Iain Glen (Brendan), David Lansbury (Larry)

A ruthless naturalist forms a lifelong attachment to gorillas, but provokes the enmity of her colleagues.

A dutiful biopic which can't make much sense of Fossey's sudden murder; the exceptional Weaver, though, is reason enough to see it.

SCR Anna Hamilton Phelan **CIN** John Seale

MUS Maurice Jarre **DES** John Graysmark **ED** Stuart Baird **PROD** Arnold Glimcher, Terence Clegg
DIST UIP/Warner

66 Can't be taken seriously. It's a feminist version of King Kong. – *Pauline Kael, New Yorker*

⚲ Sigourney Weaver (leading actress); Anna Hamilton Phelan (adapted screenplay); Stuart Baird; Maurice Jarre; Andy Nelson, Brian Saunders, Peter Handford (sound)
Ⓣ John Seale

'Tea At Four. Dinner At Eight. Murder By Midnight.'

Gosford Park ★★★★

DIR *Robert Altman*
2001 137m US/GB
[DVD] ♫

☆ Eileen Atkins (Mrs Croft), *Michael Gambon* (Sir William McCordle), *Jeremy Northam* (Ivor Novello), Clive Owen (Robert Parks), Bob Balaban (Morris Weissman), *Maggie Smith* (Constance, Countess of Trentham), Ryan Phillippe (Henry Denton), Alan Bates (Jennings), *Helen Mirren* (Mrs Wilson), Kelly Macdonald (Mary Maceachran), Richard E. Grant (George), Tom Hollander (Lt Commander Anthony Meredith), *Kristin Scott Thomas* (Lady Sylvia McCordle), *Emily Watson* (Elsie), James Wilby (The Hon. Freddie Nesbitt), Derek Jacobi (Probert), Geraldine Somerville (Louisa, Lady Stockbridge), Sophie Thompson (Dorothy), Camilla Rutherford (Isobel McCordle), Claudie Blakley (Mabel Nesbitt), Stephen Fry (Inspector Thompson), Ron Webster (Constable Dexter)

An assortment of guests and servants at a country house in the 1930s come under suspicion when their host is murdered.

Sparkling upstairs-downstairs ensemble piece, a return to Altman's observational best, with the bon mots flying back and forth irresistibly from an astounding British cast; the routine murder-mystery plot is little more than an excuse to round them all up.

SCR *Julian Fellowes* **CIN** Andrew Dunn **MUS** Patrick Doyle **DES** Stephen Altman **ED** *Tim Squyres*
PROD Robert Altman, Bob Balaban, David Levy
DIST Entertainment

66 Highly entertaining. . .But there is not much of a point; the class system is airily undisturbed, and class motivation is pretty cursory both for the rich man at his castle and the poor man at his gate. – *Peter Bradshaw, Guardian*

⚲ Julian Fellowes (original screenplay)
⚲ picture; Helen Mirren (supporting actress); Maggie Smith (supporting actress); Robert Altman; Stephen Altman; Jenny Beavan (costume design)
🛡 British film; Jenny Beavan (costume design)
Ⓣ Helen Mirren (supporting actress); Maggie Smith (supporting actress); Robert Altman; Julian Fellowes (original screenplay); Stephen Altman; Sallie Jaye, Jan Archibald (make up/hair)

The Gospel According to St Matthew ★★★

SCR/DIR Pier Paolo Pasolini
1964 142m Italy/France
[DVD]

☆ Enrique Irazoqui (Jesus Christ), Susanna Pasolini (Mary, as a woman), Mario Socrate (John the Baptist),

[DVD] Available on DVD ☆ Cast in order of importance 66 Critics' Quotes † Points of interest ⚲ Academy Award ⚲ Academy Award nomination 🛡 BAFTA Ⓣ BAFTA nomination
♫ Soundtrack on CD

Margherita Caruso (Mary, as a girl), Marcello Morante (Joseph), Settimo Di Porto (Peter), Otello Sestili (Judas)

The life of Christ seen almost as a ciné-vérité documentary.

The tone is realist, not notably iconoclastic, though it does present Christ as a rebel – a treatment that suited its time, the dawn of 1960s counter-culture. Eschewing crowd scenes and spectacle, it remains one of the most serious-minded versions of Christ's life committed to film.

CIN Tonino delli Colli   MUS Bach, Mozart, Prokofiev, Webern   ED Nino Baragli   PROD Alfredo Bini   DIST Arco/Lux

♟ Luis Enrique Bacalov (music); Luigi Scaccianoce (art direction); Danilo Donati (costume design)

The Governess ★★

SCR/DIR Sandra Goldbacher
1997   115m   GB/France
DVD ♫

☆ Minnie Driver (Rosina da Silva), Tom Wilkinson (Mr. Charles Cavendish), Harriet Walter (Mrs. Cavendish), Florence Hoath (Clementina Cavendish), Bruce Myers (Rosina's Father), Jonathan Rhys Meyers (Henry Cavendish), Arlene Cockburn (Lily Milk, the Maid), Emma Bird (Rebecca)

In the 1840s, a young London woman leaves her newly impoverished family. She becomes a governess on a remote Scottish island, where she feels the need to disguise her ethnicity, and embarks on a discreet affair with her employer.

Rather better than some of the unsavoury British reviews at the time of its release suggested; Goldbacher has a real talent for arresting imagery, and her script, which admittedly has a few loose ends, has plenty to say about the suppression of identity. There's also an agreeable sub-text about the early days of the photographer's art, which complements the film's handsome appearance.

CIN Ashley Rowe   MUS Edward Shearmur   DES Sarah Greenwood   ED Isabel Lorente   PROD Sarah Curtis   DIST Alliance/Pandora/Parallax

❝ Because the cinematography of The Governess is so richly panoramic, the movie forces you to contemplate the emotional power exerted by film. – *Stephen Holden, New York Times*

❝ The film, despite some over-obvious stretches, is mostly sad, lovely, moving, haunting. It's a striking and promising debut from a fine new filmmaker. – *Michael Wilmington, Chicago Tribune*

'For years her songs brought fame to other people. Then she found her own voice.'

Grace of My Heart ★★★

SCR/DIR Allison Anders
1996   116m   US
DVD ♫

☆ *Illeana Douglas* (Denise Waverly/Edna Buxton), John Turturro (Joel Millner), Eric Stoltz (Howard Cazsatt), Patsy Kensit (Cheryl Steed), Bridget Fonda (Kelly Porter), Matt Dillon (Jay Phillips), Bruce Davison (John Murray),

Lucinda Jenney (Marion), Jennifer Leigh Warren (Doris Shelley), Christina Pickles (Mrs. Buxton)

An aspiring singer in the 1950s and 1960s is rejected by the recording industry, but becomes a successful songwriter for others.

Bouncy and exuberant pop portrait loosely based on the story of Carole King, and giving an underused actress the part of her career.

CIN Jean-Yves Escoffier   MUS Larry Klein, Elvis Costello, Burt Bacharach   DES François Seguin   ED Thelma Schoonmaker, James Kwei, Harvey Rosenstock   PROD Ruth Charny, Daniel Hassid   DIST Universal/Gramercy/Cappa

❝ Works as a musical in its own right, and as history and critique of the pop process. – *Derek Adams, Time Out*

† Illeana Douglas's singing is dubbed by Kristen Vigard.
† Matt Dillon's character is clearly based on Beach Boy Brian Wilson, while Bridget Fonda is playing a version of singer-songwriter Lesley Gore.

'This is Benjamin . . . he's a little worried about his future!'

The Graduate ★★★★

DIR *Mike Nichols*
1967   105m   US
DVD ♫

☆ *Dustin Hoffman* (Ben Braddock), *Anne Bancroft* (Mrs Robinson), Katharine Ross (Elaine Robinson), Murray Hamilton (Mr Robinson), William Daniels (Mr Maguire), Elizabeth Wilson (Mrs Braddock), Richard Dreyfuss (Student)

A young California man from a wealthy family, recently graduated, has no idea what to do with his life or how to meet his parent's expectations He is led into an affair with an older woman, the wife of his father's best friend, then falls in love with her daughter.

Richly reflecting the disenchanted, anti-careerist mood of young people in the late sixties, this lushly-filmed sex comedy, surprisingly faithful to its excellent, concise source novel, opened a few new doors, looked ravishing, was well acted and had a popular music score. It also conferred instant stardom on Hoffman, who was older than his character: he was 30 when it opened. A comedy of its time, it has also stood the test of time.

SCR Calder Willingham, Buck Henry   CIN *Robert Surtees*   MUS Dave Grusin   DES *Richard Sylbert*   ED Sam O'Steen   PROD Lawrence Turman   DIST UA/Embassy

BENJAMIN: Mrs Robinson, if you don't mind my saying so, this conversation is getting a little strange.

❝ Seeing The Graduate is a bit like having one's most brilliant friend to dinner, watching him become more witty and animated with every moment, and then becoming aware that what one may really be witnessing is the onset of a nervous breakdown. – *Renata Adler*

❝ Yes, there are weaknesses . . . But in cinematic skill, in intent, in sheer connection with us, The Graduate is a milestone in American film history. – *Stanley Kauffmann*

♟ Mike Nichols
♟ best picture; Calder Willingham, Buck Henry (adapted screenplay); Robert Surtees; Dustin Hoffman (leading actor); Anne Bancroft (leading actress); Katharine Ross (supporting actress)

picture; Mike Nichols; Calder Willingham , Buck Henry (screenplay); Dustin Hoffman

'In the 1980's, director Lawrence Kasdan brought you "The Big Chill". Welcome to the 90's.'

Grand Canyon ★

DIR Lawrence Kasdan

1991   134m   US

[DVD] ♫

☆ Danny Glover (Simon), Kevin Kline (Mack), Steve Martin (Davis), Mary McDonnell (Claire), Mary-Louise Parker (Dee), Alfre Woodard (Jane)

A white lawyer in Los Angeles is narrowly rescued from a car-jacking by the arrival of a black tow-truck driver, and they form a friendship.

Earnest panoramic drama about social and racial divides, but one which betrays much more interest in the haves than have-nots, giving it a paranoid and reactionary tone. The plotting is haphazard and the points diffuse.

SCR Meg and Lawrence Kasdan   CIN Owen Roizman   MUS James Newton Howard   DES Bo Welch   ED Carol Littleton   PROD Lawrence Kasdan, Charles Okun, Michael Grillo   DIST TCF

66 If this disaster-packed parable often smacks of melodramatic contrivance, it does at least benefit from solid performances and direction, and a leavening line in sardonic humour. – *Geoff Andrew, Time Out*

⚱ Meg and Lawrence Kasdan (original screenplay)

'It's better to burn out than to fade away.'

Grand Theft Parsons ★

DIR David Caffrey

2003   88m   GB/US

[DVD] ♫

☆ Johnny Knoxville (Phil Kaufman), Gabriel Macht (Gram Parsons), Marley Shelton (Susie), Christina Applegate (Barbara), *Michael Shannon* (Larry Oster-Berg), *Robert Forster* (Stanley Parsons)

A country singer's corpse is stolen by his road manager in 1973 and driven out into the Mojave Desert to be cremated.

Low-budget retro road movie, based on the real-life burial of Gram Parsons, that manages a scrappy charm.

SCR Jeremy Drysdale   CIN Robert Hayes   MUS Richard Mitchell   DES Bryce Holtshousen   ED Mary Finlay, Alan Roberts   PROD Frank Mannion   DIST Redbus

66 Doesn't live up to the wondrous craziness of the legend. – *Nicholas Barber, Independent on Sunday*

La Grande Illusion ★★★★

DIR *Jean Renoir*

1937   117m   France

[DVD]

☆ *Pierre Fresnay* (Capt de Boeldieu), *Erich von Stroheim* (Von Raffenstein), *Jean Gabin* (Marechal), Julien Carette (Cartier), Marcel Dalio (Rosenthal), Gaston Modot (Surveyor), Jean Dasté (Teacher), Dita Parlo (Peasant woman)

During World War I, three captured French pilots have an uneasy relationship with their German commandant.

Celebrated mood piece, long regarded as an al-time classic of cinema, with much to say about war and mankind; more precisely, it is impeccably acted and directed, and has real tragic force.

SCR *Jean Renoir, Charles Spaak*   CIN Christian Matras   MUS Joseph Kosma   ED Marguerite Renoir, Marthe Huguet   PROD Frank Rollmer, Albert Pinkovitch   DIST Réalisations d'Art Cinématographique

66 The story is true. It was told to me by my friends in the war. . .notably by Pinsard who flew fighter planes. I was in the reconnaissance squadron. He saved my life many times when the German fighters became too persistent. He himself was shot down seven times. His escapes are the basis for the story. – *Jean Renoir*

66 Artistically masterful. – *Variety*

⚱ picture

'The thousands who have read the book will know why WE WILL NOT SELL ANY CHILDREN TICKETS to see this picture!'

The Grapes of Wrath ★★★★

DIR *John Ford*

1940   128m   US

[DVD]

☆ *Henry Fonda* (Tom Joad), *Jane Darwell* (Ma Joad), *John Carradine* (Casy), Charley Grapewin (Grandpa), Dorris Bowdon (Rosasharn), Russell Simpson (Pa Joad), Zeffie Tilbury (Grandma), O. Z. Whitehead (Al), John Qualen (Muley), Eddie Quillan (Connie), Grant Mitchell

After the dust-bowl disaster of the thirties, Oklahoma farmers trek to California in the hope of a better life.

A superb film which could scarcely be improved upon. Though the ending is softened from the book, there was too much here for filmgoers to chew on. Acting, photography, direction combine to make this an unforgettable experience, a poem of a film.

SCR *Nunnally Johnson*   CIN *Gregg Toland*   MUS Alfred Newman   ED Robert Simpson   PROD Darryl Zanuck, Nunnally Johnson   DIST TCF

TOM (HENRY FONDA) READING GRAVE MARKER: This here's William James Joad, died of a stroke, old, old man. His fokes bured him because they got no money to pay for funerls. Nobody kilt him. Just a stroke and he died.
MA (JANE DARWELL): Rich fellas come up, an' they die, an' their kids ain't no good, an' they die out. But we keep a-comin'. We're the people that live. Can't lick us. We'll go on forever, Pa, because we're the people.
MA: Well, Pa, woman can change bettern a man. Man lives – well, in jerks. Baby born or somebody dies, that's a jerk. Gets a farm or loses one, an' that's a jerk. With a woman, it's all one flow, like a stream – little eddies, little waterfalls – but the river, it goes right on. Woman looks at it that way.

66 A genuinely great motion picture which makes one proud to have even a small share in the affairs of the cinema. – *Howard Barnes*

66 The most mature motion picture that has ever been made, in feeling, in purpose, and in the use of the medium. – *Otis Ferguson*

G

[DVD] Available on DVD   ☆ Cast in order   66 Critics' Quotes   ⚱ Academy Award   BAFTA
♫ Soundtrack on CD   of importance   † Points of interest   Academy Award nomination   BAFTA nomination

263

⚜ John Ford; Jane Darwell (supporting actress)
☖ picture; Nunnally Johnson (screenplay); Henry Fonda (leading actor); Robert Simpson (editing)

'Love is a chain of love... as nature is a chain of life.'

The Grass Harp ★

DIR Charles Matthau
1995 107m US
[DVD] ♫

☆ Piper Laurie (Dolly Talbo), Sissy Spacek (Verena Talbo), Walter Matthau (Judge Charlie Cool), Edward Furlong (Collin Fenwick), Nell Carter (Catherine Creek), Jack Lemmon (Dr. Morris Ritz), Mary Steenburgen (Sister Ida), Sean Patrick Flanery (Riley Henderson), Joe Don Baker (Sheriff Junius Candle), Charles Durning (Reverend Buster), Roddy McDowall (Amos Legrand), Mia Kirshner (Maude Riordan)

In the late 30s in America's Deep South, two sisters with contrasting temperaments take in their orphaned nephew and bring him up themselves.

A pleasant, nostalgic story about life in a small town peopled with eccentrics, where insignificant events become magnified. It's slight, but pleasurable, with a welcome emphasis on anecdotes and story-telling.

SCR Sterling Silliphant, Kirk Ellis **CIN** John A. Alonzo **MUS** Patrick Williams **DES** Paul Sylbert **ED** Sidney Levin, C. Timothy O'Leary **PROD** Charles Matthau, Jerry Tokofsky, John Davis, James J. Davis **DIST** Pathé/Grass Harp/Fine Line

❝ (Matthau's) cast responds vibrantly to the invitation to tell stories as though their lives depended on them. – *Philip Strick, Sight & Sound*

Grease ★★★★

DIR Randal Kleiser
1978 110m US
♫

☆ *John Travolta, Olivia Newton-John*, Stockard Channing, Eve Arden, Frankie Avalon, Joan Blondell, Edd Byrnes, Sid Caesar, Alice Ghostley, Sha Na Na, Jeff Conaway, Barry Pearl, Michael Tucci

The path of true love in a 1950s high school does not run smoothly.

Amiable 'period' musical for teenagers: in filmic terms, it is pretty rudimentary, yet its infectious spirit overcomes technical shortcomings and suspensions of disbelief. Travolta and Newton-John make a winning couple, and almost every one of its songs has etched itself on to the public memory. It is, almost despite itself, sheer pleasure.

SCR Bronte Woodard **CIN** Bill Butler **DES** Phil Jefferies **ED** John F. Burnett **DIST** Paramount/Robert Stigwood, Allan Carr

❝ A bogus, clumsily jointed pastiche of late fifties high school musicals, studded with leftovers from West Side Story and Rebel Without A Cause. – *New Yorker*

☖ John Farrar (m,ly) (music, original song – Hopelessly Devoted to You)

'The true story of a legend.'

Great Balls of Fire! ★

DIR Jim McBride
1989 108m US
[DVD] ♫

☆ Dennis Quaid (Jerry Lee Lewis), Winona Ryder (Myra Gale Brown), John Doe (J.W. Brown), Joe Bob Briggs (Dewey 'Daddy-O' Phillips), Stephen Tobolowsky (Jud Phillips), Trey Wilson (Sam Phillips), Alec Baldwin (Jimmy Swaggart), Steve Allen (Himself), Lisa Blount (Lois Brown), Joshua Sheffield (Rusty Brown), Peter Cook (First English Reporter)

The country-rock hell-raiser Jerry Lee Lewis rises to the top, but upsets fans when he marries his 13-year-old cousin.

Colourful, engagingly performed, but ultimately thin and sanitised treatment of a controversial career.

SCR Jack Baran, Jim McBride **CIN** Affonso Beato **DES** David Nichols **ED** Lisa Day, Pembroke Herring, Bert Lovitt **PROD** Adam Fields **DIST** Rank/Orion

❝ There's a whole lotta fakin' goin' on. – *Terry Staunton, NME*

❝ It captures, perhaps for the first time on film, something of the sexual aura of rock-and-roll at its birth. I – *Caryn James, New York Times*

A Great Day in Harlem ★★

DIR Jean Bach
1994 60m US
[DVD] ♫

☆ Quincy Jones (narrator)

An account of the famous photo taken in 1958 of 57 eminent jazz musicians, assembled on a Harlem sidewalk. Many of the subjects from that day are interviewed.

Delightful, affectionate documentary, incorporating home movies of the event, footage of these jazz greats in performance and talking-head reminiscences. A spirit of celebration and generosity between the artists underpins this charming work.

SCR Jean Bach, Susan Peehl, Matthew Seig **CIN** Steve Petropoulos **ED** Susan Peehl **PROD** Jean Bach **DIST** Flo-Bert/NYFA

❝ A wonderful, warm little movie. – *Brian Case, Time Out*

† Film director Robert Benton, who was art director of Esquire magazine, commissioned the famous portrait and is among the interviewees.

☖ documentary

The Great Escape ★★★

DIR John Sturges
1963 173m US
[DVD] ♫

☆ James Garner, *Steve McQueen*, Richard Attenborough, James Donald, Charles Bronson, Donald Pleasence, James Coburn, David McCallum, Gordon Jackson, John Leyton, Nigel Stock

Allied prisoners plan to escape from a German prison camp.

Tense, exciting POW adventure that makes nearly three hours fly by. A film with a memorably jaunty theme tune that gave Steve McQueen, racing his motorbike towards the camp's barbed-wire fence, his iconic role.

SCR *James Clavell, W. R. Burnett* CIN *Daniel Fapp* MUS *Elmer Bernstein* PROD John Sturges DIST UA/Mirisch/Alpha

---

'She'll only break your heart – yet you'll still pursue her.'

Great Expectations ★

DIR *Alfonso Cuaron*
1998 111m US
DVD ♫

☆ Ethan Hawke (Finnegan Bell), Gwyneth Paltrow (Estella), Hank Azaria (Walter Plane), Chris Cooper (Joe), Ann Bancroft (Ms Dinsmoor), Robert De Niro (Prisoner/Lustig), Josh Mostel (Jerry Ragno), Kim Dickens (Magie), Nell Campbell (Erica Thrall)

An orphan in Florida helps an escaped convict, falls in love with a rich girl, and later finds his art projects in New York funded by a mysterious benefactor.

A pop, modernised Dickens adaptation which doesn't work – the characters are too blank and ennui-laden to keep the story alive. Lush design, though, makes it an interesting failure.

SCR Mitch Glazer CIN *Emmanuel Lubezki* MUS Patrick Doyle DES *Tony Burrough* ED Steven Weisberg PROD Art Linson DIST TCF

66 Capable of wonder even when its wilder ideas misfire. – *Elvis Mitchell, New York Times*

Great Expectations ★★★★

DIR *David Lean*
1946 118m GB
DVD

☆ John Mills (Pip), Bernard Miles (Joe Gargery), *Finlay Currie* (Abel Magwitch), *Martita Hunt* (Miss Havisham), Valerie Hobson (Estella), *Jean Simmons* (Young Estella), *Alec Guinness* (Herbert Pocket), Francis L. Sullivan (Jaggers), Anthony Wager (Young Pip), Ivor Barnard (Wemmick), Freda Jackson (Mrs. Joe Gargery), Hay Petrie (Uncle Pumblechook), O. B. Clarence (Aged Parent), George Hayes (Compeyson), Torin Thatcher (Betley Drummle), Eileen Erskine (Biddy)

A boy meets an escaped convict on deserted marshland, with strange long-term consequences for both of them.

Despite the inevitable simplifications, this is a superbly pictorial rendering of a much-loved novel, with all the famous characters in safe hands and masterly judgement in every department.

SCR Ronald Neame, David Lean, Kay Walsh, Cecil McGivern, Anthony Havelock-Allan CIN *Guy Green* MUS Walter Goehr ED Jack Harris PROD Anthony Havelock-Allan DIST Rank/Cineguild

66 The first big British film to have been made, a film that sweeps our cloistered virtues out into the open. – *Richard Winnington*

66 The best Dickens adaptation, and arguably David Lean's finest film. – *NFT, 1969*

⚱ Guy Green (cinematography); John Bryan (art direction) ⚱ picture; David Lean (as director); David Lean, Ronald Neame, Anthony Havelock-Allan (original screenplay)

'He'll give you the biggest heart sock, laugh shock you ever thrilled to!'

The Great McGinty ★★★

SCR/DIR *Preston Sturges*
1940 83m US

☆ *Brian Donlevy* (Dan McGinty), *Akim Tamiroff* (The Boss), Muriel Angelus (Catherine McGinty), Louis Jean Heydt (Thompson), Arthur Hoyt (Mayor Tillinghast)

A hobo and a Mob boss enter politics and have dizzying careers – initially, at least.

Lively, barbed comedy-drama which signalled the arrival of Sturges as a new and stimulating Hollywood talent.

CIN William C. Mellor MUS Frederick Hollander ED Hugh Bennett PROD Paul Jones DIST Paramount

PROLOGUE: This is the story of two men who met in a banana republic. One of them never did anything dishonest in his life except for one crazy minute. The other never did anything honest in his life except for one crazy minute. They both had to leave the country.

66 This is his first directing job and where has he been all our lives? He has that sense of the incongruous which makes some of the best gaiety. – *Otis Ferguson*

66 The tough dialogue is matched by short, snappy scenes; the picture seems to have wasted no time, no money. – *Gilbert Seldes*

⚱ Preston Sturges (original screenplay)

Greed ★★★

SCR/DIR *Erich von Stroheim*
1924 110m US

☆ *Gibson Gowland* (McTeague), Zasu Pitts (Trina Sieppe), *Jean Hersholt* (Marcus Schuler), Chester Conklin (Mr. Sieppe), Dale Fuller (Maria)

An ex-miner dentist kills his avaricious wife. Later in Death Valley he also kills her lover, but is bound to him by handcuffs.

This much-discussed film is often cited as its director's greatest folly: the original version ran eight hours. Re-edited by June Mathis, it retains considerable power sequence by sequence, but is necessarily disjointed in development. However, it must be seen to be appreciated.

CIN Ben Reynolds, William Daniels ED Erich von Stroheim, Rex Ingram, June Mathis, Jos W. Farnham PROD Erich von Stroheim, Irving Thalberg DIST MGM/Goldwyn Company

66 The end leaves one with an appalling sense of human waste, of futility, of the drabness and cruelty of lives stifled by genteel poverty. Every character in the film is overwhelmed by it. – *Gavin Lambert*

66 Von Stroheim is a genius – Greed established that beyond all doubt – but he is badly in need of a stopwatch. – *Robert E. Sherwood*

† In 1972 Herman G. Weinberg published a complete screenplay with 400 stills.

---

† The original length at the première is said to have been 420m.

'The story of two people who got married, met, and then fell in love.'

Green Card ★

SCR/DIR Peter Weir
1990 103m Australia/France
DVD ♫

☆ Gérard Depardieu (Georges), Andie MacDowell (Bronte), Bebe Neuwirth (Lauren), Gregg Edelman (Phil), Robert Prosky (Bronte's Lawyer), Jessie Keosian (Mrs. Bird), Ethan Phillips (Gorsky), Mary Louise Wilson (Mrs Sheehan), Lois Smith (Bronte's mother), Conrad McLaren (Bronte's father)

A Frenchman marries a New York horticulturalist to gain residency in the United States.

Gentle romantic comedy with a winning sincerity.

CIN Geoffrey Simpson MUS Hans Zimmer DES Wendy Stites ED William Anderson PROD Peter Weir DIST Touchstone

66 Captivating romantic bonbon. – *Peter Travers, Rolling Stone*

Ⅰ Peter Weir (original screenplay)
Ⓣ Peter Weir (original screenplay)

'Paul Edgecomb did not believe in miracles. . .until he met one.'

The Green Mile ★★

SCR/DIR Frank Darabont
1999 188m US
DVD ♫

☆ Tom Hanks (Paul Edgecomb), David Morse (Brutus 'Brutal' Howell), Bonnie Hunt (Jan Edgecomb), *Michael Clarke Duncan* (John Coffey), James Cromwell (Warden Hal Moores), Michael Jeter (Eduard Delacroix), Graham Greene (Arlen Bitterbuck), Doug Hutchison (Percy Wetmore), *Sam Rockwell* ('Wild Bill' Wharton), Barry Pepper (Dean Stanton), Jeffrey DeMunn (Harry Terwilliger), Harry Dean Stanton (Toot-Toot), Gary Sinise (Burt Hammersmith)

A retired prison warden recalls the time during the Depression when a black inmate, accused of murdering two white girls but blessed with healing powers, arrived on Death Row.

Long, often simplistic but engrossing drama that handles human interest material better than its supernatural aspects; though it can't quite reproduce on celluloid the smell of burning flesh or the agonies of passing kidney stones – both central to the plot – it at least shares one thing with its source: a deep-rooted, fundamental commitment to storytelling.

CIN David Tattersall MUS Thomas Newman DES *Terence Marsh* ED Richard Francis-Bruce PROD David Valdes, Frank Darabont DIST Warner

66 A cracking good yarn that earns its laughter, its wonder and its tears. – *Andrew O'Hehir, Salon*

66 As Darabont directs it, it tells a story with beginning, middle, end, vivid characters, humour, outrage and emotional release. Dickensian. – *Roger Ebert, Chicago Sun-Times*

Ⅰ picture; Michael Clarke Duncan (supporting actor); Frank Darabont (adapted screenplay); Robert J. Litt, Elliot Tyson, Michael Herbick, Willie D. Burton (sound)

Gregory's Girl ★★★

SCR/DIR *Bill Forsyth*
1980 91m GB
DVD

☆ *Gordon John Sinclair (later John Gordon Sinclair)* (Gregory), Dee Hepburn (Dorothy), Jake D'Arcy (Phil Menzies), Claire Grogan (Susan)

In a Scottish new town, a school football team's teenage goalkeeper is attracted to a girl who, to his amazement, is a talented striker.

Gentle-spirited comedy, written by Forsyth with humour, affection, and sympathy for the pangs of adolescence. A delightful film that became a hit on the strength of appreciative word-of-mouth.

CIN Michael Coulter MUS Colin Tully ED John Gow PROD Davina Belling, Clive Parsons DIST Lake/NFFC/STV

Ⓣ Bill Forsyth (original screenplay)

'Seduction. Betrayal. Murder. Who's Conning Who?'

The Grifters ★★★

DIR *Stephen Frears*
1990 110m US
DVD ♫

☆ *Anjelica Huston* (Lilly Dillon), John Cusack (Roy Dillon), *Annette Bening* (Myra Langtry), Pat Hingle (Bobo Justus), Henry Jones (Simms), Michael Laskin (Irv), Eddie Jones (Mintz), J. T. Walsh (Cole Langtry), Charles Napier (Hebbing)

A California conman is caught between his latest lover and his overbearing mother, who initiated him into the confidence business.

Sleek, atmospheric thriller that plays out in harsh L.A. sunlight rather than the conventional darkness of noir, notable for three excellent performances.

SCR *Donald Westlake* CIN Oliver Stapleton MUS Elmer Bernstein DES Dennis Gassner ED Mick Audsley PROD Martin Scorsese, Robert Harris, Jim Painter DIST Palace/Cineplex Odeon

66 Moves with swift unsentimental resolve towards a last act as bleak as any in recent American screen literature. In a less skilful work, it would be a downer. The Grifters is so good that one leaves the theatre on a spellbound high. – *Vincent Canby, The New York Times*

Ⅰ Stephen Frears; Anjelica Huston (leading actress); Annette Bening (supporting actress); Donald Westlake (adapted screenplay)

Ⓣ Annette Bening (supporting actress)

'In nature, there are boundaries.'

Grizzly Man ★★★

SCR/DIR *Werner Herzog*
2005 103m US/Canada
DVD

☆ Timothy Treadwell, Amie Huguenard, Warren Queeney, Willy Fulton

DVD Available on DVD ☆ Cast in order of importance 66 Critics' Quotes Ⅰ Academy Award † Points of interest Ⓣ BAFTA
♫ Soundtrack on CD Ⅰ Academy Award nomination Ⓣ BAFTA nomination

The story of Timothy Treadwell, a grizzly bear activist who lived for many months in the Alaskan wilderness, until he and his girlfriend were eaten by the bears they were trying to protect.

Intriguing portrait of a wild-child eccentric, pieced together from the footage he left behind. Herzog's severe and pessimistic view of the natural world contrasts often hilariously with Treadwell's loopy attempts to befriend it. A near-perfect documentary full of mystery, sadness and a kind of awe.

CIN Peter Zeitlinger MUS *Richard Thompson* ED Joe Bini PROD Erik Nelson DIST Revolver

66 A brilliant portrait of adventure, activism, obsession and potential madness. – *Scott Foundas, Variety*

'Even A Hit Man Deserves A Second Shot.'

Grosse Pointe Blank ★★★

DIR George Armitage
1997 107m US
[DVD] ♫

☆ *John Cusack* (Martin Q. Blank), Minnie Driver (Debi Newberry), Alan Arkin (Dr. Oatman), Dan Aykroyd (Grocer), Joan Cusack (Marcella), Jeremy Piven (Paul Spericki), Hank Azaria (Steven Lardner), Barbara Harris (Mary Blank), Mitchell Ryan (Mr. Bart Newberry)

A hit man attends his high school reunion.

The one-joke premise is unpromising, but this skilful black comedy pays off with a tone pitched somewhere between jaunty and edgy, and amusing performances all round. The lead role seems custom-built for Cusack.

SCR Tom Jankiewicz, D.V. DeVincentis, Steve Pink, John Cusack CIN Jamie Anderson DES Stephen Altman ED Brian Berdan PROD Susan Arnold, Donna Arkoff Roth, Roger Birnbaum DIST Buena Vista/Hollywood/Caravan/New Crime

66 Has enough wild-card energy to keep it bright and surprising. – *Janet Maslin, New York Times*

66 A bright burst of action and comedy with a cast that makes for rousing good company. – *Peter Travers, Rolling Stone*

'He's having the day of his life. . .over and over again.'

Groundhog Day ★★★★

DIR Harold Ramis
1993 101m US
[DVD] ♫

☆ *Bill Murray* (Phil), Andie MacDowell (Rita), Chris Elliott (Larry), Stephen Tobolowsky (Ned), Brian Doyle-Murray (Buster), Marita Geraghty (Nancy), Angela Paton (Mrs. Lancaster), Rick Ducommun (Gus)

A cynical weatherman must relive the same day over and over again until he sees the error of his ways.

A peerless conceit actually benefits from the comparatively bland, sitcom-ish direction – the main character seems trapped in the same banal episode of his life, and not even suicide works as a way out. It's the role of Murray's career and the most inspired comedy of the 1990s.

SCR *Danny Rubin, Harold Ramis* CIN John Bailey MUS George Fenton DES David Nichols ED Pembroke J. Herring PROD Trevor Albert, Harold Ramis DIST Columbia TriStar/Columbia

66 This is first and foremost a comedy of ideas, on which score it never falters. – *Geoff Andrew, Time Out*

66 For once, the audience isn't forced to surrender its intelligence (or its healthy cynicism) to embrace the film's sunny resolution. – *Hal Hinson, Washington Post*

🅣 Danny Rubin, Harold Ramis (original screenplay)

'Fight your patch.'

Grow Your Own ★★

DIR Richard Laxton
2007 97m UK

☆ Benedict Wong (Kung Sang), Eddie Marsan (Little John), Philip Jackson (Big John), Alan Williams (Kenny), Omid Djalili (Ali)

Tensions simmer on a Liverpool allotment when refugee families are given plots of land to grow their own produce.

Well-intentioned, heartfelt story about an important issue: how easy it is to regard refugees and asylum seekers as an undifferentiated mass, rather than as individuals who can bring talents to an adopted country, along with histories of pain and victimhood. Benedict Wong is affecting as a Chinese father, the victim of land grabs in his own country, rendered mute by a past trauma. The film sugars the pill of this difficult topic, thus undermining it; the comic tone sometimes sits uncomfortably beside the serious issues.

SCR Frank Cottrell Boyce, Carl Hunter CIN David Luther DES Melanie Allen ED Joe Walker PROD Luke Alkin, Carl Hunter, Barry Ryan DIST Pathe

66 An affectionate, thoughtful and sometimes amusing British ensemble piece for those who like their cinema to challenge – but not a lot. – *Dave Calhoun, Time Out*

† The story is based on a real scheme in Liverpool, the Family Refugee Support Project, which gives allotment plots to asylum seekers and refugees, and offers on-site psychotherapy.

'A fifty-year fight.'

Grumpy Old Men ★

DIR Donald Petrie
1993 103m US
[DVD]

☆ Jack Lemmon (John Gustafson), Walter Matthau (Max Goldman), Ann-Margret (Ariel Truax), Burgess Meredith (Grandpa Gustafson), Daryl Hannah (Melanie), Kevin Pollak (Jacob Goldman), Ossie Davis (Chuck), Buck Henry (Snyder), Christopher McDonald (Mike)

Relationships between two elderly neighbours, long at loggerheads, worsen further when they find themselves competing for the hand of a vivacious widow.

All the fun here is watching an affectionately regarded duo going through their familiar paces. The film bequeathed a jocular but useful phrase to the language, but it's never more than lightweight.

[DVD] Available on DVD   ☆ Cast in order   66 Critics' Quotes   🏆 Academy Award   🅣 BAFTA
♫ Soundtrack on CD   of importance   † Points of interest Academy Award nomination BAFTA nomination

267

G

SCR Mark Steven Johnson   CIN Johnny E. Jensen
MUS Alan Silvestri   DES David Chapman   ED Bonnie
Koehler   PROD John Davis, Richard C. Berman
DIST Warner/Lancaster Gate

66 If you're young enough to have missed some of the
better Lemmon-Matthau pairings, like The Fortune
Cookie or The Odd Couple, then Grumpy Old Men won't
seem so grumpy. – *Peter Rainer, Los Angeles Times*

'When lives are on the line, sacrifice everything.'

The Guardian ★★

DIR Andrew Davis
2006   139m   US
[DVD]

☆ *Kevin Costner* (Ben Randall), *Ashton Kutcher* (Jake
Fischer), Sela Ward (Helen Randall), Clancy Brown
(Captain William Hadley), Melissa Sagemiller (Emily
Thomas)

A decorated Coastguard teaches new recruits at an
elite training programme to cope in the face of
marine adversity and dangerous sea rescue
missions.

*A strong cast provide intense thrills and wrenching
human drama in an oceanic epic, using Hollywood
know-how at its most effective, engaging and exciting.*

SCR Ron L. Brinkerhoff   CIN Stephen St. John
MUS Trevor Rabin   DES Maher Ahmad   ED Thomas J.
Nordberg, Dennis Virkler   PROD Beau Flynn, Tripp
Vinson   DIST Buena Vista

66 Overlong but involving drama has obvious cross-
generational appeal. – *Joe Leydon, Variety*

Guess Who's Coming to Dinner ★★

DIR Stanley Kramer
1967   112m   US
[DVD]

☆ *Spencer Tracy, Katharine Hepburn*, Katharine Houghton,
Sidney Poitier, Cecil Kellaway, Roy E. Glenn Snr., Beah
Richards, Isabel Sanford, Virginia Christine

A well-to-do San Francisco girl announces that she
is going to marry a black man, and her parents find
they are less broad-minded than they thought.

*A problem picture that isn't really a problem, since
everyone is so nice and the prospective bridegroom is so
eligible. Yet it was significant in its way: on its release, it
was hailed as a breakthrough mainstream film for its
treatment of an inter-racial relationship. It looks like a
photographed play, but isn't based on one; the set is
unconvincing; but the acting is a dream.*

SCR William Rose   CIN Sam Leavitt   DES Robert
Clatworthy   DIST Columbia/Stanley Kramer

66 Suddenly everybody's caught up in a kind of integrated
drawing-room comedy, and unable to decide whether
there's anything funny in it or not. – *Ann Birstein, Vogue*

66 A load of embarrassing rubbish. In the circumstances
there is little that director Stanley Kramer can do but see
that his camera plod from room to room and make the
most of people sitting down and getting up again. –
Penelope Mortimer

⚲ Katharine Hepburn (leading actress); William Rose
(original screenplay)
⚲ picture; Stanley Kramer; Spencer Tracy (leading actor);
Cecil Kellaway (supporting actor); Beah Richards
(supporting actress); Frank de Vol (music)
⚲ Spencer Tracy (leading actor); Katharine Hepburn
(leading actress)

'All it took was a whisper.'

Guilty by Suspicion ★

SCR/DIR Irwin Winkler
1990   105m   US
[DVD] ♫

☆ Robert De Niro (David Merrill), Annette Bening
(Ruth Merrill), George Wendt (Bunny Baxter), Patricia
Wettig (Dorothy Nolan), Sam Wanamaker (Felix Graff),
Chris Cooper (Gary Nolan), Martin Scorsese (Joe
Lesser)

A film director in the 1950s returns to Hollywood
from Europe and is asked to testify against
his colleagues by the House Committee on
Un-American Activities.

*Worthy but fumbled drama about blacklisting,
which lets the major studios off the hook for their
involvement with HUAC, and cops out by making
its main character innocent of any communist
sympathies.*

CIN Michael Ballhaus   MUS James Newton Howard
DES Leslie Dilley   ED Priscilla Nedd   PROD Arnon
Milchan   DIST Warner

66 You want my comment? I took my name off. It violates
my aesthetics, my politics, my morality. – *Abraham
Polonsky (blacklisted screenwriter)*

66 Not only a powerful statement against the blacklist, but
also one of the best Hollywood movies I've seen. – *Roger
Ebert, Chicago Sun-Times*

† Abraham Polonsky, the original screenwriter, refused
credit when De Niro's character was made a liberal rather
than a communist.
† Martin Scorsese's character, who flees to Europe to avoid
testifying, is based on Joseph Losey.

'Prepare to visit a town you'd never want to call home.'

Gummo ★

SCR/DIR Harmony Korine
1997   89m   US
[DVD] ♫

☆ Jacob Reynolds (Solomon), Nick Sutton (Tummler),
Jacob Sewell (Bunny Boy), Darby Dougherty (Darby),
Chloë Sevigny (Dot), Carisa Glucksman (Helen), Linda
Manz (Solomon's Mom), Max Perlich (Cole)

In the wake of a devastating tornado, two alienated
small-town adolescents act out their frustrations by
thinking up ways to outrage the locals – including
torturing animals.

*Fractured story-telling and hand-held camera work,
devices employed by Korine to capture these
dysfunctional lives, often lapse into what looks like
calculated anti-style. He operates in an interesting
neighbourhood, though you wouldn't want to stick
around too long.*

CIN Jean Yves Escoffier, James Clauer   DES Dave Doernberg   ED Christopher Tellefsen   PROD Cary Woods   DIST Entertainment/Fine Line

66 The effect is as horribly funny as it is depressing, but gets pretty hard to take after a while, especially for anyone who is a committed cat lover. – *Kim Newman, Empire*

† Director Bernardo Bertolucci has described Gummo as one of the key films of the 1990s.

Gun Crazy   ★★★★

DIR *Joseph H. Lewis*
1949   87m   US

☆ *John Dall* (Bart Tare), *Peggy Cummins* (Annie Laurie Starr), Morris Carnovsky (Judge Willougby), Berry Kroeger (Packet), Anabel Shaw (Ruby Tare), Harry Lewis (Clyde Boston), Rusty Tamblyn (Bart, aged 14)

A young married couple set off on a trail of armed robbery and murder.

An updated Bonnie and Clyde story that looks like a B-movie about gangsters, but also has traces of the Western and screwball comedy about it. In fact, it's a classic of the noir genre, a superb, taut thriller that opened modestly but now has a cultish reputation, thanks to film-makers who have borrowed its central motifs, to a belated appreciation for the unconventional work of its remarkable director, and to its sheer energy, pace and wit. Several elements in the story (Annie Laurie Starr's fascination with guns, for instance) lay themselves open to a wide variety of readings, thus reinforcing the film's cult status.

SCR Dalton Trumbo, MacKinlay Kantor   CIN *Russell Harlan*   MUS Victor Young   DES Gordon Wiles

ED Harry Gerstad   DIST King Brothers/Universal-International

BART: We go together, Annie. I don't know why. Maybe like guns and ammunition go together.

† The film was a huge favourite with leading lights in the French New Wave movement. When Jean-Luc Godard and François Truffaut were considering an offer to write the script for Bonnie and Clyde (1967) they reportedly watched Gun Crazy repeatedly and had decided to make it the template for their proposed screenplay.

Guys and Dolls   ★★

SCR/DIR Joseph L. Mankiewicz
1955   149m   US
DVD

☆ Frank Sinatra, Marlon Brando, Jean Simmons, *Vivian Blaine, Stubby Kaye*, B. S. Pully, Robert Keith, Sheldon Leonard, George E. Stone

A New York gangster takes a bet that he can romance an attractive Salvation Army missionary.

A decidedly mixed experience: it rambles on far too long, and no-one will remember Brando for his singing voice. Yet it features an attractive cast, some terrific dance routines, and most of its songs are unimpeachable. For those unable to see the show on stage, this will suffice.

CIN Harry Stradling   DES Oliver Smith   DIST Samuel Goldwyn

66 Quantity has been achieved only at the cost of quality. – *Penelope Houston*

⚲ Harry Stradling (cinematography); Cyril Mockridge, Jay Blackton (music); art direction

DVD Available on DVD   ☆ Cast in order   66 Critics' Quotes   ⚲ Academy Award   🛡 BAFTA
♫ Soundtrack on CD   of importance   † Points of interest   ⚲ Academy Award nomination   Ⓣ BAFTA nomination

269

Hail the Conquering Hero ★★★

SCR/DIR *Preston Sturges*
1944　101m　US

☆ *Eddie Bracken* (Woodrow Lafayette Pershing Truesmith), *William Demarest* (Sergeant), Ella Raines (Libby), *Franklin Pangborn* (Committee Chairman), Elizabeth Patterson (Libby's Aunt), *Raymond Walburn* (Mayor Noble), *Alan Bridge* (Political Boss), Georgia Caine (Mrs. Truesmith), Freddie Steele (Bugsy), Jimmy Conlin (Judge Dennis), Torben Meyer (Mr. Schultz)

Thanks to a prank played by six sympathetic Marines, an army reject is regarded as a hero when he returns to his small-town home.

Skilfully orchestrated Preston Sturges romp, featuring his repertory of comic actors at full pitch, and with some waspish things to say about the cult of wartime heroism.

CIN John Seitz　MUS Werner Heymann　ED Stuart Gilmore　PROD Preston Sturges　DIST Paramount

66 (Sturges) uses verbal as well as visual slapstick, and his comic timing is so quirkily effective that the dialogue keeps popping off like a string of firecrackers. – *New Yorker, 1977*

66 First rate entertainment, a pattern of film making, not to be missed. – *Richard Mallett, Punch*

Å Preston Sturges (original screenplay)

'The Morning After Was Just The Beginning. . .'

La Haine ★★★

SCR/DIR *Mathieu Kassovitz*
1995　96m　France
DVD　♫

☆ *Vincent Cassel* (Vinz), *Hubert Kounde* (Hubert), *Saïd Taghmaoui* (Said), Karim Belkhadra (Samir), Edouard Montoute (Darty), Françoise Levantal (Asterix), Solo (Santo), Marc Duret (Inspector 'Notre Dame')

Three unemployed youths – one black, one Jewish, one Arab – meet up in the aftermath of a riot in which one of their contemporaries was critically injured, and debate whether or not to take revenge against the police.

Shot with grit and flair, but also an eye for moments of sink-estate poetry, this remains a time bomb of a movie, packed with explosive situations, and ticking down to its shocking and powerful denouement.

CIN *Pierre Aïm*　MUS Assassin　DES Giuseppe Ponturo
ED *Mathieu Kassovitz, Scott Stevenson*　PROD Christophe Rossignon　DIST Metro Tartan/Lazennec/Canal/La Sept/Kaso

66 Virtuoso, on-the-edge stuff, as exciting as anything we've seen from the States in ages, and more thoroughly engaged with the reality it describes. . .A vital, scalding piece of work. – *Tom Charity, Time Out*

† In 1995, Kassovitz won the best director prize at the Cannes Film Festival.

The Hairdresser's Husband ★★

DIR *Patrice Leconte*
1990　82m　France
DVD

☆ Jean Rochefort (Antoine), Anna Galiena (Mathilde), Roland Bertin (Antoine's father), Maurice Chevit (Ambroise Dupré), Philippe Clevenot (Morvoisieux), Jacques Mathou (Julien Gora), Claude Aufaure (Gay Customer), Henry Hocking (Antoine - Age 12)

A middle-aged man still treasures the erotic memory of a buxom hairdresser he encountered a boy. When he discovers an almost identical woman decades later, he impulsively marries her.

The story could be played as a story of dark obsession, but Leconte, ably assisted by the droll Rochefort, keeps the mood light until close to the end. An attractive looking film with a sly, not quite politically correct humour, and a dazzling score by Michael Nyman.

SCR Claude Klotz, Patrice Leconte　CIN *Eduardo Serra*
MUS *Michael Nyman*　DES Ivan Maussion　ED Joëlle Hache　PROD Thierry de Ganay
DIST Palace/Lambart/TFI/Investimage 2 and 3/Sofica

Ⓣ film not in the English language

'You can't stop the beat.'

Hairspray (new) ★★

DIR Adam Shankman
2007　116m　US
DVD　♫

☆ John Travolta (Edna Turnblad), Michelle Pfeiffer (Velma Von Tussle), Christopher Walken (Wilbur Turnblad), Amanda Bynes (Penny Pingleton), James Marsden (Corny Collins), Queen Latifah (Motormouth Maybelle), Nikki Blonsky (Tracy Turnblad)

A chubby teenage girl in 1960s Baltimore fights to democratise a racially segregated TV show.

Exuberant musicalisation of a cult original, based on a hit Broadway show. A riot of colour, comedy and camp, put across with élan; the trashy sensibility remains an acquired taste though.

SCR Leslie Dixon　CIN Bojan Bazelli　MUS Marc Shaiman　DES David Gropman　ED Michael Tronick
PROD Craig Zadan, Neil Meron　DIST Entertainment

66 One of the best Broadway-tuner adaptations in recent years. – *Dennis Harvey, Variety*

DVD Available on DVD　☆ Cast in order of importance　66 Critics' Quotes　† Points of interest　Å Academy Award　Ⱥ Academy Award nomination　Ⓑ BAFTA　Ⓣ BAFTA nomination
♫ Soundtrack on CD

66 Travolta is a blubbery scream. – *James Christopher, The Times*

† John Travolta donned a 30 lb fat suit for the role played by Divine in John Waters' original.

† The film features cameos by Waters and talk-show host Ricki Lake, who played Tracy in the 1988 film.

Half Moon (new) ★

DIR Bahman Ghobadi SCR/DIR Bahman Ghobadi, Behnam Behzadi

2007 114m Austria/France/Iran/Iraq

☆ Ismail Ghaffari (Mamo), Allah-Morad Rashtiani (Kako), Hedieh Tehrani (Hesho), Golshifteh Farahani (Niwemang), Hassan Poorshirazi (Police Officer)

An elderly Kurdish musician travels into Iraq with his 10 sons to perform at a concert.

Evocative road movie with much local colour and a surreal third act; the journey is evidently more important than the destination.

CIN Nigel Bluck MUS Hossein Alizadeh DES Bahman Ghobadi, Mansooreh Yazdanjoo ED Hayedeh Safiyari PROD Bahman Ghobadi DIST ICA Films

66 Fateful and funny, haunting and magical. – *Jeannette Catsoulis, New York Times*

66 It begins in a spirit of comedy and affirmation, but, as is often the case in Ghobadi's films, gets darker and darker until it reaches a level of desperation and tragedy that verges on the epic. – *Sukhdev Sandhu, Daily Telegraph*

'Secrets don't let go.'

Half Nelson ★★

DIR Ryan Fleck

2006 106m US

DVD ♫

☆ Ryan Gosling (Dan Dunne), Shareeka Epps (Drey), Anthony Mackie (Frank), Deborah Rush (Jo Dunne), Jay O. Sanders (Russ Dunne), Tina Holmes (Rachel)

An inner-city high school teacher has a heroin habit – a fact known but kept secret by one of his pupils, a 13-year-old girl. He tries to protect her from unseemly influences in her family life, and they strike up a cautious friendship.

Thinly disguised battle of wills over the future of a teenage girl between two improbable saviours, but the writing and characterisation are so strong that the story never feels reduced to a formula. Instead, the script is full of intriguing grace notes; Dan's ambivalence about growing up, Drey's wisdom that often gives way to her child-like qualities; and the pact between the two, which in context seems oddly believable. And it's rare that an actor inhabits a role as meticulously as Gosling does here.

SCR Ryan Fleck, Anna Boden CIN Andrij Parekh MUS Broken Social Scene DES Elizabeth Mickle ED Anna Boden PROD Jamie Patricof, Alex Orlovsky, Lynette Howell, Anna Boden, Rosanne Korenberg DIST Axiom

66 It's impressively adult, sure-footed film-making and that Best Actor nod was definitely deserved. – *Tim Robey, Daily Telegraph*

66 A dedicated, charismatic, crack-addicted history teacher is the most believable protagonist in an American movie this year. – *Jonathan Rosenbaum, Chicago Reader*

Ⓐ Ryan Gosling (leading actor)

'Who Is Hallam Foe?'

Hallam Foe (new) ★

DIR David Mackenzie

2007 95m UK

DVD ♫

☆ *Jamie Bell* (Hallam Foe), *Sophia Myles* (Kate Breck), Ciarán Hinds (Julius), Jamie Sives (Alasdair), Maurice Roeves (Raymond), Ewen Bremner (Andy), Clare Forlani (Verity)

A young man, disturbed by his mother's death, believes he has seen her double in an Edinburgh hotel worker, who he starts stalking.

Awkward attempt to portray an alienated outsider's view of life. Despite two workmanlike lead performances, it fails to cohere or convince.

SCR Ed Whitmore, David Mackenzie CIN *Giles Nuttgens* DES Tom Sayer ED Colin Monie PROD Gillian Berrie DIST Buena Vista

66 As a study of grief, this is silly and nonsensical. – *Dave Calhoun, Time Out*

66 A happening indie soundtrack, a nice lead performance – it's all here, and yet it can't cancel out my feeling that the film's tosh-level is considerably in excess of the EU maximum. – *Peter Bradshaw, Guardian*

'The Night He Came Home!'

Halloween ★

DIR *John Carpenter*

1978 91m US

DVD ♫

☆ Donald Pleasence, Jamie Lee Curtis, Nancy Loomis, P. J. Soles

In a small Illinois town, a psychopathic killer escapes from an asylum.

Single-minded shocker with virtually no plot, just a succession of bloody, slashing attacks in semi-darkness. Efficiently scary, and so skilfully conceived that it reinvigorated the entire horror genre in late 1970s America.

SCR John Carpenter, Debra Hill CIN Dean Cundey MUS John Carpenter DES Tommy Wallace PROD Irwin Yablans DIST Falcon International

66 One of the cinema's most perfectly engineered devices for saying Boo! – *Richard Combs, Monthly Film Bulletin*

† Jamie Lee Curtis, who became known as 'The Queen of Scream' for her roles in Halloween movies, is the daughter of Janet Leigh, who herself played a famous victim of a slasher in Psycho.

'Evil Has A Destiny.'

Halloween (new) ★

SCR/DIR Rob Zombie

2007 109m US

♫

☆ Malcolm McDowell (Dr. Samuel Loomis), Tyler Mane

DVD Available on DVD   ☆ Cast in order   66 Critics' Quotes   Ⓐ Academy Award   Ⓑ BAFTA
♫ Soundtrack on CD   of importance   † Points of interest   Ⓐ Academy Award nomination   Ⓑ BAFTA nomination

271

H

(Michael Myers), Daeg Faerch (Michael Myers, age 10), Sheri Moon Zombie (Deborah Myers), Brad Dourif (Sheriff Lee Brackett)

After murdering his family, ten year-old Michael Myers is locked away for fifteen years. Escaping he returns to hometown Haddonfield searching for his adopted younger sister Laurie, killing her college friends in the process.

A harsh, graphic, uneven blend of trailer-trash biopic and précis retread of the landmark 1978 classic.

CIN Phil Parmet   MUS Tyler Bates   DES Anthony Tremblay   ED Glenn Garland   PROD Malek Akkad, Rob Zombie, Andy Gould   DIST Paramount Pictures

66 This Myers is more problem child than bogeyman. – *Owen Gleiberman – Entertainment Weekly*

Hamlet ★★

SCR/DIR Michael Almereyda
2000   112m   US
DVD   ♫

☆ Ethan Hawke (Hamlet), Kyle MacLachlan (Claudius), Sam Shepard (Ghost), Diane Venora (Gertrude), Bill Murray (Polonius), *Liev Schreiber* (Laertes), Julia Stiles (Ophelia), Karl Geary (Horatio), Paula Malcomson (Marcella), Steve Zahn (Rosencrantz), Dechen Thurman (Guildenstern), Rome Neal (Barnardo), Jeffrey Wright (Gravedigger), Paul Bartel (Osric), Casey Affleck (Fortinbras)

The CEO of Denmark Corp is murdered, and his son plots revenge.

Interesting relocation of the play to an age of corporate ethics and techno-paranoia; the concepts intrigue, but much of the acting fails to satisfy.

CIN John De Borman   MUS Carter Burwell   DES Gideon Ponte   ED Kristina Boden   PROD Andrew Fierberg, Amy Hobby   DIST Film4

66 Cast for fun, and the whimsy is enjoyable both for its parody of heavy-handed "relevant" updates of the play. – *Ella Taylor, L.A. Weekly*

66 Much of this is amusing; virtually all of it is shallow and reductive. – *Alexander Walker, Evening Standard*

Hamlet ★

SCR/DIR Kenneth Branagh
1996   242m   US/GB
DVD   ♫

☆ Kenneth Branagh (Hamlet), *Derek Jacobi* (Claudius), Julie Christie (Gertrude), Kate Winslet (Ophelia), Richard Briers (Polonius), Nicholas Farrell (Horatio), Michael Maloney (Laertes), Brian Blessed (Ghost), Jack Lemmon (Marcellus), Billy Crystal (1st Gravedigger), Robin Williams (Osric), Gérard Depardieu (Reynaldo), Charlton Heston (Player King), Rosemary Harris (Player Queen), Judi Dench (Hecuba), John Gielgud (Priam), Rufus Sewell (Fortinbras), Ken Dodd (Yorick)

In the 19th century, Hamlet takes even longer than usual to decide on his course of revenge.

A lavish folly, pointlessly over-cast with big names in non-speaking roles, and using an unexpurgated version of the play but never finding its centre. Branagh's tactics for whipping up excitement, from swinging on

chandeliers to a crashing and tactless score, smack mainly of panic.

CIN Alex Thomson   MUS Patrick Doyle   DES Tim Harvey   ED Neil Farrell   PROD David Barron   DIST Rank/Castle Rock

66 If Branagh's ambitious film needs any compliment, it is that at around four hours it carries itself perfectly well. – *Steve Grant, Time Out*

66 Weary, stale, flat, and – in every sense of the word – unprofitable. – *Christopher Tookey, Daily Mail*

⚖ Kenneth Branagh (adapted screenplay); Patrick Doyle; Tim Harvey; Alex Byrne (costume design)
Ⓣ Tim Harvey; Alex Byrne (costume design)

'The extraordinary adaptation of Shakespeare's classic tale of vengeance and tragedy.'

Hamlet ★★

DIR Franco Zeffirelli
1990   130m   US/ France
DVD   ♫

☆ Mel Gibson (Hamlet), Glenn Close (Gertrude), Alan Bates (Claudius), Paul Scofield (Ghost), *Ian Holm* (Polonius), *Helena Bonham Carter* (Ophelia), Stephen Dillane (Horatio), Nathaniel Parker (Laertes), Sean Murray (Guildenstern), Michael Maloney (Rosencrantz), Trevor Peacock (The Gravedigger), John McEnery (Osric)

The prince of Denmark takes too long to avenge his father's death.

Workmanlike version with a strong, brooding atmosphere and surprisingly successful star casting; we've seen better, but also much worse.

SCR Christopher de Vore, Franco Zeffirelli   CIN David Watkin   MUS Ennio Morricone   DES *Dante Ferretti*   ED Richard Marden   PROD Dyson Lovell   DIST Warner/Nelson Entertainment/Icon

66 An entirely credible, middle-of-the-road production. – *Hal Hinson, Washington Post*

⚖ Dante Ferretti; Maurizio Millenotti (costume design)
Ⓣ Alan Bates (supporting actor)

Hamlet ★★★

DIR Laurence Olivier
1948   142m   GB
DVD

☆ *Laurence Olivier* (Hamlet), *Eileen Herlie* (Gertrude), *Basil Sydney* (Claudius), *Jean Simmons* (Ophelia), *Felix Aylmer* (Polonius), Norman Wooland (Horatio), Terence Morgan (Laertes), *Stanley Holloway* (Gravedigger), Peter Cushing, Esmond Knight, Anthony Quayle, Harcourt Williams, John Laurie, Niall MacGinnis, Patrick Troughton

Prince Hamlet takes his time deliberating whether to avenge his father's death.

The play is sharply cut, and the camera prowls along gloomy corridors, presumably illustrating the claustrophobic nature of the Prince's neurosis. But much of the acting is fine, some scenes compel, and the production has a splendid brooding power.

SCR Alan Dent   CIN *Desmond Dickinson*   MUS William Walton   DES *Roger Furse*   ED Helga Cranston   PROD Laurence Olivier   DIST Rank/Two Cities

DVD Available on DVD   ☆ Cast in order of importance   66 Critics' Quotes   † Points of interest   ⚖ Academy Award   ⚖ Academy Award nomination   Ⓣ BAFTA   Ⓣ BAFTA nomination
♫ Soundtrack on CD

66 Be you 9 or 90, a PhD or just plain Joe, Hamlet is the movie of the year. – *Washington Times*

66 By the end one no longer thinks of the piece as filmed Shakespeare, but accepts it simply as a splendid production of a masterpiece. – *Dilys Powell*

⚊ picture; Laurence Olivier (leading actor)

⚊ Laurence Olivier (director); Jean Simmons (supporting actress); William Walton (music); art direction

Ⓣ picture

Hamlet Goes Business ★★

SCR/DIR Aki Kaurismäki

1987 86m Finland

☆ Pirkka-Pekka Petelius (Hamlet), Esko Salminen (Klaus), Kati Outinen (Ofelia), Elina Salo (Gertrud), Esko Nikkari (Polonius), Kari Vaananen (Lauri Polonius), Hannu Valtonen (Simo), Mari Rantasila (Helena)

A son whose father is murdered takes revenge on the killer.

Kaurismäki switches the action from Elsinore to a modern Helsinki boardroom, and bizarrely the state of Denmark becomes the rubber duck industry. Darkly playful ingenuity from this provocative, droll director.

CIN Timo Salminen MUS Elmore James ED Raija Talvio PROD Aki DIST Electric/Villealfa Productions/Aki Kaurismäki

---

'Behind a beautiful face, beneath a dangerous smile, lies a revenge that can't be stopped.'

The Hand that Rocks the Cradle ★

DIR Curtis Hanson

1992 110m US

DVD ♫

☆ Annabella Sciorra (Claire Bartel), Rebecca de Mornay (Mrs. Mott / Peyton Flanders), Matt McCoy (Michael Bartel), Ernie Hudson (Solomon), Julianne Moore (Marlene Craven), Madeline Zima (Emma Bartel), John de Lancie (Dr. Victor Mott), Kevin Skousen (Marty Craven)

A woman gets herself hired as nanny to the daughter of a happily married couple, as a means to take her revenge for their part in her husband's suicide.

A formulaic thriller that hit the right buttons with audiences; it was a huge hit, and briefly made de Mornay a star. She certainly exploits her 'nanny from hell' role with gusto; yet the resolution seems predictable, even inevitable.

SCR Amanda Silver CIN Robert Elswit MUS Graeme Revell DES Edward Pisoni ED John F. Link PROD David Madden DIST Buena Vista/Hollywood Pictures/Interscope/Nomura, Babcock & Brown

---

'It's gonna be one hell of a night.'

Hangin' with the Homeboys ★

SCR/DIR Joseph B. Vasquez

1991 88m US

DVD ♫

☆ Doug E. Doug (Willie Stevens), Mario Joyner (Tom McNeal), John Leguizamo (Johnny), Nestor Serrano (Vinny / Fernando), Kimberly Russell (Vanessa), Mary B.

Ward (Luna), Reggie Montgomery (Rasta), Christine Claravall (Daria), Rose Jackson (Lila)

Four young men from the Bronx gather for a night out, and find themselves in an unfamiliar neighbourhood.

Rites-of-passage story, disguised as a hip urban movie, with decent, partly improvised performances from its young cast.

CIN Anghel Decca ED Michael Schweitzer PROD Richard Brick DIST Palace/New Line

The Hanging Garden ★

SCR/DIR Thom Fitzgerald

1997 91m Canada/GB

DVD ♫

☆ Chris Leavins (Sweet William), Kerry Fox (Rosemary), Seana McKenna (Iris), Peter MacNeill (Whiskey Mac), Christine Dunsworth (Violet), Troy Veinotte (Teen Sweet William), Sarah Polley (Teen Rosemary), Joel S. Keller (Fletcher)

A young gay man confronts his demons upon returning to his family home in Nova Scotia for his sister's wedding.

Highly literary drama, done with a certain wit that allows us to forgive the fact the main characters have all been named after plants.

CIN Daniel Jobin MUS John Roby DES Taavo Soodor ED Susan Shanks PROD Louise Garfield, Arnie Gelbart, Thom Fitzgerald DIST Triptych/Galafilm/Emotion

66 If you can forgive the self-indulgence of a debutant, this is an engaging and often darkly amusing study of repressed emotion and family angst. – *David Parkinson, Empire*

Hannah and Her Sisters ★★★★

SCR/DIR *Woody Allen*

1986 106m US

DVD

☆ *Woody Allen* (Mickey Sachs), *Mia Farrow* (Hannah), *Dianne Wiest* (Holly), *Michael Caine* (Elliot), Carrie Fisher (April), *Barbara Hershey* (Lee), Maureen O'Sullivan (Norma), Lloyd Nolan (Evan), Max von Sydow (Frederick), Daniel Stern (Dusty), Sam Waterston (David), Tony Roberts (Mickey's ex-partner), Julie Kavner (Gail)

Relationships intermingle for a New York family over a two-year period between Thanksgiving dinners.

Even though it has nowhere in particular to go, and certain scenes are over the top, this is a brilliantly assembled and thoroughly enjoyable mélange of fine acting (especially by the women in the cast), and witty one-liners, with particularly sharp editing and a nostalgic music score. One of Allen's very best films.

CIN *Carlo di Palma* MUS popular and classical extracts DES Stuart Wurtzel ED *Susan E. Morse* PROD Robert Greenhut DIST Orion/Charles R. Joffe, Jack Rollins

66 A loosely knit canvas of Manhattan interiors and exteriors. – *Sight & Sound*

66 One of Woody Allen's great films. – *Variety*

Ⓐ Woody Allen (original screenplay); Dianne Wiest (supporting actress); Michael Caine (supporting actor)
Ⓐ picture; Woody Allen (director); Susan E. Morse (film editing); art direction
Ⓑ Woody Allen (original screenplay); Woody Allen (director)

Hannah Montana/Miley Cyrus: Best of Both Worlds Concert Tour (new) ★

DIR Bruce Hendricks
2008   75m   US
♫

☆ Miley Cyrus (Hannah Montana), Billy Ray Cyrus, Kenny Ortega, The Jonas Brothers

A documentary record of 15-year-old Miley Cyrus' sell-out 2007 American concert tour as herself, and her Disney Channel pop star phenomenon alter-ego Hannah Montana.

Tweenie fans of the TV pop princess and her vanilla rock brand will be entranced – all others, bored and mystified, even in 3D, as gimmicks are kept to a minimum.

CIN Mitch Amundsen   ED Michael Tronik   PROD Bruce Hendricks, Kenny Ortega, Arthur F. Repola   DIST Buena Vista

66 Disney has discovered yet another way to print money. – *Peter Debruge, Variety*

66 Sitting through this strenuously bland floor show, I amused myself imagining all the flannel-shirted Juno misfits watching this dreary stuff aghast. – *Ella Taylor, L.A. Weekly*

The Happening (new)

SCR/DIR M. Night Shyamalan
2008   91m   US / India
DVD   ♫

☆ Mark Wahlberg (Elliot Moore), Zooey Deschanel (Alma Moore), John Leguizamo (Julian), Ashlyn Sanchez (Jess), Betty Buckley (Mrs. Jones)

When a suicide-inducing toxin wreaks havoc in America's north-eastern states, a science teacher and his wife head for the country with their friend and his young daughter.

Director Shyamalan has built a career on his empathy with the supernatural, but the connection is starting to wear thin. The plot machinations are entirely predictable; the performers look and react as if they don't believe a word.

CIN Tak Fujimoto   MUS James Newton Howard   DES Jeannine Claudia Oppewall   ED Conrad Buff IV   PROD Barry Mendel / Sam Mercer / M Night Shyamalan

66 Shyamalan's career has been going steadily downhill after peaking with The Sixth Sense in 1999. A succession of pretentious, mystical thrillers has led to The Happening, an ineffectual attempt to reprise the Cold War, nuclear-angst horror flicks of the Fifties and Sixties for the era of global warming. – *Philip French, Observer*

† The Happening is the first major joint venture for India's UTV Motion Pictures with a Hollywood company, Fox Searchlight.

Happiness ★★

SCR/DIR *Todd Solondz*
1998   134m   US
DVD

☆ Jane Adams (Joy Jordan), *Dylan Baker* (Bill Maplewood), Lara Flynn Boyle (Helen Jordan), Ben Gazzara (Lenny Jordan), Jared Harris (Vlad), Philip Seymour Hoffman (Allen), Jon Lovitz (Andy Kornbluth), Marla Maples (Ann Chambeau), Cynthia Stevenson (Trish Maplewood), Elizabeth Ashley (Diane Freed), Louise Lasser (Mona Jordan)

Three sisters in New Jersey struggle with dysfunctional relationships of different kinds.

Acutely pessimistic, cruelly funny tapestry of unfulfilled lives, in which the angst of a suburban paedophile is the standout strand. It's relentless, perhaps excessively so, in its insistence that sex destroys us.

CIN *Maryse Alberti*   MUS Robbie Kondor   DES Therese Deprez   ED Alan Oxman   PROD Ted Hope, Christine Vachon   DIST October/Good Machine/Killer Films

66 Brilliant and disturbingly jaundiced. – *Michael Wilmington, Washington Post*

66 Not just serious about life – it's downright Dostoyevskian in its moral scrutiny. – *Jonathan Romney, Guardian*

'Happy, Texas. Where even people on the run find a moment to be fabulous.'

Happy, Texas ★★

DIR Mark Illsley
1999   98m   US
DVD   ♫

☆ Jeremy Northam (Harry Sawyer), *Steve Zahn* (Wayne Wayne Wayne Jnr), William H. Macy (Sheriff Chappy Dent), Ally Walker (Josephine McLintock), Illeana Douglas (Ms Schaefer), M.C. Gainey (Bob), Ron Perlman (Nalhober), Tim Bagley (David), Michael Hitchcock (Steven), Paul Dooley (Judge)

Hiding out in a small Texas town, two runaway convicts disguise themselves as a pair of gay pageant directors.

Slight but amiable comedy in which the stakes never seem too high.

SCR Mark Illsley, Ed Stone, Phil Reeves   CIN Bruce Douglas Johnson   MUS Peter Harris   DES Maurin Scarlata   ED Norman Buckley   PROD Mark Illsley, Rick Montgomery, Ed Stone

66 A comedy of '90s sexual inclusiveness as effervescent as a cold soda pop. – *Lisa Schwarzbaum, Entertainment Weekly*

'WARNING: May cause toe-tapping.'

Happy Feet   •   ★★

DIR George Miller (with Judy Morris, Warren Coleman)
2006   108m   US/Australia
DVD   ♫

☆ Elijah Wood (Mumble), Robin Williams

(Ramon/Lovelace), Hugh Jackman (Memphis), Nicole Kidman (Norma Jean), Hugo Weaving (Noah the Elder)

In Antarctica, where fish stocks are decreasing, a penguin chick named Mumble is born. He cannot sing, unlike his peers, but to their embarrassment is a talented tap-dancer. Setting out to find out why the penguins' food is vanishing, he is captured and placed in a zoo, where his dancing makes him a sensation.

Technically a brilliant work, pushing CGI animation beyond all previous boundaries and simulating the look of a live-action epic. Some scenes (an avalanche, a dive off a high cliff) are dizzyingly well executed. But this story is a strange stew. Its one-world message feels bolted on, and the right-on, eco-friendly subplot about Mumble helping to save the penguins' declining food supply feels terribly forced. Still, overall it's clever, funny and enjoyable.

SCR George Miller, John Collee, Judy Morris, Warren Coleman   MUS John Powell   DES Mark Sexton
ED Margaret Sixel, Christian Gazal   PROD Doug Mitchell, George Miller, Bill Miller   DIST Warner Bros.

66 Schmaltzy comedy with an environmentalist message. – *Peter Bradshaw, Guardian*

66 The essence of this inventive though erratic animated feature is joyous music and eye-popping motion. – *Joe Morgenstern, Wall Street Journal*

† The film has also been screened in IMAX cinemas.

⚱ animated feature
🅣 animated feature
Ⓣ John Powell

Happy Times ★

DIR Zhang Yimou
2000   95m   China
DVD

☆ Zhao Benshan (Zhao), Dong Jie (Wu Ying), Li Xuejian (Li), Dong Lifan (Stepmother), Leng Qibin (Wu Ying's Stepbrother), Niu Ben (Old Niu), Fu Biao (Little Fu)

A retired bachelor sets up a make-believe massage parlour in order to employ a blind girl in his care.

Slender urban fairytale with Chaplinesque ambitions; the comedy seems forced, and it's unintentionally creepy.

SCR Gai Zi   CIN Hou Yong   MUS San Bao   ED Zhai Ru
PROD Zhao Yu, Yang Qinglong, Weiping Zhang
DIST TCF

66 Zhang is working in a popular sentimental mode here, but his connection to the material – and to us – is heartfelt and without a trace of condescension. As a filmmaker, he's the opposite of a con artist, and his new movie is a gentle marvel. – *Peter Rainer, New York Magazine*

66 Schmaltz served in a hand-painted cup. – *Michael Atkinson, Village Voice*

Happy Together ★★★

SCR/DIR *Wong Kar-Wai*
1997   96m   Hong Kong
DVD   ♫

☆ Leslie Cheung (Ho Po-wing), Tony Leung (Lai Yiu-fai), Chang Chen (Chang)

Two gay lovers from Hong Kong part ways in Buenos Aires.

A movie that glows like the tip of a cigarette, summoning remarkable style and energy in its portrait of a spent relationship.

CIN *Christopher Doyle*   MUS Danny Chung   DES William Chang   ED William Chang, Wong Ming-Lam
PROD Chan Ye-Cheng   DIST Artificial Eye/Block 2/Prenom H/Seawoo/Jet Tone

66 Acerbic, moody and provocatively slight. – *J. Hoberman, Village Voice*

† Wong Kar-Wai was voted best director for this film at the Cannes Film Festival in 1997.

Happy-Go-Lucky (new) ★★

SCR/DIR Mike Leigh
2008   118m   UK/US
DVD

☆ Sally Hawkins (Poppy), Eddie Marsan (Scott), Alexis Zegerman (Zoe), Stanley Townsend (Tramp)

A young London teacher maintains her cheerful attitude to life, even when confronted by its darker side.

A far brighter, more optimistic tone than is usual from Leigh, who takes pains to establish the virtues of his profoundly irritating heroine. It's a minor work for him.

CIN *Dick Pope*   MUS Gary Yershon   DES Mark Tildesley
ED Jim Clark   PROD Simon Channing Williams
DIST Momentum

66 Just occasionally the storytelling is a little glib. . .and certain plot elements demand greater depth of investigation than [Leigh] is prepared to give them. – *Geoffrey Macnab, Sight & Sound*

66 It's a funny film – a surprise, perhaps, after Vera Drake – and, crucially, it aches with truth. – *Dave Calhoun, Time Out*

† Sally Hawkins won the Silver Bear award for best actress at the 2008 Berlin Film Festival.

'As a cop, he has brains, brawn and an instinct to kill.'

Hard Boiled ★★

DIR John Woo
1992   126m   Hong Kong
DVD   ♫

☆ Chow Yun-Fat (Insp. Yuen), Tony Leung (Alan), Teresa Mo (Teresa Chang), Philip Chan (Supt. Pang), Philip Kwok (Mad Dog), Anthony Wong (Johnny Wong), Kwan Hoi-Shan (Mr Hoi), Tung Wai (Foxy)

A tough cop teams up with an undercover agent to bring down a smuggling ring.

The apex of John Woo's balletically violent style, and his last film before Hollywood came calling. Not his best-plotted thriller, but full of bravura sequences.

SCR Barry Wong   CIN Wang Wing-Heng   MUS Michael Gibbs   DES James Leung   ED John Woo, David Wu, Kai Kit-Wai, Jack Ah   PROD Linda Kuk, Terence Chang
DIST Golden Princess/Milestone

66 Infinitely more exciting than a dozen Die Hards, action cinema doesn't come any better than this. – *Mark Salisbury, Empire*

H

| DVD Available on DVD | ☆ Cast in order | 66 Critics' Quotes | ⚱ Academy Award | 🅣 BAFTA |
| ♫ Soundtrack on CD | of importance | † Points of interest | ⚱ Academy Award nomination | Ⓣ BAFTA nomination |

275

66 Mr. Woo does, in fact, seem to be a very brisk, talented director with a gift for the flashy effect and the bizarre confrontation. – *Vincent Canby, New York Times*

'Strangers shouldn't talk to little girls.'

Hard Candy

DIR David Slade
2005   104m   US
DVD

☆ Patrick Wilson (Jeff Kohlver), Ellen Page (Hayley Stark), Sandra Oh (Judy Tokuda), Odessa Rae (Janelle Rogers)

A 14-year-old girl tempts a fashion photographer into inviting her home, in the hope she can prove he is a paedophile.

Glib two-hander exploiting a topical theme for generally meretricious thrills. It leaves a nasty taste in the mouth, but the performances are fine.

SCR Brian Nelson   CIN Jo Willems   MUS Harry Escott, Molly Nyman   DES Jeremy Reed   ED Art Jones
PROD Michael Caldwell, David W. Higgins, Richard Hutton
DIST Lionsgate

66 A sardonic (rather than sadistic) celluloid fable in which Little Red Riding Hood grabs the woodman's axe and sets about turning the big bad wolf into a sacrificial lamb. – *Mark Kermode, Observer*

66 Hard Candy is impressive and effective. As for what else it may be, each audience member will have to decide. – *Roger Ebert, Chicago Sun-Times*

† The title is Internet slang for an under-age girl.
† This was the first lead part in a feature film for Page, who was Oscar-nominated for her title role performance in Juno.

A Hard Day's Night   ★★★★

DIR *Richard Lester*
1964   85m   GB
DVD   ♫

☆ *The Beatles*, Wilfrid Brambell (Grandfather), Norman Rossington (Norm), *Victor Spinetti* (TV Director)

Harassed by their manager and Paul's grandpa, the Beatles embark from Liverpool by train for a London TV show.

Comic fantasia with music; an enormous commercial success with the director trying every cinematic gag in the book, it led directly to all the kaleidoscopic Swinging London spy thrillers and comedies of the later sixties – and to the prevailing tone of pop videos decades later. At the time it was a breath of fresh air, and its playful, low-budget style, shot in black-and-white and clearly influenced by the French New Wave, faithfully captured the group's irreverent attitude to their fame, the media, and even themselves.

SCR *Alun Owen*   CIN *Gilbert Taylor*   ED John Jympson
PROD Walter Shenson   DIST UA/Proscenium

66 A fine conglomeration of madcap clowning . . . with such a dazzling use of camera that it tickles the intellect and electrifies the nerves. – *Bosley Crowther*

66 All technology was enlisted in the service of the gag, and a kind of nuclear gagmanship exploded. – *John Simon*

♪ Alun Owen; George Martin

'When good luck is a long shot, you have to hedge your bets.'

Hard Eight   ★★

SCR/DIR Paul Thomas Anderson
1996   101m   US
DVD

☆ *Philip Baker Hall* (Sydney), John C. Reilly (John Finnegan), Gwyneth Paltrow (Clementine), Samuel L. Jackson (Jimmy), F. William Parker (Hostage), Philip Seymour Hoffman (Craps player)

A veteran gambler takes a bankrupt young man under his wing, and helps him pursue a cocktail waitress.

Low-key but very promising debut from this director, who has the confidence to let its intrigue bubble up gradually.

CIN Robert Elswit   MUS Michael Penn, Jon Brion
DES Nancy Deren   ED Barbara Tulliver   PROD Robert Jones, John Lyons   DIST Entertainment/Rysher/Green Parrot

66 A subtle, understated reworking of noir conventions. – *Nick Bradshaw, Time Out*

66 Anderson, who makes as impressive a directing debut as has been seen in some time, creates a perfectly modulated mystery that doesn't even feel like one. It's a character play, and Hall, Reilly and Paltrow are so convincingly damaged they take on the properties of fine china. – *John Anderson, Los Angeles Times*

'There's only one way these two are going to get along...'

The Hard Way   ★

DIR John Badham
1991   111m   US
DVD

☆ Michael J. Fox (Nick Lang / Ray Casanov), James Woods (Detective Lt. John Moss, NYPD), Stephen Lang (Party Crasher), Annabella Sciorra (Susan), Delroy Lindo (Captain Brix, NYPD), Luis Guzman (Detective Benny Pooley, NYPD), Mary Mara (Detective China, NYPD), Penny Marshall (Angie, Nick's Agent)

A hardened New York detective reluctantly agrees to babysit a bratty Hollywood megastar researching his latest role.

Smart offering from the tail-end of the buddy-cop cycle that entertains for a couple of hours.

SCR Daniel Pyne, Lem Dobbs   CIN Robert Primes, Don McAlpine   MUS Arthur B. Rubinstein   DES Philip Harrison   ED Frank Morriss, Tony Lombardo
PROD William Sackheim, Rob Cohen
DIST UIP/Universal/Badham/Cohen

66 In addition to star chemistry and in-jokes, The Hard Way has all the required custom features, to wit: one excellent heroine who holds her own in fights and arguments, one superb villain who genuinely enjoys torturing and killing people... and a stunt-filled finale with the principals dangling from a giant model of Fox's face over Times Square. Highly recommended. – *Kim Newman, Empire*

DVD Available on DVD	☆ Cast in order	66 Critics' Quotes	♪ Academy Award	🏆 BAFTA
♫ Soundtrack on CD	of importance	† Points of interest	♪ Academy Award nomination	🏆 BAFTA nomination

'It activates it exhilarates. . .it exterminates.'

Hardware ★

SCR/DIR Richard Stanley
1990   93m   GB/US
DVD ♫

☆ Dylan McDermott (Moses Baxter), Stacey Travis (Jill), John Lynch (Shades), William Hootkins (Lincoln Wineberg Jr.), Iggy Pop (Angry Bob)

In a future desert wasteland, a scavenger unearths the head of a deadly robot which rebuilds itself and goes on a rampage.

Resourceful low-budget techno-thriller, overfiltered and overscored, but stylish.

CIN Steven Chivers   MUS Simon Boswell   DES Joseph Bennett   ED Derek Trigg   PROD Joanne Sellar, Paul Trijbits   DIST Palace/Miramax/British Screen/BSB/Wicked Films

66 An impressive assault on the senses. – *Mark Kermode, Time Out*

Harry, He's Here To Help ★★

DIR *Dominik Moll*
2000   117m   France
DVD

☆ Laurent Lucas (Michel), *Sergi Lopez* (Harry), Mathilde Seigner (Claire), Sophie Guillemin (Plum)

A psychopath persuades a new acquaintance that they went to school together, and begins to interfere in his life.

Beady, blackly comic psychological thriller with a deliberately Hitchcockian flavour.

SCR Dominik Moll, Gilles Marchand   CIN Matthieu Poirot-Delpech   MUS David Sinclair Whitaker   DES Michel Barthelemy   ED Yannick Kergoat   PROD Michel Saint-Jean   DIST Artificial Eye

66 Moll has devised a pleasing choreography of anxiety. – *Peter Bradshaw, Guardian*

66 Made with a confident grace and ironic wit. – *Philip French, Observer*

ⓣ film not in the English Language

'Dark And Difficult Times Lie Ahead.'

Harry Potter and the Goblet of Fire ★

DIR Mike Newell
2005   157m   GB/US
DVD ♫

☆ Daniel Radcliffe (Harry Potter), Rupert Grint (Ron Weasley), Emma Watson (Hermione Granger), Robbie Coltrane (Rubeus Hagrid), Ralph Fiennes (Lord Voldemort), Michael Gambon (Albus Dumbledore), Brendan Gleeson (Alastor 'Mad-Eye' Moody), Jason Isaacs (Lucius Malfoy), Gary Oldman (Sirius Black), Miranda Richardson (Rita Skeeter), Alan Rickman (Severus Snape), Maggie Smith (Minerva McGonagall), Timothy Spall (Wormtail)

Harry's life is endangered when he is selected to compete in the Tri-wizard Tournament despite being underage.

Despite a welcome focus on the youngsters' burgeoning sexuality, the film mistakes murk for darkness, and feels lumpen and overlong.

SCR Steve Kloves   CIN Roger Pratt   MUS Patrick Doyle   DES *Stuart Craig*   ED Mick Audsley   PROD David Heyman   DIST Warner

66 Handsomely made, good-natured and high-spirited family movie. – *Peter Bradshaw, Guardian*

66 A 157-minute holding pattern. – *J.R. Jones, Chicago Reader*

⅄ art direction

ⓣ Stuart Craig

ⓣ Jim Mitchell, John Richardson, Timothy Webber, Tim Alexander (special visual effects); Nick Dudman, Amanda Knight, Eithne Fennel (make up/hair)

'Journey beyond your imagination.'

Harry Potter and the Philosopher's Stone ★

DIR Chris Columbus
2001   152m   US/GB
DVD ♫

☆ Daniel Radcliffe (Harry Potter), Rupert Grint (Ron Weasley), Emma Watson (Hermione Granger), Robbie Coltrane (Hagrid), Richard Griffiths (Uncle Vernon Dursley), Richard Harris (Albus Dumbledore), Ian Hart (Professor Quirrell/Voldemort), John Hurt (Mr Ollivander), *Alan Rickman* (Professor Snape), Fiona Shaw (Aunt Petunia Dursley), Maggie Smith (Professor McGonagall), Julie Walters (Mrs Weasley), John Cleese (Nearly Headless Nick), Warwick Davis (Goblin Bank Teller/Professor Flitwick)

An 11-year-old orphan with mysterious gifts escapes the clutches of his monstrous aunt and uncle to enrol in Hogwarts School of Witchcraft and Wizardry.

Cautiously packaged for maximum appeal to the books' legions of fans, this opening salvo suffers from wanting to show off its splendid production design and star cameos at the expense of everything else, and there's not nearly enough attention to the child performances. Still, it's synthetically enjoyable.

SCR Steve Kloves   CIN John Seale   MUS John Williams   DES *Stuart Craig*   ED Richard Francis-Bruce   PROD David Heyman   DIST Warner

66 Exactly the sum of its parts, neither more nor less. – *Anthony Lane, New Yorker*

66 Is the movie any good? At the dawn of the twenty-first century, when art is defined by commerce, this question is beside the point. – *Peter Travers, Rolling Stone*

⅄ Stuart Craig; John Williams; Judianna Makovsky (costume design)

ⓣ British film

ⓣ Robbie Coltrane (supporting actor); Stuart Craig; Robert Legato, Nick Davis, John Richardson, Roger Guyett, Jim Berney (special visual effects); John Midgley, Eddy Joseph, Ray Merrin, Graham Daniel, Adam Daniel (sound); Judianna Makovsky (costume design); Amanda Knight, Eithne Fennel, Nick Dudman (make up/hair)

'Something wicked this way comes.'

Harry Potter and the Prisoner of Azkaban ★★

DIR *Alfonso Cuarón*
2004   141m   US/GB
DVD   ♫

☆ Daniel Radcliffe (Harry Potter), Rupert Grint (Ron Weasley), Emma Watson (Hermione Granger), Gary Oldman (Sirius Black), *David Thewlis* (Professor Lupin), Michael Gambon (Albus Dumbledore), Alan Rickman (Professor Severus Snape), Maggie Smith (Professor Minerva McGonagall), Robbie Coltrane (Rubeus Hagrid), Tom Felton (Draco Malfoy), Emma Thompson (Professor Sybil Trelawney), Julie Walters (Mrs Weasley), Timothy Spall (Peter Pettigrew), Julie Christie (Madame Rosmerta)

The wizard convicted of murdering Harry Potter's father escapes and heads for Hogwarts.

Easily the best in the Potter series, an altogether bolder style of adaptation handled by a sensitive director of teenagers. The whole saga comes alive here, and every aspect of the production seems newly inspired.

SCR *Steve Kloves*   CIN Michael Seresin   MUS *John Williams*   DES *Stuart Craig*   ED Steven Weisberg
PROD David Heyman, Chris Columbus, Mark Radcliffe
DIST Warner

66 Shot in spooky gradations of silver and shadow, The Prisoner of Azkaban is the first movie in the series with fear and wonder in its bones, and genuine fun, too. – *Owen Gleiberman, Entertainment Weekly*

66 Cuaron has taken the Potter story on to a matchlessly haunting level. – *Jenny McCartney, Sunday Telegraph*

⚱ John Williams; Roger Guyett, Tim Burke, John Richardson, Bill George (visual effects)

🏆 Audience Award

Ⓣ Stuart Craig; special visual effects; Amanda Knight, Eithne Fennel, Nick Dudman (make up/hair)

Harvey ★★★

DIR *Henry Koster*
1950   104m   US
DVD

☆ *James Stewart* (Elwood P. Dowd), *Josephine Hull* (Veta Louise Simmons), *Victoria Horne* (Myrtle Mae), Peggy Dow (Miss Kelly), *Cecil Kellaway* (Dr. Chumley), Charles Drake (Dr. Sanderson), *Jesse White* (Wilson), Nana Bryant (Mrs. Chumley), Wallace Ford (Lofgren)

A middle-aged drunk has an imaginary white rabbit as his friend, and his sister tries to have him certified.

An amiably batty play with splendid lines is transferred virtually intact to the screen and survives superbly.

SCR *Mary Chase (with Oscar Brodney)*   CIN William Daniels   MUS Frank Skinner   ED Ralph Dawson
PROD John Beck   DIST U-I

VETA LOUISE (JOSEPHINE HULL): Myrtle Mae, you have a lot to learn, and I hope you never learn it.
ELWOOD (JAMES STEWART): I've wrestled with reality for 35 years, and I'm happy, doctor, I finally won out over it.
ELWOOD: Harvey and I have things to do . . . we sit in the bars . . . have a drink or two . . . and play the juke box. Very soon the faces of the other people turn towards me and they smile. They say: "We don't know your name, mister, but you're all right, all right." Harvey and I warm ourselves in these golden moments. We came as strangers – soon we have friends. They come over. They sit with us. They drink with us. They talk to us. They tell us about the great big terrible things they've done and the great big wonderful things they're going to do. Their hopes, their regrets. Their loves, their hates. All very large, because nobody ever brings anything small into a bar. Then I introduce them to Harvey, and he's bigger and grander than anything they can offer me. When they leave, they leave impressed. The same people seldom come back.
ELWOOD (DESCRIBING HIS FIRST MEETING WITH HARVEY): I'd just helped Ed Hickey into a taxi. Ed had been mixing his drinks, and I felt he needed conveying. I started to walk down the street when I heard a voice saying: "Good evening, Mr Dowd". I turned, and there was this big white rabbit leaning against a lamp-post. Well, I thought nothing of that! Because when you've lived in a town as long as I've lived in this one, you get used to the fact that everybody knows your name. . .

⚱ Josephine Hull (supporting actress)
⚱ James Stewart (leading actor)

'It's not a remake. It's not a sequel. And it's not based on a Japanese one.'

Hatchet (new) ★★

SCR/DIR Adam Green
2007   85m   US
DVD

☆ Joel David Moore (Ben), Tamara Feldman (Marybeth), Deon Richmond (Marcus), Kane Hodder (Victor Crowley/Mr Crowley), Robert Englund (Sampson), Tony Todd (Reverend Zombie)

A deformed maniac terrorises tourists when their boat sinks in the Louisiana bayous.

A very bloody valentine to 80s slasher movies. Extreme brutality is balanced with hardcore humour for cheap-and-cheerful shocks.

CIN Will Barratt   MUS Andy Garfield   DES Bryan A. McBrien   ED Christopher Roth   PROD Scott Altomare, Sarah Elbert, Cory Neal   DIST The Works

66 So giddily over-the-top that you end up applauding the low-budget aplomb of it all. – *Chuck Wilson, L.A. Weekly*

'You may not believe in ghosts, but you cannot deny terror!'

The Haunting ★★★

DIR Robert Wise
1963   112m   GB

☆ Richard Johnson, Claire Bloom, Russ Tamblyn, Julie Harris, Lois Maxwell, Valentine Dyall

An anthropologist, a sceptic and two mediums spend the weekend in a haunted Boston mansion.

Genuinely frightening haunted-house drama with unbearable degrees of suspension and tension skilfully orchestrated..

SCR Nelson Gidding   CIN *David Boulton*
MUS Humphrey Searle   DES Elliot Scott   ED Ernest Walter   PROD Robert Wise   DIST MGM/Argyle

'A gambler who trusted no one. A woman who risked everything. And a passion that brought them together in the most dangerous city in the world.'

Havana ★

DIR Sydney Pollack
1990 145m US
DVD

☆ Robert Redford (Jack Weil), Lena Olin (Bobby Duran), *Alan Arkin* (Joe Volpi), *Tomas Milian* (Menocal), *Raul Julia* (Arturo Duran), Daniel Davis (Marion Chigwell), Tony Plana (Julio Ramos), Betsy Brantley (Diane)

In the dying days of the Batista era in 1950s Cuba, a slick American poker ace falls in with a radical crowd of locals.

A story that owes more than a little to Casablanca, and not one of the more memorable partnerships between Redford and Pollack, but agreeable enough, and some terrific performances in supporting roles.

SCR Judith Rascoe, David Rayfiel CIN Owen Roizman
MUS Dave Grusin DES Terence Marsh ED Frederic Steinkamp, William Steinkamp PROD Sydney Pollack, Richard Roth DIST UIP/Universal/Mirage

♪ Dave Grusin (music)

'The father, the son and the holy game.'

He Got Game

SCR/DIR Spike Lee
1998 136m US
DVD ♪

☆ Denzel Washington (Jake Shuttlesworth), Ray Allen (Jesus Shuttlesworth), Milla Jovovich (Dakota Burns), Rosario Dawson (Lala Bonilla), Hill Harper (Coleman 'Booger' Sykes), Zelda Harris (Mary Shuttlesworth), Jim Brown (Spivey), Joseph Lyle Taylor (Crudup), Ned Beatty (Warden Wyatt), Bill Nunn (Uncle Bubba), Michele Shay (Aunt Sally), Thomas Jefferson Byrd (Sweetness), Lonette McKee (Martha Shuttlesworth), John Turturro (Coach Billy Sunday)

A wife-killer is let out on parole, on the condition that he persuade his son, a highly rated basketball player, to sign up with the prison governor's alma mater.

Unconvincing combination of father–son drama and didactic fable from this provocative director, stretched out to a great length it rarely sets about earning.

CIN Malik Hassan Sayeed, Ellen Kuras DES Wynn Thomas ED Barry Alexander Brown PROD Jon Kilik, Spike Lee DIST Buena Vista/Touchstone/40 Acres and a Mule

66 A volatile combination of ambitious myth-making and nasty reality. . .it is also an inextricable combination of good and bad. – *David Denby, New York Magazine*

'Bob Maconel is about to have a very bad day.'

He Was a Quiet Man (new)

SCR/DIR Frank Cappello
2007 95m US
☆ Christian Slater (Bob Maconel), Elisha Cuthbert (Vanessa), William H. Macy (Gene Shelby), Sascha Knopf (Paula), Jamison Jones (Scott Harper)

A put-upon office worker who dreams of slaughtering his colleagues becomes a local hero after foiling a cohort who beats him to it.

Ugly black comedy with inventive fantasy sequences; like many of its ilk, its chief aim is to wrong-foot its audience.

CIN Brandon Trost MUS Jeff Beal DES Ermanno Di Febo-Orsini ED Kirk Morri PROD Michael Leahy, Frank Cappello DIST High Fliers

66 Although the budget is low and the plot uneven, it's got a certain cultish charm. – *David Edwards, Daily Mirror*

66 Too relentless for the comedy it would like to be. – *Anthony Quinn, Independent*

Head-On ★★★

SCR/DIR *Fatih Akin*
2004 121m Germany
DVD ♪

☆ *Birol Unel* (Cahit Tomruk), *Sibel Kekilli* (Sibel Guner), Catrin Striebeck (Maren), Guven Kirac (Seref), Meltem Cumbul (Selma)

Two German Turks meet in a clinic for the suicidally depressed, and agree to a marriage of convenience.

A startling, violent romance between lost souls, energised by a propulsive soundtrack, and also offering a valuable look at Turkish diaspora culture.

CIN Rainer Klausmann MUS Maceo Parker, Alexander Hacke DES Tamo Kunz ED Andrew Bird PROD Ralph Schwingel, Stefan Schubert

66 Vivid, bloody, doomed romance. – *Richard Falcon, Sight & Sound*

'There's definitely magic in the air'

Hear My Song ★★

DIR *Peter Chelsom*
1991 105m GB
DVD ♪

☆ *Ned Beatty* (Josef Locke), Adrian Dunbar (Micky O'Neill), Shirley Anne Field (Cathleen Doyle), Tara Fitzgerald (Nancy Doyle), William Hootkins (Mr. X), Harold Berens (Benny Rose), David McCallum (Jim Abbott), John Dair (Derek), Stephen Marcus (Gordon)

In the 1980s, a Liverpool club owner seeks to book the tenor Josef Locke, once a huge draw before he fled to Ireland as a tax exile. But the man he tracks down may not be the real thing.

Almost defiantly old-fashioned and unafraid to embrace whimsy, this charming, slender little tale just about scrapes by.

SCR Peter Chelsom, Adrian Dunbar CIN Sue Gibson
MUS John Altman DES Caroline Hanania ED Martin Walsh PROD Alison Owen DIST Palace/Film Four/Vision/Limelight/British Screen/Windmill Lane

66 The film's ending errs slightly on the side of excessive sunniness, but almost all the rest of it is admirably understated. – *Janet Maslin, New York Times*

Ⓣ John Altman (score); Peter Chelsom, Adrian Dunbar (original screenplay)

H

DVD Available on DVD ☆ Cast in order of importance 66 Critics' Quotes ♪ Soundtrack on CD † Points of interest ♪ Academy Award ♪ Academy Award nomination Ⓑ BAFTA Ⓣ BAFTA nomination

279

'Warning: Jealousy Seriously Damages Your Health.'

Heart ★

DIR Charles McDougall

1998   85m   GB

DVD

☆ Christopher Eccleston (Gary Ellis), Saskia Reeves (Maria Ann McCardle), Kate Hardie (Tess Ellis), Rhys Ifans (Alex Madden), Anna Chancellor (Nicola Farmer), Bill Paterson (Mr. Kreitman), Matthew Rhys (Sean McCardle)

When her son is killed in an accident, a devastated mother forms a bond with the man who received the young man's transplanted heart.

A lurid premise on paper, yet the story yields some riveting psychological insight. Straight-faced performances successfully keep the absurdity at bay for most of its length.

SCR Jimmy McGovern   **CIN** Julian Court   **MUS** Stephen Warbeck   **DES** Stuart Walker, Chris Roope   **ED** Edward Mansell   **PROD** Nicola Shindler   **DIST** Feature Film

Heartbeat Detector (new) ★★

DIR Nicolas Klotz

2008   141m   France

DVD

☆ *Mathieu Amalric* (Simon), Michael Lonsdale (Mathias Jüst), Jean-Pierre Kalfon (Karl Rose), Laetitia Spigarelli (Louisa), Valérie Dréville (Lynn Sanderson), Delphine Chuillot (Isabelle)

The boss of an in-house psychologist for a giant petro-chemical company asks him to assess its Parisian company manager's unusual behaviour. But on probing, he learns of the firm's unsavoury conduct during World War II.

Shot in stark tones of blue, black, and grey, with distinct echoes of Michael Clayton (but sadly not its brevity), director Klotz portrays the corporate machine as a ruthless steamroller of its employees' lives, sweeping all before it for profit and darker deeds. Amalric is astonishing as the investigator who uncovers a murky underbelly.

SCR Elisabeth Perceval, François Emmanuel   **CIN** Josée Deshaies   **MUS** Syd Matters   **DES** Antoine Platteau   **ED** Rose Marie Lausson   **PROD** Sophie Dulac, Michel Zana   **DIST** Trinity Filmed Entertainment

66 A fascinating collision of two fertile recent sub-genres in French cinema – the cinema of 'anxiety' and those films, such as Laurent Cantet's Human Resources, which closely examine the realities of the modern workplace. – *Wally Hammond, Time Out*

66 Intelligent, imaginative French thriller. – *Philip French, Observer*

'He waited all his life to get married. Too bad he didn't wait another week.'

The Heartbreak Kid (new)

DIR Peter Farrelly, Bobby Farrelly

2007   115m   US

DVD   ♫

☆ Ben Stiller (Eddie Cantrow), Michelle Monaghan (Miranda), Malin Akerman (Lila), Jerry Stiller (Doc), Rob Corddry (Mac), Carlos Mencia (Uncle Tito), Scott Wilson (Boo), Danny McBride (Martin)

A long-time bachelor regrets a hasty marriage after falling for another woman on his honeymoon.

Coarse, misogynist update, infused more with the juvenile sensibilities of its sibling co-directors than the spirit of the Neil Simon original.

SCR Scot Armstrong, Leslie Dixon, Bobby Farrelly, Peter Farrelly, Kevin Barnett   **CIN** Matthew F. Leonetti   **MUS** Brendan Ryan, Bill Ryan   **DES** Sidney Bartholomew   **ED** Alan Baumgarten, Sam Seig   **PROD** Ted Field, Bradley Thomas   **DIST** Paramount

66 This hit-and-miss attempt by the Farrelly brothers to up their own ante smacks of comic desperation. – *Peter Travers, Rolling Stone*

66 The cruelty and class distinctions of the original are completely lost amid the buffoonish crudity. – *Anthony Quinn, Independent*

† A shot of a donkey's erect penis was removed in the UK in order to achieve a 15 certificate.

'The magic and madness of making "Apocalypse Now."'

Hearts of Darkness: A Filmmaker's Apocalypse ★★★

SCR/DIR Fax Bahr, George Hickenlooper

1991   96m   US

A documentary account of the making of Francis Ford Coppola's Apocalypse Now, recorded by his wife.

One of the most compelling films ever made about filmmaking, delving into the chaos of a notoriously bloated production, which went so over-budget and over-schedule it was dubbed 'Apocalypse Later' in the press.

CIN Larry Carney, Shana Hagen, Igor Meglic, Steven Wacks   **MUS** Todd Boekelheide   **ED** Michael Greer, Jay Miracle   **PROD** George Zaloom, Les Mayfield   **DIST** Blue Dolphin/Zaloom Mayfield/Zoetrope

66 We had access to too much money, too much equipment, and little by little, we went insane. – *Francis Ford Coppola*

66 At once anecdotal and revealing, this excellent film both illuminates the catastrophes that beset one particular project, and shows, by way of comparison, exactly what American film has foregone since the '70s. – *Geoff Andrew, Time Out*

'A Los Angeles crime saga.'

Heat ★★★

SCR/DIR Michael Mann

1995   171m   US

DVD   ♫

☆ Al Pacino (Lt. Vincent Hanna), Robert De Niro (Neil McCauley), Val Kilmer (Chris Shiherlis), Jon Voight (Nate), Tom Sizemore (Michael Cheritto), Diane Venora (Justine Hanna), Amy Brenneman (Eady), Ashley Judd (Charlene Shiherlis), Wes Studi (Detective Casals), Natalie Portman (Lauren Gustafson)

A Los Angeles police lieutenant pursues the mastermind of a highly organised robbery outfit, and likes his style.

Virtuosically crafted but overstretched modern noir, in which Mann's idea that the cop and criminal are similar souls arbitrarily divided by law comes to seem facile, and the much-hyped face-off between De Niro and Pacino strikes disappointingly few sparks. Still, as an epic panorama of urban existence it is often breathtaking.

CIN *Dante Spinotti* MUS *Elliot Goldenthal* DES *Neil Spisak* ED Dov Hoenig, Pasquale Buba, William Goldenberg, Tom Rolf PROD Michael Mann, Art Linson DIST Warner/Monarchy/Forward Pass/Regency

NEIL MCCAULEY: 'Never have anything in your life that you can't walk out on in 30 seconds.'

66 A sleek, accomplished piece of work, meticulously controlled and completely involving. The dark end of the street doesn't get much more inviting than this. – *Kenneth Turan, Los Angeles Times*

66 A stunning crime drama that shares its protagonists' rabid attention to detail—and love of adrenalin. – *David Ansen, Newsweek*

Heathers ★★

DIR Michael Lehmann
1989 102m US
DVD ♫

☆ Winona Ryder (Veronica Sawyer), Christian Slater (Jason 'J.D.' Dean), Shannen Doherty (Heather), Lisanne Falk (Heather), Kim Walker (Heather), Penelope Milford (Pauline Fleming), Glenn Shadix (Father Ripper)

A high-school girl joins an elitist clique and realises her rebel boyfriend is a murderer.

Cutting and witty satire about the 'in' crowd, albeit one that post-Columbine audiences may find disturbingly flippant.

SCR Daniel Waters CIN Francis Kenny MUS David Newman DES Jon Hutman ED Norman Hollyn PROD Denise Di Novi DIST Premier Releasing/New World/Cinemarque Entertainment

66 As snappy and assured as it is mean-spirited. – *Elvis Mitchell, New York Times*

66 The film uses an intimate knowledge of teen-movie clichés to subvert their debased values from the inside. – *Nigel Floyd, Time Out*

'What Would You Risk For Love?'
Heaven

DIR Tom Tykwer
2002 97m Germany/US/France
DVD ♫

☆ Cate Blanchett (Philippa), Giovanni Ribisi (Filippo), Remo Girone (Father), Stefania Rocca (Regina), Matthia Sbragia (Major Pini), Alberto Di Stasio (Public Prosecutor), Stefano Santospago (Marco Vendice)

An English teacher in Turin plants a bomb to avenge her husband's death, accidentally kills four innocent people, and becomes a fugitive from justice with the Italian policeman she has fallen for.

An alarming misfire, wedding an implausible storyline to moony visuals and pseudo-metaphysical flights of fancy. Interesting exclusively because of its provenance:

one wonders what Kieslowski might have made of this material had he lived to direct it.

SCR Krzysztof Kieslowski, Krzysztof Piesiewicz CIN Frank Griebe DES Uli Hanisch ED Mathilde Bonnefoy PROD Maria Koepf, Stefan Arndt, Frédérique Dumas, William Horberg, Anthony Minghella DIST Buena Vista

66 A great deal of energy is expended on metaphysical ruminations that become ever fuzzier. The film is intended as an allegory, but it works best as a jailbreak romance. In this movie, lowbrow trumps highbrow every time. – *Peter Rainer, New York Magazine*

66 The suspense is handled slackly, as if such things didn't matter compared with the spiritual aspects. – *Philip French, Observer*

'From Vietnam to America, one woman's journey from hope, to love, to discovery.'
Heaven & Earth ★★

SCR/DIR Oliver Stone
1993 140m US
DVD ♫

☆ *Tommy Lee Jones* (Steve Butler), Joan Chen (Mama), Haing S. Ngor (Papa), Hiep Thi Le (Le Ly), Debbie Reynolds (Eugenia), Supak Pititam (Buddhist Monk), Thuan K. Nguyen (Uncle Luc)

A Vietnamese village woman survives the horrors of the war, but her hopes of a better life are dashed when the US Marine who marries her and whisks her back to America turns out to be unbalanced.

Laudable, flawed but ambitious attempt to examine the Vietnam conflict from the viewpoint of a Vietnamese character. It's not always successful, though Stone's provocative contrast between bucolic Vietnamese rural life and America's brash materialism is bracing and brave.

CIN Robert Richardson MUS Kitaro DES Victor Kempster ED David Brenner, Sally Menke PROD Oliver Stone, Arnon Milchan, Robert Kline, A. Kitman Ho DIST Warner/Regency/Canal/Alcor

66 Runs nearly two and a half hours and still manages to seem abrupt in places, thanks to the tumultuous, chameleon-like quality of Ms. Hayslip's life. – *Janet Maslin, New York Times*

'Not all angels are innocent.'
Heavenly Creatures ★★★

DIR *Peter Jackson*
1994 99m New Zealand/United Germany
DVD ♫

☆ *Melanie Lynskey* (Pauline Parker), *Kate Winslet* (Juliet Hulme), *Sarah Peirse* (Honora Parker), Diana Kent (Hilda Hulme), Clive Merrison (Henry Hulme), Simon O'Connor (Herbert Rieper), Jed Brophy (John/Nicholas)

Two schoolgirls in 1950s New Zealand form an inseparable bond, inventing a fantasy world which only they can enter, and which they will kill to continue sharing.

Horrifying but deeply compassionate account of a real-life case, in which a co-dependent teenage relationship

DVD Available on DVD ☆ Cast in order 66 Critics' Quotes ♪ Academy Award 🏆 BAFTA
♫ Soundtrack on CD of importance † Points of interest ⚐ Academy Award nomination ⓣ BAFTA nomination

281

causes a profound distortion of reality, leading to one of the most upsetting murders ever shown on screen. The girls' intense friendship is explored with a fresh and riveted eye.

SCR *Frances Walsh, Peter Jackson*　CIN *Alun Bollinger*　MUS *Peter Dasent*　DES *Grant Major*　ED *Jamie Selkirk*　PROD *Jim Booth*　DIST Buena Vista/Wingnut/Fontana/NZFC

66 Combines original vision, a drop-dead command of the medium and a successful marriage between a dazzling, kinetic techno-show and a complex, credible portrait of the out-of-control relationship between the crime's two schoolgirl perpetrators. – *David Rooney, Variety*

66 Acted with conviction, and directed and written with febrile vibrancy. – *Geoff Andrew, Time Out*

⚖ Frances Walsh, Peter Jackson (original screenplay)

Heavy ★

SCR/DIR James Mangold
1995　105m　US
[DVD]　♫

☆ *Pruitt Taylor Vince* (Victor Modino), Shelley Winters (Dolly Modino), Liv Tyler (Callie), Deborah Harry (Delores), Joe Grifasi (Leo), Evan Dando (Jeff)

The bossy mother of a shy, overweight pizza chef in his 30s sets him up with a new young waitress.

Mangold's off-kilter feature debut yields some small-scale truths beneath its patina of quirkiness.

CIN Michael Barrow　MUS Thurston Moore　DES Michael Shaw　ED Meg Reticker　PROD Richard Miller　DIST Artificial Eye/Mayfair/Available Light

66 Everyone in this lean, artful drama knows exactly how loneliness feels. – *Janet Maslin, New York Times*

Hedd Wyn ★

DIR Paul Turner
1992　123m　Wales

☆ Huw Garmon (Ellis Evans / Hedd Wyn), Sue Roderick (Lizzie Roberts), Judith Humphreys (Jini Owen), Nia Dryhurst (Mary Catherine Hughes), Gwen Ellis (Mary Evans), Grey Evans (Evan Evans), Emlyn Gomer (Morris Davies - Moi)

A young Welsh poet, killed in battle in World War I, is posthumously awarded a prize at the National Eisteddfod..

Scenes of trench warfare are expertly executed, though the story of the war's aftermath drags on too long.

SCR Alan Llwyd　CIN Ray Orton　MUS John E. R. Hardy　DES Jane Roberts, Martin Morley　ED Chris Lawrence　PROD Shân Davis　DIST S4C

† It was the first film in Welsh to receive an Oscar nomination.

⚖ foreign-language film

'It isn't love that makes the world go round.'

Heist

SCR/DIR David Mamet
2001　109m　US/Canada
[DVD]

☆ Gene Hackman (Joe Moore), Danny DeVito (Mickey Bergman), Delroy Lindo (Bobby Blane), Sam Rockwell (Jimmy Silk), Rebecca Pidgeon (Fran), Ricky Jay (Pinky Pincus), Patti LuPone (Betty Croft), Jim Frangione (D.A. Freccia)

A veteran thief is persuaded to pull off one last robbery, but his suspicious fence sends his nephew along to be on the safe side.

Humdrum caper in which the endless double-crossing has an air of fatigue, and Mamet's staccato dialogue just seems silly.

CIN Robert Elswit　MUS Theodore Shapiro　DES David Wasco　ED Barbara Tulliver　PROD Art Linson, Elie Samaha, Andrew Stevens　DIST Warner

66 Mamet is so in love with the con that he's conned himself. – *Peter Rainer, New York Magazine*

66 The thinking person's caper flick, with its endlessly clever plotting revealing character under the utmost pressure. – *Kevin Thomas, Los Angeles Times*

Hell ★

DIR Danis Tanovic
2005　98m　France/Italy/Belgium/Japan
[DVD]

☆ Emmanuelle Béart (Sophie), Karin Viard (Céline), Marie Gillain (Anne), Carole Bouquet (Mother), Guillaume Canet (Sébastien), Jacques Gamblin (Pierre)

Three estranged sisters living in Paris gradually learn more about an incident from their younger days that left their father dead and their mother crippled and dumb.

Well-acted, poised but oddly airless account of a melodramatic story that unfolds its secrets gradually, and turns out to be scarcely worth the wait. As with Heaven, the first part of this proposed trilogy, one wonders what Kieslowski, who planned to film it, might have made of it.

SCR Krzysztof Piesiewicz　CIN Laurent Dailland　MUS Dusko Segvic, Danis Tanovic　DES Aline Bonetto　ED Francesca Calvelli　PROD Cedomir Kolar, Marc Baschet, Marion Hänsel, Yuji Sadai, Rosanna Seregni　DIST Momentum

'Give Evil Hell.'

Hellboy ★★

SCR/DIR Guillermo del Toro
2004　122m　US
[DVD]　♫

☆ *Ron Perlman* (Hellboy), John Hurt (Trevor 'Broom' Bruttenholm), Selma Blair (Liz Sherman), Rupert Evans (John Myers), Karel Roden (Grigori Rasputin), Jeffrey Tambor (Tom Manning), Doug Jones (Abe Sapien)

Escaping the Nazis who conjured him, a demon grows to adulthood and joins the cause of good.

Darkly exuberant comic-book fantasy, whose impressive design honours the book's graphics while adding a dose of Del Toro's own Gothic imagination; Perlman was born to play the misshapen brute of a hero.

CIN Guillermo Navarro　MUS Marco Beltrami　DES *Stephen Scott*　ED Peter Amundson

PROD Lawrence Gordon, Mike Richardson, Lloyd Levin
DIST Columbia

66 Bizarre and loopy, romantic and dynamic. – *Peter Bradshaw, Guardian*

Hello Hemingway ★

DIR Fernando Perez
1990 90m Cuba
DVD

☆ Laura de la Uz (Larita), Raul Paz (Victor), Herminia Sanchez (Josefa), Caridad Hernandez (Rosenda), Enrique Molina (Manolo), Marta Del Rio (Doctor Martinez), Micheline Calvert (Miss Amalia)

In pre-Castro Cuba, an Elvis Presley-obsessed teenage girl tries to win the scholarship in the States that will allow her to break free of her surroundings.

Small-scale, entertaining story that thankfully only hints at the parallels between its heroine's yearnings for a new life with the story of Hemingway's The Old Man and the Sea.

SCR Maydo Royero CIN Julio Valdes MUS Edesio Alejandro ED Jorge Abello PROD Ricardo Guila
DIST Metro/ICAIC

Hell's Angels ★★★

DIR Howard Hughes
1930 135m US

☆ Ben Lyon, James Hall, Jean Harlow, John Darrow, Lucien Prival

Two American brothers become fighter pilots in World War I.

Celebrated early talkie spectacular from Howard Hughes, with zeppelin and flying sequences that still thrill. The dialogue is another matter, but all told this expensive production, first planned as a silent, is a milestone of cinema history.

SCR Howard Estabrook, Harry Behn CIN Tony Gaudio, Harry Perry, E. Burton Steene MUS Hugo Reisenfeld
DIST Howard Hughes

66 That it will ever pay off for its producer is doubtful . . . he's in so deep it can't really matter to him now. Minus blue nose interference, it can't miss, but it's up to the brim with sex. – *Variety*

66 It is not great, but it is as lavish as an eight-ring circus, and when you leave the theatre you will know you have seen a movie and not a tinny reproduction of a stage show. – *Pare Lorentz*

† The film was reissued in 1940 in a 96m version which has not survived.

† Martin Scorsese's The Aviator (2004) dealt partly with the complexities faced by Howard Hughes in making the film.

🏆 Tony Gaudio, Harry Perry, E. Burton Steene (cinematography)

Help! ★★

DIR Richard Lester
1965 92m GB
DVD

☆ John Lennon (John), Paul McCartney (Paul), George Harrison (George), Ringo Starr (Ringo), Leo McKern (Clang), Eleanor Bron (Ahme), Victor Spinetti (Foot), Roy Kinnear (Algernon), John Bluthal (Bhuta), Patrick Cargill (Superintendent)

The Beatles try to elude the leaders of a sinister Eastern cult, who desperately want a ceremonial ring worn by Ringo.

The success of A Hard Day's Night prompted this follow-up, which was more expensive, but less amusing and spontaneous. The first film's humour had a throwaway, unscripted feel: in Help! everyone is trying too hard. The locations would do credit to a Bond film – Swiss mountains, beaches in the Bahamas – but the elusive magic is gone. Happily, the songs the Fab Four contribute are, if anything, better than before.

SCR Charles Wood, Marc Behm CIN David Watkin
MUS Ken Thorne, The Beatles ED John Victor Smith
DIST UA/Walter Shenson/Suba Films

Henry: Portrait of a Serial Killer ★★

DIR John McNaughton
1990 83m US
DVD

☆ Michael Rooker (Henry), Tom Towles (Otis), Tracy Arnold (Becky)

A psychopath introduces his flatmate to serial killing, and starts dating his sister.

Profoundly disturbing because the filmmaking is so uninflected, and the off-screen deaths are almost more shocking than the ones we see; but some of its impact has ebbed away over time.

SCR Richard Fire, John McNaughton CIN Charlie Lieberman MUS John McNaughton, Ken Hale, Steven A. Jones ED Elena Maganini PROD John McNaughton, Lisa Dedmond, Steven A. Jones DIST Electric/Maljack

66 Has less suspense and more graphic violence than any Hitchcock film. Yet this intelligent, revolting, artistically made and entirely empty look at a murderer comes close to a cinema of pure technique. – *Caryn James, New York Times*

'A True Adventure More Erotic Than Any Fantasy'

Henry and June ★

DIR Philip Kaufman
1990 136m US
DVD 🎵

☆ Fred Ward (Henry Miller), Uma Thurman (June Miller), Maria de Medeiros (Anaïs Nin), Richard E. Grant (Hugo Guiler), Kevin Spacey (Richard Osborn), Jean-Philippe Ecoffey (Eduardo Sanchez), Bruce Myers (Jack), Jean-Louis Buñuel (Publisher / Editor), Feodor Atkine (Paco Miralles)

The writer Anais Nin has sexual trysts with author Henry Miller and his wife June.

Leaden account of bizarre erotic relationships in 1930s, handsomely filmed at great length, and tolerably steamy, but oddly lacking in passion.

SCR Philip Kaufman, Rose Kaufman CIN Philippe Rousselot DES Guy-Claude François ED Vivien Hillgrove Gilliam, William S. Scharf, Dede Allen
PROD Peter Kaufman DIST UIP/Universal/Walrus & Associates

DVD Available on DVD ☆ Cast in order of importance 66 Critics' Quotes † Points of interest 🏆 Academy Award Academy Award nomination 🏆 BAFTA BAFTA nomination

283

H

66 The characters' sexual abandon is so complete that it robs the story of any shape. – *Janet Maslin, New York Times*

⚑ Philippe Rousselot

Henry Fool ★

SCR/DIR Hal Hartley
1997   137m   US
[DVD]   ♫

☆ Thomas Jay Ryan (Henry Fool), James Urbaniak (Simon Grim), Parker Posey (Fay Grim), Maria Porter (Mary), James Saito (Mr. Deng), Kevin Corrigan (Warren), Liam Aiken (Ned), Miho Nikaido (Gnoc Deng), Gene Riffini (Officer Buñuel), Nicholas Hope (Father Hawkes), Diana Ruppe (Amy)

A dissolute novelist befriends a garbage man, who ends up becoming a Nobel Prize-winning poet.

A typically offbeat fable from this director, touching on themes of artistic influence, friendship and fame, but also permitting dangerous levels of grungy self-indulgence.

CIN Mike Spiller   MUS Hal Hartley   DES Steve Rosenzweig   ED Steve Hamilton   PROD Hal Hartley
DIST True Fiction/Shooting Gallery

66 Full of juice, humour and nuance. – *Jonathan Rosenbaum, Chicago Reader*

66 One has to go back to Josef von Sternberg and Yasujiro Ozu to find a compositional control within the frame as rigorous as Mr. Hartley's. – *Andrew Sarris, New York Observer*

Henry V ★★

DIR Kenneth Branagh
1989   137m   GB
[DVD]   ♫

☆ Kenneth Branagh (Henry V), Derek Jacobi (Chorus), Simon Shepherd (Gloucester), James Larkin (Bedford), Brian Blessed (Exeter), James Simmons (York), Paul Gregory (Westmoreland), Charles Kay (Archbishop of Canterbury), Alec McCowen (Bishop of Ely), Edward Jewesbury (Erpingham), Ian Holm (Fluellen), Michael Williams (Williams), Geoffrey Hutchings (Nym), Robert Stephens (Pistol), Judi Dench (Mistress Quickly), Paul Scofield, Harold Innocent, Emma Thompson, Geraldine McEwan

In 1415, King Henry leads his forces against the French at Agincourt, and must bolster their sinking morale.

Capable version, emphasising war's brutality more than Olivier's, though too much of it seems designed to show off Branagh's facility with the verse.

SCR Kenneth Branagh   CIN Kenneth MacMillan
MUS Patrick Doyle   DES Tim Harvey   ED Mike Bradsell
PROD Bruce Sharman   DIST Curzon/Renaissance Films

66 One of the things that make [Branagh's] Henry V so thrilling is his audacity in trying to turn it into an antiwar play – a view that would have astounded Shakespeare. Astonishingly, he pretty much brings it off, emerging with steadily growing power as the young king who isn't afraid to bloody his hands. – *Jay Carr, Boston Globe*

66 The more I thought about it, the more convinced I became that here was a play to be reclaimed from jingoism and its World War Two associations. – *Kenneth Branagh*

⚑ Phyllis Dalton (costume design)
⚑ Kenneth Branagh (leading actor); Kenneth Branagh (direction)

🏆 Kenneth Branagh (direction)
🏅 Kenneth Branagh (leading actor); Kenneth MacMillan; Campbell Askew, David Crozier, Robin O'Donoghue (sound); Tim Harvey; Phyllis Dalton (costume design)

Henry V ★★★★

DIR *Laurence Olivier*
1944   137m   GB
[DVD]

☆ Laurence Olivier (Henry V), *Robert Newton* (Pistol), *Leslie Banks* (Chorus), *Esmond Knight* (Fluellen), Renée Asherson (Katherine), George Robey (Falstaff), *Leo Genn* (Constable of France), Ernest Thesiger (Duke of Beri), Ivy St Helier (Alice), Ralph Truman (Mountjoy), Harcourt Williams, Max Adrian, Valentine Dyall (Duke of Burgundy), Felix Aylmer (Archbishop of Canterbury), John Laurie, Roy Emerton, Michael Shepley, George Cole

Shakespeare's historical play is initially seen in performance at the Globe Theatre in 1603; as it develops, the scenery becomes more realistic.

Immensely stirring, experimental and almost wholly successful production of Shakespeare on film, sturdy both in its stylization and its command of more conventional cinematic resources for the battle.

SCR Laurence Olivier, Alan Dent   CIN *Robert Krasker*
MUS *William Walton*   ED Reginald Beck
PROD Laurence Olivier   DIST Rank/Two Cities

66 His production – it was his first time out as a director – is a triumph of colour, music, spectacle, and soaring heroic poetry, and, as actor, he brings lungs, exultation, and a bashful wit to the role. – *Pauline Kael, 70s*

🏆 Special Award to Laurence Olivier
🏅 picture; Laurence Olivier (leading actor); William Walton; art direction

Her Name is Sabine (new) ★★

SCR/DIR Sandrine Bonnaire
2008   85m   France
[DVD]

☆ Sabine Bonnaire (Herself), Sandrine Bonnaire (Voice)

A documentary about actress Sandrine Bonnaire's autistic sister Sabine, filmed over 25 years and including her tragic stay in a psychiatric hospital and her current stay in a care home.

A moving, touching and educational odyssey and a remarkable directorial debut for actress Bonnaire.

SCR Catherine Cabrol   MUS Jefferson Lembeye, Walter N'Guyen   ED Svetlana Vaynblat   PROD Thomas Schmitt
DIST ICA

66 The documentary is intimate but never transgressive, informative but never clinical. Bonnaire has made a powerful statement about the limits of love in the face of chronic debilitating illness. – *Lisa Nesselson, Variety*

† Winner of the Fipresci award at the 2007 Cannes Film Festival.

† Director Bonnaire added snippets from her own home movies to material filmed at the home where Sabine now lives.

[DVD] Available on DVD   ☆ Cast in order of importance   66 Critics' Quotes   † Points of interest   ⚑ Academy Award   🏅 Academy Award nomination   🏆 BAFTA   🏅 BAFTA nomination
♫ Soundtrack on CD

'This land doesn't know a real hero. Yet.'

Hero ★★

DIR Zhang Yimou
2002 99m China/Hong Kong
DVD ♫

☆ Jet Li (Nameless), Tony Leung Chiu-wai (Broken Sword), Maggie Cheung (Flying Snow), Zhang Ziyi (Moon), Chen Dao Ming (King of Qin), Donnie Yen (Sky)

In feudal China, a nameless warrior goes after three assassins who have been hired to kill the king.

Ravishing martial arts epic, dressed up to the nines and impossible not to admire; but the story is distinctly mechanical, and the message about safeguarding tyrannical authority sticks in the craw.

SCR Zhang Yimou, Wang Bin, Li Feng CIN *Christopher Doyle* MUS Tan Dun DES Huo Ting Xiao, Yi Zhen Zhou ED Zhai Ru, Angie Lam PROD Bill Kong, Zhang Yimou

66 This is a leap into grandeur. – *Anthony Lane, New Yorker*

66 Zhang's characters don't sweat, lest they stain their costumes, nor do they brandish their swords too wildly, for fear of tearing the drapes. – *Mike McCahill, Sunday Telegraph*

⌁ foreign film

'One selfless act of courage can really mess up your whole day.'

Hero ★

DIR Stephen Frears
1992 117m US
DVD ♫

☆ Dustin Hoffman (Bernard 'Bernie' Laplante), Geena Davis (Gale Gayley, Channel 4 News Reporter), Andy Garcia (John Bubber), Joan Cusack (Evelyn Laplante), Kevin J. O'Connor (Chucky, Channel 4 News Cameraman), Maury Chaykin (Winston, Bernie's Landlord), Stephen Tobolowsky (James Wallace, Channel 4 Station Manager)

A two-bit thief rescues passengers after a plane crash, but a vagrant claims the credit.

Misguided and miscast attempt at a screwball satire à la Sturges or Wilder; the ironies are overstated and the laughs dry up.

SCR David Webb Peoples CIN Oliver Stapleton MUS George Fenton DES Dennis Gassner ED Mick Audsley PROD Laura Ziskin DIST Columbia TriStar

66 The movie cries out for an editor who could get it down to around 95 minutes. . .and leave out the dumb stuff and the false sentiment, and make it tough and witty. – *Roger Ebert, Chicago Sun-Times*

† After its box-office failure in the US, the film was released under the title Accidental Hero in Britain.

Hidden ★★★

SCR/DIR *Michael Haneke*
2004 117m France/Austria/Germany/Italy
DVD

☆ *Daniel Auteuil* (Georges Laurent), *Juliette Binoche* (Anne), Maurice Benichou (Majid), Annie Girardot (Mother)

The presenter of a Paris arts programme and his wife begin to receive videotapes through the mail showing their house under surveillance.

A subtly agonising thriller in Haneke's best style, using long single takes to suggest an unknown cameraman watching the couple's every move. The legacy of French misconduct in Algeria comes under scrutiny, but motivation for the tapes is finally withheld, and much depends on how we read the deliberately opaque final shot.

CIN Christian Berger DES Emmanuel De Chauvigny, Christoph Kanter ED Michael Hudecek, Nadine Muse PROD Veit Heiduschka, Andrew Colton DIST Artificial Eye

66 The movie can be dissected to reveal – as the best thrillers frequently do – an agenda. It's an extended meditation on the blood ties between colonialists and the colonized, and how they may not so easily be jettisoned when they become troublesome. – *Stephen Hunter, Washington Post*

66 A thriller all the more thrilling for its assiduously languid pace and hushed tone. – *Ken Tucker, New York Magazine*

'Murder... Torture... Corruption... The Truth Can Never Be Buried.'

Hidden Agenda ★★

DIR Ken Loach
1990 108m GB
DVD

☆ Brian Cox (Kerrigan), Frances McDormand (Ingrid Jessner), Brad Dourif (Paul Sullivan), Mai Zetterling (Moa), Bernard Bloch (Henri), John Benfield (Maxwell), Jim Norton (Brodie), Patrick Kavanagh (Alec Nevin), Bernard Archard (Sir Robert Neil)

When an American civil rights activist and Irish Republican supporter is murdered in Belfast, a police conspiracy is uncovered.

Based partly on real events, this punchy political thriller keeps the tension level high, even if we can guess, knowing this film-maker, roughly where the truth lies.

SCR Jim Allen CIN Clive Tickner MUS Stewart Copeland DES Martin Johnson ED Jonathan Morris PROD Eric Fellner DIST Enterprise/Hemdale

66 There's plenty of evidence of Loach's undiminished power as a film-maker, and equally ample evidence that something is very rotten in the state of northern Ireland. – *Steve Grant, Time Out*

† At the Cannes Film Festival in 1990, where it won the Jury prize, director Loach was openly accused by elements of the UK press of being anti-British and pro-IRA.

'Morocco 1972. It's not about escape, it's about discovery. . .'

Hideous Kinky ★

DIR Gillies MacKinnon
1998 98m GB/France
DVD ♫

☆ Kate Winslet (Julia), Said Taghmaoui (Bilal), Bella Riza (Bea), Carrie Mullan (Lucy), Pierre Clementi (Santoni), Sira Stampe (Eva)

| DVD | Available on DVD | ☆ | Cast in order | 66 | Critics' Quotes | ⌁ | Academy Award | Ⓑ | BAFTA |
| ♫ | Soundtrack on CD | | of importance | † | Points of interest | ⌁ | Academy Award nomination | Ⓑ | BAFTA nomination |

285

A hippie mother takes her two young daughters to Morocco in the late 1960s.

The backdrops are pretty, and the cast game, but there's not much else to tax the attention here.

SCR Billy MacKinnon **CIN** *John de Borman* **MUS** John Keane **DES** Louise Marzaroli, Pierre Gompertz **ED** Pia Di Ciaula **PROD** Ann Scott **DIST** Film Consortium/BBC/Arts Council/Greenpoint/L Films/AMLF

66 Never amounts to much more than a slide show of someone else's holiday snaps. – *Tom Shone, Sunday Times*

'A story of ambition, sacrifice, seduction and other career moves.'

High Art ★★

SCR/DIR *Lisa Cholodenko*

1998   101m   US

DVD ♫

☆ *Ally Sheedy* (Lucy Berliner), Radha Mitchell (Syd), *Patricia Clarkson* (Greta), Tammy Grimes (Vera), Gabriel Mann (James), Bill Sage (Arnie), Ann Duong (Dominique), David Thornton (Harry)

A bisexual magazine intern leaves her boyfriend for her upstairs neighbour, a drug-addicted fashion photographer already in a dead-end relationship with a junkie actress.

Languorous, clammily erotic story of a co-dependent lesbian affair, in which the performers bring some rather desiccated characters to life.

CIN *Tami Reiker* **MUS** Shudder to Think **DES** *Bernhard Blythe* **ED** Amy E. Duddleston **PROD** Dolly Hall, Jeff Levy-Hinte, Susan A. Stover **DIST** October Films

66 Has a subtle magnetism, and a real human pulse. – *Liam Lacey, Toronto Globe and Mail*

66 The only real disappointment in this otherwise excellent film is that the conclusion goes for childish 'live fast, die young' melodramatics instead of evolving something more provocative out of the subtle portrait that's gone before. – *Leslie Felperin, Sight & Sound*

'A comedy about fear of commitment, hating your job, falling in love and other pop favourites.'

High Fidelity ★★

DIR Stephen Frears

2000   113m   US/GB

DVD ♫

☆ John Cusack (Rob Gordon), Iben Hjejle (Laura), *Todd Louiso* (Dick), *Jack Black* (Barry), Lisa Bonet (Marie De Salle), Catherine Zeta-Jones (Charlie), Joan Cusack (Liz), Tim Robbins (Ian), Chris Rehmann (Vince), Ben Carr (Justin), Lili Taylor (Sarah), Joelle Carter (Penny), Natasha Gregson Wagner (Caroline), Sara Gilbert (Annaugh), Bruce Springsteen (Himself)

The list-obsessed owner of a record shop recounts his top five romantic break-ups, including the one in progress.

Losing little in the transfer from London to Chicago, Hornby's bestselling book about pop arcana, love and arrested adolescence is turned into a bright and engaging romcom, even if it's much better on the guys than the girls.

SCR D.V. DeVincentis, Steve Pink, John Cusack, Scott Rosenberg **CIN** Seamus McGarvey **MUS** Howard Shore **DES** David Chapman, Therese DePrez **ED** Mick Audsley **PROD** Tim Bevan, Rudd Simmons **DIST** Buena Vista

66 Movies this wry and likable rarely get made. – *Roger Ebert, Chicago Sun-Times*

66 It's hard to remember the last time guys were nailed so perceptively and dragged into adulthood so warmly and entertainingly. – *Jay Carr, Boston Globe*

ⓣ D.V DeVincentis, Steve Pink, John Cusak, Scott Rosenberg (adapted screenplay)

'A mother, a daughter, a lover. Relationships can be murder.'

High Heels ★

SCR/DIR Pedro Almodóvar

1991   112m   Spain/France

DVD

☆ Victoria Abril (Rebeca), Marisa Paredes (Becky del Páramo), Miguel Bosé (Juez Domínguez / Hugo / Letal), Feodor Atkine (Manuel (as Feodor Atkin)), Pedro Díez del Corral (Alberto), Ana Lizarán (Margarita)

A famous veteran pop singer rekindles an affair with an old flame, who is now her daughter's husband.

Campy confrontation between mother and daughter that deliberately harks back to women's pictures of the Douglas Sirk era, and throws in Almodovar's usual supporting cast of Madrid transvestites and drug pushers. It has its moments, but this transitional work, too fond of referencing other films, is generally below par.

CIN Alfredo Mayo **MUS** Ryuichi Sakamoto **DES** Pierre Thevenet **ED** José Salcedo **PROD** Agustin Almadóvar **DIST** El Deseo/Ciby 2000

66 Once again, the director as interior decorator has come up with some bold designs. – *David Thompson, Sight & Sound*

High Hopes ★★

SCR/DIR Mike Leigh

1988   112m   GB

DVD

☆ *Philip Davis* (Cyril Bender), Ruth Sheen (Shirley), Edna Dore (Mrs. Bender), Philip Jackson (Martin Burke), Heather Tobias (Valerie Burke), *Lesley Manville* (Laetitia Boothe-Brain), David Bamber (Rupert Boothe-Braine), Jason Watkins (Wayne), Judith Scott (Suzi)

Three separate couples, each prototypes in Thatcher's Britain, gather to celebrate an ageing mother's birthday.

A foretaste of things to come from Leigh: some agreeably observed dialogue, sympathy for salt-of-the earth working-class characters and cheerful slackers, and disdain for the upwardly mobile. Yet it's well-acted and mostly fun.

CIN Roger Pratt **MUS** Andrew Dixon **DES** Diana Charnley **ED** Jon Gregory **PROD** Simon Channing-Williams, Victor Glynn **DIST** Palace/Portman/Film Four International/British Screen

'When the hands point up. . .the excitement starts!'

High Noon ★★★★

DIR *Fred Zinnemann*

1952 85m US

DVD

☆ *Gary Cooper* (Will Kane), Grace Kelly (Amy Kane), Thomas Mitchell (Jonas Henderson), Lloyd Bridges (Harvey Pell), Katy Jurado (Helen Ramirez), Otto Kruger (Percy Mettrick), Lon Chaney (Martin Howe), Henry Morgan (William Fuller)

A marshal gets no help from a town's fearful citizens when he determines to defend it against a vengeful convicted killer and his cronies.

A classic Western with a simple message: stand up and be counted. It works simply because of its simplicity, and every scene is shot with laudable economy. The countdown to noon is as tense an extended sequence as any in movie history. Cinematically it was pared to the bone, and the memorable theme tune helped.

SCR *Carl Foreman* CIN *Floyd Crosby* MUS *Dimitri Tiomkin* ED *Elmo Williams, Harry Gerstad* DIST Stanley Kramer

66 The western form is used for a sneak civics lesson. – *Pauline Kael, 70s*

66 Like nearly all the Kramer productions, this is a neat, well-finished and literate piece of work, though its limitations are more conventional than most. – *Gavin Lambert*

† Director Zinnemann insisted publicly until his death he knew nothing of the parallels between the film's plot and the McCarthyite witch hunts of the time. But screenwriter Foreman was black-listed, and the parallels seem too obvious not to have some validity

⚱ Gary Cooper (leading actor); Dimitri Tiomkin; Dimitri Tiomkin (m), Ned Washington (ly) (music, original song – High Noon (Do Not Forsake Me, Oh My Darlin')); editing

⚱ picture; Carl Foreman (screenplay); Fred Zinnemann (direction)

'He's an American. She's a ghost. Vacation romances are always a hassle.'

High Spirits ★

SCR/DIR Neil Jordan

1988 96m US

DVD

☆ Peter O'Toole (Peter Plunkett), Donal McCann (Eamon), Mary Coughlan (Katie), Liz Smith (Mrs Plunkett), Steve Guttenberg (Jack Crawford), Beverly D'Angelo (Sharon Brogan Crawford), Jennifer Tilly (Miranda), Peter Gallagher (Brother Tony), Daryl Hannah (Mary Plunkett Brogan), Liam Neeson (Martin Brogan), Ray McAnally (Plunkett Senior)

The owner of an Irish castle pretends it is haunted to lure gullible American tourists. Then real poltergeists make themselves known.

Wayward comedy that lurches wildly between genres and skirts total disaster, but hangs on to its appealingly madcap spirit.

CIN Alex Thomson MUS George Fenton DES Anton Furst ED Michael Bradsell PROD Stephen Woolley, David Saunders DIST Palace/Vision PDG

High Tide ★★★

DIR *Gillian Armstrong*

1987 101m Australia

☆ *Judy Davis* (Lillie), Jan Adele (Bet), Claudia Karvan (Ally), Colin Friels (Mick), John Clayton (Col), Frankie J. Holden (Lester)

In an Australian coastal backwater, three generations of women in a single family come to terms with a mother's abandonment of her daughter.

Uncompromising, even forbidding drama about blood ties that bind, yet clash with yearnings outside the family. Davis is superb as the conflicted mother in a shamefully underrated film.

SCR Laura Jones CIN Russell Boyd MUS Peter Best DES Sally Campbell ED Nicholas Beauman PROD Sandra Levy DIST Ritzy/FGH/STL/Hemdale

66 Miss Davis isn't an actress overly interested in making audiences like her; she never makes an ingratiating move when a difficult, challenging one will do. – *Janet Maslin, New York Times*

'Question The Knowledge'

Higher Learning ★

SCR/DIR John Singleton

1995 127m US

DVD ♫

☆ Omar Epps (Malik Williams), Kristy Swanson (Kristen Connor), Michael Rapaport (Remy), Jennifer Connelly (Taryn), Ice Cube (Fudge), Laurence Fishburne (Professor Maurice Phipps), Jason Wiles (Wayne), Tyra Banks (Deja), Cole Hauser (Scott Moss)

Freshmen at a university find ways of asserting their racial, sexual and political identities, and deal with peer-pressure temptations from various established cliques.

A quieter, more consistently thoughtful piece than Singleton's dazzling debut, Boyz n The Hood. His take on America's higher education system is complex and worth hearing, but his characters, most of them stock types, prevent the story from achieving dramatic force.

CIN Peter Lyons Collister MUS Stanley Clarke DES Keith Brian Burns ED Bruce Cannon PROD John Singleton, Paul Hall DIST Columbia/New Deal

66 You won't leave the theatre arguing loudly with your partner. – *Mark Sinker, Sight & Sound*

'The true story of two sisters who shared a passion, a madness and a man.'

Hilary and Jackie ★★

DIR Anand Tucker

1998 121m GB

DVD ♫

☆ *Emily Watson* (Jacqueline Du Pré), *Rachel Griffiths* (Hilary Du Pré), James Frain (Daniel Barenboim), David Morrissey (Kiffer), Charles Dance (Derek), Celia

| DVD | Available on DVD | ☆ | Cast in order | 66 | Critics' Quotes | ⚱ | Academy Award | Ⓑ | BAFTA |
| ♫ | Soundtrack on CD | | of importance | † | Points of interest | ⚱ | Academy Award nomination | Ⓑ | BAFTA nomination |

287

Imrie (Iris), Rupert Penry-Jones (Piers), Bill Paterson (Cello teacher), Auriol Evans (Young Jackie), Keeley Flanders (Young Hilary), Nyree Dawn Porter (Dame Margot Fonteyn), Vernon Dobtcheff (Professor Bentley)

The brilliant, emotionally unstable young cellist Jacqueline Du Pré embarks on a career with her sister's husband.

Well-appointed biopic of a familiar kind, in which the complex performances compensate for a slightly plodding narrative.

SCR Frank Cottrell Boyce   CIN David Johnson
MUS Barrington Pheloung   DES Alice Normington
ED Martin Walsh   PROD Andy Paterson, Nicolas Kent
DIST Intermedia/Film Four/British Screen/Arts Council/Oxford

66 Best described as art-house comfort food. – *Russell Smith, Austin Chronicle*

66 This subjective double take transcends the limitations of the biopic to exult in the artistry of the great cellist Jacqueline du Pré, even as it poses profound troubling questions about communication, destiny and the artist's sense of her own identity. – *Tom Charity, Time Out*

⚱ Emily Watson (leading actress); Rachel Griffiths (supporting actress)

Ⓣ film; Emily Watson (leading actress); Frank Cottrell Boyce (adapted screenplay); Barrington Pheloung; Nigel Heath, Julian Slater, David Crozier, Ray Merrin, Graham Daniel (sound)

'A Land Without Boundaries. A Passion Without Limits.'

The Hi-Lo Country   ★

DIR Stephen Frears
1998   114m   US/GB
DVD ♫
☆ Woody Harrelson (Big Boy Matson), Billy Crudup (Pete Calder), Patricia Arquette (Mona), Cole Hauser (Little Brother), Penelope Cruz (Josepha O'Neil), Darren Burrows (Billy Harte), Jacob Vargas (Delfino Mondragon), James Gammon (Hoover Young), Lane Smith (Steve Shaw), Katy Jurado (Meesa), Sam Elliott (Jim Ed Love)

In the late 1940s, two cowboys who served in World War II return to their small New Mexico town and realise their way of life is on the wane.

A modest, quiet movie that makes its themes apparent gradually. The two friends have become anachronisms, and their refuge in male bonding and their dismissive attitude towards women no longer suffices in a modern community. This smart little film offers more evidence of Frears's versatility in any number of genres; though Penelope Cruz, in her American film debut, flounders in a wretchedly limited role.

SCR Walon Green   CIN Oliver Stapleton   MUS Carter Burwell   DES Patricia Norris   ED Masahiro Hirakubo
PROD Barbara De Fina/Martin Scorsese/Eric Fellner/Tim Bevan   DIST Universal

66 A rich and satisfying evocation of a culture under pressure. – *Edward Buscombe, Sight & Sound*

'In a world of breathtaking beauty unfolds a classic tale of wisdom and adventure.'

Himalaya   ★★

DIR *Eric Valli*
1999   108m   France/Switzerland/GB/Nepal
DVD ♫
☆ Thilen Lhondup (Tinle), Gurgon Kyap (Karma), Lhakpa Tsamchoe (Pema), Karma Wangel (Passang), Karma Tensing Nyima (Norbou), Labrang Tundup (Labrang), Jampa Kalsang Tamang (Jampa), Tsering Dorjee (Rabkie)

In Nepal, a wizened village chief and a young upstart battle to lead caravans of yaks across mountainous terrain to trade salt for grain.

Hugely original work, by a debutant director and former travel writer. Visually it's splendid and unique, yet its story, about one generation passing the torch to another, is universal.

SCR Eric Valli, Olivier Dazat, Jean-Claude Guillebaud, Louis Gardel, Nathalie Azoulai, Jacques Perrin   CIN *Eric Guichard, Jean Paul Meurisse*   MUS Bruno Coulais
DES Jérôme Krowicki   ED Marie-Josèphe Yoyotte
PROD Jacques Perrin, Christophe Barratier
DIST Momentum

⚱ foreign language film

Hiroshima Mon Amour   ★★★

DIR *Alain Resnais*
1959   91m   France/Japan
DVD
☆ Emmanuele Riva (She), Eiji Okada (He)

A French actress working in Hiroshima falls for a Japanese architect and remembers her tragic love for a German soldier during the occupation.

It opens stunningly, as scenes of lovers are intercut with footage of the atomic bomb blast at Hiroshima and its dazed victims. At the time, it looked like a revolutionary approach to film narrative. The remainder of the film cannot sustain this brilliance, despite outstanding camera work. Still, an important footnote in film history.

SCR Marguerite Duras   CIN Sacha Vierny, Takahashi Michio   MUS Giovanni Fusco, Georges Delerue
ED Jasmine Chasney, Henri Colpi, Anne Sarraute
DIST Argos/Comei/Pathé/Daiei

66 Suddenly a new film. Really new, first-hand: a work which tells a story of its own in a style of its own. One is almost afraid to touch it. – *Dilys Powell*

⚱ Marguerite Duras

His Girl Friday   ★★★★

DIR Howard Hawks
1940   92m   US
DVD
☆ *Rosalind Russell* (Hildy Johnson), *Cary Grant* (Walter Burns), *Ralph Bellamy* (Bruce Baldwin), Gene Lockhart (Sheriff Hartwell), Porter Hall (Murphy), Ernest Truex (Bensinger), Cliff Edwards (Endicott), *Clarence Kolb* (Mayor), *Roscoe Karns* (McCue), *Frank Jenks* (Wilson), Abner Biberman (Louis), Frank Orth (Duffy), John Qualen (Earl Williams), Helen Mack (Molly Malloy), *Billy Gilbert* (Joe Pettibone), Alma Kruger (Mrs Baldwin)

A brilliant re-working of The Front Page, with newsman Hildy Johnson turned into a woman.

Frantic, hilarious black farce with all participants at their best; possibly the fastest-talking comedy ever filmed. The interplay between Grant and Russell is dazzling, and it could scarcely be funnier.

SCR *Charles Lederer* CIN Joseph Walker MUS Sydney Cutner ED Gene Havlik PROD Howard Hawks DIST Columbia

66 The kind of terrific verbal slam-bang that has vanished from current film-making. – *New Yorker, 1975*

66 One of the fastest of all movies, from line to line and from gag to gag. – *Manny Farber, 1971*

† The Rosalind Russell role had first been turned down by Jean Arthur, Ginger Rogers, Claudette Colbert and Irene Dunne.

'Meet the boys who are making history.'

The History Boys ★★

DIR Nicholas Hytner
2006 109m UK/US
DVD ♫

☆ Richard Griffiths (Hector), Frances de la Tour (Dorothy Lintott), Stephen Campbell Moore (Irwin), Samuel Barnett (Posner), Dominic Cooper (Dakin), James Corden (Timms), Jamie Parker (Scripps), Russell Tovey (Rudge), Samuel Anderson (Crowther), Sacha Dhawan (Akhtar), Andrew Knott (Lockwood), Clive Merrison (Headmaster), Penelope Wilton (Mrs. Bibby), Adrian Scarborough (Wilkes)

In a north of England grammar school in 1983, two teachers with wildly different styles help eight sixth-formers prepare for their Oxbridge exams.

Alan Bennett's moving but uproarious play about the uses of education was a big hit in London and New York, but transfers awkwardly to the big screen: most scenes stay within the school's walls. Happily, its waspishly brilliant script saves it. Griffiths, the loveable, flawed older teacher, advocates a love of learning for its own sake. Irwin, a young, cynical careerist, urges his charges to espouse eye-catching contrarian views in their exam papers, and thus rise above the herd. Standout performances from the adult actors, and a real sense of enjoyment from the young ensemble playing the boys. Better dialogue than this is rarely heard in cinema.

SCR Alan Bennett CIN Andrew Dunn MUS George Fenton DES John Beard ED John Wilson PROD Kevin Loader, Nicholas Hytner, Damian Jones DIST TCF

MRS. LINTOTT: 'Durham was very good for history. It's where I had my first pizza. Other things too, of course, but it's the pizza that stands out.'

ASKHTAR (TO IRWIN): 'You're very young, sir. This isn't your gap year, is it, sir?'

MRS. LINTOTT: 'History is a commentary on the various and continuing incapabilities of men. What is history? History is women following behind with the bucket.'

66 A display of rich, humane and often daring writing, and some classy acting from the mature folk, that can't quite wriggle free of its formal deliberate theatrical origins. – *Ian Nathan, Empire*

Ⓣ Richard Griffiths (leading actor); Frances de la Tour (supporting actress)

'Everyone has something to hide.'

A History of Violence ★★

DIR David Cronenberg
2005 96m US/Germany
DVD ♫

☆ *Viggo Mortensen* (Tom Stall), Maria Bello (Edie Stall), William Hurt (Richie Cusack), Ed Harris (Carl Fogarty), Ashton Holmes (Jack Stall), Heidi Hayes (Sarah Stall), Peter MacNeill (Sheriff Sam Carney)

A small-town husband and father finds his past catching up with him when he stops an armed robbery.

Gripping saga of criminality rising back to the surface, subtly played and punchily directed up to the hour mark; but the last act veers into cartoonish overkill and isn't wholly satisfying.

SCR Josh Olson CIN *Peter Suschitzky* MUS Howard Shore DES Carol Spier ED *Ronald Sanders* PROD Chris Bender, J.C. Spink DIST Entertainment

66 A ticking time bomb of a movie, a gripping, incendiary, casually subversive piece of work that marries pulp watchability with larger concerns without skipping a beat. – *Kenneth Turan, Los Angeles Times*

66 A hollow story from an empty graphic novel. – *Michael Sragow, Baltimore Sun*

⚱ Josh Olson (adapted screenplay); William Hurt (supporting actor)

Ⓣ Josh Olson (adapted screenplay)

'Don't Panic'

The Hitchhiker's Guide to the Galaxy ★

DIR Garth Jennings
2005 109m US/GB
DVD ♫

☆ Martin Freeman (Arthur Dent), Mos Def (Ford Prefect), Sam Rockwell (Zaphod Beeblebrox), Zooey Deschanel (Trillian), Warwick Davis (Marvin), Alan Rickman (Voice of Marvin), John Malkovich (Humma Kavula), *Bill Nighy* (Slartibartfast)

After his planet is destroyed by aliens, an Earthling is picked up by a ragtag group touring the galaxy in search of the meaning of life.

An adaptation that gets by on sheer likability for a while, demonstrating a fondness for previous radio and TV versions, and for people over computer effects, though the zappy, channel-hopping direction, a ploy to get as much of the book in as possible, eventually proves irksome, and the comic-cosmic philosophy in Adams' writing is simply nowhere to be seen. In the end, it's somewhat like space itself: good that it's there, but terribly patchy.

SCR Douglas Adams, Karey Kirkpatrick CIN Igor Jadue-Lillo MUS Joby Talbot DES Joel Collins ED Niven Howie PROD Gary Barber, Roger Birnbaum, Nick Goldsmith, Jay Roach, Jonathan Glickman DIST Buena Vista

66 More smile-inducing than laugh-aloud funny. – *Leslie Felperin, Variety*

66 The problem is not that the film debases the book, but that movies themselves are too capacious a home for such

---

DVD Available on DVD ☆ Cast in order 66 Critics' Quotes ⚱ Academy Award Ⓑ BAFTA
♫ Soundtrack on CD of importance † Points of interest ⚱ Academy Award nomination Ⓣ BAFTA nomination

289

comedy, with its tea-steeped English musings and its love of bitty, tangential gags. – *Anthony Lane, The New Yorker*

Hitman (new)

DIR Xavier Gens
2007   93m   US/France
[DVD] ♫

☆ Timothy Olyphant (Agent 47), Dougray Scott (Mike Whittier), Olga Kurlyenko (Nika), Ulrich Thomsen (Mikhail Belicoff)

A contract assassin tries to kill a Russian politician, and then elude Interpol and the military.

Based on a video game, and it shows. Olyphant, as the titular hitman, offers no flicker of recognisable human behaviour.

SCR Skip Woods   **CIN** Laurent bares   **MUS** Geoff Zanelli   **DES** Jacques Bufnoir   **ED** Carlo Rizzo, Antoine Vareille   **PROD** Charles Gordon, Adrian Askarieh   **DIST** TCF

❝ As a movie on its own, it's simple monotony. – *Jack Mathews, New York Daily News*

❝ Xavier Gens should have stuck to making music videos rather than inflict his goldfish-like attention span on cinema. – *Wendy Ide, The Times*

'Based on the true story. Would we lie to you?'

The Hoax (new)   ★★

DIR Lasse Hallström
2006   116m   US
[DVD]

☆ Richard Gere (Clifford Irving), Alfred Molina (Dick Suskind), Marcia Gay Harden (Edith Irving), Hope Davis (Andrea Tate), Julie Delpy (Nina Van Pallandt), Eli Wallach (Noah Dietrich), Stanley Tucci (Shelton Fisher), Zelkjo Ivanek (Ralph Graves)

In one of the great literary hoaxes of the last century, Clifford Irving convinces a publisher that he has exclusive access to the reclusive billionaire Howard Hughes and can ghost his autobiography.

In playing a con artist, Gere finally surrenders to the slippery side of his considerable screen charm, and he and Molina make an entertaining pair of fraudsters. Everyone concerned seems to let their hair down, including director Hallström, thankfully less stuffy than usual.

SCR William Wheeler   **CIN** Oliver Stapleton   **MUS** Carter Burwell   **DES** Mark Ricker   **ED** Andrew Mondshein   **PROD** Bob Yari, Joshua D. Maurer, Betsy Beers, Mark Gordon, Leslie Holleran   **DIST** Momentum

❝ It's hard to believe anybody could have been persuaded this movie had to be made. – *Edward Porter, Sunday Times*

❝ Entertaining though The Hoax is, the film that I imagined before I saw it was better. – *Stanley Kauffman, New Republic*

'Some secrets are too big to keep hidden.'

Holes   ★

DIR Andrew Davis
2003   117m   US
[DVD] ♫

☆ Sigourney Weaver (Warden), Jon Voight (Mr Sir),

Patricia Arquette (Kissin' Kate Barlow), Tim Blake Nelson (Dr Pendanski), Dule Hill (Sam), *Shia LaBeouf* (Stanley Yelnats), Henry Winkler (Stanley's Father), Nate Davis (Stanley's Grandfather), Eartha Kitt (Madame Zeroni)

Falsely accused of stealing from an orphanage, a teenage boy is sent to a desert detention centre where the inmates must dig at the command of the warden.

Pleasing family movie with three good villains and a terrific lead, though its flashbacks to the Wild West are somewhat fumbled.

SCR Louis Sachar   **CIN** Stephen St. John   **MUS** Joel McNeely   **DES** Maher Ahmad   **ED** Tom Nordberg, Jeffrey Wolf   **PROD** Mike Medavoy, Andrew Davis, Teresa Tucker-Davies, Lowell Blank   **DIST** Buena Vista

❝ Unusual, intriguing and good enough to engage adults. – *Cosmo Landesman, Sunday Times*

❝ It is a funny, occasionally scary movie about family, friendship, fate, courage and redemption with some good stories to tell and several clever twists. – *Philip French, Observer*

'Bobby Taylor was on his way to becoming a star, when a funny thing happened.....'

Hollywood Shuffle   ★

DIR Robert Townsend
1987   78m   US

☆ Robert Townsend (Bobby Taylor / Jasper / Speed / Sam Ace / Rambro), Anne-Marie Johnson (Lydia / Willie Mae / Hooker #5), Starletta Dupois (Bobby's Mother), Helen Martin (Bobby's Grandmother), Craigus R. Johnson (Stevie Taylor), John Witherspoon (Mr. Jones), Keenen Ivory Wayans (Donald / Jheri Curl), Jimmy Woodard (Advanced Student / Basketball Player / Tyrone)

A struggling Afro-American actor in Hollywood is torn between his principles and the need to work.

Deft, amusing satire that rounds up Hollywood genres in vogue at the time and examines just how each one misuses and abuses black American actors. The genial Townsend keeps his anger at bay, preferring to poke fun at this sad situation. His creation of the 'Act Black' drama school is priceless.

SCR Robert Townsend, Keenen Ivory Wayans   **CIN** Peter Deming   **MUS** Patrice Rushen, Udi Harpaz   **DES** Melba Katzman Farquhar   **ED** W. O. Garrett   **PROD** Robert Townsend   **DIST** Samuel Goldwyn Company/Conquering Unicorn

---

'Living in Hollywood can make you famous. Dying in Hollywood can make you a legend.'

Hollywoodland   ★★

DIR Allen Coulter
2006   126m   US
[DVD] ♫

☆ Ben Affleck (George Reeves), Adrien Brody (Louis Simo), Diane Lane (Toni Mannix), Bob Hoskins (Edgar Mannix), Lois Smith (Helen Bessolo)

A down-at-heel private eye tries to establish whether the death by gunshot of George Reeves, who played Superman on TV, was suicide, or the result of shady studio politics.

Inconclusive and overlong, this is two stories bolted together – one broadly real, the other fictional and unsatisfactory. Period Hollywood is studiously evoked in portraying Reeves's mysterious death and his antagonism to studio bosses. But the attempts of private eye Simo to redeem himself in his young son's eyes by solving Superman's murder feels sugary and contrived. Skinny, punkish Brody fails to convince in this role, but Affleck and Lane are fine as the square-jawed, faintly dim Reeves and his older mistress, a ruthless studio executive's wife.

SCR Paul Bernbaum   CIN Jonathan Freeman
MUS Marcelo Zarvos   DES Leslie McDonald
ED Michael Berenbaum   PROD Glenn Williamson
DIST Buena Vista International

66 This film is brave enough to admit that not all failed movie careers are the result of evil corporate suits, and Affleck makes us care that this likeable but weak-minded man threw away what was solid and good in his life for the chimera of fame. – Ella Taylor, L.A. Weekly

† As with The Black Dahlia, this period film about Los Angeles was filmed elsewhere – in Toronto.

'Journey into temptation, but be sure you know your way back.'

Holy Smoke ★

DIR Jane Campion
1999   114m   US
DVD   ♫

☆ Kate Winslet (Ruth), Harvey Keitel (PJ Waters), Pam Grier (Carol), Julie Hamilton (Mum), Sophie Lee (Yvonne), Daniel Wyllie (Robbie), Paul Goddard (Tim), Tim Robertson (Dad), George Mangos (Yani)

A young Australian woman is brainwashed by an Indian guru, and her family send an American exit counsellor in to deprogramme her.

A strident treatment of an interesting topic, descending too often into over-the-top confrontations and point-scoring caricature.

SCR Anna Campion, Jane Campion   CIN Dion Beebe
MUS Angelo Badalamenti   DES Janet Patterson
ED Veronika Jenet   PROD Jan Chapman   DIST Film4

66 Filled with flashy sight gags, overwrought performances, and madly overlapping dialogue. – J. Hoberman, Village Voice

66 At once hilarious and serious, cruel and tender, and bristling with vitality, Holy Smoke is the right movie for the millennium, envisioning new possibilities in the way people view and relate to one another. – Kevin Thomas, Los Angeles Times

---

'A Family Comedy Without The Family.'

Home Alone ★

DIR Chris Columbus
1990   103m   US
DVD   ♫

☆ Macaulay Culkin (Kevin McCallister), Joe Pesci (Harry), Daniel Stern (Mary), Catherine O'Hara (Kate McCallister), John Heard (Peter McCallister), Roberts Blossom (Marley), John Candy (Gus Polinski)

The youngest child of a large family is accidentally left at home over Christmas, and defends it from a pair of inept burglars.

Ultra-commercial, ultra-successful family comedy, which briefly made a superstar of its 10-year-old lead; it's solidly put-together, but hardly inspired.

SCR John Hughes   CIN Julio Macat   MUS John Williams
DES John Muto   ED Raja Gosnell   PROD John Hughes
DIST TCF/John Hughes

66 Does have its sweet side. – Caryn James, New York Times

66 The novelty starts to wear off when a couple of burglars (Stern and Pesci, excellent) target the house. – Colette Maude, Time Out

♪ John Williams (music, original score); John Williams (m), Leslie Bricusse (ly) (music, original song – Somewhere in My Memory)

'Meet the family that put the fun in dysfunctional!'

Home for the Holidays ★★

DIR Jodie Foster
1995   103m   US
DVD   ♫

☆ Holly Hunter (Claudia Larson), Robert Downey Jnr (Tommy Larson), Anne Bancroft (Adele Larson), Charles Durning (Henry Larson), Dylan McDermott (Leo Fish), Geraldine Chaplin (Aunt Gladys), Cynthia Stevenson (Joanne Larson Wedman), Steve Guttenberg (Walter Wedman), Claire Danes (Kitt Larson), Austin Pendleton (Peter Arnold), David Strathairn (Russell Terziak)

An art restorer gets fired and goes home to her fractious family home for Thanksgiving, where her gay brother puts in a surprise appearance.

On the surface a formulaic comedy of festive dysfunction, but so imaginatively played and well-written that it emerges as a very particular portrait of a family. Quite deliberately, it's a squawking mess.

SCR W.D. Richter   CIN Lajos Koltai   MUS Mark Isham
DES Andrew McAlpine   ED Lynzee Klingman
PROD Peggy Rajski, Jodie Foster   DIST Polygram/Egg

66 Foster keeps the party hopping, although more dark humour would have helped before she winds it down with sentiment and bromides. – Peter Travers, Rolling Stone

---

'Bob Gold is a cop. A good cop. But tonight, he will betray his friends, disgrace the force, and commit an act of violence because he believes it is the only right thing to do.'

Homicide ★★★

SCR/DIR David Mamet
1991   102m   US
DVD

☆ Joe Mantegna (Bobby Gold), William H. Macy (Tim Sullivan), Natalija Nogulich (Chava), Ving Rhames (Randolph), Rebecca Pidgeon (Miss Klein), J.J. Johnston (Jilly Curran), Jack Wallace (Frank)

A Jewish cop suspects neo-Nazis were involved in the murder of a shopkeeper.

Unsettling and thoughtful thriller, arguably the director's best, about a man getting to the bottom of his own identity and being led astray in the process.

DVD Available on DVD	☆ Cast in order	66 Critics' Quotes	♙ Academy Award	♖ BAFTA
♫ Soundtrack on CD	of importance	† Points of interest	♙ Academy Award nomination	♖ BAFTA nomination

Can there be any young actor in Hollywood with aspirations to a serious career who does not look to George Clooney as a role model? It seems unlikely. In the past few years Clooney has arrived at a place where he is far more than a mere leading man. He has established himself as Hollywood's moral conscience by getting scripts made that satisfy his own ethical and political standards, while helping to subsidise them with the considerable amounts of money he makes by starring in harmless, forgettable studio films. It's a neat trick, and he seems to have pulled it off almost by stealth.

It's curious that Clooney wields such enormous influence, given that many of his films, while successful on their own terms, do not make vast sums of money at the box-office. Tom Cruise and Will Smith, for instance, would be disappointed by the business Clooney generates. True, his *Ocean's 11* trilogy and *Batman and Robin* raked in the cash (each one passing the $100 million mark in the US); money for old rope, some of us might think. But though his more personal films – *Good Night And Good Luck*, *Syriana*, and even this year's Oscar nominee *Michael Clayton* – are all excellent, thoughtful, have something worth saying, and bring him respect and critical acclaim, they don't fill huge numbers of cinemas.

This is surprising. It means that despite his enormous popularity, people still pick and choose which George Clooney films they are prepared to pay to see. And there are other holes in his screen career that he has not yet successfully plugged.

For example, given that here is a man whose gaze, charm and dapper demeanour famously make women go weak-kneed, why do those films that pit him opposite strong leading actresses feel so underpowered? Few people have much time for *One Fine Day*, which paired him with Michelle Pfeiffer. Or *The Peacemaker*, in which he was cast against Nicole Kidman. His outing with Catherine Zeta-Jones in *Intolerable Cruelty* was widely judged, well, intolerable. And this last year, his verbal jousting with Renée Zellweger in *Leatherheads* was found sorely wanting. Only in *Out of Sight* with Jennifer Lopez, by far the least accomplished of these actresses, was there any hint of screen chemistry. Clooney is routinely compared to Cary Grant for his good looks and suavity, but his track record as a romantic lead suggests he has a long way to go to justify the comparison.

Instead, Clooney operates best on screen with other men (think *Three Kings*, *The Perfect Storm*, *Good Night And Good Luck* and *O Brother Where Art Thou?*) or as a loner: he spent much of *Solaris* (uncommercial, certainly, but sadly underrated) wandering around space alone, while in *Michael Clayton*, his troubled, flawed law-firm fixer was a brooding, often solitary figure.

In his private life, Clooney has a close-knit, long-established group of jokey, sometimes raucous male friends; there doesn't seem to be much of the loner about him. Indeed, the qualities that make him so alluring in person rarely surface on screen.

Chief among these is his wit. Verbally, he is fast on his feet, and trades in wry self-deprecation. He shifts easily into charm-offensive mode, whether he is meeting the public or the media. Women admire his faintly demure gaze and his dazzling smile; it does not hurt that he is also a man who so far has become better-looking with age (he is now 47). Men, meanwhile, warm to his sly humour and view him as a potentially amiable companion with whom they might easily sink a few beers. His is a sophisticated, complex persona.

It's a shame this side of him has never been captured in his film work. There were glimpses of it in his appearances as Dr Doug Ross, the emergency ward Lothario from TV's *ER*, but they remained mere glimpses. On the big screen, Clooney has demonstrated a taste for broad, goofball humour – in *O Brother*, *Intolerable Cruelty* and *Welcome to Collinwood* – that suggests a sneaking admiration for the Three Stooges. It's fine, but a little goes a long way.

Yet that's only one of the many contradictions about him. Another is his pragmatic attitude to making hit films. It was forged with director Steven Soderbergh, with whom he collaborated on *Out of Sight*, and who shares his sceptical view of studios' priorities. The pair devised a plan: they would make one obvious commercial hit for a studio (*Ocean's 11*, say), and then use the profits to make two personal, quirky films of their own choosing. 'It seems to work,' Clooney remarked in 2003, 'though if we do a couple of *Solarises*, they'll take the toys away from us.'

Clooney is not afraid to be outspoken; indeed, it's precisely this quality that endears him to many people. He was one of the first Hollywood celebrities to voice his misgivings over the Iraq war; the conservative American commentator Bill O'Reilly, of TV's Fox News, ventured the opinion that Clooney's dissent heralded the end of his career. This turned out to be a memorably bad prediction.

For beneath the jokiness and self-deprecation, Clooney has the gift of knowing how to seize a public moment, how to make his influence count, how to be serious and, above all, how to present himself appropriately. He has been critical of public figures who do not, notably President George W Bush; he once lambasted Bush for 'winking and chuckling' in front of an audience as he was about to send young American soldiers off to war: 'Just because you have an audience yelling and cheering doesn't mean you giggle and wink,' Clooney said. 'If you're the leader of the free world, you have to be good at that stuff. But he didn't understand the moment.'

This intuitiveness and self-possession makes him a public figure who wields enormous influence. His views on global events are listened to eagerly. Earlier this year, when Clooney visited London to promote *Leatherheads,* he dropped in at 10 Downing Street and told Prime Minister Gordon Brown what he thought the western world should be doing about the humanitarian crisis in Darfur. Brown, easily Clooney's match in terms of intellect but without a smidgen of his charisma, was reported to have listened carefully.

No other figure in the film world – not Steven Spielberg, not Tom Hanks, and certainly not Tom Cruise – can do this. If he wished, Clooney could probably run for political office and achieve some success in that field; he is almost certainly smart enough not to want to.

> 'If he wished, Clooney could probably run for political office and achieve some success in that field; he is almost certainly smart enough not to want to.'

Meanwhile, he has a film career to tend to – and this year finds him at something of a crossroads. He and Soderbergh have amicably brought their partnership to an end, and Clooney is looking for projects on his own. He has already stated the sort of films he admires: titles from the 60s and 70s, such as *Klute*, *All the President's Men*, *Fail Safe*, *The Parallax View* and *Network*. In other words, films that are dramatic, gripping and entertaining, with something to say.

Emulating such work is a decent challenge for an actor, producer and director currently in a position to do anything he pleases. One would wish him well in such an endeavour. Yet is it churlish to wish that somewhere between the solemnity of his 'important' films and the almost slapstick quality of his comedies, Clooney would also find a way to represent himself on screen as dazzlingly as he does in public? At the time of writing, he seems to be an actor in search of an identity.

In this regard, actors need help – from screenwriters. Consider the gifts that Garson Kanin bestowed on Spencer Tracy with his brilliant scripts for *Adam's Rib* and *Pat and Mike*; and how eagerly Cary Grant seized on Ben Hecht's masterly dialogue in *His Girl Friday* and *Notorious*. Those screenplays helped make those actors what they were on screen. If Clooney had automatic access to such writing talent, there's no telling what he might yet achieve.

CIN Roger Deakins   MUS Alaric Jans   DES Michael
Merritt   ED Barbara Tulliver   PROD Michael Hausman,
Edward R. Pressman   DIST First Independent/J&M
Entertainment/Cinehaus

66 Portrayed with a spell-binding skill and precision, the
pace of an action-thriller off-set by unexpected patterns of
colour and speech, part documentary, part theatrical
melodrama. – *Philip Strick, Sight and Sound*

66 The movie crackles with energy and life, and with
throwaway slang dialogue by Mamet, who takes realistic
speech patterns and simplifies them into a kind of
hammer-and-nail poetry. – *Roger Ebert, Chicago
Sun-Times*

'The most astonishing, innovative, backyard adventure of
all time!'

Honey, I Shrunk the Kids   ★

DIR Joe Johnston
1989   93m   US
DVD   ♫

☆ Rick Moranis (Wayne Szalinski), Matt Frewer (Russell
'Russ' Thompson, Sr. (Big Russ Thompson), Marcia
Strassman (Diane Szalinski), Kristine Sutherland (Mae
Thompson), Thomas Brown (Russell 'Russ' Thompson, Jr.
(Little Russell Thompson)), Jared Rushton (Ronald 'Ron'
Thompson), Amy O'Neill (Amy Szalinski), Robert Oliveri
(Nick Szalinski), Carl Steven (Tommy Pervis)

A nutty scientist inadvertently shrinks his children
and must find them to reverse the process.

*Fun, frenetic Disney action comedy which never takes
itself too seriously.*

SCR Ed Naha, Tom Schulman   CIN Hiro Narita
DES Gregg Fonseca   ED Michael A. Stevenson
PROD Penney Finkelman Cox   DIST Warner/Walt
Disney/Doric

† A sequel of sorts, Honey, I Blew Up the Kid, followed
in 1992.

Honeydripper (new)   ★★★

SCR/DIR John Sayles
2007   123m   US
DVD   ♫

☆ *Danny Glover* (Tyrone Purvis), Lisa Gay Hamilton
(Delilah), Yaya DaCosta (China Doll), *Charles S. Dutton*
(Maceo), Vondie Curtis Hall (Slick), Gary Clark Jr. (Sonny
Blake), Dr. Mable John (Bertha Mae), Stacy Keach (Sheriff
Pugh), Keb' Mo' (Possum)

In the Deep South in 1950, the Honeydripper
Lounge is a struggling music bar in cotton-fields
country. To save it, owner Tyrone organises a
concert starring Guitar Sam, whose records are
radio hits. But when Sam doesn't show up, he turns
to a young stranger who has breezed into town with
his guitar case.

*Deliciously easy-paced and good-humoured film that
sheds light on a crossroads of musical and social history
– the earliest days of rock 'n' roll, when musical
instruments were going electric, guitars replaced pianos,
and big bands yielded to small groups. It's a lovely
affectionate tribute to the roots of an enduring musical
phenomenon, with generous performances to match.*

CIN Dick Pope   MUS Mason Daring   DES Toby Corbett
PROD Maggie Renzi   DIST Axiom

66 The result is one of Sayles' best films. The music, a mix
of blues, seminal rock and newcomer Gary Clark Jr.'s
performance, will be an obvious draw, as will the
performances by some leading African-American actors. –
John Anderson, Variety

66 The film is full of wonderful visual and verbal
moments. – *Philip French, Observer*

'A comedy about one bride, two grooms, and 34 flying
Elvises.'

Honeymoon in Vegas   ★★

SCR/DIR Andrew Bergman
1992   96m   US
DVD   ♫

☆ James Caan (Tommy Korman), Nicolas Cage (Jack
Singer), Sarah Jessica Parker (Betsy / Donna), Pat Morita
(Mahi Mahi), Johnny Williams (Johnny Sandwich), Anne
Bancroft (Bea Singer), Peter Boyle (Chief Orman)

A rich gambler bankrupts a New York cop at poker,
and offers to clear the debt if he can spend a
weekend in Vegas with the latter's fiancee.

*Spirited and funny comedy with a great running joke
about Elvis impersonators.*

CIN William A. Fraker   MUS David Newman
DES William A. Elliott   ED Barry Malkin   PROD Mike
Lobell   DIST First Independent/Castle Rock/New
Line/Lobell/Bergman

66 It's a romantic farce in which the explosion of the
epically earnest and funny central situation creates shock
waves that leave no person or thing untouched. Even the
film's bit players and extras are funny. – *Vincent Canby,
New York Times*

'What if Peter Pan grew up?'

Hook

DIR Steven Spielberg
1991   144m   US
DVD   ♫

☆ Dustin Hoffman (Capt. Hook), Robin Williams (Peter
Banning), Julia Roberts (Tinkerbell), Bob Hoskins (Smee),
Maggie Smith (Granny Wendy), Caroline Goodall (Moira
Banning), Charlie Korsmo (Jack 'Jackie' Banning), Amber
Scott (Maggie Banning), Laurel Cronin (Liza, Wendy's
Housekeeper), Phil Collins (Inspector Good), David
Crosby (Tickles)

The adult Peter Pan must return to Neverland to
rescue his children from the clutches of Captain
Hook.

*Indigestible and exhausting spin on a beloved book,
which doesn't unleash the child in all of us so much as
beat him or her into submission; Spielberg lets
production values smother the story, and the stars seem
flummoxed.*

SCR Jim V. Hart, Malia Scotch Marmo   CIN Dean Cundey
MUS John Williams   DES Norman Garwood (John Napier
was visual consultant)   ED Michael Kahn
PROD Kathleen Kennedy, Frank Marshall, Gerald R. Molen
DIST Columbia TriStar/Amblin

66 A failure in almost every way. . . a lumpy mess, served
up in a whopping portion. – *Terrence Rafferty, New Yorker*

66 A Disneyland nightmare people with waxwork characters. – *Sheridan Morley, Sunday Express*

♟ John Williams (m), Leslie Bricusse (ly) (music, original song – When You're Alone); Norman Garwood; Eric Brevig, Harley Jessup, Mark Sullivan, Michael Lantieri (visual effects); Anthony Powell (costume design); Christina Smith, Monty Westmore, Greg Cannom (make up)

'The Film That Stunned A Nation!'

Hoop Dreams ★★★★

DIR *Steve James*
1994 170m US
[DVD] ♫

☆ William Gates (Himself), Arthur Agee (Himself), Emma Gates (Herself, William's Mother), Curtis Gates (Himself, William's Brother), Sheila Agee (Herself, Arthur's Mother)

Two African-American teenagers from inner-city Chicago struggle to enter the world of professional basketball.

Epic, moving and intensely memorable, the movie tackles the issue of sport as an escape route from the ghetto, but heroically transcends the clichés, delving into the backgrounds of the boys and their families, detailing the obstacles they have to face over four years, and showing us what it means to them to win – a game, a place in the team, a new life. It is a truly great American documentary.

SCR Steve James, Fred Marx CIN Peter Gilbert
MUS Ben Sidran ED *Fred Marx, Steve James, Bill Haugse*
PROD Fred Marx, Steve James, Peter Gilbert
DIST Feature/FineLine/Kartemquin/KCTA-TV

66 One of the richest movie experiences of the year, a spellbinding American epic that holds you firmly in its grip for nearly three hours. – *David Ansen, Newsweek*

66 A truly great documentary. – *Kim Newman, Empire*

♟ Fred Marx, Steve James, Bill Haugse

Hope and Glory ★★★

SCR/DIR *John Boorman*
1987 113m GB
[DVD] ♫

☆ Sarah Miles, *Susan Wooldridge*, Ian Bannen, David Hayman, Derrick O'Connor, Sebastian Rice-Edwards

Adventures of a small boy and his family during the Blitz in suburban London.

A delightful account of war from an unusual viewpoint: the young boy (partly based on the young Boorman) has a good war despite the obvious dangers, finding excitement and adventure in the rubble of bombed-out buildings. A cheerful, stirring film that surprises and intrigues.

CIN Philippe Rousselot MUS Peter Martin
DES Anthony Pratt PROD John Boorman
DIST Columbia/Goldcrest/Nelson

♟ picture; John Boorman (direction); John Boorman (original screenplay); Philippe Rousselot; art direction – set decoration

🎭 Susan Wooldridge (supporting actress)

The Horse Whisperer ★

DIR Robert Redford
1998 170m US
[DVD] ♫

☆ Robert Redford (Tom Booker), Kristin Scott Thomas (Annie MacLean), Sam Neill (Robert MacLean), Dianne Wiest (Diane Booker), Scarlett Johansson (Grace MacLean), Chris Cooper (Frank Booker), Cherry Jones (Liz Hammond), Ty Hillman (Joe Booker), Catherine Bosworth (Judith)

The mother of a girl who was severely injured in a riding accident travels out west to secure the help of a gifted trainer in healing her traumatised horse.

There's a place for middlebrow romantic drama that above all looks good, and that's precisely what this overlong movie offers. Redford has an eye for sweeping landscapes, but falters with the emotional core of what was never a convincing story, even in book form.

SCR Eric Roth, Richard LaGravenese CIN *Robert Richardson* MUS Thomas Newman, Gwil Owen
DES Jon Hutman ED Tom Rolf, Freeman Davies, Hank Corwin PROD Robert Redford, Patrick Markey
DIST Buena Vista/Touchstone/Wildwood

66 Mr. Redford has found his own visually eloquent way to turn the pot-boiler into a panorama, with a deep-seated love for the Montana landscape against which his rapturously beautiful film unfolds. – *Elvis Mitchell, New York Times*

♟ Allison Moorer, Gwil Owen (m), (ly) (music – original song A Soft Place to Fall)

'Their only chance for survival was each other.'

The Horseman on the Roof ★

DIR Jean-Paul Rappeneau
1995 135m France
[DVD] ♫

☆ Olivier Martinez (Angelo Pardi), Juliette Binoche (Pauline de Théus), Isabelle Carré (The Tutor), François Cluzet (The Doctor), Jean Yanne (Le Colporteur), Claudio Amendola (Maggionari), Pierre Arditi (Monsieur Peyrolle), Gérard Depardieu (Commissaire de Police à Manosque)

In the 19th century, an Italian hussar is pursued across cholera-stricken Provence by Austrian assassins, falling into the company of a mysterious woman along the way.

Good-looking costume drama that runs out of narrative momentum long before the final showdown.

SCR Jean-Paul Rappeneau, Nina Companeez, Jean-Claude Carrière CIN *Thierry Arbogast* MUS Jean-Claude Petit
DES Jacques Rouxel, Ezio Frigerio ED Noëlle Boisson
PROD René Cleitman
DIST Hachette/France2/CEC/Canal

66 A wonderfully romantic film, arrestingly told and spectacularly realised. – *Karen McLuskey, Empire*

66 The Provencal villages and landscapes look good (as usual), but in the end there's not enough development, thematic or otherwise, to sustain interest. – *Geoff Andrew, Time Out*

[DVD] Available on DVD ☆ Cast in order 66 Critics' Quotes ♟ Academy Award 🎭 BAFTA
♫ Soundtrack on CD of importance † Points of interest ♟ Academy Award nomination 🎭 BAFTA nomination

295

'It is Lurking Behind You!'

The Host ★★★

SCR/DIR Joon-ho Bong

2006   119m   South Korea/Japan

[DVD]

☆ Kang-ho Song (Park Gang-Du), Hie-bong Byun (Park Hie-Bong), Hae-il Park (Park Nam-il), Du-na Bae (Park Nam-joo), Ah-sung Ko (Park Hyun-seo)

A mutant sea monster attacks Seoul natives.

A terrific creature feature with pulse-pounding thrills, nasty scares and a keen sense of pulp humour.

SCR Chul-Hyun Baek, Won-jun Ha, Joon-ho Bong
CIN Hyung-ku Kim   MUS Byung-woo Lee   DES Seong-hie Ryu   ED Seon Min Kim   PROD Yong-bae Choi
DIST Optimum

66 If this madly entertaining movie has a fault, it's that it's too ingenious for the genre it ostensibly inhabits. – *Richard Corliss, Time*

'Big cops. Small town. Moderate violence.'

Hot Fuzz ★★

DIR Edgar Wright

2007   120m   UK/USA/France

[DVD]   ♫

☆ Simon Pegg (Nicholas Angel), Nick Frost (PC Danny Butterman), Jim Broadbent (Inspector Frank Butterman), Paddy Considine (DC Andy Wainwright), Timothy Dalton (Simon Skinner), Billie Whitelaw (Joyce Cooper), Edward Woodward (Tom Weaver), Bill Nighy (Chief inspector)

An over-zealous London cop, transferred to a small quiet English village, uncovers a sinister secret.

Loving parody of loud, pulsating, Hollywood cop-buddy movies with a high body count. Its twist is in its unlikely setting – a village so tranquil, it's dull. Pegg and Frost are splendid as the odd-couple police heroes, and proceedings are enlivened by a fine cast of veteran British actors and a series of delightful running gags. Though overlong with an indecisive ending, its self-effacing humour wins through.

SCR Edgar Wright, Simon Pegg   CIN Jess Hall
MUS David Arnold   DES Marcus Rowland   ED Chris Dickens   PROD Nira Park, Tim Bevan, Eric Fellner
DIST Universal

DANNY BUTTERMAN: 'Have you ever fired two guns whilst jumping through the air?'

ANDY WAINWRIGHT: 'You wanna be a big cop in a small town? F*** off up the model village, then.'

66 Plenty of irrepressible fun – and big, regular laughs. – *Peter Bradshaw, Guardian*

66 Funny, inventive, furiously paced. . . – *Philip French, Observer*

'Smack destiny in the face.'

Hot Rod (new)

DIR Akiva Schaffer

2007   88m   US

[DVD]   ♫

☆ Andy Samberg (Rod Kimble), Isla Fisher (Denise), Jorma Taccone (Kevin Powell), Bill Hader (Dave), Danny McBride (Rico), Sissy Spacek (Marie Powell), Ian McShane (Frank Powell), Will Arnett (Jonathan)

A would-be daredevil with ambitions to be another Evel Knievel plans a reckless stunt to help his hated stepfather get a life-saving operation.

A goofy vehicle for Saturday Night Live regular Samberg that sets its sights as low as possible. Even so, the slender premise feels relentlessly extended.

SCR Pam Brady   CIN Andrew Dunn   MUS Trevor Rabin
DES Stephen Altman   ED Malcolm Campbell
PROD Lorne Michaels, John Goldwyn   DIST Paramount

66 High in concept, low in sophistication. – *Frank Scheck, Hollywood Reporter*

66 I laughed, then I wished it was funnier, then I just wished it would end. – *Peter Travers, Rolling Stone*

† Originally conceived as a vehicle for Will Ferrell.

'Film Noir Like You've Never Seen.'

The Hot Spot ★

DIR Dennis Hopper

1990   130m   US

[DVD]   ♫

☆ Don Johnson (Harry Madox), Virginia Madsen (Dolly Harshaw), Jennifer Connelly (Gloria Harper), Charles Martin Smith (Lon Gulick), William Sadler (Frank Sutton), Jerry Hardin (George Harshaw), Barry Corbin (Sheriff), Leon Rippy (Deputy Tate), Jack Nance (Julian Ward)

A drifter arrives in town, and finds himself falling for both a good woman and a femme fatale.

That this is director Hopper's homage to film noir soon becomes clear; but one's awareness that he is working within a genre (though with more licence to be sexually explicit) renders the story predictable.

SCR Nona Tyson, Charles Williams   CIN Ueli Steiger
MUS Jack Nitzsche   DES Cary White   ED Wende Phifer Mate   PROD Paul Lewis   DIST Rank/Orion

Hotel

SCR/DIR Mike Figgis

2001   109m   GB/Italy

[DVD]

☆ Rhys Ifans (Trent Stoken), Saffron Burrows (Duchess of Malfi), David Schwimmer (Jonathan Danderfine), Salma Hayek (Charlee Boux), Burt Reynolds (Flamenco Manager), Julian Sands (Quintus), Danny Huston (Hotel Manager), Lucy Liu (Kawika), Chiara Mastroianni (Nurse), Laura Morante (Gretta), Ornella Muti (Flamenco Manager's Wife), Heathcote Williams (Bosola), Jason Isaacs (Australian Actor), Mia Maestro (Latin Actress), John Malkovich (uncredited)

A British film crew shooting a version of The Duchess of Malfi in Venice are observed by a sleazy documentarist, while the hotel staff feast on human flesh.

An experimental in digital filmmaking without any of the point of the same director's Timecode; it's wilfully silly, but there are flashes of wit here and there.

CIN Patrick Alexander Stewart   MUS Mike Figgis, Anthony Marinelli   DES Franco Fumagalli   PROD Mike Figgis, Annie Stewart, Etchie Stroh   DIST ICA

66 All the furious improv lacks any sort of map. – *Laura Sinagra, Village Voice*

66 An addled affair. – *Philip French, Observer*

'When the world closed its eyes, he opened his arms.'

Hotel Rwanda ★★

DIR Terry George
2004 121m GB/US/South Africa/Italy
[DVD] ♫

☆ *Don Cheadle* (Paul), Sophie Okonedo (Tatiana), Joaquin Phoenix (Jack), Nick Nolte (Colonel Oliver), Jean Reno (uncredited) (Sabena Airlines President)

The owner of a hotel in Kigali opens it as a refuge for imperilled Tsutsis during the 1994 Rwandan genocide.

Powerful slant on a crisis that shook the world, but not to the extent of stepping in: it works mainly as a conventional salute to one man's bravery, but Cheadle handles the demands of his role superbly.

SCR *Keir Pearson, Terry George* CIN Robert Fraisse MUS Andrea Guerra, Rupert Gregson-Williams, Afro Celt Sound System DES Tony Burrough, Johnny Breedt ED Naomi Geraghty PROD A. Kitman Ho, Terry George DIST MGM

66 It is a powerful portrait of a slightly befuddled man who, when inhuman demands were placed on him, found within himself an unexpected response. – *Richard Schickel, Time*

66 Who cares about overdone orchestral blasts or signpost-waving lines of dialogue when such raw, naked, painful humanity is displayed by Don Cheadle in the central role? – *Dan Jolin, Empire*

⚖ Don Cheadle (leading actor); Sophie Okonedo (supporting actress); Keir Pearson, Terry George (original screenplay)

Ⓣ Keir Pearson, Terry George (original screenplay)

'Love never needed to be so blind'

The Hottie and the Nottie (new)

DIR Tom Putnam
2008 91m US

☆ Paris Hilton (Cristabell Abbott), Joel David Moore (Nate Cooper), Christine Lakin (June Phigg)

A sexy girl takes a vow of celibacy until her ugly duckling best friend gets a lover too.

A shoddy, juvenile, mirthless, tacky romp.

SCR Heidi Ferrer CIN Alex Vendler MUS David E. Russo DES John Larena ED Jeff Malmberg PROD Joshua Lekach, Myles Nestel, Victoria Nevinny, Neal Ramer, Hadeel Reda DIST Pathé

66 "Crass, shrill, disingenuous, tawdry, mean-spirited, vulgar, idiotic, boring, slapdash, half-assed and very, very unfunny". – *Nathan Lee, Village Voice*

'The time to hide is over.'

The Hours ★★★

DIR *Stephen Daldry*
2002 114m US/GB
[DVD] ♫

☆ Meryl Streep (Clarissa Vaughan), *Julianne Moore* (Laura Brown), Nicole Kidman (Virginia Woolf), Ed Harris (Richard Brown), Toni Collette (Kitty), Claire Danes (Julia Vaughan), Jeff Daniels (Louis Waters), Stephen Dillane (Leonard Woolf)

Three different women in three different times and places – the writer Virginia Woolf, a 1950s Californian housewife, and a publisher in contemporary New York – go about rituals that echo and overlap one another.

One of the few recent instances where a determined throwing of heavyweight talent at a prestige literary project hasn't entirely sunk it: shuffling back and forth to observe what connects and separates the generations – following the Mrs. Dalloway line that you can take the measure of a woman's life by examining what she does on one day – the result is a spellbinding, if eccentric, rethink of the classical women's picture.

SCR *David Hare* CIN Seamus McGarvey MUS *Philip Glass* DES Maria Djurkovic ED *Peter Boyle* PROD Scott Rudin, Robert Fox DIST Buena Vista

66 A splendid film. It uses all the resources of cinema - masterful writing, superb acting, directorial intelligence, an enveloping score, top-of-the-line production design, costumes, cinematography and editing - to make a film whose cumulative emotional power takes viewers by surprise, capturing us unawares in its ability to move us as deeply as it does. – *Kenneth Turan, Los Angeles Times*

66 There are more complex and compelling female characters in this movie than Hollywood has mustered all year. If Philip Glass's torrid score comes on a bit strong and David Hare's incisive screenplay is sometimes just too on-the-nose, these are quibbles in the face of such a boldly realised, affecting work. – *Tom Charity, Time Out*

⚖ Nicole Kidman (leading actress)

⚖ picture; David Hare (adapted screenplay); Stephen Daldry; Ed Harris (supporting actor); Julianne Moore (supporting actress); Philip Glass (music); Peter Boyle (editing); Ann Roth (costume design)

Ⓣ Nicole Kidman (leading actress); Philip Glass

Ⓣ British film; film; Meryl Streep (leading actress); Ed Harris (supporting actor); Julianne Moore (supporting actress); David Hare (adapted screenplay); Peter Boyle (editing); makeup/hair; Stephen Daldry

The Hours and Times ★★

SCR/DIR Christopher Münch
1991 60m US
[DVD]

☆ David Angus (Brian Epstein), Ian Hart (John Lennon), Stephanie Pack (Marianne), Robin McDonald (Quinones), Sergio Moreno (Miguel), Unity Grimwood (Mother)

At the height of Beatlemania, John Lennon takes a brief holiday in Spain with the group's manager Brian Epstein, who tries to seduce him.

A speculative story, based on circumstantial evidence, but an impressively stylish low-budget film with a lyrical, innocent, almost dreamy quality.

CIN Christopher Münch ED Christopher Münch PROD Christopher Münch DIST ICA/Antarctic Pictures

[DVD] Available on DVD
♫ Soundtrack on CD
☆ Cast in order of importance
66 Critics' Quotes
† Points of interest
⚖ Academy Award
⚖ Academy Award nomination
Ⓣ BAFTA
Ⓣ BAFTA nomination

297

'On the road . . . but going nowhere.'

House of America ★

DIR *Marc Evans*

1997   96m   GB/Netherlands

DVD   ♫

☆ Sian Phillips (Mam), Steven Mackintosh (Sid), Lisa Palfrey (Gwenny), Matthew Rhys (Boyo), Pascal Laurent (Clem), Richard Harrington (Cat), Islwyn Morris (Roger the Pop)

Three children grow up in a desolate Welsh mining village and long to be reunited with their father who left them for a better life in the United States.

Strikingly lit and shot, and grimly convincing for much of its length, this miserabilist account of bleak, unfulfilled lives finally topples into melodrama.

SCR Edward Thomas   **CIN** *Pierre Aim*   **MUS** John Cale   **DES** Mark Tildesley, Edward Thomas   **ED** Michiel Reichwein   **PROD** Hans De Weers   **DIST** First Independent/September/Bergen

❝ The film's tendency towards bizarre bombast is a shame, since it overshadows some genuinely effective moments. – *Liese Spencer, Sight & Sound*

House of Angels ★★

SCR/DIR Colin Nutley

1992   119m   Sweden

DVD

☆ Helena Bergström (Fanny Zander), Rikard Wolff (Zac), Sven Wollter (Axel Flogfält), Reine Brynolfsson (Henning Collmer, vicar), Ernst Gunter (Gottfrid Pettersson), Viveka Seldahl (Rut Flogfält), Per Oscarsson (Erik Zander), Tord Peterson (Ivar Pettersson), Ing-Marie Carlsson (Eva Ågren)

In rural Sweden, villagers are appalled by the arrival of a cabaret singer and her leather-clad boyfriend, who move together into a farm she has inherited.

Likable, amusing comedy about city slickers in a rural backwater, one that never takes sides or passes judgements about its characters.

CIN Jens Fischer   **MUS** Björn Isfält, Göran Martling   **DES** Ulla Herdin   **ED** Pierre Schaffer   **PROD** Lars Dahlquist   **DIST** Mayfair/Memfis/Sveriges Television/TV2/Svenska Filminstitute/Danmarks Radio/Nordisk Film and TV

❝ Nutley pictures a warm pastoral idyll, and gears his film to a suitably rural pace. – *Tom Charity, Sight & Sound*

† Director Nutley is English-born, but lives and works in Sweden.

House of Flying Daggers ★★

DIR Zhang Yimou

2004   119m   Hong Kong/China

DVD   ♫

☆ Takeshi Kaneshiro (Jin), Andy Lau (Leo), Zhang Ziyi (Mei), Song Dandan (Yee)

Two captains of the Chinese government army in the 1860s try to quash rebellion using a young blind dancer as their liaison, but both fall for her.

Splendidly upholstered as it is, with spectacular fight sequences, the movie gives into silly plot twists, and the romantic element seems sketchy and contrived.

SCR Li Feng, Zhang Yimou, Wang Bin   **CIN** *Zhao Xiaoding*   **MUS** Shigeru Umebayashi   **DES** Huo Tingxiao   **ED** Cheng Long   **PROD** Bill Kong, Zhang Yimou

❝ The most gorgeous movie of the year. This smashing martial-arts romance from Chinese director Zhang Yimou is stunning in other ways, too, like the eroticism that ripples just beneath the surface. – *Jami Bernard, New York Daily News*

❝ The end product is enough to engorge your eyes and ears; just don't look too closely at the additives, or ask: where's the beef? – *Nick Bradshaw, Time Out*

♟ Zhao Xiaoding

Ⓣ film not in the English language; Zhang Ziyi (leading actress); Zhao Xiaoding; Cheng Long; Huo Tingxiao; Angie Lam, Andy Brown, Kirsty Millar, Luke Hetherington (special visual effects); Jing Tao, Roger Savage (sound); Emi Wada (costume design); Lee-na Kwan, Xiaohai Yang, Siu-Mui Chau (make up/hair)

House of Mirth ★★★★

SCR/DIR Terence Davies

2000   140m   GB/US/United Germany

DVD

☆ *Gillian Anderson* (Lily Bart), Eric Stoltz (Lawrence Selden), *Dan Aykroyd* (Gus Trenor), Eleanor Bron (Mrs Peniston), Terry Kinney (George Dorset), Anthony LaPaglia (Sim Rosedale), *Laura Linney* (Bertha Dorset), Jodhi May (Grace Stepney), Elizabeth McGovern (Mrs. Carry Fisher)

A cash-strapped single woman in early 20th-century New York fails to marry for love or money, and finds herself stuck with a scandalous debt that threatens to bankrupt her entirely.

Stunning adaptation of Wharton's novel about a doomed social butterfly, elegantly crafted on a limited budget, and built around a piercing lead performance of Singer Sargent-esque luminosity. It makes harsh points about an even harsher social order, and makes them feel fresh.

CIN *Remi Adefarasin*   **DES** *Don Taylor*   **ED** Michael Parker   **PROD** Olivia Stewart   **DIST** FilmFour

❝ A substantial, well-upholstered picture with more sinew and power than almost any other period drama of recent times. . .a brilliant new film from a great British director. – *Peter Bradshaw, Guardian*

❝ In its own shadowed terms the film is a triumph. – *Peter Rainer, New York Magazine*

Ⓣ British film

'Some dreams can't be shared.'

House of Sand and Fog ★★

DIR Vadim Perelman

2003   126m   US/GB

DVD   ♫

☆ *Jennifer Connelly* (Kathy Nicolo), *Ben Kingsley* (Massoud Amir Behrani), Ron Eldard (Lester Burdon), Frances Fisher (Connie Walsh), Kim Dickens (Carol Burdon), *Shohreh Aghdashloo* (Nadi Behrani), Jonathan Ahdout (Esmail Behrani), Navi Rawat (Soraya Behrani)

A recovering drug addict is evicted from her San Francisco bungalow after a bureaucratic blunder, and fights to win it back from the new owner, a former colonel in the Iranian air force.

Powerfully acted piece about the competitive side of the American dream, told with force and conviction, but finally sliding into dubious melodrama.

SCR Vadim Perelman, Shawn Otto   CIN Roger Deakins   MUS James Horner   DES Maia Javan   ED Lisa Zeno Churgin   PROD Michael London, Vadim Perelman   DIST Buena Vista

66 The script of sand and fog is more like it, not to mention the acting of ham and funny accents. – *Peter Bradshaw, Guardian*

⚱ Ben Kingsley (leading actor); Shohreh Aghdashloo (supporting actress); James Horner

---

'The most astounding motion picture since motion pictures began! Man turned monster stalking show-world beauties! The ultimate dimension in terror!'

House of Wax ★★

DIR André de Toth
1953   88m   US
[DVD]

☆ *Vincent Price* (Professor Jarrod), Carolyn Jones (Cathy Gray), Paul Picerni (Scott Andrews), Phyllis Kirk (Sue Allen), Frank Lovejoy (Lt. Tom Brennan), Dabs Greer (Sgt. Jim Shane), Paul Cavanagh (Sidney Wallace)

Mutilated in a fire at his wax museum, a demented sculptor arranges a supply of dead bodies to be covered in wax for exhibition at his new showplace.

Spirited remake of Mystery of the Wax Museum (1933); as a piece of screen narrative it leaves much to be desired, but the sudden shocks are well managed, perhaps because this is the first top-grade 3-D film, packed with gimmicks irrelevant to the story, and originally shown with stereophonic sound.

SCR Crane Wilbur   CIN Bert Glennon   MUS David Buttolph   ED Rudi Fehr   PROD Bryan Foy   DIST Warner

† The director could not see the 3-D effect, being blind in one eye.

The House on Carroll Street ★★

DIR Peter Yates
1988   101m   US
[DVD]

☆ Kelly McGillis (Emily), Jeff Daniels (Cochran), Mandy Patinkin (Salwen), Christopher Rhode (Stefan), Jessica Tandy (Miss Venable), Jonathan Hogan (Alan)

In 1951, a woman forced out of her job because of her refusal to name names in the McCarthyite witch-hunt trials, takes a job reading to an old woman, and stumbles on a scheme to smuggle Nazis into the U.S...

Tense, literate thriller, well-acted, with a neat, pleasing resolution.

SCR Walter Bernstein   CIN Michael Ballhaus   MUS Georges Delerue   DES Stuart Wurtzel   ED Ray Lovejoy   PROD Peter Yates, Robert F. Colesberry   DIST Rank/Orion

† Screenwriter Walter Bernstein was himself blacklisted in the 1950s.

'If they get caught it's all over. If they don't, it's just the beginning!'

House Party

SCR/DIR Reginald Hudlin
1990   100m   US
[DVD]   ♫

☆ Christopher Reid (Kid / Christopher (as Kid N Play)), Robin Harris (Pop), Christopher Martin (Play / Peter Martin (as Kid N Play)), Martin Lawrence (Bilal), Tisha Campbell (Sidney), A. J. Johnson (Sharane), Paul Anthony (Stab)

A high school student, confined to the house by his parents, will do what it takes to get to a party thrown by his best friend, whose parents are away.

At the time, this hit movie was seen as a light-hearted corrective to dark, tragic urban black American stories. Kid N Play (as Reid and Martin were known) are exuberant and relatively innocent, and the film is affably fluffy.

CIN Peter Deming   MUS Marcus Miller, Lenny White   DES Bryan Jones   ED Earl Watson   PROD Warrington Hudlin   DIST Enterprise/Hudlin Brothers/New Line

66 Kid N Play take lead roles, and as someone says: "They've got a cute thing happening. – *Tom Charity, Time Out*

'The story of a woman slightly distracted by the possibilities of life.'

Housekeeping ★★

SCR/DIR Bill Forsyth
1987   116m   US

☆ *Christine Lahti* (Sylvie), Sara Walker (Ruth), Andrea Burchill (Lucille), Anne Pitoniak (Aunt Lilly), Barbara Reese (Aunt Nona), Bill Smillie (Sheriff), Margot Pinvidic (Helen), Wayne Robson (Pricipal)

After their mother's death, two orphaned sisters are brought up by their wayward, eccentric aunt.

In his first American feature, Forsyth strikes a more serious note, as Aunt Sylvie (brilliantly played by Lahti) comes to be viewed as less free-spirited than irresponsible and even dangerous to her young charges. A satisfyingly detailed character study.

CIN Michael Coulter   MUS Michael Gibbs   DES Adrienne Atkinson   ED Michael Ellis   PROD Robert F. Colesberry   DIST Columbia

66 The director's characteristic other-worldly charm is overshadowed by a dark intensity. . .the movie is sombre, very strange but wonderful. – *Elaine Paterson, Time Out*

'Set your dreams in motion.'

How She Move (new)

DIR Ian Iqbal Rashid
2008   91m   Canada
♫

☆ Rutina Wesley (Raya Green), Tré Armstrong (Michelle), Brennan Gademans (Quake), Clé Bennett (Garvey), Kevin Duhaney (E.C.), Tristan D. Lalla (Manny), Dwain Murphy (Bishop)

A gifted high-school student uses her dance skills to get out of the projects.

[DVD] Available on DVD   ☆ Cast in order of importance   66 Critics' Quotes   † Points of interest   ⚱ Academy Award   ⚱ Academy Award nomination   Ⓑ BAFTA   Ⓑ BAFTA nomination

Downbeat take on familiar material, its protagonist's trials being mere filler between the energetic dance sequences.

SCR Annmarie Morais **CIN** Andre Pienaar **MUS** Andrew Lockington **DES** Aidan Leroux **ED** Susan Maggi **PROD** Jennifer Kawaja, Julia Sereny, Brent Barclay **DIST** Paramount

66 The sort of film that sends you home with a spring in your step. – *Matt Zoller Seitz, New York Times*

66 She move good! – *Lisa Schwarzbaum, Entertainment Weekly*

'The Career Where Two Heads Are Better Than One'

How to Get Ahead in Advertising ★

SCR/DIR Bruce Robinson
1989   94m   GB
DVD ♫

☆ Richard E. Grant (Denis Dimbleby Bagley), Rachel Ward (Julia Bagley), Richard Wilson (John Bristol, Bagley's Boss), Jacqueline Tong (Penny Wheelstock), John Shrapnel (Psychiatrist), Susan Wooldridge (Monica), Mick Ford (Richard), Jacqueline Pearce (Maud), Roddy Maude-Roxby (Dr. Gatty)

A disillusioned advertising executive discovers a boil on his neck; it gradually grows into a second head that talks.

An all-out rant against the advertising industry from the creator of Withnail and I. A dazzling conception that sustains the film's first half, after which there's little left to say about consumerism.

CIN Peter Hannan **MUS** David Dundas, Rick Wentworth **DES** Michael Pickwoad **ED** Alan Strachan **PROD** David Wimbury **DIST** Virgin/HandMade Films

---

Howards End ★★★

DIR *James Ivory*
1992   140m   GB/Japan
DVD ♫

☆ Anthony Hopkins (Henry Wilcox), Vanessa Redgrave (Ruth Wilcox), Helena Bonham Carter (Helen Schlegel), *Emma Thompson* (Margaret Schlegel), James Wilby (Charles Wilcox), Samuel West (Leonard Bast), Jemma Redgrave (Evie Wilcox), Nicola Duffett (Jacky Bast), Prunella Scales (Aunt Juley), Simon Callow (Music Lecturer)

A widowed businessman scotches his wife's bequest of her cottage to a new but dear friend.

Engrossing, admirably lucid adaptation of Forster's own favourite among his novels; for once with Merchant–Ivory, the social critique really cuts through the pretty upholstery, and the acting is better than ever.

SCR Ruth Prawer Jhabvala **CIN** Tony Pierce-Roberts **MUS** Richard Robbins **DES** Luciana Arrighi **ED** Andrew Marcus **PROD** Ismail Merchant **DIST** Merchant Ivory/Film Four

66 Incisively witty, provocative and acted to perfection. – *Peter Travers, Rolling Stone*

⌐ Emma Thompson (leading actress); Ruth Prawer Jhabvala (adapted screenplay); Luciana Arrighi
⌐ picture; Vanessa Redgrave (supporting actress); James

Ivory; Tony Pierce-Roberts; Richard Robbins;, John Bright (costume design)

 film; Emma Thompson (leading actress)
 Samuel West (supporting actor); Helena Bonham-Carter (supporting actress); James Ivory; Tony Pierce-Roberts; Ruth Prawer Jhabvala (adapted screenplay); Andrew Marcus; Luciana Arrighi; Jenny Beavan, John Bright (costume design); Christine Beveridge (make up)

'The Man With The Barbed Wire Soul!'

Hud ★★★

DIR *Martin Ritt*
1963   112m   US
DVD

☆ *Paul Newman* (Hud Bannon), *Patricia Neal* (Alma Brown), *Melvyn Douglas* (Homer Bannon), Brandon de Wilde (Lon Bannon)

Life is hard on a Texas ranch, and the veteran owner is not helped by his sexually predatory, hard-drinking son, who is a bad influence on the household.

Superbly set in an arid landscape, this incisive character drama is extremely well directed and acted.

SCR Irving Ravetch, Harriet Frank **CIN** James Wong Howe **MUS** Elmer Bernstein **ED** Frank Bracht **PROD** Martin Ritt, Irving Ravetch **DIST** Paramount/Salem/Dover

⌐ Patricia Neal (leading actress); Melvyn Douglas (supporting actor); James Wong Howe
⌐ Paul Newman (leading actor); Martin Ritt (direction); Irving Ravetch, Harriet Frank Jr. (adapted screenplay); Hal Pereira, Tambi Larsen

 Patricia Neal (leading actress)

'For the world's greatest cat burglar nine lives may just not be enough. . .'

Hudson Hawk

DIR Michael Lehmann
1991   100m   US
DVD ♫

☆ Bruce Willis (Eddie 'Hudson Hawk' Hawkins), Danny Aiello (Tommy Five-Tone), Andie MacDowell (Anna Baragli), James Coburn (George Kaplan), Richard E. Grant (Darwin Mayflower), Sandra Bernhard (Minerva Mayflower), Donald Burton (Alfred), Don Harvey (Snickers), David Caruso (Kit Kat)

A cat burglar newly released from prison is forced to steal the works of Da Vinci as part of a world domination plot.

Excruciatingly misjudged comedy caper, unsurprisingly one of the great box-office flops of its era. Worth seeing only as an object lesson in how a studio can commit an astronomical budget to a script that was barely even a work in progress.

SCR Steven E. de Souza, Daniel Waters **CIN** Dante Spinotti **MUS** Michael Kamen **DES** Jack DeGovia **ED** Chris Lebenzon, Michael Tronick **PROD** Joel Silver **DIST** Columbia TriStar/Silver Pictures/Ace Bone

66 Ever wondered what a Three Stooges short would look like with a $40 million budget? Then meet Hudson Hawk, a relentlessly annoying clay duck that crash-lands in a sea of wretched excess and silliness. – *Variety*

---

66 Its utter failure can only be explained by some form of madness having overcome the people involved in its making. – *Philip French, Observer*

† Richard E. Grant wrote candidly and entertainingly about his part in the Hudson Hawk fiasco in his autobiographical diaries, With Nails.

The Hudsucker Proxy ★★

DIR *Joel Coen*
1994   111m   US/ GB
DVD   ♫

☆ Tim Robbins (Norville Barnes), Jennifer Jason Leigh (Amy Archer), Paul Newman (Sidney J. Mussburger), Charles Durning (Waring Hudsucker), Jim True (Buzz), John Mahoney (Chief), Bill Cobbs (Moses), Bruce Campbell (Smitty)

Plotting to lower stock prices for their own ends, the board of a major corporation elect a lowly mailroom clerk as chairman, only for their new recruit to make good – and invent the hula hoop.

Wildly stylised, beautifully designed fairytale that aspires to the comedies of Capra and Sturges; asked to mouth rat-a-tat-tat screwball dialogue, the performers can't quite get there, though the last half-hour constitutes one of the Coens' more satisfying endings.

SCR *Ethan Coen, Joel Coen, Sam Raimi*   CIN *Roger Deakins*
MUS Carter Burwell   DES *Dennis Gassner*   ED Thom Noble   PROD Ethan Coen
DIST Warner/Polygram/Silver/Working Title

66 Clever but cold, a heartless mechanical gizmo. The actors rattle around tinnily like shiny marbles inside its cavernous sets and hollow script. – *Joe Brown, Washington Post*

66 For all its technical bravado, The Hudsucker Proxy is an unsettling contradiction, a "whimsical" fable made by acerbic control freaks. It's a balloon that won't fly. – *Owen Gleiberman, Entertainment Weekly*

Hukkle ★★

SCR/DIR Gyorgy Palfi
2002   78m   Hungary
DVD

☆ Ferenc Bandi (Cseklik Bacsi), Jozsefne Racz (Bába), Jozsef Forkas (Rendõr), Ferenc Nagy (Méhész)

In a quiet, remote Hungarian village, the female population appears to be intent on poisoning their husbands.

Odd little movie with no spoken dialogue, with a cast of hapless men, hard-working women and dozens of animals, birds and insects. It doesn't add up to much – literally so, since there's no real resolution to the thin narrative – but it's not easily forgotten.

CIN Gergely Poharnok   MUS Balazs Barna, Samu Gryllus
ED Ágnes Mógor   PROD Csava Bereczki, Andras Bohm
DIST Soda

66 An engaging and distinctive debut. – *Michael Brooke, Sight & Sound*

† The title is a Hungarian rendering of the sound of a hiccup – the equivalent of 'hic!'

'The inner beast will be released.'

Hulk ★

DIR Ang Lee
2003   138m   US
DVD   ♫

☆ Eric Bana (Bruce Banner), Jennifer Connelly (Betty Ross), Sam Elliott (General 'Thunderbolt' Ross), Josh Lucas (Glenn Talbot), Nick Nolte (David Banner)

After an experiment that goes wrong, a scientist morphs into a vengeful green giant monster whenever he feels angry.

A disastrous mismatch, between Bruce Banner, a comic strip character with one over-riding characteristic, and Ang Lee, a brilliant but cerebral director whose concern was to probe Banner's psyche. Not surprisingly, the film fails, however one chooses to regard it.

SCR John Turman, Michael France, James Schamus
CIN Frederick Elmes   MUS Danny Elfman   DES Rick Heinrichs   ED Tim Squyres   PROD Avi Arad, Larry J Franco, Gale Anne Hurd, James Schamus   DIST Universal

66 The best Marvel adaptation so far. Lee's career is fast becoming the most interesting in Hollywood. – *Rob White, Sight & Sound*

† After the film's moderate box-office success, Universal retired the Hulk franchise for five years, reviving it with a new creative team.

Human Resources ★★

DIR *Laurent Cantet*
1999   103m   France/GB

☆ Jalil Lespert (Franck), Jean-Claude Vallod (Father), Chantal Barré (Mother), Véronique de Pandelaère (Sylvie), Michel Begnez (Olivier), Lucien Longueville (Boss), Danielle Mélador (Danielle Arnoux), Pascal Sémard (Personnel Manager), Didier Emile-Woldemard (Alain), Françoise Boutigny (Betty)

The son of a factory worker undergoes training as a productivity adviser at his father's plant, where tensions between the management and union are at fever pitch.

Taut, verité-style study of latent class resentment between father and son, if one whose social agenda is easily guessed.

SCR *Laurent Cantet, Gilles Marchand*   CIN Matthieu Poirot Delpech   DES Romain Denis   ED Robin Campillo, Stéphanie Leger   PROD Caroline Benjo, Carole Scotta
DIST NFT

66 Restrained, tough and subtle enough to be as engrossing on the second viewing as it was on the first. – *Amy Taubin, Village Voice*

The Hunchback of Notre Dame ★

DIR Gary Trousdale, Kirk Wise
1996   91m   US
DVD   ♫

☆ the voices of: Tom Hulce, Tony Jay, Paul Kandel, Kevin Kline, Demi Moore, Heidi Mollenhauer, Jason Alexander, David Ogden Stiers, Mary Wickes, Jane Withers

The hunchback Quasimodo rescues a gypsy girl from the clutches of an evil judge, only to lose her to a noble knight.

DVD Available on DVD   ☆ Cast in order   66 Critics' Quotes   ⚊ Academy Award   ⓦ BAFTA
♫ Soundtrack on CD   of importance   † Points of interest   ⚊ Academy Award nomination   ⓣ BAFTA nomination

301

Disney's post-Lion King confidence in its animated output was stretched by this adaptation of the Hugo novel (or remake of the 1939 Charles Laughton film): though the animation itself is as accomplished as ever, the story's adult themes don't translate easily to cartoon form, the songs are unmemorable, and humour is very much thin on the ground.

SCR Tab Murphy, Irene Mecchi, Bob Tzudiker, Noni White, Jonathan Roberts   MUS Alan Menken   ED Ellen Keneshea   PROD Don Hahn   DIST Buena Vista/Walt Disney

66 A solid, enjoyable, beautifully animated Disney movie, but one not quite out of the top drawer. – *Philip Thomas, Empire*

♪ Alan Menken, Stephen Schwartz (music)

The Hunchback of Notre Dame ★★★★

DIR *William Dieterle*
1939   117m   US
DVD

☆ *Charles Laughton* (The Hunchback), *Cedric Hardwicke* (Frollo), *Maureen O'Hara* (Esmeralda), *Edmond O'Brien* (Gringoire), *Thomas Mitchell* (Clopin), *Harry Davenport* (Louis XI), Walter Hampden (Claude), Alan Marshal (Phoebus), George Zucco (Procurator), Katherine Alexander (Mme. De Lys), Fritz Leiber (A Nobleman), Rod la Rocque (Phillipo)

A deformed bell-ringer harbours an unrequited passion for a young gypsy girl.

This superb remake is one of the best examples of Hollywood expertise at work: art direction, set construction, costumes, camera, lighting and above all direction brilliantly support an irresistible story and bravura acting.

SCR *Sonya Levien, Bruno Frank*   CIN *Joseph H. August*
MUS *Alfred Newman*   ED Robert Wise, William Hamilton
PROD Pandro S. Berman   DIST RKO

66 A super thriller-chiller. Will roll up healthy grosses at the ticket windows. – *Variety*

66 Has seldom been bettered as an evocation of medieval life. – *John Baxter, 1968*

† Other versions: Esmeralda (1906, French); Notre Dame de Paris (1911, French); The Darling of Paris (1917, US, with Theda Bara).

♪ Alfred Newman (music)

'Deadly. Silent. Stolen.'

The Hunt for Red October ★

DIR John McTiernan
1990   134m   US
DVD ♪

☆ Sean Connery (Captain Marko Ramius), Alec Baldwin (Jack Ryan), Scott Glenn (Commander Bart Mancuso), Sam Neill (Captain 2nd Rank Vasily Borodin), James Earl Jones (Admiral James Greer), Joss Ackland (Ambassador Andrei Lysenko), Richard Jordan (Dr. Jeffrey Pelt), Peter Firth (Political Officer Ivan Yurevich Putin - Red October), Tim Curry (Dr. Petrov)

In 1984, when the Soviet commander of a new super-submarine defies orders and heads for the US, it's unclear if he is trying to defect or provoke an international incident.

An effective thriller that keeps the tension ratcheted way up; director McTiernan shrewdly allows no distractions from the fast-moving central plot.

SCR Larry Ferguson, Donald Stewart   CIN Jan de Bont
MUS Basil Poledouris   DES Terence Marsh   ED Dennis Virkler, John Wright   PROD Mace Neufeld
DIST Paramount/Mace Neufeld/Jerry Sherlock

† This was the first film appearance for author Tom Clancy's character Jack Ryan, who was later played by Harrison Ford and Ben Affleck.

⚊ Cecelia Hall, George Watters II (sound effects editing)
⚊ Dennis Virkler, John Wright (film editing); Richard Bryce Goodman, Richard Overton, Kevin F. Cleary, Don J. Bassman (sound)

Ⓣ Sean Connery (leading actor); Terence Marsh (production design); Richard Bryce Goodman, Richard Overton, Kevin F. Cleary, Don J. Bassman (sound)

'Some men should not be found.'

The Hunted ★

DIR William Friedkin
2003   94m   US
DVD ♪

☆ Tommy Lee Jones (L.T. Bonham), Benicio Del Toro (Aaron Hallam), Connie Nielsen (Abby Durrell), Leslie Stefanson (Irene), John Finn (Ted Chenoweth), Jose Zuniga (Moret)

A tracker is sent to track down a rogue Special Ops agent who has been killing hunters in American forests.

Pared-down, somewhat primitive action-adventure that often resembles The Fugitive with an adult certificate: meat-and-potatoes stuff, but the meat is certainly bloody, and the potatoes are hard-boiled.

SCR David Griffiths, Peter Griffiths, Art Montersatelli
CIN *Caleb Deschanel*   MUS Brian Tyler   DES William Cruse   ED Augie Hess   PROD Ricardo Mestres, James Jacks   DIST Paramount

66 Holds fascination in its determination to trim away chat and guff and focus on tempo and filmic structure. – *Shawn Levy, Portland Oregonian*

66 What keeps you watching isn't the story or the actors, none of whom are at the top of their form, but the relentlessness of Friedkin's vision. The film has great forward thrust – Friedkin's a full-throttle guy – and the director knows where to put the camera. – *Manohla Dargis, Los Angeles Times*

'His Greatest Fight Was For Justice.'

The Hurricane ★

DIR Norman Jewison
1999   145m   US
DVD ♪

☆ *Denzel Washington* (Rubin 'Hurricane' Carter), Vicellous Reon Shannon (Lesra), Deborah Kara Unger (Lisa), Liev Schreiber (Sam), John Hannah (Terry), Dan Hedaya (Della Pesca), Debbi Morgan (Mae Thelma), Clancy Brown (Lt Jimmy Williams), David Paymer (Myron Bedlock), Harris Yulin (Leon Friedman), Rod Steiger (Judge Sarokin), Garland Witt (John Artis)

Biopic of Rubin "Hurricane" Carter, the former middleweight boxer unjustly imprisoned on a murder charge.

Well-intentioned drama let down by an unnecessary framing device reframing Carter's story through the eyes of the young black man, and the Canadian liberals, who campaigned for his release; Washington's central performance is more interesting and complex than the rest of the film.

SCR Armyan Bernstein, Dan Gordon **CIN** Roger Deakins **MUS** Christopher Young **DES** Philip Rosenberg **ED** Stephen Rivkin **PROD** Armyan Bernstein, John Ketcham, Norman Jewison **DIST** Buena Vista

66 Milks Carter's story for maximum "inspirational" value, and at times the movie skirts dangerously close to afterschool-special territory. – *Rene Rodriguez, Miami Herald*

66 Far too tepid. – *Amy Taubin, Village Voice*

⚐ Denzel Washington (leading actor)

Husbands and Wives ★★★

SCR/DIR *Woody Allen*
1992 108m US
DVD

☆ Woody Allen (Gabe Roth), *Judy Davis* (Sally), Mia Farrow (Judy Roth), Juliette Lewis (Rain), Liam Neeson (Michael), Blythe Danner (Rain's Mother), *Sydney Pollack* (Jack), Lysette Anthony (Sam)

When their best friends announce they are separating, a professor and his wife decide to spend some time apart.

Allen in top form in a piercing, astute study of spent relationships, caustically detailing the reasons to stay together and not to.

CIN Carlo Di Palma **DES** Santo Loquasto **ED** Susan E. Morse **PROD** Robert Greenhut **DIST** Columbia TriStar/TriStar

66 The film is Mr. Allen's uproarious answer to Ingmar Bergman's far more solemn but no less bleak Scenes From a Marriage. It's also an ensemble piece acted to loopy perfection by a remarkable cast. – *Vincent Canby, New York Times*

⚐ Judy Davis (supporting actress); Woody Allen (original screenplay)

Ⓣ Woody Allen (original screenplay)
Ⓣ Judy Davis (supporting actress)

'Everybody gotta have a dream.'

Hustle & Flow ★★

SCR/DIR Craig Brewer
2005 116m US
DVD ♫

☆ *Terrence Howard* (Djay), Anthony Anderson (Key), Taryn Manning (Nola), Taraji P. Henson (Shug), Paula Jai Parker (Lexus), Isaac Hayes (Arnel)

A Memphis pimp tries to get into the music business with the help of his 'ladies'.

Dubious but surprisingly credible rap drama with a terrific third act, and a magnetic performance from Howard; it surmounts its own questionable subject matter with brio.

CIN *Amelia Vincent* **MUS** Scott Bomar **DES** Keith Brian Burns **ED** Billy Fox **PROD** John Singleton, Stephanie Allain **DIST** Paramount

66 A definite crowd-pleaser, Hustle & Flow has all the makings of a massive cultural phenomenon - if only audiences can get past the whole pimp thing. – *Peter Debruge, Premiere*

66 Howard redeems this lumpy fantasy. Soft-spoken and mysterious, he presides over the movie with a dangerous, feline grace. – *David Ansen, Newsweek*

† At its premiere at the Sundance Film Festival in 2005, Paramount/MTV Films paid $9 million for distribution rights – a festival record.

⚐ Jordan Houston, Cedric Coleman, Paul Beauregard (music, original song – It's Hard Out Here for a Pimp)
⚐ Terrence Howard (leading actor)

'... maybe it's better for both of us to leave each other alone.'

The Hustler ★★★★

DIR *Robert Rossen*
1961 135m US
DVD

☆ *Paul Newman* ('Fast' Eddie Felson), *Jackie Gleason* (Minnesota Fats), *George C. Scott* (Bert Gordon), *Piper Laurie* (Sarah Packard), *Myron McCormick* (Charlie Bums), Murray Hamilton (Findlay), Michael Constantine (Big John)

A young, cocky pool room con man, Fast Eddie Felson, is matched against the legendary Minnesota Fats by a shrewd promoter; but Eddie must overcome his self-destructive impulses and keep his romantic life under control.

Downbeat melodrama that beautifully captures the seedy atmosphere of smoky, dingy pool halls and frames Fast Eddie's mission as a mythic struggle and a rite of passage into full manhood. The dialogue now seems florid and over-heated, but this was a defining role for Newman, who carries the movie.

SCR Robert Rossen, Sidney Carroll **CIN** *Eugene Schufftan* **MUS** Kenyon Hopkins **ED** Dede Allen **DIST** TCF/Robert Rossen

66 There is an overall impression of intense violence, and the air of spiritual decadence has rarely been conveyed so vividly. – *David Robinson*

66 The supreme classic of that great American genre, the low-life movie. – *Observer*

⚐ Eugene Schufftan (art direction)
⚐ picture; Robert Rossen (as director); Robert Rossen, Sidney Carroll (adapted screenplay); Paul Newman (leading actor); Piper Laurie (leading actress); Jackie Gleason (supporting actor); George C. Scott (supporting actor)

Ⓣ picture; Paul Newman

DVD Available on DVD   ☆ Cast in order   66 Critics' Quotes   ⚐ Academy Award   Ⓑ BAFTA
♫ Soundtrack on CD   of importance   † Points of interest   ⚐ Academy Award nomination   Ⓣ BAFTA nomination

303

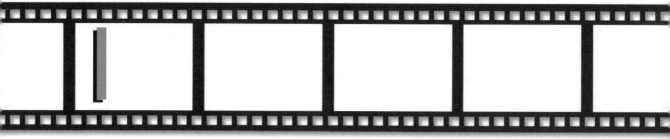

'Six sticks of dynamite that blasted his way to freedom. . .and awoke America's conscience!'

I Am a Fugitive from a Chain Gang ★★★

DIR *Mervyn LeRoy*
1932 90m US

☆ *Paul Muni* (James Allen), Glenda Farrell (Marie Woods), Helen Vinson (Helen), Preston Foster (Pete), Allen Jenkins (Barney Sykes), Edward J. Macnamara (Warden), Berton Churchill (Judge), Edward Ellis (Bomber Wells)

An innocent man is convicted and after brutal treatment with the chain gang becomes a vicious criminal on the run.

Horrifying story in the semi-documentary manner; a milestone in Hollywood history and still a fairly compelling piece of shock entertainment. Full marks, too, for the says-it-all title.

SCR *Howard J. Green, Brown Holmes* CIN *Sol Polito*
MUS Bernhard Kaun ED William Holmes PROD Hal B. Wallis DIST Warner

66 A picture with guts. . .everything about it is technically 100%. . .shy on romantic angles, but should get nice money all over. – *Variety*

66 To be enthusiastically commended for its courage, artistic sincerity, dramatic vigour, high entertainment concept and social message. – *Wilton A. Barrett*

picture; Paul Muni (leading actor)

'The last man on earth is not alone.'

I Am Legend (new) ★★

DIR Francis Lawrence
2007 100m US
♫

☆ Will Smith (Robert Neville), Alice Braga (Anna), Dash Mihok (Alpha Male), Charlie Tahan (Ethan), Salli Richardson (Zoe)

A military scientist and his dog roam desolate New York after a virus has killed most of the world's population. He holds the key to mankind's destiny, if mutant vampire night creatures do not reach him first.

A one-man-show for star Will Smith who affectingly conveys the haunted paranoia of his lonely plight. Elsewhere, the standard shocks and formula special effects reduce this would-be epic to a B-movie, despite the eerie depiction of Manhattan as an overgrown wilderness.

SCR Mark Protosevich, Akiva Goldsman CIN Andrew Lesnie MUS James Newton Howard DES Naomi

Shohan ED Wayne Wahrman PROD James Lassiter, David Heyman, Neal Moritz, Akiva Goldsman DIST Warner Bros.

66 A fascinating take on old sci-fi tale, but too CG-dependent, and an unconvincing religious ending damages its credibility. – *Kirk Honeycutt, Hollywood Reporter*

66 The problem may be that Matheson's novel has influenced so many films it's almost impossible for any new version to forge its own identity. – *Kim Newman, Sight & Sound*

'I love, I have loved, I will love.'

I Capture the Castle ★★

DIR Tim Fywell
2003 111m GB
DVD

☆ *Romola Garai* (Cassandra Mortmain), Rose Byrne (Rose Mortmain), Henry Thomas (Simon Cotton), Marc Blucas (Neil Cotton), Bill Nighy (James Mortmain), Tara Fitzgerald (Topaz Mortmain), Sinead Cusack (Mrs Cotton), Henry Cavill (Stephen Colley)

An impoverished family in the 1930s struggle to survive in their decaying castle home, and both daughters fall in love.

Gentle period romance with a great deal of charm, and making a virtue of its shoestring budget.

SCR Heidi Thomas CIN Richard Greatrex MUS Dario Marianelli DES John-Paul Kelly ED Roy Sharman PROD Anant Singh, David M. Thompson, David Parfitt DIST IDP

66 Credit has to go to the 21-year-old Garai for carrying the film so plausibly. – *Peter Bradshaw, Guardian*

I Do (new) ★★

DIR Eric Lartigau
2006 89m France
DVD

☆ Alain Chabat (Luis Costa), Charlotte Gainsbourg (Emma), Bernadette Lafont (Geneviève Costa), Wladimnir Yordanoff (Francis Bertoff), Grégoire Oestermann (Pierre-Yves), Veronique Barrault (Catherine)

Luis at 43 is happily single, and does not envisage a wife disturbing his life. Problems arise when his mother and five sisters decide he should wed. He devises a plan to find a 'fianceé' who will dump him on his wedding day and restore his freedom.

A delightful comedy, with Chabat as the bachelor and Gainsbourg as his fake fianceé. Deftly played by these

two, the story pushes the right buttons and does not overstay its welcome.

SCR Philippe Mechelen, Laurent Tirard, GrégoireVigneron, Laurent Zeitoun, Alain Chabat   **CIN** Régis Blondeau **MUS** Erwann Kermorvant   **DES** Sylvie Olivé   **ED** Juliette Welfing   **PROD** Amandine Bilot, Alain Chabat **DIST** Optimum

66 A sugary rom-com from France, thin on characterisation but carried off with brio. – *Peter Bradshaw, Guardian*

I For India (new)   ★★★

SCR/DIR Sandhya Suri
2005   70m   UK/Italy/Germany/Finland/South Africa
DVD

Yash Pal Suri, a young Indian doctor, moved to north-east England in 1965 in search of a better life. Because it was hard to maintain contact with his family back home, he bought two Super 8 cameras, two audio players and two projectors, keeping one set and sending the other home to establish an ongoing correspondence between two sets of relatives. The film consists of this home-movie footage and voiceovers.

An affecting documentary, compiled and directed by the doctor's daughter, that highlights the tension between a desire for self-improvement and the wrenching loss of homeland family ties.

CIN Sandhya Suri, Lars Lenski   **ED** Cinzia Baldessari, Brian Tagg   **PROD** Carlo Cresto-Dina, Kai Künnemann, Thomas Kufus   **DIST** ICA

66 A profound and profoundly moving film that any director could be proud of; as a debut, it's formidably accomplished. – *Kieron Corless, Sight & Sound*

66 A remarkable meditation on the agonies and enigmas of migration. – *Sukhdev Sandhu, Daily Telegraph*

I Have Never Forgotten You: The Life & Legacy of Simon Wiesenthal (new)   ★

DIR Richard Trank
2007   105m   US
DVD

☆ Nicole Kidman (Narrator), Ben Kingsley (Himself), Frederick Forsyth (Himself), Marvin Hier (Himself)

Using file footage, photographs, newsreel snippets and interviews with friends, relatives and ex-colleagues, this documentary deals with the work of Wiesenthal, who survived the concentration camps to become a celebrated, and dogged Nazi hunter.

Director Trank's treatment does its subject a disservice with its clichéd approach. Wiesenthal insisted he did not wish to be regarded as a hero, yet that is how he emerges. Celebrity tributes come from Ben Kingsley, Frederick Forsyth and others.

SCR Rabbi Marvin Hier, Richard Trank   **CIN** Jeffrey Victor **MUS** Lee Holdridge   **ED** Inbal B. Lessner **PROD** Richard Trank, Rabbi Marvin Hier   **DIST** Blue Dolphin

66 An unsurprisingly dutiful portrait of one the 20th century's most single-minded crusaders. – *Tamara Straus, San Francisco Chronicle*

I Hired a Contract Killer   ★

SCR/DIR Aki Kaurismäki
1990   79m   Finland/Sweden/ France/GB/Germany
DVD

☆ Jean-Pierre Léaud (Henri Boulanger), Margi Clarke (Margaret), Kenneth Colley (The Killer), Trevor Bowen (Department Head), Imogen Clare (Secretary), Angela Walsh (Landlady), Cyril Epstein (Taxi Driver), Nicky Tesco (Pete)

In London, a depressed civil servant hires a hit-man to murder him, then belatedly, after falling for a vivacious flower seller, changes his mind.

Oddball comedy and the English-language debut from this distinctive Finnish director. As one might expect from him, it's both melancholy and darkly funny.

CIN Timo Salminen   **DES** John Ebden   **ED** Aki Kaurismäki   **PROD** Aki Kaurismäki **DIST** Electric/Contemporary/Villealfa/Swedish Film Institute

'They're as straight as can be, but don't tell anyone.'

I Now Pronounce You Chuck and Larry (new)

DIR Dennis Dugan
2007   110m   US

☆ Adam Sandler (Chuck), Kevin James (Larry), Jessica Biel (Alex), Ving Rhames (Duncan), Steve Buscemi (Clint Fitzer), Dan Aykroyd (Captain Tucker)

Two macho New York firemen go through with a bogus gay wedding so that one of them, a widower, can secure his pension rights.

This lame, hypocritical 'comedy' exploits homophobia and racism for over an hour before peddling a message of tolerance and togetherness. No gay stereotype is overlooked, but Sandler's Larry, a loutish porn addict who beds women two or more at a time, gives heterosexuals an equal right to feel insulted.

SCR Barry Fanaro, Alexander Payne & Jim Taylor **CIN** Dean Semler   **MUS** Rupert Gregson-Williams **DES** Perry Andelin Blake   **ED** Jeff Gourson   **PROD** Adam Sandler, Jack Giarraputo, Tom Shadyac, Michael Bostick **DIST** Universal

66 As nasty a piece of sniggering homophobia as I have seen in a long time. – *Wendy Ide, The Times*

66 Relentlessly juvenile and awash in sterotypes. – *Brian Lowry, Variety*

'You only get one shot at fame.'

I Shot Andy Warhol   ★★

DIR Mary Harron
1996   106m   GB/US
DVD ♫

☆ Lili Taylor (Valerie Jean Solanas), Jared Harris (Andy Warhol), Lothaire Bluteau (Maurice Girodias), Martha

Plimpton (Stevie), Stephen Dorff (Candy Darling), Anna Thompson (Iris), Peter Friedman (Alan Burke), Tahnee Welch (Viva)

A 1960s lesbian radical tries to kill Andy Warhol when he ignores her ideas.

Clever, provocative biopic which remains aloof from its characters, offering a convincingly affectless portrait of the 1960s New York underground.

SCR Mary Harron, Daniel Minahan   CIN Ellen Kuras
MUS John Cale   DES Therese Deprez   ED Keith Reamer
PROD Tom Kalin, Christine Vachon
DIST Electric/Playhouse/Samuel Goldwyn/BBC Arena

66 Dazzling and serious, with flurries of impulse playing around a persistent core of madness. – *Stanley Kauffmann, New Republic*

'Dis-organised Crime.'

I Went Down ★★

DIR Paddy Breathnach
1997   107m   GB/Ireland/Spain
♫

☆ Brendan Gleeson (Bunny Kelly), Peter McDonald (Git Hynes), Peter Caffrey (Frank Grogan), Tony Doyle (Tom French), Antoine Byrne (Sabrina Bradley), David Wilmot (Anto)

Two incompetent crooks are instructed by a crime boss to track down a man who stole £25,000 of his money.

Action-packed road movie, little more than a series of escapes, comedy antics, plot twists and double crosses. Yet Gleeson and McDonald make an engaging double act, and the lack of a plot structure ceases to matter; the fun of this chase is enough.

SCR Conor McPherson   CIN Cian de Buitlear
MUS Dario Marianelli   DES Zoe Macleod   ED Emer
Reynolds   PROD Robert Walpole   DIST Buena
Vista/BBC/Irish Film Board/Treasure

66 Takes place in the grim Irish underworld of seedy pubs and fatalistic violence, leavened by straight-faced, Guinness-black humour. – *Philip Kemp, Sight & Sound*

'The Coolest Event In 16,000 Years.'

Ice Age ★

DIR Chris Wedge, Carlos Saldanha
2002   81m   US
DVD   ♫

☆ Voices of: Ray Romano (Manfred), John Leguizamo (Sid), Denis Leary (Diego), Goran Visnjic (Soto), Jack Black (Zeke)

A sloth, a mammoth and a sabre-toothed tiger join forces to return a lost human child to his parents.

Crude, lively prehistoric buddy comedy which will please the kids. But a bravura opening sequence featuring a sabre-toothed squirrel is the real highlight.

SCR Michael Berg, Michael J. Wilson, Peter Ackerman
MUS David Newman   DES Brian McEntee   ED John
Carnochan   PROD Lori Forte   DIST TCF

66 It yearns for Pixar-style wit without quite earning it. – *Richard Corliss, Time*

† A sequel, Ice Age: The Meltdown, followed in 2006.
⚱ animated feature

'It was 1973, and the climate was changing.'

The Ice Storm ★★★

DIR Ang Lee
1997   112m   US
DVD   ♫

☆ Kevin Kline (Ben Hood), *Joan Allen* (Elena Hood), Henry Czerny (George Clair), *Adam Hann-Byrd* (Sandy Carver), *Tobey Maguire* (Paul Hood), *Christina Ricci* (Wendy Hood), Jamey Sheridan (Jim Carver), *Elijah Wood* (Mikey Carver), *Sigourney Weaver* (Janey Carver)

In 1970s suburbia, the hedonistic antics of a set of bored and disillusioned grown-ups have a tragic impact upon their teenage offspring.

A skilful, slightly chilly but vividly atmospheric adaptation, offering a trenchant analysis of the Nixon era, and its gradual erosion of moral values; it grips as both comedy of errors and coming-of-age tragedy, with the excellent cast more than a match for the script's numerous subtleties.

SCR *James Schamus*   CIN *Frederick Elmes*   MUS *Mychael Danna*   DES Mark Friedberg   ED Tim Squyres
PROD Ted Hope, James Schamus, Ang Lee   DIST Fox
Searchlight/Good Machine

66 Unlike many dramas of middle-class family wreckage, which tilt towards soap-operatic revelations, The Ice Storm is told from an ironic, almost meditative distance that gives the movie its paradoxical power. – *David Ansen, Newsweek*

66 As frigid as its name. Burdened with a story of some of the world's least interesting people going through a holiday crisis, director Ang Lee and screenwriter James Schamus get as close as any creative team could to making matters involving, but the task is finally too much for them. – *Kenneth Turan, Los Angeles Times*

🛡 Sigourney Weaver (supporting actress)
🛡 James Schamus (adapted screenplay)

The Icicle Thief ★★

DIR *Maurizio Nichetti*
1989   90m   Italy
DVD

☆ Maurizio Nichetti (Antonio Piermattei / The Director of the Film), Caterina Sylos Labini (Maria Piermattei), Federico Rizzo (Bruno Piermattei), Renato Scarpa (Don Italo, the Priest), Heidi Komarex (The Model), Carlina Torta (TV-watching Mother), Massimo Sacilotto (TV-watching Father), Claudio G. Fava (The Film Critic)

An Italian film director watches his new film being screened on TV, and literally walks into the movie in a rage when he realises lines of dialogue are being changed, and commercials featuring the film's actors keep interrupting his masterwork.

A cry for help disguised as an amusing extended joke: the film-makers appear to be mourning the decline of

---

DVD Available on DVD   ☆ Cast in order   66 Critics' Quotes   ⚱ Academy Award   🛡 BAFTA
♫ Soundtrack on CD   of importance   † Points of interest   ⚱ Academy Award nomination   🛡 BAFTA nomination

Italy's glorious film tradition, struggling to survive against the all-powerful influence of lurid TV programming.

SCR Maurizio Nichetti, Mauro Monti   CIN Maria Battistoni   MUS Manuel de Sica   ED Rita Rossi
PROD Ernesto Di Sarro   DIST Metro/Bambú/Reitalia

'He just doesn't know it yet.'

An Ideal Husband ★

SCR/DIR Oliver Parker
1999   97m   GB/USA
DVD ♫

☆ Cate Blanchett (Lady Gertrude Chiltern), Minnie Driver (Miss Mabel Chiltern), Rupert Everett (Lord Arthur Goring), Julianne Moore (Mrs. Laura Cheveley), Jeremy Northam (Sir Robert Chiltern), John Wood (Lord Caversham), Lindsay Duncan (Lady Markby), Peter Vaughan (Phipps), Jeroen Krabbé (Baron Arnheim), Ben Pullen (Tommy Trafford), Nickolas Grace (Vicomte de Nanjac)

A government minister turns to his best friend for help when a dangerous woman blackmails him.

Unadventurous but perfectly entertaining costume romp in which the Wildean aphorisms drip from Everett's lips, though his co-stars are not universally at ease.

CIN David Johnson   MUS Charlie Mole   DES Michael Howells   ED Guy Bensley   PROD Barnaby Thompson, Uri Fruchtmann, Bruce Davey   DIST Pathé/Icon/Arts Council/Fragile/Miramax

66 However knowingly it's done, Wilde's play is treated here as heritage silverware dusted down for a big occasion. – Jonathan Romney, Guardian

† The director and Everett were reunited for The Importance of Being Earnest (2002).

Ⓣ Oliver Parker (adapted screenplay); Caroline Harris (costume); Peter King (make up/hair)

'The secret lies within.'

Identity ★

DIR James Mangold
2003   90m   US
DVD

☆ John Cusack (Ed), Ray Liotta (Rhodes), Amanda Peet (Paris), John Hawkes (Larry), Alfred Molina (Doctor), Clea DuVall (Ginny), John C. McGinley (George), Jake Busey (Robert Maine)

Ten strangers, stranded at a hotel in Nevada one stormy night, find themselves being picked off one by one.

Effective hokum with a knowing attitude to its shocks; the big twist is an outrageous gimmick, but it just about works.

SCR Michael Cooney   CIN Phedon Papamichael   MUS Alan Silvestri   DES Mark Friedberg   ED David Brenner   PROD Cathy Konrad   DIST Columbia

66 Some fancy footwork in the writing and directing can't disguise the hoary "Ten Little Indians" origins. – Todd McCarthy, Variety

'Take a long ride on the short bus.'

The Idiots ★★

SCR/DIR Lars von Trier
1998   117m
Denmark/France/Italy/Netherlands/Germany
DVD

☆ Bodil Jorgensen (Karen), Jens Albinus (Stoffer), Louise Hassing (Susanne), Troels Lyby (Henrik), Nikolaj Lie Kaas (Jeppe), Henrik Prip (Ped), Luis Mesonero (Miguel), Louise Mieritz (Josephine), Knud Romer Jorgensen (Axel), Trine Michelsen (Nana), Anne-Grethe Bjarup Riis (Katrine)

In latter-day Copenhagen, a group of bored white middle-class folk come together to stage performance art stunts, pretending to be mentally or physically handicapped.

Provocative in both form (shot according to the Dogme manifesto, which means hand-held camerawork, variable light, and improvised performances) and content, this is a sort of Animal Farm parable in which people take the place of livestock and a so-called radical revolutionary organisation proves to be just as depraved and fractious as the uncivilised world it opposes. As always with this director, the film might be understood as no more than a larkish prank, but it also has the breathtaking, confrontational immediacy of great cinema.

CIN Lars von Trier, Kristoffer Nyholm, Jesper Jargil, Casper Holm   ED Molly Malene Stensgaard   PROD Vibeke Windelov   DIST Zentropa/DRTV/DBC/Liberator/La Sept/ZDF/Arte/Argus/VPRO

66 A highly calculated act of mischief. – Owen Gleiberman, Entertainment Weekly

66 Consistently intriguing, involving, and finally quite unlike anything else. – Geoff Andrew, Time Out

If. . . ★★★★

DIR Lindsay Anderson
1968   111m   GB

☆ Malcolm McDowell (Mick Travers), David Wood (Johnny), Richard Warwick (Wallace), Robert Swann (Rowntree), Christine Noonan (The Girl), Peter Jeffrey (Headmaster), Arthur Lowe (Mr. Kemp, Housemaster), Anthony Nicholls (Gen. Denson)

Discontent at a English boys' public school escalates into rebellion.

Allegorical treatment of school life with much fashionable emphasis on obscure narrative, clever cutting, variety of pace, even an unaccountable changing from colour to monochrome and vice versa. It catches perfectly a mood of rebellion and dissatisfaction with the status quo.

SCR David Sherwin   CIN Miroslav Ondricek   MUS Marc Wilkinson   DES Jocelyn Herbert   ED David Gladwell   PROD Lindsay Anderson, Michael Medwin   DIST Paramount/Memorial

66 The school. . .is the perfect metaphor for the established system all but a few of us continue to accept. – David Wilson

66 Combines a cold and queasy view of youth with a romantic view of violence. – New Yorker

'Insanity is relative.'

Igby Goes Down

SCR/DIR Burr Steers
2002   97 minsm   US
DVD   ♫

☆ Kieran Culkin (Igby Slocumb), Susan Sarandon (Mimi Slocumb), Jeff Goldblum (DH), Ryan Phillippe (Oliver Slocumb), Bill Pullman (Jason Slocumb), Amanda Peet (Rachel), Jared Harris (Russel), Rory Culkin (Young Igby)

A privileged wastrel comes of age in New York.

Exasperatingly smug tale, owing a debt to J.D.Salinger which it fails to repay, seeming like one long champagne toast to its own sophistication.

CIN Wedigo von Schultzendorff   MUS Uwe Fahrenkrog Peterson   DES Kevin Thompson   ED William M. Anderson, Padraic McKinley, Robert Frazen   PROD Lisa Tornell, Marco Weber   DIST MGM

66 A dead-on sense of how rich kids live and talk today, a sense of the melancholy of a dysfunctional family, and some great dark laughs. – *Stephen Hunter, Washington Post*

Ikiru   ★★★

DIR *Akira Kurosawa*
1952   143m   Japan
DVD

☆ *Takashi Shimura* (Kanji Watanabe), Nobuo Kaneko (Mitsuo Watanabe), Kyoko Seki (Kazue Watanabe)

A clerk learns that he is dying of cancer and spends his last months creating a children's playground.

A moving and beautifully made humanistic personal drama which also gives an intriguing background of modern Japan.

SCR Hideo Oguni, Shinobu Hashimoto, Akira Kurosawa   CIN Asaishi Nakai   MUS Fumio Hayasaka   ED Akira Kurosawa   DIST Toho

I'll Sleep When I'm Dead

DIR Mike Hodges
2003   102m   GB/US

☆ Clive Owen (Will Graham), Charlotte Rampling (Helen), Jonathan Rhys Meyers (Davey), Malcolm McDowell (Boad), Jamie Foreman (Mickser), Ken Stott (Frank Turner), Sylvia Syms (Mrs Bartz), Geoff Bell (Arnie Ryan)

A retired gangster comes back to London to avenge the death of his brother.

Pretentious thriller from an always interesting, if often overlooked British director. But the plot doesn't add up, and the main character is a recessive blank.

SCR Trevor Preston   CIN Mike Garfath   MUS Simon Fisher Turner   DES Jon Bunker   ED Paul Carlin   PROD Michael Kaplan

66 Some effort is made to question the macho values of the crime genre, and it is this that best distinguishes I'll Sleep When I'm Dead from other recent British thrillers. – *Ryan Gilbey, Sight & Sound*

I'm Going Home   ★

SCR/DIR *Manoel de Oliveira*
2000   90m   Portugal/France
DVD

☆ *Michel Piccoli* (Gilbert Valence), Antoine Chappey (George), Catherine Deneuve (Marguerite), John Malkovich (John Crawford), Leonor Baldaque (Sylvia), Leonor Silveira (Marie)

A famous actor contemplates giving up his profession to take care of his grandson, orphaned after the rest of his family is killed in an accident.

Piccoli is superb in this essay on old age (director de Oliveira was 93 when he shot it) and the insidious advance of cheapened entertainment.

CIN Sabine Lancelin   DES Yves Fournier   ED Valerie Loiseleux   PROD Paulo Branco   DIST Artificial Eye

66 Piccoli perfectly portrays an actor of the old school, a man determined to preserve his dignity and sense of professional ethics in a world that is increasingly alien to him. – *John Mount, Sight & Sound*

'All I Can Do Is Be Me – Whoever That Is.'

I'm Not There (new)   ★★★

DIR Todd Haynes
2007   135m   US/Germany
DVD   ♫

☆ Christian Bale (Jack/Pastor John), *Cate Blanchett* (Jude), Marcus Carl Franklin (Woody), Richard Gere (Billy), Heath Ledger (Robbie), Ben Whishaw (Arthur), Charlotte Gainsbourg (Claire), Bruce Greenwood (Keenan Jones), Julianne Moore (Alice Fabian), Michelle Williams (Coco Rivington)

A rumination on the life and times of Bob Dylan, portrayed by six separate actors as a series of shifting characters at various stages of his tumultuous career.

An extraordinarily audacious, ambitious film that covers the key incidents in Dylan's life, though not necessarily in the correct order. It's a blend of what is known about this legendary figure, and what the audience thinks it knows about him. Emphatically not for the literal-minded, it's closer to a symbolist poem than to a conventional movie biography. Using various actors to 'play' Dylan is a distancing device – it's a shock to see him portrayed early on by Marcus Carl Franklin as a black folk troubadour aged 11. But the device soon seems easier to accept. It has one huge pay-off: an astonishing portrayal of Dylan in his mid-1960s electric period, with Cate Blanchett, disguised behind trademark shades, corkscrew curls, killer cheekbones, jittery amphetamine-fuelled body language and a defiant attitude. On the downside, Gere's version of Dylan as a Billy the Kid character is rambling and undramatic. Haynes shoots in different cinematic styles to capture the different Dylans, and it all adds up to an exhilarating experience. It ties up no loose factual ends: – no-one will 'understand' Dylan better, in the manner of lesser movie biographies. Instead, it lets him remain a brilliant, evasive enigma.

This may not be quite the best film of the year, but it may be the most fascinating – and one that repays repeated viewing.

SCR Todd Haynes, Oren Moverman   **CIN** Edward Lachman   **DES** Judy Becker   **ED** Jay Rabinowitz
PROD Christine Vachon, James D. Stern, John Sloss, John Goldwyn   **DIST** Paramount

66 I'm Not There is the movie of the year. – *J. Hoberman, Village Voice*

66 In Haynes's view, Dylan, through all his contradictions, was, indeed is, always his own man, if not a single man, and also a mirror in which people see their reflection or a canvas on which they write their own beliefs and longings. – *Philip French, Observer*

⚖ Cate Blanchett (supporting actress)
🅣 Cate Blanchett (supporting actress)

'People are never who they seem to be.'

Imaginary Heroes

SCR/DIR Dan Harris
2004   111m   US/Germany
DVD   ♫

☆ Sigourney Weaver (Sandy Travis), Emile Hirsch (Tim Travis), Jeff Daniels (Ben Travis), Michelle Williams (Penny Travis), Kip Pardue (Matt Travis), Deirdre O'Connell (Marge Dwyer), Ryan Donowho (Kyle Dwyer), Suzanne Santo (Steph Connors)

A young man commits suicide and his suburban family struggle to cope.

Terminally hackneyed picket-fence drama which has little to say we haven't heard umpteen times before. Weaver's subtle, detailed performance lightens the burden somewhat.

CIN Tim Orr   **MUS** Deborah Lurie   **DES** Rick Butler
ED James Lyons   **PROD** Illana Diamant, Moshe Diamant, Gina Resnick, Denise Shaw, Art Linson, Frank Hubner

66 All the hallmarks of suburban dysfunction are reassuringly in place. – *Xan Brooks, Guardian*

66 A sharply observed tragicomedy that draws laughter as genuinely as it coaxes tears, the nicely paced film tempers its themes of loss and sorrow with a cynically witty edge and is graced by a perfectly pitched Sigourney Weaver performance. – *Michael Rechtshaffen, Hollywood Reporter*

Imitation of Life   ★★★

DIR *Douglas Sirk*
1959   124m   US
☆ *Lana Turner*, Juanita Moore, John Gavin, Susan Kohner, Dan O'Herlihy, Sandra Dee, Robert Alda

An ambitious actress lives in a low-rent apartment with her black maid, but is insensitive to the pain she feels about being rejected by her lighter-skinned daughter, who tries to pass for white.

It wouldn't be a Douglas Sirk film if the prevailing tone were not one of barely suppressed hysteria, or the plot resembling a strand from a melodramatic soap opera. Yet there's much to enjoy here, not least Turner in self-parodying mood, and tragic suffering milked to the last drop.

SCR Eleanore Griffin, Allan Scott   **CIN** Russell Metty
MUS Frank Skinner   **PROD** Ross Hunter   **DIST** U-I

⚖ Juanita Moore (supporting actress); Susan Kohner (supporting actress)

'The genius behind the music. The madness behind the man. The untold love story of Ludwig Van Beethoven.'

Immortal Beloved   ★

SCR/DIR Bernard Rose
1994   120m   GB/US
DVD   ♫

☆ Gary Oldman (Ludwig van Beethoven), Jeroen Krabbe (Anton Felix Schindler), Johanna Ter Steege (Johanna Reiss/van Beethoven), Isabella Rossellini (Anna Marie Erdödy), Marco Hofschneider (Karl van Beethoven), Valeria Golino (Giulietta Guicciardi/von Gallenberg), Matthew North (Young Karl van Beethoven), Miriam Margolyes (Nanette Streicherová)

After Beethoven's death, his assistant tries to figure out the identity of the maestro's great love.

Campy biopic about the life and loves of a tortured artist, told with a degree of visual flair the script doesn't deserve.

CIN *Peter Suschitzky*   **MUS** Beethoven   **DES** Jiri Hlupy
ED Dan Rae   **PROD** Bruce Davey
DIST Entertainment/Majestic/Icon

66 Mr. Rose contributes a passionate enthusiasm for the music and an eagerness to fathom the forces that brought about its creation. At its best, his film almost brings those forces to life. – *Janet Maslin, New York Times*

Impromptu   ★

DIR James Lapine
1991   107m   GB/US/France
DVD   ♫

☆ Judy Davis (George Sand / Aurora), Hugh Grant (Frederic Chopin), Mandy Patinkin (Alfred De Musset), Bernadette Peters (Marie D'Agoult), Julian Sands (Franz Liszt), Ralph Brown (Eugene Delacroix), Georges Corraface (Felicien Mallefille), Anton Rodgers (Duke D'Antan), Emma Thompson (Duchess D'Antan), Anna Massey (George Sand's Mother)

The infamous female novelist George Sand stalks a startled Chopin at a country house gathering, and finally gets her man in Paris.

Davis's gorgeous performance as the outrageous Sand, joyously overturning social conventions, is the best reason to see this modern, calculatedly irreverent version of a true-life 19th century affair.

SCR Sarah Kernochan   **CIN** Bruno de Keyzer
ED Michael Ellis   **PROD** Stuart Oken, Daniel A. Sherkow
DIST Rank/Sovereign/Governor/Les Films Ariane

66 Not wholly successful, this is nevertheless a surprisingly perky addition to the mainly dreary catalogue of films about the loves of deadweight famous names from the past. – *Kim Newman, MFB*

† Director Lapine, whose feature debut this is, collaborated with Stephen Sondheim as the librettist on two well-regarded stage musicals, Into The Woods and Sunday in the Park With George.

DVD Available on DVD   ☆ Cast in order   66 Critics' Quotes   ⚖ Academy Award   🅑 BAFTA
♫ Soundtrack on CD   of importance   † Points of interest   ⚖ Academy Award nomination   🅣 BAFTA nomination

309

In a Lonely Place ★★★★

DIR Nicholas Ray
1950 93m US

☆ Humphrey Bogart, Gloria Grahame, Frank Lovejoy, Carl Benton Reid, Art Smith, Jeff Donnell

A jaded Hollywood scriptwriter is cleared of murdering a hat-check girl, but encounters problems with his girl-friend, who can no longer quite trust him.

A psychologically fascinating character study by Bogart, who veers between kindly and threatening. Quite apart from the main narrative, it's a knowing account of Hollywood studio politics, and where the genuinely creative types belong on the totem pole.

SCR Andrew Solt CIN Burnett Guffey MUS George Antheil PROD Robert Lord DIST Columbia/Santana

❝ It remains better than average, but lacks the penetration which would make it really interesting. – *Gavin Lambert*

In America ★★

DIR Jim Sheridan
2003 105m US/Ireland/GB
DVD ♫

☆ *Samantha Morton* (Sarah), *Paddy Considine* (Johnny), *Sarah Bolger* (Christy), *Emma Bolger* (Ariel), *Djimon Hounsou* (Mateo)

Having lost a son, a struggling Irish actor and his family move to Manhattan illegally, and befriend the AIDS-afflicted Haitian artist who lives downstairs.

Semi-autobiographical immigrant saga with a generous, fairytale spirit. The performances are wonderful, helping Sheridan achieve a heartfelt sense of hardscrabble living, though the mawkish ending is a serious problem.

SCR Jim Sheridan, Naomi Sheridan, Kirsten Sheridan CIN Declan Quinn MUS Gavin Friday, Maurice Seezer DES Mark Geraghty ED Naomi Geraghty PROD Jim Sheridan, Arthur Lappin DIST TCF

❝ A recklessly emotional film that is so committed to feelings it occasionally overflows its banks. – *Kenneth Turan, LA Times*

⌛ Samantha Morton (leading actress); Djimon Hounsou (supporting actor); Jim Sheridan, Naomi Sheridan, Kirsten Sheridan (original screenplay)

'An Out-And-Out Comedy.'

In & Out ★

DIR Frank Oz
1997 90m US
DVD

☆ Kevin Kline (Howard Brackett), *Joan Cusack* (Emily Montgomery), Matt Dillon (Cameron Drake), Debbie Reynolds (Berniece Brackett), Wilford Brimley (Frank Brackett), Bob Newhart (Tom Halliwell), Tom Selleck (Peter Malloy)

When a former student outs him in his Oscar-acceptance speech, a closeted English teacher must explain things to his fiancée.

Glib comedy about a man waking up to his sexuality

late in life; it resorts to standard jokes about Barbra Streisand, but raises a few laughs.

SCR Paul Rudnick CIN Rob Hahn MUS Mark Shaiman DES Ken Adam ED Dan Hanley, John Jympson PROD Scott Rudin DIST Paramount/Spelling Films

❝ One of the jollier comedies of the year. – *Roger Ebert, Chicago Sun-Times*

† Tom Hanks inadvertently outed one of his teachers when accepting an Academy Award for Philadelphia, thus providing the inspiration for this film.

⌛ Joan Cusack (supporting actress)

'Shoot first. Sightsee later.'

In Bruges (new) ★

SCR/DIR Martin McDonagh
2008 107m UK/Belgium
DVD ♫

☆ Colin Farrell (Ray), Brendan Gleeson (Ken), Ralph Fiennes (Harry), Clémence Poésy (Chloe), Jérémie Rénier (Eirik), Jordan Prentice (Jimmy), Ciaran Hinds (Priest)

Two Irish hitmen get up to no good after being sent to the Belgian city of Bruges.

Darkly comic, scabrously witty farce that takes a puerile glee in being casually offensive. The result is great fun, until it starts taking itself seriously.

CIN Eigil Bryld MUS Carter Burwell DES Michael Carlin ED Jon Gregory PROD Graham Broadbent, Pete Czernin DIST Universal

KEN: 'Two manky hookers and a racist dwarf!'
RAY: 'If I'd grown up on a farm and was retarded, Bruges might impress me, but I didn't, so it doesn't.'

❝ Moderately fair as a nutty character study, but overly far-fetched once the action kicks in. – *Robert Koehler, Variety*

❝ A laugh-out-loud dark comedy. – *Neil Smith, Total Film*

† Opening film at the 2008 Sundance Film Festival.

In Cold Blood ★★★

SCR/DIR *Richard Brooks*
1967 134m US
DVD

☆ *Robert Blake* (Perry Smith), Scott Wilson (Dick Hickock), John Forsythe (Alvin Dewey), Paul Stewart (Reporter), Gerald S. O'Loughlin (Harold Nye), Jeff Corey (Hickock's Father)

An account of a real life crime in which an entire family was brutally murdered on their Kansas farm by wandering gunmen.

The fatal collision between the murdered family and two rootless drifters from dysfunctional homes is given an ironic weight in this detailed reconstruction of a haphazard tragedy. It does full justice to Truman Capote's meticulous book.

CIN *Conrad Hall* MUS Quincy Jones ED Peter Zinner DIST Columbia/Richard Brooks

❝ It marks a slight step up for its director, best remembered for reducing Lord Jim to pablum and The Brothers Karamazov to pulp. – *John Simon*

⌛ Richard Brooks (direction); Richard Brooks (adapted screenplay); Conrad Hall; Quincy Jones

'The story of an American family.'

In Country ★

DIR Norman Jewison
1989 120m US
[DVD]

☆ Bruce Willis (Emmett Smith), Emily Lloyd (Samantha Hughes), Joan Allen (Irene), Kevin Anderson (Lonnie), Richard Hamilton (Grampaw), Judith Ivey (Anita), Peggy Rea (Mamaw), John Terry (Tom), Ken Jenkins (Jim Holly)

A traumatised Vietnam veteran is comforted by his young niece, as she tries to piece together details of the life of her father who died in the same war.

Decent account of bereavement, notable for Bruce Willis's first attempt at a serious dramatic role in film.

SCR Frank Pierson, Cynthia Cidre CIN Russell Boyd
MUS James Horner DES Jackson DeGovia ED Antony Gibbs, Lou Lombardo PROD Norman Jewison, Richard Roth DIST Warner

'He's rich, young and handsome. He's in love with you and he's your dad's boss.'

In Good Company ★

SCR/DIR Paul Weitz
2004 109m US
[DVD] ♫

☆ Dennis Quaid (Dan Foreman), Topher Grace (Carter Duryea), Scarlett Johansson (Alex Foreman), Marg Helgenberger (Ann Foreman), David Paymer (Morty)

A veteran advertising exec is alarmed to find himself working under a new employee half his age, who also starts dating his daughter.

Soft-core corporate comedy, never as bitter as it needs to be, but supplying an easy charm that's some compensation.

CIN Remi Adefarasin MUS Stephen Trask, Damien Rice
DES William Arnold ED Myron Kerstein PROD Paul Weitz, Chris Weitz DIST Universal

66 The scenario is stale but the actors are faultless. – *Dennis Lim, Village Voice*

66 A smooth mixture of satire and sentiment that owes an obvious debt to The Apartment, not to mention Jerry Maguire. – *David Ansen, Newsweek*

'You are invited to witness the death of a Hollywood legend.'

In Memory of My Father (new)

SCR/DIR Christopher Jaynes
2008 96m US/Austria
[DVD]

☆ Judy Greer (Judy), Jeremy Sisto (Jeremy), Christopher Jaymes (Chris), Christine Lakin (Christine), Nicholle Tom (Nicole), Matt Keeslar (Matt), Monet Mazur (Monet), Pat Healy (Pat), Eric Michael Cole (Eric)

An extended family reunites at the wake of its deceased patriarch, a Hollywood producer, to find themselves being filmed at his request.

Convoluted black comedy with characters named after the actors playing them; the ensuing shenanigans have a bleak wit but little overall impact.

CIN Abe Levy MUS Daniel Teper, Belle and Sebastian
ED Christopher Jaynes, Eric Michael Cole
PROD Christopher Jaynes DIST Scanbox Entertainment

66 This sour assault lacks sophistication and, more importantly, any real insight. – *Wendy Ide, The Times*

66 If you're a fan of jaundiced views of Hollywood or unedifying portraits of dysfunctional families, look no further. – *Wally Hammond, Time Out*

'. . .it's not just another kiss.'

In Search of a Midnight Kiss (new) ★

SCR/DIR Alex Holdridge
2008 99m US
[DVD]

☆ Scoot McNairy (Wilson), Sara Simmonds (Vivian), Brian McGuire (Jacob), Kathleen Luong (Min), Twink Caplan (Wilson's Mother), Robert Murphy (Jack)

An unsuccessful screenwriter spends New Year's Eve with a chain-smoking shrew.

Pleasing romantic comedy, filmed in black and white on a visibly low budget, that makes effective use of rarely seen Los Angeles locations.

CIN Robert Murphy ED Frank Reynolds, Jacob Vaughn
PROD Seth Caplan, Scoot McNairy DIST Vertigo Films

66 Unashamedly romantic, this is a charming and seductive piece of work. – *Peter Bradshaw, Guardian*

66 A very funny, talky and kvetchy film about loneliness and connections, mixing romance with frank sex talk and building into poignancy. – *Jason Solomons, Observer*

'A young man. An older woman. Her ex-husband. Things are about to explode. . .'

In the Bedroom ★★★

DIR *Todd Field*
2001 138m US
[DVD] ♫

☆ *Sissy Spacek* (Ruth Fowler), *Tom Wilkinson* (Matt Fowler), Nick Stahl (Frank Fowler), *Marisa Tomei* (Natalie Strout), William Mapother (Richard Strout), William Wise (Willis Grinnel), Celia Weston (Katie Grinnel), Karen Allen (Marla Keyes)

When their son is killed by his girlfriend's jealous ex-husband, a couple in Maine are let down by the justice system and find their marriage crumbling.

Devastating drama of loss without closure, whose surprise developments are meant as anything but consoling. The direction is careful and quiet, and the lead performances carry it to near-greatness.

SCR Rob Festinger, Todd Field CIN Antonio Calvache
MUS Thomas Newman ED Frank Reynolds
PROD Graham Leader, Ross Katz, Todd Field
DIST Buena Vista

66 Knows the private geography of love, grief and obsession. – *Kenneth Turan, LA Times*

66 A granola Death Wish. – *J. Hoberman, Village Voice*

⚱ picture; Tom Wilkinson (leading actor); Sissy Spacek (leading actress); Marisa Tomei (supporting actress); Rob Festinger, Todd Field (adapted screenplay)

Ⓣ Tom Wilkinson (leading actor); Sissy Spacek (leading actress)

[DVD] Available on DVD ☆ Cast in order of importance 66 Critics' Quotes † Points of interest ⚱ Academy Award ⚱ Academy Award nomination Ⓣ BAFTA Ⓣ BAFTA nomination
♫ Soundtrack on CD

311

'The drama. The passion. The intrigue. And rehearsals haven't even started.'

In the Bleak Midwinter ★

SCR/DIR Kenneth Branagh
1995 99m GB

☆ Michael Maloney (Joe Harper (Hamlet)), Richard Briers (Henry Wakefield (Claudius, the Ghost, and the Player King)), Mark Hadfield (Vernon Spatch (Polonius, Marcellus and First Gravedigger)), Julia Sawalha (Nina Raymond (Ophelia)), Nick Farrell (Tom Newman (Laertes, Fortinbras, and messengers)), Gerard Horan (Carnforth Greville (Rosencrantz, Guildenstern, Horatio, and Barnardo)), John Sessions (Terry Du Bois (Queen Gertrude)), Celia Imrie (Fadge), Hetta Charnley (Molly), Joan Collins (Margaretta D'Arcy), Jennifer Saunders (Nancy Crawford)

An out-of-work actor volunteers to save a village church by mounting a Christmas production of Hamlet.

Genial but undistinguished luvvie comedy which errs on the side of gloopy.

CIN Roger Lanser   MUS Jimmy Yuill   DES Tim Harvey
ED Neil Farrell   PROD David Barron
DIST Rank/Midwinter

66 This black-and-white film unfolds at such a lickety-split pace that at moments its snappy dialogue gets left behind in the dust. – *Stephen Holden, New York Times*

'Everything you know about desire is dead wrong.'

In the Cut ★

DIR Jane Campion
2003 119m US/Australia
DVD

☆ Meg Ryan (Frannie Avery), Mark Ruffalo (Det Giovanni A. Malloy), Jennifer Jason Leigh (Pauline), Nick Damici (Det Rodriguez), Sharrieff Pugh (Cornelius Webb)

A New York writing professor has an affair with the homicide cop investigating the murder of a woman in her neighbourhood.

An attempt to refashion the serial-killer film as a dark feminist fairytale; it fails, because of a pretentious and belligerent plot, but the dazzling cinematography is some compensation.

SCR Jane Campion, Susanna Moore   CIN *Dion Beebe*
MUS Hilmar Orn Hilmarsson   DES David Brisbin
ED Alexandre de Francheschi   PROD Laurie Parker,
Nicole Kidman   DIST Pathé

66 May be the most maddening and imperfect great movie of the year. – *Manohla Dargis, LA Times*

66 A movie that strains, and fails, to be lurid even as it wags its finger at anything that resembles sin. – *Owen Gleiberman, Entertainment Weekly*

In the Hands of the Gods (new) ★

DIR Gabe Turner, Benjamin Turner
2007 106m UK

☆ Sami Hall Bassam, Mikey Fisher, Jeremy Lynch, Danny Robinson, Paul Wood, Diego Maradona

Five young English 'freestyle' footballers busk their way though America to reach Buenos Aires and meet their hero, Diego Maradona.

The laddish 'keepy-uppy' experts are an engaging quintet, eagerly chasing a dream. The climax of their journey is certainly unexpected, yet many scenes resemble staged reality TV moments: group hugs, tears, mumbled monologues about overcoming life's obstacles. It's often sweet and touching, but is it as spontaneous as it seems?

CIN Matthew Beecroft, Diego Rodriguez   MUS Matthew Rozeik   ED Alastair Reid, Benjamin Turner   PROD Leo Pearlman, Ben Winston   DIST Lionsgate

66 If ever there was a film that celebrated the joy of existence, the heady thrill of scaling a seemingly insurmountable challenge, it's this shambling documentary. – *Wendy Ide, The Times*

† The film's title is a play on a famous comment of Maradona's: having handled before he scored a goal for Argentina against England in the 1986 World Cup, he said it was scored 'a little with the hand of God'.

'They got a murder on their hands. . .they don't know what to do with it.'

In the Heat of the Night ★★★★

DIR *Norman Jewison*
1967 109m US
DVD ♫

☆ *Sidney Poitier* (Virgil Tibbs), *Rod Steiger* (Bill Gillespie), Warren Oates (Sam Wood), Quentin Dean (Delores Purdy), William Schallert (Webb Schubert)

In a small Southern town, the bigoted and bombastic sheriff on a murder hunt grudgingly accepts the help of a black detective.

A tense and exciting thriller that also explores racism through the explosive clash of two contrasting personalities.

SCR Stirling Silliphant   CIN *Haskell Wexler*   MUS Quincy Jones   ED Hal Ashby   PROD Walter Mirisch
DIST UA/Mirisch

BILL GILLESPIE: Well, you're pretty sure of yourself, ain't you, Virgil. Virgil, that's a funny name for a nigger boy to come from Philadelphia. What do they call you up there?
VIRGIL TIBBS: They call me Mr Tibbs.

66 A very nice film and a very good film and yes, I think it's good to see a black man and a white man working together. . .but it's not going to take the tension out of New York City; it's not going to stop the riots in Chicago. – *Rod Steiger*

† Poitier subsequently starred in a couple of very inferior sequels, They Call Me Mister Tibbs and The Organization.

⌁ picture; Rod Steiger (leading actor); Stirling Silliphant (adapted screenplay); Hal Ashby; sound
⌁ Norman Jewison (direction); James A. Richard (sound effects)

⍟ Rod Steiger (leading actor)

'An assassin on the loose. A president in danger. Only one man stands between them. . .'

In the Line of Fire ★★

DIR Wolfgang Petersen
1993 128m US
DVD ♫

☆ *Clint Eastwood* (Secret Service Agent Frank Horrigan),

John Malkovich (Mitch Leary), Rene Russo (Secret Service Agent Lilly Raines), Dylan McDermott (Secret Service Agent Al D'Andrea), Gary Cole (Secret Service Presidential Detail Agent-In-Charge Bill Watts), Fred Dalton Thompson (White House Chief of Staff Harry Sargent), John Mahoney (Secret Service Director Sam Campagna), Greg Alan-Williams (Secret Service Agent Matt Wilder (as Greg Alan-Williams))

Haunted by his inability to save John F. Kennedy, a secret-service agent is taunted by a killer who means to assassinate the current President.

A superior thriller in which Eastwood is well deployed, Malkovich hammily enjoyable, and the plotting as tight as you could hope for.

SCR Jeff Maguire   **CIN** John Bailey   **MUS** Ennio Morricone   **DES** Lilly Kilvert   **ED** *Anne V. Coates*   **PROD** Jeff Apple   **DIST** Columbia

66 Works well when it works, and lazes around the rest of the time. – *Rick Groen, Toronto Globe and Mail*

66 Snappy and appealing in its fast, tense treatment. – *Angie Errigo, Empire*

John Malkovich (supporting actor); Jeff Maguire (original screenplay); Anne V. Coates

John Malkovich (supporting actor); Jeff Maguire (original screenplay); Anne V. Coates

---

'Feel the heat, keep the feeling burning, let the sensation explode.'

In the Mood for Love ★★★

SCR/DIR *Kar Wai Wong*

2000   98m   Hong Kong/ France

DVD ♫

☆ *Tony Leung Chiu-wai* (Chow Mo-wan), *Maggie Cheung* (Su Li-zhen), Lai Chin (Mr Ho), Rebecca Pan (Mrs Suen), Siu Ping-lam (Ah-ping)

Two neighbours in 1960s Hong Kong are drawn together when they discover their respective spouses are having an affair.

Ravishing retreat into love-as-reverie, lingering on every passing glance as it ponders what might have been. The story gradually dissipates, but it could hardly bewitch the senses more than it does.

CIN *Christopher Doyle, Mark Li Ping-bing*   **MUS** Michael Galasso, Umebayashi Shigeru   **DES** *William Chang*   **ED** William Chang   **PROD** Kar Wai Wong   **DIST** Metro Tartan

66 Shimmers and glows. But it also stings a little. – *Michael Wilmington, Chicago Tribune*

66 The whole thing dissolves like a paper fan in rain, an evanescent masterwork. – *Manohla Dargis, LA Weekly*

'Falsely accused. Wrongly imprisoned. He fought for justice to clear his father's name.'

In the Name of the Father ★★

DIR Jim Sheridan

1993   133m   Eire/GB

DVD ♫

☆ *Daniel Day-Lewis* (Gerry Conlon), *Pete Postlethwaite* (Giuseppe Conlon), Emma Thompson (Gareth Peirce), John Lynch (Paul Hill), Mark Sheppard (Paddy

Armstrong), Beatie Edney (Carole Richardson), Marie Jones (Sarah Conlon), Britta Smith (Annie Maguire), Corin Redgrave (Robert Dixon)

Gerry Conlon, a small-time Belfast thief, is coerced along with three of his friends into confessing to the 1994 bombing of a pub in Guildford, and spends 14 years in jail fighting to prove his innocence.

Compelling and searingly acted story of a notorious miscarriage of justice, achieving an often blistering indignation in its treatment of judicial corruption and police brutality. A major limitation, though, is that it plays fast and loose with the truth, devolving into fictionalised courtroom theatrics that undo a lot of its power.

SCR Terry George, Jim Sheridan   **CIN** *Peter Biziou*   **MUS** Trevor Jones   **DES** Caroline Amies   **ED** *Gerry Hambling*   **PROD** Jim Sheridan   **DIST** Universal/Hell's Kitchen/Gabriel Byrne

66 Letter-perfect performances from Day-Lewis and Postlethwaite do a lot more than a dozen editorials to make an unforgettable point about the miscarriage of justice. – *Kim Newman, Empire*

66 The truth was sickening enough and needed no embroidery. – *George Perry, Sunday Times*

† In preparation for his role, Daniel Day-Lewis lost 30 pounds and spent nights in the jail cell on the set as crew members threw water and verbal abuse at him.

Daniel Day-Lewis (leading actor); Pete Postlethwaite (supporting actor); Emma Thompson (supporting actress); Jim Sheridan; Terry George, Jim Sheridan (adapted screenplay); Gerry Hambling

Daniel Day-Lewis (leading actor); Terry George, Jim Sheridan (adapted screenplay)

'Remember when the world looked up.'

In the Shadow of the Moon (new) ★★★

DIR David Sington

2007   100m   UK

DVD ♫

☆ Buzz Aldrin, Alan Bean, Eugene Cernan, Michael Collins, Charles Duke, James Lovell, Edgar Mitchell, Harrison Schmitt, David Scott, John Young

Interviews with 10 of the astronauts who took part in the Apollo lunar space programme, notably the Apollo 11 mission that flew to the moon.

This thoughtful documentary stresses the awe felt by the astronauts in this wildly ambitious project. Their humility and modesty is heartening. It downplays the harsh politics of the lunar programme, and concentrates on the sense of giddy euphoria felt across the world by the moon landing.

CIN Clive North   **MUS** Philip Sheppard   **ED** David Fairhead   **PROD** Duncan Copp   **DIST** Vertigo

66 Respectful, enthusiastic and occasionally rather touching as the men, now in their seventies, recall how it felt up there. Yet the really important question never gets asked: what was it all for? – *Anthony Quinn, Independent*

66 You probably won't find a more comprehensive document of space exploration on film. – *Kevin Maher, The Times*

'A comedy about getting in over your head.'

In the Soup ★★

DIR *Alexandre Rockwell*
1992 93m US
DVD

☆ Steve Buscemi (Aldolpho Rollo), *Seymour Cassel* (Joe), Jennifer Beals (Angelica Pena), Pat Moya (Dang), Will Patton (Skippy), Jim Jarmusch (Monty), Carol Kane (Barbara)

A criminal con artist raises the money to finance a worthy, uncommercial independent film with the gains from his illegal endeavours.

Well-observed comedy about the trials and pitfalls of film-making at the no-budget end of the market. Cassel shines in the extravagant role of a hoodlum.

SCR Alexandre Rockwell, Tim Kissell   CIN Phil Parmet
MUS Mader   DES Mark Friedberg   ED Dana Congdon
PROD Jim Stark, Hank Blumenthal   DIST Will
Alliance/Pandora/Why Not/Odessa/Alta/Mikado

66 Rockwell's fourth feature succeeds wonderfully well by poking compassionate fun at his earlier efforts. – *Trevor Johnston, Sight & Sound*

'Sometimes finding the truth is easier than facing it.'

In the Valley Of Elah (new) ★★★

SCR/DIR Paul Haggis
2007 121m US

☆ *Tommy Lee Jones* (Hank Deerfield), *Charlize Theron* (Detective Emily Sanders), James Franco (Sergeant Dan Carnelli), Frances Fisher (Evie), *Susan Sarandon* (Joan Deerfield)

A Vietnam veteran's son has come home to America from the Iraq war, but gone missing. When his body is found near his army base, the father and a small-town detective try to solve the mystery, which has its roots in the war zone.

A dignified, muted commentary on the downside of the Iraq war and its aftermath for the soldiers involved. In this strong, decent film touched by melancholy, Tommy Lee Jones offers a towering performance as a man slow to be antagonised, but bristling with suppressed outrage.

CIN Roger Deakins   DES Laurence Bennett   ED Jo
Francis   PROD Patrick Wachsberger, Steven Samuels,
Darlene Caamaro Loquet, Paul Haggis, Laurence Becsey
DIST Optimum

66 Theron is excellent in a demanding role, but this is Jones's movie. He's in every scene and utterly superb. – *Philip French, Observer*

66 It's the first Hollywood Iraq movie to remind me of a Vietnam film like Coming Home, and it does more than disturb. It scalds, moves, and heals. – *Owen Gleiberman, Entertainment Weekly*

† The Valley of Elah was the place where David slew Goliath.

⚲ Tommy Lee Jones (leading actor)

'The journey to freedom has no borders.'

In This World ★★★

DIR *Michael Winterbottom*
2002 88m GB
DVD

☆ Jamal Udin Torabi (Jamal), Enayatullah (Enayat), Imran Paracha (Travel Agent), Hiddayatullah (Enayat's Brother), Kerem Atabeyoglu (Policeman), Erham Sekizcan (Factory Boss), Nabil Elouahabi (Yusif)

Two young Afghan refugees make the trek across Europe to seek asylum in Britain.

A compassionate and gripping docudrama on a timely theme, shot on digital video to afford maximum intimacy with its subjects. It doesn't flinch on the peril of their journey, but is told with a humour and humanity that makes us care all the more.

SCR Tony Grisoni   CIN *Marcel Zyskind*   MUS Dario
Marianelli   ED *Peter Christelis*   PROD Andrew Eaton,
Anita Overland   DIST ICA

66 Unfolds with the deceptive dispassion of a documentary. – *Lisa Schwarzbaum, Entertainment Weekly*

66 Beautiful, heartbreaking, fiercely affirming. . .the best British film of my lifetime. – *Sukhdev Sandhu, Daily Telegraph*

† The film is partly based on the experiences of the lead actors, real-life Afghani asylum seekers.

⚲ film not in the English language

In Which We Serve ★★★

DIR *Noël Coward, David Lean*
1942 114m GB
DVD

☆ *Noël Coward*, Bernard Miles, *John Mills*, Richard Attenborough, *Celia Johnson*, Kay Walsh, Joyce Carey, Michael Wilding, Penelope Dudley Ward, Kathleen Harrison, Philip Friend, George Carney, Geoffrey Hibbert, James Donald

Survivors from a torpedoed destroyer recall their life at sea and on leave.

Dated but splendid flag-waver; an archetypal British war film of almost limitless propaganda value.

SCR *Noël Coward*   CIN Ronald Neame   MUS Noël
Coward   PROD Noël Coward   DIST Rank/Two Cities

COMMANDER (NOËL COWARD): The Torrin has been in one scrap after another, but even when we've had men killed, the majority survived and brought the old ship back. Now she lies in 1500 fathoms and with her more than half our shipmates. If they had to die, what a grand way to go! And now they lie all together with the ship we loved, and they're in very good company. We've lost her, but they're still with her. There may be less than half the Torrin left, but I feel that we'll all take up the battle with even stronger heart. Each of us knows twice as much about fighting, and each of us has twice as good a reason to fight. You will all be sent to replace men who've been killed in other ships, and the next time you're in action, remember the Torrin! I should like to add that there isn't one of you that I wouldn't be proud and honoured to serve with again.

66 One of the screen's proudest achievements at any time and in any country. – *Newsweek*

66 Never at any time has there been a reconstruction of human experience which could touch the savage grandeur

---

and compassion of this production. – *Howard Barnes, New York Herald Tribune*

† The story and the Coward character were based on the experiences of Louis Mountbatten, whose ship, HMS Kelly, was sunk under him.

⚱ Special Award to Noël Coward
⚱ picture; Noël Coward (original screenplay)

'A global warning.'

An Inconvenient Truth ★★

DIR Davis Guggenheim
2006 96m US
DVD ♫

☆ Al Gore (Himself)

Former US vice-president Al Gore tours the world, giving lecture to heighten awareness of global warming.

There may be nothing new here for those who study environmental matters closely. And cinematically, it's little more than a filmed slide-show. Yet Gore is remarkably persuasive, addressing the public over the heads of other politicians seemingly intent on avoiding engagement with this most pressing of issues.

CIN Bob Richman, Davis Guggenheim   MUS Michael Brook   DES John Calkins   ED Jay Cassidy, Dan Swietlik   PROD Laurie David, Lawrence Bender, Scott Z. Burns   DIST UIP

AL GORE: 'Future generations may well have occasion to ask themselves, "What were our parents thinking? Why didn't they wake up when they had a chance?" We have to hear that question from them, now.'

66 Despite or perhaps because of Gore's schoolmasterly attitudes, his arguments have force. A kind of anti-charisma sees it through. – *Peter Bradshaw, Guardian*

66 It is utterly convincing, it's emotionally powerful and it makes Gore look more charming than he ever did as a presidential candidate. – *Dave Calhoun, Time Out*

⚱ documentary; Melissa Etheridge (music, original song – I Need To Wake Up)

The Incredible Hulk (new)

DIR Louis Leterrier
2008 112m US
♫

☆ Edward Norton (Bruce Banner), Liv Tyler (Betty Ross), Tim Roth (Emil Blonsky), William Hurt (General 'Thunderbolt' Ross), Tim Blake Nelson (Samuel Sterns), Ty Burrell (Dr. Samson)

On the run from the authorities, a scientist tries to control his monstrous alter-ego before another mutant creature catches up with him.

An improvement on Hulk, this playful, more action-oriented attempt to re-invigorate a comic book franchise remains dogged by unconvincing effects. Oddly, the movie is most effective when its computer-generated creations are off-screen.

SCR Zak Penn, Edward Harrison   CIN Peter Menzies Jnr   MUS Craig Armstrong   DES Kirk M. Petruccelli   ED John Wright, Rick Shaine   PROD Avi Arad, Gale Anne Hurd, Kevin Feige   DIST Universal

66 Solid and efficient, if unadventurous. – *Kenneth Turan, Los Angeles Times*

66 Perfunctory and familiar. . . a middling superhero movie. – *A.O. Scott, New York Times*

† The film features cameos from Lou Ferrigno (who played the Hulk on TV), Stan Lee (the character's creator) and Robert Downey Jnr. (reprising his Iron Man role).
† Edward Norton's contribution to the screenplay is credited to the pseudonymous Edward Harrison.

'Save The Day'

The Incredibles ★★★

SCR/DIR *Brad Bird*
2004 115m US
DVD ♫

☆ voices of: Craig T. Nelson (Bob Parr/Mr Incredible), Holly Hunter (Helen Parr/Elastigirl), Samuel L. Jackson (Lucius Best/Frozone), Jason Lee (Buddy Pine/Syndrome), Wallace Shawn (Gilbert Huph), Sarah Vowell (Violet Parr), Spencer Fox (Dashiell Parr), Brad Bird (Edna 'E' Mode)

A family of superheroes forced to cloak their special powers in order to get on in normal life come out of retirement to battle a new threat.

Thrilling computer animation, as bold in its plotting and characterisation as it is studded with glorious visual detail, which stands as one of Pixar's very best; an extension of the themes of Finding Nemo – about what we do to protect ourselves and our loved ones, and what we thus prevent ourselves from experiencing – it is, after the fashion of one of its main characters, an Elastimovie, forever finding new ways to stretch itself and the medium.

CIN Janet Lucroy, Patrick Lin, Andrew Jimenez   MUS Michael Giacchino   DES Lou Romano   ED Stephen Schaffer   PROD John Walker   DIST Buena Vista

66 The sleek beauty, crafty wit, family warmth, and impeccable slapstick suffusing The Incredibles immediately vaults it to a new, higher level of entertainment. – *Ken Tucker, New York Magazine*

66 Dazzlingly beautiful, funny, and meaningful. – *Lisa Schwarzbaum, Entertainment Weekly*

⚱ animated film; Michael Silvers, Randy Thom (sound editing)
⚱ Brad Bird (original screenplay); Randy Thom, Gary A. Rizzo, Doc Kane (sound mixing)

The Indian Runner ★

SCR/DIR *Sean Penn*
1991 127m US
DVD

☆ David Morse (Joe Roberts), Viggo Mortensen (Frank Roberts), Valeria Golino (Maria), Patricia Arquette (Dorothy), Charles Bronson (Mr. Roberts), Sandy Dennis (Mrs. Roberts), Dennis Hopper (Caesar), Jordan Rhodes (Randall)

A petty criminal and tearaway serves a tour of duty in Vietnam, then returns home to his small town, where his brother, an upright policeman, tries to mend fences with him.

Sean Penn set out his stall with this, his first effort as a writer-director: it's an extremely serious, intense, verbose

DVD Available on DVD   ☆ Cast in order   66 Critics' Quotes   ⚱ Academy Award   🅑 BAFTA
♫ Soundtrack on CD   of importance   † Points of interest   ⚱ Academy Award nomination   🅑 BAFTA nomination

315

account of men suffering anguish. Penn would follow this path again more than once. The film is obviously personal and well-intentioned, but fatally overlong: ironically, in Highway Patrolman, the song that inspired it, Bruce Springsteen managed to convey more emotion and despair in five minutes and 39 seconds.

CIN Anthony B. Richmond   **MUS** Jack Nitzsche   **DES** Michael Haller   **ED** Jay Cassidy   **PROD** Don Philips   **DIST** Columbia TriStar/Mount Film Group/Mico/NHK Enterprises

'In May, the adventure continues.'

Indiana Jones and the Kingdom of the Crystal Skull (new)   ★

DIR Steven Spielberg
2008   122m   US
DVD   ♫

☆ Harrison Ford (Indiana Jones), *Cate Blanchett* (Col. Dr. Irina Spalko), Karen Allen (Marion Ravenwood), Shia LaBeouf (Mutt Williams), Ray Winstone ('Mac' McHale), John Hurt (Professor Harold Oxley), Jim Broadbent (Dean Stanforth)

In the 1950s, Indiana Jones is called back into action to help foil a Soviet plot to locate a crystal skull, hidden deep in the Peruvian jungle; if found it will endow its owners with extraordinary power.

It's not that this fourth film in the Indiana Jones franchise, exhumed after 19 years, is bad, exactly. But it's undeniably creaky. What first made the series so fresh and amusing was its lightness of touch and its tongue-in-cheek, 'ripping yarns' spirit. That hasn't quite disappeared, but there's an awful lot of long-winded explanations of myths, legends and hieroglyphics. Thus, between a series of stunt-driven set pieces, many of them implausibly linked, the film gets bogged down in wearying talk. With a cast clearly pre-fabricated to appeal to all ages, an overstuffed plot and an ageing action hero, it feels born of commercial calculation rather than a story that needed to be told.

SCR David Koepp, George Lucas   **CIN** Janusz Kaminski   **MUS** John Williams   **DES** Guy Dyas   **ED** Michael Kahn   **PROD** Frank Marshall   **DIST** Paramount

❝ The first new chapter in the Indiana Jones saga for 20 years starts with a bang, before Spielberg's penchant for schmaltz and the supernatural leaves a permanent scar on the franchise. – *Kaleem Aftab, Independent*

❝ Set this alongside gun-wielding military bad guys and the expected conspiracy plots, and the film looks set to fit easily alongside the other Indy films. – *Mark Adams, Daily Mirror*

Indochine   ★★

DIR Régis Wargnier
1992   159m   France
DVD   ♫

☆ *Catherine Deneuve* (Eliane), Vincent Perez (Jean-Baptiste), Linh Dan Pham (Camille), Jean Yanne (Guy), Dominique Blanc (Yvette), Henri Marteau (Emile), Mai Chau (Shen)

In 1930s Indochina, the female plantation owner loves a young French naval officer; when he is sent to a remote outpost, her adopted teenage Vietnamese daughter runs away to be with him.

A lush historical romance with epic aspirations; ravishing looking, with an authoritative central performance from Deneuve that effectively burns off the opposition.

SCR Erik Orsenna, Louis Gardeal, Catherine Cohen, Régis Wargnier   **CIN** *François Catonne*   **MUS** Patrick Doyle   **DES** Jacques Bufnoir   **ED** Genevieve Winding, Agnès Schwab   **PROD** Eric Heumann, Jean Labadie   **DIST** Paradis/La Générale d'Images/BAC/Orly/Ciné Cinq

❝ The film seems to suggest that the French still do not quite understand what happened to them in Vietnam. Well, they're not alone. – *Roger Ebert, Chicago Sun-Times*

† The film won five César awards in France.

⚑ foreign language film
⚱ Catherine Deneuve (leading actress)
Ⓣ film not in the English language

Infamous   ★

SCR/DIR Douglas McGrath
2006   117m   US
DVD   ♫

☆ *Toby Jones* (Truman Capote), Sandra Bullock (Nelle Harper Lee), Daniel Craig (Perry Smith), Peter Bogdanovich (Bennett Cerf), Jeff Daniels (Alvin Dewey), Hope Davis (Slim Keith), Gwyneth Paltrow (Kitty Dean), Isabella Rossellini (Marella Agnelli), Juliet Stevenson (Diana Vreeland), Sigourney Weaver (Babe Paley)

Writer and socialite Truman Capote travels from Manhattan to Kansas to investigate the gruesome murder of a farmer's family. His reporting becomes his literary masterpiece In Cold Blood.

Unhappily for Infamous, it covers almost the same ground as Capote, released the previous year. And it suffers by comparison: it over-stresses Capote as social gadfly, gossiping madly to his frankly tiresome gang of wealthy ladies-who-lunch. The Kansas scenes are also less convincing. Its tone veers uncertainly between high-society satire, documentary, courtroom drama and doomed gay love story. Toby Jones's portrayal not only captures Capote physically but adds welcome nuance to what might have been a one-dimensional role.

CIN Bruno Delbonnel   **MUS** Rachel Portman   **DES** Judy Becker   **ED** Camilla Toniolo   **PROD** Christine Vachon, Jocelyn Hayes, Anne Walker-McBay   **DIST** Warner Bros.

❝ It's bad luck that Infamous treads the same ground as Capote, only less steadily. – *Dave Calhoun, Time Out*

❝ Jones gets everything – the gestures, the generosity, the mean streak, the bending of the ear to recitals of woe, whether across a lunch table or a prison cell. – *Anthony Lane, New Yorker*

'Loyalty. Honor. Betrayal.'

Infernal Affairs   ★★

DIR Andrew Lau, Alan Mak
2002   101m   Hong Kong
DVD

☆ Tony Leung Chiu-wai (Chan Wing-yan), Andy Lau (Insp Lau Kin-ming), Anthony Wong (Supt Wong), Eric Tsang

(Hon Sam), Chapman To (Keung), Lam Ka-tung (Insp B), Sammi Cheng (Mary)

An undercover cop in a Hong Kong mafia operation becomes aware of his opposite number, a gangster who has infiltrated the police force.

Strikingly stylish policier which grips well enough, even if the clever cat-and-mouse symmetry of the conceit isn't fully exploited.

SCR Alan Mak, Felix Chong CIN Andy Lau, Lai Yiu-fai
MUS Chan Kwong-wing ED Danny Pang, Pang Ching-hei
PROD Andrew Lau DIST Metro Tartan

66 Spins in place with aplomb. – *Dennis Lim, Village Voice*
† Remade by Martin Scorsese as The Departed.

Inherit the Wind ★★

DIR *Stanley Kramer*
1960 127m US

☆ *Spencer Tracy, Fredric March*, Florence Eldridge, Gene Kelly, Dick York, Donna Anderson, Harry Morgan, Elliott Reid, Claude Akins

A fictionalized account of the 1925 Scopes 'monkey trial', when a schoolmaster was accused of teaching the theory of evolution.

Splendid theatrics with two fine central performances, marred by meandering subplots but enhanced by a realistic portrait of a sweltering Southern town.

SCR Nathan E. Douglas (Nedrick Young), Harold Jacob Smith CIN *Ernest Laszlo* MUS Ernest Gold
ED Frederic Knudtson PROD Stanley Kramer
DIST UA/Lomitas

⚑ Spencer Tracy (leading actor); Nedrick Young, Harold Jacob Smith (adapted screenplay); Ernest Laszlo; editing

'A story of a mystery. . .A mystery inside worlds within worlds. . .Unfolding around a woman. . .A woman in love and in trouble.'

Inland Empire ★

SCR/DIR David Lynch
2006 180m US/France/Poland
DVD

☆ Laura Dern (Nikki Grace/Susan Blue), Jeremy Irons (Kingsley Stewart), Justin Theroux (Devon Berk/Billy Side), Grace Zabriskie (Visitor 1), Harry Dean Stanton (Freddie Howard)

Hollywood actress Nikki Grace accepts the lead in a new movie, then discovers its script is based on an old Polish film, abandoned after the murder of its two stars, who were illicit lovers. Alarmed by this, she descends into delusional behaviour, adopts multiple personalities and is unable to distinguish truth from fantasy.

This marks a further retreat from conventional film-making by Lynch, who seems more intrigued by the dream state induced by film rather than linear narratives. It's a test of audiences' resolve. Dense, allusive and visually stunning, its meaning remains unclear on first viewing. Time and space loop, redouble and overlap. As the realisation dawns that no rational explanations will be offered, one can relax into

experiencing it as a demented visual mood piece. Mainly for hardcore Lynch fans.

CIN David Lynch, Erik Crary, Odd Geir Saether, Ole Johan Roska MUS Angelo Badalamenti ED David Lynch
PROD Mary Sweeney, David Lynch DIST Optimum

66 Lynch's most berserk, terrifying and formally radical plunge into the unconscious since Eraserhead (1977). Hellish but extraordinary. – *Tim Robey, Daily Telegraph*
66 Inland Empire is so locked up in David Lynch's brain that it never burrows its way into ours. – *Owen Gleiberman, Entertainment Weekly*
† The title refers to an area of California, east of Los Angeles.
† Naomi Watts plays a sitcom character with a rabbit head.

'A passion beyond love. A crime beyond murder.'

The Innocent ★

DIR John Schlesinger
1993 119m GB/Germany
DVD ♫

☆ Anthony Hopkins (Bob Glass), Isabella Rossellini (Maria), Campbell Scott (Leonard Markham), Hart Bochner (Russell), Ronald Nitschke (Otto), Jeremy Sinden (Captain Lofting), James Grant (MacNamee), Richard Durden (Black)

A gauche English technician in 1950s Germany, at the height of the Cold War, becomes involved in an espionage plot orchestrated by a CIA man, and is seduced by an attractive German woman.

An intricate drama with a labyrinthine plot, featuring a hero who looks constantly confused. And with good reason; all three leading actors are of a different nationality from their characters – a factor that might account for the 'anytime, anywhere' atmosphere of the piece. By no means unwatchable, it's still the least successful adaptation of Ian McEwan's work.

SCR Ian McEwan CIN Dietrich Lohmann MUS Gerald Gouriet DES Luciana Arrighi ED Richard Marden
PROD Norma Heyman, Chris Sievernich, Wieland Schulz-Keil DIST Island Lakeheart/Sievernich/Defa

'How much will a mother sacrifice for the love of her son. . .'

Innocent Voices ★★

DIR Luis Mandoki
2005 120m Mexico/US/Puerto Rico
DVD

☆ Carlos Padilla (Chava), Leonor Varela (Kella), Gustavo Munoz (Ancha), Jose Maria Yazpik (Uncle Beto), Ofelia Medina (Mama Toya), Daniel Gimenez Cacho (Priest)

A father leaves his poor family in El Salvador at the start of the 1980s civil war to go to the US, leaving Chava, 11, as 'man of the house'. He lives in a shack with his sister, younger brother and dutiful mother. The army is already recruiting 12-year-old boys, taking them at gunpoint from their classrooms. In one year Chava will be eligible.

Mexican director Mandoki shows how a boy's indomitable spirit cannot be dulled by war and conflict. He tries to keep a sense of normality by attending school and falling in love while dodging bullets. As Chava,

DVD Available on DVD   ☆ Cast in order   66 Critics' Quotes   ⚑ Academy Award   ⚑ BAFTA
♫ Soundtrack on CD   of importance   † Points of interest   ⚑ Academy Award nomination   ⚑ BAFTA nomination

317

Carlos Padilla, with his hugely expressive face, practically carries the film.

SCR Oscar Torres, Luis Mandoki   CIN Juan Ruiz Anchia
MUS Andre Abujamra   DES Antonio Munohierro
ED Aleshka Ferrero   PROD Lawrence Bender, Alejandro Soberon Kuri, Luis Mandoki   DIST The Works

66 Effective without being overwhelming. – *Roger Ebert, Chicago Sun-Times*

66 An expert addition to a well-worn genre. – *Paul Julian Smith, Sight & Sound*

The Innocents ★★★

DIR *Jack Clayton*
1961   99m   GB

☆ *Deborah Kerr*, Megs Jenkins, Pamela Franklin, Martin Stephens, Michael Redgrave, Peter Wyngarde

In Victorian times, a spinster governess in a lonely house finds her young charges possessed by evil demons of servants now dead.

Elaborate and genuinely scary revamping of Henry James's The Turn of the Screw, the ghosts being now (possibly) the figments of a frustrated woman's imagination. The frissons lost something of their power in Cinemascope, but the decor, the shadowy lighting and impeccable black-and-white photography are exceptional.

SCR William Archibald, Truman Capote   CIN *Freddie Francis*   MUS Georges Auric   PROD Jack Clayton
DIST TCF/Achilles

'Live life like you mean it.'

Inside I'm Dancing ★

DIR Damien O'Donnell
2004   103m   GB/Ireland/Germany/France/US
DVD

☆ *James McAvoy* (Rory O'Shea), Steven Robertson (Michael Connolly), Romola Garai (Siobhan), Gerard McSorley (Fergus Connolly), Tom Hickey (Con O'Shea), Brenda Fricker (Eileen)

A rebel suffering from muscular dystrophy befriends a fellow inmate in his care home, who has cerebral palsy.

Nobly intentioned but too cosy and sitcom-ish, the picture says exactly what you expect it to say on the plight of the motor-impaired, and tiptoes around the issue of its heroes' sexual needs. But it is undeniably well-acted.

SCR Jeffrey Caine   CIN Peter J. Robertson   MUS David Julyan   DES Tom Conroy   ED Frances Parker
PROD James Flynn, Juanita Wilson   DIST Momentum

66 Moves its audience without patronising its subjects. – *Jenny McCartney, Sunday Telegraph*

'It looked like the perfect bank robbery. But you can't judge a crime by its cover.'

Inside Man ★★

DIR Spike Lee
2006   129m   US
DVD

☆ Denzel Washington (Detective Keith Frazier), Clive Owen (Dalton Russell), Jodie Foster (Madeline White), Christopher Plummer (Arthur Case), Willem Dafoe (Capt John Darius), Chiwetel Ejiofor (Detective Bill Mitchell)

A bank robber relates how he pulled off the most daring raid of his career in New York City.

A sturdy genre piece from a director who normally has bigger drums to bang. The backdrop of seething urban discontent gives it a grit the clever script might not have demanded.

SCR Russell Gewirtz   CIN Matthew Libatique
MUS Terence Blanchard   DES Wynn Thomas   ED Barry Alexander Brown   PROD Brian Grazer   DIST Universal

66 The mood is right, the twists are new. – *Lisa Schwarzbaum, Entertainment Weekly*

66 A deft and satisfying entertainment. – *Kenneth Turan, LA Times*

Inside Paris ★★

SCR/DIR Christophe Honoré
2006   93m   France
DVD   ♫

☆ Romain Duris (Paul), Louis Garrel (Jonathan), Joana Preiss (Anna), Guy Marchand (Mirko, the father), Marie-France Pisier (Mother)

The tale of two Parisian brothers, one easy-going and charming, the other suffering from depression which also had afflicted his sister – and resulted in her suicide. He tries to follow suit and jumps into the Seine but survives much to his surprise.

Far from easy viewing, but director Honoré proves adept at showing how all-consuming depression can exert such a powerful grip on the sufferer and his family. Garrel exudes accessible charm as the younger sibling, while Duris displays the pain and anguish of someone losing control.

CIN Jean-Louis Vialard   MUS Alex Beaupain
DES Samuel Deshors   ED Chantal Hymans
PROD Paulo Branco   DIST Artificial Eye

'Two Angry Men Driven To Tell The Truth...Whatever The Cost'

The Insider ★★★

DIR *Michael Mann*
1999   157m   US
DVD   ♫

☆ Al Pacino (Lowell Bergman), *Russell Crowe* (Jeffrey Wigand), *Christopher Plummer* (Mike Wallace), Diane Venora (Liane Wigand), Philip Baker Hall (Don Hewitt), Lindsay Crouse (Sharon Tiller), Debi Mazar (Debbie De Luca), Stephen Tobolowsky (Eric Kluster), Colm Feore (Richard Scruggs), Bruce McGill (Ron Motley), Gina Gershon (Helen Caperelli), Michael Gambon (Thomas Sandefur), Rip Torn (John Scanlon), Michael Moore (Himself), Wings Hauser (Tobacco Lawyer)

TV producer Lowell Bergman attempts to bring to air an interview with a tobacco executive, keen to blow the whistle on his employees and reveal the truth about cigarettes.

Both a character study and a stop-press expose, which tells a fascinating (and very modern) story with great wealth of detail; for all its technical sophistication, and

Crowe's remarkable transformation into a corpulent corporate sad-sack, what's finally amazing about it is that Mann makes gripping the business of memos and confidentiality agreements.

SCR *Eric Roth, Michael Mann*   CIN *Dante Spinotti*
MUS Lisa Gerrard, Pieter Bourke   DES Brian Morris
ED William Goldenberg, Paul Rubell, David Rosenbloom
PROD Michael Mann, Pieter Jan Brugge   DIST Buena Vista

66 A masterpiece, a brilliant dissection of recent US politics and the media by a scalpel-sharp screen sensibility. – *Mark Kermode, Sight and Sound*

66 All the visceral impact and moment-to-moment tension of a fine thriller, together with the distinctive visual style of an art film. – *Andrew O'Hehir, Salon*

⚖ picture; Russell Crowe (leading actor); Michael Mann; Eric Roth, Michael Mann (adapted screenplay); Dante Spinotti (cinematography); William Goldenberg, Paul Rubell, David Rosenbloom (editing); Andy Nelson, Doug Hemphill, Lee Orloff (sound)

Ⓣ Russell Crowe (leading actor)

'Don't close your eyes.'

Insomnia ★★★

DIR *Christopher Nolan*
2002   118m   US
DVD   ♫

☆ *Al Pacino* (Will Dormer), Robin Williams (Walter Finch), Hilary Swank (Ellie Burr), Maura Tierney (Rachel Clement), Martin Donovan (Hap Eckhart), Nicky Katt (Fred Duggar), Paul Dooley (Chief Nyback), Jonathan Jackson (Randy Stetz)

Investigating the murder of a schoolgirl in the perennially daylit town of Nightmute, Alaska, a cop under investigation for corruption shoots his partner and tries to blame it on the prime suspect.

A cunning and superbly crafted procedural thriller, remade from the Norwegian original with care and intelligence in all departments, and giving Pacino plenty of scenery to chew on; the complicity between killer and investigator gives it the quality of a queasy morality play.

SCR *Hillary Seitz*   CIN *Wally Pfister*   MUS David Julyan
DES *Nathan Crowley*   ED Dody Dorn   PROD Paul Junger Witt, Edward L. McDonnell, Broderick Johnson, Andrew A. Kosove   DIST Buena Vista

66 About as good a movie as you could have hoped for. Really good. Hole-in-one good. – *Shawn Levy, Oregonian*

66 Works up a respectable level of bleary-eyed paranoia. – *Dennis Lim, Village Voice*

'Life is what happens in between.'

interMission ★★

DIR John Crowley
2003   105m   Ireland/GB
DVD   ♫

☆ Colin Farrell (Lehiff), Shirley Henderson (Sally), Kelly Macdonald (Deidre), *Colm Meaney* (Det Jerry Lynch), Cillian Murphy (John), Ger Ryan (Maura), Brian F. O'Byrne (Mick)

Low-lifes in Dublin plan a bank robbery and struggle to hold down relationships.

Something of a riposte to the same year's treacly Love Actually, this is a refreshingly vulgar ensemble piece, full of lip and wittily scripted, even if the ending falters.

SCR *Mark O'Rowe*   CIN Ryszard Lenczewski   MUS John Murphy   DES Tom Conroy   ED Lucia Zucchetti
PROD Neil Jordan, Stephen Woolley, Alan Moloney
DIST Buena Vista

66 Snappily scripted, consistently funny and ferociously moving near the end. – *Catherine Shoard, Sunday Telegraph*

'Trust me. . .I'm a cop.'

Internal Affairs ★★

DIR *Mike Figgis*
1990   115m   US
DVD

☆ *Richard Gere* (Dennis Peck), Andy Garcia (Raymond Avila), Nancy Travis (Kathleen Avila), *Laurie Metcalf* (Amy Wallace), Richard Bradford (Grieb), William Baldwin (Van Stretch), Michael Beach (Dorian Fletcher)

Two detectives in the Internal Affairs division of the LAPD investigate a dirty colleague.

Sinuous thriller with plausibility problems but a rich atmosphere of seductive sleaze; it's also the rare movie to cast Richard Gere interestingly, as a psychopathic manipulator who uses sex to get what he wants.

SCR Henry Bean   CIN *John A. Alonso*   MUS Mike Figgis, Anthony Marinelli, Brian Banks   DES Waldemar Kalinowski   ED Robert Estrin   PROD Frank Mancuso Jnr
DIST UIP/Paramount

66 It casts a slimy-naughty spell. It's bad fun. – *Pauline Kael, New Yorker*

66 In this gutter Othello, a pair of knickers serves for the tell-tale handerchief and Gere's villain prances balletically around Garcia's bull-at-bay hero. – *Harlan Kennedy, Film Review*

Interrogation ★★

SCR/DIR Ryszard Bugajski, Janusz Dymek
1982   118m   Poland

☆ *Krystyna Janda* (Antonia Dziwisz), Adam Ferency (Morawski), Janusz Gajos (Zawada), Agnieszka Holland (Witowska), Anna Romantowska (Miroslawa "Mira" Szejnert), Bozena Dykiel (Honorata), Olgierd Lukaszewicza (Konstanty Dziwisz), Tomasz Dedek (Czesiek)

In the dying days of the Stalinist era in Poland, a female cabaret artist, suspected of consorting with an anti-government army officer, is tortured by the secret police.

Clear-eyed, detailed account of an oppressive regime's uglier side, though the irrepressibility of its heroine helps lighten the pessimistic mood.

CIN Jacek Petrycki   DES Janusz Sosnowski
ED Katarzyna Maciejko   PROD Tadeusz Drewno
DIST Gala/Zespol Filmowy 'X'

† The film was due to be released in 1982, but was banned by Poland's communist authorities for its anti-government tone. It was finally released in 1990, when Janda won the best actress prize at the Cannes Film Festival.

DVD Available on DVD   ☆ Cast in order   66 Critics' Quotes   ⚖ Academy Award   Ⓑ BAFTA
♫ Soundtrack on CD   of importance   † Points of interest   ⚖ Academy Award nomination   Ⓣ BAFTA nomination

319

'Everything you say can and will be used against you.'

Interview (new)

DIR Steve Buscemi
2007   84m   US/Canada/Netherlands
[DVD]

☆ Sienna Miller (Katya), Steve Buscemi (Pierre Peders), Michael Buscemi (Robert Peders)

A political reporter is assigned to interview a Hollywood 'It' girl, a prospect he finds distasteful.

An interview that turns into a two-way confessional. Hopelessly implausible and tedious.

SCR David Schecter, Steve Buscemi   **CIN** Thomas Kist
MUS Evan Lurie   **DES** Loren Weeks   **ED** Kate Williams
PROD Bruce Weiss, Gijs van de Westelaken   **DIST** The Works

66 A talky, tricksy but never particularly convincing or involving drama. – *Karl French, Financial Times*

66 It's really just a squib on the culture of celebrity, and the cynical conclusion that's meant to pull us up short is feeble and silly beyond patience. – *Anthony Quinn, Independent*

† This is a remake of a film by Dutch director Theo van Gogh, who was murdered in 2004 after making Submission, a documentary about Islam.

'Drink From Me And Live Forever.'

Interview with the Vampire: The Vampire Chronicles   ★

DIR Neil Jordan
1994   123m   US
[DVD]   ♫

☆ Tom Cruise (Lestat de Lioncourt), Brad Pitt (Louis de Pointe du Lac), *Antonio Banderas* (Armand), Christian Slater (Daniel Malloy), Stephen Rea (Santiago), *Kirsten Dunst* (Claudia), Virgina McCollam (Whore on Waterfront), John McConnell (Gambler), Mike Seelig (Pimp), Roger Lloyd Pack (Piano Teacher)

A vampire tells of his life as a plantation owner in the late 18th century, his conversion to bloodsucking by an older mentor and their adoption of a young girl.

Eye-catchingly designed period horror with plenty of festering, ghoulish atmosphere; but characterisation is botched quite woefully, and it stumbles in its overly coy attempts at homoerotic subtext.

SCR Anne Rice   **CIN** *Philippe Rousselot*   **MUS** *Elliot Goldenthal*   **DES** *Dante Ferretti*   **ED** Mick Audsley
PROD Stephen Woolley, David Geffen
DIST Warner/Geffen

66 Strange and mesmerising. – *Elvis Mitchell, New York Times*

66 Pretty awful – a hodgepodge of lurid spectacle and stilted, arty talk. – *Owen Gleiberman, Entertainment Weekly*

† Christian Slater's role was originally to have been played by River Phoenix, but he died shortly before production started.

⚲ Elliot Goldenthal; Dante Ferretti

♟ Philippe Rousselot; Dante Ferretti

Ⓣ Sandy Powell (costume); Stan Winston, Michèle Burke, Jan Archibald (make up/hair)

'Every Wednesday, She meets once a week.'

Intimacy

DIR Patrice Chéreau
2000   120m   GB/France/Italy/Germany
[DVD]   ♫

☆ Mark Rylance (Jay), Kerry Fox (Claire), Timothy Spall (Andy), Alastair Galbraith (Victor), Philippe Calvario (Ian), Marianne Faithfull (Betty), Susannah Harker (Susan), Rebecca Palmer (Pam)

A failed musician has anonymous sex every Wednesday afternoon with a woman in London, but puts the arrangement at risk when he asks about her life.

Grim and uninsightful drama about a loveless affair, in which the notably explicit sex scenes are offered as a badge of integrity; everything else is too bleak to be realistic.

SCR Anne-Louise Trividic, Patrice Chéreau   **CIN** Eric Gautier   **MUS** Eric Neveux   **DES** Hayden Griffin
ED Francois Gedigier   **PROD** Patrick Cassavetti, Jacques Hinstin   **DIST** Pathé

66 Fine and intelligent performances. . .but they are adrift in a film replete with false notes about sex and the city. – *Peter Bradshaw, Guardian*

'In the Spring of 1956, in a quaint little town, a crime took place that shocked a nation . . . This is the true story.'

Intimate Relations   ★

SCR/DIR Philip Goodhew
1995   105m   GB/Canada
[DVD]

☆ Julie Walters (Marjorie Beasley), Rupert Graves (Harold Guppy), Matthew Walker (Stanley Beasley), Laura Sadler (Joyce Beasley), Holly Aird (Deirdre), Les Dennis (Maurice Guppy), Elizabeth McKechnie (Iris Guppy)

In the north of England of the 1950s, a young sailor takes a room as boarder in a family home, and finds he is the sexual target of both his landlady and her teenage daughter.

Darkly comic subversion of the notion that Britain's petty bourgeoisie are genteel, appropriate and dignified. Stylised and somewhat distanced from its characters, its salvation is Walters, playing a woman of ill-concealed raging passions.

CIN Andrés Garretón   **MUS** Lawrence Shragge
DES Caroline Greville-Morris   **ED** Pia di Ciaula
PROD Angela Hart, Lisa Hope, Jon Slan
DIST TCF/Intimate Relations/Chandlertown/Handmade/Boxer/Paragon

66 Maliciously satirises the sexual hypocrisy of the time. – *Tom Charity, Time Out*

'She confused him for a therapist and told him her deepest secrets. Now, two people who never should have met are discovering there's nothing more seductive than the truth.'

Intimate Strangers   ★★★

DIR *Patrice Leconte*
2004   104m   France
[DVD]

☆ *Fabrice Luchini* (William), *Sandrine Bonnaire* (Anna),

Michel Duchaussoy (Dr Monnier), Anne Brochet (Jeanne), Gilbert Melki (Marc)

A bored wife enters a tax consultant's office, mistaking him for a psychiatrist, and keeps seeing him even when she has learned her error.

Witty two-hander, one of this director's best, in which both actors revel in the comic possibilities of the misunderstanding, and the new vistas it opens in their characters' stale lives.

SCR *Jerome Tonnerre, Patrice Leconte* CIN *Eduardo Serra* MUS Pascal Esteve DES Ivan Maussion ED Joelle Hache PROD Alain Sarde

66 Establishes its mood of playful erotic suspense in the first 10 minutes and sustains its cat-and-mouse game between therapist and patient through variations that are by turns amusing, titillating and mildly scary. – *Stephen Holden, New York Times*

Into Great Silence ★

SCR/DIR Philip Groning
2005 169m Germany/Switzerland
DVD
☆ The monks of La Grande Chartreuse (Themselves)

A record of the daily routines of Carthusian monks in a Catholic monastery in the French Alps, who have taken a vow of silence.

The sense of an ascetic life in which time passes very slowly is admirably conveyed; its virtually silent soundtrack and deliberate pace induce an almost trance-like state. Still, the rigorous silent life of the monks rarely looks like a blessed existence.

CIN Philip Groning ED Philip Groning PROD Philip Groning, Michael Weber, Andres Pfaffli, Elda Guidinetti DIST Soda Pictures

66 I hesitate. . .to call In Great Silence one of the best films of the year. I prefer to think of it as the antidote to all of the others. – *A.O. Scott, New York Times*

'Where myth and magic walk the earth.'

Into the West ★

DIR Mike Newell
1992 97m Eire/GB/US
DVD ♫
☆ Gabriel Byrne (Papa Reilly), Ellen Barkin (Kathleen), Ciarán Fitzgerald (Ossie), Ruaidhri Conroy (Tito), David Kelly (Grandfather), Johnny Murphy (Tracker), Colm Meaney (Barreller), John Kavanagh (Hartnett), Brendan Gleeson (Inspector Bolger), Jim Norton (Superintendant O'Mara)

The two young sons of an Irish traveller flee for the hills like outlaws with a white stallion, which their eccentric grandfather had tried to keep copped up in a small council flat.

An ambitious attempt to wed two narrative strands – the treatment dished out by conventional society to travelling people, and a re-creation in modern terms of an ancient Irish myth. It only partly succeeds, but its good-hearted intentions partly mask its structural faults.

SCR Jim Sheridan, David Keating CIN Tom Sigel

MUS Patrick Doyle DES Jamie Leonard ED Peter Boyle PROD Jonathan Cavendish, Tim Palmer DIST Entertainment/Little Bird/Parallel/Majestic/Miramax/Film Four/Newcomm

66 Newell's achievement is to give the horse a snorting, clattering physical presence to match the weight of myth and metaphor it carries. – *Clair Monk, Sight & Sound*

Into the Wild (new) ★★

SCR/DIR Sean Penn
2007 147m US
DVD ♫
☆ Emile Hirsch (Christopher McCandless), Marcia Gay Harden (Billie McCandless), William Hurt (Walt McCandless), Jena Malone (Carine McCandless), Catherine Keener (Jan Burres), Vince Vaughan (Wayne Westerberger), Kristen Stewart (Tracy), *Hal Holbrook* (Ron Franz), Brian Dierker (Rainey), Zach Galifianakis (Kevin)

A college graduate turned rootless drifter embarks on a peripatetic journey across America that ultimately finds him alone in Alaska.

Poignant, episodic portrait of a real-life drop-out that is perhaps too taken with its subject; for the film to work one has to find him fascinating, rather than merely foolish and narcissistic.

CIN Eric Gautier MUS Michael Brook, Kaki King, Eddie Vedder DES Derek Hill ED Jay Cassidy PROD Sean Penn, Art Linson, Bill Pohlad DIST Paramount

66 Penn's most assured and affecting work yet as director and screenwriter. – *Peter Travers, Rolling Stone*

66 Like most labours of love it's insufferably self-indulgent and long-winded. – *Christopher Tookey, Daily Mail*

⚖ Hal Holbrook (supporting actor); Jay Cassidy (editing)

Intolerance ★★★★

SCR/DIR *D. W. Griffith*
1916 115m US
DVD
☆ Mae Marsh (The Dear One), Lillian Gish (Woman Who Rocks the Cradle/Eternal Mother), Constance Talmadge (Marguerite de Valois/The Mountain Girl), Robert Harron (The Boy), Elmo Lincoln (The Mighty Man of Valour), Eugene Pallette (Prosper Latour)

Four stories – including Belshazzar's feast and the massacre of St Bartholomew – of man's inhumanity through the ages, intercut and linked by the image of a mother and her baby: 'out of the cradle, endlessly rocking'.

A massive enterprise of which audiences at the time and after were quite intolerant. Hard to take in parts, it rises to a fine climax as all the stories come to a head (including a modern one with a race between a car and train), and has been called 'the only film fugue'. At the time, by far the most expensive film ever made, and it showed: the creation of the gigantic Babylon set astounded audiences, and the huge crowds of extras marshalled for scenes in Judea spoke of a film-maker with money to burn. Cinema's first true epic.

CIN *Billy Bitzer, Karl Brown* ED Rose Smith, James Smith DIST D. W. Griffith

DVD Available on DVD ☆ Cast in order 66 Critics' Quotes ⚖ Academy Award ♛ BAFTA
♫ Soundtrack on CD of importance † Points of interest ⚖ Academy Award nomination ♛ BAFTA nomination

321

66 A mad, brilliant, silly extravaganza. Perhaps the greatest movie ever made. In it one can see the source of most of the major traditions of the screen: the methods of Eisenstein and von Stroheim, the Germans and the Scandinavians, and, when it's bad, de Mille. – *New Yorker, 1980*

'Do Not Trust Anyone. Do Not Show Emotion. Do Not Fall Asleep'

The Invasion (new)   ★

DIR Oliver Hirschbiegel
2007   99m   US
♬

☆ Nicole Kidman (Carol Bennell), Daniel Craig (Dr. Ben Driscoll), Jeremy Northam (Tucker Kaufman), Jackson Bond (Oliver), Jeffrey Wright (Dr. Stephen Galeano), Veronica Cartwright (Wendy Lenk)

When a terrifying alien infection sweeps the earth, a Washington psychiatrist tries desperately to find a cure.

Boring, unconvincing and troubled update of Invasion of the Body Snatchers that turns the classic extra-terrestrial takeover tale into predictable Hollywood schlock.

SCR David Kajganich   CIN Rainer Klausmann
MUS John Ottman   DES Jack Fisk   ED Hans Funck, Joel Negron   PROD Joel Silver   DIST Warner Bros
66 An involving sci-fi action-thriller, probably longer on chase sequences than the original director wanted and shorter on the 'ick' factor than the studio wanted. – *Kirk Honeycutt – The Hollywood Reporter*
† After director Hirschbiegel delivered his cut of the film, another director, James Teigue, was drafted in to shoot new material, written by the Wachowski brothers of Matrix fame.

'The world as they knew it was slipping away from them. Time was running out for the human race. And there was nothing to hold on to – except each other!'

Invasion of the Body Snatchers   ★★★★

DIR Don Siegel
1955   80m   US
DVD

☆ *Kevin McCarthy* (Miles Bennel), *Dana Wynter* (Becky Driscoll), Larry Gates (Dr. Dan Kauffmann), *King Donovan* (Jack), Carolyn Jones (Theodora), Virginia Christine (Wilma Lentz), Sam Peckinpah (Charlie Buckholtz)

A small Californian town is imperceptibly taken over by an alien force: pods from outer space, who capture its citizens, and replace them with motionless doubles.

Persuasive, thoroughly satisfying, low-budget science fiction, put across with subtlety and intelligence in every department. Like many sci-fi films of this era, it has been read as an allegory; the pod people may well be communists, or alternatively bigoted anti-Red propagandists. The film stands tall without such interpretation.

SCR Daniel Mainwaring   CIN Ellsworth Fredericks

MUS Carmen Dragon   ED Robert S. Eisen   DIST Allied Artists/Walter Wanger
† The story was re-made in 1979 and again in 2007; both versions were judged inferior to the original.

The Ipcress File   ★★★

DIR Sidney J. Furie
1965   109m   GB

☆ *Michael Caine*, Nigel Green, Guy Doleman, Sue Lloyd, Gordon Jackson

A Cockney intelligence agent tracks down a missing scientist and finds that one of his own superiors is a spy.

A calculated attempt to launch an Everyman James Bond, a man to whom ordinary audiences could easily relate, works rather well, courtesy of Caine's droll, matter-of-fact delivery. The plot is too convoluted for its own good, but this heralded the start of a successful franchise with an amiable hero. It found particular favour in Britain, and Caine was happy to return repeatedly.

SCR Bill Canaway, James Doran   CIN *Otto Heller*
MUS *John Barry*   PROD Harry Saltzman
DIST Rank/Steven/Lowndes

† Four sequels appeared, starring Caine as 'Harry Palmer' (never named in Deighton's books): Funeral in Berlin, Billion Dollar Brain, Bullet to Beijing and Midnight in Saint Petersburg.

🅣 British film; Ken Adam (art direction); Otto Heller (cinematography)

Iraq In Fragments   ★★

DIR James Longley
2007   94m   US
DVD

☆ Mohammed Haithem, Suleiman Mahmoud

A three-part story about an Iraqi boy of 11 whose anti-Saddam father is missing, presumed dead; a portrait of an Islamic cleric's followers; and young Kurds eager for independence.

A calm condemnation of the West's blunders in Iraq, and their plans for reconstruction. Unusually, the voices and opinions heard are those of Iraqis, and their sense of being oppressed is genuine. An intimate film that gets up close to its subjects and explains them creditably.

CIN James Longley   MUS James Longley   ED Billy McMillan, James Longley, Fiona Otway   PROD John Sinno, James Longley   DIST ICA
66 This one demands to be seen. – *Kenneth Turan, Los Angeles Times*
⚖ documentary

Irina Palm (new)

DIR Sam Garbarski
2007   103m
Belgium/Germany/Luxembourg/UK/France
DVD

☆ Marianne Faithfull (Maggie), Miki Manojlovic (Miki), Kevin Bishop (Tom), Siobhan Hewlett (Sarah), Dorka Gryllus (Luisa), Jenny Agutter (Jane), Corey Burke (Ollie)

A middle-aged woman raises money for her grandson's life-saving operation by becoming a sex worker.

Ponderous drama full of clunky dialogue, built around a central performance that borders on somnolence. Given its risqué subject matter, the film's treatment of masturbation is laughably coy.

SCR Martin Herron, Philippe Blasband CIN Christophe Beaucarne MUS Ghinzu DES Veronique Sacrez ED Ludo Troch PROD Sebastien Delloye DIST Soda Pictures

MAGGIE: 'He's dying. I'm wanking. It's a mess.'

66 A sentimental film with a raunchy premise. – *Kenneth Turan, Los Angeles Times*

66 A collector's item. . . you won't often see dramas in which a Sixties icon-turned-grandmother earns fistfuls of cash by dealing out the best hand shandies in Soho. – *Anthony Quinn, Independent*

'Her Greatest Talent Was For Life.'

Iris ★★

DIR Richard Eyre
2001 91m GB/US
DVD ♫

☆ *Judi Dench* (Iris Murdoch), *Jim Broadbent* (John Bayley), *Kate Winslet* (Young Iris), Hugh Bonneville (Young John), Penelope Wilton (Janet Stone), Juliet Aubrey (Younger Janet), Samuel West (Young Maurice), Timothy West (Older Maurice), Eleanor Bron (College Principal), Joan Bakewell (TV Presenter)

The novelist and philosopher Iris Murdoch meets her husband, John Bayley, in their student days, and in later life is diagnosed with Alzheimer's.

Not a biopic but a love story, and one which betrays little to no interest in Murdoch's literary talent or her husband's eminence as an academic; despite Dench's amazing ability to suggest a great mind aware of its own gradual erosion, it more properly belongs on TV.

SCR Richard Eyre, Charles Wood CIN Roger Pratt MUS James Horner DES Gemma Jackson ED Martin Walsh PROD Robert Fox, Scott Rudin DIST Buena Vista

66 Touching, if frustrating: it whets an appetite for the articulate, mature Murdoch who must exist somewhere between the 'bonking' and 'bonkers' phases. – *Peter Bradshaw, Guardian*

🏆 Jim Broadbent (supporting actor)
🏅 Judi Dench (leading actress); Kate Winslet (supporting actress)
🏆 Judi Dench (leading actress)
🏅 British film; Hugh Bonneville (supporting actor); Jim Broadbent (supporting actor); Kate Winslet (supporting actress); Richard Eyre, Charles Wood (adapted screenplay)

Irma Vep ★★

SCR/DIR Olivier Assayas
1996 99m France
DVD

☆ Maggie Cheung (Herself), Jean-Pierre Leaud (René Vidal), Nathalie Richard (Zoé), Antoine Basler (Journalist), Nathalie Boutefeu (Laure), Bulle Ogier (Mireille), Lou Castel (José Mirano), Arsinee Khanjian (L'américaine)

A pretentious veteran of the French New Wave plans to remake Louis Feuillade's silent film Les Vampires, and asks a leading lady of Hong Kong cinema to star.

Apparently casual satire of art-house filmmaking, but one with sly points to make about commerce, globalisation and cinema's relationship to its past.

CIN *Eric Gautier* ED Luc Barnier PROD Georges Benayoun DIST ICA/Dacia

66 Creepy and hip, fast moving and provocative. – *Jonathan Rosenbaum, Chicago Reader*

'It came from outer space'

The Iron Giant ★★★

DIR *Brad Bird*
1999 86m US
DVD ♫

☆ voices of: Jennifer Aniston, Eli Marienthal, Harry Connick Jnr, Vin Diesel, Christopher McDonald, James Gammon, Cloris Leachman, John Mahoney, M. Emmet Walsh

America, the 1950s: a young boy discovers a giant robot, and tries to defend it from suspicious government agencies.

Bright, fast and emotionally involving animation that boasts superb characterisation and design, and takes real care to preserve the pacifist message of Ted Hughes' source.

SCR *Tim McCanlies* CIN Steven Wilzbach MUS Michael Kamen DES Mark Whiting ED Darren T. Holmes PROD Allison Abbate, Des McAnuff DIST Warner

66 Neither panders to children nor sneers at them, and it beautifully, lucidly captures the giddy adventurousness of childhood. – *Cody Clark, Mr. Showbiz*

66 Both a step back and a step forward from the trends of modern animation, it feels like a classic even though it's just out of the box. – *Kenneth Turan, Los Angeles Times*

Iron Man (new) ★

DIR Jon Favreau
2008 125m US
♫

☆ Robert Downey Jnr (Tony Stark), Terrence Howard (Col. James 'Rhodey' Rhodes), Jeff Bridges (Obadiah Stane), Gwyneth Paltrow (Pepper Potts), Shaun Toub (Yinsen), Leslie Bibb (Christine Everhart), Faran Tahir (Raza)

A billionaire weapons manufacturer builds a flying metal suit to escape the terrorists who have taken him hostage in Afghanistan. Back in America, he uses the armour to fight crime.

Inventive, exciting vehicle for a lesser-known comic book character that gets much of its energy from its mercurial star. The first and better half deals with the hero's origins; what follows suffers from the lack of a suitable antagonist.

SCR Mark Fergus, Hawk Ostby, Art Marcum, Matt Holloway CIN Matthew Libatique MUS Ramin Djawadi DES J. Michael Riva ED Dan Lebental PROD Avi Arad, Kevin Feige DIST Paramount

---

66 A roaring fairground ride. . .Favreau has done a magnificent job. – *James Christopher, The Times*

66 "An unusually good superhero picture." – *A.O. Scott, New York Times*

† After the end-credit scroll, Samuel L. Jackson makes a cameo appearance as Marvel character Nick Fury.

Ironweed

DIR Hector Babenco
1987   143m   US
DVD

☆ Jack Nicholson (Francis Phelan), Meryl Streep (Helen Archer), Carroll Baker (Annie Phelan), Michael O'Keefe (Billy Phelan), Diane Venora (Margaret 'Peg' Phelan), Tom Waits (Rudy)

During America's Depression, an alcoholic drifter, haunted by the death of his baby son, returns to his home town. A sympathetic bag lady offers him the hope of redemption.

Grim, relentlessly downbeat, and true to the spirit of Kennedy's Pulitzer-winning novel. One sees why the actors might have relished their participation, but it's a tough proposition for audiences to endure.

SCR William Kennedy   CIN Lauro Escorel   MUS John Morris   DES Jeannine C. Oppewall   ED Anne Goursaud   PROD Marcia Nasatir, Keith Barish   DIST Taft Entertainment/Keith Barish/Home Box Office

66 Actors are said to like to play drunks, because it gives them an excuse for overacting. But there is not much visible "acting" in this movie; the actors are too good for that. – *Roger Ebert, Chicago Sun-Times*

⚊ Jack Nicholson (leading actor); Meryl Streep (leading actress)

'Time destroys everything.'

Irreversible

SCR/DIR Gaspar Noé
2002   97m   France
DVD   ♫

☆ Monica Bellucci (Alex), Vincent Cassel (Marcus), Albert Dupontel (Pierre), Philippe Nahon (Philippe), Jo Prestia (Le Ténia)

After his girlfriend is savagely raped in a Paris underpass, a teacher and his friend hunt the culprit down in a gay nightclub, but beat the wrong man to death.

Told backwards in the manner of Memento or Pinter's Betrayal, the movie aims to make its own violence virtually unendurable, and pretty much succeeds; beyond the fatuous idea that 'time destroys everything', it is an intellectual wasteland, as well as obscenely homophobic, pretentious and meretricious.

CIN Gaspar Noé, Benoît Debie   MUS Thomas Bangalter   DES Alain Juteau   ED Gaspar Noé   PROD Christophe Rossignon   DIST Metro Tartan

66 A genuine outlaw work of art. – *Stephen Hunter, Washington Post*

66 So formally and stylistically aggressive that this aspect overpowers what it has to say, which isn't much. – *Jonathan Rosenbaum, Chicago Reader*

'A Cop. A Waitress. A Lottery Ticket.'

It Could Happen to You   ★

DIR Andrew Bergman
1994   101m   US
DVD   ♫

☆ Nicolas Cage (Charlie Lang), Bridget Fonda (Yvonne Biasi), Wendell Pierce (Bo Williams), Rosie Perez (Muriel Lang), Isaac Hayes (Angel Dupree), Seymour Cassel (Jack Gross), Victor Rojas (Jesu), Red Buttons (Walter Zakuto)

When a cop gives a waitress half a lottery ticket in lieu of a tip, he promises her half his winnings – and sticks to it, even when her share turns out to be $2 million.

Capraesque comedy, all the more notable for being based on a true story. Light-weight to be sure, but ably directed by Bergman – and Cage has certainly never been more charming.

SCR Jane Anderson   CIN Caleb Deschanel   MUS Carter Burwell, Joe Mulherin   DES Bill Groom   ED Barry Malkin   PROD Mike Lobell   DIST Columbia TriStar/Adelson/Baumgarten/Lobell/Bergman

66 The original title, "Cop Gives Waitress $2 Million Tip," sums up the plot. – *Kenneth C. Davis, New York Times*

66 The movie is not so much about romance as about good-heartedness, which is a rarer quality, and not so selfish. – *Roger Ebert, Chicago Sun-Times*

'Together For The First Time!'

It Happened One Night   ★★★★

DIR *Frank Capra*
1934   105m   US
DVD

☆ *Clark Gable* (Peter Warne), *Claudette Colbert* (Ellie Andrews), Walter Connolly (Alexander Andrews), Roscoe Karns (Oscar Shapeley), Alan Hale (Danker), Ward Bond (Bus Driver), Jameson Thomas (King Westley), Arthur Hoyt (Zeke)

A runaway heiress falls in love with the reporter who is chasing her across America.

Highly successful and influential romance, the first to use buses and motels as background and still come up sparkling. The palpable chemistry between Gable and Colbert set the template for romantic comedies and screwball comedies in the years that followed.

SCR *Robert Riskin*   CIN Joseph Walker   ED Gene Havlick   PROD Frank Capra   DIST Columbia

66 A laughing hit that will mean important coin. – *Variety*

66 One of the most entertaining films that has ever been offered to the public. – *Observer*

† Remade 1956 (badly) as You Can't Run Away From It.
† Robert Montgomery was the first choice for the Gable role, but he refused it because he had been on a bus in Fugitive Lovers. The Colbert role was first offered to Myrna Loy, Margaret Sullavan and Constance Bennett. Colbert was lured by a 40,000-dollar fee.

⚊ picture; Clark Gable (leading actor); Claudette Colbert (leading actress); Frank Capra (direction); Robert Riskin (adapted screenplay)

It's a Gift ★★★

DIR Norman Z. McLeod
1934 73m US

☆ *W. C. Fields*, Kathleen Howard, Jean Rouverol, Julian Madison, Tommy Bupp, Baby LeRoy

A general store proprietor buys an orange ranch by mail and transports his family to California.

Roughly assembled comedy of disasters which happens to show the star more in cracking form; though the expected climax is lacking, Fields never made a better movie.

SCR Jack Cunningham   CIN Henry Sharp
PROD William Le Baron   DIST Paramount

66 An enormously amusing succession of rough and ready gags. – *Literary Digest*

† This was a reworking of Fields's 1926 silent film It's the Old Army Game.

It's a Wonderful Life ★★★★

DIR *Frank Capra*
1946 129m US
DVD ♫

☆ *James Stewart* (George Bailey), *Henry Travers* (Clarence), Donna Reed (Mary Hatch), Lionel Barrymore (Mr. Potter), Thomas Mitchell (Uncle Billy), Beulah Bondi (Mrs. Bailey), Frank Faylen (Ernie), Ward Bond (Bert), Gloria Grahame (Violet Bick), H. B. Warner (Mr. Gower), Frank Albertson (Sam Wainwright), Samuel S. Hinds (Pa Bailey), Mary Treen (Cousin Tilly)

A man is prevented from committing suicide by an elderly angel, who takes him back through his life to show him what good he has done.

Superbly assembled small-town comedy drama in a fantasy framework; arguably Capra's best and most typical work, it is certainly his most beloved. A perennial favourite, it is regularly screened on TV over the Christmas season.

SCR *Frances Goodrich, Albert Hackett, Frank Capra*
CIN *Joseph Walker, Joseph Biroc*   MUS Dimitri Tiomkin
ED William Hornbeck   PROD Frank Capra
DIST RKO/Liberty Films

CLARENCE (HENRY TRAVERS): Every time you hear a bell ring, it means that some angel's just got his wings.

66 One of the most efficient sentimental pieces since A Christmas Carol. – *James Agee*

66 The most brilliantly made motion picture of the 1940s, so assured, so dazzling in its use of screen narrative. – *Charles Higham*

↓ picture; James Stewart (leading actor); Frank Capra (direction); editing

It's Winter ★★

SCR/DIR Rafi Pitts
2006 83m Iran
DVD

☆ Mitra Hadjar (Khatoun), Ali Nicksolat (Marhab), Saeed Orkani (Ali Reza), Hashem Abdi (Mokhtar)

In Tehran, Mokhtar lives in a house by the railway. He leaves his young wife Khatoun and small daughter to seek work abroad. His family hears no word from him. Khatoun meets up with a young mechanic who declares his love for her, and she must make a choice for her daughter's future

Director Pitts depicts everyday struggles and absences with a poetic realism, coaxing amazing performances from his mainly non-professional cast.

CIN Mohammad Davoodi   MUS Hossein Alizadeh, Mohammad Reza Shajarian   DES Malak D. Khazai
PROD Mohammad Mehdi Dadgoo   DIST Artificial Eye

'There's a fine line between success and excess.'

Ivansxtc ★★★

DIR *Bernard Rose*
2000 93m US
DVD

☆ *Danny Huston* (Ivan Beckman), *Peter Weller* (Don West), Lisa Enos (Charlotte White), Joanne Duckman (Marcia Beckman), Angela Featherstone (Amanda Hill), Caroleen Feeney (Rosemary Kramer), Valeria Golino (Constanza Vero), James Merendino (Danny McTeague)

The last days of a high-flying Hollywood agent, who discovers he has terminal lung cancer but conceals the fact from his friends and colleagues.

Startlingly bleak Hollywood satire in which mortality is the ultimate taboo. Adapted from Tolstoy's Death of Ivan Ilyich and loosely based on the story of real-life agent Jay Moloney, the film's harshly day-lit, low-budget aesthetic pulls no punches, and Huston nails the boiling despair behind this character's hucksterish charisma.

SCR Bernard Rose, Lisa Enos   CIN Bernard Rose, Ron Forsythe   MUS Wagner   ED Bernard Rose   PROD Lisa Enos   DIST Metro Tartan

66 A tenacious demonstration of death as the great equaliser. – *Dennis Lim, Village Voice*

66 One wonders how much the world needs this reminder of Tinseltown turpitude. – *Anthony Quinn, Independent*

I've Heard the Mermaids Singing ★

SCR/DIR Patricia Rozema
1987 81m Canada

☆ Sheila McCarthy (Polly Vandersma), Ann-Marie MacDonald (Mary Joseph), John Evans (Warren), Brenda Kamino (Waitress), Richard Monette (Clive)

A scatter-brained woman who works in a chic art gallery falls for its owner.

Rozema's first feature of note is a slight but delightful romantic story that misses a few opportunities to show a little humour.

CIN Douglas Koch   MUS Mark Korven   ED Patricia Rozema   PROD Patricia Rozema, Alexandra Raffe
DIST Contemporary/Electric/Ontario Arts Council/Canada Council/National Film Board/Ontario Film Development Corp/Telefilm Canada

DVD Available on DVD   ☆ Cast in order   66 Critics' Quotes   ↓ Academy Award   ⬥ BAFTA
♫ Soundtrack on CD   of importance   † Points of interest   ↓ Academy Award nomination   ⬥ BAFTA nomination

325

'Terror has a new name.'

The Jacket

DIR John Maybury
2004   103m   US/Germany/Scotland
DVD

☆ Adrien Brody (Jack Starks), Keira Knightley (Jackie), Kris Kristofferson (Dr. Becker), Jennifer Jason Leigh (Dr. Lorenson), Kelly Lynch (Jean), Brad Renfro (Stranger), Daniel Craig (Mackenzie)

After being shot in the head during the first Gulf War, an amnesiac former soldier is accused of a crime he did not commit, and travels in time to unravel the mystery.

A strange, shocking mix of memory tricks, shifting chronology and a yearning to affect apparently immutable events. A striking, idiosyncratic piece of film-making, though its continual dipping in and out of genres makes it too dizzying to follow easily.

SCR Massy Tadjedin   **CIN** Peter Deming   **MUS** Brian Eno   **DES** Alan MacDonald   **ED** Emma Hickox **PROD** Peter Guber, George Clooney, Steven Soderbergh **DIST** Warner

66 The result is what you might call a mass-audience art film. It doesn't entirely succeed, but it's certainly a change from today's standard mysteries and horror movies. – *David Sterritt, Christian Science Monitor*

66 A confused attempt at headiness that feels like a poor man's Memento. – *Claudia Puig, USA Today*

'This Christmas, Santa's Got A Brand New Bag.'

Jackie Brown   ★★

SCR/DIR Quentin Tarantino
1997   154m   US
DVD   ♫

☆ *Pam Grier* (Jackie Brown), Samuel L. Jackson (Ordell Robbie), *Robert Forster* (Max Cherry), Bridget Fonda (Melanie Ralston), Michael Keaton (Ray Nicolette), Robert de Niro (Louis Gara), Michael Bowen (Mark Dargus), Chris Tucker (Beaumont Livingston)

A flight attendant becomes a cash courier for a gun-runner, and tries to outwit both sides of the law with the help of a bail bondsman.

Engaging if baggy caper, in which Tarantino graduates beyond the snappier tricks of his first two films to give the characters a more lived-in feel. It's a shame he never quite gets the plot cooking.

CIN Guillermo Navarro   **DES** David Wasco   **ED** Sally Menke   **PROD** Lawrence Bender   **DIST** Buena Vista/Miramax/A Band Apart

66 Filled with funny, gritty Tarantino lowlife gab and a respectable body count, but what is most striking is the film's gallantry and sweetness. – *David Ansen, Newsweek*

66 Becomes a who-cares proposition. – *Mick LaSalle, San Francisco Chronicle*

† The film was criticised by Spike Lee on its release for its over-use of the 'n' word.

⚱ Robert Forster (supporting actor)

'Three buddies in Vietnam. Two survived. Only one is really alive.'

Jacknife   ★

DIR David Jones
1989   102m   US
DVD

☆ Robert De Niro (Joseph 'Jacknife' Megessey), Ed Harris (David 'High School' Flannigan), Kathy Baker (Martha Flannigan), Charles Dutton (Jake, Veteran Encounter Group Leader), Elizabeth Franz (Pru Buckman), Tom Isbell (Bobby 'Red Sox' Buckman), Loudon Wainwright III (Ferretti), Sloane Shelton (Shirley), Ivan Brogger (Depot Mechanic)

A Vietnam veteran helps an old army buddy through his post-traumatic stress, and starts up an affair with his sister.

Dialogue-heavy but intriguing drama; the main pleasure is seeing De Niro and Harris, close to their best, in two-hander scenes.

SCR Stephen Metcalfe   **CIN** Brian West   **MUS** Bruce Broughton   **DES** Edward Pisoni   **ED** John Bloom **PROD** Robert Schaffel, Carol Baum   **DIST** Vestron/Kings Road Entertainment

66 This is not a movie of plot, it's a movie of character. It's about how these three people create a triangle of pain and possible healing. – *Roger Ebert, Chicago Sun-Times*

Jacquot de Nantes   ★

SCR/DIR *Agnès Varda*
1991   118m   France
☆ Philippe Maron (Jacquot 1), Edouard Joubeaud (Jacquot 2), Laurent Monnier (Jacquot 3), Brigitte de Villepoix (Marilou), Daniel Dublet (Raymond), Guillaume Navaud (Cousin Joel)

A portrait of film-maker Jacques Demy, by his wife Agnès Varda, part drama, part documentary, and including filmed interviews with him and excerpts from his films. Three actors play the young Demy at various stages.

Varda's fondness for Demy shines through this affecting biopic, yet it is effective in charting the stirrings of his life-long passion for film.

CIN Patrick Blossier, Agnes Godard, Georges Strouve MUS Joanna Bruzdowicz ED Marie-Josee Audiard PROD Agnes Varda, Perrine Baudin, Danielle Vaugon, DIST Cine-Tamaris/Canal/La Sept/La Sofiarp

Jailhouse Rock ★★

DIR Richard Thorpe
1957 96m US
DVD

☆ Elvis Presley, Judy Tyler, Mickey Shaughnessy, Vaughn Taylor, Dean Jones

An ex-convict becomes a pop star.

It's faint praise, but this is the best film in which Elvis Presley starred, the only one that does justice to his younger self in the early days of rock'n'roll when his quiff, his wiggling hips and his curled-lip sneer made him an attractive, rebellious idol. The choreography of the title song here is inventive and amusing.

SCR Guy Trosper CIN Robert Bronner PROD Pandro S. Berman DIST MGM

'When all hope was lost, he invented it.'

Jakob the Liar ★

DIR Peter Kassovitz
1999 120m US/ Germany
DVD

☆ Robin Williams (Jakob Heym), Alan Arkin (Frankfurter), Bob Balaban (Kowalsky), Hannah Taylor Gordon (Lina), Michael Jeter (Avron), Armin Mueller-Stahl (Kirschbaum), Liev Schreiber (Mischa), Nina Siemaszko (Rosa), Mathieu Kassovitz (Herschel), Justus von Dohnanyi (Preuss), Mark Margolis (Fajngold), Gregg Bello (Blumenthal)

In the Warsaw ghetto, a Jewish café owner boosts morale by claiming he owns a radio and has heard news of advances against the Nazis by Russian troops.

Williams's worst and most sentimental instincts have been reined in somewhat for this well-intentioned drama, which has its genuinely poignant moments.

SCR Peter Kassovitz, Didier Decoin CIN Elemer Ragalyi MUS Edward Shearmur DES Luciana Arrighi ED Claire Simpson PROD Marsha Garces Williams, Steven Haft DIST Columbia

66 A markedly better picture than Roberto Benigni's far more sentimental Oscar collector (Life Is Beautiful). – *Todd McCarthy, Variety*

James and the Giant Peach ★★

DIR Henry Selick
1996 79m US/GB
DVD ♫

☆ Paul Terry (James), Joanna Lumley (Aunt Spiker), Miriam Margolyes (Aunt Sponge/The Glowworm (voice)), Pete Postlethwaite (Old Man), the voices of: Simon Callow, Richard Dreyfuss, Jane Leeves, Susan Sarandon, David Thewlis

A sad orphan escapes his wicked aunts by travelling across the Atlantic inside a giant peach, with insects for company.

Dazzlingly inventive animated fantasy using the same stop-motion technique as The Nightmare Before Christmas, though it softens Dahl's bite.

SCR Karey Kirkpatrick, Jonathan Roberts, Steve Bloom CIN Pete Kozachik, Hiro Narita MUS Randy Newman DES Harley Jessup ED Stan Webb PROD Denise di Novi, Tim Burton DIST Guild/Disney/Allied Filmmakers

66 The sense of random surrealism is intact. . .a veritable nectarine of a movie. – *Neil Norman, Evening Standard*
☊ Randy Newman

'A Film Where Women Eat Men And Men Eat Ham.'

Jamón Jamón ★

DIR Bigas Luna
1992 95m Spain
DVD

☆ Stefania Sandrelli (Conchita), Anna Galiena (Carmen), Juan Diego (Manuel), Penélope Cruz (Silvia), Javier Bardem (Raul), Jordi Molla (Jose Luis)

The mother of an underwear executive hires a gigolo to seduce her son's lower-class fiancée.

Testosterone-crazed sex farce, making up in ludicrous raunch what it lacks for subtlety.

SCR Cuca Canals, Bigas Luna, Quim Monzó CIN José Luis Alcaine MUS Nicola Piovani DES Pep Olive, Gloria Martí-Palanqués ED Teresa Font PROD Andrés Vicente Gómez DIST Metro Tartan/Lolafilms/Ovideo/Sogepaq

66 Chiefly a tribute to throbbing Latin manhood. – *Rita Kempley, Washington Post*

'You don't have to know the books to be in the club.'

The Jane Austen Book Club (new)

SCR/DIR Robin Swicord
2007 105m US
DVD

☆ Kathy Baker (Bernadette), Maria Bello (Jocelyn), Marc Blucas (Dean), Emily Blunt (Prudie), Amy Brenneman (Sylvia), Hugh Dancy (Grigg), Maggie Grace (Allegra), Jimmy Smits (Daniel), Kevin Zegers (Trey), Lynn Redgrave (Sky)

Six Californians who form a book group dedicated to the English writer find their own lives beginning to resemble her romantic fictions.

Blandly inoffensive chick flick with a good-looking cast; nevertheless, one hopes this marks the end of the craze for adapting Austen's works.

CIN John Toon MUS Aaron Zigman DES Rusty Smith ED Maryann Brandon PROD John Calley, Julie Lynn, Diana Napper DIST Sony Pictures

66 Perfectly pleasant, perfectly undistinguished. – *Ella Taylor, Village Voice*

66 A twittering soap opera. – *Nigel Andrews, Financial Times*

J

Japanese Story ★★

DIR *Sue Brooks*

2003　105m　Australia/GB

DVD ♫

☆ *Toni Collette* (Sandy Edwards), Gotaro Tsunashima (Hiromitsu Tachibana), Matthew Dyktynski (Bill Baird), Lynette Curran (Mum), Yumiko Tanaka (Yukiko Tachibana)

An Australian geologist escorts an arrogant Japanese businessman on a field trip into the outback.

Impressive drama of different hues: first it's a culture-clash love story, then a portrait of bereavement and crisis. Collette handles the transition quite brilliantly.

SCR *Alison Tilson*　CIN Ian Baker　MUS Elizabeth Drake
DES Paddy Reardon　ED Jill Bilcock　PROD Sue Maslin

❝ Collette has never been better. – *Philip French, Observer*

'Welcome To The Suck.'

Jarhead ★

DIR Sam Mendes

2005　125m　Germany/US/GB

DVD ♫

☆ Jake Gyllenhaal (Swoff), Peter Sarsgaard (Troy), Lucas Black (Kruger), Brian Geraghty (Fergus), Jacob Vargas (Cortez), Chris Cooper (Lt. Col. Kazinski), Dennis Haysbert (Major Lincoln), Jamie Foxx (Staff Sgt. Sykes)

Marines in the first Gulf War wait for the fighting to start.

A tedious, inert film about the tedium and inertia of war, from a director who fawns over the iconography of crew-cut American soldiers at leisure; at least it looks good.

SCR William Broyles Jnr　CIN *Roger Deakins*
MUS Thomas Newman　DES Dennis Gassner
ED Walter Murch　PROD Douglas Wick, Lucy Fisher
DIST Universal

❝ Feels empty and tentative. – *Kirk Honeycutt, Hollywood Reporter*

❝ Too much is built on anticipation and aftermath, with nothing in the middle. – *Anthony Quinn, Independent*

Jaws ★★

DIR *Steven Spielberg*

1975　125m　US

DVD ♫

☆ *Robert Shaw, Roy Scheider, Richard Dreyfuss*, Lorraine Gary, Murray Hamilton, Carl Gottlieb

A man-eating shark causes havoc off the Long Island coast.

In the exploitation-hungry 1970s this film took more money than any other. In itself, despite genuinely suspenseful and frightening sequences, it is a slackly narrated and sometimes flatly handled thriller with an over-abundance of dialogue and, when it finally appears, a pretty unconvincing monster. But it caught the public imagination and turned the film industry on its head.

SCR Peter Benchley, Carl Gottlieb　CIN Bill Butler

MUS *John Williams*　ED Verna Fields　PROD William S. Gilmore Jnr　DIST Universal/Zanuck-Brown

❝ A mind-numbing repast for sense-sated gluttons. Shark stew for the stupefied. – *William S. Pechter*

❝ The opening sequences have few parallels in modern cinema; like the shower scene in Psycho they will haunt a whole generation. – *Les Keyser, Hollywood in the Seventies*

⚑ John Williams; Verna Fields; sound
⚐ picture
🅣 John Williams

'New songs and old favourites sung by Mr Jolson during the action of the story on the Vitaphone!'

The Jazz Singer ★★★★

DIR *Alan Crosland*

1927　89m　US

♫

☆ *Al Jolson* (Jakie Rabinowitz/Jack Robin), May McAvoy (Mary Dale), Warner Oland (Cantor Rabinowitz), Eugenie Besserer (Sara Rabinowitz), Otto Lederer (Moishe Yudelson)

A cantor's son, torn between the stage and the synagogue, chooses the secular path with success.

A sentimental tear-jerker that made history as the first talking picture. In fact, it's the singing rather than the talking that one remembers: Jolson performing My Mammy and Toot Toot Tootsie in his unbridled manner. How one reacts to the film largely depends on one's feelings for Jolson; either way, it's fascinating.

SCR Alfred A. Cohn　CIN Hal Mohr　ED Harold McCord
DIST Warner

JACK: You ain't heard nothin' yet!

❝ A beautiful period piece, extravagantly sentimental . . . yet entirely compelling in its own conviction. – *NFT, 1969*

❝ The Jazz Singer definitely establishes the fact that talking pictures are imminent. Everyone in Hollywood can rise up and declare that they are not, and it will not alter the fact. If I were an actor with a squeaky voice I would worry. – *Welford Beaton, The Film Spectator*

† The film was re-made twice, starring Danny Thomas in 1952 and Neil Diamond in 1980.
† 'Blue Skies'; 'Mother I Still Have You'; 'My Mammy'; 'Toot Toot Tootsie Goodbye'; 'Dirty Hands Dirty Face'

⚑ Special Award to Warner for producing 'the pioneer outstanding talking picture'
⚐ Alfred A. Cohn (adapted screenplay)

Jean de Florette ★★★

DIR *Claude Berri*

1986　121m　France

DVD ♫

☆ *Yves Montand* (Cesar Soubeyran/"Le Papet"), *Gérard Depardieu* (Jean de Florette/Cadoret), Daniel Auteuil (Ugolin Soubeyran/"Galignette"), Elisabeth Depardieu (Aimee Cadoret)

Elemental story of feuding over water supplies in rural France in the 20s.

Stunning performances and detailed, gorgeously photographed depiction of Provençal farming life made it a wild success not only in France, but in many other countries too.

SCR Claude Berri, Gérard Brach   CIN *Bruno Nuytten*
MUS Jean-Claude Petit   DES Bernard Vezat   ED Arlette
Langmann, Herve de Luze, Noelle Boisson
DIST Renn/Films A2/RAI2/DD

† The saga continued in Manon des Sources, from
Pagnol's sequel L'eau de collines.

🎭 picture; Daniel Auteuil (supporting actor); Claude Berri,
Gérard Brach (adapted screenplay); cinematography

Jeanne la Pucelle: Part I, Les Batailles; Part II, Les Prisons ★★

DIR *Jacques Rivette*
1994   336m   France
🎵

☆ *Sandrine Bonnaire* (Jeanne), André Marcon (Dauphin)

A comprehensive account of the rise and fall of
Joan of Arc, from her glorious role in confronting
the English, to her death at the stake.

*A towering production, in two instalments of
roughly equal length, which does full justice to Joan of
Arc's life and achievement. Director Rivette forsakes
expansive, flashy set-pieces, concentrating on intimate
scenes showing this heroine's agonising dilemmas at
close range; but he still invests her story with an epic
quality.*

SCR Christine Laurent, Pascal Bonitzer, Jacques Rivette
CIN William Lubtchansky   MUS Jordi Savall   DES Mau
de Chauvigny   ED Nicole Lubtchanksy   PROD Maurice
Tinchant, Martine Marignac,   DIST Artificial
Eye/Mayfair/La Sept/France 3/Pierre Grise

'Everybody loved him. . .Everybody disappeared.'
Jerry Maguire ★★

SCR/DIR Cameron Crowe
1996   139m   US
DVD 🎵

☆ *Tom Cruise* (Jerry Maguire), *Cuba Gooding Jnr* (Rod
Tidwell), *Renée Zellweger* (Dorothy Boyd), Kelly Preston
(Avery Bishop), Jerry O'Connell (Frank Cushman), Jay
Mohr (Bob Sugar), Regina King (Marcee Tidwell)

A sports agent grows a soul, loses his job and finds
love.

*Smart and canny romantic comedy-drama with its
heart in the right place, and three charming lead
performances; the undercurrents about professional
ethics are pleasing if never wholly persuasive, and it
all works out a little too neatly in the end.*

CIN Janusz Kaminski   DES Stephen Lineweaver   ED Joe
Hutshing   PROD James L. Brooks, Laurence Mark,
Richard Sakai, Cameron Crowe   DIST Columbia
TriStar/Gracie

66 Brashly engaging. – *Owen Gleiberman, Entertainment
Weekly*

66 Crowe is too much the good employee to spin the yarn
properly. – *Rick Groen, Toronto Globe and Mail*

⚲ Cuba Gooding Jnr (supporting actor)
⚲ picture; Tom Cruise (leading actor); Cameron Crowe
(original screenplay); Joe Hutshing

'America is being born again.'
Jesus Camp (new) ★★

DIR Heidi E. Ewing, Rachel Grady
2007   87m   US
DVD

☆ Becky Fischer, Levi, Mike Papantonio, Rachael, Tory,
Pastor Ted Haggard ((as themselves))

At a summer camp in North Dakota, Christian
children are taught to accept evangelical religion,
creationism, and to take part in anti-abortion rallies,
while rejecting mainstream culture – including the
'warlock of Satan,' Harry Potter.

*A sober documentary account of what can only be called
the brainwashing of innocents. The temptation to laugh
at the ludicrous propaganda being trotted out is stifled
by horror at its acceptance by these vulnerable, eager-to-
please children.*

CIN Mira Chang, Jenna Rosher   MUS J.J. McGeehan
ED Enat Sidi   PROD Rachel Grady   DIST ICA

66 As scary as any horror movie, but that doesn't justify
the use of creepy music – a shabby form of editorialising.
– *Edward Porter, Sunday Times*

66 A cool, deeply disturbing account of the way the
American religious right is shaping the minds of its
children to take over the nation in the name of
fundamentalism, ignorance and bigotry. – *Philip French,
Observer*

Jesus of Montreal ★★★

SCR/DIR *Denys Arcand*
1989   120m   Canada/France
DVD

☆ *Lothaire Bluteau* (Daniel), Catherine Wilkening
(Mireille), Johanne-Marie Tremblay (Constance), Rémy
Girard (Martin), Robert Lepage (Rene), Gilles Pelletier
(Fr. Leclerc), Yves Jacques (Richard Cardinal)

An actor who is to portray Christ in a radical local
passion play confronts authority figures who want
the play toned down.

*An intriguing idea: how would Jesus, a radical figure in
his own day, view our consumerist society? Yet this is
only one area that Arcand's intriguing film tackles; side
issues include artistic integrity, censorship, the misuse of
bureaucratic power and the odd instinct that wants
religious faith to be polite and socially acceptable. In
addition to that long list of topics, it's also often grimly
funny.*

CIN Guy Dufaux   MUS Yves Laferrière, François
Dompierre, Jean-Marie Benoît   DES François Séguin
ED Isabelle Dediu   PROD Roger Frappier, Pierre
Gendron, Monique Létourneau   DIST Max Films/Gérard
Mital Productions/NFB Canada

66 It's an original and uncompromising attempt to explore
what really might happen, if the spirit of Jesus were to
walk among us in these timid and materialistic times. –
Roger Ebert, Chicago Sun-Times

⚲ foreign film
🎭 film not in the English language

| DVD Available on DVD | ☆ Cast in order | 66 Critics' Quotes | ⚲ Academy Award | 🎭 BAFTA |
| 🎵 Soundtrack on CD | of importance | † Points of interest | ⚲ Academy Award nomination | 🎭 BAFTA nomination |

Jesus' Son ★★

DIR *Alison Maclean*
1999   107m   US/Canada
DVD

☆ *Billy Crudup* (FH), Samantha Morton (Michelle), Denis Leary (Wayne), Jack Black (Georgie), Will Patton (John Smith), Greg Germann (Dr. Shanis), Holly Hunter (Mira), Dennis Hopper (Bill)

A young drifter in 1970s tries to break free from his relationship with a heroin addict.

Shambling drama about deadbeats, but one with a gentle soul and a lovely sense of humour.

SCR Elizabeth Cuthrell, David Urrutia, Oren Moverman   CIN Adam Kimmel   MUS *Joe Henry*   DES David Doernberg   ED Geraldine Peroni, Stuart Levy   PROD Lydia Dean Pilcher, Elizabeth Cuthrell, David Urrutia   DIST Alliance

66 Transcends ironic grunge-glamour and achieves a beguiling combination of dark comedy and genuine sweetness. – *Jonathan Foreman, New York Post*

'He's a District Attorney. He will risk his life, the lives of his family, everything he holds dear for the one thing he holds sacred. . .the truth.'

JFK ★★

DIR *Oliver Stone*
1991   189m   US
DVD   ♫

☆ Kevin Costner (Jim Garrison), Sissy Spacek (Liz Garrison), Joe Pesci (David Ferrie), *Tommy Lee Jones* (Clay Shaw/Clay Bertrand), Gary Oldman (Lee Harvey Oswald), Jay O. Sanders (Lou Ivon), Michael Rooker (Bill Broussard), Laurie Metcalf (Susie Cox), Gary Grubbs (Al Oser), John Candy (Dean Andrews), Jack Lemmon (Jack Martin), Walter Matthau (Senator Russell Long), Ed Asner (Guy Bannister), *Donald Sutherland* (X), *Kevin Bacon* (Willie O'Keefe), Brian Doyle-Murray, Sally Kirkland, Jim Garrison

After Kennedy's assassination, New Orleans DA Jim Garrison tries to prove that a CIA conspiracy was responsible.

Flagrantly speculative but inescapably gripping, thanks to Stone's muckracking instincts and directorial verve; it certainly entertains more than it convinces, but it's increasingly hard to disentangle what's good about the film from what's just dubious.

SCR Oliver Stone, Zachary Sklar   CIN Robert Richardson   MUS John Williams   DES Victor Kempster   ED Joe Hutshing, Pietro Scalia   PROD A. Kitman Ho, Oliver Stone   DIST Warner/Le Studio Canal/Regency Enterprises/Alcor

66 A riveting marriage of fact and fiction, hypothesis and empirical proof in the edge-of-the-seat spirit of a conspiracy thriller. – *Desson Howe, Washington Post*

66 The first thing to be said about JFK is that it is a great movie, and the next is that it is one of the worst great movies ever made. It is great in spite of itself, and such greatness owes more to the moxie of the director than to his special talents. – *Norman Mailer, Vanity Fair*

⚊ Robert Richardson; Joe Hutshing, Pietro Scalia

⚊ film; Oliver Stone; Tommy Lee Jones (supporting actor); Oliver Stone, Zachary Sklar (adapted screenplay); John Williams; Michael Minkler, Gregg Landaker, Tod A. Maitland (sound)

🏆 Joe Hutshing, Pietro Scalia; Michael Minkler, Gregg Landaker, Tod A. Maitland (sound)
🏆 Tommy Lee Jones (supporting actor); Oliver Stone, Zachary Sklar (adapted screenplay)

'Under the surface of every life lies a mystery.'

Jindabyne ★★★

DIR Ray Lawrence
2006   124m   Australia
DVD   ♫

☆ Laura Linney (Claire Kane), Gabriel Byrne (Stewart Kane), Deborra-Lee Furness (Jude), John Howard (Carl), Stelios Yiakmis (Rocco), Simon Stone (Billy)

Four men from a small Australian town take a weekend fishing trip in isolated country. They find the body of an Aboriginal girl in a river. Rather than call the authorities, they continue their trip, then go home to face their community's wrath.

Rich, complex drama encompassing stormy affairs of the heart and chasms of race and gender. Superbly played by Byrne as an uncomprehending husband and Linney as his outraged wife. As in his earlier Lantana, director Lawrence shows a talent for foraging deep into characters' motives and weaknesses. A satisfying, grown-up film.

SCR Beatrix Christian   CIN David Williamson   MUS Paul Kelly, Dan Luscombe   DES Margot Wilson   ED Karl Sodersten   PROD Catherine Jarman   DIST Revolver

66 The movie is beautifully shot, and succeeds in being deeply disturbing and mysterious, with richly achieved nuances of characterisation. I have seen it two or three times now, and each time it gets better. – *Peter Bradshaw, Guardian*

† Raymond Carver's short story, the source for this film, was also adapted for a segment of Robert Altman's film Short Cuts.

'They were totally unqualified to try the case of a lifetime. . .but every underdog has his day.'

John Grisham's The Rainmaker ★

SCR/DIR Francis Ford Coppola
1997   135m   Germany/US
DVD   ♫

☆ Matt Damon (Rudy Baylor), Claire Danes (Kelly Riker), Jon Voight (Leo F. Drummond), Mary Kay Place (Dot Black), Mickey Rourke (Bruiser Stone), Danny De Vito (Deck Shifflet), Dean Stockwell (Judge Harvey Hale), Teresa Wright (Colleen 'Miss Birdie' Birdsong), Virginia Madsen (Jackie Lemancyzk), Roy Scheider (Wilfred Keeley)

An idealistic young lawyer and his partner sue a corrupt insurance company, which is withholding benefits from a leukemia victim.

Typical Grisham set-up, not unenjoyable, but shakily directed, and populated by too many stock character types with ridiculous names.

DVD Available on DVD   ☆ Cast in order of importance   66 Critics' Quotes   † Points of interest   ⚊ Academy Award   Academy Award nomination   🏆 BAFTA   BAFTA nomination

CIN John Toll MUS Elmer Bernstein DES Howard Cummings ED Barry Malkin, Melissa Kent PROD Michael Douglas, Steven Reuther, Fred Fuchs DIST UIP/Constellation/American Zoetrope

66 No Godfather, but compared with Jack, it's a masterpiece. – *Edward Porter, Sunday Times*

Journey of Hope ★★

DIR Xavier Koller
1990 110m Switzerland/GB

☆ Necmettin Çobanoglu (Haydar Sener), Nur Srer (Meryem), Emin Sivas (Mehmet Ali), Erdinç Akbas (Adama), Yaman Okay (Türkmen), Yasar Gner (Haci Baba), Hseyin Mete (Selçuk), Yaman Tarcan (Ilyas)

A Turkish family, desperate to start a new life, join a group of illegal immigrants and try to enter Switzerland across dangerous mountain terrain.

Director Koller films this story with such an eye for realism that it's easy to view it as a documentary. But the artful contrast between awe-inspiring landscapes and the grubby, grasping motives of 'guides' who prey on these unfortunates makes sobering, memorable viewing. A foreign film Oscar that was well deserved.

SCR Xavier Koller, Feride Ciçekoğlu CIN Elemer Ragalyi ED Galip Iyitanir, Daniel Gibel PROD Alfi Sinniger, Peter Fueter DIST Mainline/Catpics/Condor/SRG/RTSI/Film Four

66 It does not give much of the larger view, and never deals with the fact that Germany, Switzerland, the Scandinavian countries and other rich nations actually need these poor, cheap Southerners to do menial jobs that the locals disdain. – *Roger Ebert, Chicago Sun-Times*

⚱ best foreign film

Journey to the Beginning of the World ★

SCR/DIR Manoel de Oliveira
1997 95m Portugal/France
DVD

☆ Marcello Mastroianni (Manoel), Jean-Yves Gautier (Afonso), Leonor Silveira (Judite), Diogo Dória (Duarte), Isabel de Castro (Maria Afonso), Cecile Sanz de Alba (Christina)

Accompanied by three actors, a veteran film director takes a journey to explore his past.

So slow-moving that at times the title seems literal, it derives its power from the bitter-sweet presence of Mastroianni, cast as this veteran director's alter ego.

CIN Renato Berta MUS Emmanuel Nunes DES Zé Branco ED Valérie Loiseleux PROD Paulo Branco DIST Artificial Eye/Madragoa/Gemini

66 The star takes it like a sweet swansong that makes his performance feel like an unforced tribute to his own long career. An unusually touching obituary. – *Alexander Walker, London Evening Standard*

66 A more stupefyingly uncinematic film has probably never been made. – *Gaby Wood, Guardian*

† This was Marcello Mastroianni's final film.

'Between every mother and daughter there is a story that must be told.'

The Joy Luck Club ★★

DIR Wayne Wang
1993 139m US
DVD ♫

☆ Kieu Chinh (Suyuan Woo), Tsai Chin (Lindo Jong), France Nuyen (Ying-Ying St. Clair), Lisa Lu (An-Mei Hsu), Ming-Na Wen (Jing-Mei 'June' Woo), Tamlyn Tomita (Waverly Jong), Lauren Tom (Lena St. Clair), Victor Wong (Old Chong the Piano Teacher)

A mah-jong party provides the occasion for four Chinese-American women to reflect upon their lives, and the lives and loves of those who came before them.

Sensitive weepie that persists, not always helpfully, with a literary structure of flashbacks, and flashbacks within flashbacks. But it retains an emotional clarity and truthfulness throughout. Good for a long, indulgent wallow.

SCR Amy Tan, Ronald Bass CIN Amir Mokri MUS Rachel Portman DES Donald Graham Burt ED Maysie Hoy PROD Amy Tan, Ronald Bass, Patrick Markey DIST Buena Vista/Hollywood Pictures

66 Never has political correctness looked so sumptuously handsome as it does here, and in its pitch-perfect instinct for the cultural vibe, this sweeping movie is so immaculately dead-on that it nearly transcends criticism. – *Hal Hinson, Washington Post*

66 A sumptuous two-and-a-quarter-hour emotional epic built on one lachrymose climax after another. What little plot there is exists only to set up the next Big Cry. – *Ty Burr, Entertainment Weekly*

 Amy Tan, Ronald Bass (adapted screenplay)

Ju Dou ★★★

DIR *Zhang Yimou, Yang Fengliang*
1990 95m Japan/China
DVD

☆ Li Wei (Yang Jin-shan), Gong Li (Ju Dou), Li Baotian (Yang Tian-qing), Zhang Yi (Tianbai as child), Zheng Jian (Yang Tian-bai as a Youth)

The sadistic, infertile owner of a rural dye works in 1920s China is cuckolded by his new wife, and sets about getting his revenge through her son.

A superbly torrid melodrama with similarities to The Postman Always Rings Twice; the colours have a livid force and the storytelling holds you completely in its grip.

SCR Liu Heng CIN *Gu Changwei, Yang Lun* MUS Zhao Jiping, Ru-jin Xia DES Juiping Cao, Xia Rujin ED Du Yuan PROD Hu Jian, Yasuyoshi Tokuma, Wenze Zhang DIST ICA/Tokuma Shoten/China Film/X'ian Film Studio

66 As sumptuously cinematic as it is woefully fatalistic. – *Rita Kempley, Washington Post*

† The film was banned in China.

⚱ foreign language film

DVD Available on DVD   ☆ Cast in order of importance   66 Critics' Quotes   ⚱ Academy Award    BAFTA
♫ Soundtrack on CD   † Points of interest   Academy Award nomination   BAFTA nomination

331

'A time without pity. A society without mercy. A love without equal.'

Jude ★

DIR Michael Winterbottom
1996   123m   GB
DVD   ♫

☆ Christopher Eccleston (Jude Fawley), Kate Winslet (Sue Bridehead), Liam Cunningham (Phillotson), Rachel Griffiths (Arabella), June Whitfield (Aunt Drusilla), Ross Colvin Turnbull (Little Jude), James Daley (Jude as a Boy)

A stonemason with university ambitions is tricked into marriage by a pig farmer's daughter, and later falls for his idealistic cousin.

Fancying itself more than a period piece, this relentlessly sombre adaptation has too many modern ideas in its head, and the dialogue is often jarringly anachronistic.

SCR Hossein Amini   **CIN** Eduardo Serra   **MUS** Adrian Johnston   **DES** Joseph Bennett   **ED** Trevor Waite   **PROD** Andrew Eaton   **DIST** PolyGram/BBC Films/Revolution

66 Makes Ingmar Bergman look like Benny Hill. – *Anne Billson, Sunday Telegraph*

66 Often impressive but oddly frustrating. – *Geoff Andrew, Time Out*

J

'The things you'll see and the things you'll feel are the things that will be part of you as long as you live!'

Judgment at Nuremberg ★★★

DIR Stanley Kramer
1961   190m   US
♫

☆ *Spencer Tracy*, Marlene Dietrich, *Burt Lancaster*, Richard Widmark, *Maximilian Schell*, Judy Garland, *Montgomery Clift*, William Shatner, Edward Binns, Werner Klemperer, Torben Meyer, Alan Baxter, Ray Teal

A fictionalized version of the 1948 trial of the Nazi leaders for crimes against humanity.

It's fashionable these days to decry Stanley Kramer as a heavy-handed Hollywood liberal foisting his beliefs into his films, but he scored heavily with this courtroom drama about those men who enshrined Nazi tyranny as law. As a producer he gathered a brilliant, starry cast, while screenwriter Abby Mann provided an account of proceedings notable for its clarity. Yes, it's long, but this was an important historical event to which the film-makers have done justice. In doing so they have elicited some fine performances from big-name actors.

SCR *Abby Mann*   **CIN** *Ernest Laszlo*   **MUS** Ernest Gold   **DES** Rudolph Sternad   **PROD** *Stanley Kramer*   **DIST** UA/Roxlom

66 Some believe that by tackling such themes Kramer earns at least partial remission from criticism. How much? 20 per cent off for effort? – *Stanley Kauffmann*

† Burt Lancaster replaced Laurence Olivier, who was originally cast.

⚲ Maximilian Schell (leading actor); Abby Mann (adapted screenplay)

⚲ picture; Spencer Tracy (leading actor); Judy Garland (leading actress); Montgomery Clift (supporting actor); Stanley Kramer (direction); Ernest Laszlo

'Power. Respect.'

Juice ★

DIR Ernest R. Dickerson
1992   95m   US
DVD   ♫

☆ Omar Epps (Q), Tupac Shakur (Bishop), Jermaine Hopkins (Steel), Khalil Kain (Raheem), Cindy Herron (Yolanda), Vincent Laresca (Radames), Samuel L. Jackson (Trip), George O. Gore (Brian), Grace Garland (Q's mother), Queen Latifah (Ruffhouse M.C.)

A Harlem teenager who wants to become a DJ unwisely joins three friends intent on robbing a store.

A good-looking film, as one would expect from debutant director Ernest Dickerson, who made his name as a cinematographer; a strong young cast, led by a hugely confident Epps, do justice to this account of dashed hopes and limited options in America's urban centres.

SCR Gerard Brown, Ernest R. Dickerson   **CIN** Larry Banks   **MUS** Gary G-Wiz   **DES** Lester Cohen   **ED** Sam Pollard, Brunilda Torres   **PROD** David Heyman, Neal H. Moritz, Peter Frankfurt   **DIST** Electric/Paramount/Island World

66 Juice adapts the DJ-struggling-to-make-it scenario to put across a message of inner-city hopelessness. – *Ben Thompson, Sight & Sound*

† Queen Latifah makes a cameo appearance.

Jules et Jim ★★★

DIR *François Truffaut*
1962   105m   France
DVD   ♫

☆ *Oskar Werner* (Jules), *Jeanne Moreau* (Catherine), Henri Serre (Jim), Vanna Urbino (Gilberte), Boris Bassiak (Albert), Anny Nelsen (Lucie)

In Paris, a French and a German student simultaneously court the same young capricious woman, who keeps them both on tenterhooks. She marries one, but when the arrangement falls apart, they revert to a ménage a trois.

A film that perfectly captured the insouciant, freewheeling spirit of the New Wave in Paris at the time. It has an abundance of charm, but its most striking element is the female side of this triangle: Moreau plays a headstrong, opinionated woman whose desires, and even whims, drive the relationship and the plot.

SCR *François Truffaut, Jean Gruault*   **CIN** Raoul Coutard   **MUS** Georges Delerue   **ED** Claudine Bouche   **PROD** Marcel Berbert   **DIST** Films du Carrosse/SEDIF

66 The sense is of a director intoxicated with the pleasure of making films. – *Penelope Houston, Monthly Film Bulletin*

'Live a little first.'

Jump Tomorrow ★

SCR/DIR Joel Hopkins
2001   97m   GB/US
DVD

☆ Tunde Adebimpe (George), Hippolyte Girardot (Gerard), Natalia Verbeke (Alicia), James Wilby (Nathan), Patricia Mauceri (Consuelo), Isiah Whitlock Jnr (George's

Uncle), Kaili Vernoff (Heather Leather), Abiola Wendy Abrams (Sophie)

A young Nigerian executive considers jettisoning his arranged marriage to pursue an also-engaged Latina woman he meets at the airport.

Sweet but flawed romantic comedy in which the quirkiness seems over-determined.

CIN Patrick Cady   MUS John Kimbrough   DES John Paino   ED Susan Littenberg   PROD Nicola Usborne DIST Film4

66 Doesn't punch out its comic points but lets the story gradually reveal them. – *Roger Ebert, Chicago Sun-Times*

🇹 Nicola Usborne, Joel Hopkins (promising newcomer)

'Anywhere is possible.'

Jumper (new)

DIR Doug Liman
2008   88m   US
DVD   ♫

☆ Hayden Christensen (David Rice), Jamie Bell (Griffin), Samuel L. Jackson (Roland Cox), Rachel Bilson (Millie Harris), Diane Lane (Mary Rice), Michael Rooker (William Rice)

A man with the power to teleport himself is stalked across the globe by a secret society determined to destroy him.

Silly fantasy which quickly exhausts the possibilities of its feckless superhero's seemingly unlimited abilities.

SCR David S. Goyer, Jim Uhls, Simon Kinberg   CIN Barry Peterson   MUS John Powell   DES Oliver Scholl
ED Saar Klein, Don Zimmerman, Dean Zimmerman
PROD Arnon Milchan, Lucas Foster, Jay Sanders, Simon Kinberg   DIST TCF

66 A serviceable sci-fi thriller/videogame template that plays like The Matrix Lite. – *Brian Lowry, Variety*

66 Undernourished in its characterisations, stillborn in its action scenes. – *Richard Corliss, Time*

† Liman filmed for two months with original leads Tom Sturridge and Teresa Palmer before recasting the roles and starting from scratch.

Junebug   ★★★★

DIR *Phil Morrison*
2005   106m   US
DVD

☆ *Amy Adams* (Ashley), *Embeth Davidtz* (Madeleine), Ben McKenzie (Johnny), Alessandro Nivola (George), Frank Hoyt Taylor (David Wark), Celia Weston (Peg), Scott Wilson (Eugene)

A newlywed Chicago art dealer meets her husband's Baptist family for the first time, combining the visit with a trip to a potential client in North Carolina.

Wonderfully assured ensemble piece, starting from the reliable if tired premise of meet-the-in-laws: the culture clash is gently observed, the characterisations stealthy and somehow piercing. It is a minor picture of major sensitivity, and the acting, particularly from the astonishing Amy Adams, is near-perfect.

SCR *Angus MacLachlan*   CIN Peter Donahue   MUS Yo La Tengo   DES David Doernberg   ED *Joe Klotz*
PROD Mindy Goldberg, Mike S. Ryan   DIST Eureka

66 Fascinating and compassionate. – *Peter Bradshaw, Guardian*

66 A deceptively simple, deeply resonant film about the inherent loneliness of family. – *Carina Chocano, LA Times*

♟ Amy Adams (leading actress)

Jungle Fever   ★★

SCR/DIR Spike Lee
1991   132m   US
DVD   ♫

☆ Wesley Snipes (Flipper Purify), Annabella Sciorra (Angie Tucci), Spike Lee (Cyrus), Ossie Davis (The Good Reverend Doctor Purify), Ruby Dee (Lucinda Purify), Samuel L. Jackson (Gator Purify), Lonette McKee (Drew), John Turturro (Paulie Carbone), Frank Vincent (Mike Tucci), Anthony Quinn (Lou Carbone), Tim Robbins (Jerry), Brad Dourif (Leslie)

A married black architect has an affair with his Italian-American secretary.

Bracing drama, one of this director's strongest, which cogently addresses race taboos and prejudices without getting hysterical.

CIN Ernest Dickerson   MUS Terence Blanchard
DES Wynn Thomas   ED Sam Pollard   PROD Spike Lee
DIST UIP/Universal/Forty Acres and A Mule Filmworks

66 Funny, political, stirring and sentimental, often at the same time. – *Desson Howe, Washington Post*

'A comedy about growing up. . .and bumps along the way.'

Juno (new)   ★★

DIR *Jason Reitman*
2007   95m   US
DVD   ♫

☆ *Ellen Page* (Juno MacGuff), *Michael Cera* (Paulie Bleeker), Jennifer Garner (Vanessa Loring), Jason Bateman (Mark Loring), Allison Janney (Bren MacGuff), J.K. Simmons (Mac MacGuff), Olivia Thirlby (Leah)

An unconventional 16 year old girl faces an unplanned pregnancy, the result of a one night stand with her best friend. After considering abortion, but unable to go through with it, she decides to give the baby up for adoption, and plans auditioning suitable parents.

A witty, charming, and even wise little comedy with two young star turns from Page and Cera, and a shrewdly deployed supporting cast. Diablo Cody won an Oscar for her screenplay, which is brittle and amusing, but initially seems intent on cramming in as many one-line gags as possible. The mood (and the script) thankfully relaxes as the story continues. It's delightful, but it veers close to self-regarding whimsy, exemplified by Kimya Dawson's grating songs.

SCR *Diablo Cody*   CIN Eric Steelberg   MUS Mateo Messina   DES Steve Saklad   ED Dana E. Glauberman
PROD Lianne Halfon, John Malkovich, Mason Novick, Russell Smith   DIST Fox

---

J

66 Cody's dialogue has a definite rhythm and Reitman directs his actors to deliver the words in the rapid-fire precision of a '30s screwball comedy. Indeed all scenes develop a rhythm and inner logic that bring the movie to often startling revelations and insights. – *Kirk Honeycutt, Hollywood Reporter*

66 With its archly indie soundtrack, its Wes Anderson-inspired quirkiness and stylistic affectations (Juno's pipe-smoking, Paulie's orange Tic Tac fixation) and its sentimental ending it's closer to generic twentysomething whimsy. Still, it's whimsy done well. – *Sukhdev Sandhu, Daily Telegraph*

⚊ Diablo Cody (original screenplay)
⚊ film; Ellen Page (leading actress); Jason Reitman
Ⓣ Diablo Cody (original screenplay)
Ⓣ Ellen Page (leading actress)

Ju-on ★

SCR/DIR Takashi Shimizu
2000 89m Japan
[DVD]

☆ Yurei Yanagi (Shunsuke Kobayashi), Chiaki Kuriyama (Mizuho Tamura), Hitomi Miwa (Yuki), Asumi Miwa (Kanna Murakami), Takako Fuji (Kayako Saeki), Takashi Matsuyama (Takeo Saeki), Ryota Koyama (Toshio Saeki)

A social worker in Tokyo stumbles across a haunted house and is exposed to a deadly curse.

Creepy but unfocused chiller, the seed of a successful franchise; there are moments of considerable dread, but the jumbled narrative allows a lot of the tension to dissipate.

CIN Nobuhito Kisuki MUS Shiro Sato, Gary Ashiya
PROD Taka Ichise, Kazuo Kato, Masaaki Takashima

66 A haunted-house one-trick pony. – *Derek Elley*

'If you think you know her, think again.'

Just Another Girl on the I.R.T. ★

SCR/DIR Leslie Harris
1992 92m US
[DVD]

☆ Ariyan A. Johnson (Chantel Mitchell), Kevin Thigpen (Tyrone), Ebony Jerido (Natete), Jerard Washington (Gerard), Chequita Jackson (Paula)

A Brooklyn high school student with big ambitions must re-assess her prospects when she becomes pregnant after a one-night stand.

An affecting slice of urban American life, a dilemma well portrayed by a cast of unknowns, let down only by a contrived, pat ending.

CIN Richard Connors MUS Eric Sadler DES Michael O'Dell Green ED Jack Haigis PROD Erwin Wilson
DIST Metro Tartan/Miramax/Truth 24 F.P.S.

'In A World Of Ancient Traditions'

Kadosh ★★

DIR Amos Gitai
1999   110m   Israel/France/Italy
DVD

☆ Yoram Hattab (Meir), Yael Abecassis (Rivka), Meital Barda (Malka), Uri Klauzner (Yossef), Yussuf Abu-Warda (Rav Shimon), Lea Koenig (Elisheva), Sami Hori (Yaakov), Rivka Michaeli (Gynaecologist), Samuel Calderon (Uncle Shmouel)

A childless Israeli woman agrees that her orthodox Jewish husband can divorce her so he can have children.

Powerful portrayal of the tensions between religious doctrine and human emotions, related with sympathy and earnest deliberation. Intriguingly, the story is told from a female point of view, thus throwing down a gauntlet to rabbinical orthodoxy. But its strength lies in the human dramas it describes.

SCR Eliette Abecassis, Amos Gitai   CIN *Renato Berta*   MUS Louis Sclavis, Philippe Eidel   DES Miguel Markin   ED Monica Coleman, Kobi Netanel   PROD Amos Gitai, Michel Propper   DIST Downtown

Kafka ★

DIR Steven Soderbergh
1991   98m   US/France
DVD   ♫

☆ Jeremy Irons (Kafka), Theresa Russell (Gabriela), Joel Grey (Burgel), Ian Holm (Doctor Murnau), Jeroen Krabbé (Bizzlebek), Armin Mueller-Stahl (Grubach), Alec Guinness (The Chief Clerk), Brian Glover (Castle Henchman), Robert Flemyng (The Keeper of the Files)

An insurance worker gets involved in an underground anarchist group when a colleague disappears.

A paranoid fantasia mixing Kafka's life with his art; we soon get the impression we're going nowhere, but the design is certainly striking.

SCR Lem Dobbs   CIN *Walt Lloyd*   MUS Cliff Martinez   DES *Gavin Bocquet*   ED Steven Soderbergh   PROD Stuart Cornfeld, Harry Benn   DIST Guild/Renn/Baltimore/Pricel

66 A self-conscious and artsy fictional foray into both the real and dream worlds of Franz Kafka. – *Henry Sheehan, Variety*

66 Makes its audience suffer along with its heroes. – *Rita Kempley, Washington Post*

Kanal ★★★

DIR *Andrzej Wajda*
1956   97m   Poland

☆ Teresa Izewska (Daisy Stokrotka), Tadeusz Janczar (Corporal Korab), Emil Kariewicz (Madry), Wienczylaw Glinski (Lieutenant Zadra)

In the 1944 Warsaw uprising, a Polish anti-Nazi resistance unit take refuge from their enemies in the city's system of sewers.

An underrated entry in Wajda's war trilogy, but there is an extraordinary sense of claustrophobia in the dark, dank tunnels beneath Warsaw, and the heroism of these beleaguered partisans is stirring. Their fear of being discovered creates heart-stopping tension.

SCR Jerzy Stawinski   CIN *Jerzy Lipman*   MUS Jan Krenz   ED Halina Nawrocka   PROD Stanislaw Adler   DIST Film Polski

Kandahar ★★

SCR/DIR Mohsen Makhmalbaf
2001   85m   Iran/France
DVD

☆ Nelofer Pazira (Nafas), Hassan Tantai (Tabib Sahid), Sadou Teymouri (Khak), Hoyatalah Hakimi (Hayat)

A journalist exiled from Afghanistan returns to the country to find her suicidal sister, and joins a caravan of refugees.

Vivid snapshot of oppression under the Taliban, with an occasionally surreal tone; the semi-documentary approach excuses some iffy acting.

CIN Ebrahim Ghafouri   MUS M. R. Darvishi   ED Mohsen Makhmalbaf   PROD Mohsen Makhmalbaf   DIST ICA

66 A short, matter-of-fact visit to hell. – *Mick LaSalle, San Francisco Chronicle*

66 With its lyrical vision of oppression, it looks, if anything, milder now than it might have before the war. – *Owen Gleiberman, Entertainment Weekly*

'Kansas City, 1934. Anything could happen here. One night it did.'

Kansas City ★

DIR Robert Altman
1995   116m   US/France
DVD   ♫

☆ Jennifer Jason Leigh (Blondie O'Hara), Miranda Richardson (Carolyn Stilton), Harry Belafonte (Seldom Seen), Michael Murphy (Henry Stilton), Dermot Mulroney (Johnny O'Hara), Steve Buscemi (Johnny Flynn)

DVD Available on DVD	☆ Cast in order	66 Critics' Quotes
♫ Soundtrack on CD	of importance	† Points of interest

🏆 Academy Award   🏆 BAFTA
🏆 Academy Award nomination   🏆 BAFTA nomination

335

A hood's missus in the 1930s kidnaps the drug-addled wife of a politician in order to save her husband.

Haphazardly plotted period melodrama in which the jazzy vibe is all, but not quite enough; the mannered performances are an acquired taste. Not top-drawer Altman.

SCR Robert Altman, Frank Barhydt **CIN** Oliver Stapleton
DES Stephen Altman **ED** Geraldine Peroni
PROD Robert Altman **DIST** Electric/Sandcastle 5/CiBy
2000

66 Too silly and disjointed to be much fun. – *Ralph Novak, People Weekly*

Keane ★

SCR/DIR Lodge Kerrigan
2005 100m US
DVD

☆ Damian Lewis (William Keane), Abigail Breslin (Kira), Amy Ryan (Lynn), Tina Holmes (Michelle)

A schizophrenic New Yorker obsessively re-creates the supposed abduction of his daughter from Port Authority Bus Terminal.

A highly discomfiting portrait of mental instability, in which the truth or otherwise of the main character's convictions is purposefully withheld; it makes for an intense but alienating experience.

CIN John Foster **DES** Petra Barchi **ED** Andrew Hafitz
PROD Andrew Fierberg **DIST** TCF

66 Means to shake us, and does. – *Peter Travers, Rolling Stone*

66 Its raw hopelessness is its universality. – *Michael Atkinson, Village Voice*

† Executive producer Steven Soderbergh's alternative cut can be seen on the DVD.

'If you have to believe in something, you might as well believe in love.'

Keeping the Faith ★★

DIR *Edward Norton*
2000 128m US
DVD ♫

☆ Ben Stiller (Jake), Edward Norton (Brian), Jenna Elfman (Anna), Anne Bancroft (Ruth), Eli Wallach (Rabbi Lewis), Ron Rifkin (Larry Friedman), Milos Forman (Father Havel), Holland Taylor (Bonnie Rose), Lisa Edelstein (Ali Decker), Rena Sofer (Rachel Rose), Brian George (Indian bartender), Ken Leung (Don)

A rabbi and a Catholic priest, long-time friends, both fall in love with a girl they knew from childhood.

The premise sounds like the opening line of a corny joke, and this is an unashamedly old-fashioned set-up; Bing Crosby would not have been out of place playing this priest. For all that, it's hugely appealing, Stiller and Norton trade quips engagingly, and it's a genuinely feel-good couple of hours.

SCR *Stuart Blumberg* **CIN** Anastas Michos **MUS** Elmer Bernstein **DES** Wynn P. Thomas **ED** Malcolm Campbell **PROD** Howard Koch, Edward Norton, Stuart Blumberg **DIST** Buena Vista

66 Though it sidesteps the key issues in favour of a cop-out ending, Keeping The Faith can claim one major virtue: its wholehearted embrace, and indeed celebration, of the joys of a multi-racial society. – *Philip Kemp, Sight & Sound*

'A knight in shining overalls.'

Kenny (new)

DIR Clayton Jacobson **SCR/DIR** Clayton Jacobson, Shane Jacobson
2006 103m Australia
DVD

☆ Shane Jacobson (Kenny Smyth), Eve Von Vibra (Jackie), Ronald Jacobson (Dad)

A mock documentary about the working life of an Australian portaloo installer who takes his work extremely seriously.

Genial but over-extended one-joke comedy.

CIN Clayton Jacobson **MUS** Richard Pleasance
ED Sean Lander, Clayton Jacobson **PROD** Clayton Jacobson, Rohan Timlock **DIST** Odeon Sky Filmworks

† Lead actor Shane Jacobson and writer-director-producer Clayton Jacobson are brothers.

'They beat him. They deprived him. They ridiculed him. They broke his heart. But they couldn't break his spirit.'

Kes ★★★★

DIR *Ken Loach*
1969 109m GB
DVD

☆ David Bradley (Billy Casper), Lynne Perrie (Mrs. Casper), Colin Welland (Mr. Farthing), Freddie Fletcher (Jud), *Brian Glover* (Mr. Sugden)

In a northern industrial town, a teenage boy with family problems and who is too slightly-built to excel at sports, finds solace in his pet kestrel.

A realistic family drama, revolving around the misfortunes of a heartbreaking young boy, it became a huge popular hit and is still affectionately regarded by the British public. Loach went easy on the political message this time round, and this simple story, sad and funny in turn, feels all the better for it. Glover's ultra-keen games teacher almost steals the show in a comic turn that also suggests young Billy isn't the film's only loser.

SCR *Barry Hines, Ken Loach, Tony Garnett* **CIN** Chris Menges **MUS** John Cameron **ED** Roy Watts
PROD Tony Garnett **DIST** UA/Woodfall

66 There emerges a most discouraging picture of life in the industrial north. . .infinitely sad in its total implications, it is also immensely funny in much of its detail. – *Brenda Davies*

🅣 David Bradley (leading actor); Colin Welland (supporting actor)

'6 Reels of Joy.'

The Kid ★★★★

SCR/DIR *Charles Chaplin*
1921 52m US
DVD

☆ *Charles Chaplin* (A Tramp), *Jackie Coogan* (The Child), Edna Purviance (The Woman)

A tramp brings up an abandoned baby, and later loses him to his mother; but there is a happy ending.

Sentimental silent comedy set in the slums. The comedy is sparingly laid on, but the overall effect is much less painful than the synopsis would suggest. The production is comparatively smooth, young Coogan is sensational, and the film contains much of the quintessential Chaplin.

CIN *Rollie Totheroh*   DIST First National/Charles Chaplin

'The Story Of A Man Who Seduced Hollywood.'

The Kid Stays in the Picture ★

DIR Brett Morgen, Nanette Burstein
2002   93m   US
DVD   ♫

☆ Robert Evans (Narrator)

Producer Robert Evans gives an account of his rise and fall in the movie business.

Briskly superficial account of one Hollywood life, glossing over creative frictions or tensions in order to celebrate some undeniably accomplished end product; some of Evans' post-70s choices are explained – Sliver, for example, had the potential to be as big a pulp-lit smash as the producer's The Godfather or Love Story – but it would take more than an hour-and-a-half to justify The Phantom, Jade, or The Saint.

SCR Brett Morgen   CIN John Bailey   MUS Jeff Danna
ED Jun Diaz   PROD Graydon Carter, Brett Morgen, Nanette Burstein   DIST Momentum

❝ This stuff is golden. Directors Brett Morgan and Nanette Burstein make sure the movie goes down like potato chips. – *Peter Travers, Rolling Stone*

❝ Occasionally feels a bit suffocating, like being trapped at a party by a drunkard who won't shut up until he tells you his entire life story. – *Rene Rodriguez, Miami Herald*

Kids ★★

DIR Larry Clark
1995   91m   US
DVD   ♫

☆ Lee Fitzpatrick (Telly), Sarah Henderson (Girl #1), Justin Pierce (Casper), Jonathan S. Kim (Korean Guy), Adriane Brown (Little Girl), Sajan Bhagat (Paul), Billy Valdes (Stanly)

An HIV-positive skateboarder in New York City sets out to deflower as many virgins as possible, while one of his former conquests tries to stop him.

Potent and skilful piece of youth exploitation, in which the presentation of bored, randy and amoral teens is both convincing and clearly prurient. The movie's message about underage, unsafe sex may be designed as a wake-up call, but it often feels more like an excuse to show it.

SCR Harmony Korine   CIN Eric Edwards   MUS Lou Barlow, John Davis   DES Kevin Thompson
ED Christopher Tellefsen   PROD Cary Woods
DIST Electric/Shining Excalibur/Independent/The Guys Upstairs

❝ Simultaneously engrossing and detached, observant and just plain showy. – *Leslie Felperin, Sight and Sound*

❝ Leans towards exploitative sensationalism. – *Geoff Andrew, Time Out*

† Harmony Korine wrote the script in 1993, aged 18.

Kika ★

SCR/DIR Pedro Almodóvar
1993   114m   Spain/France
DVD   ♫

☆ Veronica Forqué (Kika), Peter Coyote (Nicholas), Victoria Abril (Andrea Caracortada), Alex Casanova (Ramón), Charo Lopez (Rafaela), Rossy de Palma (Juana), Santiago Lajusticia (Pablo), Anabel Alonso (Amparo), Bibi Andersen (Susana), Manuel Bandera (Chico Carretera)

Intersecting lives in Madrid, featuring a beautician, a photographer of lingerie models, a mentally challenged rapist, an American novelist, a lesbian maid and a former psychologist, now turned crime reporter.

Almodóvar has never made a dull movie, though this marks the end of a period. Up to this point, his films relied on in-your-face scenarios, which gave way to more reflective, mature work. It is essentially a 'greatest hits' summation of themes from his provocative early period: there is a corpse here, a pornographic film actor, a rape, a voyeur, glossy, designed interiors – and a sceptical view of trash television, which would continue to intrigue him for years to come. It does all feel faintly tired, and his decision to move on came not a moment too soon.

CIN Alfredo Mayo   ED José Salcedo   PROD Esther Garcia   DIST Electric Pictures/El Deseo/Ciby 2000

❝ Almodóvar's famed centrality of strong female roles is one of Kika's strengths. – *Rikki Morgan, Sight & Sound*

'Here comes the bride.'

Kill Bill Vol. 1 ★★

SCR/DIR Quentin Tarantino
2003   111m   US
DVD   ♫

☆ Uma Thurman (The Bride/Black Mamba), Lucy Liu (O-Ren Ishii/Cottonmouth), Vivica A. Fox (Vernita Green/Copperhead), Daryl Hannah (Elle Driver/California Mountain Snake), Michael Madsen (Budd/Sidewinder), David Carradine (Bill), Michael Parks (Earl McGraw), Sonny Chiba (Hattori Hanzo), Chiaki Kuriyama (Go Go Yubari), Gordon Liu (Johnny Mo)

Waking up after four years in a coma, an assassin wreaks her revenge on the colleagues who betrayed her.

Tarantino's homage to 1970s 'wuxia' martial arts flicks is little more than a slew of dazzlingly choreographed fight scenes, but his virtuoso technique is constantly in evidence. A self-described 'roaring rampage of revenge', this first half makes good on the promise, barely pausing for breath.

CIN *Robert Richardson*   MUS *RZA*   DES *Yohei Tanada, David Wasco*   ED *Sally Menke*   PROD Lawrence Bender
DIST Buena Vista

❝ Brutally bloody and thrillingly callous from first to last. – *Peter Bradshaw, Guardian*

337

66 Smells like the work of an aging enfant terrible incarcerated in his malodorous living room, scrabbling among the empty pizza-boxes for fresh ways to shock. – *Jenny McCartney, Sunday Telegraph*

† The film was originally intended as a single feature, but Tarantino split it into two halves rather than cutting it down.

† The long fight sequence at the House of the Blue Leaves was converted into black-and-white in order to avoid cuts for excessive violence.

Ⓣ RZA

Ⓣ Uma Thurman (leading actress); Sally Menke; Tommy Tom, Kia Kwan Tam, Wai Kit Leung, Jaco Wong' Hin Leung (speical visual effects); Michael Minkler, Myron Nettinga, Wylie Stateman, Mark Ulano (sound)

'Revenge is a dish best served cold.'

Kill Bill Vol. 2 ★

SCR/DIR Quentin Tarantino
2004   136m   US
DVD   ♫

☆ Uma Thurman (The Bride/Black Mamba), David Carradine (Bill), Michael Madsen (Budd/Sidewinder), Daryl Hannah (Elle Driver/California Mountain Snake), Gordon Liu (Pai Mei), Michael Parks (Esteban Vihaio), Perla Haney-Jardine (B.B.), Samuel L. Jackson (Rufus), Bo Svenson (Reverend Harmony)

The Bride continues her revenge against her ex-boss and his two surviving henchmen.

A much baggier proposition than Vol. 1, in which attempts at thoughtfulness and deeper characterisation fall dismayingly flat. There are good moments, but when this rampage stops roaring, it reveals itself as a bit of a sham.

CIN *Robert Richardson*   MUS Robert Rodriguez
DES David Wasco   ED *Sally Menke*   PROD Lawrence Bender   DIST Buena Vista

66 QT seems to revere every movie he's ever seen. – *Charles Taylor, Salon*

66 Mistakes collage for creativity, and, more than ever, his knee-jerk homaging feels cheap and pointless. – *Catherine Shoard, Sunday Telegraph*

'Her last request was his first mistake.'

Kill Me Again

DIR John R. Dahl
1989   94m   US
DVD

☆ Val Kilmer (Jack Andrews), Joanne Whalley-Kilmer (Fay Forrester), Michael Madsen (Vince Miller), Jonathan Gries (Alan Swayzie), Pat Mulligan (Sammy), Nick Dimitri (Marty)

A woman on the run from the mob and her psychopathic boyfriend pays a private eye to fake her death.

Surprisingly undistinguished debut from noir specialist Dahl, not helped by indifferent acting.

SCR John R. Dahl, David W. Warfield   CIN Jacques Steyn
MUS William Olvis   DES Michelle Minch   ED Frank Jiminez, Jonathan Shaw, Eric Beason   PROD David W. Warfield, Sigurjon Sighvatsson, Steve Golin
DIST Palace/Propaganda Films/ITC

'One Vicious Killer. One Relentless Cop... ...Ten Thousand Bullets.'

The Killer ★★★

SCR/DIR John Woo
1989   111m   Hong Kong
DVD

☆ Chow Yun-Fat (Ah Jong), Danny Lee (Insp. Li Ying / Little Eagle), Sally Yeh (Jennie), Chu Kong (Fung Sei), Kenneth Tsang (Sgt. Tsang Yeh), Lam Chung (Jueng Wan / Ah Jong's first victim), Shing Fui-On (Wong Hoi)

Having blinded a nightclub singer during a shootout, a contract killer takes one last job to pay for the young woman's cornea transplant, only to attract the attentions of a cop.

Landmark action movie that introduced Western viewers to the distinctive sensibility of a director as central to his genre as Ford was to the Western or Stanley Donen to the musical: between virtuoso set-pieces and balletic shootouts, it somehow manages to be genuinely, unexpectedly touching, and graceful in both senses of the word.

CIN Wong Wing-Hang, Peter Pao   MUS Lowell Lowe
ED *Fan Kung-Ming*   PROD Tsui Hark   DIST Palace/Film Workshop/Golden Princess/Magnum

66 There are half-a-dozen mega-massacres along the way, plus extraordinary spasms of sentimentality, romance and soul-searching. The tone is hysterical from start to finish, but Woo's lush visual stylings and taste for baroque detail give the whole thing an improbably serene air of abstraction. – *Tony Rayns, Time Out*

66 The excessive violence is demented, intoxicating and imaginative but never mindless, as Woo imbues the plainly preposterous material with a cartoon sensibility and an overriding sense of morality. A masterpiece indeed. – *Mark Salisbury, Empire*

'The Screen's All-Time Classic Of Suspense!'

The Killers ★★★★

DIR Robert Siodmak
1946   105m   US
DVD

☆ *Burt Lancaster* (Swede), Edmond O'Brien (Jim Reardon), *Ava Gardner* (Kitty Collins), Albert Dekker (Big Jim Colfax), Sam Levene (Lt. Sam Lubinsky), John Miljan (Jake), Virginia Christine (Lilly Lubinsky), Vince Barnett (Charleston), Charles D. Brown (Packy Robinson), Donald MacBride (Kenyon), Phil Brown (Nick Adams), Charles McGraw (Al), William Conrad (Max)

In a small sleazy town a gangster waits for two assassins to kill him, for reasons that later become apparent.

Elaborate, bleak tale of cross and double-cross, stunningly executed. It announces itself with a brilliant sequence of a murder, with the rest of the story told largely in flashback. Hugely influential film that laid down some of the guiding principles for film noir, with a weary, cynical, depressive tone, and atmospheric, downbeat locations inspired by Edward Hopper paintings. An outstanding film debut for Lancaster, established as a star from this point onwards, and a breakthrough for Gardner, a convincing, provocative femme fatale.

SCR *Anthony Veiller* **CIN** *Elwood Bredell* **MUS** *Miklos Rozsa* **ED** Arthur Hilton **PROD** Mark Hellinger **DIST** Universal-International

66 About one tenth is Hemingway's, the rest is Universal-International's. – *Richard Winnington*

66 Seldom does a melodrama maintain the high tension that distinguishes this one. – *Variety*

† John Huston contributed to the script but is not credited.

⚯ Robert Siodmak; Anthony Veiller (original screenplay); Miklos Rozsa (music); Arthur Hilton (editing)

The Killing ★★★★

SCR/DIR *Stanley Kubrick*
1956 83m US
[DVD]

☆ Sterling Hayden, *Marie Windsor*, Jay C. Flippen, Elisha Cook Jnr, Coleen Gray, Vince Edwards, Ted de Corsia, Joe Sawyer, Tim Carey

An ex-convict recruits helpers to steal $2 million from a racetrack.

Incisive, entertaining, downbeat caper movie clearly influenced by The Asphalt Jungle, Rififi and probably Rashomon. Its most remarkable feature is Kubrick's reconstruction of the narrative, telling the story of the heist from the viewpoint of individual gang members, thus assembling the truth through a gradual drip-feed of information. Enormously influential third feature by a director who by this stage clearly had talent and technique to burn.

CIN Lucien Ballard **MUS** Gerald Fried **PROD** J. B. Harris **DIST** UA/Harris-Kubrick

66 The visual authority constantly dominates a flawed script. – *Arlene Croce*

66 The camera watches the whole shoddy show with the keen eye of a terrier stalking a pack of rats. – *Time*

The Killing Fields ★★★

DIR *Roland Joffé*
1984 141m GB
[DVD] ♫

☆ *Sam Waterston* (Sidney Schanberg), *Haing S. Ngor* (Dith Pran), John Malkovich (Al Rockoff), Julian Sands (Jon Swain), Craig T. Nelson (Military Attache)

An American journalist is engulfed in the horror of Cambodia under Pol Pot's Khmer Rouge regime; his local adviser disappears and is thought to be dead.

Brilliantly filmed true story, angry, harrowing and conceived on an epic scale without losing sight of its compassion. Scenes depicting the frightened evacuation of Phnom Penh are exceptional; the ending is both rueful and optimistic, though marred by the gratuitous arrival of John Lennon's Imagine on the soundtrack.

SCR Bruce Robinson, from the article 'The Death and Life of Dith Pran' by Sidney Schanberg **CIN** *Chris Menges* **MUS** Mike Oldfield **DES** Roy Walker **ED** Jim Clark **PROD** *David Puttnam* **DIST** Goldcrest/Enigma

⚯ Haing S. Ngor (supporting actor); photography; editing
⚯ picture; Roland Joffe; Sam Waterston (leading actor); Bruce Robinson (adapted screenplay)

🎭 picture; Bruce Robinson (adapted screenplay); Haing S. Ngor (supporting actor)

'I was nobody until I killed the biggest somebody on earth.'

The Killing of John Lennon (new)

SCR/DIR Andrew Piddington
2007 114m UK

☆ Jonas Ball (Mark David Chapman), Krisha Fairchild (Chapman's Mother), Mie Omori (Gloria Chapman), Robert Kirk (Det. John Sullivan)

The former Beatle's murder, seen through the eyes of his deranged assassin.

Grim, forensic portrait of a disturbed individual; the film avoids being sensationalist but remains in dubious taste.

CIN Roger Eaton **MUS** Martin Kiszko **DES** Tora Peterson **ED** Tony Palmer **PROD** Rakha Singh **DIST** The Works

66 The power of the film is the way it charts, indeed enacts, a man losing his grip on reality. – *James Christopher, The Times*

66 A harrowing, impressionistic, widescreen tour-de-force that unfolds with the propulsive urgency of a scrapbook thrown into a howling wind. – *Eddie Cockrell, Variety*

Killing Zoe

SCR/DIR Roger Avary
1994 96m US
[DVD] ♫

☆ Eric Stoltz (Zed), Julie Delpy (Zoe), Jean-Hugues Anglade (Eric), Gary Kemp (Oliver), Bruce Ramsay (Ricardo), Tai Thai (Francois), Kario Salem

An American vault-cracker travels to Paris, sleeps with a prostitute, then meets up with a gang preparing for a bank heist.

Writer-director Avary was co-writer of Pulp Fiction, and got a movie deal as part of the Tarantino bandwagon. But this brutal gore-drenched thriller, in which one sees traces of Pulp Fiction and Reservoir Dogs, is not a patch on either. Its story is unengaging, its characters (apart from Delpy's call-girl Zoe) virtually ciphers. Avary blew his chance, and his directing career stuttered on unconvincingly from this point.

CIN Tom Richmond **MUS** Tomandandy **DES** David Wasco **ED** Kathryn Himoff **PROD** Samuel Hadida **DIST** Rank/Davis

66 One thing Avary lacks is Tarantino's ear for dialogue. – *Geoffrey Macnab, Sight & Sound*

† One French journalist unkindly dubbed this film Reservoir Frogs.

'The Daughter. The Addict. The Gossip. The Stripper. The Murder.'

The Kill-Off ★★

SCR/DIR *Maggie Greenwald*
1989 110m US

☆ Loretta Gross (Luane), Andrew Lee Barrett (Bobbie

[DVD] Available on DVD   ☆ Cast in order   66 Critics' Quotes   ⚯ Academy Award   🎭 BAFTA
♫ Soundtrack on CD   of importance   † Points of interest   ⚯ Academy Award nomination   🎭 BAFTA nomination

339

K

Ashton), Jackson Sims (Pete Pavlov), Steve Monroe (Ralph), Cathy Haase (Danny Lee), William Russell (Rags), Jorjan Fox (Myra Pavlov), Sean O'Sullivan (The Doctor), Ellen Kelly (Lily Williams)

In a small seaside town, a decision is taken to silence a vicious, bed-ridden gossip monger for good.

Effective low-budget treatment of a nasty, noirish little story, played to the hilt by a cast of unknowns.

CIN Declan Quinn   MUS *Evan Lurie*   DES Pamela Woodbridge   ED James Y. Kwei   PROD Lydia Dean Pilcher   DIST Palace/Filmworld International

Kind Hearts and Coronets ★★★

DIR *Robert Hamer*
1949   106m   GB
[DVD]

☆ *Dennis Price* (Louis Mazzini), *Alec Guinness* (Lord D'Ascoyne/Henry D'Ascoyne/Canon D'Ascoyne/General D'Ascoyne/Admiral D'Ascoyne/Ascoyne D'Ascoyne/Lady Agatha D'Ascoyne/Duke of Chalfont), *Valerie Hobson* (Edith), *Joan Greenwood* (Sibella), Miles Malleson (Hangman), Arthur Lowe (Reporter), Audrey Fildes (Mrs Mazzini), John Penrose (Lionel), Hugh Griffith (Lord High Steward), Clive Morton (Prison Governor)

An embittered heir apparent will stop at nothing to gets his hands on his fortune, so he embarks on killing eight members of the D'Ascoyne family who stand between him and the money.

Probably the jewel in the crown of Ealing comedies, this is most notable, of course, for the uncanny versatility of Guinness in playing all eight intended victims. Yet he had a splendid cast around him, and a darkly witty script – a DIY manual of inventive ways to bump off enemies. The nastiness is delivered with genteel style, and though the film might have been more visually interesting, it is overall a delight.

SCR *Robert Hamer, John Dighton*   CIN Douglas Slocombe   ED Peter Tanner   PROD Michael Relph   DIST Ealing

❝ A brilliant misfire for the reason that its plentiful wit is literary and practically never pictorial. – *Richard Winnington*

❝ Enlivened with cynicism, loaded with dramatic irony and shot through with a suspicion of social satire. – *Daily Telegraph*

'A Kind Of Loving that knew no wrong until it was too late!'

A Kind of Loving ★★★

DIR *John Schlesinger*
1962   112m   GB
[DVD]

☆ *Alan Bates* (Vic Brown), *June Ritchie* (Ingrid Rothwell), *Thora Hird* (Mrs. Rothwell), Bert Palmer (Mr. Brown), Gwen Nelson (Mrs. Brown)

A young north country draughtsman gets his girlfriend pregnant, and is forced to marry her and live with her dragon-like mother, before sorting out a relationship with his unhappy wife.

A superior example of British kitchen-sink drama of the 50s and 60s, better acted than most (especially by Hird) and with sharper dialogue. Notably, it also refuses to dwell on the misery of the couple's predicament or their surroundings.

SCR *Keith Waterhouse, Willis Hall*   CIN *Denys Coop*   MUS Ron Grainer   ED Roger Cherrill   PROD Joe Janni   DIST Anglo-Amalgamated

❝ You will be shocked by this highly moral film only if you are shocked by life. – *Evening News*

'The eighth wonder of the world.'

King Kong ★★★

DIR *Peter Jackson*
2005   187m   US/Germany/New Zealand
[DVD]   ♫

☆ *Naomi Watts* (Ann Darrow), Jack Black (Carl Denham), Adrien Brody (Jack Driscoll), Thomas Kretschmann (Capt Englehorn), Colin Hanks (Preston), Jamie Bell (Jimmy), Evan Parke (Hayes), Andy Serkis (Kong/Lumpy the Cook)

An ambitious showman leads his cast and crew to a remote island, where they discover a giant ape; captured and brought back to New York, it escapes and runs amok.

A grand spectacle and loving act of homage to a 1930s classic. The film's largesse is almost excessive at fully three hours, but it is full of wondrous sequences and derring-do, and the ape is simply astounding. Jackson's movie is a fairly magnificent beast in itself – a great tribute to the pioneers of his art form.

SCR Fran Walsh, Philippa Boyens, Peter Jackson   CIN *Andrew Lesnie*   MUS *James Newton Howard*   DES Grant Major   ED Jamie Selkirk   PROD Jan Blenkin, Carolynne Cunningham, Fran Walsh, Peter Jackson   DIST Universal

❝ The mad and magnificent brilliance of one of cinema's most extraordinary images – the giant ape's last stand atop the Empire State Building, proclaiming doomed, counter-evolutionary defiance – is thrillingly revived. – *Peter Bradshaw, Guardian*

❝ Almost too much of a good thing. – *Todd McCarthy, Variety*

⚲ Joe Letteri, Brian Van't Hul, Christian Rivers, Richard Taylor (visual effects); Christopher Boyes, Michael Semanick, Michael Hedges, Hammond Peek (sound mixing); Mike Hopkins, Ethan Van der Ryn (sound editing) ⚱ Grant Major

Ⓣ Joe Letteri, Christian Rivers, Brian Van't Hul, Richard Taylor (special visual effects)
Ⓣ Grant Major; Hammond Peek, Christopher Boyes, Mike Hopkins, Ethan Van der Ryn (sound)

'Out-leaping the maddest imaginings! Out-thrilling the wildest thrills!'

King Kong ★★★★

DIR *Merian C. Cooper, Ernest Schoedsack*
1933   100m   US
[DVD]   ♫

☆ *Robert Armstrong* (Carl Denham), *Fay Wray* (Ann Darrow), Bruce Cabot (John Driscoll), Frank Reicher (Capt. Englehorn), Sam Hardy (Charles Weston), Noble Johnson (Native Chief), Steve Clemento (Witch King)

A film producer on safari brings back a giant ape which terrorizes New York.

The greatest monster movie of all, a miracle of trick work and suspense, with some of the most memorable moments in film history, notably the ones involving the ape atop a skyscraper.

SCR James Creelman, Ruth Rose   CIN Edward Linden, Vernon Walker, L.O. Taylor   MUS Max Steiner   ED Ted Cheesman   PROD Merian C. Cooper   DIST RKO

CARL DENHAM (ROBERT ARMSTRONG): It wasn't the airplanes. It was beauty killed the beast.

† The film was re-made in 1976, then again in 2005.

'Fear and Loathing. A Study. An Approach. A Clearing. No Thing'

King Lear

SCR/DIR Jean-Luc Godard
1987   90m   US

☆ Burgess Meredith (Don Learo), Peter Sellars (William Shakespeare Junior the Fifth), Molly Ringwald (Cordelia), Jean-Luc Godard (Professor Pluggy), Norman Mailer (The Great Writer), Kate Mailer (Herself), Woody Allen (Mr. Alien)

In the wake of Chernobyl, all works of art are lost, and an American culture vulture sets about finding ways to restore them.

The cinematic equivalent of a traffic accident, conceived by a legendary director with a stellar cast, but jaw-droppingly awful and misguided at every turn.

CIN Sophie Maintigneux   ED Jean-Luc Godard
PROD Menahem Globus, Yoram Golan   DIST Cannon

† Originally, this was based on a Norman Mailer script, with Marlon Brando cast as a mafioso King Lear. At various stages of pre-production, Dustin Hoffman and Orson Welles were in the cast too.

'It's no laughing matter.'

King of Comedy   ★★★★

DIR Martin Scorsese
1983   109m   US
DVD

☆ Robert DeNiro (Rupert Pupkin), Jerry Lewis (Jerry Langford), Diahnne Abbott (Rita), Sandra Bernhard (Masha)

Obsessed with becoming a chat show host, a manic would-be stand-up comedian kidnaps his idol and ransoms him for a spot in the show.

Savage farce played for dark laughter, and an acid satire on the entire culture of fame and celebrity: how fast and randomly it can happen to you, and how fast and randomly it can disappear. De Niro and Lewis, an unlikely pairing to say the least, play off each other brilliantly.

SCR Paul D. Zimmerman   CIN Fred Shuler
MUS various   DES Boris Leven   ED Thelma Schoonmaker   PROD Arnon Milchan
DIST TCF/Embassy International

66 This is a very frightening film, and in retrospect nothing about it seems funny at all. – Variety

66 Unquestionably one of the films of the year. – Guardian

T Paul D. Zimmerman (original screenplay)

The King of Marvin Gardens   ★★★

DIR Bob Rafelson
1972   104m   US
DVD

☆ Jack Nicholson, Bruce Dern, Ellen Burstyn, Julia Anne Robinson

In Atlantic City, the pensive, reserved host of a late night radio talk show becomes involved in his brash, ambitious brother's property development schemes.

A somewhat cerebral, talky film, made at a downbeat period of American history. Its two central performances are extraordinarily strong, and Nicholson's late night radio monologues are delivered with quiet panache.

SCR Jacob Brackman   CIN Laszlo Kovacs   PROD Bob Rafelson   DIST Columbia/BBS

66 Indecipherable dark nonsense about brothers and goals and the American dream. An unqualified disaster. – New Yorker

66 Glum news from the people who made Five Easy Pieces, which had a lot of good work in it along with some pretentious flab. In their new picture the flab has taken over. – Stanley Kauffmann

† Marvin Gardens is a property in the American version of the board game Monopoly.

'Not everyone who runs a city is elected.'

King of New York   ★

DIR Abel Ferrara
1990   103m   US/Italy
DVD

☆ Christopher Walken (Frank White), David Caruso (Dennis Gilley), Larry Fishburne (Jimmy Jump), Victor Argo (Roy Bishop), Wesley Snipes (Thomas Flanigan), Janet Julian (Jennifer), Joey Chin (Larry Wong), Giancarlo Esposito (Lance)

A New York drug lord gets out of prison and sets about annihilating his rivals, intending to bankroll a hospital for the poor.

Violent and grungily stylish urban spin on Robin Hood, with Walken bringing his spectral intensity to a somewhat vague role.

SCR Nicholas St John   CIN Bojan Bazelli   MUS Joe Delia
DES Alex Tavoularis   ED Anthony Redman   PROD Mary Kane   DIST Rank/Reteitalia/Scena/Caminito

66 All soft-core lighting and music-video stylings. – Hal Hinson, Washington Post

66 A nihilistic exercise in designer pessimism. – Philip French, Observer

---

'When the world turns upside down, the trick is coming out on top.'

King of the Hill   ★

SCR/DIR Steven Soderbergh
1993   109m   US
DVD ♫

☆ Jesse Bradford (Aaron Kurlander), Jeroen Krabbé (Mr. Erich Kurlander), Lisa Eichhorn (Mrs. Kurlander), Karen Allen (Miss Mathey, Aaron's Teacher), Spalding Gray (Mr. Mungo in Room 310), Elizabeth McGovern (Lydia,

---

DVD Available on DVD   ☆ Cast in order   66 Critics' Quotes   🏆 Academy Award   T BAFTA
♫ Soundtrack on CD   of importance   † Points of interest   🏆 Academy Award nomination   T BAFTA nomination

341

K

Prostitute), Joe Chrest (Ben, Hotel Porter), Cameron Boyd (Sullivan Kurlander)

In Depression-era St. Louis, a boy of 12 is left by his parents to fend for himself in the run-down Empire Hotel.

This comes from what Soderbergh self-deprecatingly calls his 'formalist' period, when he seemed to be trying to distance himself from the enormous commercial success engendered by Sex, Lies and Videotape. This rites-of-passage movie is gentle, likable and trades on nostalgic charm – but nothing about it makes it compulsory viewing.

CIN Elliot Davis **MUS** Cliff Martinez **DES** Gary Frutkoff **ED** Steven Soderbergh **PROD** Albert Berger, Barbara Maltby, Ron Yerxa **DIST** Wildwood/Bona Fide/Gramercy

66 Take away its moody mise en scène, and King of the Hill is otherwise a purely conventional tale of a kid who wins through against the odds. – *Nick James, Sight & Sound*

The Kingdom ★★★

DIR *Lars von Trier, Morten Arnfred*
1994 279m Denmark/Sweden/Norway/Germany
DVD

☆ *Ernst Hugo Järegard* (Helmer), Kirsten Rolffes (Sigrid Drusse), Ghita Norby (Rigmor), Soren Pilmark (Krogshøj), Udo Kier (Aage Krüger), Otto Brandenburg (Hansen), Jens Okking (Bulder), *Holger Juul Hansen* (Moesgaard)

A hospital in Copenhagen is haunted by ghosts.

Originally made for Danish television in five parts, this often amazing supernatural soap opera juggles post-E.R. medical procedural, absurdist comedy and a genuine sense of the uncanny as the hospital falls under the sway of those betrayed by medical science years earlier. Visually striking in its use of off-beam camera angles and earthy brown filters, it is literally like nothing you've ever seen before.

SCR *Tómas Gislason, Lars von Trier, Nils Vorsel* **CIN** *Eric Kress* **MUS** *Joachim Holbek* **DES** *Jette Lehmann* **ED** *Jacob Thuesen, Molly Marlene Stensgaard* **PROD** Ole Reim Ib Tardini, Peter Aalbæk Jensen, Philippe Bober, Sven Abrahamsen **DIST** ICA/Zentropa/Denmark Radio TV/Swedish TV/WDR/Arte

66 This mordant blend of hospital soap, occult shocker and social satire makes David Lynch seem prim. – *Wally Hammond, Time Out*

† A second run of episodes, released internationally as The Kingdom Part II, followed in 1997.

'An elite FBI team sent to find a killer in Saudi Arabia. Now they have become the target.'

The Kingdom (new)

DIR Peter Berg
2007 109m US/Germany
DVD ♫

☆ Jamie Foxx (Ronald Fleury), Chris Cooper (Grant Sykes), Jennifer Garner (Janet Mayes), Jason Bateman (Adam Leavitt), Jeremy Piven (Damon Schmidt), Danny Huston (Gideon Young), Richard Jenkins (James Grace)

FBI operatives face official opposition and local hostility as they try to identify the terrorists behind a massacre at a western housing compound in Saudi Arabia.

Bombastic action yarn with a smattering of geopolitical awareness; the gung-ho finale settles everything with an extended shoot-out.

SCR Matthew Michael Carnahan **CIN** Mauro Fiore **MUS** Danny Elfman **DES** Tom Duffield **ED** Kevin Stitt, Colby Parker Jr. **PROD** Michael Mann, Scott Stuber **DIST** Universal

66 A realist thriller that mixes crowd-pleasing mayhem with provocative politics. – *John Anderson, Variety*

66 Syriana for dummies. – *A.O. Scott, New York Times*

'Be without fear in the face of your enemies. Safeguard the helpless, and do no wrong'

Kingdom of Heaven

DIR Ridley Scott
2005 145m GB/Spain.US/Germany
DVD ♫

☆ Orlando Bloom (Balian), Eva Green (Sibylla), Jeremy Irons (Tiberias), Brendan Gleeson (Reynald), Marton Csokas (Guy de Lusignan), Liam Neeson (Godfrey), Edward Norton (uncredited) (King Baldwin), Ghassan Massoud (Saladin)

A 12th-century blacksmith defends Jerusalem from Saladin's army during the Crusades.

A mealy-mouthed epic which reduces one of the world's most savage religious conflicts to politically correct claptrap. Scott indulges his usual eye for gorgeous spectacle, but the story is stultifying, and a terminally wooden lead performance brings it close to disaster.

SCR William Monahan **CIN** John Mathieson **MUS** Harry Gregson-Williams **DES** Arthur Max **ED** Dody Dorn **PROD** Ridley Scott **DIST** TCF

66 Everything about it looks glib and naïve. – *Peter Bradshaw, Guardian*

66 One imagined that a movie about the Crusades would be gallant and mad; one feared that it might stoke some antiquated prejudice. But who could have dreamed that it would produce this rambling, hollow show about a boy? – *Anthony Lane, New Yorker*

† A director's cut, restoring 45 minutes of footage deleted at the studio's insistence, was released on DVD.

Kings & Queen ★★★

DIR *Arnaud Desplechin*
2004 150m France
DVD

☆ *Emmanuelle Devos* (Nora Cotterelle), *Mathieu Amalric* (Ismaël Vuillard), Catherine Deneuve (Mme Vasset), Maurice Garrel (Louis Jenssens), Nathalie Boutefeu (Chloé Jenssens), Jean-Paul Roussillon (Abel Vuillard)

An art-gallery director cares for her terminally ill father, and tries to persuade her ex-lover, a musician with mental problems, to adopt her son from another man.

Strikingly ambitious drama of conflicting responsibilities and warring impulses, a complex symphony of tones in which even the main characters appear to be fighting to stay in the centre. The restless energy of the direction is fresh and exhilarating.

SCR Arnaud Desplechin, Roger Bohbot **CIN** *Eric Gautier* **MUS** Grégoire Hetzel **DES** Dan Bevan **ED** Laurence Briaud **PROD** Pascal Caucheteux **DIST** Artificial Eye

66 It insists that life is large and absurd, that we are gods and monsters, and that we stymie ourselves in our masks and guises; it's majestic movie-making. – *Nick Bradshaw, Time Out*

66 Complex, boldly experimental. – *Carina Chocano, LA Times*

'Truth Or Spin?'

King's Game ★★

DIR Nikolaj Arcel
2004 107m Denmark/Sweden/Norway
`DVD`

☆ Anders W. Berthelsen (Ulrik Torp), Søren Pilmark (Erik Dreier Jensen), Nastja Arcel (Lone Kjeldsen), Nicolas Bro (Henrik Moll), Lars Mikkelsen (Peter Schou), Ulf Pilgaard (Gunnar Torp), Charlotte Munck (Mette Torp), Lars Brygmann (Mads Kjeldsen)

A young Danish journalist is given a plum job on his paper's political beat, but gradually realises he has been set up to help downplay an ugly political plot.

Dexterous, well-plotted political thriller, well acted and cold-looking, with blues and greys dominant. But it is equally engrossing and intelligent about journalism and political spin.

SCR Rasmus Heisterberg, Nikolaj Arcel **CIN** Rasmus Videbæk **MUS** Henrik Munck, Flemming Nordkrog **DES** Niels Sejer **ED** Mikkel E.G. Nielsen **PROD** Meta Louise Foldager **DIST** Dogwoof

66 It's sparingly shot without comment and briskly edited – not a frame being wasted. – *Conan Lawrence, Sight & Sound*

'Let's talk about sex.'

Kinsey ★★

SCR/DIR Bill Condon
2004 118m US/GB/United Germany
`DVD` 🎵

☆ *Liam Neeson (Alfred Kinsey), Laura Linney* (Clara McMillen), Chris O'Donnell (Wardell Pomeroy), *Peter Sarsgaard* (Clyde Martin), Timothy Hutton (Paul Gebhard), John Lithgow (Alfred Seguine Kinsey), Tim Curry (Thurman Rice), Oliver Platt (Herman Wells), Dylan Baker (Alan Gregg), Lynn Redgrave (Final Interview Subject)

Biopic of pioneering sex researcher Dr Alfred Kinsey, whose 1948 book Sexual Behaviour in the Human Male was seminal in all senses.

Respectable, nicely acted, if overly polite portrait of a key figure in America's post-war sexual liberation, using the confusions and experimentation of Kinsey's own life to illustrate the infinitely grey area of human sexuality. The era's moral puritans are set up as priggish straw men – it's an exercise in enlightened hindsight.

CIN Frederick Elmes **MUS** Carter Burwell **DES** Richard Sherman **ED** Virginia Katz **PROD** Gail Mutrux **DIST** TCF

66 As superbly crafted – as good – as this movie is, Condon never really owns up to the cloud of pessimism at its centre. – *Ty Burr, Boston Globe*

66 Earnestly middlebrow. – *J. Hoberman, Village Voice*

⚖ Laura Linney (supporting actress)

'SeX. MurdEr. MyStery. Welcome to the party.'

Kiss Kiss Bang Bang ★

SCR/DIR Shane Black
2005 103m US
`DVD` 🎵

☆ Robert Downey Jnr (Harry Lockhart), Val Kilmer (Gay Perry), Michelle Monaghan (Harmony Faith Lane), Corbin Bernsen (Harlan Dexter), Dash Mihok (Mr Frying Pan)

A small-time thief poses as an actor in Los Angeles, teams up with a gay detective, and becomes involved in a murder investigation.

Amusingly played comic thriller with a deliberately useless narrator – but all the relentless nudging and winking verges on the conceited.

CIN Michael Barrett **MUS** John Ottman **DES** Aaron Osborne **ED** Jim Page **PROD** Joel Silver **DIST** Warner

66 A slithery treat. – *Anthony Lane, New Yorker*

66 A flashy, trifling throwaway whose surface cleverness masks a self-infatuated credulity. – *A.O. Scott, New York Times*

'I don't care what you do to me, Mike – just do it fast!'

Kiss Me Deadly ★★★

DIR Robert Aldrich
1955 105m US
`DVD`

☆ Ralph Meeker (Mike Hammer), Albert Dekker (Dr. Soberin), Cloris Leachman (Christina Bailey/Berga Torn), Paul Stewart (Carl Evello), Juano Hernandez (Eddie Yeager), Wesley Addy (Pat Chambers), Maxene Cooper (Velda), Gaby Rodgers (Gabrielle/Lily Carver)

By helping a girl who is nevertheless murdered, Mike Hammer prevents crooks from stealing a case of radio-active material.

A classic example of film noir, but with an unusual, apocalyptic climax. Aldrich shoots the film like a regular, hard-boiled black-and-white B-movie, true to the spirit of the source material by Mickey Spillane; but in his hands it becomes a strange, wonderful fable, filled with betrayals and with impossibly high stakes.

SCR A. I. Bezzerides **CIN** Ernest Laszlo **MUS** Frank de Vol **ED** Michael Luciano **PROD** Robert Aldrich **DIST** UA/Parklane

66 This meeting of "art" and pulp literature is, to say the least, curious. – *Monthly Film Bulletin*

'You know what I do to squealers? I let them have it in the belly. So they can roll around for a long time thinking it over!'

Kiss of Death ★★★

DIR Henry Hathaway
1947 98m US

☆ *Victor Mature, Richard Widmark*, Brian Donlevy, Coleen Gray, Karl Malden, Taylor Holmes

An imprisoned robber gives evidence against his partners in crime to facilitate his release, and a psychopathic killer is sent to exact vengeance.

`DVD` Available on DVD   ☆ Cast in order of importance   66 Critics' Quotes   ⚖ Academy Award   ⚖ Academy Award nomination   🅑 BAFTA   🅑 BAFTA nomination

Shot partly in a real prison, this compelling drama packs a real punch – often literally, considering its notable explicit violence.

SCR Ben Hecht, Charles Lederer CIN Norbert Brodine MUS David Buttolph PROD Fred Kohlmar DIST TCF

66 A tense, terrifying crime melodrama with an unusually authentic seamy atmosphere. – New Yorker, 1980

66 Economy of narration enhances the compactness and tautness of the whole and achieves that rarity, a picture minus unnecessary footage. – National Board of Review

† It was re-made under the same title in 1995, but previously the story was recast as a Western in The Fiend Who Walked the West (1958).

Richard Widmark (supporting actor); E. Lipsky (original screenplay)

'Lovers on the RUN . . .'

Kiss or Kill　　　　　　★

SCR/DIR Bill Bennett
1996　95m　Australia
DVD

☆ Frances O'Connor (Nikki Davies), Matt Day (Al Fletcher), Chris Haywood (Detective Hummer), Barry Otto (Adler Jones), Max Cullen (Stan), Andrew S. Gilbert (Detective Crean), Barry Langrishe (Zipper Doyle)

A couple of thieves are pursued across the Australian outback by two cops – and a football star, who appears on an incriminating sex tape they have purloined.

A decent attempt to add some zest and innovation to the classic premise of attractive young people on the run from justice. But some devices – unnecessary jump cuts, for instance – grate rather than enhance the story.

CIN Malcolm McCulloch DES Andrew Plumer ED Henry Dangar PROD Jennifer Bennett, Bill Bennett DIST AFFC/Bill Bennett

66 As the fugitive couple, Matt Day and Frances O'Connor give edgy, volatile performances. – Philip Kemp, Sight & Sound

'When it comes to love, sometimes she just can't think straight.'

Kissing Jessica Stein　　　　★

DIR Charles Herman-Wurmfeld
2001　97m　US
DVD　♫

☆ Jennifer Westfeldt (Jessica Stein), Heather Juergensen (Helen Cooper), Scott Cohen (Josh Meyers), Tovah Feldshuh (Judy Stein), Jackie Hoffman (Joan), Michael Mastro (Martin), Carson Elrod (Sebastian), David Aaron Baker (Dan Stein)

A copy editor in New York finds herself unexpectedly falling for another woman.

Breezily entertaining if skin-deep romance, in which the same-sex premise is the only ripple amid all the formulaic Woody Allen-ish one-liners and comic situations.

SCR Heather Juergensen, Jennifer Westfelt CIN Lawrence Sher MUS Marcelo Zarvos DES Charlotte Bourke

ED Kristy Jacobs Maslin, Gregory Tillman PROD Brad Zions, Eden Wurmfeld DIST TCF

66 All too content to be a comedy of surfaces and stereotypes. – Lisa Schwarzbaum, Entertainment Weekly

'There is a way to be good again.'

The Kite Runner (new)　　　　★★

DIR Marc Forster
2007　127m　US/China
DVD　♫

☆ Khalid Abdallah (Amir), Homayound Ershadi (Baba, Amir's father), Shaun Toub (Rahim Khan), Atossa Leoni (Soraya), Saïd Taghmaoui (Farid), Zekiria Ebrahimi (Young Amir), Ahmad Khan Mahoodzada (Young Hassan), Ali Danish Bakhty Ari (Sohrab)

Two boys, whose fathers are servant and master, grow up friends in 1970s Afghanistan, and fly kites together. One is victimised because of his race and caste, and his friend fails to stand up for him – a loss of nerve that haunts his adult life.

A decent, though far from thrilling adaptation of a first-rate best-seller, this film shows a different side of Afghan life from what we see on newscasts. Yet the standard of acting is mixed, the screenplay needed to be compressed, and one has the sense that the richness of Hosseini's novel simply eluded the film-makers.

SCR David Benioff CIN Roberto Schaefer MUS Alberto Iglesias DES Carlos Conti ED Matt Chessé PROD William Horberg, Walter Parkes, Rebecca Yeldham, E. Bennett Walsh DIST Paramount

66 A workmanlike, if decaffeinated version of Khaled Hosseini's best-selling novel. – Peter Bradshaw, Guardian

66 It's deeply moving, though over-emphatic and lacking variation in pace. – Philip French, Observer

† The family of the young actor who played Hassan tried to have one of his scenes, which involved sexual abuse, removed from the film.

Klute　　　　★★★

DIR Alan J. Pakula
1971　114m　US
DVD

☆ Jane Fonda (Bree Daniels), Donald Sutherland (John Klute), Charles Cioffi (Peter Cable), Roy Scheider (Frank Ligourin), Rita Gam (Trina)

A policeman leaves the force to investigate the disappearance of a research scientist, and takes up with a call girl who is involved.

Excellent adult thriller, intelligently scripted, and a career-turning performance by Fonda as a prostitute who is no victim, but a strong-minded manipulator in charge of her own destiny.

SCR Andy K. Lewis, Dave Lewis CIN Gordon Willis MUS Michael Small ED Carl Lerner PROD Alan J. Pakula DIST Warner

Jane Fonda (leading actress)
Andy K. Lewis, Dave Lewis (original screenplay)

'There are worse things than death.'

KM 31 (new)

★

SCR/DIR Rigoberto Castaneda
2007   103m   Mexico/Spain/Brazil
DVD

☆ Iliana Fox (Catalina/Agata), Raul Mendez (Omar), Adria Collado (Nuno)

Twin sisters are telepathically linked. When one is injured in a car crash and left comatose, the other returns to the accident scene to piece events together.

Efficient Mexican horror film, combining supernatural thriller elements with an ancient folk legend.

CIN Alejandro Martinez   DES Bernardo Trujillo
ED Alberto de Toro   PROD Billy Rovzar, Fernando Rovzar, Julio Fernández   DIST Yume

† On its release in February 2007, KM 31 became the third most seen film in the history of Mexican cinema.

Knife in the Water

★★★

DIR *Roman Polanski*
1962   94m   Poland
DVD   ♫

☆ Leon Niemczyk (Andrzej), Jolanta Umecka (Christine), Zygmunt Malanowicz (The Young Man)

A couple ask a young hitch-hiker to spend a weekend on their yacht, and regret it.

Detached, malevolent melodrama in a claustrophobic setting, all mind games, power trips and sexual electricity. The film introduced Polanski to a global audience and established his career in style.

SCR Jerzy Skolimowski, Roman Polanski, Jakub Goldberg
CIN Jerzy Lipman   MUS Krzystof Komeda
PROD Stanislaw Zylewicz   DIST ZRF Kamera

⚲ foreign film

'Save the due date.'

Knocked Up (new)

★★

SCR/DIR Judd Apatow
2007   128m   US
DVD   ♫

☆ *Seth Rogen* (Ben Stone), Katherine Heigl (Alison Scott), Paul Rudd (Peter), Leslie Mann (Debbie), Joanna Kerns (Alison's mother), Harold Ramis (Ben's dad)

On a drunken one-night stand, a homely young slacker impregnates an attractive TV presenter, who decides to keep the baby.

Surprisingly charming performances carry an implausible story. Rogen is a delightful, self-effacing screen presence; his scenes with his hapless slacker friends are hugely amusing despite the crudeness of their banter.

CIN Eric Edwards   MUS Loudon Wainwright III, Joe Henry   DES Jefferson Sage   ED Brent White, Craig Alpert
PROD Judd Apatow, Shauna Robertson, Clayton Townsend
DIST Universal

ALISON: 'I'm pregnant.'
BEN: 'Pregnant with emotion?'

ALISON: 'Pregnant with a baby.'

66 The sweetest, funniest, gentlest thing I have seen in such a long time. – *Peter Bradshaw, Guardian*

66 Snort-all-over-the-person-in-front-of you funny, hand-over-mouth filthy and as exhilarating as inhaling from a 10-ton oxygen tank. – *Sukhdev Sandhu, Daily Telegraph*

'The Ultimate Bachelor Has Finally Met His Match!'

Kolya

★★★

DIR Jan Sverák
1996   105m   Czech Republic/France/GB
DVD   ♫

☆ Zdenek Sverák (Frantisek Louka), Andre Chalimon (Kolya), Libuse Safránková (Klara), Ondrej Vetchy (Mr Broz), Stella Zázvorková (Mother), Ladislav Smoljak (Mr Houdek), Irina Livanova (Nadezda)

When a struggling veteran musician in Prague receives cash for marrying a Russian woman who needs immigration papers, he finds that part of the deal is taking care of her five-year-old son.

A first-class heart-string tugger, delicately acted and satisfyingly resolved – though the political backdrop to the story is a superfluous means of giving it extra significance.

SCR Zdenek Sverák   CIN Vladimir Smutny   MUS Ondrej Soukup   ED Alois Fisárek   PROD Jan Sverák, Eric Abraham   DIST Buena Vista/Portobello/Ceska Televize/Biograf Jan Sverák

66 The outlines of this story are conventional and sentimental (is there any doubt he will come to love the child?). What makes Kolya special is the way it paints the details. – *Roger Ebert, Chicago Sun-Times*

† Lead actor and screenwriter Zdenek Sverák is the father of the film's director, Jan Sverák.

⚲ foreign film

Ⓣ film not in the English language

'There's No Such Thing As A Free Ride.'

Kontroll

★★

DIR Nimrod Antal
2003   105m   Hungary
DVD

☆ Sandor Csanyi (Bulcsu), Zoltan Mucsi (Professor), Sandor Badar (Lecso), Csaba Pindroch (Muki), Zsolt Nagy (Tibi), Lajos Kovacs (Bela), Eszter Balla (Szofi)

Ticket inspectors on the Budapest underground system lose control when a serial killer threatens its passengers.

Propulsive black comedy made with a great deal of manic punk style.

SCR Jim Adler, Nimrod Antal   CIN Gyula Pados
MUS Neo   DES Balázs Hujber   ED Istvan Kiraly
PROD Tamas Hutlassa

66 A vein of humour that's blacker than the Northern Line. – *Alan Morrison, Empire*

† The film came with an anxious disclaimer from the Budapest Transport Co, explaining that its scenario is not intended realistically.

DVD Available on DVD   ☆ Cast in order   66 Critics' Quotes   ⚲ Academy Award   Ⓑ BAFTA
♫ Soundtrack on CD   of importance   † Points of interest   ⚲ Academy Award nomination   Ⓣ BAFTA nomination

'When people are afraid of you. . .You can do everything. Remember that.'

The Krays ★★

DIR Peter Medak
1990   119m   GB
[DVD]

☆ *Billie Whitelaw* (Violet Kray), Gary Kemp (Ronald Kray), Martin Kemp (Reggie Kray), Susan Fleetwood (Rose), Charlotte Cornwell (May), Jimmy Jewel (Cannonball Lee), Avis Bunnage (Helen), Kate Hardie (Frances), Alfred Lynch (Charlie Kray), Tom Bell (Jack 'The Hat' McVitie), Steven Berkoff (George Cornell)

A biopic about the East End twins who became Britain's best known criminals.

Thoughtfully conceived account of the Krays' unsavoury careers; though it sometimes gets bogged down in attempts at psychological explanation, it's at least preferable to the wave of British gang flicks that arrived a decade later, portraying violence for fun. In The Krays, nothing is fun. Whitelaw steals the picture as their overbearing mum, who, it is suggested, had much to answer for.

SCR Philip Ridley   CIN Alex Thomson   MUS Michael Kamen, Chris Rea   DES Michael Pickwoad   ED Martin Walsh   PROD Dominic Anciano, Ray Burdis
DIST Rank/Parkfield

Ⓣ Billie Whitelaw (supportitng actress)

The Kreutzer Sonata ★★

DIR Mikhail Schweitzer, Sofiya Milkina
1987   158m   USSR

☆ *Oleg Yankovsky* (Poznyshev), Aleksandr Trofimov (Pozdnyshev's fellow traveller), Irina Seleznyova (Lisa Pozdnyshev), Dmitri Pokrovsky (Trukhachevsky)

A man who murdered his wife through jealousy confess all to a traveller he meets on a train.

Excellent adaptation of Tolstoy's work, and a searing portrait of an unhappy marriage, told in flashback. Yankovsky is riveting in the lead role.

SCR Mikhail Schweitzer   CIN Mikhail Agranovich
MUS Sofia Gubaidulina   DES Igor Lemeshev, Vladimir Fabrikov   ED Lyudmila Feiginova   PROD Maria Zakharova   DIST Cannon/Mosfilm

'The destiny of a people lies in the heart of a boy.'

Kundun ★★

DIR Martin Scorsese
1997   134m   US
[DVD]   ♫

☆ Tenzin Thuthob Tsarong (Dalai Lama (Adult)), Sonam Phunstok (Reting Rimpoche), Gyatso Lukhang (Lord Chamberlain), Robert Lin (Chairman Mao), Tencho Gyalpo (Mother), Tsewang Migyur Khangsa (Father)

Tibet's 14th Dalai Lama is identified at the age of two, forced into a coalition with the Chinese government after their invasion, and ultimately exiled.

Sumptuously beautiful biopic, as bold with texture and rhythms as it is naggingly hagiographic and

sentimental in its script. It has all the décor of a great movie, but not the depth.

SCR Melissa Mathison   CIN *Roger Deakins*   MUS *Philip Glass*   DES *Dante Ferretti*   ED *Thelma Schoonmaker*
PROD Barbara de Fina   DIST Buena Vista/Touchstone

❝ At once spectacular and inert – a mosaic impersonating a movie. – *Owen Gleiberman, Entertainment Weekly*

❝ A poem of textures and silences. – *Richard Corliss, Time*

Ⓐ Roger Deakins; Philip Glass; Dante Ferretti (art direction); Dante Ferretti (costume design)

'A new comedy unlike anything you have seen before.'

Kung Fu Hustle ★

DIR *Stephen Chow*
2004   99m   Hong Kong/China
[DVD]   ♫

☆ Stephen Chow (Sing), Yuen Wah (Landlord), Yuen Qiu (Landlady), Leung Siu-lung (The Beast), Dong Zhihua (Donut), Chiu Chi-ling (Tailor), Xing Yu (Coolie), Chan Kwok-kwan (Brother Sum)

China, the 1940s: a humble locksmith defends the working-class district of Pig Sty Alley from representatives of organised crime.

Energetic knockaround nonsense that shows up how few Western filmmakers have properly exploited the cartoonish potential of computer effects (its action sequences are redrawn as though by Chuck Jones) and demonstrates a winning generosity of spirit in allowing performers of a certain age to do much of the fighting.

SCR Stephen Chow, Tsang Kan-cheong, Xin Huo, Chan Man-keung   CIN Poon Hang-seng   MUS Raymond Wong, Stephen Chow, Hang Yi, Xian Luo Zong
DES Oliver Wong   ED Angie Lam   PROD Stephen Chow, Chui Po-chu, Jeff Lau

❝ Is to House of Flying Daggers what Blazing Saddles is to Unforgiven. – *Michael Sragow, Baltimore Sun*

❝ A kung fu parody that's also a terrific kung fu movie. – *J. Hoberman, Village Voice*

Ⓣ film not in the English language

'The Film Courtney Doesn't Want You To See!'

Kurt and Courtney ★

DIR Nick Broomfield
1998   95m   GB
[DVD]

☆ Nick Broomfield (Interviewer), Kurt Cobain (Himself (archive footage)), Courtney Love (Herself)

Documentary exploration of musician Kurt Cobain's suicide and the conspiracy theories resulting from his death.

A tabloid-minded investigation, employing a ragbag of clips, sometimes wild tittle-tattle, and eventually a pair of professional celebrity stalkers to do all its dirty work; no wonder Cobain's widow Courtney Love took so forcefully against the film.

CIN Joan Churchill, Alex Vendler   ED Mark Atkins
PROD Nick Broomfield, Tine van den Brande, Michele d'Acosta   DIST Downtown/Strength

[DVD] Available on DVD   ☆ Cast in order of importance   ❝ Critics' Quotes   † Points of interest   Ⓐ Academy Award   Ⓐ Academy Award nomination   Ⓑ BAFTA   Ⓑ BAFTA nomination
♫ Soundtrack on CD

KZ ★★

DIR Rex Bloomstein
2005 95m UK
DVD

In the Austrian village of Mauthausen, the site of a Nazi concentration camp where thousands of Jews perished has now been turned into a memorial museum.

A radically different Holocaust-themed film, with no footage from death camps, testimony from survivors, voiceover commentary or mournful music. Instead TV documentary veteran Bloomstein points his camera at the bland village's residents, some of whom live in houses built for the SS, and asks if they ever consider the carnage committed there. An admirable essay about remembrance and forgetting.

CIN Alexander Boboschewski   ED Richard Rhys Davies
PROD Rex Bloomstein   DIST Shooting People

66 A beautifully understated, troubling achievement. – *Kieron Corless, Sight & Sound*

K

L

L.627 ★★

DIR *Bertrand Tavernier*
1992   145m   France
DVD   ♫

☆ Didier Bezace (Lucien 'Lulu' Marguet), Charlotte Kady (Marie), Philippe Torreton (Antoine), Nils Tavernier (Vincent), Jean-Paul Comart (Dodo), Jean-Roger Milo (Manuel), Lara Guirao (Cecile), Cécile Garcia-Fogel (Kathy Marguet), Claude Brosset (Adore)

A tenacious cop uses a video camera in his work for a new narcotics unit in Paris that tracks down drug traffickers.

Shot with enough hard-edged realism to pass for an effective documentary, this account of cops faced with an insurmountable task shows not only the tragic consequences of drug peddling but unwholesome attitudes in the narcotics unit.

SCR Michel Alexandre, Bertrand Tavernier   CIN Alain Choquart   MUS Philippe Sarde   DES Guy-Claude François   ED Ariane Boeglin   PROD Alain Sarde
DIST Artificial Eye/Little Bear

66 Doggedly unglamorous, both in terms of character and location. – *Chris Darke, Sight & Sound*

† The title refers to the statute in French law that prohibits the possession and use of drugs.
† Co-writer Michel Alexandre is a former plain-clothes drug investigator.

'Everything Is Suspect. . .Everyone Is For Sale. . .And Nothing Is What It Seems.'

LA Confidential ★★★★

DIR *Curtis Hanson*
1997   138m   US
DVD

☆ *Kevin Spacey* (Jack Vincennes), *Russell Crowe* (Bud White), *Guy Pearce* (Ed Exley), James Cromwell (Dudley Smith), David Strathairn (Pierce Patchett), *Kim Basinger* (Lynn Bracken), Danny De Vito (Sid Hudgens), Graham Beckel (Dick Stensland)

Los Angeles, the early 1950s: a by-the-book detective uncovers corruption within his own force, and enlists his brutish partner to help investigate.

A gloriously labyrinthine narrative, wrapped around half a dozen morally compromised figures worthy of films in their own right: tautly directed, lavishly produced and superlatively performed by everyone from its up-and-coming young stars to the smallest bit player, this was one of the finest – not to mention toughest – American pictures of the 1990s.

SCR *Brian Helgeland, Curtis Hanson*   CIN *Dante Spinotti*   MUS *Jerry Goldsmith*   DES *Jeannine Oppewall*   ED Peter Honess   PROD Arnon Milchan, Curtis Hanson, Michael Nathanson   DIST Warner/Regency

66 A movie bull's-eye: noir with an attitude, a thriller packing punches. It gives up its evil secrets with a smile. – *Michael Wilmington, Chicago Tribune*

66 A tough, gorgeous, vastly entertaining throwback to the Hollywood that did things right. – *Janet Maslin, New York Times*

⚲ Kim Basinger (leading actress); Curtis Hanson, Brian Helgeland (adapted screenplay)

⚱ picture; Curtis Hanson; Peter Honess; Jerry Goldsmith; Jeannine Oppewall; Dante Spinotti; Andy Nelson, Anna Behlmer, Kirk Francis (sound)

⬮ Peter Honess; Terry Rodman, Roland N. Thai, Kirk Francis, Andy Nelson, Anna Behlmer, John Levequet (sound)

⬯ film; Kevin Spacey (leading actor); Kim Basinger (leading actress); Curtis Hanson; Dante Spinotti; Jerry Goldsmith; Jeannine Oppewall; Curtis Hanson, Brian Helgeland (adapted screenplay); Ruth Myers (costume design); John M. Elliott, Scott H. Eddy, Janis Clark (make up/hair)

'Something Funny Is Happening in L.A.'

L.A. Story ★★

DIR Mick Jackson
1991   95m   US
DVD

☆ Steve Martin (Harris K. Telemacher), Victoria Tennant (Sara McDowel), Richard E. Grant (Roland Mackey), Marilu Henner (Trudi), Sarah Jessica Parker (SanDeE*), Susan Forristal (Ariel), Kevin Pollak (Frank Swan), Patrick Stewart (Mr. Perdue, Maitre D' at L'Idiot)

A TV weatherman is torn in his affections for a kooky shopgirl and a mature English journalist.

Sketchy but fun valentine to a generally unlovable city aspires to being an West Coast version of Manhattan; it's not quite that accomplished, but Martin finds more to laugh at here than most. Its most amusing sequences revolve around dating and ordering food.

SCR Steve Martin   CIN Andrew Dunn   MUS Peter Melnick   DES Lawrence Miller   ED Richard A. Harris   PROD Daniel Melnick, Michael Rachmil
DIST Guild/Rastar

66 Basically decent, intelligent and sweet. It's a fanciful romantic comedy whose wildest and craziest notion is that Los Angeles, for all of its eccentricities, is a great place to live. – *Vincent Canby, New York Times*

DVD Available on DVD   ☆ Cast in order of importance   66 Critics' Quotes   † Points of interest   ⚲ Academy Award   ⚱ Academy Award nomination   ⬮ BAFTA   ⬯ BAFTA nomination
♫ Soundtrack on CD

La Spagnola ★

DIR Steve Jacobs
2001 90m Australia
DVD

☆ Lola Marceli (Lola), Alice Ansara (Lucia), Lourdes Bartolome (Manola), Alex Dimitriades (Stefano), Simon Palomares (Ricardo), Silvio Ofria (Bruno), Gabrielle Maselli (Maria), Helen Thomson (Wendy)

In an Australian immigrant community, a Spanish mother vows vengeance on her husband's mistress, and embarrasses her teenage daughter.

Debutant Australian director Jacobs crafts a brash, sometimes over-the-top melodrama in an unusual location. Certainly, it's minor, but it jostles the memory long after larger-scale films have faded.

SCR Anna-Maria Monticelli CIN Steve Arnold
MUS Cezary Skubiszewski DES Dee Molineaux
ED Alexandre de Franceshi PROD Anna-Maria Monticelli
DIST Metro Tartan

66 So many earnest intentions have gone awry that La Spagnola becomes rather touching in its defencelessness. – *Peter Matthews, Sight & Sound*

Labyrinth of Passion

DIR Pedro Almodóvar
1982 100m Spain
DVD

☆ Cecilia Roth (Sexilia), Imanol Arias (Riza Niro), Helga Liné (Toraya), Marta Fernandez-Muro (Queti), Angel Alcazar (Eusebio), Antonio Banderas (Sadec), Agustin Almodóvar (Hassan)

A nymphomaniac rock singer and a laundry maid join forces to foil their oppressive parents and fulfil their dreams.

An early work by Almodóvar, released in the UK a whole decade after it was completed, to exploit his growing reputation. Notable mainly for the first film appearance of Antonio Banderas, it's otherwise the usual concoction of gay sex, rock music, excess and bad behaviour in Madrid's after-hours world that characterised this director's fledgling movies.

SCR Terry Lennox CIN Angel L. Fernandez
MUS Bernardo Bonezzi, Fany McNamara DES Pedro Almodóvar, Andrés Santana ED José Salcedo, Pablo Mínguez, Miguel Fernández PROD Pedro Almodóvar
DIST Metro/Alphaville/Ha Sido Producida

66 Requires a considerable dose of love from its audience to make it palatable. – *Paul Julian Smith, Sight & Sound*
† The film played at midnight every Saturday night for 10 years at Madrid's independent Alphaville cinema

'The story of two sisters who saved a stranger, and the stranger who stole their hearts.'

Ladies in Lavender ★

SCR/DIR Charles Dance
2004 104m GB
DVD ♫

☆ Judi Dench (Ursula Widdington), Maggie Smith (Janet Widdington), Daniel Bruhl (Andrea Marowski), Miriam Margolyes (Dorcas), Natascha McElhone (Olga Danilof), David Warner (Dr Francis Mead)

The relationship between two elderly spinster sisters living on the Cornish coast in the mid-1930s changes after a young Polish musician washes ashore.

Divertingly dotty period piece that might almost play as a Simpsons spoof of the quality British cinema; every scene is stocked deep with lusty yokels and other choice eccentricities, while the two Dames bicker away in engaging fashion.

CIN Peter Biziou MUS Nigel Hess DES Caroline Amies
ED Michael Parker PROD Nik Powell, Nicolas Brown, Elizabeth Karlsen DIST Entertainment

66 The film is old-fashioned because it exists. No one, to use an ever-dubious line, makes films like this anymore. – *Stanley Kauffman, New Republic*

The Lady and the Duke ★★

SCR/DIR Eric Rohmer
2001 129m France/Germany
DVD

☆ *Jean-Claude Dreyfus* (Duke of Orleans), *Lucy Russell* (Grace Elliott), Alain Libolt (Duc de Biron), Charlotte Véry (Pulcherie the Cook), Rosette (Fanchette), Léonard Cobiant (Champcenetz), François Marthouret (Dumouriez), Caroline Morin (Nanon)

A Scottish aristocrat in Paris at the time of the Revolution seeks help from her friend and former lover, the anti-Royalist Duke of Orleans.

A renewal of the period movie, using digital photography to stage bold, painterly group compositions, and capture every nuance of some intricate, close-up historical storytelling; even if you don't know your Jacobins from your sans-culottes, the human drama is more than engrossing enough, and it looks fit to hang in palatial chambers.

CIN Diane Baratier DES Antoine Fontaine ED Mary Stephen PROD Françoise Etchegaray

66 Partly a suspense drama, partly a very relevant study in how political ideas may be tainted by fanaticism, partly a typically astute moral disquisition... A splendid and remarkable achievement. – *Geoff Andrew, Time Out*

'Based on one of the most scandalous novels of our time.'

Lady Chatterley (new) ★★

DIR Pascale Ferran SCR/DIR Pascale Ferran, Roger Bohbot
2006 168m France/Belgium
DVD ♫

☆ *Marina Hands* (Constance Chatterley), Jean-Louis Culloc'h (Parkin), Hippolye Girardot (Sir Clifford Chatterley)

The wife of a paralysed ex-officer, in a sexless marriage, embarks on an affair with the gamekeeper on the family estate.

Far better than it sounds on paper, this French re-interpretation of Lawrence's story features the central love affair played tentatively against an exquisitely photographed pastoral backdrop.

CIN Julien Hirsch DES François-Renaud Labarthe
ED Yann Dedet PROD Gilles Sandoz DIST Artificial Eye

L

66 This isn't so much Beauty and the Beast but Beauty and the Dull Bloke. – *Peter Bradshaw, Guardian*

66 If Ferran is guilty of gilding the lily (the film features inter-titles, Super 8 footage, voiceover sand direct camera address) the superb cinematography and intricate costume design offer a sensual experience in their own right. – *Catherine Wheatley, Sight & Sound*

† The film won five César awards in France in 2007, including best French film, and was nominated for a further four.

† Although a French production, it was filmed in and around Sheffield.

'Prepare for the ride of your life.'

Lady Godiva (new)

SCR/DIR Vicky Jewson
2008 88m UK

☆ Phoebe Thomas (Jemima Honey/Lady Godiva), Matthew Chambers (Michael Bartle), James Wilby (Leofric), Isabelle Amyes (Mrs Bartle), Eric Carte (Mr Bartle), Simon Williams (Rupert), Petra Markham (Mother (Pink Dragon)), Nicholas Parsons (Himself)

A schoolteacher pledges to ride naked through Oxford to raise money for an arts centre.

Dim-witted, poorly scripted romantic comedy where little rings true; the action doesn't even take place in Coventry.

CIN George Stephenson, Agnès Godard **MUS** David Sinclair Whitaker **DES** Clive Crotty **ED** George Akers **PROD** Rupert Whitaker, Adam Kempton **DIST** Miracle Communications

66 A giant, steaming turd of a Brit flick. – *Ellen E. Jones, Total Film*

66 Such unintentionally hilarious tosh it's almost worth watching. – *Wendy Ide, The Times*

† At age 22, Wendy Jewson wrote, directed and raised funds for this, her debut feature, single-handed.

'Spies! Playing the game of love – and sudden death!'

The Lady Vanishes ★★★★

DIR *Alfred Hitchcock*
1938 97m GB
DVD

☆ *Margaret Lockwood* (Iris Henderson), *Michael Redgrave* (Gilbert Redman), *Dame May Whitty* (Miss Froy), *Paul Lukas* (Dr. Hartz), *Basil Radford* (Charters), *Naunton Wayne* (Caldicott), *Catherine Lacey* (The Nun), *Cecil Parker* (Eric Todhunter), *Linden Travers* (Margaret Todhunter), Googie Withers (Blanche), *Mary Clare* (Baroness), Philip Leaver (Signor Doppo)

En route back to England by train from Switzerland, an old woman disappears and two young people investigate.

The 'disappearing lady' trick brilliantly refurbished by Hitchcock and his screenwriters, who even get away with a horrid model shot at the beginning. Superb, suspenseful, brilliantly funny, meticulously detailed entertainment.

SCR *Sidney Gilliat, Frank Launder* **CIN** Jack Cox **ED** R.E. Dearing, Alfred Roome **PROD** Edward Black
DIST Gaumont British/Gainsborough

66 If it were not so brilliant a melodrama, we should class it as a brilliant comedy. – *Frank S. Nugent*

66 No one can study the deceptive effortlessness with which one thing leads to another without learning where the true beauty of this medium is to be mined. – *Otis Ferguson*

† Hitchcock was actually second choice as director. The production was ready to roll as Lost Lady, directed by Roy William Neill, with Charters and Caldicott already in place, when Neill became unavailable and Hitch stepped in.

† The film received a limited re-release in Britain in 2008, to wide acclaim. Much critical attention was paid to two minor characters, Charters and Caldicott, played by Basil Radford and Naunton Wayne. They were stuffy, cricket-loving, rather self-satisfied Englishmen who nonetheless came to represent a sort of British stoicism in the face of the Nazi threat.

Ladybird Ladybird ★★

DIR Ken Loach
1994 101m GB
DVD

☆ *Crissy Rock* (Maggie Conlan), Vladimir Vega (Jorge), Sandie Lavelle (Mairead), Mauricio Venegas (Adrian), Ray Winstone (Simon), Clare Perkins (Jill), Luke Brown (Mickey), Lilly Farrell (Serena), Jason Strachey (Sean)

A tempestuous, troubled unmarried mother, deemed an unfit parent by social workers, has her children taken into care – despite the efforts of a quiet, supportive Paraguayan exile to keep them together.

An angry attack on bureaucratic inflexibility, though Loach does not load the dice here: Maggie is her own worst enemy – a confrontational reprobate. Loach's point, which he rams home fiercely, is that for those in her position, a chance to change and improve one's life is made almost impossible. The central performance by non-actress Crissy Rock is riveting.

SCR Rona Munro **CIN** Barry Ackroyd **MUS** George Fenton **DES** Martin Johnson **ED** Jonathan Morris **PROD** Sally Hibbin **DIST** UIP/Parallax/Film Four

66 Based on a true story, Ladybird Ladybird dramatises harrowing events that would seem incredible in fiction. – *Lizzie Francke, Sight & Sound*

† Crissy Rock won the Silver Bear award for best actress at the 1994 Berlin Film Festival.

The Ladykillers ★★★

DIR *Alexander Mackendrick*
1955 97m GB
DVD ♫

☆ Alec Guinness (Professor Marcus), *Katie Johnson* (Mrs. Wilberforce), Peter Sellers (Harry), Cecil Parker (The Mayor), Herbert Lom (Louis), Danny Green (One-Round), Jack Warner (Police Superintendent), Frankie Howerd (Barrow Boy), Kenneth Connor (The Cab Driver)

An old lady takes in a sinister lodger, who with his four friends commits a robbery. When she finds out, they plot to kill her, but are hoist with their own petards.

Witty black comedy, shot in muted colours, which approaches the grotesque without damaging its acerbic

humour or sense of fantasy; it is one of the few films where death is both shocking and funny.

SCR *William Rose* CIN Otto Heller MUS Tristram Cary ED Jack Harris PROD Michael Balcon DIST Ealing

66 To be frivolous about frivolous matters, that's merely boring. To be frivolous about something that's in some way deadly serious, that's true comedy. – *Alexander Mackendrick*

66 A delicately diabolical blend of the ordinary and the brutal. – *John Powers, L.A. Weekly*

† It was re-made, to mixed reviews and indifferent box-office takings, by the Coen brothers in 2004.

⚖ William Rose (original screenplay)

Ⓣ Katie Johnson (British actress); William Rose (British screenplay)

The Lair of the White Worm ★

SCR/DIR Ken Russell
1988 93m GB
DVD

☆ Amanda Donohoe (Lady Sylvia Marsh), Hugh Grant (Lord James D'Ampton), Catherine Oxenberg (Eve Trent), Peter Capaldi (Angus Flint), Sammi Davis (Mary Trent), Stratford Johns (Peters), Paul Brooke (P.C. Erny), Imogen Claire (Dorothy Trent), Christopher Gable (Joe Trent)

In the grounds of a vast country mansion, an archaeologist unearths a skull, unleashing a series of freakish incidents.

There are those who recall this fondly as their favourite bad British film; it's an outlandish farce, consisting of eye-popping set-pieces rather than a coherent story. Naked nuns are in evidence, raping and pillaging soldiers, and (this being Russell) a crucifixion. It's not clear the director took it at all seriously; rather, there's a sense everyone made it up as they went along. Still, it's undeniably a hoot.

CIN Dick Bush MUS Stanlislas Syrewicz ED Peter Davies PROD Ken Russell DIST Vestron

'You'll never know what bit you.'

Lake Placid

DIR Steve Miner
1999 82m US
DVD ♫

☆ Bill Pullman (Jack Wells), Bridget Fonda (Kelly Scott), Oliver Platt (Hector Cyr), Brendan Gleeson (Sheriff Hank Keough), Betty White (Mrs Delores Bickerman), David Lewis (Walt Lawson), Tim Dixon (Stephen Daniel), Natassia Malthe (Janine), Mariska Hargitay (Myra Okubo), Meredith Salenger (Deputy Sharon Gare)

A trooper from the Fish and Fowl Department is sent to investigate reports of a killer crocodile in Maine.

Shrivelled horror-comedy, from the writer of TV's Ally McBeal; running to barely an hour of ho-hum humour, it has the feel of a busted small-screen pilot.

SCR David E. Kelley CIN Daryn Okada MUS John Ottman DES John Willett ED Marshall Harvey, Paul Hirsch PROD David E. Kelley, Michael Pressman DIST TCF

66 Laughably stupid, only fitfully scary, and relatively harmless. – *Michael O'Sullivan, Washington Post*

Lamerica ★★

DIR *Gianni Amelio*
1994 125m Italy/France
DVD ♫

☆ *Enrico Lo Verso* (Gino), Michele Placido (Fiore), Carmelo di Mazzarelli (Spiro), Piro Milkani (Selimi)

Two Italian capitalists head to Albania to exploit the country's failing economy, aiming to set up a false business front and pocket the proceeds.

Edgy drama that portrays a struggling nation's bleakness and loss of hope; even its villainous protagonists are forced to re-assess themselves. The film makes its points quietly and persuasively.

SCR Gianni Amelio, Andrea Porporati, Alessandro Sermoneta CIN *Luca Bigazzi* MUS Franco Piersanti DES Giuseppe M. Gaudino ED Simona Paggi PROD Mario and Vittorio Cecchi Gori DIST CGG Tiger/Arena

'A Story from the Spanish Civil War.'

Land and Freedom ★★

DIR *Ken Loach*
1995 109m GB/Germany/Spain
DVD

☆ *Ian Hart* (David Carr), *Rosana Pastor* (Blanca), Iciar Bollain (Maite), Tom Gilroy (Lawrence), Marc Martinez (Vidal), Frederic Pierrot (Bernard), Suzanne Maddock (Kim)

An unemployed Liverpudlian signs up to help fight Franco's forces in the Spanish Civil War, only to see at first hand how the Socialist resistance was undermined by in-fighting.

A memorial for those British veterans of a conflict subsequently overshadowed by WWII, opening with a present-day framing device before flashing back to a handsome, meticulous re-creation of the era. The central romance is affecting, although one extended discussion of collectivism stops the film more or less dead.

SCR *Jim Allen* CIN *Barry Ackroyd* MUS George Fenton DES Martin Johnson ED Jonathan Morris PROD Rebecca O'Brien DIST Artificial Eye/Parallax/Messidor/Road Movies

66 Loach handles what is for him an unprecedently large canvas with aplomb. The action scenes in particular have a raw, plausible immediacy. Nor is this just a movie which simply fills us in on fascinating historical details; thanks to muscular performances (especially from Hart), it also packs an emotional punch. – *Geoff Andrew, Time Out*

Ⓣ British film

'The story of three young women and the events that would change their lives... The friendships that would stay with them forever... and the loves that would change their hearts.'

The Land Girls ★

DIR David Leland
1997 111m GB/France
DVD ♫

☆ Catherine McCormack (Stella), Rachel Weisz (Ag),

DVD Available on DVD   ☆ Cast in order   66 Critics' Quotes   ⚖ Academy Award   Ⓑ BAFTA
♫ Soundtrack on CD   of importance   † Points of interest   ⚖ Academy Award nomination   Ⓣ BAFTA nomination

351

L

Anna Friel (Prue), Steven Mackintosh (Joe Lawrence), Tom Georgeson (Mr. John Lawrence), Maureen O'Brien (Mrs. John Lawrence), Lucy Akhurst (Janet)

During World War II, three young women from different backgrounds arrive at a farm in Dorset, as part of the Women's Land Army, volunteers who cover for agricultural workers fighting abroad.

A pretty-looking film, perhaps too much so; it concentrates on the girls' romantic entanglements rather than even pretending to show the hardships endured. It's agreeable, but little more.

SCR David Leland, Keith Dewhurst CIN Henry Braham MUS Brian Lock DES Caroline Amies ED Nick Moore PROD Simon Relph DIST Film Four/InterMedia/Greenpoint/West Eleven

66 Arguably (Leland's) vision of 40s rural Britain is just a little bit too cosy. – *Geoffrey Macnab, Sight & Sound*

Land of the Dead ★★

SCR/DIR *George A. Romero*
2005 93m US/Canada/France
DVD ♫

☆ Simon Baker (Riley), John Leguizamo (Cholo), Dennis Hopper (Kaufman), Asia Argento (Slack), Robert Joy (Charlie), Jennifer Baxter (Number 9)

Fast-evolving zombies, long confined to ghettos on the outskirts of town, begin to march on the homes and properties of the rich citydwellers who put them there.

In an age when most mainstream horror releases fall under the direction of first-timers who know only how to shoot and cut commercials, it's a delight to see a filmmaker who knows exactly what he's doing: Romero here juggles thrills and gore with the same high level of skill as he does his usual social concerns.

CIN Miroslaw Baszak MUS Johnny Klimek, Reinhold Heil DES Arv Grewal ED Michael Doherty PROD Mark Canton, Bernie Goldmann, Peter Grunwald DIST UIP

66 Romero's long-awaited masterpiece, a slyly suspenseful and droll thrill-ride that expounds on both the highbrow and the chewed-off-brow concepts of his previous trilogy, then flippantly dismisses the cheap scare tactics of the control-pad generation's gimmicky genre knockoffs. – *Aaron Hillis, Premiere*

66 It may be a notch down from the high watermarks of the preceding trilogy, but it still covers all the bases of the Living Dead saga: inventive suspense, spiky characters, outrageous horror and wicked satire. – *Kim Newman, Empire*

'Sometimes love isn't enough.'

Lantana ★★★

DIR *Ray Lawrence*
2001 121m Australia/Germany
DVD ♫

☆ *Anthony LaPaglia* (Leon Zat), Geoffrey Rush (John Knox), Barbara Hershey (Dr Valerie Somers), *Kerry Armstrong* (Sonja Zat), Rachael Blake (Jane O'May), Vince Colosimo (Nik Daniels), Daniela Farinacci (Paula Daniels), Peter Phelps (Patrick Phelan)

A woman's lifeless body is the end result of increasingly passive-aggressive relations in and around suburbia.

Bleak and knotty examination of modern love, more cinematic than its origins would suggest, and with moments of wit, tenderness and generosity towards its excellent ensemble that make it superior to a film like Closer.

SCR *Andrew Bovell* CIN Mandy Walker MUS Paul Kelly, Shane O'Mara, Peter Luscombe, Bruce Haymes, Steve Hadley DES Kim Buddee ED *Karl Sodersten* PROD Jan Chapman DIST Winchester

66 Sometimes has the air of a routine police procedural, sometimes the quality of a dour film noir. But this movie, so alert to mischance and dreams that don't quite work out as they should, has a good soul, a heart yearning for decency. – *Richard Schickel, Time*

66 This rare thriller insists that the most compelling mysteries are buried in human relationships. LaPaglia gives the performance of his career. – *Tom Charity, Time Out*

L'Appartement ★★

SCR/DIR *Gilles Mimouni*
1996 116m France/Spain/Italy
DVD

☆ *Romane Bohringer* (Alice), *Vincent Cassel* (Max), Jean-Philippe Ecoffey (Lucien), Monica Bellucci (Lisa), Sandrine Kiberlain (Muriel), Olivier Granier (Daniel)

In Paris, a young executive is given the runaround by three women: his fiancée, a lost love and the suicidal young woman he rescues from a rooftop.

Mimouni's only film to date – the movie equivalent of a one-hit wonder – is a shimmering jeu d'esprit, mixing elements of Hitchcock, A Midsummer Night's Dream and various ad campaigns: there's less here than meets the eye, perhaps, but an attractive young cast has great fun with its narrative chicanery.

CIN *Thierry Arbogast* MUS *Peter Chase* DES Philippe Chiffre ED Caroline Biggerstaff, Françoise Bonnot PROD Georges Benayoun DIST Artificial Eye/Ima/UGC/La Sept/M6/Mate/Cecchi Gori

66 A divertissement in the full sense of the word – an exhilarating, complex game with the viewer's perceptions, as well as the story of a man literally diverted from the course of his life. – *Jonathan Romney, Sight and Sound*

† An inferior English-language remake, Wicker Park, was released in 2004.

🎬 film not in the English language

'The search for true love begins outside the box.'

Lars and the Real Girl (new) ★★

DIR *Craig Gillespie*
2007 106m US
♫

☆ Ryan Gosling (Lars Lindstrom), Emily Mortimer (Karin Lindstrom), Paul Schneider (Gus Lindstrom), Kelli Garner (Margo), Patricia Clarkson (Dagmar), Nancy Beatty (Mrs. Gruner), Karen Robinson (Cindy)

An introverted bachelor unsettles his neighbours by falling in love with a life-sized female doll.

Beguiling and poignant comedy that deftly transcends its challenging premise.

SCR Nancy Oliver   **CIN** Adam Kimmel   **MUS** David Torn   **DES** Arv Grewal   **ED** Tatiana S. Riegel   **PROD** Sidney Kimmel, John Cameron, Sarah Aubrey   **DIST** Verve Pictures

66 What screenwriter Nancy Oliver, director Craig Gillespie and a top cast have done is construct a Frank Capra-style fable around a sex toy. – *Kenneth Turan, Los Angeles Times*

66 Part comedy, part tragedy and 100 percent pure calculation. – *Manohla Dargis, New York Times*

⚲ Nancy Oliver (original screenplay)

'Did Someone Say Action?'

Last Action Hero

DIR John McTiernan
1993   130m   US
DVD   ♫

☆ Arnold Schwarzenegger (Jack Slater / Himself), F. Murray Abraham (John Practice), Art Carney (Frank), Charles Dance (Benedict), Frank McRae (Lieutenant Dekker), Tom Noonan (Ripper / Himself), Robert Prosky (Nick), Anthony Quinn (Tony Vivaldi), Mercedes Ruehl (Irene Madigan), Ian McKellen (Death), Joan Plowright (Teacher), Tina Turner (The Mayor)

A boy's magic ticket propels him into a movie alongside his favourite action hero. But there's a catch – the killer in the film burst back through the screen into the real world, causing mayhem.

An air of desperate, cloying in-jokiness pervades this film, which has a premise that might have worked if the writing were better and if conceived in a spirit of innocence and wonder. But that would be a totally different movie: this one greedily tries to pander to every audience demographic and satisfies none. It deservedly flopped at box-offices.

SCR Shane Black, David Arnott   **CIN** Dean Semler   **MUS** Michael Kamen   **DES** Eugenio Zanetti   **ED** John Wright, Richard A. Harris   **PROD** Steve Roth, John McTiernan   **DIST** Columbia TriStar/Columbia

66 If there's one thing going for Last Action Hero, it's the construction of it all. Even if this intermixing of kid fantasy and adult shoot-'em-up, Hollywood insider jokes and cheap Arnold puns, doesn't completely bowl you over, it's clever and intriguing. – *Desson Howe, Washington Post*

66 No amount of cinematic steroids could turn this in to a muscular premise. – *Henry Sheehan, Sight & Sound*

'Sometimes justice is a crime.'

Last Dance   ★

DIR Bruce Beresford
1996   103m   US
DVD

☆ *Sharon Stone* (Cindy Liggett), Rob Morrow (Rick Hayes), Randy Quaid (Sam Burns), Peter Gallagher (John Hayes), Jack Thompson (The Governor), Don Harvey (Doug), Jayne Brook (Jill), Pamela Tyson (Linda, Legal Aid Attorney), Skeet Ulrich (Billy, Cindy's Brother)

A woman convicted of a double murder has been on Death Row for 12 years. But a young lawyer who looks into her case gives her a glimpse of hope for freedom.

A creditable, focussed, deliberately unglamorous performance by Stone in a hand-wringing, well-intentioned but underpowered plea against capital punishment.

SCR Ron Koslow   **CIN** Peter James   **MUS** Mark Isham   **DES** John Stoddart   **ED** John Bloom   **PROD** Steven Haft   **DIST** Buena Vista/Touchstone

66 Last Dance at least wears its tackiness on its sleeve, which makes it infinitely preferable to the dreary, prestige-laden Dead Man Walking. – *Peter Matthews, Sight & Sound*

Last Days of Chez Nous   ★

DIR *Gillian Armstrong*
1992   96m   Australia
DVD

☆ *Lisa Harrow* (Beth), Bruno Ganz (J.P), Kerry Fox (Vicki), Miranda Otto (Annie), Kiri Paramore (Tim), Bill Hunter (Beth's father)

The arrival of an Australian wife's love-starved sister causes intense family upheavals.

A strong cast play out an honest, psychologically authentic drama about a household falling apart.

SCR *Helen Garner*   **CIN** Geoffrey Simpson   **MUS** Paul Grabowsky   **DES** Janet Patterson   **ED** Nicholas Beauman   **PROD** Jon Chapman   **DIST** Metro/Jan Chapman/Australian Film Finance Corp.

66 Armstrong and Garner are attentive to the mundane nature of relationships that can be built on, or conversely collapse over the smallest of details. – *Lizzie Francke, Sight & Sound*

'History is made at night.'

The Last Days of Disco   ★★

SCR/DIR *Whit Stillman*
1998   113m   US
DVD   ♫

☆ Chloe Sevigny (Alice Kinnon), Kate Beckinsale (Charlotte Pingress), Chris Eigeman (Des McGrath), Matt Keeslar (Josh Neff), Mackenzie Astin (Jimmy Steinway), Matthew Ross (Dan Powers), Tara Subkoff (Holly), Burr Steers (Van), David Thornton (Bernie Rafferty), Jaid Barrymore (Francesca / Tiger Lady), Michael Weatherly (Hap), Robert Sean Leonard (Tom Platt), Jennifer Beals (Nina Moritz)

The affairs of the young, upwardly mobile but romantically confused clientele of a New York nightclub in the early 1980s.

An affectionate take on a sea change in American popular culture – when the disco movement found itself under attack from punk and new wave, and its survivors sought refuge on the dance floor – yields a sophisticated, witty comedy of manners, set to a fabulous soundtrack.

CIN John Thomas   **MUS** Mark Suozzo   **DES** Ginger Tougas   **ED** Andrew Hafitz, Jay Pires   **PROD** Whit Stillman   **DIST** Warner/Castle Rock/Westerly

TOM PLATT: Why is it that when people have sex with strangers on their mind their IQ just drops like 40 points?

L

66 A small miracle of comic social portraiture, a sometimes affectionate, sometimes ironic study of a specific group at a specific moment... deeply evocative and enjoyable. – *Dave Kehr, New York Daily News*

66 The director isn't much on orgies; he's all talk. But that's good, not bad, because his talk is so brilliant. Stillman is the Balzac of the ironic class, the Dickens of people with too much inner life. – *Stephen Hunter, Washington Post*

The Last Emperor ★★★

DIR *Bernardo Bertolucci*
1987 160m Italy/China
[DVD] ♫

☆ John Lone (Emperor Pu Yi / Henry), Joan Chen (Empress Wan Jung / Elizabeth), Peter O'Toole (Reginald F. 'R. J.' Johnston), Ying Ruocheng (Governor of Detention Center)

A biopic of Pu Yi, who acceded to the throne of China as a young child, grew up to become a reformer, and was Emperor at the point his country became a republic.

A work of epic pageantry – rivalled only, in recent years, by late Kurosawa and Farewell, My Concubine – in which the Emperor's rise to power, nimbly enacted by a trio of bright young performers, is more engaging than the decline and fall. In the age of CGI, its crowd scenes – stocked not with pixels, but living, breathing extras – have become doubly impressive.

SCR Mark Peploe, Bernardo Bertolucci CIN *Vittorio Storaro* MUS Ryuichi Sakamoto, David Byrne, Cong Su DES *Ferdinando Scarfiotti* ED Gabriella Cristiani, Anthony Sloman PROD Jeremy Thomas DIST Columbia/Yanco Films/Tao Films/Recorded Picture Company/Screenframe/AAA Soprofilm

66 Uneven, fuzzy, imperfect, and one of the reasons the movies were invented. – *Mike Clark, USA Today*

66 A genuine rarity: a blockbuster that manages to be historically instructive and intensely personal at the same time. – *Jonathan Rosenbaum, Chicago Reader*

† A 219-minute director's cut, offering more Mao for your money, opened in the US in 1998 and the UK in 2004; the extra hour allows Bertolucci and Peploe to further underline the ironies of revolution, but also allows for far too many shots of Joan Chen looking mournfully pretty.

⚲ picture; Bernardo Bertolucci; Mark Peploe, Bernardo Bertolucci (adapted screenplay); Vittorio Storaro (cinematography); Ryuichi Sakamoto, David Byrne, Cong Su (music); Gabriella Cristiani (editing); Bruno Cesari (art direction); James Acheson (costume design); sound

⚲ film; James Acheson (costume design); Fabrizio Sforza (makeup)

⚲ Peter O'Toole (supporting actor); Bernardo Bertolucci (direction); Gabriella Cristiani (editing); Ferdinando Scarfiotti (production design); score; sound; special effects

'The Novel That Shocked The World Is Now A Movie.'

Last Exit to Brooklyn ★★

DIR *Uli Edel*
1989 102m West Germany/ US
[DVD] ♫

☆ Stephen Lang (Harry Black), Jennifer Jason Leigh

(Tralala), Burt Young (Big Joe), Peter Dobson (Vinnie), Christopher Murney (Paulie), Jerry Orbach (Boyce), Alexis Arquette (Georgette)

A prostitute, a union leader and impoverished workers fend for themselves in 1950s Brooklyn, a place blighted by violence and crime.

Forceful adaptation of Hubert Selby's novel, widely thought unfilmable; a sobering, even depressing trawl through a city's low-life quarters, with every scene exploited to the full and unsparing in its detail. Yet it must be said that Edel honours the novel's intentions and outlook.

SCR Desmond Nakano CIN *Stefan Czapsky* MUS *Mark Knopfler* DES David Chapman ED Peter Przygodda PROD Bernd Eichinger DIST Guild/Neue Constantin Film Produktion/Bavaria Film/Allied Filmmakers

† Author Selby has a cameo role as a cab driver.

The Last Great Wilderness

DIR David Mackenzie
2002 95m GB/Denmark
[DVD] ♫

☆ Alastair Mackenzie (Charlie), Jonny Phillips (Vincente), David Hayman (Ruaridh), Ewan Stewart (Magnus), Victoria Smurfit (Claire)

Driving to Skye to burn down the mansion of a pop star who stole his wife, a man encounters a gigolo fleeing from vicious thugs, and they continue the journey together.

Not your average road movie, or an average movie of any kind; but writer-director Mackenzie's flair for unorthodox story-telling, and throwing in extraneous elements apparently at random, keeps things vaguely interesting.

SCR Alastair Mackenzie, Michael Tait, Gillian Berrie, David Mackenzie CIN Simon Dennis MUS The Pastels DES Tom Sayer ED Jake Roberts PROD Gillian Berrie DIST Feature Film

66 The film is possessed of distinctive energies. – *Andy Richard, Sight & Sound*

† Lead actor Alastair Mackenzie is the director's brother.

'Charming. Magnetic. Murderous.'

The Last King of Scotland ★★★

DIR Kevin Macdonald
2006 122m UK/US
[DVD] ♫

☆ Forest Whitaker (Idi Amin), James McAvoy (Nicholas Garrigan), Kerry Washington (Kay Amin), Gillian Anderson (Sarah Merrit), Simon McBurney (Stone), David Oyelowo (Dr. Junju)

An idealistic young Scottish doctor applies to work in Uganda, and becomes personal physician to the savage dictator Idi Amin.

A riveting thriller with a towering performance by Forest Whitaker as the tyrannical Amin and a hard-working, underrated one by James McAvoy. It cleverly suggests the extent of Amin's charisma and charm; McAvoy's young doctor desperately wants to approve of his employer. The fictional story has the smack of reality,

L

largely due to its Ugandan locations, and to the skill of director Macdonald, whose documentary background is evident here.

SCR Peter Morgan, Jeremy Brock   CIN Anthony Dod Mantle   MUS Alex Heffes   DES Michael Carlin   ED Justine Wright   PROD Andrea Calderwood, Lisa Bryer, Charles Steel, Chrstine Ruppert   DIST TCF

66 Amin, rather discomfitingly, is a marvellous monster. – *Sukhdev Sandhu, Daily Telegraph*

66 Macdonald has a fetching feel for the continent, and the movie has a powerful sense of what Africa looks and feels like; you can almost smell it. – *Stephen Hunter, Washington Post*

⚲ Forest Whitaker (leading actor)

🛡 British film; Forest Whitaker (leading actor); Peter Morgan, Jeremy Brock (adapted screenplay)

Ⓣ film; James McAvoy (supporting actor)

The Last Laugh   ★★★

DIR F. W. Murnau
1924   73m   Germany
DVD

☆ *Emil Jannings* (The Porter), Max Hiller (The Daughter's Fiance), Maly Delschaft (The Porter's Daughter), Hans Unterkirchen (Hotel Manager)

The old doorman of a luxury hotel is demoted to the job of lavatory attendant, but comes into a fortune and gets his revenge.

Ironic silent anecdote, made important by its virtual abandonment of dialogue and the whole-hearted adoption of a freewheeling camera technique which gives some thrilling dramatic effects.

SCR Carl Mayer   CIN Karl Freund   DIST UFA

66 A marvellous picture – marvellous in its simplicity, its economy of effect, its expressiveness, and its dramatic power. – *Life*

66 Among the finest achievements of the silent cinema. – *Ephraim Katz*

† A German remake of 1955 had Hans Albers in the lead and was of no interest.

'Before King Arthur, there was Excalibur.'
The Last Legion (new)   ★

DIR Doug Lefler
2007   102m   UK/ Italy/ France/ Slovakia/Tunisia
DVD   ♫

☆ *Colin Firth* (Aurelius), *Ben Kingsley* (Ambrosinus/Merlin), Iain Glen (Orestes), Peter Mullan (Odoacer), Thomas Sangster (Romulus Augustus)

The Arthurian legend is charted from the fall of Rome in 476 AD when the boy emperor Romulus travels to Britannia to find the fabled Dragon Legion.

More Monty Python than Camelot, this unconvincing epic on a budget with cheap-looking special effects to match is a tonally variable and confusing history lesson.

SCR Jez Butterworth, Tom Butterworth, Carlo Carlei, Peter Rader, Valerio Manfredi   CIN Marco Pontecorvo

MUS Patrick Doyle   DES Carmelo Agate   ED Simon Cozens   PROD Tarak Ben Ammar, Dino de Laurentiis, Martha de Laurentiis, Raffaella de Laurentiis   DIST Momentum

66 "Not as bad as it sounds nor as good as it might have been".. – *John Anderson, Los Angeles Times*

66 Fast-paced, diverting and unsophisticated. – *Patrick Fahy, Sight & Sound*

The Last Mistress (new)   ★★

SCR/DIR Catherine Breillat
2008   104m   France/Italy
DVD

☆ Fu'ad Aït Aattou (Ryno de Marigny), Asia Argento (Vellini), Michael Lonsdale (Le Vicomte de Prony), Roxane Mesquida (Hermangarde), Yolande Moreau (La Comtesse d'Artelles), Claude Serraute (La Marquise de Fiers)

A 19th-century love affair, set in France, between a penniless, well-bred gambler and womaniser and his tempestuous Spanish mistress, who offers him the passion missing in his recent marriage.

Beneath its literate dialogue and sumptuous costumes, Breillat's first foray into period drama maintains her familiar preoccupation with the power of female sexuality. It plays a bit like an upmarket bodice-ripper, or a close cousin of Dangerous Liaisons.

CIN Yorgos Arvanitis   ED Pascale Chavance   PROD Jean-François Lepetit   DIST Artificial Eye

66 Catherine Breillat's latest is as philosophically rigorous and psychologically revealing as anything she's made. – *Geoff Andrew, Time Out*

66 Asia Argento does a full-blown sultry-siren routine and ends up looking brattish and silly. – *Edward Porter, Sunday Times*

The Last Mitterand   ★★

DIR Robert Guédiguian
2004   116m   France/Switzerland
DVD

☆ *Michel Bouquet* (The President), Jalil Lespert (Antoine Moreau), Philippe Fretun (Doctor Jeantot), Anne Cantineau (Jeanne), Sarah Grappin (Judith), Catherine Salviat (Mado), Jean-Claude Frissung (René)

A young writer working on an authorised biography tails a former President as he fulfils various speaking engagements.

Scholarly, slightly dry character study, reputedly based on the life and times of Francois Mitterand, superbly incarnated here by Bouquet as a man of roisterous good company who is beyond the remit of spin doctors; politically true to its director's previous work, it forms an acknowledgement, more angry than sad, that globalisation will soon replace presidents of Mitterand's standing with mere pawns and pen-pushers.

SCR Gilles Taurand, Georges-Marc Benamou   CIN Renato Berta   DES Michel Vandestien   ED Bernard Sasia   PROD Frank Le Wita, Robert Guédiguian, Marc de Bayser   DIST Pathé

66 A riveting and cerebral film, replete with learning and wit. – *Peter Bradshaw, Guardian*

L

DVD Available on DVD   ☆ Cast in order   66 Critics' Quotes   ⚲ Academy Award   🛡 BAFTA
♫ Soundtrack on CD   of importance   † Points of interest   ⚲ Academy Award nomination   Ⓣ BAFTA nomination

355

'It's not the end of the world...there's still six hours left'

Last Night ★★

SCR/DIR *Don McKellar*
1998 95m Canada
[DVD] ♫

☆ Don McKellar (Patrick Wheeler), Sandra Oh (Sandra), Callum Keith Rennie (Craig Zwiller), Sarah Polley (Jennifer Wheeler), Trent McMullen (Alex), David Cronenberg (Duncan), Robin Gammell (Mr Wheeler), Roberta Maxwell (Mrs Wheeler), Tracy Wright (Donna), Michael McMurtry (Menzies), Geneviève Bujold (Mrs Carlton)

With six hours to go until the end of the world, a group of disparate-but-connected Toronto residents work out what to do with the rest of their lives.

A smart, funny and oddly moving millennial film that achieves large-scale apocalyptic effects on a lowish budget, though McKellar is more interested in characters fretting about those same irritations that would bug them on any other night. Among a more or less definitive Canadian indie cast, director Cronenberg is cast as a call-centre employee trying to finish up his work and avoid the looters.

CIN Douglas Koch MUS Alexina Louie, Alex Pauk DES John Dondertman ED Reginald Harkema PROD Niv Fichman, Daniel Iron

66 A witty, trenchant script, lots of complicated characters, and a few actors who turn human frailty into something nearly sublime. – *Amy Taubin, Village Voice*

'The first American hero'

The Last of the Mohicans ★

DIR *Michael Mann*
1992 112m US
[DVD] ♫

☆ Daniel Day-Lewis (Nathaniel Poe/Hawkeye), Madeleine Stowe (Cora Munro), Russell Means (Chingachgook), Eric Schweig (Uncas), Jodhi May (Alice Munro), Steven Waddington (Major Duncan Heyward), Wes Studi (Magua), Maurice Roeves (Colonel Munro), Patrice Chereau (General Montcalm)

The American colonies, the 18th century: a Scottish-Irish frontiersman operating as a free agent in the Anglo-French wars falls for the daughter of an English colonel.

Though beautifully shot, and done with Mann's typical intelligence, the sense is of a director trying to cover too much ground in one go: too downbeat and talky to satisfy as rousing action-adventure, it also suffers from a tacked-on and unconvincing love story.

SCR Michael Mann, Christopher Crowe CIN *Dante Spinotti* MUS Trevor Jones, Randy Edelman DES Wolf Kroeger ED Dov Hoenig, Arthur Schmidt PROD Michael Mann, Hunt Lowry DIST Warner/Morgan Creek

66 A sincere and enthralling piece of adventure moviemaking... mythic, violent and romantic in the widest possible sense. – *David Hepworth, Empire*

66 Mann's characteristic mix of rousing, profoundly physical action, lyrical interludes, and strikingly stylish

imagery serves to create superior mainstream entertainment. – *Geoff Andrew, Time Out*

🎬 sound

🎭 Dante Spinotti (cinematography), Peter Robb-King (make up)

🎭 Daniel Day-Lewis (leading actor); Elsa Zamparelli (costume design); Trevor Jones, Randy Edelman (film score); Wolf Kroeger (production design); sound

Last Orders ★★

SCR/DIR *Fred Schepisi*
2001 109m GB/Germany
[DVD] ♫

☆ *Michael Caine* (Jack), *Bob Hoskins* (Ray), *Tom Courtenay* (Vic), *David Hemmings* (Lenny), Ray Winstone (Vince), Helen Mirren (Amy), J.J. Feild (Young Jack), Anatol Yusef (Young Ray), Cameron Fitch (Young Vic), Nolan Hemmings (Young Lenny), Kelly Reilly (Young Amy), Laura Morelli (June)

Three old friends think back over their lives and relationships on their way to scatter the ashes of a contemporary off Margate Pier.

A film with many of the virtues of the best British cinema: a cast of nicely contrasting yet mutually supportive performers, a sense of time passing and final destinations being reached, a river of long-suppressed and barely articulated emotion running beneath the action proper, and above all else, a keen eye for the weather.

CIN *Brian Tufano* MUS Paul Grabowsky DES Tim Harvey ED Kate Williams PROD Fred Schepisi, Elisabeth Robinson DIST Metrodome

66 This subject matter will chime with older audiences, but everyone should take the opportunity to catch some of Britain's finest performers gathered together in the same place at the same time. – *Alan Morrison, Empire*

66 It's like Chekhov with a British accent. – *Michael Sragow, Baltimore Sun*

The Last Picture Show ★★★★

DIR *Peter Bogdanovich*
1971 118m US
[DVD] ♫

☆ Timothy Bottoms (Sonny Crawford), *Jeff Bridges* (Duane Jackson), *Cybill Shepherd* (Jacy Farrow), *Ben Johnson* (Sam the Lion), *Cloris Leachman* (Ruth Popper), Ellen Burstyn (Lois Farrow)

Teenage and adult affairs in a small Texas town in 1951, ending with the hero's embarkation for Korea and the closure of the run-down cinema.

Penetrating nostalgia, shot astutely in black-and-white, with an emphasis on matters sexual; but the details of small-town life in a particular era are shrewdly noted. Good performances all round; Bridges looked every inch a future star, while Shepherd, playing a beautiful coquettish young woman, was effortlessly convincing as a small town's primary object of desire.

SCR Larry McMurtry, Peter Bogdanovich CIN *Robert Surtees* MUS original recordings DES *Polly Platt* ED Donn Cambern PROD Stephen J. Friedman DIST Columbia/LPS/BBS

L

66 The most important work by a young American director since Citizen Kane. – *Paul D. Zimmerman*

66 So many things in it are so good that I wish I liked it more. – *Stanley Kauffmann*

† Texasville an unsuccessful sequel featuring many of the same actors, was filmed by Bogdanovich in 1990.

⚖ Ben Johnson (supporting actor); Cloris Leachman (supporting actress)

⚖ picture; Larry McMurtry, Peter Bogdanovich (adapted screenplay); Peter Bogdanovich (as director); Robert Surtees (cinematography); Jeff Bridges (supporting actor); Ellen Burstyn (supporting actress)

Ⓣ Larry McMurtry, Peter Bogdanovich (screenplay); Ben Johnson (supporting actor); Cloris Leachman (supporting actress)

Last Resort ★★

DIR *Pavel Pawlikowski*

2000   73m   GB

DVD

☆ *Dina Korzun* (Tanya), Artyom Strelnikov (Artyom), *Paddy Considine* (Alfie), Lindsey Honey (Les), Dave Bean (Frank), Perry Benson (Immigration officer), Adrian Scarborough (Council official)

After claiming political asylum in the UK, a jilted young Russian woman is transported to a seaside town, where she falls for a local arcade manager and her son slips into petty crime.

The finale sees a few too many plot points clicking into place, but up until then this is a distinctive and affecting look at aspects of Britain few others have acknowledged.

SCR Pavel Pawlikowski, Rowan Joffe   CIN *Ryszard Lenczewski*   MUS Max de Wardener   DES Tom Bowyer   ED David Charap   PROD Ruth Caleb   DIST Artificial Eye

66 Short, sharp and unerringly to the point. – *Patrick Peters, Empire*

66 This is the best class of poetic realism, the kind you can believe in without a trace of hesitation. – *Kenneth Turan, Los Angeles Times*

Ⓣ Pavel Pawlikowski (most promising newcomer)

Ⓣ British film

'In the face of an enemy, in the Heart of One Man, Lies the Soul of a Warrior.'

The Last Samurai ★

DIR Edward Zwick

2003   154m   US

DVD ♫

☆ Tom Cruise (Captain Nathan Algren), Ken Watanabe (Katsumoto), Timothy Spall (Zebulon Gant), Tony Goldwyn (Colonel Bagley), Hiroyuki Sanada (Ujio), Masato Harada (Omura), Koyuki (Taka), William Atherton (Winchester Rep)

In the 1870s, a jaded American veteran of the Civil War enlists to train the Japanese army, only to be captured by rogue warriors who teach him the ways of the samurai.

Muddled but interesting epic, a sort of Dances with Wolves gone East, which holds the attention over

two hours before disintegrating into battlefield pornography, offering no more than the redemption of Tom Cruise.

SCR John Logan, Marshall Herskovitz, Edward Zwick   CIN John Toll   MUS Hans Zimmer   DES Lilly Kilvert   ED Steven Rosenblum, Victor du Bois   PROD Edward Zwick, Marshall Herskowitz, Tom Cruise, Paula Wagner, Scott Kroopf, Tom Engelman   DIST Warner

66 An almost perfect example of mainstream Hollywood filmmaking at its most expensive, well-calculated and safe: opulent production valies, solid acting from its name star, distinguished performances from people surrounding him, Big Themes concerning sacrifice and honour, and a ridiculous finale full of superhuman achievements. – *Lawrence Toppman, Charlotte Observer*

66 There's some cool sword-fighting. But still, it's junk. – *Stephen Hunter, Washington Post*

⚖ Ken Watanabe (supporting actor); art direction; costume design; sound

The Last Seduction ★★

DIR *John Dahl*

1994   110m   US

DVD ♫

☆ *Linda Fiorentino* (Bridget Gregory), Peter Berg (Mike Swale), J. T. Walsh (Frank Griffith), Bill Nunn (Harlan), Bill Pullman (Clay Gregory)

A tough New York woman absconds with her husband's drug money, and coerces a new lover into her scam.

Clever revamping of old film noir tropes, with a performance that briefly threatened to make its leading lady a star; there's plenty of sassy dialogue and plot chicanery to enjoy, but the men seem pretty hollow, and its essential bitterness – that of the darkest chocolate – constitutes an acquired taste indeed.

SCR *Steve Barancik*   CIN Jeffrey Jur   MUS *Joseph Vitarelli*   DES Linda Pearl   ED Eric L. Beason   PROD Jonathan Shestack   DIST ITC

66 A devilishly entertaining crime story with a heroine who must be seen to be believed. – *Elvis Mitchell, The New York Times*

66 Moves inexorably, without any flat moments, toward the suspenseful, if morally indefensible, finale. – *David Stratton, Variety*

† Fiorentino was denied the chance to have her name submitted as an Oscar contender, because the film had briefly been screened on the US cable TV channel HBO before it opened in cinemas.

Ⓣ Linda Fiorentino (leading actress)

The Last Temptation of Christ ★

DIR Martin Scorsese

1988   163m   US/Canada

DVD ♫

☆ Willem Dafoe (Jesus), Harvey Keitel (Judus), Barbara Hershey (Mary Magdalene), Harry Dean Stanton (Paul), David Bowie (Pontius Pilate), Verna Bloom (Mary, mother of Jesus), Andre Gregory (John the Baptist), Juliette Caton (Girl Angel), Roberts Blossom (Aged Master), Irvin Kershner (Zebedee)

While suffering crucifixion, Jesus is stricken with

DVD Available on DVD   ☆ Cast in order of importance   66 Critics' Quotes   ⚖ Academy Award   ⚖ Academy Award nomination   Ⓣ BAFTA   Ⓣ BAFTA nomination
♫ Soundtrack on CD   † Points of interest

357

self-doubt about his destiny as the son of God, and contemplates living like an ordinary man.

Provocative and deeply-felt account of Christ's last hours, shot and written sympathetically, without resorting to sensationalism. In fact, Scorsese errs (understandably) on the side of reverence; it diligently poses a dilemma in a way that might inspire debate rather than hysteria. The acting is impeccable, and the sense of place and time, and the high drama of the situation, are all palpable.

SCR Paul Schrader   **CIN** Michael Ballhaus   **MUS** Peter Gabriel   **DES** John Beard   **ED** Thelma Schoonmaker   **PROD** Barbara De Fina   **DIST** Universal/Cineplex Odeon

† The film gained much pre-release controversy, and religious groups protested against Scorsese's insistence that it would portray Christ as a man. When it opened, the protests intensified because Jesus was shown naked, and because of his overtly sexual relationship with Mary Magdalene.

⚱ Martin Scorsese

Last Year at Marienbad ★★★

DIR *Alain Resnais*
1961   94m   France/Italy
[DVD]

☆ Delphine Seyrig (A/Woman), Giorgio Albertazzi (X/Stranger), Sacha Pitoeff (M/Escort/Husband)

In a vast old-fashioned hotel, a man meets a woman who may or may not have had an affair with him the previous year in Marienbad – or was it Frederiksbad?

A dreamy, elegant film which presents a puzzle with no solution. It is impossible to out oneself in the position of someone seeing it afresh in 1961, when its modernist trickery and juggling with time and narrative seemed utterly revolutionary. It still has its attractions for film buffs, but in fairness is not for anyone who simply wants to be told a story.

SCR *Alain Robbe-Grillet*   **CIN** Sacha Vierny   **MUS** Francis Seyrig   **ED** Jasmine Chasney, Henri Colpi
PROD Raymond Froment
DIST Terra/Tamara/Cormoran/Precitel/Como/Argos/Cinetel/Silver/Cineriz

66 Elaborate, ponderous and meaningless. – *Newsweek*
66 Clearly the film's creators know exactly what they want to do and have done it with complete success. Whether one responds to the result is entirely a matter of temperament. – *John Russell Taylor, Monthly Film Bulletin*
⚱ Alain Robbe-Grillet (original screenplay)

L'Atalante ★★★

DIR Jean Vigo
1934   89m   France
[DVD]

☆ Jean Dasté (Jean), Dita Parlo (Juliette), *Michel Simon* (Pere Jules), Giles Margarites (Peddler)

A barge captain takes his new wife down river.

Vigo's final masterpiece indicated what could be done on film: it ushered in a new realism that could be lyrical,

even poetic, and in its blend of fantasy, fairy-tale and its sober acknowledgement of the sometimes grim settings through which the barge passes, it created a new syntax for film narrative. In barebones, literal terms, little actually happens – but the inner life of its characters and their fluctuating moods, is delineated precisely by what we see. Worth seeing less in its own right than for the long, benign shadow it cast over film for the next three decades.*

SCR Jean Guinée, Jean Vigo, Albert Riera   **CIN** Boris Kaufman, Louis Berger   **MUS** Maurice Jaubert   **ED** Louis Chavance   **DIST** J. L. Nounez-Gaumont

Laura ★★★

DIR *Otto Preminger*
1944   85m   US
♫

☆ *Dana Andrews* (Mark McPherson), *Clifton Webb* (Waldo Lydecker), Gene Tierney (Laura Hunt), Judith Anderson (Ann Treadwell), *Vincent Price* (Shelby Carpenter), Dorothy Adams (Bessie Clary), James Flavin (McAvity)

A beautiful girl is murdered. . .or is she? A cynical detective investigates, and finds his tough exterior softening.

A quiet, streamlined little murder mystery that brought a new adult approach to the genre and heralded the mature film noir of the later forties. A small cast responds perfectly to a classically spare script, in Clifton Webb a new star was born, and David Raksin's haunting theme was indelible.

SCR *Jay Dratler, Samuel Hoffenstein, Betty Reinhardt*   **CIN** *Joseph LaShelle*   **MUS** *David Raksin*   **ED** Louis Loeffler   **PROD** Otto Preminger   **DIST** TCF

WALDO LYDECKER (CLIFTON WEBB): It's lavish, but I call it home.
WALDO: I shall never forget the weekend Laura died. A silver sun burned through the sky like a huge magnifying glass. It was the hottest Sunday in my recollection. I felt as if I were the only human being left in New York. . .I had just begun Laura's story when another of those detectives came to see me. I had him wait.
WALDO: In my case, self-absorption is completely justified. I have never discovered any other subject quite so worthy of my attention.

66 Everybody's favourite chic murder mystery. – *New Yorker, 1977*

† Rouben Mamoulian directed some scenes before handing over to Preminger.

⚱ Joseph LaShelle
⚱ Clifton Webb (supporting actor); Otto Preminger (direction); Jay Dretler, Samuel Hoffenstein, Elizabeth Reinhardt (screenplay); art direction

The Lavender Hill Mob ★★★★

DIR *Charles Crichton*
1951   78m   GB
[DVD]

☆ *Alec Guinness* (Henry Holland), *Stanley Holloway* (Pendlebury), Sidney James (Lackery), Alfie Bass (Shorty), Marjorie Fielding (Mrs. Chalk), Edie Martin (Miss Evesham), John Gregson (Farrow), Gibb McLaughlin

(Godwin), Sydney Tafler (Clayton), Audrey Hepburn (Chiquita)

A timid bank clerk conceives and executes a bullion robbery.

Superbly characterized and inventively detailed comedy, one of the best ever made at Ealing or in Britain.

SCR *T. E. B. Clarke*   CIN *Douglas Slocombe*
MUS Georges Auric   ED Seth Holt   PROD Michael Truman   DIST Ealing

66 Amusing situations and dialogue are well paced and sustained throughout: the climax is delightful. – *Monthly Film Bulletin*

⚊ T. E. B. Clarke (original screenplay)
⚊ Alec Guinness (leading actor)
🅣 British film

L'Avventura ★★★

DIR *Michelangelo Antonioni*
1960   145m   Italy/France
♫

☆ *Monica Vitti* (Claudia), Lea Massari (Anna), Gabriele Ferzetti (Sandro), Dominique Blanchar (Giulia), James Addams (Corrado), Lelio Luttazi (Raimondo)

Young people on a yachting holiday go ashore on a volcanic island. One of them disappears; this affects the lives of the others, but she is never found.

Antonioni, shooting in more or less real time, took a giant leap forward with this film, starting out with conventional narrative (the missing woman's lover makes a pass at her best friend with indecent haste), but then virtually dispensing with it, instead creating visual moods signalled by the volcanic landscapes. A challenging, rigorous exercise, but a fascinating one.

SCR Michelangelo Antonioni, Elio Bartolini, Tonino Guerra
CIN *Aldo Scavarda*   MUS Giovanni Fusco   ED Eraldo da Roma   PROD Amato Pennasilico   DIST Cino del Duca/PCE/Lyre

66 A film of complete maturity, sincerity and creative intuition. – *Peter John Dyer, Monthly Film Bulletin*

† The film was booed at the 1960 Cannes Film Festival (though it still won the jury prize) and was condemned as immoral by political and religious groups in several countries.

Law of Desire ★

SCR/DIR Pedro Almodóvar
1987   102m   Spain
DVD

☆ Eusebio Poncela (Pablo Quintero), Carmen Maura (Tina Quintero), Antonio Banderas (Antonio Benítez), Miguel Molina (Juan Bermúdez), Manuela Velasco (Ada), Bibi Andersen (Ada- mother), Fernando Guillen (Policeman)

A film director with two gay lovers must also cope with the crises of his transsexual brother and his complex web of affairs.

Tangled, lurid, hysterical relationship drama, involving murder, gender-swapping and a love triangle. Par for the course, in other words, for the early films of

Almodóvar before he became globally acclaimed. This is a below average example.

CIN Angel Luis Fernandez   DES José María De Cossío
ED Jose Salcedo   DIST Other Cinema/El Deseo/Laurenfilm

66 A life-affirming joy. – *Tom Charity, Time Out*

'We think we live in a rational world. . .then we screw it up.'

Lawless Heart ★★★

SCR/DIR *Neil Hunter, Tom Hunsinger*
2001   100m   GB/US
DVD   ♫

☆ Douglas Henshall (Tim), *Tom Hollander* (Nick), *Bill Nighy* (Dan), Clementine Celarie (Corinne), Josephine Butler (Leah), *Ellie Haddington* (Judy), Stuart Laing (David), *Sukie Smith* (Charlie)

Three men in an Essex coastal town adjust to life changes initiated by the death of a restauranteur.

Admirably mature, formally audacious drama, thrice returning to a wake in order to follow each of the main characters as they face up to new-found responsibilities; the screenwriters work up considerable levels of emotional complexity in their varied menages-a-trois, and the acting is universally strong.

CIN *Sean Bobbit*   MUS *Adrian Johnston*   DES Lynne Whiteread   ED *Scott Thomas*   PROD Martin Pope
DIST Optimum

66 A surprising film to be British. . .It looks great, is filled with full-bodied performances from people who usually have to settle for cameos, and fulfils every demand for intelligent entertainment. – *Alexander Walker, Evening Standard*

66 Teems with insights into the human condition revealed by an unusually smart script and a wonderfully committed cast. It's a truly fine work. – *Shawn Levy, Portland Oregonian*

'Innocence is a dangerous friend .'

Lawn Dogs ★★

DIR *John Duigan*
1997   101m   GB
DVD

☆ *Sam Rockwell* (Trent), Christopher McDonald (Morton Stockard), Kathleen Quinlan (Clare Stockard), Bruce McGill (Nash), *Mischa Barton* (Devon Stockard), David Barry Gray (Brett)

A young working-class lawnmower man who works in an affluent gated community in the American South, strikes up a relationship with the sickly daughter of one of its wealthy families.

An imaginative, stylised parable, shot in hyper-real colours, that has plenty to say about trying to banish uncertainties from life. Rockwell and Barton (in her first substantial film role) make a splendid pair of unlikely lovers.

SCR *Naomi Wallace*   CIN *Elliot Davis*   DES John Myhre
ED Humphrey Dixon   PROD Duncan Kenworthy
DIST Carlton/Rank/Toledo

66 Quirkily haunting. – *Dominic Wells, Time Out*

L

DVD Available on DVD   ☆ Cast in order   66 Critics' Quotes   ⚊ Academy Award   🅣 BAFTA
♫ Soundtrack on CD   of importance   † Points of interest   ⚊ Academy Award nomination   🅣 BAFTA nomination

359

'God Made Him Simple. Science Made Him A God.'

The Lawnmower Man

DIR Brett Leonard
1992   108m   GB/US
[DVD]

☆ Jeff Fahey (Jobe Smith), Pierce Brosnan (Dr. Lawrence Angelo), Jenny Wright (Marnie Burke), Geoffrey Lewis (Terry McKeen), Mark Bringleson (Sebastian Timms), Jeremy Slate (Father Francis McKeen), Dean Norris (The Director)

A scientist uses his retarded gardener as a guinea pig for experiments with IQ-boosting drug therapies and computer teaching aids; but the plan goes astray.

It earns an historical footnote as the first film to deal with the subject of virtual reality, and also the first to feature a 'cybersex' scene. Apart from that, it's strictly forgettable.

SCR Brett Leonard, Gimel Everett   CIN Russell Carpenter
MUS Dan Wyman   DES Alex McDowell   ED Alan Baumgarten   PROD Gimel Everett   DIST First Independent

Lawrence of Arabia   ★★★★

DIR *David Lean*
1962   221m   GB
[DVD]   ♫

☆ *Peter O'Toole* (T.E. Lawrence), *Omar Sharif* (Sherif Ali Ibn El Kharish), *Arthur Kennedy* (Jackson Bentley), Jack Hawkins (Gen Allenby), Donald Wolfit (Gen Murray), Claude Rains (Mr Dryden), Anthony Quayle (Col Harry Brighton), *Alec Guinness* (Prince Feisal), Anthony Quinn (Auda Abu Tayi), José Ferrer (Turkish Bey), Michel Ray (Ferraj), Zia Mohyeddin (Tafas)

The celebrated scholar and map-maker T.E. Lawrence's adventures and life with the Arabs, and the inspiration help he offered them in resisting the Turks, told in flashbacks after his accidental death in the thirties.

Sprawling epic that does full justice to its contradictory, remarkably complex hero. A triumph of large-scale film-making that demonstrates brain as well as budget. O'Toole is mesmerising in the title role, though the relative newcomer Sharif also rose to the occasion magnificently; it's a sign of this film's power that Sharif's first entrance on screen – a long, long fixed shot as he approaches across the hot, shimmering sands, not only holds the audience's attention but is actively spell-binding. Director Lean would never again scale such heights.

SCR Robert Bolt, Michael Wilson   CIN *Frederick A. Young*
MUS *Maurice Jarre*   DES *John Box*   ED Anne V. Coates
PROD Sam Spiegel   DIST Columbia/Horizon

❝ Grandeur of conception is not up to grandeur of setting. – *Penelope Houston*

❝ Lean has managed to market epics as serious entertainment rather than as the spectacles they are. – *Time Out, 1980*

† Albert Finney turned down the role before O'Toole was offered it.

⚱ picture; David Lean (direction); Frederick A. Young; Maurice Jarre

⚖ Peter O'Toole (Leading actor); Omar Sharif (supporting actor); Robert Bolt (adapted screenplay)

⬤ picture; British picture; Peter O'Toole (leading actor); Robert Bolt (adapted screenplay)

'Sooner or later, everything goes down.'

Laws of Gravity   ★★

SCR/DIR Nick Gomez
1992   100m   US

☆ *Peter Greene* (Jimmy), *Edie Falco* (Denise), Adam Trese (Jon), Arabella Field (Celia), Paul Schulze (Frankie), Saul Stein (Sal), James McCauley (Kenny)

A pair of small-time Brooklyn hoodlums fall out when one of them gets involved with a shady criminal who wants them to sell firearms.

Shades of Scorsese's Mean Streets here, though this ultra-low budget drama, shot guerrilla-style with hand-held cameras, has a real energy and zest of its own.

CIN Jean de Segonzac   DES Monica Bretherton
ED Tom McArdle   PROD Bob Gosse, Larry Meistrich
DIST Oasis/The Shooting Gallery

❝ The film's greatest strength is its fresh take on what are now nearly stock situations. – *Caren Myers, Sight & Sound*

† The film was shot in 12 days on a budget of just $38,000.

'Once in a lifetime you get a chance to do something different.'

A League of Their Own   ★

DIR Penny Marshall
1992   128m   US
[DVD]   ♫

☆ *Tom Hanks* (Jimmy Dugan), Geena Davis (Dottie Hinson), Madonna (Mae Mordabito), Lori Petty (Kit Keller), Jon Lovitz (Ernie Capadino), David Strathairn (Ira Lowenstein), Garry Marshall (Walter Harvey), Bill Pullman (Bob Hinson), Megan Cavanagh (Marla Hooch), Tracy Reiner (Betty Horn), Rosie O'Donnell (Doris Murphy), Ann Cusack (Shirley Baker)

In World War II, when baseball players were abroad in combat, an all-female baseball league was established. A male ex-pro is hired to coach one of its teams.

Good-natured entertainment, with spirited performances that narrowly overcome the script's uneven passages. Hanks, as a drunken ex-baseball star, steals the movie from the mostly female cast.

SCR Lowell Ganz, Babaloo Mandel   CIN Miroslav Ondricek   MUS Hans Zimmer   DES Bill Groom
ED George Bowers, Adam Bernardi   PROD Robert Greenhut   DIST Columbia/Parkway

❝ Deftly structured by director Penny Marshall and writers Lowell Ganz and Babaloo Mandel to resemble a 40s musical. – *Jonathan Rosenbaum, Chicago Reader*

† The film spawned a short-lived TV series.

'In the beginning, the rules were simple. There weren't any.'

Leatherheads (new)

DIR George Clooney
2008 113m US
♫

☆ George Clooney (Dodge Connolly), Renée Zellweger (Lexie Littleton), John Krasinski (Carter Rutherford), Jonathan Pryce (C.C. Frazier), Jack Thompson (Harvey), Stephen Root (Suds), Wayne Duvall (Coach Ferguson), Peter Gerety (Commissioner)

In 1925, a struggling American Football team enlists a war hero to save it from folding.

Old-fashioned blend of underdog sports yarn and screwball romantic comedy; neither genre is particularly well-served.

SCR Duncan Brantley, Rick Reilly CIN Newton Thomas Sigel MUS Randy Newman DES Jim Bissell ED Stephen Mirrione PROD Grant Heslov, Casey Silver DIST Universal

66 The picture labors so strenuously to approximate some of the old screwball spirit that it winds up in traction. – *A.O. Scott, New York Times*

66 The script just isn't funny enough and is far too formulaic. – *Cosmo Landesman, Sunday Times*

† Clooney downgraded his membership of the Writers Guild of America when it refused him a writing credit.

Leaving Las Vegas ★★

SCR/DIR *Mike Figgis*
1995 111m US
DVD ♫

☆ *Nicolas Cage* (Ben Sanderson), *Elisabeth Shue* (Sera), Julian Sands (Yuri), Richard Lewis (Peter), Valeria Golino (Terri), Graham Beckel (Bartender), Laurie Metcalf (Landlady), Lou Rawls (Cabbie), Carey Lowell (Bank Teller)

An alcoholic screenwriter heads to Vegas to drink himself to death, only to encounter a prostitute doing her best to stay alive.

Bleakly powerful drama about the intersection of two dead-end lives: the performers hold the attention, even as the grimness of the material threatens to send one reeling to one's own drinks cabinet.

CIN *Declan Quinn* MUS Mike Figgis DES Waldemar Kalinowski ED John Smith PROD Lila Cazes, Annie Stewart DIST Entertainment/Initial

66 At best, Leaving Las Vegas is pure alchemy – it makes of flawed humanity a hymn, and of forlorn hope a beacon. – *Rick Groen, The Globe and Mail (Toronto)*

66 Anyone who cares about ravishing filmmaking, superb acting and movies willing to dive into the mystery of unconditional love will leave this dark romance both shaken and invigorated. – *David Ansen, Newsweek*

⚊ Nicolas Cage (leading actor)

⚊ Elisabeth Shue (leading actress); Mike Figgis (director); Mike Figgis (adapted screenplay)

Ⓣ Nicolas Cage (leading actor); Elisabeth Shue (leading actress); Mike Figgis (adapted screenplay)

Legacy (new) ★

SCR/DIR Temu Babluani, Gela Babluani
2006 83m France

☆ Sylvie Testud (Patricia), Stanislaus Merhar (Jean), Olga Legrand (Céline), Pascal Bongard (Nikolaï), Georges Babluani (Young Man), Leo Gaparidze (Grandfather)

Three arrogant French tourists travel to the hinterlands of Georgia to claim a ruined castle that one of them has inherited. On the way they meet a grandfather about to sacrifice himself to end a long-running blood feud.

A story with a brilliant premise, set in a land where people have their own laws. But it falls apart in an anti-climactic final act. A disappointing follow-up to Tzameti 13, co-director Gela Babluani's assured debut.

CIN Tariel Meliava DES Claude Billois ED Gela Babluani, Noémie Moreau PROD Gela Babluani, Olivier Oursel, Jean-Marie Delbary DIST Revolver

66 The film stumbles into a blind alley of its own making. – *Peter Bradshaw, Guardian*

† The two writer-directors, Temur and Gela Babluani, are father and son.

'An Epic Story Of A Man Who Could Do Anything. . .Except Be Ordinary.'

The Legend of 1900 ★

SCR/DIR Giuseppe Tornatore
1998 165m Italy
DVD ♫

☆ Tim Roth (Danny Boodman T.D. Lemon Novecento), Pruitt Taylor Vince (Max), Melanie Thierry (The Girl), Bill Nunn (Danny Boodmann), Peter Vaughan (Music store owner), Niall O'Brien (Harbour master), Alberto Vasquez (Mexican machinist), Clarence Williams III ('Jelly Roll' Morton), Gabriele Lavia (Farmer)

An orphan, born on a cruise liner at the dawn of the 20th century, becomes a piano prodigy and spends his whole life as an entertainer on board the ship.

A curious concoction, ravishing to look at, but its imprecise central metaphor and excessive length conspire to sink the boat in dramatic terms.

CIN *Lajos Koltai* MUS Ennio Morricone DES *Francesco Frigeri* ED Massimo Quaglia PROD Francesco Tornatore DIST Fine Line

'The men of the Ludlow family. A woman's grace brought them together. Then her passion tore them apart.'

Legends of the Fall ★

DIR Edward Zwick
1994 133m US
DVD ♫

☆ Anthony Hopkins (Col. William Ludlow), Brad Pitt (Tristan Ludlow), *Aidan Quinn* (Alfred Ludlow), Henry Thomas (Samuel Ludlow), Julia Ormond (Susannah Fincannon Ludlow), Karina Lombard (Isabel Two Decker Ludlow), Gordon Tootoosis (One Stab), Tantoo Cardinal (Pet), Paul Desmond (Decker)

Two sons of an ex-army officer, one rebellious, the

other strait-laced and diligent, move with him to a Montana ranch, where they both become enamoured of the same woman.

A melodramatic throwback, this saga of a ranch family, presided over by a stern Hopkins, strains for effect. Visually it is stunning, but the human drama here is of soap opera quality. Pitt lacks the presence to play an iconic, misunderstood young man, and it's left to Quinn, in a much quieter role, to do the heavy lifting. The arrival of Ormond as the siblings' love interest is the signal for some alarmingly soggy plotting.

SCR Susan Shilliday, Bill Wittliff CIN *John Toll*
MUS James Horner DES *Lilly Kilvert* ED Steven Rosenblum PROD Edward Zwick, Bill Wittliff, Marshall Herskovitz DIST TriStar/Bedford Falls/Pangaea

66 What makes Legends such an entertaining male weepie is the star shine. Though the admirable Quinn has the toughest role, Pitt carries the picture. – *Peter Travers, Rolling Stone*

66 In all, Legends Of The Fall is a grand bore, more laughable than stirring. So big everything becomes blurry and distant, so beautiful it could be an ad for male hair products. – *Ian Nathan, Empire*

⚲ John Toll (cinematography)
⚲ Lilly Kilvert; sound

L

'Mishaps. Mayhem. Misadventures. Oh joy.'

Lemony Snicket's A Series of Unfortunate Events ★

DIR Brad Silberling
2004 108m US/Germany
DVD ♫

☆ Jim Carrey (Count Olaf), Liam Aiken (Klaus Baudelaire), Emily Browning (Violet Baudelaire), Kara and Shelby Hoffman (Sunny Baudelaire), Jude Law (Lemony Snicket), Timothy Spall (Mr Poe), Catherine O'Hara (Justice Strauss), Billy Connolly (Uncle Monty), Meryl Streep (Aunt Josephine), Luis Guzman (Bald Man)

After their parents' mysterious death in a fire, the three Baudelaire children find their inheritance – and their lives – under threat from a villainous actor.

A distinctive family movie, but one that too often substitutes arch knowingness for genuine wit: still, it rattles along, and the juvenile performers are bright and appealing.

SCR Robert Gordon CIN Emmanuel Lubezki
MUS Thomas Newman DES *Rick Heinrichs* ED Michael Kahn PROD Jim Van Wyck, Walter F. Parkes, Laurie MacDonald DIST Paramount

66 Always smart, even if it's rarely spectacular. – *Caroline Westbrook, Empire*

† Lemony Snicket is a pseudonym for author Daniel Handler, an accordion player for New York band The Magnetic Fields.

⚲ Valli O'Reilly, Bill Corso (make up)
⚲ Thomas Newman; Rick Heinrichs; Colleen Atwood (costume design)

'Now he must decide between his life of lies. . .or the truth.'

L'Emploi du Temps ★★

DIR *Laurent Cantet*
2001 134m France
DVD

☆ *Aurelien Recoing* (Vincent), Karin Viard (Muriel), Serge Livrozet (Jean-Michel), Jean-Pierre Mangeot (Vincent's father), Monique Mangeot (Vincent's mother), Nicolas Kalsch (Julien)

After he loses his job, a middle-aged man keeps up the pretence of employment to his wife, swindling money out of friends and acquaintances in order to stay afloat.

With its lead character endlessly driving around in his car, obsessively nurturing his delusions, this plays something like a white-collar Taxi Driver: suspense comes from wondering when this fantasist is going to be found out, and Recoing gives a truly chameleonic performance as a man desperately trying to keep up in a corporate world fast passing him by.

SCR Robin Campillo, Laurent Cantet CIN Pierre Milon
MUS Jocelyn Pook DES Romain Denis ED Robin Campillo, Stephanie Leger PROD Caroline Benjo
DIST Artificial Eye

66 Has the stately, well-crafted anxiety of a Hitchcock movie, except that the protagonist and antagonist are the same. – *David Ansen, Newsweek*

66 A hushed, small-scale masterpiece that moves into the realms of tragedy. – *Peter Rainer, New York Magazine*

† The film was based on a true-life case.

L'Enfer ★★

DIR Claude Chabrol
1994 100m France
DVD

☆ Emmanuelle Béart (Nelly), François Cluzet (Paul Prieur), Nathalie Cardone (Marylin), André Wilms (Doctor Arnoux), Marc Lavoine (Martineau), Christiane Minazzoli (Mme Vernon), Dora Doll (Mme Chabert), Mario David (Duhamel), Jean-Pierre Cassel (M. Vernon)

Troubles beset a charming married couple who run a lakeside hotel when the husband becomes enmeshed in pathological jealousy about his wife, who he suspects of having several affairs.

Icy, clinical portrait of a man descending into a self-imposed torment so intense it finally becomes darkly funny. An open ending feels unsatisfying, but is clearly deliberate. Yet this provocative work was Chabrol's strongest in years.

SCR Henri-Georges Clouzot, Jose-Andre Lacour, Claude Chabrol CIN Bernard Zitzermann MUS Matthieu Chabrol DES Emile Ghigo ED Monique Fardoulis
PROD Marin Karmitz DIST Mayfair/MK2/CED/France 3/Cinemanuel/Canal

66 The film simply lacks an ending. More's the pity, when it started so well. – *Philip Kemp, Sight & Sound*

† The troubled production began 30 years previously, in 1964, directed by Henri-Georges Clouzot and starring

Serge Reggiani. Shooting was halted when Reggiani fell ill, and then Clouzot suffered a heart attack. He died in 1977, and the project passed to Chabrol.

'Somewhere in the tundra lived the worst rock'n'roll band in the world. . .'

Leningrad Cowboys Go America ★★

SCR/DIR Aki Kaurismäki
1989   78m   Finland/Sweden
DVD   ♫

☆ Matti Pellonpää (Vladimir (Manager)), Kari Väänänen (Igor (Village Idiot)), Sakke Jarvenpää (The Leningrad Cowboys), Hiekki Keskinen (The Leningrad Cowboys), Pimme Oinonen (The Leningrad Cowboys), Silu Seppälä (The Leningrad Cowboys), Mauri Sumén (The Leningrad Cowboys), Mato Valtonen (The Leningrad Cowboys), Pekka Virtanen (The Leningrad Cowboys), Jim Jarmusch (Car Dealer/New York)

A ramshackle Russian folk act travel to the US in pursuit of fame and fortune, their frozen bass player in tow.

Deadpan comedy that comes at the viewer in episodic chunks: there are some big laughs to be had from its clash of cultures.

CIN Timo Salminen   MUS Mauri Sumén   ED Raija Talvio   PROD Aki Kaurismäki, Klas Olofsson, Katinka Farago   DIST Artificial Eye/Villealfa/Swedish Film Institute/Finnish Film Foundation

66 Looked at superficially, it's a one-joke movie, but as with Jarmusch, the textured images and oblique nuances take priority over the wacky premise and slender storyline. – *Nigel Floyd, Time Out*

66 One of the most splendidly silly films ever made. – *Christopher Tookey, Daily Mail*

'He Moves Without Sound, Kills Without Emotion, Disappears Without Trace.'

Leon ★★

SCR/DIR *Luc Besson*
1994   110m   France
DVD   ♫

☆ *Jean Reno* (Leon), *Gary Oldman* (Stansfield), *Natalie Portman* (Mathilda), Danny Aiello (Tony), Peter Appel (Malky), Michael Badalucco (Mathilda's Father), Ellen Greene (Mathilda's Mother), Elizabeth Regen (Mathilda's Sister)

After her family is murdered by a ruthless drug-enforcement officer, a young girl strikes up an alliance with the lonely hitman next door.

Stylish action thriller that alternates wild shoot-'em-ups with quieter, more melancholic human business.

CIN *Thierry Arbogast*   MUS Eric Serra   DES Dan Weil   ED Sylvie Landra   PROD Patrice Ledoux   DIST Buena Vista/Gaumont/Dauphin

66 A Cuisinart of a movie, mixing familiar yet disparate ingredients, making something odd, possibly distasteful, undeniably arresting out of them. – *Richard Schickel, Time*

Leon the Pig Farmer

DIR Vadim Jean, Gary Sinyor
1992   104m   GB
DVD

☆ Mark Frankel (Leon Geller), Gina Bellman (Lisa), Janet Suzman (Judith Geller), Brian Glover (Brian Chadwick), Connie Booth (Yvonne Chadwick), Maryam D'Abo (Madeleine)

A young Jewish estate agent from London discovers that his real father, a Yorkshire pig farmer, is a Gentile.

Touted as the first Jewish-British film comedy, it's essentially a mediocre, low-budget movie trading in ethnic stereotypes for laughs.

SCR Gary Sinyor, Michael Normand   CIN Gordon Hickie   MUS John Murphy, David Hughes   DES Simon Hicks   ED Ewa Lind   PROD Gary Sinyor, Vadim Jean   DIST Electric/Leon the Pig Farmer Production

66 Leon is the very model of a Jewish hero; the trouble is that the film never moves beyond dot-by-dot cultural delineation. – *Robert Yates, Sight & Sound*

Leonard Cohen: I'm Your Man ★

DIR Lian Lunson
2006   103m   USA
DVD

☆ Leonard Cohen (Himself), U2 (Themselves), Jarvis Cocker (Himself), Nick Cave (Himself), Kate and Anna McGarrigle (Themselves), Rufus Wainwright (Himself), Anthony, Beth Orton, Julie Christensen, Linda Thompson, Martha Wainwright, Perla Batalla, Teddy Thompson, The Handsome Family

Filmed concert tribute to the legendary Canadian singer-songwriter, with various artists interpreting Cohen songs, and snippets of an interview with the artist himself.

Mainly for Cohen devotees. He comes across as funny and self-deprecating, in contrast to the gushing tributes paid him, especially by members of U2. Still, Rufus Wainwright and Nick Cave acquit themselves especially well onstage with Cohen's work.

CIN John Pirozzi, Geoff Hall   MUS Leonard Cohen   ED Mike Cahill   PROD Lian Lunson, Mel Gibson, Bruce Davey

U2's THE EDGE: 'He comes down the mountain top with tablets of stone.'

66 Proves that few can manoeuvre one of Cohen's dusky, love-lorn songs like Cohen himself. – *Robert Koehler, Variety*

The Leopard ★★★★

SCR/DIR *Luchino Visconti*
1963   205m   US/Italy
DVD   ♫

☆ Burt Lancaster (Prince Don Fabrizio Salina), Claudia Cardinale (Angelica Sedara/Bertiana), Alain Delon (Tancredi), Paolo Stoppa (Don Calogero Sedara), Serge Reggiani (Don Ciccio Tumeo), Leslie French (Cavalier Chevally)

The family life of an Italian nobleman in the 1860s.

Elaborate, complex family saga, painted like an old

DVD Available on DVD   ☆ Cast in order   66 Critics' Quotes   ⚊ Academy Award   Ⓑ BAFTA
♫ Soundtrack on CD   of importance   † Points of interest   ⚊ Academy Award nomination   Ⓑ BAFTA nomination

363

master with great care and attention to detail. Visconti had asked for Lancaster, so Twentieth Century Fox picked up the international release, but couldn't make head or tail of it commercially; they even ruined its high quality by releasing a dubbed, shortened version in Cinemascope and DeLuxe colour of poor standard.

CIN *Giuseppe Rotunno*   MUS Nino Rota   ED Mario Serandrei   PROD Goffredo Lombardo
DIST TCF/Titanus/SNPC/GPC

66 The film is a glittering triumph of personal expression at its most elegant and opulent. – *Kevin Thomas, Los Angeles Times*

66 That rare thing - a great film based on a great book. – *Philip French, Observer*

'The shocking true story of an unbelievable miscarriage of justice.'

Let Him Have It ★

DIR Peter Medak
1991   115m   GB/France
[DVD]   ♫

☆ Christopher Eccleston (Derek Bentley), Paul Reynolds (Chris Craig), Tom Bell (Fairfax), Eileen Atkins (Lilian Bentley), Clare Holman (Iris Bentley), Michael Elphick (Prison Officer Jack), Mark McGann (Niven Craig), Tom Courtenay (William Bentley), Michael Gough (Lord Goddard)

The true story of Derek Bentley, an 18-year-old epileptic, who was hanged for a murder he did not commit.

An effective anti-capital punishment film, with a feel for the grim detail of post-WWII London and quietly powerful performances; only some erratic pacing lets it down.

SCR Neal Purvis, Robert Wade   CIN Oliver Stapleton
MUS Michael Kamen   DES Michael Pickwoad   ED Ray Lovejoy   PROD Luc Roeg, Robert Warr   DIST First Independent/Vivid/Le Studio Canal Plus/British Screen

66 Medak's mobile camerawork, with its subtle swirls and tracks and cranings, and [the] crisply colloquial script turn the film into a Woyzeck for austerity-era Britain. – *Nigel Andrews, Financial Times*

Let's Get Lost ★★

DIR Bruce Weber
1988   120m   US
[DVD]   ♫

Documentary about the life and drug addiction of the doomed jazz trumpeter Chet Baker.

Handsome-looking account of Baker's sad descent, including interviews with fellow musicians and acquaintances; the contrast between Baker's youthful beauty and the ravaged wreck of a man he became is painful to behold.

SCR Susan Stribling   CIN Jeff Preiss   MUS Chet Baker
ED Angelo Corrao   PROD Bruce Weber
DIST Mainline/Little Bear

† The film was re-released in the UK in 2008, and made available on DVD.

⚖ documentary

'With all my heart, I still love the man I killed!'

The Letter ★★★

DIR *William Wyler*
1940   95m   US

☆ *Bette Davis* (Leslie Crosbie), *Herbert Marshall* (Robert Crosbie), *James Stephenson* (Howard Joyce), *Sen Yung* (Ong Chi Seng), Frieda Inescort (Dorothy Joyce), Gale Sondergaard (Mrs. Hammond), Bruce Lester (John Withers), Tetsu Komai (Head Boy)

A rubber plantation owner's wife kills a man in what seems to have been self-defence; but a letter from her proves it to have been a crime of passion, and becomes an instrument of blackmail.

Excellent performances and presentation make this the closest approximation on film to reading a Maugham story of the Far East, though censorship forced the addition of an infuriating moral ending.

SCR *Howard Koch*   CIN *Tony Gaudio*   MUS *Max Steiner*
ED *Warren Low*   PROD Robert Lord   DIST Warner

66 The writing is taut and spare throughout . . . the unravelling of Maugham's story is masterly and the presentation visual and cinematic . . . the audience at the trade show did not move a finger. – *James Agate*

† Herbert Marshall played the lover in the first version and the husband in the second.

⚖ picture; William Wyler; Tony Gaudio (cinematography); Max Steiner (music); Bette Davis (leading actress); James Stephenson (supporting actor); Warren Low (editing)

'The story that will live. . .as long as there is love!'

Letter from an Unknown Woman ★★★

DIR *Max Ophüls*
1948   89m   US

☆ *Joan Fontaine* (Lisa Berndle), Louis Jourdan (Stefan Brand), Mady Christians (Frau Berndle), Art Smith (John), Marcel Journet (Johann Stauffer)

In Hapsburg-era Vienna, a woman wastes her life in unrequited love for a rakish pianist.

Superior though melodramatic 'woman's picture' which gave its director his best chance in America to recreate his beloved Vienna of long ago. Hollywood production magic at its best.

SCR *Howard Koch*   CIN *Franz Planer*   MUS Daniele Amfitheatrof   ED Ted J. Kent   PROD John Houseman
DIST Universal/Rampart

66 A film full of snow, sleigh bells, lights gleaming in ornamental gardens and trysts at night. – *Charles Higham, 1972*

66 It is fascinating to watch the sure deft means by which Ophuls sidetracks seemingly inevitable clichés and holds on to a shadowy, tender mood, half buried in the past. Here is a fragile filmic charm that is not often or easily accomplished. – *Richard Winnington*

Letters from Iwo Jima ★★★

DIR Clint Eastwood
2006   140m   US
[DVD]   ♫

☆ Ken Watanabe (Lt. General Kuribayashi), Kazunari

Ninomiya (Saigo), Tsuyoshi Ihara (Baron Nishi) (Shimizu), Shidou Nakamura (Lt. Ito), Hiroshi Watanabe (Lt. Fujita), Takumi Bando (Captain Tanida).

An account of the pivotal World War II battle, from the viewpoint of Japanese troops.

This gripping, rewarding story, almost totally spoken in Japanese, is a superior companion piece to Flags of Our Fathers. It shows Japanese troops – outnumbered, outmanoeuvred and denied reinforcements from Tokyo, fighting a rearguard action against US forces. It brilliantly depicts the waste of life common to all wars. But it strives too hard to suggest that we are all the same regardless of nationality, an argument undermined by a scene of mass suicide. A forceful document of a terrible, total defeat.

SCR Iris Yamashita, Paul Haggis CIN Tom Stern
MUS Kyle Eastwood, Michael Stevens DES Henry Bumstead, James J. Murakami ED Joel Cox, Gary D. Roach PROD Clint Eastwood, Steven Spielberg, Robert Lorenz DIST Warner Bros.

66 Eastwood has made one of the most quietly devastating war movies of our time. – *Tim Robey, Daily Telegraph*

66 A sharper account of the Iwo Jima conflict than Flags, this balances its unflinching handling of the horrors of war with its touching portrayal of those who face them. – *Dan Jolin, Empire*

⌁ Alan Robert Murray, Bub Asman (sound editing)
⌁ picture; Clint Eastwood; Iris Yamashita, Paul Haggis (original screenplay)

Liam ★

DIR Stephen Frears
2001 90m GB/Germany/Italy
DVD

☆ Ian Hart (Dad), Claire Hackett (Mam), Anthony Borrows (Liam), David Hart (Con), Megan Burns (Teresa), Anne Reid (Mrs Abernathy), Russell Dixon (Father Ryan), Julia Deakin (Auntie Aggie), Andrew Schofield (Uncle Tom), Bernadette Shortt (Lizzie)

A young boy in 1930s Liverpool grows up in a state of confusion – political, religious, sexual and social.

Authentic but forbiddingly dingy British take on the Depression years, executed more as brief snapshots of the period than as fully realised or dramatically satisfying scenes.

SCR Jimmy McGovern CIN Andrew Dunn MUS John Murphy DES Stephen Fineren ED Kristina Hetherington PROD Colin McKeown, Martin Tempia DIST Artificial Eye

66 Lets no one off the hook, least of all the audience. – *Michael O'Sullivan, Washington Post*

66 At once a heartfelt story about a family undone by violence, and an overburdened allegory of fascism. – *Manohla Dargis, L.A. Weekly*

'Trust Me.'

Liar, Liar ★★

DIR Tom Shadyac
1997 87m US
DVD ♫

☆ Jim Carrey (Fletcher Reede), Maura Tierney (Audrey Reede), Jennifer Tilly (Samantha Cole), Swoosie Kurtz (Dana Appleton), Amanda Donohoe (Miranda), Cary Elwes (Jerry).

A lawyer is forced to speak the unvarnished truth for a day after his estranged son's wish comes true.

This high-concept comedy almost does for veracity what Groundhog Day did for time: the star's face-pulling may remain an acquired taste, but here at least Carrey is at the mercy of a decent comic set-up, and working from a script with a few extra bristles to it.

SCR Paul Guay, Stephen Mazur CIN Russell Boyd
MUS John Debney DES Linda de Scenna ED Don Zimmerman PROD Brian Grazer
DIST Universal/Imagine

66 A reliably entertaining slice of comic nonsense. – *Darren Bignell, Empire*

The Libertine

DIR Laurence Dunmore
2005 114m US/GB
DVD ♫

☆ Johnny Depp (Earl of Rochester), Samantha Morton (Elizabeth Barry), John Malkovich (King Charles II), Rosamund Pike (Elizabeth Malet), Tom Hollander (Sir George Etherege), Johnny Vegas (Charles Sackville)

In the 1600s, the Earl of Rochester, a noted cad and playwright, angers Charles II with his writings, and grooms an innocent young actress to become a diva of the stage.

Intellectual bawdiness of a kind done better elsewhere by Peter Greenaway; some hand-held photography attempts to ward off the inherently static quality of a work originated for the stage, while Depp falls into syphilitic disrepair and starts to wet himself. Not, it has to be said, a great deal of fun.

SCR Stephen Jeffreys CIN Alexander Melman
MUS Michael Nyman DES Ben Van Os ED Jill Bilcock
PROD Lianne Halfon, John Malkovich, Russell Smith
DIST Entertainment

66 One of the most self-consciously grimy movies on record - it looks as if the negative were developed in a mud bath. – *Scott Foundas, LA Weekly*

66 Such a torturous mess that it winds up doing something I hadn't thought possible: it renders Johnny Depp charmless. – *Owen Gleiberman, Entertainment Weekly*

'You're only young once, but you remember forever.'

Liberty Heights ★

SCR/DIR Barry Levinson
1999 127m US
DVD ♫

☆ Adrien Brody (Van Kurtzman), Ben Foster (Ben Kurtzman), Orlando Jones (Little Melvin), Bebe Neuwirth (Ada Kurtzman), *Joe Mantegna* (Nate Kurtzman), Rebekah Johnson (Sylvia), David Krumholtz (Yussel), Richard Kline (Charlie), Vincent Guastaferro (Pete), Justin Chambers (Trey)

In 1950s Baltimore, a Jewish family is jolted when one son falls for a Protestant girl and his brother for a black classmate.

DVD Available on DVD ☆ Cast in order of importance 66 Critics' Quotes ⌁ Academy Award Ⓑ BAFTA
♫ Soundtrack on CD † Points of interest ⌁ Academy Award nomination Ⓑ BAFTA nomination

365

Levinson is at his best when tackling small, domestic-scale dramas in his home town, and this one reinforces the point: it's a wry, amusing, poignant and well-observed study of family concerns in a multi-cultural society at a time of huge changes.

CIN Chris Doyle   **MUS** Andrea Morricone   **DES** Vincent Peranio   **ED** Stu Linder   **PROD** Barry Levinson, Paula Weinstein   **DIST** Warner

66 The fourth and most ambitious film in Levinson's Proustian saga of Jewish life in post-war Baltimore, after Diner, Tin Men and Avalon. – *Andrew O'Hehir, Sight & Sound*

'First came love. . .then came Reverend Frank.'

License to Wed (new)

DIR Ken Kwapis
2007   92m   US
DVD   ♫

☆ Robin Williams (Reverend Frank), Mandy Moore (Sadie Jones), John Krasinski (Ben Murphy), Christine Taylor (Lindsey Jones), Eric Christian Olsen (Carlisle), Josh Flitter (Choir Boy), Peter Strauss (Mr. Jones)

An overzealous priest puts an engaged couple through a series of premarital trials.

Strained farce in the Meet the Parents mould, dominated by an overbearing Williams; the animatronic infant dolls are a particularly low point.

SCR Kim Barker, Tim Rasmussen, Vince Di Meglio   **CIN** John Bailey   **MUS** Christophe Beck   **DES** Gae Buckley   **ED** Kathryn Himoff   **PROD** Mike Medavoy, Arnold W. Messer, Nick Osborne, Robert Simonds   **DIST** Warner Bros

66 An astonishingly flat romantic comedy. – *Brian Lowry, Variety*

66 Working from a flawed premise with characters lacking credibility and plot turns more moronic than funny, the movie flatlines in about five minutes. – *Kirk Honeycutt, Hollywood Reporter*

Liebestraum   ★

SCR/DIR Mike Figgis
1991   112m   US
DVD   ♫

☆ Kevin Anderson (Nick Kaminsky), Pamela Gidley (Jane Kessler), Bill Pullman (Paul Kessler), Kim Novak (Lillian Anderson Munnsen), Graham Beckel (Sheriff Pete Ricker), Zach Grenier (Barnard Ralston IV), Thomas Kopache (Dr. Parker)

An architectural journalist is summoned home to his dying mother, and meets a property developer friend, about to demolish a department store that was the site of a brutal murder years before.

Suspenseful thriller, something of a departure for Figgis, that remains cerebral rather than actively exciting. A protracted scene in a brothel suggests a heavy recent exposure to David Lynch's work.

CIN Juan Ruiz Anchia   **MUS** Mike Figgis   **DES** Waldemar Kalinowski   **ED** Martin Hunter   **PROD** Eric Fellner   **DIST** UIP/MGM/Initial

The Life and Death of Colonel Blimp   ★★★

SCR/DIR Michael Powell, Emeric Pressburger
1943   163m   GB
DVD

☆ *Roger Livesey* (Clive Candy), *Anton Walbrook* (Theo Kretschmar-Schuldorff), Deborah Kerr (Edith Hunter/Barbara Wynne/Johnny Cannon), Roland Culver (Col. Betteridge), James McKechnie (Spud Wilson), Albert Lieven (Von Ritter), Arthur Wontner (Embassy Counsellor), A. E. Matthews (President of Tribunal), David Hutcheson (Hoppy), Ursula Jeans (Frau von Kalteneck), John Laurie (Murdoch), Harry Welchman (Maj. Davis)

A British soldier survives three wars and falls in love with three women.

A character adapted from a cartoon strip, but loosely so: he is a sympathetic figure in a warm, consistently interesting if idiosyncratic love story against a background of war. The producers as usual provide a sympathetic German lead in the shape of the hero's friend; quite a coup for a wartime release.

CIN *Georges Perinal*   **MUS** Allan Gray   **ED** John Seabourne   **PROD** Michael Powell, Emeric Pressburger   **DIST** GFD/Archers

66 There is nothing brilliant about the picture, but it is perceptive, witty and sweet-tempered. – *James Agee*

66 No one else has so well captured English romanticism banked down beneath emotional reticence. – *Time Out, 1985*

'Never judge a man by his cover.'

The Life and Death of Peter Sellers   ★

DIR Stephen Hopkins
2004   122m   US/GB
DVD

☆ Geoffrey Rush (Peter Sellers), Charlize Theron (Britt Ekland), Emily Watson (Anne Sellers), John Lithgow (Blake Edwards), Miriam Margolyes (Peg Sellers), Peter Vaughan (Bill Sellers), Sonia Aquino (Sophia Loren), Stanley Tucci (Stanley Kubrick), Stephen Fry (Maurice Woodruff), Heidi Klum (Ursula Andress), Edward Tudor Pole (Spike Milligan), Steve Pemberton (Harry Secombe), Nigel Havers (David Niven)

Biopic of the troubled comedian Peter Sellers, from his early days on The Goon Show to his career in movies.

True to Roger Lewis's revisionist biography, which suggested being around Sellers might not have been as much fun as one might think, the film then has to backpedal to give reasons why we might want to spend two hours in the presence of such a whiny, depressive, mother-fixated individual. Rush is neither as handsome, funny or charming as Sellers the star, and a general showbiz levity means even the film's serious moments seem pitched about the level of The Millionairess.

SCR Christopher Markus, Stephen McFeely   **CIN** Peter

Levy MUS Richard Hartley DES Norman Garwood
ED John Smith PROD Simon Bosanquet

66 Director Hopkins, it seems, has minimal faith in his audience: time and again, his film doesn't just nudge us, but rams an elbow into our ribs while chortling fruitily in our ears. – *Philip Kemp, Sight and Sound*

Life and Nothing But ★★

DIR *Bertrand Tavernier*
1989 135m France
[DVD]

☆ *Philippe Noiret* (Major Delaplane), Sabine Azéma (Irène de Courtil), Pascale Vignal (Alice), Maurice Barrier (Mercadot), François Perrot (Perrin), Jean-Pol Dubois (André), Daniel Russo (Lieutenant Trévise), Michel Duchaussoy (Général Villerieux), Arlette Gilbert (Valentine)

In northern France shortly after World War I, an officer at a military hospital checks missing soldiers' names against family descriptions. He encounters two women, one searching for her husband, the other for her fiancé.

A film of great stillness and sensitivity; the sense of loss and grief it conveys is palpable. A sharp line is drawn between individual suffering and the propagandist attempts to glorify the war. Noiret is outstanding as a patient, assiduous man, faced each day with the anguish of others.

SCR Jean Cosmos, Bertrand Tavernier CIN Bruno de Keyzer MUS Oswald d'Andrea DES Guy-Claude François ED Armand Psenny PROD René Cleitman
DIST Artificial Eye/Hachette Première et Cie/AB Films/Little Bear/A2

🏆 foreign picture

The Life Aquatic With Steve Zissou ★

DIR Wes Anderson
2004 118m US
[DVD] ♫

☆ Bill Murray (Steve Zissou), Owen Wilson (Ned Plimpton), Cate Blanchett (Jane Winslett-Richardson), Anjelica Huston (Eleanor Zissou), Willem Dafoe (Klaus Daimler), Jeff Goldblum (Alistair Hennessey), Michael Gambon (Oseary Drakoulias), Bud Cort (Bill Ubell)

An oceanographer and filmmaker in the Jacques Cousteau mould sets sail to find the shark that ate his best friend.

Brilliantly (perhaps overly) designed comic fantasia, clearly the work of a unique directorial sensibility, albeit one more often eccentric than funny, and sometimes rather haughty with it.

SCR Wes Anderson, Noah Baumbach CIN Robert Yeoman MUS Mark Mothersbaugh DES *Mark Friedberg* ED David Moritz PROD Wes Anderson, Barry Mendel, Scott Rudin DIST Buena Vista

66 Hovers frustratingly somewhere between charming and only mildly amusing. – *Desson Thomson, Washington Post*

66 A comedy that seems to have most everything going for

it but the ability to make us laugh. – *Michael Wilmington, Chicago Tribune*

† Anderson shot most of the interior scenes at the fabled Cinecittà studios in Rome.

Life is a Long Quiet River ★

DIR Etienne Chatiliez
1988 90m France

☆ Benoît Magimel (Momo Groseille), Valerie Lalande (Bernadette Le Quesnoy), Tara Romer (Million Groseille), Jérôme Floc'h (Toc-Toc Groseille), Sylvie Cubertafon (Ghislaine), Emmanuel Cendrier (Pierre Le Quesnoy)

Two babies are switched at birth, a mistake that is only discovered 12 years later, and which causes uproar in two sharply contrasting families, one affluent, one poor.

Class-divide comedy, which emphasises the fissures in bourgeois values without endorsing the fecklessness of the underclass family who stand to gain most from the mistaken identity on which the story turns. Agreeably cynical.

SCR Florence Quentin, Etienne Chatiliez CIN Pascal Lebegue MUS Gérard Kawczynski DES Geoffroy Larcher ED Chantal Delattre PROD Charles Gassot
DIST Electric/Contemporary/Téléma/MK2/FR3

'The unforgettable film that proves love, family and imagination conquer all.'

Life Is Beautiful

DIR Roberto Benigni
1997 116m Italy
[DVD] ♫

☆ Roberto Benigni (Guido Orefice), Nicoletta Braschi (Dora), Giustino Durano (Eliseo Orefice), Sergio Bustric (Ferruccio Papini), Marisa Paredes (Dora's Mother), Horst Buchholz (Dr. Lessing), Lidia Alfonsi (Guicciardini), Giuliana Lojodice (School Principal), Giorgio Cantarini (Giosue)

A Jewish father in the concentration camps pretends the events he witnesses are all part of a game, in order to better preserve the innocence of his young son.

The most reviled film ever to have been made with the best of intentions: for those whose analytical brains overruled their sobbing mechanisms, this Holocaust fantasia committed several gross lapses in taste, historical accuracy and basic human decency. Its take on the camps is an original one, to say the least, though it doesn't finally confront the horrors therein so much as run away and hide from them.

SCR Vincenzo Cerami, Roberto Benigni CIN Tonino Delli Colli MUS Nicola Piovani DES Danilo Donati ED Simona Paggi PROD Elda Ferri, Gianluigi Braschi
DIST Buena Vista/Melampo

66 That rare comedy that takes on a daring and ambitious subject and proves worthy of it. – *Michael Wilmington, Chicago Tribune*

66 I am sure Mr. Benigni is kind to children and animals. I am prepared to accept that he is a model citizen and a

[DVD] Available on DVD   ☆ Cast in order   66 Critics' Quotes   🏆 Academy Award   🏆 BAFTA
♫ Soundtrack on CD   of importance   † Points of interest   🏆 Academy Award nomination   🏆 BAFTA nomination

367

good companion. Still, Life is Beautiful is a disgrace. – *David Thomson, The New Biographical Dictionary of Film*

⚱ foreign language film; Roberto Benigni (leading actor); Nicola Piovani

⚱ picture; Roberto Benigni (director); Vincenzo Cerami, Roberto Benigni (original screenplay); Simona Paggi

📺 Roberto Benigni (leading actor)

📺 film not in the English language; Vincenzo Cerami, Roberto Benigni (original screenplay)

'A scathing new black comedy from the director of "Dim Sum" and "Chan Is Missing"'

Life Is Cheap . . . But Toilet Paper Is Expensive

DIR Wayne Wang
1990 89m US

☆ Chan Kim Wan (The duck killer), Spencer Nakasako (The-man-with-no-name), Victor Wong (The blind man), Cheng Kwan Min (Uncle Cheng), Cora Miao (Money), Lam Chung (Red Guard)

A courier goes to Hong Kong to deliver a package to a mobster, and finds himself in a violent anarchic place, a city that seems on the verge of chaos.

A thriller in style and pace, but virtually plotless, it's an astonishing series of scenes of violence, cruelty and gross-out mutilations. There's a certain droll quality to the commentary from onlookers, but Wang's mission seems to be to shock whenever possible.

SCR Spencer Nakasako CIN Amir Mokri MUS Mark Adler ED Sandy Nervig PROD Winnie Fredriksz DIST ICA/Forever Profit Investments/Far East Stars

Life Is Sweet   ★★★

SCR/DIR Mike Leigh
1990 103m GB
DVD

☆ *Alison Steadman* (Wendy), Jim Broadbent (Andy), *Claire Skinner* (Natalie), *Jane Horrocks* (Nicola), Stephen Rea (Patsy), *Timothy Spall* (Aubrey)

The travails of an ordinary family: a working-class couple and their adult daughters, both of whom cause them concern.

Leigh really found his rhythm for feature films with this affectionate study of a hapless, mildly dysfunctional family. Father Broadbent is a dreamer with useless schemes for a sweeter life, while Steadman, the mother, is a born nurturer. Yet it's Skinner and Horrocks who really take the eye: the first is a plumber whose ambivalent sexuality is never commented upon, the latter a troubled, surly binge-eater who resorts to casual sex for her only enjoyment. Spall provides comic relief as Aubrey, a clueless would-be restaurateur who wants to bring haute cuisine to Enfield. A joyous crew, and not easily forgettable. Leigh views these characters that he largely created with a fondness bordering on indulgence.

CIN Dick Pope MUS Rachel Portman DES Alison Chitty ED Jon Gregory PROD Simon Channing-

Williams DIST Palace/Thin Man/Film Four International/British Screen

66 The film is magnificent, mixing enormous fun with sad, serious subjects. – *Steve Grant, Time Out*

'A comedy for anyone who's ever been in danger. . .of falling in love.'

A Life Less Ordinary   ★

DIR Danny Boyle
1997 103m GB
DVD ♫

☆ Ewan McGregor (Robert Lewis), Cameron Diaz (Celine Naville), Holly Hunter (O'Reilly), Delroy Lindo (Jackson), Ian Holm (Naville), Ian McNeice (Mayhew), Stanley Tucci (Elliot Zweikel), Dan Hedaya (Gabriel), Maury Chaykin (Tod Johnson)

A sacked janitor takes his boss's daughter hostage while two angels contrive to make them fall in love.

Indigestible attempt at a violent and surreal screwball comedy from Britain's Trainspotting team; the whizzy stylistic flourishes owe too much to the Coen brothers, and the storytelling often seems desperate.

SCR John Hodge CIN Brian Tufano MUS David Arnold DES Kave Quinn ED Masahiro Hirakubo PROD Andrew Macdonald DIST Polygram/Figment

66 A pleasant enough ride in parts, but has too many half-realised ideas in the script to satisfy at any emotional level. – *Derek Elley, Variety*

† Shot largely in Utah, this was the first venture abroad for the creative team of Boyle, Macdonald, Hodge and McGregor. The film was a box-office flop.

Lift to the Scaffold   ★★★

DIR *Louis Malle*
1957 89m France
♫

☆ Maurice Ronet, *Jeanne Moreau*, Georges Poujouly, Yori Bertin, Lino Ventura

An executive murders his mistress's husband in his office, but becomes stuck in the lift as he departs; meanwhile his car is stolen and he is arrested for a murder committed by the thief.

Complex, watchable multi-strand story, with narratives fused together brilliantly, all accompanied by a sublime Miles Davis score that perfectly complements the look of Paris at its most dark and moody. A prodigious debut from Malle.

SCR Roger Nimier, Louis Malle CIN *Henri Decaë* MUS *Miles Davis* PROD Jean Thuillier DIST Nouvelles Editions de Films

66 Cold, clever and rather elegant. – *Penelope Houston, Monthly Film Bulletin*

'When your family is closing you in, music may be the only way out.'

Light of Day   ★

SCR/DIR Paul Schrader
1987 107m US
DVD ♫

☆ Michael J. Fox (Joe Rasnick / The Barbusters), Joan Jett

(Patti Rasnick / The Barbusters), Gena Rowlands (Jeanette Rasnick), Michael McKean (Bu Montgomery / The Barbusters)

In Cleveland a working-class family, with two siblings in a rock band, is jolted by their mother's terminal illness.

One doesn't immediately associate the ever-fascinating Paul Schrader with rock'n'roll, but this sombre family drama tries to bolt music on to his preferred theme of moral redemption. Fox is miscast, though rock musician Joan Jett, who outshines him in the band, at least looks right in the role.

CIN John Bailey   MUS Thomas Newman   DES Jeannine Claudia Oppewall   ED Jacqueline Cambas, Rose Kuo, Jill Savitt   PROD Keith Barish, Rob Cohen   DIST Taft/Keith Barish/Tri-Star

'A story about the discovery of the spirit, the Lure of Decadence, and the Chance for Escape.'

Light Sleeper ★★

SCR/DIR *Paul Schrader*
1991   103m   US
DVD   ♫
☆ *Willem Dafoe* (John LeTour), Susan Sarandon (Ann), Mary Beth Hurt (Teresa Aranow), Dana Delany (Marianne Jost), David Clennon (Robert), Victor Garber (Tis Brooke), Jane Adams (Randi Jost), Paul Jabara (Eddie)

A cocaine runner considers his future while patching up troubled relationships with his lover and employer.

Typically punchy Schrader melodrama that benefits from the compelling anguish of its central performance, and a real feel for New York streets slowly sinking into darkness and decay.

CIN Ed Lachman   MUS Michael Been   DES *Richard Hornung*   ED Kristina Boden   PROD Linda Reisman   DIST Guild/Grain of Sand

66 In film after film, for year after year, Paul Schrader has been telling this story in one way or another, but never with more humanity than this time. – *Roger Ebert, Chicago Sun-Times*

66 As in Taxi Driver and American Gigolo, there is a thriller plot – don't trust that urbane drugs-buying Swiss diplomat – but it's very much subordinated to Schrader's eerie ability to creep into a convincing netherworld where urban sleaze meets self-torturing religion. – *Kim Newman, Empire*

Lights in the Dusk ★

SCR/DIR Aki Kaurismaki
2006   77m   Finland/Germany/Italy/Sweden
☆ Janne Hyytiainen (Koistinen), Maria Jarvenhelmi (Mirja), Maria Heiskanen (Aila), Ilkka Koivula (Lindholm)

A lonely night watchman at a Helsinki shopping mall, shunned by co-workers, is set up as the fall guy in a jewel heist by a glamorous blonde woman.

Downbeat story with a central character, Koistinen, who

is a loser wronged by a femme fatale. Yet he is oddly appealing, and the film has deadpan humour and charm.

CIN Timo Salminen   DES Markku Patila   PROD Aki Kaurismaki   DIST Artificial Eye
66 A digestibly light serio-comedy. – *Peter Bradshaw, Guardian*

'A Delicious Love Story.'

Like Water for Chocolate ★★

DIR *Alfonso Arau*
1991   105m   Mexico
DVD   ♫
☆ Marco Leonardi (Pedro Muzquiz), Lumi Cavazos (Tita), Regina Torne (Mamá Elena), Mario Ivan Martinez (Doctor John Brown), Ada Carrasco (Nacha), Yareli Arizmendi (Rosaura), Claudette Maille (Gertrudis), Pilar Aranda (Chencha)

At the time of the Mexican Revolution, a passionate young woman trapped by an overbearing mother learns she has the ability to put her emotions into her cooking.

Arau and Esquivel throw ingredients of fairy tale, historical melodrama and the telenovela into a very broad pot: there's a slight off-taste to those scenes featuring the revolutionaries, but otherwise the resulting confection is delicious indeed.

SCR *Laura Esquivel*   CIN *Emmanuel Lubezki, Steve Bernstein*   MUS Leo Brouwer   DES Marco Antonio Arteaga, Emilio Mendoza Denise Pizzini   ED Carlos Bolado, Francisco Chiu   PROD Alfonso Arau   DIST Electric/Cinevista/NCCA/NTDF/Alfonso Arau

66 Flitting gracefully from high comedy to tragedy to whimsy with a sureness born of its unifying vision – a loving celebration of women and the work they do – this is original, arresting and full of visual delight, accelerating gently to an almost unbearable poignancy. – *Angie Errigo, Empire*

Ⓣ film not in the English language

Lilya 4-Ever ★

SCR/DIR Lukas Moodysson
2002   109m   Sweden/Denmark
DVD
☆ *Oksana Akinshina* (Lilya), Artyom Bogucharski (Volodya), Liliya Shinkaryova (Aunt Anna), Pavel Ponomaryov (Andrei), Tomas Neumann (Witek), Lyubov Agapova (Lilya's Mother), Tonu Kark (Sergei)

A bored Russian teenager, abandoned by her mother, is coerced into prostitution, eventually coming to ply her trade in Sweden.

Shot in tumbledown tower blocks against perpetually grey skies, this is something of an ode to joylessness, and Moodysson's crashingly tragic direction doesn't help; inside its ambitious but shaky structure, there looks to be a smaller, more affecting picture waiting to come out.

L

DVD Available on DVD   ☆ Cast in order   66 Critics' Quotes   ⚊ Academy Award   Ⓑ BAFTA
♫ Soundtrack on CD   of importance   † Points of interest   ⚊ Academy Award nomination   Ⓣ BAFTA nomination

Here's a brief film quiz. Who are the following groups of people? (a) Heather Donahue, Michael Williams, Joshua Leonard; (b) Michael Stahl-David, Jessica Lucas, T.J. Miller. Avid film fans will know – but many people would be surprised to learn they were the stars of two hugely popular, talked-about films.

The trio in group (a) were the actors who played the students filming a documentary in *The Blair Witch Project*, and (b) three of the leading cast in *Cloverfield*.

In 1999, *The Blair Witch Project* was an enormous global hit, taking $140 million in the US alone. As it had been shot on video with a budget of just $25,000, it remains the most profitable film in history.

This year's sizeable hit *Cloverfield* is its modern equivalent, and not just because its main characters were armed with video cameras. It was a disaster-horror movie (a giant monster attacks Manhattan), with a brilliant pre-release viral marketing campaign that made it irresistible to millions of filmgoers.

But to return to those two groups of names: would you know Ms Donahue, Mr Williams or Mr Leonard if they bumped into you in the street? Unlikely. As for the *Cloverfield* cast, no-one would say the film's success has elevated them to the ranks of superstardom.

So who needs stars? The question has long preoccupied Hollywood executives. Eight months after *The Blair Witch Project* opened in the States, a new film starring Julia Roberts was released. For playing the lead role in *Erin Brockovich*, she was reportedly paid $20 million. While it got rave reviews and an Oscar for Roberts, it took less money than *The Blair Witch Project* – made for one eight-hundredth of her fee. The maths made no sense.

If it was true then, it's doubly true now. In the last decade, reality TV has utterly changed the way the public regard stars – and the whole idea of celebrity and fame. Stated simply, stars and celebrities have become disposable. They have a short sell-by date. No-one expects them to endure.

Fan magazines are now devoted to the antics and lifestyle of ordinary people with no discernible talents, who manage to land themselves a place on reality TV shows For a few weeks, they're the talk of the nation. After the show ends, we're either sick to death of them, or we can barely remember who they are. Their arc of stardom is perfect for a public with a short attention span.

This has certainly shaped the attitude of younger movie audiences. They tend to be drawn by a film's pre-release buzz, its story, its attitude and overall concept, rather than by its cast.

Consider some major film hits from the last couple of years. The computer graphic epic *300*, about the Greeks battling the Persians: who starred in that, exactly? It was Gerard Butler, who played King Leonidas; yet no-one outside his own family ever went to see a film because Gerard Butler was in it.

Similarly, no-one recalls who was in *10,000 BC*. Audiences did not turn out in droves to see *Juno* because of its lead actress, Ellen Page, but because it sounded like a quirky, appealing comedy. Amy Adams is a talented, appealing actress, but it was the brilliant concept of *Enchanted* (innocent Disney princess is catapulted into gritty modern urban life) that drew the crowds.

Think, too, of those comedies that spring from the creative team around producer Judd Apatow: *Knocked Up, Superbad, Forgetting Sarah Marshall*. Their success may well stem from compelling story ideas and inspired marketing; it certainly doesn't derive from big-name casts.

> ‘Following stars has always been an agreeable part of enjoying films; a favourite actor is often the factor that hooks people on movies in the first place’

Let's turn the argument on its head. How many actors can guarantee a film huge success by starring in it? At the time of writing (summer 2008), Will Smith is about the only name that springs to mind.

Among long-standing stars, Harrison Ford's days as a big draw in his own right are over; three of his recent films, *Firewall, Hollywood Homicide* and *K-19; The Widowmaker* grossed less than $50 million in the US. But people turned out in millions this summer to see him play Indiana Jones yet again. (In fairness, young audiences may have been equally interested in teen idol Shia LaBeouf.) Tom Hanks still draws an older crowd, especially if he plays noble, dignified characters. (The title role in *Charlie Wilson's War* clearly was not, and the film was only a qualified success.) One wonders if even Tom Cruise, long regarded as box-office gold, can still command large audiences for anything other than the *Mission:Impossible* series. The jury is out on that point.

Julia Roberts's star power has clearly dimmed. Brad Pitt, playing Jesse James, starred in a notorious flop this past year. Outside the *Die Hard* franchise, Bruce Willis does not draw a crowd.

Even young stars are vulnerable to the tendency. How does Daniel Radcliffe fare when he steps outside Harry Potter's Hogwarts? Not well, judging by the Australian film *December Boys*, which played to near-empty houses. If Tobey Maguire were replaced for *Spiderman 4*, would it fatally damage the film's appeal? Not necessarily, one suspects.

Is this a bad thing? One could argue it both ways. Following stars has always been an agreeable part of enjoying films; a favourite actor is often the factor that hooks people on movies in the first place.

Yet the counter-argument is that stars have become too powerful, and not just in terms of their inflated fees. Fully aware of their influence, some have forced alterations to perfectly workable scripts to make their characters more sympathetic or heroic, and have bullied studios with 'pet projects': scripts they want to see made for private reasons, or often for pure vanity. (*Battlefield Earth*, starring John Travolta, may be the low-water mark of this tendency.)

It's also the case the actors are not necessarily the best judges of material that suits their gifts. It feels like false nostalgia to hanker

> ‘Stated simply, stars and celebrities have become disposable. They have a short sell-by date. No-one expects them to endure’

after an era in which stars were contract players for studios, and which involved them making four or five films a year. But that system didn't hurt Cary Grant, Humphrey Bogart, Gary Cooper – or for that matter Bette Davis and James Stewart, who actively fought studios over the material they were given. The roles that make actors feel good about themselves are not necessarily those that play to their strengths in the public's mind.

It's unlikely the star system will simply vanish, but lead actors and actresses may start to occupy a more realistic place in the movie business. There's no harm in that: no film was ever better than its shooting script, and if studios and producers relied more on the power of an ingenious screenplay or an intriguing premise to get a film rolling, that's better than relying on a star's charismatic presence to paper over the cracks of a leaky narrative. And if a script is so strong that it works equally well with unknown talent, audiences will clearly not complain.

CIN Ulf Brantas   MUS Nathan Larson   ED Michal Leszczylowski, Bernhard Winkler, Oleg Morgunov   PROD Lars Jönsson   DIST Metrodome

66 The season's most piercingly feel-bad movie. – *J. Hoberman, Village Voice*

66 Not without its own bleak integrity. But the movie wipes you out and leaves you with nothing, not even the feeling of exultation that can be present in the most tragic works of art. – *Charles Taylor, Salon*

'A condition of unknowable outcome.'

Limbo ★

SCR/DIR *John Sayles*
1999   126m   US/Germany
DVD   ♫

☆ *Mary Elizabeth Mastrantonio* (Donna De Angelo), *David Strathairn* (Joe Gastineau), *Vanessa Martinez* (Noelle De Angelo), Kris Kristofferson (Smilin' Jack), Casey Siemaszko (Bobby Gastineau), Kathryn Grody (Franki), Rita Taggart (Lou), Leo Burmester (Harmon King), Michael Laskin (Albright)

The relationship in a small Alaskan fishing town between a handyman and a local lounge singer is set off-course by the arrival of the man's half-brother.

A carefully drawn portrait of individuals cutting their ties with the past, and drifting accordingly; the ending can be seen as either infuriating, or the logical outcome of the film's concerns.

CIN *Haskell Wexler*   DES Gemma Jackson   ED John Sayles   PROD Maggie Renzi   DIST Columbia TriStar

66 The movie leaves conventional plot structure behind, and treks off into the wilderness itself. – *Roger Ebert, Chicago Sun-Times*

'Tell Them I'm Coming.'

The Limey ★

DIR Steven Soderbergh
1999   90m   US
DVD   ♫

☆ Terence Stamp (Wilson), Peter Fonda (Valentine), Lesley Ann Warren (Elaine), Luis Guzman (Ed), Barry Newman (Avery), Joe Dallesandro (Uncle John), Nicky Katt (Stacy), Amelia Heinle (Adhara), Melissa George (Jennifer)

An English ex-con, investigating the death of his daughter, turns up on the doorstep of a L.A. record producer.

Playfully ironic vengeance thriller that gets fair mileage out of its culture-clash between a craggy-faced Cockney and smoggy, laid-back Californians.

SCR Lem Dobbs   CIN Ed Lachman   MUS Cliff Martinez   DES Gary Frutkoff   ED Sarah Flack   PROD John Hardy, Scott Kramer

66 An art noir that courts pretension but just manages to keep from succumbing to it. – *Charles Taylor, Salon*

66 Thinly-plotted, overstylised pantomime which runs out of juice as rapidly as a clockwork toy. – *Andrew Collins, Empire*

The Lion in Winter ★★

DIR Anthony Harvey
1968   134m   GB
DVD   ♫

☆ *Katharine Hepburn, Peter O'Toole*, Jane Merrow, John Castle, Anthony Hopkins, Nigel Terry, Timothy Dalton

In 1183, King Henry II and Eleanor of Aquitaine celebrate Christmas together and have a family row.

An acting feast for two principals and assorted supports, a talking marathon in which not all the talk is good and a smart comedy with sudden lapses into melodrama. It is stimulating in parts but all rather tiresome by the end, especially as there is not much mediaeval splendour.

SCR James Goldman   CIN Douglas Slocombe   MUS *John Barry*   PROD Martin Poll   DIST Avco Embassy/Haworth

66 He is not writing a factual movie about the Plantagenets but an interpretation in which he combines their language and ours. – *Philip T. Hartung*

⚲ James Goldman (adapted screenplay); John Barry (music); Katharine Hepburn (leading actress)

⚲ picture; Anthony Harvey; Peter O'Toole (leading actor)

Ⓣ John Barry (music)

'Life's greatest adventure is finding your place in the Circle of Life.'

The Lion King ★★★

DIR *Roger Allers, Rob Minkoff*
1994   89m   US
DVD   ♫

☆ the voices of Matthew Broderick, Rowan Atkinson, Niketa Calame, Jim Cummings, Whoopi Goldberg, Jeremy Irons, Robert Guillaume, James Earl Jones, Cheech Marin, Jonathan Taylor Thomas

Upon the death of his father, the Lion King, a young cub is exiled from the jungle by his wicked uncle, who plans to ascend to the throne himself.

Reliably entertaining Disney animation that provides grown-up drama – loosely based on the plot of Hamlet – and, for light relief, excellent comic sidekicks and some memorable songs.

SCR Irene Mecchi, Jonathan Roberts, Linda Woolverton   MUS Hans Zimmer   DES Chris Sanders   ED Ivan Bilancio   PROD Don Hahn   DIST Buena Vista/Walt Disney

66 The Mickey Mouse factory at its finest, with inventive animation, stirring music, and a pride of inspired, almost-human animals. – *Desson Thomson, Washington Post*

66 A dazzling - and unexpectedly daring - addition to the Disney canon. – *Jeremy Gerard, Variety*

† The film later inspired a hit Broadway musical.

† It is to date the biggest-selling film on home video, having sold 32 million copies on VHS. In 2003, a DVD and video re-release sold more than three million copies in its first two days.

⚲ Hans Zimmer (music); Elton John (m), Tim Rice (ly) (music, original song – Can You Feel the Love Tonight) songs 'Circle of Life', 'Hakuna Matata'

Ⓣ Hans Zimmer (music); sound

L

'If you don't stand for something, you might fall for anything.'

Lions for Lambs (new)

DIR Robert Redford

2007 94m US

☆ Robert Redford (Professor Stephen Malley), Meryl Streep (Janine Roth), Tom Cruise (Senator Jasper Irving), Derek Luke (Arian Finch), Michael Peña (Ernest Rodriguez), Andrew Garfield (Todd Hayes)

A narrative about America's war on terror with three strands. In California, a political-science professor (Redford) chides a bright student whose idealism is fading. In Washington, a liberal TV journalist (Streep) interviews a smooth-talking Republican senator (Cruise). On a bleak mountain in Afghanistan, two young Army Rangers fight for their lives.

Preachy, verbose and unsatisfactory attempt to outline liberal stances on America's post 9/11 foreign policy. The scenes involving Redford are stilted and inert; Cruise is energetic and plausible in his role, but for a supposedly radical firebrand, Streep is oddly meek. The Afghanistan sequences lack credibility: how the soldiers even survived the fall from their helicopter remains unclear.

SCR Matthew Michael Carnahan   CIN Philippe Rousselot   MUS Mark Isham   DES Jan Roelfs   ED Joe Hutshing   PROD Matthew Michael Carnahan, Tracy Falco, Andrew Hauptman, Robert Redford   DIST Fox

66 There's a message behind Lions For Lambs. . .and my goodness, don't we know it at the end of a 94-minute hectoring that feels far longer. – *Wendy Ide, The Times.*

66 Liberal Hollywood sends its big guns into the 'war on terror' and winds up in a dreadful mess. – *Anthony Quinn, Independent.*

† The words in the title are said in the film to have been used to describe British infantrymen in World War I, sent to their deaths by the incompetent generals who commanded them. But the correct phrase is actually 'lions led by donkeys'.

Listen to Britain ★★★★

DIR *Humphrey Jennings*

1942 19m GB

Images of everyday life in Britain at war, with special emphasis on the part played by music in people's lives.

An astounding work of documentary art, without plot, narration or spoken dialogue, that sums up the mood of a beleaguered nation in just under 20 minutes. The music featured, from a Myra Hess piano recital to a factory workers' sing-song at the broadcast of a radio show, is profoundly moving. A succinct masterpiece about another side of life during wartime.

CIN H. E. Fowle   ED Humphrey Jennings, Stewart McAllister   PROD Crown Film Unit   DIST Ministry of Information

66 It is implicitly a utopian work, a vision of what a gentle, pluralist and decent society might look like:

exactly the kind of society Hitler wanted to destroy. – *Kevin Jackson*

† Film-maker Terence Davies insists that his documentary Of Time and the City (2008) was directly inspired by Listen to Britain.

† The film appeared on DVD in 2008 as part of Land of Promise, an outstanding collection of British documentaries from 1930-1950, distributed by the British Film Institute.

Listen Up: The Lives of Quincy Jones

SCR/DIR Ellen Weissbrod

1990 115m US

♫

Documentary on the life of a Grammy- and Oscar-winning musician, producer and composer, whose long career began in the 1940s.

A compelling topic, but a great chance squandered: with all the resources available to her – interviews music greats, home footage, newsreels and still photos, the director apparently tried to give her documentary an improvisational texture to match Jones's musical background. Consequently, opinions are heard in snippets, sometimes overlapping each other, and the film flits from one topic to another like free-form jazz. This short-changes Jones and even misunderstands his strengths – discipline, rigour and a strong sense of form and tradition.

CIN Stephen Kazmierski   MUS Quincy Jones   ED Milton Moses, Paul Zehrer, Laure Sullivan, Andrew Morreale, Pierre Kahn   PROD Courtney Sale Ross   DIST Warner/Cort

Little Buddha ★

DIR Bernardo Bertolucci

1993 123m France/GB

DVD ♫

☆ Keanu Reeves (Siddhartha), Ying Ruocheng (Lama Norbu), Chris Isaak (Dean Conrad), Bridget Fonda (Lisa Conrad), Alex Wiesendanger (Jesse Conrad), Raju Lal (Raju), Greishma Makar Singh (Gita)

A Buddhist lama searches the world to find the reincarnation of his dead teacher, and sees a young American boy as a likely candidate.

After The Last Emperor and The Sheltering Sky this was the third – and weakest – of Bertolucci's 'travelogue' films from exotic locales. It rests on two uneasily linked stories: one, which took place 2,500 years ago, relates how Prince Siddharta becomes the Buddha; in the other, a Seattle boy is named as the possible reincarnation of a Tibetan lama. Shot mainly in Bhutan, it's extraordinarily beautiful, and may have some educational value about Buddhism, but dramatically it falls short. The limited Reeves is unfortunately miscast as the Buddha-in-waiting.

SCR Rudy Wurlitzer, Mark Peploe   CIN Vittorio Storaro   MUS Ryuichi Sakamoto   DES James Acheson   ED Pietro Scalia   PROD Jeremy Thomas   DIST Buena Vista/Ciby 2000/Recorded Picture

L

66 It is unarguably fascinating to watch. – *Philip Strick, Sight & Sound*

Little Caesar ★★★

DIR *Mervyn Le Roy*

1931 77m US

DVD

☆ *Edward G. Robinson* (Cesare Enrico Bandello/"Little Caesar"), Douglas Fairbanks Jnr (Joe Massara), Glenda Farrell (Olga Strassoff), William Collier Jnr (Tony Passa), Ralph Ince (Diamond Pete Montana), George E. Stone (Otero), Thomas Jackson (Lt. Tom Flaherty), Stanley Fields (Sam Vettori), Sidney Blackmer (The Big Boy)

The rise and fall of a vicious gangster.

Its central character clearly modelled on Al Capone, this also has historical interest as vanguard of a spate of gangster films from Warner Bros. The star was forever identified with his role, and the film, though technically dated, moves fast enough to maintain interest almost 80 years later.

SCR Francis Faragoh, Robert N. Lee CIN Tony Gaudio
MUS Erno Rapee ED Ray Curtiss DIST Warner

RICO: Mother of Mercy, is this the end of Rico?

66 It has irony and grim humour and a real sense of excitement and its significance does not get in the way of the melodrama. – *Richard Dana Skinner*

66 One of the best gangster talkers yet turned out. . .a swell picture. – *Variety*

🏆 Francis Faragoh, Robert N. Lee (adapted screenplay)

Little Children ★★

DIR Todd Field

2006 136m US

DVD ♫

☆ Kate Winslet (Sarah Pierce), Jennifer Connelly (Kathy Adamson), Patrick Wilson (Brad Adamson), Jackie Earle Haley (Ronnie McGorvey), Noah Emmerich (Larry Hedges), Gregg Edelman (Richard Pierce), Phyllis Somerville (May McGorvey)

A suburban mother and an under-achieving househusband start an affair in suburbia to the disapproval of other neighbouring mothers. In the same town, an obsessive cop stalks a paedophile who lives with his elderly mother.

A smart, restrained film that starts as a satire of suburban foibles, then branches out into more interesting directions. Winslet's Sarah, this story's Madame Bovary, foolishly embarks on a love affair with the handsome but utterly vacant Brad. It takes a shocking incident involving the town paedophile (excellently played by Haley) to bring them to something like adulthood. The tone is uneven – the middle section loses its way – but it's rewarding enough.

SCR Todd Field, Tom Perrotta CIN Antonio Calvache
MUS Thomas Newman DES David Gropman ED Leo Trombetta PROD Albert Berger, Ron Yerxa, Todd Field
DIST Entertainment

66 A sharply observed and brilliantly acted study of American suburban life. – *Philip French, Observer*

66 A jolting, artfully made drama set in and around a suburban playground somewhere between 'American Beauty' and 'In the Bedroom' on America's psychic highway. – *Lisa Schwarzbaum, Entertainment Weekly*

🏆 Kate Winslet (leading actress); Jackie Earle Haley (supporting actor); Todd Field, Tom Perrotta (adapted screenplay)

🏆 Kate Winslet (leading actress)

The Little Foxes ★★★

DIR *William Wyler*

1941 116m US

DVD

☆ *Bette Davis* (Regina Hubbard Giddens), *Herbert Marshall* (Horace Giddens), *Teresa Wright* (Alexandra Giddens), Richard Carlson (David Hewitt), *Charles Dingle* (Ben Hubbard), *Dan Duryea* (Leo Hubbard), *Carl Benton Reid* (Oscar Hubbard), *Patricia Collinge* (Birdie Hubbard), Jessica Grayson (Addie), Russell Hicks (William Marshall)

A family of schemers in post-Civil War days will stop at nothing to outwit each other, especially a wife separated from her husband; though he is terminally ill, she needs his support to close a business deal..

Superb film of a brilliant play; excellent to look at and listen to, with a compelling narrative line and memorable characters.

SCR *Lillian Hellman* CIN *Gregg Toland* MUS Meredith Willson ED Daniel Mandell DIST Samuel Goldwyn

HORACE GIDDENS (HERBERT MARSHALL): Maybe it's easy for the dying to be honest. I'm sick of you, sick of this house, sick of my unhappy life with you. I'm sick of your brothers and their dirty tricks to make a dime. There must be better ways of getting rich than building sweatshops and pounding the bones of the town to make dividends for you to spend. You'll wreck the town, you and your brothers. You'll wreck the country, you and your kind, if they let you. But not me, I'll die my own way, and I'll do it without making the world any worse. I leave that to you.

66 One of the really beautiful jobs in the whole range of movie making. – *Otis Ferguson*

66 No one knows better than Wyler when to shift the camera's point of view, when to cut, or how to relate the characters in one shot to those in the next . . . you never have to wonder where you are in a Wyler picture. – *Arthur Knight*

🏆 picture; William Wyler; Bette Davis (leading actress); Teresa Wright (supporting actress); Patricia Collinge (supporting actress); Lillian Hellman (original screenplay); Meredith Willson (music); Stephen Goosson; Daniel Mandell (editing)

'It's not what he knows. It's what he understands.'

Little Man Tate ★

DIR Jodie Foster

1991 99m US

DVD ♫

☆ Jodie Foster (Dede Tate), Dianne Wiest (Jane Grierson), Adam Hann-Byrd (Fred Tate), Harry Connick Jnr (Eddie),

David Pierce (Garth), Debi Mazar (Gina), P. J. Ochlan (Damon Wells)

The future of a prodigiously gifted boy of seven is debated by his tough-talking, blue-collar single mother and a child psychologist.

Jodie Foster cut her directing teeth on this agreeable domestic drama that comes to seem too schematic: the emotional, warm mother on one side and the rigorous academic on the other, fighting, as it were, for the little boy's soul.

SCR Scott Frank   **CIN** Mike Southon   **MUS** Mark Isham   **DES** Jon Hutman   **ED** Lynzee Klingman   **PROD** Scott Rudin, Peggy Rajski   **DIST** Columbia TriStar/Orion

66 Foster draws good performances from her cast, but could have done with a better script. – *Colette Maude, Time Out*

'Where's Olive?'

Little Miss Sunshine ★★★

DIR Jonathan Dayton, Valerie Faris
2006   102m   US
DVD   ♫

☆ Greg Kinnear (Richard Hoover), Toni Collette (Sheryl Hoover), Steve Carell (Frank), Paul Dano (Dwayne), Abigail Breslin (Olive), Alan Arkin (Grandpa Hoover)

A dysfunctional American family includes a failed motivational speaker, facing financial ruin; an oversexed, drug-taking grandfather; a sulky mute teenager who communicates only by notepad; and a suicidal uncle. With the family's relatively sane mother, they travel in their dilapidated VW bus to a California beauty pageant in which their nine-year-old daughter Olive is a contestant.

An achingly funny comedy, shrewdly cast. Its script overflows with witty lines and snappy dialogue, but also speaks volumes about the American obsession with winning. The Hoover family, at first glance, are losers, but their ability to stick together through trying times makes them anything but. A joyous film that succeeds on its own terms, and even dispenses friendly wisdom.

SCR Michael Arndt   **CIN** Tim Suhrstedt   **MUS** Mychael Danna   **DES** Kalina Ivanov   **ED** Pamela Martin   **PROD** Albert Berger, Ron Yerxa, Marc Turtletaub, David T. Friendly, Peter Saraf   **DIST** TCF

66 It comes closer to the truth about the way people really live – on the edge of fantasy-driven desperation – than our sanctimonies permit us to think. – *Richard Schickel, Time*

66 A prime example of a dysfunctional family comedy that also doubles as a road movie. Even the vehicle of transport is dysfunctional. – *Peter Rainer, Christian Science Monitor*

⊥ Alan Arkin (supporting actor); Michael Arndt (original screenplay)
⊥ picture; Abigail Breslin (supporting actress)
🎭 Alan Arkin (supporting actor); Michael Arndt (original screenplay)
🎭 film; Abigail Breslin, Toni Collette (supporting actress); Jonathan Dayton, Valerie Faris

'Between good and evil and heaven and hell is. . .'

Little Odessa ★

SCR/DIR James Gray
1994   98m   US
DVD   ♫

☆ Tim Roth (Joshua Shapira), Edward Furlong (Reuben Shapira), Moira Kelly (Alla Shustervich), Vanessa Redgrave (Irina Shapira), Paul Guilfoyle (Boris Volkoff), Natasha Andreichenko (Natasha), Maximilian Schell (Arkady Shapira)

An American hitman of Russian-Jewish descent returns to his family home in the Brighton Beach area of New York and visits his family; his younger brother becomes dangerously involved in his professional life.

James Gray's feature debut, completed when he was 25, carries all the hallmarks by which he has become known: he works a specific ethnically rich area of New York, mining it for family-based stories on the fringes of a criminal world. A brisk, compelling work, with Roth a standout in the lead.

CIN Tom Richmond   **MUS** Dana Sano   **DES** Kevin Thompson   **ED** Dorian Harris   **PROD** Paul Webster   **DIST** First Independent/New Line

66 For all its contrived plotline and self-conscious solemnity, the film still exerts a grip. – *Philip Kemp, Sight & Sound*

'Every girl everywhere is a princess.'

A Little Princess ★★

DIR *Alfonso Cuaron*
1995   97m   US
DVD   ♫

☆ Eleanor Bron (Miss Minchin), Liam Cunningham (Capt. Crewe/ Prince Rama), Liesel Matthews (Sara Crewe), Rusty Schwimmer (Amelia Minchin), Arthur Malet (Charles Randolph), Vanessa Lee Chester (Becky), Errol Sitahal (Ram Dass), Heather DeLoach (Ermengarde), Taylor Fry (Lavinia)

A young English girl is forced into servitude at a New York boarding school when word comes out that her father has been killed in WWI.

Imaginative, strikingly stylised version of a children's classic.

SCR Richard LaGravenese, Elizabeth Chandler   **CIN** *Emmanuel Lubezki*   **MUS** Patrick Doyle   **DES** Bo Welch   **ED** Steven Weisberg   **PROD** Mark Johnson   **DIST** Warner/Baltimore

66 An exquisite, perfectly played serious fantasy that movingly stresses the importance of magic and the imagination in the scheme of things. A classic the moment it hits the screen, this should delight audiences of all persuasions. – *Todd McCarthy, Variety*

⊥ Emmanuel Lubezki; Bo Welch

Little Vera ★

DIR Vasili Pichul
1988   110m   USSR
DVD

☆ Natalya Negoda (Vera), Ludmilla Zaitseva (Vera's

DVD Available on DVD	☆ Cast in order of importance	66 Critics' Quotes	⊥ Academy Award	🎭 BAFTA
♫ Soundtrack on CD		† Points of interest	Academy Award nomination	BAFTA nomination

375

mother), Andrei Sokolov (Sergei), Yuri Nazarov (Vera's father), Alexander Alexeyev-Negreba (Victor), Alexandra Tabakova (Chistyakova)

In a dull Russian industrial town, a young woman without plans for her life mixes with a heavy-drinking crowd and enjoys casual sex.

This ultra-realistic look at life caused uproar in Russia on its release; it certainly marks a change from state-approved films glorifying communism and collectivism. Yet though its reputation precedes it, Little Vera seems unexceptional by western standards, though decidedly bleak.

SCR Mariya Khmelik   CIN Yefim Reznikov
MUS Vladimir Matetsky   DES Vladimir Pasternak
ED Yelena Zabolotskaya   PROD Yuri Prober
DIST Mainline/Gorky Studios

'Finding Your Own Voice Can Be Magic.'

Little Voice ★

SCR/DIR *Mark Herman*
1998   97m   GB
DVD ♫

☆ *Jane Horrocks* (L.V.), *Michael Caine* (Ray Say), *Ewan McGregor* (Billy), Jim Broadbent (Mr Boo), Brenda Blethyn (Mari Hoff), Annette Badland (Sadie), Philip Jackson (George)

A meek young woman with the uncanny ability to impersonate showbiz divas is pushed into the limelight by her overbearing mother and a sleazy agent.

Broad translation of a theatrical success: the material is strong and occasionally affecting, but more often one catches the actors playing – very loudly – to the back rows.

CIN Andy Collins   MUS John Altman   DES Don Taylor
ED Michael Ellis   PROD Elizabeth Karlsen
DIST Miramax/Scala

66 An almost perfect blend of biting wit, heart-warming comedy and perfect acting. – *Caroline Westbrook, Empire*

66 Annoyingly noisy. – *Charles Taylor, Salon*

⚲ Brenda Blethyn (supporting actress)

Ⓣ British film; Michael Caine (leading actor); Jane Horrocks (leading actress); Brenda Blethyn (supporting actress); Mark Herman (adapted screenplay); Peter Lindsay, Rodney Glenn, Ray Merrin, Graham Daniel (sound)

'The story that has lived in our hearts for generations, now comes to the screen for the holidays.'

Little Women ★★

DIR *Gillian Armstrong*
1994   115m   US
DVD ♫

☆ Winona Ryder (Jo March), Gabriel Byrne (Friedrich Bhaer), Trini Alvarado (Meg March), Samantha Mathis (Older Amy March), Kirsten Dunst (Younger Amy March), Claire Danes (Beth March), Susan Sarandon (Marmee), Eric Stoltz (John Brooke), John Neville (Mr Laurence), Mary Wickes (Aunt March)

In 19th-century New England, four young girls are raised by their doting mother.

An attractive, sensitive, nicely cast adaptation that strengthens the novel's feminist credentials.

SCR *Robin Swicord*   CIN Geoffrey Simpson
MUS Thomas Newman   DES Jan Roelfs   ED Nicholas Beauman   PROD Dennis DiNovi   DIST Columbia TriStar/Di Novi Pictures

66 It's a celebration of American female screen acting, it's a study of early feminism that feels relevant today, it's a carefully mounted exercise in period filmmaking, and it's a beloved novel come to life for the fourth time. – *Shawn Levy, Portland Oregonian*

⚲ Winona Ryder (leading actress); Thomas Newman; Colleen Atwood (costume design)

Ⓣ Colleen Atwood (costume design)

'Life, love, desire. . .and everything in between.'

Live Flesh ★★★

DIR *Pedro Almodóvar*
1997   103m   France/Spain
DVD ♫

☆ Javier Bardem (David), Francesca Neri (Elena), Liberto Rabal (Victor Plaza), Angela Molina (Clara), José Sancho (Sancho), Penelope Cruz (Isabel Plaza Caballero), Pilar Bardem (Doña Centro de Mesa)

A young man jailed for his part in a botched police raid plots to settle the score with the policeman who had him imprisoned.

Bold transposition of a Ruth Rendell novel to the streets of a post-Franco Spain: it succeeds as a historical snapshot, a gripping thriller, and as a logical maturing of its remarkable director's themes.

SCR *Pedro Almodóvar, Ray Loriga, Jorge Guerricaechevarria*   CIN *Affonso Beato*   MUS Alberto Iglesias   ED José Salcedo   PROD Agustín Almodóvar   DIST El Deseo/CiBy 2000/France 3

66 The performances are spot on, the control of pace, mood and narrative is assured, the visuals are crisp, stylish and imaginative, and the whole film has, for Almodóvar, an unprecedented weight and substance. – *Geoff Andrew, Time Out*

Ⓣ film not in the English language

'Meet The Film Crew From Hell! In The Looniest Movie About The Movies.'

Living in Oblivion ★★

SCR/DIR *Tom DiCillo*
1995   90m   US
DVD

☆ *Steve Buscemi* (Nick Reve), *Catherine Keener* (Nicole Springer), Dermot Mulroney (Wolf), Danielle von Zerneck (Wanda), James LeGros (Chad Palomino), *Peter Dinklage* (Tito)

A filmmaker at the end of his tether has to cope with a deeply insecure actress, a pretentious lead actor, a macho cameraman, and a touchy 'little person' on the set of his latest production.

Funny, savvy satire of the independent filmmaking sector, playing its characters' dreams and aspirations off against the desperate reality of a cash-strapped world those behind the camera clearly know all too well.

CIN Frank Prinzi   MUS Jim Farmer   DES Thérèse DePrez, Stephanie Carroll   ED Camilla Toniolo, Dana Congdon   PROD Michael Griffiths, Marcus Viscidi   DIST Entertainment/JDI/Lemon Sky

66 Film students should consider Living in Oblivion required viewing. Writer-director Tom DiCillo's inside view of a cinematic work-in-progress is simultaneously hair-raising and hilarious. – *Bruce Williamson, Playboy*

66 One of the truest films yet about making films. – *Alexander Walker, Evening Standard*

'A Disgrace To Criminals Everywhere.'

Lock, Stock and Two Smoking Barrels ★

SCR/DIR Guy Ritchie
1998   107m   GB
DVD ♫

☆ Jason Flemyng (Tom), Dexter Fletcher (Soap), Nick Moran (Eddie), Jason Statham (Bacon), Steven Mackintosh (Winston), Vinnie Jones (Big Chris), Sting (JD), Lenny McLean (Barry the Baptist), P.H. Moriarty ('Hatchet' Harry Lonsdale), Steve Sweeney (Plank), Frank Harper (Dog), Stephen Marcus (Nick the Greek), Peter McNicholl (Little Chris)

An East End wide boy and his friends have a week to settle their debts to a local porn magnate.

This crime caper has not a great deal of originality or heart, but displays an undeniable energy as its cast of memorable faces duck and dive between narrative entanglements. Unhappily, its massive success opened the floodgates to a wave of dismal British gangster movies.

CIN Tim Maurice-Jones   MUS David A. Hughes, John Murphy   DES Iain Andrews, Eve Mavrakis   ED Niven Howie   PROD Matthew Vaughan   DIST Polygram/Steve Tisch/SKA Films

66 Like Tarantino crossed with the Marx Brothers. – *Roger Ebert, Chicago Sun-Times*

66 Too mixed-up to synopsise easily and too rickety to think about closely, but it gets plenty of laughs as it rushes from scene to scene. – *Kim Newman, Empire*

🎭 audience award
Ⓣ British film; Niven Howie

'A forbidden love. An unthinkable attraction. The ultimate price.'

Lolita ★

DIR Adrian Lyne
1997   137m   US/France
DVD ♫

☆ *Jeremy Irons* (Humbert Humbert), *Melanie Griffith* (Charlotte Haze), Frank Langella (Clare Quilty), Dominique Swain (Dolores 'Lolita' Haze), Suzanne Shepherd (Miss Pratt), Keith Reddin (Reverend Rigger), Erin J. Dean (Mona)

A college professor falls for a 12-year-old girl.

Faithful if finally underwhelming adaptation of the novel, stronger when it concentrates on the central love triangle between man, mother and daughter than in its altogether cursory treatment of the Quilty character. Lyne's fondness for crass symbolism doesn't help. Still, it's well acted and attractively shot.

SCR Stephen Schiff   CIN *Howard Atherton*   MUS Ennio Morricone   DES Jon Hutman   ED Julie Monroe, David Bremner   PROD Mario Kassar, Joel B. Michaels   DIST Pathé

66 A pretty, gauzy Lolita that replaces the book's cruelty and comedy with manufactured lyricism and mopey romanticism. – *Charles Taylor, Salon*

66 All movie adaptations of Nabokov fall short, by definition, but this one is the most graceful failure so far. – *Anthony Lane, New Yorker*

London ★★

SCR/DIR *Patrick Keiller*
1994   85m   GB
DVD

☆ Paul Scofield (narrator)

Over images of contemporary London, a narrator recounts news of a search for the roots of English Romanticism he undertook with his university lecturer ex-lover.

Distinctive documentary-style film offering a guided tour of a city under siege from both the effects of Thatcherism and IRA terrorist attacks; Keiller possesses a keen eye for the unusual concealed within the everyday, even if his visuals are more striking and provocative than anything in the voiceover.

CIN Patrick Keiller   ED Larry Sider   PROD Keith Griffiths   DIST BFI/Channel 4

66 One of the most original British features in a long time. – *Geoff Andrew, Time Out*

London to Brighton ★★

SCR/DIR Paul Andrew Williams
2006   85m   UK
DVD

☆ Lorraine Stanley (Kelly), Johnny Harris (Derek), Alexander Morton (Duncan), Georgia Groome (Joanne), Sam Spruell (Stuart)

A prostitute flees to Brighton with an under-age runaway to protect her from a paedophile gang boss.

Grim, seedy story riddled with violence and sleaze, but an astonishingly confident debut from Williams in a virtually no-budget movie. From the opening scene, with its two female protagonists locked in a public lavatory at 3.07 a.m., and plotting their getaway, the pace never falters. Hardly pleasant viewing, but compulsive and gripping.

CIN Christopher Ross   MUS Laura Rossi   DES Jane Levick   ED Tom Hemmings   PROD Alistair Clark, Rachel Robey, Ken Marshall, Paul Andrew Williams   DIST Vertigo

66 The film's propulsive urgency barely lets up. . .a startlingly accomplished piece of work. – *Michael Brooke, Sight & Sound*

L

DVD Available on DVD   ☆ Cast in order of importance   66 Critics' Quotes   🏆 Academy Award   Ⓑ BAFTA
♫ Soundtrack on CD   † Points of interest   Academy Award nomination   BAFTA nomination

377

† Writer-director Williams has claimed he wrote the script over a single weekend.

'John Sayles invites you to return to the scene of the crime.'

Lone Star ★★

SCR/DIR *John Sayles*
1996   135m   US
[DVD]   ♫

☆ *Chris Cooper* (Sheriff Sam Deeds), *Elizabeth Peña* (Pilar Cruz), *Kris Kristofferson* (Sheriff Charlie Wade), *Matthew McConaughey* (Buddy Deeds), Jesse Borrego (Danny), Ron Canada (Otis Payne), Frances McDormand (Bunny), Joe Morton (Colonel Delmore Payne)

The sheriff of a Texan border town uncovers the remains of a racist lawman long thought to have been run out of town by the sheriff's father some four decades before.

An often astonishingly ambitious piece, exploring how the past impacts upon the present and how history comes to be written; staged with rare intelligence and skill, and blessed with several outstanding performances, it suffers only from a pace that could be described as at best measured, at worst torturously slow. The Man Who Shot Liberty Valance did it all thirty years earlier, and (crucially) fifteen minutes shorter.

CIN *Stuart Dryburgh*   MUS Mason Daring   DES Dan Bishop   ED John Sayles   PROD R. Paul Miller, Maggie Renzi   DIST Rank/Castle Rock/Turner/Rio Dulce

❝ Sayles manages to put across his ideas without a hint of didacticism, with characters who have a life of their own, and a storyline that steadily gathers momentum and power. – *Christopher Tookey, Daily Mail*

❝ Like all the best Westerns, this is at once a morality play about individual responsibility and a challenging essay about American history. You'll watch this for the third or fourth time and see fresh material. – *Kim Newman, Empire*

⚲ John Sayles (original screenplay)
Ⓣ John Sayles (screenplay)

The Loneliness of the Long Distance Runner ★★★

DIR Tony Richardson
1962   104m   GB
[DVD]

☆ *Tom Courtenay* (Colin Smith), Michael Redgrave (The Governor), James Bolam (Mike), Avis Bunnage (Mrs. Smith), Alec McCowen (Brown), Joe Robinson (Roach), Julia Foster (Gladys)

The only thing a Borstal boy does well is run, and as he trains he thinks back to his depressing life.

Class issues, typically for films of this type in this era, take centre stage here, as the troubled working-class hero competes against a team of posh boys from a boarding school. Yet the film's most striking moments show how the boy finds running a liberating force in his life, a time when he can forget his wretched life and environment.

SCR *Alan Sillitoe*   CIN Walter Lassally   MUS John

Addison   ED Anthony Gibbs   PROD Tony Richardson   DIST British Lion
Ⓣ Tom Courtenay

'Love can be murder.'

Lonely Hearts (new)

SCR/DIR Todd Robinson
2006   108m   US/Germany
[DVD]

☆ John Travolta (Elmer Robinson), James Gandolfini (Charles Hildebrandt), Jared Leto (Raymond Fernandez), Salma Hayek (Martha Beck), Scott Caan (Det. Reilly), Alice Krige (Janet Long), Laura Dern (Rene Fodie)

A dogged policeman hunts down a murderous couple who find their victims through the personal columns.

The Honeymoon Killers again, this time viewed from a cop's perspective; grimy and downbeat, with some ugly violence.

CIN Peter Levy   MUS Mychael Danna   DES Jon Gary Steele   ED Kathryn Himoff   PROD Boaz Davidson, Holly Wiersma   DIST Entertainment

❝ The film, unfortunately, never comes fully into focus or fully alive. – *Peter Travers, Rolling Stone*

† Travolta plays the director's grandfather.

The Lonely Passion of Judith Hearne ★★

DIR Jack Clayton
1987   110m   GB
[DVD]

☆ *Maggie Smith* (Judith Hearne), Bob Hoskins (James Madden), Wendy Hiller (Aunt D'Arcy), Marie Kean (Mrs. Rice), Prunella Scales (Moira O'Neill)

A middle-aged woman waits for love in a gloomy Dublin boarding house.

Maggie Smith brilliantly depicts a life of quiet desperation as a woman with few prospects, taking solace only in religion and alcohol. All the performances are superb, though because of its bleak subject matter, it's not a film to be revisited regularly.

SCR Peter Nelson   CIN Peter Hannan   MUS Georges Delerue   DES Michael Pickwood   PROD Peter Nelson, Richard Johnson   DIST HandMade

Ⓣ Maggie Smith (leading actress)

'Change your outlook. Change your life.'

Lonesome Jim (new) ★

DIR Steve Buscemi
2005   91m   US

☆ Casey Affleck (Jim), Liv Tyler (Anika), Mary Kay Place (Sally), Seymour Cassel (Don), Kevin Corrigan (Tim), Jack Rovello (Ben), Mark Boone Jr. (Evil)

A failed writer returns to his family home and receives a less than enthusiastic welcome.

Slight but pleasing character piece with a dry humour that helps compensate for an inert protagonist and a paucity of action.

[DVD] Available on DVD   ☆ Cast in order of importance   ❝ Critics' Quotes   ⚲ Academy Award   Ⓑ BAFTA
♫ Soundtrack on CD   † Points of interest   ⚲ Academy Award nomination   Ⓣ BAFTA nomination

SCR James C. Strouse   CIN Phil Parmet   MUS Evan Lurie   DES Chuck Voelter   ED Plummy Tucker   PROD Galt Niederhoffer, Celine Rattray, Daniela Taplin Lundberg, Jake Abraham, Gary Winick, Steve Buscemi   DIST Lionsgate

JIM: 'I sort of came back to have a nervous breakdown, but my brother beat me to it.'

66 I can't recall having a better time at a movie about depression. . . a deadpan delight. – *Peter Travers, Rolling Stone*

66 A modest film, but it earns its keep. – *Jan Stuart, Newsday*

† The film was shot in 16 days for $500,000.

The Long Day Closes ★★★★

SCR/DIR *Terence Davies*
1992   85m   GB
DVD

☆ Marjorie Yates (Mother), Leigh McCormack (Bud), Anthony Watson (Kevin), Nicholas Lamont (John), Ayse Owens (Helen), Tina Malone (Edna), Jimmy Wilde (Curly), Robin Polley (Mr. Nicholls)

An 11 year old boy grows up in post-war Liverpool, coping with bullying at school, regularly going to the cinema and taking part in family life.

A genuine British masterpiece, a movie in love with movies and the sense of release and escape they can bring to mundane lives. Davies re-creates in painterly detail the daily life of his 11 year old hero, and the specific time, when Britain was moving gradually away from post-war austerity and ration books, and daring to look forward to a more hopeful future. Bud's love affair with Hollywood, and the evocative, romantic pop songs that flood his house, function as more than mere nostalgia; they are formative sights and sounds in a young life. This understated but deeply emotional film captures its era with a melancholy affection.

CIN *Michael Coulter*   DES *Christopher Hobbs*
ED William Diver   PROD Olivia Stewart, Angela Topping
DIST Mayfair/Palace/Film Four/BFI

The Long Good Friday ★★★★

DIR *John Mackenzie*
1980   105m   GB
DVD   ♫

☆ *Bob Hoskins* (Harold), *Helen Mirren* (Victoria), Dave King (Parky), Bryan Marshall (Harris), Eddie Constantine (Charlie), Stephen Davis (Tony), Paul Freeman (Colin), George Coulouris (Gus), Pierce Brosnan (First Irishman)

A gangland boss faces violent reprisals from the competition.

A brutal film that re-locates the gangster film to London's Docklands with Hoskins's Harold Shand cast in the Little Caesar or Scarface mould. Hoskins is quite extraordinary, and the plot chimed with its time – the early days of the expansive, entrepreneurial Thatcher era. Yet it holds up well, and remains one of the greatest crime films to emerge from Britain.

SCR *Barrie Keefe*   CIN Phil Meheux   MUS Francis Monkman   ED Mike Taylor   PROD Barry Hanson
DIST Black Lion/Calendar

66 Much more densely plotted and intelligently scripted than most such yarns. – *Variety*

'Nothing says goodbye like a bullet!'

The Long Goodbye ★★

DIR Robert Altman
1973   111m   US
DVD

☆ Elliott Gould, Nina Van Pallandt, Sterling Hayden, Mark Rydell, Henry Gibson

Philip Marlowe helps an eccentric friend who is suspected of murdering his wife.

An amusing, radical re-working of Raymond Chandler's novel, with Gould's Marlowe a man out of time and a fish out of water in the self-regarding, paid-back L.A. of the 1970s. The film, affectionately intentioned, does no lasting harm to Chandler, but rather lacks the tautness and economy of style common to earlier film adaptations of his work. Still, a worthwhile experiment.

SCR Leigh Brackett   CIN Vilmos Zsigmond   MUS John T. Williams   PROD Jerry Bick   DIST UA/Lions Gate

66 Altman's fragmentation bomb blows up itself rather than the myths he has said he wants to lay to rest. – *Sight & Sound*

66 The trouble is that this Marlowe is an untidy, unshaven, semi-literate dimwit slob who could not locate a missing skyscraper and who would be refused service at a hot dog stand. – *Charles Champlin*

'Eight years ago she lost her memory. Now, a detective must help her remember the past before it buries them both. What's forgotten is not always gone.'

The Long Kiss Goodnight

DIR Renny Harlin
1996   120m   US
DVD   ♫

☆ Geena Davis (Samantha Caine / Charly Baltimore), Samuel L. Jackson (Mitch Henessey), Patrick Malahide (Leland Perkins), Craig Bierko (Timothy), Brian Cox (Dr. Nathan Waldman), David Morse (Luke / Daedalus), G. D. Spradlin (President)

A housewife suffering from amnesia remembers she was a CIA assassin, and is pursued by those with secrets to keep.

Wearisome attempt to send up action-movie cliches that isn't helped by some at best incoherent, at worst utterly inept direction.

SCR Shane Black   CIN Guillermo Navarro   MUS Alan Silvestri   DES Howard Cummings   ED William Goldenberg   PROD Renny Harlin, Stephanie Austin, Shane Black   DIST Entertainment/New Line/Forge/Steve Tisch

66 I liked it in the same way I might like an arcade game: it holds your attention until you run out of quarters, and then you wander away without giving it another thought. – *Roger Ebert, Chicago Sun-Times*

66 There's an excessive amount of excess - a mind-numbing plurality of firearm battles, vehicular explosions and brutally frank sexual talk. – *Desson Thomson, Washington Post*

DVD Available on DVD   ☆ Cast in order of importance   66 Critics' Quotes   † Points of interest   🏆 Academy Award   🏆 Academy Award nomination   🏆 BAFTA   🏆 BAFTA nomination

379

Longtime Companion ★★

DIR Norman René
1990 96m US
DVD

☆ Stephen Caffrey (Fuzzy), Patrick Cassidy (Howard), Brian Cousins (Bob), Bruce Davison (David), John Dossett (Paul), Mark Lamos (Sean), Dermot Mulroney (John), Mary-Louise Parker (Lisa)

The effect of AIDS on New York's gay community during the 1980s is charted through an extended circle of friends.

A noble attempt to provide a dramatic overview of an epidemic; though over-populated and skewed in favour of an East Coast elite, it manages to build a quiet, affecting power.

SCR Craig Lucas **CIN** Tony Jannelli **MUS** Greg DeBelles **DES** Andrew Jackness **ED** Katherine Wenning **PROD** Stan Wlodkowski **DIST** Palace/Companion Productions/American Playhouse

66 Puts a human face on the AIDS scare and gently coaxes general audiences (at least, the open-minded variety) into rooting for, rather than fearing, people with AIDS. – *Desson Howe, Washington Post*

🏅 Bruce Davison (supporting actor)

Look at Me ★★★

DIR Agnès Jaoui
2004 110m France/Italy
DVD 🎵

☆ *Marilou Berry* (Lolita), Agnès Jaoui (Sylvia), *Jean-Pierre Bacri* (Etienne), Laurent Grévill (Pierre), Virginie Desarnauts (Karine), Keine Bouhiza (Sebastien)

An unprepossessing teenager strives to become a classical singer in the face of the monstrous indifference of her father, a lauded, egotistical writer.

Like the filmmakers' previous collaboration Le Gout des Autres, a dry, rarefied, beautifully performed comedy of manners, gently pursuing issues of body image while insisting that the most attractive human features of all are open hearts and minds.

SCR *Agnès Jaoui, Jean-Pierre Bacri* **CIN** Stéphane Fontaine **MUS** Philippe Rombi **DES** Olivier Jacquet **ED** François Gédigier **PROD** Jean-Philippe Andraca, Christian Berard **DIST** Pathé

66 There are rollicking performances all round, and a tight script that gets laughs and doles out flaws to all the characters. – *Catherine Shoard, Sunday Telegraph*

66 Consistently funny, sometimes hilarious, and full of lovely, spot-on observations. – *Jason Solomons, Mail on Sunday*

'A four hundred year old work-in-progress.'

Looking for Richard ★

DIR Al Pacino
1996 112m US
DVD 🎵

☆ Al Pacino (Himself/Richard III), Penelope Allen (Herself/Queen Elizabeth), Harris Yulin (Himself/King Edward), Alec Baldwin (Himself/Duke of Clarence), Kevin Spacey (Himself/Earl of Buckingham), Estelle Parsons (Margaret), Winona Ryder (Lady Anne), Aidan Quinn (Richmond)

Al Pacino rounds up several thespian friends to explore what makes Shakespeare's Richard III such a compelling text.

A leisurely and engaging work, expressing a real and infectious delight in learning and literature; it will come into its own as a teaching aid.

SCR Al Pacino, Frederic Kimball **CIN** Robert Leacock **MUS** Howard Shore **ED** Pasquale Buba, William A. Anderson, Ned Bastille, Andre Betz **PROD** Michael Hadge, Al Pacino **DIST** TCF

66 A vividly annotated Shakespeare. It is as if Scarface had suddenly turned into the world's coolest English teacher. – *Brian D. Johnson, Maclean's*

'Whoever has the money has the power.'

The Lookout (new) ★

DIR Scott Frank
2007 99m US
DVD

☆ Joseph Gordon-Levitt (Chris Pratt), Jeff Daniels (Lewis), Matthew Goode (Gary Spargo), Isla Fisher (Luvlee Lemons), Bruce McGill (Robert Pratt), Carla Gugino (Janet)

A janitor with a debilitating brain injury becomes an accomplice in a robbery at the bank where he works.

Taut, engrossing noir with a vein of dark humour, held together by strong performances if compromised by an overly abrupt ending.

CIN Alar Kivilo **MUS** James Newton Howard **DES** David Brisbin **ED** Jill Savitt **PROD** Walter Parkes, Laurence Mark, Roger Birnbaum, Gary Barber **DIST** Buena Vista

LEWIS: 'I get turned down more times than the beds at the Holiday Inn.'

66 We can't avoid knowing where The Lookout is headed, but we are so deep inside its characters' heads that we wouldn't want to go anywhere else. – *Kenneth Turan, Los Angeles Times*

66 A solidly above-average thriller. – *Ruthe Stein, San Francisco Chronicle*

'The Legend Comes To Life'

The Lord of the Rings: The Fellowship Of The Ring ★★

DIR *Peter Jackson*
2001 178m US/New Zealand
DVD 🎵

☆ Elijah Wood (Frodo Baggins), Ian McKellen (Gandalf), Liv Tyler (Arwen), Viggo Mortensen (Aragorn), Sean Astin (Sam), Cate Blanchett (Galadriel), John Rhys-Davies (Gimli), Billy Boyd (Pippin), Dominic Monaghan (Merry), Orlando Bloom (Legolas), Christopher Lee (Saruman), Hugo Weaving (Elrond), Sean Bean (Boromir), Ian Holm (Bilbo Baggins), Andy Serkis (Gollum)

A young Hobbit finds a ring of immense,

corrupting power, and sets out to destroy it for the good of all mankind.

The pleasures of this first part of Jackson's ambitious trilogy lie in its painterly exteriors – using the natural wonders of New Zealand as a backdrop, it remains perhaps the most purely beautiful-looking event movie in motion picture history – and the filmmaker's ability to hold true to both Tolkien's vision and his own, early works: the villains are possessed of a ferocity to rival the zombies and cannibals in Jackson's early splatter pics. There are lulls in storytelling, but it establishes a world that would prove enchanting indeed.

SCR *Fran Walsh, Philippa Boyens, Peter Jackson*
CIN *Andrew Lesnie*   MUS Howard Shore   DES *Grant Major*   ED *John Gilbert*   PROD Barrie M. Osborne, Peter Jackson, Fran Walsh, Tim Sanders   DIST Entertainment

66 An extraordinary work, grandly conceived, brilliantly executed and wildly entertaining. It's a hobbit's dream, a wizard's delight. – *Michael Wilmington, Chicago Tribune*

66 The film is a virtuosic triumph, but parlour tricks don't make movies, and it's Jackson's unwavering sincerity that elevates The Fellowship of the Ring into the increasingly rare Valhalla of the rousing, well-told tale. – *Manohla Dargis, L.A. Weekly*

⚱ Andrew Lesnie (cinematography); Howard Shore (music); Peter Owen, Richard Taylor (make up); Jim Rygiel, Randall William Cook, Richard Taylor, Mark Stetson (visual effects)

⚱ picture; Peter Jackson; Ian McKellen (supporting actor); Grant Major; Ngila Dickson, Richard Taylor (costume design); John Gilbert (editing); Christopher Boyes, Michael Semanick, Gethin Creagh, Hammond Peek (sound); Enya, Nicky Ryan, Roma Ryan (m, ly) (music, original song – May It Be)

🎭 film; Peter Jackson; visual effects; make up/hair
Ⓣ Howard Shore; Andrew Lesnie; Ngila Dickson; John Gilbert; Ian McKellan; Grant Major; adapted screenplay; sound

The Lord of the Rings: The Return of the King ★★★

DIR *Peter Jackson*
2003   201m   New Zealand/Germany/US
DVD   🎵

☆ Elijah Wood (Frodo), *Ian McKellen* (Gandalf), Liv Tyler (Arwen), Viggo Mortensen (Aragorn), Sean Astin (Sam), Cate Blanchett (Galadriel), John Rhys-Davies (Gimli), Bernard Hill (Theoden), Billy Boyd (Pippin), Dominic Monaghan (Merry), Orlando Bloom (Legolas), Hugo Weaving (Elrond), Miranda Otto (Eowyn), *Andy Serkis* (Gollum), Ian Holm (Bilbo)

The hobbits approach the slopes of Mount Doom, preparing to dispose of the cursed Ring, while the forces of good and evil are rallied in anticipation of the ultimate battle.

The longest of the three films, which suffers from having to cut between disparate story strands, and – in its final half-hour – stacks up endings one after the other, like jetplanes waiting to land, the director visibly reluctant to let these characters go. Most audiences will forgive Jackson that, for this is a fitting conclusion to a series of films made with tremendous artistry and affection for

their subject; thrilling spectacle is underscored with palpable human drama, and it finally becomes clear why the books continue to ring such bells so loudly in the lives of so many.

SCR *Fran Walsh, Philippa Boyens, Peter Jackson*
CIN *Andrew Lesnie*   DES *Grant Major*   ED *Jamie Selkirk*
PROD *Barrie M. Osborne, Peter Jackson, Fran Walsh*
DIST Entertainment

66 The second half of the film elevates all the story elements to Beethovenian crescendo. Here is an epic with literature's depth and opera's splendour - and one that could be achieved only in movies. What could be more terrific? – *Richard Corliss, Time*

66 A miracle, an extravaganza equal to its predecessors and, in some ways, more stunning. It is a profound testament to the extraordinary power of moving images and sound. – *Gregory Weinkauf, Dallas Observer*

† The second in the Lord of the Rings trilogy, The Two Towers, was released in 2002.

⚱ picture; Peter Jackson (direction); Fran Walsh, Philippa Boyens, Peter Jackson (adapted screenplay); art direction; Jamie Selkirk (editing); Howard Shore (music); Jim Rygiel, Joe Letteri, Randall William Cook, Alex Funke (visual effects); Ngila Dickson, Richard Taylor (costume design); Christopher Boyes, Michael Semanick, Michael Hedges, Hammond Peek (sound); Richard Taylor, Peter King (makeup); Frances Walsh, Howard Shore, Annie Lennox (m, ly) (music, original song – Into the West)

🎭 film; Fran Walsh, Philippa Boyens, Peter Jackson (adapted screenplay); Andrew Lesnie; visual effects
Ⓣ Peter Jackson (direction); Ian McKellan (supporting actor); Jamie Selkirk (editing); Ngila Dickson, Richard Taylor (costume design); make up/hair; Grant Major (production design); sound

'The first and most important rule of gun-running is: never get shot with your own merchandise.'

Lord of War ★★

SCR/DIR *Andrew Niccol*
2005   122m   Germany/US
DVD   🎵

☆ Nicolas Cage (Yuri Orlov), Jared Leto (Vitaly Orlov), Bridget Moynahan (Ava Fontaine), Ian Holm (Simeon Weisz), Ethan Hawke (Valentine), Eamonn Walker (Baptiste Senior), Sammi Rotibi (Baptiste Junior)

A Ukrainian-American arms dealer, being pursued by an Interpol agent, starts re-assessing his life and values.

Smartly-written thriller that delves fearlessly into the ugly consequences of the arms trade, and maintains a high action quotient into the bargain. Cage has rarely been better, and this entire film, an underrated pleasure, is more shrewd and sophisticated than one has a right to expect.

CIN Amir Mokri   MUS Antonio Pinto   DES Jean Vincent Puzos   ED Zach Staenberg   PROD Phillippe Rousselot, Andrew Niccol, Nicolas Cage, Norman Golightly, Andy Grosch, Chris Roberts, Teri-Lin Robertson
DIST Momentum

66 With such a cynical but compelling lead character, Niccol's critique of the arms trade can't help but appear strangely ambivalent. – *Geoffrey Macnab, Sight & Sound*

DVD Available on DVD   ☆ Cast in order   66 Critics' Quotes   ⚱ Academy Award   🎭 BAFTA
🎵 Soundtrack on CD   of importance   † Points of interest   Academy Award nomination   Ⓣ BAFTA nomination

'They came from nothing to change everything.'

Lords of Dogtown

DIR Catherine Hardwicke

2005   107m   US

DVD   ♫

☆ Emile Hirsch (Jay), Victor Rasuk (Tony), John Robinson (Stacy), Michael Angarano (Sid), Nikki Reed (Kathy Alva), Heath Ledger (Skip), Rebecca De Mornay (Philaine), Johnny Knoxville (Topper Burks)

The lives of young skateboarders in the 1970s, as the sport took off.

Expensively pointless re-creation of the events portrayed in the documentary Dogtown and Z-Boys; a promising young cast play at being cardboard delinquents, sticking it to The Man.

SCR Stacy Peralta   CIN Elliot Davis   MUS Mark Mothersbaugh   DES Chris Gorak   ED Nancy Richardson   PROD John Linson   DIST Columbia TriStar

66 Shows how hard writing a fiction film can be, and what a vast artistic distance can stand between a bad fiction film and the first-rate documentary that inspired it. – *Joe Morgenstern, Wall Street Journal*

66 A wipe-out. – *Peter Bradshaw, Guardian*

'Some people make their own miracles.'

Lorenzo's Oil   ★★

DIR George Miller

1992   129m   US

DVD   ♫

☆ Nick Nolte (Augusto Odone), *Susan Sarandon* (Michaela Odone), Peter Ustinov (Professor Nikolais), Kathleen Wilhoite (Deirdre Murphy), Gerry Bamman (Doctor Judalon), Margo Martindale (Wendy Gimble), James Rebhorn (Ellard Muscatine), Ann Hearn (Loretta Muscatine), Maduka Steady (Omuori), Zack O'Malley Greenburg (Lorenzo)

When a young boy is diagnosed with a wasting disease that normally proves fatal, his parents confront medical opinion and search tirelessly for a cure.

Based on an uplifting true story, this is effectively a glossier version of a 'disease-of-the-week' TV movie, except that its emotional impact is tougher, sometimes relentlessly so. Yet within its own terms, it's impeccably performed and executed.

SCR George Miller, Nick Enright   CIN John Seale   DES Kristi Zea   ED Richard Francis-Bruce, Marcus D'Arcy   PROD Doug Mitchell, George Miller   DIST UIP/Universal/Kennedy Miller

66 An honourably compromised attempt to make medical docu-drama palatable to a wide audience. – *Tony Rayns, Sight & Sound*

🏆 Susan Sarandon (leading actress); George Miller, Nick Enright (original screenplay)

Lost Embrace   ★★

DIR Daniel Burman

2004   100m   Argentina/France/Italy/Spain/Netherlands

DVD

☆ Daniel Hendler (Ariel), Adriana Aizenberg (Sonia), Jorge D'Elia (Elias), Sergio Boris (Joseph), Rosita Londner (Grandmother)

In a seedy Buenos Aires shopping centre, a young Jewish man tries to get a Polish passport to visit Europe and learn about the effect of the Holocaust on his family.

An amiable, low-key film peopled with vivid comic characters and apparently trivial events; but finally it reveals important issues at stake.

SCR *Marcelo Birmajer, Daniel Burman*   CIN Ramiro Civita   MUS Cesar Lerner   ED Alejandro Brodersohn   PROD José María Morales   DIST Axiom

66 Strong stuff, and all the stronger for having taken itself so comically. – *Joe Morgenstern, Wall Street Journal*

66 It's a film of unexpected, almost indescribable off-centre charm that deepens as it goes on. – *Kenneth Turan, Los Angeles Times*

Lost Highway   ★

DIR *David Lynch*

1996   135m   US/France

DVD   ♫

☆ Bill Pullman (Fred Madison), Patricia Arquette (Renee Madison/Alice Wakefield), Balthazar Getty (Pete Dayton), *Robert Blake* (Mystery Man), Natasha Gregson Wagner (Sheila), Richard Pryor (Arnie), Gary Busey (Bill Dayton), Jack Nance (Phil), Henry Rollins (Guard Henry)

A jazz musician arrested on suspicion of murdering his faithless wife emerges from jail a changed man (literally): as a mechanic who falls for a gangster's moll.

A Mobius-strip movie in which narrative and screen time bends round and eventually crosses over itself into strange new (and strangely familiar) territory: some viewers will be left baffled, or repulsed by the obsessive, fetishistic close-ups of eyes, mouths and fingernails, but the director's control of mood and mystery remains unparalleled.

SCR David Lynch, Barry Gifford   CIN Peter Deming   MUS Angelo Badalamenti   DES Patricia Norris   ED Mary Sweeney   PROD Deepak Nayar, Tom Sternberg, Mary Sweeney   DIST Polygram/CiBy 2000/Asymmetrical

66 Has scattered moments of Lynch's poetry, but the film's ultimate shock is that it isn't shocking at all. – *Owen Gleiberman, Entertainment Weekly*

66 It's a soulless and dull bit of showmanship, but it sure sounds profound. – *Manohla Dargis, L.A. Weekly*

'They've got a story. . .but have lost the plot.'

Lost in La Mancha   ★★

SCR/DIR Keith Fulton, Louis Pepe

2002   93m   GB

DVD

☆ Jeff Bridges (Narrator), Terry Gilliam (Himself – Writer/Director), Johnny Depp (Himself), Jean Rochefort (Himself – Actor as Don Quixote), Bernard Bouix (Himself – Executive Producer), Rene Cleitman (Himself – Producer), Phil Patterson (Himself – First Assistant Director), Benjamin Fernandez (Himself – Production Designer)

Documentary account of director Terry Gilliam's ill-fated attempts to film The Man Who Killed Don Quixote.

Amazing footage here of the floods, NATO fly-overs and infirm Quixote that, collectively, sunk the filmmaker's dream project; the documentary makes one long to see Gilliam's completed vision, but can only leave you with images of frazzled line producers and insurance adjusters in its place.

CIN Louis Pepe MUS Miriam Cutler ED Jacob Bricca PROD Lucy Darwin DIST Optimum

66 An excruciatingly entertaining portrait of the filmmaking process that no Hollywood studio would ever allow to be shown. But Gilliam, bless his impish, obsessive heart, is anything but a Hollywood type. – *David Ansen, Newsweek*

66 Fascinating, but hardly enjoyable. It's like watching ants eat an elephant. – *Stephen Hunter, Washington Post*

T Lucy Darwin (most promising newcomer)

'Everyone wants to be found.'

Lost in Translation   ★★★

SCR/DIR *Sofia Coppola*
2003 102m US/Japan
DVD ♫

☆ *Bill Murray* (Bob Harris), *Scarlett Johansson* (Charlotte), Giovanni Ribisi (John), *Anna Faris* (Kelly), Fumihiro Hayashi (Charlie), Catherine Lambert (Jazz Singer)

A washed-up American actor in Tokyo to shoot a whisky commercial meets a bored young woman, all but ignored by her photographer husband.

A thin slip of a film, perhaps, and one that tends to view Japan as unbridgeably foreign, an approach which led to charges of racism. But its moods and textures cast a beguiling spell, and Coppola proves especially sensitive to actors: the film positioned Johansson as the face of her generation, and more significantly gave Murray several of his finest moments in years.

CIN *Lance Acord* MUS *Kevin Shields* DES Anne Ross, K.K. Barrett ED Sarah Flack PROD Ross Katz, Sofia Coppola DIST Momentum

66 Sofia Coppola's second movie as a director is more than a breakthrough: it's an insouciant triumph. . .a funky little Brief Encounter for the new century. – *Peter Bradshaw, Guardian*

66 Creeps up on you and finds its way into your heart so that you just don't want to say goodbye. – *Henry Fitzherbert, Sunday Express*

⌁ Sofia Coppola (original screenplay)
⌁ picture; Bill Murray (leading actor); Sofia Coppola (director)
T Bill Murray (leading actor); Scarlet Johansson (leading actress); Sarah Flack
⊤ film; Sofia Coppola (director); Sofia Coppola (original screenplay); Lance Acord; Kevin Shields

Lost in Yonkers   ★

DIR Martha Coolidge
1993 114m US
DVD ♫

☆ Richard Dreyfuss (Louie Kurnitz), Mercedes Ruehl (Bella Kurnitz), *Irene Worth* (Grandma Kurnitz), Mike

Damus (Arty), Brad Stoll (Jay), Robert Guy Miranda (Hollywood Harry), Jack Laufer (Eddie)

New York, 1942. Two young boys are sent to stay with their stern grandmother for the summer – but their uncle, a small-time gangster, arrives to lie low for a while, and regales them with tales of his colourful life.

A decent, if unexciting version of a Simon play, with all its snappy dialogue delivered on cue. Worth is remarkable, though, as the inflexible matriarch.

SCR Neil Simon CIN Johnny E. Jensen MUS Elmer Bernstein DES David Chapman ED Steven Cohen PROD Ray Stark DIST Columbia TriStar/Rastar

66 Exactly what you'd expect: a bitter-sweet home movie drizzled with wisecracks and dry observations. – *Caren Myers, Sight & Sound*

'From the best-seller that was talked about in whispers!'

The Lost Weekend   ★★★★

DIR *Billy Wilder*
1945 101m US
DVD ♫

☆ *Ray Milland* (Don Birnam), Jane Wyman (Helen St. James), Philip Terry (Nick Birnam), *Howard da Silva* (Nat the Bartender), *Frank Faylen* (Bim)

Two days in the life of a young alcoholic writer.

Startlingly original on its release, this stark little drama keeps its power, especially in the scenes on New York streets and in a sanatorium. It could scarcely have been more effectively filmed.

SCR *Charles Brackett, Billy Wilder* CIN *John F. Seitz* MUS Miklos Rozsa ED Doane Harrison PROD *Charles Brackett* DIST Paramount

DON BIRNAM (RAY MILLAND): It shrinks my liver, doesn't it, Nat? It pickles my kidneys, yeah. But what does it do to my mind? It tosses the sandbags overboard so the balloon can soar. Suddenly I'm above the ordinary. I'm competent, supremely competent. I'm walking a tightrope over Niagara Falls. I'm one of the great ones. I'm Michelangelo, moulding the beard of Moses. I'm Van Gogh, painting pure sunlight. I'm Horowitz, playing the Emperor Concerto. I'm John Barrymore before the movies got him by the throat. I'm Jesse James and his two brothers – all three of 'em. I'm W. Shakespeare. And out there it's not Third Avenue any longer – it's the Nile, Nat, the Nile – and down it moves the barge of Cleopatra.

66 A reminder of what celluloid is capable of achieving when used by a good director. – *Spectator*

66 A distinguished film, rich in cinematic ingenuity. – *The Times*

⌁ best picture; Charles Brackett, Billy Wilder (original screenplay); Billy Wilder (as director); Ray Milland (leading actor)
⌁ John F. Seitz (cinematography); Miklos Rozsa (music); Doane Harrison (editing)

'Something has survived'

The Lost World: Jurassic Park   ★

DIR Steven Spielberg
1997 129m US
DVD ♫

☆ Jeff Goldblum (Dr. Ian Malcolm), Julianne Moore

DVD Available on DVD ☆ Cast in order of importance 66 Critics' Quotes † Points of interest ⌁ Academy Award ⌁ Academy Award nomination T BAFTA ⊤ BAFTA nomination

383

(Dr. Sarah Harding), Pete Postlethwaite (Roland Tembo), Vince Vaughn (Nick Van Owen), Vanessa Lee Chester (Kelly Curtis Malcolm), Arliss Howard (Peter Ludlow), Richard Attenborough (John Hammond), Peter Stormare (Dieter Stark), Harvey Jason (Ajay Sidhu), Richard Schiff (Eddie Carr)

A team heads out to investigate the island used as a breeding ground for the dinosaurs of Jurassic Park.

Solid action sequel, overcoming a major plot contrivance – that there was a second island, unmentioned in the first film – with a few casual directorial flourishes.

SCR David Koepp   CIN Janusz Kaminski   MUS John Williams   DES Rick Carter   ED Michael Kahn   PROD Gerald R. Molen, Colin Wilson   DIST Universal

66 There was no way, no matter how much Spielberg flounce was imbued in this sprightly sequel, that it was going to be as good as the original. It isn't. By a long shot. But even two thirds of the way towards Jurassic Park is about a third better than your average buster of blocks. – *Ian Nathan, Empire*

visual effects

'Eight men. One summer. Figure it out.'

Love! Valour! Compassion! ★

DIR Joe Mantello
1997   108m   US
DVD ♫

☆ Jason Alexander (Buzz Hauser), Randy Becker (Ramon Fornos), Stephen Bogardus (Gregory Mitchell), John Glover (John Jeckyll, James Jeckyll), John Benjamin Hickey (Arthur Pape), Justin Kirk (Bobby Brahms), Stephen Spinella (Perry Sellars)

Eight gay men spend three weekends together at a large mansion in upstate New York.

A film that never quite shakes off its stage origins: set over three weekends, it's clearly a three-acter. It's also obvious that the eight friends are recognisable representatives for particular gay types. Still the dialogue is sharp and many of the stories, played out against the threat of Aids, are moving and well told.

SCR Terrence McNally   CIN Alik Sakharov   MUS Harold Wheeler   DES François Séguin   ED Colleen Sharp   PROD Doug Chapin, Barry Krost   DIST Entertainment/New Line/Fine Line

66 The dialogue has the sparkle worthy of the play's Tony awards. – *Paul Julian Smith, Sight & Sound*

'The ultimate romantic comedy.'

Love Actually ★

SCR/DIR Richard Curtis
2003   135m   GB/US/France
DVD ♫

☆ Hugh Grant (The Prime Minister), Alan Rickman (Harry), *Bill Nighy* (Billy Mack), Colin Firth (Jamie), *Emma Thompson* (Karen), Laura Linney (Sarah), Liam Neeson (Daniel), Martine McCutcheon (Natalie), Keira Knightley (Juliet), Rowan Atkinson (Rufus), Billy Bob Thornton (The US President), Kris Marshall (Colin Frissell), Chiwetel Ejiofor (Peter), Rodrigo Santoro (Karl), Claudia Schiffer (Carol)

Various individuals lose and find love in the run-up to Christmas.

A slick package that offers several romantic comedies for the price of one: many of the strands feel like rehashes of writer-director Curtis's previous work, a couple (notably the Marshall and Knightley stories) lapse into creepiness and a few (those involving Nighy and Thompson) hold the attention.

CIN Michael Coulter   MUS Craig Armstrong   DES Jim Clay   ED Nick Moore   PROD Duncan Kenworthy, Tim Bevan, Eric Fellner   DIST Universal

66 The movie's only flaw is also a virtue: it's jammed with characters, stories, warmth and laughs, until at times Curtis seems to be working from a checklist of obligatory movie love situations and doesn't want to leave anything out. – *Roger Ebert, Chicago Sun-Times*

66 Cloying, deceitful, and more or less irresistible. – *J.R. Jones, Chicago Reader*

Bill Nighy (supporting actor)
British film; Emma Thompson (supporting actress)

Love and Death on Long Island ★

SCR/DIR Richard Kwietniowski
1996   93m   GB/Canada
DVD   ♫

☆ *John Hurt* (Giles De'Ath), Jason Priestley (Ronnie Bostock), Fiona Loewi (Audrey), Sheila Hancock (Mrs. Barker), Maury Chaykin (Irving 'Irv' Buckmuller), Gawn Grainger (Henry), Elizabeth Quinn (Mrs. Reed)

A stuffy, highbrow British writer becomes entranced by the star of a American teen movie, and sets out to track him down.

Intriguing doodle that yields some affectionate, nicely observed moments from its clash of cultures before finally petering out into inconsequentiality.

CIN Oliver Curtis   MUS The Insects, Richard Grassby-Lewis   DES David McHenry   ED Susan Shipton   PROD Steve Clark-Hall, Christopher Zimmer   DIST Guild/Skyline/Imagex/British Screen/Telefilm Canada/Arts Council/NSFDC

66 A buoyant and elegant achievement – romantic and ruminative yet always precise, a comedy of longing propelled by a strong current of satirical observation. – *David Denby, New York Magazine*

Richard Kwietniowski (best newcomer)

Love and Human Remains ★

DIR Denys Arcand
1993   100m   Canada
DVD

☆ Thomas Gibson (David), Ruth Marshall (Candy), Cameron Bancroft (Bernie), Mia Kirshner (Benita), Joanne Vannicola (Jerri), Matthew Ferguson (Kane), Rick Roberts (Robert)

In Montreal, a group of youngish people find various ways of searching for love. But a serial killer is on the prowl.

A modern, sexually explicit series of couplings, played out against the impending threat of Aids and a killer on the loose. Very much of its time, but the

yearning of many of these characters is touchingly conveyed.

SCR Brad Fraser   **CIN** Paul Sarossy   **MUS** John McCarthy   **DES** François Seguin   **ED** Alain Baril   **PROD** Roger Frappier   **DIST** Rank/Max/Atlantis

66 With Arcand, a man whose eyebrow seems permanently raised, one can never be sure whether it is 'seriously' intended or not. – *Trevor Johnston, Sight & Sound*

'The trouble with love is, you never know where it's going to strike next.'

Love and Other Catastrophes ★

DIR Emma-Kate Croghan

1996 76m Australia

☆ Matt Day (Michael), Frances O'Connor (Mia), Alice Garner (Alice), Radha Mitchell (Danni), Matthew Dyktynski (Ari), Kim Gyngell (Professor Leach), Suzi Dougherty (Savita), Suzanne Dowling (Dr Russell), Torquil Neilson (Toby)

24 hours in the lives of five lovelorn Australian students.

Breezy romantic comedy, given a little extra pep by its attractive, up-and-coming cast.

SCR Yael Bergman, Emma-Kate Croghan, Helen Bandis   **CIN** Justin Brickle   **MUS** Oleh Witer   **ED** Ken Sallows   **PROD** Stavros Andonis Efthymiou   **DIST** TCF/Screwball Five/AFC

66 Succeeds in exerting charm and good humour, and occasional embarrassments are easily forgiven. – *George Perry, Sunday Times*

Love etc. ★

DIR Marion Vernoux

1996 105m France

DVD

☆ Charlotte Gainsbourg (Marie), Yvan Attal (Benoit), Charles Berling (Pierre), Thibault de Montalembert (Bernard), Elodie Navarre (Eleonore), Marie Adam (Bernard's girlfriend)

A love triangle between a female art restorer and two male friends: a timid business man and an indolent language teacher.

Intriguing makeover of a witty, original novel, adapted for film by making it more conventional. Yet the performances are light and skilful.

SCR Marion Vernoux, Dodine Herry   **CIN** Eric Gautier   **MUS** Alexandre Desplat   **DES** François Emmanuelli   **ED** Jennifer Auge   **PROD** Patrick Godeau   **DIST** Pathé/Aliceléo/France3/Canal+

66 There's a curiously old-fashioned aspect to the film's tone and look. – *Chris Darke, Sight & Sound*

'How long would you wait for love?'

Love in the Time of Cholera (new)

DIR Mike Newell

2007 138m US

DVD ♫

☆ Javier Bardem (Florentino Ariza), Giovanna Mezzogiorno (Fermina), Benjamin Bratt (Dr.Urbino), Catalina Sandino Moreno (Hildebranda), Hector Elizondo

(Don Leo), Liev Schreiber (Lotario), John Leguizamo (Lorenzo Daza)

An elderly man has nursed a passion for a woman who rejected him in his youth, and has seduced hundreds of other women to ease the pain of his loss. When she is finally widowed, he makes his move again.

A good-looking but uneasy adaptation of a literary classic that depends for its power on poetic language and philosophical musings. The film stays true to the story's bare outlines, but fails to convince in purely narrative terms. Bardem does his considerable best in a difficult role, but wildly varied acting in supporting roles does not help.

SCR Ronald Harwood   **CIN** Alfonso Beato   **MUS** Antonio Pinto   **DES** Wolf Kroeger   **ED** Mick Audsley   **PROD** Scott Steindorff   **DIST** Momentum

66 Stiff and stagey, Newell and Harwood's adaptation ends up reaffirming the literary and perhaps unfilmable qualities of Marquez's novel. – *Sukhdev Sandhu, Daily Telegraph*

66 A film to be strictly quarantined. – *Peter Bradshaw, Guardian*

'Study for a portrait of Francis Bacon.'

Love Is the Devil ★★

SCR/DIR *John Maybury*

1998 90m GB/France/Japan

DVD ♫

☆ *Derek Jacobi* (Francis Bacon), Daniel Craig (George Dyer), Tilda Swinton (Muriel Belcher), Anne Lambton (Isabel Hawesthorne), Adrian Scarborough (Daniel Farson), Karl Johnson (John Deakin), Annabel Brooks (Henrietta Moraes), Richard Newbold (Blonde Billy)

When gay artist discovers a small-time crook attempting to rob his home, he embarks on an affair with him.

A fierce, audacious biopic that tries to find a filmic equivalent for Francis Bacon's work. Intriguingly director Maybury seems equally influenced by videos, fine art and experimental film techniques, and subjugates all three strands into an intriguing, self-consciously stylish work. Jacobi delivers arguably the big-screen performance of his long career.

CIN *John Mathieson*   **MUS** Ryuichi Sakamoto   **DES** *Alan Macdonald*   **ED** Daniel Goddard   **PROD** Chiara Menage   **DIST** Artificial Eye/BBC/BFI/Première Heure/Uplink/Arts Council/Partners in Crime

66 Maybury creates a stifling, claustrophobic world in which post World War II society is rarely glimpsed. – *Michael O'Pray, Sight & Sound*

'Get Together. Fall Apart. Start Over.'

Love Jones ★

SCR/DIR Theodore Witcher

1997 104m US

DVD ♫

☆ Larenz Tate (Darius Lovehall), Nia Long (Nina Mosley), Isaiah Washington (Savon Garrison), Lisa Nicole Carson (Josie Nichols), Khalil Kain (Marvin Cox), Leonard Roberts (Eddie Coles), Bernadette L. Clarke (Sheila Downes)

DVD Available on DVD	☆ Cast in order	66 Critics' Quotes	Academy Award	BAFTA
♫ Soundtrack on CD	of importance	† Points of interest	Academy Award nomination	BAFTA nomination

In Chicago, a young middle-class black couple, a poet and a photographer, start dating while insisting their relationship is not the real thing.

A good example of an intriguing sub-genre – the Afro-American yuppie film. Everyone here is attractive, articulate, well-dressed and urbane: a direct, laudable riposte to stereotypical black films with a gritty, violent, inner-city feel. This romance is light, bright and easily digestible, if not exactly memorable.

CIN Ernest Holzman   MUS Darryl Jones, Wyclef Jean   DES Roger Fortune   ED Maysie Hoy   PROD Nick Wechsler, Jeremiah Samuels   DIST Entertainment/New Line

66 The cast are sexy and self-assured, the dialogue is sharp. – *John Wrathall, Sight & Sound*

Love Lessons   ★★

SCR/DIR Bo Widerberg
1995   125m   Sweden/Denmark

☆ Johan Widerberg (Stig), Marika Lagercrantz (Viola), Tomas von Brömssen (Kjell), Karin Huldt (Lisbet), Björn Kjellman (Sigge)

In Malmo, Sweden, during World War II, a 37 year old woman teacher in an unhappy marriage starts an affair with a lonely teenage pupil.

A long-awaited return to form for this director, who made his name in the 1960s with such international successes as Elvira Madigan. Like that film, this is visually stunning – one wishes as much time had been spent with the script as with the light meter. Still, it's well acted, with a fond, indulgent tone towards doomed adolescent emotions.

CIN Morten Bruus   MUS   DES Palle Arestrup   ED Bo Widerberg   PROD Per Holst   DIST Gala/Per Holst Film

66 Another period tale of young love turned sour. – *John Wrathall, Sight & Sound*

† It won the Silver Bear award at the Berlin Film Festival.
† The young lead actor, Johan Widerberg, is the director's son.

♪ foreign film

Love Me Tonight   ★★★★

DIR *Rouben Mamoulian*
1932   104m   US
[DVD]

☆ *Maurice Chevalier* (Maurice Courtelin), *Jeanette MacDonald* (Princess Jeanette), *Charles Butterworth* (Count de Savignac), *Charles Ruggles* (Vicomte Gilbert de Vareze), *Myrna Loy* (Countess Vantine), *C. Aubrey Smith* (The Duke), Elizabeth Patterson (Aunt), Ethel Griffies (Aunt), Blanche Frederici (Aunt), Robert Greig (Major-Domo Flamond)

A Parisian tailor encounters a lovesick princess and accidentally moves into the aristocracy.

A brilliant synthesis of sounds, music and lush visual images, enhanced by extravagant tracking shots and cameras swooping from all angles. Underpinned by a first-class Rodgers & Hart score, it adds up to an irresistible confection.

SCR *Samuel Hoffenstein, Waldemar Young, George Marion*

Jnr   CIN *Victor Milner*   ED William Shea   PROD Rouben Mamoulian   DIST Paramount

66 A musical frolic, whimsical in its aim and delicately carried out in its pattern. – *Variety*

66 Gay, charming, witty, it is everything that the Lubitsch musicals should have been but never were. – *John Baxter, 1968*

† 'Song of Paree'; 'Isn't It Romantic'; 'Lover'; 'Mimi'; 'A Woman Needs Something Like That'; 'Love Me Tonight'; 'The Son-of-a-Gun Is Nothing But a Tailor'; 'Poor Apache'

'If you're hoping for the perfect family, don't hold your breath. . .'

Lovely & Amazing   ★★

SCR/DIR *Nicole Holofcener*
2001   91m   US
[DVD]   ♪

☆ *Catherine Keener* (Michelle Marks), Brenda Blethyn (Jane Marks), Emily Mortimer (Elizabeth Marks), *Raven Goodwin* (Annie Marks), Aunjanue Ellis (Lorraine), Clark Gregg (Bill), Jake Gyllenhaal (Jordan), James LeGros (Paul), Michael Nouri (Dr. Crane), Dermot Mulroney (Kevin McCabe)

When their mother goes into hospital for liposuction, two troubled daughters are forced to juggle their own preoccupations with the care of an adopted black girl.

Warm, witty portrayal of various female hang-ups, with a script full of convincingly prickly conversations between characters rubbing one another up the wrong way. Given such strong material, the ensemble cast can't help but excel.

CIN Harlan Bosmajian   MUS Craig Richey   DES Devorah Herbert   ED Rob Frazen   PROD Anthony Bregman, Eric d'Arbeloff, Ted Hope   DIST Metro Tartan

66 A movie that knows its women, listens to them, doesn't give them a pass, allows them to be real. – *Roger Ebert, Chicago Sun-Times*

66 Delicate, loose-limbed and tremendously alive. – *Stephanie Zacharek, Salon*

Lucie Aubrac   ★★

SCR/DIR Claude Berri
1997   115m   France
[DVD]

☆ Carole Bouquet (Lucie Aubrac), Daniel Auteuil (Raymond), Patrice Chéreau (Max), Eric Boucher (Serge), Jean-Roger Milo (Maurice), Heino Ferch (Barbie)

After her Resistance agent husband is imprisoned and sentenced to death by the Gestapo, a pregnant French woman works to effect his escape.

Earnest and respectful where a Resistance drama like A Self-Made Hero was playful and subversive, with the intention of setting its true story in stone; it's a consistently fascinating story nonetheless, mounted in handsome fashion.

CIN Vincenzo Marano   MUS Philippe Sarde

DES Olivier Radot **ED** Hervé de Luze **PROD** Patrick Bordier **DIST** Pathé/Renn/TF1/DA/Pricel

66 Manages to take great characters and a great plot and leach them of all blood, terror, and excitement. – *Lisa Schwarzbaum, Entertainment Weekly*

66 A gripping period thriller that clicks along without resorting to hyped-up shock effects or gimmicky suspense. – *Stephen Holden, New York Times*

ⓣ film not in the English language

'Change your game. Change your life.'

Lucky You (new)

DIR Curtis Hanson
2007   123m   US
DVD   ♫

☆ Eric Bana (Huck Cheever), Drew Barrymore (Billie Offer), Robert Duvall (L.C. Cheever), Debra Messing (Suzanne Offer), Horatio Sanz (Ready Eddie), Charles Martin Smith (Roy Durucher), Jean Smart (Michelle Carson), Robert Downey Jnr (Telephone Jack)

A gambler's quest to enter a Las Vegas poker tournament is complicated by his affair with a lounge singer and his rivalry with his father.

Pallid update of The Cincinnati Kid, of little interest to anyone besides poker aficionados.

SCR Eric Roth, Curtis Hanson **CIN** Peter Deming **MUS** Christopher Young **DES** Clay A. Griffith **ED** Craig Kitson, William Kerr **PROD** Denise Di Novi, Curtis Hanson, Carol Fenelon **DIST** Warner Bros

L.C. CHEEVER: 'You got it backwards, kid. You play cards the way you should lead your life. And you lead your life the way you should play cards.'

66 Even for a poker movie, there's simply too much card-playing here with too little pay-off. – *Brian Lowry, Variety*

66 The set-up is old hat, the dialogue cliche-ridden, and the card games interminable. – *Mark Kermode, Observer*

---

† The film features cameo appearances from several real-life professional poker players.

'To kill the enemy, she would have to capture his heart. . .and break her own.'

Lust, Caution (new)   ★★★★

DIR *Ang Lee*
2007   158m   Taiwan/US/Hong Kong/China
DVD   ♫

☆ *Tony Leung* (Mr. Yee), *Tang Wei* (Wong Chia Chi), Joan Chen (Yee Tai Tai), Leehom Wang (Kuang Yu Min)

In 1942, in Japanese-occupied Shanghai, a shy young college student joins an acting troupe staging patriotic plays, then graduates to becoming part of a plot to kill a minister in the collaborationist Chinese government, after seducing him.

Lee's long, stately, gorgeous film, somewhere between a tragic romance and an espionage thriller, is a thing of beauty: a story of wartime insurrection, into which emotion of astonishing intensity intrudes. The erotic scenes between Yee and Wong are memorable, even transcendent: as a would-be actress, playing a part as her enemy's mistress simply overwhelms her. Leung is splendid as the unknowable Yee, while Tang Wei looks like the biggest discovery from this part of the world since Zhang Ziyi, or even Gong Li. The involuntary betrayal at the film's end perfectly resolves a story of great complexity and passion.

SCR Wang Hui Ling, James Schamus **CIN** *Rodrigo Prieto* **MUS** Alexandre Desplat **DES** *Pan Lai* **ED** Tim Squyres **PROD** Bill Kong, Ang Lee, James Schamus **DIST** Universal

66 It is another resounding success for Ang Lee, whose film-making has such mass and substance. – *Peter Bradshaw, Guardian*

66 Lust, Caution is a triumph for international cinema. – *Philip French, Observer*

ⓣ Foreign film; Pan Lai (costume design)

L

M

M
★★★★

DIR *Fritz Lang*
1931 118m Germany
DVD

☆ *Peter Lorre* (Franz Becker), Otto Wernicke (Inspector Karl Lohmann), Gustav Gründgens (Schraenker)

A psychopathic serial child-killer evades the police but is caught by the city's criminals who find his activities getting them a bad name.

An unmistakable classic whose oddities are hardly worth criticizing, this is part social melodrama and part satire, but entirely unforgettable, with many of its sequences brilliantly staged in expressionistic style. The bug-eyed Lorre is horribly remarkable.

SCR *Thea von Harbou, Paul Falkenberg, Adolf Jansen, Karl Vash* CIN Fritz Arno Wagner MUS Adolf Jansen ED Paul Falkenberg PROD Seymour Nebenzal DIST Nero Film

❝ Visual excitement, pace, brilliance of surface and feeling for detail. – *New Yorker, 1977*

Ma Femme Est Une Actrice
★★

SCR/DIR Yvan Attal
2001 95m France
DVD

☆ Charlotte Gainsbourg (Charlotte), Yvan Attal (Yvan), Terence Stamp (John), Noémie Lvovsky (Nathalie), Laurent Bateau (Vincent), Ludivine Sagnier (Geraldine), Keith Allen (David), Lionel Abelanski (Georges)

A sportswriter, married to a famous, glamorous actress, becomes increasingly jealous of her relationship with her suave British co-star.

Delightfully knowing comedy about the pitfalls of celebrity and the egotism of actors. An entertaining debut – written and directed by an actor.

CIN Remy Chevrin MUS Brad Mehldau DES Katia Wyszkop ED Jennifer Auge PROD Claude Berri DIST Pathé

❝ A romantic comedy for anyone in love with the movies, and anyone, for that matter, who's in love. – *Steven Rea, Philadelphia Inquirer*

Ma Saison Préferée
★★

DIR André Téchiné
1993 125m France
DVD

☆ Catherine Deneuve (Emilie), Daniel Auteuil (Antoine), Marthe Villalonga (Berthe), Jean-Pierre Bouvier (Bruno), Chiara Mastroianni (Anne), Carmen Chaplin (Khadija), Anthony Prada (Lucien), Ingrid Caven (Bar girl)

Two estranged siblings, who fell out three years previously, must confront each other as their mother lapses into serious illness.

A four-part drama, each part corresponding to a season, in which an ordinary, faintly dysfunctional family tries to heal breaches as the matriarch enters a decline. It is particularly wise about the hold that nostalgia and childhood memories exert on adults, and the need to keep them intact, despite upheavals in adult family relationships. There are no twists or surprises, but the story feels authentic and honest.

SCR André Téchiné, Pascal Bonitzer CIN Thierry Arbogast MUS Philippe Sarde DES Carlos Conti ED Martine Giordano PROD Alain Sarde DIST Arrow/TF1/DA/Alain Sarde

❝ Much of the film reads like so many clichés being strung together. But these are clichés which play upon us all. – *Martin Bright, Sight & Sound*

Ma Vie en Rose
★★

DIR *Alain Berliner*
1997 88m France/Belgium/Switzerland/GB
DVD ♫

☆ Michèle Laroque (Hanna Fabre), Jean-Philippe Ecoffey (Pierre Fabre), Hélène Vincent (Élisabeth), *Georges du Fresne* (Ludovic Fabre), Daniel Hanssens (Albert), Laurence Bibot (Lisette)

A seven-year-old boy causes consternation in his household by proclaiming himself female and wearing a dress.

Delightful contemporary fairytale, wondering whether we define ourselves by the body we have, the things we do, or the clothes we wear, and coming to the happy conclusion that each is as valid as the next.

SCR *Chris Vander Stappen, Alain Berliner* CIN Yves Cape MUS Dominique Dalcan, Zazie DES Véronique Melery ED Sandrine Deegan PROD Carole Scotta DIST Buena Vista/Haut et Court/WFE/Freeway/CAB/La Sept/RTBF/TF1

❝ Wry comedy is certainly not precluded. . .but it's the film's combination of compassion and whimsical charm that makes it utterly disarming. – *Trevor Johnston, Time Out*

Ⓣ film not in the English language

'Every success has its story. And its price.'

Mac
★

DIR John Turturro
1992 117m US
DVD

☆ *John Turturro* (Mac Viterlli), Katherine Borowitz (Alice

DVD Available on DVD ♫ Soundtrack on CD ☆ Cast in order of importance ❝ Critics' Quotes † Points of interest Academy Award Academy Award nomination BAFTA BAFTA nomination

Stunder / Vitelli), Michael Badalucco (Vico Vitelli), Carl Capotorto (Bruno Vitelli), Ellen Barkin (Oona Goldfarb), John Amos (Nat), Dennis Farina (Mr. Stunder)

When the father in a working-class New York family dies, his eldest son, a workaholic perfectionist, assumes his role, and starts his own construction company with his two easy-going brothers.

A well-observed drama about the work ethic, and how easily pride in a job well done can tip into obsession. Notably well-acted by the entire cast.

SCR John Turturro, Brandon Cole   CIN Ron Fortunato
MUS Richard Termini, Vin Tese   DES Robert Standefer
ED Michael Berenbaum   PROD Nancy Tenenbaum, Brenda Goodman   DIST Entertainment/Macfilm

66 An actors' film, and also one with a pronounced theme: the value of good work. – *Robert Yates, Sight & Sound*

'Something wicked this way comes.'

Macbeth (new)

DIR Geoffrey Wright
2006   109m   Australia
DVD

☆ Sam Worthington (Macbeth), Victoria Hill (Lady Macbeth), Lachy Hulme (Macduff), Gary Sweet (Duncan), Steve Bastoni (Banquo), Matt Doran (Malcolm)

A contemporary retelling of Shakespeare's tragedy set in Melbourne's gangland; here Macbeth packs a pistol and consorts with naked witches.

A visually impressive interpretation, let down by uneven acting and poor verse-speaking; the result falls well short of Baz Luhrmann's Romeo + Juliet.

SCR Geoffrey Wright, Victoria Hill   CIN Will Gibson
MUS John Clifford White   DES David McKay   ED Jane Usher   PROD Martin Fabinyi   DIST Revolver Entertainment

66 Shakespeare as action film – furiously paced and unapologetically cinematic. – *Megan Lehmann, Hollywood Reporter*

66 The cast can't deliver a couplet without sounding desperately camp or deeply embarrassed. – *James Christopher, The Times*

'A little guilt goes a long way...'

The Machinist ★

DIR Brad Anderson
2004   102m   Spain
DVD ♫

☆ Christian Bale (Trevor), Jennifer Jason Leigh (Stevie), Aitana Sanchez-Gijon (Marie), John Sharian (Ivan), Michael Ironside (Miller), Larry Gilliard (Jackson), Reg E. Cathey (Jones), Anna Massey (Mrs Shrike)

An insomniac factory worker unravels in the wake of a grisly workplace accident.

Oddball paranoid thriller, its dark comic aspects coming over as somewhat trivial when set against its leading man's brooding performance and (deliberately) anorexic appearance; it is certainly strange, but not substantially so: curious in the way green candyfloss is curious, and that's about all.

SCR Scott A. Kosar   CIN Xavi Gimenez   MUS Roque Banos   DES Alain Bainee   ED Luis de la Madrid
PROD Julio Fernandez   DIST Tartan

66 While the conclusion brings everything to a logical close, it also renders the movie less interesting - a stunt that didn't merit Bale's startling, and dangerous, transformation. – *Rene Rodriguez, Miami Herald*

66 Bale exists all too large under the circumstances, a well-fed actor playing at emaciation for the sake of a fiction about a character whose torment is as unreadable as his vertebrae are countable. – *Lisa Schwarzbaum, Entertainment Weekly*

'A Desperate Man. An Ambitious Reporter. A Situation Gone Mad.'

Mad City ★

DIR Costa-Gavras
1997   114m   US
DVD ♫

☆ John Travolta (Sam Baily), Dustin Hoffman (Max Brackett), Mia Kirshner (Laurie Callahan), Alan Alda (Kevin Hollander), Robert Prosky (Lou Potts), Blythe Danner (Mrs. Banks), William Atherton (Dohlen), Ted Levine (Alvin Lemke)

A tabloid-TV news reporter attempts to boost his own flagging career by stage-managing a siege at a local museum.

Hysterical satire that points a finger at falling standards within the media. The miscasting of the lead roles lets it down.

SCR Tom Matthews   CIN Patrick Blossier   MUS Thomas Newman   DES Catherine Hardwicke   ED Françoise Bonnot   PROD Arnold and Anne Kopelson
DIST Warner/Punch

66 A simplistic and obvious expose about the manipulative power of the news media that by now is so familiar that its cynical perspective is not likely to upset or provoke anyone. – *Emanuel Levy, Variety*

66 We get lots of scenes showing the vanity and hypocrisy of anchormen. This is not news. – *Roger Ebert, Chicago Sun-Times*

† The film's director and writer claimed to be inspired by the reporting of the Waco siege of 1993.

'A cop who'd rather be an artist. A mobster who'd rather be a comic. And a woman who'd rather be anywhere but between them.'

Mad Dog and Glory ★★

DIR *John McNaughton*
1993   97m   US
DVD ♫

☆ Robert De Niro (Wayne 'Mad Dog' Dobie), Uma Thurman (Glory), Bill Murray (Frank Milo), David Caruso (Mike), Mike Starr (Harold), Tom Towles (Andrew the Beater), Kathy Baker (Lee)

A sensitive Chicago forensics detective saves the life of a gangster, who returns the favour by giving the cop the 'gift' of a beautiful woman for a week.

A box-office flop despite its starry cast, this nevertheless holds up as one of the most distinctive comedies released

DVD Available on DVD   ☆ Cast in order   66 Critics' Quotes   ⅃ Academy Award   ⊕ BAFTA
♫ Soundtrack on CD   of importance   † Points of interest   ⅃ Academy Award nomination   ⊕ BAFTA nomination

389

by a major studio during the 1990s, mixing edgy laughs with brutal murder sequences that must have come much more naturally to the director of *Henry: Portrait of a Serial Killer*. Thurman has little to do but appear fetchingly distressed, but the leftfield De Niro–Murray pairing makes it worth a look.

SCR Richard Price   **CIN** Robby Müller   **MUS** Elmer Bernstein   **DES** David Chapman   **ED** Craig McKay, Elena Maganini   **PROD** Barbara DeFina, Martin Scorsese   **DIST** UIP/Universal

66 Morally difficult to justify. . .simultaneously sending up and celebrating macho bullshit. – *Angie Errigo, Empire*

66 What makes it fun is its ability to find new ways to do old things. – *Jay Carr, Boston Globe*

'A Wild And Sexy Adventure!'

Mad Love ★

DIR Antonia Bird
1995   95m   US
DVD   ♫

☆ Chris O'Donnell (Matt Leland), Drew Barrymore (Casey Roberts), Matthew Lillard (Eric), Richard Chaim (Duncan), Robert Nadir (Coach), Joan Allen (Margaret Roberts), Jude Ciccolella (Richard Roberts), Amy Sakasitz (Joanna Leland)

Two high school kids, a shy boy and a wild, mentally unstable girl, take to the road to escape parental disapproval.

A failed attempt to impose British sensibilities on a Hollywood film genre. Paula Milne's thoughtful script and Antonia Bird's individual directing voice both get lost in what becomes a conventional road movie, with characters who feel flat and uninspired. A director's cut, or better still a complete re-make, would be intriguing.

SCR Paula Milne   **CIN** Fred Tammes   **MUS** Andy Roberts   **DES** David Brisbin   **ED** Jeff Freeman   **PROD** David Manson   **DIST** Buena Vista

66 More a near miss than a failure. – *Nick James, Sight & Sound*

Madame Bovary

SCR/DIR Claude Chabrol
1991   143m   France
DVD

☆ Isabelle Huppert (Emma Bovary), Jean-François Balmer (Charles Bovary), Christophe Malavoy (Rodolphe Boulanger), Jean Yanne (M. Homais), Lucas Belvaux (Leon Dupuis), Christiane Minazzoli (Widow Lefancois)

A French doctor's wife is tempted into an affair by the ennui of her rigid rural life.

The third attempt to adapt Flaubert's masterwork for the big screen, and alas, the third failure. It's certainly a faithful rendering of his novel, but that may be the problem – Chabrol, for once, seems so awe-struck at the prospect of tampering with a beloved work that he forgets to make it interesting either in visual or narrative terms. Huppert, on paper a perfect fit for this role, looks vaguely adrift.

CIN Jean Rabier   **MUS** Matthieu Chabrol, Jean-Michel Bernard, Maurice Coignard   **DES** Michèle Abbé-Vannier   **ED** Monique Fardoulis   **PROD** Marin Karmitz   **DIST** Arrow/MK2/CED/FR3

66 Exactly the kind of faithful literary adaptation that the Nouvelle Vague once condemned as le cinéma du Papa – respectful, luxurious and eminently forgettable. – *Chris Darke, Sight & Sound*

⚚ Corinne Jorry (costume design)

'At the sperm-bank, she asked for a tall, intelligent, black man. One out of three ain't bad.'

Made in America ★

DIR Richard Benjamin
1993   111m   US
DVD   ♫

☆ Whoopi Goldberg (Sarah Mathews), Ted Danson (Halbert 'Hal' Jackson), Will Smith (Tea Cake Walters), Nia Long (Zora Mathews), Paul Rodriguez (Jose), Jennifer Tilly (Stacy), Peggy Rea (Alberta), Clyde Kusatsu (Bob Takashima)

To her horror, a young black girl discovers that owing to a mix-up at the sperm bank, her biological father is a white car salesman.

Though the plot is schematic, though the ending is guessable after the first 20 minutes, this comedy has amusing moments, and sets out its plea for racial tolerance discreetly but firmly. The film had an added frisson: Danson and Goldberg were in a relationship off-screen as it opened.

SCR Holly Goldberg Sloan   **CIN** Ralf Bode   **MUS** Mark Isham   **DES** Evelyn Sakash   **ED** Jacqueline Cambas   **PROD** Arnon Milchan, Michael Douglas, Rick Bieber   **DIST** Warner/Stonebridge/Kalola/Regency/Canal

66 Screwball comedy and social, commentary do not make comfortable bedfellows. – *Leslie Felperin, Sight & Sound*

'It takes a real man to become a maid of honour.'

Made of Honor (new)

DIR Paul Weiland
2008   101m   US/UK
DVD

☆ Patrick Dempsey (Tom Bailey), Michelle Monaghan (Hannah), Kevin McKidd (Colin McMurray), Kathleen Quinlan (Joan), Sydney Pollack (Thomas Bailey Sr.), James Sikking (Reverend Foote)

Realising he's in love with his best friend, a New Yorker sets out to sabotage her wedding to a Scottish laird.

My Best Friend's Wedding with a gender switch, no charm and a surfeit of predictable situations.

SCR Adam Sztykiel, Deborah Kaplan, Harry Elfont   **CIN** Tony Pierce-Roberts   **MUS** Rupert Gregson-Williams   **DES** Kalina Ivanov   **ED** Richard Marks   **PROD** Neal H. Moritz   **DIST** Columbia

66 Dempsey deserves a better starring vehicle than this jalopy. – *Lael Loewenstein, Variety*

66 A film to leave at the altar. – *Peter Bradshaw, Guardian*

'In an old house in Paris that was covered in vines, lived twelve little girls in two straight lines.'

Madeline ★

DIR Daisy von Scherler Mayer
1998   88m   US/Germany
[DVD] ♫

☆ Frances McDormand (Miss Clavel), Nigel Hawthorne (Lord Covington), Hatty Jones (Madeline), Stéphane Audran (Lady Covington), Ben Daniels (Leopold the Tutor), Arturo Venegas (Mr. Spanish Ambassador), Katia Caballero (Mrs. Spanish Ambassador), Chantal Neuwirth (Helene the Cook), Kristian de la Osa (Pepito)

In 1950s Paris, a young girl attempts to save her orphanage from closure.

A sometimes clumsy translation of the beloved children's books that scrabbles to put its plot lines together, but realises its heroine's world with a good deal of colour and charm.

SCR Mark Levin, Jennifer Flackett   CIN Pierre Aim
MUS Michel Legrand   DES Hugo Luczyc-Wyhowski
ED Jeffrey Wolf   PROD Allyn Stewart, Pancho Kohner, Saul Cooper   DIST Sony Pictures/TriStar Pictures/Jaffilms/Pancho Kohner/Saul Cooper

66 Bright and funny children, handsome photography, beautiful (but never showy) decor and costumes, and plain, sweet storytelling that takes its blithe time to relate a simple tale. – *Shawn Levy, Portland Oregonian*

'His Majesty was all powerful and all knowing. But he wasn't quite all there.'

The Madness of King George ★★

DIR Nicholas Hytner
1994   107m   GB
[DVD] ♫

☆ *Nigel Hawthorne* (King George III), *Helen Mirren* (Queen Charlotte), Ian Holm (Willis), Amanda Donohoe (Lady Pembroke), Rupert Graves (Greville), Rupert Everett (The Prince of Wales), Jim Carter (Fox), Geoffrey Palmer (Warren), John Wood (Thurlow), Jeremy Child (Black Rod), Cyril Shaps (Pepys)

The late 1780s: with King George III's behaviour becoming increasingly erratic, Parliament considers whether or not to vote the Prince of Wales into power.

A notable theatrical success becomes a modest cinematic affair, never quite necessitating (or filling) the bigger canvas; that said, there are funny lines and well-honed performances, and its detailed portrayal of Westminster life is enjoyable.

SCR *Alan Bennett*   CIN *Andrew Dunn*   MUS George Fenton, Handel   DES *Ken Adam*   ED Tariq Anwar
PROD Stephen Evans, David Parfitt   DIST Rank/Samuel Goldwyn/Channel 4/Close Call

66 Sturdily performed and persuasively detailed, and with a beady delight in political infighting... there's a nagging feeling that there's less here than meets the eye, but it's funny and engaging. – *Geoff Andrew, Time Out*

† The play's original title, The Madness of George III, was amended in case non-British cinemagoers thought it was the third film in a series.

♪ Ken Adam (art direction)
♦ Nigel Hawthorne (leading actor); Helen Mirren (supporting actress); Alan Bennett (adapted screenplay)
Ⓣ British picture; Nigel Hawthorne (leading actor); make up/hair
Ⓣ film; George Fenton; Ian Holm (supporting actor); Helen Mirren (leading actress); Mark Thompson (costume design); Tariq Anwar (editing); Ken Adam; Alan Bennett (adapted screenplay); sound; Nicholas Hynter

---

'In a place that defied belief their only hope was each other.'

The Magdalene Sisters ★★★

SCR/DIR *Peter Mullan*
2002   119m   GB/Ireland
[DVD]

☆ *Geraldine McEwan* (Sister Bridget), *Anne-Marie Duff* (Margaret), *Nora-Jane Noone* (Bernadette), *Dorothy Duffy* (Rose/Patricia), *Eileen Walsh* (Crispina), Mary Murray (Una), Britta Smith (Katy)

Ireland, 1964: three young women are sent to a Magdalene Laundry, run by the Catholic Church to correct those deemed to have fallen foul of the Church's moral strictures.

A powerhouse picture, based on the testimony of many real-life Magdalene sisters, that transcends the genteel boundaries of the period drama to express real anger at the way religion can be used to justify all manner of atrocities and cover a multitude of sins.

CIN Nigel Willoughby   MUS Craig Armstrong
DES Mark Leese   ED Colin Monie   PROD Frances Higson   DIST Momentum

66 A fierce, brilliant film that breaks (and then mends) your heart. – *Michael Wilmington, Chicago Tribune*

66 Celluloid incendiarism, rabble-rousing cinema with a delirious, delicious edge of black comedy... it has a kind of 120-degree proof passion which makes most other Irish and British cinema look tame and lame. – *Peter Bradshaw, Guardian*

† It won the Golden Lion for best film at the 2002 Venice film festival.

Ⓣ film; Peter Mullan (original screenplay)

The Magic Flute (new) ★

DIR Kenneth Branagh
2006   138m   UK/France

☆ Joseph Kaiser (Tamino), Amy Carson (Pamina), Benjamin Jay Davis (Papageno), Silvia Moi (Papagena), René Pape (Sarastro), Lyubov Petrova (Queen of the Night)

A soldier leaves the trenches to rescue a beautiful damsel.

Audacious staging of the Mozart opera from a film-maker better known for his Shakespeare adaptations. A baroque treat for some, an overblown bore for others; purists will no doubt prefer Ingmar Bergman's 1975 version.

SCR Kenneth Branagh, Stephen Fry   CIN Roger Lanser
DES Tim Harvey   ED Michael Parker   PROD Pierre-Olivier Bardet, Kenneth Branagh

66 Lavishly mounted and well sung, but thin on charm and spontaneity. – *Derek Elley, Variety*

M

[DVD] Available on DVD   ☆ Cast in order   66 Critics' Quotes   ♪ Academy Award   Ⓣ BAFTA
♫ Soundtrack on CD   of importance   † Points of interest   ♦ Academy Award nomination   Ⓣ BAFTA nomination

391

'Real life screened more daringly than it's ever been before!'

The Magnificent Ambersons ★★★★

SCR/DIR *Orson Welles*
1942 88m US
♫

☆ *Joseph Cotten* (Eugene Morgan), *Dolores Costello* (Isabel Amberson Minafer), *Agnes Moorehead* (Fanny Amberson), *Tim Holt* (George Amberson Minafer), *Anne Baxter* (Lucy Morgan), *Ray Collins* (Jack Amberson), *Richard Bennett* (Maj. Amberson), Erskine Sanford (Benson), Donald Dillaway (Wilbur Minafer)

A proud family loses its wealth and its control of the neighbourhood, and its youngest son gets his come-uppance.

Welles's second film, following Citizen Kane, is a fascinating period drama told in brilliant cinematic snippets; owing to studio interference, the last reels are weak, but the whole is a treat for connoisseurs, and a delight in its fast-moving control of cinematic narrative.

CIN *Stanley Cortez* MUS *Bernard Herrmann* ED Robert Wise, Mark Robson PROD Orson Welles DIST RKO/Mercury

NARRATOR (WELLES): And now Major Amberson was engaged in the profoundest thinking of his life, and he realized that everything which had worried him or delighted him during his lifetime – all his buying and building and trading and banking – that it was all a trifle and a waste beside what concerned him now, for the Major knew now that he had to plan how to enter an unknown country where he was not even sure of being recognized as an Amberson.
NARRATOR: Something had happened. A thing which years ago had been the eagerest hope of many, many good citizens of the town. And now it had come at last: George Amberson Minafer had got his come-uppance. He got it three times filled and running over. But those who had so longed for it were not there to see it, and they never knew it. Those who were still living had forgotten all about it and all about him.

66 Rich in ideas that many will want to copy, combined in the service of a story that few will care to imitate. – *C. A. Lejeune*

66 Nearly every scene is played with a casual perfection which could only come from endless painstaking planning and rehearsals, and from a wonderful sense of timing. – *Basil Wright, 1972*

† Previously filmed in 1925 as Pampered Youth.
† The credits are all at the end and all spoken, ending with: 'I wrote and directed the picture. My name is Orson Welles.'
† The studio, RKO, felt the film was too downbeat, and ordered cuts totalling 40 minutes, adding a happier ending of its own, directed by a production manager.

⚲ picture; Stanley Cortez (cinematography); Agnes Moorehead (supporting actress); Albert D'Agostino, A. Roland Fields, Darrell Silvera (art direction–interior decoration)

'They were seven – and they fought like seven hundred!'

The Magnificent Seven ★★★

DIR *John Sturges*
1960 138m US
DVD ♫

☆ *Yul Brynner*, *Steve McQueen*, *Robert Vaughn*, *James Coburn*, *Charles Bronson*, Horst Buchholz, Eli Wallach, Brad Dexter, Vladimir Sokoloff, Rosenda Monteros

A Mexican village hires seven American gunmen for protection against bandits.

Popular Western based on Kurosawa's Seven Samurai; it's a stirring story with a first-rate cast, and director Sturges takes the time to explore each one of its seven characters before the inevitable shoot-out. It also boasts one of the great Western theme tunes, courtesy of Elmer Bernstein.

SCR William Roberts CIN Charles Lang Jnr MUS *Elmer Bernstein* PROD John Sturges DIST UA/Mirisch-Alpha

† Sequels followed in 1966, 1969 and 1972.

⚲ Elmer Bernstein (music)

'Things fall down. People look up. And when it rains, it pours.'

Magnolia ★★★★

SCR/DIR *Paul Thomas Anderson*
1999 188m US
DVD ♫

☆ Jason Robards (Earl Partridge), Julianne Moore (Linda Partridge), *Tom Cruise* (Frank Mackey), *Philip Seymour Hoffman* (Phil Parma), *John C. Reilly* (Officer Jim Kurring), Melora Walters (Claudia Gator), Philip Baker Hall (Jimmy Gator), Melinda Dillon (Rose Gator), Jeremy Blackman (Stanley Spector), Michael Bowen (Rick Spector), William H. Macy (Donnie Smith), Emmanuel Johnson (Dixon)

Residents in LA's San Fernando Valley experience a day of strange coincidence, heightened emotion and freak weather.

An astounding and often breathtaking achievement, criss-crossing between disparate-yet-connected storylines with great fluency and tremendous verve, and building towards a perfectly controlled examination of those elements in life we cannot control. Anderson proves as skilled a human dramatist as he is with the cinematic tools of music and editing: conducted in three hours of what feels like more or less real time, the film never lets up its grip, and there are moments that are simply unforgettable.

CIN *Robert Elswit* MUS *John Brion* DES William Arnold, Mark Bridges ED *Dylan Tichenor* PROD Joanne Sellar, Paul Thomas Anderson DIST New Line

66 Part poem, part jungle blossom, all brilliance. – *F.X. Feeney, L.A. Weekly*

66 On a scene by scene basis, it has as much great stuff as any other picture this year. – *Kim Newman, Empire*

† The title comes from a street, Magnolia Boulevard, which crosses the San Fernando Valley from east to west.

⚲ Tom Cruise (supporting actor); Paul Thomas Anderson (original screenplay); Aimee Mann (music, original song – Save Me)

M

Malcolm X ★★

DIR Spike Lee
1992 202m US
DVD ♫

☆ *Denzel Washington* (Malcolm X), Angela Bassett (Dr. Betty Shabazz), Albert Hall (Baines), Al Freeman Jnr (Elijah Muhammad), Delroy Lindo (West Indian Archie), Spike Lee (Shorty), Theresa Randle (Laura), Kate Vernon (Sophia), Lonette McKee (Louise Little), Tommy Hollis (Earl Little)

A biopic of the black revolutionary leader.

Though wholly sincere, and with the commanding central performance it needs, this finds its director tamping down some of his usual spark to do his subject justice; at its liveliest during the early scenes of Malcolm's wartime experience as a hustler in Boston, it may ultimately be more effective as an illustrated chapter of American history than as a film.

SCR Arnold Perl, Spike Lee   CIN *Ernest Dickerson*
MUS Terence Blanchard   DES Wynn Thomas   ED Barry Alexander Brown   PROD Marvin Worth, Spike Lee
DIST Warner/Largo/Forty Acres and a Mule

66 Lee's finest, most unabashed labour of love. – *Desson Thomson, Washington Post*

66 The movie is disappointingly impersonal; it doesn't provide readers of the autobiography anything like a fresh vision of its remarkable subject. – *Terrence Rafferty, The New Yorker*

⚮ Denzel Washington (leading actor); Ruth Carter (costume design)

'Deception. Betrayal. Murder. Some Things You Never See Coming.'

Malice ★

DIR Harold Becker
1993 107m US
DVD ♫

☆ Alec Baldwin (Dr. Jed Hill), *Nicole Kidman* (Tracy Kennsinger), Bill Pullman (Andy Safian), Bebe Neuwirth (Det. Dana Harris), George C. Scott (Dr. Martin Kessler), Anne Bancroft (Mrs. Kennsinger), Peter Gallagher (Atty. Dennis Riley), Josef Sommer (Atty. Lester Adams), Tobin Bell (Earl Leemus)

An apparently innocent young bride traps her dim husband into becoming a pawn in an elaborate con-trick.

Complex, twisted and as the title suggests, malevolent in tone, this is B-movie territory with expensive production values and gloss. Still, it gave Kidman the chance to play a femme fatale with real conviction.

SCR Aaron Sorkin, Scott Frank, Jonas McCord
CIN Gordon Willis   MUS Jerry Goldsmith   DES Philip Harrison   ED David Bretherton   PROD Rachel Pfeffer, Charles Mulvehill, Harold Becker   DIST Rank/Castle Rock/New Line

66 What it implies about the current state of play between the sexes hardly bears thinking about. – *Nick James, Sight & Sound*

'A guy without a conscience! A dame without a heart!'

The Maltese Falcon ★★★★

SCR/DIR *John Huston*
1941 101m US
DVD

☆ *Humphrey Bogart* (Sam Spade), *Mary Astor* (Brigid O'Shaughnessy), *Sydney Greenstreet* (Kasper Gutman the Fat Man), *Elisha Cook Jnr* (Wilmer Cook), *Barton MacLane* (Det. Lt. Dundy), Lee Patrick (Effie Perine), *Peter Lorre* (Joel Cairo), Gladys George (Iva Archer), *Ward Bond* (Det. Tom Polhaus), *Jerome Cowan* (Miles Archer)

A private eye is hired to find a black sculpture of a bird.

A remake which shows the difference between excellence and brilliance; here every nuance is subtly stressed, and the cast is perfection. A brilliant directing debut by Huston and a transformative role for Bogart as the cynical Sam Spade; it proved he could carry a film as leading man/hero. Some brilliant supporting bad-guy roles, each played to the hilt.

CIN *Arthur Edeson*   MUS *Adolph Deutsch*   ED Thomas Richards   PROD Henry Blanke   DIST Warner

GUTMAN (SYDNEY GREENSTREET): I distrust a close-mouthed man. He generally picks the wrong time to talk and says the wrong things. Talking's something you can't do judiciously, unless you keep in practice. Now, sir, we'll talk if you like. I'll tell you right out, I'm a man who likes to talk.

SPADE (HUMPHREY BOGART) TO CAIRO (PETER LORRE): When you're slapped, you'll take it and like it!

SPADE TO BRIGID (MARY ASTOR): Don't be too sure I'm as crooked as I'm supposed to be.

GUTMAN: I distrust a man who says when. If he's got to be careful not to drink too much, it's because he's not to be trusted when he does.

66 The first crime melodrama with finish, speed and bang to come along in what seems like ages. – *Otis Ferguson*

66 A work of entertainment that is yet so skilfully constructed that after many years and many viewings, it has the same brittle explosiveness – and some of the same surprise – that it had in 1941. – *Pauline Kael, 1968*

⚮ picture; John Huston (screenplay); Sydney Greenstreet (supporting actor)

'With a suitcase full of song, hearts filled with passion, two brothers come to America in search of a dream.'

The Mambo Kings ★

DIR Arne Glimcher
1992 104m US/France/Germany
DVD ♫

☆ Armand Assante (Cesar Castillo), Antonio Banderas (Nestor Castillo), Cathy Moriarty (Lanna Lake), Maruschka (Delores Fuentes), Pablo Calogero (Ramon - The Mambo Kings Band), Scott Cohen (Bernardito - The Mambo Kings Band), Mario Grillo (Mario - The Mambo Kings Band), Desi Arnaz Jnr. (Desi Arnaz Sr.), Roscoe Lee Browne (Fernando Perez), Tito Puente (Himself)

Two Cuban brothers, both musicians, arrive in post-war New York looking for love and success.

A bare-bones adaption of an entertaining novel, but this film turned Banderas into a bankable star. The account

M

DVD Available on DVD   ☆ Cast in order of importance   66 Critics' Quotes   ⚮ Academy Award   ♫ Soundtrack on CD   † Points of interest   ⚮ Academy Award nomination   BAFTA   BAFTA nomination

393

of the band's rise to fame is routine, but it captures the flavours of its ethnic neighbourhood excitingly.

SCR Cynthia Cidre **CIN** Michael Ballhaus **MUS** Robert Kraft, Carlos Franzetti **DES** Stuart Wurtzel **ED** Claire Simpson **PROD** Arnon Milchan, Arne Glimcher **DIST** Warner/Canal/Regency/Alcor

🎵 Robert Kraft (m), Arne Glimcher (ly) (music – song Beautiful Maria of My Soul)

'A Killer Comedy.'

Man Bites Dog ★★

DIR *Rémy Belvaux, André Bonzel, Benoît Poelvoorde*
1992 95m Belgium
[DVD] 🎵

☆ *Benoît Poelvoorde* (Ben), Jacqueline Poelvoorde-Pappaert (Ben's Mother), Nelly Pappaert (Ben's Grandmother), Jenny Drye (Jenny), Malou Madou (Malou), Willy Vandenbroeck (Boby)

A documentary film crew tailing a high-minded serial killer comes to participate in their subject's grisly business.

Droll analysis of media violence that employs some very Belgian absurdist humour to cloak its integral nastiness. An unresolved structural problem means the moral viewer will become less engaged with its murderous banality the longer it goes on; for the most part, though, this remains a genuinely edgy and provocative work, if you can bear to watch.

SCR *Rémy Belvaux, André Bonzel, Benoît Poelvoorde, Vincent Tavier* **CIN** André Bonzel **MUS** Jean-Marc Chenut **ED** Rémy Belvaux, Eric Dardill **PROD** Rémy Belvaux, André Bonzel, Benoît Poelvoorde **DIST** Metro/Les Artistes Anonymes

“ One of the most ferociously disturbing films ever made. . .a sick, twisted, unbelievably depraved piece of work that haunts the consciousness long after the cinema lights have come up. – *Mark Salisbury, Empire*

“ As an exploration of voyeurism, it's one of the most resonant, caustic contributions to the cinema of violence since Peeping Tom. – *Geoff Andrew, Time Out*

A Man for All Seasons ★★★★

DIR *Fred Zinnemann*
1966 120m GB
[DVD]

☆ *Paul Scofield* (Sir Thomas More), *Wendy Hiller* (Alice More), *Susannah York* (Margaret More), *Robert Shaw* (King Henry VIII), Orson Welles (Cardinal Wolsey), Leo McKern (Thomas Cromwell), Nigel Davenport (Duke of Norfolk), John Hurt (Richard Rich), Corin Redgrave (William Roper), Cyril Luckham (Archbishop Cranmer), Jack Gwillim (Chief Justice)

Sir Thomas More opposes Henry VIII's divorce, and events lead inexorably to his execution.

Irreproachable film version of a play which has had its narrative tricks removed but stands up remarkably well. Acting, direction, sets, locations and costumes all have precisely the right touch.

SCR *Robert Bolt* **CIN** *Ted Moore* **MUS** *Georges Delerue* **DES** *John Box* **ED** Ralph Kemplen **PROD** Fred Zinnemann **DIST** Columbia/Highland

“ Mr Zinnemann has crystallized the essence of this drama in such pictorial terms as to render even its abstractions vibrant. – *New York Times*

† Reports indicate that Charlton Heston badly wanted the role of Sir Thomas More.

‡ picture; Paul Scofield (leading actor); Fred Zinnemann (direction); Robert Bolt (adapted screenplay); Ted Moore; Elizabeth Haffenden, Joan Bridge (costume design)
🎭 Wendy Hiller; Robert Shaw

Ⓓ picture; British film; Paul Scofield (leading actor); Ted Moore; John Box

---

'It's never too late to rewrite your life's story.'

Man in the Chair (new) ★

SCR/DIR Michael Schroeder
2007 109m
🎵

☆ *Christopher Plummer* (Flash Madden), M. Emmet Walsh (Mickey Hopkins), Michael Angarano (Cameron Kincaid), Robert Wagner (Taylor Moss)

A young film student decides to make a film about America's neglect of its senior citizens, and persuades a grumpy ex-film technician to enlist his friends at a retirement home for Hollywood veterans to take part.

A sweet-natured story that asserts the rights of older people to dignity and respect. Angarano's film-buff kid becomes tiresome, but Plummer is terrific in a performance that dwarfs the entire film.

CIN Dana Gonzales **MUS** Laura Karpman **DES** Carol Strober **ED** Terry Cafaro **PROD** Michael Schroeder, Sarah Schrder, Randolf Turrow **DIST** Transmedia

“ Reminiscent of Cinema Paradiso...sweet, accomplished film. – *Peter Whittle, Sunday Times*

“ Plummer gives a knockout performance. – *Philip French, Observer*

The Man in the White Suit ★★★★

DIR *Alexander Mackendrick*
1951 81m GB
[DVD]

☆ *Alec Guinness* (Sidney Stratton), *Joan Greenwood* (Daphne Birnley), *Cecil Parker* (Alan Birnley), Vida Hope (Bertha), *Ernest Thesiger* (Sir John Kierlaw), Michael Gough (Michael Corland), Howard Marion Crawford (Cranford), Miles Malleson (Tailor), *George Benson* (The Lodger), *Edie Martin* (Mrs. Watson)

A scientist produces a fabric that never gets dirty and never wears out. Unions and management are equally aghast.

Brilliant satirical Ealing comedy, played as farce and assembled with meticulous cinematic counterpoint, so that every moment counts and all concerned give of their very best.

SCR *Roger MacDougall, John Dighton, Alexander Mackendrick* **CIN** *Douglas Slocombe* **MUS** *Benjamin Frankel* **ED** Bernard Gribble **PROD** Sidney Cole **DIST** Ealing

“ The combination of an ingenious idea, a bright, funny and imaginative script, skilful playing and perceptive brisk

M

direction has resulted once more in a really satisfying Ealing comedy. – *Richard Mallett, Punch*

⚜ Roger MacDougall, John Dighton, Alexander Mackendrick (original screenplay)

Man of the West

DIR *Anthony Mann*
1958 100m US

☆ *Gary Cooper, Lee J. Cobb,* Julie London, Arthur O'Connell, Jack Lord, John Dehner, Royal Dano, Robert Wilke

In 1874 Arizona, a reformed gunman is cajoled by his old buddies to help them rob a bank.

Director Mann's reputation has risen steadily since his Westerns of the 1950s, not all of which were big box-office attractions. Many of them have a noirish quality, with heroes not unlike post-World War II American prototypes – weary, internalising their traumas, and vaguely out of step with their times. In this one, Cooper plays a man trying to escape a troubled past that keeps drawing him back.

SCR Reginald Rose **CIN** Ernest Haller **MUS** Leigh Harline **PROD** Walter M. Mirisch **DIST** UA/Ashton

The Man of the Year ★

DIR *José Enrique Fonseca*
2003 113m Brazil
DVD

☆ Murilo Benicio (Maiquel), Claudia Abreu (Cledir), Natalia Lage (Erica), Jorge Doria (Dr Carvalho), Jose Wilker (Silvio), Agildo Ribeiro (Zilmar)

Having shot the local crime boss in a spat over a new haircut, a gambler becomes an unlikely folk hero and gun-for-hire.

Scatty crime picture that goes off at unexpected plot tangents and operates in a mode of knockabout fatalism closer to the wave of post-Guy Ritchie British gangster films than to the neighbouring City of God.

SCR Ruben Fonseca **CIN** Breno Silveira **MUS** Dado Villa-Lobos **DES** Kiti Duarte **ED** Sergio Mekler **PROD** Flavio R. Tambellini, Leonardo Monteiro de Barros, Jose Enrique Fonseca **DIST** Warner

66 Falls apart almost as comprehensively as its hero... The chief problem is that Maiquel's inevitable decline lacks either tragic dimensions or satirical bite. – *Ryan Gilbey, Sight and Sound*

'Could this man be our next president?'

Man of the Year (new) ★

SCR/DIR Barry Levinson
2006 115m US
DVD

☆ Robin Williams (Tom Dobbs), Christopher Walken (Jack Menken), Laura Linney (Eleanor Green), Jeff Goldblum (Stewart), Tina Fey (Herself), Amy Poehler (Herself)

A TV talk-show host runs for president, with the intention of cleaning up politics.

This film resembles Levinson's hit-and-miss career in microcosm – some genuinely funny, telling schtick from

Williams, *bolted on to an overstuffed, tangled plot that goes nowhere but preaches cravenly, all the way to its lame ending. It's a maddening waste of real talents.*

CIN Dick Pope **MUS** Graeme Revell **DES** Stefania Celia **ED** Steven Weisberg, Blair Daily **PROD** James G. Robinson **DIST** Paramount

66 A messy jumble of comedy, soppy love story and far-fetched political thriller. – *Peter Whittle, Sunday Times*

66 Levinson made a great political comedy once, Wag the Dog, but that had a script by David Mamet. Here, Levinson seems to be torn between making a political jest and a suspense thriller. Neither works. – *Peter Rainer, Christian Science Monitor*

'A poet. A thief. Two strangers with nothing in common are about to trade their lives for a chance to cheat their destinies.'

The Man on the Train ★

DIR Patrice Leconte
2002 90m France/GB/Germany/Japan
DVD ♫

☆ *Jean Rochefort* (Manesquier), *Johnny Hallyday* (Milan), Jean-François Stévenin (Luigi), Charlie Nelson (Max), Pascal Parmentier (Sadko), Isabelle Petit-Jacques (Viviane), Édith Scob (Manesquier's sister)

An ageing bank robber and a lonely, retired schoolmaster cross paths in a small French town.

A film in a minor key, its pleasures lie in watching two very different types of screen actor together, gradually coming to form a bond; charming as this is for some while, too many scenes seem designed to let Jean and Johnny enjoy one another's company for a little while longer, and the ending is beyond all comprehension.

SCR Claude Klotz **CIN** Jean-Marie Drejou **MUS** Pascal Esteve **DES** Ivan Maussion **ED** Joëlle Hache **PROD** Philippe Carcassonne **DIST** Pathé

66 Witty and wistful, often tragic and tense, this is an impeccable example of the value of small-scale cinema. – *David Parkinson, Empire*

66 As a filmmaker, [Leconte] doesn't have anything profound to say but does say his something with craft, visual flair and professionalism. Depending on your mood, that can be either too little or just enough. – *Manohla Dargis, Los Angeles Times*

Man Push Cart ★★

SCR/DIR Ramin Bahrani
2006 86m US/ Iran
DVD

☆ Ahmad Razvi (Ahmad), Leticia Dolera (Noemi), Ali Reza (Manish), Farooq 'Duke' Muhammad (Duke), Charles Daniel Sandoval (Mohammad)

Back in Pakistan, immigrant Ahmad (Ahmad Razvi) had a hit CD and seemed to be on a roll before his luck changed. Now in New York he rises at dawn to stock his cart with coffee, doughnuts and bagels, and pushes it along traffic-congested streets to his regular corner.

Director Bahrani, an American of Iranian origin, takes us into the world of a New York coffee seller with refreshing simplicity as the man struggles to make ends

DVD Available on DVD   ☆ Cast in order   66 Critics' Quotes   ⚜ Academy Award   Ⓑ BAFTA
♫ Soundtrack on CD   of importance   † Points of interest   ⚜ Academy Award nomination   Ⓑ BAFTA nomination

395

*meet. Hope returns to his life when he meets a young
Spanish woman.*

CIN Michael Simmonds   MUS Peyman Yazdanian
ED Ramin Bahrani   PROD Ramin Bahrani/Pradip
Ghosh/Bedford T. Bentley III   DIST Dogwoof

† Actor Ahmad Razvi was himself a pushcart seller. His
experience was partly incorporated into his character.

The Man Who Cried

SCR/DIR Sally Potter
2000   100m   GB/France/US
[DVD]   ♫

☆ Christina Ricci (Suzie), Cate Blanchett (Lola), John
Turturro (Dante Dominio), Johnny Depp (Cesar), Harry
Dean Stanton (Felix Perlman), *Claudia Lander-Duke*
(Young Suzie), Oleg Yankovsky (Father)

A refugee of the Russian pogroms grows up to
become a successful nightclub singer in the Paris
of the 1930s, shortly before the Nazi occupation of
France.

*Puddingy melodrama from a hit-and-miss director that
values emotional response over logical construction, and
suffers accordingly; the leads, many of them miscast, are
asked only to inhabit infuriatingly passive roles while
Potter fetishises and exoticises around them: there
hasn't been so much Yiddisher fiddling on one
soundtrack since Topol's heyday.*

CIN Sacha Vierny   MUS Osvaldo Golijov   DES Carlos
Conti   ED Hervé Schneid   PROD Christopher Sheppard
DIST Universal

❝ The imagery is lush, but the story is pretty cornball,
with an ending that can only be called pure Hollywood. –
Jay Carr, Boston Globe

❝ There's only one performer in the movie who looks
completely at ease with what he's doing: the horse. –
Owen Gleiberman, Entertainment Weekly

The Man Who Shot
Liberty Valance   ★★★

DIR *John Ford*
1962   122m   US
[DVD]

☆ *James Stewart* (Ransom Stoddard), John Wayne (Tom
Doniphon), Vera Miles (Hallie Stoddard), *Lee Marvin*
(Liberty Valance), Edmond O'Brien (Dutton Peabody),
Andy Devine (Link Appleyard), Jeanette Nolan (Nora
Ericson), John Qualen (Peter Ericson), Ken Murray (Doc
Willoughby), Woody Strode (Pompey), Lee Van Cleef
(Reese), Strother Martin (Floyd), John Carradine (Maj.
Cassius Starbuckle)

A young lawyer becomes a hero for shooting a bad
guy, but in later life he discloses how the villain
really met his end.

*A late entry in the John Ford canon, a mature, reflective
work that is now widely hailed as one of the great
Westerns. Elegiac in tone, it deals with the founding of
the frontier, the establishing of law and order, and the
ideals to which its early inhabitants aspired.*

SCR James Warner Bellah, Willis Goldbeck   CIN William
H. Clothier   MUS Cyril Mockridge   ED Otho Lovering

PROD Willis Goldbeck   DIST Paramount/John
Ford

FAMOUS LINE: When truth becomes legend, print the
legend.

❝ Like Queen Victoria, John Wayne has become lovable
because he stayed in the saddle into a new era. – *Judith
Crist*

❝ A heavy-spirited piece of nostalgia. – *Pauline Kael, 1975*

'The Last Thing On His Mind Is Murder.'

The Man Who Wasn't There   ★★★

DIR *Joel Coen*
2001   116m   US
[DVD]   ♫

☆ *Billy Bob Thornton* (Ed Crane), Frances McDormand
(Doris Crane), Michael Badalucco (Frank), James
Gandolfini (Big Dave), Katherine Borowitz (Ann
Nirdlinger), Jon Polito (Creighton Tolliver), Scarlett
Johansson (Birdy Abundas), Richard Jenkins (Walter
Abundas), Tony Shalhoub (Freddy Riedenschneider),
Adam Alexi-Malle (Carcanogues)

Small-town America, the late 1940s: a taciturn
barber kills off his wife's lover, and sets in motion a
chain of events that lead to his own downfall.

*A striking re-creation of both the look and themes of film
noir, coolly setting itself a conundrum – what happens
when a man who talks to nobody has nobody left to talk
to? It works things out with highly attuned
performances, an emotional reticence some will
doubtless find trying, and dazzling, high-contrast
monochrome photography.*

SCR *Joel Coen, Ethan Coen*   CIN *Roger Deakins*
MUS Carter Burwell   DES *Dennis Gassner*   ED Roderick
Jaynes   PROD Ethan Coen   DIST Entertainment

ED CRANE: Me, I don't talk much. I just cut the hair.

❝ Slowly paced for a thriller and with a hero many will
find off-putting, this is nevertheless a gripping, unusual
and challenging work from the most consistently brilliant
filmmakers of the last decade. – *Kim Newman, Empire*

❝ The Coens have used the noir idiom to fashion a
haunting, beautifully made movie that refers to nothing
outside itself and that disperses like a vapour as soon as
it's over. – *Dana Stevens, The New York Times*

⚱ Roger Deakins (cinematography)
🏆 Roger Deakins (cinematography)

The Man Who Would Be King   ★★★

DIR John Huston
1975   129m   US
[DVD]   ♫

☆ Sean Connery (Daniel Dravot), Michael Caine (Peachy
Carnehan), Christopher Plummer (Rudyard Kipling),
Saeed Jaffrey (Billy Fish), Jack May (District
Commissioner), Shakira Caine

In India in the 1880s, two British ex-infantrymen
turned adventurers find themselves accepted as
kings by a remote tribe, convinced that one of them
is a god.

*Agreeable Kipling satire which creates a terrific, funny
and often combative partnership between two of
Britain's most popular actors. It has points to make*

M

about human avarice and about British imperialism, but not so clumsily that they get in the way of the fun.

SCR John Huston, Gladys Hill   CIN Oswald Morris
MUS Maurice Jarre   DES Alexander Trauner   ED Russell Lloyd   PROD John Foreman   DIST Columbia/Allied Artists/Persky-Bright/Devon

⚲ John Huston, Gladys Hill (adapted screenplay); Alexander Trauner

---

'A fatherless boy had almost given up all his dreams... until one man believed in him enough to make them come true.'

The Man without a Face ★

DIR *Mel Gibson*
1993   115m   US
DVD   ♫

☆ Mel Gibson (Justin McLeod), Margaret Whitton (Catherine Palin), Fay Masterson (Gloria Norstadt), Gaby Hoffman (Megan Norstadt), Geoffrey Lewis (Chief Wayne Stark), Richard Masur (Prof. Carl Hartley), Nick Stahl (Charles E. 'Chuck' Norstadt), Viva (Mrs. Cooper)

A young boy turns to a scarred, reclusive teacher to help him in his studies.

Modest, sentimental drama that, in its quiet emphases on literacy and scholarship, now looks like an anomaly on the filmography of the director who went on to make the bloodthirsty Braveheart and Apocalypto. Did the later Mel just devour this Mel whole for breakfast one morning?

SCR Malcolm MacRury   CIN Donald M. McAlpine
MUS James Horner   DES Barbara Dunphy   ED Tony Gibbs   PROD Bruce Davey   DIST Entertainment/Icon

❝ Nothing if not respectable, and occasionally it is something more than that. – *Julie Salamon, Wall Street Journal*

❝ Gibson, directing for the first time, presents this deeply wet material in a reasonably cool and dry manner. But his film is in desperate need of smarm-busting - something, anything that would relieve the familiarity of its characters, the predictability of its structure, the bland failure to challenge its perfect correctness of outlook. – *Richard Schickel, Time*

The Manchurian Candidate ★★★★

DIR *John Frankenheimer*
1962   126m   US
DVD   ♫

☆ Frank Sinatra (Bennett Marco), Laurence Harvey (Raymond Shaw), Janet Leigh (Rosie), James Gregory (Sen. John Iselin), Angela Lansbury (Raymond's Mother), Henry Silva (Chunjim), John McGiver (Sen. Thomas Jordon)

A Korean war 'hero' comes back to the U.S. a brainwashed zombie triggered to kill a liberal politician, his control being his own monstrously ambitious mother.

Insanely plotted but brilliantly handled political paranoia thriller, a mixture of Hitchcock, Welles and All the King's Men. Brilliant and harrowing; very much a product of its time, with its brainwashing theme, it holds up well for successive generations.

SCR George Axelrod   CIN Lionel Lindon   MUS David Amram   DES Richard Sylbert   ED Ferris Webster
PROD Howard W. Koch   DIST UA/MC

❝ The un-American film of the year. – *Penelope Houston*

❝ An intelligent, funny, superbly written, beautifully played, and brilliantly directed study of the all-embracing fantasy in everyday social, emotional and political existence. – *Philip Strick, 1973*

⚲ Angela Lansbury (supporting actress)

'This summer everything is under control.'

The Manchurian Candidate ★★

DIR *Jonathan Demme*
2004   129m   US
DVD   ♫

☆ Denzel Washington (Ben Marco), *Meryl Streep* (Eleanor Shaw), Liev Schreiber (Raymond Shaw), Jon Voight (Senator Thomas Jordan), Kimberly Elise (Rosie), Jeffrey Wright (Al Melvin), Ted Levine (Colonel Howard), Bruno Ganz (Delp), Dean Stockwell (Mark Whiting)

Upon returning from a tour of duty in the Gulf, a decorated soldier experiences terrible flashbacks, and uncovers a conspiracy involving a former comrade-in-arms running as a vice-presidential candidate.

One of the better remakes of recent years, a highly intriguing update of the original Candidate's themes for an age of spin, corporate interests and mass media blitzing; it has a strange idea of paranoia, insisting more is more, but Demme knows exactly how to get under the viewer's skin, and his film's wilder, more excessive qualities leave one (suitably) reeling.

SCR Daniel Pyne, Dean Georgaris   CIN *Tak Fujimoto*
MUS Rachel Portman   DES Kristi Zea   ED *Carol Littleton, Craig McKay*   PROD Ilona Herzberg, Jonathan Demme, Scott Rudin, Tina Sinatra   DIST Paramount

❝ The first Candidate was inspired pop art, a two-dimensional colouring book about 1962 America's subterranean political fears. Demme's film is more nuanced, less crazy-brilliant and, yes, probably less necessary, but it's still a confirmation of all the anxieties out there on the table and festering in our heads. – *Ty Burr, Boston Globe*

❝ A stylish hoot: entertainingly edgy and ludicrous all at once. – *Desson Thomson, Washington Post*

Ⓣ Meryl Streep (supporting actress)

Mandela ★

DIR *Jo Menell, Angus Gibson*
1995   118m   US
DVD   ♫

The South African leader's story, in his own words.

Given its subject's early career as a lawyer, perhaps it's no surprise long stretches of this documentary should resemble an extended deposition – resulting in more of a plod than a film on Mandela's life should have been. The man himself has much less to say on camera about his arrest and imprisonment than he does about the day of his circumcision.

M

SCR Bo Widerberg   CIN Dewald Aukema, Peter Tischhauser   MUS Cedric Gradus Samson, Hugh Masekela   ED Andy Keir   PROD Jonathan Demme, Edward Saxon, Jo Menell   DIST Nubian Tales/Island/Clinica Estetico

66 A fitting and lasting tribute to one of this century's most caring, charismatic and courageous men. – *David Parkinson, Empire*

⚖ documentary

Manhattan ★★★★

DIR *Woody Allen*

1979   96m   US

DVD   ♫

☆ *Woody Allen* (Isaac Davis), *Diane Keaton* (Mary Wilke), Meryl Streep (Jill), Mariel Hemingway (Tracy), *Michael Murphy* (Yale)

Episodes in the sex life of a TV comedy writer with an obsession about New York.

As close to a summation of Woody Allen's views and oeuvre as anybody needs; some smart jabs about the lives we lead are sometimes bogged down in earnestness and half-comic despair, while the protagonist's wildly unsuitable affair with a teenage girl is both funny and sorrowful. Allen takes Parks's lustrous black-and-white images of the city, combines them with Gershwin on the soundtrack and the result is irresistible. As funny as its immediate predecessor Annie Hall, but more sombre too.

SCR *Woody Allen, Marshall Brickman*   CIN *Gordon Willis*   ED Susan E. Morse   DIST UA/Jack Rollins/Charles H. Joffe

66 Given that the identity of his films has increasingly been determined by his compulsion to talk about the things he finds important, but also by his fear of having them come out as anything but a joke, it is not surprising that he has scarcely been able to decide on a form for his "art": from the anything-for-a-laugh skittering of his early films, to the broad parodies and pastiches of his middle period, to the recent confessional/psychoanalytical mode. – *Richard Combs, Monthly Film Bulletin*

66 A masterpiece that has become a film for the ages by not seeking to be a film of the moment. – *Andrew Sarris*

⚖ Mariel Hemingway (supporting actress); Woody Allen, Marshall Brickman (original screenplay)

Ⓣ picture

Manhattan Murder Mystery ★

DIR Woody Allen

1993   104m   US

DVD

☆ Woody Allen (Larry Lipton), Alan Alda (Ted), Anjelica Huston (Marcia Fox), Diane Keaton (Carol Lipton), Jerry Adler (Paul House), Joy Behar (Marilyn), Ron Rifkin (Sy), Lynn Cohen (Lillian House), Melanie Norris (Helen Moss)

When a neighbour drops dead of a heart attack, a married woman smells a rat and enlists her husband to investigate the possibility of foul play.

One of its director's fluffier comedies, underplaying the mystery aspect and tossing away its handful of good

lines amidst the chatter of twitty characters; a fun cast, though.

SCR Woody Allen, Marshall Brickman   CIN Carlo Di Palma   DES Santo Loquasto   ED Susan E. Morse   PROD Robert Greenhut   DIST TriStar

66 Successful lightweight Woody – no more, no less. – *Owen Gleiberman, Entertainment Weekly*

66 Both civilised filmmaking and a consistent pleasure to watch. – *Derek Malcolm, Guardian*

Ⓣ Anjelica Huston (supporting actress)

'Enter the mind of a serial killer. . .you may never come back.'

Manhunter ★★★

SCR/DIR *Michael Mann*

1986   119m   US

DVD   ♫

☆ William L. Petersen (Will Graham), Kim Greist (Molly Graham), *Joan Allen* (Reba McClane), *Brian Cox* (Dr. Hannibal Lecktor), Dennis Farina (Jack Crawford), Stephen Lang (Freddy Lounds), *Tom Noonan* (Francis Dollarhyde), David Seaman (Kevin Graham), Benjamin Hendrickson (Dr. Frederick Chilton)

An FBI agent on the trail of a serial killer turns to an incarcerated psychopath for advice.

Tremendously atmospheric thriller that provides an altogether more raw experience than the later The Silence of the Lambs or Red Dragon, establishing several of its director's key procedural themes (and its leading man's CSI credentials) while enhancing the general air of dread with dreamy, unexpected plot tangents.

CIN *Dante Spinotti*   MUS Michael Rubini   DES Mel Bourne   ED Dov Hoenig   PROD Richard Roth, Dino De Laurentiis   DIST Recorded Releasing/Red Dragon/De Laurentiis Entertainment

66 The best Hannibal Lecter movie and one of the greatest suspense movies ever made. – *Allen Barra, Salon*

66 An unpleasantly gripping thriller that rubs one's nose in a sick criminal mentality for two hours. – *Variety*

'Anything goes and does!'

Manifesto ★

SCR/DIR Dusan Makavejev

1988   96m   US

☆ Alfred Molina (Avanti), Camilla Soeberg (Svetlana Vargas), Simon Callow (Police Chief Hunt), Lindsay Duncan (Lily Sachor), Eric Stoltz (Christopher), Rade Serbedzija (Emile), Chris Haywood (Wango), Linda Marlowe (Stella Vargas), Ronald Lacey (Conductor)

In 1920, the tyrannical king of a central European country plans a visit to a small, remote village, unaware that revolutionaries are plotting his murder.

An odd, anarchic comedy, dark in tone and dependent on sexual couplings for laughter and plot advancement.

CIN Tomislav Pinter   MUS Nicola Piovani   DES Velijo Despotovic   ED Tony Lawson   PROD Yoram Globus, Menahem Golan   DIST Cannon/Menahem Golan, Yoram Globus

M

Manufactured Landsacapes (new) ★★

DIR Jennifer Baichwal
2007 86m Canada
☆ Edward Burtynsky

Canadian photographer Edward Burtynsky travels the world, recording how oilfields, mines and other industries have changed the earth's landscape.

A visually impressive and sobering account of the ravages caused to the earth's surface by advanced industrialisation. Burtynsky spent much of the time being filmed in China – but the problem he describes is a global one.

DIST BFI

66 A stunning, intelligent film. – *Andrew Pulver, Guardian*

66 There is a terrible beauty about Manufactured Landscapes. – *Philip French, Observer*

'From a Kingdom of Ice to a Land of Fire . . . A Love That Knows No Boundaries.'

Map of the Human Heart ★

DIR Vincent Ward
1992 109m GB/Australia/France/Canada
DVD ♫

☆ Patrick Bergin (Walter Russell), Anne Parillaud (Albertine), Jason Scott Lee (Avik), John Cusack (The Mapmaker), Jeanne Moreau (Sister Banville)

An old Inuit man recalls how, over several decades, he traversed the world, became involved in a world war and helped cartographers map out his region of the Arctic, all the while yearning to be reunited with the sweetheart of his adolescence.

A romantic triangle lies at the heart of this wildly ambitious would-be epic; its visual beauty sometimes overcomes the story, which sprawls to its detriment. But there are some extraordinary set-pieces, notably the consummation of the central love story atop a barrage balloon.

SCR Louis Nowra CIN Eduardo Serra MUS Gabriel Yared DES John Beard ED John Scott, Frans Vandenburg PROD Vincent Ward, Tim Bevan
DIST Rank/Working Title/Map/Sunrise/Polygram/AFFC/Vincent Ward

66 Like Ward's other work, the film is an evocative visual epic, open to many interpretations. – *Philip Strick, Sight and Sound*

Marathon Man ★★★

DIR *John Schlesinger*
1976 126m US
DVD

☆ *Dustin Hoffman* (Babe Levy), *Laurence Olivier* (Szell), *Roy Scheider* (Doc Levy), William Devane (Janeway), Marthe Keller (Elsa), Fritz Weaver (Prof. Biesenthal), Marc Lawrence (Erhard)

A vicious Nazi returns from Uruguay to New York in search of diamonds which had been kept for him by his now-dead brother, and is outwitted by the young brother of an American agent he has killed.

Complex conspiracy thriller, laced with paranoia, which

starts slowly with musings about McCarthyism and Nazism, but finally settles down to being a simple shocker with a nick-of-time climax. The presentation is dazzling. The torture scene in the dentist's chair is infamously hard to watch, but executed with style.

SCR William Goldman CIN *Conrad Hall* MUS Michael Small DES Richard MacDonald ED Jim Clark
PROD Robert Evans, Sidney Beckerman
DIST Paramount

66 A film of such rich texture and density in its construction, so fascinatingly complex in its unfolding, so engrossing in its personalities, and so powerful in its performance and pace that the seduction of the senses has physical force. – *Judith Crist, Saturday Review*

66 Fashionably violent. . .distinctly self-conscious. . .conventionally moralistic. . .and absolutely devoid of resonance. – *Tom Milne, Monthly Film Bulletin*

⚱ Laurence Olivier (supporting actor)

'In the harshest place on Earth, love finds a way.'

March of the Penguins ★★

DIR *Luc Jacquet*
2005 85m France/US
DVD ♫

☆ Morgan Freeman (Narrator)

Documentary charting the travels and travails of the Emperor Penguin during mating season in the harsh surrounds of the Antarctic.

This English-language version of a French original simplifies any zoological aspects to tell a story of love in an impossible climate, and to assert family values. But it works a peculiar magic in bringing us closer to some charismatic, visually striking creatures in locations rife with dramatic possibility.

SCR Jordan Roberts CIN *Laurent Chalet, Jerome Maison*
MUS Alex Wurman ED Sabine Emiliani PROD Yves Darondeau, Christophe Lioud, Emmanuel Priou
DIST Warner

66 A perfect family movie, a perfect date movie, and one of the most eye-ravishing documentaries ever made. – *David Denby, The New Yorker*

66 Exquisitely shot. . .a nature film built with a feel for the epic and a love of operatic narrative. – *Lisa Schwarzbaum, Entertainment Weekly*

† The film became the second highest grossing documentary at the US box office after Fahrenheit 9/11.

⚱ documentary

Ⓣ Laurent Chalet, Jerome Maison; Sabine Emiliani

Margaret's Museum ★★

DIR *Mort Ransen*
1995 114m Canada/GB
DVD

☆ *Helena Bonham Carter* (Margaret MacNeil), *Kate Nelligan* (Catherine MacNeil), Clive Russell (Neil Currie), Craig Olejnik (Jimmy MacNeil), Andrea Morris (Marilyn), Peter Boretski (Grandfather Dunald MacNeil), Kenneth Welsh (Angus MacNeil)

In 1940s Nova Scotia town, a woman in a small village is determined that her lover should not be

---

DVD Available on DVD ☆ Cast in order of importance 66 Critics' Quotes † Points of interest ⚱ Academy Award ⚱ Academy Award nomination Ⓑ BAFTA Ⓣ BAFTA nomination

399

M

forced to work down the mine that cost the lives of her father and brother.

A film that takes viewers by surprise; starting out as a tough, humorous slice of working class life, it gradually becomes a melodrama, suffused with death and madness. It's nevertheless effective, and proved a breakthrough role for Bonham Carter, hitherto better-known for being laced up tightly in Merchant Ivory costume dramas.

SCR Gerald Wexler, Mort Ransen   **CIN** Vic Sarin
MUS Milan Kymlicka   **DES** William Fleming, David McHenry   **ED** Rita Roy   **PROD** Mort Ransen, Christopher Zimmer, Claudio Luca, Steve Clark-Hall, Mike Mahoney   **DIST** Ranfilm/Imagex/Télé-Action/Skyline

---

'One family. Infinite degrees of separation.'

Margot at the Wedding (new)

SCR/DIR Noah Baumbach
2007   92m   US
DVD   ♫

☆ Nicole Kidman (Margot), Jennifer Jason Leigh (Pauline), Jack Black (Malcolm), John Turturro (Jim), Ciaran Hinds (Dick), Zane Pais (Claude), Flora Cross (Ingrid)

The arrival of one sister at another's wedding stirs up old resentments.

Waspish comedy from the talented writer-director of The Squid and the Whale; disappointingly, though, he fails to make his selfish and narcissistic antagonists either believable or likeable this time around.

CIN Harris Savides   **DES** Anne Ross   **ED** Carol Littleton
PROD Scott Rudin   **DIST** Paramount

❝ More like a collection of arresting scenes than a fully conceived and developed drama. – *Todd McCarthy, Variety*

❝ The characters are so loathsome you long for a hurricane to sweep them away. – *Wendy Ide, The Times*

† The film's original title was Nicole at the Beach, a homage to French director Eric Rohmer (who made Pauline at the Beach).

'How far will she go before she's gone too far?'

Maria Full of Grace ★★

SCR/DIR *Joshua Marston*
2004   101m   US/Colombia/Ecuador
DVD

☆ *Catalina Sandino Moreno* (Maria), Yenny Paola Vega (Blanca), Guilied Lopez (Lucy), Jhon Alex Toro (Franklin), Patricia Rae (Carla), Wilson Guerrero (Juan)

A pregnant young Colombian woman is coerced into smuggling drugs into America as a mule.

Something of a triumph in its understated, clammily gripping manner, with the camera staying close to its lead actress throughout, and observing a breakthrough performance.

CIN Jim Denault   **MUS** Jacobo Lieberman, Leonardo Heiblum   **DES** Monica Marulanda, Debbie De Villa
ED Anne McCabe, Lee Percy   **PROD** Paul Mezey
DIST Icon

❝ Sustains a documentary authenticity that is as astonishing as it is offhand. Even when you're on the edge of your seat, it never sacrifices a calm, clear-sighted humanity for the sake of melodrama or cheap moralising. – *Stephen Holden, New York Times*

❝ A simple, engrossing movie that never tells us what to think, and the acting, especially from Catalina Sandino Moreno, has the quality we used to associate with Italian neo-realism. – *Philip French, Observer*

⚱ Catalina Sandino Moreno (leading actress)

'He didn't come looking for trouble, but trouble came looking for him.'

El Mariachi ★★

SCR/DIR *Robert Rodriguez*
1993   81m   US
DVD

☆ Carlos Gallardo (El Mariachi), Consuelo Gómez (Domino), Reinol Martinez (Azul), Peter Marquardt (Moco), Jaime de Hoyos (Bigoton), Ramiro Gómez (Cantinero), Jesus Lopez (Viejo Clark), Luis Baro (Domino's Assistant)

An innocent, hard-up musician arrives in a Mexican town with his guitar in a case, and is instantly mistaken for a ruthless hit man.

Simple yet enthralling ultra-low budget thriller which comfortably compensates for what it lacks in originality with energy, humour and imagination.

CIN Robert Rodriguez   **MUS** Marc Trujillo, Alvaro Rodriguez, Chris Knudson, Cecilio Rodriguez, Eric Guthrie
ED Robert Rodriguez   **PROD** Robert Rodriguez, Carlos Gallardo   **DIST** Columbia/Los Hooligans

❝ Director Robert Rodriguez goes for broke with a breakneck pace, swarms of bullets, cinematic tricks, and a tone as playful as it is knowing of genre conventions. – *Geoff Andrew, Time Out*

❝ Juicy, adroit and likeable. – *Jonathan Rosenbaum, Chicago Reader*

† The film reportedly cost just $7,000 to shoot. Rodriguez also directed the Hollywood remake, Desperado

---

'It's the Godfather on laughing gas.'

Married to the Mob ★★

DIR *Jonathan Demme*
1988   103m   US
DVD   ♫

☆ Michelle Pfeiffer (Angela de Marco), Matthew Modine (Mike Downey), Dean Stockwell (Tony 'The Tiger' Russo), Mercedes Ruehl (Connie Russo), Alec Baldwin ('Cucumber' Frank de Marco), Trey Wilson (Regional Director Franklin), Joan Cusack (Rose)

After the murder of her gangster husband, a woman takes off to pursue a law-abiding life of her own, pursued in turn by the Mob and the FBI.

Zippy comic thriller which finds everyone both in front of and behind the camera cutting loose on a scene-by-scene basis: tremendous fun.

SCR Barry Strugatz, Mark R. Burns   **CIN** Tak Fujimoto
MUS *David Byrne*   **DES** Kristi Zea   **ED** Craig McKay
PROD Kenneth Utt, Edward Saxon
DIST Rank/Orion/Mysterious Arts

❝ Fresh, colourful and inventive. – *Variety*

⚱ Dean Stockwell (supporting actor)

'Nice Planet. We'll Take It!'

Mars Attacks! ★★

DIR Tim Burton

1955 106m US

DVD ♫

☆ Jack Nicholson (President James Dale/Art Land), Glenn Close (First Lady Marsha Dale), Annette Bening (Barbara Land), Michael J. Fox (Jason Stone), Pierce Brosnan (Professor Donald Kessler), Sarah Jessica Parker (Nathalie Lake), Martin Short (Press Secretary Jerry Ross), Lisa Marie (Martian Girl), Rod Steiger (General Decker), Danny De Vito (Rude Gambler), Lukas Haas (Richie Norris), Natalie Portman (Taffy Dale), Jim Brown (Byron Williams), Pam Grier (Louise Williams), Joe Don Baker (Richie's Dad), Tom Jones, Jerzy SkolimowskI, Barbet Schroeder

A fleet of Martians land on Earth with the intention of conquering the puny humans before them.

Something of a mixed bag, but in its best moments, the film has a rare and cherishable sense of anarchy: it's finally about as good a movie as might be gleaned from a set of bubblegum trading cards by a director big on Ed Wood.

SCR Jonathan Gems CIN Peter Suschitzky MUS Danny Elfman DES Wynn Thomas ED Chris Lebenzon PROD Tim Burton, Larry Franco DIST Warner

“ Perhaps the funniest piece of giddy schlock heartlessness ever committed to film. – *Peter Rainer, Dallas Observer*

“ Just a parade of scattershot gags, more often weird than funny and most often just flat. – *Elvis Mitchell, New York Times*

'It's the love story of an unsung hero!'

Marty ★★★★

DIR *Delbert Mann*

1955 91m US

DVD

☆ *Ernest Borgnine* (Marty), *Betsy Blair* (Clara), *Esther Minciotti* (Mrs. Pilletti), *Joe Mantell* (Angie), Karen Steele (Virginia), Jerry Paris (Thomas)

A 34-year-old Bronx butcher fears he will never get a girl because he is unattractive, but at a Saturday night dance he meets a vulnerable young schoolteacher who shares his outlook.

The first of the 'anti-epics' – filmed plays from TV which in the mid-1950s seemed like a cheap breath of spring to Hollywood, and also brought in a new wave of talent. This is one of the best, its new naturalistic dialogue falling happily on the ear; but it has been so frequently imitated since that its revolutionary appearance is hard to imagine.

SCR *Paddy Chayefsky* CIN *Joseph LaShelle* MUS Roy Webb ED Alan Crosland Jr. PROD Harold Hecht DIST UA/Hecht-Hill-Lancaster

“ Something rare in the American cinema today: a subtle, ironic and compassionate study of ordinary human relationships. – *Gavin Lambert*

“ A warm and winning film, full of the sort of candid comment on plain, drab people that seldom reaches the screen. – *Bosley Crowther, New York Times*

⚊ picture; Ernest Borgnine (leading actor); Delbert Mann (direction); Paddy Chayefsky (screenplay)

⚊ Betsy Blair (supporting actress); Joe Mantell (supporting actor); Joseph LaShelle; art direction

Ⓣ Ernest Borgnine (leading actor); Betsy Blair (supporting actress)

'A story about the years that keep us apart. . .And the moments that bring us together.'

Marvin's Room ★

DIR Jerry Zaks

1996 98m US

DVD ♫

☆ Meryl Streep (Lee), Leonardo DiCaprio (Hank), Diane Keaton (Bessie), Robert de Niro (Dr. Wally), Hume Cronyn (Marvin), Gwen Verdon (Ruth), Hal Scardino (Charlie), Dan Hedaya (Bob)

After learning she has leukaemia, a middle-aged woman who cares for her ailing father reaches out to her estranged sister for help.

An adaptation with some wit, and a fair amount of dramatic leeway for its A-list cast to work within, though it never quite transcends the feeling that one is watching a superior disease-of-the-week TV movie.

SCR Scott McPherson CIN Piotr Sobocinski MUS Rachel Portman DES David Gropman ED Jim Clark PROD Scott Rudin, Jane Rosenthal, Robert de Niro DIST Buena Vista/Miramax

“ Great actors do what they can in a simple and largely unaffecting story. – *Bob McCabe, Empire*

⚊ Diane Keaton

Mary Poppins ★★★

DIR Robert Stevenson

1964 139m US

DVD ♫

☆ *Julie Andrews* (Mary Poppins), David Tomlinson (Mr. Banks), Glynis Johns (Mrs. Banks), Dick Van Dyke (Bert/Mr. Dawes, Sr.), Reginald Owen (Adm. Boom), Ed Wynn (Uncle Albert), Matthew Garber (Michael Banks), Karen Dotrice (Jane Banks), Hermione Baddeley (Ellen), Elsa Lanchester (Katie Nanna), Arthur Treacher (Constable Jones), Jane Darwell (The Bird Woman)

In Edwardian London a prim but magical nanny teaches two slightly naughty children to make life enjoyable for themselves and others.

Sporadically a pleasant and effective entertainment for children of all ages, with plenty of brightness and charm including magic tricks, the mixing of live with cartoon adventures, and just plain fun. It suffers, however, from a wandering narrative in the second half (when Miss Poppins scarcely appears) and from Mr Van Dyke's now legendary attempt to speak like a Cockney.

SCR Bill Walsh, Don da Gradi CIN Edward Colman DES Tony Walton ED Cotton Warburton PROD Bill Walsh DIST Walt Disney

† 'Chim Chim Cher-ee'; 'Feed the Birds'; 'Fidelity Fiduciary Bank'; 'I Love to Laugh'; 'Jolly Holiday'; 'Let's Go Fly a Kite'; 'The Life I Lead'; 'The Perfect Nanny'; 'Sister Suffragette'; 'A Spoonful of Sugar'; 'Stay Awake'; 'Step in Time'; 'Supercalifragilisticexpialidocious'

| DVD Available on DVD | ☆ Cast in order | “ Critics' Quotes | ⚊ Academy Award | Ⓑ BAFTA |
| ♫ Soundtrack on CD | of importance | † Points of interest | ⚊ Academy Award nomination | Ⓣ BAFTA nomination |

⚔ Richard M. and Robert B. Sherman; Julie Andrews (leading actress); Richard M. and Robert B. Sherman (m), (ly) (music, original song – Chim Chim Cheree); special visual effects; editing

⚔ picture; Robert Stevenson (direction); Bill Walsh, Don DaGradi (adapted screenplay); Edward Colman; Irwin Kostal; art direction

Ⓣ Julie Andrews (leading actress)

Mary Shelley's Frankenstein   ★

DIR Kenneth Branagh
1994 123m US/Japan
[DVD] ♫

☆ Robert de Niro (The Creature), Kenneth Branagh (Victor Frankenstein), Tom Hulce (Henry Clerval), Helena Bonham Carter (Elizabeth), Aidan Quinn (Captain Robert Walton), Ian Holm (Baron Frankenstein), Richard Briers (Grandfather), John Cleese (Professor Waldman), Robert Hardy (Professor Krempe), Cherie Lunghi (Caroline Beaufort Frankenstein), Celia Imrie (Mrs. Moritz)

Rescued at the North Pole, a scientist recounts to a sea captain the tale of how he came to create a monster.

An ambitious staging of the novel that works well for an hour or so before tailing off in interest; allowing the creature to talk this much seems a misstep, as does a belaboured emphasis on the relationship between Victor and Elizabeth. James Whale need not feel unduly troubled.

SCR Steph Lady, Frank Darabont   CIN Roger Pratt
MUS Patrick Doyle   DES Tim Harvey   ED Andrew Marcus   PROD Francis Ford Coppola, James V. Hart, John Veitch   DIST Columbia TriStar/American Zoetrope/Japan Satellite/IndieProd

66 A work of lavish dedication and skill, yet as soon as the creature is let loose the film becomes rather listless. Branagh, for all his craftsmanship, hasn't succeeded in tapping the morbid core of the material. – *Owen Gleiberman, Entertainment Weekly*

66 Not frightening, just silly. – *Geoff Andrew, Time Out*

⚔ Daniel Parker, Paul Engelen, Carol Hemming (make up)

Ⓣ Tim Harvey

'M*A*S*H Gives A D*A*M*N.'

M*A*S*H   ★★★

DIR *Robert Altman*
1970 116m US
[DVD] ♫

☆ *Donald Sutherland* (Hawkeye Pierce), *Elliott Gould* (Trapper John McIntyre), Tom Skerritt (Duke Forrest), Sally Kellerman (Major Hot Lips Houlihan), Robert Duvall (Major Frank Burns), Jo Ann Pflug (Lt Hot Dish), René Auberjonois (Dago Red), Gary Burghoff (Radar O'Reilly), Roger Bowen (Col Henry Blake)

US surgeons at a mobile hospital during the Korean War spend what spare time they have chasing women and bucking authority.

Savage comedy of man's rebellion in the face of death, alternating sex farce with gory operation scenes; hailed as the great anti-everything film, and certainly very funny for those who can take it. It led to a long-running,

much-praised TV series which for once did not disgrace its original.

SCR *Ring Lardner Jnr*   CIN Harold E. Stine   MUS Johnny Mandel   ED Danford B. Greene   PROD Ingo Preminger, Leon Ericksen   DIST TCF/Aspen

66 Bloody funny. A hyper-acute wiretap on mankind's death wish. – *Joseph Morgenstern*

66 The laughter is blood-soaked and the comedy cloaks a bitter and terrible truth. – *Judith Crist*

⚔ Ring Lardner Jnr (adapted screenplay)

⚔ picture; Sally Kellerman (supporting actress); Robert Altman (direction); Danford B. Greene

'From Zero To Hero.'

The Mask   ★

DIR Chuck Russell
1994 97m US
[DVD] ♫

☆ Jim Carrey (Stanley Ipkiss), Peter Riegert (Lt. Mitch Kellaway), Cameron Diaz (Tina Carlyle), Peter Greene (Dorian Tyrell), Amy Yasbeck (Peggy Brandt), Richard Jeni (Charlie Schumaker), Orestes Matacena (Niko), Tim Bagley (Irv Ripley), Nancy Fish (Mrs. Peenman), Johnny Williams (Burt Ripley)

A nerdy bank clerk stumbles across a wooden mask that transforms him into a superheroic ladies' man.

Zappy effects comedy, the film equivalent of a hyperactive toddler, that pays homage to the manic energies of cartoons through the ages in an entertaining fashion; an ideal star vehicle for Carrey, it also launched the movie career of former model Cameron Diaz.

SCR Mike Werb   CIN John R. Leonetti   MUS Randy Edelman   DES Craig Stearns   ED Arthur Coburn   PROD Bob Engelman   DIST Entertainment/New Line/Dark Horse

66 Russell brings a lowbrow pulp rigour to the material that's reminiscent of vintage Roger Corman and pays lavish homage to animator Tex Avery. The design is bright as a button and the transformation scenes real eye-poppers, but the film's best special effect is Carrey with his razzle-dazzle star turn. – *Tom Charity, Time Out*

66 Carrey's a human cartoon, and his spontaneous, Avery-esque, anything-for-a-laugh outrageousness makes this otherwise blank Mask a must-see. – *Joe Brown, Washington Post*

† A regrettable sequel, Son of the Mask, followed – albeit tardily – in 2005.

⚔ visual effects

Ⓣ special effects; Craig Stearns (production design); makeup/hair

The Mask of Zorro   ★

DIR Martin Campbell
1998 136m US
[DVD] ♫

☆ Antonio Banderas (Alejandro Murrieta / Zorro), Anthony Hopkins (Don Diego de la Vega / Zorro), Catherine Zeta-Jones (Elena Montero / Elena Murrieta), Stuart Wilson (Don Rafael Montero), Matt Letscher (Capt. Harrison Love), Maury Chaykin (Prison Warden), Tony

[DVD] Available on DVD   ☆ Cast in order   66 Critics' Quotes   ⚔ Academy Award   Ⓣ BAFTA
♫ Soundtrack on CD   of importance   † Points of interest   ⚔ Academy Award nomination   Ⓣ BAFTA nomination

Amendola (Don Luiz), Pedro Armendariz (Don Pedro), L. Q. Jones (Three-Fingered Jack)

Ageing freedom fighter Zorro coaches a younger man to take up his sword and prevent California from falling under the control of a villainous Spanish governor.

Lively, big-budget pantomime which swishes its matinee origins about itself like a cape; directed with comic vigour and dramatic lassitude, it's the stunt work you come away remembering, rather than performances or plot.

SCR John Eskow, Ted Elliott, Terry Rossio   CIN Phil Meheux   MUS James Horner   DES Cecilia Montiel   ED Thom Noble   PROD Doug Claybourne, David Foster   DIST Columbia TriStar/Amblin/Zorro

66 The kind of pleasant entertainment that allows the paying customers to have as much fun as the people on screen. – *Kenneth Turan, Los Angeles Times*

66 Entertaining, but it's about one notch below being something anybody really needs to see. – *Mick LaSalle, San Francisco Chronicle*

† A sequel, The Legend of Zorro, followed in 2005.

⚱ sound; Dave McMoyler (sound effects editing)

Ⓣ Graciela Mazón (costume design)

'The Courage To Do The Impossible Lies In The Hearts of Men.'

Master and Commander: The Far Side of the World   ★★★

DIR *Peter Weir*

2003   139m   US

DVD   ♫

☆ *Russell Crowe* (Captain Jack Aubrey), *Paul Bettany* (Dr Stephen Maturin), Billy Boyd (Barrett Bonden), James D'Arcy (1st Lt Thomas Pullings), Lee Ingleby (Hollom), George Innes (Joe Plaice), Mark Lewis Jones (Mr Hogg), Chris Larkin (Captain Howard, Royal Marines), David Threlfall (Killick), Max Pirkis (Lord Blakeney)

In the year 1805, the officers and crew of the HMS Surprise are ordered to take out a rival French warship in the Atlantic.

The thinking man's Pirates of the Caribbean: a handsome, richly detailed re-creation of a life on the open waves, typical of this director's ability to create self-enclosed worlds within worlds. It is geared more towards anthropological study – the ranking of men and beast – than action, and the two lead performers give persuasive, engaging accounts of differing yet complementary personalities.

SCR Peter Weir, John Collee   CIN *Russell Boyd*   MUS Iva Davies, Christopher Gordon, Richard Tognetti   DES *William Sandell*   ED Lee Smith   PROD Samuel Goldwyn Jnr., Peter Weir, Duncan Henderson   DIST TCF

66 Rare proof that a gigantic production in contemporary Hollywood can possess a distinctive personality and its own approach to storytelling. – *Todd McCarthy, Variety*

66 An exercise in civility – a tasteful "Boy's Life" adventure with plenty of boys aboard to express their appreciation. – *J. Hoberman, Village Voice*

⚱ Russell Boyd; Richard King (sound editing)
⚱ picture; Peter Weir; Lee Smith; William Sandell, Robert Gould (art direction); Daniel Sudick, Stefen Fangmeier, Nathan McGuinness, Robert Stromberg (visual effects); Paul Massey, Doug Hemphill, Art Rochester (sound); Wendy Stites (costume design); Edouard F. Henriques, Yolanda Toussieng (make up)

Ⓣ Peter Weir; William Sandell; Richard Kirk, Doug Hemphill, Paul Massey, Art Rochester (sound); Wendy Stites (costume design)

Ⓣ Paul Bettany; special effects; film; Russell Boyd

'A hitman and a salesman walk into a bar...'

The Matador   ★★

SCR/DIR *Richard Shepard*

2004   97m   Germany/US/Ireland/Australia

DVD   ♫

☆ *Pierce Brosnan* (Julian Noble), *Greg Kinnear* (Danny Wright), *Hope Davis* (Carolyn 'Bean' Wright), Philip Baker Hall (Mr Randy), Dylan Baker (Lovell), Adam Scott (Phil Garrison)

During a stay in Mexico City, a weary middle-aged hit-man crosses paths with a visiting businessman with problems of his own.

Sophisticated comedy, nicely written and performed, which gets Brosnan out of his constraining 007 tuxedo once and for all, and lands him in a perfectly tailored character part.

CIN David Tattersall   MUS Rolfe Kent   DES Robert Pearson   ED Carole Kravetz   PROD Pierce Brosnan, Beau St Clair, Sean Furst, Bryan Furst   DIST Buena Vista

JULIAN NOBLE: 'Just consider me the best cocktail party story you ever met.'

JULIAN NOBLE: 'I'm a big fan of the "Everybody's got to pee" theory of assassination.'

66 A delightfully sly diversion. Brosnan breaks the mould and turns in what might be considered the performance of his career, the kind of witty, relaxed star portrayal that recalls those of Cary Grant and other Golden Era legends. – *Kevin Thomas, Los Angeles Times*

66 We've never seen Pierce Brosnan so liberated - he's a man reborn, and for what The Matador may lack in rounded plotting, it makes up for in funny, spiky, idiosyncratic glee. – *Ian Nathan, Empire*

Matador   ★

DIR Pedro Almodóvar

1986   110m   Spain

DVD

☆ Assumpta Serna (Maria), Antonio Banderas (Angel), Bibi Andersen (Vendedora Flores), Nacho Martinez (Diego), Eva Cobo (Eva), Julieta Serrano (Berta), Chus Lampreave (Pilar), Carmen Maura (Julia), Eusebio Poncela (Comisario)

A young trainee bullfighter, who compulsively contemplates murder, encounters other characters with obsessions of their own.

The usual cocktail of themes from Almodóvar's early period: sex, death, voyeurism and kinky fantasies – none of which get in the way of dark comedy or fabulously kitschy decor. On this evidence, his later

---

DVD Available on DVD   ☆ Cast in order of importance   66 Critics' Quotes   ⚱ Academy Award   Ⓣ BAFTA
♫ Soundtrack on CD   † Points of interest   ⚱ Academy Award nomination   Ⓣ BAFTA nomination

progress into a mature, reflective, world-class director seems even more astonishing.

SCR Jesus Ferrero, Pedro Almodóvar CIN Angel Luis Fernández MUS Bernardo Bonezzi ED Pepe Salcedo PROD Andrés Vicente Gómez DIST Iberoamericana de TV/Televisión Española

The Match Factory Girl ★★

SCR/DIR Aki Kaurismäki
1990   68m   Finland/Sweden
DVD

☆ Kati Outinen (Iris), Elina Salo (Mother), Esko Nikkari (Stepfather), Vesa Vierikko (Aarne), Reijo Taipale (The singer), Silu Seppälä (Iiris' brother)

A taciturn factory girl, abused by her lover and exploited by her bosses, wreaks revenge on everyone who has wronged her.

A sad tale, related effectively in economical fashion by this laconic, deadpan director.

CIN Timo Salminen ED Aki Kaurismäki PROD Katinka Farago, Aki Kaurismäki, Klas Olofsson DIST Electric Pictures/Swedish Film Institute/ Viillealfa/Aki Kaurismäki

'There are no little secrets.'

Match Point

SCR/DIR Woody Allen
2005   124m   GB/US/Luxembourg
DVD   ♫

☆ Scarlett Johansson (Nola Rice), Jonathan Rhys-Meyers (Chris Wilton), Emily Mortimer (Chloe Hewett Wilton), Matthew Goode (Tom Hewett), Brian Cox (Alec Hewett), Penelope Wilton (Eleanor Hewett), Ewen Bremner (Inspector Dowd), James Nesbitt (Detective Banner), Rupert Penry-Jones (Henry), Margaret Tyzack (Mrs Eastby)

A scheming coach at a London tennis club inveigles his way into a rich family by marrying one of their daughters, only to fall foul of his demanding actress lover.

The first in a run of disastrous pictures made by its exiled director on British turf: a miscast, poorly plotted, terribly written mess in which most of the players look bored, if not altogether ill-at-ease with the material presented to them.

CIN Remi Adefarasin DES Jim Clay ED Alisa Lepselter PROD Letty Aronson, Gareth Wiley, Lucy Darwin DIST Icon

❝ A modest and mildly pretentious mediocrity in the Woodman canon. – *Michael Atkinson, Village Voice*

❝ Can it really be true that our country, our capital city, and the film production company created by our national broadcaster has revitalised the career of one of America's greatest filmmakers? In a word, no. Or in seven words: I'm really sorry about this, but no. – *Peter Bradshaw, Guardian*

† Allen went on to make Scoop and Cassandra's Dream in London.

⚱ Woody Allen (original screenplay)

'Lie cheat steal rinse repeat.'

Matchstick Men ★

DIR Ridley Scott
2003   116m   US/GB
DVD   ♫

☆ Nicolas Cage (Roy Waller), Sam Rockwell (Frank Mercer), Alison Lohman (Angela), Bruce Altman (Dr. Harris Klein), Bruce McGill (Chuck Frechette), Sheila Kelley (Kathy), Beth Grant (Laundry Lady)

A con man with obsessive-compulsive disorder is confronted by the teenage daughter he never knew he had.

Breezy caper movie, updating Paper Moon for an age of mobile phones and skateboards: a spot of light relief for its director, a nice acting workout for its leading man, and an entertaining couple of hours for its audience.

SCR Nicholas Griffin, Ted Griffin CIN John Mathieson MUS Hans Zimmer DES Tom Foden ED Dody Dorn PROD Jack Rapke, Ridley Scott, Steve Starkey, Sean Bailey, Ted Griffin DIST Warner

❝ You can easily lose five minutes making sense of it – and another ten poking holes in it – but what of it? The preceding 100 minutes pass so pleasurably, the few false moves barely register – maybe the biggest con of all. – *Kimberley Jones, Austin Chronicle*

'It takes more than guns to kill a man'

Matewan ★★

SCR/DIR John Sayles
1987   135m   US
DVD   ♫

☆ Chris Cooper (Joe Kenehan), Mary McDonnell (Elma Radnor), Will Oldham (Danny Radnor), David Strathairn (Police Chief Sid Hatfield), Ken Jenkins (Sephus Purcell), Kevin Tighe (Hickey), Gordon Clapp (Griggs), James Earl Jones ('Few Clothes' Johnson), Bob Gunton (C.E. Lively), Jace Alexander (Hillard Elkins)

In 1920s West Virginia, a union rep arrives at the scene of a miners' strike to urge the workforce to stand firm against their bosses.

It's rare to see American films about organised labour, but Sayles handles this unusual material with fluent grace, even if the occasional soliloquy from the union side sounds propagandist.

CIN *Haskell Wexler* MUS Mason Daring DES Nora Chavooshian ED Sonya Polonsky PROD Peggy Rajski, Maggie Renzi DIST Enterprise/Cinecom Entertainment/Film Gallery/Red Dog

⚱ Haskell Wexler (cinematography)

'Believe the unbelievable.'

The Matrix ★★

SCR/DIR *Andy Wachowski, Larry Wachowski*
1999   136m   US/Australia
DVD   ♫

☆ Keanu Reeves (Neo), Laurence Fishburne (Morpheus), Carrie-Anne Moss (Trinity), Hugo Weaving (Agent Smith), Gloria Foster (Oracle), Joe Pantoliano (Cypher), Marcus Chong (Tank), Paul Goddard (Agent Brown), Robert Taylor (Agent Jones), Julian Arahanga (Apoc), Matt Doran

(Mouse), Belinda McClory (Switch), Anthony Ray Parker (Dozer)

A computer hacker is recruited to help expose an alternative reality designed by invading aliens to enslave humanity.

Hugely successful and influential sci-fi blockbuster – a nerd's wet dream, essentially, though less profound and original than it thinks, particularly in its representation of a dystopian futurescape. It deserves credit for at least attempting to blend state-of-the-art thrills, each set-piece insistent on topping the one before, with a more existential line of inquiry. (Or a line of inquiry as existential as a Joel Silver movie will allow.)

CIN Bill Pope   MUS Don Davis   DES Owen Paterson
ED Zach Staenberg   PROD Joel Silver   DIST Warner

66 A wonderfully enjoyable pulp classic - an unalloyed pleasure from first to last, crammed with hi-tech, high-camp action sequences and spiffy effects. And it achieves what I never dreamt was possible - it makes us fall in love with Keanu Reeves all over again. – *Peter Bradshaw, Guardian*

66 From head to tail, the deliciously inventive Wachowskis have delivered the syntax for a new kind of movie: technically mind-blowing, style merged perfectly with content, and just so damn cool the usher will have to drag you kicking and screaming back into reality. – *Ian Nathan, Empire*

† Two sequels followed: The Matrix Reloaded and The Matrix Revolutions (both 2003).

⚖ Zach Staenberg (editing); John Reitz, Gregg Rudloff, David Campbell, David Lee (sound); Dane A. Davis (sound effects editing); John Gaeta, Janek Sirrs, Steve Courtley, Jon Thum (visual effects)

🏆 special visual effects; sound
🏆 Bill Pope; Zach Staenberg; Owen Paterson

A Matter of Life and Death ★★★★
SCR/DIR *Michael Powell, Emeric Pressburger*
1946   104m   GB
DVD

☆ *David Niven* (Squadron Leader Peter D. Carter), *Roger Livesey* (Dr. Reeves), *Kim Hunter* (June), *Marius Goring* (Conductor 71), *Raymond Massey* (Abraham Farlan), *Abraham Sofaer* (The Judge)

A pilot with brain damage after bailing out is torn between this world and the next, but an operation puts things to rights.

Outrageous fantasy which seemed more in keeping after the huge death toll of a world war, and in any case learned the Hollywood lesson of eating its cake and still having it, the supernatural elements being capable of explanation. A mammoth technical job in the heavenly sequences, it deserves full marks for its sheer arrogance, wit, style and film flair.

CIN *Jack Cardiff*   MUS *Allan Gray*   DES *Hein Heckroth*
ED *Reginald Mills*   PROD Michael Powell, Emeric Pressburger   DIST GFD/Archers

66 Powell and Pressburger seem to have reached their heaven at last. . .an illimitable Wembley stadium, surrounded by tinkly music and mists, from which all men of insight, if they were ever careless enough to get

there, would quickly blaspheme their way out. – *Richard Winnington*

66 A dazzling mesh of visionary satire, postwar politics and the mystical side of English romanticism. – *Tony Rayns, Time Out, 1979*

† The film opened in the US under the title Stairway To Heaven.

'In Their Hands, A Deck Of Cards Was The Only Thing More Dangerous Than A Gun.'

Maverick ★
DIR Richard Donner
1994   127m   US
DVD ♫

☆ Mel Gibson (Bret Maverick), Jodie Foster (Annabelle Bransford), James Garner (Marshal Zane Cooper), Graham Greene (Joseph), James Coburn (Commodore Duvall), Alfred Molina (Angel)

In the Wild West, a charming card-sharper meets his match in the shape of a female con artist.

A great TV series, re-tooled for the big screen and specifically for Butch and Sundance fans, who like their western heroes handsome and self-deprecatingly funny. Gibson (who is not a patch on James Garner) flashes his grin throughout, abetted by a William Goldman script that pushes all the buttons marked 'big box-office.' A cynical exercise, maybe, but not an unenjoyable one.

SCR William Goldman   CIN *Vilmos Zsigmond*
MUS Randy Newman   DES Tom Sanders   PROD Bruce Davey, Richard Donner   DIST Warner/Icon

66 Comfortably irreverent. – *Philip Kemp, Sight & Sound*

⚖ April Ferry (costume design)

'Art + Politics = Power'

Max ★★
SCR/DIR *Menno Meyjes*
2002   106m   Hungary/Canada/GB
DVD

☆ John Cusack (Max Rothman), Noah Taylor (Adolf Hitler), Leelee Sobieski (Liselore), Molly Parker (Nina Rothman), Ulrich Thomsen (Captain Mayr), David Horovitch (Max's Father), Janet Suzman (Max's Mother), Peter Capaldi (David Cohn), Kevin McKidd (George Grosz)

Munich, 1918: a prosperous Jewish art dealer forms a relationship with a struggling young artist called Adolf Hitler.

A difficult, sometimes messy, but ultimately rich and evocative portrait of the young Hitler's life and times that flirts with a grim, edgy comedy in several places: few modern films have plunged us so into the maelstrom of art, culture and politics, and fewer still have managed to give such a sense of foreboding to the process of an artist finding his voice.

CIN Lajos Koltai   MUS Dan Jones   DES Ben Van Os
ED Chris Wyatt   PROD Andras Hamori   DIST Pathé

MAX ROTHMAN: "You're an awfully hard man to like, Hitler."

66 A peculiar and intriguing film. – *Roger Ebert, Chicago Sun-Times*

M

DVD Available on DVD   ☆ Cast in order   66 Critics' Quotes   ⚖ Academy Award   🏆 BAFTA
♫ Soundtrack on CD   of importance   † Points of interest   Academy Award nomination   BAFTA nomination

405

66 Doesn't always work, but when it fails, it does so with honour. – *Mark Kermode, Observer*

† The project was condemned by the Jewish Defamation League when news of its production first broke; the condemnation was withdrawn upon seeing the finished film.

McCabe and Mrs Miller ★★★

DIR *Robert Altman*
1971   120m   US
DVD

☆ *Warren Beatty, Julie Christie*, René Auberjonois, Shelley Duvall, John Schuck

At the turn of the century a gambling gunfighter comes to a northwest mining town and uses his money to set up lavish brothels, with his girl-friend as a madam.

Looking both muddy and bleached-out, this dirty-realist epic looks like Altman's riposte to myths about the West propagated by Hollywood; not only in deglamorising the physical conditions of frontier life, but debunking the heroism of pioneers, casting them instead as opportunists out to make a fast buck. It remains a refreshing, dissident take on an established genre.

SCR Robert Altman, Brian McKay   CIN *Vilmos Zsigmond*
DES Leon Ericksen   PROD David Foster, Mitchell Brower
DIST Warner

66 A fleeting, diaphanous vision of what frontier life might have been. – *Pauline Kael*

⚬ Julie Christie (leading actress)

'From Sandra Goldbacher, writer/director of The Governess, comes a film about the agonies and ecstasies of friendship.'

Me Without You ★

DIR Sandra Goldbacher
2001   94m   GB/Germany
DVD   ♫

☆ Anna Friel (Marina), Michelle Williams (Holly), Kyle MacLachlan (Daniel), Oliver Milburn (Nat), Trudie Styler (Linda), Marianne Denicourt (Isabel), Nicky Henson (Ray), Allan Corduner (Max)

Twenty years of friendship and bitter rivalry between two young English women, from their adolescence into their thirties.

Attractive, often caustic story with a rarely made point about friendship – the jealousy and rivalry that dare not speak its name. The underrated Goldbacher relates it in thoughtful detail, though both characters wear out their welcome before the end.

SCR Sandra Goldbacher, Laurence Coriat   CIN Denis Crossan   MUS Adrian Johnston   DES Michael Carlin
ED Michael Ellis   PROD Finola Dwyer
DIST Momentum

66 It's just Single White Female, minus the loud bangs. – *Charlotte O'Sullivan, Sight & Sound*

Ⓣ film

'Beneath the surface, everyone has a secret.'

Mean Creek ★

SCR/DIR *Jacob Aaron Estes*
2004   90m   US
DVD   ♫

☆ Rory Culkin (Sam), Ryan Kelley (Clyde), Scott Mechlowicz (Marty), Trevor Morgan (Rocky), Josh Peck (George), Carly Schroeder (Millie)

A group of classmates elect to take revenge on the school bully during a boating trip, only for their plans to go awry.

Skilfully written retread of waters previously inhabited by River's Edge and Larry Clark's Bully; the direction is just a little too cool and detached to punch up the tragedy that ensues, although a cast of actual teenagers rag and let rip on one another in a believable and largely compelling manner.

CIN Sharone Meir   MUS Tomandandy   DES Greg McMickle   ED Madeleine Gavin   PROD Rick Rosenthal, Susan Johnson, Hagai Shaham   DIST Tartan

66 Like an uncommonly artful and well-acted after-school special. I don't mean this as a put-down: its combination of realism and fretful moral inquiry is best suited to the tastes and sensibilities of young teenagers who devour young-adult fiction. – *Dana Stevens, New York Times*

66 How unusual it is to see kids this age in the movies seriously debating moral rights and wrongs and considering the consequences of their actions. – *Roger Ebert, Chicago Sun-Times*

'Watch your back'

Mean Girls ★

DIR Mark Waters
2004   97m   US
DVD   ♫

☆ Lindsay Lohan (Cady Heron), Rachel McAdams (Regina George), Tina Fey (Ms. Norbury), Tim Meadows (Mr. Duvall), Amy Poehler (Mrs. George), Ana Gasteyer (Cady's Mom)

The daughter of an anthropologist falls under the influence of a powerful clique upon starting a new school.

Certainly smarter than the average teen comedy, but not quite as clever as it could have been, or as it possibly thinks it is; the keen social observation of the earlier scenes falls away as hip-to-be-square homilies come to replace punchlines.

SCR Tina Fey   CIN Daryn Okada   MUS Rolfe Kent
DES Cary White   ED Wendy Greene Bricmont
PROD Lorne Michaels, Tony Shimkin   DIST Paramount

66 Sassy if wildly uneven. – *David Rooney, Variety*

Mean Streets ★★★★

DIR *Martin Scorsese*
1973   110m   US
DVD

☆ *Harvey Keitel* (Charlie), *Robert De Niro* (Johnny Boy), David Proval (Tony), Amy Robinson (Teresa), Richard Romanus (Teresa)

In New York's Little Italy, four young Italian-Americans use a neighbourhood bar as a base for drinking, brawling and hustling.

Melodrama with a good eye for realistic detail, featuring small-time mobsters behaving in self-destructive fashion. The first film in which Scorsese announced himself as a major talent; discovered the partly autobiographical subject matter that has served him so well; used pop music to blistering effect; and crucially, collaborated with De Niro, whose bombastic Johnny Boy is an unforgettable screen character.

SCR Martin Scorsese, Mardik Martin   CIN Kent Wakeford   ED Sid Levin   PROD Jonathan T. Taplin   DIST Taplin-Perry-Scorsese

66 Lacks a sense of story and structure . . . unless a film-maker respects the needs of his audience, he can't complain if that audience fails to show up. – *Variety*

66 A thicker-textured rot than we have ever had in an American movie, and a deeper sense of evil. – *New Yorker*

'A film dedicated to all those who are running away.'

Mediterraneo ★

DIR Gabriele Salvatores
1991   90m   Italy
DVD   ♫

☆ Diego Abatantuono (Nicola Lorusso), Claudio Bigagli (Raffaele Montini), Giuseppe Cederna (Antonio Farina), Claudio Bisio (Corrado Noventa), Gigio Alberti (Eliseo Strazzabosco), Ugo Conti (Luciano Colasanti), Memo Dini (Libero Munaron), Vasco Mirondola (Felice Munaron), Vanna Barba (Vassilissa)

A unit of Italian soldiers in World War II are sent to occupy an idyllic Greek island, and find its peaceable, sensuous atmosphere infectious.

A picture-postcard of a movie – light, undemanding, pleasant to gaze upon – and not worthy of an Oscar for best foreign film.

SCR Enzo Monteleone   CIN Italo Pettriccione   MUS Giancarlo Bigazzi, Marco Falagiani   DES Thalia Istikopoulos   ED Nino Baragali   PROD Gianni Minervini, Silvio Berlusconi, Vittorio Cecchi Gori, Mario Cecchi Gori   DIST Mayfair/Penta/AMA/Berlusconi

66 The surprisingly bitter epilogue doesn't begin to redress the balance. – *Suzi Feay, Time Out*

⊥ foreign film

'The world's most lovable monster is about to surface.'

Mee-Shee: The Water Giant (new)

DIR John Henderson
2005   94m   UK/Germany
DVD

☆ Bruce Greenwood (Sean Cambell), Daniel Magder (Mac Cambell), Rena Owen (Crazy Norma), Phyllida Law (Mrs Coogan), Joe Pingue (Jim Neilds), Shane Rimmer (Bob Anderson), Luanne Gordon (Laura Simmons)

Attempts to recover drilling equipment from the bottom of a lake are complicated by the discovery of a giant, seal-like creature.

Bland children's adventure from the director of the similar Loch Ness; effects are sub-standard, while charm is in short supply.

SCR Barry Authors   CIN John Ignatius   MUS Pol Brennan   DES Chris Wheatley   ED Bill Jones, David Yardley   PROD Barry Authors, Rainer Mockert   DIST The Works

66 A decent family adventure movie in the Spielbergian mould. – *Peter Bradshaw, Guardian*

† The titular monster was designed and built by the Jim Henson Creature Shop.

Meet Me in St Louis ★★★★

DIR Vincente Minnelli
1944   113m   US
DVD   ♫

☆ *Judy Garland* (Esther Smith), *Margaret O'Brien* ('Tootie' Smith), Tom Drake (John Truett), Leon Ames (Mr Alonzo Smith), Mary Astor (Mrs Anne Smith), Lucille Bremer (Rose Smith), June Lockhart (Lucille Ballard), *Harry Davenport* (Grandpa), Marjorie Main, Joan Carroll, Hugh Marlowe, Robert Sully, Chill Wills

A St. Louis family must decide whether to move to New York when the father earns a job promotion.

An MGM musical for the ages, featuring a sweet-natured story and enlivened by simply wonderful songs: Have Yourself A Merry Little Christmas, of course, but specifically The Trolley Song, the vehicle for a brilliant, thrillingly kinetic sequence orchestrated by Minnelli. Garand is at her most radiant, while O'Brien as the troubled Tootie is a corrective to the story's syrupy side.

SCR Irving Brecher, Fred Finklehoffe   CIN George Folsey   ED Albert Akst   PROD Arthur Freed   DIST MGM

66 A family group framed in velvet and tinsel. . .it has everything a romantic musical should have. – *Dilys Powell, 1955*

† 'Meet Me in St Louis'; 'The Boy Next Door'; 'Under the Bamboo Tree'; 'The Trolley Song'; 'You and I'; 'Have Yourself a Merry Little Christmas'

⊥ Irving Brecher Fred F. Finklehoffe (screenplay); George Folsey; Georgie Stoll; Ralph Blane, Hugh Martin (m), (ly) (music, original song – The Trolley Song)

'Think your family's weird?'

Meet the Robinsons ★★

DIR Stephen Anderson
2007   101m   US
DVD   ♫

☆ Daniel Hansen, Jordan Fry (Lewis), Angela Bassett (Mildred), Stephen John Anderson (Bowler Hat Guy), Matthew Josten (Goob), Laurie Metcalf (Lucille), Adam West (Uncle Art), Tom Selleck (Cornelius Robinson), Wesley Singerman (Wilbur Robinson)

A brilliant young inventor attends a science fair and meets a boy named Wilbur, who whisks him off to the future in a time machine.

Frenetic, funny and often dazzlingly inventive, this marks the first welcome sign of Pixar's influence on Disney animation. A story of its young hero Lewis's search for a family to call his own, it's packed with fast-paced verbal and visual gags and appealing characters. The future looks sleek, dazzling and optimistic, and the

DVD Available on DVD   ☆ Cast in order   66 Critics' Quotes   ⊥ Academy Award   🏆 BAFTA
♫ Soundtrack on CD   of importance   † Points of interest   ⊥ Academy Award nomination   🏆 BAFTA nomination

407

Robinson family's eccentricities are delightful. Primarily light-hearted fun, but also a film that applauds rational thought and patient research, and asserts the freedom to fail in pursuit of scientific advances.

SCR Jon Bernstein, Michelle Spitz, Don Hall, Nathan Greno, Aurian Redson, Joe Mateo, Stephen Anderson **MUS** Danny Elfman **ED** Ellen Keneshea **PROD** Dorothy McKim **DIST** Buena Vista

❝ A sharp-minded, plenty entertaining toon that will keep children of all ages wide-eyed and on their toes. – *Todd McCarthy, Variety*

❝ So cleverly executed that one forgives – just – the frenetic pace and absence of down time. – *Ella Taylor, L.A. Weekly*

† The film has also been screened in a 3-D version.

'The Bigger The Hit, The Harder The Fall'
Meet the Spartans (new)
SCR/DIR Jason Friedberg, Aaron Seltzer
2008   84m   US

☆ *Sean Maguire* (Leonidas), *Carmen Electra* (Queen Margo), Kevin Sorbo (Captain), Ken Davitian (Xerxes), Diedrich Bader (Traitoro)

The King of Sparta leads thirteen warriors against an invading army.

The plot of 300 is formlessly plundered for lame innuendo, dated pop-culture jokes and a barrage of gay gladiator gags.

CIN Shawn Maurer   **MUS** Christopher Lennertz **DES** William A. Elliott   **ED** Peck Prior   **PROD** Jason Friedberg, Aaron Seltzer, Peter Safran   **DIST** 20th Century Fox

❝ "The unmistakable air of desperation hangs heavily over the entire production". – *Joe Leydon, Variety*

❝ There are enough homophobic jokes to keep a Midwestern fraternity house laughing for a year. – *Philip French, Observer*

'Life can be a comedy or a tragedy, it all depends on how you look at it.'
Melinda and Melinda ★
SCR/DIR Woody Allen
2004   100m   US
DVD ♫

☆ *Radha Mitchell* (Melinda), Chloe Sevigny (Laurel), Jonny Lee Miller (Lee), Will Ferrell (Hobie), Amanda Peet (Susan), Chiwetel Ejiofor (Ellis), Wallace Shawn (Sy)

Two playwrights sitting in a Manhattan bistro tell the same story, of a single girl arriving late to a dinner party, twice over: first as tragedy, then as comedy.

Sporadically interesting work of dialectical theory, by a director somewhat out of practice, in which moderate comedy trumps moderate drama; a younger, more professionally confident Allen might have plumped for one or the other, and made much of the one integrated story, rather than telling the same one twice with lukewarm results.

CIN *Vilmos Zsigmond*   **DES** Santo Loquasto   **ED** Alisa Lepselter   **PROD** Letty Aronson   **DIST** TCF

❝ It's emotionally more alive than anything Allen has done since Sweet and Lowdown, in 1999. I was absorbed in it, and I liked parts of it. And I wish to God it was better. – *David Denby, New Yorker*

❝ Merely all right – very high-concept and on its way to interesting, but never there. – *Melissa Levine, Dallas Observer*

'Some Memories Are Best Forgotten.'
Memento ★★★
SCR/DIR *Christopher Nolan*
2000   113m   US
DVD ♫

☆ *Guy Pearce* (Leonard), *Carrie-Anne Moss* (Natalie), *Joe Pantoliano* (Teddy), Mark Boone Jnr (Burt), Stephen Tobolowsky (Sammy), Harriet Sansom Harris (Mrs. Jankis), Callum Keith Rennie (Dodd)

In LA an insurance agent with the inability to form short-term memories attempts to avenge the rape and murder of his wife.

An astonishingly ambitious feature for a young British director to undertake as his first American production, attempting – at the end of the movies' first century – to rewrite the rules of narrative cinema in some way: much of what we see takes place in reverse, as dictated by the hero's condition. That it succeeds in not only being comprehensible – thanks to bold, indelible performances – but a resonant musing on identity makes the film even more astounding. Hugely influential among aspiring screenwriters, this is a film that demands fullest attention.

CIN Wally Pfister   **MUS** David Julyan   **DES** Patti Podesta **ED** *Dody Dorn*   **PROD** Suzanne Todd, Jennifer Todd **DIST** Pathé

❝ A provocatively structured and thrillingly executed film noir, an intricate, inventive use of cinema's possibilities that pushes what can be done on screen in an unusual direction. – *Kenneth Turan, Los Angeles Times*

❝ Operates in an orbit somewhere between Oliver Sacks and Lewis Carroll. I can't remember when a movie has seemed so clever, strangely affecting and slyly funny at the same time. – *Joe Morgenstern, Wall Street Journal*

† The DVD offers the chance to view scenes in chronological order.

⚖ Christopher Nolan (original screenplay); Dody Dorn

Memoirs of a Geisha ★
DIR Rob Marshall
2005   145m   US
DVD ♫

☆ *Ziyi Zhang* (Sayuri), Ken Watanabe (The Chairman), Michelle Yeoh (Mameha), Koji Yakusho (Nobu), Youki Kudoh (Pumpkin), Kaori Momoi (Mother), Tsai Chin (Auntie), Cary-Hiroyuki Tagawa (The Baron), Gong Li (Hatsumomo)

A young girl is sold by her father into the life of a geisha, overcoming her rivals to become to the most desired woman in 1940s Japan.

Good-looking but clunky epic of the old Hollywood school, with Chinese actors speaking Japanese and a heroine left to sell her virginity off to the highest bidder; the whole is as fluid as a Sumo wrestler, and as authentically oriental as Sunny Delight.

SCR Robin Swicord CIN Dion Beebe MUS John Williams DES John Myhre ED Pietro Scalia PROD Lucy Fisher, Douglas Wick, Steven Spielberg DIST Columbia TriStar

66 One of those bad Hollywood films that by virtue of their production values nonetheless afford a few dividends, in this case, fabulous clothes and three eminently watchable female leads. – *Manohla Dargis, New York Times*

66 Deluxe orientalist kitsch, a would-be cross between Showgirls and Raise the Red Lantern, too dumb to cause offence though falling short of the oblivious abandon that could have vaulted it into high camp. – *Dennis Lim, Village Voice*

† There were widespread protests in Japan on the film's release over the casting of Chinese actors to play Japanese roles.

⚐ Dion Beebe; John Myhre; Colleen Atwood (costume design)

⚐ John Williams; Kevin O'Connell, Greg P. Russell, Rick Kline, John Pritchett (sound); Wylie Stateman (sound editing)

Ⓣ Dion Beebe; John Williams; Colleen Atwood (costume design)

Ⓣ Ziyi Zhang leading actress); John Myhre; Noriko Watanabe, Kate Biscoe, Lyndell Quiyou, Kelvin R. Trahan (make up/hair)

Memories of Matsuko (new)   ★

SCR/DIR Tetsuya Nakashima
2006 129m Japan
DVD

☆ Miki Nakatani (Matsuko Kawajiri), Yuseke Iseya (Ryu Yoichi), Teruyuki Kagawa (Norio Kawajiri), Eita (Sho Kawajiri), Asuka Kurosawa (Megumi Sawamura), Akira Emoto (Tsenehiro Kawajiri)

The nephew of a murdered bag lady investigates how the former teacher turned prostitute met such a sorry end.

Kaleidoscopic tragi-comedy, structured like Citizen Kane and stylistically redolent of Amélie; the result is a vibrant visual spectacle, albeit one that rather outstays its welcome.

CIN Shoichi Ato MUS Gabriele Roberto DES Towako Kuwashima ED Yoshiyuki Koike PROD Yuji Ishida, Hidemi Satami DIST Third Window Films

66 A strange, candy-coloured and rather beguiling confection. – *Sukhdev Sandhu, Telegraph*

66 Sleek but soulless. – *Russell Edwards, Variety*

Memphis Belle   ★

DIR Michael Caton-Jones
1990 107m GB
DVD ♫

☆ Matthew Modine (Capt. Dennis Dearborn), Eric Stoltz (Sgt. Danny 'Danny Boy' Daly), Tate Donovan (1st Lt. Luke Sinclair), D. B. Sweeney (Lt. Phil Lowenthal), Billy Zane

(Lt. Val 'Valentine' Kozlowski), Sean Astin (Sgt. Richard 'Rascal' Moore), Harry Connick Jnr (Sgt. Clay Busby), Reed Edward Diamond (Sgt. Virgil Hoogesteger), Courtney Gains (Sgt. Eugene McVey), Neil Giuntoli (Sgt. Jack Bocci)

In World War II, the American crew of a B-17 bomber prepare to fly their 25th and last mission over Germany.

An exercise in nostalgia, with aerial footage of dog-fights that surpasses the human drama within the plane. This deliberate homage to earlier war films did not appeal to as wide an audience as was anticipated.

SCR Monte Merrick CIN David Watkin MUS George Fenton DES Stuart Craig ED Jim Clark PROD David Puttnam, Catherine Wyler DIST Warner/Enigma

66 For the most part, sensitive, gripping, oddly old-fashioned cinema. – *Geoff Andrew, Time Out*

Ⓣ George Fenton (original film score)

'A completely new experience between men and women!'

The Men   ★★★

DIR Fred Zinnemann
1950 85m US
DVD

☆ *Marlon Brando* (Ken), *Teresa Wright* (Ellen), *Everett Sloane* (Dr. Brock), Jack Webb (Norm), Howard St John (Ellen's Father)

Paraplegic war veterans are prepared for civilian life; the fiancée of one of them helps overcome his problems.

Vivid semi-documentary melodrama, at the time rather shocking in its no-holds-barred treatment of sexual problems. Serous-minded work, best remembered as Brando's film debut.

SCR *Carl Foreman* CIN Robert de Grasse MUS Dimitri Tiomkin DES Edward G. Boyle ED Harry Gerstad DIST Stanley Kramer

66 Don't be misled into feeling that to see this film is merely a duty; it is, simply, an experience worth having. – *Richard Mallett, Punch*

⚐ Carl Foreman (original screenplay)

Men Don't Leave   ★

DIR Paul Brickman
1990 115m US

☆ *Jessica Lange* (Beth Macauley), Arliss Howard (Charles Simon), Joan Cusack (Jody), Kathy Bates (Lisa Coleman), Tom Mason (John Macauley), Chris O'Donnell (Chris Macauley), Charlie Korsmo (Matt Macauley), Belita Moreno (Mrs. Buckley), Jim Haynie (Mr. Buckley), Cory Carrier (Winston Buckley), Shannon Moffett (Dale Buckley)

A depressed widow with two young sons tries to piece her life back together after her husband's accidental death.

Unjustly neglected but soundly scripted film, with a terrific performance by Lange.

DVD Available on DVD   ☆ Cast in order   66 Critics' Quotes   ⚐ Academy Award   Ⓣ BAFTA
♫ Soundtrack on CD   of importance   † Points of interest   ⚐ Academy Award nomination   Ⓣ BAFTA nomination

409

SCR Barbara Benedek, Paul Brickman   CIN Bruce Surtees
MUS Thomas Newman   DES Barbara Ling   ED Richard
Chew   PROD Jon Avnet   DIST Warner

'Protecting The Earth From The Scum Of The
Universe.'

Men in Black ★★

DIR *Barry Sonnenfeld*
1997 98m US
DVD ♫

☆ *Tommy Lee Jones* (K), Will Smith (J), Linda Fiorentino
(Laurel), *Vincent D'Onofrio* (Edgar), Rip Torn (Zed), Tony
Shalhoub (Jeebs), Siobhan Fallon (Beatrice)

A young cop is recruited by a top-secret government
organisation charged with monitoring the
behaviour of alien life forms on Earth.

*Lively, fast-moving event movie that takes great care not
to drown the engaging human players under its layers of
(often witty) out-of-this-world effects.*

SCR Ed Solomon   CIN Don Peterman   MUS Danny
Elfman   DES Bo Welch   ED Jim Miller   PROD Walter F.
Parkes, Laurie MacDonald   DIST Columbia/Amblin

66 Behind its mask of deadpan goofiness, it's a friendly,
clever picture, one that doesn't feel untouched by human
hands. And at an hour-and-a-half, it doesn't wear out its
welcome. – *Charles Taylor, Salon*

† A sequel, widely deemed inferior, was released in
2002.

⚱ Rick Baker, David LeRoy Anderson (make up)
⚱ Danny Elfman; Bo Welch
Ⓣ Eric Brevig, Rick Baker, Rob Coleman, Peter Chesney
(special effects)

Men with Guns ★★

SCR/DIR *John Sayles*
1997 127m US
DVD ♫

☆ Federico Luppi (Dr. Fuentes), Damian Delgado
(Domingo, the Soldier), Dan Rivera (Conejo, the Boy),
Tania Cruz (Graciela, the Mute Girl), Damian Alcazar
(Padre Portillo, the Priest), Mandy Patinkin (Andrew),
Kathryn Grody (Harriet), Iguandili Lopez (Mother), Nandi
Luna Ramirez (Daughter), Rafael de Quevedo (General),
Roberto Sosa (Bravo)

An aged doctor in a Mexican city takes a sabbatical
to track down former students working in the wilds
of South America, becoming aware of various
atrocities en route.

*Powerful Spanish-language road movie that addresses
one continent's turbulent history and the need for
greater political vigilance in the West; despite the
bloodshed we witness, it arrives at a hopeful place.*

CIN Slawomir Idziak   MUS Mason Daring   DES Felipe
Fernandez Del Paso   ED John Sayles   PROD R. Paul
Miller, Maggie Renzi   DIST Lexington Road/Clear Blue
Sky/IFC/Anarchists' Convention

66 Immensely moving and sad, and yet because it dares
so much, it is an exhilarating film. – *Roger Ebert, Chicago
Sun-Times*

66 A film of beauty, integrity, power and compassion. –
Geoff Andrew, Time Out

'This is the truth. This is what's real.'

Menace II Society ★

DIR Allen Hughes, Albert Hughes
1993 97m US
DVD ♫

☆ Tyrin Turner (Caine 'Kaydee' Lawson), Jada Pinkett
(Ronnie), Larenz Tate (Kevin 'O-Dog'), Arnold Johnson
(Grandpapa), MC Eiht (A-Wax), Marilyn Coleman
(Grandmama), Vonte Sweet (Sharif), Clifton Powell (Lew-
Loc), Samuel L. Jackson (Tat Lawson)

A young black man in the Watts district of LA lives a
double life, attempting to graduate and care for his
girlfriend while dealing drugs and evading the law.

*Middleweight entry in the 'hood' movie cycle of the early
1990s, getting at some of the social realities of the time
while heading towards a schematically tragic outcome.*

SCR Tyger Williams, Allen Hughes, Albert Hughes
CIN Lisa Rinzler   MUS QD III   DES Penny Barrett
ED Christopher Koefoed   PROD Darin Scott   DIST First
Independent/New Line

66 One chillingly authentic scene after another. – *Brad
Laidman, Film Threat*

66 A compendium of clichés. . .photographed, scored and
performed with more flair than the material deserves. –
Geoff Andrew, Time Out

† The film's UK video release was delayed due to concerns
over its violent content.

Mephisto ★★★

DIR *István Szabó*
1981 144m Hungary
DVD

☆ *Klaus Maria Brandauer* (Hendrik Hofgen), Ildikó
Bánsági (Nicoletta Von Niebuhr), Krystyna Janda (Barbara
Bruckner)

In 1920s Germany, an actor committed to the idea
of a workers' theatre ends up becoming a puppet of
the Nazis.

*Brandauer is a standout as a man who all too willingly
compromises his beliefs for career advancement in a
troubling, compelling drama; it reveals the sly strategies
employed by the Nazis to ensnare people by locating
their weaknesses.*

SCR Peter Dobai, István Szabó   CIN *Lajos Koltai*
MUS Zdenko Tamassy   ED Zsuzsa Csakany
DIST Mafilm/Manfred Durniok

⚱ foreign film

Merci Pour Le Chocolat ★

DIR Claude Chabrol
2000 99m France/Switzerland
DVD

☆ Isabelle Huppert (Marie-Claire 'Mika' Muller), Jacques
Dutronc (André Polonski), Anna Mouglalis (Jeanne
Pollet), Rodolphe Pauly (Guillaume Polonski), Michel
Robin (Dufreigne), Brigitte Catillon (Louise Pollet),
Mathieu Simonet (Axel)

A concert pianist remarries his first wife, a
chocolate company heiress, and a young piano
student starts to believe she may be his daughter.

Chabrol, a fervent Hitchcock disciple, channels the Master in this enjoyable, noirish thriller set among the bourgeoisie – scrupulously polite and proper on the surface, but seething with wayward passions and murderous thoughts inside.

SCR Caroline Eliacheff, Claude Chabrol   **CIN** Renato Berta   **MUS** Matthieu Chabrol   **DES** Ivan Niclass   **ED** Monique Fardoulis   **PROD** Marin Karmitz   **DIST** Artificial Eye

66 Chabrol, French cinema's definitive Comeback Kid, has done it again. – *Keith Reader, Sight & Sound*

Metropolis   ★★★

DIR *Fritz Lang*
1926   120m   Germany
DVD   ♫

☆ *Brigitte Helm* (Maria/The Robot), Alfred Abel (Joh Frederson), Gustav Fröhlich (Freder Frederson), Rudolf Klein-Rogge (Rotwang), Fritz Rasp (The Man of Black)

In the year 2000, the workers in a modernistic city live underground. Unrest is quelled by the persuasion of a saintly girl, Maria; but a demented inventor creates an evil Maria to incite them to revolt.

Overlong and heavy-going in places, this futuristic fantasy not only has many brilliant sequences which created genuine excitement and terror, but inspired many Hollywood clichés, notably the Frankenstein theme.

SCR *Thea von Harbou*   **CIN** *Karl Freund, Günther Rittau*   **PROD** Erich Pommer   **DIST** UFA

66 It goes too far and always gets away with it. – *New Yorker, 1978*

66 A wonderful, stupefying folly. – *New Yorker, 1982*

† In 1984 Giorgio Moroder put out his own new version, with tinted sequences and a re-edited running time of 83 minutes. It was received with a mixture of distaste, respect and caution.

'Finally. . .A film about the downwardly mobile.'

Metropolitan   ★★★

SCR/DIR *Whit Stillman*
1989   98m   US
DVD   ♫

☆ Carolyn Farina (Audrey Rouget), Edward Clements (Tom Townsend), *Christopher Eigeman* (Nick Smith), Taylor Nichols (Charlie Black), Allison Parisi (Jane Clarke), Dylan Hundley (Sally Fowler), Isabel Gillies (Cynthia McClean), Bryan Leder (Fred Neff), Will Kempe (Rick Von Sloneker)

New York, the late 1980s: a cash-strapped young man falls in with a group of rich socialites.

Graceful portrait of a social set insistent on putting the world to rights while singularly failing to cope with any world other than their own; an intelligent, civilised comedy of manners, it is not a million miles away from the Jane Austen novels so beloved by the characters.

CIN John Thomas   **MUS** Mark Suozzo, Tom Judson   **ED** Christopher Tellefsen   **PROD** Whit Stillman   **DIST** Mainline/Westerly Film-Video/Allagash Films

66 A film F. Scott Fitzgerald might have been comfortable with, a film about people covering their own insecurities

with a facade of social ease. – *Roger Ebert, Chicago Sun-Times*

Whit Stillman (original screenplay)

'Lipstick and attitude – the girls from Echo Park are hard!'

Mi Vida Loca   ★

SCR/DIR Allison Anders
1993   92m   US
DVD   ♫

☆ Angel Aviles (Sad Girl), Seidy Lopez (Mousie), Jacob Vargas (Ernesto), Marlo Marron (Giggles), Nelida Lopez (Whisper), Jessie Borrego (El Duran), Magali Alvarado (La Blue Eyes)

Hispanic teenage girls, with their brothers and boyfriends either dead, disabled or in prison, form a bond on the streets.

Some naïve acting performances, a scattered narrative and intrusive voice-overs prevent an otherwise revealing, decent film from realising its potential.

CIN Rodrigo Garcia   **MUS** John Taylor   **DES** Jane Ann Stewart   **ED** Kathryn Himoff, Tracy Granger, Richard Chew   **PROD** Carl Colpaert, Daniel Hassid

66 Brilliant study of girl gangs in Los Angeles' Echo Park. – *Hal Hinson, Washington Post*

'Real badge. Real gun. Fake cop.'

Miami Blues   ★★

SCR/DIR George Armitage
1990   97m   US
DVD

☆ Fred Ward (Sgt. Hoke Moseley), *Jennifer Jason Leigh* (Susie Waggoner), *Alec Baldwin* (Frederick J. Frenger Jr.), Cecilia Perez-Cervera (Stewardess), Georgie Cranford (Little Boy at Miami Airport), Edward Saxon (Krishna Ravindra at Miami Airport), Jose Perez (Pablo), Obba Babatunde (Blink Willie, Informant)

A sociopath, freed from jail, steals the gun and badge of a detective who is tailing him, and goes on a murderous shoot-out, while pretending to be a cop.

The work of pulp-influenced novelist Charles Willeford is as elusive in adaptation as Elmore Leonard's, and this screen version narrowly misses capturing the source book's wayward tone. Yet it's enjoyable enough, with colourful performances, notably Baldwin, playing a baddie with real relish, and Leigh as a child-like prostitute.

CIN Tak Fujimoto   **MUS** Gary Chang   **DES** Maher Ahmad   **ED** Craig McKay   **PROD** Jonathan Demme, Gary Goetzman   **DIST** Rank/Orion/Tristes Tropiques

'Love is great. Marriage is a completely different affair.'

Miami Rhapsody   ★

SCR/DIR David Frankel
1995   105m   US
DVD   ♫

☆ *Sarah Jessica Parker* (Gwyn Marcus), Gil Bellows (Matt), Antonio Banderas (Antonio), Mia Farrow (Nina Marcus), Paul Mazursky (Vic Marcus), Kevin Pollak (Jordan Marcus), Barbara Garrick (Terri), Naomi Campbell (Kaia)

DVD Available on DVD   ☆ Cast in order of importance   66 Critics' Quotes   † Points of interest   Academy Award   Academy Award nomination   BAFTA   BAFTA nomination

411

Before she accepts a marriage proposal, a woman surveys the chaotic, wrecked relationships of those closest to her.

Widely criticised for being over-derivative of Woody Allen, this is nevertheless a sharp, smart, attractive comedy with deft one-liners and careful avoidance of sentimentality. Parker really shines in the lead role; in retrospect, it's surprising that she only emerged as a major star via television.

CIN Jack Wallner MUS Mark Isham DES J. Mark Harrington ED Steven Weisberg PROD Barry Jossen, David Frankel DIST Buena Vista/Hollywood/Cantaloupe

66 High-gloss comedy of manners. – *Jonathan Romney, Sight & Sound*

'The truth can be adjusted.'

Michael Clayton (new) ★★★★

SCR/DIR *Tony Gilroy*
2007 119m US
DVD ♫

☆ *George Clooney* (Michael Clayton), *Tom Wilkinson* (Arthur Edens), *Tilda Swinton* (Karen Crowder), *Sydney Pollack* (Marty Bach), Michael O'Keefe (Barry Grissom)

Clayton, an in-house fixer at a New York corporate law firm, with a disastrous private life, must rescue one of the firm's clients, a shady chemical company being sued for poisoning people with weed-killer. He suffers a crisis of conscience.

Intelligent, literate thriller, blessed with a near-faultless script and boasting superb performances down to the minor roles. Extraordinarily satisfying.

CIN Robert Elswit MUS James Newton Howard DES Kevin Thompson ED John Gilroy PROD Sydney Pollack, Steven Samuels, Jennifer Fox, Kerry Orent DIST Pathé

CLAYTON: 'Do I look like I'm negotiating?'
CLAYTON: 'You're a manic depressive.'
EDENS: 'I am Shiva, the god of death!'
CLAYTON: 'I'm not a miracle worker, I'm a janitor.'

66 What we have at the heart of this excellent thriller is a story of greed, the misuse of the law, the contempt of the powerful for the weak, and the small window of decency through which such things can be corrected. – *Philip French, Observer*

66 The movie is not so much a paranoia thriller, more a character study – showing the corrosive effect of years of swallowed disappointment. – *Peter Bradshaw, Guardian*

Tilda Swinton (supporting actor)
Best picture; Tony Gilroy (direction); Tony Gilroy (original screenplay); George Clooney; Tom Wilkinson; James Newton Howard

Tilda Swinton
Tony Gilroy (screenplay); George Clooney; Tom Wilkinson; editing

---

'An Epic Tale Of Passion And Destiny.'

Michael Collins ★★

SCR/DIR *Neil Jordan*
1996 133m US
DVD ♫

☆ *Liam Neeson* (Michael Collins), Aidan Quinn (Harry Boland), Stephen Rea (Ned Broy), Alan Rickman (Eamon de Valera), Julia Roberts (Kitty Kiernan), Ian Hart (Joe O'Reilly), Richard Ingram (British Officer), John Kenny (Patrick Pearse)

Biopic of the Irish Republican leader, covering the years between the Easter Rising in 1916 and his assassination six years later.

Given the controversial subject matter, perhaps it's inevitable the film's portrayal of actual historical events – notably Collins's dealings with the British – should provoke such heated debate, but on a purely cinematic level, it remains one of its director's finest achievements: a work of evident passion and conviction, with a skilful lead performance.

CIN *Chris Menges* MUS Elliot Goldenthal DES Antony Pratt ED J. Patrick Duffner, Tony Lawson PROD Stephen Woolley DIST Warner/Geffen

66 A thriller with a real sense of scale, pace, menace and moral import. – *Geoff Andrew, Time Out*

66 Rousing, rough-hewn and raw, like its subject. – *Tom Shone, Sunday Times*

† The film won prizes for Best Actor and Best Film at the 1996 Venice film festival.
† Before its release, it was the subject if a sustained attack by sections of the British tabloid press, which charged that it was anti-British, and might even derail the peace process in Northern Ireland.

Chris Menges; Elliot Goldenthal
Alan Rickman (supporting actor); Chris Menges

'A Romantic Comedy You Can't Refuse.'

Mickey Blue Eyes ★

DIR Kelly Makin
1999 103m US/GB
DVD ♫

☆ Hugh Grant (Michael Felgate), James Caan (Frank Vitale), Jeanne Tripplehorn (Gina Vitale), Burt Young (Vito Graziosi), James Fox (Philip Cromwell), Joe Viterelli (Vinnie), Gerry Becker (Agent Connell), Maddie Corman (Carol), Tony Darrow (Angelo), Paul Lazar (Ritchie Vitale)

In New York, a well-spoken English auctioneer falls in love with a teacher whose mobster father is the local don.

A fish-out-of-water comedy, ideal for Grant, with his diffident, hesitant Englishman act, to rub up against the more forthright social manners of mobsters. Enjoyable while it lasts, though not remotely memorable.

SCR Adam Scheinman, Robert Kuhn CIN Donald E. Thorin MUS Basil Poledouris DES Gregory Keen ED David Freeman PROD Elizabeth Hurley, Charles Mulvehill DIST Universal

---

Microcosmos ★

SCR/DIR Claude Nuridsany, Marie Pérennou
1996 80m France/Switzerland/Italy
DVD ♫

☆ Jacques Perrin (Narrator (French version)), Kristin Scott Thomas (Narrator (English version))

Documentary study of 24 hours in the life of a French meadow.

DVD Available on DVD ☆ Cast in order of importance 66 Critics' Quotes † Points of interest Academy Award Academy Award nomination BAFTA BAFTA nomination

Diverting look at the world beneath our feet: its photography of stag beetles fighting a duel or caterpillars tripping over one another is rarely less than extraordinary. But certain sequences look more than a little contrived.

CIN *Claude Nuridsany, Marie Pérennou, Hugues Ryffel, Thierry Machado* MUS Bruno Coulais ED Marie-Josèphe Yoyotte, Florence Ricard PROD Jacques Perrin, Christophe Barratier, Yvette Mallet
DIST Guild/Galatée/France 2/Bac/Delta/JMH/Urania

66 I can't recall a documentary which has done more to reveal the beauty, strangeness and horror of the natural world. – *Christopher Tookey, Daily Mail*

Midnight ★★★

DIR *Mitchell Leisen*
1939 95m US

☆ *Claudette Colbert* (Eve Peabody/'Baroness Czerny'), Don Ameche (Tibor Czerny), *John Barrymore* (George Flammarion), Francis Lederer (Jacques Picot), Mary Astor (Helene Flammarion), Elaine Barrie (Simone), Hedda Hopper (Stephanie), Rex O'Malley (Marcel)

A cash-strapped young American woman arrives in Paris at midnight, is courted by a Hungarian cab driver, who helps her pass herself off as a Hungarian countess, hired by a wealthy man to seduce the gigolo chasing his wife.

Sparkling, sophisticated, and for its time sexually candid comedy which gallops along at a relentless pace, with the whole cast in effervescent form. As co-writer, Wilder brought a touch of European knowingness to English-speaking audiences.

SCR *Billy Wilder, Charles Brackett* CIN Charles Lang MUS Frederick Hollander ED Doane Harrison PROD Arthur Hornblow Jnr DIST Paramount

66 Leisen's masterpiece, one of the best comedies of the thirties. – *John Baxter, 1968*

66 One of the authentic delights of the thirties. – *New Yorker, 1976*

'To tell you the truth, I ain't a real cowboy. But I'm one helluva stud!'

Midnight Cowboy ★★★★

DIR *John Schlesinger*
1969 113m US
DVD ♫

☆ *Jon Voight* (Joe Buck), *Dustin Hoffman* (Enrico 'Ratso' Rizzo), Brenda Vaccaro (Shirley), Sylvia Miles (Cass), John McGiver (Mr. O'Daniel)

A dim-witted Texan comes to New York to offer his services as a stud for rich women, but to his distaste is forced by economic hardship to service gay men too. He falls in with a tubercular con artist, and they form an unlikely friendship.

An unblinking gaze at Manhattan's seedy side, where harshness can co-exist with surprising tenderness. At the time, the film looked like a stern response to the consequence-free ethos of drop-out culture. Hoffman and Voight, two very different actors playing contrasting characters, constitute a dream team; by its end, this

harrowing account feels more like a rites-of-passage story.

SCR *Waldo Salt* CIN *Adam Holender* DES John Robert Lloyd ED Hugh A. Robertson DIST UA/Jerome Hellman

66 If only Schlesinger's directorial self-discipline had matched his luminous sense of scene and his extraordinary skill in handling actors, this would have been a far more considerable film. – *Arthur Schlesinger Jnr. (no relation)*

66 A great deal besides cleverness, a great deal of good feeling and perception and purposeful dexterity. – *Stanley Kauffmann*

† It was the only film released with an X certificate in the US to win a best picture Oscar.

🏆 picture; John Schlesinger (direction); Waldo Salt (adapted screenplay)
Ⓐ Dustin Hoffman (leading actor); Jon Voight (leading actor); Sylvia Miles (supporting actress)

🅑 picture; Dustin Hoffman (leading actor); Jon Voight (leading actor); John Schlesinger (direction); Waldo Salt (adapted screenplay)

Midnight Express ★★★

DIR Alan Parker
1978 121m GB
DVD ♫

☆ Brad Davis, Randy Quaid, John Hurt, Irene Miracle, Bo Hopkins

An American student is caught trying to smuggle drugs out of Turkey, and thrown into a nightmarish jail.

Bombastic, emotionally manipulative but undeniably effective account of a harrowing story. Stone's script may take a superficial approach to its subject, and it may be guilty of xenophobia, but none of that makes it unwatchable; Parker at his best can bend an audience to his will.

SCR Oliver Stone CIN Michael Seresin MUS Giorgio Moroder PROD Alan Marshall, David Puttnam DIST Columbia/Casablanca

66 One of the ugliest sado-masochistic trips, with heavy homosexual overtones, that our thoroughly nasty movie age has yet produced. – *Richard Schickel, Time*

66 The film details all [the horrors] so relentlessly on one screaming note that it is rather like being hit in the gut until you no longer feel a thing. – *Derek Malcolm, Guardian*

🏆 Oliver Stone (adapted screenplay); music
Ⓐ picture; John Hurt (supporting actor); Alan Parker (direction)

🅑 John Hurt (supporting actor); Alan Parker (direction)

'Welcome To Savannah, Georgia. A City Of Hot Nights And Cold Blooded Murder.'

Midnight in the Garden of Good and Evil ★

DIR Clint Eastwood
1997 155m US
DVD ♫

☆ Kevin Spacey (James 'Jim' Williams), John Cusack (John Kelso), *Jack Thompson* (Sonny Seiler), *The Lady*

					413

DVD Available on DVD ☆ Cast in order 66 Critics' Quotes 🏆 Academy Award 🅑 BAFTA
♫ Soundtrack on CD   of importance † Points of interest   Ⓐ Academy Award nomination ⓑ BAFTA nomination

Chablis (as herself), Alison Eastwood (Mandy Nichols), Irma P. Hall (Minerva), Paul Hipp (Joe Odom), Jude Law (Billy Carl Hanson), Dorothy Loudon (Serena Dawes), Anne Haney (Margaret Williams), Kim Hunter (Betty Harty), Geoffrey Lewis (Luther Driggers)

A New York journalist visiting Savannah, Georgia becomes caught up in the story of a wealthy socialite charged with murdering a rent boy.

Florid rendering of a true-life story, based on a compelling book. It manages plenty of atmosphere and colour at the expense of any real narrative drive; Cusack's reporter has only to keep from tripping over his dropped jaw as he stumbles between the assembled eccentrics.

SCR John Lee Hancock   CIN Jack N. Green   MUS Lennie Niehaus   DES Henry Bumstead   ED Joel Cox
PROD Clint Eastwood, Arnold Stiefel
DIST Warner/Malpaso/Silver

66 An outstanding lean film trapped in a fat film's body. – *Todd McCarthy, Variety*

Midnight Movies: From the Margin to the Mainstream ★★

DIR Stuart Samuels
2005   88m   US/Canada
DVD

☆ *George Romero, John Waters, Alejandro Jodorowsky, David Lynch, Perry Henzell, Richard O'Brien*

The talent behind six movies, including El Topo and Eraserhead, discuss how their cutting-edge work changed the way 1970s audiences viewed cult movies.

Engaging, informative clip-and-interview round-up of key players in the Midnight Movie trend that found its unlikely apotheosis in The Rocky Horror Picture Show.

SCR Victor Kushmaniuk, Stuart Samuels   CIN Richard Fox   MUS Eric Cadesky, Nick Dyer   ED Michael Bembenek; Robert J. Coleman, John Dowding, Lorenzo Massa, Kevin Rollins   PROD Stuart Samuels
DIST Metrodome

66 An enjoyable, if blandly celebratory documentary. – *Peter Bradshaw, Guardian*

'Robert De Niro has to get the FBI off his case, the mob off his trail, and Charles Grodin off his back!'

Midnight Run ★★★

DIR Martin Brest
1988   126m   US
DVD   ♫

☆ *Robert De Niro* (Jack Walsh), *Charles Grodin* (Jonathan Mardukas), Yaphet Kotto (FBI Agent Alonzo Mosely), John Ashton (Marvin Dorfler), Dennis Farina (Jimmy Serrano), Joe Pantoliano (Eddie Moscone)

A bounty hunter captures a bail-hopping swindler in New York; handcuffed together they cross America to L.A., chased by gangsters and lawmen.

First rate amalgam of three distinct genres: road movie, action thriller and comedy. Terrifically enjoyable on all fronts, with De Niro and Grodin an outstanding, genuinely funny 'odd couple.'

SCR George Gallo   CIN Donald Thorin   MUS Danny Elfman   DES Angelo Graham   ED Billy Weber, Chris Lebenzon, Michael Tronick   PROD Martin Brest
DIST UIP/Universal

66 Here and there, director Brest succumbs to the car chase, but overall, the movie is way above average for the genre. – *Brian Case, Time Out*

Mifune ★★

DIR Soren Kragh-Jacobsen
1999   98m   Denmark/Sweden
DVD

☆ Anders W. Berthelsen (Kresten), Iben Hjejle (Liva), Jesper Asholt (Rud), Emil Tarding (Bjarke), Anders Hove (Gerner), Sofie Grabol (Claire), Paprika Steen (Pernille), Mette Bratlann (Nina)

An ambitious young businessman marries his boss's daughter, all the while disguising his humble rural origins. When his father dies back home, and he cannot take care of his retarded brother, he hires a housekeeper, who turns out to be a prostitute.

Subtly delightful story about human frailty, pretence and honesty, that winds its way to a not unexpected resolution.

SCR Soren Kragh-Jacobsen, Anders Thomas Jensen
CIN Anthony Dod Mantle   MUS Thor Backhausen, Karl Bille, Christian Sievert   ED Valdis Oskarasdottir
PROD Brigitte Hald, Morten Kaufmann   DIST Alliance

66 If the story is immensely satisfying in a traditional way, the style has its own delights. – *Roger Ebert, Chicago Sun-Times*

'The quest for friendship is the noblest cause of all.'

The Mighty ★★

DIR *Peter Chelsom*
1998   100m   US
DVD

☆ Sharon Stone (Gwen Dillon), Gena Rowlands (Gram), Harry Dean Stanton (Grim), *Kieran Culkin* (Kevin Dillon), *Elden Hanson* (Maxwell Kane), *Gillian Anderson* (Loretta Lee), James Gandolfini (Kenny Kane), Joe Perrino (Blade), Meat Loaf (Iggy), Jenifer Lewis (Mrs. Addison)

A bright but physically fragile boy befriends a hulking classmate who has learning difficulties.

Charming family movie that communicates its themes of loyalty and mutual understanding with great intelligence, making optimum use of a tremendous (and tremendously diverse) cast: a real gem.

SCR *Charles Leavitt*   CIN John de Borman   MUS Trevor Jones   DES Caroline Hanania   ED Martin Walsh
PROD Jane Startz, Simon Fields
DIST Miramax/Scholastic

66 Although it's ruthlessly after your heartstrings, The Mighty is distinctive for the grimness of its worldview - the Cincinnati setting is squalid in the extreme, the bad kids aspiring Scorsese extras, and there's much trauma that Chelsom is tough enough not to bowdlerise... superior, thoughtful teenage entertainment. – *Jonathan Romney, Guardian*

66 Keeps the story true to life and grounded in the everyday reality of its working-class setting through many

moods, while disease-of-the-week cliches are dodged with rare sensitivity. – *Angie Errigo, Empire*

Mighty Aphrodite ★

SCR/DIR Woody Allen
1995 95m US
DVD ♫

☆ Woody Allen (Lenny), Helena Bonham Carter (Amanda), *Mira Sorvino* (Linda Ash), Michael Rapaport (Kevin), F. Murray Abraham (Leader), Claire Bloom (Amanda's Mother), Olympia Dukakis (Jocasta), David Ogden Stiers (Laius), Jack Warden (Tiresias), Peter Weller (Jerry Bender)

A sportswriter and his wife adopt a baby, only to discover that the child's mother is a prostitute and amateur porn star.

Frothy comedy, lent some distinction by Sorvino's deeper-than-required performance and the use of a Greek chorus to comment on some very contemporary action.

CIN Carlo DiPalma DES Santo Loquasto ED Susan E. Morse PROD Robert Greenhut
DIST Miramax/Seetland/Jean Doumanian

❝ It treads enjoyably over old ground, and it has a surprisingly foul mouth, though rather than cruising along with the ease of Allen's best work it tends to hobble, and it closes in a flurry of undecided endings. – *Anthony Lane, The New Yorker*

⚲ Mira Sorvino (supporting actress)
⚱ Woody Allen (original screenplay)
Ⓣ Mira Sorvino (supporting actress)

'It was an event that shocked the world. This is the story you haven't heard.'

A Mighty Heart (new) ★★

DIR Michael Winterbottom
2007 100m US/UK
DVD ♫

☆ Angelina Jolie (Mariane), Dan Futterman (Daniel), Archie Panjabi (Asra), *Irrfan Khan* (Captain), Denis O'Hare (John Bussey), Will Patton (Randall Bennett), Adnan Siddiqui (Dost Aliani), Gary Wilmes (Steve LeVine)

An account of the 2002 kidnapping and execution of American journalist Daniel Pearl by Islamic militants in Karachi, as experienced by his wife Mariane.

Director Winterbottom brings his usual bristling energy, pace and sense of detail to depicting the chaotic, teeming, apparently unknowable streets of Karachi. Yet perhaps because we know the outcome of this awful story, the film lacks tension. Jolie's performance as Mariane Pearl is a trifle flat, until her agonised keening when she accepts her husband is dead. But creditably she always seems part of an ensemble than a star actress doing an isolated turn.

SCR John Orloff CIN Marcel Zyskind MUS Harry Escott, Molly Nyman DES Mark Digby ED Peter Christelis PROD Dede Gardner, Brad Pitt, Andrew Eaton
DIST Paramount

❝ Despite the best of intentions, an actress who makes her own headlines gets in the way of the big picture. – *Lisa Schwarzbaum, Entertainment Weekly*

❝ It doesn't reduce the Daniel Pearl story to a plot, but elevates it to a tragedy. – *Roger Ebert, Chicago Sun-Times*

'Back together for the first time, again.'

A Mighty Wind ★

DIR Christopher Guest
2003 90m US
DVD ♫

☆ Bob Balaban (Jonathan Steinbloom), Christopher Guest (Alan Barrows), John Michael Higgins (Terry Bohner), Eugene Levy (Mitch Cohen), Jane Lynch (Laurie Bohner), Michael McKean (Jerry Palter), *Catherine O'Hara* (Mickey Devlin Crabbe), Parker Posey (Sissy Knox)

A 1960s folk trio prepare for a memorial concert.

Pleasant mockumentary, a tribute to earnest 1960s folk music without much underlying satirical bite; it's amusing enough, but a so-so effort for this crowd.

SCR Christopher Guest, Eugene Levy CIN Arlene Donnelly Nelson MUS Christopher Guest, Michael McKean, Harry Shearer, Eugene Levy, Annette O'Toole, Catherine O'Hara, C.J. Vanston, John Michael Higgins
DES Joseph T. Garrity ED Robert Leighton
PROD Karen Murphy DIST Warner

❝ An amusing gallery of incisively observed characters, riffing off each other with enjoyment levels that frequently prove contagious. – *David Rooney, Variety*

⚲ Michael McKean, Annette O'Toole (music, original song – A Kiss at the End of the Rainbow)

'Milagro, New Mexico. Population 426. Nothing had changed here for 300 years. But there's something about this day...'

The Milagro Beanfield War ★★

DIR Robert Redford
1988 117m US
DVD

☆ Ruben Blades (Sheriff Bernabe Montoya), Richard Bradford (Ladd Devine), Sonia Braga (Ruby Archuleta), Julie Carmen (Nancy Mondragon), James Gammon (Horsethief Shorty), John Heard (Charlie Bloom), M. Emmet Walsh (Governor)

Farmers in New Mexico unite to take a stand against the development of a leisure resort on their land.

An early entry in Hollywood's green cycle, this beguiling, sun-kissed drama takes a laidback, whimsical, largely amiable approach to the altogether serious issue of land exploitation; something like a cornball, whitebread version of a John Sayles movie, it remains watchable all the same.

SCR *David Ward, John Nichols* CIN *Robbie Greenberg*
MUS *Dave Grusin* DES Tom Roysden, Joe Aubel
ED Dede Allen, Jim Miller PROD Robert Redford, Moctesuma Esparza DIST Universal

❝ Ostensibly a celebration of the triumph of community over exploitation and injustice, Redford's film sustains a slow mood of simpatico amiability and photographs the landscape with moony or golden washes that are perhaps hard to dislike, but is slain by its adherence to an outdated populist mythology. – *Wally Hammond, Time Out*

M

66 Corny, you bet. But that's to be admired in an old war horse on the last frontier. – *Rita Kempley, Washington Post*

♪ Dave Grusin (music)

'The kind of woman most men want. . .and shouldn't have!'

Mildred Pierce ★★★

DIR *Michael Curtiz*
1945 113m US

☆ *Joan Crawford*, Jack Carson, Zachary Scott, *Eve Arden*, *Ann Blyth*, Bruce Bennett, George Tobias, Lee Patrick, Moroni Olsen

A housewife splits up with her husband, works hard to pay for her daughters' education, and becomes the successful owner of a restaurant chain before she suffers a setback.

A woman's picture par excellence, glossily and moodily photographed, but with noirish undertones. It is lifted considerably by a remarkably strong turn from Crawford, latching gratefully on to a role that would reinvigorate her career.

SCR Ranald MacDougall, Catherine Turney **CIN** *Ernest Haller* **MUS** *Max Steiner* **PROD** Jerry Wald
DIST Warner

66 Constant, lambent, virulent attention to money and its effects, and more authentic suggestions of sex than one hopes to see in American films. – *James Agee*

♫ Joan Crawford (leading actress)
♫ picture; Eve Arden (supporting actress); Ann Blyth (supporting actress); Ronald MacDougall (screenplay); Ernest Haller

Miles from Home ★

DIR Gary Sinise
1988 108m US
[DVD]

☆ Richard Gere (Frank Roberts), Kevin Anderson (Terry Roberts), Brian Dennehy (Frank Roberts Sr.), Jason Campbell (Young Frank Roberts), Austin Bamgarner (Young Terry Roberts), Larry Poling (Nikita Khrushchev), Terry Kinney (Mark), Penelope Ann Miller (Sally), Helen Hunt (Jennifer), John Malkovich (Barry Maxwell)

In the mid-west two brothers, who tried to maintain a struggling farm, raze it to the ground rather than let the bank re-possess it, then hit the road.

Part road movie, part rural drama in which there is at least something at stake, But Gere's character is so unattractive it's hard to sympathise with his eventual fate.

SCR Chris Gerolmo **CIN** Elliot Davis **MUS** Robert Folk
DES David Gropman **ED** Jane Schwartz Jaffe
PROD Frederick Zollo, Paul Kurta
DIST Fox/Braveworld/Cinemcom/J & M Entertainment

'Up is down, black is white, and nothing is what it seems.'

Miller's Crossing ★★★★

DIR *Joel Coen*
1990 115m US
[DVD] ♫

☆ *Gabriel Byrne* (Tom Reagan), Marcia Gay Harden (Verna Bernbaum), John Turturro (Bernie Bernbaum), Jon Polito

(Johnny Caspar), J. E. Freeman (Eddie Dane), *Albert Finney* (Liam 'Leo' O'Bannon), Mike Starr (Frankie), Al Mancini (Tic-Tac), Richard Woods (Mayor Dale Levander)

In a Prohibition-era war between Irish and Italian gangs, the aide to a shady politician tries to broker a peace – but then he and his employer fall for the same woman.

Here are the Coens at the top of their game, with a dark saga, almost operatic in tone, that pays homage to the movies of the time it depicts, and also to the stories of Dashiell Hammett. The acting is spell-binding, with Byrne and Finney both mesmeric, and the sense of menace the brothers conjure up is squirmingly uncomfortable – especially when the action reaches that remote part of the woods named in the title, a favoured location for assassinations.

SCR Joel Coen, Ethan Coen **CIN** Barry Sonnenfeld
MUS Carter Burwell **DES** Dennis Gassner **ED** Michael Miller **PROD** Ethan Coen **DIST** Fox/Circle Films/Ted and Jim Pedas/Ben Barenholtz/Bill Durkin

66 As disturbing and densely beautiful as its opening image, a lofty forest that dwarfs the gangsters as they laugh over their kill. – *Rita Kempley, Washington Post*

66 The Coens are artists too, and their cool dazzler is an elegy to a day when Hollywood could locate moral gravity in a genre film for grownups. – *Richard Corliss, Time*

'Beyond his silence, there is a past. Beyond her dreams, there is a feeling. Beyond hope, there is a memory. Beyond their journey, there is a love.'

Million Dollar Baby ★

DIR Clint Eastwood
2004 132m US
[DVD] ♫

☆ Clint Eastwood (Frankie Dunn), *Hilary Swank* (Maggie Fitzgerald), Morgan Freeman (Eddie Scrap-Iron Dupris), Anthony Mackie (Shawrelle Berry), Jay Baruchel (Danger Barch), Mike Colter (Big Willie Little)

A veteran boxing coach reluctantly takes a plucky waitress under his wing, and trains her until tragedy strikes.

Creaky, cantankerous melodrama that often feels like a round-up of Hollywood (and specifically Hollywood Irish) clichés from pictures of the 1930s and 40s; you're meant to be distracted from the film's patronising, if not entirely contemptuous, attitude towards the lower classes by a talking-point plot twist, but even here Eastwood pulls a lukewarm potato out of the fire only to smother it with kid oven gloves. Swank alone merits praise: her strenuously lank hair is the truest thing in the picture.

SCR Paul Haggis **CIN** Tom Stern **MUS** Clint Eastwood
DES Henry Bumstead **ED** Joel Cox **PROD** Clint Eastwood, Albert S. Ruddy, Tom Rosenberg, Paul Haggis
DIST Warner

66 Eastwood takes the audience to raw, profoundly moving places. If you fear strong emotions, this is not for you. But if you want to see Hollywood filmmaking at its most potent, Eastwood has delivered the real deal. – *David Ansen, Newsweek*

66 Perhaps the director's most touching, elegiac work yet. – *Kenneth Turan, Los Angeles Times*

🏆 picture; Hilary Swank (leading actress); Morgan Freeman (supporting actor); Clint Eastwood (director)
🏆 Clint Eastwood (leading actor); Paul Haggis (adapted screenplay); Joel Cox

'Can anyone be truly good?'

Millions ★★

DIR *Danny Boyle*
2004 98m GB/US
DVD 🎵

☆ Alex Etel (Damian Cunningham), Lewis McGibbon (Anthony Cunningham), James Nesbitt (Ronnie Cunningham), Daisy Donovan (Dorothy), Christopher Fulford (The Poor Man), Pearce Quigley (Community Policeman), Alun Armstrong (St Peter)

With only days to go until the UK converts to the Euro, two young brothers find an abandoned holdall full of £20 and £50 notes, and wonder how best to spend it.

A gorgeous twist on a familiar narrative device: Boyle, one of Britain's most versatile directors, had already employed (for darker purposes) a plot that hinged on a found bag full of money in Shallow Grave. In contrast, this is a terrific family feature that manages to be profoundly moral without ever patronising either its young audience or any grown-ups looking on.

SCR *Frank Cottrell Boyce* CIN Anthony Dod Mantle MUS John Murphy DES Mark Tildesley ED Chris Gill PROD Andrew Hauptman, Graham Broadbent, Damian Jones DIST Pathé

66 Vibrant and verdant and heartbreakingly inviting, begging you to escape into a lovely tale in which children, through a simple act of faith, find their own heaven on Earth. – *Robert Wilonsky, Dallas Observer*

66 Millions most recalls pictures from the golden age of Ealing; it succeeds in holding up a mirror to the nation in order to make it not merely laugh but pause for self-scrutiny. It is likely to amuse both children and adults. And, best of all, to enchant them. – *Sukhdev Sandhu, Daily Telegraph*

Milou in May ★★★

DIR *Louis Malle*
1989 107m France/Italy
DVD 🎵

☆ *Michel Piccoli* (Milou), Miou-Miou (Camille), Michel Duchaussoy (Georges), Dominique Blanc (Claire), Harriet Walter (Lily), Bruno Carette (Grimaldi), François Berléand (Daniel), Martine Gautier (Adele), Paulette Dubost (Mme. Vieuzac)

When a family matriarch dies, her 60-year-old son gathers the family for a funeral in the grounds of their idyllic rural vineyard.

The underlying joke in this gentle, wry comedy of manners is its date: in May 1968, urban France was upended by revolutionary fervour and les evènements, but in another France completely, life went on much as it ever did. The events depict greed, jealousy and a distinct absence of grief, but Malle treats his characters indulgently. A delight.

SCR Louis Malle, Jean-Claude Carrière CIN Renato Berta MUS Stéphane Grappelli DES Willy Holt, Philippe Turlure ED Emmanuelle Castro PROD Louis Malle Jean-Yves Asselin DIST Gala/Nouvelles Editions de Films/TF1/Ellepi Film

66 Has the same slight, poignant lyricism as its Stéphane Grappelli score. – *Geoff Andrew, Time Out*
ⓣ film not in the English language

'For thousands of years, man has been evolution's greatest creation... until now.'

Mimic ★

DIR Guillermo Del Toro
1997 105m US
DVD

☆ Mira Sorvino (Dr. Susan Tyler), Jeremy Northam (Dr. Peter Mann), Josh Brolin (Josh), Giancarlo Giannini (Manny), Charles S. Dutton (Leonard), Alexander Goodwin (Chuy), Alix Koromzay (Remy), F. Murray Abraham (Dr. Gates)

Giant mutant insects, their DNA tampered with by humans when they were found to carry a disease that afflicted children, stalk and terrorise the New York subway system.

Efficient horror flick, intelligently conceived, but mainly of interest as the first American film from Guillermo del Toro. Even in this unexceptional outing, he shows considerable flair for creating unease and dread.

SCR Matthew Robbins, Guillermo Del Toro CIN Dan Laustsen MUS Marco Beltrami DES Carol Spier ED Patrick Lussier, Peter Devaney Flanagan PROD Bob Weinstein, B. J. Rack, Ole Bornedal DIST Buena Vista/Dimension

66 A stylish B horror movie about giant insects in the catacombs of Manhattan, it's by turns queasy, gross, terrifying, and – never underestimate this one – enthusiastically dumb. It's everything you want in a big-bug thriller. – *Owen Gleiberman, Entertainment Weekly*

Mina Tannenbaum ★★

SCR/DIR Martine Dugowson
1993 128m France/Belgium/Netherlands
🎵

☆ Romane Bohringer (Mina Tannenbaum), Elsa Zylberstein (Ethel Benegui), Hugues Quester (Choumachere), Nils Tavernier (François), Stéphane Slima (Didier), Chantal Krief (Delsy), Florence Thomassin (The cousin), Eric Defosse (Serge), Jean-Philippe Ecoffey (Jacques Dana)

Two Jewish girls, born on the same day in Paris, grow up and go their separate ways. One thrives in journalism; the other becomes a successful artist, but takes her own life when her love life falls apart.

A 'women's picture' quite literally, in that all the crucial characters are female. It's a skilled exploration of friendship, jealousy and rivalry between its two female leads, and its tone becomes more sombre as it progresses. It employs a range of stylistic devices – characters address the camera directly, their 'shadow selves' pass comment on events – adding up to an intriguing, complex whole.

M

DVD Available on DVD	☆ Cast in order	66 Critics' Quotes	🏆 Academy Award	🅱 BAFTA
🎵 Soundtrack on CD	of importance	† Points of interest	Academy Award nomination	ⓣ BAFTA nomination

CIN Dominique Chapuis   MUS Peter Chase
DES Philippe Chiffre   ED Martine Barraqué, Dominique
Gallieni   PROD Paul Rosenberg, Georges Benayoun
DIST Mayfair/IMA/UGC/Christian Bourgois/La
Sept/SFPC/L'Etang/Belbo/RTBF

66 What awkwardness and lack of subtlety there may be
are compensated for by the sense of enthusiasm and
experiment that permeates the film. – *Ginette Vincendeau,
Sight & Sound*

'What would you do if you were accused of a murder you
had not committed. . .yet?'

Minority Report   ★★

DIR *Steven Spielberg*
2002   144m   US
DVD   ♫

☆ Tom Cruise (Chief John Anderton), Colin Farrell
(Danny Witwer), Samantha Morton (Agatha), Max von
Sydow (Director Lamar Burgess), Lois Smith (Dr. Iris
Hineman), Peter Stormare (Dr. Solomon Eddie), Tim
Blake Nelson (Gideon), Steve Harris (Jad)

In the future, a police unit is dedicated to tracking
down criminals before they commit their crimes. A
cop in the unit learns he himself is about to murder
somebody.

*Another to add to the cinema's long list of almost-
great works derived from Philip K. Dick novels: though
it can't finally get round the miscasting of a blankly
heroic Cruise in the lead role, Yet Spielberg displays
tremendous technical mastery, and enough grasp
of human frailty, to make this enthralling science-
fiction.*

SCR Scott Frank, Jon Cohen   CIN Janusz Kaminski
MUS John Williams   DES *Alex McDowell*   ED Michael
Kahn   PROD Jan De Bont, Bonnie Curtis, Gerald R.
Molen, Walter F. Parkes   DIST TCF

66 A virtuoso high-wire act, daring so much, achieving it
with such grace and skill. Minority Report reminds us why
we go to the movies in the first place. – *Roger Ebert,
Chicago Sun-Times*

66 Spielberg's sharpest, brawniest, most bustling
entertainment since Raiders of the Lost Ark. – *Richard
Corliss, Time*

♪ Richard Hymns, Gary Rydstrom (sound editing)

Ⓣ Scott Farrar, Michael Lantieri, Nathan McGuinness,
Henry LaBounta (special visual effects)

The Miracle   ★

SCR/DIR Neil Jordan
1990   97m   GB/Ireland
☆ *Beverly D'Angelo* (Renee Baker), Donal McCann (Sam),
Niall Byrne (Jimmy), Lorraine Pilkington (Rose), J. G.
Devlin (Mr. Beausang), Cathleen Delany (Miss Strange),
Tom Hickey (Tommy), Shane Connaughton (Rose's
Father)

When a glamorous actress arrives in a small Irish
town, she enlivens the days of two imaginative
teenagers.

*Jordan's films often have an elusive quality, and this is
no exception. While awaiting its outcome, there's much
to admire: the conviction of the acting, the interplay
between the engaging adolescents, and the sense of an
agreeable place that time, and modern life, forgot.*

CIN Philippe Rousselot   MUS Anne Dudley
DES Gemma Jackson   ED Joke Van Wijk   PROD Stephen
Woolley, Redmond Morris
DIST Palace/Promenade/British Screen/Film Four

'50 minutes and counting. . .'

Miracle Mile   ★

SCR/DIR Steve DeJarnatt
1988   87m   US
DVD   ♫

☆ Anthony Edwards (Harry Washello), Mare
Winningham (Julie Peters), John Agar (Ivan Peters), Lou
Hancock (Lucy Peters), Mykel T. Williamson (Wilson),
Kelly Jo Minter (Charlotta), Kurt Fuller (Gerstead), Denise
Crosby (Landa)

A man in L.A. misses a late-night date with his
waitress girlfriend, picks up a ringing pay phone
outside the diner where she works, and learns that
the end of the world is literally nigh.

*A modestly-budgeted nuclear thriller with a terrific
premise, shot atmospherically and played to the max
by Edwards as a man with the ultimate dilemma.*

CIN Theo Van de Sande   MUS Tangerine Dream
DES Christopher Horner   ED Stephen Semel, Kathie
Weaver   PROD John Daly, Derek Gibson   DIST Hemdale
† The title refers to a section of Wilshire Boulevard
in Los Angeles, where exteriors for the film were actually
shot.

The Miracle of
Morgan's Creek   ★★★

SCR/DIR *Preston Sturges*
1943   99m   US
☆ Betty Hutton (Trudy Kockenlocker), Eddie Bracken
(Norval Jones), William Demarest (Officer Kockenlocker),
Diana Lynn (Emmy Kockenlocker), Porter Hall (Justice of
the Peace), Akim Tamiroff (The Boss), Brian Donlevy
(Governor McGinty), Alan Bridge (Mr. Johnson)

Chaos results when a stuttering hayseed tries to
help a girl accidentally pregnant by a soldier whom
she met hazily at a dance.

*Weird and wonderful one-man assault on the would-be
censors in the Hays Office and sundry other American
institutions such as motherhood and politics; an
indescribable, tasteless, roaringly funny mêlée, as
unexpected at the time as it was effective, like a kick in
the pants to all other film comedies.*

CIN John Seitz   MUS Leo Shuken, Charles Bradshaw
ED Stuart Gilmore   PROD Preston Sturges
DIST Paramount

OFFICER KOCKENLOCKER (WILLIAM DEMAREST): Daughters.
They're a mess no matter how you look at 'em. A headache
till they get married – if they get married – and after that
they get worse . . . Either they leave their husbands and
come back with four kids and move into your guest room
or the husband loses his job and the whole caboodle
comes back. Or else they're so homely that you can't get

rid of them at all and they sit around like Spanish moss and shame you into an early grave.

EMILY KOCKENLOCKER (DIANA LYNN): If you don't mind my mentioning it, father, I think you have a mind like a swamp.

66 Like taking a nun on a roller coaster. – *James Agee*

66 This film moves in a fantastic and irreverent whirl of slapstick, nonsense, farce, sentiment, satire, romance, melodrama – is there any ingredient of dramatic entertainment except maybe tragedy and grand opera that hasn't been tossed into it? – *National Board of Review*

⚐ Preston Sturges (original screenplay)

Miracle on 34th Street ★★★

SCR/DIR *George Seaton*
1947 94m US
DVD

☆ *Edmund Gwenn* (Kris Kringle), Maureen O'Hara (Doris Walker), John Payne (Fred Gailey), Natalie Wood (Susan Walker), Gene Lockhart (Judge Henry X. Harper), Porter Hall (Mr. Sawyer), William Frawley (Charles Halloran), Jerome Cowan (Thomas Mara), Thelma Ritter (Mother)

In New York, a department store Santa Claus claims to be the real thing.

Charming comedy fantasy which quickly became an American classic, and is still a staple of Christmastime TV programming.

CIN Charles Clarke, Lloyd Ahern MUS Cyril Mockridge ED Robert Simpson PROD William Perlberg DIST TCF

66 Altogether wholesome, stimulating and enjoyable. – *Motion Picture Herald*

⚑ Edmund Gwenn (supporting actor); George Seaton (screenplay); Valentine Davies
⚐ picture

'Discover the Miracle.'
Miracle on 34th Street ★★

DIR Les Mayfield
1994 114m US
DVD ♫

☆ *Richard Attenborough* (Kris Kringle), Elizabeth Perkins (Dorey Walker), Dylan McDermott (Bryan Bedford), Mara Wilson (Susan Walker), Robert Prosky (Judge Henry Harper), J. T. Walsh (Ed Collins), James Remar (Jack Duff), William Windom (C.F. Cole)

One Christmas, the manageress of a department store hires an old man who believes he's Santa Claus to work in the store's grotto, only for a rival store owner to cast doubt on the man's authenticity.

Very acceptable (if overlong) remake, making perfect use of Attenborough's beardy charm as the Santa figure.

SCR George Seaton, John Hughes CIN Julio Macat MUS Bruce Broughton DES Doug Kraner ED Raja Gosnell PROD John Hughes DIST TCF

66 If you're after an entirely pleasant, inoffensive, feel-good movie at Christmas, this is it: the kind of innocent, utterly charming, hanky-wringing fare that they aren't supposed to be making any more. – *Angie Errigo, Empire*

'A story about just how wrong two people can be before they can be right. . .'
The Mirror Has Two Faces ★

DIR Barbra Streisand
1996 126m US
DVD ♫

☆ Barbra Streisand (Rose Morgan), Jeff Bridges (Gregory Larkin), Pierce Brosnan (Alex), George Segal (Henry Fine), Mimi Rogers (Claire), Brenda Vaccaro (Doris), *Lauren Bacall* (Hannah Morgan), Austin Pendleton (Barry), Elle Macpherson (Candice)

A homely university professor, wooed by a dull colleague for her brains, reinvents herself in order to spark his passion.

Glossy romantic nonsense entirely out of time in the 1990s, enjoyment of which depends heavily on one's fondness for/tolerance of the composer-director-star.

SCR Richard LaGravenese CIN Dante Spinotti, Andrzej Bartkowiak MUS Marvin Hamlisch, Barbra Streisand DES Tom John ED Jeff Werner PROD Barbra Streisand, Arnon Milchan DIST Columbia TriStar/Phoenix/Arnon Milchan/Barwood

66 The overkill of The Mirror Has Two Faces is partly offset by Ms. Streisand's genuine diva appeal. The camera does love her, even with a gun to its head. And she's able to wring sympathy and humor from the first half of this role. The film also has a big asset in Ms. Bacall, though she plays a mother so targeted for disapproval that she might as well be wearing a bull's-eye on her back. – *Janet Maslin, New York Times*

⚑ Lauren Bacall (supporting actress); Barbra Streisand, Marvin Hamlisch, Bryan Adams, Robert 'Mutt' Lange (m, ly) (music, original song – I Finally Found Someone)
Ⓣ Lauren Bacall (supportting actress)

'In a time of chaos, in a world of change, he was moved by a book he could not read to become a hero he never imagined.'
Les Misérables ★★★

SCR/DIR *Claude Lelouch*
1995 175m France
DVD

☆ *Jean-Paul Belmondo* (Henri Fortin/Jean Valjean), Michel Boujenah (Andre Ziman), Alessandra Martines (Elise Ziman), Annie Girardot (Farmer Woman), Philippe Leotard (Farmer), Clementine Celarie (Catherine/Fantine), Rufus (Farmer), Ticky Holgado (The Kind Hoodlum)

After aiding a Jewish couple escape Nazi-occupied France, an illiterate boxer-turned-removal man learns of Victor Hugo's novel, and starts to see unexpected parallels with his own life.

A vast and masterly piece of storytelling, juggling the novelist's concerns with those of a more contemporary era, and in doing so shedding new light on both Hugo's fiction and a particular dark chapter in French history.

CIN Claude Lelouch, Philippe Pavans de Ceccatty MUS Francis Lai, Didier Barbelivien, Philippe Servain, Erik Berchot, Michel Legrand DES Laurent Tesseyre, Jacques

DVD Available on DVD   ☆ Cast in order of importance   66 Critics' Quotes   ⚑ Academy Award   Ⓑ BAFTA
♫ Soundtrack on CD   † Points of interest   ⚐ Academy Award nomination   Ⓣ BAFTA nomination

Bufnoir   ED Hélène de Luze   PROD Claude Lelouch
DIST Warner/Films 13/TF1/Canal

66 It is all shameless pace and jostle, a compendium of evil (war, suicide, poverty, injustice, exploitation) that yet asks us to believe that common decency (and a strong back) can eventually triumph over it. Maybe so, maybe not. But how pretty it is to believe it may. And how pleasurable it is to be absorbed into the bloodstream of this movie and be borne along on its racing pulse. – *Richard Schickel, Time*

Ⓣ film not in the English language

'Paul Sheldon used to write for a living. Now he's writing to stay alive.'

Misery ★★★

DIR *Rob Reiner*
1990   107m   US
DVD   ♫

☆ *James Caan* (Paul Sheldon), *Kathy Bates* (Annie Wilkes), Richard Farnsworth (Buster), Frances Sternhagen (Virginia), Lauren Bacall (Marcia Sindell), Graham Jarvis (Libby), Jerry Potter (Pete)

A deranged nurse cares for her hero, a romantic novelist, when she finds him injured in a road accident. But when she learns he is about to kill off her favourite heroine, she starts torturing him in an attempt to change his mind.

One of the very best adaptations of Stephen King's work – a long, dark look at the price of celebrity and the wilder shores of fan worship. Bates and Caan make an unlikely but outstandingly effective pairing, and Bates's wild fits of anger are discomfiting, as well as very funny.

SCR William Goldman   CIN Barry Sonnenfeld
MUS Marc Shaiman   DES Norman Garwood
ED Robert Leighton   PROD Andrew Scheinman, Rob Reiner   DIST Medusa/Castle Rock/Nelson

66 Reiner captures just the right level of physical tension, but for the most part wisely emphasises the mental duels. – *Colette Maude, Time Out*

⚲ Kathy Bates (leading actress)

'Worlds apart. . .bound by desire.'

Miss Julie

DIR *Mike Figgis*
1999   103m   GB/US
DVD   ♫

☆ Saffron Burrows (Miss Julie), Peter Mullan (Jean), Maria Doyle Kennedy (Christine)

An aristocrat's flirty daughter attempts to woo her valet away from his fiancée, a cook.

Low-budget, one-set adaptation shot on digital video, with occasional split-screen photography and a surfeit of close-ups. At its best, it offers the sight of good actors chewing over a rather gristly piece of writing, though indifferent handling soon makes the play seem like rather more of an antiquated slog than it perhaps is.

SCR Helen Cooper   CIN Benoit Delhomme   MUS Mike Figgis   DES Michael Howells   ED Matthew Wood
PROD Mike Figgis, Harriet Cruikshank   DIST Optimum

66 Fiery but turgid. – *Phoebe Flowers, Miami Herald*

---

66 It would appear that Dogme 95 has spawned another fellow traveller. – *Peter Matthews, Sight & Sound*

'Loyalty Without Question. Friendship Without Equal.'

Mrs Brown ★★★

DIR *John Madden*
1997   103m   GB
DVD   ♫

☆ *Judi Dench* (Queen Victoria), *Billy Connolly* (John Brown), Geoffrey Palmer (Henry Ponsonby), *Anthony Sher* (Disraeli), Gerard Butler (Archie Brown), Richard Pasco (Doctor Jenner), David Westhead (Bertie, Prince of Wales)

John Brown, a gruff, outspoken Scottish servant, helps a newly widowed Queen Victoria through her sadness, and sparks rumours of a romance.

Handsome, enjoyable drama that benefits from a thoughtful, knowing script that finally remains discreet about its intriguing central relationship. Dench and Connolly, in a real odd-couple piece of casting, balance each other out exquisitely.

SCR *Jeremy Brock*   CIN *Richard Greatrex*   MUS Stephen Warbeck   DES *Martin Childs*   ED Robin Sales
PROD Sarah Curtis   DIST Miramax/Ecosse

66 The film is an entertaining history lesson that wisely leaves the true nature of the relationship open to interpretation. – *William Mager, BBC*

⚲ Judi Dench (leading actress); Lisa Westcott, Veronica Brebner, Beverly Binda (make up)

Ⓣ Judi Dench (leading actress); Deidre Clancy (costume design)

Mrs Dalloway ★★

DIR *Marleen Gorris*
1997   97m   GB/US/Netherlands
DVD   ♫

☆ *Vanessa Redgrave* (Clarissa Dalloway), Natascha McElhone (Young Clarissa), Rupert Graves (Septimus), Michael Kitchen (Peter Walsh), John Standing (Richard Dalloway), Alan Cox (Young Peter), Lena Headey (Young Sally), Sarah Badel (Lady Rossiter)

A day in the life of a middle-aged English socialite, who finds her comfortable life in the 1920s deeply disturbed by the surprise arrival of a former lover, and rocked by the fate of a shell-shocked young war veteran.

Virginia Woolf's tricky, intricate novel is intelligently adapted by Eileen Atkins, though Mrs. Dalloway's airy complacency is harder to accept in a leading film character than within the context of a literary device. Redgrave captures Clarissa with assured skill.

SCR Eileen Atkins   CIN Sue Gibson   MUS Ilona Sekacz
DES David Richens   ED Michiel Reichwein
PROD Stephen Bayly, Lisa Katselas Paré   DIST Artificial Eye/First Look

66 Mrs Dalloway is a rich work, an insightful consideration of the nature of civilisation in the wake of the 'war to end all wars'. – *Kevin Thomas, Los Angeles Times*

DVD Available on DVD   ☆ Cast in order of importance   66 Critics' Quotes   ⚲ Academy Award   Ⓣ BAFTA
♫ Soundtrack on CD   † Points of interest   Academy Award nomination   Ⓣ BAFTA nomination

'A Woman Ahead Of Her Time. A Movie That Can't Be Missed.'

Mrs Parker and the Vicious Circle ★

DIR Alan Rudolph
1994   124m   US
♬

☆ Jennifer Jason Leigh (Dorothy Parker), Matthew Broderick (Charles MacArthur), Campbell Scott (Robert Benchley), Andrew McCarthy (Eddie Parker)

Hollywood scriptwriter and famous wit Dorothy Parker looks back on her younger days with members of the famous Algonquin circle in New York.

An honest and workmanlike bid to portray the hard-drinking humorists in this literary coterie. But director Rudolph unwisely indulges the excesses of Jennifer Jason Leigh, whose mannered monotone soon grates – and even obscures Parker's best and most stinging one-liners.

SCR Alan Rudolph, Randy Sue Coburn   CIN Jan Kiesser
MUS Mark Isham   DES François Séguin   ED Suzy Elmiger   PROD Robert Altman   DIST Artificial Eye/Miramax/Fine Line

66 The film wants to make a case for Dorothy Parker as the first modern woman. It gets the look and the attitude right, but it can't find her heart. – *Peter Travers, Rolling Stone*

Mrs Ratcliffe's Revolution (new)

DIR Bille Eltringham
2007   103m   UK/Hungary
☆ Catherine Tate (Dorothy Ratcliffe), Iain Glen (Frank Ratcliffe), Jessica Barden (May Ratcliffe), Brittany Ashworth (Alex Ratcliffe), Katharina Thalbach (Anna), Nigel Betts (Uncle Phillip), Heike Makatsch (Fraulein Unger)

A Yorkshire housewife becomes a dissident after her socialist husband moves his family to communist East Germany.

Fact-inspired comedy with a dated feel; senior audiences might appreciate its sitcom-style humour.

SCR Bridget O'Connor, Peter Straughan   CIN Sean Bobbitt   MUS Rob Lane   DES Malcolm Thornton
ED John Wilson   PROD Leslee Udwin   DIST Warner Bros

DOROTHY: 'I've helped two boys defect, the Stasi are after us and we have to escape right now or we'll be arrested.'

66 Presumably this seemed like a funny idea before The Lives of Others filled the world in about the details of living under communism in East Germany. Now it just seems like an embarrassing, bad-taste sneer. – *Andrew Pulver, Guardian*

† Based on the story of Brian Norris, an English teacher from Bolton who left the UK in 1968 to take up a job at the University of Halle in East Germany. He lasted nine months.

'How far would you go, how much would you sacrifice to get back what you have lost?'

The Missing ★

DIR Ron Howard
2003   137m   US
DVD   ♬

☆ Tommy Lee Jones (Samuel Jones), Cate Blanchett (Maggie Gilkeson), Eric Schweig (Chidin), Evan Rachel Wood (Lilly Gilkeson), Jenna Boyd (Dot Gilkeson), Steve Reevis (Two Stone), Ray McKinnon (Russell J. Wittick), Val Kilmer (Lt. Jim Ducharme)

New Mexico, 1885: a mother and her estranged, Apache-bred husband search for their daughter after she is kidnapped by an Apache warrior.

Though well-assembled, this fails to do anything especially distinctive with its themes and Western backdrop; in the end, it's a much less provocative work than The Searchers was nearly a half-century before it.

SCR Ken Kaufman   CIN Salvatore Totino   MUS James Horner   ED Dan Hanley, Mike Hill   PROD Brian Grazer, Daniel Ostroff, Ron Howard   DIST Columbia

66 It is as if The Searchers has been rewritten in keeping with strict rules of political correctness: the hunters, the hunted, and their captives are all evenly split between white folks and Injuns so that no offence on grounds of race or culture can be given or received. – *Peter Bradshaw, Guardian*

66 Has a little for fans of all kinds of movies: embattled but empowered womenfolk, crusty old gunslingers, a horror film villain, panoramic landscapes, horses, fractured family values, historical nuggets, massacres, rescue attempts, shoot-outs and honest-to-John Wayne cowboy heroics. However, ultimately, it proves neither compelling nor resonant. – *Kim Newman, Empire*

Missing ★★★

DIR *Costa-Gavras*
1982   122m   US
☆ *Jack Lemmon*, Sissy Spacek, Melanie Mayron, John Shea, Charles Cioffi, Richard Bradford

A conservative American father and his liberal wife investigate the disappearance of their son in Chile during the military coup that brought General Pinochet to power; but they find themselves rebuffed by US diplomats.

Trenchant thriller from this most politically-minded of directors. It's hugely compelling, and Lemmon is a stand-out as a decent patriot, appalled by the duplicity of US foreign policy. But the nagging feeling persists that in narrative terms, the dice are loaded.

SCR Costa-Gavras, Donald Stewart   CIN Ricardo Aronovich   MUS Vangelis   DES Peter Jamison
ED Françoise Bonnot   PROD Edward and Mildred Lewis
DIST Universal/Polygram/Peter Guber, Jon Peters

66 Provocation and entertainment prove to be uneasy allies. – *Tom Milne, Monthly Film Bulletin*

⚜ Costa-Gavras, Donald Stewart (adapted screenplay)
⚜ picture; Jack Lemmon (leading actor); Sissy Spacek (leading actress)

🏆 Costa-Gavras, Donald Stewart (adapted screenplay)

DVD Available on DVD   ☆ Cast in order   66 Critics' Quotes   ⚜ Academy Award   🏆 BAFTA
♬ Soundtrack on CD   of importance   † Points of interest   ⚜ Academy Award nomination   🏆 BAFTA nomination

421

'Expect the impossible.'

Mission: Impossible ★★

DIR Brian de Palma
1996   110m   US
[DVD]   ♫

☆ Tom Cruise (Ethan Hunt), Jon Voight (Jim Phelps), Emmanuelle Beart (Claire Phelps), Henry Czerny (Eugene Kittridge), Jean Reno (Franz Krieger), Ving Rhames (Luther Stickell), Kristin Scott-Thomas (Sarah Davies), Vanessa Redgrave (Max)

After witnessing the deaths of the rest of his team during a failed mission, a spy attempts to find out who betrayed them.

An explosive, kinetic updating of an old television series; not a tremendously interesting film for its director to have on his CV, but there's a good deal of fun to be derived from its array of gadgets, disguises and relentless chicanery.

SCR David Koepp, Robert Towne, Steven Zaillian
CIN Stephen H. Burum   MUS Danny Elfman
DES Norman Reynolds   ED Paul Hirsch   PROD Tom Cruise, Paula Wagner   DIST Paramount

❝ De Palma is having too much fun zipping around curves and hitting the accelerator to slow down. He's a supremely confident engineer, and if you're game enough to make a jump for it and hold on, he offers the giddy excitement of watching the ground rush by beneath your dangling feet. – *Charles Taylor, Salon*

❝ A movie of profoundly complicated pop pleasures. Between dazzling suspense sequences, it invites the audience to work for a good time. – *Owen Gleiberman, Entertainment Weekly*

† The film features a remix of Lalo Schifrin's series theme by Adam Clayton and Larry Mullen from the band U2.

Mission: Impossible III ★

DIR J.J. Abrams
2006   126m   US/Germany/China
[DVD]   ♫

☆ Tom Cruise (Ethan Hunt), Philip Seymour Hoffman (Owen Davian), Ving Rhames (Luther), Billy Crudup (Musgrave), Michelle Monaghan (Julia), Jonathan Rhys Meyers (Declan), Keri Russell (Lindsey Farris), Laurence Fishburne (Theodore Brassel)

A spy on the brink of settling down to married life is called back in to rescue from a fellow agent from capture, only to attract the murderous attentions of a global arms dealer.

After two films, not to mention the similar True Lies and the TV series 24, the franchise threatens to look rather stale, but Lost creator Abrams does a respectable job assembling the formula's nuts and bolts – action, gadgets and disguise – and has fun allowing two very different screen presences to play off one another.

SCR Alex Kurtzman, Roberto Orci, J.J. Abrams   CIN Dan Mindel   MUS Michael Giacchino   DES Scott Chambliss   ED Mary Jo Markey, Maryann Brandon   PROD Tom Cruise, Paula Wagner   DIST Paramount

❝ Yes, it's fundamentally business as usual, but it's the best kind of business as usual, and it finds everyone working in top form. – *Keith Phipps, The Onion*

❝ Big and fast and silly, but it's never dumb, and it's certainly never boring. – *Rene Rodriguez, Miami Herald*

† The second film in the series was released in 2000.

'1964. When America was at war with itself.'

Mississippi Burning ★★

DIR Alan Parker
1988   128m   US
[DVD]   ♫

☆ *Gene Hackman* (Agent Rupert Anderson), Willem Dafoe (Agent Alan Ward), Frances McDormand (Mrs. Pell), Brad Dourif (Deputy Clinton Pell), R. Lee Ermey (Mayor Tilman), Gailard Sartain (Sheriff Ray Stuckey), Stephen Tobolowsky (Clayton Townley), Michael Rooker (Frank Bailey), Pruitt Taylor Vince (Lester Cowans)

In 1964, three civil rights activists go missing in Mississippi, and two FBI agents with directly opposing methods pursue their murderers.

A film much garlanded with awards, yet the charge about its uneasy focus on the fate of white activists is one that sticks. However, it is shot exquisitely, moves along with relentless power, and at least conveys an unequivocal message about racism, however unexceptional and self-congratulatory that may be. Hackman's turn as the pragmatic FBI man, prepared to spout racial hatred in order to catch his perpetrators, is mesmerising.

SCR Chris Gerolmo   CIN *Peter Biziou*   MUS Trevor Jones   DES Philip Harrison, Geoffrey Kirkland   ED *Gerry Hambling*   PROD Frederick Zollo, Robert F. Colesberry   DIST Rank/Orion

⌗ Peter Biziou
⌗ picture; Alan Parker; Gene Hackman; Frances McDormand; Gerry Hambling; sound

Ⓣ Peter Biziou
Ⓣ Alan Parker; Trevor Jones; Peter Biziou; Gerry Hambling; sound

'Romeo And Juliet Had It Easy.'

Mississippi Masala ★

DIR Mira Nair
1991   118m   US/ GB
[DVD]   ♫

☆ Denzel Washington (Demetrius Williams), Roshan Seth (Jay), Sarita Choudhury (Meena), Charles S. Dutton (Tyrone Williams), Joe Seneca (Williben Williams), Sharmila Tagore (Kinnu), Ranjit Chowdhry (Anil)

A young Asian woman living in Mississippi, her family having been expelled from Uganda by Idi Amin's regime, falls for a black American who runs a carpet-cleaning business, to the consternation of her parents and the local Asian community.

Mira Nair's second feature after the remarkable success of Salaam Bombay takes the unusual step of portraying suspicions between two minority ethnic groups in the U.S.. It's hardly earth-shattering, though the two leads have an appealingly shy chemistry.

SCR Sooni Taraporevala   CIN Ed Lachman   MUS L.
Subramaniam   DES Mitch Epstein   ED Roberto Silvi
PROD Michael Nozick, Mira Nair
DIST SCS/Odyssey/Cinecom/Film
Four/Mirabai/Movieworks/Black River

66 What's different here is the exclusion of any
overarching white perspective or white characters. –
Farrah Anwar, Sight & Sound

Mr & Mrs Bridge ★★

DIR *James Ivory*
1990   126m   US
DVD   ♫

☆ *Paul Newman* (Walter Bridge), *Joanne Woodward*
(India Bridge), Robert Sean Leonard (Douglas Bridge
(grown-up)), Margaret Walsh (Carolyn Bridge), Kyra
Sedgwick (Ruth Bridge), Blythe Danner (Grace Barron),
Simon Callow (Dr. Alex Sauer), Saundra McClain
(Harriet)

The marriage between a warm-hearted woman and
her emotionally closed lawyer husband goes into a
slow decline as their relationship, their children,
then life itself all fall short of expectations.

*A respectful rendition of twin novels, both written with
intimacy and care. The film stands and falls on its two
performances, which are first-rate. Unhappily, its
stunning photography – every scene is beautifully
composed and lit – tends to soften the subtle agonies at
the story's heart.*

SCR Ruth Prawer Jhabvala   CIN *Tony Pierce-Roberts*
MUS Richard Robbins   DES *David Gropman*
ED Humphrey Dixon   PROD Ismail Merchant
DIST Palace/Cineplex Odeon/Merchant Ivory/Robert
Halmi

⚱ Joanne Woodward (leading actress)

'There's Something About.'

Mr Brooks (new) ★★

SCR/DIR Bruce A. Evans
2007   120m   US
DVD   ♫

☆ Kevin Costner (Earl Brooks), Demi Moore (Detective
Tracy Atwood), William Hurt (Marshall), Marg
Helgenberger (Emma Brooks), Dane Cook (Mr. Smith)

A successful Portland businessman with an
imaginary alter ego is a notorious killer, wanted by
police for years. But a blackmail plot looks set to
ensure his capture.

*Tense, gripping psychodrama relying on well-drawn
characters, narrative precision, smart twists and terrific
performances.*

SCR Raynold Gideon   CIN John Lindley   MUS Ramin
Djawadi   DES Jeffrey Beecroft   ED Miklos Wright
PROD Kevin Costner, Raynold Gideon, Jim Wilson
DIST Verve Pictures

66 Watching Costner and Hurt share grim laughs is
one of the pleasures of this totally absurd and equally
entertaining psychological thriller. – *Jack Matthews – New
York Daily News*

66 Costner's double-act with Hurt is a wicked pleasure,
like The Odd Couple with a psychopathic twist. –
Anthony Quinn, Independent

Mr Deeds Goes to Town ★★★

DIR *Frank Capra*
1936   118m   US
DVD

☆ *Gary Cooper* (Longfellow Deeds), Jean Arthur (Babe
Bennett), Raymond Walburn (Walter), Lionel Stander
(Cornelius Cobb), Walter Catlett (Morrow), George
Bancroft (MacWade), Douglass Dumbrille (John Cedar),
H. B. Warner (Judge Walker), Ruth Donnelly (Mabel
Dawson), *Margaret Seddon* (Jane Faulkner), *Margaret
McWade* (Amy Faulkner)

A small-town poet inherits a vast fortune and
shocks all New York by his stated desire to give it
away.

*What once was fresh and charming now seems rather
laboured in spots, and the production is parsimonious,
but the courtroom scene still works, and the good
intentions conquer all.*

SCR *Robert Riskin*   CIN Joseph Walker   MUS Adolph
Deutsch   ED Gene Havlick   PROD Frank Capra
DIST Columbia

66 I have an uneasy feeling he's on his way out. He's
started to make pictures about themes instead of people. –
Alistair Cooke

66 Everywhere the picture goes, from the endearing to the
absurd, the accompanying business is carried through
with perfect zip and relish. – *Otis Ferguson*

⚱ Frank Capra (direction)
⚱ picture; Gary Cooper (leading actor); Robert Riskin
(screenplay)

Mister Lonely (new)

DIR Harmony Korine   SCR/DIR Harmony Korine, Avi
Korine
2008   112m   France/Ireland/UK/US

☆ Diego Luna (Michael Jackson), Samantha Morton
(Marilyn Monroe), Denis Lavant (Charlie Chaplin),
James Fox (The Pope), Anita Pallenberg (The Queen
of England), Werner Herzog (Father Umbrillo), Esme
Creed-Miles (Shirley Temple)

A Michael Jackson lookalike falls for a Marilyn
Monroe mimic and follows her to a Scottish
commune populated by celebrity impersonators.

*Bizarre, whimsical curio from a director intent on
dividing his audience; it's certainly a long haul once
the novelty wears off.*

CIN *Marcel Zyskind*   MUS Jason Spaceman, The Sun
City Girls   DES Richard Campling   ED Paul Zucker,
Valdis Oskarsdottir   PROD Nadja Romain   DIST Tartan
Films

66 Korine's most lavishly produced pic to date falls short
of its ambition to say something meaningful about the
obsessive nature of celebrity culture. – *Scott Foundas,
Variety*

66 So pointless and irritating that after a while I
literally found it difficult to breathe. – *Peter Bradshaw,
Guardian*

M

DVD Available on DVD   ☆ Cast in order   66 Critics' Quotes   ⚱ Academy Award   🏆 BAFTA
♫ Soundtrack on CD   of importance   † Points of interest   ⚱ Academy Award nomination   🛡 BAFTA nomination

423

'You have to believe it to see it.'

Mr Magorium's Wonder Emporium (new)

SCR/DIR Zach Helm
2007   94m   US/Canada
[DVD]   ♫

☆ Dustin Hoffman (Mr. Magorium), Natalie Portman (Molly Mahoney), Jason Bateman (Henry), Zach Mills (Eric Applebaum)

The 243-year-old proprietor of a magical toyshop is finally facing his own mortality, and offers to turn the store over to Molly, his assistant, who is a piano prodigy.

Less objectionable than many children's films – it is devoid of product placement, and smug grown-up gags aimed over kids' heads. But it's strained and whimsical, with too many references to childhood wonder.

CIN Roman Osin   MUS Alexandre Desplat, Aaron Zigman   DES Therese DePrez   ED Sabrina Plisco, Steven Weisberg   PROD Richard N. Gladstein, James Garavente   DIST Icon

66 Helm gets huge bonus points for noticing everything that's annoying about modern children's films and including none of those things in his movie. – *Peter Hartlaub, San Francisco Chronicle*

66 Helm achieves bursts of charm and whimsy, but not quite enough magic to elicit a consistent sense of wonderment. – *Claudia Puig, USA Today*

Mr North   ★

DIR Danny Huston
1988   93m   US
[DVD]

☆ Anthony Edwards (Theophilus North), Robert Mitchum (Mr. Bosworth), Lauren Bacall (Mrs. Cranston), Harry Dean Stanton (Henry Simmons), Anjelica Huston (Persis Bosworth-Tennyson), Mary Stuart Masterson (Elspeth Skeel), Virginia Madsen (Sally Boffin), Tammy Grimes (Sarah Baily-Lewis), David Warner (Doctor McPherson)

In the 1920s, a young man arrives in the wealthy New England resort of Newport and makes a name as a miracle healer – much to the local doctor's chagrin.

There's not much to this agreeable fable, but watch it for the names: Mitchum and Bacall on screen together in a film co-scripted by one Huston (John), directed by a second (Danny) and co-starring a third (Anjelica). It's recommendation enough.

SCR Janet Roach, John Huston, James Costigan
CIN Robin Vidgeon   MUS David McHugh   DES Eugene Lee   ED Roberto Silvi   PROD Steven Haft, Skip Steloff
DIST Columbia TriStar/Heritage Entertainment/Showcase Productions

'It's lonely at the middle.'

Mr Saturday Night   ★★

DIR Billy Crystal
1992   119m   US
[DVD]   ♫

☆ Billy Crystal (Buddy Young, Jr.), David Paymer (Stan),

Julie Warner (Elaine), Helen Hunt (Annie Wells), Ron Silver (Larry Meyerson)

An old stand-up comedian looks back, partly with regret, at the ups and downs of his 50-year career.

A hugely underrated comedy, a portrait apparently owing something to Milton Berle and various stand-ups on the Jewish borscht-belt circuit. Crystal, who understands precisely the comic tradition in which he follows, is in fine form as a complex, driven, publicly funny man, seething with malice and self-regard once he steps off stage. It should be added: many of Buddy Young Jr.'s jokes are out of the top drawer.

SCR Billy Crystal, Lowell Ganz, Babaloo Mandel   CIN Don Peterman   MUS Marc Shaiman   DES Albert Brenner
ED Kent Beyda   PROD Billy Crystal
DIST Columbia/Castle Rock/New Line

66 There are probably enough sharp one-liners, hilarious routines and clever mimicry to see most people through the soggier patches. – *Nigel Floyd, Time Out*

🏃 David Paymer (supporting actor)

'Stirring – in the seeing! Precious – in the remembering'

Mr Smith Goes to Washington   ★★★★

DIR *Frank Capra*
1939   130m   US
[DVD]

☆ *James Stewart* (Jefferson Smith), *Claude Rains* (Sen. Joseph Paine), *Jean Arthur* (Saunders), *Thomas Mitchell* (Diz Moore), *Edward Arnold* (Jim Taylor), Guy Kibbee (Gov. Hubert Hopper), Eugene Pallette (Chick McGann), Beulah Bondi (Ma Smith), *Harry Carey* (President of the Senate), H. B. Warner (Sen. Fuller), Astrid Allwyn (Susan Paine), Ruth Donnelly (Mrs. Emma Hopper), Charles Lane (Nosey), Porter Hall (Sen. Monroe)

Washington's youngest senator exposes corruption in high places, almost at the cost of his own career.

Archetypal high-flying Capra vehicle, with the little man coming out top as he seldom does in life. Supreme gloss hides the corn, helter-skelter direction keeps one watching, and all concerned give memorable performances. A cinema classic.

SCR *Sidney Buchman*   CIN *Joseph Walker*   MUS *Dimitri Tiomkin*   ED Al Clark, Gene Havlick   PROD Frank Capra
DIST Columbia

SMITH (JAMES STEWART): I wouldn't give you two cents for all your fancy rules if, behind them, they didn't have a little bit of plain, ordinary kindness – and a little looking out for the other fella, too.

66 Timely and absorbing drama presented in best Capra craftsmanship. – *Variety*

66 More fun, even, than the Senate itself. . .not merely a brilliant jest, but a stirring and even inspiring testament to liberty and freedom. – *Frank S. Nugent, New York Times*

🏆 Lewis R. Foster

🏃 picture; James Stewart (leading actor); Claude Rains (supporting actor); Harry Carey (supporting actor); Frank Capra (direction); Sidney Buchman (screenplay); Dimitri Tiomkin; Lionel Banks

'Sometimes the wrong person is the only right person for you.'

Mr Wonderful ★

SCR/DIR Anthony Minghella from original screenplay by Amy Schor, Vicki Polon
1992 97m US
`DVD`

☆ Matt Dillon, Annabella Sciorra, Mary-Louise Parker, William Hurt, Vincent D'Onofrio, David Barry Gray, Dan Hedaya

Hard-up New York electrician hopes to cut his alimony payments by finding a new man for his ex-wife, only to fall in love with her again.

Minghella made his American debut with this formulaic rom-com, and found it hard to overcome the script's limitations. Its charm, which is considerable, comes from his careful directing of the performances.

CIN Geoffrey Simpson **MUS** Michael Gore **DES** Doug Kraner **ED** John Tintori **PROD** Marianne Moloney **DIST** Buena Vista/Samuel Goldwyn

66 A thoughtful romantic comedy with a snappy hook. – *Channel 4*

'Letting Go Of Your Past Is Hard...Especially When It's Dating Your Mom.'

Mr Woodcock (new)

DIR Craig Gillespie
2007 87m US/Germany
`DVD`

☆ Billy Bob Thornton (Mr. Woodcock), Seann William Scott (John Farley), Susan Sarandon (Beverly Farley), Melissa Sagemiller (Tracy), Melissa Leo (Sally Jansen), Bill Macy (Mr. Woodcock's dad), Amy Poehler (Maggie)

The young author of a self-help book about letting go of one's past is alarmed to learn his mother is marrying the bullying gym teacher from his school days.

A promising premise, undermined by a scarcity of witty dialogue and a predictable ending.

SCR Michael Carnes Josh Gilbert **CIN** Tami Reiker **DES** Alison Sadler **ED** Alan Baumgarten, Kevin Tent **PROD** Bob Cooper, David Dobkin **DIST** Entertainment

66 Disappointing. – *Peter Bradshaw, Guardian*

'Everybody's trying to get their girlfriend into the movies. . .'

Mistress ★

DIR Barry Primus
1992 110m US
`DVD`

☆ Robert Wuhl (Marvin Landisman), Martin Landau (Jack Roth), Robert DeNiro (Evan M. Wright), Jace Alexander (Stuart Stratland Jr.), Laurie Metcalf (Rachel Landisman), Danny Aiello (Carmine Rasso), Christopher Walken (Warren Zell), Eli Wallach (George Lieberhof), Tuesday Knight (Peggy), Sheryl Lee Ralph (Beverly), Ernest Borgnine (Himself)

When a screenwriter tries to get financing to film his new script, he finds all the money men want roles for their mistresses, and insist on alterations to accommodate them.

It caused smirks of approval at the time, and it offers knowing insights into the movie biz, but the conceit of producers insisting on roles for their mistresses has receded with time. The film now has a faintly sleazy, decidedly 1980s feel.

SCR Barry Primus, Jonathan L. Lawton **CIN** Sven Kirsten **MUS** Galt MacDermot **DES** Phil Peters **ED** Steve Weisberg **PROD** Meir Teper, Robert DeNiro **DIST** Tribeca

66 In Hollywood everyone ends up prostituting themselves – it's the old laboured joke at the centre of the film. – *Lizzie Francke, Sight & Sound*

'A Spike Lee joint.'

Mo' Better Blues ★

SCR/DIR Spike Lee
1990 129m US
`DVD` 🎵

☆ Denzel Washington (Bleek Gilliam), Spike Lee (Giant), Wesley Snipes (Shadow Henderson (Sax)), Joie Lee (Indigo Downes), Cynda Williams (Clarke Bentancourt), Giancarlo Esposito (Left Hand Lacey (Piano)), Robin Harris (Butterbean Jones), Bill Nunn (Bottom Hammer (Bass))

A gifted, ambitious, single-minded jazz trumpeter forms a band, becomes successful, but burns bridges with everyone in his life before seeing the error of his ways.

An overstuffed piece about a relatively simple theme, which is lent no extra significance by its excessive length. Its resolution is meant to be a satisfying release, but Washington's Bleek and those close to him all feel somewhat diminished. Far from Lee's finest moment.

CIN Ernest Dickerson **MUS** Bill Lee **DES** Wynn Thomas **ED** Sam Pollard **PROD** Spike Lee **DIST** UIP/40 Acres and a Mule Filmworks/Spike Lee

66 This lengthy indulgence succeeds neither as jazz movie nor as cautionary tale. – *Geoff Andrew, Time Out*

'You'll never laugh as long and as loud again as long as you live! The laughs come so fast and so furious you'll wish it would end before you collapse!'

Modern Times ★★★

SCR/DIR Charles Chaplin
1936 87m US
`DVD`

☆ *Charles Chaplin* (A Worker), *Paulette Goddard* (Gamine), Henry Bergman (Gamine), Chester Conklin (Mechanic), Tiny Sandford (Big Bill/Worker)

An assembly-line worker goes berserk but can't get another job.

Silent star comedy produced in the sound period; flashes of genius alternate with sentimental sequences and jokes without punch. But it is best known for its scathing critique of a mechanised, impersonal society, ruled by the relentless assembly line – which gives it fresh resonance in the 21st century.

CIN Rollie Totheroh, Ira Morgan **MUS** Charles Chaplin **DIST** Charles Chaplin

66 A natural for the world market. . .box office with a capital B. – *Variety*

66 A feature picture made out of several one- and two-reel shorts, proposed titles being The Shop, The Jailbird, The Singing Waiter. – *Otis Ferguson*

The Moderns ★★

DIR *Alan Rudolph*
1988 126m US
DVD ♫

☆ Keith Carradine (Nick Hart), Linda Fiorentino (Rachel Stone), Geneviève Bujold (Libby Valentin), Geraldine Chaplin (Nathalie de Ville), Wallace Shawn (Oiseau), John Lone (Bertram Stone), Kevin O'Connor (Hemingway), Elsa Raven (Gertrude Stein), Ali Giron (Alice B. Toklas)

A knowing study of the 'lost generation' bon vivants who clustered around Hemingway, Gertrude Stein and other literary figures in 1920s Paris.

Americans in Paris at their most superficial and pretentious, viewed acerbically (and a little snobbishly) by Rudolph, who nevertheless creates a Paris to which anyone might aspire: its cafes, restaurants, salons and galleries seem the most desirable places on earth to gossip, sit near the famous and talented, and hope their veneer rubs off. The film isn't about very much, but it dazzles nonetheless.

SCR Alan Rudolph, Jon Bradshaw CIN Toyomichoi Kurita MUS Mark Isham DES Steven Legler ED Debra T. Smith, Scott Brock PROD Carolyn Pfeiffer, David Blocker, Shep Gordon DIST Rank/Alive Films/Nelson

Mojo ★

SCR/DIR *Jez Butterworth*
1997 90m GB

☆ Ian Hart (Mickey), Ewen Bremner (Skinny), Aiden Gillen (Baby), Martin Gwynn Jones (Sweets), Hans Matheson (Silver Johnny), Andy Serkis (Potts), Ricky Tomlinson (Ezra), Harold Pinter (Sam Ross)

In 1958 Soho, a gangster murders a club-owner to take over the career of an emerging rock 'n' roll star.

A striking success on stage, enlivened by its vivid use of street language, this story dissipates on screen. The carefully stylised production design – probably a means of disguising the film's modest budget – overpowers the characters, with one exception: Pinter shows a sleek, malevolent grace as the menacing gangster Mr. Ross.

CIN Bruno de Keyzer MUS Murray Gold DES Hugo Luczyc-Wyhowski ED Richard Milward PROD Eric Abraham DIST Portobello/BBC/British Screen/Mojo

66 Fab performances, exuberance and style ensure that it works, but only in spurts. – *Tom Charity, Time Out*

Molière (new) ★

DIR *Laurent Tirard*
2007 120m France
DVD ♫

☆ Romain Duris (Jean-Baptiste Poquelin, aka Moliere), Fabrice Luchini (M. Jourdain), Laura Morante (Elmire Jourdain), Edouard Baer (Dorante), Ludivine Sagnier (Célimene), Fanny Valette (Henriette Jourdain)

The young playwright agrees to teach a rich businessman how to woo, only to fall in love with his patron's wife.

Robust costume romp, played with gusto; Shakespeare in Love seems the obvious comparison, though it helps to know a little about its subject's work.

SCR Laurent Tirard, Grégoire Vigneron CIN Gilles Henry MUS Frédéric Talgorn DES Françoise Dupertuis ED Valérie Deseine PROD Olivier Delbosc, Marc Missonnier DIST Pathé

66 Sumptuous, touching and often laugh-out-loud funny. – *Lisa Nesselson, Variety*

66 A very satisfying film. – *Philip French, Observer*

† The plot incorporates elements from Tartuffe and Le Bourgeois Gentilhomme, among other plays.

Mona Lisa ★★★

DIR *Neil Jordan*
1986 104m GB
DVD

☆ *Bob Hoskins*, Cathy Tyson, Michael Caine, Robbie Coltrane, Clarke Peters, Sammi Davis

An ex-con is hired as a chauffeur by a gangster and falls for a troubled prostitute who he drives to meet clients. She begs him to help her find a friend whose disappearance seems sinister.

A crime thriller, viewed from the lower echelons of the gang underworld. Hoskins, in perhaps his best ever role, is touching as a minor pawn out of his depth in a bigger game. An effective story, directed and told with assurance.

SCR Neil Jordan, David Leland CIN Roger Pratt MUS Michael Kamen DES Jamie Leonard ED Lesley Walker PROD Stephen Woolley, Patrick Cassavetti DIST HandMade/Palace

66 A film to see again, with the certainty that each viewing will add something new. – *Monthly Film Bulletin*

🎭 Bob Hoskins (leading actor)

'Greatness comes to those who take it.'

Mongol (new) ★

DIR *Sergei Bodrov*
2007 125m Germany/Kazakhstan/Russia
♫

☆ Asano Tadanobu (Temudgin), Honglei Sun (Jamukha), Khulan Chuluun (Borte), Odnyam Odsuren (Young Temudgin), Amarbold Tuvinbayar (Young Jamukha), Bayartsetseg Erden (Young Borte), Amadu Mamadakov (Tartugai)

The young Genghis Khan survives a perilous childhood and the betrayal of his best friend to become the warrior and ruler we know today.

Epic chronicle with a multi-ethnic cast that strives to give a human side, and a love interest, to the legendary figure.

SCR Arif Aliyev, Sergei Bodrov CIN Sergey Trofimov, Rogier Stoffers MUS Tuomas Kantelinen, Altan Urag DES Dashi Namdakov ED Zach Staenberg, Valdis Oskarsdottir PROD Sergey Selyanov, Sergei Bodrov, Anton Melnik DIST The Works

66 I don't know the Mongolian word for panache, but Mongol's got plenty of it. The battle scenes are as notable for their clarity as their intensity; we can follow the strategies, get a sense of who's losing and who's winning. – *Joe Morgenstern, Wall Street Journal*

66 Long on ethnographic detail and visual splendor but short on narrative coherence. – *Frank Scheck, Hollywood Reporter*

† Kazakhstan's official submission in the Foreign Language Film category for the 2008 Academy Awards.

⚱ Foreign Language Film

Monkey Shines ★

SCR/DIR George A. Romero
1988   113m   US
DVD

☆ Jason Beghe (Allan Mann), John Pankow (Geoffrey Fisher), Kate McNeil (Melanie Parker), Joyce Van Patten (Dorothy Mann), Christine Forrest (Maryanne Hodges)

A quadriplegic student, paralysed in an accident, is given a trained capuchin monkey to help him with his daily tasks, but the creature becomes so attuned to his master's mental state that he begins enacting violent revenge.

A lesser-known title in the Romero canon, but well worth investigating; it's trashy, creepy and outrageously funny in more or less equal parts.

CIN James A. Contner   MUS David Shire   DES Cletus Anderson   ED Pasquale Buba   PROD Charles Evans DIST Rank/Orion

66 Romero's is a formidable talent that others can only hope to ape. – *Nigel Floyd, Time Out*

Monsieur Hire ★

DIR Patrice Leconte
1989   81m   France
DVD

☆ Michel Blanc (Monsieur Hire), Sandrine Bonnaire (Alice), André Wilms (Police Inspector), Luc Thuillier (Emile)

A middle-aged outcast, suspected by the police of involvement in a murder, strikes up a relationship with the female neighbour he spies upon.

Stylish update of Hitchcockian themes to contemporary France, but so cold in its appreciation of human weakness you can practically see the goose pimples forming on the screen.

SCR Patrice Leconte, Patrick Dewolf   CIN Denis Lenoir MUS Michael Nyman   DES Ivan Mausson   ED Joelle Hache   PROD René Cleitman, Philippe Carcassonne DIST Palace/Cinea/Hachette Premiere/FR3

66 Goes way beyond Blue Velvet in exploring 'the dark side of the moon' of human nature, its mixtures of obstinacy and masochism, self-destruction and chilly shame. – *Raymond Durgnat, Film Review*

66 It's a great film to look at, stylish and inventive.. . .but you just can't respect a film that so completely backs out of all its commitments. It's a tour de force in a vacuum: all dressed up and no place to go. – *Julie Phillips, Village Voice*

'The Rain Is Coming. And So Is The Family.'

Monsoon Wedding ★★★

DIR Mira Nair
2001   114m   US/Italy/Germany/France
DVD   ♫

☆ Naseeruddin Shah (Lalit Verma), Lillete Dubey (Pimmi Verma), Shefali Shetty (Ria Verma), Vasundhara Das (Aditi Verma), Parvin Dabas (Hemant Rai), Vijay Raaz (P. K. Dubei), Tillotama Shome (Alice), Rajat Kapoor (Tej Puri)

An extended family gathers in Delhi to celebrate an arranged marriage.

Broad, crowd-pleasing comedy, with a tremendous generosity of spirit, and enough distinct types amongst its sizeable cast for everyone watching to have someone to identify with. Despite all the jollity, Nair is careful to remind the audience of this family's privileges, and the broader context in which they can be enjoyed.

SCR Sabrina Dhawan   CIN *Declan Quinn*   MUS *Mychael Danna*   DES Stephanie Carroll   ED Allyson C. Johnson PROD Caroline Baron, Mira Nair   DIST Film4

66 Has an engaging warmth and an effortless sense of life. It also has an instinct for the humanity and universality of situations that are comic, romantic and quite seriously dramatic by turns. – *Kenneth Turan, Los Angeles Times*

66 An optimistic and luscious film. – *Emma Cochrane, Empire*

† It won the Golden Lion award for best film at the Venice Film Festival in 2001.

ⓣ film not in the English language

'Based on a true story.'

Monster ★

SCR/DIR Patty Jenkins
2003   109m   Germany/US
DVD

☆ *Charlize Theron* (Aileen Wuornos), Christina Ricci (Selby Wall), Bruce Dern (Thomas), Scott Wilson (Horton), Pruitt Taylor Vince (Gene), Lee Tergesen (Vincent Corey), Annie Corley (Donna Tentler)

Biopic of Aileen Wuornos, who emerged from a broken home to work as a prostitute, killing several of her clients before being executed.

An honourable, well-acted attempt to do right by a woman who was wronged (and did wrong) for much of her existence, hamstrung by having to explain away its heroine's crimes, often in shockingly moralistic terms; in the end, it's hard not to feel Wuornos's life and ambiguity were better served by the two Nick Broomfield documentaries she inspired.

CIN Steven Bernstein   MUS BT   DES Edward T. McAvoy ED Jane Kurson, Arthur Coburn   PROD Charlize Theron, Mark Damon, Clark Peterson, Donald Kushner, Brad Wyman   DIST Metrodome

66 One of the greatest performances in the history of the cinema. – *Roger Ebert, Chicago Sun-Times*

66 I don't think it's a great movie - though Theron's is a near-great performance - but it's not one you can easily forget. – *Michael Wilmington, Chicago Tribune*

DVD Available on DVD   ☆ Cast in order   66 Critics' Quotes   ⚱ Academy Award   ⓑ BAFTA
♫ Soundtrack on CD   of importance   † Points of interest   ⚱ Academy Award nomination   ⓣ BAFTA nomination

427

† Wuornos appeared in the Broomfield documentaries Aileen Wuornos: The Selling of a Serial Killer (1992) and Aileen: Life and Death of a Serial Killer (2003).

⚊ Charlize Theron (leading actress)

Ⓣ Charlize Theron (leading actress)

'A lifetime of change can happen in a single moment.'

Monster's Ball ★

DIR Marc Forster

2001 111m US

[DVD] ♫

☆ Billy Bob Thornton (Hank Grotowski), Heath Ledger (Sonny Grotowski), Halle Berry (Leticia Musgrove), Peter Boyle (Buck Grotowski), Sean Combs (Lawrence Musgrove), Mos Def (Ryrus Cooper), Will Rokos (Warden Velasco), Milo Addica (Tommy Roulaine)

A death-row guard at a prison facility in Georgia starts a relationship with the widow of a man he escorted to his death.

Spare, elliptical character piece, more convincing in its brooding evocation of place and atmosphere than when the narrative starts exhorting us all to get along.

SCR Milo Addica, Will Rokos CIN Roberto Schaefer MUS Asche and Spencer DES Monroe Kelly ED Matt Chesse PROD Lee Daniels DIST Entertainment

❝ A very adult, very humane drama. – *Angie Errigo, Empire*

❝ A traffic map of calls and responses, lessons and homework, wishes and fulfillment. All roads lead to acting-award nominations, but none lead to truth. – *Lisa Schwarzbaum, Entertainment Weekly*

⚊ Halle Berry (leading actress)

⚊ Milo Addica, Will Rokos (original screenplay)

Ⓣ Halle Berry (leading actress)

'We Scare Because We Care.'

Monsters, Inc. ★

DIR Pete Docter

2001 92m US

[DVD] ♫

☆ voices of: John Goodman (Sulley), Billy Crystal (Mike Wazowski), Steve Buscemi (Randall Boggs), Mary Gibbs (Boo), James Coburn (Henry J. Waternoose), Jennifer Tilly (Celia), John Ratzenberger (Yeti), Frank Oz (Fungus)

Two monsters' attempt to break the all-time record for scaring children after dark is halted when a little girl accidentally ends up in their world.

Middle-ranking Pixar, enjoyable and achieving technological firsts with its detailed generation of the monsters' furry exteriors, but prone to easy sentiment; up until an inspired finale, the corporate corridors where much of the action takes place also seem too familiar and unimaginative an environment to sustain any visual wonder.

SCR Andrew Stanton, Daniel Gerson MUS Randy Newman DES Harley Jessup, Bob Pauley ED Jim Stewart PROD Darla K. Anderson DIST Buena Vista

❝ The movie may not be perfect, but it's jam-packed with goodies - like a breakfast cereal fun-pack with a prize on every box-top. – *Michael Sragow, Baltimore Sun*

❝ It's a nice movie. But Disney has never learned that "nice", especially in comedy, is a negative virtue. – *Charles Taylor, Salon*

⚊ Randy Newman (music, original song – If I Didn't Have You)

⚊ animated feature film; Randy Newman; Gary Rydstrom, Michael Silvers (sound editing)

'See the movie that's controversial, sacrilegious, and blasphemous. But if that's not playing, see The Life of Brian.'

Monty Python's Life of Brian ★★★

DIR Terry Jones

1979 93m GB

☆ Graham Chapman (Brian etc), John Cleese (Reg etc), Terry Gilliam, Eric Idle (Stan/Loretta etc.), Michael Palin (Pontius Pilate etc), Terry Jones (The Virgin Mandy etc), Kenneth Colley (Jesus the Christ), Gwen Taylor (Mrs. Big Nose etc.), Carol Cleveland (Mrs Gregory)

A contemporary of Jesus is mistaken for him and crucified.

Controversial romp that offended some religious groups, and led to the film being banned in parts of the UK and US. It is, though, the Pythons' best film by far, with a wealth of quotable lines and sequences: remember the big difference between the Judean People's Front and the People's Front of Judea? As for the hilarious Spartacus-like finale, with a crucified choir singing 'Always Look on the Bright Side of Life,' it must be admitted that when the Pythons were in peak form, their talent seemed, well, God-given.

SCR John Cleese, Graham Chapman, Eric Idle, Michael Palin, Terry Gilliam, Terry Jones CIN Peter Biziou MUS Geoffrey Burgon ED Julian Doyle PROD John Goldstone DIST Hand Made Films

BRIAN'S MOTHER: He's not the Messiah. He's a very naughty boy!

❝ The more things change, the more we have to laugh if we are to have a prayer of remaining sane, and the Pythons are the best possible step in that direction. – *Kenneth Turan, Los Angeles Times*

Moolaadé ★★

SCR/DIR *Ousmane Sembene*

2004 124m Senegal

[DVD]

☆ Fatoumata Coulibaly (Colle), Maimouna Helene Diarra (Hadjatou), Salimata Traore (Amsatou), Dominique T. Zeida (Mercenaire), Mah Compaore (Circumcision Elder), Aminata Dao (Alima Ba)

In a village in Burkina Faso, a spirited older woman offers a refuge to four young girls who have escaped from a circumcision ritual – to the dismay of the local men.

Surprisingly upbeat and vibrant film on a tough subject, playing off tradition and modernity with a rich comic brio, and finding many reasons to cheer the women's spirited resistance.

CIN Dominique Gentil MUS Boncana Maiga DES Joseph Kpobly ED Abdellatif Raiss PROD Ousmane Sembene

M

[DVD] Available on DVD	☆ Cast in order	❝ Critics' Quotes	⚊ Academy Award	Ⓑ BAFTA
♫ Soundtrack on CD	of importance	† Points of interest	⚊ Academy Award nomination	Ⓣ BAFTA nomination

This richly textured parable feels every inch the work of a master. – *Scott Foundas, Variety*

A movie about contemporary sexual politics in which there is something very real at stake. – *Peter Bradshaw, Guardian*

† At the time of the film's release, the genital mutilation of young girls was still a practice in 38 of 54 member states of the African Union.

'In life and love, expect the unexpected.'

Moonlight Mile ★

SCR/DIR Brad Silberling
2002   117m   US
DVD   ♫

☆ Jake Gyllenhaal (Joe Nast), Dustin Hoffman (Ben Floss), Susan Sarandon (JoJo Floss), Holly Hunter (Mona Camp), Ellen Pompeo (Bertie Knox), Richard T. Jones (Ty), Allan Corduner (Stan Michaels), Dabney Coleman (Mike Mulcahey)

A young man grieving over the accidental death of his fiancée goes to stay with her grieving parents, but to his surprise, he is swiftly attracted to another woman in town.

A heavy-hitting cast for a story that looks promising in theory, but somehow fails to capitalise on the best part of its theme: the unpredictability of emotions.

CIN Phedon Papamichael   MUS Mark Isham
DES Missy Stewart   ED Lisa Zeno Churgin   PROD Mark Johnson, Brad Silberling   DIST Buena Vista

Though its conclusion is too tidily therapeutic, and though elements of its story strain credibility, Moonlight Mile has an understated, lived-in quality and a wry, unforced sense of the absurd. – *Dana Stevens, New York Times*

What's on screen is too honest and from the heart to totally dismiss but too slick and contrived to completely embrace. This is a film that cares about genuine emotion but also wants to tame it, to tidy it up and keep it confined to quarters. – *Kenneth Turan, Los Angeles Times*

'Life. Family. Love.'

Moonstruck ★

DIR Norman Jewison
1987   102m   US
DVD   ♫

☆ Cher (Loretta Castorini), Nicolas Cage (Ronny Cammareri), Vincent Gardenia (Cosmo Castorini), Olympia Dukakis (Rose Castorini), Danny Aiello (Mr. Johnny Cammareri)

A widow in her late thirties is torn between two brothers, one dependable but dull, the other wild and crazy.

Lightweight romantic comedy, tarted up with Oscars but not exactly short on broad ethnic stereotypes.

SCR John Patrick Shanley   CIN David Watkin   MUS Dick Hyman   DES Philip Rosenberg   PROD Patrick Palmer, Norman Jewison   DIST Patrick Palmer/Norman Jewison

A great big beautiful valentine of a movie, an intoxicating romantic comedy set beneath the biggest, brightest Christmas moon you ever saw. It's a monster moon, a Moby Dick of a moon, whose radiance fills the winter sky and every cranny of this joyous love story. – *Rita Kempley, Washington Post*

⚎ Cher (leading actress); Olympia Dukakis (supporting actress); John Patrick Shanley (original screenplay)
⚎ picture; Norman Jewison; Vincent Gardenia (supporting actor)
⚎ Olympia Dukakis (supporting actress)
⚎ Cher (leading actress); John Patrick Shanley (original screenplay); Dick Hyman

Morvern Callar ★

DIR Lynne Ramsay
2001   98m   GB/Canada
DVD   ♫

☆ *Samantha Morton* (Morvern Callar), *Kathleen McDermott* (Lanna), Raife Patrick Burchell (Boy in Room 1022), Dan Cadan (Dazzer), Carolyn Calder (Sheila Tequila), Jim Wilson (Tom Boddington), Dolly Wells (Susan), Ruby Milton (Couris Jean)

A supermarket shelf-stacker passes off her dead boyfriend's manuscript as her own writing, and heads with a friend to Spain.

Shot in its director's trademark pointilist fashion, a thoroughly offbeat and dreamy fantasy of escapism, grounded in the believable friendship of its two female leads, but exasperatingly static in narrative terms.

SCR Lynne Ramsay, Liana Dognini   CIN *Alwin Kuchler*
DES Jane Morton   ED Lucia Zucchetti   PROD Robyn Slovo, Charles Pattinson, George Faber   DIST Momentum

Ramsay is experimental, unconventional, and forever reaching at the gorgeousness in grief and despair. Her film moves slow as molasses, slow as paint drying – and all the better to see the colours and the complexities. – *Kimberley Jones, Austin Chronicle*

Ramsay's confidence is what is so absorbing: her confidence in her own visual language, her mastery of the material and her address to the audience. – *Peter Bradshaw, Guardian*

Mostly Martha ★★

SCR/DIR Sandra Nettelbeck
2001   109m   Germany/Austria/Switzerland/Italy
DVD

☆ *Martina Gedeck* (Martha Klein), *Sergio Castellito* (Mario), Maxime Foerste (Lina), August Zirner (Therapist), Ulrich Thomsen (Sam Thalberg)

The ordered existence of a workaholic German chef is overturned when she has to become a mother to her orphaned eight year old niece, and deal at work with a new flamboyant Italian sous-chef.

It follows a wave of food-centred movies, but this one has extra zest in its delightful ingredients – the route map to the insecure heart of an emotionally closed control freak.

CIN Michael Bertl   DES Thomas Freudenthal   ED Mona Brauer   PROD Karl Baumgartner, Christoph Friedel
DIST Optimum

This is better than good, it's wonderful: if facial expressions can be compared to colours, Gedeck works with an unusually broad palette, constantly surprising us, and she helps her co-stars shine. – *Jonathan Rosenbaum, Chicago Reader*

 M

DVD Available on DVD   ☆ Cast in order   66 Critics' Quotes   ⚎ Academy Award   ⚎ BAFTA
♫ Soundtrack on CD   of importance   † Points of interest   ⚎ Academy Award nomination   ⚎ BAFTA nomination

429

66 Little gem. – *Mick LaSalle, San Francisco Chronicle*

† A vastly inferior American remake of the film, No Reservations, opened in 2007.

'It can take a lifetime to feel alive.'

The Mother

DIR Roger Michell

2003   112m   GB

DVD

☆ Anne Reid (May), Daniel Craig (Darren), Steven Mackintosh (Bobby), Cathryn Bradshaw (Paula), Oliver Ford Davies (Bruce), Anna Wilson Jones (Helen), Peter Vaughn (Toots)

A recently widowed grandmother has her sex life reawakened by the handyman with whom her married daughter has been having an affair.

A stiflingly tasteful account of menopausal blossoming, making melodramatic mountains out of the molehill issue that seniors are still having sex; despite Craig's best efforts, the characterisation of the Jabberwocky-reading stud-builder hardly rings true, and the whole is guilty of that very British crime of being utterly po-faced in and around the bedroom.

SCR Hanif Kureishi   CIN Alwin Kuchler   MUS Jeremy Sams   DES Mark Tildesley   ED Nicolas Gaster
PROD Kevin Loader   DIST Momentum

66 Feels like life itself, sharpened to its finest points. – *Melissa Levine, Dallas Observer*

66 It's a remarkable film – one to gnaw at you and keep you up at night. – *David Edelstein, Slate*

Ⓣ Anne Reid (leading actress)

Mother and Son   ★★

DIR *Alexandr Sokurov*

1997   73m   Russia/Germany

DVD

☆ Gudrun Geyer (Mother), Alexei Ananishov (Son)

A young man and his dying mother spend their remaining days together in a house in a forest close to the coast.

Amazingly delicate, barely hour-long evocation of final words and last gasps, full of sequences – ravishing landscapes, deathbed pietás – that strive for the quality of portraiture; remarkable as it is, it belongs to that school of cinema that wants to be something else entirely, an aspiration that will strike viewers as either admirable or antithetical.

SCR Yuri Arabov   CIN *Aleksei Fyodorov*   MUS Mikhail Ivanovich   DES Vera Zelinskaya, Esther Ritterbusch
ED Leda Semyonova   PROD Thomas Kufus
DIST Zero/O-Film/Severnij Fond/Lenfilm

66 Manifests such fundamental disengagement from the dramatic conventions of the medium as to make Peter Greenaway, or even Robert Bresson, look like naturals for the next Hollywood dinosaur picture. – *Nick Bradshaw, Sight and Sound*

66 Sokurov turns life into art, and back again. He has a control I haven't seen exercised so relentlessly over actors since Carl Dreyer was alive. Will it move you?

I'm not sure. But you'll marvel at a film so far out of our time. – *Alexander Walker, Evening Standard*

† A spiritual sequel, Father and Son, followed in 2004.

'Howard W. Campbell, Jr. Is The Most Patriotic American In The Third Reich.'

Mother Night   ★★

DIR Keith Gordon

1996   114m   US

DVD   ♫

☆ *Nick Nolte* (Howard Campbell), Sheryl Lee (Helga Noth/Resi Noth), *Alan Arkin* (George Kraft), John Goodman (Major Frank Wirtanen), Kirsten Dunst (Young Resi Noth), Arye Gross (Dr. Abraham Epstein), Frankie Faison (Robert Sterling Wilson), David Strathairn (Lieutenant Bernard B. O'Hare), Bernard Behrens (Reverend Dr. Lionel Jones), Henry Gibson (Adolf Eichmann (voice))

In the late 1930s, an American playwright living in Berlin is recruited to deliver coded Allied messages under the cover of pro-Nazi propaganda.

Fiercely intelligent and ironic drama that suffers from erratic pacing; it's the punchy middle section – set in the post-war years, with the hero having been made persona non grata by US authorities – which provides the best showcase for the superior acting personnel.

SCR Robert B. Weide   CIN Tom Richmond
MUS Michael Convertino   DES François Seguin   ED Jay Rabinowitz   PROD Keith Gordon, Robert B. Weide
DIST Fine Line/Whyaduck

66 Well-played and handsomely realised, Mother Night is a true movie rarity – an attempt to grapple seriously yet entertainingly with some of the complexities of modern morality. – *Richard Schickel, Time*

'Let the world change you... and you can change the world.'

The Motorcycle Diaries   ★★★

DIR *Walter Salles*

2004   126m   US/Argentina/Chile/France/GB

DVD   ♫

☆ *Gael Garcia Bernal* (Ernesto Guevara de la Serna), *Rodrigo de la Serna* (Alberto Granado), Mia Maestro (Chichina), Gustavo Bueno (Dr Hugo Pesce), Jorge Chiarella (Dr Bresciani)

The young Che Guevara, a rugby-playing medical student, and his best friend travel by motorbike through South America, observing the poverty and suffering of the people.

A romanticised account of the young Guevara's life, this boisterously played and good-looking picture suggests his growing radical fervour through the varying landscapes of a continent and the detail of incidents that point to institutionalised injustice all across it. Still, its appeal is more nostalgic than political.

SCR José Rivera   CIN *Eric Gautier*   MUS Gustavo Santaolalla   DES Carlos Conti   ED Daniel Rezende
PROD Michael Nozik, Edgard Tenembaum, Karen Tenkhoff

66 Nothing like a full picture of Che - nor of Granado and his eventual scientific career in Cuba, for that matter. But it exhilarates with the spirit of these young men in Act One of their lives. – *Stanley Kauffmann, The New Republic*

M

66 Much of the film glides past with a slightly purposeless elegance. Astounding landscapes rise and fall away; enticing women glance and dance and disappear. – *Anthony Lane, The New Yorker*

♪ Jorge Dexler (m, ly) (music, original song – Al Otro Lado Del Rio)

♪ José Rivera (adapted screenplay)

🅣 film not in the English language; Gustavo Santaolalla
🅣 film; Eric Gautier; Gael Garcia Bernal (leading actor); Rodrigo de la Serna (supporting actor); José Rivera (adapted screenplay)

'Some Things Are Worth The Risk.'

Moulin Rouge! ★

DIR Baz Luhrmann
2001   127m   Australia/US
DVD   ♪

☆ Nicole Kidman (Satine), Ewan McGregor (Christian), John Leguizamo (Toulouse-Lautrec), Jim Broadbent (Zidler), Richard Roxburgh (Duke of Worcester), Garry McDonald (The Doctor), Matthew Whittet (Satie), Kerry Walker (Marie), Kylie Minogue (Green Fairy)

Paris, the Summer of Love, 1899: a penniless writer falls for a beautiful nightclub courtesan.

A post-modern musical in which deconstructing the form subtracts more than it adds: the pop cover versions sounded better in their original versions, while relentless editing reduces the film to visual confetti; on its release in September 2001, many viewers did, however, take refuge in its camp humour, hokey, insincere romance, and dazzling costumes and sets.

SCR Baz Luhrmann, Craig Pearce   CIN Donald M. McAlpine   MUS Craig Armstrong   DES *Catherine Martin*   ED Jill Bilcock   PROD Martin Brown, Baz Luhrmann, Fred Baron   DIST TCF

66 A landmark musical movie – controversial, mercurial, even cheeky. – *Michael Wilmington, Chicago Tribune*

66 Diverting, energetic and even reasonably satisfying, so long as you aren't looking for a real musical to take its place. – *Jonathan Rosenbaum, Chicago Reader*

† 'Nature Boy'; 'Lady Marmalade'; 'Children of the Revolution'; 'Diamonds Are a Girl's Best Friend'; 'Material Girl'; 'Your Song'; 'Sound of Music'; 'One Day I'll Fly Away'; 'All You Need is Love'; 'Like a Virgin'; 'Come What May'; 'Fool To Believe'; 'The Show Must Go On'

♪ Catherine Martin; Catherine Martin, Angus Strathie (costume)

♪ picture; Nicole Kidman (leading actress); Donald M. McAlpine; Jill Bilcock; Andy Nelson, Anna Behlmer, Roger Savage, Guntis Sics (sound); Maurizio Silvi, Aldo Signoretti (make up)

🅣 Jim Broadbent (supporting actor); Craig Armstrong; Andy Nelson, Anna Behlmer, Roger Savage, Guntis Sics, Gareth Vanderhope, Anthony Gray (sound)
🅣 film; Baz Luhrmann; Donald McAlpine; Jill Bullock; Catherine Martin; Chris Godfrey, Andy Brown, Nathan McGuinness, Brian Cox (special visual effects); Catherine Martin, Angua Strathie (costume design); Maurizio Silvi, Aldo Signoretti (make up/hair); Baz Zuhrmann, Craig Pearce (orignal screenplay)

Mountains of the Moon ★★

DIR Bob Rafelson
1989   136m   US
DVD   ♪

☆ Patrick Bergin (Richard Francis Burton), Iain Glen (John Hanning Speke), Richard E. Grant (Larry Oliphant), Fiona Shaw (Isabel Arundell), John Savident (Lord Murchison), James Villiers (Lord Oliphant), Adrian Rawlins (Edward), Peter Vaughan (Lord Houghton), Delroy Lindo (Mabruki), Bernard Hill (Dr. David Livingstone)

Captain Richard Burton and Lieutenant John Hanning Speke, two Victorian-era explorers, set off to find the source of the Nile for the glory of the British Empire.

Male bonding under extreme duress is the overriding theme of this old-fashioned adventure story. More fascinating is the aftermath: how two dissimilar men drifted apart when they had no grand project on which to collaborate. Thanks to its ravishing photography, the film is almost absurdly good-looking.

SCR William Harrison, Bob Rafelson   CIN *Roger Deakins*   MUS Michael Small   DES Norman Reynolds   ED Thom Noble   PROD Daniel Melnick
DIST Guild/Carolco/IndieProd

66 Despite longueurs, this handsome epic has a spark of intelligence and a pleasing wit. – *Nigel Floyd, Time Out*

'The squeak shall inherit the earth'

Mouse Hunt ★★

DIR *Gore Verbinski*
1997   98m   US
DVD   ♪

☆ Nathan Lane (Ernie Smuntz), Lee Evans (Lars Smuntz), Vicki Lewis (April Smuntz), Maury Chaykin (Alexander Falko), Eric Christmas (Lawyer), Michael Jeter (Quincy Thorpe), *Christopher Walken* (Caesar), Debra Christofferson (Ingrid), Camilla Soeberg (Hilde), William Hickey (Rudolf Smuntz)

Having inherited their late father's mansion, two scheming brothers attempt to rid themselves of the rodent that stands in the way of their making a sizeable profit on the property.

An enjoyable live-action cartoon, given zip by witty, agile direction, and darker shading by some of the performances.

SCR Adam Rifkin   CIN *Phedon Papamichael*   MUS Alan Silvestri   DES *Linda DeScenna*   ED Craig Wood
PROD Alan Riche, Tony Ludwig, Bruce Cohen
DIST DreamWorks

66 Comes over as a mix of Laurel and Hardy, Home Alone and Tom and Jerry, and it works very well. – *Derek Adams, Time Out*

'Close your eyes and picture the perfect world.'

Mouth to Mouth (new)

SCR/DIR Alison Murray
2006   103m   UK/Germany
DVD

☆ Ellen Page (Sherry), Eric Thal (Harry), Natasha Wightman (Rose), August Diehl (Tiger), Maxwell McCabe-

---

DVD Available on DVD   ☆ Cast in order   66 Critics' Quotes   ♪ Academy Award   🅣 BAFTA
♪ Soundtrack on CD   of importance   † Points of interest   ♪ Academy Award nomination   🅣 BAFTA nomination

431

M

Lokos (Mad Ax), Beatrice Brown (Nancy), Diana Greenwood (Dog), Jefferson Guzman (Blade)

A rebellious teen joins a travelling cult in Berlin but begins to have second thoughts after its charismatic leader recruits her mother as well.

Overwrought rite-of-passage drama, interspersed with weird interpretative dance sequences; its belated British release came off the back of its young star's Oscar nomination for Juno.

CIN Barry Stone   MUS Rowan Oliver   DES Ulrika Andersson   ED Christian Lonk   PROD Anne Beresford, Judy Tossell   DIST Dogwoof Pictures

66 Uneven, occasionally vivid, ultimately unsatisfactory. – *Dennis Harvey, Variety*

66 Page's performance is developmental at best. Though she shows flashes of strong-willed, seductive decisiveness, she mostly looks confused and under-directed. – *Mark Olsen, Los Angeles Times*

† Murray based the script on her own experiences as a member of a radical group.

'A Romantic Comedy For Anyone Who's Ever Been In Love.'

Much Ado about Nothing ★★

SCR/DIR Kenneth Branagh
1993   111m   GB
DVD   ♫

☆ Kenneth Branagh, *Richard Briers*, Michael Keaton, Denzel Washington, Robert Sean Leonard, Keanu Reeves, *Emma Thompson*, Kate Beckinsale, Brian Blessed, Patrick Doyle, Imelda Staunton, Phyllida Law, Ben Elton

As soldiers take a welcome break from war in Sicily, sexual dalliances begin, and two confirmed singletons toy with each other.

Shakespeare's romantic comedy is staged in almost aggressively jolly mood, with the sense that the cast are grimly determined to have a good time. The American contingent strikes a jarring note, though Branagh and Thompson (then still married) add some bite and spark to their stormy courtship.

CIN Roger Lanser   MUS Patrick Doyle   DES Tim Harvey   ED Andrew Marcus   PROD Steven Evans, David Parfitt, Kenneth Branagh   DIST Samuel Goldwyn/Renaissance

66 The key to the film's success is in the acting, especially in the sparks that fly between Branagh and Thompson. – *Roger Ebert, Chicago Sun-Times*

66 The picture is overripe, and with few exceptions, so are the performances. – *Peter Travers, Rolling Stone*

'A Love Story In The City Of Dreams.'

Mulholland Dr. ★★

SCR/DIR David Lynch
2001   146m   US/France
DVD   ♫

☆ Justin Theroux (Adam Kesher), Naomi Watts (Betty Elms), Laura Elena Harring (Rita), Ann Miller (Coco Lenoix), Dan Hedaya (Vincenzo Castigliane), Mark Pellegrino (Joe), Brian Beacock (Studio Singer), Robert Forster (Det. Harry McKnight)

A fame-seeking starlet arrives in Hollywood and gets involved with a beautiful young girl who has lost her memory.

Originally planned as a TV series, this idiosyncratic story flatters to deceive. It promises much, it's forcefully atmospheric, and has the air of an enigmatic masterpiece. But ultimately it simply bewilders; it's a spooky dead end.

CIN Peter Deming   MUS Angelo Badalamenti   DES Jack Fisk   ED Mary Sweeney   PROD Mary Sweeney, Alain Sarde, Neal Edelstein, Michael Polaire, Tony Krantz   DIST Pathé

66 Creepy, fascinating and dreamily self-indulgent. – *Peter Bradshaw, Guardian*

66 Every scene groans with oppressive dread and glitters with black humour. – *Paul Arendt, Teletext*

⚲ David Lynch (director)

Ⓣ Mary Sweeney

'A New Kind Of Law Enforcement.'

Mulholland Falls ★

DIR Lee Tamahori
1996   107m   US
DVD   ♫

☆ *Nick Nolte*, Melanie Griffith, Chazz Palminteri, Michael Madsen, Chris Penn, Treat Williams, Jennifer Connelly, Daniel Baldwin, Andrew McCarthy, John Malkovich, Bruce Dern, Ed Lauter

Set in 1950s Los Angeles in the 50s, a tough, old-school detective investigates the death of his ex-lover, while trying to preserve his marriage.

This lovingly staged and photographed evocation of post-war LA hardly pushes back any barriers; its script is too convoluted for that. But it's watchable enough, and Nolte, like a roaring angry bull, gives it his all.

SCR Pete Dexter, Floyd Mutrux   CIN *Haskell Wexler*   MUS Dave Grusin   DES *Richard Sylbert*   ED Sally Menke   PROD Richard D. Zanuck, Lili Fini Zanuck   DIST Polygram/MGM/Largo/Zanuck

66 Mulholland Falls is a provocative crime drama with a limp script and a forced feeling. But Nick Nolte is a ticking time bomb as a brutal Los Angeles police detective with a hulking, gasping sense of pain and meanness. He gives the film an odd, askew tone that keeps it tough and alive. – *Peter Stack, San Francisco Chronicle*

'The world was watching in 1972 as 11 Israeli athletes were murdered at the Munich Olympics. This is the story of what happened next.'

Munich ★★

DIR Steven Spielberg
2005   164m   US/Canada
DVD

☆ Eric Bana (Avner), Daniel Craig (Steve), Ciaran Hinds (Carl), Mathieu Kassovitz (Robert), Hanns Zischler (Hans), Ayelet Zurer (Daphna), Geoffrey Rush (Ephraim), Michael Lonsdale (Papa)

Israel's secret-service agency Mossad assembles a team of assassins to kill the Palestinian terrorists responsible for the massacre of Israeli athletes at the 1972 Olympic Games in Munich.

Grimly convincing and largely forceful thriller that manages to develop a great deal of tension around the

hit team's deadly missions, but falters in its attempt to analyse the morality of their actions.

SCR Tony Kushner, Eric Roth **CIN** Janusz Kaminski **MUS** John Williams **DES** Rick Carter **ED** Michael Kahn **PROD** Kathleen Kennedy, Steven Spielberg, Barry Mendel, Colin Wilson **DIST** DreamWorks

66 Gripping, intelligent and sadly all too relevant. – *David Edwards, Daily Mirror*

66 It's a brutal, merciless, sombre picture, utterly devoid of the heart-tugging sentimentality that always creeps into Spielberg's best films. It is also, unfortunately, timid when it should be bold and clunky when it should be eloquent. – *Rene Rodriguez, Miami Herald*

† The documentary One Day in September dealt with the same incident at the 1972 Olympics.

picture; Steven Spielberg; Tony Kushner, Eric Roth (adapted screenplay); Michael Kahn; John Williams

'One Broke His Silence. The Other Broke The System.'

Murder in the First ★

DIR Marc Rocco
1995 122m US

☆ Christian Slater, *Kevin Bacon*, Gary Oldman, Embeth Davidtz, Bill Macy, Stephen Tobolowsky, Brad Dourif, Mia Kirshner, Kyra Sedgwick

Henry Young is jailed in the 1930s for stealing five dollars and so badly brutalised inside that he becomes a killer. An ambitious young lawyer convinces Young to plead not guilty and put the prison system on trial.

This compelling courtroom drama is based on a true story, which makes the narrative so shocking. There is some fine acting on view but the direction is at times heavy-handed.

SCR Dan Gordon **CIN** Fred Murphy **MUS** Christopher Young **DES** Kirk M. Petruccelli **ED** Russell Livingstone **PROD** Marc Frydman, Mark Wolper **DIST** Guild/Canal/Wolper

66 Though based on a true story, this gruelling drama is peopled by characters that have been fictionalised into big house clichés. – *Rita Kempley, Washington Post*

'A Story of Love, Laughter and the Pursuit of Matrimony.'

Muriel's Wedding ★★

SCR/DIR P.J. Hogan
1994 105m Australia
DVD ♫

☆ *Toni Collette*, Bill Hunter, Rachel Griffiths, Jeanie Drynan, Gennie Nevinson, Matt Day, Daniel Lapaine, Sophie Lee, Chris Haywood

A chubby, miserable young Australian woman, who dreams of a spectacular wedding day, lives her life in the fantasy world of Abba songs. She steals her parents' life savings and heads to Sydney to find a husband.

Small-town ugly duckling Muriel is sympathetically portrayed by Toni Collette in this amiable comedy. Thought it's awkward, uneven, and chokes on its own melancholy in a sub-plot involving Muriel's best friend (Griffiths), it mainly good-hearted and amusing.

CIN Martin McGrath **MUS** Peter Best **DES** Patrick Reardon **ED** Jill Bilcock **PROD** Lynda House, Jocelyn Moorhouse **DIST** Buena Vista/CIBY 2000/AFFC

66 Muriel's Wedding runs into trouble when it looks for poignancy too openly, working better at giddy moments than in its occasional sad ones. – *Elvis Mitchell, New York Times*

66 Ultimately, the comedy here is grounded in self-hatred, hostility and despair. Nearly everyone who wanders through this brash and deliberately tasteless film is stupid, ungainly or grotesquely tragic. – *Michael Forstrom, TV Guide*

'In Goddess we trust.'

The Muse ★★

DIR Albert Brooks
1999 97m US
DVD ♫

☆ Albert Brooks (Steven Philips), Sharon Stone (Sarah), Andie MacDowell (Laura Phillips), Jeff Bridges (Jack Warrick), Mark Feuerstein (Josh Martin), Steven Wright (Stan Spielberg), Bradley Whitford (Hal), Mario Opinato (European Man), Dakin Matthews (Dr. Jacobson), Concetta Tomei (Nurse Rennert)

In Hollywood, a blocked screenwriter meets a woman who claims to be a 'muse,' and promises she will help his problem if he obeys her completely.

Brooks's humour is so bone-dry that it may have blocked the success he richly deserves; but his funny, astute, sometimes savage take on Hollywood excess and tastelessness is sadly underrated. Stone does a nice comic turn as his muse, and such luminaries as Martin Scorsese and James Cameron have walk-on roles as her 'clients.'

SCR Albert Brooks, Monica Johnson **CIN** Thomas Ackerman **MUS** Elton John **DES** Dina Lipton **ED** Peter Teschner **PROD** Herb Nanas **DIST** Entertainment

66 A real gem: a deadpan fantasy that turns into one of the best pictures ever about the post-Star Wars studio moviemaking era. – *Michael Wilmington, Chicago Tribune*

66 The sharpest insider Hollywood comedy in quite a while. – *Kenneth Turan, Los Angeles Times*

'As a lawyer all she wanted was the truth. As a daughter all she wanted was his innocence. How well do you really know your father?'

Music Box ★

DIR Costa-Gavras
1989 126m US
♫

☆ *Jessica Lange, Armin Mueller-Stahl*, Frederic Forrest, Donald Moffat, Lukas Haas, Cheryl Lynn Bruce, Mari Torocsik, J.S. Block, Sol Frieder

A successful Chicago lawyer defends her kindly Hungarian father when he is charged with Nazi war crimes.

A striking premise that devolves into a competent courtroom drama; the performances of the two leads are rather better than the script merits.

M

DVD Available on DVD   ☆ Cast in order of importance   66 Critics' Quotes   Academy Award   Academy Award nomination   BAFTA   BAFTA nomination
♫ Soundtrack on CD   † Points of interest

433

SCR Joe Eszterhas   CIN Patrick Blossier   MUS Philippe Sarde   DES Jeannine Claudia Oppewall   ED Joelle Van Effenterre   PROD Irwin Winkler   DIST Guild/Carolco

66 Although the movie is about suffering, trust and family love, it has no heart. – *Roger Ebert, Chicago Sun-Times*

⚖ Jessica Lange (leading actress)

The Music Man   ★★★

DIR *Morton da Costa*
1962   151m   US
DVD   ♫

☆ *Robert Preston* (Harold Hill), *Shirley Jones* (Marian Paroo), Buddy Hackett (Marcellus Washburn), *Hermione Gingold* (Eulalie MacKechnie Shinn), Pert Kelton (Mrs. Paroo), Paul Ford (Mayor Shinn)

A confidence trickster persuades a small-town council to start a boys' band, with himself as the agent for all the expenses.

Reasonably cinematic, thoroughly invigorating transference to the screen of a hit Broadway musical. Splendid period 'feel', standout performances, especially the dynamic Preston's, and some exuberant, rousing, show-stopping numbers.

SCR Marion Hargrove   CIN Robert Burks   ED William Ziegler   PROD Morton da Costa   DIST Warner

66 This is one of those triumphs that only a veteran performer can have; Preston's years of experience and his love of performing come together joyously. – *Pauline Kael*

† It was remade for television in 2003, with Matthew Broderick in the lead.
† 'Rock Island'; Iowa Stubborn'; 'Ya Got Trouble'; '76 Trombones'; 'Pick-a-Little, Talk-a-Little'; 'The Sadder But Wiser Girl'; 'Wells Fargo'; 'Will I Ever Tell You?'; 'It's You'; 'Being in Love'; 'Till There Was You'

⚖ Ray Heindorf (music)
⚖ picture

'Jack Pozzi is about to take the biggest gamble of his life...'

The Music of Chance   ★★

DIR *Philip Haas*
1993   98m   US
DVD

☆ James Spader (Jack Pozzi), Mandy Patinkin (Jim Nashe), M. Emmet Walsh (Calvin Murks), Charles Durning (Bill Flower), Joel Grey (Willy Stone), Samantha Mathis (Tiffany), Christopher Penn (Floyd)

A drifter and a gambler lose at poker to a pair of millionaires, and are asked to build a wall in the latter's estate to pay off their debt.

Coolly intriguing latter-day fable about the choices we make in life and the responsibilities we bear, put across by a cast with an eye and ear for the ambiguities of the piece.

SCR *Philip Haas, Belinda Haas*   CIN Bernard Zitzermann   MUS Philip Johnston   DES Hugo Luczyc-Wyhowski   ED Belinda Haas   PROD Frederick Zollo, Dylan Sellers   DIST Feature film/I.R.S. Media/American Playhouse

66 Haas handles his droll, resonant parable admirably, balancing its philosophical and dramatic dynamics with assurance and wit. Crucially, he has a good eye for an

element of mystery. Minor, but unexpectedly engrossing. – *Geoff Andrew, Time Out*

† Auster makes a cameo appearance as the motorist in the final scene.

'The secret life of architectural genius Louis Kahn.'

My Architect   ★★★

SCR/DIR Nathaniel Kahn
2003   116m   US
DVD

☆ Nathaniel Kahn (narrator)

Nathaniel Kahn sets out to find out more about his famous architect father Louis, who died deep alone and in debt at New York's Penn Station in 1974.

Fascinating psychological insight of a son bewildered by a philandering father, who could create public buildings of such formal beauty while making such a monumental mess of his life.

CIN Bob Richman   MUS Joseph Vitarelli   ED Sabine Krayenbuehl   PROD Susan Rose Behr, Nathaniel Kahn

66 A personal but enlightening documentary monument to a father from his estranged son. – *David Parkinson, Empire*

66 This is above all a fascinating, touching human story: when was the last time you cried at an architecture documentary? – *Time Out*

⚖ documentary

My Beautiful Laundrette   ★★★

DIR *Stephen Frears*
1985   97m   GB
DVD

☆ Saeed Jaffrey, Roshan Seth, *Daniel Day-Lewis*, Gordon Warnecke, Shirley Anne Field, Rita Wolf

In south London, a gay young Asian manages his uncle's launderette and falls for a white racist boy.

This charming, off-kilter story somehow evoked the spirit of its Thatcherite times, embracing racism, sexism and entrepreneurialism, all wrapped up in an improbably tender romance. Day-Lewis is a revelation as a bleached-blond object of desire.

SCR *Hanif Kureishi*   CIN Oliver Stapleton   MUS Ludus Tonalis   PROD Sarah Radclyffe, Tim Bevan   DIST Working Title/SAF/Channel 4

† The film was originally broadcast on TV but secured a cinema release after being shown at the Edinburgh Film Festival, to critical raves.

⚖ Hanif Kureishi (original screenplay)

'Julianne fell in love with her best friend the day he decided to marry someone else.'

My Best Friend's Wedding   ★

DIR P.J. Hogan
1997   105m   US
DVD   ♫

☆ Julia Roberts (Julianne Potter), Dermot Mulroney (Michael O'Neal), Cameron Diaz (Kimmy Wallace), *Rupert Everett* (George Downes), Philip Bosco (Walter Wallace), M. Emmet Walsh (Joe O'Neal), Rachel Griffiths (Samantha Newhouse)

M

Best friends Julianne and Michael agree to marry by the age of 28, unless they fall for someone else. When she discovers he's engaged, she tries to undermine the wedding plans.

An adequate comedy which fails to come alive – until Everett, as Roberts's gay chum, starts shamelessly stealing the show.

SCR Ronald Bass   CIN Laszlo Kovacs   MUS James Newton Howard   DES Richard Sylbert   ED Garth Craven, Lisa Fruchtman   PROD Jerry Zucker, Ronald Bass   DIST Columbia TriStar

66 My Best Friend's Wedding feels repetitive at times, but its star power and willingness to undercut convention come through at the end. – *Kenneth Turan, Los Angeles Times.*

⚊ James Newton Howard

Ⓣ Rupert Everett (supporting actor)

'Love is here to stay. . .So is her family.'

My Big Fat Greek Wedding   ★

DIR Joel Zwick

2002   95m   US/Canada

DVD   ♫

☆ Nia Vardalos (Toula), John Corbett (Ian), Michael Constantine (Gus), Lainie Kazan (Maria), Andrea Martin (Aunt Voula), Joey Fatone (Angelo), Gia Carides (Nikki), Louis Mandylor (Nick)

The large family of an outspoken Greek-American woman is devastated when she announces she is to wed a non-Greek.

An agreeable comedy that grew from small beginnings to become a huge hit through its word-of-mouth reputation. Yet it is devoid of any surprise, suspense, or a sense that anything is at stake.

SCR Nia Vardalos   CIN Jeffrey Jur   MUS Chris Wilson, Alexander Janko   DES Gregory Keen   ED Mia Goldman   PROD Rita Wilson, Tom Hanks, Gary Goetzman   DIST Entertainment

66 It's a poorly drilled parade of clichés familiar from pictures about force-of-life immigrants running ethnic restaurants. – *Philip French, Observer*

66 There is nothing subtle or original about this film, but it is well- intentioned and cute. – *Jean Lowerison, San Diego Metropolitan*

† A TV sitcom, My Big Fat Greek Life, went into production after the film's success.

⚊ Nia Vardalos (original screenplay)

'How do you say goodbye to someone you can't imagine living without?'

My Blueberry Nights (new)   ★

DIR Wong Kar-Wai

2007   95m   Hong Kong/France/China

DVD   ♫

☆ Norah Jones (Elizabeth), Jude Law (Jeremy), David Strathairn (Arnie), Rachel Weisz (Sue Lynne), Natalie Portman (Leslie), Chan Marshall (Katya)

Every night a New York woman, stunned by a broken love affair, visits a café where an English waiter serves her blueberry pie and listens to her sob story. She takes a road trip across America, and meets other victims of heartbreak.

Two debuts here: the first English-language film for this visionary director, and the acting debut of singer Jones. Sadly, its promise remains unfulfilled: Law's accent is imprecise; Jones looks uncomfortable. It looks pretty enough, but it's all atmosphere and no plot.

SCR Wong Kar-Wai, Lawrence Block   CIN Darius Khondji   MUS Ry Cooder   DES William Chang Suk Ping   ED William Chang Suk Ping   PROD Wong Kar-Wai, Jean-LouisPiel, Wang Wei   DIST Optimum

66 Most of its tropes and motifs are transplanted from Hong Kong, its chamber-piece exchanges neglecting any real engagement with US life. – *Ben Walters, Time Out*

66 Law, bigger-haired than usual, and at times guilty of frantic mugging, ladles up a wide-boy charm that leaves you longing for Tony Leung and his infinitely more subtle appeal. – *Sukhdev Sandhu, Daily Telegraph*

'Sometimes the things we fight about are what bring us closest together.'

My Brother is an Only Child (new)   ★

DIR Daniele Luchetti

2007   103m   Italy/France

☆ Elio Germano (Accio), Riccardo Scamarcio (Manrico), Angela Finocchiaro (Amelia), Luca Zingaretti (Mario), Massimo Popolizio (Ettore), Ascanio Celestini (Padre Cavalli), Diane Fleri (Francesca), Alba Rohrwacher (Violetta), Vittorio Emanuele Propizio (Younger Accio), Anna Bonaiuto (Bella)

In 1970s Italy, two brothers are distanced by their political and ideological beliefs.

A more manageable slice of sociological drama from the writers of The Best of Youth that effectively evokes nostalgia for the period and affection for its protagonists.

SCR Sandro Petraglia, Stefano Rulli, Daniele Luchetti   CIN Claudio Collepiccolo   MUS Franco Piersanti   DES Francesco Frigeri   ED Mirco Garrone   PROD Riccardo Tozzi, Giovanni Stabilini, Marco Chimenz   DIST Revolver Entertainment

66 As lively, witty, funny and intelligent a meditation on Italy's Fascist inheritance as we're likely to get. – *Wally Hammond, Time Out*

66 A lively minor addendum to the grand tradition of Italian fraternal cinema. – *A.O. Scott, New York Times*

'Rambo. Terminator. Indiana Jones. Vinny Gambini.'

My Cousin Vinny   ★★

DIR Jonathan Lynn

1992   120m   US

DVD   ♫

☆ *Joe Pesci* (Vincent 'Vinny' Gambini), Ralph Macchio (William 'Billy' Gambini), *Marisa Tomei* (Mona Lisa Vito), Mitchell Whitfield (Stan Rothenstein), Fred Gwynne (Judge Chamberlain Haller), Lane Smith (D.A. Jim Trotter, III), Austin Pendleton (John Gibbons), Bruce McGill (Sheriff Dean Farley), Maury Chaykin (Sam Tipton)

A newly qualified, barely competent New York lawyer goes to the deep South to speak up for his cousin who is wrongly accused of murder.

DVD Available on DVD   ☆ Cast in order   66 Critics' Quotes   ⚊ Academy Award   Ⓑ BAFTA
♫ Soundtrack on CD   of importance   † Points of interest   ⚊ Academy Award nomination   Ⓣ BAFTA nomination

Low laughs here in a shambling story that becomes a courtroom comedy, with Pesci good-humouredly playing against type, and Tomei a stand-out as his tough-talking but far smarter girlfriend.

SCR Dale Launer **CIN** Peter Deming **MUS** Randy Edelman **DES** Victoria Paul **ED** Tony Lombardo, Stephen E. Rivkin **PROD** Dale Launer, Paul Schiff **DIST** TCF/Peter V. Miller Investment Corp.

„ My Cousin Vinny is a movie that meanders along going nowhere and then lightning strikes. – *Roger Ebert, Chicago Sun-Times*

⊥ Marisa Tomei (supporting actress)

'She was everything the west was – young, fiery, exciting!'

My Darling Clementine ★★★

DIR *John Ford*
1946 98m US
DVD

☆ *Henry Fonda* (Wyatt Earp), *Victor Mature* (Doc Holliday), *Walter Brennan* (Old Man Clanton), Linda Darnell (Chihuahua), Cathy Downs (Clementine), Tim Holt (Virgil Earp), Ward Bond (Morgan Earp), *Alan Mowbray* (Granville Thorndyke), John Ireland (Billy Clanton), Jane Darwell (Kate)

Wyatt Earp, along with Doc Holliday, cleans up Tombstone and wipes out the Clanton gang at the OK Corral.

Archetypal Western mood piece, full of nostalgia for times gone by. Shot exquisitely in black-and-white, and making good use of director Ford's favoured Monument Valley locations, it crackles with memorable scenes and characterizations.

SCR Samuel G. Engel, Winston Miller **CIN** *Joe MacDonald* **MUS** *Cyril Mockridge* **ED** Dorothy Spencer **PROD** Samuel G. Engel **DIST** TCF

„ Every scene, every shot is the product of a keen and sensitive eye. – *Bosley Crowther*

„ Considerable care has gone to its period reconstruction, but the view is a poetic one. – *Lindsay Anderson*

'Every Family Needs An Optimist.'

My Dog Skip ★

DIR Jay Russell
2000 95m US
DVD

☆ Frankie Muniz (Willie Morris), Diane Lane (Ellen Morris), Luke Wilson (Dink Jenkins), Kevin Bacon (Jack Morris), Caitlin Wachs (Rivers Applewhite), Bradley Coryell (Big Boy Wilkinson), Daylan Honeycutt (Henjie Henick), Cody Linley (Spit McGee), Peter Crombie (Junior Smalls), Clint Howard (Millard), Harry Connick Jnr (Narrator)

In small-town America in 1942, a perky Jack Russell terrier puppy teaches his troubled and withdrawn nine-year-old owner some valuable lessons in life.

Gentle, nostalgic movie that recalls the agonies of growing up with welcome charm and perception. It's generous with its helpings of sentimentality.

SCR Gail Gilchriest **CIN** James L. Carter **MUS** William Ross **DES** David J. Bomba **ED** Harvey Rosenstock, Gary

Winter **PROD** Broderick Johnson, Andrew A. Kosove, Mark Johnson, John Lee Hancock **DIST** Warner

„ Though sincerely, often tenderly filmed for good humour and credible life lessons, My Dog Skip walks an uneasy path between nostalgic reverie and gut-grabbing melodrama. – *David Elliott, San Diego Union-Tribune*

† Muniz went on to star in the TV series Malcolm in the Middle.

My Fair Lady ★★★

DIR George Cukor
1964 175m US
DVD ♫

☆ *Rex Harrison* (Prof. Henry Higgins), Audrey Hepburn (Eliza Doolittle), Stanley Holloway (Alfred P. Doolittle), Wilfrid Hyde-White (Col. Hugh Pickering), Gladys Cooper (Mrs. Higgins), Jeremy Brett (Freddy Eynsford-Hill), Theodore Bikel (Zoltan Karpathy), Isobel Elsom (Mrs. Eynsford-Hill), Mona Washbourne (Mrs. Pearce), Walter Burke (Main Bystander)

Musical version of Pygmalion, about a flower girl trained by an arrogant elocutionist to pass as a lady.

Careful, cold transcription of a stage success; cinematically quite uninventive when compared with Pygmalion itself, but it's sumptuously presented, with opulent sets and Cecil Beaton's astonishing costumes. Harrison is as authoritative here as he had been throughout the musical's long stage run; Hepburn, somewhat shaky as a Cockney flower girl, comes into her own with a vengeance in the second half, when she becomes a lady. And of course, a good three-quarters of the songs are unforgettable.

SCR Alan Jay Lerner **CIN** *Harry Stradling* **MUS** Frederick Loewe **ED** William Ziegler **PROD** Jack L. Warner **DIST** CBS/Warner

„ The property has been not so much adapted as elegantly embalmed. – *Andrew Sarris*

† Audrey Hepburn's singing was famously dubbed by Marni Nixon.
† 'Why Can't the English'; 'Wouldn't It Be Luverly'; 'I'm an Ordinary Man'; 'With a Little Bit of Luck'; 'Just You Wait'; 'The Rain in Spain'; 'I Could Hve Danced All Night'; 'Ascot Gavotte'; 'On the Street Where You Live'; 'Get Me to the Church on Time'; 'I've Grown Accustomed to Her Face'

⊥ picture; Rex Harrison (leading actor); George Cukor (direction); Harry Stradling; André Previn (scoring of music); Cecil Beaton (costume design); sound
⊥ Stanley Holloway (supporting actor); Gladys Cooper (supporting actress); Alan Jay Lerner (adapted screenplay); editing
Ⓑ picture

'A film about life, laughter, and the occasional miracle.'

My Left Foot ★★

DIR Jim Sheridan
1989 103m GB
DVD ♫

☆ *Daniel Day-Lewis* (Christy Brown), *Ray McAnally* (Mr. Brown), *Brenda Fricker* (Mrs. Brown), Ruth McCabe (Mary), Fiona Shaw (Dr. Eileen Cole), Eanna MacLiam (Benny), Alison Whelan (Sheila), Declan Croghan (Tom),

Hugh O'Conor (Young Christy Brown), Cyril Cusack (Lord Castlewelland)

Account of the life of Irish writer and painter Christy Brown, who became successful despite being crippled from birth by cerebral palsy.

Acceptable film version of Christy Brown's astonishing autobiography perfectly complemented by an electrifying performance from Daniel Day-Lewis, with steadfast support from the main cast.

SCR Shane Connaughton, Jim Sheridan **CIN** Jack Conroy **MUS** Elmer Bernstein **DES** Austen Spriggs **ED** J. Patrick Duffner **PROD** Noel Pearson **DIST** Palace/Fernadale Films/Granada TV International/Radio Telefis Eireann

66 An intelligent, beautifully acted adaptation of Christy Brown's first book. – *Vincent Canby, New York Times*

Daniel Day-Lewis (leading actor); Brenda Fricker (supporting actress)

picture; Jim Sheridan; Shane Connaughton, Jim Sheridan (adapted screenplay)

Daniel Day-Lewis (leading actor); Ray McAnally (supporting actor)

film; Shane Connaughton, Jim Sheridan (adapted screenplay); Ken Jennings (make up)

My Life as a Dog ★★★

DIR Lasse Hallström
1985   101m   Sweden
DVD   ♫

☆ Anton Glanzelius (Ingemar Johansson), Manfred Serner (Erik), Anki Lidén (His Mother), Tomas von Bromssen (Uncle Gunnar), Melinda Kinnaman (Saga), Ing-Marie Carlsson (Berit)

A lonely 12-year-old Swedish boy learns to cope with his mother's illness and death, and retreats into a vivid fantasy life while staying with his aunt and uncle in the country.

A delightful rites-of-passage movie that manages to be warm and appealing without lapsing into gooey sentimentality – a trick that would sometimes elude director Hallström after Hollywood embraced his undoubted talents.

SCR Lasse Hallström, Reidar Jonsson, Brasse Brännström, Per Berglund **CIN** Jörgen Persson, Rolf Lindström **MUS** Björn Isfält **ED** Christer Furubrand, Susanne Linnman

Lasse Hallström (direction); Lasse Hallström, Reidar Jönsson, Brasse Brännström, Per Berglund (adapted screenplay)

'Fear Is Not Knowing. Terror Is Finding Out.'

My Little Eye ★

DIR Marc Evans
2002   95m   GB/France/US/Canada
DVD

☆ Sean CW Johnson (Matt), Kris Lemche (Rex), Stephen O'Reilly (Danny), Laura Regan (Emma), Jennifer Sky (Charlie), Bradley Cooper (Travis Patterson), Nick Mennell (Cop)

Five attractive young people agree to stay in a remote house for six months for a TV show. They start to panic when one of them is murdered.

Heavy-handed low-budget horror film promisingly introduces a TV reality show from hell. But it's about as scary as Big Brother, and equally preposterous.

SCR David Hilton, James Watkins **CIN** Hubert Taczanowski **MUS** Bias **DES** Crispian Sallis **ED** Marguerite Arnold **PROD** Jonathan Finn, Jane Villiers, David Hilton, Alan Greenspan **DIST** Momentum

66 Witless and utterly pointless. – *Moira Macdonald, Seattle Times*

My Name Is Joe ★★★

DIR *Ken Loach*
1998   105m   GB/Germany/France/Italy/Spain
DVD   ♫

☆ *Peter Mullan* (Joe Kavanagh), Louise Goodall (Sarah Downie), David McKay (Liam), Annemarie Kennedy (Sabine), David Hayman (McGowan), Gary Lewis (Shanks), Lorraine McIntosh (Maggie)

In Glasgow, a recovering alcoholic and amateur soccer coach embarks on a fragile relationship with a nurse. Their happiness is threatened when he agrees to a dangerous favour to help a friend in trouble.

As often with Loach, these characters are shaped and trapped by poverty, and vulnerable to the temptations and trouble it brings. It's a grim story, though Mullan (in a defining role) succeeds in making it warm and funny too.

SCR Paul Laverty **CIN** Barry Ackroyd **MUS** George Fenton **DES** Martin Johnson **ED** Jonathan Morris **PROD** Rebecca O'Brien **DIST** Parallax/Road Movies

66 The performances are uniformly superb, though Peter Mullan is especially charismatic, and the direction discreet but wonderfully telling. – *Time Out*

British film

'Wherever, Whatever, Have a nice day.'

My Own Private Idaho ★★

SCR/DIR Gus Van Sant
1991   104m   US
DVD

☆ River Phoenix (Mike Waters), Keanu Reeves (Scott Favor), James Russo (Richard Waters), William Richert (Bob Pigeon), Rodney Harvey (Gary), Michael Parker (Digger), Udo Kier (Hans)

A narcoleptic male prostitute searches for his long-lost mother, with help from a rich friend.

A loose adaptation of Shakespeare's Henry IV opens on the mean streets of Seattle's sleazier side, and turns into a bizarre road movie brim full of emotional surprises and dream sequences.

CIN Eric Alan Edwards, John Campbell **MUS** Bill Stafford **DES** David Brisbin **ED** Curtiss Clayton **PROD** Laurie Parker **DIST** New Line

66 This exquisite, cinematic poem is about the eternal search to belong somewhere, and the lonely landscape of the soul. – *Desson Howe, Washington Post*

M

DVD Available on DVD   ☆ Cast in order   66 Critics' Quotes   Academy Award   BAFTA
♫ Soundtrack on CD   of importance   † Points of interest   Academy Award nomination   BAFTA nomination

437

My Son the Fanatic ★★

DIR Udayan Prasad
1997 87m GB
[DVD]

☆ Om Puri (Parvez), Rachel Griffiths (Bettina/Sandra), Stellan Skarsgard (Schitz), Akbar Kurtha (Farid), Gopi Desai (Minoo), Harish Patel (Fizzy), Sarah Jane Potts (Madeline Fingerhut)

A Pakistani taxi driver, who has cheerfully abandoned his religion in order to assimilate in Britain, is astonished when his son embraces Muslim fundamentalism.

Well-observed and original family drama that tackles questions of tolerance and bigotry with flair and empathy.

SCR Hanif Kureishi **CIN** Alan Almond **MUS** Stephen Warbeck **DES** Grenville Horner **ED** David Gamble **PROD** Chris Curling **DIST** BBC/UGC/Arts Council/Zephyr

66 Intelligent, poignant and witty. – *Kenneth Turan, Los Angeles Times*

'The most dangerous thing to want is more.'

My Summer of Love ★★★

DIR *Pawel Pawlikowski*
2004 86m GB
[DVD] ♫

☆ Nathalie Press (Mona), Emily Blunt (Tamsin), Paddy Considine (Phil), Dean Andrews (Ricky)

Two teenage girls from opposite sides of the tracks develop a crush for each other over a long, hot summer in Yorkshire.

A delicate coming-of-age love story from across the class divide, with a strong sense of place and temperature, and a yearning, melancholy atmosphere that foreshadows disappointments ahead.

SCR Pawel Pawlikowski, Michael Wynne **CIN** Ryszard Lenczewski **MUS** Alison Goldfrapp, Will Gregory **DES** John Stevenson **ED** David Charap **PROD** Tanya Seghatchian, Chris Collins **DIST** ContentFilm

66 An exquisite exploration into the realms of seduction, obsession, deception and disillusionment. – *Stephen Rea, Philadelphia Inquirer*

🅣 British film

My Sweet Little Village ★

DIR Jiri Menzel
1985 98m Czechoslovakia

☆ Janos Ban (Otík), Marian Labuda (Pávek), Rudolf Hrusinsky (Skruzn), Milena Dvorska (Pávková), Ladislav Zupanic (Rumlena), Petr Cepek (Turek)

A simple Czechoslovakian villager triumphs over a greedy bureaucrat who wants to take over his cottage.

Gentle, lovingly crafted comedy that paints a wonderful picture of big-hearted yet cunning country folk outsmarting a cynical city slicker. There's political satire bubbling under, but it doesn't obtrude.

SCR Zdenek Sverak **CIN** Jaromir Sofr **MUS** Jiri Sust

DES Zbyner Hoch **ED** Jiri Brozeck **PROD** Jan Suster
DIST Cannon/Barrandov Film Studio '85

66 This movie is joyful from beginning to end – a small treasure but a real one. – *Roger Ebert, Chicago Sun Times*

⚍ foreign film

'Two boys. One can't remember. The other can't forget.'

Mysterious Skin ★★★

SCR/DIR Gregg Araki
2004 99m US/Netherlands
[DVD] ♫

☆ Brady Corbett (Brian), Joseph Gordon-Levitt (Neil), Michelle Trachtenberg (Wendy), Jeff Licon (Eric), Bill Sage (Coach), Mary Lynn Rajskub (Avalyn Friesen), Elisabeth Shue (Mrs. McCormick)

Two teenage boys in small-town Kansas discover that childhood 'memories' of abduction by aliens are blocking out histories of sexual abuse.

A disturbing account of paedophilia, told calmly, graphically and with impressive authority.

CIN Steve Gainer **MUS** Harold Budd, Robin Guthrie **DES** Devorah Herbert **ED** Gregg Araki **PROD** Mary Jane Skalski, Jeffrey Levy-Hinte, Gregg Araki **DIST** Tartan

66 Mysterious Skin may be a brave piece of movie-making but its unblinking look at paedophilia and male rape never makes for easy viewing. – *David Edwards, Daily Mirror*

66 The only thing Mysterious Skin will do is make yours crawl. – *Neil Smith, BBC*

Mystery Train ★★

SCR/DIR Jim Jarmusch
1989 110m US/Japan
[DVD] ♫

☆ Masatoshi Nagase (Jun), Youki Kudoh (Mitsuko), Screamin' Jay Hawkins (Night Clerk), Cinque Lee (Bellboy), Rufus Thomas (Man in Station), Nicoletta Braschi (Luisa), Elizabeth Bracco (Dee Dee), Joe Strummer (Johnny aka Elvis), Rick Aviles (Will Robinson), Steve Buscemi (Charlie the Barber)

Two Japanese teenagers obsessed by Elvis Presley and Carl Perkins visit Sun Studios in Memphis, Tennessee on an eventful pilgrimage.

Director Jarmusch in his trademark deadpan mode, surveying naïve tourists searching for memories of their American musical heroes. It's a low-key delight.

CIN Robby Müller **MUS** John Lurie **DES** Dan Bishop **ED** Melody London **PROD** Jim Stark **DIST** Palace/JVC

66 The best thing about Mystery Train is that it takes you to an America you feel you ought to be able to find for yourself, if only you knew where to look. – *Roger Ebert, Chicago Sun-Times*

† The film takes its title from an Elvis Presley track, first recorded in 1953 by Little Junior Parker.

'A romantic comedy with the works.'

Mystic Pizza ★

DIR Donald Petrie
1988 104m US
[DVD]

☆ Vincent Phillip D'Onofrio (Bill), Annabeth Gish (Kat

Arujo), William R. Moses (Tim Travers), Julia Roberts (Daisy Arujo), Adam Storke (Charles Gordon Windsor, Jr.), Lili Taylor (Jojo), Conchata Ferrell (Leona), Porscha Radcliffe (Phoebe Travers)

Two young sisters and their girlfriend work in a pizza parlour in Mystic, Connecticut. When all fall in love for the first time, they make different plans for the future.

Inoffensive light comedy about three winning young women girls experiencing their first romances. Roberts is splendid in what proved to be a breakthrough role.

SCR Amy Jones, Perry Howze, Randy Howze, Alfred Uhry **CIN** Tim Suhrstedt **MUS** David McHugh **DES** David Chapman **ED** Marion Rothman, Don Brochu **PROD** Mark Levinson, Scott Rosenfelt **DIST** Virgin/Samuel Goldwyn Company

66 A thoroughly involving movie that doesn't resort to violence, sex or schmaltz to pack an emotional punch. – *Time Out*

'We bury our sins, we wash them clean.'

Mystic River ★★★

DIR Clint Eastwood
2003 137m US/Australia
[DVD] ♫

☆ *Sean Penn* (Jimmy Markum), *Tim Robbins* (Dave Boyle), *Kevin Bacon* (Sean Devine), Laurence Fishburne (Whitey

Powers), Marcia Gay Harden (Celeste Boyle), Laura Linney (Annabeth Markum), Kevin Chapman (Val Savage), Thomas Guiry (Brendan Harris), Emmy Rossum (Katie Markum)

Three childhood friends from Boston share a dark secret from their youth. Their lives intersect again when an innocent young girl is murdered.

Sinister, brooding story with a strong sense of place. Despite its failed aspirations to tragic grandeur, it succeeds as a whole, thanks to some fine acting in the lead roles, and director Eastwood's ability to maintain dramatic tension.

SCR Brian Helgeland **CIN** Tom Stern **MUS** Clint Eastwood **DES** Henry Bumstead **ED** Joel Cox **PROD** Robert Lorenz, Judie G. Hoyt, Clint Eastwood **DIST** Warner

66 Eastwood's drama is substantial, but monolithic, like a handsome, well-made piece of traditional American furniture. – *Peter Bradshaw, Guardian*

66 Works as a straight-up detective story, and the acting is often breathtaking. – *Bill Muller, Arizona Republic*

⚊ Sean Penn (leading actor); Tim Robbins (supporting actor)

⚊ picture; Marcia Gay Harden (supporting actress); Clint Eastwood; Brian Helgeland (adapted screenplay)

Ⓣ Sean Penn (leading actor); Tim Robbins (supporting actor); Laura Linney (supporting actress); Brian Helgeland (adapted screenplay)

[DVD] Available on DVD ☆ Cast in order 66 Critics' Quotes ⚊ Academy Award Ⓑ BAFTA
♫ Soundtrack on CD of importance † Points of interest ⚊ Academy Award nomination Ⓣ BAFTA nomination

439

Nadine ★

SCR/DIR Robert Benton
1987 78m US
DVD ♫

☆ Jeff Bridges (Vernon Hightower), Kim Basinger (Nadine Hightower), Rip Torn (Buford Pope), Gwen Verdon (Vera), Glenne Headly (Renée Lomax), Jerry Stiller (Raymond Escobar)

An unhappily married couple are forced to flee together after they stumble into a murder scene.

An attempt to revive a broader, old-fashioned vein of caper comedy does not quite succeed, though it's tolerable fun watching everyone try.

CIN Nestor Almendros MUS Howard Shore DES Paul Sylbert ED Sam O'Steen PROD Arlene Donovan
DIST Columbia TriStar/ML Delphi

66 A curiously flat, unfinished, low-energy comedy. – *Roger Ebert, Chicago Sun-Times*

Naked ★★

SCR/DIR Mike Leigh
1993 131m GB
DVD

☆ *David Thewlis* (Johnny), Lesley Sharp (Louise Clancy), Katrin Cartlidge (Sophie), Greg Cruttwell (Jeremy G. Smart), Claire Skinner (Sandra), Peter Wight (Brian), Ewen Bremner (Archie), Susan Vidler (Maggie)

A manic misogynist runs away from Manchester to London to move in with an old girlfriend before his life spirals out of control.

David Thewlis is electrifying in this saga of violence and self-hatred. It isn't director Leigh's best work – he's on firmer ground when dealing with groups and communities rather than individuals – but Thewlis's jolting conviction sees the film through.

CIN Dick Pope MUS Andrew Dickson DES Alison Chitty ED Jon Gregory PROD Simon Channing-Williams DIST First Independent/Thin Man/Film Four

66 Raw, haunting and indelible. Where's David Thewlis's Oscar? – *Jonathan R. Perry, Tyler Morning Telegraph, Texas*

66 Hilarious, but sometimes hard to stomach, Leigh's picaresque tale is his most troubling and intriguing work since Meantime; it's also by far his most cinematic. – *Time Out*

Ⓣ British film

'The Most Exciting Story Of The World's Most Exciting City!'

The Naked City ★★★

DIR *Jules Dassin*
1948 96m US
DVD

☆ *Barry Fitzgerald* (Lt. Dan Muldoon), *Don Taylor* (Jimmy Halloran), Howard Duff (Frank Niles), Dorothy Hart (Ruth Morrison), Ted de Corsia (Garzah), Adelaide Klein (Mrs. Batory)

New York police track down the killer of a woman found murdered in her bath.

Highly influential documentary thriller which, shot on location in New York's teeming streets, claimed to be giving an impression of city life; actually its real mission was to tell an ordinary murder tale with an impressive accumulation of detail and humour. The narrator's last words became a cliché: 'There are eight million stories in the naked city. This has been one of them.'

SCR *Malvin Wald, Albert Maltz* CIN *William Daniels* MUS Frank Skinner, Miklos Rozsa ED *Paul Weatherwax* PROD Mark Hellinger DIST Universal

♣ William Daniels (cinematography); Paul Weatherwax (editing)
♣ Malvin Wald (original story)

'The Villain. Even Mother Teresa wanted him dead.'

The Naked Gun: From the Files of Police Squad ★★★

DIR *David Zucker*
1988 85m US
DVD

☆ *Leslie Nielsen* (Lt. Frank Drebin), Priscilla Presley (Jane Spencer), Ricardo Montalban (Vincent Ludwig), George Kennedy (Capt. Ed Hocken), O. J. Simpson (Det. Nordberg), Susan Beaubian (Wilma Nordberg), Nancy Marchand (Mayor Barkley), Raye Birk (Papshmir), Jeannette Charles (Her Majesty, Queen Elizabeth II)

A hapless detective uncovers a plot to assassinate the Queen of England during a royal visit to Los Angeles.

Neither big, clever, artful nor especially profound – but, for silly-minded slapstick delivered with the straightest of faces, this probably is about as good as it gets.

SCR *Jerry Zucker, Jim Abrahams, David Zucker, Pat Proft* CIN Robert Stevens MUS Ira Newborn DES John J. Lloyd ED Michael Jablow PROD Robert K. Weiss
DIST UIP/Paramount

66 More juvenile than a Mel Brooks movie, wittier than Get Smart, almost as low as Animal House and close to

---

DVD Available on DVD ☆ Cast in order of importance 66 Critics' Quotes ♣ Academy Award Ⓑ BAFTA
♫ Soundtrack on CD † Points of interest ♣ Academy Award nomination Ⓑ BAFTA nomination

the laugh count of Airplane! – *Desson Thomson, Washington Post*

66 It will help if, while watching The Naked Gun, viewers can assume a mental age of about 14. The jokes will seem fresher that way, and they will also, much to the writers' credit, seem screamingly funny at times. – *Elvis Mitchell, The New York Times*

† Two sequels followed: The Naked Gun 2$^1/_2$: The Smell of Fear in 1991, and The Naked Gun 33 1/3: The Final Insult in 1994.

'Frank Drebin is back. Just accept it.'

Naked Gun 2$^1/_2$: The Smell of Fear ★

DIR David Zucker
1991 85m US
DVD ♫

☆ Leslie Nielsen (Lt. Frank Drebin), Priscilla Presley (Jane Spencer), George Kennedy (Captain Ed Hocken), O.J. Simpson (Nordberg), Robert Goulet (Quentin Hapsburg), Richard Griffiths (Dr. Albert S. Meinheimer/Earl Hacker), Jacqueline Brookes (Commissioner Anabell Brumford), Anthony James (Hector Savage), Lloyd Bochner (Terence Baggett)

Clueless cop investigates a devious plot to kidnap the US President's energy expert with a lookalike who will ignore environmental concerns.

The familiar formula returns with good jokes slightly thinner on the ground; but it's still laugh-out-loud funny at its best.

SCR David Zucker, Pat Proft **CIN** Robert Stevens **MUS** Ira Newborn **DES** John J. Lloyd **ED** James Symons, Chris Greenbury **PROD** Robert K. Weiss **DIST** UIP/Paramount/Zucker/Abrahams/Zucker

66 A feeble sequel to The Naked Gun that's about one and a half rungs down from its predecessor and a good four or five down from Airplane! – *Jonathan Rosenbaum, Chicago Reader*

66 A perfect 90 minutes of goofball fun. – *John F. Kelly, Washington Post*

Naked Gun 33$^1/_3$: The Final Insult ★★

DIR Peter Segal
1994 82m US
DVD

☆ Leslie Nielsen (Lt. Frank Drebin), Priscilla Presley (Jane Spencer), George Kennedy (Captain Ed Hocken), O.J. Simpson (Nordberg), Fred Ward (Rocco Dillon), Kathleen Freeman (Muriel Dillon), Anna Nicole Smith (Tanya Peters), Ellen Greene (Louise), Ed Williams (Ted Olsen)

Retired detective Frank Drebin is persuaded to return as an undercover cop to catch a crazed bomber planning a terrorist attack.

Sparkling gags and Nielsen at his straight-faced best make this an inspired piece of silliness.

SCR Pat Proft, David Zucker, Robert LoCash **CIN** Robert Stevens **MUS** Ira Newborn **DES** Lawrence G. Paull **ED** Jim Symons **PROD** Robert K. Weiss, David Zucker **DIST** Paramount

66 Still funny. – *Jeffrey M. Anderson, San Francisco Examiner*

66 Any film that can rescue Pia Zadora from obscurity, if only to plunk a tuba on her head and toss her off a stage, deserves some kind of award. – *TV Guide's Movie Guide*

'Exterminate all rational thought.'

Naked Lunch ★★

SCR/DIR David Cronenberg
1991 115m Canada/GB
DVD ♫

☆ Peter Weller (Bill Lee), Judy Davis (Joan Frost/Joan Lee), Ian Holm (Tom Frost), Julian Sands (Yves Cloquet), Roy Scheider (Doctor Benway), Monique Mercure (Fadela), Nicholas Campbell (Hank), Michael Zelniker (Martin), Robert A. Silverman (Hans), Joseph Scorsiani (Kiki)

A drug-addled pornography writer shoots his wife dead while doing a party trick, and escapes to a paranoid fantasy world.

The bizarre hallucinations of William S. Burroughs are compelling in print, though fearsomely hard to adapt. But Cronenberg has a decent stab in this wildly inventive version that becomes a long contemplation on the process of writing itself. Admirable enough, though the very antithesis of mainstream entertainment.

CIN Peter Suschitzky **MUS** Howard Shore, Ornette Coleman (alto sax solos) **DES** Carol Spier **ED** Ronald Sanders **PROD** Jeremy Thomas **DIST** First Independent

66 A twisted, brilliant masterpiece. One of Cronenberg's best. – *Jeffrey M Anderson, San Francisco Examiner*

66 There is so much dryness, death and despair here, in a life spinning itself out with no joy. – *Roger Ebert, Chicago Sun-Times*

'Two worlds. One journey.'

The Namesake ★★★

DIR Mira Nair
2007 121m US/India/Japan
DVD ♫

☆ Irrfan Khan (Ashoke Ganguli), Tabu (Ashima), Kal Penn (Gogol Ganguli), Jacinda Barrett (Maxine), Zuleikha Robinson (Moushumi Mazumdar), Brooke Smith (Sally), Sahira Nair (Sonia)

An Indian couple leave Calcutta for a new life in New York. Their son, torn between his Bengali roots and his American peers, struggles to find his identity – a problem that affects his romantic relationships.

A classic immigrant story about cultural clashes. Nair astutely contrasts the warm, exuberant colours of Calcutta with the bleached-out tones of wintry but more affluent New York: a perfect visual metaphor for what Ashoke and Ashima have lost and gained. This delicate balance recurs throughout: there's laughter through tears, hope mixed with sadness, pride in achievement laced with melancholy. It's ravishing to look at, genuinely moving, with a wisdom touched by poignancy. The romantic life of the son, Gogol, takes a surprising, welcome twist near the end.

N

DVD Available on DVD   ☆ Cast in order of importance   66 Critics' Quotes   ⌇ Academy Award   ⌇ Academy Award nomination   † Points of interest   🅱 BAFTA   🅱 BAFTA nomination

441

SCR Sooni Taraporevala   CIN Frederick Elmes
MUS Nitin Sawhney   DES Stephanie Carroll   ED Allyson
C. Johnson   PROD Lydia Dean Pilcher, Mira Nair
DIST TCF

66 A considerable achievement, assured, moving, often
very funny. – *Philip French, Observer*

66 Making you feel the presence of absences – of the
distant and the departed, of dreams that never quite come
true – is the key thing that this uneven film gets exactly
right. – *Michael Sragow, Baltimore Sun*

'Small Town Girl. Big Time Adventure.'

Nancy Drew (new)

DIR Andrew Fleming
2007   99m   US
♫

☆ Emma Roberts (Nancy Drew), Josh Flitter (Corky), Max
Thieriot (Ned Nickerson), Rachael Leigh Cook (Jane
Brighton), Tate Donovan (Carson Drew), Barry Bostwick
(Dashiel Biedermeyer), Laura Elena Harring (Dehlia
Draycott)

After moving to Los Angeles with her father, teen
sleuth Nancy Drew gets drawn into a mystery
involving a long-dead starlet and a haunted
Hollywood mansion.

*Flat-footed stab at giving a moribund property a
modern makeover; next to the high-school antics and
romantic subplot, the mystery element seems almost
incidental.*

SCR Andrew Fleming, Tiffany Paulsen   CIN Alexander
Gruszynski   MUS Ralph Sall   DES Tony Fanning
ED Jeff Freeman   PROD Jerry Weintraub   DIST Warner
Bros

66 Purportedly an attempt to modernise the young
detective's adventures for a new generation of tweens, the
pic instead serves up stale mystery-movie clichés and
overcooked red herrings. – *Lael Loewenstein, Variety*

66 The whole thing caused my cerebellum to seize up with
a killer combo of resentment, boredom and misery. – *Peter
Bradshaw, Guardian*

† Bruce Willis makes a cameo appearance as the star of the
film whose shooting Nancy interrupts.

'A comedy about life at the top, as seen from the
bottom.'

The Nanny Diaries (new)

SCR/DIR Robert Pulcini, Shari Springer Berman
2007   104m   US
DVD   ♫

☆ Scarlett Johansson (Annie Braddock), Laura Linney
(Mrs X), Alicia Keys (Lynette), Chris Evans ('Harvard
Hottie'), Donna Murphy (Judy Braddock), Paul Giamatti
(Mr X), Nicholas Reese Art (Grayer)

A would-be anthropology student is hired to mind
the child of a wealthy New York couple who make
her life a misery.

*Glossy comedy in the Devil Wears Prada mould; as
before, the villainess of the piece, here played by Laura
Linney, is infinitely more interesting than the nominal
heroine.*

CIN Terry Stacey   MUS Mark Suozzo   DES Mark Ricker
ED Robert Pulcini   PROD Richard N. Gladstein, Dany
Wolf   DIST Paramount

ANNIE BRADDOCK: 'In Africa they have a saying: it takes a
village to raise a child. But for the tribe of the Upper East
Side of Manhattan, it takes just one.'

66 The clash between a supposedly working-class girl and
the preppy rich parents never gets beyond a couple of
token putdowns, not least because the actress looks
infinitely classier than her tormentors. – *James Christopher,
The Times*

66 As shallow as the Upper East Side society it skewers. –
Geoff Berkshire, Chicago Tribune

Nanook of the North   ★★★

1921   57m   US
DVD

The life of an Eskimo and his family.

*Primitive but trail-blazing documentary, astonishingly
photographed under the most severe conditions. A
genuinely historic film.*

DIST Revillon Frères

66 In a day of emotional and artistic deliquescence on the
screen, a picture with the fresh strength and pictorial
promise of Nanook of the North is in the nature of a
revolution. – *Frances Taylor Patterson*

† Nanook himself died of starvation in Hudson Bay shortly
after the film's release.

† The film was re-edited in 1948, with music and a
voiceover narrative added.

† It was wholly financed by a company of furriers.

Napoleon   ★★★★

SCR/DIR *Abel Gance*
1927   378m   France

☆ Albert Dieudonné (Napoleon Bonaparte), Antonin
Artaud (Marat), Pierre Batcheff (General Lazare Hoche)

The early life of Napoleon.

*A cinematic epic which, although brilliant in most
particulars, owes its greatest interest to its narrative
sweep, its flair for composition and its use of triptych
screens which at the end combine to show one giant
picture, the clear precursor of Cinerama. In 1934
Gance cut his film to 140 minutes and added
stereophonic sound.*

CIN various   MUS Arthur Honegger   ED *Abel Gance*
DIST WESTI/Société Générale de Films

† A version restored to 235 minutes by film historian
Kevin Brownlow was released in 1981, the year of
Gance's death, with a new musical score by Carmine
Coppola.

'He's out to prove he's got nothing to prove.'

Napoleon Dynamite   ★

DIR Jared Hess
2004   86m   US
DVD   ♫

☆ Jon Heder (Napoleon Dynamite), Jon Gries (Uncle
Rico), Aaron Ruell (Kip), Efren Ramirez (Pedro), Tina
Majorino (Deb), Diedrich Bader (Rex)

DVD Available on DVD   ☆ Cast in order   66 Critics' Quotes   ♪ Academy Award   🅑 BAFTA
♫ Soundtrack on CD   of importance   † Points of interest   ♫ Academy Award nomination   🅑 BAFTA nomination

Oddball high-school pupil campaigns to get his misfit chum elected as class president.

It wears its kooky attitude like a badge of honour, and consequently seems a little smug. Yet this slab of adolescent whimsy struck a chord with younger audiences, and the lead characters' extreme nerdiness comes to seem faintly touching.

SCR Jared and Jerusha Hess   CIN Munn Powell   MUS John Swihart   DES Cory Lorenzen   ED Jeremy Coon   PROD Jeremy Coon, Sean C. Covel, Chris Wyatt   DIST Fox Searchlight

66 Debut director Jared Hess's wonderfully offbeat movie revels in its own kookiness and is the most engaging teen movie to emerge from the States for many a year. – *Adrian Hennigan, BBC*

66 As long as you don't mind making fun of the afflicted there are some killer comic moments. – *Empire Magazine*

Narc ★

SCR/DIR Joe Carnahan
2002   105m   US
DVD   ♫

☆ Ray Liotta (Lt. Henry Oak), Jason Patric (Nick Tellis), Chi McBride (Capt. Cheevers), Busta Rhymes (Beery), Anne Openshaw (Katherine Calvess), Richard Chevolleau (Steeds), John Ortiz (Ruiz)

Undercover detectives in Detroit work fearlessly to capture the drug dealers who killed one of their colleagues.

Unshowy thriller that breaks little ground, but holds the attention from start to finish.

CIN Alex Nepomnischy   MUS Cliff Martinez   DES Taava Sooder, Greg Beale   ED John Gilroy   PROD Diane Nabatoff, Ray Liotta, Michelle Grace, Julius R. Nasso   DIST UIP

66 Ferociously gritty and unsentimentally tough, Joe Canahan's movie is drenched with a cynicism that permeates the celluloid itself. – *Peter Bradshaw, Guardian*

'The damnedest thing you ever saw!'

Nashville ★★★

DIR *Robert Altman*
1975   161m   US
DVD   ♫

☆ Geraldine Chaplin (Opal), David Arkin (Norman Chauffeur), Barbara Baxley (Lady Pearl), Ned Beatty (Delbert Reese), Karen Black (Connie White), *Keith Carradine* (Tom Frank), *Henry Gibson* (Haven Hamilton), Keenan Wynn (Mr. Green), *Lily Tomlin* (Linnea Reese), Ronee Blakley (Barbara Jean)

A political campaign in Nashville organizes a mammoth pop concert to gain support.

Kaleidoscopic, fragmented, multi-storied musical melodrama, a mammoth movie which only occasionally over-reaches itself in its audacious attempt to analyse the various strata of a complex, colourful American city.

SCR *Joan Tewkesbury*   CIN Paul Lohmann   ED Sidney Levin, Dennis M. Hill   PROD Robert Altman   DIST Paramount/ABC

66 A gigantic parody. . .crammed with samples taken from every level of Nashville society, revealed in affectionate detail bordering on caricature in a manner that would surely delight Norman Rockwell. – *Philip Strick*

66 A wonderful mosaic which yields up greater riches with successive viewings. – *Tom Milne, Time Out*

⚱ Keith Carradine (m), (ly) (music, original song – I'm Easy)

⚱ picture; Lily Tomlin (supporting actress); Ronee Blakley (supporting actress); Robert Altman (direction)

The Nasty Girl ★★

SCR/DIR *Michael Verhoeven*
1990   92m   West Germany
DVD

☆ Lena Stolze (Sonja), Monika Baumgartner (Maria), Michael Gahr (Paul Rosenberger), Fred Stillkrauth (Uncle), Elisabeth Bertram (Grandmother), Robert Giggenbach (Martin), Karin Thaler (Nina), Hans-Reinhard Muller (Dr. Juckenack)

A young Bavarian woman becomes a social outcast in her town after ostentatiously researching its activities during the Nazi era, in order to write an essay on the subject in a national essay competition.

Alternately funny and biting, this deft satire chimed with the times in Germany, coinciding with the rise of a young generation examining their consciences and their legacy. Almost documentary in style, it makes its points effectively.

CIN Axel de Roche   MUS Mike Hertung, Elmar Schloter, Billy Gorlt, Lydie Auvray   DES Hubert Popp   ED Barbara Hennings   PROD Michael Senftleben   DIST Mainline/Sentana/ZDF

⚱ best foreign film

🅣 best foreign film

National Treasure: Book of Secrets (new)

DIR Jon Turteltaub
2007   124m   US
DVD

☆ Nicolas Cage (Ben Gates), Jon Voight (Patrick Gates), Harvey Keitel (Sadusky), Ed Harris (Mitch Wilkinson), Diane Kruger (Abigail Chase), Justin Bartha (Riley Poole), Bruce Greenwood (The President), Helen Mirren (Emily Appleton)

Treasure hunter Ben Gates seeks a city of gold to prove his ancestors had nothing to do with Lincoln's assassination.

Strained sequel which mistakes haste for urgency as it tears across the globe to little coherent purpose.

SCR Cormac Wibberley, Marianne Wibberley   CIN John Schwartzman, Amir Mokri   MUS Trevor Rabin   DES Dominic Watkins   ED William Goldenberg, David Rennie   PROD Jerry Bruckheimer, Jon Turteltaub   DIST Buena Vista

66 Sometimes entertaining but mostly pretty tired. – *Peter Bradshaw, Guardian*

66 The riddles are conspicuously less clever, the humour more obvious, the stabs at educational value even more perfunctory. – *Justin Chang, Variety*

DVD Available on DVD   ☆ Cast in order of importance   66 Critics' Quotes   ⚱ Academy Award   🅣 BAFTA
♫ Soundtrack on CD   † Points of interest   ⚱ Academy Award nomination   🅣 BAFTA nomination

443

† Dame Helen Mirren was prevented by filming from accepting an invitation to meet Queen Elizabeth II, whom she played on screen in The Queen.

'In The Media Circus Of Life, They Were The Main Attraction.'

Natural Born Killers ★★

DIR Oliver Stone
1994 118m US
[DVD] ♫

☆ Woody Harrelson (Mickey), Juliette Lewis (Mallory), Robert Downey Jnr (Wayne Gale), Tommy Lee Jones (Dwight McClusky), Rodney Dangerfield (Mallory's Dad), Edie McClurg (Mallory's Mom)

A murderous young couple go on a slaying spree and become instant media celebrities.

While it was widely castigated as a glorious hymn to violence, this is a forceful satire about the American media's fascination with colourful criminals. Owing more than a little to Badlands and Bonnie and Clyde, it is not remotely in the same class, yet it has a real visceral kick. That piledriver effect on audiences may be its only message; certainly its moralising amounts to little.

SCR David Veloz, Richard Rutowski, Oliver Stone
CIN Robert Richardson **MUS** Brent Lewis **DES** Victor Kempster **ED** Hank Corwin, Brian Berdan **PROD** Jame Hamsher, Don Murphy, Clayton Townsend
DIST Warner/Regency/Alcor/JD/Ixtlan/New Regency

66 The actors are given no space to build up characters and the film's main 'virtue' is that it's nowhere near as explicit as the tabloids suggested. Turgid. – *Time Out*

66 Welcome to Natural Born Killers, Stone's empty, manic meditation on society's glorification of violence and the ugly heroes it loves to hate. – *Desson Howe, Washington Post*

† Brad Pitt reportedly turned down the role of Mickey.
† The UK release of the video was cancelled after mass killings in Dunblane, Scotland in 1996. It finally became available in 2001.

The Navigators ★★

DIR Ken Loach
2001 96m GB/Spain/Germany
[DVD]

☆ Dean Andrews (John), Tom Craig (Mick), Joe Duttine (Paul), Steve Huison (Jim), Venn Tracey (Gerry), Andy Swallow (Len), Sean Glenn (Harpic), Charlie Brown (Jack), Juliet Bates (Fiona), Angela Saville (Tracy)

The privatisation of British Rail leads to disillusionment amongst the company's workforce, and puts the lives of track workers at risk.

Potent, polemical but always human drama, a return to British shores for its director after a trilogy of films set in the Americas (Land and Freedom, Carla's Song, Blood and Roses) – and, in those scenes featuring the navvies themselves, a return to the salty-funny blue-collar banter of Riff-Raff and Raining Stones. The tragedy that unfolds is lent extra force by the good humour expressed before it.

SCR *Rob Dawber* **CIN** Mike Eley, Barry Ackroyd
MUS George Fenton **DES** Martin Johnson
ED Jonathan Morris **PROD** Rebecca O'Brien **DIST** BFI

66 Simply the final word on the evils of private industry. – *Maria Garcia, Film Journal International*

66 Loach has a way of capturing the offhand, unspectacular way people live, with social comedy but minus any sociology. – *Wesley Morris, Boston Globe*

† Screenwriter Rob Dawber worked on the railways in Sheffield for eighteen years; he died of asbestos-related cancer shortly before the film's release.

'You Can Kill A Man. But Not A Legend.'

Ned Kelly ★

DIR Gregor Jordan
2003 110m Australia/GB/US/France
[DVD] ♫

☆ Heath Ledger (Ned Kelly), Orlando Bloom (Joe Byrne), Naomi Watts (Julia Cook), Geoffrey Rush (Superintendent Francis Hare), Rachel Griffiths (Mrs Scott), Laurence Kinlan (Dan Kelly), Philip Barantini (Steve Hart), Joel Edgerton (Aaron Sherritt)

In Australia in the 1870s, a farmhand, handy with his fists, becomes a famous outlaw after police persecute his family.

A film in two minds about its ambitions: it is an action-heavy biopic, or a superficial psychological study of a man whose character is now clouded by legend? It cannot decide, yet it's watchable enough, its terrain lovingly filmed, and its hero always given the benefit of the doubt.

SCR John Michael McDonagh **CIN** Oliver Stapleton
MUS Klaus Badelt, Bernard Fanning **DES** Steven Jones-Evans **ED** Jon Gregory **PROD** Lynda House, Nelson Woss **DIST** Universal

66 Ultimately (director Gregor) Jordan's film is so murky that Ned Kelly remains as foreign to us as wombat stew. – *Janice Page, Boston Globe*

66 A leaden retelling of the legend of Australia's Jesse James that has understandably been sitting on the shelf for a couple of years. – *Lou Lumenick, New York Post*

Neil Young: Heart of Gold ★★

DIR Jonathan Demme
2006 103m US
[DVD]

☆ Neil Young, Emmylou Harris, Ben Keith, Spooner Oldham, Rick Rosas, Karl Himmel, Chad Cromwell, Wayne Jackson, Pegi Young, Grant Boartwright

Singer-songwriter Neil Young premieres his album Prairie Wind at Nashville's Ryman Auditorium.

The indefatigable Young covers his almost 40-year career in this lovely concert film. Demme films him discreetly, mostly in unobtrusive long takes. The stage is bathed in gold – appropriately for an artist whose life has now reached the season of mellow fruitfulness.

CIN Ellen Kuras **DES** Michael Zansky **ED** Andy Keir
PROD Jonathan Demme, Ilona Herzberg **DIST** UIP

66 The concert film has never looked or sounded classier. – *Robert Koehler, Variety*

N

[DVD] Available on DVD   ☆ Cast in order   66 Critics' Quotes   ⏐ Academy Award   🅱 BAFTA
♫ Soundtrack on CD   of importance   † Points of interest   ⏐ Academy Award nomination   Ⓑ BAFTA nomination

66 All in all, a visual and musical feast. – *Peter Rainer, Christian Science Monitor*

† Neil Young's album Prairie Wind was released in 2005.

Nelly and M Arnaud ★★

DIR Claude Sautet
1995   106m   France/Germany/Italy
DVD

☆ *Emmanuelle Béart* (Nelly), *Michel Serrault* (M. Pierre Arnaud), Jean-Hugues Anglade (Vincent Granec), Claire Nadeau (Jacqueline), Françoise Brion (Lucie), Michèle Laroque (Isabelle), Michel Lonsdale (Dolabella)

After a chance meeting with a rich, elderly businessman in a Paris café, an attractive young wife walks out on her dull, unemotional husband.

An insightful, cerebral drama featuring the most restrained of relationships.

SCR Claude Sautet, Jacques Fieschi, Yves Ulmann
CIN Jean-François Robin   MUS Philippe Sarde
DES Carlos Conti   ED Jacqueline Thiedot   PROD Alain Sarde   DIST Guild/TFI/Cecchi Gori/Prokino/Canal/Alain Sarde

66 It's reserved, polished and challengingly intelligent. – *Hal Hinson, Washington Post*

Ⓣ film not in the English language

The Neon Bible ★★

SCR/DIR Terence Davies
1995   91m   GB

☆ Gena Rowlands (Mae Morgan), Jacob Tierney (David, aged 15), Diana Scarwid (Sarah), Denis Leary (Frank), Leo Burmester (Bobbie Lee Taylor), Frances Conroy (Miss Scover), Peter McRobbie (Reverend Watkins), Drake Bell (David, aged 10)

In 1940s Georgia, a young boy endures a miserable domestic life with his violent, racist father and his deranged mother. Only when his worldly aunt moves in does his life improve.

Another vastly underrated film by Davies, leaving Liverpool to make his American debut. But he imports his style with him: each shot is meticulously composed, his eye for detail remains keen, and his preoccupations are not so different: in this case a boy's dreary family existence is cheered considerably by the arrival of his flamboyant aunt, a glamorous night-club singer. This isn't really Davies's milieu, but his attentiveness lifts what might otherwise be a mundane film. As the aunt, Rowlands is radiant.

CIN Mick Coulter   DES Christopher Hobbs   ED Charles Rees   PROD Elizabeth Karlsen, Olivia Stewart
DIST Artificial Eye/Mayfair/Scala/Channel 4

'Television will never be the same!'

Network ★★★

DIR Sidney Lumet
1976   121m   US
DVD

☆ *Peter Finch* (Howard Beale), *William Holden* (Max Schumacher), Faye Dunaway (Diana Christensen), Robert Duvall (Frank Hackett), Wesley Addy (Nelson Chaney), Ned Beatty (Arthur Jensen), Beatrice Straight (Louise Schumacher), John Carpenter (George Bosch)

A network TV news commentator begins to say what he thinks about the world, thereby becoming a new messiah to his viewers and an embarrassment to his sponsors.

A deliberately melodramatic satire on media corruption, it is passionate and compulsively watchable in its attack on demagoguery and in its depiction of the dangerous madness exploited by the mass media. What once seemed overheated satire now looks eerily prescient. Yet the film's very existence in a commercial system was as remarkable as its box-office success.

SCR *Paddy Chayefsky*   CIN Owen Roizman   MUS Elliot Lawrence   ED Alan Heim   PROD Howard Gottfried, Fred Caruso   DIST MGM/UA

HOWARD BEALE (PETER FINCH) ON LIVE TELEVISION: I don't know what to do about the depression and the inflation and the Russians and the crime in the streets. All I know is that first you've got to get mad. You've got to say: "I'm a human being, god damn it, my life has some value!" So I want you to get up now. I want all of you to get up out of your chairs. I want you to get up right now and go to the window, open it and stick your head out and yell "I'm mad as hell, and I'm not going to take this any more!"
HOWARD BEALE: Ladies and gentlemen, I would like at this moment to announce that I will be retiring from this programme in two weeks' time because of poor ratings. Since this show was the only thing I had going for me in my life, I have decided to kill myself. I'm going to blow my brains out right on this programme a week from today.
MAX SCHUMACHER (WILLIAM HOLDEN): You're television incarnate, Diana, indifferent to suffering, insensitive to joy. All of life is reduced to the common rubble of banality. War, murder, death – all the same to you as bottles of beer, and the daily business of life is a corrupt comedy. You even shatter the sensations of time and space into split seconds and instant replays. You're madness, Diana.

66 The cast of this messianic farce take turns yelling at us soulless masses. – *New Yorker*

66 Too much of this film has the hectoring stridency of tabloid headlines. – *Michael Billington, Illustrated London News*

† The theme was taken up a year later in the shortlived TV series W.E.B.

⬗ Peter Finch (leading actor); Faye Dunaway (leading actress); Beatrice Straight (supporting actress); Paddy Chayefsky (original screenplay)
⬗ picture; William Holden (leading actor); Ned Beatty (supporting actor); Sidney Lumet (direction); Owen Roizman

Ⓣ Peter Finch (leading actor)

'Win or lose. . .everyone has their fight.'

Never Back Down (new)

DIR Jeff Wadlow
2008   113m   US

☆ Sean Faris (Jake Tyler), Amber Heard (Baja Miller), Cam Gigandet (Ryan McCarthy), Evan Peters (Max Cooperman), Leslie Hope (Margot Tyler), Djimon Hounsou (Jean Roqua), Wyatt Smith (Charlie Tyler)

DVD Available on DVD   ☆ Cast in order of importance   66 Critics' Quotes   ⬗ Academy Award   Ⓣ BAFTA
♫ Soundtrack on CD   † Points of interest   ⬗ Academy Award nomination   Ⓣ BAFTA nomination

445

A fatherless teenager learns Mixed Martial Arts so he can avenge himself on a school bully.

Unconscionably violent update of The Karate Kid that attempts to suggest vendettas are character-building.

SCR Chris Hauty **CIN** Lukas Ettlin **MUS** Michael Wandmacher **DES** Ida Random **ED** Victor DuBois **PROD** Craig Baumgarten, David Zelon **DIST** Momentum

66 Basically a love-letter to buff guys with tight abs beating the crap out of each other while adoring bikini babes look on, whooping with adoration. – *Peter Bradshaw, Guardian*

66 Everyone's a model, everyone beats each other half to death, and no one looks as if they've ever suffered so much as a cold sore. – *John Anderson, Variety*

'They're a new breed of gangster. The new public enemy. The new family of crime.'

New Jack City ★

DIR Mario Van Peebles
1991   101m   US
DVD   ♫

☆ Wesley Snipes (Nino Brown), Ice T (Scotty Appleton), Allen Payne (Gee Money), Chris Rock (Pookie), Mario Van Peebles (Stone), Michael Michele (Selina Thomas), Bill Nunn (Duh Duh Duh Man), Russell Wong (Park), Bill Cobbs (Old Man)

An arrogant, out of control crime boss in Harlem is targeted by a determined undercover detective.

Fast-paced thriller credited with helping the breakthrough of hip-hop inflected movies, it features memorably extravagant acting from Snipes.

SCR Thomas Lee Wright, Barry Michael Cooper **CIN** Francis Kenny **MUS** Michel Colombier, Vassal Benford **DES** Charles C. Bennett **ED** Steven Kemper **PROD** Doug McHenry, George Jackson **DIST** Warner

66 A brash, unconvincing crime thriller. – *Ian Nathan, Empire*

'Once discovered, it was changed forever.'

The New World ★

SCR/DIR Terrence Malick
2005   150m   US
DVD   ♫

☆ Colin Farrell (Captain John Smith), Q'orianka Kilcher (Pocahontas), Christopher Plummer (Captain Newport), Christian Bale (John Rolfe), August Schellenberg (Powhatan), Wes Studi (Opechancanough), David Thewlis (Wingfield), Ben Mendelsohn (Ben), Noah Taylor (Selway), Jonathan Pryce (King James)

A British captain arriving in Virginia in 1607 falls for a native girl and has to choose between the old world and new.

Malick's long-awaited return to the cinema, and an equally long disappointment: a hotch-potch of Sealed Knot re-creationism, muddled manifesto for minority groups (greens, native Americans, those who still think Colin Farrell should be on the A-list) and perfume-commercial aesthetic. Its thesis – isn't nature great? – can't sustain the film past the two-hour mark, and some might say making the case against progress in Dolby surround sound is naive in the extreme.

CIN *Emmanuel Lubezki* **MUS** James Horner **DES** Jack Fisk **ED** Richard Chew, Hank Corwin, Saar Klein, Mark Yoshikawa **PROD** Sarah Green

66 A work of breathtaking imagination, less a movie than a mode of transport, and in every sense a masterpiece. – *Carina Chocano, Los Angeles Times*

66 Many have tried, but none can match Malick's touch for shuffling a deck of elegiac images (water/sky/clouds/rain) and fanning out the hand to express what speech cannot. – *Lisa Schwarzbaum, Entertainment Weekly*

⚱ Emmanuel Lubezki (cinematography)

New York Stories ★

DIR Martin Scorsese, Francis Coppola, Woody Allen
1989   124m   US
DVD   ♫

☆ Nick Nolte (Lionel Dobie), Patrick O'Neal (Phillip Fowler), Rosanna Arquette (Paulette), Heather McComb (Zoe), Talia Shire (Charlotte), Gia Coppola (Baby Zoe), Giancarlo Giannini (Claudio), Woody Allen (Sheldon), Marvin Chatinover (Psychiatrist), Mae Questel (Mother), Mia Farrow (Lisa)

An anthology of three short films by different directors. Scorsese's Life Lessons casts a beady gaze on the art world. Coppola's Life Without Zoë sees a young girl helping to reunite her parents. In Allen's Oedipus Wrecks, a 50-year-old man is mortified when his domineering mother materialises in the sky over Manhattan.

A curate's egg here: Allen's Jewish mother joke is splendid, Scorsese's drama works up a powerful head of steam, but Coppola's syrupy little film is utterly unwatchable.

SCR Richard Price, Francis Coppola, Sofia Coppola, Woody Allen **CIN** Nestor Almendros, Vittorio Storaro, Sven Nykvist **MUS** Carmine Coppola **DES** Kristi Zea, Dean Tavoularis, Santo Loquasto **ED** Thelma Schoonmaker, Barry Malkin, Susan E. Morse **PROD** Robert Greenhut **DIST** Warner/Touchstone

66 New York Stories consists of three films; one good, one bad, one disappointing. – *Roger Ebert, Chicago Sun-Times*

'Every family needs a hero.'

Nicholas Nickleby ★

SCR/DIR Douglas McGrath
2002   132m   US/GB/Germany/Netherlands
DVD   ♫

☆ Charlie Hunnam (Nicholas Nickleby), *Christopher Plummer* (Ralph Nickleby), Jim Broadbent (Wackford Squeers), Juliet Stevenson (Mrs Squeers), *Tom Courtenay* (Newman Noggs), Jamie Bell (Smike), Edward Fox (Sir Mulberry Hawk), Romola Garai (Kate Nickleby), Nathan Lane (Vincent Crummles), Barry Humphries (Mrs Crummles), Alan Cumming (Mr Folair), Anne Hathaway (Madeline Bray), Timothy Spall (Charles Cheeryble)

A young schoolteacher battles to prevent his malevolent uncle from forcing his sister into a doomed marriage in order to settle a debt.

Dickens' novel is ruthlessly boiled down to its essential linear narrative for this decent, workmanlike

production. *A field day for veteran actors, with Plummer in his pomp as the vile Uncle Ralph.*

CIN Dick Pope   MUS Rachel Portman   DES Eve Stewart   ED Lesley Walker   PROD Simon Channing Williams, John N. Hart, Jeffrey Sharp   DIST MGM

66 It doesn't help that in a movie packed with perky cameos [director Douglas] McGrath's stripped-down story centres in so squarely on Nicholas, a dullard too handsome to be interesting, as embodied by the beach-blond Charlie Hunman, and too decent to be believable. – *Mark Kermode, Observer*

Night and the City   ★★★

DIR *Jules Dassin*
1950   101m   GB
☆ *Richard Widmark*, Gene Tierney, Googie Withers, Hugh Marlowe, Herbert Lom

In London, a crooked wrestling promoter is tracked down by an underworld gang.

An ambitious, unusual project: to import the look and style of film noir from urban America to London with an imported star cast, and British actors in support. It pays off: London lends itself perfectly to the menacing, dark, expressionist look required. Originally conceived by director Dassin as a way to exploit his success with Naked City from two years earlier, but in its way this is the more intriguing film. Widmark is outstanding as a hustler living on his wits.

SCR Jo Eisinger   CIN *Max Greene*   MUS Benjamin Frankel   PROD Samuel G. Engel   DIST TCF

66 Brilliantly photographed, it is an example of neo-expressionist techniques at their most potent. – *Richard Roud, 1964*

† An inferior, unsuccessful remake starring Robert de Niro was released in 1992. It was set in New York City.

A Night at the Opera   ★★★★

DIR *Sam Wood*
1935   96m   US
DVD
☆ *Groucho Marx* (Otis B. Driftwood), *Chico Marx* (Fiorello), *Harpo Marx* (Tomasso), *Margaret Dumont* (Mrs. Claypool), Kitty Carlisle (Rosa Castaldi), Allan Jones (Riccardo Baroni), Walter Woolf King (Rodolfo Lassparri), *Sig Rumann* (Herman Gottlieb)

Three zanies first wreck, then help an opera company.

Certainly among the best of the Marx Brothers' extravaganzas, and the first to give them a big production to play with, as well as musical interludes by other than themselves for a change of pace. The mix plays beautifully.

SCR *George S. Kaufman, Morrie Ryskind*   CIN Merritt Gerstad   ED William LeVanway   PROD Irving Thalberg   DIST MGM

66 Corking comedy with the brothers at par and biz chances excellent. . .songs in a Marx picture are generally at a disadvantage because they're more or less interruptions, the customers awaiting the next laugh. – *Variety*

'In a city of nine million people is there room for one honest man?'

Night Falls on Manhattan   ★

SCR/DIR Sidney Lumet
1997   114m   US
DVD
☆ Andy Garcia (Sean Casey), Richard Dreyfuss (Sam Vigoda), Lena Olin (Peggy Lindstrom), Ian Holm (Liam Casey), James Gandolfini (Joey Allegretto), Colm Feore (Elihu Harrison), Ron Liebman (Morgenstern)

Outspoken young New York lawyer probes the shooting of his policeman father and discovers high-level corruption and real danger.

Tense, fascinating thriller; familiar territory for Lumet, who makes a decent fist of it, despite a script with a distracting romantic sub-plot that almost derails it.

CIN David Watkin   MUS Mark Isham   DES Philip Rosenberg   ED Sam O'Steen   PROD Thom Mount, Josh Kramer   DIST Paramount/Spelling

66 [Director Sidney] Lumet creates, with warmth, wisdom and humour, a vibrant world in which good and evil are in constant combat and in which possibilities in relationships between people are fluid and infinite. – *Kevin Thomas, Los Angeles Times*

'The scenes! The story! The stars! But above all – the suspense!'

The Night of the Hunter   ★★★★

DIR *Charles Laughton*
1955   93m   US
DVD   ♫
☆ *Robert Mitchum* (Preacher Harry Powell), Shelley Winters (Willa Harper), Lillian Gish (Rachel), Don Beddoe (Walt Spoon), Evelyn Varden (Icey Spoon), Peter Graves (Ben Harper), James Gleason (Birdie)

A psychopathic preacher goes on the trail of hidden money, the secret of which is held by two children.

Weird, manic fantasy in which evil is pitted against the forces of sweetness and light (the children, an old lady, water, animals). Although the narrative does not flow smoothly there are splendidly imaginative moments, and no other film has ever quite achieved its texture. As for Mitchum, he was never better – or more menacing.

SCR *James Agee*   CIN *Stanley Cortez*   MUS Walter Schumann   ED Robert Golden   DIST UA/Paul Gregory

PREACHER (ROBERT MITCHUM): Lord, you sure knew what you was doing when you brung me to this very cell at this very time. A man with ten thousand dollars hid somewhere, and a widder in the makin'.

66 One of the most frightening movies ever made. – *Pauline Kael, 1968*

66 A genuinely sinister work, full of shocks and over-emphatic sound effects, camera angles and shadowy lighting. – *NFT, 1973*

'Pits the dead against the living in a struggle for survival!'

The Night of The Living Dead   ★★★

DIR *George A. Romero*
1968   98m   US
DVD
☆ Judith O'Dea (Barbara), Duane Jones (Ben), Karl

DVD Available on DVD   ☆ Cast in order of importance   66 Critics' Quotes   ⚊ Academy Award   ⚊ Academy Award nomination   ⬤ BAFTA   ⓣ BAFTA nomination
♫ Soundtrack on CD

447

Hardman (Harry Cooper), Keith Wayne (Tom), Russell Streiner (Johnny)

Flesh-eating zombies, activated by radiation from a space rocket, ravage the countryside.

Gruesome horror comic with effective moments; the director was still doing the same schtick 10 years later. One of the most influential, and most imitated, of modern horror movies.

SCR John A. Russo   CIN George A. Romero   ED George Romero   DIST Image Ten

66 Casts serious aspersions on the integrity of its makers . . . the film industry as a whole and exhibs who book the pic, as well as raising doubts about the future of the regional cinema movement and the moral health of filmgoers who cheerfully opt for unrelieved sadism. – *Variety*

'Five Taxis. Five Cities. One Night.'

Night on Earth   ★★

SCR/DIR Jim Jarmusch
1991   129m   US
DVD   ♫

☆ Winona Ryder (Corky), Gena Rowlands (Victoria Snelling), Giancarlo Esposito (YoYo), Armin Mueller-Stahl (Helmut Grokenberger), Rosie Perez (Angela), Isaach de Bankolé (Driver (Paris)), Béatrice Dalle (Blind Woman), Roberto Benigni (Driver (Rome)), Paolo Bonacelli (Priest), Matti Pellonpää (Mika)

Five people take very different taxi rides in five cities: Los Angeles, New York, Paris, Rome and Helsinki.

Essentially a series of minor, quirky stories, each turning on the interaction between passenger and driver. Jarmusch clearly set himself the exercise: keeping the drama inside the cabs. He just about carries it off.

CIN Frederick Elmes   MUS Tom Waits   ED Jay Ribinowitz   PROD Jim Jarmusch   DIST Electric/Locus Solus/Victor/Victor Musical Industries/Pyramide/Canal/Pandora/Channel 4

66 [Director Jim] Jarmusch is a true visionary; he knows his films can't bring order to the ravishing chaos around him, but he can't resist the fun of trying. – *Peter Travers, Rolling Stone*

Night Sun   ★

DIR Paolo and Vittorio Taviani
1990   112m   Italy/France/Germany
DVD   ♫

☆ Julian Sands (Sergio Giuramondo), Charlotte Gainsbourg (Matilda), Nastassja Kinski (Cristina), Massimo Bonetti (Prince Santobuono), Margarita Lozano (Sergio's Mother), Patricia Millardet (Aurelia), Rudiger Vogler (King Charles), Pamela Villoresi (Giuseppina Giuramondo)

An aristocrat in 18th-century Italy refuses to marry the king's mistress and instead becomes a hermit.

High-minded, rigorous and haunting, it's beautifully executed though its ascetic tone makes it feel more daunting than the story warrants.

SCR Paolo and Vittorio Taviani, Tonino Guerra
CIN Giuseppe Lanci   MUS Nicola Piovani   DES Gianni Sbarra   ED Roberto Perpignani   PROD Giuliani G. de Negri   DIST Artificial Eye/Filmtre/Raiuno/Capoul/Interpool/Sara/Direkt

66 The way the Tavianis pare down composition, dialogue, narrative and performance to essentials ensures a clarity of purpose and effect rarely encountered in contemporary cinema. – *Time Out*

'A comedy with room for romance.'

The Night We Never Met   ★

SCR/DIR Warren Leight
1993   99m   US
DVD

☆ Matthew Broderick (Sam Lester), Annabella Sciorra (Ellen Holder), Kevin Anderson (Brian McVeigh), Jeanne Tripplehorn (Pastel), Justine Bateman (Janet Beehan), Michael Mantell (Aaron Holder), Christine Baranski (Lucy)

A boorish Wall Street trader sublets his apartment to two other New Yorkers, a man recovering from a broken heart and a woman considering a extra-marital fling.

A very 90s romantic comedy, both in its casting and its emphasis on the vagaries of the Manhattan property market; all very episodic, but there's fun to be had around the edges of the plot, and from Tripplehorn's casually nude French performance artist in particular.

CIN John A. Thomas   MUS Evan Lurie   DES Lester Cohen   ED Camilla Toniolo   PROD Michael Peyser   DIST Guild/Miramax

66 Has three amiable leads and doesn't overstay its welcome. – *Tom Charity, Time Out*

'Lori thought she knew everything about her boyfriend. . .Lori was wrong.'

Nightbreed   ★

SCR/DIR Clive Barker
1990   102m   US
DVD   ♫

☆ Craig Sheffer (Aaron Boone/Cabal), Anne Bobby (Lori Desinger), David Cronenberg (Dr. Philip K. Decker), Charles Haid (Captain Eigerman), Hugh Quarshie (Detective Joyce), Hugh Ross (Narcisse), Doug Bradley (Dirk Lylesberg), Catherine Chevalier (Rachel), Malcolm Sith (Ashberry), Bob Sessions (Pettine), Oliver Parker (Peloquin)

A man on the run seeks sanctuary in a tiny Canadian town, where he finds a strange underground world peopled by monsters.

An imaginative horror movie, with director David Cronenberg doing notable acting work as an ill-intentioned psychiatrist. It's not exactly scary, or even thrilling, but Barker at least carves out a niche for himself in a genre that often settles for the tried and tested.

CIN Robin Vidgeon   DES Steve Hardie   ED Richard Marden, Mark Goldblatt   PROD Gariella Martinelli   DIST Fox/Morgan Creek

66 In the end [director Clive] Barker seems to have expended all his energies on masks that cannot hide the terminal deficiencies of his script. – *Richard Harrington, Washington Post*

'Tim Burton's classic returns in 3-D so real, it's scary.'

The Nightmare before Christmas ★★★

DIR *Henry Selick*
1993 76m US
[DVD] ♫

☆ the voices of Danny Elfman, Chris Sarandon, Catherine O'Hara, William Hickey, Glenn Shadix, Paul Reubens

The Pumpkin King of Halloween Town tries to take over Christmas, with disastrous consequences.

One-of-a-kind stop-motion musical fantasia, clearly the work of someone who spent a lot of constructive time alone in their bedroom growing up; zippy direction, fine songs and witty visuals make for something of a modern classic.

SCR Caroline Thompson, Michael McDowell CIN *Pete Kozachik* ED Stan Webb PROD Tim Burton, Denise Di Novi DIST Buena Vista/Touchstone

66 A treat from Hollywood's most unlikely Midas. . .this beautifully realised confection will delight grown-ups of all ages. – *Tom Charity, Time Out*

66 Don't be put off by its ostensibly ghoulish content – this spine-ticklingly funny fright show is terrific fun for kids and adults alike. – *Mark Salisbury, Empire*

† An excellent digital 3-D version of the film was released in 2006.

⚚ Pete Kozachik, Eric Leighton, Ariel Velasco-Shaw, Gordon Baker (visual effects)

Nightshift ★★

DIR *Philippe Le Guay*
2001 95m France
[DVD]

☆ Gerald Laroche (Pierre), Marc Barbe (Fred), Bernard Ballet (Franck), Alexandre Carriere (Danny), Jean-Francois Lapalus (Mickey), Sabri Lahmer (Farid), Luce Mouchel (Carole), Bastien Le Roy (Victor)

A timid newcomer to the night shift in a bottling factory is harassed and bullied by a co-worker.

An unsettling psychological drama that seeks to establish a co-dependent relationship between bully and victim. An intriguing slant on an unusual theme for film.

SCR Philippe Le Guay, Regis Franc, Olivier Dazat CIN Jean-Marc Fabre MUS Yann Tiersen DES Jimmy Vansteenkiste ED Emmanuelle Castro PROD Bertrand Faivre, Adeline Lecallier DIST Metro Tartan

66 This extraordinarily involving study of workplace bullying in a French factory is, as the Hollywood suits say, a 'tough watch'. – *Peter Bradshaw, The Guardian*

† The film's French title, Trois Huit, refers to a working day divided into three eight-hour shifts.

'The Hit of Paris and London Has Come to America.'

Nikita ★

SCR/DIR Luc Besson
1990 115m France/Italy
[DVD] ♫

☆ Anne Parillaud (Nikita), Jean-Hugues Anglade (Marco), Tcheky Karyo (Bob), Jeanne Moreau (Amande), Jean Reno (Victor), Marc Duret (Rico)

Savage young woman killer in France is turned into a trained assassin by the government's cynical intelligence services.

Preposterous plot is stylishly delivered and eventually made enjoyable by Parillaud's iconic title role performance.

CIN Thierry Arbogast MUS Eric Serra DES Dan Weil ED Olivier Mauffroy PROD Patrice Ledoux DIST Palace/Gaumont/Cecci/Tiger

66 Nikita begins with the materials of a violent thriller but transcends them with the story of the heroine's transformation. – *Roger Ebert, Chicago Sun-Times*

† In 1993 the film was re-made as Point of No Return in America, with Bridget Fonda in the main role, and released in the UK under the title The Assassin. Besson was offered the chance to direct it, but declined. John Badham took the reins instead.

Nil by Mouth ★★

SCR/DIR *Gary Oldman*
1997 128m GB
[DVD]

☆ *Ray Winstone* (Ray), *Kathy Burke* (Valerie), Charlie Creed-Miles (Billy), Laila Morse (Janet), Edna Doré (Kath), Chrissie Cotterill (Paula), Jon Morrison (Angus), Jamie Forman (Mark)

A vicious alcoholic ex-convict terrorises his south London family.

A grim, harrowing view of underclass life, rendered even more sobering by writer-director Oldman's admission that it is partly autobiographical. The outstanding acting fails to alleviate the bleakness, but makes the rough ride worthwhile.

CIN Ron Fortunato MUS Eric Clapton DES Hugo Luczyc-Wyhowski ED Brad Fuller PROD Luc Besson, Douglas Urbanski, Gary Oldman DIST TCF/SE8

66 [Director Gary] Oldman's key achievement is to make you feel for people you wouldn't want to know in real life. – *Kevin Thomas, Los Angeles Times*

🇬 British film; Gary Oldman (original screenplay)
🇹 Ray Winstone (leading actor); Kathy Burke (leading actress)

'Be the hero of your own story.'

Nim's Island (new)

DIR Mark Levin, Jennifer Flackett
2008 95m US

☆ Abigail Breslin (Nim Rusoe), Jodie Foster (Alexandra Rover), Gerard Butler (Jack Rusoe/Alex Rover), Michael Carman (Captain), Mark Brady (Purser), Christopher Baker (Ensign)

[DVD] Available on DVD   ☆ Cast in order   66 Critics' Quotes   ⚚ Academy Award   🇬 BAFTA
♫ Soundtrack on CD   of importance   † Points of interest   ⚚ Academy Award nomination   🇹 BAFTA nomination

449

Can it really be only two years ago that a fierce campaign was being waged to protest against the casting of Daniel Craig as the sixth actor to play James Bond on film? So much water has since passed under the bridge that it seems an eternity ago.

Yet for several months before the release of the last Bond film, *Casino Royale*, in November 2006, a committed band of Bond fans wrote angry blogs about Craig being cast as the suave British spy. They created a website as a means of expressing their grievances, and even threatened to boycott the movie when it opened.

These fans had an enormous advantage that fuelled their evangelical zeal: they had not seen *Casino Royale*, nor did they have any idea how Craig would rise to the challenge of playing this iconic hero.

As it turned out, they were wrong. Not just slightly wide of the mark, but hopelessly, laughably, 180 degrees wrong. *Casino Royale* went on to become the highest grossing Bond movie ever, taking some $594 million worldwide. It also attracted some of the most positive reviews for a Bond film since the long distant days when Sean Connery was synonymous with 007. Far from undermining the extraordinary Bond franchise, which now stretches back 46 years, Craig has given it a whole new lease of life.

Until his arrival, Bond films had dutifully been making big money for their studio MGM (the question arises whether MGM would even have survived over the past four decades had it not been for the Bond franchise). Under Pierce Brosnan's stewardship of 007 in four films (*GoldenEye, Tomorrow Never Knows, The World Is Not Enough* and *Die Another Day*) the global box-office totals rose gradually. Yet many of us who recall with affection the earliest Bond films starring Connery (*Dr No, From Russia With Love, Goldfinger*) found it hard to raise much enthusiasm for the Brosnan years. Those four films seemed like a series of hugely elaborate stunts – and the big stunt before the title sequence was usually the highlight of the entire film – with a flimsy story nailed on almost as an afterthought.

In truth, the Bond films have succeeded almost despite themselves since Connery hung up his Walther PPK. The perfect replacement for Connery was never found, and chopping and changing actors has been a consistent feature of the franchise's history. The short-lived George Lazenby was clearly not the right man (though his one film, *On Her Majesty's Secret Service* (1969), was slightly above average).

Roger Moore held down the franchise for seven films between 1973 and 1985, making Bond more ironic and light-hearted; he was quick with a quip, a flirtatious gaze from baby blue eyes, and sexual innuendo accompanied by innocently raised eyebrows. Ian Fleming, who died in 1964, never saw Moore in action as Bond, though it's safe to say Moore's was not the interpretation he had in mind for his fictional creation.

Timothy Dalton may have been technically the most gifted actor to play Bond, and laudably tried to return the character closer to Fleming's conception of him. But his two films (*The Living Daylights* and *Licence to Kill*) were among the worst in the franchise's history.

Brosnan is a competent actor. Yet one felt he almost belonged to another age. He can do suave, but in a rather old-fashioned way – with a twinkle of the eye and an ability to look well-groomed, his pompadour unruffled, even under severe physical duress. In this respect, the movie Bond he most resembled was Roger Moore, and by the turn of the century, that was starting to look like a retrograde step.

Craig's arrival and the release of *Casino Royale* solved these problems at a stroke. First, Craig himself looks every inch a modern, 21st-century Bond – yet paradoxically he is also a throwback, all the way to Connery. Craig is tough, buff, attractive, just this side of handsome, with a cool, dry manner and a strong, almost bull-like physique. His hair is short, virtually cropped; he looks ready for action. And crucially, there's a touch of cruelty and ruthlessness about him – something Connery clearly recognised as an essential ingredient in Bond's character, but which his successors had been encouraged to play down.

> '*Craig looks every inch a modern, 21st century Bond – yet paradoxically he is also a throwback, all the way to Connery.*'

Casino Royale is by no means a perfect film, but there are three things I like about it very much – and all of them have positive repercussions for the continuing health of the Bond franchise.

The first is the opening scene, an ugly, brutal murder in a public lavatory, shot in grainy black and white. One need not be a fan of movie violence to admit that this scene does its job brilliantly; it announces *Casino Royale* as a very different kind of Bond film, one that will not be weighed down by flippancy, double entendres or lead actors who look unsuited to the physical, often grim job of espionage.

The second is a chase scene, on a construction site in Madagascar, featuring Bond and a bad guy indulging in 'free-running' across steel girders, and even, heart-poundingly, up the jib of a crane. (One wonders if the film's producers, ever alert to changing cultural trends, might have been influenced by the enjoyable 2004 French film *District 13*, featuring two remarkably agile free-running heroes.) As you watch Craig straining every sinew in his ascent along that jib, you think: now here is a Bond of whom Fleming might have approved.

Last, is a brief snatch of significant dialogue:

Bond: 'Vodka martini.'
Waiter: 'Shaken or stirred?'
Bond: 'Do I look like I give a damn?'

Hearing this exchange makes you want to punch the air in triumph. At last, an end to all that prescriptive brand-name fetishism about suits, weaponry, drinks and other accoutrements deemed crucial for a fictional British spy first imagined during the height of the Cold War, way back in the early 1950s. It feels like an enormous relief.

There's even a sense that a new leaf has been turned over by the Bond producers in the treatment of women characters. Judi Dench has been installed as M for years now, but casting Eva Green as *Casino Royale's* female protagonist Vesper Lynd was an especially shrewd move; her brains are as important as her beauty, and 007 treats her with appropriate respect. It represents a welcome progression from the tired notion of 'Bond girls' – crowds of interchangeable bikini-clad lovelies, mooching around the pool, and squealing with delight whenever Roger Moore ambled on screen. They had begun to look as if they belonged in a Benny Hill sketch.

All of this is good news, and the commercial success of *Casino Royale* had its intriguing aspects. Its global box-office total of $594 million puts it way ahead of the previous Bond film, *Die Another Day* ($424 million). Yet the US box-office result for both films tells a different story: *Casino Royale* narrowly squeezes home with $167 million to around $161 million. What this tells us is that while Craig's presence has not deterred American Bond fans, he has been embraced in huge numbers by new non-American audiences; overnight, as it were, he has become an international star.

And one could add that it's a huge sign of confidence on the part of a studio to release a film with the title *Quantum of Solace*, the 22nd Bond film, which opens in November 2008. What does *Quantum of Solace* mean? Prior to its release, no-one has a clue. But if there were any doubts about the viability of Craig as Bond, a blander, less curious title would surely have been commissioned.

Daniel Craig, then, will do for now. His tenure as James Bond will probably last until the middle of the next decade (by which time he will be 47 or so), and he shows every sign of being the right man to last the course. At some stage, inevitably, a successor will be announced – and doubtless the protests from Bond fans will start all over again.

After her scientist father goes missing at sea, a little girl alone on a desert island enlists the help of an agoraphobic novelist she mistakenly believes to be the male hero of her best-selling adventure novels.

Inconsequential adventure whose disparate parts never gel; Jodie Foster is particularly miscast in a rare comedic role.

SCR Joseph Kwong, Paula Mazur, Mark Levin, Jennifer Flackett CIN Stuart Dryburgh MUS Patrick Doyle DES Barry Robison ED Stuart Levy PROD Paula Mazur DIST Universal

66 Picturesque adventure-comedy that quickly capsizes under the weight of its obnoxious slapstick, pedestrian dialogue and general unwillingness to rise above stock ideas and situations. – *Justin Chang, Variety*

66 Strictly for the 8-and-under crowd. – *Lou Lumenick, New York Post*

Nine Queens ★★

SCR/DIR *Fabian Bielinsky*
2000 114m Argentina
DVD

☆ *Ricardo Darin* (Marcos), *Gaston Pauls* (Juan), Leticia Bredice (Valeria), Tomas Fonzi (Federico), Ignasi Abadal (Vidal Gandolfo), Alejandro Awada (Washington), Antonio Ugo (D'Agostino), Oscar Nunez (Sandler)

Two con artists, one smoothly experienced, the other incompetent, join forces to swindle their way to success in Buenos Aires, and become involved in a complex scam involving forged copies of rare stamps.

Slick, cynical movie that casts a resigned, weary gaze on Argentinian society, its social problems and financial troubles. It's intelligently written, always stays a step ahead of the audience, and adds up to sheer pleasure.

CIN Marcelo Camorino MUS Cesar Lerner DES Daniela Passalaqua ED Sergio Zottola PROD Pablo Bossi DIST Optimum

66 Terrific performances, snappy photography and a razor-sharp script combine to make this one of the most enjoyable films of the year. – *Matthew Turner, Empire*

66 When you think you've figured out Bielinsky's great game, that's when you're in the most trouble: He's the con, and you're just the mark. – *Stephen Hunter, Washington Post*

'Y9u never kn9w when y9ur number is up.'

The Nines (new) ★

SCR/DIR John August
2007 99m US
DVD

☆ Ryan Reynolds (Gary/Gavin/Gabriel), Hope Davis (Sarah/Susan/Sierra), Melissa McCarthy (Margaret/Melissa/Mary), Elle Fanning (Noelle)

An actor, writer and videogame designer begin to question their respective realities.

Smart, tricksy thriller with a metaphysical hook, let down by a drab ending; the three leads all portray three different characters.

CIN Nancy Schreiber MUS Alex Wurman ED Douglas

Crise PROD Dan Jinks, Bruce Cohen, Dan Etheridge DIST Optimum Releasing

GARY: 'There's something wrong with the world!'

66 An adventuresome gizmo for grown-ups. – *Dennis Harvey, Variety*

66 An intriguing post-modern take on TV, film and gaming culture. – *Damon Wise, Empire*

'The picture that kids the commissars!'

Ninotchka ★★★

DIR *Ernst Lubitsch*
1939 110m US
DVD

☆ *Greta Garbo* (Lena Yakushova, 'Ninotchka'), *Melvyn Douglas* (Count Leon Dolga), *Sig Rumann* (Michael Ironoff), *Alexander Granach* (Kopalski), *Felix Bressart* (Buljanoff), Ina Claire (Grand Duchess Swana), Bela Lugosi (Commissar Razinin)

A Paris playboy falls for a communist emissary sent to sell some crown jewels.

Sparkling comedy on a theme which has been frequently explored; delicate pointing and hilarious character comedy sustain this version perfectly until the last half hour, when it certainly sags; but it remains a favourite Hollywood example of this genre. In retrospect, the influence of co-writer Billy Wilder, sophisticated and cynical, is all over this film.

SCR *Charles Brackett, Billy Wilder, Walter Reisch* CIN *William Daniels* MUS *Werner Heymann* ED Gene Ruggiero PROD Ernst Lubitsch DIST MGM

PROLOGUE: This picture takes place in Paris in those wonderful days when a siren was a brunette and not an alarm – and if a Frenchman turned out the light it was not on account of an air raid!

NINOTCHKA (GRETA GARBO): I must have a complete report of your negotiations and a detailed expense account
BULJANOFF (FELIX BRESSART): No, non, Ninotchka. Don't ask for it. There is an old Turkish proverb that says, if something smells bad, why put your nose in it?
NINOTCHKA: And there is an old Russian saying, the cat who has cream on his whiskers had better find good excuses.
NINOTCHKA: The last mass trials were a great success. There are going to be fewer but better Russians.

66 High calibre entertainment for adult audiences, and a top attraction for the key de-luxers. – *Variety*

66 The Lubitsch style, in which much was made of subtleties – glances, finger movements, raised eyebrows – has disappeared. Instead we have a hard, brightly lit, cynical comedy with the wisecrack completely in control. – *John Baxter, 1968*

† William Powell and Robert Montgomery were formerly considered for the Melvyn Douglas role.

⏷ picture; Greta Garbo (leading actress); Charles Brackett, Walter Reisch, Bill Wilder (screenplay); story

'Leave the unknown alone.'

The Ninth Gate ★

DIR Roman Polanski
1999 133m France/Spain/US
DVD ♫

☆ Johnny Depp (Dean Corso), Frank Langella (Boris

Balkan), Lena Olin (Liana Telfer), Emmanuelle Seigner (The Girl), Barbara Jefford (Baroness Kessler), Jack Taylor (Victor Fargas), Jose Lopez Rodero (Pablo and Pedro Ceniza), James Russo (Bernie)

A rare book collector is drawn into the search for the fabled Book of the Nine Gates, said to be the Devil's work.

Half modern noir, half Satanic horror movie, all enjoyably preposterous, though it somehow manages to make something momentarily fascinating out of the business of folios.

SCR Enrique Urbizu, John Brownjohn, Roman Polanski **CIN** *Darius Khondji* **MUS** *Wojciech Kilar* **DES** Dean Tavoularis **ED** Herve de Luze **PROD** Roman Polanski **DIST** Artisan

66 Amusing, ultra-deadpan entertainment. The director was lucky enough to have a cast who were in on the joke and tuned in to his wavelength. – *Charles Taylor, Salon.com*

66 Euro-kitsch of the highest order. – *Manohla Dargis, Los Angeles Times*

'He had greatness within his grasp.'

Nixon ★★★

DIR Oliver Stone
1995 192m US
DVD ♫

☆ *Anthony Hopkins* (Nixon), *Joan Allen* (Pat Nixon), Powers Boothe (Alexander Haig), Ed Harris (E. Howard Hunt), E.G. Marshall (John Mitchell), David Paymer (Ron Ziegler), David Hyde Pierce (John Dean), Paul Sorvino (Henry Kissinger), J.T. Walsh (John Erlichman), James Woods (H.R. Haldeman), Mary Steenburgen (Hannah Nixon)

As the Watergate scandal begins to unfold, US President Richard Nixon's looks back over his past.

Nixon's spectacular fall from power makes fascinating viewing. From the moment we first see him, on a stormy night in 1973, listening to the tapes that are to drive him from office, through memorable moments in his life and career, right up to the inevitable end game, few moments are less than compelling. This is Stone at his best – bold, provocative, striving for an epic scale, but in confident control of his material. Hopkins is excellent as Nixon, but then so is the whole supporting cast.

SCR Stephen J. Rivele, Christopher Wilkinson, Oliver Stone **CIN** Robert Richardson **MUS** John Williams **DES** Victor Kempster **ED** Brian Berdan, Hank Corwin **PROD** Clayton Townsend, Oliver Stone, Andrew G. Vajna **DIST** Entertainment/Illusion/Cinergi

66 What it finally adds up to is a huge mixed bag of waxworks and daring, a film that is furiously ambitious even when it goes flat and startling even when it settles for eerie, movie-of-the-week mimicry. – *Janet Maslin, New York Times*

66 It is possible to watch this entire three hour and ten minute movie and not feel you understand this president any better than when you came in. – *Kenneth Turan, Los Angeles Times*

⚊ Anthony Hopkins (leading actor); Joan Allen (supporting actress); Stephen J. Rivele, Christopher Wilkinson, Oliver Stone (original screenplay); John Williams

Ⓣ Joan Allen (supporting actress)

'There are no clean getaways.'

No Country For Old Men (new) ★★★★

SCR/DIR *Joel Coen, Ethan Coen*
2007 122m US
DVD

☆ *Tommy Lee Jones* (Sheriff Ed Tom Bell), *Javier Bardem* (Anton Chigurh), *Josh Brolin* (Llewellyn Moss), *Woody Harrelson* (Carson Wells), *Kelly Macdonald* (Carla Jean Moss), Garret Dillahunt (Wendell), Tess Harper (Loretta Bell)

In 1980, near the Rio Grande in Texas, a hunter stumbles on a drug deal gone wrong: dead bodies, and a briefcase full of cash, which he takes. He is then hunted down by a sociopath, hired to retrieve the money, while a veteran local sheriff investigates the crime scene.

A pitch-perfect piece of film-making, all at one with its complex, dark subject matter: a nightmarish scenario of unfettered, unstoppable evil descending on a dry, desolate land, sweeping aside notions of decency as old-fashioned and irrelevant. As is often the case, the Coens twist and bend genre rules to their own ends, and the story crackles with dry humour and surprises: one character meets his end off screen in what, in other hands, would seem anti-climactic. Jones is the voice of decency here, a weary man nearing retirement age and fearful of an impending doom in which evil would become routine. He has good cause: as the relentless Chuigurh, Bardem is utterly terrifying. This is a remarkably assured work, stunningly photographed, with music that sounds like a light wind across an arid landscape. The Coens have never been better.

CIN *Roger Deakins* **MUS** Carter Burwell **DES** Jess Gonchor **ED** Roderick Jaynes **PROD** Scott Rudin, Ethan Coen, Joel Coen **DIST** Paramount

WENDELL: It's a mess, ain't it, Sheriff?
SHERIFF: If it ain't, it'll do till the mess gets here.
CHIGURH (TO GAS STATION PROPRIETOR): Call it, friendo!

66 Perhaps the Coens' finest achievement to date. Like the not dissimilar Fargo, it's one of their least eccentric and laid-back, but it does contain characteristically unforgettable moments and images. – *Philip French, Observer*

66 The most measured, classical film of their (Coen Brothers) 23-year career, and maybe the best. – *Scott Foundas, Village Voice*

⚊ film; Javier Bardem (supporting actor); Joel and Ethan Coen (direction); Joel and Ethan Coen (adapted screenplay)
⚊ Roger Deakins; Roderick Jaynes (pseudonym for Joel and Ethan Coen) sound; sound editing.

Ⓣ Javier Bardem (supporting actor); Joel and Ethan Coen (direction); Roger Deakins
Ⓣ film; Tommy Lee Jones (supporting actor); Kelly Macdonald (supporoting actress); Joel and Ethan Coen (adapted screenplay); Joel and Ethan Coen (editors); sound

---

No Direction Home ★★★

DIR *Martin Scorsese*
2005 208m US/UK/Japan
DVD

☆ Bob Dylan (Himself)

DVD Available on DVD ☆ Cast in order 66 Critics' Quotes ⚊ Academy Award Ⓑ BAFTA
♫ Soundtrack on CD of importance † Points of interest ⚊ Academy Award nomination Ⓣ BAFTA nomination

453

A documentary account of the crucial period in the life and career of Bob Dylan from 1961 to 1966, when he moved away from his folk music roots and embraced electric rock.

Outstandingly comprehensive survey of Dylan's radical change of style, which affected all of popular music for decades to come. Scorsese uses archival footage and candid interviews, a few of them not flattering to Dylan, that indicate his pre-eminence at the time and the magnitude of the artistic leap he was making. This fills in the gaps left by the documentary Don't Look Back and the sequences featuring Cate Blanchett in the feature film I'm Not There. A labour of love that feels more personal than a few of Scorsese's recent works.

ED *David Tedeschi* **PROD** *Susan Lacy, Jeff Rosen, Martin Scorsese, Nigel Sinclair, Anthony Wall*

66 It has taken me all this time to accept Bob Dylan as the extraordinary artist he clearly is, but because of a new documentary by Martin Scorsese, I can finally see him freed from my disenchantment. – *Roger Ebert, Chicago Sun-Times*

† The film's title comes from a line in Dylan's song Like A Rolling Stone.

No Man's Land ★★

SCR/DIR Danis Tanovic
2001   98m   France/Italy/Belgium/UK/Slovenia
DVD

☆ Brancko Djuric (Chiki), Rene Bitoraja (Nino), Filip Sovagovic (Cera), Georges Siatidis (Marchand), Katrin Cartlidge (Jane Livingstone), Simon Callow (Col. Soft), Serge-Henri Valcke (Capt. Dubois)

During bitter fighting in the Balkans in 1993, two enemy soldiers, a Bosnian and a Serb, are trapped in a trench with another, booby-trapped soldier.

Angry, articulate and often humorous satire on the reductive lunacy of war, cleverly staged.

CIN Walther Vanden Ende   **MUS** Danis Tanovic
DES Dusko Milavec   **ED** Francesca Calvelli
PROD Frederique Dumas-Zajdela, Marc Baschet, Cedomir Kolar   **DIST** Momentum

66 An absorbing, deeply affecting, well-acted – and remarkably even-handed – antiwar statement. – *Lou Lumenick, New York Post*

⌁ foreign film

'Life isn't always made to order.'

No Reservations (new)

DIR Scott Hicks
2007   104m
DVD   ♫

☆ Catherine Zeta-Jones (Kate Armstrong), Aaron Eckhart (Nick Palmer), Abigail Breslin (Zoe), Patricia Clarkson (Paula), Bob Balaban (Therapist)

A controlling, emotionally closed female master chef in a swish Manhattan restaurant is wooed by an exuberant, spontaneous sous-chef.

There's not an unpredictable moment in this plodding, syrupy story. Misconceived from start to finish.

SCR Carol Fuchs   **CIN** Stuart Dryburgh   **MUS** Philip Glass   **DES** Barbara Ling   **ED** Pip Karmel   **PROD** Kerry Heysen, Sergio Aguero   **DIST** Warners

66 It's a fantastically smug and boring movie about food and romance, pumped with artificial sweeteners. – *Anthony Quinn, Independent*

66 Utterly phoney baloney. – *Angie Errigo, Empire*

† This is a remake of the 2001 German film Mostly Martha.

'Is it a crime of passion, or an act of treason?'

No Way Out ★

DIR Roger Donaldson
1987   114m   US
DVD   ♫

☆ Kevin Costner (Lt. Cmdr. Tom Farrell), Gene Hackman (Defence Secretary David Brice), Sean Young (Susan Atwell), Will Patton (Scott Pritchard), Howard Duff (Senator William 'Billy' Duvall), George Dzundza (Sam Hesselman)

A navy officer is assigned to the Pentagon, where he secretly shares a mistress with his boss. When she is found dead, suspicions arise that she was murdered by a foreign agent.

A decent revision of The Big Clock (1947), though set in Washington rather than the business world. It capably keeps the audience guessing until the final reel; a sex scene in a limousine between Costner and Young, an eyebrow-raiser at the time, seems rather tame now.

SCR Robert Garland   **CIN** John Alcott   **MUS** Maurice Jarre   **DES** Dennis Washington   **PROD** Laura Ziskin, Robert Garland   **DIST** Orion/Neufeld/Ziskin/Garland

66 Emotions overrule good sense in Roger Donaldson's No Way Out. The film makes such good use of Washington and builds suspense so well that it transcends a plot bordering on the ridiculous. – *Desson Howe, Washington Post*

'In A Town Where Nothing Ever Happens. . .Everything Is About To Happen To Sully.'

Nobody's Fool ★

SCR/DIR Robert Benton
1994   110m   US
DVD   ♫

☆ Paul Newman (Sully Sullivan), Jessica Tandy (Beryl Peoples), Bruce Willis (Carl Roebuck), Melanie Griffith (Toby Roebuck), Dylan Walsh (Peter Sullivan), Pruitt Taylor Vince (Rub Squeers), Gene Saks (Wirf Wirfley), Philip Bosco (Judge Flatt)

A grouchy small-town handyman who has shirked responsibility all his life faces a major rethink when his estranged son shows up for Thanksgiving.

To his credit, Newman embraces his advancing years for this grumpy old man role – as he also does in Twilight. Even more to his credit is his refusal to make Sully Sullivan one bit more likable than he really is. In fact, he's irksome – which pays off dramatically in this story, infused as it is with low-key charm.

CIN John Bailey   **MUS** Howard Shore   **DES** David Gropman   **ED** John Bloom   **PROD** Scott Rudin, Arlene

Donovan   DIST TCF/Paramount/Capella/Scott Rudin/Cinehaus

66 Nobody's Fool functions mostly as a character study, but it's also (director Robert) Benton's elegy to America's endangered small towns. It's a gem. – *Edward Guthmann, San Francisco Chronicle*

⚐ Paul Newman (leading actor); Robert Benton (screenplay)

Noi Albinoi ★★

SCR/DIR Dagur Kari
2002   93m   Iceland/Germany/GB/Denmark
DVD

☆ Tomas Lemarquis (Noi), Throstur Leo Gunnarsson (Kiddi), Elin Hansdottir (Iris), Anna Fridriksdottir (Lina), Hjalti Rognvaldsson (Oskar)

In Iceland, a 17-year-old albino slacker yearns to escape the snowy wastes of his tiny, remote village.

This unusual story, with its apocalyptic ending, has the power of timeless myth; young director Kari, a talent to watch, supplies a real sense of isolation and anomie.

CIN Rasmus Videbaek   MUS Dagur Kári, Orri Jonsson
DES Jon Steinar Ragnarsson   ED Daniel Dencik
PROD Philippe Bober, Kim Magnusson, Skuli Fr. Malmquist, Thorir Snaer Sigurjonsson, Lene Ingemann   DIST Artificial Eye

66 Beautifully paced and played with charm, this is a fond evocation of a unique place and a sympathetic take on teenage insecurity. – *David Parkinson, Empire*

Norma Rae ★★

DIR Martin Ritt
1979   114m   US

☆ *Sally Field*, Beau Bridges, Ron Leibman, Pat Hingle, Barbara Baxley

A young Southern widow working in a textiles factory becomes a staunch union organizer.

Well-intentioned and well-acted pamphlet of political enlightenment with an inevitably ambivalent attitude; it would be rather unremarkable, however, but for a gritty lead performance by Field, cast against type as a serious-minded woman increasingly drawn to feminism and workplace equality.

SCR Irving Ravetch, Harriet Frank Jnr   CIN John A. Alonzo
MUS David Shire   DES Walter Scott Herndon
PROD Tamara Asseyev, Alex Rose   DIST TCF

⚐ Sally Field (leading actress); David Shire (m), Norman Gimbel (ly) (music, original song – It Goes Like It Goes)
⚐ picture; Irving Ravetch, Harriet Frank Jr. (adapted screenplay)

North by Northwest ★★★★

DIR *Alfred Hitchcock*
1959   136m   US
DVD ♫

☆ *Cary Grant* (Roger O. Thornhill), Eva Marie Saint (Eve Kendall), James Mason (Phillip Vandamm), Leo G. Carroll (Professor), Martin Landau (Leonard), Jessie Royce Landis (Clara Thornhill), Adam Williams (Valerian)

A businessman is mistaken for a spy, and enemy agents then try to kill him because he knows too much.

A delightful mixture: a gorgeous-looking chase comedy-thriller with a touch of sex, a kind of compendium of its director's best work. Grant is suave and dashing even by his own standards, and two scenes, one involving the crop-dusting plane, the other set at Mount Rushmore, will be deemed peerless for as long as cinema exists.

SCR *Ernest Lehman*   CIN *Robert Burks*   MUS *Bernard Herrmann*   ED *George Tomasini*   PROD Alfred Hitchcock
DIST MGM

66 It is only when you adopt the basic premise that Cary Grant could not possibly come to harm that the tongue in Hitchcock's cheek becomes plainly visible. – *Hollis Alpert, Saturday Review*

⚐ Ernest Lehman (original screenplay); art direction; editing

'All She Wanted Was To Make A Living. Instead She Made History.'

North Country ★★

DIR Niki Caro
2005   126m   Germany/US
DVD ♫

☆ Charlize Theron (Josey Aimes), Frances McDormand (Glory), Sean Bean (Kyle), Richard Jenkins (Hank), Jeremy Renner (Bobby Sharp), Michelle Monaghan (Sherry), Woody Harrelson (Bill White), Sissy Spacek (Alice)

An outspoken single mother, abused by her male colleagues in a Minnesota iron mine becomes the first American woman to file a class-action lawsuit for sexual harassment.

A flawed attempt to adapt a genuinely fascinating story. It has its moments, primarily those scenes between Theron and McDormand – who plays a much tougher and more interesting character. The film pulls too many punches: one has the sense its producers just wanted to send all sections of the audience home feeling good about themselves.

SCR Michael Seitzman   CIN Chris Menges
MUS Gustavo Santaolalla   DES Richard Hoover
ED David Coulson   PROD Nick Weschler   DIST Warner

66 In real life it's an inspiring story, but this movie is pathetically scared of alienating the male audience demographic and makes Theron's victory entirely contingent on being extravagantly forgiven by her father and her son. – *Peter Bradshaw, The Guardian*

⚐ Charlize Theron (leading actress); Frances McDormand (supporting actress)
Ⓣ Charlize Theron (leading actress); Frances McDormand (supporting actress)

Nosferatu ★★★

DIR *F. W. Murnau*
1921   72m   Germany
DVD ♫

☆ *Max Schreck* (Count Orlok, Nosferatu the Vampire), Gustav von Wangenheim (Thomas Hutter), Greta Schröder (Ellen), Alexander Granach (Knock)

DVD Available on DVD   ☆ Cast in order of importance   66 Critics' Quotes   † Points of interest   ⚐ Academy Award   ⚐ Academy Award nomination   🏆 BAFTA   Ⓣ BAFTA nomination

Count Dracula goes to Bremen and is destroyed by sunlight.

An unauthorised treatment of the Bram Stoker novel, with a terrifying Count and several genuinely chilling moments. Schreck is extraordinary, the film dutifully terrifies – and Murnau ended up in the embrace of Hollywood.

SCR Henrik Galeen   **CIN** Fritz Arno Wagner   **DIST** Prana

Not Here to be Loved ★★

SCR/DIR Stephane Brizé
2005   93m   France
[DVD]   ♫

☆ Patrick Chesnais (Jean-Claude Delsart), Anne Consigny (Françoise), Lionel Abelanski (Thierry), Georges Wilson (Jean-Claude's father)

Jean-Claude, a 50-year-old bailiff, has given up on life's pleasures. But he decides to join a tango club across from his office, and meets Françoise. A whole new world opens up for him via music and dance.

Affecting, touching portrait of late-blooming love in an unlikely place, rendered believable by the excellent playing of hangdog Chesnais and the delightful Consigny.

SCR Stephane Brizé/Juliette Sales   **CIN** Claude Garnier   **MUS** Christoph H Muller, Eduardo Makaroff   **DES** Valerie Saradjian   **ED** Anne Klotz   **PROD** Milena Poylo/Gilles Sacuto   **DIST** Artificial Eye

'In her village, she was the teacher... In the city, she discovered how much she had to learn.'

Not One Less ★★

DIR Zhang Yimou
1999   106m   China
[DVD]

☆ Wei Minzhi (Wei Minzhi), Zhang Huike (Zhang Huike), Tian Zhenda (Village chief), Gao Enman (Teacher Gao), Sun Zhimei (Sun Zhimei), Feng Yuying (TV receptionist), Li Fanfan (TV host)

A 13-year-old girl is pressed into service as a teacher at a school in rural China and promised a bonus if she keeps all her 28 pupils. When one runaway student jeopardises this arrangements, she hunts the pupil down.

Amateur actors bring refreshing authenticity to a film that starts out with a deft light-hearted comic tone, but also condemns China's rural education system – and eventually, exploitative child labour.

SCR Shi Xiangsheng   **CIN** Hou Yong   **MUS** San Bao   **DES** Cao Jiuping   **ED** Zhai Ru   **PROD** Zhao Yu   **DIST** Columbia

66 Zhang's work is always worth watching, but this is the first of his films in which the sorrows are so heart-rending, its many comic moments so laugh-out-loud human. – *F.X. Feeney, L.A. Weekly*

† It won the Golden Lion for best film at the 1999 Venice Film Festival.

'Behind every great love is a great story.'

The Notebook

DIR Nick Cassavetes
2004   123m   US
[DVD]   ♫

☆ Ryan Gosling (Noah), Rachel McAdams (Allie), James Garner (Duke), Gena Rowlands (Allie Calhoun), James Marsden (Lon Hammond), Kevin Connolly (Fin), Sam Shepard (Frank Calhoun), Joan Allen (Anne Hamilton)

A man reads to his mentally incapacitated wife the story of how they first met in the summer of 1941.

Tortuous tosh that has somehow picked up a cult reputation, perhaps for its sheer, unrelentingly gormless sincerity – encapsulated in Gosling's doltish lead performance – or its mistaken faith in the power of that most Hollywood of placebos, a spoonful of sugar, as a cure for senile dementia.

SCR Jeremy Leven   **CIN** Robert Fraisse   **MUS** Aaron Zigman   **DES** Sarah Knowles   **ED** Alan Heim   **PROD** Mark Johnson, Lynn Harris

66 Has a single goal: to prod your tear ducts to open up. It is very, very good at this task. Whether The Notebook is good in any other respect is a bit more complicated. – *M.E. Russell, Portland Oregonian*

66 Handsome, thoughtful, and frankly rather mawkish. – *Mark Kermode, Observer*

'One woman's mistake is another's opportunity.'

Notes on a Scandal ★★

DIR Richard Eyre
2006   91m   UK/US
[DVD]   ♫

☆ Judi Dench (Barbara Covett), Cate Blanchett (Sheba Hart), Bill Nighy (Richard Hart), Andrew Simpson (Steven Connelly), Phil Davis (Brian Bangs), Julia McKenzie (Marjorie)

Barbara, a lonely middle-aged London teacher, befriends Sheba, a new younger colleague who embarks on a secret affair with one of her pupils, aged 15.

Entertaining adaptation of an ingenious story about an older woman's friendship gradually revealed as menacing manipulation. It might have been wan, judgemental or wistful, but director Eyre chooses an amused, melodramatic approach; the dominant tone is barely suppressed hysteria, complemented perfectly by Glass's insistent, fever-dreamlike score. The novel's 'unreliable narrator' device fails to translate, partly because the disparity between Barbara's musings and what we see on screen is clear. But it's an enjoyable ride, with Dench doing some of the best film work in her long career.

SCR Patrick Marber   **CIN** Chris Menges   **MUS** Philip Glass   **DES** Tim Hatley   **ED** John Bloom, Antonia Van Drimmelen   **PROD** Scott Rudin, Robert Fox   **DIST** TCF

66 A sensationally stylish and tense drama. Great

[DVD] Available on DVD   ☆ Cast in order of importance   66 Critics' Quotes   † Points of interest   ♩ Academy Award   ♪ Academy Award nomination   🅱 BAFTA   Ⓑ BAFTA nomination
♫ Soundtrack on CD

performances all round make this a movie to remember. – *Mark Adams, Sunday Mirror*

66 There are brilliantly handled scenes of anger, embarrassment and humiliation, and brutal physical and emotional confrontations of great power. – *Philip French, Observer*

Judi Dench (leading actress); Cate Blanchett (supporting actress); Patrick Marber (adapted screenplay); Philip Glass

British film; Judi Dench (leading actress); Patrick Marber (adapted screenplay)

'Fateful Fascination! Electric Tension!'

Notorious ★★★

DIR *Alfred Hitchcock*
1946   101m   US
DVD   ♫

☆ *Cary Grant* (Devlin), *Ingrid Bergman* (Alicia Huberman), *Claude Rains* (Alexander Sebastian), Louis Calhern (Paul Prescott), Leopoldine Konstantin (Mme. Sebastian), Reinhold Schünzel (Dr. Anderson)

In Rio, a notorious lady marries a Nazi renegade to help the US government but finds herself falling in love with her contact.

Superb romantic suspense thriller, impeccably scripted by Ben Hecht and containing some of Hitchcock's best direction.

SCR *Ben Hecht*   CIN Ted Tetzlaff   MUS Roy Webb   ED Theron Warth   PROD Alfred Hitchcock   DIST RKO

66 Velvet smooth in dramatic action, sharp and sure in its characters, and heavily charged with the intensity of warm emotional appeal. – *Bosley Crowther*

66 The suspense is terrific. – *New Yorker, 1976*

Claude Rains (supporting actor); Ben Hecht (original screenplay)

'Can the most famous film star in the world fall for just an ordinary guy?'

Notting Hill ★★★

DIR Roger Michell
1999   124m   US/GB
DVD   ♫

☆ Julia Roberts (Anna Scott), Hugh Grant (William Thacker), Hugh Bonneville (Bernie), Emma Chambers (Honey), James Dreyfus (Martin), Rhys Ifans (Spike), Tim McInnerny (Max), Gina McKee (Bella), Richard McCabe (Tony), Alec Baldwin (Jeff King)

A shy English bookseller in a chic part of London is launched into a sudden, surprising fling with a beautiful and famous American film star.

The most satisfying collaboration between screenwriter Curtis and leading man Grant – a thoughtful, well-crafted script that wears its ideas lightly and sparkles with genuine wit. It has much to say about the condition of fame, and the price paid by those who encounter it. More crucially, it is a first-class romantic comedy in the classic traditions of the genre.

SCR Richard Curtis   CIN Michael Coulter   MUS Trevor Jones   DES Stuart Craig   ED Nick Moore   PROD Duncan Kenworthy   DIST Polygram/Working Title

ANNA: After all...I'm just a girl, standing in front of a boy, asking him to love her.

66 A smartly cast and consistently amusing romantic comedy. – *Kenneth Turan, Los Angeles Times*

66 The film has this weird postmodernist taint: It has a self-aware script that cleverly plays off the reality of its own cast and their famous real-life contretemps. It's smart and knowing. – *Stephen Hunter, Washington Post*

audience award

'It happens in the best of families.'

Now Voyager ★★★

DIR *Irving Rapper*
1942   117m   US
DVD   ♫

☆ *Bette Davis* (Charlotte Vale), *Claude Rains* (Dr. Jaquith), *Paul Henreid* (Jerry D. Durrance), Gladys Cooper (Mrs. Henry Windle Vale), John Loder (Elliott Livingston), Bonita Granville (June Vale), Ilka Chase (Lisa Vale), Lee Patrick ('Deb' McIntyre), Charles Drake (Leslie Trotter), Franklin Pangborn (Mr. Thompson), Janis Wilson (Tina Durrance)

A plain single woman goes into therapy, impulsively embarks on a love affair, throws off her inhibitions and starts behaving like a vivacious socialite.

A basically soggy script still gets by thanks to the romantic magic of its stars, who were all at their best. Also, suffering while wearing mink went over big with wartime audiences.

SCR Casey Robinson   CIN Sol Polito   MUS Max Steiner   ED Warren Low   PROD Hal B. Wallis   DIST Warner

CHARLOTTE (BETTE DAVIS): Oh, Jerry, don't let's ask for the moon. We have the stars!

66 If it were better, it might not work at all. This way, it's a crummy classic. – *New Yorker, 1977*

Max Steiner

Bette Davis (leading actress); Gladys Cooper (supporting actress)

'1938. One family's story of a homeland lost and a new one found...'

Nowhere in Africa ★★

SCR/DIR Caroline Link
2001   141m   Germany
DVD   ♫

☆ Juliane Koehler (Jettel Redlich), Merab Ninidze (Walter Redlich), Matthias Habich (Suesskind), Sidede Onyulo (Owuor), Lea Kurka (Regina Redlich (younger)), Karoline Eckertz (Regina Redlich (older)), Gerd Heinz (Max), Hildegard Schmahl (Ina)

A Jewish lawyer, his wife and daughter flee Germany just before World War II, abandoning their comfortable existence for a hard life running a remote farm in Kenya.

A story that relates to the Holocaust in an oblique but significant manner: the family's struggle to survive in their new environment involves questions of rootlessness and identity, and even touches on survivor guilt. The

---

DVD Available on DVD   ☆ Cast in order   66 Critics' Quotes   Academy Award   BAFTA
♫ Soundtrack on CD   of importance   † Points of interest   Academy Award nomination   BAFTA nomination

457

African landscapes make an appealing foreground, but the really absorbing action takes place inside characters' heads.

CIN Gernot Roll   **MUS** Niki Reiser   **DES** Susann Bieling, Uwe Szielasko   **ED** Patricia Rommel   **PROD** Peter Herrmann   **DIST** Optimum

66 Easy on the eye and effortlessly entertaining across almost 2½ hours. – *Derek Elley, Variety*

66 Audience empathy for the displaced Redlichs, coupled with the filmmaker's proffered charms of wise natives and their mysterious rituals, goes a long way toward making this lyrical travelogue a crowd pleaser. – *Lisa Schwarzbaum, Entertainment Weekly*

↓ foreign film

'She's chasing a dream...they're chasing her.'

Nurse Betty ★

DIR Neil LaBute

2000   110m   US

DVD   ♫

☆ Renée Zellweger (Betty Sizemore), Morgan Freeman (Charlie), Chris Rock (Wesley), Greg Kinnear (Dr. David Ravell/George McCord), Aaron Eckhart (Del), Tia Texada (Rosa), Crispin Glover (Roy), Pruitt Taylor Vince (Ballard), Allison Janney (Lyla), Kathleen Wilhoite (Sue Ann), Harriet Sanson Harris (Ellen), Laird Macintosh (Dr. Lonnie Walsh)

A waitress, traumatised by witnessing the brutal murder of her cheating husband, sets out from her Kansas home to Hollywood, to consult the TV soap opera doctor with whom she has fallen in love.

A darkish comedy which heavy-handedly pokes fun at lives dominated by TV values. It has moments of unpredictable wit, but there's a sense of condescension by the writers towards their characters.

SCR John C. Richards, James Flamberg   **CIN** Jean Yves Escoffier   **MUS** Rolfe Kent   **DES** Charles Breen   **ED** Joel Plotch, Steven Weisberg   **PROD** Gail Mutrux, Steve Golin

66 A slick, clever, heartless satire on a society whose dreams, ambitions and mores are influenced at every turn by the deceptive blandishments of TV culture. – *Time Out*

66 All in all, Nurse Betty is a wonderful movie, unpredictably alive to the fact that the American citizenry is a lot stranger than we like to admit. – *Richard Schickel, Time*

'A magnificent Christmas spectacular'

Nutcracker – The Motion Picture ★

DIR Carroll Ballard

1986   89m   US

DVD

☆ Hugh Bigney (Herr Drosselmeier), Vanessa Sharp (Clara (in reality)), Patricia Barker (Clara - in dream/Ballerina Doll), Wade Walthall (Nutcracker/Prince)

Tchaikovsky's classic ballet is brought to screen life by the Pacific Northwest Ballet.

Given the limits of adapting ballet for the screen, this is charming and faithful to its source – though Ballard's habit of zooming in close to dancers' feet and limbs does grate a little.

CIN Stephen M. Burum   **MUS** Tchaikovsky   **DES** Maurice Sendak   **ED** John Nutt, Michael Silvers   **PROD** Thomas L. Wilhite, Peter Locke, Donald Kushner, Willard Carroll   **DIST** Entertainment/Hyperion/Kushner/Locke

66 Great family entertainment. – *BBC*

'Mad As In Angry. Or Just Plain... NUTS'

Nuts ★

DIR Martin Ritt

1987   116m   US

DVD

☆ Barbra Streisand (Claudia Draper), Richard Dreyfuss (Aaron Levinsky), Maureen Stapleton (Rose Kirk), Karl Malden (Arthur Kirk), Eli Wallach (Herbert A. Morrison)

High-priced hooker goes on trial for murdering a client, and finds herself fighting to prove she is not mentally incompetent.

Streisand fans will have a ball here, with their heroine in the feistiest of form. It's not much of a courtroom drama. It's not even much of a story. But the lure of Barbra, should you succumb to it, renders such considerations moot. Dreyfuss, another actor with a bullying screen presence, holds his own; but it's clear who the real star is.

SCR Tom Topor, Alvin Sargent, Darryl Ponicsan   **CIN** Andrzej Bartkowiak   **MUS** Barbra Streisand   **DES** Joel Schiller   **ED** Sidney Levin   **PROD** Barbra Streisand   **DIST** Warner

66 It wants to be a movie with a message, but in the end it's just a melodrama. – *Rita Kempley, Washington Post*

DVD Available on DVD   ☆ Cast in order of importance   66 Critics' Quotes   † Points of interest   ↓ Academy Award   ⚱ Academy Award nomination   Ⓣ BAFTA   Ⓣ BAFTA nomination
♫ Soundtrack on CD

'Everything Comes Full Circle...'

O

DIR Tim Blake Nelson
2001 95m US
`DVD` ♫

☆ Mekhi Phifer (Odin James), Josh Hartnett (Hugo Goulding), Julia Stiles (Desi Brable), Elden Henson (Roger Rodriguez), Andrew Keegan (Michael Cassio), Rain Phoenix (Emily), John Heard (Dean Brable), Anthony 'A. J.' Johnson (Dell), Martin Sheen (Coach Duke Goulding)

The only black pupil at an elite American prep school, a basketball star, stirs up dangerous jealousies when he romances a white girl.

A brave, well-meaning attempt to adapt Othello for high-schoolers founders from the word go, stripping all the passion and fury from Shakespeare's tragedy. O dear.

SCR Brad Kaaya **CIN** Russell Lee Fine **MUS** Jeff Danna **DES** Dina Goldman **ED** Kate Sanford **PROD** Eric Gitter, Anthony Rhulen **DIST** Buena Vista

66 It's highly enjoyable and well acted, with the Iago figure better motivated than in the original play. – *Philip French, Observer*

66 This arty melodrama is not likely to make teenage America get down with Shakespeare. – *David Ansen, Newsweek*

† The film was completed in 1999, but its release coincided with the shooting at Columbine High School, and was delayed for more than two years.

'They have a plan, but not a clue.'

O Brother, Where Art Thou? ★★★

DIR *Joel Coen*
2000 106m US
`DVD` ♫

☆ *George Clooney* (Everett Ulysses McGill), John Turturro (Pete), Tim Blake Nelson (Delmar), Charles Durning (Pappy O'Daniel), John Goodman (Big Dan Teague), Michael Badalucco (George Nelson), Holly Hunter (Penny), Stephen Root (Radio Station Man), Chris Thomas King (Tommy Johnson), Wayne Duvall (Homer Stokes), Daniel Von Bargen (Sheriff Cooley)

Three convicts, two of them dimwits, the other dapper, vain and smooth-talking, escape from a chain gang in 1930s Mississippi, go searching for buried treasure, and experience wildly varied adventures.

Extremely loosely based on Homer's Odyssey, this very funny road movie (with hillbilly music thrown in) ticks off more cultural references than you can shake a stick at, yet still carves out its own shambling, goofy identity. T-Bone Burnett supplied an impeccable collection of traditional country and bluegrass songs for the soundtrack.

SCR *Ethan and Joel Coen* **CIN** *Roger Deakins* **MUS** *T Bone Burnett* **DES** Dennis Gassner **ED** Roderick Jaynes, Tricia Cooke **PROD** Ethan Coen **DIST** Universal

66 It's a wild, whacked-out wonder. Coenheads rejoice. – *Peter Travers, Rolling Stone.*

66 This is the Coen brothers' most emotionally felt movie, and that's not meant as faint praise. – *Peter Rainer, New York Magazine*

† The title comes from Preston Sturges's Sullivan's Travels. It is the name of the serious, harrowing social drama that its director hero wanted to make.

† Though the film was only a moderate success – it grossed $45 million in the US – its soundtrack album was an enormous surprise hit, selling four million copies.

⅄ Ethan Coen, Joel Coen (adapted screenplay)

Ⓣ Roger Deakins; Dennis Gassner; Monica Howe (costume design); (screenplay) (music)

'Sometimes The Most Desirable Relationship Is The One You Can't Have.'

The Object of My Affection ★★

DIR Nicholas Hytner
1998 111m US
`DVD` ♫

☆ Jennifer Aniston (Nina Borowski), Paul Rudd (George Hanson), Alan Alda (Sidney Miller), Nigel Hawthorne (Rodney Fraser), John Pankow (Vince McBride), Tim Daly (Dr. Robert Joley), Allison Janney (Constance Miller), Steve Zahn (Frank Hanson), Amo Gulinello (Paul James), Bruce Altman (Dr. Goldstein), Kevin Carroll (Louis Crowley)

A gay man and his best friend, a pregnant woman dumped by her lover, become closer when she asks him to help raise her child.

A new twist on the romantic comedy genre, which only partly works: Aniston and Rudd work well together on screen, but either way they lose. Director Hytner is not about to settle for compromise, so 'happily ever after' is never on the cards, at least not that simply. Very fine support work from veterans Hawthorne and Alda helps make this a witty, if light-weight treat.

SCR Wendy Wasserstein **CIN** Oliver Stapleton **MUS** George Fenton **DES** Jane Musky **ED** Tariq Anwar **PROD** Laurence Mark **DIST** TCF

`DVD` Available on DVD   ☆ Cast in order   66 Critics' Quotes   ⅄ Academy Award   Ⓣ BAFTA
♫ Soundtrack on CD   of importance   † Points of interest   ⅄ Academy Award nomination   Ⓣ BAFTA nomination

'Are You In Or Out?'

Ocean's Eleven

DIR Steven Soderbergh
2001 116m US/Australia
[DVD] ♫

☆ George Clooney (Danny Ocean), Matt Damon (Linus), Andy Garcia (Terry Benedict), Brad Pitt (Rusty Ryan), Julia Roberts (Tess Ocean), Casey Affleck (Virgil Malloy), Scott Caan (Turk Malloy), Don Cheadle (Basher Tarr), Elliott Gould (Reuben Tishkoff), Eddie Jemison (Livingston Dell), Bernie Mac (Frank Catton), Shaobo Qin (Yen), Carl Reiner (Saul Bloom)

A charismatic conman, freed from prison, recruits a crack criminal gang to rob a casino boss and win back his wife.

This remake of Frank Sinatra's Rat Pack film of 1960 is an improvement on the original in every department – which isn't saying much. Clooney plays Danny Ocean's affectless cool very convincingly, and it's glossy, good-looking and essentially harmless. But it doesn't end a minute too soon.

SCR Ted Griffin CIN Peter Andrews MUS David Holmes DES Philip Messina ED Stephen Mirrione PROD Jerry Weintraub DIST Warner

66 Ocean's Eleven raises the benchmark for all future blockbusters and is guaranteed to put a grin on your face from ear to ear. – *Jamie Russell, BBC*

66 The movie is more like an elegant journey in a hot-air balloon than a trip on a rollercoaster and is that rare thing, a thriller without any violence, sex or profanity. – *Philip French, Observer*

† After its box-office success – $183 million in the US, and $267 million in other territories, two sequels followed: Ocean's Twelve in 2004 and Ocean's Thirteen in 2007.

October ★★★★

DIR *Sergei M. Eisenstein*
1927 95m USSR
[DVD]

☆ Vasili Nikandrov (Lenin), N. Popov (Kerensky), Boris Livanov (Minister Tereschenko)

In 1917, the short-lived Kerensky regime is overthrown by the Bolsheviks.

A propaganda masterpiece whose images have all too often been mistaken and used for genuine newsreel. Cinematically, an undoubted masterpiece.

SCR Sergei M. Eisenstein, Grigory Alexandrov
CIN Edouard Tissé, V. Popov DIST Sovkino

66 The film lacks excitement and may leave you cold. – *Pauline Kael*

66 Some of the action scenes are genuinely stirring–when he wasn't editorializing, the man really could cut film. – *David Kehr, Chicago Reader*

† On Stalin's orders, the film was re-edited to remove any reference to Trostky's contribution to the 1917 revolution.

The Odd Couple ★★

DIR Gene Saks
1968 105m US
☆ *Jack Lemmon, Walter Matthau,* John Fiedler, Herb

Edelman, David Sheiner, Larry Haines, Monica Evans, Carole Sheely, Iris Adrian

A nervous, fastidious, tidy man, still reeling from his divorce, moves in with his slobbish friend, and they get on each other's nerves.

Straight filming of a funny play which sometimes seems lost on the wide screen, but the performances from two seasoned veterans are fine.

SCR *Neil Simon* CIN Robert B. Hauser MUS Neal Hefti
PROD Howard W. Koch DIST Paramount

OSCAR (WALTER MATTHAU): I can't take it anymore, Felix. I'm crackin' up. Everything you do irritates me. And when you're not here, the things I know you're gonna do when you come in irritate me. You leave me little notes on my pillow. I told you 158 times I cannot stand little notes on my pillow. "We are all out of cornflakes, F.U." It took me three hours to figure out that F.U. was Felix Ungar. It's not your fault, Felix. It's a rotten combination, that's all.

⚱ Neil Simon (adapted screenplay)

Of Freaks and Men ★★

DIR Alexei Balabanov
1998 93m Russia
[DVD]

☆ Sergei Makovetskii (Johan), Dinara Drukarova (Lisa), Lika Nevolina (Ekaterina Kirillovna), Victor Sukhorukov (Victor Ivanovich), Dyo Alyosha (Kolya), Chingiz Tsydendabayev (Tolya), Vadim Prokhorov (Pytilov), Alexandr Mezentsev (Dr Stasov), Dariya Lesnikova (Grunya), Igor Shibanov (Radlov), Tatyana Polonskaya (Darya)

Ruthless Russian pornographer in St. Petersburg at the start of the last century destroys lives by trading photographs of naked women being whipped and spanked.

An odd, deeply original film, shot in both black and white and sepia, thus underlining its sense of period and subject matter. It is partly a send-up of early cinema styles, and also a rebuke to Russian cinema's high-minded theorists; it's telling that the pornographer's assistant, his photographer, becomes a successful director. Balabanov is an equal-opportunity offence-giver in this satire of Russian society – the rich are feckless, the poor are grasping, and foreigners are after influence and money. Finally, though, it's also a tribute to cinema's life-affirming possibilities.

CIN Sergei Astakhov DES Vera Zelinskaya ED Marina Lipartia PROD Sergei Selyanov, Oleg Botogov
DIST Metro Tartan

66 Director Alexei Balabanov combines luridly perverse subject matter – pornography, madness, the sex life of Siamese twins – with a style that draws both on Russian literary fabulism and on early-cinema pastiche. – *Jonathan Romney, Sight & Sound*

'We have a dream. Someday we'll have a little house and a couple of acres. A place to call home.'

Of Mice and Men ★

DIR Gary Sinise
1992 115m US
[DVD] ♫

☆ John Malkovich (Lennie Small), Gary Sinise (George

[DVD] Available on DVD	☆ Cast in order	66 Critics' Quotes	⚱ Academy Award	⊕ BAFTA
♫ Soundtrack on CD	of importance	† Points of interest	⚱ Academy Award nomination	⊕ BAFTA nomination

Milton), Ray Walston (Candy), Casey Siemaszko (Curley), Sherilyn Fenn (Curley's Wife), John Terry (Slim)

Two farmhands' dreams of finding better lives in a place of their own are wrecked when one of them kills the farmer's flirtatious wife.

Steinbeck's novel is treated respectfully in this sensitive, workmanlike adaptation.

SCR Horton Foote **CIN** Kenneth MacMillan **MUS** Mark Isham **DES** David Gropman **ED** Robert L. Sinise **PROD** Russell Smith, Gary Sinise **DIST** UIP/MGM

66 A quiet triumph. – *Roger Ebert, Chicago Sun-Times*

† Malkovich and Sinise first played Lennie and George on stage, when they were regulars at Chicago's Steppenwolf Theatre.

'Romance never dies.'

Offending Angels

DIR Andrew Rajan

2000 93m GB

DVD

☆ Susannah Harker (Paris), Andrew Lincoln (Sam), Shaun Parkes (Zeke), Andrew Rajan (Baggy), Paula O'Grady (Alison), Marion Bailey (Mentor), Michael Cochrane (Mentor), Sophie Dix (Mandy)

Two dropouts who use drugs and pornography to pass the time are surprised when two guardian angels enter their lives.

A film with but one point of interest: according to its producer, it had the lowest ever box-office gross in the British cinema history: £79. Furthermore, in one of the few cinemas where it was exhibited, in Croydon, it played for an entire week with not a single person paying to see it. Given that history, it may be of perverse interest to some.

SCR Andrew Rajan, Tim Moyler **CIN** Alvin Leong **MUS** Martin Ward **ED** Roger Burgess, Catherine Fletcher **PROD** Andrew Rajan **DIST** Guerrilla Films

66 Drivel. . .avoid at all costs. – *Jamie Russell, BBC*

The Officers' Ward ★★

SCR/DIR François Dupeyron

2001 135m France

DVD

☆ *Eric Caravaca* (Adrien), Denis Podalydes (Henri), Gregori Derangere (Pierre), Sabine Azema (Anais), Andre Dussollier (The Surgeon), Isabelle Renauld (Marguerite), Geraldine Pailhas (Clemence), Jean-Michel Portal (Alain)

A lieutenant disfigured by a bomb during World War I tries to piece his life back together during a stay in a sanatorium on the outskirts of Paris.

Restrained period piece that takes pride in its own literariness, exploring the very European idea of 'losing face'; its lead does a lot with a strange role, off-screen for much of the first half and then stuck with one expression for the remainder.

CIN Tetsuo Nagata **MUS** Jean-Michel Bernard **DES** Patrick Durand **ED** Dominique Faysse **PROD** Michele and Laurent Petin **DIST** Optimum

66 A richly emotional and deeply considered film. No one with an interest in the Great War should miss it. – *Peter Bradshaw, Guardian*

Offside ★★

DIR Jafar Panahi

2006 92m Iran

DVD

☆ Sima Mobarak-Shahi (First girl), Shayesteh Irani (Smoking girl), Ayda Sadeqi (Soccer girl), Golnaz Farmani (Girl with tchador), Mahnaz Zabihi (Female Soldier), Nazanin Sediq-zadeh (Young girl), Safdar Samandar (Soldier from Azerbaijan)

A group of soccer-loving teenage girls decide to pass themselves off as boys to gate-crash the Iran–Bahrain game at Tehran stadium, a 2006 World Cup qualifying match.

Director Panahi provides a sharp, fast-paced comedy about the deprivation of women's basic human rights under Iran's strict policy of segregation between sexes. Lively ensemble playing from the soccer 'boys', all non-professional, enhances its appeal.

SCR Jafar Panahi/Shadmehr Rastin **CIN** Mahmoud Kalari **ED** Jafar Panahi **PROD** Jafar Panahi **DIST** Artificial Eye

66 It's a wisp of a movie, but it has stayed with me longer than much supposedly weightier fare. – *Peter Rainer, Christian Science Monitor*

66 The amateur ensemble cast and superb satire make this one of the best football films going. – *David Parkinson, Empire*

Old Joy ★

DIR Kelly Reichardt

2006 76m US

DVD

☆ Will Oldham (Kurt), Daniel London (Mark), Tanya Smith (Tanya)

Two old friends spend a weekend camping in the Pacific Northwest.

Thoughtful, unhurried meditation on memory, friendship and the passing of time.

SCR Kelly Reichardt, Jonathan Raymond **CIN** Peter Sillen **MUS** Yo La Tengo **ED** Kelly Reichardt **PROD** Lars Knudsen, Neil Kopp, Anish Savjani, Jay Van Hoy **DIST** Soda Pictures

KURT: 'Sorrow is nothing but worn-out joy.'

66 A spare and satisfying experience. – *Steve Rose, Guardian*

66 Visually stunning, quietly insightful and more than a little hard to endure. – *Frank Scheck, Hollywood Reporter*

† Will Oldham is better known in the US as alternative country singer Bonnie 'Prince' Billy.

'15 years forced in a cell, only 5 days given to seek revenge.'

Oldboy ★★

DIR Park Chan-wook

2003 120m South Korea

DVD ♫

☆ Choi Min-sik (Oh Daesu), Yu Ji-tae (Woo Jin), Kang Hye-jeong (Mido)

DVD Available on DVD ☆ Cast in order 66 Critics' Quotes Academy Award BAFTA
♫ Soundtrack on CD of importance † Points of interest Academy Award nomination BAFTA nomination

461

A Korean man goes after revenge after being kidnapped and unjustly imprisoned for 15 years.

This brutally violent thriller combines bizarre comedy with chilling savagery in a highly individual way. Constantly fascinating, though it's hard to watch a tongue being snipped out with scissors, and other acts of mutilation.

SCR Hwang Jo-yun, Lim Jun-hyeong, Park Chan-wook **CIN** Jeong Jeong-hun **MUS** Yeong-wook Jo **DES** Ryu Seong-heui **ED** Kim Sang-beom **PROD** Seung-yong Lim **DIST** Tartan

66 This plays like Titus Andronicus shot through the fixed and beady lens of Jim Jarmusch. Park has all the while been crafting a Grand Guignol masterpiece of fiendish, shattering power. Don't miss it. – *Tim Robey, Daily Telegraph*

66 A sadistic masterpiece. – *Jamie Russell, BBC*

'Much much more than a musical!'

Oliver!   ★★★

DIR *Carol Reed*
1968   146m   GB
DVD   ♫

☆ *Ron Moody* (Fagin), Oliver Reed (Bill Sikes), Harry Secombe (Mr. Bumble), Mark Lester (Oliver Twist), Shani Wallis (Nancy), *Jack Wild* (The Artful Dodger), Hugh Griffith (The Magistrate), Joseph O'Conor (Mr. Brownlow), Leonard Rossiter (Mr. Sowerberry), Hylda Baker (Mrs. Sowerberry), Peggy Mount (Widow Corney), Megs Jenkins (Mrs. Bedwin)

A musical version of Oliver Twist.

This hugely popular and successful British musical drags a little in spots, but on the whole does credit both to the show and the original novel, though it is eclipsed in style by David Lean's straight version.

SCR Vernon Harris **CIN** Oswald Morris **MUS** Lionel Bart **DES** John Box **ED** Ralph Kemplen **PROD** John Woolf **DIST** Columbia/Warwick/Romulus

66 Only time will tell if it is a great film but it is certainly a great experience. – *Joseph Morgenstern*

66 There is a heightened discrepancy between the romping jollity with which everyone goes about his business and the actual business being gone about. . .such narrative elements as the exploitation of child labour, pimping, abduction, prostitution and murder combine to make Oliver! the most non-U subject ever to receive a U certificate. – *Jan Dawson*

† 'Food Glorious Food'; 'Where Is Love'; 'Boy for Sale'; 'Consider Yourself'; 'You've Got to Pick a Pocket'; 'It's a Fine Life'; 'I'd Do Anything'; 'Be Back Soon'; 'Who Will Buy'; 'As Long As He Needs Me'; 'Reviewing the Situation'; 'Oom-Pah-Pah'; 'Oliver'

⚊ picture; Carol Reed (direction); John Green; Onna White; sound

⚊ Ron Moody (leading actor); Jack Wild (supporting actor); Vernon Harris (adapted screenplay); Oswald Morris; Phyllis Dalton (costume design); editing

Oliver Twist   ★

DIR Roman Polanski
2005   130m   GB/France/Czech Republic
DVD

☆ Ben Kingsley (Fagin), Barney Clark (Oliver Twist),

Jamie Foreman (Bill Sykes), Harry Eden (Artful Dodger), Leanne Rowe (Nancy), Edward Hardwicke (Mr Brownlow), Ian McNeice (Mr Limbkins), Mark Strong (Toby Crackit)

Underfed London orphan flees the workhouse and falls in with bad company.

Competent, if uninspired, version of Charles Dickens' classic novel which edits out much of the more colourful parts of the story, as well as the author's wit and restrained rage about social conditions.

SCR Ronald Harwood **CIN** Pawel Edelman **MUS** Rachel Portman **DES** Allan Starski **ED** Herve de Luze **PROD** Robert Benmussa, Alain Sarde, Roman Polanski **DIST** Pathé

66 It's noble, high-minded and safe, and I can't help thinking that I would have preferred an audacious but honest failure. – *Ann Hornaday, Washington Post*

66 It's as though Polanski had set the story's foolproof motor on cruise control and left the room; the tale is well told but told without personality. – *Ty Burr, Boston Globe*

Oliver Twist   ★★★★

DIR *David Lean*
1948   116m   GB
DVD   ♫

☆ *Alec Guinness* (Fagin), *Robert Newton* (Bill Sikes), *Francis L. Sullivan* (Mr Bumble), *John Howard Davies* (Oliver Twist), *Kay Walsh* (Nancy), *Anthony Newley* (The Artful Dodger), *Henry Stephenson* (Mr Brownlow), *Mary Clare* (Mrs Corney), *Gibb McLaughlin* (Mr Sowerberry), *Diana Dors* (Charlotte)

A foundling falls among thieves but is rescued by a benevolent old gentleman.

Simplified, brilliantly cinematic version of the voluminous Dickens novel, beautiful to look at and memorably played, with every scene achieving the perfect maximum impact.

SCR *David Lean, Stanley Haynes* **CIN** *Guy Green* **MUS** *Arnold Bax* **DES** *John Bryan* **ED** Jack Harris **PROD** Ronald Neame **DIST** GFD

66 A thoroughly expert piece of movie entertainment. – *Richard Winnington*

66 A brilliant, fascinating movie, no less a classic than the Dickens novel which it brings to life. – *Time*

'Life is never as innocent as it seems.'

Olivier, Olivier   ★★

DIR Agnieszka Holland
1992   110m   France
DVD   ♫

☆ François Cluzet (Serge Duval), Brigitte Roüan (Elisabeth Duval), Jean-François Stévenin (Druot), Grégoire Colin (Olivier), Marina Golovine (Nadine), Frédéric Quiring (Marcel)

A French family is stunned when a 15-year-old male prostitute appears at their door, claiming to be their son who vanished six years earlier.

Compelling drama, based on a true story, and reminiscent of the central dilemma in The Return of Martin Guerre: is the boy for real, or an impostor? Yet the reaction of the rest of the family to his arrival proves more fascinating than the answer to that question.

SCR Agnieszka Holland, Yves Lapointe, Régis Debray
CIN Bernard Zitzermann   MUS Zbigniew Preisner
DES Helene Bourgy   ED Isabelle Lorente   PROD Marie-Laure Reyre   DIST Gala/Oliane/A2

66 Part intimate melodrama, part mystery story, the film delves with confidence into some dark areas and takes the scalpel to the nuclear family as pitilessly as anything since Bergman's heyday. – *Time Out*

66 Though the scenes of incest, rape and murder are disturbing (director Agnieszka) Holland's exploration of the destructive and healing powers of family touches a raw nerve. – *Peter Travers, Rolling Stone*

Los Olvidados ★★★

DIR *Luis Buñuel*
1951   88m   Mexico
DVD

☆ Alfonso Mejia (Pedro), Miguel Inclan (The Blind Man), Estela Inda (The Mother), Roberto Cobo (Jaibo)

A good boy is contaminated by the young thugs in Mexico City's slums, and both he and his tormentor die violently.

Sober but penetrating analysis of social conditions leading to violence, shot in almost documentary style. Bunuel shows his hand by refusing to sentimentalise the subject matter or the young protagonists; it's a bleak view of humanity.

SCR Luis Buñuel, Luis Alcoriza, Oscar Dancigers
CIN Gabriel Figueroa   MUS Gustavo Pitaluga
ED Carlos Savage   DIST Utramar/Oscar Dancigers

'Anything is possible.'

On a Clear Day

DIR Gaby Dellal
2004   98m   GB
DVD

☆ *Peter Mullan* (Frank), Brenda Blethyn (Joan), Sean McGinley (Eddie), Jamie Sives (Rob), Ron Cook (Norman)

A Glasgow shipbuilder, depressed by being laid off after 40 years, finds a new purpose in life–-trying to swim across the English Channel.

Formulaic little-man-against-the-odds Britflick, blending weepy emotions and broad humour. Mullan, the main, and maybe the only reason for watching, gives it all he's got.

SCR Alex Rose   CIN David Johnson   MUS Stephen Warbeck   DES Mark Leese   ED John Wilson, Robin Sales   PROD Dorothy Berwin, Sarah Curtis   DIST Icon

66 Another variation of the British feel-good, inspirational dramedy, this time concerning a laid-off shipbuilder who finds new purpose in life. – *Glenn Whipp, Los Angeles Daily News*

† It was chosen as opening film at the Sundance Film Festival in 2004.

'They Paint The Town With Joy!'

On the Town ★★★★

DIR Gene Kelly, Stanley Donen
1949   98m   US
DVD

☆ *Gene Kelly* (Gabey), *Frank Sinatra* (Chip), *Jules Munshin*

(Ozzie), *Vera-Ellen* (Ivy Smith), *Betty Garrett* (Brunhilde Esterhazy), *Ann Miller* (Claire Huddesen), Tom Dugan (Officer Tracy), Florence Bates (Mme. Dilyovska), Alice Pearce (Lucy Shmeeler)

Three sailors enjoy 24 hours' shore leave in New York.

Most of this brash location musical counts as among the best things ever to come out of Hollywood; the serious ballet towards the end slows things down, but finally it's the film's sheer joy and vitality, and its astonishingly exuberant opening sequence that stick in the memory.

SCR *Betty Comden, Adolph Green*   CIN *Harold Rosson*
MUS Saul Chaplin, Roger Edens, Leonard Bernstein
ED Ralph E. Winters   PROD Arthur Freed   DIST MGM

66 A film that will be enjoyed more than twice. – *Lindsay Anderson*

66 So exuberant that it threatens at moments to bounce right off the screen. – *Time*

† 'New York, New York'; 'Prehistoric Man'; 'I Can Cook Too'; 'Main Street'; 'You're Awful'; On the Town'; 'Count on Me'; 'Pearl of the Persian Sea'

⚱ Lennie Hayton, Roger Edens

On the Waterfront ★★★★

DIR *Elia Kazan*
1954   108m   US
DVD

☆ *Marlon Brando* (Terry Malloy), *Eva Marie Saint* (Edie Doyle), *Lee J. Cobb* (Johnny Friendly), Rod Steiger (Charley Malloy), Karl Malden (Father Barry), Pat Henning ('Kayo' Dugan), Leif Erickson (Glover), James Westerfield (Big Mac), John Hamilton ('Pop' Doyle)

After the death of his brother, a young longshoreman breaks the hold of a Mob-connected waterfront gang boss.

Intense, broody dockside thriller with 'method' performances; very powerful of its kind, and much imitated.

SCR *Budd Schulberg*   CIN *Boris Kaufman*   MUS Leonard Bernstein   ED Gene Milford   DIST Columbia/Sam Spiegel

TERRY (MARLON BRANDO): It was you, Charley. You and Mickey. Like the night the two of you's come in the dressing room and says, "Kid, this ain't your night. We're going for the price on Wilson." It ain't my night. I'd of taken Wilson apart that night! I was ready. Remember the early rounds throwing them combinations? So what happens? This bum Wilson he gets the title shot. Outdoors in the ball park! And what do I get? A couple of bucks and a one-way ticket to Palookaville. 'It was you, Charley. You was my brother. You should have looked out for me instead of making me take them dives for the short end money.
CHARLEY (ROD STEIGER): I always had a bet down for you. You saw some money.
TERRY: See! You don't understand! I could've been a contender. I could've had class and been somebody. Real class. Instead of a bum. It was you, Charley.

66 An uncommonly powerful, exciting and imaginative use of the screen by gifted professionals. – *New York Times*

66 A medley of items from the Warner gangland pictures of the thirties, brought up to date. – *Steven Sondheim, Films in Review*

O

DVD Available on DVD   ☆ Cast in order   66 Critics' Quotes   ⚱ Academy Award   🎭 BAFTA
♫ Soundtrack on CD   of importance   † Points of interest   ⚱ Academy Award nomination   🎭 BAFTA nomination

463

picture; Marlon Brando (leading actor); Eva Marie Saint (supporting actress); Elia Kazan (direction); Budd Schulberg (screenplay); Boris Kaufman; Richard Day; editing

Lee J. Cobb (supporting actor); Rod Steiger (supporting actor); Karl Malden (supporting actor); Leonard Bernstein;

Marlon Brando (leading actor)

'How often do you find the right person?'

Once (new) ★★

SCR/DIR John Carney
2007 86m Ireland/US

☆ Glen Hansard (The guy), Markéta Inglová (The girl), Bill Hodnett (Guy's dad), Danuse Ktrestova (Girl's mother)

A busker on the streets of Dublin meets and falls for a young mother, an immigrant from the Czech Republic. Together they start to make music.

Charming, poignant and sentimental, this low-budget music-drenched film carries a disproportionate punch. The shy manner of the two leads works in the film's favour, and their songs, while not world-beating, at least underpin the narrative.

CIN Tim Fleming DES Tamara Conboy ED Paul Mullen
PROD Martina Niland DIST Icon

66 A largely successful attempt to present something old-fashioned – a romantic musical – in a modern way and on a budget that stops some distance short of six figures. – *Karl French, Financial Times*

† Glen Hansard was a member of the fictional band The Commitments assembled by Alan Parker for his 1991 film. He has since been the leader of a Dublin-based group, the Frames.

† Once was shot in just three weeks on a budget of £80,000. It grossed $9.5 million in the US alone.

Glen Hansard, Markéta Inglová (music – original song Falling Slowly)

'As boys they said they would die for each other. As men, they did.'

Once Upon a Time in America ★★★★

DIR Sergio Leone
1984 228m US
DVD ♫

☆ *Robert De Niro* (Noodles), *James Woods* (Max), Elizabeth McGovern (Deborah), Treat Williams (Jimmy O'Donnell), Tuesday Weld (Carol), Burt Young (Joe), Danny Aiello (Police Chief Aiello), William Forsythe (Cockeye)

An account of the lives of two gangster friends from the Roaring Twenties to 1968.

Vast, sprawling, violent crime saga with a neat circularity about its rags-to-riches-to-rags narrative. It is operatic in style, often brutal in tone, nostalgic in mood and mesmerising to watch. A stunning, towering achievement, not afraid to stray into lurid territory when the plot demands it, that taps into audiences' guilty fascination with dangerous, sociopathic characters. Woods and De Niro could hardly be improved upon, and Morricone's score is exquisitely fitting.

SCR Leonardo Benvenuti, Piero de Bernardi, Enrico Medioli, Franco Arcalli, Franco Ferrini, Sergio Leone
CIN *Tonino Delli Colli* MUS *Ennio Morricone* ED Nino Baragli PROD Arnon Milchan
DIST Warner/Embassy/Ladd/PSO

66 It is, finally, a heart-breaking story of mutual need. By matching that need with his own need to come to terms with his own cultural memories, Leone has made his most oneiric and extraordinary film. – *Tony Rayns, Monthly Film Bulletin*

† Leone's full version, running close to four hours, was cut by the studio for its US release to 139 minutes. The flashback sequences were virtually excised, which made a virtual nonsense of what remained. Predictably, the film fared badly at the US box-office, though in other territories, where the director's preferred cut was exhibited, it was widely hailed as a masterpiece.

music

'The time has come.'

Once Upon a Time in Mexico ★

SCR/DIR Robert Rodriguez
2003 102m US
DVD ♫

☆ Antonio Banderas (El Mariachi), Salma Hayek (Carolina), Johnny Depp (Sands), Mickey Rourke (Billy), Eva Mendes (Ajedrez), Danny Trejo (Cucuy), Ruben Blades (Jorge FBI), Willem Dafoe (Barillo)

An American secret agent persuades a legendary gunman to come out of retirement to save the president of Mexico from being killed.

Depp and Rodriguez play cowboys south of the border. It's an amiable shambles, really, more a cartoon than any kind of human drama, driven by gaudy, sometimes funny set-pieces. Everyone involved looked as if they enjoyed making it: half the audience may feel the same about watching.

CIN Robert Rodriguez MUS Robert Rodriguez
DES Robert Rodriguez ED Robert Rodriguez
PROD Elizabeth Avellan, Carlos Gallardo, Robert Rodriguez DIST Buena Vista

66 Boisterously entertaining stuff, but whenever Johnny Depp's off screen the energy levels plummet. – *Peter Bradshaw, The Guardian*

66 It's a grisly, chuckling cartoon made on shots of tequila, Red Bull, and Sergio Leone. – *Wesley Morris, Boston Globe*

Once Upon a Time in the West ★★★

DIR Sergio Leone
1969 165m Italy/US
DVD ♫

☆ *Henry Fonda* (Frank), Claudia Cardinale (Jill McBain), *Jason Robards* (Cheyenne), Charles Bronson (The Man "Harmonica"), Gabriele Ferzetti (Morton), Keenan Wynn (Sheriff), Paolo Stoppa (Sam), Lionel Stander (Barman), Jack Elam (Knuckles), Woody Strode (Stony)

In the old west a gunfighter, with ambitions to be a wealthy businessman, prepares to drive a woman off her land, which is sought after by the railroad company.

DVD Available on DVD   ☆ Cast in order   66 Critics' Quotes   Academy Award   BAFTA
♫ Soundtrack on CD   of importance   † Points of interest   Academy Award nomination   BAFTA nomination

Immensely long and convoluted epic Western, Leone's first within the Hollywood studio system, in which he revisits the motives, most of them less than noble, that led to the opening up and exploitation of the West. In this context, casting Fonda, a revered American icon, as a grasping, violent opportunist was a counter-intuitive master stroke. A beautiful-looking film that takes its sweet time in getting where it wants to go, but riveting all the same.

SCR Sergio Leone, Sergio Donati   CIN Tonino Delli Colli   MUS Ennio Morricone   DES Carlo Simi   ED Nino Baragli   PROD Fulvio Morsella   DIST Paramount

66 The paradoxical, but honest 'fun' aspect of Leone's previous preoccupation with elaborately-stylized violence is here unconvincingly asking for consideration in a new 'moral' light. – Variety

66 Akira Kurosawa once said that Toshiro Mifune could give him in three feet of film the emotion any other actor would take 10 to deliver, but in a single flash of Fonda's electric turquoise orbs, Leone (Kurosawa's first and sincerest flatterer-imitator) managed to say as much about John Ford, the devil, and the corruptions of the Way Out Western world as the genre ever would. – Chuck Stephens, Village Voice

† The film's credits sprawl through the first 12 minutes.
† Two future directors of note, Bernardo Bertolucci and Dario Argento, received story credits on the film.

'Her only chance for the future is to embrace the power of her past.'

Once Were Warriors ★★

DIR Lee Tamahori
1994   103m   New Zealand
DVD ♫

☆ Rena Owen (Beth Heke), Temuera Morrison (Jake Heke), Mamaengaroa Kerr-Bell (Grace Heke), Julian Arahanga (Nig Heke), Taungaroa Emile (Boogie Heke), Rachael Morris (Polly Heke), Joseph Kairau (Huata Heke), Clifford Curtis (Bully)

A Maori wife and mother must endure violent assaults from her drunken husband as she labours to keep her troubled family together.

The underbelly of New Zealand life, never featured on the travel posters, is graphically and disturbingly displayed. It's also an account of cultural displacement; these Maoris unhappily inhabit shoddy housing in a hostile urban environment.

SCR Riwia Brown   CIN Stuart Dryburgh   MUS Murray Grindley, Murray McNabb   DES Michael Kane   ED Michael Horton   PROD Robin Scholes   DIST Entertainment/Communicado/NZFC/Avalon/New Zealand On Air

66 Domestic violence has never been more savagely portrayed on screen. – David Ansen, Newsweek

66 A gut-grabber from New Zealand that stays with you for days afterward. – Edward Guthmann, San Francisco Chronicle

† It took more money at the New Zealand box-office than any other film so far.
† A sequel What Becomes of the Broken-Hearted? followed in 1999.

† A Region 1 DVD release includes commentary by Lee Tamahori.

A One and a Two. . . ★★★★

SCR/DIR Edward Yang
2000   173m   Taiwan/Japan
DVD

☆ Wu Nien-jen (NJ Jian), Elaine Jin (Min-Min), Issei Ogata (Mr Ota), Kelly Lee (Ting-Ting), Jonathan Chang (Yang-Yang), Chen Hsi-sheng (Ah-Di), Ko Su-Yun (Sherry), Michael Tao (Da-Da), Hsiao Shu-shen (Hsiao Yen), Adriene Lin (Li-Li)

A family in Taipei question their lives as they deal with an assortment of crises.

Marvellous multi-generational drama from one of the leading lights of Taiwanese cinema, hovering at a delicate remove from its characters but conveying volumes about their hopes and disappointments.

CIN Yang Wei-han   MUS Peng Kai-li   DES Peng   ED Chen Bo-wen   PROD Shinya Kawai, Naoko Tsukeda   DIST ICA

66 Three light-on-its-feet hours long, it starts with a wedding, ends with a funeral and in between captures what seems like a lifetime of experience. – David Ansen, Newsweek

66 Although dense with incident and motif, the movie has an effortless flow. – J. Hoberman, Village Voice

† In 2000, the Cannes Film Festival jury awarded it the Palme D'Or for best film.

'September 5, 1972. The Munich Games. On This Day, There Would Be No Winners.'

One Day in September ★★

DIR Kevin Macdonald
1999   94m   GB
DVD

☆ Michael Douglas (Narrator)

Documentary about the terrorist attack at the 1972 Olympic Games in Munich, when 11 Israeli athletes were taken hostage and massacred.

Absorbing factual film that re-tells the story of the killings and hostage-taking and includes an interview with the one surviving Palestinian hostage-taker, Jamal Al Gashey, who is seen in the original footage. The film calmly but firmly emphasises how ineptly the German authorities handled the unfolding crisis.

CIN Alwin Kuchler, Neve Cunningham   MUS Alex Heffes   ED Justine Wright   PROD Arthur Cohn, John Battsek   DIST Redbus

66 It could be described as the most gripping political thriller to hit the big screen in many years, although given the events it depicts through interviews, photographs, and news footage, the words 'gripping' and 'thriller' have inappropriately frivolous and commercial associations. – Amy Taubin, Village Voice

66 Macdonald's singular achievement is to restore – through interviews and archival footage – the dead to such vivid life, you weep for them and for their families, who have only memories to live off. – Ella Taylor, L.A. Weekly

⚊ documentary

DVD Available on DVD   ☆ Cast in order   66 Critics' Quotes   ⚊ Academy Award   ⚊ BAFTA
♫ Soundtrack on CD   of importance   † Points of interest   ⚊ Academy Award nomination   ⚊ BAFTA nomination

465

'All it takes to bring him down is one bullet... one woman or... One False Move.'

One False Move ★★★

DIR *Carl Franklin*

1992 105m US

[DVD]

☆ Bill Paxton (Dale 'Hurricane' Dixon), Cynda Williams (Fantasia/Lila), Billy Bob Thornton (Ray Malcolm), Michael Beach (Pluto), Jim Metzler (Dud Cole), Earl Billings (McFeely), Natalie Canerday (Cheryl Ann)

Three murderous thieves set off from L.A. with the gains from a drug heist, and head for a small Arkansas town, where the local police chief and two LAPD detectives await them.

A tense, taut, neatly constructed thriller with a narrative that constantly reminds us the final meeting between these parties will not be pleasant. A small gem from a talented, under-used director.

SCR Billy Bob Thornton, Tom Epperson **CIN** James L. Carter **MUS** Peter Haycock, Derek Holt **DES** Gary T. New **ED** Carole Kravetz **PROD** Jesse Beaton, Ben Myron **DIST** Metro/I.R.S. Media

66 A road trip through America's bloodstained heartland. . .it's an eerie and horrifying experience. – *Desson Howe, Washington Post*

66 One of the finest American movies in recent years. – *Time Out*

One Flew over the Cuckoo's Nest ★★★★

DIR *Milos Forman*

1975 134m US

[DVD] ♫

☆ *Jack Nicholson* (Randle Patrick McMurphy), *Louise Fletcher* (Nurse Mildred Ratched), William Redfield (Harding), *Will Sampson* (Chief Bromden), *Brad Dourif* (Billy Bibbit), Christopher Lloyd (Taber), Scatman Crothers (Turkle), Danny DeVito (Martini)

A charismatic rebel in a psychiatric hospital enlists the help of his fellow patients in stirring up trouble against the authorities, personified by a dictatorial nurse.

Wildly and unexpectedly commercial film of a project which had lain dormant for 14 years, this amusing and horrifying work captured the dissident spirit of its time, with a beguiling central performance from Nicholson that immediately marshals audience sympathy. Impeccably thought through in every department, it swept all the major Academy Awards, and understandably so: it's impossible to ignore.

SCR Lawrence Hauben, Bo Goldman **CIN** *Haskell Wexler, Bill Butler, William Fraker* **MUS** Jack Nitzsche **DES** *Paul Sylbert* **ED** *Richard Chew, Sheldon Kahn, Lynzee Klingman* **PROD** *Saul Zaentz, Michael Douglas* **DIST** UA/Fantasy Films

66 Lacks the excitement of movie art, but the story and the acting make the film emotionally powerful. – *New Yorker*

66 A comedy that can't quite support its tragic conclusion, which is too schematic to be honestly moving, but it is acted with such a sense of life that one responds to its

demonstration of humanity if not to its programmed metaphors. – *Vincent Canby, New York Times*

⚲ picture; Jack Nicholson (leading actor); Louise Fletcher (leading actress); Milos Forman (direction); Lawrence Hauben, Bo Goldman (adapted screenplay)

⚲ Brad Dourif (supporting actor); Haskell Wexler; Jack Nitzsche; editing

⚲ picture; Jack Nicholson (leading actor); Louise Fletcher (leading actress); Brad Dourif (supporting actor); Milos Forman (direction); editing

One for the Road ★

SCR/DIR Chris Cooke

2003 94 minsm GB

[DVD]

☆ Rupert Proctor (Paul), Greg Chisholm (Jimmy), Mark Devenport (Mark), Hywel Bennett (Richard), Julie Legrand (Liz), Micaiah Dring (Eve), Johann Myers (Dave)

Four convicted drunk drivers meet at a rehabilitation course, but refuse to take it seriously – and get a few more rounds in.

Perceptive blackish comedy about male self-denial, with a sharp script and actors unafraid to portray losers.

CIN N.G. Smith **MUS** Steve Blackman **DES** Jason Carlin **ED** Nick Fenton **PROD** Kate Ogborn

66 A slender plot takes a back seat to the enjoyable interplay among these used-up men. – *Miles Fielder, Empire*

66 An entertaining shaggy-dog tale, One For the Road builds on the pleasures of incidental detail to conclude with yet another anti-climax. – *Liese Spencer, Sight & Sound*

'There's nothing more dangerous than a familiar face.'

One Hour Photo ★★

SCR/DIR Mark Romanek

2002 96m US

[DVD] ♫

☆ *Robin Williams* (Seymour 'Sy' Parrish), Connie Nielsen (Nina Yorkin), Michael Vartan (Will Yorkin), Gary Cole (Bill Owens), Dylan Smith (Jake Yorkin), Eriq La Salle (Detective Van Der Zee), Erin Daniels (Maya Burson)

A lonely bachelor who develops photos in a discount store develops an unhealthy interest in a happy suburban family from their many snapshots.

Stylised, deftly directed chiller, with Williams thankfully reined-in, but in genuinely creepy form.

CIN *Jeff Cronenweth* **MUS** Reinhold Heil, Johnny Klimek **DES** Tom Foden **ED** Jeffrey Ford **PROD** Christine Vachon, Pamela Koffler, Stan Wlodkowski **DIST** TCF

66 This is a very effective, distinctive thriller, and incidentally one of those rare films that give a diverting, well-informed insight into the mundane world of work. – *Peter Bradshaw, Guardian*

'This Time The Magic Is Real.'

101 Dalmatians

DIR Stephen Herek

1996 103m US

[DVD] ♫

☆ *Glenn Close* (Cruella De Vil), Jeff Daniels (Roger), Joan

[DVD] Available on DVD ☆ Cast in order of importance 66 Critics' Quotes † Points of interest ⚲ Academy Award ⚲ Academy Award nomination ⚲ BAFTA ⚲ BAFTA nomination
♫ Soundtrack on CD

Plowright (Nanny), Joely Richardson (Anita), Hugh Laurie (Jasper), Mark Williams (Horace), John Shrapnel (Skinner) Two Dalmatian owners get married, while their pets try to escape an insane villainess who wants to make a fur coat out of them.

Crass live-action remake of the 1961 animated hit, flaunting some fun scenery-chewing from Glenn Close, and Anthony Powell's exuberant costumes, but not much else.

SCR John Hughes CIN Adrian Biddle MUS Michael Kamen DES Assheton Gorton ED Larry Bock, Trudy Ship PROD John Hughes, Ricardo Mestres DIST Buena Vista/Walt Disney/Great Oaks

66 Relentlessly cuddlesome enough to make this, if not enchanting, then sufficiently chucklesome and likeable to send family audiences home with their tails wagging. – *Angie Errigo, Empire*

† A sequel, 102 Dalmatians, followed in 2000.

'What will it sound like when you die?'

One Missed Call (new)

DIR Eric Valette
2008 87m USA
DVD

☆ Shannyn Sossamon (Beth Raymond), Ed Burns (Jack Andrews), Ray Wise (Ted Summers), Jason Beghe (Ray Purvis)

College students die soon after receiving messages on their mobile phones from their future selves in the throes of violent death.

A shock-less, scare-less, lifelessly directed mess of Japanese horror clichés, watered down further by the American remake industry.

SCR Andrew Klavan CIN Glen MacPherson MUS Reinhold Heil, Johnny Klimek DES Laurence Bennett ED Steve Mirkovich PROD Broderick Johnson, Scott Kroopf, Andrew A. Kosove, Jenny Lew Tugend, Lauren Weissman DIST Warner Bros.

66 "Originally a so-so Takashi Miike freak-out. Now it's a worse-worse American eyesore". – *Wesley Morris, Boston Globe*

'It was just one night that changed everything.'

One Night Stand ★

SCR/DIR Mike Figgis
1997 102m US
DVD ♫

☆ Wesley Snipes (Max Carlyle), Nastassja Kinski (Karen), Robert Downey Jnr (Charlie), Ming-Na Wen (Mimi Carlyle), Kyle MacLachlan (Vernon), Glenn Plummer (George), Amanda Donohoe (Margaux), Thomas Haden Church (Don), Julian Sands (Chris)

A married British commercials director visits an HIV-positive friend when staying overnight in New York,. He then sleeps with a woman he meets, and regrets it.

Shallow, contrived movie involving a crowd of characters, many of them not quite substantial enough to qualify as cardboard.

CIN Declan Quinn MUS Mike Figgis DES Waldemar

Kalinowski ED John Smith PROD Mike Figgis, Annie Stewart, Ben Myron DIST Entertainment/New Line/Red Mullet

66 A lukewarm confection that is just plain dreary. – *BBC*

† Figgis has a cameo role as a hotel clerk.

'From Alexander Pushkin's timeless masterpiece of love and obsession.'

Onegin ★

DIR Martha Fiennes
1998 106m US
DVD ♫

☆ Ralph Fiennes (Evgeny Onegin), Liv Tyler (Tatyana Larin), Toby Stephens (Vladimir Lensky), Lena Headey (Olga Larin), Martin Donovan (Prince Nikitin), Alun Armstrong (Zaretsky), Harriet Walter (Mme Larina), Irene Worth (Princess Alina), Jason Watkins (Guillot), Francesca Annis (Katiusha)

A Russian aristocrat, who inherits a country estate, rejects romantic advances from an attractive young neighbour.

Pushkin's classic novel is handled with kid gloves: it's striking to look at and certainly well-acted (though Tyler is miscast). But no-one involved seems able to locate the passion that drove Pushkin to create the story.

SCR Peter Ettedgui, Michael Ignatieff CIN Remi Adefarasin MUS Magnus Fiennes DES Jim Clay ED Jim Clark PROD Ileen Maisel, Simon Bosanquet DIST Entertainment

66 Onegin strikes a timeless note of eternal love and loss. – *Kevin Thomas, Los Angeles Times*

66 The film suffers from some lapses of emotional tension. . .but even if grand pathos isn't achieved (director) Martha Fiennes makes a brave and welcome stab at it. – *Time Out*

Ⓣ British film

'A love story written in the stars'

Only You ★

DIR Norman Jewison
1994 115m US
DVD

☆ Marisa Tomei (Faith Corvatch), Robert Downey Jnr (Peter Wright), Bonnie Hunt (Kate Corvatch), Billy Zane (Harry, The False Damon Bradley), Joaquim de Almeida (Giovanni), Fisher Stevens (Larry Corvatch)

On advice from a fortune teller, a Pittsburgh woman abandons her wedding plans and flies to Europe to meet the stranger she believes will be the love of her life.

Light-hearted and light-weight romantic comedy that recalls 1950s films feature constant southern European sunshine and happy endings. Modest, likable, old-fashioned escapism.

SCR Diane Drake CIN Sven Nykvist MUS Rachel Portman DES Luciana Arrighi ED Stephen Rivkin PROD Norman Jewison, Cary Woods, Robert N. Fried, Charles Mulvehill DIST Columbia TriStar/Fried/Woods Films/Yorktown

66 It is total fantasy, light as a feather, contrary to all notions of common sense, it features a couple of stars who

DVD Available on DVD   ☆ Cast in order   66 Critics' Quotes   ⚊ Academy Award   Ⓑ BAFTA
♫ Soundtrack on CD   of importance   † Points of interest   ⚋ Academy Award nomination   Ⓣ BAFTA nomination

467

are really good kissers – and it takes place mostly in Venice, Rome and the glorious Italian hillside town of Positano. What more do you want? – *Roger Ebert, Chicago Sun-Times*

Open Hearts ☆

DIR Susanne Bier
2002 113m Denmark
DVD

☆ Sonja Richter (Cecilie), Nikolaj Lie Kaas (Joachim), Mads Mikkelsen (Niels), Paprika Steen (Marie), Stine Bjerregaard (Stine), Birthe Neumann (Hanne), Niels Olsen (Finn), Ulf Pilgaard (Thomsen)

A doctor and a cook are thrown together emotionally after his wife causes a road accident that paralyses her fiancé.

An unusual drama, convincingly acted, charting the unpredictable patterns of attraction.

SCR Anders Thomas Jensen **CIN** Morten Soborg
MUS Jesper Winge Leisner **DES** William Knuttel
ED Pernille Bech Christensen, Thomas Krag
PROD Vibeke Windelov, Jonas Frederiksen **DIST** Icon

66 The canny observations of relationships and sexual politics would hold true in much less melodramatic circumstances. – *Vicky Wilson, Sight & Sound*

† It was a huge hit in Denmark, where an estimated 10 per cent of the adult population saw it in its first few weeks of release.

'No place to run. No reason to hide.'

Open Range ★★

DIR Kevin Costner
2003 139m US/GB
DVD ♫

☆ Robert Duvall (Boss Spearman), Kevin Costner (Charley Waite), Annette Bening (Sue Barlow), Michael Gambon (Denton Baxter), Michael Jeter (Percy), Diego Luna (Button), James Russo (Sheriff Poole), Abraham Benrubi (Mose), Dean McDermott (Doc Barlow)

Two cowboys, who tend cattle on the free range, are told by a landowner that they are unwelcome in the area.

Costner deserves full credit for keeping the Western alive when everyone else seems to have deserted the genre. This one has a gentle, courteous air; it could be more viscerally exciting but it's conceived and shot with affection and care.

SCR Craig Storper **CIN** James Muro **MUS** Michael Kamen **DES** Gae Buckley **ED** Michael J. Duthie, Miklos Wright **PROD** David Valdes, Kevin Costner, Jake Eberts **DIST** Winchester

66 Costner is likeable as a good and honest man, and Annette Bening splendid in a rare romantic part for a woman over 40. – *Edward Buscombe, Sight & Sound*

Opera Jawa (new) ☆

DIR Garin Nugroho
2007 120m Indonesia/Netherlands/Austria
☆ Eko Supriyanto (Ludiro), Martinus Miroto (Setio), Artika Sari Devi (Siti)

A sung-through work with gamelan music, based on an epic poem in Sanskrit. The attractive wife of a potter is torn between her husband and a scheming butcher.

Visually ravishing, though niche entertainment by any standard.

SCR Garin Nugroho, Aramantono **CIN** Teoh Gay Hian **ED** Andhy Pulung **PROD** Garin Nugroho **DIST** Yume

---

'You'll laugh, you'll cry, you'll be offended.'

The Opposite of Sex ★★★

SCR/DIR Don Roos
1998 105m US
DVD ♫

☆ *Christina Ricci (Dede Truitt), Martin Donovan (Bill Truitt), Lisa Kudrow (Lucia DeLury), Lyle Lovett (Sheriff Carl Tippett), Johnny Galecki (Jason Bock), Ivan Sergei (Matt Mateo)*

A teenager runs off with, and becomes pregnant by, her gay brother's lover.

Savagely funny attack on modern American mores and viewer preconceptions alike that provides a field day for actors who delight in spitting out barbed, adult dialogue; though the whole is drenched in irony, everybody works hard to ensure the emotional and (briefly) physical violence hurts, and indeed that we care how this unlikely scenario unfolds.

CIN Hubert Taczanowski **MUS** Mason Daring
DES Michael Clausen **ED** David Codron **PROD** David Kirkpatrick, Michael Besman **DIST** Sony/Rysher

66 The smartest, edgiest, most human and handsomely acted romantic comedy in elephant years. – *Richard Corliss, Time*

66 Holds in perfect tonal balance, and without cynicism, a brew of maliciously transgressive comedy and tender sympathy for its tortured characters, all gripped by terror of love, or sex, or both. – *Ella Taylor, L.A. Weekly*

Orlando ★★★

SCR/DIR Sally Potter
1992 93m GB/Russia/France/Italy/Netherlands
DVD ♫

☆ *Tilda Swinton (Orlando), Billy Zane (Shelmerdine), Lothaire Bluteau (The Khan), John Wood (Archduke Harry), Charlotte Valandrey (Princess Sasha), Heathcote Williams (Nick Greene/Publisher), Quentin Crisp (Queen Elizabeth I), Peter Eyre (Pope), Thom Hoffman (King William of Orange), Jimmy Somerville (Falsetto/Angel), Dudley Sutton (King James I), Anna Healy (Euphrosyne)*

A young nobleman lives for 400 years, from his days as a constant presence at the court of Queen Elizabeth I, through his decision to change sex, and finally as a smart modern business woman in a sleek office..

Swinton is astonishing as Orlando, regardless of gender – a charismatic hero/heroine who literally stares her audience in the eye. The film is visually dazzling, perfectly complementary in spirit to Woolf's playful fantasia. A career high for this maddeningly inconsistent director.

CIN *Alexsei Rodionov*　MUS David Motion, Sally Potter
DES *Ben Van Os, Jan Roelfs*　ED Herve Schneid
PROD Christopher Sheppard　DIST Electric/Adventure Pictures/Lenfilm/Mikado/Sigma/British Screen

66 The film is also a romp through British history, which it presents as richly textured spectacle. – *Lizzie Francke, Sight & Sound*

🎬 Ben Van Os, Jan Roelfs; Sally Potter (costume design)
🎭 Morag Ross (make up)
🎭 Sandy Powell (costume design)

The Orphanage (new)　★★
DIR Juan Antonio Bayona
2007　105m　Spain
DVD　🎵

☆ *Belén Rueda* (Laura), Fernando Cayo (Carlos), Roger Princep (Simon), Montserrat Carulla (Benigna), Andrés Gertrudix (Enrique), Geraldine Chaplin (Aurora), Mabel Rivera (Pilar)

After moving into the old orphanage where she lived as a child, a mother fears the ghosts of her erstwhile playmates have kidnapped her son.

Superior ghost story reminiscent of The Innocents, all the more effective for rooting its chills – of which there are several – in psychological truth.

SCR Sergio G. Sanchez　CIN Oscar Faura
MUS Fernando Velazquez　DES Josep Rosell　ED Elena Ruiz　PROD Mar Targarona, Joaquin Padro, Alvaro Augustin　DIST Optimum Releasing

66 A beautifully told, terrifying ghost story that lingers with you long after the shivers have stopped. – *Olly Richards, Empire*

66 This Spanish supernatural thriller begins interestingly and finishes intriguingly. But what lies between drags. – *Richard James Havis, Hollywood Reporter*

† Guillermo del Toro was the film's executive producer.

Orphans　★
DIR Alan J. Pakula
1987　115m　US

☆ Albert Finney (Harold), Matthew Modine (Treat), Kevin Anderson (Phillip), John Kellogg (Barney)

Two adult brothers live alone off the proceeds of petty crime, until a career criminal moves in, and adopts the role of father figure.

Adapted for film by its playwright, this piece sits more comfortably on stage – but it's ferociously well acted and ultimately moving.

SCR Lyle Kessler　CIN Donald McAlpine　MUS Michael Small　DES George Jenkins　ED Evan A. Lottman
PROD Susan Solt, Alan J. Pakula　DIST Lorimar

'Are Your Parents A Burden?'
Orphans　★★
SCR/DIR *Peter Mullan*
1997　101m　GB
DVD

☆ Gary Lewis (Thomas), Douglas Henshall (Michael), Rosemarie Stevenson (Sheila), Stephen McCole (John), Frank Gallagher (Tanga), Malcolm Shields (Duncan)

Three brothers and their sister, who has cerebral palsy, spend an eventful night before their mother's funeral mourning her in various ways.

Glaswegian comedy of the darkest hue, which asserts that grief can strike in different, even inappropriate ways. Apart from being a tough-minded account of working-class life, it has the courage to find humour in bleak moments, and vice versa. Mullan marshals a talented cast with vigour.

CIN Grant Scott Cameron　MUS Craig Armstrong
DES Campbell Gordon　ED Colin Monie　PROD Frances Higson　DIST Downtown/Channel 4

66 Orphans makes for difficult viewing. – *Edward Lawrenson, Sight & Sound*

Osama　★★★
SCR/DIR *Siddiq Barmak*
2003　83m　Afghanistan/Japan/Ireland
DVD

☆ *Marina Golbahari* ('Osama'), Arif Herati (Espandi), Zubaida Sahar (Mother)

In Afghanistan, the mother of a 12-year-old girl disguises her as a boy so she can find work – thus risking the wrath of the ruling Taliban..

An astonishing film, and one that rests on the slender shoulders of its non-professional lead actress. The story sheds more insight into the terror engendered by the Taliban regime than a thousand political lectures could.

CIN Ebrahim Ghafuri　MUS Mohammad Reza Darwishi
DES Akbar Meshkini　ED Siddiq Barmak　PROD Julie LeBrocquy, Siddiq Barmak, Makoto Ueda, Julia Fraser
DIST ICA

66 The movie is a rare uncensored postcard from a ruined place, a document at once depressing and hideously beautiful that sketches the real hardships of trampled people – specifically women – with authority and compelling simplicity. – *Lisa Schwarzbaum, Entertainment Weekly*

66 The performances are credible, but set-pieces like the water-cannoning of a procession of burkha-clad protesters are also impeccably judged. – *David Parkinson, Empire*

Oscar and Lucinda　★★
DIR Gillian Armstrong
1997　132m　Australia/US
DVD　🎵

☆ Ralph Fiennes (Oscar Hopkins), Cate Blanchett (Lucinda Leplastrier), Ciaran Hinds (Reverend Dennis Hasset), Tom Wilkinson (Hugh Stratton), Richard Roxburgh (Mr. Jeffries), Clive Russell (Theophilus), Barry Otto (Jimmy D'Abbs), Geoffrey Rush (Narrator (voice))

In the Victorian era a pair of eccentrics, an Anglican minister and a rich Australian woman, are both in thrall to gambling. He wagers that he can transport a delicate glass chapel across the outback.

An attractive-looking costume drama that just about conveys the novel's subtle contrasts between obsession and faith, and the role fate and destiny play in shaping lives.

SCR Laura Jones   CIN Geoffrey Simpson   MUS Thomas Newman   DES *Luciana Arrighi*   ED Nicholas Beauman   PROD Robin Dalton, Timothy White   DIST Fox/AFFC/Meridian

66 Everything a costume drama should be. – *Trevor Johnston, Time Out*

⚖ Janet Patterson (costume design)

'Envy greed jealousy and love.'

Othello ★

SCR/DIR Oliver Parker
1995   123m   US/GB
[DVD] ♫

☆ Laurence Fishburne (Othello), Irene Jacob (Desdemona), Kenneth Branagh (Iago), Nathaniel Parker (Cassio), Michael Maloney (Roderigo), Anna Patrick (Emilia), Nicholas Farrell (Montano), Indra Ove (Bianca)

Othello's courtship of Desdemona is undermined by the jealous, vengeful Iago.

Compact version of Shakespeare's play, its dialogue cruelly curtailed. Director Parker seems unconcerned that some of his cast gabble their lines, as if in an attempt to maintain the film's lively pace. Branagh alone emerges with credit – though the Tuscan locations give the film a warm, expensive sheen.

CIN David Johnson   MUS Charlie Mole   DES Tim Harvey   ED Tony Lawson   PROD Luc Roeg, David Barron   DIST Columbia/Castle Rock/Dakota/Imminent

66 A highly engaging attempt at Shakespeare's most domestic tragedy. – *Steve Grant, Time Out*

'The only thing that could come between these sisters...is a kingdom.'

The Other Boleyn Girl (new)

DIR Justin Chadwick
2008   115m   UK/US
[DVD] ♫

☆ Natalie Portman (Anne Boleyn), Scarlett Johansson (Mary Boleyn), Eric Bana (Henry Tudor), Kristin Scott Thomas (Lady Elizabeth Boleyn), Mark Rylance (Sir Thomas Boleyn)

In 16th-century England, two sisters from a wealthy, ambitious family compete to be the wife of King Henry VIII.

Good-looking, fast-paced costume drama that takes liberties with history, and briefly veers into soap-opera territory before politely correcting itself. It lacks both dignity and authority, and might have worked better as a knowing, amusing romp; as it is, it falls between two stools.

SCR Peter Morgan   CIN Kieran McGuigan   MUS Paul Cantelon   DES *John Paul Kelly*   ED Paul Knight, Carol Littleton   PROD Alison Owen   DIST Universal

66 It can't decide whether to be serious or comic. It is tasteful, but unappetising. – *Sukhdev Sandhu, Daily Telegraph*

66 After covering much of its ground at a stylish canter, The Other Boleyn Girl finishes at a plod. – *Joe Morgenstern, Wall Street Journal*

'Meet Larry the Liquidator. Arrogant. Greedy. Self-centered. Ruthless. You gotta love the guy.'

Other People's Money ★

DIR Norman Jewison
1991   103m   US
[DVD]

☆ *Danny DeVito* (Lawrence Garfield), Gregory Peck (Andrew Jorgenson), Penelope Ann Miller (Kate Sullivan), Piper Laurie (Bea Sullivan), Dean Jones (Bill Coles), R. D. Call (Arthur), Mo Gaffney (Harriet), Bette Henritze (Emma)

A wheeler-dealer who styles himself 'Larry the Liquidator' targets a prudent, family-run, debt-free company, aiming to strip its assets.

A comedy of its time, coming as it did at the tail-end of the 80s, a decade defined by greed and self-interest. Peck's liberal paternalist company boss is a cipher, and the romance involving Miller as the company's in-house lawyer never quite ignites. Yet there's much to enjoy in de Vito's performance as the gleefully malicious Larry.

SCR Alvin Sargent   CIN Haskell Wexler   MUS David Newman   DES Philip Rosenberg   ED Lou Lombardo, Michael Pacek, Hubert de la Bouillerie   PROD Norman Jewison, Ric Kidney   DIST Warner/Yorktown

'Sooner Or Later They Will Find You.'

The Others ★★★

SCR/DIR Alejandro Amenábar
2001   104m   Spain/US
[DVD] ♫

☆ *Nicole Kidman* (Grace), Christopher Eccleston (Charles), Fionnula Flanagan (Mrs Mills), Elaine Cassidy (Lydia), Eric Sykes (Mr Tuttle), *Alakina Mann* (Anne), *James Bentley* (Nicholas), Renée Asherson (Old lady)

During the last days of WWII, the governess of a mansion on Jersey becomes unnerved by her young charges' claims to have seen ghostly apparitions.

Handsomely mounted, well-told ghost story with superior performances and an affecting, tender undertow.

CIN *Javier Aguirresarobe*   MUS Alejandro Amenábar   DES *Benjamin Fernandez*   ED Nacho Ruiz Capillas   PROD Fernando Bovaira, Jose Luis Cuerda, Sunmin Park   DIST Buena Vista

66 An elegantly crafted entertainment, balanced between the psychological and the supernatural, that gets extra credit for not relying on computer effects. – *Andrew O'Hehir, Salon*

66 What a relief to have a scary movie instead of a Scary Movie – no boring irony, no tiresome inverted commas. It is well constructed, as opposed to incompetently deconstructed. Whether or not you are actually scared depends on a willing susceptibility. But providing that submission is accomplished – well, many is the pleasureable and invigorating frisson to be had. – *Peter Bradshaw, Guardian*

Ⓣ Nicole Kidman (leading actress); Alejandro Amenábar (original screenplay)

'Opposites attract.'

Out of Sight ★★★

DIR Steven Soderbergh

1998 123m US

`DVD` ♫

☆ George Clooney (Jack Foley), Jennifer Lopez (Karen Sisco), Vingh Rhames (Buddy Bragg), Don Cheadle (Maurice (Snoopy) Miller), Dennis Farina (Marshall Sisco), Albert Brooks (Richard Ripley)

A bank robber escapes from prison and falls in love with a female federal marshal on the way out.

A good-looking film with a sparkling script; Clooney has never enjoyed the degree of on-screen sizzle and chemistry with another lead actress as he does here with Lopez. A gorgeous film, with wry throwaway humour, and a genuinely intricate thriller plot.

SCR Scott Frank CIN Elliot Davis MUS Cliff Martinez DES Gary Frutkoff ED Anne V. Coates PROD Danny de Vito, Michael Shamberg, Stacey Sher DIST Universal/Jersey

66 This isn't a profound film, or even an important one, but then it isn't trying to be. It's so diverting and so full of small satisfying pleasures, you don't realize how good it is until it's over. – *Manohla Dargis, L.A. Weekly*

66 Lucky for us there are no ordinary circumstances in this smart, tasty adaptation of the Elmore Leonard novel and it gets quirkier, funnier and sexier as it goes. – *David Ansen, Newsweek*

⌇ Scott Frank; Anne V. Coates

'From the last place on earth comes a true story of courage and survival.'

Out of the Blue (new) ★★

DIR Robert Sarkies

2006 103m New Zealand

`DVD`

☆ Karl Urban (Nick Harvey), Matthew Sunderland (David Gray), Lois Lawn (Helen Dickson), Simon Ferry (Garry Holden), Tandi Wright (Julie-Anne Bryson), Paul Glover (Paul Knox), William Kircher (Sgt. Stu Guthrie)

Residents of a small town in New Zealand are astonished when one of their number goes on a killing spree.

Sobering re-creation of a 1990 tragedy, told with skill and commendable restraint.

SCR Graham Tetley, Robert Sarkies CIN Greig Fraser MUS Victoria Kelly DES Phil Ivey ED Anne Collins PROD Tim White, Steven O'Meager DIST Metrodome

66 Harrowing and heartbreaking. – *David Edwards, Mirror*

66 An inspiring film on a bleak subject. – *Matt Zoller Seitz, New York Times*

† The Aramoana massacre, in which 13 people died, is the largest mass murder in New Zealand history.

'You're no good and neither am I. We deserve each other!'

Out of the Past ★★★★

DIR Jacques Tourneur

1947 97m US

☆ *Robert Mitchum, Jane Greer, Kirk Douglas*, Rhonda Fleming, Richard Webb, Steve Brodie, Virginia Houston, Dickie Moore

A gang boss hires a detective to track down his girlfriend, who has run off with his fortune; the private eye succeeds, but falls for the woman himself.

One of the greatest of all films noir, tense, moody and with an outstanding cast: Mitchum, all heavy-lidded insouciance, might have been born to play the lead role, and Greer is perhaps cinema's most underrated femme fatale. Immensely satisfying.

SCR Geoffrey Homes CIN *Nicholas Musuraca* MUS Roy Webb PROD Warren Duff DIST RKO

66 Is this not an outcrop of the national masochism induced by a quite aimless, newly industrialized society proceeding rapidly on its way to nowhere? – *Richard Winnington*

66 Mitchum is so sleepily self-confident with the women that when he slopes into clinches you expect him to snore in their faces. – *James Agee*

† It was unsuccessfully re-made in 1984 under the title Against All Odds, with Greer neatly cast as the mother of the femme fatale character, played by Rachel Ward.

'The First Film Made In Outer Space.'

Out of the Present ★★

SCR/DIR Andrei Ujica

1995 96m Germany/France/Belgium/Russia

☆ Anatoli Artesbarski, Sergei Krikalev, Helen Sharman, Viktor Afanasiev, Musa Monarov

A filmed account of life in space on board the Russian Mir station in 1991.

Cosmonaut Sergei Krikalev spent ten months aboard Mir and returned to find a completely new Russia, with Boris Yeltsin having replaced Mikhail Gorbachev. It includes breath-taking photography of Earth and the heavens, shot by Krikalev himself.

CIN Vadim Yusov ED Ralf Henninger, Heldi Leihbecher, Svetlana Ivanova, Andrei Ujica PROD Elke Peters DIST Downtown/Bremer Institut/Fernsehen

66 A profoundly affecting work. – *Kim Newman, Sight & Sound*

The Outlaw Josey Wales ★★★

DIR Clint Eastwood

1976 135m US

`DVD` ♫

☆ *Clint Eastwood*, Chief Dan George, Sondra Locke, John Vernon, Bill McKinney

Near the end of the Civil War, a peaceable farmer turns vengeful when renegade Union soldiers murder his wife.

A violent, action-packed, tautly constructed and well acted; one of Eastwood's better Westerns.

SCR Phil Kaufman, Sonia Chernus CIN Bruce Surtees MUS Jerry Fielding PROD Robert Daley DIST Warner/Malpaso

⌇ Jerry Fielding (music)

O

`DVD` Available on DVD	☆ Cast in order	66 Critics' Quotes	⌇ Academy Award	Ⓑ BAFTA
♫ Soundtrack on CD	of importance	† Points of interest	⌇ Academy Award nomination	Ⓑ BAFTA nomination

'You can't kill what's already dead.'

Outpost (new)

★

DIR Steve Barker
2008   89m   UK

☆ Julian Wadham (Hunt), Ray Stevenson (DC), Richard Brake (Prior), Julian Rivett (Voyteche), Paul Blair (Jordan)

Mercenaries fight an unstoppable zombie force at an East European outpost where Nazis once carried out time-bending experiments.

A few eerie moments carry a stylishly suspenseful charge, but unoriginality dooms the incessant creeping about dark tunnels.

SCR Rae Brunton   CIN Gavin Struthers   MUS James Seymour Brett   DES Max Berman, Gordon Rogers   ED Chris Gill, Alastair Reid   PROD Arabella Page Croft, Kieran Parker   DIST Sony Pictures Entertainment

66 "Never quite seems to gel; the script fails to bring it all together". – *Phelim O'Neill, The Guardian*

66 British director Steve Barker has used a trusted template for low-budget horror: a group of soldiers up against something nasty in a confined space. – *Edward Porter, Sunday Times*

'Just because she's passed on. . .doesn't mean she's moving on.'

Over Her Dead Body (new)

SCR/DIR Jeff Lowell
2008   94m   US
DVD

☆ Eva Longoria Parker (Kate), Paul Rudd (Henry), Lake Bell (Ashley), Jason Biggs (Dan), Lindsay Sloane (Chloe), William Morgan Sheppard (Father Marks)

A woman killed on her wedding day does all she can from beyond the grave to stop her intended falling for another.

Laboured spin on Blithe Spirit that has as much life as its obnoxious ghostly heroine.

CIN John Bailey   MUS David Kitay   DES Cory Lorenzen   ED Matthew Friedman   PROD Paul Brooks, Peter Safran   DIST Entertainment

66 Even the weakest Desperate Housewives episode packs more heat than this tepid romantic comedy-fantasy. – *Dennis Harvey, Variety*

66 Not only have we been there, done that, we didn't want to go there, do that in the first place. – *Roger Ebert, Chicago Sun-Times*

† The film's original title was Ghost Bitch.

Overlord

★★★

DIR *Stuart Cooper*
1975   83m   GB
DVD

☆ Brian Stirner, Davyd Harries, Nicholas Ball, Julie Neesam

In early 1944, an 18-year-old youth is called up and takes part in the D-Day landings.

Intriguing, unusual semi-documentary that incorporates newsreel footage into a story tracing a young recruit's first experience of love and war in a lyrical, almost poetic manner.

SCR Stuart Cooper, Christopher Hudson   CIN *John Alcott*   MUS Paul Glass   PROD James Quinn   DIST EMI/Jowsend

† It received a limited but well-received exhibition in British cinemas in 2008, to accompany its DVD release.

'There's More Than One Way To Shoot Yourself.'

Overnight

★

DIR Tony Montana, Mark Brian Smith
2003   115m   US
DVD

☆ Troy Duffy, Jeff 'Skunk' Baxter, Willem Dafoe, Billy Connolly

Documentary on bartender Troy Duffy, who gets a $1 million deal to make a movie that falls apart disastrously.

Enthralling factual feature on the rise and fall of a briefly legendary loudmouth. Watching the risibly over-confident Duffy become another Hollywood casualty is not pretty, but it's entertaining, even educational.

CIN Mark Brian Smith   MUS Peter Nashel, Jack Livesey   ED Mark Brian Smith, Tony Montana, Jonathan Nixon   PROD Tony Montana

66 A disturbing, sad and blisteringly funny cautionary tale. I reckon this is the documentary of the year. – *David Edwards, Daily Mirror*

66 His story is instructive, as well as chilling and occasionally hilarious – a brief, probably foredoomed career during which a would-be Orson Welles, playing shamelessly to the camera, draws from a bottomless cesspool of hubris, bile and rage. – *Joe Morgenstern, Wall Street Journal*

The Ox

★★

DIR Sven Nykvist
1991   92m   Sweden/ Denmark

☆ Max von Sydow (Vicar), Stellan Skarsgård (Helge Roos), Ewa Fröling (Elfrida Roos), Erland Josephson (Sigvard Silver), Liv Ullmann (Mrs. Gustafsson)

In 19th-century rural Sweden, a father kills his boss's ox to feed his starving family and is imprisoned for life.

In this impossibly harsh setting (which led many Swedes to emigrate to America), a harrowing tale finally arrives, incredibly, at a point of reconciliation and forgiveness. It ends in springtime, which suggests renewal and survival. Debutant director Nykvist, the long-time cinematographer for Ingmar Bergman, predictably makes the film look striking.

SCR Sven Nykvist, Lasse Summanen   CIN Sven Nykvist   MUS Lubos Fiser   DES Peter Høimark   ED Lasse Summanen   PROD Jean Doumanian   DIST Artificial Eye/Sweetland

⚱ best foreign film

The Oxford Murders (new)

★

SCR/DIR Alex de la Iglesia
2008   107m   Spain/France/UK
♫

☆ *John Hurt* (Arthur Seldom), *Elijah Wood* (Martin),

Leonor Watling (Lorna), Julie Cox (Beth), Anna Massey (Mrs. Eagleton)

An Oxford philosopher and one of his students try to solve killings linked by mathematical formulas.

A bland, pretentious old-fashioned mystery, lacking suspense or drama.

SCR Jorge Guerricaechevarria   **CIN** Kiko de la Rica

MUS Roque Banos   **DES** Cristina Casali   **ED** Alejandro Lazaro, Cristina Pastor   **PROD** Alvaro Augustin, Alex de la Iglesia, Gerado Herrera, Elena Manrique, Mariela Besuievski   **DIST** Odeon Sky Filmworks

66 "You can get better ridiculous whodunits on TV". – *Kim Newman, Empire*

DVD Available on DVD   ☆ Cast in order   66 Critics' Quotes   Ⓐ Academy Award   Ⓑ BAFTA
♫ Soundtrack on CD   of importance   † Points of interest   Ⓐ Academy Award nomination   Ⓑ BAFTA nomination

473

P

'Sometimes there's only one thing left to say.'

P.S. I Love You (new)

DIR Richard LaGravenese
2007   125 minsm   US
♫

☆ Hilary Swank (Holly Kennedy), Gerard Butler (Gerry Kennedy), Lisa Kudrow (Denise Hennessey), Harry Connick, Jr. (Daniel Connelly), Gina Gershon (Sharon McCarthy), Jeffrey Dean Morgan (William Gallagher), Kathy Bates (Patricia Rawley), James Marsters (John McCarthy)

A grieving widow receives letters from her late husband that help her rebuild her life and find new love.

Mawkish comedy drama with an uncertain tone; an odd vehicle for a female star better known for tragic dramas, complete with a detour to Ireland that's pure Gaelic cliché.

SCR Richard LaGravenese, Steven Rogers   CIN Terry Stacey   MUS John Powell   DES Shepherd Frankel
ED David Moritz   PROD Wendy Finerman, Broderick Johnson, Andrew A. Kosove, Molly Smith
DIST Momentum

❝ The film is not a beautiful object or a memorable cultural one, and yet it charms, however awkwardly. – *Manohla Dargis, New York Times*

❝ Ghost with a brogue. – *John Anderson, Variety*

† Cecilia Ahern, author of the 1994 source novel, is the daughter of Irish Taoiseach Bertie Ahern.

'A new level of fear.'

P2 (new)   ★★★

DIR Franck Khalfoun
2007   97m   US
DVD

☆ Wes Bentley (Thomas), Rachel Nichols (Angela Bridges), Philip Akin (Karl), Stephanie Moore (Lorraine), Miranda Edwards (Jody), Simon Reynolds (Bob Harper)

A young female executive is terrorised in an underground garage by a psychotic parking attendant and his Rottweiler.

Generic thriller with few actual scares and a fair degree of camp; the under-lit locale is well utilised though.

SCR Franck Khalfoun, Alexandre Aja, Gregory Levasseur
CIN Maxime Alexandre   MUS Tomandandy   DES Oleg Savytski   ED Patrick McMahon   PROD Alexandre Aja, Gregory Levasseur, Patrick Wachsberger, Erik Feig
DIST Tartan Films

❝ Unscary, uninteresting tosh. – *Dan Jolin, Empire*

❝ A canny exploitation of one of the urban woman's greatest fears. – *Jeannette Catsoulis, New York Times*
† The title stands for Parking Level 2.

'Sometimes the greatest journey is the distance between two people.'

The Painted Veil   ★★★

DIR John Curran
2006   124m   US/China
DVD   ♫

☆ *Edward Norton* (Walter Fane), Naomi Watts (Kitty Fane), Liev Schreiber (Charlie Townsend), Toby Jones (Deputy Commissioner Waddington), Diana Rigg (Mother Superior), Anthony Wong (Colonel Yu)

In 1925 China, a stern idealistic English doctor takes his glamorous young wife on a mission to save a remote village ravaged by cholera, threatening to expose her adultery if she declines.

A large-scale epic, ravishing to behold. It's old-fashioned in many ways; the code of behaviour automatically linking adultery with public shame is of its time. So are the body language and emotional reticence of Walter Fane, well played by Norton with clipped accent and stiff-backed rectitude. His courtship of the frivolous Kitty (Watts) is cursory; the initial bond between them does not quite convince. But their fractured relationship shifts under duress; it's a grown-up view of human behaviour and forgiveness. The film has a majestic sweep; scenes along China's Li River are jaw-droppingly beautiful, proving cinema can still stun without recourse to CGI trickery.

SCR Ron Nyswaner   CIN *Stuart Dryburgh*
MUS Alexandre Desplat   DES Tu Juhua   ED Alexandre de Franceschi   PROD Jean-Francois Fonlupt, Sara Colleton, Bob Yari, Edward Norton, Naomi Watts
DIST Momentum

❝ It bears almost no resemblance to the current crop of mostly rat-a-tat movies. To view it is to enter a time warp, and there is some pleasure in stepping back into the languor. – *Peter Rainer, Christian Science Monitor*

❝ Combine[s] a strong-limbed narrative about marital frustration with a painstaking account of the British imperial presence in 1920s China. – *Peter Bradshaw, Guardian*

The Palm Beach Story   ★★★

SCR/DIR Preston Sturges
1942   88m   US
DVD

☆ *Claudette Colbert* (Gerry Jeffers), *Joel McCrea* (Tom

DVD Available on DVD   ☆ Cast in order   ❝ Critics' Quotes   ⚊ Academy Award   Ⓑ BAFTA
♫ Soundtrack on CD   of importance   † Points of interest   ⚊ Academy Award nomination   Ⓣ BAFTA nomination

Jeffers), *Rudy Vallee* (J.D. Hackensacker III), Mary Astor (Princess Centimillia), Sig Arno (Toto), Robert Warwick (Mr. Hinch), Torben Meyer (Dr. Kluck), Jimmy Conlin (Mr. Asweld), William Demarest (Member of Ale and Quail Club), Jack Norton (Member of Ale and Quail Club), Robert Greig (Member of Ale and Quail Club), Roscoe Ates (Member of Ale and Quail Club), Chester Conklin (Member of Ale and Quail Club), Franklin Pangborn (Manager), Alan Bridge (Conductor), Robert Dudley

The wife of a hard-up engineer takes off for Florida to set her sights on a millionaire.

Flighty comedy, inconsequential in itself, but decorated with scenes, characters and zany touches typical of its creator, here at his most brilliant if uncontrolled.

CIN Victor Milner   MUS Victor Young   ED Stuart Gilmore   PROD Paul Jones   DIST Paramount

HACKENSACKER (RUDY VALLEE): That's one of the tragedies of this life, that the men most in need of a beating up are always enormous.

WEENIE KING (ROBERT DUDLEY): Anyway, I'd be too old for you. Cold are the hands of time that creep along relentlessly, destroying slowly but without pity that which yesterday was young. Alone, our memories resist this disintegration and grow more lovely with the passing years. That's hard to say with false teeth.

66 Surprises and delights as though nothing of the kind had been known before . . . farce and tenderness are combined without a fault. – *William Whitebait*

66 Minus even a hint of the war . . . packed with delightful absurdities. – *Variety*

'In A Town This Bad It's No Use Being Good.'

Palmetto

DIR Volker Schlöndorff
1998   114m   US/Germany
DVD   ♫

☆ Woody Harrelson (Harry Barber), Elisabeth Shue (Mrs. Donnelly/Rhea Malroux), Gina Gershon (Nina), Rolf Hoppe (Felix Malroux), Michael Rapaport (Donnely), Chloe Sevigny (Odette), Tom Wright (John Renick), Marc Macauley (Miles Meadows)

A muck-raking Florida reporter is tricked by the trophy wife of a tycoon into kidnapping a young girl.

An unconvincing attempt to convert a James Hadley Chase novel into film noir; it specifically seems to be modelling itself on The Big Sleep. It proceeds at too leisurely a pace, and finally lacks a certain rigour. Harrelson plays the surly 'hero' with a faint air of puzzlement. One sees why.

SCR E. Max Frye   CIN Thomas Kloss   MUS Klaus Dolinger   DES Clare Jenora Bowin   ED Peter Przygodda   PROD Mathias Wendlandt   DIST Warner/Castle Rock/Rialto

66 Palmetto has a satisfyingly deceptive plot that ultimately takes one too many turns. – *Owen Gleiberman, Entertainment Weekly*

66 There is nothing reprehensible about Palmetto; it simply falls short of conviction because you're too aware you've seen it all a hundred times before. – *Angie Errigo, Empire*

'One foot in the door. The other one in the gutter.'

Palookaville   ★★

DIR Alan Taylor
1995   92m   US
DVD

☆ William Forsythe (Sid Dunleavy), Vincent Gallo (Russell Pataki), Adam Trese (Jerry), Gareth Williams (Ed the Cop), Lisa Gay Hamilton (Betty, Jerry's Wife), Bridgit Ryan (Enid), Kim Dickens (Laurie, Russell's Girlfriend)

In New Jersey, three dead-end friends turn to a life of crime to alleviate their boredom; but their efforts founder.

There's not much new or unpredictable here, but director Taylor, making his screen debut, injects some atmosphere, and brings the best out of his three leads, who really do seem to know each other – and their faults – inside out.

SCR David Epstein   CIN John Thomas   MUS Rachel Portman   DES Anne Stuhler   ED David Leonard   PROD Uberto Pasolini   DIST Metrodome/Playhouse International/Samuel Goldwyn/Redwave

66 A refreshing and hilarious alternative to the cool-guys-with-guns flick. – *Empire*

66 A benevolent, even sweet-centred, piece of story-telling. – *Geoffrey Macnab, Sight & Sound*

Pandora's Box   ★★★

DIR G. W. Pabst
1929   97m   Germany
DVD

☆ *Louise Brooks* (Lulu), Fritz Kortner (Dr Peter Schon), Franz Lederer (Alwa Schön), Gustav Diessl (Jack the Ripper)

A woman murders her lover, becomes a prostitute, and is murdered in London by Jack the Ripper.

Curious silent fantasy on a few favourite German themes: very watchable, brilliantly photographed in expressionistic style, and benefiting from a charismatic performance by the remarkable Brooks. An unquestioned classic of the pre-talkies era.

SCR G. W. Pabst, Laszlo Wajda   CIN *Günther Krampf*   DIST Nero Film

66 A disconnected melodramatic effusion. – *Mordaunt Hall, New York Times*

† Remade in Austria in 1962 as No Orchids for Lulu, with Nadja Tiller.

'It was supposed to be the safest room in the house.'

Panic Room   ★

DIR David Fincher
2002   112m   US
DVD   ♫

☆ Jodie Foster (Meg Altman), Forest Whitaker (Burnham), Dwight Yoakam (Raoul), Jared Leto (Junior), Kristen Stewart (Sarah Altman), Ann Magnuson (Lydia Lynch), Ian Buchanan (Evan Kurlander), Patrick Bauchau (Stephen Altman)

Three robbers break into a house to recover cash hidden in a bunker-style safe room – where a mother and her young daughter are hiding.

P

DVD Available on DVD   ☆ Cast in order of importance   66 Critics' Quotes   † Points of interest   ⚊ Academy Award   ⚊ Academy Award nomination   BAFTA   BAFTA nomination

475

Fincher's hyper-active, jittery cameras swoop and spin through tiny, claustrophobic spaces, making a routine thriller seem rather better than it is. In fact, it's all-action all the time; check your brains in at the door. More evidence that Foster's career has taken an unexpected, and hardly welcome detour.

SCR David Koepp   **CIN** Conrad W. Hall, Darius Khondji   **MUS** Howard Shore   **DES** Arthur Max   **ED** James Haygood, Angus Wall   **PROD** Gavin Polone, Judy Hofflund, David Koepp, Cean Chaffin   **DIST** Columbia TriStar

66 Ultimately, this is just a big, dumb, commercial suspenser – but it's one of the best for ages, reminding us that it is still possible to make a high quality piece of popcorn entertainment. – *Empire*

66 A fairly standard exercise in claustrophobic menace. It is also an exercise in style. – *Richard Schickel, Time*

'Innocence has a power evil cannot imagine.'

Pan's Labyrinth   ★★★

SCR/DIR *Guillermo del Toro*
2006   119m   Spain/Mexico/US
DVD   ♫

☆ *Sergi Lopez* (Captain Vidal), *Maribel Verdu* (Mercedes), *Ivana Baquero* (Ofelia), Alex Angulo (Dr. Ferreiro), Ariadna Gil (Carmen)

In 1944 Spain, the imaginative stepdaughter of a cruel Fascist army captain takes refuge in a fantasy world, and meets a faun, a monstrous toad and a pale, death-like man.

Supernatural drama set against the real-life aftermath of the Spanish Civil War, when victorious Fascists were hunting down resistance fighters. The fantasy elements, superbly realised through brilliant CGI work and set design, illuminate the stark horrors, explicitly portrayed, that occur in Ofelia's real world. Outstanding performances by Lopez and Baquero, and Verdu as the gallant, courageous housekeeper Mercedes. But the major credit is del Toro's; from disparate elements he has forged a monumental work of visually breathtaking art.

CIN Guillermo Navarro   **MUS** Javier Navarrete   **DES** *Eugenio Caballero*   **ED** Bernat Vilaplana   **PROD** Bertha Navarro, Alfonso Cuaron, Frida Torresblanco, Alvaro Augustin   **DIST** Optimum

66 A brilliant work of the imagination, capable of truly seizing and igniting our fantasies. – *Michael Wilmington, Chicago Tribune*

♙ Guillermo del Toro; Eugenio Caballero; David Marti, Montse Ribe (make up)

♙ foreign language film; Guillermo del Toro (original screenplay)

♟ film in a foreign language; Lala Huete (costume design); Jose Quetglas, Blanca Sanchez (make up and hair); Javier Navarrete (music, original score)

♟ Guillermo del Torro (original screenplay); Guillermo Navarro; Eugenio Caballero; Martin Hernandez, Miguel Polo, Jaime Bashkt (sound)

'The People Called Them Heroes. The F.B.I. Called Them Public Enemy Number One.'

Panther   ★

DIR Mario Van Peebles
1995   124m   US
DVD   ♫

☆ Kadeem Hardison (Judge), Bokeem Woodbine (Tyrone), Joe Don Baker (Brimmer), Courtney B. Vance (Bobby Seale), Tyrin Turner (Cy), Marcus Chong (Huey Newton), James Russo (Rodgers), Chris Rock (Yuck Mouth), Richard Dysart (J. Edgar Hoover), M. Emmet Walsh (Dorsett), Jenifer Lewis (Rita), Wesley Johnson (Little Bobby Hutton), Nefertiti (Alma)

In the mid-60s, a member of the radical Black Panthers is approached by the FBI as the authorities desperately try to work out how to deal with the fast-growing, increasingly influential movement.

Known facts about the Panthers' history are blended with imagined scenarios in this dramatic but inadequate account of a crucial time in the history of America's racial struggles.

SCR Melvin Van Peebles   **CIN** Edward J Pei   **MUS** *Stanley Clarke*   **DES** Richard Hoover   **ED** Earl Watson   **PROD** Mario Van Peebles, Melvin Van Peebles, Preston L. Holmes, Robert De Niro   **DIST** Polygram/Working Title/Tribeca/MVP

66 A frustrating amalgam of truth, violence, supposition and inspiration. – *Kenneth Turan, Los Angeles Times*

'They put together New York's fastest moving newspaper. They search for truth, they strive for justice. . .then print what they can get away with.'

The Paper   ★★

DIR Ron Howard
1994   112m   US
DVD   ♫

☆ Michael Keaton (Henry Hackett), Glenn Close (Alicia Clark), Marisa Tomei (Martha Hackett), Robert Duvall (Bernie White), Randy Quaid (Michael McDougal), Jason Alexander (Marion Sandusky), Spalding Gray (Graham Keighley), Catherine O'Hara (Susan), Lynne Thigpen (Janet)

Life in the offices of a New York newspaper, on the day two young black men are falsely arrested on charges of murder.

A pacy entertainment that takes a light-hearted view of contemporary journalism; not quite The Front Page, but an engaging supplement, very enjoyably staffed.

SCR David Koepp, Stephen Koepp   **CIN** John Seale   **MUS** *Randy Newman*   **DES** Todd Hallowell   **ED** Daniel Hanley, Michael Hill   **PROD** Brian Grazer, Frederick Zollo   **DIST** Universal/Imagine

66 It's come to something when a newspaper movie casts the cynical journalist as the villain, and the big moral dilemma here would scarcely support a sitcom. Even so, quite watchable, with whip pans and fast tracks, and one eye constantly on the clock. – *Tom Charity, Time Out*

♙ Randy Newman (m), (ly) (music, original song – Make Up Your Mind)

DVD Available on DVD   ☆ Cast in order   66 Critics' Quotes   ♙ Academy Award   ♟ BAFTA
♫ Soundtrack on CD   of importance   † Points of interest   ♙ Academy Award nomination   ♟ BAFTA nomination

Paradise Now ★★★

DIR Hany Abu-Assad
2005   90m   Netherlands/Israel/Germany/France
DVD   ♫

☆ Kais Nashef (Said), Ali Suliman (Khaled), Lubna Azabal (Suha), Amer Hlehel (Jamal), Ashraf Barhoum (Abu-Karem)

Two young Palestinian suicide bombers prepare to blow themselves up in an Israeli city but one of them has second thoughts.

A calm, analytical, even-handed film, the very antithesis of propaganda; director Abu-Assad goes out of his way to demystify the ghastly rituals that accompany preparations for such a mission. And it undermines the supposed heroism of such missions; when Khaled records his last will and testament, while brandishing an AK-47, the video camera keeps breaking down. An eloquent work of real value.

SCR Hany Abu-Assad, Bero Beyer, Pierre Hodgson
CIN Antoine Heberle   DES Olivier Meidinger
ED Sander Vos   PROD Bero Beyer, Amir Harel, Gerhard Meixner, Hengameh Panahi, Roman Paul   DIST Warner

66 A deeply humanistic and compassionate work that avoids moralising or dogma. – *Ali Jaafar, Sight & Sound*

66 At the stunning conclusion, you feel as if the weight of the Israeli-Palestinian conflict has come down on your head. – *Jack Mathews, New York Daily News*

⚱ foreign film

'Courage echoes forever.'

Paradise Road ★

SCR/DIR Bruce Beresford
1997   122m   Australia/US
DVD   ♫

☆ Glenn Close (Adrienne Pargiter), Pauline Collins (Daisy 'Margaret' Drummond), Cate Blanchett (Susan Macarthy), Frances McDormand (Dr. Verstak), Julianna Margulies (Topsy Merritt), Jennifer Ehle (Rosemary Leighton-Jones), Wendy Hughes (Mrs. Dickson), Johanna Ter Steege (Sister Wilhelminia), Elizabeth Spriggs (Mrs. Roberts), Clyde Kusatsu (Sergeant Tomiashi, 'The Snake')

In World War II, female survivors of a Japanese prison camp in Sumatra form a voice orchestra, and sing to keep up their morale.

Something of a missed opportunity: though the film is based on actual events, the reality in the camp was surely worse than the well-scrubbed, well-nourished prisoners on screen might lead us to believe. This sanitising process extends to the script, which has a whiff of soap opera rhythms.

CIN Peter James   MUS Ross Edwards   DES Herbert Pinter   ED Tim Wellburn   PROD Sue Milliken, Greg Coote   DIST TCF/YTC/Village Roadshow

66 If Paradise Road has a fault, it's that it is altogether too lush. . .[Director Bruce] Beresford shies away from the pain of the prison camp. – *Edvins Beitiks, San Francisco Examiner*

66 In trying to keep track of everybody while providing enough melodrama to sustain an atmosphere of controlled

---

terror, Paradise Road stumbles all over itself and never really finds its centre. – *Stephen Holden, New York Times*

'There is no conspiracy. Just twelve people dead.'

The Parallax View ★★★

DIR Alan J. Pakula
1974   102m   US
DVD

☆ Warren Beatty (Joseph Frady), Paula Prentiss (Lee Carter), William Daniels (Austin Tucker), Hume Cronyn (Editor Edgar Rintels), Walter McGinn (Parallax Agent Jack Younger)

Witnesses to a political assassination are systematically killed, despite the efforts of a crusading journalist.

Stylish, persuasive conspiracy thriller with a paranoiac edge, sufficiently confident of itself not to engineer a contrived ending.

SCR David Giler, Lorenzo Semple Jnr   CIN Gordon Willis
MUS Michael Small   DES George Jenkins   ED Jack Wheeler   PROD Alan J. Pakula
DIST Paramount/Gus/Harbour/Doubleday

66 Pakula at his best . . . the test sequence is one of the most celebrated, manipulating the audience as it bombards Beatty's psyche. – *Les Keyser, Hollywood in the Seventies*

66 It is terribly important to give an audience a lot of things they may not get as well as those they will, so that finally the film does take on a texture and is not just simplistic communication. – *Alan J. Pakula*

Paranoid Park (new) ★★

SCR/DIR Gus Van Sant
2007   85m   US/France
DVD   ♫

☆ Gabe Nevins (Alex), Taylor Momsen (Jennifer), Lauren McKinney (Macy), Dan Liu (Detective Liu), Jake Miller (Jared), Grace Carter (Alex's mother)

A teenage boy from a broken home accidentally kills a security guard near Paranoid Park, a haven for skateboarders in Portland, Oregon, and decides to keep his guilt a secret.

Working with cinematographer Christopher Doyle, who films the trance-like skateboarding sequences in gritty Super 8, and using a cunning sound design by Leslie Shatz, Van Sant succeeds in making the damaged Alex a three-dimensional character with unexpressed desires. This is sympathetic story-telling about affectless kids in the 'whatever' generation.

CIN Christopher Doyle, Rain Kathy Li   DES John Pearson-Denning   ED Gus Van S ant   PROD Neil Kopp, David Cress   DIST Tartan

66 The story is from a novel by Portland author Blake Nelson, but the choppy chronology and editing are Van Sant's own. The soundtrack matches the feel: Nino Rota gives way to Elliott Smith, then Beethoven. It's as if an iPod has been left on shuffle. – *Ben Walters, Sight & Sound*

66 This may be credible, and it may (as Van Sant evidently thinks) be a valid metaphor for the present state of America's youth, but it's not much to look at for an hour and a half. – *Edward Porter, Sunday Times*

P

DVD Available on DVD   ☆ Cast in order   66 Critics' Quotes   ⚱ Academy Award   Ⓑ BAFTA
♫ Soundtrack on CD   of importance   † Points of interest   ⚱ Academy Award nomination   Ⓣ BAFTA nomination

477

† Van Sant allegedly reportedly recruited his mostly non-professional cast of high schoolers from the My Space website, though all the leading young actors who accompanied him to the film's world premiere at the 2007 Venice Film Festival denied that this was how he discovered them.

'It could happen to you.'

Parenthood ★★

DIR Ron Howard
1989   124m   US
DVD   ♫

☆ Steve Martin (Gil Buckman), Tom Hulce (Larry Buckman), Rick Moranis (Nathan Huffner), Martha Plimpton (Julie Buckman), Keanu Reeves (Tod Higgins), Jason Robards (Frank Buckman), Mary Steenburgen (Karen Buckman), Dianne Wiest (Helen Buckman)

A middle-class American family suffers disruption as fathers and sons from three generations fail to agree on rules of behaviour.

Competent and sometimes amusing comedy about the joys and travails of raising children. It has a strong feelgood factor, which, coming from director Howard, is hardly a surprise.

SCR Lowell Ganz, Babaloo Mandel   CIN Donald McAlpine   MUS Randy Newman   DES Todd Hallowell   ED Michael Hill, Daniel Hanley   PROD Brian Grazer   DIST UIP/Imagine Entertainment

66 A funny and touching look at the joys of family life. – *Caroline Westbrook, Empire*

66 There is something brave and original about piling up most of our worst parental nightmares in one movie and then daring to make a midsummer comedy out of them. It really shouldn't work, but it does. – *Richard Schickel, Time*

⚘ Dianne Wiest; song 'I Love To See You Smile' (m/l Randy Newman)

'There's A New Name For Terror.'

Parents ★

DIR Bob Balaban
1988   81m   US
DVD

☆ Randy Quaid (Nick Laemle), Mary Beth Hurt (Lily Laemle), Sandy Dennis (Millie Dew), Bryan Madorsky (Michael Laemle), Juno Mills-Cockell (Sheila Zellner), Kathryn Grody (Miss Baxter), Deborah Rush (Mrs. Gladys Zellner), Graham Jarvis (Mr. Zellner)

A disturbed boy in 1950s small-town America discovers to his horror that his parents are cannibals.

Ink-black comedy in the cosiest of suburban settings. Funny and provocative on its own limited terms, though not a movie to discuss afterwards over dinner.

SCR Christopher Hawthorne   CIN Ernest Day, Robin Vidgeon   MUS Jonathan Elias   ED Bill Pankow   PROD Bonnie Palef   DIST Vestron/Parents Productions

66 The movie degenerates into a dumb horror show. – *Hal Hinson, Washington Post*

Paris, Texas ★★★

DIR *Wim Wenders*
1984   148m   West Germany/France
DVD   ♫

☆ *Harry Dean Stanton* (Travis Clay Henderson), Dean Stockwell (Walt Henderson), Aurore Clement (Anne), Hunter Carson (Hunter), Nastassja Kinski (Jane), Bernhard Wicki (Dr. Ulmer)

After separating from his family, a man goes missing in the hinterlands of America, and turns up years later to reunite with his son – and his wife, now working as a stripper.

The plot meanders and sometimes strays from logic, but this movie is all about appearances: Wenders and cinematographer Müller linger on the arid, desolate stretches of Texas landscape, shooting it with an intense curiosity that may be the preserve of outsiders. Stanton, cast unusually in a lead role, is suitably enigmatic, a description that holds good for the whole picture. Still, it exerts a certain hypnotic fascination, reinforced by Ry Cooder's admirably sparse score.

SCR Sam Shepard   CIN *Robby Müller*   MUS Ry Cooder   ED Peter Pryzgodda   PROD Don Guest, Anatole Dauman   DIST Road Movies/Argos

🛡 Wim Wenders (direction)

Paris by Night ★

SCR/DIR David Hare
1988   103m   GB
DVD   ♫

☆ Charlotte Rampling (Clara Paige), Michael Gambon (Gerald Paige), Robert Hardy (Adam Gillvray), Iain Glen (Wallace Sharp), Jane Asher (Pauline), Andrew Ray (Michael Swanton), Niamh Cusack (Jenny Swanton), Jonathan White (Simon Paige), Linda Bassett (Janet Swanton), Robert Flemyng (Jack Sidmouth), Robert David MacDonald (Sir Arthur Sanderson)

A Tory Euro MP's life, already troubled by a failing marriage and threats from a blackmailer, is complicated further on a trip to Paris.

David Hare, a world-class playwright and skilful adapter of other people's source material for film, labours to create original stories that convince on screen. This story is all atmosphere and subtext, but it lacks dramatic punch and plausibility. A film that feels classy, but flatters to deceive.

CIN Roger Pratt   MUS Georges Delerue   DES Anthony Pratt   ED George Akers   PROD Patrick Cassavetti   DIST Virgin/British Screen/Film Four International/Zenith

'Stories of Love. From the City of Love.'

Paris Je T'Aime (new) ★

DIR Bruno Podalydès, Gurinder Chadha, Gus Van Sant, Joel and Ethan Coen, Walter Salles, Daniela Thomas, Christopher Doyle, Isabel Coixet, Suwa Nobuhiro, Sylvain Chomet, Alfonso Cuarón, Olivier Assayas, Oliver Schmitz, Richard LaGravenese, Vincenzo Natali, Wes Craven, Tom Tykwer, Frédéric Auburtin, Gérard Depardieu, Alexander Payne
2006   120m
DVD   ♫

☆ Marianne Faithfull, Steve Buscemi, Catalina Sandino

Moreno, Miranda Richardson, Juliette Binoche, Willem Dafoe, Nick Nolte, Ludivine Sagnier, Maggie Gylenhaal, Fanny Ardant, Bob Hoskins, Elijah Wood, Emily Mortimer, Rufus Sewell, Natalie Portman, Gena Rowlands, Ben Gazzard, Gérard Depardieu, Margo Martindale.

Eighteen short films set in Paris, one for each of the city's arrondissements.

The quality of contributions in this portmanteau movie varies wildly. Its more memorable moments include Margo Martindale as a wistful American tourist in Alexander Payne's segment, a topical inter-racial romance written and directed by Gurinder Chadha, and Gena Rowlands and Ben Gazzara reunited on screen for Gérard Depardieu.

SCR Tristan Carné (idea), Emmanuel Benbihy (feature concept)   PROD Claudie Ossard, Emmanuel Benbihy   DIST The Works

66 Some of the shorts, as is to be expected in a project of this kind, fall a little flat; many more, though, are charming and socially pertinent. – *Sukhdev Sandhu, Daily Telegraph*

66 All in all, the films are a heap of canapés that doesn't constitute a proper meal, but there are some interesting morsels. – *Edward Porter, Sunday Times*

'A brutal murder in a small town. A triangle of passion, power and rage.'

Paris Trout ★★★

DIR Stephen Gyllenhaal
1991   99m   US
☆ Dennis Hopper (Paris Trout), *Barbara Hershey* (Hanna Trout), *Ed Harris* (Harry Seagraves), Ray McKinnon (Carl Bonner), Tina Lifford (Mary Sayers), Darnita Henry (Rosie Sayers), Eric Ware (Henry Ray Sayers), Ronreaco Lee (Chester Sayers), Gary Bullock (Buster Devonne)

In 1949 Georgia, a malevolent racist loan shark shoots the sister of a black man who reneged on a debt and faces a murder trial.

The title character is a nasty piece of work, even by the standards of characters Hopper has played, but he attacks the role with relish, with fine support work from Hershey and Harris. A handsomely photographed, disturbing and under-rated film that encapsulates the insidious attitudes in easy-paced southern towns of the time.

SCR Pete Dexter   CIN *Robert Elswit*   MUS David Shire
DES Richard Sherman   ED Harvey Rosenstock
PROD Frank Konigsberg, Larry Sanitsky
DIST Palace/Viacom

66 Some times the pace is as slow as watching cotton grow, but at others the rage and bigotry on Dennis Hopper's face spills out dreadfully across the screen. – *Steve Grant, Time Out*

Une Partie de Campagne ★★★

SCR/DIR *Jean Renoir*
1936   40m   France
DVD
☆ Sylvia Bataille (Henriette Dufour), Georges Darnoul (Henri), Jane Marken (Mme. Juliette Dufour), Paul Temps (Anatole)

Around 1880, a Parisian tradesman and his family picnic one Sunday in the country, and one of the daughters falls in love.

An unfinished film which was much admired for its local colour, like an impressionist picture come to life.

CIN *Claude Renoir, Jean Bourgoin*   MUS *Joseph Kosma*
ED Marinette Cadix, Marguerite Renoir
DIST Pantheon/Pierre Braunberger

Pascali's Island ★

SCR/DIR James Dearden
1988   104m   GB/US
♫
☆ *Ben Kingsley* (Basil Pascali), *Charles Dance* (Anthony Bowles), *Helen Mirren* (Lydia Neuman), Stefan Gryff (Izzet Effendi), George Murcell (Herr Gesing), Nadim Sawalha (Pasha), T. P. McKenna (Dr. Hogan), Sheila Allan (Mrs. Marchant)

On a beautiful Aegean island in 1908, a Turkish spy and a phoney English archaeologist try to outwit each other for the favours of a beautiful woman.

Exquisite looking period drama, given flavour by its low-key sexual tension – and in Kingsley's case, sexual ambivalence. Well-acted by the three leads, and an absorbing historical subtext.

CIN Roger Deakins   MUS Loek Dikker   DES Andrew Mollo   ED Edward Marnier   PROD Mirella Sklavounou, Paul Raphael, Tania Windsor Blunden
DIST Virgin/Avenue Pictures/Initial/Film Four International

66 It is Ben Kingsley's performance as the despairing victim of his own actions that makes this island worth a visit. – *Desson Howe, Washington Post*

† The film was shot on the island of Rhodes.

'I used to be somebody else; but I traded myself in. . .'

The Passenger ★★★

DIR Michelangelo Antonioni
1975   119m   Italy/France/Spain
☆ Jack Nicholson, Maria Schneider, Jenny Runacre, Ian Hendry

A burnt-out TV reporter in a Sahara desert hotel swaps identities with a dead man and finds he is now an African gun runner being drawn irresistibly towards his own death.

Pretty much in the style of Blow Up, but with a more rigorous air about it. Fascinating study of identity and of the west's attitude to the Third World, seen through eyes of a character who feels detached and alienated. The long closing shot, hinting at his state of mind, is a stunning coup.

SCR Mark Peploe, Peter Wollen, Michelangelo Antonioni
CIN Luciano Tovoli   PROD Carlo Ponti
DIST MGM/CCC/Concordia/CIPI

66 A film of real romance, depth and power . . . the very quintessence of cinema. – *Michael Billington, Illustrated London News*

P

Passion Fish ★★

SCR/DIR *John Sayles*
1992 135m US
DVD ♫

☆ *Mary McDonnell* (May-Alice Culhane), *Alfre Woodard* (Chantelle), David Strathairn (Rennie), Vondie Curtis-Hall (Sugar LeDoux), Nora Dunn (Ti-Marie), Sheila Kelley (Kim), Angela Bassett (Dawn/Rhonda), Leo Burmester (Reeves)

A TV soap star paralysed in a road accident, returns to her family home in the Deep South, and behaves like the patient from Hell – until a new carer shows her she's not the only one with problems.

Nicely judged, female dominated drama; it benefits from a thoughtful script that starts at the point most inspirational TV movies leave off. The two lead performances are impeccable.

CIN Roger Deakins MUS Mason Daring DES Dan Bishop, Dianna Freas ED John Sayles PROD Sarah Green, Maggie Renzi DIST Atchafalaya

66 It's a damning comment on the sexism of movies today that (director John) Sayles's plain good sense now seems revolutionary. – *Peter Travers, Rolling Stone*

⚖ Mary McDonnell (leading actress); John Sayles (original screenplay)

'By his wounds, we were healed.'

The Passion of The Christ ★

DIR Mel Gibson
2004 127m US
DVD ♫

☆ Jim Caviezel (Jesus), Monica Bellucci (Magdalen), Hristo Naumov Shopov (Pontius Pilate), Maia Morgenstern (Mary), Francesco De Vito (Peter), Luca Lionello (Judas), Mattia Sbragia (Caiaphas), Rosalinda Celentano (Satan)

The final twelve hours of Christ's life, during which he is arrested, tried, beaten and finally crucified.

A real anomaly – the first US box-office hit to be performed entirely in pig Latin and Aramaic – that works better as a forceful show of faith than as a film per se, though Gibson attempts to rouse the masses with slo-mo action scenes, horrific effects work and a buff Jesus; what's missing from its blunt-force theology is any real sense of grace.

SCR Benedict Fitzgerald, Mel Gibson CIN Caleb Deschanel MUS John Debney DES Francesco Frigeri ED John Wright PROD Mel Gibson, Bruce Davey, Stephen McEveety DIST Icon

66 This is not a sermon or a homily, but a visualisation of the central event in the Christian religion. Take it or leave it. – *Roger Ebert, Chicago Sun-Times*

66 If an age produces the renditions of classic stories that reflect those times, then The Passion of the Christ, which is violent, contentious, emotional, extreme and highly proficient, must be the Jesus movie for this era. – *Todd McCarthy, Variety*

† The film was reissued at Easter 2005 as The Passion Recut, a version which excised some of the more extreme gore.

† It was a surprising world-wide hit, grossing $370 million in the US and a further $241 million in other territories.

⚖ Caleb Deschanel; John Debney; Keith Vanderlaan, Christien Tinsley (make up)

Passport to Pimlico ★★★★

DIR Henry Cornelius
1949 84m GB
DVD

☆ Stanley Holloway (Arthur Pemberton), *Margaret Rutherford* (Prof. Hatton-Jones), Basil Radford (Gregg), Naunton Wayne (Straker), Hermione Baddeley (Eddie Randall), John Slater (Frank Huggins), Paul Dupuis (Duke of Burgundy), Jane Hylton (Molly), Raymond Huntley (Mr. Wix), Betty Warren (Connie Pemberton), Barbara Murray (Shirley Pemberton), Sydney Tafler (Fred Cowan)

In the post-war years, part of a London district is discovered to belong to the Duchy of Burgundy, and the inhabitants free themselves from rationing restrictions, set up border controls and adopt continental airs.

A cleverly detailed little shaggy-dog story which ushered in the best period of Ealing comedy, its preoccupation with suburban man and his foibles. Not exactly satire, but great fun, and kindly with it.

SCR T. E. B. Clarke CIN Lionel Banes MUS *Georges Auric* ED Michael Truman PROD E. V. H. Emmett DIST Ealing

66 One of the most felicitous and funny films since the age of the René Clair comedies. – *C. A. Lejeune*

⚖ T. E. B. Clarke (screenplay)

'Not much meat on her, but what there is is cherce!'

Pat and Mike ★★★

DIR George Cukor
1952 95m US

☆ *Spencer Tracy, Katharine Hepburn*, Aldo Ray, William Ching, Sammy White, Jim Backus, Phyllis Povah

A jaded small-time sports promoter takes as a client an intellectual sportswoman.

Pretty much everything we have come to expect from Tracy-Hepburn comedies: fast, whip-smart repartee, exasperation and tenderness in close proximity, and real sexual chemistry. With all that going for it, it scarcely matters that the Kanin-Gordon script compares unfavourably with their more fluent and satisfying Adam's Rib.

SCR Ruth Gordon, Garson Kanin CIN William Daniels MUS David Raksin PROD Lawrence Weingarten DIST MGM

66 They do not, like the Lunts, give the impression of a rigid calculated effect; rather, they complement and stimulate each other. – *Monthly Film Bulletin*

⚖ Ruth Gordon, Garson Kanin (screenplay)

Pather Panchali ★★★★

SCR/DIR *Satyajit Ray*
1955 115m India
DVD

☆ Kanu Banerjee (Harihar), Karuna Banerjee (Sarbajaya),

Uma Das Gupta (Durga), Subir Bannerjee (Apu), Chunibala (Indir Thakrun)

In a small Bengal village, the son of a would-be writer grows up in poverty and tragedy before setting off with what remains of the family to seek a living in Benares.

An extraordinary debut from an Indian director that immediately became a classic of world cinema: clearly influenced by the Italian neo-realists, Ray employed a non-professional cast to film this story of extreme hardship and separation, viewed largely through a child's eyes.

CIN Subrata Mitra   **MUS** *Ravi Shankar*   **ED** Dulal Dutta   **PROD** Satyajit Ray   **DIST** Government of West Bengal

† This film, the first part of the 'Apu trilogy,' was followed by Aparajito (1956) and The World of Apu (1959).
† The title means 'Song of the road.'
† Ray shot the ultra-low budget film over four years, on weekends and Indian public holidays.

Paths of Glory   ★★★★

DIR *Stanley Kubrick*
1957   86m   US
[DVD]

☆ *Kirk Douglas* (Col. Dax), *Adolphe Menjou* (Gen. Broulard), *George Macready* (Gen. Mireau), Wayne Morris (Lt. Roget), Richard Anderson (Maj. Saint-Auban), Ralph Meeker (Cpl. Paris), Timothy Carey (Pvt. Ferol)

In 1916 in the French trenches, three soldiers are court-martialled for cowardice by officers who want to use their case to instil discipline into the ranks.

Incisive melodrama chiefly depicting the corruption and incompetence of the high command; the plight of the soldiers is less interesting. The trench scenes are unforgettably vivid, and the rest is shot in genuine castles, with resultant difficulties of lighting and recording; the overall result is an overpowering piece of cinema.

SCR Stanley Kubrick, Calder Willingham, Jim Thompson   **CIN** *Georg Krause*   **MUS** Gerald Fried   **ED** Eva Kroll   **PROD** James B. Harris   **DIST** UA/Bryna

❝ A bitter and biting tale, told with stunning point and nerve-racking intensity. – *Judith Crist*
❝ Beautifully performed, staged, photographed, cut and scored. – *Colin Young*

'What would you do if they destroyed your home, threatened your family? Where would you draw the line?'

The Patriot

DIR Roland Emmerich
2000   165m   US/Germany
[DVD] ♫

☆ Mel Gibson (Benjamin Martin), Heath Ledger (Gabriel Martin), Joely Richardson (Charlotte Selton), Jason Isaacs (Col William Tavington), Chris Cooper (Col Harry Burwell), Tcheky Karyo (Jean Villeneuve), Rene Auberjonois (Rev Oliver), Lisa Brenner (Anne Howard), Tom Wilkinson (Gen Cornwallis), Donal Logue (Dan Scott), Leon Rippy (John Billings), Adam Baldwin (Loyalist/Captain Wilkins), Gregory Smith (Thomas Martin), Mika Boorem (Margaret Martin)

After one of his sons is killed and another wounded in the War of Independence, a plantation owner in America's South seeks revenge on the British colonel responsible.

Regrettable period drama which rewrites or ignores huge swathes of history for its own ends, and reduces the complex politics of secession to a petty vengeance drama; it's not helped by Gibson's humourless, heavy-handed screen presence and an insanely long running time.

SCR Robert Rodat   **CIN** Caleb Deschanel   **MUS** John Williams   **DES** Kirk M. Petruccelli   **ED** David Brenner   **PROD** Dean Devlin, Mark Gordon, Gary Levinsohn   **DIST** Columbia

❝ Takes us by the hand and leads us through its phoney American landscape. To one side lies the smoky battlefields where the English are bested and, to the other, long sentimental tracts where the corn is as high as an elephant's eye. Everything else has simply been airbrushed out of the picture. – *Xan Brooks, Guardian*
❝ Has a flag-waving dumbness at its core. – *William Arnold, Seattle Post-Intelligencer*
† The film was widely criticised in the UK media for its anti-British bias.
⌁ Caleb Deschanel; John Williams (music score); Kevin O'Connell, Greg P. Russell, Lee Orloff (sound)

'Get Ready To Root For The Bad Guy.'

Payback   ★

DIR Brian Helgeland
1999   100m   US
[DVD] ♫

☆ Mel Gibson (Porter), Gregg Henry (Val), Maria Bello (Rosie), Deborah Kara Unger (Lynn), David Paymer (Stegman), Bill Duke (Detective Hicks), Jack Conley (Detective Leary), William Devane (Carter), Kris Kristofferson (Bronson), John Glover (Phil), Lucy Alexis Liu (Pearl)

A ruthless robber is double-crossed by his wife and his partner-in-crime after a botched hold-up, and resolves to obtain his share of the spoils – with interest.

It's not Point Blank, of course, and never could be. But there's no harm in using the same source novel as a template, and Gibson does a fair job as a single-minded avenger. This murky, violent film's uneven quality may stem from the fact that a sizeable proportion of it is the work of an anonymous director; Helgeland declined to re-shoot several scenes at the bidding of its producer (Gibson's business partner).

SCR Brian Helgeland, Terry Hayes   **CIN** Ericson Core   **MUS** Chris Boardman   **DES** Richard Hoover   **ED** Kevin Stitt   **PROD** Bruce Davey   **DIST** Paramount/Icon

❝ In the popcorn sense it certainly delivers on mindless escapism. In the artistic sense, let's just say that Payback is a long way from Point Blank. – *Peter Travers, Rolling Stone*
† In 2006, a DVD of a 'Director's Cut' version was released, for which Helgeland restored his original scenes that had been excised.

P

'In the fall of 1997, every nuclear device in the world will be accounted for . . . Except one.'

The Peacemaker ★

DIR Mimi Leder
1997   124m   US
[DVD]   ♫

☆ George Clooney (Lt. Col. Thomas Devoe), Nicole Kidman (Dr. Julia Kelly), Marcel Iures (Dusan Gavrich), Alexander Baluev (General Aleksandr Kodoroff), Rene Medvesek (Vlado Mirich), Gary Werntz (Terry Hamilton), Randall Batinkoff (Ken), Jim Haynie (General Garnett), Armin Mueller-Stahl (Dimitri Vertikoff)

A military man and a scientist join forces to track down a nuclear warhead set to be detonated somewhere in New York.

Reasonably tough action-adventure yarn attempts to identify a threat to American interests emerging from the new nations of Eastern Europe, only to fall away into stock missile-touting villainy; the Manhattan scenes, at least, have a certain immediacy in their favour.

SCR Michael Schiffer   CIN Dietrich Lohmann
MUS Hans Zimmer   DES Leslie Dilley   ED David Rosenbloom   PROD Walter Parkes, Branko Lustig
DIST DreamWorks

66 It looks great. The technical credits are impeccable, and Clooney and Kidman negotiate assorted dangers skilfully. But it's mostly spare parts from other thrillers. – *Roger Ebert, Chicago Sun-Times*

† The first release from the newly-formed DreamWorks studio, it performed indifferently at the US box-office, grossing only $41 million. Its leading man Clooney subsequently criticised its script.

'More horrible than horror! More terrible than terror!'

Peeping Tom ★★★

DIR *Michael Powell*
1959   109m   GB
[DVD]

☆ Carl Boehm (Mark Lewis), Moira Shearer (Vivian), Anna Massey (Helen Stephens), Maxine Audley (Mrs. Stephens), Esmond Knight (Arthur Baden), Michael Goodliffe (Don Jarvis), Shirley Anne Field (Diane Ashley), Jack Watson (Inspector Gregg)

A young amateur film-maker has a compulsion to murder women, and photograph the fear on their faces as they realise their fate.

Reviled by many critics on its release as depraved and perverted, this infamous film effectively halted Powell's British career. It is now regarded as a masterpiece, addressing directly the voyeurism of cinema audiences and implicitly posing questions of why and for how long they will keep their gaze fixed to the screen. All that aside, it's a psychologically intricate horror film, if a nasty one.

SCR Leo Marks   CIN *Otto Heller*   MUS Brian Easdale
ED Noreen Ackland   DIST Anglo Amalgamated/Michael Powell

66 Of enormous and deserved reputation. – *Time Out, 1982*

† Powell's original title was The Film Maker.
† Martin Scorsese, together with other admirers of Powell and the film, found an intact print, restored it and had it re-released in 1979, when the critical response was mixed, but more measured.

Pelle the Conqueror ★★

SCR/DIR *Bille August*
1987   157m   Denmark/Sweden
[DVD]   ♫

☆ *Max von Sydow* (Pappa Lasse), *Pelle Hvenegaard* (Pelle), Erik Paaske (Farm Foreman), Kristina Tornqvist (Little Anna), Morten Jørgensen (Farming trainee), Axel Strøbye (Kongstrup), Astrid Villaume (Mrs. Kongstrup), Björn Granath (Farmhand Erik)

At the start of the 20th century, a meek old Swedish widower and his son emigrate to Denmark, where they struggle to survive hardships and even injustices.

Beautifully filmed, finely detailed account of an agricultural year in Denmark, with a warm, convincing bond between father and son. The film finally achieves epic quality by stealth, from the rich accumulation of events.

CIN *Jörgen Persson*   MUS Stefan Nilsson   DES Anna Asp
ED Janus Billeskov Jansen   PROD Per Holst
DIST Curzon/Danish Film Institute/Swedish Film Institute/Svensk Filmindustri/Per Holst

66 Despite occasional lapses into sentimentality, the film is saved by its performances and its uncluttered depiction of a man cowed by age and servitude. – *Colette Maude, Time Out*

† The film won the Palme D'Or at the 1988 Cannes Film Festival, nine months before winning its Oscar.

⚊ foreign film
⚊ Max von Sydow (leading actor)
Ⓣ film not in the English language

'What makes us different makes us beautiful'

Penelope (new) ★

DIR Mark Palansky
2008   93m   UK/US/Germany

☆ Christina Ricci (Penelope Wilhern), James McAvoy (Max), Catherine O'Hara (Jessica Wilhern), Reese Witherspoon (Annie), Peter Dinklage (Lemon), Richard E. Grant (Franklin Wilhern)

A wealthy socialite, born with a pig's snout, the result of a secret family curse, searches for her Prince Charming.

An oddly stilted modern fairytale, too bland for adults, too shackled by reality for kids.

SCR Leslie Caveny   CIN Michel Amathieu   MUS Joby Talbot   DES Amanda McArthur   ED Jon Gregory
PROD Reece Witherspoon, Scott Steindorff, Jennifer Simpson   DIST Momentum

66 Director Palansky wishes he was Tim Burton. So will you. – *Peter Travers, Rolling Stone.*

66 At best an oddity, and, like most oddities, a distributor's nightmare – it has been sitting on the shelf since 2006. The reason is not the cast – Christina Ricci and James McAvoy as romantic leads, producer Reese Witherspoon in a

modest best-friend role – but that Ricci is sporting a pig's snout. – *Tim Robey, Daily Telegraph*

The People vs. Larry Flynt ★★

DIR *Milos Forman*
1996 129m US
DVD ♫

☆ *Woody Harrelson* (Larry Flynt), *Courtney Love* (Althea Leasure), *Edward Norton* (Isaacman), James Cromwell (Charles Keating), Crispin Glover (Arlo), James Carville (Simon Leis), Brett Harrelson (Jimmy Flynt), Donna Hanover (Ruth Carter Stapleton)

Biopic of the porn entrepreneur and publisher of *Hustler* magazine, focusing on his battles with the US authorities over issues of indecency.

Another of Forman's left-of-centre biopics, a maniacally funny, even touching portrait of a tireless thorn in the side of the moral majority, given substance by wholly committed turns from performers unafraid of showing these characters' horny, needy or seedier sides. As tracts on free speech go, it's a winner: Flynt may come out of it a sleazeball, but you have, surely, to respect his right to be a sleazeball.

SCR *Scott Alexander, Larry Karaszewski* CIN Philippe Rousselot MUS Thomas Newman DES Patrizia von Brandenstein ED Christopher Tellefsen PROD Oliver Stone, Janet Yang, Michael Hausman DIST Columbia TriStar/Ixtlan/Phoenix

66 Smart, funny, shamelessly entertaining and perfectly serious too. – *Elvis Mitchell, The New York Times*

66 Full of outrageous material that will offend liberals and conservatives alike, but it's positioned on the cutting edge of contemporary debates about free speech, feminism, and the effects of mass media on modern society. – *David Sterritt, Christian Science Monitor*

† The real-life Flynt has a cameo as a judge.

⚲ Woody Harrelson (leading actor); Milos Forman (direction)

Pepi, Luci, Bom

SCR/DIR Pedro Almodóvar
1980 82m Spain
DVD

☆ Carmen Maura (Pepi), Félix Rotaeta (Policeman), Olvido 'Alaska' Gara (Bom), Eva Siva (Luci), Pedro Almodóvar (Master of ceremonies)

During the punk era in Madrid, a Spanish rape victim gets her revenge by luring her attacker's wife into a lesbian fling with a sadistic singer.

Pedro Almodóvar's first full-length feature, and one that set the tone of his films for the next few years: a lurid mixture of kitschy interiors, camp performances, transgressive sexual acts and a relaxed attitude to drugs. More significantly, he gives three actresses the lead roles, foreshadowing his fascination with female characters. That aside, it's minor Almodóvar, of interest mainly to his completist fans.

CIN Paco Femenia ED Pepe Salcedo PROD Pepón Corominas, Pastora Delgado, Ester Rambal DIST Metro/Figaro

66 Most notable for its bathroom jokes, humorous rape scenes and abysmal home-movie cinematography, the film is a reputation-dimming mess. – *Janet Maslin, New York Times*

'On the way to finding a family, she found love.'

The Perez Family ★

DIR Mira Nair
1995 113m US
DVD ♫

☆ Marisa Tomei (Dorita Evita Perez), Alfred Molina (Juan Raul Perez), Chazz Palminteri (Lt. John Pirelli), Anjelica Huston (Carmela Perez), Trini Alvarado (Teresa Perez), Celia Cruz (Luz Pat), Diego Wallraff (Angel Diaz), Angela Lanza (Flavia)

A Cuban dissident flees to the US, where he's caught between his wife and the new woman in his life.

Slight but colourful soap opera, with attractive Miami locations. One of this director's minor works.

SCR Robin Swicord CIN Stuart Dryburgh MUS Alan Silvestri DES Mark Friedberg ED Robert Estrin, Greg Finton PROD Michael Nozik, Lydia Dean Pilcher DIST Film Four/Samuel Goldwyn

66 Crammed with histrionic performances and ersatz mise en scene, and it looks like a musical after all the songs have been cut out. – *Tom Charity, Time Out*

The Perfect Storm

DIR Wolfgang Petersen
2000 129m US
DVD ♫

☆ George Clooney (Billy Tyne), Mark Wahlberg (Bobby Shatford), John C. Reilly (Dale 'Murph' Murphy), Diane Lane (Christine Cotter), William Fichtner (David 'Sully' Sullivan), John Hawkes (Michael 'Bugsy' Moran), Allen Payne (Alfred Pierre), Mary Elizabeth Mastrantonio (Linda Greenlaw), Karen Allen (Melissa Brown), Cherry Jones (Edie Bailey), Bob Gunton (Alexander McAnally III), Christopher McDonald (Todd Gross), Michael Ironside (Bob Brown)

The last voyage of the Andrea Gail, a small fishing boat caught up in violent storms in the North Atlantic.

Bombastic recreation of an everyday maritime tragedy, featuring beardy actors splashing about in studio water tanks for much of the duration, and – back on dry land – several fine actresses given very little to do.

SCR Bill Wittliff CIN John Seale MUS James Horner DES William Sandell ED Richard Francis-Bruce PROD Paula Weinstein, Wolfgang Petersen, Gail Katz DIST Warner

66 While its roiling collision of weather systems is pulled off with cinematic deftness, the actors who stand there getting lashed and splashed don't have anything terribly interesting to say. – *Steve Rea, Philadelphia Inquirer*

66 By the end, I felt like a beetle going round and round in a toilet bowl that wouldn't stop flushing. – *Lawrence Toppman, Charlotte Observer*

† The film was a huge hit in the States, grossing $182 million.

P

A Perfect World ★

DIR Clint Eastwood
1993 138m US
♫

☆ Kevin Costner (Robert 'Butch' Haynes), Clint Eastwood (Chief Red Garnett), Laura Dern (Sally Gerber), T.J. Lowther (Phillip 'Buzz' Perry), Keith Szarabajka (Terry Pugh), Leo Burmester (Tom Adler), Paul Hewitt (Dick Suttle), Bradley Whitford (Bobby Lee)

An escaped convict develops fatherly feelings for the seven-year-old boy he has kidnapped, while they flee across Texas from the authorities.

Old-fashioned slice of outlaw sentimentality on the road, off-puttingly corny and overlong but with graceful moments. Notably features two male leads who rarely share top billing.

SCR John Lee Hancock   CIN Jack N. Green   MUS Lennie Niehaus   DES Henry Bumstead   ED Joel Cox, Ron Spang   PROD Mark Johnson, David Valdes, Clint Eastwood   DIST Warner/Malpaso

66 While this lacks the class and assured blend of genre traditions and subversion that marks Eastwood's best work, it is very entertaining. – *Geoff Andrew, Time Out*

'See them all in a film about fantasy. And reality. Vice. And versa.'

Performance ★★★

DIR *Nicolas Roeg, Donald Cammell*
1970 105m GB
♫

☆ *James Fox* (Chas Devlin), *Mick Jagger* (Turner), Anita Pallenberg (Pherber), Michèle Breton (Lucy), Stanley Meadows (Rosebloom), Allan Cuthbertson (The Lawyer)

A vicious gangster moves in with an ex-pop star in his chic Chelsea basement flat, where they both indulge in power plays, drugs, sexual antics with groupies and identity-swapping.

This dense, Pinteresque melodrama about alter egos was regarded as unreleasable by the studio, and shelved for two years, before it saw the light of day. Propelled by Fox's jolting tough-guy act and Jagger's androgynous charisma, it's a hallucinatory journey into parallel lives, fragmented in style, and basking in a kind of decadent haze. Word of mouth has turned it into a cult classic, though it wears its literary influences a little obviously; no accident that a Jorge Luis Borges paperback was left around for all to see.

SCR Donald Cammell   CIN *Nicolas Roeg*   MUS Jack Nitzsche   ED Antony Gibbs, Brian Smedley-Aston   PROD Donald Cammell   DIST Warner/Goodtimes

66 A humourless, messy mixture of crime and decadence and drug-induced hallucination. – *New Yorker, 1980*

66 You don't have to be a drug addict, pederast, sado-masochist or nitwit to enjoy it, but being one or more of these things would help. – *John Simon*

'The film Iran didn't want the world to see.'

Persepolis (new) ★★★

SCR/DIR Marjane Satrapi, Vincent Paronnaud
2007 96m France/US
DVD ♫

☆ Chiara Mastroianni (Voice of Marjane), Catherine Deneuve (Voice of Tadji), Danielle Darrieux (Voice of Marjane's Grandmother), Simon Akbarian (Voice of Ebi), Gabrielle Lopes (Voice of Marjane as a child), Francois Jerosme (Voice of Uncle Anouche)

A rebellious Iranian girl looks on as her country undergoes an Islamic revolution.

Beautifully rendered, mostly black-and-white adaptation of an autobiographical graphic novel that succeeds both as a rite-of-passage story and a Middle East history primer.

MUS Olivier Bernet   DES Marisa Musy   ED Stephane Roche   PROD Marc-Antoine Robert, Xavier Rigault   DIST Optimum Releasing

66 Any stragglers still unconvinced that animation can be an exciting medium for both adults and kids will run out of arguments in the face of Persepolis. – *Lisa Nesselson, Variety*

66 Full of warmth and surprise, alive with humour and a fierce independence of spirit. – *A.O. Scott, New York Times*

† Joint winner of the Jury Prize at the 2007 Cannes Film Festival.
† A dubbed version featuring Gena Rowlands, Sean Penn and Iggy Pop was released in English-speaking territories.
🏆 animated feature

Persona ★★★

SCR/DIR *Ingmar Bergman*
1966 81m Sweden
DVD

☆ *Liv Ullmann* (Actress Elisabeth Vogler), *Bibi Andersson* (Nurse Alma), Margaretha Krook (Dr. Lakaren), Gunnar Björnstrand (Mr. Vogler)

A nurse begins to identify with her mentally ill patient, a stage actress, and herself has a nervous breakdown.

Intense clinical study presented in a complex, hallucinatory manner which complements but also obscures the main theme. An audacious, fascinating experiment; opinions about its effectiveness tend to polarise.

CIN Sven Nykvist   MUS Lars Johan Werle   ED Ulla Ryghe   PROD Lars-Owe Carlberg   DIST Svensk Filmindustri

66 Reactions have ranged from incomprehension to irritation with what is dismissed as a characteristic piece of self-indulgence on Bergman's part – Bergman talking to himself again. – *David Wilson, Monthly Film Bulletin*

66 A puzzling, obsessive film that Bergman seems not so much to have worked out as to have torn from himself. – *New Yorker, 1977*

Personal Velocity: Three Portraits ★

SCR/DIR Rebecca Miller
2001　86m　US
[DVD]

☆ Jon Ventimiglia (Narrator), Kyra Sedgwick (Delia), David Warshofsky (Kurt), Brian Tarantina (Pete), Parker Posey (Greta), Tim Guinee (Lee), Wallace Shawn (Mr Gelb), Joel de la Fuente (Thavi), Fairuza Balk (Paula), Lou Taylor Pucci (Kevin), Seth Gilliam (Vincent), David Patrick Kelly (Peter), Patti D'Urbanville (Celia)

Three short films about women facing big decisions: One leaves her abusive husband, another faces up to fidelity issues, and a third picks up a hitchhiker, but pays a price for her charitable deed.

This was adapted by director Miller from her own short stories, and the literary source of these stories is evident. All of them are tasteful, literate and plodding to varying degrees, and none of them leaps from the screen; Miller may well have done better to find an objective collaborator at some stage.

CIN Ellen Kuras　MUS Michael Rohaytn　DES Judy Becker　ED Sabine Hoffman　PROD Gary Winick, Lemore Syvan, Alexis Alexanian　DIST Optimum

66 I just wish a ruthless editor had been let loose on this script before it was made into a film, which frankly, fails to deliver the goods. – *Jonathan Ross, Daily Mirror*

66 This isn't a movie – it's an author in love with the sound of her own voice. – *Ty Burr, Boston Globe*

† The film won the Grand Jury prize at Sundance in 2002.

'It's never too late for true love.'

Persuasion ★★★

DIR Roger Michell
1995　107m　GB
[DVD]

☆ Amanda Root (Anne Elliot), Ciaran Hinds (Captain Wentworth), Susan Fleetwood (Lady Russell), Corin Redgrave (Sir Walter Elliot), Fiona Shaw (Mrs. Croft), John Woodvine (Admiral Croft), Samuel West (Mr. Elliot), Phoebe Nicholls (Elizabeth Elliot), Judy Cornwell (Mrs. Musgrove)

A young woman is persuaded not to accept a marriage proposal from a dashing but cash-strapped naval officer; years later, with her own family in dire financial straits, she gets another chance to revive the romance.

BBC period drama, with all the customary virtues: consistently good acting and attractive visuals within a modest budget. This film also benefits from Michell's insistence on dirty realism: muddy hems, no wigs, minimal make-up, and clothes rather than 'costumes'. He also brings the story home at a brisk 90 minutes, when it could have stretched to five episodes; that the film still feels rich and complete says much for screenwriter Dear's skilled, witty adaptation.

SCR Nick Dear　CIN John Daly　MUS Jeremy Sams
DES William Dudley, Brian Sykes　ED Kate Evans
PROD Fiona Finlay　DIST BBC-TV/WGBH/Boston and Millesime/France2

---

66 Literate, sophisticated, bitingly funny, it's a Cinderella romance so delicious you want it never to end. – *Kenneth Turan, Los Angeles Times*

† The film was originally made for BBC television, and broadcast in 1995, but given a cinema release in the rest of the world..

'Her voice became his passion. Her love became his obsession. Her refusal became his rage. . .'

The Phantom of the Opera

DIR Joel Schumacher
2004　143m　GB/US
[DVD]　♫

☆ Gerard Butler (The Phantom), Emmy Rossum (Christine Daae), Patrick Wilson (Raoul de Chagny), Miranda Richardson (Madame Giry), Minnie Driver (Carlotta), Simon Callow (André), Ciaran Hinds (Firmin)

A disfigured music lover, who has a lair beneath the Opera Populaire in Paris, is smitten by a young girl singer. When she rebuffs his advances in favour of another man, he abducts her.

The most hotly anticipated of all the filmed versions of this story, this adaptation of the phenomenally successful stage musical crashes to earth like the chandelier in its most famous scene. One sees the logic in casting virtual unknowns in the lead roles – the play's the thing, after all – but Schumacher fails to establish why any of them got the job. The singing is adequate at best, so for want of anything better to do, one ends up looking at the garish sets and costumes. A massively misjudged effort.

SCR Andrew Lloyd Webber, Joel Schumacher　CIN John Mathieson　DES Anthony Pratt　ED Terry Rawlings
PROD Andrew Lloyd Webber　DIST Warner

66 This most expensive and lavish of Phantoms is the least felt, least impressive of them all. – *Kim Newman, Sight & Sound*

66 So lifeless and soulless it's almost scary, with actors who glide slowly around, warbling away in their silly outfits, as if being towed on roller-skates. – *Peter Bradshaw, Guardian*

♪ John Mathieson; art direction; Andrew Lloyd Webber (m), Charles Hart (ly) (music – song Learn to be Lonely)

'No One Would Take On His Case. . .Until One Man Was Willing To Take On The System.'

Philadelphia ★★

DIR Jonathan Demme
1993　125m　US
[DVD]　♫

☆ Tom Hanks (Andrew Beckett), Denzel Washington (Joe Miller), Jason Robards (Charles Wheeler), Mary Steenburgen (Belinda Conine), Antonio Banderas (Miguel Alvarez), Ron Vawter (Bob Seidman), Robert Ridgely (Walter Kenton), Charles Napier (Judge Garnett), Joanne Woodward (Sarah Beckett)

An openly gay lawyer with AIDS is suddenly sacked for having an attitude problem, but suspects the truth lies elsewhere and sues his firm for unfair dismissal. In court, the dying man is represented by

---

P

[DVD] Available on DVD　☆ Cast in order　66 Critics' Quotes　⚊ Academy Award　Ⓑ BAFTA
♫ Soundtrack on CD　of importance　† Points of interest　⚊ Academy Award nomination　Ⓣ BAFTA nomination

485

a lawyer who dislikes the gay lifestyle but stand up for justice.

Stirring courtroom drama about a brave man confronting discrimination. A fine central performance from Hanks in a breakthrough film – the first major Hollywood movie to tackle the subject of Aids. Yet it feels de-fanged – a treatment of gay life made acceptable for suburbanites. Thus there seems to be alarmingly little passion between Hanks's Beckett and his smouldering boy-friend Miguel. A laudable effort, sunk by its own timidity.

SCR Ron Nyswaner CIN Tak Fujimoto MUS Howard Shore DES Kristi Zea ED Craig McKay PROD Edward Saxon, Jonathan Demme DIST TriStar/Clinca Estetico

66 In terms of the ugly, debilitating truth about AIDS, or in terms of homosexual life – both of which this movie purports to portray – Philadelphia is lost and floating somewhere on the far side of Pluto. – *Washington Post*

66 For all its weaker aspects it is to be recommended as a denunciation of intolerance made with understanding, compassion and some honour. – *Angie Errigo, Empire*

⚱ Tom Hanks (leading actor); Bruce Springsteen (m/ly song 'Streets of Philadelphia')

⚱ Ron Nyswaner (original screenplay); Neil Young (m/ly song 'Philadelphia'); Carl Fullerton, Alan D'Angerio (make up)

Ⓣ Ron Nyswaner (original screenplay)

'Uncle Leo's bedtime story for you older tots! The things they do among the playful rich – oh, boy!'

The Philadelphia Story ★★★★

DIR *George Cukor*

1940 112m US

DVD

☆ *Katharine Hepburn* (Tracy Lord), *Cary Grant* (C.K. Dexter Haven), *James Stewart* (Macauley Connor), *Ruth Hussey* (Elizabeth Imbrie), *Roland Young* (Uncle Willie), *John Halliday* (Seth Lord), *Mary Nash* (Margaret Lord), *Virginia Weidler* (Dinah Lord), *John Howard* (George Kittredge), *Henry Daniell* (Sidney Kidd)

A stuffy heiress, about to be married for the second time, turns human and considers returning gratefully to husband number one.

Hollywood's most wise and sparkling comedy, with a script which is even an improvement on the original play. Cukor's direction is so discreet you can hardly sense it, and all the performances are just perfect.

SCR *Donald Ogden Stewart* CIN Joseph Ruttenberg MUS *Franz Waxman* ED Frank Sullivan PROD Joseph L. Mankiewicz DIST MGM

66 There are just not enough superlatives sufficiently to appreciate this show. – *Hollywood Reporter*

† Cary Grant donated his salary to war relief.

⚱ Donald Ogden Stewart (original screenplay); James Stewart (leading actor)

⚱ picture; George Cukor; Katharine Hepburn (leading actress); Ruth Hussey (supporting actress)

'Your life is on the line.'

Phone Booth ★★

DIR Joel Schumacher

2002 81m US

DVD ♫

☆ Colin Farrell (Stu Shepard), Kiefer Sutherland (The Caller), Forest Whitaker (Captain Ramey), Radha Mitchell (Kelly Shepard), Katie Holmes (Pamela McFadden), Richard T. Jones (Sergeant Cole)

A cocky public relations man is cornered in a New York telephone booth by a sniper who threatens to kill him if he hangs up.

It engenders a real sense of being trapped in a confined space, even in outdoors Manhattan. Farrell plays frustration and dismay to the hilt; but even with a short running time, the film's central gimmick does not quite sustain itself to the end.

SCR Larry Cohen CIN Matthew Libatique MUS Harry Gregson-Williams DES Andrew Laws ED Mark Stevens PROD Gil Netter, David Zucker DIST TCF

66 What gives the film a special interest is the way the phone kiosk becomes a cross between a glass coffin and a confessional. – *Philip French, Observer*

'Faith in chaos.'

Pi ★

SCR/DIR Darren Aronofsky

1998 84m US

DVD ♫

☆ Sean Gullette (Maximillian Cohen), Mark Margolis (Sol Robeson), Ben Shenkman (Lenny Meyer), Pamela Hart (Marcy Dawson), Stephen Pearlman (Rabbi Cohen), Samia Shoaib (Devi)

An obsessive mathematician and computer genius searches for a number that will explain the universe, and finds himself pursued by ruthless Wall Street traders and religious fanatics.

A clever but fatiguing film that renders the hero's warped, compulsive view of the world in images that are designed to disorientate. It's a shortish film that feels far longer.

CIN Matthew Libatique MUS Clint Mansell DES Matthew Marraffi ED Oren Sarch PROD Eric Watson DIST Live Entertainment/Truth & Soul/Harvest/Plantain/Protozoa

66 As smart as it is, Pi is awfully hard to watch. Filmed with hand-held cameras in splotchy black and white and crudely edited, it has the style and attitude of a no-budget midnight movie. – *Stephen Holden, New York Times*

'Music was his passion. Survival was his masterpiece.'

The Pianist ★★★

DIR Roman Polanski

2002 150m France/Poland/Germany/GB/US

DVD ♫

☆ *Adrien Brody* (Wladyslaw Szpilman), Thomas Kretschmann (Captain Wilm Hosenfeld), Frank Finlay (The Father), Maureen Lipman (The Mother), Emilia Fox (Dorota), Ed Stoppard (Henryk), Julia Rayner (Regina), Jessica Kate Meyer (Halina), Ruth Platt (Janina)

A talented pianist flees the Warsaw ghetto after his family is rounded up, and attempts to stay out of the hands of the Nazis.

A vivid Holocaust movie that shows up the 'directedness' of Schindler's List by sticking closely to Szpilman's first-person perspective; no museum piece, it is instead a living, breathing, haunting experience, shot through with omissions, elisions, and nagging details which refuse to be tidied up easily and thus carry an inherent aura of truth about them. The film's Babelian mix of languages and accents is a minor weakness, but it's a film where the words spoken mean so much less than the sounds heard and the sights seen: what use have we for words when faced with such indescribable horror?

SCR *Ronald Harwood*   CIN *Pawel Edelman*
MUS *Wojciech Kilar*   DES *Allan Starski*   ED Hervé de Luze   PROD Roman Polanski, Roman Benmussa, Alain Sarde   DIST Pathé

66 Polanski's strongest and most personally felt movie. – *Peter Rainer, New York Magazine*

66 Never before has a fiction film so clearly and to such devastating effect laid out the calculation of the Nazi machinery of death, and its irrationality. – *Manohla Dargis, Los Angeles Times*

† The film won the Palme D'Or at the 2002 Cannes film festival.

† The Pianist may be the most heavily-awarded film in history. Apart from its three Oscars, it won 43 awards and was nominated for 42 others.

⚊ Adrien Brody (leading actor); Roman Polanski (direction); Ronald Harwood (adapted screenplay)

⚊ picture; Pawel Edelman; Anna B. Sheppard (costume design); Hervé de Luze

Ⓣ film; Roman Polanski (direction)

Ⓣ Adrien Brody (leading actor); Wojciech Kilar; Pawel Edelman; Ronald Harwood (adapted screenplay); sound

The Piano   ★★★

SCR/DIR *Jane Campion*
1992   121m   Australia/France
DVD   ♫

☆ *Holly Hunter* (Ada McGrath), *Harvey Keitel* (George Baines), Sam Neill (Stewart), *Anna Paquin* (Fiona McGrath), Kerry Walker (Aunt Morag), Genevieve Lemon (Nessie), Tungia Baker (Hira), Ian Mune (Reverend)

A mute Scottish woman arrives with her daughter in 19th century New Zealand for an arranged marriage to a local landowner, only to have to enter into negotiations with a half-Maori settler to retrieve her beloved piano from the beach.

Unusual period piece that combines music, imagery and performance in ways that are tremendously atmospheric; for its otherworldly seriousness, the film could be (and has been) easily mocked, and the interiority of its characters means it remains a romance easier to admire from distance than to embrace wholeheartedly. But there are grand passions beneath its starkly beautiful surface, of a kind the cinema had scarcely witnessed before.

CIN *Stuart Dryburgh*   MUS *Michael Nyman*   DES *Andrew McAlpine*   ED Veronika Jenet   PROD Jan Chapman
DIST Entertainment/CIBY 2000/Jan Chapman

66 The Piano plays itself with such contrapuntal richness, it resonates in you forever. – *Desson Thomson, Washington Post*

66 One of those rare movies that is not just about a story, or some characters, but about a whole universe of feeling. – *Roger Ebert, Chicago Sun-Times*

† The film shared the Palme d'Or as best film at Cannes in 1993; Campion became the first female film-maker to win the award. Hunter won the award for best actress.

⚊ Holly Hunter (leading actress); Anna Paquin (supporting actress); Jane Campion (original screenplay)

⚊ picture; Jane Campion (direction); Stuart Dryburgh; Veronika Jenet; Janet Patterson (costume design)

Ⓣ Holly Hunter (leading actress); Andrew McAlpine; Janet Patterson (costume design)

Ⓣ film; Stuart Dryburgh; Veronika Jenet; Michael Nyman; Jane Campion (original screenplay); Jane Campion (direction); sound

The Piano Teacher   ★★★

SCR/DIR *Michael Haneke*
2001   131m   France/Austria
DVD   ♫

☆ *Isabelle Huppert* (Erika Kohut), *Annie Girardot* (The Mother), *Benoit Magimel* (Walter Klemmer), Anna Sigalevitch (Anna Schober), Susanne Lothar (Mrs Schober), Udo Samel (Dr Blonskij)

A professor at the Viennese Conservatory, repressed for years under the roof of her demanding mother, enters into a sado-masochistic relationship with a boyish student.

Bravura adaptation of a tough, uncompromising novel. Haneke uses the film as a high-brow particle collision chamber, smashing together notions of high and low culture, denial and gratification, youth and maturity: it is inevitable that somebody gets hurt, and that the audience leaves reeling, but this is cinema at its most rigorous and serious-minded.

CIN Christian Berger   MUS Francis Haines
DES Christoph Kanter   ED Monika Willi, Nadine Muse
PROD Veit Heiduschka   DIST Artificial Eye

66 A film experience that those with a strong stomach should not miss. – *Alexander Walker, Evening Standard*

66 Seems less like a fictional story than a tour through Freud's forgotten files. – *Ann Hornaday, Washington Post*

† Huppert and Magimel won the top acting awards at the Cannes Film Festival in 2001.

Ⓣ film not in the English language

'How the law took a chance on a B-girl. . .and won!'

Pickup on South Street   ★★★

SCR/DIR *Samuel Fuller*
1953   80m   US
DVD

☆ *Richard Widmark* (Skip McCoy), Jean Peters (Candy), *Thelma Ritter* (Moe), Richard Kiley (Joey), Murvyn Vye (Captain Dan Tiger)

P

DVD Available on DVD   ☆ Cast in order of importance   66 Critics' Quotes   ⚊ Academy Award / Academy Award nomination   Ⓣ BAFTA / BAFTA nomination   ♫ Soundtrack on CD   † Points of interest

487

A pickpocket steals a young woman's purse on the New York subway, discovers micro-film, and becomes embroiled in a Soviet espionage plot.

Director Fuller lobbed this grenade of a B-movie at the height of the McCarthyite era and anti-Communist witch-hunts in America. Intriguingly, it stays neutral in terms of its political allegiances, though it casts a wry gaze at those willing to see evidence of the Red Menace everywhere. Apart from that, it benefits from a neat premise and a fine performance from the reliably excellent Widmark.

CIN Joe MacDonald   **MUS** Leigh Harline   **ED** Nick de Maggio   **PROD** Jules Schermer   **DIST** TCF

† Remade 1968 as Capetown Affair.

⚰ Thelma Ritter (supporting actress)

'A recollection of evil. . .'

Picnic at Hanging Rock ★★★

DIR *Peter Weir*

1975   115m   Australia

DVD

☆ Rachel Roberts (Mrs. Appleyard), Dominic Guard (Michael Fitzhubert), Helen Morse (Dianne De Poiters), Jacki Weaver (Minnie), Vivean Gray (Miss Greta McGraw), Kirsty Child (Dora Lumley)

In 1900, schoolgirls set out with a teacher for a picnic at an aboriginal sacred site; three of them disappear and are never found.

A genuinely tantalising film that brushes up against supernatural elements but offers no resolution to its central mystery. It certainly alludes to white colonialism, and its atmosphere evokes burgeoning sexuality, but its 'meaning' remains an open question – a factor that burnishes its mystique.

SCR Cliff Green   **CIN** Russell Boyd   **MUS** Bruce Smeaton   **ED** Max Lemon   **PROD** Hal and Jim McElroy   **DIST** Picnic Productions/Australia Film Corporation

❝ Atmospherically vivid, beautifully shot, and palpably haunting. – *Michael Billington, Illustrated London News*

❝ If this film had a rational and tidy conclusion, it would be a good deal less interesting. But as a tantalizing puzzle, a tease, a suggestion of forbidden answer just out of earshot, it works hypnotically and very nicely indeed. – *Roger Ebert*

† Those expected Weir's 'director's cut' in 1998 to reveal the film's central mystery were disappointed: it adds no material, and is actually eight minutes shorter.

Ⓣ Russell Boyd

'She's the one in every family.'

Pieces of April ★

SCR/DIR Peter Hedges

2003   80m   US

DVD   ♫

☆ Katie Holmes (April Burns), *Patricia Clarkson* (Joy Burns), Oliver Platt (Jim Burns), Derek Luke (Bobby), Alison Pill (Beth Burns), John Gallagher Jnr (Timmy Burns), Alice Drummond (Grandma Dottie)

A rebellious young woman of changeable moods tries to reach out to her dysfunctional family –

including her mother, who is terminally ill – by preparing them Thanksgiving dinner.

An acid little comedy, with Clarkson sweeping all before her as the cold-hearted, cancer-stricken mother. It includes insightful glimpses about the ease with which blood relations, no matter how distant, can instantly rub each other up the wrong way, especially over a meal that turns out to be heroically disastrous.

CIN Tami Reiker   **MUS** Stephin Merritt   **DES** Rick Butler   **ED** Mark Livolsi   **PROD** John Lyons, Gary Winick, Alexis Alexanian   **DIST** Optimum

❝ (Writer/director) Peter Hedges's intelligent and touching farce makes an important contribution to a small and insignificant subgenre: Thanksgiving Day failure. – *Elvis Mitchell, New York Times*

⚰ Patricia Clarkson

Pierrepoint ★

DIR Adrian Shergold

2005   90m   GB/US

DVD

☆ *Timothy Spall* (Albert Pierrepoint), Juliet Stevenson (Annie Pierrepoint), Cavan Clerkin (George Cooper), Eddie Marsan (James 'Tish' Corbitt)

A grocery deliveryman, following in his family's footsteps, becomes Britain's last public hangman,

Striking biopic based on the story of Albert Pierrepoint, who executed some 600 people in a quarter of a century. It's completely Spall's show; he gives an internal performance, appropriate for a man unable to talk shop casually. Stevenson gives sterling support as his pursed-lipped wife, and the action, again fittingly, takes place in a permanent dusk-like gloom.

SCR Jeff Pope, Bob Mills   **CIN** Danny Cohen   **MUS** Martin Phipps   **DES** Candida Otton   **ED** Tania Reddin   **PROD** Christine Langan   **DIST** Lionsgate

❝ Grim and disturbing yet perversely riveting. – *Ruthe Stein, San Francisco Chronicle*

Ⓣ Christine Langan (newcomer)

'Things that make the heart beat faster.'

The Pillow Book ★

SCR/DIR Peter Greenaway

1995   126m   GB/Netherlands/France/Luxemburg

DVD   ♫

☆ Vivian Wu (Nagiko), Yoshi Oida (The Publisher), Ken Ogata (The Father), Hideko Yoshida (The Aunt / The Maid), Ewan McGregor (Jerome), Judy Ongg (The Mother), Ken Mitsuishi (The Husband)

A Japanese woman who invites her lovers to write on her naked form vows revenge on the publisher who abused her father and her current beau.

A brainiac's rather sterile idea of exotica, ultimately, though one which gains in interest from some state-of-the-art montage techniques, and its director's willingness to experiment with diverse narrative and musical forms.

CIN Sacha Vierny   **DES** Wilbert van Dorp, Andree Putman, Noriyuki Tanaka, Hiroto Oonogi, Willemijn Loivers, Koichi Hamamura   **ED** *Chris Wyatt, Peter*

Greenaway **PROD** Kees Kasander **DIST** Film Four/Kasander & Wigman/Alpha/Woodline

66 The film is best watched as a richly sensual stylistic exercise filled with audaciously beautiful imagery, captivating symmetries and brilliantly facile tricks. – *Janet Maslin, The New York Times*

66 For all its desperate fashion and layered imagery, it's a staggering bore – as vacantly petulant as Kate Moss's stare. – *J. Hoberman, Village Voice*

'Out of a dream world into yours!'

Pinocchio ★★★★

DIR Hamilton Luske, Ben Sharpsteen
1940 77m US
DVD ♫

☆ voices of: Dickie Jones (Pinocchio), Christian Rub (Geppetto), *Cliff Edwards* (Jiminy Cricket), Evelyn Venable (The Blue Fairy), Walter Catlett (J. Worthington Foulfellow), Frankie Darro (Lampwick)

The blue fairy breathes life into a puppet, which has to prove itself before it can turn into a real boy.

Charming, fascinating, superbly organized and streamlined cartoon feature without a single second of boredom.

DIST Walt Disney

66 A film of amazing detail and brilliant conception. – *Leonard Maltin*

66 A work that gives you almost every possible kind of pleasure to be got from a motion picture. – *Richard Mallett, Punch*

† 'When You Wish Upon A Star'; 'Give a Little Whistle'; 'Hi-Diddle-Dee-Dee (An Actor's Life for Me)'; 'I've Got No Strings'

⚐ Leigh Harline, Ned Washington, Paul J. Smith; Leigh Harline (m), Ned Washington (ly) (music, original song – When You Wish Upon a Star)

'Prepare to be blown out of the water.'

Pirates of the Caribbean: The Curse of the Black Pearl ★

DIR Gore Verbinski
2003 143m US
DVD ♫

☆ Johnny Depp (Jack Sparrow), Geoffrey Rush (Barbossa), Orlando Bloom (Will Turner), Keira Knightley (Elizabeth Swann), Jack Davenport (Norrington), Kevin R. McNally (Joshamee Gibbs), Zoe Saldana (Anamaria), Jonathan Pryce (Governor Weatherby Swann)

An eccentric pirate rushes to the rescue when the British governor's daughter is kidnapped by his former shipmates.

Enjoyable action adventure, based on a Disney theme-park ride, barely has a coherent plot but still hits the spot – especially as Depp's Jack Sparrow, in this first film of the franchise, has the advantage of surprise. His mascara-lidded, swaggering, Cockney pirate, a rock star by any other name, is a truly original creation.

SCR Ted Elliott, Terry Rossio **CIN** Dariusz Wolski
MUS Klaus Badelt **DES** Brian Morris **ED** Craig Wood,

Stephen Rivkin, Arthur Schmidt **PROD** Jerry Bruckheimer
DIST Buena Vista

66 Audiences aren't cajoled into feeling they should be having fun; they simply are having fun because the movie is too. – *Alan Morrison, Empire*

66 Letting any other actor run wild like this could have been a disaster, but Depp's peculiar buccaneer is an instant classic of actorly charisma. – *Jami Bernard, New York Daily News*

† The film took $305 million at the US box-office and a further $348 million in other territories.

⚐ Johnny Depp (leading actor); John Knoll, Hal T. Hickel, Charles Gibson, Terry D. Frazee (visual effects); Ve Neill, Martin Samuel (makeup); Christopher Boyes, David Parker, David E. Campbell, Lee Orloff (sound); Christopher Boyes, George Watters II (sound editing)

ⓑ makeup
ⓣ Johnny Depp (leading actor); Penny Rose (costume design); Christopher Boyes, David Parker, David E. Campbell, Lee Orloff (sound); John Knoll, Hal T. Hickel, Charles Gibson, Terry D. Frazee (visual effects)

'Seldom has the screen so captured the fire and fever of today's youth! Seldom has a film boasted three such exciting star performances!'

A Place in the Sun ★★

DIR *George Stevens*
1951 122m US
DVD

☆ Montgomery Clift, Elizabeth Taylor, Shelley Winters, Anne Revere, Keefe Brasselle, Fred Clark, Raymond Burr, Frieda Inescort, Shepperd Strudwick, Kathryn Givney, Walter Sande

A poor young man, offered the chance of a rich wife, allows himself to be convicted and executed for the accidental death of his former fiancée.

Serious-minded adaptation of a classic American novel, and all too often trying to impress its importance on the audience. Yet it is beautifully crafted, with striking photography, notably when Taylor enters the frame. It fudges some of the class issues laid out by Dreiser's work, but at times it feels sumptuous.

SCR Michael Wilson, Harry Brown **CIN** *William C. Mellor*
MUS Franz Waxman **ED** William Hornbeck
DIST Paramount/George Stevens

66 An almost incredibly painstaking work. . .mannered enough for a very fancy Gothic murder mystery. This version gives the story a modern setting, but the town is an arrangement of symbols of wealth, glamour and power versus symbols of poor, drab helplessness – an arrangement far more suitable to the thirties than to the fifties. – *Pauline Kael*

⚐ script; George Stevens; William C. Mellor; Franz Waxman; editing
⚐ picture; Montgomery Clift (leading actor); Shelley Winters (leading actress)

Place Vendôme ★

DIR Nicole Garcia
1998 117m France/Belgium/GB
DVD ♫

☆ *Catherine Deneuve* (Marianne), Jean-Pierre Bacri (Jean-

| DVD | Available on DVD | ☆ | Cast in order | 66 | Critics' Quotes | ⚐ | Academy Award | ⓑ | BAFTA |
| ♫ | Soundtrack on CD | | of importance | † | Points of interest | ⚐ | Academy Award nomination | ⓣ | BAFTA nomination |

Pierre), Emmanuelle Seigner (Nathalie), Jacques Dutronc (Battistelli), Bernard Fresson (Vincent Malivert), François Berléand (Eric Malivert), Philippe Clévenot (Kleiser)

An alcoholic widow attempts to sell the jewels left by her husband, and must sober up fast to outsmart circling creditors.

Stylish French thriller (directed by a former actress) that gives Deneuve a chance to shine as a woman under pressure, trying to reclaim her sense of self-worth.

SCR Jacques Fieschi, Nicole Garcia   CIN Laurent Dailland
MUS Richard Robbins   DES Thierry Flamand   ED Luc Barnier, Francoise Bonnot, Jean-François Naudon
PROD Alain Sarde   DIST Artificial Eye

66 Catherine Deneuve plays the alcoholic widow of a debt-ridden diamond merchant and she's captivatingly seedy. – *Peter Rainer, New York Magazine*

'Steve Martin had no reason to panic...until John Candy came along.'

Planes, Trains and Automobiles ★

SCR/DIR John Hughes
1987   93m   US
DVD ♫

☆ Steve Martin (Neal Page), John Candy (Del Griffith), Michael McKean (State Trooper), Kevin Bacon (Taxi Racer), Dylan Baker (Owen), Carol Bruce (Joy Page), Olivia Burnette (Marti Page), Diana Douglas (Peg), William Windom (Bryant)

A harassed advertising executive, desperate to get home to Chicago for Thanksgiving, finds himself re-routed to Kansas and stuck with a nightmarish travelling companion – an intrusive, relentlessly cheerful salesman.

Amiable comedy, with plot obstacles provided by the erratic US transport system, that allows Martin and Candy to establish a reluctant odd-couple act.

CIN Don Peterman   MUS Ira Newborn   DES John W. Corso   ED Paul Hirsch   PROD John Hughes
DIST UIP/Paramount

66 A screwball comedy with a heart, and after the laughter is over the film has generated a lot of good feeling. – *Roger Ebert, Chicago Sun-Times*

'Humanity's last hope. . .Rests on a high-power machine gun'

Planet Terror (new) ★★

SCR/DIR Robert Rodriguez
2007   105m   US
DVD ♫

☆ Rose McGowan (Cherry Darling), Freddy Rodriguez (El Wray), Josh Brolin (Dr. William Block), Marley Shelton (Dr. Dakota Block), Jeff Fahey (J T Hague), Bruce Willis (Lt. Muldoon), Michael Biehn (Sheriff Hague), Quentin Tarantino (Rapist No. 1), Naveen Andrews (Abby)

In a Texas town, a ragtag group of survivors, including a one-legged go-go dancer, battle armies of flesh-eaters, damaged by the government's chemical experiments.

An expert recreation of over-the-top grindhouse artlessness using grimy sex, showcase splatter, hard-hitting stereotypes, explosive action for its own sake and

dubious sensationalism to comment on the exploitation genre while cleverly lampooning it. Complete with a missing reel, burns, jumps and scratches.

CIN Robert Rodriguez   MUS Graeme Revell, Carl Thiel
DES Steve Joyner   ED Robert Rodriguez, Ethan Maniquis
PROD Robert Rodriguez, Elizabeth Avellan, Quentin Tarantino   DIST Momentum Pictures

66 Rodriguez's devil-may-care style embraces the spirit of trash rather than trying to embalm it, and the random frenzy he unleashes is ridiculously gory and very funny. – *Tim Robey, Daily Telegraph*

† In the US, the film was released as part of a 'grindhouse' double bill with Death Proof.

'The first casualty of war is innocence.'

Platoon ★★★

SCR/DIR *Oliver Stone*
1986   120m   US
DVD ♫

☆ Tom Berenger, Willem Dafoe, Charlie Sheen, Forest Whitaker, Francesco Quinn

New arrivals replace infantrymen wounded or killed in the Vietnam war, and undergo a tour of duty.

Written and directed by a man who had seen active service combat in Vietnam, this is effectively a battle of wills between two hardened soldiers (Berenger and Dafoe) for the soul of a young recruit (Sheen, more or less an Oliver Stone surrogate). A tense, effective drama, it was a box-office hit in America, where the public may have been finally ready to consider the war's legacy.

CIN *Robert Richardson*   MUS Georges Delerue
ED Claire Simpson   DIST Hemdale

⚊ picture; Oliver Stone (direction); Claire Simpson
⚊ Tom Berenger (supporting actor); Willem Dafoe (supporting actor); Oliver Stone (original screenplay); Robert Richardson

Ⓣ Oliver Stone (direction)

'Making movies can be murder.'

The Player ★★★

DIR *Robert Altman*
1992   124m   US
DVD ♫

☆ Tim Robbins (Griffin Mill), Greta Scacchi (June Gudmundsdottir), Fred Ward (Walter Stuckel), Whoopi Goldberg (Detective Avery), Peter Gallagher (Larry Levy), Brion James (Joel Levison), Cynthia Stevenson (Bonnie Sherow), Vincent D'Onofrio (David Kahane), Dean Stockwell (Andy Civella), Richard E. Grant (Tom Oakley), Sydney Pollack (Dick Mellen)

A Hollywood studio executive is plagued by threatening missives from a disgruntled writer, and is driven to murder.

Clever satire on the movie business, garlanded with star cameos and all its director's considerable filmmaking savvy – though subsequent Oscar nods would suggest the showbiz community didn't take its line of attack too personally.

SCR *Michael Tolkin*   CIN *Jean Lepine*   MUS *Thomas Newman*   DES Stephen Altman   ED Geraldine Peroni,

Maysie Hoy **PROD** David Brown, Michael Tolkin, Nick Wechsler **DIST** Guild/Avenue

66 Combines intelligence, wit, drama, humour and downright brilliance to such winning effect that, even for the man who has given us M*A*S*H, Nashville and Thieves Like Us, this could well be the crowning glory of a remarkable career. – *Philip Thomas, Empire*

66 The film is sublime entertainment, at once ticklish and suspenseful, cynical and sincere. By its very existence, Altman's comedy about the death of Hollywood lets you know that movies are still alive and kicking. – *Owen Gleiberman, Entertainment Weekly*

† Amongst the stars playing themselves are Bruce Willis, Julia Roberts, Burt Reynolds, Susan Sarandon, John Cusack, Nick Nolte, Harry Belafonte, James Coburn, Peter Falk, Teri Garr, Angelica Huston, Rod Steiger and Jack Lemmon.

🎖 Robert Altman (direction); Michael Tolkin (adapted screenplay); Geraldine Peroni

🏆 Robert Altman (direction); Michael Tolkin (adapted screenplay)

Ⓣ film; Tim Robbins (leading actor); Geraldine Peroni

'Nothing is as simple as black and white.'

Pleasantville ★★★

SCR/DIR Gary Ross
1998   124m   US
DVD   ♫

☆ *Tobey Maguire* (David), *Jeff Daniels* (Bill Johnson), *Joan Allen* (Betty Parker), William H. Macy (George Parker), J. T. Walsh (Big Bob), Don Knotts (TV Repairman), Reese Witherspoon (Jennifer)

A teenage boy and his sister, fighting over the TV remote, are sucked back through the screen into becoming characters on a black-and-white 1950s sitcom.

A genuinely smart fantasy comedy that makes brilliant use of its switch between monochrome and colour, but also has wise insights about selective nostalgia, tolerance of others, sexual oppressiveness, philistinism and the decline of deference. Yet even on a light-hearted adventure level, it works a treat.

CIN John Lindley   **MUS** Randy Newman   **DES** Jeannine Oppewall   **ED** William Goldenberg   **PROD** Gary Ross, Jon Kilik, Robert J. Degus, Steven Soderbergh   **DIST** New Line/Larger Than Life

66 Overcomes its moralising and occasional pomposity with magical photographic effects. – *Andrew O'Hehir, Sight and Sound*

66 The kind of parable that encourages us to re-evaluate the good old days and take a fresh look at the new world we so easily dismiss as decadent. – *Roger Ebert, Chicago Sun-Times*

🎖 Randy Newman; Jeannine Oppewall; Judianna Makovsky (costume design)

'Detective Jerry Black has made a promise he can't break, to catch a killer he can't find.'

The Pledge ★★

DIR *Sean Penn*
2000   123m   US
DVD   ♫

☆ *Jack Nicholson* (Jerry Black), Patricia Clarkson (Margaret

Larsen), Benicio Del Toro (Toby Jay Wadenah), Dale Dickey (Strom), Aaron Eckhart (Stan Krolak), Costas Mandylor (Monash Deputy), Helen Mirren (Doctor), Robin Wright Penn (Lori), Vanessa Redgrave (Annalise Hansen), Mickey Rourke (Jim Olstand), Sam Shepard (Eric Pollack), Lois Smith (Helen Jackson), Harry Dean Stanton (Floyd Cage)

On the day of his retirement, a detective makes a pledge to a grieving mother that he will find the killer of her child.

A sombre and serious work which often feels like a film in perpetual slow-motion, labouring under the dramatic and philosophical weight of its source material; worth seeing, though, for the extraordinary performance Penn digs out of an actor threatening to coast through the rest of his career.

SCR *Jerzy Kromolowski, Mary Olson-Kromolowski*
CIN Chris Menges   **MUS** Hans Zimmer, Klaus Badelt
DES Bill Groom   **ED** Jay Cassidy   **PROD** Michael Fitzgerald, Sean Penn, Elie Samaha   **DIST** Warner

66 Not a pleasant film, but it is deeply, scarily rewarding. – *Stephen Holden, The New York Times*

66 A rare thriller – and a rare American film – that centres on both dramatic and moral issues, crises of confidence. And thanks to a superb central performance, it's a film that compels, thrills and ends up coming very close to tragedy. – *Michael Wilmington, Chicago Tribune*

Point Blank ★

DIR *John Boorman*
1967   92m   US

☆ Lee Marvin, Angie Dickinson, Keenan Wynn, Carroll O'Connor, Lloyd Bochner, Michael Strong, John Vernon, Sharon Acker

In Los Angeles, a criminal is cheated out of money by his wife and mobsters, and he goes to extraordinary lengths to retrieve it.

Violent gangster thriller, stunningly shot on location and showing sides of the city rarely seen on film. Its cult reputation has endured, largely because of its fragmented atmosphere and its convincing sense of unease and angst. Marvin lands the role of his career as an unstoppable force of nature.

SCR Alexander Jacobs, David Newhouse, Rafe Newhouse
CIN *Philip Lathrop*   **MUS** Johnny Mandel
DIST MGM/Judd Bernard, Irwin Winkler

66 The fragmentation was necessary to give the characters and the situation ambiguity, to suggest another meaning beyond the immediate plot. – *John Boorman*

† It was re-made in 1999 as Payback.

'Every Friendship Has Its Limits. Every Man Has His Breaking Point. Together They Take Adventure Past The Point Of No Return.'

Point Break ★★

DIR Kathryn Bigelow
1991   120m   US
DVD   ♫

☆ Patrick Swayze (Bodhi), Keanu Reeves (FBI Special Agent John 'Johnny' Utah), Gary Busey (FBI Agent Angelo Pappas), Lori Petty (Tyler Ann Endicott), John McGinley

---

DVD Available on DVD   ☆ Cast in order   66 Critics' Quotes   🎖 Academy Award   🏆 BAFTA
♫ Soundtrack on CD   of importance   † Points of interest   🎖 Academy Award nomination   Ⓣ BAFTA nomination

491

P

(FBI Agent Ben Harp), James Le Gros (Roach), John Philbin (Nathanial), Bojesse Christopher (Grommet), Julian Reyes (Alvarez)

An FBI agent, on the trail of a gang of bank robbers who wear presidential masks on their raids, is forced to go undercover among Californian surfers.

Enjoyable though frankly daft thriller with a preposterous plot and some risible mystical nonsense about being at one with the waves. Best to concentrate on Bigelow's shrewd handling of action scenes, and some great surfing footage.

SCR W. Peter Iliff   CIN Donald Peterman   MUS Mark Isham   DES Peter Jamison   ED Howard Smith, Burt Lovitt   PROD Peter Abrams, Robert L. Levy   DIST TCF/Largo/Tapestry

66 The hinted spirituality of the film is plainly silly, but it's quickly swallowed by the undertow of crashing spectacle. – *Nick Hilditch, BBC*

'The Film That Shocked America! Denounced As ''Obscene'' and ''Pornographic'' by the Moral Majority.'

Poison ★

SCR/DIR Todd Haynes

1990 85m US

DVD

☆ 'Hero': Edith Meeks (Felicia Beacon), Millie White (Millie Sklar), Buck Smith (Gregory Lazar), Anne Giotta (Evelyn McAlpert), Scott Renderer (John Broom), James Lyons (Jack Bolton), John R. Lombardi (Rass), Tony Pemberton (Young Broom), Andrew Harpending (Young Bolton), Tony Gigante (Inspector), Larry Maxwell (Dr. Graves), Susan Norman (Nancy Olsen), Al Quagliata (Deputy Hansen), Michelle Sullivan (Deputy Hansen)

Three separate stories: In 'Hero' a seven-year-old boy kills his father and runs away. 'Homo' features a male prison rape. 'Horror' introduces a doctor who drinks his own sex drive serum and becomes a monster.

Todd Haynes's provocative first feature shows different aspects of prejudice and stereotyping, with limited success.

CIN Maryse Alberti, Barry Ellsworth   MUS James Bennett   DES Sarah Stollman   ED James Lyons, Todd Haynes   PROD Christine Vachon   DIST Mainline/Bronze Eye

66 The acting is uneven, the lighting sometimes dim, the tone at time deliberately awkward. But this suggestive, discordant movie takes you places you haven't been. – *David Ansen, Newsweek*

66 Compelling and quirkily intelligent. – *Time Out*

'Journey Beyond Your Imagination.'

The Polar Express ★★

DIR Robert Zemeckis

2004 99m US

DVD ♫

☆ Tom Hanks (Hero Boy/Father/Conductor/Hobo/Scrooge/Santa Claus), Michael Jeter (Smokey/Steamer), Nona Gaye (Hero Girl), Peter Scolari (Lonely Boy), Eddie Deezen (Know-it-All), Charles Fleischer (Elf General), Steven Tyler (Elf Lieutenant/Elf Singer)

A sceptical boy's belief in Santa Claus is restored when he takes an extraordinary journey to the North Pole to meet him, on board a magical train.

If nothing else, a technical breakthrough, with all its sets entirely computer-generated, and its actors digitally re-created in an animation process known as 'performance capture.' The story feels over-extended, and viewed conventionally, this is an underwhelming experience. But in 3-D, it comes alive for audiences in remarkable fashion, sweeping all reservations away. Likely to be a Christmas staple at IMAX cinemas for years to come.

SCR Robert Zemeckis, William Broyles Jnr   CIN Don Burgess, Robert Presley   MUS Alan Silvestri   DES Rick Carter, Doug Chiang   ED Jeremiah O'Driscoll, R. Orlando Duenas   PROD Steve Starkey, Robert Zemeckis, Gary Goetzman, William Teitler   DIST Warner

66 This movie, which aspires to be a Christmas movie classic on the It's a Wonderful Life level, is overwhelming, enjoyable and impressive, without being really entrancing. – *Michael Wilmington, Chicago Tribune*

66 Like the coolest train set a kid ever had. It's not real and the faces on the toy people don't look human, but it has bells and whistles galore and will take you as far as your imagination allows. – *Chris Kaltenbach, Baltimore Sun*

† It cost some $165m to make and took around the same amount at the US box-office.

⚲ Glen Ballard, Alan Silvestri (m), (ly) (music – song Believe); Randy Thom, Dennis Leonard (sound editing); Randy Thom, Tom Johnson, Dennis Sands, William B. Kaplan (sound mixing)

The Polish Bride ★★

DIR Karim Traidia

1998 90m Netherlands

☆ Jaap Spijkers (Henk Woldring), Monic Hendrickx (Anna), Rudi Falkenhagen (Pimp), Roef Ragas (Son), Hakim Traidia (Postman), Soraya Traidia (Krystyna)

A cash-strapped Dutch farmer takes in a Polish prostitute, who is fleeing from her abusive pimps; she becomes his housekeeper and they fall in love.

An understated account of an implausible romance, with an impact that accumulates gradually, as if by stealth. Its austere shooting style complements these two characters, both understandably suspicious of joy entering their lives; but its emotional restraint pays off satisfyingly.

SCR Kees van de Hulst   CIN Jacques Laureys, Daniel Reeves   MUS Fons Merkies   ED Chris Teerink   PROD Marc Bary, Ilana Netiv, Jeroen Beker, Frans van Gestel   DIST Artificial Eye

---

'A True Portrait of Life and Art.'

Pollock ★★★

DIR Ed Harris

2000 122m US

DVD ♫

☆ Ed Harris (Jackson Pollock), Marcia Gay Harden (Lee Krasner), Amy Madigan (Peggy Guggenheim), Jennifer Connelly (Ruth Kligman), Jeffrey Tambor (Clement Greenberg), Bud Cort (Howard Putzel), John Heard (Tony Smith), Val Kilmer (William DeKooning)

Life story of acclaimed abstract expressionist artist Jackson Pollock, including his surrender to alcohol which led to his untimely death.

A superior biopic about an artist, one that really does try seriously to find a way of conveying the wellspring of creativity. The uncompromising Pollock is played with ferocity by Harris, and his supporting cast do the picture justice. Apart from its other virtues, the film sheds light on the bitchiness and jealousies rampant in the art world – and how some artists play the games of that world more readily than others.

SCR Barbara Turner, Susan J. Emshwiller   CIN Lisa Rinzler   MUS Jeff Beal   DES Mark Friedberg   ED Kathryn Himoff   PROD James Francis Trezza, Jon Kilik, Ed Harris   DIST Columbia TriStar

66 This is a quietly excellent movie, clearly a labour of love for (director and star, Ed) Harris, and far superior to much of the current Hollywood product. It is aimed at educated adults. – *Peter Bradshaw, The Guardian*

66 Confident, insightful work – one of the year's best films. – *Roger Ebert, Chicago Sun-Times*

⚱ Marcia Gay Harden (supporting actress)
⚱ Ed Harris (leading actor)

Ponette ★★

SCR/DIR Jacques Doillon
1996   97m   France
DVD

☆ *Victoire Thivisol* (Ponette), Marie Trintignant (The mother), Claire Nebout (The aunt), Xavier Beauvois (The father), Matiaz Bureau Caton (Matiaz), Delphine Schiltz (Delphine), Léopoldine Serre (Ada), Luckie Royer (Luce), Carla Ibled (Carla), Antoine du Merle (Antoine)

A four-year-old girl attempts to cope with her sense of loss after she is injured in a car crash that causes the death of her mother.

The uncanny performance by the young star moved many people, but was also troubling: what methods does a director employ to elicit grief from a child actress so young? Still, it's a memorable, sensitive effort.

CIN Caroline Champetier   MUS Philippe Sarde   DES Henri Berthon   ED Jacqueline Lecompte   PROD Alain Sarde   DIST Les Films Alain Sarde/Rhône-Alpes Cinéma

66 One of the most sensitive, luminous films about the young ever made. – *Kevin Thomas, Los Angeles Times*

† Victoire Thivisol, then aged 5, was named best actress at the Venice Film Festival in 1996.

The Portrait of a Lady

DIR Jane Campion
1996   144m   GB/US
DVD ♫

☆ Nicole Kidman (Isabel Archer), John Malkovich (Gilbert Osmond), Martin Donovan (Ralph Touchett), Barbara Hershey (Madame Serena Merle), Mary-Louise Parker (Henrietta Stackpole), Shelley Winters (Mrs. Touchett), Richard E. Grant (Lord Warburton), Shelley Duvall (Mrs. Touchett), Viggo Mortensen (Caspar Goodwood), Christian Bale (Edward Rosier), John Gielgud (Mr. Touchett)

Europe, the late 19th century: an American heiress is manipulated into an unhappy marriage.

Misguided attempt to deconstruct and renovate the period drama simultaneously: oddly colourless to look at, and dramatically inert, with inexplicable inserts involving talking kidney beans; a major disappointment after the director's previous The Piano, it simply doesn't work.

SCR Laura Jones   CIN Stuart Dryburgh   MUS Wojciech Kilar   DES Janet Patterson   ED Veronika Jenet   PROD Monty Montgomery, Steve Golin   DIST Polygram

66 I think if you care for James, you must see it. It is not an adaptation but an interpretation. – *Roger Ebert, Chicago Sun-Times*

66 Intelligent but exasperating, its monotonous tone will wear down even viewers who started out in its corner. – *Mike Clark, USA Today*

⚱ Barbara Hershey (supporting actress); Jane Patterson (costume design)

'The untold story of the wild west.'

Posse

DIR Mario Van Peebles
1993   111m   GB/US
DVD ♫

☆ Mario Van Peebles (Jesse Lee), Stephen Baldwin (Jimmy J. 'Little J' Teeters), Charles Lane (Weezie), Tiny Lister (Obobo (as Tiny Lister)), Big Daddy Kane (Father Time), Billy Zane (Colonel Graham), Blair Underwood (Carver), Melvin Van Peebles (Papa Joe), Tone Loc (Angel), Isaac Hayes (Cable)

In the Wild West of the 1890s, an intrepid band of black cowboys outwit the Ku Klux Klan and a racist sheriff.

A film that deserves a footnote, as the first Western with black heroes. Apart from that, this Leone-inspired adventure is strictly routine.

SCR Sy Richardson, Dario Scardapane   CIN Peter Menzies Jnr   MUS Michel Colombier   DES Catherine Hardwicke   ED Mark Conte, Seth Flaum   PROD Preston Holmes, Jim Steel   DIST Rank/Polygram/Working Title

66 A rousing entertainment directed by Van Peebles with a rare sense of purpose and mischief. – *Peter Travers, Rolling Stone*

'Having a wonderful time, wish I were here.'

Postcards from the Edge ★

DIR Mike Nichols
1990   101m   US
DVD

☆ Meryl Streep (Suzanne Vale), Shirley MacLaine (Doris Mann), Dennis Quaid (Jack Faulkner), Gene Hackman (Lowell Kolchek), Richard Dreyfuss (Doctor Frankenthal), Rob Reiner (Joe Pierce), Mary Wickes (Grandma), Conrad Bain (Grandpa), Annette Bening (Evelyn Ames), Simon Callow (Simon Asquith)

A famous actress with a drug problem is ordered by the insurers of her latest movie to stay with someone who can look after her during production. She ends up with her mother, a domineering, alcoholic film star.

DVD Available on DVD   ☆ Cast in order of importance   66 Critics' Quotes   ⚱ Academy Award   ⚱ Academy Award nomination   🅱 BAFTA   🅑 BAFTA nomination
♫ Soundtrack on CD   † Points of interest

An entertaining adaptation of Carrie Fisher's acerbic, more than semi-autobiographical novel; it lacks the book's bite, but is still shrewdly entertaining.

SCR Carrie Fisher **CIN** Michael Ballhaus **MUS** Carly Simon **DES** Patrizia von Brandenstein **ED** Sam O'Steen **PROD** Mike Nichols, John Calley **DIST** Columbia

66 Postcards From The Edge contains too much good writing and too many good performances to be a failure, but its heart is not in the right place. – *Roger Ebert Chicago Sun-Times*

Ⅹ Meryl Streep (leading actress); original song 'I'm Checkin' Out' (m/ly Shel Silverstein)

Ⓣ Carly Simon; Shirley MacLaine; (screenplay)

'A shy postman didn't stand a chance with the island's most beautiful woman until the great poet of love gave him the courage to follow his dreams. . .and the words to win her heart.'

Il Postino ★★

DIR Michael Radford
1994 108m Italy/France
DVD ♫

☆ *Massimo Troisi* (Mario Ruoppolo), Philippe Noiret (Pablo Neruda), Maria Grazia Cucinotta (Beatrice Russo), Linda Moretti (Donna Rosa), Renato Scarpa (Telegrapher)

Encouraged by the exiled Chilean poet Pablo Neruda, an Italian postman sets about winning the heart of a beautiful woman.

Gentle, sun-kissed romance, the epitome of a Miramax Films release, but at the more sincere end of its touristy genre.

SCR Anna Pavignano, Michael Radford, Furio Scarpelli, Giacomo Scarpelli, Massimo Troisi **CIN** Franco di Giacomo **MUS** Luis Enrique Bacalov **DES** Lorenzo Baraldi **ED** Roberto Perpignani **PROD** Gaetano Daniele, Vittorio Cecchi Gori, Mario Cecchi Gori **DIST** Buena Vista/Cecchi Gori/Tiger/Pentafilm/Mediterraneo/Blue Dahlia/Canal

66 A rueful, warmly affecting film featuring a wonderful performance by Mr. Troisi, The Postman would be attention-getting even without the sadness that overshadows it. – *Elvis Mitchell, New York Times*

† Massimo Troisi, who had postponed heart surgery so he could finish his work in the film, died of a heart attack within days of its completion.

Ⅹ Luis Enrique Bacalov

Ⓧ picture; Massimo Troisi (leading actor); Michael Radford; Anna Pavignano, Michael Radford, Furio Scarpelli, Giacomo Scarpelli, Massimo Troisi (adapted screenplay)

Ⓣ film not in the English language; Michael Radford; Luis Enríquez Bacalov

Ⓣ Massimo Troisi (leading actor) Anna Pavignano, Michael Radford, Furio Scarpelli, Giacomo Scarpelli, Massimo Troisi (adapted screenplay)

'It is 2013. War has crippled the Earth. Technology has been erased. Our only hope is an unlikely hero.'

The Postman

DIR Kevin Costner
1997 177m US
DVD ♫

☆ Kevin Costner (The Postman), Will Patton (General

Bethlehem), Larenz Tate (Ford Lincoln Mercury), Olivia Williams (Abby), James Russo (Idaho), Daniel von Bargen (Pineview Sheriff Briscoe), Tom Petty (Bridge City Mayor), Scott Bairstow (Luke)

In a future America desolated by war, an actor sets himself up in opposition to the ruling totalitarian forces by assuming the guise of a postman, and vowing to deliver the mail.

Waffly mix of sci-fi and Western that would almost certainly have been improved by substantial cutting; at three hours, there's no end, and very little point, to it. Return to sender.

SCR Eric Roth, Brian Helgeland **CIN** Stephen Windon **MUS** James Newton Howard **DES** Ida Random **ED** Peter Boyle, Regina Prosi-Bassman **PROD** Jim Wilson, Steve Tisch, Kevin Costner **DIST** Warner/Tig

66 A curious result, one that may or may not have an audience, but is nonetheless compelling in the heartfelt way it is presented. – *Todd McCarthy, Variety*

66 Aims for an uncomfortable compromise between the dramatic sincerity of Dances with Wolves and the epic spectacle of Waterworld, but lacks the explanatory detail and narrative fluency to achieve either. – *Nick Bradshaw, Time Out*

† The film has gone down in history as one of Hollywood's biggest ever bombs, having reportedly cost more than $100 million, but grossing just $17.6 million. It ended Costner's run as a leading man in big-budget, self-directed movies.

'Radio like you've never seen it before.'

A Prairie Home Companion ★★

DIR Robert Altman
2006 105m US
DVD ♫

☆ Garrison Keillor (Garrison Keillor), Meryl Streep (Yolanda Johnson), Lily Tomlin (Rhonda Johnson), Lindsay Lohan (Lola Johnson), Tommy Lee Jones (The Axeman), Woody Harrelson (Dusty), John C. Reilly (Lefty), Kevin Kline (Guy Noir), Virginia Madsen (The Dangerous Woman)

Frenetic comings and goings backstage as the last-ever performance of a long-running radio show, featuring country music and variety acts, gets under way.

A delectable swan song to the career of its great director; Altman died in November 2006. Minor in both key and stature, it's corny, good-natured and old-fashioned, rather like Keillor's real radio show that gives the film its title. Still, it has a decent story: the show is about to be taken over by a philistine Texas corporation and closed down. Fittingly, the shadow of death hovers gently over the story. It seems faintly shambolic, but Altman's camera drifts around backstage, peeking through curtains, nosing into nooks and crannies: a systematic way to convey information. Impeccable timing and effortless grace are the watchwords for this gentle, middlebrow delight.

SCR Garrison Keillor **CIN** Ed Lachman **MUS** Richard Dworsky **DES** Dina Goldman **ED** Jacob Craycroft **PROD** Robert Altman, Wren Arthur, Joshua Astrachan, Tony Judge, David Levy **DIST** The Works

66 What a lovely film this is, so gentle and whimsical, so simple and profound. – *Roger Ebert, Chicago Sun-Times*

A Prayer for the Dying ★

DIR Mike Hodges
1987 107m GB

☆ Mickey Rourke (Martin Fallon), Bob Hoskins (Father Michael Da Costa), Alan Bates (Jack Meehan), Sammi Davis (Anna), Christopher Fulford (Billy Meehan)

A priest agonises over whether to identify an IRA gunman who has alluded to a crime during confession, while the terrorist is torn about silencing the priest.

Somewhere in this convoluted mess may be a first-rate thriller by a talented director. But the film was re-edited against Hodges's wishes, and he disowned the released version, having tried in vain to get his name removed from the credits. It now survives as an intriguing 'what-if?'

SCR Edmund Ward, Martin Lynch **CIN** Mike Garfath **MUS** Bill Conti **DES** Evan Hurcules **ED** Peter Boyle **PROD** Peter Snell, Samuel Goldwyn Jr **DIST** Peter Snell/Samuel Goldwyn Co

'If it bleeds, we can kill it...'

Predator

DIR John McTiernan
1987 107m US
DVD ♫

☆ Arnold Schwarzenegger (Dutch), Carl Weathers (Dillon), Bill Duke (Mac), Elpidia Carrillo (Anna), Jesse Ventura (Blain)

A team of US commandos, sent to eliminate gun-running in South America, find they are being targeted by a deadly alien.

Action thriller that more or less dispenses with human interaction completely, and concentrates on chases, combat and special effects. Still, director McTiernan keeps the tension ratcheted up efficiently.

SCR Jim and John Thomas **CIN** Donald McAlpine **MUS** Alan Silvestri **DES** John Vallone **ED** John F. Link, Mark Helfrich **PROD** John Davis, Joel Silver, Lawrence Gordon **DIST** TCF/Lawrence Gordon/Joel Silver/John Davis

66 It is so lean, so exciting and so imaginative that you can watch it every month or two, year in year out, and never get tired of it. – *Douglas Pratt, Hollywood Reporter*

'Attraction. Desire. Deception. Murder. No one is ever completely innocent.'

Presumed Innocent ★★

DIR Alan J. Pakula
1990 127m US
DVD

☆ *Harrison Ford* (Rusty Sabich), Brian Dennehy (Raymond Horgan), Raul Julia (Sandy Stern), Bonnie Bedelia (Barbara Sabich), Paul Winfield (Judge Larren Lyttle), Greta Scacchi (Carolyn Polhemus), John Spencer (Det. Lipranzer), Joe Grifasi (Tommy Molto), Sab Shimono ('Painless' Kumagai), Jesse Bradford (Nat Sabich)

A successful prosecuting attorney investigates the murdering of a colleague, his ex-mistress, but comes under suspicion himself.

Glossy, confident courtroom drama with high production values; Ford is near the top of his game as the man in the dock, and the twists keep coming with reliable regularity.

SCR Frank Pierson, Alan J. Pakula **CIN** Gordon Willis **MUS** John Williams **DES** George Jenkins **ED** Evan Lottman **PROD** Sydney Pollack, Mark Rosenberg **DIST** Warner/Mirage

66 Even readers with reservations about the ways the film fails to measure up to the book should appreciate a smart, passionate, steadily engrossing thriller in a summer of mindless zap. – *Peter Travers, Rolling Stone*

'The fashion world laid bare.'

Prêt-à-Porter

DIR Robert Altman
1994 133m US
DVD

☆ Anouk Aimée (Simone Lowenthal), Lauren Bacall (Slim Chrysler), Kim Basinger (Kitty Potter), Michael Blanc (Inspector Forget), Sophia Loren (Isabella de la Fontaine), Marcello Mastroianni (Sergei/Sergio), Anne Canovas (Violetta Romney), Jean-Pierre Cassel (Isabella de la Fontaine), Rossy de Palma (Pilar), François Cluzet (Nina's Assistant), Rupert Everett (Jack Lowenthal), Teri Garr (Louise Hamilton), Richard E. Grant (Cort Romney), Sally Kellerman (Sissy Wanamaker), Ute Lemper (Albertine), Linda Hunt, Lyle Lovett, Stephen Rea, Tim Robbins, Julia Roberts, Jean Rochefort, Tracey Ullman, Forest Whitaker

Everyone in the fashion industry converges upon Paris for the most important gathering of the year – the fashion shows.

In the wake of two Robert Altman masterpieces, The Player and Short Cuts, this supposed satire of the fashion industry landed with a dull thud. It features a fabulous cast, but the coherent script this multi-strand vehicle cried out for obviously failed to arrive. Some sub-plots simply fall flat; while a few are faintly amusing, this can be written off as one of Altman's interesting failures.

SCR Robert Altman, Barbara Shulgasser **CIN** Pierre Mignot, Jean Lépine **MUS** Michel Legrand **DES** Stephen Altman **ED** Geraldine Peroni, Suzy Elmiger **PROD** Robert Altman **DIST** Buena Vista/Miramax

66 Though it credits Mr Altman and Barbara Shulgasser as writers, this film seems practically scriptless, to the point where much of it plays like a first rehearsal. – *Janet Maslin, New York Times*

66 The picture is not a social satire. It's a mess. – *Rita Kempley, Washington Post*

'Revenge knows no mercy.'

Pretty Persuasion ★

DIR Marcos Siega
2005 110m US
DVD

☆ Evan Rachel Wood (Kimberly Joyce), Ron Livingston (Percy Anderson), *James Woods* (Hank Joyce), Jane

Krakowski (Emily Klein), Elisabeth Harnois (Brittany), Selma Blair (Grace Anderson), Danny Comden (Roger Nicholl), Adi Schnall (Randa)

A precocious teenage schoolgirl in a Beverly Hills private school persuades two classmates to make false allegations about a drama teacher's sexual abusiveness.

A thoroughly nasty little piece, with the most repellent father-daughter tag team in memory. Yet there's something bracing about its surly, curled-lip dismissal of political correctness and consensus values. Woods, as the girl's profane, racist father, is in his element.

SCR Skander Halim **CIN** Ramsey Nickell **MUS** Gilad Benamram **DES** Paul Oberman **ED** Nicholas Erasmnus **PROD** Todd Dagres, Carl Levin, Marcos Siega, Matthew Weaver

66 Too flip to be serious and too smug to be rousing. – *Carina Chocano, Los Angeles Times*

66 A hand grenade lobbed at no place in particular. – *Ben Koenigsberg, Village Voice*

Pretty Village Pretty Flame ★★★

DIR Srdan Dragojevic
1996 115m Serbia
DVD

☆ Dragan Bjelogrlic (Milan), Nikola Kojo (Velja), Dragan Maksimovic (Petar), Velimir Bata Zivojlinovic (Gvozden), Zoran Cvijanovic (Brzi), Milorad Mandic (Viljuska), Dragan Petrovic (Laza)

In the former Yugoslavia, the bond between two childhood friends, a Serb and a Muslim, is fractured by a civil war.

A sobering anti-war film that highlights the sheer insanity of the conflict all the way to a numbing climax. Despite the over-liberal use of flashback sequences, it has rare power.

SCR Vanja Bulic, Srdan Dragojevic, Nikola Pejakovic **CIN** Dusan Joksimovic **MUS** Aleksandar Habic, Lazar Ristovski **DES** Milenko Jeremic **ED** Petar Markovic **PROD** Goran Bjelogrlic, Dragan Bjelogrlic, Nikola Kojo, Milko Josifov **DIST** Guild Pathé/Cobra/RTV/MCRC

66 Boldly shot and edited, the film quite rightly puts you through the wringer. – *Tom Charity, Time Out*

'Who knew it was so much fun to be a hooker?'

Pretty Woman ★

DIR Garry Marshall
1990 119m US
DVD ♫

☆ Richard Gere (Edward Lewis), *Julia Roberts* (Vivian Ward), Ralph Bellamy (James Morse), Jason Alexander (Philip Stuckey), Laura San Giacomo (Kit De Luca), Hector Elizondo (Barney Thompson)

In Los Angeles, a successful asset stripper is charmed by a perky prostitute he hires for a night as an escort, invites her to spend a week with him, and falls for her.

A modern fairy tale with shades of Pygmalion, so deftly written and directed and with such a radiant lead actress that it became a huge hit. One can find fault

with the dubious sexual politics on display here, but it says much for Roberts's overwhelming screen charm that audiences have overlooked that aspect of the story. This was the role that kick-started, and even defined her stellar career.

SCR J. F. Lawton **CIN** Charles Minsky **MUS** James Newton Howard **DES** Albert Brenner **ED** Priscilla Nedd, Raja Gosnell **PROD** Arnon Milchan, Steven Reuther **DIST** Buena Vista/Touchstone

66 It's the sweetest and most openhearted love fable since The Princess Bride. Here is a movie that could have marched us down mean streets into the sinks of iniquity, and it glows with romance. – *Roger Ebert, Chicago Sun-Times*

† The film was a massive global hit, grossing $178 million in the US, and $285 million elsewhere.
† The script was originally titled '$3,000' – the fee charged by Vivian for a whole night.

⚱ Julia Roberts (leading actress)

Ⓣ film Julia Roberts (leading actress); Marilyn Vance (costume design); screenplay

'She's stealing his heart. He's paying for it.'

Priceless ⓝⓔⓦ ★

DIR Pierre Salvadori
2006 105m France
DVD

☆ Audrey Tautou (Irene), Gad Elmaleh (Jean), Marie-Christine Adam (Madeleine), Vernon Dobtcheff (Jacques), Jacques Spiesser (Gilles), Annelise Hesme (Agnes)

A gold-digger on the French Riviera teaches a waiter she initially mistakes for a millionaire to be a male gigolo.

Likeable trifle that generates frothy entertainment from the oldest profession.

SCR Pierre Salvadori, Benoit Graffin. **CIN** Gilles Henry **MUS** Camille Bazbaz **DES** Yves Fournier **ED** Isabelle Devinck **PROD** Philippe Martin **DIST** Icon

66 An amusing ball of fluff that refuses to judge its characters' amoral high jinks. – *Stephen Holden, New York Times*

66 A cheap-looking, tiresomely tawdry tale of two prostitutes, neither of whom you'd want to spend more than a night with. – *Emma Morgan, Total Film*

'In A World Of Rituals, In A Place Of Secrets, A Man Must Choose Between Keeping The Faith And Exposing The Truth.'

Priest ★★

DIR Antonia Bird
1994 105m GB
DVD

☆ *Linus Roache* (Father Greg Pilkington), *Tom Wilkinson* (Father Matthew Thomas), Cathy Tyson (Maria Kerrigan), *Robert Carlyle* (Graham), James Ellis (Father Ellerton), Lesley Sharp (Mrs. Unsworth), Robert Pugh (Mr. Unsworth), Christine Tremarco (Lisa Unsworth)

A new Catholic priest arrives in a working-class Liverpool parish determined to do something about its lax standards, until it is publicly revealed that he is gay.

Enthralling critique of Catholic attitudes to sexuality; the senior parish priest (Wilkinson) shares a bed with his housekeeper, while the new disciplinarian (Roache) leads a tortured double life, unhappily frequenting gay bars by night. It's a fascinating mess that resolves itself movingly. Screenwriter Jimmy McGovern (the creator of TV's Cracker) does it justice with a hard-hitting script.

SCR *Jimmy McGovern* CIN Fred Tammes MUS Andy Roberts DES Raymond Langhorn ED Susan Spivey PROD George Faber, Josephine Ward DIST Electric/BBC/Polygram

66 Wickedly sardonic and very moving, with an outstanding performance from Linus Roache at the centre of a fine cast it clearly works a treat for cinema audiences. – *Tom Charity, Time Out*

Ⓣ British film

'Sooner or later a man who wears two faces forgets which one is real.'

Primal Fear

DIR Gregory Hoblit
1996 129m US
DVD ♫

☆ Richard Gere (Martin Vail), Laura Linney (Janet Venable), John Mahoney (John Shaughnessy), Alfre Woodard (Judge Miriam Shoat), Frances McDormand (Dr. Molly Arrington), *Edward Norton* (Aaron Stampler), Terry O'Quinn (Bud Yancy), Andre Braugher (Tommy Goodman)

When a shy choirboy is accused of murdering an archbishop, a hotshot publicity conscious lawyer steps in to defend him.

A routine whodunit with a preposterous twist in the tail. A bad film, yes, but one with a single glittering performance: Norton is a revelation here as the accused young man – stuttering, brooding and sullen.

SCR Steve Shagan, Ann Biderman CIN Michael Chapman MUS James Newton Howard DES Jeannine Oppewall ED David Rosenbloom PROD Gary Lucchesi DIST UIP/Paramount/Rysher

66 If you're in the mood for a tense, chilling mystery, by all means pass on Primal Fear. – *Peter Travers, Rolling Stone*

66 The plot is as good as crime procedurals get, but the movie is really better than its plot because of the three-dimensional characters. – *Roger Ebert, Chicago Sun-Times*

⚱ Edward Norton (supporting actor)
Ⓣ Edward Norton (supporting actor)

'What Went Down On The Way To The Top.'

Primary Colors ★★

DIR Mike Nichols
1998 143m US
DVD ♫

☆ John Travolta (Governor Jack Stanton), Emma Thompson (Susan Stanton), Billy Bob Thornton (Richard Jemmons), Adrian Lester (Henry Burton), Maura Tierney (Daisy Green), Paul Guilfoyle (Howard Ferguson), Larry Hagman (Gov. Fred Picker), Kathy Bates (Libby Holden), Diane Ladd (Mamma Stanton), Caroline Aaron (Lucille Kaufman), Mykelti Williamson (Dewayne Smith)

A charismatic, promiscuous US governor from the South runs for presidential office, helped by his ambitious, pragmatic wife.

Joe Klein's best-seller, a smart, insider roman á clef about the Clintons, is defanged in this film version, with Travolta doing a passable imitation of Bill Clinton's good-ol'-boy charm, but with much of the intriguing detail conveyed by Klein sadly missing. American politics is still presented as both entertaining and distasteful, but it's a film one can forget within 10 minutes of its end credits rolling.

SCR Elaine May CIN Michael Ballhaus MUS Ry Cooder DES Bo Welch ED Arthur Schmidt PROD Mike Nichols DIST Universal/Mutual/Icarus

66 A great cast – led by a charming John Travolta, an effectively steely Emma Thompson and a perfectly foul-mouthed Kathy Bates – relishes the lines and bites the hand that governs them. – *Bob McCabe, Empire Magazine*

⚱ Kathy Bates (supporting actress); Elaine May (screenplay)
Ⓑ Elaine May (screenplay)
Ⓣ Kathy Bates (supporting actress)

'A therapeutic new comedy.'

Prime ★

SCR/DIR Ben Younger
2005 105m US
DVD ♫

☆ *Meryl Streep* (Lisa Metzger), *Uma Thurman* (Rafi Gardet), *Bryan Greenberg* (David Bloomberg), Jon Abrahams (Morris), Zak Orth (Randall), Annie Parisse (Katherine)

A lonely divorcee in New York begins an affair with a much younger man, who turns out to be the son of her Jewish therapist.

A minor film with a delightful premise, diligently and enthusiastically played by all three leads.

CIN William Rexer MUS Ryan Shore DES Mark Ricker ED Kristina Boden PROD Jennifer Todd, Suzanne Todd DIST Universal

66 There are a few memorable moments. . .alas the odd chortle in two hours in not enough to make Prime anything like essential viewing. – *David Edwards, Daily Mirror*

66 A prime example of a solid romantic comedy. – *Kirk Honeycutt, Hollywood Reporter*

'If you always want what you can't have, what do you want when you can have anything?'

Primer ★★

SCR/DIR Shane Carruth
2004 77m US
DVD

☆ Shane Carruth (Aaron), David Sullivan (Abe), Casey Gooden (Robert), Anand Upadhyaya (Phillip), Carrie Crawford (Kara)

Two bright young inventors are shocked to discover that they have constructed a time machine.

This ultra low-budget movie might look amateurish by Hollywood standards but the ideas and energy behind it are bracing and sometimes electrifying.

DVD Available on DVD ☆ Cast in order 66 Critics' Quotes ⚱ Academy Award Ⓑ BAFTA
♫ Soundtrack on CD of importance † Points of interest ⚱ Academy Award nomination Ⓣ BAFTA nomination

497

P

CIN Anand Upadhyaya, Daniel Bueche   MUS Shane Carruth   DES Shane Carruth   ED Shane Carruth   PROD Shane Carruth   DIST Tartan

66 It is maddening, fascinating and completely successful. – *Roger Ebert, Chicago Sun-Times*

† It was made for just $7,000, and most of that money went towards film stock.

'The Power Is Real. The Story Is Forever. The Time Is Now.'

The Prince of Egypt ★★

DIR Brenda Chapman, Steve Hickner, Simon Wells
1998   99m   US
DVD   ♫

☆ the voices of: Val Kilmer, Ralph Fiennes, Michelle Pfeiffer, Sandra Bullock, Jeff Goldblum, Danny Glover, Patrick Stewart, Helen Mirren, Steve Martin, Martin Short

After being raised as the son of a Pharoah in Ancient Egypt, Moses learns he is Hebrew and must accept his destiny as the leader of his people out of slavery.

A full-length animated musical feature version of the biblical story. It boasts technical brilliance and spectacular design, but it rather grandly announces itself as an epic, and there's a faint whiff of worthiness about it.

SCR Philip LaZebnik   MUS Hans Zimmer   DES *Darek Gogol*   ED Nick Fletcher   PROD Penney Finkelman Cox, Sandra Rabins   DIST DreamWorks

66 As epic, emotionally satisfying spectacle, it's way up there with the very best in mainstream animation. – *Time Out*

† This was the first feature from DreamWorks' animation division, and much was expected of it. But its US box-office takings of $101 million were judged disappointing.
† A sequel, Joseph: King of Dreams, went straight to video.

⚬ (music – original song When You Believe) Stephen Schwartz

⚬ Stephen Schwartz, Hans Zimmer (music – original score)

'A story about the memories that haunt us, and the truth that sets us free.'

The Prince of Tides ★★

DIR Barbra Streisand
1991   132m   US
DVD   ♫

☆ Barbra Streisand (Susan Lowenstein), *Nick Nolte* (Tom Wingo), *Blythe Danner* (Sally Wingo), *Kate Nelligan* (Lila Wingo Newbury), Jeroen Krabbé (Herbert Woodruff), Melinda Dillon (Savannah Wingo), George Carlin (Eddie Detreville), Jason Gould (Bernard Woodruff), Brad Sullivan (Henry Wingo)

A coastal state in America's south. The unhappy brother of a suicidal woman falls in love with her married psychiatrist.

Southern discomfort and dysfunction, beautifully shot and played to the hilt with real conviction. Nolte is a credibly tortured soul, while Streisand, for once, resists every chance to upstage him. Soap opera of the highest order.

SCR Pat Conroy, Becky Johnston   CIN *Stephen Goldblatt*   MUS James Newton Howard   DES Paul Sylbert   ED Don Zimmerman   PROD Barbra Streisand, Andrew Karsch   DIST Columbia/Barwood/Longfellow

66 Barbra Streisand proves she is a good director with an assured and very serious love story that allows neither humour nor romance to get in the way of its deeper and darker subject. – *Roger Ebert, Chicago Sun-Times*

66 An emotionally satisfying film. – *Rita Kempley, Washington Post*

† Jason Gould, who plays Streisand's character's son, is her real-life son from her marriage to Elliott Gould.

⚬ film; Nick Nolte (leading actor); Kate Nelligan (supporting actress); Pat Conroy, Becky Johnston (adapted screenplay); Stephen Goldblatt; James Newton Howard; Paul Sylbert

Princess (new) ★

SCR/DIR Anders Morgenthaler
2007   90m   Denmark/Germany
☆ Thure Lindhardt (August), Stine Fischer Christensen (Christina 'Princess'), Mira Hilli Moller Hallund (Mia), Tommy Kenter (Preben)

A priest exacts revenge on pornographers responsible for his sister's death and the abuse of her 5-year-old daughter.

Crude anime style animation (with live action flashbacks) and an even cruder moral stance makes for a distasteful muddle of gory, sensationalised exploitation.

SCR Mette Heeno   MUS Mads Brauer, Casper Clausen   DES Rune Fisker   ED Mikkel E.G. Nielsen   PROD Sarita Christensen   DIST Tartan Films

66 Takes a high and mighty line on the sex industry, but revels in gory violence. – *Leslie Felperin - Variety*

'Scaling the Cliffs of Insanity, Battling Rodents of Unusual Size, Facing torture in the Pit of Despair – True love has never been a snap.'

The Princess Bride ★★

DIR Rob Reiner
1987   98m   US
DVD   ♫

☆ Cary Elwes (Westley), Mandy Patinkin (Inigo Montoya), Chris Sarandon (Prince Humperdinck), Christopher Guest (Count Tyrone Rugen), Peter Falk (The Grandfather/Narrator), Wallace Shawn (Vizzini)

A bedridden boy listens to a fairy tale from his grandfather, a modern fable of the kidnap of a beautiful princess.

Inventive, hyperactive fantasy from veteran screenwriter Goldman which polarises opinions. If you're in the mood to be enchanted by a land where monsters, sword fights and damsels in distress compete for space with knowing comic gags, then sit tight. If you're not prepared to suspend disbelief at least a little, then steer clear.

SCR William Goldman   CIN Adrian Biddle   MUS Mark Knopfler   DES Norman Garwood   ED Robert Leighton   PROD Andrew Scheinmann, Rob Reiner   DIST Act III

66 Occasionally a bit too clever for its own good, but it's all so cheerful and has so many ingenious set-pieces that you can forgive it any excess. – *Caroline Westbrook, Empire*

♟ Willy DeVillec (music – original song Storybook Love)

Prisoner of the Mountains ★★

DIR Sergei Bodrov
1996 99m Russia/Kazakhstan
DVD

☆ Oleg Menshikov (Sacha Kostylin), Sergei Bodrov Jnr (Ivan (Vanya) Zhilin), Susanna Mekhralieva (Dina), Alesandr Bureev (Hasan), Valentina Fedotova (Zhilin's Mother), Aleksei Zharkov (Maslov, the Russian Commander)

Two Russian soldiers are captured by a Chechen father determined to exchange them for his son, but the prisoners escape.

This off-centre war story concentrates less on the horror of conflict than the humanity, even across cultural and national divides, and successfully sustains interest.

SCR Arif Aliev, Sergei Bodrov, Boris Giller **MUS** Leonid Desiatnikov **DES** Valerii Kostrin **ED** Olga Grinshpun, Vera Kruglova, Alan Baril **PROD** Boris Giller, Sergei Bodrov, Eduard Krapivsky, Carolyn Cavallero **DIST** Metro/Tartan/Karavan/BG

66 Simple, powerful, convincing. – *Kenneth Turan, Los Angeles Times*

† This was the first fiction film to deal with the Chechnya conflict.

♟ foreign language film

'The Immortal Lovers All The World Loves!'

The Prisoner of Zenda ★★★

DIR *John Cromwell*
1937 101m US

☆ *Ronald Colman* (Rudolph Rassendyl/King Rudolf V), *Douglas Fairbanks Jnr* (Rupert of Hentzau), Madeleine Carroll (Princess Flavia), David Niven (Capt. Fritz von Tarlenheim), Raymond Massey (Black Michael), Mary Astor (Antoinette De Mauban), *C. Aubrey Smith* (Col. Zapt), Byron Foulger (Johann), Montagu Love (Detchard)

An Englishman on holiday in Ruritania finds himself helping to defeat a rebel plot by impersonating the kidnapped king at his coronation.

A splendid schoolboy adventure story is perfectly transferred to the screen in this exhilarating swashbuckler, one of the most entertaining films to come out of Hollywood.

SCR *John Balderston, Wells Root, Donald Ogden Stewart* **CIN** *James Wong Howe* **MUS** *Alfred Newman* **ED** Hal C. Kern, James E. Newcom **DIST** David O. Selznick

66 The most pleasing film that has come along in ages. – *New York Times*

66 One of those rare movies that seem, by some magic trick, to become more fascinating and beguiling with each passing year. – *John Cutts, 1971*

† Previously filmed in 1913 and 1922.

♟ Alfred Newman (music); Lyle Wheeler (art direction)

'For six strangers in search of love, the City of Lights can be a very lonely place.'

Private Fears in Public Places (new) ★★

DIR Alain Resnais
2006 120m France/Italy
DVD

☆ Sabine Azéma (Charlotte), Isabelle Carré (Gaelle), Laura Morante (Nicole), Pierre Arditi (Lionel), André Dussollier (Thierry), Lambert Wilson (Dan), Claude Rich (Arthur)

Romantic misunderstandings blight various lives in Paris.

An English play transplanted virtually intact into a French setting; where the original was a bitter-sweet comedy, this is more of a melancholy mood piece.

SCR Alain Resnais, Jean-Michel Ribes, Alan Ayckbourn **CIN** Eric Gautier **MUS** Mark Snow **DES** Jacques Saulnier, Solange Zeitoun **ED** Hervé de Luze **PROD** Bruno Pesery **DIST** Artificial Eye

66 A masterpiece by any measure. – *Kevin Thomas, Los Angeles Times*

66 Where Ayckbourn's play might have made frothy fun of this comedie humaine, on screen this feels a poor, airless thing. – *Anthony Quinn, Independent*

† Resnais' Smoking/No Smoking was also adapted from an Alan Ayckbourn play.

'The things I do for England!'

The Private Life of Henry VIII ★★★

DIR Alexander Korda
1933 97m GB
DVD

☆ *Charles Laughton* (Henry VIII), *Elsa Lanchester* (Anne of Cleves), Robert Donat (Thomas Culpepper), Merle Oberon (Anne Boleyn), Binnie Barnes (Katherine Howard), Franklin Dyall (Thomas Cromwell), Miles Mander (Wriothesley), Wendy Barrie (Jane Seymour), Claud Allister (Cornell), Everley Gregg (Catherine Parr)

How Henry beheaded his second wife and acquired four more.

This never was a perfect film, but certain scenes are very funny and its sheer sauciness established the possibility of British films making money abroad, as well as starting several star careers. It now looks very dated and even amateurish in parts.

SCR *Lajos Biro, Arthur Wimperis* **CIN** Georges Périnal **MUS** Kurt Schroeder **ED** Harold Young, Stephen Harrison **PROD** Alexander Korda **DIST** London Films

66 Among the best anywhere and by far the top British picture . . . figures a sock entry, especially for the best houses. – *Variety*

♟ Charles Laughton (leading actor)
♟ picture

Private Property (new) ★★

DIR Joachim Lafosse
2008 95m Luxembourg/Belgium/France
DVD

☆ Isabelle Huppert (Pascale), Jérémie Renier (Thierry),

DVD Available on DVD ☆ Cast in order 66 Critics' Quotes ♟ Academy Award 🏆 BAFTA
♫ Soundtrack on CD of importance † Points of interest ♟ Academy Award nomination 🏆 BAFTA nomination

499

Yannick Renier (François), Kris Cuppens (Jan), Raphaelle Lubansu (Anne), Patrick Descamps (Luc)

When a divorced mother finds a new lover, her grown-up twin sons react with hostility.

Directed with tightly coiled, slow-burning intensity, this family drama plays like a claustrophobic thriller. Hypnotic performance from Huppert as a mother under siege from her offspring and her emotional past.

SCR Joachim Lafosse, François Pirot CIN Hichame Alaouie DES Anna Falguere ED Sophie Vercruysse PROD Joseph Rouschop DIST Soda Pictures

66 An impressive low-key family drama. – *Ginette Vincendeau, Sight & Sound*

† Belgian director Lafosse felt 'it was very important to have real life brothers [Jeremie and Yannick Renier] playing in the film because they bring a real credibility to it. You cannot make up that kind of relationship.'

The Producers ★★★★

SCR/DIR Mel Brooks
1968 88m US
DVD ♫

☆ Zero Mostel (Max Bialystock), Gene Wilder (Leo Bloom), Kenneth Mars (Franz Liebkind), Estelle Winwood (Old Lady), Renee Taylor (Eva Braun), Dick Shawn (Lorenzo St. Du Bois)

A Broadway producer seduces elderly widows to obtain finance for his new play, sells 25,000 per cent of the stake in the confident expectation that it will flop, and is horrified when it succeeds.

A cult success that became a public favourite through its brilliantly funny premise and a script insanely overstuffed with great gags. Mostel and Wilder are an inspired example of odd-couple casting, and the appalling bad-taste musical Springtime for Hitler, with its Busby Berkeley-inspired routine showing dancers in a swastika formation, is imperishable.

CIN Joseph Coffey MUS John Morris ED Ralph Rosenbloom PROD Sidney Glazier DIST Avco

MAX: That's it, baby, when you've got it, flaunt it, flaunt it!
FRANZ: Not many people know it, but the Fuhrer was a terrific dancer.
FRANZ: Hitler... there was a painter! He could paint an entire apartment in ONE afternoon! TWO coats!

66 One of the funniest movies ever made. – *Roger Ebert*

66 An almost flawless triumph of bad taste, unredeemed by wit or style. – *Arthur Schlesinger Jnr*

† A re-make followed in 2005, in the wake of Brooks re-shaping the screenplay into a hugely successful Broadway and West End musical.

⚰ Mel Brooks (original screenplay)
⚰ Gene Wilder (supporting actor)

The Producers ★★

DIR Susan Stroman
2005 134m US
DVD ♫

☆ Nathan Lane (Max Bialystock), Matthew Broderick (Leo Bloom), Uma Thurman (Ulla), Will Ferrell (Franz Liebkind), Gary Beach (Roger De Bris), Roger Bart (Carmen Ghia), Eileen Essell (Hold Me-Touch Me)

A cash-strapped producer learns from his timid accountant that he could recoup his losses by staging a flop – then to his horror finds he has a hit on his hands with a camp musical about Hitler.

To recap: the film version of the Broadway musical of the original film. No-one can accuse Mel Brooks of not exploiting a property; Max Bialystock would be proud. The wonderful gags arrive like old friends, and overall it's a treat, but in truth it lacks the theatrical panache of the musical and the dark, inspired shock value of the first film.

SCR Mel Brooks, Thomas Meehan CIN John Bailey, Charles Minsky MUS Glen Kelly DES Mark Friedberg ED Steven Weisberg PROD Mel Brooks, Jonathan Sanger DIST Universal

66 It's springtime for musical fans as the ultimate bad taste comedy goosesteps into cinemas in this appallingly funny film. – *David Edwards, Daily Mirror*

66 Barely adequate. – *Paul Byrnes, Sydney Morning Herald*

'A night to die for.'

Prom Night (new)

DIR Nelson McCormick
2008 87m US/Canada
DVD ♫

☆ Brittany Snow (Donna Keppel), Scott Porter (Bobby), Jessica Stroup (Claire), Dana Davis (Lisa Hines), Collins Pennie (Ronnie Heflin), Kelly Blatz (Michael), James Ransone (Det. Nash), Brianne Davis (Crissy Lynn), Johnathon Schaech (Richard Fenton), Idris Elba (Det. Winn)

Three years after seeing her family slaughtered by a crazed teacher, a high school student learns her stalker is after her again.

Boring horror that has little in common with the cult 1980 slasher whose name it shares; even the violence feels half-hearted.

SCR J.S. Cardone CIN Checco Varese MUS Paul Haslinger DES Jon Gary Steele ED Jason Ballantine PROD Neal H. Moritz, Toby Jaffe DIST Columbia Pictures

66 Knife, stab, blood, screaming. – *Xan Brooks, Guardian*

66 As spine-tingling as an algebra exam. – *Michael Rechtshaffen, Hollywood Reporter*

Promised Land ★

SCR/DIR Michael Hoffman
1987 102m US
DVD ♫

☆ Kiefer Sutherland (Danny 'Senator' Rivers), Meg Ryan (Beverly 'Bev' Sykes), Jason Gedrick (Davey Hancock), Tracy Pollan (Mary Daley), Googy Gress (Baines), Deborah Richter (Pammie)

The lives of two high-school pals in a small town diverge dramatically on either side of the law.

Decently acted and beautifully shot account of limited lives in the sticks. The film became a calling card for novice director Hoffman, and his engaging young cast give it their all.

CIN *Ueli Steiger, Alexander Gruszynski*   MUS James Newton Howard   DES Eugenio Zanetti   ED David Spiers   PROD Rick Stevenson   DIST Vestron/Wildwood/Oxford Film Company

66 The American Dream hasn't a prayer in the small town of Ashville. . .the film has a lot going for it though, with its beautiful snowy landscapes, empty highways, and committed playing from the cast. – *Time Out*

'Before Love Comes Trust. Before Trust Comes. . .'

Proof ★★

SCR/DIR Jocelyn Moorhouse
1991   90m   Australia
[DVD]

☆ Hugo Weaving (Martin), Genevieve Picot (Celia), Heather Mitchell (Martin's Mother), Jeffrey Walker (Young Martin), Daniel Pollock (Punk), Frankie J. Holden (Brian), Frank Gallacher (Vet), Saskia Post (Waitress), Russell Crowe (Andy)

A blind photographer rejects the amorous advances of his sexually voracious housekeeper, and becomes friends with a male dishwasher who describes his photographs to him.

A delicately played three-cornered psychological drama which marked a notable debut for director Moorhouse.

CIN Martin McGrath   MUS Not Drowning, Waving   DES Patrick Reardon   ED Ken Sallows   PROD Lynda House   DIST Artificial Eye/House & Moorhouse Films/Australian Film Commission/Film Victoria

66 If there is a kind of movie I like better than any other, it is this kind, the close observation of particular lives, perhaps because it exploits so completely the cinema's potential for voyeurism. – *Roger Ebert, Chicago Sun-Times*

'This land will be civilized.'

The Proposition ★★

DIR *John Hillcoat*
2005   104m   GB/Australia
[DVD] ♫

☆ *Guy Pearce* (Charlie Burns), *Ray Winstone* (Captain Stanley), Danny Huston (Arthur Burns), John Hurt (Jellon Lamb), David Wenham (Eden Fletcher), Emily Watson (Martha Stanley), Noah Taylor (Brian O'Leary), David Gulpilil (Jacko)

A captured outlaw in the Australian bush of the 1880s is given an agonising choice – hunt down and kill his murderous older brother or watch his 14-year-old younger brother hang.

Tough, unsympathetic, joltingly violent account of how the outback was won shows the bleaker side of the Australian dream. Excellent acting, particularly from Winstone, helps hold the attention on some deeply unpleasant characters.

SCR Nick Cave   CIN Benoit Delhomme   MUS Nick Cave, Warren Ellis   DES Chris Kennedy   ED John Gregory   PROD Chris Brown, Chiara Menage, Jackie O'Sullivan, Cat Villiers   DIST Tartan

66 Brutal, bloody and brilliant, this is superior film-making, and more evidence of the renaissance of the Australian film industry. – *Adam Smith, Empire*

'A magician's spell, the innocence of young love and a dream of revenge unite to create a tempest.'

Prospero's Books ★

SCR/DIR Peter Greenaway
1991   129m   Netherlands/France/Italy/GB/Japan
♫

☆ John Gielgud (Prospero), Michael Clark (Caliban), Michel Blanc (Alonso), Erland Josephson (Gonzalo), Isabelle Pasco (Miranda), Tom Bell (Antonio), Kenneth Cranham (Sebastian), Mark Rylance (Ferdinand), Gérard Thoolen (Adrian), Pierre Bokma (Francisco), Michiel Romeyn (Stephano)

A filmed record of Sir John Gielgud playing Prospero in The Tempest.

A colourful, extraordinary adaptation of Shakespeare's play, in which Greenaway focuses his attention on Prospero's library. The director includes textual marginalia on screen, and overlays multiple images, perhaps as a means of showing the decisions that led him to create this work in this fashion. It's reasonably intriguing, though the suspicion lingers that Greenaway is bored with film, and needs extramural input from other artistic forms to sustain him. Whatever the reason, the film finally feels like a trial to be endured, though it finds Gielgud in spellbinding form.

CIN Sacha Vierny   MUS Michael Nyman   DES Ben van Os, Jan Roelfs   ED Marina Bodbyl   PROD Kees Kasander   DIST Palace/Allarts/Cinea/Camera One/Penta/Elsevier Vendex/Film Four/VPRO/Canal Plus/NHK

66 Lock up the tots and blindfold Granny – Peter Greenaway is at it again. – *Peter Travers, Rolling Stone*

66 An unfathomable flood of intoxicating imagery, a banquet of beauty so rich and overripe it is ultimately indigestible. – *Joe Brown, Washington Post*

† This is the first film to be shot completely in high definition video.

Ⓣ visual effects

Protégé (new)

SCR/DIR Derek Yee
2007   108m   Hong Kong
☆ Daniel Wu (Nick), Andy Lau (Banker), Zhang Jing Chu (Jane), Anita Yuen (Banker's Wife), Louis Koo (Jane's Husband)

An undercover cop is torn between his dedication to duty and his growing affection for the Hong Kong drug lord he is trying to bring to justice.

Watchable if preachy thriller in the Infernal Affairs vein, with rather too much time spent on the minutiae of drug running.

CIN Venus Keung   MUS Peter Kam   DES Yee Chung-man   ED Kwong Chi-leung   PROD Peter Ho-sun Chan, Andre Morgan   DIST Liberation Entertainment

66 A faintly overblown but pungent and compelling thriller. – *Tim Robey, Telegraph*

66 Moderately efficient. – *Philip French, Observer*

[DVD] Available on DVD   ☆ Cast in order of importance   66 Critics' Quotes   🏆 Academy Award / Academy Award nomination   Ⓑ BAFTA / Ⓣ BAFTA nomination
♫ Soundtrack on CD   † Points of interest

'Check in. Unpack. Relax. Take a shower.'

Psycho

DIR Gus Van Sant
1998   105m   US
`DVD`   ♫

☆ Vince Vaughn (Norman Bates), Julianne Moore (Lila Crane), Viggo Mortensen (Samuel 'Sam' Loomis), William H. Macy (Milton Arbogast), Anne Heche (Marion Crane)

A woman on the run is brutally murdered in the shower in a lonely motel.

Alfred Hitchcock's classic is lovingly, if pointlessly, re-created scene for scene, except with less inspired casting. Quite what Van Sant was thinking remains unclear.

SCR Joseph Stefano   **CIN** Chris Doyle   **MUS** Bernard Herrmann   **DES** Tom Foden   **ED** Amy Duddleston
PROD Brian Grazer, Gus Van Sant
DIST Universal/Imagine

❝ It remains the most structurally elegant and sneakily playful of thrillers. – *Janet Maslin, New York Times*

❝ [Director Gus] Van Sant has cranked up the realism about 20 points, but somehow what he achieves for the effort is a larger sense of banality. – *Stephen Hunter, Washington Post*

'The screen's master of suspense moves his camera into the icy blackness of the unexplained!'

Psycho   ★★★★

DIR *Alfred Hitchcock (and Saul Bass)*
1960   109m   US
`DVD`   ♫

☆ *Anthony Perkins* (Norman Bates), Vera Miles (Lila Crane), John Gavin (Sam Loomis), Janet Leigh (Marion Crane), John McIntire (Sheriff Chambers), Martin Balsam (Milton Arbogast), Simon Oakland (Dr. Richmond)

At a lonely motel, vicious murders take place and are attributed to the manic mother of the young owner.

Curious shocker devised by Hitchcock as a tease and initially received by most critics as an unpleasant horror piece in which the main scene, the shower stabbing, was allegedly directed not by Hitchcock but by Saul Bass. After enormous commercial success it achieved classic status over the years; despite effective moments of fright, it has a childish plot and script, yet it remains a hugely successful confidence trick, made for very little money by a TV crew.

SCR Joseph Stefano   **CIN** John L. Russell   **MUS** *Bernard Herrmann*   **ED** George Tomasini   **DIST** Shamley/Alfred Hitchcock

❝ Probably the most visual, most cinematic picture he has ever made. – *Peter Bogdanovich*

❝ I think the film is a reflection of a most unpleasant mind, a mean, sly, sadistic little mind. – *Dwight MacDonald*

† When asked by the press what he used for the blood in the bath, Mr Hitchcock said: 'Chocolate sauce.'

† This is the whole text of Hitchcock's trailer, in which he audaciously wandered round the sets and practically gave away the entire plot: 'Here we have a quiet little motel, tucked away off the main highway, and as you see perfectly harmless looking, whereas it has now become known as the scene of a crime. . .This motel also has an adjunct, an old house which is, if I may say so, a little more sinister looking. And in this house the most dire, horrible events took place. I think we can go inside because the place is up for sale – though I don't know who would buy it now. In that window in the second floor, the one in front, that's where the woman was first seen. Let's go inside. You see, even in daylight this place looks a bit sinister. It was at the top of these stairs that the second murder took place. She came out of that door there and met the victim at the top. Of course in a flash there was the knife, and in no time the victim tumbled and fell with a horrible crash. . .I think the back broke immediately it hit the floor. It's difficult to describe the way. . .the twisting of the. . .I won't dwell on it. Come upstairs. Of course the victim, or should I say victims, hadn't any idea of the kind of people they'd be confronted with in this house. Especially the woman. She was the weirdest and the most. . .well, let's go into her bedroom. Here's the woman's room, still beautifully preserved. And the imprint of her body on the bed where she used to lie. I think some of her clothes are still in the wardrobe. [He looks, and shakes his head.] Bathroom. This was the son's room but we won't go in there because his favourite spot was the little parlour behind the office in the motel. Let's go down there. This young man. . .you have to feel sorry for him. After all, being dominated by an almost maniacal woman was enough to. . .well, let's go in. I suppose you'd call this his hideaway. His hobby was taxidermy. A crow here, an owl there. An important scene took place in this room. There was a private supper here. By the way, this picture has great significance because. . .let's go along into cabin number one. I want to show you something there. All tidied up. The bathroom. Oh, they've cleaned all this up now. Big difference. You should have seen the blood. The whole place was. . .well, it's too horrible to describe. Dreadful. And I tell you, a very important clue was found here. [Shows toilet.] Down there. Well, the murderer, you see, crept in here very slowly – of course, the shower was on, there was no sound, and. . .' Music wells up fiercely, shower curtain swishes across, blackout. Voice: 'The picture you must see from the beginning – or not at all.' Janet Leigh's book *Psycho: Behind the Scenes of the Classic Thriller* (1995) chronicles the making of the film.

† It was re-made, virtually frame for frame, by director Gus Van Sant in 1998, but was not received enthusiastically.

⚐ Janet Leigh (supporting actress); Alfred Hitchcock (direction); John L. Russell; art direction

---

'Drama that hurls a mighty challenge to all humanity!'

The Public Enemy   ★★★

DIR *William Wellman*
1931   84m   US
`DVD`   ♫

☆ *James Cagney* (Tom Powers), Edward Woods (Matt Doyle), Jean Harlow (Gwen Allen), Joan Blondell (Mamie), Beryl Mercer (Ma Powers), Donald Cook (Mike Powers), Mae Clarke (Kitty), Leslie Fenton (Nails Nathan)

Two slum boys begin as bootleggers in the Prohibition era, get too big for their boots, and receive their just desserts.

Although it doesn't flow as a narrative, this early gangster film still has vivid and startling scenes and was influential in the development of the urban American crime film.

`DVD` Available on DVD   ☆ Cast in order of importance   ❝ Critics' Quotes   † Points of interest   ⚐ Academy Award   ⚐ Academy Award nomination   BAFTA   BAFTA nomination
♫ Soundtrack on CD

SCR Harvey Thew   CIN *Dev Jennings*   MUS David Mendoza   ED Ed McCormick   DIST Warner

66 Roughest, most powerful and best gang picture to date. So strong as to be repulsive in some aspects, plus a revolting climax. No strong cast names but a lot of merit. – *Variety*

66 The real power of The Public Enemy lies in its vigorous and brutal assault on the nerves and in the stunning acting of James Cagney. – *James Shelley Hamilton*

⚱ Kubec Glasmon, John Bright

'Murder. Scandal. Crime. No matter what he was shooting, Bernzy never took sides he only took pictures. . .Except once.'

The Public Eye ★

SCR/DIR Howard Franklin
1992   99m   US
♫

☆ Joe Pesci (Leon Bernstein), Barbara Hershey (Kay Levitz), Stanley Tucci (Sal), Jerry Adler (Arthur Nabler), Jared Harris (Danny the Doorman), Richard Riehle (Officer O'Brien), Bryan Travis Smith (Young Cop)

In the 1940s, a member of the New York paparazzi before the term was coined, falls in love with a beautiful woman who is in trouble with the Mafia.

Stylised, decent attempt to create a film-noir atmosphere. It looks better than the script merits, though Hershey and the perfectly cast Pesci pull it through.

CIN Peter Suschitzky   MUS Mark Isham   DES Marcia Hinds-Johnson   ED Evan Lottman   PROD Sue Baden-Powell   DIST UIP/Universal

66 There are moments in The Public Eye that made me think a little about Casablanca, especially the earlier scenes when Bogart is still mad at Bergman. Higher praise is not necessary. – *Roger Ebert, Chicago Sun-Times*

† Largely inspired by the life of the New York photographer Weegee, whose stark black-and-white street images were the genesis of the film The Naked City.

'Girls like me don't make invitations like this to just anyone.'

Pulp Fiction ★★★★

DIR *Quentin Tarantino*
1994   154m   US
DVD ♫

☆ *John Travolta* (Vincent Vega), *Samuel L. Jackson* (Jules Winfield), *Uma Thurman* (Mia Wallace), Harvey Keitel (The Wolf), Tim Roth (Pumpkin), Amanda Plummer (Honey Bunny), Ving Rhames (Marsellus Wallace), Maria de Madeiros (Fabienne), Eric Stoltz (Lance), Rosanna Arquette (Jody), Christopher Walken (Captain Koons), Bruce Willis (Butch Coolidge)

Interlocking stories from the seedy side of Los Angeles include ruthless hitmen, a gangster's beautiful wife with a roaming eye and a boxer who refuses to take a fall.

The defining film of the 1990s, playfully mixing up its chronology, packed with memorable, snappy, cute dialogue and showing a genuine zest for the art of film-making. Tarantino's film-literacy, learned obsessively during his stint as a video-store assistant, pays off

handsomely here; almost every line is quotable, a sense *of fun pervades, there's a host of delightful set-pieces (including Travolta and Thurman's sexy dance) and generous screen time is given to characters rarely considered at length in film, such as Travolta and Jackson's stolid hitmen. Briefly, Tarantino shone brighter than anyone else in the industry, and this film justifies his accolades.*

SCR Quentin Tarantino, Roger Avary   CIN Andrzej Sekula   DES David Wasco   ED Sally Menke   PROD Lawrence Bender   DIST Buena Vista/Miramax/A Band Apart/Jersey

66 (Director Quentin) Tarantino lacks the maturity to invest his work with anything that might provoke a heartfelt emotional response to his characters. Very entertaining, none the less. – *Time Out*

66 Brilliantly written and unfathomably cool, this would make a good case for most quotable crime movie of all time. – *Ian Freer, Empire*

† It won the Palme d'Or at the Cannes Film Festival in 1994.

⚱ Quentin Tarantino, Roger Avary (screenplay)
⚱ picture; Quentin Tarantino; John Travolta (leading actor); Samuel L. Jackson (supporting actor); film editing
🅣 Quentin Tarantino, Roger Avary (original screenplay); Samuel L. Jackson (supporting actor)
🅣 John Travolta (leading actor); Uma Thurman (supporting actress); screenplay; Sally Menke; film; sound; direction; Andrzej Sekula

---

'The Voice of a Generation.'

Pump Up the Volume ★

SCR/DIR Allan Moyle
1990   102m   US
DVD ♫

☆ Christian Slater (Mark Hunter (Hard Harry)), Ellen Greene (Jan Emerson), Annie Ross (Loretta Creswood), Samantha Mathis (Nora Diniro), Scott Paulin (Brian Hunter)

A shy but determined teenager starts his own pirate radio station and transforms himself into an outrageous 'shock jock' DJ.

Perceptive youth movie, a cut above the average, about a young man who becomes an unlikely mentor to his peers.

CIN Walt Lloyd   DES Robb Wilson King   ED Janice Hampton, Larry Bock   PROD Rupert Harvey, Sandy Stern   DIST New Line/SC Entertainment

66 Surprising success with what could have been a formulaic disgruntled teen movie. Fast-paced with a satisfyingly unhappy ending. – *Lloyd Bradley, Empire*

Punch-Drunk Love ★

SCR/DIR Paul Thomas Anderson
2002   95m   US
DVD ♫

☆ Adam Sandler (Barry Egan), Jason Andrews (Operator Carter (voice)), Don McManus (Plastic (voice)), Emily Watson (Lena Leonard), Luis Guzmán (Lance)

A depressed bathroom novelties salesman falls in love, but the owner of a phone-sex business starts harassing him.

DVD Available on DVD   ☆ Cast in order of importance   66 Critics' Quotes   ⚱ Academy Award   ⚱ Academy Award nomination   🅣 BAFTA   🅣 BAFTA nomination

503

P

The one misfire to date in Paul Thomas Anderson's canon: a supposedly romantic comedy with a dramatic edge and an uneasy tone. Sandler milks his hero's dysfunctional qualities to little effect; while the story is set in L.A's San Fernando Valley, its characters seem to inhabit no recognisable universe.

CIN Robert Elswit   MUS Jon Brion   DES William Arnold   ED Leslie Jones   PROD Joanne Sellar, Daniel Lupi, Paul Thomas Anderson   DIST Columbia

66 It's a romantic comedy on the verge of a nervous breakdown – *David Ansen, Newsweek*

66 I wouldn't have minded even the Hollywood schlock lurking behind the studied weirdness if I'd believed in any of the characters on any level. – *Jonathan Rosenbaum, Chicago Reader*

'Dying's easy. Comedy's hard.'

Punchline ★

SCR/DIR David Seltzer
1988   128m   US
DVD   ♫

☆ Sally Field (Lilah Krytsick), Tom Hanks (Steven Gold), John Goodman (John Krytsick), Mark Rydell (Romeo), Kim Greist (Madeline Urie), Paul Mazursky (Arnold), Pam Matteson (Utica Blake)

A housewife and a failed medical student both dream of becoming successful stand-up comics.

The hard work and tension that goes into attempting to make people laugh is well demonstrated in a rather dull movie.

CIN Reynaldo Villalobos   MUS Charles Gross   DES Jack De Govia   ED Bruce Green   PROD Daniel Melnick, Michael Rachmil   DIST Columbia TriStar

66 A pathetic movie into which a great deal of energy and talent has disappeared. – *Roger Ebert, Chicago Sun-Times*

'There is always someone pulling the strings.'

The Puppetmaster ★

DIR Hsiao-hsien Hou
1993   142m   Taiwan
DVD

☆ Li Tianlu (Himself), Chung Lin (Li Tianlu)

An old man in Taiwan recalls his rise to become a celebrated puppeteer during the fraught 50-year occupation of the island by the Japanese.

Detailed, stylised, deliberately-paced biopic, narrated by Li Tianlu at age 84. His painful memories are viewed through an often static camera, which sometimes enhance the drama and sometimes feel over-important.

SCR T'ien-wen Chu, Nien-Jen Wu   CIN Pin Bing Lee   MUS Ming Chang Chen, Hongda Zhang   DES Ming-Ching Lu, Chang Hung   ED Ching-Song Liao   PROD Fu-Sheng Chiu, Huakun Zhang   DIST Electric Pictures/Nian Dai

66 Slow-moving, but visually stunning. – *Channel 4*

66 Long term admirers will come out of the film with a vivid sense of Chinese folk-culture. – *Time Out*

'You don't have a chance. Seize it!'

Pusher ★

DIR Nicolas Winding Refn
1996   105m   Denmark
DVD   ♫

☆ Kim Bodnia (Frank), Zlatko Buric (Milo), Laura Drasbaek (Vic), Slavko Labovic (Radovan), Mads Mikkelsen (Tonny), Peter Andersson (Hasse), Vanja Bajicic (Branko)

A heroin dealer in Denmark has two days to pay off his debt to a local gangster or he will be killed.

Murky, grungy thriller about a side of Copenhagen rarely seen on film; the tension moves up a few notches as the desperate anti-hero's exit routes are closed off. It's effectively dramatic, and in a deadpan manner, even funny.

SCR Nicolas Winding Refn, Jens Dahl   CIN Morten Soborg   MUS Povl Kristian, Peter Peter   DES Kim Lovetand Julebaek   ED Anne Osterud   PROD Henrik Danstrup   DIST Metrodome/Balboa

66 The film practically vibrates with youthful aggression, sly humour and gathering tension, hurling itself forward like a junkie to the next fix. – *Robert Abele, Los Angeles Times*

'I'm the Angel of Death.'

Pusher 3

SCR/DIR Nicolas Winding Refn
2005   90m   Denmark
DVD

☆ Zlatko Buric (Milo), Marinela Dekic (Milena), Slavko Labovic (Radovan), Ramadan Huseini (Rexho), Kujtim Loki (Luan)

A middle-aged Serbian drug baron without a pension plan realises his criminal empire in Copenhagen is vulnerable to a new generation of violent gangsters.

Stomach-churning savagery, brutal killings and mutilated corpses set the tone, though a strain of darkest black humour is a slightly mitigating factor. Still, it's a long way down from this director's first Pusher movie.

CIN Morten Soborg   MUS PeterPeter   DES Rasmus Thjellesen   ED Anne Osterud, Miriam Norgaard   PROD Henrik Danstrup   DIST Vertigo

66 The third and final part of Nicolas Winding Refn's startling gangster trilogy is a crunching disappointment. – *Peter Bradshaw, The Guardian*

'Comedy about Life, Love, Airplanes and Other Bumpy Rides.'

Pushing Tin ★★

DIR Mike Newell
1999   124m   US
DVD   ♫

☆ *John Cusack* (Nick Falzone), *Billy Bob Thornton* (Russell Bell), *Cate Blanchett* (Connie Falzone), Angelina Jolie (Mary Bell), Vicki Lewis (Tina Leary), Kurt Fuller (Barry Plotkin), Matt Ross (Ron Hewitt), Jerry Grayson (Leo Morton), Michael Willis (Pat Feeney)

DVD Available on DVD   ☆ Cast in order of importance   66 Critics' Quotes   † Points of interest   ⚊ Academy Award   ⚊ Academy Award nomination   🛡 BAFTA   🛡 BAFTA nomination

A hotshot air traffic controller in New York feels his supremacy threatened by an ultra-cool new colleague.

A light, shambling comedy, a little ragged around the edges and all the more appealing for it. It never quite dazzles, yet it's also never less than amusing.

SCR Glen Charles, Les Charles CIN Gale Tattersall
MUS Anne Dudley, Chris Seefried DES Bruno Rubeo
ED Jon Gregory PROD Art Linson DIST TCF

66 It's frustrating to see such a promising premise, and such a delightful cast, wasted. – *David Ansen, Newsweek*

66 It's an intriguing film, one of the year's most interesting, but involving as it is, it leaves an unsatisfied taste when it's over. – *Kenneth Turan, Los Angeles Times*

Pygmalion ★★★★

DIR *Anthony Asquith, Leslie Howard*
1938 96m GB
DVD

☆ *Leslie Howard* (Henry Higgins), *Wendy Hiller* (Eliza Doolittle), *Wilfrid Lawson* (Alfred Doolittle), *Scott Sunderland* (Colonel Pickering), *Marie Lohr* (Mrs Higgins), *David Tree* (Freddy Eynsford-Hill), *Esmé Percy* (Count Aristid Karpathy), *Everley Gregg* (Mrs Eynsford-Hill), *Jean Cadell* (Mrs Pearce)

A professor of phonetics takes a bet that within six months he can turn a Cockney flower seller into a lady who can pass as a duchess.

Perfectly splendid Shavian comedy of bad manners, extremely well filmed and containing memorable lines and performances; subsequently turned into the musical My Fair Lady. One of the most heartening and adult British films of the 1930s.

SCR Anatole de Grunwald, W.P. Lipscomb, Cecil Lewis, Ian Dalrymple CIN Harry Stradling MUS *Arthur Honegger*
ED David Lean DIST Gabriel Pascal

HIGGINS (LESLIE HOWARD): Yes, you squashed cabbage leaf, you disgrace to the noble architecture of these columns, you incarnate insult to the English language, I can pass you off as the Queen of Sheba.
HIGGINS: Where the devil are my slippers, Eliza?

66 Ought to have big potentialities in the US, with some cutting. . .An introductory title briefly gives the source of the play, which was Shakespeare's Pygmalion.' (!) – *Variety*
'An exhibition of real movie-making – of a sound score woven in and out of tense scenes, creating mood and tempo and characterization. – *Pare Lorentz*

66 Every possible care has been taken in the presentation of what may well prove to have a significant effect on future British film production, for it is live, human entertainment, flawlessly presented and making an obvious appeal to all kinds of audiences. – *The Cinema*

⚎ Bernard Shaw; Ian Dalrymple, Cecil Lewis, W. P. Lipscomb (screenplay)
⚎ picture; Leslie Howard (leading actor); Wendy Hiller (leading actres)

P

DVD Available on DVD ☆ Cast in order 66 Critics' Quotes ⚎ Academy Award ⚈ BAFTA
♫ Soundtrack on CD of importance † Points of interest ⚎ Academy Award nomination ⚈ BAFTA nomination

505

'When the questions are dangerous, the answers can be deadly.'

Q & A ★

SCR/DIR Sidney Lumet
1990   132m   US
DVD

☆ *Nick Nolte* (Captain Michael Brennan), Timothy Hutton (Asst. Dist. Atty. Aloysius 'Al' Francis Reilly), *Armand Assante* (Roberto 'Bobby Tex' Texador), Patrick O'Neal (Kevin Quinn (Chief of Homicide)), Lee Richardson (Leo Bloomenfeld), Luis Guzman (Det. Luis Valentin), Charles Dutton (Det. Sam 'Chappie' Chapman), Jenny Lumet (Nancy Bosch / Mrs. Bobby Texador), Paul Calderon (Roger Montalvo)

A naïve new assistant D.A. probes the killing of a Puerto Rican dope dealer by a veteran cop, and discovers corruption throughout the legal and law enforcement systems.

A decent crime drama, with Nolte in roaring, rampaging form, that changes tack in midstream and focuses on racist attitudes in the NYPD.

CIN Andrezej Bartkowiak   **MUS** Ruben Blades
DES Philip Rosenberg   **ED** Richard Cirincione
PROD Arnon Milchan, Burtt Harris
DIST Virgin/Regency/Odyssey

66 This is (director Sidney) Lumet's boldest film in years – a combustible drama with a vivid shocking immediacy. – *Peter Travers, Rolling Stone*

'Tradition prepared her. Change will define her.'

The Queen ★★★

DIR *Stephen Frears*
2006   102m   UK/USA/France/Italy
DVD   ♫

☆ *Helen Mirren* (The Queen), *Michael Sheen* (Tony Blair), James Cromwell (Prince Philip), Helen McCrory (Cherie Blair), Alex Jennings (Prince Charles), *Roger Allam* (Robin Janvrin), Sylvia Syms (Queen Mother)

In the days after Princess Diana's death, Queen Elizabeth tries to maintain a dignified silence, staying at Balmoral Castle without meeting her subjects and joining in their grief. But persuaded by the new young Prime Minister, Tony Blair, she comes to accept times have changed.

Intriguing and provocative, with a brilliant script by Peter Morgan along the lines of Shakespearean history plays: the staging of known public facts and events, combined with deliciously imagined conversations behind closed doors. Director Frears maintains a brisk pace, interspersing speculative events with TV news footage. The story shifts subtly: the Queen concedes that public emotion is the modern mode of mass mourning, while Blair, initially wary, comes to admire the monarch. The lead actors are unimprovable: Helen Mirren suggests multiple facets of the Queen's personality, including vulnerability, pathos and humanity beneath a forbidding surface. Michael Sheen captures Blair's eager-to-please manner and Cheshire-cat grin perfectly. The only gripe is that the film's TV origins are a little too obvious. But remarkably, it conveys the complex, contradictory feelings shared by British subjects of The Queen, whatever their opinion about the monarchy.

SCR *Peter Morgan*   **CIN** Alfonso Beato   **MUS** Alexandre Desplat   **DES** Alan MacDonald   **ED** Lucia Zucchetti
PROD Andy Harries, Christine Langan, Tracey Seaward
DIST Pathe

66 An immensely entertaining and seemingly acute chronicle of the week Diana died. – *Richard Corliss, Time*

66 It is intelligent, hilariously funny and ultimately rather moving. – *Philip French, Observer*

♀ Helen Mirren (leading actress)
♀ picture; Stephen Frears; Peter Morgan; Alexandre Desplat; Consolata Boyle (costume design)
film; Helen Mirren (leading actress)
British film; Michael Sheen (supporting actor); Stephen Frears; Lucia Zucchetti; Alexandre Desplat; Consolata Boyle (costume design); Daniel Phillips (make up and hair)

'The Wild West Just Got A Little Wilder.'

The Quick and the Dead ★

DIR Sam Raimi
1995   107m   US
DVD   ♫

☆ Gene Hackman (John Herod), Sharon Stone (Ellen 'The Lady'), Leonardo DiCaprio (Fee Herod 'The Kid'), Russell Crowe (Cort), Tobin Bell (Dog Kelly), Roberts Blossom (Doc Wallace), Lance Henriksen (Ace Hanlon), Pat Hingle (Horace), Gary Sinise (The Marshal), Woody Strode (Charlie Moonlight)

Assorted gunmen and one angry gunwoman gather in a one-horse Western town for a gun-fighting contest in which the winner is the only person left alive.

Framed as a classic western, with gender politics thrown into the mix, and resulting in zany, straight-faced fun. The elegant Stone is a deeply unconvincing female gunfighter; but if viewed as a tongue-in-cheek feminist homage to spaghetti westerns, it passes the time amusingly.

SCR Simon Moore   CIN Dante Spinotti   MUS Alan
Silvestri   DES Patrizia von Brandenstein   ED Pietro
Scalia   PROD Joshua Donen, Allen Shapiro, Patrick
Markey   DIST Columbia TriStar

66 Although Sharon Stone may be pleasing to some eyes,
she's pretty small in the saddle here – just an innocuous
gender twist on the reluctant cowboy hero. And her story
of hell-bent revenge is about as compelling as a 30-second
fragrance commercial. – *Desson Howe, Washington Post*

'The bank robbery was easy. But getting out of New York
was a nightmare.'

Quick Change ★

DIR Howard Franklin, Bill Murray
1990   89m   US
DVD

☆ Bill Murray (Grimm), Geena Davis (Phyllis Potter),
Randy Quaid (Loomis), Jason Robards (Chief Rotzinger),
Bob Elliott (Bank Guard), Kimberleigh Aarn (Bank Teller),
Ron Ryan (Bank Customer), Brian McConnachie (Bank
Manager), Jack Gilpin (Yuppie Hostage)

Three robbers stage a spectacular bank job in New
York, but then struggle to make their escape out of
the city.

*Murray, whose character Grimm is dressed as a clown
to stage the robbery, co-directed this warm, faintly
poignant little comedy, and is easily its strongest selling
point. But it's uniformly well acted and has a strong,
affectionate sense of place.*

SCR Howard Franklin   CIN Michael Chapman
MUS Randy Edelman   DES Speed Hopkins   ED Alan
Heim   PROD Robert Greenhut, Bill Murray
DIST Warner/Devoted

66 A funny, but not inspired, comedy. – *Roger Ebert,
Chicago Sun-Times*

'In war, the most powerful weapon is seduction.'

The Quiet American ★★★

DIR *Phillip Noyce*
2002   101m   US/Germany/GB
DVD   ♫

☆ *Michael Caine* (Thomas Fowler), Brendan Fraser
(Alden Pyle), Do Thi Hai Yen (Phuong), Rade Sherbedgia
(Inspector Vigot), Tzi Ma (Hinh), Robert Stanton (Joe
Tunney), Holmes Osborne (Bill Granger), Pham Thi Mai
Hoa (Phuong's Sister), Quang Hai (The General)

A cynical British newspaper reporter and an
idealistic American doctor clash in Vietnam in the
early 1950s over politics and the love of a beautiful
woman.

*A more clear-eyed and politically astute version of
Greene's great novel than the 1957 film. Caine is
deeply moving as the wary, cynical journalist, and the
various betrayals, public and private, have a
devastating force.*

SCR Christopher Hampton, Robert Schenkkan
CIN Christopher Doyle   MUS Craig Armstrong
DES Roger Ford   ED John Scott   PROD William
Horberg, Staffan Ahrenberg   DIST Buena Vista

66 Michael Caine's performance as an English reporter
goaded out of his comfortable, opium-clouded, ex-pat

lifestyle ranks among the very best of his career. – *Alan
Morrison, Empire*

66 The reason I found myself finally unmoved by this film,
which is immaculately produced and has serious things to
say, is that it comes across rather too plainly as allegory. –
Christopher Tookey, Daily Mail

⚊ Michael Caine (leading actor)
Ⓣ Michael Caine (leading actor)

The Quiet Man ★★★

DIR *John Ford*
1952   129m   US
DVD   ♫

☆ *John Wayne* (Sean Thornton), *Maureen O'Hara* (Mary
Kate Danaher), *Barry Fitzgerald* (Michaeleen Flynn), *Victor
McLaglen* (Red Will Danaher), *Ward Bond* (Fr. Peter
Lonergan), Mildred Natwick (Mrs. Sarah Tillane), Francis
Ford (Dan Tobin), Arthur Shields (Rev. Cyril Playfair),
Eileen Crowe (Mrs. Elizabeth Playfair), Sean McClory
(Owen Glynn), Jack MacGowran (Feeney)

An Irish village version of The Taming of the Shrew,
the tamer being an ex-boxer retired to the land of his
fathers and in need of a wife. Archetypal John Ford
comedy, as Irish as can be, with everything but
leprechauns and the Blarney Stone on hand.

*Despite some poor sets the film has a gaiety about it,
with much brawling vigour and broad comedy, while
the actors all give their roistering best.*

SCR *Frank Nugent*   CIN *Winton C. Hoch, Archie Stout*
MUS *Victor Young*   ED Jack Murray   PROD John Ford,
Merian C. Cooper   DIST Republic/Argosy

66 Ford's art and artifice . . . are employed to reveal a way
of life – stable, rooted, honourable, purposeful in nature's
way, and thereby rhythmic. Everyone is an individual, yet
everyone and everything has a place. – *Henry Hart, Films
in Review*

⚊ John Ford; Winton C. Hoch, Archie Stout
(cinematography)
⚊ picture; Frank Nugent (original screenplay); Victor
McLaglen (supporting actor)

The Quince Tree Sun ★★

DIR Victor Erice
1992   133m   Spain
♫

☆ Antonio López (Himself)

A documentary follows artist Antonio López Garcia
for 10 weeks as he meticulously paints a tree of
yellow, ripening quinces, while reminiscing about
his life and talking to friends.

*A meticulous account of an artist's creative process that
commands the attention gradually and subtly. A rare
film for which the phrase 'watching paint dry' can be
expressed as a compliment.*

SCR Víctor Erice, Antonio López García   CIN Javier
Aguirresarobe, Angel Luis Fernandez   MUS Pascal Gaigne
ED Juan Ignacio San Mateo   DIST Artificial Eye/Maria
Moreno

66 More analytical than contemplative, never less than
straightforward, Dream of Light makes no showy bid for
the sublime. – *Village Voice*

Q

DVD Available on DVD   ☆ Cast in order   66 Critics' Quotes   ⚊ Academy Award   Ⓣ BAFTA
♫ Soundtrack on CD   of importance   † Points of interest   ⚊ Academy Award nomination   Ⓣ BAFTA nomination

507

'Fifty million people watched, but no one saw a thing.'

Quiz Show ★★★

DIR *Robert Redford*
1994 133m US
[DVD]

☆ John Turturro (Herbie Stempel), Ralph Fiennes (Charles Van Doren), Rob Morrow (Dick Goodwin), *Paul Scofield* (Mark Van Doren), David Paymer (Dan Enright), Hank Azaria (Albert Freedman), Christopher McDonald (Jack Barry), Griffin Dunne (Account Guy), Mira Sorvino (Sandra Goodwin), Martin Scorsese (Martin Rittenhome)

A scandal breaks in 1950s America when television's most famous quiz show is found to be rigged in a bid to attain higher ratings.

An outstandingly smart, incisive account of a famous example of corruption in network TV. On the quiz show 21 Fiennes plays a smooth-talking, affable, and above all telegenic professor who the network honchos want to cultivate; effectively, he's a perfect front man for their brand. Turturro is a sweating, gauche immigrant with an awkward manner – equally knowledgeable, but ratings suicide. This talky, absorbing drama touches on race, class and media values. Attanasio's script is a model of poise and wit. Recommendable, especially as the symptoms of malaise in TV land keep recurring.

SCR *Paul Attanasio* CIN Michael Ballhaus MUS Mark Isham DES Jon Hutman ED Stu Linder PROD Robert Redford, Michael Jacobs, Julian Krainin, Michael Nozik DIST Buena Vista/Hollywood/Wildwood/Baltimore

66 Acutely observed, beautifully performed, lovingly directed morality tale that resonates far beyond its 1950s setting. – *Kim Newman, Empire*

66 Perfectly pitched, the film brims with insight and wit. – *Time Out*

⚵ picture; Robert Redford; Paul Scofield (supporting actor); Paul Attanasio (screenplay)

ⵣ Paul Attanasio (screenplay)
ⵙ film; Paul Scofield (supporting actor)

Q

'A Daring Escape. An Epic Journey. The True Story Of 3 Girls Who Walked 1500 Miles To Find Their Way Home...'

Rabbit-Proof Fence ★★

DIR Phillip Noyce
2002   94m   Australia/GB
DVD ♫

☆ Everlyn Sampi (Molly Craig), Tianna Sansbury (Daisy Kadibill), Laura Monaghan (Gracie Fields), David Gulpilil (Moodoo), Kenneth Branagh (A. O. Neville), Deborah Mailman (Mavis), Jason Clarke (Constable Riggs), Ningali Lawford (Maud)

In 1930s Australia, three young mixed-race girls are taken from their aborigine mothers to be trained as servants for whites. But they escape and trek for 1,500 miles, along a rabbit-proof fence dividing the continent, to reach home.

This affecting film, based on a true story, is both a captivating adventure and an eloquent condemnation of a shameful government policy. Strikingly photographed against sparse terrain, with winning, natural performances from the children.

SCR Christine Olsen   **CIN** *Christopher Doyle*   **MUS** Peter Gabriel   **DES** Roger Ford   **ED** John Scott, Veronika Jenet   **PROD** Phillip Noyce, Christine Olsen, John Winter   **DIST** Buena Vista

66 This is a moving and fascinating look at a piece of recent history that most Australians would prefer to forget. – *Jo Berry, Empire*

† The government policy that allowed mixed-race children to be taken from their families and forced into servitude was not repealed until the 1970s.

A Rage in Harlem ★★

DIR Bill Duke
1991   108m   GB/US
DVD ♫

☆ *Forest Whitaker* (Jackson), Gregory Hines (Goldy), Robin Givens (Imabelle), Zakes Mokae (Big Kathy), Danny Glover (Easy Money), Badja Djola (Slim), John Toles-Bey (Jodie), Ron Taylor (Hank), Samm-Art Williams (Gus Parsons)

A gangster's mistress arrives in 1950s Harlem with a bag full of stolen booty. An innocent, pious undertaker's assistant gives her shelter.

Fast-moving and enjoyable thriller, though its violence jars with its mainly comic tone.

SCR John Toles-Bey, Bobby Crawford   **CIN** Toyomichi Kurita   **MUS** Elmer Bernstein, Jeff Vincent   **DES** Steven Legler   **ED** Curtiss Clayton   **PROD** Stephen Woolley, Kerry Rock   **DIST** Palace/Miramax

66 The film is less gritty noir than ebullient, good-natured fantasy. – *Geoff Andrew, Time Out*

Raging Bull ★★★★

DIR *Martin Scorsese*
1980   119m   US
DVD

☆ *Robert De Niro* (Jake LaMotta), Cathy Moriarty (Vickie LaMotta), *Joe Pesci* (Joey), Frank Vincent (Salvy), Nicholas Colasanto (Tommy Como)

The rise to fame of an unlikeable but virtually unstoppable middle-weight boxer, based on the autobiography of Jake La Motta, nicknamed the Bronx Bull.

Filmed largely in black-and-white, this tough, compelling, powerfully made melodrama takes us uncomfortably close to the jarring action in the ring. An astonishing performance from De Niro, who inhabits the role to an eerie extent, and Scorsese orchestrates events with the aim of capturing the crunching reality of this world. It's brutal, and not a single character truly engages one's sympathy, but there's undeniably a visual poetry about it.

SCR Paul Schrader, Mardik Martin   **CIN** *Michael Chapman*   **MUS** from library sources   **DES** Gene Rudolf   **ED** *Thelma Schoonmaker*   **DIST** UA/Chartoff-Winkler

66 Scorsese makes pictures about the kind of people you wouldn't want to know. – *Variety*

66 One of the bloodiest and most beautiful reflections on atonement in the Scorsese canon...It is still one of cinema's most breathtaking films. – *Sheila Benson, Los Angeles Times*

⌐ Robert De Niro (leading actor); Thelma Schoonmaker (editing)
⌐ film; Cathy Moriarty (supporting actress); Joe Pesci (supporting actor); Martin Scorsese (direction); Michael Chapman; Donald O. Mitchell, Bill Bicholson, David J. Kimball, Les Lazarowitz (sound)
⍟ Joe Pesci (supporting actor); editing

Raiders of the Lost Ark ★★★

DIR *Steven Spielberg*
1981   115m   US
DVD ♫

☆ Harrison Ford (Indiana Jones), Karen Allen (Marion Ravenwood), Ronald Lacey (Toht), Paul Freeman (Belloq), John Rhys-Davies (Sallah), Denholm Elliott (Brody), Wolf Kahler (Dietrich), Anthony Higgins (Gobler), Alfred Molina (Satipo)

DVD Available on DVD   ☆ Cast in order   66 Critics' Quotes   ⌐ Academy Award   ⍟ BAFTA
♫ Soundtrack on CD   of importance   † Points of interest   ⌐ Academy Award nomination   ⍟ BAFTA nomination

509

In the 1930s, an American archaeologist and explorer beats the Nazis to a priceless artefact, the magical box containing fragments of the stones on which God wrote his laws.

Commercially very successful, this attempted wrap-up of pre-war Saturday morning serials spends a great deal of money and expertise on frightening rather than exciting us. Second time round, one can better enjoy the ingenious detail of the hero's exploits; still, there are boring bits in between, and the story doesn't make a lot of sense. Yet this was the genesis of the modern action-adventure blockbuster for all the family, and few of its successors have a fraction of its wit, verve or sense of fun.

SCR Lawrence Kasdan   CIN Douglas Slocombe
MUS John Williams   DES *Norman Reynolds*   ED Michael Kahn   PROD Frank Marshall
DIST Paramount/Lucasfilm

66 Both de trop and not enough. – *Sight & Sound*

66 Children may well enjoy its simple-mindedness, untroubled by the fact that it looks so shoddy and so uninventive. – *Observer*

† Tom Selleck was the first choice for the lead, but was tied up with his TV series Magnum.
† It was followed by three sequels: Indiana Jones and the Temple of Doom, Indiana Jones and the Last Crusade and Indiana Jones and the Kingdom of the Crystal Skull.

⚊ Michael Kahn (editing); visual effects
⚊ picture; Steven Spielberg (direction); Douglas Slocombe; John Williams
Ⓣ Norman Reynolds

Rain Man ★★★

DIR *Barry Levinson*
1988   133m   US
[DVD]   ♬

☆ *Dustin Hoffman* (Raymond Babbitt), *Tom Cruise* (Charlie Babbitt), Valeria Golino (Susanna), Jerry Molen (Dr. Bruner), Jack Murdock (John Mooney), Michael D. Roberts (Vern), Ralph Seymour (Lenny), Lucinda Jenney (Iris), Bonnie Hunt (Sally Dibbs)

On his father's death, a young wheeler-dealer, heavily in debt, discovers to his chagrin that all the money is left to an autistic elder brother, unknown to him.

A road movie with a difference, featuring one of the most showy, and admittedly memorable leading performances in recent years. Hoffman is remarkably meticulous in his portrayal of the immutable, repetitive idiot savant. Yet the film stands and falls on Cruise: it later became a cliché that he chose characters who progressed from arrogant egotism to selflessness, yet that is precisely what is required here. Working from a script that pushes all the right buttons, Levinson directs with snap, energy and a good deal of wit.

SCR *Ronald Bass, Barry Morrow*   CIN John Seale
MUS Hans Zimmer   DES Ida Random   ED Stu Linder
PROD Mark Johnson   DIST UIP/United Artists/Guber-Peters

RAYMOND: (REPEATEDLY): I'm an excellent driver.
RAYMOND: (REPEATEDLY): Three minutes to Wapner.

66 Somehow, Hoffman makes all this hypnotically interesting, and, through impeccable timing, sometimes terribly funny– a sweet humour which never betrays Raymond's unalterable character. – *Sheila Benson, Los Angeles Times*

66 How can you make a movie about a man who cannot change, whose whole life is anchored and defended by routine? Few actors could get anywhere with this challenge, and fewer still could absorb and even entertain us with their performance, but Hoffman proves again that he almost seems to thrive on impossible acting challenges. – *Roger Ebert, Chicago Sun-Times*

† A film that had a hugely troubled pre-production period, with various leading actors and directors coming and going, while the budget spiralled.

⚊ picture; director; original screenplay; Dustin Hoffman (leading actor)
⚊ original score; cinematography; film editing; art direction
Ⓣ Dustin Hoffman (leading actor); Stu Linder; screenplay

Raining Stones ★★

DIR Ken Loach
1993   90m   GB
[DVD]

☆ Bruce Jones (Bob), Julie Brown (Anne), Gemma Phoenix (Coleen), Ricky Tomlinson (Tommy), Tom Hickey (Father Barry), Mike Fallon (Jimmy), Ronnie Ravey (Butcher), Lee Brennan (Irishman)

In the north of England, a hard-up unemployed Catholic father frantically tries to raise the cash for a communion dress for his young daughter, rather than accept a loan from a priest.

Grim, unblinking glance at British life below the poverty line, where loan sharks hover menacingly. Bruce Jones is moving, in the lead role, and his scenes with Ricky Tomlinson as his clueless best friend are minor masterpieces of comic timing. An uneven film that scores its political points effectively.

SCR Jim Allen   CIN Barry Ackroyd   MUS Stewart Copeland   DES Martin Johnson   ED Jonathan Morris
PROD Sally Hibbin   DIST First Independent/Parallax/Channel 4

66 The picture doesn't break any new ground – this sort of kitchen-sink realism has been a British speciality since the 50s. Yet Loach creates a story that is so gripping and sadly true to life that the need to stretch the genre, or transcend it, seems beside the point. – *Hal Hinson, Washington Post*

66 People laugh along with Raining Stones, even before it's started, because it is a Ken Loach film above all else. – *Jenny Turner, Sight & Sound*

† Bruce Jones later became nationally known as Les Battersby, a comic character on the TV soap opera Coronation Street.

Ⓣ British film

'China, 1920's. One master, four wives . . . One fate.'

Raise the Red Lantern ★★★

DIR *Zhang Yimou*
1991   125m   Hong Kong
[DVD]   ♬

☆ Gong Li (Songlian), Ma Jingwu (Master Chen Zuoqian), He Caifei (Meishan), Cao Cuifen (Zhuoyun), Jin Shuyuan

(Yuru), Kong Lin (Yan'er), Ding Weimin (Songlian's mother), Cui Zhihgang (Doctor Gao), Chu Xiao (Feipu)

Against her family's wishes, a teenage girl in 1920s China becomes the fourth wife of a rich merchant, and finds herself competing for her husband's goodwill against his other wives.

An enthralling examination of a male-dominated society; Zhang Yimou uses colour schemes, meticulously symmetrical compositions and stylised interiors to evoke an inflexible society. It is a film of ravishing formal beauty – to the extent that its look threatens to soften the ugly aspects of the society it depicts

SCR Ni Zhen   CIN Zhao Fei, Yang Lun   MUS Zhao Jiping, Naoki Tachikawa   ED Du Yuan   PROD Chiu Fu-Sheng   DIST Palace/Era/China Film

66 A beautifully crafted and richly detailed feat of consciousness-raising and a serious drama with the verve of a good soap opera. – *Janet Maslin, New York Times*

⚲ foreign film

🇹 foreign film

'When Jenny cheated on her husband, he didn't just leave . . . he split.'

Raising Cain ★

SCR/DIR Brian de Palma
1992   91m   US
DVD   ♫

☆ John Lithgow (Carter/Cain/Dr. Nix/Josh/Margo), Lolita Davidovich (Jenny), Steven Bauer (Jack Dante), Frances Sternhagen (Dr. Lynn Waldheim), Gregg Henry (Lt. Terri), Tom Bower (Sgt. Cully), Mel Harris (Sarah), Teri Austin (Karen), Gabrielle Carteris (Nan)

A child psychologist with multiple personality disorder becomes a suspect when several children go missing.

Brian de Palma sometimes makes bad films, though never dull ones. This time he's in Hitchcock-fan mode, with Lithgow offering a virtuoso, if tongue-in-cheek performance as the various identities of a single individual. Best viewed for its sly, straight-faced excess, it also springs some chilling shocks.

CIN Stephen H. Burum   MUS Pino Donaggio
DES Doug Kraner   ED Paul Hirsch, Bonnie Koehler, Robert Dalva   PROD Gale Anne Hurd
DIST UIP/Universal

66 Shallow, derivative, misogynous and heartless, in Raising Cain, (director Brian) De Palma seems to be buying his own bad press. His film is a sorry and cynical exercise in self-loathing. – *Peter Travers, Rolling Stone*

66 A sterile, tail-chasing admission of defeat. – *Jonathan Romney, Sight & Sound*

Raising Victor Vargas ★★

SCR/DIR Peter Sollett
2002   88m   US/France
DVD

☆ Victor Rasuk (Victor Vargas), Judy Marte (Judy Gonzalez), Melonie Diaz (Melonie), *Altagracia Guzman* (Grandma), Silvestre Rasuk (Nino Vargas), Krystal Rodriguez (Vicki Vargas), Kevin Rivera (Harold), Wilfree Vasquez (Carlos)

A macho teenage boy on New York's Lower East Side is determined to enjoy a lively love-life, but his strict, devout grandmother thinks otherwise.

An appealing debut from writer/director Sollett that covers a lot of ground, both in terms of its social setting and its domestic tensions. A cast of mainly amateur actors reinforce the feeling of authenticity.

CIN Tim Orr   MUS Roy Nathanson, Brad Jones
DES Judy Becker   ED Myron Kerstein   PROD Peter Sollett, Alain de la Mata, Robin O'Hara, Scott Macaulay
DIST Momentum

66 This gentle family comedy is thoroughly likeable, thanks to its host of charming characters and poignant, upbeat ending. – *Empire*

66 Tender and funny. – *J. Hoberman, Village Voice*

'Innocence has never been so seductive.'

Rambling Rose ★★

DIR Martha Coolidge
1991   112m   US
DVD   ♫

☆ Laura Dern (Rose), Robert Duvall (Daddy Hilyer), Diane Ladd (Mother), Lukas Haas (Buddy), John Heard (Willcox Hillyer), Kevin Conway (Dr. Martinson), Robert Burke (Dave Wilkie), Lisa Jakub (Doll), Evan Lockwood (Waski), Matt Sutherland (Billy)

A young boy growing up in an affluent household in the deep South of the 1930s is bowled over by the arrival of a troubled, apparently promiscuous young girl hired as a housekeeper.

Delicate, but ultimately upbeat story about a troubling new presence within an eccentric, essentially kindly family.

SCR Calder Willingham   CIN Johnny E. Jensen
MUS Elmer Bernstein   DES John Vallone   ED Steven Cohen   PROD Renny Harlin   DIST Guild/Carolco

66 Here is a movie as light as air, as delicate as a flower. Breathe on it and it will wither. It tells the story of a strange Southern family and the troubled teenage girl who comes to live with them and brings a sharp awareness of carnality under their roof, with only the most cheerful of results. – *Roger Ebert, Chicago Sun-Times*

⚲ Laura Dern (leading actress); Diane Ladd (supporting actress)

'Heroes never die – they just reload.'

Rambo (new)

DIR Sylvester Stallone
2008   91m   US/Germany
DVD

☆ Sylvester Stallone (Rambo), Julie Benz (Sarah), Matthew Marsden (Schoolboy), Graham McTavish (Lewis)

John Rambo is retired from combat and living near a Thai river. But he agrees to take a group of American charity workers upstream into a Burmese war zone.

Little more than a cartoon, the film caters only for those still smitten by the rat-a-tat of continuous gunfire. Yet it works on its own impoverished terms: a film that knows

R

DVD Available on DVD   ☆ Cast in order   66 Critics' Quotes   ⚲ Academy Award   🇹 BAFTA
♫ Soundtrack on CD   of importance   † Points of interest   ⚲ Academy Award nomination   🇹 BAFTA nomination

511

what it is, with a star content to embrace his limitations.

SCR Art Monterastelli, Sylvester Stallone CIN Glen MacPherson MUS Brian Tyler DES Franco Giacomo Carbone ED Sean Albertson PROD Avi Lerner, Kevin King-Templeton, John Thompson DIST Columbia

66 This is 90 minutes of violence. No more, no less. – *David Jenkins, Time Out*

66 What it can't quite do is gloss over the preposterous centre-stage presence of its 61 year-old star. – *Xan Brooks, Guardian*

† It has been estimated that a record 236 characters are killed in the course of this film.

Ran ★★★

DIR *Akira Kurosawa*
1985 161m Japan
DVD ♫

☆ Tatsuya Nakadai (Lord Hidetora Ichimonji), Satoshi Terao (Tarotakatora Ichimonji), Jinpachi Nezu (Jiromasatora Ichimonji), Daisuke Ryu (Saburonaotora Ichimonji), Peter (Kyoami)

A Japanese version of King Lear, with three sons instead of three daughters.

Predictable bloodshed and tremendous style are evident in this oriental epic from a master film-maker at the age of 75.

SCR Akira Kurosawa, Hideo Oguni, Masato Ide CIN *Takao Saito* MUS Toru Takemitsu ED Akira Kurosawa PROD Masato Hara, Serge Silberman DIST Herald-Ace/Nippon-Herald/Greenwich

66 Prepare to be astonished. . .a towering achievement in any language. – *People*

66 The triumphant masterpiece of Akira Kurosawa's fertile twilight. – *Desmond Ryan, Philadelphia Inquirer*

⌇ Emi Wada (costume design)
⌇ Akira Kurosawa (direction); photography; art direction
ⓣ foreign film

R

'Rapture (rap'chur) 1. ecstatic joy or delight. 2. a state of extreme sexual ecstasy. 3. the feeling of being transported to another sphere of existence. 4. the experience of being spirited away to Heaven just before the Apocalypse.'

The Rapture ★★

SCR/DIR *Michael Tolkin*
1991 100m US
DVD ♫

☆ *Mimi Rogers* (Sharon), David Duchovny (Randy), Patrick Bauchau (Vic), Kimberly Cullum (Mary), Terri Hanauer (Paula), Dick Anthony Williams (Henry), James LeGros (Tommy)

A telephone operator with a taste for unconventional sex suddenly hears a message from God, turns to fundamentalist religion and heads for the desert, where she awaits the Second Coming.

A thoughtful provocative debut from writer-director Tolkin, who treats the subject of evangelical sects in a materialist, godless society with intelligence and irreverent wit.

CIN Bojan Bazelli MUS Thomas Newman DES Robert Standefer ED Suzanne Fenn PROD Karen Koch, Nancy

Tenenbaum, Nick Wechsler DIST Electric/New Line/Wechsler/Tenenbaum/Parker

66 Without question, it's a nutty piece of work, and it gets nuttier as it goes along. – *Hal Hinson, Washington Post*

66 Though this controversial movie has been screened at several prestigious film festivals, The Rapture isn't art— it's misery. – *Peter Travers, Rolling Stone*

Rashomon ★★★★

SCR/DIR *Akira Kurosawa*
1951 83m Japan
DVD ♫

☆ Toshiro Mifune (The bandit), Machiko Kyo (Masago, the samurai's wife), Masayuki Mori (The samurai), Takashi Shimura (The woodcutter), Minoru Chiaki (The priest)

In mediaeval Japan, four people have different versions of a violent incident, when a bandit attacks a nobleman in the forest.

Indescribably vivid in itself, and genuinely strange (one of the versions is told by a ghost), Rashomon reintroduced Japanese films to the world market and was remade (badly) in Hollywood as The Outrage in 1964. But its device of an incident re-told from different perspectives and memories is so potent and compelling that it has echoes in any number of subsequent films.

CIN *Kazuo Miyagawa* MUS Fumio Hayasaka PROD Jingo Minoura DIST Daiei

66 A masterpiece, and a revelation. – *Gavin Lambert, Monthly Film Bulletin*

⌇ foreign film
⌇ art direction

'A comedy with great taste.'

Ratatouille (new) ★★★

SCR/DIR Brad Bird
2007 111m US
DVD ♫

☆ Patton Oswalt (Voice of Remy), Ian Holm (Voice of Skinner), Lou Romano (Voice of Alfredo Linguini), Brian Dennehy (Voice of Remy's father), *Peter O'Toole* (Voice of Anton Ego)

Remy, a Parisian rat who wants to be a gourmet chef, teams up with a young underling in a five-star restaurant.

Brilliant animation executed with deft skill. Witty and funny, though some jokes are too knowing and subtle for younger audiences.

CIN Sharon Calahan, Robert Anderson MUS Michael Giacchino DES Harley Jessup ED Darren Holmes PROD Brad Lewis DIST Buena Vista

66 Brad Bird and Pixar recapture the charm and winning imagination of classic Disney animation. – *Kirk Honeycutt, Hollywood Reporter*

66 Bird clearly knows the great silent clowns: the slapstick he devises is balletic. – *David Edelstein, New York Magazine*

⌇ animated feature film
⌇ Brad Bird (original screenplay); Michael Giacchino; Randy Thom, Michael Semarick, Doc Kane (sound); Randy Thom, Michael Silvers (sound editing)
ⓣ animated film

DVD Available on DVD	☆ Cast in order of importance	66 Critics' Quotes	⌇ Academy Award	ⓣ BAFTA
♫ Soundtrack on CD		† Points of interest	⌇ Academy Award nomination	ⓣ BAFTA nomination

Ratcatcher ★★★

SCR/DIR *Lynne Ramsay*
1999   94m   GB/France
DVD ♫

☆ William Eadie (James), Tommy Flanagan (Da), Mandy Matthews (Ma), Michelle Stewart (Ellen), Lynne Ramsay Jnr (Anne Marie), Leanne Mullen (Margaret Anne), John Miller (Kenny), Jackie Quinn (Mrs Quinn)

In 1970s Glasgow, a 12-year-old boy keeps quiet after he accidentally drowns a friend in a canal. Haunted by the memory, he daydreams of moving from his city slum to a new housing estate, near green fields on the edge of town.

A breakthrough movie from a young film-maker with a sharp eye for dreamy, lyrical imagery. The 1973 dustbin men's strike provides a suitably grim contrast to the escapist pastoral dreams of the guilt-stricken boy. Unusually for a British film, it's a wildly successful marriage of gritty reality and visual poetry.

CIN *Alwin Küchler*   MUS Rachel Portman   DES Jane Morton   ED *Lucia Zucchetti*   PROD Gavin Emerson
DIST Pathé

❝ (Director Lynne) Ramsay's imaginative shot-making gifts make for a sublime result, creating a different sort of magical realism than we're used to seeing. – *Kenneth Turan, Los Angeles Times*

❝ A film of a unique kind. I could never love anyone who did not love Ratcatcher. – *Andrew O'Hagan, Daily Telegraph*

Ⓣ Lynne Ramsay (newcomer)
Ⓣ British film

'The extraordinary life story of Ray Charles. A man who fought harder and went farther than anyone thought possible.'

Ray ★★★

DIR *Taylor Hackford*
2004   152m   US
DVD ♫

☆ *Jamie Foxx* (Ray Charles), Kerry Washington (Della Bea Robinson), Regina King (Margie Hendricks), Clifton Powell (Jeff Brown), Aunjanue Ellis (Mary Ann Fisher), Harry Lennix (Joe Adams), Terrence Dashon Howard (Gossie McKee), Larenz Tate (Quincy Jones), Bokeem Woodbine (Fathead Newman)

Film biography of the great singer and pianist Ray Charles, and his struggles with blindness and drug addiction.

Foxx's astonishing performance anchors a biopic that evokes a particular era of music with visual brilliance, and faithfully tracks the roots of Charles's creative genius – combining as he did the sacred and profane into a fresh musical genre. As happens so often in such biopics, there's a heavy-handed attempt to pin all Charles's problems on one traumatic incident – in this case, the tragic death of a sibling. And the film concludes with the bland comment that once Charles kicked drugs, he went on to become a national treasure, omitting to add that his music went into decline from this precise point; this leaves open the question of whether his musical genius was actually liberated by narcotics. Still, it's a vivid, sometimes joyous insider view of what was then called 'race music'.

SCR James L. White   CIN Pawel Edelman   MUS Craig Armstrong   DES Stephen Altman   ED *Paul Hirsch*
PROD Howard Baldwin, Karen Baldwin, Taylor Hackford, Stuart Benjamin   DIST Universal

❝ Ambitious, honest, music-drenched, handsomely mounted, wonderfully acted biopic of the great Ray Charles. – *David Ansen, Newsweek*

⚱ Jamie Foxx (leading actor); John Dykstra, Scott Stokdyk, Anthony LaMolinara, John Frazier (visual effects); Scott Millan, Greg Orloff, Bob Beemer, Steve Cantamessa (sound mixing)

⚱ film; Taylor Hackford; Paul Hirsch; Sharen Davis

Ⓣ Jamie Foxx (leading actor); sound
Ⓣ Craig Armstrong; screenplay

'Who said saving the world can't be entertaining?'

Razzle Dazzle (new) ★

DIR Darren Ashton
2007   91m   Australia

☆ *Ben Miller* (Mr. Jonathon), Kerry Armstrong (Justine), Shayni Notelovitz (Tenille), Sheridan Rynne (Vanessa), Kerry-Ann Thoo (Millie)

In this mock documentary, an Australian film crew follows and interviews rival teams preparing for the grand finale of a major children's ballroom dancing competition.

Strictly over-familiar camp territory lacking any real point, surprise or laughs, but redeemed by a strong lead performance.

SCR Robin Ince, Carolyn Wilson   CIN Garry Phillips
MUS Roger Mason   DES Karen Harborow   ED Julie-Ann De Ruvo   PROD Andrena Finlay, Jodi Matterson
DIST Sony Pictures

❝ "Easy to like...understated and wry". – *Megan Lehmann, The Hollywood Reporter*

❝ British comic Ben Miller is brilliant as pretentious choreographer Mr. Jonathon, who devises dances with social significance, like a prize-winning number dramatising the liberation of Afghan women from their Taliban oppressors. – *Philip French, Observer*

'She taught him good manners, he taught her bad ones.'

Read My Lips ★★★

DIR *Jacques Audiard*
2001   118m   France
DVD

☆ Vincent Cassel (Paul Angeli), *Emmanuelle Devos* (Carla Behm), Olivier Gourmet (Marchand), Olivia Bonamy (Annie), Olivier Perrier (Masson), Bernard Alane (Morel), Céline Samie (Josie Marchand), David Saracino (Richard Carambo)

A secretary with hearing problems uses her ability to lip-read in assisting a petty thief she has hired as a trainee.

A smart psychological two-hander about office duplicity, benefiting from Audiard's taut direction and a terrific performance from Devos.

DVD Available on DVD   ☆ Cast in order of importance   ❝ Critics' Quotes   † Points of interest   ⚱ Academy Award   Academy Award nomination   Ⓣ BAFTA   Ⓣ BAFTA nomination

513

SCR Tonino Benacquista, Jacques Audiard   CIN Mathieu Vadepied   MUS Alexandre Desplat   DES Michel Barthélémy   ED *Juliette Welfling*   PROD Jean-Louis Livi, Philippe Carcassonne   DIST Pathé

66 Expertly sinister. – *Lisa Schwarzbaum, Entertainment Weekly*

66 A wholly amoral movie, but it's honestly amoral. – *Charles Taylor, Salon*

'What you see isn't always what you get.'

The Real Blonde ★

SCR/DIR Tom DiCillo
1997   105m   US
DVD ♫

☆ Matthew Modine (Joe), Catherine Keener (Mary), Daryl Hannah (Kelly), Maxwell Caulfield (Bob), Elizabeth Berkley (Tina), Marlo Thomas (Blair), Bridgette Wilson (Sahara)

Two struggling New York actors, their relationships troubled by money and pregnancy, compromise their ideals and finally make good.

Lightweight satire on life in media circles, with fashion photographers and TV soap opera stars most cruelly targeted. Hardly original, but sharply amusing.

CIN Frank Prinzi   MUS Jim Farmer   DES Christopher A. Nowak   ED Camilla Toniolo, Keiko Deguchi   PROD Marcus Viscidi, Tom Rosenberg   DIST Paramount/Lakeshore

66 Media superficiality and the cult of pretty have been fair game since the dawn of the photo age, maybe since the first cave-wall centrefold. But by interweaving a very contemporary love story into these themes [director Tom] DiCillo has at least given it a fresh spin. – *Jack Mathews, Los Angeles Times*

'A Comedy About Love In The '90s.'

Reality Bites ★

DIR Ben Stiller
1993   99m   US
DVD ♫

☆ Winona Ryder (Lelaina Pierce), Ethan Hawke (Troy Dyer), Ben Stiller (Michael Grates), Janeane Garofalo (Vickie Miner), Steve Zahn (Sammy Gray), Swoosie Kurtz (Charlane McGregor), Joe Don Baker (Tom Pierce), John Mahoney (Grant Gubler), Harry O'Reilly (Wes McGregor), Barry Sherman (Grant's Producer)

A young graduate with a musician boy-friend makes a video documentary about her friends and ambitions and is torn when she learns a TV executive has fallen for her.

Ryder is plausible in the central role, and if much of this rambling love story now seems contrived and shallow, it chimed with its times.

SCR Helen Childress   CIN Emmanuel Lubezki   MUS Karl Wallinger   DES Sharon Seymour   ED Lisa Churgin, John Spence   PROD Danny DeVito, Michael Shamberg   DIST Universal/Jersey

66 There's probably a moderate little romantic comedy crying to get out here, but the film's vain striving for casual hip proves suffocatingly obtrusive. – *Trevor Johnston, Time Out*

66 Reality Bites begins as a promising and eccentric tale of contemporary youth but evolves into a banal love story as predictable as any lush Hollywood affair. – *Leonard Klady, Variety*

Rear Window ★★★★

DIR *Alfred Hitchcock*
1954   112m   US
DVD

☆ *James Stewart* (L.B. 'Jeff' Jeffries), *Grace Kelly* (Lisa Carol Fremont), *Raymond Burr* (Lars Thorwald), Judith Evelyn (Miss Lonely Hearts), Wendell Corey (Det. Thomas J. Doyle), *Thelma Ritter* (Stella)

A photo-journalist, confined to his room by a broken leg, is convinced he has seen a murder committed in a room on the other side of the court.

Artificial but gripping suspense thriller, which has plenty to say about voyeurism and the reality of what is observed from a distance. Delightfully, each window opposite provides a glimpse of a miniature drama that resolves itself (or not) during the film's course. Intriguingly, Hitchcock added a sexually knowing romance between Stewart and Kelly to this intriguing premise. It all adds up to one of the director's most brilliant movies.

SCR *John Michael Hayes*   CIN Robert Burks   MUS Franz Waxman   ED George Tomasini   DIST Paramount/Alfred Hitchcock

† The film's theme was lifted wholesale in Disturbia (2006)

⚱ Alfred Hitchcock (direction); John Michael Hayes (screenplay); Robert Burks

---

'The shadow of this woman darkened their love.'

Rebecca ★★★★

DIR *Alfred Hitchcock*
1940   130m   US
DVD ♫

☆ *Laurence Olivier* (Maxim de Winter), *Joan Fontaine* (Mrs. de Winter), *George Sanders* (Jack Favell), *Judith Anderson* (Mrs. Danvers), *Nigel Bruce* (Maj. Giles Lacy), *Gladys Cooper* (Beatrice Lacy), *Florence Bates* (Mrs. Van Hopper), *Reginald Denny* (Frank Crawley), *C. Aubrey Smith* (Col. Julyan), Melville Cooper (Coroner), Leo G. Carroll (Dr. Baker), Leonard Carey (Ben)

The naïve young second wife of a Cornish landowner is haunted by the image of his glamorous first wife Rebecca.

The supreme Hollywood entertainment package, set in Monte Carlo and Cornwall, with generous helpings of romance, comedy, suspense, melodrama and mystery, all indulged in by strongly-drawn characters, and directed by the English wizard from a novel which sold millions of copies. It really couldn't miss, and it didn't.

SCR *Robert E. Sherwood, Joan Harrison*   CIN *George Barnes*   MUS *Franz Waxman*   ED *Hal C. Kern*   DIST David O. Selznick

NARRATOR: Last night I dreamed I went to Manderley again. . .

FAVELL (GEORGE SANDERS) TO MRS DE WINTER: I say, marriage with Max is not exactly a bed of roses, is it?

MRS DANVERS (JUDITH ANDERSON): You're overwrought, madam. I've opened a window for you. A little air will do you good. Why don't you go? Why don't you leave Manderley? He doesn't need you. He's got his memories. He doesn't love you – he wants to be alone again with her. You've nothing to stay for. You've nothing to live for, have you, really? Look down there. It's easy, isn't it? Why don't you? Go on, go on. Don't be afraid. . .

MAXIM (LAURENCE OLIVIER): You thought I loved Rebecca? You thought that? I hated her. Oh, I was carried away by her – enchanted by her, as everyone was – and when I was married, I was told I was the luckiest man in the world. She was so lovely, so accomplished, so amusing. "She's got the three things that really matter in a wife," everyone said, "breeding, brains and beauty." And I believed them completely. But I never had a moment's happiness with her. She was incapable of love, or tenderness, or decency.

66 A carefully considered trying out of the superior technical resources now at Hitchcock's disposal. – *George Perry, 1965*

66 Hitchcock fans will have to put up with a surprising lack of the characteristic Hitchcock improvisations in the way of salty minor personages and humorous interludes, and satisfy themselves with a masterly exhibition of the Hitchcock skill in creating suspense and shock with his action and his camera. – *National Board of Review*

† Original casting thoughts, all rejected, were Ronald Colman, William Powell and Leslie Howard for Maxim; Anne Baxter, Margaret Sullavan, Loretta Young, Vivien Leigh and Olivia de Havilland (for the second Mrs de Winter).

picture; George Barnes

Laurence Olivier (leading actor); Joan Fontaine (leading actress); Judith Anderson (supporting actress); Alfred Hitchcock (direction); Robert E. Sherwood, Joan Harrison (screenplay); Franz Waxman; Lyle Wheeler; Hal C. Kern

---

'The bad boy from a good family!'

Rebel without a Cause ★★★

DIR *Nicholas Ray*
1955 111m US
[DVD] ♫

☆ *James Dean* (Jim), Natalie Wood (Judy), Jim Backus (Jim's Father), *Sal Mineo* (Plato), Ann Doran (Jim's Mother), Dennis Hopper (Goon)

The adolescent son of a well-to-do family gets into trouble with other kids and the police.

The first Hollywood film to suggest that juvenile violence is not necessarily bred in the slums, this melodrama also catapulted James Dean to stardom as the prototype 1950s rebel – less than articulate, but neurotically sensitive.

SCR *Stewart Stern* CIN Ernest Haller MUS Leonard Rosenman ED William Ziegler PROD David Weisbart
DIST Warner

JIM (TO HIS PARENTS): You're tearing me apart!

† Dean died in a car accident before the film's opening.

Natalie Wood (supporting actress); Sal Mineo (supporting actor); Nicholas Ray (original story)

[Rec] (new) ★★★

DIR Jaume Balaguero, Paco Plaza
2007 85m Spain

☆ Manuela Velasco (Angela), Ferrán Terraza (Manu), Jorge Serrano (Sergio), Pablo Rosso (Marcos), David Vert (Alex)

Crew of a Spanish reality TV show are caught up in a rabid virus outbreak while accompanying firemen on a routine call. All they can do is tape the unfolding nightmare so the actual events will eventually be seen.

Working the Blair Witch documentary aesthetic to urgent perfection, this well-sustained, often terrifying shocker twists into totally unexpected territory.

SCR Luiso Berdejo, Jaume Balaguero, Paco Plaza
CIN Pablo Rosso DES Gemma Fauria ED David Gallart
PROD Julio Fernández DIST Odeon Sky Filmworks

66 Strictly-by-the-numbers Spanish horror flick. – *Alissa Simon, Variety*

66 The edge-of-the-seat tension is sustained to the very last second. – *Nigel Floyd, Time Out*

The Red Balloon ★★★★

SCR/DIR *Albert Lamorisse*
1955 34m France

☆ Pascal Lamorisse (Pascal)

A lonely boy finds a balloon which becomes his constant companion and finally lifts him to the skies.

Absorbing and quite perfectly timed fantasy, one of the great film shorts. Without dialogue.

CIN *Edmond Sechan* MUS *Maurice Le Roux* ED Pierre Gillette DIST Films Montsouris

Albert Lamorisse (original screenplay)

'An Explosive Love Story.'

Red Firecracker, Green Firecracker ★★

DIR He Ping
1994 115m China/Hong Kong
[DVD]

☆ Ning Jing (Cai Chunzhi), Zhao Xiaorui (Dihong), Gao Yang (Butler), Xu Zhengyun (Old Master Xu), Zhao Liang (Hei Liu)

A young woman in early 1920s China pretends to be a man in order to run the family firework factory – but then falls for a macho artist.

An intriguing story of forbidden love and hidden sexuality in an oppressed society. Vivid and colourful, it could also be subtler.

SCR Da Ying Ye CIN Yang Lun MUS Zhao Jiping, Zhang When, Changning Gu DES Qian Yunxiu
ED Yuan Hong PROD Chan Chun-Keung, Yung Naiming
DIST Electric/Yung/Xi'an Studio/Beijing Salon

66 With his eye for gorgeous, haunting visuals and two exceptionally attractive stars to play tormented lovers, Chinese director He Ping works a lovely magic with his moodily romantic film. – *Peter Stack, San Francisco Chronicle*

R

[DVD] Available on DVD   ☆ Cast in order   66 Critics' Quotes   Academy Award   BAFTA
♫ Soundtrack on CD   of importance   † Points of interest   Academy Award nomination   BAFTA nomination

Red River ★★★

DIR *Howard Hawks*
1948   133m   US
DVD

☆ *John Wayne* (Tom Dunson), *Montgomery Clift* (Matthew Garth), Joanne Dru (Tess Millay), Walter Brennan (Groot Nadine), Coleen Gray (Fen), John Ireland (Cherry Valance), Noah Beery Jnr (Buster McGee), Harry Carey Jnr (Dan Latimer)

The young ward of a dictatorial cattle boss rebels against him in the course of an all-important cattle drive.

A brilliantly cinematic production which looks terrific on a big screen, and thanks to Tiomkin's score, feels stirring. Wayne fares better than one might expect in an unsympathetic role, and the young Clift is an arresting, dramatic presence. The film's mood accurately captures the rough-and-tumble nature of a cattle drive, and its action sequences are splendid.

SCR Borden Chase, Charles Schnee   CIN *Russell Harlan*
MUS *Dimitri Tiomkin*   ED *Christian Nyby*
PROD Howard Hawks   DIST UA/Monterey

⚱ Borden Chase (original story); editing

Red Road ★★

SCR/DIR *Andrea Arnold*
2006   113m   UK/Denmark
DVD

☆ *Kate Dickie* (Jackie), Tony Curran (Clyde), Martin Compston (Stevie), Natalie Press (April)

Jackie, a Glasgow woman working as a CCTV operator, is shocked to see a man on camera who instigated a dreadful episode in her past. Obsessively, she tracks him down.

Grim, utterly uncompromising viewing, including a remarkably explicit sex scene that turns out to be crucial to the plot. The narrative, gripping and propulsive for much of the film, loses focus towards the end. But this ravaged inner-city quarter is shot with brilliance and honesty; Arnold announces herself as a possible inheritor to Ken Loach's realist crown. In the lead, deadpan Kate Dickie is mesmerising.

CIN Robbie Ryan   DES Helen Scott   ED Nicholas Chaudeurge   PROD Carrie Comerford   DIST Verve

66 A slow-burning but enticing thriller, it captures its working-class Glaswegian setting in absorbing detail. – *Anna Smith, Empire*

66 Sensual, dark in every sense, but a touch derivative, Red Road reps an impressive feature debut for Andrea Arnold. – *Leslie Felperin, Variety*

🏆 Andrea Arnold (most promising newcomer)

'...All Roads Lead To Intrigue.'

Red Rock West ★★★

DIR *John Dahl*
1993   98m   US
DVD

☆ Nicolas Cage (Michael Williams), Lara Flynn Boyle (Suzanne Brown / Ann McCord), *Dennis Hopper* (Lyle from Dallas), *J. T. Walsh* (Wayne Brown / Kevin McCord), Craig Reay (Jim), Vance Johnson (Mr. Johnson), Robert Apel (Howard)

A lonely drifter in a vintage Cadillac arrives in a small town, he is mistaken for a hitman and accepts a payment from a husband to kill his wife. Then the real hitman shows up.

Stylish, dark, unpredictable comedy with Hopper in fine, malevolent form. A playful slice of modern noir that clinches director Dahl's mastery of the genre.

SCR John Dahl, Rick Dahl   CIN *Marc Reshovsky*
MUS William Olvis   DES Robert Pearson   ED Scott Chestnut   PROD Sigurjon Sighvatsson, Steve Golin
DIST Rank/Red Rock

66 Beautifully shot by Marc Reshovsky, Red Rock West canters along, often to a dry, reverb-laden guitar track that underscores the Wyoming atmosphere and the film's wit. It is a treasure waiting to be discovered. – *Richard Harrington, Washington Post*

The Red Shoes ★★★★

SCR/DIR *Michael Powell, Emeric Pressburger*
1948   136m   GB
DVD   ♫

☆ *Anton Walbrook* (Boris Lermontov), *Moira Shearer* (Victoria Page), Marius Goring (Julian Craster), Robert Helpmann (Ivan Boleslawsky), Albert Basserman (Sergei Ratov), Frederick Ashton, Leonide Massine (Grischa Ljubov), Ludmilla Tcherina (Irina Boronskaja), Esmond Knight (Livy)

A young ballerina becomes a great star but comes under stress when torn between love and her career.

Never was a better film made from such a plain story so unpersuasively written and performed; the splendour of the production is in the intimate view it gives of life backstage in the ballet world with its larger-than-life characters. The ballet excerpts are very fine, and the colour distinctive; the whole film is charged with excitement.

CIN *Jack Cardiff*   MUS *Brian Easdale*   DES *Hein Heckroth*
ED *Reginald Mills*   PROD Michael Powell, Emeric Pressburger   DIST GFD/The Archers

66 In texture, like nothing the British cinema has ever seen. – *Time Out, 1981*

⚱ Brian Easdale; Hein Heckroth
⚱ picture; Michael Powell, Emeric Pressburger (original story); editing

Red Sorghum ★★★

DIR Zhang Yimou
1987   91m   China
DVD

☆ Gong Li (Nine, the Grandmother), Jiang Wen (Yu, the Grandfather), Teng Rujun (Luohan), Liu Jia (Father, as child), Ji Chunhua (Sanpao, the Bandit Chief)

A Chinese man recounts a love story from his grandparents' era that was blighted by the invasion of Japanese forces.

Zhang Yimou's strong, colourful debut film swiftly propelled him into the pantheon of world cinema; a story of epic proportions, boldly photographed, with a

full spectrum of emotional involvement and an underlying tribute to Chinese resilience.

SCR Chen Jianyu, Zhu Wei   CIN Gu Changwei   MUS Jiping Zhao   ED Yuan Du   PROD Tian-Ming Wu   DIST Palace/Xi'an Film Studio

66 There is a strength in the simplicity of this story, in the almost fairy-tale quality of the images and the shocking suddenness of its violence that Hollywood, in its sophistication, has lost. – *Roger Ebert, Chicago Sun-Times*

'Passion Is Timeless.'

The Red Violin ★

DIR François Girard
1998   131m   Canada/Italy/GB/US
DVD ♫

☆ *Samuel L. Jackson* (Charles Morritz (Montréal)), Don McKellar (Evan Williams (Montréal)), Carlo Cecchi (Nicolo Bussotti (Cremona)), Irene Grazioli (Anna Bussotti (Cremona)), Jean-Luc Bideau (Georges Poussin (Vienna)), Christoph Koncz (Kaspar Weiss (Vienna)), Jason Flemyng (Frederick Pope (Oxford)), Greta Scacchi (Victoria Byrd (Oxford)), Sylvia Chang (Xiang Pei (Shanghai)), Liu Zi Feng (Chou Yuan (Shanghai)), Colm Feore (Auctioneer (Montréal)), Monique Mercure (Mme. Leroux (Montréal))

A unique 300-year-old violin, which was the last work of a master craftsman who added his wife's blood to its varnish, travels through various hands until the present day, when it is sought after at an auction.

Handsome looking, with appealing music, but despite its long, episodic, multi-lingual, trans-continental story, it holds the interest only sporadically. Jackson's energetic turn as a possibly crooked valuer perks up the narrative considerably.

SCR Don McKellar, François Girard   CIN *Alain Dostie*   MUS *John Corigliano*   DES François Séguin   ED Gaëtan Huot   PROD Niv Fichman   DIST Film4/New Line/Téléfilm Canada/Rhombus Media/Mikado/Sidecar

66 A good score can only do so much and too often here it is undercut by an overly sentimental story. – *Ed Kelleher, Film Journal International*

⚱ John Corigliano

'Truth is the first casualty of war.'

Redacted (new) ★★

SCR/DIR Brian de Palma
2007   90m   US/Canada
DVD

☆ Patrick Carroll (Reno), Rob Devaney (Lawyer McCoy), Izzy Diaz (Angel Salazar), Mike Figueroa (Sergeant Jim Vasquez), Ty Jones (Master Sergeant Sweet)

In Iraq in 2006, a soldier makes a video diary of his tour of duty, including the rape of a teenager Iraqi girl by his fellow soldiers.

Boldly using a variety of forms – blogs, YouTube posts, internet videologs and the video diary the soldier in the film is shooting, de Palma crafts a raw, jolting film that carries a real emotional punch, even if his methods and approach seem lurid and exploitative.

CIN Jonathon Cliff   DES Philip Barker   ED Bill Pankow   PROD Jennifer Weiss, Simone Urdl, Jason Kliot, Joana Vicente   DIST Optimum

66 A brilliantly unsettling film. – *Nigel Andrews, Financial Times*

66 Redacted is hell to sit through, but I think de Palma is bravely trying to imagine his way inside an atrocity, and that he's on to something powerful with his multisided approach. – *David Denby, New Yorker*

† The plot is almost identical to an earlier Brian de Palma film, Casualties of War.

† The word 'redacted' means edited or excised.

La Règle du Jeu ★★★★

DIR *Jean Renoir*
1939   113m   France
DVD

☆ *Marcel Dalio* (Robert de la Chesnaye), Nora Gregor (Christine de la Chesnaye), Jean Renoir (Octave), Mila Parély (Genevieve de Marrast), Julien Carette (Marceau), Gaston Modot (Schumacher), Roland Toutain (Andre Jurieu)

An aristocrat in a country house organizes a weekend shooting party, resulting in complex romantic intrigues among servants as well as the ruling classes.

Celebrated satirical comedy with a uniquely bleak outlook. It performed disastrously at the box-office on release and was not seen again for some 15 years, when critics the world over hailed it as a masterpiece.

SCR *Jean Renoir, Carl Koch*   CIN Jean Bachelet, Alain Renoir   MUS Joseph Kosma, Roger Desormières   ED Marguerite Renoir, Marthe Huguet   PROD Claude Renoir   DIST La Nouvelle Edition Française

66 It is a question of panache, of preserving a casual indifference to the workings of fate. – *The Times*

66 How brilliantly Renoir focuses the confusion! The rather fusty luxury of the chateau, the constant mindless slaughter of wild animals, the minuets of adultery and seduction, the gavottes of mutual hatred or mistrust. . . – *Basil Wright, 1972*

† The film was originally banned as indicting the corruption of France, and during the war the negative was destroyed during an air raid; but eventually a full version was pieced together from various materials.

Regular Lovers ★★

DIR Philippe Garrel
2005   183m   France
DVD

☆ Louis Garrel (François), Clotilde Hesme (Lilie), Julien Lucas (Antoine)

In 1968 Paris, a student revolutionary and his friends throw bombs, have free-wheeling sex, recite poetry and dodge military service in an effort to keep the real world at bay.

Director Garrel, the lead actor Louis's father, pays authentic homage to the New Wave in this overlong, monochrome attempt to recapture the heady spirit of the times. It improves with perseverance.

SCR Philippe Garrel, Marc Cholodenko, Arlette Langmann   CIN William Lubtchansky   MUS Jean-Claude Vannier   DES Nikos Meletopoulos, Mathieu Menut   ED Francoise Collin, Philippe Garrel   PROD Gilles Sandoz   DIST Artificial Eye

R

DVD Available on DVD   ☆ Cast in order of importance   66 Critics' Quotes   ⚱ Academy Award   Ⓑ BAFTA
♫ Soundtrack on CD   † Points of interest   Academy Award nomination   Ⓑ BAFTA nomination

† Louis Garrel, a rising star of new French cinema, played a similar role in Bernardo Bertolucci's The Dreamers, also about the events in Paris of May 1968.

'Let in the unexpected.'

Reign Over Me ★★

SCR/DIR *Mike Binder*

2007 124m US

[DVD] ♫

☆ *Adam Sandler* (Charlie Fineman), *Don Cheadle* (Alan Johnson), Jada Pinkett Smith (Janeane Johnson), Liv Tyler (Angela Oakhurst), Saffron Burrows (Donna Remar), Donald Sutherland (Judge Raines), Robert Klein (Jonathan Timpleman), Melinda Dillon (Ginger Timpleman), Mike Binder (Bryan Sugarman)

A grief-stricken man who lost his family in the 9/11 attacks reunites with an old college room-mate who helps him rebuild his life.

A real surprise: Sandler, best known for broad, insufferable low-IQ comedies, is outstanding here as the devastated Charlie. So is the reliably splendid Don Cheadle as affluent, unhappy Alan. The story's key is their mutually liberating friendship. This is a ramshackle, rambling piece, but a satisfying one. Together with The Upside of Anger, it marks a return from long years in the wilderness for writer-director Binder, who scripted Coupe de Ville.

CIN Russ Alsobrook MUS Rolfe Kent DES Christian Wintter ED Steve Edwards, Jeremy Roush PROD Jack Binder DIST Sony

66 This film manages to be not just bearable, but on occasion quite affecting. – *Sukhdev Sandhu, Daily Telegraph*

66 It's a courageous, moving, organically funny picture. – *Michael Sragow, Baltimore Sun*

† The title is adapted from the song Love Reign O'er Me by the Who, which is heard on the soundtrack.

'She was the daughter of a King, the sister of a King, the wife of a King . . . and the lover of an enemy.'

La Reine Margot ★★

DIR *Patrice Chéreau*

1994 162m France/Germany/Italy

[DVD] ♫

☆ Isabelle Adjani (Margot), Daniel Auteuil (Henri de Navarre), Jean-Hugues Anglade (Charles IX), Vincent Perez (La Môle), Virna Lisa (Catherine de Médicis), Dominique Blanc (Henriette de Nevers), Pascal Greggory (Anjou), Asia Argento (Charlotte de Sauve), Jean-Claude Brialy (Coligny)

In 1572, the sister of the Catholic King of France reluctantly agrees to marry the Protestant Duke of Navarre, an event that leads to the Saint Bartholomew's Day Massacre of Protestants and causes turmoil in the kingdom.

Engagingly vivid account of power struggles on personal, political and religious levels, involving bloodshed, poison, lust and betrayal.

SCR Danièle Thompson, Patrice Chereau CIN *Philippe Rousselot* MUS Goran Bregovic DES Richard Peduzzi,

Olivier Radot ED François Gédiger, Hélène Viard PROD Claude Berri DIST Guild/Renn/France 2/DA/NEF/Degeto/RCS

66 Close to the bone, this is the shocking, slightly cold but undeniably powerful apotheosis of the French heritage film. – *Chris Darke, Sight & Sound*

⚱ costume design

Ⓣ film not in the English language

The Remains of the Day ★★★

DIR James Ivory

1993 134m GB

[DVD] ♫

☆ *Anthony Hopkins* (James Stevens), Emma Thompson (Mary Kenton), James Fox (Lord Darlington), Christopher Reeve (Jack Lewis), Peter Vaughan (William Stevens), Hugh Grant (Reginald Cardinal), Michel Lonsdale (Dupont D'Ivry), Tim Piggot-Smith (Thomas Benn), Patrick Godfrey (Spencer)

Just before World War II, a loyal and dedicated butler slowly comes to doubt his long-held respect for his master, a Nazi-sympathiser aristocrat, was misplaced.

A master class in minimalist acting from Anthony Hopkins, reining himself in to convey deeply repressed emotions and unhappy denial of the world around him. Jhabvala's literate adaptation underpins a triumphant period piece in a high-water mark era for Merchant Ivory.

SCR *Ruth Prawer Jhabvala* CIN *Tony Pierce-Roberts* MUS Richard Robbins DES *Luciana Arrighi* ED Andrew Marcus PROD Ishmail Merchant, Mike Nichols, John Calley DIST Columbia/Merchant Ivory

66 Playing a man pitiably incapable of expressing his emotions, Anthony Hopkins demonstrates what a great physical actor he's become. – *David Ansen, Newsweek*

66 The actors keep this interesting, but as a story it drifts and rambles. – *Jonathan Rosenbaum, Chicago Reader*

⚱ picture; Anthony Hopkins (leading actor); Emma Thompson (leading actress); James Ivory; Ruth Prawer Jhabvala (adapted screenplay); Richard Robbins; Luciana Arrighi; Jenny Beavan, John Bright (costume design)

Ⓣ film; Anthony Hopkins (leading actor); Emma Thompson (leading actress); James Ivory; Ruth Prawer Jhabvala (adapted screenplay); Tony Pierce-Roberts

---

'What if someone you love...just disappeared?'

Rendition (new) ★★

DIR Gavin Hood

2007 122m US

[DVD] ♫

☆ Jake Gyllenhaal (Douglas Freeman), Reese Witherspoon (Isabella Fields El-Ibrahim), Alan Arkin (Senator Hawkins), Peter Sarsgaard (Alan Smith), J.K. Simmons (Lee Mayer), Omar Metwally (Anwar El-Ibrahim)

An Egyptian chemical engineer, who lives with his wife and son in America, is suspected of involvement in a terrorist bomb in North Africa. On his return home from a conference abroad, he is

R

---

apprehended by the CIA and flown to Egypt, where he is thrown into prison and tortured.

An issue film with a story that never soars to match the importance of the issue. Having set out its stall as unsympathetic to the vile practice of rendition, little room remains for drama or tension.

SCR Kelley Sane **CIN** Dion Beebe **MUS** Paul Hepker, Mark Kilian **DES** Barry Robinson **ED** Megan Gill **PROD** Steve Golin, Marcus Viscidi **DIST** Entertainment

66 This certainly isn't dull, but it is a touch uncinematic and more than a little preachy. – *Karl French, Financial Times*

66 About two-thirds of the way through, Rendition takes a bad turn and sells out most of what made it worth watching in the first place. Witherspoon is given little to do except look weepy, Freeman's change of heart is Q.E.D., and the radical Islamist subplot overwhelms the action, which becomes so confusingly structured that I thought the projectionist had misplaced a reel. – *Peter Rainer, Christian Science Monitor*

Reprise (new) ★★

DIR Joachim Trier
2006   105m   Norway/Sweden

☆ Anders Danielsen Lie (Philip), Espen Klouman Høiner (Erik), Viktoria Winge (Kari)

Two troubled young writers who frequent Oslo's club scene compete to become famous.

An assured debut from director Tier, influenced by the French New Wave and suffused with a newcomer's verve and excitement. There's a playful, amused quality to the story and its characters' immature preoccupations; it's an agreeable pleasure.

SCR Eskil Vogt, Joachim Trier **CIN** Jakob Ihre **MUS** Ola Fløttum **DES** Roger Rosenberg **ED** Olivier Bugge Coutté **PROD** Karin Julsrud **DIST** Diffusion

66 Has the elegant exuberance of a display of indoor fireworks. – *Philip French, Observer*

'The nightmare world of a virgin's dreams becomes the screen's shocking reality!'

Repulsion ★★★

DIR *Roman Polanski*
1965   105m   GB
DVD

☆ *Catherine Deneuve* (Carol Ledoux), Ian Hendry (Michael), John Fraser (Colin), Patrick Wymark (Landlord), Yvonne Furneaux (Helen Ledoux)

In 1960s London, a Belgian manicurist living with her promiscuous sister becomes increasingly terrified of physical contact. She enters a state of neurotic withdrawal and holes up in a dark shadowy flat, ready to commit murder rather than let herself be approached.

An anti-Swinging London film, using distorted imagery and exaggerated sound to convey the heroine's state of mind. Coolly controlled by director Polanski, and chillingly effective.

SCR Roman Polanski, Gerard Brach **CIN** *Gilbert Taylor* **MUS** Chico Hamilton **ED** Alastair McIntyre **PROD** Gene Gutowski **DIST** Compton/Tekli

66 An unashamedly ugly film, but as a lynx-eyed view of a crumbling mind it is a masterpiece of the macabre. – *Daily Mail*

Requiem ★★★

DIR Hans-Christian Schmid
2006   93m   Germany
DVD

☆ Sandra Huller (Michaela Klingler), Burghart Klaussner (Karl Klingler), Imogen Kogge (Marianne Klingler), Anna Blomeier (Hanna Imhof), Nicholas Reinke (Stefan Weiser), Jens Harzer (Exorcist Martin Borchert)

A teenage epileptic is convinced she is possessed by a demonic spirit.

Inspired by a real-life case, an evocatively dispassionate study in psychological breakdown with a brilliant central performance by Huller.

SCR Bernd Lange **CIN** Bogumil Godfrejow **DES** Christian Goldbeck **ED** Berns Schlegel, Hansjorg Weibrich **PROD** Hans-Christian Schmid **DIST** Soda Pictures

66 Just as haunting as a horror film, but far more heartrending. – *Gene Seymour, Newsday*

† Inspired by the same 1976 events dramatized in The Exorcism of Emily Rose (2005).

Requiem for a Dream ★★

DIR Darren Aronofsky
2000   102m   US
DVD   ♫

☆ Ellen Burstyn (Sara Goldfarb), Jared Leto (Harry Goldfarb), Jennifer Connelly (Marion Silver), Marlon Wayans (Tyrone C. Love), Christopher McDonald (Tappy Tibbons), Louise Lasser (Ada), Keith David (Big Tim), Sean Gullette (Arnold the Shrink)

A Coney Island mother and son both become addicted to drugs hell.

A bleak drama about four wasted lives, shot in a manner that mirrors their alienation and despair. Craftsmanlike, and a laudable attempt to extend the grammar of film, but one feels cornered by its pervasive hopelessness.

SCR Hubert Selby Jnr, Darren Aronofsky **CIN** Matthew Libatique **MUS** Clint Mansell (string quartets performed by Kronos Quartet) **DES** James Chinlund **ED** Jay Rabinowitz **PROD** Eric Watson, Palmer West

66 A superbly acted tale of hopelessness and despair. – *Philip French, Observer*

66 Be warned, this is not for the faint-hearted. It's brutal, stark, stomach-churning and unglamorous. – *Ben Falk, BBC*

� Ellen Burstyn (leading actress)

'A true story of survival...declassified.'

Rescue Dawn (new) ★★

SCR/DIR Werner Herzog
2007   125m   US/Luxembourg
DVD   ♫

☆ *Christian Bale* (Dieter Dengler), Steve Zahn (Duane), Jeremy Davies (Gene), Zach Grenier (Squad leader), Pat Healy (Norman)

R

| DVD Available on DVD | ☆ Cast in order | 66 Critics' Quotes | ⌐ Academy Award | ⍟ BAFTA |
| ♫ Soundtrack on CD | of importance | † Points of interest | ⍨ Academy Award nomination | ⍟ BAFTA nomination |

519

A German-American navy pilot is shot down in a secret US mission over Laos, where he is captured, imprisoned and tortured before staging a remarkable escape.

A compelling, if often gruelling story, given value-added force by the sheer conviction of Bale's performance as Dengler. The film's unexamined, aw-shucks pro-Americanism is an anomaly that is curious, but not ruinous.

CIN Peter Zeitlinger MUS Klaus Badelt DES Ann Pinijvararak ED Joe Bini PROD Steve Marlton, Elton Brand, Harry Knapp DIST Pathé

66 Dengler's stubborn, crazy life-force lights up the entire film like an electric storm. – *Jenny McCartney, Sunday Telegraph*

66 Rescue Dawn is a tale of heroism untainted by political scepticism. In an age when U.S. soldiers are seen as villains or victims, the movie offers a GI who bravely, or madly, simply refuses to die. – *Richard Corliss, Time*

† Dengler's imprisonment and escape were the subject of Herzog's 1997 documentary Little Dieter Needs To Fly.

'Let's go to work.'

Reservoir Dogs ★★★★

SCR/DIR *Quentin Tarantino*
1991 99m US
DVD ♫

☆ *Harvey Keitel* (Mr. White/Larry), Tim Roth (Mr. Orange/Freddy), Michael Madsen (Mr. Blonde/Vic), Chris Penn (Nice Guy Eddie), Steve Buscemi (Mr. Pink), Lawrence Tierney (Joe Cabot), Randy Brooks (Holdaway), Kirk Baltz (Marvin Nash), Eddie Bunker (Mr. Blue), Quentin Tarantino (Mr. Brown)

A gang's robbery of a jewellery store goes disastrously wrong, and as one of them bleeds to death, the others try to establish which one of them is a police informer.

Electrifying directorial debut by Tarantino: a tense, almost hysterical gangster movie stuffed with colourful vernacular, male posturing, deadpan humour and jaw-dropping violence. Its influence on other young film-makers would prove inestimable.

CIN Andrzej Sekula DES David Wasco ED Sally Menke PROD Lawrence Bender DIST Rank/Live America/Dog Eat Dog

66 A remarkable macho crime caper that is at once violent, sickeningly funny and utterly compelling....the hippest crime flick this side of Goodfellas, Reservoir Dogs has all the hallmarks of a modern classic. – *Jeff Dawson, Empire*

66 A small, modestly budgeted crime movie of sometimes dazzling cinematic pyrotechnics and over-the-top dramatic energy. – *Vincent Canby, New York Times*

† The film was shot in five weeks on a budget of $1.5 million.

'Experimentation. . .Evolution. . . Extinction'

Resident Evil: Extinction (new) ★

DIR Russell Mulcahy
2007 95m France/Australia/ Germany/ UK/ US
♫
☆ Milla Jovovich (Alice), Oded Fehr (Carlos Olivera), Ali

Larter (Claire Redfield), Iain Glen (Dr. Isaacs), Ashanti (Betty)

Guided by the super-powered Alice, T-Virus survivors flee across the zombie-infested desert terrain towards a safe Alaskan haven.

A franchise as mindless as the zombies it depicts gets a much-needed lift with Mulcahy adding Mad Max-style visual flash to a yawningly routine living-dead script.

SCR Paul W.S. Anderson CIN David Johnson MUS Charlie Clauser DES Eugenio Caballero ED Niven Howie PROD Bernd Eichinger, Samuel Hadida, Robert Kulzer, Jeremy Bolt, Paul W.S. Anderson DIST Sony

66 One or two good action sequences keep boredom at bay for a while, but so little of it is fresh that extinction can't come too soon. – *Anthony Quinn, Independent*

† This is the third film in the Resident Evil series.

Respiro ★★

SCR/DIR Emanuele Crialese
2002 95m Italy/France
DVD

☆ *Valeria Golino* (Grazia), Vincenzo Amato (Pietro), Francesco Casisa (Pasquale), Veronica D'Agostino (Marinella), Filippo Pucillo (Filippo)

A free-spirited mother on a small, remote Italian island upsets her husband with her unconventional behaviour and her family decide she needs medical help.

A canny blend of fantasy and hard-edged realism underpins this fable of a woman determined to rise above an insular society's structures. A great star turn for the vivacious Golino, climaxing in a lovely underwater representation of dreamy escape.

CIN Fabio Zamarion MUS John Surman, Andrea Guerra ED Didier Ranz PROD Domenico Procacci DIST Metro Tartan

66 An arresting, but occasionally disconcerting mix of fiercely tough realism and sentimentally soft magic realism...watchable. – *Peter Bradshaw, The Guardian*

66 Not since Y Tu Mamá También has a movie so palpably captured the down-to-earth, flesh-and-blood reality of high-spirited people living their lives without self-consciousness. – *Stephen Holden, New York Times*

'In a world of seduction and power, temptation has its price.'

Restoration ★

DIR Michael Hoffman
1995 117m US/GB
DVD ♫

☆ *Robert Downey Jnr* (Robert Merivel), Sam Neill (King Charles II), David Thewlis (John Pearce), Polly Walker (Celia Clemence), Meg Ryan (Katharine), Ian McKellen (Will Gates), Hugh Grant (Elias Finn), Ian McDiarmid (Ambrose), Mary Macleod (Midwife)

A philandering young doctor is one of Charles II's favourites at the English court, until he falls in love with one of the monarch's mistresses.

A lavish period drama, in which everything seems to flow from its extraordinary, extravagant production

design. *The subtleties and sub-texts of the source novel are somewhat lost in the transition to the screen, though it's an amusing, if patchy movie, with Downey an agreeable central presence. The memory of Meg Ryan, disastrously miscast as a mad Irishwoman, still causes shudders.*

SCR Rupert Walters **CIN** *Oliver Stapleton* **MUS** James Newton Howard **DES** *Eugenio Zanetti* **ED** Garth Craven **PROD** Cary Brokaw, Andy Paterson, Sarah Ryan Black **DIST** Buena Vista/Segue/Avenue/Oxford Film Company

66 The film is overcome by the rumbling workings of a creaky plot as the story grows more serious. – *Kevin Thomas, Los Angeles Times*

66 Restoration prefers farce to irony, and its tragedy is entirely melodramatic. – *Nick James, Sight & Sound*

♏ Eugenio Zanetti; James Acheson (costume design)
Ⓣ James Acheson (costume design)

Resurrected ★

DIR Paul Greengrass
1989   96m   GB

☆ David Thewlis (Kevin Deakin), Tom Bell (Mr. Deakin), Rita Tushingham (Mrs. Deakin), Michael Pollitt (Gregory Deakin), Rudi Davies (Julie), William Hoyland (Captain Sinclair), Ewan Stewart (Corporal Byker), Christopher Fulford (Slaven), David Lonsdale (Hibbert)

A British soldier, gone AWOL and believed killed in the Falklands War, turns up alive after the fighting is over and is beaten, shunned and 'tried' by his fellow soldiers.

The first fiction film by the estimable Greengrass, this fact-based story embraces jingoism, loyalty, a media quick to jump to conclusions, and the cost of fighting for one's country. The title is no accident: religious imagery abounds, sometimes obtrusively and inappropriately so. But it's a jolting experience.

SCR Martin Allen **CIN** Ivan Strasburg **MUS** John Keane **DES** Christopher Burke **ED** Dan Rae **PROD** Tara Prem, Adrian Hughes **DIST** Hobo/St Pancras Films/Film Four International/British Screen

66 In high-quality acting company, David Thewlis shone out as a major talent in this strident film. – *Time Out*

The Return ★★★★

DIR *Andrei Zvyagintsev*
2003   105m   Russia
DVD

☆ Ivan Dobronravov (Ivan), Vladimir Garin (Andrei), Konstantin Lavronenko (Father), Natalia Vdovina (Mother)

Two young brothers in Russia are astonished when the father they can hardly remember returns home after 12 years absence. He takes the boys on a fishing trip, but they all struggle to get along.

A strange, intriguing rites-of-passage drama with an overpowering sense of menace. Its story alludes to religious and political parallels without ever clarifying them. A chilly, brilliant film from a startlingly talented debutant director that fascinates from its first frame.

SCR Vladimir Moiseenko, Alexandre Novototsky
CIN *Mikhail Krichman* **MUS** Andrei Dergachev

DES Zhanna Pakhomova   **ED** Vladimir Mogilevsky
PROD Dmitri Lesnevsky

66 A quiet and disquieting masterpiece which gets under your skin and stays there long after you leave the cinema. – *David Hughes, Empire*

† It won the Golden Lion for best film at the 2003 Venice Film Festival.
† Vladimir Garin, who played one of the young brothers, was drowned in an accident soon after filming was completed. He was 16.

Revengers Tragedy

DIR Alex Cox
2002   109m   GB
DVD   ♫

☆ Christopher Eccleston (Vindici), Eddie Izzard (Lussurioso), Derek Jacobi (The Duke), Diana Quick (The Duchess), Carla Henry (Castiza), Andrew Schofield (Carlo), Antony Booth (Lord Antonio)

In a post-apocalyptic Liverpool in 2011, an angry man returns to the city to take revenge on the ruling Duke, who killed his wife on their wedding night.

Director Cox, toiling away in the regions, tries laudably to make British films with a different viewpoint, but this is a botched attempt to update a classic Jacobean drama, with alarmingly mixed acting and showy, ill-judged camera work.

SCR Frank Cottrell Boyce **CIN** Len Gowing **MUS** ChumbaWumba **DES** Cecilia Montiel **ED** Ray Fowlis **PROD** Margaret Matheson, Tod Davies **DIST** Metro Tartan

'The Case of Claus Von Bülow. An American Saga of Money and Mystery.'

Reversal of Fortune ★★

DIR Barbet Schroeder
1990   111m   US
DVD   ♫

☆ Glenn Close (Sunny von Bülow/Narrator), *Jeremy Irons* (Claus von Bülow), Ron Silver (Professor Alan Dershowitz), Annabella Sciorra (Sarah), Uta Hagen (Maria, Sunny's Personal Maid), Fisher Stevens (David Marriott), Christine Baranski (Andrea Reynolds, Claus' Girlfriend), Jack Gilpin (Peter MacIntosh, Dershowitz's Student Staff), Stephen Mailer (Elon Dershowitz)

European aristocrat Claus von Bülow hires a brilliant American lawyer to handle his appeal when he is convicted of attempting to murder his wife.

Irons is mesmerising as the embattled if unknowable von Bülow; even though this true story's outcome is well-known, the film works both as courtroom drama and irresistible gossip.

SCR *Nicholas Kazan* **CIN** Luciano Tovoli **MUS** Mark Isham **DES** Mel Bourne **ED** Lee Percy **PROD** Oliver Stone, Edward R. Pressman **DIST** Warner/Shochiku Fuji/Sovereign Pictures/Edward R. Pressman, Oliver Stone

66 This is a movie rich in moral ambiguities and one which should thoroughly please voyeurs and detective story enthusiasts alike. – *Robyn Karney, Empire*

♏ Jeremy Irons (leading actor)
♏ Barbet Schroeder; Nicholas Kazan (screenplay)

R

DVD Available on DVD   ☆ Cast in order   66 Critics' Quotes   ♏ Academy Award   Ⓣ BAFTA
♫ Soundtrack on CD   of importance   † Points of interest   ♏ Academy Award nomination   Ⓣ BAFTA nomination

521

3-D FILMS: GOODBYE TO GOOFY GLASSES

For half a century or more, 3-D films have been regarded as examples of whimsical nostalgia. We associate them with 1950s America, a nation in the long shadow of the Cold War. Photographs of 3-D film audiences now seem comical: rows of people, wearing curious cardboard or plastic-framed glasses, with red cellophane for one eye, green or blue for the other. Expressionless behind their glasses, they stare up in unison at the screen. Typically, such 1950s photos are found in history books, beside pictures of American children cowering beneath their school desks in drills designed to protect them from the impending nuclear threat. It was a different time.

Few people, then, would have expected 3-D to be talked about in 2008 as the Next Big Thing. Yet many shrewd film executives now speak of 3-D in almost evangelical terms. What happened to give a promising future to a phenomenon that seemed years past its sell-by date? There are many factors, all relating to technological innovations.

The most significant is the recent advances in digital projection. Shooting stereoscopic 3-D requires two lenses, set the same distance apart as human eyes – about two and a half inches. The spectacles worn by audiences ensure that one image goes to one eye, and the image from the second camera to the other. The human brain processes two different but similar pieces of visual information, and links them together, allowing the illusion of 3-D images.

But the two images need to be synchronised precisely for the effect to work properly. The sequence of images and their colour need to match exactly and meet the viewer's eyes simultaneously. If not, watching 3-D can be uncomfortable and unpleasant. As the brain struggles to correct the differences between the incoming images, the pictures blur. This was the problem with the post-war generation of 3-D: in the 1950s, audiences complained that watching gave them headaches.

Digital projection is now so advanced that such problems are obsolete. At its best, 3-D offers crisp, bright, detailed visual images and digital projectors are perfectly equipped to provide them. They can accommodate a high rate of frames (144 per second) that maximise the experience, and deliver them in perfect sync.

Computer animation has also progressed in leaps and bounds in recent years. The first *Toy Story* film was rightly regarded as a huge breakthrough on its release in 1995, as the first animated movie to consist solely of computer-generated imagery (CGI). Yet already it looks somewhat dated. Such advances reinforce the 3-D revival: CGI is the ideal medium for the stereoscopic process.

The clincher has been the growing popularity of cinema's enormous IMAX screens; there are now more than 300 world-wide. These all-encompassing screens, combined with the 3-D process, make for a memorable experience.

The Polar Express (2004), which employed 'performance capture' animation to re-create human actors in digital form, was pleasant but unremarkable when viewed in normal cinemas; on IMAX screens, seen from behind giant spectacles, it became intriguing. Never was it easier to believe that you could simply extend a hand and catch a falling snowflake, or grasp one of the actors by the arm.

Word of the phenomenon spread, and many people who saw the film in its original format returned to see it in 3-D. Grosses for *The Polar Express* were around $180 million, of which a whopping 10 per cent came from IMAX cinema revenues. Yet the proportion of IMAX screens to ordinary screens was miniscule.

This lesson was not lost on Hollywood studio bosses, who sought to create 3-D projects, and even re-issue films in 3-D at IMAX venues. Tim Burton's *The Nightmare Before Christmas* was first released in 1993, and grossed $50 million. But when reissued in 3-D in 2006 and 2007, the takings were almost half as much again.

Special 3-D editions of new films were no longer an exception. Pixar's *Monsters Inc.* received the treatment, as did Disney's *Chicken Little* and *Meet the Robinsons*. Meanwhile Robert Zemeckis, director–producer of *The Polar Express*, gave *Beowulf* a run in 3-D at IMAX venues in 2007.

Still, the notion that 3-D could again become commercially significant only truly surfaced this year, with the release of two much-vaunted 3-D concert films.

One of these, *Hannah Montana & Miley Cyrus: The Best of Both Worlds* (about a teenager who is a schoolgirl by day and popstar by night), topped the US box-office chart in February 2008, and finally grossed $65 million. It was a staggering sum, given that it played on fewer than 700 screens, around 20 per cent of the average for a major studio release.

The veteran rock group U2 co-operated in the release of a film of stadium concerts they had played in South America. *U2 3-D* was less successful commercially, but it created a huge stir from the day of its world premiere at the 2007 Cannes Film Festival. Clearly, new-generation 3-D would not be some passing fad.

Attempts have been made to perfect 3-D since the start of cinema history. By 1900 projectors for stereoscopic still photographs were commonplace, though none proved viable. In 1939 a colour stereoscopic process was exhibited at the World's Fair in New York – the first time the trademark glasses with red and green 'lenses' were introduced. But again there was no immediate commercial application.

This changed in the early 1950s. Hollywood studios were worried about the advent of TV: if audiences could receive moving pictures in their homes for the price of a TV set, they might never again pay to see them in cinemas.

'The notion that 3-D could again become commercially significant only truly surfaced this year, with the release of two much-vaunted 3-D concert films.'

So 3-D movies were marketed as offering something that could not be experienced in living rooms. This was true, though not quite the same as saying the actual films were any good. In truth, most 3-D movies from that era were of poor quality, and the public soon tired of what was often a badly executed gimmick.

The prognosis for 3-D looks far more optimistic now. The technology has finally caught up with the concept, and in America, some 10,000 cinema screens are being converted to digital projection (thus making them 3-D friendly).

In Britain, the UK Film Council has created a network of 240 digital screens (out of 3,440). In Liverpool, the Picturehouse at FACT cinema now markets itself as a venue, where feature films can be seen in 3-D.

Jeffrey Katzenberg, who oversees the animation division of DreamWorks, calls 3-D 'the single most revolutionary change since colour pictures,' and believes 3-D films can boost box-office takings. He argues that they are special events, so audiences will pay more to see them. So far, the mark-up on tickets in the US has been about 50 per cent.

He has also added $15 million to the budget of every DreamWorks animated title, so they can be released in 3-D. Other studios, including Disney, Fox and Universal (all of which have animation divisions) have pooled resources to help convert US cinema screens to digital.

This summer, the release of *Journey to the Centre of the Earth 3-D*, starring Brendan Fraser, was advertised as 'the first 3-D live action digital movie ever,' with the significant warning: 'only in theatres'. Sound familiar? Fifty years on, Hollywood is still trying to protect its core business.

Yet 3-D will inevitably be a reality in homes, and soon. Many manufacturers (including Samsung, Philips and Mitsubishi) have already developed stereoscopic TVs, and 3-D broadcasts have been trialled in Asia. This wave of 3-D seems sure to spill over beyond cinema screens and into living rooms.

And if anyone can devise some way to enable audiences to watch 3-D films and programmes without the need for those wretched glasses, its continuing popularity seems assured.

'I can smile . . . and murder while I smile.'

Richard III
★★★

DIR *Richard Loncraine*

1995   104m   GB

DVD   ♫

☆ *Ian McKellen* (Richard III), Annette Bening (Queen Elizabeth), Jim Broadbent (Buckingham), Robert Downey Jnr (Earl Rivers), Nigel Hawthorne (Clarence), Kristin Scott Thomas (Lady Anne), Maggie Smith (The Duchess of York), John Wood (King Edward IV), Adrian Dunbar (Corporal James Tyrell), Dominic West (Richmond)

The setting of Shakespeare's history play moves up to the 1930s after an imagined fascist coup in England, and the King's younger brother attaining the throne through murder, and attempting to hold on to it as civil war rages.

A striking, audacious re-working, based on a production first staged at London's National Theatre. McKellen is in imperious form, and the new updating is convincing – though the play's spirit and its rich dialogue remain largely intact. The famous cry: 'A horse! A horse! My kingdom for a horse!' delivered when Richard's jeep gets stuck in mud, is an amusing but apposite moment.

SCR *Ian McKellen, Richard Loncraine*   CIN Peter Biziou   MUS Trevor Jones   DES *Tony Burrough*   ED Paul Green   PROD Liza Katselas Pare, Stephen Bayly   DIST UA/British Screen/First Look

᠅᠅ It is all in the grand manner of Shakespearean tragedies. – *Andrew Geller, New York Times*

᠅᠅ This is Shakespeare exciting enough for even the most dubious, which, after all, is no less than the man deserves. – *Kenneth Turan, Los Angeles Times*

⚱ Tony Burrough; Shuna Harwood (costume design)

Ⓣ Tony Burrough; Shuna Harwood (costume design)

Ⓣ British film; Ian McKellen (adapted screenplay)

'In a No-man's Land between North and South, You didn't fight for the Blue or the Grey... You fought for your friends and family.'

Ride With The Devil
★★

DIR Ang Lee

1999   138m   US

DVD   ♫

☆ Skeet Ulrich (Jack Bull Chiles), Tobey Maguire (Jake Roedel), Jewel (Sue Lee Shelley), Jeffrey Wright (Daniel Holt), Simon Baker (George Clyde), Jonathan Rhys Meyers (Pitt Mackeson), James Caviezel (Black John), Thomas Guiry (Riley Crawford), Tom Wilkinson (Orton Brown), Jonathan Brandis (Cave Wyatt), Matthew Faber (Turner Rawls), Stephen Mailer (Babe Hudspeth), John Ales (Quantrill)

In Missouri in the 1860s, two young 'bushwhacker' friends fight for the Southern cause in the American Civil War, ambush Yankee combat units, but have to hide out in a cave during a bleak winter.

Director Lee ticks off another western genre that he masters with seemingly effortless ease. This film has an epic sweep, but manages to keep its central relationships intimate and vital: the conversations between the two

leads are as compelling as the deft staging of the massacre at Lawrence, Kansas. Handsomely shot, with a thoughtful script, it amounts to an experience that satisfies the emotions and the brain.

SCR James Schamus   CIN *Frederick Elmes*   MUS Mychael Danna   DES Mark Friedberg   ED Tim Squyres   PROD Ted Hope, Robert Colesberry, James Schamus   DIST Entertainment

᠅᠅ While the movie intermittently revs up for some showy combat scenes, its real metier is a texture of fine-grained observation that brings history to life on the molecular level. – *Peter Matthews, Sight and Sound*

'Wit is the ultimate weapon.'

Ridicule
★★

DIR Patrice Leconte

1996   102m   France

DVD   ♫

☆ Fanny Ardant (Madame de Blayac), Charles Berling (Le Marquis Grégoire Ponceludon de Malavoy), Bernard Giraudeau (L'Abbée de Vilecourt), Judith Godrèche (Mathilde de Bellegarde), Jean Rochefort (Le Marquis de Bellegarde), Carlo Brandt (Le Chevalier de Milletail)

A young engineer arrives at the court of Louis XVI at Versailles in the 1780s seeking help to save his region from mosquito infestation. But the indolent courtiers care more for rhetoric and wit than real-world problems.

Pre-revolutionary French royalty at its most decadent point, splendidly portrayed in this sharp period piece that cunningly overturns the conventions of costume drama.

SCR Remi Waterhouse, Michel Fessler, Eric Vicaut   CIN Thierry Arbogast   MUS Antoine Duhamel   DES Ivan Maussion   ED Joëlle Hache   PROD Gilles Legrand, Frédérick Brillion, Philippe Carcassonne   DIST Electric/Epithète/Cinéa/France 3

᠅᠅ It is an unusually involving costume drama that takes us into a decadent world few will know existed. – *Kenneth Turan, Los Angeles Times*

⚱ film not in the English language

Ⓣ foreign film

'Those that live on the edge sometimes fall.'

Riff-Raff
★★

DIR Ken Loach

1990   95m   GB

DVD

☆ *Robert Carlyle* (Steve), Emer McCourt (Susan), Jimmy Coleman (Shem), George Moss (Mo), Ricky Tomlinson (Larry), David Finch (Kevin), Richard Belgrave (Kojo), Ade Sapara (Fiaman), Derek Young (Desmonde), Bill Moores (Smurph)

A mixed group of labourers toiling on a London building site laugh, joke, but get deadly serious when their employers' lax safety standards provoke a crisis.

More upbeat than some of Loach's work, though its serious intent does not stay hidden for long. A star-making role for Robert Carlyle, and a cheerfully

R

DVD Available on DVD   ☆ Cast in order of importance   ᠅᠅ Critics' Quotes   † Points of interest   ⚱ Academy Award   ⚱ Academy Award nomination   Ⓣ BAFTA   Ⓣ BAFTA nomination
♫ Soundtrack on CD

enthusiastic ensemble cast make the widespread affection for the film thoroughly deserved.

SCR Bill Jesse   **CIN** Barry Ackroyd   **MUS** Stewart Copeland   **DES** Martin Johnson   **ED** Jonathan Morris   **PROD** Sally Hibbin   **DIST** BFI/Parallax

66 (Director Ken) Loach's vision, cutting and compassion makes Riff-Raff black comedy of a high order. – *Peter Travers, Rolling Stone*

† Scriptwriter Bill Jesse died before the film was completed.

Rififi ★★★

DIR *Jules Dassin*
1955   116m   France
☆ *Jean Servais*, Carl Mohner, Robert Manuel, Marie Sabouret, Perlo Vita (Jules Dassin)

After an elaborate raid on a jewellery store, thieves fall out and the caper ends in bloodshed.

A film that inadvertently has much to answer for, in the form of hundreds of inferior imitations showing detailed accounts of robberies. In its time it was crisp and exciting, and the 25-minute silent robbery sequence is brilliantly executed.

SCR René Wheeler, Jules Dassin, Auguste le Breton   **CIN** Philippe Agostini   **MUS** Georges Auric   **DIST** Indus/Pathé/Prima

66 I sometimes ask myself whether so much of the film is silent because of my own lack of French. – *Jules Dassin*

† Several 'sequels' were made using the word rififi (criminal argot for 'trouble') in the title, but in plot terms they were entirely unrelated.

The Right Stuff ★★★

SCR/DIR *Philip Kaufman*
1983   193m   US
[DVD] ♫
☆ *Sam Shepard*, Scott Glenn, *Ed Harris*, Dennis Quaid, Fred Ward, Barbara Hershey, Kim Stanley, Veronica Cartwright

In the 1950s and 60s, test pilots are recruited and trained as astronauts.

A reasonably factual account of the Mercury programme: extremely well made, and not too noble to take some satirical sideswipes at the bizarre aspects of the US space programme, while remaining respectful of these heroes of a new frontier.

CIN Caleb Deschanel   **MUS** Bill Conti   **DES** Geoffrey Kirkland   **ED** Glenn Farr, Lisa Fruchtman, Stephen A. Rotter, Douglas Stewart, Tom Rolf   **PROD** Irwin Winkler, Robert Chartoff   **DIST** Warner/Ladd

⊥ Bill Conti (music); editing; sound; sound editing
⊥ Picture; Sam Shepard (supporting actor); Caleb Deschanel (cinematography)

'One curse, one cure, one week to find it'

Ringu ★

DIR Hideo Nakata
1998   96m   Japan
[DVD]
☆ Nanako Matsushima (Reiko Asakawa), Miki Nakatani

(Mai Takano), Hiroyuki Sanada (Ryuji Takayama), Yuko Takeuchi (Tomoko Oishi), Hitomi Sato (Masami Kurahashi), Yoichi Numata (Takashi Yamamura), Yutaka Matsushige (Yoshino), Katsumi Muramatsu (Koichi Asakawa), Rikiya Otaka (Yoichi Asakawa), Masako (Shizuko Yamamura)

A reporter investigates the sudden death of a teenager staying at a remote cabin, then finds she must deal with a vengeful ghost.

A traditional-looking detective story that gradually gives way to supernatural elements, short on real shocks but well told.

SCR Hiroshi Takahashi   **CIN** Junichiro Hayashi   **MUS** Kinji Kawai   **DES** Iwao Saito   **ED** Nobuyuki Takahashi   **PROD** Shinya Kawai, Takashige Ichise, Takenori Sento

66 A landmark in horror cinema, Japan's Ringu is arguably the most chilling piece of popular, supernatural cinema of the 90s – *Channel 4*

Rio Bravo ★★★

DIR *Howard Hawks*
1959   141m   US
[DVD]
☆ *John Wayne, Dean Martin*, Ricky Nelson, Angie Dickinson, Walter Brennan, Ward Bond, John Russell, Pedro Gonzalez-Gonzalez, Claude Akins, Harry Carey Jnr, Bob Steele

A sheriff tries to protect a Western town against marauding outlaws, with only a drunk, a crippled man and a callow young gunfighter to support him.

A stately Western, full of fine individual turns, and with a boisterous spirit that sets it apart from the sombre, similarly-themed High Noon. It was underrated at the time, and dismissed cursorily by Hawks himself, but it now seems an essential part of the Western canon.

SCR Jules Furthman, Leigh Brackett   **CIN** Russell Harlan   **MUS** *Dimitri Tiomkin*   **PROD** Howard Hawks   **DIST** Warner/Armada

66 After we finished we found we could have done it a lot better . . . and that's why we went ahead and made El Dorado. – *Howard Hawks*

† More or less remade in 1966 as El Dorado and in 1970 as Rio Lobo.

'Older. Wiser. More talented.'

Ripley's Game

DIR Liliana Cavani
2002   110m   Italy/GB/US
[DVD] ♫
☆ John Malkovich (Tom Ripley), Dougray Scott (Jonathan Trevanny), Ray Winstone (Reeves), Lena Headey (Sarah Trevanny), Chiara Caselli (Luisa Harari)

An ailing art collector in an Italian village is insulted by a neighbour and starts plotting murderous revenge, goaded by Ripley, a wealthy sociopath with a secret agenda.

One of the less effective film renderings of Patricia Highsmith's anti-hero, though it's fascinating to compare and contrast. This one suffers from a mannered, self-indulgent performance by a lisping,

R

languid Malkovich. Director Cavani cannot or will not rein him in, and makes scarcely more impact on the rest of this oddly uninvolving film.

SCR Charles McKeown, Liliana Cavani   CIN Alfio Contini   MUS Ennio Morricone   DES Francesco Frigeri   ED Jon Harris   PROD Ileen Maisel, Simon Bosanquet, Riccardo Tozzi   DIST Entertainment

66 Trashy and supercilious, it's a guilty pleasure. – *Time Out*

Rise of the Footsoldier (new)

DIR Julian Gilbey
2007   119m   UK

☆ Ricci Harnett (Carlton Leach), Craig Fairbrass (Pat Tate), Billy Murray (Mickey Steele), Terry Stone (Tony Tucker)

A criminal progresses from football hooliganism to becoming a violent bouncer and a sidekick in a murderous gang.

Ugly, dim-witted account of a bit-player's career in gangland, featuring macho strutting, foul language, rage-fuelled mayhem and big guns.

SCR Julian Gilbey, William Gilbey   CIN Ali Asad   MUS Sandy McLelland, Ross Cullum, Nigel Champion   DES Matthew Button   ED Julian Gilbey, Wiliam Gilbey   PROD Michael Loveday   DIST Optimum

66 A repugnant gangland romp. . .the direction smacks of sadism. – *David Jenkins, Time Out*

River Queen (new)

DIR Vincent Ward   SCR/DIR Vincent Ward, Toa Fraser
2006   113m   New Zealand/UK
DVD ♫

☆ Samantha Morton (Sara O'Brien), Kiefer Sutherland (Doyle), Cliff Curtis (Wiremu), Temuera Morrison (Te Kai Po), Anton Lesser (Baine), Stephen Rea (Francis O'Brien), Rawiri Pene (Boy)

An Irish woman in 19th-century New Zealand travels up river to find her half-breed son after he is kidnapped by a Maori tribe.

Muddled historical epic full of stunning scenery, unlikely accents and improbable behaviour.

CIN Alun Bollinger   MUS Karl Jenkins   DES Rick Kofoed   ED Ewa J. Lind   PROD Don Reynolds, Chris Auty   DIST The Works

66 A choppy mess with gorgeous moments. – *Tim Robey, Daily Telegraph*

66 Contrived and unreal. – *Peter Bradshaw, Guardian*

† Vincent Ward was replaced by cinematographer Alun Bollinger during shooting. He returned to the project when filming was completed.

A River Runs through It   ★

DIR Robert Redford
1992   123m   US
DVD ♫

☆ Craig Sheffer (Norman Maclean), Brad Pitt (Paul Maclean), *Tom Skerritt* (Rev Mclean), Brenda Blethyn (Mrs Maclean), Emily Lloyd (Jessie Burns), Edie McClurg (Mrs Burns), Stephen Shellen (Neal Burns), Nicole Burdette (Mabel), Susan Traylor (Rawhide)

The two sons of a Presbyterian clergyman, though bitter rivals, sink their differences in the calming pursuit of fly-fishing.

A beautifully photographed film, hardly eventful, but with a tranquil, earnest, old-fashioned appeal.

SCR Richard Friedenberg   CIN *Philippe Rousselot*   MUS Mark Isham   DES Jon Hutman   ED Lynzee Klingman, Robert Estrin   PROD Robert Redford, Patrick Markey, Amalia Mato   DIST Guild/Allied Filmmaker/Columbia

66 Here are two things I never thought I'd say: I like a movie about fly fishing, and Robert Redford has directed one of the most ambitious, accomplished films of the year. – *Caryn James, New York Times*

⚱ Philippe Rousselot
⚱ Richard Friedenberg (adapted screenplay); Mark Isham

'The vacation is over.'

The River Wild   ★★

DIR *Curtis Hanson*
1994   108m   US
DVD ♫

☆ *Meryl Streep* (Gail Hartman), *Kevin Bacon* (Wade), David Strathairn (Tom), Joseph Mazzello (Roarke), John C. Reilly (Terry), Benjamin Bratt (Ranger Johnny)

A family on a white-water rafting expedition are hijacked into helping armed robbers use the river ride to escape the police.

Enjoyable action drama, with Meryl Streep, in an unusual role for her, demonstrating rangy athleticism, and the reliable Bacon suitably sinister. The white-water action is expertly directed by Hanson. Hardly ground-breaking, but splashing good fun.

SCR Denis O'Neill   CIN *Robert Elswit*   MUS Jerry Goldsmith   DES Bill Kenney   ED Joe Hutshing, David Brenner   PROD David Foster, Lawrence Turman   DIST UIP/Turman-Foster

66 We haven't seen this sturdy, physical, macho Meryl Streep before, yet she seems totally in her element. – *David Ansen, Newsweek*

66 The perfect high old time for audiences in the mood to be tossed into the spin cycle for a pulse-pounding thrill ride. – *Peter Travers, Rolling Stone*

The Road Home   ★★

DIR Zhang Yimou
1999   89m   China/Hong Kong
DVD

☆ Zhang Ziyi (Young Zhao Di), Sun Honglei (Luo Yusheng), Zheng Hao (Luo Changyu), Zhao Yuelin (Old Zhao Di), Li Bin (Grandmother), Chang Guifa (Old Mayor), Sung Wencheng (Mayor), Liu Qi (Old Carpenter Xia), Ji Bo (Carpenter Xia), Zhang Zhongxi (Crockery Repairman)

A Chinese businessman returns home for the funeral of his teacher father, and is deeply moved when many ex-pupils arrive to pay tribute as he recalls his parents' lives.

The importance of traditional rural values in a materialist world underpins this gentle, affecting story about family life and Chinese history.

SCR Bao Shi   CIN Hou Yong   MUS San Bao   ED Zhai Ru   PROD Zhao Yu   DIST Columbia

66 A deeply eloquent film about an especially difficult period in China's past. – *Michael Thomson, BBC*

'Every Father Is A Hero To His Son.'

Road to Perdition ★★

DIR Sam Mendes
2002   117m   US
DVD ♫

☆ Tom Hanks (Michael Sullivan), Paul Newman (John Rooney), Jude Law (Maguire), Jennifer Jason Leigh (Annie Sullivan), Stanley Tucci (Frank Nitti), Daniel Craig (Connor Rooney), Tyler Hoechlin (Michael Sullivan Jnr), Liam Aiken (Peter Sullivan), Dylan Baker (Alexander Rance), Ciaran Hinds (Finn McGovern)

A professional hit man in Chicago seeks revenge after a betrayal by an Irish-American Mob boss, who treated him like a son.

An absorbing crime thriller, handsome in a self-conscious way, and with a faint air of self-importance. Hanks squeaks by as a vengeful assassin, cast against type; Newman, all chummy malevolence, excels.

SCR David Self   CIN *Conrad L. Hall*   MUS Thomas Newman   DES Dennis Gassner   ED Jill Bilcock   PROD Richard D. Zanuck, Dean Zanuck, Sam Mendes   DIST TCF

66 This is supremely crafted, grown-up moviemaking that never escapes its pulp origins. – *Ian Nathan, Empire*

66 What the film lacks, though not fatally, is human warmth, something to engage us emotionally, rather than just aesthetically and viscerally. – *Philip French, Observer*

⚱ Conrad L. Hall
⚱ Paul Newman (supporting actor); Thomas Newman; Dennis Gassner (with Nancy Haigh); Scott Millan, Bob Beemer, John Pritchett (sound); Scott Hecker (sound editing)

🏆 Conrad L. Hall; Dennis Gassner
🏆 Paul Newman (supporting actor)

'A little magic goes a long way.'

Roald Dahl's Matilda

DIR Danny DeVito
1996   98m   US
DVD

☆ Danny DeVito (Harry Wormwood / Narrator), Rhea Perlman (Zinnia Wormwood), Embeth Davidtz (Miss Jennifer 'Jenny' Honey), Pam Ferris (Agatha Trunchbull), Mara Wilson (Matilda), Paul Reubens (FBI Agent Bob), Tracey Walter (FBI Agent Bill), Brian Levinson (Michael 'Mikey' Wormwood)

A precocious young girl neglected by her ghastly parents uses her special powers to terrify her headmistress.

One of the better film adaptations of Dahl's work; in DeVito, a kindred spirit with a taste for dark comedy was unearthed, and happily not all the author's edgy humour was removed in the transition.

SCR Nicholas Kazan, Robin Swicord   CIN Stefan Czapsky   MUS David Newman   DES Bill Brzeski   ED Lynzee Klingman, Brent White   PROD Danny DeVito, Michael Shamberg, Stacey Sher, Liccy Dahl   DIST Columbia TriStar

66 Slick kids' movie that preserves Roald Dahl's gleeful nastiness. – *Jeffrey M Anderson, San Francisco Examiner*

'Honour made him a man. Courage made him a hero. History made him a legend.'

Rob Roy ★★

DIR Michael Caton-Jones
1995   139m   US
DVD ♫

☆ Liam Neeson (Robert Roy McGregor), Jessica Lange (Mary McGregor), John Hurt (John Graham, Marquis of Montrose), *Tim Roth* (Archibald Cunningham), Eric Stoltz (Alan MacDonald), Andrew Keir (Duke of Argyll), Brian Cox (Killearn), Brian McCardie (Alasdair McGregor), Gilbert Martin (Will Guthrie), Vicki Masson (Betty)

In Scotland at the start of the 18th century Rob Roy McGregor turns outlaw and fights to avenge his wife's honour.

Decent, worthy adaptation of Sir Walter Scott's novel that never quite takes flight; Neeson is a brooding, introverted hero and in general there's a lack of excitement. It features a fine, literate script, far superior to that of Braveheart which was shot in the same year, even using some of the same locations. But that felt like a rousing movie; this does not.

SCR *Alan Sharp*   CIN Karl Walter Lindenlaub   MUS Carter Burwell   DES Assheton Gorton   ED Peter Honess   PROD Peter Broughan, Richard Jackson   DIST UIP/UA/Talisman

66 Liam Neeson simply has no spark here. He is good and honest and honourable until your face turns blue. He's just no fun. – *Barbara Shulgasser, San Francisco Examiner*

⚱ Tim Roth (supporting actor)
🏆 Tim Roth (supporting actor)

Roberto Succo ★★

SCR/DIR Cedric Kahn
2001   124m   France/ Switzerland
DVD

☆ Stefano Cassetti (Kurt), Isild Le Besco (Lea), Patrick Dell'Isola (Thomas), Vincent Deneriaz (Denis), Aymeric Chauffert (Aelaunay), Viviana Aliberti (Swiss schoolteacher), Estelle Perron (Celine)

An Italian murderer escapes from a mental asylum and goes on a savage two-year killing spree in France with his teenage girlfriend.

This chilling reconstruction of real events, featuring a horrific catalogue of vicious murders as police mount a massive manhunt, is fascinating but grim. Cassetti, the non-professional lead, is wholly convincing.

CIN Pascal Marti   MUS Julien Civange   DES François Abelanet   ED Yann Dedet   PROD Gilles Sandoz, Patrick Sobelman   DIST Artificial Eye

66 Understated and restrained, but scary as hell. – *Empire*

R

DVD Available on DVD   ☆ Cast in order   66 Critics' Quotes   ⚱ Academy Award   🏆 BAFTA
♫ Soundtrack on CD   of importance   † Points of interest   ⚱ Academy Award nomination   🏆 BAFTA nomination

527

'For the good of all men, and the love of one woman, he fought to uphold justice by breaking the law'

Robin Hood: Prince of Thieves ★★

DIR Kevin Reynolds
1991 143m US
[DVD] ♫

☆ Kevin Costner (Robin of Locksley), Morgan Freeman (Azeem), Mary Elizabeth Mastrantonio (Marian Dubois), Christian Slater (Will Scarlett), *Alan Rickman* (Sheriff of Nottingham), Sean Connery (uncredited) (King Richard), Geraldine McEwan (Mortianna), Michael McShane (Friar Tuck), Brian Blessed (Lord Locksley), Michael Wincott (Guy of Gisborne), Nick Brimble (Little John)

Robin Hood returns from the Crusades to find that the Sheriff of Nottingham has killed his father, and becomes an outlaw to launch his revenge.

Widely panned, but an undemanding, enjoyable swashbuckler, even if it's clear most of the creative input came from Hollywood rather than anywhere near Sherwood Forest. Rickman, hamming it up for fun, does much scene-stealing as the sinister sheriff.

SCR Pen Densham, John Watson CIN Douglas Milsome MUS Michael Kamen DES John Graysmark ED Peter Boyle PROD John Watson, Pen Densham, Richard B. Lewis DIST Warner

66 Kevin Costner is so boyishly lightweight that it seems he'd be better equipped with a bag of fairy dust than a quiver of arrows on his back. – *Hal Hinson, Washington Post*

♪ song '(Everything I Do) I Do For You' (mMichael Kamen, lyBryan Adams, Robert John Lange)

🏆 Alan Rickman (supporting actor)
🏅 John Bloomfield (costume design)

Robinson in Space ★

SCR/DIR Patrick Keiller
1997 82m GB
[DVD]

☆ Paul Scofield (narrator)

An art lecturer delivers a highly personal verdict on 'the problem of England' and the slow death of the country's traditional industries.

A film touring England's non-touristic locations, from crowded motorways to derelict factories, with a commentary studded with historical and political references. Weirdly enthralling.

CIN Patrick Keiller DES Jacqui Timberlake ED Larry Sider PROD Keith Griffiths DIST BBC/BFO/Koninck

66 Provocative, determinedly left-field film-making: bright, adventurous, engrossing and. . .well, very English. – *Time Out*

'Part man. Part machine. All cop.'

Robocop ★★

DIR *Paul Verhoeven*
1987 103m US
[DVD] ♫

☆ Peter Weller (Alex J. Murphy/Robocop), Nancy Allen (Anne Lewis), Ronny Cox (Richard 'Dick' Jones), Kurtwood Smith (Clarence J. Boddicker), Dan O'Herlihy (The Old Man), Miguel Ferrer (Robert Morton)

In Detroit of the near future, a cop is shot to pieces and reconstructed by science to battle the forces of evil.

Colourfully bleak, futuristic, violence-packed crime thriller brightened by frequent shafts of unexpected humour and even satire.

SCR Edward Neumeier, Michael Miner CIN Jost Vacano, Sol Negrin MUS Basil Poledouris DES William Sandell ED Frank J. Urioste PROD Arne Schmidt DIST Rank

66 There's a brooding, agonized quality to the violence that seems almost subversive, as if (director Paul) Verhoeven were both appalled and fascinated by his complicity in the toxic action rot. – *Pat Graham, Chicago Reader*

66 Paul Verhoeven, a Dutch director ('Soldier of Orange'), doesn't let the furiously futuristic plot get in the way of the flaming explosions, shattering glass and hurtling bodies. – *Walter Goodman, New York Times*

† Two sequels followed, in 1990 and 1993.

🏅 Frank J. Urioste (editing), Robert Wald, Aaron Rochin, Carlos Delarios, Michael J. Kohut(sound); John Pospisil & Stephen Hunter Flick (special achievement award for sound effects)

🏅 Carla Palmer (makeup); Rob Bottin, Rocco Gioffre, Phil Toppitt, Peter Kuran (special effects)

Rocket Science (new) ★

SCR/DIR Jeffrey Blitz
2007 101m US
[DVD] ♫

☆ Reece Daniel Thompson (Hal Hefner), Anna Kendrick (Ginny), Nicholas D'Agosto (Ben Wekselbaum), Vincent Piazza (Earl Hefner), Margo Martindale (Coach Lumbly), Aaron Yoo (Heston), Josh Kay (Lewis)

A stuttering teenager falls in love after he is invited to join his high-school debating team.

Charming and disarming if rather inconsequential comedy; its humour may be sporadic, but at least it's intelligent.

CIN Jo Willems MUS Eef Barzelay DES Rick Butler ED Yana Gorskaya PROD Effie T. Brown, Sean Welch DIST Optimum Releasing

66 This unusually voluble comedy is as eloquent about love, self-realisation and adolescent angst as its protagonist is endearingly tongue-tied. – *Justin Chang, Variety*

66 Needlessly cruel. – *Tim Robey, Daily Telegraph*

† The first fiction feature from Blitz, director of 2002 documentary Spellbound.

'His whole life was a million-to-one shot!'

Rocky ★★★

DIR *John G. Avildsen*
1976 119m US
[DVD] ♫

☆ *Sylvester Stallone* (Rocky Balboa), Burgess Meredith (Mickey), Talia Shire (Adrian), Burt Young (Paulie), Carl Weathers (Apollo Creed), Thayer David (Miles Jergens)

A slightly dim-witted Philadelphia boxer makes good.

An uplifting, likable underdog film that came after a traumatic decade for America, with an apparently average Ordinary Joe for a hero, a character who might have been a minor sidekick in an urban pre-war movie. Stallone wrote himself a part with grit, wit and a little self-deprecation, and showed an indomitability in getting it made that recalled Rocky's unlikely rise through the rankings.

SCR Sylvester Stallone   CIN James Crabe   MUS Bill Conti   DES Bill Cassidy   ED Scott Conrad, Richard Halsey   PROD Gene Kirkwood   DIST UA/Chartoff-Winkler

† Five sequels followed between 1979 and 2006.

⌶ picture; John G. Avildsen (direction)

⌷ Sylvester Stallone (leading actor); Burgess Meredith (supporting actor); Talia Shire (supporting actress); Burt Young (supporting actor); Sylvester Stallone (original screenplay); Bill Conti (m), Carol Connors, Ayn Robbins (ly) (music, original song – Gonna Fly Now)

'The story of a rebel and his mike.'

Roger & Me ★★

SCR/DIR Michael Moore
1989   91m   US
DVD

☆ Michael Moore (himself)

Outraged at the devastation caused to his home town, journalist Michael Moore tries to interview General Motors chairman Roger Smith about his decision to close a car factory, putting thousands of people out of work.

This was where Moore's persona was hatched: an ordinary-looking, pudgy fellow in a baseball cap, asking tricky questions in an ingenuous manner. It worked well here, though Smith's elusiveness is all that holds the film together.

CIN Christopher Beaver, John Prusak, Kevin Rafferty, Bruce Schermer   ED Wendy Stanzler, Jennifer Beman   PROD Michael Moore   DIST Warner/Dog Eat Dog Films/Michael Moore

66 A hilariously cranky bit of propaganda. One part home movie, one part editorial, one part letter bomb, the film is a one-man insurrection. – *Hal Hinson, Washington Post*

'Sex is everywhere.'

Roger Dodger ★

SCR/DIR Dylan Kidd
2002   106m   US
DVD

☆ Campbell Scott (Roger), Jesse Eisenberg (Nick), Isabella Rossellini (Joyce), Elizabeth Berkley (Andrea), Jennifer Beals (Sophie)

An arrogant New York adman thinks he can seduce any woman, but a night out teaching his dating skills to his 16 year-old nephew brings him down to earth.

Delightful plot in which New York's singles scene is shown up as a garish nightmare and a sweet innocent gives a rapacious alpha male his comeuppance. Minor but amusing.

CIN Joaquin Baca-Asay   MUS Craig Wedren   DES Stephen Beatrice   ED Andy Kier   PROD Anne Chaisson, George VanBuskirk, Dylan Kidd   DIST Optimum

66 This is Sex and the City – man-style, with the sour tang of testosterone lingering in the air. – *Peter Bradshaw, The Guardian*

66 The dramatic arc of Roger Dodger may be banal but (director Dylan) Kidd manages some marvellous moments. – *Peter Rainer, New York Magazine*

Roman Holiday ★★★

DIR William Wyler
1953   118m   US

☆ Gregory Peck, Audrey Hepburn, Eddie Albert, Hartley Power, Harcourt Williams

A princess on an official visit to Rome slips away incognito and falls in love with a newspaperman.

Wispy, charming, old-fashioned romantic comedy shot in Rome and a little obsessed by the locations; one feels that a studio base would have resulted in firmer control of the elements. The stars, however, made it memorable.

SCR Ian McLellan Hunter, John Dighton   CIN Franz Planer, Henri Alekan   MUS Georges Auric   ED Robert Swink   PROD William Wyler   DIST Paramount

66 Witty, warm and beautifully filmed by Franz Planer and Henri Alekan, it remains an unabashed romantic delight, with Hepburn particularly luminescent. – *David Parkinson, Empire*

⌶ Audrey Hepburn (leading actress); Ian McLellan Hunter (original story); Edith Head (costume design)

⌷ picture; Eddie Albert (supporting actor); William Wyler (direction); Ian McLellan Hunter, John Dighton (screenplay); Franz Planer, Henri Alekan; art direction; editing

🏆 Audrey Hepburn (leading actress)

Romance

SCR/DIR Catherine Breillat
1999   99m   France
DVD

☆ Caroline Ducey (Marie), Sagamore Stévenin (Paul), François Berléand (Robert), Rocco Siffredi (Paolo), Reza Habouhossein (Man on stairs), Fabien de Jomaron (Claude), Emma Colberti (Charlotte), Ashley Wanninger (Ashley)

A French schoolteacher, irritated by her boyfriend's refusal to have sex with her, starts sleeping around.

A joyless, drab confection, masquerading as a feminist tract. It's relentlessly dull, even including its revenge-themed coda. This movie caused a scandal for its sexual explicitness and the presence in the cast of porn star Rocco Siffredi. The real scandal was how the film obtained a release.

CIN Giorgos Arvanitis   MUS Raphael Tidas, DJ Valentin   DES Frédérique Belvaux   ED Agnès Guillemot   PROD Jean-François Lepetit   DIST Blue Light

66 Who could have imagined that sex on screen could be so unbearably dull? – *Kenneth Turan, Los Angeles Times*

R

DVD Available on DVD   ☆ Cast in order   66 Critics' Quotes   ⌶ Academy Award   🏆 BAFTA
♫ Soundtrack on CD   of importance   † Points of interest   ⌷ Academy Award nomination   🏆 BAFTA nomination

529

'A Savage Musical.'

Romance & Cigarettes ★

SCR/DIR John Turturro
2005   105m   US/GB
DVD

☆ James Gandolfini (Nick Murder), Susan Sarandon (Kitty), Kate Winslet (Tula), Steve Buscemi (Angelo), Christopher Walken (Cousin Bo), Mary-Louise Parker (Constance), Barbara Sukowa (Gracie), Elaine Stritch (Nick's Mother)

A construction worker starts an affair, which makes his wife and daughters turn angrily against him.

A foul-mouthed blue-collar opera, in which a stellar cast sing along to familiar pop songs to convey their feelings; Walken's version of Delilah is a highlight, though Dennis Potter virtually copyrighted this device. Overall, it's spicy and original with rough-hewn charm, but distinctly patchy.

CIN Tom Stern   **DES** Donna Zakowska   **ED** Ray Hubley
PROD John Penotti, John Turturro   **DIST** Icon

66 An uneven, but sporadically entertaining movie. – *Peter Bradshaw, The Guardian*

Romanzo Criminale ★★

DIR Michele Placido
2005   152m   Italy/France/UK
DVD   ♫

☆ Kim Rossi Stuart (Freddo ('Ice')), Anna Mougialis (Patrizia), Pierfrancesco Favino (Lebanese), Claudio Santamaria (Dandy), Riccardo Scamarcio (Nero)

In 1970s Rome, a group of small-time criminals, friends since childhood, plot to take over the city's underworld.

An old-fashioned, action-packed story about gangsters on the rise, packaged sleekly, and looking terrific. Despite its long-running length, the narrative rarely falters, and the large cast of characters are economically but interestingly drawn. Hugely satisfactory within the limits it sets itself.

SCR Stefano Rulli, Sandro Petraglia, Giancarlo de Cataldo
CIN Luca Bigazzi   **MUS** Paolo Buonvino   **ED** Esmeralda Calabria   **PROD** Riccardo Tozzi, Giovanni Stabilini, Marco Chimenz   **DIST** Icon

66 An ambitious, bloody and engrossing work. – *Alan Morrison, Empire*

Rome, Open City ★★★

DIR *Roberto Rossellini*
1945   101m   Italy
DVD

☆ Aldo Fabrizi (Don Pietro Pellegrini), *Anna Magnani* (Pina), Marcello Pagliero (Giorgio Manfredi), Maria Michi (Marina)

Italian underground workers defy the Nazis in Rome towards the end of the war.

A vivid newsreel quality is achieved by this nerve-stretching melodrama in which all the background detail is as real as care could make it. It effectively launched Rossellini's career, and remains a foundation stone in the history of Italian neo-realism.

SCR Sergio Amidei, Federico Fellini   **CIN** Ubaldo Arata
MUS Renzo Rossellini   **DIST** Minerva

† Apart from Magnani and Fabrizi, the supporting cast were mostly non-professionals.

⌇ Sergio Amidei, Federico Fellini (screenplay)

'The story of a cop who wanted it bad and got it worse.'

Romeo Is Bleeding

DIR Peter Medak
1993   100m   US
DVD   ♫

☆ Gary Oldman (Jack Grimaldi), Lena Olin (Mona Demarkov), Annabella Sciorra (Natalie Grimaldi), Juliette Lewis (Sheri), Roy Scheider (Don Falcone), David Proval (Scully), Will Patton (Martie)

A corrupt cop is ordered to protect a Russian hitwoman.

Chaotic, slyly comic thriller in which sexual and violent interactions between its amoral characters trump any attempt at story-telling.

SCR Hilary Henkin   **CIN** Dariusz Wolski   **MUS** Mark Isham   **DES** Stuart Wurtzel   **ED** Walter Murch
PROD Hilary Henkin, Paul Webster
DIST Rank/Polygram/Working Title

66 For all its promise, and for all the brittle beauty of Darius Wolski's cinematography, Romeo is Bleeding eventually collapses under the weight of its violent affectations. – *Janet Maslin, New York Times*

Romero ★

DIR John Duigan
1989   102m   US
DVD

☆ Raul Julia (Archbishop Oscar Romero), Richard Jordan (Father Rutilio Grande), Ana Alicia (Arista Zelada), Eddie Velez (Lt. Columa), Alejandro Bracho (Father Alfonzo Osuña), Tony Plana (Father Manuel Morantes), Harold Gould (Francisco Galedo), Lucy Reina (Lucia)

Events in El Salvador radicalise a politically neutral cleric, who starts fighting for human rights and speaking out against the country's death squads.

A worthy but ponderous biopic that never quite engages with the fascination of the story it has to tell.

SCR John Sacret Young   **CIN** Geoff Burton   **MUS** Gabriel Yared   **DES** Roger Ford   **ED** Frans Vandenburg
PROD Ellwood E. Kieser   **DIST** Warner/Paulist Pictures

66 The film has a good heart and Raul Julia's performance is an interesting one, restrained and considered. . .The film's weakness is a certain implacable predictability. We can feel at every moment what must happen next. – *Roger Ebert, Chicago Sun-Times*

'You've never seen anything like it.'

Romper Stomper ★

SCR/DIR Geoffrey Wright
1992   94m   Australia
DVD   ♫

☆ Russell Crowe (Hando), Daniel Pollock (Davey), Jacqueline McKenzie (Gabe), Alex Scott (Martin), Leigh Russell (Sonny Jim)

R

A gang of neo-Nazi skinheads in Melbourne routinely attack Vietnamese immigrants.

An early sight here of Russell Crowe's potential, harnessed to a powerful, thoughtfully shot and edited glimpse of Australia's meanest streets.

CIN Ron Hagen   MUS John Clifford White   DES Steven Jones-Evans   ED Bill Murphy   PROD Daniel Scharf, Ian Pringle   DIST Seon/Australian Film Commission/Film Victoria

66 Ignore the prudes who think you shouldn't make films that scare you. It's a first line of defence. This Aussie Reservoir Dogs opens up a brutal world that needs to be understood. – *Peter Travers, Rolling Stone*

66 The cheap 'message' of the ending fails to salvage a film that at best is well-meant but misguided, at worst, flashy and garbled. – *Time Out*

Romuald et Juliette ★★

SCR/DIR Coline Serreau
1989   111m   France
[DVD]

☆ Daniel Auteuil (Romuald Blindet), Firmine Richard (Juliette Bonaventure), Pierre Vernier (Blache), Maxime Leroux (Cloquet), Gilles Privat (Paulin), Muriel Combeau (Nicole), Catherine Salviat (Françoise Blindet)

Romuald's yoghurt company is being undermined by conniving colleagues until his black cleaning woman comes to his emotional rescue – and helps save the business.

Shakespeare might struggle to recognise these characters, yet this civilised romantic comedy, played and directed with admirable lightness, is a small triumph.

CIN Jean-Noël Ferragut   DES Jean-Marc Stehle   ED Catherine Renault   PROD Jean-Louis Piel, Philippe Carcassonne   DIST Gala/Cinéa/Eniloc/FR3

66 Spirited performances and some fine blues on the soundtrack help to make this warm comedy a real pleasure. – *Time Out*

† best film not in the English language

La Ronde ★★★

DIR *Max Ophüls*
1950   100m   France

☆ *Anton Walbrook* (Master of Ceremonies), Simone Signoret (Leocadie, the Prostitute), Serge Reggiani (Franz, the Soldier), Simone Simon (Marie, the Chambermaid), Daniel Gélin (Alfred, the Young Man), *Danielle Darrieux* (Emma Breitkopf, the Married Lady), Fernand Gravey (Charles, the Husband), Odette Joyeux (The Grisette), Jean-Louis Barrault (Robert Kuhlenkampf, the Poet), Isa Miranda (The Actress), Gérard Philipe (The Count)

In 1900 Vienna, an elegant compère shows that love is a merry-go-round: prostitute meets soldier meets housemaid meets master meets married woman meets husband meets salesgirl meets poet meets actress meets officer meets prostitute meets soldier. . .

Superb stylized comedy with a fine cast, subtle jokes, rich decor and fluent direction; not to mention a haunting theme tune.

SCR Jacques Natanson, Max Ophüls   CIN Christian Matras   MUS Oscar Straus   ED Leonide Azar, S. Rondeau   DIST Sacha Gordine

66 One of the most civilized films to have come from Europe in a long time. – *Gavin Lambert, Monthly Film Bulletin*

66 A film that drags on and on by what seems like geometric progression. – *John Simon, 1968*

⚖ Jacques Natanson, Max Ophuls (screenplay)

🎭 film

'Loyalty Is Bought. Betrayal Is A Way Of Life. . .'

Ronin ★★

DIR John Frankenheimer
1998   121m   US
[DVD]   ♫

☆ Robert de Niro (Sam), Jean Réno (Vincent), Natascha McElhone (Deirdre), Stellan Skarsgard (Gregor), Sean Bean (Spence), Skipp Sudduth (Larry), Michael Lonsdale (Jean-Pierre), Jan Triska (Dapper Gent), Jonathan Pryce (Seamus O'Rourke)

A gang of six secret agents assembles in France to steal a briefcase for Irish revolutionaries, but they start betraying each other.

Suspenseful, if seriously improbable, thriller, with a plot so convoluted that its lack of internal logic ceases to matter. The beauty is in the caper, the hint of menace and not least the adrenalin-fuelled car chase. De Niro just about wins the tough-guy honours, while the virtual narrative just about holds the attention.

SCR J. D. Zeik, Richard Weisz (David Mamet)   CIN Robert Fraisse   MUS Elia Cmiral   DES Michael Z. Hanan   ED Tony Gibbs   PROD Frank Mancuso Jnr   DIST UA/FGM

66 Ronin is devoted to the panache of tough-looking men in black who chase one another in fast cars and then retire to cafes, where they sit around grimly smoking. – *David Denby, New York Magazine*

'He took a new kid and made a hero out of him.'

The Rookie ★

DIR Clint Eastwood
1990   121m   US
[DVD]

☆ Clint Eastwood (Nick Pulovski), Charlie Sheen (David Ackerman), Raul Julia (Strom), Sonia Braga (Liesl), Tom Skerritt (Eugene Ackerman), Lara Flynn Boyle (Sarah), Pepe Serna (Lt. Ray Garcia), Marco Rodriguez (Loco), Pete Randall (Cruz)

Veteran cop needs rescuing from sadistic villains by his new young partner.

Above average example of an unloved sub-genre – the old-cop-young-cop partnership. Violent, packed with action and stunts, with agreeably world-weary cynicism from Eastwood thrown in.

SCR Boaz Yakin, Scott Spiegel   CIN Jack N. Green   MUS Lennie Niehaus   DES Judy Cammer   ED Joel Cox   PROD Howard Kazanjian, Steven Siebert, David Valdes   DIST Warner/Malpaso

66 The Rookie plays like an anthology of stuff that has worked before in action pictures. It's jammed with

[DVD] Available on DVD   ☆ Cast in order of importance   66 Critics' Quotes   ⚖ Academy Award   🎭 BAFTA
♫ Soundtrack on CD   † Points of interest   ⚖ Academy Award nomination   🎭 BAFTA nomination

531

material and the budget was obviously large, but somehow not much pays off. It's all there on the screen, but lifeless. – *Roger Ebert, Chicago Sun-Times*

66 Cops again. Clint again. The pits again. – *Hal Hinson, Washington Post*

'A savage story of lust and ambition.'

Room at the Top ★★★

DIR *Jack Clayton*
1958   117m   GB
DVD

☆ Laurence Harvey (Joe Lampton), *Simone Signoret* (Alice Aisgill), Heather Sears (Susan Brown), Donald Wolfit (Mr. Brown), Ambrosine Philpotts (Mrs. Brown), Donald Houston (Charles Soames), Raymond Huntley (Mr. Hoylake), John Westbrook (Jack Wales), Allan Cuthbertson (George Aisgill), Hermione Baddeley (Elspeth), Mary Peach (June Samson)

In the north of England, an ambitious young civil servant causes the death of his real love, an older Frenchwoman, but manages to marry into a rich family.

One of the first and best-known British 'kitchen sink' dramas, portraying regional working-class life with some realism. It is not quite the best; Harvey is miscast, but his character's calculated rise is fascinating to behold. The excellent Signoret seems to have stepped in from another film entirely.

SCR Neil Paterson   CIN *Freddie Francis*   MUS Mario Nascimbene   ED Ralph Kemplen   PROD John and James Woolf   DIST Remus

66 A drama of human drives and torments, told with maturity and precision. – *Stanley Kauffmann*

⚊ Simone Signoret (leading actress); Neil Paterson (adapted screenplay)

⚊ picture; Jack Clayton (direction); Laurence Harvey (leading actor); Hermione Baddeley (supporting actress)

⚊ film; British film; Simone Signoret (leading actress)

A Room for Romeo Brass ★★★

DIR *Shane Meadows*
1999   90m   GB/ Canada
DVD ♫

☆ Andrew Shim (Romeo Brass), Ben Marshall (Knock Knock), *Paddy Considine* (Morell), Frank Harper (Joe Brass), Julia Ford (Sandra Woolley), James Higgins (Bill Woolley), Vicky McClure (Ladine Brass), Ladene Hall (Carol Brass), Bob Hoskins (Steven Laws)

Two 12-year-old boys who are neighbours in the East Midlands have their friendship disrupted by the arrival of a volatile and dangerous adult.

Winning, truthful and unpredictable comedy about the lessons of growing up, pulling off a potentially jarring shift into melodrama. It's this fine director's best film to date.

SCR Paul Fraser, Shane Meadows   CIN Ashley Rowe
MUS Nick Hemming   DES Crispian Sallis   ED Paul Tothill   PROD George Faber, Charles Pattinson

66 This is a small picture with a deceptively big kick. – *Geoff Andrew, Time Out*

'Ali wants to be loved, inspired – and to belong. But first he needs a. . .[Room To Rent]'

Room to Rent ★

DIR Khaled Al Haggar
2000   95m   GB/France
DVD ♫

☆ Said Taghmaoui (Ali), Juliette Lewis (Linda), Rupert Graves (Mark), Anna Massey (Sarah Stevenson), Clementine Celarie (Vivienne), Karim Belkhadra (Ahmed)

A young Egyptian with ambitions to be a screenwriter is about to be deported from Britain. He considers marriage as a means to stay, and has two choices of bride, a Marilyn Monroe impersonator or an elderly blind woman, convinced he is the reincarnation of her dead lover.

A wry appraisal of immigrant life that underplays darker realities in favour of light comedy. But its amiability and sharp sense of location do not make it memorable.

SCR Khaled Al Haggar, Amanda Mackenzie Stuart
CIN Romain Winding   MUS Safy Boutella   DES Eli Bo
ED John Richards   PROD Ildiko Kemeny   DIST UIP

66 A tad unrealised, despite some great performances this film feels like a whole lot of preparation and not a lot of pay out. – *Bob McCabe, Empire*

A Room with a View ★★★

DIR *James Ivory*
1985   115m   GB
DVD ♫

☆ Maggie Smith (Charlotte Bartlett), Denholm Elliott (Mr. Emerson), Helena Bonham Carter (Lucy Honeychurch), Julian Sands (George Emerson), Daniel Day-Lewis (Cecil Vyse), Simon Callow (Rev. Beebe), Judi Dench (Miss Lavish), Rosemary Leach (Mrs. Honeychurch), Rupert Graves (Freddy Honeychurch)

An innocent Edwardian girl travelling in Italy has her eyes opened to real life and romance.

This film marked the start of Merchant Ivory's peak years of commercial success, and established the firm's trademarks: gorgeous locations and costumes, and detailed period production design, all in the service of quality literary adaptations. This attractive version of Forster's novel established Bonham Carter as a staple in the genre, and featured a remarkable performance by Day-Lewis as the foppish Vyse.

SCR Ruth Prawer Jhabvala   CIN Tony Pierce-Roberts
MUS Richard Robbins   DES Gianna Quaranta, Brian Ackland-Snow   ED Humphrey Dixon   PROD Ismail Merchant   DIST Merchant Ivory/Goldcrest

66 Quality-starved filmgoers will welcome it. – *Variety*

⚊ art direction; Ruth Prawer Jhabvala (adapted screenplay); Jenny Beavan, John Bright (costume design)

⚊ picture; Denholm Elliott (supporting actor); Maggie Smith (supporting actress); James Ivory (direction); Tony Pierce-Roberts

⚊ picture; Maggie Smith (leading actress); Judi Dench (supporting actress) production design

DVD Available on DVD   ☆ Cast in order   66 Critics' Quotes   ⚊ Academy Award   ⚊ BAFTA
♫ Soundtrack on CD   of importance   † Points of interest   ⚊ Academy Award nomination   ⚊ BAFTA nomination

Les Roseaux Sauvages ★★

DIR André Techiné
1994   110m   France
`DVD`

☆ Élodie Bouchez (Maïté Alvarez), *Gaël Morel* (François Forestier), Stephane Rideau (Serge Bartolo), Frederic Gorny (Henri Mariani), Michele Moretti (Madame Alvarez)

In 1962, in the dying days of the Algerian War, two 18 year old schoolboys in rural France face dilemmas about military service, duty and their sexuality.

A delicate rites-of-passage film, sensitively written and portrayed; the passionate emotions on display make a bold contrast with the idyllic landscape.

SCR André Techiné, Gilles Taurand, Olivier Massart   CIN Jeanne Lapoirie   DES Pierre Soula   ED Martine Giordano   PROD Alain Sarde, Georges Benayoun   DIST Gala/Ima/Alain Sarde

66 Politics and post-pubescent sex are the interlocking elements in this well-crafted and sober study of provincial French youth in the early 1960s. – *Alexander Walker, London Evening Standard*

Rosemary's Baby ★★★

SCR/DIR Roman Polanski
1968   137m   US
`DVD`

☆ *Mia Farrow* (Rosemary Woodhouse), John Cassavetes (Guy Woodhouse), Ruth Gordon (Minnie Castevet), Sidney Blackmer (Roman Castevet), Patsy Kelly (Laura-Louise), Ralph Bellamy (Dr Sapirstein), Maurice Evans (Hutch), Angela Dorian (Terry Fionoffrio), Elisha Cook (Mr Nicklas), Charles Grodin (Dr Hill)

After unwittingly becoming friendly with devil-worshippers, an actor's innocent wife is impregnated by the Devil.

Seminal gothic melodrama, suffused with psychological menace – and topped by a streak of dark humour, courtesy of its director.

CIN William Fraker   MUS Krzysztof Komeda   DES Richard Sylbert   ED Sam O'Steen, Bob Wyman   DIST Paramount

66 It may not be for the very young, and perhaps pregnant women should see it at their own risk. – *Motion Picture Herald*

66 Tension is sustained to a degree surpassing Alfred Hitchcock at his best. – *Daily Telegraph*

† William Castle, the producer, is glimpsed outside a phone booth.
† A TV sequel followed: Look What Happened to Rosemary's Baby.

⚐ Ruth Gordon (supporting actress)
⚐ Roman Polanski (adapted screenplay)

Rosencrantz and Guildenstern Are Dead ★

SCR/DIR Tom Stoppard
1990   117m   US
`DVD`

☆ Gary Oldman (Rosencrantz), Tim Roth (Guildenstern),

Richard Dreyfuss (The Player), Joanna Roth (Ophelia), Iain Glen (Hamlet), Donald Sumpter (Claudius), Joanna Miles (Gertrude), Ljubo Zecevic (Osric), Ian Richardson (Polonius), Sven Medvesck (Laertes)

Two minor rogues from Shakespeare's Hamlet are summoned to the King of Denmark's court to snoop on the unhappy Prince.

Tom Stoppard's dazzling stage play transfers unhappily to the cinema screen. Disappointing.

CIN Peter Biziou   MUS Stanley Myers   DES Vaughan Edwards   ED Nicolas Gaster   PROD Michael Brandman, Emanuel Azenburg   DIST Hobo/Brandenburg

66 As a movie, this material freely adapted by Tom Stoppard, is boring and endless. It lies flat on the screen, hardly stirring. – *Roger Ebert, Chicago Sun-Times*

Rosetta ★★★

SCR/DIR Luc and Jean-Pierre Dardenne
1999   95m   Belgium/France
`DVD`

☆ *Emilie Dequenne* (Rosetta), Fabrizio Rongione (Riquet), Anne Yernaux (Rosetta's mother), Olivier Gourmet (Boss)

A jobless young woman, living with her alcoholic mother on a grim Belgian caravan site, dreams of finding work and a life of her own.

An intense work, about a mundane life so downtrodden and so close to the loss of hope that it can be uncomfortable to watch. The film offers no artificially concocted resolution, nor does it seem tied to a political message; it's about one individual, and it is heart-breaking.

CIN Alain Marcoen   MUS Jean-Pierre Cocco   DES Igor Gabriel   ED Marie-Hélène Dozo   PROD Luc and Jean-Pierre Dardenne, Michele and Laurent Petin   DIST Artificial Eye

66 It's so finely empathetic and insightful it tears at your heart. A triumph of humanistic cinema. – *Kenneth Turan, Los Angeles Times*

66 Ultimately there is little respite in Rosetta, and that's what makes it a film of such eviscerating emotional intensity. – *Lizzie Francke, Sight & Sound*

† The film won the Palme d'Or at the 1999 Cannes Film Festival, where Emilie Dequenne was named best actress.

'Family Isn't A Word. . .It's A Sentence.'

The Royal Tenenbaums ★★★

DIR Wes Anderson
2001   110m   US
`DVD` ♫

☆ *Gene Hackman* (Royal Tenenbaum), Anjelica Huston (Etheline Tenenbaum), Ben Stiller (Chas Tenenbaum), Gwyneth Paltrow (Margot Tenenbaum), Luke Wilson (Richie Tenenbaum), Owen Wilson (Eli Cash), Danny Glover (Henry Sherman), Bill Murray (Raleigh St Clair), Seymour Cassel (Dusty), Kumar Pallana (Pagoda), Alec Baldwin (Narrator)

An affluent family of gifted high achievers falls apart spectacularly as the disgraced patriarch returns to the fold to redeem himself.

Enormously imaginative comedy with Hackman in fine form as a hugely flawed father. It's more effective

`DVD` Available on DVD   ☆ Cast in order of importance   66 Critics' Quotes   ⚐ Academy Award   ⚑ BAFTA
♫ Soundtrack on CD   † Points of interest   ⚐ Academy Award nomination   ⚑ BAFTA nomination

533

around its margins – in characters' eccentricities or matching clothes – than at its centre, where the story feels faintly rickety. Anderson establishes his fondness for strategically placed pop music on the soundtrack, and occasional bravura camera sequences. It's brainy and entertaining, though in retrospect one also detects traits that later bogged him down, including his weakness for screwed-up, self-absorbed privileged people.

SCR Wes Anderson, Owen Wilson   CIN Robert Yeoman
MUS Mark Mothersbaugh   DES David Wasco   ED Dylan Tichenor   PROD Wes Anderson, Barry Mendel, Scott Rudin   DIST Buena Vista

66 It's one of the cleverest comedies to happen along in ages. – *Caroline Westbrook, Empire*

⚏ Wes Anderson, Owen Wilson (original screenplay)
Ⓣ Wes Anderson, Owen Wilson (original screenplay)

Ruby

DIR John MacKenzie
1992   111m   US
DVD   ♫

☆ Danny Aiello (Jack Ruby), Sherilyn Fenn (Sheryl Ann DuJean/Candy Cane), Frank Orsatti (Action Jackson), Jeffrey Nordling (Hank), Maurice Bernard (Diego), Joe Viterelli (Joseph Valachi), Robert S. Telford (Senator)

Jack Ruby, a strip club owner, shoots dead Lee Harvey Oswald, the assassin of President Kennedy, to expose a conspiracy to murder JFK.

Sympathetic biopic of Jack Ruby that purports to show that he was trapped into killing Oswald. It's wise to regard the film as entertaining, gossipy speculation rather than rigorously documented fact, though Aiello makes a convincing Ruby.

SCR Stephen Davis   CIN Phil Meheux   MUS John Scott
DES David Brisbin   ED Richard Trevor   PROD Sigurjon Sighvatsson, Steve Golin   DIST Rank/Propaganda

66 Rife with audacious conjecture and titillating improbabilities. . .a wonderfully gossipy biography. – *Rita Kempley, Washington Post*

Ruby Blue (new)

SCR/DIR Jan Dunn
2008   107m   UK

☆ Bob Hoskins (Jack), Josiane Balasko (Stephanie), Jody Latham (Ian), Josef Altin (Frankie), Jessica Stewart (Florrie), Shannon Tomkinson (Stacey), Sean Wilton (Dick)

A lonely widower comes under suspicion when the young girl he has befriended goes missing.

Modest drama from the makers of Gypo that takes its name from its main character's prize racing pigeon; despite some initial promise, the film fails to take flight.

CIN Ole Birkeland   MUS Janette Mason   DES Stevie Stewart   ED Emma Collins   PROD Elaine Wickham
DIST Medb Films

66 Despite a nicely nuanced performance from Hoskins, the limitations of the threadbare budget are a little too evident. – *Andrew Pulver, Guardian*

66 The film comes unstuck too quickly, descending into

amateurish contrivance and hackneyed melodrama. – *Tom Huddleston, Time Out*

† K.T. Tunstall wrote the theme tune.

'Terror has evolved.'

The Ruins (new)

DIR Carter Smith
2008   90m   US/Australia
DVD

☆ Jonathan Tucker (Jeff), Jena Malone (Amy), Shawn Ashmore (Eric), Laura Ramsay (Stacy), Joe Anderson (Mathias), Dimitri Baveas (Dimitri), Sergio Calderon (Lead Mayan)

Young American tourists vacationing in Mexico find themselves trapped in an ancient Mayan temple at the mercy of lethal vines.

Grimly effective horror that might be read as an ecological cautionary tale, at least by those who haven't seen The Day of the Triffids. It could sure use a third act though.

SCR Scott B. Smith   CIN Darius Khondji   MUS Graeme Revell   DES Grant Major   ED Jeff Betancourt
PROD Stuart Cornfield, Jeremy Kramer, Chris Bender
DIST Paramount

JEFF: 'Four Americans on vacation don't just disappear!'

66 A movie that is nowhere near as original as its monster. – *Matt Zoller Seitz, New York Times*

66 Give neophyte director Carter Smith an A for making an effort to evolve a fresh horror flick, but a C for execution and a D for too many cheap thrills. – *Kirk Honeycutt, Hollywood Reporter*

'Love. Commitment. Responsibility. There's nothing he won't run away from.'

Run Fat Boy Run (new)

DIR David Schwimmer
2007   100m   UK/US
DVD   ♫

☆ Simon Pegg (Dennis), Thandie Newton (Libby), Hank Azaria (Whit), Dylan Moran (Gordon), Harish Patel (Mr. Goshdashtidar), Simon Day (Vincent), Ruth Sheen (Claudine), Matthew Fenton (Jake)

A hapless loser tries to win back the woman he deserted at the altar by entering a London marathon.

Broad, sports-based comedy, originally set in America but rather awkwardly relocated to Britain; entertaining enough, if riddled with clichés and stereotypes.

SCR Michael Ian Black, Simon Pegg   CIN Richard Greatrex   MUS Alex Wurman   DES Sophie Becher
ED Michael Parker   PROD Robert Jones, Sarah Curtis
DIST Entertainment

66 Deserves some sort of award for being so perfectly, impeccably average. – *David Edwards, Daily Mirror*

66 Might have been something more had its original concept as a New York-set comedy not been changed into a laboured London travelogue. – *Martin Hoyle, Financial Times*

† Originally conceived as a vehicle for Jack Black.

Run Lola Run ★★★

SCR/DIR *Tom Tykwer*
1998 80m Germany
DVD ♫

☆ *Franka Potente* (Lola), Moritz Bleibtreu (Manni), Herbert Knaup (Lola's Father), Armin Rohde (Mr Schuster), Joachim Krol (Nortbert von Au), Nina Petri (Jutta Hansen), Heino Ferch (Ronnie)

An attractive young woman has a terrifying ultimatum: if she doesn't bring her boyfriend a bag of money in 20 minutes, he will be killed by gangsters.

Exhausting, exhilarating thriller which shows Lola's life-or-death run three times, with three different outcomes. A brilliant idea, and filmed to perfection by Tykwer, using speeded-up action, jump cuts, extreme angles, all in the service of cranking up the suspense. The hard-working, impressively athletic Potente makes an outstanding heroine.

CIN Frank Griebe MUS Tom Tykwer, Johnny Klimek, Reinhold Hei DES Alexander Manasse ED Mathilde Bonnefoy PROD Stefan Arndt DIST Columbia TriStar

66 Cleverly juggling the elements and encounters of a simple thriller scenario by using multiple viewpoints and a domino effect to create different destinies. – *David Rooney, Variety*

Ⓣ film not in the English language

'Sometimes, the most daring step to freedom is out the front door.'

The Run of the Country ★

DIR *Peter Yates*
1995 106m US/Ireland

☆ Albert Finney (Danny's Father), Matt Keeslar (Danny), Victoria Smurfit (Annagh), Anthony Brophy (Prunty), David Kelly (Father Gaynor), Dearbhla Molloy (Danny's Mother)

In rural Ireland, a mother's death devastates a family, and her widower, a policeman and his teenage son clash bitterly in the aftermath.

A modest but well-crafted, intense family drama, with a cross-border romance and the 'Troubles' looming darkly in the background.

SCR *Shane Connaughton* CIN Mike Southon MUS Cynthia Millar DES Mark Geraghty ED Paul Hodgson PROD Peter Yates, Ruth Boswell DIST Rank/Castle Rock/One Two Nine

66 The Run of the Country unfolds gracefully on the screen while possessing the rich substance of a fine novel. – *Kevin Thomas, Los Angeles Times*

'The year is 2019. The finest men in America don't run for President. They run for their lives.'

The Running Man ★

DIR *Paul Michael Glaser*
1987 101m US
DVD ♫

☆ Arnold Schwarzenegger (Ben Richards), Maria Conchita Alonso (Amber Mendez), Yaphet Kotto (William Laughlin), Jim Brown (Fireball), Jesse Ventura (Captain Freedom), Erland Van Lidth (Dynamo), Marvin J. McIntyre (Harold Weiss), Mick Fleetwood (Mic), Richard Dawson (Damon Killian)

In a virtual police state in 2019, a cop framed on a murder charge is forced to take part in a TV game show in which trained assassins hunt him down across Los Angeles.

Inventive futuristic romp which combines good action with bad jokes and deft satire about the downward direction of TV. Undeniably watchable.

SCR Steven E. de Souza CIN Thomas Del Ruth MUS Harold Faltermeyer, Harold Faltermeyer DES Jack T. Collis ED Mark Roy Warner, Edward A. Warschilka, John Wright PROD Tim Zinnemann, George Linder DIST Rank/Braveworld

66 The Running Man has the manners and the gadgetry of a sci-fi adventure film but is, at heart, an engagingly mean, cruel, nasty, funny send-up of television. It's not quite Network but then it also doesn't take itself too seriously. – *Vincent Canby, New York Times*

'In 1971, Arthur and Annie Pope blew up a napalm lab to protest the war. . .Ever since then they have been on the run from the FBI. They chose their lives. Now their son must choose his.'

Running on Empty ★

DIR Sidney Lumet
1988 116m US
DVD

☆ Christine Lahti (Annie Pope/Cynthia Manfield), River Phoenix (Danny Pope/Michael Manfield), Judd Hirsch (Arthur Pope/Paul Manfield), Jonas Abry (Harry Pope/Stephen Manfield), Martha Plimpton (Lorna Phillips), Ed Crowley (Mr. Phillips), L. M. Kit Carson (Gus Winant), Steven Hill (Donald Patterson), Augusta Dabney (Abigail Patterson), David Margulies (Dr. Jonah Reiff)

A teenage boy, whose radical parents have moved from place to place, evading the FBI for 17 years, wants to settle in one place and forge a career as a musician.

Thoughtful family drama that puts a new spin on the aftermath of the 60s, and those affected by the fallout from that turbulent decade. Phoenix is a stand-out in this earnest, minor work.

SCR Naomi Foner CIN Gerry Fisher MUS Tony Mottola DES Philip Rosenberg ED Andre Mondshein PROD Amy Robinson, Griffin Dunne DIST Warner/Lorimar/Double Play

River Phoenix (supporting actor); Naomi Foner (original screenplay)

'This summer, they're kicking it in Paris.'

Rush Hour 3 ⓝⓔⓦ

DIR Brett Ratner
2007 91m US
DVD ♫

☆ Chris Tucker (Carter), Jackie Chan (Lee), Hiroyuki Sanada (Kenji), Youki Kudoh (Dragon Lady), Max Von Sydow (Reynard), Yvan Attal (George), Noémie Lenoir (Genevieve), Roman Polanski (Revi)

Carter and Lee hunt Chinese Triads in Paris with the help of a sultry nightclub singer.

DVD Available on DVD | ☆ Cast in order of importance | 66 Critics' Quotes | † Points of interest | ⓘ Academy Award | ⓘ Academy Award nomination | ⓣ BAFTA | ⓣ BAFTA nomination

♫ Soundtrack on CD

R

More of the same, only less; from the unexciting action to the strained comedy, it seems everyone involved is merely going through the motions.

SCR Jeff Nathanson **CIN** J. Michael Muro **MUS** Lalo Schifrin **DES** Edward Verreaux **ED** Don Zimmerman, Dean Zimmerman, Mark Helfrich **PROD** Arthur Sarkissian, Roger Birnbaum, Jay Stern, Jonathan Glickman, Andrew Z. Davis **DIST** Entertainment

❝ The division of labour is the same as in the first two films. Jackie kicks ass; Chris kicks sass. – *Richard Corliss, Time*

❝ Junky, clunky, grimly unfunny. – *Manohla Dargis, New York Times*

'All's fair when love is war.'

Rushmore ★★★

DIR *Wes Anderson*
1998 93m US
DVD ♫

☆ Jason Schwartzman (Max Fischer), *Bill Murray* (Herman Blume), *Olivia Williams* (Rosemary Cross), Seymour Cassel (Bert Fischer), Brian Cox (Dr Guggenheim), Mason Gamble (Dirk Calloway), Sara Tanaka (Margaret Yang), Stephen McCole (Magnus Buchan), Ronnie McCawley (Ronny Blume), Keith McCawley (Donny Blume), Connie Nielsen (Mrs Calloway), Kim Terry (Mrs Blume)

A precocious 15-year-old falls for one of his teachers, but turns vicious when she prefers a local businessman.

Genre-defying indie comedy with passages of superb, zany slapstick. But it is more often rueful and melancholy, particularly when Murray – in one of his great sad-sack performances – is in the frame.

SCR Wes Anderson, Owen Wilson **CIN** Robert Yeoman **MUS** Mark Mothersbaugh **DES** David Wasco **ED** David Moritz **PROD** Barry Mendel, Paul Schiff **DIST** Buena Vista

❝ Creates its own category of stealth comedy. – *Mick LaSalle, San Francisco Chronicle*

❝ Stylistically fresh and full of sweetness that never cloys. – *Jonathan Rosenbaum, Chicago Reader*

'A Spy Story. . .A Love Story. . .A Story to Cross all Boundaries.'

The Russia House ★

DIR Fred Schepisi
1990 122m US
DVD ♫

☆ Sean Connery (Bartholomew 'Barley' Scott Blair), Michelle Pfeiffer (Katya Orlova), Roy Scheider (Russell), James Fox (Ned), John Mahoney (Brady), Michael Kitchen (Clive), J.T. Walsh (Colonel Quinn), Ken Russell (Walter), David Threlfall (Wicklow), Klaus Maria Brandauer (Dante)

Heavy-drinking British publisher who works for western intelligence organisations in Moscow falls for a beautiful Russian editor.

A thriller with impeccably classy credits throughout, which makes it all the more puzzling that it somehow fails to cohere. Le Carré's novel loses something en route to the big screen; Stoppard's script is literate but hardly exciting. And while Connery and especially Pfeiffer do their best to keep it afloat, it remains an intriguing, largely watchable failure.

SCR Tom Stoppard **CIN** Ian Baker **MUS** Jerry Goldsmith **DES** Richard MacDonald **ED** Peter Honess, Beth Jochem Besterveld **PROD** Paul Maslansky, Fred Schepisi **DIST** UIP/Pathé Entertainment

❝ At its best The Russia House offers a rare and enthralling spectacle: the resurrection of buried hopes. – *Peter Travers, Rolling Stone*

'The first live-action one-take feature film ever made.'

Russian Ark ★★

DIR *Alexander Sokurov*
2002 99m Russia/Germany
DVD

☆ Sergei Dreiden (The Marquis), Maria Kuznetsova (Catherine the Great), Leonid Mozgovoy (Spy), David Giorgobiani (Orbeli), Alexander Chaban (Boris Piotrovsky), Maxim Sergeyev (Peter the Great)

A 19th-century French aristocrat wanders around the Russian State Hermitage Museum in St Petersburg and encounters various historical figures.

There's no denying the technical feat here, as Sokurov's camera weaves through dozens of rooms and past hundreds of costumed extras in a single 87-minute take. As a pageant of Russian history it is abstruse and impenetrable to say the least, but for many this is the ne plus ultra of the 21st-century art film.

SCR Anatoly Nikiforov, Alexsandr Sokurov, Boris Khaimsky, Svetlana Proskurina **CIN** *Tilman Buttner* **MUS** Sergei Yevtushenko **DES** Yelena Zhukova, Natalia Kochergina **ED** Sergey Ivanov, Betina Kuntzsch, Stefan Ciupek **PROD** Andrey Deryabin, Jens Meurer, Karsten Stoter **DIST** Artificial Eye

❝ Audacious, gorgeous and unique. – *Shawn Levy, Portland Oregonian*

❝ A gladsome cavalcade of music, dance, colour and costume. – *Sukhdev Sandhu, Daily Telegraph*

† The production had one day to shoot, and the fourth take was successful.
† The final dance sequence re-creates the last ball ever held in Czarist Russia, in 1913, in the very same ballroom.

'If you're sad, and like beer, I'm your lady.'

The Saddest Music in the World ★

DIR Guy Maddin
2003   100m   Canada
DVD

☆ Mark McKinney (Chester Kent), Isabella Rossellini (Lady Port-Huntley), Maria de Medeiros (Narcissa), David Fox (Fyodor), Ross McMillan (Roderick Kent)

In Winnipeg, gripped by the Depression of the 1930s, a literally legless 'Beer Queen' organises a contest to find the world's saddest music.

Plenty of absurd wit and bizarre situations, but a shade too desperate in its provocation. It's a surreal mess, though a hugely original one, that shifts between colour and black-and-white in a nod to its silent movie roots.

SCR Guy Maddin, George Toles   CIN Luc Montpellier
MUS Christopher Dedrick   DES *Matthew Davies*
ED David Wharnsby   PROD Niv Fichman, Jody Shapiro

66 Despite a charismatic performance from ms Rossellini, the surreal nature of this bizarre tale creates an emotional distance from the characters. – *Anna Smith, Empire*

'In the 21st Century Nobody Is. . .'

Safe ★★★

SCR/DIR *Todd Haynes*
1995   119m   US/GB
DVD   ♫

☆ *Julianne Moore* (Carol White), Xander Berkeley (Greg White), Dean Norris (Mover), Julie Burgess (Aerobics instructor), Ronnie Farer (Barbara), Jodie Markell (Anita)

A California housewife contracts a mysterious allergy to her environment, and moves to a New Age-style retreat in the desert.

A movie about a chilling illness and an equally disconcerting 'cure', playing off ideas of bourgeois consumerism but never settling for an easy satirical tone. It explores the subtle horrors and delusions of modern living in deadly earnest.

CIN Alex Nepomniaschy   MUS *Ed Tomney*   DES David Bomba   ED James Lyons   PROD Christine Vachon, Lauren Zalaznick   DIST Metro Tartan/American Playhouse/Chemical/Good Machine/Kardana/Channel 4/Arnold Semler

66 As seductive as the sherbety decor of Carol's home, as mysterious as the illness that seizes her. – *Richard Corliss, Time*

66 A chic post-modern chiller. – *Rita Kempley, Washington Post*

Salaam Bombay! ★★★★

DIR *Mira Nair*
1988   113m   India/France/GB
DVD   ♫

☆ Shafiq Syed (Krishna/Chaipau), Raghubir Yadav (Chillum), Nana Patekar (Baba), Aneeta Kanwar (Rekha), Hansa Vithal (Manju)

An 11-year-old country boy's adventures among thieves, prostitutes and drug addicts in a large city.

A dazzling feature debut for Nair, who immediately joined the ranks of world-class film-makers with this affecting, documentary-style dissection of a teeming, often dangerous city. A brilliant study of street life, acted by a cast of mainly homeless children, it is moving and harrowing, and has genuine poignancy.

SCR Sooni Taraporevala   CIN Sandi Sissel   MUS L. Subramaniam   DES Mitch Epstein   ED Barry Alexander Brown   PROD Mira Nair   DIST Mainline/Mirabai Films/NFDC/Cadrage/La SEPT/Channel 4

† It was only the second Indian film to be nominated for an Oscar.
† Filmed on the tightest of budgets, it employed 52 locations in a 52-day shoot.

⚱ foreign film
Ⓣ film not in the English language

Saltwater ★

SCR/DIR Conor McPherson
1999   97m   Ireland/GB/Spain

☆ Peter McDonald (Frank Beneventi), Brian Cox (George Beneventi), Conor Mullen (Dr Raymond Sullivan), Laurence Kinlan (Joe Beneventi), Brendan Gleeson ('Simple' Simon McCurdie), Eva Birthistle (Deborah McCeever), Valerie Spelman (Carmel Beneventi), David O'Rourke (Damien Fitzgibbon), Caroline O'Boyle (Tara), Gina Moxley (Sgt Duggan)

In Ireland, a cafe owner's son turns to robbery to rescue his debt-bedevilled father from the clutches of a loan shark.

Writer-director McPherson is best known for his stage work, and this script lacks the right rhythms for cinema – lacking in focus, it is essentially a pleasing series of mostly male character studies.

CIN Oliver Curtis   MUS Plague Monkeys   DES Luana Hanson   ED Emer Reynolds   PROD Robert Walpole
DIST Artificial Eye

Salvador ★★★

DIR Oliver Stone
1986 123m US
[DVD] ♬

☆ James Woods, James Belushi, Michael Murphy, John Savage

An American photo-journalist, looking for a wild time, drives south of the border with a friend and encounters a bloody war in Central America.

One of director Stone's best films, and his most underrated: this is an indictment of US policy and CIA meddling in a troubled region. The excellent Woods starts out cynical and ready to remain unaffected by anything he sees, but gets drawn into the treachery and bloodshed despite himself. An outstanding, deeply-felt work.

SCR Oliver Stone, Richard Boyle **CIN** Robert Richardson **MUS** Georges Delerue **DIST** Hemdale/Gerald Green, Oliver Stone

66 As raw, difficult, compelling, unreasonable, reckless and vivid as its protagonist. – *Variety*

⌘ James Woods (leading actor); Oliver Stone, Rick Boyle (original screenplay)

The Samurai ★★★

SCR/DIR *Jean-Pierre Melville*
1967 95m France

☆ *Alain Delon* (Jef Costello), François Périer (The Inspector), Nathalie Delon (Jan Lagrange), Caty Rosier (Valerie), Jacques Le Roy (The Gunman), Michel Boisrond (Wiener), Robert Favart (Barman)

A hired assassin who lives by a code of self-sufficiency betrays himself by falling in love with the woman who witnessed his murder of a night-club owner.

Moodily atmospheric, engrossing, low-key thriller with a laconic, smouldering hero and minimal dialogue, beautifully shot in tones of greys and blues.

CIN *Henri Decaë* **MUS** François de Roubaix **DES** Georges Casati **ED** Monique Bonnot, Yo Maurette **PROD** Raymond Borderie, Eugene Lepicier **DIST** Filmel/CICC/Fida

Saturday Night and Sunday Morning ★★★★

DIR *Karel Reisz*
1960 89m GB
[DVD]

☆ *Albert Finney* (Arthur Seaton), Shirley Anne Field (Doreen Gretton), *Rachel Roberts* (Brenda), Bryan Pringle (Jack), Norman Rossington (Bert), Hylda Baker (Aunt Ada)

A Nottingham factory worker, dissatisfied with his lot, gets into trouble through his affair with a married woman, but finally settles for convention.

Startling when it emerged, this raw working-class melodrama, with its sharp detail and strong comedy asides, delighted the mass audience chiefly because of its

strong central character thumbing his nose at authority. Matching the mood of the times, and displaying a new attitude to sex, it transformed British cinema and was much imitated.

SCR *Alan Sillitoe* **CIN** *Freddie Francis* **MUS** Johnny Dankworth **ED** Seth Holt **PROD** Harry Salzman, Tony Richardson **DIST** Bryanston/Woodfall

ARTHUR SEATON: I'm out for a good time – all the rest is propaganda!

66 Here is a chance for our own new wave. – *Evening Standard*

66 This study of working-class energies and frustrations has been overdirected. – *Pauline Kael*

Ⓣ British film; Albert Finney (leading actor); Rachel Roberts (leading actress)

Saturday Night Fever ★★★

DIR *John Badham*
1977 119m US
[DVD] ♬

☆ *John Travolta* (Tony Manero), Karen Lynn Gorney (Stephanie), Barry Miller (Bobby C.), Joseph Cali (Joey), Paul Pape (Double J), Bruce Ornstein (Gus)

Italian roughnecks in Brooklyn live for their Saturday night disco dancing, and one of them falls in love with a girl who makes him realize there are better things in life.

Foul-mouthed, fast-paced slice of life which made a movie star of Travolta, a terrific dancer. It capitalised on, and indeed reinforced the disco boom. A phenomenal box-office success that despite some of its flaws – its minor characters are not well sketched, and Tony Manero isn't exactly multi-dimensional – seemed entirely predictable.

SCR Norman Wexler **CIN** Ralf D. Bode **MUS** David Shire **DES** Charles Bailey **ED** David Rawlins **PROD** Milt Felsen **DIST** Paramount/Robert Stigwood

66 A stylish piece of contemporary anthropology, an urban safari into darkest America, a field study of the mystery cults among the young braves and squaws growing up in North Brooklyn. – *Alan Brien, Sunday Times*

66 One minute into Saturday Night Fever you know this picture is on to something, that it knows what it's talking about. – *Gene Siskel, Chicago Tribune*

⌘ John Travolta (leading actor)

'1986. Passion, Rage, Liberty and Love.'

Savage Nights ★

SCR/DIR Cyril Collard
1992 126m France/ Italy
♬

☆ Cyril Collard (Jean), Romane Bohringer (Laura), Carlos Lopez (Samy), Corine Blue (Laura's Mother), Claude Winter (Jean's Mother), René-Marc Bini (Marc), Maria Schneider (Noria), Clémentine Célarié (Marianne)

A bisexual, HIV- positive cameraman lives life to the full, continuing to have unsafe sex, though he is aware of the consequences.

A blazingly honest film full of unsympathetic characters who make bad decisions in ways ranging from trivial to

lethal. There's a touch of hysteria about this work that finds an echo in the behaviour on screen.

CIN Manuel Téran   MUS Cyril Collard, René-Marc Bini
ED Lise Beaulieu   PROD Nella Banfi   DIST Banfilm
Ter/La Sept/Erre/Canal/Sofinergie II/CNC

† The film won four César awards in France in 1993, days after Collard died of Aids.

The Savages (new)   ★★★

SCR/DIR Tamara Jenkins
2007   114m
DVD

☆ *Laura Linney* (Wendy Savage), *Philip Seymour Hoffman* (Jon Savage), *Philip Bosco* (Lenny Savage), Peter Friedman (Larry), Gbenga Akinnagbe (Jimmy), Cara Seymour (Kasia), Debra Monk (Nancy Lachman)

On the east coast of America, an estranged brother and sister, both around 40, and struggling respectively in academia and the theatre, reunite to bring back their dying father to a nursing home nearer to them.

A warm, affecting story that never underplays the ordeal of caring for a dying relative; the siblings confront their own mortality and grow up a little in the process. This is a minor gem, made even more sparkling by three great acting performances.

CIN Mott Hupfel   MUS Stephen Trask   DES Jane Ann Stewart   ED Brian A. Kates   PROD Ted Hope, Anne Carey, Erica Westheimer

66 It's socially and psychologically well observed and the performances are beyond reproach. – *Philip French, Observer*

66 Decent, sweet-natured movie. – *Peter Bradshaw, Guardian*

⚖ Laura Linney; Tamara Jenkins (screenplay)

'Heaven Help Us.'

Saved!   ★

DIR Brian Dannelly
2004   92m   US
DVD

☆ Jena Malone (Mary), Mandy Moore (Hilary Faye), Macaulay Culkin (Roland), Patrick Fugit (Patrick), Heather Matarazzo (Tia), Eva Amurri (Cassandra), Martin Donovan (Pastor Skip), Mary-Louise Parker (Lillian)

A girl at a Christian high school in America starts to doubt her faith after her boyfriend tells her he is gay, and becomes pregnant in her attempts to convert him.

Taking on religious hypocrisy is a fine idea for satire, especially within the confines of a high school movie, but while this makes a promising start, it runs out of steam and ultimately pulls no punches.

SCR Brian Dannelly, Michael Urban   CIN Bobby Bukowski
MUS Christophe Beck   DES Tony Devenyi   ED Pamela Martin   PROD Michael Stipe, Sandy Stern, Michael Ohoven, William Vince   DIST MGM

66 This lame movie is far too timorous. – *David Jays, Sight & Sound*

'The mission is a man.'

Saving Private Ryan   ★★★

DIR *Steven Spielberg*
1998   170m   US
DVD   ♫

☆ Tom Hanks (Captain Miller), Edward Burns (Private Reiben), Tom Sizemore (Sergeant Horvath), Jeremy Davies (Corporal Upham), Vin Diesel (Private Caparzo), Adam Goldberg (Private Mellish), Barry Pepper (Private Jackson), Giovanni Ribisi (T/4 Medic Wade), Matt Damon (Private Ryan), Dennis Farina (Lieutenant Colonel Anderson), Ted Danson (Captain Hamill), Harve Presnell (General Marshall), Harrison Young (Ryan as Old Man)

During the D-Day landings, a squad of eight soldiers is sent on a mission to rescue the sole survivor of four brothers, who is trapped behind enemy lines.

The battle sequences, particularly the Omaha beach landing, are among the most stunningly powerful of Spielberg's career. But the episodic plotting is naggingly formulaic, and the coda in a graveyard tips this nearly great movie into unfortunate mawkishness.

SCR Robert Rodat   CIN *Janusz Kaminski*   MUS John Williams   DES Tom Sanders   ED *Michael Kahn*
PROD Steven Spielberg, Ian Bryce, Mark Gordon, Gary Levinsohn   DIST Paramount/Amblin/Mutual

66 A movie of staggering virtuosity and raw lyric power, a masterpiece of terror, chaos, blood, and courage. – *Owen Gleiberman, Entertainment Weekly*

66 Nothing that suggests an independent vision, unless you count seeing more limbs blown off than usual. – *Jonathan Rosenbaum, Chicago Reader*

† Edward Norton was offered the role of Private Ryan, but turned it down.

⚖ Steven Spielberg; Janusz Kaminski; Michael Kahn; Gary Rydstrom, Richard Hymns (sound); Gary Rydstrom, Gary Summers, Andy Nelson, Ron Judkins (sound effects editing)

⚖ picture; Tom Hanks (leading actor); Robert Rodat (original screenplay); John Williams; Tom Sanders; Lois Burwell, Conor O'Sullivan, Daniel C. Striepeke (make up)

🅱 Stefen Fangmeier, Roger Guyett, Neil Corbould (special visual effects); Gary Rydstrom, Ron Judkins, Gary Summers, Andy Nelson, Richard Hymns (sound)

🅑 film; Tom Hanks (leading actor); Steven Spielberg; Janusz Kaminski; Michael Kahn; John Williams; Tom Sanders; Lois Burwell, Jeanette Freeman (make up/hair)

'Hope is worth fighting for.'

Savior   ★

DIR Peter Antonijevic
1998   103m   US
DVD

☆ Dennis Quaid (Joshua Rose/Guy), Nastassja Kinski (Maria Rose), Stellan Skarsgard (Peter Dominic), Natasa Ninkovic (Vera), Sergej Trifunovic (Goran), Nebojsa Glogovac (Vera's Brother), Vesna Trivalic (Woman on Bus)

An American mercenary, numbed after losing his family in a terrorist attack, fights for the Serbs in Bosnia, and rediscovers his humanity when he helps a pregnant rape victim.

S

DVD Available on DVD   ☆ Cast in order   66 Critics' Quotes   ⚖ Academy Award   🅱 BAFTA
♫ Soundtrack on CD   of importance   † Points of interest   ⚖ Academy Award nomination   🅑 BAFTA nomination

539

Earnest and well-intentioned war film, with Quaid in excellent form as a man who comes to appreciate the universality of suffering.

SCR Robert Orr   **CIN** Ian Wilson   **MUS** David Robbins   **DES** Vladislav Lasic, Zoé Sakellaropoulo   **ED** Ian Crafford, Gabriella Cristiani   **PROD** Oliver Stone, Janet Yang   **DIST** First Independent/Initial Entertainment

66 As you might expect from a film produced by Oliver Stone, Savior doesn't bother with political correctness. – *John Wrathall, Sight & Sound*

'Every piece has a puzzle'

Saw

DIR James Wan
2004   103m   US
[DVD]   ♫

☆ Cary Elwes (Dr. Lawrence Gordon), Danny Glover (Detective David Tapp), Monica Potter (Alison Gordon), Michael Emerson (Zep Hindle), Tobin Bell (John)

Two men wake chained up in the lair of a serial killer, their only means of escape being to kill each other or saw their own feet off.

'Torture porn' was notably born in this grimly inventive thriller, which shows off its series of ingenious deathtraps but can't drum up the faintest interest in who survives or doesn't: gloating sadism is the only objective.

SCR Leigh Whannell   **CIN** David Armstrong   **MUS** Charlie Clouser   **DES** Julie Berghoff   **ED** Kevin Greutert   **PROD** Oren Koules, Mark Burg, Gregg Hoffman   **DIST** Entertainment

66 Impressively loathsome and extravagantly twisted. – *Peter Bradshaw, Guardian*

66 Nasty, nasty, nasty. – *Jason Solomons, Mail on Sunday*

† The film cost $1.2m and made $55 at the US box office. Three sequels followed.

'It's a Trap.'

Saw IV (new)   ★

DIR Darren Lynn Bousman
2007   92 minsm   USA

☆ Tobin Bell (Jigsaw/John), Costas Mandylor (Hoffman), Scott Patterson (Agent Strahm), Betsy Russell (Jill), Lyriq Bent (Rigg)

Deceased Jigsaw sets a test from beyond the grave that puts a justice-obsessed SWAT team member through a maze of moral choices.

Drawing on all previous episodes for its brain-numbing twists and micro-detailed flashbacks fleshing out Jigsaw's past, the frantic action is so convoluted it's hard to remain emotionally connected to anyone involved in the clinically grisly torture scenarios.

SCR Patrick Melton, Marcus Dunstan, Thomas Fenton   **CIN** David A. Armstrong   **MUS** Charlie Clouser   **DES** David Hackl   **ED** Kevin Greutert   **PROD** Gregg Hoffman, Oren Koules, Mark Burg   **DIST** Lions Gate Films

66 Since the thing is increasingly impatient to jump forward to the next big torture set piece, there isn't any time to establish anyone's character. Butcher shops are bloody, too, but they're not scary. – *Kyle Smith – New York Post*

'To know Lloyd Dobler is to love him. Diane Court is about to know Lloyd Dobler.'

Say Anything. . .   ★★

SCR/DIR Cameron Crowe
1989   100m   US
[DVD]   ♫

☆ John Cusack (Lloyd Dobler), Ione Skye (Diane Court), John Mahoney (James Court), Lili Taylor (Corey Flood), Amy Brooks (D.C.), Pamela Segall (Rebecca), Jason Gould (Mike Cameron), Joan Cusack (Constance Dobler), Lois Chiles (Diane's Mother)

An underachieving student falls in love with a beautiful brain-box, but must win over her father too.

Disarming, influential teen romance, which wears its heart on its sleeve.

CIN Laszlo Kovacs   **MUS** Richard Gibbs, Anne Dudley, Nancy Wilson   **DES** Mark Mansbridge   **ED** Richard Marks   **PROD** Polly Platt   **DIST** TCF

66 A teen movie that transcends its teen limitations. – *Hal Hinson, Washington Post*

'The Story That Seduced The World Is Now The Most Controversial Film Of The Year.'

Scandal

DIR Michael Caton-Jones
1988   115m   GB/US
[DVD]   ♫

☆ John Hurt (Stephen Ward), Joanne Whalley-Kilmer (Christine Keeler), Ian McKellen (John Profumo), Bridget Fonda (Mandy Rice-Davies), Leslie Phillips (Lord Astor (Bill)), Britt Ekland (Mariella Novotny), Daniel Massey (Mervyn Griffith-Jones), Roland Gift (Johnnie Edgecombe), Jeroen Krabbé (Eugene Ivanov)

Osteopath Stephen Ward introduces call-girl Christine Keeler to the cabinet minister John Profumo in the 1960s, causing an uproar when their affair is made public.

Flat-footed dramatisation of the era's most notorious tabloid sex scandal.

SCR Michael Thomas   **CIN** Mike Molloy   **MUS** Carl Davis   **DES** Simon Holland   **ED** Angus Newton   **PROD** Stephen Woolley   **DIST** Palace/Miramax/British Screen

66 A soft-centred fairytale, with Ward more or less whitewashed. – *Ken Russell*

66 Seedy piece of half-baked exploitation. – *Christopher Tookey, Daily Mail*

† Two extras during the Cliveden House orgy sequence were discovered to have been actually having sex on camera, causing the scene to be trimmed.

'He loved the American Dream. With a vengeance.'

Scarface   ★★★

DIR Brian de Palma
1983   170m   US
[DVD]

☆ Al Pacino (Tony Montana), Steven Bauer (Manny Ray), Michelle Pfeiffer (Elvira), Mary Elizabeth Mastrantonio (Gina), Robert Loggia (Frank Lopez), Paul Shenar

(Alejandro Sosa), Harris Yulin (Bernstein), F. Murray Abraham (Omar)

The rise and fall of a Cuban immigrant who becomes a big-time drug dealer.

Brutalized remake, with detailed violence and a superabundance of foul language; yet Pacino is mesmerising, and Pfeiffer and Bauer both lend first-rate support. Miami, superbly photographed, looks all too likely a location for such nefarious dealings. With this film, De Palma made a shocking statement about the advanced state of the narcotics trade in America's cities.

SCR Oliver Stone   CIN John A. Alonzo   MUS Giorgio Moroder   ED Jerry Greenberg, David Ray   PROD Martin Bregman   DIST Universal

TONY MONTANA: In this country, you gotta make the money first. Then when you get the money, you get the power. Then when you get the power, then you get the woman.

66 An efficient gangster picture, a good nasty entertainment. – *Terrence Rafferty, Sight and Sound*

66 The picture is peddling macho primitivism and at the same time making it absurd. – *Pauline Kael, New Yorker*

'I'm going to run the whole works. There's only one law: do it first, do it yourself, and keep doing it!'

Scarface ★★★

DIR *Howard Hawks*
1932   99m   US
DVD

☆ *Paul Muni* (Tony Camonte), *Ann Dvorak* (Cesca Camonte), *George Raft* (Guino Rinaldo), Boris Karloff (Gaffney), Osgood Perkins (Johnny Lovo), Karen Morley (Poppy), C. Henry Gordon (Inspector Guarino), Vince Barnett (Angelo), Henry Armetta (Pietro), Edwin Maxwell (Commissioner)

The life and death of a Chicago gangster of the 1920s.

Obviously modelled on Al Capone, with an incestuous sister thrown in, this was perhaps the most vivid film of the gangster cycle, and its revelling in its own sins was not obscured by its sub-title, The Shame of a Nation.

SCR Ben Hecht, Seton I. Miller, John Lee Mahin, W. R. Burnett, Fred Pasley   CIN *Lee Garmes, L. W. O'Connell*   MUS Adolph Tandler, Gus Arnheim   ED Edward Curtiss   DIST Howard Hughes

66 Presumably the last of the gangster films, on a promise, it is going to make people sorry that there won't be any more. Should draw wherever it can play. – *Variety*

66 More brutal, more cruel, more wholesale than any of its predecessors. – *James Shelley Hamilton*

† On original release added scenes showed Tony tried, convicted and hanged, though since Muni is never seen, it appears that they were an afterthought made when he was not available.

'Based on a private diary of Catherine the Great!'

The Scarlet Empress ★★★

DIR *Josef von Sternberg*
1934   109m   US
DVD

☆ *Marlene Dietrich* (Sophia Frederica), *John Lodge* (Count Alexei), *Sam Jaffe* (Grand Duke Peter), Louise Dresser (Empress Elizabeth), C. Aubrey Smith (Prince August), Gavin Gordon (Gregory Orloff), Jameson Thomas (Lt. Ostvyn)

A fantasia on the love life of Catherine the Great.

An overwhelming, dramatically insubstantial but pictorially brilliant homage to a star; it now seems presciently camp, kitschy and oddly suggestive in a surprisingly modern manner, and is none the worse for it.

SCR Manuel Komroff   CIN *Bert Glennon*   ED Josef von Sternberg   DIST Paramount

66 She's photographed behind veils and fishnets, while dwarfs slither about and bells ring and everybody tries to look degenerate. – *New Yorker, 1975*

66 A ponderous, strangely beautiful, lengthy and frequently wearying production. – *Mordaunt Hall, New York Times*

'No mercy. No shame. No sequel.'

Scary Movie

DIR Keenen Ivory Wayans
2000   88m   US
DVD ♫

☆ Shawn Wayans (Ray), Marlon Wayans (Shorty), Cheri Oteri (Gail Hailstorm), Shannon Elizabeth (Buffy), Anna Faris (Cindy Campbell), Jon Abrahams (Bobby), Lochlyn Munro (Greg), Regina Hall (Brenda), Dave Sheridan (Doofy), Dan Joffre (Kenny)

A bumbling serial killer stalks a group of high school students.

Truly lame, crass and witless spoof of the slasher-movie conventions Wes Craven had already sent up in Scream; the sequels are if anything a slight improvement. Its success opened the door for more spoof movies that were barely spoofs at all.

SCR Shawn Wayans, Marlon Wayans, Buddy Johnson, Phil Beauman, Jason Friedberg, Aaron Seltzer   CIN Francis Kenny   MUS David Kitay   DES Robb Wilson King   ED Mark Helfrich   PROD Eric L. Gold, Lee R. Mayes

66 Is it funny? Yes, it is. – *Roger Ebert, Chicago Sun-Times*

† Followed by Scary Movie 2 (2001), Scary Movie 3 (2003) and Scary Movie 4 (2006), the last two without the involvement of the Wayans brothers.

Scenes from the Class Struggle in Beverly Hills

DIR Paul Bartel
1989   95m   US
DVD

☆ Jacqueline Bisset (Clare Lipkin), Ray Sharkey (Frank), Mary Woronov (Lisabeth Hepburn-Saravian), Robert Beltran (Juan), Ed Begley Jnr (Peter), Wallace Shawn (Howard), Arnetia Walker (To-Bel), Paul Bartel (Dr. Mo Van De Kamp), Paul Mazursky (Sidney), Rebecca Schaeffer (Zandra)

Characters from various classes and backgrounds swap beds in an affluent neighbourhood.

Great title, shame about the movie. It sets itself up as a knowing satire of the rich and famous in L.A., but effectively it's little more than an acid little comedy

S

about sexual liaisons that straddle social strata. At the time it was thought faintly daring; but subversive it's not.

SCR Bruce Wagner   **CIN** Steven Fierberg   **MUS** Stanley Myers   **DES** Alex Tavoularis   **ED** Alan Toomayan   **PROD** C. Katz   **DIST** Rank/North Street Films/Cinecom Entertainment

The Scent of Green Papaya   ★★

SCR/DIR *Tran Anh Hung*
1993   104m   France
[DVD]   ♫

☆ Yên-Khê Tran Nu (Mui Age 20), Man San Lu (Mui Age 10), Thi Lôc Truong (The mother), Anh Hoa Nguyen (Ti), Hoa Hôi Vuong (Khuyen), Ngoc Trung Tran (The father)

A young village girl in 1950s Vietnam works as a maid for a struggling family and finds herself falling in love.

Slow-paced, beautifully observed treatment of a moving, emotional domestic drama, crafted with great care.

CIN *Benoît Delhomme*   **MUS** Tiêt Ton-That   **DES** Alain Nègre   **ED** Nicole Dedieu, Jean-Pierre Roques   **PROD** Christophe Rossignon   **DIST** Artificial Eye/Lazennec/La Sept/Canal

66 Here is a film so placid and filled with sweetness that watching it is like listening to soothing music. – *Roger Ebert, Chicago Sun-Times*

66 A lovely experience in the dreamily exotic. – *Peter Stack, San Francisco Chronicle*

⚖ foreign language film

'The List Is Life. The Man Was Real. The Story Is True.'

Schindler's List   ★★★★

DIR *Steven Spielberg*
1993   195m   US
[DVD]   ♫

☆ *Liam Neeson* (Oskar Schindler), *Ben Kingsley* (Itzhak Stern), *Ralph Fiennes* (Amon Goeth), Caroline Goodall (Emilie Schindler), Jonathan Sagalle (Poldek Pfefferberg), Embeth Davidtz (Helen Hirsch), Malgosha Gebel (Victoria Klonowska), Shmulik Levy (Wilek Chilowicz), Mark Ivanir (Marcel Goldberg)

The Austrian entrepreneur Oskar Schindler starts a factory during the war using Jews as slave labour, witnesses the horrors of the Holocaust and compiles a list of over 1,100 Jews to save from death, bribing an SS commandant.

Not a perfect film but still a masterpiece, an unforgettably moving drama on the theme of conscience, told in a stark, unflinching and consistently brave way. It is the traces of sentimentality that actually make it bearable – we watch the movie not to relive the Holocaust, but to bear emotional witness to it.

SCR *Steven Zaillian*   **CIN** *Janusz Kaminski*   **MUS** *John Williams*   **DES** *Allan Starski*   **ED** *Michael Kahn*   **PROD** Steven Spielberg, Gerald R. Molen, Branko Lustig   **DIST** Universal/Amblin

66 One of the great films in the history of the cinema. – *Iain Johnstone, Sunday Times*

66 A welcome astonishment from a director who has given us much boyish esprit, much ingenuity, but little seriousness. – *Stanley Kauffmann, New Republic*

† Spielberg approached Billy Wilder, Roman Polanski and Martin Scorsese to direct the film, worried that he would not do the story justice.

† Stellan Skarsgård, Bruno Ganz and Harrison Ford were all considered for the role of Schindler.

† It was the first black-and-white film since The Apartment (1960) to win the Best Picture Oscar.

🏆 picture; Steven Spielberg; Steven Zaillian (adapted screenplay); Janusz Kaminski; Michael Kahn; John Williams; Allan Starski

⚖ Liam Neeson (leading actor); Ralph Fiennes (supporting actor); Anna Biedrzycka-Sheppard (costume design); Andy Nelson, Steve Pederson, Scott Millan, Ron Judkins (sound); Christina Smith, Matthew W. Mungle, Judith A. Cory (make up)

🅑 film; Steven Zaillian (adapted screenplay); Steven Spielberg; Ralph Fiennes (supporting actor); Janusz Kaminski; John Williams; Michael Kahn

🅣 Liam Neeson (leading actor); Ben Kingsley (supporting actor); Anna Biedrzycka-Sheppard (costume sesign); Allan Starski, Louis Edemann, Robert Jackson, Ron Judkins, Andy Nelson Steve Pederson, Scott Millan (sound); Christina Smith, Matthew W. Mungle, Judith A. Cory (make up)

'We don't need no education.'

School of Rock   ★★

DIR *Richard Linklater*
2003   108m   US/Germany
[DVD]   ♫

☆ *Jack Black* (Dewey Finn), *Joan Cusack* (Rosalie Mullins), Mike White (Ned Schneebly), Sarah Silverman (Patty Di Marco), Joey Gaydos Jnr (Zack), Robert Tsai (Lawrence), Maryam Hassan (Tomika), Kevin Clark (Freddy Jones)

A slobbish musician poses as a temp teacher and instructs a class of posh ten-year-olds in the ways of rock.

Inspired mainstream comedy, the perfect vehicle for its star, crunching out big laughs like power-chords and infused with a spirit of gentle rebellion. Rarely has such an obvious premise made for quite such sterling entertainment.

SCR *Mike White*   **CIN** Rogier Stoffers   **MUS** Craig Wedren   **DES** Jeremy Conway   **ED** Sandra Adair   **PROD** Scott Rudin   **DIST** Paramount

66 Alive and well-acted and smart and perceptive and funny. – *Roger Ebert, Chicago Sun-Times*

'There are no partners in crime.'

The Score   ★

DIR Frank Oz
2001   124m   US/Germany
[DVD]   ♫

☆ Robert De Niro (Nick), Edward Norton (Jack/Brian), Marlon Brando (Max), Angela Bassett (Diane), Gary Farmer (Burt), Paul Soles (Danny)

In Montreal, a veteran thief, tempted by the prospect of one last big heist that will enable him to leave crime behind, teams up with his former partner and a brash young novice.

The glittering cast make this relatively mundane robbery movie worth watching, but it is still too familiar.

SCR Kario Salem, Lem Dobbs, Scott Marshall Smith CIN Rob Hahn MUS Howard Shore DES Jackson De Govia ED Richard Pearson PROD Gary Foster, Lee Rich DIST Pathé

66 It does nothing you haven't seen before, but it does it quickly, cleanly and efficiently, an in-and-out job, like all the best heists. – *Jason Solomons, Observer*

† This was Brando's last completed film.

'Protection Is The Job, Justice Is The Goal, Death Is The Price.'

La Scorta ★

DIR *Ricky Tognazzi*
1993 92m Italy
DVD ♫

☆ Claudio Amendola (Angelo Mandolesi), Enrico Lo Verso (Andrea Corsale), Carlo Cecchi (Judge Michele de Francesco), Ricky Memphis (Fabio Muzzi), Tony Sperandeo (Raffaele Frasca), Francesca D'Aloja (Anna Spano), Angelo Infanti (Judge Barresi), Leo Gullotta (Policeman)

A Sicilian judge is assigned a police escort after ordering an investigation into links between the Mafia and local politicians.

Reasonably gripping thriller, somewhat over-involved, but with fluid camerawork and a sense of the constant threat lawmakers face in a place of Mob law.

SCR Graziano Diana, Simona Izzo CIN *Alessio Gelsini* MUS *Ennio Morricone* DES Mariangela Capuano ED Carla Simoncelli PROD Claudio Bonivento DIST Claudio Bonivento

66 A serviceable thriller, and basically an enjoyable B-movie. – *Christopher Tookey, Daily Mail*

'Don't Answer The Phone. Don't Open The Door. Don't Try To Escape.'

Scream ★★

DIR *Wes Craven*
1996 111m US
DVD ♫

☆ Drew Barrymore (Deputy Dwight 'Dewey' Riley), Neve Campbell (Sidney Prescott), Skeet Ulrich (Billy Loomis), Courteney Cox (Gale Weathers), Rose McGowan (Tatum Riley), David Arquette (Deputy Dwight 'Dewey' Riley)

A cine-literate serial killer stalks and murders a series of teenage girls.

A 'meta' slasher movie, and one which certainly knows whereof it shrieks, functioning as a superior example of the genre it's spoofing. The in-jokes will please fans; the only downside is that it's a little too pleased with itself.

SCR Kevin Williamson CIN Mark Irwin MUS Marco Beltrami DES Bruce Alan Miller ED Patrick Lussier PROD Cary Woods, Cathy Konrad DIST Buena Vista/Miramax/Dimension

66 Amusingly twisted. – *Peter Stack, San Francisco Chronicle*

66 Like most navel-gazing jokes it rapidly begins to induce a sense of pointlessness. – *Kevin Jackon, Independent on Sunday*

† Two sequels followed in 1997 and 2000.

The Sea Inside ★★★

DIR *Alejandro Amenabar*
2004 125m Spain/France/Italy
DVD ♫

☆ *Javier Bardem* (Ramon Sampedro), Belen Rueda (Julia), Lola Duenas (Rosa), Mabel Rivera (Manuela), Celso Bugallo (Jose), Clara Segura (Gene), Joan Dalmau (Joaquin)

In Spain, a quadriplegic man, who broke his neck in a diving accident as a young man, fights for the right to die after living paralysed for three decades.

Based on a true story, this unsentimental, sometimes funny film is more than a plea for euthanasia; it questions whether life can ever stop being worth living, and airs both sides of the argument. Bed-ridden Bardem is stunning in the central role, conveying more with a sideways glance than most actors do with their entire bodies.

SCR Alejandro Amenabar, Mateo Gil CIN *Javier Aguirresarobe* MUS Alejandro Amenabar DES Benjamin Fernandez ED Alejandro Amenabar PROD Fernando Bovaira, Alejandro Amenabar

66 It's a polished, thought-provoking, poignant melodrama, and Javier Bardem is superb. – *Time Out*

66 The film is worth seeing, but only if you're prepared to set aside your aversion to its polemic in order to experience its compassion. – *Ron Reed, Christianity Today*

† Ramon Sampedro eventually committed suicide by drinking cyanide, with the help of 10 supporters. His death was videotaped and broadcast on Spanish TV.
† At the 2004 Venice Film Festival, Bardem was named best actor.

⏳ foreign language film
⏳ Jo Allen, Manolo Garcia (make up)

'In search of a killer, he found someone who's either the love of his life. . .or the end of it.'

Sea of Love ★★

DIR Harold Becker
1989 112m US
DVD ♫

☆ Al Pacino (Det. Frank Keller), Ellen Barkin (Helen Cruger), John Goodman (Det. Sherman), William Hickey (Frank Keller Sr.), Michael Rooker (Terry), Richard Jenkins (Gruber)

A serial killer is targeting men who advertise in the lonelyhearts columns, and the New York detective on the case begins a relationship with the prime suspect.

Decent thriller, a return to form for Pacino after a string of turkeys, even if it's bigger on sexiness than sense.

SCR Richard Price CIN Ronnie Taylor MUS Trevor Jones DES John Jay Moore ED David Bretherton PROD Martin Bregman, Louis A. Stroller DIST Universal

S

DVD Available on DVD   ☆ Cast in order of importance   66 Critics' Quotes   † Points of interest   ⏳ Academy Award   ⏳ Academy Award nomination   🅑 BAFTA   🅣 BAFTA nomination

543

66 The script's complexities are buried too deep. – *Neil Norman, Evening Standard*

'The True Story Of A Longshot Who Became A Legend.'

Seabiscuit ★★

SCR/DIR *Gary Ross*
2003   141m   US
DVD

☆ Tobey Maguire (Red Pollard), Jeff Bridges (Charles Howard), Chris Cooper (Tom Smith), Elizabeth Banks (Marcela Howard), Gary Stevens (George Woolf), William H. Macy ('Tick-Tock' McGlaughlin), Kingston DuCoeur (Sam), Eddie Jones (Samuel Riddle)

A crippled old nag in Depression-era America comes good, along with its bereaved owner, washed-up trainer and one-eyed jockey.

A metaphorical epic about America picking itself back up, but one which only occasionally works, thanks to a windy self-importance, and the dramatic cheesiness of managing so many comebacks at once. Still, the races are nicely mounted.

CIN John Schwartzman   MUS Randy Newman
DES Jeannine Oppewall   ED William Goldenberg
PROD Kathleen Kennedy, Frank Marshall, Gary Ross, Jane Sindell   DIST Universal

66 A proudly cornball sentimental epic. – *J. Hoberman, Village Voice*

66 It's deluxe and handsome and has no soul. – *Charles Taylor, Salon*

picture; Gary Ross (adapted screenplay); John Schwartzman; William Goldenberg; Jeanninee Oppewall (costume design); Judianna Makovsky, Andy Nelson, Anna Behlmer, Tod A. Maitland (sound mixing)

'He had to find her . . . he had to find her. . .'

The Searchers ★★★★

DIR *John Ford*
1956   119m   US
DVD

☆ John Wayne (Ethan Edwards), Jeffrey Hunter (Martin Pawley), Natalie Wood (Debbie Edwards), Vera Miles (Laurie Jorgensen), Ward Bond (Capt. Rev. Samuel Clayton), John Qualen (Lars Jorgensen), Henry Brandon (Chief Scar), Antonio Moreno (Emilio Figueroa)

A Confederate war veteran tracks down the Indians who have slaughtered his brother and sister-in-law and carried off their daughter.

Disturbing Western about obsession and racism which has become Ford's most influential film. Wayne gives his most ambiguous performance, being no longer a simple gung-ho hero, but a tormented loner out of step with his society. Its themes of loss and reconciliation are echoed in many films that followed.

SCR Frank S. Nugent   CIN Winton C. Hoch   MUS Max Steiner   ED Jack Murray   PROD Merian C. Cooper
DIST Warner/C. V. Whitney

66 You can read a lot into it, but it isn't very enjoyable. – *Pauline Kael, 70s*

66 A rip-snorting Western, as brashly entertaining as they come. – *Bosley Crowther, New York Times*

The Secret Adventures of Tom Thumb ★★

SCR/DIR *Dave Borthwick*
1993   60m   GB
DVD

☆ Nick Upton (Pa Thumb), Deborah Collard (Ma Thumb), Frank Passingham (Man), John Schofield (Man)

Two sinister strangers take a tiny child from his poor parents to a laboratory full of mutants. But the miniature person escapes into a rubbish dump where he discovers little people like himself.

Live action and animation is cleverly combined in this fascinating allegory on the human race. Innovative, imaginative and challenging, this is anything but a fairy tale.

CIN Dave Borthwick, Frank Passingham   MUS John Paul Jones, Startled Insects   DES Dave Borthwick   ED Dave Borthwick   PROD Richard 'Hutch' Hutchison
DIST Bolex Brothers/BBC Bristol/La Sept/Manga/Lumen

66 Too intense for small children The Secret Adventures of Tom Thumb is an unexpected pleasure for sophisticated adults. – *Kevin Thomas, Los Angeles Times*

† The animation team, known as the Bolex Brothers, were based in Bristol, and became part of that city's animation wave in the wake of Aardman's success.

'The timeless tale of a special place where magic, hope and love grow.'

The Secret Garden ★★

DIR *Agnieszka Holland*
1993   101m   US
DVD   ♫

☆ Maggie Smith (Mrs. Medlock), Kate Maberly (Mary Lennox), Heydon Prowse (Colin Craven), Andrew Knott (Dickon), Laura Crossley (Martha), John Lynch (Lord Archibald Craven), Walter Sparrow (Ben Weatherstaff), Irene Jacob (Mary's Mother/Lilias Craven)

A young girl is sent to live in England with her aristocratic uncle when her parents are killed in India, helps her sickly invalid cousin back to life.

An imaginative rendering of a children's classic, strikingly shot, with an appropriately Gothic feel.

SCR Caroline Thompson   CIN Roger Deakins
MUS Zbigniew Preisner   DES Stuart Craig   ED Isabelle Lorente   PROD Fred Fuchs, Fred Roos, Tom Luddy
DIST Warner/American Zoetrope

66 The Secret Garden has the feel of a classic . . . it would be a shame if adults felt they needed a child in tow to see this movie. They'd be missing out on a rich cinematic treat. – *David Ansen, Newsweek*

Ⓣ Maggie Smith (supporting actress)

The Secret Laughter of Women ★

DIR *Peter Schwabach*
1998   99m   GB/Canada

☆ Colin Firth (Matthew Field), Nia Long (Nimi Da Silva), Dan Lett (John), Joke Silva (Nene), Ariyon Bakare (Reverend Fola), Joy Elias-Rilwan (Mama Fola), Hakeem Kae-Kazim (Doctor Ade), Bella Enahoro (Madame Rosa), Fissy Roberts (Sammy), Rakie Ayola (Talking Drum),

---

DVD Available on DVD   ☆ Cast in order of importance   66 Critics' Quotes   † Points of interest   Academy Award   Academy Award nomination   Ⓑ BAFTA   Ⓣ BAFTA nomination
♫ Soundtrack on CD

Caroline Goodall (Jenny Field), Ellen Thomas (Bitter Leaf), Thomas Baptiste (Papa Fola)

On the French Riviera, a diffident comic-book writer begins a tentative romance with a beautiful exiled Nigerian widow, who is also being courted by her priest.

A flimsy romantic comedy that deceptively seems to be going somewhere, though it dwells too often on culture-clash misunderstandings. Still, it has its charms.

SCR O.O. Sagay, Misan Sagay **CIN** Martin Fuhrer **MUS** Yves Laferriere **DES** Christopher J. Bradshaw **ED** Michael Pacek **PROD** Misan Sagay, Jon Slan **DIST** Optimum

66 Despite the exotic setting – a Nigerian community in a seaside town in southern France – and the issue-driven narrative, Peter Schwabach's aimless drama struggles to get going. – *Sunday Times*

'Between Land And Sea There Is A Place Where Myths Are Real. . .'

The Secret of Roan Inish ★

SCR/DIR John Sayles
1993 103m US
DVD ♫

☆ Mick Lally (Hugh), Eileen Colgan (Tess), John Lynch (Tadhg), Jeni Courtney (Fiona), Richard Sheridan (Eamon), Cillian Byrne (Jamie)

A young girl sent to live with her grandparents in coastal Ireland is fascinated by local myths about half-human, half-seal creatures called selkies. She is convinced these myths hold clues to the whereabouts of her little dead brother.

A sensitively conveyed take on an ancient Celtic myth of loss and salvation. A complete change of pace for director Sayles, it is moving and haunting.

CIN *Haskell Wexler* **MUS** Mason Daring **DES** Adrian Smith **ED** John Sayles **PROD** Sarah Green, Maggie Renzi **DIST** Metro Tartan/Skerry/Jones Entertainment

66 Not so much a children's film as an adult film in which the children and animals are graceful presences, this is a charming, genuinely moving gem. – *Angie Errigo, Empire*

The Secret Rapture ★

DIR Howard Davies
1993 97m GB
DVD

☆ Juliet Stevenson (Isobel Coleridge), Joanne Whalley-Kilmer (Katherine Coleridge), Penelope Wilton (Marion French), Alan Howard (Tom French), Neil Pearson (Patrick Steadman), Robert Stephens (Max Lopert), Hilton McRae (Norman), Robert Glenister (Jeremy)

Two sisters clash bitterly after the death of their father and struggle to cope with their wild young, alcoholic stepmother.

David Hare's adaptation of his own perceptive stage play seeks to draw broader social and political points from this claustrophobic drama. It has its moments, but theatre may be a more suitable medium for it.

SCR David Hare **CIN** Ian Wilson **MUS** Richard Hartley **DES** Barbara Gosnold **ED** George Akers **PROD** Simon Relph **DIST** Oasis/Greenpoint/Channel 4

66 Wrenching performances and dark, clammy atmosphere cast an unsettling chill. – *Stephen Holden, New York Times*

Secret Wedding ★★

SCR/DIR Alejandro Agresti
1989 95m Argentina/Netherlands/Canada
DVD

☆ Tito Haas (Fermin), Mirtha Busnelli (Tota), Sergio Poves Campos (Pipi), Nathan Pinzon (Pastor), Floria Bloise (Dona Patricia), Elio Marchi (Leandro)

A political dissident who became one of the 'disappeared' in Argentina returns home after 13 years, but is viewed with suspicion and even shunned.

A righteously angry, sobering film about the aftermath of an oppressive regime's brutal persecution.

CIN Ricardo Rodriguez, Alejandro Agresti **MUS** Paul Michael Van Brugge **DES** Juan Collini **ED** Rene Wiegmans **PROD** Andre Bennett, Juan Collini, Kees Kasander, Denis Wigman, Brigitte Young **DIST** Allarts/Cogurccio/Cinéphile

'A comedy for everybody who's been tied up at work.'

Secretary ★★★

DIR Steven Shainberg
2002 104m US
DVD ♫

☆ James Spader (E. Edward Grey), *Maggie Gyllenhaal* (Lee Holloway), Jeremy Davies (Peter), Patrick Bauchau (Dr. Twardon), Stephen McHattie (Burt Holloway), Oz Perkins (Jonathan), Jessica Tuck (Tricia O'Connor), Amy Locane (Lee's Sister), Lesley Ann Warren (Joan Holloway)

A woman given to self-harm embarks on a sado-masochistic relationship with her new boss.

Kinky, smart, provocative and unexpectedly affirming tale of the twisted play between two consenting adults. The power games are addictive, and Gyllenhaal's performance is a marvel.

SCR Erin Cressida Wilson **CIN** Steven Fierberg **MUS** Angelo Badalamenti **DES** Amy Danger **ED** Pam Wise **PROD** Steven Shainberg, Andrew Fierberg, Amy Hobby **DIST** Metro Tartan

66 Freshly conceived, small-scale and daring. – *Alexander Walker, Evening Standard*

'Roxanne drives her mother crazy. Maurice never speaks to his niece. Cynthia has a shock for her family. Monica can't talk to her husband. Hortense has never met her mother.'

Secrets and Lies ★★★

SCR/DIR *Mike Leigh*
1995 142m GB
DVD

☆ *Timothy Spall* (Maurice), Phyllis Logan (Monica), *Brenda Blethyn* (Cynthia), Claire Rushbrook (Roxanne), *Marianne Jean-Baptiste* (Hortense), Elizabeth Berrington (Jane), Michele Austin (Dionne), Lee Ross (Paul)

After the death of her adoptive parents, an upwardly mobile young black optician goes in search of her birth mother, who she discovers is working-class and white.

S

DVD Available on DVD   ☆ Cast in order   66 Critics' Quotes   ⚱ Academy Award   🏆 BAFTA
♫ Soundtrack on CD   of importance   † Points of interest   Academy Award nomination   BAFTA nomination

545

A generous picture in every sense, a superbly meaty look at the pretences in ordinary lives, with perhaps this director's finest ensemble giving their parts a real workout. The acting does get a little broad, and the script lunges unsubtly at catharsis, but it is a film of real heart and intelligence all the same.

CIN Dick Pope   **MUS** Andrew Dickson   **DES** Alison Chitty   **ED** Jon Gregory   **PROD** Simon Channing-Williams   **DIST** Film Four/CiBy 2000/Thin Man/Channel 4

66 A whirl of comedy and soap opera, of bruising tenderness and bravura acting, with the immediacy of real life heightened into the craft of movie art. – *Richard Corliss, Time*

66 The soul-baring and communal hugging drift perilously close to Hollywood-style sentimentality. – *Anne Billson, Sunday Telegraph*

† At the Cannes Film Festival in 1996, it won the Palme d'Or, and Brenda Blethyn was named best actress.

⚲ picture; Brenda Blethyn (leading actress); Marianne Jean-Baptiste (supporting actress); Mike Leigh (director); Mike Leigh (original screenplay)

Ⓣ British film; Brenda Blethyn (leading actress) Mike Leigh (original screenplay)

Ⓣ film; Marianne Jean-Baptiste (supporting actress); Mike Leigh (director)

See How They Fall ★

DIR Jacques Audiard
1993   90m   France
DVD   ♫

☆ Jean-Louis Trintignant (Marx), Jean Yanne (Simon), Mathieu Kassovitz (Johnny), Bulle Ogier (Louise), Christine Pascal (Sandrine), Yvon Back (Mickey)

An ageing con man divulges the secrets of his craft to a young upstart, who turns the tables on him. They meet a salesman bent on revenge for the murder of his boy-friend, an undercover cop.

Two separate and apparently unrelated stories that finally merge in this intriguing film, a noirish thriller with gay undertones.

SCR Alain Le Henry, Jacques Audiard   **CIN** Gérard Sterin   **MUS** Alexandre Desplat   **DES** Jacques Rouxel   **ED** Juliette Welfling   **PROD** Didier Haudepin
DIST MIHK/Bloody Mary/France3/CEC

'Les vies les plus belles sont celles qu'on invente.'

A Self-Made Hero ★★★

DIR Jacques Audiard
1995   107m   France
DVD   ♫

☆ Mathieu Kassovitz (Albert Dehousse), Anouk Grinberg (Servane), Sandrine Kiberlain (Yvette), Jean-Louis Trintignant (Albert, Present), Albert Dupontel (Dionnet), Nadia Barentin (Madame Louvier/Madame Revuz/The General's Wife), Bernard Bloch (Ernst)

After World War II, a shy, cowardly fantasist, the son of French collaborators, passes himself off as a Resistance hero.

Brilliantly funny story about opportunism, fame and assumed identity. The story also hints at the wishful

thinking with which the French regard their wartime legends.

SCR Alain Le Henry, Jacques Audiard   **CIN** Jean-Marc Fabre   **MUS** Alexandre Desplat   **DES** Michel Vandestien   **ED** Juliette Welfling   **PROD** Patrick Godeau
DIST Artificial Eye/Alicélo/Lumière/France 3/M6/Initial

66 The story of a man for whom everything is equally unreal, who distrusts his own substance so deeply that he must be somebody else to be anybody at all. – *Roger Ebert, Chicago Sun-Times*

'Putting the funk into the dunk.'

Semi-Pro (new)

DIR Kent Alterman
2008   91m   US
DVD   ♫

☆ Will Ferrell (Jackie Moon), Woody Harrelson (Ed Monix), Andre Benjamin (Clarence Withers), Maura Tierney (Lynn), Will Arnett (Lou Redwood), David Koechner (Commissioner), Andrew Daly (Dick Pepperfield), Rob Corddry (Kyle)

The player-owner of a struggling 1976 basketball team tries to turn his ramshackle outfit into a going concern.

Flaccid vehicle on a par with its star's other sports-based comedies, elevated slightly by its attention to period detail.

SCR Scot Armstrong   **CIN** Shane Hurlbut   **MUS** Theodore Shapiro   **DES** Clayton Hartley   **ED** Debra Neil-Fisher, Peter Teschner   **PROD** Jimmy Miller
DIST Entertainment

66 Semi-Pro finds the sweet spot between sports melodrama and parody and hammers it for 90 diverting minutes. – *Matt Zoller Seitz, New York Times*

66 Chillingly devoid of laughs. – *Peter Bradshaw, Guardian*

† Rocky, the grizzly bear Ferrell's character wrestles in the film, later killed the handler who had doubled for the actor in the sequence.

'Lose your heart and come to your senses.'

Sense and Sensibility ★★★

DIR *Ang Lee*
1995   136m   GB/US
DVD   ♫

☆ *Emma Thompson* (Elinor Dashwood), Alan Rickman (Colonel Brandon), *Kate Winslet* (Marianne Dashwood), Hugh Grant (Edward Ferrars), James Fleet (John Dashwood), *Harriet Walter* (Fanny Dashwood), Gemma Jones (Mrs Dashwood), Elizabeth Spriggs (Mrs Jennings), Robert Hardy (Sir John Middleton), Greg Wise (John Willoughby), *Hugh Laurie* (Mr. Palmer), Imelda Staunton (Charlotte Palmer), Imogen Stubbs (Lucy Steele), Emile François (Margaret Dashwood)

Two sisters, one careful and pragmatic, the other younger and more reckless, hope to make matches that will save their family from penury.

Gorgeously spirited and shrewd Jane Austen adaptation that marries the virtues of its title, taking liberties with the novel – doubling Elinor's age for instance – that pay off in every instance. Thompson's script is a gem.

S

SCR Emma Thompson   CIN Michael Coulter
MUS Patrick Doyle   DES Luciana Arrighi   ED Tim
Squyres   PROD Lindsay Doran   DIST Columbia/Mirage

66 Crisp, merry and timeless. – *Dana Kennedy,
Entertainment Weekly*

66 Poised, delicate, powerful, hovering between poignancy
and pealing laughter, it is a feast formed by skill and
serendipity. – *Liam Lacey, Toronto Globe and Mail*

† In 1996, it won the Golden Bear as the best film at the
Berlin Film Festival.

⚊ Emma Thompson (adapted screenplay)
⚊ picture; Emma Thompson (leading actress); Kate
Winslet (supporting actress); Michael Coulter; Patrick
Doyle; Jenny Beavan, John Bright (costume design)
⚊ film; Emma Thompson (leading actress); Kate Winslet
(supporting actress)
⚊ Alan Rickman (supporting actor); Elizabeth Spriggs
(supporting actress); Ang Lee; Emma Thompson (adapted
screenplay); Michael Coulter; Patrick Doyle; Luciana
Arrighi; Jenny Beavan, John Wright (costume design);
Morag Rees, Jan Archibold (make up/hair)

Separate Lies ★

SCR/DIR Julian Fellowes
2004   87m   GB/US
DVD

☆ *Tom Wilkinson* (James Manning), Emily Watson
(Anne Manning), Rupert Everett (Bill Bule), Linda
Bassett (Maggie), David Harewood (Inspector Marshall),
John Neville (Lord Rawlston), Hermione Norris
(Priscilla)

A lawyer's wife confesses to her affair with a local
playboy, and their involvement in a hit and run
killing.

*Overly genteel drama about the way we British do
things. The parochial detail is amusingly observed,
and there's an impeccable lead performance worthy
of Michael Redgrave, but it never achieves enough
force.*

CIN Tony Pierce-Roberts   MUS Stanislas Syrewicz
DES Alison Riva   ED Alex Mackie, Martin Walsh
PROD Christian Colson, Steven Clark-Hall   DIST TCF

66 A souffle that begins promisingly but never quite rises.
– *Lou Lumenick, New York Post*

66 Presents a moral morass involving betrayal, illicit sex,
hypocrisy and a crime, yet the film feels tidy. – *Kirk
Honeycutt, Hollywood Reporter*

September ★

SCR/DIR Woody Allen
1987   82m   US
DVD

☆ Denholm Elliott (Howard), Dianne Wiest (Stephanie),
Mia Farrow (Lane), Elaine Stritch (Diane), Sam Waterston
(Peter)

On a country weekend in a New England mansion,
half a dozen highly-strung intellectuals vent their
angst at each other and consider embarking on
illicit affairs.

*At those times when Allen tired of trying to make
amusing, witty movies, he retreated to the wintry, more*
cerebral pleasures of Chekhov and Bergman. Both
influences are evident in this creakingly artificial rondo
of desire that never seems to get anywhere. It is, however,
photographed exquisitely.

CIN Carlo Di Palma   DES Santo Loquasto   ED Susan E.
Morse   PROD Robert Greenhut   DIST Orion

66 Looks like Hannah and her Sisters, without the laughs.
– *Geoff Andrew, Time Out*

'Never turn your back on the past.'

Seraphim Falls (new) ★★

DIR David Von Ancken
2007   111m   US
DVD

☆ Piece Brosnan (Gideon), Liam Neeson (Colonel
Carver), Michael Wincott (Hayes), Ed Lauter (Parsons),
Kevin J. O'Connor (Henry), Anjelica Huston (Madame
Louise)

Three years after the end of the Civil War, a fugitive
is hunted down by a vengeful pursuer and his
posse.

*Superior western with a gripping, virtually wordless first
half hour, consisting of a chase through snowy
mountainous landscapes. The tension dissipates when
the reason for the manhunt becomes clear.*

SCR David Von Ancken, Abby Everett Jaques   CIN John
Toll   MUS Harry Gregson-Williams   DES Michael Hanan
ED Conrad Buff   PROD Bruce Davey, David Flynn
DIST Icon

66 After decades of revisionist westerns, this drama by TV
veteran David Von Ancken is impressive for its stubborn
classicism. – *J.R. Jones, Chicago Reader*

66 A psychological drama with an intriguing ambiguity
that challenges the viewer's loyalties and preconceived
notions. – *Claudia Puig, USA Today*

'Can't stop the signal.'

Serenity ★★

SCR/DIR Joss Whedon
2005   119m   US
DVD   ♫

☆ Nathan Fillion (Mal), Gina Torres (Zoe), Alan Tudyk
(Wash), Morena Baccarin (Inara), Adam Baldwin (Jayne),
Jewel Staite (Kaylee), Sean Maher (Simon)

The crew of a space freighter try to evade a
government agent sent to capture the telepathic
refugee they are harbouring.

*Giddily enjoyable space western, a spin-off from a
cancelled TV show, which has enough of a retro zing to
give it cult appeal.*

CIN Jack N. Green   DES Barry Chusid   ED Lisa Lassek
PROD Barry Mendel

66 A sci-fi action picture with more energy in its little
finger than Revenge of the Sith had in its whole, bloated
body. – *Peter Bradshaw, Guardian*

† Whedon's TV series Firefly was cancelled by Fox after
just 11 episodes, but DVD sales were brisk enough for him
to get the film financed by Universal.

DVD Available on DVD   ☆ Cast in order   66 Critics' Quotes   ⚊ Academy Award   Ⓣ BAFTA
♫ Soundtrack on CD   of importance   † Points of interest   ⚊ Academy Award nomination   Ⓣ BAFTA nomination

547

'A loving mother. A caring wife. A model citizen. So what's the problem?'

Serial Mom ★★

SCR/DIR John Waters
1994 95m US
DVD ♫

☆ *Kathleen Turner* (Beverly R. Sutphin), Sam Waterston (Eugene Sutphin, D. D. S), Ricki Lake (Misty Sutphin), Matthew Lillard (Chip Sutphin), Mary Jo Catlett (Rosemary Ackerman), Patricia Hearst (Birdie), Mink Stole (Dottie Hinkle), Suzanne Somers (herself)

A sweetly devoted middle-class mother starts killing anyone who causes her or her family offence.

Gleeful black comedy, surprisingly tame given the director and concept, but charged up nicely by its excellent star turn.

CIN Robert M. Stevens   MUS Basil Poledouris
DES Vincent Peranio   ED Janice Hampton, Erica Huggins
PROD John Fiedler, Mark Tarlov   DIST Guild/Savoy/Polar

66 Endearing in its cheeky irreverence, but also rather mild and scattershot in its satiric marksmanship. – *Todd McCarthy, Variety*

'Real People In Real Danger.'

Series 7: The Contenders ★

SCR/DIR Daniel Minahan
2000 86m US
DVD

☆ Brooke Smith (Dawn), Glenn Fitzgerald (Jeff), Marylouise Burke (Connie), Richard Venture (Franklin), Michael Kaycheck (Tony), Merritt Wever (Lindsay), Angelina Phillips (Doria), Nada Despotovich (Michelle)

A reality-TV show gives guns to six contestants, chosen by lottery, who must kill all the others to win.

Clever satire, prescient about the way competitive TV formats are heading, but sometimes irritatingly smug in its rebukes to the audience.

CIN Randy Drummond   MUS Girls Against Boys
DES Gideon Ponte   ED Malcolm Jamieson, Alan Miller
PROD Jason Kliot, Joana Vicente, Christine Vachon, Katie Roumel   DIST Film4

66 Unpretentious and brashly exploitative. – *Michael Sragow, Baltimore Sun*

'Don't bury me. . .I'm not dead!'

The Serpent and the Rainbow ★

DIR Wes Craven
1987 98m US
DVD ♫

☆ Bill Pullman (Dennis Alan), Cathy Tyson (Marielle Duchamp), Zakes Mokae (Dargent Peytraud), Paul Winfield (Lucien Celine), Brent Jennings (Louis Mozart), Conrad Roberts (Christophe), Badja Djola (Gaston), Theresa Merritt (Simone), Michael Gough (Schoonbacher)

A scientist journeys to Haiti to try to find a mysterious potion which represses human nervous and respiratory systems and could explain the phenomenon of zombies. He becomes seduced by the power of voodoo but falls foul of local corruption.

Creepy horror film distinguished by an off-kilter story; the reality depicted is as scary as the deliberate shock effects.

SCR Richard Maxwell, Adam Rodman   CIN John Lindley
MUS Brad Fiedel   DES David Nichols   ED Glenn Farr
PROD David Ladd, Doug Claybourne
DIST UIP/Universal

66 Take a powerful, revealing non-fiction book, sift through it for its most cliche'd elements and you've got The Serpent and The Rainbow. – *Richard Harrington, Washington Post*

The Servant ★★

DIR Joseph Losey
1963 116m GB
DVD

☆ *Dirk Bogarde, James Fox, Sarah Miles*, Wendy Craig, Catherine Lacey, Richard Vernon

A rich, ineffectual playboy hires a manservant, but during a series of power plays, the relationship between them gradually changes.

A spiky drama that has much to do with British class structures, viewed dispassionately by its American director. The changing role of the two lead characters seems somewhat schematic, but the portrayal of decadence and moral laxity remains chilling.

SCR Harold Pinter   CIN *Douglas Slocombe*   MUS Johnny Dankworth   PROD Joseph Losey, Norman Priggen
DIST Elstree

66 Moodily suggestive, well acted, but petering out into a trickle of repetitious unmeaningful nastiness. – *John Simon*

🏆 Dirk Bogarde; James Fox; Douglas Slocombe

Seul contre Tous ★

SCR/DIR Gaspar Noé
1998 93m France
DVD ♫

☆ Philippe Nahon (The Butcher), Frankye Pain (His Mistress), Blandine Lenoir (His Daughter, Cynthia), Martine Audrain (His Mother-in-Law)

An out-of-work butcher moves to Lille with his pregnant mistress, assaults her when it doesn't work out, and returns to the Paris slums to find his mentally handicapped daughter.

Remorselessly nihilistic, in-your-face character study owing a debt to Taxi Driver, but forgoing irony or distance in favour of increasingly bludgeoning shock tactics.

CIN Dominique Colin   ED Lucille Hadzihalilovic, Gaspar Noé   PROD Gaspar Noé, Lucile Hadzihalilovic
DIST Alliance/Cinémas de la Zone/Lovestreams/CNC

66 Not for the faint-hearted. . .a movie whose shocks fall like assaults on human complacency and whose bile-filled content congeals on the surface. – *Marjorie Baumgarten, Austin Chronicle*

† British censors insisted that scenes from a pornographic film being watched by the central character be shown blurred.

'Seven deadly sins. Seven ways to die.'

Seven ★★★

DIR *David Fincher*

1995 127m US

DVD ♫

☆ Brad Pitt (Detective David Mills), *Morgan Freeman* (Lieutenant William Somerset), Richard Roundtree (Talbot), R. Lee Ermey (Police Captain), John C. McGinley (California), Julie Araskog (Mrs. Gould), Kevin Spacey (John Doe), Gwyneth Paltrow (Tracy)

A veteran detective and a hot-headed trainee take on the case of a serial killer inspired by the seven deadly sins.

A grippingly realised thriller set in a modern-day equivalent of Dante's inferno, full of doomed wretches whom the killer is virtually putting out of their misery; it gains more from its darkly stylised direction and design than from its somewhat pretentious screenplay, though the ending remains one of the most shattering in memory.

SCR Andrew Kevin Walker   CIN *Darius Khondji*
MUS *Howard Shore*   DES *Arthur Max*   ED *Richard Francis-Bruce*   PROD Arnold Kopelson, Phyllis Carlyle
DIST Entertainment/New Line

66 Stands up as the most complex and disturbing entry in the serial killer genre since Manhunter. – *John Wrathall, Sight and Sound*

66 Remarkably raw and unsettling. – *Stephen Amidon, Sunday Times*

† Brad Pitt smashed his arm through a car windscreen while filming, and his injury was written into the script.

⌕ Richard Francis-Bruce

Ⓣ Andrew Kevin Walker (original screenplay)

Seven Days in May ★★★

DIR *John Frankenheimer*

1964 120m US

DVD

☆ *Kirk Douglas* (Col. Martin "Jiggs" Casey), Burt Lancaster (Gen. James M. Scott), *Fredric March* (President Jordan Lyman), Ava Gardner (Eleanor Holbrook), Martin Balsam (Paul Girard), *Edmond O'Brien* (Sen. Raymond Clark), George Macready (Christopher Todd), John Houseman (Adm. Barnswell)

An American general's aide discovers that his boss intends a military takeover because he considers the President's pacifism traitorous.

An outlandish but hugely entertaining conspiracy thriller, well acted, with the entire cast keeping laudably straight faces.

SCR *Rod Serling*   CIN *Ellsworth Fredericks*   MUS Jerry Goldsmith   ED Ferris Webster   PROD Edward Lewis
DIST Seven Arts/Joel/John Frankenheimer

66 A political thriller which grips from start to finish. – *Penelope Houston*

66 It is to be enjoyed without feelings of guilt, there should be more movies like it, and there is nothing first class about it. – *John Simon*

⌕ Edmond O'Brien (supporting actor)

The Seven Samurai ★★★★

DIR *Akira Kurosawa*

1954 155m Japan

DVD ♫

☆ *Toshiro Mifune* (Kikuchiyo), Takashi Shimura (Kambei), Kuninori Kodo (Gisaku), Yoshio Inaba (Gorobei), Seji Miyaguchi (Kyuzo), Minoru Chiaki (Heihachi)

In 16th-century Japan, villagers hire samurai to defend their property against an annual raid by bandits.

Superbly strange, vivid and violent mediaeval adventure which later served as the basis for the Western, The Magnificent Seven. Kurosawa keeps the audiences waiting for the first confrontation, but when it comes, it comes with a vengeance.

SCR Akira Kurosawa, Shinobu Hashimoto, Hideo Oguni   CIN Asaichi Nakai   MUS Fumio Hayasaka   ED Akira Kurosawa   PROD Shojiro Motoki   DIST Toho

66 It is as sheer narrative, rich in imagery, incisiveness and sharp observation, that it makes its strongest impact . . . It provides a fascinating display of talent, and places its director in the forefront of creative film-makers of his generation. – *Gavin Lambert, Sight & Sound*

66 This, on the surface, is a work of relentless, unmitigated action, as epic as any film ever made, and, again on the surface, sheer entertainment. Yet it is also an unquestionable triumph of art. – *John Simon*

⌕ So Matsuyama (art direction)

The Seventh Seal ★★★★

SCR/DIR *Ingmar Bergman*

1957 95m Sweden

DVD

☆ *Max von Sydow* (Antonius Block), *Bengt Ekerot* (Death), Gunnar Bjornstrand (Jons), Nils Poppe (Jof), Bibi Andersson (Mia), Gunnel Lindblom (Girl)

Death comes for a knight, who challenges him to a game of chess while trying to postpone his end by showing him illustrations of goodness in mankind.

A modestly budgeted minor classic which, because of its international success and its famous shots – the chess on the beach and the dance of death sequences – is seldom analysed in detail. It is kept going by its splendid cinematic feel, and its atmosphere is that of a dark world irrationally sustained by religion.

CIN *Gunnar Fischer*   MUS Erik Nordgren   DES P. A. Lundgren   ED Lennart Wallen   PROD Allan Ekelund
DIST Svensk Filmindustri

66 The most extraordinary mixture of beauty and lust and cruelty, Odin-worship and Christian faith, darkness and light. – *Alan Dent, Illustrated London News*

66 You know where they dance along the horizon? We'd packed up for the evening and were about to go home. Suddenly I saw a cloud, and Fischer swung his camera up. Some actors had gone, so grips had to stand in. The whole scene was improvised in ten minutes flat. – *Ingmar Bergman*

DVD Available on DVD   ☆ Cast in order   66 Critics' Quotes   ⌕ Academy Award   Ⓑ BAFTA
♫ Soundtrack on CD   of importance   † Points of interest   ⌕ Academy Award nomination   Ⓣ BAFTA nomination

549

sex, lies and videotape ★★

SCR/DIR *Steven Soderbergh*
1989 100m US
`DVD` ♫

☆ James Spader (Graham Dalton), Andie MacDowell (Ann Bishop Mullany), Peter Gallagher (John Mullany), Laura San Giacomo (Cynthia Patrice Bishop), Ron Vawter (Therapist)

A young voyeur, who enjoys taping interviews with women about their sex lives, visits an old schoolfriend who is having an affair with his wife's sister.

Sharp study of insecurities and peccadilloes in and outside marriage; a highly promising debut, very much of its time, which was a little over-praised on its first appearance.

CIN Walt Lloyd MUS Cliff Martinez ED Steve Soderbergh PROD Robert Newmyer, John Hardy DIST Virgin/Outlaw Productions

66 It has more intelligence than heart, and is more clever than enlightening. – *Roger Ebert, Chicago Sun-Times*

66 What amazes is that at just 26, Soderbergh displays the three qualities associated with mature filmmakers: a unique authorial voice, a spooky camera assurance, and the easy control of ensemble acting. – *Richard Corliss, Time*

† The film won the Palme D'Or for best film at the Cannes Film Festival in 1989.

🏆 Steven Soderbergh (original screenplay)

Ⓣ Laura San Giacomo (supporting actress); Steven Soderbergh (original screenplay)

Sex and Lucia ★

SCR/DIR *Julio Medem*
2001 128m Spain/France
`DVD` ♫

☆ Paz Vega (Lucia), Tristan Ulloa (Lorenzo), Najwa Nimri (Elena), Daniel Freire (Carlos/Antonio), Elena Anaya (Belen), Silvia Llanos (Luna), Javier Camara (Pepe)

A waitress seeks refuge on an isolated Mediterranean island after the loss of her novelist boyfriend, and learns a lot more of his history.

A tantalising but frustrating erotic saga, in which the balmy visuals do most of the seducing; the story, which may or may not be the work of the writer character, is coy with its revelations and low on sense.

CIN Kiko de la Rica MUS Alberto Iglesias ED Ivan Aledo PROD Fernando Bovaira, Enrique Lopez Lavigne DIST Metro Tartan

66 Elegant and sometimes inscrutable. – *Joe Morgenstern, Wall Street Journal*

66 The plot remains as guarded as a virgin with a chastity belt. – *Marta Barber, Miami Herald*

'Get carried away.'

Sex and the City (new)

SCR/DIR *Michael Patrick King*
2008 145m US
`DVD` ♫

☆ Sarah Jessica Parker (Carrie Bradshaw), Kim Cattrall (Samantha Jones), Kristin Davis (Charlotte York), Cynthia Nixon (Miranda Hobbes), Jennifer Hudson (Louise),

Candice Bergen (Enid Frick), Chris Noth (Mr. Big)

After four years, four female friends reunite in New York to find their love lives as complicated and eventful as ever.

Slickly assembled spin-off from a popular US TV sitcom that makes few concessions to the uninitiated. Awash with sentimentality and designer labels, the result is little more than a glossy advert for hedonistic materialism. In tone and form, though, it is clearly a direct descendant of the classic 'women's pictures' from the 1940s and '50s.

CIN John Thomas MUS Aaron Zigman DES Jeremy Conway ED Michael Berenbaum PROD Sarah Jessica Parker, Michael Patrick King, Darren Star, John Melfi DIST Entertainment

66 Girly, whirly and twirly. . . a cut above the usual sinister romcom slush. – *Peter Bradshaw, Guardian*

66 Vulgar, shrill, deeply shallow and overlong. – *Manohla Dargis, New York Times*

'The search for the lowest form of life on the planet is over.'

Sex Lives of the Potato Men

SCR/DIR *Andy Humphries*
2003 82m GB
`DVD`

☆ Johnny Vegas (Dave), Mackenzie Crook (Ferris), Mark Gatiss (Jeremy), Dominic Coleman (Tolly), Julia Davis (Shelley), Lucy Davis (Ruth)

In Birmingham, four working-class men have sex lives that leave much to be desired.

Vile, grubby little movie about the brutish, joyless couplings of four foul-mouthed Brummies who deliver potatoes to fish and chip shops. It was the most critically reviled British film in memory, with some observers speculating about the usefulness of the UK Film Council, which partly funded it with public money. Interesting to watch only in that context of waste and bad judgement.

CIN Andy Collins MUS Super Preachers DES Patrick Lyndon-Stanford, Adam Zoltowski ED Guy Bensley PROD Anita Overland DIST Entertainment

66 A master-class in film-making ineptitude, a squalid waste of lottery money. – *James Christopher, The Times*

66 A film about coitus at its most squalid and undignified. – *Nicholas Barber, Independent*

'Sometimes It's Hard To Say No.'

Sexy Beast ★★

DIR *Jonathan Glazer*
2000 89m GB/Spain/US
`DVD` ♫

☆ *Ray Winstone* (Gary 'Gal' Dove), *Ben Kingsley* (Don 'Malky' Logan), Ian McShane (Teddy Bass), Amanda Redman (Deedee), Cavan Kendall (Aitch), Alvaro Monje (Enrique), James Fox (Harry), Darkie Smith (Stan Higgins)

A retired London thief living on the Costa del Sol is confronted by a psychopathic associate who insists he come back to do one last job.

Strikingly off-kilter gangster movie, a welcome departure from the usual dross. The story is thin and the heist uninteresting, but it works very well as an actors' showcase, allowing Kingsley to combust with OTT menace and Winstone to develop a stereotypical role into one of some substance.

SCR Louis Mellis, David Scinto   **CIN** Ivan Bird
MUS Roque Baños   **DES** Jan Houllevigue   **ED** John Scott, Sam Sneade   **PROD** Jeremy Thomas
DIST FilmFour

66 A corking debut, enlivening natty, Pinter-like dialogue with terrific editing. – *Jason Solomons, Mail on Sunday*

66 Offers a serious and intriguing portrait of the gangland sunset, a bleak elegy to a wild life of crime. – *Xan Brooks, Guardian*

⚱ Ben Kingsley (supporting actor)

Ⓣ British film

A Shadow of a Doubt ★★

SCR/DIR Aline Issermann,
1993   106m   France
☆ Mireille Perrier (Mother), Alain Bashung (Father), Sandrine Blancke (Alexandrine), Emmanuelle Riva (Grandmother), Michel Aumont (Grandfather), Luis Issermann (Pierre), Roland Bertin (Judge), Dominique Lavanant (Teacher), Thierry L'hermitte (Alexandrine's Lawyer)

When an 11-year-old girl claims her father has sexually molested her, a social worker is the one person who believes her.

Potentially lurid material, handled with calm and thoughtfulness by writer-director Aline Issermann. What interests her in the story is the doubt; she allows it to linger, and concentrates on the hellish situation in which this child and her father find themselves. Quietly accomplished.

CIN Darius Khondji   **MUS** Reno Isaac   **DES** Cyr Boitard
ED Hervé Schneid   **DIST** CIBY 2000/TF1

Shadow of the Vampire ★

DIR E. Elias Merhige
2000   92m   GB/US/Luxemburg
DVD ♫
☆ John Malkovich (F. W. Murnau), Willem Dafoe (Max Schreck), Cary Elwes (Fritz Wagner), John Aden Gillet (Henrick Galeen), Eddie Izzard (Gustav von Wangerheim), Udo Kier (Albin Grau), Catherine McCormack (Greta Schroeder), Ronan Vibert (Wolfgang Muller)

The film director F. W. Murnau hires a real vampire, Max Schreck, to play the leading role in his film Nosferatu.

A enjoyable fantasia on horror-movie legend with a clever inversion up its sleeve – the director is the real blood-sucker – and a scenery-chewing performance from Dafoe. Sadly, it descends into silly camp.

SCR Steven Katz   **CIN** Lou Bogue   **MUS** Dan Jones
DES Assheton Gorton   **ED** Chris Wyatt   **PROD** Nicolas Cage, Jeff Levine   **DIST** Metrodome

66 A bit of a one-joke wonder. – *Steven Rea, Philadelphia Inquirer*

⚱ Willem Dafoe (supporting actor); Ann Buchanan, Amber Sibley (make up)

'He thought that magic only existed in books, and then he met her.'

Shadowlands ★★★

DIR Richard Attenborough
1993   131m   GB
DVD ♫
☆ Anthony Hopkins (Jack Lewis), Debra Winger (Joy Gresham), John Wood (Christopher Riley), Edward Hardwicke (Warnie Lewis), Joseph Mazzello (Douglas Gresham), Julian Fellowes (Desmond Arding), Roddy Maude-Roxby (Arnold Dopliss), Michael Denison ("Harry" Harrington), Peter Firth (Dr. Craig)

The Oxford don and children's author C. S. Lewis grows to love his wife, the American poet Joy Gresham, before discovering that she is dying of cancer.

Beautifully acted tearjerker which does a good job repressing emotion until the final opening of the floodgates; it is conventionally done, but well done.

SCR William Nicholson   **CIN** Roger Pratt   **MUS** George Fenton   **DES** Stuart Craig   **ED** Lesley Walker
PROD Richard Attenborough, Brian Eastman
DIST UIP/Showlands/Spelling/Pirce/Savoy

66 When the force of the emotion hits you, it's an unstoppable tidal wave. – *Nick James, Sight and Sound*

66 Brims with substance and wit, though it's essentially a soap opera with a Rhodes scholarship. – *Rita Kempley, Washington Post*

⚱ Debra Winger (leading actress); William Nicholson (adapted screenplay)

Ⓣ British film; Anthony Hopkins (leading actor)
Ⓣ film; Debra Winger (leading actress); Richard Attenborough; William Nicholson (adapted screenplay)

Shadows and Fog ★

SCR/DIR Woody Allen
1991   85m   US
DVD
☆ Woody Allen (Kleinman), Mia Farrow (Irmy), John Malkovich (Clown), Madonna (Marie), Donald Pleasence (Doctor), Lily Tomlin (Prostitute), Jodie Foster (Prostitute), Kathy Bates (Prostitute), John Cusack (Student Jack), Kate Nelligan (Eve), Julie Kavner (Alma), Fred Gwynne (Hacker's Follower)

In an eastern European town, a mild-mannered man is coerced into joining a group of vigilantes stalking a murderer.

An attempted homage to German expressionist films that only intermittently gets the look right (they were about more than mere shadows and fog) and settles into a vaguely Kafkaesque drama with a stunning cast list that never quite satisfies. Another of Allen's upwardly mobile detours from sophisticated comedy that failed to pay off.

CIN Carlo Di Palma   **DES** Santo Loquasto   **ED** Susan E. Morse   **PROD** Robert Greenhut   **DIST** Columbia TriStar/Orion

S

DVD Available on DVD   ☆ Cast in order   66 Critics' Quotes   ⚱ Academy Award   Ⓑ BAFTA
♫ Soundtrack on CD   of importance   † Points of interest   ⚱ Academy Award nomination   Ⓣ BAFTA nomination

551

66 An inconclusive charade for celebrity guests. – *Brian Case, Time Out*

'A comedy about the greatest love story almost never told.'

Shakespeare in Love ★★★

DIR *John Madden*
1998   123m   US
[DVD]   ♫

☆ *Gwyneth Paltrow* (Viola De Lesseps), Joseph Fiennes (Will Shakespeare), Geoffrey Rush (Philip Henslowe), Colin Firth (Lord Wessex), Ben Affleck (Ned Alleyn), *Judi Dench* (Queen Elizabeth), Rupert Everett (Christopher Marlowe), Simon Callow (Tilney, Master of the Revels), Jim Carter (Ralph Bashford), Martin Clunes (Richard Burbage), Antony Sher (Dr. Moth), Imelda Staunton (Nurse), Tom Wilkinson (Hugh Fennyman), Mark Williams (Wabash)

Broke and stuck in a creative rut, Shakespeare falls in love with a cross-dressing heiress who wants to act, and is inspired to write Romeo and Juliet (and Twelfth Night).

A vibrantly romantic entertainment for Bard-lovers, which finds a pleasing match for our Will and strews their union with the usual romcom obstacles; possibly as a result of extensive re-writes, it sometimes seems a tad over-stuffed, manically attempting to cram in all the in-jokes.

SCR *Marc Norman, Tom Stoppard*   **CIN** *Richard Greatrex*   **MUS** *Stephen Warbeck*   **DES** *Martin Childs*   **ED** *David Gamble*   **PROD** David Parfitt, Donna Gigliotti, Harvey Weinstein, Edward Zwick, Marc Norman   **DIST** UIP/Miramax/Universal/Bedford Falls

66 That rare thing – a literate crowd-pleaser. – *Owen Gleiberman, Entertainment Weekly*

66 Falls some way short of infinite jest. – *Jonathan Romney, Guardian*

⚱ picture; Gwyneth Paltrow (leading actress); Judi Dench (supporting actress); Marc Norman, Tom Stoppard (original screenplay); Stephen Warbeck; Martin Childs; Sandy Powell (costume design)

⚱ Geoffrey Rush (supporting actor); John Madden; Richard Greatrex; David Gamble; Robin O'Donoghue, Dominic Lester, Peter Glossop (sound); Lisa Westcott, Veronica Brebner (make up)

Ⓣ film; Judi Dench (supporting actress); David Gamble
Ⓣ Joseph Fiennes (leading actor); Gwyneth Paltrow (leading actress); Geoffrey Rush (supporting actor); Tom Wilkinson (supporting actor); John Madden; Marc Norman, Tom Stoppard (original screenplay); Richard Greatrex; Stephen Warbeck; Martin Childs; Sandy Powell (costume design); Robin O'Donoghue, Dominic Lester (sound); Lisa Westcott (make up/hair)

'He's An Overworked Accountant. She's An Accomplished Dancer. Passion Is About To Find Two Unlikely Partners.'

Shall We Dance? ★★★

SCR/DIR *Masayuki Suo*
1995   118m   Japan
[DVD]

☆ *Koji Yakusho* (Shohei Sugiyama), Tamiyo Kusakari (Mai Kishikawa), Naoto Takenaka (Tomio Aoki), Eriko Watanabe (Toyoko Takahashi), Akira Emoto (Tôru Miwa), Yu Tokui (Tokichi Hattori), Hiromasa Taguchi (Masahiro Tanaka), Reiko Kasamura (Tamako Tamura), Hideko Hara (Masako Sugiyama)

A Japanese salaryman, feeling jaded by work and bored with his family life, joins a ballroom dancing class.

A delightful comedy, dealing with a modest, humble man's search for exuberance, spontaneity and passion in a life he finds restrained and crushing. It has a sweetness that is remarkably unforced.

CIN Naoki Kayano   **MUS** Yoshikazu Suo   **DES** Kyoko Heya   **ED** Junichi Kikuchi   **PROD** Tetsuya Ikeda   **DIST** Buena Vista/Altamura/Daiei/NTV/Hakuhodo/Nippon Shuppan

66 There are no villains in Shall We Dance?, and its sense of the ridiculous never precludes sympathy. – *Philip Kemp, Sight & Sound*

† A disastrous American remake, starring Richard Gere, was released in 2004.

'What's a little murder between friends?'

Shallow Grave ★★★

DIR *Danny Boyle*
1994   93m   GB
[DVD]   ♫

☆ Kerry Fox (Juliet Miller), Christopher Eccleston (David Stephens), Ewan McGregor (Alex Law), Ken Stott (Detective Inspector McCall), Keith Allen (Hugo), Colin McCredie (Cameron)

Three friends in Edinburgh find their new flatmate dead with £1m in cash, and decide to keep the money and dispose of the body.

Brisk and stylish thriller which keeps its energy up, even when the plotting frays and characterisation takes a turn for the loopy. It heralded a new wave in high-impact pop filmmaking from Britain.

SCR John Hodge   **CIN** Brian Tufano   **MUS** Simon Boswell   **DES** Kave Quinn   **ED** Masahiro Hirakubo   **PROD** Andrew Macdonald   **DIST** Rank/Figment/Channel 4/Glasgow Film Fund

66 A tar-black comedy that zings along on a wave of visual and scripting inventiveness. – *Derek Elley, Variety*

66 Shallow Grave is not about class or society, or people being crushed by forces they can't control. There are no victims in the story. Everyone takes responsibility for their decisions, which I think people do in real life anyway. – *Danny Boyle*

† The film broke house records at four of the eight London cinemas that showed it in its opening weekend.

Ⓣ British film

Shane ★★★

DIR *George Stevens*
1953   118m   US
[DVD]

☆ *Alan Ladd* (Shane), Jean Arthur (Marion Starrett), Van Heflin (Joe Starrett), *Jack Palance* (Wilson), Brandon de Wilde (Joey), Ben Johnson (Chris), Edgar Buchanan (Lewis), Emile Meyer (Ryker), Elisha Cook Jnr (Torrey), John Dierkes (Morgan)

A mysterious stranger helps a family of homesteaders.

S

Archetypal family Western, but much slower and statelier than most, as though to emphasize its own quality, which is evident anyway. It's told from a boy's point of view, but it's also the role of Ladd's career, with a final scene that causes a lump in the throat.

SCR A. B. Guthrie Jnr   CIN Loyal Griggs   MUS Victor Young   ED Tom McAdoo, William Hornbeck   PROD George Stevens   DIST Paramount

66 A kind of dramatic documentary of the pioneer days of the west. – *Monthly Film Bulletin*

66 Westerns are better when they're not too self-importantly self-conscious. – *New Yorker, 1975*

🏆 Loyal Griggs

🏆 picture; Jack Palance (supporting actor); Brandon de Wilde (supporting actor) George Stevens (direction); A. B. Guthrie Jnr (screenplay)

'In 1930's Shanghai violence was not the problem. It was the solution.'

Shanghai Triad   ★★

DIR *Zhang Yimou*

1995   108m   Hong Kong/ France

DVD   ♫

☆ *Gong Li* (Xiao Jingbao), Li Baotian (Tang, the Gang Boss), Wang Xiaoxiao (Shuisheng, the boy), Li Xuejian (Liu, 6th Uncle), Sun Chun (Song, Tang's No. 2), Fu Biao (Zheng, Tang's No.3), Chen Shu (Shi Ye), Liu Jiang (Fat Yu)

In the 1930s, the uncle of a 14-year-old boy from rural China finds him work with a triad – taking care of the needs of the boss's mistress, a nightclub singer. In her company, he learns of all the deceptions and betrayals rife within the triad.

The film's English title promises a feast of violent mobster action, but it's more of a character study; Gong Li is a radiant presence as a woman who gradually comes to see that she's not just a deceiver, but deceived in her own right. It's a visual treat with a dazzling colour palette, though it loses narrative focus well before the end. This was the seventh and last collaboration between Zhang Yimou and Gong Li as both personal and professional partners. They would not work together again for another decade.

SCR Bi Feiyu   CIN Lu Yue   MUS Zhang Guangtian   DES Cao Jiuping   ED Du Yuan   PROD Jean-Louis Piel, Yigong Wu, Yves Marmion   DIST Electric/Shanghai Studio/Alpha/UGC-Images/La Sept

🏆 Lu Yue

'Kick some grass!'

Shaolin Soccer   ★

DIR Stephen Chow

2001   113m   Hong Kong/China/US

DVD   ♫

☆ Stephen Chow (Mighty Steel Leg Sing), Zhao Wei (Mui), Ng Mang-tat (Golden Leg Fung), Patrick Tse (Team Evil Coach Hung), Cecilia Cheung (Team Moustache Player 1), Karen Mok (Team Moustache Player 2)

A Shaolin monk meets a down-on-his-luck football player, and they form a team.

Bumptious action comedy blending kung fu with soccer games; some of the computer effects are woeful, but it's shameless fun.

SCR Stephen Chow, Tsang Ken-cheong   CIN Kwong Ting-wo, Kwen Pak-huen   MUS Raymond Wong, Lowell Lo, Jacky Chan   ED Kai Kit-wai   PROD Yeung Kwok-Fai   DIST Buena Vista

66 A screwy treat. – *Catherine Shoard, Sunday Telegraph*

66 Piffle, yes, but superior piffle. – *Roger Ebert, Chicago Sun-Times*

'A love he can't forget. A murder he can't remember.'

Shattered   ★

SCR/DIR Wolfgang Petersen

1991   98m   US

DVD   ♫

☆ Tom Berenger (Dan Merrick), Greta Scacchi (Judith Merrick), Bob Hoskins (Gus Klein), Joanne Whalley-Kilmer (Jenny Scott), Corbin Bernsen (Jeb Scott), Debi A. Monahan (Nancy Mercer), Bert Robario (Rudy Costa), Scott Getlin (Jack Stanton), Kellye Nakahara (Lydia)

A property developer awakes from a car crash with amnesia, begins to question his wife's version of events, and hires a private investigator.

Preposterously plotted thriller which nonetheless keeps us guessing.

CIN Laszlo Kovacs   MUS Alan Silvestri   DES Gregg Fonseca   ED Hannes Nikel, Glenn Farr   PROD Wolfgang Petersen, John Davis, David Korda   DIST Palace/Capella/Davis Entertainment

66 A shadowy modern noir that's cynical to its marrow. – *Hal Hinson, Washington Post*

'Read between the lies.'

Shattered Glass   ★★

SCR/DIR Billy Ray

2003   94m   US/Canada

DVD   ♫

☆ Hayden Christensen (Stephen Glass), *Peter Sarsgaard* (Chuck Lane), Chloe Sevigny (Caitlin Avey), Rosario Dawson (Andie Fox), Melanie Lynskey (Amy Brand), Steve Zahn (Adam Penenberg), Hank Azaria (Michael Kelly), Ted Kotcheff (Marty Peretz)

A young journalist rises to the top on New Republic magazine, until his stories are revealed to be fabrications.

Compelling study of a wormy fabulist. It lacks completely convincing psychology, but compensates with gripping newsroom dynamics, and a terrific performance from Sarsgaard as the editor who pulled the plug.

CIN Mandy Walker   MUS Mychael Danna   DES François Seguin   ED Jeffrey Ford   PROD Adam Merims, Gaye Hirsch, Tove Christensen, Craig Baumgarten

66 Carefully constructed, intently played, and shot with creepy calm. – *Anthony Lane, New Yorker*

66 Smart about journalism because it is smart about offices; the typical newsroom is an open space filled with desks, and journalists are actors on this stage; to see a good writer on deadline with a big story is to watch not

DVD Available on DVD   ☆ Cast in order of importance   66 Critics' Quotes   † Points of interest   🏆 Academy Award   🏆 Academy Award nomination   🏆 BAFTA   🏆 BAFTA nomination

♫ Soundtrack on CD

553

simply work but performance. – *Roger Ebert, Chicago Sun-Times*

† After leaving journalism, Stephen Glass spent time in therapy, graduated from Georgetown Law School and wrote a novel, The Fabulist, about an ambitious young reporter who is a pathological liar.

'A romantic comedy. With zombies.'

Shaun of the Dead ★★

DIR Edgar Wright
2004   99m   GB/US/France
DVD   ♫

☆ Simon Pegg (Shaun), Kate Ashfield (Liz), Lucy Davis (Dianne), Nick Frost (Ed), Dylan Moran (David), Bill Nighy (Philip), Penelope Wilton (Barbara), Jessica Stevenson (Yvonne)

Zombies run amok in North London, and a shop assistant tries to rescue his ex-girlfriend.

Spirited zombie spoof, an unusually satisfying British comedy with plenty of laughs.

SCR Simon Pegg, Edgar Wright   **CIN** David M. Dunlap **MUS** Daniel Mudford, Pete Woodhead   **DES** Marcus Rowland   **ED** Chris Dickens   **PROD** Nira Park **DIST** Universal

66 The romantic zombie comedy we've all been waiting for. – *Jason Solomons, Mail on Sunday*

Ⓣ British film; interactive award (DVD); Nira Park (promising newcomer)

'Fear can hold you prisoner. Hope can set you free.'

The Shawshank Redemption ★★★

SCR/DIR Frank Darabont
1994   142m   US
DVD   ♫

☆ *Tim Robbins* (Andy Dufresne), *Morgan Freeman* (Ellis Boyd 'Red' Redding), Bob Gunton (Warden Norton), William Sadler (Heywood), Clancy Brown (Captain Hadley), James Whitmore (Brooks Hatlen), Gil Bellows (Tommy), Mark Rolston (Bogs Diamond), Jeffrey DeMunn (1946 D.A.)

A banker, wrongly convicted of killing his wife and her lover, finds the strength to deal with the brutality of prison, thanks to a murderer serving a life term.

A tense drama of injustice and male dignity, brilliantly adapted from Stephen King's story, with Robbins and Freeman at their peak. A satisfying, audience-pleasing movie.

CIN Roger Deakins   **MUS** Thomas Newman **DES** Terence Marsh   **ED** Richard Francis-Bruce **PROD** Niki Marvin   **DIST** Rank/Castle Rock

66 A throwback to the kind of serious, literate drama Hollywood used to make. – *Derek Adams, Time Out*

66 It's a simple story elegantly, cleverly told, not to mention expertly acted. – *Boston Globe*

† The film has enjoyed a curious after-life. On its release in 1994, it had mixed reviews and grossed just $28 million in the US; it did not make the list of Top 50 films at the box-office for that year. Yet in 2001, Channel 4 TV viewers voted it their third favourite movie of all time, behind only the Star Wars and Godfather films. Readers of Time Out

and Empire magazines have also named it among their very favourites.

⚱ picture; Morgan Freeman (leading actor); Frank Darabont (adapted screenplay); Roger Deakins; Richard Francis-Bruce; Thomas Newman; Robert J. Litt, Elliot Tyson, Michael Herbick, Willie D. Burton (sound)

'One heterosexual male. 18 lesbians. His fee $10,000 . . . each.'

She Hate Me

DIR Spike Lee
2004   138m   US/France
DVD   ♫

☆ Anthony Mackie (John Henry Armstrong), Kerry Washington (Fatima Goodrich), Ellen Barkin (Margo Chadwick), Monica Bellucci (Simona Bonasera), Jim Brown (Geronimo Armstrong), Ossie Davis (Judge Buchanan), Brian Dennehy (Chairman Church), Woody Harrelson (Leland Powell)

A penniless biotech executive, fired for exposing corruption at his firm, takes to impregnating lesbians for cash.

Catastrophic would-be satire on corporate ethics and sexual politics. Straining to be provocative, Lee provides something here to offend everyone, and it goes on for ever.

SCR Michael Genet, Spike Lee   **CIN** Matthew Libatique **MUS** Terence Blanchard   **DES** Brigitte Broch   **ED** Barry Alexander Brown   **PROD** Spike Lee, Preston Holmes, Fernando Sulichin   **DIST** Columbia TriStar

66 When a Spike Lee film doesn't fly, it sinks like a stone. This one is Gibraltar. – *Peter Travers, Rolling Stone*

'A woman's dangerous and erotic journey beneath. . .'

The Sheltering Sky ★★

DIR Bernardo Bertolucci
1990   138m   GB/Italy/US
DVD   ♫

☆ Debra Winger (Kit Moresby), John Malkovich (Port Moresby), Campbell Scott (George Tunner), Jill Bennett (Mrs. Lyle), Timothy Spall (Eric Lyle), Eric Vu-An (Belqassim), Amina Annabi (Mahrnia), Philippe Morier-Genoud (Captain Broussard), Paul Bowles (Narrator)

A married American couple travel through North Africa in search of themselves and the desert, and find their relationship threatened by the vastness of the strange landscapes – and by a lecherous companion.

Bertolucci captures the forbidding beauty of the Sahara quite stunningly, but while the film is utterly ravishing to look at, its characters are stiff, self-regarding and unlikable, their predicament is far from compelling, and the psychological drama of Bowles's novel never quite surfaces.

SCR Mark Peploe, Bernardo Bertolucci   **CIN** *Vittorio Storaro*   **MUS** *Ryuichi Sakamoto*   **DES** *Gianni Silvestri, Ferdinando Scarfiotti*   **ED** Gabriella Cristiani **PROD** *Jeremy Thomas*   **DIST** Palace/Sahara Company/TAO Film/Recorded Picture Company/Aldrich Group

S

66 A frustratingly, monotonously obscure movie. – *Hal Hinson, Washington Post*

66 Those who haven't read the book will be left bewildered. – *Variety*

🅣 Vittorio Storaro
🅣 Gianni Silvestri; Ferdinando Scarfiotti

'No-one makes it alone.'

Sherrybaby (new)   ★★

SCR/DIR Laurie Collyer
2006 95m US

☆ *Maggie Gyllenhaal* (Sherry Swanson), Brad William Henke (Bobby Swanson), Giancarlo Esposito (Parole Officer Hernandez), Sam Bottoms (Bob Swanson Sr.), Bridget Barkan (Lynette Swanson)

Released from prison, Sherry (Gyllenhaal), a former drug addict struggles to stay on the straight and narrow and become a good mother to her young daughter.

Affecting story with a flawed but sympathetic heroine finally and reluctantly reaching out to others for the help she needs. Gyllenhaal's remarkably well-observed and detailed performance carries the entire film.

CIN Russell Lee Fine MUS Jack Livesey DES Stephen Beatrice ED Curtiss Clayton, Joe Landauer PROD Marc Turtletaub, Lemore Syvan DIST Metrodome

66 Gyllenhaal's sympathetic and charismatic performance binds us to the horror of Sherry's personal demons. – *Duane Byrge, Hollywood Reporter.*

66 Emotionally arresting. – *Owen Gleiberman, Entertainment Weekly*

Shine   ★★★

DIR Scott Hicks
1996 105m Australia/GB
DVD 🎵

☆ *Geoffrey Rush* (David Helfgott as an Adult), *Armin Mueller-Stahl* (Peter), *Noah Taylor* (David Helfgott as a Young Man), Lynn Redgrave (Gillian), Googie Withers (Katharine Susannah Prichard), Sonia Todd (Sylvia), Nicholas Bell (Ben Rosen), John Gielgud (Cecil Parkes), Chris Haywood (Sam)

An aspiring pianist, pushed too hard by his Holocaust-survivor father, undergoes a mental breakdown, but recovers and makes a comeback in later life.

Genuinely inspiring biopic which soft-pedals its subject's mental instability ever so slightly; as an expressionistic portrait of the artist though, it is vital and memorable, and the acting's marvellous.

SCR Jan Sardi CIN *Geoffrey Simpson* MUS David Hirschfelder DES Vicki Niehus ED *Pip Karmel*
PROD Jane Scott DIST Buena Vista

66 My idea of a truly feelgood film – one that doesn't shirk its responsibilities and never short-changes us on realism. – *Anne Billson, Sunday Telegraph*

66 He is mad – schizophrenic, to be exact – but it's a nice mad, not angry or morose. – *Richard Corliss, Time*

† In the wake of the film's release, pianist David Helfgott enjoyed a surge of popularity and undertook an international concert tour.

🏆 Geoffrey Rush (leading actor)
🏆 picture; Armin Mueller-Stahl (supporting actor);Scott Hicks; Jan Sardi (original screenplay); Pip Karmel; David Hirschfelder;

🅣 Geoffrey Rush (leading actor)
🅣 film; John Gielgud (supporting actor); Lynn Redgrave (supporting actress); Scott Hicks; Jan Sardi (original screenplay); Pip Karmel; David Hirschfelder

---

Shine a Light (new)   ★★

DIR Martin Scorsese
2008 122m US/UK
DVD 🎵

☆ Mick Jagger, Keith Richards, Charlie Watts, Ronnie Wood, Buddy Guy, Jack White III, Christina Aguilera, Bill Clinton, Hillary Clinton, Martin Scorsese

A Rolling Stones concert, filmed at New York's Beacon Theatre in 2006.

Scorsese opted to film the Stones up close and personal, showing their lined faces and the ravages of age. His policy of fast cutting and constant close-ups short-changes the Stones as an interdependent unit. But their songs are timeless, and their energy and exuberance is phenomenal.

CIN Robert Richardson DES Star Theodos ED *David Tedeschi* PROD Victoria Pearman, Michael Cohl, Steve Bing, Zane Weiner DIST TCF

66 Scorsese spends much of the film lingering on the latter-day Jagger. – *John Lewis, Sight & Sound*

† Scorsese hired a stellar team of 18 cinematographers to film the concert, including six Oscar winners: Robert Richardson, John Toll, Andrew Lesnie, Stuart Dryburgh, Robert Elswit and Emmanuel Lubezki.

'All work and no play make Jack a dull boy...'

The Shining   ★★

DIR Stanley Kubrick
1980 119m GB
DVD

☆ Jack Nicholson, Shelley Duvall, Danny Lloyd, Barry Nelson, Scatman Crothers, Philip Stone

Under the influence of a desolate hotel where murders had occurred, a caretaker goes berserk and threatens his family.

Genuinely scary ghost story that polarises opinions; devotees find it the greatest horror film ever, while nay-sayers deride its over-the-top histrionics. Admittedly, it gets the heart pounding, and there's a truly disturbing edge to Nicholson's performance, but between the highlights, there's not enough to maintain one's enthusiasm.

SCR Stanley Kubrick, Diane Johnson CIN *John Alcott*
MUS Bela Bartok (on record) DES *Roy Walker*
DIST Warner/Stanley Kubrick

JACK TORRANCE: Heeere's Johnny!

66 Ostensibly a haunted house story, it manages to traverse a complex world of incipient madness, spectral murder and supernatural visions ... and also makes you jump. – *Ian Nathan, Empire*

66 Meticulously detailed and never less than fascinating, The Shining may be the first movie that ever made its audience jump with a title that simply says "Tuesday." – *Janet Maslin, New York Times*

'No one thought she had the courage. The nerve. Or the lingerie.'

Shirley Valentine ★★

DIR Lewis Gilbert
1989 108m US/GB
[DVD] ♫

☆ *Pauline Collins* (Shirley Valentine-Bradshaw), Tom Conti (Costas Caldes), Julia McKenzie (Gillian), Alison Steadman (Jane), Joanna Lumley (Marjorie Majors), Sylvia Syms (Headmistress), Bernard Hill (Joe Bradshaw)

A Liverpool housewife leaves her boor of a husband for a holiday in Greece, where she has a fling with a local man.

Pleasing slice of sentimental escapism, in which Russell's tart one-liners are knocked for six by the wonderful Collins.

SCR *Willy Russell* CIN Alan Hune MUS Willy Russell DES John Stoll ED Lesley Walker PROD Lewis Gilbert DIST UIP/Paramount

66 Fast-feminism for the masses. – *Christopher Tookey, Daily Mail*

⚱ Pauline Collins; song 'The Girl Who Used to be Me' (m Marvin Hamlisch; l Alan and Marilyn Bergman)
🏆 Pauline Collins (leading actress)
🏆 film; Willy Russell (adapted screenplay)

Shoah ★★★★

DIR Claude Lanzmann
1985 566m France
[DVD]

Massive documentary history of the Holocaust, using survivors' testimony and some re-enactment but no historical footage. The sheer accumulation of detail and witness testimony makes this one of the most important documents in film history.

DIST Aleph/Historia

† Part 1 is 274m, Part 2 292m.

'Just another family man making a living.'

Shoot 'Em Up (new)

SCR/DIR Michael Davis
2007 86m US
☆ Clive Owen (Smith), Paul Giamatti (Hertz), Monica Bellucci (Donna)

A mysterious, hard-boiled gunman (Owen) rescues a heavily pregnant woman from a shoot-out, delivers the baby – then has to care for it, with the help of a prostitute (Bellucci).

A rollicking parody of gun-crazy Hong Kong action movies with sky-high body counts. The belated attempt at a plot need not detain us: the cartoonish violence and dark, amoral humour are the entire point.

CIN Peter Pau MUS Paul Haslinger DES Gary Frutkoff ED Peter Amundson PROD Susan Mountford, Don Murphy, Rick Benattar DIST Entertainment

66 A deliberately excessive homage to John Woo. – *Philip French, Observer*

66 A witless, soulless, heartless movie that mistakes noise for bravura and tastelessness for wit. – *A.O. Scott, New York Times*

Shoot the Pianist ★★★

DIR *François Truffaut*
1960 80m France
☆ Charles Aznavour, Nicole Berger, Marie Dubois, Michèle Mercier, Albert Rémy

A bar-room piano player becomes involved with gangsters through his disreputable brother.

Fair New Wave copy of an American film noir, but with playful little distancing devices, including jump cuts and blatant homages to other films in the genre. None of this spoils the central story, which has a melancholy, rough-edged charm.

SCR Marcel Moussy, François Truffaut CIN Raoul Coutard MUS Jean Constantin, Georges Delerue PROD Pierre Braunberger DIST Films de la Pléiade

66 Pictorially it is magnificent, revealing Truffaut's brilliant control over his images; emotionally, it is all a little jejune. – *John Gillett, Monthly Film Bulletin*

'1994, 800,000 killed in 100 days. Would you risk your life to make a difference?'

Shooting Dogs ★

DIR Michael Caton-Jones
2005 115m GB/Germany/France
[DVD]

☆ John Hurt (Father Christopher), Hugh Dancy (Joe Connor), Dominique Horwitz (Captain Delon), Louis Mahoney (Sibomana), Nicola Walker (Rachel), Steve Toussaint (Roland)

A British priest and a teacher try to provide refuge for victims of the Rwandan genocide.

The white perspective isn't a problem in and of itself, but the dramatic drift of this handsome production is towards gratefulness to the non-African characters, which is surely wrong-headed.

SCR David Wolstencroft CIN Ivan Strasburg MUS Dario Marianelli DES Bertram Strauss ED Christian Lonk PROD David Belton, Pippa Cross, Jens Meurer DIST Metrodome

66 All we get are white people shaking their heads and cursing Western governments. – *Kirk Honeycutt, Hollywood Reporter*

† The film was released in the US under the title Beyond the Gates.

🏆 David Belton (promising newcomer)

Short Cuts ★★★

DIR *Robert Altman*
1993 187m US
[DVD] ♫

☆ Andie MacDowell (Ann Finnigan), Bruce Davison (Howard Finnigan), Jack Lemmon (Paul Finnegan), Zane Cassidy (Casey Finnigan), Julianne Moore (Marian Wyman), Matthew Modine (Dr. Ralph Wyman), Anne

S

Archer (Claire Kane), Fred Ward (Stuart Kane), Jennifer Jason Leigh (Lois Kaiser), Chris Penn (Jerry Kaiser), Joseph C. Hopkins (Joe Kaiser), Josette Macario (Josette Kaiser), Robert Downey Jnr (Bill Bush), Madeleine Stowe (Sherri Shepard), Tim Robbins (Gene Shepard), Lily Tomlin, Tom Waits, Frances McDormand, Peter Gallagher, Annie Ross, Lori Singer, Lyle Lovett, Buck Henry

The everyday lives of some two dozen Los Angeles residents collide and intertwine.

A superbly achieved panoramic drama in the tradition of Altman's own Nashville, and just as sour; the vast majority of the characters are too self-absorbed to appreciate their place in the wider scheme of things. Altman provides a clever nexus between Carver's stories of lovelessness and dissatisfaction, even if his own contribution – Ross and Singer's troubled mother-and-daughter musicians – strikes the one false note.

SCR *Robert Altman, Frank Barhydt* **CIN** *Walt Lloyd* **MUS** Mark Isham **DES** Stephen Altman **ED** Geraldine Peroni, Suzy Elmiger **PROD** Cary Brokaw **DIST** Artificial Eye/Spelling/Fine Line/Avenue

66 A rich, unnerving film, as comic as it is astringent, that in its own quiet way works up a considerable emotional charge. – *Kenneth Turan, L.A. Times*

66 Uses Carver's writing partly to hack away at, and re-shape, the soap opera tradition's spreading empire on the modern screen. . .[Its] brilliance. . .lies in its surgical casualness, at once blithe and precise. – *Nigel Andrews, Financial Times*

⚱ Robert Altman

A Short Film about Killing ★★★★

DIR *Krzysztof Kieslowski*
1988 84m Poland
[DVD]

☆ Miroslaw Baka (Jacek Lazar), Krzysztof Globisz (Piotr Balicki), Jan Tesarz (Waldemar Rekowski), Zbigniew Zapasiewicz (Bar Examiner)

After senselessly and brutally killing a taxi driver, a disturbed young man has his case defended by an idealistic lawyer opposed to the death penalty.

Two acts of killing – one criminal, one state-approved – rendered almost equally excruciating. The film is stark and implacable in its moral condemnation of both.

SCR Krzysztof Piesiewicz, Krzysztof Kieslowski **CIN** *Slawomir Idziak* **MUS** Zbigniew Preisner **DES** Halina Dobrowolska **ED** Ewa Small **PROD** Ryszard Chutkowski **DIST** Gala/Film Unit 'Tor'/Zespoly Filmowe

66 The depiction of violence is far removed from the usual camera choreography, and is, in consequence, truly appalling. – *Brian Case, Time Out*

† The film is part of Dekalog, a 10-part TV series about the Ten Commandments.

A Short Film about Love ★★

DIR Krzysztof Kieslowski
1988 86m Poland
[DVD]

☆ Grazyna Szapolowska (Magda), Olaf Lubaszenko (Tomek), Stefania Iwinska (Godmother), Piotr Machalica (Roman), Artur Barcis (Young Man)

A teenage boy spies on a woman who lives across from his city apartment and becomes obsessed by her sex life.

As one might expect from this director, the title has a whiff of irony about it. Obsession and voyeurism are the themes here, and the film hearkens back to Michael Powell's Peeping Tom and Hitchcock's Rear Window. As an examination of dashed romantic hopes, it's sad and downbeat.

SCR Krzysztof Piesiewicz, Krzysztof Kieslowski **CIN** Witold Adamek **MUS** Zbigniew Preisner **DES** Halina Dobrowolska **ED** Ewa Smal **PROD** Ryszard Chutkowski **DIST** Gala/Polish Film Producers' Corporation

66 Its picture of a world where people spy on one another reverberates with a post-cold-war paranoia, evoking the chilling notion that privacy, like love, may also be just an illusion. – *Stephen Holden, New York Times*

'Two families, one feud, no going back.'

Shotgun Stories (new) ★

SCR/DIR Jeff Nichols
2008 90m US
[DVD]

☆ Michael Shannon (Son Hayes), Douglas Ligon (Boy Hayes), Barlow Jacobs (Kid Hayes), Michael Abbott Jnr (Cleaman Hayes), Travis Smith (Mark Hayes), Lynsee Provence (Stephen Hayes), David Rhodes (John Hayes), Glenda Pannell (Annie Hayes)

In rural Arkansas, three brothers begin a feud with the four children their late father had with his second wife.

Grimly compelling tragedy on a Biblical theme; violence is used sparingly but effectively.

CIN Adam Stone **MUS** Ben Nichols, Lucero Pyramid **DES** Lindsay Millar **ED** Steven Gonzales **PROD** David Gordon Green, Lisa Muskat, Jeff Nichols **DIST** Vertigo Films

66 A point-blank buckshot blast of inarticulate American rage. – *Eddie Cockrell, Variety*

66 A rural tragedy with the capacity to surprise. – *Philip French, Observer*

Show Me Love ★★

SCR/DIR Lukas Moodysson
1998 89m Sweden/Denmark
[DVD]

☆ Alexandra Dahlström (Elin), Rebecca Liljeberg (Agnes Ahlberg), Mathias Rust (Johan Hult), Erica Carlson (Jessica), Stefan Hörberg (Markus), Josefin Nyberg (Viktoria), Ralph Carlsson (Olof), Maria Hedborg (Karin), Axel Widegren (Oskar), Jill Ung (Birgitta)

A much-teased teenage girl in a boring Swedish suburb shares an accidental kiss with the most popular girl in the school, and falls in love with her.

Promising debut from poet-director Moodysson, but by no means the finished article; such rites-of-passage films may have been an event in Sweden (where it was a huge hit), but it looks familiar material from this vantage point, despite the nuances of the two lead performers.

S

CIN Ulf Brantas   DES Heidi Saikkonen, Lina Strand
ED Michal Leszczylowski, Bernhard Winkler   PROD Lars
Jönsson   DIST Alliance

66 Director Moodysson's story may be an old one – the
taboo between lovers from different ends of the school
spectrum – but his sharp script refreshes old themes. –
Liese Spencer, Sight and Sound

66 This lively comedy should strike a chord with bored
teenagers everywhere. – *David Parkinson, Empire
Magazine*

'Leave Your Inhibitions At The Door.'

Showgirls ★

DIR Paul Verhoeven
1995   131m   US
[DVD]

☆ Elizabeth Berkley (Nomi Malone), Kyle MacLachlan
(Zack Carey), Gina Gershon (Cristal Connors), Glenn
Plummer (James Smith), Robert Davi (Al Torres), Alan
Rachins (Tony Moss), Gina Ravera (Molly Abrams)

A stripper in Las Vegas claws her way up the pole to
stardom.

*Sleazy, tawdry, exhibitionistic fiasco, one of the most
damningly reviewed films of all time; but the movie is
full of perverse pleasures, because it refuses to be
contemptuous of its own tacky milieu. Simply put, it's
every bit as bad as you want it to be.*

SCR Joe Eszterhas   CIN Jost Vacano   MUS David A.
Stewart, Rena Riffel   DES Allan Cameron   ED Mark
Goldblatt, Mark Helfrich   PROD Alan Marshall, Charles
Evans   DIST Guild/United Artists/Chargeurs/Carolco

66 Has the distinction of being the first movie about Las
Vegas that is actually more vulgar than Las Vegas. –
Anthony Lane, New Yorker

66 Offers a slumming party inside the filmmakers' libidos.
– *Richard Corliss, Time*

'The greatest fairy tale never told.'

Shrek ★★

DIR Andrew Adamson, Vicky Jenson
2001   90m   US
[DVD]   ♫

☆ Mike Myers (Shrek), Eddie Murphy (Donkey), Cameron
Diaz (Princess Fiona), John Lithgow (Lord Farquaad),
Vincent Cassel (Monsieur Hood)

To reclaim his swamp, an ugly green ogre agrees to
rescue a princess, and falls in love with her.

*Slick and often hilarious computer-animated fantasy,
which makes a lot of hay at the expense of button-
pushing Disney magic. It's hard not to come away
entertained, and the sugary uplift works fine, but it's a
slightly hypocritical business, more a covert reinvention
of the Disney formula than an outright riposte to it.*

SCR Ted Elliott, Terry Rossio, Joe Stillman, Roger S. H.
Schulman   MUS Harry Gregson-Williams, John Powell
DES James Hegedus   ED Sim Evan-Jones   PROD Aron
Warner, John H. Williams, Jeffrey Katzenberg
DIST DreamWorks

66 You'll be hard pressed to find a funnier 90 minutes. –
Ian Nathan, Empire

66 Beating up on the irritatingly dainty Disney trademarks
is nothing new; it's just that it has rarely been done with
the demolition-derby zest of Shrek. – *Elvis Mitchell, New
York Times*

† Two sequels followed: Shrek 2 (2004) and Shrek the
Third (2007)

⚱ animated feature film
⚱ Ted Elliott, Terry Rossio, Joe Stillman, Roger S. H.
Schulman (adapted screenplay)
Ⓣ Ted Elliott, Terry Rossio, Joe Stillman, Roger S. H.
Schulman (adapted screenplay)
Ⓣ film; Eddie Murphy (supporting actor); Harry Gregson-
Williams, John Powell; Ken Bielenberg (special visual
effects); Andy Nelson, Anna Behlmer, Wylie Stateman, Lon
Bender (sound)

'Once upon another time. . .'

Shrek 2 ★★

DIR Andrew Adamson, Kelly Asbury, Conrad Verno
2004   93m   US
[DVD]   ♫

☆ voices of: Mike Myers (Shrek), Eddie Murphy (Donkey),
Cameron Diaz (Princess Fiona), Julie Andrews (Queen
Lillian), Antonio Banderas (Puss in Boots), John Cleese
(King Harold), Rupert Everett (Prince Charming), Jennifer
Saunders (Fairy Godmother)

Newlyweds Shrek and Princess Fiona visit her
parents, while a bitter Fairy Godmother and her
son, Prince Charming, try to break up the marriage.

*Both better and worse than its predecessor: the
storytelling is a lot more deft, with some lively new
characters, but it's even more dependent on snarky in-
jokes for its laughs.*

SCR Andrew Adamson, Joe Stillman, J. David Stern, David
N. Weiss   MUS Harry Gregson-Williams
DES Guillaume Aretos   ED Michael Andrews, Sim Evan-
Jones   PROD Aron Warner, David Lipman, John H.
Williams

66 Rambunctious fun. – *A. O. Scott, New York Times*

66 The helter-skelter story and throwaway gags emerge
from a sensibility that confuses gossipy knowingness and
jadedness with wit. – *Michael Sragow, Baltimore Sun*

† The film was one of the biggest box-office hits of all time,
grossing $919m internationally.

⚱ animated film; Adam Duritz, Charles Gillingham, Jim
Bogios, David Immergluck, Matthew Malley, David Bryson
(m), Adam Duritz, Daniel Vickrey (ly) (music–original song
Accidentally in Love)

'Get ready to get wasted.'

Shrooms (new)

DIR Paddy Breathnach
2007   84m   Ireland/UK/Denmark
☆ Lindsey Haun (Tara), Jack Huston (Jake), Max Kasch
(Troy), Maya Hazen (Lisa), Alice Greczyn (Holly), Robert
Hoffman (Bluto), Don Wycherley (Ernie), Sean McGinley
(Bernie)

American teenagers come a cropper after ingesting
magic mushrooms in rural Ireland.

*Low-budget horror with a psychedelic flavour, a surfeit
of clichés and a silly climactic twist.*

S

SCR Pearse Elliott   CIN Nanu Segal   MUS Dario
Marianelli   DES Mark Geraghty   ED Dermot Diskin
PROD Robert Walpole, Paddy McDonald   DIST Vertigo

66 Every element of Paddy Breathnach's Irish slasher
movie is so familiar that it feels like a dog-eared horror
anthology found down the back of the sofa. – *Nigel Floyd,
Time Out*

66 As scary as the adventures of Noddy. – *David Edwards,
Daily Mirror*

† Jack Huston is the grandson of director John and the
nephew of actress Anjelica.

'Freedom of speech is fine, as long as you don't do it in
public.'

Shut Up & Sing   ★★

DIR Barbara Kopple, Cecilia Peck
2006   93m   US
DVD

☆ Natalie Maines (Herself), Emily Robison (Herself),
Martie McGuire (Herself), Simon Renshaw (Himself),
Adrian Pasdar (Himself), Rick Rubin (Himself)

An American female country music trio is vilified
for attacking President George W. Bush on foreign
soil.

*Compelling look at what can happen when celebs
mouth off; though unlikely to appeal beyond the band's
fan base, it remains a cut above the usual
rockumentary.*

CIN Christine Burrill, Joan Churchill, Seth Gordon, Gary
Griffin, Luis Lopez   MUS Dixie Chicks   ED Bob
Eisenhardt, Aaron Kuhn, Emma Morris, Jean Tsien
PROD David Cassidy, Claude Davies, Barbara Kopple,
Cecilia Peck   DIST Momentum

NATALIE: 'Just so you know, we're ashamed the President
of the United States is from Texas.'

66 A bracingly candid documentary portrait of the artists
in a career-defining transition, the film simultaneously
offers a unique perspective of a nation at a similarly
significant crossroads. It also happens to be a lot of fun. –
Michael Rechtshaffen, Hollywood Reporter

† Natalie Maines made her controversial remark during a
concert at London's Shepherd's Bush Empire.

'The most terrifying images are the ones that are real.'

Shutter (new)

DIR Masayuki Ochiai
2008   84m   US
DVD

☆ Joshua Jackson (Ben Shaw), Rachael Taylor (Jane Shaw),
Megumi Okina (Megumi Tanaka), David Denman
(Bruno), John Hensley (Adam), Maya Hazen (Seiko)

A pair of American newly-weds are hounded in
Tokyo by mysterious apparitions that appear in their
photographs.

*Workmanlike, formulaic reprise of a superior Thai
original that suggests the Hollywood craze for J-horror
remakes may have finally run its course.*

SCR Luke Dawson   CIN Katsumi Yanagijima
MUS Nathan Barr   DES Norifumi Ataka   ED Michael N.

Knue, Tim Alverson   PROD Taka Ichise, Roy Lee, Doug
Davison   DIST TCF

66 Low on real scares, atmosphere and character, both
human and directorial. – *Dennis Harvey, Variety*

66 Derivative, predictable and slightly dull. – *Tony Horkins,
Empire*

'This might hurt a little.'

Sicko (new)   ★★

SCR/DIR Michael Moore
2007   123m   US
DVD

☆ Michael Moore

Michael Moore interviews victims of the US health-
care system, and compares health provision in
Britain, France, Canada and Cuba.

*As ever, Moore is provocative, angry and howlingly
funny, sometimes in the same scene. Only he would
devise scenes suggesting Guantánamo Bay detainees
enjoy better health care than average Americans. His
reporting of US health care injustices is diligent, but his
selective view of the virtues of health services elsewhere
undermines his case.*

CIN Tony Hardmon, Peter Nelson, Jonathan Weaver, Andy
Black, Daniele Marracino, Jayme Roy   MUS Erin O'Hara
ED Dan Swietlik, Geoffrey Richman, Christopher Seward
PROD Michael Moore, Meghan O'Hara   DIST Optimum

66 You do wish Moore would tie up his arguments a bit
more sensibly. – *Tim Robey, Daily Telegraph*

66 Moore is rightly celebrated for his elaborately staged
stunts and this film's highlight, involving a boat-trip to
Cuba, is as hilarious as it is disturbing. – *Karl French,
Financial Times*

⚱ documentary

'In search of wine. In search of women. In search of
themselves.'

Sideways   ★★★

DIR *Alexander Payne*
2004   126m   US
DVD   ♫

☆ *Paul Giamatti* (Miles Raymond), *Thomas Haden Church*
(Jack Lopate), *Virginia Madsen* (Maya), Sandra Oh
(Stephanie), Marylouise Burke (Miles' Mother), Jessica
Hecht (Victoria)

Two middle-aged buddies, one a failed novelist
and the other a failed actor about to get married,
go on a road trip through California's wine
country.

*Very adroit comedy of male hopelessness, sparkling with
insight, bitter humour and fine performances, and
offering some light at the end of the tunnel.*

SCR *Alexander Payne, Jim Taylor*   CIN Phedon
Papamichael   MUS Rolfe Kent   DES Jane Ann Stewart
ED Kevin Tent   PROD Michael London   DIST TCF

66 A road movie of impeccably slack structure,
effervescent but with a strong bouquet of melancholy and
more than a faint trace of bawdy. – *Sukhdev Sandhu, Daily
Telegraph*

66 Deliciously bitter-sweet. – *David Ansen, Newsweek*

S

DVD Available on DVD   ☆ Cast in order   66 Critics' Quotes   ⚱ Academy Award   🅱 BAFTA
♫ Soundtrack on CD   of importance   † Points of interest   ⚱ Academy Award nomination   🅣 BAFTA nomination

559

🏆 Alexander Payne, Jim Taylor (adapted screenplay)
🎬 film; Alexander Payne; Thomas Haden Church (supporting actor); Virginia Madsen (supporting actress)
Ⓣ Alexander Payne, Jim Taylor (adapted screenplay)

'To enter the mind of a killer she must challenge the mind of a madman.'

The Silence of the Lambs ★★★

DIR *Jonathan Demme*
1990   118m   US
DVD   🎵

☆ *Jodie Foster* (Clarice Starling), *Anthony Hopkins* (Dr. Hannibal Lecter), Scott Glenn (Jack Crawford), Ted Levine (Jame Gumb), Anthony Heald (Dr. Frederick Chilton), Lawrence A. Bonney (FBI Instructor), Kasi Lemmons (Ardelia Mapp), Lawrence J. Wrentz (Agent Burroughs), Frankie Faison (Barney), Roger Corman (FBI Director Hayden Burke)

Naive young female FBI agent, trying to gain an insight into the mind of a serial killer, seeks the help of imprisoned serial killer and psychiatrist Hannibal 'The Cannibal' Lecter to track him down.

These vivid characters, brilliantly acted, linger in the mind for a long time. Hopkins approaches his role as Lecter with something like gleeful gratitude; he makes it look like an actor's long-awaited dream come true. In its way, this tense thriller is a masterpiece, even if viewed from behind the sofa.

SCR Ted Tally   CIN Tak Fujimoto   MUS Howard Shore
DES Kristi Zea   ED Craig McKay   PROD Edward Saxon, Kenneth Utt, Ron Bozman   DIST Rank/Orion/Strong Heart/Demme

66 At first unmissable, then enduring, but always unmissable. – *Empire*

66 This is a bloody tale, with a finale that's make you think twice about entering a dark room without a sturdy weapon to defend yourself. – *Ben Falk, BBC*

† The character of Hannibal Lecter first made his appearance on film in Michael Mann's Manhunter.

🏆 film; Anthony Hopkins (leading actor); Jodie Foster (leading actress); Jonathan Demme; Ted Tally (adapted screenplay)
🎬 Craig Mckay; Tom Fleischman, Christopher Newman (sound)
Ⓑ Anthony Hopkins (leading actor); Jodie Foster (leading actress)
Ⓣ film; Jonathan Demme; Ted Tally; Tak Fujimoto; Craig McKay; Howard Shore; Tom Fleischman, Christopher Newman (sound)

Silent Light (new) ★

SCR/DIR Carlos Reygadas
2007   136m   Mexico/France/Netherlands
DVD

☆ Cornelio Wall (Johan), Miriam Toews (Esther), Maria Pankratz (Marianne), Peter Wall (Johan's father)

In Mexico, a Mennonite farmer with a wife and children, falls in love with another woman, with tragic consequences for his faith and his life.

An austere, slow-moving film that reflects the harshness and simplicity of this community's life. Its ending gives the solemn story the quality of a parable. Strictly for art-house audiences with a taste for the rigorous.

PROD Jaime Romandia, Carlos Reygadas   DIST Tartan

66 Shots in Silent Light are held for a very long time . . . Reygadas admits (this) is one way of making a film harder to forget. – *Nick James, Sight & Sound*

† It won the jury prize at the 2007 Cannes Film Festival.
† Reygadas's cast is composed of non-professional actors.

'Come back, or I shall die.'

Silk (new)

DIR François Girard
2007   108m   US/Canada/Italy/Japan

☆ Michael Pitt (Hervé Joncour), Keira Knightley (Hélène Joncour), Alfred Molina (Baldabiou), Koji Yakusho (Hara Jubei), Sei Ashina (The Girl), Miki Nakatani (Madame Blanche)

A 19th-century trader sent from France to Japan to buy silkworm eggs falls for a warlord's concubine.

Tedious travelogue based on an exotic bestseller; a miscast Pitt in the lead doesn't help, though it would be hard to see how any actor could energise such airless material.

SCR François Girard, Michael Golding   CIN Alain Dostie
MUS Ryuichi Sakamoto   DES François Séguin, Emita Frigato, Fumio Ogawa   ED Pia Di Ciaula   PROD Niv Fichman, Nadine Luque, Domenico Procacci, Sonoko Sakai
DIST Entertainment

66 Vacuous, arid and terminally dull. – *Todd McCarthy, Variety*

66 By neglecting its characters and narrative, it winds up as little more than an exercise in expert cinematography. – *Anna Smith, Empire*

'Vote early. Vote often.'

Silver City ★

SCR/DIR John Sayles
2004   128m   US
DVD

☆ Chris Cooper (Dickie Pilager), Richard Dreyfuss (Chuck Raven), Cajardo Lindsey (Lloyd), John C. Ashton (Director), Elizabeth Rainer (Leslie), Tim Roth (Mitch Paine), Thora Birch (Karen Cross)

When the dim-witted son a of a wealthy, powerful Colorado family runs for state governor, his aides hire an ex-reporter to investigate who is trying to derail his campaign. But the investigator inadvertently uncovers dirty deeds and shady deals, traceable to the candidate and his family.

The normally consistent Sayles comes a cropper with this heavy-handed political satire of an obvious target: Cooper's inarticulate family puppet is a dead ringer for George W. Bush. And could the family's surname, Pilager, be any less subtle? The film isn't funny enough: it has a resigned, petulant air, taking time to observe that the voters routinely support the Pilager clan, despite their glaring faults. It's as if Sayles, as a liberal, is too exhausted to harangue real-life conservative demagogues with any conviction.

S

CIN Haskell Wexler   MUS Mason Daring   DES Toby Corbett   ED John Sayles   PROD Maggie Renzi
DIST Tartan

'A Haunting Story Of Earthly Reason And Divine Intervention.'

Simon Magus ★

SCR/DIR Ben Hopkins
1999   101m   GB/France/Germany/Italy/US
DVD

☆ Noah Taylor (Simon), Stuart Townsend (Dovid Bendel), Sean McGinley (Maximillian Hase), Embeth Davidtz (Leah), Amanda Ryan (Sarah), Rutger Hauer (Count Albrecht), Ian Holm (Sirius/Boris/The Devil), Terence Rigby (Bratislav), Ursula Jones (Rebecca), Cyril Shaps (Chaim), David De Keyser (Rabbi)

In 19th century Silesia, a slow-witted outcast in a Jewish community, convinced he is possessed by Satan, becomes a pawn in a land deal that would bring a railway to the village.

Initially it has the look of a silent movie, and as it progresses it assumes the air of a folk fable. An ambitious debut from director Hopkins, but its blend of fantastical elements, superstition and hard-headed business deals adds up to an unfocused whole.

CIN Nicholas Knowland   MUS Deborah Mollison
DES Angela Davies   ED Alan Levy   PROD Robert Jones

66 It's a shame that Simon Magus is populated with so many stock characters. From Simon's holy fool to the patrician, dutiful squire, all seem overly familiar. – *Ken Hollings, Sight & Sound*

'There is no such thing as adventure and romance. There's only trouble and desire.'

Simple Men ★

SCR/DIR Hal Hartley
1992   105m   GB/US/Italy
DVD

☆ Robert Burke (Bill McCabe), William Sage (Dennis McCabe), Karen Sillas (Kate), Elina Löwensohn (Elina), Martin Donovan (Martin), Mark Chandler Bailey (Mike), Chris Cooke (Vic)

Two brothers take to the road to track down their father, an ex-radical and former baseball star, wanted by the authorities for his part in a bombing. On their travels the brothers meet intriguing women and larger-than-life characters.

Hartley's skewed view of human behaviour can look like studied eccentricity, and here he's too busy detailing every quirk of every character to move the story along as briskly as one might wish. That said, it has a certain shambling charm.

CIN Michael Spiller   MUS Ned Rifle, Yo La Tengo
DES Daniel Ouellette   ED Steve Hamilton   PROD Ted Hope, Hal Hartley, Bruce Weiss, Jerome Brownstein
DIST Metro/Zenith/American Playhouse/Fine Line/Film Four/BIM

66 Simple Men, in its best moments, seems like a carbon copy of its predecessors. – *Geoffrey Macnab, Sight & Sound*

'Sometimes good people do evil things.'

A Simple Plan ★★★

DIR Sam Raimi
1998   121m   France/UK/Germany/USA/Japan
DVD   ♫

☆ Bill Paxton (Hank Mitchell), *Billy Bob Thornton* (Jacob Mitchell), Bridget Fonda (Sarah Mitchell), Brent Briscoe (Lou Chambers), Gary Cole (Baxter), Becky Ann Baker (Nancy), Chelcie Ross (Carl), Jack Walsh (Tom Butler)

Two brothers and a friend in Minnesota find $4.4m in a crashed plane, and decide to keep it.

Bracing thriller in a John Huston-ish mode, exploring the sad and shocking effect of an illicit windfall on ordinary lives, and doing so with real craftsmanship and intelligence.

SCR *Scott B. Smith*   CIN Alar Kivilo   MUS *Danny Elfman*
DES Patrizia von Brandenstein   ED Arthur Coburn, Eric L. Beason   PROD James Jacks, Adam Schroeder
DIST Paramount/Mutual/Savoy

66 One of the year's best films for a lot of reasons, including its ability to involve the audience almost breathlessly in a story of mounting tragedy. – *Roger Ebert, Chicago Sun-Times*

⚱ Billy Bob Thornton (supporting actor); Scott B. Smith (adapted screenplay)

'Michael McCann Is About To Find Wealth Beyond His Imagination . . . A Real Family.'

A Simple Twist of Fate ★

DIR Gillies MacKinnon
1994   106m   US
DVD   ♫

☆ Steve Martin (Michael McCann), Gabriel Byrne (John Newland), Laura Linney (Nancy Lambert Newland), Catharine O'Hara (April Simon), Stephen Baldwin (Tanny Newland), Byron Jennings (Keating), Michael des Barres (Bryce), Amelia Campbell (Marsha Swanson), Kellen Crosby (Lawrence age 11)

A miser and recluse finds a way to make some sense of his grim life when he adopts an illegitimate motherless girl.

This update of George Eliot's Victorian novel Silas Marner has some poignant moments, due in part to Steve Martin's intelligent adaptation. Whether Martin should have played the miser himself is another matter; a stronger dramatic actor might have fitted the bill more comfortably.

SCR Steve Martin   CIN Andrew Dunn   MUS Cliff Eidelman   DES Andy Harris   ED Humphrey Dixon
PROD Ric Kidney   DIST Buena Vista/Touchstone

66 [It] may have a classical provenance, but it plays like a tawdry weepie from the '40s. – *Hal Hinson, Washington Post*

'See our family. And feel better about yours.'

The Simpsons Movie (new) ★★

DIR David Silverman
2007   87m   US
DVD

☆ Featuring the voices of: Dan Castellaneta, Julie Kavner,

DVD Available on DVD   ☆ Cast in order   66 Critics' Quotes   ⚱ Academy Award   BAFTA
♫ Soundtrack on CD   of importance   † Points of interest   Academy Award nomination   BAFTA nomination

S

561

Nancy Cartwright, Yeardley Smith, Harry Shearer, Hank Azaria, Tress MacNeille

The cartoon family get involved in various scrapes in their hometown, involving pollution in the lake, Springfield being sealed off under a glass dome, Homer adopting a pig, a romance for Lisa and Bart skateboarding naked through town.

Astute, witty adaptation of the wildly successful TV series, with its 22-minute episodes, to feature-length. The pace is a little more relaxed, the gags arrive reliably and the complicated story is just about sustained.

SCR James L.Brooks, Matt Groening, Al Jean, Ian Maxtone-Graham, George Meyer, David Mirkin, Mike Reiss, Mike Scully, Matt Selman, John Swartzwelder, Jon Vitti
MUS Hans Zimmer, Danny Elfman (theme) ED John Carnochan DIST TCF

HOMER (IN CINEMA): 'I can't believe we're paying to see something we get on TV for free! If you ask me, everybody in this theatre is a giant sucker!'
TODD FLANDERS: 'I wish Homer was my father.'
NED FLANDERS: 'And I wish you didn't have the devil's curly hair.'
HOMER (LEAFING THROUGH THE BIBLE): 'This book doesn't have any answers!'

66 The movie crams in so many jokes around the edges of the frame that it'll need a DVD pause facility to appreciate them all. – *Kim Newman, Sight & Sound*

66 I laughed sporadically at this enjoyable film. – *Philip French, Observer*

'Walk down the right back alley in Sin City and you can find anything.'

Sin City ★

DIR Frank Miller, Robert Rodriguez
2005 124m US
DVD ♫

☆ Jessica Alba (Nancy), Devon Aoki (Miho), Alexis Bledel (Becky), Powers Boothe (Senator Roark), Rosario Dawson (Gail), Benicio Del Toro (Jackie Boy), Michael Clarke Duncan (Manute), Carla Gugino (Lucille), Josh Hartnett (The Man), Rutger Hauer (Cardinal Roark), Jaime King (Goldie/Wendy), Michael Madsen (Bob), Clive Owen (Dwight), Mickey Rourke (Marv), Bruce Willis (Hartigan), Elijah Wood, Brittany Murphy

Three tough guys in depraved Basin City try to save the women they love.

One of the truest transfers of comic-book to film, a ferociously stylised piece which successfully creates its own pulp universe. Still, it's a singularly repellent one, in which the women are prostitutes across the board, and the violence is unredeemed by any underlying humanity.

SCR Frank Miller CIN Robert Rodriguez MUS Robert Rodriguez, John Debney, Graeme Revell ED Robert Rodriguez PROD Elizabeth Avellan DIST Buena Vista

66 The comic-book style, the stark framing, the Runyonesque dialogue, the hallucinatory design and strange mix of heartless gore and choked-up sentiment are all meticulously imitated rather than lived. – *Peter Bradshaw, Guardian*

66 Pure pulp meta-fiction. – *Stephen Hunter, Washington Post*

'For a mother, a sister and a niece, nothing is the same . . . Since Otar Left'

Since Otar Left. . . ★★

DIR Julie Bertuccelli
2003 103m France/Belgium
DVD

☆ *Esther Gorintin* (Eka), Nino Khomasuridze (Marina), Temour Kalandadze (Tengiz), Dinara Drukarova (Ada), Roussoudan Bolkvadze (Rusiko)

A grandmother in Tbilisi is unaware of her son's death, because her daughter and granddaughter keep the news from her, inventing fake letters to keep him alive.

Beautifully acted melodrama about the difficulty of being cruel to be kind. It is well handled on a tiny scale, though the final act becomes implausibly forgiving of all the subterfuge.

SCR Julie Bertuccelli, Bernard Renucci, Roger Bohbot CIN Christophe Pollock DES Emmanuel de Chauvigny ED Emmanuelle Castro PROD Yael Fogiel

66 The final effect of this movie about absence and loss is unsentimentally affirmative. – *Philip French, Observer*

'What a Glorious Feeling!'

Singin' in the Rain ★★★★

DIR Gene Kelly, Stanley Donen
1952 102m US
DVD ♫

☆ *Gene Kelly* (Don Lockwood), *Donald O'Connor* (Cosmo Brown), *Debbie Reynolds* (Kathy Seldon), *Millard Mitchell* (R.F. Simpson), *Jean Hagen* (Lina Lamont), Rita Moreno (Zelda Zanders), Cyd Charisse (Dancer), *Douglas Fowley* (Roscoe Dexter)

When talkies are invented, the reputation of one female star shrivels while another grows.

Brilliant comic musical, the best picture by far of Hollywood in transition, with the catchiest tunes, the liveliest choreography, the most engaging performances and the most hilarious jokes of any musical.

SCR *Adolph Green, Betty Comden* CIN *Harold Rosson* MUS *Nacio Herb Brown* ED Adrienne Fazan PROD Arthur Freed DIST MGM

66 Perhaps the most enjoyable of all movie musicals. – *New Yorker, 1975*

66 I thought it the greatest thing I'd ever seen – joyous, witty, life-enhancing. There is a succession of imaginatively staged, beautiful numbers starting with the title song performed behind the opening credits by Kelly, Debbie Reynolds and Donald O'Connor. The finest is Kelly and Reynolds performing 'You Were Meant for Me' on an empty sound stage, an explicit statement about, and expression of, the cinema's ability to use technology to create romantic magic. – *Philip French, Observer*

† 'Make 'Em Laugh; Moses'; 'Fit as a Fiddle'; 'Singin' in the Rain'; 'All I Do Is Dream of You'; 'I've Got a Feelin' You're Foolin'; 'Should I'; 'You Were Meant For Me'; 'Good Morning'; 'Would You'; 'You Are My Lucky Star'

⚬ Jean Hagen (supporting actress); Lennie Hayton

'Love is a game. Easy to start. Hard to finish.'

Singles ★★

SCR/DIR *Cameron Crowe*
1992 99m US
DVD ♫

☆ Bridget Fonda (Janet Livermore), Campbell Scott (Steve Dunne), Kyra Sedgwick (Linda Powell), Sheila Kelley (Debbie Hunt), Jim True (David Bailey), Matt Dillon (Cliff Poncier), Ally Walker (Pam), Eric Stoltz (The Mime), Tom Skerritt (Mayor Weber)

A group of twentysomethings search for love in grunge-era Seattle.

Smart and touching comedy about the yearning of young people for greater fulfilment, in a sub-culture where singleness is cool.

CIN Ueli Steiger, Tak Fujimoto MUS Paul Westerberg
DES Stephen Lineweaver ED Richard Chew
PROD Cameron Crowe, Richard Hashimoto
DIST Warner/Atkinson/Knickerbocker

66 Witty, perceptive, refreshing. – *Hugo Davenport, Daily Telegraph*

66 Too many plots competing for one charm franchise. . .However I liked the safe sex party that enjoins guests to come dressed as your favourite contraceptive. – *Nigel Andrews, Financial Times*

'A Seductive New Comedy.'

Sirens ★

SCR/DIR John Duigan
1994 94m Australia/GB
DVD

☆ Hugh Grant (Anthony Campion), Tara Fitzgerald (Estella Campion), Sam Neill (Norman Lindsay), Elle Macpherson (Sheela), Portia de Rossi (Giddy), Kate Fischer (Pru), Pamela Rabe (Rose Lindsay), Ben Mendelsohn (Lewis), Mark Gerber (Devlin), Tom Polson (Tom)

A priggish vicar and his wife are sent to visit a loose-living Australian painter, and find their inhibitions challenged.

Pleasant, if inconsequential comedy of bohemianism clashing with prudish mores.

CIN Geoff Burton MUS Rachel Portman DES Roger Ford ED Humphrey Dixon PROD Sue Milliken
DIST Buena Vista/WGM/AFFC/British Screen/Samson/Sarah Radclyffe

66 A good-bad movie. . .to sit through in a state of benign indolence. – *John Simon, National Review*

66 Does have its lulling, sensual moments. – *Tom Gliatto, People Weekly*

Sisters in Law ★★

DIR Florence Ayisi, Kim Longinotto
2006 104m UK
DVD

☆ Vera Ngassa, Veraline, Judge Beatrice Ntuba

Three women working in Cameroon's legal system – a prosecutor, a lawyer and a judge – work to bring sexual equality to the country.

Stirring account of women who help female victims of rape, spousal abuse and abandonment. Fascinating, richly detailed and often amusing, but above all a triumph for human rights in a male-dominated society.

CIN Kim Longinotto MUS D'Gary ED Oliver Huddleston PROD Kim Longinotto DIST ICA

66 Some cases are harrowing, but the film is never grim. The formidable Ngassa shows such resilience, kindness and common sense that the effect is oddly uplifting. – *Geoffrey Macnab, Guardian*

'For Paul, every person is a new door to a new world.'

Six Degrees of Separation ★★★

DIR *Fred Schepisi*
1993 112m US
DVD ♫

☆ *Stockard Channing* (Louisa ('Ouisa') Kittredge), *Will Smith* (Paul), Donald Sutherland (John Flanders ('Flan') Kittredge), Mary Beth Hurt (Kitty), Bruce Davison (Larkin), Heather Graham (Elizabeth), Anthony Michael Hall (Trent Conway), Eric Thal (Rick), Richard Masur (Dr. Fine), Ian McKellen (Geoffrey Miller)

A young impostor, claiming to be the son of actor Sidney Poitier, inveigles his way into the lives of a rich couple on Manhattan's Upper East Side, giving them an anecdote to dine out on for months.

Dazzlingly witty and teasing account of unexpected connections between the rarefied strata of New York society, based on a true story plucked from the papers. It is about more than a con artist taking advantage of rich fools, because the episode forces Channing's character to reconsider her whole take on life. This was Smith's first attempt at 'serious' acting, and he's a knockout, too.

SCR *John Guare* CIN Ian Baker MUS Jerry Goldsmith DES *Patrizia von Brandenstein* ED Peter Honess PROD Fred Schepisi, Arnon Milchan
DIST MGM/Maiden Movies/New Regency

66 Offers no simple answers but cleverly weaves its questions into a guilt-edged parlour game. – *Bruce Williamson, Playboy*

66 Clever, facile, hermetic – a highly accomplished crock. – *Owen Gleiberman, Entertainment Weekly*

† The title refers to the idea that if a person is one step away from each person he or she knows, and two steps away from each person known by one of the people he or she knows, then everyone is an average of six 'steps' away from each person on Earth.

⚱ Stockard Channing (leading actress)

Sixteen Years of Alcohol

SCR/DIR Richard Jobson
2003 102m GB
DVD

☆ Kevin McKidd (Frankie Mac), Laura Fraser (Helen), Susan Lynch (Mary), Stuart Sinclair Blyth (Miller), Jim Carter (Director), Ewen Bremner (Jake)

An Edinburgh lad takes to the bottle and falls in with some violent types.

Danny Boyle meets Terence Davies in a sodden bar encounter: a miserabilist cocktail of cod philosophy,

DVD Available on DVD ☆ Cast in order of importance 66 Critics' Quotes ⚱ Academy Award ⚱ Academy Award nomination 🏆 BAFTA 🏆 BAFTA nomination
♫ Soundtrack on CD † Points of interest

563

S

violence and pub ditties which never begins to get past its influences or illuminate what it claims to be about. Still, a deeply personal debut from this writer-director.

CIN John Rhodes MUS Keith Atack DES Adam Squires ED Ioannis Chalkiadakis PROD Richard Jobson, Mark Burton DIST Metro Tartan

66 A rich density of mood and texture. – *Edward Porter, Sunday Times*

66 Two things ruin it: the absurdly wordy voice-over, in which someone isn't just "dead", he's "dead, dead, dead, no longer living, lifeless", and a soundtrack of pedal-heavy piano chords of the sort you might knock out during Grade 2 practice. – *Catherine Shoard, Sunday Telegraph*

'Not every gift is a blessing.'

The Sixth Sense ★★★

SCR/DIR *M. Night Shyamalan*
1999 107m US
DVD ♫

☆ *Bruce Willis* (Malcolm Crowe), Toni Collette (Lynn Sear), Olivia Williams (Anna Crowe), *Haley Joel Osment* (Cole Sear), Donnie Wahlberg (Vincent Gray), Glenn Fitzgerald (Sean), Mischa Barton (Kyra Collins), Trevor Morgan (Tommy Tammisimo), Bruce Norris (Stanley Cunningham)

A Philadelphia child psychologist struggles to save his marriage as he treats a disturbed young boy who can see the dead.

Smashing debut from a director who failed to live up to this early promise. A fascinating, haunting movie with genuine power and presence. Willis and young Osment carry off the leading roles with great aplomb; the story is challenging and unpredictable.

CIN Tak Fujimoto MUS James Newton Howard DES Larry Fulton ED Andrew Mondshein PROD Frank Marshall, Kathleen Kennedy, Barry Mendel DIST Buena Vista

COLE SEAR: 'I see dead people.'

66 What finally elevates the film above its shaggy dog tale roots. . .is a performance from Haley Joel Osment that is simply one of the finest given by a child in any film. – *Adam Smith, Empire*

66 Too often the film gets lost in overlit opulence and the soundtrack going 'boo'. – *Michael Atkinson, Village Voice*

⚱ picture; Haley Joel Osment (supporting actor); Toni Collette (supporting actress); M. Night Shyamalan (direction); M. Night Shyamalan (original screenplay); Andrew Mondshein

Ⓣ film; M. Night Shyamalan (direction); M. Night Shyamalan (original screenplay); Andrew Mondshein

---

Sketches of Frank Gehry ★★

DIR Sydney Pollack
2006 83m US
DVD

☆ Frank Gehry, Sydney Pollack, Michael Eisner, Bob Geldof, Barry Diller, Michael Ovitz, Philip Johnson, Julian Schnabel, Dennis Hopper, Ed Ruscha

An exploration of the life and work of the celebrated architect.

Pollack does not try to be objective about Gehry, a long-time friend. In this admiring investigation into his work methods, special emphasis is given to the Guggenheim Museum in Bilbao, which Pollack shoots with something approaching awe. Intrusively, the director often appears in shot. Still, there's intriguing material here: Gehry's name change (through a fear of anti-Semitism); his years in psychoanalysis; his unusually close association with a group of Los Angeles artists; and his refusal to recognise architecture's traditional boundaries. A decent account of a complex, sublimely talented man.

CIN Ultan Guilfoyle, Sydney Pollack MUS Sorman & Nystrom ED Karen Schmeer PROD Ultan Guilfoyle DIST Artificial Eye

66 Too much of the film is taken up with gushy, self-serving talking-head testimonials. – *Peter Rainer, Christian Science Monitor*

'Who will save us?'

Sky Captain and the World of Tomorrow

SCR/DIR Kerry Conran
2004 106m US/Italy/GB
DVD

☆ Gwyneth Paltrow (Polly Perkins), Jude Law (Sky Captain), Angelina Jolie (Franky), Giovanni Ribisi (Dex), Michael Gambon (Editor Paley), Bai Ling (Mysterious Woman), Dr. Totenkopf (Laurence Olivier)

When giant flying robots attack New York City, a flying ace and his ex-wife, a reporter, team up to investigate their origin.

Hollow feat of retro stylisation, with literally every scene digitally composited to resemble sci-fi adventures of the 1930s. Hyped as a technological breakthrough, but offering little in the way of real excitement.

CIN Eric Adkins MUS Edward Shearmur DES Kevin Conran ED Sabrina Plisco PROD Jon Avnet, Marsha Oglesby, Sadie Frost, Jude Law DIST Paramount

66 Arresting at first but gradually trails off under the weight of its hyper-derivativeness and anxiety to please. – *Todd McCarthy, Variety*

66 Never escapes the flatness of pastiche. – *Edward Porter, Sunday Times*

† Olivier's 'performance' was collated by using extracts of his roles in previous films.

Slab Boys ★

SCR/DIR John Byrne
1997 97m GB
♫

☆ Robin Lang (Phil McCann), Duncan Ross (Alan Downie), Russell Barr (George 'Spanky' Farrell), Bill Gardiner (Hector McKenzie), Louise Berry (Lucille Bentley), Anna Massey (Miss Elsie Walkinshaw), Tom Watson (Willie Curry), Moray Hunter (Jack Hogg), David O'Hara (Terry Skinnedar)

In the early rock 'n' roll era, three young paint-mixers in a Glasgow carpet factory dream of escaping their working-class environment.

Byrne attempted to transfer the energy and snap of his two plays to film; but shackled by a low budget that apparently kept the production largely studio-bound, the work feels too constricted for the big screen.

CIN Seamus McGarvey **MUS** Jack Bruce **DES** Luana Hanson **ED** John Macdonnell **PROD** Simon Relph, Lauren Lowenthal **DIST** Channel 4/Skreba/Wanderlust

66 The Slab Boys highlights (Byrne's) talents as writer and designer, but Scotland's most famous polymath hasn't yet proved that he can direct films to the same standard. – *Geoffrey Macnab, Sight & Sound*

Slacker ★★

SCR/DIR *Richard Linklater*
1991 97m US
DVD

☆ Richard Linklater (Should Have Stayed at Bus Station), Rudy Basquez (Taxi Driver), Jean Caffeine (Roadkill), Jan Hockey (Jogger), Stephan Hockey (Running Late), Mark James (Hit-and-run Son)

A succession of young citizens of Austin, Texas, move round the city, the ongoing story being continued like a relay race as individuals' paths cross.

A film with a title that coined an attitude for a particular generation: appropriately, it is virtually plotless (though not formless) and speaks eloquently to its target demographic. It embraces a leisurely way of approaching life, a weakness for conspiracy theories, and a tendency to record one's every move on video. It has an artless charm.

CIN Lee Daniel **DES** Deborah Pastor **ED** Scott Rhodes **PROD** Richard Linklater **DIST** Feature/Detour

66 What is absent from Slacker is any significant political dimension...there's little sense of economic deprivation, nor any suggestion that these marginal characters are the victims of callous economic policy. – *Philip Kemp, Sight & Sound*

'Four friends made a mistake that changed their lives forever.'

Sleepers ★

SCR/DIR Barry Levinson
1996 147m US
DVD ♫

☆ Kevin Bacon (Sean Nokes), Robert de Niro (Father Bobby), Dustin Hoffman (Danny Snyder), Bruno Kirby (Shakes' Father), Jason Patric (Lorenzo 'Shakes' Carcaterra), Brad Pitt (Michael Sullivan), Brad Renfro (Young Michael Sullivan), Ron Eldard (John Reilly), Billy Crudup (Tommy Marcano), Vittorio Gassman (King Benny), Minnie Driver (Carol Martinez)

A group of teenagers in New York's Hell's Kitchen are brutalised by a sadistic guard in a detention centre, and plot revenge 10 years later with the help of a lawyer and a priest.

Glossy but dubious melodrama, with a touch of old-style Warner Bros. 1930s gangster pictures, and the added ingredient of male rape; though stylishly assembled, it becomes a jerry-rigged justification for vigilantism.

CIN *Michael Ballhaus* **MUS** John Williams **DES** Kristi Zea **ED** Stu Linder **PROD** Barry Levinson, Steve Golin **DIST** Polygram/Warner/Propaganda/Baltimore

66 Rigged, and horribly manipulative. . .What really sticks in the craw is that another mainstream Hollywood movie, hot on the heels of A Time To Kill, has championed the acquittal of murderers. – *Anthony Quinn, Mail on Sunday*

† The factual basis for the story, based on journalist Lorenzo Carcaterra's memoir, has been challenged, after the New York legal community disputed the existence of any such case.

♪ John Williams

'What if someone you never met, someone you never saw, someone you never knew was the only someone for you?'

Sleepless in Seattle ★

DIR Nora Ephron
1993 105m US
DVD ♫

☆ *Tom Hanks* (Sam Baldwin), *Meg Ryan* (Annie Reed), Ross Malinger (Jonah Baldwin), Rita Wilson (Suzy), Victor Garber (Greg), Tom Riis Farrell (Rob), Carey Lowell (Maggie Abbott Baldwin), Bill Pullman (Walter)

A widower's eight-year-old son calls a radio phone-in show hoping he can find a partner for his dad; a journalist, engaged but harbouring doubts, listens in and sets about finding him.

Fluffy, desexualised, though hugely successful romcom, full of nostalgic references to the 1950s weepie An Affair to Remember, thereby encouraging comparisons it never merits. It is so sweet you could rot your teeth on it.

SCR Nora Ephron, David S. Ward, Jeff Arch **CIN** Sven Nykvist **MUS** Marc Shaiman **DES** Jeffrey Townsend **ED** Robert Reitano **PROD** Gary Foster **DIST** TriStar

66 A pre-coitus interruptus of gigantic dimensions. – *John Simon, National Review*

66 Magical. – *Christopher Tookey, Daily Mail*

♪ Nora Ephron, David S. Ward, Jeff Arch (original screenplay); Marc Shaiman, original song (m) Ramsey McLean (ly) (music – A Wink and a Smile)

Ⓣ Nora Ephron, David S. Ward, Jeff Arch (original screenplay); Marc Shaiman

'Heads will roll.'

Sleepy Hollow ★

DIR Tim Burton
1999 105m US/Germany
DVD ♫

☆ Johnny Depp (Ichabod Crane), Christina Ricci (Katrina Van Tassel), Miranda Richardson (Lady Van Tassel/Crone), Michael Gambon (Baltus Van Tassel), Caspar Van Dien (Brom Van Brunt), Jeffrey Jones (Rev Steenwyck), Christopher Lee (Burgomaster), Richard Griffiths (Magistrate Philipse), Ian McDiarmid (Doctor Lancaster), Michael Gough (Notary Hardenbrook), Christopher Walken (Hessian Horseman), Lisa Marie (Lady Crane), Steven Waddington (Killian), Claire Skinner (Beth Killian), Alun Armstrong (High Constable)

In 1799, an eccentric constable from New York is sent to the village of Sleepy Hollow to investigate a series of unexplained beheadings.

| DVD | Available on DVD | ☆ | Cast in order | 66 | Critics' Quotes | ♪ | Academy Award | Ⓣ | BAFTA |
| ♫ | Soundtrack on CD | | of importance | † | Points of interest | ♪ | Academy Award nomination | Ⓣ | BAFTA nomination |

565

Lavishly designed homage to Hammer horror, dripping with picture-book foreboding; but the plot lacks suspense and just goes through the motions, rather like an overlong period episode of Scooby Doo.

SCR Andrew Kevin Walker, Kevin Yagher **CIN** *Emmanuel Lubezki* **MUS** *Danny Elfman* **DES** *Rick Heinrichs* **ED** Chris Lebenzon, Joel Negron **PROD** Scott Rudin, Adam Schroeder **DIST** Paramount

66 History will recognize the rich imagination and secret tenderness of Burton's best films. – *Janet Maslin, New York Times*

66 A ferocious yet lyrical piece of filmmaking – an enchanted bloodbath. – *David Edelstein, Slate*

⚱ Rick Heinrichs

⚱ Emmanuel Lubezki; Colleen Atwood (costume designed)

Ⓣ Rick Heinrichs, Colleen Atwood (costume design)

Ⓣ Jim Mitchell, Kevin Yagher, Joss Williams, Paddy Eason (special visual effects)

'Obey the rules.'

Sleuth (new)

DIR Kenneth Branagh
1998 88m UK/US
[DVD] ♫

☆ Michael Caine (Andrew Wyke), Jude Law (Milo Tindle), Harold Pinter (Man on TV), Carmel O'Sullivan (Maggie)

A wealthy crime novelist and the struggling actor for whom his wife has left him conspire to stage a burglary.

Inadequate remake of the 1972 film which was itself hampered by its stage origins. This time, it's hard to see why anyone thought the enterprise worthwhile.

SCR Harold Pinter **CIN** Haris Zambarloukos
MUS Patrick Doyle **DES** *Tim Harvey* **ED** Neil Farrell
PROD Jude Law, Simon Halfon, Tom Sternberg, Marion Pilowsky, Kenneth Branagh, Simon Moseley
DIST Paramount

66 If you consider what the exalted quartet of Branagh, Pinter, Caine and Law might have done with the project, and what they did to it, Sleuth has to be the worst prestige movie of the year. – *Richard Corliss, Time*

66 The result is that what was once insignificant is now insufferable. – *Manohla Dargis, New York Times*

'There are two sides to every story. Helen is about to live both of them . . . at the same time. Romance was never this much fun.'

Sliding Doors   ★

SCR/DIR Peter Howitt
1998 99m GB/US
[DVD] ♫

☆ Gwyneth Paltrow (Helen Quilley), John Hannah (James Hammerton), John Lynch (Gerry), Jeanne Tripplehorn (Lydia), Zara Turner (Anna), Douglas McFerran (Russell), Paul Brightwell (Clive), Nina Young (Claudia), Virginia McKenna (James's Mother)

The live of a London PR executive hinges on whether she catches a tube train – if she does, she catches her boyfriend cheating on her; if not, she doesn't.

Nice idea, brightly done, but her life is fairly dull either way.

CIN Remi Adfarasin **MUS** David Hirschfelder
DES Maria Djurokovic **ED** John Smith **PROD** Sydney Pollack, Philippa Braithwaite, William Horberg
DIST Paramount/Miramax

66 As sweet as sherbet, and dissolves just as speedily on the tongue. – *Anthony Quinn, Mail on Sunday*

66 Sometimes looks more like an advert inviting people to come and film in Britain than a film in its own right. – *Tom Shone, Sunday Times*

Ⓣ British film

'A simple man. A difficult choice.'

Sling Blade   ★★

SCR/DIR Billy Bob Thornton
1996 135m US
[DVD] ♫

☆ *Billy Bob Thornton* (Karl Childers), Dwight Yoakam (Doyle Hargraves), *J. T. Walsh* (Charles Bushman), *John Ritter* (Vaughan Cunningham), *Lucas Black* (Frank Wheatley), Natalie Canderday (Linda Wheatley), Robert Duvall (Karl's Father), Jim Jarmusch (Frostee Cream Boy)

A simple man, hospitalised since killing his mother and her lover in childhood, is released to start a new life with a widow and her unhappy son in a small Southern town.

Impressive, deliberately paced character piece which is sometimes a little too much of an actors' showcase, allowing the plot to drag.

CIN Barry Markowitz **MUS** Daniel Lanois **DES** Clark Hunter **ED** Hughes Winborne **PROD** Brandon Rosser, David L. Bushell **DIST** Miramax/Shooting Gallery

KARL: Some folks call it a sling blade. I call it a kaiser blade.

66 You don't see too many first-rate movies about lovable axe-murderers. – *Guy Flatley, Cosmopolitan*

66 Suffers from something one might call Forrest Gump syndrome, that is, a weakness for sentimentalising damaged minds as a kind of higher soulfulness. – *Anthony Quinn, Mail on Sunday*

† A feature-length remake of a 25-minute short, Some Call It a Sling Blade, also written by and starring Thornton. It was directed by George Hickenlooper, and co-starred Molly Ringwald in a role that was excised in the longer version.

⚱ Billy Bob Thornton (adapted screenplay)

⚱ Billy Bob Thornton (leading actor)

'What's gotten into you?'

Slither   ★★

SCR/DIR James Gunn
2006 95m US
[DVD] ♫

☆ Nathan Fillion (Sheriff Pardy), Elizabeth Banks (Starla Grant), Gregg Henry (Jack MacReady), Tania Saulnier (Kylie Strutemeyer), Brenda James (Brenda Gutierrez), Don Thompson (Wally), Michael Rooker (Grant Grant)

Inhabitants of American small-town are infected by worm-like parasites from outer space.

S

About as dryly witty as any alien-horror-zombie movie can possibly be. It revels in being repellent and slimy, but Gunn's cheap, cheerful wit makes it an unexpected treat.

CIN Gregory Middleton   MUS Tyler Bates   DES Andrew Neskoromny   ED John Axelrad   PROD Paul Brooks, Eric Newman   DIST Entertainment

66 A gross, disgusting but undeniably amusing treat, laden with homages and in-jokes. – *Kevin Crust, Los Angeles Times*

'Take it from Vivian . . . the biggest problem in the country isn't money or drugs. It's breasts.'

Slums of Beverly Hills   ★★

SCR/DIR Tamara Jenkins

1998   91m   US

DVD   ♫

☆ *Alan Arkin* (Murray Samuel Abromowitz), *Marisa Tomei* (Rita Abromowitz), *Natasha Lyonne* (Vivian Abromowitz), Kevin Corrigan (Eliot Arenson), Eli Marienthal (Rickey Abromowitz), David Krumholtz (Ben Abromowitz), Jessica Walter (Doris Zimmerman), Carl Reiner (Mickey Abromowitz), Rita Moreno (Belle Abromowitz)

A teenage girl in the mid-1970s moves from one cheap flat to another with her family in Beverly Hills.

Sparky semi-autobiographical comedy with a slightly sitcom-ish feel, but fresh performances.

CIN Tom Richmond   MUS Rolfe Kent   DES Dena Roth   ED Pamela Martin   PROD Michael Nozik, Stan Wlodkowski   DIST Fox Searchlight/South Fork

66 Keeps the small surprises frequent and the coming-of-age perspective sharp. – *Elvis Mitchell, New York Times*

† Writer-director Jenkins waited nine years to make her next full-length film, The Savages.

'Some things are better left unsaid.'

Small Engine Repair (new)

SCR/DIR Niall Heery

2007   98m   Ireland/UK

☆ Iain Glen (Doug), Steven Mackintosh (Bill), Stuart Graham (Burley), Laurence Kinlan (Tony), Kathy Kiera Clarke (Agnes)

A diffident middle-aged Irishman (Glen) dreams of country-music stardom, while helping out his best friend (Mackintosh) who opens a repair shop for any trucks that happens to pass their remote backwoods locale.

Poignant but inconsequential little story that never soars. Glen's country songs are distinctly sub-par.

CIN Tim Fleming   MUS Niall Byrne   DES Mark Lowry   ED Emer Reynolds   PROD Tristan Orpen-Lynch, Dominic Wright   DIST Guerilla

---

'They took a bite out of crime.'

Small Time Crooks   ★

SCR/DIR Woody Allen

2000   94m   US

DVD

☆ Woody Allen (Ray Winkler), Tracey Ullman (Frenchy Winkler), Tony Darrow (Tommy), Hugh Grant (David), George Grizzard (George Blint), Jon Lovitz (Benny), Elaine May (May), Michael Rapaport (Denny), Elaine Stritch (Chi Chi Potter)

A loser thief and his wife open a shop next to a bank they plan to rob, and strike it rich by selling cookies.

More laughs in this straightforward romp than in Allen's previous few films, but there's a lot of snobbery towards the nouveau riche characters.

CIN Zhao Fei   DES Santo Loquasto   ED Alisa Lepselter   PROD Jean Doumanian   DIST DreamWorks

66 Very, very lightweight stuff. – *Robert W. Butler, Kansas City Star*

66 Sour, broadly comic and yet the most financially successful film he's made in years. – *Leslie Felperin, Sight & Sound*

† This marked a rare appearance by screenwriter Elaine May; it was only her second film-acting role in 22 years.

Smalltime   ★

SCR/DIR *Shane Meadows*

1996   60m   GB

☆ Mat Hand (Malc), Dena Smiles (Kate), Shane Meadows (Jumbo), Gena Kawecka (Ruby), Jimmy Hynd (Big Willy), Leon Lammond (Bets), Tim Cunningham (Lenny the Fence), Dominic Dillon (Mad Terry)

Two petty thieves in the Midlands struggle to hang on to girlfriends while they plan their biggest job yet.

Ultra-low-budget debut, barely at feature length, displaying the skilful realism and comic dialogue of director Meadows's later work.

CIN Helene Whitehall   MUS Gavin Clarke   ED David Wilson   PROD Shane Meadows   DIST BFI/Big Arty

66 Though often very funny, this proudly parochial tale never opts for knowing caricature. – *Geoff Andrew, Time Out*

'Sometimes the smartest people have the most to learn.'

Smart People (new)   ★

DIR Noam Murro

2008   94m   US

DVD

☆ Dennis Quaid (Lawrence Wetherhold), Sarah Jessica Parker (Dr. Janet Hartigan), Ellen Page (Vanessa Wetherhold), Thomas Haden Church (Chuck Wetherhold), Ashton Holmes (James Wetherhold), Christine Lahti (Nancy), Camille Mana (Missy Chin)

A misanthropic professor with an overachieving daughter is forced to rely on his feckless brother after an accident.

Tepid comedy drama about a dysfunctional family, centred around a disillusioned hero similar to that of Wonder Boys. This time, alas, the characters simply don't ring true.

SCR Mark Jude Poirier   CIN Toby Irwin   MUS Nuno Bettencourt   DES Patti Podesta   ED Robert Frazen, Yana Gorskaya   PROD Bridget Johnson, Michael Costigan, Michael London, Bruna Papandrea   DIST Icon

S

DVD Available on DVD   ☆ Cast in order of importance   66 Critics' Quotes   † Points of interest   ⚱ Academy Award   ⚱ Academy Award nomination   Ⓑ BAFTA   Ⓑ BAFTA nomination

567

66 It ends up less a dark comedy than a medium-gray one. – *Dennis Harvey, Variety*

66 Droll, watchable but strangely humdrum. – *Tim Robey, Telegraph*

'Snow covers everything . . . except the truth.'

Smilla's Feeling for Snow

DIR Bille August
1997   121m   Germany/Denmark/Sweden
☆ Julia Ormond (Smilla Jasperson), Gabriel Byrne (The Mechanic), Richard Harris (Dr. Andreas Tork), Vanessa Redgrave (Elsa Lübing), Robert Loggia (Moritz Jasperson), Jim Broadbent (Dr. Lagermann), Mario Adorf (Capt. Sigmund Lukas), Bob Peck (Ravn), Tom Wilkinson (Prof. Loyen), Emma Croft (Benja), Peter Capaldi (Birgo Lander)

A small boy falls off a roof in Copenhagen, and his neighbour investigates if it was really an accident.

An elegant novel turned into a flat, opaque film with only the snowy visuals to recommend it.

SCR Ann Biderman   **CIN** Jörgen Persson   **MUS** Harry Gregson-Williams   **DES** *Anna Asp*   **ED** Janus Billeskov-Jansen   **PROD** Bernd Eichinger, Martin Moszkowicz   **DIST** TCF/Constantin/Greenland/Bavaria

66 A mixed bag of blessings and blunders. – *Bruce Williamson, Playboy*

Smoke ★★

DIR Wayne Wang
1995   112m   US/ Japan
DVD   ♬
☆ William Hurt (Paul Benjamin), Harvey Keitel (Augustus 'Auggie' Wren), Forest Whitaker (Cyrus Cole), Harold Perrineau Jnr (Thomas 'Rashid' Cole), Victor Argo (Vinnie), Erica Gimpel (Doreen Cole), Clarice Taylor (Grandma Ethel), Malik Yoba (The Creeper), Mary Ward (April Lee the Bookstore Clerk), Jared Harris (Jimmy Rose)

Customers at a Brooklyn cigar store shoot the breeze and tell their stories.

Nicely rambling ensemble piece, well-performed, and making the world seem small.

SCR Paul Auster   **CIN** Adam Holender   **MUS** Rachel Portman   **DES** Kalina Ivanov   **ED** Maisie Hoy, Christopher Tellefsen   **PROD** Greg Johnson, Peter Newman, Hisami Kuriowa, Kenzo Hurikoshi   **DIST** Miramax/Nippon

66 Unimpeachably hipper-than-thou. – *Anne Billson, Sunday Telegraph*

66 A symphony of chance and coincidence. – *Derek Malcolm, Guardian*

† Director Wang shot Blue in the Face on completion of this film, using some of its existing characters improvising with new actors.

Smoking/No Smoking ★

DIR Alain Resnais
1993   298 (2 parts)m   France
☆ Sabine Azéma (Celia Teasdale/Sylvie Bell/Irene Pridworthy/Rowena Coombes/Josephine Hamilton), Pierre Arediti (Toby Teasdale/Miles Coombes/Lionel Hepplewick/Joe Hepplewick)

Two parallel stories with the same characters in a Yorkshire village that diverge as a result of a single incident: whether or not the local headmaster's wife decides to quit smoking.

An intriguing idea, and one that playwright Alan Ayckbourn employed with some success in his plays Intimate Exchanges. But it's a decidedly theatrical device, and it fits uneasily on the big screen. Impressively, the two lead actors get to play all 15 characters between them, though cinematic close-ups take the edge off their versatility. It's also unusual to see a French film about characters from Yorkshire; its notion of how the English look, dress and behave misses the mark.

SCR Jean-Pierre Bacri, Agnes Jaoui   **CIN** Renato Berta   **MUS** John Pattison   **DES** Jacques Saulnier   **ED** Albert Jurgenson   **PROD** Bruno Persey, Michel Seydoux   **DIST** Mainline/Arena/Camera One/France 2

'Believe everything except your eyes.'

Snake Eyes ★

DIR Brian de Palma
1998   98m   US
DVD   ♬
☆ Nicolas Cage (Rick Santoro), Gary Sinise (Commander Kevin Dunne), John Heard (Gilbert Powell), Carla Gugino (Julia Costello), Stan Shaw (Lincoln Tyler), Kevin Dunn (Lou Logan), Michael Rispoli (Jimmy George), Joel Fabiani (Charles Kirkland), Luis Guzman (Cyrus), David Anthony Higgins (Ned Campbell)

A corrupt Atlantic City detective investigates a political assassination at a boxing match.

Flashy but brainless thriller, opening with a bravura Steadicam shot in this director's best style, but quickly spiralling into absurdity.

SCR David Koepp   **CIN** Stephen H. Burum   **MUS** Ryuichi Sakamoto   **DES** Anne Pritchard   **ED** Bill Pankow   **PROD** Brian de Palma   **DIST** Buena Vista/DeBart

66 This director has evolved into a cinematic serial killer of common sense. – *Owen Gleiberman, Entertainment Weekly*

66 It's the worst kind of bad film: the kind that gets you all worked up and then lets you down, instead of just being lousy from the first shot. – *Roger Ebert, Chicago Sun-Times*

† Will Smith turned down the role eventually played by Gary Sinise.

† Not to be confused with the 1993 Abel Ferrara film starring Madonna and Harvey Keitel, which carries the same title in many territories, but is more widely known as Dangerous Game.

'Sit back. Relax. Enjoy the fright.'

Snakes on a Plane ★

DIR David R. Ellis
2006   105m   US/Germany
DVD   ♬
☆ Samuel L. Jackson (Neville Flynn), Julianna Margulies (Claire Miller), Nathan Phillips (Sean Jones), Bobby Cannavale (Hank Harris), Flex Alexander (Three G's), Todd Louiso (Dr. Steven Price)

A consignment of poisonous snakes causes havoc on a commercial airliner.

A film that began as a joke ends up having the last laugh: a trashy slice of knowing exploitation with the good sense to acknowledge the banality of its concept.

SCR John Heffernan, Sebastian Gutierrez **CIN** Adam Greenberg **MUS** Trevor Rabin **DES** Jaymes Hinkle **ED** Howard E. Smith **PROD** Gary Levinsohn, Don Granger, Craig Berenson **DIST** Entertainment

NEVILLE FLYNN: 'Enough is enough! I have had it with these motherf**king snakes on this motherf**king plane!'

66 An entertaining B-movie gleefully stuffed with bad tough-guy dialogue, obvious stock characters, cheap titillation and lots and lots of snake attacks. – *Tim Grierson, Screen International*

66 Of its kind, the movie's surprisingly good. – *Philip French, Observer*

† The producers took advantage of pre-release internet interest, inviting suggestions for scenes and dialogue before bringing the cast back for re-shoots. Contrary to expectations, however, the film underperformed at the US box-office, grossing only half of what had been predicted in its opening weekend.

† Samuel L. Jackson accepted his role without reading the script on the basis of the title alone. When New Line Cinema changed it to Pacific Air Flight 121, he threatened to pull out unless they changed it back.

'We could tell you what it's about. But then, of course, we would have to kill you.'

Sneakers ★★★

DIR *Phil Alden Robinson*
1992   126m   US
DVD   ♫

☆ Robert Redford (Martin 'Marty' Bishop), Dan Aykroyd (Mother), Ben Kingsley (Cosmo), Mary McDonnell (Liz), River Phoenix (Carl Arbegast), Sidney Poitier (Donald Crease), David Strathairn (Erwin 'Whistler' Emory), James Earl Jones (NSA Agent Bernard Abbott), Stephen Tobolowsky (Dr. Werner Brandes)

A ragtag group of security analysts are pressured by the government into stealing a top-secret black box from a former partner in crime.

Droll, light-hearted thriller with a likeable cast all enjoying themselves.

SCR Phil Alden Robinson, Lawrence Lasker, Walter F. Parkes **CIN** John Lindley **MUS** *James Horner* **DES** Patrizia von Brandenstein **ED** Tom Rolf **PROD** Walter F. Parkes, Lawrence Lasker **DIST** UIP/Universal

66 A highly polished film that gives the caper comedy tradition a thorough work-out, and never puts the brain cells to sleep. – *Geoff Brown, The Times*

'Sometimes stopping is the most important part of the journey. . .'

Snow Cake ★★

DIR Marc Evans
2006   111m   UK/Canada/Natherlands
DVD

☆ Alan Rickman (Alex Hughes), *Sigourney Weaver* (Linda Freeman), Carrie-Anne Moss (Maggie), Emily Hampshire

(Vivienne Freeman), Callum Keith Rennie (John Neil), James Allodi (Clyde)

A middle-aged British man on a Canadian road trip finds it hard to leave an autistic woman after informing her of her daughter's death.

A delicate chamber piece with a stand-out performance from Weaver that recalls Dustin Hoffman's in Rain Man.

SCR Angela Pell **CIN** Steve Cosens **MUS** Broken Social Scene **DES** Matthew Davies **ED** Marguerite Arnold **PROD** Gina Carter, Jessica Daniel, Andrew Eaton, Niv Fichman **DIST** Momentum Pictures

66 The film's main flaw is that Angela Pell's script, though sometimes pleasantly acidic, often lays on the quirkiness with a trowel. – *Jonathan Romney, Screen International*

Snow White and the Seven Dwarfs ★★★

1937   82m   US
DVD   ♫

☆ the voices of Adriana Caselotti, Harry Stockwell, Lucille La Verne, Billy Gilbert

An animated fairy tale featuring a princess, a wicked queen, and a handsome prince.

Disney's first feature cartoon was a mammoth enterprise which no one in the business thought would work. The romantic leads were wishy-washy but the splendid songs and the marvellous comic and villainous characters turned the film into a worldwide box-office bombshell which remains almost as fresh as when it was made.

SCR Ted Sears, Otto Englander, Earl Hurd, Dorothy Ann Blank, Richard Creedon, Dick Richard, Merrill de Maris, Webb Smith, from the fairy tale by the brothers Grimm **MUS** Frank Churchill, Leigh Harline, Paul Smith **DIST** Walt Disney

66 The first full-length animated feature, the turning point in Disney's career, a milestone in film history, and a great film. – *Leonard Maltin*

† 'Bluddle-Uddle-Um-Dum'; 'Heigh Ho'; 'I'm Wishing'; 'One Song'; 'Some Day My Prince Will Come'; 'Whistle While You Work'; 'With a Smile and a Song'

⚲ Special Award to Walt Disney for 'a significant screen innovation'. He was given one Oscar and seven miniature statuettes.

⚲ Frank Churchill, Leigh Harline, Paul Smith

'All that glitter . . . All that glamour . . . All that dirt.'

Soapdish ★

DIR Michael Hoffman
1991   97m   US
DVD   ♫

☆ Sally Field (Celeste Talbert/Maggie), Kevin Kline (Jeffrey Anderson/Dr. Rod Randall), Robert Downey Jnr (David Seton Barnes), Whoopi Goldberg (Rose Schwartz), Carrie Fisher (Betsy Faye Sharon), Cathy Moriarty (Montana Moorehead/Nurse Nan), Teri Hatcher (Ariel Maloney/Dr. Monica Demonico), Paul Johansson (Blair Brennan/Bolt), Elisabeth Shue (Lori Craven/Angelique), Garry Marshall (Edmund Edwards)

DVD Available on DVD   ☆ Cast in order   66 Critics' Quotes   ⚲ Academy Award   BAFTA
♫ Soundtrack on CD   of importance   † Points of interest   ⚲ Academy Award nomination   BAFTA nomination

569

A soap-opera queen finds her position threatened by a jealous co-star, who arranges for the old flame she had fired from the show to make a comeback.

Broad behind-the-scenes parody of a daytime American TV soap, not a bad time, but pushing the tone too far into frenzied histrionics.

SCR Robert Harling, Andrew Bergman   CIN Ueli Steiger
MUS Alan Silvestri   DES Eugenio Zanetti   ED Garth Craven   PROD Aaron Spelling, Alan Greisman
DIST UIP/Paramount

66 A treat for the thinking addict. – *Alexander Walker, Evening Standard*

66 Come back Dynasty, all is forgiven. – *Colette Maude, Time Out*

Sofie ★

DIR Liv Ullmann
1992   152m   Denmark/Norway/Sweden
DVD

☆ Karen-Lise Mynster (Sofie), Ghita Norby (Frederikke), Erland Josephson (Sofie's Father), Jesper Christensen (Hojby), Torben Zeller (Jonas), Henning Moritzen (Frederick Philipson), Stig Hoffmeyer (Gottlieb), Kirsten Rolffes (Jonas' Mother)

In late 19th-century Denmark, a Jewish couple urge their daughter to spurn her Gentile lover and marry her unstable cousin.

This was Liv Ullmann's debut as a feature-film director, and unsurprisingly Ingmar Bergman's influence is writ large. It's a richly textured saga of assimilation (represented by Sofie's meek parents) and rebellion, suppressed in Sofie's case, acted upon by her son. High-minded, austere, faintly bleak and overlong, it represents a strand of European art-house cinema that was just passing its peak.

SCR Liv Ullmann, Peter Poulsen   CIN Jörgen Persson
DES Peter Hoimark   ED Grete Moldrup   PROD Lars Kolvig   DIST Arrow/Nordisk/Norsk/Svensk Filmindustri

66 Ullmann's original script was just over eight hours long, and it feels as though she's expanded rather than cut it. – *Ben Thompson, Sight & Sound*

'There are some places man is not ready to go.'

Solaris ★★★

SCR/DIR *Steven Soderbergh*
2002   99m   US
DVD   ♫

☆ George Clooney (Dr. Chris Kelvin), Natascha McElhone (Rheya), Jeremy Davies (Snow), Viola Davis (Dr. Helen Gordon), Ulrich Tukur (Gibarian)

A widowed psychologist is sent to a remote space-station to investigate unexplained phenomena, and receives visits from his dead wife.

Fascinating remake of Tarkovsky's philosophical space parable, in many ways improving on it with a crystalline economy, and offering a traumatic post-mortem on a failed relationship.

CIN *Peter Andrews (Steven Soderbergh)*   MUS *Cliff Martinez*   DES *Philip Messina*   ED Mary Ann Bernard (Steven Soderbergh)   PROD James Cameron, Rae

Sanchini, Jon Landau   DIST TCF

66 A real, repeatable experience, a likely cult movie for decades to come. – *John Patterson, Guardian*

66 Beneath a pretence of profundity, we get meaningless ambiguity. – *Edward Porter, Sunday Times*

† Clooney said of the film: "Solaris? It's a bomb. The great thing was, Fox agreed to make it but they didn't commit to the idea of how to sell it. You make a $47 million art film, and you have to agree that's the film you've made and not mislead and not steal opening weekend. That's always dangerous. They sold it on me being naked and the ratings board being upset. Such a dumb thing to do. They sold it as a space film, which it isn't. It wasn't just that it bombed, people hated it. So we were playing to the wrong audience, that's what that tells you." Solaris grossed just $14.97 million in the US.

'The planet where nightmares come true. . .'

Solaris ★★★

DIR Andrei Tarkovsky
1972   165m   USSR
DVD   ♫

☆ Natalya Bondarchuk (Harey), Donatas Banionis (Kris), Yuri Yarvet (Snaut), Anatoli Sonlonitsin (Sartorius)

A psychologist is sent to investigate the many deaths in a space station orbiting a remote planet.

Heavy-going but highly imaginative space fiction in which the menaces are ghosts materialized from the subjects' guilty pasts. The technology is superbly managed, but it is all somewhat ponderous.

SCR Andrei Tarkovsky, Friedrich Gorenstein   CIN Vadim Yusov   MUS Eduard Artemyev   DIST Mosfilm

'Their tragedy was to fall in love.'

Solomon and Gaenor ★★

SCR/DIR *Paul Morrison*
1998   102m   GB
DVD

☆ *Ioan Gruffudd (Solomon Levinsky), Nia Roberts (Gaenor Rees), Sue Jones Davies (Gwen), William Thomas (Idris Rees), Mark Lewis Jones (Crad Rees), Maureen Lipman (Rezl), David Horovitch (Isaac), Cyril Shaps (Ephraim)*

In the Welsh valleys in 1911, a Jewish door-to-door salesman and a young woman from a chapel-going family fall in love, causing ructions in their families.

It's rather more than Romeo and Juliet in the Rhondda, as Morrison's script describes racial prejudice in the valleys as well as the families' opposition. Well-acted, directed and photographed, it's a sufficiently mature work not to strain for an artificially upbeat resolution.

CIN *Nina Kellgren*   MUS Ilona Sekacz   DES Hayden Pearce   ED Kant Pan   PROD *Sheryl Crown*
DIST Film4/S4C/Arts Council/APT

66 Its pleasures aren't so much in the inevitable plot complications, but in the passion of the performances and the spare beauty of the elegant framing and photography. – *Stephen Hunter, Washington Post*

† It was filmed in both English and Welsh.

⚱ foreign film

S

'The movie too HOT for words!'

Some Like It Hot ★★★★

DIR *Billy Wilder*

1959 122m US

DVD ♫

☆ *Jack Lemmon* (Jerry/Daphne), *Tony Curtis* (Joe/Josephine), *Marilyn Monroe* (Sugar Kane), *Joe E. Brown* (Osgood E. Fielding III), George Raft (Spats Columbo), Pat O'Brien (Mulligan), Nehemiah Persoff (Little Bonaparte), George E. Stone (Toothpick Charlie), Joan Shawlee (Sweet Sue)

Two unemployed musicians accidentally witness the St Valentine's Day Massacre and flee to Miami disguised as girl musicians.

A milestone of film comedy which keeps its central situation alive with constant and fresh invention; its wit, combined with a sense of danger, has rarely been duplicated and never equalled.

SCR *Billy Wilder, I. A. L. Diamond* CIN Charles Lang Jnr MUS Adolph Deutsch ED Arthur P. Schmidt PROD Billy Wilder DIST UA/Mirisch

CLOSING LINE: OSGOOD: Well . . . nobody's perfect.

⚱ Orry-Kelly (costume design)

⚱ Jack Lemmon (leading actor); Billy Wilder (direction); Billy Wilder, I.A.L. Diamond (adapted screenplay); Charles Lang Jnr; art direction

Ⓣ Jack Lemmon (leading actor)

'Between love and loyalty... Between life and death... Lies a choice no mother should have to make.'

Some Mother's Son ★

DIR Terry George

1996 112m US/Ireland

♫

☆ *Helen Mirren* (Kathleen Quigley), Fionnula Flanagan (Annie Higgins), Aiden Gillen (Gerard Quigley), David O'Hara (Frank Higgins), John Lynch (Bobby Sands), Tom Hollander (Farnsworth), Tim Woodward (Harrington), Ciaran Hinds (Danny Boyle)

A widowed pacifist teacher in Northern Ireland is shocked to learn her son is involved with the IRA, but supports him when he is arrested, jailed and goes on hunger strike.

Based on a script that falls just short of propaganda, the film is saved by Mirren's unsparing portrait of a woman whose blood ties trump her political outlook.

SCR Terry George, Jim Sheridan CIN Geoffrey Simpson MUS Bill Whelan DES David Wilson ED Craig McKay PROD Jim Sheridan, Arthur Lappin, Edward Burke DIST Rank/Castle Rock/Turner/Hell's Kitchen

66 The film-makers are able to honour the memory of the hunger strikers without becoming bogged down in the settling of old scores. – *Geoffrey Macnab, Sight & Sound*

Someone Else (new)

DIR Col Spector

2007 78m UK

☆ Stephen Mangan (David), Susan Lynch (Lisa), Lara Belmont (Nina), John Henshaw (Paul)

A commitment-phobic man (Mangan) dumps his girl-friend (Lynch) for a younger woman, who then goes off with another man.

In this morose little fable, every dramatic sequence fizzles and every comic scene falls flat. Impossible to recommend.

SCR Col Spector, Radha Chakraborty CIN Trevor Forrest DES Clive Howard ED Matthew McKinnon PROD Radha Chakraborty DIST Soda

'He's a streetwise cop who just made detective. She's a stunning sophisticate who just saw a murder. A killer is the only thing they had in common. Until tonight.'

Someone to Watch Over Me ★

DIR Ridley Scott

1987 106m US

DVD

☆ Tom Berenger (Det. Mike Keegan), Mimi Rogers (Claire Gregory), Lorraine Bracco (Ellie Keegan), Jerry Orbach (Lt. Garber), John Rubinstein (Neil Steinhart), Andreas Katsulas (Joey Venza)

A married New York cop falls for a socialite who witnessed a murder.

Competent if forgettable thriller, mainly an excuse for Scott's ornate command of atmosphere.

SCR Howard Franklin CIN Steven Poster MUS Michael Kamen DES Jim Bissell ED Claire Simpson PROD Thierry de Ganay, Harold Schneider DIST Columbia/Thierry de Ganay

66 The haze is so thick, you'll need to bring a defogger. – *Rita Kempley, Washington Post*

'Love can turn you upside down.'

Somersault ★

SCR/DIR Cate Shortland

2004 106m Australia

DVD ♫

☆ *Abbie Cornish* (Heidi), Damian de Montemas (Adam), Olivia Pigeot (Nicole), Alex Babic (Brian the barman)

An Australian teenager runs away from home after a fling with her mother's boyfriend.

Moody but unpersuasive drama of disaffected adolescence, with a promising lead performance.

CIN Robert Humphreys MUS Decoder Ring DES Melinda Doring ED Scott Gray PROD Anthony Anderson

66 Less than the sum of its parts. – *Peter Bradshaw, Guardian*

'A story about husbands, wives, parents, children and other natural disasters.'

Something to Talk About ★

DIR Lasse Hallström

1995 106m US

DVD ♫

☆ *Julia Roberts* (Grace King Bichon), Dennis Quaid (Eddie Bichon), Robert Duvall (Wyly King), Gena Rowlands (Georgia King), *Kyra Sedgwick* (Emma Rae King), Brett Cullen (Jamie Johnson), Haley Aull (Caroline 'Doodlebug' Bichon), Muse Watson (Hank Corrigan)

DVD Available on DVD ☆ Cast in order ⁶⁶ Critics' Quotes ⚱ Academy Award Ⓑ BAFTA
♫ Soundtrack on CD of importance † Points of interest ⚱ Academy Award nomination Ⓣ BAFTA nomination

571

In a southern US state, a wife who manages the family's successful riding stable learns her husband has been having an affair – and is appalled when her parents urge her to patch things up.

An amusing character piece that feels faintly unreal. The behaviour of every character but one (Roberts's feisty sister, played gloriously by Sedgwick) seems artificial and contrived. It's also curious to see Roberts, at the peak of her stardom, opting for an ensemble role. Yet there's a polish and touch of class here, with Duvall and Rowlands using their long experience to great effect. It's a film one can like without being able to justify why.

SCR Callie Khouri   **CIN** Sven Nykvist   **MUS** Hans Zimmer, Graham Preskett   **DES** Mel Bourne   **ED** Mia Goldman   **PROD** Anthea Sylbert, Paula Weinstein   **DIST** Warner/Spring Creek

66 On its own pointedly reduced terms, it's an honest job. – *Peter Matthews, Sight & Sound*

'She knew his face. His touch. His voice. She knew everything about him . . . But the truth.'

Sommersby ★

DIR Jon Amiel
1993   114m   US/France
DVD   ♫

☆ Richard Gere (John Robert 'Jack' Sommersby), Jodie Foster (Laurel Sommersby), Bill Pullman (Orin Meecham), James Earl Jones (Judge Barry Conrad Issacs), Lanny Flaherty (Buck), William Windom (Reverend Powell), Wendell Wellman (Travis), Brett Kelley (Little Rob)

A missing-in-action Civil War veteran returns home to his wife, but arouses suspicions about his identity.

Handsome costumer without any urgent need to unravel its central mystery.

SCR Nicholas Meyer, Sarah Kernochan   **CIN** Philippe Rousselot   **MUS** *Danny Elfman*   **DES** Bruno Rubeo   **ED** Peter Boyle   **PROD** Arnon Milchan, Steven Reuther   **DIST** Warner/Regency/Canal

66 Belles wring and bosoms heave in a manner most pleasing. – *Rita Kempley, Washington Post*
66 Unabashedly romantic and morally intricate. – *Variety*
† An English-language remake of the 1982 French film The Return of Martin Guerre.

Son Of Man (new) ★★

DIR Mark Dornford-May
2008   91m   South Africa/UK
☆ Andile Kosi (Jesus), Andries Mbali (Satan), Pauline Malefane (Mary), James Anthony (Gabriel)

A version of the Gospel story, set in a turbulent fictional African country wracked by civil war.

An imaginative re-telling of Christ's life and death, using mediaeval mystery plays as a template. Herod rules with a murderous, rifle-toting militia; Christ is conceived during a bloody attack on an infants' school. It's vivid storytelling that uses southern Africa's startling landscapes to terrific effect.

SCR Mark Dornford-May, Pauline Malefane, Andiswa Kedama   **PROD** Mark Dornford-May   **DIST** Spier Films
66 A thoughtful and stirring experiment. – *Tim Robey, Daily Telegraph*
66 It could as easily be footage from Rwanda or Darfur. – *Cath Clarke, Guardian*

'Make Believe. Not War.'

Son of Rambow (new) ★★★

SCR/DIR *Garth Jennings*
2008   95m   UK/France/Germany/US
☆ Bill Milner (Will Proudfoot), Will Poulter (Lee Carter), Jules Sitruk (Didier), Neil Dudgeon (Brother Joshua), Jessica Stevenson (Mary Proudfoot)

Two very different boys at the same school in 1982 form an unlikely alliance. One is from a sheltered religious family that shuns worldly pleasures, including books, music and TV; the other, badly-behaved, is from a broken home and makes bizarre home movies. Together they embark on a low-tech home video remake of Sly Stallone's First Blood.

Winning, utterly charming British film that wears its modest budget and ambitions on its sleeve; in describing the ups and downs of unlikely friendship, it tips its hat to the film-makers' own early experiments in the creative arena.

CIN Jess Hall   **MUS** Joby Talbot   **DES** Joel Collins   **ED** Dominic Leung   **PROD** Nick Goldsmith   **DIST** Optimum

66 A sweet, slight and vaguely disappointing movie. – *Tim Robey, Daily Telegraph*

'He's Japan's best kept secret – unleashed on America for the first time.'

Sonatine ★

SCR/DIR Takeshi Kitano
1993   94m   Japan
DVD

☆ 'Beat' Takeshi (Takeshi Kitano) (Aniki Murakawa), Aya Kokumai (Miyuki), Tetsu Watanabe (Uechi), Masanobu Katsumura (Ryoji), Susumu Terashima (Ken), Ren Ohsugi (Katagiri), Tonbo Zushi (Kitajima), Kenichi Yajima (Takahashi)

A world-weary Yakusa gangster, sent to settle a gang war in Okinawa, realises he has been set up.

Sometimes violent, more often languid gangster movie with a somewhat pretentious quality.

CIN Katsumi Yanagishima   **MUS** Joe Hisaishi   **ED** Takeshi Kitano   **PROD** Masayuki Mori, Hisao Nabeshima, Takio Yoshida   **DIST** ICA/Bandai/Shochiku Dai-ichi Kogyo

66 Ends up stepping in knee-jerk nihilism. – *Sam Adams, Philadelphia City Paper*

Songs From the Second Floor ★★★

SCR/DIR *Roy Andersson*
2000   98m   Sweden/France/Denmark/Norway/Germany
DVD

☆ Lars Nordh (Kalle), Stefan Larsson (Stefan), Torbjörn

Fahlström (Pelle Wigert), Sten Andersson (Lasse), Lucio Vucina (Magician), Hanna Eriksson (Mia), Peter Roth (Tomas), Tommy Johansson (Uffe), Sture Olsson (Sven)

In a nameless European city, a man burns down his own furniture store for the insurance money, while other individuals shuffle their way through bizarre situations.

Astonishingly barbed vignettes of personal despair and white-collar alienation, shot like deadpan comedy sketches despite their often morbid content – a magician accidentally saws into his volunteer's stomach, and a young child is ritually pushed off a cliff. It is a brilliantly original, if bleak, work.

CIN *Istvan Borbas, Jesper Klevenas, Robert Komarek* MUS Benny Andersson ED Roy Andersson PROD Lisa Alwert, Roy Andersson DIST ICA

66 Depressive, slow, darkly funny, unyielding in its formal rigor, and unsettlingly beautiful. – *Ty Burr, Boston Globe*

66 Very funny and very despairing. – *Nigel Andrews, Financial Times*

Sons of the Desert ★★★★

DIR *William A. Seiter*
1934 68m US
DVD

☆ *Stan Laurel* (Himself), *Oliver Hardy* (Himself), *Charley Chase* (Himself), Mae Busch (Mrs. Lottie Chase Hardy), Dorothy Christie (Mrs. Betty Laurel), Lucien Littlefield (Dr. Horace Meddick)

Laurel and Hardy want to go to a Chicago convention, but kid their wives that they are going on a cruise for health reasons.

Archetypal Stan and Ollie comedy, unsurpassed for gags, pacing and sympathetic characterization.

SCR *Frank Craven, Byron Morgan* CIN Kenneth Peach ED Bert Jordan DIST Hal Roach

The Son's Room ★★★★

DIR *Nanni Moretti*
2001 99m Italy/France
DVD ♫

☆ Nanni Moretti (Giovanni), Laura Morante (Paola), Jasmine Trinca (Irene), Giuseppe Sanfelice (Andrea), Claudia Della Seta (Raffaella), Stefano Accorsi (Tommaso), Sofia Vigliar (Arianna)

A close-knit family unit begins to unravel when the teenage son dies in an accident.

Subtle, gentle study of bereavement, sharp on the distinction between public and private grief, that mixes its director's usual wry humour with a new-found profundity: the results are both funny and sad, but always lively and inquisitive. Its ending is all the more moving for being discreet and understated.

SCR Linda Ferri, Nanni Moretti, Heidrun Schleef CIN Giuseppe Lanci MUS Nicola Piovani DES Giancarlo Basili ED Esmeralda Calabria PROD Angelo Barbagallo, Nanni Moretti, Lorenzo Luccarini, Vincenzo Galluzzo, Federico Fabrizio DIST Momentum

66 Isn't bold or daring, but it is delicately distinctive; it's the kind of picture that stirs subterranean rumbles of empathy in us rather than flashy, gushing waves. – *Stephanie Zacharek, Salon*

66 This affecting and beautiful film really is a very accomplished piece of work from Moretti, superbly acted, refreshingly direct and blessed with an ingenious, unexpected final act. – *Peter Bradshaw, Guardian*

'In 1943, one young woman stood up to the Nazis, her courage made her a legend, this is her story.'

Sophie Scholl: The Final Days ★

DIR Marc Rothemund
2005 117m Germany/France
DVD

☆ *Julia Jentsch* (Sophie Scholl), Alexander Held (Robert Mohr), Fabian Hinrichs (Hans Scholl), Johanna Gastdorf (Else Gebel), André Hennicke (Richter Dr Roland Freisler)

In 1943, the anti-Nazi protester Sophie Scholl and her brother are arrested and tried for distributing pamphlets in Munich.

Creditably acted account of a famous resistance figure's last days, but one which is too stolid and stagey to add up to more.

SCR Fred Breinersdorfer CIN Martin Langer MUS Johnny Klimek, Reinhold Heil DES Jana Karen-Brey ED Hans Funck PROD Chistoph Muller, Sven Burgemeister, Fred Breinersdorfer, Marc Rothemund DIST ICA

66 Instils respect for the Scholl of history, but not a direct fascination with the young woman on the screen. – *Edward Porter, Sunday Times*

† Julia Jentsch won the Silver Bear for Best Actress at the Berlin Film Festival in 2005.

⅃ foreign film

Le Souffle ★

SCR/DIR Damien Odoul
2001 77m France
DVD

☆ Pierre-Louis Bonnetblanc (David), Dominique Chevalier (Jacques), Maxime Dalbrut (Paul), Jean-Claude Lecante (Jean-Claude), Jean Milord (M'sieur Milord), Stéphane Terpereau (Stef), Laurent Simon (Matthieu)

A bored teenager is forced to spend a summer on his uncle on a ramshackle farm, a setting that lacks excitement for him.

Rites-of-passage drama in a rural setting, in which a bored teenager lets rip, with drunken and sadistic behaviour that mirrors that of the boozy, gluttonous farmhands. The ugliness of their actions is contrasted with the beauty of the surroundings, which are conveyed in visually poetic terms. It's a one-off: not what one might call enjoyable, but striking nonetheless.

CIN Pascale Granel DES Hélène Melani ED Gwenola Heaulme PROD Gérard Lacroix, Gérard Pont, Edgard Tenenbaum DIST Metro Tartan

66 Even with so much beauty to please the eye, a person will eventually question the purpose of a film in which

DVD Available on DVD ☆ Cast in order 66 Critics' Quotes ⅃ Academy Award Ⓑ BAFTA
♫ Soundtrack on CD of importance † Points of interest ⅃ Academy Award nomination Ⓣ BAFTA nomination

573

S

violence engenders in its perpetrator no apparent emotion, not even pleasure. – *Ryan Gilbey, Sight & Sound*

'The Happiest Sound In All The World!'

The Sound of Music ★★★

DIR *Robert Wise*
1965   172m   US
[DVD]   ♫

☆ *Julie Andrews* (Maria), *Christopher Plummer* (Capt. Von Trapp), Richard Haydn (Max Detweiler), Eleanor Parker (The Baroness), *Peggy Wood* (Mother Abbess), Anna Lee (Sister Margaretta), Marni Nixon (Sister Sophia)

In 1938 Austria, a trainee nun becomes governess to the Trapp family, falls in love with the widower father, and helps them all escape from the Nazis.

Slightly muted, very handsome version of an enjoyably old-fashioned stage musical, with a host of splendid songs. Hugely successful for a reason: it is custom-built to please.

SCR Ernest Lehman   **CIN** *Ted McCord*   **DES** *Boris Leven*
ED William Reynolds   **PROD** Robert Wise
DIST TCF/Argyle

66 …sufficient warning to those allergic to singing nuns and sweetly innocent children. – *John Gillett*

† 'The Sound of Music'; 'Morning Hymn'; 'Alleluia'; 'Maria'; 'I Have Confidence In Me'; 'Sixteen Going on Seventeen'; 'My Favorite Things'; 'Do-Re-Mi'; 'The Lonely Goatherd'; 'Edelweiss'; 'So Long Farewell'; 'Climb Every Mountain'; 'Something Good'

⚊ picture; Robert Wise; Irwin Kostal (music)
⚊ Julie Andrews (leading actress); Peggy Wood (supporting actress); Ted McCord (cinematography)

'A hilarious comedy from the co-creator of "Seinfeld"'

Sour Grapes

SCR/DIR Larry David
1998   91m   US
[DVD]

☆ Steven Weber (Evan Maxwell), Craig Bierko (Richie Maxwell), Matt Keeslar (Danny Pepper), Karen Sillas (Joan), Robyn Peterman (Roberta), Viola Harris (Selma Maxwell), Orlando Jones (Digby), Jennifer Leigh Warren (Millie)

When a man hits the $400,000 slots jackpot at a casino, his cousin insists he deserves half, having lent him the quarters to play.

A barely-released rarity with one overwhelming point of interest: it's the sole venture into feature films of Larry David, co-creator of the peerless Seinfeld and writer-star of the acidly comic TV series Curb Your Enthusiasm. You'd expect great things, but it's alarmingly mixed, with the few amusing moments adrift in a sea of stale plotting.

CIN Victor Hammer   **DES** Charles Rosen   **ED** Priscilla Nedd-Friendly   **PROD** Laurie Lennard
DIST Columbia/Castle Rock

66 Provides dispiriting evidence that material rooted in the conventions of the 22-minute TV sitcom is not easily

accommodated to the expanses of a feature film. – *Andy Richards, Sight & Sound*

'Warning: This movie will warp your fragile little minds.'

South Park: Bigger Longer & Uncut ★★★

DIR Trey Parker
1999   81m   US
[DVD]   ♫

☆ voices of: Matt Stone, Trey Parker, Mary Kay Bergman, Isaac Hayes, George Clooney, Brent Spiner, Minnie Driver, Eric Idle

Discovering that their children have snuck into an R-rated Canadian comedy and learned to swear, the mothers of South Park incite a war against Canada.

Breathtakingly rude satire on America's culture of censorship, a step up in every department from the TV show. It is wickedly funny from the first musical number, and the sequences with Satan and Saddam Hussein as homosexual lovers in Hell hit a peak of surreal invention. For all the crude animation, it may be the one essential American film musical of its decade.

SCR *Trey Parker, Matt Stone, Pam Brady*   **MUS** Marc Shaiman, James Hetfield   **ED** John Venzon   **PROD** Trey Parker, Matt Stone   **DIST** Paramount/Warner

66 So gleefully vulgar, it's tough not to get on all fours and beg for more. – *John Anderson, L.A. Times*

66 Their assault on pop-culture pieties can be as acidly funny as it is indiscriminate and offensive. – *Rod Dreyer, New York Post*

† Unsurprisingly, the film was banned in Iraq.
† Mountain Town; Uncle Fucka; Wendy's Song; It's Easy Mmmkay; Hell Isn't Good; Blame Canada; Kyle's Mom's a Bitch; What Would Brian Boitano Do?; Up There; I Can Change; I'm Super; Eyes of a Child

⚊ Trey Parker, Marc Shaiman (music, original song – Blame Canada)

'No Ordinary Day Trip.'

South West Nine ★

DIR Richard Parry
2001   90m   GB/Ireland
[DVD]

☆ Wil Johnson (Freddy), Stuart Laing (Jake), Mark Letheren (Mitch), Amelia Curtis (Kat), Orlessa Edwards (Helen), Nicola Stapleton (Sal), Frank Harper (Douser)

A Brixton drug dealer organises a rave in a disused church to pay off his debts.

Promising look at a multicultural underclass in a melting-pot area of London; but it's hard to get too involved, and the rave sequence sends the film into a druggy trance for its duration.

SCR Richard Parry, Steve North   **CIN** Graham Fowler
DES Rob Lunn   **ED** Christine Pancott   **PROD** Allan Niblo
DIST Fruit Salad

66 A comedy-thriller with its own two-way get-out clause: the "comedy" excusing the absence of plausible thrills, and the "thriller" acting as an alibi for the lack of laughs. – *Peter Bradshaw, Guardian*

[DVD] Available on DVD   ☆ Cast in order of importance   66 Critics' Quotes   ⚊ Academy Award   🏆 BAFTA
♫ Soundtrack on CD   † Points of interest   ⚊ Academy Award nomination   🏆 BAFTA nomination

66 A colourful and energetic work. – *Jason Solomons, Observer*

ⓣ Richard Parry (promising newcomer)

'Have a nice apocalypse.'

Southland Tales ⓝⓔⓦ

SCR/DIR Richard Kelly
2007   144m   US
♫

☆ Dwayne Johnson (Boxer Santaros), Seann William Scott (Roland Taverner/Ronald Taverner), Sarah Michelle Gellar (Krysta Kapowski/Krysta Now), Nora Dunn (Cyndi Pinziki), Christopher Lambert (Walter Mung), John Larroquette (Vaughn Smallhouse), Bai Ling (Serpentine), Jon Lovitz (Bart Bookman), Mandy Moore (Madeline Frost Santaros), Miranda Richardson (Nana Mae Frost), Justin Timberlake (Abilene)

Various individuals scattered across Los Angeles hold the key to the end of the world.

An incomprehensible folly from the director of Donnie Darko whose aims remain a mystery known only to him; its fleeting moments of inventive satire are not worth enduring the shamefully self-indulgent whole.

CIN Steven Poster   MUS Moby   DES Alexander Hammond   ED Sam Bauer   PROD Sean McKittrick, Bo Hyde, Kendall Morgan, Matthew Rhodes   DIST Universal

KRYSTA NOW: 'Scientists are saying the future is going to be far more futuristic then they originally predicted.'

66 A pretentious, overreaching, fatally unfocused fantasy about American fascism, radical rebellion, nuclear terrorism and apocalypse. – *Todd McCarthy, Variety*

66 One of those rare, impossible oddities that cinema would be poorer without. – *Jonathan Crocker, Time Out*

† The film was originally screened at the 2006 Cannes Film Festival in a version running 160 minutes that drew almost universal derision.
† The film is divided into three sections – Temptation Waits, Memory Gospel and Wave of Mutilation.
† Three comic-book 'prequels' were published in the run-up to the film's US release.

'Dreams are the only thing worth fighting for.'

Southpaw ★★

DIR Liam McGrath
1998   79m   Ireland/GB
DVD

☆ Francis Barrett, Chick Gillen, Tom Humphries, Colum Flynn, Nicolas Cruz Hernandez, Gerry Callan, Jim McGee, Eamonn Hunt (narrator)

An account of the surprising rise of a young Irish boxer from a family of travellers. He represents his country at the 1996 Atlanta Olympics, where he carries the Irish flag at the opening ceremony.

A restrained, thoughtful documentary about a young man's exposure to sporting glory and celebrity, for which nothing in his humble background prepared him.

CIN Cian De Buitlear   MUS Dario Marianelli   ED James E. Dalton   PROD Paddy Breathnach, Robert Walpole

66 That same irrepressible enthusiasm he shows in the ring is what makes him such an engaging subject. – *Geoffrey Macnab, Sight & Sound*

'Space Will Never Be The Same.'

Space Cowboys ★★

DIR Clint Eastwood
2000   130m   US/Australia
DVD   ♫

☆ Clint Eastwood (Frank Corvin), Tommy Lee Jones (Hawk Hawkins), Donald Sutherland (Jerry O'Neill), James Garner (Tank Sullivan), James Cromwell (Bob Gerson), Marcia Gay Harden (Sara Holland), William Devane (Eugene Davis), Loren Dean (Ethan Grace), Courtney B. Vance (Roger Hines), Barbara Babcock (Barbara Corvin), Rade Sherbedgia (General Vostov), Blair Brown (Dr. Anne Caruthers)

A retired engineer and his old test-pilot colleagues are sent into space to fix a degraded Russian satellite.

Fond Howard Hawks-style geriatric adventure with the stars gruffly proving they've still got what it takes; thanks to state-of-the-art special effects, it's a pleasing blend of old and new.

SCR Ken Kaufman, Howard Klausner   CIN Jack N. Green   MUS Lennie Niehaus, Clint Eastwood   DES Henry Bumstead   ED Joel Cox   PROD Clint Eastwood, Andrew Lazar   DIST Warner

66 A solid, professionally paced salute to grey power. – *Xan Brooks, Guardian*

66 Eastwood works the crowd better than he has in years. – *Wesley Morris, San Francisco Examiner*

⚲ Alan Robert Murray and Bub Asman (sound editing)

'Can you really trust anyone?'

The Spanish Prisoner ★★

SCR/DIR David Mamet
1997   110m   US
DVD

☆ Campbell Scott (Joseph A. 'Joe' Ross), Rebecca Pidgeon (Susan Ricci), Steve Martin (Julian 'Jimmy' Dell), Ricky Jay (George Lang), Ben Gazzara (Mr. Klein), Felicity Huffman (Pat McCune), Ed O'Neill (FBI Team Leader)

A scientist invents a potentially priceless formula and instantly becomes intensely suspicious about whether he can trust his friends, colleagues and acquaintances.

A film that, like Mamet's earlier House of Games, hinges on scams, con tricks and double bluffs. Much of the pleasure for the audience lies in knowing that they too are being conned by the plot. For all that, it's more clever and intricate than substantial.

CIN Gabriel Beristain   MUS Carter Burwell   DES Tim Galvin   ED Barbara Tulliver   PROD Jean Doumanian   DIST Sweetland

66 Completely engaging from start to finish. – *Chris Grunden, Film Journal International*

66 The problem with The Spanish Prisoner is not so much, as one character says, 'If I told you this story, would

DVD Available on DVD   ☆ Cast in order of importance   66 Critics' Quotes   † Points of interest   ⚲ Academy Award   Academy Award nomination   ⓣ BAFTA   BAFTA nomination

575

you believe it?' as 'Even if you believed it, would you care? – *Kenneth Turan, Los Angeles Times*

'A Darkly Humorous Suburban Tale Creeping Beyond Normality. . .'

Spanking the Monkey ★★
SCR/DIR *David O. Russell*
1994 100m US
DVD

☆ Jeremy Davies (Ray Aibelli), *Alberta Watson* (Susan Aibelli), Benjamin Hendrickson (Tom Aibelli), Carlo Gallo (Toni Peck), Matthew Puckett (Nicky), Judette Jones (Aunt Helen)

A medical student spends the summer looking after his suicidal mother, who has broken her leg, and finds their level of physical intimacy disturbing.

A controlled and promising debut, treating the theme of potential incest quite seriously, in its black way.

CIN Michael Mayers MUS David Carbonara
DES Susan Block ED Pamela Martin PROD Dean Silvers DIST Metro Tartan/Buckeye/Swelter

66 A twisted suburban Oedipal knot seen through a sardonic, yet deeply involved eye. – *Marjorie Baumgarten, Austin Chronicle*

Sparkle (new) ★★
SCR/DIR Neil Hunter, Tom Hunsinger
2007 104m UK

☆ Stockard Channing (Sheila), Shaun Evans (Sam), Anthony Head (Tony), *Bob Hoskins* (Vince), Lesley Manville (Jill), Amanda Ryan (Kate)

Sam, 22, gets a job at a PR agency, sleeps with his boss, an older woman, then falls in love with a young girl, unaware she is his mistress's daughter.

Amiable comedy of manners, with a handful of amusing subplots. Bob Hoskins is excellent as the melancholic suitor of Sam's mother Jill, an aspiring lounge singer.

CIN Sean Van Hales MUS Adrian Johnston
DES Cristina Casali ED Martin Brinkler PROD Martin Pope, Michael Rose DIST Vertigo

66 Sparkle it doesn't, but it's well performed. – *Philip French, Observer*

66 A bittersweet joy. – *James Christopher, The Times*

Spartacus ★★★
DIR *Stanley Kubrick*
1960 196m US
DVD ♫

☆ *Kirk Douglas*, Laurence Olivier, Charles Laughton, Tony Curtis, Jean Simmons, Peter Ustinov, John Gavin, Nina Foch, Herbert Lom, John Ireland, John Dall, Charles McGraw, Woody Strode

A gladiator in ancient Rome sparks a slaves' revolt.

Long, well-made, downbeat epic, rather talky in its first half, but with deeper than usual characterization and several bravura sequences. About as good as the sword-and-sandals genre got in this era.

SCR Dalton Trumbo CIN *Russell Metty* MUS Alex North
DES Alexander Golitzen ED Robert Lawrence
PROD Edward Lewis DIST U-I/Bryna

66 One comes away feeling rather revolted and not at all ennobled. – *Alan Dent, Illustrated London News*

66 A lot of first-rate professionals have pooled their abilities to make a first-rate circus. – *Stanley Kauffmann*

⚐ Peter Ustinov (supporting actor); Russell Metty; art direction
⚑ Alex North; editing

'She's missing.'

Spartan ★
SCR/DIR David Mamet
2003 102m US/Germany
DVD

☆ Val Kilmer (Scott), Derek Luke (Curtis), William H. Macy (Stoddard), Ed O'Neill (Burch), Kristen Bell (Laura Newton), Said Taghmaoui (Tariq Asani), Linda Kimbrough (Donny), Tia Texada (Jackie)

The daughter of the US President is abducted and sold into a Middle-Eastern sex-slavery ring, and government agents track her down.

Initially intriguing thriller, with a political cover-up replacing the cons in Mamet's other films, but the mannered talk distracts and the formulaic ending is a bust.

CIN Juan Ruiz Anchia MUS Mark Isham DES Gemma Jackson ED Barbara Tulliver PROD Art Linson, Moshe Diamant, Elie Samaha, David Bergstein DIST Warner

66 When it's good, it's surprisingly gripping and fresh, and when it's bad, it's just another overcooked Hollywood paranoid thriller. – *Ty Burr, Boston Globe*

66 The macho one-liners are sufficiently adolescent to produce the desired snickers. – *Jonathan Rosenbaum, Chicago Reader*

'Get ready for rush hour.'

Speed ★★★
DIR *Jan de Bont*
1994 116m US
DVD ♫

☆ Keanu Reeves (Jack Traven), Dennis Hopper (Howard Payne), Sandra Bullock (Annie), Joe Morton (Captain McMahon), Jeff Daniels (Harry), Alan Ruck (Stephens), Glenn Plummer (Jaguar Owner), Richard Lineback (Norwood), Beth Grant (Helen), Hawthorne James (Sam), Carlos Carrasco (Ortiz)

A psychopath with a grudge against the LAPD plants a bomb on a bus, which will explode if the speedometer drops below 50 mph.

Living up to its title as an adrenalised thrill-ride, this set a benchmark for dumb fun at 1990s blockbusters, spinning enough hair-raising suspense out of its gimmicky scenario to satisfy perfectly on a popcorn level.

SCR Graham Yost CIN Andrzej Bartkowiak MUS Mike Mancina DES Jackson de Govia ED *John Wright*
PROD Mark Gordon DIST TCF

HOWARD PAYNE: Pop quiz, hotshot. There's a bomb on a bus. Once the bus goes 50 miles an hour, the bomb is armed. If it drops below 50, it blows up. What do you do? What do you do?

66 Executed with panache and utter conviction. – *Richard Schickel, Time*

66 Like The Wages of Fear redone at rollercoaster tempo. – *Owen Gleiberman, Entertainment Weekly*

⚐ Gregg Landaker, Steve Maslow, Bob Beemer, David R. R. MacMillan (sound); (Stephen Hunter Flick sound effects editing)

⚐ John Wright

🇹 John Wright

'From the creators of the Matrix trilogy comes a world built for speed.'

Speed Racer (new)

SCR/DIR Andy Wachowski, Larry Wachowski

2008   135m   US

♫

☆ Emile Hirsch (Speed Racer), Christina Ricci (Trixie), John Goodman (Pops Racer), Susan Sarandon (Mom Racer), Matthew Fox (Racer X), Benno Fürmann (Inspector Detector), Hiroyuki Sanada (Mr. Musha), Roger Allam (Royalton), Richard Roundtree (Ben Burns)

In a hi-tech future, a young race-car driver faces enemies on and off the track.

Visually arresting, dramatically incoherent fantasy, painted in primary colours; the result is more video game than film and is far too long for its target audience.

CIN David Tattersall   **MUS** Michael Giacchino **DES** Owen Paterson   **ED** Zach Staenberg, Roger Barton **PROD** Joel Silver, Grant Hill, Andy Wachowski, Larry Wachowski   **DIST** Warner Brothers

66 Its furious pace and movement make the Road Runner seem narcoleptic. – *Dave Calhoun, Time Out*

66 I can't begin to describe how creepy this futuristic movie is. The famous actors look more plastic than the sets. – *James Christopher, The Times*

'Little kids. Big words. American dreams.'

Spellbound ★★★

DIR Jeffrey Blitz

2002   97m   US

DVD

☆ Nupur Lala, Angela Arenivar, Ted Brigham, Ashley White, Neil Kadakia, April DeGideo, Paige Kimble, Harry Altman, George Thampy, Balu Natarajian, Jonathan Knisely, Frank Neuhauser

Eight children from across the US prepare for the final of the National Spelling Bee.

Delightful doc about kids competing head-to-head in one of their country's most treasured pageants; many of them seem borderline autistic, and are driven by the pride and ambition of their parents. It presents a fascinating panorama of America's competitive diversity, and could hardly be more entertaining.

CIN Jeffrey Blitz   **MUS** Daniel Hulsizer   **ED** Yana Gorskaya   **PROD** Sean Welch, Jeffrey Blitz **DIST** Metrodome

66 An unpretentious classic of the form. – *Ty Burr, Boston Globe*

66 Hilarious and often unwatchably tense. – *Peter Bradshaw, Guardian*

⚐ documentary

'Terror Can Fill Any Space.'

Sphere

DIR Barry Levinson

1998   134m   US

DVD   ♫

☆ Dustin Hoffman (Dr. Norman Goodman), Sharon Stone (Dr. Elizabeth 'Beth' Halperin), Samuel L. Jackson (Dr. Harry Adams), Peter Coyote (Captain Harold C. Barnes), Liev Schreiber (Dr. Ted Fielding), Queen Latifah (Alice 'Teeny' Fletcher), Marga Gomez (Jane Edmunds)

A team of scientists are deployed to explain the discovery of a huge metal vessel beneath the Pacific ocean floor.

Like Contact, it has enthusiastic adherents, especially in the US, but this bizarre, empty and mostly dull deep-sea sci-fi thriller spends most of a very long running time getting nowhere at all.

SCR Stephen Hauser, Paul Attanasio   **CIN** Adam Greenberg   **MUS** Elliot Goldenthal   **DES** Norman Reynolds   **ED** Stu Linder   **PROD** Michael Crichton, Andrew Wald, Barry Levinson **DIST** Warner/Baltimore/Constant/Punch

66 All meaning is simply lost in the hubbub. – *Richard Schickel, Time*

'The only thing worse than losing your mind . . . is finding it again.'

Spider ★★★

DIR *David Cronenberg*

2002   98m   Canada/GB/Japan/France

DVD

☆ *Ralph Fiennes* (Spider), *Miranda Richardson* (Yvonne/Mrs. Cleg), *Gabriel Byrne* (Bill Cleg), Bradley Hall (Young Spider), Lynn Redgrave (Mrs Wilkinson), John Neville (Terrence), Gary Reineke (Freddy), Philip Craig (John)

A paranoid schizophrenic is released into a halfway home after some 20 years in a mental institution, and has flashbacks to his traumatic childhood.

A brilliantly managed psychological thriller, one of this director's best, in which we're placed inside the mindscape of a seriously disturbed individual, and must puzzle out his past with the few clues we're given. The performances from Fiennes, and Richardson and Byrne as his parents, are exceptional.

SCR *Patrick McGrath*   **CIN** *Peter Suschitzky* **MUS** *Howard Shore*   **DES** *Andrew Sanders*   **ED** Ronald Sanders   **PROD** David Cronenberg, Samuel Hadida, Catherine Bailey   **DIST** Helkon SK

66 Lasts in the mind and it's built to last. – *J. Hoberman, Village Voice*

66 I was floored by Cronenberg's mastery of the material. – *Jonathan Rosenbaum, Chicago Reader*

DVD Available on DVD   ☆ Cast in order   66 Critics' Quotes   ⚐ Academy Award   🇹 BAFTA
♫ Soundtrack on CD   of importance   † Points of interest   ⚐ Academy Award nomination   🇹 BAFTA nomination

577

'With great power comes great responsibility.'

Spider-Man ★★

DIR Sam Raimi

2002 121m US

DVD ♫

☆ Tobey Maguire (Spider-Man/Peter Parker), Willem Dafoe (Green Goblin/Norman Osborn), Kirsten Dunst (Mary Jane Watson), James Franco (Harry Osborn), Cliff Robertson (Ben Parker), Rosemary Harris (May Parker), J. K. Simmons (J. Jonah Jameson), Joe Manganiello (Flash Thompson)

Bitten by a genetically-altered spider, a nerd develops special powers and uses them to combat a mad scientist.

Fairly enjoyable franchise-starter, in which the limited effects and dull, cartoony design are problems; but the warm chemistry between Spidey and his girl (somewhat squandered in its sequels) keeps it nicely afloat.

SCR David Koepp CIN Don Burgess MUS Danny Elfman DES Neil Spisak ED Bob Murawski, Arthur Coburn PROD Laura Ziskin, Ian Bryce DIST Columbia TriStar

66 What holds the movie together is its modest, sweet spirit. – *Charles Taylor, Salon*

66 With spider-like timidity, scuttles into a corner and freezes. – *Anthony Lane, New Yorker*

⚭ John Dykstra, Scott Stokdyk, Anthony LaMolinara, John Frazier (visual effects); Kevin O'Connell, Greg P. Russell, Ed Novick (sound)

Ⓣ John Dykstra, Scott Stokdyk, John Frazier, Anthony LaMolinara (special visual effects)

'The battle within.'

Spider-Man 3 ★★

DIR Sam Raimi

2007 138m US

DVD ♫

☆ Tobey Maguire (Peter Parker/Spider-Man), Kirsten Dunst (Mary Jane Watson), James Franco (Harry Osborn/New Goblin), Thomas Haden Church (Flint Marko/Sandman), Topher Grace (Eddie Brock/Venom), Bryce Dallas Howard (Gwen Stacy), Rosemary Harris (Aunt May Parker)

Peter Parker is comfortable, even self-satisfied, about Spider-Man's fame and success, but then his character comes under scrutiny when an alien organism morphs itself into a black suit that envelops him.

A decent addition to the franchise, with some nice moments: self-effacing Peter Parker developing a swagger as he enjoys new-found celebrity, and a terrific new villain, the Sandman, who can turn at will into a fearsome monster made of grains of sand. A couple of other villains might have been excised from the script, but the special effects are often dazzling, and while overlong, the film could be said to represent super-sized value.

SCR Sam Raimi, Ivan Raimi, Alvin Sargent CIN Bill Pope MUS Christopher Young, Danny Elfman DES Neil Spisak,

J. Michael Riva ED Bob Murawski PROD Laura Ziskin, Avi Arad, Grant Curtis DIST Sony

66 The tone is ultimately more subdued than your average superhero movie. Kudos to Raimi for making it feel justified. – *Ben Walters, Time Out*

66 The main flaw is an over-abundance of villains, a bout of narrative greediness that sees them marching out of their lairs like so many evildoers-on-parade. – *Rick Groen, Toronto Globe and Mail*

Ⓣ Scott Stokdyk, Peter Nofz, John Frazier, Spencer Cook (special visual effects)

The Spider's Stratagem ★★★

DIR *Bernardo Bertolucci*

1970 97m Italy

☆ *Giulio Brogi*, Alida Valli, Tino Scotti, Pino Campanini

Revisiting the Italian village where his father was killed by in 1936, and puzzled by the defacement of his statue, his son learns he was really a traitor executed by his own men.

Elaborately mysterious puzzle, which gradually reveals itself to intriguing effect. A dense, assured script, brilliantly extended from a very short Borges story, that offers the lead character increasing psychological awareness in his search for truth. Beautifully photographed on location in the Po Valley.

SCR *Bernardo Bertolucci, Eduardo de Gregorio, Marilu Parolini* CIN *Vittorio Storaro, Franco di Giacomo* PROD Giovanni Bertolucci DIST Radiotelevisione Italiana/Red Film

'Their World Is Closer Than You Think.'

The Spiderwick Chronicles ⓝⓔⓦ ★★

DIR Mark Waters

2008 96m US

DVD ♫

☆ Freddie Highmore (Jared Grace/Simon Grace), Mary-Louise Parker (Helen Grace), Nick Nolte (Mulgarath), Joan Plowright (Aunt Lucinda), David Strathairn (Arthur Spiderwick), Seth Rogen (Voice of Hogsqueal), Martin Short (Voice of Thimbletack), Sarah Bolger (Mallory Grace)

Three siblings find their new home sits beside a secret kingdom of goblins, fairies and ogres.

Imaginative fantasy with excellent effects that wastes no time establishing its mythological universe.

SCR Karey Kirkpatrick, David Berenbaum, John Sayles CIN Caleb Deschanel MUS James Horner DES James Bissell ED Michael Kahn PROD Mark Canton, Larry Franco, Ellen Goldsmith-Vein, Karey Kirkpatrick DIST Paramount

HOGSQUEAL: 'Vengeance or death!. . .Hopefully vengeance.'

66 A work of both modest enchantment and enchanting modesty, grounded in a classically Spielbergian realm where childlike wonderment crosses paths with the tough realities of young adulthood. – *Justin Chang, Variety*

66 The most enjoyable PG fantasy this side of Hogwarts. – *James Christopher, The Times*

S

The Spirit of the Beehive ★★★

DIR *Victor Erice*

1973   98m   Spain

[DVD]

☆ Fernando Fernan Gomez, Teresa Gimpera, *Ana Torrent*, Isabel Telleria

In 1940 in a remote Spanish village, two children, forcibly relocated from their home by the Civil War, see a travelling film show of Frankenstein, and their imaginations run riot.

Sensitive story of childish fears and mysteries, set during the rising wave of Fascism, but keeping its political subtext firmly in place. This perfect sense of balance results in a delightful, if unsettling film.

SCR Francisco J. Querejeta   CIN *Luis Cuadrado*
MUS Luis de Pablo   DIST Elias Querejeta

66 The Spirit of the Beehive, like Cinema Paradiso, also takes place at the particular intersection of reality and fantasy defined by youthful movie-going. – *Dana Stevens, New York Times*

66 A graceful and potent lyric on children's vulnerable hunger, but also a sublime study on cinema's poetic capacity to reflect and hypercharge reality. – *Michael Atkinson, Village Voice*

Spirited Away ★★★

SCR/DIR *Hayao Miyazaki*

2001   125m   Japan

[DVD]   ♫

☆ voices of: Rumi Hiiragi (Chihiro), Miyu Irino (Haku), Mari Natsuki (Yubaba/Zeniba), Takashi Naito (Akio), Yasuko Sawaguchi (Yugo)

A forlorn 10-year-old girl sees her parents turned into pigs in a mysterious town full of gods and spirits, and must work in a bathhouse to earn her freedom.

Wildly imaginative and compellingly strange animated feature, not unlike being lost in a waking dream; the story is often confounding, but there are moments of extraordinary wonder and delicacy.

MUS Joe Hisaishi   DES Norobu Yoshida   ED Takeshi Seyama   PROD Toshio Suzuki   DIST Optimum

66 A triumph of psychological depth and artistic brilliance. – *Lisa Schwarzbaum, Entertainment Weekly*

66 Weird and wonderful. Mostly wonderful. – *Peter Bradshaw, Guardian*

† The movie was released in two versions, one subtitled and the other dubbed into English.

⌁ animated feature

Ⓣ film not in the English language

Spring, Summer, Autumn, Winter . . . and Spring ★★★

SCR/DIR *Kim Ki-duk*

2003   103m   South Korea/Germany

[DVD]

☆ Oh Yeong-su (Old Monk), Kim Ki-duk (Adult Monk), Kim Yeong-min (Young Adult Monk), Seo Jae-gyeong

(Boy Monk), Ha Yeo-jin (The Girl), Kim Jung-ho (Child Monk)

On a island monastery in the middle of a remote Korean lake, a monk's apprentice learns lessons at each stage in life, and eventually takes over from his master.

A beguiling distillation of Buddhist philosophy, rich with a glistening natural beauty and unfolding with Zen calm, despite vigorous bursts of sex and cruelty. The episodic structure represents life as a cycle of perpetual renewal, like the seasons.

CIN Baek Dong-hyeon   MUS Ji-woong Park   ED Kim Ki-duk   PROD Karl Baumgartner, Seung-jae Lee

66 Persuasively transmits a Buddhist conviction that time, age and youth are an illusion. – *Peter Bradshaw, Guardian*

66 As meditative and beautiful as its title would indicate. – *Kenneth Turan, L.A. Times*

Springtime in a Small Town ★★★

DIR *Tian Zhuangzhuang*

2002   116m   China/Hong Kong/France

[DVD]

☆ Hu Jingfan (Yuwen), Wu Jun (Dai Liyan), Xin Baiqing (Zhang Zhichen), Ye Xiaokeng (Lao Huang), Lu Sisi (Dai Xiu)

An ailing landowner and his bored wife in 1946 provincial China find their marriage shaken up by a visit from a Shanghai doctor, who used to know them both intimately.

Chinese Chekhov: a stately drama of waning love and reawakened passion, in which post-war fatigue is a metaphor for the characters' ennui and vice versa. It's sumptuously done, if slightly too static for its own good.

SCR Ah Cheng   CIN Mark Li   MUS Zhao Li
DES Cheng Kuangming, Tim Yip Kam-tim   ED Xu Jiangping   PROD Li Xiaowan, Bill Kong, Tang Yatming
DIST Artificial Eye

66 An intensely insular drama that cares about what's not said, what doesn't happen, who sighs first. – *Catherine Shoard, Sunday Telegraph*

66 The kind of deeply intelligent, humane cinema with heart and sinew. – *Peter Bradshaw, Guardian*

'Real Spies . . . only smaller.'

Spy Kids ★

SCR/DIR *Robert Rodriguez*

2001   88m   US

[DVD]   ♫

☆ Antonio Banderas (Gregorio Cortez), Carla Gugino (Ingrid Cortez), Alexa Vega (Carmen Cortez), Daryl Sabara (Juni Cortez), Alan Cumming (Fegan Floop), Tony Shalhoub (Alexander Minion), Teri Hatcher (Ms. Gradenko), Cheech Marin (Felix Gumm), Robert Patrick (Mr. Lisp), Danny Trejo (Machete)

The children of two spies must rescue their parents from a techno-wizard and his sidekick.

Scrappily engaging Bond-lite caper for kids, full of the desired gadgetry and crowd-pleasing humour.

[DVD] Available on DVD	☆ Cast in order of importance	66 Critics' Quotes	⌁ Academy Award · Ⓐ Academy Award nomination	Ⓑ BAFTA · Ⓣ BAFTA nomination
♫ Soundtrack on CD	† Points of interest		

579

S

CIN Guillermo Navarro   MUS Danny Elfman, Marcel Rodriguez, John Debney, Robert Rodriguez, Los Lobos   DES Cary White   ED Robert Rodriguez   PROD Robert Rodriguez, Elizabeth Avellan   DIST Buena Vista

66 A piece of almost Dadaist filmmaking. . .great fun with its constant spirit of invention. – *Stephen Hunter, Washington Post*

† Spy Kids 2: Island of Lost Dreams followed in 2002, and Spy Kids 3D: Game Over the next year.

'Joint Custody Blows.'

The Squid and the Whale ★★★★

SCR/DIR *Noah Baumbach*
2005   81m   US
DVD   ♫

☆ *Jeff Daniels* (Bernard), *Laura Linney* (Joan), Jesse Eisenberg (Walt), Owen Kline (Frank), William Baldwin (Ivan), Anna Paquin (Lili), Halley Feiffer (Sophie)

Two teenage boys in 1980s Brooklyn watch with horror as their writer parents' once happy marriage slowly collapses into bitterness. After their split, the boys are coerced into taking sides.

A coming-of-age story as well as an account of a failing marriage; superlatively well-acted, with Daniels and Linney in peak form. Director Baumbach also wrote the perceptive, acutely observed and loosely autobiographical script, which is wonderfully literate and witty.

CIN Robert D. Yeoman   MUS Dean Wareham, Britta Phillips   DES Anne Ross   ED Tim Streeto   PROD Wes Anderson, Peter Newman, Clara Markowicz, Charlie Corwin   DIST Columbia TriStar

66 An extremely funny, deeply painful account of the break-up in 1986 of the marriage between middle class intellectuals and its effect on their teenage sons. – *Philip French, Observer*

66 Bitterly funny about divorce, it's even sharper and more original about intellectuals and their discontent. – *Michael Sragow, Baltimore Sun*

⚲ Noah Baumbach (original screenplay)

'School can be a riot.'

St Trinian's (new)

DIR Oliver Parker, Barnaby Thompson
2007   100m   UK
♫

☆ Rupert Everett (Miss Fritton/Carnaby Fritton), Colin Firth (Geoffrey Thwaites), Lena Headey (Miss Dickinson), Jodie Whittaker (Beverly), Russell Brand (Flash Harry), Anna Chancellor (Miss Bagstock), Stephen Fry (Himself), Celia Imrie (Matron), Toby Jones (Bursar), Mischa Barton (J.J. French), Girls Aloud (Themselves)

The rebellious pupils of a floundering school for girls steal a famous painting to solve a financial crisis.

Game attempt to resurrect a British comedy staple; energy and irreverence, however, are no substitutes for plain old-fashioned wit.

SCR Piers Ashworth, Nick Moorcroft   CIN Gavin Finney   MUS Charlie Mole   DES Amanda McArthur   ED Alex

Mackie   PROD Oliver Parker, Barnaby Thompson   DIST Entertainment

66 The original films' anti-establishment tone has morphed into a celebration of dumbed-down 'yoof' culture. – *Derek Elley, Variety*

66 Nowhere near the calamity it should have been. – *David Edwards, Daily Mirror*

† The film features an animated sequence in the style of Ronald Searle's original cartoons.

Stagecoach ★★★★

DIR *John Ford*
1939   99m   US
DVD

☆ *Claire Trevor* (Dallas), *John Wayne* (The Ringo Kid), *Thomas Mitchell* (Dr. Josiah Boone), *George Bancroft* (Sheriff Curly Wilcox), Andy Devine (Buck Rickabaugh), *Berton Churchill* (Henry Gatewood), Louise Platt (Lucy Mallory), *John Carradine* (Hatfield), *Donald Meek* (Mr. Samuel Peacock), Tim Holt (Lt. Blanchard), Chris-Pin Martin (Chris)

Various Western characters board a stagecoach which is besieged by an Indian war party.

What might have been a minor Western became a classic by virtue of its firm characterization, restrained writing, exciting climax, the scenery of Monument Valley – and some world-class stunt work by the great Yakima Canutt. Whatever the reasons, it works.

SCR Dudley Nichols   CIN Bert Glennon   MUS Richard Hageman, W. Frank Harling, John Leopold, Leo Shuken, Louis Gruenberg   ED Otho Lovering, Dorothy Spencer   PROD UA

66 It displays potentialities that can easily drive it through as one of the surprise big grossers of the year. – *Variety*

66 The basic western, a template for everything that followed. – *John Baxter, 1968*

⚲ Thomas Mitchell (supporting actor); music
⚲ picture; John Ford (direction); Bert Glennon; art direction; editing

---

'Till the last man.'

Stalingrad ★★

DIR Joseph Vilsmaier
1993   138m   Germany
DVD

☆ Dominique Horwitz (Obergefreiter Fritz Reiser), Jochen Nickel (Unteroffizier Manfred Rohleder), Sebastian Rudolph (GeGe Müller), *Thomas Kretschmann* (Lt. Hans von Witzland), Martin Benrath (Gen. Hentz), Dana Vavrova (Irina)

A German platoon is decimated during the Battle of Stalingrad in 1942–3, and attempts to escape.

Harrowing and relentless war film from a grunt's eye view, in which the Russian winter is as deadly a force as the enemy.

SCR Johannes Heide, Jürgen Büscher, Joseph Vilsmaier   CIN Peter von Haller, Klaus Moderegger, Rolf Greim   MUS Norbert J. Schneider   DES Wolfgang Hundhammer, Jindrich Goetz   ED Hannes Nikel   PROD Hanno Huth,

Günter Rohrbach **DIST** Entertainment/Royal/Bavaria/BA/Perathon

66 Renders a bitter, almost choking sense of the futility of war. – *Peter Stack, San Francisco Chronicle*

'In 1982, a new troublemaker hit Garfield High. He was tough. He was wild. He was willing to fight. He was the new math teacher.'

Stand and Deliver ★★

DIR Ramon Menendez
1988 102m US
[DVD] ♫

☆ *Edward James Olmos* (Jaime A. Escalante), Lou Diamond Phillips (Angel Guzman), Rosana de Soto (Fabiola Escalante), Andy Garcia (Dr. Ramirez), Ingrid Oliu (Guadalupe 'Lupe' Escobar), Karla Montana (Claudia Camejo), Vanessa Marquez (Ana Delgado), Mark Eliot (Tito)

An inner-city maths teacher adopts unconventional methods to interest his listless pupils in passing their exams.

Rousing true story about a triumph over the odds, with a terrific character turn in the lead.

SCR Ramon Menendez, Tom Musca **CIN** Tom Richmond **MUS** Craig Safan **ED** Nancy Richardson **PROD** Tom Musca **DIST** Warner/American Playhouse

66 A dramatic story, and this is a worthy movie for telling it. I only wish I hadn't been reminded, so often, that the movie was making it feel just a little better than life. – *Roger Ebert, Chicago Sun-Times*

⌇ Edward James Olmos (leading actor)

'Every generation has a legend. Every journey has a first step. Every saga has a beginning.'

Star Wars: Episode I – The Phantom Menace ★

SCR/DIR George Lucas
1999 133m US
[DVD] ♫

☆ Liam Neeson (Qui-Gon Jinn), Ewan McGregor (Obi-Wan Kenobi), Natalie Portman (Queen Padmé Amidala), Jake Lloyd (Anakin Skywalker), Pernilla August (Shmi Skywalker), Frank Oz (Yoda (voice)), Ian McDiarmid (Senator Palpatine), Oliver Ford Davies (Gov. Sio Bibble), Hugh Quarshie (Capt. Panaka), Ahmed Best (Jar Jar Binks (voice)), Samuel L. Jackson (Mace Windu), Ray Park (Darth Maul), Peter Serafinowicz (Darth Maul (voice)), Ralph Brown (Ric Olié), Terence Stamp (Supreme Chancellor Valorum), Brian Blessed, Sofia Coppola

Two Jedi knights help a young queen save her planet from the predations of a greedy trade federation.

Clunky, much-criticised prologue to the original saga with a few spectacular effects sequences. It's aimed squarely at young children, and fans of the series hoping for a deepening of its mythology were severely disappointed. Lucas gives the whole movie over to his digital background artists, the script feels several drafts off coherent, and the cast fail to make sense of it all. Two further episodes of the prologue only added to the sense of overall anti-climax.

CIN David Tattersall **MUS** John Williams **DES** Gavin Bocquet **ED** Paul Martin Smith, Ben Burtt **PROD** Rick McCallum **DIST** TCF/Lucasfilm

66 After waiting 16 years for the overture to this epic saga, this is what we get? An in-progress trade war? – *Marc Caro, Chicago Tribune*

66 Many of the scenes feel shapeless and flat – they're not ended, but abandoned. – *David Ansen, Newsweek*

† Episodes II and III in the Star Wars cycle were released in 2002 and 2005 respectively.

⌇ Gary Rydstrom, Tom Johnson, Shawn Murphy, John Midgley (sound); Ben Burtt, Tom Bellfort (sound effects editing); John Knoll, Dennis Muren, Scott Squires, Rob Coleman (visual effects)

ⓣ John Knoll, Dennis Muren, Scott Squires, Rob Coleman (special visual effects); Ben Burtt, Tom Bellfort, John Midgley, Gary Rydstrom, Tom Johnson, Shawn Murphy (sound)

Star Wars: Episode IV – A New Hope ★★★★

SCR/DIR George Lucas
1977 121m US
[DVD] ♫

☆ Mark Hamill (Luke Skywalker), *Harrison Ford* (Han Solo), Carrie Fisher (Princess Leia Organa), Peter Cushing (Grand Moff Tarkin), *Alec Guinness* (Obi-Wan Kenobi), *Anthony Daniels* (C3 PO), *Kenny Baker* (R2-D2), Dave Prowse (Darth Vader), Phil Brown (Owen Lars)

A rebel princess in a distant galaxy escapes, and with the help of her robots and a young farmer overcomes the threatening forces of evil.

Flash Gordon rides again, but with timing so impeccably right that the movie became a phenomenon and one of the top grossers of all time; at the time, that could hardly have been foreseen, and certainly not by the studios. Good harmless fun, put together with style and imagination.

CIN Gilbert Taylor **MUS** *John Williams* **DES** John Barry **ED** Paul Hirsch, Marcia Lucas, Richard Chew **PROD** Gary Kurtz **DIST** TCF/Lucasfilm

66 A great work of popular art, fully deserving the riches it has reaped. – *Time*

66 Acting in this movie I felt like a raisin in a giant fruit salad. And I didn't even know who the coconuts or the cantaloupes were. – *Mark Hamill*

⌇ John Williams; John Barry; editing; John Mollo (costume design); John Stears, John Dykstra and others (visual effects); sound
⌇ picture; Alec Guinness (supporting actor); George Lucas (direction); George Lucas (original screenplay)
ⓣ John Williams

Star Wars: Episode V – The Empire Strikes Back ★★★★

DIR Irvin Kershner
1980 124m US
[DVD] ♫

☆ Mark Hamill (Luke Skywalker), *Harrison Ford* (Han Solo), Carrie Fisher (Princess Leia), Billy Dee Williams (Lando Calrissian), Anthony Daniels (C-3PO), Peter

[DVD] Available on DVD   ☆ Cast in order   66 Critics' Quotes   ⌇ Academy Award   ⓣ BAFTA
♫ Soundtrack on CD   of importance   † Points of interest   ⌇ Academy Award nomination   ⓣ BAFTA nomination

581

Mayhew (Chewbacca), Kenny Baker (R2-D2), Frank Oz (Yoda), *Alec Guinness* (Obi-Wan Kenobi)

The Rebel Alliance takes refuge from Darth Vader on a frozen planet.

More exhilarating interplanetary adventures, with better production values than its predecessor Star Wars and just as enjoyable for aficionados.

SCR Leigh Brackett, Lawrence Kasdan CIN Peter Suschitzky MUS *John Williams* DES *Norman Reynolds* ED Paul Hirsch PROD Gary Kurtz DIST TCF

66 Slightly encumbered by some mythic and neo-Sophoclean overtones, but its inventiveness, humour and special effects are scarcely less inspired than those of its phenomenally successful predecessor. – *New Yorker*

⏃ John Williams; art direction

Ⓣ music

Star Wars: Episode VI – Return of the Jedi ★★★★

DIR Richard Marquand

1983 132m US

DVD ♫

☆ Mark Hamill, Harrison Ford, Carrie Fisher, Billy Dee Williams, Anthony Daniels, Peter Mayhew, Kenny Baker

In this Star Wars episode, our heroes combat Darth Vader and Jabba the Hutt.

More expensive fantasy for the world's children of all ages, especially the undemanding ones.

SCR Lawrence Kasdan, George Lucas CIN Alan Hume MUS *John Williams* DES Norman Reynolds ED Sean Barton, Duwayne Dunham, Marcia Lucas, Arthur Repola PROD Howard Kazanjian DIST TCF/Lucasfilm

66 I admire the exquisite skill and talent which have been poured into these films, while finding the concepts behind these gigantic video games in the sky mindlessly tedious. – *Margaret Hinxman, Daily Mail*

66 An impersonal and rather junky piece of moviemaking. – *Pauline Kael, New Yorker*

⏃ John Williams; art direction

'This summer a star falls. The chase begins.'

Stardust (new) ★

DIR Matthew Vaughn

2007 128m UK/US

♫

☆ Charlie Cox (Tristan), Claire Danes (Yvaine), Michelle Pfieffer (Larnia), Peter O'Toole (The King), Robert de Niro (Captain Shakespeare), Ricky Gervais (Ferdy the Fence)

An English lad crosses into a supernatural parallel universe and endures perils to bring a fallen star back to his true love. But the celestial creature's pure heart is also being sought by a witch to gain eternal youth.

An unwieldy mash-up of dark fable, saccharine romance and broad farce that never coalesces into a convincing whole. It remains the sum of mostly silly, occasionally magical parts.

SCR Jane Goldman, Matthew Vaughn CIN Ben Davis MUS Ilan Eshkeri DES Gavin Bocquet ED Jon Harris PROD Lorenzo di Bonaventura, Matthew Vaughn, Michael Dreyer, Neil Gaiman DIST Paramount Pictures

66 Floating in on an airy breeze of dreams and true love, the lively adventure-romance offers that elusive quality summer movies are supposed to possess but rarely do – total escape. – *Kevin Crust – Los Angeles Times*

Starter for Ten ★★

DIR Tom Vaughan

2006 96m UK/US

DVD ♫

☆ James McAvoy (Brian Jackson), Alice Eve (Alice Harbinson), Rebecca Hall (Rebecca Epstein), Catherine Tate (Julie Jackson), Dominic Cooper (Spencer), Benedict Cumberbatch (Patrick Watts), James Corden (Tone), Mark Gatliss (Bamber Gascoigne)

In 1985, a brainy working-class student with a remarkable memory for facts is offered a place at university.

Amiable comedy, with an appealing hero: Brian Jackson is gauche, naïve and a compulsive joker. At Bristol University, confronted by the class system, he is tragically out of his depth in all respects but one: his ability to recall facts helps him sail into the University Challenge team. A strong cast, alert to comic nuance, carries the film, which suffers from a harsh plot twist. Its romantic outcome is predictable, if pleasing. A comedy that refreshingly applauds knowledge, rather than the lack of it.

SCR David Nicholls CIN Ashley Rowe MUS Blake Neely DES Sarah Greenwood ED Jon Harris, Heather Persons PROD Tom Hanks, Gary Goetzman, Pippa Harris DIST Icon

BRIAN: 'Epstein? That's a Jewish name, isn't it? I've never met a Jew before. Which is odd, because lots of my heroes. . .'

PATRICK: 'Let's quiz!'

66 If there are life lessons here, they're harsh ones – although they're taught with a gentle, forgiving spirit. – *Leslie Felperin, Variety*

'Loneliness is much better when you have got someone to share it with.'

The Station Agent ★

SCR/DIR Tom McCarthy

2003 88m US

DVD

☆ Peter Dinklage (Finbar McBride), Patricia Clarkson (Olivia Harris), Bobby Cannavale (Joe Oramas), Raven Goodwin (Cleo), Paul Benjamin (Henry Styles), Michelle Williams (Emily)

A lonely dwarf inherits an abandoned railway station in rural New Jersey from a co-worker and starts to form relationships with some unlikely friends.

Unusual rural drama that asserts people's right not to be prejudged by their appearance – or size. Quietly delightful.

CIN Oliver Bokelberg MUS Stephen Trask DES John Paino ED Tom McArdle PROD Mary Jane Skalski, Robert May, Kathryn Tucker DIST Buena Vista

66 The brilliance of Peter Dinklage's performance as the ironclad loner is that he doesn't much care. – *James Christopher, The Times*

🛡 Tom McCarthy (original screenplay)

Steamboat Bill Jnr ★★★

DIR Charles Riesner
1928 71m US
DVD

☆ *Buster Keaton*, Ernest Torrence, Marion Byron

A student takes over his father's old Mississippi steamboat, and wins the daughter of his rival.

Mixed comedy redeemed by a few scenes of absolute brilliance, including the one where Keaton stands still as the front of a house falls around him.

SCR Carl Harbaugh, Buster Keaton CIN J. Devereaux Jennings, Bert Haines DIST UA/Buster Keaton/Joseph Schenck

'Sometimes laughter is a matter of life and death.'

Steel Magnolias ★

DIR Herbert Ross
1989 117m US
DVD 🎵

☆ Sally Field (M'Lynn Eatenton), Dolly Parton (Truvy Jones), Shirley MacLaine (Ouiser Boudreaux), Daryl Hannah (Annelle Dupuy Desoto), Olympia Dukakis (Clairee Belcher), Julia Roberts (Shelby Eatenton Latcherie), Tom Skerritt (Drum Eatenton), Sam Shepard (Spud Jones)

In a Deep South beauty parlour, a group of women gather to gossip and discuss men, marriage, motherhood and life's ups and downs.

A showcase for some of the hottest actresses in Hollywood at the time, this piece, based on a stage play, dutifully delivers regular one-line zingers and laughter through tears. It's always sentimental, occasionally maudlin, and men are virtually absent from the universe it depicts; but it's a safe bet for those who find Terms of Endearment insufficiently weepy.

SCR Robert Harling CIN John A. Alonzo MUS Georges Delerue DES Gene Callahan, Edward Pisoni ED Paul Hirsch PROD Ray Stark DIST Columbia TriStar/Rastar/Ray Stark

⚖ Julia Roberts (supporting actress)
🛡 Shirley MacLaine (supporting actress)

Stella

DIR John Erman
1990 109m US
DVD

☆ Bette Midler (Stella Claire), John Goodman (Ed Munn), Trini Alvarado (Jenny Claire), Stephen Collins (Stephen Dallas), Marsha Mason (Janice Morrison), Eileen Brennan (Mrs. Wilkerson), Linda Hart (Debbie Whitman)

A waitress does whatever she can to secure the marriage of her illegitimate daughter to an upper-class suitor.

This misjudged remake of the Barbara Stanwyck classic Stella Dallas – with a new, 'modern' ending – cannot withstand even gentle analysis. But Midler, in the manner of Streisand, is an artist whose screen presence transcends the notions of quality and good taste one might apply to more retiring talents. She gives the role her all, and it's good campy fun.

SCR Robert Getchell CIN Billy Williams MUS John Morris DES James Hulsey ED Jerrold L. Ludwig, Bud Molin PROD Samuel Goldwyn Jr. DIST Rank/Samuel Goldwyn Company/Touchstone

'Sure, I Like A Good Time!'

Stella Dallas ★★★

DIR *King Vidor*
1937 106m US
DVD

☆ *Barbara Stanwyck*, John Boles, *Anne Shirley*, Barbara O'Neil, Alan Hale, Marjorie Main, Tim Holt

A social climber finds herself a rich suitor and marries him, but though her humble background proves a stumbling block, she resolves to make something of herself for her daughter's sake.

Melodrama that strays into soap opera territory, but still eminently watchable, with Stanwyck in imperious form in the title role.

SCR Victor Heerman, Sarah Y. Mason CIN Rudolph Maté MUS Alfred Newman DIST Samuel Goldwyn

66 A tear-jerker of A ranking. There are things about the story that will not appeal to some men, but no one will be annoyed or offended by it. And the wallop is inescapably there for femmes. – *Variety*

† Goldwyn's premier choices for the lead were Ruth Chatterton and Gladys George.

⚖ Barbara Stanwyck (leading actress); Anne Shirley (supporting actress)

Stella Does Tricks ★

DIR Coky Giedroyc
1996 99m GB
DVD

☆ Kelly Macdonald (Stella), James Bolam (Mr. Peters), Hans Matheson (Eddie), Ewan Stewart (McGuire), Lindsay Henderson (Young Stella)

A young teenage prostitute in London yearns to start a new life in her Glasgow hometown with her boy-friend, but struggles to escape the cycle of abuse and exploitation.

A minor film, and by no means a great one, yet it confirmed Macdonald as one of the Britain's most accomplished young actresses; her portrayal of rough-humoured resilience is almost inspiring.

SCR A. L. Kennedy CIN Barry Ackroyd MUS Nick Bicat DES Lynne Whiteread ED Budge Tremlett PROD Adam Barker DIST BFI/Channel 4/Compulsive/Sidewalk

S

DVD Available on DVD ☆ Cast in order 66 Critics' Quotes ⚖ Academy Award 🛡 BAFTA
🎵 Soundtrack on CD of importance † Points of interest ⚖ Academy Award nomination 🛡 BAFTA nomination

Sight & Sound
THE INTERNATIONAL FILM MAGAZINE

July 08
Volume 18 Issue 7 £3.95

BFI

PLUS
David Lean
revisited

Charles Burnett
interview

Errol Morris'
*Standard Operating
Procedure*

CANNES
SPECIAL

STEVE McQUEEN'S
HUNGER

PLUS THE REST OF THE FESTIVAL, INCLUDING:
Steven Soderbergh's *Che*, Terence Davies' *Of Time and the City*, *Maradona by Kusturica*,
James Toback's *Tyson*, Nuri Bilge Ceylan's *Three Monkeys*, Atom Egoyan's *Adoration*,
Charlie Kaufman's *Synecdoche, New York*, Woody Allen's *Vicky Cristina Barcelona*

Serious film publications, such as the monthly magazine *Sight & Sound*, continue to be influential and approach their subject with a rigorous, critical perspective. But in the blogging era, is traditional film criticism under threat?

What, exactly, is the point of film critics? To pose the question in public, as a film critic, sounds like talking oneself out of a job. Yet it's an issue that has been troubling critics both in Britain and the US this year.

Signs abound that the traditional role of the film critic is in decline. In Britain, several magazines and regional newspapers have dispensed with their film critics. In America, the trend has reached epidemic proportions: this year, Sean P. Means, the film critic of the *Salt Lake Tribune*, compiled a list of American movie critics who had lost their jobs in the previous two years. He listed 28 critics who had been laid off, re-assigned, seen their position eliminated, learned their contract was not renewed, or had taken early retirement.

Some publications he named were regional or minor – but startlingly, several leading newspapers and magazines had joined in the cull of critics: *The Los Angeles Times, The New York Daily News* and the *Village Voice* among them.

Two reasons are cited for this state of affairs. Firstly, the newspaper industry is contracting and in decline on both sides of the Atlantic. The business model of many newspapers is simply no longer working, and employing a full range of critics who cover film and other arts has come to seem an ideal that is hard to justify.

Secondly, the Internet has played its part. There's no reason to buy a publication just to see how a film critic rates a new release; dozens of movie bloggers will do that for you, for no charge. Given that many of these solo bloggers will be younger than the average professional film critic, their tastes are also more likely to be in tune with the largest core audience for films today: the 15–24 age group.

It would be unfortunate if movie bloggers hastened the total demise of professional film critics. Yet their rise should be welcomed, if cautiously. The British critic Lee Marshall argues persuasively that teenage film fans regularly visit such websites as Metacritic or Rotten Tomatoes to judge what films to see. Some may simply note the consensus approval ratings of critics featured on these sites, but who knows how many click a second or third time, and read full reviews? Marshall points out that in the past, few of these young people would have visited a library to compare the views of a dozen newspaper critics; now more people – especially young people – are reading film reviews than ever before.

I'm certainly not about to castigate movie bloggers. Clearly, they help to democratise opinions about film. It's also clearly not the fashion for young film enthusiasts to receive prescriptive opinions in a 'top-down' manner from veteran mentors (Andrew Sarris, say, in America; Derek Malcolm in the UK).

Yet the movie-related blogosphere is still in its infancy, and as yet it's hard to sort the wheat from the chaff. This remains the problem with much of the Internet: solo blogs have no 'cues' that swiftly indicate the value of what you are reading, in the way that the title of a publication does – the *New Yorker* on one hand, say, and the *Sun* on the other.

> ‘I'm surprised by how many movie bloggers I've read are deferential to the movie industry and to the films themselves, especially given the blogosphere's sceptical dismissal of "the traditional media".’

I'm surprised by how many movie bloggers I've read are deferential to the movie industry and to the films themselves, especially given the blogosphere's sceptical dismissal of 'the traditional media.' Many bloggers (though this is true of modern mainstream journalism too) are distinguished by the stridency rather than the quality of their opinions. And too many online reviewers fall short in the areas of perspective and expertise.

That's not a dig at the young. I've been inspired by the wisdom, wit, and sharpness of thought and expression in film critics of all ages. Some have been veterans: the late, irreplaceable Pauline Kael, of course; Nigel Andrews of *The Financial Times*; the *Observer's* Philip French. Others are currently are in their 40s: Anthony Lane of the *New Yorker*, the *Independent's* Anthony Quinn. But two of the most astute, incisive British film critics today are in the '30 and under' age range: Tim Robey and Mike McCahill of the *Daily* and *Sunday Telegraph* respectively. I'm delighted that both have contributed reviews to this volume.

So film criticism as we have traditionally known it is under threat. Does any of this matter? That depends on how much you care about films. It also depends on how much publications that carry film-related coverage care about them. If films are merely vehicles for celebrity gossip, or a means for the publication to market itself to a target audience, then it doesn't matter much at all.

In the short term, it doesn't matter much to studios and film distributors, either. There has recently been a worrying trend in films being released, both here and in America, without pre-release screenings for critics.

As things stand, reviews for a film are the one unpredictable factor in its pre-release strategy. Get rid of reviews – and the risk that some will be negative – and you can let your advertising and marketing work their spell, and accurately calculate a film's profitability.

> ‘Once you start side-stepping critics by withholding films from them, you are simply touting films like any other commodity – widgets or baked beans.’

But that's a narrow view. If a distributor willingly exposes a film to critical comment, it is a way of asserting it as a means of creative expression, liable to succeed or fail. Once you start side-stepping critics by withholding films from them, you are simply touting films like any other commodity – widgets or baked beans.

And the public may respond accordingly; a traditional chain of affection for films may be broken. This would be an unwise strategy, now that films must fight hard in the marketplace against entertainment delivered by TV, video games, the Internet and mobile phones. They need all the help they can get – and thoughtful criticism is one form of help.

To answer my opening question: what is the point of film critics? The answer, if nothing else, must be: to keep movies – and the people who make them – honest.

66 A mature work, bold enough to resist both unnecessary irony and resolution, and wise enough to be honest without being earnest. – *Melanie McGrath, Sight & Sound*

'It's not where you're from. It's where you're at.'

Step Up 2 The Streets (new)

DIR John M. Chu
2008   97m   US
DVD   ♫

☆ Briana Evigan (Andie), Robert Hoffman (Chase Collins), Will Kemp (Blake Collins), Sonja Sohn (Sarah), Adam G. Sevani (Moose), Cassie Ventura (Sophie), Channing Tatum (Tyler Gage)

A rebellious teen finds her true calling while competing in a street dance competition.

Spectacular choreography fitfully energises this thoroughly predictable gender-switch sequel.

SCR Toni Ann Johnson, Karen Barna   CIN Max Malkin
MUS Aaron Zigman   DES Devorah Herbert   ED Andrew Marcus, Nicholas Erasmus   PROD Patrick Wachsberger, Erik Feig, Adam Shankman, Jennifer Gibgot
DIST Universal

66 Like its predecessor, this follow-up takes place in a gritty neighbourhood, has a white lead, posits a universe where racial and class differences are minor obstacles to fun and pretends its clichés aren't clichés. – *Matt Zoller Seitz, New York Times*

66 Channing Tatum's brief appearance only serves to highlight his successors' lack of charisma. – *Anna Smith, Empire*

Still Life (new)   ★★★

SCR/DIR Zhangke Jia
2006   112m   Hong Kong/China
DVD

☆ Zhao Tao (Shen Hong), Han Sanming (Han Sanming), Wang Hongwei (Architect)

Two people with missing partners arrive in the Three Gorges region where a new dam is under construction on the Yangtze River. A nurse, looking for her husband, gradually realises he may have abandoned her. A miner seeks his child – and his mail-order wife, whom he bought 16 years previously.

With stunning visuals and a compelling narrative, Jia Zhangke's fifth feature shows how ordinary people being evacuated from their homes and forced to live in an alien urban environment. Given the political climate and social and economic changes, it's courageous and touching.

CIN Nelson Yu Lik-wai   MUS Giong Lim   DES Jing Dong Liang, Qiang Liu   ED Jing Lei Kong   PROD Tianyun Wang, PengleXu, Jiong Zhu   DIST BFI

66 A quiet, subtle picture of social turmoil in a country currently enjoying the worst aspects of capitalism and communism. – *Philip French, Observer*

† Still Life was voted one of the ten best pictures of 2007 by the French film magazine Cahiers du Cinéma. It was the surprise winner of the Golden Lion at the Venice Film Festival.

'All it takes is a little confidence!'

The Sting   ★★

DIR *George Roy Hill*
1973   129m   US
DVD   ♫

☆ Paul Newman (Henry Gondorff/Mr. Shaw), *Robert Redford* (Johnny Hooker/Kelly), Robert Shaw (Doyle Lonnegan), Charles Durning (Lt. William Snyder), Ray Walston (J.J. Singleton), Eileen Brennan (Billie)

In Depression-era Chicago, two con men stage an elaborate revenge on a big-time gangster who caused the death of a friend.

Bright, likeable and suspenseful comedy, reuniting its director with the two leads from Butch Cassidy and the Sundance Kid. Yet it isn't in the earlier film's class; its central scam is well executed, but it takes too long arriving at its climax. None of this prevented its huge success.

SCR David S. Ward   CIN *Robert Surtees*   MUS Scott Joplin (arranged by Marvin Hamlisch)   ED William Reynolds   PROD Tony Bill, Michael S. Phillips
DIST Universal/Richard Zanuck, David Brown

66 A visually claustrophobic, mechanically plotted movie that's meant to be a roguishly charming entertainment. – *New Yorker*

66 It demonstrates what can happen when a gifted young screenwriter has the good fortune to fall among professionals his second time out. – *Judith Crist*

⚊ picture; George Roy Hill; David S. Ward (original screenplay); Marvin Hamlisch (music)
⚊ Robert Redford (leading actor); Robert Surtees (cinematography)

'In every mind there is a door that has never been opened.'

Stir of Echoes   ★★★

SCR/DIR *David Koepp*
1999   99m   US
DVD   ♫

☆ *Kevin Bacon* (Tom Witzky), *Kathryn Erbe* (Maggie Witzky), *Illeana Douglas* (Lisa), Liza Weil (Debbie Kozac), Kevin Dunn (Frank McCarthy), Conor O'Farrell (Harry Damon), Jennifer Morrison (Samantha), Zachary David Cope (Jake Witzky), Lisa Lewis (Debbie's Mother), Eddie Bo Smith Jnr (Neil the Cop)

A telephone repair man in Boston is hypnotised by his sister-in-law at a party, and finds himself plagued by psychic visions about a local killing.

Intense, well-crafted, terrifically acted supernatural thriller, which morphs from ghostly shocks into a compelling study of obsession and a fraying marriage – it is one of the more underrated Hollywood films of its decade.

CIN Fred Murphy   MUS James Newton Howard
DES Nelson Coates   ED Jill Savitt   PROD Gavin Polone, Judy Hofflund   DIST TCF

66 A scream-out-loud movie, upsetting and deliriously effective. – *Phoebe Flowers, Miami Herald*

DVD Available on DVD   ☆ Cast in order   66 Critics' Quotes   ⚊ Academy Award   🅑 BAFTA
♫ Soundtrack on CD   of importance   † Points of interest   ⚊ Academy Award nomination   🅣 BAFTA nomination

The Stolen Children ★

DIR *Gianni Amelio*
1992   114m   Italy/France
DVD

☆ Enrico Lo Verso (Antonio), Valentina Scalici (Rosetta), Giuseppe Ieracitano (Luciano), Renato Carpentieri (Chief of Police), Vitalba Andrea (Antonio's Sister), Fabio Alessandrini (Grignani), Massimo de Lorenzo (Papaleo)

An inexperienced Italian cop finds himself in charge of two young children – an 11-year-old girl, forced to become a prostitute by her mother, and her younger brother.

Sentimental story, efficiently told, and brimming with compassion – though its employment of a child's point of view to focus on society's shortcomings sometimes seems facile.

SCR Sandro Petraglia, Stefano Rulli, Gianni Amelio
CIN Tonino Nardi, Renato Tafuri   **MUS** Franco Piersanti
DES Andrea Crisanti   **ED** Simona Paggi   **PROD** Angelo Rizzoli   **DIST** Mayfair/Erre/Alia/RAIDUE/Arena/Vega

66 Decently acted, but alarmingly bereft of originality or analytical insights, it's a well-meaning dirge of a film. – *Time Out*

66 Here is a movie with the spontaneity of life; watching it is like living it. – *Roger Ebert, Chicago Sun-Times*

Stolen Kisses ★★

DIR François Truffaut
1968   91m   France
DVD

☆ *Jean-Pierre Léaud* (Antoine Doinel), Delphine Seyrig (Fabienne Tabard), Michel Lonsdale (Georges Tabard), Claude Jade (Christine Darbon)

A private eye, hired by a store owner to discover why his employees are disaffected, falls for the boss's wife while trying to keep his girlfriend happy.

An inconsequential little comedy, handled with such delicacy and a sense of playfulness that one easily forgives its shortcomings.

SCR François Truffaut, Claude de Givray, Bernard Revon
CIN Denys Clerval   **MUS** Antoine Duhamel
PROD Marcel Berbert   **DIST** Films du Carrosse/Artistes Associés

⚐ foreign film

'Between maleness and femaleness there is fabulousness.'

Stonewall ★

DIR Nigel Finch
1996   98m   GB
DVD ♫

☆ Guillermo Diaz (La Miranda), Frederic Weller (Matty Dean), Brendan Corbalis (Ethan), Duane Boutté (Bostonia), Bruce MacVittie (Vinnie), Peter Ratray (Burt), Dwight Ewell (Helen Wheels), Matthew Faber (Mizz Moxie)

A re-creation of New York's historic Stonewall riots in 1969, triggered by a police raid on a gay bar. The events are seen through the eyes of a gay man who becomes radicalised by the event.

A low-budget 'factionalised' drama, bankrolled by the BBC, that might have worked better as documentary; its invented central story feels crudely bolted on. Yet it does convey the riots' pivotal importance in the advance of gay rights. Terrific soundtrack, on which girl groups dominate.

SCR Rikki Beadle Blair   **CIN** Chris Seager   **MUS** Michael Kamen   **DES** Therese DePrez   **ED** John Richards
PROD Christine Vachon, Ruth Caleb   **DIST** Metro Tartan/BBC

66 The movie seizes on social history in order to consecrate it as legend. – *Peter Matthews, Sight & Sound*

Stop Making Sense ★★★

DIR Jonathan Demme
1984   87m
DVD

☆ David Byrne, Jerry Harrison, Chris Frantz, Tina Weymouth

A documentary account of the rock group Talking Heads in concert.

One if the great concert documentaries, of a performance that actually has a narrative arc: the stage starts almost bare and gradually fills with musicians as the concert joyously progresses. The cerebral group's front man David Byrne is unquestionably the star, with his jerky movements, tortured singing voice, and his resorts to shadow mime and the donning of a giant suit to perform some numbers. He is mesmerising, as is the film, which confirms both director and singer-songwriter share an interest in pushing back artistic boundaries.

CIN Jordan Cronenweth   **ED** Lisa Day   **PROD** Gary Goetzman   **DIST** Palace

66 One of those miracle movies, a picture that seems to have come together by laws unto itself. It doesn't seem "made." It merely exists, like some inexplicable and wonderful quirk of nature. – *Stephanie Zacharek, salon.com*

Stop-Loss (new) ★

DIR Kimberley Peirce
2008   112m   US

☆ Ryan Philippe (Brandon King), Abbie Cornish (Michele), Channing Tatum (Steve Shriver), Joseph Gordon-Levitt (Tommy Burgess), Ciarán Hinds (Roy King), Timothy Olyphant (Lt. Col.Boot Miller), Mamie Gummer (Jeanie)

A young army sergeant commands a unit in Iraq, returns to his small-town Texas home, and learns that a loophole allows the US government to send him back to combat duty. He rebels and hits the road.

A premise with terrific potential, but a script that instead zeroes in on the post-traumatic stress suffered by returning soldiers. As a result, the film feels muddled and overwrought, forever skittering in different directions and succumbing unhappily to lapses of judgement.

SCR Kimberley Peirce, Mark Richard   **CIN** Chris Menges
MUS John Powell   **DES** David Wasco   **ED** Claire Simpson   **PROD** Scott Rudin, Mark Roybal, Kimberley Peirce, Gregory Goodman   **DIST** Paramount

S

'The Most Dangerous Choices Are Made With The Heart'

Stormy Monday ★

SCR/DIR Mike Figgis
1988 93m GB/US
DVD ♫

☆ Melanie Griffith (Kate), Tommy Lee Jones (Cosmo), Sting (Finney), Sean Bean (Brendan), James Cosmo (Tony), Mark Long (Patrick), Brian Lewis (Jim)

The owner of a club in Newcastle is pressured to sell up by American mobsters.

A routine story is lifted by Figgis's moody urban style and gritty performances.

CIN *Roger Deakins* MUS *Mike Figgis* DES Andrew McAlpine ED Dave Martin PROD Nigel Stafford-Clark DIST Palace/Moving Picture Company/Film Four International/Atlantic Entertainment/British Screen

66 All style and promise, a come-on that keeps coming on but never satisfies. – *Rita Kempley, Washington Post*

The Story of Qiu Ju ★★★

DIR Zhang Yimou
1992 100m China/Hong Kong
DVD

☆ Gong Li (Wan Qiu Ju), Quesheng Lei (Wan Shantang, Village Head), Liu Peiqi (Wan Qing Lai, Husband), Yang Liuchun (Meizi)

The outraged pregnant wife of an injured Chinese peasant appeals to the highest courts in the land to force a village elder to apologize for injuring her husband.

Qiu Ju takes it personally when the local chief kicks her husband in the groin over a planning dispute, triggering her quietly tenacious quest for justice, told in almost documentary style. Her mission sheds light on the tangled mess of China's legal system, and the huge gap between life in the cities and rural areas.

SCR Liu Heng CIN Chi Xiaoning, Yu Xiaoqun, Hongyi Lu MUS Zhao Jiping ED Du Yuan PROD Ma Fung Kwok, Yiting Feng, DIST Sil-Metropole/Beijing Film Academy Youth Film Studio

66 An odd drama of near-contemporary China, with a heroine whose admirable indomitability doesn't make her any less irritating. – *Empire*

† The film won the Golden Lion award for best film and Gong Li won the award for best actress at the 1992 Venice Film Festival.

'Some fairy tales are true . . . some legends are real.'

The Story of the
Weeping Camel ★★

DIR Byambasuren Davaa, Luigi Falorni
2003 90m Germany, Mongolia
DVD

☆ Janchiv Ayurzana (Janchiv), Chimed Ohin (Chimed), Amgaabazar Gonson (Amgaa), Zeveljamz Nyam

(Zevel), Ikhbayar Amgaabazar (Ikchee), Odgerel Ayisch (Odgoo)

In the remote Gobi desert, a Mongolian family of herders is distraught when a baby camel is rejected by its mother, and try everything to save the newly born creature's life.

An astute documentary that focuses on the neglected calf, but also examines the threat of modern life to nomadic communities.

SCR Byambasuren Davaa, Luigi Falorni, Batbayar Davgadorj CIN Luigi Falorni, Juliane Gregor MUS Marcel Leniz, Marc Riedinger, Choigiw Sangidorj ED Anja Pohl PROD Tobias N. Siebert

66 A cinematic oasis, both refreshing and thoroughly life-affirming. – *Stella Papamichael, BBC*

⚖ documentary

Storytelling ★

SCR/DIR Todd Solondz
2001 87m US
DVD ♫

☆ Selma Blair (Vi), Leo Fitzpatrick (Marcus), Aleksa Palladino (Catherine), Robert Wisdom (Gary Scott), Noah Fleiss (Brady Livingston), Paul Giamatti (Toby Oxman), John Goodman (Marty Livingston), Julie Hagerty (Fern Livingston), Lupe Ontiveros (Consuelo), Jonathan Osser (Mikey Livingston), Franka Potente (Editor)

A film of two halves. In Fiction, a creative writing student allows herself to be sexually exploited by her professor; in Nonfiction, a self-styled documentarist makes a film about a rich teenager and his dysfunctional family.

A clever point-scoring exercise in which Solondz answers back his critics, exploring the vexed relationship between truth and storytelling; but his sour worldview is hardly broadened in the process.

CIN Frederick Elmes MUS Belle & Sebastian, Nathan Larson DES James Chinlund ED Alan Oxman PROD Ted Hope, Christine Vachon DIST Entertainment

66 No more likely than Happiness or Welcome to the Dollhouse to resolve the question of whether [Solondz] is a serious artist or a nasty little man with a perversely glum view of the universe. – *Ella Taylor, LA Weekly*

66 A minor Solondz movie, a faltering misstep. – *Peter Bradshaw, Guardian*

La Strada ★★★

DIR *Federico Fellini*
1954 94m Italy
DVD ♫

☆ *Giulietta Masina (Gelsomina), Anthony Quinn (Zampano), Richard Basehart (Matto "The Fool")*

A half-witted peasant girl is sold to an itinerant strong man and ill-used by him.

Curious attempt at a kind of poetic neo-realism, saved by style and performances. Masina's waif-like heroine perfectly complements Quinn's muscular dolt, and together they create and oddly moving story that has much to say – much of it critical – about the state of humanity. Long regarded as a cinematic classic, yet to

S

some modern eyes it now looks over-sentimental and winsome.

SCR Federico Fellini, Ennio Flaiano, Tullio Pinelli
CIN Otello Martelli   MUS Nino Rota   ED Leo Catozzo, Lina Caterini   DIST Ponti/de Laurentiis

🏆 foreign film
🏅 Federico Fellini, Tullio Pinelli (orignal Screenplay)

Straight out of Brooklyn ★

SCR/DIR Matty Rich
1991   91m   US
DVD

☆ George T. Odom (Ray Brown), Ann D. Sanders (Frankie Brown), Lawrence Gilliard Jnr (Dennis Brown), Barbara Sanon (Carolyn Brown), Reana E. Drummond (Shirley), Matty Rich (Larry), Mark Malone (Kevin)

A young black man in a slum area makes a rash bid to escape his environment, by organising an armed robbery.

Rough-edged, powerful debut feature by a young film-maker who seems to know the mean streets surveyed here.

CIN John Rosnell   MUS Harold Wheeler   ED Jack Haigis
PROD Matty Rich   DIST Artificial Eye/Blacks N'Progress/American Playhouse

66 Not a glittering debut, but it does have a low-budget, first-time energy which sets it apart from much mainstream work. – *Michael O'Pray, Sight and Sound*

66 Rudimentary in every way, from writing to acting to camerawork, and covers all-too-familiar ground with no particular flair. – *Variety*

† Director Matty Rich was only 19 when he completed the film.

The Straight Story ★★★

DIR *David Lynch*
1999   112m   France/US/GB
DVD ♫

☆ *Richard Farnsworth* (Alvin Straight), Sissy Spacek (Rose), Jane Galloway Heitz (Dorothy), Everett McGill (Tom the Dealer), Jennifer Edwards-Hughes (Brenda), John Farley (Thorvald), John Lordan (Priest), Harry Dean Stanton (Lyle)

When a lonely old man gets word that his estranged brother has suffered a stroke, he leaps on his lawnmower and drives 300 miles to visit.

This most unusual of road movies is astonishingly based on a true story. Gentle, folksy, eccentric, and quite unlike anything else in Lynch's body of work, it has charm to burn.

SCR *John Roach, Mary Sweeney*   CIN *Freddie Francis*
MUS Angelo Badalamenti   DES Jack Fisk   ED Mary Sweeney   PROD Mary Sweeney, Neal Edelstein
DIST Buena Vista

66 A slow-moving, folksy-looking, profoundly spiritual film. – *Janet Maslin, New York Times*

66 Lyrical, sweet and brimming with optimism about the human condition. – *Lou Lumenick, New York Post*

🏅 Richard Farnsworth (leading actor)

'You know you want it.'

Strange Days ★★

DIR *Kathryn Bigelow*
1995   145m   US
DVD ♫

☆ Ralph Fiennes (Lenny Nero), Angela Bassett (Lornette 'Mace' Mason), Juliette Lewis (Faith Justin), Tom Sizemore (Max Peltier), Vincent D'Onofrio (Burton Steckler), Michael Wincott (Philo Gant), Glenn Plummer (Jeriko One)

On the eve of the millennium in riot-torn Los Angeles, a dealer in bootleg recorded memories stumbles on a police conspiracy involving the murder of a prostitute.

Dazzlingly appointed, if messy, future noir, with plenty of Sturm und Drang to recommend it and a terrifically depraved, derelict setting; the thoughts on voyeurism and technology don't congeal into anything like coherence, but the film's jittery overkill is half its point.

SCR James Cameron, Jay Cocks   CIN Matthew F. Leonetti
MUS Graeme Revell   DES *Lilly Kilvert*   ED Howard Smith   PROD James Cameron, Steven-Charles Jaffe
DIST UIP/Lightstorm

66 It's as if Philip K Dick had re-circuited Brian De Palma's brain. – *Owen Gleiberman, Entertainment Weekly*

66 A hectic, atrocious movie that tries to drill its own hole into your cortex and fill it with a rich impasto of doomsday glop. – *Peter Rainer, LA Times*

Strange Wilderness (new)

DIR Fred Wolf
2008   84m   United States
DVD

☆ Steve Zahn (Peter Gaulke), Allen Covert (Fred Wolf), Ashley Scott (Cheryl), Justin Long (Junior), Kevin Heffernan (Bill Whitaker), Harry Hamlin (Sky Pierson), Jonah Hill (Cooker), Ernest Borgnine (Milas)

When an incompetent wildlife TV producer's show is threatened with cancellation, he takes his accident-prone crew to the Andes in search of Bigfoot to boost its ratings.

The combination of comic actors may seem promising, but they flounder with flimsy material and weak direction. Many scenes start off with good intentions but go nowhere.

SCR Peter Gaulke, Fred Wolf   CIN David Hennings
MUS Waddy Wachtel   DES Perry Andelin Blake   ED Tom Costain   PROD Peter Gaulke   DIST Paramount Pictures UK

66 Instead of releasing this picture, it would have been better to lock up the producers. – *Philip French, Observer*

† The script is loosely based on a series of sketches written for the American TV show Saturday Night Live in the early 90s.

The Stranger ★

SCR/DIR Satyajit Ray
1991   120m   India/France
☆ Dipankar De (Sudhindra Bose), Mamata Shankar (Anila Bose), Bikram Bhattacharya (Satyaki/Bablu), Utpal

DVD Available on DVD   ☆ Cast in order   66 Critics' Quotes   🏅 Academy Award   🏆 BAFTA
♫ Soundtrack on CD   of importance   † Points of interest   🏅 Academy Award nomination   🏆 BAFTA nomination

589

Dutt (Manomohan Mitra), Dhritiman Chatterjee (Prithwish Sen Gupta), Robi Ghosh (Ranjan Rakshit), Subrata Chatterjee (Chhanda Rakshit)

In a story of a newly arrived prodigal that echoes the themes of The Return of Martin Guerre, a Calcutta family start to wonder whether a long-estranged uncle who comes to stay may be an impostor.

Satyajit Ray's final film constituted a quiet end to a distinguished career. It's a subtle low-key delight that his fans will admire, yet in truth it's lacking in dynamism.

CIN Barun Raha   MUS Satyajit Ray   ED Dulal Dutt
PROD Satyajit Ray   DIST Artificial Eye/National Film Development Corporation of India/Erato/DD/Soprofilms/Canal

66 It shows all the virtues of a master artist in full maturity. – *Hal Hinson, Washington Post*

'It begins with the scream of a train whistle – and ends with screaming excitement!'

Strangers on a Train ★★★

DIR *Alfred Hitchcock*
1951   101m   US
DVD   ♫

☆ Farley Granger (Guy Haines), *Robert Walker* (Bruno Antony), Ruth Roman (Anne Morton), Leo G. Carroll (Sen. Morton), Patricia Hitchcock (Barbara Morton), *Marion Lorne* (Mrs. Antony), Howard St John (Capt. Turley), Jonathan Hale (Mr. Antony), Laura Elliot (Miriam)

On a train, a tennis star is pestered by a psychotic man who wants to swap murders, and proceeds to carry out his part of the bargain.

This quirky melodrama has the director at his best, sequence by sequence, even if the story is implausible. Still, it is unbeatably suspenseful and entertaining.

SCR Raymond Chandler, Czenzi Ormonde   CIN *Robert Burks*   MUS *Dimitri Tiomkin*   ED William Ziegler
PROD Alfred Hitchcock   DIST Warner

BRUNO (ROBERT WALKER): Some people are better off dead – like your wife and my father, for instance.

66 You may not take it seriously, but you certainly don't have time to think about anything else. – *Richard Mallett, Punch*

66 The construction seems a little lame, but Hitch takes delight in the set pieces. – *Time Out, 1985*

† Remade 1970 as Once You Kiss A Stranger.

⚱ Robert Burks

'Distant Dreams and Passionate Lovers.'

Strawberry and Chocolate ★★

DIR Tomás Gutiérrez Alea, Juan Carlos Tabío
1994   108m   Cuba/Mexico/Spain
DVD   ♫

☆ *Jorge Perugorria* (Diego), Vladimir Cruz (David), Mirta Ibarra (Nancy), Francisco Gattorno (Miguel), Joel Angelino (German), Marilyn Solaya (Vivian)

In Havana, a naïve and conformist university student, a Communist Party member, reluctantly becomes friends with a cultured homosexual, who is persecuted for his subversive views.

The first gay-themed Cuban film, which ironically, given the US trade embargo against Cuba, was Oscar-nominated. It concerns an odd-couple friendship between an apolitical, cultured gay man and a straight Marxist who cares little for the arts. It asserts its tolerance lightly, in an often playful manner.

SCR Senel Paz   CIN Mario Garcia Joya   MUS José Maria Vitier   DES Fernando Pérez O'Reilly   ED Miriam Talavera, Osvaldo Donatien, Rolando Martínez
PROD Miguel Mendoza   DIST Metro Tartan/ICAIC/IMC/Telemadrid/Co. Tabasco

66 The overall tenor of the film's argument – that just being gay doesn't mean you're not a nice person – seems culpably naive. – *Philip Kemp, Sight & Sound*

⚱ foreign language film

'Good cop. Bad cop. Nothing is that simple.'

Street Kings (new)

DIR David Ayer
2008   108m   US

☆ Keanu Reeves (Det. Tom Ludlow), Forest Whitaker (Capt. Jack Wander), Hugh Laurie (Capt. James Biggs), Chris Evans (Det. Paul Diskant), Cedric 'The Entertainer' Kyles (Scribble), Jay Mohr (Sgt. Mike Clady), Terry Crews (Det. Terrence Washington), Naomie Harris (Linda Washington)

A Los Angeles cop implicated in the death of his former partner uncovers corruption in his department.

Formulaic crime thriller with some effective action, lots of gratuitous violence and a leading man perhaps unsuited to roles involving moral ambiguity.

SCR James Ellroy, Kurt Wimmer, Jamie Moss   CIN Gabriel Beristain   MUS Graeme Revell   DES Alec Hammond
ED Jeffrey Ford   PROD Lucas Foster, Alexandra Milchan, Erwin Stoff   DIST TCF

66 Another mean, violent and decently acted slab of Ellroy-flavoured criminality. – *Ian Nathan, Empire*

66 Depressing and sickeningly violent. . .dismal. – *James Christopher, The Times*

† The first film in which James Ellroy contributed to an film adaptation of one of his stories.

A Streetcar Named Desire ★★

DIR *Elia Kazan*
1951   122m   US
DVD   ♫

☆ *Vivien Leigh, Marlon Brando*, Kim Hunter, Karl Malden

A neurotic Southern widow is harassed, taunted and violated by her ferocious brother-in-law.

Reasonably successful, decorative picture from a highly theatrical but influential play. It's recalled most often now as the breakthrough film for Brando as the mumbling, brutal Stanley Kowalski; his performance (ironically, he was the only one of the four leads not to win an Oscar) inspired generations of young actors.

SCR Tennessee Williams   CIN *Harry Stradling*
MUS Alex North   PROD Charles K. Feldman
DIST Warner/Elia Kazan

⚱ Vivien Leigh (leading actress); Kim Hunter (supporting actress); Karl Malden (supporting actor)

---

picture; Marlon Brando (leading actor); Tennessee Williams; Elia Kazan; Harry Stradling; Alex North; Richard Day

Ⓣ Vivien Leigh (leading actress)

'There's something in the air. It might be love – but it isn't.'

Strictly Ballroom ★★★

DIR *Baz Luhrmann*

1992 94m Australia

[DVD] ♫

☆ *Paul Mercurio* (Scott Hastings), *Tara Morice* (Fran), Bill Hunter (Barry Fife), Pat Thomson (Shirley Hastings), Gia Carides (Liz Holt), Peter Whitford (Les Kendall), Barry Otto (Doug Hastings), John Hannan (Ken Railings), Sonia Kruger (Tina Sparkle), Kris McQuade (Charm Leachman), Antonio Vargas (Rico), Armonia Benedito (Ya Ya)

A ballroom dancer falls out with the establishment by coming up with his own steps, and looks for a new partner he can work with.

Class-act romance, directed with a showman's intoxicating flair, and leaving us with no doubt who to root for.

SCR Baz Luhrmann, Craig Pearce **CIN** Steve Mason **MUS** David Hirschfelder **DES** *Catherine Martin* **ED** Jill Bilcock **PROD** Tristam Miall **DIST** Rank/M&A/Australian Film Finance Corp

66 Begins as straightfaced baroque, shifts up into rococo and ends as a roaring essay in comical-romantic glitz. – *Nigel Andrews, Financial Times*

† Both the film's forgotten stars had cameos in the mockumentary Razzle Dazzle (2007).

Ⓣ David Hirschfelder; Catherine Martin; Angus Strathie, Catherine Martin (costume design)

Ⓣ film; Tara Morice (leading actress); Jill Bilcock (editing); Tristam Miall, Baz Luhrmann (adapted screenplay); sound

---

'Some people get into trouble . . . No matter what they wear.'

Striptease

SCR/DIR Andrew Bergman

1996 117m US

[DVD] ♫

☆ Demi Moore (Erin Grant), Burt Reynolds (Congressman David Dilbeck), Armand Assante (Lt. Al Garcia), Ving Rhames (Shad), Robert Patrick (Darrell Grant), Paul Guilfoyle (Malcolm Moldovsky), Jerry Grayson (Orly), Rumer Willis (Angela Grant)

A single mother turned Miami stripper is dragged into a murder case involving a corrupt Congressman who has taken a shine to her.

Depressingly botched adaptation of a much-liked satirical novel, turned into pure Hollywood cheese thanks to its off-key script and casting. Moore's plastic surgery is better showcased, shall we say, than her acting. Along with Showgirls it eloquently demonstrates the taste-free desperation prevalent in Hollywood in the mid-90s.

CIN Stephen Goldblatt **MUS** Howard Shore **DES** Mel Bourne **ED** Anne V. Coates **PROD** Mike Lobell, Andrew Bergman **DIST** Rank/Castle Rock/Turner

66 Can't decide whether to be sexy or safe or campy or cuddly. So it comes close to being nothing at all. – *Owen Gleiberman, Entertainment Weekly*

† Won six Razzies, including Worst Picture, Worst Director and Worst Actress.

Stuart Little ★★

DIR Rob Minkoff

1999 84m US/Germany

[DVD] ♫

☆ Geena Davis (Mrs. Little), Hugh Laurie (Mr Little), Jonathan Lipnicki (George Little), Brian Doyle-Murray (Cousin Edgar), Estelle Getty (Grandma Estelle), Julia Sweeney (Mrs. Keeper), Dabney Coleman (Dr Beechwood), voices of: Michael J. Fox (Stuart Little), Nathan Lane, Chazz Palminteri, Steve Zahn, Jim Doughan, David Alan Grier, Jennifer Tilly, Bruno Kirby

A New York family adopt a mouse, which earns the love of its human big brother, but not the family cat.

Pleasant children's entertainment, with endearingly old-fashioned values wedded to state-of-the-art animation effects.

SCR M. Night Shyamalan, Greg Brooker **CIN** Guillermo Navarro **DES** Bill Brzeski **ED** Tom Finan, Julie Rogers **PROD** Douglas Wick **DIST** Columbia

66 Alternately a sentimental celebration of family life and a quite savage comedy. – *Philip French, Observer*

† A sequel, Stuart Little 2, followed in 2002.

visual effects (John Dykstra, Jerome Chen, Henry F. Anderson III, Eric Allard)

The Stunt Man ★★★

DIR *Richard Rush*

1980 129m US

[DVD]

☆ Peter O'Toole, Steve Railsback, Barbara Hershey, Allen Goorwitz, Alex Rocco, Sharon Farrell

A Vietnam veteran on the run from the police finds refuge on a film set as a star stunt man for a sinister director, and ends up seducing the leading lady.

Something of a cult grew up around director Rush, who has worked infrequently in recent years. He was Oscar-nominated for this curious, enigmatic drama which plays around with illusion and reality while satirising the movie business. It's a bold, distinctive effort that sometimes misfires, but largely works well.

SCR Lawrence B. Marcus **CIN** Mario Tosi **MUS** Dominic Frontière **PROD** Richard Rush **DIST** Melvin Simon

66 It's like one of those sets of Chinese boxes, each one with another box inside, growing smaller and smaller until finally there is nothing left at all. – *Roger Ebert*

Richard Rush; Peter O'Toole (leading actor); Richard Rush, Lawrence B. Marcus (adapted screenplay)

Sugarhouse (new)

DIR Gary Love

2007 90m UK

[DVD]

☆ Steven Mackintosh (Tom), Ashley Walters (D), Andy

[DVD] Available on DVD   ☆ Cast in order of importance   66 Critics' Quotes   Academy Award   Academy Award nomination   Ⓑ BAFTA   Ⓣ BAFTA nomination

591

Serkis (Hoodwink), Tolga Safer (Sef), Teddy Nygh (Gary), Adam Deacon (Ray), Tracy Whitwell (Tina)

A cuckolded husband buys a stolen handgun from a drug addict, much to the displeasure of its unhinged owner.

Grim and grimy three-hander, adapted from a stage play; one admires the commitment far more than the end result.

SCR Dominic Leyton   CIN Dan Bronks   MUS Michael Price   DES Caroline Story   ED Peter Davies   PROD Oliver Milburn, Michael Riley, Arvind Ethan David, Matthew Justice, Ben Dixon, Rachel Connors   DIST SlingShot

66 An hour-and-a-half of cuss-heavy New British Brutalism. – *Derek Elley, Variety*

66 A static slice of ghetto hell. – *Tom Hawker, Total Film*

'There's no speed limit and no brake when Sullivan travels with Veronica Lake!'

Sullivan's Travels ★★★★

SCR/DIR *Preston Sturges*
1941   90m   US
[DVD]

☆ *Joel McCrea* (John L. Sullivan), *Veronica Lake* (The Girl), *Robert Warwick* (Mr. Lebrand), William Demarest (Mr. Jones), Franklin Pangborn (Mr. Casalais), Porter Hall (Mr. Hadrian), Byron Foulger (Mr. Valdelle), Eric Blore (Sullivan's Valet), Robert Greig (Sullivan's Butler), Torben Meyer (The Doctor), *Jimmy Conlin* (Trusty), Margaret Hayes (Secretary)

A successful Hollywood director tires of comedy and, frustrated in his wish to make a searing social drama, goes out to find real life.

Marvellously sustained tragi-comedy which ranges from pratfalls to the chain gang and never loses its grip or balance.

CIN *John Seitz*   MUS *Leo Shuken*   ED Stuart Gilmore   PROD Paul Jones   DIST Paramount

DEDICATION: To all the funny men and clowns who have made people laugh.

66 A brilliant fantasy in two keys – slapstick farce and the tragedy of human misery. – *James Agee*

66 The most witty and knowing spoof of Hollywood movie-making of all time. – *Film Society Review*

† The deadly serious film Sullivan wished to make was called O Brother, Where Art Thou?, a title lifted by the Coen brothers more than half a century later.

'NYC '77. Disco In The Clubs. Panic In The Streets.'

Summer of Sam ★★

DIR Spike Lee
1999   142m   US
[DVD]   ♫

☆ John Leguizamo (Vinny), Adrien Brody (Ritchie), Mira Sorvino (Dionna), Jennifer Esposito (Ruby), Anthony LaPaglia (Det Lou Petrocelli), Bebe Neuwirth (Gloria), Patti LuPone (Helen), Ben Gazarra (Luigi), Joe Lisi (Tony Olives), Michael Badalucco (Son of Sam), Michael Rispoli (Joey T), John Savage (Simon), Spike Lee (John Jeffries)

In the Bronx in 1977, the notorious serial killer dubbed 'Son of Sam' is at large, and members of the Italian-American community start pointing fingers at each other.

A melting-pot movie, and one which doesn't always nail its time and place convincingly, but builds up plenty of friction between the characters in a climate of unease; the fleeting glimpses of the killer at work chill the marrow.

SCR Victor Colicchio, Michael Imperioli, Spike Lee   CIN *Ellen Kuras*   MUS Terence Blanchard   DES Therese DePrez   ED Barry Alexander Brown   PROD Jon Kilik, Spike Lee   DIST Downtown

66 A thick stew of sex, violence and suspicion. – *David Ansen, Newsweek*

66 Has plenty of chutzpah and raunch. – *Peter Bradshaw, Guardian*

† Co-screenwriter Michael Imperioli is best known for his role in the TV series The Sopranos, playing Tony Soprano's nephew Christopher.

A Summer Story ★

DIR Piers Haggard
1988   95m   GB
♫

☆ James Wilby (Mr Ashton), *Imogen Stubbs* (Megan David), Ken Colley (Jim), Sophie Ward (Stella Halliday), Susannah York (Mrs Narracombe), Jerome Flynn (Joe Narracombe)

While recovering from an accident, a lawyer falls for a working-class girl in Devon, and recalls the experience.

Beautifully filmed account of a restrained early 20th-century romance. A superior example of material that was par for the course in the British film industry at the time.

SCR Penelope Mortimer   CIN *Kenneth MacMillan*   MUS Georges Delerue   DES Leo Austin   ED Ralph Sheldon   PROD Danton Rissner   DIST Warner/ITC

'It's about three decent people. They will break your heart!'

Sunday, Bloody Sunday ★★★

DIR *John Schlesinger*
1971   110m   GB
[DVD]

☆ *Glenda Jackson* (Alex Greville), *Peter Finch* (Dr. Daniel Hirsh), Murray Head (Bob Elkin), Peggy Ashcroft (Mrs. Greville), Maurice Denham (Mr. Greville), Vivian Pickles (Alva Hodson), Frank Windsor (Bill Hodson), Tony Britton (George Harding), Harold Goldblatt (Daniel's Father)

A young designer shares his sexual favours equally between two loves of different sexes, a Jewish doctor and a divorced woman executive.

Stylishly made character study with melodramatic leanings, rather self-conscious about the then risky subject of homosexuality; but, scene by scene, both adult and absorbing, with an overpowering mass of sociological detail about the way we live.

SCR *Penelope Gilliatt*   CIN *Billy Williams*   MUS Ron Geesin   DES Luciana Arrighi   ED Richard Marden   PROD Joseph Janni   DIST UA/Vectia

66 This is not a story about the loss of love, but about its absence. – *Roger Ebert*

♟ Glenda Jackson (leading actress); Peter Finch (leading actor); John Schlesinger (direction); Penelope Gilliatt (original screenplay)

🅣 picture; Peter Finch (leading actor); Glenda Jackson (leading actress) John Schlesinger (direction)

Sunrise ★★★★

DIR *F. W. Murnau*

1927 97m US

DVD ♫

☆ Janet Gaynor (The Wife), George O'Brien (The Man), Margaret Livingston (The Woman From the City), Bodil Rosing (The Maid), J. Farrell MacDonald (The Photographer)

A villager in love with a city woman tries to kill his wife, but then repents and spends a happy day with her.

Lyrical melodrama, superbly handled: generally considered among the finest Hollywood productions of the 1920s.

SCR Carl Mayer   CIN *Karl Struss, Charles Rosher*   MUS (sound version) Hugo Riesenfeld   ED Harold D. Schuster   DIST Fox

OPENING TITLE: This story of a man and his wife is of nowhere and everywhere, you might hear it anywhere and at any time.

66 It is filled with intense feeling and in it is embodied an underlying subtlety. . .exotic in many ways for it is a mixture of Russian gloom and Berlin brightness. – *Mordaunt Hall, New York Times*

66 Not since the earliest, simplest moving pictures, when locomotives, fire engines and crowds in streets were transposed to the screen artlessly and endearingly, when the entranced eye was rushed through tunnels and over precipices on runaway trains, has there been such joy in motion as under Murnau's direction. – *Louise Bogan, The New Republic*

♟ Janet Gaynor (leading actress); Karl Struss, Charles Rosher; Unique and Artistic Picture

♟ Rochas Gliese

'It happened in Hollywood . . . a love story . . . a drama real and ruthless, tender and terrifying!'

Sunset Boulevard ★★★★

DIR *Billy Wilder*

1950 110m US

DVD

☆ *Gloria Swanson* (Norma Desmond), *William Holden* (Joe Gillis), *Erich von Stroheim* (Max von Mayerling), *Fred Clark* (Sheldrake), *Nancy Olson* (Betty Schaefer), Jack Webb (Artie Green), Lloyd Gough (Morino), *Cecil B. de Mille* (Himself), H. B. Warner (Himself), Anna Q. Nilsson (Herself), Buster Keaton (Himself), Hedda Hopper (Herself)

A luckless Hollywood scriptwriter goes to live with a wealthy older woman, a slightly dotty and extremely possessive relic of the silent screen.

Incisive melodrama with marvellous moments but a tendency to overstay its welcome; the first reels are certainly the best, though the last scene is worth waiting for, and the malicious observations about Hollywood are a treat.

SCR *Charles Brackett, Billy Wilder, D. M. Marshman Jnr*   CIN *John F. Seitz*   MUS *Franz Waxman*   ED *Arthur Schmidt, Doane Harrison*   PROD Charles Brackett   DIST Paramount

JOE: You're Norma Desmond. You used to be in silent pictures. You used to be big.

NORMA: I am big. It's the pictures that got small.

66 That rare blend of pungent writing, expert acting, masterly direction and unobtrusively artistic photography which quickly casts a spell over an audience and holds it enthralled to a shattering climax. – *New York Times (T.M.P.)*

66 Miss Swanson's performance takes her at one bound into the class of Boris Karloff and Tod Slaughter. – *Richard Mallett, Punch*

♟ Charles Brackett, Billy Wilder, D.M. Marshman Jr. (screenplay); Franz Waxman; art direction

♟ picture; William Holden (leading actor); Erich von Stroheim (supporting actor); Nancy Olson (leading actres); Billy Wilder (direction); John F. Seitz; Gloria Swanson; editing

'Three generations. One dream.'

Sunshine ★★★

DIR *István Szabó*

1999 181m Austria/Canada/Germany/Hungary/GB

DVD ♫

☆ *Ralph Fiennes* (Ignatz Sonnenschein/Adam Sors/Ivan Sors), Rosemary Harris (Valerie Sors), Rachel Weisz (Greta Sors), Jennifer Ehle (Valerie Sonnenschein), Molly Parker (Hannah Wippler), Deborah Kara Unger (Carole Kovaks), James Frain (Gustave Sonnenschein), John Neville (Gustave Sors), Miriam Margolyes (Rose Sonnenschein), David de Keyser (Emmanuel Sonnenschein), Mark Strong (Istvan Sors), William Hurt (Andor Knorr), Bill Paterson (Minister of Justice), Rudiger Vogler (General Jakofalvy)

A century of Hungarian history, involving imperial, Nazi and communist subjugation, as viewed through the eyes of three successive patriarchs of a single Jewish family.

A laudably ambitious film, ravishing looking, epic in scale, and for Szabo, clearly a summation of themes about his native country he has touched on in earlier films. The casting of Fiennes as all three family heads is equally audacious, though to non-Hungarians not all the events depicted have emotional resonance.

SCR István Szabó, Israel Horovitz   CIN *Lajos Koltai*   MUS Maurice Jarre   DES Atilla Kovacs   ED Dominique Fortin, Michael Arcand   PROD Robert Lantos, Andras Hamori   DIST Alliance

66 This is a movie of substance and thrilling historical sweep, and its three hours allow Szabo to show the family's destiny forming and shifting under pressure. – *Roger Ebert, Chicago Sun-Times*

66 Leaves you with a sense of quiet, chastened grace. – *Dana Stevens, New York Times*

'If the sun dies, so do we.'

Sunshine ★★

DIR Danny Boyle

2007 107m

☆ Cillian Murphy (Capa), Michelle Yeoh (Corazon), Rose Byrne (Cassie), Benedict Wong (Trey), Troy Garity

---

DVD Available on DVD   ☆ Cast in order of importance   66 Critics' Quotes   ♟ Academy Award   ♟ Academy Award nomination   🅣 BAFTA   🅣 BAFTA nomination

† Points of interest

♫ Soundtrack on CD

S

(Harvey), Cliff Curtis (Searle), Chris Evans (Mace), Hiroyuki Sanada (Captain Kaneda)

In the mid-21st century, a team of astronauts goes on a mission to save Earth by launching a bomb at the dying sun, thus reviving it. A first mission had failed seven years earlier. But it is unclear whether the new team can achieve their objective and return safely.

For the first two-thirds, a sturdy piece of science-fiction, with interactions between the crew on this uncertain mission astutely portrayed. A fine collaboration between production design, photography and model work combines to convey the sun's deadly beauty. The script, too, has a stubborn logic, with real tension generated around these characters' fates. But things go badly wrong in the final act, with a plot twist that seems directly lifted from Alien, and it descends into slasher-movie territory.

SCR Alex Garland   CIN *Alwin Kuchler*   MUS John Murphy, Underworld   DES *Mark Tildesley*
PROD Andrew Macdonald   DIST TCF

66 It's in the relationship between the crew and the sun that Sunshine really shines. – *Ben Walters, Time Out*

66 A thrilling sensual spectacle. – *Peter Bradshaw, Guardian*

† Sunshine was shot almost entirely at 3 Mills Studios in London's East End.

'Take a vacation with John Sayles'

Sunshine State ★★

SCR/DIR *John Sayles*
2002   141m   US
DVD   ♫

☆ *Edie Falco* (Marly Temple), Angela Bassett (Desiree Perry), Jane Alexander (Delia Temple), Ralph Waite (Furman Temple), James McDaniel (Reggie), Timothy Hutton (Jack Meadows), Mary Alice (Eunice Stokes), Bill Cobbs (Dr Lloyd), Mary Steenburgen (Francine Pickney), Miguel Ferrer (Lester)

Land developers descend on a tiny seaside town in Florida, and meet resistance from the locals.

A talky, ruminative movie about people whose energy is failing them in the struggle against corporate steamrollers; the story drifts, and is marred by a Greek chorus of rich golfers, but it is one of Sayles's more rewarding efforts.

CIN Patrick Cady   MUS Mason Daring   DES Mark Ricker   ED John Sayles   PROD Maggie Renzi
DIST Columbia

66 Moves among a large community of characters with grace, humour and a forgiving irony. – *Roger Ebert, Chicago Sun-Times*

66 Less than the sum of its parts, but the parts are often lovely, and always true. – *Jessica Winter, Village Voice*

'A film of epic portions.'

Super Size Me ★★

SCR/DIR Morgan Spurlock
2004   100m   US
DVD   ♫

☆ Morgan Spurlock

The director subjects himself to a month-long diet of McDonald's burgers in super-sized portions to demonstrate their health risks.

Crudely effective stunt documentary, which makes its points simply but entertainingly: as a result of his experiment, Spurlock gains 25 lbs, experiences liver and cholesterol problems, and gets struck off one corporation's Christmas card list.

CIN Scott Ambrozy   ED Stela Gueorguieva, Julie 'Bob' Lombardi   PROD Morgan Spurlock   DIST Tartan

66 A funny, frightening and salutary film. – *Philip French, Observer*

66 A compelling cautionary tale hot-wired to your gag reflex. – *Desson Thomson, Washington Post*

† McDonald's withdrew their Super Size option following the release of the documentary.

⅄ documentary

'Come and Get Some.'

Superbad (new) ★

DIR Greg Mottola
2007   112m   US
DVD   ♫

☆ Michael Céra (Evan), Jonah Hill (Seth), Seth Rogen (Officer Michaels), Bill Hader (Officer Slater), Kevin Corrigan (Mark), Christopher Mintz-Plasse (Fogell)

When their friend gets a fake ID, two high school boys promise a girl throwing a party in her parents' empty house that they will be able to secure alcohol for the evening.

Junior league version of Knocked Up from the Judd Apatow comedy factory, though coarser and only fitfully amusing.

SCR Seth Rogen, Evan Goldberg   CIN Russ Alsobrook   MUS Lyke Workman   DES Chris Spellman   ED William Kerr   PROD Judd Apatow, Shauna Robertson   DIST Sony

EVAN (EXAMINING FOGELL'S FAKE ID): 'McLovin? What kind of a stupid name is that? What are you trying to be, an Irish r-and-b singer?'

66 Some of the patter is funny, but the movie lacks the clever plot developments and the character nuances of a classic like "American Graffiti." And it's missing the belly laughs of earlier raunchfests "American Pie" and "There's Something About Mary." – *Stephen Farber, Hollywood Reporter*

66 Horny is as horny does in the sweetly absurd high school comedy Superbad. – *Manohla Dargis, New York Times*

'The greatest Superhero movie of all time! (not counting all the others)'

Superhero Movie (new)

SCR/DIR Craig Mazin
2008   85m   US
DVD

☆ Drake Bell (Rick Riker), Sara Paxton (Jill Johnson), Christopher McDonald (Lou Landers), Kevin Hart (Trey), Brent Spiner (Dr. Strom), Jeffrey Tambor (Dr. Whitby), Robert Joy (Dr. Stephen Hawking), Regina Hall (Mrs. Xavier), Pamela Anderson (Invisible Girl), Leslie Nielsen (Uncle Albert Adams)

A teenager becomes a superhero after being bitten by a radioactive dragonfly.

Lame and laboured spoof of a genre many might consider beyond parody; this vulgar affair certainly fails to suggest otherwise.

CIN Thomas E. Ackerman MUS James L. Venable DES Bob Ziembicki ED Craig Herring, Daniel A. Schalk, Andrew S. Eisen PROD Robert K. Weiss, David Zucker, Craig Mazin DIST Momentum

66 A pudding-headed Spider-Man redux spackled with John Hughes nods and slathered with banana peels. – *Ken McIntyre, Total Film*

66 Though marginally better than recent skits on Hollywood staples, this scattergun comedy still has only one in a dozen jokes that are passably funny. – *Derek Malcolm, Evening Standard*

'A major ocean picture.'

Surf's Up (new) ★

DIR Ash Brannon, Chris Buck
2007 85m US
DVD ♫

☆ Shia LaBeouf (Cody Maverick), Jeff Bridges (Big Z/Geek), Zooey Deschanel (Lani Aliikai), Jon Heder (Chicken Joe), James Woods (Reggie), Diedrich Bader (Tank Evans)

A hot-headed penguin gets surfing lessons from a former champion.

Likeable, if overlong animation with a mock-documentary format that may be too sophisticated for its target audience.

SCR Don Rhymer, Ash Brannon, Chris Buck, Christopher Jenkins CIN Andres Martinez MUS Mychael Danna DES Paul Lasaine ED Ivan Bilancio PROD Christopher Jenkins DIST Sony Pictures

66 A charming computer cartoon. – *Andrew Osmond, Empire*

66 Kids, I'm afraid, will love it. – *James Christopher, The Times*

'No matter the cost. No matter the danger. They will find the truth.'

Suspect ★

DIR Peter Yates
1987 121m US
DVD ♫

☆ Cher (Kathleen Riley), Dennis Quaid (Eddie Sanger), Liam Neeson (Carl Wayne Anderson), John Mahoney (Judge Matthew Bishop Helms), Joe Mantegna (Charlie Stella), Philip Bosco (Paul Gray), E. Katherine Kerr (Grace Comisky), Fred Melamed (Morty Rosenthal), Lisbeth Bartlett (Marilyn), Paul D'Amato (Michael)

A public defender, working to acquit a deaf-mute vagrant of murder, exposes corruption in high places with the help of a jury member.

Preposterous thriller which has its tense moments.

SCR Eric Roth CIN Billy Williams MUS Michael Kamen DES Stuart Wurtzel ED Ray Lovejoy PROD Daniel A. Sherkow DIST Columbia/Tri-Star

66 Breaks down under cross-examination like those cornered witnesses at the end of Perry Mason. – *Desson Howe, Washington Post*

'Never forget. Never forgive.'

Sweeney Todd: The Demon Barber of Fleet Street (new) ★★

DIR Tim Burton
2007 116m UK/US
DVD ♫

☆ Johnny Depp (Sweeney Todd/Benjamin Barker), *Helena Bonham Carter* (Mrs.Lovett), Alan Rickman (Judge Turpin), Timothy Spall (Beadle Barnford), Sacha Baron Cohen (Signor Adolfo Pirelli), Jamie Campbell Bower (Anthony Hope), Laura Michelle Kelly (Lucy/Beggar woman), Jayne Wisener (Johanna), Edward Sanders (Toby)

A musical about a Victorian London barber who, in revenge for the murder of his sweetheart as a young man, slices his victims' throats and drops them down a chute, where his accomplice processes them into pie fillings.

A wonderful, impressionistic version of a shadowy, sinister London. Director Burton creates a specific, thrilling world, in which he does not spare the brightly-coloured gore, though the shock of Sweeney's behaviour lessens with repetition. Depp and Bonham Carter sing passably well, but they're not trained to sing musicals, and some of the intricate brilliance of Sondheim's lyrics is lost in garbled or slurred enunciation. An impressive feat, but a failure as a Sondheim production.

SCR John Logan CIN *Dariusz Wolski* DES Dante Ferretti ED Chris Lenenzon PROD Richard Zanuck, Walter Parkes, Laurie MacDonald, John Logan DIST Warners

66 The film is jaunty, beautifully rhythmic in its camera movement and editing, extraordinarily rapid without being hasty. – *Philip French, Observer*

66 An engaging but rather flat spectacle. – *Edward Porter, Sunday Times*

⚑ Dante Ferretti (art direction)

⚑ Johnny Depp (leading actor); Colleen Atwood (costume design)

Ⓣ Costume design; Ivana Primorac (make up and hair)

Sweet and Lowdown ★★

SCR/DIR *Woody Allen*
1999 95m US
DVD ♫

☆ *Sean Penn* (Emmet Ray), *Samantha Morton* (Hattie), Uma Thurman (Blanche), Brian Markinson (Bill Shields), Anthony LaPaglia (Al Torrio), Gretchen Mol (Ellie), Vincent Guastaferro (Sid Bishop), John Waters (Mr Haynes), Constance Shulman (Hazel), Kellie Overbey (Iris)

A narcissistic jazz guitarist in the 1930s dreams of fame and mistreats his half-wit girlfriend.

A rose-tinted period comedy of the jazz era, in love with the guitar music of Django Reinhardt, and loosely modelling its love story on Fellini's La Strada; not one of Allen's more urgent pictures, it has an air of picturesque harmlessness.

DVD Available on DVD ♫ Soundtrack on CD ☆ Cast in order of importance 66 Critics' Quotes † Points of interest ⚑ Academy Award ⚑ Academy Award nomination Ⓑ BAFTA Ⓣ BAFTA nomination

CIN *Zhao Fei* MUS Dick Hyman DES Santo Loquasto ED Alisa Lepselter PROD Jean Doumanian DIST Columbia TriStar

66 Has a nostalgic burnish that perfectly complements the anecdotal tenderness of the story. – *Anthony Quinn, Independent*

† Sean Penn's playing was dubbed by the eminent jazz guitarist Howard Alden.

⚐ Sean Penn (leading actor); Samantha Morton (supporting actress)

'There is no such thing as the simple truth.'

The Sweet Hereafter ★★★

SCR/DIR *Atom Egoyan*
1997 112m Canada
DVD ♫

☆ *Ian Holm* (Mitchell Stephens), Maury Chaykin (Wendell Walker), Gabrielle Rose (Dolores Driscoll), Peter Donaldson (Schwartz), Bruce Greenwood (Billy), David Hemblen (Abbott), Brooke Johnson (Mary), Arsinée Khanjian (Wanda), *Sarah Polley* (Nicole Burnell)

An ambulance-chasing lawyer arrives in a small Canadian town to convince grieving parents of 14 children killed in a school-bus accident to let him represent them.

A moving investigation of a terrible tragedy that uses a sophisticated fragmented narrative, re-told and going back and forth in time, to reflect various residents' viewpoints. The anger, guilt or resignation they display eloquently underlines the complexity of grief.

CIN Paul Sarossy MUS Mychael Danna DES Philip Barker ED Susan Shipton PROD Camelia Frieberg, Atom Egoyan DIST Electric/Speaking Parts/Alliance/Ego

66 It's a tactfully acted film, beautifully shot in snowy widescreen, subtly scripted and directed with a rare touch. – *Kim Newman, Empire*

66 A rich, complex meditation on the impact of a terrible tragedy on a small town. – *Brendan Kelly, Variety*

† The film won the Grand Jury prize at the 1997 Cannes Film Festival.

† Russell Banks, who wrote the original novel, has a small cameo role as a doctor. His daughter Caerthan appears as Zoe Stevens.

⚐ Atom Egoyan (direction); Atom Egoyan (adapted screenplay)

'It's you and Liam, against the world.'

Sweet Sixteen ★★★

DIR Ken Loach
2002 106m GB/Germany/Spain/Italy/France
DVD

☆ *Martin Compston* (Liam), William Ruane (Pinball), Annmarie Fulton (Chantelle), Michelle Abercromby (Suzanne), Michelle Coulter (Jean), Gary McCormack (Stan), Tommy McKee (Rab)

Awaiting his mother's release from prison, a teenager near Glasgow starts dealing drugs to raise money for their new home.

Thoroughly persuasive drama which makes crime seem like the only way out of a desperate, poverty-stricken

situation; *Loach extends his usual compassion to tough lives and tougher choices, leavens it with lovely touches of humour, and coaxes a wonderful performance from Compston, a novice actor aged 17.*

SCR *Paul Laverty* CIN Barry Ackroyd MUS George Fenton DES Martin Johnson ED Jonathan Morris PROD Rebecca O'Brien DIST Icon

66 Miraculously catches life on the fly, without apparent embellishment, cliché or melodrama. – *Michael Wilmington, Chicago Tribune*

66 Superb and viscerally powerful. – *Sukhdev Sandhu, Daily Telegraph*

† The film received a much-criticised 18 certificate in the UK because of the amount of swearing.

† Because of the broad Scottish accents used by many characters, it opened in the US with sub-titles.

† It was filmed in Compston's home town of Greenock.

'This is the story of J.J. – but not the way he wants it told!'

Sweet Smell of Success ★★★★

DIR *Alexander Mackendrick*
1957 96m US
DVD ♫

☆ *Burt Lancaster* (J.J. Hunsecker), *Tony Curtis* (Sidney Falco), Martin Milner (Steve Dallas), Sam Levene (Frank D'Angelo), Susan Harrison (Susan Hunsecker), Barbara Nichols (Rita), *Emile Meyer* (Harry Kello)

A crooked press agent helps a megalomaniac New York columnist break up his sister's romance.

Moody, brilliant, Wellesian melodrama put together with great artificial style; the plot matters less than the photographic detail and the skilful manipulation of decadent characters, bigger than life-size.

SCR *Clifford Odets, Ernest Lehman* CIN *James Wong Howe* MUS *Elmer Bernstein* ED Alan Crosland Jnr PROD James Hill DIST UA/Norma/Curtleigh

J.J. HUNSECKER: Match me, Sidney.

66 A sweet slice of perversity, a study of dollar and power worship. – *Pauline Kael*

66 The last of the great films noirs, and among the sharpest, most uncompromisingly dark Manhattan street movies. – *Peter Bogdanovich*

'On the surface, all is calm.'

Swimming Pool ★

DIR François Ozon
2002 103m France/GB
DVD ♫

☆ Charlotte Rampling (Sarah Morton), Ludivine Sagnier (Julie), Charles Dance (John Bosload), Marc Fayolle (Marcel), Jean-Marie Lamour (Franck), Mireille Mosse (Marcel's Daughter)

A mystery novelist with writer's block goes to stay at her publisher's house in France, where his highly-sexed teenage daughter provokes her.

A slick but superficial tease in which the central pas de deux depends largely on caricature, and the twist merely annoys.

SCR François Ozon, Emmanuele Bernheim   CIN Yorick Le Saux   MUS Philippe Rombi   ED Monica Coleman   PROD Olivier Delbosc, Marc Missonnier   DIST UGC

66 Less a thriller than a comedy, and a formulaic one at that, predicated on a bizarrely simplistic clash of personalities and cultures. – *Dennis Lim, Village Voice*

66 As subtle as a belly flop. – *Anthony Quinn, Independent*

'Life is not a movie.'

Swimming with Sharks ★★

SCR/DIR George Huang
1994   101m   US
DVD ♫

☆ *Kevin Spacey* (Buddy Ackerman), Frank Whaley (Guy), Benicio del Toro (Rex), Michelle Forbes (Dawn Lockard), T. E. Russell (Foster Kane), Roy Dotrice (Cyrus Miles), Matthew Flynt (Manny)

A naive Hollywood studio assistant gets his own back on his appalling boss.

Caustic satire on Tinseltown mores, albeit a film that's better setting up its conflicts than resolving them.

CIN Steven Finestone   MUS Tom Heil   DES Veronika Merlin, Cecil Gentry   ED Ed Marx   PROD Steve Alexander, Joanne Moore   DIST Starlight

66 The picture's raison d'être has to be Spacey's 'loud and nasty' performance: he's the sort of actor who grabs you by the throat and beats you about the head without ever lifting his feet from the desk. And when he's off screen, you miss him. – *Tom Charity, Time Out*

'Get a nightlife.'

Swingers ★

DIR Doug Liman
1996   96m   US
DVD ♫

☆ Jon Favreau (Mike Peters), Vince Vaughn (Trent Walker), Ron Livingston (Rob), Patrick Van Horn (Sue), Alex Desert (Charles), Deena Martin (Christy), Katherine Kendall (Lisa), Heather Graham (Lorraine)

A failed comedian and his friends party in Hollywood and try to pick up girls.

Engaging comedy which nails a particular brand of brash male camaraderie, and gave the dating game a whole new vocabulary.

SCR Jon Favreau   CIN Doug Liman   MUS Justin Reinhardt   DES Brad Halvorson   ED Stephen Mirrione   PROD Victor Simpkins   DIST Miramax

TRENT: Excuse me darling. I'm sorry. Wow. I want you to remember this face here, OK, this is the guy behind the guy behind the guy.

TRENT: There's nothing wrong with letting the girls know that you're money and that you want to party.

66 Sweet, funny, observant and goofy. – *Roger Ebert, Chicago Sun-Times*

66 It often happens that Mike means to be suave and winds up totally misunderstood. That's the basis for this film's inverted sense of high style, which has such fun with its characters' awkwardness that it turns their square-peg ethos into counter-cool. – *Janet Maslin, New York Times*

'Leopold and Loeb. The Perfect Crime. A Deadly Love Affair.'

Swoon ★

DIR Tom Kalin
1992   80m   US
DVD

☆ Daniel Schlachet (Richard Loeb), Craig Chester (Nathan Leopold Jr.), Ron Vawter (State's Attorney Crowe), Michael Kirby (Detective Savage), Michael Stumm (Doctor Bowman), Valda Z. Drabla (Germaine Reinhardt), Natalie Stanford (Susan Lurie)

In 1924 Chicago, two wealthy gay college students kill a schoolboy for kicks, and face a trial.

Other films about the Leopold and Loeb thrill murders have downplayed their homosexuality. Kalin foregrounds it, but seems more interested in making a stylish-looking film, all breathlessly dramatic monochrome, than exploring in depth the homophobic attitudes that made their case infamous.

SCR Tom Kalin, Hilton Als   CIN Ellen Kuras   MUS James Bennett   DES Thérèse DePrez   ED Tom Kalin   PROD Christine Vachon   DIST Argos Films

66 Decadent and economical, subjective and detached, fascinating and appalling. – *Tom Charity, Time Out*

'Revenge Was Never This Sweet'

Sympathy for Mr Vengeance ★★★

DIR *Park Chan-wook*
2002   129m   South Korea
DVD

☆ Song Kang-ho (Park Dong-jin), Shin Ha-kyun (Ryu), Bae Du-na (Cha Yeong-mi), Lim Ji-eun (Ryu's Sister), Han Bo-bae (Yu-sun), Kim Se-dong (Chief of Staff), Lee Dae-yeon (Choe)

A young deaf-mute in Seoul kidnaps a businessman's daughter to raise money for his ailing sister's kidney transplant.

Impressively twisted little number with the flavour of Jacobean tragedy or Titus Andronicus: everything goes hideously, bloodily wrong. Shot through a fixed and beady lens, the movie is a technical tour de force, and announced Park as a major name on the international film circuit.

SCR Lee Yong-jong, Lee Jae-soon, Lee Mu-yeong, Park Chan-wook   CIN Kim Byung-il   DES Choe Jung-hwa   ED Kim Sang-beom   PROD Lim Jin-gyu, Lee Jae-sun   DIST Metro Tartan

66 Jangles in the mind long after the final credits. – *Peter Bradshaw, Guardian*

† This was the first part of Park's Vengeance Trilogy, which continued with Oldboy and Sympathy for Lady Vengeance.

Syndromes and a Century (new) ★★

SCR/DIR Apichatpong Weerasethakul
2007   105m   Thailand/France/Austria/Netherlands
DVD

☆ Nantarat Sawaddikul (Dr. Tei), Jaruchai Iamaram (Dr. Nohng), Nu Nimsomboon (Toa)

S

DVD Available on DVD   ☆ Cast in order   66 Critics' Quotes   🏆 Academy Award   🎭 BAFTA
♫ Soundtrack on CD   of importance   † Points of interest   🏆 Academy Award nomination   🎭 BAFTA nomination

597

A story in two halves about the director's parents, both of whom were doctors.

Curious formal structure, in which many incidents and scenes seem to be repeated. It exerts an odd fascination between longueurs.

CIN Sayombhu Mukdeeprom   MUS Kantee Anantagant   ED Lee Chatametikool   PROD Apichatpong Weerasethakul   DIST BFI

66 Fragmented and elliptical to the point of being bewildering. – *Sukhdev Sandhu, Daily Telegraph*

66 There are times when the proceedings cross over from restfulness to plain dullness. – *Edward Porter, Sunday Times*

'Everything is connected.'

Syriana   ★★

SCR/DIR Stephen Gaghan
2005   126m   US
[DVD]   ♫

☆ George Clooney (Bob Barnes), Matt Damon (Bryan Woodman), Jeffrey Wright (Bennett Holiday), Chris Cooper (Jimmy Pope), William Hurt (Stan), Mazhar Munir (Wasim Khan), Tim Blake Nelson (Danny Dalton), Amanda Peet (Julie Woodman), Christopher Plummer (Dean Whiting)

A washed-up CIA agent becomes the fall guy in a botched plot to assassinate a progressive Arab prince, while the anti-competitive merger of two American oil companies is investigated by the Department of Justice in Washington.

A hugely ambitious political thriller, with much to say about the labyrinthine corruption of the global oil industry. The film's weakness is that it explores everyone's culpability except the consumer's, and the sheer obscurity of the plotting can feel a little high-handed.

CIN *Robert Elswit*   MUS *Alexandre Desplat*   DES Dan Weil   ED *Tim Squyres*   PROD Jennifer Fox, Michael Nozik, Georgia Kacandes   DIST Warner

66 A fearless and ambitious piece of work, made with equal parts passion and calculation. – *Kenneth Turan, L.A. Times*

66 Impresses as an all-round entertainment and thought-provoker... [but] it's possible to come away from the film feeling unimplicated. – *Jonathan Romney, Independent on Sunday*

† Harrison Ford was offered the role of Bob Barnes, but turned it down, a decision he subsequently admitted regretting.

♟ George Clooney (supporting actor)
♟ Stephen Gaghan (original screenplay)
Ⓣ George Clooney (supporting actor)

'Everyone says he should date girls his own age. Oscar respectfully disagrees.'

Tadpole ★★

DIR Gary Winick

2002 78m US

DVD

☆ Sigourney Weaver (Eve), Aaron Stanford (Oscar Grubman), John Ritter (Stanley Grubman), *Bebe Neuwirth* (Diane), Robert Iler (Charlie), Adam Lefevre (Phil)

A 15-year-old boy on the Upper East Side falls in love with his stepmother, but is seduced by her best friend.

Smart, if slight, New York comedy with a debt to The Graduate, via Woody Allen.

SCR Heather McGowan, Niels Mueller **CIN** Hubert Taczanowski **MUS** Renaud Pion **DES** Anthony Gasparro **ED** Susan Littenberg **PROD** Dolly Hall, Alexis Alexanian, Gary Winick **DIST** Buena Vista

66 As sweet and unassuming a film as they come. – *Jessica Winter, Village Voice*

† The film was shot in just 14 days.

'In a place this treacherous, what a good spy needs is a spy of his own.'

The Tailor of Panama ★★

DIR John Boorman

2001 109m US/Ireland

DVD ♫

☆ Pierce Brosnan (Andy Osnard), Geoffrey Rush (Harry Pendel), Jamie Lee Curtis (Louisa Pendel), Brendan Gleeson (Mickie Abraxas), Catherine McCormack (Francesca), Leonor Varela (Marta), Harold Pinter (Uncle Benny), Daniel Radcliffe (Mark Pendel), Lola Boorman (Sarah Pendel), David Hayman (Luxmore), Mark Margolis (Rafi Domingo), Martin Ferrero (Teddy), John Fortune (Ambassador Maltby)

An out-of-favour British spy agent is banished to the backwater of post-Noriega Panama, where he recruits a pretentious, possibly treacherous expatriate tailor to provide the intelligence he needs to rescue his floundering career.

Brosnan slips out of his James Bond tuxedo to play a much nastier kind of spy: a malevolent, sleazy womaniser. It's a grown-up, unsentimental story of two men blatantly using each other, but the personal cat-and-mouse game never quite meshes with the complex political backdrop. It has its moment, but finally this is another Le Carré story that lost its way en route to the big screen.

SCR Andrew Davies, John Le Carré, John Boorman **CIN** Philippe Rousselot **MUS** Shaun Davey **DES** Derek Wallace **ED** Ron Davis **PROD** John Boorman **DIST** Columbia

66 This film, for all its earnestness, snaky comedy, and would-be intelligence, never manages any real fizz. – *Ian Nathan, Empire*

66 If you think the spy-thriller genre has been streamlined and spoofed and subvert until nothing new can be done to it, think again. – *Peter Rainer, New York Magazine*

The Tale of the Fox ★★★

DIR Wladyslaw Starewicz

1931 65m France

DVD

☆ the voices of Claude Dauphin, Romain Bouquet, Sylvain Itkine, Léon Larive, Robert Seller, Edy Debray, Nicolas Amato

Renard, a cunning fox causes so much trouble that the king (a lion) orders him to be arrested and brought before the throne.

A brilliant pioneering animated film which was Wladyslaw Starevicz's only feature. Its eventual British release in 1994 helped bring belated recognition to an early master of the art.

SCR Wladyslaw Starewicz, Irène Starewicz, Jean Nohain, Antoinette Nordmann, Roger Richebé **MUS** Vincent Scotto **DES** Wladyslaw Starewicz **ED** Laura Séjounré **PROD** Louis Nalpas, Roger Richebé **DIST** BFI/Wladyslaw Starewicz

† Starewicz reportedly took 10 years to prepare the film, and 18 months to shoot it.

'How Far Would You Go To Become Someone Else?'

The Talented Mr Ripley ★★★

SCR/DIR Anthony Minghella

1999 139m US

DVD ♫

☆ Matt Damon (Tom Ripley), *Jude Law* (Dickie Greenleaf), Gwyneth Paltrow (Marge Sherwood), *Cate Blanchett* (Meredith Logue), *Philip Seymour Hoffman* (Freddie Miles), Jack Davenport (Peter Smith-Kingsley), James Rebhorn (Herbert Greenleaf), Sergio Rubini (Inspector Roverini), Philip Baker Hall (Alvin MacCarron), Rosario Fiorello (Fausto), Stefania Rocca (Silvana)

A young men's room attendant in New York is hired by a wealthy man to bring back his wayward playboy son from Italy; but instead he decides to kill him and assume his identity.

DVD Available on DVD ☆ Cast in order 66 Critics' Quotes 🏆 Academy Award 🏆 BAFTA
♫ Soundtrack on CD of importance † Points of interest 🏆 Academy Award nomination 🏆 BAFTA nomination

An audacious take on Patricia Highsmith's pitch-dark novel, and director Minghella (whose best film this is) made an inspired choice: moving the setting forward a few years, closer to an era of cool jazz, the dawning of Italy's dolce vita, and a more relaxed attitude to sexuality. Shot to mirror the dazzle and glamour of Dickie Greenleaf's shrill, superficial social set, it also has an undertow of homosexual longing and disappointment. A brilliantly conceived adaptation.

CIN John Seale   MUS Gabriel Yared   DES Roy Walker
ED Walter Murch   PROD William Horberg, Tom Sternberg
DIST Paramount

66 On balance worth seeing more for its undeniably delightful journey than its final destination. – Andrew Sarris, New York Observer

66 An elegantly polished affair, with top notch performances all round. – Geoff Andrew, Time Out

† Highsmith's novel was first filmed in 1960 by René Clément under the title Plein Soleil.

⚊ Jude Law (supporting actor); Anthony Minghella (adapted screenplay); Gabriel Yared; Roy Walker; Ann Roth, Gary Jones (costume design)

Ⓣ Jude Law (supporting actor)
Ⓣ film; Cate Blanchett (supporting actress); Anthony Minghella (direction); Anthony Minghella (adapted screenplay); John Seale; Gabriel Yared

Tales from Earthsea (new)

DIR Goro Miyazaki
2006   115m   Japan
DVD ♫

☆ Timothy Dalton (Ged/Sparrowhawk (voice)), Mariska Hargitay (Tenar (voice)), Matt Levin (Prince Arren (voice)), Willem Dafoe (Cob (voice)), Cheech Marin (Usagi (voice))

In a mythical world of magic and dragons, a young prince joins forces with a wandering sage to fight an evil wizard.

Flatly drawn and dully dubbed adaptation of a celebrated fantasy series; it might have worked better in the original Japanese.

SCR Goro Miyazaki, Keiko Niwa   MUS Tamiya Terashima
ED Takeshi Seyama   PROD Toshio Suzuki
DIST Optimum Releasing

66 A mishmash of Celtic mysticism, Mediterranean architecture and cartoon villainy. – Anthony Quinn, Independent

66 Compressed and confusing. – Tim Robey, Daily Telegraph

† The first film to be directed by Goro Miyazaki, son of acclaimed animation director Hayao.
† The film is released in two versions: Dubbed into English, and in Japanese with English sub-titles.

'The last neighbourhood in America.'

Talk Radio   ★★

DIR Oliver Stone
1988   110m   US
DVD ♫

☆ Eric Bogosian (Barry Champlain), Alec Baldwin (Dan), Ellen Greene (Ellen), Leslie Hope (Laura), John C.

McGinley (Stu), John Pankow (Dietz), Michael Wincott (Kent / Michael / Joe)

An abusive radio talk-show host, who relentlessly taunts his listeners, is threatened by neo-Nazis on the eve of being nationally syndicated.

Loosely based on the murder of Denver DJ Alan Berg, this is a dark and oppressive drama about the dangers of free speech, charged up by the monologues of an incessantly obnoxious protagonist.

SCR Eric Bogosian, Oliver Stone   CIN Robert Richardson
MUS Stewart Copeland   DES Bruno Rubeo   ED David
Brenner   PROD Edward R. Pressman, A. Kitman Ho
DIST Fox/Cineplex Odeon/Ten-Four Productions

'Inspired by a true story.'

Talk To Me (new)   ★★

DIR Kasi Lemmons
2007   118m   US
DVD ♫

☆ Don Cheadle (Petey Greene), Chiwetel Ejiofor (Dewey Hughes), Cedric the Entertainer ('Nighthawk' Bob Terry), Taraji P. Henson (Vernell Watson), Mike Epps (Milo Hughes), Vondie Curtis Hall (Sunny Jim Kelsey), Martin Sheen (E.G. Sonderling)

An Afro-American jailbird finds his true calling, as a disc-jockey, and becomes a star turn at a Washington D.C. radio station.

A decent re-telling of a notable but hardly astonishing story, enlivened by Cheadle, often cast as a model of restraint, letting rip as the motor-mouthed Petey. A terrific soundtrack of Stax soul hits adds to the raucous enjoyment.

SCR Michael Genet, Rick Famuyiwa   CIN Stephane
Fontaine   MUS Terence Blanchard   DES Warren Alan
Young   ED Terilyn A. Shropshire   PROD Mark Gordon,
Sidney Kimmel, Joe Fries, Josh McLaughlin   DIST Verve

66 Don Cheadle, in the lead role, gets to play a charismatic, funny, never-lost-for-words kind of guy. This he does entertainingly, adding zest to what is otherwise a routine Hollywood life story. – Edward Porter, Sunday Times

66 A rowdy, richly offbeat biopic. – Owen Gleiberman, Entertainment Weekly

† More than 10,000 people lined the streets of Washington at Petey Greene's funeral in 1984.

The Tall T   ★★★

DIR Budd Boetticher
1957   78m   US

☆ Randolph Scott, Richard Boone, Maureen O'Sullivan, Arthur Hunnicutt, Skip Homeier, John Hubbard, Henry Silva

Three bandits hold up the wrong stagecoach and take a woman hostage; a rancher tries to rescue her.

Splendidly terse, economical Western by a fine director who excelled in this genre; with several characters more complex than one has a right to expect, this tense drama is intensified by the harsh, arid landscapes.

SCR Burt Kennedy   CIN Charles Lawton Jnr   MUS Heinz
Roemheld   PROD Harry Joe Brown
DIST Columbia/Scott-Brown

T

Tampopo ★★

SCR/DIR Juzo Itami
1986   114m   Japan
DVD

☆ Tsutomu Yamazaki (Goro), Nobuko Miyamoto (Tampopo), Koji Yakuso (Man in White Suit), Ken Watanabe (Gun), Rikiya Yasouka (Pisuken)

A Japanese trucker helps a woman chef turn her roadside noodle bar into one of Tokyo's most popular restaurants.

A wacky, good-hearted tribute to the widely-ranging powers of good food, with some very funny parodies of western movie genres thrown in as a side dish.

CIN Masaki Tamura   MUS Kinihiko Murai   ED Akira Suzuki   PROD Juzo Itami, Yashushi Tamaoki, Seigo Hosogoe   DIST Itami Productions/New Century Producers

---

'A comedy that keeps women hopping.'

Tango ★★

DIR *Patrice Leconte*
1993   88m   France
DVD ♫

☆ *Philippe Noiret* (L'Elégant), Richard Bohringer (Vincent Baraduc), Thierry Lhermitte (Paul), Miou Miou (Marie), Judith Godreche (Madeleine), Carole Bouquet (Female Guest), Jean Rochefort (Bellhop)

A stunt pilot is acquitted of murdering his wife and her lover, then blackmailed by the misogynistic judge into carrying out a further killing.

Stylish, splendidly acted comedy of male prejudice, albeit one which gives too little space to a female rejoinder.

SCR Patrice Leconte, Patrick Dewolf   CIN *Eduardo Serra*   MUS Angelique and Jean-Claude Nachon   DES Ivan Maussion   ED Genevieve Winding   PROD René Cleitman, Philippe Carcassonne   DIST Cinea/Hachette Premiere/TF1/Zoulou

The Tango Lesson ★

SCR/DIR Sally Potter
1997   102m   GB/France/Argentina/Japan/Germany
DVD ♫

☆ Sally Potter (Sally), Pablo Veron (Pablo), Gustavo Naveira (Gustavo), Fabian Salas (Fabian), David Toole (Fashion Designer), Carolina Lotti (Pablo's partner)

An English film director becomes obsessed with the tango and falls in love with her dance partner.

It's hard to tell what true and what's invention in this odd, semi-autobiographical story. Potter and Veron were clearly having a good time, rather more so, in fact, than the audience. Neither is a skilled actor, and the film veers giddily between moments of embarrassment and sequences that feel laudable in their sincerity and audacity.

CIN Robby Müller   MUS Sally Potter, Fred Frith   DES Carlos Conti   ED Harvé Schneid   PROD Christopher Sheppard   DIST Artificial Eye

66 The dance sequences are pleasurable enough to watch but in the end tango is the movie's only strength. – *Jack Mathews, Los Angeles Times*

66 It's smoothly directed, nicely written and falters only in the performance that [director Sally] Potter was able to squeeze out of herself while performing her multiple tasks. – *Edward Guthmann, San Francisco Chronicle*

Ⓣ film not in the English language

Tape ★★

DIR *Richard Linklater*
2001   86m   US
DVD

☆ *Ethan Hawke* (Vince), *Robert Sean Leonard* (Johnny), *Uma Thurman* (Amy)

A drug-dealer invites his old school friend to a Michigan motel room, where he secretly tapes him admitting to the possible date-rape of a girl they both knew.

Intentionally claustrophobic, digitally filmed play, crackling with hidden resentments and paranoia – it is a somewhat constricted exercise, but one Linklater and his actors pull off admirably.

SCR *Stephen Belber*   CIN Maryse Alberti   DES Stephen J. Beatrice   ED Sandra Adair   PROD Gary Winick, Alexis Alexanian, Anne Walker-McBay

66 Crackles with unpredictability. – *Ryan Gilbey, Observer*

66 May not be a great movie, but it's a great demonstration of creativity within severe limitations. – *Michael Wilmington, Chicago Tribune*

'Your greatest creation is the life you lead.'

Tarnation ★★

SCR/DIR Jonathan Caouette
2004   88m   US
DVD

☆ Jonathan Caouette (Himself)

An intensely personal collage of the filmmaker's life, growing up as a flamboyantly gay teenager with an extremely disturbed, schizophrenic mother.

An artful video diary, pieced together from home-movie footage, that pushes the possibilities of DIY filmmaking, functioning as both performance art and confessional therapy for the director; but his exhibitionism is difficult to warm to, and the picture becomes acutely hard to watch when Caouette's mentally ill mother and other family members are dragged in.

CIN Jonathan Caouette   ED Jonathan Caouette   PROD Stephen Winter, Jonathan Caouette   DIST Optimum

66 A tale of sadness and hysteria so raw that it bleeds. – *J. Hoberman, Village Voice*

66 A daunting blend of head trip, cinema vérité, music video, and auto-therapy. – *Anthony Lane, New Yorker*

† The total budget for the film was originally stated to be just $218.32, but it came to $400,000 when the cost of music and video clip royalties were included.

† Caouette edited the film with Apple Computer's "iMovie" - a free DV editing program for Macintosh computers.

T

DVD Available on DVD   ☆ Cast in order of importance   66 Critics' Quotes   † Points of interest   🏆 Academy Award   Academy Award nomination   Ⓑ BAFTA   Ⓣ BAFTA nomination

♫ Soundtrack on CD

601

A Taste of Cherry ★★★

SCR/DIR Abbas Kiarostami
1977 95m Iran
[DVD]

☆ Homayoun Ershadi (Mr. Badiei), Abdol Hossain Bagheri (Taxidermist)

In the suburbs of Tehran, a middle-aged man looks for someone to break Islamic laws by burying him after he commits suicide.

Fascinating story, a road movie of sorts, told in a series of episodes that shed light on the people Mr Badiei propositions. It's about life, mortality and a society's strict, even perverse, moral codes. This brilliant film-maker is close to his best here.

CIN Homayun Payvar   ED Abbas Kiarostami
PROD Abbas Kiarostami   DIST Artificial Eye/Abbas Kiarostami

66 A deceptively simple parable of the meaning and value of life. – *Andrew Sarris, New York Observer*

† The film shared the Palme d'Or at Cannes in 1997 with The Eel.

'The Sexy Comedy About Good Taste. . .And Bad Manners!'

The Taste of Others ★★★

DIR Agnès Jaoui
2000 112m France
[DVD] ♫

☆ *Jean-Pierre Bacri* (Castella), *Anne Alvaro* (Clara Devaux), Agnès Jaoui (Manie), Gerard Lanvin (Moreno), *Alain Chabat* (Bruno Deschamps), Brigitte Catillon (Beatrice), Christiane Millet (Angelique), Wladimir Yordanoff (Antoine)

A coarse industrialist falls for an actress, and has his eyes opened to the arts.

Nicely played French comedy in which a philistine falls for an intellectual, and audiences' sympathies are neatly re-aligned.

SCR Agnès Jaoui, Jean-Pierre Bacri   CIN Laurent Dailland
MUS Jean-Charles Jarrell   DES François Emmanuelli
ED Herve de Luze   PROD Christian Berard, Charles Gassot   DIST Pathé

66 This is what Woody Allen movies might be like if they were not ruled by narcissism, pretentious point-scoring, cheap observations, and Woody's peculiar speech patterns. – *Michael Atkinson, Mr. Showbiz*

† A huge hit in France, where it registered 3.5 million admissions. Jaoui and Bacri became famous as a screenwriting team, and were given the collective nickname 'Jabac'.

⚖ foreign language film

Taxi Driver ★★★★

DIR *Martin Scorsese*
1976 114m US
[DVD] ♫

☆ *Robert De Niro* (Travis Bickle), Jodie Foster (Iris Steensman), Cybill Shepherd (Betsy), Peter Boyle (Wizard), Leonard Harris (Charles Palantine), Harvey Keitel (Sport)

A lonely Vietnam veteran becomes a New York taxi driver and allows the violence and squalor around him to explode in his mind.

The epitome of the sordid realism of the 70s, this unlovely but brilliantly made film haunts the mind and paints a most vivid picture of a hell on earth. Herrmann's haunting, almost slurred music captures the desolate mood to perfection.

SCR Paul Schrader   CIN Michael Chapman
MUS Bernard Herrmann   ED Tom Rolf, Melvin Shapiro, Marcia Lucas   PROD Michael and Julia Philips
DIST Columbia/Italo-Judeo

66 I don't question the truth of this material. I question Scorsese's ability to lift it out of the movie gutters into which less truthful directors have trampled it. – *Stanley Kauffmann*

66 A vivid, galvanizing portrait of a character so particular that you may be astonished that he makes consistent dramatic sense. – *Vincent Canby, New York Times*

† Schrader says the story was modelled after the diaries of would-be assassin Arthur Bremer.

⚖ picture; Robert De Niro (leading actor); Jodie Foster (supporting actress); Bernard Herrmann

🇹 Jodie Foster (supporting actress); Bernard Herrmann

Taxi to the Dark Side (new) ★★★

SCR/DIR Alex Gibney
2007 106m US
[DVD]

☆ Alex Gibney (Narrator), Maan Kaassamani (Detainee), Greg d'Agistino, Brian Keith Allen, Karyn Plonsky (soldiers)

Taking the death in custody of an innocent Afghan taxi driver, this documentary analyses the brutal, even illegal interrogation techniques used by the US government since 9/11.

Sobering and illuminating account of scandalous, torturous practices, routinely carried out in the name of freedom.

CIN Maryse Alberti, Greg Andracke   MUS Ivor Guest, Robert Logan   ED Sloane Klevin   PROD Alex Gibney, Eva Omer, Susannah Shipman   DIST Revolver

66 One of the most important films of the past five years. It's already out on DVD. See it. – *Philip French, Observer*

66 A taut, well-assembled and very disturbing analysis. – *Sukhdev Sandhu, Daily Telegraph*

⚖ documentary

'Three stories. Three generations. Three men. One bizarre and shocking universe.'

Taxidermia (new)

DIR Gyorgy Palfi
2006 91m France/Hungary/Austria
[DVD]

☆ Csaba Czene (Morosgovanyi Vendel), Gergely Trocsanyi (Balatomy Kalman), Piroska Molnar (Hadnagyne), Adel Stanczel (Aczel Gizi)

Three male generations in a troubled Hungarian family each feature in three tales depicting raw human activities of sex, eating and death.

T

A repulsive art-house assault on the senses and stomach using surreal imagery, graphic hardcore sex, excessive bloodletting and all manner of extreme grossness to shock for no apparent reason.

SCR Zsofia Ruttkay, Gyorgy Palfi **CIN** Gergely Pohamok **MUS** Amon Tobin **DES** Adrienn Asztalos **ED** Reka Lemhenyi **PROD** Alexander Dumreicher-Ivanceanu, Emile Georges, Gabriele Kranzelbinder, Alexandre Mallet-Guy **DIST** Tartan Films

66 Raucous, body-horror flick. . .that might give even David Cronenberg a bad night's sleep. – *Philip French, Observer*

'He has a Yen for her, but he won't tell her where it's hidden. . .'

A Taxing Woman ★★

SCR/DIR Juzo Itami
1987 127m Japan
DVD

☆ Nobuko Miyamoto (Ryoko Itakura), Tsutomu Yamazaki (Hideki Gondo), Masahiko Tsugawa (Hanamura), Hideo Murota (Ishii)

A shy but tenacious female tax inspector attempts to bring down a seedy embezzler.

Delightful satire of consumerist society that hit home hard in Japan. Telling and entertaining in equal parts.

CIN Yonezo Maeda **MUS** Toshiyuki Honda **ED** Akira Suzuki **PROD** Seigo Hosogoe, Yasushi Tamaoki **DIST** Itami Productions

---

'A story of civilised disobedience.'

Tea with Mussolini

DIR Franco Zeffirelli
1999 117m GB/Italy
DVD ♫

☆ Judi Dench (Arabella), Joan Plowright (Mary Wallace), Maggie Smith (Lady Hester Random), Cher (Elsa Morganthal Strauss-Armistan), Lily Tomlin (Georgie Rockwell), Baird Wallace (Luca), Charlie Lucas (Luca (Child)), Massimo Ghini (Paolo), Paolo Seganti (Vittorio Fanfanni), Paul Checquer (Wilfred Random, aka Miss Lucy), Tessa Pritchard (Connie Raynor)

An Italian boy, born out of wedlock, is raised by a gaggle of elderly Englishwomen in pre-WWII Tuscany, who gradually become aware that fascism is not nice.

Absurd nostalgic melodrama, a testament to Anglophilia in beautiful surroundings, asking little of its grandes dames but to wobble around haughtily and preserve the local artworks. It tips right into camp and stays there.

SCR John Mortimer **CIN** David Watkin **MUS** Alessio Vlad, Stefano Arnaldi **ED** Tariq Anwar **PROD** Clive Parsons, Riccardo Tozzi, Giovannella Zannoni **DIST** UIP/Medusa/Universal

66 Embarrassingly awkward, like a dilettante playing the doyenne. – *Steve Davis, Austin Chronicle*

66 An old queen's film, awash with a rapt savouring of stellar femininity and endearingly predictable in its

casting of inept but decorative young men. – *Andy Medhurst, Sight & Sound*

🏆 Maggie Smith (supporting actress)
🏆 Jenny Beavan, Anna Anni, Alberto Spiazzi (costume design)

'Putting the "F" back in Freedom.'

Team America World Police ★★

DIR Trey Parker
2004 98m US/Germany
DVD ♫

☆ voices of: Trey Parker (Gary, Joe, Kim Jong Il, Hans Blix), Matt Stone (Chris), Kristen Miller (Lisa), Masasa (Sarah), Daran Norris (Spottswoode), Phil Hendrie (I.N.T.E.L.L.I.G.E.N.C.E.), Maurice LaMarche (Alec Baldwin)

Members of an elite American military squad blow up most of Paris to rescue it from a terrorist threat, and then take on North Korean dictator Kim Jong-Il.

Scattershot puppet satire, sometimes hilarious, often breathtakingly offensive, and taking no prisoners – Hollywood liberals take the brunt of the abuse. The musical parodies are brilliant: it could have done with more of them, and more of a point, which is somewhat lost amid all the equal-opportunity mockery.

SCR Trey Parker, Matt Stone, Pam Brady **CIN** Bill Pope **MUS** Harry Gregson-Williams **DES** Jim Dultz **ED** Thomas M. Vogt **PROD** Scott Rudin, Trey Parker, Matt Stone **DIST** Paramount

66 An explosion of hilarious bad taste and ambiguous political satire. – *Peter Bradshaw, Guardian*

66 Stuck between point-blank ridicule and the obligations of a weary plot. – *Wesley Morris, Boston Globe*

Tears of the Black Tiger ★★★

SCR/DIR *Wisit Sasanatieng*
2000 110m Thailand
DVD ♫

☆ Chartchai Ngamsan (Black Tiger), Stella Malucchi (Rumpoey), Supakorn Kitsuwon (Mahesuan), Arawat Ruangvuth (Police Captain Kumjorn), Sombat Metanee (Fai), Pairoj Jaisingha (Phya Prasit), Naiyana Sheewanun (Rumpoey's maid), Kanchit Kwanpracha (Kamnan Dua), Chamloen Sridang (Sergeant Yam)

A Thai peasant, determined to win the love of a rich man's daughter, becomes a notorious bandit.

Luridly-styled and extravagantly camp western pastiche, playing homage to Leone and Peckinpah, but with touches of Jacques Demy too; it's fabulously entertaining in its peculiar way.

CIN Nattawat Kittikhun **MUS** Amornpong Methakunawut **DES** Ek Lemchuen **ED** Dusanee Puinongpho **PROD** Nonzee Nimibutr **DIST** Pathé

66 In a barking world of its own. – *Peter Bradshaw, Guardian*

66 This is a scrapbook, a happy jumble, of many of the things we instinctively respond to in movies: colour, shape, sound and movement, all intensified by heightened emotion. – *Stephanie Zacharek, Salon.com*

DVD Available on DVD   ☆ Cast in order   66 Critics' Quotes   🏆 Academy Award   🏆 BAFTA
♫ Soundtrack on CD   of importance   † Points of interest   🏆 Academy Award nomination   🏆 BAFTA nomination

T

603

'Every rose has its thorns.'

Teeth (new)

SCR/DIR Mitchell Lichtenstein

2008 93m US

☆ Jess Weixler (Dawn), John Hensley (Brad), Josh Pais (Dr. Godfrey), Hale Appleman (Tobey), Ashley Springer (Ryan), Lenny Von Dohlen (Bill)

A high school student discovers she has a toothed vagina.

Bizarre horror comedy that takes satirical sideswipes at censorship, feminism and sexual abstinence. The result is certainly bold and provocative, if tonally erratic and prone to gore.

CIN Wolfgang Held **MUS** Robert Miller **DES** Paul Avery **ED** Joe Landauer **PROD** Joyce Pierpoline, Mitchell Lichtenstein **DIST** Momentum

66 Teenage horror-movie spoof, John Waters parody, No Nukes protest movie, twisted sex-education film, quasi-feminist fable: Mitchell Lichtenstein's clever, crude comedy is all these and more. – *Stephen Holden, New York Times*

66 Few guys' notion of an ideal date movie. – *Todd McCarthy, Variety*

'A brutal crime. A man accused. But nothing is what it seems.'

Tell No One ★★

DIR Guillaume Canet

2006 130m France

☆ Francois Cluzet (Alex Beck), Marie-Josee Croze (Margot Beck), Andre Dussollier (Jacques Laurentin), Kristin Scott Thomas (Helene Perkins), Francois Berleand (Eric Levkowitch), Nathalie Baye (Elisabeth Feldman), Jean Rochefort (Gilbert Neuville), Guillaume Canet (Philippe Neuville)

A Paris paediatrician is perturbed to receive e-mails from the wife he believed to have died eight years previously.

Polished adaptation of an American novel; implausible and talkative in parts but generally intriguing and exciting, with a fine cast to boot.

SCR Guillaume Canet, Philippe Lefebvre **CIN** Christophe Offenstein **MUS** Mathieu Chedid **DES** Philippe Chiffre **ED** Herve de Luze **PROD** Alain Attal **DIST** Revolver Entertainment

66 Canet directs with a muscular swagger that occasionally borders on arrogance. – *Wendy Ide, The Times*

66 An intricate, intelligent and very watchable thriller. – *Andrew Pulver, Guardian*

'What the heart hides, the moon reveals.'

Temptress Moon ★

DIR Chen Kaige

1996 127m Hong Kong/China

DVD

☆ Leslie Cheung (Temptress Moon), Gong Li (Pang Ruyi), Kevin Lin (Pang Duanwu), He Seifei (Yu Xiuyi), Xian Xie (Boss), Shih Chang (Li Niangjiu), David Wu (Jingyun)

A wealthy but dysfunctional Shanghai family, ravaged by opium addiction. A boy and a girl, both raised in an ancestral palace, whose lives take sharply different turns. The changing face of China in the wake of the 1911 revolution..

Melodramatic, almost soap-opera style story with multiple strands. Received coolly at the Cannes Film Festival, its US distributor ordered 15 minutes of cuts; but it remains a rambling mess, though a lavishly good-looking one.

SCR Shu Kei, Wang Anyi, Chen Kaige **CIN** Christopher Doyle **MUS** Zhao Jiping **DES** Huang Qiagui **ED** Pei Xianzhi **PROD** Tong Cunlin, Hsu Feng **DIST** Artificial Eye/Tomson/Shanghai Film

10 ★★★

SCR/DIR *Abbas Kiarostami*

2002 93m France/Iran/US

DVD

☆ Mania Akbari (Driver), Amin Maher (Amin), Roya Arabshahi, Katayoun Taleidzadeh, Mandana Sharbaf, Amene Moradi

A female driver in Tehran gives ten lifts to different passengers.

Kiarostami's minimalist filmmaking at its most pared-down, with just two camera angles. Up close, the characters' often fractious conversations – and silences – make it one of his most revealing works about Iranian society.

CIN Abbas Kiarostami **MUS** Howard Blake **ED** Abbas Kiarostami, Vahid Ghazi, Bahman Kiarostami **PROD** Abbas Kiarostami, Marin Karmitz **DIST** ICA

66 By the end you feel that the lives of the characters, and the complicated society they inhabit, have been illuminated. – *A.O. Scott, New York Times*

66 There's no doubt that this movie is, as the network executives say, a tough watch. But it repays the investment of attention a thousandfold. – *Peter Bradshaw, Guardian*

† The making of this film is the subject of the documentary 10 on Ten.

'It takes a hero to change the world.'

10,000 B.C. (new) ★

DIR Roland Emmerich

2008 109m US/South Africa/New Zealand

♫

☆ Steven Strait (D'Leh), Camille Belle (Evolet), Cliff Curtis (Tic'Tic), Joel Virgel (Nakudu), Affif Ben Badra (Warlord), *Omar Sharif* (Narrator)

A young hunter from a mountain tribe embarks on a quest to find the girl he loves, and frees the slaves of a lost civilization.

Bland, over-blown prehistoric epic constructed around mindless spectacle. Inaccurate po-faced nonsense that isn't entertainingly silly enough.

SCR Roland Emmerich, Harald Kloser **CIN** Ueli Steiger **MUS** Harald Kloser, Thomas Wander **DES** Jean-Vincent Puzos **ED** Alexander Berner **PROD** Roland Emmerich, Mark Gordon, Michael Wimer **DIST** Warner Bros.

66 "Conventional where it should be bold, and mild where it should be wild". – *Todd McCarthy, Variety*

T

DVD Available on DVD ☆ Cast in order 66 Critics' Quotes ⏐ Academy Award Ⓑ BAFTA
♫ Soundtrack on CD of importance † Points of interest Ⓐ Academy Award nomination Ⓣ BAFTA nomination

'Ten canoes, three wives, 150 spears. . .trouble.'

Ten Canoes ★★

DIR Rolf de Heer, Peter Djigirr

2006   91m   Australia

DVD

☆ Crusoe Kurddal (Ridjimiraril), Jamie Dayindi Gulpilil (Dayindi), Richard Birrinbirrin (Birrinbirrin), David Gulpilil (The Storyteller)

A storyteller relates the history and mythology of the Yolngu people of Australia's Northern Territory.

Charming but calmly authoritative account of the Yolngu that becomes a comment on the power of story-telling itself. Occasional forays into delightfully broad humour confirm the film as utterly original.

SCR Rolf de Heer   **CIN** Ian Jones   **ED** Tania Nehme **PROD** Rolf de Heer, Julie Ryan   **DIST** The Works

66 Wise, warm, witty fare. – *Geoff Andrew, Time Out*

66 It's rather wonderful. – *Wendy Ide, The Times*

† Director de Heer acknowledged the consultation of the aboriginal people of Ramingining in writing his script.

'What a story it tells! What majesty it encompasses! What loves it unveils! What drama it unfolds!'

The Ten Commandments ★★

DIR Cecil B. de Mille

1956   219m   US

DVD   ♫

☆ *Charlton Heston*, Yul Brynner, Edward G. Robinson, Anne Baxter, Nina Foch, Yvonne de Carlo, John Derek, H. B. Warner, Henry Wilcoxon, Judith Anderson, John Carradine, Douglass Dumbrille, Cedric Hardwicke, Martha Scott, Vincent Price, Debra Paget

The life of Moses and his leading of the Israelites to the Promised Land.

Popular but incredibly stilted and verbose bible-in-pictures spectacle. Charlton Heston gets to part the Red Sea, and the sheer size (and imagined cost) of the spectacle is intriguing. But it's fatally overlong and pedestrian. Still, this passed for a state-of-the-art epic in 1950s Hollywood.

SCR Aeneas Mackenzie, Jesse L. Lasky Jnr, Jack Gariss, Fredric M. Frank   **CIN** Loyal Griggs   **MUS** Elmer Bernstein   **ED** Anne Bauchens   **PROD** Henry Wilcoxon **DIST** Paramount/Cecil B. de Mille

66 De Mille not only moulds religion into a set pattern of Hollywood conventions; he has also become an expert at making entertainment out of it. – *Gordon Gow, Films and Filming*

66 The result of all these stupendous efforts? Something roughly comparable to an eight-foot chorus girl – pretty well put together, but much too big and much too flashy . . . What de Mille has really done is to throw sex and sand into the moviegoers' eyes for almost twice as long as anyone else has ever dared to. – *Time*

⊥ John Fulton (special effects)

⊥ picture; Loyal Griggs; art direction; editing; sound; Edith Head and others (costume design)

Ten Rillington Place ★★★

DIR Richard Fleischer

1971   111m   GB

DVD

☆ Richard Attenborough, *John Hurt*, Judy Geeson, Pat Heywood, Isobel Black, Geoffrey Chater, André Morell, Robert Hardy

An account of serial killer Reginald Christie's deeds in London in the 1940s.

Agreeably seedy reconstruction of a cause célèbre, carefully built around the star part of a murderous aberrant landlord. A sombre story set in an austere era, related with clarity.

SCR Clive Exton   **CIN** Denys Coop   **MUS** Johnny Dankworth   **ED** Ernest Walter   **PROD** Leslie Linder **DIST** Columbia/Filmways

'How do I loathe thee? Let me count the ways.'

10 Things I Hate about You ★★

DIR Gil Junger

1999   97m   US

DVD   ♫

☆ *Heath Ledger* (Patrick Verona), *Julia Stiles* (Katarina Stratford), Joseph Gordon-Levitt (Cameron James), Larisa Oleynik (Bianca Stratford), *David Krumholtz* (Michael Eckman), Andrew Keegan (Joey Donner), Susan May Pratt (Mandella), Gabrielle Union (Chastity), *Larry Miller* (Walter Stratford)

A high-school girl isn't allowed to date until her older sister gets a boyfriend.

Shakespeare's The Taming of the Shrew redone as a teen comedy. It's one of the best of this wave of adaptations, thanks to the charming cast.

SCR Karen McCullah Lutz, Kirsten Smith   **CIN** Mark Irwin **MUS** Richard Gibbs   **DES** Carol Winstead Wood   **ED** O. Nicholas Brown   **PROD** Andrew Lazar   **DIST** Buena Vista/Touchstone/Mad Chance/Janet Entertainment

66 A bright little romantic comedy, nicely and sharply written, which wears its learning winningly and lightly. – *Peter Bradshaw, Guardian*

† This was Heath Ledger's Hollywood debut.

The Terminator ★★

DIR James Cameron

1984   108m   US

DVD   ♫

☆ Arnold Schwarzenegger, Michael Biehn, Linda Hamilton, Paul Winfield, Rick Rossovich, Lance Henriksen

An android from the future is sent back to the present time on a mission of extermination.

Slick, rather nasty but undeniably compelling comic book adventure. This cemented Schwarzenegger's action man career and gave him his career-defining role.

SCR James Cameron, Gale Anne Hurd   **CIN** Adam Greenberg   **MUS** Brad Fiedel   **ED** Mark Goldblatt **PROD** Gale Anne Hurd   **DIST** Orion/Hemdale/Pacific Western

T

'It's Nothing Personal.'

Terminator 2: Judgment Day ★★★

DIR *James Cameron*
1991 137m US
DVD ♫

☆ Arnold Schwarzenegger (The Terminator), *Linda Hamilton* (Sarah Connor), Edward Furlong (John Connor), Robert Patrick (T-1000), Earl Boen (Dr. Silberman), Joe Morton (Miles Dyson), S. Epatha Merkerson (Tarissa Dyson), Castulo Guerra (Enrique Salceda)

Two android assassins from the future fight to murder or save a teenage boy who will become the leader of a resistance movement.

A stunning advance on its predecessor, mounting a state-of-the-art apocalypse full of action, sound and fury, and signifying more than you might think: amid all the time-travelling and effects coups, this is a nightmare vision of corporations owning our post-nuclear future.

SCR James Cameron, William Wisher CIN *Adam Greenberg* MUS *Brad Fiedel* DES *Joseph Nemec* ED *Richard A. Harris, Mark Goldblatt, Conrad Buff* PROD James Cameron DIST Guild/Carolco/Pacific Western/Lightstorm

66 Imagines things you wouldn't even be likely to dream, and puts these visions on to the screen with a seamlessness that's mind-boggling. – *Mick LaSalle, San Francisco Chronicle*

66 Visceral to the point of overkill (and beyond). – *Joe Brown, Washington Post*

⚐ Dennis Murren, Stan Winston, Gene Warren Jnr, Robert Skotak (visual effects); Stan Winston, Jeff Dawn (make up); sound; sound effects editing

⚐ Adam Greenberg (cinematography); editing

⚐ sound; visual effects

⚐ Joseph Nemec (production design)

'Her death will not be ordinary.'

The Terrorist ★★

DIR Santosh Sivan
1998 95m India/US
DVD

☆ *Ayesha Dharkar* (Malli), Vishnu Vardhan (Thyagu), Bhanu Prakash (Perumal), K. Krishna (Lover), Sonu Sisupal (Leader), Vishwas (Lotus)

A politically committed teenage girl begins to have last-minute doubts about her deadly mission as a suicide bomber.

Taut, compact little film that never deviates from its narrative path, nor lets up on the suspense it creates. It creates extraordinary tension right until its final frame.

SCR Santosh Sivan, Ravi Deshpande, Vijay Deveshwar CIN Santosh Sivan MUS Sonu Sisupal, Rajamani DES Shyam Sunder ED A. Skreekar Prasad PROD A. Sriram, Abhijit Joshi, A. Sreekar Prasad, Shree Prasad DIST Metro Tartan

66 Almost unbearably suspenseful. – *A.O. Scott, New York Times*

66 Ayesha Dharkar is extremely good at intense, quiet power and communicates a great deal of depth without saying a word. – *Michael Thomson, BBC*

'Dictators. Terrorists. War Criminals. Meet the man who defended them all.'

Terror's Advocate (new) ★

DIR Barbet Schroeder
2007 137m France
DVD

☆ Jacques Verges (Himself), Barbet Schroeder (Narrator)

Urbane French lawyer Jacques Verges fields questions about a controversial career that has seen him represent terrorists, befriend dictators and defend Klaus Barbie.

Intriguing portrait of a fascinating character too slippery to incriminate himself; the archive footage adds both context and length.

CIN Caroline Champetier, Jean-Luc Perreard MUS Jorge Arriagada ED Nelly Quettier PROD Rita Dagher DIST Artificial Eye

66 One of the most engaging, morally unsettling political thrillers in quite some time, with the extra advantage of being true. – *A.O. Scott, New York Times*

66 Queasily fascinating. – *Sukhdev Sandhu, Telegraph*

'It's not a place . . . it's a state of mind'

Texasville

SCR/DIR Peter Bogdanovich
1990 123m US
DVD

☆ Jeff Bridges (Duane Jackson), Cybill Shepherd (Jacy Farrow), Annie Potts (Karla Jackson), Cloris Leachman (Ruth Popper), Timothy Bottoms (Sonny Crawford), Eileen Brennan (Genevieve Morgan), Randy Quaid (Lester Marlow), Harvey Christiansen (Old Man Balt), Pearl Jones (Minerva), Loyd Catlett (Lee Roy)

An indebted oil man cheats on his alcoholic wife, and is reunited with his teenage sweetheart, who has returned to her small-town home after the end of her acting career.

Much-anticipated but disappointingly flat, misguided sequel to The Last Picture Show, resurrecting characters whose lives are somehow much less interesting 30 years on.

CIN Nicholas von Sternberg DES Phedon Papamichael ED Richard Fields PROD Barry Spikings, Peter Bogdanovich DIST Guild/Nelson Films/Cine-Source

66 Comes off like an exceptionally slow episode of Dallas. – *Rolling Stone*

'America is living in spin.'

Thank You for Smoking ★★

SCR/DIR Jason Reitman
2006 92m US
DVD ♫

☆ Aaron Eckhart (Nick Naylor), Maria Bello (Polly Bailey), Cameron Bright (Joey Naylor), David Koechner (Bobby Jay Bliss), Sam Elliott (Lorne Lutch), Katie Holmes (Heather Holloway), Rob Lowe (Jeff Megall), Robert Duvall (The Captain), William H. Macy (Senator Finistirre)

A ruthlessly persuasive Washington lobbyist for tobacco companies makes a handsome living spreading lies about the virtues of cigarettes.

T

Darkly funny and dead set against political correctness. Scenes between Nick and his fellow 'merchants of death' – lobbyists for the alcohol and firearms industries – are cynical but hilarious. Nick's attempt to prove his principles to his son brings the script perilously close to sentimentality. But its blistering irony narrowly survives.

CIN James Whitaker   MUS Rolfe Kent   DES Steve Saklad   ED Dana E. Glauberman   PROD David O. Sacks   DIST TCF

NICK NAYLOR: 'Michael Jordan plays ball. Charles Manson kills people. I talk.'

NICK (TO HIS SON JOEY): 'If you argue correctly, you're never wrong.'

66 A nifty but slight movie. . .but Eckhart, in a sure-handed performance holds the picture together. – *David Denby, New Yorker*

That Obscure Object of Desire ★★

DIR Luis Buñuel
1977   103m   France/Spain
☆ Fernando Rey, Carole Bouquet, Angela Molina, Julien Bertheau

A wealthy, middle-aged businessman recounts his attempts to seduce his maid, only to be constantly rebuffed.

Unrecognizable remake of a novel previously filmed as a vehicle for Dietrich and Bardot. Despite the tricking out with surrealist touches (the girl is played by two different actresses) this final film of Buñuel's revisits some of his preferred themes rather than striking out for new territory. Intriguing, nonetheless.

SCR Luis Buñuel, Jean-Claude Carrière   CIN Edmond Richard   MUS from Richard Wagner   PROD Serge Silberman   DIST Greenwich/Galaxie/In Cine

foreign film; Luis Buñuel, Jean-Claude Carrière (adapted screenplay)

'In every life there comes a time when that dream you dream becomes that thing you do.'

That Thing You Do! ★

SCR/DIR Tom Hanks
1996   108m   US
DVD ♫
☆ Tom Everett Scott (Guy Patterson), Liv Tyler (Faye Dolan), Johnathon Schaech (Jimmy Mattingly), Steve Zahn (Lenny Haise), Ethan Embry (T. B. Player), Tom Hanks (Mr. White), Chris Isaak (Uncle Bob), Kevin Pollak (Victor 'Boss Vic Koss' Kosslovich), Jonathan Demme (Major Motion Picture Director)

A Pennsylvania rock band scores a hit in 1964, and tries to parlay it into long-term fame with the help of their manager.

Nostalgic 1960s rock movie with a wholesome appeal, but no real bite.

CIN Tak Fujimoto   MUS Howard Shore   DES Victor Kempster   ED Richard Chew   PROD Gary Goetzman, Jonathan Demme, Edward Saxon   DIST TCF/Clinica Estetico

66 May be inconsequential, but in some ways that's a strength. – *Roger Ebert, Chicago Sun-Times*

Adam Schlesinger (m, ly) (music, original song – That Thing You Do!)

'The living will always be more dangerous than the dead.'

The Devil's Backbone ★★

DIR Guillermo del Toro
2001   108m   Spain/Mexico
DVD
☆ Marisa Paredes (Carmen), Eduardo Noriega (Jacinto), Federico Luppi (Casares), Fernando Tielve (Carlos), Irene Visedo (Conchita), Inigo Garces (Jaime)

A young boy is orphaned in the Spanish Civil War and sent to a remote and threatening monastery, haunted by the ghost of an unknown child.

Beautifully constructed, allegorical story, full of chilling twists and turns, and set against the backdrop of a nation wrestling with a cruel internal conflict.

SCR Guillermo del Toro, Antonio Trashorras, David Munoz   CIN Guillermo Navarro   MUS Javier Navarrete   ED Luis de la Madrid   PROD Pedro Almodovar, Guillermo del Toro   DIST Optimum

66 It's a striking film and further good news for the Spanish cinema. – *Philip French, Observer*

66 A finely acted, atmospheric period piece with a strong streak of mystery and the supernatural. Both chilling and rewarding. – *Channel 4*

The Family Friend ★★

SCR/DIR Paolo Sorrentino
2006   102m   Italy / France
DVD ♫
☆ Giacomo Rizzo (Geremia), Fabrizio Bentivoglio (Gino), Laura Chiatti (Rosalba), Gigi Angelillo (Saverio), Clara Bindi (Geremia's mother)

Geremia, an odious money lender in a small town, tries to seduce a young bride with a financial incentive, then finds his world turned upside down as she professes love and reveals she is carrying his child.

Sorrentino, the Neapolitan director who made The Consequences of Love, consolidates his reputation as one of Italy's most original new talents. Rizzo proves inspired casting as the unsavoury loan shark who inhabits a dank, dark world and revels in the suffering of others while considering himself their 'friend'.

CIN Luca Bigazzi   MUS Teho Teardo   DES Lino Fiorito   ED Giogio Franchini   PROD Domenico Procacci, Nicola Giuliano, Francesca Cima   DIST Artificial Eye

66 All the surface style is properly wrapped around ideas of substance. – *Geoff Andrew, Time Out*

† After this film, Domenico Procacci, one of Italy's most prolific producers, founded Last Kiss Productions, a company in New York, to make films in English.

'Before the fall of the Berlin wall, East Germany's police listened to your secrets.'

The Lives of Others ★★★★

SCR/DIR Florian Henckel von Donnersmarck
2006   137m   Germany
DVD ♫
☆ Martina Gedeck (Christa-Maria Sieland), Ulrich Mühe

T

(Captain Gerd Wiesler), Sebastian Koch (Georg Dreyman), Ulrich Tukur (Lt. Col. Anton Grubitz), Thomas Thieme (Minister Bruno Hempf), Volkmar Kleinert (Albert Jerska), Hans-Uwe Bauer (Paul Hauser)

In 1980s Communist East Germany, the Ministry of State Security (Stasi) has an army of officers who spy on every aspects of citizens' lives. Stasi captain Wiesler, an expert in breaking down suspected dissidents under interrogation, is assigned to spy on Dreyman, a successful playwright, and his actress girlfriend Christa. Wiesler gradually comes to realise they are decent people with enviable lives.

A fascinating, sad but electrifying film about betrayed friendships, ruined lives and dashed expectations. The atmosphere of paranoia, distrust and fear in East Germany at the time is brilliantly evoked. Von Dommersmarck maintains the pace of a thriller, while conveying the universal distrust that permeated this society. The acting is superlative, notably Koch's suave, agreeable Dreyman, and the remarkable Mühe as the unmemorable-looking Wiesler, working doggedly but silently in crisis. The final line, comprising four short words, is unutterably moving. A rare film that can subtly alter the way one looks at life.

CIN Hagen Bogdanski MUS Gabriel Yared, Stéphane Moucha ED Patricia Rommel PROD Quirin Berg, Max Wiedemann DIST Lionsgate

66 It is a tribute to the richness of this film that one cannot say for sure who the hero is. – *Anthony Lane, New Yorker*

66 You should take pains not to miss this outstanding, and astounding German film. . .the layered ironies and bitter compromises of the story resonate as satisfyingly as a great novel. – *Anthony Quinn, Independent*

† Ulrich Mühe died in July 2007. On the film's release, he claimed he had discovered in an old Stasi file that his second wife had kept him under surveillance in the 1980s. She denied the allegation.

⚊ foreign language film

Ⓣ film not in the English language

Ⓣ Florian Henckel von Donnersmarck; Ulrich Mühe (leading actor); Florian Henckel von Donnersmarck (original screenplay)

The Page Turner ★★

DIR Denis Dercourt
2006 84m France
DVD ♫

☆ Catherine Frot (Ariane Fouchécourt), Deborah Francois (Mélanie Prouvost), Pascal Greggory (Jean Fouchécourt), Clotilde Mollet (Virginie), Xavier de Guillebon (Laurent), Christine Citti (Madame Prouvost)

A former music student takes elaborate revenge on the concert pianist she blames for her failure to progress.

Sophisticated psychological thriller in the Hitchcock mould; the kind of film Hollywood has forgotten how to make, or maybe just doesn't want to.

SCR Denis Dercourt, Jacques Sotty CIN Jerome Peyrebrune MUS Jerome Lemonnier ED Francois Gedigier PROD Michel Saint-Jean DIST Artificial Eye

66 A treat for lovers of intelligent cinema. – *Peter Bradshaw, Guardian*

The Right of the Weakest (new) ★★★

SCR/DIR Lucas Belvaux
2006 116m France/Belgium
DVD

☆ Lucas Belvaux (Marc), Eric Caravaca (Patrick), Patrick Descamps (Jean-Pierre), Claude Semal (Robert), Elie Belvaux (Steve), Natacha Régnier (Carole), Gilbert Melki (Scrap iron dealer)

A group of desperate unemployed men gathers regularly in a café to play cards. The men find in Marc, a newcomer freshly released from prison, hope to escape their sad fate. Together they decide to rob a local factory. Their improbable plan is crazy enough to work. Now a new moral code applies between them.

Belvaux's much anticipated sixth feature does not disappoint. Setting it in the urban landscape of Liège, he mixes the social realism of Ken Loach and the gritty underworld sagas of Jean-Pierre Melville to provide drama of the highest order – partly through the performances and partly through a powerful sense of place: factories, pubs, dismal housing projects.

CIN Pierre Milon MUS Riccardo Del Fra ED Ludo Troch PROD Patrick Sobelman, Diana Elbaum DIST Tartan

66 Dour and schematic drama about disenfranchised factory workers. Think Belgian Ken Loach. – *Tim Robey, Daily Telegraph*

† The Right of the Weakest is the 6th feature film by the Belgian filmmaker, winner of the 2003 Louis-Delluc Prize for his trilogy An Amazing Couple, On the Run and After the Life.

'Vincent's life is being destroyed. Now he must find out why.'

The Serpent (new) ★

SCR/DIR Eric Barbier
2007 119m France

☆ Yvan Attal (Vincent), Clovis Cornillac (Plender), Pierre Richard (Cendras), Simon Abkarian (Sam), Olga Kurylenko (Sofia)

A fashion photographer (Attal) is accused of rape by one of his models. But it turns out she is setting him up in a vengeful scam masterminded by a private eye (Cornillac) who Vincent bullied in their school days.

Taut, stylish, engrossing film that falls apart dramatically in the last reel as the action is ratcheted up alarmingly and it comes to resemble a cheap, routine Hollywood thriller.

CIN Jerome Robert MUS Renaud Barbier DES Pierre Renson ED Véronique Lange PROD Olivier Delbosc, Eric Jehelmann, Pierre Rambaldi, Marc Missonier DIST Metrodome

66 The more overblown the film becomes, the less it engages our emotions. – *Tom Dawson, BBC*

66 Pretty effective in the manner of Cape Fear. – *Philip French, Observer*

† English crime writer Ted Lewis, who wrote the novel on which this is based, also authored Get Carter.

The Singer (new)   ★★★

SCR/DIR Xavier Giannoli
2006   113m   France/Belgium
DVD   ♫

☆ Gérard Depardieu (Alain Moreau), Cécile de France (Marion), Mathieu Amalric (Bruno), Christine Citti (Michèle), Patrick Pineau (Daniel), Alain Chanone (Philipppe Mariani)

Ageing entertainer Alain Moreau wins the hearts of pensioners and middle-aged ladies with heart-rending songs he performs at village discos, retirement homes and local festivals. After the 'glamour' of the concerts, he goes home to his empty house, where a jukebox, a goat and a self-tanning machine are his only companions. His life changes when he meets cool, pretty Marion, an energetic estate agent many years his junior.

Dépardieu shows off his vocal skills as a lonely dance-hall singer in a film that nostalgically portrays a profession threatened by DJs and karaoke bars. It is unashamedly sentimental but no less affecting for that. Dépardieu, sporting garish shirts and a fake tan, gives one of his best performances, full of tenderness and humility.

CIN Yorick Le Saux   MUS Alexandre Desplat
DES François-Renaud Labarthe   ED Martine Giordano
PROD Pierre-Ange Le Pogam, Edouard Weil
DIST Artificial Eye

66 Giannoli's film is as bitter as it is sweet and paints the scene with masterly precision, even if the usual comforting ending is at odds with what has gone before. – *Derek Malcolm, London Evening Standard*

† Director Giannoli went to see real dance hall singers in and around the French city of Clermont-Ferrand. 'The universe touched me. I'm Parisian, but I was very moved by this world,' he was quoted as saying.

The Umbrellas of Cherbourg   ★★★

SCR/DIR *Jacques Demy*
1964   92m   France/West Germany
DVD   ♫

☆ *Catherine Deneuve, Anne Vernon*, Nino Castelnuovo

A French shopgirl loves a gas station attendant, but when he goes off to the Algerian War, she finds she is pregnant and marries another man. Years later the couple reunite briefly and accidentally.

Unique, delightfully colourful piece, with sung-through dialogue and camera work that enhances its faintly magical, fairy-tale quality. This was Deneuve's breakthrough film role, and she makes the most of it. In a category all by itself, this admittedly flimsy narrative has remained a perennial favourite, partly for its swooningly lovely music and for its moving, tear-jerking qualities.

CIN *Jean Rabier*   MUS *Michel Legrand, Jacques Demy*
DIST Parc/Madeleine/Beta

66 Poetic neo-realism. – *Georges Sadoul*

66 We are told that in Paris the opening night audience wept and the critics were ecstatic. It would have made a little more sense the other way round. – *John Simon*

⚲ foreign film; Jacques Demy (origianl screenplay); Michel Legrand, Jacques Demy; Michel Legrand (m), Jacques Demy (ly) (music, original song – I Will Wait for You); scoring

The Witnesses (new)   ★★★

DIR André Téchiné
2007   112m   France/Spain
DVD   ♫

☆ Michel Blanc (Adrien), Emmanuelle Béart (Sarah), Sami Bouajila (Mehdi), Julie Depardieu (Julie), Johan Libéreau (Manu)

The dramatic emergence of the AIDS epidemic in the early 1980s is witnessed at first hand by a diverse collection of characters. Manu arrives in Paris to move in with his sister Julie in a squalid hotel room. His encounter at a favourite cruising spot with Adrien, a 50-year-old doctor, introduces him to a varied group of friends and lovers.

Veteran Téchiné, despite the serious subject and dark finale, maintains an optimistic tone without resorting to sentiment. He tracks the first stories about the outbreak of AIDS and its effect on individuals, communities and the medical establishment. From the cast, newcomer Johan Libéreau impresses.

SCR André Téchiné, with Laurent Guyot, Viviane Zingg
CIN Julien Hirsch   MUS Philippe Sarde
DES MichèleAbbe   ED Martine Giordano   PROD Said Ben Said   DIST Artificial Eye

66 One cares about what happens, despite some characters being thoroughly unlikeable. – *Peter Whittle, Sunday Times*

'Somebody said get a life. . .so they did.'

Thelma and Louise   ★★★★

DIR *Ridley Scott*
1991   129m   US
DVD   ♫

☆ *Susan Sarandon* (Louise), *Geena Davis* (Thelma), Harvey Keitel (Hal), Michael Madsen (Jimmy), Christopher McDonald (Darryl), Stephen Tobolowsky (Max), Brad Pitt (J.D.)

Two bored small-town women go on the run after a fun weekend together goes horribly wrong, and one of them shoots a man who was trying to rape the other.

Exhilarating, adrenalin-fuelled road movie with Sarandon and Davis making the most of the exuberant characters gifted to them by writer Khouri; it's a welcome aberration in director Scott's career, but he doesn't put a foot wrong, and the film's elevation to classic feminist tract seems utterly merited.

SCR *Callie Khouri*   CIN Adrian Biddle   MUS Hans Zimmer   DES Norris Spencer   ED Thom Noble

T

| DVD Available on DVD | ☆ Cast in order | 66 Critics' Quotes | ⚲ Academy Award | Ⓑ BAFTA |
| ♫ Soundtrack on CD | of importance | † Points of interest | ⚱ Academy Award nomination | Ⓣ BAFTA nomination |

PROD Ridley Scott, Mimi Polk   **DIST** UIP/Pathé Entertainment

66 It may look like just another girl-buddy road picture, but in director Ridley Scott's hands it's propulsively more. – *Desson Howe, Washington Post*

66 This brilliant road movie puts women in the driving seat. – *Channel 4*

⚲ Callie Khouri (original screenplay)

⚲ Geena Davis (leading actress); Susan Sarandon (leading actress); Ridley Scott (direction); Adrian Biddle; editing

Ⓣ film; Geena Davis (leading actress); Susan Sarandon (leading actress); Ridley Scott (direction); Adrian Biddle; editing; Callie Khourib (original screenplay); Hans Zimmer

---

'Kill one and two others take its place! Don't turn your back or you're doomed! And don't tell anyone what Them are!'

Them!   ★★

DIR *Gordon Douglas*
1954 94m US
[DVD]

☆ *Edmund Gwenn*, James Whitmore, Joan Weldon, James Arness, Onslow Stevens

Spawned by atomic bomb radiation, giant ants breed in the New Mexico desert and head west.

Among the first, and certainly the best, of the post-atomic monster animal cycle, this durable thriller starts with several eerie desert sequences and builds up to a shattering climax in the Los Angeles sewers. A general air of understatement helps a lot, and it's a first-class mutant bug movie.

SCR Ted Sherdeman   **CIN** *Sid Hickox*   **MUS** Bronislau Kaper   **PROD** David Weisbart   **DIST** Warner

66 I asked the editor: How does it look? And he said: Fine. I said: Does it look honest? He said: As honest as twelve-foot ants can look. – *Gordon Douglas*

'When ambition meets faith.'

There Will Be Blood (new)   ★★★★

SCR/DIR Paul Thomas Anderson
2007 158m US
[DVD] ♫

☆ *Daniel Day-Lewis* (Daniel Plainview), Paul Dano (Eli Sunday/Paul Sunday), Kevin J. O'Connor (Henry), Ciaran Hinds (Fletcher), Dillon Freasier (H.W. Plainview)

In 1898, prospector Daniel Plainview strikes silver. It marks the start of his rapidly growing empire and his move into the oil business. Her and his young son H.W. (nominally his partner) visit a tract of land in California, said to be oil-rich. On striking oil, Plainview crosses swords with a young local preacher who disapproves of his voracious greed.

An historical epic that has the power of timeless myth, a story with Biblical overtones about a man who became immensely rich and powerful but lost his humanity on that journey. Day-Lewis's portrayal of Plainview, a solitary misanthrope with an appalling, barely concealed fury, is an astonishing master-class in acting. Dano as the young preacher Eli – calm but smug and manipulative makes an effective foil. But it's writer-director Anderson's conception that carries the

day; he has fashioned a story that surveys the wellspring of American business and entrepreneurialism and finds it morally wanting. This is an angry, roaring discordant film, and you emerge feeling genuinely jolted.

CIN Robert Elswit   **MUS** Jonny Greenwood   **DES** Jack Fisk   **ED** Dylan Tichenor   **PROD** Joanne Sellar, Paul Thomas Anderson, Daniel Lupi   **DIST** Buena Vista

66 There Will Be Blood is ferocious, and it will be championed and attacked with an equal ferocity. When the dust settles, we may look back on it as some kind of obsessed classic. – *David Ansen, Newsweek*

66 A creation myth for American capitalism, blazingly mounted against barren California landscapes. – *Hannah McGill, Sight & Sound*

⚲ Daniel Day-Lewis (leading actor); Robert Elswit
⚲ film; Paul Thomas Anderson (direction); Paul Thomas Anderson (adapted screenplay); Dylan Tichenor; Jack Fisk; sound editing

Ⓣ Daniel Day-Lewis (leading actor)
Ⓣ film; Paul Thomas Anderson (direction); Paul Thomas Anderson (adapted screenplay); Paul Dano; Jonny Greenwood; Jack Fisk; sound

---

They Live by Night   ★★★

DIR *Nicholas Ray*
1948 96m US

☆ Farley Granger, Cathy O'Donnell, Howard da Silva, Helen Craig

A young man, imprisoned for an accidental killing, escapes with two hardened criminals, then meets a girl but has to keep running.

Well-made drama, a notable debut from this fine director, that established the pattern for movies about a boy and a girl on the run from the law. Its realistic yet impressionist style drew attention on its first release.

SCR Charles Schnee   **CIN** *George E. Diskant*   **MUS** Leigh Harline   **ED** Sherman Todd   **PROD** Dore Schary   **DIST** RKO

† Robert Altman re-made this story in 1974, titled Thieves Like Us.

The Thief   ★★

SCR/DIR Pavel Chukhrai
1997 96m Russia/France
[DVD]

☆ Vladimir Mashkov (Tolyan), Ekaterina Rednikova (Katya), Misha Philipchuk (Sanya), Dima Chigaryov (Sanya, 12 years-old), Amaliya Mordvinova (Doctor's Wife), Lidiya Savchenko (Baby Sanya)

After World War II, a fatherless Russian boy gradually discovers that the Red Army soldier he and his mother love is a deserter, a cheat and a thief.

Sensitive drama about the shattering of childhood dreams; the story also mirrors political disillusionment in post-Soviet Russia, but not too obviously.

CIN Vladimir Klimov   **MUS** Vladimir Dashkevich   **DES** Victor Petrov   **ED** Marina Dobrianskaja, Natalia Kucherenko   **PROD** Igor Tolstunov

66 This is a moving, decent and worthy film. even so, it's deeply conventional. – *Time Out*

[DVD] Available on DVD   ☆ Cast in order   66 Critics' Quotes   ⚲ Academy Award   Ⓣ BAFTA
♫ Soundtrack on CD   of importance   † Points of interest   ⚲ Academy Award nomination   Ⓣ BAFTA nomination

T

† Pavel Chukrai's father is the legendary director Grigory Chukhrai, best known for Ballad of a Soldier (1959)

⚖ foreign language film

The Thief of Bagdad ★★★

DIR *Raoul Walsh*

1924   135m   US

DVD

☆ *Douglas Fairbanks* (The Thief), Snitz Edwards (Evil Associate of the Thief), Charles Belcher (The Holy Man), Anna May Wong (The Mongol Slave), Julanne Johnston (The Princess), Etta Lee (The Slave of the Sand Board), Brandon Hurst (The Caliph), Sojin (The Mongol Prince)

In old Bagdad, a thief uses magic to outwit the evil Caliph.

Celebrated silent version of the old fable, its camera tricks a little timeworn now, but nevertheless maintaining the air of a true classic by virtue of its leading performance and driving narrative energy.

SCR Lotta Woods, Douglas Fairbanks   **CIN** *Arthur Edeson*
MUS Mortimer Wilson   **ED** William Nolan
DIST Douglas Fairbanks

66 An entrancing picture, wholesome and compelling, deliberate and beautiful, a feat of motion picture art which has never been equalled. – *New York Times*

66 Here is magic. Here is beauty. Here is the answer to cynics who give the motion picture no place in the family of the arts . . . a work of rare genius. – *James Quirk, Photoplay*

'A laugh tops every thrilling moment!'

The Thin Man ★★★

DIR *W. S. Van Dyke*

1934   93m   US

DVD

☆ *William Powell* (Nick Charles), *Myrna Loy* (Nora Charles), Maureen O'Sullivan (Dorothy Wynant), Nat Pendleton (Lt. John Guild), Minna Gombell (Mimi Wynant), Edward Ellis (Clyde Wynant), Porter Hall (MacCauley), Henry Wadsworth (Tommy), William Henry (Gilbert Wynant), Harold Huber (Nunheim), Cesar Romero (Chris Jorgenson), Edward Brophy (Joe Morelli)

In New York over Christmas, a tipsy detective, with his wife and dog, solves the murder of an eccentric inventor.

Fast-moving, charming, alternately comic and suspenseful mystery drama developed in brief scenes and fast wipes. It set a sparkling comedy career for two stars previously known for heavy drama, it was frequently imitated, and it showed a wisecracking, affectionate married relationship almost for the first time.

SCR *Frances Goodrich, Albert Hackett*   **CIN** James Wong Howe   **MUS** William Axt   **ED** Robert J. Kern
PROD Hunt Stromberg   **DIST** MGM/Cosmopolitan

66 A strange mixture of excitement, quips and hard-boiled sentiment . . . full of the special touches that can come from nowhere but the studio, that really make the feet a movie walks on. – *Otis Ferguson*

† Sequels, on the whole of descending merit, included the following, all made at MGM with the same star duo: 1936: After the Thin Man (V*, L; 110m). 1939: Another Thin Man (V*, L; 102m). 1941: Shadow of the Thin Man (V*, L; 97m). 1944: The Thin Man Goes Home (V*, L; 100m). 1947: Song of the Thin Man (V*, L; 86m).

† It became a popular TV series in 1957, starring Peter Lawford and Phyllis Kirk.

⚖ picture; W. S. Van Dyke; Frances Goodrich, Albert Hackett (adapted screenplay); William Powell (leading actor)

'Every Man Fights His Own War.'

The Thin Red Line ★★★★

SCR/DIR *Terrence Malick*

1998   170m   US

DVD   ♫

☆ *Sean Penn* (First Sergeant Welsh), Adrien Brody (Corporal Fife), *Jim Caviezel* (Pvt. Witt), Ben Chaplin (Bell), George Clooney (Bosche), John Cusack (Gaff), Woody Harrelson (Keck), *Elias Koteas* (Captain "Bugger" Staros), Jared Leto (Whyte), Dash Mihok (Doll), Tim Blake Nelson (Tills), Nick Nolte (Colonel Tall), John C. Reilly (Storm), Larry Romano (Mazzi), John Savage (McCron), John Travolta, Arie Verveen, Miranda Otto

US soldiers in C-for-Charlie army rifle company discover disturbing truths about each other in the tropics as they desperately fight the Japanese on Guadalcanal in 1943.

A philosophical, beautiful film about war, constantly surveying the ravishing landscape and the place of natural life within it, and contrasting it with the brutish horrors of battle. At times, it's almost a dreamy meditation. Visually, it is quite unforgettable. A unique masterpiece.

CIN *John Toll*   **MUS** Hans Zimmer   **DES** Jack Fisk
ED Billy Weber, Leslie Jones, Saar Klein   **PROD** Robert Michael Geisler, John Roberdeau, Grant Hill
DIST TCF/Fox 2000/Phoenix

66 One of the most curious and perversely brilliant films ever made in the American studio system. It's a shining example of qualities we don't normally see in our big theatrical pictures: vast ambition, huge resources and technical genius mated to a unique and compelling vision of life. – *Michael Wilmington, Chicago Tribune*

66 An art film to the core. If it's an epic, it's an intimate, dream-time epic, an elliptical, episodic film, dependent on images and reveries, that treats war as the ultimate nightmare, the one you just cannot awaken from no matter how hard you try. – *Kenneth Turan, Los Angeles Times*

† The film was shot in the Solomon Islands, close to the site of Guadalcanal.

⚖ picture; Terrence Malick (direction); Terrence Malick (adapted screenplay); John Toll; Hans Zimmer; Billy Weber, Leslie Jones, Saar Klein; sound

The Thing ★★

DIR Christian Nyby

1951   87m   US

☆ Robert Cornthwaite (Dr Arthur Carrington), Kenneth Tobey (Capt. Pat Hendry), Margaret Sheridan (Nikki Nicholson), William Self (Cpl Barnes), Dewey Martin (Bob), James Arness (The Thing), Douglas Spencer (Ned Scott), Robert Nichols (Lt Ken Erickson)

DVD Available on DVD   ☆ Cast in order   66 Critics' Quotes   ⚖ Academy Award   Ⓑ BAFTA
♫ Soundtrack on CD   of importance   † Points of interest   ⚖ Academy Award nomination   Ⓑ BAFTA nomination

A US scientific expedition in the Arctic is menaced by a ferocious being they inadvertently thaw out from a spaceship.

Pioneering sci-fi thriller that shows the first space monster on film, and is quite nimbly made, though perhaps for budgetary reasons it relies on suspense and a creepy atmosphere rather than overtly scary scenes featuring the alien. Hawks is credited as producer, though it is widely believed he partly directed too.

SCR Charles Lederer   CIN Russell Harlan   MUS Dimitri Tiomkin   ED Roland Gross   PROD Howard Hawks
DIST RKO/Winchester

LAST SPEECH OF FILM: I bring you warning – to every one of you listening to the sound of my voice. Tell the world, tell this to everyone wherever they are: watch the skies, watch everywhere, keep looking – watch the skies!

66 There seems little point in creating a monster of such original characteristics if he is to be allowed only to prowl about the North Pole, waiting to be destroyed by the superior ingenuity of the US Air Force. – *Penelope Houston*

66 A monster movie with pace, humour and a collection of beautifully timed jabs of pure horror. – *NFT, 1967*

'Dealing with the mob is always a gamble.'

Things Change   ★★

DIR David Mamet
1988   100m   US
[DVD]

☆ Don Ameche (Gino), Joe Mantegna (Jerry), Robert Prosky (Joseph Vincent), J. J. Johnston (Frankie), Ricky Jay (Mr. Silver), Mike Nussbaum (Mr. Greene), Jack Wallace (Repair Shop Owner), Dan Conway (Butler)

An accident-prone criminal, guarding an elderly shoeshine man who has been persuaded to take the rap for a Mafia murder, agrees to take him on a gambling trip to Nevada.

Light-hearted comic charm isn't a quality often associated with David Mamet, but the writer-director scores heavily here with a delightful two-hander. The casting of the veteran Ameche was inspired; there's a kindly quality about the film, with undertones of wry wisdom.

SCR David Mamet, Shel Silverstein   CIN Juan Ruiz Anchia
MUS Alaric Jans   DES Michael Merritt   ED Trudy Ship
PROD Michael Hausman   DIST Columbia TriStar/Filmhaus

66 A film of enormous charm and beguiling sentimentality. – *Time Out*

† Ameche died in 1993. This film came near the end of a career spanning more than 50 years.

Things to Come   ★★★

DIR *William Cameron Menzies*
1936   113m   GB
[DVD]

☆ *Raymond Massey* (John Cabal/Oswald Cabal), Edward Chapman (Pippa Passworthy/Raymond Passworthy), Ralph Richardson (The Boss), Margaretta Scott (Roxana/Rowena), Cedric Hardwicke (Theotocopulos), Sophie Stewart (Mrs. Cabal), Derrick de Marney (Richard Gordon), John Clements (The Airman)

War in 1940 is followed by plague, rebellion, a new class-based society, and the first rocketship to the moon.

Fascinating, chilling and dynamically well-staged vignettes tracing mankind's future for a century hence. It feels like a British riposte to Fritz Lang's Metropolis. Bits of the script and acting may be wobbly, but the sets and music are magnificent, the first part of the prophecy chillingly accurate, and the whole mammoth undertaking almost unique in film history.

SCR H. G. Wells   CIN *Georges Périnal*   MUS *Arthur Bliss*
DES *William Cameron Menzies*   ED Charles Crichton, Francis Lyon   PROD Alexander Korda   DIST London Films

CABAL (RAYMOND MASSEY): It is this or that – all the universe or nothing. Which shall it be, Passworthy? Which shall it be?

THEOTOCOPULOS (CEDRIC HARDWICKE): What is this progress? What is the good of all this progress onward and onward? We demand a halt. We demand a rest . . . an end to progress! Make an end to this progress now! Let this be the last day of the scientific age!

66 Successful in every department except emotionally. For heart interest Mr Wells hands you an electric switch . . . It's too bad present-day film distribution isn't on a Wells 2040 basis, when the negative cost could be retrieved by button pushing. It's going to be harder than that. It's going to be almost impossible. – *Variety*

66 An amazingly ingenious technical accomplishment, even if it does hold out small hope for our race . . . the existence pictured is as joyless as a squeezed grapefruit. – *Don Herold*

'They Can Die Quickly Or They Can Die Slowly But They Have To Die.'

Things to Do in Denver When You're Dead   ★★★

DIR Gary Fleder
1995   115m   US
[DVD] ♫

☆ Andy Garcia (Jimmy 'The Saint' Tosnia), Christopher Lloyd (Pieces), William Forsythe (Franchise), Bill Nunn (Easy Wind), Treat Williams (Critical Bill), Jack Warden (Joe Heff), Steve Buscemi (Mister Shhh), Fairuza Balk (Lucinda), Gabrielle Anwar (Dagney), Christopher Walken (The Man with the Plan)

An allegedly reformed criminal agrees to carry out one last job and recruits a gang of veteran helpers with disastrous results.

The elderly dream team of villains may be too calculatingly oddball to make this stylish thriller perfect; but there's a cool, loose feel about it, and writer Rosenberg's arcane criminal slang enhances the sense that we're in on a delicious in-joke.

SCR Scott Rosenberg   CIN Elliot Davis   MUS Michael Convertino   DES Nelson Coates   ED Richard Marks
PROD Cary Woods   DIST Woods Entertainment

DAGNEY (TO JIMMY): My, aren't we the sultan of segue?
FRANCHISE: (RECURRING): It is what it is.
FRANCHISE: (RECURRING): Give it a name!
EASY WIND: Franchise, my brother from another mother!
FRANCHISE: Gentlemen, we have boat drinks!

66 A very cool soundtrack and more hip lingo than two ears can absorb, but, like the air in Denver, this movie is spread awfully thin. – *Marjorie Baumgarten, Austin Chronicle*

'Hope comes with letting go.'

Things We Lost in the Fire (new)   ★

DIR Susanne Bier
2007   117m   US/UK
DVD   ♫

☆ Halle Berry (Audrey Burke), Benicio Del Toro (Jerry Sunborne), David Duchovny (Brian Burke), Alison Lohman (Kelly), Omar Benson Miller (Neal), John Carroll Lynch (Howard Glassman), Alexis Llewellyn (Harper Burke), Micah Berry (Dory Burke)

A grieving widow invites her late husband's best friend, a recovering drug addict, to live in her garage.

Thoughtful melodrama boasting committed performances, compromised somewhat by the clash between its Danish director's art-house sensibilities and the commercial dictates of studio movie-making.

SCR Allan Loeb   CIN Tom Stern   MUS Johan Soderqvist, Gustavo Santaolalla   DES Richard Sherman   ED Pernille Bech Christensen, Bruce Cannon   PROD Sam Mendes, Sam Mercer   DIST Paramount

66 Worth seeing despite its unevenness. – *Kenneth Turan, Los Angeles Times*

66 The kind of awards-seeking Hollywood movie that bends over backward to prove that serious American movies can hold their own with the best films from overseas. – *Stephen Holden, New York Times*

'Hunted by men... Sought by women!'

The Third Man   ★★★★

DIR *Carol Reed*
1949   100m   GB
DVD

☆ *Joseph Cotten* (Holly Martins), *Trevor Howard* (Maj. Calloway), *Alida Valli* (Anna Schmidt), *Orson Welles* (Harry Lime), *Bernard Lee* (Sgt. Paine), *Wilfrid Hyde-White* (Crabbin), Ernst Deutsch (Baron Kurtz), Siegfried Breuer (Popescu), Erich Ponto (Dr. Winkel), Paul Hoerbiger (Porter)

A writer of Westerns arrives in post-war Vienna to join his old friend Harry Lime, who seems to have met with an accident.

Totally memorable and irresistible romantic thriller. Stylish from the first to the last, with inimitable backgrounds of zither music and war-torn buildings pointing up a then-topical black market story, full of cynical, corrupt characters, but not without humour. A dazzling creation.

SCR *Graham Greene*   CIN *Robert Krasker*   MUS *Anton Karas*   ED *Oswald Hafenrichter*   PROD Carol Reed   DIST British Lion/London Films/David O. Selznick/Alexander Korda

HARRY LIME (ORSON WELLES): Look down there. Would you really feel any pity if one of those dots stopped moving for ever? If I offered you twenty thousand pounds for every dot that stopped, would you really, old man, tell me to keep

my money, or would you calculate how many dots you could afford to spare? Free of income tax, old man, free of income tax. It's the only way to save money nowadays.
LIME: In Italy for thirty years under the Borgias they had warfare, terror, murder and bloodshed, but they produced Michelangelo, Leonardo da Vinci and the Renaissance. In Switzerland, they had brotherly love; they had five hundred years of democracy and peace – and what did that produce? The cuckoo clock.

66 Sensitive and humane and dedicated, [Reed] would seem to be enclosed from life with no specially strong feelings about the stories that come his way other than that they should be something he can perfect and polish with a craftsman's love. – *Richard Winnington*

66 Crammed with cinematic plums which could do the early Hitchcock proud. – *Time*

⚊ Robert Krasker (cinematography)
⚊ Carol Reed; Oswald Hafenrichter (editing)
Ⓣ British film

'It's happening so fast.'

Thirteen   ★

DIR Catherine Hardwicke
2003   100m   US
DVD   ♫

☆ *Holly Hunter* (Melanie), Evan Rachel Wood (Tracy), Nikki Reed (Evie Zamora), Jeremy Sisto (Brady), Brady Corbett (Mason), Deborah Kara Unger (Brooke), Kip Pardue (Luke), Sarah Clarke (Birdie), D.W. Moffett (Travis)

Thirteen-year-old Los Angeles girls descend into a spiral of bad behaviour that includes sex, drugs and shoplifting.

A sobering story of spoiled adolescents and clueless parents that often seems to revel in its controversy. Still, it feels authentic, and Hunter is splendid as a desperate mother.

SCR Catherine Hardwicke, Nikki Reed   CIN Elliot Davis   MUS Mark Mothersbaugh, Brian Zarate   DES Carol Strober   ED Nancy Richardson   PROD Michael London, Jeffrey Levy-Hinte   DIST UIP

66 With an authenticity that is tender and merciless, the movie shows you what it looks like when youth rebellion becomes a form of fascism. – *Owen Gleiberman, Entertainment Weekly*

† The film is based on the teenage experiences of its actress Nikki Reed, who plays the troubled Evie, and shared writing credit with director Hardwicke.

⚊ Holly Hunter (supporting actress)
Ⓣ Holly Hunter (supporting actress)

Thirteen Conversations about One Thing   ★★

DIR Jill Sprecher
2001   104m   US
DVD

☆ Matthew McConaughey (Troy), John Turturro (Walker), *Alan Arkin* (Gene), Clea DuVall (Beatrice), Amy Irving (Patricia), Barbara Sukowa (Helen), David Connolly (Owen), Frankie Faison (Dick Lacey)

Lawyers celebrating a big win in a New York bar are brought down to earth by a gloomy fellow drinker,

---

DVD Available on DVD   ☆ Cast in order of importance   66 Critics' Quotes   ⚊ Academy Award   Ⓣ BAFTA
♫ Soundtrack on CD   † Points of interest   ⚊ Academy Award nomination   Ⓣ BAFTA nomination

T

sparking 13 intersecting discussions about happiness.

A bizarre baker's dozen conversations just about gel as the basis of four connected stories. Well constructed, but maybe too complex for its own good; not a single story feels satisfyingly rounded out.

SCR Karen Sprecher, Jill Sprecher **CIN** Dick Pope **MUS** Alex Wurman **DES** Mark Ricker **ED** Stephen Mirrione **PROD** Ben Atoori, Gina Resnick **DIST** Arrow

66 It's entertaining, well-written, slice of life stuff, but I'd rather spend 90 minutes with one of these stories than flit between several in a manner that does little to illuminate any of them. – *Time Out*

66 A small, but highly polished, gem. – *Jonathan Romney, The Independent*

'In 1962 America and Russia took their nations to the brink of war and the planet to the edge of extinction. . .'

Thirteen Days ★★

DIR Roger Donaldson
2000 145m US
DVD ♫

☆ *Kevin Costner* (Kenneth P. O'Donnell), *Bruce Greenwood* (John F. Kennedy), Steven Culp (Robert F. Kennedy), Dylan Baker (Robert McNamara), Michael Fairman (Adlai Stevenson), Henry Strozier (Dean Rusk), Frank Wood (McGeorge Bundy), Kevin Conway (Gen Curtis LeMay), Tim Kelleher (Ted Sorensen), Len Cariou (Dean Acheson), Bill Smitrovich (Gen Maxwell Taylor), Dakin Matthews (Arthur Lundahl), Ed Lauter (Gen Marshall Carter), Olek Krupa (Andrei Gromyko), Stephanie Romanov (Jacqueline Kennedy)

The Cuban missile crisis of 1962 is viewed from inside the Pentagon, with President Kennedy agonising about triggering a third world war.

Captivating re-creation of a literally crucial historical event; despite its talky, essentially static and barely cinematic nature, the material generates real suspense and tension, even though we know how events were resolved. Greenwood and Costner do sterling work in the lead roles.

SCR David Self **CIN** Andrzej Bartkowiak, Christopher Duddy, Roger Deakins **MUS** Trevor Jones **DES** Dennis Washington **ED** Conrad Buff **PROD** Armyan Bernstein, Peter O. Almond, Kevin Costner **DIST** New Line

66 A good movie about a profound moment in world history. – *Mick LaSalle, San Francisco Chronicle*

66 Keeps you hanging on every twist and turn of its wilder-than-fiction plot. – *David Ansen, Newsweek*

13 Tzameti ★★★

SCR/DIR Gela Babulani
2005 93m France
DVD

☆ Georges Babulani (Sebastien), Aurelien Recoing (Player No. 6), Pascal Bongard (Master of Ceremonies)

Sebastien, a young man, steals an envelope with a train ticket and a hotel reservation. He travels, checks in and is given directions to a meeting place where he becomes involved in a murderous game run by wealthy gamblers.

Astonishingly assured, stylish debut by French-Georgian Babulani. Sebastien's descent into an unimaginable hell is truly jolting. A suspenseful thriller of the first order: the audience never knows more than the terrified lead character himself.

CIN Tariel Meliava **MUS** East (Troublemakers) **DES** Bernard Peault **ED** Noemia Moreau **PROD** Gela Babulani **DIST** Revolver

66 Babulani creates a fear so bottomless, a bad dream so plausible that its hooks tear into your consciousness. – *Michael Wilmington, Chicago Tribune*

30 Days of Night (new) ★★

DIR David Slade
2007 113 minsm USA/New Zealand
♫

☆ Josh Hartnett (Sheriff Eben Oleson), Melissa George (Stella Oleson), Danny Huston (Marlow), Ben Foster (The Stranger), Mark Boone Jr, (Beau Brower)

A pack of feral vampires terrorise an Alaskan town that spends a polar winter month in darkness cut off from the outside world.

A classic siege-by-blood-crazed-monsters plot gets an excitingly visceral update. Snowy landscapes add to the chill of the slow-building premise, leading to a bleak ending.

SCR Steve Niles, Stuart Beattie, Brian Nelson **CIN** Jo Willems **MUS** Brian Reitzell **DES** Paul Denham Austerberry **ED** Art Jones **PROD** Sam Raimi, Robert G. Tapert **DIST** Icon Films

66 Doing little more than drenching the centuries-old vampire myth in just a little more gore. – *Robert Wilonsky, The Village Voice*

The 39 Steps ★★★★

DIR *Alfred Hitchcock*
1935 81m GB
DVD

☆ *Robert Donat* (Richard Hannay), *Madeleine Carroll* (The Airman), Godfrey Tearle (Prof. Jordan), Lucie Mannheim (Miss Smith/Annabella), Peggy Ashcroft (Margaret), John Laurie (John), *Wylie Watson* (Mr. Memory), *Helen Haye* (Mrs. Jordan), Frank Cellier (Sheriff Watson)

A spy is murdered; the man who becomes an immediate suspect eludes the police, becomes handcuffed to a fetching woman he meets on a train, until a chase across Scotland produces the real villains.

Marvellous comedy thriller with most of the gimmicks found not only in Hitchcock's later work but in anyone else's who has tried the same vein. Donat and Carroll have a sizzling on-screen chemistry rarely seen in British films of this era. The film has little to do with John Buchan's original novel, and barely sets foot outside the studio, but it makes every second count, and is unparalleled in its use of timing, atmosphere and comedy relief.

SCR *Charles Bennett, Ian Hay, Alma Reville* **CIN** *Bernard Knowles* **MUS** Hubert Bath, Jack Beaver **ED** Derek Twist **PROD** Ivor Montagu **DIST** Gaumont British

T

66 A narrative of the unexpected – a humorous, exciting, dramatic, entertaining, pictorial, vivid and novel tale told with a fine sense of character and a keen grasp of the cinematic idea. – *Sydney W. Carroll*

66 A miracle of speed and light. – *Otis Ferguson*

32 Short Films about Glenn Gould ★★

DIR *François Girard*
1993   98m   Canada/Portugal/Finland/Netherlands
DVD   ♫
☆ Colm Feore (Glenn Gould), Derek Keurvorst (Gould's father), Katya Ladan (Gould's mother)

The life of the famously eccentric Canadian concert pianist Glenn Gould, partly acted out and partly captured in documentary footage.

The restless, fragmentary nature of this biopic is meant to reflect the man's mercurial talents. Frustratingly bitty at times, but interesting even when not wholly successful.

SCR François Girard, Don McKellar   CIN Alain Dostie
MUS Bach, Beethoven and others, played by Glenn Gould
ED Gaétan Huot   PROD Niv Fichman, Michael Allder, Barbara Willis Sweete, Larry Weinstein
DIST Electric/Rhombus Media

66 Manages to hold the watcher in its grip from start to finish. – *Derek Malcolm, Guardian*

66 A uniquely entertaining venture. One need not know Gould's artistry or be attuned to the music to respond to the material. – *Leonard Klady, Variety*

'He looked like the ideal husband. He seemed like the perfect father. That's just what they needed. But that's not what they got.'

This Boy's Life

DIR Michael Caton-Jones
1993   115m   US
DVD   ♫
☆ Robert DeNiro (Dwight Hansen), Ellen Barkin (Caroline Wolff Hansen), *Leonardo DiCaprio* (Tobias 'Toby' Wolff), Jonah Blechman (Arthur Gayle), Eliza Dushku (Pearl), Chris Cooper (Roy), Carla Gugino (Norma), Zack Ansley (Skipper)

In the 1950s, a rebellious teenage boy finds life tough when his divorced mother moves to Seattle and starts a new life with a bullying new husband.

Moving drama, intelligently adapted from a grim real-life memoir, and elevated beyond its source material by a gifted, cohesive cast. DiCaprio, who was just 17 when he made the film, is an arresting presence as the helpless young rebel.

SCR *Robert Getchell*   CIN David Watkin   MUS Carter Burwell   DES Stephen J. Lineweaver   ED Jim Clark
PROD Art Linson   DIST Warner

66 The movie is successful largely because Leonardo DiCaprio is a good enough actor to hold his own in his scenes with Robert De Niro. – *Roger Ebert, Chicago, Sun-Times*

'You can't exchange family.'

This Christmas (new)

SCR/DIR Preston A. Whitmore II
2007   118m   US
♫
☆ Delroy Lindo (Joseph Black), Idris Elba (Quentin Whitfield), Loretta Devine (Ma'Dere), Chris Brown (Michael Whitfield), Mekhi Phifer (Gerald), Regina King (Lisa)

Members of an African-American family, each one with a story or something to hide, reunite over Christmas.

Writer-director Whitmore ruthlessly wraps up every loose end of this overstuffed, multi-strand plot. Laboured and obvious.

CIN Alexander Gruszynski   MUS Marcus Miller
DES Dawn Snyder   ED Paul Seydor   PROD Preston A. Whitmore II, Will Packer   DIST Sony

66 It's redemption through sentimentality, salvation through schmaltz. – *Josh Rosenblatt, Austin Chronicle*

66 This is good-natured, determinedly aspirational African-American entertainment, but did it have to be quite so heavy on the clichés? – *Trevor Johnston, Time Out*

'Censorship, uncensored.'

This Film Is Not Yet Rated ★★

DIR Kirby Dick
2006   97m   US
DVD
☆ Kirby Dick, Ben Affleck, Kevin Bacon, Alec Baldwin, Christian Bale, Pierce Brosnan, Tom Cruise, Robert De Niro

An expose of the MPAA, the non-profit US ratings board which is supposedly impartial but seemingly bolsters the interests of major studios while treating the independent film sector less leniently.

A funny, entertaining but serious attack on the chicanery at large in the ratings system. Using clips, interviews, animation and a private investigator, the filmmakers uncover the corruption behind America's tolerance to film violence but puritanical view of sex.

SCR Kirby Dick, Eddie Schmidt, Matt Patterson
CIN Shana Hagan, Kirsten Johnson, Michael Parry, Amy Vincent, Ben Wolf   MUS Michael S. Patterson
ED Matthew Clarke, Simon B. Veredon   PROD Eddie Schmidt   DIST ICA

66 Matter of public concern. – *J. Hoberman – The Village Voice*

This Is England ★★

SCR/DIR *Shane Meadows*
2007   102m   UK
DVD   ♫
☆ *Thomas Turgoose* (Shaun Fields), Stephen Graham (Combo), Jo Hartley (Cynth), Andrew Shim (Milky), Vicky McClure (Lol), Joe Gilgun (Woody)

In 1983, a 12-year-old boy in the north of England, whose father has died in the Falkands War, falls in with a gang of skinheads who introduce him to racist members of the far-right National Front.

Blistering account of grim, working-class 1980s life, and the easy temptations to blame immigrants for economic hardship. The first two-thirds look like the film the talented Meadows has threatened to make for years – potent, funny and visceral. In child actor Thomas Turgoose, he has found a real gem. Yet some characters are inconsistent: Shaun's mother, concerned at first for her son's well-being, simply disappears from sight. And the final shot, all high-flown melodrama, seems to belong to a different film. Still, it is defiantly alive; its hostility and violence are jolting.

CIN Danny Cohen   MUS Ludovico Einaudi   DES Mark Leese   ED Chris Wyatt   PROD Mark Herbert   DIST Optimum

66 An affecting but uneven memoir of council-estate Britain in the summer of 1983. – *Anthony Quinn, Independent*

66 This is English cinema. – *Peter Bradshaw, Guardian*

🇬🇧 British film

Ⓣ Shane Meadows (original screenplay)

'It's 10 p.m. Do you know where your mother is?'

This Is My Life ★★

DIR Nora Ephron
1992   105m   US
♫

☆ Julie Kavner (Dottie Ingels), Samantha Mathis (Erica Ingels), Gaby Hoffman (Opal Ingels), Carrie Fisher (Claudia Curtis), Dan Aykroyd (Arnold Moss), Bob Nelson (Ed), Marita Geraghty (Mia Jablon)

A single mother with two young daughters makes her dream of becoming a stand-up comedian come true.

Ephron's directorial debut and her most underrated movie. Kavner is excellent as a driven mother who re-works her real neglect of her daughters as material for stand-up comedy. Its pace flags here and there, but it feels more honest and authentic than many films on Ephron's CV.

SCR Nora Ephron, Delia Ephron   CIN Bobby Byrne   MUS Carly Simon   DES David Chapman   ED Robert Reitano   PROD Lynda Obst   DIST TCF

66 Like her character, Julie Kavner struggles valiantly to reconcile the demands of comedy and domestic drama, but ultimately succumbs to a surfeit of schmaltz and Carly Simon songs. – *Time Out*

66 A gentle burp of a movie. – *Rita Kempley, Washington Post*

† Kavner is best-known as the voice of Marge on The Simpsons.

'A life taken, now Spike and Heaton are running for their own...'

This is not a Love Song

DIR Bille Eltringham
2002   94m   GB
DVD

☆ Michael Colgan (Spike), Kenneth Glenaan (Heaton), David Bradley (Mr. Bellamy), John Henshaw (Arthur), Adam Pepper (William), Keri Arnold (Gerry)

Two thieves, released from prison, soon encounter trouble when a man is killed on a remote farm, and the anger of locals forces them to flee.

The basic premise – two losers hounded across moors by enraged vigilantes – makes for a movie that fails to live up to its ground-breaking method of distribution. Another perplexing milestone in writer Beaufoy's post-Full Monty career, characterised by his steadfast rejection of anything that smacks of commercial appeal.

SCR Simon Beaufoy   CIN Robbie Ryan   MUS Mark Rutherford, Adrian Johnston   DES Jon Henson   ED Ewa J. Lind   PROD Mark Blaney

66 A bracing B-movie thriller with a dash of repressed male-on-male romance. – *Xan Brooks, The Guardian*

† On September 5, 2003, this became the first British film to be released on the Internet and in cinemas on the same day.

This Is Spinal Tap ★★★★

DIR Rob Reiner
1984   82m   US
DVD   ♫

☆ Christopher Guest (Nigel Tufnel), Michael McKean (David St. Hubbins), Harry Shearer (Derek Smalls), Rob Reiner (Marty DiBergi), R. J. Parnell (Mick Shrimpton), David Kaff (Viv Savage), Tony Hendra (Ian Faith), Bruno Kirby (Tommy Pischedda)

A hapless British heavy metal rock group tour America, and find disappointments and setbacks along the way.

A 'mockumentary,' as it announces itself, about rock musicians, their acolytes, their vanity and crassness, and their inability to function in anything like the real world. Clever, sharp and consistently hilarious from start to finish.

SCR Christopher Guest, Michael McKean, Harry Shearer, Rob Reiner   CIN Peter Smokler   MUS Christopher Guest, Michael McKean, Harry Shearer, Rob Reiner   DES Dryan Jones   ED Robert Leighton   PROD Karen Murphy   DIST Mainline/Embassy

66 A heady flow of brilliant stupidity. – *Jay Carr, Boston Globe*

66 One of the funniest, most intelligent, most original films. – *Roger Ebert, Chicago Sun-Times*

† The Regions 1 and 2 special edition DVD releases include an hour of extra footage, audio commentary by the band (in character) and an interview with the director. It was also available on an interactive CD-ROM, which included extra audio commentary on the film and out-takes.

† This Is Spinal Tap: The Official Companion, edited by Karl French, was published by Bloomsbury in 2000.

This Is the Sea

SCR/DIR Mary McGuckian
1996   103m   US/Ireland/GB
♫

☆ Richard Harris (Old Man Jacobs), Gabriel Byrne (Rohan), John Lynch (Padhar McAliskey), Dearbhla Molloy (Ma Stokes), Ian McElhinney (Da Stokes), Samantha Morton (Hazel Stokes), Ross McDade (Malachy McAliskey)

In the Northern Ireland ceasefire of 1995, a young Protestant woman falls in love with a Catholic man with IRA connections.

A strained re-telling of Romeo and Juliet set against a modern backdrop of real warring communities. It must have seemed like a good idea; on this evidence, it wasn't, though it did offer Morton her biggest film role to date.

CIN Des Whelan   MUS Mike Scott, the Waterboys, Brian Kennedy   DES Claire Kenny   ED Kant Pan, Alan Duffy
PROD Michael Garland, Mary McGuckian
DIST Polygram/Pembridge/Overseas

66 Unfortunately the two young leads are weak while the older hands, Richard Harris and Gabriel Byrne, are given too little to do. Sometimes sincerity and goodwill are not enough. – *Channel 4*

This Sporting Life ★★★

DIR *Lindsay Anderson*
1963   134m   GB
DVD

☆ *Richard Harris* (Frank Machin), *Rachel Roberts* (Mrs. Hammond), Alan Badel (Weaver), William Hartnell (Johnson), Colin Blakely (Maurice Braithwaite), Vanda Godsell (Mrs. Weaver), Arthur Lowe (Slomer)

A tough miner becomes a successful Rugby League player, but his inner crudeness and violence keep contentment at bay.

Director Anderson's debut film was notable for its treatment of the theme of class, and the possibility of escape, however temporary, offered by sport from a dreary routine existence. Harris offers a brutally honest portrait of a man who can articulate his feelings most eloquently through violence, while Roberts, his landlady, is equally unflinching in a blistering portrayal of a desperate life. A fitting conclusion to the cycle of kitchen sink dramas that had been popular in British cinema in the previous few years.

SCR David Storey   CIN *Denys Coop*   MUS Roberto Gerhard   ED Peter Taylor   PROD Karel Reisz
DIST Rank/Independent Artists

⚱ Richard Harris (leading actor); Rachel Roberts (leading actress)

🏆 Rachel Roberts

'How do you get the man who has everything?'

The Thomas Crown Affair ★★

DIR John McTiernan
1999   113m   US
DVD   ♫

☆ Pierce Brosnan (Thomas Crown), Rene Russo (Catherine Banning), Denis Leary (Det Michael McCann), Ben Gazzara (Andrew Wallace), Frankie Faison (Det Paretti), Fritz Weaver (John Reynolds), Charles Keating (Golchan), Mark Margolis (Knutzhorn), Faye Dunaway (Psychiatrist)

Bored billionaire steals a priceless painting from New York's Metropolitan Museum of Art, because he can, and is tracked by an attractive female insurance agent determined to snare him.

Not quite as memorable as the 1968 original, but a decidedly elegant copy with strong James Bond overtones.

SCR Leslie Dixon, Kurt Wimmer   CIN Tom Priestley
MUS Bill Conti   DES Bruno Rubeo   ED John Wright
PROD Pierce Brosnan, Beau St. Clair   DIST MGM

66 Hard to believe that real emotion was involved anywhere in this story. – *Elvis Mitchell, New York Times*

Those Who Love Me Can Take The Train ★★

DIR Patrice Chéreau
1998   122m   France
DVD

☆ Pascal Greggory (François), Jean-Louis Trintignant (Lucien/Jean-Baptiste), Valeria Bruni-Tedeschi (Claire), Charles Berling (Jean-Marie), Bruno Todeschini (Louis), Sylvain Jacques (Bruno), Vincent Perez (Viviane), Roschdy Zem (Thierry), Dominique Blanc (Catherine), Nathan Cogan (Sami), Marie Daems (Lucie)

The death of a wealthy artist brings together people whose lives he has touched on a train journey from Paris to the funeral in Limoges.

An enthralling assembly of oddballs clash and emote as they assess their feelings about the mischievous artist's demise. Delicious plot twists, and the intimacy of hand-held cameras on board the train, make for a gossipy, campy treat.

SCR Danièle Thompson, Patrice Chereau, Pierre Trividic
CIN Eric Gautier   DES Richard Peduzzi, Sylvain Chauvelot
ED François Gedigier   PROD Charles Gassot
DIST Artificial Eye

66 Unfolding like an autopsy on a collection of flawed, apathetic or deeply unpleasant characters the film is earnest and heavy, a plodding drama that throws light into corners some of us would prefer not to look in. – *Anwar Brett, BBC*

'Best friends. Bitter rivals. Sisters.'

A Thousand Acres ★

DIR Jocelyn Moorhouse
1997   105m   US
DVD   ♫

☆ Michelle Pfeiffer (Rose Cook Lewis), Jessica Lange (Ginny Cook Smith), Jason Robards (Larry Cook), Jennifer Jason Leigh (Caroline Cook), Colin Firth (Jess Clark), Keith Carradine (Ty Smith)

An elderly farmer in Iowa divides his estate among three daughters.

Pallid, rather cowed adaptation of Jane Smiley's Pulitzer Prize-winning novel, a transposition of King Lear to the American Midwest. The leads do their best with a stilted script.

SCR Laura Jones   CIN Tak Fujimoto   MUS Richard Hartley   DES Dan Davis   ED Maryann Brandon
PROD Marc Abraham, Lynn Arost, Steve Golin, Kate Guinzburg, Sigurjon Sighvatsson   DIST Buena Vista/Touchstone/Beacon/Propaganda/Via Rosa/Prairie

66 Breast cancer, infertility, adultery, wife beating – it seems as if someone's ticking off a list of female 'issues'. – *Tom Charity, Time Out*

T

DVD Available on DVD   ☆ Cast in order of importance   66 Critics' Quotes   ⚱ Academy Award   🏆 BAFTA
♫ Soundtrack on CD   † Points of interest   ⚱ Academy Award nomination   🏆 BAFTA nomination

617

A Thousand Months ★★

SCR/DIR Faouzi Bensaidi
2003   124m   France/Morocco/Belgium/Germany
DVD

☆ Fouad Labied (Mehdi), Nezha Rahil (Amina), Mohammed Majd (Grandfather), Abdelati Lambarki (Caid), Mohamed Bastaoui (Caid's Brother)

A young boy in 1980s Morocco is introduced into the ways of village life, while remaining unaware that his dissident father has been jailed.

This impressive directorial debut is a little rough around the edges, which adds to its charm. Nothing much seems to happen in individual scenes, but in the end the story is drawn together expertly.

SCR Emmanuelle Sardou   CIN Antoine Hebérlé
DES Naima Bouanani, Veronique Melery   ED Sandrine Deegen   PROD Laurent Lavole, Isabelle Pragier, Benedicte Bellocq, Souad Lamriki, Diana Elbaum

66 We're left in no doubt that this is a narrow, censorious society, where religion serves largely as a source of fear and a means of coercion. – *Philip Kemp, Sight & Sound*

3.10 to Yuma ★★

DIR *Delmer Daves*
1957   92m   US
DVD   ♫

☆ *Glenn Ford* (Ben Wade), *Van Heflin* (Dan Evans), Felicia Farr (Emmy), Leora Dana (Mrs. Alice Evans), Henry Jones (Alex Potter), Richard Jaeckel (Charlie Prince), Robert Emhardt (Mr. Butterfield)

A sheriff has to get his prisoner on to a train despite the threatening presence of the prisoner's outlaw friends.

Tense, well-directed but rather talky low-budget Western: excellent performances and atmosphere flesh out an unconvincing physical situation.

SCR Halsted Welles   CIN *Charles Lawton Jnr.*
MUS George Duning   ED Al Clark   PROD David Heilwell   DIST Columbia

66 A vivid, tense and intelligent story about probable people, enhanced by economical writing and supremely efficient direction and playing. – *Guardian*

66 We experimented by not filling the shadows with reflected light. – *Delmer Daves*

† The film was re-made exactly half a century later, directed by James Mangold, and starring Christian Bale and Russell Crowe.

'Time waits for one man.'

3.10 to Yuma (new) ★★

DIR James Mangold
2007   122m   US
DVD   ♫

☆ *Russell Crowe* (Ben Wade), *Christian Bale* (Dan Evans), Ben Foster (Charlie Prince), Gretchen Moi (Alice Evans), *Peter Fonda* (Byron McElroy)

A small-time rancher agrees to accompany a captured outlaw to a train taking him to trial.

A decent western, well-acted, but with character

motivations blurred and a surprisingly implausible ending.

SCR Stuart Beattie, Michael Brandt, Derek Haas, James Mangold   CIN Phedon Papamichael   MUS Marco Beltrami   DES Andrew Menzies   ED Michael McCusker   PROD Cathy Konrad   DIST Lionsgate

66 A riveting remake of a pretty terrific 1957 western about manhood, fatherhood and honour. – *Carrie Rickey, Philadelphia Inquirer*

66 New Zealand's Russell Crowe and Britain's Christian Bale don the hats and accents to play outlaw and escort with grizzled assurance. – *Nigel Andrews, Financial Times*

⌇ Marco Beltrami, Paul Massey, David Giammarco, Jim Stuebe (sound)

'A comedy about how far you would go to change your life.'

Three and Out (new)

DIR Jonathan Gershfield
2008   108m   UK

☆ Mackenzie Crook (Paul Callow), Colm Meaney (Tommy Cassidy), Gary Lewis (Callaghan), Annette Badland (Maureen), Imelda Staunton (Rosemary Cassidy), Gemma Arterton (Frankie Cassidy)

A London Tube driver, despairing after two passengers fall under his train, is told that a third death would entitle him a to a lucrative payoff. He seeks out suicide volunteers.

The 'comic' premise would make anyone wince, and director Gershfield doesn't waste time handling it sensitively. Meaney brings a little grace to what turns into a mismatched buddy movie, but it's still a second-rate mess.

SCR Steve Lewis, Tony Owen   CIN Richard Greatrex   MUS Trevor Jones   DES Amanda McArthur   ED Jon Gregory   PROD Ian Harries, Wayne Godfrey   DIST Worldwide Bonus Entertainment

66 It's too gauche, too derivative and merely sporadically amusing. – *Wally Hammond, Time Out*

'For justice. For loyalty. For friendship.'

The Three Burials of Melquiades Estrada ★★

DIR Tommy Lee Jones
2005   121m   US/France
DVD   ♫

☆ Tommy Lee Jones (Pete Perkins), Barry Pepper (Mike Norton), Julio Cesar Cedillo (Melquiades Estrada), Dwight Yoakam (Belmont), January Jones (Lou Ann Norton), Melissa Leo (Rachel), Levon Helm (Old Man With Radio)

A principled Texas ranch hand kidnaps the border patrolman who killed his illegal immigrant friend, forces him to dig up the body, and makes him take them both back to Mexico for a family burial.

Enthralling, atmospheric Western with Tommy Lee Jones mightily convincing in a tricky leading role. It has an extraordinary feel for the dead-end quality of Texas border towns, but the corpse's journey becomes gradually less credible.

SCR Guillermo Arriaga   CIN Chris Menges   MUS Marco Beltrami   DES Merideth Boswell   ED Roberto Silvi

PROD Michael Fitzgerald, Luc Besson, Pierre-Ange Le Pogam, Tommy Lee Jones **DIST** Optimum

66 Incisive yet supple, wrenching yet deeply pleasurable, The Three Burials of Melquiades Estrada easily ranks among the year's best pictures. – *Kevin Thomas, Los Angeles Times*

Three Colours: Blue ★★★★

DIR *Krzysztof Kieslowski*

1993 100m France/Switzerland/Poland

DVD ♫

☆ Juliette Binoche (Julie), Benoît Régent (Olivier), Florence Pernel (Sandrine), Charlotte Véry (Lucille), Hélène Vincent (Journalist), Philippe Volter (Estate Agent), Claude Duneton (Doctor), Hugues Quester (Patrice), Emmanuelle Riva (The Mother)

Shocked by the death of her composer husband and their young daughter in a car crash, a woman destroys his final work, but draws back from killing herself.

The first part of Kieslowski's magisterial trilogy is a harrowing experience, as Binoche's Julie first attempts suicide, then strives for the freedom to cope with her suffering by retreating within herself. Discreetly, brilliantly and closely observed.

SCR Krzysztof Pisiewicz, Krzysztof Kieslowski **CIN** *Slawomir Idziak* **MUS** *Zbigniew Preisner* **DES** Claude Lenoir **ED** Jacques Witta **PROD** Marin Karmitz **DIST** Artificial Eye/MK2/CED/France 3/CAB/TOR/Canal

66 The rehabilitation of a human spirit after painful tragedy is given stunning, aesthetic dimension. – *Desson Howe, Washington Post*

Three Colours: Red ★★★★

DIR *Krzysztof Kieslowski*

1994 99m France/Switzerland/Poland

DVD ♫

☆ Irene Jacob (Valentine), Jean-Louis Trintignant (Judge Joseph Kern), Jean-Pierre Lorit (Auguste), Frédérique Feder (Karin), Juliette Binoche (Julie), Julie Delpy (Dominique)

In Geneva, a beautiful but insecure model confides her worries to a lonely, snooping old judge, who turns match-maker and secretly arranges a meeting for her with a young lawyer.

This final part of Kieslowski's trilogy is an intriguing examination of solitude, destiny, chance and connectedness. Its deployment of colour, sound and music is overwhelming.

SCR *Krzysztof Piesiewicz, Krzysztof Kieslowski* **CIN** *Piotr Sobocinski* **MUS** *Zbigniew Preisner* **DES** Claude Lenoir **ED** Jacques Witta **PROD** Marin Karmitz **DIST** Artificial Eye/MK2/France 3/CAB/Tor

66 Takes its audience on an enchanting journey of discovery. – *BBC*

† It is the last part of a trilogy based on the French tricolour and dealing with fraternity.

⚲ Krzysztof Kieslowski (direction); Krzysztof Piesiewicz (screenplay); Piotr Sobocinski

⚲ Krzysztof Kieslowski (direction); Krzysztof Piesiewicz (original screenplay); film not in the English language; Irene Jacob (leading actress)

Three Colours: White ★★

DIR *Krzysztof Kieslowski*

1993 91m France/Poland/Switzerland

DVD ♫

☆ Zbigniew Zamachowski (Karol Karol), Julie Delpy (Dominique), Janusz Gajos (Mikolaj), Jerzy Stuhr (Jurek), Juliette Binoche (Julie)

In Paris, a Frenchwoman divorces her impotent Polish hairdresser husband, then burns down his salon and frames him for arson. He returns to Warsaw, determined to get rich and win back his wife.

Unlikely black comedy, with a nod to Charlie Chaplin's treatment of underdog characters. Amusing and humane, it remains the weakest link in Kieslowski's trilogy – though at this level of brilliance, 'weak' is a relative term..

SCR *Krzysztof Piesiewicz, Krzysztof Kieslowski* **CIN** Edward Klosiński **MUS** Zbigniew Preisner **DES** Halina Dobrowolska, Claude Lenoir **ED** Urszula Lesiak **PROD** Marin Karmitz **DIST** Artificial Eye/MK2/France 3/Cab/TOR/Canal

66 Though the second film in Krysztof Kieslowski's Three Colours trilogy lacks the power of the first and third instalments, White's story of obsessive love is originally told and surprisingly funny. – *TV Guide*

'His code name is Condor. In the next twenty-four hours everyone he trusts will try to kill him.'

Three Days of the Condor ★★★

DIR *Sydney Pollack*

1975 118m US

DVD ♫

☆ *Robert Redford*, Faye Dunaway, Cliff Robertson, Max von Sydow, John Houseman, Walter McGinn

An innocent researcher for a branch of the CIA finds himself marked for death by assassins employed by another branch.

Entertaining New York-based thriller dealing in conspiracy theories, which were fashionable fodder for film scripts in the 1970s. It is just possible to follow its complexities, and the dialogue is smart.

SCR *Lorenzo Semple Jnr, David Rayfiel* **CIN** Owen Roizman **MUS** Dave Grusin **PROD** Stanley Schneider **DIST** Paramount/Dino de Laurentiis/Wildwood

'They're Deserters, Rebels And Thieves. But In The Nicest Possible Way.'

Three Kings ★★★

SCR/DIR David O. Russell

1999 114m US/Australia

DVD ♫

☆ George Clooney (Archie Gates), Mark Wahlberg (Troy Barlow), Ice Cube (Chief Elgin), Spike Jonze (Conrad Vig), Jamie Kennedy (Walter Wogaman), Mykelti Williamson (Colonel Horn), Cliff Curtis (Amir Abdulah), Said

---

DVD Available on DVD ☆ Cast in order 66 Critics' Quotes ⚲ Academy Award Ⓣ BAFTA
♫ Soundtrack on CD of importance † Points of interest ⚲ Academy Award nomination Ⓣ BAFTA nomination

Taghmaoui (Captain Said), Judy Greer (Cathy Daitch), Liz Stauber (Debbie Barlow)

As the first Gulf War ends, a determined, unscrupulous band of American soldiers try to steal Saddam Hussein's gold, buried behind Iraqi lines.

Classy if cynical caper movie that uses labyrinthine Middle East politics as a dark, unlikely yet amusing backdrop for the shameless behaviour on display.

CIN Newton Thomas Sigel   MUS Carter Burwell
DES Catherine Hardwicke   ED Robert K. Lambert
PROD Charles Roven, Paul Junger Witt, Edward L. McDonnell   DIST Warner

66 Not a great picture, but a very good one, perhaps the first feature of merit to come out of the Gulf War. – *Rick Groen, Toronto Globe and Mail*

66 The tone's a little shaky, veering across merry black humour, denunciatory polemic and high octane thrills. – *Time Out*

'Prepare for glory.'

300

DIR Zach Snyder
2007   116m   US/Canada
DVD   ♫

☆ Gerard Butler (King Leonidas), Lena Headey (Queen Gorgo), Dominic West (Theron), David Wenham (Dilios), Vincent Regan (Captain), Andrew Tiernan (Ephialtes), Rodrigo Santoro (Xerxes)

In ancient Sparta, King Leonidas leads his army against a vastly superior Persian force.

Spectacularly violent sword-and-sandal epic utilising the latest in computerised trickery; the result delights the eye, though the ear quickly tires of bombastic dialogue, more often yelled than spoken.

SCR Zach Snyder, Kurt Johnstad, Michael B. Gordon
CIN Larry Fong   MUS Tyler Bates   DES James Bissell
ED William Hoy   PROD Gianni Nunnari, Mark Canton, Bernie Goldmann, Jeffrey Silver   DIST Warner

LEONIDAS: 'Spartans! Ready your breakfast and eat hearty. For tonight, we dine in hell!'

66 A movie blood-drunk on its own artful excess. – *Peter Travers, Rolling Stone*

66 Possibly nowhere outside of gay porn have so many broad shoulders, bulging biceps and ripped torsos been seen on screen. – *Todd McCarthy, Variety*

Thumbsucker   ★★

SCR/DIR *Mike Mills*
2005   96m   US
DVD   ♫

☆ Lou Pucci (Justin Cobb), Tilda Swinton (Audrey Cobb), Vincent D'Onofrio (Mike Cobb), Vince Vaughn (Mr Geary), *Keanu Reeves* (Perry Lyman), Benjamin Bratt (Matt Schramm), Kelli Garner (Rebecca), Chase Offerle (Joel Cobb)

A teenage American boy still sucks his thumb; aware of the effect on his family and love life, he tries hypnosis therapy.

Quirky coming-of-age movie that has nowhere to go in narrative terms, but features delightful performances

from the adults in the cast – notably Reeves, unusually cast as a cheerfully insensitive New Age dentist who urges the boy to find his 'inner animal'.

CIN Joaquin Baca-Asay   MUS Tim DeLaughter with Polyphonic Spree   DES Judy Becker   ED Angus Wall, Haines Hall   PROD Anthony Bregman, Bob Stephenson
DIST Columbia TriStar

66 Doesn't live up to its early promise and slips into a meandering tale of high school angst. – *The Independent*

66 It feels fresh, almost improvised, mainly because Mills doesn't drive his scenes toward an obvious resolution. – *David Denby, New Yorker*

'Two Men From Different Worlds. Two Cops After The Same Killer. Together They Must Uncover The Secrets. Together They Must Discover The Truth.'

Thunderheart   ★

DIR Michael Apted
1992   119m   US
DVD   ♫

☆ Val Kilmer (Ray Levoi), Sam Shepard (Frank Coutelle), Graham Greene (Walter Crow Horse), Fred Ward (Jack Milton), Fred Dalton Thompson (William Dawes), Sheila Tousey (Maggie Eagle Bear), Chief Ted Thin Elk (Grandpa Sam Reaches), John Trudell (Jimmy Looks Twice), Julius Drum (Richard Yellow Hawk), Sarah Brave (Maisy Blue Legs)

A brave young FBI agent has to confront his own Indian heritage when he discovers a cover-up of a murder on a Sioux reservation.

A lively thriller with an unusual theme and some intelligent musings about split identity and its consequences.

SCR *John Fusco*   CIN Roger Deakins   MUS James Horner   DES Dan Bishop   ED Ian Crafford
PROD Robert DeNiro, Jane Rosenthal, John Fusco
DIST Columbia TriStar/Tribeca/Waterhorse

66 The story boasts integrity and serves as a forceful indictment of on-going injustice. – *Time Out*

'A Titled Family. A Missing Heir. A Fortune At Stake.'

The Tichborne Claimant   ★

DIR David Yates
1998   98m   GB
DVD

☆ Robert Pugh (Tichborne claimant), John Kani (Andrew Bogle Tiyonga), Stephen Fry (Sir Henry Hawkins), Robert Hardy (Lord Rivers), John Gielgud (Cockburn), Rachael Dowling (Mary Anne), Paola Dionisotti (Dowager Lady Tichborne), Charles Gray (Lord Arundell), James Villiers (Uncle Henry), Anita Dobson (Fanny Loder), Dudley Sutton (Onslow Onslow)

A rich 19th-century English family send their black servant to Australia to find the missing heir to the Tichborne fortune, but he returns home with an impostor set on a swindle.

Preposterous but frequently funny period romp, with cast members apparently competing in a private over-acting contest. Based, remarkably, on a true story.

SCR Joe Fisher CIN Peter Thwaites MUS Nicholas Hooper DES Brian Sykes ED Jamie Trevill PROD Tom McCabe DIST Redbus

66 Bristling with such old-fashioned delights as well-turned dialogue, urbane wit, neat but unflashy lensing and even a courtroom finale. – *Derek Elley, Variety*

Tickets ★

DIR Ken Loach, Ermanno Olmi, Abbas Kiarostami
2005 109m Italy/GB
DVD

☆ Carlo Delle Piane (Professor), Valeria Bruni Tedeschi (PR Lady), Silvana De Santis (Italian Lady), Filippo Trojano (Filippo), Martin Compston (Jamesy), William Ruane (Frank), Gary Maitland (Spaceman)

A trio of short stories take place on a train to Rome. First an old scientist recalls an early love; an angry widow of a general is escorted to a memorial service; and three Celtic fans clash with an Albanian family.

In this portmanteau comedy-drama, three very different world-class directors try to have fun on the railway – with mixed results. Loach's story about soccer fans is telling and amusing – but much of the material is strictly narrow-gauge.

SCR Paul Laverty, Ermanno Olmi, Abbas Kiarostami
CIN Fabio Olmi, Mahmoud Kalari, Chris Menges MUS George Fenton ED Giovanni Ziberna, Babak Karimi, Jonathan Morris PROD Carlo Crest-Dina, Babak Karimi, Rebecca O'Brien, Domenico Procacci DIST Artificial Eye

66 Warm, vital and gut-achingly hilarious. – *Matthew Leyland, BBC*

'A highly strung love story. . .'

Tie Me Up! Tie Me Down! ★

DIR Pedro Almodóvar
1989 111m Spain
DVD ♫

☆ Victoria Abril (Marina Osorio), Antonio Banderas (Ricky), Loles Leon (Lola), Francisco Rabal (Máximo Espejo), Julieta Serrano (Alma), Maria Barranco (Médica), Rossy de Palma (Camello en Vespa), Lola Cardona (Psychiatrist)

Drug-addicted porn actress is kidnapped by a patient recently released from a psychiatric hospital, who assaults her and keeps her tied up.

Almodóvar never embraced bad taste quite as fervently as in this lurid, camp and often unsettling melodrama. It needs to be seen as a riposte to Spanish institutions: the church, the government – and indeed, marriage. Those looking for finger-wagging lectures on morality must look elsewhere.

SCR Yuyi Beringola, Pedro Almodóvar CIN José Luis Alcaine MUS Ennio Morricone DES Esther García ED Jose Salcedo PROD Enrique Posner DIST Enterprise/El Deseo

66 A very black comedy in the vein of Bunuel's Belle de Jour, and worthy of the comparison. – *Rupert Smith, Time Out*

'The system wanted them to become soldiers. One soldier just wanted to be human.'

Tigerland ★

DIR Joel Schumacher
2000 100m US/Germany
DVD

☆ Colin Farrell (Roland Bozz), Matthew Davis (Jim Paxton), Clifton Collins Jnr (Miter), Thomas Guiry (Cantwell), Shea Whigham (Wilson), Russell Richardson (Johnson), Cole Hauser (Staff Sergeant Cota)

A reluctant young soldier makes trouble at a Louisiana training camp before being shipped off to Vietnam.

Farrell's charismatic presence announced itself in this vibrant, intimately-shot movie, which feels familiar but remains watchable.

SCR Ross Klavan, Michael McGruther CIN *Matthew Libatique* MUS Nathan Larsen DES Andrew Laws ED Mark Stevens PROD Arnon Milchan, Steven Haft, Beau Flynn DIST TCF

66 Though it doesn't break much new ground thematically, Tigerland is a tautly focused, well-executed drama. – *Variety*

66 Consistently fresh, engrossing and unpredictable. – *Kevin Thomas, Los Angeles Times*

'Loving You Is Like Loving The Dead.'

Tim Burton's Corpse Bride ★★

DIR Mike Johnson, Tim Burton
2005 76m US/GB
DVD

☆ voices of: Johnny Depp (Victor Van Dort), Helena Bonham Carter (Corpse Bride), Emily Watson (Victoria Everglot), Tracey Ullman (Nell Van Dort/Hildegarde), Paul Whitehouse (William Van Dort/Mayhew/Paul the Head Waiter), Albert Finney (Finis Everglot), Richard E. Grant (Barkis Bittern), Christopher Lee (Pastor Galswells)

In a mystical 19th-century European village a shy man is whisked away to the underworld and mistakenly weds a dead girl while his real bride waits bewildered.

A gorgeous example of stop-motion animation, in the service of a story that veers effortlessly between Gothic horror and moments of lyricism and real sweetness.

SCR John August, Caroline Thompson, Pamela Pettler CIN Pete Kozachik MUS Danny Elfman DES *Alex McDowell* ED Jonathan Lucas, Chris Lebenzon PROD Tim Burton, Allison Abbate DIST Warner

66 A wondrous flight of fancy, a stop-motion-animated treat brimming with imaginative characters, evocative sets, sly humour, inspired songs and a genuine whimsy that seldom finds its way into today's movies. – *Kirk Honeycutt, Hollywood Reporter*

⚲ animated feature film

'Prey for the victims'

Timber Falls (new) ★

DIR Tony Giglio
2008 100m US

☆ Josh Randall (Mike), Brianna Brown (Sheryl), Nick Searcy (Clyde), Beth Broderick (Ida), Sascha Rosemann (Deacon)

A couple go camping in West Virginia woods where they are tortured into procreating by religious fanatics desperate to continue their family line.

Lacking any real plot surprises, genuinely scary suspense rebounds to the terrified couple's plight, due to taut direction and high-end production values.

SCR Daniel Kay **CIN** Toby Moore **MUS** Henning Lohner **DES** John Welbanks **ED** Peter Mergus **PROD** Christopher Eberts, Kia Jam, Steve Markoff, Bruce McNall, Arnold Rifkin **DIST** Scanbox Entertainment

66 "A leering, bloody, sadistic affair made by people who understand the audience". – *Philip French, Observer*

66 The most ridiculous horror flick in months, as well as the least subtle parable of America's secular/religious divide. – *Tim Robey, Daily Telegraph*

A Time for Drunken Horses ★★★

SCR/DIR *Bahman Ghobadi*
2000 80m Iran
DVD

☆ Amaneh Ekhtiar-Dini (Ameneh), Madi Ekhtiar-Dini (Madi), Ayoub Ahmadi (Ayoub), Rojin Younessi (Rojin)

A group of Kurdish street children shuttle back and forth over the Iran–Iraq border on smuggling expeditions for their guardians.

Vivid portrait of a community on the edge, never allowing itself to get dragged down by the poverties it observes, but instead resolving to make something poetic and affecting of them; performed by a cast of youngsters who've clearly been through enough to look several years older than they actually are, it's a film Western world cinema buffs might reasonably show children of their own, should those children ever complain how hard or unfair their lives are.

CIN *Saed Nikzat* **MUS** Hossein Alizadeh **ED** Samad Tavazoi **PROD** Bahman Ghobadi **DIST** Porter Frith

66 A central work in the new, boldly politicised Iranian cinema. – *Manohla Dargis, L.A. Weekly*

66 A very remarkable film: a blazingly passionate, spiritual bulletin from a contemporary frontline of almost unimaginable hardship. – *Peter Bradshaw, Guardian*

Time of the Gypsies ★

DIR Emir Kusturica
1989 136m Yugoslavia
♫

☆ Davor Dujmovic (Perhan), Bora Todorovic (Ahmed), Ljubica Adzovic (Khaditza (Grandmother)), Husnija Hasmovic (Merdzan (Uncle)), Sinolicka Trpkova (Azra (girlfriend)), Zabit Memedov (Zabit (neighbour))

An orphaned young gypsy boy with telekinetic powers desperately tries to flee a band of thieves and beggars with the girl he loves.

This agreeable story of young love and ambition provides an enthralling insight into gypsy culture; it's moderately entertaining, and capably juxtaposes fantasy elements and harsh realities. But it's overlong, its structure is ramshackle, and too many characters in a large cast are mere sketches.

SCR Emir Kusturica, Gordan Mihic **CIN** Vilko Filac **MUS** Goran Bregovic **DES** Miljen Kreka Kljakovic **ED** Andrija Zafranovic **PROD** Mirza Pasic **DIST** Enterprise/Forum Film/Sarajevo TV

66 The very richness of the film is a handicap. There are so many people here, and so many places and things happening to them, that it is possible to lose track. – *Roger Ebert, Chicago Sun-Times*

† The film is reduced from a TV series in six parts that ran for 270 minutes.

† Kusturica used a mixture of professional and non-professional actors in his cast. He was named best director at the 1989 Cannes Film Festival.

Time of the Wolf ★★

SCR/DIR Michael Haneke
2003 113m France/Austria/Germany
DVD

☆ Isabelle Huppert (Anne), Maurice Benichou (Mr Azoulay), Lucas Biscombe (Ben), Patrice Chereau (Thomas Brandt), Beatrice Dalle (Lise Brandt), Anais Demoustier (Eva), Daniel Duval (Georges), Maryline Even (Mrs Azoulay)

After a non-specified apocalypse has devastated Europe, desperate families fight it out over food and shelter.

Cheerless vision of a calamitous future and a population out of control. The film's inky blackness underscores its grim theme, though some green shoots of potential survival finally mitigate the gloom.

CIN Jurgen Jurges **DES** Christoph Kanter **ED** Monika Willi, Nadine Muse **PROD** Margaret Menegoz, Veit Heiduschka **DIST** Artificial Eye

66 In today's digital bog of empty light and marketing deceptions, this is what early-millennium Euro art-film masterpieces feel like – lean, qualmish, abstracted to the point of parable but as grounded as a grave-digging. – *Michael Atkinson, Village Voice*

Time Regained ★★

DIR *Raúl Ruiz*
1999 158m France/Italy/Portugal
DVD

☆ Catherine Deneuve (Odette), Emmanuelle Beart (Gilberte), Vincent Perez (Morel), John Malkovich (Charlus), Pascal Greggory (Saint-Loup), Marie-France Pisier (Madame Verdurin), Chiara Mastroianni (Albertine), Arielle Dombasle (Madame de Farcy), Marcello Mazzarella (Narrator)

An ailing author dictates his final novel from his sickbed in Paris, unlocking from his memory many intriguing events from his long life.

A smoothly crafted adaptation of Proust's seminal work, using shifting time frames to conjure up emotions, memories and stories from the past. Attractively staged, with a script that has a brave stab at adapting a towering, formidable literary classic.

SCR Gilles Taurand, Raúl Ruiz **CIN** Ricardo Aronovich **MUS** Jorge Arriagada **DES** Bruno Beauge **ED** Denise de Casabianca **PROD** Paulo Branco

66 A mesmerizing, shimmering and amazingly successful adaptation. – *Kevin Thomas, Los Angeles Times*

DVD Available on DVD ☆ Cast in order of importance 66 Critics' Quotes † Points of interest ⚱ Academy Award ⚱ Academy Award nomination 🏆 BAFTA 🏆 BAFTA nomination
♫ Soundtrack on CD

T

Time to Leave ★★

SCR/DIR François Ozon
2005 81m France
DVD
☆ *Melvil Poupaud* (Roman), *Jeanne Moreau* (Laura), Valeria Bruni-Tedeschi (Jany), Daniel Duval (Father), Marie Rivière (Mother), Christian Sengewald (Sasha)

A successful, gay young fashion photographer in Paris appears to have the world at his feet, until he is diagnosed with cancer and given only weeks to live.

A strikingly unsentimental look at coping with mortality, one that involves cutting off ties and affections. Still it's rewarding enough; Poupaud makes the most of a great lead role and Moreau supplies bristling authority as the hero's grandmother and sole confidante.

CIN Jeanne Lapoirie DES Katia Wyszkop ED Monica Coleman PROD Olivier Delbosc, Marc Missonnier
DIST Artificial Eye

66 Explains very little, choosing instead to emphasise the essential paradox that an individual's life is never complete and always over too soon. – *A O Scott, New York Times*

The Time to Live and the Time to Die ★★

DIR Hsiao-Hsien Hou
1985 137m Taiwan
☆ An Shun Yu (Ah-Hsiao as a teenager), Tian Feng (Fen Ming), Mei Fang (mother), Jü-Yün Tang (grandmother), Ai Hsiao (Hui-Lan), Shu Fen Hsin (Wu Shu-Mei), Hsieng-P'ing Hu (teacher)

A Chinese man recalls his troubled family life growing up on Taiwan in the 1950s and 60s with a grandmother and her doomed plans of returning to the mainland.

Poignant, beautifully shot, semi-autobiographical film of the director's intriguing family struggling to come to terms with financial crises and political change. Deceptively simple, yet enthralling.

SCR T'ian-Wen Chu, Hsiao-Hsien Hou CIN Ping Bin Li
MUS Chu Chu Wu ED Ch'i-Yang Wang PROD Hua-K'un Chang, Wan-LiYue DIST Central Motion Pictures

66 A subtle, deeply moving picture of Taiwanese history seen through the eyes of a boy whose family has recently emigrated from the mainland. – *Time Out*

'4 Cameras. No Edits. Real Time.'
Timecode ★★

SCR/DIR Mike Figgis
2000 97m US
DVD ♫
☆ Xander Berkeley (Evan Watz), Golden Brooks (Onyx Richardson), Saffron Burrows (Emma), Viveka Davis (Victoria Cohen), Richard Edson (Lester Moore), Aimee Graham (Sikh Nurse), Salma Hayek (Rose), Glenne Headly (Therapist), Andrew Heckler (Auditioning Actor), Holly Hunter (Executive), Danny Huston (Randy), Kyle MacLachlan (Bunny Drysdale), Julian Sands (Quentin),

Stellan Skarsgard (Alex Green), Jeanne Tripplehorn (Lauren Hathaway)

Assorted agents, actors – and ambitious chancers desperate to be in on the movie business – compete to get through the door at the offices of a production company.

An audacious experiment in which interlinking, largely improvised stories, shot in real time without cuts, appear on four split screens. None of the stories is quite strong enough to stand alone, but it's an enjoyable gimmick, and one is never short of somewhere to look.

CIN Patrick Alexander Stewart MUS Mike Figgis, Anthony Marinelli DES Charlotte Malmlof PROD Mike Figgis, Annie Stewart DIST Screen Gems

66 It adds up to a properly jaundiced satire of Hollywood on the roves. – *Time Out*

† Figgis reportedly shot the film 15 times – once a day for a fortnight, in one continuous 90-minute take.

'Golf pro. Love amateur.'
Tin Cup ★★★

DIR Ron Shelton
1996 135m US
DVD ♫
☆ Kevin Costner (Roy 'Tin Cup' McAvoy), Rene Russo (Dr. Molly Griswold), Cheech Marin (Romeo Posar), Don Johnson (David Simms), Linda Hart (Doreen), Dennis Burkley (Earl), Rex Linn (Dewey), Lou Myers (Clint)

Shiftless, trailer-inhabiting, golf professional suddenly tries to revive his game when he falls for the beautiful girlfriend of a sneering, successful rival.

It may cleave to the predictable template of sports movies, but this is a feel-good hoot, with any number of appealing, faintly disreputable characters. Shelton's amiable touch as a writer, which underpinned the earlier Bull Durham, is strongly apparent. Costner radiates shambling charm and generates real chemistry with the formidable Russo. It's all topped by generous portions of genial Tex-Mex music on the soundtrack. Not quite a hole in one, but by no means a slice into a bunker, either.

SCR John Norville, Ron Shelton CIN Russell Boyd
MUS William Ross DES James Bissell ED Paul Seydor, Kimberly Ray PROD Gary Foster, David Lester
DIST Warner/Monarchy/Regency

66 Kevin Costner hasn't been this charming and spontaneous for years. – *Time Out*

The Tit and the Moon ★★

DIR Bigas Luna
1994 90m Spain/France
DVD
☆ Biel Duran (Tete), Mathilda May (Estrellita), Gérard Darmon (Maurice), Miguel Poveda (Miquel), Abel Folk (Father), Genis Sanchez (Stallone)

A young Catalan boy is jealous when he sees his newborn baby brother being breast-fed and forms a fixation for the ample breasts of a cabaret performer.

T

DVD Available on DVD	☆ Cast in order of importance	66 Critics' Quotes	Ⅰ Academy Award	Ⓣ BAFTA
♫ Soundtrack on CD		† Points of interest	Ⅰ Academy Award nomination	Ⓣ BAFTA nomination

623

Touching little story of a boy coming to terms with the adult world – though once Luna's premise is stated, the story has nowhere to go.

SCR Cuca Canals, Bigas Luna   **CIN** José Luis Alcaine   **MUS** Nicola Piovani   **DES** Irene Montcada   **ED** Carmen Frias   **PROD** Andrés Vicente Gómez   **DIST** Metro Tartan/Lolafils/Cartel/Sogepaq

66 It's a riot. . .visually amazing and utterly unlike anything ever made in North America. – *John Doyle, Toronto Globe and Mail*

'Nothing On Earth Could Come Between Them.'

Titanic ★★

SCR/DIR *James Cameron*
1997   194m   US
[DVD]   ♫

☆ Leonardo DiCaprio (Jack Dawson), *Kate Winslet* (Rose DeWitt Bukater), Billy Zane (Caledon 'Cal' Hockley), Kathy Bates (Molly Brown), Frances Fisher (Ruth Dewitt Bukater), Gloria Stuart (Old Rose), Bill Paxton (Brock Lovett), Bernard Hill (Captain Smith), Jonathan Hyde (Bruce Ismay), Victor Garber (Thomas Andrews), David Warner (Spicer Lovejoy), Danny Nucci (Fabrizio), Suzy Amis (Lizzy Calvert), Bernard Fox (Col. Archibald Gracie)

As the Titanic sails off on its ill-fated voyage across the Atlantic, a rich girl, engaged to a bullying bore in first class, falls for a penniless young man in steerage.

A film of two distinct halves. Its love story is dreary and hardly credible: DiCaprio looks too callow and polite to be an artist with a bohemian history. As for its treatment of the class divide on board, the hideous cod-Irish music that accompanies each appearance on screen of those fun-loving, life-affirming lower orders below decks virtually amounts to a racial slur. The entire film is book-ended by a sentimental memory from one of the vessel's few remaining survivors; it is absolute tosh. But once that boat hits the iceberg, things take a turn for the better: the final hour is a thrilling, nail-biting fight for survival against the clock, and the technical brilliance of Cameron and his crew (and the computer-generated effects) ensure it is executed brilliantly. Effectively, there's something for everyone, which may explain its astonishing success: but at the time, its popularity was driven by DiCaprio's brief but spectacular reign as the film world's leading object of young desire.

CIN *Russell Carpenter*   **MUS** *James Horner*   **DES** *Peter Lamont*   **ED** Conrad Buff, James Cameron, Richard A. Harris   **PROD** *James Cameron, Jon Landau*   **DIST** TCF/Lightstorm

66 It leaves the port of enterprise and arrives on the far shore of art. – *Dave Kehr, New York Daily News*

66 It is flawlessly crafted, intelligently constructed, strongly acted, and spellbinding. – *Roger Ebert, Chicago Sun-Times*

† The film, with world-wide box-office receipts of $1.84 billion, is the highest-grossing in history.

† Its release, originally scheduled for summer 1997, was delayed for six months, after reports that the production had been troubled and hit by cost overruns. Winslet had also complained publicly of insensitive treatment of the actors by director Cameron, especially in difficult underwater scenes.

⚊ picture; James Cameron (direction); Russell Carpenter (cinematography); Peter Lamont; James Horner (music); Deborah Lynn Scott (costume design); editing; visual effects; sound; sound effects editing; James Horner (m), Will Jennings (ly) (music, original song – My Heart Will Go On)

⚊ Kate Winslet (leading actress); Gloria Stuart (supporting actress); make-up

Ⓣ film; James Cameron (direction); Russell Carpenter (cinematography); Peter Lamont; James Horner; Deborah Lynn Scott (costume design); editing; visual effects; sound; make-up

Titanic Town ★

DIR Roger Michell
1998   100m   GB
♫

☆ Julie Walters (Bernie McPhelimy), Ciaran Hinds (Aidan McPhelimy), Nuala O'Neill (Annie McPhelimy), James Loughran (Thomas McPhelimy), Barry Loughran (Brendan McPhelimy), Elizabeth Donaghy (Sinead McPhelimy), Ciaran McMenamin (Dino / Owen), Jaz Pollock (Patsy French), Aingeal Grehan (Deirdre)

A Catholic housewife and mother of four in early 1970s Belfast leads a group of women who band together to put an end to violence.

Alternately grim and darkly amusing drama, based on real events, with Walters in ebullient form as a plain-talking freedom fighter who employs words rather than weapons to achieve her ends.

SCR Anne Devlin   **CIN** John Daly   **MUS** Trevor Jones   **DES** Pat Campbell   **ED** Kate Evans   **PROD** George Faber, Charles Patterson   **DIST** Pandora/BBC/British Screen/Company Pictures

66 Covers some very dark ground indeed but in its heart burns the indomitable flame of the human spirit. – *Michael O'Sullivan, Washington Post*

'If You Think Revenge Is Sweet, Taste This.'

Titus ★

SCR/DIR Julie Taymor
1999   162m   US/GB
[DVD]   ♫

☆ Anthony Hopkins (Titus Andronicus), Jessica Lange (Tamora), Alan Cumming (Saturninus), Colm Feore (Marcus), James Frain (Bassianus), Laura Fraser (Lavinia), Harry Lennix (Aaron), Angus Macfadyen (Lucius), Matthew Rhys (Demetrius), Jonathan Rhys Meyers (Chiron), Geraldine McEwan (Nurse)

A ruthless Roman general and the proud queen of the Goths clash bitterly in a bloody battle to the death in 400AD Italy.

Shakespeare's most vengeful and bloodthirsty play, with a few modern touches added to period costumes. Taymor typically emphasises its overall look, which is pleasing and striking. Also typically, she seems less concerned about the actors' interpretations of their roles, which range from efficient to eccentric.

[DVD] Available on DVD   ♫ Soundtrack on CD   ☆ Cast in order of importance   66 Critics' Quotes   † Points of interest   ⚊ Academy Award   ⚊ Academy Award nomination   Ⓣ BAFTA   Ⓣ BAFTA nomination

CIN *Luciano Tovoli*　MUS *Elliot Goldenthal*　DES *Dante Ferretti*　ED *Françoise Bonnot*　PROD *Jody Patton, Conchita Airoldi, Julie Taymor*

66 This wild tale of a savage cycle of revenge in imperial Rome is accessible and exceedingly vivid. – *Todd McCarthy, Variety*

† The film was mostly shot in and around Rome.

♔ Milena Canonero (costume design)

To Be or Not to Be　★★★★

DIR *Ernst Lubitsch*

1942　99m　US

DVD

☆ *Jack Benny* (Joseph Tura), *Carole Lombard* (Maria Tura), *Robert Stack* (Lt. Stanislav Sobinski), *Stanley Ridges* (Prof. Alexander Siletsky), *Felix Bressart* (Greenberg), *Lionel Atwill* (Rawitch), *Sig Rumann* (Col. Erhardt), *Tom Dugan* (Bronski), Charles Halton (Dobosh)

Warsaw actors get involved in an underground plot and an impersonation of invading Nazis, including Hitler.

Marvellous free-wheeling entertainment which starts as drama and descends through romantic comedy and suspense into farce; accused of bad taste at the time, but now seen as an outstanding example of Hollywood moonshine, kept alight through sheer talent and expertise.

SCR *Edwin Justus Mayer*　CIN *Rudolph Maté*
MUS *Werner Heymann*　ED *Dorothy Spencer*
DIST *Alexander Korda/Ernst Lubitsch*

TURA IN DISGUISE (JACK BENNY): That great, great Polish actor Joseph Tura – you must have heard of him.

ERHARDT (SIG RUMANN): Ah, yes . . . what he did to Shakespeare, we are now doing to Poland!

ERHARDT (AND OTHERS): So they call me Concentration Camp Erhardt!

66 The comedy is hilarious, even when it is hysterically thrilling. – *Commonweal*

66 As effective an example of comic propaganda as The Great Dictator and far better directed. – *Charles Higham, 1972*

♔ Werner Heymann (music)

'She knew what it took to get to the top. A lot of heart. And a little head.'

To Die For　★★★

DIR *Gus Van Sant*

1995　106m　US/GB

DVD　♫

☆ *Nicole Kidman* (Suzanne Stone Maretto), *Matt Dillon* (Larry Maretto), *Joaquin Phoenix* (Jimmy Emmett), *Casey Affleck* (Russel Hines), *Illeana Douglas* (Janice Maretto), *Dan Hedaya* (Joe Maretto), *Kurtwood Smith* (Earl Stone), *Buck Henry* (Mr. H. Finlaysson), *David Cronenberg* (Man at Lake), George Segal (uncredited) (Conference Speaker)

When a ruthlessly ambitious TV weather presenter realises her husband is impeding her career, she hires three teenagers to kill him.

A breakout role for Kidman, a total knockout as a

small-town girl who will literally stop at nothing to make it big in television. This skilfully constructed satire on the lunacy of celebrity worship and the values of ratings-driven TV is tremendous fun.

SCR *Buck Henry*　CIN *Eric Alan Edwards*　MUS *Danny Elfman*　DES *Missy Stewart*　ED *Curtiss Clayton*
PROD *Laura Ziskin*　DIST *Rank/Columbia*

66 Director Gus Van Sant's black satirical riff on fame, television and tabloid fever asks you to giggle with pleasure at being hip enough to like it. – *Owen Gleiberman, Entertainment Weekly*

Ⓣ Nicole Kidman (leading actress)

To Have and Have Not　★★★

DIR *Howard Hawks*

1945　100m　US

DVD

☆ *Humphrey Bogart* (Steve), *Lauren Bacall* (Slim), Walter Brennan, Hoagy Carmichael, Dolores Moran, Sheldon Leonard, Dan Seymour, Marcel Dalio

An American charter boat captain in Martinique gets involved with Nazis.

Fairly routinely made studio adventure notable as an imitation of Casablanca, for its consistent though not outstanding entertainment value – and for the first pairing of Bogart and Bacall (making her film debut), who showed immediate screen chemistry..

SCR *Jules Furthman, William Faulkner*　CIN *Sid Hickox*
MUS *Franz Waxman* (uncredited)　PROD *Howard Hawks*
DIST *Warner*

SLIM: You know you don't have to act with me, Steve. You don't have to say anything, and you don't have to do anything. Not a thing. Oh, maybe just whistle. You know how to whistle, don't you, Steve? You just put your lips together and... blow.

66 Remarkable for the ingenuity and industry with which the original story and the individualities of Ernest Hemingway have been rendered down into Hollywood basic. – *Richard Winnington*

66 Sunlight on the lattice, sex in the corridors, a new pianist at the café, pistol shots, the fat Sureté man coming round after dark. – *William Whitebait*

'It takes a traitor and a hero...'

To Kill A King　★

DIR *Mike Barker*

2003　102m　GB/Germany

DVD　♫

☆ *Tim Roth* (Oliver Cromwell), *Dougray Scott* (Thomas Fairfax), *Rupert Everett* (Charles I), *Olivia Williams* (Lady Anne), *James Bolam* (Holles), *Corin Redgrave* (Lord de Vere), *Finbar Lynch* (Cousin Henry)

As England slowly recovers from the Civil War, Oliver Cromwell and army leader General Fairfax clash angrily over the fate of the vanquished King Charles I.

For historians it's a powerful political drama set at a crucial point in time, and the script discusses some intriguing ideas. But the dialogue is leaden, and the whole enterprise looks faintly cheap.

DVD Available on DVD　☆ Cast in order of importance　66 Critics' Quotes　♔ Academy Award　Ⓑ BAFTA
♫ Soundtrack on CD　† Points of interest　♔ Academy Award nomination　Ⓣ BAFTA nomination

SCR Jenny Mayhew   CIN Eigil Bryld   MUS Richard G. Mitchell   DES Sophie Becher   ED Guy Bensley   PROD Kevin Loader   DIST Pathé

66 There are some great scenes but also far too many unintentionally hilarious moments. – *Jamie Russell, BBC*

† This was a troubled production, and shooting was halted for two weeks while producers raised the finds to continue.

Ⓣ Jenny Mayhew (writer)

To Kill a Mockingbird ★★★

DIR *Robert Mulligan*
1962   129m   US
DVD   ♫

☆ *Gregory Peck* (Atticus Finch), *Mary Badham* (Scout), Philip Alford, John Megna, Frank Overton, Rosemary Murphy, Ruth White, Brock Peters, *Robert Duvall* (Boo Radley)

A lawyer in a small Southern town defends a black man accused of rape.

Familiar dollops of social conscience, very well presented with child interest and excellent atmosphere. Peck is magisterial as the upright liberal lawyer, while Robert Duvall makes his film debut as the disturbed outsider Boo Radley. One caveat: the film is a mite overlong.

SCR Horton Foote   CIN Russell Harlan   MUS Elmer Bernstein   PROD Alan Pakula   DIST U-I

† The narrator is Kim Stanley.

⚊ Horton Foote (adapted screenplay); Gregory Peck (leading actor)

⚊ picture; Robert Mulligan; Mary Badham (supporting actress); Russell Harlan; Elmer Bernstein

To Live ★★

DIR *Zhang Yimou*
1994   125m   Hong Kong
DVD

☆ *Ge You* (Xu Fugui), Gong Li (Xu Jiazhen), Niu Ben (Town Chief), Guo Tao (Chunsheng), Jiang Wu (Wan Erxi), Ni Dahong (Long'er)

Three decades in the life of a once affluent Chinese family; it starts when the head of the household loses the family mansion and his inheritance in gambling debts. The now impoverished family struggles to survive through the oppressive era of Chairman Mao.

A fascinating family drama set against 'interesting' times; less an overt criticism of China's successive communist governments than a tribute to the resilience of the country's people.

SCR Yu Hua, Lu Wei   CIN Lu Yue   MUS Zhao Jiping   ED Du Yuan   PROD Chiu Fu-sheng, Funhong Kow, Christophe Tseng   DIST Electric/Century/Era/Shanghai Film Studios

66 Scenes of misfortune are leavened with surprising incursions of black comedy. – *Time Out*

Ⓕ film not in the English language

'When Harry comes to town, he brings good times, bad times... And a lot of trouble!'

To Sleep with Anger ★★

SCR/DIR *Charles Burnett*
1990   102m   US
DVD

☆ Danny Glover (Harry), Paul Butler (Gideon), Mary Alice (Suzie), Carl Lumbly (Junior), Vonetta McGee (Pat), Richard Brooks (Babe Brother), Sheryl Lee Ralph (Linda), Ethel Ayler (Hattie), Julius Harris (Herman)

A hard-working black family is happily settled in Los Angeles until a old friend with strange powers arrives from the Deep South, and causes tensions..

Glover merits attention as the malevolent drifter who claims to have a hot line to the dark side. His presence sets up an intriguing contrast between past and present, superstition and modernity. Quietly effective.

CIN Walt Lloyd   MUS Stephen James Taylor   DES Penny Barrett   ED Nancy Richardson   PROD Caldecot Chubb, Thomas S. Byrnes, Darin Scott   DIST Metro/SVS Films

66 This is highly engaging and enjoyable storytelling, but just when you want the supernatural action to ratchet up a notch or two, the tale takes a left turn into family drama. – *Channel 4*

† Writer-director Burnett was given a retrospective at London's BFI Southbank in 2008, and his earlier film Killer of Sheep (1977) received a limited re-release in cinemas.

Together ★★

SCR/DIR *Lukas Moodysson*
2000   106m   Sweden/Denmark/Italy
DVD

☆ Lisa Lindgren (Elisabeth), Mikael Nyqvist (Rolf), Gustaf Hammarsten (Goran), Anja Lundqvist (Lena), Jessica Liedberg (Anna), Ola Norell (Lasse), Shanti Roney (Klas), Sam Kessel (Stefan)

In the mid '70s, a mother leaves her abusive husband and moves into a disorganised, vegetarian commune with her two children.

At first it looks like a ringing endorsement for laissez-faire liberal values, dope-smoking and rejection of mean-minded capitalist society. But director Moodysson turns that scenario on its head, and shows the problems of sustaining such a lifestyle when human nature, in all its competitive selfish glory, intrudes. An agreeable, even-handed social comedy that scores a few well-argued points.

CIN Ulf Brantas   ED Michal Leszczylowski, Fredrik Abrahamsen   PROD Lars Jonsson   DIST Metrodome

66 Moodysson captures exactly the preening narcissism and gumption of these frazzled would-be revolutionaries trying to wriggle out of their bourgeois straitjackets. – *Peter Rainer, New York Magazine*

66 Terrifically funny and remarkably wise, a comedy that speaks volumes, without a polemical word, about the tension between rigid politics of any stripe and the imperatives of life and love. – *Joe Morgenstern, Wall Street Journal*

Tokyo Story ★★★★

DIR *Yasujiro Ozu*
1953   135m   Japan
[DVD]

☆ *Chishu Ryu* (Shukishi Hirayama), *Chieko Higashiyama* (Tomi Hirayama), Setsuko Hara (Noriko), Haruko Sugimura (Shige Kaneko), Nobuo Nakamura (Kurazo Kaneko), So Yamamura (Koichi), Kuniko Miyake (Fumiko), Eijiro Tono (Sanpei Numata)

An ageing Japanese couple visit Tokyo to see their ungrateful grown-up children, but discover they are too busy to spend time with them.

Poignant domestic drama that recounts a heart-breaking domestic family rift. Ozu may be making a point about a self-regarding younger generation, and about urban life being too hectic for old-fashioned family loyalties to survive. This is a quiet, subtle, tenderly observed masterpiece.

SCR Kogo Noda, Yasujiro Ozu   **CIN** Yuharu Atsuta
MUS Kojun Saito   **ED** Yoshiyasu Hamamura
PROD Takeshi Yamamoto   **DIST** Shochiku

'The whole world loves him!'

Tom Jones ★★★

DIR *Tony Richardson*
1963   129m   GB
[DVD]

☆ *Albert Finney* (Tom Jones), Susannah York (Sophie Western), Hugh Griffith (Squire Western), Edith Evans (Miss Western), Joan Greenwood (Lady Bellaston), Diane Cilento (Molly Seagrim), George Devine (Squire Allworthy), Joyce Redman (Mrs. Waters/Jenny Jones), David Warner (Blifil), Wilfrid Lawson (Black George), Freda Jackson (Mr. Seagrim), Rachel Kempson (Bridget Allworthy)

In 18th-century England, a foundling is brought up by the squire and marries his daughter after many adventures.

Fantasia on Old England, at some distance from the original novel, with the director trying every possible jokey approach against a meticulously realistic physical background. Despite industry fears, its frantic, sexy, flamboyant style made it an astonishing box-office success, and it was much imitated.

SCR *John Osborne*   **CIN** *Walter Lassally, Manny Wynn*
MUS *John Addison*   **DES** Ralph Brinton   **ED** Antony Gibbs   **PROD** Tony Richardson   **DIST** UA/Woodfall

66 Uncertainty, nervousness, muddled method . . . desperation is writ large over it. – *Stanley Kauffmann*

66 Much of the time it looks like a home movie, made with sporadic talent by a group with more enthusiasm than discipline. – *Tom Milne*

† The narrator was Michael MacLiammoir.

⚱ picture; John Osborne (adapted screenplay); Tony Richardson; John Addison (music)

⚱ Albert Finney (leading actor); Hugh Griffith (supporting actor); Edith Evans (supporting actress); Diane Cilento (supporting actress); Joyce Redman (supporting actress); production design

Ⓣ picture; British film; John Osborne

'Justice is coming.'

Tombstone ★

DIR George P. Cosmatos
1993   130m   US
[DVD] ♫

☆ *Kurt Russell* (Wyatt Earp), Val Kilmer (Doc Holliday), Sam Elliott (Virgil Earp), Bill Paxton (Morgan Earp), Powers Boothe (Curly Bill Brocius), Michael Biehn (Johnny Ringo), Charlton Heston (Henry Hooker), Jason Priestley (Deputy Billy Breckinridge), Jon Tenney (John Behan, Cochise County Sheriff), Stephen Lang (Ike Clanton), Robert Mitchum (narrator)

Wyatt Earp and his family ride into Tombstone, Arizona in 1879, hoping to open a business and settle down. But they soon discover the lawless community needs taming first.

Colourful (and reasonably accurate) reconstruction of the events that led up to the infamous gunfight at the OK Corral, and made like an old-fashioned western. It sprawls, it's ragged around the edges, but at least you feel it's trying to keep a tradition alive.

SCR Kevin Jarre   **CIN** William A. Fraker   **MUS** Bruce Broughton   **DES** Catherine Hardwicke   **ED** Frank J. Urioste, Roberto Silvi, Harvey Rosenstock   **PROD** James Jacks, Sean Daniel, Bob Misiorowski
DIST Entertainment/Cinergi

66 There are some truly classic scenes here, but the film is a mess. – *Austin Chronicle*

Tony Takitani ★★

SCR/DIR *Jun Ichikawa*
2005   76m
[DVD]

☆ Issey Ogata (Tony Takitani), Rie Miyazawa (Konuma Eiko/Saito Hisako), Takahumi Shinohara (Young Tony), Hidetoshi Nishijima (Narrator)

A lonely, widowed illustrator advertises for a look-alike to model his dead wife's expensive collection of haute couture clothes.

Quiet and subtle to the point of self-effacement, this gentle film is shot in muted earth tones, with a spare, haunting piano score by Ryuichi Sakamoto. Ingeniously the story, which nods towards Hitchcock's Vertigo, unfolds as a series of lateral tracking shots. It's the equivalent of tasteful, uncluttered minimalist décor, yet it is surprisingly moving. A stylish exercise in restraint.

CIN Taishi Hirokawa   **MUS** Ryuichi Sakamoto
ED Tomoh Sanjyo   **PROD** Motoki Ishida

66 A delicate wisp of a film with a surprisingly sharp sting. – *Manohla Dargis, New York Times*

† Actress Rie Miyazawa plays both Tony's wife and the look-alike he hires.

Tootsie ★★★

DIR *Sydney Pollack*
1982   116m   US
[DVD] ♫

☆ *Dustin Hoffman* (Michael Dorsey/Dorothy Michaels), Jessica Lange (Julie), Teri Garr (Sandy), Dabney Coleman

---

[DVD] Available on DVD   ☆ Cast in order of importance   66 Critics' Quotes   ⚱ Academy Award   ⚱ Academy Award nomination   Ⓑ BAFTA   Ⓣ BAFTA nomination
♫ Soundtrack on CD   † Points of interest

627

T

(Ron), Charles Durning (Les), Sydney Pollack (George Fields), George Gaynes (John Van Horn)

An out-of-work actor pretends to be a woman in order to get a job in a soap opera.

An unlikely comedy subject that makes an instant classic. Hoffman is sensational in his detailed interpretation of an actor literally living two lives, and he gets fine support from Lange (as his secret love interest), director Pollack, also on screen as his dismissive agent, and an uncredited Bill Murray as his incredulous best pal. A reportedly tempestuous production, with perfectionists yelling incessantly at each other. But the end result proves well worth it.

SCR *Larry Gelbart, Murray Shisgal* CIN Owen Roizman MUS Dave Grusin DES Peter Larkin ED Frederic and William Steinkamp PROD Sydney Pollack, Dick Richards DIST Columbia/Mirage/Punch

⚊ Jessica Lange (supporting actress)
⚊ picture; Dustin Hoffman (leading actor); Teri Garr (supporting actress); Sydney Pollack (director); Larry Gelbart, Murray Shisgal (original screenplay); Owen Roizman (cinematography); Frederic Steinkamp, William Steinkamp (editing); Dave Grusin, Marilyn Bergman (ly) Alan Bergman (m) (music, original song – It Might Be You); sound
Ⓣ Dustin Hoffman

'They're Dancing Cheek-To-Cheek Again!'

Top Hat ★★★★

DIR *Mark Sandrich*
1935   100m   US
DVD

☆ *Fred Astaire* (Jerry Travers), *Ginger Rogers* (Dale Tremont), *Edward Everett Horton* (Horace Hardwick), *Helen Broderick* (Madge Hardwick), *Eric Blore* (Bates), *Erik Rhodes* (Alberto Beddini)

The path of true love is roughened by mistaken identities.

Marvellous Astaire-Rogers musical, with a more or less realistic London supplanted by a totally artificial Venice, and show-stopping numbers from Irving Berlin, separated by amusing plot complications lightly handled by a team of deft farceurs.

SCR *Dwight Taylor, Allan Scott* CIN *David Abel, Vernon Walker* ED William Hamilton PROD Pandro S. Berman DIST RKO

† 'No Strings'; 'Isn't This a Lovely Day'; 'Top Hat, White Tie and Tails'; 'Cheek to Cheek'; 'The Piccolino'
⚊ picture; Irving Berlin (music, original song – Cheek to Cheek); Hermes Pan; art direction

'The Egos. The Battles. The Words. The Music. The Women. The Scandal. Gilbert & Sullivan & So Much More'

Topsy-Turvy ★★★

SCR/DIR *Mike Leigh*
1999   160m   GB
DVD

☆ *Jim Broadbent* (W.S. Gilbert), *Allan Corduner* (Sir Arthur Sullivan), Lesley Manville (Lucy Gilbert), Eleanor David (Fanny Ronalds), Ron Cook (Richard D'Oyly Carte),

Timothy Spall (Richard Temple), Martin Savage (Grossmith), Kevin McKidd (Lely), Shirley Henderson (Leonora Braham), Dorothy Atkinson (Jessie Bond), Wendy Nottingham (Helen Lenoir)

Inside story of the creation of The Mikado, with much drama and division between the gifted composers Gilbert and Sullivan.

A one-off on director Leigh's CV: a backstage view of the working methods of, and mutual tensions in one of the greatest artistic collaborations of all time, two men sinking their differences to create operettas of dizzying grace. Lit as if for an intimate stage play, the film luxuriates in a burnished glow. Broadbent and Corduner are exceptional.

CIN *Dick Pope* MUS Carl Davis, based on the works of Arthur Sullivan DES *Eve Stewart* ED Robin Sales PROD Simon Channing-Williams DIST Pathé

❝ Though ultimately pic creaks a little under the weight of massive historical research into its characters, a consistently persuasive cast keeps it alive and relevant to their modern-day stage and film descendants. – *Deborah Young, Variety*

⚊ Lindy Hemming (costume design); Christine Blundell, Trefor Proud (make up)
⚊ Mike Leigh (original screenplay); Eve Stewart
Ⓣ Christine Blundell (make up/hair)
Ⓣ British film; Jim Broadbent (leading actor); Timothy Spall (supporting actor); Mike Leigh (original screenplay)

'It takes a lot of guts and a helluva sense of humour to live life in Arnold's shoes.'

Torch Song Trilogy ★

DIR Paul Bogart
1988   120m   US
DVD   ♫

☆ Harvey Fierstein (Arnold Beckoff), Anne Bancroft (Ma Beckoff), Matthew Broderick (Alan Simon), Brian Kerwin (Ed Reese), Karen Young (Laurel), Eddie Castrodad (David), Ken Page (Murray), Charles Pierce (Bertha Venation), Axel Vera (Marina Del Rey)

Middle-aged drag artiste finds and loses love, and eventually repairs his relationship with his overbearing mother.

Not all the ground-breaking appeal of Fierstein's Tony-winning Broadway play carried over into this film version; but with Bancroft firing (loudly) on all cylinders it remains memorable.

SCR Harvey Fierstein CIN Mikael Salomon MUS Peter Matz DES Richard Hoover ED Nicholas C. Smith PROD Howard Gottfried DIST Palace/New Line

❝ Bancroft and Fierstein break the sound barrier, as well as hearts. – *Rita Kempley, Washington Post*

Torremolinos 73 ★

SCR/DIR *Pablo Berger*
2003   91m   Spain/Denmark
DVD

☆ Javier Camara (Alfredo), Candela Pena (Carmen), Juan Diego (Don Carlos), Thomas Bo Larson (Dennis), Fernando Tejero (Juan Luis)

A hapless Spanish encyclopaedia salesman and his wife are tricked into making a pornographic film. It ignites his passion to be a filmmaker, and makes her a star.

A bold, bawdy little farce that pokes fun at Franco's Spain, the sex industry and the loftier end of the film business, while negotiating emotional highs and lows.

CIN Kiko de la Rica   MUS Mastretta   PROD Tomas Cimadevilla, Mohamed Khashoggi   DIST Buena Vista

❝ Dismissed in some quarters as a suburban Spanish take on Boogie Nights, this is a gentle, camp but nonetheless revealing satire on how a nation circumvented the social strictures imposed upon it by Franco's fading fascist regime. – *Empire*

'They stole his mind. Now he wants it back.'

Total Recall ★★

DIR Paul Verhoeven
1990   113m   US
[DVD] ♫

☆ Arnold Schwarzenegger (Douglas Quaid / Hauser), Rachel Ticotin (Melina), *Sharon Stone* (Lori), Ronny Cox (Vilos Cohaagen), Michael Ironside (Richter), Marshall Bell (George / Kuato), Mel Johnson Jnr (Benny), Michael Champion (Helm), Roy Brocksmith (Dr. Edgemar), Ray Baker (Bob McClane), Rosemary Dunsmore (Dr. Lull), Priscilla Allen (Fat lady)

In 2084, a construction worker has a dream and remembers he had a previous existence as a secret agent on Mars.

Over-excitable, science-fiction fantasy film that introduces bone-crunching violence when it stumbles over its overlapping ideas. The plot takes dizzying turns at regular intervals, as it tries to keep up with Dick's overstuffed original story. But the film can be watched as an effects-driven spectacle, its themes reduced to background incidental mood music. Under such circumstances, if you've half a mind to watch, that's all you'll need.

SCR Ronald Shusett, Dan O'Bannon, Gary Goldman   CIN Jost Vacano   MUS Jerry Goldsmith   DES William Sandell   ED Frank J. Urioste, Carlos Puente   PROD Buzz Feitshans, Ronald Shusett   DIST Guild/Carolco

❝ Ugly, stupid, loud, offensive, and pointlessly violent – let's not mince words – this film should be called Total Reject. – *TV Guide*

⚲ Stephen Hunter Flick (sound effects editing); Nelson Stoll, Michael J. Kohut, Carlos Delarios, Aaron Rochin (sound)

Ⓣ visual effects

Toto le Héros ★★

DIR Jaco van Dormael
1991   91m   Belgium/France/Germany
[DVD] ♫

☆ Michel Bouquet (Thomas, as an old man), Jo de Backer (Thomas, as an adult), Thomas Godet (Thomas, as a child), Gisela Uhlen (Evelyne as an old woman), Mireille Perrier (Evelyne as young woman), Sandrine Blancke (Alice), Peter Böhlke (Alfred as an old man), Didier Ferney

(Alfred, as an adult), Hugo Harold Harrisson (Alfred, as a child)

A grumpy old man, convinced he was swapped with another baby in a fire in the maternity ward, plots the murder of a childhood enemy who married the woman he loved.

Acute, joyously offbeat story, viewing the strangeness of the adult world through a child's eyes, eventually becoming a successful blend of a young boy's fantasy and droll adult humour.

SCR Jaco van Dormael, Laurette Vankeerberghen, Pascal Lonhay, Didier de Neck   CIN Walther van den Ende   MUS Pierre van Dormael   DES Herbert Pouille   ED Susana Rossberg   PROD Dany Geys, Luciano Gloor   DIST Electric/Ibis/Metropolis/RTBF/FRZ/ZDF/Canal Plus

❝ An immensely vibrant, inventive, compassionate movie. – *Geoff Andrew, Time Out*

† The infectious song that recurs throughout the film is Boom, sung and performed by Charles Trenet.

Ⓣ film not in the English language

'When It Comes To Fame And Fortune, Heaven Knows He's Got The Touch. . .'

Touch ★

SCR/DIR Paul Schrader
1996   96m   US/France
[DVD] ♫

☆ Bridget Fonda (Lynn Marie Faulkner), Christopher Walken (Bill Hill), Skeet Ulrich (Juvenal aka Charlie Lawson), Tom Arnold (August Murray), Gina Gershon (Debra Lusanne), Lolita Davidovich (Antoinette Baker), Paul Mazursky (Artie), Janeane Garafalo (Kathy Worthington), Breckin Mayer (Greg Czarnicki), John Doe (Elwin Worrel), Conchata Ferrell (Virginia Worrel)

A young man with apparently miraculous powers of healing is targeted for exploitation by chancers and religious zealots.

One could programme an intriguing film festival from attempts to adapt Elmore Leonard's droll novels; intriguing, but mostly flawed. This one takes a running jump at the excellent source material and misses by a country mile. Uneven in tone and execution, this is not one of Schrader's happier efforts.

CIN Ed Lachman   MUS David Grohl   DES David Waso   ED Cara Silverman   PROD Lila Cazès, Fida Attieh   DIST Pathé/Lumière

❝ The only reason to see Touch is to witness for yourself the birth of a star. Skeet Ulrich, playing a serene young man with healing hands and bleeding stigmata, is Johnny Depp, Tom Cruise and Tom Hanks all in one. – *Barbara Shulgasser, San Francisco Examiner*

Touch of Evil ★★★★

SCR/DIR *Orson Welles*
1958   95m   US
[DVD] ♫

☆ Charlton Heston (Ramon Miguel "Mike" Vargas), Orson Welles (Hank Quinlan), Janet Leigh (Susan Vargas), Marlene Dietrich (Tanya), Akim Tamiroff ("Uncle Joe" Grandi), Joseph Calleia (Pete Menzies), Ray Collins (District Attorney Adair), Dennis Weaver (Motel Clerk)

A Mexican narcotics investigator honeymooning in a border town clashes with the local police chief over a murder.

Self-consciously seedy story with strong noir touches, set near the Mexican border, announcing itself with a five-minute tracking shot of extraordinary style and dexterity. It's an overpoweringly atmospheric, convoluted melodrama crammed with Wellesian touches, but very cold and unsympathetic, with rather restrained performances (especially his). Re-cut by an unimpressed studio after it was delivered, it has gone on to be regarded as a classic, and easily the best example of Welles's mid-career work.

CIN *Russell Metty* MUS Henry Mancini ED Virgil Vogel, Aaron Stell PROD Albert Zugsmith DIST U-I

66 Pure Orson Welles and impure balderdash, which may be the same thing. – *Gerald Weales, Reporter*

'The closer you are to death. The more you realize you are alive.'

Touching the Void ★★★

DIR *Kevin Macdonald*
2003 106m GB/US
DVD

☆ Brendan Mackey (Joe Simpson), Nicholas Aaron (Simon Yates), Ollie Ryall (Richard Hawking), Joe Simpson (as himself), Simon Yates (as himself), Richard Hawking (as himself)

A pair of intrepid mountaineers look back at a disastrous accident during a dangerous climb in Peru, where one was left for dead and endangered both their lives.

A remarkable film, using an original blend of documentary, interviews and dramatic reconstruction to revisit a real mountaineering emergency in all its terrifying detail. Much of the pair's behaviour on the mountain appears to be beyond bravery, and speaks instead to obsessive ambition. But it's their indomitable survival instinct that takes centre stage.

CIN Mike Eley, Keith Partridge MUS Alex Heffes DES Patrick Bill ED Justine Wright PROD John Smithson DIST Pathé

66 By the end of this white-knuckle movie, you stand in awe at the depth of man's will to survive. – *David Ansen, Newsweek*

🇬🇧 British film

Tough Enough (new) ★

DIR Detlev Buck
2006 98m Germany

☆ David Kross (Michael), Jenny Elvers (Miriam Poliscka), Hans Löw (Detective Gerber), Jan Henrik Stalberg (Klaus)

A teenage boy moves to a seedier, multi-ethnic part of Berlin after his mother's lover kicks them out of his upscale flat. In his new life he becomes involved in drugs and murder.

Nothing desperately new here, but director Buck has a smart, sympathetic touch and young Kross is appealing.

SCR Zoran Drvenkar, Gregor Tessnow CIN Kolja Brandt MUS Bert Wrede DES Udo Kramer ED Dirk Grau PROD Claus Boje DIST Dogwoof

66 First-rate job, well acted, scored and paced. – *Steve Rose, Guardian*

Tous les matins du monde ★

DIR Alain Corneau
1992 115m France
DVD ♫

☆ Gérard Depardieu (Marin Marais), Jean-Pierre Marielle (Monsieur de Sainte Colombe), Anne Brochet (Madeleine), Guillaume Depardieu (Young Marin Marais), Caroline Sihol (Mme. de Sainte Colombe), Carole Richert (Toinette), Violaine Lacroix (Young Madeleine), Nadege Teron (Young Toinette)

Monsieur de Sainte Colombe, a master of the viola and a remote musical mentor at Louis XIV's court, is recalled affectionately by musician and composer Marin Marais, who remembers the vital musical values he learned, as well as his troubled romance with his teacher's daughter.

Elegantly produced, handsome period drama; its baroque music is exquisite to listen to, but the stately pace often feels self-indulgent.

SCR Pascal Quignard, Alain Corneau CIN Yves Angelo MUS Jordi Savall DES Bernard Vezat ED Marie-Josephe Yoyotte PROD Jean-Louis Livi DIST Electric/FilmParFilm/D.D./Divali/Sedif/FR3/C.N.C./Canal/Para

66 It reminds us that music, like any art, is a gift sometimes bestowed on those who do not deserve it. – *Roger Ebert, Chicago Sun-Times*

'Hang on for the comedy that goes to infinity and beyond!'

Toy Story ★★★★

DIR *John Lasseter*
1995 81m US
DVD ♫

☆ voices of: Tom Hanks (Woody), Tim Allen (Buzz Lightyear), Don Rickles (Mr Potato Head), Jim Varney (Slinky Dog), Wallace Shawn (Rex), John Ratzenberger (Hamm)

A toy astronaut refuses to accept that he is simply a plaything and becomes the favourite of a small boy – which makes his previous preferred toy, a cowboy, deeply jealous.

Sensational animated feature, a milestone in this specific genre. It was the first such film to be completely computer-generated, and fully exploited this technological advance to the maximum to tell its tale with great humour and conviction. A rare 'family film' that everyone in the family will genuinely enjoy; adults for its sophisticated charm, and children for its affectionate, imaginative fantasy about what toys get up to when humans leave the room.

SCR *Joss Whedon, Andrew Stanton, Joel Cohen, Alec Sokolow* MUS Randy Newman ED Robert Gordon, Lee Unkrich PROD Ralph Guggenheim, Bonnie Arnold DIST Buena Vista/Walt Disney/Pixar

WOODY: What chance does a toy like me have against a Buzz Lightyear action figure?

T

66 A deceptively simple story 'peopled' with charming, funny, and well-realised characters and highly enjoyable fare for anyone who ever owned a toy. – *Nick Hilditch, BBC*

66 Although its computer-generated imagery is impressive, the major surprise of this bright foray into a new kind of animation is how much cleverness has been invested in story and dialogue. – *Kenneth Turan, Los Angeles Times*

⚲ John Lasseter (special achievement)
⚲ Randy Newman; Randy Newman (m), (ly) (music, origianl song – You've Got a Friend); Joss Whedon, Andrew Stanton, Joel Cohen, Alec Sokolow (original screenplay)
Ⓣ special effects

'The Toys Are Back!'

Toy Story 2 ★★★

DIR John Lasseter, Lee Unkrich, Ash Brannon
1999 92m US
DVD ♫

☆ voices of: Tom Hanks, Tim Allen, Joan Cusack, Kelsey Grammer, Don Rickles, Jim Varney, Wallace Shawn, John Ratzenberger, Wayne Knight, John Morris, Laurie Metcalf

A cynical, greedy toyshop owner steals the cowboy Woody in order to cash in by selling a complete set of toys a Japanese museum.

This cleverly crafted sequel, which did not quite emulate the scintillating script or the wondrous technical surprises of its brilliant predecessor, remains exceptionally entertaining.

SCR Andrew Stanton, Rita Hsiao, Doug Chamberlin, Chris Webb, John Lasseter, Pete Docter, Ash Brannon
CIN Sharon Calahan MUS Randy Newman
DES William Cone, Jim Pearson ED Edie Bleiman, David Ian Salter, Lee Unkrich PROD Helene Plotkin, Karen Robert Jackson DIST Buena Vista

66 In the realm of sequels, Toy Story 2 is to Toy Story what The Empire Strikes Back was to its predecessor, a richer, more satisfying film in every respect. – *Todd McCarthy, Variety*

66 It's a great, IQ-flattering entertainment, both wonderful and wise. – *Lisa Schwarzbaum, Entertainment Weekly*

⚲ Randy Newman (m), (ly) (music, original song – When She Loved Me)

'Laughter Is A State of Mind.'

Toys

DIR Barry Levinson
1992 118m US
DVD ♫

☆ Robin Williams (Leslie Zevo), Michael Gambon (Lt. General Leland Zevo), Joan Cusack (Alsatia Zevo), Robin Wright (Gwen Tyler), LL Cool J (Captain Patrick Zevo), Donald O'Connor (Kenneth Zevo), Jack Warden (Old General Zevo)

Military maniac inherits a toy factory and orders a total change in production from harmless cuddly toys to miniature fighting weapons.

A fascinating failure from this maddeningly inconsisten director: an elegantly staged extravaganza, dazzling to behold, but fatally sure of its merits. Its unlikely (and unlikable) concept is allowed to get completely out of control.

SCR Valerie Curtin, Barry Levinson CIN Adam Greenberg
MUS Hans Zimmer DES *Ferdinando Scarfiotti* ED Stu Linder PROD Mark Johnson, Barry Levinson DIST TCF

66 There's a curious residue of dissatisfaction after Toys is over. It opened so well and promised so much that we're confused: Is that all there is? The production creates a wonderful world but doesn't make its purpose clear. – *Roger Ebert, Chicago Sun-Times*

⚲ Ferdinando Scarfiotti (art direction); Albert Wolsky (costume design)

Track 29 ★

DIR Nicolas Roeg
1987 91m GB
DVD

☆ Theresa Russell (Linda Henry), Gary Oldman (Martin), Christopher Lloyd (Henry Henry), Sandra Bernhard (Nurse Stein), Colleen Camp (Arlanda), Seymour Cassel (Dr. Bernard Fairmont)

An attractive but sexually frustrated wife, whose husband is more interested in playing with his electric train-set than being attentive to her, finds herself drawn to a mysterious stranger who claims to be her long-lost son.

This intriguing, unique collaboration between screenwriter Potter and director Roeg fails to cohere: it's a bizarre, unconvincing psychological drama that starts badly and quickly falls away.

SCR Dennis Potter CIN Alex Thomson MUS Stanley Myers DES David Brockhurst, Mark Fincannon
ED Tony Lawson PROD Rick McCullum
DIST Recorded Releasing/Handmade

66 There's nothing really to be done but throw up your hands and give in. Though preposterous, the movie is watchable. – *Hal Hinson, Washington Post*

† The title comes from the 1940 song Chattanooga Choo-Choo, made famous by Glenn Miller.

'No One Gets Away Clean'

Traffic ★★

DIR Steven Soderbergh
2000 147m US
DVD ♫

☆ Michael Douglas (Robert Wakefield), Don Cheadle (Montel Gordon), *Benicio Del Toro* (Javier Rodriguez), Luiz Guzman (Ray Castro), Dennis Quaid (Arnie Metzger), Catherine Zeta-Jones (Helena Ayala), Steven Bauer (Carlos Ayala), Benjamin Bratt (Juan Obregon), James Brolin (General Ralph Landry), Erika Christensen (Caroline Wakefield), Clifton Collins Jnr (Francisco Flores), Miguel Ferrer (Eduardo Ruiz), Albert Finney (Chief of Staff), Topher Grace (Seth Abrahms), Amy Irving (Barbara Wakefield), Tomas Milian, D.W. Moffett, Peter Riegert

A conservative American judge, appointed to lead a new national initiative against drug trafficking, learns that his own daughter has become an addict.

In this multi-strand drama, Douglas strives to invest his drugs czar with nuance and complexity; but he must carry the weight of one of the two less convincing stories.

T

The other features Zeta-Jones, implausibly calculating as the pregnant wife of an elusive drug kingpin. Del Toro fares far better as an ethical Mexican cop, beset by temptation. Soderbergh directs events with both the immediacy of a documentary and the genuine tension of a superior thriller; but in terms of story, it's decidedly mixed.

SCR Stephen Gaghan   **CIN** Peter Andrews   **MUS** Cliff Martinez   **DES** Philip Messina   **ED** Stephen Mirrione   **PROD** Edward Zwick, Marshall Herskovitz, Laura Bickford   **DIST** Entertainment

66 Traffic is a real cannonball, a hard-ass drama about the drug trade that Steven Soderbergh directs like a thriller – it comes out blazing. – *Peter Travers, Rolling Stone*

⚊ Steven Soderbergh; Benicio Del Toro (supporting actor); Stephen Gaghan (adapted screenplay); Stephen Mirrione (editing)

⚊ picture

Ⓣ Stephen Gaghan (adapted screenplay); Benicio Del Toro (supporting actor)

Ⓣ Stephen Mirrione (editing); Steven Soderbergh

'The only thing more dangerous than the line being crossed, is the cop who will cross it.'

Training Day   ★★

DIR Antoine Fuqua

2001   120m   US/Australia

DVD   ♫

☆ *Denzel Washington* (Alonzo Harris), Ethan Hawke (Jake Hoyt), Scott Glenn (Roger), Tom Berenger (Stan Gursky), Harris Yulin (Doug Rosselli), Raymond J. Barry (Lou Jacobs), Cliff Curtis (Smiley), Dr Dre (Paul), Snoop Dogg (Blue), Macy Gray (Sandman's Wife), Charlotte Ayanna (Lisa)

A naïve young cop is proud to become a member of an elite drugs unit, until he finds out his senior officer is corrupt.

Fast-paced thriller which persistently plunges Denzel Washington, who appears to relish being cast against type as a bad guy, into a series of increasingly violent situations. A pessimistic, beady-eyed view of law enforcement; sour and harsh, but oddly watchable.

SCR David Ayer   **CIN** Mauro Fiore   **MUS** Mark Mancina   **DES** Naomi Shohan   **ED** Conrad Buff   **PROD** Jeffrey Silver, Bobby Newmyer   **DIST** Warner

66 A brutal, fierce, and tense political thriller, Training Day takes a well-worn format and infuses it with freshness and verve. – *Nev Pierce, BBC*

⚊ Denzel Washington (leading actor)

⚊ Ethan Hawke (supporting actor)

'Choose life. Choose a job. Choose a starter home. Choose dental insurance, leisure wear and matching luggage. Choose your future. But why would anyone want to do a thing like that?'

Trainspotting   ★★★★

DIR *Danny Boyle*

1996   94m   GB

DVD   ♫

☆ *Ewan McGregor* (Mark Renton), Ewen Bremner (Spud), Jonny Lee Miller (Sick Boy), Kevin McKidd (Tommy),

Robert Carlyle (Begbie), Kelly Macdonald (Diane), Peter Mullan (Swanney), Irvine Welsh (Mikey)

Heroin addiction seen through the experiences of four young Scottish friends whose lives are coloured by petty crime, sex, alcohol and violence – sometimes simultaneously.

With its memorable opening, the iconic 'Choose life' monologue and the scene of Renton haring down Edinburgh's Princes Street, being chased by cops, Trainspotting announces itself as a jolting, amoral, adrenalin-fuelled departure from the British film tradition. Its high-energy performances ooze conviction and almost casually convey the bleak reality and dangers of drugs. It's brave, fearless, sickening, relentlessly offensive – and impossible to ignore.

SCR *John Hodge*   **CIN** Brian Tufano   **DES** Kave Quinn   **ED** Masahiro Hirakubo   **PROD** *Andrew Macdonald*   **DIST** Polygram/Channel 4/Figment/Noel Gay

RENTON: Choose your future. Choose life... But why would I want to do a thing like that? I chose not to choose life. I chose somethin' else. And the reasons? There are no reasons. Who needs reasons when you've got heroin?

66 The reason there is a fierce joy in Trainspotting, despite the appalling things that happen in it, is that it's basically about friends in need. – *Roger Ebert, Chicago Sun-Times*

66 A movie that shines with unusual ambition despite its British roots. – *Almar Haflidason, BBC*

⚊ John Hodge (adapted screenplay)

Ⓣ John Hodge (adapted screenplay)

Ⓣ British film

'Life is more than the sum of its parts.'

Transamerica   ★★

SCR/DIR Duncan Tucker

2005   103m   US

DVD   ♫

☆ *Felicity Huffman* (Bree), Kevin Zegers (Toby), Fionnula Flanagan (Elizabeth), Elizabeth Pena (Margaret), Graham Greene (Calvin), Burt Young (Murray)

A transsexual man, preparing for his final transformation into a woman, is shocked to meet his/her long-lost son, who was conceived on a one-night stand 17 years previously.

Felicity Huffman's dominant, affecting central performance was about another kind of transformation: this movie, which started out as an intriguing premise, became a warm, witty, life-affirming experience.

CIN Stephen Kazmierski   **MUS** David Mansfield   **DES** Mark White   **ED** Pam Wise   **PROD** Linda Moran, Rene Bastian, Sebastian Dungan   **DIST** Pathé

66 Felicity Huffman is perfectly tuned to the character of Bree so that even in her most selfish moments her vulnerability is laid bare, along with other thing. – *Stella Papamichael, BBC*

66 Like all good road movies, Transamerica is both a journey in space and time and a journey of the mind and spirit. – *Philip French, Observer*

⚊ Felicity Huffman (leading actress); Dolly Parton (m, ly) (music, original song – Travelin' Thru')

T

'Their war. Our world.'

Transformers (new) ★

DIR Michael Bay
2007 143m US

☆ Shia LaBeouf (Sam Witwicky), Tyrese Gibson (Sergeant Epps), Josh Duhamel (Captain Lennox), John Turturro (Agent Simmons), Megan Fox (Mikaela), Jon Voight (Defence Secretary Keller)

Two factions of robots from a distant planet, the evil Decepticons and the heroic Autobots, wage war, using Earth as a battlefield. They can turn themselves into various vehicles, and their struggle impacts on the life of Sam, a suburban teenager.

The light-hearted story surrounding Sam, played by the appealing LaBeouf, finally gives way to a series of collisions, explosions, and exhaustingly relentless action sequences. The film's juvenile premise cannot be sustained over its disproportionate length.

SCR Roberto Orci, Alex Kurtzman **CIN** Mitchell Amundsen **MUS** Steve Jablonsky **DES** Jeff Mann **ED** Paul Rubell, Glen Scantlebury, Thomas Muldoon **PROD** Lorenzo di Bonaventura, Tom DeSanto, Don Murphy, Ian Bryce **DIST** Paramount

66 A classic Michael Bay mega-movie. Interested in plot and character development? Move along. You're blocking the view. – *Elizabeth Weitzman , New York Daily News*

66 The surprise is the lightness of touch. Treat as a comedy for best results. – *Ian Nathan, Empire*

Transylvania (new) ★

SCR/DIR Tony Gatlif
2006 103 minsm France
[DVD] ♫

☆ Asia Argento (Zingarina), Amira Casar (Marie), Birol Unel (Tchangalo), Marco Castoldi (Milan Agustin)

A pregnant Parisian arrives in Transylvania to find the father of her child. Disguised as a gypsy, she wanders through the countryside with a petty crook.

A hopelessly unstructured and pretentiously picaresque Romany road trip through rough emotional terrain. Not much happens between ethnic musical interludes.

CIN Céline Bozon **MUS** Tony Gatlif, Delphine Mantoulet **DES** Brigitte Brassart **ED** Monique Dartonne **PROD** Tony Gatlif **DIST** Peccadillo Pictures

ASIA ARGENTO/ZINGARINA: 'Imagine anything you like, I've done it.'

66 A little of it goes quite a long way. – *Peter Bradshaw, Guardian*

'Greed, gold and gunplay on a Mexican mountain of malice!'

The Treasure of the Sierra Madre ★★★

SCR/DIR John Huston
1948 126m US
[DVD] ♫

☆ *Humphrey Bogart, Walter Huston*, Tim Holt, Alfonso Bedoya, John Huston, Bruce Bennett, Barton MacLane

Three gold prospectors travel south of the border, and seem to strike it lucky.

Barbed adventure story, almost Biblical in its stern attitude towards human greed and fallibility, with great starring turns from Bogart and a grizzled Walter Huston. It ends as effectively as it opens; this is satisfying, popular film-making by any standard.

CIN Ted McCord **MUS** Max Steiner **PROD** Henry Blanke **DIST** Warner

66 This bitter fable is told with cinematic integrity and considerable skill. – *Henry Hart*

66 The faces of the men, in close-up or in a group, achieve a kind of formal pattern and always dominate the screen. – *Peter Ericsson*

⚊ John Huston (original screenplay, director); Walter Huston (supporting actor)

⚊ picture

'One man's search for . . . who knows what.'

Trees Lounge ★

SCR/DIR Steve Buscemi
1996 95m US
[DVD] ♫

☆ Steve Buscemi (Tommy), Chloe Sevigny (Debbie), Michael Buscemi (Raymond), Anthony LaPaglia (Rob), Elizabeth Bracco (Theresa), Mark Boone Jnr (Mark Boone Junior), Danny Baldwin (Jerry), Seymour Cassel (Uncle Al), Carol Kane (Connie), Bronson Dudley (Bill), Samuel L. Jackson (Wendell), Mimi Rogers (Patty)

An unemployed motor mechanic stalks a neighbourhood in an ice-cream van and gets drunk in his favourite bar to ease the pain of his problems.

Writer-director Buscemi plays a bottle fatigue victim with weary conviction, but though it's a well-observed character study, there's little at stake in the regretful story.

CIN Lisa Rinzler **MUS** Evan Lurie **DES** Steve Rosenzweig **ED** Kate Williams **PROD** Brad Wyman, Chris Hanley **DIST** Electric/Live Film/Mediaworks

66 The most accurate portrait of the daily saloon drinker I have ever seen. – *Roger Ebert, Chicago Sun-Times*

Tremors ★

DIR *Ron Underwood*
1989 96m US
[DVD]

☆ Kevin Bacon (Valentine McKee), Fred Ward (Earl Bassett), Finn Carter (Rhonda LeBeck), Michael Gross (Burt Gummer), Reba McEntire (Heather Gummer), Bobby Jacoby (Melvin Plug), Charlotte Stewart (Nancy Sterngood), Tony Genaro (Miguel)

Man-eating worms, each the size of a house and with multiple serpents' tongues, burst out from under the earth and threaten a small Western town.

Amusing monster movie with strong echoes of the 1950s; it's unclear if it's tongue-in-cheek or genuinely intent on scaring audiences. Either way, it's fine.

SCR S. S. Wilson, Brent Maddock, Ron Underwood **CIN** Alexander Gruszynski **MUS** Ernest Troost **DES** Ivo Cristante **ED** O. Nicholas Brown **PROD** S. S. Wilson,

---

[DVD] Available on DVD   ☆ Cast in order of importance   66 Critics' Quotes   † Points of interest   ⚊ Academy Award   ⚊ Academy Award nomination   🅱 BAFTA   🅱 BAFTA nomination

♫ Soundtrack on CD

T

Brent Maddock   DIST UIP/Universal/No Frills/Brent
Maddock, S. S. Wilson

66 An affectionate send-up of schlocky 1950s monster
pics, but with better special effects. – *Variety*

† A sequel, Tremors II: Aftershocks, was released in 1995.

Triple Agent   ★

SCR/DIR Eric Rohmer

2003   115m   France/Italy/Spain/Greece/Russia
DVD

☆ Katerina Didaskalou (Arsinoe Voronin), Serge Renko
(Fiodor Voronin), Cyrielle Clair (Maguy), Grigori
Manoukov (Boris), Dimitri Rafalsky (Gen Dobrinsky),
Nathalia Krougly (The General)

A Paris-based White Russian army general is
suspected of being a Nazi and a Soviet spy in the
1930s.

*A literate, elegantly constructed espionage tale so riddled
with duplicity that the truth stays well hidden. Yet it's a
fascinating exploration of private and public deceptions.*

CIN Diane Baratier   DES Antoine Fontaine   ED Mary
Stephen   PROD Françoise Etchegaray, Jean-Michel Rey,
Philippe Liegeois   DIST Artificial Eye

66 Thanks to the splendid leads, the film is a beautifully
played exercise in political and ethical speculation,
although its Hitchcockian air of everyone acting guilty
leads to cool and aloof characters. – *Ian Johns, The Times*

Triumph of the Spirit   ★

DIR Robert M. Young

1989   120m   US
DVD   ♫

☆ Willem Dafoe (Salamo Arouch), Edward James Olmos
(Gypsy), Robert Loggia (Father Arouch), Wendy Gazelle
(Allegra), Kelly Wolf (Elena), Costas Mandylor (Avram
Arouch), Kario Salem (Jacko), Edward Zentara (Janush),
Hartmut Becker (Maj. Rauscher)

In World War II, a young Jewish boxer is forced by
the Nazis to fight in a series of boxing matches in
Auschwitz; losers were sent to the gas chambers.

*Harrowing drama, based on appalling real events,
which, though well-intentioned, never quite does justice
to the memories of those involved, and veers close to
melodrama.*

SCR Andrzej Krakowski, Laurence Heath   CIN Curtis
Clark   MUS Cliff Eidelman   DES Jerzy Maslowska
ED Arthur Coburn, Norman Buckley   PROD Arnold
Kopelson, Shimon Arama   DIST Guild/Nova
International

66 Earnest, but woefully misguided. – *Peter Travers, Rolling
Stone*

† Dafoe lost 20 pounds in weight to replicate Arouch's
skeletal appearance.

Triumph of the Will   ★★★

DIR *Leni Riefenstahl*

1936   120m   Germany
DVD

The official record of the Nazi party congress held at
Nuremberg in 1934.

*A devastatingly brilliant piece of filmmaking – right
from the opening sequence of Hitler descending from the
skies, his plane shadowed against the clouds. The rally
scenes are a terrifying example of the camera's power of
propaganda. After World War II it was banned for
many years because of general fears that it might inspire
a new Nazi party.*

CIN Sepp Allgeier and 36 assistants   MUS Herbert Windt
ED Leni Riefenstahl   DIST Leni Riefenstahl/Nazi Party

66 Its length and lack of variety scream incompetence...
Interminable, self-indulgent, repetitive – in a word, turgid.
– *Brian Winston, Sight & Sound, 2002*

Trojan Eddie   ★

DIR Gillies MacKinnon

1996   105m   GB/Ireland
DVD

☆ Richard Harris (John Power), Stephen Rea (Trojan
Eddie), Brendan Gleeson (Ginger), Sean McGinley
(Raymie), Angeline Ball (Shirley), Brid Brennan (Betty),
Stuart Townsend (Dermot), Aislin McGuckin (Kathleen)

An amiable Irish chancer, caught between his
miserable wife, nagging girlfriend and bullying
boss somehow triumphs over adversity.

*Stephen Rea and Richard Harris work an entertaining
odd-couple act together, but the world depicted here is
the trump card: Irish society's rough edges, where
everything feels temporary, the scenery is gorgeous and
any stupid thing might happen. A film like this really
shouldn't be fast-paced; but maybe not this slow, either.*

SCR Billy Roche   CIN John de Borman   MUS John Keane
DES Frank Conway   ED Scott Thomas   PROD Emma
Burge   DIST Film Four/Channel 4/IFB/Initial/Irish Screen

66 Takes a while to reveal its qualities but ends up deeply
satisfying on all levels, thanks to well-rounded characters
and performances down the line. – *Derek Elley, Variety*

Trop Belle pour Toi!   ★

SCR/DIR Bertrand Blier

1989   91m   France
DVD

☆ Gérard Depardieu (Bernard Barthélémy), *Josiane
Balasko* (Colette Chevassu), Carole Bouquet (Florence
Barthélémy), Roland Blanche (Marcello), François Cluzet
(Pascal Chevassu), Didier Benureau (Léonce), Philippe
Loffredo (Tanguy)

A French man with a successful career and a
fetching wife has a midlife crisis and begins an
affair with his dowdy secretary.

*Occasionally amusing romantic comedy that risks
charges of sexism, but overcomes them with ease, thanks
to a forceful, moving performance from Balasko. It's an
intriguing idea, but it runs out of steam before the end.*

CIN Philippe Rousselot   DES Theobald Meurisse
ED Claudine Merlin   PROD Bernard Marescot
DIST Artificial Eye/Cine Valse/DD Productions/Orly
Films/SEDIF/TF1

66 A thoughty, pouty broken valentine pervaded with
comic melancholia and Schubert. – *Rita Kempley,
Washington Post*

DVD Available on DVD   ☆ Cast in order   66 Critics' Quotes   ♦ Academy Award   Ⓑ BAFTA
♫ Soundtrack on CD   of importance   † Points of interest   ♦ Academy Award nomination   Ⓑ BAFTA nomination

'For Honour'

Troy ★

DIR Wolfgang Petersen
2004   163m   GB/Malta/US
DVD   ♫

☆ Brad Pitt (Achilles), Eric Bana (Hector), Orlando Bloom (Paris), Diane Kruger (Helen), Brian Cox (Agamemnon), Sean Bean (Odysseus), Brendan Gleeson (Menelaus), Saffron Burrows (Andromache), *Peter O'Toole* (Priam), Julie Christie (Thetis), Rose Byrne (Briseis), John Shrapnel (Nestor)

The young Trojan prince Paris seduces beautiful Queen Helen during a peace mission to Sparta, which irritates her husband and sparks the siege of Troy.

Vast, computer-generated Greek armies lay siege to the fortress city of Troy with the underwhelming assistance of Brad Pitt, looking faintly embarrassed as the warrior Achilles. An expensive-looking epic, let down by dismal dialogue and only mildly diverting action scenes. O'Toole's big scene as King Priam, begging Achilles for his son's body, introduces a jolting touch of real class; it could belong to a different movie.

SCR David Benioff   **CIN** Roger Pratt   **MUS** James Horner   **DES** Nigel Phelps   **ED** Peter Honess
PROD Wolfgang Petersen, Diana Rathbun, Colin Wilson
DIST Warner

66 I doubt there has ever been a more spectacular folly than Wolfgang Petersen's Troy, a hugely entertaining and utterly preposterous tilt at Homer's mythical siege. – *James Christopher, The Times*

66 Homer's estate should sue. – *Roger Ebert, Chicago Sun-Times*

⚇ Bob Ringwood

True Crime ★

DIR Clint Eastwood
1999   127m   US
DVD   ♫

☆ Clint Eastwood (Steve Everett), Isaiah Washington (Frank Louis Beechum), Denis Leary (Bob Findley), Lisa Gay Hamilton (Bonnie Beechum), James Woods (Alan Mann), Bernard Hill (Warden Luther Plunkitt), Diane Venora (Barbara Everett), Michael McKean (Rev Shillerman), Michael Jeter (Dale Porterhouse), Mary McCormack (Michelle Ziegler), Hattie Winston (Angela Russel)

An old hack reporter lands the scoop of a lifetime in a race against the clock to prove that a man about to be hanged for murder is innocent.

Eastwood at his most gnarled and bear-like enlivens this formula thriller. Its story is unlikely – beyond unlikely, in truth. Yet somehow it's perfectly watchable, and even fun.

SCR Larry Gross, Paul Brickman, Stephen Schiff   **CIN** Jack N. Green   **MUS** Lennie Niehaus   **DES** Henry Bumstead
ED Joel Cox   **PROD** Clint Eastwood, Richard D. Zanuck, Lili Fini Zanuck   **DIST** Warner/Zanuck/Malpaso

66 Claptrap. – *Peter Travers, Rolling Stone*

66 It's hokey, implausible and packed with red herrings, and yet it's a lot of fun. – *Edward Guthmann, San Francisco Chronicle*

'If All You Want To Do Is Have A Good Time . . . Why Get Married?'

True Love ★★

DIR Nancy Savoca
1989   104m   US
DVD   ♫

☆ Annabella Sciorra (Donna), Ron Eldard (Michael), Aida Turturro (Grace), Roger Rignack (Dom), Star Jasper (JC), Michael J. Wolfe (Brian), Kelly Cinnante (Yvonne), Rick Shapiro (Kevin)

In the Bronx, an inconsiderate heavy drinker prepares to marry a hopelessly romantic young woman.

Wry, witty, sharply observed comedy, sympathetically directed by debutant Savoca, which manages to be a little funny and a little wise. The radiant Sciorra takes the acting plaudits.

SCR Nancy Savoca, Richard Guay   **CIN** Lisa Rinzler
DES Lester W. Cohen   **ED** John Tintori   **PROD** Richard Guay, Shelley Houis   **DIST** Oasis/UA

66 This is a subtle movie that invites us to read between the lines. It suggests that a lot of couples may be married to marriage rather than to each other. – *Roger Ebert, Chicago Sun-Times*

True North (new) ★

SCR/DIR Steve Hudson
2007   96m   UK/Germany/Ireland
DVD

☆ Peter Mullan (Riley), Gary Lewis (Skipper), Martin Compston (Sean)

A trawler captain and his crew smuggle illegal Chinese immigrants across the North Sea to stay afloat financially.

Tense story, efficiently related for the most part, before a late lapse into melodrama.

CIN Peter Robertson   **MUS** Edmund Butt   **DES** John Hand, Bettina Schmidt   **ED** Andrea Mertens
PROD Sonja Ewers, Benjamina Mimik, Eddie Dick, David Collins   **DIST** Cinefile

66 Its visual and physical immediacy and its unsparing moral acuity suggest a considerable talent in the making. – *Philip Kemp, Sight & Sound*

'. . .Stealing . . . Cheating . . . Killing . . . who says romance is dead?'

True Romance ★★

DIR Tony Scott
1993   120m   US
DVD   ♫

☆ Christian Slater (Clarence Worley), Patricia Arquette (Alabama Whitman), *Dennis Hopper* (Clifford Worley), Val Kilmer (Elvis, Mentor), *Gary Oldman* (Drexl Spivey), Brad Pitt (Floyd), *Christopher Walken* (Vincenzo Coccotti)

A shop assistant marries a hooker, steals cocaine from her pimp, and the couple go on the run, chased by angry gangsters.

A thriller with distinctly comic undertones, enlivened by Tarantino's smart, confident dialogue, and bravura

---

DVD Available on DVD   ☆ Cast in order   66 Critics' Quotes   ⚇ Academy Award   🎭 BAFTA
♫ Soundtrack on CD   of importance   † Points of interest   ⚇ Academy Award nomination   🎭 BAFTA nomination

performances way down the cast list. It tips its hat to *Badlands* and *Bonnie and Clyde*, but it's truly one of a kind, hurtling along at a tremendous clip, with violence imminent at every turn. Cruel, nasty and tasteless, it's a deeply guilty pleasure – none of which implies you'll want to look away for a second.

SCR *Quentin Tarantino*   **CIN** Jeffrey L. Kimball   **MUS** Hans Zimmer   **DES** Benjamin Fernandez   **ED** Michael Tronick, Christian Wagner   **PROD** Bill Unger, Steve Perry, Samuel Hadida, Gary Barber   **DIST** Warner/Morgan Creek/Davis

66 True Romance aims to be a Bonnie and Clyde for the '90s, but its aim isn't true – it's just Bonnie and Clyde for an MTV generation with a short attention span and an even shorter emotional range. – *Richard Harrington, Washington Post*

66 Everyone shines, right down to the smallest bits from Brad Pitt as a stoned innocent to Val Kilmer as the ghost of Elvis. But it's Tarantino's gutter poetry that detonates True Romance. This movie is dynamite. – *Rolling Stone*

Truly, Madly, Deeply ★★
SCR/DIR *Anthony Minghella*
1990   106m   GB
DVD

☆ *Juliet Stevenson* (Nina), *Alan Rickman* (Jamie), Bill Paterson (Sandy), Michael Maloney (Mark), Jenny Howe (Burge), Carolyn Choa (Translator), Christopher Rozycki (Titus), Keith Bartlett (Plumber), David Ryall (George)

A bereaved London woman, who wills her partner back from the grave, is visited by his ghost.

Warm, emotional yet intelligent account of the grieving process, frequently witty but also raw with sorrow. Stevenson offers an astonishingly uninhibited portrayal of a woman suffering a crushing loss. This is the thinking moviegoer's Ghost.

CIN Remi Adefarasin   **MUS** Barrington Pheloung   **DES** Barbara Gosnold   **ED** John Stothart   **PROD** Robert Cooper   **DIST** Samuel Goldwyn Company/Winston/BBC/Lionheart

66 Sans special effects, pic manages to suspend disbelief through fine ensemble playing and sheer strength of the main performances. – *Variety*

🎭 original screenplay
🎭 Alan Rickman (leading actor); Juliet Stevenson (leading actress)

'All the world's a stage...'
The Truman Show ★★★
DIR *Peter Weir*
1998   103m   US
DVD 🎵

☆ *Jim Carrey* (Truman Burbank), *Laura Linney* (Meryl), Noah Emmerich (Marlon), Natascha McElhone (Lauren/Sylvia), Holland Taylor (Truman's Mother), *Ed Harris* (Christof)

A baby boy is adopted by a television company and made the subject of a 24-hour soap opera. He grows up and discovers his wife, friends and neighbours are all acting their parts in his life.

Dazzling, smart satire on the media, which now seems less implausible, and even prophetic in the era of reality TV. The creation of Seahaven, the idyllic town that is really a studio set, is a breathtaking coup; and the character of Truman finally does justice to Carrey's scattershot talents.

SCR *Andrew Niccol*   **CIN** Peter Biziou   **MUS** Burkhard Dallwitz   **DES** *Dennis Gassner*   **ED** William Anderson, Lee Smith   **PROD** Scott Rudin, Andrew Niccol, Edward S. Feldman, Adam Schroeder   **DIST** Paramount

66 That rare cinematic experience – a movie so close to pure perfection that it seems a shame to spoil it by even reading a review beforehand. – *Michael O'Sullivan, Washington Post*

🏆 Ed Harris (supporting actor); Peter Weir (direction); Andrew Niccol (original screenplay)

🎭 Peter Weir (direction); Andrew Niccol (original screenplay); Dennis Gassner

🎭 film; Ed Harris (supporting actor); Peter Biziou; special effects

'A slightly twisted comedy.'
Trust ★
SCR/DIR *Hal Hartley*
1990   107m   GB/USA
DVD

☆ Adrienne Shelly (Maria Coughlin), Martin Donovan (Matthew Slaughter), Marritt Nelson (Jean Coughlin), John MacKay (Jim Slaughter), Edie Falco (Peg Coughlin), Gary Sauer (Anthony), Matt Malloy (Ed)

A schoolgirl gets pregnant and breaks the news to her father, who collapses and dies. Her mother blames her, her boyfriend dumps her and she turns for solace to a surly, grenade-carrying electronics expert.

Hartley's comic manner is relentlessly deadpan, which is amusing for a while, but sometimes comes to look like condescension to his characters. Still, it's a passable if small-scale story, dependent on quirks of character and dysfunction.

CIN Michael Spiller   **MUS** Phillip Reed   **DES** Dan Ouellette   **ED** Nick Gomez   **PROD** Bruce Weiss, Hal Hartley   **DIST** Palace/Zenith/True Fiction/Film Four

66 Bleak, off-center comedy about dysfunctional families in working-class suburbia. – *Variety*

'Everybody has a secret'
The Truth About Charlie ★
DIR Jonathan Demme
2002   104m   US/Germany
DVD 🎵

☆ Mark Wahlberg (Joshua Peters), Thandie Newton (Regina Lambert), Tim Robbins (Mr Bartholomew), Joong-Hoon Park (Il-Sang Lee), Ted Levine (Emil Zadapec), Lisa Gay Hamilton (Lola Jansco), Stephen Dillane (Charlie), Charles Aznavour (Himself), Anna Karina (Karina), Agnès Varda (The Widow Hyppolite)

A young woman returns home to Paris to find her husband has been mysteriously murdered and their apartment and bank accounts emptied. A mysterious man comes to her help.

This oddly-conceived remake of the 1963 thriller *Charade* leaves one wondering: why? Wahlberg is no Cary Grant, nor is Newton any more than a shadow of Audrey Hepburn. One waits in vain to see what Demme was trying to achieve.

SCR Jonathan Demme, Steve Schmidt, Peter Joshua, Jessica Bendinger **CIN** Tak Fujimoto **MUS** Rachel Portman, Leigh Gorman **DES** Hugo Luczyc-Wyhowski **ED** Carol Littleton **PROD** Jonathan Demme, Peter Saraf, Edward Saxon **DIST** Universal

66 Chalk this razzle-dazzle chase picture up as effective Friday-night entertainment, not the heart-stirring romantic thriller it might have been. – *David Sterritt, Christian Science Monitor*

66 It's a movie for movie lovers – playful, hip and light as a feather. – *David Ansen, Newsweek*

'Like you've never seen her before.'

Truth or Dare ★

DIR Alek Keshishian
1991   114m   US
DVD

☆ Madonna (herself), Warren Beatty (himself)

Madonna's international concert tour of 1990, covered in a documentary.

Mildly interesting glance inside a world which reveals Madonna's high work-rate and shows how much careful preparation goes into projecting an image of wild and spontaneous sexuality. An ego trip that encircles the globe.

CIN Robert Leacock **ED** Barry Alexander Brown **PROD** Tim Clawson, Jay Roewe **DIST** Rank/Propaganda/Boy Toy

WARREN BEATTY: She doesn't want to live off-camera, much less talk. There's nothing to say off-camera. Why would you say something if it's off-camera? What point is there existing?

66 This is a backstage documentary with a vengeance, an authorized invasion of privacy in which the camera follows Madonna even during intimate moments with her family and childish sex games with her backup dancers. – *Roger Ebert, Chicago Sun-Times*

'In this world... redemption just comes once.'

Tsotsi ★★

SCR/DIR Gavin Hood
2005   94m   South Africa/GB
DVD   ♫

☆ Presley Chweneyagae (Tsotsi), Terry Pheto (Miriam), Kenneth Nkosi (Aap), Mothusi Magano (Boston), Zenzo Ngqobe (Butcher)

A vicious young gangster in Johannesburg ruthlessly shoots a woman motorist and steals her car but then finds a baby in the back seat. He dumps the car but cares for the helpless child.

Nicely judged story about a young hoodlum who seems beyond redemption unexpectedly getting a shot at it. The story has the feel of a parable rather than a slab of realism, but is none the worse for that. Director Hood captures the colours and rhythms of the townships to great effect.

CIN Lance Gewer **MUS** Mark Kilian, Paul Hepker **DES** Emelia Weavind **ED** Megan Gill **PROD** Peter Fudakowski **DIST** Momentum

66 An earnest film about the South African shantytowns at some pains to show that its heart is in the right place – that is right up on its sleeve. – *Peter Bradshaw, The Guardian*

† 'Tsotsi' means 'thug' in South African township slang.

⅃ foreign film

Ⓣ film not in the English language; Peter Fudakowski

'When they tried to buy him, he refused. When they tried to bully him, he resisted. When they tried to break him, he became an American legend. The true story of Preston Tucker.'

Tucker: The Man and His Dream ★★

DIR Francis Ford Coppola
1988   110m   US
DVD   ♫

☆ Jeff Bridges (Preston Thomas Tucker), Joan Allen (Vera Tucker), Martin Landau (Abe Karatz / Voice of Walter Winchell), Frederic Forrest (Eddie Dean), Mako (Jimmy Sakuyama), Elias Koteas (Alex Tremulis), Christian Slater (Junior Tucker), Lloyd Bridges (Senator Homer Ferguson), Dean Stockwell (Howard Hughes)

A brilliant designer creates a wonderful, revolutionary new car, but is put out of business by rival vested interests.

Are we being invited to see Coppola in Tucker, a man too far ahead of his time for the business in which he toils to appreciate his genius? The thought does occur. This fact-based story seems an aberration in Coppola's career, but it's rather affecting and involving – as well as sumptuous looking.

SCR Arnold Schulman, David Seidler **CIN** *Vittorio Storaro* **MUS** Joe Jackson **DES** Dean Tavoularis **ED** Priscilla Nedd-Friendly **PROD** Fred Roos, Fred Fuchs **DIST** UIP/Lucasfilm

66 Automotive innovator Preston Tucker built his dream machine from used parts and grand schemes. Francis Ford Coppola built Tucker The Man and His Dream from the same basic materials. Tucker came up with a classic but poor Coppola has turned a great American tragedy into a gas-guzzling human comedy. – *Rita Kempley, Washington Post*

⅄ Martin Landau (supporting actor); Dean Tavoularis, Armin Ganz (costume design)

Ⓣ Dean Tavoularis

'They ran away from everything. . .but each other'

Tumbleweeds ★

DIR Gavin O'Connor
1999   102m   US
DVD   ♫

☆ *Janet McTeer* (Mary Jo Walker), Kimberly J. Brown (Ava Walker), Gavin O'Connor (Jack Ranson), Jay O'Sanders (Dan Miller), Lois Smith (Ginger), Laurel Holloman (Laurie Pendleton), Michael J. Pollard (Mr Cummings), Noah Emmerich (Vertis Dewey), Ashley Buccille (Zoe Brussard), Cody McMains (Adam Riley)

T

Ratatouille (2007) is one of those rare family films that successfully manages to appeal to children and adults, without patronising either.

If there's one unquestioned growth area in current mainstream filmmaking, it would be family movies. Once they were the sole province of Disney, but recently every studio in Hollywood has been getting in on the act. One would like to speculate that their motives are altruistic, but the truth is, there's gold in family movies.

Hollywood's relationship with adult audiences has shifted considerably in the past decade, and grown-ups have been squeezed out of their considerations, for economic reasons. In the typical studio business model, making middle-budget dramas or romantic comedies specifically aimed at audiences over 30 has ceased to make sense. These films are inevitably one-offs, with no sequel opportunity attached. They do not lend themselves to merchandising. And because they target a relatively discerning audience, there's no real way of knowing how successful, and therefore profitable, they might be.

Yet Hollywood has found a way to bring adults back into cinemas – with their children. Research showed that adults were perfectly content to take their kids to see films that were appropriate for their age-range. But until the mid-1990s, many of these films were faintly dull for anyone over primary school age. It was clear to the studios that parents would be even happier if they felt there was something in family-friendly films to tickle their adult tastes too.

Thus the modern hybrid family film was devised – with an innocent storyline that looks and feels like a children's story, but with amusing pop-culture references and sly, sophisticated jokes attached. They're to keep the parents happy, and to increase the likelihood that they'll bring their children back to more family-friendly films.

The idea may have come from the crossover appeal of the great animated TV series *The Simpsons*, which proved adults and children could watch a story together and derive completely different pleasures from it. Children clearly enjoyed the antics and tomfoolery of Bart, Homer *et al*, but the clever, throwaway humour of *The Simpsons* – much of which went over children's heads – delighted adults.

The first time this strategy first became evident in Hollywood was in 1992, with Disney's animation film *Aladdin*. Certainly it featured some outstanding animation, and some decent songs – but it was Robin Williams who completely stole the show, voicing a hyperactive genie with a non-stop barrage of

> '**It was clear to the studios that parents would be even happier if they felt there was something in family-friendly films to tickle their adult tastes too.**'

The first time this strategy first became evident in Hollywood was in 1992, with Disney's animation film *Aladdin*. Certainly it featured some outstanding animation, and some decent songs – but it was Robin Williams who completely stole the show, voicing a hyperactive genie with a non-stop barrage of motor-mouthed gags, many of them faintly mystifying to younger audience members. Yet kids giggled, adults roared, and word of mouth spread fast.

Aladdin went on to exceed Disney's wildest expectations, becoming the highest-earning film to open in the US that year. (It grossed an astonishing $217 million, a cool $43 million clear of its nearest rival.) In every Hollywood studio, executives exchanged meaningful looks: something was happening here.

Three years later, *Toy Story* proved that *Aladdin* was more than a fluke. It had its own unique selling point: the first wholly computer-generated animation feature. It looked new, shiny and exciting. But it also followed the template: an enchanting story centred on a children's toy box, with a smattering of topical jokes for baby-boomer parents. Yet *Toy Story* held huge appeal for adults. I recall seeing it in New York, at a midweek afternoon screening. The cinema was two-thirds full, the audience was appreciative, and there wasn't a child in the house. In America, it grossed $191 million, making it the biggest hit of 1995.

> '*The making and marketing of family-friendly films has evolved into a craft. Their success has been astonishing.*'

Since then, the making and marketing of family-friendly films has evolved into a craft. Their success has been astonishing. In 2007, seven of the top 20 grossing films in America were PG or G-rated. These included *Shrek the Third, Enchanted, Ratatouille, Alvin and the Chipmunks* and *National Treasure: Book of Secrets*. This leaves no room for doubt: family-friendly films are a significant commercial force.

Their advantages to studios are manifold. Children are not deterred by repetition, and many of them will pester their parents to see the film a second time. (Then when the DVD is released, they will typically watch it again and again.) And if a parent can be tempted to take the family along to such films, they will buy three, four or five tickets at a time.

There is even an argument that family-friendly films have brought back into cinemas a significant number of adults who had given up the film-going habit. In America, for example, conservative Christian adults, who had found the violence and sexual candour of many films distasteful, find themselves back in the cinemas to see movies they can feel confident will be inoffensive. So everyone wins.

Well, almost everyone. Getting the balance right between enchanting children and amusing adults is a tricky business. When film-makers get it right (as they did, for example, in the first *Shrek* film, *Finding Nemo, Wallace & Gromit in the Curse of the Were-Rabbit* and *Meet the Robinsons*), the results leave everyone with a glow of delighted satisfaction. But when the balance is wrong, and the scales are tipped in favour of keeping the parents from fidgeting, the outcome can be queasy. For me the low water mark of this tendency came in 2004, with the release of the animated DreamWorks film *Shark Tale*. Reviewing it in the *Daily Telegraph*, I wrote:

'There's more smarmy irony in *Shark Tale* than in a week of David Letterman shows . . . all the film's humour is equally airless and narrow – most gags are about show business or consumerism . . . it's a trainspotterish form of enjoyment for grown-ups, sitting there in the dark, joylessly ticking off *Shark Tale*'s smirking pop-culture references.'

> '*Family-friendly films have brought back into cinemas a significant number of adults who had given up the film-going habit.*'

These complaints can be applied to any number of family-friendly films. *Shrek the Third* is an example: the progression, if that's the word, from the first *Shrek* film to the third has been a depressing one.

And the success of family-friendly films has predictably led to a glut in the market. There are simply too many of them, and the good ones shine like beacons. The mediocre, slapdash ones, which form the great majority, tend to fall into the same trap – slyly winking at the adults in the audience while maintaining the pretence of targeting the kids.

Over-strenuous attempts to broaden the appeal of such movies will have only one outcome: short-changing their core audience. Children should remain the primary concern of family-friendly films. Film-makers and studios need to keep that in mind.

A feckless mother lurches thoughtlessly from town to town and man to man until her sparky 12-year-old daughter starts to rebel.

A beautifully performed relationship drama with a level-headed child teaching a clueless adult a few life lessons. One of the few films properly to utilise the talents of the statuesque McTeer, a thoughtful, compelling, strangely underrated actress.

SCR Gavin O'Connor, Angela Shelton **CIN** Dan Stoloff **MUS** David Mansfield **DES** Bryce Holtshousen **ED** John Gilroy **PROD** Greg O'Connor **DIST** Entertainmeny

66 Janet McTeer doesn't imitate Mary Jo Walker, and she doesn't act her. She becomes her. It's almost spooky. – *Stephen Hunter, Washington Post*

66 Tumbleweeds is gorgeously nuanced. – *David Edelstein, Slate*

Janet McTeer (leading actress)

Twelfth Night ★

SCR/DIR Trevor Nunn
1996 134m US/GB
DVD ♫

☆ Helena Bonham Carter (Olivia), Richard E. Grant (Sir Andrew Aguecheek), Nigel Hawthorne (Malvolio), Ben Kingsley (Feste), Mel Smith (Sir Toby Belch), Imelda Staunton (Maria), Toby Stephens (Duke Orsino), Imogen Stubbs (Viola), Steven MacKintosh (Sebastian), Nicholas Farrell (Antonio), Sid Livingstone (Captain)

Shakespeare's play moves up to the 18th century, with shipwrecked boy and girl twins causing misunderstandings and romantic problems.

This comedy of sexual confusion just about squeaks by, though Nunn is clearly more comfortable directing on stage than on a film set. Stubbs lifts proceedings with her spirited performance.

CIN Clive Tickner **MUS** Shaun Davey **DES** Sophie Becher **ED** Peter Boyle **PROD** Stephen Evans, David Parfitt **DIST** Entertainment/Fine Line/Twelfth Night/Renaissance

66 Trevor Nunn's new film version of Twelfth Night, a lighthearted comedy of romance and gender confusion, creates a romantic triangle out of the same sorts of mistaken sexual identities that inspired Some Like It Hot. And Nunn directs it in something of the same spirit; the film winks at us while the characters fall in love. To be sure, Imogen Stubbs makes a better boy than Jack Lemmon made a girl, but nobody's perfect. – *Roger Ebert, Chicago Sun-Times*

12.08 East of Bucharest (new) ★★

SCR/DIR Corneliu Porumboiu
2006 88m Romania
DVD

☆ Teodor Corban (Virgil Jderescu), Ion Sapdaru (Tiberiu Manescu), Mircea Andreescu (Emanoil Piscoci)

A small-town TV presenter hosts a live phone-in show to establish if the community was genuinely part of the revolution that overthrew the dictator Ceaucescu 16 years previously. But neither of his two guests are his first choice, and one turns out to be an unreliable witness.

Agreeably dark comedy with serious points to make about history and remembrance. The fun palls in the last half-hour as the disastrous programme is played out in real time.

CIN Marius Panduru **MUS** Grupul Rotaria **DES** Daniel Raduta **ED** Roxana Szel **PROD** Daniel Burlac **DIST** Artificial Eye

66 A terrifically droll and slyly incisive comedy. – *Sukhdev Sandhu, Daily Telegraph*

66 A deadpan delight that offers further proof of Romania's cinematic ascendance. – *David Jenkins, Total Film*

† It was named the best debut film at the 2006 Cannes Festival.

12 Angry Men ★★★★

DIR *Sidney Lumet*
1957 95m US
DVD

☆ *Henry Fonda* (Juror No. 8), *Lee J. Cobb* (Juror No. 3), *E. G. Marshall* (Juror No. 4), *Jack Warden* (Juror No. 7), *Ed Begley* (Juror No. 10), *Martin Balsam* (Juror No. 1), *John Fiedler* (Juror No. 2), *Jack Klugman* (Juror No. 5), *George Voskovec* (Juror No. 11), *Robert Webber* (Juror No. 12), *Edward Binns* (Juror No. 6), *Joseph Sweeney* (Juror No. 9)

A murder case jury about to vote guilty is convinced otherwise by one doubting member.

Though unconvincing in detail, this is a brilliantly tight character melodrama which is never less than absorbing to experience. Acting and direction are superlatively right, and the film was important in helping to establish television talents in Hollywood.

SCR *Reginald Rose)* **CIN** *Boris Kaufman* **MUS** Kenyon Hopkins **ED** Carl Lerner **PROD** (UA) Orion-Nova (Henry Fonda, Reginald Rose)

† Lumet shot the film in just 19 days.

picture; Reginald Rose; Sidney Lumet

Henry Fonda (leading actor)

'The Future Is History.'

Twelve Monkeys ★★★

DIR Terry Gilliam
1995 129m US
DVD ♫

☆ Bruce Willis (James Cole), Brad Pitt (Jeffrey Goines), Madeleine Stowe (Kathryn Railly), Christopher Plummer (Dr. Goines), Joseph Melito (Young Cole), Jon Seda (Jose), Michael Chance (Scarface), Vernon Campbell (Tiny)

In the middle of the 21st century, when most of the earth's population has been wiped out by a deadly virus and the few remaining people alive exist underground, a convict is sent to travel back in time to find a cure.

Gilliam's hit-and-miss genius is in full flower here, a perfect match for this fascinating story. Willis gives one of his best dramatic performances, while Pitt certainly extended his range with his comic, if self-consciously showy turn as a nervously twitchy asylum inmate. It's a terrific thrill ride, with visual touches and sharp narrative turns that are utterly inspired.

SCR David Peoples, Janet Peoples   **CIN** Roger Pratt   **MUS** Paul Buckmaster   **DES** Jeffrey Beecroft   **ED** Mick Audsley   **PROD** Charles Roven
DIST Polygram/Universal/Atlas/Classico

❝ Solving the riddle of Twelve Monkeys is an exhilarating challenge. – *Peter Travers, Rolling Stone*

❝ A complex and rewarding fantasy. – *BBC*

⚱ Brad Pitt (supporting actor); Julie Weiss (costume design)

'The Days Are Numbered.'

28 Days Later. . .   ★★

DIR Danny Boyle
2002   113m   GB
DVD   ♫

☆ Cillian Murphy (Jim), Noah Huntley (Mark), Naomie Harris (Selena), Brendan Gleeson (Frank), Megan Burns (Hannah), Christopher Eccleston (Major West)

A hospital patient wakes up to discover a deserted London, wiped out by a virus that has turned the British populace into zombies.

Managing an impressively apocalyptic feel for a low-budget digital production, this home-grown zombie romp is tense and thrilling in patches, but succumbs to a few too many half-baked ideas.

SCR Alex Garland   **CIN** Anthony Dod Mantle   **MUS** John Murphy   **DES** *Mark Tildesley*   **ED** *Chris Gill*
PROD Andrew Macdonald   **DIST** TCF

❝ Shows a rather arrogant disdain for its audience in between occasional flashes of flair. – *Derek Elley, Variety*

❝ The best purely British horror/science-fiction film in decades. And the first great apocalypse movie of the new millennium. – *Empire*

† The film was released in the US with two endings, one upbeat and the other downbeat.
† Followed by the sequel 28 Weeks Later.

'Can you change your whole life in a day?'

25th Hour   ★

DIR Spike Lee
2002   135m   US
DVD   ♫

☆ Edward Norton (Monty Brogan), Philip Seymour Hoffman (Jacob Elinsky), Barry Pepper (Francis Xavier Slaughtery), Rosario Dawson (Naturelle Riviera), Anna Paquin (Mary D'Annunzio), Brian Cox (James Brogan), Tony Siragusa (Kostya Novotny)

Before starting a seven-year stint in jail, a Manhattan drug dealer spends his last free day with the important people in his life.

A peculiarly solemn slog from the provocative Spike Lee, irrelevantly set against a post-9/11 backdrop. There are scattered points of interest, but the central character study and performances are not among them.

SCR David Benioff   **CIN** Rodrigo Prieto   **MUS** Terence Blanchard   **DES** James Chinlund   **ED** Barry Alexander Brown   **PROD** Spike Lee, Jon Kilik, Tobey Maguire, Julia Chasman   **DIST** Buena Vista

---

❝ For all the trauma of 9/11, the atmosphere isn't markedly different from that of any other Spike Lee joint. . .Perhaps the tone is slightly chastened, and the conciliatory spirit of its ending is untypically earnest, but for the rest, it's another square yard of New York attitude. – *Anthony Quinn, Independent*

❝ A turgid, bombastic and outrageously self-satisfied movie. – *Peter Bradshaw, Guardian*

'The unbelievably true story of one man, one movement, the music and madness that was Manchester.'

24 Hour Party People   ★★

DIR Michael Winterbottom
2002   117m   GB
DVD   ♫

☆ *Steve Coogan* (Tony Wilson), Lennie James (Alan Erasmus), Shirley Henderson (Lindsay Wilson), Paddy Considine (Rob Gretton), Andy Serkis (Martin Hannett), *Sean Harris* (Ian Curtis), John Simm (Bernard Sumner), Ralf Little (Peter Hook), Keith Allen (Roger Ames)

The story of Manchester rock label Factory Records and its smug impresario, Tony Wilson.

The supercilious narration is wittily tailored to Coogan, and the film finds clever ways to puncture the ballooning pomposity of its own true story. Highly enjoyable, but some interest in the era is essential.

SCR *Frank Cottrell Boyce*   **CIN** Robby Muller   **DES** Mark Tildesley   **ED** Trevor Waite   **PROD** Andrew Eaton
DIST Pathé

❝ Reasonably entertaining stuff – but haven't we seen and heard it all before? It makes no serious attempt to find convincing or compelling human stories behind the legends. – *Peter Bradshaw, Guardian*

TwentyFourSeven   ★★

DIR Shane Meadows
1997   96m   GB
DVD   ♫

☆ Bob Hoskins (Alan Darcy), Mat Hand (Wesley Fangash), Sun Hand (Jordon Fangash), Sarah Thom (Fangash's Girl (Louise)), Sammy Pasha (Jimmy Marsh), Gina Aris (Sharon), James Corden (Tonka (Carl Marsh)), Frank Harper (Ronnie Marsh), Anthony Clarke (Youngy)

An ex-boxer tries to inspire the alienated youths of his small Midlands town by starting a boxing club.

A low-budget British movie, shot in black and white, that references kitchen-sink dramas from half a century previously. Hoskins, for once playing an uncomplicated nice guy holds together a production largely populated with first-timers. A promising debut for Meadows.

SCR Shane Meadows, Paul Fraser   **CIN** Ashley Rowe
MUS Neill MacColl, Boo Hewerdine   **DES** John-Paul Kelly
ED Bill Diver   **PROD** Imogen West
DIST Pathé/BBC/Scala

❝ Director Shane Meadows' film's scope and ambitions may be small, but its heart is large. – *Edward Guthmann, San Francisco Chronicle*

† .

Ⓣ British film

DVD Available on DVD   ☆ Cast in order   ❝ Critics' Quotes   ⚱ Academy Award   🅑 BAFTA
♫ Soundtrack on CD   of importance   † Points of interest   ⚱ Academy Award nomination   Ⓣ BAFTA nomination

641

'Inspired by the true story of five students who changed the game forever.'

21 (new)

DIR Robert Luketic
2008 123m US
♫

☆ Jim Sturgess (Ben Campbell), Kevin Spacey (Mickey Rosa), Laurence Fishburne (Cole Williams), Kate Bosworth (Jill Taylor)

A group of gifted maths students, led by their brilliant but greedy professor (Spacey), head for Vegas each weekend to try and get rich on blackjack tables by counting cards.

Lame, implausible gambling movie, based very loosely on a true story. It seems aimed at audiences too young to play the tables legally. So smug and disagreeable are the students, one roots for the casino to take all their money.

SCR Peter Steinfeld, Allan Loeb   CIN Russell Carpenter
MUS David Sardy   DES Missy Stewart   ED Elliot Graham   PROD Dana Brunetti, Michael de Luca, Kevin Spacey   DIST Columbia

66 It's nearly as much fun as watching an insurance professional compute actuarial tables. – *Jim Emerson, Chicago Sun-Times*

'How much does life weigh?'

21 Grams ★

DIR Alejandro Gonzalez Inarritu
2003 124m US/Germany
DVD ♫

☆ Sean Penn (Paul Rivers), *Benicio Del Toro* (Jack Jordan), *Naomi Watts* (Cristina Peck), Charlotte Gainsbourg (Mary Rivers), Melissa Leo (Marianne Jordan), Clea DuVall (Claudia), Danny Huston (Michael), Paul Calderon (Brown)

A hit-and-run accident brings together a grieving widow with the recipient of her husband's transplanted heart.

Though the performances have some power, this is a bullying and portentous exercise, hiding its melodramatic essence under the tricksy, fractured style typical of this writer and director.

SCR Guillermo Arriaga   CIN Rodrigo Prieto
MUS Gustavo Santaolalla   DES Brigitte Broch
ED Stephen Mirrione   PROD Alejandro Gonzalez Inarritu, Robert Salerno   DIST Icon

66 Strives for greatness, and that's precisely what it achieves. – *Rob Fraser, Empire*

66 It's forceful, to be sure, but in a lurid way that suggests a telenovela that's been baking in the sun too long. – *Peter Rainer, New York*

† The title refers to the weight a person's body supposedly loses at the moment of death.

⚱ Naomi Watts (leading actress); Benicio Del Toro (supporting actor)

Ⓣ Sean Penn (leading actor); Naomi Watts (leading actress); Benicio Del Toro (supporting actor); Guillermo Arriaga (original screenplay); Stephen Mirrione (editing)

'This January, always a bridesmaid, never a bride.'

27 Dresses (new)

DIR Anne Fletcher
2008 110m US
DVD ♫

☆ Katherine Heigl (Jane Nichols), James Marsden (Kevin Doyle), Malin Akerman (Tess Nichols), Judy Greer (Casey), Edward Burns (George), Melora Hardin (Maureen), Brian Kerwin (Hal Nichols)

A serial bridesmaid is forced to arrange a wedding for her sister to the man she secretly loves.

Formulaic rom-com with an appealing lead too charismatic to convince as a lovelorn spinster.

SCR Aline Brosh McKenna   CIN Peter James
MUS Randy Edelman   DES Shepherd Frankel
ED Priscilla Nedd Friendly   PROD Roger Birnbaum, Gary Barber, Jonathan Glickman   DIST TCF

66 This by-the-numbers romantic comedy is the kind of rote exercise that can give a genre a bad name. – *Carina Chocano, Los Angeles Times*

66 The film's credibility crumbles like stale wedding cake. – *Wendy Ide, The Times*

'Some people can buy their way out of anything. Except the past.'

Twilight ★

DIR Robert Benton
1998 94m US
DVD

☆ *Paul Newman* (Harry Ross), Susan Sarandon (Catherine Ames), Gene Hackman (Jack Ames), Reese Witherspoon (Mel Ames), Stockard Channing (Verna), James Garner (Raymond Hope), Giancarlo Esposito (Reuben), Liev Schreiber (Jeff Willis), Margo Martindale (Gloria Lamar), John Spencer (Captain Phil Egan), M. Emmet Walsh (Lester Ivar)

An elderly semi-retired detective, living in Los Angeles off the charity of his film star friends, almost unwittingly finds himself investigating a 20-year-old murder.

A thoughtful thriller, very clearly aimed at older audiences and appropriately conducted at a gentle pace with no gratuitous violence, still makes its mark as a richly textured whodunnit.

SCR Robert Benton, Richard Russo   CIN Piotr Sobocinski
MUS Elmer Bernstein   DES David Gropman   ED Carol Littleton   PROD Arlene Donovan, Scott Rudin
DIST Paramount

66 Paul Newman is a class act in great company and the movie is a joy. – *Time Out*

'A different kind of love story.'

Twin Falls Idaho ★

DIR Michael Polish
1999 111m US
DVD ♫

☆ Michael Polish (Francis Falls), Mark Polish (Blake Falls), Michele Hicks (Penny), Jon Gries (Jay), Patrick Bauchau (Miles), Garrett Morris (Jesus), William Katt (Surgeon), Lesley Ann Warren (Francine), Teresa Hill (Sissy), Ant (Tre), Holly Woodlawn (Flamboyant at Party)

DVD Available on DVD   ☆ Cast in order   66 Critics' Quotes   ⚱ Academy Award   Ⓑ BAFTA
♫ Soundtrack on CD   of importance   † Points of interest   ⚱ Academy Award nomination   Ⓣ BAFTA nomination

Conjoined twin brothers fall out badly when one of them falls for a hooker.

A gentle movie, and an eccentric one, to say the least, made by and starring identical though not conjoined twins. After it lays out its basic premise, it really has nowhere to go dramatically. But no-one could accuse it of being run-of-the-mill.

SCR Mark and Michael Polish CIN M. David Mullen MUS Stuart Matthewman DES Warren Alan Young ED Leo Trombetta PROD Marshall Persinger, Rena Ronson, Stephen J. Wolfe

66 Surprisingly formulaic. So many scenes seem lifted from a 1950s melodrama, from Blake and Francis' repentant mother (Lesley Ann Warren) to the film's tearjerker of a final scene. – *Ann Hornaday, Baltimore Sun*

'The Dark Side of Nature.'

Twister   ★

DIR Jan de Bont
1996 113m US
DVD ♫

☆ Helen Hunt (Dr. Jo Harding), Bill Paxton (Bill Harding), Jami Gertz (Dr. Melissa Reeves), Cary Elwes (Dr. Jonas Miller), Lois Smith (Meg Greene), Philip Seymour Hoffman (Dustin Davis), Alan Ruck (Robert 'Rabbit' Nurick)

Divorcing meteorologists are blown back together by a series of gargantuan cyclones.

Super special effects enhance this visit to Oklahoma's Tornado Alley. Unfortunately any memorable pages in the script must have been blown away too. But it's just unpretentious fun that makes you cackle with glee.

SCR Michael Crichton, Anne-Marie Martin CIN Jack N. Green MUS Mark Mancina DES Joseph Nemec III ED Michael Kahn PROD Kathleen Kennedy, Ian Bryce, Michael Crichton DIST Warner/Universal/Amblin

66 The hackneyed chatter and half-baked personal histories are enough to make you scream into the wind. – *Desson Howe, Washington Post*

⚱ visual effects; sound

🎭 Stefen Fangmeier, John Frazier, Henry LaBounta, Habib Zargarpour (special visual effects)

'Two infant tiger cubs, separated from their parents and each other.'

Two Brothers   ★

DIR Jean-Jacques Annaud
2004 109m France/GB
DVD ♫

☆ Guy Pearce (Aidan McRory), Jean-Claude Dreyfus (Administrator Normandin), Freddie Highmore (Raoul), Philippine Leroy-Beaulieu (Mathilde Normandin), Moussa Maaskri (Saladin), Vincent Scarito (Zerbino), Mai Anh Le (Nai-Rea), Oanh Nguyen (His Excellency)

Two tiger cubs are captured in Indo-china. One is sold off to a circus and the other becomes the pet of a rich Frenchman; but thanks to their amazing survival instincts, the tigers are eventually reunited.

The human acting? Eminently forgettable. The themes of colonialism, hunting and looting? It's padding. But

the patiently-amassed footage of the exquisite tigers Kumal and Sangha is extraordinary; they're the real stars here. Superior family viewing.

SCR Alain Godard, Jean-Jacques Annaud CIN Jean-Marie Dreujou MUS Stephen Warbeck DES Pierre Queffelean ED Noelle Boisson PROD Jake Eberts, Jean-Jacques Annaud DIST Pathé

66 It's tigers who steal the headlines in an epic worthy of the most popular children's stories a la Rudyard Kipling. – *Judith Prescott, The Hollywood Reporter*

'He knew Paris was for lovers. He just didn't think they were all hers.'

Two Days in Paris (new)   ★★

SCR/DIR Julie Delpy
2007 96m France/Germany
DVD

☆ Julie Delpy (Marion), Adam Goldberg (Jack), Marie Pillet (Anna), Albert Delpy (Jeannot), Adan Jodorowsky (Mathieu), Alex Nahon (Manu)

An argumentative French photographer and her boyfriend, a neurotic American interior designer, visit her parents in Paris en route for New York. But their stay in this romantic city is marked by jealousies and arguments.

Smart, funny and often well observed; Delpy is merciless about the drawbacks to her home city, especially its racist, homophobic cab drivers. The spiky humour finally becomes wearisome, however.

CIN Lubomir Bakchev MUS Julie Delpy DES Barbara Marc ED Julie Delpy PROD Christophe Mazodier, Thierry Potok DIST The Works

66 Neatly balances stabs at both America and the French. – *Dave Calhoun, Time Out*

† Marion's parents are Delpy's in real life.

'You have one minute to decide the rest of your life.'

2 Days in the Valley   ★

SCR/DIR John Herzfeld
1996 105m US
DVD ♫

☆ Danny Aiello (Dosmo Pizzo), Greg Cruttwell (Allan Hopper), Jeff Daniels (Alvin Strayer), Teri Hatcher (Becky Foxx), Glenne Headly (Susan Parish), Peter Horton (Roy Foxx), Marsha Mason (Audrey Hopper), Paul Mazursky (Teddy Peppers), James Spader (Lee Woods), Eric Stoltz (Wes Taylor), Keith Carradine (Detective Creighton), Louise Fletcher (Evelyn), Austin Pendleton (Ralph Crupi), Lawrence Tierney (Older man), Charlize Theron (Helga Svelden)

Assorted denizens of Los Angeles cross paths in 48 hours of violent intrigue.

An unsavoury crime comedy with everyone out for themselves, it's mainly notable for featuring Charlize Theron's first credited role.

CIN Oliver Wood MUS Anthony Marinelli DES Catherine Hardwicke ED Jim Miller, Wayne Wahrman PROD Jeff Wald, Herb Nanas DIST Entertainment/Rysher/Redemption

66 Marked by a wearying amount of hostile and antisocial behavior by its criminal and civilian characters alike. . .Pic

---

DVD Available on DVD   ☆ Cast in order   66 Critics' Quotes   ⚱ Academy Award   🎭 BAFTA
♫ Soundtrack on CD   of importance   † Points of interest   ⚱ Academy Award nomination   🎭 BAFTA nomination

does offer some entertainment value for mainstream audiences. – *Todd McCarthy, Variety*

'They say money makes the world go round. But sex was invented before money.'

The Two Jakes ★

DIR Jack Nicholson
1990   138m   US
[DVD]

☆ Jack Nicholson (J.J. 'Jake' Gittes), Harvey Keitel (Julius 'Jake' Berman), Meg Tilly (Kitty Berman), Madeleine Stowe (Lillian Bodine), Eli Wallach (Cotton Weinberger), Ruben Blades (Michael 'Mickey Nice' Weisskopf), Frederic Forrest (Chuck Newty), David Keith (Det. Lt. Loach), Richard Farnsworth (Earl Rawley)

Successful private detective finds his plans to marry and settle down are interrupted when he investigates the murder of an old lover.

Interesting primarily because it's a sequel to Chinatown. It's not bad, exactly, but the elusive brilliance of the first film never settles on this one. Nicholson has his moments, but the film's all mood, without a coherent narrative to sustain it.

SCR Robert Towne   CIN Vilmos Zsigmond   MUS Van Dyke Parks   DES Jeremy Railton, Richard Sawyer   ED Anne Goursaud   PROD Robert Evans, Harold Schneider   DIST Blue Dolphin/Paramount

66 It's an exquisite short story about a mood, and a time, and a couple of guys who are blind-sided by love. – *Roger Ebert, Chicago Sun-Times*

† An infamously troubled production, long delayed, with Robert Towne originally set to direct. On the first day, Towne fired producer Evans, who was playing the role of Berman. Eventually Nicholson took over the directing reins, and Keitel replaced Evans.

'Where everything ends. . .and begins' (Spanish translation).'

2046 ★

SCR/DIR Kar Wai Wong
2004   129m   Hong Kong/France/Italy/China/Germany
[DVD]   ♫

☆ Tony Leung Chiu Wai (Chow Mo-Wan), Li Gong (Su Li Zhen), Takuya Kimura (Tak), Faye Wong (Wang Jing Wen/Android on 2046 train), Ziyi Zhang (Bai Ling), Carina Lau (Lulu/Mimi), Chen Chang (Mimi's boyfriend), Wang Sum (Mr Wang/Train captain), Ping Lam Siu (Ping), Maggie Cheung (Su Lie Zhen 1960), Thongchai McIntyre (Bird), Jie Dong (Wang Jie Wen)

A sexually promiscuous novelist imagines a future in which memories of his lost loves can be rekindled.

A compendium of this director's pet obsessions, showcase for his favourite actresses and sequel of sorts to In the Mood for Love. An almost cosmic sense of heartbreak pervades it, but the narrative appears to have been lost on the cutting-room floor.

CIN Christopher Doyle, Lai Yiu-fai, Kwan Pun-leung   MUS Peer Raben, Shigeru Umebayashi   DES *William Chang*   ED William Chang   PROD Kar Wai Wong   DIST TCF

66 Because of its passion, its craft, its belief in the grace and pain of love – 2046 is the film of 2004. – *Richard Corliss, Time*

66 It's a swirling brew of lyrical images contrasting soft and acid colours, merging real-life encounters with their transformation into often bizarre fictions. – *Philip French, Observer*

2001: A Space Odyssey ★★★★

DIR *Stanley Kubrick*
1968   141m   GB
[DVD]   ♫

☆ Gary Lockwood (Frank Poole), Keir Dullea (David Bowman), William Sylvester (Dr. Heywood Floyd), Leonard Rossiter (Smyslov), Robert Beatty (Halvorsen), Daniel Richter (Moon-watcher), Douglas Rain (voice of HAL), Margaret Tyzack (Elena)

From ape to modern space scientist, mankind has striven to reach the unattainable.

A lengthy montage of brilliant model work and obscure symbolism, this curiosity slowly gathered commercial momentum and came to be cherished by those who used it as a trip without LSD.

SCR Stanley Kubrick, Arthur C. Clarke   CIN *Geoffrey Unsworth, John Alcott*   MUS Richard Strauss, Johann Strauss and other classics   DES *Tony Masters, Harry Lange, Ernie Archer*   ED Ray Lovejoy   PROD Victor Lyndon   DIST MGM

66 Somewhere between hypnotic and immensely boring. – *Renata Adler*

66 Morally pretentious, intellectually obscure and inordinately long. . .intensely exciting visually, with that peculiar artistic power which comes from obsession. . .a film out of control, an infuriating combination of exactitude on small points and incoherence on large ones. – *Arthur Schlesinger Jnr.*

⚊ Stanley Kubrick (special visual effects)
⚊ Stanley Kubrick (original screenplay); art direction
Ⓣ cinematography; production design

'Sex. Murder. Betrayal. Everything That Makes Life Worth Living.'

U Turn ★

DIR Oliver Stone
1997 125m US/France
DVD ♫

☆ Sean Penn (Bobby Cooper), Nick Nolte (Jake McKenna), Jennifer Lopez (Grace McKenna), Powers Boothe (Sheriff Virgil Potter), Claire Danes (Jenny), Joaquin Phoenix (Toby N. Tucker a.k.a. TNT), Billy Bob Thornton (Darrell), Jon Voight (Blind Man), Julie Haggerty (Flo), Bo Hopkins (Ed), Liv Tyler (Girl in Bus Station)

A shiftless gambler arrives in a small Arizona town, where he becomes involved with a married couple who each want him to kill the other.

Stone is never knowingly dull, and even on a routine genre exercise such as this one, he creates a taut little thriller. If Penn and Nolte are slumming – and they truly are – they never let on.

SCR John Ridley **CIN** Robert Richardson **MUS** Ennio Morricone **DES** Victor Kempster **ED** Hank Corwin, Thomas J. Nordberg **PROD** Dan Halsted, Clayton Townsend **DIST** TriStar/Phoenix/Illusion/Clyde is Hungry

66 Only Oliver Stone knows what he was trying to accomplish by making U Turn, and it is a secret he doesn't share with the audience. This is a repetitive, pointless exercise in genre filmmaking. – *Roger Ebert, Chicago Sun-Times*

U2 3D (new) ★

DIR Catherine Owens, Mark Pellington
2008 85m Ireland/US

☆ Bono, The Edge, Adam Clayton, Larry Mullen Jr.

Live concert footage of U2's 2005-6 tour, filmed at seven shows in South America with 3-D cameras

Diverting and different, for the first few minutes; 3-D requires better subjects. On stage, U2 are static and unexciting; it feels as if the cameras, not the band, are doing all the work. They seem close yet far away; inadvertently, U2 3D mimics perfectly the empty, intimacy-free spectacle that is stadium rock.

CIN Tom Kreuger **ED** Olivier Wicki **PROD** Jon Shapiro, Peter Shapiro, John Modell, Catherine Owens **DIST** Revolver

66 You could almost be among those fans; the swaying arms in the film's foreground seem to be just a couple of rows in front of you. Of course, this is not reason enough for anybody to see the film if they don't care for U2. – *Edward Porter, Sunday Times*

66 Some of the more full-bodied 3-D shots make the band look like toy models. – *Derek Adams, Time Out*

U2 Rattle and Hum ★

DIR Phil Joanou
1988 99m US
DVD

Documentary on U2, the Irish rock group – claimed to be the world's most popular, recording a new album and touring performing at home and in the States.

A decent account of the group on the road, in the days before they regularly pontificated on matters of global importance. Shot in both black-and-white and in colour, it's thoughtfully compiled – though ironically an appearance by legendary blues veteran B. B. King is the real stand-out sequence.

CIN Jordan Cronenweth (colour), Robert Brinkman (bw) **ED** Phil Joanou **PROD** Michael Hamlyn **DIST** Paramount/Midnight

66 An exercise in rock 'n' roll hagiography. It's a fanzine on celluloid. – *Hal Hinson, Washington Post*

U-Carmen Ekyayelitsha ★★

DIR Mark Dornford-May
2005 127m South Africa
DVD

☆ Pauline Malefane (Carmen), Andile Tshoni (Jongikhaya), Andries Mbali (Bra Nkomo), Zorro Sidloyi (Lulamile)

A staging of Bizet's opera Carmen, transposed to a modern South African township.

In this version, the love story between Carmen and Don Jose flourishes in a society scarred by poverty, security, police, gangsters and illegal drinking clubs. Bright, vibrant primary colours dominate, its locations teem with life, and it is spoken in Xhosa, with its distinctive tongue-clicks. A remarkable document of the arresting all-black South African theatre company Dimpho di Kopane, this may not be for opera purists – but it's hugely invigorating.

SCR Mark Dornford-May, Pauline Malefane, Andiswa Kedama **CIN** Giulio Biccari **MUS** Georges Bizet **ED** Ronelle Loots **PROD** Mark Dornford-May, Ross Garland, Camilla Driver **DIST** Tartan

66 A vivacious film that is a treat for eyes and ears. – *V.A. Musetto, New York Post*

Ugetsu Monogatari ★★★

DIR *Kenji Mizoguchi*
1953 94m Japan

☆ Masayuki Mori (Genjuro), Machiko Kyo (Lady Wukasa), Sakae Ozawa (Tobei), Mitsuko Mito (Ohama)

During a 16th-century civil war two potters find a way of profiteering, but their ambitions bring disaster on their families.

Unique mixture of action, comedy and the supernatural, with strong, believable characters participating and a delightfully delicate touch in script and direction. On its first release it began to figure in many top ten lists, but has faded from public approbation.

SCR *Matsutaro Kawaguchi, from 17th-century collection by Akinara Ueda, Tales of a Pale and Mysterious Moon after the Rain* CIN *Kazuo Miyagawa* MUS Fumio Hayasaka ED Mitsuji Miyata PROD Masaichi Nagata DIST Daiei

'The story of a family on the edge, and a man who brought them back.'

Ulee's Gold ★

SCR/DIR *Victor Nuñez*
1997 113m US
DVD ♫

☆ *Peter Fonda* (Ulee Jackson), Patricia Richardson (Connie Hope), Jessica Biel (Casey Jackson), J. Kenneth Campbell (Sheriff Bill Floyd), Christine Dunford (Helen Jackson), Steven Flynn (Eddie Flowers), Dewey Weber (Ferris Dooley)

A brave beekeeper, a Vietnam veteran, fights to keep his fractured family together and girds himself for a confrontation with his son's shady ex-associates.

Fonda delivers a towering central performance, arguably the finest of his career, though this funereally-paced drama never truly soars.

CIN Virgil Mirano MUS Charles Engstrom DES Robert 'Pat' Garner ED Victor Nuñez PROD Peter Saraf, Sam Gowan (co-producers) DIST Orion

❝ Thrill junkies out for a rush from Ulee's Gold should find another summer flick pronto. This low-budget indie from writer and director Victor Nuñez limps like a tortoise on Prozac. – *Peter Travers, Rolling Stone*

⊿ Peter Fonda (leading actor)

Ulysses' Gaze ★

DIR Theo Angelopoulos
1995 176m Greece/France/Italy/Germany/GB
DVD ♫

☆ Harvey Keitel (A), Maia Morgenstern (Ulysses' wife), Erland Josephson (S., film-museum curator), Thanassis Vengos (Taxi driver), Yorgos Michalokopoulos (Friend and Journalist), Dora Volonaki (Old Woman)

A Greek film director returns to his homeland, after 35 years in exile in America, to find three missing film reels and make a historic documentary.

It's a long journey home to the film-maker's Balkan roots, and it feels like it. Clearly it's a story that needs to reveal itself gradually, but Angelopoulos tests the audience's patience with protracted scenes that do little

to advance the story. Still, it's a film with the courage of its deep convictions.

SCR Theo Angelopoulos, Tonino Guerra, Petros Markaris CIN *Yorgos Arvanitis, Andreas Sinanos* MUS Eleni Karaindrou DES Yorgos Patsas, Miodrag Nicolic ED Yannis Tsitsopoulos PROD Theo Angelopoulos, Eric Heumann, Dragan Ivanovic, Herbert G. Kloiber, Ivan Milovanovic, Giorgio Silvagni, Marc Soustras DIST Theo Angelopoulos/GFC/Paradis/La Generale d'Images/La Sept/Basic/RAI

❝ This grim travelogue through a landscape of despair lacks internal power. It feels laboured and portentous. – *Desson Howe, Washington Post*

'A Lovers' Story.'

The Unbearable Lightness of Being ★★

DIR *Philip Kaufman*
1987 171m US
DVD ♫

☆ Daniel Day-Lewis (Tomas), Juliette Binoche (Tereza), Lena Olin (Sabina), Erland Josephson (The Ambassador), Daniel Olbrychski (Interior Ministry Official)

A philandering Czech brain surgeon becomes trapped in a tumultuous love triangle against the backdrop of the 1968 Soviet invasion of Prague.

Bold, and captivating adaptation of Milan Kundera's tragic-comic novel; it benefits enormously from fine acting performances, particularly from Day-Lewis.

SCR Jean-Claude Carrière, Philip Kaufman CIN Sven Nykvist MUS Mark Adler DES Pierre Guffroy ED Walter Murch, Michael Magill, Vivien Hillgrove PROD Saul Zaentz DIST Saul Zaentz

❝ It's a rich, ambitious film, repetitive and voyeuristic in its eroticism, but exhilarating in its blend of documentary and fictional re-creation to depict the Soviet invasion. – *Time Out*

⊿ Sven Nykvist; Jean-Claude Carrière, Philip Kaufman (adapted screenplay)

Ⓣ Jean-Claude Carrière, Philip Kaufman (adapted screenplay)

Unbelievable Truth ★

SCR/DIR Hal Hartley
1989 90m US
DVD

☆ *Adrienne Shelly* (Audry Hugo), *Robert Burke* (Josh Hutton), Christopher Cooke (Vic Hugo), Julia McNeal (Pearl), Mark Bailey (Mike), Gary Sauer (Emmet), Katherine Mayfield (Liz Hugo)

A killer serves his time in prison and is released to return home to Long Island, where he begins a controversial affair with a discontented, cerebral young woman.

Off-kilter drama, marked by quirky backchat, that sustains its central intrigue: is the new stranger in town all he seems, or maybe something even more sinister? This was the feature debut for Hartley, and his trademark deadpan style is already in evidence. The jokes at the expense of sheltered small-town dwellers are overdone, though.

U

CIN Michael Spiller MUS Jim Coleman, Philip Reed, Kendall Brothers, Wild Blue Yonder DES Carla Gerona ED Hal Hartley PROD Bruce Weiss, Hal Hartley DIST Electric/Contemporary/Action

66 Though undeniably low-key The Unbelievable Truth still succeeds as a perceptive comment on the mores of small-town life. – *David Wood, BBC*

'Some things are only revealed by accident.'

Unbreakable ★

SCR/DIR M. Night Shyamalan
2000 106m US
DVD ♫

☆ Bruce Willis (David Dunn), Samuel L. Jackson (Elijah Price), Robin Wright Penn (Audrey Dunn), Charlayne Woodard (Elijah's Mother), Spencer Treat Clark (Joseph Dunn), James Handy (Priest), Eamonn Walker (Dr Mathison), Elizabeth Lawrence (School Nurse), Leslie Stefanson (Kelly)

A security guard, the sole survivor of an horrific accident, is convinced by a handi-capped dealer in comics that he has genuine superpowers.

The follow-up to The Sixth Sense, and an inferior one; this marks the first stage of director Shyamalan's long slow decline. Still, there is enough here to hold the attention: a subtle, serious performance from Willis, and a story that promises much and holds disbelief at bay until the last act.

CIN Eduardo Serra MUS James Newton Howard DES Larry Fulton ED Dylan Tichenor PROD M. Night Shyamalan, Barry Mendel, Sam Mercer DIST Buena Vista

66 A muddled, self-serious snoozer. – *Edward Guthmann, San Francisco Chronicle*

Under Satan's Sun ★

DIR Maurice Pialat
1987 93m France

☆ Gérard Depardieu (Donissan), Sandrine Bonnaire (Mouchette), Maurice Pialat (Menou-Segrais), Alain Artur (Cadignan), Yann Dedet (Gallet), Brigitte Legendre (Mouchette's Mother)

A tortured Catholic priest in rural France becomes convinced that Satan is humanity's controlling force.

Austere, rigorous film that functions as a debate about the nature of religious belief.

SCR Sylvie Danton, Maurice Pialat CIN Willy Kurant MUS Henri Dutilleux DES Katia Vischkof ED Yann Dedet PROD Daniel Toscan du Plantier DIST Cannon/Erato films/A2/Action Films

66 Here's your choice: You can spend however many dollars it takes to see Maurice Pialat's Under Satan's Sun. Or you can stay at home and hit yourself over the head with a hammer. – *Hal Hinson, Washington Post*

⚐ It won the Palme d'Or at the Cannes Film Festival in 1987, though director Pialat was booed and heckled when he received the awards.

'How close can you get to a killer before you're too close?'

Under Suspicion ★★

SCR/DIR Simon Moore
1992 99m GB
DVD

☆ Liam Neeson (Tony Aaron), Kenneth Cranham (Frank), Laura San Giacomo (Angeline), Maggie O'Neill (Hazel Aaron), Alan Talbot (Powers), Malcolm Storry (Waterston), Martin Grace (Colin), Kevin Moore (Barrister)

In Brighton in 1959, a disgraced cop turned private detective is accused of murder when a couple of corpses are found in a hotel room.

Home-grown noir: a British thriller with a seedy background (Brighton looks as disreputable as it did in Brighton Rock). Neeson acquits himself well as the down-at-heel gumshoe, and the moody atmosphere is skilfully sustained.

CIN Vernon Layton MUS Christopher Gunning DES Tim Hutchinson ED Tariq Anwar PROD Brian Eastman DIST Rank/Carnival/Columbia/LWT

66 Slick and professionally produced mystery thriller that is almost a very fine film. – *BBC*

Under the Bombs (new) ★★

DIR Philippe Aractingi
2007 98m

☆ *Nada Abou Farhat (Zeina), Georges Khabbaz (Tony), Rawya El Chab (Hotel receptionist), Bsharra Atallah (Journalist)*

In 2006, on the day of the cease-fire ending Israel's invasion of Lebanon, a wealthy woman arrives at Beirut airport, and hires the only taxi-driver willing to drive to the country's war-torn south, in search of her missing son.

Guerrilla film-making, much of it shot without a script, in the middle of real-life destruction in Lebanon. The people Zeina and Tony meet on their journey are playing themselves, and they speak heart-breakingly about the losses genuinely suffered during the bombing raids. Though the story struggles to sustain its momentum after its dazzling, dramatic opening, this is a gutsy, memorable piece of film that stuns the senses.

SCR Michel Leviant, Philippe Aractingi CIN Nidal Abdel Khalek MUS René Aubry, Lazare Boghossian ED Deena Charara PROD Hervé Chabalier, Paul Raphael, François Cohen-Séat, Philippe Aractingi

66 Its stated aim is to 'tell the suffering of the innocents', and it does that with upsetting success. – *Sukhdev Sandhu, Daily Telegraph*

66 A heartfelt road movie with lacerating images of Israel's recent war in Lebanon. – *Peter Bradshaw, Guardian*

'Can love vanish without a trace?'

Under the Sand ★★

DIR François Ozon
2000 92m France
DVD

☆ *Charlotte Rampling (Marie Drillon), Bruno Cremer (Jean Drillon), Jacques Nolot (Vincent), Alexandra Stewart*

U

(Amanda), Pierre Vernier (Gerard), Andrée Tainsy (Suzanne)

After the disappearance of her husband on a beach holiday, a university teacher refuses to accept his death.

Haunting, low-key study of grief and the aftermath of intimacy – lingering, here, beyond the grave – which Rampling carries superbly.

SCR François Ozon, Emmanuele Bernheim, Marina De Van, Marcia Romano   CIN Jeanne Lapoirie, Antoine Heberle   MUS Philippe Rombi   DES Sandrine Canaux   ED Laurence Bawedin   PROD Olivier Delbosc, Marc Missonnier

66 Creepily evocative. – *Peter Rainer, New York Magazine*
66 An exquisite reflection on personal bereavement. – *Derek Elley, Variety*

'Your body betrays your soul.'

Under the Skin ★★

SCR/DIR Carine Adler
1997   82m   GB
DVD

☆ *Samantha Morton* (Iris Kelly), Claire Rushbrook (Rose Kelly), Rita Tushingham (Mum), Mark Womack (Frank), Matthew Delamere (Gary), Christine Tremarco (Vron), Stuart Townsend (Tom)

Two sisters in Liverpool are both devastated when their mother dies from a brain tumour, but deal with their grief differently, the younger one taking refuge in casual, spontaneous sex.

A powerful, passionate film about tragedy and grief, elevated by remarkable work from Samantha Morton, making her feature film debut at age 20.

CIN Barry Ackroyd   MUS Ilona Sekacz   DES John-Paul Kelly   ED Ewa J. Lind   PROD Kate Ogborn   DIST BFI/Channel 4/Strange Dog/Rouge/MFP

66 Despite occasional stumbles, Under the Skin is an impressive, highly involving feature debut by writer-director Carine Adler. – *Derek Elley, Variety*

'One Nation, Under Dog'

Underdog (new) ★

DIR Frederik Du Chau
2008   84m   US
DVD

☆ Jason Lee (voice) (Underdog), James Belushi (Dan Unger), Alex Neuberger (Jack Unger), Peter Dinklage (Dr. Simon Barsinister), Patrick Warburton (Cad)

A mad scientist's lab accident turns a pet beagle into a talking, flying, crime-fighting caped crusader.

Silly but cute canine Superman send-up veering between squirm-inducing childishness and smart parody.

SCR Adam Rifkin, Joe Piscatella, Craig A. Williams, W. Watts Biggers   CIN David Eggby   MUS Randy Edelman   DES Garreth Stover   ED Tom Finan   PROD Gary Barber, Roger Bimbaum, Jonathan Glickman, Jay Polstein   DIST Buena Vista

66 "Clumsy, fast moving and thoroughly inoffensive". – *Justin Chang, Variety*

66 As superhero movies go, Underdog is a damn sight better than Spider-Man 3. – *Edward Porter, Sunday Times*

Underground ★

DIR Emir Kusturica
1995   170m   France/Germany/Hungary
DVD ♫

☆ Miki Manojlovic (Marko), Lazar Ristovski (Crni), Mirjana Jokovic (Natalija), Slavko Stimac (Ivan), Ernst Stotzner (Franz)

Two Yugoslav partisans take refuge in a cellar during World War II, and it becomes their established home for years.

A tortuous examination of the rivalries repressed in Tito's Yugoslavia which still have resonance today. Yet the motivations of many characters remain impenetrable, and the narrative is rambling and confused.

SCR Dusan Kovacevic, Emir Kusturica   CIN Vilko Filac   MUS Goran Bregovic   DES Miljan Kljakovic   ED Branka Ceperac   PROD Pierre Spengler   DIST Artificial Eye/Mayfair/CiBy 2000/Pandora/Novo

66 I suppose director Emir Kusturica can justify the 167-minute length by the historical breadth of the movie, but it simply doesn't sustain one's interest, significant or not. – *Barbara Shulgasser, San Francisco Examiner*

† Kusturica won his second Palme d'Or at the Cannes Film Festival with this in 1995.
† The director came under fire in his native Bosnia for the film's reluctance to condemn Serb aggression.

'For passion, betrayal and murder. . .there's still no place like home.'

The Underneath ★

DIR Steven Soderbergh
1995   99m   US
DVD ♫

☆ Peter Gallagher (Michael Chambers), Alison Elliott (Rachel), William Fichtner (Tommy Dundee), Adam Trese (David Chambers), Joe Don Baker (Clay Hinkle), Paul Dooley (Ed Dutton), Elisabeth Shue (Susan Crenshaw), Anjanette Comer (Mrs. Chambers)

A deep in debt security guard plots to rob his own armoured car to fund a new life with his girlfriend.

Thoughtful re-working of a film noir classic that employs three overlapping time frames. A difficult, demanding movie – and it isn't always clear that it's worth the effort.

SCR Sam Lowry, Daniel Fuchs   CIN Elliot Davis   MUS Cliff Martinez   DES Howard Cummings   ED Stan Salfas   PROD John Hardy   DIST UIP/Gramercy

66 There is one twist too many for my taste; I like to be fooled but I don't like to be toyed with. – *Roger Ebert, Chicago Sun-Times*

† A remake of Robert Siodmak's Criss Cross, starring Burt Lancaster, Yvonne de Carlo and Dan Duryea.
† Soderbergh once said of this, his fourth feature film: "I was in danger of becoming a formalist."

U

DVD Available on DVD   ☆ Cast in order of importance   66 Critics' Quotes   † Points of interest   Academy Award   Academy Award nomination   BAFTA   BAFTA nomination
♫ Soundtrack on CD

Undertow ★

DIR David Gordon Green
2004   108m   US
DVD   ♫

☆ *Jamie Bell* (Chris Munn), Devon Alan (Tim Munn), Dermot Mulroney (John Munn), Josh Lucas (Deel Munn), Shiri Appleby (Violet), Pat Healey (Grant)

In the backwoods of Georgia, two young brothers flee their home when their uncle kills their father in a dispute over their inheritance.

A derivative chase movie that builds up considerable tension, which is dissipated by a limp ending. Bell seems more than comfortable in an American role.

SCR Joe Conway, David Gordon Green   CIN Tim Orr
MUS Philip Glass   DES Richard A. Wright   ED Zene Baker, Steven Gonzales   PROD Terrence Malick, Lisa Muskat, Edward R. Pressman   DIST Feature Film

66 The film is stronger on mood than narrative drive and ends up as a pale imitation of Charles Laughton's 1955 classic, Night of the Hunter, which it consciously reworks. – *Philip French, Observer*

'Revolvers bark! Figures steal slowly among the shadows of the night! Then all is still . . . That's just a bit of the underworld!'

Underworld ★★

DIR *Josef von Sternberg*
1927   82m   US

☆ George Bancroft, Evelyn Brent, Clive Brook, Larry Semon

A gangster is rescued from prison by his moll and his lieutenant, and when he realizes they are in love he allows them to escape when the law closes in.

An innovative film in its time, this melodrama was the first to look at crime from the gangsters' point of view. Its main appeal now lies in its lush direction.

SCR Ben Hecht, Robert N. Lee, Josef von Sternberg
CIN Bert Glennon   PROD Hector Turnbull
DIST Paramount

† The film was a great international success and had an influence on the pessimistic French school of the thirties.

⌶ Ben Hecht (original screenplay)

'Where do you go when you've gone too far?'

Unfaithful ★

DIR Adrian Lyne
2002   124m   US
DVD   ♫

☆ Richard Gere (Ed Sumner), *Diane Lane* (Connie Sumner), Olivier Martinez (Paul Martel), Erik Per Sullivan (Charlie Sumner), Zeljko Ivanek (Detective Dean), Dominic Chianese (Frank Wilson), Kate Burton (Tracy), Chad Lowe (Bill Stone)

A happily married New York housewife launches into a passionate affair with a suave Frenchman.

Stylish relationship drama, directed painstakingly, with Lane in top form as the adulterous wife. Not up to

Chabrol's original film, but it insults no-one's intelligence either.

SCR Alvin Sargent, William Broyles Jnr   CIN Peter Biziou
MUS Jan A. P. Kaczmarek   DES Brian Morris   ED Anne V. Coates   PROD Adrian Lyne, G. Mac Brown   DIST TCF

66 What's intriguing about the film is that instead of pumping up the plot with recycled manufactured thrills, it's content to contemplate two reasonably sane adults who get themselves into an almost insoluble dilemma. – *Roger Ebert, Chicago Sun-Times*

66 Slick, sleek and genteelly erotic – *Kenneth Turan, Los Angeles Times*

⌶ Diane Lane (leading actress)

Unforgiven ★★★★

DIR *Clint Eastwood*
1992   131m   US
DVD   ♫

☆ *Clint Eastwood* (William Munny), *Gene Hackman* (Sheriff 'Little Bil' Daggett), *Morgan Freeman* (Ned Logan), *Richard Harris* (English Bob), Jaimz Woolvett (The Schofield Kid), Saul Rubinek (W.W. Beauchamp), Frances Fisher (Strawberry Alice), Anna Thomson (Delilah Fitzgerald), David Mucci (Quick Mike), Rob Campbell (Davey Bunting), Anthony James (Skinny Dubois)

A hired gunman, now eking out a living as a farmer, is tempted back for one last job – to collect a reward for the thugs who carved up a prostitute.

One of the all-time great Westerns, a film aware of the historical tradition in which it operates, and one that finds something new to say within its genre. Eastwood is superb as William Munny, weary of life and especially weary of violence. He is buttressed by a wonderful supporting cast, notably Hackman as a callous sheriff and Freeman as his former partner. At a point when it was widely assumed Westerns were movie-making history, Eastwood proved them spectacularly wrong.

SCR *David Webb Peoples*   CIN Jack N. Green
MUS Lennie Niehaus   DES Henry Bumstead   ED Joel Cox   PROD Clint Eastwood   DIST Warner

66 That implacable moral balance, in which good eventually silences evil, is at the heart of the western, and Clint Eastwood is not shy about saying so. – *Roger Ebert, Chicago Sun-Times*

66 Clint Eastwood gives Unforgiven a tragic stature that puts his own filmmaking past in critical and moral perspective. In three decades of climbing into the saddle, Eastwood has never ridden so tall. – *Rolling Stone*

† Regions 1 and 2 two-disc special edition DVDs include a commentary by Richard Schickel, documentaries on Eastwood and the making of the film and Duel at Sundown, an episode of the TV series Maverick.

⌶ picture; Gene Hackman; (supporting actor); Clint Eastwood (direction); Joel Cox
⌇ Clint Eastwood (leading actor); Henry Bumstead; Jack N. Green; David Webb Peoples; (sound)
◉ Gene Hackman (supporting actor)
◎ best film; Clint Eastwood (direction); Jack N. Green (sound); David Webb Peoples (screenplay)

'September 11, 2001. Four planes were hijacked. Three of them reached their target. This is the story of the fourth'

United 93 ★★★★

SCR/DIR *Paul Greengrass*
2006 111m US/GB/France
DVD ♫

☆ David Alan Basche (Todd Beamer), Richard Bekins (William Joseph Cashman), Susan Blommaert (Jane Folger), Ray Charleson (Joseph DeLuca), Christian Clemenson (Thomas E. Burnett Jnr), Khalid Abdalla (Ziad Jarrah), Lewis Alsamari (Saeed Al Ghamdi), Ben Sliney (Himself), Major James Fox (Himself), Gregg Henry (Colonel Robert Marr)

Passengers and crew on board a hijacked United Airlines Flight 93 on September 11, 2001 unsuccessfully struggle with four terrorists to take back control of the plane.

An astonishing documentary-style drama that tracks in scrupulous detail the known events on the ground and acts of bravery inside the doomed plane. Understandably, it is often painful to watch, but is never exploitative, and does justice to those who died on board. Greengrass's decision to cast lesser-known actors, so as not to distract audiences with star sightings, proves impeccably correct.

CIN *Barry Ackroyd* **MUS** John Powell **DES** Dominic Watkins **ED** *Clare Douglas, Christopher Rouse, Richard Pearson* **PROD** *Tim Bevan, Eric Fellner, Lloyd Levin, Paul Greengrass* **DIST** Universal

66 An honourable attempt to confront something many would rather forget; it is emotionally raw yet unsentimental; it shows people at their most pained and inspirational; it is both brilliant and troubling. – *Nev Pierce, BBC*

66 This staggering, draining film is exceptionally accomplished but extremely difficult to watch. It turns out to be easier to admire from whatever distance you can manage than to embrace with any kind of emotional intimacy. – *Kenneth Turan, Los Angeles Times*

† The scenes on board the plane were shot in a British studio.

⚲ Paul Greengrass (direction); (editing)

🅣 Paul Greengrass (direction); (editing)

🅣 British film; Barry Ackroyd; (screenplay); (sound)

'Trust No One. Fear Everyone.'

Unknown ★★

DIR Simon Brand
2006 85m US
DVD

☆ Jim Caviezel (Jean Jacket), Greg Kinnear (Broken Nose), Joe Pantoliano (Bound Man), Barry Pepper (Rancher Shirt), Jeremy Sisto (Handcuffed Man)

Five men wake up in a locked warehouse and cannot remember their names, whether they are good guys or bad, or why they are there.

An irresistible premise, terrifically played out by an able cast, it grips right up until the very last plot swerve.

SCR Matthew Waynee **CIN** Steve Yedlin **MUS** Angelo Milli **DES** Chris Jones **ED** Luis Carballar, Paul Trejo

PROD Rick Lashbrook, Darby Parker, John S. Schwartz
DIST Optimum

66 A nifty little psychological crime thriller that suggests a Treasure of the Sierra Madre for the post-industrial age. – *Ann Hornaday – Washington Post*

'Sometimes you find your heroes in the most unlikely places.'

Unstrung Heroes ★★

DIR Diane Keaton
1995 93m US
DVD ♫

☆ Andie MacDowell (Selma Lidz), John Turturro (Sid Lidz), Michael Richards (Danny Lidz), Maury Chaykin (Arthur Lidz), Nathan Watt (Steven / Franz Lidz), Kendra Krull (Sandy Lidz)

When a 12-year-old boy's mother contracts a terminal illness, he goes to live with his two eccentric uncles and struggles to cope with his father's sudden emotional distance.

As director, Keaton keeps the quirkiness firmly (and thankfully) in check. Certainly the boy's relatives are oddballs, but it's their affection for him, sometimes shown obliquely that finally counts. As a result, this is a sweet-natured, amusing take on sensitive, serious issues.

SCR Richard LaGravenese **CIN** Phedon Papamichael **MUS** Thomas Newman **DES** Garreth Stover **ED** Lisa Churgin **PROD** Susan Arnold, Donna Roth, Bill Badalato **DIST** Buena Vista/Hollywood

66 Diane Keaton's kooky sensibilities as a director are ideally suited to the sweet madness of Unstrung Heroes, a sensitive coming of age story in the sublime tradition of My Life as a Dog. – *Rita Kempley, Washington Post*

⚲ Thomas Newman

The Untouchables ★★★

DIR *Brian de Palma*
1987 119m US
DVD ♫

☆ *Kevin Costner, Sean Connery, Robert DeNiro*, Charles Martin Smith, Andy Garcia, Richard Bradford

Law enforcers in 1920s Chicago go after Al Capone and other mobsters.

The long-running TV show is given a new polish in this showy, violent and widely popular gangster picture. Director de Palma stages some spectacular sequences, most famously a re-creation of the Odessa Steps sequence in Battleship Potemkin, but at a railway station. It looks lavish, Morricone's score ensures it sounds wonderful and Mamet reins himself in with some crisp, pointed dialogue. Costner's stardom was confirmed by his portrayal of Eliot Ness, while De Niro as a menacing Capone and Connery as a veteran cop lend first-class support. A hugely entertaining treat.

SCR *David Mamet* **CIN** Stephen H. Burum **MUS** *Ennio Morricone* **DES** *Patrizia von Brandenstein* **ED** Jerry Greenberg, Bill Pankow **DIST** Paramount/Art Linson

66 Time honoured mayhem in the windy city. – *Time Out*

⚲ Sean Connery (supporting actor)

DVD Available on DVD ☆ Cast in order of importance
♫ Soundtrack on CD
66 Critics' Quotes † Points of interest
⚲ Academy Award
⚲ Academy Award nomination
🅣 BAFTA
🅣 BAFTA nomination

'The FBI Cyber Crimes Division hunts down vicious criminals online . . . But the most dangerous one is hunting them.'

Untraceable (new)

DIR Gregory Hoblit
2008   101m   US
[DVD]   ♫

☆ Diane Lane (Jennifer Marsh), Billy Burke (Det. Eric Box), Colin Hanks (Griffin Dowd), Joseph Cross (Owen Reilly), Mary Beth Hurt (Stella Marsh), Peter Lewis (Richard Brooks)

A resourceful FBI agent pursues a killer who streams his murders online.

Efficient thriller with a hi-tech gimmick that does not stop it resorting to lurid excesses and generic woman-in-peril clichés.

SCR Robert Fyvolent, Mark R. Brinker, Allison Burnett   **CIN** Anastas Michos   **MUS** Christopher Young   **DES** Paul Eads   **ED** David Rosenbloom, Gregory Plotkin   **PROD** Steven Pearl, Andy Cohen, Tom Rosenberg, Gary Lucchesi, Hawk Koch   **DIST** Universal

66 A satisfying slice of solidly crafted meat-and-potatoes filmmaking. – *Joe Leydon, Variety*

66 The problem with Hollywood films condemning the public appetite for torture is that they frequently pander to it. – *Anthony Quinn, Independent*

'Sometimes what tears us apart helps us put it back together.'

The Upside of Anger   ★★

SCR/DIR Mike Binder
2005   116m   US/Germany
[DVD]

☆ Joan Allen (Terry Wolfmeyer), Kevin Costner (Denny Davies), Erika Christensen (Andy), Evan Rachel Wood (Lavender), Keri Russell (Emily), Alicia Witt (Hadley), Mike Binder (Shep Goodman)

A housewife whose adulterous husband disappeared three years ago is raising four daughters, drinking heavily and venting her fury on the world. She gets involved with a neighbour, a former baseball star, also a drunk and bored with his job as a radio host.

Joan Allen's anger in this film is magnificent to behold, yet Costner's washed-up sports hero takes it calmly on the chin, setting the stage for an unlikely romance. Both actors are on top form. This role marks a comeback for Costner, who has never before strayed so far from obvious leading man territory. A surprisingly effective story with a rueful undertow; not even a jarring plot twist in the final reel spoils the enjoyment.

CIN Richard Greatrex   **MUS** Alexandre Desplat   **DES** Chris Roope   **ED** Steve Edwards, Robin Sales   **PROD** Alex Gartner, Jack Binder, Sammy Lee   **DIST** The Works

66 As this matron on the loose, Allen is rancorously funny. – *David Denby, New Yorker*

66 For its top-drawer acting, and Allen's brittle fury in particular, this is well worth investigating. – *Tim Robey, Daily Telegraph*

† Though the story is set in Detroit, the interiors of Terry's home were shot at a house in Hampstead, north London.

Urga   ★★

DIR Nikita Mikhalkov
1991   119m   France/USSR
♫

☆ Bayaertu (Gombo), Badema (Pagma), Vladimir Gostukhin (Sergei), Babushka (Grandma)

A Mongolian herdsman and his wife live a simple yet idyllic life which is interrupted when he rescues a Russian lorry-driver who has crashed into a river and brings him home to his family.

Gentle, almost dreamy movie that contrasts consumerism and the stress of modern living with a less cluttered way of life that scarcely exists in the developed world. Many subsequent movies (some of them also set in Mongolia) have taken their cues from the themes here.

SCR Nikita Mikhalkov, Roustam Ibragimbekov   **CIN** Vilen Kaluta   **MUS** Eduard Artemyev   **DES** Aleksei Levchenko   **ED** Joelle Hache   **PROD** Michel Seydoux   **DIST** Hachette Première/Studio Trite

66 As slight as a breeze, as charming as a sly old con man. . .one of the strongest qualities in the film is the joy of living shared by husband and wife, who love each other. – *Roger Ebert, Chicago Sun-Times*

⚖ foreign language film

'A story about love, family and other embarrassments.'

Used People   ★

DIR Beeban Kidron
1992   116m   US/Japan
♫

☆ Shirley MacLaine (Pearl Berman), Marcello Mastroianni (Joe Meledandri), Bob Dishy (Jack), Kathy Bates (Bibby Berman), Jessica Tandy (Freida), Marcia Gay Harden (Norma), Lee Wallace (Uncle Harry), Louis Guss (Uncle Normy)

In 1960s New York, an Italian widower makes a move to court a Jewish woman rather soon after her husband dies.

A warm, rambling romantic comedy, clearly aimed at older audiences, which sees Marcello Mastroianni upstage the rest of the formidable cast with what looks like effortless ease.

SCR Todd Graff   **CIN** David Watkin   **MUS** Rachel Portman   **DES** Stuart Wurtzel   **ED** John Tintori   **PROD** Peggy Rajski   **DIST** TCF/Largo

66 From the Fried Green Tomatoes school of indigestible tragic-comedies comes this family saga. – *Peter Travers, Rolling Stone*

66 A modern, absurdist sensibility informs the soap opera Used People, which harks back to 50s weepies. – *Variety*

U

| [DVD] Available on DVD | ☆ Cast in order | 66 Critics' Quotes | ⚖ Academy Award | 🇹 BAFTA |
| ♫ Soundtrack on CD | of importance | † Points of interest | ⚖ Academy Award nomination | 🇹 BAFTA nomination |

651

'Five Criminals. One Line Up. No Coincidence.'

The Usual Suspects ★★★★

DIR Bryan Singer
1995   106m   US/Germany
DVD

☆ Gabriel Byrne (Dean Keaton), Stephen Baldwin (McManus), Chazz Palminteri (Kujan), Kevin Pollak (Hockney), Pete Postlethwaite (Kobayashi), *Kevin Spacey* (Roger 'Verbal' Kint), Suzy Amis (Edie), Giancarlo Esposito (Jack Baer), Dan Hedaya (Sgt. Rabin), Benicio del Toro (Fenster), Paul Bartel (Smuggler)

A story related in flashbacks, of five petty crooks, wrongly accused of a crime, who meet in a police line-up and unwittingly plan robberies together, before it dawns on them that a master criminal may (or may not) be controlling their every move.

A fabulous con-trick of a movie, playfully tweaking the traditions of story-telling, raising expectations and encouraging assumptions before changing tack with dizzying grace, and finally resolving itself with an explanatory tour de force that leads audiences to question everything they have already seen. Spacey steals the show as the hangdog Verbal, but everyone in this literal rogue's gallery plays his part. The brilliance of the story's structure encouraged a whole generation of screenwriters to emulate its feat. Commercial gold dust, in the sense that people were drawn to see it again, to pick up on the clues they missed first time round.

SCR Christopher McQuarrie   **CIN** Newton Thomas Sigel
MUS John Ottman   **DES** Howard Cummings   **ED** John Ottman   **PROD** Bryan Singer, Michael McDonnell
DIST Polygram/Spelling/Blue Parrot/Bad Hat Harry/Rosco

66 Goes straight to cult status without quite touching one important base: the audience's emotions. This movie finally isn't anything more than an intricate feat of gamesmanship, but it's still quite something to see. – *Elvis Mitchell, New York Times*

66 The Usual Suspects filled me with a highly unusual urge – to be a true 'reviewer', to rewind the projector and figure out this humdinger once and for all. – *Rick Groen, Toronto Globe & Mail*

⚱ Kevin Spacey (supporting actor); Christopher McQuarrie (original screenplay)

🛡 film; Christopher McQuarrie (original screenplay); (editing)

Uzak ★★★

SCR/DIR *Nuri Bilge Ceylan*
2003   110m   Turkey/Netherlands
DVD

☆ Muzaffer Ozdemir (Mahmut), Emin Toprak (Yusuf), Zuhal Gencer Erkaya (Nazan), Nazan Kirilmis (Lover), Feridun Koc (Janitor)

An unemployed young Turk travels from his rural home to Istanbul to find work, and stays with his miserable middle-aged photographer cousin.

A strangely fascinating examination of solitude and an inability to communicate. Discarding music, and sparing with dialogue, Ceylan still manages to convey entire worlds.

CIN Nuri Bilge Ceylan   **DES** Ebru Yapici   **ED** Ayhan Ergusel   **PROD** Nuri Bilge Ceylan

66 Superlatives are entirely warranted for immensely assured Turkish art-house drama Uzak, which is filled with a palpable sense of loss and yearning. – *Tom Dawson, BBC*

† Ozdemir and Toprak shared the best actor prize at the 2003 Cannes Film Festival for their performances.

U

DVD Available on DVD
♫ Soundtrack on CD
☆ Cast in order of importance
66 Critics' Quotes
† Points of interest
⚱ Academy Award
⚱ Academy Award nomination
🛡 BAFTA
🛡 BAFTA nomination

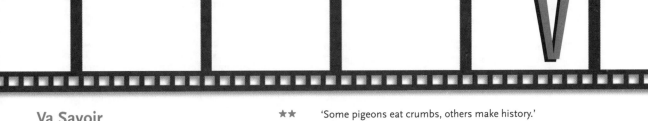

Va Savoir ★★

DIR *Jacques Rivette*

2001   154m   France/Italy/Germany

DVD

☆ Jeanne Balibar (Camille), Sergio Castellitto (Ugo), Jacques Bonnaffe (Pierre), Marianne Basler (Sonia), Helene de Fougerolles (Do), Bruno Todeschini (Arthur), Catherine Rouvel (Mother)

Six actors appearing in Pirandello's play As You Desire Me in Paris enjoy changes of relationships both in and out of characters

A literate rondo, charming and brilliantly executed. The veteran Rivette's practised assurance permeates every frame of this comic charade, which has plenty to say about the impact of art on life and love.

SCR Christine Laurent, Pascal Bonitzer, Jacques Rivette   **CIN** William Lubtchansky   **DES** Manu de Chauvigny   **ED** Nicole Lubtchansky   **PROD** Martine Marignac   **DIST** Artificial Eye

66 A farce in waltz time. – *Roger Ebert, Chicago Sun-Times*

66 Veteran French filmmaker Jacques Rivette shows that at 73 he can still skilfully craft an intricate tale. – *Sandi Chaitram, BBC*

Vagabonde ★★

SCR/DIR *Agnès Varda*

1985   104m   France

☆ Sandrine Bonnaire (Mona), Macha Meril (Madame Landier), Stéphane Freiss (Jean-Pierre), Laurence Cortadellas (Elaine), Marthe Jarnais (Aunt Lydie), Yolande Moreau (Yolande), Joel Fosse (Paulo)

When an attractive young Frenchwoman is found frozen to death in a ditch, acquaintances trace her decision to give up her home and her job to live a vagrant's life.

Starkly unsentimental profile of a wasted young life, and its alarming decline, born out of an unknowable alienation.

CIN Patrick Blossier   **MUS** Joanna Bruzdowicz   **ED** Agnès Varda, Patricia Mazuy   **PROD** Oury Milshtein   **DIST** Cine-Tamaris/A2/Ministère de la Culture

66 What a film this is. Like so many of the greatest films, it tells us a very specific story, strong and unadorned. . .it is only many days later that we reflect the story of the vagabond could also be the story of our lives. – *Roger Ebert, Chicago Sun-Times*

† It won the Golden Lion award for best film at the Venice Film Festival in 1985.

'Some pigeons eat crumbs, others make history.'

Valiant ★

DIR Gary Chapman

2005   76m   GB/US

DVD   ♫

☆ voices of: Ewan McGregor (Valiant), Ricky Gervais (Bugsy), Tim Curry (General Von Talon), Jim Broadbent (Sergeant), Hugh Laurie (Gutsy), John Cleese (Mercury), John Hurt (Felix)

A brave woodpigeon joins an RAF squadron in World War II, flying secret Allied plans to safety from under the beak of a Nazi falcon.

Animated movie combining technical wizardry with Boys' Own-style heroics. It has entertaining and genuinely exciting moments, but its calculatedly old-fashioned story-telling and its cheerfully corny gags grate at times.

SCR Jordan Katz, George Webster, George Melrod   **CIN** John Fenner   **MUS** George Fenton   **DES** John Byrne   **ED** Jim Stewart   **PROD** John H. Williams   **DIST** Entertainment

66 This patriotic salute to the homing pigeon is an amiable but doggedly old-fashioned affair, wedding wartime nostalgia to a rash of computer graphics and pantomime antics to a stiff-upper-lip sensibility. – *Xan Brooks, The Guardian*

Valmont

DIR Milos Forman

1989   137m   France/GB

DVD

☆ Colin Firth (Valmont), Annette Bening (Merteuil), Meg Tilly (Madame de Tourvel), Fairuza Balk (Cecile), Sian Phillips (Madame de Volanges), Jeffrey Jones (Gercourt), Henry Thomas (Danceny), Fabia Drake (Madame de Rosemonde), T. P. McKenna (Baron), Isla Blair (Baroness), Ronald Lacey (José)

Two jaded 18th century French aristocrats enjoy sexual adventures and conspire in the seduction of an innocent young bride-to-be.

A lavish, light-hearted adaptation of the novel Les Liaisons Dangereuses, which underplays the cynicism of these characters, renders their machinations as almost frolicsome, and lingers approvingly on the beauty of the mansions and lawns where they disport themselves. There's a faint sense it misses the entire point.

SCR Jean-Claude Carrière, Milos Forman   **CIN** Miroslav Ondricek   **MUS** Christopher Palmer   **DES** Pierre Guffroy

---

DVD Available on DVD   ☆ Cast in order of importance   66 Critics' Quotes   † Points of interest   ♪ Soundtrack on CD   Ⓐ Academy Award   Ⓐ Academy Award nomination   Ⓑ BAFTA   Ⓑ BAFTA nomination

653

ED Alan Heim, Nena Danevic   **PROD** Paul Rassam,
Michael Hausman   **DIST** Orion/Claude Berri/Renn

66 It's a naughty costume dramedy in which the erotic
conquests of bored libertines are transformed into
children's kissing games. – *Rita Kempley, Washington
Post*

† The film's British release was delayed for six months so
as not to clash with another filmed version of the same
novel, Dangerous Liaisons. Valmont consequently
suffered in box-office terms.

⌀ (costume design)

Ⓣ (costume design)

'A large portion of life. . .'

The Van

DIR Stephen Frears
1996   100m   Eire/GB
DVD

☆ Colm Meaney (Larry), Donal O'Kelly ('Bimbo'), Ger
Ryan (Maggie), Caroline Rothwell (Mary), Neili Conroy
(Diane), Ruaidhri Conroy (Kevin), Brendan O'Carroll
(Weslie)

A sacked Dublin baker uses his redundancy money
to buy an old van, go into the mobile fish-and-chip
business with a friend, and cash in on the 1990
World Cup euphoria hitting Ireland.

*A quirky comedy about two men battling against a cruel
world to make a decent living. But despite its jocular
tone, it feels forced and formulaic.*

SCR Roddy Doyle   **CIN** Oliver Stapleton   **MUS** Eric
Clapton, Richard Hartley   **DES** Mark Geraghty   **ED** Mick
Audsley   **PROD** Lynda Myles   **DIST** TCF

66 A jauntily enjoyable comedy about unemployment. –
Time Out

Van Gogh   ★★

SCR/DIR Maurice Pialat,
1991   158m   France
DVD

☆ *Jacques Dutronc* (Van Gogh), Alexandra London
(Marguerite (Gachet)), Bernard Le Coq (Théo), Gerard Sety
(Gachet), Corinne Bourdon (Jo), Elsa Zylberstein (Cathy),
Leslie Azoulai (Adeline), Jacques Vidal (Ravoux), Chantal
Barbarit (Madame Chevalier)

In the last months of his life, the great painter
Vincent Van Gogh instigates an affair with a local
doctor's young daughter quarrels with his brother
Theo, and commits suicide.

*Masterly biopic, as good as any about this artist, that
leaves Dutronc to convey the agony of a dying flawed
man rather than some rarefied genius. Raw,
uncomfortable, fascinating.*

CIN Gilles Henry, Emmanuel Machuel   **MUS** A. Bernot, J.
M. Bourget, J. Dutronc, P. Revedy   **DES** Philippe Pallut,
Katia Vischkof   **ED** Yann Dedet, Nathalie Hubert, Hélène
Viard   **PROD** Daniel Toscan du Plantier   **DIST** Artificial
Eye/Erato/Canal/A2/Livradois

66 It brings off the considerable trick of describing an
artist's life without trundling out the hammy, lust-for-life
clichés. – *Peter Bradshaw, The Guardian*

The Vanishing   ★

DIR George Sluizer
1988   107m   Netherlands/France
DVD

☆ Bernard-Pierre Donnadieu (Raymond Lemorne), Gene
Bervoets (Rex Hofman), Johanna Ter Steege (Saskia
Wagter), Gwen Eckhaus (Lieneke), Bernadette Le Sache
(Simone Lemorne), Tania Latarjet (Denise Lemorne)

Three years after a Dutch girl is snatched at a
French petrol station, her boyfriend is approached
by the kidnapper.

*Unconventional, cleverly crafted chiller which reveals
much of its mystery early on, but still manages a jolting
ending.*

SCR Tim Krabbé   **CIN** Toni Kuhn   **MUS** Henry Vrienten
ED George Sluizer, Lin Friedman   **PROD** Anne Lordo,
George Sluizer   **DIST** Metro/Golden Egg Film/Ingrid
Productions/MGS Film

66 An extraordinary, gripping film. The conclusion will
stay with you for a long time. – *Hal Hinson, Washington
Post*

'All's fair in love and war.'

Vanity Fair   ★★

DIR Mira Nair
2004   141m   GB/US
DVD   ♫

☆ Reese Witherspoon (Becky Sharp), Eileen Atkins (Miss
Matilda Crawley), Jim Broadbent (Mr Osborne), Gabriel
Byrne (The Marquess of Steyne), Romola Garai (Amelia
Sedley), Bob Hoskins (Sir Pitt Crawley), Rhys Ifans
(William Dobbin), Geraldine McEwan (Lady Southdown),
Jonathan Rhys Meyers (George Osborne), James Purefoy
(Rawdon Crawley), Douglas Hodge (Pitt Crawley)

Bright, attractive young woman is so ambitious to
make a mark in London's high society that she
finally over-reaches herself.

*Ambitious adaptation, composed of telling set-pieces,
with a subtle Indian influence in the background. It
lacks the viciousness of the social climbing detailed in
the novel, but hangs together as a cohesive, satisfying
and literally colourful story.*

SCR Matthew Faulk, Mark Skeet, Julian Fellowes
CIN Declan Quinn   **MUS** Mychael Danna   **DES** Maria
Djurkovic   **ED** Allyson C. Johnson   **PROD** Janette Day,
Donna Gigliotti, Lydia Dean Pilcher   **DIST** UIP

66 The peculiar quality of Vanity Fair, which sets it aside
from the Austen adaptations such as 'Sense and
Sensibility' and 'Pride and Prejudice,' is that it's not about
very nice people. That makes them much more
interesting. – *Roger Ebert, Chicago Sun-Times*

66 Witherspoon's simply terrific, and it's amazing how
quickly and easily she sheds speculation that she was too
modern for the role. – *Stephen Hunter, Washington Post*

'8 strangers. 8 points of view. 1 truth.'

Vantage Point   (new)

DIR Pete Travis
2008   89m   US
DVD   ♫

☆ Dennis Quaid (Thomas Barnes), Matthew Fox (Kent

Taylor), Forest Whitaker (Howard Lewis), Sigourney Weaver (Rex Brooks), William Hurt (President Ashton), Edgar Ramirez (Javier), Ayelet Zurer (Veronica), Said Taghmaoui (Suarez), Zoe Saldana (Angie Jones), Bruce McGill (Phil McCullough)

An attempt on the US President's life in Spain is viewed from various perspectives.

Overcooked spin on Rashomon that tests the patience before culminating in a seemingly endless car chase.

SCR Barry L. Levy **CIN** Amir Mokri **MUS** Atli Orvarsson **DES** Brigitte Broch **ED** Stuart Baird **PROD** Neal H. Moritz **DIST** Sony Pictures

66 All gimmick and not a lot of substance. – *Wendy Ide, The Times*

66 Initially intriguing and energetic, this film ends up demonstrating that a good script needs to be more than a clever concept. – *Kenneth Turan, Los Angeles Times*

† Though set in the Spanish town of Salamanca, almost all of the film was shot in Mexico City.

Vanya on 42nd Street ★

DIR *Louis Malle*
1994 119m US
DVD

☆ Wallace Shawn (Vanya), Julianne Moore (Yelena), Brooke Smith (Sonya), Larry Pine (Dr. Astrov), George Gaynes (Serybryakov), Phoebe Brand (Nanny), Madhur Jaffrey (Mrs. Chao), André Gregory (himself), Lynn Cohen (Maman)

The cast and small invited audience assemble in a relic of a theatre in New York for a rehearsal of a production of Chekhov's Uncle Vanya.

This partly documentary film re-creates an intriguing theatrical occasion; accessible and enjoyable, even to non-actors, than one might imagine.

SCR David Mamet, Andre Gregory **CIN** Declan Quinn **MUS** Joshua Redman **DES** Eugene Lee **ED** Nancy Baker **PROD** Fred Berner **DIST** Artificial Eye/Laura Pels/Mayfair

66 The performances are precise, the language is alive and well spoken and the setting is striking, but Vanya on 42nd Street still suffers heavily from the limitations of filmed theatre. – *Todd McCarthy, Variety*

† This was the last film Malle directed. He died in 1995.

Vendredi Soir ★★

DIR *Claire Denis*
2002 90m France
DVD

☆ *Valerie Lemercier* (Laure), *Vincent Lindon* (Jean)

A Parisian woman prepares to move in with her boyfriend but, stuck in a traffic jam caused by a public transport strike, she impulsively gives a lift to a stranger, with whom she spends the night in a hotel room.

A fascinating, somewhat chilling look at the impersonality of relationships in modern city life. Director Denis shrewdly refuses to offer glimpses of the precise motivations here – which adds to the intrigue. The two leads are impeccably unknowable.

SCR Emmanuele Bernheim, Claire Denis **CIN** Agnes Godard **MUS** Dickon Hinchliffe **DES** Katia Wyszkop **ED** Nelly Quettier **PROD** Bruno Pesery **DIST** Metro Tartan

66 Vendredi Soir may seem surprisingly discreet, yet its warmth and tenderness help make for a deeply romantic experience. – *Tom Dawson, BBC*

Venus ★★

DIR Roger Michell
2006 94m UK/US
DVD

☆ Peter O'Toole (Maurice Russell), Leslie Phillips (Ian), Jodie Whitaker (Jessie), Richard Griffiths (Donald), Vanessa Redgrave (Valerie)

Maurice and Ian, two veteran British actor friends, find their cosy lives are jolted when Ian's sullen grand-niece Jessie arrives to live with him – and Maurice attempts an outrageous seduction.

A film that polarises opinion along the divide of one's reaction to the spectacle of a young woman being pawed by an elderly man. Distasteful lust on his part, or an indirect rage against the dying of the light? O'Toole's skill and charm help audiences to take the broader, less obvious view. Kureishi's script is funny and bawdy, though the overall tone is melancholic. Phillips does sterling work as a grouchy sidekick, while O'Toole's scenes with Vanessa Redgrave, who plays his ex-wife, are acting masterclasses.

SCR Hanif Kureishi **CIN** Haris Zambarloukos **MUS** David Arnold **DES** John Paul Kelly **ED** Nicolas Gaster **PROD** Kevin Loader **DIST** Buena Vista

66 An affirmation of pleasure and generous-mindedness as well as credible takes on the different aches of adolescence and senescence. – *Ben Walters, Time Out*

66 Venus may be a leering male fantasy but it is also, improbably but persuasively, a love story as tender as it is transgressive. – *Ella Taylor, L.A. Weekly*

Ⅰ Peter O'Toole (leading actor)

Ⓣ Peter O'Toole (leading actor); Leslie Phillips (supporting actor)

'Welcome to the Venus Beauty Institute where love, innocence and sex are a sight to behold.'

Vénus Beauté (institut) ★★

DIR Tonie Marshall
1999 105m France
DVD

☆ Nathalie Baye (Angèle), Bulle Ogier (Madame Nadine), Samuel LeBihan (Antoine), Jacques Bonnaffé (Jacques), Mathilde Seigner (Samantha), Audrey Tautou (Marie), Robert Hossein (Pilot), Edith Scob (Customer with spots on her hands), Marie Rivière (Customer), Hélène Fillières (Antoine's fiancée), Brigitte Roüan (Madame Marianne), Claire Nebout (Asthmatic customer), Elli Medeiros (Mlle Evelyne), Micheline Presle (Tante Maryse), Emmanuelle Riva (Tante Lyda)

An ageing French beautician with a promiscuous attitude to relationships finally meets a man who really cares for her.

Baye is in splendid form, as a woman embittered by a string of one-night stands now thawing gently at the prospect of happiness. A wry romantic comedy, with some sharp sideswipes at the beauty industry.

SCR Tonie Marshall, Marion Vernoux, Jacques Audiard
CIN Gérard De Battista   MUS Khalil Chahine
DES Michel Vandestien   ED Jacques Comets
PROD Gilles Sandoz

66 An uneven film, but one of considerable charm. – Mick LaSalle, San Francisco Chronicle

---

'Wife. Mother. Criminal.'

Vera Drake   ★★★

SCR/DIR Mike Leigh
2004   125m   GB/France/US
[DVD]

☆ Imelda Staunton (Vera Drake), Phil Davis (Stan), Peter Wight (Det Inspector Webster), Adrian Scarborough (Frank), Heather Craney (Joyce), Daniel Mays (Sid), Alex Kelly (Ethel), Sally Hawkins (Susan), Eddie Marsan (Reg)

A working-class mother with a heart of gold performs illegal abortions in post-war London as an act of charity to desperate young girls.

Brilliant, detailed re-creation of humble lives in the ration-book era, with Staunton making the most of the role of a lifetime as the kindly but dimly naive Vera. Outstanding performances from a hard-working cast, though the faint suspicion lingers that Leigh loads the dramatic dice by making Vera just a little too innocent.

CIN Dick Pope   MUS Andrew Dickson   DES Eve Stewart
ED Jim Clark   PROD Alain Sarde   DIST Momentum

66 It's clear why actors clamour to work with Mike Leigh – this wrenchingly powerful picture has as its lifeblood the kind of performances that don't just happen, they have to be lovingly, patiently nurtured. – Wendy Ide, The Times

⚱ Imelda Staunton (leading actress); Mike Leigh (direction); Mike Leigh (screenplay);

Ⓣ Imelda Staunton (leading actress); Mike Leigh (direction); Jacqueline Durran

Ⓣ British film; Mike Leigh (screenplay); Jim Clark; Heather Craney; Phil Davis; Eve Stewart; (make up/hair)

'Frank Galvin has one last chance to do something right'

The Verdict   ★★★

DIR Sidney Lumet
1982   128m   US

☆ Paul Newman, James Mason, Charlotte Rampling, Jack Warden, Milo O'Shea, Lindsay Crouse, Edward Binns, Wesley Addy

In Boston, an ageing, booze-sodden attorney, regarded by acquaintances as little more than an ambulance chaser, is unexpectedly handed an important case of medical malpractice and has a chance to redeem himself.

Sombre story about a flawed man clinging on to a final hope, brilliantly portrayed by Newman, making the most of the best role in his latter career. He is helped

tremendously by an outstanding Mamet script that details the complex legal and medical ethics involved, while never losing sight of the main narrative thrust – the human story of the attorney.

SCR David Mamet   CIN Andrzej Bartkowiak
MUS Johnny Mandel   DES Edward Pisoni
PROD Richard D. Zanuck, David Brown
DIST TCF/Zanuck-Brown

⚱ picture; Paul Newman (leading actor); James Mason (supporting actor); Sidney Lumet; David Mamet (adapted screenplay)

'Why would anyone want to kill Veronica Guerin?'

Veronica Guerin   ★

DIR Joel Schumacher
2003   98m   US/GB/Ireland
[DVD]   ♫

☆ Cate Blanchett (Veronica Guerin), Gerard McSorley (John Gilligan), Ciaran Hinds (John 'The Coach' Traynor), Brenda Fricker (Bernadette Guerin), Barry Barnes (Graham Turley), Joe Hanley (Holland), Colin Farrell (Tattooed Boy)

A fearless Dublin investigative journalist exposes the cynical criminals running the city's drug trade, before she is ruthlessly murdered in retaliation.

Glossy production of a true story which was anything but glossy. Only Blanchett's assiduous performance saves it from being a complete misfire.

SCR Carol Doyle, Mary Agnes Donoghue   CIN Brendan Galvin   MUS Harry Gregson-Williams   DES Nathan Crowley   ED David Gamble   PROD Jerry Bruckheimer
DIST Buena Vista

66 The film crams in every modern Oirish cliche in the book and Cate Blanchett gives a supercilious and queenly impersonation of what she and director Joel Schumacher imagine to be a twinkle-eyed force of nature, exasperating police and employers with her obstinate yet lovable ways, neglecting her husband and child a teeny bit, yet not so much that the audience won't like her. – Peter Bradshaw, The Guardian

---

Vertigo   ★★★★

DIR Alfred Hitchcock
1958   128m   US
[DVD]   ♫

☆ James Stewart (John Ferguson), Kim Novak (Madeleine Elster/Judy Barton), Barbara Bel Geddes (Midge), Tom Helmore (Gavin Elster), Henry Jones (Coroner)

A detective with a fear of heights is drawn into a complex plot in which a girl he loves apparently falls to her death. Then he meets her double.

Double identity thriller which has many sequences in Hitchcock's best style. A film as unsettling as the phobia it deals with, keeping its audience dizzy and off balance throughout. This ranks among his very best work.

SCR Alec Coppel, Samuel Taylor   CIN Robert Burks
MUS Bernard Herrmann   ED George Tomasini
PROD Alfred Hitchcock   DIST Paramount

[DVD] Available on DVD   ☆ Cast in order of importance   66 Critics' Quotes   ⚱ Academy Award   Ⓣ BAFTA
♫ Soundtrack on CD   † Points of interest   ⚱ Academy Award nomination   Ⓣ BAFTA nomination

66 It is about how Hitchcock used, feared and tried to control women. – *Roger Ebert, Chicago Sun-Times*

66 With less playfulness and much more overt libido than other Hitchcock classics, Vertigo was always anomalous. – *Janet Maslin, New York Times*

⚖ art direction; George Dutton (sound)

'About to be very big in a very small town.'

Very Annie-Mary ★

SCR/DIR Sara Sugarman
2001   104m   GB/France
DVD   ♫

☆ Rachel Griffiths (Annie-Mary), Jonathan Pryce (Jack Pugh), Ioan Gruffudd (Hob), Matthew Rhys (Nob), Kenneth Griffiths (Minister), Ruth Madoc (Mrs Ifans), Joanna Page (Bethan Bevan), Rhys Miles Thomas (Colin Thomas)

In a small Welsh village, a gauche, dependent young woman blossoms after her domineering widowed father suffers a stroke, and finds the confidence to air her impressive singing voice.

There's a decent script somewhere in there, but director Sugarman cannot tease it out from writer Sugarman. Nothing seems to have been excised in the name of quality control. But there are shamefully, bleakly funny sequences about raising money for a terminally ill village to visit Disneyland. Otherwise, it's too determined to be quirky. Still, Griffiths gives her considerable all as Mary, while Rhys and Gruffudd have a blast as the only two gays in the village.

CIN Barry Ackroyd   MUS Stephen Warbeck   DES Alice Normington   ED Robin Sales   PROD Graham Broadbent, Damian Jones   DIST FilmFour

66 More a collection of comical vignettes than a fleshed-out narrative. – *Neil Smith, BBC*

A Very British Gangster (new) ★

DIR Donal MacIntyre
2007   101m   UK
DVD

☆ Dominc Noonan, Donal MacIntyre, Bugsy Noonan, Sean Noonan, Paddy Noonan

A portrait of a Manchester gang boss, his sidekicks and extended family.

The film raises awkward questions about MacIntyre's methods, as well as whether 'documentary' is the right word. There's a constant sense of the gang playing up for him; it's as if he told them they could star in their own gangster movie and strut their stuff for his cameras.

CIN Nick Manley, Mike Turnbull   ED Sally Hilton
PROD Donal MacIntyre, Lil Cranfield   DIST Contender

66 As ever, you sense that MacIntyre is half-seduced by the hard-man lifestyle, flattered to be included and content to peddle excitable gangland tourism in the guise of a criminal exposé. – *Xan Brooks, Guardian*

66 A deeply unnerving exposé. – *James Christopher, The Times*

'Never let go.'

A Very Long Engagement ★★

DIR Jean-Pierre Jeunet
2004   133m   France/US
DVD   ♫

☆ Audrey Tautou (Mathilde), Gaspard Ulliel (Manech), Jean-Pierre Becker (Esperanza), Dominique Bettenfeld (Ange Bassignano), Clovis Cornillac (Benoit Notre Dame), Marion Cotillard (Tina Lombardi), Jean-Pierre Daroussin (Benjamin Gordes), Jodie Foster (Elodie Gordes), Ticky Holgado (Germain Pire), Tcheky Karyo (Favourier), Denis Lavant (Six Sous)

A polio-crippled Frenchwoman clings to the slim hope that her fiancé survived World War One.

Risky stab at a whimsical romantic epic against the backdrop of trench chaos. Though the characters lack vitality, it comes off surprisingly well on the whole, and the sumptuous design is nothing if not eye-grabbing.

SCR Jean-Pierre Jeunet, Guillaume Laurant   CIN *Bruno Delbonnel*   MUS Angelo Badalamenti   DES *Aline Bonetto*   ED Herve Schneid   PROD Francis Boespflug   DIST Warner

66 There are many ways to say that war is hell, but few filmmakers have said it with as much imagination, humour, intrigue and humanity. – *Jack Mathews, New York Daily News*

66 Can a movie have too much good stuff? Not when it's stuffed like this one. – *Richard Corliss, Time*

⚖ Bruno Delbonnel; Aline Bonetto
Ⓣ film not in the English language

'Fear is the oxygen of blackmail. If Barrett was paying, others are. Find me one!'

Victim ★★★

DIR *Basil Dearden*
1961   100m   GB
DVD

☆ *Dirk Bogarde* (Melville Farr), Sylvia Syms (Laura Farr), John Barrie (Detective Inspector Harris), Norman Bird (Harold Doe), Peter McEnery (Jack Barrett), Anthony Nicholls (Lord Fullbrook), Dennis Price (Calloway), *Charles Lloyd Pack* (Henry), Derren Nesbitt (Sandy Youth), John Cairney (Bridie), Hilton Edwards (P.H.), Peter Copley (Paul Mandrake), Donald Churchill (Eddy Stone), Nigel Stock (Phip)

A barrister with homosexual inclinations tracks down a blackmailer despite the risk to his own reputation.

A plea for a change in the law is very smartly wrapped up as a murder mystery which allows all aspects to be aired, and the London locations are vivid.

SCR Janet Green, John McCormick   CIN Otto Heller   MUS Philip Green   ED John D. Guthridge   PROD Michael Relph   DIST Rank/Allied Filmmakers/Parkway

66 Ingenious, moralistic, and moderately amusing. – *Pauline Kael, 70s*

V

DVD Available on DVD   ☆ Cast in order   66 Critics' Quotes   ⚖ Academy Award   Ⓑ BAFTA
♫ Soundtrack on CD   of importance   † Points of interest   ⚖ Academy Award nomination   Ⓣ BAFTA nomination

657

'The extraordinary life of Edith Piaf.'

La Vie en Rose ★★

SCR/DIR Olivier Dahan
2007   140m   France/Czech Republic/UK
DVD ♫

☆ Marion Cotillard (Edith Piaf), Sylvie Testud (Mômone), Pascal Greggory (Louis Barrier), Emmanuelle Seigner (Titine), Jean-Pierre Martins (Marcel Cerdan), Gérard Depardieu (Louis Leplée)

A biography of French singer Edith Piaf, from her childhood to her death at age 47.

Thankfully, one need not be a fan of Piaf's melodramatic, self-regarding singing style to enjoy this sprightly biography, which zips back and forth in time, covering most aspects of her life. Structurally, the film is flawed; a crucial piece of information about Piaf is tossed in very late, almost as an afterthought. Yet it's a triumph for Cotillard, who embodies Piaf perfectly, miming skilfully, and capturing the singer's creepy extremes to perfection.

CIN Tetsuo Nagata   **MUS** Christopher Gunning
ED Richard Manzy   **PROD** Ilan Goldman   **DIST** Icon

66 Anyone looking for scandal or salacious revelations will be disappointed. This over-long film does not probe or analyse; it is an exercise in heightened feeling, an opportunity for us to revel in emotion. – *Sukhdev Sandhu, Daily Telegraph*

⚊ Marion Cotillard (leading actress); Didier Lavergne, Jan Archibald (makeup)
⚊ Marit Allen (costume design)
⚊ Marion Cotillard (leading actress); Christopher Gunning; Marit Allen (costume design); Didier Lavergne, Jan Archibald (makeup and hair)
⚊ Film not in the English language; Olivier Raoux, Stanislas Reydellet (production design); Laurent Zeilig, Pascal Villard, Jean-Paul Hurier, Marc Doisne (sound)

Vigo: Passion for Life ★

DIR Julien Temple
1997   106m   GB/France/Japan/Spain/Germany

☆ Romane Bohringer (Lydu), James Frain (Jean Vigo), Jim Carter (Bonaventure), Diana Quick (Emily), William Scott-Masson (Marcel), James Faulkner (Dr Gerard), Francine Bergé (Mama Lozinska), Vernon Dobtcheff (Papa Lozinska), Adolfo Fernandez (Almereyda)

An account of the short life of French director Jean Vigo, who died at age 29 after making just three films.

A laudable but faintly misguided labour of love, which tries to locate the wellspring of Vigo's creativity, but settles for interpreting him as another misunderstood artist.

SCR Peter Ettedgui, Anne Devlin, Julien Temple   **CIN** John Mathieson   **MUS** Bingen Mendizabal   **DES** Caroline Greville-Morris   **ED** Marie-Thérèse Boiché
PROD Amanda Temple, Jeremy Bolt   **DIST** Channel Four

66 Playing fast and loose with its subject's life, Julien Temple's stylised attempt to capture the anarchic free spirit that was French director Jean Vigo won't win any prizes for authenticity but gets full marks for passion. – *Total Film*

Vincent: The Life and Death of Vincent van Gogh ★

SCR/DIR Paul Cox
1987   105m   Australia
DVD

☆ John Hurt (narrator)

The sad story of the life and eventual suicide of van Gogh is told in his letters to his brother Theo.

A worthy documentary, greatly enhanced by John Hurt's impeccable readings; the great man, though, remains elusive and enigmatic.

CIN Peter Levy   **MUS** Norman Kaye   **ED** Paul Cox
PROD Tony Llewellyn-Jones
DIST Illumination/Look/Daska

66 A chore to sit through. – *Hal Hinson, Washington Post*

Vincent and Theo ★

DIR Robert Altman
1990   138m   France/GB/Netherlands/Italy
DVD

☆ *Tim Roth* (Vincent Van Gogh), *Paul Rhys* (Theodore 'Theo' Van Gogh), Johanna Ter Steege (Jo Bonger), Wladimir Yordanoff (Paul Gauguin), Jip Wijngaarden (Sien Hoornik), Anne Canovas (Marie)

Film following the tormented life of painter Vincent Van Gogh and his supportive, but equally disaffected brother.

Gently paced, beautifully acted movie that sheds some light on the conflicting tensions between family relationships and artistic expression.

SCR Julian Mitchell   **CIN** Jean Lepine   **MUS** Gabriel Yared   **DES** Stephen Altman   **ED** Françoise Coispeau, Geraldine Peroni   **PROD** Ludi Boeken, Emma Hayter
DIST Blue Dolphin/Belbo Films/Central Films

66 A film that generates the feeling that we are in the presence of a man in the act of creation. – *Roger Ebert, Chicago Sun-Times*

Violent Cop ★

DIR Takeshi Kitano
1989   103m   Japan
DVD

☆ 'Beat' Takeshi (Takeshi Kitano) (Azuma), Maiko Kawakami (Akari), Makoto Ashigawa (Kikuchi), Haku Ryu (Kiyohiro), Ken Yoshizawa (Shinkai), Shiro Sano (Yoshinari), Ittoku Kishibe (Nito), Shigeru Hiraizumi (Iwaki)

Unconventional Japanese detective teaching his new rookie partner about the job while other cops are involved in pushing drugs.

Stylish, violent, occasionally funny crime thriller set in Tokyo; strong on chase sequences, less so in terms of character development.

SCR Hisashi Nozawa   **CIN** Yasushi Sasakibara
MUS Daisaku, Kume   **ED** Nobutake Kamiya
PROD Hisao Nabeshima, Takio Yoshida, Shozo Ichiyama
DIST ICA/Bandai/Shochiku-Fuji

66 Grim and exhilarating at the same time. – *Bob Graham, San Francisco Chronicle*

V

DVD Available on DVD   ☆ Cast in order of importance   66 Critics' Quotes   † Points of interest   ⚊ Academy Award   ⚊ Academy Award nomination   ⚊ BAFTA   ⚊ BAFTA nomination
♫ Soundtrack on CD

'Love. Sex. Passion. Fear. Obsession.'

Virgin Suicides ★★

SCR/DIR Sofia Coppola
1999   97m   US
DVD   ♫

☆ James Woods (Mr Lisbon), Kathleen Turner (Mrs Lisbon), Kirsten Dunst (Lux), John Hartnett (Trip Fontaine), Hanna Hall (Cecilia), Chelse Swain (Bonnie), A.J. Cook (Mary), Leslie Hayman (Therese), Danny DeVito (Dr Hornicker), Scott Glenn (Father Moody), Jonathan Tucker (Tim), Anthony DeSimone (Chase), Giovanni Ribisi (Narrator)

A group of male friends become obsessed by mysterious sister who are sheltered by their strict and religious parents after one of them commits suicide.

Sofia Coppola proved her screenwriting and directing outstripped her acting ability in this odd, sweet, almost ethereal story from the heart of 1970s suburban America.

CIN Edward Lachman   **MUS** Air   **DES** Jasna Stefanovic   **ED** James Lyon, Melissa Kent   **PROD** Francis Ford Coppola, Julie Costanzo, Chris Hanley, Dan Halsted

66 There's a melancholy sweetness here, a gentle humour that speaks to the angst and awkwardness of girls turning into women, and the awe of boys watching the transformation from afar. – *Stephen Rea, Philadelphia Inquirer*

66 An artful blend of '70s detail and dreamlike moodiness makes Coppola's first movie an exceptionally promising directorial debut. – *David Sterritt, Christian Science Monitor*

Viridiana ★★★★

DIR *Luis Buñuel*
1961   91m   Spain/Mexico
☆ Silvia Pinal (Viridiana), Francisco Rabal (Jorge), Fernando Rey (Don Jaime), Jose Calvo (The Beggar), Margarita Lozano (Ramona), José Manuel Martin (The Beggar), Victoria Zinny (Lucia)

A novice about to take her vows is corrupted by her lascivious uncle; she later gives shelter to outcasts in his house.

Often hilarious surrealist melodrama packed with double meanings, targeting the Catholic church and Spain's fascist regime. It is truly extraordinary and outlandish.

SCR Luis Buñuel, Julio Alajandro   **CIN** José F. Agayo   **MUS** Gustavo Pittaluga   **DES** Francisco Canet   **ED** Pedro del Rey   **PROD** Munoz Suay   **DIST** Uninci/Films 59/Gustavo Alatriste

66 One of the cinema's few major philosophical works. – *Robert Vas*

† It won the Palme D'Or at the 1961 Cannes Film Festival, though the Spanish government, having first nominated it without seeing it, tried to have it withdrawn from competition.

† It was censured by the Vatican. A spokesman described it as 'an insult to Christianity.'

Visions of Light ★★★★

DIR Arnold Glassman, Todd McCarthy, Stuart Samuels
1992   92m   US/Japan
DVD

☆ Todd McCarthy (interviewer)

A collection of cinematographers discuss their art and trace its development of cinematography from The Birth of a Nation in 1915 to the present day.

A lyrical hymn to the art of cinematography, too often overlooked by casual filmgoers, but given its rightful pride of place here. A must for anyone remotely interested in the effect and beauty of film, and the capacity of visual images to move hearts and minds.

SCR Todd McCarthy   **CIN** Nancy Schreiber   **ED** Arnold Glassman   **PROD** Stuart Samuels   **DIST** City Screen/American Film Institute/NHK

66 Will cause everyone who sees it to look at movies a little differently in future. – *Roger Ebert, Chicago Sun-Times*

Volver ★★★

SCR/DIR *Pedro Almodóvar*
2006   121m   Spain
DVD   ♫

☆ *Penélope Cruz* (Raimunda), Carmen Maura (Irene), Lola Dueñas (Sole), Blanca Portillo (Agustina), Yohana Cobo (Laura), Chus Lampreave (Aunt Paula)

A story of three generations of Spanish woman: a dead grandmother (Maura), an impoverished Madrid mother in an unhappy marriage (Cruz) and her vulnerable teenage daughter (Cobo). It involves ghosts, a murder and a terrible family secret.

The most mature work yet from this world-class director. Volver means 'return', and Almodóvar has come back from the urban settings of his earlier films to the Spanish region of his childhood: La Mancha, flat, rural and windswept, where superstition abounds and belief in ghosts still flourishes. A brilliant opening tracking shot of widows scrupulously sweeping their husbands' graves swiftly establishes the mood. The story feels loose and flexible, and nothing is quite what it seems. The film's strength lies in the performances of the largely female cast, notably Cruz as the beleaguered mother Raimunda – feisty, smart and voluptuous. Volver is a treat: a wise, reflective, wistful story, masterfully told.

CIN José Luis Alcaine   **MUS** Alberto Iglesias   **ED** José Salcedo   **PROD** Esther García   **DIST** Pathé

66 Richly entertaining fantasy from a cinematic master. – *Ray Bennett, Hollywood Reporter*

66 Enchanting, gentle, transgresssive. . .what a distinctive film-maker Almodóvar has become. – *Roger Ebert, Chicago Sun-Times*

† At the 2006 Cannes Film Festival, the six leading members of the ensemble cast shared the best actress award.

⌁ Penélope Cruz (leading actress)

Ⓣ film not in the English language; Penélope Cruz (leading actress)

V

'Even the darkest secret couldn't keep them apart.'

Voyager ★

DIR Volker Schlöndorff

1991   117m   Germany/France/Greece

☆ Sam Shepard (Walter Faber), Julie Delpy (Sabeth), Barbara Sukowa (Hannah), Dieter Kirchlechner (Herbert Hencke), Traci Lind (Charlene), Deborah Lee-Furness (Ivy), August Zirner (Joachim), Thomas Heinze (Kurt)

A middle-aged engineer survives a plane crash in Mexico, embarks on a transatlantic voyage, and starts a passionate affair with a teenage girl, only to learn she is the daughter of his ex-mistress.

Convoluted drama, with some intriguing political and philosophical ideas fighting – not always successfully – to make themselves heard.

SCR Rudy Wurlitzer   CIN Yorgos Arvanitis, Pierre L'homme   MUS Stanley Myers   DES Nicos Perakis   ED Dagmar Hirtz   PROD Eberhard Junkersdorf   DIST Palace/Bioskop/Action/Stefi 2/Hellas

66 The problem with Voyager is that it never amounts to anything more than a philosophical fashion show, with Shepard as its stylish mannequin. – *Hal Hinson, Washington Post*

V

'A comedy about truth, justice and other special effects.'

Wag the Dog ★★

DIR *Barry Levinson*
1997 97m US
`DVD` ♫

☆ Dustin Hoffman (Stanley Motss), Robert de Niro (Conrad Brean), Anne Heche (Winifred Ames), Woody Harrelson (Sergeant William Schumann), Denis Leary (Fad King), Willie Nelson (Johnny Dean), Andrea Martin (Liz Butsky), Kirsten Dunst (Tracy Lime), William H. Macy (CIA Agent Charles Young)

US presidential aides hire a Hollywood producer to help invent a fake war in order to divert attention from a sexual scandal in the Oval Office.

Riotously funny satire that takes for granted the lack of integrity in political life. Both the sexual scandal it describes and the phony reasons for engaging in a distracting war had a resonance with real-life events. But the movie, shot by Levinson with sprightly, light-footed haste, is valid and telling in its own right.

SCR *Hilary Henkin, David Mamet* CIN Robert Richardson MUS Mark Knopfler DES Wynn Thomas ED Stu Linder PROD Jane Rosenthal, Robert de Niro, Barry Levinson DIST Entertainment/New Line/Tribeca/Baltimore/Punch

66 A funny movie about something serious. – *Mick LaSalle, San Francisco Chronicle*

† Hoffman reportedly modelled his performance as a Hollywood mogul on Robert Evans.

♟ Dustin Hoffman (leading actor); Hilary Henkin, David Mamet

Ⓣ (screenplay)

The Wages of Fear ★★★

SCR/DIR *Henri-Georges Clouzot*
1953 140m France/Italy
`DVD`

☆ *Yves Montand* (Mario), Folco Lulli (Luigi), Peter Van Eyck (Bimba), *Charles Vanel* (Jo), Vera Clouzot (Linda), William Tubbs (Bill O'Brien)

The manager of a Central American oilfield offers big money to drivers who will take an explosive cargo of nitro-glycerine into the jungle to put out an oil well fire.

After too extended an introduction to the less than admirable characters, this fascinating film resolves itself into a suspense shocker with one craftily managed bad moment after another.

CIN *Armand Thirard* MUS Georges Auric DES Rene Renoux ED Henri Rust, Madeleine Gug, Etienne Muse DIST Filmsonor/CICC/Vera

66 As skilful as, in its preoccupation with violence and its unrelieved pessimism, it is unlikeable. – *Penelope Houston, Sight and Sound*

66 It has some claim to be the greatest suspense thriller of all time; it is the suspense not of mystery but of Damocles' sword. – *Basil Wright, 1972*

† Sorcerer (1977) was a lamentable remake.

† Unusually, it was named best film at both the Cannes and Berlin film festivals in 1953.

Ⓣ picture

Wagonmaster ★★

DIR *John Ford*
1950 86m US

☆ Ben Johnson, Joanne Dru, Harry Carey Jnr, Ward Bond, Charles Kemper, Alan Mowbray, Jane Darwell, Russell Simpson

Adventures of a Mormon wagon train journeying towards Utah in 1879.

Low-key, simple John Ford Western, essentially a collection of incidents, fondly and enjoyably presented.

SCR Frank Nugent, Patrick Ford CIN Bert Glennon MUS Richard Hageman PROD John Ford, Merian C. Cooper DIST RKO/Argosy

66 The feel of the period, the poetry of space and of endeavour, is splendidly communicated. – *Lindsay Anderson*

66 What emerges at the end is nothing less than a view of life itself, the view of a poet. – *Patrick Gibbs, 1965*

The Waiting Room (new) ★

SCR/DIR *Roger Goldby*
2008 105m UK

☆ Anne-Marie Duff (Anna), Ralf Little (Stephen), Rupert Graves (George), Frank Finlay (Roger), Zoe Telford (Jem), Phyllida Law (Helen), Christine Bottomley (Fiona), Adrian Bower (Toby)

Two strangers involved in unhappy relationships meet by chance in a railway station waiting room and spend the rest of the film wondering if they are meant to be together.

Slight but appealing romantic drama, set in south London; the occasional truthful insight can't quite dispel the overall reliance on sentimentality.

`DVD` Available on DVD
♫ Soundtrack on CD
☆ Cast in order of importance
66 Critics' Quotes
† Points of interest
♟ Academy Award
♟ Academy Award nomination
Ⓣ BAFTA
Ⓣ BAFTA nomination

CIN James Aspinall   MUS Edmund Butt   DES Ana Viana
ED David Thrasher   PROD Sarah Sulick   DIST Lionsgate

66 A Britflick with European urges. – *Kevin Maher, The Times*

66 At last: an intelligent British ensemble relationship drama that feels the real deal. – *James Mottram, Marie Claire*

'If only life were as easy as pie.'

Waitress (new)   ★

SCR/DIR Adrienne Shelly
2007   108m   US
[DVD]

☆ Keri Russell (Jenna), Nathan Fillion (Dr. Pomatter), Cheryl Hines (Becky), Adrienne Shelly (Dawn), Jeremy Sisto (Earl)

In a southern state in America, a waitress hoarding her money in order to free herself of her malevolent husband discovers she is pregnant, and starts an affair with the new doctor in town.

Charming, likable but a little halting in its comic tone, the film finally stands and falls with its lead actress, who is a shade too bland to carry the narrative's weight.

CIN Matthew Irving   MUS Andrew Hollander
DES Ramsey Avery   ED Annette Davey   PROD Michael Roiff   DIST TCF

66 The film is laced with lovely moments, from the leads and from Shelly as a waitress friend. – *Peter Rainer, Christian Science Monitor*

66 Washed in a honeyed 1950s glow, Waitress has a mildly puckish way with outlandish baked goods and pert dialogue, but the movie is memorable largely for the contrast between its innocent sweetness and the savagery of its maker's premature death. – *Ella Taylor, L.A. Weekly*

† Writer-director Shelly was murdered by a construction worker who entered her Manhattan apartment in November 2006. She was 40 years old.

Waking Life   ★

SCR/DIR Richard Linklater
2001   100m   US
[DVD] ♫

☆ Wiley Wiggins (Main Character), Trevor Jack Brooks (Young Boy Playing Paper Game), Lorelei Linklater (Young Girl Playing Paper Game), Glover Gill (Accordion Player), Lara Hicks (Violin Player), Ames Asbell (Viola Player), Leigh Mahoney (Viola Player), Sara Nelson (Cello Player)

A man is run over and begins to shuffle through his dreams, searching for the meaning of the universe.

Live actors are shot on video, every frame of which is 'painted' over to produce a vivid, visually dazzling animated film. This effect is far more interesting than the content, which quickly descends into self-indulgent musings about life, mortality and the dream state.

CIN Richard Linklater, Tommy Pallotta   MUS Glover Gill
ED Sandra Adair   PROD Anne Walker-McBay, Tommy Pallotta, Palmer West, Jonah Smith   DIST TCF

66 Audiences looking for something fresh and different, not to mention a head trip, will find it in Waking Life, an appealing new work from Richard Linklater. – *Todd McCarthy, Variety*

'There are 6,894,620 reasons for... Waking Ned.'

Waking Ned   ★★

SCR/DIR Kirk Jones
1998   91m   GB/France/US
[DVD]   ♫

☆ Ian Bannen (Jackie O'Shea), David Kelly (Michael O'Sullivan), Fionnula Flanagan (Annie O'Shea), Susan Lynch (Maggie O'Toole), James Nesbitt (Pig Finn), Maura O'Malley (Mrs. Kennedy), Robert Hickey (Maurice O'Toole), Paddy Ward (Brendy O'Toole), James Ryland (Dennis Fitzgerald), Fintan McKeown (Pat Mulligan), Matthew Devitt (Tom Toomey)

Two elders of a small Irish village plot to claim a dead neighbour's substantial Lottery fortune as their own.

Nicely written and amusingly played comedy in the Ealing tradition; a jovial timewaster.

CIN Henry Braham   MUS Shaun Davey   DES John Ebden   ED Alan Strachan   PROD Glynis Murray, Richard Holmes   DIST TCF/Fox Searchlight/Tomboy

66 A passable entertainment - call it The Half Monty. – *David Edelstein, Slate*

† Though the film is set in Ireland, it was shot on the Isle of Man.

Ⓣ Kirk Jones (screenplay)

'Life made him tough. Love made him strong. Music made him hard.'

Walk Hard: The Dewey Cox Story (new)   ★

DIR Jake Kasdan
2007   95m   US
[DVD]   ♫

☆ John C. Reilly (Dewey Cox), Jenna Fischer (Darlene Madison), Tim Meadows (Sam), Kristen Wiig (Edith), Raymond J. Barry (Pa Cox), Margo Martindale (Ma Cox), Chris Parnell (Theo), Matt Besser (Dave)

The life and times of a fictional country singer, from tragic youth to debauched manhood.

Entertaining mock biopic modelled on Walk the Line and Ray; the musical parodies are ingenious, though the script runs out of steam.

SCR Judd Apatow, Jake Kasdan   CIN Uta Briesewitz
MUS Michael Andrews   DES Jefferson D. Sage   ED Tara Timpone, Steve Welch   PROD Judd Apatow, Jake Kasdan, Clayton Townsend   DIST Sony Pictures

PA COX: 'The wrong kid died!'

66 A pitch-perfect musical comedy. – *Michael Rechtshaffen, Hollywood Reporter*

66 Veers from smart, on-the-money send-ups to broad, crude visual gags. – *Peter Whittle, Sunday Times*

† The film features cameos from Jack White (Elvis Presley), Jack Black (Paul McCartney), Paul Rudd (John Lennon) and Frankie Muniz (Buddy Holly).

'It was the summer of Woodstock . . . when she became the woman she always wanted to be.'

A Walk on the Moon ★★

DIR Tony Goldwyn
1998 107m US
DVD ♫

☆ *Diane Lane* (Pearl Kantrowitz), *Liev Schreiber* (Marty Kantrowitz), Anna Paquin (Alison Kantrowitz), Viggo Mortensen (Walker Jerome), Tovah Feldshuh (Lilian Kantrowitz), Bobby Boriello (Daniel Kantrowitz), Stewart Bick (Neil Leiberman), Jess Platt (Herb Fogler)

In 1969, at the time of the first moon landings, an American woman and her teenage daughter go on a holiday without her husband. She takes a lover, and they go off together to Woodstock, to the daughter's chagrin.

Beautifully observed drama with a strong sense of place (the upstate New York vacation resort for Jewish families) and a quietly satisfactory conclusion. Something of a turning point in Lane's career; she plays wifely ennui to the hilt.

SCR Pamela Gray CIN Anthony Richmond
MUS Mason Daring DES Dan Leigh ED Dana Congdon PROD Dustin Hoffman, Tony Goldwyn, Jay Cohen, Neil Koenigsberg, Lee Gottsegan, Murray Schisgal
DIST Miracle

66 A film of exceptional emotional honesty. – *Kevin Thomas, Los Angeles Times*
66 A nostalgia movie that doesn't get sticky with false sentiment. – *Michael Wilmington, Chicago Tribune*

'Love is a burning thing.'

Walk the Line ★★

DIR James Mangold
2005 136m Germany/US
DVD ♫

☆ *Joaquin Phoenix* (John R. Cash), *Reese Witherspoon* (June Carter), Ginnifer Goodwin (Vivian Cash), Robert Patrick (Ray Cash), Dallas Roberts (Sam Phillips), Dan John Miller (Luther Perkins), Tyler Hilton (Elvis Presley), Waylon Malloy Payne (Jerry Lee Lewis), Shooter Jennings (Waylon Jennings)

The life of singer Johnny Cash, from his childhood in Arkansas to his celebrated Folsom Prison gig in 1968.

A resolutely linear biopic, coy about Cash's experiences with sex and drugs, and prone to cod psychology in scenes with the singer's distant father. But the coyness seems deliberate, so as not to spoil what's at the film's heart: one of the most enduring romances in all popular culture, between Johnny and his wife June. The stars give an object lesson in screen chemistry.

SCR Gill Dennis, James Mangold CIN Phedon Papamichael MUS *T-Bone Burnett* DES David J. Bomba
ED Michael McCusker PROD Cathy Konrad, James Keach DIST TCF

66 A big, juicy, enjoyable wide-canvas biography with a handful of indelible moments. – *Owen Gleiberman, Entertainment Weekly*

66 It all depends on how black you like it: as a psychological study of the complex Cash, Walk the Line is perfectly pat; as a celebration of the romance between Cash and Carter, it is perfectly sweet. – *Colin Kennedy, Empire*

⚊ Reese Witherspoon (leading actress)
⚊ Joaquin Phoenix (leading actor); Michael McCusker; Paul Massey, Doug Hemphill, Peter F. Kurland (sound); Arianne Phillips (costume design)

ⓣ Reese Witherspoon (leading actress); Paul Massey, Doug Hemphill, Peter F. Kurland, Donald Sylvester (sound)

ⓣ Joaquin Phoenix (leading actor); T- Bone Burnett

'In a strange and horrifying playground the innocents act out their game of life and death. . .'

Walkabout ★★★

DIR Nicolas Roeg
1970 100m Australia
DVD ♫

☆ *Jenny Agutter* (Girl), Lucien John (Boy), David Gulpilil (Aborigine), John Meillon (Father)

A man kills himself in the desert, and his teenage daughter and her young brother trek among the aborigines to safety.

Eerily effective contrast of city with aboriginal life, a director's and photographer's experimental success.

SCR Edward Bond CIN *Nicolas Roeg* MUS John Barry
DES Brian Eatwell ED Antony Gibbs, Alan Pattillo
DIST Max L. Raab/Si Litvinoff

'Everyone loves a scandal.'

The Walker (new) ★

SCR/DIR Paul Schrader
2007 108m UK/Germany/US
DVD

☆ *Woody Harrelson* (Carter Page III), Kristin Scott Thomas (Lynn Lockner), Lauren Bacall (Natalie Van Miter), Lily Tomlin (Abigail Delorean), Ned Beatty (Jack Delorean), Moritz Bleibtreu (Emek)

A middle-aged, superficial, gay man who squires gossipy, wealthy society women in Washington DC makes a rare moral decision: to shield a friend involved in a politically motivated murder.

First-rate acting and occasional bursts of sparkling dialogue cannot quite disguise the threadbare plot, and it is hard to believe in the central character's sudden redemption. There are unwelcome echoes of this director's American Gigolo.

CIN Chris Seager MUS Anne Dudley DES James Merifield ED Julian Rodd PROD Deepak Nayar
NATALIE: 'You know the Washington wisdom, Carter – never stand between your friend and a firing squad.'
CARTER: 'I am the gay weathervane!'

66 What we care most about in this daring, glitteringly intelligent murder mystery is the moral fate of its unexpected, persecuted hero. – *Philip Horne, Daily Telegraph*

66 As a portrait of a man who finds 'doors closing all over town', it does offer some pleasures; but they are

W

DVD Available on DVD ☆ Cast in order 66 Critics' Quotes ⚊ Academy Award ⓣ BAFTA
♫ Soundtrack on CD of importance † Points of interest ⚊ Academy Award nomination ⓣ BAFTA nomination

663

simply too few and far between. – *Roger Clarke, Sight & Sound*

'Eating & sleeping, fighting & joking, dating & cheating. . .'

Walking & Talking ★★

SCR/DIR *Nicole Holofcener*
1996   86m   GB/US
[DVD] ♫

☆ *Catherine Keener* (Amelia), *Anne Heche* (Laura), Todd Field (Frank), Liev Schreiber (Andrew), Kevin Corrigan (Bill), Randall Batinkoff (Peter)

A single woman living in Manhattan is panicked by news of her best friend's engagement.

Charming, witty romantic comedy making optimum use of one of the definitive mid-90s indie casts.

CIN Michael Spiller   MUS Billy Bragg   DES Anne Stuhler
ED Alisa Lepselter   PROD Ted Hope, James Schamus
DIST Electric/Zenith

66 Concentrating on the fine-tuned trivia that fuels so much television comedy, it also creates two bright, appealing heroines and watches them face life's little insults with fresh, disarming humour. – *Elvis Mitchell, The New York Times*

'Every dream has a price.'

Wall Street ★★

DIR *Oliver Stone*
1987   125m   US
[DVD] ♫

☆ Charlie Sheen (Bud Fox), *Michael Douglas* (Gordon Gekko), Martin Sheen (Carl Fox), Daryl Hannah (Darien Taylor), Terence Stamp (Sir Larry Wildman), Sean Young (Kate Gekko), Sylvia Miles (Realtor), James Spader (Roger Barnes), Hal Holbrook (Lou Mannheim), Saul Rubinek (Harold Salt)

In a Manhattan brokerage house, an ambitious young upstart finds his loyalties torn between his father, an ethical mechanic and union boss, and a charismatic corporate raider, always willing to cut corners in pursuit of wealth and power.

A very 1980s morality tale, with Sheen's Bud caught between hard-working collective decency embodied by his father and the irresistible glamour of financial wheeler-dealing. Inevitably, the devil has all the best lines, and Douglas seizes the role with relish. Guiltily, we side with Gekko, if only it means seeing more of Douglas chewing the scenery.

SCR Stanley Weiser, Oliver Stone   CIN Robert Richardson
MUS Stewart Copeland   DES Stephen Hendrickson
ED Claire Simpson   PROD Edward R. Pressman
DIST Edward R. Pressman/American Entertainment

GEKKO: 'Lunch is for wimps.'
GEKKO: 'Greed is good.'

66 As with Platoon, Stone captures the horrific essence of an environment and transfers it to us without the need for prior knowledge. Dazzling filmmaking. – *Angie Errigo, Empire*

66 Douglas plays Gekko with a terrible intensity. He raves

and rants, but he has a rascal's humour. – *Rita Kempley, Washington Post*

⚱ Michael Douglas (leading actor)

Wallace & Gromit: Curse of the Were-Rabbit ★★★

DIR *Steve Box, Nick Park*
2005   85m   GB/US
[DVD] ♫

☆ *voices of: Peter Sallis*, Ralph Fiennes, Helena Bonham Carter, Peter Kay, Nicholas Smith, Liz Smith

A hapless inventor comes up with a machine to keep rabbits off nearby allotments, only to unleash a monstrous, all-devouring mega-bunny.

Triumphant step up to full-feature level for the Aardman animation team, shot and lit with real dynamism, plotted with ingenuity and voice-cast to perfection; there are jokes and in-jokes here to satisfy tots and grown-ups alike.

SCR Nick Park, Bob Baker, Steve Box, Mike Burton
CIN *Tristan Oliver, Dave Alex Riddett*   MUS Julian Nott
DES *Phil Lewis*   ED *David McCormick, Gregory Perler*
PROD David Sproxton, Carla Shelley, Nick Park, Peter Lord, Claire Jennings   DIST UIP

66 A lovely family film packed with cheeky gags and buoyant fun, like the best-ever Bumper Holiday edition of the Beano, with the merest hint of Viz. – *Peter Bradshaw, Guardian*

66 So much modern animation is technically brilliant and yet comes off as cold and indifferent. But Wallace, Gromit and the people and creatures in their world always look warm to the touch. Someone made, and moved, all those bunnies by hand. It's impossible not to believe in them. – *Stephanie Zacharek, Salon*

⚱ animated film

🛡 British film

'Choose Your Destiny.'

Wanted (new) ★★

DIR *Timur Bekmambetov*
2008   110m   US
♫

☆ *James McAvoy* (Wesley Gibson), *Morgan Freeman* (Sloan), *Angelina Jolie* (Fox), *Terence Stamp* (Pekwarsky), Thomas Kretschmann (Cross)

A meek office worker learns he is an elite member of an ancient fraternity of super-powered assassins, pledged to carry out the unbreakable orders of Fate.

Hyper-kinetic action, brilliantly choreographed stunts and a turbo-driven visual style all contribute to an ultra-violent, spectacular thrill-ride.

SCR Michael Brandt, Derek Haas, Chris Morgan
CIN Mitchell Amundsen   MUS Danny Elfman
DES John Myhre   ED David Brenner   PROD Marc Platt, Jim Lemley, Jason Netter, Iain Smith   DIST Universal Pictures

66 Effectively hits the ground running with a steady flow of wildly inventive CGI-infused action sequences. – *Michael Rechtshaffen, The Hollywood Reporter*

[DVD] Available on DVD   ☆ Cast in order of importance   66 Critics' Quotes   ⚱ Academy Award   🛡 BAFTA
♫ Soundtrack on CD   † Points of interest   ⚱ Academy Award nomination   🛡 BAFTA nomination

'Vengeance is the ultimate weapon.'

War (new) ★

DIR Philip G Atwell

2007   103m   US/Canada

DVD   ♪

☆ Jet Li (Rogue), Jason Statham (Special Agent Jack Crawford), John Lone (Li Chang), Devon Aoki (KiraYanagawa), Luis Guzman (Benny), Saul Rubinek (Dr. Sherman)

When his partner is killed by an infamous assassin who has set off a bloody crime war between rival Asian mobs, an FBI agent starts a deadly game of cat and mouse to settle the score.

Despite its pretensions to be more than an action film, War creates few frissons and remains a routine crime drama with martial-arts pyrotechnics thrown in. Statham meets his match in Jet Li, who mercifully is not required to utter many lines.

SCR Lee Anthony Smith, Gregory J Bradley   CIN Pierre Morel   MUS Brian Tyler   DES Chris August   ED Scott Richter   PROD Steven Chasman, Christopher Petzel, Jim Thompson   DIST Lionsgate

66 Next to Li's character, Matt Damon in The Bourne Ultimatum looks like he's remaking My Dinner With Andre. – *Peter Hartlaub, San Francisco Chronicle*

'Once in a lifetime comes a motion picture that makes you feel like falling in love all over again. This is not that movie.'

The War of the Roses ★

DIR Danny DeVito

1989   116m   US

DVD

☆ Michael Douglas (Oliver Rose), Kathleen Turner (Barbara Rose), Danny DeVito (Gavin D'Amato), Marianne Sägebrecht (Susan), Sean Astin (Josh at 17), Heather Fairfield (Carolyn at 17), G. D. Spradlin (Harry Thurmont), Trenton Teigen (Josh at 10), Bethany McKinney (Carolyn at 10)

A 'perfect' couple decide to divorce and battle bitterly over who gets their luxurious house.

Spiky, cruel comedy, a satire on the acquisitive mood of the 1980s. The leads throw themselves gleefully into the pitched battle, but they overstay their welcome, as does the flimsy story.

SCR Michael Leeson   CIN Stephen H. Burum   MUS David Newman   DES Ida Random   ED Lynzee Klingman   PROD James L. Brooks, Arnon Milchan   DIST Fox/Gracie Films

66 Wildly funny and deeply disturbing, The War of the Roses never hesitates to go for the jugular and succeeds more often than not in its valiant attempts to draw blood. – *Robyn Karney, Empire*

Ⓣ Michael Leeson (adapted screenplay)

'They're already here.'

War of the Worlds ★

DIR Stephen Spielberg

2005   116m   US

DVD   ♪

☆ Tom Cruise (Ray Ferrier), Dakota Fanning (Rachel Ferrier), Miranda Otto (Mary Ann), Justin Chatwin (Robbie Ferrier), Tim Robbins (Ogilvy), Rick Gonzalez (Vincent), Yul Vazquez (Julio), Morgan Freeman (Narrator)

A single father attempts to protect his children after Earth is invaded by alien life forms in giant, human-killing machines.

For all its vast spectacle and post-9/11 imagery – tumbling buildings, cities in dust – this mechanical exercise feels like Spielberg reductio ad absurdum: flashes of light and noise, intermittently muffled by large dollops of marshmallow. Given the lack of significant human interest – and casting Cruise as a blue-collar everyman really doesn't wash – you could be forgiven for starting to cheer for the aliens.

SCR Josh Friedman, David Koepp   CIN Janusz Kaminski   MUS John Williams   DES Rick Carter   ED Michael Kahn   PROD Kathleen Kennedy, Colin Wilson   DIST Paramount/Dreamworks

66 It is, simply, the alien-invasion movie to beat all alien-invasion movies: meticulously detailed and expertly paced and photographed, with sights so spectacular and terrible that viewers will have to consciously remind themselves to close their mouths when their jaws drop open. – *Mick LaSalle, San Francisco Chronicle*

66 A voracious big-budget action-spectacular with a pleasingly ravenous bite. – *Mark Kermode, Observer*

♙ Dennis Muren, Pablo Helman, Randy Dutra, Daniel Sudick (visual effects); Andy Nelson, Anna Behlmer, Ron Judkins (sound); Richard King (sound editing)

Warm Water under the Red Bridge ★

DIR Shohei Imamura

2001   120m   Japan/France

DVD

☆ Koji Yakusho (Yosuke Sasano), Misa Shimizu (Saeko Aizawa), Mitsuko Baisho (Mitsu Aizawa), Mansaku Fuwa (Gen), Kazuo Kitamura (Taro), Isao Natsuyagi (Masayuki Uomi), Yukiya Kitamara (Shintaro Uomi), Hijiri Kojima (Mika Tagami)

An erotic comedy about a young woman who expels torrents of water when she approaches a sexual climax.

Curious, engaging and ravishingly handsome film that's far more accessible and charming than any brief synopsis could suggess.

SCR Motofumi Tomikawa, Daisuke Tengan, Shohei Imamura   CIN Shigeru Komatsubara   MUS Shinichiro Ikebe   DES Hisao Inagaki   ED Hajime Okayasu   PROD Hisa Iino   DIST Metro Tartan

66 Seeing it as a Westerner is an enlightening, even liberating, experience. – *Roger Ebert, Chicago Sun-Times*

The Warrior ★

DIR Asif Kapadia

2001   86m   GB/France/Germany

DVD

☆ Irfan Khan (Lafcadia), Puru Chhibber (Katiba, His Son), Mandakini Goswami (Shawl Seller), Sunita Sharma (The Girl), Noor Mani (Riaz the Thief), Damayanti Marfatia

DVD Available on DVD   ☆ Cast in order of importance   66 Critics' Quotes   ♙ Academy Award   ♙ Academy Award nomination   Ⓑ BAFTA   Ⓣ BAFTA nomination

♪ Soundtrack on CD

665

(Blind Woman), Aino Annuddin (Biswas), Anupam Shyam (The Lord)

A warrior develops a conscience and decides to stop killing, but is hunted down by his ruthless masters.

This handsome Western-style story set in ancient India has a raw, brutal appeal, though its characters are archetypes with barely a hint of nuance.

SCR Asif Kapadia, Tim Miller   CIN *Roman Osin*
MUS Dario Marianelli   DES Adrian Smith   ED Ewa J. Lind   PROD Bertrand Faivre   DIST FilmFour

66 With its stark narrative simplicity, its timeless setting and cipher characters, the epic mode may not produce psychological complexity, but it does score in terms of scale, sweep and sheer panache. – *Time Out*

🅣 British film; Asif Kapadia (most promising newcomer)
🅣 film not in the English language

'Every big secret starts small.'

The Water Horse: Legend of the Deep (new)

DIR Jay Russell
2007   111m   US/UK
[DVD]   ♫

☆ Emily Watson (Anne MacMorrow), Alex Etel (Angus MacMorrow), Ben Chaplin (Lewis Mowbray), David Morrissey (Capt. Hamilton), Brian Cox (Old Angus), Priyanka Xi (Kirstie MacMorrow)

In Scotland during World War Two, a young boy finds an egg that hatches the Loch Ness Monster.

Old-fashioned fantasy with cutting-edge effects; the mix is an appealing one, though there's not much plot to speak of.

SCR Robert Nelson Jacobs   CIN Oliver Stapleton
MUS James Newton Howard   DES Tony Burrough
ED Mark Warner   PROD Robert Bernstein, Douglas Rae, Barrie M. Osborne, Charlie Lyons   DIST Columbia Pictures

66 Family-friendly escapist fare. – *Laura Kern, New York Times*

66 The film looks and feels like one of those nice British movies from the Fifties. – *Derek Malcolm, Evening Standard*

Water Lilies (new)

SCR/DIR Celine Sciamma
2007   83m   France
[DVD]   ♫

☆ Pauline Acquart (Marie), Adele Haenel (Floriane), Louise Blachere (Anne), Warren Jacquin (Francois), Barbara Renard (Natacha)

In a suburb of Paris, a teenaged girl develops a crush on a member of her school's synchronised swimming team.

Well-observed, sympathetic portrait of adolescent angst, self-doubt and nascent sexuality.

CIN Crystel Fournier   MUS Para One   DES Gwendal Bescond   ED Julien Lacheray   PROD Jerome Dopffer, Benedicte Couvreur   DIST Slingshot

66 Successfully illustrates the anxiety, worry and cruelty experienced on the road to adulthood. – *Richard James Havis, Hollywood Reporter*

66 A nice, attractive, watchable, minor work. What it lacks is a sense of purpose, a commitment not just to its characters but also to its own reason for being. – *Manohla Dargis, New York Times*

† The film's French title means Birth of Octopuses.

'Imagine being trapped inside your own body. Imagine being set free.'

The Waterdance   ★★

DIR Neal Jimenez, Michael Steinberg
1991   106m   US
[DVD]

☆ Eric Stoltz (Joel Garcia), Wesley Snipes (Raymond Hill), William Forsythe (Bloss), Helen Hunt (Anna), Elizabeth Pena (Rosa), William Allen Young (Les), Henry Harris (Mr. Gibson), Tony Genaro (Victor), Eva Rodriguez (Victor's Wife), Grace Zabriskie (Pat)

Three permanently paralysed men in a rehabilitation centre struggle to cope with their conditions.

Engaging drama deals unsentimentally with a difficult subject, never shying from dark, savage humour to underline its points.

SCR Neal Jimenez   CIN Mark Plummer   MUS Michael Convertino   DES Robert Ziembicki   ED Jeff Freeman   PROD Gale Anne Hurd, Marie Cantin   DIST Samuel Goldwyn/No Frills

66 The film's strength lies in the relationships among the three men, who help one another navigate the treacherous waters outside. Fear makes their humour as explosive as their anger. – *Peter Travers, Rolling Stone*

66 The streak of autobiographical earnestness is the movie's most memorable trait. – *Hal Hinson, Washington Post*

† Writer-director Neal Jimenez was himself paralysed in an accident in 1984.

'Beyond The Horizon Lies A Secret To A New Beginning.'

Waterworld

DIR Kevin Reynolds
1995   136m   US
[DVD]   ♫

☆ Kevin Costner (Mariner), Dennis Hopper (Deacon), Jeanne Tripplehorn (Helen), Tina Majorino (Enola), Michael Jeter (Old Gregor), Gerard Murphy (Nord), Zakes Mokae (Priam)

After the melting of the polar ice caps, a mutant human sails the globe in search of land, accompanied by a woman and her young daughter.

Misbegotten mega-budget action movie, overlong and dramatically uninvolving; the Dennis Hopper own-brand of villainy is quite fun, but everybody else is badly at sea here.

SCR Peter Rader, David Twohy   CIN Dean Semler, Scott Fuller   MUS James Newton Howard   DES Dennis Gassner, Artie Kane   ED Peter Boyle   PROD Charles Gordon, John Davis, Kevin Costner, Lawrence Gordon   DIST UIP/Universal

[DVD] Available on DVD   ☆ Cast in order   66 Critics' Quotes   🏆 Academy Award   🅑 BAFTA
♫ Soundtrack on CD   of importance   † Points of interest   🏆 Academy Award nomination   🅣 BAFTA nomination

66 If the story seems a little waterlogged, it's still big, loud and fun to watch. – *Desson Thomson, Washington Post*

66 A not-bad futuristic actioner with three or four astounding sequences, an unusual hero, a nifty villain and less mythic and romantic resonance than might be desired. – *Todd McCarthy, Variety*

† The film was, at the time, the most expensive made in Hollywood, with a reported cost of $175m.

⌁ Steve Maslow, Gregg Landaker, Keith A. Webster (sound)

Ⓣ Michael J. McAlister, Brad Kuehn, Robert Spurlock Martin Bresin (special effects)

'In the real world there are no happy endings.'

A Way of Life   ★

SCR/DIR Amma Asante

2004   91m   GB

DVD

☆ *Stephanie James* (Leigh-Anne), Nathan Jones (Gavin), Gary Sheppeard (Robbie), Dean Wong (Stephen), Sara Gregory (Julie), Oliver Haden (Hassan Osman), Brenda Blethyn (Annette)

When the council threatens to take her baby into care, a single mother in South Wales instigates a hate campaign against the Turkish man across the street.

Forcefully grim drama finding the seeds of racism in poverty and unemployment. Though unflinchingly observed, it has the slight feel of a government information broadcast.

CIN Ian Wilson   MUS David Gray   DES Hayden Pearce ED Steve Singleton, Clare Douglas   PROD Charlie Hanson, Patrick Cassavetti, Peter Edwards   DIST Verve

66 As a first film this is bleak but brilliant stuff. Asante is definitely one to watch. – *Anna Smith, Empire*

Ⓣ Amma Asante
Ⓣ David Gray

The Way of the Gun   ★

SCR/DIR Christopher McQuarrie

2000   119m   US

DVD   ♫

☆ Ryan Phillippe (Parker), Benicio Del Toro (Longbaugh), James Caan (Joe Sarno), Juliette Lewis (Robin), Taye Diggs (Jeffers), Nicky Katt (Obecks), Dylan Kussman (Dr Allen Painter), Scott Wilson (Hale Chidduck), Kristin Lehman (Francesca Chidduck), Geoffrey Lewis (Abner)

Two small-time villains kidnap a pregnant woman and discover she is carrying a child for a powerful and ruthless gangster.

Disappointing follow-up from the writer of The Usual Suspects; its plotting is equally complex, but needlessly so.

CIN Dick Pope   MUS Joe Kraemer   DES Maia Javan ED Stephen Semel   PROD Kenneth Kokin DIST Momentum

66 The much-signposted childbirth finale goes seriously off the rails and Ryan Phillippe's badass credentials never really persuade. – *Time Out*

Way Out West   ⌁   ★★★★

DIR James Horne

1937   66m   US

DVD

☆ *Stan Laurel* (Himself), *Oliver Hardy* (Himself), *James Finlayson* (Mickey Finn), *Sharon Lynne* (Lola Marcel), Rosina Lawrence (Mary Roberts)

Laurel and Hardy come to Brushwood Gulch to deliver the deed to a gold mine.

Perfect joy, with the comedians at their very best in brilliantly-timed routines, plus two songs as a bonus.

SCR *Jack Jevne, Charles Rogers, James Parrott, Felix Adler* CIN *Art Lloyd, Walter Lundin*   MUS Marvin Hatley ED Bert Jordan   PROD Stan Laurel   DIST Hal Roach

66 The film is leisurely in the best sense; you adjust to a different rhythm and come out feeling relaxed as if you'd had a vacation. – *New Yorker, 1980*

66 Not only one of their most perfect films, it ranks with the best screen comedy anywhere. – *David Robinson, 1962*

⌁ Marvin Hatley (music)

The Way to the Stars   ★★★

DIR Anthony Asquith

1945   109m   GB

DVD

☆ *John Mills* (Peter Penrose), *Rosamund John* (Miss Toddy Todd), *Michael Redgrave* (David Archdale), *Douglass Montgomery* (Johnny Hollis), Basil Radford (Tiny Williams), Stanley Holloway (Palmer), Joyce Carey (Miss Winterton), Renée Asherson (Iris Winterton), Felix Aylmer (Rev. Charles Moss), Bonar Colleano (Joe Friselli), Trevor Howard (Squadron Leader Carter), Jean Simmons (Singer)

An account of the lives of members of an RAF squadron in World War II, and the flamboyant US pilots who are dispatched to the same aerodrome.

Generally delightful comedy-drama suffused with tragic atmosphere but with very few flying shots; one of the few films which instantly brought back the atmosphere of the war in Britain for anyone who was involved.

SCR *Terence Rattigan, Anatole de Grunwald*   CIN Derick Williams   MUS *Nicholas Brodszky*   ED Fergus McDonell PROD Anatole de Grunwald   DIST Two Cities

66 Not for a long time have I seen a film so satisfying, so memorable, or so successful in evoking the precise mood and atmosphere of the recent past. – *Richard Mallett, Punch*

66 Humour, humanity, and not a sign of mawkishness . . . a classic opening sequence, with the camera wandering through an abandoned air base, peering in at each detail in the nissen huts, the sleeping quarters, the canteens, noting all the time a procession of objects each of which will have its own special significance in the action of the film. – *Basil Wright, 1972*

'You'll laugh. You'll cry. You'll hurl.'

Wayne's World   ★★

DIR Penelope Spheeris

1992   95m   US

DVD   ♫

☆ Mike Myers (Wayne Campbell), Dana Carvey (Garth

W

Algar), Rob Lowe (Benjamin Kane), Tia Carrere (Cassandra), Brian Doyle-Murray (Noah Vanderhoff), Lara Flynn Boyle (Stacy), Michael DeLuise (Alan), Dan Bell (Neil)

A cable-access show presented by two friends is bought up by a sleazy executive with ulterior motives.

Character-based comedy, coasting by on an affectionate, inclusive humour that was to prove immensely popular amongst young audiences; it is narratively threadbare but directed and performed with compensatory enthusiasm. Of all the films derived from Saturday Night Live sketches, this is the one with the most memorable lines and moments.

SCR Mike Myers, Bonnie Turner, Terry Turner   CIN Theo Van de Sande   MUS J. Peter Robinson   DES Gregg Fonseca   ED Malcolm Campbell   PROD Lorne Michaels   DIST UIP/Paramount

WAYNE: No way!
GARTH: Way!
GARTH: I'm having a good time . . . not!

66 Isn't much more than an amiable goof, yet it's carried along by the flaked-out exuberance of its two stars. – *Owen Gleiberman, Entertainment Weekly*

† A sequel, in which the characters attempt to stage their own rock festival, followed in 1994.

Waz (new)

DIR Tom Shankland
2008   92m
☆ Stellan Skarsgård (Eddie Argo), Melissa George (Helen Westcott), Ashley Walters (Daniel), Tom Hardy (Pierre Jackson), Selma Blair (Jean Lerner)

A bereaved woman, forced by a gang of rapists to shoot her own mother, avenges herself on the gang's loved ones.

Grungy serial killer saga, efficiently directed and interestingly photographed, but a little too close to torture-porn for most tastes.

SCR Clive Bradley   CIN Morten Soborg   MUS David Julyan   DES Ashleigh Jeffers   ED Tim Murrell   PROD Allan Niblo, James Richardson

† Though set in New York, the film was partly shot in Northern Ireland.

'The musical journey of a lifetime.'

We Are Together (new)   ★

DIR Paul Taylor
2007   86m   UK/US
DVD   ♫

A group of musical children at a South African orphanage, many of whose parents died of Aids, plan to make a CD and perform in London to raise money. Though the plan backfires, they end up singing in New York.

A touching, inspirational account of children dealt a harsh hand by life, and their communal struggles against adversity.

SCR Paul Taylor, Slindile Moya   CIN Paul Taylor   MUS Dario Marianelli   ED Masahiro Hirakubo, Ollie

Huddleston   PROD Teddy Leifer, Paul Taylor
DIST EMI/Shooting People

'Ordinary lives. Extraordinary emotions.'

We Don't Live Here Anymore   ★★

DIR John Curran
2004   101m   US/Canada
DVD

☆ Mark Ruffalo (Jack Linden), *Laura Dern* (Terry Linden), Peter Krause (Hank Evans), Naomi Watts (Edith Evans), Sam Charles (Sean Linden), Haili Page (Natasha Linden), Jennifer Bishop (Sharon Evans)

In a New England college town, two academics and their wives swap sexual partners.

A chamber piece of agonising intensity, showing the unhappiness that betrayal and infidelity can bring. It has some dark humour, but the overall mood is brooding and brackish. The acting is top-notch, though Linney, as an alcoholic, is the standout.

SCR Larry Gross   CIN Maryse Alberti   MUS Michael Convertino   DES Tony Devenyi   ED Alexandre de Franceschi   PROD Harvey Kahn, Naomi Watts, Jonas Goodman   DIST Redbus

66 If you're looking for a film to put you off marriage, children, affairs, and indeed life itself, look no further than this melancholic ensemble piece. – *Anna Smith, Empire*

66 All four performances are strong and nuanced, which makes the film oddly compelling. At the same time, all four characters are hard to like, difficult to care about. They're like car-crash victims in a demolition derby of narcissism and lies. – *Steven Rea, Philadelphia Inquirer*

'Two brothers on opposite sides of the law. Beyond their differences lies loyalty.'

We Own The Night (new)   ★

SCR/DIR James Gray
2007   117m   US
DVD   ♫

☆ Joaquin Phoenix (Bobby Green), Mark Wahlberg (Joseph Grusinsky), Eva Mendes (Amanda Juarez), Robert Duvall (Burt Grusinsky)

A Polish-American police chief and his son, an NYPD captain, are trying to keep a gang of Russian criminals out of Manhattan. But the chief's other son runs a disco that caters for these shady types.

Gray's third feature is again set in the Brighton Beach neighbourhood of New York, and while he can conjure up a strong sense of location, he rarely creates nuanced characters who can do more than drive a plot forward. The film's air of gloom suggests a self-importance it never merits. One strikingly shot car chase lifts the spirits, but only briefly.

CIN Joaquin Baca-Asay   MUS Wojciech Kilar   DES Ford Wheeler   ED John Axelrad   PROD Nick Wechsler, Marc Butan, Mark Wahlberg, Joaquin Phoenix   DIST Universal

66 A little cumbersome, with plenty of macho-sentimentalism, and the ending is frankly contrived. – *Peter Bradshaw, Guardian*

66 The film has considerable weight but little depth. – *Philip French, Observer*

W

'Everyone Wants To Kiss The Bride. . .Except The Groom.'

The Wedding Banquet ★★★

DIR Ang Lee

1993   106m   Taiwan/US

DVD   ♫

☆ Mitchell Lichtenstein (Simon), Winston Chao (Wai Tung), May Chin (Wei-Wei), Sihung Lung (Mr. Gao), Ah-Lei Gua (Mrs. Gao), Dion Birney (Andrew), Jeanne Kuo Chang (Wai Tung's Secretary)

A gay estate agent in New York struggles to hide his sexuality and his boyfriend when his mother and father arrive to celebrate his arranged marriage to a Chinese woman.

Lightweight, undemanding comedy of modern manners and culture clashes that now seems familiar, but retains immense charm and poignancy.

SCR Ang Lee, Neil Peng, James Schamus   CIN Jong Lin
MUS Mader   DES Steve Rosenzweig   ED Tim Squyres
PROD Ang Lee, Ted Hope, James Schamus
DIST Mainline/Central Motion Picture/Good Machine

❝ The Wedding Banquet is being presented as a zany comedy, complete with promotional fortune cookie giveaways in theater lobbies. But it's really a sweet, perceptive story about the cost of deception and the power of family rituals. – *Megan Rosenfeld, Washington Post*

⚱ foreign-language film

'He's gonna party like it's 1985.'

The Wedding Singer ★

DIR Frank Coraci

1998   95m   US

DVD   ♫

☆ Adam Sandler (Robbie), Drew Barrymore (Julia), Christine Taylor (Holly), Allen Covert (Sammy), Matthew Glave (Glenn), Ellen Albertini Dow (Rosie), Angela Featherstone (Linda), Alexis Arquette (George), Christina Pickles (Angie), Jon Lovitz (uncredited) (Jimmie Moore), Steve Buscemi (uncredited) (David 'Dave' Veltri)

A New Jersey singer is jilted at the altar but finds true love with a waitress planning to marry another man.

This romantic comedy is set in the mid 1980s, but most of the jokes are much older. Yet it's Sandler's finest comic performance in movies to date; his shuffling, romantic loser is surprisingly delightful.

SCR Tim Herlihy   CIN Tim Suhrstedt   MUS Teddy Castellucci   DES Perry Andelin Blake   ED Tom Lewis
PROD Robert Simonds, Jack Giarraputo
DIST Entertainment/New Line

❝ Finally, an Adam Sandler comedy that you can sit through without wanting to throw a mallet through the screen. – *Liam Lacey, Toronto Globe and Mail*

'Five guys. One safe. No brains.'

Welcome to Collinwood ★

SCR/DIR Joe Russo, Anthony Russo

2002   86m   US/Germany

DVD   ♫

☆ Sam Rockwell (Pero), William H. Macy (Riley), Isaiah Washington (Leon), Michael Jeter (Toto), George Clooney

(Jerzy), Luis Guzman (Cisimo), Patricia Clarkson (Rosalind)

A crooked gang's plans to rob a pawnbroker's shop go awry when one of their number falls for the girl across the way.

Sporadically amusing comedy that assumes the form of an indie pantomime before petering out into insubstantiality; given the talent involved, a likely reaction will be 'Is that it?'

CIN Lisa Rinzler, Charles Minsky   MUS Mark Mothersbaugh   DES Tom Meyer   ED Amy Duddleston
PROD Steven Soderbergh, George Clooney   DIST Warner

❝ It takes us about half the film to adjust to its quirkiness, and we leave the theatre with both laughter cramps and the feeling that it should have been funnier a lot longer. – *Jack Mathews, New York Daily News*

† The original film, Big Deal on Madonna Street, (1958), itself partly a spoof of the robbery classic Rififi (1955), was first remade by Louis Malle as Crackers (1984).

'For this celebrated, outrageous, adrenaline-loving bunch of reporters, home is the latest war zone. Now, one of them is about to do the unthinkable – get emotionally involved.'

Welcome to Sarajevo ★

DIR Michael Winterbottom

1997   103m   GB/US

DVD   ♫

☆ *Stephen Dillane* (Michael Henderson), Woody Harrelson (Flynn), Marisa Tomei (Nina), Emira Nusevic (Emira), Kerry Fox (Jane Carson), *Goran Visnjic* (Risto Bavic), James Nesbitt (Gregg), Emily Lloyd (Annie McGee), Juliet Aubrey (Helen Henderson)

A British news reporter in war-torn Yugoslavia to report upon the siege of Sarajevo helps smuggle an orphaned Bosnian girl out of the country.

Principled if patchy drama, more compelling as a study of journalists under fire than when it goes looking for human interest stories of its own. Yet the thought also occurs that a TV reporter's plight pales beside the ordeals of the locals.

SCR Frank Cottrell Boyce   CIN Daf Hobson
MUS Adrian Johnston   DES Mark Geraghty   ED Trevor Waite   PROD Graham Broadbent, Damian Jones
DIST Film Four/Channel 4/Miramax

❝ Winterbottom has never before done such potent work; he's created a fiction film about the siege of Sarajevo that bristles with the raw, unnerving textures of a battlefield documentary. – *Michael Sragow, Dallas Observer*

❝ Startling and repellent – a challenge to filmgoers accustomed to fake gunfire, fake wounds and cosmeticised death. – *Edward Guthmann, San Francisco Chronicle*

'Not all girls want to play with dolls.'

Welcome to the Dollhouse ★

SCR/DIR Todd Solondz

1995   88m   US

DVD   ♫

☆ Heather Matarazzo (Dawn Wiener), Victoria Davis (Lolita), Christina Brucato (Cookie), Christina Vidal (Cynthia), Siri Howard (Chrissy), Brendan Sexton Jnr

W

DVD Available on DVD   ☆ Cast in order of importance   ❝ Critics' Quotes   ⚱ Academy Award   Ⓦ BAFTA
♫ Soundtrack on CD   † Points of interest   ⚱ Academy Award nomination   Ⓦ BAFTA nomination

669

(Brandon McCarthy), Daria Kalinina (Missy Wiener), Matthew Faber (Mark Wiener)

An unprepossessing pre-teen has her life made hell by bullies both at school and closer to home.

Bleakly funny fable, though its unwavering tone of irony begins to pall towards the end.

CIN Randy Drummond   **MUS** Jill Wisoff   **DES** Susan Block   **ED** Alan Oxman   **PROD** Todd Solondz   **DIST** Artificial Eye/Suburban

66 Admirably unsentimental exploration of the bewildering, cruel nightmare that is early adolescence: astutely perceptive, darkly comic and often profoundly and provocatively unsettling. – *Geoff Andrew, Time Out*

66 The subject is powerful, but the film-making often seems slapdash, and the final half-hour dithers. – *Jonathan Rosenbaum, Chicago Reader*

Welcome to the Land of the Ch'tis (new)   ★

SCR/DIR Danny Boon
2008   106m   France

☆ Dany Boon (Antoine Bailleul), Kad Merad (Philippe Abrams), Zoe Felix (Julie Abrams), Anne Marivin (Annabelle Deconnick), Philippe Dusquene (Fabrice Canoli)

A postal executive is relocated to a bleak Northern French province against his wishes. But in time he comes to like their strange ways and vernacular.

Hugely popular in France, but the unfathomable culture clashes and local references simply refuse to travel.

SCR Franck Magnier, Alexandre Charlot   **CIN** Pierre Aim   **MUS** Philippe Rombi   **DES** Alain Veyssier   **ED** Luc Barnier   **PROD** Claude Berri, Jerome Seydoux   **DIST** Pathe

66 It makes fun of regional prejudices yet still gets comic mileage out of rube characters and a nearly impenetrable dialect. – *Kirk Honeycutt, The Hollywood Reporter*

Went the Day Well?   ★★★

DIR Alberto Cavalcanti
1942   92m   GB

☆ Leslie Banks, Elizabeth Allan, Frank Lawton, Basil Sydney, Valerie Taylor, Mervyn Johns, Edward Rigby, Marie Lohr, C. V. France, David Farrar

Villagers resist when German paratroopers invade an English village and the squire proves to be a collaborator.

Intriguing could-it-happen melodrama which made excellent wartime propaganda, but has been the subject of increased critical interest recently. Smartly executed with a foreigner's eye by its Brazilian-born director, it shows the British as they wanted to be shown – peaceable but staunch and stubborn.

SCR Angus MacPhail, John Dighton, Diana Morgan   **CIN** Wilkie Cooper   **MUS** William Walton   **PROD** S. C. Balcon   **DIST** Ealing

66 At last, it seems, we are learning to make films with our own native material. – *Sunday Times*

66 It has the sinister, freezing beauty of an Auden prophecy come true. – *James Agee*

Werckmeister Harmonies   ★★

DIR Bela Tarr
2000   145m
Hungary/Germany/France/Switzerland/Italy
[DVD]

☆ Lars Rudolph (Janos Valuska), Peter Fitz (Gyorgy Eszter), Hanna Schygulla (Tunde Eszter), Janos Derzi (Man In the Broadcloth Coat), Djoko Rossich (Man in the Western Boots)

In a small, cold town on a Hungarian plain, a circus comes to town. Its main attraction is the carcass of a whale, which, when revealed, causes violent scenes and anarchy.

A rigorous, nightmarish, film from the austere end of the art-house spectrum. It moves slowly in lengthy takes, makes do with sparse dialogue and yields up its possible meanings gradually, if at all. It seems to be a parable about some coming dread, or at least the replacement of some fatigued established order by new energies, long repressed. Is it a metaphor for the cataclysmic shifts of power in Europe? Or a representation of a nihilistic, defeatist philosophy? Either way, it is hugely challenging, sometimes arduous, but surprisingly rewarding.

SCR Laszlo Krasznahorkai, Bela Tarr   **CIN** Gabor Medvigy, Rob Tregenza, Emil Novák, Erwin Lanzensberger, Miklós Gurbán, Patrick de Ranter   **MUS** Mihaly Vig   **ED** Agnes Hranitzky   **PROD** Miklos Szita, Franz Goess, Paul Saadoun, Joachim von Vietinghoff

66 Mysterious, poetic and allusive, The Werckmeister Harmonies beckons filmgoers who complain of the vapidity of Hollywood movie making and yearn for a film to ponder and debate. – *Lawrence Van Gelder, New York Times*

66 A stunning feature – another hypnotic meditation on popular demagogy and mental manipulation. – *Derek Elley, Variety*

West Beirut   ★★

SCR/DIR Ziad Doueiri
1998   105m   France/Lebanon/Belgium/Norway
[DVD]

☆ Rami Doueiri (Tarek), Mohamad Chamas (Omar), Rola Al Amin (May), Carmen Lebbos (Hala Noueiri), Joseph Bou Nassar (Riad Noueiri), Liliane Nemry (Neighbour), Leila Karam (Oum Walid), Hassan Frahat (Roadblock Militiaman)

The Lebanon, early 1975: two pop-loving teenagers have their friendship tested by a renewed outbreak of fighting.

Highly accessible political coming-of-age tale that necessarily simplifies to present the Arab–Israeli conflict in terms its young protagonists would understand, but evokes its particular time and place most persuasively.

CIN Ricardo Jacques Gale   **MUS** Stewart Copeland   **DES** Hamzé Nasrallah   **ED** Dominique Marcombe   **PROD** Rachid Bouchareb, Jean Brehat   **DIST** Metrodome

66 A funny, artful picture about family life and growing up in a disturbed yet oddly liberating place. – *Philip French, Observer*

66 Succeeds by offering up sturdy performances, attention to detail, humour, drama and a refusal to sermonise and take sides. It marks Doueiri as a talent to watch. – *Geoff Andrew, Time Out*

West Side Story ★★★★

DIR *Robert Wise, Jerome Robbins*
1961   155m   US
DVD ♫

☆ *Natalie Wood (sung by Marni Nixon)* (Maria), Richard Beymer (sung by Jimmy Bryant) (Tony), Russ Tamblyn (Riff), *Rita Moreno (sung by Betty Wand)* (Anita), *George Chakiris* (Bernardo), Simon Oakland (Lt Schrank), Bill Bramley (Officer Krupke), Tucker Smith (Ice), Tony Mordente, Tony Winters, Eliot Feld

The Romeo and Juliet story in a New York dockland setting.

The essentially theatrical conception of this entertainment is nullified by determinedly realistic settings, but its production values are fine, the dancing electrifying and the songs almost without exception sensational.

SCR *Ernest Lehman*   CIN *Daniel L. Fapp*   DES *Boris Leven*   ED *Thomas Stanford*   PROD UA Mirisch/Seven Arts Robert Wise

66 The opening finger-snapping sequence is one of the best uses of dance in movie history. – *Roger Ebert, Chicago Sun-Times*

66 Nothing short of a film masterpiece. – *Bosley Crowther, New York Times*

⚱ picture; Robert Wise, Jerome Robbins; Daniel L. Fapp; Rita Moreno (supporting actress); George Chakiris (supporting actor); Thomas Stanford (editing); Irene Sharaff (costume design); Saul Chaplin, Johnny Green, Sid Ramin, Irwin Kostal (musical direction); art direction; sound

⚱ Ernest Lehman (adapted screenplay)

'One young girl dared to confront the past, change the present and determine the future.'

Whale Rider ★★★

SCR/DIR *Niki Caro*
2002   101m   New Zealand/Germany
DVD ♫

☆ *Keisha Castle-Hughes* (Paikea), *Rawiri Paratene* (Koro), Vicky Haughton (Nanny Flowers), Cliff Curtis (Porourangi), Grant Roa (Uncle Rawiri)

A young Maori girl tries to prove herself to her grandfather, who insists that a male should replace him as community leader.

An enchanting film, alert to the workings of the human heart and the mysteries of the deep blue sea, with the clarity and resonance of a timeless campfire legend; beautifully shot against a backdrop of serene coastal locations, it features a tremendously expressive central performance.

CIN *Leon Narbey*   MUS *Lisa Gerrard*   DES Grant Major   ED David Coulson   PROD John Barnett, Tim Sanders, Frank Hubner   DIST Icon

66 Caro roots her characters in a landscape equal parts mundane and boundless, incorporates tantalising sea photography and Lisa Gerrard's ambient soundtrack, and lifts off into a sublime, Elysian ending. – *Nick Bradshaw, Time Out*

⚱ Keisha Castle-Hughes (leading actress)

The Whales of August ★

DIR *Lindsay Anderson*
1987   90m   US
DVD

☆ *Bette Davis* (Libby Strong), *Lillian Gish* (Sarah Webber), Vincent Price (Mr. Maranov), Ann Sothern (Tisha Doughty), Harry Carey Jnr (Joshua Brackett), Mary Steenburgen (Young Sarah), Tisha Sterling (Young Tisha)

Two elderly sisters recall their summers on the Maine coast and look back over their lives.

Two veteran actors strut their stuff in curmudgeonly fashion, their immense screen presence still palpable. Anderson directs this two-hander tactfully, letting the stars do what stars do.

SCR David Berry   CIN Mike Fash   MUS Alan Price   DES Joselyn Herbert   ED Nicolas Gaster   PROD Carolyn Pfeiffer, Mike Kaplan   DIST Circle/Nelson

66 A dignified, if frail, wave goodbye. – *Channel 4*

† Gish was 91 when she made this film, the last before her death in 1993.

⚱ Ann Sothern (supporting actress)

'Bob's a special kind of friend. The kind that drives you crazy!'

What about Bob? ★★

DIR *Frank Oz*
1991   99m   US
DVD

☆ *Bill Murray* (Bob 'Bobby' Wiley), Richard Dreyfuss (Dr. Leo Marvin), Julie Hagerty (Fay Marvin), Charlie Korsmo (Sigmund 'Siggy' Marvin), Kathryn Erbe (Anna Marvin), Tom Aldredge (Mr. Guttman), Susan Willis (Mrs. Guttman)

A manipulative obsessive-compulsive patient tracks down his psychiatrist, who is on holiday with his family.

Murray is close to the top of his form here, and let loose to play havoc with Dreyfuss's control-freak tendencies. A dark, sceptical view of the therapy business makes for some bracingly nasty, but smart humour.

SCR Tom Schulman   CIN Michael Ballhaus   MUS Miles Goodman   DES Les Dilley   ED Anne V. Coates   PROD Laura Ziskin   DIST Warner/Touchstone/Touchwood Pacific Partners I

66 Rests entirely on Murray's shoulders. But he more than takes the weight. – *Desson Howe, Washington Post*

66 What makes the film work is the double act between the two actors, and some great one-liners that pepper the script and cover up the fact there isn't a great deal of originality in the plot. – *Jo Berry, Empire*

W

DVD Available on DVD   ☆ Cast in order of importance   66 Critics' Quotes   ⚱ Academy Award   Ⓑ BAFTA
♫ Soundtrack on CD   † Points of interest   ⚱ Academy Award nomination   Ⓑ BAFTA nomination

'Get lucky.'

What Happens in Vegas (new)

DIR Tom Vaughan

2008 98m US

☆ Cameron Diaz (Joy McNally), Ashton Kutcher (Jack Fuller), Rob Corddry (Stever 'Hater' Hader), Lake Bell (Tipper), Treat Williams (Jack Fuller Snr.), Dennis Farina (Banger), Queen Latifah (Dr. Twitchell), Dennis Miller (Judge Whopper)

Two strangers who drunkenly wed in Las Vegas are forced to cohabit after one wins $3m with the other's money.

Obnoxious romantic comedy with a pair of unappealing leads; they may well deserve each other, but we certainly don't deserve them.

SCR Dana Dox **CIN** Matthew F. Leonetti **MUS** Christophe Beck **DES** Stuart Wurtzel **ED** Matthew Friedman **PROD** Michael Aguilar, Shawn Levy, Jimmy Miller **DIST** TCF

66 This two-seated star vehicle wrings a respectable number of laughs from a formulaic scenario. – *Joe Leydon, Variety*

66 Gives vulgarity a bad name. – *Philip French, Observer*

What Have I Done to Deserve This? ★

SCR/DIR Pedro Almodóvar

1984 101m Spain

DVD

☆ Carmen Maura (Gloria), Luis Hostalot (Polo), Angel de Andres-Lopez (Antonio), Gonzalo Suarez (Lucas Villalba), Veronica Forque (Cristal), Juan Martinez (Toni), Miguel Angel Harranz (Miguel)

In Madrid, an unhappy mother and cleaning woman, who takes drugs just to keep awake, becomes increasingly depressed by the chaotic antics of her wayward family.

Another darkly farcical piece from Almodóvar's early period; he throws in more outrageous sub-plots than the film can bear, though one sees Maura's nascent star presence even in such flimsy material as this.

CIN Angel Luis Fernandez **MUS** Bernardo Bonezzi **DES** Pin Morales, Román Arango **ED** Jose Solcedo **PROD** Tadeo Villabla **DIST** Metro/Tesauro/Kaktus

'Sister, sister, oh so fair, why is there blood all over your hair?'

Whatever Happened to Baby Jane? ★★

DIR Robert Aldrich

1962 132m US

DVD

☆ *Bette Davis* (Baby Jane), *Joan Crawford* (Blanche), *Victor Buono*, Anna Lee

In middle age, a demented ex-child star lives in an old Hollywood mansion with her invalid sister, and tension leads to murder.

Famous for marking the first time Hollywood's ageing first ladies turned to horror. This melodrama only

occasionally grabs the attention and has enough plot for about half its length, though a decent smattering of memorable lines, most of them snarled put-downs. The performances are striking and memorable.

SCR Lukas Heller **CIN** Ernest Haller **MUS** Frank de Vol **PROD** Robert Aldrich **DIST** Warner Seven Arts/Associates and Aldrich

JANE: You mean all this time we could have been friends?

66 It goes on and on, in a light much dimmer than necessary, and the climax, when it belatedly arrives, is a bungled, languid mingling of pursuers and pursued. . . – *New Yorker*

⚱ Ernest Haller; Bette Davis (leading actress); Victor Buono (supporting actor)

'A Delicious Comedy Of Table Manners.'

What's Cooking? ★

DIR Gurinder Chadha

2000 109m US/GB

DVD ♫

☆ Alfre Woodard (Audrey Williams), Dennis Haysbert (Ronald Williams), Ann Weldon (Grace Williams), Mercedes Ruehl (Elizabeth Avila), Victor Rivers (Javier Avila), Douglas Spain (Anthony Avila), A. Martinez (Daniel), Lainie Kazan (Ruth Seeling), Maury Chaykin (Herb Seeling), Kyra Sedgwick (Rachel Seeling), Julianna Margulies (Carla), Estelle Harris (Aunt Bea), Joan Chen (Trinh Nguyen)

In latter-day Los Angeles, four families – one black, one white, one Latino, one Asian – prepare Thanksgiving dinner.

Likable ensemble piece in which characters of an ethnic diversity rarely seen in American-made films come to be united through ritual, good food and lively conversation.

SCR Gurinder Chadha, Paul Mayeda Berges **CIN** Jong Lin **MUS** Craig Pruess **DES** Stuart Blatt **ED** Janice Hampton **PROD** Jeffrey Taylor **DIST** Redbus

66 For so brisk and entertaining a film, sharp in its observations but light in its touch, Cooking has unexpected substance, and is a formidable accomplishment in that it brings dimension to its nearly 40 principal characters. – *Kevin Thomas, Los Angeles Times*

66 It's a meal you may feel you've eaten before, but you nonetheless walk away stuffed and happy. – *Dana Stevens, The New York Times*

'A film about the love you find. . .in the last place you look.'

What's Eating Gilbert Grape? ★

DIR Lasse Hallström

1993 118m US

DVD

☆ Johnny Depp (Gilbert Grape), Juliette Lewis (Becky), Mary Steenburgen (Betty Carver), *Leonardo DiCaprio* (Arnie Grape), Darlene Cates (Bonnie Grape), Laura Harrington (Amy Grape), Mary Kate Schellhardt (Ellen Grape), Crispin Glover (Bobby McBurney), Kevin Tighe (Ken Carver)

A young man yearning to escape his family and small town finds hope in a relationship with a female drifter.

W

DVD Available on DVD ☆ Cast in order of importance 66 Critics' Quotes † Points of interest ⚱ Academy Award Academy Award nomination BAFTA BAFTA nomination

Offbeat drama with a good young cast (notably a teenage DiCaprio) and some striking imagery; but too often its gentleness strays into inertia.

SCR Peter Hedges   **CIN** *Sven Nykvist*   **MUS** Alan Parker, Björn Isfält   **DES** Bernt Capra   **ED** Andrew Mondshein   **PROD** Meir Teper, Bertil Ohlsson, David Matalon   **DIST** Paramount

❝ As odd and funny a collection of cares as ever beset the youthful protagonist of a movie... more than sweetly offbeat without becoming whimsical, cloying or cute. – *Angie Errigo, Empire*

❝ Hallström and Nykvist do their best to disguise the predictability with their own grace notes. But all the music in the world can't hide a tone this false. – *Desson Thomson, Washington Post*

⚷ Leonardo DiCaprio (supporting actor)

'Not just the story of a life –The movie of a lifetime.'

What's Love Got to Do with It ★

DIR Brian Gibson
1993   118m   US
[DVD] ♫

☆ *Angela Bassett* (Anna Mae Bullock/Tina Turner), *Laurence Fishburne* (Ike Turner, Sr.), Vanessa Bell Calloway (Jackie), Jenifer Lewis (Zelma Bullock), Phyllis Yvonne Stickney (Alline Bullock), Khandi Alexander (Darlene), Rae'ven Kelly (Young Anna Mae Bullock)

The life of rock singer Tina Turner, charting her turbulent relationship with her abusive husband Ike and subsequent solo success.

Rounded performances are the best thing about this frenzied biopic, which hurries to cram overnight success, pregnancy, depressions, overdoses, spousal abuse, Buddhism, and Nutbush City Limits into two hours: 'It's all happening too fast,' remarks a pre-stardom Tina, and the lady's right.

SCR Kate Lanier   **CIN** Jamie Anderson   **MUS** Stanley Clarke   **DES** Stephen Altman   **ED** Stuart Pappé   **PROD** Doug Chapin, Barry Krost   **DIST** Buena Vista/Touchstone

❝ Never just a story of hit records, but the hip, compelling tale of a showbiz and hard life survivor. – *Angie Errigo, Empire*

⚷ Laurence Fishburne (leading actor); Angela Bassett (leading actress)

'Through the good times. Through the bad times.'

When a Man Loves a Woman

DIR Luis Mandoki
1994   126m   US
[DVD] ♫

☆ Andy Garcia (Michael Green), Meg Ryan (Alice Green), Philip Seymour Hoffman (Gary), Lauren Tom (Amy), Tina Majorino (Jessica Green), Mae Whitman (Casey Green), Ellen Burstyn (Emily)

A husband is troubled by his wife's alcoholism, and she goes to a clinic to dry out.

A film that announces itself as serious-minded, but still takes the shortest route to an implausibly happy resolution.

SCR Ronald Bass, Al Franken   **CIN** Lajos Koltai   **MUS** Zbigniew Preisner   **DES** Stuart Wurtzel   **ED** Garth Craven   **PROD** Jordan Kerner, Jon Avnet   **DIST** Buena Vista/Touchstone

❝ Noteworthy for casting Meg Ryan as an alcoholic – an interesting deviation from her usual flighty wholesomeness. – *Woody Haut, Sight & Sound*

❝ A coruscating dissection of a marriage built on shifting sand. – *Nigel Floyd, Time Out*

'Can two friends sleep together and still love each other in the morning?'

When Harry Met Sally ★★

DIR Rob Reiner
1989   96m   US
[DVD] ♫

☆ *Billy Crystal* (Harry Burns), Meg Ryan (Sally Albright), Carrie Fisher (Marie), Bruno Kirby (Jess), Steven Ford (Joe), Lisa Jane Persky (Alice), Michelle Nicastro (Amanda)

Two long-standing acquaintances wonder if it's possible for men and women to enjoy friendship without sex.

A very talky, slightly clinical examination of that particular quandary – something like three-quarter strength Woody Allen – though not without good lines and appealing performances.

SCR Nora Ephron   **CIN** Barry Sonnenfeld   **DES** Jane Musky   **ED** Robert Leighton   **PROD** Rob Reiner, Andrew Scheinman   **DIST** Palace/Castle Rock/Nelson Entertainment

WOMAN CUSTOMER IN RESTAURANT (AFTER SALLY SHOWS HOW TO FAKE AN ORGASM): I'll have what she's having.

❝ Destined to join Annie Hall, The Graduate, Alfie and a few others of that ilk, films which are guaranteed a long shelf life as TV movies because of the way they imperfectly frame the sexual dilemmas of their time. And make us laugh. – *David Hepworth, Empire*

❝ The kind of little film you can get cosy with, laugh at in odd places even when nobody else is laughing – and yet people will not turn around to glower at you because they understand. – *Peter Stack, San Francisco Chronicle*

⚷ Nora Ephron (original screenplay)
Ⓣ Nora Ephron (original screenplay)
Ⓣ film

'The Untold Story Of The Rumble In The Jungle.'

When We Were Kings ★★★

DIR *Leon Gast*
1996   89m   US
[DVD] ♫

☆ Muhammad Ali, George Foreman, Don King, President Mobutu Sese Seko, Spike Lee, Norman Mailer

Documentary account of the so-called "Rumble in the Jungle" – the heavyweight boxing clash between Muhammad Ali and George Foreman, held in Zaire in October 1974.

Highly impressive chronicle of not just a memorable hour in sporting history, but the media circus that pitched its tents around the event, and the awesome power, verbal dexterity and physical beauty of the young

[DVD] Available on DVD	☆ Cast in order	❝ Critics' Quotes	⚷ Academy Award	Ⓣ BAFTA
♫ Soundtrack on CD	of importance	† Points of interest	⚷ Academy Award nomination	Ⓣ BAFTA nomination

673

Ali; though prone to cheap shots at Foreman's expense, it recreates the era most vividly.

CIN Maryse Alberti, Paul Goldsmith, Kevin Keating, Albert Maysles, Roderick Young.   **ED** *Leon Gast, Taylor Hackford, Jeffrey Levy-Hinte, Keith Robinson*   **PROD** Taylor Hackford, Leon Gast   **DIST** Polygram/DAS

66 One of the best and most emotionally affecting documentaries ever made. – *David Parkinson, Empire*

66 A wonderfully entertaining, at times thrilling, film. Ali is magnificent, Foreman oddly touching, and their fight, which is shown almost in total, makes for superb, nail-biting suspense - even two decades after the fact. – *Manohla Dargis, L.A. Weekly*

documentary

'From the guy who brought you Super Size Me comes the next great big adventure!'

Where in the World is Osama Bin Laden? (new)

DIR Morgan Spurlock
2008   89m   US

☆ Morgan Spurlock (Himself), Alexandra Jamieson (Herself)

The star of Super Size Me heads to the Middle East, ostensibly to find the al-Qaeda leader, but also to explore attitudes to America and its war on terror.

Spurlock's scattershot approach feels unsuited to material best left to serious filmmakers; the result is as facile as its title, though not without some amusing sequences.

SCR Jeremy Chilnick, Morgan Spurlock   **CIN** Daniel Marracino   **MUS** Jon Spurney   **ED** Gavin Coleman, Julie 'Bob' Lombardi   **PROD** Jeremy Chilnick, Stacey Offman   **DIST** Optimum Releasing

66 A supersized problem gets the superficial treatment. – *Justin Lowe, Hollywood Reporter*

66 Frustratingly soft. – *Damon Wise, Empire*

Where the Heart Is   ★

DIR John Boorman
1990   107m   US
DVD

☆ Dabney Coleman (Stewart McBain), Uma Thurman (Daphne McBain), Joanna Cassidy (Jean), Crispin Glover (Lionel), Suzy Amis (Chloe McBain), Christopher Plummer (Shitty)

A wealthy demolition expert orders his three indulged children out of their comfortable home to live in a derelict Brooklyn house.

Part comedy, partly a satire about the shortcomings of capitalist individualism, Boorman's film is uncertain in tone, and loses its bearings. Its amusing to see the kids prosper in a collective ethos, while their tycoon Dad hits trouble. But whatever the over-arching idea was here, it stays hidden from view.

SCR John Boorman, Telsche Boorman   **CIN** Peter Suschitzky   **MUS** Peter Martin   **DES** Carol Spier   **ED** Ian Crafford   **PROD** John Boorman   **DIST** Buena Vista/Touchstone

66 Real issues are softened and sentimentalised. – *Geoff Andrew, Time Out*

'Another con. Another sting. Another day.'

Where The Money Is   ★

DIR Marek Kanievska
1999   89m   US/Germany/GB
DVD

☆ *Paul Newman* (Henry Manning), *Linda Fiorentino* (Carol), Dermot Mulroney (Wayne), Susan Barnes (Mrs Foster), Anne Pitoniak (Mrs Tetlow), Bruce MacVittie (Karl), Irma St Paul (Mrs. Galer), Michel Perron (Guard), Dorothy Gordon (Mrs Norton)

A retirement home nurse persuades one of the home's residents, a retired bank robber, to assist her in a heist.

Slight but pleasant caper movie, distinguished by the easy chemistry between its two leads.

SCR E. Max Frye, Topper Lilien, Carroll Cartwright   **CIN** Thomas Burstyn   **MUS** Mark Isham   **DES** Andre Chamberland   **ED** Sam Craven, Garth Craven, Dan Lebental   **PROD** Ridley Scott, Charles Weinstock, Chris Zarpas, Christopher Dorr

66 It's just another modest, unsurprising little heist flick. So why is it so much fun? Newman. – *Ann Hornaday, Baltimore Sun*

66 Coasts to a smooth, frictionless stop, but its star doesn't; he works as if his career depended on this movie. – *A.O. Scott, New York Times*

'A story about love at second sight.'

While You Were Sleeping   ★

DIR Jon Turteltaub
1995   103m   US
DVD   ♫

☆ *Sandra Bullock* (Lucy Eleanor Moderatz), Bill Pullman (Jack Callaghan), Peter Gallagher (Peter Callaghan), Peter Boyle (Ox Callaghan), Jack Warden (Saul), Glynis Johns (Elsie), Ally Walker (Ashley Bartlett Bacon)

A railway employee rescues the lawyer she longs for after he is mugged and left for dead on the tracks, only to be mistaken for his fiancée when his family arrive at the hospital.

Modest, unpretentious, surprisingly entertaining comedy with a fun supporting cast and a gem of a leading performance that instantly made Bullock a star; perhaps a last hurrah for old-fashioned screen romance before the genre slipped into cynicism.

SCR Daniel G. Sullivan, Frederic Lebow   **CIN** Phedon Papamichael   **MUS** Randy Edelman   **DES** Garreth Stover   **ED** Bruce Green   **PROD** Joe Roth, Roger Birnbaum   **DIST** Buena Vista/Hollywood/Caravan

66 What is startling is how well While You Were Sleeping recaptures the true spirit of the best kind of modern fairytale — classic romantic comedy. – *Richard Schickel, Time*

66 The required resolution is a long time in coming, but there's plenty to keep you diverted, including the light backchat amongst the semi-weirdos who make up the brothers' family, and Bullock's ridiculously watchable performance. – *Anthony Lane, The New Yorker*

W

Whisky Galore ★★★★

DIR *Alexander Mackendrick*
1948 82m GB
DVD

☆ Basil Radford (Capt. Paul Waggett), Joan Greenwood (Peggy Macroon), Jean Cadell (Mrs. Campbell), Gordon Jackson (George Campbell), James Robertson Justice (Dr. MacLaren), Wylie Watson (Joseph Macroon), John Gregson (Sammy MacConrum), Morland Graham (The Biffer), Duncan Macrae (Angus MacCormac), Catherine Lacey (Mrs. Waggett), Bruce Seton (Sgt. Odd), Henry Mollinson (Mr. Farquharson), Compton Mackenzie (Capt. Buncher), A. E. Matthews (Col. Linsey-Woolsey)

During World War II, a ship full of whisky is wrecked on a small Hebridean island, and the local customs and excise man has his hands full.

Marvellously detailed, fast-moving, well-played and attractively photographed comedy which firmly established the richest Ealing vein.

SCR *Compton Mackenzie, Angus MacPhail* CIN *Gerald Gibbs* MUS *Ernest Irving* ED Joseph Sterling PROD Monja Danischewsky DIST Ealing

66 Basil Radford gives a flawless performance of the misunderstood Home Guard chief whose zealousness leads to trouble in high quarters. – *Variety*

'Pick up the pieces, folks, Jimmy's in action again!'

White Heat ★★★

DIR *Raoul Walsh*
1949 114m US
DVD

☆ *James Cagney* (Arthur Cody Jarrett), Edmond O'Brien (Hank Fallon/Vic Pardo), *Margaret Wycherly* (Ma Jarrett), Virginia Mayo (Verna Jarrett), Steve Cochran (Big Ed Somers), John Archer (Phillip Evans)

A violent, mother-fixated gangster gets his come-uppance when a government agent is infiltrated into his gang.

This searing melodrama reintroduced the old Cagney and then some: spellbinding suspense sequences complemented his vivid and hypnotic portrayal.

SCR Ivan Goff, Ben Roberts CIN Sid Hickox MUS Max Steiner ED Owen Marks PROD Louis F. Edelman DIST Warner

CODY (JAMES CAGNEY): Made it, Ma! Top of the world!

66 The most gruesome aggregation of brutalities ever presented under the guise of entertainment. – *Cue*

66 In the hurtling tabloid traditions of the gangster movies of the thirties, but its matter-of-fact violence is a new post-war style. – *Time*

🏅 Virginia Kellogg (screenplay)

'An adventure in obsession. . .'

White Hunter Black Heart ★★

DIR Clint Eastwood
1990 110m US
DVD

☆ Clint Eastwood (John Wilson), Jeff Fahey (Pete Verrill), Charlotte Cornwell (Miss Wilding), Norman Lumsden (Butler George), George Dzundza (Paul Landers), Edward Tudor Pole (Reissar), Roddy Maude-Roxby (Thompson), Richard Warwick (Basil Fields)

A director visits Africa to shoot a movie but is more interested in the chance of shooting an elephant.

Eastwood acts in a style rarely seen on screen: he is patrician, pretentious, utterly self-centred – and quite insouciant enough to let his film go hang while he pursues his prey. He's channelling John Huston directing The African Queen; the author of the source novel here was an uncredited screenwriter on that film.

SCR Peter Viertel, James Bridges, Burt Kennedy CIN Jack N. Green MUS Lennie Niehaus DES John Graysmark ED Joel Cox PROD Clint Eastwood DIST Warner/Malpaso/Rastar

66 Eastwood constructs a marvellously pacy, suspenseful movie which is deceptively easy on both eye and ear. – *Geoff Andrew, Time Out*

'In England they were the elite, but bound by rules of society. In Kenya there were no rules, only glamour, decadence. . .and murder.'

White Mischief ★

DIR Michael Radford
1987 107m GB
DVD 🎵

☆ Charles Dance (Josslyn Hay: Earl of Erroll), Greta Scacchi (Lady Diana Broughton), Joss Ackland (Sir Henry 'Jock' Delves Broughton), Sarah Miles (Alice de Janzé), John Hurt (Gilbert Colvile), Trevor Howard (Jack Soames)

An aristocratic lothario, who seduces bored expatriate women in Kenya's infamous Happy Valley, is found murdered.

A real-life story about a murder that exposed the hanky-panky rampant among the Valley's wealthy gin-swilling colonial set. Director Radford has a sharp eye for this milieu, and the film holds the interest until it becomes clear that there's not a single sympathetic character to guide the audience through the unfolding drama.

SCR Michael Radford, Jonathan Gems CIN Roger Deakins MUS George Fenton DES Roger Hall ED Tom Priestley PROD Simon Perry DIST Umbrella

🎭 Joss Ackland (supporting actor); Marit Allen (costume design)

'The story of a younger man, and a bolder woman.'

White Palace ★★

DIR Luis Mandoki
1990 103m US
DVD 🎵

☆ *Susan Sarandon* (Nora Baker), James Spader (Max Baron), Jason Alexander (Neil), Kathy Bates (Rosemary), Eileen Brennan (Judy), Steven Hill (Sol Horowitz), Rachel Levin (Rachel)

An upwardly mobile young advertising executive falls for a fortysomething waitress.

A sensitive, well-observed odd-couple romance, rare in Hollywood terms for offering the sight of an older

---

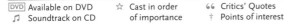

DVD Available on DVD   🎵 Soundtrack on CD   ☆ Cast in order of importance   66 Critics' Quotes   † Points of interest   🏅 Academy Award   🏅 Academy Award nomination   🎭 BAFTA   🎭 BAFTA nomination

woman wooing a younger man in all sincerity, and with an outrageously sexy performance from Sarandon as one of the few truly real-seeming women – passionate, hard-working, troubled – in recent American cinema.

SCR *Ted Tally, Alvin Sargent* **CIN** *Lajos Koltai*
MUS *George Fenton* **DES** *Jeannine C. Oppewall*
ED *Carol Fischer, Carol Littleton* **PROD** *Mark Rosenberg, Amy Robinson, Griffin Dunne*
DIST *UIP/Universal/Mirage/Double Play*

66 Part love story, part comedy of manners. . .a thoroughly entertaining – if quite obviously far-fetched – yarn. – *Tom Tunney, Empire*

66 There's an unmistakable charge between the two leads, and an acute sense of their mutual confusion. – *Colette Maude, Time Out*

'It's the story of a man, a woman, and a rabbit in a triangle of trouble.'

Who Framed Roger Rabbit ★★

DIR *Robert Zemeckis*
1988　103m　US
DVD　♫

☆ *Bob Hoskins (Eddie Valiant), Christopher Lloyd (Judge Doom), Joanna Cassidy (Dolores), Stubby Kaye (Marvin Acme), the voices of Charles Fleischer, Kathleen Turner, Amy Irving, Lou Hirsch, Mel Blanc*

A film studio detective teams up with a rabbit accused of murder to clear the latter's name.

In an age where live action and animation are routinely integrated, the novelty of the effects has gone, and what's left looks like a very canny, albeit solidly entertaining, extension of the Disney brand; there are fun cameos from Dumbo, Betty Boop and Daffy and Donald Duck, but it's Hoskins who increasingly holds the attention, effortlessly good in what was one of the toughest assignments of that decade: acting opposite empty space.

SCR *Jeffrey Price, Peter S. Seaman* **CIN** *Dean Cundey*
MUS *Alan Silvestri* **DES** *Elliot Scott, Roger Cain*
ED *Arthur Schmidt* **PROD** *Robert Watts, Frank Marshall*
DIST *Warner/Touchstone/Amblin*

66 Virtually faultless on the technological front, it also excels in terms of a breathless, wisecracking script, deft characterisation (both human and Toon), and rousing action. At its best, the humour is as cruel, violent and surreal as vintage Chuck Jones. – *Geoff Andrew, Time Out*

66 A film whose best moments are so novel, so deliriously funny, and so crazily unexpected that they truly must be seen to be believed. – *Elvis Mitchell, The New York Times*

⚲ Arthur Schmidt; Ken Ralston, Richard Williams, Ed Jones, George Gibbs (visual effects); Charles L. Campbell, Louis L. Edemann (sound effects)

⚲ Dean Cundey; George Gibbs (art direction); (sound); Richard Williams

Ⓣ George Gibbs, Richard Williams, Ken Ralston, Ed Jones (special effects); Dean Cundey; Arthur Schmidt; (production design); (screenplay)

'You are cordially invited to George and Martha's for an evening of fun and games!'

Who's Afraid of Virginia Woolf? ★★★★

DIR *Mike Nichols*
1966　129m　US
DVD　♫

☆ *Richard Burton (George), Elizabeth Taylor (Martha), George Segal (Nick), Sandy Dennis (Honey)*

A college professor and his wife have an all-night shouting match and embarrass their guests.

As a film of a play, fair to middling; as a milestone in cinematic permissiveness, very important; as an entertainment, sensational for those in the mood.

SCR *Ernest Lehman* **CIN** *Haskell Wexler* **MUS** *Alex North* **DES** *Richard Sylbert* **ED** *Sam O'Steen* **PROD** *Ernest Lehman* **DIST** *Warner*

66 A magnificent triumph of determined audacity. – *Bosley Crowther*

66 One of the most scathingly honest American films ever made. – *Stanley Kauffmann*

⚲ Elizabeth Taylor (leading actress); Sandy Dennis (supporting actress); Haskell Wexler

⚲ picture; Richard Burton (leading actor); George Segal (supporting actor); Ernest Lehman (adapted screenplay); Mike Nichols; Alex North (music)

Ⓣ picture; Richard Burton; Elizabeth Taylor

Why We Fight ★★★★

1942　US

A series of feature-length compilations released during 1942–5, primarily for showing to the armed forces, these were superbly vigorous documentaries which later fascinated the public at large.

DIST *Frank Capra*

⚲ documentary (Prelude to War)

'Flesh to touch...Flesh to burn! Don't keep the Wicker Man waiting!'

The Wicker Man ★★★

DIR *Robin Hardy*
1973　100m　GB
DVD　♫

☆ *Edward Woodward (Sgt Howie), Britt Ekland (Willow), Christopher Lee (Lord Summersisle), Ingrid Pitt (Librarian), Diane Cilento (Miss Rose), Lindsay Kemp (Alder MacGregor), Russell Waters (Harbour Master)*

A policeman flies to a remote Scottish isle to investigate the death of a child, and finds himself in the hands of devil-worshippers.

A virtually unconsidered B-movie at the time of release, the reputation of this old-fashioned but remarkably well made scare story has grown to a point where it is now regarded as a horror classic. Woodward is outstanding as the devout cop from the Scottish mainland, confronted by pagans. The story's religious and sexual overtones add complexity, and the final conflagration is deeply creepy.

DVD Available on DVD　　☆ Cast in order of importance　　66 Critics' Quotes　　⚲ Academy Award　　Ⓣ BAFTA
♫ Soundtrack on CD　　† Points of interest　　⚲ Academy Award nomination　　Ⓣ BAFTA nomination

SCR *Anthony Shaffer* CIN Harry Waxman MUS Paul Giovanni ED Eric Boyd-Perkins PROD Peter Snell DIST British Lion

66 An encouraging achievement for those who had begun to despair of the British cinema. – *David McGillivray*

† It was re-made disastrously in the US in 2006, with Nicolas Cage in the lead role.

'Nine men who came too late and stayed too long!'

The Wild Bunch ★★★★

DIR *Sam Peckinpah*
1969 145m US
[DVD] ♫

☆ William Holden (Pike Bishop), Ernest Borgnine (Dutch Engstrom), Robert Ryan (Deke Thornton), Edmond O'Brien (Sykes), Warren Oates (Lyle Gorch), Jaime Sanchez (Angel), Ben Johnson (Tector Gorch), Strother Martin (Coffer), L. Q. Jones (T.C.), Albert Dekker (Pat Harrigan)

In 1914, Texas bandits are ambushed by an old enemy and die bloodily in defence of one of their number against a ruthless Mexican revolutionary.

Arguably the director's best film, and one which set a fashion for blood-spurting violence in Westerns. Peckinpah made a point of dwelling on the violence in slow-motion, choreographed shootings – believed at the time to be a comment on the violence being inflicted in Vietnam. Yet it also an elegy for the Old West, a mournful funeral rite for a way of life. Undeniably stylish, thoughtful, and in places very exciting.

SCR Walon Green, Sam Peckinpah CIN *Lucien Ballard* MUS Jerry Fielding ED Lou Lombardo DIST Warner Seven Arts/Phil Feldman

66 A western that enlarged the form aesthetically, thematically, demonically. – *Stanley Kauffmann, 1972*

66 We watch endless violence to assure us that violence is not good. – *Judith Crist, 1976*

⅃ original screenplay; Jerry Fielding (music)

Wild Man Blues ★★

DIR *Barbara Kopple*
1997 105m US
[DVD]

☆ Letty Aronson, Soon-Yi Previn, Dan Barrett, Simon Wettenhall, John Gill, Greg Cohen, Cynthia Sayer, Eddy Davis, Woody Allen, Nettie Konigsberg, Martin Konigsberg

Documentary following Woody Allen and his New Orleans jazz band as they tour Europe.

An essential footnote in the Allen filmography: a candid and often very funny exercise which catches its subject relatively off-guard – playing live, flirting with (as he introduces her) 'the notorious' Soon-Yi Previn, and speaking over the phone with his mother – but underlines exactly where the glass-half-empty worldview of his stand-up and film comedy comes from.

CIN Tom Hurwitz ED Lawrence Silk PROD Jean Doumanian DIST Film Four/Magnolia/Sweetland

66 Kopple never manages to find an answer to the question 'how do you make a film with Woody Allen in it

that isn't a Woody Allen film?'. . .One begins to wonder how many of the apparently candid moments in the documentary are actually performances. – *Kevin Macdonald, Sight and Sound*

66 Although cynics might label this a glorified PR job, it adds up to a colourful portrait of the man and his music. – *Trevor Lewis, Empire*

'That streetcar man has a new desire!'

The Wild One ★★

DIR *Laslo Benedek*
1954 79m US
[DVD]

☆ *Marlon Brando*, Lee Marvin, Mary Murphy, Robert Keith, Jay C. Flippen

Hoodlum motorcyclists terrorize a small town.

Brooding, compulsive, well-made little melodrama which was much banned because there was no retribution for the gang's actions. As a narrative it does somewhat lack dramatic point, yet the leather-clad Brando was terrific, a genuinely iconic figure, the first young rebel of what would become the rock 'n' roll era.

SCR John Paxton CIN Hal Mohr MUS Leith Stevens DIST Columbia/Stanley Kramer

WAITRESS: What are you rebelling against, Johnny?
JOHNNY (BRANDO): Whaddaya got?

66 A picture that tries to grasp an idea, even though the reach falls short. – *New York Times*

† Sharpness of photography was achieved by the Garutso lens

'The true story of a bohemian St Francis and his remarkable relationship with a flock of wild red and green parrots'

The Wild Parrots of Telegraph Hill ★

DIR Judy Irving
2005 83m US
[DVD] ♫

☆ Mark Bittner

Documentary about a self-confessed vagabond who cares for a flock of some 40 parrots, mostly abandoned or escaped, in San Francisco.

Inoffensive curio about an amiable oddball, though his colourful feathered friends upstage him at every turn.

CIN Judy Irving MUS Chris Michie ED Judy Irving PROD Judy Irving DIST ICA

Wild Strawberries ★★★

SCR/DIR *Ingmar Bergman*
1957 93m Sweden
[DVD]

☆ *Victor Sjostrom* (Prof. Isak Borg), *Ingrid Thulin* (Marianne Borg), Gunnar Bjornstrand (Evald Borg), Bibi Andersson (Sara), Naima Wifstrand (Isak's Mother), Jullan Kindahl (Agda)

An elderly professor, Isak Borg, has a nightmare and thinks back over his long life.

A beautifully paced and acted, but somewhat obscure piece; Borg's nightmares are characterised by visually

[DVD] Available on DVD   ☆ Cast in order   66 Critics' Quotes   ⅃ Academy Award   ⊕ BAFTA
♫ Soundtrack on CD   of importance   † Points of interest   ⅃ Academy Award nomination   ⊕ BAFTA nomination

677

arresting but often unfathomable symbols. More effective by far are his idyllic pastoral memories of his cousin Sara, exquisitely shot.

CIN *Gunnar Fischer* MUS Erik Nordgren ED Oscar Rosendar PROD Allan Ekelund DIST Svensk Filmindustri

66 The work of a man obsessed by cruelty, especially spiritual cruelty, trying to find some resolution. – *Kenneth Cavander, Monthly Film Bulletin*

66 In Borg, Sjostrom and Bergman created cinema's domestic, bourgeois, 20th-century answer to Lear. – *Peter Bradshaw, Guardian*

† It won the 1958 Golden Bear award at the Berlin Film Festival.

⚖ Ingmar Bergman (original screenplay)

'They're dying to play with you.'

Wild Things

DIR John McNaughton
1998   108m   US
DVD   ♫

☆ Kevin Bacon (Sgt. Ray Duquette), Matt Dillon (Sam Lombardo), Neve Campbell (Suzie Marie Toller), Theresa Russell (Sandra Van Ryan), Denise Richards (Kelly Lanier Van Ryan), Robert Wagner (Tom Baxter), Bill Murray (Kenneth Bowden), Carrie Snodgress (Ruby), Daphne Rubin-Vega (Det. Gloria Perez)

A high-school guidance counsellor is undone when two young women accuse him of rape.

Glib, knowingly trashy thriller from a director capable of much better.

SCR Stephen Peters   CIN Jeffrey L. Kimball MUS George S. Clinton   DES Edward T. McAvoy ED Elena Maganini   PROD Rodney Liber, Steven A. Jones DIST Columbia

66 A tricky-bordering-on-gimmicky film noir with a glaze of softcore kink. – *Owen Gleiberman, Entertainment Weekly*

66 It's like a three-way collision between a soft-core sex film, a soap opera and a B-grade noir. I liked it. – *Roger Ebert, Chicago Sun-Times*

Wild West   ★★

DIR David Attwood
1992   85m   GB
DVD

☆ Naveen Andrews (Zaf), Sarita Choudhury (Rifat), Ronny Jhutti (Kay), Ravi Kapoor (Ali Ayub), Ameet Chana (Gurdeep), Bhasker Patel (Jagdeep), Lalita Ahmed (Mrs. Ayub), Shaun Scott (Tony)

A bunch of young London-based Pakistanis form a country band and dream of forging a career that will take them all the way to Nashville. Trouble looms when one of them courts a young Asian woman unhappily married to a white taxi driver.

The West in the title is west London – Southall, to be precise, home of the Asian lads who constitute the Honky Tonk Cowboys. That doesn't prevent director Attwood from referencing a few classic westerns in this scrappy, amiable comedy about culture clashes and improbable musical tastes. In retrospect, it was a little ahead of its time.

SCR Harwant Bains   CIN Nic Knowland   MUS Dominic Miller   DES Caroline Hanania   ED Martin Walsh PROD Eric Fellner   DIST Initial/Channel 4/British Screen

66 Colourful, packed with comic detail, it certainly works well as a feelgood movie along the lines of The Commitments. – *Geoffrey Macnab, Sight & Sound*

'We are all in the gutter, but some of us are looking at the stars.'

Wilde   ★★

DIR Brian Gilbert
1997   118m   GB/US/Japan/Germany
DVD   ♫

☆ *Stephen Fry* (Oscar Wilde), Jude Law (Bosie), Vanessa Redgrave (Lady Speranza Wilde), Jennifer Ehle (Constance Lloyd Wilde), Gemma Jones (Lady Queensberry), Michael Sheen (Robbie Ross), Zoe Wanamaker (Ada Leverson), Tom Wilkinson (Marquess of Queensberry)

The final years of the playwright and humorist Oscar Wilde, centring on his doomed liaison with Lord Alfred 'Bosie' Douglas.

Sincere, well-appointed account of a great literary life, drawing out the biographical resonances in Wilde's bedtime story The Selfish Giant, and conveying both the writer's timeless wit and the torment of his last days.

SCR *Julian Mitchell*   CIN Martin Fuhrer   MUS Debbie Wiseman, Arthur Sullivan   DES Maria Djurkovic ED Michael Bradsell   PROD Mark Samuelson, Peter Samuelson   DIST Polygram/Samuelson/Dove/NDF-/Pony Canyon/Pandora/BBC

66 Fry is utterly convincing. He speaks the witty lines as if he invented them, and manages to square Wilde's weakness and arrogance with his immense generosity of spirit. – *Steve Grant, Time Out*

66 Apart from a sprinkling of Wilde's legendary bons mots and a few fleeting visits to theatres where audiences cheer Lady Windermere's Fan, there is disappointingly little here to suggest the complexity of his mind, the range of his writing or, crucially, the importance of being Oscar. – *Angie Errigo, Empire*

† The playwright's life inspired two earlier films: Oscar Wilde and The Trials of Oscar Wilde (both 1960).

Ⓣ Zoe Wanamaker (supporting actress); Jennifer Ehle (supporting actress)

'Hope & Despair. Tragedy & Love. Romeo & Juliet.'

William Shakespeare's
Romeo and Juliet   ★★

DIR *Baz Luhrmann*
1996   120m   US
DVD   ♫

☆ Leonardo DiCaprio (Romeo), Claire Danes (Juliet), Brian Dennehy (Ted Montague), John Leguizamo (Tybalt), Pete Postlethwaite (Father Laurence), Paul Sorvino (Fulgencio Capulet), Diane Venora (Gloria Capulet)

In latter-day Verona Beach, two teenagers from warring families fall for one another against their parents' objections.

The film that kick-started a whole cycle of re-doing the classics for kids: a flashy, exuberant, thoroughly

DVD Available on DVD   ☆ Cast in order of importance   66 Critics' Quotes   ⚖ Academy Award   Ⓑ BAFTA
♫ Soundtrack on CD   † Points of interest   ⚖ Academy Award nomination   Ⓣ BAFTA nomination

cinematic, occasionally clever but more often self-consciously cute modernisation of the play, relocated amongst California's gang culture, with a soundtrack of pop hits; sporadically diverting, and an obvious boon for students unenthused by the original text, but its foolish passion is still no substitute for the real thing.

SCR Craig Pearce, Baz Luhrmann   CIN Donald McAlpine
MUS *Nellee Hooper*   DES *Catherine Martin*   ED Jill Bilcock   PROD Gabriella Martinelli, Baz Luhrmann
DIST TCF

66 A unique ride through one of the Bard's best-known texts, illuminating the story, occasionally subjugating the language but always delivering a vision that is bold, brassy, hugely inventive and, in a strange way, just right. – *Bob McCabe, Empire*

66 The movie, a frenetic, explosive experience full of car crashes and gun battles, is original and exhilarating. But more often, it's so overwhelming, it'll make you want to watch Die Hard with a Vengeance for peace and quiet. – *Desson Thomson, Washington Post*

† DiCaprio won the prize for best actor at the Berlin Film Festival in 1997.

⚱ Catherine Martin

Ⓑ Baz Luhrmann; Catherine Martin; Nellee Hooper; screenplay

Ⓣ sound; Donald McAlpine; Jill Bilcock

The Wind ★★★

DIR *Victor Sjostrom*
1928   75m   US

☆ *Lillian Gish* (Letty), Lars Hanson (Lige), Montagu Love (Roddy Wirt), Dorothy Cummings (Cora)

A sheltered Virginia girl goes to live on the rough and windy Texas prairie, marries a man she doesn't love and kills a would-be rapist.

Heavy melodrama with a strong visual sense.

SCR Frances Marion   CIN John Arnold   ED Conrad A. Nervig   DIST MGM

66 So penetrating is the atmosphere that one can almost feel the wind itself and taste the endless dust. – *Georges Sadoul*

66 Unrelieved by the ghost of a smile . . . but its relentlessness is gripping . . . a fine and dignified achievement. – *Pictureplay*

'There Are Worse Things Than Dying.'
Wind Chill (new) ★★

DIR Gregory Jacobs
2007   91m   USA/UK

☆ Emily Blunt (Girl), Ashton Holmes (Guy), Martin Donovan (Highway Patrolman), Ned Bellamy (Snow Plough Driver), Ian Wallace (Priest)

Two strangers involved in a car crash on a remote country road develop an intense relationship braving winter elements and mysterious ghostly encounters.

Familiar supernatural elements are served up in an eerie package with understated acting contrasting with the fright factors.

SCR Joe Gangemi, Steven Katz   CIN Dan Laustsen

MUS Clint Mansell   DES Howard Cummings   ED Lee Percy   PROD Peter Czernin, Steven Soderbergh
DIST Sony Pictures

66 Intermittently effective thriller serves as a rickety vehicle for its two perfectly cast leads, working better as a slow-thawing two-hander than as a chilly ghost story. – *Justin Chang , Variety*

The Wind that Shakes the Barley ★★

DIR Ken Loach
2006   126m
UK/Ireland/Germany/Italy/Spain/Switzerland
DVD

☆ Cillian Murphy (Damien), Liam Cunningham (Dan), Padraic Delaney (Teddy), Orla Fitzgerald (Sinead), Roger Allam (Sir John Hamilton)

In 1920, a radical young Irish doctor cancels plans to practise medicine in London when he witnesses British troops brutalising volunteers waging a guerrilla campaign. He is arrested and tortured, and later keeps fighting, though a treaty has been signed between the Irish and British governments.

A skilful account of a pivotal period in Irish history, told by a director and screenwriter who make no secret of their sympathies. Loach portrays the Irish volunteers as innocents in an unsullied pastoral paradise – until the troops move in, of course. Still, the film has undeniable narrative power, and Laverty makes complicated counter-arguments between the Irish rebels perfectly palatable. Beautifully shot by Barry Ackroyd, with a fine, dignified performance by Murphy as an idealist prepared to fight to the death for his beliefs and country.

SCR Paul Laverty   CIN Barry Ackroyd   MUS George Fenton   DES Fergus Clegg   ED Jonathan Morris
PROD Rebecca O'Brien   DIST Pathe

66 A stirring lament for good human beings caught in the crossfire of history. – *Dave Calhoun, Time Out*

66 The history presented in The Wind that Shakes the Barley hardly feels like a closed book or a museum display. It is as alive and as troubling as anything on the evening news, though far more thoughtful and beautiful. – *A.O. Scott, New York Times*

† The film won the 2006 Palme d'Or at Cannes.
† The title comes from an old Irish folk song.

The Wind Will Carry Us ★★★★

SCR/DIR Abbas Kiarostami
1999   118m   France/Iran
DVD

☆ Behzad Dourani (Engineer), Farzad Sohrabi, Shahpour Ghobadi, Masood Mansouri, Masoameh Salimi, Bahman Ghobadi, Noghre Asadi, Ali Reza Naderi

Mysterious visitors arrive at a remote Kurdistani village and reveal enormous interest in an old dying woman.

Intriguing and ambiguous, this film mixes witty and absurdist comedy with an unexpected thriller element, while contrasting traditional rural life with urban modernity. The answers to the questions it poses reveal

DVD Available on DVD   ☆ Cast in order of importance   66 Critics' Quotes   ⚱ Academy Award   † Points of interest   ⚱ Academy Award nomination   Ⓑ BAFTA   Ⓣ BAFTA nomination

679

themselves gradually, and seem to lie in the very landscape. A film of poetic depth that alludes to questions of life and mortality almost by stealth.

CIN Mahmoud Kalari   **MUS** Peyman Yazdanian   **ED** Abbas Kiarostami   **PROD** Marin Karmitz, Abbas Kiarostami   **DIST** ICA

66 Abbas Kiarostami reinforces his claim to be world cinema's most challenging director with this non-drama, that is more interested in the sights and rhythms of the everyday than narrative. – *Empire*

Winged Migration ★

DIR Jacques Perrin

2001   98m   France/Germany/Spain/Italy/Switzerland

[DVD]   ♫

☆ Philippe Labro (Narrator (English version)), Jacques Perrin (Narrator (voice))

Documentary study of the migrating habits of various birds.

A spectacularly shot exercise in birdwatching, but one which simply never provides enough context for the images shown: a film which should bring us closer to understanding our feathered friends instead only emphasises how far removed and alien they are to us.

SCR Jacques Perrin, Stephane Durand, Jean Dorst, Guy Jarry, Francis Roux   **CIN** *Olli Barbe, Michel Benjamin, Sylvie Carcedo, Laurent Charbonnier, Luc Drion, Laurent Fleutot, Philippe Garguil, Dominique Gentil, Bernard Lutic, Thierry Machado, Stephane Martin, Fabrice Moindrot, Ernst Sasse, Michel Terasse, Thierry Thomas*   **MUS** Bruno Coulais   **DES** Regis Nicolino   **ED** Marie-Josephe Yoyotte   **PROD** Jacques Perrin, Christophe Barratier   **DIST** Columbia TriStar

66 Favours boggling over exploring or explaining; regrettably, despite impressive camerawork, it doesn't even boggle that well... both the narrative and the images get a little tedious. Couldn't we at least have had a swallow, a warbler, or a bottleneck of massed raptors soaring over the Bosphorus or the Strait of Gibraltar? A wasted opportunity. – *Geoff Andrew, Time Out*

⚷ documentary

'There are angels on the streets of Berlin.'

Wings of Desire ★★★

DIR *Wim Wenders*

1987   127m   France/West Germany

[DVD]   ♫

☆ *Bruno Ganz* (Damiel), Solveig Dommartin (Marion), Otto Sander (Cassiel), Curt Bois (Homer), Peter Falk (Himself)

A guardian angel watching over Berlin falls for a trapeze artist, and expresses a wish to become human.

Swooning metaphysical fantasia, filtering its director's keynote existentialism through the heightened aesthetic of the then-ascendant cinema du look; it strikes such chords in places that one can forgive it its longueurs and pretensions everywhere else, and its use of pre-unification Berlin is always resonant. A gorgeous car commercial for the soul.

SCR Wim Wenders, Peter Handke, Richard Reitinger   **CIN** *Henri Alekan*   **MUS** Jürgen Knieper   **DES** Heidi Ludi   **ED** Peter Przygodda   **PROD** Wim Wenders, Anatole Dauman   **DIST** Road Movies/Argos films

66 A sublimely beautiful, deeply romantic film for our times. – *Variety*

66 Masterpiece? Maybe not, but few films are so rich, so intriguing, or so ambitious. – *Geoff Andrew, Time Out*

ⓣ film not in the English language

'A couple with everything but money. An heiress with everything but love. A temptation no one could resist.'

The Wings of the Dove ★★

DIR Iain Softley

1997   102m   GB/US

[DVD]   ♫

☆ *Helena Bonham Carter* (Kate Croy), Linus Roache (Merton Densher), Alison Elliott (Millie Theale), Elizabeth McGovern (Susan 'Susie' Stringham), Charlotte Rampling (Aunt Maude), Alex Jennings (Lord Mark), Michael Gambon (Lionel Croy, Kate's Father)

An idealistic, cash-strapped journalist is persuaded by his beautiful lover to seduce a wealthy dying heiress, and marry her for her money.

An updated treatment of a Henry James novel becomes an entertaining, tantalising period love triangle that succeeds on its own terms.

SCR *Hossein Amini*   **CIN** Eduardo Serra   **MUS** Edward Shearmur   **DES** John Beard   **ED** Tariq Anwar   **PROD** David Parfitt, Stephen Evans   **DIST** Miramax/Renaissance Dove

66 A luscious, surprisingly complex adaptation of the Henry James novel. – *Edward Guthmann, San Francisco Chronicle*

⚷ Helena Bonham Carter (leadinf actress); Hossein Amini (adapted screenplay); Eduardo Serra; Sandy Powell (costume design)

ⓣ Eduardo Serra; Sallie Jaye, Jan Archibald (make up/hair)
ⓣ Helena Bonham Carter (leading actress); Hossein Amini (adpated screenplay); Sandy Powell (costume design)

The Winslow Boy ★★

SCR/DIR David Mamet

1998   104m   US

[DVD]   ♫

☆ Nigel Hawthorne (Arthur Winslow), *Jeremy Northam* (Sir Robert Morton), Rebecca Pidgeon (Catherine Winslow), Gemma Jones (Grace Winslow), Guy Edwards (Ronnie Winslow), Colin Stinton (Desmond Curry), Sarah Flind (Violet), Neil North (First Lord of the Admiralty), Sara Stewart (Miss Barnes), Perry Fenwick (Fred), Alan Polonsky (Mr Michaels)

A furious father fights to clear the family name in England in 1910 when his son is expelled from naval college for stealing a five shilling postal order.

Elegant, eloquent evocation of an excellent stage play, which David Mamet, surprisingly, adapts and directs completely straight. A first-rate cast helps him reveal the precision of the play's inner workings.

CIN Benoit Delhomme   **MUS** Alaric Jans   **DES** Gemma Jackson   **ED** Barbara Tulliver   **PROD** Sarah Green   **DIST** Columbia TriStar

66 This is the kind of movie that literate viewers pine for, laced with gracefulness and wit. – *David Sterritt, Christian Science Monitor*

'No matter where you hide, life will always find you.'

The Winter Guest ★

DIR Alan Rickman
1996 108m GB/US
DVD ♫

☆ Phyllida Law (Elspeth), Emma Thompson (Frances), Sheila Reid (Lily), Sandra Voe (Chloe), Arlene Cockburn (Nita), Gary Hollywood (Alex), Sean Biggerstaff (Tom), Douglas Murphy (Sam)

In snowy, remote Scotland, a mother tries to re-build her relationship with her depressed, recently widowed daughter.

This glum story of the impact of bereavement on a family never quite escapes its theatrical roots. Rickman makes much of the icy exteriors, but the drama indoors lacks heat too.

SCR Sharman MacDonald, Alan Rickman **CIN** Seamus McGarvey **MUS** Michael Kamen **DES** Robin Cameron Don **ED** Scott Thomas **PROD** Ken Lipper, Edward R. Pressman, Steve Clark-Hall **DIST** Film Four/Fine Line/Channel 4/Capitol/Scottish Arts Council/Lottery Fund

'For John Belushi Every Night Was Saturday Night.'

Wired

DIR Larry Peerce
1989 112m US
♫

☆ Michael Chiklis (John Belushi), Patti D'Arbanville (Cathy Smith), J. T. Walsh (Bob Woodward), Lucinda Jenney (Judy Belushi), Gary Groomes (Dan Aykroyd), Ray Sharkey (Angel Velasquez), Alex Rocco (Arnie Fromson), Jere Burns (Lou Connors)

Biopic that relates how the comic actor John Belushi met his death from a heroin and cocaine cocktail overdose in Hollywood's Chateau Marmont hotel in 1982.

Convoluted account, which includes the appearance of Walsh playing Bob Woodward, the author of the account on which this film is based. It's not afraid to embrace the lurid, tabloid aspects of Belushi's death. Chiklis makes a decent fist of portraying Belushi, without ever capturing his inspired comic talents.

SCR Earl MacRauch **CIN** Tony Imi **MUS** Basil Poledouris **DES** Brian Eatwell **ED** Eric Sears **PROD** Edward A. Feldman, Charles R. Meeker **DIST** Entertainment/Lion Screen Entertainment

† After this film, Michael Chiklis worked steadily in minor roles until emerging as a genuine TV star in 2002, when he played the unconventional Detective Vic Mackey in the series The Shield.

The Witches ★★

DIR Nicolas Roeg
1989 91m US
DVD

☆ Anjelica Huston (Miss Eva Ernst / Grand High Witch),

Mai Zetterling (Helga Eveshim), Jasen Fisher (Luke Eveshim), Rowan Atkinson (Mr. Stringer), Bill Paterson (Mr. Jenkins), Brenda Blethyn (Mrs. Jenkins), Charlie Potter (Bruno Jenkins), Anne Lambton (Woman in Black), Jane Horrocks (Miss Irvine)

A small boy and his brave grandmother fight to prevent the witches from turning children into mice by feeding them poisonous chocolate.

The master of the macabre for minors scores again. Roald Dahl's preferred ending might be changed, but this adaptation of his source material counts as a screen triumph.

SCR Allan Scott **CIN** Harvey Harrison **MUS** Stanley Myers **DES** Andrew Sanders **ED** Tony Lawson **PROD** Mark Shivas **DIST** Warner/Lorimar

66 A gutsy version of Roald Dahl's story. . .strange and scary enough to fascinate parents and offspring alike. – *Time Out*

† Roald Dahl strenuously objected to the ending of his story being changed, and denounced the film in strong terms.

Ⓣ Christine Beveridge (make up)

'If you can't remember the 60's, ...don't worry. Neither can they.'

Withnail and I ★★★

SCR/DIR *Bruce Robinson*
1987 107m GB
DVD ♫

☆ *Richard E. Grant* (Withnail), *Paul McGann* (Marwood), *Richard Griffiths* (Monty), *Ralph Brown* (Danny), Michael Elphick (Jake)

London, circa 1969: two unemployed actors leave their grotty flat behind to holiday in a country cottage.

Much-loved comedy that conjures a genuine poetry from its tumbledown locations and stunted characters: its fans are keen to recall the sometimes profane, always witty dialogue, but it's the film's melancholy air – its lament for lost friendships and a bygone Britain – which stays with you even longer.

CIN Peter Hannan **MUS** *David Dundas, Rick Wentworth* **DES** *Michael Pickwoad* **ED** Alan Strachan **PROD** Paul M. Heller **DIST** Recorded Releasing/HandMade Films

WITHNAIL: We want the finest wines available to humanity. And we want them here, and we want them now!
WITHNAIL: There must and shall be aspirin!
DANNY: I don't advise a haircut, man. All hairdressers are in the employment of the government. Hairs are your aerials. They pick up signals from the cosmos, and transmit them directly into the brain. This is the reason bald-headed men are uptight.

66 Robinson's debut as writer/director exhibits the value of the old virtues: characterisation, detail, and engagement... Beautifully scripted, indecent, honest and truthful, it's a true original. – *Wally Hammond, Time Out*

66 An even rarer pleasure than it at first seems: a comedy that truly comes from the heart. – *Adam Smith, Empire*

† The film was co-executive produced by Beatle George Harrison. A consultant credit for 'Richard Starkey, MBE' refers to Harrison's bandmate Ringo Starr.

W

† In 2006, a 15-minue short film was released as a 'homage' to all the drinks consumed during Withnail And I.

'A big city cop who knows too much. His only witness – a small boy who's seen too much!'

Witness ★★★★

DIR *Peter Weir*

1985   112m   US

[DVD] ♫

☆ *Harrison Ford* (John Book), Kelly McGillis (Rachel), Josef Sommer (Schaeffer), *Lukas Haas* (Samuel), Jan Rubes (Eli Lapp), Alexander Godunov (Daniel Hochleitner)

A young Amish boy witnesses a murder, and a big-city detective hides out in this community to protect him.

As much about the meeting of cultures as about cops and robbers, this is one of those lucky movies which works out well on all counts and shows that there are still craftsmen lurking in Hollywood.

SCR *Earl W. Wallace, William Kelley*   CIN *John Seale*   MUS Maurice Jarre   DES Stan Jolley   ED Thom Noble   DIST Paramount/Edward S. Feldman

❝ It's pretty to look at and it contains a number of good performances, but there is something exhausting about its neat balancing of opposing manners and values. – *Vincent Canby*

❝ Witness arrives like a fresh new day. It is a movie about adults, whose lives have dignity and whose choices matter to them. And it is also one hell of a thriller. – *Roger Ebert, Chicago Sun-Times*

⚱ Thom Noble (editing); original screenplay

⚱ picture; Peter Weir; Harrison Ford (leading actor); photography; music; art direction

Ⓣ music

Witness for the Prosecution ★★★

DIR *Billy Wilder*

1957   114m   US

[DVD]

☆ *Charles Laughton* (Sir Wilfrid Robarts), Tyrone Power (Leonard Stephen Vole), Marlene Dietrich (Christine Helm/Vole), John Williams (Brogan Moore), Henry Daniell (Mayhew), Elsa Lanchester (Miss Plimsoll), Norma Varden (Mrs. Emily French), Una O'Connor (Janet MacKenzie), Ian Wolfe (Carter)

A convalescent QC takes on a murder defence and finds himself in a web of trickery.

Thoroughly likeable though relentlessly over-expanded movie version of a clever stage thriller. Some miscasting and artificiality is condoned by smart dialogue and handling, one celebrated performance, and a handful of surprises.

SCR *Billy Wilder, Harry Kurnitz*   CIN Russell Harlan   MUS Matty Melneck   ED Daniel Mandell   PROD Arthur Hornblow Jnr   DIST UA/Theme/Edward Small

SIE WILFRID: The question is whether you were lying then or are you lying now... or whether in fact you are a chronic and habitual LIAR!

⚱ picture; Billy Wilder; Charles Laughton (leading actor); Elsa Lanchester (supporting actress); Daniel Mandell (editing)

Wittgenstein ★★

DIR *Derek Jarman*

1993   75m   GB/Japan

[DVD]

☆ Karl Johnson (Ludwig Wittgenstein), Michael Gough (Bertrand Russell), Tilda Swinton (Lady Ottoline Morrell), John Quentin (Maynard Keynes), Kevin Collins (Johnny), Clancy Chassay (Young Wittgenstein), Jill Balcon (Leopoldine Wittgenstein)

Biopic of the philosopher Ludwig Wittgenstein.

A film making up for its limited financial means with vast intellectual and visual resources; though likely to be most fully appreciated by fans of the director, or students of his subject, the altogether austere world of Wittgenstein's studies in linguistics is evoked, using bold colours that wouldn't look out of place in a Vincente Minnelli film.

SCR *Derek Jarman, Terry Eagleton, Ken Butler*   CIN James Welland   MUS Jan Latham-Koenig   ED Budge Tremlett   PROD Tariq Ali   DIST BFI/Channel 4/Uplink/Bandung

❝ If it ranges wide rather than deep – the philosophy is either dropped into conversation or presented like a blackboard primer – Jarman still manages to capture the spirit and complexity of his fascinating subject. – *Wally Hammond, Time Out*

The Wizard of Oz ★★★★

DIR *Victor Fleming*

1939   102m   US

[DVD] ♫

☆ *Judy Garland* (Dorothy), *Frank Morgan* (Prof. Marvel/The Wizard/Guard/Coachman), *Ray Bolger* (Hunk/The Scarecrow), *Jack Haley* (Hickory/The Tin Woodsman), *Bert Lahr* (Zeke/The Cowardly Lion), *Margaret Hamilton* (Miss Gulch/The Wicked Witch), Billie Burke (Glinda), Charley Grapewin (Uncle Henry), Clara Blandick (Auntie Em)

Unhappy Dorothy runs away from home, has adventures in a fantasy land, but finally decides that happiness was in her own back yard all the time.

Classic fairy tale given vigorous straightforward treatment, made memorable by performances, art direction and hummable tunes. Perhaps the most beloved family film of all time.

SCR Noel Langley, Florence Ryerson, Edgar Allan Woolf   CIN Harold Rosson   ED Blanche Sewell   PROD Mervyn Le Roy   DIST MGM

SCARECROW (RAY BOLGER): I could while away the hours Conversin' with the flowers Consultin' with the rain. And perhaps I'd deserve you And be even worthy erv you If I only had a brain. . .

COWARDLY LION (BERT LAHR): Oh, it's sad to be admittin' I'm as vicious as a kitten Widout de vim and voive; I could show off my prowess Be a lion, not a mowess If I only had de noive.

GLINDA, THE GOOD WITCH (BILLIE BURKE): Close your eyes and tap your heels together three times. And think to yourself, there's no place like home.

W

[DVD] Available on DVD   ☆ Cast in order of importance   ❝ Critics' Quotes   † Points of interest   ⚱ Academy Award   ⚱ Academy Award nomination   Ⓣ BAFTA   Ⓣ BAFTA nomination

♫ Soundtrack on CD

DOROTHY (JUDY GARLAND): If I ever go looking for my heart's desire again, I won't look any further than my own back yard, because if it isn't there, I never really lost it to begin with.

DOROTHY, LION, SCARECROW, TIN MAN: We're off to see the Wizard The wonderful Wizard of Oz. We hear he is a whiz of a wiz If ever a wiz there was. If ever a wever a wiz there was The Wizard of Oz is one because Because of the wonderful things he does. . .

66 There's an audience for it wherever there's a projection machine and a screen. – *Variety*

66 I don't see why children shouldn't like it, but for adults there isn't very much except Bert Lahr. – *Richard Mallett, Punch*

† Ray Bolger was originally cast as the tin man but swapped roles with Buddy Ebsen who was to have been the scarecrow. Ebsen then got sick from the aluminium dust and was replaced by Jack Haley. Edna May Oliver was originally cast as the wicked witch. For Dorothy MGM wanted Shirley Temple, but Twentieth Century Fox wouldn't loan her.

† The sepia scenes at beginning and end were directed by King Vidor.

† 'Over the Rainbow'; 'Ding Dong the Witch is Dead'; 'We're Off to See the Wizard'; 'Follow the Yellow Brick Road'; 'If I Only Had a Brain'; 'The Merry Old Land of Oz'; 'If I Were King of the Forest'

🏆 Harold Arlen (m), E.Y. Harburg (ly) (music, original song – Over the Rainbow); Herbert Stothart (music); Judy Garland (special award)

🏆 picture; art direction

'The Animal Is Out.'

Wolf ★

DIR Mike Nichols
1994   125m   US
DVD ♫

☆ Jack Nicholson (Will Randall), Michelle Pfeiffer (Laura Alden), James Spader (Stewart Swinton), Kate Nelligan (Charlotte Randall), Christopher Plummer (Raymond Alden), Richard Jenkins (Det. Bridger), Eileen Atkins (Mary), David Hyde Pierce (Roy), Prunella Scales (Maude)

After a cerebral editor-in-chief at a publishing house is bitten by a wolf, he begins to exhibit wolf-like characteristics, hunting and killing a deer, savaging muggers and howling at the moon.

A strange concoction, this: a werewolf film that isn't remotely scary. Indeed, there's something comical about this civilised, tweedy publishing type suddenly growing hair and loping around on all fours. What persuaded Nicholson to play Wolfman Jack? It's a bigger mystery than any contained in the film.

SCR Jim Harrison, Wesley Strick   CIN Giuseppe Rotunno
MUS Ennio Morricone   DES Bo Welch, Jim Dultz
ED Sam O'Steen   PROD Douglas Wick   DIST Columbia

66 Never quite getting its conventions in focus, Wolf plays mix-and-match with werewolf lore from a dozen sources. – *Philip Kemp, Sight & Sound*

66 It's simply too ridiculous for a mainstream audience and too familiar for horror fans. – *Kim Newman, Empire*

Woman of the Dunes ★★★

DIR Hiroshi Teshigahara
1964   127m   Japan
DVD ♫

☆ Eiji Okada (The man), Kyoko Kishoda (The woman)

An insect expert on a deserted beach finds an attractive young widow living in a shack at the bottom of a huge sand pit, and spends the night with her.

Unique sex melodrama, all shifting sand and picturesque angles. The story is open to a number of interpretations, relating to the woman's outcast status and the social undesirability of their tryst. Oblique and strikingly unusual.

SCR Kobo Abe   CIN Hiroshi Segawa   MUS Toru Takemitsu   ED F. Susui   PROD Kiichi Ichikawa
DIST Teshigahara

66 Teasingly opaque, broodingly erotic. – *Monthly Film Bulletin*

🏆 Hiroshi Teshigahara; foreign language film

A Woman under the Influence ★

SCR/DIR John Cassavetes
1974   155m   US
DVD

☆ Peter Falk, Gena Rowlands, Matthew Cassel, Matthew Laborteaux, Christina Grisanti, Katherine Cassavetes

A highly-strung housewife and mother of three indulges in eccentric behaviour, much to the frustration of her husband, who drives her towards a nervous breakdown and a spell in a psychiatric hospital.

Even a truly extraordinary performance by Rowlands cannot overshadow the film's absurdly excessive length.

CIN Mitch Breit, Caleb Deschanel   MUS Bo Harwood
ED Tom Cornwell   PROD Sam Shaw   DIST Faces International

🏆 John Cassavetes (direction); Gena Rowlands (leading actress)

Women in Love ★★★

DIR Ken Russell
1969   130m   GB
DVD

☆ Glenda Jackson (Gudrun Brangwen), Jennie Linden (Ursula Brangwen), Alan Bates (Rupert Birkin), Oliver Reed (Gerald Crich), Michael Gough (Tom Brangwen), Alan Webb (Thomas Crich)

Two young women have their first sexual encounters in a Nottinghamshire mining community in the 1920s.

Satisfactory rendering of a celebrated novel, with excellent period detail atoning for rather irritating characters. The nude male wrestling scene between Bates and Reed was a famous first.

SCR Larry Kramer   CIN Billy Williams   MUS Georges Delerue   ED Michael Bradsell   PROD Larry Kramer
DIST UA/Brandywine

W

DVD Available on DVD   ☆ Cast in order   66 Critics' Quotes   🏆 Academy Award   🅑 BAFTA
♫ Soundtrack on CD   of importance   † Points of interest   🏆 Academy Award nomination   🅑 BAFTA nomination

683

They should take all the pretentious dialogue off the soundtrack and call it Women in Heat. – *Rex Reed*

Two-thirds success, one-third ambitious failure. – *Michael Billington, Illustrated London News*

🏆 Glenda Jackson (leading actress)

🏅 Larry Kramer (adapted screenplay); Ken Russell; Billy Williams

Women on the Verge of a Nervous Breakdown ★★★

SCR/DIR *Pedro Almodóvar*
1988　90m　Spain
DVD

☆ *Carmen Maura* (Pepa), Antonio Banderas (Carlos), Julieta Serrano (Lucía), Maria Barranco (Candela), Rossy de Palma (Marisa), Guillermo Montesinos (Taxista), Kiti Manver (Paulina Morales)

After learning she is pregnant, a woman in Madrid runs into her married lover's family, amongst other unhinged individuals.

Wonderfully inventive, endlessly colourful farce that somehow manages to encompass burning beds, mambo taxi drivers, spiked gazpacho and Shi'ite terrorists.

CIN Jose Luis Alcaine　MUS Bernardo Bonezzi　ED Jose Salcedo　PROD Pedro Almodóvar　DIST Rank/El Deseo/Lauren Film/Orion

An explosion of garish colour, wacky detail and surreal complications. – *David Parkinson, Empire*

The women here aren't afraid to get extreme about love, but in the end, you sense that they are too sound to destroy themselves over the worthless man they have allowed to personify it. That's what lifts Women on the Verge of a Nervous Breakdown from the amusing to the sublime. – *Jay Carr, Boston Globe*

† The film is loosely based on Jean Cocteau's play La Voix Humaine.

🏅 foreign film

Ⓣ film not in the English language

'Undependable. Unpredictable. Unforgettable.'

Wonder Boys ★★

DIR Curtis Hanson
2000　111m　US/Germany/GB/Japan
DVD ♫

☆ *Michael Douglas* (Grady Tripp), Tobey Maguire (James Leer), Frances McDormand (Sara Gaskell), *Robert Downey Jnr* (Terry Grabtree), Katie Holmes (Hannah Green), Richard Thomas (Walter Gaskell), Rip Torn (Q), Philip Bosco (Hank Winters), Jane Adams (Oola), Richard Knox (Vernon Hardapple), Michael Cavaias (Miss Sloviak/Tony)

An academic suffering from writer's block spends an eventful weekend with a morbid young literary prodigy.

A meandering, though often very funny, account of one man's midlife crisis that puts on screen a collection of interesting characters, but doesn't entirely know what to do with them.

SCR *Steve Kloves*　CIN Dante Spinotti　MUS Christopher Young　DES Jeannine Oppewall　ED Dede Allen　PROD Scott Rudin, Curtis Hanson　DIST Paramount

With a cast this terrific and a story this rich and wry, Wonder Boys really can't miss, even if it thumps to an underwhelming and moralistic ending that undoes a fair amount of its goodwill. – *Andrew O'Hehir, Salon*

Sweet, flaky, and more than a little aimless. – *Owen Gleiberman, Entertainment Weekly*

🏆 Bob Dylan (song 'Things Have Changed')

🏅 Steve Kloves (screenplay); Dede Allen

Ⓣ Michael Douglas (leading actor); Steve Kloves (screenplay)

'Everybody's looking for something.'

Wonderland ★

DIR Michael Winterbottom
1999　108m　GB
DVD ♫

☆ Shirley Henderson (Debbie), Gina McKee (Nadia), Molly Parker (Molly), *Ian Hart* (Dan), John Simm (Eddie), Stuart Townsend (Tim), Kika Markham (Eileen), Jack Shepherd (Bill), Enzo Cilenti (Darren), Sarah-Jane Potts (Melanie), David Fahm (Franklyn)

The problems of three sisters come to a head over one weekend in contemporary London.

Despairing mosaic of modern life, full of characters making wrong or incomplete connections to a soundtrack grimly parodying Queen's 'We Are The Champions'; skilfully done, though it makes for altogether chilly viewing.

SCR Laurence Coriat　CIN *Sean Bobbitt*　MUS Michael Nyman　DES Mark Tildesley　ED Trevor Waite　PROD Andrew Eaton, Michele Camarda　DIST Universal

A subtle, moving and evocative document of capital life at the end of the 90s. – *Tom Doyle, Empire*

Its superb performances, music, photography, dialogue, its rhythms of tone and theme all complement each other perfectly. – *Jonathan Foreman, New York Post*

Ⓣ British film

'A wide-eyed boy in a narrow-minded world.'

Wondrous Oblivion ★

SCR/DIR *Paul Morrison*
2003　106m　GB/Germany
DVD

☆ Sam Smith (David Wiseman), *Delroy Lindo* (Dennis Samuels), Emily Woof (Ruth Wiseman), Stanley Townsend (Victor Wiseman), Angela Wynter (Grace Samuels), Leonie Elliott (Judy Samuels), Naomi Simpson (Dorothy Samuels)

The summer of 1960: a young, cricket-mad Jewish boy living in South London is fascinated by his new Jamaican neighbours.

Likable, capably performed drama that, while never straying too far from a Billy Elliot-in-cricket-pads formula, touches on several interesting social and historical themes.

CIN Nina Kellgren　MUS Ilona Sekacz　DES *Eve Stewart*　ED David Freeman　PROD Jonny Persey　DIST Momentum

Somewhat contrived and occasionally sentimental. But it's warm, kindly, and has a heart the size of the Oval. – *Philip French, Observer*

W

'What's the worst thing you ever did?'

The Woodsman ★

DIR Nicole Kassell
2004   87m   US
DVD

☆ *Kevin Bacon* (Walter), Kyra Sedgwick (Vicki), Eve (Mary-Kay), Mos Def (Sgt Lucas), David Alan Grier (Bob), Benjamin Bratt (Carlos), Michael Shannon (Rosen)

A paedophile is paroled after 12 years in prison, and struggles on the outside to suppress his instincts and cope with public hostility.

Sobering account of a flawed, dangerous man's long journey to redemption. Full marks to the ever-reliable Bacon for investing such a character with humanity.

SCR Nicole Kassell, Steven Fechter   **CIN** Xavier Pérez Grobet   **MUS** Nathan Larson   **DES** Stephen Beatrice   **ED** Brian A. Kates, Lisa Fruchtman   **PROD** Lee Daniels

66 Walter is a study in agonised self-loathing, both aware of the horror of his desires and at times utterly and apparently helplessly in their grip. – *Empire*

'For anyone who's ever won. For anyone who's ever lost. And for everyone who's still in there trying.'

Working Girl ★★

DIR *Mike Nichols*
1988   113m   US
DVD   ♫

☆ *Harrison Ford* (Jack Trainer), *Sigourney Weaver* (Katharine Parker), Melanie Griffith (Tess McGill), Alec Baldwin (Mick Dugan), Joan Cusack (Cyn), Philip Bosco (Oren Trask), Nora Dunn (Ginny), Oliver Platt (Lutz), James Lally (Turkel), Olympia Dukakis (Personnel Director)

A secretary discovers her boss has been stealing her ideas, so takes revenge by stealing her man.

Smashing comedy, generally performed smartly, though Griffith's turn as a naive secretary is a little too eager to please.

SCR Kevin Wade   **CIN** Michael Ballhaus   **DES** Patrizia von Brandenstein   **ED** Sam O'Steen   **PROD** Douglas Wick   **DIST** Fox

66 One of those entertainments where you laugh a lot along the way, and then you end up on the edge of your seat at the end. – *Roger Ebert, Chicago Sun-Times*

66 A delectable reworking of the ultimate girl's myth, a corporate Cinderella story with shades of a self-made Pygmalion. – *Rita Kempley, Washington Post*

† It later became a US TV series.

♪ song (Let The River Run by Carly Simon)
♪ picture; Mike Nichols; Melanie Griffith; Joan Cusack; Sigourney Weaver
Ⓣ Sigourney Weaver; Melanie Griffith; Carly Simon

'South Africa, 1963. A mother's love. A family's courage.'

A World Apart ★★★

DIR *Chris Menges*
1987   112m   GB/Zimbabwe
DVD   ♫

☆ *Jodhi May* (Molly Roth), Jeroen Krabbé (Gus Roth), *Barbara Hershey* (Diana Roth), Linda Mvusi (Yvonne

Abelson), David Suchet (Elsie), Paul Freeman (Kruger), Tim Roth (Harold), Yvonne Bryceland (Bertha), Albee Lesotho (Solomon), Rosalie Crutchley (Mrs Harris), David Suchet (Muller)

Anti-apartheid drama about a white woman jailed for supporting the ANC, from the viewpoint of her 13-year-old daughter.

Excellent account of a story with important themes that never tips over into excessive worthiness. Excellently acted and moving mix of political and domestic drama. May, in her film debut, and Hershey are outstanding.

SCR Shawn Slovo   **CIN** Peter Biziou   **MUS** Hans Zimmer   **DES** Brian Morris   **ED** Nicolas Gaster   **PROD** Sarah Radclyffe   **DIST** Palace/British Screen/Atlantic/Working Title

66 Intelligent, unsensational and painful, it's a film to applaud. – *Brian Case, Time Out*

† Shawn Slovo is the daughter of Ruth First, on whose life the story is based.

Ⓑ Shawn Slovo (original screenplay)
Ⓣ David Suchet (supporting actor)

'Some men want to rule the world... Some women ask for the world... Some believe the world is theirs for the taking... But for one man, The World Is Not Enough'

The World Is Not Enough ★★

DIR Michael Apted
1999   128m   US/GB
DVD   ♫

☆ Pierce Brosnan (James Bond), Sophie Marceau (Elektra), Robert Carlyle (Renard), Denise Richards (Christmas Jones), Robbie Coltrane (Valentin Zukovsky), Judi Dench (M), Desmond Llewelyn (Q), John Cleese (R), Maria Grazia Cucinotta (Cigar Girl), Samantha Bond (Moneypenny), Michael Kitchen (Tanner), Colin Salmon (Robinson), Goldie (Bull), David Calder (Sir Robert King), Serena Scott Thomas (Dr Molly Warmflash)

James Bond saves the world from destruction at the hands of a villain with a bullet in his brain which makes it impossible for him to feel pain.

Not so much a film, more a road-tested formula. Preposterous plot plus appalling acting (notably from Richards, risibly cast as a nuclear scientist) and spectacular stunts equals a form of entertainment that ticks all the boxes.

SCR Neal Purvis, Robert Wade, Bruce Feirstein   **CIN** Adrian Biddle   **MUS** David Arnold   **DES** Peter Lamont   **ED** Jim Clark   **PROD** Michael G. Wilson, Barbara Broccoli   **DIST** MGM

66 Like glue, Bond sticks around. Familiar and competent, the last Bond film of the millennium adheres to the formula and mostly succeeds in meeting the ritualistic demands of the series. – *Toronto Globe and Mail*

The World of Apu ★★★★

SCR/DIR *Satyajit Ray*
1959   106m   India
DVD

☆ Soumitra Chatterjee (Apu), Sarmila Tagore (Aparna), Alok Chakravarti (Kajal), Swapan Mukherjee (Pulu), Dhiresh Majumdar (Sasinarayan), Sefalika Devi

W

DVD Available on DVD   ☆ Cast in order of importance   66 Critics' Quotes   ♪ Academy Award   Ⓑ BAFTA
♫ Soundtrack on CD   † Points of interest   Academy Award nomination   Ⓣ BAFTA nomination

685

(Sasinarayan's Wife), Dhires Ghosh (Landlord)

In India, a would-be writer, stuck in a tedious clerical job, struggles to accept the son of his wife, who died in childbirth.

The last part of a monumental trilogy, and a sense that events have moved full circle over the three separate stories. This final episode brings a sense of closure for the members of a troubled family who have known immense hardship and struggle.

CIN Subrata Mitra   **MUS** *Ravi Shankar*   **ED** Dulal Dutta
DIST Satyajit Ray Productions

66 Rich and contemplative, and a great, convincing affirmation. – *Pauline Kael, New Yorker*

† The film is the final part of a trilogy that began with Pather Panchal and continued with Aparajito

'Life is a trip, but the afterlife is a hell of a ride.'

Wristcutters: A Love Story (new)

SCR/DIR Goran Dukic
2006   88m
DVD   ♫

☆ Patrick Fugit (Zia), Shannyn Sossamon (Mikal), Shea Whigham (Eugene), Leslie Bibb (Desiree), Tom Waits (Kneller)

A young slacker, distressed at breaking up with his girl-friend, slashes his wrists and finds himself in a parallel purgatory for suicides.

Leaden fantasy that strives for goofy charm in vain. The purgatory on view also seems to be limited to slack-jawed young inside types with artfully dishevelled hair.

CIN Vanja Cernjul   **MUS** Bobby Johnston   **DES** Linda Sena   **ED** Jonathan Alberts   **PROD** Adam Sherman, Chris Coen, Tatiana Kelly, Mikal P. Lazarev

DIST Miracle/Halcyon

66 Falls victim to its washed-out mood, and limps bloodlessly to a close. – *Cath Clarke, Guardian*

'The Epic Story Of Love And Adventure In A Lawless Land.'

Wyatt Earp   ★★

DIR Lawrence Kasdan
1994   191m   US/Canada
DVD   ♫

☆ *Kevin Costner* (Wyatt Earp), *Dennis Quaid* (Doc Holliday), Gene Hackman (Nicholas Earp), Jeff Fahey (Ike Clanton), Mark Harmon (Johnny Behan), Michael Madsen (Virgil Earp), Catherine O'Hara (Allie Earp), Bill Pullman (Ed Masterson), Isabella Rossellini (Big Nose Kate)

A detailed account of the career of western lawman Wyatt Earp, culminating in his role at the gunfight at the OK Corral.

Serous-minded, beautifully shot, comprehensive Western, with one eye apparently set on being the film of record about Earp. Certainly it concentrates on him as a flawed human being rather than a legend, and Costner, again volunteering for a role that keeps the Western genre alive and kicking, is excellent. Quaid, as the tubercular Doc Holliday, makes a perfect, sometimes comic foil. It's overlong, but its intentions are noble – and it's certainly superior to Tombstone, another film about Earp released the previous year.

SCR Dan Gordon, Lawrence Kasdan   **CIN** *Owen Roizman*
MUS James Newton Howard   **DES** Ida Random
ED Carol Littleton   **PROD** Jim Wilson, Kevin Costner, Lawrence Kasdan   **DIST** Warner/Tig/Kasdan

† The film was originally intended as an eight-hour TV mini-series.

♟ Owen Roizman

'The time has come for those who are different to stand united.'

X2 ☆

DIR Bryan Singer
2003   133m   US
DVD   ♫

☆ Patrick Stewart (Professor Charles Xavier), Hugh Jackman (Logan/Wolverine), Ian McKellen (Eric Lensherr/Magneto), Halle Berry (Storm), Famke Janssen (Jean Grey), James Marsden (Scott Summers/Cyclops), Rebecca Romijn-Stamos (Mystique), Brian Cox (William Stryker), Alan Cumming (Kurt Wagner/Nightcrawler), Bruce Davison (Senator Kelly), Shawn Ashmore (Bobby Drake/Iceman), Anna Paquin (Rogue)

The leaders of rival schools of mutant superheroes team up to counter a hawkish general intent on waging war against all those with the mutant gene.

A typically crowded blockbuster sequel, offering so many superheroes that pretty much every narrative eventuality is covered; what it gains in diversity and spectacle, it lacks in threat, and those unfamiliar with the comic books, or the first X-Men outing, may well have cause to find themselves lost in its labyrinthine plotting.

SCR Michael Dougherty, Dan Harris, David Hayter
CIN Newton Thomas Sigel   MUS John Ottman
DES Guy Hendrix Dyas   ED John Ottman, Elliot Graham
PROD Lauren Shuler Donner, Ralph Winter   DIST TCF

66 Bigger and more ambitious in every respect, from its action and visceral qualities to its themes. – *Todd McCarthy, Variety*

66 The real distinction of Singer's X-films is that he understands the comic-book dictate that something cool or affecting has to happen on every page. No other filmmaker has better dramatised superpowers in action and yet remembered the human cost of all the trickery. – *Kim Newman, Sight and Sound*

XXY (new) ★★

SCR/DIR Lucia Puenzo
2008   86m   Argentina/ Spain/ France

☆ Ines Efron (Alex), Martin Piroyansky (Alvaro), Ricardo Darin (Kraken), Valeria Bertuccelli (Suli), Germán Palacios (Ramiro)

An Argentine family are torn between letting their 15 year old hermaphrodite daughter make up her mind over her eventual sexuality or make the surgical decision for her.

A beautifully judged balancing act between quiet subtlety and resonant directness, this emotional drama about gender politics explores themes of fears, prejudice and acceptance uniquely.

CIN Natasha Braier   MUS Andrés Goldstein, Daniel Tarrab   DES Roberto Samuelle   ED Hugo Primero, Alex Zito   PROD José Maria Morales, Luis Puenzo
DIST Peccadillo Pictures

66 "Lucia Puenzo tackles a dicey subject with sensitivity and taste". – *V A Musetto, New York Post*

DVD Available on DVD   ☆ Cast in order   66 Critics' Quotes   ⏲ Academy Award   🏆 BAFTA
♫ Soundtrack on CD   of importance   † Points of interest   🏆 Academy Award nomination   ⓣ BAFTA nomination

687

Y Tu Mamá También ★★★

DIR *Alfonso Cuarón*

2001   105m   Mexico

[DVD] ♫

☆ *Maribel Verdu* (Luisa Cortes), *Gael Garcia Bernal* (Julio Zapata), *Diego Luna* (Tenoch Iturbide), Diana Bracho (Silvia Allende de Iturbide), Emilio Echevarria (Miguel Iturbide), Ana Lopez Mercado (Ana Morelos), Maria Aura (Cecilia Huerta), Andres Almeida (Diego 'Saba' Madero)

Two Mexican teenagers from different backgrounds head off with a bored older woman in search of an idyllic beach.

Remarkably successful hybrid of teen road movie and social realism that resembles what might have happened if the Godard of Weekend had been brought in to pep up an American Pie script; as engaged as it is by the boys' raunchy antics, it also finds time – through the use of a narrator, and the sad eyes of the boys' travelling companion – to observe the cruel and beautiful world beyond their windscreen. The performances are truly effervescent.

SCR *Alfonso and Carlos Cuarón*   **CIN** *Emmanuel Lubezki*   **DES** Miguel Alvarez, Marc Bedia   **ED** Alfonso Cuarón, Alex Rodriguez   **PROD** Jorge Vergara, Alfonso Cuarón   **DIST** Icon

66 It's a movie where people are rendered more alive by, rather than reduced to, the contexts that surround them. It's beautiful to look at; more importantly, it's invigorating to experience. – *José Arroyo, Sight & Sound*

66 One of the most joyous movies I've ever seen, and one of the handful of great erotic films the movies have given us. – *Charles Taylor, Salon.com*

🏆 Carlos Cuarón; Alfonso Cuarón (screenplay)

Ⓣ film not in the English language; (screenplay)

Yaaba ★★★

SCR/DIR Idrissa Ouédraogo

1989   90m   Burkina Faso/France/Switzerland

[DVD]

☆ Fatima Sanga (Yaaba), Noufou Ouédraogo (Bila), Barry Roukietou (Nopoko), Adama Ouédraogo (Kougri), Amade Toure (Tibo), Sibidou Ouédraogo (Poko), Adame Sidibe (Razougou)

In an African village, a 10-year-old boy remains loyal to an old woman, dismissed as a witch by the community. When his young cousin falls ill, it is her medicine that cures him.

A spellbinding account of life in a setting too rarely seen on western cinema screens. Director Ouédraogo uses a cast of non-professionals, working in an almost documentary style to present the boy's torn loyalties between individual friendship and community duty. The film also subtly comments on the tensions between tradition and modernity. Its tone is wry and gentle, but it's a work of remarkable value. This was the film that put Burkina Faso on the map of world cinema.

CIN Matthias Kalin   **MUS** Francis Bebey   **ED** Loredana Cristelli   **PROD** Idrissa Ouédraogo, Michel David   **DIST** Oasis/Les Films de l'Avenir/Thelma Film/Arcadia Films

† At the 1989 Cannes Film Festival, it won the FIPRESCI prize, awarded by the international press, jointly with sex, lies and videotape.

The Yacoubian Building (new) ★

DIR Marwan Hamed

2006   171m   Egypt

A variety of stories that effect inhabitants of a Cairo apartment building, touching on drugs, corruption, homosexuality, fundamentalism and prostitution.

Based on a runaway best-selling book that fairly teems with life, and is a fond nostalgic memory for a more secular and louche Cairo, this film faithfully imports the agreeable soap-opera quality of its source material, but even at more than three hours cannot do justice to the complexity of these intersecting stories.

SCR Waheed Hamed   **CIN** Sameh Salim   **MUS** Khaled Hammad   **DES** Fawzy El Awamry   **ED** Khaled Marei   **PROD** Emad Al Din Adeeb   **DIST** ICA

66 This adaptation, which, although attractively shot by Sameh Salim, can never fully give order to its teeming tales of the diverse inhabitants of a Cairo apartment block. – *Sukhdev Sandhu, Daily Telegraph*

† At $4 million, this was the most expensive film ever made in Egypt at the time of its completion in 2006.
† Islamist members of Egypt's parliament, already aware of the contents of the novel, tried unsuccessfully to have the film banned.

'There's nothing more dangerous than an innocent man.'

The Yards ★

DIR James Gray

2000   115m   US

[DVD] ♫

☆ Mark Wahlberg (Leo Handler), Joaquin Phoenix (Willie Gutierrez), Charlize Theron (Erica Stoltz), James Caan (Frank Olchin), Ellen Burstyn (Val Handler), Faye Dunaway (Kitty Olchin), Chad Aaron (Bernard Stoltz),

Andrew Davoli (Raymond Price), Steve Lawrence (Arthur Mydanick), Tony Musante (Seymour Korman), Victor Argo (Paul Lazarides), Tomas Milian (Manuel Sequiera), Robert Montano (Hector Gallardo), Victor Arnold (Albert Granada)

An ex-convict who works for his corrupt uncle's subway company and finds himself framed for murder.

Suspense-studded New York thriller full of intricate deviousness and brutal violence. Its sense of place and milieu is strong and bold, though its story never quite convinces.

SCR James Gray, Matt Reeves   CIN Harris Savides   MUS Howard Shore   DES Kevin Thompson   ED Jeffrey Ford   PROD Nick Wechsler, Paul Webster, Kerry Orent   DIST Film4

66 Better in execution than in content. . .the writing is full of ideas but gloomily ambiguous and lacking in originality or excitement. – *Empire*

'It was incredible. It was the year that changed everything. Forever.'

The Year My Voice Broke ★★

SCR/DIR *John Duigan*
1987   103m   Australia
DVD

☆ *Noah Taylor* (Danny Embling), Loene Carmen (Freya Olson), Ben Mendelsohn (Trevor Leishman), Graeme Blundell (Nils Olson), Lynette Curran (Anne Olson), Malcolm Robertson (Bruce Embling), Judi Farr (Sheila Embling)

A shy teenager is traumatised when the girl he loves falls for the local bad boy in 1950s small-town Australia.

Coming-of-age drama that deals with sexual awakening and teenage angst sensitively and without condescension. It's enhanced by gutsy performances from emerging young Australian actors.

CIN Geoff Burton   MUS Christine Woodruff   DES Roger Ford   ED Neil Thumpston   PROD Terry Hayes, Doug Mitchell, George Miller   DIST Palace/Kennedy Miller Productions

66 Director John Duigan's gift for characterization and feel for period give the film its haunting and evocative mood, and hint at something altogether darker than the average teen flick. – *Channel 4*

† Flirting is a sequel that continues the adventures of young Danny Embling, the alter ego of writer-director Duigan.

'Has the world left you a stray?'

Year of the Dog (new) ★

SCR/DIR Mike White
2007   96m   US
DVD

☆ Molly Shannon (Peggy), Laura Dern (Bret), Regina King (Layla), John C. Reilly (Al), Peter Sarsgaard (Newt)

A depressive Los Angeles secretary is distraught at the death of her pet dog, and obsessively takes in hordes of stray dogs who wreck her home.

A dark-hued comedy with unusual subject matter. But Shannon is of one of nature's sidekicks rather than a lead actress, and a sentimental ending undermines the tone.

CIN Tim Orr   MUS Christophe Beck   DES Daniel Bradford   ED Dody Dorn   PROD Mike White, Ben Leclair, Dede Gardner   DIST Paramount

66 The best evocation I've seen of how much worse it is to be depressed in a sunny climate. – *Ella Taylor, L.A. Weekly*

66 Loses its way, as if uncertain how to point out its moral and make us laugh at the same time.' – *Derek Malcolm, Evening Standard*

'Crank it up.'

Year of the Horse ★★

DIR Jim Jarmusch
1997   106m   US
DVD

☆ Neil Young, Frank 'Poncho' Sempedro, Billy Talbot, Ralph Molina

Concert footage of the 1996 tour by Neil Young and his group Crazy Horse, intercut with archive material from earlier days of their long history together.

An affectionate documentary tribute to one of the most enduring and restless talents of the rock era, and his talented but frequently troubled backing band. They certainly play better than they explain themselves on camera, but director Jarmusch ably nails their faintly renegade spirit.

CIN L. A. Johnson, Jim Jarmusch, Arthur Rosato, Steve Onuska   MUS Crazy Horse   ED Jay Rabinowitz   PROD L. A. Johnson   DIST October/Shakey Pictures

Yella (new) ★★

SCR/DIR Christian Petzold
2007   89m   Germany
DVD

☆ Nina Hoss (Yella), Devid Striesow (Philipp), Hinnerk Schoenemann (Ben), Burghart Klaussner (Dr. Gunthen), Barbara Auer (Barbara Gunthen), Christian Redl (Yella's Father)

A young woman from the former East Germany finds her attempts to get ahead in business complicated by surreal events.

Chilly, oblique drama with a supernatural twist; one might also read it as a critique of the new Europe.

CIN Hans Fromm   DES Kade Gruber   ED Bettina Bohler   PROD Florian Koerner von Gustorf, Michael Weber   DIST Artificial Eye

66 Petzold's portrait of the intricate and erotic dynamics of high finance is unusually sophisticated. – *Sukhdev Sandhu, Daily Telegraph*

66 Exquisitely frigid, menacing, disquieting. – *Peter Bradshaw, Guardian*

DVD Available on DVD   ☆ Cast in order   66 Critics' Quotes   ⚜ Academy Award   BAFTA
♫ Soundtrack on CD   of importance   † Points of interest   ⚜ Academy Award nomination   BAFTA nomination

Yojimbo ★★★

DIR *Akira Kurosawa*
1961 110m Japan
`DVD`

☆ Toshiro Mifune (Sanjuro Kuwabatake), Eijiro Tono (Gonji the Sake Seller), Kamatari Fujiwara (Tazaemon), Takashi Shimura (Tokuemon), Seizaburo Kawazu (Seibei), Isuzu Yamada (Orin), Hiroshi Tachikawa (Yoichiro)

A wandering samurai offers his fighting skills to two rival gangs of cutthroats, to trick them into destroying one other.

Masterful, beautifully composed, witty movie that inspired the 'spaghetti Western' cycle when it was remade by Sergio Leone as A Fistful Of Dollars.

SCR Ryuzo Kikushima, Akira Kurosawa **CIN** *Kazuo Miyagawa* **MUS** Masuru Sato **DIST** Toho

66 Dark humour is balanced in the film by other moments approaching slapstick. – *Roger Ebert, Chicago Sun-Times*

You, the Living (new) ★

SCR/DIR Roy Andersson
2007 93m
Sweden/Germany/France/Denmark/Norway/Japan
☆ Jessika Lundberg (Anna), Elisabet Helander (Mia), Bjorn Englund (Tuba Player), Leif Larsson (Carpenter), Ollie Olson (Consultant), Kemal Sener (Barber)

Against a faceless urban landscape, lonely city dwellers use music, alcohol and dreams to deal with their lives.

Bleak tableau of human despair, made up of long and static compositions and shot through with absurdist humour.

CIN Gustav Danielsson **MUS** Robert Hefter **ED** Anna Marta Waern **PROD** Roy Andersson, Philippe Bober, Susanne Marian, Carsten Brandt, Hakon Overas
DIST Artificial Eye

66 Andersson's movie reveals poetic ironies, surreal slapstick and melancholy truths, often all wrapped up together. – *Tom Charity, Total Film*

66 Grim but amusing. – *David Parkinson, Empire*

† The film begins with an epigram by Goethe: 'Be pleased then, you the living, in your delightfully warmed bed, before Lethe's ice-cold wave will lick your escaping foot.'
† Funding difficulties caused the production to close down twice.

You Can Count On Me ★★

SCR/DIR *Kenneth Lonergan*
2000 111m US
`DVD` ♫

☆ *Laura Linney* (Sammy Prescott), *Mark Ruffalo* (Terry Prescott), Rory Culkin (Rudy), *Matthew Broderick* (Brian), Jon Tenney (Bob), J. Smith-Cameron (Mabel), Kenneth Lonergan (Ron)

The life of a hard-working single mother in a small town is changed when her brother returns from jail.

A quietly impressive, well-written and very capably performed drama of reconciliation, if finally a bit too familiar to many others of its type: it all ends in the expected hugs and tears.

CIN Stephen Kazmierski **MUS** Lesley Barber
DES Michael Shaw **ED** Anne McCabe **PROD** John Hart, Jeff Sharp, Larry Meistrich, Barbara De Fina

66 A film in which much is confronted and little resolved, and it is played to something like perfection. – *Philip French, Observer*

66 Maybe these lives are, objectively speaking, inconsequential. But they have a resonance that big, sappy 'relationship' pictures ought to envy. – *Richard Schickel, Time*

⚱ Kenneth Lonergan (script); Laura Linney

'A killer comedy by John Dahl.'

You Kill Me (new) ★

DIR John Dahl
2007 92m US
☆ Ben Kingsley (Frank Falenczyk), Téa Leoni (Laurel Pearson), Luke Wilson (Tom), Dennis Farina (Edward O'Leary), Philip Baker Hall (Roman Krzeminski), Bill Pullman (Dave), Marcus Thomas (Stef Czyprynski)

An alcoholic Buffalo hitman sent to San Francisco to dry out finds love, sobriety and a new calling.

Jet-black comedy with a sentimental streak; performances are a delight, though the material feels familiar.

SCR Christopher Markus, Stephen McFeely **CIN** Jeffrey Jur **MUS** Marcelo Zarvos **DES** John Dondertman
ED Scott Chestnut **PROD** Al Corley, Bart Rosenblatt, Eugene Musso, Carol Baum, Mike Marcus, Zvi Howard Rosenman **DIST** Revolver

66 You Kill Me is never less than mildly entertaining, and it's almost never more than that. – *Mick LaSalle, San Francisco Chronicle*

66 An inert, tone-deaf melange of The Sopranos and Six Feet Under. – *Scott Foundas, Village Voice*

Young Adam

SCR/DIR David Mackenzie
2002 98m GB/France
`DVD` ♫

☆ Ewan McGregor (Joe Taylor), Tilda Swinton (Ella Gault), Peter Mullan (Les Gault), Emily Mortimer (Cathie Dimly), Jack McElhone (Jim Gault), Therese Bradley (Gwen), Ewan Stewart (Daniel Gordon), Stuart McQuarrie (Bill)

Scotland, the 1950s: a frustrated writer encounters sex and death while working as a bargehand on the boat of a married couple.

An altogether grim and joyless experience that seems determined to keep its audience in a dark place from which nothing useful can be learned; what begins as a writer's callow, self-regarding fantasy drifts off into mopey nihilism.

CIN Giles Nuttgens **MUS** David Byrne **DES** Laurence Dorman **ED** Colin Monie **PROD** Jeremy Thomas
DIST Warner

66 A film in which mood matters more than plot, while the hero's heroic stature steadily shrinks. – *Jonathan Rosenbaum, Chicago Reader*

66 There are movies that are important, and then there are movies that simply look and act as if they're important. With its arthouse cast, hipster credentials and ominous

atmosphere, Young Adam never bothers to reach for real significance. – *Elizabeth Weitzman, New York Daily News*

'Six reasons why the west was wild.'

Young Guns ★

DIR Christopher Cain

1988   107m   US

DVD

☆ Emilio Estevez (William H. 'Billy the Kid' Bonney), Kiefer Sutherland (Josiah Gordon 'Doc' Scurlock), Lou Diamond Phillips ('Jose' Chavez y Chavez), Charlie Sheen (Richard 'Dick' Brewer), Dermot Mulroney (Dirty Steve Stephens), Casey Siemaszko (Charles 'Charley' Bowdre), Terence Stamp (John Tunstall), Jack Palance (Lawrence G. Murphy), Patrick Wayne (Patrick Floyd 'Pat' Garrett)

A gang of young ranch hands, led by Billy 'the Kid' Bonney, seek revenge on the men who murdered their employer.

Evidence of the increased financial viability of the teen pic in the 1980s, resurrecting with some success a genre that had been left for dead after Heaven's Gate; the result is shallow, good-looking fun, pacily directed, but bigger on the violence of the West than any of its attendant myths.

SCR John Fusco   CIN Dean Semler   MUS Anthony Marinelli, Brian Banks   DES Jane Musky   ED Jack Hofstra   PROD Joe Roth, Christopher Cain   DIST Vestron/Morgan Creek Productions

❝ A mixed homage to the craggy Arizona landscape and the pert boyishness of the Brat Pack cast. Little more than a flawed romp, but energetic and enjoyable, with sterling performances. – *Elaine Paterson, Time Out*

'The Story Of Abraham Lincoln That Has Never Been Told!'

Young Mr Lincoln ★★★

DIR *John Ford*

1939   100m   US

DVD

☆ *Henry Fonda* (Abraham Lincoln), *Alice Brady* (Abigail Clay), Marjorie Weaver (Mary Todd), Arleen Whelan (Hannah Clay), Eddie Collins (Efe Turner), Richard Cromwell (Matt Clay), Donald Meek (John Felder), Eddie Quillan (Adam Clay), Spencer Charters (Judge Herbert A. Bell)

Abraham Lincoln as a young country lawyer stops a lynching and proves a young man innocent of murder.

Splendid performances and period atmosphere, with Honest Abe played as an idealised hero. But this is a marvellous old-fashioned entertainment with its heart in the right place.

SCR *Lamar Trotti*   CIN *Bert Glennon*   MUS Alfred Newman   ED Walter Thompson   PROD Kenneth MacGowan   DIST TCF

❝ A dignified saga of early Lincolniana, paced rather slowly . . . lack of romance interest is one of the prime factors which deter the film from interpreting itself into big box office. – *Variety*

❝ Its simple good faith and understanding are an

expression of the country's best life that says as much as 40 epics. – *Otis Ferguson*

⚲ Lamar Trotti (original screenplay)

'Nothing's More Deadly Than A Poisoned Mind'

The Young Poisoner's Handbook ★

DIR Benjamin Ross

1994   99m   GB/Germany/France

DVD

☆ Hugh O'Conor (Graham Young), Anthony Sher (Dr. Ernest Zeigler), Ruth Sheen (Molly), Roger Lloyd Pack (Fred), Charlotte Coleman (Winnie), Paul Stacey (Dennis), Samantha Edmonds (Sue)

A 14-year-old English boy poisons his stepmother and uncle and is sent to a hospital for the criminally insane. Later he is declared cured, but kills more people.

A jaw-dropping true story is dramatised with style, witty observations about suburbia – and the darkest of humour, though friends and relatives of Graham Young's victims would doubtless fail to see the joke. A notable debut from a director whose promise seems largely unfulfilled.

SCR Jeff Rawle, Benjamin Ross   CIN Hubert Taczanowski   MUS Robert Lane, Frankie Strobel   DES Maria Djorkovic   ED Anne Sopel   PROD Sam Taylor   DIST Electric/Mass/Kinowelt/Haut et Court

❝ A dark comedy of questionable taste. – *Edward Guthmann, San Francisco Chronicle*

Young Soul Rebels

DIR Isaac Julien

1991   105m   GB/France/Germany/Spain

DVD   ♫

☆ Valentine Nonyela (Chris), Mo Sesay (Caz), Dorian Healy (Ken), Frances Barber (Ann), Sophie Okonedo (Tracy), Jason Durr (Billibud), Gary McDonald (Davis), Debra Gillet (Jill)

In 1977, at the time of the Silver Jubilee, two young black friends who run a pirate radio station from a high-rise tower block in London set out to investigate a gay friend's murder.

A film that for years commanded extraordinary loyalty in certain British industry circles, probably because it ticked so many boxes: the first feature from a gay black British director, and one that dealt with identity, Britishness and the treatment of minority groups. But it simply doesn't work: director Julien clearly has a long agenda, and he tries to cover all its points in a story of under two hours. In the end, this is pamphleteering rather than movie-making.

SCR Paul Hallam, Derrick Saldaan McClintock, Isaac Julien   CIN Nina Kellgren   MUS Simon Boswell   DES Derek Brown   ED John Wilson   PROD Nadine Marsh-Edwards   DIST BFI/Film Four/Sankofa/La Sept/Kinowelt/Iberoamericana

❝ The film suffers from weak performances and an undernourished script that never frames its ideas within a gripping narrative. – *Geoff Andrew, Time Out*

DVD Available on DVD   ☆ Cast in order of importance   ❝ Critics' Quotes   ⚲ Academy Award   Ⓑ BAFTA

♫ Soundtrack on CD   † Points of interest   ⚲ Academy Award nomination   Ⓑ BAFTA nomination

Youth Without Youth (new)

SCR/DIR Francis Ford Coppola
2007　124m　Romania/France/Italy/US
[DVD] ♫

☆ Tim Roth (Dominic Matei), Alexandria Maria Lara (Veronica/Laura/Rupini), Bruno Ganz (Professor Stanciulescu)

An elderly professor is struck by lightning and finds his body is mysteriously rejuvenated. He rediscovers the love of his life, who has multiple identities.

A baffling, rambling story, incorporating secrets of eternal youth, lost love, Nazi spy rings, hunts for treasure and philosophical dialogue. Even more baffling is why this great but exasperating film-maker chose to adapt it.

CIN Mihai Malaimare Jr.　**MUS** Osvaldo Golijov
DES Calin Papura　**ED** Walter Murch　**PROD** Francis Ford Coppola　**DIST** Pathé

❝ A very minor work, self-indulgent beyond belief. – *Roger Clarke, Sight & Sound*

❝ Not quite a complete write-off, but basically a folly. – *Kim Newman, Empire*

† This was Coppola's first official directing work for a decade, since The Rainmaker (1997)

'Someone you pass on the street may already be the love of your life.'

You've Got Mail　　　　　　　　　　★

DIR Nora Ephron
1998　119m　US
[DVD] ♫

☆ Tom Hanks (Joe Fox), Meg Ryan (Kathleen Kelly), Parker Posey (Patricia Eden), Greg Kinnear (Frank Navasky), Jean Stapleton (Birdie Conrad), Steve Zahn (George Pappas), David Chappelle (Kevin Jackson), Dabney Coleman (Nelson Fox), John Randolph (Schuyler Fox), Heather Burns (Christina Plutzker)

The owner of an independent bookstore in New York begins an online relationship with the corporate raider trying to put her out of business.

Bizarre attempt at rethinking The Shop Around the Corner for the age of viral marketing: it wants to be wistful and old-fashioned at the same time as being plugged-in and mercenary, and – despite occasionally funny screenwriting and appealing performers – can't quite reconcile the two aims.

SCR Nora Ephron, Delia Ephron　**CIN** John Lindley
MUS George Fenton　**DES** Dan Davis　**ED** Richard Marks　**PROD** Nora Ephron, Lauren Shuler Donner
DIST Warner

❝ The movie, without seeming to realise it, turns into a romantic parable about the joys of being absorbed by a conglomerate. – *David Edelstein, Slate*

❝ Filmmaking as a minor feat of engineering, the kind where even the gossamer emotions seem like prefab components – charm, whimsy, serendipity, all so many discs plugged into the hard drive. – *Rick Groen, Toronto Globe and Mail*

† Laszlo's play had previously inspired both Lubitsch's 1940 film and the 1949 musical In the Good Old Summertime.

Y

Z

★★★★

DIR *Costa-Gavras*

1968 125m France/Algeria

DVD ♫

☆ Jean-Louis Trintignant (The Examining Magistrate), Jacques Pérrin (Photojournalist), Yves Montand (The Deputy), François Périer (Public Prosecutor), Irene Papas (Helene), Charles Denner (Manuel)

In Greece, a leading opposition MP is murdered at a rally. The police are anxious to establish the event as an accident, but the examining magistrate proves otherwise.

An exciting police suspense drama which also recalls events under the Greek colonels and was therefore highly fashionable for a while both as entertainment and as a political roman à clef.

SCR *Costa-Gavras, Jorge Semprun* CIN Raoul Coutard
MUS Mikis Theodorakis DES Jacques D'Ovidio
ED Françoise Bonnot DIST Reggane/ONCIC/Jacques Pérrin

66 These would seem to be completely political events, but the young director Costa-Gavras has told them in a style that is almost unbearably exciting. Z is at the same time a political cry of rage and a brilliant suspense thriller. – *Roger Ebert, Chicago Sun-Times*

⚲ foreign language film
⚲ picture; Costa-Gavras (director); Costa-Gavras, Jorge Semprun (adapted screenplay)
Ⓣ Mikis Theodorakis

Zatoichi

★

SCR/DIR Takeshi Kitano

2003 116m Japan

DVD ♫

☆ Beat Takeshi (Zatoichi), Tadanobu Asano (Hattori), Michiyo Ogusu (Aunt Oume), Yui Natsukawa (Hattori's Wife), Gadarukanaru Taka (Shinkichi), Daigoro Tachibana (Osei, the Geisha), Yuuko Daike (Okinu, the Geisha), Ittoku Kishibe (Ginzo)

A blind masseur and swordsman helps two siblings avenge the slaying of their family by a penny-pinching overlord.

Larky post-modern revival of a frequently recurring character in Japanese cinema, delighting in all manner of digressions – stand-up routines, magic tricks, balancing acts, musical numbers – and comical, fountain-like sprays of computer-generated blood. The director/star goes through it all with his eyes firmly closed.

CIN Katsumi Yanagishima MUS Keiichi Suzuki
DES Norihiro Isoda ED Takeshi Kitano, Yoshinori Oota
PROD Masayuki Mori, Tsunehisa Saito DIST Artificial Eye

66 Uses exaggerated acting, choreographed violence and, most radically, the rhythms of everyday life – farmers pounding the earth, the syncopated plop of falling rain – to turn this genre story into a crypto-Kabuki play and one blissfully idiosyncratic diversion. – *Manohla Dargis, Los Angeles Times*

66 Despite the bizarre mix of ingredients, nothing feels forced or uncomfortable, and it all looks like the simple result of Kitano's boisterous mission to entertain – by any means necessary. – *Peter Bradshaw, Guardian*

Zéro de Conduite

★★★

SCR/DIR *Jean Vigo*

1933 45m France

DVD

☆ Jean Dasté (Monitor Huguet), Louis Lefébvre (Caussat), Gilbert Pruchon (Colin), le nain Delphin (Principal)

Boys return from the holiday to a nasty little boarding school, where the headmaster is an unpleasant dwarf and all the staff are hateful. A revolution breaks out.

A clear forerunner of If . . . and one of the most famous of surrealist films, though it pales beside Buñuel and is chiefly valuable for being funny.

CIN Boris Kaufman MUS Maurice Jaubert ED Jean Vigo DIST Gaumont/Franco Film/Aubert

66 One of the most poetic films ever made and one of the most influential. – *New Yorker, 1978*

66 A wholly original creation, the film walks a narrow line between surrealist farce and social realism. – *Dave Kehr, Chicago Reader*

'3% Body Fat. 1% Brain Activity.'

Zoolander

★

DIR Ben Stiller

2001 89m US/Germany/Australia

DVD ♫

☆ *Ben Stiller* (Derek Zoolander), *Owen Wilson* (Hansel), Will Ferrell (Mugatu), Christine Taylor (Matilda Jeffries), Milla Jovovich (Katinka), Jerry Stiller (Maury Ballstein), Jon Voight (Larry Zoolander), David Duchovny (J. P. Prewitt), Judah Friedlander (Scrappy Zoolander)

A vain, famous male model, renowned for his 'blue steel' stare at fashion shoots, finds his position usurped by a new supermodel.

Stiller and Wilson inhabit their roles with true conviction, and the results are intermittently amusing. But satirising the fashion industry is a bit like shooting fish in a barrel, and the laughs come too easily. As for a bizarre subplot in which Zoolander is brainwashed to assassinate the Prime Minister of Malaysia, it smacks of crass insensitivity and xenophobia: did no-one connected with the film know that Malaysia is a real country?

SCR Drake Sather, Ben Stiller, John Hamburg **CIN** Barry Peterson **MUS** David Arnold **DES** Robin Standefer **ED** Greg Hayden **PROD** Scott Rudin, Ben Stiller, Stuart Cornfeld **DIST** Paramount

ZOOLANDER: I'm pretty sure there's a lot more to life than being really, really, ridiculously good looking. And I plan on finding out what that is.

66 What Zoolander does have, and this was enough for me, is a sublime comic performance by Owen Wilson, as the supermodel Hansel, positively radiant in its dimness. – *Carrie Rickey, Philadelphia Inquirer*

66 There have been articles lately asking why the United States is so hated in some parts of the world. As this week's Exhibit A from Hollywood, I offer Zoolander. – *Roger Ebert, Chicago Sun-Times*

ACADEMY AWARD WINNERS

1927/28
Picture: *Wings*
Unique and Artistic Picture: *Sunrise* (F. W. Murnau)
Director: Frank Borzage (*Seventh Heaven*)
Comedy Director: Lewis Milestone (*Two Arabian Knights*)
Actor: Emil Jannings (*The Last Command, The Way of All Flesh*)
Actress: Janet Gaynor (*Seventh Heaven, Street Angel, Sunrise*)
Original Screenplay: Ben Hecht (*Underworld*)
Adapted Screenplay: Benjamin Glazer (*Seventh Heaven*)
Title Writing: Joseph Farnham (*Telling the World*)

1928/29
Picture: *Broadway Melody*
Director: Frank Lloyd (*The Divine Lady, Weary River, Drag*)
Actor: Warner Baxter (*Old Arizona*)
Actress: Mary Pickford (*Coquette*)
Writing Achievement: Hans Kraly (*The Patriot*)

1929/30
Picture: *All Quiet on the Western Front*
Director: Lewis Milestone (*All Quiet on the Western Front*)
Actor: George Arliss (*Disraeli*)
Actress: Norma Shearer (*The Divorcee*)
Writing Achievement: Frances Marion (*The Big House*)

1930/31
Picture: *Cimarron*
Director: Norman Taurog (*Skippy*)
Actor: Lionel Barrymore (*A Free Soul*)
Actress: Marie Dressler (*Min and Bill*)
Original Screenplay: John Monk Saunders (*The Dawn Patrol*)
Adapted Screenplay: Howard Eastabrook (*Cimarron*)

1931/32
Picture: *Grand Hotel*
Director: Frank Borzage (*Bad Girl*)
Actor: Wallace Beery (*The Champ*), Fredric March (*Dr Jekyll and Mr Hyde*)
Actress: Helen Hayes (*The Sin of Madelon Claudet*)
Original Screenplay: Francis Marion (*The Champ*)
Adapted Screenplay: Edwin Burke (*Bad Girl*)

1932/33
Picture: *Cavalcade*
Director: Frank Lloyd (*Cavalcade*)
Actor: Charles Laughton (*The Private Life of Henry VIII*)
Actress: Katharine Hepburn (*Morning Glory*)
Original Screenplay: Robert Lord (*One Way Passage*)
Adapted Screenplay: Victor Heerman, Sarah Y. Mason (*Little Women*)

1934
Picture: *It Happened One Night*
Director: Frank Capra (*It Happened One Night*)
Actor: Clark Gable (*It Happened One Night*)
Actress: Claudette Colbert (*It Happened One Night*)
Original Screenplay: Arthur Caesar (*Manhattan Melodrama*)
Adapted Screenplay: Robert Riskin (*It Happened One Night*)

1935
Picture: *Mutiny on the Bounty*
Director: John Ford (*The Informer*)
Actor: Victor McLaglen (*The Informer*)
Actress: Bette Davis (*Dangerous*)
Original Screenplay: Ben Hecht, Charles MacArthur (*The Scoundrel*)
Adapted Screenplay: Dudley Nichols (*The Informer*)

1936
Picture: *The Great Ziegfeld*
Director: Frank Capra (*Mr Deeds Goes to Town*)
Actor: Paul Muni (*The Story of Louis Pasteur*)
Actress: Luise Rainer (*The Great Ziegfeld*)
Supporting Actor: Walter Brennan (*Come and Get It*)
Supporting Actress: Gale Sondergaard (*Anthony Adverse*)
Original Screenplay: Pierre Collings, Sheridan Gibney (*The Story of Louis Pasteur*)

1937
Picture: *The Life of Emile Zola*
Director: Leo McCarey (*The Awful Truth*)
Actor: Spencer Tracy (*Captains Courageous*)
Actress: Luise Rainer (*The Good Earth*)
Supporting Actor: Joseph Schildkraut (*The Life of Emile Zola*)
Supporting Actress: Alice Brady (*In Old Chicago*)
Original Story: William A. Wellman, Robert Carson (*A Star Is Born*)
Original Screenplay: Heinz Herald, Geza Herczeg, Norman Reilly Raine (*The Life of Emile Zola*)

1938
Picture: *You Can't Take It with You*
Director: Frank Capra (*You Can't Take It with You*)
Actor: Spencer Tracy (*Boys' Town*)
Actress: Bette Davis (*Jezebel*)
Supporting Actor: Walter Brennan (*Kentucky*)
Supporting Actress: Fay Bainter (*Jezebel*)
Original Story: Eleanore Griffin, Dore Schary (*Boys' Town*)
Screenplay: George Bernard Shaw, adapted by Ian Dalrymple, Cecil Lewis, W. P. Liscomb (*Pygmalion*)

1939
Picture: *Gone with the Wind*
Director: Victor Fleming (*Gone with the Wind*)
Actor: Robert Donat (*Goodbye Mr Chips*)
Actress: Vivien Leigh (*Gone with the Wind*)
Supporting Actor: Thomas Mitchell (*Stagecoach*)
Supporting Actress: Hattie McDaniel (*Gone with the Wind*)
Original Story: Lewis R. Foster (*Mr Deeds Goes to Washington*)
Screenplay: Sidney Howard (*Gone with the Wind*)

1940
Picture: *Rebecca*
Director: John Ford (*The Grapes of Wrath*)
Actor: James Stewart (*The Philadelphia Story*)
Actress: Ginger Rogers (*Kitty Foyle*)
Supporting Actor: Walter Brennan (*The Westerner*)
Supporting Actress: Jane Darwell (*The Grapes of Wrath*)
Original Story: Benjamin Glazer, John S. Toldy (*Arise My Love*)

Original Screenplay: Preston Sturges (*The Great McGinty*)
Screenplay: Donald Ogden Stewart (*The Philadelphia Story*)

1941

Picture: *How Green Was My Valley*
Director: John Ford (*How Green Was My Valley*)
Actor: Gary Cooper (*Sergeant York*)
Actress: Joan Fontaine (*Suspicion*)
Supporting Actor: Donald Crisp (*How Green Was My Valley*)
Supporting Actress: Mary Astor (*The Great Lie*)
Original Story: Harry Segall (*Here Comes Mr Jordan*)
Original Screenplay: Herman J. Mankiewicz, Orson Welles (*Citizen Kane*)
Screenplay: Sidney Buchman, Seton I. Miller (*Here Comes Mr Jordan*)

1942

Picture: *Mrs Miniver*
Director: William Wyler (*Mrs Miniver*)
Actor: James Cagney (*Yankee Doodle Dandy*)
Actress: Greer Garson (*Mrs Miniver*)
Supporting Actor: Van Heflin (*Johnny Eager*)
Supporting Actress: Teresa Wright (*Mrs Miniver*)
Original Story: Emeric Pressburger (*The Invaders*)
Original Screenplay: Michael Kanin, Ring Lardner Jnr (*Woman of the Year*)
Screenplay: George Froeschel, James Hilton, Claudine West, Arthur Wimperis (*Mrs Miniver*)

1943

Picture: *Casablanca*
Director: Michael Curtiz (*Casablanca*)
Actor: Paul Lukas (*Watch on the Rhine*)
Actress: Jennifer Jones (*Song of Bernadette*)
Supporting Actor: Charles Coburn (*The More the Merrier*)
Supporting Actress: Katina Paxinou (*For Whom the Bell Tolls*)
Original Story: William Saroyan (*The Human Comedy*)
Original Screenplay: Norman Krasna (*Princess O'Rourke*)
Screenplay: Julius J. Epstein, Philip G. Epstein, Howard Koch (*Casablanca*)

1944

Picture: *Going My Way*
Director: Leo McCarey (*Going My Way*)
Actor: Bing Crosby (*Going My Way*)
Actress: Ingrid Bergman (*Gaslight*)
Supporting Actor: Barry Fitzgerald (*Going My Way*)
Supporting Actress: Ethel Barrymore (*None but the Lonely Heart*)
Original Story: Leo McCarey (*Going My Way*)
Original Screenplay: Lamar Trotti (*Wilson*)
Screenplay: Frank Butler, Frank Cavett (*Going My Way*)

1945

Picture: *The Lost Weekend*
Director: Billy Wilder (*The Lost Weekend*)
Actor: Ray Milland (*The Lost Weekend*)
Actress: Joan Crawford (*Mildred Pierce*)
Supporting Actor: James Dunn (*A Tree Grows in Brooklyn*)
Supporting Actress: Anne Revere (*National Velvet*)
Original Story: Charles G. Booth (*The House on 92nd Street*)
Original Screenplay: Richard Schweizer (*Marie-Louise*)
Screenplay: Charles Brackett, Billy Wilder (*The Lost Weekend*)

1946

Picture: *The Best Years of Our Lives*
Director: William Wyler (*The Best Years of Our Lives*)
Actor: Fredric March (*The Best Years of Our Lives*)
Actress: Olivia de Havilland (*To Each His Own*)
Supporting Actor: Harold Russell (*The Best Years of Our Lives*)
Supporting Actress: Anne Baxter (*The Razor's Edge*)
Original Story: Clemence Dane (*Vacation from Marriage*)
Original Screenplay: Muriel Box, Sydney Box (*The Seventh Veil*)
Screenplay: Robert E. Sherwood (*The Best Years of Our Lives*)

1947

Picture: *Gentleman's Agreement*
Director: Elia Kazan (*Gentleman's Agreement*)
Actor: Ronald Colman (*A Double Life*)
Actress: Loretta Young (*The Farmer's Daughter*)
Supporting Actor: Edmund Gwenn (*Miracle on 34th Street*)
Supporting Actress: Celeste Holm (*Gentleman's Agreement*)
Original Story: Valentine Davies (*Miracle on 34th Street*)
Original Screenplay: Sidney Sheldon (*The Bachelor and the Bobby-Soxer*)
Screenplay: George Seaton (*Miracle on 34th Street*)

1948

Picture: *Hamlet*
Director: John Huston (*The Treasure of the Sierra Madre*)
Actor: Laurence Olivier (*Hamlet*)
Actress: Jane Wyman (*Johnny Belinda*)
Supporting Actor: Walter Huston (*The Treasure of the Sierra Madre*)
Supporting Actress: Claire Trevor (*Key Largo*)
Motion Picture Story: Richard Sweizer, David Wechsler (*The Search*)
Screenplay: John Huston (*The Treasure of the Sierra Madre*)

1949

Picture: *All the King's Men*
Director: Joseph L. Mankiewicz (*A Letter to Three Wives*)
Actor: Broderick Crawford (*All the King's Men*)
Actress: Olivia de Havilland (*The Heiress*)
Supporting Actor: Dean Jagger (*Twelve O'Clock High*)
Supporting Actress: Mercedes McCambridge (*All the King's Men*)
Motion Picture Story: Douglas Morrow (*The Stratton Story*)
Screenplay: Joseph L. Mankiewicz (*A Letter to Three Wives*)
Story & Screenplay: Robert Pirosh (*Battleground*)

1950

Picture: *All About Eve*
Director: Joseph L. Mankiewicz (*All About Eve*)
Actor: José Ferrer (*Cyrano de Bergerac*)
Actress; Judy Holliday (*Born Yesterday*)
Supporting Actor: George Sanders (*All About Eve*)
Supporting Actress: Josephine Hull (*Harvey*)
Motion Picture Story: Edna Anhalt, Edward Anhalt (*Panic in the Streets*)
Screenplay: Joseph L. Mankiewicz (*All About Eve*)
Story & Screenplay: Charles Brackett, Billy Wilder, D. M. Marshman Jnr (*Sunset Boulevard*)

1951

Picture: *An American in Paris*
Director: George Stevens (*A Place in the Sun*)
Actor: Humphrey Bogart (*The African Queen*)
Actress: Vivien Leigh (*A Streetcar Named Desire*)
Supporting Actor: Karl Malden (*A Streetcar Named Desire*)

Supporting Actress: Kim Hunter (*A Streetcar Named Desire*)
Motion Picture Story: Paul Dehn, James Bernard (*Seven Days to Noon*)
Screenplay: Michael Wilson, Harry Brown (*A Place in the Sun*)
Story & Screenplay: Alan Jay Lerner (*An American in Paris*)

1952

Picture: *The Greatest Show on Earth*
Director: John Ford (*The Quiet Man*)
Actor: Gary Cooper (*High Noon*)
Actress: Shirley Booth (*Come Back Little Sheba*)
Supporting Actor: Anthony Quinn (*Viva Zapata!*)
Supporting Actress: Gloria Grahame (*The Bad and the Beautiful*)
Motion Picture Story: Frederic M. Frank, Theodore St John, Frank Cavett (*The Greatest Show on Earth*)
Screenplay: Charles Schnee (*The Bad and the Beautiful*)
Story & Screenplay: T. E. B. Clarke (*The Lavender Hill Mob*)

1953

Picture: *From Here to Eternity*
Director: Fred Zinnemann (*From Here to Eternity*)
Actor: William Holden (*Stalag 17*)
Actress: Audrey Hepburn (*Roman Holiday*)
Supporting Actor: Frank Sinatra (*From Here to Eternity*)
Supporting Actress: Donna Reed (*From Here to Eternity*)
Motion Picture Story: Ian McLellan Hunter, fronting for the blacklisted Dalton Trumbo (*Roman Holiday*)
Screenplay: Daniel Taradash (*From Here to Eternity*)
Story & Screenplay: Charles Brackett, Walter Reisch, Richard Breen (*Titanic*)

1954

Picture: *On the Waterfront*
Director: Elia Kazan (*On the Waterfront*)
Actor: Marlon Brando (*On the Waterfront*)
Actress: Grace Kelly (*The Country Girl*)
Supporting Actor: Edmond O'Brien (*The Barefoot Contessa*)
Supporting Actress: Eva Marie Saint (*On the Waterfront*)
Motion Picture Story: Philip Yordan (*Broken Lance*)
Screenplay: George Seaton (*The Country Girl*)
Story & Screenplay: Budd Schulberg (*On the Waterfront*)

1955

Picture: *Marty*
Director: Delbert Mann (*Marty*)
Actor: Ernest Borgnine (*Marty*)
Actress: Anna Magnani (*The Rose Tattoo*)
Supporting Actor: Jack Lemmon (*Mister Roberts*)
Supporting Actress: Jo Van Fleet (*East of Eden*)
Motion Picture Story: Daniel Fuchs (*Love Me or Leave Me*)
Screenplay: Paddy Chayevsky (*Marty*)
Story & Screenplay: William Ludwig, Sonya Levien (*Interrupted Melody*)

1956

Picture: *Around the World in Eighty Days*
Director: George Stevens (*Giant*)
Actor: Yul Brynner (*The King and I*)
Actress: Ingrid Bergman (*Anastasia*)
Supporting Actor: Anthony Quinn (*Lust for Life*)
Supporting Actress: Dorothy Malone (*Written on the Wind*)
Motion Picture Story: Dalton Trumbo (as Robert Rich) (*The Brave One*)
Original Screenplay: Albert Lamorisse (*The Red Balloon*)
Adapted Screenplay: James Poe, John Farrow, S. J. Perelman (*Around the World in Eighty Days*)

1957

Picture: *The Bridge on the River Kwai*
Director: David Lean (*The Bridge on the River Kwai*)
Actor: Alec Guinness (*The Bridge on the River Kwai*)
Actress: Joanne Woodward (*The Three Faces of Eve*)
Supporting Actor: Red Buttons (*Sayonara*)
Supporting Actress: Miyoshi Umeki (*Sayonara*)
Original Story & Screenplay: George Wells (*Designing Woman*)
Adapted Screenplay: Pierre Boulle, Michael Wilson, Carl Foreman (*The Bridge on the River Kwai*)

1958

Picture: *Gigi*
Director: Vincente Minnelli (*Gigi*)
Actor: David Niven (*Separate Tables*)
Actress: Susan Hayward (*I Want to Live*)
Supporting Actor: Burl Ives (*The Big Country*)
Supporting Actress: Wendy Hiller (*Separate Tables*)
Original Story & Screenplay: Nathan E. Douglas (the blacklisted Ned Young), Harold Jacob Smith (*The Defiant Ones*)
Adapted Screenplay: Alan Jay Lerner (*Gigi*)

1959

Picture: *Ben-Hur*
Director: William Wyler (*Ben-Hur*)
Actor: Charlton Heston (*Ben-Hur*)
Actress: Simone Signoret (*Room at the Top*)
Supporting Actor: Hugh Griffith (*Ben-Hur*)
Supporting Actress: Shelley Winters (*The Diary of Anne Frank*)
Original Story & Screenplay: Russell Rouse, Clarence Greene, Stanley Shapiro, Maurice Richlin (*Pillow Talk*)
Adapted Screenplay: Neil Paterson (*Room at the Top*)

1960

Picture: *The Apartment*
Director: Billy Wilder (*The Apartment*)
Actor: Burt Lancaster (*Elmer Gantry*)
Actress: Elizabeth Taylor (*Butterfield 8*)
Supporting Actor: Peter Ustinov (*Spartacus*)
Supporting Actress: Shirley Jones (*Elmer Gantry*)
Original Story & Screenplay: Billy Wilder, I. A. L. Diamond (*The Apartment*)
Adapted Screenplay: Richard Brooks (*Elmer Gantry*)

1961

Picture: *West Side Story*
Director: Jerome Robbins, Robert Wise (*West Side Story*)
Actor: Maximilian Schell (*Judgment at Nuremberg*)
Actress: Sophia Loren (*Two Women*)
Supporting Actor: George Chakiris (*West Side Story*)
Supporting Actress: Rita Moreno (*West Side Story*)
Original Story & Screenplay: William Inge (*Splendor in the Grass*)
Adapted Screenplay: Abby Mann (*Judgment at Nuremberg*)

1962

Picture: *Lawrence of Arabia*
Director: David Lean (*Lawrence of Arabia*)
Actor: Gregory Peck (*To Kill a Mockingbird*)
Actress: Anne Bancroft (*The Miracle Worker*)
Supporting Actor: Ed Begley (*Sweet Bird of Youth*)
Supporting Actress: Patty Duke (*The Miracle Worker*)
Original Story & Screenplay: Ennio de Concini, Alfredo Gianetti, Pietro Germi (*Divorce Italian Style*)
Adapted Screenplay: Horton Foote (*To Kill a Mockingbird*)

1963

Picture: *Tom Jones*
Director: Tony Richardson (*Tom Jones*)
Actor: Sidney Poitier (*Lilies of the Field*)
Actress: Patricia Neal (*Hud*)
Supporting Actor: Melvyn Douglas (*Hud*)
Supporting Actress: Margaret Rutherford (*The VIPs*)
Original Story & Screenplay: James R. Webb (*How the West Was Won*)
Adapted Screenplay: John Osborne (*Tom Jones*)

1964

Picture: *My Fair Lady*
Director: George Cukor (*My Fair Lady*)
Actor: Rex Harrison (*My Fair Lady*)
Actress: Julie Andrews (*Mary Poppins*)
Supporting Actor: Peter Ustinov (*Topkapi*)
Supporting Actress: Lila Kedrova (*Zorba the Greek*)
Original Story & Screenplay: S. H. Barnett, Peter Stone, Frank Tarloff (*Father Goose*)
Adapted Screenplay: Edward Anhalt (*Becket*)

1965

Picture: *The Sound of Music*
Director: Robert Wise (*The Sound of Music*)
Actor: Lee Marvin (*Cat Ballou*)
Actress: Julie Christie (*Darling*)
Supporting Actor: Martin Balsam (*A Thousand Clowns*)
Supporting Actress: Shelley Winters (*A Patch of Blue*)
Original Story & Screenplay: Frederic Raphael (*Darling*)
Adapted Screenplay: Robert Bolt (*Dr Zhivago*)

1966

Picture: *A Man for All Seasons*
Director: Fred Zinnemann (*A Man for All Seasons*)
Actor: Paul Scofield (*A Man for All Seasons*)
Actress: Elizabeth Taylor (*Who's Afraid of Virginia Woolf?*)
Supporting Actor: Walter Matthau (*The Fortune Cookie*)
Supporting Actress: Sandy Dennis (*Who's Afraid of Virginia Woolf?*)
Original Story & Screenplay: Claude Lelouch, Pierre Uytterhoeven (*A Man and a Woman*)
Adapted Screenplay: Robert Bolt (*A Man for All Seasons*)

1967

Picture: *In the Heat of the Night*
Director: Mike Nichols (*The Graduate*)
Actor: Rod Steiger (*In the Heat of the Night*)
Actress: Katharine Hepburn (*Guess Who's Coming to Dinner*)
Supporting Actor: George Kennedy (*Cool Hand Luke*)
Supporting Actress: Estelle Parsons (*Bonnie and Clyde*)
Original Story & Screenplay: William Rose (*Guess Who's Coming to Dinner*)
Adapted Screenplay: Sterling Silliphant (*In the Heat of the Night*)

1968

Picture: *Oliver!*
Director: Carol Reed (*Oliver!*)
Actor: Cliff Robertson (*Charly*)
Actress: Katharine Hepburn (*The Lion in Winter*), Barbra Streisand (*Funny Girl*)
Supporting Actor: Jack Albertson (*The Subject Was Roses*)
Supporting Actress: Ruth Gordon (*Rosemary's Baby*)
Original Story & Screenplay: Mel Brooks (*The Producers*)
Adapted Screenplay: James Goldman (*The Lion in Winter*)

1969

Picture: *Midnight Cowboy*
Director: John Schlesinger (*Midnight Cowboy*)
Actor: John Wayne (*True Grit*)
Actress: Maggie Smith (*The Prime of Miss Jean Brodie*)
Supporting Actor: Gig Young (*They Shoot Horses, Don't They?*)
Supporting Actress: Goldie Hawn (*Cactus Flower*)
Original Story & Screenplay: William Goldman (*Butch Cassidy and the Sundance Kid*)
Adapted Screenplay: Waldo Salt (*Midnight Cowboy*)

1970

Picture: *Patton*
Director: Franklin J. Schaffner (*Patton*)
Actor: George C. Scott (*Patton*)
Actress: Glenda Jackson (*Women in Love*)
Supporting Actor: John Mills (*Ryan's Daughter*)
Supporting Actress: Helen Hayes (*Airport*)
Original Story & Screenplay: Francis Ford Coppola, Edmund H. North (*Patton*)
Adapted Screenplay: Ring Lardner Jnr (*M*A*S*H*)

1971

Picture: *The French Connection*
Director: William Friedkin (*The French Connection*)
Actor: Gene Hackman (*The French Connection*)
Actress: Jane Fonda (*Klute*)
Supporting Actor: Ben Johnson (*The Last Picture Show*)
Supporting Actress: Cloris Leachman (*The Last Picture Show*)
Original Story & Screenplay: Paddy Chayevsky (*The Hospital*)
Adapted Screenplay: Ernest Tidyman (*The French Connection*)

1972

Picture: *The Godfather*
Director: Bob Fosse (*Cabaret*)
Actor: Marlon Brando (*The Godfather*)
Actress: Liza Minnelli (*Cabaret*)
Supporting Actor: Joel Grey (*Cabaret*)
Supporting Actress: Eileen Heckart (*Butterflies Are Free*)
Original Story & Screenplay: Jeremy Larner (*The Candidate*)
Adapted Screenplay: Mario Puzo, Francis Ford Coppola (*The Godfather*)

1973

Picture: *The Sting*
Director: George Roy Hill (*The Sting*)
Actor: Jack Lemmon (*Save the Tiger*)
Actress: Glenda Jackson (*A Touch of Class*)
Supporting Actor: John Houseman (*The Paper Chase*)
Supporting Actress: Tatum O'Neal (*Paper Moon*)
Original Story & Screenplay: David S. Ward (*The Sting*)
Adapted Screenplay: William Peter Blatty (*The Exorcist*)

1974

Picture: *The Godfather Part II*
Director: Francis Ford Coppola (*The Godfather Part II*)
Actor: Art Carney (*Harry and Tonto*)
Actress: Ellen Burstyn (*Alice Doesn't Live Here Any More*)
Supporting Actor: Robert de Niro (*The Godfather Part II*)
Supporting Actress: Ingrid Bergman (*Murder on the Orient Express*)
Original Story & Screenplay: Robert Towne (*Chinatown*)
Adapted Screenplay: Francis Ford Coppola, Mario Puzo (*The Godfather Part II*)

1975
Picture: *One Flew over the Cuckoo's Nest*
Director: Milos Forman (*One Flew over the Cuckoo's Nest*)
Actor: Jack Nicholson (*One Flew over the Cuckoo's Nest*)
Actress: Louise Fletcher (*One Flew over the Cuckoo's Nest*)
Supporting Actor: George Burns (*The Sunshine Boys*)
Supporting Actress: Lee Grant (*Shampoo*)
Original Screenplay: Frank Pierson (*Dog Day Afternoon*)
Adapted Screenplay: Lawrence Hauben, Bo Goldman (*One Flew over the Cuckoo's Nest*)

1976
Picture: *Rocky*
Director: John G. Avildsen (*Rocky*)
Actor: Peter Finch (*Network*)
Actress: Faye Dunaway (*Network*)
Supporting Actor: Jason Robards (*All the President's Men*)
Supporting Actress: Beatrice Straight (*Network*)
Original Screenplay: Paddy Chayevsky (*Network*)
Adapted Screenplay: William Goldman (*All the President's Men*)

1977
Picture: *Annie Hall*
Director: Woody Allen (*Annie Hall*)
Actor: Richard Dreyfuss (*The Goodbye Girl*)
Actress: Diane Keaton (*Annie Hall*)
Supporting Actor: Jason Robards (*Julia*)
Supporting Actress: Vanessa Redgrave (*Julia*)
Original Screenplay: Woody Allen, Marshall Brickman (*Annie Hall*)
Adapted Screenplay: Alvin Sargent (*Julia*)

1978
Picture: *The Deer Hunter*
Director: Michael Cimino (*The Deer Hunter*)
Actor: Jon Voight (*Coming Home*)
Actress: Jane Fonda (*Coming Home*)
Supporting Actor: Christopher Walken (*The Deer Hunter*)
Supporting Actress: Maggie Smith (*California Suite*)
Original Screenplay: Nancy Dowd, Waldo Salt, Robert C. Jones (*Coming Home*)
Adapted Screenplay: Oliver Stone (*Midnight Express*)

1979
Picture: *Kramer versus Kramer*
Director: Robert Benton (*Kramer versus Kramer*)
Actor: Dustin Hoffman (*Kramer versus Kramer*)
Actress: Sally Field (*Norma Rae*)
Supporting Actor: Melvyn Douglas (*Being There*)
Supporting Actress: Meryl Streep (*Kramer versus Kramer*)
Original Screenplay: Steve Tesich (*Breaking Away*)
Adapted Screenplay: Robert Benton (*Kramer versus Kramer*)

1980
Picture: *Ordinary People*
Director: Robert Redford (*Ordinary People*)
Actor: Robert de Niro (*Raging Bull*)
Actress: Sissy Spacek (*Coal Miner's Daughter*)
Supporting Actor: Timothy Hutton (*Ordinary People*)
Supporting Actress: Mary Steenburgen (*Melvin and Howard*)
Original Screenplay: Bo Goldman (*Melvin and Howard*)
Adapted Screenplay: Alvin Sargent (*Ordinary People*)

1981
Picture: *Chariots of Fire*
Director: Warren Beatty (*Reds*)
Actor: Henry Fonda (*On Golden Pond*)

Actress: Katharine Hepburn (*On Golden Pond*)
Supporting Actor: John Gielgud (*Arthur*)
Supporting Actress: Maureen Stapleton (*Reds*)
Original Screenplay: Colin Welland (*Chariots of Fire*)
Adapted Screenplay: Ernest Thompson (*On Golden Pond*)

1982
Picture: *Gandhi*
Director: Richard Attenborough (*Gandhi*)
Actor: Ben Kingsley (*Gandhi*)
Actress: Meryl Streep (*Sophie's Choice*)
Supporting Actor: Louis Gossett Jnr (*An Officer and a Gentleman*)
Supporting Actress: Jessica Lange (*Tootsie*)
Original Screenplay: John Briley (*Gandhi*)
Adapted Screenplay: Costa-Gavras, Donald Stewart (*Missing*)

1983
Picture: *Terms of Endearment*
Director: James L. Brooks (*Terms of Endearment*)
Actor: Robert Duvall (*Tender Mercies*)
Actress: Shirley Maclaine (*Terms of Endearment*)
Supporting Actor: Jack Nicholson (*Terms of Endearment*)
Supporting Actress: Linda Hunt (*The Year of Living Dangerously*)
Original Screenplay: Horton Foote (*Tender Mercies*)
Adapted Screenplay: James L. Brooks (*Terms of Endearment*)

1984
Picture: *Amadeus*
Director: Milos Forman (*Amadeus*)
Actor: F. Murray Abraham (*Amadeus*)
Actress: Sally Field (*Places in the Heart*)
Supporting Actor: Haing S. Ngor (*The Killing Fields*)
Supporting Actress: Peggy Ashcroft (*A Passage to India*)
Original Screenplay: Robert Benton (*Places in the Heart*)
Adapted Screenplay: Peter Shaffer (*Amadeus*)

1985
Picture: *Out of Africa*
Director: Sydney Pollack (*Out of Africa*)
Actor: William Hurt (*Kiss of the Spider Woman*)
Actress: Geraldine Page (*The Trip to Bountiful*)
Supporting Actor: Don Ameche (*Cocoon*)
Supporting Actress: Anjelica Huston (*Prizzi's Honor*)
Original Screenplay: William Kelley, Pamela Wallace, Earl W. Wallace (*Witness*)
Adapted Screenplay: Kurt Luedtke (*Out of Africa*)

1986
Picture: *Platoon*
Director: Oliver Stone (*Platoon*)
Actor: Paul Newman (*The Color of Money*)
Actress: Marlee Matlin (*Children of a Lesser God*)
Supporting Actor: Michael Caine (*Hannah and Her Sisters*)
Supporting Actress: Dianne Wiest (*Hannah and Her Sisters*)
Original Screenplay: Woody Allen (*Hannah and Her Sisters*)
Adapted Screenplay: Ruth Prawer Jhabvala (*A Room with a View*)

1987
Picture: *The Last Emperor*
Director: Bernardo Bertolucci (*The Last Emperor*)
Actor: Michael Douglas (*Wall Street*)
Actress: Cher (*Moonstruck*)

Supporting Actor: Sean Connery (*The Untouchables*)
Supporting Actress: Olympia Dukakis (*Moonstruck*)
Original Screenplay: John Patrick Shanley (*Moonstruck*)
Adapted Screenplay: Mark Peploe, Bernardo Bertolucci (*The Last Emperor*)

1988
Picture: *Rain Man*
Director: Barry Levinson (*Rain Man*)
Actor: Dustin Hoffman (*Rain Man*)
Actress: Jodie Foster (*The Accused*)
Supporting Actor: Kevin Kline (*A Fish Called Wanda*)
Supporting Actress: Geena Davis (*The Accidental Tourist*)
Original Screenplay: Ronald Bass, Barry Morrow (*Rain Man*)
Adapted Screenplay: Christopher Hampton (*Dangerous Liaisons*)

1989
Picture: *Driving Miss Daisy*
Director: Oliver Stone (*Born on the Fourth of July*)
Actor: Daniel Day-Lewis (*My Left Foot*)
Actress: Jessica Tandy (*Driving Miss Daisy*)
Supporting Actor: Denzel Washington (*Glory*)
Supporting Actress: Brenda Fricker (*My Left Foot*)
Original Screenplay: Tom Schulman (*Dead Poets Society*)
Adapted Screenplay: Alfred Uhry (*Driving Miss Daisy*)

1990
Picture: *Dances with Wolves*
Director: Kevin Costner (*Dances with Wolves*)
Actor: Jeremy Irons (*Reversal of Fortune*)
Actress: Kathy Bates (*Misery*)
Supporting Actor: Joe Pesci (*Goodfellas*)
Supporting Actress: Whoopi Goldberg (*Ghost*)
Original Screenplay: Bruce Joel Rubin (*Ghost*)
Adapted Screenplay: Michael Blake (*Dances with Wolves*)

1991
Picture: *Silence of the Lambs*
Director: Jonathan Demme (*Silence of the Lambs*)
Actor: Anthony Hopkins (*Silence of the Lambs*)
Actress: Jodie Foster (*Silence of the Lambs*)
Supporting Actor: Jack Palance (*City Slickers*)
Supporting Actress: Mercedes Ruehl (*The Fisher King*)
Original Screenplay: Callie Khouri (*Thelma and Louise*)
Adapted Screenplay: Ted Tally (*Silence of the Lambs*)

1992
Picture: *Unforgiven*
Director: Clint Eastwood (*Unforgiven*)
Actor: Al Pacino (*Scent of a Woman*)
Actress: Emma Thompson (*Howards End*)
Supporting Actor: Gene Hackman (*Unforgiven*)
Supporting Actress: Marisa Tomei (*My Cousin Vinny*)
Original Screenplay: Neil Jordan (*The Crying Game*)
Adapted Screenplay: Ruth Prawer Jhabvala (*Howards End*)

1993
Picture: *Schindler's List*
Director: Steven Spielberg (*Schindler's List*)
Actor: Tom Hanks (*Philadelphia*)
Actress: Holly Hunter (*The Piano*)
Supporting Actor: Tommy Lee Jones (*The Fugitive*)
Supporting Actress: Anna Paquin (*The Piano*)
Original Screenplay: Jane Campion (*The Piano*)
Adapted Screenplay: Steven Zaillian (*Schindler's List*)

1994
Picture: *Forrest Gump*
Director: Robert Zemeckis (*Forrest Gump*)
Actor: Tom Hanks (*Forrest Gump*)
Actress: Jessica Lange (*Blue Sky*)
Supporting Actor: Martin Landau (*Ed Wood*)
Supporting Actress: Dianne Wiest (*Bullets over Broadway*)
Original Screenplay: Quentin Tarantino, Roger Avary (*Pulp Fiction*)
Adapted Screenplay: Eric Roth (*Forrest Gump*)

1995
Picture: *Braveheart*
Director: Mel Gibson (*Braveheart*)
Actor: Nicolas Cage (*Leaving Las Vegas*)
Actress: Susan Sarandon (*Dead Man Walking*)
Supporting Actor: Kevin Spacey (*The Usual Suspects*)
Supporting Actress: Mira Sorvino (*Mighty Aphrodite*)
Original Screenplay: Christopher McQuarrie (*The Usual Suspects*)
Adapted Screenplay: Emma Thompson (*Sense and Sensibility*)

1996
Picture: *The English Patient*
Director: Anthony Minghella (*The English Patient*)
Actor: Geoffrey Rush (*Shine*)
Actress: Frances McDormand (*Fargo*)
Supporting Actor: Cuba Gooding Jr (*Jerry Maguire*)
Supporting Actress: Juliette Binoche (*The English Patient*)
Original Screenplay: Ethan Coen, Joel Coen (*Fargo*)
Adapted Screenplay: Billy Bob Thornton (*Slingblade*)

1997
Picture: *Titanic*
Director: James Cameron (*Titanic*)
Actor: Jack Nicholson (*As Good As It Gets*)
Actress: Helen Hunt (*As Good As It Gets*)
Supporting Actor: Robin Williams (*Good Will Hunting*)
Supporting Actress: Kim Basinger (*LA Confidential*)
Original Screenplay: Matt Damon, Ben Affleck (*Good Will Hunting*)
Adapted Screenplay: Curtis Hanson, Brian Helgeland (*LA Confidential*)

1998
Picture: *Shakespeare in Love*
Director: Steven Spielberg (*Saving Private Ryan*)
Actor: Roberto Begnini (*Life is Beautiful*)
Actress: Gwyneth Paltrow (*Shakespeare in Love*)
Supporting Actor: James Coburn (*Affliction*)
Supporting Actress: Judi Dench (*Shakespeare in Love*)
Original Screenplay: Marc Norman, Tom Stoppard (*Shakespeare in Love*)
Adapted Screenplay: Bill Condon (*Gods and Monsters*)

1999
Picture: *American Beauty*
Director: Sam Mendes (*American Beauty*)
Actor: Kevin Spacey (*American Beauty*)
Actress: Hilary Swank (*Boys Don't Cry*)
Supporting Actor: Michael Caine (*The Cider House Rules*)
Supporting Actress: Angelina Jolie (*Girl, Interrupted*)
Original Screenplay: Alan Ball (*American Beauty*)
Adapted Screenplay: John Irving (*The Cider House Rules*)

2000
Picture: *Gladiator*
Director: Stephen Soderbergh (*Traffic*)

Actor: Russell Crowe (*Gladiator*)
Actress: Julia Roberts (*Erin Brockovich*)
Supporting Actor: Benicio Del Toro (*Traffic*)
Supporting Actress: Marcia Gay Harden (*Pollock*)
Original Screenplay: Cameron Crowe (*Almost Famous*)
Adapted Screenplay: Stephen Gaghan (*Traffic*)

2001
Picture: *A Beautiful Mind*
Director: Ron Howard (*A Beautiful Mind*)
Actor: Denzel Washington (*Training Day*)
Actress: Halle Berry (*Monster's Ball*)
Supporting Actor: Jim Broadbent (*Iris*)
Supporting Actress: Jennifer Connelly (*A Beautiful Mind*)
Original Screenplay: Julian Fellowes (*Gosford Park*)
Adapted Screenplay: Akiva Goldsman (*A Beautiful Mind*)
Animated Feature: *Shrek*

2002
Picture: *Chicago*
Director: Roman Polanski (*The Pianist*)
Actor: Adrien Brody (*The Pianist*)
Actress: Nicole Kidman (*The Hours*)
Supporting Actor: Chris Cooper (*Adaptation*)
Supporting Actress: Catherine Zeta-Jones (*Chicago*)
Original Screenplay: Pedro Almodovar (*Talk to Her/Hable con Ella*)
Adapted Screenplay: Ronald Harwood (*The Pianist*)
Animated Feature: *Spirited Away/Sen Yo Chihiro No Kamikakushi*

2003
Picture: *The Lord of the Rings: The Return of the King*
Director: Peter Jackson (*The Lord of the Rings: The Return of the King*)
Actor: Sean Penn (*Mystic River*)
Actress: Charlize Theron (*Monster*)
Supporting Actor: Tim Robbins (*Mystic River*)
Supporting Actress: Renée Zellweger (*Cold Mountain*)
Original Screenplay: Sofia Coppola (*Lost in Translation*)
Adapted Screenplay: Fran Walsh, Philippa Boyens, Peter Jackson (*The Lord of the Rings: The Return of the King*)
Animated Feature: *Finding Nemo*

2004
Picture: *Million Dollar Baby*

Director: Clint Eastwood (*Million Dollar Baby*)
Actor: Jamie Foxx (*Ray*)
Actress: Hilary Swank (*Million Dollar Baby*)
Supporting Actor: Morgan Freeman (*Million Dollar Baby*)
Supporting Actress: Cate Blanchett (*The Aviator*)
Original Screenplay: Charlie Kaufman, Michel Gondry, Pierre Bismuth (*Eternal Sunshine of the Spotless Mind*)
Adapted Screenplay: Alexander Payne, Jim Taylor (*Sideways*)
Animated Feature: *The Incredibles*

2005
Picture: *Crash*
Director: Ang Lee (*Brokeback Mountain*)
Actor: Philip Seymour Hoffman (*Capote*)
Actress: Reese Witherspoon (*Walk The Line*)
Supporting Actor: George Clooney (*Syriana*)
Supporting Actress: Rachel Weisz (*The Constant Gardener*)
Original Screenplay: Paul Haggis, Bobby Moresco (*Crash*)
Adapted Screenplay: Larry McMurtry, Diana Ossana (*Brokeback Mountain*)
Animated Feature: *Wallace & Gromit: Curse of the Were-Rabbit*

2006
Picture: *The Departed*
Director: Martin Scorsese (*The Departed*)
Actor: Forest Whitaker (*The Last King of Scotland*)
Actress: Helen Mirren (*The Queen*)
Supporting Actor: Alan Arkin (*Little Miss Sunshine*)
Supporting Actress: Jennifer Hudson (*Dreamgirls*)
Original Screenplay: Michael Arndt (*Little Miss Sunshin*)
Adapted Screenplay: William Monahan (*The Departed*)
Animated Feature: *Happy Feet*

2007
Picture: *No Country For Old Men*
Director: Joel and Ethan Cohen (*No Country For Old Men*)
Actor: Daniel Day-Lewis (*There Will be Blood*)
Actress: Marion Cotillard (*La Vie en Rose*)
Supporting Actor: Javier Bardem (*No Country For Old Men*)
Supporting Actress: Tilda Swinton (*Michael Clayton*)
Original Screenplay: Diablo Cody (*Juno*)
Adapted Screenplay: Joel and Ethan Cohen (*No Country For Old Men*)
Animated Feature: *Ratatouille*

FOUR-STAR FILMS — BY YEAR

1915
The Birth of a Nation

1916
Intolerance

1917
Easy Street

1921
The Kid

1925
The Battleship Potemkin

1926
The General

1927
The Jazz Singer
Napoleon
October
Sunrise

1929
Big Business

1930
All Quiet on the Western Front
The Blue Angel

1931
Frankenstein
M

1932
Love Me Tonight

1933
Duck Soup
King Kong

1934
It Happened One Night
Sons of the Desert

1935
The Bride of Frankenstein
A Night at the Opera
The 39 Steps
Top Hat

1937
A Day at the Races
La Grande Illusion
Way Out West

1938
The Adventures of Robin Hood
Alexander Nevsky
The Lady Vanishes
Pygmalion

1939
Destry Rides Again
Gone with the Wind
The Hunchback of Notre Dame
Mr Smith Goes to Washington
La Règle du Jeu
Stagecoach
The Wizard of Oz

1940
The Grapes of Wrath
His Girl Friday
The Philadelphia Story
Pinocchio
Rebecca

1941
All that Money Can Buy
Citizen Kane
The Maltese Falcon
Sullivan's Travels

1942
Bambi
Casablanca
Listen to Britain
The Magnificent Ambersons
To Be or Not to Be
Why We Fight

1944
Double Indemnity
Henry V
Meet Me in St Louis

1945
Brief Encounter
Les Enfants du Paradis
The Lost Weekend

1946
The Best Years of Our Lives
Great Expectations
It's a Wonderful Life
The Killers
A Matter of Life and Death

1947
Brighton Rock
Out of the Past

1948
Bicycle Thieves
Oliver Twist
The Red Shoes
Whisky Galore

1949
Gun Crazy
On the Town
Passport to Pimlico
The Third Man

1950
All About Eve
In a Lonely Place
Sunset Boulevard

1951
An American in Paris
The Lavender Hill Mob
The Man in the White Suit
Rashomon

1952
High Noon
Singin' in the Rain

1953
The Band Wagon
Tokyo Story

1954
On the Waterfront
Rear Window
The Seven Samurai

1955
Bad Day at Black Rock
Invasion of the Body Snatchers
Marty
The Night of the Hunter
Pather Panchali
The Red Balloon

1956
The Killing
The Searchers

1957
Paths of Glory
The Seventh Seal
Sweet Smell of Success
12 Angry Men

1958
Ashes and Diamonds
Touch of Evil
Vertigo

1959
The Four Hundred Blows
North by Northwest
Some Like It Hot
The World of Apu

1960
A Bout de Souffle
The Apartment
La Dolce Vita
Psycho
Saturday Night and Sunday Morning

1961
The Hustler
Viridiana
West Side Story

1962
The Exterminating Angel
Lawrence of Arabia
The Manchurian Candidate

1963
Dr Strangelove; or, How I Learned to Stop Worrying and Love the Bomb
The Leopard

1964
A Hard Day's Night

1965
The Battle of Algiers

1966
Andrei Rublev
A Man for All Seasons
Who's Afraid of Virginia Woolf?

1967
Bonnie and Clyde
Don't Look Back
The Graduate
In the Heat of the Night

1968
If. . .
The Producers
2001: A Space Odyssey
Z

1969
The Army in the Shadows
Le Boucher
Butch Cassidy and the Sundance Kid
The Conformist
Easy Rider
Kes
Midnight Cowboy
The Wild Bunch

1971
The Last Picture Show

1972
Aguirre, Wrath of God
Cabaret
Cries and Whispers
The Discreet Charm of the Bourgeoisie
The Godfather

1973
Badlands
Don't Look Now
Mean Streets

1974
Chinatown
The Godfather Part II

1975
One Flew over the Cuckoo's Nest

1976
All the President's Men
Taxi Driver

1977
Annie Hall
Star Wars: Episode IV – A
    New Hope

1978
Grease

1979
Alien
Apocalypse Now
Manhattan

1980
The Long Good Friday
Raging Bull
Star Wars: Episode V – The
    Empire Strikes Back

1982
E.T. The Extra-Terrestrial
Fanny and Alexander
Fitzcarraldo

1983
King of Comedy
Star Wars: Episode VI –
    Return of the Jedi

1984
Once Upon a Time in
    America
This Is Spinal Tap

1985
Back to the Future
Brazil
Come and See
Shoah
Witness

1986
Blue Velvet
Hannah and Her Sisters

1987
Au Revoir Les Enfants

1988
Cinema Paradiso
Salaam Bombay!
A Short Film about Killing

1989
Cinema Paradiso
Do the Right Thing

1990
Goodfellas
Miller's Crossing

1991
City of Hope
Reservoir Dogs
Thelma and Louise

1992
The Long Day Closes
Unforgiven
Visions of Light

1993
Groundhog Day
Schindler's List
Three Colours: Blue

1994
Hoop Dreams
Pulp Fiction
Three Colours: Red

1995
Babe
Toy Story
The Usual Suspects

1996
Fargo
Trainspotting

1997
LA Confidential

1998
The Big Lebowski
Central Station
The Thin Red Line

1999
All About My Mother
Magnolia
The Wind Will Carry Us

2000
Amores Perros
Atanarjuat the Fast Runner
House of Mirth
A One and a Two. . .

2001
Gosford Park
The Son's Room

2002
Être et Avoir
Far from Heaven

2003
The Return

2004
Downfall

2005
Brokeback Mountain
Capote
Junebug
The Squid and the Whale

2006
The Lives of Others
United 93

2007
The Assassination of Jesse
    James by the Coward
    Robert Ford
Atonement
Before The Devil Knows
    You're Dead
Lust, Caution
Michael Clayton
No Country For Old Men
There Will Be Blood

FOUR-STAR FILMS – BY TITLE

A Bout de Souffle
The Adventures of Robin Hood
Aguirre, Wrath of God
Alexander Nevsky
Alien
All About Eve
All About My Mother
All Quiet on the Western Front
All that Money Can Buy
All the President's Men
An American in Paris
Amores Perros
Andrei Rublev
Annie Hall
The Apartment
Apocalypse Now
The Army in the Shadows
Ashes and Diamonds
The Assassination of Jesse James by the Coward Robert Ford
Atanarjuat the Fast Runner
Atonement
Au Revoir Les Enfants
Babe
Back to the Future
Bad Day at Black Rock
Badlands
Bambi
The Band Wagon
The Battle of Algiers
The Battleship Potemkin
Before The Devil Knows You're Dead
The Best Years of Our Lives
Bicycle Thieves
Big Business
The Big Lebowski
The Birth of a Nation
The Blue Angel
Blue Velvet
Bonnie and Clyde
Le Boucher
Brazil
The Bride of Frankenstein
Brief Encounter
Brighton Rock
Brokeback Mountain
Butch Cassidy and the Sundance Kid
Cabaret
Capote
Casablanca
Central Station
Chinatown
Cinema Paradiso
Citizen Kane
City of Hope
Come and See
The Conformist

Cries and Whispers
A Day at the Races
Destry Rides Again
The Discreet Charm of the Bourgeoisie
Do the Right Thing
Dr Strangelove; or, How I Learned to Stop Worrying and Love the Bomb
La Dolce Vita
Don't Look Back
Don't Look Now
Double Indemnity
Downfall
Duck Soup
E.T. The Extra-Terrestrial
Easy Rider
Easy Street
Les Enfants du Paradis
Être et Avoir
The Exterminating Angel
Fanny and Alexander
Far from Heaven
Fargo
Fitzcarraldo
The Four Hundred Blows
Frankenstein
The General
The Godfather
The Godfather Part II
Gone with the Wind
Goodfellas
Gosford Park
The Graduate
La Grande Illusion
The Grapes of Wrath
Grease
Great Expectations
Groundhog Day
Gun Crazy
Hannah and Her Sisters
A Hard Day's Night
Henry V
High Noon
His Girl Friday
Hoop Dreams
House of Mirth
The Hunchback of Notre Dame
The Hustler
If. . .
In a Lonely Place
In the Heat of the Night
Intolerance
Invasion of the Body Snatchers
It Happened One Night
It's a Wonderful Life
The Jazz Singer
Junebug
Kes
The Kid
The Killers

The Killing
King Kong
King of Comedy
LA Confidential
The Lady Vanishes
The Last Picture Show
The Lavender Hill Mob
Lawrence of Arabia
The Leopard
Listen to Britain
The Long Day Closes
The Long Good Friday
The Lost Weekend
Love Me Tonight
Lust, Caution
M
The Magnificent Ambersons
Magnolia
The Maltese Falcon
A Man for All Seasons
The Man in the White Suit
The Manchurian Candidate
Manhattan
Marty
A Matter of Life and Death
Mean Streets
Meet Me in St Louis
Michael Clayton
Midnight Cowboy
Miller's Crossing
Mr Smith Goes to Washington
Napoleon
A Night at the Opera
The Night of the Hunter
No Country For Old Men
North by Northwest
October
Oliver Twist
On the Town
On the Waterfront
Once Upon a Time in America
A One and a Two. . .
One Flew over the Cuckoo's Nest
Out of the Past
Passport to Pimlico
Pather Panchali
Paths of Glory
The Philadelphia Story
Pinocchio
The Producers
Psycho
Pulp Fiction
Pygmalion
Raging Bull
Rashomon
Rear Window
Rebecca
The Red Balloon
The Red Shoes

La Règle du Jeu
Reservoir Dogs
The Return
Salaam Bombay!
Saturday Night and Sunday Morning
Schindler's List
The Searchers
The Seven Samurai
The Seventh Seal
Shoah
A Short Film about Killing
Singin' in the Rain
Some Like It Hot
Sons of the Desert
The Son's Room
The Squid and the Whale
Stagecoach
Star Wars: Episode IV – A New Hope
Star Wars: Episode V – The Empire Strikes Back
Star Wars: Episode VI – Return of the Jedi
Sullivan's Travels
Sunrise
Sunset Boulevard
Sweet Smell of Success
Taxi Driver
The Lives of Others
Thelma and Louise
There Will Be Blood
The Thin Red Line
The Third Man
The 39 Steps
This Is Spinal Tap
Three Colours: Blue
Three Colours: Red
To Be or Not to Be
Tokyo Story
Top Hat
Touch of Evil
Toy Story
Trainspotting
12 Angry Men
2001: A Space Odyssey
Unforgiven
United 93
The Usual Suspects
Vertigo
Viridiana
Visions of Light
Way Out West
West Side Story
Whisky Galore
Who's Afraid of Virginia Woolf?
Why We Fight
The Wild Bunch
The Wind Will Carry Us
Witness
The Wizard of Oz
The World of Apu
Z

THREE-STAR FILMS – BY YEAR

1919
The Cabinet of Dr Caligari

1921
Nanook of the North
Nosferatu

1922
Doctor Mabuse the Gambler

1924
Greed
The Last Laugh
The Thief of Bagdad

1925
The Big Parade
The Gold Rush

1926
Metropolis

1928
The Crowd
Steamboat Bill Jnr
The Wind

1929
Pandora's Box

1930
Earth
Hell's Angels

1931
City Lights
Little Caesar
The Public Enemy
The Tale of the Fox

1932
I Am a Fugitive from a
    Chain Gang
Scarface

1933
42nd Street
The Private Life of Henry
    VIII
Zéro de Conduite

1934
The Gay Divorcee
It's a Gift
L'Atalante
The Scarlet Empress
The Thin Man

1936
Modern Times
Mr Deeds Goes to Town
Things to Come
Triumph of the Will
Une Partie de Campagne

1937
The Prisoner of Zenda

Snow White and the Seven
    Dwarfs
Stella Dallas

1938
Angels with Dirty Faces
Bringing Up Baby

1939
Goodbye Mr Chips
Midnight
Ninotchka
Young Mr Lincoln

1940
The Bank Dick
Fantasia
The Great McGinty
The Letter

1941
Dumbo
The Little Foxes

1942
In Which We Serve
Now Voyager
The Palm Beach Story
Went the Day Well?

1943
The Life and Death of
    Colonel Blimp
The Miracle of Morgan's
    Creek

1944
Hail the Conquering Hero
Laura

1945
Detour
Mildred Pierce
Rome, Open City
To Have and Have Not
The Way to the Stars

1946
The Big Sleep
Gilda
My Darling Clementine
Notorious

1947
Black Narcissus
Body and Soul
Crossfire
Kiss of Death
Miracle on 34th Street

1948
Criss Cross
Easter Parade
The Fallen Idol
Force of Evil
Hamlet
Letter from an Unknown
    Woman

The Naked City
Red River
They Live by Night
The Treasure of the Sierra
    Madre

1949
Kind Hearts and Coronets
White Heat

1950
The Asphalt Jungle
The Diary of a Country
    Priest
Father of the Bride
Harvey
La Ronde
The Men
Night and the City

1951
Ace in the Hole
The African Queen
Los Olvidados
Strangers on a Train

1952
Ikiru
Pat and Mike
The Quiet Man

1953
Calamity Jane
From Here to Eternity
Genevieve
Pickup on South Street
Roman Holiday
Shane
Ugetsu Monogatari
The Wages of Fear

1954
The Dam Busters
Les Diaboliques
La Strada

1955
All that Heaven Allows
The Big Combo
Kiss Me Deadly
The Ladykillers
Rebel without a Cause
Rififi

1956
Around the World in Eighty
    Days
Bob Le Flambeur
Funny Face
Kanal

1957
The Bridge on the River
    Kwai
A Face in the Crowd
Lift to the Scaffold
The Tall T

Wild Strawberries
Witness for the Prosecution

1958
Gigi
Room at the Top

1959
Anatomy of a Murder
Hiroshima Mon Amour
Imitation of Life
Peeping Tom
Rio Bravo

1960
L'Avventura
The Magnificent Seven
Shoot the Pianist
Spartacus

1961
The Innocents
Judgment at Nuremberg
Last Year at Marienbad
Victim
Yojimbo

1962
Dr. No
Jules et Jim
A Kind of Loving
Knife in the Water
The Loneliness of the Long
    Distance Runner
The Man Who Shot Liberty
    Valance
The Music Man
To Kill a Mockingbird

1963
The Birds
8 and a Half
The Great Escape
The Haunting
Hud
This Sporting Life
Tom Jones

1964
Fail-Safe
A Fistful of Dollars
Goldfinger
The Gospel According to St
    Matthew
Mary Poppins
My Fair Lady
Seven Days in May
The Umbrellas of
    Cherbourg
Woman of the Dunes

1965
Darling
The Ipcress File
Repulsion
The Sound of Music

1966
Closely Observed Trains
The Good, the Bad and the
  Ugly
Persona

1967
Belle de Jour
The Firemen's Ball
In Cold Blood
The Samurai

1968
Bullitt
La Femme Infidèle
The Night of The Living
  Dead
Oliver!
Rosemary's Baby

1969
Once Upon a Time in the
  West
Women in Love

1970
Five Easy Pieces
The Go-Between
M*A*S*H
Performance
The Spider's Stratagem
Walkabout

1971
A Clockwork Orange
The French Connection
Get Carter
Klute
McCabe and Mrs Miller
Sunday, Bloody Sunday
Ten Rillington Place

1972
Deliverance
The King of Marvin Gardens
Solaris

1973
Amarcord
American Graffiti
The Spirit of the Beehive
The Wicker Man

1974
The Conversation
Fear Eats the Soul
The Parallax View

1975
Dog Day Afternoon
The Man Who Would Be
  King
Nashville
Overlord
The Passenger
Picnic at Hanging Rock
Three Days of the Condor

1976
Assault on Precinct 13
Marathon Man
Network

The Outlaw Josey Wales
Rocky

1977
Saturday Night Fever

1978
Days of Heaven
The Deer Hunter
Midnight Express

1979
Monty Python's Life of
  Brian

1980
The Big Red One
'Breaker' Morant
Gregory's Girl
The Stunt Man

1981
Atlantic City
Chariots of Fire
Das Boot
Mephisto
Raiders of the Lost Ark

1982
Blade Runner
Diner
The Draughtsman's
  Contract
Gandhi
Missing
Tootsie
The Verdict

1983
Blood Simple
The Right Stuff
Scarface

1984
Amadeus
Broadway Danny Rose
The Killing Fields
Paris, Texas
Stop Making Sense

1985
My Beautiful Laundrette
My Life as a Dog
Ran
A Room with a View

1986
Jean de Florette
Manhunter
Mona Lisa
Platoon
Salvador

1987
The Dead
Empire of the Sun
High Tide
Hope and Glory
The Last Emperor
Red Sorghum
The Untouchables
Wings of Desire

Withnail and I
A World Apart

1988
Akira
Au Revoir Les Enfants
Dangerous Liaisons
Distant Voices, Still Lives
Eight Men Out
A Fish Called Wanda
Midnight Run
The Naked Gun: From the
  Files of Police Squad
Rain Man
Women on the Verge of a
  Nervous Breakdown

1989
Born on the Fourth of July
Casualties of War
Creature Comforts
Crimes and Misdemeanors
The Fabulous Baker Boys
Jesus of Montreal
The Killer
Metropolitan
Milou in May
Yaaba

1990
Cyrano de Bergerac
Delicatessen
The Grifters
Ju Dou
Life Is Sweet
Misery
The Silence of the Lambs

1991
Autobus
Barton Fink
Beauty and the Beast
La Belle Noiseuse
Boyz N the Hood
A Brighter Summer Day
The Commitments
Hearts of Darkness: A
  Filmmaker's Apocalypse
Homicide
Paris Trout
Raise the Red Lantern
Terminator 2: Judgment Day

1992
Aladdin
And Life Goes On. . .
The Best Intentions
The Fencing Master
Glengarry Glen Ross
Howards End
Husbands and Wives
One False Move
Orlando
The Piano
The Player
Sneakers
The Story of Qiu Ju
Strictly Ballroom

1993
The Blue Kite
Farewell My Concubine

Fearless
The Fugitive
Germinal
The Nightmare before
  Christmas
Red Rock West
The Remains of the Day
Shadowlands
Short Cuts
Six Degrees of Separation
The Wedding Banquet

1994
Before the Rain
Chungking Express
Four Weddings and a
  Funeral
Heavenly Creatures
The Kingdom
The Lion King
Quiz Show
Shallow Grave
The Shawshank
  Redemption
Speed

1995
Antonia's Line
Casino
Dead Man Walking
Get Shorty
Heat
La Haine
Les Misérables
Nixon
Persuasion
Richard III
Safe
Secrets and Lies
A Self-Made Hero
Sense and Sensibility
Seven
Shall We Dance?
Things to Do in Denver
  When You're Dead
To Die For
Twelve Monkeys

1996
Big Night
Brassed Off
The English Patient
Grace of My Heart
Kolya
Pretty Village Pretty Flame
Shine
Tin Cup
When We Were Kings

1997
Abre Los Ojos
The Apple
Boogie Nights
Donnie Brasco
The Full Monty
The Game
Grosse Pointe Blank
Happy Together
The Ice Storm
Live Flesh
Mrs Brown

The Sweet Hereafter
A Taste of Cherry

1998

After Life
Bulworth
Elizabeth
Eternity and a Day
Festen
My Name Is Joe
The Opposite of Sex
Out of Sight
Pleasantville
Run Lola Run
Rushmore
Saving Private Ryan
Shakespeare in Love
A Simple Plan
The Truman Show

1999

American Beauty
Being John Malkovich
The Blair Witch Project
Boys Don't Cry
Bringing Out the Dead
Election
Fight Club
The Insider
The Iron Giant
Notting Hill
Ratcatcher
A Room for Romeo Brass
Rosetta
The Sixth Sense
South Park: Bigger Longer
    & Uncut
Stir of Echoes
The Straight Story
Sunshine
The Talented Mr Ripley
Three Kings
Topsy-Turvy
Toy Story 2

2000

Billy Elliot
Code Unknown
Erin Brockovich
Gladiator
In the Mood for Love

Ivansxtc
Memento
O Brother, Where Art Thou?
Pollock
Songs From the Second
    Floor
The Taste of Others
Tears of the Black Tiger
A Time for Drunken Horses

2001

Amélie
Donnie Darko
In the Bedroom
Lantana
Lawless Heart
The Man Who Wasn't There
Monsoon Wedding
The Others
The Piano Teacher
Read My Lips
The Royal Tenenbaums
Spirited Away
Y Tu Mamá También

2002

Abouna
Adaptation
Bloody Sunday
Bowling for Columbine
City of God
Divine Intervention
Gangs of New York
The Hours
Insomnia
In This World
The Magdalene Sisters
The Pianist
The Quiet American
Secretary
Solaris
Spellbound
Spider
Springtime in a Small Town
Sweet Sixteen
Sympathy for Mr Vengeance
10
Whale Rider

2003

Aileen: Life and Death of a
    Serial Killer

Finding Nemo
The Lord of the Rings: The
    Return of the King
Lost in Translation
Master and Commander:
    The Far Side of the World
My Architect
Mystic River
Osama
Spring, Summer, Autumn,
    Winter. . .and Spring
Touching the Void
Uzak

2004

The Aviator
The Bourne Supremacy
Collateral
Fahrenheit 9/11
Finding Neverland
Head-On
Hidden
The Incredibles
Intimate Strangers
Kings & Queen
Look at Me
The Motorcycle Diaries
Mysterious Skin
My Summer of Love
Ray
The Sea Inside
Sideways
Vera Drake

2005

Ballets Russes
Batman Begins
The Beat That My Heart
    Skipped
The Child
The Constant Gardener
Fateless
Forty Shades of Blue
Grizzly Man
I For India
King Kong
No Direction Home
Paradise Now
13 Tzameti
Wallace & Gromit: Curse of
    the Were-Rabbit

2006

Babel
Children of Men
Climates
Days of Glory
The Departed
The Good Shepherd
The Host
Jindabyne
The Last King of Scotland
Letters from Iwo Jima
Little Miss Sunshine
The Painted Veil
Pan's Labyrinth
The Queen
Requiem
The Right of the Weakest
The Singer
Still Life
Volver

2007

4 Months, 3 Weeks and 2
    Days
Beowulf
The Bourne Ultimatum
Control
The Counterfeiters
The Diving Bell and the
    Butterfly
Don't Touch the Axe
Enchanted
Ghosts
Ghosts of Cité Soleil
Gone Baby Gone
Honeydripper
I'm Not There
In the Shadow of the
    Moon
In the Valley Of Elah
The Namesake
P2
Persepolis
Ratatouille
[Rec]
The Savages
Taxi to the Dark Side
The Witnesses

2008

Son of Rambow

THREE-STAR FILMS – BY TITLE

Abouna
Abre Los Ojos
Ace in the Hole
Adaptation
The African Queen
After Life
Aileen: Life and Death of a
  Serial Killer
Akira
Aladdin
All that Heaven Allows
Amadeus
Amarcord
Amélie
American Beauty
American Graffiti
Anatomy of a Murder
And Life Goes On. . .
Angels with Dirty Faces
Antonia's Line
The Apple
Around the World in Eighty
  Days
The Asphalt Jungle
Assault on Precinct 13
Atlantic City
Au Revoir Les Enfants
Autobus
The Aviator
Babel
Ballets Russes
The Bank Dick
Barton Fink
Batman Begins
The Beat That My Heart
  Skipped
Beauty and the Beast
Before the Rain
Being John Malkovich
Belle de Jour
La Belle Noiseuse
Beowulf
The Best Intentions
The Big Combo
Big Night
The Big Parade
The Big Red One
The Big Sleep
Billy Elliot
The Birds
Black Narcissus
Blade Runner
The Blair Witch Project
Blood Simple
Bloody Sunday
The Blue Kite
Bob Le Flambeur
Body and Soul
Boogie Nights
Das Boot
Born on the Fourth of
  July
The Bourne Supremacy
The Bourne Ultimatum
Bowling for Columbine

Boys Don't Cry
Boyz N the Hood
Brassed Off
'Breaker' Morant
The Bridge on the River
  Kwai
A Brighter Summer Day
Bringing Out the Dead
Bringing Up Baby
Broadway Danny Rose
Bullitt
Bulworth
The Cabinet of Dr Caligari
Calamity Jane
Casino
Casualties of War
Chariots of Fire
The Child
Children of Men
Chungking Express
City Lights
City of God
Climates
A Clockwork Orange
Closely Observed Trains
Code Unknown
Collateral
The Commitments
The Constant Gardener
Control
The Conversation
The Counterfeiters
Creature Comforts
Crimes and Misdemeanors
Criss Cross
Crossfire
The Crowd
Cyrano de Bergerac
The Dam Busters
Dangerous Liaisons
Darling
Days of Glory
Days of Heaven
The Dead
Dead Man Walking
The Deer Hunter
Delicatessen
Deliverance
The Departed
Detour
Les Diaboliques
The Diary of a Country
  Priest
Diner
Distant Voices, Still Lives
Divine Intervention
The Diving Bell and the
  Butterfly
Doctor Mabuse the
  Gambler
Dr. No
Dog Day Afternoon
Donnie Brasco
Donnie Darko
Don't Touch the Axe

The Draughtsman's
  Contract
Dumbo
Earth
Easter Parade
8 and a Half
Eight Men Out
Election
Elizabeth
Empire of the Sun
Enchanted
The English Patient
Erin Brockovich
Eternity and a Day
The Fabulous Baker
  Boys
A Face in the Crowd
Fahrenheit 9/11
Fail-Safe
The Fallen Idol
Fantasia
Farewell My Concubine
Fateless
Father of the Bride
Fear Eats the Soul
Fearless
La Femme Infidèle
The Fencing Master
Festen
Fight Club
Finding Nemo
Finding Neverland
The Firemen's Ball
A Fish Called Wanda
A Fistful of Dollars
Five Easy Pieces
Force of Evil
Forty Shades of Blue
42nd Street
4 Months, 3 Weeks and 2
  Days
Four Weddings and a
  Funeral
The French Connection
From Here to Eternity
The Fugitive
The Full Monty
Funny Face
The Game
Gandhi
Gangs of New York
The Gay Divorcee
Genevieve
Germinal
Get Carter
Get Shorty
Ghosts
Ghosts of Cité Soleil
Gigi
Gilda
Gladiator
Glengarry Glen Ross
The Go-Between
The Gold Rush
Goldfinger

Gone Baby Gone
The Good, the Bad and the
  Ugly
The Good Shepherd
Goodbye Mr Chips
The Gospel According to St
  Matthew
Grace of My Heart
The Great Escape
The Great McGinty
Greed
Gregory's Girl
The Grifters
Grizzly Man
Grosse Pointe Blank
Hail the Conquering Hero
La Haine
Hamlet
Happy Together
Harvey
The Haunting
Head-On
Hearts of Darkness: A
  Filmmaker's Apocalypse
Heat
Heavenly Creatures
Hell's Angels
Hidden
High Tide
Hiroshima Mon Amour
Homicide
Honeydripper
Hope and Glory
The Host
The Hours
Howards End
Hud
Husbands and Wives
I Am a Fugitive from a
  Chain Gang
I For India
The Ice Storm
Ikiru
I'm Not There
Imitation of Life
In Cold Blood
In the Bedroom
In the Mood for Love
In the Shadow of the Moon
In the Valley Of Elah
In This World
In Which We Serve
The Incredibles
The Innocents
The Insider
Insomnia
Intimate Strangers
The Ipcress File
The Iron Giant
It's a Gift
Ivansxtc
Jean de Florette
Jesus of Montreal
Jindabyne
Ju Dou

Judgment at Nuremberg
Jules et Jim
Kanal
The Killer
The Killing Fields
Kind Hearts and Coronets
A Kind of Loving
King Kong
The King of Marvin Gardens
The Kingdom
Kings & Queen
Kiss Me Deadly
Kiss of Death
Klute
Knife in the Water
Kolya
The Ladykillers
Lantana
The Last Emperor
The Last King of Scotland
The Last Laugh
Last Year at Marienbad
L'Atalante
Laura
L'Avventura
Lawless Heart
The Letter
Letter from an Unknown
    Woman
Letters from Iwo Jima
The Life and Death of
    Colonel Blimp
Life Is Sweet
Lift to the Scaffold
The Lion King
Little Caesar
The Little Foxes
Little Miss Sunshine
Live Flesh
The Loneliness of the Long
    Distance Runner
Look at Me
The Lord of the Rings: The
    Return of the King
Lost in Translation
The Magdalene Sisters
The Magnificent Seven
The Man Who Shot Liberty
    Valance
The Man Who Wasn't
    There
The Man Who Would Be
    King
Manhunter
Marathon Man
Mary Poppins
M*A*S*H
Master and Commander:
    The Far Side of the
    World
McCabe and Mrs Miller
Memento
The Men
Mephisto
Metropolis
Metropolitan
Midnight
Midnight Express
Midnight Run
Mildred Pierce
Milou in May

The Miracle of Morgan's
    Creek
Miracle on 34th Street
Les Misérables
Misery
Mrs Brown
Missing
Mr Deeds Goes to Town
Modern Times
Mona Lisa
Monsoon Wedding
Monty Python's Life of
    Brian
The Motorcycle Diaries
The Music Man
My Architect
My Beautiful Laundrette
My Darling Clementine
My Fair Lady
My Life as a Dog
My Name Is Joe
My Summer of Love
Mysterious Skin
Mystic River
The Naked City
The Naked Gun: From the
    Files of Police Squad
The Namesake
Nanook of the North
Nashville
Network
Night and the City
The Night of The Living
    Dead
The Nightmare before
    Christmas
Ninotchka
Nixon
No Direction Home
Nosferatu
Notorious
Notting Hill
Now Voyager
O Brother, Where Art Thou?
Oliver!
Los Olvidados
Once Upon a Time in the
    West
One False Move
The Opposite of Sex
Orlando
Osama
The Others
Out of Sight
The Outlaw Josey Wales
Overlord
P2
The Painted Veil
The Palm Beach Story
Pandora's Box
Pan's Labyrinth
Paradise Now
The Parallax View
Paris, Texas
Paris Trout
Une Partie de Campagne
The Passenger
Pat and Mike
Peeping Tom
Performance
Persepolis

Persona
Persuasion
The Pianist
The Piano
The Piano Teacher
Pickup on South Street
Picnic at Hanging Rock
Platoon
The Player
Pleasantville
Pollock
Pretty Village Pretty
    Flame
The Prisoner of Zenda
The Private Life of Henry
    VIII
The Public Enemy
The Queen
The Quiet American
The Quiet Man
Quiz Show
Raiders of the Lost Ark
Rain Man
Raise the Red Lantern
Ran
Ratatouille
Ratcatcher
Ray
Read My Lips
Rebel without a Cause
Red River
Red Rock West
Red Sorghum
The Remains of the Day
Repulsion
Requiem
Richard III
Rififi
The Right Stuff
Rio Bravo
Rocky
Roman Holiday
Rome, Open City
La Ronde
Room at the Top
A Room for Romeo Brass
A Room with a View
Rosemary's Baby
Rosetta
The Royal Tenenbaums
Run Lola Run
Rushmore
Safe
Salvador
The Samurai
Saturday Night Fever
The Savages
Saving Private Ryan
Scarface (1983)
Scarface (1932)
The Scarlet Empress
The Sea Inside
Secretary
Secrets and Lies
A Self-Made Hero
Sense and Sensibility
Seven
Seven Days in May
Shadowlands
Shakespeare in Love
Shall We Dance?

Shallow Grave
Shane
The Shawshank
    Redemption
Shine
Shoot the Pianist
Short Cuts
Sideways
The Silence of the Lambs
A Simple Plan
Six Degrees of Separation
The Sixth Sense
Sneakers
Snow White and the Seven
    Dwarfs
Solaris (2002)
Solaris (1972)
Son of Rambow
Songs From the Second
    Floor
The Sound of Music
South Park: Bigger Longer &
    Uncut
Spartacus
Speed
Spellbound
Spider
The Spider's Stratagem
The Spirit of the Beehive
Spirited Away
Spring, Summer, Autumn,
    Winter. . .and Spring
Springtime in a Small Town
Steamboat Bill Jnr
Stella Dallas
Still Life
Stir of Echoes
Stop Making Sense
The Story of Qiu Ju
La Strada
The Straight Story
Strangers on a Train
Strictly Ballroom
The Stunt Man
Sunday, Bloody Sunday
Sunshine
The Sweet Hereafter
Sweet Sixteen
Sympathy for Mr Vengeance
The Tale of the Fox
The Talented Mr Ripley
The Tall T
A Taste of Cherry
The Taste of Others
Taxi to the Dark Side
Tears of the Black Tiger
10
Ten Rillington Place
Terminator 2: Judgment Day
The Right of the Weakest
The Singer
The Umbrellas of
    Cherbourg
The Witnesses
They Live by Night
The Thief of Bagdad
The Thin Man
Things to Come
Things to Do in Denver
    When You're Dead
13 Tzameti

This Sporting Life
Three Days of the Condor
Three Kings
A Time for Drunken Horses
Tin Cup
To Die For
To Have and Have Not
To Kill a Mockingbird
Tom Jones
Tootsie
Topsy-Turvy
Touching the Void

Toy Story 2
The Treasure of the Sierra Madre
Triumph of the Will
The Truman Show
Twelve Monkeys
Ugetsu Monogatari
The Untouchables
Uzak
Vera Drake
The Verdict
Victim
Volver

The Wages of Fear
Walkabout
Wallace & Gromit: Curse of the Were-Rabbit
The Way to the Stars
The Wedding Banquet
Went the Day Well?
Whale Rider
When We Were Kings
White Heat
The Wicker Man
Wild Strawberries
The Wind

Wings of Desire
Withnail and I
Witness for the Prosecution
Woman of the Dunes
Women in Love
Women on the Verge of a Nervous Breakdown
A World Apart
Y Tu Mamá También
Yaaba
Yojimbo
Young Mr Lincoln
Zéro de Conduite

TOP 10 FILMS BY GENRE

Each of these films is subjectively selected as an excellent example of its particular genre. Not all of them receive the maximum four-star rating in this guide; indeed one or two are harshly reviewed. But within their genre, they can be agreed to be outstanding. It should also be stressed that some films straddle categories: for instance, *The Philadelphia Story* is as much a romance as a comedy, and any of *The Lord of the Rings* films could count as fantasy as well as action-adventure.

ACTION-ADVENTURE
The Adventures of Robin Hood (1938)
Back to the Future (1985)
Batman Begins (2005)
Children of Men (2006)
Crouching Tiger, Hidden Dragon (2000)
Dr No (1962)
King Kong (1933)
The Lord of the Rings – The Fellowship of the Ring (2001)
Raiders of the Lost Ark (1981)
Spider-Man (2002)

BRITISH FILMS
Brighton Rock (1947)
Don't Look Now (1973)
Kes (1969)
Kind Hearts and Coronets (1949)
Listen to Britain (1941)
The Long Day Closes (1992)
A Matter of Life and Death (1946)
Performance (1970)
Secrets and Lies (1995)
Trainspotting (1996)

COMEDY
Annie Hall (1977)
Duck Soup (1933)
The General (1926)
Groundhog Day (1993)
His Girl Friday (1940)
The Philadelphia Story (1940)
The Producers (1968)
Some Like It Hot (1959)
Sullivan's Travels (1941)
This is Spinal Tap (1984)

CRIME/GANGSTER
Bonnie and Clyde (1967)
The Godfather (1972)
The Godfather Part II (1974)
Goodfellas (1990)
L.A. Confidential (1997)
The Long Good Friday (1980)

Mean Streets (1973)
Once Upon A Time in America (1984)
Reservoir Dogs (1991)
Scarface (1932)

HORROR
The Blair Witch Project (1999)
Dawn of the Dead (2004)
The Exorcist (1973)
Frankenstein (1931)
Invasion of the Body Snatchers (1955)
Halloween (1978)
Night of the Living Dead (1968)
Rosemary's Baby (1968)
The Thing (1951)
The Wicker Man (1973)

MUSICALS
An American in Paris (1951)
Calamity Jane (1953)
Easter Parade (1948)
Grease (1978)
A Hard Day's Night (1964)
Meet Me in St Louis (1944)
Singin' in the Rain (1952)
Top Hat (1935)
West Side Story (1961)
The Wizard of Oz (1939)

ROMANCE
Adam's Rib (1949)
Brief Encounter (1945)
Casablanca (1942)
Far From Heaven (2002)
Gone with the Wind (1939)
It Happened One Night (1934)
Lost in Translation (2003)
Notting Hill (1999)
Manhattan (1979)
To Have and Have Not (1944)

SCIENCE-FICTION
Alphaville (1965)
Blade Runner (1982)
The Day the Earth Stood Still (1951)

The Empire Strikes Back (1980)
Metropolis (1926)
Solaris (2002)
Star Wars (1977)
Sunshine (2007)
The Thing (1951)
2001: A Space Odyssey (1968)

THRILLER
Psycho (1960)
Vertigo (1958)
Touch of Evil (1958)
Memento (2000)
Heat (1995)
Wages of Fear (1953)
Chinatown (1974)
The French Connection (1971)
The Conversation (1974)
Fargo (1996)

WAR
All Quiet on the Western Front (1930)
Apocalypse Now (1979)
The Battle of Algiers (1965)
The Big Red One (1980)
The Bridge on the River Kwai (1957)
Come and See (1985)
Paths of Glory (1957)
Saving Private Ryan (1998)
Schindler's List (1993)
The Thin Red Line (1998)

WESTERNS
High Noon (1952)
The Magnificent Seven (1960)
Man of the West (1958)
The Man Who Shot Liberty Valance (1962)
Once Upon a Time in the West (1984)
Red River (1948)
Rio Bravo (1959)
The Searchers (1956)
Stagecoach (1939)
Unforgiven (1992)